Origen: New Fragments from the Commentary on Matthew

Panayiotis Tzamalikos

Origen: New Fragments from the Commentary on Matthew

Codices Sabaiticus 232 & Holy Cross 104, Jerusalem

BRILL | **Ferdinand Schöningh**

Bibliographic information published by the Deutsche Nationalbibliothek.

The Deutsche Nationalbibliothek lists this publication in the Deutsche Nationalbibliografie; detailed bibliographic data available online: http://dnb.d-nb.de

www.schoeningh.de

Cover design: Evelyn Ziegler, Munich
Production: Brill Deutschland GmbH, Paderborn

ISBN 978-3-506-70280-7 (hardback)
ISBN 978-3-657-70280-0 (e-book)

To
the holy and indelible memory of
Professor Jan den Boeft

Grates tibi maximas ago

Χάριτας πλείστας ὁμολογῶ σοι,
ὦ ψυχὰ κρατίστη,
χαρίτων πλεῖστον ἔχουσα μέρος

Contents

Preface

All too often we speak about 'evolution' in Origen's theology. However, this is an exaggeration. While bearing a tremendous erudition in his luggage as a formerly illustrious Greek philosopher, Origen's approach was clear: God had already revealed to the heathen his 'invisible things', no matter if the Greeks misunderstood those and spoke of theories of 'Ideas' or kept on worshipping idols, as Paul wrote in Rom. 1:19-22: the Greeks 'knew God' but 'did not glorify Him, and became vain in their reasoning, and professing themselves to be wise, they became fools.' For even in the case of those simple fishermen, who were taught by Jesus 'privately and especially in places of retreat', it was because they 'received those thoughts by the grace of God' that 'they saw better than Plato what thoughts should be committed to writing and how they should be written' (*Cels*, VI.6). However, along with frequently recalling Paul's words, Origen (unlike other Christians who saw Hellenism as a daemon) did not dismiss the first part of Paul's statement, namely, that the Greeks somehow '*knew* God'. Whatever part of this 'somehow' could be rescued and taken advantage of, Origen did not despise, although he did so tacitly. This was one aspect of what both his contemporary and later inquisitors saw as his scandalous and unpardonable sin.

Already at the time when he wrote the preface to his *De Principiis*, Origen explicated the need for a codified 'corpus of doctrine' to be constructed. To this purpose, he did not count on Christians prior to him, on whom he commented very seldom, let alone that excoriated some of them as heretics on various grounds, such as Melito of Sardis and, more importantly, Tatian, whom Clement on Alexandria had criticised exactly on the same issue and grounds.

Consequently, in reality Origen's work was not *evolution*: it was *revolution*. This means that, upon his conversion to Christianity, he had clear ideas concerning certain aspects of doctrine, such as his Anaxagorean theory of generation (that I have expounded as 'Theory of logoi'), in light of which he explained the narrative of Genesis without allowing room for being blamed in the least. And yet, he was inculpated (or calumniated) by uninformed fanatics, but this did not deter Gregory of Nyssa from following Origen's theory suit, with remarkable diligence and impressive knowledgeability.

However, Origen's Theology was a different matter: for whereas as a formerly Anaxagorean Greek philosopher he departed from his fundamental monotheistic notion of God being an entirely simple *Nous*, he had to move to the notion of the Trinity being an absolutely simple *Nous* and yet threeness of distinct Persons in oneness. This he did right from the very start, when he argued that the Trinitarian God is 'altogether one and simple' (πάντη ἓν καὶ ἁπλοῦν), using the same expression which Plotinus used exclusively for the supreme and unfathomable One ontologically standing above the Nous (the Intellect, which is not 'altogether simple', but 'one many', ἓν πολλά). Against this, even as a Greek philosopher, Origen believed that there is nothing superior to the *Nous* (therefore, he dismissed the Neoplatonic One), for which Proclus criticised him severely and averred that Plato could have never included Origen among his pupils for that matter.

Hence, the 'evolution' in Origen's thought is far more attenuated than what many believe, since some fundamentals were there right from the start of his Christian life. Besides, in effect he set out to explain scripture from scratch. He only felt he could avail himself sparingly and cautiously of a few earlier Christians, such as Clement of Alexandria and Hippolytus, which though did not involve cardinal points of doctrine.

The present codex-text reveals (actually, confirms) that, at a later stage of his life, Origen overcame his inhibitions concerning use of the Gnostic term *homoousios* about the Trinity. He did so also upon writing the commentary on Matthew and some other works – a point that Pamphilus arguably explained in his *Apology for Origen*. As it happens, scholars are loath to accept facts, one of which is that Origen's use of *homoousios* does not come to light now for the first time: this is also in Klostermann's texts, and, prior to those, this term has been there ever since Migne's *Scholia on Matthew*.

In any case, however, to Origen this was just a word among the many figurative terms and expressions he used in order to adumbrate the mystery of God being *Triune* and yet absolutely *One*. This means that he did not make *homoousios* a 'banner' or catchword, as the followers of Nicaea zealously and contentiously did later, although, to begin with, most of them could hardly account for the import of the notion of God's *ousia*.

Athanasius eagerly and honestly assured that the term *homoousios* was not a novelty invented at Nicaea; instead, 'eminent bishops and scholars of old' had already used this. Eusebius used the selfsame words explaining to his flock why was it that he eventually signed up for this term – and those words were repeated as a sort of appeal to authority by later Christians, such as the historians Socrates, Gelasius of Cyzicus, and Nicephorus Callistus, as well as Theodoret. Beyond hypotheses about who those 'bishops of old' possibly were (discussed in the Introduction), one should wonder about this: in an era when both doctrinal faultlessness and aberration were determined by the pulpit, who those laymen 'scholars of old' could possibly have been? And if Origen were excluded in the teeth of so much evidence, who else could be a possible alternative?

At any rate, what should be realised is this: a scandal and logical inconsistency could be there if Origen did *not* theorise the Trinity as *homoousios*, once he posited the Trinitarian God as a *Nous* 'altogether one and simple', while styling not only the Trinity *in toto* but also each Trinitarian Person *Nous*, a formula of which Cyril of Alexandria could not have enough (and I should not mention Origen's expression styling the Son 'homoousios king', because this appears in one of his fragments on the Psalms, which are vulnerable to being impugned as untrustworthy).

Perhaps this explains why, after three quarters of a century, Klostermann's honourable collection of Origen's fragments from the commentary on Matthew is stubbornly snubbed. The twenty-four codices that this great and industrious scholar explored contain material that calls for perusal, which though never really took place. Unfortunately, Klostermann missed *Codex Sabaiticus 232*, which is the most important of all since it contains more material not found in other codices – indeed material that questions current prejudice by means of facts. Nevertheless, the present edition is meant to remain side by side with Klostermann's work, which will never be displaced or outdated. Instead, my hope is that the present edition will stimulate renewed attention to Klostermann's volume and to the study it deserves.

If Origen's commentary on Matthew is rightly considered a 'mature' work of his, this is not because it contains new *ideas* that Origen developed step by step; rather, it is his different *spirit*, which evinces a man who is now set free and expresses himself more courageously, notwithstanding the gloomy circumstances (indeed the pandaemonium) surrounding him and despite avowed enemies that lay in wait, of whom he was fully aware.

As I have argued earlier (and discuss further in the present Introduction with respect to John Chrysostom), Epiphanius was a quarrelsome zealot, yet he cared to be an accurate scholar, and his testimony that Origen lived in Caesarea for two years only and then moved to Tyre for the rest twenty-eight years of his life must be given credit. Once Origen decamped from Alexandria to Caesarea, he continued to write his commentary on John (from the sixth book onwards) and it is hardly coincidence that he implied that, at that time, he himself was 'a man of the church', i.e. a clergyman. However, in the thirty-second book of the same commentary, he speaks of 'bishops and presbyters, who hold these superior posts as clergymen', in the same way he speaks of 'those who hold other secular offices', as if placing both groups on the same par, which probably suggests that he was no longer a member of any of those privileged élites. Above all, at Tyre Origen was at odds with the local bishop, as careful study of his commentary on Matthew bespeaks. I should have thought that this bishop was no other than Methodius, known as 'of Olympus'. As nasty and unfettered as Jerome oftentimes was towards his enemies, yet, whenever he wanted to, he was an accurate scholar, and his testimony about Methodius having been 'bishop of Olympus, then of Tyre' should not be dismissed lightheartedly. After all, Jerome knew far more about the historically obscure Methodius than we do, and he was not sparing of characterisations, such as styling Methodius 'most dialectical' (disertissimum) and his exposition 'brilliant' (nitidum).

There are many who take it as mere coincidence that a bishop 'of Olympus' was all out to confront two eminent intellectuals of Tyre, namely, its native Porphyry and the immigrant Origen, while this prelate was located as far as Cilicia is from Palestine. Given Jerome's testimony (embraced by Photius, too), I myself do not think that Methodius' arduous invective was motivated merely by the obsession of a bishop whose see was located hundreds of miles away from Tyre. In fact, Methodius' rancour against Origen turned out a chronic situation once both of them lived in the same city and the illustrious Alexandrian was a thorn in the local bishop's side. In this context, Origen's vehement attacks (only in the commentary on Matthew, i.e. after Methodius had moved to Tyre from Olympus) on bishops (meaning the local bishop par excellence) whom at numerous points he identified with the Gospel's Pharisees (whom Jesus evicted violently from the Temple, the self-righteous hypocrites, etc.) have not as yet been properly assessed and understood as to their real historical setting.

I should also have thought that Methodius was a much younger contemporary of Origen, and when the former held the office of bishop at Tyre, Origen lived there but was no longer a presbyter, and the title he had received at Caesarea was but a waned memory of the past. Whether by that time Methodius had written his *Symposium* (or, *On Chastity*) is hard to say, although this is known as one of his early works. But in case Origen (the most relentless critic of Gnosticism) had read this, he could have been dismayed at Methodius styling the Son of God 'most senior of all aeons' (πρεσβύτατος αἰών), 'firstling' (πρωτόγονον βλάστημα), and 'the first of all archangels' (πρῶτον τῶν ἀρχαγγέλων). Little wonder that, when Photius reviewed this book, he was appalled at 'the Arianist malice and the mythical narratives' which he read therein. On the other hand, Methodius' obloquy against Origen in reality had nothing to do with the ideas that Origen himself systematically and forcefully had expounded. For he laid at Origen's door the theory of beginningless creation (or, eternity of the world), pre-existence of souls, and transmigration – that is, all those theories that Origen forcefully confuted through the whole of his writings.

In the commentary on Matthew Origen is different in *mood*, not in *ideas*: he is highly critical of the ecclesiastical establishment of his city, with which his relations could have not been worse; he deplores their moral quality and their penchant for mundane pleasures, goods, and power; he rebukes the mentality of regarding converted Christians, such as Origen himself, as inferior to those who were born to Christian parents, and argues extensively against this attitude. Moreover, he certainly has no inhibitions about using such bold terms as *homoousios* in the context of his Trinitarian theology, a term already defamed and precarious because of its Gnostic usage, as Origen's arguments against the Gnostics in his commentary on John evince, too.

All in all, when Origen wrote his commentary on Matthew, in some respects he was a different *person*, sometimes disillusioned, often disheartened, yet, concerning his fundamental ideas, he was not a different *theologian*.

The manuscript of *Sabaiticus 232* presented in this volume has the merit of offering not only 'fragments', but also extensive ratiocination in ample context, which can be considered critically. The Greek language is exquisite and the author every now and then feels it necessary to make analyses concerning the etymology and appositeness of the terms used either by the scripture or by himself, to explain their significance, or clear up possible polysemic imports and consider meaningful nuances. Alongside the explicit attributions made to Origen, all of these texts are very much like his style and methodology, which is a feature abundantly making its mark throughout all of his works.

I wish to express my gratitude to Professor Martin Illert for making this book a tenant of the historic house of Ferdinand Schöningh. His knowledgeable approach to the content of this work, and subsequently his noble collaboration he offered me, has profoundly touched me. In the person of Production Manager Lisa Sauerwald, I found a partner at all times ready to make things as easy as possible. In thanking her, I extend my appreciation also to all the members of her highly professional team.

Dedication of this book to the late Professor Jan den Boeft (Rotterdam, 13 October 1935 – † Leiden, 10 August 2019) falls short of expressing what I really feel and think of this man. He was a respectable figure that made this world a better place to live in, and a person whose role in my scholarly career has been decisive and unforgettable. As the editor-in-chief of the *Vigiliae Christianae Supplements* (1990-2014) he considered four volumes of mine that have been published therein. He was Professor of Latin literature, but he had also a profound knowledge of Greek since the times he was a teacher of Greek and Latin at the City Gymnasium in Leiden (1958-1976), then, during his lectureship in Latin at the University of Utrecht, then, as Professor Extraordinarius in the History of ancient religions in the Theological Faculty of the University of Utrecht, and finally, as Professor holding the chair of Latin at the Vrije Universiteit, Amsterdam (since 1994), where he taught until his retirement in 2000.

I have always admired his love for both the Classical and the Christian traditions. Nevertheless, to me, he was always a wise mentor, whose opinion on various matters weighed over the direction of my pursuits, and his advice has always turned out to be invaluable. I cherish the hope that, to the noble and compassionate Jan den Boeft, the gates of Paradise have been already wide open.

Abbreviations

CHRISTIAN AUTHORS

ORIGEN

adDeut	*Adnotationes in Deuteronomium*
adGen	*Adnotationes in Genesim*
adLev	*Adnotationes in Leviticum*
adNum	*Adnotationes in Numeros*
Cels	*Contra Celsum*
comm1Cor	*Fragmenta ex commentariis in Epistulam i ad Corinthios*
commEph	*Fragmenta ex Commentariis in Epistulam ad Ephesios*
commGen	*Commentarii in Genesim (fragmenta)*
commJohn	*Commentarii in Evangelium Joannis*
commMatt	*Commentarium in Evangelium Matthaei*
commRom	*Commentarii in Epistulam ad Romanos*
commSerMatt	*Commentariorum Series in Evangelium Matthaei*
deOr	*De Oratione*
Dial	*Dialogus cum Heraclide*
excPs	*Excerpta in Psalmos*
exhMar	*Exhortatio ad Martyrium*
expProv	*Expositio in Proverbia*
fr1Cor	*Fragmenta ex commentariis in Epistulam i ad Corinthios*
frEph	*Fragmenta ex commentariis in epistulam ad Ephesios*
frJer	*Fragmenta in Jeremiam*
frJohn	*Fragmenta in Evangelium Joannis*
frLam	*Fragmenta in Lamentationes*
frLuc	*Fragmenta in Lucam*
frMatt	*Fragmenta in Evangelium Matthaei*
frProv	*Fragmenta ex commentariis in Proverbia*
frPs	*Fragmenta in Psalmos*
homEz	*Homiliae in Ezechielem*
homGen	*Homiliae in Genesim (in catenis)*
homJer	*In Jeremiam (homiliae 1–11)*
homJob	*Homiliae in Job*
homLev	*Homiliae in Leviticum*
homLuc	*Homiliae in Lucam*
homPs	*Homiliae in Psalmos (15, 36, 67, 83, 74, 75, 76, 77, 80, 81)*
Princ	*De Principiis*
schLuc	*Scholia in Lucam*

schMatt	*Scholia in Matthaeum*
selDeut	*Selecta in Deuteronomium*
selEz	*Selecta in Ezechielem*
selEx	*Fragmenta ex commentariis in Exodum (In illud: Induravit dominus cor Pharaonis)*
selGen	*Selecta in Genesim*
selPs	*Selecta in Psalmos*
selNum	*Selecta in Numeros*

OTHER CHRISTIAN AUTHORS

Panarion	Epiphanius of Salamis, *Panarion* (*Adversus Haereses*)
frPs(al)	Didymus, *Fragmenta in Psalmos Altera*
commZacch	Didymus, *Commentarii in Zacchariam*
commJob	Didymus, *Commentarii in Job*
–	Olympiodorus, the deacon of Alexandria, *Commentarii in Job*
–	Julian the Arian, *Commentarius in Job*
–	John Chrysostom, *Commentarius in Job*
frProv	Didymus, *Fragmenta in Proverbia*
De Providentia	Theodoret, *De Providentia Orationes Decem*
Curatio	*Graecarum Affectionum Curatio*
In Joannem	Cyril of Alexandria, *Commentarii in Joannem*
In Isaiam	Cyril of Alexandria, *Commentarius in Isaiam Prophetam*
–	Eusebius, *Commentarius in Isaiam*
–	Theodoret, *Commentarius in Isaiam*
commLuc	Cyril of Alexandria, *Commentarii in Lucam*
commMatt	Jerome, *Commentarium in Evangelium Matthaei*
–	Photius, *Commentarii in Matthaeum*
commProphXII	Cyril of Alexandria, *Commentarius in xii Prophetas Minores*
–	Theodoret, *Interpretatio in xii Prophetas Minores*
–	Theodore of Mopsuestia, *Commentarius in xii prophetas minores*
De Adoratione	Cyril of Alexandria, *De Adoratione et Cultu in Spiritu et Veritate*
De Spiritu Sancto i	Gennadius Scholarius, *Tractatus De Processu Spiritus Sancti i*
De Spiritu Sancto ii	*Gennadius Scholarius, Tractatus De Processu Spiritus Sancti i*
epitSummae	*Gennadius Scholarius, Epitome Primae Partis Summae Theologicae Thomae Aquinae*
frMatt	Cyril of Alexandria, *Commentarii in Matthaeum* (*in catenis*) (J. Reuss)
–	Theodore of Heraclea, *Fragmenta in Matthaeum* (*in catenis*) (J. Reuss)

–	Theophilus of Alexandria, *Fragmenta in Matthaeum* (*in catenis*) (J. Reuss)
–	Photius, *Commentarii in Matthaeum* (*in catenis*) (J. Reuss)
–	John of Damascus, *Fragmenta in Matthaeum* (e catena Nicetae), (Migne)
Opuscula i	Michael Psellus, *Opuscula Logica, Physica, Allegorica, Alia*
Catena in Matthaeum	*Catena in Matthaeum* (*catena integra*) (*e cod. Paris. Coislin. gr. 23*)
Catena in Marcum	*Catena in Marcum* (*recensio ii*) (*e codd. Oxon. Bodl. Laud. 33 + Paris. Coislin. 23 + Paris. gr. 178*)
Catena in Lucam	*Catena in Lucam* (*typus B*) (*cod. Paris. Coislin. 23 & Oxon. Bodl. Misc. 182*)
HE	*Historia Ecclesiastica*

(Eusebius, Theodoret, Sozomenus, Socrates Scholasticus, Gelasius of Cyzicus, Nicephorus Callistus Xanthopulus)

GREEK AUTHORS

commAnalPost	John Philoponus, *In Aristotelis Analytica Posteriora Commentaria*
–	*Eustratius of Nicaea, In Aristotelis Analyticorum Posteriorum Librum Secundum Commentarium*
commAnalPr	John Philoponus, *In Aristotelis Analytica Priora Commentaria*
–	Alexander of Aphrodisias, *In Aristotelis Analyticorum Priorum Librum i Commentarium*
–	Ammonius of Alexandria, *In Aristotelis Analyticorum Priorum Librum i Commentarium*
commAnim	John Philoponus, *In Aristotelis Libros De Anima Commentaria*
–	Simplicius, *In Aristotelis Libros De Anima Commentaria*
–	Gennadius Scholarius, *Translatio Commentarii Thomae Aquinae De Anima Aristotelis*
commCael	Simplicius, *In Aristotelis Quattuor Libros De Caelo Commentaria*
commCateg	Dexippus, *In Aristotelis Categorias Commentarium*
–	Porphyry, *In Aristotelis Categorias Expositio per Interrogationem et Responsionem*
–	Porphyry, *In Aristotelis Categorias Commentarium*
–	Ammonius of Alexandria, *In Aristotelis Categorias Commentarius*
–	Simplicius, *In Aristotelis Categorias Commentarium*
–	John Philoponus, *In Aristotelis Categorias Commentarium*
–	Olympiodorus of Alexandria, *In Aristotelis Categorias Commentarium*

–	Elias of Alexandria, *In Aristotelis Categorias Commentarium,*
–	Arethas of Caesarea, *Scholia in Aristotelis Categoria*
commCrat	Proclus, *In Platonis Cratylum Commentaria*
commDeInterpr	Stephanus of Alexandria, *In Aristotelis Librum De Interpretatione Commentarium*
	Ammonius of Alexandria, *In Aristotelis Librum De Interpretatione Commentarius*
commEpict	Simplicius, *Commentarius in Epicteti Enchiridion*
commEthNic	Aspasius, *In Ethica Nichomachea Commentaria*
–	Michael of Ephesus, *In Ethica Nicomachea ix-x Commentaria*
–	Eustratius of Nicaea, *In Aristotelis Ethica Nicomachea*
–	Anonymous, *In Aristotelis Ethica Nicomachea*
–	Anonymous, *In Ethica Nicomachea Paraphrasis*
–	John Philoponus, *In Aristotelis Categorias Commentarium*
commEucl	Proclus, *In Primum Euclidis Elementorum Librum Commentarii*
commGorg	Olympiodorus of Alexandria, *In Platonis Gorgiam Commentaria*
commPhaed	Olympiodorus of Alexandria, *In Platonis Phaedonem Commentaria*
schPhaedr	Hermias of Alexandria, *In Platonis Phaedrum Scholia*
commPhaed	*In Platonis Phaedonem Commentaria*
commGenAnim	John Philoponus, *In Libros De Generatione Animalium Commentaria*
commGenCorr	John Philoponus, *In Aristotelis Libros De Generatione et Corruptione Commentaria*
commMetaph	Syrianus, *In Aristotelis Metaphysica Commentaria*
–	Alexander of Aphrodisias, *In Aristotelis Metaphysica Commentaria*
–	Asclepius of Tralles, *In Aristotelis Metaphysicorum Libros Commentaria*
commMeteor	John Philoponus, *In Aristotelis Meteorologicorum Librum Primum Commentarium*
–	Alexander of Aphrodisias, *In Aristotelis Meteorologicorum Libros Commentaria*
commPhys	John Philoponus, *In Aristotelis Physicorum Libros Commentaria*
–	Simplicius, *In Aristotelis Physicorum Libros Commentaria*
–	Michael Psellus, *In Aristotelis Physicorum Libros Commentarium*
–	Alexander of Aphrodisias, *Commentaria In Aristotelis Physica*
commRep	Proclus, *In Platonis Rem Publicam Commentarii*
commTim	Porphyry, *In Platonis Timaeum Commentaria (fragmenta)*
–	Proclus, *In Platonis Timaeum Commentaria*
commTop	Alexander of Aphrodisias, *In Aristotelis Topicorum Libros Octo Commentaria*

De Providentia	Proclus, *De Decem Dubitationibus Circa Providentiam*
paraphrAnalPost	Themistius, *Analyticorum Posteriorum Paraphrasis*
paraphrAnim	Sophonias, *In Aristotelis Libros De Anima Paraphrasis*
–	Themistius, *In Aristotelis Libros De Anima Paraphrasis*
paraphrPhys	Themistius, *In Aristotelis Physica Paraphrasis*
Princ	Damascius, *De Principiis*
Vitae	Diogenes Laertius, *Vitae Philosophorum*

OTHER VOLUMES

ACO	Schwartz, E., *Acta Conciliorum Oecumenicorum*
GCS	Die Griechischen Christlichen Schriftsteller der ersten drei Jahrhunderte
TU	Texte und Untersuchungen zur Geschichte der altcristlichen Literatur
PG	J. P. Migne, *Patrologia Graeca* (volume / page / line)
PL	J. P. Migne, *Patrologia Latina* (volume / page / line)
Analecta Hymnica Graeca	Day / Canon / Ode
SVF	J. von Arnim, *Stoicorum Veterum Fragmenta* (volume, page, verse)
COT	P. Tzamalikos, *Origen: Cosmology and Ontology of Time*
PHE	P. Tzamalikos, *Origen: Philosophy of History and Eschatology*
RCR	P. Tzamalikos, *The Real Cassian Revisited*
NDGF	P. Tzamalikos, *A Newly Discovered Greek Father*
Scholia in Apocalypsin	P. Tzamalikos, *An Ancient Commentary on the Book of Revelation*
Anaxagoras	*P. Tzamalikos, Anaxagoras, Origen, and Neoplatonism: The Legacy of Anaxagoras to Classical and Late Antiquity*
L&S	Liddell, H.G. – Scott, R., *A Greek – English Lexicon*

Psalms are numbered after LXX

Introduction

The Aim

The commentary on Matthew is probably the last of Origen's works[1] and much later than the *Contra Celsum*,[2] although both of them belong to the latest and most difficult stage of his life. It is quite telling that all those who condemned him did not cite a single word from those accomplished works; instead, they were obsessed only with the extant, and largely tampered, version of his *De Principiis*. The aim of publication of this codex is to shed light on the *real* Origen as a contribution to doing justice to this tragic figure of early Christianity.

When I came to read *Codex Sabaiticus 232*, not only did I find out that almost all of Klostermann's (universally shunned) fragments from Origen's commentary on Matthew were there, but also at several points this manuscript provided the hitherto unknown wider context of those. As a matter of fact, most of the passages contained in the present volume are no 'fragments', but extensive sections from a flowing text revealing Origen's mentality and his approach to the gospel on Matthew.

Moreover, this manuscript contains commentary beyond the point of Matthew's gospel at which Klostermann's fragments stop. Hence, the present volume is an opportunity not simply to unearth and probe the contents of a codex, but also to cast light on Klostermann's conscientious work and to go beyond this by presenting new textual evidence and resolve on several dubious points of that work, to which multiple attributions have been made in catenae that leave matters moot.

On that account, parts of this manuscript corroborate certain passages of Origen's that are already known, but now the new text provides their context by demonstrating how these 'fragments' worked in Origen's full commentary and argument, which is one of the good reasons for the contents of this ancient manuscript to be trusted along with critical and comparative study of them.

Bringing the content of a certain ancient manuscript to light takes more than just transcribing the text, plus philological emendation of this: it takes critical discussion of the ideas involved therein, interrelations, connections, dependencies, influence, and sometimes refutation of uninformed assertions.

To this purpose, beside picking up those texts tagged with the name of Origen, I have included and considered some of the 'unattributed' passages (ἀνεπίγραφα), as well as a few ones appearing under the name of other authors

1 Unless Origen wrote a commentary on Luke subsequent to this; see *infra*, p. CXCIV.

2 See *infra*, pp. CLIII-CLXII.

 | DOI:10.30965/9783657702800_002

(such as Theodore of Heraclea,[3] or Severus of Antioch, or Photius), for which critical and comparative analysis reveals that they should have been written by Origen himself. For example, an extensive *anepigraphon* on folios 4r-v turns out to be a copy from Origen's *Contra Celsum*, I.34-35. Why some of Origen's passages appear as *anepigrapha* in later codices (such as *Sabaiticus 232*) is all but mystery: he had been branded 'heretic' and it was rather natural for earlier catenists to delete his name while quoting his words. Subsequently, such passages thereafter passed on as 'unattributed', and later anthologers had no choise but copy this designation in texts transmitted to them. This means that, whereas the initial catenist did not *want* to cite Origen's name, subsequent scribes did not *know* the name of the author. This phenomenon is as old as to be pointed out by Pamphilus.

> In order that the contentious bias [of Origen's detractors], or (in order to speak the truth) their prejudiced insanity, may come to light more easily, [I should add that] it usually happens during either by chance or sometimes on purspose, that his name is absent from the title of the codex while something of his [Origen's] is read in the hearing of his slanderers, as if this were [written] by another author. This delights them, and they praise and admire it very much for as long a time as his name is not mentioned (quandiu nomen non fuerit indicatum). However, once it becomes known that those things that gratified them were written by Origen, they forthwith dislike them and say that these are heretical; and the things that a short while before they extolled to heaven, by the same voices and the same tongues they plunge into hell.[4]

A pertinent instance is pretty telling: a copyist of codex Great Laura Athos 184[5] juxtaposed the scriptural passages of the Ephesians in that codex with the corresponding ones in Origen's commentary on the Ephesians. Then, he wrote some notes on the margin indicating where each of Origen's commentaries on Paul's epistles began. However, a later scribe erased many of those marginal references to Origen, as if he wished to 'purge' this codex from Origen's name.[6]

---

3 See Jerome, *De Viris Illustribus*, XC: "Theodore, bishop of Heraclea in Thrace, published in the reign of the emperor Constantius commentaries on Matthew and John, on the Epistles and on the Psalter. These are written in a polished and clear style and show an excellent historical sense." J. Reuss published some alleged fragments from Theodore's presumed commentary on Matthew; see discussion *infra*, pp. XXXII ff.

4 Pamphilus, *Apologia pro Origene*, PG.17.546A-B.

5 Some scholars tagged this 'Codex von der Goltz'.

6 F. von der Goltz, *Eine textkritische Arbeit des zehnten bezw. sechsten Jahrbunderts*, TU 2.4, Leipzig, 1899, p. 95. Cf. C.P. Bammel, "A New Witness to the Scholia from Origen in the Codex von der Goltz", in *Origeniana Rufiana*, Vetus Latina 29, Freiburg, 1996, pp. 137-138. K. Lake – S. New (eds.), *Six Collections of New Testament Manuscripts*, Harvard Theological Studies, 17, Cambridge Mass. 1932, pp. 141-219. J.N. Birdsall, "The Text and Scholia of the Codex von der

A case in point is also the spurious Hippolytus fragment 7, from the introduction to the commentary on the Psalms: H. Achelis came upon three manuscripts in which this extensive text is unattributed, but the Syrian *Ambrosianus* ascribes this to Origen – and indeed the style is all too characteristic of and like Origen.[7] Similarly, fragment 9 of Achelis belongs to Origen, and this has been attributed to him because codex *Barberinus Graecus III 59* did so, and yet this is 'left anonymous by three other codices'.[8]

Why should the present codex be deemed more trustworthy than others? In the first place, it is of course hard to argue that a certain codex is more truthful than another one, especially whenever we have 'fragments' ascribed to different authors at the same time (either in a specific codex or in different ones). However, the present case is not about a certain passage being attributed to Origen whereas other manuscripts ascribe this to another: this is about *text* of Origen's in which a specific passage ascribed to another author is only a tiny portion. The case of John Chrysostom is intruiging in that respect, indeed this is like a 'patchwork': we have Chrysostom's points from his homilies on Matthew juxtaposed with the present text, and it turns out that there are passages of several lines that are a case of copy-and-paste, whereas the surrounding context in either author is different.

Accordingly, in *Codex Sabaiticus 232*, we have uninterrupted pages of extensive text, which here and there includes passages that have been ascribed to several other authors, such as Apollinaris, Chrysostom, Cyril of Alexandria, Theodore of Heraclea, Theodore of Mopsuestia, Severus of Antioch, even to Origen's pupil Gregory Thaumaturgus, of whom only a single passage allegedly from his commentary of Matthew is extant, but now this appears under Origen's name.

It should be emphasised, therefore, that this manuscript contains not simply 'fragments' but also extensive flowing text, in which Klostermann's portions (including those ascribed to other Christian authors) are seamed here and there, like varicoloured patches revealing how Origen's commentary was

---

Goltz and its Allies, and their bearing upon the Texts of the Words of Origen, especially the Commentary on Romans", in *Origeniana: Premier colloque international des études origeniennes*, Montserrat, 18-21, Septembre 1973, in H. Crouzel – G. Lomiento – J. Rius-Camps (eds), *Quaderni di Vetera Christianorum*, 12, Bari, 1975, pp. 215-222.

7 See Karl Praechter, "Die griechischen Aristotelescommentare" in *Byzantinische Zeitschirift*, 1909, pp. 516-518; p. 47. This is a review of the *Commentaria in Aristotelem Graeca*, published by the Berlin Academy in twenty-six volumes. See an English translation of Praechter's review by B. Caston in R. Sorabji (ed.), *Aristotle Transformed: The Ancient Commentators and Their Influence*, Ithaca, NY, 1990, pp. 31-54. My references pertain to the English translation. See *infra*, pp. CLXII-CLXXX, discussion of Origen's prologues to his commentaries.

8 Karl Praechter, *loc. cit.*

availed of by later authors, some of whom, such as Jerome, took pride at both having copied from Origen's commentary and being his indicter.

Moreover, Klostermann's last fragment (fr. 572) is a comment on Matthew, 28:18 (yet even this is stated as a dubious one), but *Codex Sabaiticus 232* contains commentary down to Matthew's concluding phrase, namely, 28:20.

Thus, on the one hand, we have Origen's extensive text; on the other, Klostermann's few lines here and there, which are included in the same text, having been ascribed to other authors.

In several cases discussed below, this phenomenon can arguably mean that certain later authors copied different points from Origen's commentary on Matthew, but this phenomenon has not to do only with the commentary on Matthew. For example, a text of Origen's from the commentary on Job cannot be disputed since he expounds his fundamental doctrine concerning the difference between ποίησις[9] suggesting Actual creation and πλάσις[10] which points to Providential creation.[11] The passage goes on thus: 'Ικετεύω δὴ μνησθῆναι καὶ τοῦ τῆς φύσεως εὐτελοῦς καὶ ὀλιγοχρονίου.[12] Now, we have the text by John Chrysostom which is the same: ἱκετεύων μνησθῆναι τοῦ τῆς φύσεως εὐτελοῦς καὶ ὀλιγοχρονίου.[13] Moreover, the phrase that precedes this phrase of Chrysostom[14] is but the one from Didymus.[15] In short, when Chrysostom commented on the book of Job, he wholeheartedly drew on the Origenian tradition, namely both Origen's and Didymus' commentaries on Job.[16] This is a phenomenon that we shall come upon at several points of critical consideration of the present manuscript.

The case is particularly revealing in Chrysostom's sermons on Matthew: they exist as a whole, and most of them are recognisably dotted by passages picked up from Origen's commentary; otherwise, the context in either Chrysostom and Origen is different both before and after such points, at which all too often do we come upon Chrysostom's usual flowery prose. The case on folio 112v is illuminating, although this is only one of numerous ones: in the *Catena on*

---

9 Cf. Gen. 1:26.

10 Cf. Gen. 2:7.

11 See *COT*, pp. 84-86; *Anaxagoras*, pp. 909-911.

12 Origen, *homJob*, p. 363.

13 John Chrysostom, *Fragmenta in Job*, PG.64.605.47-38.

14 John Chrysostom, *op. cit.* PG.64.605.35-37: 'Ακολούθως δὲ καὶ τῆς δημιουργίας καὶ τῆς προνοίας αὐτὸν ἐπιστάμενος ἀρχηγὸν καὶ κύριον, εἰς εὐχὴν τρέπει τὸν λόγον, ἱκετεύων etc. as above.

15 Didymus, *commJob* (*7.20c-11*), codex p. 275, lines 13-17.

16 Later, the deacon Olympiodorus of Alexandria copied from Origen and Chrysostom to the letter, too. *commJob*, p. 106: 'Ικετεύω δὲ μνησθῆναί σε καὶ τοῦ τῆς φύσεως εὐτελοῦς καὶ ὀλιγοχρονίου.

Matthew,[17] there is a very extensive text of Origen's explaining Matthew 13:33. In Chrysostom's homily, some of Origen's phrases are just copy-pasted while Chrysostom's words either before or those points are different.[18]

Another reason for publishing parts of *Codex Sabaiticus 232* is that there are texts of Origen which are heretofore unknown and come to light for the first time. Moreover, although we come upon almost all of Klostermann's fragments, now we have the context for numerous of them, which turns consideration of 'fragment' to study of an integrated *text*. Actually, almost all of Klostermann's portions would be footnotes to the present and much wider text – this excellent scholar just missed the present codex, which though happens to be the most rich and informative of all those that Klostermann used.

My own ambition has not been simply, as it frequently happens, to transcribe the contents of a codex that are ascribed to Origen: instead, as I did with the *Scholia in Apocalypsin*, I have thought it incumbent upon me to demonstrate, as incontestably as possible, by means of an accompanying critical commentary, the interrelation and the interplay, on the one hand, between Origen and his enormous philosophical background, and, on the other, between Origen and the vast number of illustrious and less illustrious posterior authors. For it is a monotonously repeated truism that all of subsequent authors copied from Origen. Both before and after his official condemnation, authors conveniently styled Origen 'erudite' (πολυμαθὴς) or indeed 'most erudite' (πολυμαθέστατος).[19] However, *specific* and argued instances of this phenomenon almost never appear in scholarship, let alone that Origen's commanding presence and effect on his posterity is overlooked, obscured, unnamed, and certainly undetermined – mostly because of inability to recognise the tremendous impact of his thought.

Modern times hardly deviated from the hackneyed asseverations about *who* and *what* Origen was: monographs, theses, articles, and certainly class-teaching, decided that he was one of the 'Christian Platonists of Alexandria', not to mention allegations about him being a 'Gnostic' or a 'Pythagorean', and the list is all but short. No one was moved by Eusebius being flabbergasted

17 Origen, *apud Catena in Matthaeum*, p. 107.

18 John Chrysostom, *In Matthaeum*, PG.58.478.25-27; p. 197, endnote cmlxxxviii.

19 Athanasius, *In Illud: Qui Dixerit Verbum In Filium*, PG.26.649.21-22 & *Epistulae Quattuor Ad Serapionem*, epistle 4.2.1: Παλαιοὶ μὲν οὖν ἄνδρες, ᾿Ωριγένης ὁ πολυμαθὴς καὶ φιλόπονος. Theodoret, *Haereticarum Fabularum Compendium*, PG.83.345.47-48: ᾿Ωριγένης, ὁ πολυμάθειαν ἀσκήσας. Cf. a later testimony by a catenist of Papias of Hierapolis, *Fragmenta*, fr. 12: οὕτω δὲ καὶ ὁ πολυμαθὴς ᾿Ωριγένης ἐν τῇ κατὰ Ματθαῖον ἑρμηνείᾳ. Also, John Malalas, *Chronologica*, p. 12. George Monachus, *Chronicon*, p. 53; *Chronicon Breve*, PG.110: 84.12 & 96.33-34. Nicetas David, *Orationes ii De Fine Mundi*, oration 1, lines 99-100. Synodicon Vetus, sections 17 & 18. Nicephorus Callistus Xanthopulus, *HE*, 4.5; 5.1.

at Marcellus's claim associating Origen with Plato only because the former allegedly borrowed the first words of *De Principiis* from Plato's *Gorgias*. This was Eusebius' refutation of Marcellus, who anyway did not actually claim that Origen was a Platonist: he only remarked that Origen took up the first words of *De Principiis* (οἱ πεπιστευκότες καὶ πεπεισμένοι) from Plato's *Gorgias*.[20] Opposite this, Eusebius pointed out that 'Origen's fundamental premisses were sheer different', and exclaimed, 'what has Origen to do with Plato?'[21]

However, this tradition of not disputing the allegations of Origen's official condemnation stands side by side with another phenomenon: while the assertion about Origen being a heretic is not disputed, whenever his name comes up in discussions by scholars who have neither specialised interest in, or consummate knowledge of, his work, their comment made in passing is that almost all of 'orthodox' Christian authors drew on his ideas. This is a tralaticious opinion reproduced anemophilously, although what the *particular* dues to Origen have been remains in the dark, and hardly are specific instances adduced in order to demonstrate *who* and *how* and *in what extent* they embraced or borrowed from or swept up or seized upon, or indeed appropriated Alexandrian's work. But as it happens with the great yet tragic figures of all History, and no matter whether deservedly or not, the bigger they come, the harder they fall.

Nevertheless, this is a correct remark and represents what the state of affairs concerning this tragic figure has always been: he is both generally damned as a 'heretic' and generally praised as a source of inspiration. More specifically, once Justinian decided that Origen should be anathematised (although the alleged 'Origenism' of the sixth century had too little to do with Origen's real ideas),[22] his denunciation became part of the politically correct conduct, even by authors who reproduced Origen's ideas and analyses – actually they stigmatised his name mostly unconsciously, while at the same time they drew on authors such as the Cappadocians who had embraced and reproduced important facets of Origen's ideas and locution. In reality, Justinian had signed a document against Origen that had been prepared at the Laura of Sabas by abbot Gelasius and his band at the behest of Peter, Patriarch of Jerusalem.[23] His signature made this deplorable obloquy an edict, and then a synodical decision by obliging prelates. Justinian of course had no idea of what this all was about: he was not a theologian (as many moderns cheerfully style him); at best,

---

20 Cf. Plato's *Gorgias*, 454e: Ἀλλὰ μὴν οἵ τέ γε μεμαθηκότες πεπεισμένοι εἰσὶν καὶ οἱ πεπιστευκότες.

21 Eusebius, *Contra Marcellum*, 1.4.26-27: ποία γὰρ πρὸς ταῦτα κοινωνία γένοιτ᾽ ἄν ποτε Πλάτωνι; οὐδὲν Πλάτωνος *Περὶ Ἀρχῶν* μνημονεύεται βιβλίον, οὐδὲ Ὠριγένης ὁμοίως περὶ ἀρχῶν ἐδόξασεν Πλάτωνι.

22 *RCR*, 'The sixth-Century Origenism', pp. 259-321.

23 See *RCR*, pp. 78; 258-259; 267; 271; 280; 323. *NDGF*, pp. 7; 407.

he was as much of a theologian as Joseph II, the Holy Roman Emperor and Mozarts' patron, was a musician.

Origen's Commentary on Matthew

At Tyre,[24] Origen wrote the commentary on Matthew comprising twenty-five books[25] during the very last period of his life, when he was stripped not just of the recognition of the ecclesiastical establishment, but also of his illusions concerning the real quality of the prelates of that city, whom he criticised severely in this work of his. Once again, we are reminded that what drives the most sublime meditation is contempt for ingratiation. At the same time, it is this masterpiece that teaches us that the very greatest philosophy is not limited by time or place or the taste of the powerful of the day.

Of this commentary, there are eight books (10-17) extant in Greek commenting on Matthew 13:36-22:33, plus a larger portion in an ancient Latin translation (by an unknown translator, perhaps, late fifth or early sixth century), traditionally called *Commentariorum Series*, which begins with book 12.9, covering Matthew 16:13-27:63. This overlaps only a part of the preserved Greek text, but as it develops (Matthew 22:24-27:66), there is no way to tell how it tallies with the original Greek volume structure; actually, this has no corresponding Greek original. A comparative assessment of this *Series* indicates that the translator used portions from Origen's commentary 12.9, and although it carries well through Matthew's gospel (Matthew 27:66; scriptural quotations being followed by comments), this does not reach Origen's comments on the end of it, namely, on Matthew 28. *Codex Sabaiticus 232* is the only manuscript known to me which contains text from the very end of Origen's commentary on Matthew (commenting on Matthew 28:20, 'and, lo, I am with you ...'). This text has no parallel and has been heretofore unknown. This alone could suffice for engaging in a critical publication of this codex, but there are more reasons to it, which I discuss below.

The text of Migne's *Patrologia Graeca* (volume 13) is a re-edited publication of that by the Maurist Charles De La Rue and his nephew Vincent De La Rue (eighteenth century; commentary on Matthew in 1759), which subsequently was printed by Klostermann.[26] Modern publication of what is extant from this commentary in both Greek and Latin owes much to German scholarship: there

24 Epiphanius of Salamis, *Panarion*, v. 2, p. 406.

25 Eusebius, *HE*, 6.36.2.19. Jerome, *Epistulae*, 33.4. Nicephorus Callistus Xanthopulus, who largely copied from Eusebius, wrote that Origen's commentary comprised 'five books'. *HE*, 5.19. This is a mistake, probably a scribal one.

26 GCS 41.1, *Origenes Werke* X, 1935.

are four volumes in the *GCS* series.[27] The edition of Lommatzsch[28] was mainly used by the series of *Ante Nicene Fathers.*

It is believed that the Greek text of books 10-17 has survived complete. The main codices that preserve the text are, (1) Codex Monacensis gr. 191, bombycin, thirteenth century (containing also the *Commentary on John*). (2) Codex Venice, Marcianus, 43 (1374), which was copied from Codex Monacensis (and contains some folia that have otherwise perished). (3) Cambridge, Trinity College, 194-B-8-10 (known also as Codex Holmiensis, used for the *editio princeps* of 1668), paper, fourteenth century.

The Latin *Commentariorum Series* is arranged into 145 chapters and has been reproduced in the form of two sections: the first one, which follows the Greek text (on Matthew 16:13-22:33) is known as the *Vetus Interpretatio;* the other (to which there is no corresponding Greek original) is commentary on Matthew 22:24-27:66. In short, whether in Greek or Latin, Origen's commentary on Matthew is extant in so far as his text refers to Matthew 13:36-27:66.

Did this happen because of the size of the commentary or of its content? The normal explanation opts for its size. However, were it for that to be so, why was the *Contra Celsum* preserved in impeccable form notwithstanding its size? My own surmise is that certain dark aspects of human nature that bluntly were expressed after Jerome's shift of attitude towards Origen should be taken into account.

Concerning modern times, the story of translation of the commentary on Matthew is weird on the face of it, but decipherable and revealing nonetheless.

We owe a complete German one of the extant commentary on Matthew to H.J. Vogt.[29] The English translation in the series of *Ante Nicene Fathers* (1885) was largely based on De La Rue's edition and contains only fragments from Books 1, 2, and 10-14. Books 15-17 are absent. The translator John Patrick wrote a short introduction, which suggests that he knew of Books 15-17, but he opted

27 Ernst Benz – Erich Klostermann (eds.), *Origenes Matthäuserklärung*, Leipzig, 1937. GCS 40: *Origenes Werke X, Commentarius in Matthaeum I* (Greek text of books 10-17). GCS 38: *Origenes Werke XI, Commentarius in Matthaeum II* (Latin *Commentariorum Series*, a cluster of homilies translated in some way from the commentary, and considerably referring to points of the lost books). GCS 41.1, 41.2: *Origenes Werke XII, Commentarius in Matthaeum III* (quotations from other Christians works, as well as fragments from catenae).

28 *Origenis Opera Omnia*, Berlin 1831-1848.

29 H.J. Vogt: *Origenes: Der Kommentar zum Evangelium nach Mattäus. Eingeleitet, übersetzt und mit Anmerkungen versehen.* Stuttgart, 1983-1993; Erster Teil: Buch X – XIII *Bibliothek der griechischen Literatur*, v. 18, Abt. Patristik), 1983. Zweiter Teil: Buch XIV – XVII (*Bibliothek der griechischen Literatur*, v. 30, Abt. Patristik), 1990. Dritter Teil: *Die Commentariorum Series* (*Bibliothek der griechischen Literatur*. v. 38, Abt. Patristik), 1993.

for not translating them, and so he did with some Latin portions. In 1970, the *Sources Chretiennes* series published a French translation of books 10-11 by Robert Girod, but translation of Books 12-17 never appeared in this series. Presumably, it was deemed that this part of Origen's work should not be rendered in French, as indeed it never was.

It appears then that there has been a characteristic aversion to presenting Origen's Books 15-17 in either English[30] or French translation, and no reason has ever been given for this exclusion. Why is that so? Is this mere coincidence? My opinion is that this is hardly so.

1. In this (very mature) part of his work, Origen expounds his most vigorous attack on the theory of transmigration of souls. This he did throughout his entire work anyway,[31] but now he engages in a more detailed and robust *philosophical* argument in order to make this point. At the same time, in this part (Books 15-17) he also explains the parable of 'labourers' (hired workers, of Matthew 20:1-16), which to those who lacked the background would have appeared as suggesting transmigration or at least pre-existence *of souls* (§27). However, were that so, Origen could be but a schizophrenic who expounded diametrical views in the same part of his commentary, in which he engaged in extensive analyses rebutting (actually, rebuking) the 'folly of transmigration'.[32] In any event, comprehension of his analysis of the parable of 'labourers' presupposes grasp of his theory of soul as a whole (that 'was more sublime that Plato's one'),[33] which heretofore unfortunately has not happened.[34] It was probably because this was beyond the ken of his translators that they opted for thwarting rendering of this part of Origen's in modern languages – which appears as a combination of sanctimony, philosophical ignorance, and bigotrous fearfulness supposedly aiming at 'sparing Origen's heretical views' from being communicated to modern audience.

Moreover, commenting on the three kinds of eunuchs, he began his exegesis with criticising himself for having committed self-castration. On this, my only

30 At the time when these lines were written, an English translation R. Heine was announced: *The Commentary of Origen on the Gospel of St Matthew*, 2 vols. Oxford, 2018. I have not read this yet, but in view of this translator's 'introductions' to earlier translations of Origen's works, in which he virtually embraced all ancient obloquy about 'the Platonist Origen', I am hardly optimistic about this work.

31 See pp. LXXXII-XCII; CLIX; 488, endnote mli.

32 Origen, *commMatt*, 10.20: τὴν μετενσωματώσεως ψευδοδοξίαν. Cf. *op. cit.* 13.1-2.

33 Origen, *Cels*, IV.17: οὐ κατὰ τὴν Πλάτωνος μετενσωμάτωσιν ἀλλὰ κατ᾽ ἄλλην τινὰ ὑψηλοτέραν θεωρίαν.

34 I have discussed Origen' theory of soul in my *Anaxagoras*, vol. 2, chapter 13, pp. 1178-1462. This chapter alone is as long as a book, but it had to be there, so that arguments should be supported by those in the preceding chapters.

remark is that it would take staggering ignorance in order not to realise that which is blindingly obvious, namely, that we are upon a mature intellectual, who, now well on in age, declares that 'when he was young' he committed this 'unwise' act because he was a zealot, and partially (but determinately) was influenced by specific propositions of two of his favourite intellectuals, namely Sextus and Philo. In other words, this is about personal and *auto-biographical* remarks made by the contrite-hearted aged Origen.[35]

Besides, commenting on Jesus' teaching in relation to the little children brought to him,[36] his criticism is directed on those who despised those who were 'little children', referring either to those heathen who had joined the faith when they were already adult (as it happened with Origen himself) or those who are considered advanced in knowledge of the profound truths of the Gospel.[37]

Furthermore, he criticises copies of the gospel of Matthew that are 'incompatible with each other' (μὴ συνᾴδειν ἀλλήλοις), 'either because of scribes's sluggishness or evil-minded boldness or neglect concerning editing of the text or interpolation of personal views which led to either adding text to the gospel or omitting parts of it.' This was one of the reasons for him to engage in textual criticism and composition of the *Hexapla*, in order to 'cure' (ἰάσαθαι) such detriment to Matthew's text.[38] Nevertheless, earlier, in the reply to Celsus, Origen had written that he did 'not know of people who tampered with the gospel other than the Marcionites and Valentinians, perhaps also the folowers of Lucan (οἱ ἀπὸ Λουκάνου)'.[39] At that point, however, he meant to rebut Celsus' claim that he knew of 'some believers, who engaged in altering the original text of the Gospel three and four and several times over, and they rephrased it so as to enable themselves to contradict criticism'. Now, in the later commentary on Matthew, Origen admits that the text of the gospel had indeed been tampered with for the sundry reasons that he mentions.

---

35 Origen, *commMatt*, 15.1-5 (on Matt 19.12).

36 Origen, *op. cit.* 15.6-9. Cf. Matt. 18:2-10.

37 Origen, *op. cit.* 15.6, to which he returns with more explicit remarks in 15.26.

38 Origen, *op. cit.* 15.14.

39 *Cels*, II.27. Whether this 'Lucan' had anything to do with the pupil of Marcion and teacher of the Marcionite church is not certain. Hippolytus mentioned such a pupil by the name 'Lucian', not 'Lucan'. *Refutatio Omnium Haeresium*, 7 (table of contents) and 7.37.2 (H. Chadwick's reference to this being a reference to 'Lucan' is wrong, since Hippolytus wrote 'Lucian'. See Chadwick's translation of *Contra Celsum*, p. 91, note 1; as for the reference to Hippolytus *op. cit.* 'vii.11', this is simply a nonexistent *locus*). Otherwise, one is dependent on Tertullian's reference to a certain 'Lucan' having been a pupil of Marcion (*De Resurrectione Carnis*, 2; also Pseudo-Tertullian, *Adversus Haereses*, 6.3).

It is in this part of his commentary that he explains his theory of Restoration, although he warns that this doctrine just like that of Creation is 'a great mystery' (τὸ περὶ τῆς γενέσεως μυστήριον).[40]

He also refers to other 'ineffable mysteries',[41] such as the primeval Fall,[42] his notion of recurrent worlds (which was sheer different from the Stoic one),[43] his explanation of allegorical method,[44] his notion of *kairos*,[45] his Eschatology,[46] and his relentless attacks on debauched bishops,[47] which involves autobiographical allusions, but I postpone discussion of these until publication of Origen's biography.

Copying from Origen while Forgetting his Name: a Prefatory Annotation

In *Codex Sabaiticus 232*, there are several continuous extensive texts by Origen, most of which are heretofore unknown. However, portions of some of them have been ascribed to other authors or to no author at all (as it happens with the entire Catena on Mark), but in terms of methodology two points resolve

40 Origen, *commMatt*, 15.23; 16.6.

41 Origen, *op. cit.* 11.7: Τάχα δὲ καὶ δηλοῦταί τι ἀπόρρητον καὶ κεκρυμμένον μυστήριον. Cf. *Princ*, IV.2.3 (*Philocalia*, 1.10): τὴν ἐπίκρυψιν τῶν ἀπορρήτων μυστηρίων … βίβλους περιεχούσας τὰ ἀπόρρητα τῆς γνώσεως καὶ παντελῆ μυστήρια. *Op. cit.* IV.2.7 (*Philocalia*, 1.14): περὶ τῶν ἀπορρήτων μυστηρίων. *commJohn*, VI.4.24: Χριστοῦ … διδάξαντος τὰ ἀπόρρητα τῆς θεοσεβείας μυστήρια … τὰ περὶ τοῦ θεοῦ μυστήρια καὶ ἄρρητα δόγματα. *Fragmenta in Librum Primum Regnorum*, fr. 20: καὶ εὕρῃ *πρὸς κεφαλῆς* ἀπόρρητα μυστήρια. *Dial*, 28: τὰ ἀπόρρητα μυστήρια. *homJer*, homily 18.5: τοῖς δυναμένοις ἀκούειν ἀπορρήτων μυστηρίων. *fr1Cor*, fr. 49: ἐν μέρει γὰρ τῆς γνώσεως ἡ τῶν μυστηρίων ἐστὶν ἐπιστήμη. τὸ δὲ περὶ τῶν ἀπορρητοτέρων καὶ θειοτέρων εἰδέναι τοῦτ' εἶναι τὸ *μυστήριον* γινώσκειν, ὡς εἶναι γενικὸν μὲν λόγον τῆς γνώσεως οὐκέτι δὲ πάσης τῆς γνώσεως εἶναι τὴν κατάληψιν μυστηρίων. *commEph*, fr. 5: τὸ τῶν μυστηρίων ὄνομα ἐπὶ τῶν θείων καὶ ἀπορρήτων καὶ μὴ ἐπιτηδείων φθάνειν εἰς πολλοὺς παραλαμβάνεται. *frPs*, on Psalm 4:4: θαύμασι προσαχθέντες τῶν ἀποῤῥήτων μυστηρίων καὶ τῶν ἁγίων θεωρημάτων. *Op. cit.* on Psalm 22:5 & *selPs*, PG.12.1261.36-37: Ἔχει τι μυστήριον ἀπόῤῥητον, ἵνα τις εὔχηται θλίβεσθαι. *selPs*, PG.12.1185.50-52: Κρύφιά ἐστι γνῶσις ἀπόῤῥητος τῶν περὶ Χριστοῦ τοῦ ἀληθινοῦ Θεοῦ μυστηρίων. *homJob*, PG.17.89.56-92.1: ὑπεραπόῤῥητα τὰ ἔνδον μυστήρια τὰ ἅγια τοῦ Θεοῦ. *Scholia in Canticum Canticorum*, PG.17.268.54-56: Περὶ τῶν πρὸ τοῦ γάμου μυστηρίων … ἀποῤῥητοτέρων ἐθέλων κοινωνεῖν.

42 Origen, *commMatt*, 15.27; 17.2. He repeats that explicating this doctrine is a 'dangerous' thing to do (παρακεκινδυνευκέναι): *commMatt*, 17.30 (comm. on Gen. 6:2) σαφῶς δὲ τὰ κατὰ τὸν τόπον ἐπαπορῆσαι καὶ τὴν ἀκολουθίαν αὐτῶν ἐπισκοπῆσαι καὶ χάρτῃ πιστεῦσαι τὴν τῶν τηλικούτων σαφήνειαν, μήποτε οὐκ ἀσφαλὲς ᾖ. ἀρκεῖ γὰρ καὶ ἐπὶ τοῖς εἰρημένοις ἡμᾶς ἐπὶ τοσοῦτον παρακεκινδυνευκέναι.

43 Origen, *op. cit.* 15.31.

44 Origen, *op. cit.* 15.4; 15.15; 15.17-21; 15.25; 16.20; 17.22; 17.27-28; 17.34-35.

45 Origen, *op. cit.* 15.34-36; 16.29; 17.6-9. See discussion of this in *PHE*, pp. 134-141.

46 Origen, *op. cit.* 16.1-5; 17.14-19; 17.29-30; 17.33-35.

47 Origen, *op. cit.* 16.8; 16.22; 16.25.

the case in point easily: (1) along with the present codex-text, Klostermann's fragments from Origen's commentary on Matthew confirm his authorship of many of them; (2) unlike spurious parallel attributions to other authors, now we have a largely continuous text, of which several of Klostermann's fragments are merely excerpts and their context abundantly illuminates Origen's train of argument.

I have included a few 'unattributed' passages from the first folios of the codex, because critical study of them shows that it is impossible to disregard Origen's commanding influence. The Greek text begins with a passage providing a definition of the term 'gospel' (εὐαγγέλιον = εὖ + ἀγγέλειν = 'announcing good news'). Klostermann tagged this 'fragment 1', but this is actually from the commentary on John, of which the editor was aware. Nevertheless, Origen could have used this definition also in the commentary on Matthew, since the term εὐαγγέλιον appears in two of the synoptic gospels.[48] I subsumed this text not only because this is a befitting introduction to the commentary, but also in order to show how Cyril of Alexandria and John Chrysostom conveniently copied from Origen (as discussed below), which is an abundantly recurring phenomenon in this volume.

A case in point is the fragments ascribed to Theodore of Heraclea, which turn out to be mere copies from Origen's commentary on Matthew. For instance, on folio 5r, there is an *anepigraphon*, yet J. Reuss came upon another codex ascribing this to Theodore of Heraclea. However, critical consideration of this reveals that this is Origen's, who also expounded the same idea when he wrote his *First Principles*. The context was a series of arguments concerning prophecies about the advent of Christ that were eventually fulfilled.

> Moreover, the place of his birth is foretold by Micah: And you Bethlehem, it says, land of Judah, are in no way least among the rulers of Judah; for out of you shall come a governor, who shall shepherd my people Israel.[49] And the seventy weeks[50] until the coming of Christ the governor were fulfilled in accordance with Daniel's prophecy.[51]

The passage of Daniel was taken as implying that Christ should appear after a period of 'seventy weeks', which was promptly embraced by Origen's student

48 Matthew 4:23; 9:35; 24:14; 26:13; Mark, 1:1; 1:14; 8:35; 10:29; 13:10; 14:9; 16:15. Matthew spoke of 'the evangelium of the kingdom' and Mark of 'the evangelium of God'.

49 Micah, 5:2, quoted in Matthew 2:6.

50 Daniel, 9:24-25.

51 Origen, *Princ*, IV.1.5 (*Philocalia*, 1.5). This appears also in the Latin translation.

Julius Africanus.[52] This would be regarded as extrapolation, given that neither Clement of Alexandria nor Hippolytus advanced such an idea; actually, they treated Daniel's passage differently.[53] However, Theodoret availed himself of this,[54] and the extremely anti-Origenist[55] *Chronicon Paschale* considered Julius Africanus' idea seriously.[56]

The tenor of the passage allegedly written by Theodore of Heraclea in a commentary on Matthew is exactly the same: it considers both prophecies (by Micah and Daniel) as indicating the advent of Christ,[57] while reviling the 'faithlessness' of the Jews who 'refused to believe' that Jesus was the expected 'governor' of the prophecies. In Origen's extant writings, the notion of 'faithlessness of the Jews' (ἀπιστία Ἰουδαίων) appears (for the first time in Christian literature, so far as sources go) in his *Contra Celsum*,[58] which is a late work, yet earlier than the commentary on Matthew.[59] Later, his devotees such as Gregory of Nyssa, Eusebius, Athanasius, Didymus, and others, used this formula, too. Nevertheless, the Greek text of Origen's commentary on Matthew starts with an exegesis of Matthew 13:36. This means that commentary on the passage of Matthew 2:6 quoting Micah, 5.2, in which also Daniel's portion should have been considered (as in *De Principiis*) is not extant. Moreover, since Origen's rather far-fetched exegesis did not win the day, nor did this enjoy any currency by authors who otherwise copied from him abundantly, it would be plausible to assume that the present 'unattributed' passage is Origen's – although in the present edition I maintain the siglum ANE (*anepigraphon*) of the codex. Besides, given that in this manuscript there are numerous attributions to Theodore of Heraclea, it is strange that this specific one remained an orphan as to its authorship. On the other hand, as far as Origen is concerned, this lack of attribution should not be irrelevant to the loss of the first nine books of his commentary on Matthew. Besides, it is all but surprise that the immediately ensuing text on the same folio (5v) continues to be 'unattributed'; however, Klostermann's fragment 24 reveals that not only is this Origen's, but also that Jerome copied from this; actually, he did so at numerous points of his

52 Julius Africanus, *Chronographia*, fr. 50. Then, Eusebius (considering the text of Julius Africanus), *Demonstratio Evangelica*, 8.2.43-50; endorsing the idea, *Eclogae Propheticae*, p. 96.

53 Clement of Alexandria, *Stromateis*, 1.21.12.5. Hippolytus, *Commentarium in Danielem*, 4.30.

54 Theodoret, *Interpretatio in Danielem*, PG.81.1489-1473.

55 Cf. *Chronicon Paschale*, p. 635.

56 *Chronicon Paschale*, p. 307.

57 See Greek text, fr. 4e, pp. 12-13.

58 Origen, *Cels*, I.44; II.8; II.75; II.78-79; cf. *homJer*, homily, 15.5; *frLuc*, fr. 246; *commSerMatt*, p. 54; *commMatt*, 16.23.

59 See *infra*, pp. CLIII-CLXII.

own commentary on Matthew, which he never denied: actually, but took pride at this practice.[60] Likewise, on folio 53r, a felicitous addition on the margin provides an expanded text from Origen's commentary, of which Klostermann's fragment 141 is only a part.

Origen is the sole author who averred that John the Baptist 'is the last of prophets and the beginning of the Gospel'. He did so in the commentary on John, but it now turns out that he wrote this also in his preamble to his commentary on Matthew.[61] This unique exegesis was employed by the compiler of the catena on Mark, but by no other author ever. The catenist provides an interesting little story concerning Mark's biblical quotation upon the beginning of his gospel: in the first place, he endorses Origen's exegesis to the letter ('John is the last of prophets and the beginning of the Gospel'). However, he subsequently mentions Eusebius' point, who argued that Mark's quotation is a saying that belonged not 'to Isaiah', as the evangelist wrote, but to Malachi, which Eusebius pointed out 'in his exegesis addressed to Marinus', and opined that this is a scribal error (γραφέως ἐστὶ σφάλμα).[62]

Nevertheless, Mark's catenist goes on with adducing Origen's analysis made 'in the sixth volume of his commentary on John'. Origen did not consider this prophetic citation as a 'mistake', whether scribal or whatever: he argued that Mark made a combined abridged compilation (ἐπιτεμόμενος) of Isaiah, 40:3 and Malachi, 3:1, thus representing this assemblage as a saying by Isaiah (ἐπιτεμόμενος οὖν ὁ Εὐαγγελιστὴς ὡς ὑπὸ Ἡσαΐου εἰρημένας τὰς δύο χρήσεις παρέθηκεν).[63] In order to bolster his point, he adduces a similar example of such an 'incision' (he uses the term ἐπιτεμόμενος ['one who abridges a text'] and its derivative ἐπιτομή, *epitome*). The catenist copied this section to the letter from Origen's[64] commentary on John, in which he argued that there is nothing wrong with Mark's 'epitomising' and combining different prophetic sayings, and then he adduces similar examples from the gospel of John.

Furthermore, a twofold attribution appears in an illuminating manner: on folios 11v-12r, a passage is ascribed to both Origen and Theodore of Mopsuestia, which is otherwise known as the latter's one,[65] although the ideas and vocabulary of this are the same as the preceding 'unattributed' one, which arguably

---

60 See discussion *infra*, pp. LXXVIII-XCII.

61 Origen, *commJohn*, I.4.22, quoted in endnote viii to the Greek text.

62 In the extant text of Eusebius' treatise this remark does not exist, but see Eusebius, *Supplementa Minora ad Queastiones ad Marinum*, PG.22.1008.37-41 (excerpted from this catena).

63 *Catena in Marcum*, pp. 266-267.

64 Origen, *commJohn*, VI.24.127-131.

65 Theodore of Mopsuestia, *frMatt*, fr. 12 (Reuss).

turns out to be Origen's, and it is written between two passages plainly ascribed to Origen. In this, the analysis about John the Baptist being 'the last of prophets' carries further, and the passage has a unique anonymous parallel in the *Catena in Marcum*. Presumably, the anthologist[66] abode by Cyril's guideline 'not all propositions by heretics should be sidestepped and waived' (οὐ πάντα ὅσα λέγουσιν οἱ αἱρετικοὶ φεύγειν καὶ παραιτεῖσθαι χρή).[67]

This 'unattributed' passage advances the same exegesis about the Baptist: the catenist of the gospel of Mark used it in relation to Mark, 1:6, and the catenist of *Codex Sabaiticus 232* in relation to Matthew 3:4 –both scriptural instances are the same: 'John's food was locusts and wild honey'. The distinctly idiomatic (actually, very uncommon) phraseology makes its mark in both texts, and it is all too evident that they derive from the same original.[68] The composer of the *Catena in Marcum* cites Origen's name[69] and the selfsame text that now occurs in the present codex makes it clear that, in that section, the catenist drew entirely on Origen's work. This would also explain why is it that so many fragments on the commentary of Matthew attributed to Theodore of Mopsuestia in J. Reuss' chain are in fact Origen's, as parallel quotations of them in the present volume demonstrate – but at several points it is only now that we have Origen's extensive context, not simply fragments.

Likewise, in the present *Codex Sabaiticus 232*, there is a text designated 'Unattributed' in which it is explained that 'it took two years for the Magi to reach the new-born Jesus and prostrate themselves before him',[70] which is why Herod 'killed all the male children who were in Bethlehem and in all the surrounding countryside, from two years old and under'.[71] However, this text is

66 The catenist declares in title that his compilation is based on Cyril's commentary on Mark, since no one other than Cyril did ever write a commentary on Mark (*Catena in Marcum*, p. 263).

67 This is from Cyril's *Epistle to Eulogius* (see *Catena in Matthaeum*, p. 4) quoted in ACO, *Concilium universale Ephesenum anno 431*, tome 1.1.4, p. 35, and Justinian, *Contra Monophysitas*, 157. Quoted also by the the sixth-seventh century theologian Pamphilus, *Diversorum Capitum seu Difficultatum Solutio*, Question 12, lines 222-225, and Photius, *Bibliotheca*, Codex 230, p. 270b. Quoted also in the prologue of Origen's *Philocalia* by a later editor of this, who declared himself hostile to Origen's thought.

68 Cf. folio 12r: λόγῳ μετεωροπόρῳ, οὐ βεβηκότι ὑπὲρ τῶν πτερύγων, μέλι ἄγριον ... μὴ γεωργούμενον ... διὰ ... ζητήσεως). *Catena in Marcum* (*recensio ii*), p. 269: Ἡ δὲ τροφὴ αὐτοῦ, ὡς ἡγοῦμαι, σύμβολον ἦν τῆς λογικῆς τοῦ λαοῦ τότε τροφῆς, οὐκ ἐσθίοντός τι τῶν καθαρῶν πετεινῶν τοῦ οὐρανοῦ, τρεφομένου δὲ τῷ μὲν δοκοῦντι λόγῳ μετεωροπόρῳ, ἀλλ᾽ οὐ βεβηκότι ὑπὲρ τῶν πτερύγων.

69 See *Catena in Marcum*, citing Origen's name on p. 266; so it does on pp. 314 & 418.

70 Cf. Matthew 2:11.

71 Matthew 2:16.

attributed to 'Origen and Eusebius' in three codices explored by Klostermann[72] and so it is in the *Catena on Matthew.*[73] I just wonder whether it would be too much of extrapolation to surmise that Eusebius took up a point from his creative flare.

By the same token, Klostermann footnoted a passage to his 'fragment 81' from Codex *Parisinus suppl. gr. 612* (written before the year 1164), in which this passage is 'Unattributed' ('Ανεπίγραφος). However, this is ascribed to Origen in the present *Codex Sabaiticus 232.*[74] What Klostermann did not notice is that Gregory of Nyssa once again copied from Origen while slightly paraphrasing his source.[75] So did Gregory with the text occurring on folio 26r, but only *Sabaiticus 232* attributes this to Origen. What is more, this provides more and hitherto unknown context.[76] The same goes with Origen's text on folia 36v-37r, which Gregory copied to the letter, too.[77] Likewise, Gregory replicated Origen's text on folia 25r-v, which is also Klostermann's fr. 79.[78] I discuss those instances in the pertinent endnotes. More striking still is Origen's continuous text on folia 19v-20r, most of which comes to light for the first time: while we have the entire flowing text, two small portions of this have appeared as allegedly written by the anti-Chalcedonian Severus of Antioch and another one by Gregory of Nyssa, whereas other portions of this are confirmed as Origen's ones by Klostermann's chain. However, now the text is continuous and carries

72 Origen, fr. 23 (Klostermann).

73 Eusebius & Origen, *apud Catena in Matthaeum*, p. 15. Cf. Eusebius, *Ad Stephanum*, PG.22.933.19-36. Epiphanius followed once again. *Panarion*, v. 1, pp. 372-373; v. 2, p. 287. Likewise, John Chrysostom, *In Matthaeum*, PG.57.76.21-34. Michael Glycas, *Annales*, pp. 387-388 (drawing on Chrysostom). Nicephorus Callistus Xanthopulus, *HE*, 1.13. So Theodore of Heraclea or Theodore of Mopsuestia, *Fragmenta in Matthaeum*, fr. 8 (Reuss).

74 See folio 26v (p. 51): Ἢ ἐπειδὴ πλεονάζει κατὰ τὴν φύσιν ἡ πρὸς τὰ κακὰ ταχυτής, καλῶς τὸ ἐν τοῖς τοιούτοις ἠρεμοῦν μακάριον.

75 Gregory of Nyssa, *Orationes viii De Beatitudinibus*, PG.44.1213.41-43: Οὐκοῦν ἐπειδὴ πλεονάζει κατὰ τὴν φύσιν ἡμῶν ἡ πρὸς τὰ κακὰ ταχύτης, καλῶς τὸ ἐν τοῖς τοιούτοις ἠρεμοῦν μακαρίζεται.

76 The text on folios 25v-26r reads thus: Ὅ τε γὰρ διάβολος, οὐκ ὢν πρὸ τούτου τοιοῦτος, οὕτω διάβολος γέγονεν, ὅτε πρῶτος ἄνθρωπος, ἰσοθεΐαν φαντασθεὶς καὶ τοιαύταις ἐλπίσι παρὰ τοῦ διαβόλου φυσηθείς, ἐξετραχηλίσθη [Cf. Job, 15:25]. Then (also attributed to Origen): καὶ ἐπεὶ ἐμπέφυκέ πως τὸ κατὰ τὴν ἔπαρσιν πάθος παντὶ ἀνθρώπῳ, which Gregory of Nyssa copied to the letter. *Orationes viii De Beatitudinibus*, PG.44.1201.12-14. In his ensuing text, Gregory kept on copying from Origen. See the whole of passage in PG.44.1201.1-21. The text of *Sabaiticus 232* (also 'by Origen') goes on thus: Ἢ καὶ οὕτως. ὁ πάντων τῶν κατὰ κακίαν νοουμένων ἑκουσίως πτωχεύων, εἴη ἂν οὗτος ἐν τῇ τῶν μακαριζομένων πτωχείᾳ, which comes to light for the first time.

77 See Gregory of Nyssa, *op. cit.* PG.44.1216.21-30 and Gregory of Nyssa, *apud Catena in Matthaeum*, pp. 37-38.

78 Gregory of Nyssa, *op. cit.* PG.44.1196.9-17.

through folio 27r, most of which is original and appears nowhere else than *Sabaiticus* 232.

Consequently, I have included some of the 'unattributed' passages of this codex because the compelling evidence that those were written by Origen could not be overlooked. Nevertheless, I maintain the codex's tag 'unattributed' and leave it for readers to assess their authorship taking into account my critical remarks and the adduced parallel passages, and feeling free to either endorse or dismiss them.

On folios 7r-v, the text, Ἀλλόκοτος ὁ Ἡρώδης ... Ἡρώδης ἦρξε τοῦ Ἰουδαίων ἔθνους, is attributed to Theodore of Heraclea.[79] However, the present codex attributes to Theodore only *part* of this (Ἀλλόκοτος ὁ Ἡρώδης ... ἐπιβουλεῦσαι τῷ βρέφει;). Now we have (heretofore unknown) more of text beyond Reuss' one, and the present codex *ipso facto* disputes attribution of all of Reuss' text to Theodore. However, the text that Reuss ascribed to Theodore of Heraclea is Origen's, since the latter's seal is incontrovertibly therein, which of course calls for argument. The critical point is Origen's consideration of 'Jacob's prophecy' (Gen. 49:1-30), particularly its apostrophe, *A ruler shall not fail from Judah, nor a prince from his loins, until there come the things stored up for him; and he is the expectation of nations.*[80]

Origen remarked that, on the face of it, this portion runs contrary to Hosea's saying, *For the children of Israel shall abide many days without a king, and without a prince, and without a sacrifice, and without an altar, and without a priesthood, and without oracles.*[81] Being a Greek philosopher of exquisitely consistent logic, Origen recognised that those apparently conflicting passages could disconcert and 'baffle' readers of the Bible (literally: 'cause distress' to them, τοὺς ἐν τῷ θλίβεσθαι).[82] The idea he advanced in *De Principiis* was that the Jewish expectation of an 'ethnarch' (ἐθνάρχην)[83] was realised through Christ's advent, yet in a way far different from that which those people visualised. Justin had already explained Jacob's words in Gen 49:10 as pointing to the advent of Jesus Christ.[84] All those who cared for explaining this specific dictum / prophecy wrote much later, and they all sided with Justin's and Origen's exegesis.[85]

79 Theodore of Heraclea, *frMatt*, fr. 9.

80 Gen. 49:10: οὐκ ἐκλείψει ἄρχων ἐξ Ἰούδα καὶ ἡγούμενος ἐκ τῶν μηρῶν αὐτοῦ, ἕως ἂν ἔλθῃ τὰ ἀποκείμενα αὐτῷ, καὶ αὐτὸς προσδοκία ἐθνῶν.

81 Hosea, 3:4.

82 *Princ*, IV.1.3 & *Philocalia*, 1.3.

83 Origen, *loc. cit.*

84 Justin Martyr, *Apologia*, 31.1-3; *Dialogus cum Tryphone*, 52.

85 Anonymous, *Dialogus cum Judaeis*, chapter 12. Anonymous, *Papisci et Philonis Iudaeorum cum Monacho Colloquium*, p. 58. Pseudo-Anastasius of Sinai, *Disputatio adversus*

However, in the immediately preceding paragraph, Origen's argument is that Hosea's prophecy was fulfilled when Jerusalem was destroyed in AD 70. Cyril of Alexandria explained Hosea's passage as generally pointing to the predicament of the Jews from the first century AD onwards.[86] On the other hand, Theodore of Mopsuestia resolved that Hosea's saying pointed to the Jews' captivity at Babylon.[87] Nevertheless, at the same point of *De Principiis*, Origen quotes the prophecy of Gen. 49:10 once again, but now he associates its fulfillment with the advent of Christ.[88] It is evident that he regards the particle ἕως (= until, till) of Gen. 49:10 as having a different meaning from the ἕως in Matthew 16:28; Mark, 9:1; Luke, 9:27, as well as in Matthew 20:20. In the former case, ἕως means 'until such a time as' (Christ appears); in the latter, it suggests infinite and endless time.[89]

In any event, Origen was the first and sole writer who reformulated the phrase of Gen. 49:10: instead of the scriptural Future tense's *affirmation* (οὐκ ἐκλείψει ἄρχων ἐξ Ἰούδα), he argued that this Aorist bespeaks *negation* (ἐξέλιπεν ἄρχων ἐξ Ἰούδα) in order to signify the realisation of this prophecy upon and after the advent of Jesus Christ.[90] No other author did ever reformulate this prophetic announcement of Gen. 49:10 in order to declare that this has been fulfilled.

Bearing this in mind, now we are upon Origen's *unique* meaningful formulation in a passage allegedly by Theodore of Heraclea (*frMatt*, fr. 9) making

---

Judaeos, p. 1220. George Syncellus, *Ecloga Chronographica*, p. 362. Neophytus Inclusus, *Commentarius in Hexaemeron Genesim*, chapter 16. Nicolas Hydruntinus, *Disputatio contra Judaeos*, p. 201. Gennadius Scholarius, *De Prophetiis Principalibus Jesu Christi*, p. 305.

86 Cyril of Alexandria, *commProphXII*, v. 1, pp. 87; 97; 310; v. 2, p. 563; *Epistulae Paschales*, PG.77: 468; 872; *De Adoratione*, PG.68.74; *Glaphyra in Pentateuchum*, PG.69.576; *In Isaiam*, PG.70, pp. 29; 1140.

87 Theodore of Mopsuestia, *commProphXII* (on prophet Hosea, 3:4); (on prophet Amos 8:4-6); (on prophet Zachariah, 2:13).

88 *Princ*, IV.1.3 (& *Philocalia*, 1.3): σαφῶς γὰρ ἐκ τῆς ἱστορίας δῆλον … ἐπληρώθη γὰρ ἡ λέγουσα προφητεία (then, he quotes Hosea 3:4). Likewise, *commJohn*, I.23.143; XIII.26.154; *selPs*, PG.12.1496.3-9; *homPs*, homily 26.5; *frLam*, fr. 42; *Cels*, I.53; *commMatt*, 10.21.

89 Cf. Origen, *schLuc*, PG.17.341.25-29, commenting on the particle ἕως (= until, till) as in Matthew 16:28; Mark, 9:1; Luke, 9:27 in apposition with Matthew 20:20. See Origen's passages considering the particle ἕως at the end of the present Greek text (folio 240v).

90 *Princ*, IV.1.3 (& *Philocalia*, 1.3); *frLam*, fr. 42. Likewise, Origen, *apud Catena in Lucam* (Cramer), p. 28 (I have corrected some diacritics): ἐν τοῖς τῆς ἐνανθρωπήσεως χρόνοις τοῦ Κυρίου ἡμῶν καὶ Θεοῦ Ἰησοῦ Χριστοῦ, ἐκλελοίπει καθόλου ἄρχων καὶ ἡγούμενος ἐξ Ἰουδαίων. ἀλλόφυλοι δὲ ἦρχον, Ῥωμαίων μέν, οἱ δὲ λοιποὶ Ἡρώδου υἱοί, Ἀσκαλωνίτης τὸ γένος, *ἦλθε γὰρ ᾧτινι τὸ ἄρχειν ἀπόκειται*, τουτέστι Χριστῷ τῷ Θεῷ ἡμῶν. Ἐξέλιπον δὲ οἱ Ἰουδαίων ἄρχοντες κατὰ τοὺς λόγους Ἰακὼβ τοῦ πατριάρχου. τούτου χάριν τοῦτο γέγονε. The information that Herod was from Ascalon originates in Justin Martyr, *Dialogus cum Tryphone*, 52.3; then, Origen's pupil Julius Africanus, *Chronographia*, fr. 48; *Epistula ad Aristidem*, p. 60.

the same point, of which though the last four-line portion is *not* ascribed to Theodore in the present *Codex Sabaiticus 232*. I am not surprised in the least: for the entire fragment is now arguably shown to be Origen's, and similar cases are so many that I have come to doubt if a single fragment of Reuss' collection supposedly written by Theodore of Heraclea was indeed written by that author. For in the present critical edition every now and then it turns out that one after another of Theodore's alleged 'fragments' coincide with sections from Origen's published work, not to mention that this anti-Nicene champion and personal opponent of Athanasius on that score has been attributed impeccable Nicene formulations in Reuss' compilation – which of course is absurd and uncritical. This is why I shun the idolised 'international standards' of presenting ancient manuscripts, by which moden egomaniac mediocre 'powerful' editors mean, 'no matter how implausible the attribution, just present the text! -and leave all critical considerations of this aside'.

Folios 16v-26r contain an unbroken text by Origen, which is a uniquely valuable confirmation of Klostermann's fragments attesting to Origen's Trinitarian theology being unerringly Nicene, which after all confirms Athanasius' testimony, but in fact these are inexorable corollaries of Origen's Anaxagorean inspiration, as I have argued. However, the evidence that we have now is no longer a 'fragment': it is an ample text from the commentary on Matthew, which (1) reveals the wider context of Klostermann's very short fragments; (2) shows that the specific portions from theologians such as Gregory of Nyssa, Theodore of Heraclea, Theodore of Mopsuestia, Cyril of Alexandria, and Severian of Gabala, were copied from Origen.

From folio 26r to 31v, there is a text attributed to the anti-Chalcedonian Severus of Antioch. However, every now and then this passage contains portions that are Origen's known ones, especially from Klostermann's collection of fragments on Matthew. Therefore, I have included this section of the codex, of course maintaining attribution to Severus of Antioch, as in the codex. Nevertheless, all too often does critical assessment of this point to Origen, although several portions of that have been published by J. Reuss as fragments of Apollinaris.[91]

Moreover, numerous segments of these sections are Chrysostom's known ones, which I have quoted in apposition and have left for readers to make up their own mind. In my view, the common source of all this is Origen's commentary

91 See Bibliography. Apollinaris was bishop of Laodicea and teacher of Jerome during his stay in Antioch in 378 (*Epistulae*, 84.3). He taught that the human and divine natures of Christ were fused into one, for which the Council of Ephesus condemned him in 431, and that of Chalcedon in 451.

on Matthew, on which all of the foregoing authors drew, no matter whether the catenist either emended the text or drew on Origen's one. This means nothing really important: for example, I have shown how Origen formed his theory of Time[92]: from the Stoics he took up the *natural* concept of time as 'extension' (διάστημα); from Alexander of Aphrodisias he employed the *existential* adumbration of this as 'co-extended alongside with' (συμπαρεκτεινόμενος);[93] and he himself composed a *theological* theory instituting Time as teleological, and seeing History as the dramatic milieu in which divine and creaturely free will ceaselessly interact with each other. The Cappadocians took up this theory to the letter, but later lexica copied from Nazianzen's slightly and insignificantly different phrasing.

In any case, identical passages of a text ostensibly written by Severus appear also in authors earlier to him, but comparative study of Severus' alleged text has turned out to be a compilation of statements by authors earlier to Severus himself, and these happen to be authors who took their cue and inspiration from Origen. In this category (passages attributed to Severus in the present codex) fall fourteen fragments from Klostermann's chain quoted to the letter,[94] three from Origen's commentary on John, three from his commentary on Matthew; then, four excerpts from Gregory of Nyssa's homilies on the Blessings of Jesus, in which Gregory abundantly availed himself of Origen, as discussed in detail; six passages from John Chrysostom's sermons on Matthew; four from Cyril of Alexandria's commentary on Matthew; one passage of Didymus following Origen suit; six fragments currently attributed to Apollinaris (there are plenty of those fragments coinciding with Origen's passages, as shown in due course) and two fragments attributed to Theodore of Heraclea from his commentary on Matthew, but following textual evidence I have argued throughout this volume that I could hardly bet that even a single alleged passage of Theodore's in Reuss' chain is not in fact Origen's.[95] Finally, there is also a passage from

92 See *COT*, pp. 218; 262-265; 309; *Anaxagoras*, pp. 299.

93 Alexander of Aphrodisias, *commMetaph*, p. 699; cf. *op. cit.* pp. 449; 818; *commTop*, p. 80; *commMeteor*, p. 78. Cf. Galen, *De Anatomicis Administrationibus*, p. 370; *De Ossibus ad Tirones*, p. 777; *Venarum Arteriarumque Dissectione*, p. 823; *De Usu Partium*, v. 3, p. 710; v. 4, pp. 59; 202; *De Difficultate Respirationis*, p. 915; *De Locis Affectis*, p. 323. Pseudo-Galen, *Introductio*, p. 716. Cf. *COT*, pp. 210-218; 262–265; 308 *Anaxagoras*, pp. 229; 992.

94 Origen, *frMatt* (Klostermann), frs. 81; 82; 83; 85; 86; 87; 88; 91; 92; 93; 94; 95 I; 95 II; 96.

95 Nevertheless, Jerome declared that he wrote his own commentary on Matthew after having read the commentaries of some authors including Theodore (Prologue, 4). The others were Theophilus of Antioch, Hippolytus, Apollinaris of Laodicea, Didymus of Alexandria, Hilary, Victorinus, and Fortunatianus. However, critical study of Jerome's commentary suggests that in reality first and foremost he drew on Origen, which is also the case with his commentary on the Ephesians. In both commentaries he was all but coy to present

Clement of Alexandria's *Stromateis*, which Origen could well have availed himself of.

Therefore, the question is, what remains out of the supposed attribution to Severus in those folios? My simple reply would be 'nothing'.

Likewise, on folio 35v, we have an extensive text by Origen; a small part of this is confirmed as Origen's, in Klostermann's fr. 102II from the commentary on Matthew. The editor notes that in other codices he came upon this being tagged either 'unattributed' or 'by Severus'. However, the context makes Origen's seal upon it clear once the notion of παροδεύειν τὸν βίον (meaning, 'living this life as a temporary state' in view of the eternal one) is persused: this formula was introduced by Origen and then taken up by his devotees, as well as by some of his detractors.[96] The same goes for a few lines of another extensive text of Origen's on folio 41r: those few lines were attributed to Severus in the *Catena on Matthew*, but now we are upon additional text providing a wider context, in which Origen develops his argument fully.

At several points, we come along portions of the present codex having been attributed to Theodore of Heraclea in J. Reuss' edition, although in this manuscript they are ascribed to Origen. However, now we have a much wider context available containing fuller development of an argument, whereas Reuss' text gives us only partial phrases that are simply tiny portions out of context.

Besides, there is only one fragment commenting on the gospel of Matthew which is attributed to Origen's pupil Gregory Thaumaturgus, but its (definitely, plausible) ascription to Origen in the present codex (folio 45v) sets things in order,[97] since this portion now appears as only a few phrases that are part of an extensive analysis by Origen, which comes to light for the first time.

Multiple Attributions

It goes without saying that, in collections of 'fragments', attribution of a certain passage to more than one author is not uncommon.[98] For example, a text commenting of the Epistle to the Hebrews is attributed to Athanasius in a

Origen's ideas and propositions as ones of his own. Whenever he appears to expound more than one view allegedly by different authors, catena-fragments reveal that in fact he repeated different interpretations by Origen. See H. Bammel, "Die Pauluskommentare des Hieronymus: Die ersten wissenchaftlichen lateinnischen Bibelkommentare?", in *Christianesimo Latino e cultura Greca sino al sec. IV*, Studia Ephemeridis 'Augustinianum', 42, Rome, 1993, pp. 187-207, esp. pp. 197-198 & 205-206.

96 See text, p. 68, and endnotes ccclix; ccclxvi.

97 Cf. Gregory Thaumaturgus, *Fragmentum in Evangelium Matthaei 6.22-23*, PG.10.1189.25-41.

98 For example, the passage attributed to Diodore of Tarsus in K. Staab's *Fragmenta in Epistulam ad Romanos*, p. 92 (commenting on Rom. 8:11) is the selfsame one ascribed to 'Theodore' (of Mopsuestia?) in J.A. Cramer's *Catena in Epistulam ad Romanos*, p. 129.

catena,[99] even though this is found in an epistle allegedly written by Basil,[100] whereas a later monk of Constantinople preferred to present this as one of his own.[101] Therefore, I am all but suggesting that passages by authors found here and there should be used uncritically – far for the contrary. For otherwise one should allow oneself to be 'informed' by authors such as Anastasius of Sinai, who cheerfully reported that 'Origen postulated that Christ was but a bare man' (!),[102] or by the chronographer who 'advised' that 'a certain Father revealed that Clement of Alexandria was an Origenist',[103] although the same author had no problem with writing that 'Origen was a student of Clement'.[104]

Nevertheless, part of the value of the present codex lies in this: portions that in various collections have been published as mere 'fragments', now emerge as parts of an ample *continuous* text, which allows for their context to be perused and the points made to be considered arguably.

In the chains of fragments, the phenomenon of joint attributions to more than one author is usual;[105] hence, the next question is, what should scholar-

99 *Catena in Epistulam ad Hebraeos* (Cramer), p. 343: ἤδη ποτὲ τοῦ ἐν τῇ νεφέλῃ τόξου τὴν λαμπηδόνα κατὰ τὸ ἔαρ τεθέασαι, ... etc.

100 Basil, *Epistulae* (Y. Courtonne), 38.5.

101 Jacob (monk, twelfth century), *Epistulae*, epistle 43.

102 Anastasius of Sinai, *Viae Dux*, 21.1: καὶ Ὠριγένης ψιλὸν ἄνθρωπον τὸν Χριστὸν ἐδογμάτισεν. He claimed this about Origen, the man who used the term Θεοτόκος for Mary a good 180 years before this was sanctioned by the council of Ephesus (431). Quite simply (as it usually happened), Anastasius blindly followed Justinian's allegations which had been promptly and ridiculously endorsed by the synod Justian had convened against Origen. In *Codex Sabaiticus 232*, Origen scorned the Jews for seeing Jesus 'as a bare man' (folio 116r, comm. on Matth. 13:54): τὸν μὲν ἄνδρα ἐθεώρουν ὡς ψιλὸν ὄντα. The same, in Origen, *frMatt*, fr. 312 (Klostermann). Likewise, folio 177v: Ἐπειδὴ ψιλὸν ἄνθρωπον ᾤοντο εἶναι τὸν Χριστόν, ἀνατρέπει αὐτῶν τὴν δόξαν. ... Εἰπόντων γὰρ τῶν Φαρισαίων ὅτι *υἱός* ἐστι *τοῦ Δαυὶδ* ὁ Χριστός, ψιλὸς ἄνθρωπος. ... ἀλλὰ δείκνυσιν ὅτι οὐ ψιλός ἐστιν ἄνθρωπος, ἀλλὰ καὶ Θεός. Also, folio 218v: Οἰκονομικῶς εἶπε τοῦτο, ... πρὸς τὸ ἀπατηθῆναι τὸν διάβολον καὶ ὡς ψιλῷ ἀνθρώπῳ ἐπιπηδῆσαι αὐτῷ καὶ καταλυθῆναι σὺν τῷ θανάτῳ. See more evidence and discussion of the Greek text, in the commentary, endnote lv.

103 George Monachus (monk, ninth century, Alexandria,), *Chronicon Breve*, PG.110.84.5-6: Κλήμης δὲ ὁ Στρωματεύς, Ὠριγενιαστὴς ὤν, ὥς τινι τῶν Πατέρων ἀπεκαλύφθη.

104 About Origen being a student of Clement, see Eusebius, *HE*, 6.6.1. Also, George Monachus, *op. cit.* PG.110.532.20 (copied by Symeon Logothetes, *Chronicon*, 66.3 & George Cedrenus, *Compendium Historiarum*, v. 1, p. 441): Κλήμεντος δὲ φοιτητὴς Ὠριγένης ἐγένετο. Cf. Philip of Side, *Historia Christiana*, lines 9-16. Nicephorus Callistus Xanthopulus, *HE*, 5.18. Dositheus II (Dositheus Notaras, 1641-1707, Patriarch of Jerusalem, 1669-1707), *Δωδεκάβιβλος Δοσιθέου Α'-Β'*, Book 1, p. 97: καθὼς ἤθελεν ὁ Ὠριγένης καὶ ὁ Κλήμης ὁ διδάσκαλος αὐτοῦ στερεωμένοι ἐπάνω στὰ κυριακὰ λόγια τοῦ κατὰ Ματθαῖον.

105 See *Catena in Matthaeum*, p. 12: 'Basil [of Caesarea]. Chrysostom'. *Op. cit.* pp. 12 & 15: 'Eusebius. Origen'. *Op. cit.* p. 13: 'Eusebius. Origen. Isidore of Pelusium'. *Op. cit.* p. 39: 'Origen. Cyril [of Alexandria]'. *Op. cit.* p. 39: 'Cyril. John [Chrysostom]. Isidore [of Pelusium].

ship make of such cases? Although this could not be set forth as a rule, I believe that once the selfsame text is ascribed in such a way, it would be plausible to assume than the oldest of authors was the most likely source of this. In any case, however, such an editorial assertion would call for argument.

As far as Origen is concerned, his authorship is often confirmed by comparative study of his own texts. For example, on folio 2r of *Sabaiticus 232*, there is a passage attributed to both 'Eusebius and Cyril'. However, this was written by Eusebius;[106] nevertheless, minor phrasal variations reveal that Cyril had indeed copied this text, although this is not found in Cyril's extant writings.[107] Klostermann's work (fr. 15) reveals[108] that this was indeed a passage of Eusebius who once again had taken up Origen's exegesis using the same distinctive terms.

Theodore of Heraclea'. *Op. cit.* p. 48: 'Theodore of Heraclea. Cyril [of Alexandria] (but this is Origen's idea in *frPs*, on Psalm 118:148). *Loc. cit.* 'Theodore Monachus [of Mopsuestia, see *frMatt*, fr. 5]. Clement [of Alexandria]'. *Op. cit.* p. 85: 'Isidore [of Pelusium]. Theodore of Heraclea. Cyril.' *Loc. cit.* 'Isidore. Cyril. Theodore of Heraclea' (but this is from Origen, *homLuc*, homily 28, p. 64). *Op. cit.* p. 87: 'Chrysostom. Theodore of Heraclea'. *Loc. cit.* 'Theodore of Heraclea. Theodore Monachus [of Mopsuestia]'. *Op. cit.* pp. 122 & 235: 'Cyril [of Alexandria. Origen']. *Supplementum et Varietas Lectionis ad Commentarium Chrysostomi in Evangelium Sancti Matthaei*, p. 452: 'Eusebius Pamphili and Isidore of Pelusium'. *Catena in Lucam*, p. 121: 'Cyril and Chrysostom'. *Catena in Joannem*, p. 257: 'Theodore of Heraclea and Apollinaris'. *Op. cit.* pp. 339 & 353 & 365: 'Apollinaris and Theodore of Heraclea'. *Op. cit.* p. 351: 'Theodore of Heraclea, Apollinaris and Cyril'. *Catena in Epistulam ad Romanos*, p. 7: 'Apollinaris, John [Chrysostom], Theodore'. *Op. cit.* p. 15: 'Eusebius and Severian'. *Op. cit.* p. 23: 'Severian [of Gabala]. Theodoret'. *Op. cit.* p. 66. 'Diodore [of Tarsus] and Theodoret'. *Op. cit.* pp. 117 & 219 & 220: 'Severian and Theodore'. *Op. cit.* p. 128: 'Gennadius and Theodoret'. *Op. cit.* p. 520: 'Chrysostom and Theodoret'. *Catena in Epistulam i ad Corinthios*, p. 18: 'Both Theodore and Theodoret'. *Op. cit.* p. 30: 'Theodore and Theodoret'. *Op. cit.* p. 44: 'Chrysostom and Theodoret and Severian'. *Op. cit.* p. 102: 'Origen and Cyril [of Alexandria]'. *Op. cit.* p. 141: 'Theodoret and Cyril'. *Op. cit.* p. 156: 'Theodore and Theodoret'. *Op. cit.* pp. 167 & 226: 'Theodoret and Theodore'. *Catena in Epistulam ad Hebraeos*, p. 365: 'Basil and Gregory, his brother'. *Op. cit.* p. 454: 'Isidore [of Pelusium] and Chrysostom'.

106 Eusebius, *Ad Stephanum*, PG.22.884.30-36.

107 Eusebius *loc. cit.*: εἰ μὴ ἐξ ἁγίου Πνεύματος πέπειστο αὐτὴν συνειληφέναι, ἀκριβῶς εἰδὼς ὅτι μηδὲ ἐξ αὐτοῦ τὸ κατὰ γαστρὸς ἔφερε, τί δῆτα δίκαιος ὢν ὁ ἀνήρ, οὐκ εἰς πάντας ἐξάγων τὴν διαφθαρεῖσαν πρὸ γάμου τὴν ὥραν [Cod. τῆς ὥρας], τοῖς τὰ τοιαῦτα λαχοῦσι κρίνειν παρεδίδου δράσασαν δειγματίσαι; [in Cod. δράσασαν δειγματίσαι is not there] πῶς δὲ δίκαιος ὁ τὴν παράνομον πρᾶξιν ἐπισκιάζειν καὶ ἐπικρύπτειν προθυμούμενος; [Cod. πῶς δὲ δίκαιος ὁ μὴ θέλων τοῦτο αὐτὰ δράσασαν δειγματίσαι ἀλλ' ἐπισκιάζειν καὶ ἐπικρύπτειν βουλόμενος;]. See Greek text (folio 2r), and the same ideas in Eusebius, *apud Catena in Matthaeum*, p. 10.

108 Origen, fr. 15 (Klostermann).

Likewise, there are multiple attributions in the Catena on Matthew.[109] This chain contains under the header 'Unattributed' ('Ἐξ ἀνεπιγράφου)[110] an indisputable text of Origen's, which is confirmed not only by the present codex (folia 227r-v), but also by Klostermann's collection (fr. 556), as well as by Migne's Patrology;[111] and yet, the same passage has been attributed also to Apollinaris,[112] which is a recurring phenomenon concerning Origen's texts in *Codex Sabaiticus 232*. For example, on folio 240v, the text ascribed to Origen has been attributed also to John Chrysostom,[113] and elsewhere the same text is recorded also as 'Unattributed' ('Ἐξ ἀνεπιγράφου).[114] Likewise, Origen's comment on Matthew, 19:1-2, has been attributed to both him and John Chrysostom.[115] Klostermann noted that this shared designation appears in Codex *Coislianus 195* (tenth century)[116] and Cramer in his catena on Matthew included this as Origen's one.[117] However, in Cramer's catena on Mark, this text is unattributed,[118] but in fact this is part of John Chrysostom's homilies on Matthew,[119] and this is how it appeared in two other codices, namely, Codex *Coislianus 23* (eleventh century) and Codex *Coislianus 187* (eleventh century).

There are several portions of Origen's text which have been also attributed to both John Chrysostom and Cyril of Alexandria. However, in the present codex these appear as only portions of extensive texts ascribed to Origen alone. As argued below, there are points at which parts of Origen's passages were attributed to Chrysostom as 'fragments' – but now we have Origen's texts demonstrating that Chrysostom had copied a few lines from an otherwise continuous text written by Origen.[120]

---

109 *Catena in Matthaeum*, pp. 39-40 ('by Origen and Cyril'). See also the same double attribution in *op. cit.* pp. 122; 235.

110 *Op. cit.* pp. 236-237.

111 Origen, *schMatt*, PG.17.308.44-309.33.

112 Apollinaris, *frMatt*, fr. 143.

113 John Chrysostom, *In Matthaeum*, PG.58.789.40-49.

114 *Catena in Matthaeum*, p. 242.

115 See the same text in Origen, fr. 384 (Klostermann); also, Origen, *apud Catena in Matthaeum*, p. 150. John Chrysostom, *In Matthaeum*, PG.58.595.52-54. I have included this in the present publication although this is not found in *Codex Sabaiticus 232*. See p. 261.

116 Klostermann, *frMatt*, 384, p. 164.

117 *Catena in Matthaeum*, p. 150.

118 *Catena in Marcum*, p. 371.

119 John Chrysostom, *In Matthaeum*, PG.58.595.52-54.

120 The cases are numerous; nevertheless, cf. John Chrysostom, *In Matthaeum*, PG.58.473.5-8: Οὐ γὰρ μόνον οὐκ ἤκουον, ἀλλὰ καὶ *Βαρέως ἤκουον*. ἐποίησαν δὲ τοῦτο, φησί, *Μήποτε ἐπιστρέψωσι, καὶ ἰάσωμαι αὐτούς*. τὴν ἐπιτεταμένην αὐτῶν λέγων πονηρίαν, καὶ τὴν μετὰ σπουδῆς ἀποστροφήν. Here is Origen's selfsame passage in the *Catena in Matthaeum*, p. 102 (which is part of an extensive text – hence, we have also the context): τὸ δὲ *μή ποτε ἐπιστρέψωσι καὶ*

The case of Cyril of Alexandria is similar, yet not identical: for the passages ascribed to him do not appear in known texts of his (as it happens with Chrysostom's sermons on Matthew): these are simply alleged 'fragments' attributed to him by catenists. This is far too strange for a prelate of the Byzantine establishment, indeed one from whose writings official councils quoted all too often. To surmise that there are texts of his that have perished (from which the catenist of *Sabaiticus 232* or any previous codex purportedly copied) would be impossible to sustain by any sort of argument.

At several points of critical consideration of the present text, I quote texts by either John Chrysostom or Cyril of Alexandria (or by both of them) and argue that those theologians copied them from Origen's commentary on Matthew, which places an onus on me to explain a point that calls for demonstration.

Cyril of Alexandria and John Chrysostom Seizing on Origen

Neither Cyril of Alexandria nor John Chrysostom did ever mention Origen by name. However, perusal of their work evinces that both of them *knew* what Origen wrote and drew on his ideas and certainly on his texts. It now turns out that both of them copied from Origen's commentary on Matthew.

It would be interesting to wonder why was it that of Cyril's 'commentary on Matthew' there are only fragments scattered in various chains but not the entire text of his (if he ever wrote one, which I doubt) given that his works were highly cherished by the guardians of the imperial orthodoxy. Could it be reasonably surmised that Cyril wrote a commentary on a cardinal scriptural text and this did not survive?

On the other hand, Chrysostom commented on this gospel only in his thirty-four sermons, in which he used Origen's portions hither and thither, yet the preceding and ensuing textual context is different: on the one hand, we have Origen's pithy analyses; on the other, Chrysostom rehashes them in his usual turgid style, which was not unbefitting an oration. In view of so many 'coincidences' appearing in this codex, it would be plausible to surmise that most of John's alleged 'fragments' are in fact excerpts from the Origen's commentary – only now we have a much wider context of the pertinent points. Little wonder then that there are relevant catena-fragments being attributed to *both* Origen

ἰάσομαι αὐτους [Isaiah, 6:10; Matthew 13:15], τὴν ἐπιτεταμένην πονηρίαν αὐτῶν σημαίνει, καὶ τὴν μετὰ σπουδῆς ἀποστροφήν. Moreover, Klostermann (in footnote to *frMatt*, fr. 284, p. 127) advises that he found this in *Codex Vaticanus 757* (eleventh century) being attributed to Origen. However, the *Catena in Acta* (*catena Andreae*), p. 419, insisted on attributing this to Chrysostom.

and John Chrysostom, or to *both* Origen and Cyril of Alexandria.[121] After all, it was Cyril himself who had declared that 'not all propositions by heretics should be sidestepped and waived' (οὐ πάντα ὅσα λέγουσιν οἱ αἱρετικοὶ φεύγειν καὶ παραιτεῖσθαι χρή).[122]

The anthologer who compiled the catena on the gospel of Matthew, in his prologue quoted this guideline from Cyril's *Epistle to Eulogius*, which explains why so many points made by Origen are found therein.[123] So did the anonymous editor who wrote a preamble to Origen's *Philocalia;* he was extremely hostile to Origen, and quoted this as if he wanted to justify the great Cappadocian compilers of this anthology and certainly to protect himself for publishing a work containing thoughts of a 'heretic'.[124] This remark by Cyril enjoyed a rather wide currency. The council of Ephesus quoted it,[125] but authors felt comfortable with this only once Justinian did so. This probably explains why was it that all of the authors who promptly appealed to Cyril's *Epistle to Eulogius* were either sixth-century ones or later.[126]

Moreover, Origen offered a pithy definition of 'knavery' (πονηρία), which was paid no attention by posterity: "knavery is willful evil-doing".[127] But it is precisely because of this that Cyril of Alexandria's use of it constitutes a serependitous confirmation that he had read Origen's commentary on Matthew

---

121 For example, *Catena in Matthaeum*, pp. 39; 122; 235; *Catena in Epistulam i ad Corinthios* (*typus Vaticanus*) (*e cod. Paris. gr. 227*), p. 102. John Chrysostom, *Fragmenta in Jeremiam*, PG.64.917.44-50. Cyril of Alexandria, *Expositio in Psalmos*, PG.69.940.11-32. Also, Chrysostom followed Origen's *commEph*, fr. 15 (comm. on Eph. 3:15).

122 See his epistle in ACO, *Concilium Universale Ephesenum anno 431*, tome, 1.1.4, p. 35 & Justinian, *Contra Monophysitas*, 157. Somehow, this became a guidline quoted by subsequent apprehensive commentators who came upon useful analyses in otherwise allegedly heretical writings. Pamphilus (theologian, sixth-seventh century), *Difficultatum Solutio*, question 12, line 22-223. Photius, *Bibliotheca*, Codex 230, p. 270b; *Epistulae et Amphilochia*, epistle 284, line 1734-1736. Nilus Cabasilas, *Orationes Quinque De Spiritu Sancto*, 4.16.

123 *Catena in Matthaeum*, p. 4.

124 Origen, *Philocalia*, Prologue, 1b.

125 ACO, *Concilium Universale Ephesenum Anno 431*, tome 1.1.1, pp. 8; 12; tome 1.1.4, p. 35; tome 1.1.7, pp. 12; 165; 171; 173.

126 Eustathius (monk, Constantinople, sixth century), *Epistula ad Timotheum Scholasticum De Duabus Naturis Adversus Severum*, line 80. Leontius (monk, Jerusalem, sixth century), *Testimonia Sanctorum*, pp. 8; 56; 84. Pamphilus (theologian, sixth-seventh century), *Difficultatum Solutio*, Question 6, lines 186; 206; Question 12, line 219. Anastasius of Sinai, *Viae Dux*, 8.1; 9.2; 10.1.2; 10.2.5; 10.5.21; 13.2. Also, *Doctrina Patrum*, p. 149. Photius, *Bibliotheca*, Codex 196, p. 160a; Codex 229, pp. 251a; 257a; 261b; Codex 230, pp. 270b; 273a; *Epistulae et Amphilochia*, epistle 284, lines 1734-1736. Nilus Cabasilas, *Orationes Quinque De Spiritu Sancto*, oration 4.16.

127 Origen, *commMatt*, 12.4: ἔστι δὲ ἡ πονηρία ἑκούσιος κακοποιία. See also *Codex Sabaiticus 232:* Origen's text runs parallel to that of folio 99v.

and copied from this abundantly (not necessarily in an *ad hoc* commentary on that gospel). He quoted Origen's definition that made reference to 'certain ones who, not low-mindedly (οὐκ ἀγεννῶς) gave this definition of knavery'.[128] There is no textual evidence that would allow to determine who those 'certain ones' were. However, the vocabulary is Origen's own, especially the turn of phrase 'not low-mindedly' (οὐκ ἀγεννῶς), which was as old as Plato, and had been abundantly used by two of the cardinal philological sources of Origen,[129] namely, Galen and Plutarch.[130] As it normally happened, a later lexicographer used Origen's definition drawing on its second-hand usage by Cyril.[131] At this point, a remark is necessary: in the newly published anonymous comments on the Psalms that editors attributed to Origen, the selfsame text of Cyril[132] appears as having been written by Origen,[133] which is one more indication that Cyril copied from Origen to the letter.

On the other hand, Chrysostom's homilies on Matthew, as well as other ones,[134] are like a patchwork containing Origen's passages every now and then, whereas in between there are Chrysostom's own sermonical instructions. I should have thought that his drawing on Origen now confirmed by textual

128 Cyril of Alexandria, *Expositio in Psalmos*, PG.69.929.5-9: Ὡρίσαντο δέ τινες τὴν πονηρίαν οὐκ ἀγεννῶς εἶναι ἑκούσιον κακοποιΐαν. ἄλλο γάρ ἐστι κατὰ ἄγνοιαν κακοποιεῖν καὶ οἱονεὶ νικώμενον, καὶ ἄλλο αὐτὸ τοῦτο θέλειν κακῶς ποιῆσαι. ὅπερ ἐστὶ καὶ πονηρία, δι' ἣν καὶ ὁ διάβολος πονηρὸς λέγεται. Likewise, Origen, *commMatt*, 10.11: οὐ γὰρ φύσις ἐν ἡμῖν αἰτία τῆς πονηρίας, ἀλλὰ προαίρεσις ἑκούσιος οὖσα κακοποιητική. *frPs*, on Psalm 9:36: πονηρὸς δὲ ὁ ἑκουσίως κακοποιητικός. *homPs*, homily 4.4: Ὡρίσαντο δέ τινες τὴν πονηρίαν οὐκ ἀγεννῶς εἶναι ἑκούσιον κακοποιΐαν. Ἄλλο γάρ ἐστι κατὰ ἄγνοιαν κακοποιεῖν καὶ οἱονεὶ νικώμενον, ἄλλο αὐτὸ τοῦτο θέλειν κακῶς ποιῆσαι. ὅπερ ἐστὶ καὶ πονηρία, δι' ἣν καὶ ὁ διάβολος πονηρὸς λέγεται.

129 See *infra*, notes 329; 581; 722.

130 Cf. Plato, *Phaedrus*, 264b; *Charmides*, 158c; *Gorgias*, 492d; *Respublica*, 529a. Plutarch, *Timoleon*, 15.2; *Comparatio Pelopidae et Marcelli*, 3.3; *Cimon*, 13.2; *Tiberius et Gaius Gracchus*, 12.4; *Antonius*, 77.7; *Conjugalia Praecepta*, p. 141C. Galen, *De Naturalibus Facultatibus*, p. 52; *De Diebus Decretoriis*, p. 856; *De Methodo Medendi*, p. 307; *De Simplicium Medicamentorum Temperamentis Ac Facultatibus*, pp. 437; 438; 800; *et passim* galore. Origen, *Cels*, IV.52; IV.56; VI.4 (& *Philocalia*, 15.6;); VI.35; *commMatt*, 15.18. Naturally, later Christian authors (notably, Origen's admirers) followed him on this, too. Eusebius, *HE*, 4.7.8; 4.24.1. Gregory Nyssa, *Contra Eunomium*, 3.3.13; *Dialogus De Anima et Resurrectione*, PG.46.145.20. Gregory of Nazianzus, *Epistulae*, epistle 228.2. Basil of Caesarea, *Homilia Exhortatoria ad Sanctum Baptisma*, PG.31.432.18. Theodoret, *Quaestiones in Libros Regnorum et Paralipomenon*, PG.80.540.33. Cyril of Alexandria, *De Adoratione*, PG.68.480.23; *et passim*. Sozomenus, *HE*, 6.14.3. *Et. al.*

131 Pseudo-Zonaras, *Lexicon*, letter pi, p. 1566: Πονηρία. ἑκούσιος κακοποιΐα, δι' ἣν καὶ ὁ διάβολος πονηρὸς λέγεται. No other author did ever use this definition.

132 Cyril of Alexandria, *Expositio in Psalmos*, PG.69.929.5-9, quoted *supra*, note 128.

133 Origen, *homPs*, homily 4.4; quoted *supra*, note 128.

134 See *supra*, p. XXIII.

analysis is neither fortuitous nor unexpected once some events of Chrysostom's turbulent life are considered – and in those events Origen's shadow was commanding. As a brief preamble to those events, a few points concerning the role of Epiphanius and Jerome in Origen's incrimination should be recalled.

Epiphanius (died in 403) was the man who stirred up the Origenistic controversies. In 393, he launched a campaign which aimed at formal condemnation of Origen as a heretic. He sent one of his monks (named Atarbius) to Palestine with a document to be signed by Jerome (living in Bethlehem) and Rufinus (living in the monastery of Mount of Olives). Jerome signed up to the document, whereas Rufinus reacted furiously and refused even to admit the envoy. The inflamed Jerome (who was out to gratify his octogenarian friend Epiphanius) turned against both Rufinus and Patriarch John of Jerusalem, who supported his priest Rufinus. Consequently, Jerusalem became the theatre of a public encounter between John and Epiphanius. Once John did not yield to Epiphanius' plan, Epiphanius impugned him as a heretic and ordained Jerome's younger brother Paulinian a priest in John's see. Epiphanius would later replicate this uncanonical procedure in John's Chrysostom's diocese and play a key role (along with Bishop Theophilus of Alexandria) in having Chrysostom, Patriarch of Constantinople, deposed and exiled. Epiphanius had determined that Jerome's monks could not receive Communion from clergymen whose head (namely John of Jerusalem) was a heretic. In response, the latter banned Jerome from entering the Cave and the Church of the Nativity. Although Melania along with Paulinian mediated a temporary reconciliation between the two men in 397, a more rancorous Origenistic controversy erupted in late 398, shortly after Rufinus had translated Origen's *De Principiis*. Theophilus of Alexandria was somehow there once again, since Jerome strove to defame John Chrysostom and Rufinus of Aquileia for heresy as a service to that man.

In 400, Theophilus of Alexandria condemned Origen at a synod convened at Alexandria, which would explain why his nephew Cyril never identified Origen by name in his writings despite heavily copying from him as well as seizing on some of his cardinal terms and ideas. Naturally, it was not difficult for Theophilus (no less a pillar of the imperial establishment than Cyril was shortly after him) to obtain imperial endorsement of this resolution: the emperor vested this decision with the imperial authority, which proscribed Origen's works. Subsequently, Theophilus sent a letter to Pope Anastasius of Rome recounting the proceedings and alleged heretical propositions in detail. Anastasius issued a condemnation of the Origenist theses along with other alleged ones, taking for granted that those ran contrary to the ecclesiastical faith. He passed those decisions on to Simplicius, Bishop of Milan. The man who obliged serving as a messenger between the Pope and the Bishop of Milan was Eusebius of Cremona, Jerome's dedicatee of the commentary on Matthew, which he wrote in Bethlehem in March 398 –that is, about one year after his reconciliation with John of Jerusalem and a few months before the outbreak of a renewed row between them, following translation of Origen's *De Principiis*.

No matter how distorted Origen's thought was upon such a presentation, no room for any bishop of the era to give them thoughtful contemplation was allowed whatsoever: the *Zeitgeist* was already there, indeed it had been established since the year 380, when Emperor Theodosius I (347-395) declared 'the triumph of Orthodoxy', and after the Second Oecumenical Council (381) an all out war was waged against anything considered 'pagan' or 'heretical'. In 387, mere study of mathematics was a cause for death penalty; in 389, a mob of monks destroyed pagan temples, set libraries on fire, stoned pagan priests, and lynched heathen; in 392, persecution of everything real or imagined 'Greek' resulted in slaughter of priests of the Cabeirian Mysteries at Samothrace, destruction of the temple of Amos Zeus at Aphytos of Chalcidice, and, as Libanius wrote, 'in courts of law, blood flows as if in a rushing stream'.[135]

What could Origen's fate have possibly been amidst this 'spirit of the times', given that writing to his pupil Gregory Thaumaturgus he had declared his method of education in the most explicit terms?

> Therefore, your shrewdness has the potential of making you a perfect Roman doctor of law and a Greek philosopher in one of the schools that are held in high repute. However, I wished to make the most of the power of your acumen so as to direct you to Christianism. This is why in reality my desire has been to teach you also those tenets of the philosophy of the Greeks which could serve as general education and preparatory teaching towards Christianism (εἰς χριστιανισμόν), such as those parts of geometry and astronomy which will be useful in the interpretation of the holy scriptures, so that, what the pupils of philosophers say about geometry and music, grammar, rhetoric and astronomy (i.e. that they are aides of philosophy, ὡς συνερίθων φιλοσοφία), we may say of philosophy itself in relation to Christianism (περὶ αὐτῆς φιλοσοφίας πρὸς χριστιανισμόν).[136]

135 Libanius, *Orationes*, oration 45.29: ὅταν δὲ ἄνθρωποι ῥύακας μὲν αἵματος ἐν τοῖς δικαστηρίοις διὰ τῶν μαστίγων ποιῶσι.

136 Origen, *Epistula ad Gregorium Thaumaturgum*, 1 (*Philocalia*, 13.1). Against Origen's own words pronounced during an advanced age, Eusebius' mythology had it that the young Origen 'considered the teaching of language and literature as being at odds with training in sacred studies and without hesitation he broke away from the school of language as useless and inimical to divine learning. Then, on the same grounds, in order not to be in need of help by others [i.e. Greek literature], he disposed of ... whatever works he had of ancient literature ... and received four obols a day from him who bought them.' *HE*, 6.3.8-9. And yet, although the adolescent Origen allegedly 'got rid of all his heathen books', after several decades, when he wrote the *Contra Celsum*, he was able to quote *verbatim* from a stupendously large number of Greek and Oriental authors!

Quite evidently, Origen marched to the beat of a different drum. However, all of those developments did not prevent Rufinus from keeping on translating and publishing Origen's works into Latin during and after those condemnations, indeed doing so under the auspices of his own bishop. This is highly telling of the feelings towards that which was called 'Origenism', all the more so since Rufinus' scholarly activity did not provoke the slightest protest. In reality, Jerome's transferring the allegation about 'heretic Origenism' in the West succeeded only as far as a perfunctory papal signature of 'condemnation' was obtained; otherwise, the uproar that Jerome stirred became a matter of politics and personal likes and dislikes rather than actual theology. On this, a remark by Hans von Campenhausen referring to Jerome summarised the truth of the matter: "It was only his own interests, by no means unselfish, his private embarrassments, entanglements, and whims which forced him, almost against his will, to this public polemic and heresy-hunt. Jerome cannot be excused in this case."[137]

It is telling that Augustine declined taking sides with Jerome while lamenting the way in which those fruitless quarrels shattered friendships between orthodox churchmen.[138] How could possibly Augustine have done otherwise, given that he would have thought highly of Origen, from whom he had borrowed cardinal points such as Origen's Theory of Time?[139] I should have thought that Augustine learned much about Origen after having sent his pupil Paul Orosius to the East in order to form an idea of what the alleged 'Origenism' was about. Orosius had contact also with Jerome, but presumably Augustine wished to have an account as impartial as possible, hence Orosius' visit to Palestine.[140] Apparently, Augustine knew Jerome's character, he knew that he had been embroiled in hostile polemic with monks and priests because of the insulting and defamatory style of his satirical writings, for which (following the death of

137 Hans von Campenhausen, *The Fathers of the Church*, Peabody, MA, 1999, pp. 178-179.

138 Cf. Augustine, *Epistle 73*, to Jerome: "Where is the friend who may not be feared as possibly a future enemy, if the breach that we deplore could arise between Jerome and Rufinus? Oh, sad and pitiable is our portion!". Cf. Augustine, Epistle 82.1.

139 See P. Tzamalikos, "Origen, The Source of Augustine's Theory of Time", *Philosophia*, Yearbook of the Research Center for Greek Philosophy at the Academy of Athens, v. 17-18, 1989, pp. 396-418.

140 Paulus Orosius (born c. 375, died after 418 AD) was a Gallaecian Chalcedonian priest, historian, and theologian. He wrote a book intended for Augustine, entitled *Consultatio sive Commonitorium ad Augustinum De Errore Priscillianistarum et Origenistarum* (*Assessment and Reminders to Augustine Against the Errors of the Priscillians and the Origenists*). Its content makes it clear that Orosius was rather baffled at the claims he heard, so he asked for Augustine's advice regarding those theological issues. Augustine responded by writing the book *Liber Ad Orosium contra Priscillianistas et Origenistas*.

his protector Pope Damasus, December 384) an official ecclesiastical inquiry was conducted wherefore Jerome was condemned in formal judgment, and (in 385) he was forced to leave the city.

The events at Constantinople were pretty similar to those that took place at Jerusalem between Jerome and Bishop John. Given that Theophilus,[141] the Patriarch of Alexandria, accused Chrysostom of being a follower of Origen, it is hard not to assume that he had read much of Origen's words and ideas into Chrysostom's teaching, both sermons and treatises. Actually, this was one of the accusations by Theophilus (accompanied by his nephew Cyril), and by other enemies of Chrysostom's, that made its mark in the Synod of the Oak, convened in 403 by Empress Eudoxia at that suburb of Constantinople in which resided a considerable number of people from Egypt.

Moreover, the impetuous Epiphanius, who challenged Chrysostom by asking from him to denounce Origen's teaching, had espoused these charges about 'Origenism' only because he had noticed that Chrysostom's works were full of excerpts from Origen's own words, which now becomes evident from Chrysostom's parallel texts quoted in apposition to Origen's ones found in this manuscript.

The censure about 'Origenism' by Theophilus against Chrysostom is vividly attested by Photius reviewing a book by a certain 'George, Bishop of Alexandria', of whom Photius declared that otherwise he knew nothing. This George wrote that he resisted the empress' pressure to consent to Chrysostom's deposition, and reported that Theophilus denounced Chrysostom's use of Origen's works 'because he [i.e. Chrysostom] did not stop to study those works, for which Theophilus censured him' (Ὁ δὲ Θεόφιλος … τῶν Ὠριγενείων ἀναγνωσμάτων, ἐν οἷς ἐκεῖνον διέβαλλεν, οὐκ ἀπείχετο).[142]

When Theophilus convinced Epiphanius (in c. 401/2) that Chrysostom was 'an Origenist',[143] the bishop of Cyprus came to be a more formidable foe of Chrysostom's than Theophilus himself. What if the historian Socrates deemed that Theophilus convinced Epiphanius because the latter 'was too pious and simple-minded' (ἁπλοϊκὸς ὤν)? The fact is that the acerbic Epiphanius convened an assembly of the bishops of Cyprus and banned reading of Origen's works

141 Edward Gibbon described Theophilus as 'the perpetual enemy of peace and virtue, a bold, bad man, whose hands were alternately polluted with gold and with blood.' *The Decline and Fall of the Roman Empire*, New York, 1983, v. 3, p. 171.

142 Photius, *Bibliotheca*, Codex 96, pp. 78b-83a.

143 Socrates Scholasticus, *HE*, 6.10 & Nicephorus Callistus Xanthopulus, *HE*, 13.11-12: Ὡς Θεόφιλος κατὰ Ἰωάννου γενόμενος, καὶ Ἐπιφάνιον τὸν Κύπρου προσεταιρισάμενος, τὰ πρῶτα ἐκείνῳ διάφορος ὤν, ὡς Ὠριγενιαστὴν τὸν Ἰωάννην διέβαλε, καὶ συνόδους ἐποίει ἀθετούσας τὰ Ὠριγένους συγγράμματα, Ἰωάννην καὶ τοὺς Μακροὺς δῆθεν ἐπαιτιώμενος.

altogether.[144] Besides, he caused a great deal of turmoil at Constantinople by challenging Chrysostom in front of the congregation at another gathering into the church of the Holy Apostles.[145] Besides, vexed as he was at Chrysostom's nonchalance, he relentlessly declined not only Chrysostom's invitation to stay in a house belonging to the Church, but also to join him in common prayer, unless Chrysostom 'denounced Origen's books in public and in front of all the people'.[146]

The fact of the matter is that Epiphanius shared Theophilus rage against Origen not just because he was 'simple-minded': actually, he had read Origen's books, which 'he carried with him when he set sail for Constantinople' in order to lobby for condemnation of Chrysostom as an 'Origenist'. This explains why was it that, in Epiphanius' writings, so many peculiar notions and expressions clearly originate in Origen's work, as shown at several points of this volume, as well in earlier monographs of mine. Nevertheless, it is noteworthy that (unlike Theophilus) Epiphanius did not seek condemnation of Origen's *person*, but only of his *writings*.[147]

Against all of this turbulence, although Chrysostom could have won his personal peacefulness in a walk by simply denouncing Origen's teaching, he did not yield to this Faustian bargain by selling his own convictions for shares in mundane power and influence: naturally then, he ignored Epiphanius' raucous voice.[148] He accused Epiphanius of breaching the ecclesiastical laws through his various non-canonical actions at the capital, but shunned the latter's bill of indictment,[149] which first and foremost denigrated Origen.[150]

Of course, beside monks whose minds were inaccessible to mercy or reason, Chrysostom had not only enemies: he had also defenders. One of them was a legendary figure, namely, bishop Theotimus of Scythia, a saintly man

---

144 Socrates Scholasticus, *loc. cit.*

145 Socrates Scholasticus, *op. cit.* 6.14; Sozomenus, *HE*, 8.14.

146 Sozomenus, *op. cit.* 8.14.9. Cf. Socrates Scholasticus, *HE*, 6.12.3: Καὶ τὴν μὲν προτροπὴν Ἰωάννου ἐξέκλινεν Θεοφίλῳ χαριζόμενος, ἐν ἰδιαζούσῃ δὲ καταλύει μονῇ.

147 Socrates Scholasticus, *HE*, 6.12: Μετ᾽ οὐ πολὺ δὲ ἐκ τῆς Κύπρου ὁ ἐπίσκοπος Ἐπιφάνιος ἐπὶ τὴν Κωνσταντινούπολιν ἔρχεται, ταῖς ὑποθήκαις Θεοφίλου πεισθείς, ἐπικομιζόμενος ἐν ταὐτῷ τὰ καθαιρετικὰ τῶν Ὠριγένους βιβλίων, δι᾽ ὧν οὐκ αὐτὸν Ὠριγένην ἀκοινώνητον εἶναι ἀπέφηνεν, ἀλλὰ τὰ βιβλία μόνον διέβαλλεν.

148 Leo VI Sapiens, emperor, *Homiliae*, homily 38, lines 1004-1008: Πείθει [sc. Theophilus] τὸν Ἐπιφάνιον γράψαι τῷ Ἰωάννῃ τῶν Ὠριγένους βίβλων ἀπέχεσθαι καὶ μηδαμῶς συμφρονεῖν αὐταῖς. Ὁ δὲ μέγας ὄντως οὗτος Χρυσόστομος ταῦτα δεξάμενος, τῷ καθαρῷ τοῦ φρονήματος οὐκ ἐφρόντιζε τῶν ἐπεμβαινόντων, μόνα δὲ τὰ τῆς κοινῆς σωτηρίας διεμερίμνα διὰ παντός.

149 Sozomenus, *op. cit.* 8.14.9.

150 Socrates Scholasticus, *op. cit.* 6.14.

of acclaimed piousness,[151] who stood up against Epiphanius by bringing forward some of Origen's writings in order to demonstrate that there was nothing wrong with them.

Socrates recorded Theotimus' reaction to Epiphanius' obloquy against Origen. At the time when Epiphanius strove to lobby Theotimus in order to engineer a condemnation of Origen, Theotimus upbraided Epiphanius: he declared that he would not go along, and he 'will not excommunicate people and works that our predecessors did not reject' (ἐκβάλλων ἃ οἱ πρὸ ἡμῶν οὐκ ἠθέτησαν).[152] Moreover, Theotimus avowed that he himself had read Origen's books, yet had found nothing wrong in them, and then he went on with a devastating argument: there were four prelates accusing Origen, namely, Methodius of Olympus, Eustathius of Antioch, Apollinaris of Laodicea, and Theophilus of Alexandria, all of whom Theotimus styled 'the slanderous tetrad' (ἡ τῶν κακολόγων τετρακτύς):[153] all this was but connivance to condemn Origen's theology as heretical, but none of them had the slightest modicum of ken to grasp what this theology was about. Theotimus grasped and made the real point: since none of them was able to produce any noteworthy theological work of their own, they sought fame by speaking evil of those who were superior to them – a remark that reminds a similar one by Hierocles the Stoic, who had pointed out, 'To be sure, selfishness can magnify one's own things and glorify them greatly, while belittling and disparaging those of others. It is because of this [selfishness] that paltry people oftentimes represent themselves as more eminent than others who are in fact far more superior.'[154]

Theotimus' point was this: each one of 'the slanderous tetrad' accused Origen of different specific things, which suggested that they found the rest of Origen's doctrines orthodox. Not a single doctrine of Origen's was incriminated by at least two of them – and none of them found any fault in Origen's Trinitarian doctrine.[155]

Therefore, no alleged heresy by Origen was pointed out by all four of them or indeed even by two. This 'tetrad' spearheaded the campain aiming to stab Origen in the back, but they were unable to agree on which the stagger point

151 Socrates Scholasticus, *op. cit.* 6.12: ὁ ἐπ᾽ εὐλαβείᾳ καὶ βίου ὀρθότητι περιβόητος Θεότιμος.

152 Socrates Scholasticus, *loc. cit.*

153 Socrates Scholasticus, *op. cit.* 6.13.

154 Hierocles the Stoic (second century AD), *Fragmenta Ethica*, p. 59, *apud* Stobaeus, *Anthologium*, 4.27.20.

155 Socrates, *HE*, 6.13: Οἱ γὰρ κινήσαντες ὅσαπερ ᾤοντο κινήσεως ἄξια, δι᾽ ὧν ὡς κακῶς δοξάζοντα περὶ τῆς ἁγίας τριάδος οὐδ᾽ ὅλως ἐμέμψαντο δείκνυνται περιφανῶς τὴν ὀρθὴν εὐσέβειαν μαρτυροῦντες αὐτῷ.

should be. Too assorted an invective to make the case of 'heretical Origen', let alone coax unprejudiced parties.

In addition, Theotimus reminded that, after Methodius had rebuked Origen, he eventually turned an admirer of his and wrote favourably of him in a certain a dialogue of his entitled 'the Guest-Chamber' (Ξενών). Therefore, Theotimus declared, 'in my eyes, their calumny against Origen is in fact a praise of him'. 'These men made a mistake, because by accusing Origen they also accused Athanasius, the man who paid tribute to Origen as a great defender of orthodoxy'.[156] All of those detractors were unmoved by the fact that, when Gregory of Nazianzus (died 389) met Jerome at Constantinople and the latter was glad to make himself Gregory's pupil, the Theologian urged him to study Origen's scriptural exegesis – obviously he did not admonish a young Latin-speaking aspirant to be educated by a 'heretic', and, anyway, Jerome did so and would draw upon and indeed appropriate Origen's exegesis for the rest of his life.

A few decades later, the church historian Sozomenus recorded these accounts of Socrates: he was evidently impressed by the latter's empathy for Origen, as well as by Theotimus' vigorous attack on Epiphanius in defense of Origen. Sozomenus was somewhat more explicit in recording Epiphanius' malicious lobbying for condemnation of Origen with the bishops that happened to sojourn in Constantinople at that time: he had managed to persuade some prelates, but the majority of them did not go along.[157] Moreover, Sozomenus' personal view was that Basil and Gregory of Nazianzus strengthened the faith of those who followed the Nicene Creed only because they had studied Origen's works.[158]

As late as the fifteenth century, shortly after the fall of Constantinople to the Turks, Cardinal Bessarion named Origen as one of the 'Greek Fathers and masters', alongside with the names of Chrysostom and Cyril of Alexandria.[159] Writing to a friend of his, he told him that there is no need for the addressee to send Origen's *Contra Celsum* to Bessarion, 'since we have this book, too'.[160]

Photius reviewed 'the acts of the synod that was illegally convened against John Chrysostom' (namely, that of Oak) and remarked that the bishops that had the upper hand during that event ('Theophilus of Alexandria, Acacius of Veroia, Antiochus of Ptolemais, and Severian of Gabala') were at the same time

156 On Theotimus' staunch resistance against Epiphanius, see also Theodore Anagnostes, *Epitome Historiae Tripartitae*, 4.288-291.

157 Sozomenus, *HE*, 8.14.

158 Sozomenus, *op. cit.* 6.17.2.

159 Bessarion, *In Verbum Evangelii: sic eum volo manere, quid ad te?*, 5.3.

160 Bessarion, *Epistulae*, 37, p. 489.

both 'men that hated' Chrysostom and 'judges and witnesses' during that trial. Moreover, he reported some incredibly mean instances of behaviour against Chrysostom. What matters at this point is that one of Chrysostom's detractors was his deacon called John, and part of his obloquy was that 'he suffered a lot for the sake of the Origenists because of Sarapion' (ὡς πολλὰ κακὰ παθὼν χάριν τῶν Ὠριγενειαστῶν).[161]

John of Damascus quoted from a *Chronographia* written by 'deacon Isidore', in which Isidore assured that 'Theophilus sinned by reviling John Chrysostom to empress Eudoxia as allegedly embracing the doctrines of Origen's heresy.'[162]

Posterity condemned the synod of Oak, some authors lampooned Theophilus of Alexandria as being the one who wooed the Anthropomorphist monks[163] and hated Origen on that score, too.[164] However, the theme that recurred in relation to those events was different from what subsequent, as well as modern, Origen-scholars could have expected: there was absolutely no effort by anyone to prove that Chrysostom *was not* an admirer of Origen. For indeed beneath the sesquipedalian bells and whistles of John Chrysostom there is plenty of Origen's ideas and locution, which is why the vitriolic Epiphanius of Salamis held Chrysostom to obloquy for using Origen's works, but Chrysostom ignored Epiphanius' conniption and bill of indictment, which first and foremost denigrated Origen, and unabashedly he kept on flaunting his rhetorical skill. Origen's commanding influence was an undeniable fact, which both Epiphanius and Theophilus had demonstrated by using Origen's books and juxtaposing the teaching of Origen and Chrysostom. Therefore, the retort was *that there was nothing wrong* about Origen's ideas, hence, if Chrysostom had availed himself of them, then, well done!

Theotimus presented Origen's books to Epiphanius in order to demonstrate that drawing on them would be beneficial; and if there was any offence

161 Photius, *Bibliotheca*, Codex 59, pp. 17b-19b. Sarapion was Chrysostom's archdeacon. Theodore Anagnostes, *op. cit.* 4.287.

162 John of Damascus, *Orationes De Imaginibus Tres*, 3.124.

163 Socrates Scholasticus, *op. cit.* 6.10. Theodore Anagnostes, *op. cit.* 4.289. Nicephorus Callistus Xanthopulus, *HE*, 13.10; 13.12. John of Damascus quoted from 'the *Chronicon* by deacon Isidore', in which the author rebuked Theophilus' assault against Chrysostom and his conspiracy with the empress to his purposes. *Orationes De Imaginibus Tres*, 3.124.

164 In the first place, Theophilus had opposed John's appointment as Patriarch of Constantinople. When Theophilus had disciplined four Egyptian monks (known as 'the Tall Brothers') over their support of Origen's teaching, they fled to John, who welcomed them.

involved in that commotion, this was not to be found in Origen's ideas but in Epiphanius' shameful actions.[165]

In the turn of the fifth to sixth century, Procopius of Gaza composed his anthology on the Song of Songs quoting conveniently from Origen, as well as from Gregory of Nyssa, Cyril of Alexandria, Didymus, Eusebius, Theodoret, and others.[166]

The historian Socrates reported that Athanasius used Origen's books in the battle against Arianism,[167] and that both Pamphilus and Eusebius defended Origen.[168]

Later, the historian Nicephorus Callistus remarked that 'Theophilus, who previously believed different things from Epiphanius, took into partnership with the latter and vilified John [Chrysostom] as being an Origenist'; but 'he cast blame upon Origen's books, which a man of many labours such as Athanasius himself used very often in order to establish the system of his own faith in the treatises he wrote against the Arianists'.[169]

Besides, Nicephorus Callistus was perplexed upon reporting the views of two Arianist erudite scholars, called Timothy and George: how could it have been possible for Timothy to have appealed to Origen for support of his heretical views, given that, 'in all of his works, Origen explicitly teaches that the Son is co-eternal with the Father'? ('Ἀλλὰ καὶ 'Ωριγένης ἁπανταχοῦ τῶν λόγων διαῤῥήδην συναΐδιόν φησι τὸν Υἱὸν Πατρί).[170] For to those who 'were able to comprehend the depth of Origen's books' (οἱ τῶν 'Ωριγένους βιβλίων τὸ βάθος κατανοῆσαι δυνάμενοι), 'never did Origen teach any beginning of the Son's existence'; instead, he taught that 'the Son was born from the Father',[171] which

165 Nicephorus Callistus Xanthopulus, *HE*, 13.13 (copying from Sozomenus, *HE*, 8.14): Ταῦτα λέγων, καί τι τῶν 'Ωριγένους συγγραμμάτων εἰς μέσον προῆγε. καὶ ὡς ἀναγκαῖα καὶ χρειώδη ἐκεῖνα ταῖς ἐκκλησίαις ἀποδείξας, *Ἄτοπον, ἔλεγε, πράττουσιν οἳ ταῦτα διαβάλλειν ἐπιτηδεύουσιν. οὐ ταῦτα γάρ, ἀλλὰ περὶ ὧν οἱ λόγοι κινδυνεύουσι καθυβρίζειν.* Theodore Anagnostes reporting Socrates Scholasticus wrote that 'Theotimus staunchly argued against Epiphanius in defense of Origen'. *Op. cit.* 4.290. Cf. Socrates Scholasticus, *HE*, 6.12.

166 Procopius of Gaza, *Catena in Canticum Canticorum*, p. 1545.

167 Socrates Scholasticus, *HE*, 6.9; 6.13.

168 Socrates Scholasticus, *op. cit.* 3.7; 4.27.

169 Nicephorus Callistus Xanthopulus, *op. cit.* 13.12: τοῖς 'Ωριγένους δὲ βιβλίοις ἐπιμεμφόμενος. οἷς δὴ πρὸς αὐτοῦ ὁ πολύαθλος 'Αθανάσιος τῆς οἰκείας πίστεως εἰς σύστασιν ἀπεχρήσατο πλειστάκις ἐν τοῖς κατὰ 'Αρειανῶν αὐτῷ πονηθεῖσι συγγράμμασι.

170 Nicephorus Callistus Xanthopulus, *op. cit.* 14.14.

171 Socrates Scholasticus, *op. cit.* 2.22 & Nicephorus Callistus Xanthopulus, *op. cit.* 9.13: τῶν 'Ωριγένους βιβλίων, ἐν οἷς πανταχοῦ τὸν Υἱὸν ἐκ τοῦ Πατρὸς γεννηθέντα εὑρίσκουσιν οἱ τῶν 'Ωριγένους βιβλίων τὸ βάθος κατανοῆσαι δυνάμενοι.

was but the Nicene formula[172] set forth as tantamount to the proposition 'born from the essence of the Father'[173] -an equivalent first introduced by Origen.[174]

Little wonder that Nicephorus Callistus styled Origen 'most wise' (ὁ τὴν σοφίαν πολὺς 'Ωριγένης),[175] which was a designation that scholars began to accord Origen after no less than four centuries had passed since his condemnation by Justinian and by the torrent of 'theologians' ingratiating the emperor's wishes by means of their suave reproduction of his unscholarly allegations.[176] Later

---

172 τὸν υἱὸν τοῦ θεοῦ, γεννηθέντα ἐκ τοῦ πατρὸς μονογενῆ, τουτέστιν ἐκ τῆς οὐσίας τοῦ πατρός. *Concilium Universale Ephesenum Anno 431*, tome 1.1.1, p. 31; tome 1.1.2, p. 12; tome 1.1.3, p. 39; tome 1.1.4, p. 54; tome 1.1.6, p. 29; *et passim*. Eusebius, *Epistula ad Caesarienses*, 8; 9. Epiphanius of Salamis, *Ancoratus*, 118.10; *Panarion*, v. 3, p. 266. Athanasius, *De Decretis Nicaenae Synodi*, 19.4; 33.7-8; 37.2; *De Synodis Arimini in Italia et Seleuciae in Isauria*, 35.3-4; 54.1; *Oratio I Contra Arianos*, 15.6; 16.1; *Epistula ad Jovianum et Epistula Joviani ad Athanasium*, 1.3.1. Basil of Caesarea, *Epistulae*, epistles 125.2; 140.2. Socrates Scholasticus, *HE*, 1.8; 4.12. Theodoret, *HE*, pp. 50-51; 215. Cyril of Alexandria, *Thesaurus De Sancta Consubstantiali Trinitate*, PG.75.45.20-37.

173 ACO, *Concilium Universale Ephesenum Anno 431*, tome 1.1.6, p. 28; tome 1.1.7, p. 65. *Concilium Universale Chalcedonense Anno 451*, tome 2.1.1, p. 108; tome 2.1.2, pp. 80; 127-128. *Synodus Constantinopolitana et Hierosolymitana Anno 536*, tome 3, p. 4. *Concilium Lateranense a. 649 Celebratum*, Act 3, p. 158; Act 4, p. 218. *Concilium Universale Constantinopolitanum Tertium (680-681)*, Document 10, pp. 390; 392; Document 18, p. 770. Athanasius, *De Synodis Arimini in Italia et Seleuciae in Isauria*, 25.3; 26.1.2; 27.2. Epiphanius of Salamis, *Ancoratus*, 118.10. Cyril of Jerusalem, *Catecheses ad Illuminandos*, 11.3; 11.14; 11.21. Socrates Scholasticus, *HE*, 2.18; 2.30. Justinian, *Contra Monophysitas*, 39; 72. *Edictum Rectae Fidei*, p. 130; *Contra Nestorianos*, p. 32. John of Damascus, *Expositio Fidei*, 8; *Contra Nestorianos*, 35; 41. Photius, *Epistulae et Amphilochia*, epistle 1. Also, *Florilegium Cyrillianum*, p. 105 & *Chronicon Paschale*, p. 631; 637.

174 *commJohn*, XX.24.211: Τοσαῦτα καὶ πρὸς τὸν Ἡρακλέωνος λόγον εἰπόντος τὸ *Ἐκ τοῦ πατρὸς τοῦ διαβόλου* ἀντὶ τοῦ ἐκ τῆς οὐσίας τοῦ πατρὸς εἰρῆσθω. Cf. Socrates Scholasticus, *HE*, 3.7, who reported that, 'according to Pamphilus and Eusebius replying to those that detested Origen', he formed his Trinitarian doctrine (including the *homoousion*) 'not out of his own, but only because he interpreted the secret tradition of the church' (οὐ πρῶτον 'Ωριγένην ἐπὶ ταύτην τὴν πραγματείαν ἐλθεῖν φασιν, ἀλλὰ τὴν τῆς ἐκκλησίας μυστικὴν ἑρμηνεῦσαι παράδοσιν). Cf. Nicephorus Callistus Xanthopulus, *HE*, 10.14 (by and large copying from Socrates): οὗτοι δὴ πάντες καὶ ἕτεροι τοῖς πεπονημένοις τούτων συγγράμμασιν ἔμψυχον τὸν ἐνανθρωπήσαντα Λόγον, ἅτε δὴ αὐτοῖς ὁμοούσιον, ἐκδεδώκασι.

175 Nicephorus Callistus Xanthopulus, *op. cit.* 1.1; 10.14.

176 George Monachus, *Chronicon*, p. 53 & *Chronicon Breve*, PG.110.96.33-34: τοῦ σοφωτάτου καὶ πολυμαθοῦς 'Ωριγένους. Michael Glycas, *Quaestiones in Sacram Scripturam*, chapter 13, p. 166: ὁ τὰ θεῖα πρότερον σοφὸς 'Ωριγένης. Nicetas Seides, *Oratio Contra Eustratium Nicaeensem*, 16: Ἄκουσον καὶ τρίτου μάρτυρος τοῦ σοφοῦ 'Ωριγένους. Ephraem of Aenus (Thrace, thirteenth-fourteenth century), *Historia Chronica*, lines 166-167: Μαμαίας πιστευσάσης διδασκαλίαις ταῖς σοφαῖς 'Ωριγένους. Nilus Cabasilas, *De Processione Spiritus Sancti*, 14.219: Καὶ μὴν 'Ωριγένης, σοφώτατος ἐν Χριστιανοῖς γεγονὼς καὶ περὶ τὰς γραφὰς σπουδαιότατος. Nicephorus Gregoras, *Explicatio in Librum Synesii De Insomniis*, p. 13: ὡς καὶ 'Ωριγένει δοκεῖ τῷ σοφῷ.

still, when intellectuals were free from the ghost of Justinian's caesaropapism, Bessarion had no difficulty with appealing to 'Greek fathers and masters' and explaining this designation by citing three names: 'Origen, Chrysostom, Cyril, and the rest of them' (καὶ οἱ Ἕλληνες πατέρες τε καὶ διδάσκαλοι Ὠριγένης, Χρυσόστομος, Κύριλλος καὶ οἱ λοιποὶ πάντες), and styling them 'most wise and most holy ones' (σοφωτάτοις καὶ ἁγιωτάτοις).[177]

It is quite telling that, although Nicephorus Callistus posed as a defender of orthodoxy, he was struck by the sarcastic, and witty nonetheless, remark of Socrates Scholasticus: whereas malicious envy (ὁ φθόνος) struck Origen after he was dead, Chrysostom escaped this only just. For Origen was excommunicated by Theophilus of Alexandria nearly two hundred years after his death, whereas Chrysostom was restored only thirty five years after his death by Proclus of Constantinople.[178] 'However, it does not elude prudent people how do these things happened and always happen' (Ἀλλὰ ταῦτα μὲν ὅπως γέγονέ τε καὶ ἀεὶ γίνεται, τοὺς εὖ φρονοῦντας οὐ διαφεύγει).[179]

This is what the wise Theotimus had seen in the acts of 'the slanderous tetrad' of Methodius of Olympus, Eustathius of Antioch, Apollinaris of Laodicea, and Theophilus of Alexandria. This is also what the nearly-contemporary emperor Julian was appalled to notice in connection with some Christian bishops, when he said that 'no wild beasts are such enemies to mankind as most Christians in their deadly hatred for one another are.'[180] Celsus had described dissenting Christians in like terms: 'they speak evil of each other with dreadful and unspeakable words of abuse' and 'they utterly hate each other'.[181]

Nevertheless, the foregoing approaches were sequestered ones against the flurry of allegations claiming that Origen was the father of every possible and impossibly heresy, especially after his official condemnation during the sixth century: due to a number of assorted reasons, in the ensuing centuries when 'great theologians' was a scarce commodity and only a memory of the past, the allegations against Origen that Justinian had sanctioned were reproduced to the letter by theologisers seldom better than competent and normally worse.

I believe that Epiphanius was irritated not simply at Chrysostom's use of Origen's words, but in the latter's disposition to the Greek letters. The tradition

---

177 Bessarion, *In Verbum Evangelii: Sic Eum Volo Manere, Quid ad Te?*, 5.3.

178 In 438, Proclus transferred the relics of his old master, Saint John Chrysostom, from Comana back to Constantinople, where he interred them with great honour in the Church of the Twelve Apostles.

179 Socrates Scholasticus, *HE*, 7.45, quoted by Nicephorus Callistus Xanthopulus, *HE*, 14.43.

180 Ammianus Marcellinus (c. 330 – c. 400), *Res Gestae*, 22.4.4.

181 *Cels*, V.63.

had began with Clement of Alexandria, who (in his first *Stromateus*) argued for a view and attitude which later would have appeared as sheer scandal: Greek philosophy is not a fabrication by the daemons, but a gift given by God – therefore, this is highly valuable in order to comprehend Christian faith.

Origen had made 'the tenets of the philosophy of the Greeks' part of his syllabus, and so he did with geometry, astronomy, music, grammar, and rhetoric – all of which he valued as 'preparatory teaching towards understanding Christianism' (εἰς χριστιανισμόν).[182]

Epiphanius could not attack men such as Basil of Caesarea, who wrote provocative works, such as urging the youth to study of the Greek letters and instructed them how to benefit from this.[183] For Basil was a very tough proposition, because of not only his powerful advocation for the Nicene Creed but also his political connections. By the same token, Gregory of Nazianzus, although an orator and philosopher by training who infused Hellenism into the early church, was too prestigious to become a target. By contrast, Chrysostom was undeterred in his sympathy and respect for Origen: even after the commotion caused by Epiphanius at Constantinople, Chrysostom was as brave as to grant asylum to the four monks known as the 'Tall Brothers', who were leaders of the Nitrian community that had been expelled by Theophilus – the man who, one year later (July of 403), orchestrated John's condemnation and deposition at the Synod of Oak.

The allegation that Chrysostom was an 'Origenist' or that 'he embraced Origen's doctrines' was reproduced as hearsay by later authors. However none of them did ever say *what* was exactly that which could by branded 'heretical' view. Gregory Palamas wrote that he was prepared to bear the unfair charges against him as heretic, because he had in mind the case of 'a great man such as Chrysostom', who 'although surely and clearly expressed the [Christian] piety by means of his speeches that were as sweet as honey', he 'was cut-off from the Church on the grounds that he espoused the ideas of Origen, and was condemned to exile'.[184]

Certainly, such hearsay did not prevent intellectuals such as the illustrius pupil of George Gemistus, namely, Basil Bessarion (1403-1472) to speak

182 Origen, *Epistula ad Gregorium Thaumaturgum*, 1 (*Philocalia*, 13.1); see quotation on p. XLIX and note 136.

183 Basil of Caesarea, *De Legendis Gentilium Libris*, ed. by F. Boulenger, *Saint Basile. Aux jeunes gens sur la manière de tirer profit des lettres Helléniques*, Paris, 1935 (repr. 1965), pp. 41-61.

184 Gregory Palamas, *Orationes Asceticae*, 3.5: Τί γάρ, οὐχὶ καὶ ὁ Χρυσόστομος πατήρ, ὁ καὶ σῶμα περικείμενος ἔτι τῇ Ἐκκλησίᾳ τῶν πρωτοτόκων ἐν οὐρανοῖς συνημμένος, εἴπερ ἀσφαλῶς ἅμα καὶ σαφῶς καὶ μελιχρῶς λογογραφῶν τὴν εὐσέβειαν, οὐχ οὗτος τοίνυν ὁ τηλικοῦτος, ὡς τὰ Ὠριγένους γράφων καὶ φρονῶν, ἐξεκόπη τῆς Ἐκκλησίας καὶ ὑπερορίαν κατεδικάσθη;

respectfully of Origen and include him among 'the fathers and doctors of the Church'.[185]

Later still, when Patriarch Dositheus II of Jerusalem (1641-1707) wrote his twelve-volume *History of the Patriarchate of Jerusalem* (1715), he remarked that 'Chrysostom was accused only because he used to read Origen's works',[186] and this was why he was incriminated as a defender of Origen's doctrines not only by Theophilus but also by Epiphanius' (ὡς ὑπερασπιστὴς τῶν δογμάτων τοῦ 'Ωριγένους), which was a 'false pretext' (τὸ εἶναι δῆθεν 'Ωριγενιαστὴν τὸν Χρυσόστομον).[187] Nevertheless, Dositheus had no problem with appealing to various exegeses by Origen.[188] And when Dositheus reported a certain exegesis that Origen expounded in his commentary on the epistle to the Galatians, he added that both 'Theodoret and Chrysostom embraced this in their commentaries on the same epistle', and so did 'Cassiodorus, Augustine,[189] and Jerome, and the rest of the authoritative fathers'.[190]

The nebulous report always was that 'Chrysostom used to read Origen's works', but what exactly was wrong that either of them said was never declared or at least hinted at.[191]

Therefore, the dispute was not really about Origen's passages being used by Chrysostom, since his case was not the same as that of, say, Gregory of Nyssa (and, to a lesser extent, Nanianzen) who was accused of upholding Origenian doctrines, such as that of universal restoration. In Chrysostom's case, it was his *attitude* rather than Origen's specific *ideas* or theories that were intolerable to his detractors.

The altercation was more profound and critical, since it touched on the contentious Christian assessment and treatment of Hellenism. Chrysostom was just one of those enlightened theologians who did not see Hellenism as a daemon that should be exorcised – an attitude which in Justinian's dark era became a daemon in itself. After all, Chrysostom was born to Greek parents, he was a pupil of Libanius, and never did he disown his love for both the Greek art of rhetoric and the benefits inherent in Greek language and literature.

---

185 Bessarion, *In verbum evangelii: Sic eum volo manere, quid ad te?*, section 5.3.

186 Dositheus II of Jerusalem, *Δωδεκάβιβλος*, book 1, p. 143.

187 *Op. cit.* Book 3, p. 95; see also pp. 102; 104.

188 Dositheus, *op. cit.* book 10, pp. 404; 497.

189 On Augustine seizing on Origen's ideas, see my "Origen, The Source of Augustine's Theory of Time", in *Philosophia*, Yearbook of the Research Center for Greek Philosophy at the Academy of Athens, v. 17-18, 1989, pp. 396-418.

190 Dositheus, *op. cit.* book 1, p. 72.

191 See Michael Glycas, *Annales*, pp. 130; 414. Leo VI the Wise, *Homiliae*, homily 38, lines 1000-1008. John Zonaras, *Epitome Historiarum*, p. 102: 'Ωριγενιαστὴς γὰρ ὁ εὐσεβέστατος ἐκεῖνος πατὴρ καὶ ἐκαλεῖτο καὶ ἐνομίζετο. Dositheus, *op. cit.* book 1, p. 143.

This was not just about mere predilection: Origen's works demonstrably show that Greek lore is indispensable to formulating Christian propositions, especially the abstruse ones. Siding with Origen (and ultimately with Paul) Chrysostom would have never endorsed Tertullian's "What has Athens to do with Jerusalem? (Quid ergo Athenis et Hierosolymis?) What concord is there between the Academy and the Church?'. As a matter of fact, he knew full well that Athens had a lot to do with Jerusalem. 'Athens' and 'Jerusalem' were all but two mutually exclusive entities.

In the epistle to the Romans, 1:18-25, Paul granted that the Greeks received by God an inkling of the divine grandeur and yet they did not glorify Him as God. Nevertheless, the 'things' that 'God revealed to them' could not be overlooked. However, in order for this study to bring about fruits, a certain background was necessary. The 'sin' of Origen and Chrysostom was that they were knowledgeable enough as to recognise the seeds that God had granted the Hellenes. This is why in Origen's work there is a great deal of 'Athens' – only this is not recognised by his readers. This comes as no surprise, given that 'Athens' is a very expensive commodity to gain possession of. The virtuous Athenian statesman and general Phocion (c. 402 – c. 318 BC; nicknamed The Good) was condemned to die by drinking the hemlock; but when Phocion had drunk the hemlock that was given to him, the dose proved insufficient to be lethal and the public executioner refused to prepare more unless he was paid 12 drachmas, Phocion said to one of his friends (on May 19, 318 BC), 'In Athens, it is hard for a man even to die without paying for it' (εἰ μηδ' ἀποθανεῖν Ἀθήνησι δωρεάν ἐστιν).[192] Like Origen, Chrysostom *could* afford to 'visit' Athens and enjoy the goods that the city could offer, because he *could* afford the 'money' required and appreciate the value of those 'goods'. This was in reality the intolerable sin which he was not forgiven for – although it turned out that, to the Church, he remained an orthodox father.

As a result, anthologists who either ignored Origen's work, or apprehensively sought to suppress his name while quoting his words, attributed extensive parts from the present commentary to stars of Christian theology, only because the latter had copied from Origen without mentioning his name – some of them in good will, others not quite so. Glaring examples of this practice which emerges in the present book are John Chrysostom, Cyril of Alexandria, as well as authors either prior of posterior to sixth century, such as Gregory Thaumaturgus, Gregory of Nyssa (exclusively in his *Orationes viii De Beatitudinibus*), Basil of Caesarea, Theodore of Heraclea, Apollinaris,

192 Plutarch, *Phocion*, 36.7.

Theodore of Mopsuestia, Theodoret, Isidore of Pelusium, Maximus Confessor, Philagathus (Philip Cerameus, twelfth century), and Photius.

Common allegiances to Origen certainly do not mean mutual good relations. Cyril of Alexandria always 'felt utter repugnance towards John' Chrysostom (ἀπεχθῶς μάλα ἔχοντι πρὸς Ἰωάννην) because the latter had opposed Cyril's uncle, bishop Theophilus of Alexandria.[193] Patriarch Alexander of Antioch was the first who decided to include Chrysostom's name in the ecclesiastical tabulae, but Cyril took a strong stand against this. Patriarch Atticus of Constantinople wrote a letter to Cyril imploring him to relent, but Cyril sent a reply confirming that he adamantly abode by his repugnance for Chrysostom.[194] Actually, Cyril (who had accompanied his uncle Theophilus at the synod of Oak) until his last breath muttered that Chrysostom had been justly condemned. Anastasius of Sinai styled Cyril 'the seal of all the Fathers' (σφραγὶς τῶν πατέρων),[195] but the Oriental synod of fifty Eastern bishops convened at Ephesus by Patriarch John I of Antioch (429-441) which sympathised with Nestorius, described the Alexandrian primate as 'a monster, born and educated for the destruction of the church' (ὁ δὲ ἐπ᾽ ὀλέθρῳ τῶν ἐκκλησιῶν καὶ τεχθεὶς καὶ τραφείς, ὡς ἔοικε, Κύριλλος ὁ τῆς Ἀλεξανδρέων).[196] Anyway, Christian writings, especially documents of synods that dignified themselves with the name 'oecumenical', are full of such heinous declarations and wishes.

Consequently, it is all but chance that many passages of Origen occur *verbatim* in Chrysostom's work, who he never denied this (and Epiphanius was all too quick to walk all over it) and certainly Chrysostom never succumbed to the demand to denounce Origen and his ideas.

Nevertheless, the present codex displays some interesting characteristics and there are some telling recurring phenomena.

For one, later catenists (normally, monks in scriptoria of monasteries) sometimes attributed passages of Origen to stars of orthodoxy, mainly Cyril of Alexandria and John Chrysostom, especially if they came upon such portions in both authors. Therefore, especially in the case of Chrysostom, there is nothing strange about passages attributed to both him and Origen – which is but the case of Chrysostom using Origen's words in his own homilies,[197] for which the Archbishop of Constantinople paid a heavy price.

193 Nicephorus Callistus Xanthopulus, *HE*, 14.25.

194 Nicephorus Callistus Xanthopulus, *op. cit.* 14.25-27.

195 Anastasius of Sinai, *Viae Dux*, 7.1.

196 ACO, *Concilium Universale Ephesenum anno 431*, tome 1.1.5, p. 129.

197 For example, fragment 15 from Origen's commentary on the Ephesians was attributed also to Chrysostom. By the same token, Chrysostom's fragment on Jeremiah (PG.64.917.46-50) was ascribed also to Origen.

Secondly, once Origen had introduced a term and used it moderately, some conspicuous posterior authors took this up and used it obsessively, sometimes promiscuously. The difference between Chrysostom and Cyril was that the former conveniently used passages of Origen to the letter, whereas Cyril abided by the philosophical ideas and characteristic philosophical terminology of his predecessor, and applied them to numerous points repeatedly. A few examples hopefully will convince even those who still doubt Cyril's allegiances to Origen. After all, the fact that Cyril's education included study of Origen, of Didymus the Blind, and of Eusebius, is not new knowledge.

1. Cyril felt it necessary to denounce the notion of God being an anthropomorphous material body.[198] But whose view did he possibly renounce other than that of his immediate predecessor (and uncle) Theophilus, who had switched his view of incorporeal God to the anthropomorphic one held by the local monks that were hostile to his pastoral letter of 399, and then he turned on the followers of Origen after having supported them for a time?[199]

2. The notion of Logos being envisaged as a 'stark-naked' one (γυμνὸς) is a recurring motif in Origen: it suggests the Logos not only as incorporeal but also as not being involved with, or engaging in, generating the material reality.[200] On this, Philo influenced him.[201] Two of the most faithful followers of Origen imbibed this trope moderately,[202] but Cyril of Alexandria was obsessed

---

198 Cyril of Alexandria rejected the doctrine, while caring not to mention its author; *Ad Calosyrium*, p. 604: οὐκοῦν οὐκ ἐνσώματος, εἰ πνεῦμά ἐστιν. In the twelfth century, Michael Glycas recalled that 'some of our own people posited God as corporeal'; *Quaestiones in Sacram Scripturam*, chapter 11, p. 145: Οἱ μὲν γὰρ ἐνσώματον εἶναι τὸν Θεὸν καθ' ἡμᾶς ἐδογμάτισαν.

199 Socrates Scholasticus, *HE*, 6.7. See *supra*, note 141.

200 Cf. *commJohn*, II.8.61: Οὐ γυμνὸς δὲ τῷ Ἰωάννῃ ὁρᾶται τῷ ἵππῳ ὀχούμενος ὁ τοῦ θεοῦ λόγος. *Op. cit.* VI.35.179: ἵνα ταῦτά τις λύσας τὸν χωρὶς τῶν ὑποδημάτων ἴδῃ λόγον γυμνὸν τῶν ὑποδεεστέρων καθ' αὑτόν. *Op. cit.* XIX.22.147: ὅσῳ διαφέρει γυμνὸς πάσης ὕλης τοῦ ὅλου κόσμου λόγος τοῦ ἐνύλου κόσμου. *frJohn*, 63: ἀλλ' ἐπεὶ ὁ τοιοῦτος λόγος οὐ γυμνὸς ὕλης καὶ σωματικῶν παραδειγμάτων εἰς ἀνθρώπους ἔρχεται.

201 Philo, *De Opificio Mundi*, 24: εἰ δέ τις ἐθελήσειε γυμνοτέροις χρήσασθαι τοῖς ὀνόμασιν, οὐδὲν ἂν ἕτερον εἴποι τὸν νοητὸν κόσμον εἶναι ἢ θεοῦ λόγον ἤδη κοσμοποιοῦντος. *Quod Deus Sit Immutabilis*, 83: οὐ γάρ ἐστιν ὁ λόγος αὐτῷ γεγονὼς ἀέρος πλῆξις ἀναμιγνύμενος ἄλλῳ τὸ παράπαν οὐδενί, ἀλλὰ ἀσώματός τε καὶ γυμνός.

202 Gregory Thaumaturgus, *In Origenem Oratio Panegyrica*, 15: γυμνὸς καὶ ἀσκεπὴς ὁ θεῖος εἰσίῃ λόγος. Gregory of Nyssa, *De Deitate Filii et Spiritus Sancti*, PG.46.564.50-53 (quoted also by Theodoret, *Eranistes*, p. 105): Κατέβη τοίνυν καὶ ἐφάνη οὐ γυμνὸς ὁ Λόγος, ἀλλὰ σὰρξ γενόμενος. Much later, Anastasius of Sinai, *Sermo ii in Constitutionem Hominis Secundum Imaginem Dei*, 3 (τοῦ γυμνοῦ θεοῦ λόγου); cf. *Sermo i in Constitutionem Hominis Secundum Imaginem Dei*, 1 (τῆς γυμνῆς θεότητος). John of Damascus, *De Fide Contra Nestorianos*, 19.

with the metaphor and could not have enough of it.[203] Subsequently, Maximus Confessor (who knew what Origen's Theory of *logoi* was about)[204] spoke not only of the 'stark-naked Logos', but also of the 'stark-naked logoi',[205] meaning the incorporeal *causes* that give rise to all aspects of reality. The participants of the council of Ephesus employed the expression 'stark-naked Logos' (γυμνὸς Λόγος) only because Cyril had used the expression, but they had no inkling of the fact that the Christian source of it was Origen.[206] So did those who took part in a sixth-century synod,[207] and the irony was that both of those assemblies treated Origen as a damned heretic while unconsciously using his legacy – a usual sixth-century phenomenon, anyway.[208]

In any event, seizing on of Origen's inventive and innovative formulas was always a convenient practice. For example, considering the 'grace' granted by the Holy Spirit, he introduced the expression ἐνοίκησις τοῦ ἁγίου Πνεύματος ('dwelling of the Holy Spirit') in apposition with the biblical term χρίσμα ('anointing'). He had in mind such scriptural points as Acts, 10:38 and Psalm 44:8 quoted in Heb. 1:9 (for 'anointing'), as well as Ezekiel 37:27 paraphrased in 2 Cor. 6:16 (for 'dwelling'), but the set expression itself was not scriptural: it was new, indeed and it was his own.[209] Origen's devout admirers promptly took

203 Cyril of Alexandria, *In Joannem*, v. 1, pp. 257; 277; 283; 489; *Responsiones ad Tiberium Diaconum Sociosque Suos*, pp. 591-592; *De Sancta Trinitate Dialogi*, pp. 516; *De Incarnatione Unigeniti*, 705; *Quod Unus Sit Christus*, pp. 748; 755; 764; 772; *Epistulae Paschales*, PG.77.568.38-39; *Expositio in Psalmos*, PG.69.1040.28; *Commentarius in Isaiam Prophetam*, PG.70.1045.1; *Commentarii in Lucam*, PG.72.509.41-42; *Thesaurus De Sancta Consubstantiali Trinitate*, PG.75.429.33-34.

204 Maximus was aware of, and inspired by, Origen's theory of creation almost as much as Gregory of Nyssa was. The difference was that Gregory elaborated on Origen's theory and expanded it by using philosophical exposition which we do not see in Origen's extant works, although what Gregory said was neither new nor different. On the other hand, Maximus abode by Origen's terminology.

205 Maximus Confessor, *Quaestiones ad Thalassium*, 25; 27: γυμνοὺς θεάσασθαι τοὺς λόγους τῶν αἰσθητῶν.

206 ACO, *Concilium Universale Ephesenum Anno 431*, v. 1.1.1, pp. 64; 66; v. 1.1.4, p. 56; v. 1.1.5, pp. 52; 59; 70; 85; v. 1.1.6, pp. 47; 63; v. 1.1.7, p. 58.

207 ACO, *Synodus Constantinopolitana et Hierosolymitana Anno 536*, v. 3, pp. 7; 217.

208 *RCR*, 'The sixth-century Origenism', pp. 259-321.

209 Origen, *selEz*, PG.13.812.5-6 (comm. on Ez. 16:9): Χρίσμα ἐστὶν ἐνοίκησις τοῦ ἁγίου Πνεύματος ἐν γνώσει τῆς ἀληθείας.

this up,[210] so did later theologians galore,[211] and, as it happened, his detractor Epiphanius of Salamis did so once again.[212]

3. With the exception of Eusebius who made extensive quotations from the *Enneads*,[213] during the next two hundred years after Origen's death no author did ever mention the novel Plotinian notion and formula 'being beyond the Intellect' (ἐπέκεινα νοῦ). One would be surprised at finding out that the author after Origen who did so was not a Neoplatonist[214] enthusiast: it was Cyril of Alexandria, the celebrated authority of Christian orthodoxy, who was obsessed with applying Plotinus' expression ἐπέκεινα νοῦ.[215] As a rule, Christian authors

---

210 Athanasius, *Oratio I Contra Arianos*, 46.5 & *Catena in Epistulam ad Hebraeos* (*catena Nicetae*), p. 338; quoted also by Gennadius Scholarius, *De Spiritu Sancto ii*, Part 2, p. 289: ὅμως δὲ λέγεται νῦν *χρίεσθαι*, ἵνα πάλιν ὡς ἄνθρωπος λεγόμενος τῷ πνεύματι χρίεσθαι ἡμῖν τοῖς ἀνθρώποις, καθάπερ τὸ ὑψωθῆναι καὶ ἀναστῆναι, οὕτως καὶ τὴν τοῦ πνεύματος ἐνοίκησιν καὶ οἰκειότητα κατασκευάσῃ. Basil of Caesarea, *Adversus Eunomium*, PG.29.725.18-30 & *Catena in Epistulam ad Romanos* (*typus Monacensis*), p. 242: τὴν τοῦ Πνεύματος ἐνοίκησιν ἀποφαίνοντος Χριστοῦ. … Χρίσμα δὲ τὸ Πνεῦμα ἐφ' ἡμῖν, ὡς 'Ιωάννης λέγει. Cf. Gregory of Nyssa, *De Instituto Christiano*, p. 61: τὴν ἐνοίκησιν τοῦ ἁγίου πνεύματος. *Op. cit.* p. 79: καὶ τοῦ πνεύματος δι' ἔργων ἀγαθῶν προκοπῆς ἐνοίκησις.

211 Pseudo-Macarius, *Sermones 64*, homily 25.2.5: ἡ πληρεστάτη τοῦ ἁγίου πνεύματος καὶ ἐνεργὴς ἐνοίκησις. *Epistula Magna*, p. 277 (& Ephraem Syrus, *Institutio ad Monachos*, p. 353): ἀπολαύσει ὁ τοιοῦτος διὰ τὴν ἐνεργῆ ἐνοίκησιν τοῦ ἁγίου πνεύματος. *Op. cit.* p. 278 (& Ephraem Syrus, *op. cit.* p. 354): ἡ γὰρ τοῦ ἁγίου πνεύματος εἰς αὐτοὺς πληρεστάτη ἐνοίκησις. Theodore of Mopsuestia, *Fragmenta in Epistulam i ad Corinthios*, p. 192: ὁ δὲ προφητεύων τοὺς ἀκούοντας ὠφελεῖ καὶ ἐκ τῆς προγνώσεως δείκνυσι τὴν ἐνοίκησιν τοῦ ἁγίου πνεύματος τὴν ἐν αὐτῷ. Ammonius of Alexandria (presbyter), *Fragmenta in Joannem*, fr. 27: ὁ Χριστὸς διὰ τοῦ λουτροῦ δέδωκεν ἡμῖν πνεύματος ἁγίου ἐνοίκησιν. Likewise, numerous later Byzantine authors.

212 Epiphanius of Salamis, *Panarion*, v. 3, p. 331: ναὸς θεοῦ καλούμεθα δι' ἐνοίκησιν ἁγίου πνεύματος.

213 Eusebius, *Praeparatio Evangelica*, 11.17.10.9.

214 Damascius used the expression ἐπέκεινα τῶν πάντων in the opening of his tract in order to endorse the standard tenet that the One is transcendent to Being (i.e. to *Nous*). *Princ*, p. 1. Simplicius described Aristotle's First Immovable Mover in the same terms (πάντων ὄντος ἐπέκεινα). *commCael*, p. 432.

215 Cyril of Alexandria, *De Incarnatione Unigeniti*, p. 683: Θεὸς δὲ ὁ παντὸς ἐπέκεινα νοῦ, γενέσεως καὶ φθορᾶς τὴν ὕπαρξιν ἔχων ἐξῃρημένην τε καὶ ὑπερίσχουσαν. *Op. cit.* p. 685: ὁ ὢν ἐν ἀρχῇ τῇ παντὸς ἐπέκεινα νοῦ. *Epistulae Paschales*, PG.77.725.34: Τροπὴν γὰρ οὐκ οἶδεν ἡ παντὸς ἐπέκεινα νοῦ καὶ ἀνωτάτω φύσις. *Op. cit.* PG.77.769.46: 'Αποδέχεται τὸν λόγον, ὡς Λόγου Πατήρ, ὁ παντὸς ἐπέκεινα νοῦ, φημὶ δὴ Θεός. *Op. cit.* PG.77.773.33. καὶ ὁ πρὸ παντὸς αἰῶνος καὶ χρόνου τὴν ἐκ Θεοῦ τοῦ καὶ Πατρὸς ἀπότεξιν ἔχων, τὴν ἐπέκεινα νοῦ καὶ λόγου παντός. *Op. cit.* PG.77.885.45: καὶ ἀναμορφοῦσθαι τρόπον τινὰ δι' εὐαγοῦς πολιτείας πρὸς τὸν παντὸς ἐπέκεινα νοῦ. *Op. cit.* PG.77.893.18: τὴν θείαν τε καὶ ἀκήρατον φύσιν, τὴν παντὸς ἐπέκεινα νοῦ, καὶ πέραν λόγου καὶ θαύματος. *Op. cit.* PG.77.924.20: 'Ο γὰρ ἐπέκεινα νοῦ παντός, ὁ δι' οὗ τὰ πάντα παρήχθη πρὸς γένεσιν, ὁ ἐξ αὐτῆς ἀναφὺς τῆς οὐσίας τοῦ Θεοῦ καὶ Πατρὸς Λόγος. *Glaphyra in Pentateuchum*, PG.69.465.46: Ἄποπτος γὰρ παντελῶς, καὶ μὴν καὶ ἐπέκεινα νοῦ

refrained from using the precarious Platonic catchphrase,[216] until Michael Psellus did so in the eleventh century. This, however, did not prevent the council of Ephesus from employing it conveniently, only because they copied from Cyril's writings.[217]

Once Cyril took his cue from Origen, he became obsessed with identifying God as *Nous*, indeed the Anaxagorean one. There is reference to a work of his entitled 'Against the Synousiasts', which is not extant, but we learn of this from a quotation by Justinian writing against the Monophysites. There are subsequent references to this work, all of them drawing on Justinian, but the fact that this work is not extant is strange: how was it possible for a tract by a pillar of the Byzantine establishment and a powerful bishop to be lost? Perhaps this quotation from Justinian provides the answer: not only did Cyril see the Christian God as 'Nous', but now he described Him in sheer Anaxagorean terms: the Supreme Nature is 'pure' (καθαρός),[218] 'simple' (ἁπλοῦς),[219] and 'unmixed (ἀμιγής)[220] with anything else'.[221]

παντός, καὶ λόγου δύναμιν ὑπερφέρεται. *Commentarius in Isaiam Prophetam*, PG.70.896.47: ἀλλὰ αὐτὸς ἡ πάντων ἀρχὴ καὶ παντὸς ἐπέκεινα νοῦ, καὶ μετ' αὐτὸν οὐκ ἔσται. Μένει γὰρ ὁ αὐτός, καὶ ἀναλλοίωτον ἔχει τὴν φύσιν, καὶ ἀκράδαντον τὴν κατὰ πάντων ὑπεροχήν, καὶ διηνεκῆ βασιλείαν. *De Sancta Trinitate Dialogi*, p. 383: καὶ τὰ παντὸς ἐπέκεινα νοῦ καὶ γοῦν ἐν ἐσόπτρῳ καὶ αἰνίγματι βλέπειν. *Op. cit.* p. 506: τὴν ἀπόρρητον καὶ παντὸς ἐπέκεινα νοῦ τοῦ Θεοῦ φύσιν. *Op. cit.* p. 558: πρὸς τὰ ἐπέκεινα νοῦ παντὸς ἀναμύειν οὐ παραιτούμεθα.

216 By annexing 'beyond nous' (ἐπέκεινα νοῦ, *Enneades*, I.7.1; III.8.9; V.3.11&12; V.4.2; V.8.1) to Plato's 'beyond essence' (ἐπέκεινα οὐσίας), Plotinus augmented Plato's expression as in *Respublica*, 509b. Otherwise, Plotinus used Plato's phrase itself abundantly.

217 ACO, *Concilium Universale Ephesenum Anno 431*, 1.1.1, p. 48 (quoting from Cyril's *De Incarnatione Unigeniti*, p. 683): θεὸς δὲ ὁ παντὸς ἐπέκεινα νοῦ γενέσεως καὶ φθορᾶς τὴν ὕπαρξιν ἔχων ἐξῃρημένην τε καὶ ὑπερίσχουσαν. *Op. cit.* tome 1.1.1, p. 50 (*apud* Cyril, *op. cit.* p. 685): ὁ ὢν ἐν ἀρχῇ τῇ παντὸς ἐπέκεινα νοῦ.

218 Plotinus, *Enneades*, V.1.9. Asclepius of Tralles, *commMetaph*, p. 62.

219 Aristotle, *De Anima*, 429b. Plotinus, *Enneades*, V.1.9; and commentators (Themistius, Simplicius, John Philoponus, Sophonias).

220 Aristotle, *Physica*, 256b; *De Anima*, 429a. Plotinus, *Enneades*, V.1.9; so did Aristotle's commentators, Themistius, Syrianus, Simplicius, John Philoponus, Asclepius of Tralles, Michael Psellus, and Sophonias.

221 Justinian, *Contra Monophysitas*, 68 (quoting from Cyril's *Against the Synousiasts*): ἐν ἁγίοις Κύριλλος ... λέγει γὰρ ἐν τῷ κατὰ τῶν Συνουσιαστῶν λόγῳ ταῦτα ... δεῖ γὰρ τῇ πάντων ἐπέκεινα καὶ ἀνωτάτω φύσει σῴζεσθαι καθαρῶς τὸ ἁπλοῦν καὶ ἀσυμμιγὲς ἑτέρῳ. Cyril's work entitled Κατὰ Συνουσιαστῶν is mentioned by Justinian also in *op. cit.* 9; also in the *Florilegium Cyrillianum*, pp. 138; 141, and in the *Doctrina Patrum*, pp. 33; 59; 125. So did Eustathius (monk, Constantinople, sixth century), *Epistula ad Timotheum Scholasticum De Duabus Naturis Adversus Severum*, line 954; Nicephorus I of Constantinople (Patriarch, eighth-ninth century), *Eusebii Caesariensis Confutatio*, 66; Photius, *Bibliotheca*, Cod. 229, p. 253a. 'Synousiasts' were styled those who sustained (or so Justinian claimed) that, in Christ, the divine and human natures were made one.

Of course, Justinian had no idea what all this was about, but presumably it was later realised that Cyril had gone too far. Nevertheless, styling God Platonically as being 'beyond everything' (ἐπέκεινα πάντων), became a recurrent theme in Christian literature because of Cyril of Alexandria, who championed this usage at legion of points. However, Origen had refrained from such a formula.[222] It goes without saying that this was precarious and would be easily seen as verging on heresy. Nevertheless, a late Byzantine author, obviously taking his cue from this, figured out the Trinity analogously to a human being: the Father is Intellect; the Son is Logos; the Spirit is like a translucent aether smoothly gliding around the Father and Son, as if a light breezy breath.[223]

4. In the treatise 'On the Three Primary Hypostases', Plotinus explained the 'lineage'[224] of the Intellect, saying that this lineage is 'befitting the purest Intellect' (ὁ νοῦς οὗτος ἄξιος[225] νοῦ τοῦ καθαρωτάτου), since it springs from the first principle'.[226]

This instance is more than an occasional linguistic loan from Anaxagoras. For although Plotinus identified his Intellect with Plato's Demiurge and strove to convince that his source was Plato, in fact, he wrote having in mind Anaxagoras' Nous. This is why, shortly after that point,[227] he felt it necessary to mention Anaxagoras by name in order to acknowledge that this Presocratic did not really say anything different, even though 'his exposition was not very accurate, because of his ancientness'. However, the fact of the matter is that the source of Plotinus' expression καθαρώτατος νοῦς ('most pure Intellect')

---

222 Cf. *Cels*, VI.64: whether God is 'beyond essence' (quoting Plato, *Respublica*, 509b) or He is essence himself, is a question that Origen opted for leaving moot. Likewise, in VI.64. In VII.45, πάντων ἐπέκεινα ὤν are Celsus' words. More interesting is a reference made nearly ten years before *Cels* was composed. In the *exhMar*, 47, he seems to allow for comprehension of the incomprehensible God: as every instrument of the body is akin to grasping specific kinds of stimuli (e.g. an eye can see things that are visible and an ear can hear sounds), so mind is akin to grasping both 'intelligible things, and God, who is beyond intelligible things' (ὥσπερ ἕκαστον μέλος ἡμῶν πρός τι πέφυκεν οἰκειότητα σῴζειν, οἱ ὀφθαλμοὶ πρὸς τὰ ὁρατὰ καὶ ὦτα πρὸς τὰ ἀκουστά, οὕτω νοῦς πρὸς τὰ νοητὰ καὶ τὸν ἐπέκεινα τῶν νοητῶν θεόν). In *Cels*, VII.45, he is explicit on this, too: 'although God is beyond everything, He can be grasped intellectually, by means of a certain ineffable power' (πάντων ἐπέκεινα ὤν, ἀρρήτῳ τινὶ δυνάμει νοητός).

223 *apud* Anonymous, *Vita Sancti Andreae Sali*, 36, lines 3018-3027: νοῦς γὰρ ὁ πατήρ, λόγος ὁ υἱός, πνεῦμα ἐκείνη ἡ εὔπνοια, δι᾽ ἧς τὸν αἰθέρα ἀναπνέομεν. ... καὶ εὑρήσεις νοῦν τὸν πατέρα καὶ λόγον τὸν μονογενῆ αὐτοῦ υἱὸν καὶ πνεῦμα τὸ πνεῦμα τὸ ἅγιον. διὰ γὰρ τῶν τριῶν τούτων ὑποστάσεων εἷς θεὸς καὶ ὁρᾶται καὶ κηρύσσεται θεοπρεπῶς. Likewise, *op. cit.* 13, lines 842-844.

224 Using the expression of Homer's *Ilias*, VI.211.

225 I opt for the known alternative ἄξιος, not ἀξίας which makes no sense.

226 Plotinus, *Enneades*, V.1.7.

227 Plotinus, *op. cit.* V.1.9.

was Anaxagoras, not Plato. Cyril of Alexandria, who was fascinated by the Anaxagorean vocabulary and applied the designation Nous to the Father, did so once again: the Father is a simple, incorporeal, and most pure Nous.[228] To say that the Father begot the Son is the same as saying that the Nous generated the Logos.[229] Presumably he wrote having in mind his own reception of Anaxagoras, since he conveniently entertained into his Trinitarian exposition characteristic expressions associated with the Presocratic philosopher, who regarded the Mind as 'simple' (ἁπλοῦς), 'incorporeal' (ἀσώματος), and 'most pure' (καθαρώτατος).[230]

Origen had entertained the idea of a 'First Nous' (τοῦ πρώτου νοῦ, meaning the *supreme* one), which he also styled 'perfect Nous' (τέλειος νοῦς), and argued that everything, including 'qualities', was created by this 'Nous'.[231] It is certainly not fortuitous that Gregory Thaumaturgus in his farewell panegyric address to his master Origen entertained the notion of 'First Nous' meaning the Father of

---

228 Cyril of Alexandria, *Thesaurus De Sancta Consubstantiali Trinitate*, PG.75.76.21-23: ἁπλοῦς δὲ καὶ ἀσώματος, καὶ αὐτὸ δὴ τοῦτο νοῦς ὁ πάντων καθαρώτατος.

229 Cyril of Alexandria, *In Joannem*, v. 1, pp. 69-70: διὰ τὸ λόγον καὶ σοφίαν καὶ ἀπαύγασμα καὶ χαρακτῆρα καὶ δύναμιν τοῦ Πατρὸς ἀποκαλεῖσθαι τὸν Υἱόν. λόγος μὲν γὰρ καὶ σοφία, διὰ τὸ ἐκ νοῦ καὶ ἐν νῷ προσεχῶς καὶ ἀδιαστάτως, καὶ τὴν εἰς ἄλληλα τῶν σημαινομένων, ὡς ἂν εἴποι τις, ἀντεμβολήν. νοῦς γὰρ ἐν λόγῳ καὶ σοφίᾳ, καὶ λόγος εἰς νοῦν ἀμοιβαδὸν ὀφθήσονται, καὶ τὸ μεσολαβοῦν οὐδὲν ἢ χωρίζον τοῦ ἑτέρου τὸ ἕτερον. *Op. cit.* v. 1, pp. 604-605: ἀπεστάλη δὲ οὕτως ὡς λόγος ἐκ νοῦ, ὡς ἀπαύγασμα τὸ ἡλιακὸν ἐξ αὐτοῦ. ... οὐ γὰρ ἐπειδήπερ ἐξεδόθη λόγος ἐκ νοῦ, καὶ ἀπαύγασμα τυχὸν ἐξ ἡλίου, διὰ τοῦτο χρὴ πάντως οἴεσθαι τῶν ἐκβεβηκότων ὑπάρχειν ἔρημα τὰ γεννήσαντα. *De Sancta Trinitate Dialogi*, pp. 450-451: Ἔστι γὰρ ἐκ νοῦ καὶ εἰς νοῦν ὁ λόγος ἀεί, καὶ μὴν καὶ ὁ νοῦς ἐν λόγῳ. Ἦ εἰ τοῦτο φαῖεν ἂν ὡς οὐκ ἄριστα ἔχοι, νοῦς μὲν ἄλογος ἔσται, λόγος δὲ ἄνους ... Νοῦς μὲν γὰρ ἀεὶ λόγου ῥίζα τε καὶ γένεσις, νοῦ δὲ αὖ λόγος καρπός τε καὶ κύημα. Ὁ μὲν γὰρ ἄλογος οὐδαμῶς, καὶ εἰ λόγον ἐκτέκοι, ὁ δὲ τὴν τοῦ τεκόντος ποιότητα καὶ ἰδέαν φύσιν ὥσπερ ἰδίαν διεκληρώσατο, πρόεισί τε τὸν τεκόντα παραβλάψας οὐδέν. ... νοῦς ὅτι λόγον ἔχει, λόγος δὲ αὖ πάλιν ὅτι μεμέστωται νοῦ, πῶς ἂν νοοῖτό ποτε δίχα μὲν λόγου νοῦς, λόγος δὲ νοῦ τητώμενος. *Op. cit.* p. 452: Ὅτι λόγου μὲν ἡ ἐκ νοῦ πρὸς τὸ ἔξω φορὰ καὶ τὸ ἀπαθὲς τῆς γεννήσεως καὶ μὴν ὅτι τὸ γεννηθὲν οὐ διατετμήσεται, μενεῖ δὲ μᾶλλον αὐτό τε ἐν τῷ γεννήσαντι νῷ καὶ τὸν γεννήσαντα νοῦν ἕξει που πάντως ἐν ἑαυτῷ. *Op. cit.* p. 462: Ἀποπληξία γάρ, οἶμαι, νοῦ καὶ παρακοπὴ Θεὸν μὲν οὐκ εἶναι λέγειν κατὰ φύσιν καὶ ἀληθινὸν τὸν ἐκ Θεοῦ πεφηνότα Υἱόν, ὡς λόγον ἐκ νοῦ.

230 Cyril of Alexandria, *Thesaurus De Sancta Consubstantiali Trinitate*, PG.75.76.19-26: Ἐπειδὴ δὲ οὔτε σῶμα Θεός, οὔτε μὴν τὴν ἐν τοῖς σώμασιν ἔχει διαφορὰν (ἄρσεν γὰρ καὶ θῆλυ μόνον ἐν τοῖς τῶν σωμάτων ζητεῖται σχήμασιν), ἁπλοῦς δὲ καὶ ἀσώματος, καὶ αὐτὸ δὴ τοῦτο νοῦς ὁ πάντων καθαρώτατος, διὰ ταύτην οἶμαι τὴν αἰτίαν χρῆναι δεῖν τοὺς ὅσοι τὴν ἐπ᾽ αὐτοῦ γέννησιν ἐξετάζειν βούλονται, τὰς ἐκ νοῦ καρποφορίας ζητεῖν, καὶ ταύταις μᾶλλον ἐξομοιοῦν ἐπείγεσθαι τοῦ Λόγου τὴν γέννησιν. *Op. cit.* PG.75.80.28-31: Ὑποδείγματα μερικῶς σημαίνοντα τὸ πῶς ἀμερίστως ἐκ Πατρὸς προῆλθεν ὁ Υἱός. Ὁ λόγος οὗτος ὁ προφορικὸς ᾧ κεχρήμεθα, εἰς νοῦν καὶ ἐκ νοῦ γεννᾶται.

231 *Cels*, IV.54; cf. *op. cit.* IV.56-57.

the Son,[232] just as Cyril later did abundantly.[233] Nevertheless, Origen made it clear that 'First Nous' (πρῶτος νοῦς) was yet another designation of that which Zeno of Citium used speaking of the Stoic universal Logos,[234] and I cannot see why too many scholars are obsessed with associating Origen with Numenius on this issue.

5. The proposition 'The Father generated the Son' became the norm for Christian theology to express the Trinitarian doctrine of the Son having been born from the Father. However, it is hardly common knowledge that the same notion was expressed in equivalent terms that had a characteristic Anaxagorean tenor, namely, 'the Nous [Mind] generated the Logos'. Eminent Christian theologians expounding the same doctrine imbibed this proposition, which Plotinus used, too.[235]

The fact that avowed admirers of Origen used this formula is not susrpirising: Gregory of Nazianzus assured that 'the Unbegotten Father is always a Nous, and so is His begotten Son'.[236] To another author, who signed 'Athanasius', 'the Father is an Unbegotten Nous and the Son is a Logos that was begotten' from Him.[237] This was also Theodoret's formulation: the Uncreated Nous begot his Logos, and from this Nous the Holy Spirit proceeded, too.[238] Later, Gennadius Scholarius summarised the idea as being one maintained also by Thomas Aquinas: the Christian God is 'the First Nous' (ὁ Θεὸς πρῶτος ἐστὶ νοῦς).[239] Likewise, 'God is a Nous (ὁ Θεὸς νοῦς ἐστιν), and the Three, namely, Nous and Logos and Spirit, are one God'.[240] However, less known are other

---

232 Gregory Thaumaturgus, *In Origenem Oratio Panegyrica*, 4: λόγος ... ὕμνους ὁμολογείσθω, τελειότατος ὢν καὶ ζῶν, καὶ αὐτοῦ τοῦ πρώτου νοῦ λόγος ἔμψυχος ὤν.

233 See notes 215; 241.

234 *Cels*, IV.54.

235 Plotinus, *Enneades*, III.2.2: ἐξ ἑνὸς νοῦ καὶ τοῦ ἀπ' αὐτοῦ λόγου ἀνέστη τόδε τὸ πᾶν καὶ διέστη.

236 Gregory of Nazianzus, *De Dogmate et Constitutione Episcoporum* (*orat.* 20), PG.35.1077.9-12: ἀλλ' ὁμοῦ τῷ τὸν Πατέρα εἶναι ἀγεννήτως (ἀεὶ δὲ ἦν, οὐχ ὑπερπίπτει γὰρ εἰς τὸ μὴ εἶναί ποτε ὁ νοῦς) καὶ ὁ Υἱὸς ἦν γεννητῶς.

237 Pseudo-Athanasius, *Sermo in Annuntiationem Deiparae*, PG.28.921.39-40: τὸν μὲν Πατέρα ὡς νοῦν ἀγέννητον, τὸν δὲ Υἱὸν ὡς Λόγον γεννητόν. Also, 'the Son came forth as Logos from a Mind'. Pseudo-Athanasius, *Syntagma Ad Quendam Politicum*, PG.28.1404.15-16: ὁ δὲ Υἱὸς καὶ γέννημα τοῦ Πατρός, ὡς ἐξ ἡλίου φῶς καὶ ἐκ νοῦ λόγος.

238 Theodoret, *Curatio*, 2.107: Εἰ δὲ πιστεύομεν εἶναί τι καὶ ἀγέννητον καὶ ἄναρχον καὶ ἀναίτιον, πιστευτέον ἄρα, ὡς ἐκ τούτου νοῦ γε ὄντος ἐγεννήθη ὁ Λόγος καὶ προῆλθε τὸ Πνεῦμα τὸ ἅγιον. Likewise, *op. cit.* 2.109: ἐξ ἐκείνου γε τοῦ ἀγεννήτου φῦναι τὸν Λόγον καὶ τὸ πανάγιον Πνεῦμα, τὸν μέν, ὡς λόγον, ἐκ τοῦ νοῦ γεννώμενον, τὸ δέ, ὡς πνεῦμα, ἐκπορευόμενον.

239 Gennadius Scholarius, *Epitome Summae contra gentiles Thomae Aquinae*, 1.62. Cf. *Epistulae Diversae I*, epistle 2, p. 128: ὁ Θεὸς ... νοῦς ὤν.

240 Gennadius Scholarius, *Expositio Brevis Fidei Christianae*, 3: ἐπεὶ ὁ Θεὸς νοῦς ἐστιν, ὡς προείρηται. καὶ ταῦτα τὰ τρία, νοῦς καὶ λόγος καὶ πνεῦμα, εἷς θεός ἐστιν. ... αὐτὸν δὲ τὸν

facets of Origen's influence on Cyril, who did not mention his source's name at all, but in the present volume I hope it will become evident how heavily he drew on his illustrious predecessor.

In view of this, it is hard to attribute the same idea to Athanasius, since a pertinent text was ascribed both to him and Cyril, and in view of the present discussion the latter ascription is more likely.[241] On the other hand, the later Byzantine theologian Marcus Eugenicus (1392-1444, archbishop of Ephesus) noted that the Council of Nicaea, where Athanasius was a protagonist, entertained the analogy of human mind producing its own logos in Trinitarian accounts.[242] Likewise, an anonymous author, who aspired to convincing his readers by signing 'Athanasius', applied the same analogy, too.[243] No matter who he really was, the shadow of Origen was there once again.

Cyril lent himself easily to monistic views, and had no inhibition about identifying the First and Second Persons of the Trinity as 'minds'. This idea was condemned only when the great inquisitors of Christian doctrine realised that they discovered it in alleged heretics, but, of course, no one touched Cyril. This happened when Justinian's libel against Origen[244] fancifully laid at his door the idea that God could have never remained idle, hence he had to be Creator beginninglessly.[245] Cyril, for his part, who saw in Christian Trinity the Anaxagorean Nous (although he often put it inarticulately), declared that 'the Logos who proceeded from the Father proclaimed that the nature of the Father is ever-moving and ever-acting', which is assumed from Jesus' words, 'My Father

---

νοῦν καλοῦμεν Πατέρα, διότι αὐτός ἐστιν ἀγέννητος καὶ ἀναίτιος, αἴτιος δὲ τοῦ Υἱοῦ καὶ τοῦ Πνεύματος. Cf. *Quaestiones et Responsiones De Divinitate Domini Nostri Jesu Christi*, p. 467: αὐτὸς γὰρ ὁ ἀΐδιος καὶ νοητὸς Λόγος καὶ Υἱὸς τοῦ Θεοῦ τοῦ ἀγεννήτου νοῦ καὶ Πατρός.

241 Cyril of Alexandria, *Expositio in Psalmos*, PG.69.1028.1-5 (comm. on Psalm, 44:2): Ἐνταῦθά μοι νόει τοῦ ἐκ τῆς οὐσίας τοῦ Θεοῦ καὶ Πατρὸς Θεοῦ Λόγου πρόοδον, ἤτοι γέννησιν, οὐχ ὡς σῶμα ἐκ σώματος, ἀλλὰ ἀσύνθετον, ἄϋλόν τε καὶ νοητήν, ὡς λόγον ἐκ νοῦ, οὐ κατὰ μερισμὸν ἢ διαίρεσιν. In PG.27.564.40-46 (Athanasius, *Expositiones in Psalmos*), the catenist wrote that this idea and expression belonged to both 'Athanasius and the great and divine Cyril': Ἀθανάσιος δὲ ὁ πάνυ καὶ ὁ θεῖος Κύριλλος.

242 Marcus Eugenicus, *Testimonia Spiritum Sanctum ex Patre Procedere Probantia*, Testimonium 118: Παραδείγματα τῆς πρώτης ἁγίας καὶ οἰκουμενικῆς συνόδου. Ἀνάλογον γὰρ λαμβάνουσι τῷ Πατρὶ μὲν τὸν ἐν ἡμῖν νοῦν, τὸ πῦρ, τὴν πηγήν. τῷ Υἱῷ δὲ τὸν λόγον, τὸ ἀπαύγασμα, τὸν ποταμόν.

243 Pseudo-Athanasius, *Syntagma ad Quendam Politicum*, PG.28.1404.15-16: ὁ δὲ Υἱὸς καὶ γέννημα τοῦ Πατρός, ὡς ἐξ ἡλίου φῶς καὶ ἐκ νοῦ λόγος.

244 The libel against Origen was written at the Laura of Sabas by abbot Gelasius and his band. Justinian just signed the document without changing a word of it, not even its peculiar colloquialisms. See *NDGF*, pp. 385; 407; *RCR*, pp. 258-260; 267; 324-325.

245 I have shown the folly of these allegations in *COT*, chapter 4, "Beginningless world: a myth reconsidered", pp. 165-175.

works hitherto, and I work',[246] and 'the words which I speak unto you, I speak not of myself: but the Father that dwells in me, he does the works.'[247] However, Cyril was a pillar of the imperial faith and a powerful lobbyist in the political and religious establishment of his day; hence, he was at liberty to make statements that the administration was quick to anathematise only when they were pronounced by lips from outside the chambers of political power.

6. To Origen 'sin' was but 'irrationality' (ἀλογία), which is one more point on which he followed a Stoic rather than Platonic rationale.[248] Actually, he saw 'irrationality' (ἀλογία),[249] or indeed 'utter irrationality' (ἐσχάτη ἀλογία)[250] as the main existential characteristic of daemonic condition; 'ignorance' is only a consequence of wickedness, in contrast to Plato who posited wickedness as but ignorance.[251] Consequently, one's moral quality is 'proportionate'

---

246 John, 5:17.

247 John, 14:10. Cyril of Alexandria, *De Sancta Trinitate Dialogi*, p. 524: Καὶ [Μωσῆς] ἀναπείσει μειζόνως, ἀεικίνητόν τε καὶ ἐνεργῆ τὴν τοῦ Πατρὸς φύσιν ἀνακηρύττων ὁ Λόγος ὁ ἐξ αὐτοῦ πεφηνώς.

248 *Cels*, IV.32: τῆς ἀλόγου καὶ πονηρᾶς τῶν δαιμόνων ἐνεργείας. *selPs*, PG.12.1664.33-36: τὰ φαῦλα νοήματα πολλάκις οἱ δαίμονες οὐ γυμνὰ ἀποτίθενται ἡμῖν, ἵνα μὴ ὁ νοῦς ἄντικρυς τὸ ἄλογον αὐτῶν θεασάμενος, τοὺς λογισμοὺς ἀποῤῥίψῃ. *schLuc*, PG.17.348.30-34: Ἔστι δὲ ἄλαλον καὶ κωφὸν δαιμόνιον αἱ ἄλογοι πρὸς τὸ δοκοῦν καλὸν ὁρμαὶ ὑπὸ τοῦ λόγου ἐκβαλλόμεναι, ἃς αὐτὸς ἐποίει ἀλόγῳ φορᾷ, νομιζόμεναι ὑπὸ τῶν βλεπόντων κατὰ λόγον ταῦτα πράττειν τῆς Ἰησοῦ διδασκαλίας. In reference to Matt. 16:25-26, and to Mark, 8:35-37 ('what will it profit a man, if he gains the whole world, and forfeits his life?'), his comment was that by 'forfeiting knowledge' one incurs 'damage', which is but 'utter irrationality' (τὴν ἐσχάτην ἀλογίαν). Origen, *expProv*, PG.17.209.9-14. Cf. 'irrationality' being considered as concomitant with sin. *Cels*, II.79; III.75; IV.85-86 (*Philocalia*, 2.20); *homLuc*, homily 17, pp. 103-104; *frLuc*, 216. Cf. Plutarch, *De Stoicorum Repugnantiis*, p. 1042C (Chrysippus, *Fragmenta Moralia*, fr. 760): ἡ δὲ κακία λογικόν ἐστι, μᾶλλον δὲ λόγος ἡμαρτημένος.

249 *Cels*, II.79; III.75 (& *Philocalia*, 20.12): ἐν κολάσεως μοίρᾳ τῷ φαύλῳ ἀποδίδοσθαι ἀναισθησίαν ἢ ἀλογίαν. *Op. cit.* IV.85; *homLuc*, homily 17, pp. 103-104: Ἐὰν μὴ πέσῃ ἡ πορνεία, ἡ σωφροσύνη οὐκ ἀνίσταται, ἐὰν μὴ ἡ ἀλογία συντριβῇ, τὸ λογικὸν τὸ ἐν ἡμῖν οὐκ ἀνθήσει. οὕτως οὖν ἡ πτῶσις καὶ ἡ ἀνάστασις πολλῶν. *frLuc*, 216: ἡ λογικὴ φύσις ἐν ἀλογίᾳ γενομένη ἐπιθυμεῖ, κἂν μὴ ἐν κρείττοσι λόγοις, ἐν ὁποίοις γοῦν καταντῆσαι. *selEz*, PG.13.817.28-29: Παραπίπτει δὲ ὁ καθεὶς ἀπολλύων τὸν λόγον εἰς ἀλογίαν.

250 *expProv*, PG.17.209.6-13: τὴν δὲ προσθήκην τῆς ψυχῆς, ἀφανισμὸν τῶν φυσικῶν περὶ Θεοῦ ἐννοιῶν, παντάπασιν αὐτῆς εἰς ἀλογίαν καταπεσούσης. … Ἐνταῦθα ἡ ἀπώλεια τὴν ἄγνοιαν σωμάτων καὶ ἀσωμάτων ἐμφαίνει. ἡ δὲ ζημία τὴν ἐσχάτην ἀλογίαν παρίστησιν.

251 Plato, *Timaeus*, 86d7-e2; cf. *Theaetetus*, 176c4-5; *Sophista*, 228d1-11; *Philebus*, 48b-49e.

(ἀνάλογον)[252] to one's 'participation in reason' (μετοχὴν τοῦ λόγου),[253] and so is one's knowledge of God,[254] since the entire world participates in the Logos.[255]

The notion of 'irrationality' as inherently being involved with 'wickedness' is central to Origen's thought, who, for that matter, maintained that this state is reversible by means of exercising free will. Sins have many names and different manifestations, yet the head of all predicables is always the same, namely, 'irrationality' (ἀλογία).[256] This term assumed its full philosophical significance with the Stoics, to whom ἀλογία meant anything done or thought to be contrary to the Logos, which involved not only wicked action but also all kinds of passion (τοῦ πάθους ἀλογίαν).[257] Consequently, to them, 'anyone

---

252 *Cels*, IV.16: Εἰσὶ γὰρ διάφοροι οἱονεὶ τοῦ λόγου μορφαί, καθὼς ἑκάστῳ τῶν εἰς ἐπιστήμην ἀγομένων φαίνεται ὁ λόγος, ἀνάλογον τῇ ἕξει τοῦ εἰσαγομένου ἢ ἐπ' ὀλίγον προκόπτοντος ἢ ἐπὶ πλεῖον ἢ καὶ ἐγγὺς ἤδη γινομένου τῆς ἀρετῆς ἢ καὶ ἐν ἀρετῇ γεγενημένου. *Op. cit.* VII.60 (& *Philocalia*, 15.4): Καὶ τῷ τυχόντι γὰρ δῆλον, ταύτα ἀναγινώσκοντι, ὅτι πολλὰ βαθύτερον τοῦ αὐτόθεν ἐμφαινομένου ἔχειν δύναται νοῦν, τοῖς ἀνατιθεῖσιν αὐτοὺς τῇ ἐξετάσει τοῦ λόγου φανερούμενον, καὶ φανερούμενον κατὰ τὴν ἀναλογίαν τῆς εἰς τὸν λόγον σχολῆς καὶ εἰς τὴν ἄσκησιν αὐτοῦ προθυμίας.

253 Origen, *op. cit.* V.1: *νοῦν δὲ Χριστοῦ* λαβόντες ἀπὸ τοῦ μόνου διδόντος αὐτὸν πατρὸς αὐτοῦ καὶ πρὸς τὴν μετοχὴν τοῦ λόγου τοῦ θεοῦ βοηθηθέντες *πᾶν ὕψωμα ἐπαιρόμενον κατὰ τῆς γνώσεως τοῦ θεοῦ* καθέλοιμεν.

254 Origen, *op. cit.* VI.17: Οὔτε γὰρ τὸν ἀγένητον καὶ πάσης γενητῆς φύσεως πρωτότοκον κατ' ἀξίαν εἰδέναι τις δύναται ὡς ὁ γεννήσας αὐτὸν πατήρ, οὔτε τὸν πατέρα ὡς ὁ ἔμψυχος λόγος καὶ σοφία αὐτοῦ καὶ ἀλήθεια. οὗ μετοχῇ περιαιροῦντος ἀπὸ τοῦ πατρὸς τὸ λεγόμενον *σκότος*, ὃ *ἔθετο ἀποκρυφὴν αὐτοῦ*, [Psalm, 17:12; 2 Kings, 22:12] καὶ τὸ λεγόμενον *περιβόλαιον* [Psalm 103:6] αὐτοῦ, τὴν *ἄβυσσον*, καὶ ἀποκαλύπτοντος οὕτω τὸν πατέρα ὅστις ποτ' ἂν χωρῇ γινώσκειν αὐτὸν γινώσκει. *commJohn*, II.241.156: ζωὴ ἐνταῦθα οὐχ ἡ κοινὴ λογικῶν καὶ ἀλόγων λέγεται, ἀλλ' ἡ ἐπιγινομένη τῷ ἐν ἡμῖν συμπληρουμένῳ λόγῳ, τῆς μετοχῆς ἀπὸ τοῦ πρώτου λαμβανομένης λόγου.

255 *COT*, 'The Place of the Logos', pp. 165-172.

256 *Cels*, II.79: Καὶ οὐ θαυμαστὸν εἰ τῶν φρονίμων ἀλλὰ καὶ τῶν ἀλογωτάτων καὶ τοῖς πάθεσιν ἐγκειμένων καὶ ὅσον ἐπὶ τῇ ἀλογίᾳ χαλεπώτερον μετατιθεμένων εἰς τὸ σωφρονέστερον. *Op. cit.* III.75: πῶς οὐ βελτίονας ταῖς ψυχαῖς κατασκευάσομεν τοὺς πειθομένους λόγῳ, οὐ διδάσκοντι μὲν ἐν κολάσεως μοίρᾳ τῷ φαύλῳ ἀποδίδοσθαι ἀναισθησίαν ἢ ἀλογίαν, παριστάντι δὲ εἶναι τινα φάρμακα ἐπιστρεπτικὰ τοὺς ἀπὸ θεοῦ τοῖς φαύλοις προσαγομένους πόνους καὶ τὰς κολάσεις; *homLuc*, homily 17, quoted *supra*, note 249. *frLuc*, fr. 216: Νοήσεις δὲ καὶ οὕτως τὸ ἐπιθυμεῖν, κορεσθῆναι τὸν ἄσωτον ἐκ τῶν κερατίων. ἡ λογικὴ φύσις ἐν ἀλογίᾳ γενομένη ἐπιθυμεῖ, κἂν μὴ ἐν κρείττοσι λόγοις, ἐν ὁποίοις γοῦν καταντῆσαι. *selEz*, PG.13.817.28-29: Παραπίπτει δὲ ὁ καθεὶς ἀπολλύων τὸν λόγον εἰς ἀλογίαν. *expProv*, PG.17.209.5-13: τῆς ψυχῆς ... παντάπασιν αὐτῆς εἰς ἀλογίαν καταπεσούσης. ... ἡ δὲ ζημία τὴν ἐσχάτην ἀλογίαν παρίστησιν. *commMatt*, 11.12: Εἰ δὲ χρὴ ὑπογράψαι τὰ κατὰ τὸ εὐαγγέλιον ἀκάθαρτα βρώματα, φήσομεν ὅτι τοιαῦτά ἐστι τὰ ἀπὸ πλεονεξίας πεπορισμένα καὶ ἀπὸ αἰσχροκερδείας περιγεγενημένα καὶ ἀπὸ φιληδονίας λαμβανόμενα καὶ ἀπὸ τοῦ θεοποιεῖσθαι τιμωμένην τὴν γαστέρα, ὅταν αὐτὴ καὶ αἱ κατ' αὐτὴν ὀρέξεις καὶ μὴ ὁ λόγος ἄρχη τῆς ψυχῆς ἡμῶν.

257 Galen, *De Placitis Hippocratis et Platonis*, 4.7.27 (*SVF*, III.118.32). I have argued several times about Galen being a main source of Origen's terminology, and about Origen's influence on

who is grieved or scared or desirous, he sins'.[258] This is the sense in which they identified 'irrationality' with 'sin' (ἁμάρτημα).[259] Accordingly whenever Origen exalted righteous action or conduct of life, he described that as having taken place 'according to reason' (κατὰ λόγον),[260] whereas any sin was an affront to

---

Porphyry's nomenclature and some ideas. On the present point, see Origen, *commMatt*, 53: χοϊκοὺς γεγονότας καὶ πάθεσιν ἀλόγοις ἐνιδρυθέντας κατὰ λόγον ἔτι μηδὲν ἐνεργεῖν. *adLev*, PG.17.21.47-48 & *schLuc*, PG.17.365.40-41: ἡγοῦμαι γὰρ τὴν λέπραν ἀντὶ ἀλόγων λαμβάνεσθαι τῆς ψυχῆς παθημάτων. *expProv*, PG.17.161.29-30: παιδεία ἐστὶ μετριοπάθεια παθῶν περὶ τὸ παθητικὸν ἢ ἄλογον τῆς ψυχῆς μέρος θεωρουμένη. Porphyry, *De Abstinentia*, 1.44: ἀπὼν δὲ καὶ ὡς φασίν τινες πρὸς τοῖς ἑαυτοῦ ὤν, εἰ μὲν καὶ τὴν ἡμετέραν πρόσεξιν ἔχει παρ' ἑαυτῷ, οὐδ' ἐπιτρέπει τῇ ἀλογίᾳ παθαίνεσθαι οὐδ' ὅλως τι ἐνεργεῖν. Iamblichus, *Protrepticus*, p. 35: καταργητέον οὖν εἰς δύναμιν τῆς ἀλογίας τὰ πάθη, ταῖς δὲ τοῦ νοῦ καθαραῖς ἐνεργείαις καὶ εἰς ἑαυτὸν καὶ τὸ θεῖον ἀφορώσαις χρηστέον καὶ ταῖς διεξόδοις τοῦ νοῦ ζῆν μελετητέον.

258 Plutarch (one of Origen's most favourite authors; see *infra*, note 732), *De Virtute Morali*, p. 449D (*SVF*, III.119.21-32): πᾶν μὲν γὰρ πάθος ἁμαρτία κατ' αὐτούς ἐστι, καὶ πᾶς ὁ λυπούμενος ἢ φοβούμενος ἢ ἐπιθυμῶν ἁμαρτάνει. Epictetus, *Dissertationes Ab Arriano Digestae*, 2.1.23-25: οὐδεὶς τοίνυν ἁμαρτάνων ἐλεύθερός ἐστιν. Βούλεσθε ζῆν φοβούμενοι, βούλεσθε λυπούμενοι, βούλεσθε ταρασσόμενοι; οὐδαμῶς. οὐδεὶς ἄρα οὔτε φοβούμενος οὔτε λυπούμενος οὔτε ταρασσόμενος ἐλεύθερός ἐστιν, ὅστις δ' ἀπήλλακται λυπῶν καὶ φόβων καὶ ταραχῶν, οὗτος τῇ αὐτῇ ὁδῷ καὶ τοῦ δουλεύειν ἀπήλλακται. Cf. Origen, *frLam*, fr. 52: *πύλαι* δὲ ψυχῆς αἱ αἰσθήσεις, αἵτινες ἁμαρτανούσης κατακλύζονταί τε πάθεσι καὶ γίνονται *γηΐναι*. καὶ αἱ ταύτας δὲ τηροῦσαι τῆς ψυχῆς δυνάμεις ἐκλύονται ἀπολωλότος νοῦ τε *βασιλεύοντος* καὶ λογισμῶν *ἀρχικῶν ἐν* τοῖς πάθεσιν. *commMatt*, 15.20: ἀντιστῆναι τοῖς πάθεσι καὶ ταῖς ἁμαρτίαις. *Op. cit.* 17.19: ζήλου καὶ ἔριδος καὶ τῶν λοιπῶν παθῶν καὶ ἁμαρτημάτων. *commEph*, fr. 22: τὰ δὲ περὶ ἡμῶν ὀνομαζόμενα ὁμολογουμένως πάθη ἐστὶ καὶ ἁμαρτήματα. *commRom* (*I.1–XII.*21), fr. 38: ἀμήχανον γὰρ ἀνθρωπίνην ψυχὴν μὴ ὑποπεσεῖν πάθεσι, κἂν ἐξ ἐπιμελείας ὕστερον οἱονεὶ ἐν ἀπαθείᾳ γένηται. *Loc. cit.*: ὧδε δὲ ὁ Παῦλος *πᾶσαν ἐπιθυμίαν* λέγει παθητικὴν καὶ ἁμαρτωλόν, ἣν ὁ νόμος ἀπαγορεύει.

259 Clement of Alexandria, *Paedagogus*, 1.13.101.1 (Chrysippus, *Fragmenta Moralia*, fr. 445): Πᾶν τὸ παρὰ τὸν λόγον τὸν ὀρθὸν τοῦτο ἁμάρτημά ἐστιν. Αὐτίκα γοῦν τὰ πάθη τὰ γενικώτατα ὧδέ πως ὁρίζεσθαι ἀξιοῦσιν οἱ φιλόσοφοι, τὴν μὲν ἐπιθυμίαν ὄρεξιν ἀπειθῆ λόγῳ, τὸν δὲ φόβον ἔκκλισιν ἀπειθῆ λόγῳ, ἡδονὴν δὲ ἔπαρσιν ψυχῆς ἀπειθῆ λόγῳ, ‹λύπην δὲ συστολὴν ψυχῆς ἀπειθῆ λόγῳ›. *Stromateis*, 4.22.146.1: ἀλλ' εἰ καὶ λήσεσθαι τὸν θεὸν ἐφ' οἷς πράττει πεισθείη, ὅπερ ἀδύνατον, πρᾶξαί τι παρὰ τὸν λόγον τὸν ὀρθὸν ἐθελῆσαι ποτ' ἄν. Also, Chrysippus, *op. cit.* fr. 500 (*apud* Stobaeus, *Anthologium*, 2.7.11a): κατόρθωμα δ' εἶναι λέγουσι καθῆκον πάντας ἐπέχον τοὺς ἀριθμούς, ἢ τέλειον καθῆκον. ἁμάρτημά τε τὸ παρὰ τὸν ὀρθὸν λόγον πραττόμενον ἢ ἐν ᾧ παραλέλειπταί τι καθῆκον ὑπὸ λογικοῦ ζῴου. Chrysippus, *op. cit.* fr. 501 (*apud* Stobaeus, *op. cit.* 2.7.11e, *apud* Arius Didymus): ἁμαρτήματα δ' εἶναι τό τε ἀφραίνειν καὶ τὸ ἀκολασταίνειν καὶ τὸ ἀδικεῖν καὶ τὸ λυπεῖσθαι καὶ τὸ φοβεῖσθαι καὶ τὸ κλέπτειν καὶ καθόλου ὅσα παρὰ τὸν ὀρθὸν λόγον πράττεται.

260 *commJohn*, XXXII.2.6: τοῖς ἤδη ἐπὶ πλεῖον προκεκοφόσι παρατιθεμένη κατὰ λόγον. *deOr*, 28.8: καὶ γενόμενος πνευματικὸς τῷ ὑπὸ τοῦ πνεύματος ἄγεσθαι τρόπον υἱοῦ θεοῦ ἐφ' ἕκαστον τῶν κατὰ λόγον πρακτέων. *commSerMatt*, pp. 146-147: λαμπάδες δὲ τὰ ὄργανα τοῦ καλῶς καὶ κατὰ λόγον βιοῦντος ἢ ἐναντίως. *commMatt*, 11.12: καὶ τὰ λεγόμενα ἀκάθαρτα δυνατὸν κατὰ λόγον ἐν χρήσει ἡμῖν γινόμενα λογίζεσθαι καθαρά. *Op. cit.* 11.18: ἄλλους δὲ *τυφλοὺς* τὴν ψυχὴν καὶ μὴ βλέποντας τὸ *ἀληθινὸν φῶς*, καὶ ἄλλους *χωλοὺς* καὶ μὴ δυναμένους κατὰ λόγον πορεύεσθαι, καὶ

reason,[261] i.e. to the Logos / Son. Perhaps the most felicitous précis of this is the following expression, which was ascribed to Cyril of Alexandria:

> Every sinful action is wrong-doing against the rational essence (πᾶν ἁμάρτημα ὡς πρὸς τὴν λογικὴν οὐσίαν παρόραμά ἐστι).[262]

Conclusion: the points on which Cyril wrote as a student of Origen's are too many to doubt influence, which explains why so many catena-passages were attributed jointly to Cyril and Origen. Besides, there are several sections of this commentary that are ascribed to Origen, with some short portions having been attributed to Cyril's as isolated 'fragments'. I should add that a vast number of other passages explicitly ascribed to Cyril of Alexandria *are* included in *Codex Sabaiticus 232*, but editing them was out of my scope.

Origen's Commentary and Other Authors

The phenomenon of theologians having presented themselves as champions against 'the heretic Origen' and yet copying from him is typical of how his *person* and his *work* were treated. Little wonder then that in *Codex Sabaiticus 232* there are passages attributed to Apollinaris (one of 'the slanderous tetrad'), even though Origen's authorship of them if confirmed by more than one sources. I myself would not consider such instances as misattributions: rather, these cases were ones of Apollinaris having copied from Origen's commentary on Matthew. However, as it happens, the well-known psychological complex functioned once again: the more one copied from the damned genius, the more one had a yen for Origen's burial along with his work into a flurry of revilement and calumny, not to mention ignorance, which resulted in the sixth-century

ἄλλους *κυλλοὺς* καὶ μὴ δυναμένους κατὰ λόγον ἐργάζεσθαι. *schMatt*, PG.17.304.26-29: *Φρόνιμοι* μὲν οὖν αἱ τοῦ κατὰ λόγον βιοῦντος αἰσθήσεις. *μωραὶ* δὲ αἱ τοῦ ἐναντίως καὶ παρὰ τὸν ὀρθὸν λόγον πολιτευομένου. *comm1Cor*, 23: ὅλῃ γὰρ τῇ ἐκκλησίᾳ ἐγκαλεῖ περὶ ἑνὸς πορνεύσαντος, καὶ τῇ φυσιώσει αὐτῶν ἐγκαλεῖ ὡς οὐ κατὰ λόγον γινομένῃ. *commEph*, fr. 29: τὰ τοῦ γάμου κατὰ λόγον οἰκονομεῖ, μιμουμένου Χριστὸν τὸν τῆς ἐκκλησίας νυμφίον. *selPs*, PG.12.1133.50-51. ἡ εὔρυθμος καὶ κατὰ λόγον ἐξεταστικὴ πολιτεία εἰς δόξαν Θεοῦ γινομένη.

261 *commJohn*, XX.37.344: *Καὶ ὑμεῖς ἀτιμάζετέ με*, οὐχὶ καὶ ἐκείνοις μόνοις εἰρῆσθαι τότε ἀλλὰ καὶ τοῖς ἀεὶ ἀτιμάζουσι, δι᾽ ὧν πράττουσι παρὰ τὸν ὀρθὸν λόγον τὸν τοῦ θεοῦ, καὶ ἀτιμάζουσιν δι᾽ ὧν ἀδικοῦσιν τὸν Χριστόν, ὅς ἐστιν δικαιοσύνη. *homJer*, homily 9.4: Μήποτε γὰρ ἐπεὶ ἐν ἡμῖν εἰσιν ἁμαρτωλοί τινες καὶ παρὰ τὸν ὀρθὸν λόγον πράττοντες. *Philocalia*, 18.21: ἀποτρέποντες δ᾽ ἀπὸ τοῦ καταφρονεῖν τοῦ θείου καὶ πάντων τῶν παρὰ τὸν ὀρθὸν λόγον πραττομένων. *frPs*, on Psalm 54:3-4 & *selPs*, PG.12.1464.27-29: Πάντα ὅσα πράττομεν παρὰ τὸν ὀρθὸν λόγον ἢ τὸν νόμον, ἀδολεσχία ἐστι, καὶ ὅσα εἰκῆ λαλοῦμεν. *Cels*, III.50: ἀποτρέποντες δ᾽ ἀπὸ τοῦ καταφρονεῖν τοῦ θείου καὶ πάντων τῶν παρὰ τὸν ὀρθὸν λόγον πραττομένων. *Op. cit.* V.23: εἰ δὲ τὰ κατὰ λόγον θεοῦ καὶ βούλησιν αὐτοῦ γινόμενα, ἀναγκαῖον εὐθέως εἶναι μὴ παρὰ φύσιν.

262 *Catena in Epistulam Joannis i* (*catena Andreae*), p. 141. Cf. *supra*, note 259.

phenomenon of authors excoriating the *name* of Origen while embracing and entertaining his *ideas*.[263]

Nevertheless, there were also gross misattributions, of which the most arrant case is that of Theodore of Heraclea. Long before the present codex was written, several 'fragments' had been attributed to him, but the most conspicuous is one in which this anti-Nicene champion, and Athanasius' personal enemy for that matter, is represented as a devout exponent of the Nicene Creed. Likewise, there are fragments jointly attributed to him and Origen, but now we are upon a text of the commentary being attributed to Origen, of which those 'fragments' are only out-of-context small bits of Origen's extensive text.[264] At best, when Theodore wrote (if indeed it was he who wrote this), 'certain ones say', and then quoted from Origen, this only means that this 'Theodore' wrote his own commentary on Matthew while having Origen's work in front of him. However, the question persists: how could a staunch opponent of Nicaea ever have embraced Nicence propositions?

In *Codex Sabaiticus 232*, folia 239v-240v, the text from ἀρχὴν τῆς διδασκαλίας to μία δὲ οὐσία (commenting on Matthew 28:19-20) has been attributed also to Theodore of Heraclea as 'fragment 133',[265] which is one more token of the mess surrounding attributions of catena-fragments. However, this particular ascription, which once again is a Nicene statement, reaches its most far-fetched absurdity once one considers who that author was: for Theodore of Heraclea[266] was a leader of the anti-Nicene party and a personal opponent of Athanasius, against whom he never ceased to conspire and lobby. Theodore was notorious for his Arian views, or, at best, as a reactionary who sided with Eusebius opposing the term *homoousios*, for which he was condemned and expelled from the Church. Furthermore, Origen's expression was in effect refuted by Theodore's companion Basil of Ancyra (who was also condemned on the same grounds)[267]

263 I have canvassed this in *RCR*, 'The sixth-century Origenism', pp. 259-321.

264 See Origen's fr. 126 (Klostermann) being attributed also to Theodore; folio 44v.

265 *Fragmenta in Matthaeum*, ed. J. Reuss, *Matthäus-Kommentare aus der griechischen Kirche* [Texte und Untersuchungen 61. Berlin: Akademie Verlag, 1957], pp. 55-95.

266 During old times, Heraclea was called Perinthus, which is mentioned by several historians: Theodoret, *HE*, p. 82. Sozomenus, *HE*, 3.5.10; 6.7.1. Zosimus, *Historia Nova*, 1.62.1. Theodore Anagnostes, *Epitome Historiae Tripartitae*, 2.60; 3.159. Procopius of Caesarea, *De Bellis*, 3.12.6; *De Aedificiis*, 4.9.14. Anonymous, *Chronicon Paschale*, p. 510. Michael Attaliates, *Historia*, p. 250. *Et. al.*

267 About Theodore of Heraclea's confrontation with Athanasius, his sharing the same Arian ideas with Basil of Ancyra, and the condemnation of them both, see Athanasius, *Apologia Contra Arianos* (*Apologia Secunda*), 36.6; 46.1; *Epistula ad Episcopos Aegypti et Libyae*, 7.3 (Theodore and Basil). Theodoret, *HE*, pp. 82; 87; 97; 109; 111; 286. Socrates Scholasticus, *HE*, 2.12. Sozomenus, *HE*, 2.25.19; 3.3.1; 3.5.10; 3.7.4; 3.10.4. Gelasius of Cyzicus,

who used the expression (as in the present codex, folio 240r) ἀσυνάρτητοι οὐσίαι (= 'essences, or beings, of different ontological orders'), which was appealed to and quoted by Eunomius arguing that 'uncreatedness' (ἀγεννησίαν) of the Father should be taken as bespeaking a different essence. No other author did ever use this phraseology whatsoever.[268]

Therefore, to ascribe to Theodore of Heraclea fragments representing him as a champion of the Nicene Creed would be nothing short of absurd. Quite simply, the attribution to Origen made in this manuscript should be accepted as being correct, since this abundantly fits with his entire theology (as discussed below). No matter how embarrassing to certain religious allegiances, in my previous books, I have repeatedly demonstrated that Origen paved the way to Nicaea (which Athanasius was the first to acknowledge). In any event, it can be shown that other fragments ascribed to Theodore were mere copies from Origen's text. Moreover, the sentence, καὶ ὥσπερ οὔκ ἐστιν συναγέννητος ἕτερος θεός, οὕτως οὐδὲ συγγεγεννημένος ἕτερος θεός, υἱός, was used by Basil of Caesarea in order to make the same point, and in the same context as Origen's present text does.[269] Likewise, Eusebius had employed Origen's language of the present text to an even wider extent, and the scarcity (indeed distinctiveness) of the locution makes it impossible to claim that this was not copied from any author other than Origen.[270]

Furthermore, the passage of fragment 131, which was ascribed to Theodore of Heraclea, is the selfsame text as that in Origen's already known commentary on Matthew. This is included also in Migne's edition and was rightly attributed

HE, 2.7.43. Theodore Anagnostes, *Epitome Historiae Tripartitae*, 2.54; 2.60; 2.66; 2.72. Photius, *Homiliae*, homily 16, p. 154 (Theodore of Heraclea was one of the heretics who conspired against Athanasius); 158. Nicephorus Callistus Xanthopulus, *HE*, 9.5; 9.7; 9.10; 9.12 (Theodore of Perinthus and Basil of Ancyra were expelled from the Church); 9.14; 11.48.142 & 12.2 & 12.6 (Theodore was an Arian). Anonymous, *Synodicon Vetus*, 37; 45 (Basil of Ancyra was deposed during his lifetime; Theodore of Heraclea was deposed posthumously); 77 (Theodore was condemned as heretic by the Second Oecumenical Council of Constantinople).

268 Gregory of Nyssa, *Contra Eunomium*, 1.1.474-475 (quoting Eunomius who quoted Basil of Ancyra): τὴν ἀγεννησίαν οὐσίαν ἀποφηνάμενος καὶ τὴν τῆς οὐσίας ἑτερότητα διαθρυλήσας, οὑτωσὶ λέγων ταῦτα κατὰ τὴν λέξιν. *ἢ καθὼς νομοθετεῖ Βασίλειος, ἀπ' αὐτῶν ἄρξασθαι τῶν ζητουμένων ἔδει ἀσυναρτήτως τὴν ἀγεννησίαν οὐσίαν λέγοντας καὶ τὴν τῆς οὐσίας ἑτερότητα θρυλεῖν ἢ ταὐτότητα.*

269 Cf. Basil of Caesarea, *Adversus Eos Qui per Calumniam Dicunt Dici a Nobis Tres Deos*, PG.31.1493.11-13: Ὥσπερ οὐκ ἔνι συναγέννητος Θεὸς ἕτερος, οὕτως οὐδὲ συγγεγεννημένος Υἱὸς ἕτερος.

270 Eusebius, quoted by Gelasius of Cyzicus, *HE*, 2.19.9: ὥσπερ οὖν οὐκ ἔστι συναγέννητος τῷ θεῷ καὶ πατρὶ θεὸς ἕτερος, οὕτως οὐδὲ συγγεγεννημένος ἢ προγεγεννημένος ἢ μεταγεγεννημένος υἱός ἕτερος τοῦ θεοῦ τῷ μονογενεῖ υἱῷ αὐτοῦ θεῷ λόγῳ.

to him according to another manuscript. Fragment 131 allegedly attributed to Theodore is simply an inveterate Origen's text.[271] It refers to the philosopher Flegon, who reportedly recorded the eclipse that took place during Jesus' crucifixion. Origen mentions Φλέγων by name also in the *Contra Celsum*, II.14 and II.33, and makes it clear that he had read Flegon's work entitled *Χρονικά*,[272] which he cites confidently.

In brief, almost all of the 'fragments' that are allegedly Theodore of Heraclea's turn out to be Origen's passages, which is also what already published parallel ones indisputably show. Consequently, the least that could be said about editor J. Reuss is that he was not very discriminating as regards consistency between the *views* expressed in 'fragments' he came upon and the *person* that allegedly expounded them.

This is not the only circumstance in which known passages of Origen's have been attributed to Theodore of Heraclea without critical consideration: false attribution of Origen's statements to Theodore appear as a too flagrantly far-fetched practice. For example, the largest part of Fragment 18 allegedly from Theodore's commentary on Matthew is Clement of Alexandria's.[273] Besides, a portion attributed to 'Theodore of Heraclea or Theodore of Mopsuestia' (J. Reuss)[274] makes it evident that this 'Theodore' copied Origen's words, quoting what 'others said' (φασί τινες). But it can be indubitably authenticated that those 'others' were but Origen himself, which can be easily validated from his *On Prayer*, 27.8 (confirmed also by his commentary on Luke)[275] concerning a unique etymology of the *epiousios bread* (ἐπιούσιος ἄρτος), the phrase used in the Dominical Prayer.[276] This is now confirmed by both *Codex Sabaiticus*

---

271 Origen, *schMatt*, PG.17.309.2-26.

272 Flegon of Tralles (76-138 AD), a freedman of Emperor Hadrian, was a historian. Actually, his chronicle was entitled *Olympiads*, and it expounded history in sixteen books from the first Olympiad until his own times.

273 The text, οὕτως οὖν καὶ ὅτε ἂν ὁ θεὸς λέγηται *πῦρ καταναλίσκον* … ἔχει δὲ καὶ φόβον τὸ πῦρ καὶ διάχυσιν τὸ φῶς is but Clement of Alexandria's *Eclogae Propheticae*, 26.1.

274 Theodore of Heraclea or Theodore of Mopsuestia, *Fragmenta in Matthaeum*, fr. 123 (Reuss).

275 Origen, *frLuc*, fr. 181: ταπεινοὶ δὲ οἱ νομίζοντες περὶ σωματικοῦ ἄρτου λέγειν τὸν διδάσκοντα μὴ μεριμνᾶν *περὶ τῆς αὔριον*, μάλιστα εἰ *τὸν ἐπιούσιον* ἀντὶ τοῦ *τὸν ἐπιόντα καὶ ἐπερχόμενον* λαμβάνουσιν. τοῦτο δὲ δῆλον ἐκ τοῦ εἰπεῖν. *οὐ γὰρ οἶδας, τί τέξεται ἡ ἐπιοῦσα*, τοῦτ᾽ ἔστιν ἡ αὔριον ἡ ἐπερχομένη.

276 Origen, *deOr*, 27.13: ἐρεῖ δέ τις τὸ *ἐπιούσιον* παρὰ τὸ ἐπιέναι κατεσχηματίσθαι, ὥστε αἰτεῖν ἡμᾶς κελεύεσθαι *τὸν ἄρτον* τὸν οἰκεῖον τοῦ μέλλοντος αἰῶνος, ἵνα προλαβὼν αὐτὸν ὁ θεὸς ἤδη ἡμῖν δωρήσηται, ὥστε τὸ οἱονεὶ αὔριον δοθησόμενον *σήμερον* ἡμῖν δοθῆναι, *σήμερον* μὲν τοῦ ἐνεστῶτος αἰῶνος λαμβανομένου αὔριον δὲ τοῦ μέλλοντος. Theodore of Heraclea or Theodore of Mopsuestia, *frMatt*, fr. 23 (Reuss): Ὡς τρέφεται εἰς ζωὴν ὁ ἄνθρωπος, οὕτω καί φασί τινες τὸ *ἐπιούσιον* παρὰ τὸ ἐπιέναι καὶ ἐπέρχεσθαι, ἵν᾽ ᾖ τοιοῦτον τὸ λεγόμενον. *τὸν μὴ τοῦ ἐνεστῶτος*

232 (folio 44r) and Klostermann's chain of Origen's fragments from the commentary on Matthew.[277] This correlation which is made possible thanks to the the present codex also authenticates that Apollinaris wrote his commentary on Matthew largely copying from Origen's one,[278] if indeed Apollinaris ever wrote a commentary on Matthew at all.

Jerome's Commentary on Matthew

That translations of Origen's works have been a point of hot dispute even during the ancient times is now only a platitude. Origen's translator Rufinus was an old-time Jerome's friend,[279] who came to be a bitter enemy, and sided with another adversary of Jerome's, Bishop John of Jerusalem (Jerome wrote a tract against John, which is informative of the Origenistic background of their mutual hostility). The permanent estrangement of the two friends seems to have begun with their respective translations of Origen's *De Principiis*. Jerome apparently believed that Origen was a brilliant scholar but an untrustworthy teacher of doctrine.[280] Nevertheless, it was Jerome, in his prologue to Origen's Homilies on Ezekiel, who had said that he intended to translate all of the homilies, since he regarded the Alexandrian a teacher of the Church second only to the apostles. Anyway, once he changed his mind, Jerome pointed the finger at Rufinus for allegedly having adjusted Origen's translation to orthodoxy.[281] In

---

αἰῶνος οἰκεῖον ἄρτον, ἀλλὰ τοῦ μέλλοντος καὶ μετὰ ταῦτα ἀποδοθησόμενον ὑπό σου τοῖς ἀξίοις λαβεῖν ἤδη δὸς ἡμῖν σήμερον καὶ καθ' ἡμέραν.

277 Origen, fr. 122 (Klostermann), *op. cit.* p. 64. The editor came upon this in Codex B113 of the Great Laura of Mount Athos (eleventh century), and the fact that this is ascribed to 'Theodore and Origen' is telling once again. Klostermann notes that the text begins with attribution to Origen alone and assumes that this 'Theodore' perhaps appealed to Origen.

278 Cf. Apollinaris, *frMatt*, fr. 134: *καὶ ἄρτος ἐπιούσιος τὸ πνεῦμα τοῦτ' ἔστιν τροφὴ ζωοποιὸς εἰς τὸν ἐπιόντα αἰῶνα.*

279 Cf. Jerome, *Letter* 3 to him, and Jerome's references to him in *Letter* 4 to Florentinus.

280 Cf. Jerome, *Letter* 82.7 to Theophilus, *Letter* 84 to Pammachius and Oceanus, and his *Apology Against Rufinus*, 2.34.

281 Jerome, *Apology Against Rufinus*, 1.3-7, and *Letter* 84.7.

turn, Rufinus castigated Jerome for smuggling heretical views under the guise of accurate translation[282] into Origen's works.[283]

Melania, a Roman widow and follower of Rufinus, had an important involvement in this controversy. Consequently, although she was once highly praised by Jerome,[284] later he vituperated her for allegedly having aided the cause of Rufinus by approving and favouring him during the translation controversy.[285]

In his own exegesis of Matthew, Jerome defiantly appropriated large portions of Origen's commentary on Matthew – and I deemed a substantial facet of the present edition that Jerome's allegiances should be brought to the fore by means of full quotations. It was the time when Jerome highly valued Origen as a commentator and seized both on his thoughts and on fundamental points of his exegetical method, such as (against Gnostic allegations) the doctrine that God of the Old Testament is as benevolent and gracious as the God of the New one,[286] or philologically perusing New Testament terms in comparison with their usage in the Old one.

When Jerome wrote his commentary on Matthew as an admirer of Origen (398), his polemics with Rufinus was yet to take place in the future (400-402). However, this work is illuminating of how Jerome felt deep down about Origen *before* he engaged in polemics with Rufinus: just like all plagiarists, on the one hand, he appropriated Origen's work, while, on the other, he hated the genious he encroached on.

Rufinus wrote his *Apology* in 400, adducing seventeen passages exposing Jerome as a hypocrite and demonstrating that he had endorsed and appropriated Origen's views expressed in the commentary on Ephesians. Besides, whereas Origen had set forth some views tentatively, Jerome expounded them as conclusive ones. Jerome wrote his *Apology against Rufinus* in 402. As it happens, whereas such theologians as Rufinus and Ambrose would have had no

---

282 Cf. James Albert DeLater, *Theory in the Age of Louis XIV: The 1683 De Optimo Genere Interpretandi* [on the Best Kind of Translating) by the cleric Pierre Daniel Huet (1630-1721)], Oxford, 2002, note 230: "Aside from Jerome's and Rufinus' mutual charges of inaccuracy and unfaithfulness to orthodox dogma, Jerome's admission in *Letter* 82.7 to Theophilus that he retrenched what he believed heretical parts of Origen's work (see *De Optimo Genere Interpretandi*, 85, for a reference to these excisions) raises the broad question of censorship (self-censorship or otherwise) in translating." The author refers to his note on Huet's *De Optimo Genere Interpretandi*, 4, concerning the charge that Huet himself had omitted a line in Origen's commentaries on Matthew in the interests of Catholic orthodoxy.

283 Rufinus, *Apologia*, 1.22, PL.21.559-560; 2.46-47, PL.21.621-624.

284 See the above-mentioned *Letters* 3 and 4, as well as *Letter* 39.5 to Paula and 45.5 to Ascella.

285 Jerome, *Letter* 133.3 to Ctesiphon and 143.2 to Augustine.

286 Cf. Jerome, *op. cit.* 5.1; 10.1; 10.40; 11.30; 13.1-2; 17.7.

problem with admitting to having used Origen's writings, his belated enemy Jerome had all the reasons to care for making sure that pertinent works Origen's should be underrated or indeed extinguished as much as possible, under the pretext of a host of disingenuous claims. Nevertheless, he did not refuse that he had availed himself of Origen's commentary on Matthew; actually, he declared himself proud for having done so.

The case of Jerome's commentary on Matthew is illuminating, since he did not just take notice of Origen's commentary nor did he simply depend on his ideas: at several points, he copied from that work word for word. He said that he had read 'Origen's twenty-five books on Matthew many years ago and just as many of his homilies and a kind of verse interpretation.'[287] In general, while he admitted that he had translated several *tomes* (i.e. commentaries) of Origen's ('multa de tomis'),[288] none of his Biblical commentaries is presented as a translation – which could only mean that he went as far as to present (at least some) commentaries of Origen as ones of his own, perhaps with minor alterations or omission of points that he deemed too precarious to reproduce. Presumably, this would have happened after 393, once Epiphanius spearheaded the dispute over Origen, and Jerome was all too quick to laid the first stone on him and set foot on his vitriolic attacks aiming at annulling his former praise on Origen while alleging that he did not wish to retract them.

Jerome dictated this commentary in just two weeks (as he explains in his prologue addressed to Eusebius of Cremona) and he used exactly the same pattern as Origen: he wrote lemmas from the gospel of Matthew and then glossed them by means of ensuing brief exegeses. Origen himself had taken up this method from Alexander of Aphrodisias' commentaries on Aristotle: he did not need any specific edition of Aristotle's work since all of the text was there, lemma after lemma, accompanied by Alexander's comments. He employed the same methodology in his rebuttal of Celsus, thanks to which the largest part of the latter's text has been saved.

This is as far as scholarly similarities of Jerome's commentary with Origen's work go. For the *qualitative* difference between the two commentaries is abysmal. Perusing Jerome's commentary is a frustrating job to engage in, since this is a paltry text which contributes nothing to the germane tradition. His (mostly brief) comments are platitudes and regularly mere paraphrases of the scriptural text.

While having Origen's commentary in front of him, and copying from this every now and then, Jerome was always on his guard to besmirch his

287 Jerome in the Preface to his commentary on Matthew.

288 Jerome, *Apology against the Books of Rufinus*, I.8.

predecessor whenever he deemed it possible to do so. Commenting on Matthew 8:29 (about 'two people possessed by daemons'), he remarked, 'Some people ridiculously think that the daemons know the Son of God, but the devil is ignorant of him, because they are less evil than he whose satellites they are' (Ridiculeque putant quidam daemones scire Filium Dei, et diabolum ignorare; eo quod minoris malitiae sint isti quam ille cujus satellites sunt). Of course, he had in mind Origen, who had commented on instances of daemons speaking to Jesus and saying, *You are the Son of God,*[289] or when they addressed him *Son of God.*[290] Naturally, Origen's comment was that 'daemons knew that he was Christ' (ᾔδεισαν αὐτὸν Χριστὸν εἶναι).[291] On the other hand, he had commented on the Son's saying to those damned, *I never knew you* (οὐδέποτε ἔγνων ὑμᾶς).[292] He explained that this is so because *the Lord knows those who are his own ones*;[293] therefore, 'he does not know those who are not his'.[294] Hence, the expression *I never knew you* betokens 'the Saviour's greater rather than lesser power', which is why 'a sinner is not known by God.'[295]

The point Jerome actually had in mind was from Origen's Homilies on Luke, which should have been part of his commentary on Matthew, too.[296] Having made all of the foregoing remarks (some of them as early as in the commentary on John), it was Origen himself who posited the question with his proverbial consistency: since the daemons knew that Jesus was the Son of God, why was it that Paul wrote, *But we speak God's wisdom in a mystery, ... which none of the rulers of this world has known. For had they known it, they wouldn't have crucified the Lord of glory.*[297] His reply was that 'the economy of passion took place while the adverse activity was in a state of lapse of memory' (τὴν τοῦ πάθους οἰκονομίαν κατὰ λήθην φησὶ γεγονέναι τῆς ἀντικειμένης ἐνεργείας). However, 'since there was no forgetfulness in a specific daemon, who had said, *we know who you are: you are the Son of God,*[298] you should pay attention to the fact that the

289 Mark, 3:11; Luke, 4:41.
290 Matthew 8:29; Mark, 5:7; Luke, 8:28.
291 *commJohn*, X.11.57; *commMatt*, 11.17; cf. *homLuc*, homily 6, p. 36.
292 Matthew 7:23.
293 2 Tim. 2:19; cf. Num. 16:5.
294 *commJohn*, XXXII.14.154.
295 *homJer*, homily 1.8. In *op. cit.* 1.10, Origen adduced the example of men: the more they advance in quality, the less they want to know whatever is unworthy of being known'; likewise, 'God does not want to know Pharaoh, or the Egyptians; instead, he wants to know Moses and Jeremiah'.
296 The texts of those two works largely coincide, which is natural for two of the synoptic gospels to happen, in which numerous instances are the same. See discussion on p. CXCIV.
297 1 Cor. 2:7-8.
298 Cf. Mark, 1:24 & Luke, 4:34: "I know you who you are: the Holy One of God!"

one [daemon] who was lesser as regards wickedness knew the Saviour, whereas the worse in respect of this [wickedness, that is, the devil] was hindered from beholding him [sc. the Saviour] because of the magnitude of his [sc. the devil's] wickedness.'[299]

To Jerome, all of these appeared 'ridiculous', simply because, while he was plundering Origen's work, he was haunted by the shadow of that genius nonetheless. He would have used Origen's *Hexapla* in order to pose as a man who knew Hebrew, hence, one who (against Augustine's advice) could use Hebrew Bible instead of the *Septuaginta*.

This is an opportunity to resolve a point which appears baffling to some scholars, although it should not: on the one hand, Jerome shunned the *Septuaginta* and composed his translations of Old Testament on Hebrew exemplars; besides, he appeared dismissive of the Alexandrian canon of the Old Testament, that is, of deuterocanonicals, such as Wisdom of Solomon, Wisdom of Sirach, Tobit, Judith, Maccabees, and additions to Daniel, Esther, and Baruch. On the other, in his commentary on Matthew, most of scriptural quotations do not harmonise with Jerome's own Vulgate. The same goes for his quotations from the other gospels. However, the case is not that 'Jerome had no particular respect for his own version even when he was writing a commentary on a gospel', as A. Souter put it.[300] It was not a matter of 'respect' for his own work: it was only one of appropriation[301] according to Jerome's habit. This is evident also in his commentary on Ephesians, which in effect he copied from Origen's commentary: he used the same scriptures as Origen did, in the same order, and in the same way, even fusing passages in a single text as Origen did. Thus, he could not have had the time to consult his own rendering of the Scripture once scriptural quotations were there for him to copy from, along with Origen's own comments. According to L. Doutreleaux, Jerome did exactly the same in his commentary on Zachariah while copying from Didymus' commentary.[302]

His comment on Matthew 13:31-32 ('The kingdom of heaven is like a grain of mustard seed') is but Origen's one and it is all too evident that Jerome copied uninhibitedly.

---

299 Origen, *homLuc*, homily 6, pp. 36-37: ὅρα, ὅτι ὁ ἐλάττων ἐν τῇ κακίᾳ ᾔδει τὸν σωτῆρα, ὁ δὲ χείρων ἐν αὐτῇ ἀπὸ τοῦ μεγέθους τῆς κακίας ἐνεποδίζετο αὐτὸν θεωρεῖν.

300 A. Souter, "Notes on Incidental Gospel Quotations", *Journal of Theological Studies*, 42 (1941), p. 13.

301 I can only agree with G. Bardy who argued that all of what Jerome claimed to have learned first hand from the Jews in fact he had taken from Origen. "Saint Jérôme et ses maîtres hébreux", *Revue Bénedictine*, 46 (1934), pp. 145-164.

302 L. Doutreleaux, *Didyme l'aveugle sur Zacharie*, vol. I, Paris, 1962, pp. 230-231.

On who Zachariah (as in Matthew 23:35) really was,[303] Jerome assured that he had conducted independent research ('I have read diverse things in diverse sources'). In fact, however, he reproduced different testimonies ('some say … others want this Zachariah to be understood as … others want this Zachariah to be …) that had been set forth by Origen.[304]

Jerome copied from Origen while being unfit to grasp his predecessor's overall theological scope. For example, he insisted that, 'based on diversity of hopes, diverse rewards will be received';[305] however, he was unable to assess the difference between the doctrine of eschatological universal restoration and the state of things following the present age (aeon).[306] Accordingly, he was confounded at Origen maintaining both the notion of 'different degrees of punishment' (which Jerome himself seized on) and the final state of restitution, only because he wished to controvert such mediocre thinkers as Jovinian, who allegedly opposed a hierarchical interpretation of the 'diversity of gifts' among Christians and rejected differentiation of heavenly rewards. Thus, Jerome pulled back from Origen's idea of eschatological universal unity while embracing the latter's idea about different degrees of punishment – only the irony was that Jerome's intransigence stemmed from his viewing those two harmonious notions of Origen as incompatible. Consequently, in his treatise *Against Jovinian*, Jerome (based on Matthew 13:8) propounded the idea of different degrees of reward (concerning either virgins and chaste widows, or married women), although Augustine wrote that it was possible to praise virginity without vilifying marriage – a thesis that medieval authors in effect ignored and praised virginity at the expense of marriage. In turn, this gave rise to another bafflement of some modern Roman Catholic theologians, who pointed out that their 'doctrine of merit' is about a performed duty owed to God's favour rather than something humans either 'stockpile' or 'count'.

However, Jerome followed Origen suit in considering human deeds as *accumulation* and *calculation* of deeds in this life,[307] which was an idea of Origen's[308]

303 Cf. Origen, *commSerMatt*, pp. 42-43; *commMatt*, 10:18. Jerome, *commMatt*, 23.235-236.

304 Origen, *commSerMatt*, pp. 42-43; *commMatt*, 10.18; 10.20; *Epistula ad Africanum*, PG.11.69.7-10.

305 Jerome, *commEph*, PL.26.559, comm. on Eph. 1:12. Rufinus rightly pinpointed this passage as an example of Jerome's adoption of Origen's doctrines.

306 See *PHE*, chapter 9, pp. 237-356.

307 Jerome wrote (*commMatt*, 11.23) that Capernaum will be 'struck with worse punishments', because the city was unwilling to receive Jesus' teaching although the city had been dignified with the privilege of 'being exalted up to heaven by witnessing' Jesus' 'signs and miracles'.

308 See Origen, *commMatt*, in *Codex Sabaiticus* 232, folio 90r: διδάσκει δὲ διαφορὰς εἶναι κολάσεων (see endnote dccciv); *op. cit.* folio 181v: Εἰ γὰρ πᾶς ὁ ποιῶν κακὸν ἄξιός ἐστι

abundantly supported by numerous scriptural passages,[309] on which Origen commented several times. Whether this makes Jerome 'a good Catholic', or not, is not for me to assess, and I really do not care about this. The fact is that Origen clearly and confidently propounded the notion of 'different degrees of punishment', which is why he made Jesus' following words an important theme undergirding his idea:

> Do not lay up treasures for yourselves on the earth, where moth and rust consume, and where thieves break through and steal, but lay up for yourselves treasures in heaven, where neither moth nor rust consume, and where thieves do not break through and steal.[310]

Origen returned to this in order to bolster his fundamental thesis:

> And if you crave to learn from Scripture who is it who is *from beneath*, and who is it who is *from above*,[311] pay attention; for each person's treasure is where his heart is:[312] if someone stores up treasure, he is *from beneath*; but if someone stores up *treasure in heaven*,[313] that person is born *from above*[314] and assumes *the image of the heavenly*.[315] Besides, and above all, once this person has passed through all the heavens, he has attained to the most blessed end. And his works would be [the treasure],[316] of which I spoke, so that it would be said that the one who is *from beneath* does *the works of flesh*,[317] but the one who is *from above* produces *the fruit of the spirit*.[318]

τιμωρίας, ὁ ἐν προσχήματι εὐλαβείας τοῦτο ποιῶν χαλεπωτέρας ἐστὶ τιμωρίας ὑπεύθυνος. In reference to Matthew 25:41, Pamphilus in his *Apology* (PG.17.616), appealed to this by quoting from Origen's *Commentary on the Wisdom of Solomon*: "He thus shows that the same kind of punishment has been prepared for human sinners and for the devil and his angels, although in the same punishment the amount of punishment may be different: one is tormented more heavily and more austerely in proportion to the magnitude of his sins; another, however, is punished more lightly, because his sins were less grave and less severe."

309 Cf. Matthew 5:12; 6:1; 6:19-23; 13:8; Luke, 6:23; 6:35; 12:47-48; John 14:2.

310 Matthew 6:19-20. Cf. Luke, 12:21: "So is he who lays up treasure for himself, and is not rich toward God".

311 John, 8:23.

312 Cf. Matt. 6:21.

313 Cf. Matt. 6:20.

314 Cf. John, 3:3.

315 Cf. 1 Cor. 15:49.

316 At this point the text is irremediably corrupt. I restore as follows: Εἴη δ' ἂν καὶ τὰ ἑκάστου ἔργα ‹θησαυρὸς› οἷον εἶπα.

317 Cf. Gal. 5:19.

318 Gal. 5:22. Origen, *commJohn*, XIX.21.138-139. Cf. *commMatt*, 10.14: Καὶ ἔστι γε ἀληθῶς ὁρίσασθαι περὶ τοῦ ὡς ἀποδεδώκαμεν ἐν οὐρανοῖς θησαυρίζοντος.

Likewise,

> Each one is the cause of himself being *written about.*[319] If you pursue the *things of the earth*, you do not pursue *the heavenly* ones.[320] If your soul has inclined to the things that are here, you yourself will be the cause of [what will happen to] you (σὺ σεαυτῷ αἴτιος γίνῃ). For Jesus said, *Do not lay up treasures for yourselves on the earth, where moth and rust consume, and where thieves break through and steal, but lay up for yourselves treasures in heaven.*[321] Do you treasure in heaven? You yourself are the cause for you name to be written in the heavens.[322]

In the commentary on Matthew, he reiterated the same theory by reminding Jesus' concluding words in that scriptural instance ('and you will have treasure in heaven')[323] along with his own previous exegesis of what 'laying treasures in heaven' means. In any event, any 'treasure' is liable not only to increasing but also to decreasing. The latter is the consequence of what Origen styled 're-crucifixion of the Body of of Logos'[324] following the 'irrationality' that imbues any human 'sin'.

This interactive relationship between the Bridegroom and a Bride adumbrates the precariousness of this rapport: once the 'woman' is faithful to her 'husband', she accumulates 'treasures' in heaven; if she is not, the deposit account abates. Therefore, this is all about human *freedom* being able to affect the Body of Logos. Origen saw this idea also in the passage of Matthew 11:12 ('From the days of John the Baptist until now, the kingdom of heavens suffers violence, and the violent take it by force'). A hardly known portion from Klostermann's collection casts light on how Origen understood this.

> Therefore, once one who is still at the initial stages of training, firstly comes upon the words of Jesus, while walking along the road (which, to the beginners, appears harsh and uphill), he seizes the kingdom of heavens by force, which [kingdom of heavens] admits of violence (ἁρπάζει βίᾳ τὴν βασιλείαν τῶν οὐρανῶν, βίαν ὑπομένουσαν). For in this case, the [scriptural verb] *βιάζεται* is not active (οὐ γὰρ ἐνεργητικόν): instead, it is used in a passive sense (ἀντὶ δὲ παθητικοῦ εἴληπται).[325]

319 Commenting on Jer. 17:13: "Let them be written about on the earth."
320 Cf. John, 3:12; 1 Cor. 15:40.
321 Matt. 6:19-20.
322 Origen, *homJer*, homily 17.4. Similarly, *homJer*, homily 8.2 (Latin).
323 Matt. 16:21; Mark, 10:21.
324 Heb. 6:6. *commJohn*, XX.12.89-90; XXVIII.15.126. See discussion in *Anaxagoras*, p. 1371.
325 Origen, *frMatt*, fr. 227 (Klostermann).

This is how the 'heavenly treasures' are accumulated (and, by parity of reason, dissipated). For 'the violent' are 'those who believe sincerely and exercise violence by means of utter asceticism'.[326]

Jerome left no doubt about his copying from Origen: the following example is unique, since he refers to 'Crates the philosopher' who 'relinquished everything' by abandoning all of his paternal property.[327] Most of copyists emended Jerome's 'Crates' to 'Socrates' because, for lack of background, they did not realise what was this all about. However, Origen mentioned Crates in his own commentary on Matthew, indeed he attested to a proverbial phrase by Crates, of which variants (but not the precise phrase as attested by Origen, which appears as the most ancient witness to this information) can be found in E. Diehl's pertinent collection and its update.[328] Crates said those words when he donated all of his fortune to the people of Thebes and chose to live a life of poverty on the streets of Athens.

> Today, Crates sets Crates free (σήμερον ὁ Κράτης Κράτητα ἐλευθεροῖ).[329]

Moreover, it is quite surprising that, although Jerome's copying from Origen has been recognised, particular points of this 'method' were not noticed, and

---

326 Origen, *frMatt*, fr. 228 (Klostermann): *Βιασταί* εἰσιν οἱ εἰλικρινῶς πιστεύοντες καὶ δι' ἄκρας ἀσκήσεως βιαζόμενοι.

327 Jerome, *commMatt*, 19.28.

328 E. Diehl, *Anthologia Lyrica Graeca*, fasc. 1, 3rd ed., Leipzig, 1949, pp. 120-126. H. Lloyd-Jones – P. Parsons, *Supplementum Hellenisticum*, Berlin, 1983, pp. 164-172.

329 Origen, *commMatt*, 15.15: Κράτητα γὰρ τὸν Θηβαῖον ἐλόμενον δι' ἐλευθερίαν ‹τῆς ψυχῆς αὐτοῦ› καὶ παράδειγμα εὐτελοῦς βίου καὶ (ὡς ᾤετο) μακάριον ἑαυτὸν παραστῆσαι βουλόμενον τοῖς Ἕλλησι μηδενὸς *‹τοῦ κόσμου τούτου›* χρῄζοντα, φασὶν ἀποδόμενον πᾶσαν τὴν οὐσίαν τῷ Θηβαίων δήμῳ δεδωρῆσθαι, μετὰ τοῦ εἰρηκέναι ὅτι *σήμερον ὁ Κράτης Κράτητα ἐλευθεροῖ*. This testimony was taken up by the following authors: Eusebius, *Demonstratio Evangelica*, 3.6.22. Gregory of Nazianzus, *Funebris Oratio in Laudem Basilii Magni Caesareae in Cappadocia Episcopi*, 60.4; *Contra Julianum*, PG.35.596.12-16; *Carmina Moralia*, column 697. Isidore of Pelusium, *Epistulae De Interpretatione Divinae Scripturae*, Book 2, epistle 146. Procopius of Gaza, *Epistulae*, epistle 159. Epiphanius of Salamis, *Panarion*, v. 3, p. 507. Crates of Thebes (c. 365 – c. 285 BC) was a Cynic philosopher who married Hipparchia of Maroneia who lived in the same manner he did. Respected by the people of Athens, he is remembered for being the teacher of Zeno of Citium, the founder of Stoicism. See references to Crates and / or Hipparchia: *Suda*, letter kappa, entry 2341; letter theta, entry 150; letter eta, entry 448; letter iota, entry 517. Diogenes of Sinope, *Epistulae*, epistles 3.1; 43.1. Crates of Thebes, *Epistulae*, epistle 28.1. Epictetus, *Dissertationes ab Arriano Digestae*, 3.22.76. Diogenes Laertius, *Vitae*, 2.118. Pseudo-Nonnus, *Scholia Mythologica*, 4.28. Simplicius, *commEpict*, p. 29. Plutarch, *De Vitando Aere Alieno*, pp. 830C; 831E; *et passim*. Constantine Manasses, *Monodia in Nicephorum Comnenum*, line 148. Pseudo-Zonaras, *Lexicon*, letter beta, p. 414. Michael Apostolius, *Collectio Paroemiarum*, 10.5.

scholars (who otherwise argued for Jerome's poor contribution to modern exegesis) received his interpretation of the mustard-seed (Matthew 13:31-32) in admiration for its eloquence.[330] In fact, however, in Jerome's commentary there is nothing that could be styled inspired or eloquent or erudite[331] since this is only a prosaic humdrum, and at many points what is supposed to be a comment is simply a tautological rendering of Matthew's text. Except for one point referring to 'others', he thought that there is nothing in Matthew that would be explained as concurrent with Christian Trinitarian doctrine – in contrast to Origen, in whose commentary analyses of this kind abound, especially references to the equality of Father and Son, and of the Three Persons being 'consubstantial', as discussed below. Jerome appropriated numerous ideas of Origen and all too often did he so with his words *verbatim*. However, he had no inkling of Origen's philosophical background. A case in point is his comment, 'the whole rational creation of angels and human souls constitutes one body',[332] which is but Origen's notion of Body of Logos. But whereas to Origen this was an Anaxagorean notion put to fresh use,[333] Jerome had not the faintest or foggiest idea of this was all about.

The reason why I am considering this unimaginative text is because all too often its attacks on Origen are out of proportion compared to its alleged scope: while looting the latter's commentary on Matthew, he was plagued by Origen's personality and sought points that could appear helpful to the purpose of attacking him. For example, if one reads Jerome's short comment on Matthew 14:1-2 (when Herod heard about Jesus, he asked his servant if he was John the Baptist having risen from the dead), one would be definitely baffled: once again, concealing his venom behind general reference ('some of the ecclesiastical interpreters'), he refers to Origen's text in *Codex Sabaiticus 232* (folio 117r), in which he surmised that Herod posed this question because he was reflecting 'in accordance with the heresy of transmigration' (Κατὰ αἵρεσιν

330 See J. Steinmann, *Hieronymus: Ausleger der Bibel. Weg und Werk eines Kirchenvaters*, Leipzig, 1958, p. 247.

331 For example, the comment on Matthew 9:9 is but Origen's *frLuc*, 108. The comment on Matthew 10:37 is a copy from Origen's fr. 216 (Klostermann). The comment on Matthew 11:2-3 is based on Origen's fr. 220 I (Klostermann). The comment on Matthew 13:45-46 bears on Origen's *commMatt*, 10.9, and that on Matthew 13:47-47 bears on Origen's *commMatt*, 10.13. The comment on Matthew 14:14 is but Origen's exegesis in *commMatt*, 10.23. And so on at several other points, but I have not deemed worth considering and pointing out too much of Jerome's looting.

332 See Rufinus's *Apologiae in sanctum Hieronymum*, Book 2.42, in Philip Schaff – Henry Wallace, *Nicene and Post-nicene Fathers: Second Series (vol. III): Theodoret, Jerome, Gennadius, Rufinus*, New York, 2007, p. 479.

333 See *Anaxagoras*, 'The First Body', pp. 781-790.

μετεμψυχώσεως), and then he made some additional remarks. In reality, Jerome commented on Origen's comment rather than on Matthew's text: he excoriateed 'those interpreters' who sought to explain why was it that Herod was suspicious, 'as if we need to account for the error of an alien (erroris alieni)! Or as if the sect of μετεμψύχωσις were occasioned from these words!'[334]

Origen had expounded his exegesis of this, speaking about 'the false doctrine of transmigration' (τὴν τῆς μετενσωματώσεως ψευδοδοξίαν),[335] but at that point he used the term μετεμψύχωσις. In general, the terms he used for transmigration are μετενσωμάτωσις[336] and μετεμψύχωσις[337] but never do both terms appear in the same work.

The term μετενσωμάτωσις appears for the first time in the sixth book of his commentary on John (the first book that he wrote in Caesarea), then, in the *Contra Celsum* and, later, in the commentary on Matthew. Interestingly, the term μετεμψύχωσις appears only in the homilies on Luke (considerably coinciding with catena fragments on Matthew) and on Ezekiel, which would suggest that they belong to the latest works of his, since he used μετεμψύχωσις instead of μετενσωμάτωσις by the end of his life.[338]

It is remarkable that the term μετεμψύχωσις is very scarce and appears in texts of his rendered by third hands, whereas in the texts indisputably reproducing the original he used μετενσωμάτωσις. As I have argued several times, Galen considerably influenced Origen,[339] but this is out of my present scope. I just note that only Origen and Galen were those who pointed out the distinction between 'incarnation' and 'transmigration' (Origen: ἐνσωμάτωσις / μετενσωμάτωσις,[340] Galen: ἐμψύχωσις / μετεμψύχωσις).[341]

---

334 Jerome, *commMatt*, 14.1-2.

335 *commMatt*, 10.20.

336 Cf. μετενσωμάτωσις: *commJohn*, VI: 10.64; 11.66; 11.70; 12.72; 12.73; 14.86; *commMatt*, 10.20; 13.1-2; *Cels*, I: 13; 20; III.75; IV.17; V: 29; 49; VI.36; VII.32; VIII.30.

337 Cf. μετεμψύχωσις: *homLuc*, homily 4; *selEz*, PG.13.808.2.

338 Origen did not end up his life in Caesarea, nor did he remain there for a long time, namely, for more than two years. Cf. Epiphanius of Salamis, *Panarion*, v. 2, p. 406. However, this issue is beyond of my present scope, and I postpone discussion of it until a new biography of his is published.

339 On Galen and Origen, see *Anaxagoras*, pp. 397-398; 658; 676-677; 849; 865; 929; 954; 1049; 1230; 1244-1245; 1258; *COT*, pp. 169; 200-201; 219; 245; 323; 373; *PHE*, pp. 169; 368-369; *NDGF*, pp. 218; 239; 397; *Scholia*, pp. 40; 84; 320; 323; 402. See Galen and Alexander of Aphrodisias considered in apposition: *NDGF*, p. 597; *Scholia*, pp. 212; 242; 262; 307; 320; 386; 402. On alleged common ideas in Galen and Plutarch, see *Anaxagoras*, pp. 1438; 1503.

340 *commJohn*, IV.14.86: Ἐν οἷς καὶ τί ἐστι κυρίως μετενσωμάτωσις ἐξετάσαι δεήσει, τί τε αὕτη διαφέρει ἐνσωματώσεως.

341 Galen, *De Substantia Facultatum Naturalium Fragmentum* (*De Propriis Placitis fragmentum*), p. 763: καὶ κατά γε τοῦτο πρὸς τὴν ἰατρικὴν τέχνην οὐδὲν ἡγοῦμαι βλαβήσεσθαι διὰ τὴν

I have also argued that all too often is translation of Greek texts in English frustrating, since almost always something of the meaning involved is missing. In this case, both terms normally are rendered 'transmigration of souls'. However, there is a remarkable difference between them: μετεμψύχωσις is used in consideration of a *body* being animated by a soul coming in from another body. On the other hand, μετενσωμάτωσις mainly bespeaks a *soul* changing place and being confined in another body.[342] It is quite remarkable, that whereas all scathing statements against Origen during and after the sixth century attributed to him μετεμψύχωσις, Origen himself used μετενσωμάτωσις far more extensively.[343] In any event, Origen was the only Christian author ever to point out the need for the important distinction to be made between the terms ἐνσωμάτωσις and μετενσωμάτωσις. The former is translated 'incarnation', the latter 'transmigration', but this misses the fact that this is about the *same* noun (ἐν-σωμάτωσις), only the second one is prefixed by one more preposition (μετ-εν-σωμάτωσις). Nevertheless, the root-noun is the same and (as I have argued upon perusing Origen's doctrine of soul[344]) Origen suggests that a soul is *generated* (which is why he speaks of 'the origin of its constitution'),[345] by which he meant concurrence of principles / causes / *logoi* that are 'embodied', that is, involved with matter and generate matter itself, too. This is why physical parents are only the *means* for offspring to be generated; in reality, any soul comes from God (i.e. from the constitutive *logoi* stemming from the Body of Logos), which is why 'there is neither father nor mother of any human soul; it is God alone who is its creator and father'. This is the meaning of God's saying 'all souls are mine' and 'each soul has a standing of its own, and it is not possible to say that a soul pays for sins committed by another one'.[346]

ἄγνοιαν τῆς καλουμένης ἐμψυχώσεώς τε καὶ μετεμψυχώσεως. The only other case of the distinction ἐμψύχωσις / μετεμψύχωσις appears in the Corpus Hermeticum, *Fragmenta*, fr. 26 (*apud* Stobaeus, *Anthologium*, 1.49.69).

342 I have argued that speaking of the incorporeal soul (and any incorporeal, in general) and expressions such as 'coming' or 'going' to another 'place', or being 'included' in something, are self-defeating ones.

343 See μετεμψύχωσις. Origen, *homLuc*, homily 4, p. 27; *frLuc*, frs. 17c; 17e; *Philocalia*, Prologue; *selEz*, PG.13.808.2; *commMatt*, in *Codex Sabaiticus 232*, folio 117r: Κατὰ αἵρεσιν μετεμψυχώσεως. See μετενσωμάτωσις, in *Cels*, I.13 (& *Philocalia*, 18.7); I.20 (& *Philocalia*, 18.5); III.75; IV.17; V.29 (& *Philocalia*, 22.8); V.49; VI.36; VII.32; VIII.30; *commJohn*, VI: 11.66; 11.70; 12.72; 12.73; 14.86; *commMatt*, 10.20; 13.1-2; *frMatt*, frs. 4-8.

344 *Anaxagoras*, chapter 13, pp. 1279-1462.

345 *Cels*, IV.17; Εἰ δὲ ἦν ἐννοήσας, τί ἀκολουθεῖ ψυχῇ ἐν αἰωνίῳ ἐσομένῃ ζωῇ καὶ τί χρὴ φρονεῖν περὶ τῆς οὐσίας αὐτῆς καὶ περὶ τῶν ἀρχῶν αὐτῆς.

346 Origen, *selEz*, PG.13.817.16-22: Ἡ γένεσις ἡμῶν κατὰ σάρκα οὖσα, ταύτης καὶ πατέρας καὶ μητέρας ἔχομεν. Οὐ γάρ ἐστι ψυχῆς μήτηρ ἢ πατήρ· ταύτης γὰρ ὁ Θεὸς μόνος ἐστὶ ποιητὴς καὶ πατήρ. Καὶ τοῦτο διδάσκων ὁ Θεὸς λέγει, ὅτι, *Πᾶσαι αἱ ψυχαὶ ἐμαί εἰσι.* Καὶ ἑκάστη ψυχὴ

The pristine reality and *object of creation* is not souls, but logoi / 'seeds', which can produce *also* souls just like everything else in the world. A soul is *not* a primeval reality, as falsely believe those who speak about 'fall of souls' or 're-uinification of souls with God' in reference to Origen. This means that there is not a definite number of souls, which normally was a reason for those who believed so to maintain transmigration, and certainly the so-called 'traducianism' was too ridiculous a notion for a scholar such as Origen to dignify with any particular consideration. Anyway, the scholastic problem of whether the number of souls is finite or infinite (of which Thomas Aquinas made much disputing Averroes) has no place and makes no sense in Origen, since that pseudo-problem took for granted the assumption that a soul is a certain personal self-subsistent *quid*. Against such idle talking, to Origen, the soul is but a result of different existential modes of concurring incorporeal logoi, which appear involved with the corporeal hypostasis of a human being and cause it to be animated, as much as do they cause all of its physiological operations to come to pass.

Therefore, μετεμψύχωσις and μετενσωμάτωσις (both of which Origen staunchly dismissed[347]) have an implication in common, which is lost upon

ἰδίαν ὑπόστασιν ἔχει, ἐν τῷ ἰδίῳ λόγῳ ἱσταμένη, καὶ οὐκ ἐν ἄλλῳ. See analysis in *Anaxagoras*, pp. 1317-1319; 1351-1352.

347 *commJohn*, VI.10.64: τάχα τούτῳ χρήσονται οἱ ἐκ τούτων τῷ περὶ μετενσωματώσεως παριστάμενοι λόγῳ, ὡς τῆς ψυχῆς μεταμφιεννυμένης σώματα καὶ οὐ πάντως μεμνημένης τῶν προτέρων βίων. *Op. cit.* VI.11.66. Ἕτερος δέ τις ἐκκλησιαστικὸς τὸν περὶ τῆς μετενσωματώσεως ἀποπτύων ὡς ψευδῆ λόγον. *Op. cit.* VI.11.70: ἐκκλησιαστικὸς ... ἑτέρως παρὰ τὸν ὑπολαμβάνοντα μετενσωμάτωσιν ἀπολογούμενος ἐρεῖ. *Op. cit.* VI.12.72: Ὁ δὲ πρῶτος, οὗ τὸν νοῦν παρεθήκαμεν οἰομένου μετενσωμάτωσιν ἐντεῦθεν κατασκευάζεσθαι. *Op. cit.* VI.12.73: τὸ *Σὺ Ἠλίας εἶ*; [John, 1.21] δῆλον ὅτι τοῦτο ἔλεγον τὸ περὶ μετενσωματώσεως δόγμα οἰόμενοι εἶναι ἀληθὲς ὡς πάτριον τυγχάνον καὶ οὐκ ἀλλότριον τῆς ἐν ἀπορρήτοις διδασκαλίας αὐτῶν ... καὶ εἰ ἀκολουθεῖ τῷ λέγοντι μετενσωμάτωσιν ἄφθαρτον τηρεῖν τὸν κόσμον. *homLuc*, homily 4 & *frLuc*, fr. 17c: Οὐ γὰρ ἐν ψυχῇ Ἡλίου φησὶν (οὐ γὰρ ἦν μετεμψύχωσις) ἀλλ᾽ *ἐν πνεύματι καὶ δυνάμει Ἡλίου*. *frLuc*, fr. 17e: ἀλλ᾽ οὐδὲ τοῖς πρὸς μετεμψύχωσιν βουλομένοις τὸ ῥῆμα βιάζεσθαι χώραν δίδωσιν ἡ ἱστορία. ἐτόλμησαν γὰρ πολλοὶ ταύτην ἐπιρρῖψαι τὴν θεωρίαν τῇ τοῦ κυρίου φωνῇ. *Philocalia*, Prologue, section c & 20.1 (title): ἐν οἷς καὶ κατὰ μετεμψυχώσεως, καὶ περὶ οἰωνιστικῆς καὶ τῆς κατ᾽ αὐτὴν ἀπάτης. *selEz*, PG.13.808.1-2: Εἰ γὰρ τοῦτο δώσομεν, ὥρα τὰ πάντα λέγειν ἔμψυχα, καὶ συνηγορεῖν τοῖς τὰς μετεμψυχώσεις εἰσάγουσι. *commMatt*, 10.20: τὴν τῆς μετενσωματώσεως ψευδοδοξίαν. *Op. cit.* 13.1 & *frMatt*, p. 4: τὸ ἀλλότριον τῆς ἐκκλησίας τοῦ θεοῦ περὶ τῆς μετενσωματώσεως δόγμα. ... ἕκαστον δὲ τούτων τῷ ἐνορᾶν δυναμένῳ τοῖς πράγμασιν ἀνατρεπτικόν ἐστι τῆς μετενσωματώσεως. *Op. cit.* 13.2: οὐκ εἶπεν *ἐν ψυχῇ Ἠλίου*, ἵν᾽ ἔχῃ τόπον ἡ μετενσωμάτωσις, ἀλλ᾽ *ἐν πνεύματι καὶ δυνάμει Ἠλίου*. *Cels*, I.20 & *Philocalia*, 18.5: ὑπὲρ τὴν μυθικὴν μετενσωμάτωσιν, τὴν περὶ τῆς πιπτούσης ἀπὸ τῶν ἁψίδων τοῦ οὐρανοῦ ψυχῆς. *Op. cit.* III.75: τοὺς πεπονθότας τὴν περὶ μετενσωματώσεως ἄνοιαν. *Op. cit.* IV.17: οὐ κατὰ τὴν Πλάτωνος μετενσωμάτωσιν ἀλλὰ κατ᾽ ἄλλην τινὰ ὑψηλοτέραν θεωρίαν. *Op. cit.* V.29 & *Philocalia*, 22.8: ἵνα μὴ εἰς τὰς τυχούσας ἀκοὰς ὁ περὶ ψυχῶν οὐκ ἐκ μετενσωματώσεως εἰς σῶμα ἐνδουμένων λόγος

their English translation: this is all about *embodiment*, that is, *embodiment of logoi* operating *in matter* and acting upon it, thus determining its different forms, qualities, and all sorts of functions.

The more Jerome drew on Origen the more he was always on his alert to criticise points of Origen's commentary on Matthew as much as he was so upon heavily copying from him. For example, he thought it worthy to shed his venom on Origen's comments[348] on points such as Matthew 16:14, but Jerome's own comments were but paraphrases of the same points as those in Origen's commentary on Matthew.[349]

Whenever Jerome felt like adding something of his own in the commentary, this was either trivial rehashing of Matthew's text or tralaticious information that Origen had already reported. For instance, in reference to Jesus' departure to a desert place following the death of the Baptist, Jerome copies from Origen, yet he adds one reason of his own as to why did Jesus do so: 'He did so ... in order to spare his enemies from adding one murder to another'.[350] But this was only a banality that had been attributed to Aristotle, when he decamped from Athens to his mother's estate at Chalcis, 'so that the Athenians should not be given a chance to commit a second crime against philosophy'.[351] Unless anonymous *Lives* of Aristotle had already circulated (probably they had) by the third century, Origen is perhaps the only known source to attest to this;[352] actually, he did so upon discussing the portion of Matthew, 10:23, 'when they persecute you in this city, flee into the next'.

In Jerome's commentary there is nothing theologically significant, let alone new. We are only once again upon manifestations of his character, as it were,

ῥιπτῆται. *Op. cit.* V.29: Ἐκεῖνοι μὲν γὰρ διὰ τὸν περὶ ψυχῆς μετενσωματουμένης μῦθον ἐμψύχων ἀπέχονται. *Op. cit.* VI.36: Κάθοδον δὲ αὖθις στενὴν τάχα οἱ τὴν μετενσωμάτωσιν εἰσάγοντες φήσουσιν. *Op. cit.* VII.32: οὐχ, ὡς οἴεται Κέλσος, τῆς μετενσωματώσεως παρακούσαντες τὰ περὶ ἀναστάσεώς φαμεν. *Op. cit.* VIII.30: Οὐδαμῶς μέντοι γε λέγοντες μετενσωμάτωσιν εἶναι ψυχῆς.

348 Jerome, *commMatt*, 16.14: "I marvel that certain interpreters inquire about the causes of these errors. They compose extensive argumentation about why was it that some people were thinking that our Lord Jesus Christ was John, others Elias, and others Jeremiah or one of the prophets".

349 For example, see Origen, *commMatt*, Book 12, sections 14, 16, 17, 21, 22, 24, etc. – but I am not going to follow this nauseating juxtaposition all the way through.

350 Jerome, *commMatt*, 14.13.

351 Anonymous, *Vita Aristotelis*, *Vita Marciana*, 41: Ἐπαναστάντων δ' αὐτῷ τῶν Ἀθηναίων ὑπεχώρησεν εἰς Χαλκίδα, τοσοῦτον ὑπειπὼν ὡς *Οὐ συγχωρήσω Ἀθηναίοις δὶς ἁμαρτεῖν εἰς φιλοσοφίαν*. *Vita Vulgata*, 19: μετέπειτα ἀνταρσίας γενομένης ἐν τοῖς Ἀθηναίοις, ἦλθεν ὁ Ἀριστοτέλης ἐν Χαλκίδι, εἰρηκὼς τοῖς Ἀθηναίοις ὅτι *Οὐκ ἂν ἐάσω ὑμᾶς δὶς εἰς φιλοσοφίαν ἁμαρτεῖν*.

352 See *Cels*, I.65 (& *Philocalia*, 18.14). Elias of Alexandria, *commCateg*, p. 123.

'persisting' in belying his modern hagiographers; a character that was the sheer antipode to whatever Christianity stands for.

Beyond his vitriolic attacks on Rufinus and Rufinus' bishop John of Jerusalem, Jerome had exerted his twisted Ciceronian rhetoric skills and embittered sarcasm in order to defame such personalities as Ambrose of Milan and John Chrysostom (presumably, also because of Chrysostom's undisguised and profuse use of Origen's ideas, and indeed of selfsame words and expressions as Origen's). It seems that, deep down, what Jerome needed in the first place in order to regard someone favourably was to be able himself to look down on him. Quite simply, he was was constitutionally undeferential to superior genius. And, speaking of his knowledge of languages, Jerome is the eternal exemplar of Paul's paradigmatic cases: "If I speak with the languages of men and of angels, but don't have love, I have become sounding brass, or a clanging cymbal. If I have the gift of prophesy, and know all mysteries and all knowledge, and if I have all faith, so as to remove mountains, but don't have love, I am nothing."[353]

The Term and Notion of ὁμοούσιος

In *Sabaiticus 232*, and in reference to Trinitarian relations, Origen uses the term ὁμοούσιος[354] confidently. Full discussion of this term in regard to his overall theology is beyond my present scope, but some discussion is called for, since

353 1 Cor. 13:1-2.

354 Origen, *commMatt*, *Codex Sabaiticus 232*, folio 1v (& Kl. fr. 14): Τὸ λεγόμενον πνευματικὴ *γέννησις*, τὸ δὲ *ἐκ* τὸν ‹ἁγια›σμὸν δηλώσει καὶ τὴν δύναμιν· ναὶ μὴν καὶ τὸ ὁμοούσιον. Folio 18v (& Klostermann fr. 58): Εἷς τῆς Τριάδος ἐβαπτίσθη. εἷς ἐν εἴδει περιστερᾶς ὤφθη. εἷς ἄνωθεν ἐπεφώνει. Τρεῖς οὖν ὑποστάσεις, μία δὲ οὐσία τῶν τριῶν. *Loc. cit.* Δεικνὺς δὲ τὸ ὁμοούσιον τὸ πρὸς τὸν πατέρα τῷ *ἐστὶ* πρὸς ῥήματι κέχρηται. Folio 19r: Ὁ γὰρ ὁμοούσιον ἔχων τὸ Πνεῦμα τὸ Ἅγιον, καθὸ Θεὸς ἦν καὶ ὁμοούσιος τῷ Πατρί, πῶς ἔμελλε πνευματικῆς δεῖσθαι καὶ ἀνηγμένης ζωῆς; Folio 91r-v (& Kl. fr. 244): Ἐπειδὴ δὲ ἔδειξεν ὅ τι πάντων ἐστὶ δεσπότης, δείκνυσι καὶ ἕτερον μεῖζον, τὸ εἰδέναι τὸν πατέρα καὶ τῆς αὐτῆς οὐσίας εἶναι. Folio 95r (& Kl. fr. 257): Ὁ Πατὴρ λέγει τῷ Υἱῷ *τὸ Πνεῦμα* καταπέμπειν. Οὐκοῦν προσκυνοῦμεν Τριάδα ὁμοούσιον, Θεὸν τὸν Πατέρα, Θεὸν τὸν Υἱόν, Θεὸν τὸ Πνεῦμα τὸ Ἅγιον. Μίαν φύσιν ἐν τρισὶν ἰδιότησι νοεραῖς, τελείαις, καθ' ἑαυτὰς ὑφεστώσαις, ἀριθμῷ διαιρεταῖς καὶ οὐ διαιρεταῖς θεότητι. Folio 194v: Εἴπερ γάρ ἐστι καὶ ὁμοούσιος, καὶ τὸ γινώσκειν ἔχει. Folio 195v: ὅτι οὗπερ ἐστὶν ὁμοούσιος ἐξ αὐτοῦ καὶ τὸ γινώσκειν ἔχει καὶ τὸ ἐν πάσῃ σοφίᾳ καὶ δόξῃ τῇ πρεπούσῃ αὐτοῦ τῇ θεότητι θεωρεῖσθαι. Folio 239v (& Kl. fr. 572 & Origen, *schMatt*, PG.17.309.37-53): Εἷς ὁ ζῶν, Πατὴρ καὶ Υἱὸς καὶ Ἅγιον Πνεῦμα. Εἷς ἐστιν, οὐ συναλοιφῇ τῶν τριῶν, ἀλλ' οὐσία μία. Τρεῖς δὲ ὑποστάσεις τέλειαι ἐν πᾶσι καὶ κατάλληλοι. Κατὰ φύσιν ἐγέννησεν ὁ Θεός. διόπερ ὁμοούσιος ὁ γεννηθείς. Οὐ σῶμα ὁ Θεός, καὶ οὐ κατὰ ῥεῦσιν ἢ κίνησιν ἤ τι τῶν τοιούτων ἃ ἐν τοῖς σώμασι θεωρεῖται. Ὁ Θεὸς ὁ ἀσώματος ἐγέννησεν. Ἐνυπόστατος ἡ γέννησις. Ἀπετέχθη ἐκ τῆς οὐσίας τοῦ Πατρὸς ὁ Υἱός. Folio 240r: Τριάδα τοίνυν τοῖς μαθηταῖς ὁμοούσιον τοῖς βαπτιζομένοις διδόναι παρεγγυᾷ. *Op. cit.* folio 240v: Ἔστι γὰρ καθ' ὑπόστασιν ἰδίαν Πνεῦμα Ἅγιον, ὁμοούσιον τῷ Πατρὶ καὶ τῷ Υἱῷ. Folio 240v: Ἔστι γὰρ καθ' ὑπόστασιν ἰδίαν Πνεῦμα Ἅγιον, ὁμοούσιον τῷ Πατρὶ καὶ τῷ Υἱῷ, ἐκ

this codex contains highly important portions from Origen's work which, however, have been almost entirely and persistently overlooked by scholars refusing to see the indisputable evidence about the great Alexandrian having preceded Nicaea.

The fact that Origen's Trinitarian theology did not deviate from the Nicene Creed was proclaimed by Athanasius paying tribute to his illustrious predecessor and declaring that use of *homoousios* was not an invention of Nicaea, but this had been already set forth by earlier 'erudite men',[355] indeed not only 'bishops' but also 'scholars' (λόγιοι).

In relation to the Father and Son, Athanasius defended the expression 'from the essence of the Father' (ἐκ τῆς οὐσίας τοῦ Πατρὸς) by using the example of the sun emitting its light. He drew on Theognostus, the late-third century Alexandrian theologian (c. 210-270), who reportedly was a disciple of Origen, he presided over the school of Alexandria after Pierius (265 AD), and wrote a seven-volume work called *Hypotyposes*, which was extant at the time of Photius, who reviewed it. Athanasius quoted from Theognostus,[356] who maintained that the Son's substance was not made out of nothing, nor was this produced by 'partition' of the paternal substance (οὐ μερισμὸν ὑπομεινάσης τῆς τοῦ πατρὸς οὐσίας). The Son was generated 'from the essence of the Father' (ἐκ τῆς οὐσίας), in like a manner the sun emits its light, which causes no diminution of sun's own substance itself. This is why the Son is 'the image' of the Father (εἰκόνα ἑαυτῆς ἔχουσα τὸν υἱόν) which caused no alteration to the paternal

τοῦ Πατρὸς ἐκπορευόμενον, δι᾽ Υἱοῦ πεφηνός, ἀχώριστον τοῦ Πατρὸς καὶ τοῦ Υἱοῦ, ὡς ἴδιον. Τρεῖς οὖν τετελειωμέναι ὑποστάσεις *Πατρὸς καὶ Υἱοῦ καὶ Ἁγίου Πνεύματος*, μία δὲ οὐσία.

355 Athanasius, *Epistula ad Afros Episcopos*, PG.26.1040.27–38 (the same, in the edition by Brennecke, von Stockhausen, and Heil, 6.3-4): Ἐπίσκοποι γὰρ ἀρχαῖοι πρὸ ἐτῶν ἐγγύς που ἑκατὸν τριάκοντα τῆς μεγάλης Ῥώμης καὶ τῆς ἡμετέρας πόλεως γράφοντες ᾐτιάσαντο τοὺς ποίημα λέγοντας τὸν Υἱὸν καὶ μὴ ὁμοούσιον τῷ Πατρί. καὶ τοῦτο ἐγίνωσκεν Εὐσέβιος ὁ γενόμενος ἐπίσκοπος τῆς Καισαρείας, πρότερον μὲν συντρέχων τῇ Ἀρειανῇ αἱρέσει, ὕστερον δὲ ὑπογράψας ἐν αὐτῇ τῇ ἐν Νικαίᾳ συνόδῳ, ἔγραψε τοῖς ἰδίοις διαβεβαιούμενος, ὅτι καὶ τῶν παλαιῶν τινας λογίους καὶ ἐπιφανεῖς ἐπισκόπους καὶ συγγραφέας, ἔγνωμεν ἐπὶ τῆς τοῦ Πατρὸς καὶ Υἱοῦ θεότητος τῷ τοῦ *ὁμοουσίου* χρησαμένους ὀνόματι. Athanasius, *De Decretis Nicaenae Synodi*, 27.1: Περὶ δὲ τοῦ ἀϊδίως συνεῖναι τὸν λόγον τῷ πατρὶ καὶ μὴ ἑτέρας οὐσίας ἢ ὑποστάσεως, ἀλλὰ τῆς τοῦ πατρὸς ἴδιον ‹γέννημα› αὐτὸν εἶναι, ὡς εἰρήκασιν οἱ ἐν τῇ συνόδῳ, ἐξέστω πάλιν ὑμᾶς ἀκοῦσαι καὶ παρὰ τοῦ φιλοπόνου Ὠριγένους. See further (*op. cit.* 27.2-3), Athanasius' quotation from Origen having introduced the Nicene catchphrase οὐκ ἔστιν ὅτε οὐκ ἦν ('there was no [state of the Deity] in which he [sc. the Son] was not').

356 Athanasius praises and appeals to 'men of old', mentioning Origen and Theognostus by name (παλαιοὶ ἄνδρες, Ὠριγένης ὁ πολυμαθὴς καὶ φιλόπονος καὶ Θεόγνωστος ὁ θαυμάσιος καὶ σπουδαῖος). *In illud: Qui Dixerit Verbum in Filium*, PG.26.649.21 ff & 38 ff; the same in the *Epistulae Quattuor ad Serapionem*, 4.2.1; 4.3.1.

essence (οὕτως οὐδὲ ἡ οὐσία τοῦ πατρὸς ἀλλοίωσιν ὑπέμεινεν).[357] This was a lesson that Origen had taught right from the start of his Christian life, when he scolded those who believed that 'the Son has been begotten of the Father's essence in like a manner one might understand this in the case of pregnant women, and that God, once he has begotten the Son, is diminished and lacking, as it were, in terms of the essence [substance] that he formerly had (οἱονεὶ μειουμένου καὶ λείποντος τῇ οὐσίᾳ ἣ πρότερον εἶχεν τοῦ Θεοῦ).'[358]

Pamphilus made much of Origen's arguments in this context by quoting from both *De Principiis* and the commentary on John, and advising that Origen's analyses were mainly directed against Valentinus, who taught that the Son was generated from the Father as a 'projection' (προβολὴ) which entailed no 'division' of the Father.[359]

Once again, Gregory of Nyssa followed suit: the case of the Father having begotten the Son should not be understood as analogous to the order according to which Nature operates (τὴν ἐκ φύσεως τάξιν).[360]

The essential point about this is not mere usage of the Valentinian term *homoousios* while Origen attacked Valentinian Gnosticism[361] vehemently: rather, it is its implications, which were grasped by such admirers of his as Athanasius, who assured that the *auctoritas vetustatis* of the term *homoousios* came from illustrious 'bishops and scholars of old.' This was a phrase that Eusebius also used explaining to his flock why was it that he shifted from his Arianising views to signing up to the Nicene resolution.[362] Hence, Athanasius is the authority who had declared that Origen's theology was orthodox – a fact which has always been stubbornly overlooked, and so is to date.

357 Athanasius, *De Decretis Nicaenae Synodi*, 25.2. The same in the *Catena in Epistulam ad Hebraeos* (*catena Nicetae*) (e cod. Paris. gr. 238), p. 361, which, at this point, goes on with Athanasius's text (*De Decretis Nicaenae Synodi*, 27.1-4) quoting from Origen and arguing for Origen's Trinitarian orthodoxy.

358 *commJohn*, XX.18.157. Cf. *Princ*, I.2.6: "For it is not only the utmost impiety, but also the depth of folly, to entertain the slightest suspicion that such a thing would happen to an incorporeal being; nor is at all consistent with our intelligence to think that a physical division of an incorporeal being is possible." *Op. cit.* IV.4.1; *Cels*, VII.27.

359 Pamphilus, *op. cit.* PG.17.582A-584A.

360 Gregory of Nyssa, *Contra Eunomium*, 3.1.139.

361 The term *homoousios* was not a term generally used by the Gnostics: only the 'Valentinian Christians' used this.

362 Athanasius, *Epistula ad Afros Episcopos*, PG.1040.24-38 (the same in the edition by H.C. Brennecke – U. Heil – A. von Stockhausen, 6.3-4): καὶ τοῦτο ἐγίνωσκεν Εὐσέβιος ὁ γενόμενος ἐπίσκοπος τῆς Καισαρείας, πρότερον μὲν συντρέχων τῇ ᾿Αρειανῇ αἱρέσει, ὕστερον δὲ ὑπογράψας ἐν αὐτῇ τῇ ἐν Νικαίᾳ συνόδῳ, ἔγραψε τοῖς ἰδίοις διαβεβαιούμενος, ὅτι καὶ τῶν παλαιῶν τινας λογίους καὶ ἐπιφανεῖς ἐπισκόπους καὶ συγγραφέας ἔγνωμεν ἐπὶ τῆς τοῦ Πατρὸς καὶ Υἱοῦ θεότητος τῷ τοῦ ὁμοουσίου χρησαμένους ὀνόματι.

> As for the Logos co-existing with the Father eternally (ἀϊδίως συνεῖναι) and not being of a different essence or [being] an [ontologically] different hypostasis (μὴ ἑτέρας[363] οὐσίας ἢ ὑποστάσεως), but He [sc. the Logos] is a progeny born from the Father himself (which is what the fathers at the synod also said), it is possible to learn from the industrious Origen. For whatever he wrote as questions set forth for investigation or as a mental exercise should not be regarded as his own views, but as propositions aimed at those who made conjectural claims in a polemical mood (τῶν πρὸς ἔριν φιλονεικούντων ἐν τῷ ζητεῖν). But whatever he determines unreservedly, these are the [real] views of the Industrious.[364]

Besides, Athanasius assured that the term *homoousios* was nothing new: "For we are aware of certain distinguished bishops and *scholars* of old who wrote 'nearly a hundred and thirty years ago, both in the great city of Rome and in our city' and used the term *homoousios* upon writing about the theology of the Father and Son.[365] Those bishops had censured those who urged that the Son is a creature and not *homoousios* with the Father."[366] This was a reason why the men of the cloth at Nicaea employed the term.[367] Accordingly, Athanasius paying his dues to Origen as a predecessor, confirmed that, to Origen, not only is the Son co-eternal with the Father but also the Son's *ousia* is not different from that of the Father.[368]

Little wonder that Athanasius used Origen's commentary on John in order to explain that this critical term applied to the Father and the Son had nothing

363 The editorial addition μὴ [ἐξ] ἑτέρας by H.G. Opitz is not wrong, but it is superfluous. Cf. Pseudo-Athanasius, *Liber De Definitionibus*, PG.28.545.21-22: Ἑτερούσιον δὲ λέγεται τὸ ἑτέρας οὐσίας ὑπάρχον.

364 Athanasius, *De Decretis Nicaenae Synodi*, 27.1-2. The text continues with reporting that the catchphrase οὐκ ἦν ὅτε οὐκ ἦν positing the co-eternity of the Son originated with Origen. I have discussed the Greek sources of Origen's usage of this elegant philological formula in *Anaxagoras*, pp. 843; 991-992.

365 Cf. Athanasius appealing to 'men of old' (παλαιοὶ ἄνδρες), mentioning Origen by name. *In Illud: Qui Dixerit Verbum In Filium*, PG.26.649.21 ff & 38 ff; the same in *Epistulae Quattuor ad Serapionem*, 4.2.1; 4.3.1.

366 Athanasius, *loc. cit.*: Ἐπίσκοποι γὰρ ἀρχαῖοι πρὸ ἐτῶν ἐγγύς που ἑκατὸν τριάκοντα τῆς μεγάλης Ῥώμης καὶ τῆς ἡμετέρας πόλεως γράφοντες ᾐτιάσαντο τοὺς ποίημα λέγοντας τὸν Υἱὸν καὶ μὴ ὁμοούσιον τῷ Πατρί.

367 Athanasius, *op. cit.* 33.13: ᾧ καὶ αὐτῷ τοῦτον ἑρμηνευθέντι τὸν τρόπον καλῶς ἔχειν ἐφάνη συγκαταθέσθαι, ἐπεὶ καὶ τῶν παλαιῶν τινας λογίους καὶ ἐπιφανεῖς ἐπισκόπους καὶ συγγραφεῖς ἔγνωμεν ἐπὶ τῆς τοῦ πατρὸς καὶ υἱοῦ θεολογίας τῷ τοῦ ὁμοουσίου χρησαμένους ὀνόματι.

368 Athanasius, *De Decretis Nicaenae Synodi*, 27.1-4. Ironically, John Zonaras used Athanasius' selfsame vocabulary in order to argue that Arius simply repeated the teaching of Origen, since it was 'Origen who first pronounced that the Son is a creature and alien to the *ousia* of the Father'. *Epitome Historiarum* (T. Büttner-Wobst), p. 20.

to do with any *corporeal* implication whatsoever,[369] which was an argument that Origen used not only against those outside the faith, but also against bishops such as Melito of Sardis who claimed that God is a corporeal body and had written a tract under this title.[370] Thus, Athanasius reported that one of the reasons why Eusebius changed his mind and eventually concurred and signed up to the Nicene resolution was that 'he knew of certain scholars and bishops who used the term *homoousios* in relation to the theology of Father and Son'; and those 'ancient bishops and scholars' who wrote so were located 'somehow near both the great city of Rome and Alexandria ('our own city').[371] The former is probably a reference to Hippolytus[372] or perhaps Tertullian,[373] who had spoken of "tres autem, non statu sed gradu, nec substantia des forma, nec potestate sed specie, unius autem substantiae et unius status et unius potestatis";[374] also, "alium ... personae, non substantiae, nomine, ad distinctionem, non ad divisionem," "unam substantiam in tribus cohaerentibus".[375] One thing is for sure: hardly could Tertullian's theology have entirely escaped Origen's attention. However, the question is not whether Nicaea took up the *term homoousios* from the West (to J.F. Bethune-Baker, yes; to C. Stead, no);[376] but if the the term *homoousios* was taken up by the Eastern theology as one that *conceptually* originated in the West. For a Westerner could have used the term more conveniently that an Easterner (who could have been deterred by its Gnostic usage) – which is a fact supporting the hypothesis that Origen was encouraged to use the *term* (not the *notion*, which he maintained, anyway) after Tertullian rather than the other way around. J.F. Bethune-Baker noted that

---

369 Athanasius, *op. cit.* 33.12: Οὕτω δὲ καὶ τὸ ὁμοούσιον εἶναι τοῦ πατρὸς τὸν υἱὸν ἐξεταζόμενος ὁ λόγος συνίστησιν, οὐ κατὰ τὸν τῶν σωμάτων τρόπον οὐδὲ τοῖς θνητοῖς ζῴοις παραπλησίως, οὔτε γὰρ κατὰ διαίρεσιν τῆς οὐσίας οὔτε κατὰ ἀποτομήν, ἀλλ᾽ οὐδὲ κατά τι πάθος ἢ τροπὴν ἢ ἀλλοίωσιν τῆς τοῦ πατρὸς οὐσίας τε καὶ δυνάμεως. Quite evidently, Athanasius had in mind Origen's statements in *commJohn*, XX.18.157 and *Princ*, I.2.6 (quoted *supra*, note 358), and perhaps other ones that are not extant.

370 Origen, *selGen*, PG.12.93.7-13. Melito's treatise was also mentioned by Eusebius, *HE*, 4.26.2 and Nicephorus Callistus Xanthopulus, *HE*, 4.10.

371 Athanasius, *Epistula ad Afros Episcopos*, PG.26.1040.27-38 (& *Epistula ad Afros Episcopos*, 6.4 in H.C. Brennecke – U. Heil – A. von Stockhausen, *Athanasius: Werke*, Zweiter Band. *Die "Apologien"*, 8. Lieferung, Berlin – New York, 2006, pp. 322-339).

372 Cf. Hippolytus using the term *homoousios* in relation to Father and Son. *In Canticum Canticorum* (*paraphrasis*), 1.6.

373 However, Tertullian was not a bishop, and whether he was actually a priest is a matter of ongoing dispute.

374 Tertullian, *Ad Praxeam*, 2.

375 Tertullian, *op. cit.* 12.

376 J.F. Bethune-Baker, *The Meaning of Homoousios in the 'Constantinopolitan' Creed*, Cambridge, 1901, p. 11. C. Stead, *Divine Substance*, Oxford, 1977, pp. 190-266.

'the theology of Tertullian was accepted in Rome'[377] and 'that Origen really held the doctrine for which ὁμοούσιος stands seems certain',[378] which is why 'the theologians who had studied Origen regarded it with favour', and mentions the Cappadocians and Athanasius.[379] In Christopher Stead's view, it is possible that Origen heard of 'una substantia' when he visited Rome, perhaps he heard also in Greek of μία οὐσία, and probably of the term ὁμοούσιος itself, since Greek was the language of the educated, and Tertullian's theology would have gained considerable currency in Rome.[380]

Athanasius' second reference ('and Alexandria') was presumably one to Origen – which becomes abundantly clear with the present codex, yet not for the first time, since in Klostermann's collection of Origen's fragments on Matthew the term is clearly there, yet scholars have opted for turning a blind eye to this and ignore Klostermann's work rather than coming to terms with such 'disturbing' facts. Actually, Origen speaks of *homoousios* not only in relation to the theology of Father and Son but of all the three Trinitarian Persons.[381]

All of this meant to secure that the authority of the *homoousios* was in fact supported by means of scriptural considerations, against the Arians who rejected it as a non-scriptural novelty (ἄγραφον).[382] The retort by Athanasius and a host of later authors was that if non-scriptural terms maintain pious doctrines they should be accepted, whereas distorted interpretation of scriptural portions might well be impious, which the Arians did along with their own use of non-scriptural propositions about the Son, such as 'he came to being from

377 J.F. Bethune-Baker, *op. cit.* p. 24.

378 J.F. Bethune-Baker, *op. cit.* p. 26. Charles Bigg (*The Christian Platonists of Alexandria*, Oxford, 1886, p. 179) had argued that this could not have been Origen's definite opinion, and engaged in some considerations as to what this meant to Origen, which though proves nothing.

379 J.F. Bethune-Baker, *op. cit.* p. 10.

380 Christopher Stead, *op. cit.* p. 253.

381 See Klostermann, frs. 14; 257; 572 (also, in Origen, *schMatt*, PG.17.309.37-53). Also, abundantly in the present *Codex Sabaiticus 232*, passages most of which come to light the first time. See folia 1v; 18v; 19r; 95r; 194v; 239v; 240r; 240v. *Supra*, note 354.

382 Cf. Photius, *Homiliae*, homily 16, p. 155: Οἱ ἀρειανοί, ἄγραφός ἐστιν ἡ τοῦ ὁμοουσίου φωνή. ... Οἱ ἀρειανοί, οὔτε γὰρ ἐν τοῖς εὐαγγελίοις τὰ κυριακὰ λόγια, οὔτε οἱ θεῖοι ἀπόστολοι, οὔτε ἡ παλαιὰ γραφὴ παραδέδωκεν ὁμοούσιον ἢ ὁμοιοούσιον ἢ οὐσίαν λέγειν ὅλως ἐπὶ πατρὸς καὶ υἱοῦ. Arethas, *Scholia Arethae in Cyrilli Apologiam xii Anathematismorum contra Theodoretum et in Theodoreti Impugnationem*, p. 114: τοῦτο ὁμοία πλημμέλεια τῇ Ἀρίου μανίᾳ, ἐπὶ τῇ τοῦ ὁμοουσίου λέξει μὴ παρὰ τοῖς παλαιοῖς πατράσιν εὑρημένῃ διατεινομένῳ, ἀλλὰ νεαρῶς καινολογουμένῳ.

non-being' (ἐξ οὐκ ὄντων) and 'there was [a state] when he was not' (ἦν ποτε ὅτε οὐκ ἦν).[383]

In the ninth century, George Monachus of Alexandria felt that he could claim that the *notion* of *homoousios* (though not the *term* itself) was 'in a secret manner' present not only in the New Testament but also in the Old one. He pushed his argument as far as to urge that it was because these doctrines existed in the Old Testament that a devout Jew such as Philo 'was compelled' to speak about God the Logos in a manner showing the Logos to be a separate person, and he realised that God should be understood in terms of the mystery of the Holy Trinity.[384]

This was the end of a process that stretched from Athanasius right down to the end of the first millennium. Meanwhile, John of Damascus had admitted that neither the Old nor the New Testament mention either the name 'Trinity' itself or speak explicitly of the *homoousion*, or of one nature of the Deity, or of Three Hypostases, or of one hypostasis of Christ, or of 'two natures' of his.

---

383 Athanasius, *De Decretis Nicaenae Synodi*, 1.2; *Epistula ad Afros Episcopos*, PG.26.1040.18-23: καὶ ὁ γογγυσμὸς δὲ αὐτῶν, ὅτι ἄγραφοί εἰσιν αἱ λέξεις, ἐλέγχεται παρ᾽ αὐτῶν μάταιος. ἐξ ἀγράφων ἀσεβήσαντες (ἄγραφα δὲ τὸ *ἐξ οὐκ ὄντων* καὶ τὸ *ἦν ποτε ὅτε οὐκ ἦν*), αἰτιῶνται, ὅτι ἐξ ἀγράφων μετ᾽ εὐσεβείας νοουμένων λέξεων κατεκρίθησαν. Likewise, in *De Synodis Arimini in Italia et Seleuciae in Isauria*, 37.2. Theodoret, *HE*, pp. 97; 161. Cyril of Alexandria, *De Sancta Trinitate Dialogi*, pp. 391-392. Theodore Anagnostes, *Epitome Historiae Tripartitae*, 2.54. Symeon Logothetes, *Chronicon*, p. 91. Michael Psellus, *Historia Brevis*, 56. Nicephorus Callistus Xanthopulus, *HE*, 6.37; 8.18; 8.21-22; 9.5; 9.20. Gregory Palamas quoted a passage allegedly by Basil of Caesarea, in which this view of Athanasius in effect is reiterated. However, this passage (italics) does not exist in Basil's extant work. Gregory Palamas, *Orationes Antirrheticae Contra Acindynum*, 1.13.63: καθάπερ ἀρειανοί ποτε τὸ ὁμοούσιον καὶ τὸ ἐκ τῆς οὐσίας, ἄηθες καὶ ἄγραφον καὶ τὰ τοιαῦτα λέγοντες, ἐροῦμεν πρὸς αὐτοὺς τὸ τοῦ μεγάλου Βασιλείου, ὅτι *κἂν ἀγράφους τις λέγῃ λέξεις, οὐδὲν διαφέρει, ἕως ἂν εὐσεβῆ τὴν διάνοιαν ἔχῃ. οἱ δὲ αἱρετικοί, κἂν τοῖς ἀπὸ τῶν Γραφῶν χρήσωνται, οὐδὲν ἧττον ὕποπτοι καὶ τὸν νοῦν διεφθαρμένοι.*

384 George Monachus, *Chronicon*, p. 527 & *Chronicon Breve*, PG.110.645.35-648.7 (& George Cedrenus, *Compendium Historiarum*, v. 1, p. 507): Ἰστέον τοίνυν ὡς ἐν τῇ Παλαιᾷ Διαθήκῃ περὶ τῆς ἁγίας καὶ ὁμοουσίου Τριάδος μυστικῶς ἡ διδασκαλία ἐγκατέσπαρται, ὡς καὶ Φίλωνα, καίτοι Ἰουδαῖον ἄνδρα ὑπάρχοντα καὶ ζηλωτήν, δι᾽ ὧν καταλέλοιπε συγγραμμάτων, ἀπομάχεσθαι τῇ οἰκείᾳ θρησκείᾳ. Βασανίζων γὰρ τὸ εἰρημένον. *Ἐν εἰκόνι Θεοῦ ἐποίησα τὸν ἄνθρωπον* ἠναγκάσθη ὑπὸ τῆς ἀληθείας, καὶ ἐξεβιάσθη καὶ τὸν τοῦ Θεοῦ Λόγον θεολογῆσαι. Τί γάρ; Εἰ καὶ δεύτερον τὸν συναΐδιον τῷ Πατρὶ καὶ ἀριθμοῦ καὶ χρόνων ἀνώτερον ὄντα καλεῖ, τῆς ἀληθείας μὴ ἐφικνούμενος, ὅμως ἔννοιαν ἔσχε καὶ ἑτέρου προσώπου. Οὐκ ἐνταῦθα δὲ μόνον ἔπαθε τοῦτο, ἀλλὰ καὶ τὸ *θεός* καὶ τὸ *κύριος* ἑρμηνεῦσαι πειρώμενος τῆς βασιλικωτάτης τριάδος ἔννοιαν ἔσχεν. φάσκων γὰρ ὅτι εἷς ἐστιν ὁ θεὸς οὐ πρὸς τὸν ἀριθμὸν κατέδραμε τῆς μονάδος, ἀλλὰ πρὸς τὸ μυστήριον τῆς ἁγίας τριάδος.

However, 'the holy fathers' derived all these doctrines from equivalent words which obtain in the Scripture.[385]

The commentary on Matthew was one of Origen's last works, and the term ὁμοούσιος appears there, too, along with his care to point out that, since God is not corporeal, the notion of the Son having been 'begotten' should be understood accordingly, that is, in terms befitting incorporeality. He felt it necessary to emphasise that corporeal analogies should be excluded from considerations of God (which could be entirely superfluous to do, had he been addressing a Greek audience), since Melito of Sardis claimed that God is corporeal, for which Origen censured him.[386]

This was the reason why Eunomius used Origen's expression οὐ κατὰ ῥεῦσιν,[387] but he had a different agenda: he argued that the term ὁμοούσιος should be rejected exactly on the grounds that 'essence' and generation 'from the essence' bespeak corporeal manner of procreation.[388] This was the argument of the five bishops who rejected the term ὁμοούσιος which was included in the Nicene resolution, wherefore they did not sign up to the acts.[389]

This was exactly the ground on which Gregory of Nyssa rebuked Eunomius who composed his Trinitarian arguments about the Son's generation 'by having recourse and reflecting according to the order of Nature' (καταφεύγουσι πρὸς τὴν ἐκ τῆς φύσεως τάξιν).[390] Basil of Caesarea wrote likewise;[391] in fact, he

385 John of Damascus, *Orationes De Imaginibus Tres*, 3.11: Ποῦ εὗρες ἐν τῇ παλαιᾷ ἢ ἐν τῷ εὐαγγελίῳ ὄνομα τριάδος ἢ ὁμοούσιον ἢ μίαν φύσιν θεότητος τρανῶς ἢ τρεῖς ὑποστάσεις αὐτολεξεὶ ἢ μίαν ὑπόστασιν τοῦ Χριστοῦ ἢ δύο φύσεις αὐτολεξεί; Ἀλλ' ὅμως, ἐπειδὴ ἐκ τῶν ἰσοδυναμουσῶν λέξεων τῶν ἐν τῇ γραφῇ κειμένων ὥρισαν ταῦτα οἱ ἅγιοι πατέρες, δεχόμεθα καὶ τοὺς μὴ δεχομένους ἀναθεματίζομεν.

386 Origen, *selGen*, PG.12.93.10-13.

387 In *Codex Sabaiticus 232*, folio 239v. Also, in Origen, fr. 572 (Klostermann *apud* five codices), and Origen, *schMatt*, PG.17.309.37-53.

388 Eunomius, quoted by Gregory of Nyssa in *Contra Eunomium*, 3.2.28: λέγων γεγεννῆσθαι παρὰ τοῦ πατρὸς τοῦ υἱοῦ τὴν οὐσίαν, οὐ κατὰ ἔκτασιν προβληθεῖσαν, οὐ κατὰ ῥεῦσιν ἢ διαίρεσιν τῆς τοῦ γεννήσαντος συμφυΐας ἀποσπασθεῖσαν. Cf. Eusebius, *Demonstratio Evangelica*, 4.3.13, who in fact copied from Origen: καὶ τῷ πατρὶ ὡς υἱὸν διὰ παντὸς συνόντα, καὶ οὐκ ἀγέννητον ὄντα, γεννώμενον δ' ἐξ ἀγεννήτου πατρός, μονογενῆ ὄντα, λόγον τε καὶ θεὸν ἐκ θεοῦ, οὐ κατὰ διάστασιν ἢ τομὴν ἢ διαίρεσιν ἐκ τῆς τοῦ πατρὸς οὐσίας προβεβλημένον, ἀρρήτως δὲ καὶ ἀνεπιλογίστως ἡμῖν.

389 Socrates Scholasticus, *HE*, 1.8.171. Those were Eusebius of Nicomedia, Theognis of Nicaea, Maris of Chalcedon, Theonas of Marmarike, Secundus of Ptolemais. They were banished to exile on Emperor Constantine's order. To this list, Nicephorus Callistus Xanthopulus added the names of three more bishops. *HE*, 8.18.

390 Gregory of Nyssa, *Contra Eunomium*, 3.1.139.

391 Basil of Caesarea, *Epistulae*, epistle 52.3: Ὅταν δὲ ἐκ τῆς οὐσίας τοῦ Πατρὸς τὸν Υἱὸν εἶναι διδασκώμεθα καὶ γεννηθέντα, ἀλλὰ οὐχὶ ποιηθέντα, μὴ καταπίπτωμεν ἐπὶ τὰς σωματικὰς τῶν παθῶν ἐννοίας. Οὐ γὰρ ἐμερίσθη ἡ οὐσία ἀπὸ Πατρὸς εἰς Υἱόν, οὐδὲ ῥυεῖσα ἐγέννησεν, οὐδὲ

recapitulated Origen's idea banning any notion of 'effluence' (ῥεῦσις) or 'projection' (προβολή) in relation to Son's generation.[392] Later, Cyril of Alexandria copied from Origen's specific text almost to the letter, and although he wrote in different times, he felt it necessary to emphasise that God is not corporeal.[393]

In any event, it was Origen that had taught a fundamental lesson, which should have been obvious, but this was not always the case: to read the proposition 'the Son was begotten from the Father's essence' analogously to 'the case of women that are pregnant', which could entail that 'once God begot the Son, His essence was diminished and somehow lacked in the essence that he formerly had', is just ridiculous and had been advanced by 'people who had not even dreamed of what invisible and incorporeal essence' really is.[394]

The source of the expression ἐκ τῆς οὐσίας τοῦ Πατρὸς is Origen's,[395] from whom Athanasius borrowed his own formulations that eventually became the doctrine of Nicaea, and certainly this is one of the reasons why Athanasius averred that Origen's Trinitarian theory was impeccable by Nicene standards.[396] The historian Socrates reports that Athanasius used Origen's books in the battle against Arianism.[397] Nevertheless, since a principal meaning of the polysemous term οὐσία was 'matter', Origen introduced the caveat that being 'from the essence' should be understood far apart from any corporeal analogy.[398] Consequently, he advised understanding the generation of the Son not in terms of matter flowing from another matter, namely, οὐ κατὰ ῥεῦσιν,[399]

προβαλοῦσα, ὡς τὰ φυτὰ τοὺς καρπούς, ἀλλ' ἄρρητος καὶ ἀνεπινόητος λογισμοῖς ἀνθρώπων τῆς θείας γεννήσεως ὁ τρόπος. Likewise, using the same terminology, Athanasius, *Oratio i contra Arianos*, 28.1-6. Cyril of Alexandria, *Thesaurus De Sancta Consubstantiali Trinitate*, PG.75.360.1-20.

392 Marcellus, *Fragmenta*, fr. 37, allegedly quoting from Origen's *De Principiis* (*Fragmenta De Principiis*, fr. 31), *apud* Eusebius, *Contra Marcellum*, 1.4.20.

393 Cyril of Alexandria, *In Joannem*, v. 1, p. 190: αὐτὸν εἶναι κυρίως καὶ μόνον ἀληθῶς Υἱόν, οὐ νόθον οὐδὲ ψευδώνυμον, ἀλλ' ἐκ τῆς οὐσίας τοῦ Θεοῦ καὶ Πατρὸς οὐ κατὰ ἀποκοπήν, ἢ ῥεῦσιν, ἢ μερισμόν, ἢ τομήν. ... καὶ ἐξ αὐτοῦ προελθόντα ἀμερίστως καὶ ἀδιαστάτως, ἐπεὶ μηδὲ κατὰ σῶμα τὸ θεῖον.

394 *commJohn*, XX.18.157-158. See *supra*, p. XCIV and note 358.

395 Cf. Origen, in the present manuscript, folio 239v, and in the *schMatt*, PG.17.309.52-53: Ἐνυπόστατος ἡ γέννησις. ἀπετέχθη ἐκ τῆς οὐσίας τοῦ Πατρὸς ὁ Υἱός. *frJohn*, fr. 9: Τὸ *Ὡς μονογενοῦς παρὰ πατρὸς* νοεῖν ὑποβάλλει ἐκ τῆς οὐσίας τοῦ πατρὸς εἶναι τὸν υἱόν.

396 Athanasius, *De Decretis Nicaenae Synodi*, 27.1: Περὶ δὲ τοῦ ἀϊδίως συνεῖναι τὸν λόγον τῷ πατρὶ καὶ μὴ ‹ἐξ› ἑτέρας οὐσίας ἢ ὑποστάσεως, ἀλλὰ τῆς τοῦ πατρὸς ἴδιον ‹γέννημα› αὐτὸν εἶναι, ὡς εἰρήκασιν οἱ ἐν τῇ συνόδῳ, ἐξέστω πάλιν ὑμᾶς ἀκοῦσαι καὶ παρὰ τοῦ φιλοπόνου Ὠριγένους.

397 Socrates, *op. cit.* 6.9; 6.13.

398 See his analysis in *commJohn*, XX.18.157-159 (*supra*, p. XCIV and note 357), lampooning those who argued for such a line of explanation.

399 Migne's ἀσταρεῦσιν makes no sense since this is not a Greek word.

as explained above. However, in spite of this warning, the danger of misunderstanding was lurking. For, in the first place, mere reference to divine 'essence', indeed to ὁμοούσιος alone, takes for granted that there is a certain essence *of* God, along with its inevitable connotations (such as 'divine substance' taken as ontologically prior to the Trinitarian Persons).[400] Little wonder then that employment of this term caused prolonged dispute.

Pamphilus wrote an entire section in order to demonstrate that Origen expounded the *homoousion* of the Father and Son in his commentaries on the epistles to the Romans and to the Hebrews,[401] and emphasised the implications of the terms 'effluence' (ἀπόρροια) and 'moist vapour' (ἀτμὶς) used of the Wisdom / Son.[402] However, this was not 'projection' (προβολή) as it happens with separation during the birth of animals,[403] which was a perception verging on the Gnostic one, which Origen condemned.[404] The *Apology for Origen* by Pamphilus (extant in a translation by Rufinus) possibly was written c. 309 AD, that is, a short while before the outbreak of the Arian controversy. He appears as an authoritative source for Origen's uses of the *homoousios* in his lost Commentary of Hebrews.[405] Moreover, it is clear that Pamphilus himself was ready to endorse this usage, in noticeable contrast to the reserve shown a little later by his friend Eusebius. Why was that so? Presumably because the 'simpleton' Pamphilus had grasped Origen's essential reasoning, whereas the learned Eusebius saw the hardly tractable implications of speaking about 'God's *ousia*': since by definition the most fundamental meaning of *ousia* indicates that which is prior to existence proper, the difficulties involved in such a usage to him were all too evident. I believe that Eusebius signed up to the Nicene

400 Cf. Basil of Caesarea arguing against such misunderstanding; *Contra Sabellianos et Arium et Anomoeos*, PG.31.605.23-27.

401 Pamphilus, *op. cit.* 759C-582A.

402 In like a manner 'breath' proceeds from bodily substance, likewise Wisdom proceeds from the very substance of God. Cf. Wisdom of Solomon, 7:25. The second simile of 'effluence' (ἀπόρροια) has the same import: it bespeaks a common substance between the Father and the Son. In fact, 'effluence' implies that the Son is of the same substance (ὁμοούσιος) with the Father. This is one more forerunning appearance of the term ὁμοούσιος, which later became the key-word of the Creed of Nicaea.

403 Origen, *Fragmenta De Principiis*, fr. 31, *apud* Eusebius, *Contra Marcellum*, 1.4.19. Cf. Socrates Scholasticus, *HE*, 1.8.32 & Nicephorus Callistus Xanthopulus, *HE*, 8.18.

404 *commJohn*, XX.18.157-159. Also, *Princ*, I.2.6, quoted *supra*, note 358; *op. cit.* IV.4.1; *Cels*, VII.27. On the Gnostic view, see also Epiphanius, *Panarion*, v. 3, pp. 158-159, and Athanasius, *De Synodis Arimini in Italia et Seleuciae in Isauria*, 16.3-5. Also, John Grammaticus (presbyter, theologian, grammarian, Palestine, sixth century), *Disputatio cum Manichaeo*, lines 20-31.

405 Karl Heinrich Eduard Lommatzsch, ed., *Origenes Opera Omnia*, V, Berlin, 1835, p. 297. One should wonder why did Jerome not include this work in Origen's list.

resolution as a concession to the emperor, but I also believe that he never rid himself of his reservations – and, in my view, rightly so, and little wonder that 'the followers of Origen were not agreed as to the value of the phrase *from God's substance*.'[406]

It is all but chance that Eusebius held fast to Origen's caveat banning analogy of proposition 'the Son was begotten from the Father's essence' to 'the case of women that are pregnant'.[407] Hence, the disclaimers that Eusebius himself made every now and then (also upon explaining his changing of mind to his diocese),[408] in fact had taken their cue from Origen's warning against any material perception of God.[409]

In his *Apology*, Pamphilus rejected the obloquy that Origen saw the Son as 'ingenerate' (*innatum* = ingenerate or underived = ἀγέννητον), which would rob the Father from his principal characteristic (for he could not be a Father unless he had generated a Son). But his reply was formed as a demonstration of the notion that not simply is the Son generated from the Father, but the Son is *homoousios* with the Father, for which Pamphilus adduced and quoted Origen's texts from the commentary on the Romans, the commentary on the epistle to the Hebrews,[410] and the commentary on John.[411] He starts with quoting a passage from Origen's commentary on the epistle to the Romans and concertedly considering the portions 'God is love' (1 John, 4:8&16) and 'Love is of God' (1 John, 4:7): he identifies the second 'love' with the Son and pronounces him as 'Love begotten of Love, as God of God' (sicut Deum ex Deo, ita caritatem ex caritatem progenitum). This asseveration proximately follows suit his header,

406 Christopher Stead, *Divine Substance*, p. 230; *op. cit.* p. 231: "On the other hand Pamphilus, who quotes the passage from Origen in support of the *homoousion*, seems to have no hesitation about the phrase *from God's substance.*"

407 See *supra*, Origen, *commJohn*, XX.18.157-158; *Princ*, I.2.6 (quoted *supra*, note 358); *op. cit.* IV.4.1.

408 Eusebius, *Epistula ad Caesarienses*, 7 (allegedly so said by Constantine – in fact, Eusebius' usual lip service to the emperor): ὅτι μὴ κατὰ τῶν σωμάτων πάθη λέγοιτο ὁμοούσιος [ὁ Υἱός], οὔτ᾽ οὖν κατὰ διαίρεσιν οὔτε κατά τινα ἀποτομὴν ἐκ τοῦ Πατρὸς ὑποστῆναι. *Op. cit.* 12-13: καὶ τὸ ὁμοούσιον εἶναι τοῦ Πατρὸς τὸν Υἱὸν ... οὔτε γὰρ κατὰ διαίρεσιν τῆς οὐσίας οὔτε κατὰ ἀποτομήν, ἀλλ᾽ οὐδὲ κατά τι πάθος ἢ τροπὴν ἢ ἀλλοίωσιν τῆς τοῦ Πατρὸς οὐσίας τε καὶ δυνάμεως.

409 Eusebius, *Demonstratio Evangelica*, 4.3.11: οὔτι πω κατὰ στέρησιν ἢ μείωσιν ἢ τομὴν ἢ διαίρεσιν τοῦ προϋποκειμένου. *Op. cit.* 4.3.13: οὐ κατὰ διάστασιν ἢ τομὴν ἢ διαίρεσιν ἐκ τῆς τοῦ Πατρὸς οὐσίας προβεβλημένον. *Op. cit.* 4.15.52: οὐ κατὰ προβολὴν ἢ κατὰ διαίρεσιν ἢ τομὴν ἢ μείωσιν ἢ κατά τι τῶν ἐν σώμασιν ὑπονουμένων. *Op. cit.* 5.1.8: μήτε κατὰ προβολὴν μήτε κατὰ διάστασιν ἢ διαίρεσιν ἢ μείωσιν ἢ τομὴν ἢ κατά τι ὅλως τῶν ἐπὶ τῆς θνητῆς γενέσεως ἐπιτελουμένων, τὴν ἀπόρρητον αὐτοῦ γενεσιουργίαν ἐπινοοῦμεν. *Op. cit.* 5.1.9: οὐδὲ ... οὐσίαν ἐξ οὐσίας κατὰ πάθος ἢ διαίρεσιν μεριστὴν καὶ χωριστὴν ἐκ τοῦ Πατρὸς προεληλυθέναι τὸν Υἱὸν φάναι ὅσιον.

410 Pamphilus, *op. cit.* PG.17.579B-584A.

411 Pamphilus, *op. cit.* PG.17.583C.

"That the Son is born of God the Father, and is of one substance (unius substantiae) with the Father, but distinct from the substances of created things."

The term *homoousios* appears at two points, now in Greek: first, in the header, which introduced a series of portions from Origen's commentary on the epistle to the Hebrews, in much the same terms as before (quomodo ὁμοούσιος est cum Patre Filius ... alienus autem a substantia creaturae); secondly, in Pamphilus' confident concluding comment on this section, which Rufinus rendered *'Satis manifeste, ut opinor, et valde evidenter ostensum est, quod Filium Dei de ipsa Dei substantia natum dixerit, id est ὁμοούσιον, quod est eiusdem cum Patre substantiae; et non esse creaturam, neque per adoptionem, sed natura Filium verum, ex ipso Patre generatum.'* We may note once again how closely is the word ὁμοούσιος associated with phrases describing the Son's derivation 'from the *ousia'* of the Father. It was all too natural for Pamphilus to say so: for according to Origen, the Son's consubstantiality is par excellence gathered from the fact of the Son's *generation* (not creation) from the Father. It is *generation* itself that authenticates and confirms the Son's consubstantiality.

> God begot in accordance with His own nature, which is why the one who was born is *homoousios* [with Him]. God is not a body; therefore, notions which pertain to bodies, such as flowing, or motion, or anything of the sort [do not apply to God]. It was the incorporeal God who begot. The birth was substantial. The Son was born from the essence of the Father.[412]

Even in *De Principiis*, Origen recalls the biblical reference to Adam who begot Seth 'according to his image',[413] and his comment is that 'generation' from a father entails that the offspring is of the same nature and essence as the progenitor (quae imago etiam naturae et substantiae patris et filii continet uniatatem).[414]

Likewise, he wrote that 'everyone who shares in anything is undoubtedly of one substance and one nature (unius substantiae est uniusque naturae) with him who shares the same thing.'[415]

---

412 Origen, *commMatth*, in *Codex Sabaiticus*, 232, folio 239v. Also, *schMatt*, PG.17.309.49-53 (on Matt. 28:19); also *frMatt* (Klostermann). fr. 572: Κατὰ φύσιν ἐγέννησεν ὁ Θεός, διόπερ ὁμοούσιος ὁ γεννηθείς. Οὐ σῶμα ὁ Θεός, καὶ οὐ κατὰ ῥεῦσιν ἢ κίνησιν ἤ τι τῶν τοιούτων ἃ ἐν τοῖς σώμασι θεωρεῖται. Ὁ Θεὸς ὁ ἀσώματος ἐγέννησεν. Ἐνυπόστατος ἡ γέννησις. Ἀπετέχθη ἐκ τῆς οὐσίας τοῦ Πατρὸς ὁ Υἱός.

413 Gen. 5:3.

414 *Princ*, I.2.6.

415 *Princ*, IV.4.9. Once again, H. Crouzel and M. Simonetti were quick to dismiss this 'substance and one nature' (evidently, οὐσία καὶ φύσις in the Greek original) alleging that this is an interpolation by Rufinus (*Traité des Principes*, v. 2, pp. 40-41, note 35), on the ground

This idea is also confirmed by the statement that 'the Son is God not by participation, but by essence'[416] – and if wilful doubts are still there about Origen's surviving commentaries on the Psalms, let doubters read once again Pamphilus' phrase, *neque per adoptionem, sed natura Filium verum, ex ipso Patre generatum.*

Origen reprimanded those who posited the Son as merely 'thought' of the Father and they dismissed his being a real individual Person.[417] It is evident

---

that Origen 'used οὐσία καὶ ὑπόστασις in an individual sense'. Actually, Origen frequently used οὐσία in the sense of a real individual being (e.g. in *commJohn*, II.2.16 [of the Son]; II.10.74 [of the Holy Spirit]), but these editors forgot that Origen used this also in the sense of 'common substratum' that characterises something par excellence. For example, *commJohn*, XIII.21.123 (the οὐσία of God); *exhMar*, 47 ('the οὐσία of rational soul'). Actually, in *deOr*, 27.8, Origen gave a lecture on the sundry senses of οὐσία according to various Greek schools. See also his reference to οὐσία καὶ φύσις in *commMatt*, 17.27 ('substance and nature of the soul'), or his investigative reference to 'the nature God' being 'beyond essence', in *commJohn*, XIX.6.37. Above all, see his Trinitarian proposition in the *schMatt*, PG.17.309.46-53 (& Klostermann, *frMatt*, fr. 572 & the present *Codex Sabaiticus 232*, folio 239v): εἷς ἐστιν οὐ συναλοιφῇ τῶν τριῶν, ἀλλ' οὐσία μία, τρεῖς δὲ ὑποστάσεις τέλειαι ἐν πᾶσι καὶ κατάλληλοι. Κατὰ φύσιν ἐγέννησεν ὁ Πατήρ, διόπερ ὁμοούσιος ὁ γεννηθείς. ... Ἀπετέχθη ἐκ τῆς οὐσίας τοῦ Πατρὸς ὁ Υἱός. By contrast, when Origen spoke of οὐσία καὶ ὑπόστασις, he meant individual existence along with its specific characteristics (e.g. *Cels*, I.23; VIII.67). Of these, the aforestated editors appear as having no inkling. Instead, they concentrated on the expression οὐσία καὶ ὑπόστασις, which is *not* used at this point of *De Principiis*, and they ignored Origen's meaningful usage of οὐσία καὶ φύσις, which *is* indeed used at this point. See Origen positing that the Father and Son are of one nature, *commJohn*, II.11.81; XIX.2.6; *Selecta in Exodum*, PG.12: 284.12; 289.29. Actually, he spoke of 'one divine physis' (which is but an equivalent to *homoousion*): *commJohn*, II.1076; X.6.24; XIX.2.10; XIX.6.37; XX.8.56; XXXII.27.338; *et passim; Homiliae in Exodum*, p. 222; *commEph*, fr. 9; *Cels*, II.49; VII.60 (& *Philocalia*, 15.10); IV.79 (& *Philocalia*, 20.6); IV.81 (& *Philocalia*, 20.8); II: 49; 51; 53; 68; 76; 79; 81; 90; III.28; VII.17; *commSerMatt*, p. 206; and countless other points, *passim*. Such editorial mistakes sometimes have serious implications. For if Origen used *ousia* only in order to indicate individual existence, then, when Athanasius reported Origen's orthodox Trinitarian views which posited that the Son is not ἑτέρας οὐσίας from the Father, this would entail the absurd claim that Origen maintained that the Son is not an individual Person – which is a view that he rebutted frequently and staunchly.

416 Cf. Origen, *selPs*, PG.12.1656.12-13. ὁ δὲ Σωτὴρ οὐ κατὰ μετουσίαν, ἀλλὰ κατ' οὐσίαν ἐστὶ Θεός. *commEph*, fr. 3 (on Eph. 1:5): οὐκ ἂν γοῦν ταχθείη τὸ ὄνομα τῆς υἱοθεσίας ἐπὶ τοῦ Σωτῆρος. Also, see my *Scholia in Apocalypsin*, compiled by the newly discovered father Cassian the Sabaite. Scholion XX: Ἅγιος, ἀληθινὸς ὁ μὴ μετουσίᾳ, ἀλλὰ οὐσίᾳ ὢν τοιοῦτος, αὐτός ἐστιν ὁ Θεὸς Λόγος. See in the *Scholia*, pp. 132-135; 279-281. This scholion XX was written by the compiler Cassian the Sabaite, following Didymus and Origen. Cf. similar statements by Origen's admirers, such as Gregory of Nyssa, *Antirrheticus Adversus Apollinarium*, p. 220, and Athanasius, *De Synodis Arimini in Italia et Seleuciae in Isauria*, 53.4-5.

417 *commJohn*, I.34.243: "For his wisdom does not merely exist in the mental images of God and Father of the universe in a way analogous to the images of human thoughts." (Οὐ γὰρ ἐν ψιλαῖς φαντασίαις τοῦ θεοῦ καὶ πατρὸς τῶν ὅλων τὴν ὑπόστασιν ἔχει ἡ σοφία αὐτοῦ κατὰ

that his statement was made apropos of Christians of his time who were attracted by the bid of some Middle-Platonists to save Plato's theory of Ideas (which could hardly survive the attacks from various quarters, indeed as different ones as Aristotle, the later Peripatetics, and Stoicism): thus, it was argued that Plato's Ideas are 'thoughts of God', but discussion of this is outside my present scope.

Moreover, Origen referred to certain heretics as those who urged that 'the Son is not simply of the same essence as the Father, but also that the Son is not a different Subject (ἓν οὐ μόνον οὐσίᾳ ἀλλὰ καὶ ὑποκειμένῳ τυγχάνοντας ἀμφοτέρους).' He did not object to the claim of oneness of the essence of Father and Son (which those heretics maintained because they saw God as one single Subject); he rebutted only their denial of the Son's real individual personal existence. This is the idea also in the fragment 9 from the same (early) commentary,[418] as well as in the commentary on Matthew, which is one of his latest works, perhaps the very last one.[419]

Moreover, Pamphilus appealed to Origen's first book of the commentary on the epistle to the Romans, and his argument on Origen's theory was summarised through the phrase, *Quod not sit Pater antequam Filius, sed coeternus sit Filius Patre: quod eadem sit incovertibilitas Patris, et Filii, et Spiritus Sancti: quod sicut Pater novit initia omnium et fines, sic et Filius, sic et Spiritus sanctus: quod ex Deo Patre natus est Filius, ac unius et ejusdem cum Patre substantiae; alienus vero a substantis creaturarum.* Evidently, this rebutted any hint of Arianism, which was a theory diametrically opposite to that of Origen's (*quae a diametro haeresi Arianae adversantur*).[420]

τὰ ἀνὰ λόγον τοῖς ἀνθρωπίνοις ἐννοήμασι φαντάσματα). Cf. *op. cit.* X.37.246. *Princ*, I.2.1: the wisdom of God has hypostatic existence (aliquid insubstantivum) ... 'once it is rightly accepted that the only-begotten Son of God is God's wisdom hypostatically existing'. *Op. cit.* I.2.5: "The Wisdom of God has her subsistence (substistentian habere) nowhere else but in Him who is the beggining of everything (initio omnium), from whom also she was born (ex quo nata est)." *Op. cit.* I.2.9: "The strength of all this power, so great and so immence, comes to have a subsistence of its own; ... There comes into existence another power (virtus altera) subsisting in itself (in sua proprietate subsistens) ... and there is not time when she did not exist (non est autem quando non fuerit)". Likewise, *op. cit.* IV.4.1. This ran sheer contrary to Philo, who identified the totality of Ideas with the Logos (styling him 'Idea of Ideas'), *De Opificio Mundi*, 25; cf. *op. cit.* 16.

418 *frJohn*, fr. 9: Τὸ Ὡς μονογενοῦς παρὰ πατρὸς νοεῖν ὑποβάλλει ἐκ τῆς οὐσίας τοῦ πατρὸς εἶναι τὸν υἱόν. Likewise, Origen, *commMatt* in the present *Codex 232*, folio 239v (&Kl. fr. 572 & Origen, *schMatt*, PG.17.309.37-53):): Ἀπετέχθη ἐκ τῆς οὐσίας τοῦ Πατρὸς ὁ Υἱός.

419 See pp. CLIII-CLXIII.

420 PG.17.529.

Of course, there is always the easy 'explanation' that such phrases were interpolated by Rufinus, which has served as a factotum that spared cheerful 'scholars' from further research and argument. However, what should be made of the ensuing six quotations demonstrating that Pamphilus was out to defend Origen opposite the charge of Subordinationism, since the converse charge had already been rebutted in chapter III ('On the divinity of the Son of God')? Three of those quotations are independently attested (one from the commentary on Romans, two from the commentary on John); hence, there is no room for alleging that these are not authentic, which grants credibility to the ensuing three that are excerpted from the commentary on the epistle to the Hebrews. In those three portions, Origen criticises 'those who are loath to confess that the Son of God is God'. Shortly below, he comments on the phrase *splendor gloriae* (i.e. Heb. 1:3, ἀπαύγασμα τῆς δόξης) and compares this with the description of Wisdom as 'a breath of the power of God, and a pure effluent (ἀπόρροια) of the glory of Almighty.'[421] Apropos of this, Origen remarks that Scripture teaches us by means of 'mysteries' and subtle methods: it uses the notion of 'vapour' (ἀτμίς), which is taken from the natural reality only in order to illustrate that, in like a manner a vapour proceeds from a physical substance, so Christ (who is the Wisdom) proceeds from the actual substance of God. Then, following his reference to the metaphor *corporalis aporrhea*, he concludes:

> These two metaphors show most plainly that the Son has a community of substance with the Father; for an emanation appears to be *homoousios*, that is of one substance, with the body from which it is a emanation or vapour (*Quae utraeque similitudines manifestissime ostendunt, communionem substantiae esse Filio cum Patre. Aporrhea enim ὁμοούσιος videtur, id est, unius substantiae cum illo corpore, ex quo est vel aporrhea, vel vapor*).

Thus, Origen adumbrates the generation of the Son from the Father by means of the term *ὁμοούσιος*, and he does so in a context designed to demonstrate (1) that the Son is superior to 'all rule and all authority and power'[422] – consequently, the Son is superior to any *created* being; (2) that the Son proceeds from the Father while maintaining a communion of substance – which communion of substance is illustrated by means of the Son being a vapour or effluence from his source.

Moreover, in the Twelfth homily on the Numbers, we read that 'the Holy Spirit is no different from the Father and from the Son ... So there is this

421 Wisdom of Solomon, 7:25.

422 1 Cor. 15:24; Eph. 1:21; 3:10; 6:12; Col. 1:16; 2:10; 2:15.

distinction of three Persons in the Father and the Son and the Holy Spirit, which is recalled in the plural number of the wells. Yet of these wells there is one spring.[423] For the substance and nature of the Trinity is one' (Alius enim et ipse est spiritus a patre et filio ... Est ergo haec trium distinctio personarum in patre et filio et spiritu sancto ... sed ... unus est fons; una enim substantia est et natura trinitatis).[424] The Trinitarian accounts in this Homily are determined by the juxtaposed notions of *unity* and *plurality*, suggested by the image of several wells fed by a single spring.[425] In this case, the single essence of the Trinity is gathered from the fact that the Father is the source of the Trinity, which became a common theme in Christian theology.[426] This is the only sense in which Origen styles the Father αὐτόθεος ('the very God'),[427] and efforts to see this as ringing a subordinationist ring are only a token of unfamiliarity with philosophy.[428]

---

423 Commenting on Num. 21:16-23.

424 Origen, *Homilia 12.1.4 in Numeris*, PG.12.657B. It is hard to imagine that the Latin word 'substantia' at this point rendered any term other than οὐσία.

425 Prov. 5:15-16. *Princ*, I.3.7: The Father is the single fount of the Trinity.

426 Origen, *commJohn*, I.17.102: ἀρχὴ υἱοῦ ὁ πατὴρ καὶ ἀρχὴ δημιουργημάτων ὁ δημιουργὸς καὶ ἁπαξαπλῶς ἀρχὴ τῶν ὄντων ὁ θεός. ... εἴπερ εἰκὼν τοῦ θεοῦ τοῦ ἀοράτου ὁ πρωτότοκος πάσης κτίσεως, ἀρχὴ αὐτοῦ ὁ πατήρ ἐστιν. *Op. cit.* II.3.20: ἀμφότερα γὰρ πηγῆς ἔχει χώραν, ὁ μὲν πατὴρ θεότητος, ὁ δὲ υἱὸς λόγου. Cf. Origen styling the Father 'root and well' (ῥίζαν καὶ πηγὴν) of the Son. *frJohn*, fr. 69. Cyril of Alexandria used the selfsame phraseology, *De Sancta Trinitate Dialogi*, p. 501. See also, Eusebius, *Praeparatio Evangelica*, 7.15; *De Laudibus Constantini*, 13.1. Pseudo-Athanasius, *Contra Sabellianos*, PG.28.97.32. Pseudo-Dionysius the Areopagite, *De Divinis Nominibus*, p. 128. Nicolas of Methone, *Ad Magnum Domesticum*, p. 209. Gregory II (Cyprus, Patriarch, thirteenth century), *Tomus Fidei*, p. 241. Gennadius Scholarius, *Disputationes Florentinae ad Quaestionem Religiosam*, 7.1; *Tractatus De Processu Spiritus Sancti i*, Part 3, p. 123; Part 4, p. 180; *et passim*. Also, Documenta Concilii Secundi Lugduno, *Synopsis Canonum contra Latinos*, p. 565. *Synodicon contra Joannem Beccum*, section 2, pp. 575; 578.

427 *commJohn*, II.2.17: αὐτόθεος ὁ θεός ἐστι. *Op. cit.* II.3.20: Ὁ γὰρ ἐν ἑκάστῳ λόγος τῶν λογικῶν τοῦτον τὸν λόγον ἔχει πρὸς τὸν ἐν ἀρχῇ λόγον πρὸς τὸν θεὸν ὄντα λόγον θεόν, ὃν ὁ θεὸς λόγος πρὸς τὸν θεόν. ὡς γὰρ αὐτόθεος καὶ ἀληθινὸς θεὸς ὁ πατὴρ πρὸς εἰκόνα καὶ εἰκόνας τῆς εἰκόνος, ... οὕτως ὁ αὐτόλογος πρὸς τὸν ἐν ἑκάστῳ λόγον. Once again, both admirers and detractors alike followed Origen. Cf. Eusebius, *De Ecclesiastica Theologia*, 2.14.6; 3.17.14. Epiphanius of Salamis, *Panarion*, v. 3, pp. 368; 447; 518. Gregory of Nazianzus, *De Pace 2* (*orat. 22*), PG.35.1132.13. Pseudo-Dionysius the Areopagite, *De Divinis Nominibus*, p. 222. Eustratius of Nicaea, *commEthNic*, p. 287. Nicolas of Methone, *Refutatio Institutionis Theologicae Procli*, 114. Gregory Palamas, *Orationes Dogmaticae*, orationes 4.21; 5.8; 6.7; *et passim* (abundantly). John Cyparissiotes, *Expositio Materiaria*, 5.5; 10.3; (quoting Maximus Confessor) *Contra Tomum Palamiticum*, 6.11; 7.6; *Orationes antirrheticae quinque contra Nilum Cabasilam*, oration 5.6.

428 Cf. Proclus, of whom I have shown that influence by Origen in his work is evident. He considered αὐτόθεος as a possible attribution to the One assumed as 'a source of Deity

According to this conception, the Monarchian basis of the Trinitarian Monotheism is not only the common substance of the Three Persons: it is also the Person of God the Father as the unique Cause of the mode of existence of the other two Persons. We can speak of a three-Person Monad (τρισυπόστατος μονάς)[429] only once those *two* premisses concur, namely, (1) identity of substance, and (2) the Father is the single source and cause of the existence of the persons of the Son and of the Holy Spirit.[430]

Moreover, in the Commentary on Romans,[431] Origen argued that Christ's death is a proof of divine goodness: *Nisi enim esset hic ex illa veniens substantia.*[432] And in the Commentary on Hebrews, as quoted by Pamphilus, a slightly more apologetic note appears when Origen cites Wisdom 7:25, explaining that the Scripture uses corporeal metaphors to express spiritual truths, and concluding, *sic et sapientia ex eo procedens, ex ipsa Dei substantia generatur.*

Of course, whenever facts are disturbing, there is always the easy way-out argument: all of these are interpolations using a post-Nicene language, mainly by Rufinus. However, the notion of *homoousios* being an integral notion of Origen's theology is not based simply on Latin truffle hunting: Greek texts attest to this, too, above all, the present *Codex Sabaiticus 232* –and so do his cardinal philosophical conceptions, which will be briefly mentioned at the end of this section.

proper', although he preferred to believe that no name could be attributed to the One. *In Platonis Parmenidem*, pp. 1108-1009: οὕτως ἄρα καὶ τὸ ἓν ἡ πηγὴ θεότητος πάσης, καὶ ὅ ἐστιν αὐτόθεος (πᾶς γὰρ θεός, καθὸ θεός, ἀπὸ τοῦ 'Ενὸς ὑφέστηκεν). *Op. cit.* pp. 1096: τὸ δὲ Αὐτοέν οὐδὲν ἄλλο ἐστὶ ἢ αὐτοθεότης. *commTim*, v. 3, p. 207: τὸ μὲν οὖν αὐτοὲν μόνως θεὸς καὶ αὐτόθεος, οὐδενὸς ὂν οὐδὲ μεθεκτὸν ὑπάρχον, τὸ δὲ ἓν ὄν, ἐν ᾧ πρώτη μέθεξις, θεοῦ θεός.

429 Cf. Ephraem Syrus, *Sermo in Transfigurationem Domini et Dei Salvatoris Nostri Jesu Christi*, p. 30. Pseudo-Dionysius the Areopagite, *De Caelesti Hierarchia*, p. 32. Maximus Confessor, *Quaestiones ad Thalassium*, 55; *Mystagogia*, 3; *Ambigua ad Thomam*, 1; *Ambigua ad Joannem*, 67.10. John Carpathius, *Capita Theologica*, 2. Theodore Studites, *Canon In Requiem Monachi*, line 30. Anonymous, *Dissertatio contra Judaeos*, 10. Symeon the New Theologian, *Hymni*, hymn 28; *Orationes Theologicae*, oration 1. Michael Glycas, *Proverbia*, 19. Nicolas of Methone, *Refutatio Institutionis Theologicae Procli*, 64; 97. John Cyparissiotes, *Contra Tomum Palamiticum*, 8.17; *Orationes Antirrheticae Quinque contra Nilum Cabasilam*, 2.3; 5.8-9; *Expositio Materiaria*, 9.2; 9.10. Gennadius Scholarius, *Precatio ad Deum per Salutem Peloponnesi*, ode 4.

430 Cf. *Princ*, I.3.7: "Nothing in the Trinity can be called greater or less, for there is but one fount of deity, ... the power of the Trinity is one and the same."

431 On Rom. 4:10; Origen, PG.14.998A.

432 Cf. Origen, *Commentary of Romans*, in *Enchiridion Patristicum*, edited by Marie Joseph Rouët de Journel, Freiburg, 1946, pp. 1911 ff: "naturam Trinitatis et substantiam unam".

It should also be observed that Origen's references to the *homoousion* of the Three Persons are made apropos of commenting on different scriptural instances.

His reference to the Son having been begotten 'from the substance of the Father' (ἐκ τῆς οὐσίας τοῦ Πατρὸς) refers either to John 1:14 (*frJohn*, fr. 9) or to John 8:42 and 16:27 (*commJohn*, XX.18.157), or to Matthew 28:18 (*schMatt*, PG.17.309.52-53). The comment positing that the Father and Son are one in terms of essence (ἓν οὐσίᾳ τυγχάνοντας)[433] comments on John 1:17. In Klostermann's collection on Matthew, Fragment 14 speaking of 'the homoousion of the Trinity' (τὸ ὁμοούσιον τῆς Τριάδος) is a comment on Matthew 1:18. Fragment 58 ('Hence, there are Three Hypostases and one substance of the Three [Persons]') comments on Matthew 3:16-17. Fragment 244 ('the Son knows the Father and is of the same substance with Him') is on Matthew 11:27. Fragment 257 positing 'homoousios Trinity' (Τριάδα ὁμοούσιον) is a comment on Matthew 12:18-20. Fragment 572 on Matthew (Klostermann) ('the Father begot according to His nature, hence the Begotten is *homoousios*, indeed from the essence of the Father') comments on Matthew 28:18-20.

In the present codex *Sabaiticus 272*, we come upon not only some of Klostermann's fragments (e.g. frs. 58; 244; 382; 572), but also new ones which are not really 'fragments' but parts of a more detailed and argued exposition.[434]

Origen does not say that the substance of each Person is '*like* that of the Other': he says that this is *one ousia*, thus introducing a conception of one *identical* essence. This makes clear that the *ousia* of God is not to be understood as an abstract species, but as a single undifferentiated substance, identically expressed in each of the three Persons. It is indeed through the doctrine of *identity of ousia* that Origen safeguards his fundamental conception of God as a Single Being: God is without parts, since he 'is entirely one and simple' (ὁ θεὸς μὲν οὖν πάντῃ ἕν ἐστιν καὶ ἁπλοῦν).[435] Thus, God is a Single Being in three Subjects of presentation. As seen and thought of, He is three; as seeing and thinking and acting, he is one. Given that the polysemous *ousia* could suggest, among other significations, either a real individual being or a common substratum (Origen conveniently entertained both of these senses), it is not surprising that Eusebius initially tried to thwart this, and seems to have thought that the independent reality of the Three Persons could properly be stated not only in terms of three distinct *hypostases*, but also of three distinct *οὐσίαι*. Perhaps, in

433 *commJohn*, X.37.246.

434 Cf. for example, folio 240v: Τρεῖς οὖν τετελειωμέναι ὑποστάσεις *Πατρὸς καὶ Υἱοῦ καὶ Ἁγίου Πνεύματος*, μία δὲ οὐσία.

435 *commJohn*, I.20.119. See p. CXXIX, and note 537.

this way the doctrines surrounding this pivotal conception (such as those of the unity and singularity of all divine nature, will, operation and energy) could be made more clear and less disputed.

When Origen averred that it is not possible for two beings to be 'one' unless they are of the same οὐσία, in fact he expressed a plausible corollary of what *homoousion* really means. Thus, he confirmed accordingly that the Son and the Father 'are *one*, because they are neither one flesh nor one spirit: they are one God' (εἷς Θεός),[436] which means that the two Persons are of the same *ousia*.[437]

If one wished to employ the Aristotelian logic and ask of this ousia τὸ τί[438] Origen did in fact determine the framework of this analysis: once we wonder about God's τὸ τί, then, we should analyse how the Father and Son are both one and two. That is, if there is any room for perusing the divine ousia at all, this should concentrate on an endeavour to cast some light and comprehend so far as possible the *relation* between the Trinitarian Persons.

However, Origen did not make such an analysis *ad hoc*, obviously because he believed that any analysis of the mystery of the Trinitarian God by means of Greek philosophical methods and terms could lead nowhere. Once 'no one knows the Father except the Son',[439] 'who else other than the Son could possible teach us about God?'[440] This means that only God himself can teach God.[441]

If there is such a thing as 'God's essence' at all, this should be something 'more divine and more glorious and more blessed' (θειοτέρα καὶ ἐνδοξοτέρα καὶ μακαριωτέρα),[442] and entirely unlike the ousia we know of, namely, the ousia of created beings.[443] Definitely, this is not a generic 'substratum' (ὑποκείμενον), i.e. a prior one from which the Three proceed: ousia is something pertaining

436 *Dial*, section 3: οὕτω ὁ Σωτήρ ἡμῶν καὶ Κύριος πρὸς τὸν Πατέρα καὶ Θεὸν τῶν ὅλων ἐστὶν οὐ μία σάρξ, οὐχὶ ἓν πνεῦμα, ἀλλὰ τὸ ἀνωτέρω καὶ σαρκὸς καὶ πνεύματος, εἷς Θεός. Cf. *op. cit.* section 2: καὶ δεῖ δεῖξαι κατὰ τί δύο εἰσὶν καὶ κατὰ τί εἷς θεός εἰσιν οἱ δύο.

437 Athanasius wrote that to speak of 'being like in terms of essence' (ὅμοιον κατ' οὐσίαν) is the same as suggesting that this involves the Son being what he is 'by means of participation', since similarity' suggests 'quality', not essence – which is unacceptable. *De Synodis Arimini in Italia et Seleuciae in Isauria*, 53.3. Cf. *Epistula ad Afros Episcopos*, PG.26.1044.7-16.

438 Aristotle, *Analytica Posteriora*, 92a34; *De Anima*, 402a13; Cf. *ousia* defined as τὸ τί ἦν εἶναι. *Analytica Posteriora*, 91b7-8; *Metaphysica*, 983a27-28; 988a34-35; *et passim*.

439 Matt. 11:27; Luke, 10:22.

440 *commJohn*, XIII.24.146.

441 *deOr*, 24.3; *frLuc*, fr. 163: ἐγὼ γὰρ παρὰ ἀνθρώπου οὐ δύναμαι μαθεῖν, ἐὰν μὴ παρὰ σοῦ μάθω. τίς γὰρ ὀφείλει διδάσκειν περὶ θεοῦ ἢ θεός; ἄνωθεν τοίνυν ἡ ἀποκάλυψις μετὰ τὴν κατ' ἀξίαν πρόθεσιν.

442 *Dial*, 3. Cf. *commJohn*, XIII.21.123; XIX.6.37; *frJohn*, fr. 6.

443 *deOr*, 23.5.

to the relation between the three Persons, which though is ineffable and incomprehensible. Nevertheless, we know that the Father begot the Son, and as it happens in this case (even with respect to human beings and all animals) *begetting* means producing a progeny of the *same ousia.*

Origen did not offer any further analysis of this (which could be impossible to do, anyway), but he emphasised that the Trinitarian character of God is immanent in the Divine Nature itself: there is no way to envisage God the Father in the absence of the Son (for how could possibly the Father be ontologically *Father* unless He was always Father of a Son?), and the same goes for the Holy Spirit.

> For if God is eternally perfect, and in Him there is the inherent power to be a Father, and it is good to be the Father of such a Son, why should he postpone this and deprives Himself of such a good thing, out of which (as it were) he can be Father of a Son? And certainly, the same should be said of the Holy Spirit.[444]

Athanasius took notice of Origen's warning against any material understanding of generation ἐκ τῆς οὐσίας τοῦ Πατρός, and emphasised this in the selfsame terms in his own writings. The irony is that he ascribed this explanation of the term ὁμοούσιος to emperor Constantine, which only means paying lip service to a rude despot who had no idea of theology and did not care about anything other than his own power and the stability and coherence of the empire.[445]

Eusebius reproduced Origen's cautious qualifications,[446] and so did Cyril of Alexandria,[447] but such instances are only a tiny fragment of references compared to the vast number of cases where ἐκ τῆς οὐσίας τοῦ Πατρός was used unreservedly. It is also irony that Abbot Gelasius of the Laura of Sabas in Palestine, and the other leaders of the monastery, who composed Justinian's

---

444 Origen, *commGen*, PG.12.45.34-39 (*apud* Eusebius, *Contra Marcellum*, 1.4.22 [Marcellus, *Fragmenta*, fr 39]).

445 Athanasius, *De Decretis Nicaenae Synodi*, 33.7: ἑνὸς μόνου προσεγγραφέντος ῥήματος τοῦ ὁμοουσίου, ὃ καὶ αὐτὸς ἑρμήνευε λέγων. ὅτι μὴ κατὰ τῶν σωμάτων πάθη λέγοιτο ὁμοούσιος ‹ὁ υἱός›, οὔτ᾽ οὖν κατὰ διαίρεσιν οὔτε κατά τινα ἀποτομὴν ἐκ τοῦ πατρὸς ὑποστῆναι. μηδὲ γὰρ δύνασθαι τὴν ἄϋλον καὶ νοερὰν καὶ ἀσώματον φύσιν σωματικόν τι πάθος ὑφίστασθαι … καὶ ὁ μὲν σοφώτατος ἡμῶν καὶ εὐσεβέστατος βασιλεὺς τοιάδε ἐφιλοσόφει. Also 33.11; 33.13. Eusebius promptly quoted the text of Athanasius, evidently being in panic terror, and thus hoping to exorcise his reservations about signing up to the *homoousion.* Eusebius, *Epistula ad Caesarienses*, 7.

446 See *supra*, p. XCIV and note 358. Eusebius, *Demonstratio Evangelica*, 4.3.13; 5.1.9; *Epistula ad Caesarienses*, 8; 11.

447 Cyril of Alexandria, *In Joannem*, v. 1, p. 190: ἀλλ᾽ ἐκ τῆς οὐσίας τοῦ Θεοῦ καὶ Πατρὸς οὐ κατὰ ἀποκοπήν, ἢ ῥεῦσιν, ἢ μερισμόν, ἢ τομήν. So in *Epistulae Paschales*, PG.77.664.18; *Thesaurus De Sancta Consubstantiali Trinitate*, PG.75: 44.15-20; 45.26-32.

text against the Monophysites, used Origen's phraseology (whom otherwise they condemned!)[448] upon making this point, without having the foggiest inkling of who their actual source was.[449] Nevertheless, it is characteristic that those who cared to reproduce Origen's expression ἐκ τῆς οὐσίας τοῦ Πατρὸς were Origen's followers, such as Cassian the Sabaite in the sixth century.[450]

More to the point, there is a uncharacteristic obstinacy to consider (even read) points where Origen styled the Trinity *homoousios* in the teeth of the fact that Athanasius modestly reported that this term was not his own invention (as normally urged by the hackneyed shibboleth), but the bishops of Nicaea received this 'from eminent bishops and scholars of old' – in fact, they 'consented to using' this term of old.[451]

We know that the term *homoousios* was used in a dispute between Bishop Dionysius of Alexandria and Pope Dionysius of Rome, c. 255-260, when the latter defended himself against the charge that he maintained subordinationist views (drawn from his anti-Sabellian criticism that thrived at Pentapolis) and not endorsing the doctrine that 'Christ is *homoousios* with the Father'.[452] Athanasius, Hilary, and Basil reported that *homoousios* was condemned through a (not extant) Synodic Letter of Antioch, but the reasons for that are not clear since Athanasius and Hilary give conflicting accounts.

---

448 The same monks composed Justinian's edict against Origen, and the emperor just signed it. See *NDGF*, pp. 385; 407; *RCR*, pp. 258-260; 267; 324-325.

449 Justinian, *Contra Monophysitas*, 87; 125; 141.

450 Cassian the Sabaite (Pseudo-Caesarius), *Quaestiones et Responsiones*, chapter 3: Ἀλλ' οὐχ ἴσα βροτοῖς κατὰ ῥεῦσιν ἢ τομὴν ἢ διάστασιν ὁ υἱὸς καὶ τὸ πνεῦμα ἐκ τοῦ πατρὸς προῆλθον. *Op. cit.* chapter 37: οὐ γὰρ σῶμα τὸ θεῖον ὑπάρχει ὄγκῳ ἢ συστολῇ ὑποκείμενον ἢ ῥεύσει ἢ τομῇ ἢ ὅλως πάθει τινὶ χειρούμενον. καθὸ οὖν ὁ πατὴρ πνεῦμα ὑπάρχων τὸν υἱὸν θεὸν λόγον πνευματικῶς, ἀχρόνως, ἀφράστως γεγέννηκεν. ... ἐπὶ τοῦ ἀπαθῶς γεννῆσαι τὸ θεῖον οὐ ῥεῦσιν, οὐ τομὴν ὑφιστάμενον. Cassian the Sabaite (Pseudo-Didymus), *De Trinitate*, 15.82. Pseudo-Basil of Caesarea (*forsan* Cassian the Sabaite), *Enarratio in Prophetam Isaiam*, 13.264: ὁ ἐκ τῆς οὐσίας τοῦ Πατρὸς τὴν ὕπαρξιν ἔχων. Pseudo-Justin, *Expositio Rectae Fidei*, p. 380B. On Cassian the Sabaite being the actual author of the foregoing works by Pseudo-Caesarius and Pseudo-Didymus, see my *NDGF*, Appendices I and II.

451 Athanasius, *De Decretis Nicaenae Synodi*, 33.13: ᾧ καὶ αὐτῷ τοῦτον ἑρμηνευθέντι τὸν τρόπον καλῶς ἔχειν ἐφάνη συγκαταθέσθαι, ἐπεὶ καὶ τῶν παλαιῶν τινας λογίους καὶ ἐπιφανεῖς ἐπισκόπους καὶ συγγραφεῖς ἔγνωμεν ἐπὶ τῆς τοῦ Πατρὸς καὶ Υἱοῦ θεολογίας τῷ τοῦ ὁμοουσίου χρησαμένους ὀνόματι. See the same text in Eusebius explaining to his flock why did he eventually assent to using that term. *Epistula ad Caesarienses*, 13. See this important testimony also in Socrates Scholasticus, *HE*, 1.8 (lines 299-303); Theodoret, *HE*, pp. 37 & 52; Gelasius of Cyzicus, *HE*, 2.35.13; Nicephorus Callistus Xanthopulus, *HE*, 8.21-22; and Theodore Dexius (theologian, Constantinople, fourteenth century), *Appelatio adversus Joannem Cantacuzenum*, section 52.

452 Athanasius, *De Sententia Dionysii*, 18.

Furthermore, the author of the Introduction to Pamphilus' *Apology for Origen* quoted a testimony from the anti-heretical treatise *Praedestinatus*, in which the author ('perhaps either Arnobius the Younger or Primasius') 'in the first book of his *On Heresies*' ('Heresy 22, on the Apellites' – followers of the Gnostic Apelles) wrote this:

> Origen defeated all of those [heretics] as perfectly as to end up becoming himself a 'Traveller' (περιοδευτής), and walking over the cities of the East one after the other, he taught all of them [the right faith]. And since the volumes of his treatises are countless, the defeated heretics, being driven by the most devious of presumptions, distorted his books at their own liking, so that they could say to all those that they sought to deceive that this was how Origen had set forth his own exegeses.
>
> This is the reason why, once anyone who reads Origen's books until today is able to read his books correctly and perspicaciously, is able to grasp the passages that the heretics defiled.
>
> Pamphilus the Martyr made it clear in his *Apology* that this is quite the case. Actually, writing about the Heresy 43, he says that there had been different persons named 'Origen': one of them was a most impious Syrian who taught wicked things; also another one, who rejected the resurrection of the dead and claimed that the Holy Spirit is a creature created by Christ. … and then, he [sc. Pamphilus] added this: "Everything that those two persons wrote under the name Origen[453] was malicious, and Origen's orthodox works were mingled [with those interpolations] by heretical and perverted teachers." … However, anyone who is endowed with a healthy spirit and the eyes of his mind are clear-sighted, he can see that all those dreadful things were interpolated into Origen's works, and he learns how to discern those [interpolations] as pieces of cloth coloured white, or having any other tincture, having been seamed on a red mattress." This is what the holy martyr Pamphilus teaches … who published his *Apology* excluding all those lies that the uninformed orthodox (because of ignorance) attribute to Origen, and demonstrating that all those reprehensible [views] that occur in his works are not in fact Origen's [views] but ones maintained by those whom Origen overthrew. For all those [interpolated passages] that are entirely debauched were written by the other two persons who had Origen's name, but they had neither his faith nor his conscience.[454]

Although the author of this introductory Latin *Admonitio* quoted Jacques Sirmond's *Praedestinatus*[455] (who in turn quoted from an anonymous author),

453 Thus, according to this testimony, there were *three* Origens. On two different Origens, see also Epiphanius of Salamis, *Panarion*, v. 1, pp. 158; 160; v. 2, pp. 398; 403; 409; 522-523; *Ancoratus*, 13.6. Pseudo-Epiphanius of Salamis, *Anacephalaeosis*, v. 2, pp. 213-214.

454 Pamphilus, *op. cit.* PG.17.539-540 (Introduction).

455 Jacques Sirmond (Jacobus Sirmundus, 1559-1651) was a French scholar and Jesuit priest. See his *Praedestinatus, seu Praedestinatorum haeresis et libris*, MDCXLV (1645, no place of publication), pp. 35-36. Likewise, Sirmond's source defended Pamphilus' *Apology for*

this author of the *Admonitio* himself (probably a medieval monk faithful to the imperial orthodoxy) did not place reliance on this testimony as a true one.[456] Nevertheless, he knew of the anonymous author whose five volumes arguing that 'Origen said nothing wrong about the Trinity' Photius had reviewed,[457] as well as of Rufinus' *De Adulteratione librorum Origenis.*[458]

A glaring example of such malevolent interpolation is the passage positing the Holy Spirit as creature created by Christ (exactly as reported in the foregoing passage by the anonymous author repudiating this as a malicious adulteration), and yet, this has been unstudiously used in the modern editions of the commentary on John.[459]

This point is one of the more striking cases of 'pieces of cloth coloured white which are seamed on a red mattress.' Once again, we are upon the question of credibility of apparently incoherent passages in the second book of the commentary on John, which reminds us not only of Origen having taken exception to the adulteration of his books during his lifetime, but also of Rufinus' text itself on the same subject, in which he says what is evident: Origen was not as

---

Origen (*op. cit.* p. 31) and praised him for having countered the Marcionites along with Tertullian (*op. cit.* p. 26).

456 In his edition of Origen's commentary on John (pp. xxiv-xxvi), Erwin Preuschen included a prologue by the scribe, which is as long as two pages of text. In this, the scribe quotes a prologue by a certain emperor (Preuschen conjectured that this could have been Justinian), who could not have enough of blaming Origen for every heresy. This quotation aimed at reassuring the scribe himself against the blame that he reproduced the text of a damned heretic. The prologue concentrates on Origen having been 'the leader of Arianism' – and 'Aetius [of Antioch] and Arius the Libyan [who though was an Alexandrian] and Eunomius of Libya [who though was from Cyzicus!] were merely Origen's followers'. For example (p. xxiv), this 'emperor' argued *against Origen* (allegedly having made the Son a creature) that the Logos was beginningless in the Wisdom / Son, since it could be impossible for the Son ever to have been without logos [rationality], i.e. to be 'irrational' (ἄλογος). But this was exactly the argument that Origen himself expounded against those who claimed that the Son had been created, of which this fanatic of those dark times of course had no idea. Cf. Origen, *commJohn*, II.10.130 (ref. to John, 1:1): Ἀλλὰ *Λόγος μὲν ἐν ἀρχῇ* οὐκ ἐγένετο· οὐκ ἦν γὰρ ὅτε ἀρχὴ ἄλογος ἦν.

457 Photius, *Bibliotheca*, Codex 117, pp. 91b-92b.

458 Rufinus exposing this adulteration wondered, 'how is it possible for Origen to declare that the Father and Son are *homoousioi*, and yet, in the ensuing chapters, to claim that these are of different substance – although Origen a short while ago wrote that the Son was born from the Father's nature itself?' Rufinus, *op. cit.* PG.17.619.

459 E. Preuschen, *Origenes, Commentarii in evangelium Joannis*, II.75-76 (f. 136r) as in *Origenes Werke*, vol. 4 (Die griechischen christlichen Schriftsteller 10), Leipzig, 1903, p. 65. C. Blanc followed Preuschen blindly. *Origène, Commentaire sur saint Jean*, 5 vols. (Sources chrétiennes 120, 157, 222, 290, 385), Paris, vol. 1: 1966; vol. 2:1970; vol. 3:1975; vol. 4:1982; vol. 5:1992.

schizophrenic as to contradict himself within different points which are close to each other in the same work. Pamphilus pointed out that that this was a recurrent case concerning allegations about *De Principiis*, and every sane reader who read such allegations could have thought likewise (although, not so long ago, there have been modern 'scholars' [!] who urged that 'everything in *De Principiis* has also its antithesis therein' – in other words, Origen was but an inconsistent schizophrenic).

But let me give an example, which shows the quality of some of Origen's modern editions.

In the second book of the commentary on John, we read the following *interpolated* passage, which is apparently a tentative proposition set forth for investigation,[460] yet the tenor of this 'white piece of cloth' appears as a *conclusive* resolution.

> Besides, once the statement *all things were made through him*[461] is true, it should be examined whether also the Holy Spirit *was made through him*, too. For I think that, for anyone who professes that this [sc. the Holy Spirit] was created (γενητὸν αὐτὸ εἶναι) and upholds the [statement] *all things was made through him*, it is also necessary to accept that the Holy Spirit was also made through the Logos, whereby the Logos is senior to this [sc. the Holy Spirit]. For once one does not concede that the Holy Spirit has been created through Christ (διὰ τοῦ Χριστοῦ γεγονέναι), it follows that this should be posited as 'uncreated' (ἀγένητον).[462] ... However, we who are persuaded that the Father, the Son, and the Holy Spirit are three hypostases, and believe that no [hypostasis] apart from the Father is unbegotten, admit also (as more pious and as true doctrine) that, of all those that

460 Origen called this 'propositions set forth for the purpose of γυμνασία ('mental exercise')'; *commMatt*, 14.12; 15.5; 15.33; cf. *frLuc*, fr. 186. See Athanasius attesting to Origen's method (τὰ ὡς ἐν γυμνασίᾳ λεγόμενα), and warning against taking those points as Origen's definitive views; *De Decretis Nicaenae Synodi*, 27.2; also, referring to Theognostus who likewise proposed tentative views just for the sake of logical examination of them (ἐν γυμνασίᾳ ἐξετάσας), *op. cit.* 25.2. This kind of 'mental exercise' had been encouraged (indeed prescribed) by Plato, in *Parmenides*, 135c-136c; *Alcibiades i*, 132b (all ancient authors treated this as a genuine Plato's work).

461 John, 1:3.

462 C. Blanc following E. Preuschen wrote ἀγέννητον, which is an editorial mistake. For the discussion at this point is about the Holy Spirit being either created or uncreated, not begotten or unbegotten. On ἀγένητος in reference to God, see Origen, *commJohn*, I.17.103; II.2.14; II.14.104; XX.22.184 (τοῦ μὲν πρώτως ἁγίου Πατρὸς ἀγενήτου τυγχάνοντος -οὗτος δέ ἐστιν ὁ Θεός). Likewise, *Dial*, 1; *Commentarii in Romanos* (*III.5-V.7*), p. 226; *Cels*, II.51; IV.38; VI.17 (ref. to the Son: τὸν ἀγένητον καὶ πάσης γενητῆς φύσεως πρωτότοκον); VI.66. All of these refer to the 'uncreated God' (or, to the 'uncreated divine nature'). There are also other points referring to theories about the 'uncreated cosmos', the 'uncreated matter', etc. The notion of 'unbegotten' appears after two sections (II.10.75), which I quote forthwith.

> were made through the Logos, the Holy Spirit is the most honourable and first in rank of all those that have been created by the Father through Christ.[463]

Hence, Origen is represented as maintaining that the Holy Spirit is a creature made by the Logos just like the cosmos and everything in it.[464] It should be observed that this alleged text of Origen is exactly the same as that Pamphilus reported and denounced as gross interpolation in Origen's works by 'another [Origen], who rejected the resurrection of the dead and claimed that the Holy Spirit is a creature created by Christ.' The use of the term 'Christ' instead of Logos at some points of the foregoing text is quite characteristic. The idea that the Son was created by the Father, and the Holy Spirit by the Father and the Son, came to be synonymous with the Arians and Eunomians.[465]

Let *all* of modern scholars take these editions seriously. However, there are disturbing facts that persistently demand answers.

For one thing, these things appear only in the beginning of his commentary on John, that is, upon Origen's conversion to Christianity, and more or less simultaneously with his commentary on Genesis and *De Principiis*, as he reveals in the latter.[466] Nowhere else throughout his works do such statements appear, which reminds of the caveat, 'But whosoever is sane and has clear eyes of mind, can see that these terrible things were added to the works of Origen, and learns to distinguish them just as pieces of cloth coloured white or having any other tincture having been seamed on a red mattress'.[467]

Besides, the least one should do (which his modern self-assured editors evidently did not) is read what else did Origen write on the same topic during the same period when he wrote the second book on the commentary on John. Here is then what he wrote in *De Principiis*.

---

463 Origen, *commJohn*, II.10.73 & 75 – a flagrant interpolation.

464 See further, *op. cit.* II.11.79: Ἔχει δὲ ἐπαπόρησιν διά τε τὸ *Πάντα δι᾽ αὐτοῦ ἐγένετο* καὶ τὸ ἀκολουθεῖν τὸ πνεῦμα γενητὸν ὂν διὰ τοῦ λόγου γεγονέναι, πῶς οἱονεὶ προτιμᾶται τοῦ Χριστοῦ ἔν τισι γραφαῖς, ... etc. Also, *op. cit.* II.11.86: Ταῦτα δὲ ἐπὶ πολὺ ἐξήτασται σαφέστερον ἰδεῖν βουλομένοις, πῶς, εἰ *πάντα δι᾽ αὐτοῦ ἐγένετο*, καὶ τὸ πνεῦμα διὰ τοῦ λόγου ἐγένετο, ἓν τῶν πάντων τυγχάνον ὑποδεέστερον τοῦ δι᾽ οὗ ἐγένετο νοούμενον, εἰ καὶ λέξεις τινὲς περισπᾶν ἡμᾶς εἰς τὸ ἐναντίον δοκοῦσιν. And yet, scholars are unmoved by such interpolations.

465 See Bessarion, *Ad Alexium Lascarem Philanthropenum De Processione Spiritus Sancti*, 4.74: οἱ ταῦτα λέγοντες ἅγιοι πρὸς ἀρειανοὺς καὶ εὐνομιανοὺς μαχόμενοι ἔλεγον ταῦτα. οἵ τὸν μὲν υἱὸν ἐκ τοῦ πατρὸς εἶναι, τὸ δὲ πνεῦμα ἐκ τοῦ πατρὸς καὶ υἱοῦ ὡμολόγουν. ἠρνοῦντο δὲ τὸ ἐκ τῆς οὐσίας λέγοντες τὸν υἱὸν ἐκ τοῦ πατρὸς μέν, ἀλλ᾽ οὐκ οὐσιωδῶς, ἀλλὰ θελήσει τοῦ πατρὸς γεννηθῆναι. τὸ δὲ πνεῦμα καὶ αὐτὸ ἐκ τοῦ υἱοῦ, οὐκ οὐσιωδῶς, ἀλλὰ θελήσει. ... ὡς τρεῖς οὐσίας ποιεῖν ἐν θεότητι.

466 *Princ*, I.2.13.

467 Introduction to the text of Pamphilus' *Apology for Origen*. PG.17.540.

Of the existence of the Holy Spirit, however, we are taught in many passages of scripture. ... From all of which we learn that the person of the Holy Spirit is of so great authority and dignity that saving baptism is not complete except when performed with the authority of the whole most excellent Trinity, that is, by the naming of Father, Son and Holy Spirit; and that the name of the Holy Spirit must be joined to that of the unbegotten God the Father and his only-begotten Son.[468]

But up to the present we have not been able to find any passage in the holy scriptures which would warrant us in saying that the Holy Spirit was a being made or created.[469]

The Holy Spirit would have never been included in the unity of the Trinity, that is, along with the unchangeable Father and with his Son, unless he had always been the Holy Spirit.[470]

He who is *born again through God*[471] needs [all the Three, namely], the Father and Son and Holy Spirit, and will not attain to salvation apart from the entire Trinity and ... it is not possible to become partaker of the Father or the Son without the Holy Spirit.[472]

Nothing in the Trinity can be called greater or less, for there is but one fount of deity, ... the power of the Trinity is one and the same.[473]

The power of the Trinity is one and the same. ... there is no separation in the Trinity, but that which is called the *gift of the Spirit*[474] is ministered through the Son and worked by God the Father. ... This then is the testimony we bear to the unity of Father, Son, and Holy Spirit.[475] ... This blessed and ruling power, therefore, that is, the power that exercises control of all things, we call the Trinity.[476]

The nature of the Trinity is one and incorporeal.[477]

We have proved ... that all things that exist were made by God, and there is nothing that was not made except the nature of the Father, the Son, and the Holy Spirit.[478]

---

468 *Princ*, I.3.2.

469 *Op. cit.* I.3.3. This passage was quoted as evidence also by Pamphilus in his *Apology*, PG.17.567A.

470 *Op. cit.* I.3.4.

471 1 Peter, 1:3.

472 *Op. cit.* I.3.5.

473 *Op. cit.* I.3.7.

474 Cf. 1 Cor. 12:4-11.

475 *Princ*, I.3.7.

476 *Op. cit.* I.4.2.

477 *Op. cit.* IV.4.5.

478 *Op. cit.* IV.4.8.

> Unless we thirst after the three wells of the waters, we shall not find the one source of the waters either. For the Jews appeared as having thirsted for the one well, namely for God, but since they did not thirst for Christ and the Holy Spirit, they cannot drink from God either. … And those who believe in one God but they dismiss the prophecies, they did not thirst for the Holy Spirit which is present in the prophecies; hence, they shall drink neither from the Fatherly well nor from Him who at the Temple said, 'If one is thirsty, let him come to me and drink' (John, 7:37).[479]

> When you hear about 'ranks' being applied to the Trinity, you should understand this as pertaining to our [human] condition. Once you hear about greatness of the Father and smallness of the Son, you should take this as reference not to [the divine] nature and hypostasis, but to our condition.[480]

Moreover, Pamphilus wrote an *ad hoc* chapter in order to demonstrate Origen's doctrine about the Holy Spirit, and took particular care to show that never did Origen regard the the Holy Spirit as a creature. To this purpose, Pamphilus quoted an array of passages from *De Principiis* (books I and IV) at which Origen's view could not have been more clear and categorical.[481]

Therefore, the (current deplorable) text of the commentary on John should be edited: the foregoing interpolation should be cast away, since the text II.10.73-76 is but a flagrantly coarce interpolation of the kind reported above. The text should continue from II.10.77, onwards.

Moreover, here is what Origen wrote in the commentary on Matthew in *Codex Sabaiticus 232*:

> Folio 1v (& Kl. fr. 14 I; and II, as below): Τὸ λεγόμενον, πνευματικὴ *γέννησις*, τὸ δὲ *ἐκ* τὸν ‹ἁγια›σμὸν δηλώσει καὶ τὴν δύναμιν. ναὶ μὴν καὶ τὸ ὁμοούσιον.

> Folio 19r: Ὁ γὰρ ὁμοούσιον ἔχων τὸ Πνεῦμα τὸ Ἅγιον, καθὸ Θεὸς ἦν καὶ ὁμοούσιος τῷ Πατρί, πῶς ἔμελλε πνευματικῆς δεῖσθαι καὶ ἀνηγμένης ζωῆς;

> Folio 95r (& Kl. fr. 257): Ὁ Πατὴρ λέγει τῷ Υἱῷ *τὸ Πνεῦμα* καταπέμπειν. Οὐκοῦν προσκυνοῦμεν Τριάδα ὁμοούσιον. Θεὸν τὸν Πατέρα, Θεὸν τὸν Υἱόν, Θεὸν τὸ Πνεῦμα τὸ Ἅγιον. Μίαν φύσιν ἐν τρισὶν ἰδιότησι νοεραῖς, τελείαις, καθ᾽ ἑαυτὰς ὑφεστώσαις, ἀριθμῷ διαιρεταῖς καὶ οὐ διαιρεταῖς θεότητι.

> Folio 240r: Διόπερ ἀναγκαία τῆς Τριάδος ἡ ὀνομασία. Καὶ ὅπερ ἂν ὑπεξαιρῇ τις ὄνομα, κολοβὸν ποιεῖ τὸ τῆς θεολογίας. Ἀτελὲς μέν, ἐὰν τὸ Πνεῦμα περιαιρῇ· διεστῶσαν δὲ τοῦ τέλους τὴν ἀρχὴν ἐὰν τὸ μέσον ἐξαιρῇ, τὸν Υἱόν. Ἀδύνατον δὲ τὸν κατὰ μίαν ἐνέργειαν γινόμενον ἁγιασμὸν ἐκ διαφόρων καὶ ἀσυναρτήτων οὐσιῶν ἐπιτελεῖσθαι. Ἀσεβὲς γὰρ

---

479 *homJer*, homily 19.9.

480 Origen, *frMatt* (Klostermann), fr. 404 (comm. on Matt. 20:23).

481 Pamphilus, *op. cit.* PG.17.564C-571A; chapter 4: 'On the Holy Spirit'.

> τὸ τὰ ἑτεροφυῆ καὶ ἀσύναπτα μιᾷ τῇ ἐνεργείᾳ περιλαβεῖν. Τριάδα τοίνυν τοῖς μαθηταῖς ὁμοούσιον τοῖς βαπτιζομένοις διδόναι παρεγγυᾷ, οὐχ ἕτερος ὢν αὐτῆς, ἀλλ᾽ ἑαυτὸν Υἱὸν ἀορίστως προσονομάζων ...
>
> Folio 240v: Ἔστι γὰρ καθ᾽ ὑπόστασιν ἰδίαν Πνεῦμα Ἅγιον, ὁμοούσιον τ‹ῷ› Πατρ‹ὶ› καὶ τ‹ῷ› Υἱ‹ῷ›, ἐκ τοῦ Πατρὸς ἐκπορευόμενον, δι᾽ Υἱοῦ πεφηνός, ἀχώριστον τοῦ Πατρὸς καὶ τοῦ Υἱοῦ, ὡς ἴδιον. Τρεῖς οὖν τετελειωμέναι ὑποστάσεις *Πατρὸς καὶ Υἱοῦ καὶ Ἁγίου Πνεύματος*, μία δὲ οὐσία.

Beyond these, Klostermann quoted another version of his Fragment 14 (just quoted above) which goes thus: τοῦτο δὲ *ἐκ* τὸν ἁγιασμὸν δηλοῖ καὶ τὸ ὁμοούσιον τῆς τριάδος καὶ τὸ μίαν εἶναι τὴν δύναμιν.[482]

The interesting thing about this that the expression ὁμοούσιος Τριὰς (that is, application of the adjective *homoousios* to the Trinity *in toto* as unity of Persons) does not show before Epiphanius of Salamis[483] and his more or less contemporary Basil of Caesarea,[484] and in *spuria* under the names of both authors, which are much later.[485] But it is hard to overlook that this expression appears in Origen's distinguished followers, namely, Didymus and Evagrius,[486] and later in the newly discovered moderate Origenist Cassian the Sabaite, in the turn of the fifth to sixth century.[487] I am aware that scholars are loath[488] to accept that Origen used this expression about the Trinity, only because they do not realise that this was only one of Origen's numerous statements about the Trinity, which to him was the perfect adumbration of the true God. Throughout decades, in the mind of the Greek philosopher Origen, God was the absolutely

482 Klostermann, p. 12, attributed to Origen from 'a single thirteen-century codex containing a catena on the gospel of Matthew edited by Petrus Possinus (Hs. Paris. 194).'

483 Epiphanius of Salamis, *Panarion*, v. 2, pp. 49; 349; v. 3, pp. 255; 332; 399; 514; *Ancoratus*, 64.3.

484 Basil of Caesarea, *Adversus Eunomium*, PG.29.712.11.

485 Pseudo-Epiphanius of Salamis, *Homilia in Laudes Mariae Deiparae*, PG.43.501.38. Pseudo-Basil of Caesarea, *Sermo 12* (*De Ascetica Disciplina*), PG.31.649.30; *Orationes* (*Exorcismi*), PG.31.1684.54.

486 Didymus, *Commentarii in Zachariam*, 3.261. Evagrius of Pontus, *Tractatus ad Eulogium*, PG.79.1140.14-15; *Institutio*, PG.79.1237.32-33.

487 Cassian the Sabaite (Pseudo-Didymus), *De Trinitate*, 1.2; 4.10; 6.9; 7.8(8); 17.1; 18.49; 20.1; 22 (title); 24 (title); 25 (title); PG.39: 604.22; 713.4-5; 728.27.

488 For example, Mark Edwards, in his review of Panayiotis Tzamalikos, *Anaxagoras, Origen, and Neoplatonism, The Legacy of Anaxagoras to Classical and Late Antiquity*, vol. I and II, De Gruyter, 2016. *Journal of Ecclesiastical History*, v. 69 / 3, 2018, pp. 610-612: This "study demands our attention, though it asks us to swallow too much when it credits Origen, or any third-century Christian, with the proclamation of a homoousios Trinity".

simple Anaxagorean *Nous*.[489] Nevertheless, once he converted to Christianity, he never disowned this cardinal concept of Deity.

Put simply, the expression ὁμοούσιος Τριὰς is only a paraphrastic alternative equivalent couched in Christian theological terms, which is but one of Origen's expressions that stand for his fundamental doctrine positing that 'God is altogether one and simple' (πάντῃ ἓν καὶ ἁπλοῦν).[490] Had he not said so, this could only mean that the Trinity comprises *three* different ontological orders – in which case how could the Trinity be 'entirely one and simple'? For this could introduce three different *essences* within the Trinity, that is, three ontological levels – which was the Arian argument.[491]

One of the invaluable contributions of *Codex Sabaiticius 232* is that it offers the argument precisely bolstering Origen's relevant outlook.

In various instances, as discussed in previous works of mine, theologians (including the detractor Epiphanius) drew on Origen. Therefore, the fact that the same expression appears in an extensive section of Origen's commentary on Matthew in the present *Codex Sabaiticus 232* should not come as a surprise.[492] What would be a surprise (although it should not) is rather the fact that Origen's influence on his posterity perpetually turns out to be more extensive than numerous modern scholars could imagine.

It would be utterly naive to believe that Origen's evolution of thought could be understood as a process from maintaining (as a Greek philosopher)

489 The fundamental ontological characteristic of Anaxagoras' *Nous* was 'simple, and unmixed' with anything else (ἁπλοῦς καὶ ἀμιγής). Cf. Aristotle, *De Anima*, 405a; *Metaphysica*, 989b. Alexander of Aphrodisias, *commMetaph*, p. 69. Plotinus, *Enneades*, V.1.9. Themistius, *paraphrAnim*, pp. 14; 97. Simplicius, *commPhys*, pp. 235; 1227; *commAnim*, p. 235. John Philoponus, *commAnim*, p. 86. Asclepius of Tralles, *commMetaph*, p. 62. Sophonias, *commAnim*, p. 134. Gennadius Scholarius, *Epitome Summae contra Gentiles Thomae Aquinae*, 2.59.

490 *commJohn*, I.20.119; likewise, *Cels*, IV.14. See discussion *infra*.

491 To 'sever the Trinity into three essences' (τρεῖς οὐσίας) was aberration associated with the name of Arius and Eunomius, and seen as tantamount to tritheism. See ACO, *Concilium Universale Ephesenum anno 431*, tome 1.1.7, p. 98: μὴ τρεῖς τινας οὐσίας διαφόρους νομίζειν. Justinian, *Edictum Rectae Fidei*, p. 130 (& *Chronicon Paschale*, p. 637): κατὰ τὴν Αρείου μανίαν εἰς τρεῖς διαφόρους οὐσίας κατατέμνοντος τὴν θεότητα. ACO, *Concilium Lateranense a. 649 celebratum*, Act 3, p. 156. Cf. Gregory of Nazianzus, *In Laudem Athanasii (orat. 21)*, PG.35.1125.1-10. Theodoret, *Eranistes*, p. 116. Anastasius of Sinai, *Viae Dux*, 6.2; 8.5; 9.1; 9.2; 11.1. Pamphilus (theologian, sixth-seventh century), *Diversorum Capitum seu Difficultatum Solutio*, Question 11, lines 109-122. John of Damascus, *Contra Jacobitas*, 2; 76. Photius, *Bibliotheca*, Codex 230, p. 283b; *Epistulae et Amphilochia*, epistle 34. Anonymous, *Adversus Haereses* (e cod. Coisl. 299, saec. XI), p. 279 (Eunomius τρεῖς μὲν μερικὰς οὐσίας ἐπὶ τῆς τριάδος ὁρίζοντα). Also, Bessarion, *supra*, note 465.

492 Origen, *Codex Sabaiticus 232*, folio 240r: Τριάδα τοίνυν τοῖς μαθηταῖς ὁμοούσιον τοῖς βαπτιζομένοις διδόναι παρεγγυᾷ, οὐχ ἕτερος ὢν αὐτῆς, ἀλλ' ἑαυτὸν Υἱὸν ἀορίστως προσονομάζων.

the Anaxagorean God as an utterly simple *Nous*, and upon converting to Christianity he employed the crude assertion that this *Nous* 'begot' a Son / Logos, who in turn 'created' the Holy Spirit – hence, Origen allegedly made up his Christian God a weird mingling of an *uncreated* Father, a 'born' (to Origen's detractors: 'created') Son, and a Holy Spirit *created* by the Son – and yet he argued (from the very start to the very end of his Christian life) that this grotesque conglomeration is a 'God absolutely one and simple',[493] and 'the nature of God is altogether incorruptible and simple and incomposite and indivisible'[494]

If anyone who presumes that has understood even a modicum of *who* Origen really was, believed that *this* Origen was bowled head over heals by such a madness, it could be better for them to abandon Origen altogether and spare their time and exertions to things better suited their talents.

The following story is quite indicative of Origen's unending historical plight. Pope Anastasius I, bishop of Rome (399-401), sent a letter to John, bishop of Jerusalem. In this letter, the pope approved of the condemnation of Origen's writings – a condemnation that had been decreed by a synod of anti-Origenist bishops in Egypt. The pope claimed that Origen's objective was to disintegrate the Christian faith, and virtually he anathematised Rufinus, the translator of Origen's works rather than Origen as an author himself (although Origen himself did not escape condemnation, too). Why was that so? Because, amazingly, the same pope admitted that he had never read Origen's works, and, what is more, he had never heard of Origen – that is, the man he was convicting by that 'Letter'!

This was all about ecclesio-political intrigues rather than theology: the case was simply that this bishop of Rome was acting under the influence of Jerome and Marcella (an anti-Origenist friend of Jerome's) and wrote this letter just for the sake of satisfying Jerome's and Marcella's behests. In order to obtain the letter, Marcella had supplied the pope with a fraudulent edition of Rufinus translation of Origen's *De Principiis*, overfull with faked forgeries.[495]

Notwithstanding all of this vicious vilification, Anastasius was satisfied that Origen's condemnation was 'condemnation by the Church'!

This incident happened nearly one century after Pamphilus' death. It seems, however, that this was a practice which was earlier and favourite to Origen's detractors. Pamphilus knew of this, as his testimony reveals.

493 *commJohn*, I.20.119: ὁ Θεὸς μὲν οὖν πάντῃ ἕν ἐστι καὶ ἁπλοῦν.

494 *Cels*, IV.14: τὴν φυσικὴν ἔννοιαν τοῦ Θεοῦ ὡς πάντῃ ἀφθάρτου καὶ ἀσυνθέτου καὶ ἀδιαιρέτου.

495 On this incident, see Rufinus declaiming against Jerome, in his *Apology Against Jerome*, 1.19.

> Besides, it is possible to come upon the following [situation], namely, that there are such indicters that do not even know Greek; others are ignorant in every respect (omnimodis imperiti); some of them, even if they appear as having some experience, nevertheless it turns out that they did not care at all to deal with his books; or, if they happened to read them, they did not have such a sufficient education as to be able to grasp the height of his ideas (ut altitudinem sensus ejus)[496] and pay attention to those points which he used to consider from different points of view in accordance with the [specific scriptural] portions and the [specific scriptural] instance (quo ea quae ille diverso prospectu pro locis et causis disserere solet). You will find many who, if you ask them in which books or at which passages did he say those things of which they accuse him, they admit that they neither have knowledge of the issues they make claims about nor did they ever read them, but they heard others talking about them. Consequently, everyone will believe that their opinion is ridiculous, since they pass judgements and condemn those things that they have been unable either to learn or familiarise themselves with in the first place (que nec discere quidem prius ac nosse potuerunt).[497]

I have not seen many modern scholars being as to lest this account should touch on themselves. The case is rather that too many of them relish discrediting the authenticity of Origen's thought whenever his texts happen to conform to their 'orthodoxy'. For example, Pierre Nautin alleged[498] that Rufinus' translation of the *Apology* by Pamphilus altered on the occasion of the Trinity – which however is blatantly groundless, all the more so since the same scholar admitted that this translation is faithful in other passages which can be compared with Greek fragments where the doctrine of the Trinity is not discussed. Nevertheless, the scholarly avocation taking pleasure in discrediting everything 'orthodox' contained in Origen's works has taken root since a long time ago, and uprooting this is a tough yet worthwhile proposition bound to destroy the insouciant nirvana of the vast majority of modern Origen scholars.

In view of such captious trifling against Origen, anyone can appreciate the value and authority of many condemnations passed against him. In reality, modern editions of the Latin *De Principiis* came to be a conspectus not of Origen's actual theology but of what any detractor fantasised this to be, or concocted as 'interpretation'. At all events, and for good or ill, the obscure initial text of that treatise will remain unknown for ever; scholars will be overly

496 Concerning Origen's concept of soul, this applies par excellence to his ancient and modern detractors alike: he declared that his own 'doctrine was more sublime (ὑψηλοτέρα θεωρία) which had nothing to do with Plato's transmigration' (*Cels*, IV.17). However, those who persist in branding him a Platonist also on this score, 'do not have such a sufficient education as to be able to grasp the height of his ideas'.

497 Pamphilus, *op. cit.* PG.17.546B-C.

498 Pierre Nautin, *Origène, Sa vie et son oeuvre*, Paris, 1977, pp. 150-152.

concerned with the extant text that has reached us – a text compiled from several sources, and at points heavily interpolated by both the arguments against the later so-called *Origenism* and by uninformed opponents.

How little had this 'Origenism' to do with Origen's real views is a question which still waits for a comprehensive argued answer; an answer which could be reached only as an upshot of a thorough research of his works extant in both Greek and Latin. As long as this task is not fulfilled, much room remains open to the current unschooled tragic historic bias against the authentic views of a brilliant pioneer of Christian thought.

Concerning the present topic, it is evident that is takes a suicidal jump to conclusion to assert that the points which Rufinus reformulated are those pertaining to the Trinity,[499] the extreme version of which (yet a cliché in the modern historical-critical mindset of theology) has been the claim that statements about 'the Trinity and the resurrection of the body are suspicious if they agree with the fourth-century church dogma'![500]

Hence, we are asked to believe modern uninformed scholars rather than Athanasius himself, who not only assured that Origen's theology was the same as the Nicene one, but also quoted Origen's phrase about the Son being co-eternal with the Father: οὐκ ἔστιν ὅτε οὐκ ἦν[501] – a formula which, as I have demonstrated, was one of the numerous loans that Origen took up from Alexander of Aphrodisias.[502]

Annie Jaubert rightly pointed out that the very fact that translations of Origen's homilies are concerned with edification rather than dogmatic controversies is exactly what makes them essentially reliable.[503] In her own words, 'La comparaison avec la *Philocalie* est donc très positive en faveur de Rufin'.[504] Anyway, even during his lifetime, Origen had been charged of heresy by forgers who tampered with his writings.[505] This is why, in *De Principiis*, 1.6.1, he warned

499 Thomas P. Scheck (tr.), *Origen, Commentary on the Epistle to the Romans, Books 1-5*, Washington, 2001, p. 19.

500 R. E. Heine, *Origen, Homilies on Genesis and Exodus*, Washington, 1981, p. 38.

501 Athanasius, *De Decretis Nicaenae Synodi*, 27.2 (Origen, *Fragmenta De Principiis*, fr. 33).

502 See *Anaxagoras*, pp. 991-992; cf. pp. 843; 890; 910; 1016. Cf. Simplicius, *commPhys*, p. 1169: ὅτι ἀγένητός ἐστιν ἡ κίνησις καὶ οὐκ ἦν ὅτε οὐκ ἦν κίνησις καὶ ὅτι οὐκ ἔσται ὅτε οὐκ ἔσται κίνησις. John Philoponus used the same blueprint exactly as Athanasius did quoting Origen (*De Aeternitate Mundi*, p. 24). Philoponus quoted Proclus having used this formula, too (*op. cit.* p. 103).

503 Annie Jaubert (ed. and trans.), *Origène: Homélies sur Josué*, Sources Chrétiennes, 71, Paris, 1960, p. 68.

504 *Op. cit.* p. 81.

505 Origen, *Homilies in Luke*, homily 25.6: "Others, however, criticise our homilies unfairly and reproach us with holding positions that we never knew we held." *Homilies on Genesis*

his readers that now (speaking 'On the End or Consummation') he did not set forth definitive doctrines but only subjects that call for discussion rather than for definition. By contrast, he declared that he made definitive statements only on the doctrine of the Trinity.

> Now we ourselves speak on these subjects with great fear and caution, discussing and investigating rather than laying down fixed and certain affirmations. For we have pointed out above[506] what are the subjects which clearly determined by the doctrine, which we have done to the best of our ability, when we spoke about the Trinity. Now, however, we are dealing, as a sort of exercise[507] with subjects in order to discuss rather than define them [as definitive doctrines].[508]

Once again, Gregory of Nyssa turns out to be the most faithful of Origen's admirers. He repeatedly set forth his thoughts 'for the sake of mental exercise' (γυμνασία)[509] and warned against 'guilefully' taking them as definitive views of his, all the more so he knew that there were several enemies that lay in wait in order to spread slander against him.[510]

(Latin), homily 13.3: "I am indeed digging wells. However, those who love the letter will forthwith stir up malicious accusations against me and will lie in wait for me. They will contrive hostilities straight off and shall cause persecutions, because they refuse to accept that truth can stand except upon earth." Likewise, in *op. cit.* 7.2; *homJer*, homily 16.1. Cf. Origen's fragment on the Epistle to Titus PG.14.1306. See also, Pamphilus, *op. cit.* PG.17.539-540 (Introduction); quoted *supra*, p. CXIII and note 454. Cf. Jerome, *Epistulae*, 62.2; 84.10.

506 See *Princ*, I.1-4.

507 This should have been Origen's favourite term γυμνασία.

508 *Princ*, I.6.1 ('On the End or Consummation').

509 Gregory of Nyssa, *In Christi Resurrectionem oratio i*, p. 286: οὐ γὰρ ἀπόφασις ὁ λόγος ἐστίν, ἀλλὰ γυμνασία καὶ ζήτησις. *De Opificio Hominis*, PG.44.185.11-15: Ἡμεῖς δέ, καθὼς ἔστι δυνατόν, διὰ στοχασμῶν τινων καὶ εἰκόνων φαντασθέντες τὴν ἀλήθειαν, τὸ ἐπὶ νοῦν ἐλθὸν οὐκ ἀποφαντικῶς ἐκτιθέμεθα, ἀλλ' ὡς ἐν γυμνασίας εἴδει τοῖς εὐγνώμοσι τῶν ἀκροωμένων προσθήσομεν. Cf. *In Ecclesiasten*, p. 318.

510 Gregory of Nyssa, *Ad Graecos ex Communibus Notionibus*, p. 28: καὶ τοὺς ἀκροωμένους, ὡς ἔγωγε φαίην ἄν, φιλοπόνως γυμνάσαι παρορῶντες τὸ παρ' ἡμῶν λελεγμένον καὶ τὸ μὴ δεδομένον ὡς ὁμολογούμενον λαμβάνοντες παραλογισμῷ τε χρώμενοι τὸ δοκοῦν κατασκευάζουσι. *Dialogus De Anima et Resurrectione*, PG.46.57.39-42: ὁ δὲ δὴ περὶ τούτων λόγος ἡμῖν ὡς ἐν γυμνασίῳ προκείσθω, ὡς ἂν διαφύγοι τῶν συκοφαντικῶς ἀκουόντων τὰς ἐπηρείας. *Apologia in Hexaemeron*, p. 68: τὰ δὲ ἡμέτερα ὡς ἐν γυμνασίῳ τινὶ σχολαστικῶς ἐπιχειρούμενα τοῖς ἐντυγχάνουσι προκείσθω, μηδεμιᾶς μηδενὶ διὰ τούτων βλάβης προσγινομένης εἴτι παρὰ τὴν κοινὴν ὑπόληψιν ἐν τοῖς λεγομένοις εὑρίσκοιτο. Οὐ γὰρ δόγμα τὸν λόγον ποιούμεθα, ὥστε ἀφορμὴν δοῦναι τοῖς διαβάλλουσιν, ἀλλ' ὁμολογοῦμεν ἐγγυμνάζειν μόνον ἑαυτῶν τὴν διάνοιαν τοῖς προκείμενοις νοήμασιν, οὐ διδασκαλίαν ἐξηγητικὴν τοῖς ἐφεξῆς ἀποτίθεσθαι. Gennadius Scholarius quoted this telling passage as one of the numerous ones he compiled from several authors. This anthology aimed to show that sometimes Fathers of the Church expounded their ideas tentatively and for the sake of mental exercise, which would

Now, although it was Origen himself who had rejected attacks based on falsification of his works, there is a current persistent stubbornness to brand everything 'an interpolation by Rufinus'. This first paragraph of *Princ*, I.6.1 has been dismissed by Franz Heinrich Kettler as 'interpolation by Rufinus'[511] while overlooking the fact that Origen himself repeatedly denounced falsification of his thought long before Rufinus. As it happens, Kettler (just like so many others) ignored Athanasius' statement who appealed to the orthodoxy of Origen's definitive statements while caveating that other ones that were set forth only as 'exercise' should not be read as his definitive views.[512]

It all began with Rufinus' honest statement that, in his translation of *De Principiis*, he altered some points in order to make them familiar to his Latin audience, plus his conviction about the (all too evident!) fact that Origen's texts had been tampered with by his opponents.[513] Rufinus' prefaces are truthful and trustworthy reports of how he worked in each case – but scholars have made this a banner. However, wherever Rufinus thought that heretics had tampered with the Greek text, he said so and he did not hide his intention to eliminate what he thought to be malicious distortions.[514] Against this, the modern obsession is that Rufinus altered Origen's expressed views so as to deceive his audience. However, I do not see why he should not be given the credit of honesty in making the statements he made in each of his prefaces. It is good, nevertheless, that there are studies by unbiased scholars who have argued that some of Rufinus' points were paraphrastic, but they saw that the changes were made for the sake of clarity and the import of the text remained faithful to the Greek.[515]

---

appear as views deviating from the official dogma. *Tractatus de Processu Spiritus Sancti ii*, Part 1, p. 284; *Tractatus de Processu Spiritus Sancti iii*, p. 484.

511 Franz Heinrich Kettler, *Der ursprüngliche Sinn der Dogmatik des Origenes*, Berlin, 1966, pp. 33-39.

512 Athanasius, *Epistula ad Afros Episcopos*, PG.26.1040.27–38; *De Decretis Nicaenae Synodi*, 27.1. See both of these quoted *supra*, note 355.

513 In his *Apology against Jerome*, and in his *Book on the Adulteration of Origen's Writings*, Rufinus expresses his conviction that heretics have falsified some passages in Origen's works. In the Preface to the *Commentary on the Epistle to the Romans*, Rufinus tells us that Origen's works had been 'interpolated'. So he does in the Preface to *De Principiis*.

514 Rufinus, *Liber De Adulteratione Librorum Origenis; Praefatio ad Heraclium; Praefatio De Principiis* 1.3.

515 Cf. Monica Wagner, *Rufinus the Translator. A Study of His Theory and Practice as Illustrated in His Version of the Apologetica of St. Gregory Nazianzen*, Washington DC, 1945, p. 11; cf. pp. 29; 35; 98. J. E. L. Oulton, "Rufinus's Translation of the Church History of Eusebius", *Journal of Theological Studies*, 30, 1929, p. 157. Also, Annie Jaubert, *op. cit.* pp. 81-82.

Moreover, it has turned out that points which caused 'suspicion' to more or less the same 'suspicious' scholars were not in fact expansions by Rufinus: instead, fragments that were discovered later demonstrated that extracts and fragments preserved in the *Philocalia* and Procopius' *Catena on the Octateuch* had been thought to be trustworthy only because they were highly compressed. Hence, the case was *compression* by Origen's anthologisers rather than *expansion* by Rufinus.

This analysis is far from exhausting Origen's use of *homoousion*, far less his Trinitarian theology, which hopefully I will present in another work. It is only a short reply to the obstinacy of several fast and furious scholars who cannot stomach the fact that Origen was the real predecessor of Nicaea – and let Athanasius, Origen's works themselves, and stubborn facts persist in annoying them and pressing to the opposite direction.

I should, therefore, just remind of analyses made in previous works of mine: to Origen, there are three clear and distinct ontological levels – the corporeal, the created incorporeals (the logoi / causes that comprise the Body of Logos), and the Holy Trinity. There is no room for introducing a *fourth* ontological status, which should make either the Second or the Third, or both, Trinitarian Persons belong to that. Beyond searching for passages and seeking to reveal 'crooks' such as the 'devious' Rufinus, who allegedly interpolated them so as to hoax us and exonerate Origen, we should point out the fundamental *sine qua non* reasons on account of which Origen could have not thought otherwise. For example, if (contrary to facts, texts, and trustworthy witnesses) it were claimed (as indeed it is) that his Trinity is not *homoousios*, the least one should expect would be an explanation of how could it be possible for Origen's Trinity to be postulated as 'absolutely one and simple Trinity'.

However, to Origen, any ontological differentiation within the Trinity is simply unthinkable since his theology allows no room whatsoever for a fourth ontological level, this time within the Trinity. This is exactly what the present codex reveals, and, what is more, now we see this sustained by means of impeccable philosophical argument.

Origen went to great lengths in order to demonstrate the inscrutable idea that God is both simple Oneness[516] and yet Three Hypostatic Persons,[517] and

516 *commJohn*, I.20.119.

517 Origen maintained this fundamental doctrine ever since he converted to Christianity, because monotheism was the gist of his earlier Anaxagorean convictions. Cf. *Princ*, I.2.8 (interpreting Phil. 2:6-7): 'It is by such likeness as this that the Son, in emptying himself of his equality with the Father, and showing to us a way by which we may know him, becomes an *express image* of God's substance [Heb. 1:3]; so that, through this fact of his becoming to us the brightness, we who were not able to look at the glory of pure light while

that the Trinitarian ontology is all but a process of demultiplication and fragmentation of the divine unity. His stress on God being 'altogether one and simple' (ὁ θεὸς πάντῃ ἕν ἐστι καὶ ἁπλοῦν),[518] coupled with statements such as, God is 'simple, invisible, and incorporeal,[519] was applied to God as *Nous*, whereas Neoplatonists reserved absolute simplicity for the One standing above the Nous.[520] Origen dismissed this classification as fanciful: there is nothing above the Nous / God, a claim at which Proclus declared himself astonished.[521] Given this, how could it be possible for Origen's God to be 'absolutely simple oneness' and yet to comprise three Persons of *different* ontological order? No author other than Origen could have embraced more willingly scriptural statements such as 'I and the Father are one',[522] and 'That they may be one, even as we are one',[523] and 'The Father is in me, and I in the Father',[524] and to read these in terms of the Father's essence being one and the same as the Son's.[525]

Not only did Origen apply the expression 'God is altogether one and simple' (πάντῃ ἓν καὶ ἁπλοῦν)[526] to this Nous; he also reprimanded the Stoics who did not manage to apprehend God as being 'simple, invisible, and incorporeal',[527]

---

it remained in the greatness of his godhead, may find a way of beholding the divine light through looking at the brightness. … witness the words which he said to his disciples." Subsequently, he quotes John, 14:9, 10:30, and 10:38. *Op. cit.* I.2.10: "the omnipotence of the Father and the Son is one and the same." *Op. cit.* I.2.13: "Nor has the goodness that is in him [sc. in the Son] any dissimilarity or divergence from that of the Father."

518 *commJohn*, I.20.119. Little wonder that Origen made this statement upon his conversion to Christianity. Likewise, Gregory of Nyssa, *Antirrheticus Adversus Apollinarium*, p. 133: "By its nature, Deity is simple and incomposite" (ἁπλοῦν γὰρ τῇ φύσει τὸ θεῖον). See the same in *Contra Eunomium*, 2.1.25; 2.1.27; *Orationes viii De Beatitudinibus*, PG.44.1289.52. So Theodoret, *Curatio*, 5.51; *De Incarnatione Domini*, PG.75.1432.20-21. *Et. al.*

519 *Cels*, VII.38.

520 *Enneades*, V.3.11(26-27); V.3.13(16-17); V.9.14(1-3). Proclus, *commTim*, v. 1, p. 384; v. 3, p. 211. Damascius, *Princ*, pp. 37; 42; 47; 58-59; 65; 76; 79; 84; 90. Naturally, since the Nous comprises all the 'intelligible things' (τὰ νοητά), Damascius declared that 'unlike the One, the Nous is not simple' (*op. cit.* p. 25).

521 Proclus, *Theologia Platonica*, v. 2, p. 31.

522 John, 10:30. Cf. *Princ*, I.2.8; III.6.1; *commJohn*, XIII.36.228; XIX.2.6; *frLuc*, fr. 212; *Dial*, 4; *selGen*, PG.12.109.45-48; *Cels*, VIII.12.

523 John, 17:30. Cf. *Princ*, III.6.4.

524 John, 10:38. Cf. *Princ*, I.2.8; *Cels*, VIII.17; *frJohn*, fr. 7; *selPs*, PG.12.1241.45-47.

525 Cf. *Princ*, IV.4.3, speaking of the Son's deity during the Incarnation: "The reverent confession of piety" is not "supposing that there took place any separation whatever from the essence of the Father (et nulla penitus a paterna substantia facta putetur esse divulsio), which exists everywhere (que ubique est)."

526 *commJohn*, I.20.119; likewise, *Cels*, IV.14.

527 *Cels*, VII.38.

indeed 'entirely simple and incomposite and indivisible'.[528] Of all Presocratics, Anaxagoras was the first who propounded this doctrine in the selfsame terms.[529] Origen knew of course that both Plato[530] and Aristotle[531] had seized on Anaxagoras' cardinal idea (as well as on the term *Nous*), but he drew on the real source rather than on followers. The Neoplatonists reserved absolute simplicity for the One standing above the Nous,[532] which is 'one many' (ἓν πολλά) and was contrasted with the One for that matter.[533] Origen dismissed this classification as fanciful: there is nothing above the absolutely simple Nous / God, for which Proclus declared himself perplexed and flabbergasted: of all the 'exegetes of Plato', he cited only Origen and argued that, although he was an outstanding intellectual (καὶ διαφερόντως Ὠριγένην), his view that posited the Nous as the Supreme Principle could be the reason why 'Plato could have

528 *Op. cit.* IV.14 (ref. to the Stoics): "For they have not been able to grasp the natural concept of God (τὴν φυσικὴν τοῦ Θεοῦ ἔννοιαν) as being entirely incorruptible and simple and incomposite and indivisible (ὡς πάντῃ ἀφθάρτου καὶ ἁπλοῦ καὶ ἀσυνθέτου καὶ ἀδιαιρέτου)." The expression τὴν φυσικὴν ἔννοιαν is crucial: it means a concept formed in one's mind by means of *a priori* direct apprehension (also called πρόληψις), not cognition by means of cerebral process or following instruction by a teacher. See this explanation by Posidonius, *Fragmenta*, fr. 460, *apud* Diogenes Laertius, *Vitae*, 7.54. Later, the *Suda* attributed this to Chrysippus; letter pi, entry 2495. Likewise, Albinus, *Epitome Doctrinae Platonicae*, 4.6 & 4.8. Alexander of Aphrodisias, *De Mixtione*, p. 218. Themistius, *paraphrAnalPost*, p. 7. Simplicius, *commCateg*, p. 154. Likewise, Athenagoras of Athens, *De Resurrectione*, 14.1-2. Clement of Alexandria, *Stromateis*, 1.19.94.2. Basil of Caesarea, *Adversus Eunomium*, PG.29.513.45. Nemesius of Emesa, *De Natura Hominis*, chapter 13, p. 69. John of Damascus, *Expositio Fidei*, 34.

529 Themistius, *paraphrAnim*, p. 14: Ἀναξαγόρας … πάντῃ ἀμιγῆ καὶ ἁπλοῦν φησι εἶναι τὸν νοῦν. Likewise, Plotinus, *Enneades*, V.1.9.

530 Plato (acknowledging Anaxagoras as the origin of the notion), *Phaedo*, 97c-d; *Phaedrus*, 270a; *Cratylus*, 396c; 400a; 413c; *Philebus*, 30c-d; 58d; (as if the idea were his own); 59d; *Phaedo*, 98a; *Timaeus*, 39e; 47b; 47e; 48a; 51e; *Leges*, 714a; 897c; 898a; 966e; 967b.

531 Aristotle (ref. to Anaxagoras), *De Anima*, 404b; 405a-b; 429b; 430a; *Metaphysica*, 1065b; 1069b; 1072a; 1075b; 1091b; *Physica*, 203a; 256b; 265b; *Protrepticus*, fr. 110; (no ref. to Anaxagoras), *De Anima*, 407a-408b; 431b; 432a; *Ethica Eudemia*, 1217b; *Ethica Nicomachea*, 1096a; *Physica*, 198a; *Fragmenta Varia*, Category 1 (*apud De Anima*), fr. 38; Category 1 (*apud On Prayer*), fr. 49.

532 Plotinus, *Enneades*, V.3.11(26-27); V.3.13(16-17); V.9.14(1-3). Proclus, *commTim*, v. 1, p. 384; v. 3, p. 211. Damascius, *Princ*, pp. 1; 37; 42; 47; 58-59; 65; 76; 79; 84; 90.

533 Plotinus, *Enneades*, V.1.8; V.3.15; VI.2.9&10&15&17; VI.6.12&13; VI.7.14. Porphyry, *Sententiae*, sententia 43 (Stobaeus, *Anthologium*, 1.48.5). Proclus, *Theologia Platonica*, v. 1, p. 47; *In Platonis Parmenidem*, pp. 768; 930; 1089; *commTim*, v. 1, p. 305. Damascius, *Princ*, p. 7: οὐδὲ αὐτὸς ὁ νοῦς ἁπλοῦς, ὥστε πάντῃ ἄγνωστόν τε καὶ ἄρρητον τὸ ἕν. *Op. cit.* p. 37: πρὸ ταύτης ἄρα τὸ ἁπλοῦν καὶ πάντῃ ἀσύνθετον. *Op. cit.* p. 42: οἷον τὸ πάντα ἓν κατὰ τὸ πάντῃ ἁπλούστατον. *Op. cit.* p. 65: ἐκεῖνο δὲ πάντῃ ἁπλοῦν. *Op. cit.* p. 90: τὸ πάντῃ ἁπλούστατον καὶ πάντων ἐπέκεινα.

never included Origen among his pupils'.[534] Consequently, against inveterate verdicts, to Origen, use of the precarious (Gnostic) term *homoousios* with reference to the ontology of the Three Persons[535] was useful in order to adumbrate the inscrutable notion of the oneness of the threeness and yet unalloyed simplicity of Nous. This is why, to Origen, the generation of the Son is patently neither expansion nor division of the divine nature.

> He who saves is One; there is one salvation. He who lives is One, the Father, and the Son, and the Holy Spirit. He is one; He is not a fusion of the three, but [He is] one in essence. There are three Hypostases, which are perfect and appropriate in all respects. God begot in accordance with His own nature, which is why the one who was born is consubstantial (ὁμοούσιος).[536]

The Monad turned to Triad – and Origen's enthusiast Gregory of Nazianzus did not hesitate to state his master's proposition unqualifiedly and explicitly:

> This is why the Monad originally moved to Dyad and then it became a Trinity. This is what the Father and the Son and the Holy Spirit are to us (διὰ τοῦτο μονὰς ἀπ' ἀρχῆς εἰς δυάδα κινηθεῖσα, μέχρι τριάδος ἔστη. Καὶ τοῦτό ἐστιν ἡμῖν ὁ πατὴρ καὶ ὁ υἱὸς καὶ τὸ ἅγιον πνεῦμα).[537]

No doubt, this statement is precarious. Were it for Origen to have said this, he could have been excoriated as a Pythagorean, and the like (which he did not escape, anyway). But it was Gregory of Nazianzus who said so in his emblematic homily *On the Son* – which is why later authors quoted this abundantly, confidently, and fearlessly. However, it should be noticed that no author did ever dare to use Nazianzen's statement *prior* to the end of the seventh century – whereas, afterwards, all of them cared to cite Gregory's name.[538] It is telling

534 Proclus, *Theologia Platonica*, v. 2, p. 31.

535 Origen, *frMatt*, fr. 14 (Klostermann), columns 1 & 2; frs. 257; 572. *commMatt, Codex Sabaiticus 232*, folios 18v (bis: Son and Father; Three Persons); 94v (Three Persons); 194v (Son and Father); 195v (Three Persons); 240v (Three Persons). Athanasius (*De Decretis Nicaenae Synodi*, 33.13, quoted *supra* note 451) reported that he was 'aware of certain scholars and bishops of old that had used the term *homoousios* in reference to the theology of Father and Son', but no one paid attention to this acknowledgement. Of course, he had Origen in mind, too. At least, in the case of the Nicene shibboleth οὐκ ἦν ὅτε οὐκ ἦν, he cited Origen by name as the Source of this.

536 Origen, *schMatt*, PG.17.309.42-52 (on Matt. 28:19); also, *frMatt* (Klostermann), fr. 572; also, in *Codex Sabaiticus 232*, folio 239v.

537 Gregory of Nazianzus, *De Filio* (*orat.* 29), 2. Cf. *supra*, p. CIX.

538 See Maximus Confessor, *Epistula Secunda ad Thomam*, 1; *Ambigua ad Thomam*, 1; *Ambigua ad Joannem*, 23.1 7 23.4. John of Damascus, *Epistula De Hymno Trisagio*, 28. Michael Psellus, *Theologica*, opuscula 20; 27. John Italus, *Quaestiones Quodlibetales*, 69 (bis). Eustratius

that, when Photius reviewed Maximus Confessor's *Ambigua ad Thomam* (just cited), he cared to make reference to that 'Thomas' as the person who had been alarmed by Gregory's statement and asked Maximus for explanation and guidance. Maximus offered this by mentioning also another similar statement by Nazianzen about 'the Monad that moved because of its own prolificness' (Μονάδος κινηθείσης διὰ τὸ πλούσιον).[539] If one recalled the Neoplatonic 'effluence' (ἀπόρροια) upon reading this, hardly could one be blamed – I have argued several times for Nazianzen's Platonism, anyway.

Thus, the absolute monotheism of Anaxagoras and the Pythagorean Monad turned to Trinitarianism without compromising the unity of God as Nous. Pamphilus cast light on a matter which should have been grasped without second thoughts – and yet it was not. The Arians claimed that the Son was produced not from the Father's essence but from the Father's will.[540] However, never did Origen say anything of the kind. All he did was to struggle simply to adumbrate (not expound, which he deemed impossible) how the One Nous / God was Three. His main concern was to preclude any implication of 'division' of this Nous and his oneness. Thus, Pamphilus quoted Origen's words from *De Principiis* (first book, chapter two) in which the 'will' is just used as an example in his struggle to show that 'generation of the Son' does not entail division of the Father: this is *something like* 'the [human] will, which stems from the mind and yet it does not cut-off or divide the mind' (Magis ergo sicut voluntas procedit e mente, et neque partem aliquam mentis sacat, neque ab ea separatur aut divitur, tali quadam specie putandus est Patre filium ginuisse,

of Nicaea, *Orationes*, oration 6, p. 152. Andronicus Camaterus, *Sacrum Armamentarium*, 3.34. Nicolas of Methone, *Refutatio Institutionis Theologicae Procli*, Proem, lines 119-20; section 14, line 26. Jacob of Constantinople (monk, twelfth century), *De Fide*, lines 132-133. John Beccus, *In Andronici Camateri Animadversiones*, pp. 461; 516. George Acropolites, *In Gregorii Nazianzeni Sententias*, 3. John Cyparissiotes, *Expositio Materiaria*, 3.2; 8.1. Joseph Bryennius, *Orationes*, oration 1, lines 278-279. This author saw the precariousness of the statement and explained that, 'if anyone is embarrassed by this, one should know that by *Monad* Nazianzen did not mean any prior common 'divine essence', but the Father himself' (*op. cit.* lines 290 ff). Manuel Calecas, *De Essentia et Operatione*, column 425. Marcus Eugenicus, *Testimonia Spiritum Sanctum ex Patre Procedere Probantia*, testimonium 54.

539 Gregory of Nazianzus, *De Pace*, PG.35.1160.38-44. Maximus Confessor, *Ambigua ad Thomam*, 1; *Epistula Secunda ad Thomam*, 1; *Quaestiones et Dubia*, 105. Photius, *Bibliotheca*, Codex 194, p. 159a, and *op. cit.* Codex 222, p. 192a. Likewise, later authors, too.

540 Cf. Athanasius, *Oratio iii contra Arianos*, 59.1; 65.2-3; *De Synodis Arimini in Italia et Seleuciae in Isauria*, 42.1. Didymus, *frPs(al)*, fr. 1061. Maximus Confessor, *Ambigua ad Joannem*, 24.2-4. Cassian the Sabaite, *Scholia in Apocalypsin*, scholion XXVI (see my *Scholia*, pp. 145-147 & 313-319).

imaginem scilicet suam).[541] Moreover, Pamphilus quoted a passage 'from the second book of the commentary on John', in which the same analogy is used:

> Therefore, the Only-Begotten God and our Saviour is the only one who was born from the Father and is Son by nature, not by adoption. Nevertheless, he was born from the Father's mind itself, like [human] will stems from the mind (Unigenitus ergo Deus Salvator noster solus a Patre generatus, natura et non adoptione Filius est. Natus est autem ex ipsa Patris mente, sicut voluntas ex mente). For the divine nature (that is, the one of the ungenerated Father) is indivisible; consequently, we cannot think that the Son was born by means of division or subtraction of the essence of the Father.[542]

All of these should be read in the light of Origen's fundamental axioms, (1) the birth of the Son could not be compared with that of men or animals, which 'could be impious', and (2) 'there must be some exceptional process, to which we can find no comparison whatsoever, not merely in things, but even in thought and imagination, so that by its aid human thought could apprehend how the unbegotten God becomes Father of the only-begotten Son.'[543]

Origen was out for securing a notion of divine generation befitting the incorporeal nature of God; he had no reason to be concerned with making the Son born 'from the will of the Father' –which he never actually did or said. And yet Justinian decided that Origen believed that 'the Son was born from the will of the Father' (ὁ υἱὸς ἐκ θελήματος τοῦ πατρὸς γεννηθείς), and naturally this became one of the reasons for his official condemnation.[544] I should have thought that it was more precarious to stipulate that 'the Son *himself* is the will of the Father', which though became a usual theme among orthodox authors, starting with Gregory of Nyssa, and then Cyril of Alexandria.[545]

Origen has been blamed for *subordinationism*, even though his Anaxagorean premisses harmoniously compounded with the Biblical ones and *ab ovo* precluded, indeed fended off, such a line of thinking. In fact, there was a stark disconnect between Origen's recurrent propositions and the pertinent stricture. The indictment stemmed from unawareness of his background, which

541 Pamphilus, *op. cit.* PG.17.582A-B. See *Princ*, I.2.6.

542 Pamphilus, *op. cit.* PG.17.583B-583C.

543 *Princ*, I.2.4; cf. Pamphilus, *op. cit.* PG.17.562C-563A.

544 Justinian, *Edictum contra Origenem*, p. 108; subsequently, this was copied and became part of synodical acts. ACO, *Synodus Constantinopolitana et Hierosolymitana anno 536*, tome 3, p. 209.

545 Gregory of Nyssa, *Contra Eunomium*, 2.1.216. Cyril of Alexandria, *In Joannem*, v. 1, pp. 294-295; *Thesaurus De Sancta Consubstantiali Trinitate*, PG.75.92.7-17; also in the *Catena in Joannem* (Cramer), p. 223. ACO, *Concilium universale Constantinopolitanum tertium (680-681)*, Document 9, pp. 272; Document 10, p. 320.

owed much to the Anaxagorean philosophy. It was because of this that his Trinitarian concept was diametrical to Plotinus' ontologically classified pattern, which Origen regarded as untenable, for which Proclus found fault with Origen.[546] Damascius in effect demolished the Plotinian pattern much later.[547] This was a seismic shift that could have reformed the course of Neoplatonism, but it was too late for this to make any impact in an era of persecution of Greeks by the State. Besides, there was a flood of commentaries on Plato by various commentators who either saw him through the eyes of Plotinus, or essayed to reconcile Plato with Aristotle by arguing that the two masters did not really dissent from each other *au fond*. However, although modern times dignified Plotinus as the 'founder of Neoplatonism', hardly did the *Enneads* receive *ad hoc* commentaries.[548] For ancient scholiasts mostly saw Plotinus in the way he had seen himself, namely, as a mere follower of Plato.[549]

Origen could have never entertained an idea of vertical ontological classification of the Supreme Principle, since the crux of his ontology was the monotheism of Anaxagoras,[550] and the absolute simplicity of the Trinity.[551] I have argued several times, and hopefully shown, that he was the real and incisive

---

546 Proclus, *Theologia Platonica*, v. 2, p. 31.

547 See *Anaxagoras*, pp. 732; 817-823; 996-997; 1093-1094.

548 It seems that it was only Proclus who did so. See testimonies by (Pseudo-?) Palchus, an Egyptian astrologer (fifth-sixth century), *Dodecaeteris Chaldaica*, p. 189, and Pseudo-David of Alexandria, *In Porphyrii Isagogen*, Praxis 12, p. 15. Stobaeus commented only on a passage from that work; *Anthologium*, 1.49.35&37. According to Proclus, Iamblichus accused Porphyry of virtually having contravened the thought of Plotinus. *commTim*, v. 1, p. 307. A later scribe of Iamblichus' *De Mysteriis* wrote that 'Proclus, in his commentary on Plotinus' *Enneads*, wrote that Porphyry's addressee [of the *Epistle to Anebo*] was in fact Iamblichus'. Iamblichus, *De Mysteriis*, Prologue, section 1.

549 Stobaeus saw Plotinus as merely one 'of the Platonists'. *Anthologium*, 1.49: 32; 35; 37; 38; 39; 40; 41; 43; 65; 67. Likewise, Dexippus, *commCateg*, p. 5. Proclus, *commTim*, v. 2, p. 88. Simplicius, *commCateg*, p. 284. John Philoponus, *De Aeternitate Mundi*, p. 481. Of Christians, Socrates Scholasticus, *HE*, 7.15. George Syncellus, *Ecloga Chronographica*, p. 443. Michael Psellus, *Theologica*, opusculum 79. Nicephorus Callistus Xanthopulus, *HE*, 14.16. Bessarion, *In Calumniatorem Platonis*, 2.5.6; 2.6.17. In the acts of Christian synods, Plotinus' name was never honoured with any deprecatory reference.

550 *Princ*, I.1.6: God is 'a nature simple which is sheer mind' (natura illa simplex et tota mens). *commJohn*, I.20.119: "God is altogether one and simple" (Ὁ θεὸς μὲν οὖν πάντῃ ἕν ἐστι καὶ ἁπλοῦν). *Op. cit.* I.3.7: "The power of the Trinity is one and the same. ... there is no separation in the Trinity". *Op. cit.* I.4.2: "This blessed and ruling power, therefore, that is, the power that exercises control of all things, we call the Trinity". *Cels*, IV.14: "The Stoics have been unable to demonstrate the natural concept of God as being altogether indestructible and simple and incomposite and indivisible" (τὴν φυσικὴν ἔννοιαν τοῦ Θεοῦ ὡς πάντῃ ἀφθάρτου καὶ ἁπλοῦ καὶ ἀσυνθέτου καὶ ἀδιαιρέτου). *Op. cit.* VII.38: God 'is simple'.

551 *commJohn*, I.20.119; see discussion forthwith.

predecessor of the doctrine of Nicaea. Concerning the Trinitarian theory and terminology, I did not rest the case too much by such references as those of Athanasius who assured that the Nicene Fathers took up the term *homoousios* 'from bishops and scholars of old', or reported that Origen maintained that 'the Son co-exists with the Father beginninglessly' and 'the Son does not differ from the Father in terms of essence' (μὴ ἑτέρας οὐσίας), as well as that it was Origen who introduced the proverbial catchphrase, 'there was not when the Son was not' (οὐκ ἦν ὅτε οὐκ ἦν).[552] Nor did I appeal too much to Origen's texts in which either the term *homoousios* is used,[553] or it is stated that the Father and the Son are 'of one essence' or 'of the same essence'.[554] Rather, I have called attention to his fundamental concept of the Trinity: Origen employed Anaxagoras' innovative concept of God as *Nous*,[555] but he went beyond that: this Nous is absolute unity and yet three hypostatic persons; accordingly, this threeness is sheer oneness,[556] which is why he styled *nous* either the Trinity *in toto* or each one of the Trinitarian Persons.[557]

Origen converted to Christianity when he was almost fifty years of age. Up to that time, his conception of God was plain and altogether Anaxagorean: God is but *Nous*. Once he was 'convinced and believed'[558] in the new religion, his

---

552 Athanasius, *De Decretis Nicaenae Synodi*, 27.1. I have perused the origins of this phrase in my *Anaxagoras* and shown that Origen took up this turn from Alexander of Aphrodisias and applied it to an entirely different (i.e. theological) context.

553 *frMatt*, frs. 14; 257; 572 (Klostermann); *schMatt*, PG.17.309.37-53.

554 *frMatt*, frs. 244; 572 (Klostermann); *commJohn*, II.2.16; X.37.246; XX.18.157; *frJohn*, fr. 9.

555 *Princ*, I.1.6: "God ... is ... the mind and fount from which originates all intellectual existence and mind. *Cels*, IV.54: God is 'the Supreme Mind' and the 'Nous'. *Op. cit.* VII.38: God is 'Nous'.

556 *commJohn*, I.20.119: "God is altogether one and simple". *Princ*, I.1.6: "God ... is a simple intellectual existence ... simple and wholly mental existence ... the simplicity of its divine nature". *Op. cit.* I.3.7: "The power of the Trinity is one and the same. ... there is no separation in the Trinity". *Op. cit.* I.4.2: "This blessed and ruling power, therefore, that is, the power that exercises control of all things, we call the Trinity. *Cels*, IV.14: God is 'simple and incomposite and indivisible'. *Op. cit.* VII.38: God 'is simple. *Op. cit.* VIII.38: God 'is the creator and father of each and every mind."

557 *Princ*, I.1.6; I.1.7; *Cels*, IV.54 ('the Supreme Nous' created everything, and all qualities were bestowed on matter by 'a certain Perfect Nous').

558 The opening of the lost Greek original of *De Principiis* started with the phrase, 'Those who have believed and been convinced' (οἱ πεπιστευκότες καὶ πεπεισμένοι). See Eusebius, *Contra Marcellum*, 1.4.26 (attested by Marcellus, *Fragmenta*, fr. 88). Origen converted to Christianity when he was nearly fifty years of age, because he 'was convinced and believed'. He was not born a Christian: he was 'a Greek who had been educated in the Greek letters' (Ἕλλην ἐν Ἕλλησιν παιδευθεὶς λόγοις); Porphyry, *Contra Christianos*, fr. 39, *apud* Eusebius, *HE*, 6.19.7 (copied by Nicephorus Callistus Xanthopulus, *HE*, 5.13).

primary concern was to understand and then render how was it that the One and simple and indivisible Nous was also Three.

Therefore, since 'God is absolutely one and simple', how could it be possible for him also to maintain that there is an ontological classification of the Persons of this absolute unity?

Once again, he was not as schizophrenic as to maintain both Subordinationism and advance the theory of *homoousios* Trinity at the same time. Quite simply, following the formula of Heb. 1:3 (the Son is 'image of the Father's being'), he explained that the Logos is the true God equal with the Father[559] and through the Son and the Holy Spirit the *ad extra* manifestation of God is realised.[560]

---

559 See *Codex Sabaiticus 232*, folio 119r: καίπερ ἐπὶ τῶν ἄλλων σημείων αὐθεντικῶς ποιῶν ὡς ἴσος ὢν τῶ πατρί, ἵνα πείσῃ τοὺς ὄχλους ὅτι ἐκ τοῦ πατρὸς ἦν. *Op. cit.* 131v: ‹Εἰ› ο‹ὖ›ν φιλεῖται παρ᾽ ἐμοῦ, μὴ φοβοῦ τὸ πάθος· ἴσος γάρ μου ἐστί. *Op. cit.* folio 91v: Ἐπειδὴ δὲ ἄνω ἐπὶ τοῦ Πατρὸς ἔταξε τὸ τῆς ἀποκαλύψεως, νῦν τῷ Υἱῷ αὐτὸ προσάπτει, ἵνα γνῶμεν ὅτι κοινὰ τὰ τῆς θεότητος. Διὰ γὰρ τούτου καὶ τοῦ ἀκαταλήπτου δηλοῦνται αὐτῶν αἱ ἰσότητες. Cf. Origen, *frMatt*, fr. 362 (Klostermann): οὐ γὰρ ἐπειδὴ ἐγέννησε μόνον φιλεῖ, ἀλλ᾽ ἐπειδὴ ἴσος αὐτῷ καὶ ὁμογνώμων κατὰ πάντα. *Princ*, I.2.6: "It is by such likeness as this that the Son, in *emptying himself of his equality with the Father* [Phil. 2:7], and showing to us a way by which we may know him, becomes *an express image of God's being* [Col. 1:15; cf. Heb. 1:3]".

560 Cf. Origen, *Princ*, I.2.3 (styling the Father by means of the Anaxagorean term *Nous*): the Logos and Wisdom 'is an interpreter of the secrets of Nous'. *Op. cit.* I.2.6: the Logos is a 'mediator', who 'makes God understood and known'. Further (*op. cit.* I.2.8) using the example of 'statues', he explains that the Logos is the true God through whom the *ad extra* manifestation of God is realised. *commMatth*, 19.68: νῦν μὲν γάρ, κἂν ἀξιωθῶμεν βλέπειν τὸν θεὸν τῷ νῷ καὶ τῇ καρδίᾳ, οὐ βλέπομεν *αὐτὸν καθώς ἐστιν* ἀλλὰ καθὼς διὰ τὴν ἡμετέραν οἰκονομίαν ἡμῖν γίνεται. ἐπὶ δὲ τέλει τῶν πραγμάτων καὶ τῆς *ἀποκαταστάσεως πάντων ὧν ἐλάλησε διὰ στόματος τῶν ἁγίων ἐξ αἰῶνος προφητῶν αὐτοῦ* [Acts, 3:21], *ὀψόμεθα αὐτόν*, οὐχ ὡς νῦν, ὃ οὐκ ἔστιν, ἀλλ᾽ *ὡς* πρέπει τότε, *ὅ ἐστιν* [1 John, 3:2]. *frPs*, on Psalm 20:7: πρόσωπον δὲ Θεοῦ, *ὁ χαρακτὴρ τῆς ὑποστάσεως* αὐτοῦ. [Heb. 1:3]. *selPs*, PG.12.1296.37-39: τὸ πρόσωπον τοῦ Θεοῦ οἱ λόγοι εἰσὶ τῶν ἐπὶ γῆς, οἱ χαρακτηρίζοντες τὸν δημιουργικὸν αὐτοῦ λόγον. *Op. cit.* PG.12.1424.11-13: Τὸν γὰρ Σωτῆρά φησι χεῖρα, δεξιάν, βραχίονα καὶ φωτισμόν. Πρόσωπον δὲ Πατρός, ὡς χαρακτὴρ ὑποστάσεως αὐτοῦ. *Op. cit.* PG.12.1600.16-17: Πρόσωπον Θεοῦ ὁ χαρακτὴρ τῆς ὑποστάσεως αὐτοῦ, ὡς πολλάκις εἴρηται. See the same idea recurring in Didymus, *Commentarii in Psalmos 29-34*, codex p. 149; *Commentarii in Ecclesiasten* (*3-4.12*), codex p. 89; *frPs*(*al*), frs. 21; 98; 167; 676a; 887; 922; 1001; 1101; 1227. Cf. Basil of Caesarea drawing on Origen. *Epistulae*, epistle 38.8: εἰκόνα τοῦ Θεοῦ τοῦ ἀοράτου καὶ τῆς ἀγαθότητος αὐτοῦ πάλιν εἰκόνα φησίν, οὐχὶ τῷ διαφέρειν τοῦ ἀρχετύπου τὴν εἰκόνα κατὰ τὸν τῆς ἀορασίας καὶ τῆς ἀγαθότητος λόγον, ἀλλ᾽ ἵνα δειχθῇ ὅτι ταὐτὸν τῷ πρωτοτύπῳ ἐστί, κἂν ἕτερον ᾖ. Οὐ γὰρ ἂν ὁ τῆς εἰκόνος διασωθείη λόγος, εἰ μὴ διὰ πάντων τὸ ἐναργὲς ἔχοι καὶ ἀπαράλλακτον. … Ὥστε ἡ τοῦ Υἱοῦ ὑπόστασις οἱονεὶ μορφὴ καὶ πρόσωπον γίνεται τῆς τοῦ Πατρὸς ἐπιγνώσεως, καὶ ἡ τοῦ Πατρὸς ὑπόστασις ἐν τῇ τοῦ Υἱοῦ μορφῇ ἐπιγινώσκεται, μενούσης αὐτοῖς τῆς ἐπιθεωρουμένης ἰδιότητος εἰς διάκρισιν ἐναργῆ τῶν ὑποστάσεων.

Further, the point is not simply about this or that term that Origen used: more importantly, the term *homoousios* was an inexorable corollary of his fundamental premisses, even though portions of the New Testament[561] could give the superficial impression of Subordinationism.[562] Moreover, since the Trinity has one energy,[563] it is necessary that the Trinitarian Persons should be ontologically equal.[564]

Alongside the notion of being 'simple', Origen had also a clear grasp of what 'to be composite' meant: once something is composite, there is no way for this to be either 'simple' or 'one' (τὰ σύνθετα μὴ οἷόν τε ἐξ ἑνὸς τὴν σύστασιν ἔχειν); for the very notion of being '*composite* suggests that this is a mixture of simple components' (τὸ γὰρ σύνθετον ἁπλῶν τινων μῖξιν μηνύει ... τὰ σύνθετα ἐξ ἁπλῶν τὴν σύστασιν ἔχει).[565]

Any composite entity is patently in need of a superior factor that should hold the components together. For example, since 'the composite man' (σύνθετος ἄνθρωπος) comprises body, soul, and spirit (or mind), it is the spirit that holds the entity 'man' together.[566] Were it for the Trinity to be 'composite', this could entail that there should be something *superior* to the Trinity, which would keep the Three together.[567] To any Christian, and to Origen par excellence, this could have been utter folly to suggest.

561 Matthew 19.17; Mark, 10:18; Luke, 18:19.

562 Cf. Origen, *commMatt.* 15.10.

563 Cf. Origen, *selNum*, PG.12.576.22-23: Ἓν γὰρ ἐν Χριστῷ τὸ Πνεῦμα καὶ μία διὰ πάντων ἡ ἐνέργεια.

564 There is a quotation in the acts of the *Concilium Universale Constantinopolitanum Tertium (680-681)*, p. 848, attributed 'to Basil, from his *Contra Eunomium*': τῶν ἑτερογενῶν οὐκ ἔστιν ἐνέργεια μία. In other words, if the Trinitarian Persons are not ontologically equal, it would follow that the Trinitarian action would not be *one*. This quotation attributed to Basil is not found in his extant diatribe against Eunomius.

565 Origen, *Philocalia*, 20.8. Eusebius wrote that he found this in a certain Maximus. *Praeparatio Evangelica*, 7.22.57. But Eusebius could have taken this up from Methodius of Olympus' *On Free Will* (whom he did not feel like citing, anyway), which Methodius could have copied from Origen, for which see Photius, *Bibliotheca*, Codex 236, p. 304b. Ultimately, this is an analysis that Aristotle had made in his *De Coloribus*, 792a. See a relevant analysis using the selfsame locution in Pseudo-Alexander of Aphrodisias, *Ἀπορίαι καὶ Λύσεις*, p. 64.

566 Cf. Origen, *homPs*, homily 23.2: σύνθετοι μέν ἐσμεν ἐκ πνεύματος καὶ ψυχῆς καὶ σώματος. σύνθετοι δὲ ὄντες δέον κρατεῖσθαι ἡμᾶς ὑπὸ τοῦ κρείττονος πνεύματος. Cf. *deOr*, 14.5: τοῦ πνεύματος ὡς κρείττονος ὄντος. *commICor*, fr. 10: ἀλλ' ἔδει γενέσθαι κρεῖττον ἐν ἡμῖν πνεῦμα. So in *op. cit.* fr. 24.

567 Gennadius Scholarius, *Epitome Primae Partis Summae Theologicae Thomae Aquinae*, 1.3. Gennadius using Origen's formula wrote of God, πάντῃ ἁπλοῦς ἐστιν. Furthermore, he explained that 'any composite is posterior to its components; any composite stems from a certain cause which causes its different components to come together; always, any

Furthermore, once the notion of God being 'a whole consisted of parts' is banned,[568] how could it be possible for God to be both 'absolutely one and simple' (πάντῃ ἓν καὶ ἁπλοῦν)[569] and yet to comprise three components (Trinitarian Persons) belonging to different ontological orders? Consequently, to Origen, use of the precarious term *homoousios* with reference to the ontology of the Three Persons[570] was serviceable in order to adumbrate the inscrutable notion of the *oneness* of the *threeness* and yet unalloyed *simplicity* of the Nous being Trinity.

One of the reasons why the present codex is particularly important is that we find for the first time exposition arguing exactly for this: a simple entity such as the Deity could not comprise components which are ontologically irrelevant, i.e. of different ontological orders.[571] Once the notion of God being

---

composite exists first potentially, then actually; and any composite cannot be predicated by means of any of its components.'

568 *Cels*, I.23: πάντα γὰρ μέρη κόσμου, οὐδὲν δὲ μέρος ὅλου θεός. … Τάχα δὲ βαθύτερος λόγος δείξει ὅτι κυρίως θεὸς ὥσπερ οὐκ ἔστι μέρος οὕτως οὐδὲ ὅλον, ἐπεὶ τὸ ὅλον ἐκ μερῶν ἐστι. καὶ οὐχ αἱρεῖ λόγος παραδέξασθαι τὸν ἐπὶ πᾶσι θεὸν εἶναι ἐκ μερῶν, ὧν ἕκαστον οὐ δύναται ὅπερ τὰ ἄλλα μέρη. To be sure, Origen was well aware of Plato's analyses in *Theaetetus* (from which he quoted in *Cels*, IV.62), especially 204b-205e, treating the difference between 'the whole' (τὸ ὅλον) and 'the all' (τὸ πᾶν). Cf. Neoplatonists building on this. Proclus, *Theologia Platonica*, v. 3, p. 71; *Institutio Theologica*, 69; 74. Damascius, *Princ*, pp. 116; 120; 140; 146. Cf. Michael Psellus, *Theologica*, opusculum 11 (considering the nature of Christ, and yet appealing to Porphyry in relation to the issue of 'whole' and 'parts'), lines 126-141.

569 *commJohn*, I.20.119.

570 *frMatt*, fr. 14 (Klostermann), columns 1 & 2; frs. 257; 572; also, *Codex Sabaiticus 232*, folios 18v (bis: Son and Father; Three Persons); 94v (Three Persons); 194v (Son and Father); 195v (Three Persons); 240v (Three Persons). See *supra*, note 525.

571 Origen, in *Codex Sabaiticus 232*, folio 240r: Ἀδύνατον δὲ τὸν κατὰ μίαν ἐνέργειαν γινόμενον ἁγιασμὸν ἐκ διαφόρων καὶ ἀσυναρτήτων οὐσιῶν ἐπιτελεῖσθαι. *Op. cit.* folio 240r: Ἀσεβὲς γὰρ τὸ τὰ ἑτεροφυῆ καὶ ἀσύναπτα μιᾷ τῇ ἐνεργείᾳ περιλαβεῖν. This became a cardinal doctrine. See Athanasius, *Epistulae Quattuor ad Serapionem*, epistle 1.31.1. Basil of Caesarea, *Adversus Eunomium*, PG.29.713.14-15. Theodoret, *Interpretatio in Psalmos*, PG.80.1684.32-33 (see the same text in Pseudo-John Chrysostom, *In Psalmos 101-107*, PG.55.640.69). Procopius of Gaza, *Commentarii in Genesim*, 2.3. John of Damascus, *Contra Nestorianos*, 21; *Expositio Fidei*, 59. John Cyparissiotes, *Contra Tomum Palamiticum*, 6.12. See also Origen's argument expounded by the newly discovered moderate Origenist Cassian the Sabaite (c. 475-20 July, 548) (Pseudo-Didymus), *De Trinitate*, PG.39.601.12-15: Καὶ διὰ τοῦτο ἓν θέλημα καὶ μίαν ἐξουσίαν καὶ δύναμιν τῆς Τριάδος εἶναι λέγομεν. Ὧν δὲ θέλησις καὶ ἐξουσία καὶ ἐνέργεια μία, ἄρα μία καὶ ἡ Θεότης. Cyril of Alexandria, *Thesaurus De Sancta Consubstantiali Trinitate*, PG.75.105.22-23: Τὰ ἑτερογενῆ τε καὶ ἑτεροφυῆ τὴν αὐτὴν ἐνέργειαν ἔχειν οὐκ ἄν τις δῴη σωφρονῶν. The same, in ACO, *Concilium Lateranense a. 649 celebratum*, Act 5, pp. 266 & 316; *Concilium Universale Constantinopolitanum Tertium (680-681)*, Document 19, p. 848. Also, in the *Doctrina Patrum*, p. 74. Meletius of Tiberiopolis, *De Natura Hominis*, p. 155. Photius, *Bibliotheca*, Codex 229, p. 261a (slightly paraphrased).

'a whole consisted of parts' is ruled out,[572] it is impossible for God to be both 'absolutely one and simple' (πάντῃ ἓν καὶ ἁπλοῦν)[573] and ontologically manifold Personal Subjects. This is a main reason that makes the notion of *homoousios* Trinity inexorable.

From this cardinal thesis he did not deviate a bit, while unremittingly sticking up for the idea that the generation of the Son is neither expansion nor division of the divine nature.[574] To him, the Son 'could not have remained God, unless he had bided in perpetual sight of the Father's depth' (καὶ οὐκ ἂν μείνας θεός, εἰ μὴ παρέμενε τῇ ἀδιαλείπτῳ θέᾳ τοῦ πατρικοῦ βάθους);[575] wherefore, the Father can be seen only through the Son,[576] which is a fundamental doctrine that he made one of the pillars of his theology.[577] In the teeth of all these, he has been fancifully attributed the notion that 'the Son cannot see the Father',[578] although he wrote exactly the opposite already during the period of his life at Alexandria.

It is for sure that the bishops of Nicaea did not have any clear conception of the word *homoousios*. They did not even know whether they used the word in the same sense as Origen did. Perhaps this is why some otherwise ardent anti-Arians were so wary in their use of the term. Did this term mean that Father and Son had all the characteristics of Godhead, whatever these are – which leads to two (or three) Gods? Did it mean (in a more Aristotelian fashion) that Father and Son were numerically one actual entity – which leads to modalism? This was feared much more, after a chief Nicene anti-Arian, Marcellus of

572 Origen, *Cels*, I.23; see *supra*, note 568.

573 *commJohn*, I.20.119.

574 *Princ*, I.2.6: "For it is not only the utmost impiety, but also the depth of folly, to entertain the slightest suspicion that such a thing would happen to an incorporeal being; nor is at all consistent with our intelligence to think that a physical division of an incorporeal being is possible." Likewise, *commJohn*, XX.18.157; *Princ*, IV.4.1.

575 *commJohn*, II.2.18; cf. XX.7.47; XX.18.157-158.

576 *commJohn*, XIX.6.35; XXI.7.47. Of course, he had in mind, and endorsed, John, 14:9.

577 See for example, *Cels*, VI.17: Ἀλλὰ καὶ ὁ σωτὴρ ἡμῶν καὶ κύριος λόγος τοῦ θεοῦ τὸ μέγεθος παριστὰς τῆς γνώσεως τοῦ πατρός, ὅτι κατ' ἀξίαν προηγουμένως αὐτῷ μόνῳ λαμβάνεται καὶ γινώσκεται.

578 Cf. Epiphanius of Salamis, *Panarion*, v. 2, p. 412; *Ancoratus*, 63.3; copied by John Zonaras, *Epitome Historiarum*, v. 3, p. 133. Ironically, this was a teaching by Arius (Athanasius, *Epistula ad Episcopos Aegypti et Libyae*, 12.10), for the rebuttal of which Origen's theology turned out the main weapon used by Athanasius and others. Despite these facts, defiant chroniclers had no problem with claiming that 'Arius took his cue from Origen'. George Monachus, *Chronicon*, p. 457, copied by Constantine Porphyrogenitus, *De Virtutibus et Vitiis*, v. 2, p. 139; *Suda*, letter omega, entry 183; and George Cedrenus, *Compendium Historiarum*, v. 1, p. 446.

Ancyra, turned out to be a modalist, which was a horror example for all those who did not have any clear grasp of *ὁμοούσιος* after Nicaea.

This demonstrates the magnitude of Origen's achievement in employing the precarious Gnostic term *ὁμοούσιος*. What he has not been given credit for is that he used his Trinitarian terminology in such a manner as to declare, on the one hand, that the Father, the Son and the Holy Spirit are *one*, without lapsing to modalism, while, on the other, to distinguish the Three Persons without classifying them to different ontological levels.

For Origen *homoousios* meant that whatever means to be God, the Son is. The Son is not a halfway being of the Late Antiquity religiosity sort; neither is he a mediator between time and timelessness; nor is he a personal saviour, a mediator of grace, or a semi-god of any kind. The Son is constitutive of God, not merely revelatory. The divinity of the Son is not seen as derived, because the essence of the Trinity is not to be found in any ontological level surpassing the hypostatic character of the three Persons (such as, for example, 'Deity'). To Origen, no matter what the 'essence' of God means, it is not the Trinity that is the essence of Deity, it is not Deity which is the essence of the Trinity. Essence is the relation of the Three Persons. God's Being is exactly the hypostatic character of the Three and their communion so as to be One. Hence, the difference and distinction of the Three exists in a single existence. Accordingly, Origen based his theology on two bedrocks, both of which he emphasised equally: the *distinction* as well as the *unity* of the Three Persons. The term *homoousios* itself expresses this twofold and balanced concept of both the oneness and distinction. For nothing can be *co-substantial* with itself: it has to be consubstantial with something *else*.[579]

When Arius wrote his *Thalia* and used the expression 'not consubstantial' (μὴ ὁμοούσιος) in order to dismiss the notion of the Father and Son being of the same ontological order, in fact he contradicted Origen. The real opponent of Arius was Origen, who, nevertheless, used *homoousios* as just one word out of many other terms and periphrases in order to couch his conception of the Trinitarian God. However, never did he make this a 'banner', as it were, nor could he have imagined that this term was destined to become a catchword loaded with such a critical importance by the bishops of Nicaea. My point is that the term had entered Christian mindset long before, and Origen was one of the 'scholars' whom Athanasius mentioned as the source of it (perhaps, he was the only 'scholar', along with 'bishops'). Athanasius acknowledged this. Historians still do not want to see this point.

579 Cf. Basil of Caesarea, *Epistulae*, epsitle 52.3: οὐ γὰρ αὐτό τι ἐστὶν ἑαυτῷ ὁμοούσιον, ἀλλ' ἕτερον ἑτέρῳ.

The exertions of Erich Klostermann[580] to edit fragments from Origen's commentary on Matthew resulted in publication of them in 1941. Hardly could he have imagined that this conscientious work was destined to be largely ignored by scholars. However, it turned out that in *Codex Sabaiticus 232*, several of Klostermann's brushed-aside fragments were there, plus a wider context of several of them. Besides, his last fragment (fr. 572) refers to Matthew, 28:18, yet he saw this as a dubious one, despite the fact that this is entirely consonant with Origen's Nicene propositions[581] already published but hitherto shunned.[582]

Who was Celsus?

I should add a few things concerning the identity of Celsus, although I am afraid this question is bound to remain obscure. When Ambrose asked Origen to confute Celsus' treatise entitled *True Discourse*, Origen was not sure as to who that opponent actually was. In the first place, he thought that this person was an Epicurean philosopher of the end of second century AD. He styled Celsus 'Epicurean' at several points,[583] which subsequent authors mentioning *Contra Celsum* did so, too,[584] yet without giving this point much consideration. A remark by Philip of Side (c. 380 – died after 431) is interesting: he reported that Athenagoras of Athens (when he was still a philosopher of the Academy) wrote against the Christians before Celsus did so.[585] Later, another author wrote that

580 Erich Klostermann (unter Mitwirkung von Ernst Benz), *Origenes Matthäuserklärung III*, (erste Hälfte: Fragmente und Indices), *Origenes Werke XII*, GCS 41.1, Leipzig, 1941.

581 Gunnar af Hällström, "More than initiation? Baptism according to Origen of Alexandria", in David Hellholm – Tor Vegge – Øyvind Norderval – Christer Hellholm (eds.) *Ablution, Initiation, and Baptism: Late Antiquity, Early Judaism, and Early Christianity*, Berlin, 2011, p. 993. He mentions Klostermann's fr. 572, but he underrates it because Origen perused Matthew 28:18-20 in order to expound his (impeccably Nicene) Trinitarian theology.

582 Cf. Origen, *schMatt*, PG.17.309.35-53: *Ἐδόθη μοι πᾶσα ἐξουσία ἐν οὐρανῷ καὶ ἐπὶ γῆς*. Τὸ *Ἐδόθη μοι πᾶσα ἐξουσία*, καὶ ἑξῆς, εἰς τὴν ἐνανθρώπησιν νόει. Εἰ δὲ καὶ εἰς τὴν θεότητα [βούλει] θεωρεῖν, καὶ οὕτω λήψῃ τὸ *Ἐδόθη μοι ἐξουσία*, ἀντὶ τοῦ *Ἐχωρήθη*. *Ἐδόθη*, ἠνέχθη μοι, περὶ τοῦ αὐτεξουσίου ἐπιστεύθην. Χώραν ἔσχεν ἡ ζωὴ πρῶτον μὲν ἐν τοῖς ἄνω, εἶτα νῦν καὶ ἐν τοῖς κάτω. Οὓς θαῤῥοῦντες βαπτίσατε εἰς τὸ ὄνομα τοῦ Πατρὸς καὶ τοῦ Υἱοῦ καὶ τοῦ ἁγίου Πνεύματος. Εἷς ὁ σώζων, μία ἡ σωτηρία. Εἷς ὁ ζῶν Πατήρ, ὁ Υἱός, καὶ τὸ ἅγιον Πνεῦμα. Εἷς ἐστιν, οὐ συναλοιφῇ τῶν τριῶν, ἀλλ' οὐσία μία. Τρεῖς δὲ ὑποστάσεις τέλειαι ἐν πᾶσι, καὶ κατάλληλοι. Κατὰ φύσιν ἐγέννησεν ὁ Πατήρ. Διόπερ ὁμοούσιος ἐγεννήθη. Οὐ σῶμα ὁ Θεός. Διὰ τοῦτο οὐκ κατὰ ῥεῦσιν ἢ κίνησιν, ἤ τι τῶν τοιούτων, ἃ ἐν τοῖς σώμασι θεωρεῖται. Ὁ Θεὸς ὁ ἀσώματος ἐγέννησεν. Ἐνυπόστατος ἡ γέννησις. Ἀπετέχθη ἐκ τῆς οὐσίας τοῦ Πατρὸς ὁ Υἱός.

583 *Cels*, I: 8; 10; 20 (& *Philocalia*, 18.5); II.60; III: 35; 49; 75; 80; IV: 4; 36; 54; 75 (& *Philocalia*, 20.3); 86 (& *Philocalia*, 20.13); V.3.

584 Eusebius, *HE*, 6.36.2. Arethas of Caesarea, *Scripta Minora*, opus 20, p. 198. Michael Psellus, *Orationes Forenses et Acta*, oration 1, line 792. Nicephorus Callistus Xanthopulus, *HE*, 5.19.

585 Philip of Side, *Historia Christiana*, line 4. Athenagoras lived c. 133 – c. 190 AD.

Eustathius of Antioch ('in the twenty-sixth chapter of his commentary on the gospel of John') also engaged in some confutation of Celsus' claims.[586]

Origen knew of two intellectuals named Celsus, both of whom were Epicurean: one lived 'in the age of Nero (54-68 AD), the other in the age of Hadrian (117-138) and later', and this 'later' could have made it possible for that 'Epicurean Celsus' to have been the man to whom Galen wrote a letter.[587] Besides, the name 'Celsus' had appeared in a work by Lucian of Samosata (c. 125 AD – died after 180 AD).[588] A much later (and evidently Christian) commentator of Lucian wrote that 'Celsus', whom Lucian addressed in that work, was the same person as that 'which the highly versed Origen contradicted.'[589] Although Lucian (who admired Democritus and Epicurus, both of whom advocated naturalistic cosmologies) frequently mocked superstition, certain religious leaders, and traditional stories about the gods, he nonetheless professed belief in existence of gods. Besides, I have pointed out that it is more than probable that Origen had read Lucian's works and he was not untouched by some exquisite turns of Lucian's vocabulary.[590]

Besides, since Origen was a diligent student of Galen's works[591] (to whose style and terminology he owed a great deal), perhaps he had read a reference to 'Celsus the Epicurean' by Galen (129 AD – c. 200 / c. 216), to whom Galen himself had written a letter.[592]

Origen implies that he was aware of 'other books' by Celsus, which were 'Epicurean' ones. However, in this specific treatise against Christianity, this philosophy could hardly be traced: Celsus often appealed to Plato and quoted from him, while also arguing on the basis of Stoic doctrines and terminology,

---

586 Pseudo-Anastasius of Sinai, *Florilegium Adversus Monotheletas*, 1. Eustathius of Antioch became Patriarch of Antioch shortly before the Council of Nicaea.

587 *Cels*, I.8. This portion appears only in the *Papyrus Cairo 88747* (seventh century), which contains excerpts from books I and II.

588 Lucian of Samosata, *Alexander*, sections 1; 17; 21. This satirical work is about Alexander Abonoteichus (Ἀλέξανδρος ὁ Ἀβωνοτειχίτης, also known as Alexander the Paphlagonian, c. 105 – c. 170 AD), whom Lucian portrayed as the master of fraud and deceit. Lucian explained why Alexander, an avowed enemy of Epicurus, was a pseudo-prophet and charlatan (*Alexander*, 17; 25; 38; 43-47). The same Alexander had burned a book of Epicurus in public (*Alexander*, 47).

589 Anonymous, *Scholia in Lucianum*, comm. on *Alexander*, section 1.

590 Cf. *RCR*, pp. 162-163; *NDGF*, pp. 71; 158; 163; 218; 220; 565; *Scholia in Apocalypsin*, pp. 30; 40; 70; 178; 220; 259; 284; 310-312; 403.

591 On Galen and Origen, see *Anaxagoras*, pp. 397-398; 658; 676-677; 849; 865; 929; 954; 1049; 1230; 1244-1245; 1258; *COT*, pp. 169; 200-201; 219; 245; 323; 373; *PHE*, pp. 169; 368-369; *NDGF*, pp. 218; 239; 397; *Scholia in Apocalypsin*, pp. 40; 84; 320; 323; 402.

592 Galen listed this 'epistle to Celsus the Epicurean' in a short treatise about his own books. *De Libris Propriis*, p. 48.

as discussed below. In reality, the allegedly 'Epicurean' philosophical identity is virtually absent from the treatise that Origen set out to confute; hence, his passing remarks insinuating his doubts as to whether his opponent was actually an Epicurean.[593] And when he thought that Celsus, who 'in his desire to demolish our doctrines, throughout all his treatise has not admitted that he is an Epicurean, now is proven to change sides and employs the opinions of Epicurus',[594] it was Origen's inference through agonistic argument rather than Celsus' own words that supported such an alleged like-mindedness. For although Origen liked to think that Celsus was an Epicurean (presumably, because Galen had written so), in fact the statements of Celsus hardly bear on Epicurus' philosophy, whereas all too often do they ring a Platonic bell – in which case Origen wondered whether Celsus concealed his Epicurean convictions or, at a subsequent stage, he had changed his views and embraced more sublime ones, or other he was simply a namesake of the Epicurean that Origen had assumed him to be. In view of such remarks, Origen sometimes opted for claiming that Celsus was an Epicurean who 'pretended' not to be one and took heed of not declaring his philosophical identity openly:[595] Celsus refrained from expounding the doctrines of that school, 'because, had he done so, his criticisms could not be trustworthy'.[596] At any rate, Origen realised (IV.54) that Celsus' casual assaults on divine intervention did not originate with Epicurus' atomic materialism.

> Let us briefly deal with this, and prove either that he is pretending not to avow his Epicurean opinion, or, as someone might say, he has changed views for the better (ὕστερον μεταθέμενον ἐπὶ τὰ βελτίω), or other, as might be said, that he is only a namesake of the Epicurean (τὸν ὁμώνυμον τῷ Ἐπικουρείῳ).

Sometimes Origen argued against Celsus on the basis of books that he had read, written by 'the Epicurean Celsus'.[597] In reality, however, deep down he was never sure as to *who* that high-handed Celsus really was, namely, whether it was 'the Epicurean who had written two more books against the Christians',

---

593 *Cels*, III.49 (& *Philocalia*, 18.20): 'To say this is more appropriate for us than for Celsus, particularly *if* he turns out to be an Epicurean' (ἐὰν ἐπικούρειος ὢν ἐλέγχηται). *Op. cit.* IV.4: Celsus does 'not appear from his treatise to be an Epicurean at all, but pretends to believe in Providence' (μὴ πάνυ ἐμφαίνοντι διὰ τοῦ συγγράμματος τὸν Ἐπικούρειον ἀλλὰ προσποιουμένῳ πρόνοιαν εἰδέναι).

594 Origen, *op. cit.* V.3.

595 *Op. cit.* I.8; III: 22; 35; 80; IV: 4; 54; V.3.

596 *Op. cit.* I.8.

597 *Cels*, I.8: Εὑρίσκεται γὰρ ἐξ ἄλλων συγγραμμάτων ἐπικούρειος ὤν.

or he was another person.[598] The latter was not likely, since *this* Celsus wrote that he intended 'to compose another treatise, in which' he promised 'to teach the [proper] way of living those who are willing and able to be persuaded' about following such a conduct of life – to which Origen declared himself prepared to reply, too.[599]

No matter what Celsus' identity was, his text was a mixture of hubristic and often distortive allegations lacking basic virtues of Greek art of rhetoric, such as not failing to consider facts, no matter what a rhetor's personal assessment of them. For example, he pointed out that 'when they [sc. Christians] were in the beginning, they were few and were of one mind; but since they have spread to become a multitude, they are divided and rent asunder, and each wants to have his own party. For they wanted to have this from the beginning. They are divided again by becoming too numerous and condemn one another; they only have one thing still in common, so to speak, if indeed they have that – the name. And yet, in spite of their divisions, they are ashamed to give up this name. As for the rest, they are at sixes and sevens.'[600]

Origen could not have contradicted this out of hand. He only replied that 'any doctrine that has had serious origin and is beneficial to life has caused different sects'.[601] Actually, he would have endorsed some of those remarks – yet never in his reply to Celsus. Otherwise, in another text addressing his pupils, he was pretty harsh concerning the state of affairs in the Christian communities.

> But in reality, if we assess things by means of truth and not by [means of] mobs [gathered in churches] ... we will realise that now we are not faithful. ... now, when we have become many, since there cannot be many elect,[602] ... there are very few who attain the selection by God and the blessedness.[603]

Celsus simply ignored the (sometimes irreconcilable) dissent among those who styled themselves 'Platonists' (and the lesser one among Peripatetics and Stoics).[604] For concerning 'division' in sundry sects, Celsus should have known that his invective would have applied perfectly to a far more ancient tradition,

---

598 *Op. cit.* IV.39: ὁ ἐπικούρειος Κέλσος, εἴγε οὗτός ἐστι καὶ ὁ κατὰ Χριστιανῶν ἄλλα δύο βιβλία συντάξας. Cf. *op. cit.* III.49 ('if he is an Epicurean'): Καὶ ἡμῖν μᾶλλον πρέπει τοῦτο λέγειν τῷ Κέλσῳ, καὶ μάλιστ' ἐὰν ἐπικούρειος ὢν ἐλέγχηται.

599 *Op. cit.* VIII.76.

600 *Cels*, III.10; III.12 (& *Philocalia*, 16.1).

601 *Cels*, III.12.

602 Cf. Matt. 22:14.

603 *homJer*, homily 4.3.

604 See testimonies by Stobaeus, *Anthologium*, 1.49.37. Galen, *De Libris Propriis*, p. 41; *De Placitis Hippocratis et Platonis*, 5.7.10.

which at points appeared as his favourite,[605] namely, Platonism. Origen certainly believed that Plato taught sublime things,[606] he posited incorporeal principles, he revered Deity,[607] he dismissed those Greek myths that were debauched,[608] he 'spoke well' by positing God as 'the Supreme Good' (πρῶτον ἀγαθὸν)[609] and affirmed a universal Nous who 'decorated everything',[610] which Plato himself acknowledged that he had learned it from Anaxagoras.[611] All in all then, Plato 'has been serviceable to many people'.[612] Therefore, along with Stoicism, it was Platonism that Origen had also in mind when he spoke of doctrines that 'had serious origin and are beneficial to life'. Nevertheless, when he addressed Christians, not Celsus' arguments, he did not conceal his frustration at the state of things among Christians, and wrote, as above, 'now that we have become many, since there cannot be many elect,[613] there are very few who attain to selection by God and to blessedness.'

Besides, by Celsus' time (second century AD) there had been four different 'Academies'. All of them pleaded allegiance to Plato, and all of their members dignified themselves with the designation 'Platonist'. However, in the dialogues *Parmenides* and *Sophist*, Plato's concerns about his own theory of Ideas are plain; hence, the tantalised Academy moved through the waves of Pythagoreanism, and then of Scepticism. From the Pythagoreanism of Xenocrates (396-314 BC) to the Scepticism of Philo of Larissa (c. 154 – c. 84 BC) things had evolved 'at sixes and sevens', and yet all of them (as Celsus would have put it) 'had one thing still in common' – the name 'Platonist', which 'they were ashamed to disown'. Moreover, Antiochus of Ascalon (c. 130 – c. 68 BC) was a member of the Academy under Philo of Larissa (c. 154 – c. 84 BC) at a period when Philo had allowed his Platonism to degenerate into arid Scepticism. He went to great lengths to show that the Stoic doctrines were present already in Plato. But when he argued that talk of immaterial substances (such as the Platonic Ideas) was 'unintelligible' and that he saw 'no possibility … of existence of anything immaterial, transcendent or external to the material universe',[614] he himself

605 Cf. *Cels*, IV.83; VI.47.

606 *Cels*, I.10.

607 *Op. cit.* I.15 (& *Philocalia*, 17.2); *op. cit.* IV.48 (& *Philocalia*, 17.6), referring to *Philebus*, 12c.

608 *Op. cit.* IV.50; cf. VII.6, once again, contradicting Plato. *Respublica*, 334b; 377d; 378d; 379c; 383a; 387b; 389a; 595b; 600e.

609 *Op. cit.* VI.11. Cf. Mark, 10:18; Luke, 18:18.

610 *Philebus*, 28c; 28e; 30d; *Phaedrus*, 98a-b; *Timaeus*, 36d; 47e; *Leges*, 963a; 967b.

611 *Phaedo*, 97c; *Cratylus*, 400a; 413c; cf. *op. cit.* 396b. Aristotle, *De Anima*, 405a. Plutarch, *Pericles*, 4.6.

612 *Cels*, VI.2.

613 Ref. to Matt. 22:14.

614 A quotation from Cicero, *De Finibus*, *apud* J.M. Dillon, *The Middle Platonists*, p. 84.

actually moved into Stoicism, instead of forcing the Stoa into the Academy, as Sextus Empiricus had claimed somehow mourning the eviction of Scepticism from the late Academy.[615] Just like Aristotle, Antiochus saw that the notions of self-existent individuality and incorporeality are mutually exclusive. This is why later Platonists, such as Eratosthenes of Alexandria (born in Cyrene, c. 275 – c. 194 BC) and Ptolemy (c. 90 – c. 168 AD) sustained that 'a soul is always in a body' and it transmigrates 'from subtle bodies to other ones that are oyster-like' (ἀπὸ σωμάτων αὐτὴν λεπτοτέρων εἰς τὰ ὀστρεώδη πάλιν εἰσοικίζει σώματα). Although Iamblichus (as reported by Stobaeus) claimed that 'Eratothenes, Ptolemy, and others' belonged to 'another Platonist sect' (ἄλλη αἵρεσις τῶν Πλατωνικῶν), in reality Ptolemy was a polymath prone to Aristotelian empiricism and Stoicism, even though Platonism is evident in his writings. Both intellectuals were reported as having sustained that different souls 'dwell in a certain part of the perceptible world' (διατρίβειν μὲν γὰρ αὐτὴν εἰς μοῖράν τινα τοῦ αἰσθητοῦ), they exchange 'solid bodies, moving intermittently to different places of the entire world' (καθήκειν γε μὴν εἰς τὸ στερεὸν σῶμα ἄλλοτε ἀπ' ἄλλων τοῦ παντὸς τόπων), and they come into this world from different places (ἀπὸ τῶν διαφερόντων τόπων καταβάσεις τῶν ψυχῶν).[616] However, this in not Platonism: it is an eclectic attitude employed by disillusioned Platonists. Galen at least had declared himself openly an 'eclecticist'.

In effect then, five schools claimed the title 'Platonic Academy' that stretched out to three main periods (Old, under Plato; Middle, of Arcesilaus; and New, of Carneades and Clitomachus, followed by a Fourth Academy under Philo and Charmidas)[617] and countless heresies, all of which claimed for themselves the authority of rendering Plato's theories authentically: from Xenocrates' Pythagoreanism down to Philo of Larissa's moderate scepticism and the Stoicism of his pupil, Antiochus of Ascalon, 'Platonism' was claimed by different sorts of intellectuals, including Scepticism (called the Fifth Academy, under Sextus Empiricus).[618] Cardinal ideas of the Late Antiquity were new (within the Greek mindset, at least), but everyone sought to hallow them as mere revisitation of the 'authentic' Plato. Antiochus of Ascalon embraced Stoic ideas representing them as return to the real Platonism,[619] and Numenius felt

615 Sextus Empiricus, *Pyrrhoniae Hypotyposes*, 1.235: ἀλλὰ καὶ ὁ Ἀντίοχος τὴν Στοὰν μετήγαγεν εἰς τὴν Ἀκαδημίαν, ὡς καὶ εἰρῆσθαι ἐπ' αὐτῷ ὅτι ἐν Ἀκαδημίᾳ φιλοσοφεῖ τὰ Στωικά. ἐπεδείκνυε γὰρ ὅτι παρὰ Πλάτωνι κεῖται τὰ τῶν Στωικῶν δόγματα. ὡς πρόδηλον εἶναι τὴν τῆς σκεπτικῆς ἀγωγῆς διαφορὰν πρός τε τὴν τετάρτην καὶ τὴν πέμπτην καλουμένην Ἀκαδημίαν.

616 Iamblichus, *De Anima*, fr. 26, *apud* Stobaeus, *Anthologium*, 1.49.39.

617 Sextus Empiricus, *Pyrrhoniae Hypotyposes*, 1.220; *Adversus Rhetores*, 2.20.

618 Sextus Empiricus, *Pyrrhoniae Hypotyposes*, 1.235.

619 *Cels*, IV.51.

no less so when he amalgamated Platonism, Pythagoreanism, and Gnosticism: while pointing out the dissent among those who claimed themselves to be Plato's heirs, he believed that he was himself the orthodox exponent of this philosophy,[620] to which Origen would have agreed since he regarded Numenius as 'by far the best exegete of Pythagoras and Plato.'[621]

When Longinus praised Plotinus (along with Amelius) for being an assiduous thinker, he believed that Plotinus in essence expounded Platonic and Pythagorean doctrines in his own way (τρόπῳ θεωρίας ἰδίῳ),[622] not original ideas of Plotinus' own. However, the dissent among the pupils of Plotinus as to what Plato really believed was by no means of no essential consequence.

Who was Celsus then? Although it was easy for Origen to recall the name of an earlier Epicurean, or two ones (which Origen did, if tentatively), the problem was that hardly did Celsus' treatise itself ring any Epicurean bell. The fragments of this quoted by Origen reveal not only that Celsus was pretty well informed on Greek philosophy, but also that had done his homework with Christian sources. Opposite this, Origen was all too prompt to toss his hat into the ring and felt he should exhibit his superior knowledge of pagan sources in order to discredit what he saw as insolent attempt of derogation. Accordingly, since the peremptory Celsus appeared as having clashed the cymbal against Christianity on philosophical rather than political grounds (which, nevertheless, is not absent), Origen sought not so much to refute as to overwhelmingly take him by storm, by quoting from several pagan sources in order to show Celsus' ineptness to grasp the meaning not only of Christian sources but also of Greek ones, his lack of dialectical skill, and his logical inconsistencies. Not only did he refute Celsus' diatribe, but also cared to show that he was superior to his adversary on that score, frequently by turning his opponent's argument against Celsus himself. In short, during a period when the Greek intellegentia treated Christian mindset contumeliously, Origen sought to disgrace his adversary, while bolstering up his own image as both a highly schooled Greek scholar and a learned Christian philosopher.

In fact, there is no such thing as 'the philosophy of Celsus', and certainly the case is all but that 'Celsus' philosophy is that of an eclectic Platonist' and 'his affinities are with the Middle Platonists like Albinus'.[623] Celsus had read

620 The title of Numenius' treatise was *Περὶ τῆς τῶν Ἀκαδημαϊκῶν πρὸς Πλάτωνα διαστάσεως*. Cf. Eusebius, *PE*, 14.4.16; 15.5.1. Numenius, *Fragmenta*, 3, fr. 24.

621 *Op. cit.* IV.51.

622 Porphyry, *Vita Plotini*, 20. This is from the Proem (quoted by Porphyry) of Longinus' treatise, *On the End: to Plotinus and Gentilianus Amelius.* Porphyry highlighted the expression τρόπῳ θεωρίας ἰδίῳ, quoting this also in *op. cit.* 21.

623 H. Chadwick (tr.), *Origen, Contra Celsum*, Cambridge, 1953; p. xxvi.

philosophy, but he was not a philosopher. Origen clearly suggests that Celsus 'fell short of education in argument and had absolutely no knowledge about it' (δεόμενος τῆς διὰ λόγου παιδεύσεως καὶ μηδαμῶς ἐπαΐων αὐτῆς).[624] He was just a bookworm unable to make his own mind and fathom the depths of the sundry theories, who contented himself with pedant exhibitionism of awareness of his scattered readings. On that account, he was not a philosopher, not even an 'eclectic' one: at best, he was just a lettered imperial court-fawner who pretended to defend the state's observation of laws of worship (τὰ σφέτερα νόμιμα θρησκεύειν),[625] and to urge that the aloofness of Christians from the social and political life was tantamount to subversion of the empire during times that this was threatened by the barbarians. It was then hardly surprising that Celsus concluded his polemic by arguing for the need to observe the Roman religion[626] and, if an oath were to be taken, this should be done 'by the emperor's name'.[627]

He had read some books and was fascinated by various, no matter how conflicting, Greek theories, which he had neither assimilated nor made his own. This is why at points he contradicted himself, and of course Origen could not have left this unexploited. Celsus was seeing himself just as a *tout court* eclectic Hellene, who admired this cultural phenomenon as a versed *fan* rather than as a *philosopher* who arguably had opted for this or that philosophical school. He was not even one 'who chose to be either a Stoic, or a Platonist, or a Peripatetic, or an Epicurean, or a follower of another philosophical sect' once he would have been impelled to become such a follower by an irrational impulse' (ἀλόγῳ τινὶ φορᾷ).[628] He was fascinated by everything 'Hellenic', while caring little to make out the (sometimes unyielding) differences between some Greek schools. But as Oscar Wilde put it, 'It is only an auctioneer who can equally and impartially admire all schools of art'. Celsus was just a bumptious aficionado who rollicked through 'Hellenism' with the excitement of a tourist and described its virtues and rectitude with the enthusiasm of an auctioneer.

Perplexed as Origen was about his opponent's real identity, first he saw him as an Epicurean,[629] later he styled him one 'who, at many points, wants to be Platonising'.[630] But as he went on with reading his opponent's treatise and came upon Celsus appealing to Plato, he saw Celsus as one 'who at many points

624 *Cels*, IV.83.
625 *Op. cit.* V.36.
626 *Op. cit.* VIII.66-75.
627 *Op. cit.* VIII.67.
628 *Op. cit.* I.10.
629 *Op. cit.* I: 8; 10; 20; II.20; III: 22; 35; 49; 75; 80; IV: 4; 36; 54; 75; 86; V: 3. After that point, Origen attacks the 'Epicureans' rather than the 'Epicurean' Celsus: VII.63.
630 *Cels*, IV.83.

exalted Plato'.[631] Perhaps Celsus did so also in the text which Origen's quotations did not save, but at points of the extant one, he indeed treated Plato as an authority,[632] he 'quoted much from' him,[633] and so he did with 'theologians' of old (Pherecydes, Pythagoras, Socrates),[634] including Persians (Mithras),[635] at which Origen expressed his surprise,[636] given that Celsus posed as an exponent not of the barbaric wisdom, but of the Hellenic letters. Origen realised this,[637] and pointed out Celsus' superficial reading of Plato[638] and his inability to render Plato's views consistently.[639] On no account, however, did Origen see Celsus as a follower of Plato, whether an eclectic one or not, notwithstanding Celsus' desultory use of Platonic propositions.[640]

As a matter of fact, Celsus' arguments were sometimes too erratic: on the one hand, he represented Jesus as an ignorant carpenter,[641] while, at another, he accused Jesus as one who had read yet misunderstood Plato.[642] Otherwise, he selected from whatever quarter he thought it fit in order to bolster his polemic. He could move conveniently from Plato to Stoicism so as to defend Providence,[643] or the universal interrelation and interdependent coherence

---

631 *Op. cit.* VI.47.

632 *Op. cit.* I.32; IV.36; VI: 7-8; 13; 16-19; 21; 47; 64; VII: 28; 30-31; 42; 45; 58-59.

633 *Op. cit.* VI.8.

634 *Op. cit.* IV.97.

635 *Op. cit.* VII.62.

636 *Op. cit.* VI.22.

637 *Op. cit.* IV.56: "But perhaps in this case, because he is in difficulties, Celsus would turn away from Plato … and flee for refuge to Aristotle and the Peripatetics."

638 *Op. cit.* IV.62: "I think he has not even heard accurately of Plato's view – he who subsumes (ἐκπεριλαμβάνων) all the truth in this one treatise and entitles his book against us *True Discourse*. The verb ἐκπεριλαμβάνω appears to be Origen's coinage, which only his devout pupil Gregory of Nyssa used. Cf. *Cels*, VI.45 (ἐκπεριλαβών). Gregory of Nyssa, *In Inscriptiones Psalmorum*, p. 62 (ἐκπεριλαβών); *Orationes viii De Beatitudinibus*, PG.44.1284.20 (ἐκπεριλαβών). Naturally, this is absent from L&S lexicon.

639 *Op. cit.* VII.43: "Subsequently, as if [Celsus] had forgotten the words of Plato which he quoted, he says that [to Plato and theologians of old] god is unnameable."

640 *Cels*, I.32: "Moreover, as addressing Greeks and Celsus in particular, whether he upholds Plato's doctrines or not, nevertheless he quotes them, I would ask this question."

641 *Op. cit.* VI.34; VI.36.

642 *Op. cit.* VI.16; VII.68 (& *Philocalia*, 15.8).

643 *Op. cit.* IV.99: "And God cares about the universe and never does his providence fail this".

of all things (the Stoic 'sympathy'),[644] or the idea of periodic conflagration – cataclysm,[645] and identical recurrence of worlds).[646]

Naturally, Origen noticed Celsus' Stoicising twisting shifts, and apropos of treating the figure Zeus / Logos acting upon formless matter / Hera, he seized the opportunity to denounce a Stoic allegorical exegesis of a 'despicable picture' of Zeus and Hera at Samos.[647] Likewise, Celsus demeaned the Christian view of God being 'spirit' by arguing that this was but a Stoic theory,[648] and used the characteristic Stoic term 'administration [of the universe] by God' (διοίκησις Θεοῦ).[649] And when Celsus spoke generally (i.e. what 'men of olden times' believed) of the world being 'god's child and demigod', Origen gave a short lecture about the various Greek theories of the world being regarded as god.[650] According to Proclus, Numenius posited three gods, namely, the Father as 'first God', the Demiurge as 'second God ', and the world as 'third god', and he attributed the creative act to both the First and second God.[651] Origen knew of this theory.[652] However, Theodoret reported that, according to Numenius, 'the first God does not have to create, and one should think that the first God is the father of the second God.'[653] Alongside these variations, the teaching attributed to Hermes Trismegistus posited the 'world' as 'second God' in order to argue that no thing actually perishes: what appears as death is only mutation from one form to another.[654] This is an Anaxagorean approach par excellence, which maintains that all things are made of principles and are dissolved into principles – but the principles themselves never perish. Therefore, the world

644 *Op. cit.* IV.5 (Celsus): "For if you changed any one quite insignificant thing on earth, you would upset and destroy everything". *Op. cit.* IV.70: "Even if something seems to you to be evil, it is not yet clear whether it actually is evil; for you do not know what is advantageous either for you or for someone else or for the universe."

645 *Op. cit.* IV.11: "after the last flood in the time of Deucalion, the cycle demands a conflagration in accordance with the alternating succession of the universe". Likewise, Celsus, in *op. cit.* I.19-20; IV.69; IV.79. Cf. Chrysippus, *Fragmenta Logica et Physica*, frs. 608; 628; 1174.

646 Celsus, in *op. cit.* IV.62; IV.65.

647 *Op. cit.* IV.48; cf. VI.42.

648 *Op. cit.* VI.71.

649 *Op. cit.* VII.68.

650 *Op. cit.* V.7; cf. v.7; VI.47.

651 Proclus, *commTim*, v. 1, p. 304.

652 *Cels*, V.7.

653 Theodoret, *Curatio*, 2.81.

654 Cf. *Corpus Hermeticum*, *῞Οτι οὐδὲν τῶν ὄντων ἀπόλλυται, ἀλλὰ τὰς μεταβολὰς ἀπωλείας καὶ θανάτους πλανώμενοι λέγουσιν*, 1: ὁ γὰρ θάνατος ἀπωλείας ἐστίν. οὐδὲν δὲ τῶν ἐν τῷ κόσμῳ ἀπόλλυται. εἰ γὰρ δεύτερος θεὸς ὁ κόσμος καὶ ζῷον ἀθάνατον, ἀδύνατόν ἐστι τοῦ ἀθανάτου ζῴου μέρος τι ἀποθανεῖν. πάντα δὲ τὰ ἐν τῷ κόσμῳ μέρη ἐστὶ τοῦ κόσμου, μάλιστα δὲ ὁ ἄνθρωπος, τὸ λογικὸν ζῷον.

is a 'second God' made by 'God, who is eternal, unborn, and creator of all', and this world 'was not made just once, but it is perpetually being made (οὔποτε δὲ ἐγένετο, ἀλλὰ ἀεὶ γίνεται)'.[655] In this setting, man is made 'in the image of the world' (that is, of the second God) yet is related not only to the second God, but also to the first one, whom actually man can grasp. What kind of apprehension is this? Whereas the second God (the world) is grasped as a body, the first one is perceived as 'incorporeal and as Mind and as Good', in contrast to Numenius who did not allow for grasp of the First God at all.[656]

Nevertheless, there are points on which Origen and Celsus could have agreed with each other. For example, this could have happened on the question of 'idolatry', which in fact was a mutual reproach. Celsus rightly pointed out that never did the Greeks believe that the statues of gods themselves are gods,[657] and quoted Heraclitus who wrote that 'those who approach lifeless things as gods are like a man who holds conversations with walls'.[658] Porphyry likewise argued that only a fool could believe that gods dwell in the statues of them, which are only like images of friends that are cherished, while certainly no one believes that any such friend is himself present in those images: these (like temples themselves) are simply reminders of persons that are held dear. And if gods are pictorialised as men, this is so only because man is the best of all animals and an image of God.[659] Anyway, the term 'idolatry' (εἰδωλολατρεία) was coinded by Christians, starting with Paul.[660]

Besides, Celsus argued that the gospel had been adulterated, 'so as to evade difficulties in face of criticism', meaning the sometimes discrepant texts of different manuscripts. In his reply, Origen claimed that the only ones of whom he knew that had falsified the text were the Marcionite and Valentinians, 'and, I think also the followers of Lucan'.[661] However, when Origen (much later) wrote his commentary on Matthew, he criticised copies of that gospel that were 'incompatible with each other' (μὴ συνᾴδειν ἀλλήλοις), 'either because of scribe's sluggishness or evil-minded boldness or neglect concerning editing of the text

655 *Op. cit.* 2.

656 *Op. cit.* 5: τὸ δὲ τρίτον ζῷον, ὁ ἄνθρωπος, κατ᾽ εἰκόνα τοῦ κόσμου γενόμενος, νοῦν κατὰ βούλησιν τοῦ πατρὸς ἔχων παρὰ τὰ ἄλλα ἐπίγεια ζῷα, οὐ μόνον πρὸς τὸν δεύτερον θεὸν συμπάθειαν ἔχων, ἀλλὰ καὶ ἔννοιαν τοῦ πρώτου. τοῦ μὲν γὰρ αἴσθεται ὡς σώματος, τοῦ δὲ ἔννοιαν λαμβάνει ὡς ἀσωμάτου καὶ νοῦ, τοῦ ἀγαθοῦ.

657 *Op. cit.* VII.36; cf. Origen's reply in VII.40.

658 *Op. cit.* I.5. Heraclitus' maxim is quoted also in *op. cit.* VII.62 & 65. Earlier, this had been quoted by Clement of Alexandria, *Protrepticus*, 4.50.5.

659 Porphyry, *Contra Christianos*, frs. 76 & 77, *apud* Macarius of Magnesia, *Apocriticus*, Book 4, pp. 200-202 (Blondel).

660 1 Cor. 5:11; 6:9; 10:7&14; *et passim*.

661 *Op. cit.* II.27.

or interpolation of personal views which led to either adding text to the gospel or omitting text of it.' This was one of the reasons for him to engage in textual criticism, in order to 'cure' (ἰάσαθαι) such detriment to Matthew's text, as he did with the Biblical *Hexapla*.[662]

Celsus made it fairly clear that he came from the region of Phoenice and Palestine;[663] and he made even more clear that he was the sort of the well-read person who was not content with rebutting Christinity by means of cultured argument alone: he went out to the agora, he watched real or fake Christians preaching, and was always highly strung and predisposed to argue with them in public, which he did with 'alleged [Christian] prophets' too.[664] Likewise, he cared to learn what sort of books some Christian presbyters happened to hold in their hands, and he felt triumphant in alleging that he saw presbyters making use of books that 'contained barbarian names of daemons and magical formulas'.[665]

It is all but sure that 'Celsus was lying', as Origen put it. For one thing, Origen disagreed with Aristotle (and the Epicureans) who thought that 'magic' is nonexistent and mere superstition; instead, he maintained that magic was a real thing to deal with.[666] Moreover, when Origen made reference to 'the doctrine about daemons' (τὸν περὶ δαιμόνων λόγον) and 'magic', clearly he had in mind a structured and disciplined doctrine, which could be comprehended only if this were taught systematically.

> And no one who has not grasped the truth about the so-called devil and his angels, and who he was before he became a devil, and how he became a devil, and what was the cause for his so-called angels to have apostasised along with him (τίς ἡ αἰτία τοῦ συναποστῆναι αὐτῷ τοὺς καλουμένους αὐτοῦ ἀγγέλους), will be able to know the origin of evils. Anyone who aspires to behold this [cause] and possesses a more accurate perception of daemons (περὶ δαιμόνων ἀκριβέστερον διειληφέναι) must know that they are God's creatures not in so far as they are daemons, but only in so far as they are rational beings of some sort (καθὸ λογικοί τινες). [And he must perceive] how they came to be such that their mind was caused to subsist in a state of daemons (ὡς ἐν καταστάσει δαιμόνων αὐτῶν ὑποστῆναι τὸ ἡγεμονικόν). Accordingly, if there is any subject of those that need to be perused among men, which is hard for our [human] nature to grasp (δυσθήρατός ἐστι τῇ φύσει ἡμῶν), the origin of evils must be classed as one of them (ἡ τῶν κακῶν ταχθείη ἂν γένεσις).[667]

---

662 *commMatt*, 15.14.
663 *Cels*, VII: 3; 8-9; 11.
664 *Op. cit.* VII.11.
665 *Op. cit.* VI.40.
666 *Op. cit.* I.24; cf. I.68; II.51; VI.32; VI.41; *selNum*, PG.12.584.16-19.
667 *Cels*, IV.65.

Also:

> Then, he next says about Christians that although they will agree that these things are intended for the honour of certain beings, whether they resemble their shape or not, yet they think that those to whom they are dedicated are not gods but daemons, and that no one who worships God ought to serve daemons. But if he knew the doctrine about daemons (τὸν περὶ δαιμόνων λόγον) and the activity of each of them, whether each one is invoked by the experts in these matters, or if it is of its own choice that it devotes itself to the activity which it desires and can perform, and if he had grasped the different aspects of the doctrine about daemons (καὶ διειλήφει τὸν περὶ δαιμόνων λόγον),[668] which is profound and hard for human nature to understand (πολὺν ὄντα καὶ δύσληπτον τῇ ἀνθρωπίνῃ φύσει), he would not have made it a censure against us that we say that no one who reveres the supreme God ought to worship daemons. We are indeed so far from worshiping daemons, that by prayers and by lessons [that we have learned] from the holy scriptures (καὶ τοῖς ἀπὸ τῶν ἱερῶν γραμμάτων μαθήμασιν) we even expel them from human souls and from places where they have established themselves, and sometimes even from animals. For frequently the daemons act to the detriment of those, too.[669]

Origen had given an example of such 'lessons' earlier in the same work:

> It is clear that the Jews trace their genealogy back to the three fathers, Abraham, Isaac, and Jacob. Their names are so powerful when linked with the name of God that the formula, 'the God of Abraham, and the God of Isaac, and the God of Jacob', is used not only by people of this [Jewish] nation in their prayers to God and when they subdue daemons by conjuration (καὶ ἐν τῷ κατεπᾴδειν δαίμονας), but also by almost all those who engage in magic and spells (τοὺς τὰ τῶν ἐπῳδῶν καὶ μαγειῶν πραγματευομένους). For this invocation of, and appeal to (ἐπίκλησις καὶ παράληψις), the name of God is found at numerous points of magical treatises (εὑρίσκεται γὰρ ἐν τοῖς μαγικοῖς συγγράμμασι πολλαχοῦ ἡ τοιαύτη τοῦ θεοῦ ἐπίκλησις), since this is held to be affiliated with the names of these men in respect to [fight] against daemons (εἰς τὰ κατὰ τῶν δαιμόνων).[670]

Beyond the fact that Origen speaks conveniently of his readings of 'magical treatises', more important to notice is that he speaks of 'the doctrine about daemons' as an authority who feels superior to his opponent on that score, and he demonstrates this every now and then: this doctrine is 'profound' and Celsus simply has no idea of this. The foregoing expression, 'if he had grasped

668 For example, an aspect of this profound doctrine in about 'the daemons who live on the earth'. *Cels*, IV.32: τὸν περὶ τῶν ἐπὶ γῆς δαιμόνων λόγον.

669 *Cels*, VII.67.

670 *Op. cit.* IV.33. The same knowledge he expounds in I.22&24; V.45 (& *Philocalia*, 17.4); *exhMar*, 46. In *Cels*, VIII.59, he appears aware of 'thirty-six barbarian daemons, which the Egyptian magicians invoke', which Celsus mentioned.

the different aspects of the doctrine about daemons' (καὶ διειλήφει τὸν περὶ δαιμόνων λόγον) is not made is passing: rather, it shows that this is one more topic on which Origen was superior to his opponent. He had said so earlier in the same book, speaking of the Scythians, the Nomads of Libya, the Persians, the 'godless' Seres, and the Persians: all of them are 'intolerant of altars and images', but they are so because 'they want to avoid degrading or debasing the worship of God to matter, which has been modelled in a particular way' as a certain statue; 'nor is it because they have grasped [truth] about daemons (οὐδὲ διὰ τὸ διειληφέναι περὶ δαιμόνων), namely, that they have occupied these images and places either because they have been invoked by certain magical spells, or because they have managed to get possession of places for themselves, where greedily they partake of the portions of the sacrifices[671] and seek for illicit pleasure and for lawless men.'[672] In short, once again, he speaks as an expert and implies that he has studied, comprehended, and expounded this 'profound' doctrine.

Celsus was not the ordinary literate man in the street: although not exactly a scholar, he was well-informed on Greek tradition and apparently *au courant* concerning Christian religion. He made use of that as much as he could, and I should have thought that he was a proud Roman citizen who held the ancestral lore in high regard. I surmise this because he made use of an extremely rare turn of phrase: 'it is best to compare things that are homologous' (τὰ ἴσα τοῖς ἴσοις παραβάλλειν κράτιστον), meaning, arguments could be applied to different situations only once those situations are logically cognate and susceptible of being compared on commensurate terms.

Celsus took this up from the only man who had entertained this elegant scheme, namely, Aelius Aristides (117-181 AD), the orator and star of the Second Sophistic.[673] Besides, this is a subtle point which could provide some safe ground for Celsus' chronology and allow for determining that of the two 'Celsi' that Origen knew, this one was the second, namely, the one who lived in the age of Hadrian (117-138) and later', still the designation 'Epicurean' could hardly fit Origen's interlocutor.

In any event, Celsus' attack on Christianity was passionate, literate if considered fractionally – yet as a whole it points to a lettered person who had

671 *Cels*, VIII.63: Of those things that Celsus said about 'daemons needing burnt-offering and blood' which 'they long for', Origen authoritatively grants that 'Celsus spoke the truth'.

672 *Cels*, VII.64.

673 Aelius Aristides, *Ῥώμης Ἐγκώμιον*, p. 208: οὐκ ἴσα ἴσοις παραβάλλων δίειμι, ἀλλ᾽ οὐκ ὄντων ἑτέρων παραδειγμάτων ἀναγκάζομαι τοῖς οὖσι χρῆσθαι ('I am not escaping from comparing things that are homologous, but in the absence of other examples, I am bound to use those that are available').

read much but could not go as far as to side with any particular philosophical school. His motives were evidently those of the highbrowed intelligentsia of his day: pride for the Greek lore and contempt for the new religion. In this respect, Celsus was a fanatic, to whom Christianity was a thorn that had become a monomania – which was perhaps his fatal weakness. Origen evidently had realised this, wherefore he knew that his opponent could be beaten: for any fanatic is deep down tantalised by a doubt, which he desperately strives to conceal and overcome by means of swelling his own zealotry.

The Commentary on Matthew is later than the Contra Celsum

When Origen decided to convert to Christianity, he was already a famous Greek philosopher of nearly fifty years of age. In the new religion, he came upon the story of a man who was born in Bethlehem of Galilee, taught in the region of Palestine, and demonstrated signs of being God. The notion of men being gods had made a mark in both Greek and Oriental history, as well as in the Roman one. It was a widespread belief that Greek gods in fact were prominent men of old that had been deified,[674] and the Cretans claimed that a certain site in the region was the tomb of Zeus.[675] However, as against the notion of a man being God, the idea of *God being man* was different and far more hard to grasp, all the more so once this involved the notion of a suffering God who was 'crucified', or 'wounded', or he 'mourned', a God who felt fear, anguish, ignorance, hunger, fatigue, or thirst. This idea permeated the gospel of John par excellence. It was then rather natural for him to start his production of Christian writings with commenting on the gospel of John.[676]

This is presumably the reason why the commentary on John (which foregrounds Jesus' divinity) was written at a very early stage of Origen's Christian life, whereas the commentary on Matthew (which accentuates Jesus' humanity) belongs to the latest period of his works. It was all but coincidence that the

---

674 Cf. Origen, *Cels*, III.21-22; III.35; VIII.9.

675 Lucian of Samosata, *Philopseudes*, 3. Pseudo-Lucian of Samosata, *Philopatris*, 10. Tatian, *Oratio ad Graecos*, 27.1. On whether the satirist and the Christian 'Lucian' were two persons or one, see discussion in my *Scholia*, pp. 30-31. Athenagoras, *Legatio*, 30.3. Origen, *Cels*, III.43. Eusebius, *Praeparatio Evangelica*, 3.10.21. Gregory of Nazianzus, *Contra Julianum*, PG.35.705.17-18. Severian of Gabala, *Fragmenta in Epistulam ad Titum*, p. 344. John Chrysostom, *In Epistulam ad Titum*, PG.62.676.55-57. Theodoret, *Interpretatio in xiv Epistulas sancti Pauli*, PG.82.861.20-26. Photius, *Bibliotheca*, Codex 190, p. 147b. Cf. Pausanias, *Graeciae Descriptio*, 2.22.5.

676 Origen started writing the commentary on John shortly after he had set out to compose his *De Principiis*, and then he wrote those two works more or less simultaneously. Cf. *Princ*, I.2.3-4; I.2.13. Besides, when he wrote the second book of *De Principiis*, he had already written a comment of Genesis, 1:1. See *Princ*, II.3.6.

Ebionites, who maintained that Jesus was a bare human being (ψιλὸς ἄνθρωπος), such as Akylas of Pontus, Theodotion, and Symmachus, appealed to the gospel of Matthew in order to support their belief,[677] which evolved further with Origen's contemporary Paul of Samosata, whose adoptionist theories ran sheer contrary to those of Origen's.[678]

> If the immortal divine Logos assumes both a human body and a human soul, and by so doing appears to Celsus to be subject to change and reshaping, let him learn that, while the Logos remains Logos in essence, he suffers nothing of the suffering of the body or of the soul. Nevertheless, sometimes he comes down to the level of him who is unable to look upon the radiance and brilliance (τὰς μαρμαρυγὰς καὶ τὴν λαμπρότητα)[679] of the Deity, and, as it were, becomes flesh by being spoken of in physical terms, until he who has accepted him in this form is able to look also upon, so to speak, his most sublime form by being gradually elevated by the Logos. There are, so to speak, different forms of the Logos corresponding to how the Logos appears to each of those who are led to know him, which is analogous to the acquired habit of either one who is a beginner, or one that has made a little progress, or is more advanced, or has nearly attained to virtue already, or has in fact attained it.[680]

Origen made this point mainly (yet not exclusively) in relation to the event of Jesus' transfiguration and to the reference[681] in Isaiah, 53:2-3. So he did also in the sixth book of *Contra Celsum*. His remark was that he had 'explained more extensively' (διὰ πλειόνων ἐν τοῖς πρὸ τούτων ἀπελογησάμεθα ... ὃ ἀποδεδώκαμεν) what 'different forms of Logos' means in relation to Jesus 'bringing' his three disciples 'into a high mountain apart'.[682]

Nevertheless, the instance of transfiguration narrated in Matthew 17:1-6 called for *ad hoc* exegesis in the context of his commentary on that gospel. This he did in the twelfth book of that work. Now, he used not only the expression

---

677 *Suda*, letter omega, entry 182. Cf. Eusebius, *HE*, 6.17.1. Nicephorus Callistus Xanthopulus, *HE*, 5.12.

678 Little wonder that the bishops who controverted Paul of Samosata were of Origenian kinship, such as Gregory Thaumaturgus, Firmilian of Caesarea, Dionysius of Alexandria, Theotecnus of Caesarea, *et. al.* Paul of Samosata was convicted by a council held at Antioch in 268. See *supra*, note 102 (Anastasius of Sinai claimed that Origen maintained the idea about Christ being 'a bare man', καὶ Ὠριγένης ψιλὸν ἄνθρωπον τὸν Χριστόν)!

679 Cf. Plato, *Respublica*, 581a. Origen, *Cels*, VI:17; 66; 67; *homJob*, PG.17.92.44-48.

680 *Cels*, IV.15-16.

681 Matthew 17:1-6; Mark, 9:2-8. Cf. *Philocalia*, 15.18-20, quoting *Cels*, VI.77, explaining Isaiah, 53:2-3 (Prologue, section c: καὶ τίς ὁ λόγος τῶν διαφόρων τοῦ λόγου μορφῶν).

682 He had in mind his statement in IV.15-16, which I have just quoted. Cf. *Cels*, II.65; VI.68: σκηνώσας δὲ καὶ γενόμενος ἐν ἡμῖν οὐκ ἔμεινεν ἐπὶ τῆς πρώτης μορφῆς, ἀλλ' ἀναβιβάσας ἡμᾶς ἐπὶ τὸ λογικὸν *ὑψηλὸν ὄρος* ἔδειξεν ἡμῖν τὴν ἔνδοξον μορφὴν ἑαυτοῦ καὶ τὴν λαμπρότητα τῶν ἐνδυμάτων αὐτοῦ.

'different forms of Logos' (διαφόρους μορφάς),[683] but also 'differences of Logos' (τὰς τοῦ λόγου διαφοράς).[684] As always, he quoted the evangelical passage first, and then expounded his own comment on this, in just the same way Alexander of Aphrodisias did with Aristotle's commentaries, from which Origen had learned not only Alexander's own comments but also Aristotle's text itself. I will ponder for a moment on the introductory phrase of his specific comment, which follows quotation of Matthew 17:1-2.

> Let this exegesis of the [scriptural] passage, so far as its phraseology is concerned, be set forth, in addition to the one that we have offered a long time ago as this had appeared to us [to be correct].[685]

Since 'those remarks' are found only in the *Contra Celsum*, it follows that this work had been written 'a long time' before the commentary on Matthew.[686] Nevertheless, the *Contra Celsum* itself is one of Origen's later works. This means that he did not die in 254/5, as currently believed, but later – which though is beyond the scope of the present book and will be demonstrated in my forthcoming biography of Origen.[687]

One more point of Origen's foregoing remark deserves discussion. When he wrote, 'Let this exegesis of the [scriptural] passage so far as its phraseology is concerned be set forth',[688] he used the verbal form γεγονέτω, which is

683 Origen, *Cels*, VI.77; *commMatt*, 12.32; 12.36-38; *schLuc*, PG.17: 340.28-56; 344.33-54; *frLuc*, fr. 139c.

684 Origen, *commMatt*, 12.30.

685 Origen, *op. cit.* 12.36: Τοῦτο δὲ καὶ πρὸ‹ς τοῖς› τῆς κατὰ ταῦτα φαινομένης ἡμῖν διηγήσεως γεγονέτω πάλαι καὶ ὡς πρὸς τὴν λέξιν. Read: Τοῦτο δὲ καὶ ὡς πρὸς τὴν λέξιν γεγονέτω καὶ πρὸ‹ς τοῖς› πάλαι τῆς κατὰ ταῦτα φαινομένης ἡμῖν διηγήσεως. See also *infra*, note 678. As strange as it appears, the expression ὡς πρὸς τὴν λέξιν (meaning concentration of the phraseology of a passage) apparently was introduced by Origen and appears only in two of his admirers, namely, Eusebius (*Commentaria in Psalmos*, PG.23: 493.18 & 645.37 864.12-13) and Didymus (*Commentarii in Psalmos 29-34*, codex p. 218). Later, only John Philoponus used this; *commGenCorr*, p. 81. I have argued that John Philoponus was aware of Origen's work and availed himself of this. See *Anaxagoras*, pp. 954; 1491; 1560; *COT*, p. 266; *PHE*, pp. 118; 126-127; 171; 214-215; 311; 398-399; 423; 429; *NDGF*, pp. 413; 516; 567; *RCR*, pp. 350; *Scholia*, pp. xv; 50; 166; 211; 213; 226; 240; 380-382.

686 Eusebius simply reported: "They say that Origen wrote the *Contra Celsum* and the commentary on Matthew when he was over sixty years old'. *HE*, 6.36.1-2. On Origen's *commMatt* being his latest work, see my *Anaxagoras*, pp. 1300; 1145; 1582.

687 Nevertheless, see *Anaxagoras*, pp. 1032-1040: 'Origen writing after 265 AD'.

688 Origen, *commMatt*, 12.36: "Let the following be added to the exegesis as this appeared to us [to be correct] which we have offered a long time ago, the following one, also so far as the scriptural wording is concerned" (τοῦτο δὲ καὶ πρὸς τοῖς τῆς κατὰ ταῦτα φαινομένης ἡμῖν διηγήσεως γεγονέτω πάλαι καὶ ὡς πρὸς τὴν λέξιν). See Origen using the expression, ὡς

the Present Perfect Imperative of the verb γίγνομαι. This Imperative form is alternative to the periphrastic (third person) γεγονὼς ἔστω (second person: γεγονὼς ἴσθι).[689] The non-periphrastic form of this Present Perfect appeared only during the third century BC, but what is most characteristic about it is that this Imperative was used almost exclusively by Geometricians. Prior to Origen, this had been used by Apollonius of Perga (Greek geometer and astronomer, late third – early second centuries BC),[690] Archimedes,[691] Euclides,[692] Heron of Alexandria,[693] Claudius Ptolemy,[694] Pappus of Alexandria,[695] Theon of Alexandria,[696] Serenus of Antinopolis.[697] Also, by mathematicians, such as Eutocius of Ascalon.[698] Proclus used this, too, yet he did so almost exclusively in context of mathematical considerations.[699] So did Simplicius,[700] and several anonymous commentators, mainly of Euclides.[701] In the few cases that Christian intellectuals made use of this verbal form, this only reflected their knowledge of mathematics, especially of Geometry.[702]

Consequently, it turns out that when Origen used this form of Present Perfect Imperative (γεγονέτω) he was the only one (excluding Geometricians

---

πρὸς τὴν λέξιν, meaning 'concerning the literal meaning'. *Cels*, VII.19; *commJohn*, X.5.21; XIII.27.162; *frLam*, fr. 162; *commGen*, PG.12.81.22 (*Philocalia*, 23.19); *commMatt*, 17.26; *selGen*, PG.12.133.8; *selPs*, PG.12.1125.34&39. See also *supra*, note 675.

689 Cf. Plato, *Leges*, 951c: ὁ θεωρὸς ὁ τοιοῦτος ἡμῖν γεγονὼς ἔστω πλειόνων ἐτῶν ἢ πεντήκοντα. *Op. cit.* 953c: πρῶτον μὲν ἔλαττον ἐτῶν μηδὲν πεντήκοντα γεγονὼς ἔστω. Pappus of Alexandria, *Synagoge*, Book 7, p. 700: Ἔστω γεγονός. Didymus, *frPs*(*al*), fr. 1175: Ἴσθι δὲ ἐν τούτοις γεγονὼς ὑπὸ κυρίου εὐλογίαν ἔχειν.

690 Apollonius of Perga, *Conica*, 2.4; 2.44. 2.26; *et passim* (at nearly two dozens of points).

691 Archimedes, *De Sphaera et Cylindro*, v. 1, pp. 109; 121; *De Planorum Aequilibriis*, v. 2, p. 96.

692 Euclides, *Elementa*, Book 10, Demonstratio 105; Book 12, Demonstratio 2; *et passim* (at more than fifty points).

693 Heron of Alexandria, *Χειροβαλλίστρας Κατασκευὴ καὶ Συμμετρία*, 1.7; 2.2; 4.1; *Pneumatica*, 1.2; *et passim* (at more than thirty points).

694 Claudius Ptolemy, *Geographia*, 1.11.1; *Harmonica*, 2.7; 3.8.

695 Pappus of Alexandria, *Synagoge*, Book 2, p. 2; *et passim* (at more than thirty points).

696 Theon of Alexandria, *Commentaria in Ptolemaei Syntaxin Mathematicam*, pp; 985; 1009; *et passim.*

697 Serenus of Antinouplis (geometrician), *De Sectione Coni*, p. 150.

698 Eutocius of Ascalon (c. 480 – c. 540 AD), *Commentarii in Libros De Sphaera et Cylindro*, pp. 16; 40; *et passim* (at more than twenty points).

699 Proclus, *Hypotyposis Astronomicarum Positionum*, 3.16; 3.18; 3.19; 5.101; *Institutio Physica*, 2.8; *et passim; commEucl*, v. 3, pp. 75; 224; 344; *commTim*, v. 2, pp. 176; 237.

700 Simplicius, *commPhys*, p. 1149.

701 Anonymous, *Scholia in Euclidis Elementa*, Book 5, scholion 61; *et passim.*

702 Cf. Michael Psellus, *Opuscula ii*, p. 7. George Pachymeres, *Quadrivium*, 1.26; 3.10; 3.24; 3.25; 3.26; 3.27; 3.28. Barlaam of Calabria, *Λογιστική*, 1.26; 5.6; 5.7; 5.11; 5.13; 5.14; 6.6; *et passim.* Didymus, *Commentarii in Psalmos 40-44.4*, codex p. 323.

both prior and posterior to him) to make this part of his own vocabulary. No doubt, this is one more token of his vast erudition, which he used as introductory course in order to train his pupils to theology, which is what he wrote to Gregory Thaumaturgus.[703]

Careful reading of certain points of the *Contra Celsum* makes it clear that, when Origen wrote this work, composition of a commentary on Matthew was a plan placed in the *future*. In the second book of the *Contra Celsum*, he briefly considered Jesus' suffering, death, and burial (also quoting Paul's statement, 'for we are buried together with him by baptism'[704]), but wrote this:

> But *we will explain* (διηγησόμεθα) at length the points concerning his burial and the tomb and the man who buried him *at a more suitable time in another work* (εὐκαιρότερον διὰ πλειόνων ἐν ἄλλοις), in which our primary purpose will be to discuss these matters.[705]

As a matter of fact he did so – but it is only now that the text of the commentary on on Matthew that contains this analysis comes to light, which reveals that he had more to say on the meaning of Jesus' 'burial' and its significance for those 'saints' who opt for participating in this burial, that is, for the significance of Jesus' burial into the tomb in the context of Origen's own Philosophy of History.[706] Nevertheless, he did so also in the extant commentary on Matthew, because he needed to peruse this in relation both to his own Eschatology and to his theory of Restoration.[707]

Likewise, in his reply to Celsus, Origen argued that it would be absurd to accept the Stoic theory of recurrence of identical worlds, in which 'Socrates, Xanthippe, Anytus, and Melitus' will re-appear identically and act invariably in an indistinguishable world, which 'will be the same'. Once again, he postponed discussion of this:

> However, the primary argument in reply to the words of both Celsus and the Stoics *will be discussed in another work* at a more convenient time (εὐκαιρότερον ἐν ἄλλοις ἐξετασθήσεται), since, saying more about these (πλεονάσαι) *at the present moment* (κατὰ τὸν παρόντα καιρὸν) is out of keeping with our present purpose (τὴν ἐνεστηκυῖαν πρόθεσιν).[708]

---

703 Origen, *Epistula ad Gregorium Thaumaturgum*, 1 (*Philocalia*, 13.1). See quotation *supra*, p. XLIX and note 136.

704 Rom. 4:4.

705 Origen, *Cels*, II.69; italics are mine.

706 Origen, *apud Codex Sabaiticus 232*, folios 230r-v.

707 Origen, *commMatt*, 15.23.

708 Origen, *op. cit.* II.69; italics are mine.

Why was that so? Because these matters involved exposition of theories such as transmigration of souls, which he discussed extensively in the commentary on Matthew.[709] Furthermore, he declared that this topic was part of a broader scope, which he intended to consider at a later stage of his life.

> But whether or not there is reason to suppose that after evil has disappeared it rises again, or not, such a problem *will be discussed* in a treatise dealing predominantly with this subject (ἐν προηγουμένῳ λόγῳ τὰ τοιαῦτα ἐξετασθήσεται).[710]

Why? Because it is also in the commentary on Matthew that he treated the question of eventual abolition of evil and his theory of universal restoration, and it is also in that commentary that cardinal ideas of his Eschatology are expounded.[711] It is certainly all but coincidence that, when Pamphilus came to considering the allegations attributing 'transmigration of souls' to Origen, he started the pertinent section with quoting from the latter's commentary on Matthew.[712]

Moreover, there is a telling difference of temper between those two treatises, which also reveals that, although *Contra Celsum* and the *Commentary on Matthew* were late works, the former was written long since the latter was composed during the dusk of Origen's life.

His tenor in the *Contra Celsum* makes it clear that he felt he had plenty of time to live and write more works in order to advance or elaborate on critical points of his theology. Upon concluding the last book of *Contra Celsum*, he wrote that, since Celsus had announced that he was going to write one more refutation of Christian faith, he was himself prepared to write one more refutation of Celsus' allegations, and asked Ambrose to send a copy of them to him, should such a treatise by Celsus appear at all.[713]

Earlier in the same work, he announced that whether evil would rekindle after its total abolition, or not, was a topic that he intended to peruse in a subsequent *ad hoc* treatise.[714] As for the doctrine of recurrence of identical worlds, although he had already set forth a lot of arguments in the *Contra Celsum*, he also wrote that this 'should be examined in more length in future works' of his,

709 Cf. Origen, *commMatt*, 10.20; 13.1-2; *frMatt* (Benz – Klostermann), pp. 4-8. Also, *commMatt* in the present *Codex Sabaiticus*, *232*, folio 117r.

710 *Cels*, IV.69; italics are mine.

711 Cf. Origen, *commMatt*, 13.2; 15.24; 16.5; 16.18; 17.15-16; 17.19. *commMatt* in *Codex Sabaiticus*, *232*, folio 174v;

712 Pamphilus, *Apologia pro Origene*, PG.17.608-616.

713 Origen, *Cels*, VIII.76.

714 Origen, *op. cit.* IV.69

because this did not entirely fit with his present purpose'.[715] Why did he need to expound this more extensively? The reason can be found only in the commentary on Matthew: he wanted to examine this idea of recurrence of identical worlds in relation to the theory of transmigration.[716]

By contrast, in the commentary on Matthew,[717] the feeling that he has plenty of time in front of him for composing new works is entirely gone: Origen appears lonely and disheartened, a man who felt that the end is hovering. This is why he did not mince his words concerning the putrefaction of the clergy at his town (i.e. Tyre), especially that of bishops.[718] Moreover, he appeared determined to finish off with the 'false doctrine of transmigration' (τῆς μετενσωματώσεως ψευδοδοξίαν)[719] 'which is alien to the Church of God' (τὸ ἀλλότριον τῆς ἐκκλησίας τοῦ θεοῦ περὶ τῆς μετενσωματώσεως δόγμα),[720] and to explain that scriptural points which would apparently lend themselves to such an assumption (e.g. the parable of hired labourers in Matthew, 20) had a very different meaning.[721] It is certainly because he wrote in this melancholic mood that he allowed himself to express his regret for having committed castration upon himself when he was 'young in the faith' and to explain his motives, as well as the reasons why he 'unwisely' committed that act.[722]

All too often Origen's critical terms pass unnoticed, although they tellingly point to his vast background and reveal his philosophical predilections. One of them is relevant to the present discussion.

Despite his dualism, Plato maintained that the human identity is not the soul / body entity: it is the soul alone that should be identified with the human person. The soul is only a prisoner incarcerated in a body, and it is eager to get rid of its bonds and return to its natural abode in the Beyond. The human soul may transmigrate to other living beings, such as fishes or oysters, still it is the *same* soul. This is only about a prisoner having changed prison and decamped to a worse one. The point was about what kind of prison is a living being

715 Origen, *op. cit.* IV.68.

716 Origen, *commMatt*, 13.1.

717 Therefore, I disagree with Ronald Heine's assumption, 'Origen's commentary on Matthew seems to have been written before the *Against Celsus*, but Vogt thinks Origen had not yet finished it when he was working on the *Against Celsus*.' R. Heine, *Origen: Scholarship in the Service of the Church*, pp. 219-220. Cf. H.J. Vogt, *Origenes als Exegete*, Paderborn, 1999, pp. 179-185. Lately, Heine has reversed his thesis.

718 Origen, *commSerMatt*, fr. 138; *commMatt*, 11.15; 12.14; 14.22; 15.26; 16.8; 16.19; 16.21-23; 16.25; *schMatt*, PG.17.301.41-52.

719 Origen, *commMatt*, 10.20.

720 Origen, *op. cit.* 13.1 & *frMatt* (Benz – Klostermann), p. 4.

721 Origen, *op. cit.* 15.34. See discussion of this in *Anaxagoras*, pp. 1343-1348.

722 Origen, *commMatt*, 15.1.

condemned to live in. But this was only mere adaptation of Pythagoreanism and of the subsequent theory of Empedocles.

In Plato's *Timaeus*, we are told that 'one who has failed shall be changed into woman's nature at the second birth; and if, in that shape, he still does not refrain from wickedness, he shall be changed every time, according to the nature of his wickedness, into some bestial form after the similitude of his own nature'. He classified degradation of men through reincarnation to women, then to 'the tribe of birds', then to 'the wild species of animal that goes on foot', and, worst of all, to 'the tribe of fishes and of shell-fish (or, oysters) and to all creatures of the waters'.[723] However, this involves the idea that 'living creatures keep passing into one another in all these ways, as they undergo transformation by the loss or by the gain of reason and unreason' (νοῦ καὶ ἀνοίας ἀποβολῇ καὶ κτήσει μεταβαλλόμενα).[724] This is all about transmutation of existence within this world, not about different ranks of life. In any case, Plato did not say anything about reincarnation into plants. Moreover, he did not explain what is the kind of 'sin' that a bird would commit so as to incur reincarnation into the worse condition of a wild animal or an oyster.

It was this point on which Origen implicitly criticised Plato's idea.

> For it is impossible to see aquatic genera of being transformed from being mean, as, for example, genera of fishes [being transformed] to honourable ones, or from superior to lower ones. In contrast, it is always possible to see men either righteous or wicked either to attain to virtue from vice, or from being fallen from progressing in virtue to abundance of wickedness.[725]

Likewise,

> Let then others, who are estranged from the teaching of the church, believe that souls transmigrate from human bodies to bodies of dogs in accordance with different degrees of wickedness.[726]

In general, Origen put his vast philosophical background to use in order to take Christian philosophy through the surrounding challenges of his Greek environment, although the vast majority of Christian authors during and after the sixth century could not tolerate Origen's gestation of Greek notions (if

723 Plato, *Timaeus*, 42a; cf. *op. cit.* 90e.

724 Plato, *op. cit.* 91d-92b.

725 Origen, *commMatt*, 10.11.

726 Origen, *op. cit.* 11.17. He commented on the instance of Matt. 15:22-28 and referred to Exodus, 22:20, 'And you shall be holy men to me; and you shall not eat flesh taken of beasts, you shall cast it to the dog'.

not propositions) and his putting them into service to the purpose of forming a coherent Christian doctrine. Despite frustration caused especially by his Christian environment, he persevered in his quest for truth until the end. His analyses are full of meaningful technical philosophical turns, yet normally these pass unnoticed only because most often his students lack the background to recognise them. One of the aims of the present volume is to shed light on the telling implications of such points.

A postscript to this subsection is necessary. In 2017, I sent the manuscript of the present book to an acquisitions editor at Turnhout, Belgium, who, in the preceding years, had expressed interest in publishing some work of mine. His anonymous reader, while praising the quality of the critical editing and of my commentary, passed the verdict that 'the value of the Greek text of *Sabaiticus* 232 itself is nil' [!]. Subsequently, I sent this work to another far more prestigious publisher: their assessment as to the value of *Sabaiticus 232* was diametrical, and they expressed keen interest in publishing this – all the more so since they recognised that *Sabaiticus 232* happens to be a most valuable and revealing witness to Origen's commentary on Matthew, and that unfortunately Klostermann missed this. However, I could not accept their demand to follow hackneyed 'international standards' concerning presentation of the critical apparatus, which means to present the Greek text alone without my comments that cast light on the serious philosophical and theological implications of this valuable text. Instead, I insisted on maintaining the present scheme, which is the same as that of my previously published edition volumes, only because I am satisfied that this is far more serviceable, more informative, and more beneficial to those interested in this new Greek text – indeed in any newly discovered Greek text. Consequently, I decided to withdraw my proposal. Much later, in 2018, while enjoying one of those lovely summer nights of Thessaloniki upon dinner with the same Turnhout acquisitions editor, he did not reveal the identity of his anonymous reader (of which I would have never asked, of course), but made the passing remark (as a retrospective comment on a long past case) that his reader who assessed this project is 'a scholar who is a specialist on the Greek text of Origen's commentary on Matthew'. Not long after that, an announcement of an English translation of Origen's commentary on Matthew came to my knowledge. In 2019, I read some of the Introduction to that translation, and I came upon a brief subsection expounding the argument that the commentary on Matthew is later than the *Contra Celsum*. Incidentally, by making this claim, the same author (while refraining from explicating this) reversed the thesis he had argued for in an earlier book of his (see note 717), namely, that 'Origen's commentary on Matthew seems to have been written before the *Against Celsus*'. Most of his new argument adduces Origen's own cross-reference to other works of his – all of which is long known stuff and nothing new. The only supposedly new in this section is the argument based on Origen's references to his comments on Jesus' burial, just as discussed above. I want to believe that this happenstance is accidental – but I will certainly not disown important results of my personal research, also preserved and dated in my electronic 'sent-mail' box.

Origen's Proem from Codex Holy Cross 104

Codex Holy Cross 104 reveals a portion from the proem of Origen's commentary on Matthew, which is partially unique,[727] given that the extant Greek text of the commentary starts with the tenth book of it, commenting on Matthew 13:36. Jerome reproduced this, although at that point his expression is somewhat obscure, because he copied from Origen hastefully.[728]

What is important about this short text is that it reveals Origen's adherence to writing Prologues introducing readers to a commentary by treating general questions surrounding the work that he was about to comment upon. This topic calls for discussion of a specific aspect of Origen's methodology that evinces his Greek lore being put to use when he wrote as a Christian.

It is known that in some of his extant works Origen wrote prologues; these works are his commentaries on Genesis, Leviticus, the Lamentations, the Psalms, the Song of Songs, the gospels of John and Matthew, and the epistle to the Romans. The topics treated in such prologues more or less follow the pattern of commentaries by Greek authors, especially Aristotelian commentators (notably, Alexander of Aphrodisias), as well as Galen.[729]

---

727 The first part of this appears in a quotation by Eusebius and is quoted forthwith. The rest is heretofore unknown and comes to light for the first time.

728 "Tertius Lucas medicus natione Syrus Antiochensis (cujus laus in Evangelio) qui et ipse discipulus apostolic Pauli" (The third is Luke, the physician, of Syrian descent born in Antioch [whose praise is in the Gospel], who was himself also a disciple of apostle Paul). But the 'praise' of Luke (in a rather attenuated sense) is in the epistles of Paul (cf. Gal. 2:7; Col. 4:14; 2 Tim. 4:11), not in the 'Gospel' –by which presumably at this point Jerome indicated all of the New Testament.

729 See Ilsetraut Hadot, "Les Introductions aux commentaires exégétiques chez les Auteurs Néoplatoniciens et les auteurs chrétiens", in Michel Tardieu (ed.), *Les règles de l'interprétation*, Paris, 1989, pp. 99-122. Bernard Neuschäfer, *Origenes als Philologe*, Schweizerische Beiträge zur Altertumswissenschaft 18/1-2, Basel, 1987, pp. 57-84. Jaap Mansfeld, *Prolegomena: Questions to Be Settled before the Study of an Author, or a Text*, Philosophia Antiqua 61, Leiden, 1994. Alfons Fürst, "Origen: exegesis and Philosophy in early Christian Alexandria", in Josef Löss – John W. Watt (eds.), *Interpreting the Bible and Aristotle in Late Antiquity: The Alexandrian Commentary tradition Between Rome and Baghdad*, Burlington, 2011, pp. 13-32.

Origen himself used the works of Greek authors of Late Antiquity, particularly those by Alexander of Aphrodisias,[730] Galen,[731] and Plutarch.[732] From those his picked up critical expressions and terms which he adapted to his own objectives. His work makes it evident that, a Greek philosopher as he was until he converted to Christianity at the age of nearly fifty, he was aware of the Greek techniques concerning prefatory schemata, but he followed them only to the extent they suited his purposes.

More than a hundred years ago, Karl Praechter proposed a schematic reconstruction of the topics included in commentary prologues. Praechter's range of consideration starts with Alexander of Aphrodisias and concludes with the commentaries by Michael of Ephesus (twelfth century). He drew attention to the *schemata isagogica* of such commentaries, and believed that what are now known as 'commentaries' were largely transcripts from class lectures by the 'commentator'.[733] Besides, he pointed out the ten particular topics ('which are enumerated by Ammonius, Simplicius, Olympiodorus, Philoponus and Elias') that any commentator felt incumbent upon him to address upon writing a preamble.

(1) How many and in what sorts of ways did the philosophical schools get their names? (κατὰ πόσους καὶ ποίους τρόπους τὰς ὀνομασίας ἔσχον αἱ κατὰ φιλοσοφίαν αἱρέσεις;)

(2) What is the division of the Aristotelian treatises, so that it should become clear where in their sequence we should place the present book? (τίς ἡ διαίρεσις τῶν Ἀριστοτελικῶν συγγραμμάτων, ἵνα καὶ τὸ προκείμενον ὅπου χοροῦ τάξωμεν γένηται δῆλον;)

(3) Where should one begin Aristotle's treatises from? (πόθεν ἀρκτέον τῶν Ἀριστοτέλους συγγραμμάτων;)

(4) What is the goal of Aristotle's philosophy? (τί τὸ τέλος ἐστὶν τῆς Ἀριστοτέλους φιλοσοφίας;)

(5) What leads us to this goal? (τίνα τὰ ἄγοντα ἡμᾶς πρὸς τὸ τέλος;)

---

730 On Alexander of Aphrodisias and Origen, see, *Anaxagoras*, pp. 354; 397-398; 512; 522; 597; 658; 672; 676; 843; 869; 927 (God styled αὐτοζωή); 928-929; 978; 991-992; 996-997. *RCR*, pp. 173; 313; 368; 377; *PHE*, pp. 269; 404; *NDGF*, pp. 305-306; 352; 516; 581; *Scholia*, pp. 40; 147; 166; 199; 262; 265-268; 277; 279; 294; 300; 304; 330; 337; 345; 385; 397; 402-404. Eusebius expressed explicitly his respect for Alexander of Aphrodisias. *Praeparatio Evangelica*, 6.8.39–6.9.32.

731 See *supra*, note 591.

732 On Plutarch and Origen see, *Anaxagoras*, pp. 676; 854; *COT*, pp. 122; 201; 219; *PHE*, pp. 15; 45; *NDGF*, pp. 220; 238-239; 371-372; *RCR*, pp. 80; 326; 343; 377; *Scholia*, pp. 40; 267-268; 294; 322; 337; 368. See joint considerations of Galen and Plutarch, in *NDGF*, pp. 218; 239; 289; 345; 405; *RCR*, p. 163; *Scholia*, pp. 73; 97; 246; 262; 388.

733 Praechter, *op. cit.* (note 7), pp. 38-40.

(6) What is the genre (εἶδος) of the Aristotelian treatises? (τί τὸ εἶδος τῶν Ἀριστοτελικῶν συγγραμμάτων;)

(7) Why did the Philosopher practice obscurity? (διὰ τί τὴν ἀσάφειαν ἐπετήδευσεν ὁ φιλόσοφος;) It was Alexander of Aphrodisias who first pointed out Aristotle's 'obscurity', yet he did not essay too much to justify this (allegedly, deliberate) practice.[734] Likewise, later commentators saw this as an intentional practice aiming to stir students to reflection and cause the 'sluggish' or less perceptive ones to withdraw.[735]

(8) What sort of interpreter do such arguments require? (ποῖον δεῖ τὸν ἐξηγητὴν εἶναι τῶν τοιούτων λόγων;)

(9) What is the sort of a pupil who should be granted access? (ποῖον δεῖ τὸν ἀκροατὴν παραλαμβάνεσθαι;)

(10) Of how many chapters from each Aristotelian treatise should one provide a preconception to his readers? Of what sort are these, and why? (πόσα δεῖ προλαμβάνειν ἑκάστης Ἀριστοτελικῆς πραγματείας κεφάλαια καὶ ποῖα καὶ διὰ ποίαν αἰτίαν;)[736]

It has been assumed that the origin of this classification was Ammonius of Alexandria,[737] which is what Praechter thought, too. There were differences of expression in this list, yet by and large those were immaterial. However, in Elias' similar list these are not quite so. For example, Elias did not see 'the τέλος of Aristotle's philosophy' (fourth clause) as meaning 'goal'; instead, he saw this as 'end' distinguished from 'beginning' and 'middle'.[738] Besides, Elias was

734 Alexander of Aphrodisias, *commMetaph*, p. 673 (on 1069b26): Πάνυ τεταραγμένως καὶ φύρδην καὶ οὐ τεταγμένως οὐδ' ἀκολούθως ἐπάγει τὰ ἐν τῷ βιβλίῳ τούτῳ λεγόμενα, δι' οὐδὲν ἕτερον ἢ δι' ἣν ἀρχῆθεν ἐπετήδευσεν ἀσάφειαν.

735 Simplicius, *commPhys*, p. 8. John Philoponus, *commCateg*, p. 6; *commAnalPr*, p. 52. David of Alexandria, *In Porphyrii Isagogen*, p. 105. Arethas of Caesarea, *Scholia in Porphyrii Isagogen*, scholion 22. Ammonius of Alexandria thought that Aristotle 'practiced obscurity' because he sought to use terms that should be as appropriate as possible (διὰ τὸ βούλεσθαι αὐτὸν οἰκειοτέροις ὀνόμασι χρῆσθαι). *commCateg*, pp. 1 & 25 copied by John Philoponus, *commCateg*, p. 29). I believe Ammonius had in mind Aristotle's expression in the *Magna Moralia*, 1185a: ᾧ οὐθὲν ἔχομεν οἰκειότερον ὄνομα ἐπιθεῖναι ἢ θρεπτικόν.

736 Simplicius, *commCateg*, p. 3; cf. p. 60. Dionysius of Halicarnassus wrote that giving in advance an idea of what the 'ensuing chapters' are about was part of the art of rhetoric. *De Thucydide*, 19. Cf. Theon of Alexandria, *Commentaria in Ptolemaei Syntaxin Mathematicam i-iv*, p. 435. Ammonius of Alexandria, *commDeInterpr*, p. 1. Elias of Alexandria, *commCateg*, pp. 108; 107; 127.

737 Ammonius of Alexandria, *commCateg*, p. 1. Later commentators followed suit: John Philoponus, *commCateg*, p. 1. Elias of Alexandria, *commCateg*, p. 124. Olympiodorus of Alexandria, *Prolegomena*, p. 1, but see next how he nuanced this.

738 Elias of Alexandria, *commCateg*, p. 107: καὶ ἐπειδὴ ὅπου ἀρχὴ καὶ τέλος, ἔστι τι καὶ μεταξύ.

confident that this tabulation had been introduced not by Ammonius, but by the latter's teacher, namely, Proclus.[739]

As a matter of fact, this can be confirmed by Proclus' own analysis in his proem to the commentary on Plato's *Republic:* he puts his students on their notice about the importance of Plato's prologues (τοὺς προλόγους τῶν Πλατωνικῶν διαλόγων) and the special consideration that those should be given. Moreover, he was aware that composition of prologue involved a certain 'method', which should be perused as much as the main body of the treatise, and in the same way (τὸν αὐτὸν καὶ ἐπὶ τῶν ἄλλων τρόπον μετιόντες τὰς ἐξηγήσεις στοχάζοισθε ἂν τῆς περὶ ταῦτα μεθόδου). He speaks scrornfully of 'many exegetes' who 'passed over' this section without bringing its merits to light (ξηρὸν καὶ ἐλλιπῆ τὸν τόπον παραλείπειν), and warns against 'imitating' them (τοὺς πολλοὺς τῶν ἐξηγητῶν μιμουμένους). He would have had in mind lessons he had attended at Alexandria, where 'he followed and enjoyed both the lessons on Aristotle by Olympiodorus' and the company of Heron, who introduced him in the 'knowledge of mathematical science' (τῶν κατὰ παίδευσιν ὁδῶν).[740] However, 'when he heard someone explaining Plato in class (ἐν τῇ συναναγνώσει) in a manner not worthy of Plato', he came to despise that school and went to Athens, accompanied by many scholars'.[741]

Accordingly, Proclus points out seven topics that should be discussed in prologue (τῶν ἑπτὰ τούτων), which are the following: (1) the aim (πρῶτον μέν, ... τὴν πρόθεσιν, then, ὁ σκοπός); (2) the material (τὴν ὕλην), by which he meant the kind of the treatise (τὸ εἶδος, then, δεύτερον δέ, ... ποῖόν ἐστιν τῶν λόγων εἶδος); (3) precursory explanation of the content, such as identifying the persons involved, as well as the places and the times of the setting (τρίτον δὲ ... ἣν ἔν τε προσώποις καὶ τόποις καὶ καιροῖς θεωρεῖσθαι συμβέβηκεν) always in relation to the aim of this or any other dialogue (πρὸς τὸν ἑκάστου διαλόγου σκοπόν); (4) analysis of how did Plato categorise different States (τέταρτον, ... διελέσθαι τὰς πολιτείας κατὰ Πλάτωνα) and determining which one he speaks about (καὶ εἰπεῖν

739 Elias of Alexandria, *loc. cit.*: Ταῦτα πάντα τοῦ Πρόκλου λέγοντος δεῖν προλαμβάνειν ἀρχομένους τῶν Ἀριστοτελικῶν συνταγμάτων ἐν τῇ συναναγνώσει (σύνταγμα δὲ τούτου Πρόκλειον).

740 The expression τῶν κατὰ παίδευσιν ὁδῶν is actually Plato's (*Timaeus*, 53c) and is sometimes rendered 'the methods of science' (R.G. Bury's translation 'the technical method', Loeb, v. 234, is wrong). Proclus understood this expression of *Timaeus* as meaning 'knowledge of mathematical science' (*commEucl*, p. 20), and this is what he meant when he used this himself in his *Theologia Platonica* (v. 1, p. 11): in order to understand theology one should have a good command of mathematics, 'since this is how one could comprehend immaterial realities'. Likewise, Simplicius explained this as 'mathematical science' (*commCael*, p. 641). Proclus' discipleship with Heron is also recorded by the *Suda*, letter eta, entry 553, copying from Marinus.

741 Marinus of Neapolis (Proclus' pupil), *Vita Procli*, lines 212-239.

ὑπὲρ τῆς ποίας ἐστὶν αὐτῷ πολιτείας ὁ λόγος); (5) while focusing on the specifics of a certain State, it should be examined if there are kinds of States that are deficient, which and how many they are, and which of them should be given precedence in the discussion (πέμπτον … περὶ ποίας τῶν πολλῶν τούτων ἔσται προηγουμένως ἡ θεωρία τῷ λογισμῷ λαβεῖν); (6) explanation of how did Plato peruse the State he opted for, and figuring out if there are aspects of the topic that eluded his analysis (εἰ μηδένα τρόπον ἀδιερεύνητον ἀφῆκεν τῆς περὶ αὐτὴν θεωρίας); (7) pointing out the ideas permeating Plato's analysis, and bringing to light and demonstrating their congruent coherence (τὰ δόγματα, then, τὴν δι' ὅλου τοῦ συγγράμματος διήκουσαν τῶν λόγων ὑπόθεσιν, then, ἕβδομον τὴν δι' ὅλου τοῦ συγγράμματος διήκουσαν τῶν δογμάτων ἀκολουθίαν ὑπ' ὄψιν ἀγαγεῖν καὶ ἐπιδεῖξαι).

These are the 'chapters' (κεφάλαια)[742] Proclus determined that should constitute the prefatory discussion 'of Plato's *Republic*' (τῆς Πολιτείας Πλάτωνος) by 'those who set out to explain this correctly' (τοὺς ὀρθῶς ἐξηγουμένους αὐτήν), prior to engaging in reading Plato's dialogue itself (ἐν τοῖς πρὸ τῆς λέξεως) and prior to 'reading together' (πρὸ τῆς συναναγνώσεως) the relevant comments in class to those who share the concern for learning what this dialogue is about (τοῖς συσχολάζουσιν).

Why did he set forth this methodolocical *schema isagogicum*? Because he knew of 'others that hold Plato dear', who engage 'in enormous interminable argument' (ἀμήχανον ὅσην ἀπεραντολογίαν) in order to rebut the gainsaying of the heterodox, but they put forward only the main body of the treatise (αὐτὸ μόνον τὸ προκείμενον σύγγραμμα προστησαμένους)' while omitting consideration of those important prefatory issues. Accordingly, Proclus began his teaching with explaining those seven topis (ἑπτὰ ταῦτα) that should be considered 'prior to reading' (πρὸ τῆς ἀναγνώσεως) 'of Plato's *Republic*'.

What is more, Proclus tells us that his own *modus operandi*, which he just propounded, is not anything new: he has 'explained many times how the aims of Plato's dialogues should be pointed out' (κατ' ἐκείνους, οὓς πολλάκις οἶδα κανόνας εἰπὼν περὶ τῆς εὑρέσεως τῶν ἐν τοῖς Πλατωνικοῖς διαλόγοις σκοπῶν). Concerning the kind of the treatise, he immediately reminds that 'this should be all too obvious to those who remember' his 'earlier lessons on this' (δῆλον δὲ ἔσται καὶ τοῦτο τοῖς μεμνημένοις τῶν ἐν τοῖς διαλόγοις εἰδῶν), indeed his teaching about 'which and how many these kinds are' (ποῖά τε καὶ πόσα τυγχάνει ὄντα).[743]

742 The term κεφάλαιον was taken as an alternative for 'proem'. John of Sicily, *Commentarium in Hermogenis Librum Περὶ Ἰδεῶν*, p. 323: κεφαλὴν μὲν τὰ προοίμια λέγων [sc. Hermogenes].

743 Proclus, *commRep*, v. 1, pp. 5-6. Nevertheless, Proclus pointed out that intellectuals 'of old held various opinions about Plato's prologues'. *In Platonis Parmenidem*, p. 658: τῶν παλαιῶν περὶ τῶν Πλατωνικῶν προοιμίων διαφόρους δόξας ἐχόντων.

Proclus' expressions 'prior to reading' (πρὸ τῆς ἀναγνώσεως), or 'prior to reading together' (πρὸ τῆς συναναγνώσεως), was not anything new.

The former (πρὸ τῆς ἀναγνώσεως) had been used by the (probably first century AD) historian Thrasyllus, in the title of his book, *[Issues] preceding the reading of Democritus books'* (*Τὰ πρὸ τῆς ἀναγνώσεως τῶν Δημοκρίτου βιβλίων*).[744] Later, Gregory of Nyssa also used this, meaning his prefatory section to the exegesis of the Song of Songs,[745] obviously imitating Origen who, among other works, had writen a prologue also to this biblical book.

As for the latter (πρὸ τῆς συναναγνώσεως), there are only two authors who used it: one was Proclus, as already discussed, in the title to his Prologue.[746] The other was Origen concluding his prologue to the commentary on John.[747] By the way, the proem of Proclus in his *Theologia Platonica* addressing his friend 'Pericles, the most dear of all friends' is an exemplar which is reminiscent of Origen addressing Ambrose in the prologues of the books of *Contra Celsum*.[748]

However, this 'reading together' (συνανάγνωσις) as a method of teaching was not a novelty. Plutarch made mention of gatherings for the study of Plato as a matter of course,[749] and Nicomachus of Gerasa (second century AD) refers to such gatherings 'of old' in like spirit,[750] by which he had in mind those of the Platonists who engaged in such gatherings.[751] The term is peculiar as much as is it informative; the fact is that, after Plutarch and Nicomachus, it was only Origen who used this in the first book of his commentary on John upon his conversion to Christianity, which suggests that his exegesis of that gospel was delivered as class lectures, in like a manner the exegesis of Plato usually

---

744 Diogenes Laertius, *Vitae*, 9.41 (Life of Democritus); Thrasyllus, *Fragmenta*, fr. 4.

745 Gregory of Nyssa, *In Canticum Canticorum*, p. 3: Ὅσα πρὸ τῆς παρούσης ἀναγνώσεως ἐν τοῖς προοιμίοις τοῦ Ἄσματος τῶν ᾀσμάτων ἡμῖν τεθεώρηται. Anonymous, *Ὀνομασίαι τῶν Κατὰ Ἄνθρωπον*, section 2: Ἔτι μὴν καὶ οἱ γραμματισταὶ πρὸ τῆς ἀναγνώσεως καὶ τῆς ἄλλης διδασκαλίας, καὶ τὴν τῶν στοιχείων ὀνομασίαν ὁμοίως προδιδάσκουσιν.

746 Proclus, *commRep*, v. 1, p. 1 (in his table of contents); then, on p. 5, as title of his preface: περὶ τοῦ τίνα χρὴ καὶ πόσα πρὸ τῆς συναναγνώσεως τῆς Πολιτείας Πλάτωνος κεφάλαια διαρθρῶσαι τοὺς ὀρθῶς ἐξηγουμένους αὐτήν.

747 *commJohn*, I.15.88: αὐτοῦ που καταπαύσομεν τὰ πρὸ τῆς συναναγνώσεως τῶν γεγραμμένων. Cf. *op. cit.* X.11.60: Καὶ ἡμεῖς δὲ θεοῦ διδόντος γενόμενοι κατὰ τὰ τοιαῦτα χωρία τῆς συναναγνώσεως ὅπου δόξαι ἂν μηδὲν ἠνυκέναι ἐπιδημήσας χωρίοις τισίν, πειρασόμεθα τὸ μὴ μάταιον τῆς ἐπιδημίας αὐτοῦ τρανῶσαι.

748 Cf. Proclus, *Theologia Platonica*, v. 1, pp. 4-8. Origen, *Cels*, Prologue.

749 Plutarch, *Quaestiones Convivales*, p. 700C: Ἐν ταῖς Πλατωνικαῖς συναναγνώσεσιν.

750 Nicomachus of Gerasa, *Introductio Arithmetica*, 2.21.1: καὶ εἰς τὰς τῶν παλαιῶν συναναγνώσεις.

751 Nicomachus of Gerasa, *op. cit.* 2.24.11: ἐν τῇ Πλατωνικῇ συναναγνώσει.

took place.[752] After him, Eusebius used the same noun,[753] and then its scarce usage passed over to Neoplatonists and was taken up Photius, only to fade soon afterwards.[754] It is quite telling that those who mostly used this term in Prologues were Neoplatonists.

Therefore, Praechter erroneously argued that this prefatory schema reappeared suddenly with Ammonius. Moreover, although Praechter thought that reading of Aristotle's work *always* started with the *Categories*, Olympiodorus argued that study of Aristotle should not start with the *Categories*,[755] but 'with the *premisses* of the *Categories*, and indeed with those of all of Aristotle's philosophy' (τὰ προλαμβανόμενα τῶν Κατηγοριῶν καὶ πάσης τῆς Ἀριστοτέλους φιλοσοφίας). This is why the twenty-five pages of his *Prolegomena* are in fact discussion of these προλαμβανόμενα themselves. Furthermore, although Simplicius and the other Aristotelian commentators (mentioned above) posited the aforementioned ten points upon prefacing their commentaries on the *Categories*, Olympiodorus' approach was different: although he did not dispute this layout of the points that should be considered in advance, he argued that this should apply to 'the whole of Aristotle's philosophy' (διὰ δὲ πᾶσαν τὴν Ἀριστοτέλους φιλοσοφίαν δέκα τινά). For 'Aristotle's philosophy is more catholic[756] than the Logic, and Logic is more catholic that the Categories' (καὶ γὰρ αὕτη καθολικωτέρα μέν ἐστι τῆς λογικῆς, ἡ δὲ λογικὴ τῶν Κατηγοριῶν). Once this takes place, study of the *Categories* could follow, in which case there are

---

752 See *supra*, note 749.

753 Eusebius, *Eclogae Propheticae*, p. 1: ἐπεὶ μὴ ῥᾴδιον ἀλλ' ὡς ἐκ τῆς ‹ἀπο›τάδην τῶν γραφῶν συναναγνώσεως τὰς πάσας ὑποπίπτειν τοῖς ἀνὰ στόμα καὶ διὰ μνήμης φέρειν αὐτὰς βουλομένοις. Codex has it "... απο". I restore to ‹ἀπο›τάδην (= extensively). Cf. Eusebius, *In Isaiam*, 1.71.

754 Ammonius of Alexandria, *commDeInterpr*, p. 1: ἐν τοῖς προλαμβανομένοις τῆς συναναγνώσεως τῶν Κατηγοριῶν. Proclus, *commRep*, v. 1, pp. 1; 5. Marinus, *Vita Procli*, line 234. John Philoponus, *In Nicomachi Arithmeticam Introductionem*, 70 (quoting from Nicomachus): ἐν ταῖς τῶν παλαιῶν συναναγνώσεσιν. Elias of Alexandria, *commCateg*, p. 107: Ταῦτα πάντα τοῦ Πρόκλου λέγοντος δεῖν προλαμβάνειν ἀρχομένους τῶν Ἀριστοτελικῶν συνταγμάτων ἐν τῇ συναναγνώσει (σύνταγμα δὲ τούτου Πρόκλειον). Anonymus, *Prolegomena Philosophiae Platonicae*, 28: Καὶ μέχρι μὲν τούτων ἔστω τὰ προτέλεια τῆς συναναγνώσεως τῆς Πλάτωνος φιλοσοφίας ἐν ἕνδεκα κεφαλαίοις περικλεισθέντα. Photius, *Bibliotheca*, Codex 150, p. 99b (ref. to classes studying rhetorics): Δῆλον δ' ὅτι εἰς τὰς τῶν ῥητορικῶν λόγων συναναγνώσεις τὰ μέγιστα ἡ πραγματεία συμβάλλοιτ' ἄν. *Op. cit.* Codex 153, p. 100a: εἰς τὰς ἀττικὰς συναναγνώσεις χρήσιμον, εἰ μὴ καὶ μᾶλλον. *Op. cit.* Codex 168, p. 116a: Καὶ τῆς τροπῆς δὲ ἡ κατ' ἔμφασιν καὶ οἰκείωσιν μεταχείρισις τῆς Ἰωάννου [Chrysostom] συνουσίας καὶ συναναγνώσεως οὐκ ἐλάχιστον ὑπάρχει τεκμήριον.

755 Olympiodorus of Alexandria, *Prolegomena*, p. 1: λέγω τοίνυν ὅτι δεῖ προηγεῖσθαι τὰ ζητούμενα κατὰ τῆς Ἀριστοτέλους φιλοσοφίας ἤπερ τὰ τῶν Κατηγοριῶν καὶ τῆς μεθόδου διὰ δύο αἰτίας τινάς, διὰ τὰς ἐπιστήμας καὶ τὰς τέχνας.

756 That is, it has a wider scope.

six points (ἕξ τινα) that should be considered, namely, (1) the goal (τὸν σκοπόν); (2) the utility (τὸ χρήσιμον); (3) the order (τὴν τάξιν); (4) the title (τὴν ἐπιγραφήν); (5) the author (τὸν συγγραφέα); (6) the structure or arrangement of the book (τὴν διασκευὴν τοῦ βιβλίου).

Consequently, the generalisation described by Simplicius was not in fact a strict 'rule'. In reality, how many of those points should be treated in prologue depended on the specific character and title of each particular treatise. Despite having endorsed the list, Philoponus remarks that one should discuss 'the title' only if this happens to be unclear (ἀδήλου τῆς ἐπιγραφῆς οὔσης); for example, Aristotle's titles such as *Categories* or *On Interpretation* call for elucidation in proem; others, however, such as *On the Soul* or *On Heaven*, do not.[757]

This is from Philoponus' own proem setting out to comment on the *Categories*, where he calls attention to *ten* topics (κεφάλαια δέκα) about that treatise he should discuss: (1) 'How many philosophical schools are there, and how do they get their name, so that we should know which school this philosopher belongs to'; (2) the division of Aristotle's works; (3) which of them should a certain study of Aristotle begin with; (4) the goal of Aristotle's philosophy; (5) the way to attain this goal; (6) the genre of the Aristotelian narrative; (7) why did Aristotle practice obscurity; (8) what is the student's required quality; (9) who is the proper (i.e. qualified) exegete; (10) what are the topics that a prologue to an Aristotelian treatise should comprise.[758]

John Philoponus argued that, 'concerning each of Aristotle's treatise, prefatory discussion should consider six topics, unless one of them is self-evident'; these topics are (1) the aim, (2) the utility, (3) the order of reading, (4) the cause of title, (5) whether this is a genuine work, (6) its division into chapters. However, he immediately adds, 'to them, I should add a seventh one, namely, which part of philosophy this work belongs to, and whether this is determined on account of the entire treatise or of part of this'.[759] Simplicius said exactly the same, determining six topics (the same as Philoponus, if in different order), and likewise added, 'it would not be pointless also to inquire which part of philosophy this work belongs to'.[760] However, Philoponus, in his commentary

757 John Philoponus, *commCateg*, p. 7.

758 John Philoponus, *op. cit.* p. 1.

759 John Philoponus, *commAnalPr*, p. 1: ἕξ ἐστι τὰ ὀφείλοντα προλέγεσθαι ἑκάστου Ἀριστοτελικοῦ συγγράμματος, εἰ μή τι τῶν κεφαλαίων αὐτόθεν εἴη φανερόν, σκοπός, χρήσιμον, τάξις ἀναγνώσεως, αἰτία ἐπιγραφῆς, εἰ γνήσιον τοῦ φιλοσόφου τὸ βιβλίον, ἡ εἰς τὰ κεφάλαια διαίρεσις. προσθήσω δὲ καὶ ἕβδομον, ὑπὸ ποῖον τῆς φιλοσοφίας μέρος ἀνάγεται, καὶ εἰ ὅλως ὑπό τι τῶν μερῶν ἢ οὔ.

760 Simplicius determined seven points. *commCateg*, p. 8: Δέκατον λοιπὸν ἦν τῶν προτεθέντων, πόσα χρὴ κεφάλαια καὶ τίνα τῶν Ἀριστοτέλους πραγματειῶν προδιαρθροῦσθαι. καὶ ἔστι ταῦτα

on the *Categories*, 'concerning all of Aristotle's treatises', was content with setting forth the *six* out of those seven points, and stated them in different order.[761]

Ammonius of Alexandria, upon setting out to comment on Porphyry's *Introduction*, determined *six* 'so-called topics which philosophers call *prolegomena*, or [topics] treated technically in advance': (1) the aim; (2) the utility; (3) whether this is a genuine work; (4) the order of reading; (5) the cause of title; (6) its division into chapters'.[762] Importantly, Ammonius himself does not pose as the source of this methodology (as Praechter thought), but advises that these prefatory topics have been 'invented' by philosophers of the past (ταῦτα δὲ ἐπενόησαν οἱ φιλόσοφοι προλέγειν) so as to 'make readers more keen to study' a treatise.[763]

On the other hand, Asclepius of Tralles, upon beginning with his commentary on *Metaphysics*, felt he should treat only *three* questions in advance as far this particular work was concerned (the aim, the order *of the work* [not of the *reading*], and the cause of the title),[764] but then he set forth these criteria differently: 'concerning the present treatise', one should consider its 'aim, utility, order, the cause of the title', plus, 'to consider the [authorship] of Alpha Major and Alpha Minor'.[765]

This exploration could go further to Olympiodorus, Elias, David, Pseudo-David, even Arethas, who pointed out *eight* prefatory points that call for consideration prior to embarking on commentary of Porphyry's *Introduction*: (1) the aim; (2) the utility; (3) if the work is genuine; (4) the cause of the title; (5) the order of the work; (6) its division into chapters; (7) the way of teaching

---

ὁ σκοπός, τὸ χρήσιμον, ἡ τῆς ἐπιγραφῆς αἰτία, ἡ τάξις τῆς ἀναγνώσεως, εἰ γνήσιον τοῦ φιλοσόφου τὸ βιβλίον, ἡ εἰς τὰ κεφάλαια διαίρεσις. οὐκ ἄτοπον δὲ ἴσως ζητεῖν καὶ ὑπὸ ποῖον μέρος αὐτοῦ τῆς φιλοσοφίας ἀνάγεται.

761 John Philoponus, *commCateg*, p. 7: Πασῶν δὲ τῶν Ἀριστοτέλους πραγματειῶν τὰ προλέγεσθαι ὀφείλοντα ἕξ ἐστιν, ὁ σκοπὸς τὸ χρήσιμον ἡ αἰτία τῆς ἐπιγραφῆς ἡ τάξις τῆς ἀναγνώσεως ἡ εἰς τὰ κεφάλαια διαίρεσις καὶ εἰ γνήσιον τοῦ φιλοσόφου τὸ βιβλίον.

762 Ammonius of Alexandria, *In Porphyrii Isagogen*, p. 21: ὁ σκοπὸς τὸ χρήσιμον τὸ γνήσιον ἡ τάξις τῆς ἀναγνώσεως ἡ αἰτία τῆς ἐπιγραφῆς ἡ εἰς τὰ κεφάλαια διαίρεσις καὶ ὑπὸ ποῖον μέρος ἀνάγεται τὸ παρὸν σύγγραμμα.

763 Ammonius of Alexandria, *loc. cit.*

764 Asclepius of Tralles, *commMetaph*, p. 1: Δεῖ ἡμᾶς ἀρχομένους τῆς παρούσης πραγματείας εἰπεῖν τὸν σκοπόν, τὴν τάξιν, τὴν αἰτίαν τῆς ἐπιγραφῆς.

765 Asclepius of Tralles, *op. cit.* p. 2: Δεῖ ἡμᾶς ἀρχομένους τῆς παρούσης πραγματείας εἰπεῖν τὸν σκοπόν, τὸ χρήσιμον, τὴν τάξιν, τὴν αἰτίαν τῶν ἐπιγραφῶν (πολλαὶ γὰρ ἐπιγραφαὶ φέρονται, αἷς δείκνυμεν τὸν τρόπον τοῦ συγγράμματος ὅλου) καὶ περὶ τοῦ μεγάλου ἄλφα καὶ τοῦ μικροῦ ἄλφα, καὶ πόθεν ὥρμησεν εἰς ἔννοιαν τῆς πρώτης φιλοσοφίας Ἀριστοτέλης.

this treatise; (8) the kind of philosophy this belongs to.[766] In fact, Arethas followed David of Alexandria.

Thus, the prefatory topics and their number became 'famous' (literally: much-spoken-of, πολυθρύλλητα)[767] as a methodology, which was deemed rather perfunctory and a 'matter of prestige' (κῦρος), but hardly was there any consensus about *which* and *how many* those topics should be. It seems, nevertheless, that authors later to Arethas (ninth century) made mention of this practice while having in mind his remark, which Arethas himself had learned from David's commentary on Porphyry's *Introduction*.[768]

Thus, against Praechter's claim that Ammonius' scheme was an 'established pattern', in reality, authors such as Stephanus of Alexandria (the medical doctor and philosopher, sixth-seventh century) did not treat this as a sacrosanct stereotype; rather, what he saw as 'traditional treatment' was a prefatory scheme comprising *eight* points, not ten.[769] Philoponus already had made a reasonable remark: what is the need for treating the topic of 'cause of the title'

766 Arethas of Caesarea, *Scholia in Porphyrii Isagogen*, scholion 1: Ὀκτώ τινα ἐπὶ παντὸς συγγράμματος ὑπὸ τῶν ἐξηγητῶν ζητεῖται κεφάλαια, ἃ οὕτως ὠνόμασται διότι τὸ κῦρος τοῦ παντὸς λόγου ἐπέχουσιν. εἰσὶ δὲ ταῦτα. ὁ σκοπός, τὸ χρήσιμον, τὸ γνήσιον, ἡ αἰτία τῆς ἐπιγραφῆς, ἡ τάξις, ἡ εἰς τὰ κεφάλαια διαίρεσις, ὁ διδασκαλικὸς τρόπος, καὶ ἡ ὑπὸ τί μέρος ἀναφορά.

767 Pseudo-David of Alexandria, *In Porphyrii Isagogen*, p. 80: Μέλλοντες σὺν θεῷ ἄρχεσθαι τοῦ παρόντος συγγράμματος τὰ εἰωθότα ὑπὸ τῶν ἐξηγητῶν ζητεῖσθαι κεφάλαια, ὀκτὼ τὸν ἀριθμὸν ὄντα, ζητήσωμεν. κεφάλαια δὲ ταῦτα λέγονται, διότι τὸ κῦρος παντὸς τοῦ λόγου ἐπέχουσιν. εἰσὶ δέ, ὡς εἴρηται, τὰ ὀκτὼ τὸν ἀριθμὸν κεφάλαια ταῦτα. οἷον ὁ σκοπός, τὸ χρήσιμον, τὸ γνήσιον, ἡ αἰτία τῆς ἐπιγραφῆς, ἡ εἰς τὰ κεφάλαια διαίρεσις, ἡ τάξις, ὁ διδασκαλικὸς τρόπος καὶ ἡ ὑπὸ τί μέρος ἀναφορά. Cf. Pseudo-David, *In Porphyrii Isagogen*, Praxis 24, p. 49: φέρε θεὸν προστησάμενοι σύμμαχον εἴπωμεν καὶ τὰ προτέλεια τῆς παρούσης πραγματείας, φημί δε τὰ πολυθρύλλητα ὀκτὼ κεφάλαια. τὸν σκοπὸν τοῦ παρόντος βιβλίου, τὸ χρήσιμον αὐτοῦ, καὶ τὰ λοιπά. κεφάλαια δὲ λέγονται παρὰ τὸ τὸ κῦρος ἐν ἑαυτοῖς ἔχειν. Anonymous, *Scholia ad Hermogenis Librum Περὶ Στάσεων*, pp. 62-63: λέγω δὴ περὶ διαιρέσεως ῥητορικῆς. πολιτικῶν δὲ εἴπομεν ζητημάτων, ἐπειδή ἐστι καὶ φιλόσοφα, λεγόμενα δὲ κεφάλαια, ὅτι ὥσπερ ἡ κεφαλὴ τὸ κῦρος τοῦ σώματος ἔχει παντός, οὕτω καὶ ταῦτα τὸ κῦρος τοῦ σύμπαντος λόγου ἔχοντα εἰκότως κεφάλαια λέγονται ἢ ἀντὶ τοῦ βοώμενα καὶ θρυλούμενα κεφάλαια.

768 Accordingly, in the eleventh century, John Doxapatres of Constantinople (not without some irony) felt he should treat *eight* points, because he thought this was the standard number for those 'celebrated [introductory] chapters'. *Prolegomena in Aphthonii Progymnasmata*, pp. 127-128: Ἔλθωμεν λοιπὸν καὶ ἐπὶ τὴν τῶν πολυθρυλήτων κεφαλαίων ζήτησιν ὀκτὼ τὸν ἀριθμόν, ὥς φασι, τυγχανόντων. ἔστι δὲ ταῦτα. ὁ σκοπός, τὸ χρήσιμον, τὸ γνήσιον, ἡ τάξις τῆς ἀναγνώσεως, ἡ αἰτία τῆς ἐπιγραφῆς, ἡ εἰς τὰ μέρη διαίρεσις, ὁ διδασκαλικὸς τρόπος, καὶ ἀντὶ τῆς ὑπὸ τί μέρος ἀναφορᾶς, ἥτις ἐν τοῖς κατὰ φιλοσοφίαν ὡς ἐπὶ τὸ πολὺ εἴωθε ζητεῖσθαι συγγράμμασι. John Argyropulos just copied this; *Prolegomena ad Progymnasmata Rhetoricae*, p. 177. See the same text in Anonymous, *Expositio Artis Rhetoricae*, p. 728.

769 Stephanus, *Scholia in Hippocratis De Fracturis*, p. 17: Τὰ εἰωθότα προλέγεσθαι ὀκτὼ κεφάλαια παντὸς βιβλίου.

in treatises of which the title is all too clear concerning the content?[770] Hence, what Praechter saw as standard pattern was not so standard after all.

When Origen wrote Prologues to his works, he all but had the impression that he introduced any novelty. There were such precedents as Alexander of Aphrodisias and Galen, and, to me, it is hardly a surpise that those two authors were the only ones who cared to explain the title of Aristotle's *On Sense Perception.*[771] It seems that Alexander thought highly of his contemporary Galen,[772] and Galen felt likewise.[773] Both of them commented on, and paid particular attention to, the prologues by Aristotle[774] and by Hippocrates respectively. Galen refers to earlier authors who had pointed out that a proem should treat such topics as 'the method of teaching' and what was the need that a treatise was supposed to meet. Galen's opinion is that 'a proem must be informative of the topics that are to be treated in the book' (χρὴ γὰρ τὸ προοίμιον οἰκεῖον εἶναι τῶν κατὰ τὸ βιβλίον εἰρησομένων), and that those who cared to compose such proems 'were more knowledgeable than the others'.[775] Galen's reference to 'the method of teaching' (τὸν τρόπον τῆς διδασκαλίας) is important since this appears in Ammonius as one of the indispensable virtues of a prologue, along with other ones, such as its 'goal' (τὸν σκοπὸν) and 'utility' (τὸ χρήσιμον).[776]

770 John Philoponus, *commCateg*, p. 7.

771 Galen, *De Instrumento Odoratus*, 5.3. Alexander of Aphrodisias, *commMeteor*, p. 142.

772 Alexander of Aphrodisias, *commTop*, p. 549; *commPhys*, 7.1432. Nevertheless, Alexander supposedly wrote a treatise *Against Galen On Motion*, attested in the Arab tradition.

773 Galen, *De Praenotione ad Posthumum*, p. 627; *De Anatomicis Administrationibus*, p. 218. I will not discuss some dissent as to whether 'Alexander the Damascene' mentioned by Galen was a different person from Alexander of Aphrodisias. It appears that Galen himself confused things, since he wrote that 'Alexander the Damascene' was appointed teacher of philosophy at Athens, and we know that Alexander of Aphrodisias held this post. Anyway, it is all but coincidence that Galen took up Alexander's innovative (and at points, idiosyncratic) term συμπαρεκτεινόμενος, which Origen was happy to come upon in both authors. I discuss this term in the commentary to the Greek text (endnote cdlxxxv). In this section, see *infra*, notes 801, 804, 805.

774 Alexander of Aphrodisias, *commMetaph*, pp. 12; 137; 539: καὶ ὅρα πῶς ἐκ προοιμίων τὸ οἰκεῖον ὑποφαίνει βούλημα.

775 Galen, *In Hippocratis Aphorismos*, p. 351: ὅσοι τοίνυν ἢ τοῦ τρόπου τῆς διδασκαλίας ἢ ὅλως τῆς χρείας τῶν συγγραμμάτων αἰτίαν ἀποδίδοσθαι κατὰ τὸ προοίμιόν φασιν, οὗτοί μοι δοκοῦσιν ἄμεινόν τι τῶν ἄλλων γινώσκειν. See also, *op. cit.* p. 352.

776 Ammonius, *In Porphyrii Isagogen*, p. 23: πρὸ δὲ τούτων ἐν τῷ προοιμίῳ προανακρούεται τὸν σκοπὸν τοῦ βιβλίου καὶ τὸ χρήσιμον διδάσκει καὶ τὸν τρόπον τῆς διδασκαλίας. Elias of Alexandria followed suit. *In Porphyrii Isagogen*, p. 40: τὸ τοίνυν προοίμιον αὐτῆς τρία διδάσκει, τὸν σκοπόν, τὸ χρήσιμον καὶ τὸν τρόπον τὸν διδασκαλικόν, μᾶλλον δὲ τὸ ἔμπαλιν τὸ χρήσιμον, τὸν σκοπὸν καὶ τὸν τρόπον τὸν διδασκαλικόν. Likewise, David of Alexandria, *In Porphyrii Isagogen*, p. 95: ἐν μὲν γὰρ τῷ πρώτῳ προοιμίῳ τρία τινὰ παραδίδωσι, τὸν σκοπὸν τὸ χρήσιμον καὶ τὸν τρόπον τῆς διδασκαλίας, ἐν δὲ τῷ δευτέρῳ προοιμίῳ αἰτίας τινὰς παραδίδωσι

Anyway, not only did Galen praise Hippocrates' proems,[777] but also he wrote ones of his own.[778] However, the same virtues were detected back to Aristotle himself, which is what Gennadius Scholarius pointed out.[779]

Of particular importance is Praechter's reference to Origen: he considered 'the inauthentic Hippolytus fragment 7 from the introduction to the commentary on the Psalms', noting that H. Achelis came upon three manuscripts in which this extensive text is unattributed, but the Syrian *Ambrosianus* ascribes this to Origen – and indeed the style is very like him.[780]

Besides, Origen explains 'the aim and utility' of the book (τῆς βίβλου ὁ σκοπὸς καὶ τὸ χρήσιμον), as well as the reason why the specific title for the Psalms was used (ἡ δὲ αἰτία τῆς ἐπιγραφῆς). This passage explains why the Psalter was not actually written *only* by David (μόνου τοῦ Δαυίδ, 'because former heathen who have become believers entitle the book *Psalms of David*') 'although the Acts accord this simply the title *Book of the Psalms*'. The aim of this analysis was to explain the assorted *titles* of various Psalms and the reason for having been ordered the way they are.[781] Once again, Origen availed himself of Alexander of Aphrodisias (as he did on numerous occasions) who had pointed out the need to determine 'the reason of title' (αἰτία τῆς ἐπιγραφῆς).[782]

Moreover, the designation 'the aim and utility' of a book (ὁ σκοπὸς καὶ τὸ χρήσιμον) stated by Origen could have been originated also in Alexander of Aphrodisias (commenting on the *Topica*), who associated this with the 'intention' (ἡ πρόθεσις) of a certain intellectual activity, whether a treatise or

τῶν λεχθησομένων. Arethas of Caesarea, *Scholia in Porphyrii Isagogen*, scholion 11: Ὅτι τὸ παρὸν προοίμιον τρία παραδίδωσι· τὸν σκοπόν, τὸ χρήσιμον, τὸν διδασκαλικὸν τρόπον.

777 Galen, *In Hippocratis Prognosticum*, p. 23; *In Hippocratis Librum De Fracturis*, p. 318.

778 Galen, *In Hippocratis Aphorismos*, p. 561; *In Hippocratis Librum De Articulis et Galeni in Eum*, p. 300; *In Hippocratis Prognosticum*, p. 17; *In Hippocratis Librum De Fracturis*, p. 318; *Dictionum Exoletarum Hippocratis Explicatio*, p. 62.

779 Gennadius Scholarius, *Translatio Commentarii Thomae Aquinae De Anima Aristotelis*, 1.3: Θεὶς ὁ Φιλόσοφος πρότερον τὸ προοίμιον, ἐν ᾧ καὶ τὸν σκοπὸν αὐτοῦ καὶ τὸν τῆς διδασκαλίας τρόπον καὶ τὴν δυσχέρειαν τούτου τοῦ ἔργου ἔδειξεν ἱκανῶς. This is probably Gennadius' own comment.

780 Karl Praechter, *supra*, p. XXIII, and note 7.

781 Pseudo-Hippolytus, *Fragmenta in Psalmos*, fr. 9 (Achelis). Ὠριγένους περὶ τῶν ρν' ψαλμῶν. … Καὶ τὰ τοιαῦτα δ' ἣν ἐπὶ πλεῖόν τις διατρίψας τηρήσῃ, τῆς ἱστορίας καὶ τῶν ἐπιγραφῶν ἀκριβέστερον εὑρήσει τὰς αἰτίας τῆς τάξεως τῶν ψαλμῶν.

782 Alexander of Aphrodisias, *commAnalPr*, p. 42: αὕτη γὰρ καὶ ἡ τῆς ἐπιγραφῆς αἰτία τῆς τῶν Προτέρων Ἀναλυτικῶν καὶ Ὑστέρων ἐπιγράφεσθαι τάσδε τὰς πραγματείας. Then, Ammonius of Alexandria, *In Porphyrii Isagogen*, p. 21; *commCateg*, pp. 7; 66. Palladius of Alexandria, *Scholia in Hippocratis De Fracturis*, p. 16. Simplicius, *commCateg*, pp. 8; 15; *commPhys*, p. 4. John Philoponus, *commCateg*, pp. 7; 8; 133.

'a method'.[783] He offered a well-argued account of both this idea and the terminology in his commentary on the *Metaphysics* (nevertheless, once again, appealing to the *Topica*).[784] Subsequently, 'the aim and utility' became a technical expression with and after Ammonius of Alexandria,[785] but its usage by Origen points to this having been used earlier, if indeed this was not actually introduced by Origen himself being inspired by Alexander of Aphrodisias. Philoponus also used this formula also in relation to justifying the 'title' of the book (ἡ ἐπιγραφή).[786]

When Origen argued that to explain such things as the order, numbering, or titles of Psalms is 'most difficult and hard to achieve' (χαλεπώτατον καὶ δυσέφικτον), he used an expression from the Proem of Ptolemy to his *Harmonica*,[787] which is the first instantiation of this turn being used. Naturally, after Origen, his usual followers such as Basil, or imitators such as Cyril of

783 Alexander of Aphrodisias, *commTop*, p. 34: Εἰπὼν πρῶτον τὰ περὶ τῆς διαλεκτικῆς (ταῦτα δὲ ἦν ἡ πρόθεσις τῆς μεθόδου, ἡ πρὸς τὰς ἄλλας τὰς συλλογιστικὰς μεθόδους αὐτῆς διαφορά, τὸ χρήσιμον τὸ ἀπ' αὐτῆς, ἡ τοῦ τέλους ἐπίκρισις).

784 Alexander of Aphrodisias, *commMetaph*, pp. 173-174 (italics are mine): προστίθησι δὲ τούτοις τὸ τοὺς ζητοῦντας περί τινος χωρὶς τοῦ ἀπορῆσαι μηδέποτε εἰ εὐπόρηταί τε καὶ τέλος ἔχει τὸ ζητούμενον γνωρίζειν δύνασθαι. οὗ αἰτίαν ἀποδέδωκε τὸ τοῖς μὲν οὕτω ζητοῦσι περί τινος μὴ εἶναι γνώριμον τὸ τέλος τοῦ ζητουμένου. διὰ τοῦτο γὰρ ἐοικέναι εἶπεν αὐτοὺς καὶ ὁμοίους εἶναι τοῖς ποῖ δεῖ βαδίζειν ἀγνοοῦσιν, οἷς ἀγνοεῖται τὸ τέλος. τούτοις δὲ οὐδ' εἴ ποτε εὕρηται γνώριμον τὸ τέλος καὶ *ὁ σκοπός*. ἡ γὰρ τῶν ἀπορεῖσθαι δυναμένων περί τινα λύσις τὸ τέλος τε καὶ εὕρεσις αὐτοῦ. … ἀληθὲς ἄρα τὸ ἐν τοῖς Τοπικοῖς εἰρημένον *τὸ χρήσιμον* εἶναι τὴν διαλεκτικὴν πρὸς τὰς κατὰ φιλοσοφίαν ζητήσεις.

785 Ammonius of Alexandria, *In Porphyrii Isagogen*, pp. 23; 47. Palladius of Alexandria, *Commentarii in Hippocratis Librum Sextum De Morbis Popularibus*, p. 3. Simplicius, *commCateg*, p. 8. John Philoponus, *commCateg*, pp. 7-8. Olympiodorus of Alexandria, *Prolegomena*, pp. 1; 12. Elias of Alexandria, *In Porphyrii Isagogen*, pp. 40-41. David of Alexandria, *In Porphyrii Isagogen* pp. 87; 91; 95-96. Stephanus of Alexandria, *Scholia in Hippocratis Prognosticon*, 1.1. Arethas of Caesarea, *Scholia in Porphyrii Isagogen*, scholia 11; 14.

786 John Philoponus, *commCateg*, p. 8: πολλάκις γὰρ τῷ σκοπῷ συναναφαίνεται καὶ τὸ χρήσιμον, οἷον ἐν τῇ *Περὶ οὐρανοῦ* ἢ ἐν τῇ *Περὶ ψυχῆς* δῆλος καὶ ὁ σκοπὸς καὶ τὸ χρήσιμον καὶ ἡ ἐπιγραφή. Ἐν μέντοι γε τοῖς *Τόποις* οὐδὲ ἓν τούτων δῆλον. Ἀλλ' οὐδὲ τοῦ σκοποῦ γνωσθέντος εὐθὺς καὶ τὸ χρήσιμον συναναφαίνεται. … ἐν μέντοι γε ταῖς *Κατηγορίαις* καὶ ἐν τῷ *Περὶ ἑρμηνείας* ἅμα τῷ σκοπῷ τὸ χρήσιμον συναναφαίνεται, ὡς ἑξῆς δείξομεν. Εἴπωμεν δὲ καὶ περὶ τοῦ προκειμένου τῶν Κατηγοριῶν βιβλίου τίς τε ὁ σκοπὸς καὶ τὸ χρήσιμον καὶ ἡ αἰτία τῆς ἐπιγραφῆς καὶ ἡ τάξις τῆς ἀναγνώσεως καὶ εἰ γνήσιον τοῦ φιλοσόφου τὸ παρὸν βιβλίον καὶ ἡ εἰς τὰ κεφάλαια διαίρεσις. Cf. *commMeteor*, p. 53: Ἐπεξελθὼν ὡς ἐν προοιμίοις ὅσα προδιδάξαι τῆς τῶν μετεώρων θεωρίας χρήσιμον ἦν, τουτέστι τόν τε σκοπὸν τῆς προκειμένης ἀφορισάμενος πραγματείας καὶ τὴν τάξιν, ἣν ἐν τοῖς φυσικοῖς αὐτοῦ συγγράμμασιν εἴληχε, τίνα τε διδάξαι πρὸ αὐτῆς ὡς προηγούμενα φυσικῶς ἀκόλουθον ἦν, καὶ τίνα μετ' αὐτὴν ὡς ἑπόμενα μέλλει διδάσκειν.

787 Ptolemaeus, *Harmonica*, 1.1: τὸ τρίτον δὲ ἢ λαβεῖν ἢ τριπλασίαν θεῖναι χαλεπώτερον, … καὶ κατὰ λόγον ἀεὶ δυσεφικτότερον.

Alexandria, seized on this. It is characteristic that both of them used this in a proem, too.[788] That Proclus used this phrase[789] and he was the only commentator to do so, is hardly a surprise, since I have argued for Origen's influence upon Proclus' technical locution.[790]

Against all these critical data, of which Praechter was only partially aware (not aware in respect of Origen, anyway) and being also unaware of Origen's background as an illustrious philosopher of note (let alone his allegiances to Alexander of Aphrodisias), he opted for dismissing attribution of the passages to Origen (despite clear ascription to his name occurring in codices). Instead, he treated them as simply 'forgery', on the grounds that 'the prolegomena schematism is unlikely, even thus abridged, for the beginning of the third century'.[791] Whereas Ammonius declared that this practice was one by philosophers of old, and Proclus had used this already, Praechter decided to make Origen's text spurious only because he had no inkling of the antiquity of this practice by commentarors. Although he knew of F. Littig's finds attesting to the first instantiation of this practice in Andronicus of Rhodes (first century BC), he decided that 'the schema would have disappeared from the literature for centuries, only to surface again in Ammonius' time'.[792] Granted, Praechter could not have known later works rebutting his hypothesis,[793] but he ought to have been aware that Ammonius himself wrote that such a practice was one of old, and Elias of Alexandria reported that Proclus, Ammonius' teacher, had practiced this prior to Ammonius himself.

Quite simply (as he did every now and then in his writings), Origen opted for adopting a philological and oratorical prefatory formula he had come upon in Alexander of Aphrodisias, from whom he had taken up also a vast number of terms and some idiosyncratic expressions. Even so, nevertheless, he never felt that he should mould his prefaces so as to fit a hallowed corset: instead, it was

788 Cf. Basil of Caesarea, *In illud: In Principio Erat Verbum*, PG.31.472.45 (Proem): τοῦτο χαλεπὸν καὶ δυσέφικτον. Cyril of Alexandria, *De Sancta Trinitate Dialogi*, p. 468: ἔν γε δὴ τούτῳ τὸ χαλεπὸν ἢ δυσέφικτον. *Thesaurus De Sancta Consubstantiali Trinitate*, PG.75.9.15-16 (Proem): Τί γὰρ ἂν οὕτω γένοιτο δυσέφικτόν τε καὶ χαλεπὸν εἰς κατάληψιν;

789 Proclus, *commTim*, v. 1, p. 302 (comm. on *Timaeus*, 28c): αὕτη γὰρ ἔργον ἂν προσρηθείη κυρίως, ἢ ὡς χαλεπὴ καὶ δυσέφικτος.

790 *RCR*, 'Christian influence on Neoplatonism', pp. 333-366.

791 Praechter, *op. cit.* p. 47.

792 Praechter, *op. cit.* p. 46.

793 Cf. Ilsetraut Hadot, "Les Introductions aux commentaires exégétiques chez les Auteurs Néoplatoniciens et les auteurs chrétiens", in Michel Tardieu (ed.), *Les règles de l'interprétation*, Paris, 1989, pp. 99-122. Hans B. Gottschalk, "The earliest Aristotelian commentators", in R. Sorabji (ed.), *Aristotle Transformed: The Ancient Commentators and Their Influence*, Ithaca, NY, 1990, pp. 55-81.

the theme of the treatise that determined the prologue – which is why hardly has his proem to *Contra Celsum* anything to do with the ancient pattern.

Karl Praechter, like other philologists of his lot, times, and mentality, had a tendency for generalisations, which their audience were happy to embrace as authoritative. However, they were not. One more example is his analyses of the designation *ἀπὸ φωνῆς* ('from the voice of' someone) appearing in titles of commentaries, including Neoplatonic ones on Aristotle or on Porphyry. He decided that this tag meant 'that a *viva vox* of a lecturer is recorded'.[794] However, when Procopius of Gaza composed his catena on the Song of Song, and wrote in title, 'From the voice of ...' and cited eleven names (including Origen's), he simply meant 'according to ...' (i.e. culling from the works of ...').[795] The same goes for the catenist who wrote 'from the voice of Origen, the blessed John [Chrysostom], Severian, Theodore'.[796] Accordingly, the label *ἀπὸ φωνῆς* was simply an oft-conventional way for an author's name to be put on the header of his work,[797] which would have suggested that this had been later 'dictated' to scribes. After all, Origen made it clear that his thoughts and exposition materialised through his *voice*, not by means of his personal *calamus*.[798]

794 Karl Praechter, *op. cit.* pp. 38 ff.

795 Procopius of Gaza, *Catena in Canticum Canticorum*, p. 1545. Likewise, in the title of his *Catena in Ecclesiasten* (citing six names of authors of old, again including Origen).

796 *Catena in Epistulam ad Ephesios* (*typus Parisinus*), p. 255.

797 Cf. Palladius of Alexandria, *Commentarii in Hippocratis Librum Sextum De Morbis Popularibus*, p. 1. John of Alexandria (medical doctor, seventh century), *Commentarii in Hippocratis Librum De Natura Pueri*, (title of Lecture 1) ('from the voice of John'). Stephanus of Alexandria, *In Aristotelis Librum De Interpretatione*, p. 1 ('from the voice of Stephen the philosopher'); likewise, *Scholia in Hippocratis Prognosticon*, (title). John of Damascus, *Institutio Elementaris*, Proem ('from the voice of John, the humble monk, to John the most hallowed bishop of Laocicea'). Photius, *Bibliotheca*, Codex 241, p. 323b ('[the book] *On Apollonius* from the voice of Philostratus has been read'). George Choeroboscus, *Prolegomena et Scholia in Theodosii Alexandrini Canones Isagogicos De Flexione Nominum*, pp. 1 & 103 & 118 ('from the voice of George Choeroboscus'); *De Orthographia* (epitome), p. 167 ('from the voice of George Choeroboscus'); *Scholia in Hephaestionem*, p. 177 ('from the voice of the grammarian George Choeroboscus'); *Epimerismi in Psalmos*, p. 1; *Scholia in Hephaestionem*, p. 177. John of Sicily, *Prolegomena in Hermogenis Librum Περὶ Ἰδεῶν*, p. 393 ('from the voice of John of Sicily'). Bessarion, *In Calumniatorem Platonis*, 1.2.6 (ref. to 'those things that have reached us from the voice of exegetes' (τὸ ἐκμανθάνειν τὰ ἀπὸ φωνῆς τῶν ἐξηγητῶν παραδιδόμενα). Notice that he wrote 'from the voice', not 'from the voices'.

798 Origen frequently spoke of his 'dictating' (ὑπαγορεύειν) his works. *commJohn*, XX.1.1 (ὑπαγορεύοντες); *op. cit.* V.2.1 (& *Philocalia*, V.2); V.8.1; VI.2.9; VI.2.10; XX.1.1; XXXII.1.2&3; XXXII.7.74; *Epistula ad Africanum*, PG.11.85.44-45; *Exhortatio ad Martyrium*, 51; *Cels*, Prologue.3-6 (πεπειράμεθα ὑπαγορεῦσαι ... ἐλογισάμεθα ... ὑπαγορεῦσαι ... μετὰ τὸ ὑπαγορεῦσαι πάντα); τὰ πρὸς Κέλσον ἡμῖν ὑπαγορευθέντα ... ὅτι ἄλλῃ μὲν προθέσει τὴν ἀρχὴν

It goes without saying that the case could have been one of a modest commentator notifying his readers that this was his authority's ideas,[799] which might have been a record of oral teaching in class. However, Praechter's postulating a universal meaning of *ἀπὸ φωνῆς* as an invariable rule is a quite different matter, indeed an extrapolation.[800]

Alexander of Aphrodisias was the philosopher from whom Origen took up the term 'to be co-extended alongside with' (συμπαρεκτεινόμενος),[801] since this was introduced by Alexander discussing Aristotle's proposition concerning the divine life of 'the First Mind'.[802] Origen made this a cardinal notion of his own theory of Time, a theory nevertheless that was different from Alexander's: in fact, in terms of natural conception it was Stoic (time posited as 'extension', διάστημα).[803] As always, later Christian authors (starting with the Cappadocians)

τῶν πρὸς Κέλσον ὑπηγορεύσαμεν ...... τοῖς κατὰ τὴν ἀρχὴν οὕτως ὑπαγορευθεῖσιν. *Op. cit.* II.1; VII.11; VIII.1; VIII.76; *commMatt*, 14.6; 15.27; 15.36; 16.9; 16.20.

799 Cf. Asclepius of Tralles, *commMetaph*, p. 1 (on 'A Major' 'by Asclepius, from the voice of Ammonius Hermiae'; likewise 'on A Minor', and on Books B, Γ). Olympiodorus of Alexandria, *commCateg*, p. 148 & *In Platonis Alcibiadem*, 1 (in both, 'from the voice of Olympiodorus'). Nevertheless, other commentaries ascribed to Olympiodorus (such as the *In Platonis Gorgiam*) could have been written by a pupil, since the designation is, 'by Olympiodorus, the great philosopher' (in prologue, and in chapter 50.17).

800 The case of Elias attributing a commentary 'to David' is one of its own. Cf. *commCateg*, p. 107. Nevertheless, see the label *ἀπὸ φωνῆς* in Elias of Alexandria, *Commentarius in Aristotelis Analytica Priora*, p. 134. David of Alexandria, *Prolegomena Philosophiae*, p. 1; *In Porphyrii Isagogen*, pp. 80; 95.

801 Alexander of Aphrodisias, *commMetaph*, p. 699: αἰὼν γάρ ἐστιν ἡ ἑκάστῳ συμπαρεκτεινομένη ζωή. Origen, *commJohn*, I.29.204: οὐκ ἔνι γὰρ ἑσπέρα θεοῦ, ἐγὼ δὲ ἡγοῦμαι, ὅτι οὐδὲ πρωΐα, ἀλλὰ ὁ συμπαρεκτείνων τῇ ἀγενήτῳ καὶ ἀϊδίῳ αὐτοῦ ζωῇ, ἵν' οὕτως εἴπω, χρόνος *ἡμέρα* ἐστὶν αὐτῷ *σήμερον*. Cf. Galen, *De Anatomicis Administrationibus*, p. 370: παράκειται συμπαρεκτεινόμενος αὐτῷ μέχρι τῆς ἐπὶ τὸν καρπὸν φορᾶς. *De Ossibus ad Tirones*, p. 777: καὶ αὐτοῖς ἔξωθεν συμπαρεκτείνεται τὸ κυβοειδές. *De Venarum Arteriarumque Dissectione*, p. 823: ταύταις συμπαρεκτείνονταί τε καὶ συγκατασχίζονται. *De Usu Partium*, v. 3, p. 710: ὅπως, ... καὶ ὁ ἀδὴν αὐταῖς συμπαρεκτείνηται. *Op. cit.* v. 4, p. 59: ἤτοι μὴ συμπαρεκτεινόμενον ὅλῳ τῷ μήκει τῆς ῥάχεως. *Op. cit.* v. 4, p. 202: ἀγγείοις συμπαρεκτείνεταί τε καὶ συγκατασχίζεται. *De Difficultate Respirationis*, p. 915: ἐπεὶ γὰρ συμπαρεκτείνεται τῷ μήκει τοῦ χρόνου τῆς ἀναπνοῆς ὁ πόνος. *De Locis Affectis*, p. 323: ἀλλήλοις συμπαρεκτείνεται ταῦτα τὰ τρία. Pseudo-Galen, *Introductio*, p. 716: συμπαρεκτείνεται μὲν τῇ τραχείᾳ ἀρτηρίᾳ. See discussion in the commentary to the Greek text (endnote cdlxxxv).

802 Cf. Aristotle, *Metaphysica*, 1072b28-31, describing God's 'life' as 'a continuous eternal existence belonging to God'. See discussion in Greek text, endnote cdlxxxv.

803 See *COT*.

seized on Origen's terminology (Chrysostom did so abundantly[804]) while having no inkling of the fact that the source was Alexander of Aphrodisias.[805]

Besides, it was from Alexander of Aphrodisias that Origen learned almost everything about Aristotle, indeed Aristotle's text itself along with Alexander's comments on this, lemma after lemma. Alexander was the man from whom Origen received the expression οὐκ ἦν ὅτε οὐκ ἦν[806] and applied this at

804 John Chrysostom, *In Sanctum Julianum Martyrem*, PG.50.668.2-4: ἵνα ... ἡ ἀπόλαυσις μένῃ διαρκὴς καὶ ἀτελεύτητος, τῇ τῶν ἀπείρων αἰώνων ἐκείνων ἀθανασίᾳ συμπαρεκτεινομένη. *In Genesim*, PG.53.147.52-54: ὅτι διηνεκῆ καὶ τῷ παντὶ αἰῶνι συμπαρεκτεινομένην αὐτῷ τὴν τιμωρίαν ἐπήγαγε. *Op. cit.* PG.53.254.23-24: καὶ σημεῖον παρέχει τὸ δυνάμενον παντὶ τῷ αἰῶνι συμπαρεκτεινόμενον. *Op. cit.* PG.53.278.47: καὶ ἵνα παντὶ τῷ αἰῶνι συμπαρεκτείνηται. *Op. cit.* PG.53.279.16-17: ὥστε τὴν μνήμην παντὶ τῷ αἰῶνι συμπαρεκτείνεσθαι. *Op. cit.* PG.53.288.11: ὡς παντὶ τῷ αἰῶνι συμπαρεκτείνεσθαι αὐτήν. *Op. cit.* PG.54.386.25: οὐδὲ ἐν τῷ αἰῶνι τούτῳ συγκαταλυόμενον, ἀλλὰ διηνεκής, ἀθάνατος, ἅπασι τοῖς αἰῶσι συμπαρεκτεινόμενος. *Expositiones in Psalmos*, PG.55.62.1-3: τὰ δὲ ἀγαθὰ ἐν τῷ μέλλοντι ἐταμιεύσατο αἰῶνι, ὥστε τῷ ἀγήρῳ συμπαρεκτείνεσθαι τὰς ἀμοιβάς. *Catecheses ad Illuminandos*, Catechesis 7.14: τὰ ἐν τοῖς οὐρανοῖς, τὰ ἀκίνητα, τὰ τῷ διηνεκεῖ αἰῶνι συμπαρεκτεινόμενα.

805 Evagrius of Pontus, *expProv*, p. 91: αἰῶνα τὸ συμπαρεκτεινόμενον τῇ συστάσει τῆς ζωῆς αὐτοῦ διάστημα ὀνομάζων. Then, Gregory of Nazianzus followed suit: *In Theophania*, PG.36.320.14–18 & *In Sanctum Pascha*, PG.36.628.30–34 (quoted also by Michael Psellus, *Opuscula i*, opusculum 41 & John Cyparissiotes, *Contra Tomum Palamiticum*, 6.7): Αἰὼν γὰρ οὔτε χρόνος, οὔτε χρόνου τι μέρος. οὐδὲ γὰρ μετρητόν. ἀλλ' ὅπερ ἡμῖν ὁ χρόνος, ἡλίου φορᾷ μετρούμενος, τοῦτο τοῖς ἀϊδίοις, αἰών, τὸ συμπαρεκτεινόμενον τοῖς οὖσιν, οἷόν τι χρονικὸν κίνημα καὶ διάστημα. This became a lemma: Pseudo-Zonaras, *Lexicon*, letter alpha, p. 63. I have discussed this in *COT*, p. 265. Pseudo-Basil of Caesarea (*forsan*, Cassian the Sabaite), *Enarratio in Prophetam Isaiam*, 1.31: Τὴν ἡμέραν Κυρίου τὴν μεγάλην, ... ἥτις μία ἔσται καὶ διηνεκής, διάδοχον νύκτα μὴ ἔχουσα, ἀλλὰ τῷ αἰῶνι παντὶ συμπαρεκτεινομένη. *Op. cit.* 9.227: ἡ δὲ παρὰ τοῦ Κυρίου εἰρήνη τῷ αἰῶνι παντὶ συμπαρεκτείνεται, ἀπεριόριστος οὖσα καὶ ἀτερμάτιστος. Basil of Caesarea, *Asceticon Magnum*, PG.31.912.5-6: εὐχὴν ἐποιοῦντο πάσῃ τῇ αἰωνίᾳ ζωῇ συμπαρεκτείνεσθαι τὴν θεωρίαν τῆς τερπνότητος τοῦ Κυρίου. Anonymus, *Dialogus cum Judaeis*, chapter 1, lines 141-142: εἰς αἰῶνας τὲ τοῖς δικαίοις συμπαρεκτείνεσθαι τῶν ἀγαθῶν τὴν ἀπόλαυσιν. Olympiodorus the deacon of Alexandria, *Commentarii in Ecclesiasten*, PG.93.481.24-25: Τῶν γεγονότων τὰ μὲν ἀδιάδοχα, συμπαρεκτεινόμενα τῷ ἐνεστῶτι αἰῶνι, ὡς οὐρανός, καὶ γῆ, καὶ ἥλιος, καὶ ἄστρα. *Op. cit.* PG.93488.14-17: Τῶν κτισμάτων τὰ μέν εἰσι μονογενῆ καὶ ἀδιάδοχα, οἷον ἥλιος, καὶ σελήνη, καὶ τὰ τῷ αἰῶνι συμπαρεκτεινόμενα. John of Damascus, *apud Catena in Epistulam ad Romanos*, p. 494: οὐκ ἦν αἰὼν μεριστός, ἀλλὰ τὸ συμπαρεκτεινόμενον τοῖς ἀϊδίοις, οἱονεὶ χρονικὸν κίνημα καὶ διάστημα. καὶ κατὰ μὲν τοῦτο, εἷς αἰών ἐστι καθὸ καὶ λέγεται ὁ Θεὸς αἰώνιος καὶ προαιώνιος. *Expositio fidei*, 15: Πρὸ δὲ τῆς τοῦ κόσμου συστάσεως, ... οὐκ ἦν αἰὼν μετρητός, ἀλλὰ τὸ συμπαρεκτεινόμενον τοῖς ἀϊδίοις οἷόν τι χρονικὸν κίνημα καὶ διάστημα. καὶ κατὰ μὲν τοῦτο εἷς αἰών ἐστι, καθὸ καὶ λέγεται ὁ θεὸς αἰώνιος, ἀλλὰ καὶ προαιώνιος. George Syncellus, *Ecloga Chronographica*, p. 2: τοῖς γὰρ ἀϊδίοις ἤγουν ταῖς ἀΰλοις οὐσίαις αἰών τις ἀνεπισκότιστος συμπαρεκτείνεται. Nicetas David, *Commentarii in Psalmos*, lines 314-316: ἀμείωτα μένει παντελῶς καὶ ἀκατάβλητα, τῷ μακρῷ τοῦ αἰῶνος συμπαρεκτεινόμενα διαστήματι. Further, Theodore Studites, *Parva Catechesis*, Catechesis 16, lines 33-36.

806 Alexander of Aphrodisias, *commMetaph*, p. 449: ἀλλ' ἦν ποτε ὅτε οὐκ ἦν. *Op. cit.* p. 450: εἰ πᾶν ὅπερ ἤδη ἐστίν, ἦν δέ ποτε ὅτε οὐκ ἦν, ἄρα γέγονεν. *Op. cit.* p. 818: ἀΐδιον γάρ ἐστιν ὃ

various points, including the relation of the Son to the Father (as Athanasius attested),[807] which became the catchphrase of Nicaea. Arius used Origen's expression without negativing the whole proposition, thus claiming the opposite of what Origen maintained: by ἦν ὅτε οὐκ ἦν,[808] Arius meant that there was a state in which the Son was not yet, and was subsequently created by the Father. Later uninformed fanatics attributed Arius' expression to Origen.

Origen's dues to Alexander are too many to recapitulate now, and the same goes for Galen, which is anyway out of my scope. What I am suggesting is that there is nothing strange about Origen, upon constructing some proems to his own commentaries, having gone along those predecessors by following a schema that those eminent intellectuals had espoused.

Concerning the prologue of the commentary on Matthew, there are two heretofore known fragments of this: Klostermann's fragment 1, which is about the designation εὐαγγέλιον, that is, the *title* – a question discussed also in the prologue of the commentary on John.[809] The other is an excerpt from Eusebius,[810] which considers the *division* of the one Gospel into four narratives by the four evangelists, and since their names are enumerated ('first ... second .. third .., and ...'), this could be taken as consideration of the Gospel's *order*, too.

Now, the text of *Codex Holy Cross* (*Τιμίου Σταυροῦ*) *104* provides more of this part of the prologue. Since it considers the reason of the sequence of the four

---

ἀδύνατον εἰπεῖν ὡς ἦν ποτε ὅτε οὐκ ἦν καὶ ἔσται ὁμοίως ὅτε οὐκ ἔσται, τὸ δὲ γεγονὸς ἦν ὅτε οὐκ ἦν. *commTop*, p. 80: οὐ γὰρ ἀεὶ ἦν ὁ μουσικὸς γραμματικός, ἀλλ' ἦν ποτε ὅτε οὐκ ἦν. *commMeteor*, p. 78: ἀλλ' ἦν τέ τις χρόνος ὅτε οὐκ ἦν θάλασσα, καὶ ἔσται τις πάλιν ὅτε οὐκ ἔσται.

807 Cf. Origen quoted by Athanasius, *De Decretis Nicaenae Synodi*, 27.2: [the Son] ὁμοιότης τυγχάνων τοῦ πατρὸς οὐκ ἔστιν ὅτε οὐκ ἦν. Origen, *commJohn*, II.19.130: οὐκ ἦν γὰρ ὅτε ἡ ἀρχὴ ἄλογος ἦν. *Op. cit.* XX.12.94-5: ἡ κατὰ τὸν Ἰησοῦν πνευματικὴ οἰκονομία οὐκ ἔστιν ὅτε τοῖς ἁγίοις οὐκ ἦν. *Op. cit.* XX.17.137-138: Παῦλος δὲ ἦν ὅτε οὐκ ἠγάπα τὸν Ἰησοῦν, ἦν ἄρα καιρὸς ὅτε ὁ θεὸς Παύλου πατὴρ οὐκ ἦν. *Philocalia*, 24.8: ἦν ποτε καιρὸς ὅτε ἡ ὕλη οὐκ ἦν, τουτέστι πρὶν τὰ ἁπλᾶ [sc. the Anaxagorean principles] συνελθεῖν. εἰ δὲ ἦν ποτε καιρὸς ὅτε ἡ ὕλη οὐκ ἦν, οὐκ ἦν δέ ποτε καιρὸς ὅτε τὸ ἀγένητον οὐκ ἦν, οὐκ ἔσται ἀγένητος ἡ ὕλη. *selPs*, PG.12.1601.1-2: Ὥσπερ ὁ τυρὸς ἦν ὅτε οὐκ ἦν τυρός, οὕτως οἱ δαίμονες ἦσάν ποτε ὅτε οὐκ ἦσαν πονηροί. *expProv*, PG.17.173.33-34: Ἦν ὅτε οὐκ ἦν κακόν, καὶ ἔσται ὅτε οὐκ ἔσται. Also, in texts incriminating Origen (allegedly from *Princ*): Justinian, *Edictum contra Origenem*, p. 110 & ACO, *Synodus Constantinopolitana et Hierosolymitana anno 536*, tome 3, p. 210: οὐκ ἔστιν ὅτε παντοκράτωρ οὐκ ἦν. Justinian, *op. cit* p. 214 & ACO, *op. cit.* tome 3, p. 212: ὥσπερ τὸ ἀπολωλὸς ἦν ὅτε οὐκ ἀπολώλει καὶ ἔσται ποτὲ ὅτε οὐκ ἔσται ἀπολωλός, οὕτω καὶ ἡ ψυχὴ ἦν ὅτε οὐκ ἦν ψυχὴ καὶ ἔσται ὅτε οὐκ ἔσται ψυχή.

808 Pamphilus in his *Apology* mentioned this, too. *Op. cit.* PG.17.561B: nunquam est quando Filius non Filius fuit. *Op. cit.* 562C: non est auterm quando non fuerit.

809 See both fragments quoted in the beginning of the Greek text.

810 Eusebius, *HE*, 6.25.4-6; copied by Nicephorus Callistus Xanthopulus, *HE*, 5.16.

gospels, it can be argued that Origen's had in mind their *order*. As a matter of fact, this is the word that he used (λόγον τινὰ ἔχει ἡ τῶν εὐαγγελίων τάξις).

Thus, in this prologue there is discussion of the *title*, the *order*, the *authors*, and (in Olympiodorus' words[811]) the *structure* or arrangement of the book (τὴν διασκευὴν τοῦ βιβλίου).

Moreover, in the second short passage of this codex that immediately follows, Origen suggests how the four evangelists should be pictorialised: river Geon represents Matthew; river Phison, Mark; river Tigris, Luke; river Euphrates, John. This is important, because it is unique: none of Origen's admirers or any other author did ever take this up. Even Jerome, who copied from this commentary of Origen's abundantly, did not employ this adumbration either; rather, he toed the line of those who saw Matthew standing for a man, Mark for a lion, Luke for a calf, John for an eagle.[812]

In *Codex Holy Cross 104* (folio 17v), this passage occupies just a little less than four lines – and then it breaks off. However, Klostermann's fragment 11 from Origen's commentary on Matthew (which I quote immediately after that passage) amazingly makes it all too clear that the small portion of *Holy Cross* 104 is in fact the hitherto unknown text that preceded Klostermann's one: once Origen explained which 'river' each evangenlist stands for, he cut his text short reminding that 'we have perused these things in length' ('Αλλὰ ταῦτα μὲν ἱκανῶς ἐξήτασται), and then he went on with the exegesis of Matthew's text. Where did he explain this idea of this adumbration he did not say – but where else could he possibly have done so other than in his commentary on Genesis 2:10-14? Hence, the two portions that are found in different codices make up Origen's one flowing text.[813]

The Present Edition

Codex Sabaiticus 232 (Commentary on Matthew, beginning of eleventh century, parchment; folia 128-135 linen paper) comprises 242 folia (484 pages). This is the only one which contains text from the very end of Origen's commentary on Matthew (commenting on Matt. 28:20, 'And, lo, I am with you ...'). This text has no parallel and has been heretofore unknown. During the fifteenth century,

811 Olympiodorus of Alexandria, *Prolegomena*, p. 1. See *supra*, p. CLXIX.

812 Jerome, *commMatt*, Prologue.

813 This is a turn of phrase that (naturally) Gregory of Nyssa took up – and he was the only one to do so. *Contra Eunomium*, 3.4.23: ἤδη μὲν ἱκανῶς διὰ τῶν εἰρημένων ἐξήτασται. Nevertheless, it would be interesting to notice this turn in another case, which was used also in a *proem*. Pseudo-David and Pseudo-Elias, *In Porphyrii Isagogen*, Praxis 24, p. 49: 'Επειδὴ τὰ προτέλεια τῆς φιλοσοφίας ἱκανῶς ἡμῖν διεξήτασται.

this codex was preserved at the monastery of Abba Gerasimus. The initial folios are mutilated, but the portion with which extant Sabaiticus 232 begins is not a mystery: I have identified the missing text as being one from Eusebius' *Evangelical Questions to Stephen*.[814]

This codex contains comments on the gospel of Matthew ascribed to the following authors: Origen, Theodore of Heraclea, Eusebius of Caesarea, John Chrysostom, Cyril of Alexandria, Severus of Antioch, Theodore of Mopsuestia, Gregory of Nyssa, and Photius. I have transcribed and edited all of the texts under the name of Origen. Of passages tagged ΑΝΕ[ΠΙΓΡΑΦΟΝ] ('Unattributed'), I have selected only a few ones. I show that they are Origen's, by means of subsequent quotations of Origen's known parallel texts (in smaller fonts), in which I maintain the (not always correct) published editorial orthography.

Nevertheless, the 'Unattributed' passages that I have edited are only a handful compared to the vast number of those under his name occurring in this manuscript. In all of those cases, I have maintained the attribution as in codex.

Codex Holy Cross (*Τιμίου Σταυροῦ*) *104*, Jerusalem, is a twelfth-century parchment manuscript comprising 330 folia. Origen's introductory comments from the commentary on Matthew appear only on folia 16v-17v, which I have used in the beginning of the present edition.

Arabic figures have been used for footnotes and Latin ones for endnotes.

Italics in the edited codex text fonts indicate quotations from the gospel of Matthew. Then, smaller fonts are used for (1) Klostermann's fragments on Origen's commentary on Matthew; (2) Origen's indisputable texts on the same subject from other existing publications, yet not included in this codex; (3) texts by other Christian authors running parallel to Origen's commentary on Matthew; (4) Jerome's portions from his commentary on Matthew which demonstrably are loans from Origen's commentary.

At several points (e.g. folios 89r-97r), there is Origen's continuous text against scattered known fragments from other publications, which are quoted in smaller fonts at the proper points below the pertinent portions. At points such as this, although Origen's text is continuous, I have written the ensuing codex text in the next line (without paragraph) so as to highlight an ensuing parallel portion quoted from already known publications and make comparative study easier.

814 Eusebius, *Quaestiones Evangelicae ad Stephanum*, PG.22.896.56-897.7. The extant text at the beginning of the codex is the sequel, namely, Eusebius, *op. cit.* PG.22.897.7-10. The same text, with a couple of slight phrasal variations, appears in Eusebius, *Supplementa ad Quaestiones ad Stephanum*, PG.22.964.33-44.

Coming upon a certain passage being attributed either to Origen in a certain codex or to another (normally, later) author in another, does not have by all means to entail that the subsequent author copied from Origen. I have worked on the assumption that each case should be considered *ad hoc*, taking into account historical circumstances, a certain author's beliefs, tenets, interrelations, dependencies, et cetera. For example, when a passage expounding a thoroughly Nicene Trinitarian doctrine is attributed to Theodore of Heraclea, who was a fierce anti-Nicene theologian and personal opponent of Athanasius on that score, there is good reason to doubt this. When a single short passage from a commentary on Matthew is attributed to Origen's devout acolyte Gregory Thaumaturgus, which is the only one under his name, and the present codex supplies Origen's text of which Gregory's passage is only a portion,[815] why should the present codex that attributes this entirely to Origen not be given credit?

However, there are cases of authors having availed themselves of Origen, which can be arguably demonstrated. Jerome, for one, not only admitted to having copied from Origen's commentary on Matthew but also declared himself proud for having done so.[816] John Chrysostom was well-known (to Epiphanius, he was notorious, as discussed earlier) for being an assiduous reader of Origen and for using his writings, and the former's homilies on Matthew are full of numerous verbatim passages (as a sort of patchwork) from the latter's commentary.[817]

I should provide one more example out of dozens that could be adduced in order to show how Origen as a source of inspiration for later Christian authors has been treated. At the outset of his second homily on Exodus, Origen wrote about the devil always essaying to avert men from recalling their 'fatheland of paradise'. Once a modern translator read this, he felt it necessary to make a note cheerfully mimicking the inveterate verdict discovering 'Platonism' in Origen.[818] The ignorance diplayed by such statements is all too egregious,

815 Gregory Thaumaturgus, *Fragmentum in Evangelium Matthaei 6.22-23*, PG.10.1189.25-41. *Codex Sabaiticus 232*, folio 45v.

816 See Jerome's reply to Rufinus, when the latter accused Jerome of having plagiarised form Origen; pp. LXXIX-LXXXVIII.

817 The examples are legion, and many of them will appear in my commentary to this Greek text. For now and for example, see Origen, *selPs*, PG.12.1584.20-40 & John Chrysostom, *Expositiones in Psalmos*, PG.55.337.1-9 (he copied lines 27-35 from Origen's text): Τί γὰρ τῆς ἡμέρας ταύτης ἴσον γένοιτο ἄν, ἐν ᾗ ... τὴν ἀρχαίαν ἀπελάβομεν πατρίδα, καὶ κατάρα ἠφανίσθη καὶ ἡ ἁμαρτία ἐλύθη; But Origen spoke of 'the fatherland of paradise' also in his *Homilies on Exodus*, 1.1. Subsequently, later authors took up the phrase. See *infra*, notes 831; 832.

818 R. Heine, *Origen, Homilies on Genesis and Exodus*, p. 240, note 14: "Origen (see *De Princ.* 1.4.1, 2.8.3-4, 2.9.1-2.6) believed that all souls existed originally as pure souls in the presence

which is why I have spoken of deplorable state of modern Origenian studies. Actually, I wonder why was it that, in the first place, this person toiled for translating Origen's homilies once he accompanied them with an array of flagrantly misleading comments, which do not deserve to be dignified with any discussion whatsoever, but this becomes an almost inevitable disagreeable digression in view of the plaguing distortion that imbues alleged 'interpretations' of Origen's thought.

(1) The portion of Plato's *Phaedrus* 246b-d is exactly the one Origen himself explicitly kept at bay; actually, he quoted this only to dismiss it, declaring that his own doctrine of the soul was 'more sublime' than that of Plato's.[819] It is quite obvious that this translator cited this only because he saw it at the pertinent point of G. Butterworth's translation of *De Principiis*,[820] thus perpetuating a flagrant error of fact, which misleads younger scholars even today. It is astonishing that he copied Butterworth's note but did not care to read Plato's portion, which Origen explicitly confuted!

This translator cited three points of *De Principiis*. All of them are shamefully hoaxing and far from making such a point. The first one (*Princ*, I.4.1) is but an interpolation by Koetschau quoting Jerome, who, however, notwithstanding his usual spitefulness, did not argue that such an opinion was maintained by Origen: he only wrote, 'We wish to know ... whether the doctrine of Origen is true, who said that ... etc.'. The second point (*Princ*, II.8.3-4) is once again an interpolation by Koetschau quoting from Origen's detractor, Epiphanius of Salamis, with parallel reference by Jerome[821] alleging that, to Origen, 'souls lived in paradise' and thereafter they have been 'bound in this body as in a prison' –a nescient nonsense to which I return in a moment. Besides, the same section has it, 'All these considerations seem to show that, when the mind departed from its original condition and dignity, it became or it was termed a soul, and if ever it is restored and corrected it returns to the condition of being a mind'. As for the third point (*Princ*, II.9.1-2), again this is about an interpolation by Koetschau quoting from Justinian's obloquy,[822] and then some text of

---

of God before their existence in bodies in this earthly life. His Platonism is obvious in this doctrine (See Plato, *Phaed.* 246 B-D)."

819 *Cels*, IV.40: Καὶ ὁ ἐκβαλλόμενος δὲ ἐκ τοῦ παραδείσου ἄνθρωπος μετὰ τῆς γυναικός, τοὺς *δερματίνους* ἠμφιεσμένος *χιτῶνας*, οὓς διὰ τὴν παράβασιν τῶν ἀνθρώπων ἐποίησε τοῖς ἁμαρτήσασιν ὁ θεός, ἀπόρρητόν τινα καὶ μυστικὸν ἔχει λόγον, ὑπὲρ τὴν κατὰ Πλάτωνα κάθοδον τῆς ψυχῆς, πτερορρυούσης καὶ δεῦρο φερομένης, *ἕως ἂν στερεοῦ τινος λάβηται.* Cf. Plato, *Phaedrus*, 245b6-c3: ἡ δὲ πτερορρυήσασα φέρεται ἕως ἂν στερεοῦ τινος ἀντιλάβηται.

820 Butterworth, p. 41, note 1.

821 Butterworth, p. 124, note 8.

822 Butterworth, p. 129, note 1.

the Latin translation follows. Even so, however, this part of *De Principiis* does *not* make mention of primeval 'souls', but of 'minds'; anyway, echoes and hints of Origen's real doctrine of creation are there, since the text is about creation of 'seeds' and 'causes'.[823] Worse still, *De Principiis*, II.9.6, speaks about God having 'gathered the diversities of minds into the harmony of a single world, so as to furnish, as it were, out of these diverse vessels or souls or minds, one house.'[824] Of course, Origen could have never spoken of 'souls or minds' as alternative terms, since he robustly pointed out the sheer ontological difference between those two states.[825] Anyhow, the text subsequently speaks about 'rational creatures' and 'their minds', and certainly there is no such reference as 'all souls existed originally as pure souls in the presence of God', for which the aforestated translator misleadingly cited '*De Princ.* II.9.1-2,6'.

To finish off with this: Origen never wrote that 'all souls existed originally as pure souls in the presence of God before their existence in bodies', because souls are *not* a primal reality. The obloquy against him was that he spoke of 'minds' that *fell* and became 'souls'.[826] Even garbled fragments by Koetschau at some points are his own construction, which he formed by partially drawing on John of Damascus allegedly rendering the accusations by Antipater of Bostra, on which Justinian's second-hand edict was based.[827] And yet, this translator advised those who read his translation that 'Origen believed that all souls existed originally as pure souls in the presence of God before their existence in bodies in this earthly life.'

2. The expression 'ancient fatherland' (of ἀρχαία πατρὶς)[828] is indeed Origen's and it appears in a comment on Psalm 127:24, which John Chrysostom copied to the letter.[829] To the same translator, this appeared 'Platonism', wherefore he

823 See analysis of Origen's doctrine of creation, which is the selfsame as that of Gregory of Nyssa, in my *COT* and *Anaxagoras*.

824 Butterworth, p. 134.

825 See *Anaxagoras*, pp. 946-947; 1311-1313; 1330-1336; 1371; 1437-1439; 1446.

826 See Butterworth, pp. 67-68: reference is made to primeval 'minds', in an otherwise self-defeating passage. Likewise, Koetschau's fr. 23a (Butterworth, pp. 125-126) is an excerpt from the anathemas against Origen, and it is about 'minds', not 'souls'. ACO, *Canones xv* (*contra Origenem sive Origenistas*), tome 4.1, p. 248. Likewise, Koetschau's fr. 24 (from Justinian letter to Menas) is about 'minds', too. Likewise, Justinian, *Edictum contra Origenem*, p. 116. 'His' synod spoke about 'souls that were formerly minds'. ACO, *Synodus Constantinopolitana et Hierosolymitana anno 536*, tome 3, p. 213. Likewise, Barsanuphius and John, *Quaestiones et Responsiones ad Coenobitas*, epistle 600, line 3. Nicephorus Callistus Xanthopulus, *HE*, 5.33.

827 See *NDGF*, pp. 385; 407; *RCR*, pp. 258-260; 267; 324-325.

828 See *PHE*, pp. 87-88; 288-290.

829 Origen, *selPs*, PG.12.1584.20-40 & John Chrysostom, *Expositiones in Psalmos*, PG.55.337.1-9. See *supra*, note 817.

felt he should made a note on that expression making this claim. However, he had no inkling of the fact that Basil of Caesarea had taken a fancy to this figure, too.[830] Besides, once John Chrysostom followed Origen suit, he could not have enough of it,[831] and both authors (like all subsequent ones) used this in exactly the same context (return to Paradise).[832] In view of such quality of 'evidence' aspiring to 'prove' that Origen maintained pre-existence of souls, which 'existed originally', and that Origen's 'Platonism is evident', it is for scholars to decide how they should select the quality of their readings. Although out of my present scope, I should briefly note only the following:

To Origen, the 'Prime Body' of Anaxagoras[833] was the *living* Body of the personal Logos that comprises all of the generative, sustaining, cognitive *logoi* / causes, and is adumbrated by means of figurative scriptural terms, such as

830 Basil of Caesarea, *Homiliae in Hexaemeron*, homily 6.1: Ἐν τῇ πόλει ταύτῃ, ἐν ᾗ ἡ ἀρχαία πατρὶς ἡμῶν, ἧς μετανέστησεν ἡμᾶς ὁ ἀνθρωποκτόνος δαίμων. *De Spiritu Sancto*, 27.66: τὴν ἀρχαίαν ἐπιζητοῦμεν πατρίδα, τὸν παράδεισον. *Homilia Dicta in Lacisis*, PG.31.1456.9-15, esp. Μὴ τοίνυν συνεμπέσῃς εἰς τὴν ἀπάτην τοῦ διαβόλου. ἐβάσκηνέ σοι, ἐβάσκηνεν. ἐξώρισέ σε τοῦ παραδείσου. ... μὴ ἐπιλάθῃ τῆς πατρίδος τῆς ἀρχαίας. Μέμνησο τῆς εὐγενείας τῆς σεαυτοῦ. μέμνησο τῆς πατρίδος ὅθεν ἐξωρίσθης.

831 John Chrysostom, *De Cruce et Latrone* (homily 1), PG.49.401.15-18: Σήμερον ἀπέδωκεν ἡμῖν τὴν ἀρχαίαν πατρίδα, σήμερον ἐπανήγαγεν ἡμᾶς ἐπὶ τὴν πατρῴαν πόλιν, καὶ τὴν οἰκίαν ἐχαρίσατο τῇ κοινῇ τῶν ἀνθρώπων φύσει. *Op. cit.* PG.49.409: *Op. cit.* PG.49.409.38-39: ἀπέδωκεν αὐτῷ τὴν ἀρχαίαν πατρίδα, ἐπανήγαγεν αὐτὸν [i.e. τὸν λῃστὴν] ἐπὶ τὴν πατρῴαν πόλιν. *De Futurae Vitae Deliciis*, PG.51.350.46-51: Ἐπειδὴ γὰρ ἐκ παραδείσου τὸ πρᾶγμα ἀπέπτη, ... καθάπερ φυγάδα πρὸς τὴν ἀρχαίαν ἐπαναγαγὼν πατρίδα, καὶ τῆς μακρᾶς ἐξορίας ἀπαλλάττων. *Expositiones in Psalmos*, PG.55.214.22-24: πρὸς τὴν ἀρχαίαν πατρίδα, μᾶλλον δὲ πρὸς πολλῷ βελτίονα, τὴν φύσιν ἀναγαγὼν τὴν ἡμετέραν. *Expositiones in Psalmos*, PG.55.273.3-4: λῃστὴς εἰς τὴν ἀρχαίαν ἐπανήει πατρίδα. *In Joannem*, PG.59.152.5-6: δέον τὴν ἀρχαίαν πατρίδα ἀπολαβεῖν. *Contra Ludos et Theatra*, PG.59.264.9: καὶ λῃστὴς εἰς τὴν ἀρχαίαν ἐπανήγετο πατρίδα.

832 Origen, *selPs*, PG.12.1584.20-40; *Homilies on Exodus* (Lat.), 2.1. Pseudo-Athanasius, *Quaestiones Ad Antiochum Ducem*, PG.28.620.25-28: πρὸς τὸν παράδεισον ἀφορῶμεν, ὅθεν καὶ ἐξεπέσαμεν πρὸς τὴν ἀρχαίαν ἡμῶν πατρίδα καὶ χώραν, αἰτούμενοι τὸν Θεὸν καὶ Δεσπότην ἀποκαταστῆσαι ἡμᾶς, ὅθεν ἐξωρίσθημεν. Cassian the Sabaite (Pseudo-Didymus), *De Trinitate*, PG.39.697.46-47: καὶ τὴν προτέραν ἀποδέχεσθαι χάριν, καὶ τὴν ἀρχαίαν ἀπολαμβάνειν πατρίδα. Cassian the Sabaite (Pseudo-Caesarius), *Quaestiones et Responsiones*, 121: τὴν ἀρχαίαν τοῦ παραδείσου ἐπιζητοῦσα πατρίδα. Also, Basil of Caesarea, *Homiliae in Hexaemeron*, homily 6.1; *De Spiritu Sancto*, 27.66; *Homilia Dicta in Lacisis*, PG.31.1456.11-13. Pseudo-Basil of Seleucia, *De Vita et Miraculis Sanctae Theclae*, 1.7 (line 75). John Chrysostom, *De Cruce et Latrone* (homily 1), PG.49.401.16; 409.38-39; *et passim.* Romanus Melodus, *Cantica*, hymn 39.12. John of Damascus, *Expositio Fidei*, 85. Theodore Studites, *Μεγάλη Κατήχησις*, catechesis 58, p. 413. Michael Psellus, *Orationes Hagiographicae*, 1a (lines 8 & 65); *Orationes Funebres*, oration 10.3; *Epistulae*, epistle 5. Michael Glycas, *Proverbia*, section 8, line 163; *Quaestiones in Sacram Scripturam*, Chapter 11, p. 143. Analecta Hymnica Graeca, *Canones Martii*, 6.10.9. See this discussed in *PHE*, pp. 287-91; also, in *NDGF*, p. 400.

833 See *Anaxagoras*, p. 366.

'paradise', 'kingdom of heavens', 'precious stones', 'luxurious stones', 'decoration of Wisdom / Logos', 'upper Jerusalem', 'heavenly Jerusalem', 'Mount Zion', 'holy mountain', 'city of God', 'city of the living God', 'city of the Great King', 'pleroma', 'sons of the kingdom', 'Church of the firstborn'. This is why the 'heavenly Jerusalem'[834] is 'our mother'[835] that 'begets' all souls, which is what happened with the soul of Jesus, too.[836] To those figurative names, Origen added some of his own, styling this reality 'our ancient fatherland' (ἀρχαία πατρίς, which numerous later authors employed) and 'Body of Logos' (σῶμα τοῦ Λόγου).[837]

At various points, Origen's context could leave no doubt that the 'heavenly Jerusalem' that 'gives birth' to souls is no other than the Anaxagorean 'Prime Body', and his expression *Body of Logos* is more meaningful than at face value, since this is pregnant with a rich philosophical legacy. Prior to him, it appears that Clement of Alexandria initiated the formula 'Body of Logos' in its abstract *philosophical* purport,[838] which though did not enjoy currency among later Christian authors, except in the context of speaking about the Holy Eucharist, which bears on the present point only in an attenuated sense.[839] The analogous expression 'Body of Christ' in essence adumbrates the same notion, and Origen employed this abundantly, all the more so since this obtains in the New Testament.[840] Maximus Confessor was the only one who (as he did on numerous issues) followed Origen suit by employing the critical phrase 'Body of Logos' and styled Christ 'the essence of virtues' (σῶμα οὖν τοῦ Λόγου ἐστὶν ἡ

834 Heb. 12:22. Cf. Origen, *Princ*, IV.3.8; *homJer*, homilies 5.13; 12.3; *Cels*, VII.29; VIII.5.

835 Gal. 4:26. Cf. Origen, *Princ*, IV.3.8; *homJer*, homily 5.13; *Cels*, IV.44; *commMatt*, 14.13; 16.15.

836 *commMatt*, 14.17.

837 *commJohn*, I.13.79; X.35.220 & 229; X.36.235 & 236 & 286; *commMatt*, 13.21; 11.18; 13.21; 13.24; 14.1; 14.17; 14.23; *commSerMatt*, pp. 126; 146; *Libri x in Canticum Canticorum* (*fragmenta*), p. 175; *commEph*, frs. 5; 9; 16; 17; 33. Cf. Gregory of Nyssa, *Oratio Catechetica*, 37, copied by Bessarion, *De Sacramento Eucharistiae*, section 10.7.

838 Clement of Alexandria, *Paedagogus*, 6.47.3: ἐν τῷ αἵματι τῷ αὐτοῦ κοσμήσειν λέγει τὸ σῶμα τοῦ Λόγου.

839 For example, see the notion of the 'Body of Logos' (σῶμα τοῦ Λόγου) in Gregory of Nyssa, *Oratio Catechetica*, 37; copied by Bessarion, *De Sacramento Eucharistiae*, section 10.7.

840 1 Cor. 12:27; Eph. 4:12; Col. 2:17. Cf. Origen, *commJohn*, I.13.79: τῆς κεφαλῆς τοῦ ὅλου τῶν σῳζομένων σώματος, Χριστοῦ Ἰησοῦ. *Op. cit.* X.35.229: ὥστε καὶ τὴν γενομένην ἀνάστασιν ... περιέχειν μυστήριον τῆς ἀναστάσεως τοῦ παντὸς Χριστοῦ σώματος. *Op. cit.* X.35.220: οὕτως τὸ ὅλον τῶν ἁγίων Χριστοῦ σῶμα συνεσταύρωται καὶ οὐκέτι ζῇ. *Op. cit.* X.36.235: ποίοις γὰρ ὀστοῖς ... ἅτε οὖσιν οἴκῳ Ἰσραὴλ ἢ τῷ Χριστοῦ σώματι. *Op. cit.* X.36.236: ὅτε δὲ γίνεται ἡ ἀνάστασις τοῦ ἀληθινοῦ καὶ τελειοτέρου Χριστοῦ σώματος ... τοῦ σώματος τοῦ Χριστοῦ. Likewise, *op. cit.* X.36.286; XX.11.81&82; *commMatt*, 13.21; 11.18; 13.21; 13.24; 14.1; 14.17; 14.23; *commSerMatt*, pp. 126; 146; *Libri x in Canticum Canticorum* (fragmenta), p. 175; *commEph*, frs. 5; 9; 16; 17; 33.

τῶν ἀρετῶν οὐσία).[841] As for Cyril of Alexandria, it can be demonstrably shown that he took up cardinal ideas and notions from Origen and entertained them in an historical milieu in which mere reference to Origen's name would have been lethal danger – which is why he never did so albeit he drew abundantly on his predecessor.

It would be superfluous to point it out, yet, to my experience, this is necessary for some scholars to know this: when in my commentary I refer to authors having 'copied from Origen', on no account does 'copy from' have the pejorative connotation of doing something illegal or immoral, and especially getting caught doing something that one should not have done. Christian authors knew full well that all of them fought for a common cause, and there was nothing reprehensible about availing themselves of a common stock, which after all would have made their source author proud.

Therefore, to have recourse to ostensibly alternative well-meant expressions, such as 'borrowed from', 'is dependent on', 'is verbally dependent on', etc. could make no sense. For all the instances I point out and quote are not about 'borrowing' or being 'verbally dependent on': these are carbon copies of a few or several lines of text, especially in Chrysostom, in a context which otherwise is different either in this author's or in Origen's corresponding textual context. Once one is aware of how avid preachers such as the authors just mentioned felt, there is no room for assumptions about 'disparagement' or 'denigration' of those who confidently and proudly copied from Origen's present commentary, as well from other works of his. To assume that, when a twenty-first century author writes about fourth-century Christians having 'copied from Origen' involves a 'pejorative sense' suggesting plagiarism would only mean unawareness of the aims and disposition of those early Christians. Not only did later Christian authors feel free to employ Origen's ideas, but also they had no inhibitions about copying from him *literatim*, because they felt that there was nothing wrong about them doing so.

Besides, why should later catenists incorrectly attribute the authorship of a particular quotation to Origen, once he was a notorious damned heretic? Perhaps, because they were 'Origenists'? But the compiler of the catena on Matthew was all too anxious to declare his allegiance to orthodoxy right

841 Maximus Confessor, *Quaestiones et Dubia*, 191, lines 53-54. Cf. Origen, *apud Catena in Matthaeum*, p. 180: καὶ ἐνδυσάμενος τὸ ὕφασμα τῆς ἀρετῆς, Χριστόν. *commMatt*, 12.14: ὁ Χριστὸς γὰρ ἡ πᾶσα ἀρετή. *commSerMatt*, pp. 145-147: αἱ ἀρεταὶ τῇ ὑποστάσει ὁ Χριστός. *frMatt*, fr. 83 (Klostermann): αὕτη γοῦν ἐστιν (κατά γε τὸν ἐμὸν λόγον) ἡ ἀληθὴς ἀρετή, τὸ ἀμιγὲς τοῦ χείρονος ἀγαθόν, αὐτὸς ὁ θεός. *schMatt*, PG.17.304.15-18: Εἰσὶ γὰρ αἱ κοινῶς νοούμεναι … ἀρεταὶ τῆς ὑποστάσεως Χριστοῦ. *commEph*, fr. 33: ἢ τὴν ἀρετὴν ἥτις ἐστὶν ὁ Χριστός. *selNum*, PG.12.583: ὁ Χριστός, ἡ οὐσιώδης ἀρετή. Cf. *Cels*, VI.6; 8; *commMatt*, 12.14; *commEph*, fr. 33.

from the start, and so did the anonymous writer of the prologue to Origen's *Philocalia*.[842] Quoting from 'heretics' in catenae was a practice allowed only as a concession, which is is what the compiler of the *Catena on Matthew* also did, yet taking heed to appeal to Cyril of Alexandria having made allowance for such a practice.[843]

Therefore, this is the point for me to explain my methodology concerning the edited presentation of the Greek text at hand.

By exploring twenty-four codices attesting to Origen's commentary on Matthew, Klostermann did a toilsome job which deserves respect. However, his practice was the same as that of almost all those who complied similar works: he just transcribed the paleographic text, emended egregious errors of language, added scriptural references and, if not always, he cited (not quoted) parallel passages by other authors. This is supposed to be 'critical apparatus', but in my view it is all but 'critical'.

Klostermann followed this method of work, and, whenever he found a passage attributed to other authors in one or more other codices, he advised accordingly by means of a footnote. In some cases, when a passage was attributed also to another author, he opted for placing this in brackets, as if he himself doubted the attribution, albeit this was ascribed also to Origen, normally in more than one codex. I mention such cases *ad hoc* in my commentary to the present text, but at this point the question is this: unless there is unsurmountable obscurity and impossibility of comparative study, once an editor is ambivalent as to *critically* assessing the authorship of a text, what is the use of such a presentation in the first place? Is it the fact of transcribing passages, many of which are known already? This use could not be doubted, but hardly does such a presentation make an edition and its 'apparatus' a *critical* one.

In this edition, I opted for going beyond this conveniently established practice. In order for an edition to be really *critical*, I saw as the editor's task to assess the implications of the language involved, to explore all of the parallel instances of either the text itself or its ideas appearing in other authors, and sometimes to more or less risk determining a passage's real authorship while always maintaining the attribution made in the codex itself. Of course, no reader of this analysis has to agree in every respect, let alone entirely. Nevertheless, the editor's arguments and parallel textual evidence is there: I did not opt for the labour-saving stereotype, 'here is the text of this or that codex; one codex ascibes this to A, the other to B' – and that is all. Of course, anyone is welcome

842 Origen, *Philocalia*, Prologue, 1b.
843 *Catena in Matthaeum* (Cramer), p. 4.

to disagree; but this cannot be done on the basis of an ostentatious 'hermeneutics of suspicion', which normally is only the refuge of half-learnedness, at best.

Reading excerpts from Origen's commentary does not by all means have to suggest that a catenist (especially if he happened to be an intellectual) felt that he should copy everything to the letter. It should be expected that at points he abbreviated the text by omitting or skipping some of Origen's digressions, which usually are learned and useful, but not essential to the instructive character a catena was meant to have. Thus, comparing the exegesis of a certain scriptural point with the extant commentary on Matthew and expecting to see the selfsame text would be utopic, and sometimes absurd. For example, the treatment of Matthew 13:44 (on the kingdom of heaven being a treasure hidden in the field, folio 114r) is found in Book 10.4-7. Quite reasonably, the catenist did not deem it necessary to copy Origen's analyses of the difference between 'parable' (παραβολή) and 'resemblance' (ὁμοίωσις), by which Origen resolved that the former is a particular case of the latter. Rather, the catenist concentrated on the core of Origen's exegesis of the scriptural point itself, of which I have provided parallel texts from his commentary.

Likewise, the comment on Matthew 22:3 (folio 173r) appears to have somewhat summarised the exposition in Book 17.15. So what? – all the more so, once we have the parallel to this both from Klostermann's fr. 433 and Origen's extant text in the catena on Matthew? Is there any real need for discussion of 'how close' the parallels are to the preserved commentary text, or to get 'suspicious' because a small explanatory sentence was omitted by the catenist in an otherwise parallel text? Examples of this kind would go a long way, but this would be useless. I only note that excerpts of Origen's commentary on Matthew could have obtained not in one work of his, but in *three* relevant compositions of his explaining the gospel of Matthew, as discussed earlier.

I have to declare that this is not exactly my own conception of scholarship. To come upon the same *ideas*, the same *vocabulary*, the selfsame *text* – and yet to 'suspect' that a passage is not Origen's (while being unable to suggest any alternative) only because a catenist omitted some intervening or concluding explanatory sentences, in my view would be absurd. Besides, the fact is that there was too much of shortage of space in the specific *Codex 232* (a usual case with codices, anyway), which is all too evident also from the numerous additional passages appearing on the margins, written in a highly abbreviated manner, which adds to the difficulty of reading the palaeographic text. Consequently, to expect to see, for example, analysis of the children pericope as in Matthew 19:13-15 (folia 150v-151r) which occupies nine (one-column) pages instead of the nearly twenty-lines in this codex would be no less absurd.

It is always possible that, when a superior of a monastery recited from the lectern, he could have slightly amended scriptural quotations in accordance with knowledge from his own manuscript. For example, the clause quoted from Matthew 19:9 (καὶ ὁ ἀπολελυμένην γαμήσας μοιχᾶται, folio 149v) perhaps was not the same as in the manuscript Origen himself used. Nevertheless, this was a known one and had been so used by eminent authors.[844]

Moreover, to expect that a florilegium of Matthew's gospel (which *ipso facto* was meant to be used as an edifying companion) would engage in copying Origen's discussion (folia 151v-154v) as to whether Matthew 13:19 ('You shall love your neighbour as yourself') was part of the original text, or not (which Origen did in *commMatt*, 15.14), could only betray unawareness of *why* such catenae were written in the first place.

Likewise, the codex text does not engage in the lengthy explanation of the Jewish practice of Corban from which Origen said he had learned 'from one of the Hebrews';[845] but the reference to Corban and explanation of this is there nonetheless (folios 122v-123r), and my commentary can show if the attribution of part of Origen's text to Photius could stand up to any modicum of logic.

To claim that the clear attribution of such catena-fragments should be disputed on the grounds of 'suspicion' that the catenist treated the text of Origen freely, adding, omitting, and rewriting the material, would just be not arguable. Why should the one who allegedly did so be the catenist and not Origen himself? For, as discussed in a moment, Jerome wrote that he drew on Origen who expounded his exegesis in the gospel of Matthew not only in a commentary, but also in homilies, as well as 'in a kind of verse interpretation'.

In addition, any 'suspicious' reader could not just get away with simply casting doubt on a testimony and then remain silent and idle: this doubt should be accompanied by an explanation of why would a catenist have cared to attribute to the 'damned' Origen such a text, which perfectly conforms with his extant analyses. For this is not about ascribing a passage to this or that orthodox author: it is attribution to a 'heretic'. In order for such passages to be perused properly, my endnotes / commentary provide Origen's relevance with the points made, the technical expressions used, and quote texts running parallel to them. This is why some of the endnotes are long, but this is also what makes Origen's seal on critical points all too evident. For instance, discussion

844 Basil of Caesarea, *Regulae Morales*, PG.31.852.12-25. John Chrysostom, *Encomium ad Maximum*, PG.51.225.51. Cyril of Alexandria, *commProphXII*, v. 2, p. 589. John of Damascus, *Sacra Parallela*, PG.96.244.14. Matthaeus Blastares, *Collectio Alphabetica*, letter gamma, chapter 13. The Nestle-Aland edition notes that this version of the text is found in three codices.

845 Origen *commMatt*, 11.9.

of the term συμπαρεκτείνειν (in endnote cdlxxxv) is illuminating, since normally this is passed by indifferently due to unawareness of its history and crucial implications.

The same goes for such notes as ccix, in which the notion of 'guardian power' (φρουροῦσα δύναμις) having been introduced by Origen is discussed. This demonstrates not only that his acolytes took this up, but also how Origen himself made use of his stupendous Greek background. As for note mcclxxviii, this is not just the study of a word (the verb τροποφορῶ): it is demonstration of how Origen's background resulted in his *reasoned* use of a term, thus revealing him as author of the text. The same goes for endnote mcdliii providing the story of the bread and wine of the Holy Eucharist being styled 'material' existence of the Body of the Logos, which reveals Origen's relevance with the present codex text once again.

No matter who the catenist was, he had access to all three compositions of Origen's commentary on Matthew, and copied from all of them, thus saving for posterity text from those works.

I know of no other codex that has preserved Origen's commentary on the very last phrase of Matthew, namely, 28:19-20. This means that *Sabaiticus 232* is a (thus far, unique) source filling the gap of points of the manuscript tradition of Origen's commentary, or indeed commentaries, on Matthew. The points that are made therein and the terms used are critical with respect to the Nicene Creed (robustly and explicitly endorsed), which allows no room for ambiguity or ambivalence as to Origen's real views, which, once again, are inexorably harmonious with his overall theology.

It appeared that someone dignified himself as 'specialist on catenae fragments' and yet decided that 'the value of fragments that appear in the present manuscript is nil'. No doubt, considering 'fragments' always takes a higher degree of considerate alertness, sometimes risk, but such views only imply that the exertions of such scholars as Cramer, Reuss, Klostermann, Benz, Diekamp, Leanza, Constantinescu, and others, were pointless.

To me, such 'specialists' are like eunuchs looking through the keyhole a man and a woman having sexual intercourse, and subsequently criticising the male for his defection on that score and giving advice for improvement. To such 'eunuchs', catenists were writing their own commentaries, and drew on the commentaries of earlier Christian authors for their material, but they were not interested primarily in preserving those texts precisely: they were only interested in shaping their own interpretation of the scriptural text through what earlier authors had said about it; allegedly, they just omitted, altered, summarised, and the like; sometimes they were working with a manuscript of the Christian author they were quoting, and sometimes the later ones were drawing on earlier catena commentaries, which had already gone through an alteration process to which they added their own when necessary.

Were it for such views of men who, once they are given an opportunity, criticise (which can hardly conceal spitefulness) but are unable to produce anything really contributing to our knowledge of a fertile past, to prevail in scholarship, it would follow that all editions of catenae-fragments should be thrown to the wastebin, and a cloud of inconclusive 'suspicion' would render all those testimonies absolutely sterile. It was exactly because of this 'conspiracy of mediocrity' that I followed a method different from previous editions of fragmentary testimonies, although in this case we are mostly upon not mere 'fragments' but extensive sections of Origen's exegeses: I perused every technical term or expression to the minutest detail, so as to shed as much light as possible on the itinerary of ideas; I sought to pinpoint *all* parallel texts and assess the plausibility or implausibility of correlation, which is not the case with extant similar editions. Upon editing the present text, I have deemed it necessary to ponder not only on the ideas, but also on the technical vocabulary, which undergirds Origen's authorship, as well as its roots, including prior and posterior usage by specific authors both Greek and Christian. I could think of no other way to make a stand against the 'hermeneutics of suspicion', which is otherwise 'invincible', just like some other well-known human traits which do not happen to belong to man's higher qualities.

Nevertheless, when all is said and done, the readers of this volume remain free to assess for themselves the value of these testimonies and decide whether, and to what extent, these could be used as evidence.

The range of assessing the text of the present codex with Origen's extant commentary on Matthew is limited by the fact that, of this we have only Books 10-17 commenting on Matthew 13:36-22:33, whereas *Codex Sabaiticus 232* covers Matthew 1:18-28:20. Consequently, parallel study should take into account also Klostermann's 572 fragments (covering Matthew from 1:1 to 28:18-20), which is what I have done, too. In Klostermann's collection, parallel study is possible only from fragment 303 (on Matthew 13:36) to fragment 444 (on Matthew 22:22). It can be easily noticed that those portions contain comments which cannot be paralleled to Origen's extant text.[846] Naturally, a number of them have appeared under dual ascriptions, as explained above. As for several others that were deemed susceptible of comparative reading, Klostermann indicated

846 Cf. Klostermann, frs. 327; 331; 332 [used by Jerome]; 333; 334 [used by Jerome]; 337 [used by Jerome]; 338; 342; 362; 384; 386; 390; 393; 395; 401; 404-406; 411-416; 418; 420; 422-424; 426; 427; 431; 432; 440.

parallel *loci* in Origen's commentary, without being deterred by the fact that the language was not a carbon copy one.

Whether this was the reason why earlier scholars (as well as certain modern ones of the quality I indicated above) treated Klostermann's conscientious work almost with contempt, I do not know. What I do know is that once, in a fragment, we come upon a term used by Origen which does not appear elsewhere, this should not be a reason for dismissing it out of hand. Perhaps an example would suffice at this point: suppose that the *Contra Celsum* had been preserved only partially, in catena-fragments, and one came upon him arguing that Jesus' disciples wrote their scriptural texts without any intention of trickery and that their intentions were 'guileless' (ἀπάνουργος). Were it for not all of the *Contra Celsum* to have survived, the modern claim would be that this is a word that does not occur elsewhere in Origen's extant writings – therefore, the statement is not Origen's. But it *was* – indeed it was taken up not only by Origen's admirers (including Porphyry) and detractors alike,[847] and it can be arguably shown that Origen drew on one of his favourite authors, namely, Plutarch.[848]

The question then is this: what should we make of those of Origen's fragments collected by Klostermann, which apparently have no parallel in the extant commentary on Matthew? To this question two possible alternatives should be taken into account.

1. Since Jerome wrote[849] that he used 'Origen's twenty-five books on Matthew many years ago and just as many of his homilies and a kind of verse interpretation', it is clear that Origen offered his analyses of that gospel not only in his 'commentary' but also in pertinent 'homilies' and in a sort of 'verse interpretation' nonetheless (legisse me fateor ante annos plurimos in Matthaeum Origenis viginti quinque volumina, et totidem ejus Homilias, commaticumque interpretationis genus). This makes it all too clear that Origen's exegeses on the gospel of Matthew were expounded not in just *one* work of his, but in *three.*

To determine *which* catena-passage belongs to either of those expositions is just impossible, and the claim that this 'kind of verse interpretation' along with those homilies have not survived is simply a lighthearted red herring.

847 Origen, *Cels*, III.24. Porphyry, *Contra Christianos*, fr. 7. Eusebius, *Demonstratio Evangelica*, 1.1.9; 3.5.96. Epiphanius of Salamis, *Panarion*, v. 1, p. 430. Didymus, *Commentarii in Psalmos 22-26.10*, codex p. 91. Pseudo-John Chrysostom, *In Sanctum Pascha*, 14; 17. Cyril of Alexandria, *commProphXII*, v. 1, p. 596; v. 2, p. 76; *In Joannem*, v. 1, p. 11.

848 Plutarch, *Quaestiones Convivales*, p. 716B; *De Sollertia Animalium*, p. 966B. Athenaeus, *Deipnosophistae*, 3.53. Sextus Empiricus, *Adversus Rhetores*, 2.77.

849 See *supra*, p. LXXX reference to Jerome's Preface to his commentary on Matthew.

At the same time, however, it is this fact that renders scholastic juxtaposition of catena fragments *only* with Origen's extant commentary nonsenical. To say that a fragment makes a specific point by quoting this or that scriptural passage, whereas the extant commentary on Matthew does not include citation of any of them, is just inutile scholarship.

2. There is also another possibility that should be considered. Eusebius' account of Origen's life and writings, and those who copied from him (Jerome, Nicephorus Callistus Xanthopulus) mentioned the twenty-five volumes of the commentary on Matthew, but not any commentary on Luke. However, catenae that were written in the ensuing centuries purportedly quoted from the latter commentary, too. Given that Origen wrote the commentary on Matthew when he was well on in age, it would appear that subsequently he set on to write a commentary on Luke. In Cramer's catena on the commentary on Luke there are numerous passages attributed to Origen.[850] What is characteristic is that the catenist all too often wrote a specific phrase here and there: "As for the pericope [which he quotes], the exegesis of this has been written earlier in the catena on the gospel according to Matthew" (προεγράφη εἰς τὸ κατὰ Ματθαῖον), and this remark was made also in fragments attributed to Origen.[851] This was all too natural to do, since the case was about two synoptic gospels in which several points, instances, and phrases, are almost identical. Anyhow, beyond Cramer's collection, we have those by M. Rauer,[852] and prior to him, those by Migne.[853] Study of Origen's fragments on both gospels makes it immediately evident that, at several points, the exposition is identical in terms of not only ideas but also language.

Although I cannot be categorical, my own surmise is that catenists of subsequent times came upon scriptural pericopes that were more or less the same in both gospels (let alone differences of manuscripts concerning each one of them) followed by exegeses, in which it was easy to come upon one referring to Matthew's gospel and taking this as exegesis on a more or less identical pericope by Luke. Of course, this made no essential difference whatsoever, but it would also explain why is it that several fragments on Matthew

---

850 J.A. Cramer, *Catena in Lucam (typus B) (e codd. Paris. Coislin. 23 & Oxon. Bodl. Misc. 182)*, pp. 29 & 30 (ref. to Origen's *commMatt*), pp. 6; 10; 20; 26; 30 (bis); 34; 35; 36; 37; 54; 84; 86; 93; 103; 108; 140; 147; 148.

851 J.A. Cramer, *op. cit.* pp. 29 & 30 (ref. to Origen's *commMatt*); 30 (bis); 32; 49; 81; 86; 90; 91; 94 (ref. to Origen's *commMatt*); 96; 101; 102; 103; 105; 108; 109; 111; 117; 123; 127; 128; 130; 133; 151; 153; 159; 160; 165; 167; 170; 171. *Supplementum et Varietas Lectionis ad Catenam in Evangelium Sancti Lucae (e cod. Oxon. Bodl. Laud. 33)*, pp. 422; 423; 428 (bis).

852 M. Rauer, *Fragmenta in Lucam (in catenis)*, 257 frs. *Homiliae in Lucam*, from homiles 1-39.

853 Origen, *Scholia in Lucam (fragmenta e cod. Venet. 28)*, PG.17.312-369.

in Klostermann's collection have no parallel in the extant text of Origen's commentary. In any event, this tentative explanation is not applicable to points that are exclusive to Matthew's gospel, such as his concluding phrase (28:18-20). This explanation, however, can also show that seeking to correspond all of Origen's fragments with the surviving text of his commentary on Matthew could make sense only to a certain extent.

The aim of the present edition is not to supersede Klostermann's edition, which should and will remain with its value intact, always valid, and serviceable. Thus, my methodology has been determined by my aim not to outdate Klostermann's great work comprising fragments from Origen's commentary on Matthew found in twenty-four codices.[854] I do believe that there is neither need nor possibility for Klostermann's collection to be outdated. Instead, my wish has been to supplement this volume with the text of a codex that Klostermann missed, which contains unparalleled text and happens to cast new light on Origen's thought for that matter. In this context, I deemed it necessary to quote (not just cite) for synoptic reading parallel texts that have been ascribed either to other authors, or Origen's one's from extant editions. Klostermann just *cited* some yet not all of them. But since *Codex Sabaiticus 232* is mutilated in the beginning, I only quoted the first three of Klostermann's fragments simply for reasons of completeness.

Nevertheless, in the cases that portions of *Codex Sabaiticus 232* coincide with Klostermann's fragments, readers that are interested should consult also with his edition in order to find out which are the codices that attest to those points. For example, I deemed it unnecessary to cite other codices, such as the group labelled by Klostermann C^1 (Catena prima Ps.-Petri Laodiceni) and its subgroups. As for the three Codices Mosquensis Sinod. gr. 47 (Vlad. 91) [Clb 1 in Klostermann], Parisinus suppl. gr. 612 [Clb 5], and Parisinus Coisl. 24 [Clb 2], Klostermann's volume is always there to consult with. The same goes for some other manuscripts beside those three from Moscow and Paris, for which likewise there was no reason to be included in the apparatus – far less has it been deemed necessary to deal with information on the other manuscripts. As for an assumed stemma of them, which is always too a tentative and hardly reliable undertaking, Klostermann was as wise as not to engage in such a thankless and fruitless job at all.

854 *Matthäus-Erklärung III* (Origenes Werke, XII 3), eds. E. Benz – E. Klostermann, Leipzig 1941.

Commentary on the Gospel of Matthew

Εὐαγγέλιόν ἐστι λόγος περιέχων ἀπαγγελίαν πραγμάτων κατὰ τὸ εὔλογον καὶ διὰ τὸ ὠφελεῖν εὐφραίνων τὸν ἀκούοντα, ἐπὰν παραδέξηται τὸ ἀπαγγελλόμενον· ἢ λόγος ἀπαγγέλλων παρεῖναι ἀγαθὸν τὸ προσδοκώμενον.[i]

Ἔστι τοίνυν τὸ εὐαγγέλιον λόγος περιέχων ἀπαγγελίαν πραγμάτων κατὰ τὸ εὔλογον διὰ τὸ ὠφελεῖν εὐφραινόντων τὸν ἀκούοντα, ἐπὰν παραδέξηται τὸ ἀπαγγελλόμενον· οὐδὲν δ' ἧττον ὁ τοιοῦτος λόγος εὐαγγέλιόν ἐστιν, ἂν καὶ πρὸς τὴν σχέσιν τοῦ ἀκούοντος ἐξετάζηται.[1]

Ἢ εὐαγγέλιόν ἐστι λόγος περιέχων ἀγαθοῦ τῷ πιστεύοντι παρουσίαν ἢ λόγος ἐπαγγελλόμενος παρεῖναι ἀγαθὸν τὸ προσδοκώμενον.[ii]

Ἕκαστον γὰρ εὐαγγέλιον, σύστημα ἀπαγγελλομένων ὠφελίμων τῷ πιστεύοντι καὶ μὴ παρεκδεξαμένῳ τυγχάνον ὠφέλειαν ἐμποιοῦν, κατὰ τὸ εὔλογον εὐφραίνει, διδάσκον τὴν δι' ἀνθρώπους τοῦ πρωτοτόκου πάσης κτίσεως Χριστοῦ Ἰησοῦ σωτήριον αὐτοῖς ἐπιδημίαν.[iii]

Ἀπὸ τοῦ κεφαλαίου καλέσας. τοῦτο γὰρ παραδίδωσιν ὡς ἀρχὴ καὶ ῥίζα τῶν ἀγαθῶν τὸ θεὸν γενέσθαι ἄνθρωπον. ἀκολούθως ἕψεται τὸ ἑξῆς ὡς καὶ *βίβλος γενέσεως οὐρανοῦ*[2] *καὶ γῆς*.[iv]

Ἡ τοῦ Χριστοῦ γένεσις οὐχὶ ὁδός ἐστιν ἐκ τοῦ μὴ ὄντος εἰς τὸ εἶναι, ὡς οἴονταί τινες ἐπ' ἀνθρώπων, ἀλλ' ὁδὸς ἀπὸ τοῦ *ἐν μορφῇ Θεοῦ* ὑπάρχειν εἰς τὸ ἀναλαβεῖν τὴν τοῦ *δούλου*[3] *μορφήν*.[v]

Codex Holy Cross (*Τιμίου Σταυροῦ*) *104*, Jerusalem

1

16v (Ὠριγένους) Πρῶτος δὲ τῶν λοιπῶν εὐαγγελιστῶν γεγράφηκεν ὁ θεῖος οὗτος ἀνὴρ τὸ παρ‹όν›[4] | **17r** εὐαγγέλιον ἑβραΐδι φωνῇ[vi] τοῖς ἐκ περιτομῆς‹,› καὶ γράμμασιν ἑβραϊκοῖς συντεταγμένον. Δεύτερον δὲ τὸ κατὰ Μᾶρκον ὡς Πέτρος ὑφηγήσατο αὐτῷ,

---

1 Origen, *commJohn*, I.5.27. Cf. John Chrysostom, *Catena in Lucam*, p. 6: (Τοῦ ἁγίου Ἰωάννου τοῦ Χρυσοστόμου) Εὐαγγέλιον δέ ἐστι λόγος περιέχων ἐπαγγελίαν πραγμάτων κατὰ τὸ Εὐαγγέλιον, διὰ τὸ ὠφελεῖν εὐφραίνων τὸν ἀκούοντα, ἐπὰν παραδέξηται τὸ ἐπαγγελλόμενον.

2 Gen. 2:4.

3 Rom. 1:3.

4 Cod. παρ´΄.

 | DOI:10.30965/9783657702800_003

ὃν καὶ υ‹ἱὸ›ν[5] ἐν τῇ καθολικῇ προσαγορεύει ἐπιστολῇ.[6] Τρίτον δὲ τὸ κατὰ Λουκᾶν τὸ ὑπὸ Παύλ‹ου›[7] ἐπαινούμενον εὐαγγέλιον τοῖς ἀπὸ τῶν *ἐθνῶν*.[8] Καὶ ἐπὶ πᾶσι τὸ[9] [κατὰ] Ἰωάννην.[10]

> Ὡς ἐν παραδόσει μαθὼν περὶ τῶν τεσσάρων εὐαγγελίων, ἃ καὶ μόνα ἀναντίρρητά ἐστιν ἐν τῇ ὑπὸ τὸν οὐρανὸν ἐκκλησίᾳ τοῦ θεοῦ, ὅτι πρῶτον μὲν γέγραπται τὸ *κατὰ* τόν ποτε τελώνην ὕστερον δὲ ἀπόστολον Ἰησοῦ Χριστοῦ *Ματθαῖον*, ἐκδεδωκότα αὐτὸ τοῖς ἀπὸ Ἰουδαϊσμοῦ πιστεύσασιν, γράμμασιν Ἑβραϊκοῖς συντεταγμένον. δεύτερον δὲ τὸ κατὰ Μᾶρκον, ὡς Πέτρος ὑφηγήσατο αὐτῷ, ποιήσαντα, ὃν καὶ υἱὸν ἐν τῇ καθολικῇ ἐπιστολῇ διὰ τούτων ὡμολόγησεν φάσκων. *ἀσπάζεται ὑμᾶς ἡ ἐν Βαβυλῶνι συνεκλεκτὴ καὶ Μᾶρκος ὁ υἱός μου*[11]. καὶ τρίτον τὸ κατὰ Λουκᾶν, τὸ ὑπὸ Παύλου ἐπαινούμενον εὐαγγέλιον τοῖς ἀπὸ τῶν ἐθνῶν πεποιηκότα. ἐπὶ πᾶσιν τὸ κατὰ Ἰωάννην.[vii]

Εἰ δὲ γέγραπται ταῦτα *πν‹εύματ›ι*,[12] εἴποιμι δ' ἂν ὅτι καὶ λόγον τινὰ ἔχει ἡ τῶν εὐαγγελίων τάξις. Καὶ ὅρα εἰ δυνάμεθα λέγειν ὅτι πρῶτος εἰκότως ἔγραψεν ὁ εἰς γένεσιν ἀνθρωπίνην καταβιβάζων αὐτ‹ὸ›ν[13] τῷ λόγῳ, καὶ γενεαλογῶν αὐτὸν *ἀπὸ τοῦ Ἀβραὰμ ἕως Δα‹υὶ›δ*,[14] καὶ *ἀπὸ τοῦ Δα‹υὶ›δ*[15] *ἕως τῆς μετοικεσίας Βαβυλῶνος*, καὶ *ἀπὸ τῆς μετοικεσίας Βαβυλῶνο‹ς›*[16] *ἕως* αὐτοῦ *τοῦ Χ‹ριστοῦ›*.[17] Διὸ καὶ τὰ πλεῖστα ἀνθρώπινα ὁ Ματθαῖος διηγήσατο καὶ μετὰ τοῦτον Μᾶρκος, φάσκων | **17v** ἀρχὴν εἶναι *τοῦ εὐαγγελίου*[18] Ἰωάννην[19] τὸν[20] τελευταῖον τῶν προφητῶν.[viii] Καὶ τρίτο‹ς›[21] ὁ Λουκᾶς ὁμολογεῖ μεθ' ἑτέρους ἐπιβεβληκέναι τὸ γράφειν εὐαγγέλιον, λέγων. *Ἐπειδήπερ πολλοὶ ἐπεχείρησαν ἀνατάξασθαι διήγησιν περὶ τῶν πεπληροφορημένων ἐν ἡμῖν πραγμάτων*,[22] ἀλλ' ἔοικε μὴ ἐγκεῖσθαι τὰ τῶν πολλῶν.

Τοῦ αὐτοῦ.

---

5 Cod. ῦν.
6 1 Peter, 1:13.
7 Cod. παύλ.
8 Cf. Gal. 2:7.
9 Cod. τὸν.
10 Cf. Gal. 2:9.
11 1 Peter, 5:13.
12 Cod. πνῑ. Cf. 2 Cor. 3:3.
13 Cod. ἀυτ̀.
14 Cod. δα̱δ.
15 Cod. δα̱δ.
16 Cod. βαβυλῶνο.
17 Cod. χ̄ῡ. Cf. Matt. 1:12-17.
18 Mark, 1:1.
19 Cf. Mark, 1:1-4.
20 Cod. τ̀.
21 Cod. τρῖτο.
22 Luke, 1:1.

᾿Απεικαστέον δὲ *Γηών*, τῷ Ματθαίῳ. *Φυσ‹ών›*,[23] τῷ Μάρκῳ. *Τίγρις*, τῷ Λουκᾷ. *Εὐφράτης*, τῷ ᾿Ιωάννῃ.[24] Ταῦτα κατὰ νοῦν ζήτει· εἰσί γαρ καὶ ἄλλοι λόγοι ἐν τούτοις.[ix]

᾿Αλλὰ ταῦτα μὲν ἱκανῶς ἐξήτασται,[x] σὺ δὲ πρὸς τούτοις ζήτει ὅτι πῶς ποτε ἄρα ὧδε μὲν γεννήσεως μέμνηται ὁ εὐαγγελιστής, κατ᾿ ἀρχὰς δὲ τοῦ εὐαγγελίου τῆς γενέσεως. ᾿Ενταῦθα μὲν γὰρ λέγει *τοῦ δὲ ᾿Ιησοῦ Χριστοῦ ἡ γέννησις οὕτως ἦν*,[25] ἐκεῖ δὲ *βίβλος γενέσεως*.[26] Τίς οὖν ἡ διαφορὰ τῆς γεννήσεως καὶ τῆς γενέσεως, καὶ πῶς ἀμφότερα ἐπὶ Χριστοῦ λαμβάνεται; Ὥσπερ ὁ λόγος οὗτος ὁ προφορικὸς κατὰ τὴν οἰκείαν φύσιν ἀναφής ἐστι καὶ ἀόρατος, ὅταν δὲ ἐν βιβλίῳ γραφῇ καὶ οἱονεὶ σωματωθῇ τότε καὶ ὁρᾶται καὶ ψηλαφᾶται, οὕτως καὶ ὁ ἄσαρκος τοῦ θεοῦ λόγος καὶ ἀσώματος, οὔτε ὁρώμενος οὔτε γραφόμενος κατὰ τὴν θεότητα, ἐπειδὴ ἐσαρκώθη, καὶ ὁρᾶται καὶ γράφεται. Διὰ τοῦτο, ὡς σαρκωθέντος, καὶ *βίβλος* ἐστὶ τῆς αὐτοῦ *γενέσεως*. ᾿Αλλ᾿ οὐκ ἐζήτηται ἐνθάδε τὸ διὰ τί εἶπε *βίβλος* καὶ οὐκ εἶπεν ὅρασις ἢ λόγος (τοῦτο γὰρ εἴρηται). ἀλλὰ τὸ πῶς ὄπισθεν *γενέσεως* ἐμνημόνευσεν ὁ Ματθαῖος ὧδε δὲ γεννήσεως, καὶ τί ἐστι *γέννησις*, καὶ τί γένεσις. Διαφέρει γένεσις καὶ *γέννησις*. Γένεσις μὲν γάρ ἐστιν ἡ ἐκ θεοῦ πρώτη πλάσις, *γέννησις* δὲ ἡ ἐκ καταδίκης τοῦ θανάτου διὰ τὴν παράβασιν ἐξ ἀλλήλων διαδοχή. Καὶ ἔτι ἡ μὲν γένεσις τὸ ἄφθαρτον ἔχει καὶ ἀναμάρτητον, ἡ δὲ *γέννησις* τὸ παθητὸν καὶ ἁμαρτητικόν. ῾Ο μὲν οὖν κύριος τῆς μὲν γενέσεως τὸ ἀναμάρτητον φυσικῶς λαβὼν τὸ ἄφθαρτον οὐ προσέλαβε, τῆς δὲ γεννήσεως τὸ παθητὸν εἰληφὼς τὸ ἁμαρτητικὸν οὐ προσέλαβε, τὸν πρῶτον τοῖς κατ᾿ ἄμφω μέρεσιν ᾿Αδὰμ φέρων ἀμείωτον. Οὐκοῦν εἴη ἂν ἐπὶ Χριστοῦ γένεσις μὲν οὐκ ἐκ τοῦ μὴ ὄντος εἰς τὸ εἶναι πρόοδος, ἀλλ᾿ ὁδὸς ἀπὸ τοῦ *ἐν μορφῇ θεοῦ* ὑπάρχειν εἰς τὸ ἀναλαβεῖν τὴν τοῦ *δούλου μορφήν*.[27] ῾Η δὲ *γέννησις* αὐτοῦ διπλῆ γέγονε, καθ᾿ ἡμᾶς καὶ ὑπὲρ ἡμᾶς. Τὸ μὲν γὰρ *ἐκ γυναικός*[28] γεννηθῆναι καθ᾿ ἡμᾶς, τὸ δὲ μὴ *ἐκ θελήματος σαρκὸς* ἢ *ἀνδρός*[29] *ἀλλ᾿ ἐκ πνεύματος ἁγίου*[30] ὑπὲρ ἡμᾶς· ὅπερ καὶ τὴν μέλλουσαν προανεφώνει γέννησιν, ἣν ἡμῖν ἔμελλεν ἐκ πνεύματος χαρίσασθαι.[xi]

Codex Sabaiticus 232, Jerusalem

2

| **1r** (ΩΡΙΓΕΝΟΥΣ) *Τοῦ δὲ ᾿Ιησοῦ Χριστοῦ ἡ γέννησις οὕτως ἦν*.[31] ᾿Επηγγείλατο καὶ τὸν τρόπον ἡμῖν ἐκθέσθαι καθ᾿ ὃν γεγέννηται, καὶ φησί· *τοῦ δὲ ᾿Ιησοῦ Χριστοῦ ἡ γέννησις οὕτως ἦν*· ἀντὶ τοῦ οὐχ ὁμοίως ἐτέχθη τοῖς λοιποῖς, ἀλλ᾿ ἑτέρως.

23 Cod. φῑσ̄.
24 Cf. Gen. 2:10-14.
25 Matt. 1:18.
26 Matt. 1:1.
27 Phil. 2:6-7.
28 Gal. 4:4.
29 Cf. John, 1:13.
30 Matt. 1:18; 1:20.
31 Matt. 1:18.

Γενεαλογεῖται μὲν *Ἰωσὴφ* κατὰ τὴν γενεαλογίαν τῶν γραφῶν ἄνδρας γενεαλογουσῶν καὶ οὐ γυναῖκας, πληροῖ δὲ ἐν πολλοῖς ὁ ἀνὴρ τῆς γυναικὸς τὸ λεῖπον, ὡς Ἰακὼβ τῆς Ῥαχὴλ ἐν προσκυνήσει τοῦ Ἰωσὴφ κατὰ τὰ ὀνείρατα.[xii]

An attentive reader might pose the question: since Joseph is not the father of the Lord and Saviour, how does the sequence of genealogy descending to Joseph pertain to the Lord? Our first response to this is that it is not a custom of Scripture to trace out the genealogies of women.[xiii]

Ἄλλο γένεσις, καὶ ἄλλο γέννησις.[xiv] καὶ ἀμφότερα ληπτὰ ἐν ὁσιότητι εἰς Χριστὸν Ἰησοῦν.

Τοῦ δὲ Ἰησοῦ ἡ γέννησις οὕτως ἦν........ Ὧδε μὲν γεννήσεως μέμνηται ὁ εὐαγγελιστής, κατ᾽ ἀρχὰς δὲ τοῦ Εὐαγγελίου, *τῆς γενέσεως*. Ἐνταῦθα μὲν γὰρ λέγει. *Τοῦ δὲ Ἰησοῦ Χριστοῦ ἡ γέννησις οὕτως ἦν*, [Matt. 1:18] ἐκεῖ δὲ, *Βίβλος γενέσεως Ἰησοῦ Χριστοῦ*. [Matt. 1:1] Τίς οὖν ἡ διαφορὰ τῆς γεννήσεως καὶ τῆς γενέσεως; καὶ ὡς ἀμφότερα ἐπὶ Χριστοῦ λαμβάνεται; Ὥσπερ ὁ λόγος οὗτος ὁ προφορικὸς κατὰ τὴν οἰκείαν φύσιν ἀναφὴς ἐστι καὶ ἀόρατος. ὅταν δὲ ἐν βιβλίῳ γραφῇ, καὶ οἱονεὶ σωματωθῇ, τότε καὶ ὁρᾶται καὶ ψηλαφᾶται. οὕτως καὶ ὁ ἄσαρκος τοῦ Θεοῦ Λόγος καὶ ἀσώματος, οὔτε ὁρώμενος, οὔτε γραφόμενος κατὰ τὴν θεότητα, ἐπειδὴ ἐσαρκώθη, καὶ ὁρᾶται καὶ γράφεται. Διὰ τοῦτο, ὡς σαρκωθέντος, καὶ βίβλος ἐστὶ τῆς αὐτοῦ γενέσεως. Ἀλλ᾽ οὐκ ἐξήτηται ἐνθάδε τὸ διὰ τί εἶπε *βίβλος*, καὶ οὐκ εἶπεν ὅρασις, ἢ λόγος. ἀλλὰ τὸ τί ἐστι γέννησις καὶ τί γένεσις; Διαφέρει γένεσις καὶ γέννησις. Γένεσις μὲν γάρ ἐστι παρὰ Θεοῦ πρώτη πλάσις. γέννησις δὲ ἡ ἐκ καταδίκης τοῦ θανάτου διὰ τὴν παράβασιν ἐξ ἀλλήλων διαδοχή. Καὶ ἔτι, ἡ μὲν γένεσις τὸ ἄφθαρτον ἔχει καὶ ἀναμάρτητον, ἡ δὲ γέννησις τὸ παθητὸν καὶ ἁμαρτητικόν. Ὁ οὖν Κύριος, τῆς μὲν γενέσεως τὸ ἀναμάρτητον φυσικῶς λαβών, τὸ ἄφθαρτον οὐ προσέλαβε. τῆς δὲ γεννήσεως τὸ παθητὸν εἰληφώς, τὸ ἁμαρτητικὸν οὐ προσέλαβε, τὸν πρῶτον τοῖς κατ᾽ ἄμφω μέρεσιν Ἀδὰμ φέρων ἀμείωτον. Οὐκοῦν εἴη ἂν ἐπὶ Χριστοῦ γένεσις μὲν οὐκ ἐκ τοῦ μὴ ὄντος εἰς τὸ εἶναι πρόοδος, ἀλλ᾽ ὁδὸς ἀπὸ τοῦ ἐν μορφῇ Θεοῦ ὑπάρχειν εἰς τὸ ἀναλαβεῖν τὴν τοῦ δούλου μορφήν. ἡ δὲ γέννησις αὐτοῦ διπλῆ γέγονε, καθ᾽ ἡμᾶς καὶ ὑπὲρ ἡμᾶς. Τὸ μὲν γὰρ ἐκ γυναικὸς γεννηθῆναι καθ᾽ ἡμᾶς. τὸ δὲ μὴ ἐκ θελήματος σαρκὸς ἢ ἀνδρὸς ἀλλ᾽ ἐκ Πνεύματος ἁγίου, ὑπὲρ ἡμᾶς. Ὅπερ καὶ τὴν μέλλουσαν προανεφώνει γέννησιν, ἣν ἡμῖν ἔμελλεν ἐκ Πνεύματος χαρίσεσθαι.[xv]

Ἄλλο γένεσις, καὶ ἄλλο γέννησις. καὶ ἀμφότερα ληπτὰ ἐν ὁσιότητι εἰς Χριστὸν Ἰησοῦν.[xvi] Καὶ ἀμφότερα, τήν τε γένεσιν ἅμα καὶ τὴν γέννησιν λέγειν ἐπὶ Χριστοῦ ὁσίως ἅμα καὶ εὐσεβῶς οὐ λυμαίνεται τῷ λόγῳ τῆς ἀληθείας, κἂν πολὺ ἀλλήλοις διαφέρωσιν. ἐπειδὰν εἴ τι *γέννησις*, καὶ γένεσίς ἐστιν, οὐ μὴν εἴ τι γένεσις καὶ *γέννησις*. Καὶ ἔοικε καθολικώτεον εἶναι τὸ τῆς γενέσεως ὄνομα, διὸ καὶ ἐπὶ τῆς γεννήσεως λέγεται ἀδιαβλήτως.[xvii]

Μνηστευθείσης γὰρ τῆς μητρὸς αὐτοῦ.[32] Διὰ τρεῖς αἰτίας μετὰ τὴν μνηστείαν συνέλαβεν· ἵνα δόξῃ ἐξ αὐτοῦ κεκυηκέναι καὶ μὴ ἀποθάνῃ καὶ ἵνα ἐξ αὐτοῦ γενεαλογηθῇ[xviii] καὶ ἵνα σχῇ κηδεμόνα τῆς ἀπὸ Ἡρώδου ἐπιβουλῆς, συναντιλαμβανόμενον αὐτῆς.

---

32 Matt. 1:18.

> Τίνος ἕνεκεν μετὰ τὴν μνηστείαν συνέλαβεν; τὴν παρθένον οἶμαι τρισὶ ταύταις αἰτίαις περιέχεσθαι, τῷ τε δοκεῖν πᾶσιν ἐκ τοῦ Ἰωσὴφ γενέσθαι τὴν κύησιν καὶ διὰ τοῦτο πεφευγέναι τὸν κίνδυνον καὶ τῷ ἐξ αὐτοῦ τούτου γενεαλογηθῆναι τὸν Χριστὸν καὶ ἔτι τῷ κηδεμόνα ἔχειν αὐτὸν καὶ διάκονον ἐν ταῖς περιστάσεσιν, ὅτε ὑπὸ τοῦ Ἡρώδου ἐδιώκοντο.[xix]

2a

| **1v** (ΑΝΕΠ)[xx] Μετὰ τὴν μνηστείαν συλλαμβάνει ἵνα δόξῃ ἐξ αὐτοῦ κεκυηκέναι καὶ σχῇ κηδεμόνα ἐν ταῖς ἐπιβουλαῖς καὶ ἵνα μὴ ἐν τῷ οἴκῳ τῶν γονέων τοῦτο παθοῦσα κινδυνεύσῃ. Ἄλλως τε δέ· οὐκ ἐπὶ ἀμνηστεύτου[xxi] ἐγένετο τῆς παρθένου[xxii] ἡ σύλληψις διὰ τὸ συνεσκιασμένως[xxiii] γενέσθαι τὴν τοῦ Χριστοῦ γέννησιν, ἵνα λάθῃ τὸν ἄρχοντα τοῦ κόσμου τούτου, γεννωμένου τοῦ καταλύσαντος αὐτόν.[xxiv]

> Τί δήποτε κρίνας ὁ θεὸς ἐκ παρθένου γεννῆσαι τὸν σωτῆρα οὐκ ἐπελέξατο παρθένον ἀμνήστευτον;[xxv]

> καὶ ἔλαθε τὸν ἄρχοντα τοῦ αἰῶνος τούτου ἡ παρθενία Μαρίας… . Ἐβούλετο δὲ ὁ σωτὴρ καθ' ὅλην τὴν οἰκονομίαν λανθάνειν τὸν διάβολον.[xxvi]

> Why is he conceived not from a simple virgin but from one betrothed? First, so that the origin of Mary would be shown through the genealogy of Joseph; second, to prevent her from being stoned by the Jews as an adulteress; third, so that when she fled to Egypt, she might have solace. The martyr Ignatius[xxvii] added even a fourth reason why he was conceived from a betrothed woman, saying that it was in order that his birth would be concealed from the devil, so long as he thought that the baby was not of a virgin but of a wife.[xxviii]

Εὑρέθη ἐν γαστρὶ ἔχουσα.[33] Τίνι[xxix] δὲ ἄρα εὑρέθη, ἀλλ' ἢ τῷ Ἰωσὴφ μόνῳ; Πῶς δὲ καὶ τίνα τρόπον εὕρηται τῷ Ἰωσὴφ ὁ λόγος διδάσκει λέγων *ἐκ Πνεύματος Ἁγίου* γνωστὸν γέγονεν. Ὡς γὰρ τῇ *Ἐλισάβετ ἐκ Πνεύματος Ἁγίου*[34] γνωστὸν γέγονεν, οὕτω καὶ τῷ Ἰωσήφ· *δίκαιος* γὰρ ἦν. *Δίκαιος* δὲ τυγχάνων οὐ θαυμαστὸν εἰ καὶ Πνεύματος Ἁγίου ἠξίωτο πρὸς τὸ συνεῖναι μὲν τὴν τῆς μελλούσης γαμετῆς κύησιν, ἐπισχεῖν δὲ τὴν κατὰ ἄνδρα κοινωνίαν. Αὐτίκα συνεὶς καὶ καταπλαγείς, *ἐβουλήθη λάθρα ἀπολῦσαι αὐτήν*, μείζονα ἢ κατὰ τὴν σὺν αὐτῷ διατριβὴν τὰ πεπραγμένα εἶναι λογισάμενος. Καὶ τοῦτο ἄρα ἦν τὸ αἴτιον. Διὸ *δίκαιος ὢν* οὐκ ἔκρινε μὲν εἶναι δίκαιον *δειγματίσαι αὐτήν, ἠβουλήθη δὲ λάθρᾳ ἀπολῦσαι αὐτήν.*[35]

33 Matt. 1:18.
34 Luke 1:41.
35 Matt. 1:19.

Καὶ ἵνα (καθὼς Ἰγνάτιος ὁ Ἐφέσιος γράφει) ἡ παρθενία τῆς Μαρίας λάθῃ τὸν ἄρχοντα τοῦ κόσμου τούτου, γεννωμένου τοῦ καταλύσαντος αὐτόν. ἐπέστη γὰρ ἂν τῇ τῆς γενέσεως καινότητι καὶ ἀντεστρατεύετο.[xxx]

3

1v (ΩΡΙΓΕΝΟΥΣ) *Ἐκ Πνεύματος Ἁγίου.*[36] Τὸ λεγόμενον, πνευματικὴ *γέννησις*, τὸ δὲ *ἐκ* τὸν ‹ἁγια›σμὸν δηλώσει καὶ τὴν δύναμιν, ναὶ μὴν καὶ τὸ ὁμοούσιον.

Τὸ λεγόμενον πνευματικὴ *γέννησις*, τὸ δὲ *ἐκ* τὸν ἁγιασμὸν δηλοῖ καὶ τὴν δύναμιν, ναὶ μὴν καὶ τὸ ὁμοούσιον.[xxxi]

Ἐπειδὴ *ἐκ πνεύματος ἁγίου* ἐλέγετο, ἀνάγκη καὶ πνευματικὴν εἶναι τὴν γέννησιν. τοῦτο δὲ τὸν ἁγιασμὸν δηλοῖ καὶ καὶ τὸ ὁμοούσιον καὶ τὸ μίαν εἶναι τὴν δύναμιν.[xxxii]

3a

2r (ΑΝΕΠ)[xxxiii] *Ἰωσὴφ δὲ ὁ ἀνὴρ αὐτῆς δίκαιος ὤν.*[37] *Ἀνὴρ* διὰ τὴν μνηστείαν *δίκαιος*. Ἐπεὶ παρὰ τὸν Μωσέως νόμον δοκῶν ποιεῖν εἰ δὴ κρύπτει τὰ ἀπόρρητα, *ἐβουλήθη λάθρα ἀπολῦσαι* τὴν παρθένον. Διὸ οὐκ ἤθελεν *αὐτὴν* παραδειγματίσαι, ὡς ἐννοήσας ὅτι *ἐκ Πνεύματος Ἁγίου*[38] συνείληφεν· ἤτοι ἐπεὶ οὐκ ἔκρινεν ἑαυτὸν ἄξιον εἶναι τοῦ συνοικεῖν αὐτῇ. Γνοὺς καὶ ἐκ Πνεύματος Ἁγίου τὴν σύλληψιν *ἐβουλήθη λάθρα* | **2v** *ἀπολῦσαι αὐτήν*, μὴ θέλων αὐτὴν καταισχῦναι ἢ κινδυνεῦσαι. Τοῦτο γάρ ἐστιν τὸ *παραδειγματίσαι*. Δειγματίσαι μὲν γάρ ἐστιν τὸ ἁπλῶς ἀπολῦσαι· *παραδειγματίσαι* δὲ τὸ ἐπὶ κακῷ φανερῶσαι καὶ παραδοῦναι εἰς θάνατον ὡς μοιχαλίδα.

Ὠριγένης δὲ καὶ Εὐσέβιος ὁ Καισαρείας ἀντὶ τοῦ μὴ *θέλων αὐτὴν παραδειγματίσαι δειγματίσαι* φασίν, οὕτως ἐκτιθέμενοι τὸ ῥητὸν *Ἰωσὴφ δὲ ὁ ἀνὴρ αὐτῆς δίκαιος ὢν μὴ θέλων δειγματίσαι αὐτὴν* καὶ οὕτως ἐξηγούμενοι. πρὸ γὰρ τοῦ *συνελθεῖν αὐτοὺς εὑρέθη ἐν γαστρὶ ἔχουσα*. [τίνι δὲ *εὑρέθη ἀλλ'* ἢ τῷ Ἰωσὴφ μόνῳ; πῶς δὲ καὶ τίνα τρόπον εὕρηται τῷ Ἰωσήφ, ὁ λόγος διδάσκων φασίν. *ἐκ πνεύματος ἁγίου* γνωστὸν γέγονεν. ὡς γὰρ τῇ Ἐλισάβετ γνωστὸν γέγονεν *ἐκ πνεύματος ἁγίου*, οὕτω καὶ τῷ Ἰωσήφ. *δίκαιος* γὰρ ἦν, *δίκαιος* δὲ τυγχάνων οὐ θαυμαστὸν εἰ καὶ *πνεύματος ἁγίου* ἠξίωτο πρὸς τὸ συνεῖναι μὲν τὴν τῆς μελλούσης γαμετῆς κύησιν, ἐπισχεῖν δὲ τὴν κατὰ ἄνδρα κοινωνίαν. αὐτίκα συνεὶς καὶ καταπλαγεὶς *ἐβουλήθη λάθρα ἀπολῦσαι αὐτήν*, μείζονα ἢ κατὰ τὴν σὺν αὐτῷ διατριβὴν τὰ πεπραγμένα εἶναι λογισάμενος. καὶ τοῦτο ἄρα ἦν τὸ αἴτιον· διὸ *δίκαιος ὢν* οὐκ ἔκρινε ‹μὲ›ν εἶναι δίκαιον *δειγματίσαι* ‹αὐτήν, *ἠβουλήθη* δὲ λάθρα *ἀπολῦσαι*› *αὐτήν*. καὶ μὴν εἰ μὴ *ἐξ ἁγίου πνεύματος* ἐπεπίστευτο αὐτὴν συνειληφέναι, ἀκριβῶς εἰδὼς

36 Matt. 1:18.
37 Matt. 1:19.
38 Matt. 1:18-20.

ὅτι μηδὲ ἐξ αὐτοῦ τὸ κατὰ γαστρὸς ἔφερεν, τί δῆτα *δίκαιος ὢν* ἀνὴρ οὐχὶ εἰς πάντας ἐξαγαγὼν τὴν διαφθαρεῖσαν πρὸ γάμου τὴν ὥραν τοῖς ‹ἱκανοῖς› τοιαῦτα κρίνειν παρεδίδου; πῶς δὲ *δίκαιος ὁ μὴ θέλων* τὴν τοιαῦτα δράσασαν *δειγματίσαι*, ἀλλ᾽ ἐπισκιάζειν καὶ ἐπικρύπτειν βουλόμενος; ἀλλ᾽ οὐκ εἰκὸς τὸν εὐαγγελιστὴν δίκαιον αὐτὸν ἐπὶ τούτοις φάναι, ἀλλὰ γὰρ συναισθόμενον δι᾽ *ἁγίου πνεύματος* θειοτέραν τὴν τῆς παρθένου γεγονέναι κύησιν καὶ κρείττονα τῆς σὺν αὐτῷ διατριβῆς ἡγησάμενον εἶναι τὴν οἰκονομίαν εἰκότως αὐτόν φησιν διανενοῆσθαι *λάθρα ἀπολῦσαι αὐτὴν* μὴ δειγματισθεῖσαν ὑπ᾽ αὐτοῦ μηδὲ φανερὰν τοῖς πολλοῖς γενομένην. εὖ γοῦν μοι καὶ τὸ *μὴ θέλων αὐτὴν δειγματίσαι* ‹εἰρῆσθαι δοκεῖ ὑπὸ τοῦ εὐαγγελιστοῦ. οὐ γὰρ ἔφησεν *μὴ θέλων αὐτὴν παραδειγματίσαι*, ἀλλὰ *μὴ θέλων δειγματίσαι*›, πολλῆς οὔσης ἐν τούτοις τῆς διαφορᾶς. ὡς γὰρ οὐ ταὐτὸν σημαίνει ‹τὸ› γράψαι καὶ παραγράψαι καὶ τὸ λογίσασθαι καὶ παραλογίσασθαι ‹καὶ τὸ ψηφίσαι καὶ παραψηφίσαι›, οὕτως οὐδὲ τὸ *δειγματίσαι* καὶ *παραδειγματίσαι*. τὸ μὲν γὰρ *παραδειγματίσαι* τὴν ἐπὶ κακῶς πράξαντι εἰς πάντας φανέρωσίν τε καὶ διαβολὴν ὑποβάλλει νοεῖν, τὸ δὲ *δειγματίσαι* τὸ φανερὸν ἁπλῶς ποιῆσαι.] *δίκαιος* τοίνυν ὑπάρχων οὐκ *ἐβουλήθη* τοῖς πᾶσιν φανερὰν ποιῆσαι. δειγματισμὸς γὰρ ἡ ἄκαιρος τῆς οἰκονομίας παρρησία, γέλωτα μᾶλλον καὶ ἀπιστίαν παρέχουσα.[xxxiv]

(ΕΥΣΕΒΙΟΥ, ΩΡΙΓΕΝΟΥΣ)[xxxv] Εὖ γοῦν μοι καὶ τὸ μὴ θέλειν αὐτὴν δειγματίσαι εἰρῆσθαι δοκεῖ ὑπὸ τοῦ Εὐαγγελιστοῦ. οὐ γὰρ ἔφησεν μὴ θέλειν αὐτὴν δειγματίσαι, ἀλλὰ *μὴ παραδειγματίσαι θέλων*, πολλῆς οὔσης ἐν τούτοις διαφορᾶς. ὡς γὰρ οὐ ταυτὸν σημαίνει τὸ γράψαι καὶ τὸ παραγράψαι, καὶ τὸ λογίσασθαι καὶ τὸ παραλογίσασθαι, καὶ ψηφίσαι καὶ παραψηφίσαι, οὕτως οὔτε τὸ δειγματίσαι καὶ παραδειγματίσαι. τὸ μὲν γὰρ παραδειγματίσαι τὴν ἐπὶ κακῷ πράξαντι πάντας φανέρωσίν τε καὶ διαβολὴν ὑποβάλλει νοεῖν. ὁ τοίνυν *Ἰωσὴφ δίκαιος ὤν, καὶ μὴ θέλων αὐτὴν παραδειγματίσαι*, τουτέστιν εἰς φανερὸν τοῖς πᾶσιν ἀγαγεῖν, *ἐβουλήθη λάθρα ἀπολῦσαι αὐτήν*.[xxxvi]

4

4r (ΩΡΙΓΕΝΟΥΣ) *Ἵνα πληρωθῇ τὸ ῥηθέν.*[39] Προφητεία ἐστὶν πρόρρησις μελλόντων, ὧν περατουμένων τέλος ἔχει τὸ ῥηθέν. Οὐκ ἐπειδὴ δὲ ἐρρέθη ἐγένετο (τὸ γὰρ τοιοῦτον οὐ προφητεία) ἀλλ᾽ ἐπειδὴ ἔμελλε γίνεσθαι ἐρρέθη· καὶ τοῦτο ἡ προφητεία.

Προφητεία ἐστὶν πρόρρησις μελλόντων, ὧν περατουμένων τέλος ἔχει τὸ ῥηθέν. οὐκ ἐπειδὴ δὲ ἐρρέθη ἐγένετο. τὸ γὰρ τοιοῦτον οὐ προφητεία, ἀλλ᾽ ἐπειδὴ ἔμελλε γίνεσθαι ἐρρέθη. καὶ τοῦτο ἡ προφητεία.[xxxvii]

4a

4r (ΑΝΕΠ) *Ἰδοὺ ἡ παρθένος ἐν γαστρί.*[40] Παρθένον εἰπὼν τὴν Μαρίαν ὁ ἄγγελος ἀτάραχον ἐποίησε τὸν Ἰωσὴφ περὶ τῆς σωφροσύνης αὐτῆς.[xxxviii] Ἐπειδὴ δὲ Ἰουδαῖοι

39 Matt. 1:22.
40 Matt. 1:23.

φασὶν ὅτι ὁ χρησμὸς οὗτος ἐδόθη τῷ Ἄχαζ περὶ Ἐζεκίου τοῦ υἱοῦ αὐτοῦ ἐλέγχεται τὸ ψεῦδος αὐτῶν ἐκ τῆς τῶν Βασιλειῶν ἱστορίας. Μετὰ γὰρ τὸ μεῖναι Ἄχαζ ἐν τῇ βασιλείᾳ πεντεκαιδεκαετῆ χρόνον, τελευτήσαντος αὐτοῦ ἐβασίλευσεν Ἐζεκίας ὁ υἱὸς αὐτοῦ ὢν ἐτῶν κδ', ὡς εἶναι αὐτὸν πρὸ τοῦ χρησμοῦ τεχθέντα πρὸ θ' ἐτῶν εἰ ‹δ›ῶμεν[41] ἐν πρώτῳ ἔτει τοῦ πατρὸς αὐτοῦ Ἄχαζ λελέχθαι τὸν χρησμόν, ὅπερ οὐκ ἴσμεν.[xxxix] Λέγουσι δὲ ὅτι οὐ κεῖται ἐν Ἠσαΐᾳ *ἰδοὺ ἡ παρθένος*,[42] ἀλλ' ἡ νεᾶνις.[xl] Λέγομεν οὖν ὅτι ἴσον δύναται τὸ εἰπεῖν *ἰδοὺ ἡ παρθένος* καὶ τὸ ἰδοὺ ἡ νεᾶνις. Εἰ δὲ τὸ νεᾶνις ἐπὶ τῆς καθ' ἡλικίαν ἀκμαζούσης εἴρηται, ὡς Ἰουδαῖοι φασί, οὐχὶ δὲ ἐπὶ τῆς ἀπειρογάμου,[xli] ποῖον τοῦτο σημεῖον; Τί γάρ ἐστιν θαυμαστὸν μίαν τῶν πολλῶν γυναῖκα ἀνδρὶ συνοικοῦσαν μητέρα γενέσθαι παιδίου; Τίνι δὲ ἁρμόζει ‹τὸ› γεννήσει *Ἐμμανουήλ*; Γυναικὶ συνουσιασθείσῃ καὶ διὰ | **4v** πάθους συλλαβούσῃ ἢ καθαρᾷ καὶ ἁγνῇ παρθένῳ;

Ἵνα δὲ μὴ δοκῶμεν ἀπὸ λέξεως ἑβραϊκῆς τοῖς μὴ καταλαμβάνουσι, πότερον συγκαταθετέον αὐτῇ ἢ μή, φέρειν παραμυθίαν περὶ τοῦ προφήτην εἰρηκέναι ἐκ παρθένου τεχθήσεσθαι τοῦτον, ἐφ' οὗ τῇ γενέσει λέλεκται τὸ *μεθ' ἡμῶν ὁ θεός*,[43] φέρε ἀπ' αὐτῆς τῆς λέξεως παραμυθησώμεθα τὸ λεγόμενον. Ὁ μὲν κύριος ἀναγέγραπται εἰρηκέναι τῷ Ἄχαζ. *Αἴτησαι σεαυτῷ σημεῖον παρὰ κυρίου τοῦ θεοῦ σου εἰς βάθος ἢ εἰς ὕψος*,[44] ἑξῆς δὲ τὸ διδόμενον σημεῖον τὸ *Ἰδοὺ ἡ παρθένος ἐν γαστρὶ ἕξει καὶ τέξεται υἱόν*.[45] Ποῖον οὖν σημεῖον τὸ νεάνιδα μὴ παρθένον τεκεῖν; Καὶ τίνι μᾶλλον ἁρμόζει γεννῆσαι *Ἐμμανουήλ*, τουτέστι *μεθ' ἡμῶν ὁ θεός*, ἆρα γυναικὶ συνουσιασθείσῃ καὶ διὰ πάθους γυναικείου συλλαβούσῃ ἢ ἔτι καθαρᾷ καὶ ἁγνῇ καὶ παρθένῳ; Ταύτῃ γὰρ πρέπει γεννᾶν γέννημα, ἐφ' ᾧ τεχθέντι λέγεται τὸ *μεθ' ἡμῶν ὁ θεός*.

Ἐὰν δὲ καὶ οὕτως εὑρεσιλογῇ λέγων ὅτι τῷ Ἄχαζ εἴρηται *Αἴτησαι σεαυτῷ σημεῖον παρὰ κυρίου τοῦ θεοῦ σου*,[46] ἀπαντήσομεν. Κατὰ τοὺς χρόνους τοῦ Ἄχαζ τίς ἐγεννήθη, ἐφ' οὗ τῇ γενέσει λέγεται τὸ *Ἐμμανουήλ, ὅ ἐστι μεθ' ἡμῶν ὁ θεός*;[47] Εἰ γὰρ οὐδεὶς εὑρεθήσεται, δηλονότι τὸ τῷ Ἄχαζ εἰρημένον τῷ οἴκῳ εἴρηται Δαυὶδ διὰ τὸ *ἐκ σπέρματος Δαυὶδ* ἀναγεγράφθαι τὸν σωτῆρα γεγονέναι τὸ *κατὰ σάρκα*.[48] Ἀλλὰ καὶ τὸ σημεῖον τοῦτο εἰς βάθος ἢ εἰς ὕψος λέγεται εἶναι, ἐπεὶ *Ὁ καταβὰς αὐτός ἐστι καὶ ὁ ἀναβὰς ὑπεράνω πάντων τῶν οὐρανῶν, ἵνα πληρώσῃ τὰ πάντα*.[49] Ταῦτα δὲ λέγω ὡς πρὸς τὸν Ἰουδαῖον συγκατατιθέμενον τῇ προφητείᾳ.[xlii]

Οὐκ ἔστι δὲ διαφωνία τὸ τὸν μὲν εἰπεῖν *καὶ καλέσεις τὸ ὄνομα αὐτοῦ Ἰησοῦν*,[50] τὸν δὲ προφήτην εἰπεῖν *καὶ καλέσουσι τὸ ὄνομα αὐτοῦ Ἐμμανουήλ*.[51] Οὐδὲ γὰρ ὁ Ἰωσὴφ

41 Cod. θῶμεν.
42 Is. 7:14.
43 Matt. 1:23.
44 Is. 7:11.
45 Is. 7:14.
46 Is. 7:11.
47 Matt. 1:23.
48 Rom. 1:3.
49 Eph. 4:10.
50 Matt. 1:21.
51 Matt. 1:23; cf. Is. 7:14.

τοῦτο αὐτὸν ὠνόμασεν, ἀλλ' ἐκ τῆς τῶν πραγμάτων ἐκβάσεως οἱ ὄχλοι οὕτως αὐτὸν ἐκάλουν, τουτέστιν ὄψονται Θεὸν μετὰ ἀνθρώπων.[xliii]

4b

Καὶ παρέλαβε τὴν γυναῖκα αὐτοῦ.[52] (ΑΝΕΠ) Ἐξ ὧν ὁ Ἰωσὴφ φαίνεται παραλαβὼν τὴν Μαρίαν καὶ μετὰ τὸν τόκον θεραπεύων καὶ μὴ ζηλοτυπῶν. Δῆλός ἐστι πληροφορηθεὶς ὅτι οὐκ ἐξ ἀνθρώπου ἐκύησεν, ἀλλ' *ἐκ Πνεύματος Ἁγίου.* Κατέσχεν οὖν αὐτὴν οὐχ ὡς γυναῖκα, ἀλλὰ μόνον συνῴκει, ὡς ὁ εὐαγγελιστής φησι, ὅτι *οὐκ ἐγίνωσκεν αὐτὴν ἕως οὗ ἔτεκε.*[53]
Τὸ δὲ ἕως οὐκ ἔστιν ἐνταῦθα χρονικόν. Οὐ γὰρ πρὸς τὸν παρεληλυθότα χρόνον τάσσεται, ἀλλ' ἐπὶ ἀπεράντου ἐτέθη.[xliv]

> Τὸ ἕως ἐν τῇ γραφῇ πολλάκις ἐπὶ διηνεκοῦς εὑρίσκεται,[xlv] ὡς τὸ *ἕως ἂν θῶ τοὺς ἐχθρούς σου, ὑποπόδιον τῶν ποδῶν σου*[54] καὶ τὸ *ἕως ἂν καταγηράσητε*[55] *ἐγώ εἰμι* καὶ τὸ *οὐκ ἀνέστρεψεν ἡ περιστερὰ πρὸς τὸν Νῶε, ἕως τοῦ ξηρανθῆναι τὸ ὕδωρ*·[56][xlvi] ἅπερ εἰσὶ διηνεκῶς εἰρημένα. νοητέον δὲ καὶ οὕτως· οὐκ ἐγίνωσκεν αὐτήν, πόθεν συνέλαβεν, ἕως οὗ ἔτεκε, καὶ εἶδεν τὰ γενόμενα σημεῖα.[xlvii]

> Τὸ δὲ ἕως, ἐνταῦθα δηλοῖ τὸν κατεπείγοντα περὶ τοῦ δηλουμένου χρόνον, οὐ περιοριζόμενον, ὥστε γενέσθαι μετὰ τὸ ἕως τὸ ἐν αὐτῷ τῷ δηλουμένῳ, ὡς τό, *Καὶ ἰδοὺ ἐγὼ μεθ' ὑμῶν εἰμι ἕως τῆς συντελείας τοῦ αἰῶνος.*[xlviii]

Οὕτως δὲ δεῖ αὐτὸ ἀναγνῶναι· *καὶ οὐκ ἐγίνωσκεν αὐτὴν ἕως οὗ ἔτεκε τὸν υἱὸν αὐτῆς.*[57] Ἐνταῦθα ὑποστικτέον.[xlix] Εἶτα ἀορίστως δεῖ ἐπαγαγεῖν, *τὸν πρωτότοκον*, οὐ πρὸς ἀντιδιαστολὴν δευτέρου τόκου. Πρωτότοκος δὲ καλεῖται ἐπειδὴ πρῶτος καὶ μόνος ἐτέχθη ἐκ Πατρὸς καὶ πρῶτος καὶ μόνος ἐκ παρθένου *τὸ κατὰ σάρκα.*[58]

> Based upon this passage, certain people most perversely surmise that Mary had also other sons. They claim that there would be no talk of a firstborn unless there are brothers, although it is the custom of the holy scriptures to call *firstborn* not one who is followed by brothers, but the first to be born.[l]

> Some conjecture that the brothers of the Lord are sons of Joseph by another wife. They follow apocryphal nonsense, fabricating some little woman called Escha.

52 Matt. 1:24.
53 Matt. 1:25.
54 Psalm 109:1.
55 Is. 46:4.
56 Gen. 8:7.
57 Matt. 1:25.
58 Cf. John, 7:42; Rom. 1:3; 2 Tim. 2:8.

But as the book that we have written against Helvidius shows, we understand the brothers of the Lord to be not sons of Joseph but first cousins of the Saviour.[li]

Ἔστι γὰρ ὁ *αὐτός*,[59] ὡς μὲν φύσει Θεὸς *πρωτότοκος*[60] *πρὸ τῶν αἰώνων*,[61] | **5r** ὡς δὲ *ἀπαρχὴ*[62] δευτέρα τοῦ γένους ἡμῶν πρῶτος ἐκ *παρθένου*[63] σαρκωθείς.

Καὶ οὐκέτι ἐγίνωσκεν αὐτήν.[64] Ὅτι[65] οὐ συνῆλθεν αὐτῇ πρὸς γάμου κοινωνίαν. Πῶς γὰρ ἂν τούτου μετὰ θείαν σύλληψιν[lii] κατ[...]ησεν. Οὐ λέγω *δίκαιος ὢν*, ἀλλὰ καὶ ε[...]δρα[66] τίς ὑπῆρχεν ἄθεσμος[67] καὶ παράνομος. Φρίκῃ καὶ ἀγωνίᾳ πολλῇ συνεχόμενος εἰς τὸ ἐννοῆσαι μόνον μή τι γε δὴ καὶ ἐργάσασθαι μαρτυρεῖ γράψας σαφῶς ὁ Λουκᾶς σὺν Μαριὰμ *τῇ μεμνηστευμένῃ αὐτῷ γυναικὶ οὔσῃ ἐγκύῳ*.[68] Καὶ πῶς εἰ ἔγκυος ἐμεμνήστευτο διὰ τὸ μὴ ἐξ αὐτοῦ τὴν κύησιν, ἀλλ' *ἐκ Πνεύματος* ὑπάρχειν *Ἁγίου* γέγραφε δὲ πάλιν ὁ αὐτὸς εὐαγγελιστής· *καὶ αὐτὸς ἦν ὁ Ἰησοῦς ὡς ἐτῶν τριάκοντα ἀρχόμενος ὤν, ὡς ἐνομίζετο υἱὸς Ἰωσήφ*.[69] Ἀλλ' ὅμως χρεία ἦν τούτου τοῦ νομίζεσθαι. Εἰ γὰρ ἐξ ἀρχῆς ἔγνωσαν οἱ φονῶντες Ἰουδαῖοι[liii] κατὰ παντὸς αἵματος εὐσεβοῦς τὴν παρθενίαν καὶ τὴν *ἐκ Πνεύματος Ἁγίου*[70] σύλληψιν, πάντες ἂν τὴν παρθένον ἀνεῖλον καὶ μυρία εἰργάσαντο δεινά. Καὶ τούτων ἐγγὺς ἡ ἀπόδειξις, ὅτι διὰ τῶν θαυμάτων ὡς θεομάχοι μᾶλλον πρὸς μιαιφονίαν[liv] διηρεθίζοντο. *Τὸν γὰρ Λάζαρον*, ἐπείπερ ἐκ νεκρῶν ὑπὸ τοῦ Ἰησοῦ παραδόξως ἐγερθέντα εἶδον, ἀποκτεῖναι διενοοῦντο.[71] Καὶ αὐτὴν δὲ τὴν θεοτόκον παρθένον[lv] εὑρίσκομεν τῇ οἰκονομίᾳ ἐνδιατιθεμένην καὶ ταῦτα παρὰ πάντας ἀνθρώπους ἐπισταμένην ὡς οἷόν τε τὸ ἐν αὐτῇ τελεσθὲν μέγα μυστήριον | **5v** καὶ λέγουσαν πρὸς τὸν Ἰησοῦν ἔτι νεάζοντα κατὰ σάρκα· *τέκνον, τί ἐποίησας ἡμῖν οὕτως; ἰδοὺ ὁ πατήρ σου κἀγὼ ὀδυνώμενοι ἐζητοῦμεν σε*.[72] Μὴ τοίνυν ‹θαυ›μάσῃς ἄνδρα τῆς παρθένου τὸν Ἰωσὴφ ‹κηρυκ›εύων[lvi] μαθὼν τῆς οἰκονομίας τὸ βά‹θος›.

(ΑΝΕΠ, cont.) Σκοπὸς γὰρ ἦν οὐκ Ἰουδαίοις μόνον λαθεῖν τὴν παρθενίαν καὶ τὸ τοῦ τόκου παράδοξον, ἀλλὰ καὶ τὸν πατέρα τούτων διάβολον,[73][lvii] βασκαίνοντα μὲν τῇ ἡμετέρᾳ σωτηρίᾳ,[lviii] τὴν δὲ τούτων ἔκβασιν ἀγνοήσαντα. Καὶ ὅτι σπέρμα τοῦ

59 Heb. 13:8.

60 Cf. Col. 1:15; Heb. 1:6.

61 Cf. Psalm 54:20; 1 Cor. 2:7.

62 Cf. 1 Cor. 15:20&23.

63 Luke, 1:27.

64 Matt. 1:25.

65 Cod. Ὅτι δὲ.

66 *Loci desperati*, due to a smirch from melted candle (presumably, lighting at the time of transcribing the codex) obscuring some letters of the text.

67 Cf. 3 Macc. 5:12; 6:26; 2 Peter, 2:7; 3:17.

68 Luke, 2:5.

69 Luke, 3:23.

70 Matt. 1:20.

71 John, 12:10.

72 Luke, 2:48.

73 Cf. John, 8:44.

παντὸς ὑπῆρχε σωτηρία τοῦτο καὶ ὁ θεοφόρος Ἰγνάτιος[lix] Ἐφεσίοις ἐπιστέλλων ἔγραφεν οὕτως· *καὶ ἔλαθε τὸν ἄρχοντα τοῦ αἰῶνος τούτου ἡ παρθενία Μαρίας καὶ ὁ τόκος αὐτῆς. ὁμοίως καὶ ὁ θάνατος τοῦ Κυρίου. τρία μυστήρια κραυγῆς, ἅτινα ἐν ἡσυχίᾳ Θεοῦ ἐπράχθη.*[lx]

(ΑΝΕΠ, cont.)[lxi] *Τοῦ δὲ Ἰησοῦ γεννηθέντος ἐν Βηθλεὲμ τῆς Ἰουδαίας.*[74] Ἀκολούθως τῇ προφητείᾳ ὁ Ἰησοῦς *ἐν Βηθλεὲμ* ἐτέχθη. Μέμνηται δὲ ὁ εὐαγγελιστὴς καὶ τῶν *τοῦ Ἡρῴδου χρόνων*, ὅπως ἀπὸ τῆς τοῦ Δανιὴλ προφητείας ἕως τοῦ Χριστοῦ ἀριθμοῦντες τὰς *ἑβδομήκοντα* ἑβδομάδας[75] τῶν ἐτῶν εὑρήσωμεν τὴν συμπλήρωσιν τῶν ἐτῶν. Καὶ ἐπείπερ διὰ τὴν αὐτῶν ἀπιστίαν οἱ Ἰουδαῖοι οὐκ ἔγνωσαν τὸν χρόνον τῆς γεννήσεως, ἐκ τῶν μάγων αὐτοὺς καταισχύνει ὡς ἀμελεῖς.

4c

5v (ΑΝΕΠ) *Ἰδοὺ μάγοι ἀπὸ ἀνατολῶν.*[76] Τούτους λέγουσί τινες τοῦ γένους εἶναι τοῦ Βαλαάμ, οἳ καὶ εὑρόντες παρ᾽ ἑαυτοῖς ὡς εἰκὸς τὴν τοῦ Βαλα |**6r** άμ[77] χρησμῳδίαν τὴν λέγουσαν, *ἀνατελεῖ ἄστρον ἐξ Ἰακὼβ*[78] καὶ τὰ ἑξῆς σωζομένην, ἰδόντες τὸν ἀστέρα δρομαῖοι ἦλθον εἰς Ἱερουσαλήμ.

> *Μάγοι* Περσῶν σοφοί, ὧν εἷς ἦν Βαλαάμ.[lxii] καὶ τάχα ‹εἶχον› οὗτοι τὰ προφητευθέντα τῷ Βαλάκ, ὅτε ἀντὶ τοῦ ἀρᾶσθαι τὸν Ἰσραὴλ εὐλόγει λέγων *ἀνατελεῖ ἄστρον ἐξ Ἰακὼβ καὶ ἀναβήσεται ἄνθρωπος ἐξ Ἰσραὴλ* καὶ τὰ ἑξῆς. ταῦτα τοίνυν κατέχοντες καὶ προσδοκῶντες βασιλέα μέγαν γεγεννῆσθαι Ἰουδαίοις καὶ κρείττονα ἐπιδεδημηκέναι δύναμιν τῷ μηκέτι ὁμοίως δαίμονας ὑπακούειν ἢ τελετὰς τελεῖσθαι ἔγνωσαν καὶ τὰς ἐπῳδίας. ὡς κομῆται δὲ καὶ τ‹οι›αῦτα περὶ τὸν αἰθέρα καινόν τι τῷ βίῳ σημαίνουσιν, οὕτω πολὺ πλέον παράδοξος ἀστὴρ ἐφαίνετο μεγάλου βασιλέως Ἰησοῦ Χριστοῦ.[lxiii]

> Πρὸς ἕκαστον χρῆται ὁ θεὸς τοῖς συνηθέσιν αὐτοῦ, ὁδηγῶν αὐτὸν πρὸς ἀλήθειαν, καθάπερ καὶ τοὺς μάγους ἄγων ἀπὸ τῆς οἰκείας χώρας ἐπὶ τὴν προσκύνησιν Χριστοῦ δι᾽ ἀστρολογίας. οὗτοι γὰρ τὴν τοῦ Βαλαὰμ ἔχοντες πρόρρησιν καὶ ταύτῃ πιστεύσαντες ἐπέτυχον τοῦ ποθουμένου καὶ τῷ Χριστῷ *προσεκύνησαν.*[lxiv]

> They [sc. the Magi] had known that this would happen by the prediction of Balaam, whose successors they were.[lxv]

---

74 Matt. 2:1.
75 Daniel, 9:24-25.
76 Matt. 2:1.
77 I deleted the repeated, οἳ καὶ εὑρόντες παρ᾽ ἑαυτοῖς ὡς εἰκὸς τὴν τοῦ Βαλαάμ.
78 Num. 24:17.

Ὡς ὡς πρέσβεις δὲ ἦλθον πρὸς τὸν βασιλέα τοῦ Ἰσραήλ, ἵνα γένηται μεταξὺ αὐτῶν καὶ Ἰουδαίων εἰρήνη δι' αὐτοῦ. Ἀφ' οὗ δὲ εἶδον *τὸν ἀστέρα*[79] ἕως φθάσουσιν εἰς Ἱεροσόλυμα ὡς διετὴς ἀναλώθη χρόνος. Διὰ τοῦτο δὲ ἐκρύβη πρὸς καιρὸν ὁ ἀστήρ, ἵνα ἀναγκασθῶσιν ἐρωτῆσαι, καὶ γένηται πᾶσι κατάδηλον τὸ περὶ τῆς γεννήσεως τοῦ Χριστοῦ μυστήριον. Ἐκ δὲ τούτου δῆλον ὅτι οὐκ ἦν τῶν συνήθων ὁ ἀστήρ, ὅτι καὶ ἐν ἡμέρᾳ ἐφαίνετο. Συγκαταβάσει δὲ χρώμενος ὁ Θεὸς διὰ τὸ ἔθος ἔχειν Χαλδαίους τοῖς ἄστροις προσέχειν, διὰ τούτου αὐτοὺς εἵλκυσεν.[lxvi]

Εἴδομεν γὰρ αὐτοῦ τὸν ἀστέρα.[80] Ὡς κομῆται[lxvii] δὲ καὶ τοιαῦτα περὶ τὸν αἰθέρα καινόν τι τῷ βίῳ σημαίνουσιν, οὕτω πολὺ πλέον παράδοξος ὁ ἀστὴρ ἐφαίνετο τοῦ μεγάλου βασιλέως Ἰησοῦ. Οὔτε δὲ Ἡρώδῃ οὔτε ἱερεῦσιν οὔτε γραμματεῦσιν, ἀλλ' ἁπλῶς ἐν τῇ πόλει λέγουσιν οἰόμενοι φανερὸν εἶναι τὸν ἀστέρα καὶ τὸν βασιλέα τοῖς εἰδόσι τὴν προφητείαν· ὅπερ ἐστὶν ἔλεγχος Ἰουδαίοις.

4d

7r (ΘΕΟΔΩΡΟΥ ΗΡΑΚΛΕΙΑΣ)[81] Ἀλλόκοτος[lxviii] ὁ Ἡρώδης πῇ μὲν πιστεύων τοῖς προφητικοῖς, ὅτι ἔσται Χριστὸς ὁ βασιλεὺς πάντων, πῇ δὲ νομίζων δύνασθαι αὐτὸν ἀνελεῖν καὶ τὰς προφητείας ἀνατρέψαι. Μανίας δὲ τεκμήριον. Εἰ γὰρ ἐπίστευσε τοῖς λεχθεῖσιν, ὤφειλεν ἐννοεῖν ὅτι ὑπὲρ ἄνθρωπον ἦσαν τὰ λεχθέντα καὶ γεγονότα καὶ οὐχ οἷός τε ἦν ἀνατρέψαι τὰ τῷ θεῷ δόξαντα· ἢ εἰ οὐκ ἐπίστευσεν, τί ἐδειλία καὶ ἤθελεν ἐπιβουλεῦσαι τῷ βρέφει;[lxix] Οὗτος ὁ Ἡρώδης Ἰδουμαῖος ἦν τὸ γένος· ἐπειδὴ γὰρ *ἐξέλιπεν ἐξ Ἰούδα ἄρχων*[82] κατὰ τὴν τοῦ Ἰακὼβ προφητείαν καὶ λοιπὸν οἱ Ῥωμαῖοι ἦρξαν, ἔκτοτε καὶ ὁ Ἡρώδης ἦρξε τοῦ Ἰουδαίων ἔθνους.

4e

(ΑΝΕΠ) Βασιλέα δὲ ζητούντων τῶν μάγων, ὡς νομομαθεῖς Φαρισαῖοι Χριστὸν ἐπευφήμιζον. Διὸ καὶ *Ἡρώδης* ἐάσας τοὺς μάγους Ἰουδαίους ἐρωτᾷ *ποῦ ὁ Χριστὸς γεννᾶται· οἱ δὲ εἶπον αὐτῷ· ἐν Βηθλεὲμ τῆς Ἰουδαίας.*[83] Οἱ *γραμματεῖς* δὲ τὴν προφητείαν προβάλλονται καὶ *ἐν Βηθλεέμ* φησι *τῆς Ἰουδαίας*, εἰ καί τινες τῶν Ἰουδαίων εἰς Ζοροβάβελ τὴν προφητείαν[84] εἰρῆσθαί φασιν κακῶς λέγοντες. Ὁ γὰρ Ζοροβάβελ

79 Matt. 2:2.
80 Matt. 2:2.
81 In reality, however, this passage, along with the ensuing 'Unattributed' one, belongs to Origen. See Introduction.
82 Cf. Gen. 49:10.
83 Matt. 2:4-5.
84 Ref. to Micah, 5:1-3; quoted in Matt. 2:6.

οὐκ *ἐν Βηθλεὲμ ἀλλ'* ἐν Βαβυλῶνι γεννᾶται.[lxx] οὔτε | **7v** δὲ εἰς Ζοροβάβελ ἁρμόζει τὸ ἐπενεχθὲν τῇ προφητείᾳ, τὸ *καὶ αἱ ἔξοδοι αὐτοῦ ἀπ' ἀρχῆς ἐξ ἡμερῶν αἰῶνος.*[85]

4f

| **7v** (ΑΝΕΠ)[lxxi] *Τότε Ἡρώδης λάθρα καλέσας.*[86] Οἰόμενος ἀπατᾶν τοὺς μάγους ὁ *Ἡρώδης λάθρα* καλεῖ αὐτοὺς ἐπειδὴ ὑπώπτευε τοὺς Ἰουδαίους ἀποκρύπτειν τὸν Χριστόν, ὡς ἴδιον βασιλέα βουλομένους αὐτὸν διασῶσαι. Διὰ δύο δὲ ἐτῶν οἱ μάγοι ἦλθον ἀπὸ τῆς χώρας αὐτῶν, διὸ καὶ τὰ ἀπὸ διετοῦς ἀνεῖλε βρέφη κατὰ *τὸν χρόνον* ὃν *ἠκρίβωσε παρὰ* τῶν μάγων ἐντεῦθεν δῆλον, ὅτι οὐ πάραυτα[87] ἐν τῷ σπηλαίῳ *προσεκύνησαν*[88] οἱ μάγοι τὸ βρέφος ὑπὸ τοῦ ἀστέρος δηλούμενον. Μετὰ γὰρ τὸ εὐλογηθῆναι ὑπὸ Συμεὼν ἐν Ἱερουσαλὴμ, καταβάντων πάλιν ἐν τῇ Βηθλεὲμ τῶν γονέων, τοῦ βρέφους ἐν ἀγκάλαις τῆς τεκούσης φερομένου καὶ παροικούσης ἐν οἴκῳ ξενίας, εἰς ὃν οἶκον ἐλθόντες οἱ μάγοι, κἀκεῖ προσενέγκαντες αὐτῷ τὰ δῶρα, *προσεκύνησαν* ἰδόντες αὐτὸν μετὰ Μαρίας τῆς μητρὸς αὐτοῦ, ὡς φαίνεσθαι Ἰησοῦν ὄντα ἐτῶν δύο, πάραυτα[89] τῆς γεννήσεως αὐτοῦ ἀνατείλαντος τοῦ ἀστέρος, διετοῦς ὄντος χρόνου ἐξ οὗ ἐφαίνετο ὁ ἀστὴρ τοῖς μάγοις. Τινές δέ φασιν ὅτι ἐν σπαργάνοις ὄντα εἶδον Ἰησοῦν ἐν τῶ σπηλαίῳ. Τὸν γὰρ ἀστέρα πρὸ τοῦ τόκου εἶδον.[lxxii] Πρὸς δὲ πλείονα ἀσφάλειαν τοῦ λῦσαι τὴν ἑαυτοῦ δειλίαν *ἀνεῖλε* καὶ τοὺς *ἀπὸ διετοῦς ὁ Ἡρώδης*[90] κατὰ *τὸν χρόνον* ὃν *ἠκρίβωσε παρὰ* τῶν μάγων.[91] Ἰδόντες οὖν *τὸ* | **8r** *παιδίον* Ἰησοῦν, μὴ θέλοντες ἐνώπιον αὐτοῦ ριφθῆναι κενοί, προσφέρουσιν ἃ φέρουσι· χρυσὸν μέν, ὡς βασιλεῖ· λίβανον δέ, ὡς Θεῷ· σμύρναν δέ, ὡς μαθόντες ἀπὸ Βαλαὰμ περὶ αὐτοῦ, τὸ *κατακλιθεὶς ἀνεπαύσατο ὡς λέων, τίς ἐγερεῖ αὐτόν;*[92] δηλοῦν αὐτοῦ τὴν ταφὴν καὶ τὴν ἐκ νεκρῶν ἔγερσιν.

> Ὁ χρόνος, ὃν *ἠκρίβωσεν* ὁ Ἡρώδης παρὰ τῶν μάγων, διετὴς ἦν. μετὰ γὰρ τὸ γεννηθῆναι τὸν σωτῆρα διὰ δύο ἐτῶν ἦλθον ἀπὸ τῆς χώρας αὐτῶν. τὰ γοῦν *ἀπὸ διετοῦς* βρέφη ἀνεῖλεν.
>
> Καὶ μετ' ὀλίγον.
>
> Ἐντεῦθέν σοι ἡ γνῶσίς ἐστιν ὅτι οὐ παραυτὰ τοῦ κυρίου *γεννηθέντος* ἐν τῷ σπηλαίῳ *προσεκύνησαν* οἱ μάγοι τὸ βρέφος τὸ ὑπὸ τοῦ ‹ἀστέρος δηλούμενον› μηνύοντος ἐν τῇ φάτνῃ, ἀλλ' ὅτι μὲν οἱ ποιμένες εὐθέως ἐν ἐκείνῃ τῇ νυκτὶ μετὰ τῶν ἀγγέλων

85 Micah, 5:1.
86 Mat. 2:7.
87 Cod. παρ' αὐτά.
88 Matt. 2:11.
89 Cord. παραυτά.
90 Matt. 2:16.
91 Matt. 2:7.
92 Num. 24:9.

θέαν δρομαῖοι ἀπήεσαν ἰδεῖν τὸ ἀληθές, ἅτε γειτνιῶντος τοῦ σπηλαίου αὐτοῖς· οἱ δὲ μάγοι συμπεριλαβόντος ἔτους δευτέρου μετὰ τὸ εὐλογηθῆναι αὐτὸν ὑπὸ Συμεὼν (καταβάντων πάλιν ἐν τῇ Βηθλεὲμ ‹τῶν γονέων› τοῦ βρέφους φερομένου [τε] ἐν ἀγκάλαις τῆς τεκούσης) καὶ παροικῆσαι ἐν οἰκίᾳ ξενίας ἡμέρας πολλάς. εἰς [ὃν] οἶκον κατὰ μὲν τὸν αὐτὸν ἐλθόντες οἱ *μάγοι ἐκ τῆς ἀνατολῆς*, κἀκεῖ προσενεγκάντες αὐτῷ τὰ *δῶρα*, θεαταὶ γεγόνασι τοῦ αἰωνίου βασιλέως.[lxxiii] φησὶ γὰρ ὁ εὐαγγελιστὴς τὸν Ἡρώδην κελεύσαντα τοῖς δημίοις *ἀπὸ διετοῦς* μόνον *καὶ κατωτέρω* κατακτεῖναι τὰ βρέφη *κατὰ τὸν χρόνον ὃν ἠκρίβωσε παρὰ τῶν μάγων*. φεύγει δὲ τὴν Ἡρώδου μανίαν μετὰ τῶν κατὰ σάρκα γονέων εἰς Αἴγυπτον ὢν ἐτῶν δύο, καὶ καταμένει ἐκεῖ σὺν αὐτοῖς ἕτερα ἔτη δύο, μέχρι τοῦ πρώτου ἔτους τῆς Ἀρχελάου βασιλείας, ἐν τῇ καλουμένῃ Πανός. εἰθ᾽ οὕτως κακῶς τὸν βίον μετελθόντος Ἡρώδου, διὰ χρηματισμοῦ πάλιν ἄνεισιν ἐξ Αἰγύπτου ὁ κύριος σὺν αὐτοῖς *εἰς γῆν Ἰσραήλ*, ὢν ἐτῶν τεσσάρων τὸ κατὰ σάρκα, ἔτους με´ τῆς βασιλείας Αὐγούστου. μετὰ δὲ τὴν ἐξ Αἰγύπτου ἐπάνοδον, εὑρήσεις τὸν Λουκᾶν λέγοντά σοι τὰ καθεξῆς ἀκόλουθα.[lxxiv]

5

8r (ΩΡΙΓΕΝΟΥΣ)[lxxv] *Καὶ ἰδοὺ ‹ὁ› ἀστήρ*.[93] Δύναμίς τις ἦν ἡ τοὺς μάγους ὁδηγοῦσα ἐν ἀστέρος εἴδει. Αὕτη δὲ οὐ μακρὰν τῆς γῆς βαδίζουσα ὡδήγει τοὺς μάγους· ἥτις δύναμις, σοφὸς διδάσκαλος οὖσα, ἔγνω κρυβῆναι, τὴν ὑπακοὴν τοῖς ἀνηκόοις παρασκευάζουσαι. Ὅτι δὲ οὐχ ‹εἷ›ς[94] τῶν πολλῶν ὁ ἀστήρ, φανερὸν ἐκ τοῦ *ἔ‹σ›τη*[95] *ἐπάνω οὗ ἦν τὸ παιδίον*.[96]

> Δύναμίς τις ἦν ἡ τοὺς μάγους ὁδηγοῦσα ἐν ἀστέρος εἴδει, αὕτη δὲ οὐ μακρὰν τῆς γῆς βαδίζουσα ὡδήγει τοὺς μάγους, ἥτις σοφὸς διδάσκαλος οὖσα, ἔγνω κρυβῆναι, τὴν ὑπακοὴν τοῖς ἀνηκόοις παρασκευάζουσαι. ὅτι δὲ οὐχ εἷς τῶν πολλῶν ὁ ἀστήρ, φανερὸν ἐκ τοῦ *ἔστη ἐπάνω οὗ ἦν τὸ παιδίον*.[lxxvi]

5a

8v (ΑΝΕΠ)[lxxvii] *Ἀναχωρησάντων δὲ αὐτῶν*.[97] Φεύγει τὴν Ἡρώδου μανίαν μετὰ τῶν κατὰ σάρκα γονέων εἰς Αἴγυπτον Ἰησοῦς ὢν ἐτῶν δύο καὶ καταμένει σὺν αὐτοῖς, ἕτερα ἔτη δύο μέχρι τοῦ πρώτου ἔτους τῆς Ἀρχελάου βασιλείας. Εἶθ᾽ οὕτως κακῶς τὸν βίον μετελθόντος Ἡρώδου, διὰ χρηματισμοῦ πάλιν ἄνεισιν ἐξ Αἰγύπτου ὢν ἐτῶν τεσσάρων τὸ κατὰ σάρκα, ἔτους $\overline{\text{ΜΕ}}$ τῆς βασιλείας Αὐγούστου.

---

93 Matt. 2:9.
94 Cod. ἧς.
95 Cod. ἔτη.
96 Matt. 2:9.
97 Matt. 2:13.

φεύγει δὲ τὴν Ἡρώδου μανίαν μετὰ τῶν κατὰ σάρκα γονέων εἰς Αἴγυπτον ὢν ἐτῶν δύο, καὶ καταμένει ἐκεῖ σὺν αὐτοῖς ἕτερα ἔτη δύο, μέχρι τοῦ πρώτου ἔτους τῆς Ἀρχελάου βασιλείας, ἐν τῇ καλουμένῃ Πανός. εἶθ᾽ οὕτως κακῶς τὸν βίον μετελθόντος Ἡρώδου, διὰ χρηματισμοῦ πάλιν ἄνεισιν ἐξ Αἰγύπτου ὁ κύριος σὺν αὐτοῖς *εἰς γῆν Ἰσραήλ*, ὢν ἐτῶν τεσσάρων τὸ κατὰ σάρκα. ἔτους με᾽ τῆς βασιλείας Αὐγούστου. μετὰ δὲ τὴν ἐξ Αἰγύπτου ἐπάνοδον, εὑρήσεις τὸν Λουκᾶν λέγοντά σοι τὰ καθεξῆς ἀκόλουθα.[lxxviii]

(Εὐσεβίου. Ὠριγένους). φεύγει δὲ τὴν Ἡρώδου μανίαν μετὰ τῶν κατὰ σάρκα γονέων εἰς Αἴγυπτον ὢν ἐτῶν δύο, καὶ καταμένει ἐκεῖ σὺν αὐτοῖς ἕτερα ἔτη δύο, μέχρι τοῦ πρώτου ἔτους τῆς Ἀρχελάου βασιλείας, ἐν τῇ καλουμένῃ Πανός. εἶθ᾽ οὕτως κακῶς τὸν βίον μετελθόντος Ἡρώδου, διὰ χρηματισμοῦ πάλιν ἄνεισιν ἐξ Αἰγύπτου ὁ Κύριος σὺν αὐτοῖς εἰς γὴν Ἰσραήλ, ὢν ἐτῶν τεσσάρων τὸ κατὰ σάρκα. ἔτους με᾽ τῆς βασιλείας Αὐγούστου. μετὰ δὲ τὴν ἐξ Αἰγύπτου ἐπάνοδον, εὑρήσεις τὸν Λουκᾶν λέγοντά σοι τὰ καθεξῆς ἀκόλουθα.[lxxix]

Φεύγει[lxxx] δὲ Θεὸς ὢν ὁ Χριστὸς δι᾽ οἰκονομίαν, ἵνα δειχθῇ ὅτι καὶ ἄνθρωπος ἦν ἡμῖν ὁμοιοπαθής. Εἰ γὰρ ἔμεινεν ὡς Θεὸς ἀπαθὴς κατακόψαντος αὐτὸν τοῦ Ἡρώδου καὶ μὴ ἀπέθανεν, ἔλεγον ἂν τινες ὅτι οὐ | **9r** κ ἀνέλαβε σάρκα ἀνθρώπου, ἀλλὰ φαντασίᾳ ἦν ἄνθρωπος. Εἰσῆλθε τοίνυν εἰς Αἴγυπτον δεικνὺς ὅτι τὴν Βαβυλῶνα καὶ Αἴγυπτον (αἳ ἦσαν δεισιδαιμονέστεραι πάντων)[lxxxi] εἵλκυσε. Τὸ δὲ *ἐξ Αἰγύπτου ἐκάλεσα τὸν υἱόν μου*,[98] εἰ καὶ Ἰουδαῖοι φασὶ ὅτι ἐπ᾽ αὐτῶν ἐλέχθη, ὡς ἐν τύπῳ ἐλέχθη. Ἐπὶ γὰρ Χριστοῦ ὅς ἐστι φύσει υἱὸς τοῦ Θεοῦ[lxxxii] ἀπέβη τὸ ρητόν, διὸ ὡς πέρας τότε λαβούσης τῆς προφητείας εἶπε τοῦτο ὁ εὐαγγελιστής.

Λουκᾶς μὲν[lxxxiii] τὸν καιρὸν ἱστορῶν τῆς τοῦ Σωτῆρος ἡμῶν γενέσεως, τῆς Αὐγούστου βασιλείας μνημονεύει καὶ τῆς κατ᾽ αὐτὸν ἀπογραφῆς. φησί τε μηδὲ ἐσχηκέναι αὐτοὺς ἐν τῇ Βηθλεὲμ κατάλυμα, πλήθους συνόντος ὡς εἰκὸς ἐν τῇ Βηθλεὲμ τῶν ἀπὸ γένους Δαβὶδ τῆς ἀπογραφῆς ἕνεκεν. διὸ μηδὲ οἴκου τὸν Ἰωσὴφ εὐπορεῖν. ὅθεν τεκοῦσάν φησι τὴν Μαρίαν σπαργανῶσαι τὸ βρέφος καὶ ἀποθέσθαι ἐν φάτνῃ, διὰ τὸ μὴ εἶναι αὐτοῖς τόπον ἐν τῷ καταλύματι. καὶ εἰκός γε ἦν πλείστων συνόντων διὰ τὴν ἀπογραφὴν μὴ εὐπορεῖν καταγωγίου, ἀλλὰ καί, *Ὅτε*, φησίν, *αἱ ἡμέραι ἐπλήσθησαν τοῦ περιτεμεῖν αὐτὸν* (*χρὴ δὲ τοῦτο γίνεσθαι ὀγδόῃ μετὰ τὴν ἀπότεξιν ἡμέρᾳ*), *ἀνήγαγον τὸ παιδίον εἰς Ἱεροσόλυμα, καὶ τελέσαντες ἐπ᾽ αὐτῷ τὰ νενομισμένα, ἀπίασιν εἰς Ναζαρέθ*. Τούτων παρὰ τῷ Λουκᾷ κειμένων οὐδενὸς μνημονεύσας ὁ Ματθαῖος, παραχωρήσας δὲ τῷ Λουκᾷ τὰ εἰρημένα, ἕτερα αὐτὸς διηγεῖται. τίνα δὲ ἦν ταῦτα, ἀλλ᾽ ἢ τῶν Μάγων ἀπὸ Ἀνατολῆς ἄφιξις; κινησάντων μὲν ἀπὸ τῆς οἰκείας γῆς ἅμα τῷ γεννηθῆναι τὸν Ἰησοῦν, ἀστέρος αὐτοῖς τὴν γνῶσιν τῆς γεννήσεως ὑποφήναντος, οὐδήπου δὲ τὴν τοσαύτην στειλαμένων πορείαν καιρῷ βραχεῖ. οὐ γὰρ ἐν ἡμέραις ὀκτὼ τὴν ἀπὸ Ἀνατολῶν ὁδὸν εἰκὸς αὐτοῖς ἐπὶ τὴν Ἰουδαίαν ἠνῦσθαι, ὡς τὸν αὐτὸν νομίσαι εἶναι καιρὸν τῆς τε τούτων ἀφίξεως, καὶ τῆς τοῦ Σωτῆρος ἡμῶν γενέσεως. εἰ δὲ καὶ πυνθανόμενοι λέγουσι, *Ποῦ ἐστιν ὁ τεχθεὶς βασιλεὺς τῶν Ἰουδαίων; εἴδομεν γὰρ αὐτοῦ τὸν ἀστέρα, καὶ ἤλθομεν προσκυνῆσαι αὐτῷ*, οὐ τὸν σήμερον τεχθέντα, ὡς ἂν τις ὑπολάβοι, καθ᾽ ὃν ταῦτα ἐπυνθάνοντο χρόνον δηλοῦσιν, ἀλλὰ τὸν τότε γενόμενον ὅτε αὐτοῖς ὁ ἀστὴρ ἐπέφανε.

98 Matt. 2:15; cf. Hosea, 11:1.

Πόσος δὲ ἦν οὗτος ὁ μεταξὺ χρόνος, τοῦ τε φανέντος τοῖς Μάγοις ἐπὶ τῆς τοῦ Σωτῆρος ἡμῶν γενέσεως ἀστέρος, καὶ τῆς αὐτῶν εἰς τὰ Ἱεροσόλυμα παρουσίας, αὐτός σε διδάξει ὁ εὐαγγελιστὴς λέγων. *Τότε Ἡρώδης λάθρα καλέσας τοὺς Μάγους, ἠκρίβωσε παρ᾽ αὐτῶν τὸν χρόνον τοῦ φαινομένου ἀστέρος.* Καὶ ὡς ἂν ἀκριβώσας παρ᾽ αὐτῶν, μαθὼν ὅστις ἦν οὗτος, μετὰ τὸ ἀναχωρῆσαι λάθρα τοὺς Μάγους, ἰδὼν ὅτι ἐνεπαίχθη ὑπ᾽ αὐτῶν, *ἐθυμώθη λίαν, καὶ ἀποστείλας ἀνεῖλε πάντας τοὺς παῖδας ἐν Βηθλεέμ, καὶ ἐν πᾶσι τοῖς ὁρίοις αὐτῆς, ἀπὸ διετοῦς καὶ κατωτέρω, κατὰ τὸν χρόνον ὃν ἠκρίβωσε παρὰ τῶν Μάγων.* Οὐκοῦν διετὴς χρόνος ἤδη παρεληλύθει ἀπὸ τῆς Ἰησοῦ γενέσεως καὶ ἐπὶ τὴν ἄφιξιν τῶν εἰρημένων. οὐκ ἄρα διαφωνεῖ τὰ παρὰ τοῖς ἱεροῖς εὐαγγελισταῖς, εἰ ὁ μὲν Λουκᾶς ὀγδόῃ τῆς γενέσεως ἡμέρᾳ ἀνάγει αὐτὸν ἅμα τοῖς γονεῦσιν εἰς Ἱερουσαλὴμ τῆς τῶν νομίμων ἐκπληρώσεως ἕνεκα, κἀκεῖθεν ἀπάγει ἐπὶ τὴν Ναζαρέθ. ὁ δὲ Ματθαῖος μετὰ διετῆ χρόνον γενομένους πάλιν ἐν Βηθλεὲμ ἀναγράφει, ἐντεῦθέν τε εἰς Αἴγυπτον ἀπεληλυθέναι φησὶ διὰ τὴν τοῦ βασιλέως ἐπιβουλήν. καὶ ἦν εἰκὸς οὐ μόνον δεύτερον, ἀλλὰ καὶ πλειστάκις ἐπιφοιτᾷν αὐτοὺς τῷ τόπῳ, μνήμης τοῦ παραδόξου χάριν. δείκνυται γοῦν ἀναμφιβόλως οὐχ ὁ αὐτὸς ὢν καιρὸς ἐν ᾧ γεγέννηται κατὰ τὸν Λουκᾶν ὁ Σωτὴρ ἡμῶν, ἐν ᾧ τε κατὰ τὸν Ματθαῖον ὑπήντησαν οἱ ἐξ Ἀνατολῶν Μάγοι.

Ὅτι δὲ μὴ εἷς ἦν ὁ παρ᾽ ἀμφοτέροις τοῖς εὐαγγελισταῖς χρόνος, καὶ ἄλλως ἐστὶ συλλογίσασθαι. Λουκᾶς φησι μὴ εὐπορῆσαι αὐτοὺς καταγωγίου ἐν τῇ Βηθλεέμ. διὸ καὶ τεκοῦσαν ἀνακλῖναι τὸ παιδίον ἐν φάτνῃ, διὰ τὸ μὴ εἶναι τόπον ἐν τῷ καταλύματι, ὡς εἰκός, τῆς ἀπογραφῆς ἕνεκεν πάντων πανταχόθεν τῶν ἐξ οἴκου καὶ πατριᾶς Δαβὶδ συντρεχόντων εἰς τὴν εἰρημένην πόλιν, διά τε τὸ πλῆθος τῶν ἐπιξενουμένων αὐτόθι μὴ εὐπορούντων καταλύματος. ὁ δὲ Ματθαῖος *Ἀκούσαντες, φησίν, οἱ Μάγοι τοῦ βασιλέως Ἡρώδου, ἐπορεύθησαν εἰς Βηθλεέμ. καὶ ἰδοὺ ὁ ἀστὴρ ὃν εἶδον ἐν τῇ Ἀνατολῇ προῆγεν αὐτούς, ἕως οὗ ἦν τὸ παιδίον μετὰ Μαρίας τῆς μητρὸς αὐτοῦ. καὶ πεσόντες προσεκύνησαν αὐτῷ.* Ἀλλ᾽ οὐκ ἐν φάτνῃ κείμενον οὗτοι καταλαμβάνουσι τὸ παιδίον ὁμοίως τοῖς ποιμέσιν, ἀλλ᾽ ἔνδον ἐν οἰκίᾳ μετὰ τῆς μητρὸς αὐτὸ θεωροῦσι, καίτοι Λουκᾶς ἔφησε μὴ εἶναι τόπον αὐτοῖς ἐν τῷ καταλύματι. Πῶς οὖν ὁ Ματθαῖος οἰκίαν αὐτοῖς ἀφορίζει; Ἀλλ᾽ ἐπεὶ Λουκᾶς τὸν καιρὸν ἱστορεῖ τῆς γενέσεως, οὗτος δ᾽ ἦν ὁ τῆς ἀπογραφῆς, καθ᾽ ὃν πανδημεὶ συνέτρεχον οἱ τῷ αὐτῷ γένει προσήκοντες ἐν τῇ τοῦ Δαβὶδ πόλει, ὁ δὲ Ματθαῖος τὰ μετὰ δύο ἐτῶν χρόνους ἱστορεῖ (τοσοῦτος γὰρ ἦν ὁ χρόνος ὃν Ἡρώδης παρὰ τῶν Μάγων ἠκρίβωσεν). ὥστε σχολῆς οὔσης ἐν τῇ Βηθλεέμ, κατὰ τὸν Ματθαῖον εὐπόρουν καταγωγίου. διὸ εἰσελθόντες οἱ Μάγοι εἰς τὴν οἰκίαν, εἶδον τὸ παιδίον μετὰ Μαρίας τῆς μητρὸς αὐτοῦ. καὶ πεσόντες προσεκύνησαν αὐτῷ. καὶ αὕτη μὲν ἡ τοῦ ζητηθέντος λύσις.[lxxxiv]

Ἕτεροι δέ φασιν[lxxxv] ταῦτα διαφωνεῖν πρὸς τὰ παρὰ τῷ Λουκᾷ κείμενα. εἰ γὰρ ἀπὸ τῆς Βηθλεὲμ κατὰ τὸν Λουκᾶν ἀνῆλθεν εἰς Ἱερουσαλὴμ κἀκεῖθεν εἰς τὰ Νάζαρα,[99] πῶς κατὰ τὸν Ματθαῖον ἀπὸ τῆς Βηθλεὲμ χρηματισθεὶς ὁ Ἰωσὴφ ἀπήρθη εἰς Αἴγυπτον;[100] Λουκᾶς μὲν γὰρ τὸν καιρὸν ἱστορῶν τῆς τοῦ σωτῆρος ἡμῶν γεννήσεως τῆς *Αὐγούστου*[101] βασιλείας μνημονεύει καὶ τῆς κατ᾽ αὐτὸν *ἀπογραφῆς* καὶ τὰ συμβάντα ἐπὶ τῇ τοῦ σωτῆρος γεννήσει, ἀλλὰ καὶ *ὅτε*, φησίν, *ἐπλήσθησαν αἱ ἡμέραι τοῦ περιτεμεῖν αὐτόν, ἀνήγαγον* τὸ παιδίον *εἰς Ἱεροσόλυμα*[102] καὶ τελέσαντες ἐπ᾽ αὐτῷ τὰ νενομισμένα ἀπίασιν εἰς *Ναζαρέθ.*[103] ὁ δὲ Ματθαῖος οὐδ᾽ ὅλως τῶν παρὰ τῷ Λουκᾷ μέμνηται, τίθησι δὲ τὰ

99 Luke, 2:22-39.
100 Matt. 2:13.
101 Luke, 2:1.
102 Luke, 2:21-22.
103 Luke, 2:34.

παρὰ τούτῳ σεσιγημένα, λέγω δὴ τὰ κατὰ τοὺς μάγους, κινησάντων μὲν ἴσως ἀπὸ τῆς οἰκείας γῆς ἅμα τῷ γεννηθῆναι τὸν Ἰησοῦν οὔπω δὲ τὴν τοσαύτην στειλαμένων πορεί-αν ἐν καιρῷ βραχεῖ. πόσος δὲ ἦν οὗτος ὁ μεταξὺ χρόνος τοῦ τε φανέντος ἀστέρος καὶ τῆς τῶν μάγων ἀφίξεως, αὐτὸς ἐδίδαξεν ὁ εὐαγγελιστὴς λέγων *ἀπὸ διετοῦς καὶ κατὰ τὸν χρόνον ὃν ἠκρίβωσεν παρὰ τῶν μάγων*.[104] οὐκοῦν διετὴς ἤδη χρόνος παρελήλυθεν ἀπὸ τῆς τοῦ κυρίου γεννήσεως καὶ ἐπὶ τὴν ἄφιξιν τῶν εἰρημένων. οὔκουν διαφωνεῖ τὰ παρὰ τοῖς ἱεροῖς εὐαγγελισταῖς, εἰ μὲν ὁ Λουκᾶς ὀγδόῃ τῆς γεννήσεως ἡμέρᾳ ἀνάγει αὐτὸν ἅμα τοῖς γονεῦσιν εἰς Ἰερουσαλὴμ κἀκεῖθεν ἀπάγει ἐπὶ τὴν Ναζαρέθ, Ματθαῖος δὲ μετὰ διετῆ χρόνον γενόμενον πάλιν ἐν Βηθλεὲμ ἀναγράφει, ἐντεῦθέν τε εἰς Αἴγυπτον ἀπεληλυθέναι διὰ τὴν τοῦ βασιλέως ἐπιβουλήν. καὶ ἦν εἰκὸς οὐ μόνον δεύτερον, ἀλλὰ καὶ πλειστάκις ἐπιφοιτᾶν αὐτοὺς τῷ τόπῳ μνήμης τοῦ παραδόξου χάριν. ὅτι δὲ μὴ εἷς ἦν παρ᾽ ἀμφοτέροις χρόνος, καὶ ἄλλως ἔστι συλλογίσασθαι. Λουκᾶς φησι μὴ εὐπορῆσαι αὐτοὺς καταγωγείου ἐν τῇ Βηθλεὲμ διὰ τὸ πλῆθος τῶν ἐπιξενουμένων αὐτόθι προφάσει τῆς ἀπογραφῆς, ὁ δὲ Ματθαῖος, ὅτι *ἐλθόντες εἰς τὴν οἰκίαν εἶδον τὸ παιδίον μετὰ Μαρίας τῆς μητρὸς αὐτοῦ, καὶ πεσόντες προσεκύνησαν αὐτῷ*.[105] ἀλλ᾽ οὐκ ἐν *φάτνῃ* κείμενον αὐτοὶ καταλαμβάνουσι τὸ παιδίον ὁμοίως τοῖς ποιμέσιν, ἀλλ᾽ ἔνδον ἐν *οἰκίᾳ μετὰ τῆς αὐτοῦ μητρὸς* θεωροῦσιν. ἐκεῖ μὲν γὰρ διὰ τὸ μὴ εἶναι *τόπον ἐν τῷ καταλύματι ἐν φάτνῃ* τίθεται,[106] ἐνταῦθα δὲ μετὰ διετῆ χρόνον ἐν *οἰκίᾳ* εὑρίσκεται ὑπὸ τῶν μάγων *μετὰ τῆς μητρὸς αὐτοῦ* σχολῆς οὔσης ἐν τῇ Βηθλεὲμ *καὶ πεσόντες προσεκύνησαν αὐτῷ*.[lxxxvi]

Ῥαμὰ σημαίνει τόπον ὑψηλόν, ὅθεν ἔν τισι τῶν ἀντιγράφων τοῦ προφήτου γέγραπται, *φωνὴ ἐν τῇ ὑψηλῇ ἠκούσθη*, καὶ τὰ ἑξῆς. καὶ ἔστιν ὁ τῆς *Ῥαχὴλ* τάφος κατὰ τὸν Ἱππόδρομον περὶ τὴν Βηθλεέμ. διὸ *Ῥαχὴλ* λέγεται κεκλαυκέναι *τὰ τέκνα αὐτῆς*. *** οἱ ἐν τῷ τόπῳ τῆς Ῥαχήλ, οἵτινες οὐδὲ *παρακληθῆναι* ἤθελον ἐπὶ τοῖς τέκνοις αὐτῶν, ὡς *οὐκ εἰσίν*. οὐδέπω γὰρ ἦσαν μεμαθηκότες ἀπὸ τοῦ ἐναργῶς παραστῆσαι δυναμένου τῇ αὐτοῦ ἀναστάσει τὴν ἀνάστασιν τῶν νεκρῶν, ὅτι οὐκ *εἰσὶν* οἱ νομιζόμενοι τοῖς κλαίουσι καὶ ὀδυρομένοις μὴ εἶναι.[lxxxvii]

Ἡ *Ῥαχὴλ* εἰς τύπον τῆς Ἐκκλησίας τῆς κάτω καὶ τῆς ἄνω τηρεῖται, εἰπεῖν δὲ μᾶλλον θεωρεῖται.[lxxxviii]

Φωνὴ ἐν Ῥαμὰ ἠκούσθη. (Ὠριγένους) *Ῥαμὰ* σημαίνει τόπον ὑψηλόν, ὅθεν ἔν τισι τῶν ἀντιγράφων τοῦ προφήτου γέγραπται, *φωνὴ ἐν τῇ ὑψηλῇ ἠκούσθη*, καὶ τὰ ἑξῆς. καὶ ἔστιν ὁ τῆς *Ῥαχὴλ* τόπος κατὰ τὸν Ἱππόδρομον περὶ τὴν Βηθλεέμ. διὸ Ῥαχὴλ λέγεται κεκλαυκέναι τὰ τέκνα αὐτῆς. οἷον ἐν τῷ τόπῳ τῆς Ῥαχήλ, οἵ τινες οὐδὲ παρακληθῆναι ἤθελον ἐπὶ τοῖς τέκνοις αὐτῶν, ὡς οὐκ εἰσίν. οὐδέ πω γὰρ ἦσαν μεμαθηκότες ἀπὸ τοῦ ἐναργῶς παραστῆσαι δυναμένου τῇ ἑαυτοῦ ἀναστάσει τὴν ἀνάστασιν τῶν νεκρῶν, ὅτι οὐκ εἰσὶν οἱ νομιζόμενοι τοῖς κλαίουσι καὶ ὀδυρομένοις μὴ εἶναι.[lxxxix]

Ἡ *Ῥαχιὴλ* εἰς τύπον τῆς Ἐκκλησίας τῆς κάτω καὶ τῆς ἄνω τηρεῖται, εἰπεῖν δὲ μᾶλλον θεωρεῖται.[xc]

Τελευτήσαντος δὲ τοῦ Ἡρώδου, ἰδοὺ Ἄγγελος Κυρίου κατ᾽ ὄναρ φαίνεται τῷ Ἰωσὴφ ἐν Αἰγύπτῳ.[107] Φανεὶς δὲ ὁ Ἄγγελος τῷ Ἰωσὴφ μετὰ θάνατον τοῦ Ἡρώδου, διὰ τοῦτο τὸ

---

104 Matt. 2:16.
105 Matt. 2:11.
106 Luke, 2:7.
107 Matt. 2:19.

οὐκ ἔτι φεῦγε φησίν, ἀλλὰ *πορεύου*. ἵνα μετὰ τὸν πειρασμὸν ἄνεσιν εὕρωσιν. ὅμως οὖν διὰ τὸ βασιλεύειν ἀντὶ Ἡρώδου Ἀρχέλαον υἱὸν αὐτοῦ, τὴν μὲν Ἰουδαίαν ἐδεδοίκει καταλαβεῖν, εἰς δὲ τὴν Ναζαρὲτ ἔρχεται, ὁμοῦ τε τὸν κίνδυνον φεύγων, ὁμοῦ τὲ ἐμφιλοχωρῶν τῇ πατρίδι, ἵνα μᾶλλον θαρρῇ καὶ χρηματισμὸν δέχεται παρὰ τοῦ Ἀγγέλου τούτου. πληροῦται δὲ καὶ τὸ ρηθὲν ὑπὸ τῶν προφήτων, *ὅτι Ναζωραῖος κληθήσεται*. τὸ δὲ ποῖοι προφῆται τοῦτο εἶπον, μὴ περιεργάζου. πολλὰ γὰρ τῶν προφητικῶν ἠφανίσθη βιβλίων. καὶ ταῦτα ἀπὸ τῆς ἱστορίας τῶν Παραλειπομένων ἴδοι τίς ἄν. εἰς ἀσέβειαν γὰρ οἱ Ἰουδαῖοι συνεχῶς ἐμπίπτοντες, τὰ μὲν ἠφίεσαν τῶν βιβλίων ἀπόλλυσθαι, τὰ δὲ αὐτοὶ κατέκαιον. καὶ τὸ μὲν Ἱερεμίας διηγεῖται, τὸ δὲ ὁ τὴν τετάρτην συντεθεικὼς τῶν Βασιλειῶν, λέγων μετὰ πολὺν χρόνον τὸ Δευτερονόμιον εὑρεθῆναι κατορωρυγμένον ποῦ καὶ ἠφανισμένον. ἐπεὶ ὅτι γε προεῖπον οἱ προφῆται πολλαχοῦ, καὶ οἱ Ἀπόστολοι Ναζωραῖον καλοῦσιν. διὰ δὲ τὸ λέγειν τὸν Λουκᾶν οὐ κατὰ χρησμὸν αὐτὸν ἐληλυθέναι ἐκεῖ, ἀλλ᾽ ὅτι τὸν καθαρισμὸν πληρώσαντες πάντα, ὑπέστρεψαν εἰς Ναζαρέτ, χρὴ νοεῖν, ὅτι τὸν χρόνον τὸν τῆς καθόδου τῆς εἰς Αἴγυπτον μὴ ἱστορῶν ὁ Λουκᾶς ταῦτα λέγει. οὐδὲ γὰρ ἂν πρὸ τοῦ καθαρμοῦ κατήγαγεν αὐτοὺς εἰς Αἴγυπτον ὁ Ἄγγελος διὰ τὸ μηδὲν ὅλως γενέσθαι παράνομον. πληρώσαντες δὲ ἅπαντα, κατῆλθον εἰς Ναζαρέτ.

Ὅτι Ἀρχέλαος βασιλεύει ἐπὶ τῆς Ἰουδαίας, ἐφοβήθη ἐκεῖ ἀπελθεῖν.[108] Εἰς τὴν Ἰουδαίαν, φησίν, ἐδεδοίκει ἀπελθεῖν, διὰ τὸν Ἀρχέλαον. ἀλλ᾽ ἔδει καὶ τὴν Γαλιλαίαν διὰ τὸν Ἡρώδην φοβηθῆναι. ἀλλ᾽ ἐπεὶ τὸ χωρίον ἤμειψεν, τὸ πρᾶγμα συνεσκιάζετο λοιπόν. ἡ γὰρ ὁρμὴ πᾶσα κατὰ τῆς Βηθλεὲμ ἦν, καὶ τῶν ὁρίων αὐτῆς. τῆς τοίνυν σφαγῆς γενομένης, ᾤετο λοιπὸν ὁ παῖς Ἀρχέλαος τέλος ἐσχηκέναι τὸ πᾶν καὶ ἐν τοῖς πολλοῖς καὶ τὸν ζητούμενον ἀνῃρῆσθαι.[xci]

5b

| **10r** (ΑΝΕΠ)[xcii] *Τελευτήσαντος δὲ τοῦ Ἡρώδου.*[109] Πολλοῖς καὶ ἀνηκέστοις περιπεσὼν πάθεσιν ὁ Ἡρώδης ἀποθνήσκει ἐξ ἐπιβουλῆς τῆς ἰδίας γυναικός. *Χρηματισθεὶς* δὲ τὸ τηνικαῦτα ὁ *Ἰωσὴφ* παραλαβεῖν *τὸ παιδίον* καὶ ἀπελθεῖν *εἰς γῆν Ἰσραήλ*,[110] *ἀκούσας ὅτι Ἀρχέλαος βασιλεύει τῆς Ἰουδαίας ἀντὶ Ἡρώδου τοῦ πατρὸς αὐτοῦ*,[111] δεδιὼς τὴν πατρῴαν ἔχθραν, ὡς ἐνυπόπτου[xciii] οὔσης τῆς Βηθλεὲμ οὐκ ἦλθεν εἰς τὴν Ἰουδαίαν. Διαπορουμένου δὲ αὐτοῦ ποῦ δεῖ οἰκεῖν ἀφόβως ἐχρηματίσθη πάλιν, ἀπελθεῖν εἰς *Ναζαρέτ*.[112] Εἰ δὲ καὶ ὁ Λουκᾶς φησι ὅτι μετὰ τὸ πληρῶσαι τὸν καθαρισμὸν ἀπῆλθεν εἰς *Ναζαρέτ*,[113] ἀλλὰ πάλιν ἦλθεν εἰς τὴν Βηθλεέμ. Εἶτα φυγὼν εἰς Αἴγυπτον καὶ ἐπανελθὼν πάλιν ᾤκησε τὴν *Ναζαρὲτ* διὰ χρηματισμοῦ.[114] Ἡ δὲ *Ναζαρὲτ* πόλις ἐστὶ τῆς Γαλιλαίας ἧς ἐκράτει Ἡρώδης, ὁ υἱὸς μὲν Ἡρώδου ἀδελφὸς δὲ Ἀρχελάου. Ἀποθανὼν γὰρ ὁ πρῶτος Ἡρώδης δύο μόνους κατέλιπεν | **10v** υἱούς, ὧν ὁ μὲν Ἀρχέλαος ἦρξε τῆς Ἰουδαίας ἀντὶ Ἡρώδου τοῦ πατρὸς αὐτοῦ, ὁ δὲ Ἡρώδης τῆς Γαλιλαίας. Δυνάμενος

108 Matt. 2:22.
109 Matt. 2:19.
110 Matt. 2:20.
111 Matt. 2:22.
112 Matt. 2:22-23.
113 Cf. Luke, 2:29.
114 Matt. 2:19-23.

δὲ καὶ ἀλλαχοῦ λαθεῖν ἐκεῖ *κατῴκησε*, πληρῶν τὴν προφητείαν καὶ δεικνὺς ὅτι μέλλει τὴν Ἰουδαίαν καταλιπεῖν καὶ *εἰς τὰ ἔθνη*[115] ἀπελθεῖν ἵνα πιστεύσωσιν εἰς αὐτόν. Οὐ κεῖται[xciv] δὲ ἡ λέξις παρ᾽ οὐδενὶ τῶν προφητῶν ὅτι *Ναζωραῖος κληθήσεται*[116] ὁ Χριστός, ἀλλ᾽ ὁ νοῦς. Διὸ πληθυντικῶς εἶπε, *τῶν προφητῶν*[117] (τὸ γὰρ *Ναζωραῖος* ἑρμηνεύεται ὁ ἅγιος τοῦ Θεοῦ καὶ ἄνθος), ἤτοι διὰ τὸ ἐν ταῖς πολλαῖς αἰχμαλωσίαις ἀπολέσθαι τὰς βίβλους ἢ διὰ τὸ καυθῆναι ἐν τῇ ἁλώσει. Οὐχ εὑρίσκεται παρὰ τίνι τῶν προφητῶν κεῖται ἡ χρῆσις. Εἰ δὲ ἴσον ἐστι τὸ *Ναζωραῖος* τῷ ἡγιασμένος, πολλοὶ προφῆται εἰρήκασι τὸν Χριστὸν Ναζωραῖον, τουτέστιν ἅγιον. Καὶ ὁ Δανιὴλ *ἅγιον ἁγίων*[118] αὐτὸν καλεῖ.

> Τοῦτο οὐχ εὑρίσκεται λεχθέν. εἰ δὲ ἴσον ἐστι τῷ ἡγιασμένῳ, πολλοὶ προφῆται εἰρήκασι Χριστὸν ναζωραῖον τουτέστι ΑΓΙΟΝ. καὶ γὰρ τοὺς ΗΓΙΑΣΜΕΝΟΥΣ ἔθος τῇ γραφῇ καλεῖν ναζωραίους.[xcv]

> Εἰ δὲ ὁ *Ναζωραῖος* ἅγιος ἑρμηνεύεται ἢ κατά τινας[xcvi] ἄνθος, εὑρίσκεται τοῦτο παρὰ πολλοῖς τὸ ὄνομα. *ἅγιον γὰρ ἁγίων* ὁ Δανιὴλ αὐτὸν ὀνομάζει[119] καὶ ὁ Ἠσαΐας *ῥάβδον ἐκ τῆς ῥίζης Ἰεσσαὶ καὶ ἄνθος* ἐξ αὐτῆς.[120] καὶ αὐτὸς δὲ ὁ κύριος περὶ ἑαυτοῦ λέγει ἐν τῷ ᾄσματι τῶν ᾀσμάτων. *ἐγὼ ἄνθος πεδίου, κρίνον τῶν κοιλάδων.*[xcvii]

> If he had recorded an exact citation from the scriptures, he never would have said, *what has been spoken through the prophets*, but simply, 'what has been spoken through the prophet'. But now, by saying *prophets*, in the plural, he is showing that he has not taken the words from the scriptures, but rather the sense.[xcviii] Nazarene is translated 'holy'. All scripture relates that the Lord was to be holy. We can also explain this in another way, that according to the Hebrew truth, it is written in Isaiah, indeed in the same words, *And there shall come forth a rod out of the root of Jesse, and a blossom shall come up from his root.*[xcix]

5c

(ΑΝΕΠ, cont.)[c] *Ἐν ταῖς ἡμέραις ἐκείναις παραγίνεται Ἰωάννης ὁ βαπτιστής.*[121] Ἔθος τοῦτο τῇ γραφῇ τὰ μετὰ χρόνον ὡς εὐθὺς συμβάντα λέγειν. Διὸ ἀντὶ τοῦ παρεγένετο εἴρηται τὸ *παραγίνεται.* Ἰωάννης δὲ ἐξελληνίζεται ἀπὸ τοῦ ἑβραϊκοῦ τοῦ Ἰωνᾶς, καὶ ἑρμηνεύεται Ἰαὼ χάρις αὐτοῖς.[ci]
Πρῶτος δὲ Ἰωάννης κηρύσσει βασιλείαν οὐρανῶν, ἥτις ἦν ὁ Χριστός.[cii]

---

115 Cf. Gal. 3:14.
116 Matt. 2:23.
117 Cf. Matt. 2:23.
118 Daniel, 9:24.
119 Daniel, 9:24.
120 Is. 11:1.
121 Matt. 3:1.

(᾿Ωριγένους) Πρῶτον ᾿Ιωάννην εὑρίσκομεν ὀνομάζοντα βασιλείαν οὐρανῶν, ἥτις ἦν ὁ Χριστός.[ciii]

Πρῶτον ᾿Ιωάννην εὑρίσκομεν ὀνομάζοντα βασιλείαν *οὐρανῶν*, ἥτις ἦν ὁ Χριστός.[civ]

First John the Baptist proclaims the kingdom of heaven, so that the Lord's precursor might be honoured with this privilege.[cv]

Κηρύσσει δὲ οὐκ ἐν θορύβῳ πόλεων, ἀλλ᾿ ἐν ἡσυχίᾳ.[cvi]

Εἰς τὸ ὄρος ἄνεισιν, ἵνα ἐκτὸς ὄχλου καθ᾿ ἡσυχίαν διδάξῃ.[cvii]

(ΑΝΕΠ, cont.)[cviii] | **11r** Λέγεται δὲ *βασιλεία οὐρανῶν* οὐ μόνον τὸ ζῆν θεαρέστως,[cix] ἀλλὰ καὶ ἡ πρώτη καὶ δευτέρα Χριστοῦ παρουσία[cx] καὶ ἡ ἀπόλαυσις τῶν μελλόντων ἀγαθῶν.[cxi]

Ἔστι δὲ *βασιλεία οὐρανῶν* καὶ ὁ Χριστὸς καὶ ἡ ἐνάρετος ζωή.[cxii]

Βασιλεία δὲ Θεοῦ, ὥς φησιν ᾿Ωριγένης, αὐτὸς ἂν εἴη ὁ Χριστός, ἑκάστου τῶν ἐν τῇ ἐπινοίᾳ αὐτοῦ λαμβανομένων, οἷον σοφίας λόγων ἀληθείας ὄντος οὐρανοῦ μὴ παρερχομένου μὴ ἀπολλυμένου.[cxiii]

Βασιλεία οὐρανῶν αὐτὸς ἂν εἴη ὁ Χριστός, ἑκάστου τῶν ἐν ἐπινοίᾳ αὐτοῦ λαμβανομένων ἰδίων (σοφίας, λόγου, ἀληθείας) ὄντος οὐρανοῦ μὴ παρερχομένου μὴ ἀπολλυμένου. ἢ ἡ παρουσία αὐτοῦ. αὕτη γὰρ ἡμῖν χαρίζεται τὴν τοῦ Πνεύματος μετάληψιν καὶ τὴν εἰς οὐρανοὺς ἄνοδον καὶ τὸ εἰς ἀγαθὸν τοῖς ἁγίοις ἐν τῷ ἐσομένῳ αἰῶνι ἄτρεπτον.[cxiv]

Ἡ *βασιλεία τῶν οὐρανῶν* αὐτός ἐστιν ᾿Ιησοῦς ὁ Χριστὸς προτρεπόμενος πάντας εἰς μετάνοιαν καὶ ἕλκων εἰς ἑαυτὸν διὰ τῆς χάριτος.[cxv]

Βασιλεία τῶν οὐρανῶν καὶ βασιλεία τοῦ θεοῦ λέγεται μὲν ἡ πρώτη τοῦ δεσπότου Χριστοῦ παρουσία ... λέγεται δὲ *βασιλεία τῶν οὐρανῶν* καὶ αὕτη ἡ ἀπόλαυσις καὶ ἡ κτῆσις τῶν αἰωνίων ἀγαθῶν ... λέγεται βασιλεία ἡ ἀνάστασις ... λέγεται δὲ *βασιλεία τῶν οὐρανῶν* καὶ αὕτη ἡ ἀπόλαυσις καὶ ἡ κτῆσις τῶν αἰωνίων ἀγαθῶν ... λέγεται *βασιλεία* καὶ ἡ δευτέρα παρουσία τοῦ Χριστοῦ.[cxvi]

(ΑΝΕΠ, cont.) *Κηρύσσων ἐν τῇ ἐρήμῳ.* Ὁ ᾿Ιωάννης ἅπαντα τὸν προλαβόντα χρόνον ἐν τῇ ἐρήμῳ διῆγεν ἀσκούμενος ἐπὶ τῷ γενέσθαι τοιοῦτος οἷον ἐχρῆν εἶναι τὸν μέλλοντα τοσαύτῃ διακονῆσαι λειτουργίᾳ. Οὕτω γὰρ ἡ θεία χάρις ᾠκονόμησε γενέσθαι, ὡς ἂν μηδὲ μία φαύλη τις ἐγγένηται τοῖς ἀνθρώποις ὑπόνοια περὶ τοῦ μέλλοντος μαρτυρεῖν τῷ δεσπότῃ Χριστῷ, ὡς ἢ διὰ συγγένειαν ἢ διὰ τὴν ἐκ παίδων συνήθειαν, ὃ καὶ αὐτὸς ἔλεγε, *κἀγὼ οὐκ ᾔδειν αὐτόν.*[122]

---

122 John, 1:31&33.

(ΑΝΕΠ, cont.) *Μετανοεῖτε.*[123] Τὸ *μετανοεῖτέ* φησιν ἀντὶ τοῦ μεταβάλλετε τὸν τρόπον ἀπὸ τῆς ἰουδαϊκῆς συνηθείας. Διὰ τοῦτο δὲ ἦλθεν *Ἰωάννης βαπτίζων*,[124] ἵν᾽ ὁδοποιήσῃ τῷ Χριστοῦ βαπτίσματι ἐθίζων αὐτοὺς εἰς τοῦτο δραμεῖν εὐκόλως, τὸ παρέχον *ἄφεσιν ἁμαρτιῶν.*[125] Τὸ γὰρ Ἰωάννου οὐ παρεῖχεν ἄφεσιν.[cxvii] Εἶτα ἐπάγει καὶ ῥῆσιν Ἡσαΐου τοῦ προφήτου δεικνὺς ὁ εὐαγγελιστὴς καὶ αὐτὸν τὸν Ἰωάννην κηρυσσόμενον ὑπὸ Ἡσαΐου καὶ φωνὴν προσαγορευόμενον.[126] Ἀναλόγως γὰρ Χριστῷ καὶ Ἰωάννῃ ἐστι φωνή. Πρεσβύτερος γοῦν τῇ γενέσει (φωνῆς γὰρ πρὸ λόγου ἀντιλαμβανόμεθα) δείκνυσι Χριστόν. Φωνῇ γὰρ παρίσταται λόγος. Ἄνευ Ἰωάννου φωνῆς οὐχ ἑτοιμάζεται ὁδὸς *Κυρίου.*[127] Εἰς δὲ τὴν μὴ ἑτοιμασθεῖσαν ἐν τῇ ψυχῇ *ὁδὸν* τῷ Υἱῷ τοῦ Θεοῦ οὐκ ἂν ἥκοι *ἡ ὁδός*,[128] *ὁ Λόγος.*[129] Μὴ ποιήσαντες δὲ ἡμεῖς *εὐθείας τὰς τρίβους*, οὐ δυνάμεθα χω | **11v** ρῆσαι τὸν ἀ‹λη›θῆ[130] Κύριον.
Πέμπεται δὲ ἡ *φωνὴ* οὐ βοῶσα, *ἀλλὰ βοῶντος*· καὶ οὐ λέγοντος ἁπλῶς, κεκραγότος δέ,[cxviii] ἵνα καὶ οἱ μακρὰν καὶ οἱ δυσήκοοι τῷ μεγέθει τῶν λεγομένων ἀκούσωσιν.

Οὗτος δὴ συνιεὶς τὴν περὶ ἑαυτοῦ προφητείαν παρὰ τῷ Ἡσαΐᾳ εἰρημένην φησὶν εἶναι φωνὴ οὐχὶ βοῶσα *ἐν τῇ ἐρήμῳ*,[131] *ἀλλὰ βοῶντος ἐν τῇ ἐρήμῳ*, τοῦ ἑστῶτος καὶ κεκραγότος. *Ἐάν τις διψᾷ, ἐρχέσθω πρὸς μὲ καὶ πινέτω.*[cxix]

6

11v (ΩΡΙΓΕΝΟΥΣ) *Ἤγγικε γὰρ ἡ βασιλεία τὸν οὐρανῶν.*[132] Βασιλεία Θεοῦ αὐτὸς ἂν εἴη ὁ Χριστός, ἑκάστου τῶν ἐν ἐπινοίᾳ αὐτοῦ λαμβανομένων ἰδίων. σοφίας, λόγου, ἀληθείας, ὄντος οὐρανοῦ μὴ παρερχομένου[133] μὴ δὲ ἀπολλυμένου.[cxx]

Ἢ ἡ παρουσία αὐτοῦ· αὕτη γὰρ ἡμῖν χαρίζεται τὴν τοῦ Πνεύματος μετάληψιν καὶ τὴν εἰς οὐρανοὺς ἄνοδον καὶ τὸ εἰς ἀγαθὸν τοῖς ἁγίοις ἐν τῷ ἐσομένῳ αἰῶνι ἄτρεπτον.

---

123 Matt. 3:2.
124 Mark, 1:4; John, 1:28; 3:23.
125 Mark, 1:4; Luke, 3:3; cf. Luke, 24:47; Acts, 2:38; 5:31; 10:43; 10:38; 24:18; Col. 1:14.
126 Cf. Is. 40:3; Matt. 3:3; Mark, 1:3; Luke, 3:4; John, 1:23.
127 Cf. Matt. 3:3.
128 Cf. John, 14:4.
129 John, 1:1.
130 Cod. ἀθῆ.
131 Matt. 3:3; Mark, 1:3; Luke 3:4; John, 1:23 (quoting Is. 40:3).
132 Matt. 3:2.
133 Cf. Matt. 24:35; Mark, 13:31; Luke, 21:33.

6a

11v (ΑΝΕΠ) *Εἶχε τὸ ἔνδυμα αὐτοῦ ἀπὸ τριχῶν καμήλου.*[134] Καὶ ἡ στολὴ καὶ ἡ τροφὴ Ἰωάννου αἰνίγματι ἐδήλου τὴν σκολιότητα καὶ ἀκαρπίαν τοῦ τότε λαοῦ. Ἤτοι ὡς μέσος παλαιᾶς καὶ τῆς τῶν ἐθνῶν κλήσεως,[135] τῶν τέως ἀκαθάρτων. Ἡ ἡ γὰρ κάμηλος καθὸ μὲν μηρυκίζεται καθαρά ἐστι, καθὸ δὲ μὴ διχηλὴν ἔχει τὴν *ὁπλήν*, ἀκάθαρτος.[136] Καὶ ὡς πενθῶν *Ἰακὼβ* τὸν Ἰωσὴφ *ἐπέθετο σάκκον ἐπὶ τὴν ὀσφὺν αὐτοῦ,*[137] οὕτως καὶ ὁ Ἰωάννης πενθῶν τὸν τότε καρπὸν τῆς ὀσφύος τοῦ Ἰσραὴλ τῇ περιθέσει τοῦ νεκροῦ δέρματος ἐνέκρου τὴν ὀσφύν. Εἰ δὲ καὶ καθό *ἐστιν Ἠλίας,*[138] ὅπερ ἐκεῖνος περιεζώσατο[139] κἀκεῖνος ἐπενόει τὸν λαὸν πενθῶν ζηλῶν τῷ Κυρίῳ. Καὶ ὡς ἐν ἔργῳ ὢν καὶ *ὁδοιπορίαις*[140] καὶ ὡς *δοῦλος Χριστοῦ,*[141] διὰ τὸ ἐπιγινώσκειν τὰ οἰκεῖα μέτρα καὶ διὰ τὸ ὑπερορᾶν παντὸς καλλωπισμοῦ καὶ σκληραγωγίαις σχολάζειν.

It says that his clothing was made *of hair*, not of wool. The former is an indication of austere dress, the latter of luxury and smoothness. Also, the leathern girdle, with which Elias was girded, is a σύμβολον of mortification.[cxxi]

7

(ΩΡΙΓΕΝΟΥΣ, ΘΕΟΔΩΡΟΥ ΜΟΨΟΥΕΣΤΙΑΣ) Τρί |**12r** χες γὰρ *καμήλου* λαμβάνονται εἰς σκληραγωγίαν ἀρετῆς. Καὶ τοῦτο δὲ οὐ παρέργως,[cxxii] ἀλλ᾽ ὡς ἐν μυστηρίῳ καὶ τύπῳ. Καὶ γὰρ ἡ κάμηλος οὔτε τοῖς ἀκαθάρτοις τελείως κτήνεσιν οὔτε τοῖς καθαροῖς συνηρίθμηται, μέσην δέ τινα τάξιν ἔχει καὶ ἐπαμφοτερίζει τοῖς ἰδιώμασι. Τὸ μὲν γὰρ ἀνάγειν μηρυκισμόν, τοῦτ᾽ ἔστιν ἀναφέρειν τὴν ἅπαξ καταποθεῖσαν τροφὴν καὶ πάλιν τοῖς ὀδοῦσι παραπέμπειν καὶ ἀναμασᾶσθαι τῶν καθαρῶν ἴδιον ζῴων, ὃ καὶ τῇ καμήλῳ πρόσεστι· τὸ δὲ μὴ δίχηλον τὴν ὁπλὴν ἔχειν, τοῖς ἀκαθάρτοις προσπέφυκε. Καὶ ἡ τῆς καμήλου δὲ βάσις κατὰ τὴν τῶν ὀνύχων προσβολὴν οὐ διῄρηται. Ταύτης οὖν ἕνεκα τῆς αἰτίας ὁ Ἰωάννης τὰς τρίχας τοῦ ζῴου τούτου περιεβάλλετο, δεικνὺς ὡς ἡ εὐαγγελικὴ κλῆσις καὶ ἣν ἐγγίζειν ἔλεγε βασιλείαν θεοῦ καὶ τοὺς ἐκ τοῦ Ἰσραὴλ τοῦ καθαροῦ λαοῦ καὶ τοὺς ἐκ τῶν ἀκαθάρτων ἐθνῶν παραδέξεται, καὶ ὅτι καὶ τούτοις κἀκείνοις ὁμοτίμως ἐκήρυττε τὴν μετάνοιαν.[cxxiii]

134 Matt. 3:4.
135 Cf. Rom. 9:24-25.
136 Cf. Lev. 11:4; Deut. 14:6-7.
137 Gen. 37:34.
138 Cf. Matt. 11:14.
139 Cf. 4 Kings (2 Kings, in Masoretic text), 1.8.
140 Cf. 2 Cor. 11:26.
141 Cf. Rom. 1:1; 1 Cor. 7:22; Gal. 1:10; Eph. 6:6; Phil. 1:1; Col. 4:12; James, 1:1; 2 Peter, 1:1; Judas, 1:1.

Ἤσθιε δὲ ἀκρίδας καὶ μέλι.[142] Καὶ οἱ μὲν φαύλια[cxxiv] τὰ τῶν ἀκροδρύων ἀκρίσματα,[cxxv] καὶ *μέλι ἄγριον*, τὴν βοτάνην ἢ τὸ ἐν ἀγρίοις τόποις εὑρισκόμενον μέλι, ἤτοι τὸ κηρίον ἀγεώργητον ὄν. Τινὲς δὲ *ἀκρίδας* τὰ ζῷα φασίν, ἐπεὶ καὶ ὁ λαὸς ἐτρέφετο λόγῳ μετεωροπόρῳ[cxxvi] μέν, οὐ βεβηκότι δὲ *ἐπὶ πτερύγων*,[143] οὐδὲ ὑπερβαίνοντι τὴν γῆν. *μέλι* ἦν τὸ ὑπ᾽ ἀνθρώπων ἀγεώργητον, ἐπεὶ τὸ γενόμενον ὑπὸ *νόμου καὶ προφητῶν*[144] *μέλι* οὐκ ἐγεώργουν μὴ ἐξετάζοντες τὸ βούλημα[cxxvii] αὐτοῦ μηδὲ ἐρευνῶντες *τὰς γραφάς*,[145] καὶ |**12v** ἐπειδὴ τὸ ἤρεμον μέλι ἐτηρεῖτο τῷ Χριστῷ.[cxxviii]

7a

13r (ΑΝΕΠ)[cxxix] *Γεννήματα ἐχιδνῶν.*[146] Ὡς φονικοὺς διασύρων αὐτούς, *γεννήματα ἐχιδνῶν* ἔφη ὁ Ἰωάννης. Ὅμως ἔχει καὶ ἔπαινον ἡ ὕβρις. Θαυμάζει γὰρ αὐτῶν τὴν νῦν μεταβολὴν διὰ τὸ καταλεῖψαι αὐτοὺς ὡσεὶ νεκρὰν τὴν ἑαυτῶν μητέρα *Ἱερουσαλὴμ*[147] καὶ δραμεῖν πρὸς αὐτὸν καὶ σωθῆναι ἀπὸ τῆς μελλούσης | **13v** αὐτοῖς ἐπενεχθῆναι ὀργῆς, ἢ τῆς ἀπὸ τῶν Ῥωμαίων ἢ τῆς ἐν τῇ συντελείᾳ. Οὕτω δὲ καλεῖ τοὺς ἐρχομένους πρὸς τὸ βάπτισμα αὐτοῦ ὁ Ἰωάννης, ὡς πρὸς τὴν τῶν ἰοβόλων ἐχιδνῶν πικρίαν κατενεχθέντας, ἐπειδὴ ἐφόνευον τοὺς πνευματικοὺς αὐτῶν πατέρας, τοὺς προφήτας. Καὶ γὰρ αἱ ἔχιδναι τὰς τῶν μητέρων γαστέρας ἐσθίουσαι ἐξερχόμεναι κατὰ τὸν τοῦ τόκου καιρόν· καὶ αἱ θήλειαι ὅταν συγγένωνται αὐταῖς οἱ ἄρρενες τὰς κεφαλὰς αὐτῶν δεχόμεναι ἐν τοῖς ἑαυτῶν στόμασιν ὑπὸ φιληδονίας ἀποτέμνουσιν. Οὕτω καὶ οἱ ἐπὶ κοιλίας ἕρποντες καὶ τὰ σαρκικὰ τοῦ βίου πράττοντες καὶ φιλήδονοι τὰς ἀλλήλων κεφαλὰς ἀποτέμνουσι διὰ τὰς κοσμικὰς ἐπιθυμίας. Καρποὶ δὲ *μετανοίας*[148] προηγουμένως μὲν ἡ εἰς Χριστὸν πίστις, ἔπειτα δὲ καὶ ἡ εὐαγγελικὴ πολιτεία.[cxxx] *Ποιήσατε* οὖν φησι καρποὺς ἀξίους *τῆς μετανοίας*· τουτέστι μὴ μόνον τὴν ψυχὴν τῇ μετανοίᾳ καθάρητε, ἀλλὰ καὶ ἔργα ποιήσατε χρηστά. Εἶτα τοῖς κατὰ σάρκα αὐχοῦσι τὸν Ἀβραὰμ τὴν καθαίρεσιν προφητεύει καὶ τὴν κλῆσιν τῶν ἐθνῶν (τῶν ἀναισθήτων δίκην λίθων,[cxxxi] καὶ *λίθοις καὶ ξύλοις*[149] πεπιστευκότων[cxxxii]) τῷ εἰπεῖν, *καὶ μὴ δόξητε λέγειν ἐν ἑαυτοῖς, πατέρα ἔχομεν τὸν Ἀβραάμ.*[150] Διὰ δὲ τούτου προτρέπεται αὐτοὺς ἀποστῆναι τῆς κατὰ σάρκα συγγενείας[151] καὶ ἕλκει ἐπὶ τοὺς *ἐκ πίστεως.*[152]

---

142 Cf. Matt. 3:4; Mark, 1:6.
143 Cf. Exodus, 19:4; Psalms 17:11; 103:3; Job, 37:3.
144 Acts, 13:15; Rom. 3:21; cf. Matt. 7:12; 11:13; 22:40; Luke, 24:44; John, 1:45.
145 Cf. John, 5:39.
146 Matt. 3:7; Luke, 3:7.
147 Cf. Gal. 4:26.
148 Matt. 3:8; Luke, 3:8.
149 Cf. Deut. 4:28; 28:36; 28:64; Ez. 20:32.
150 Matt. 3:9; cf. Luke, 3:8.
151 Cf. Rom. 9:3.
152 Cf. Gal. 3:7-11; 3:8-9; Rom. 4:16.

Εἶτα προφητεύει καὶ τὴν παρουσίαν τοῦ Χριστοῦ ἤδη γεγενῆσθαι. Ἀξίνη γάρ ἐστιν ὁ Χριστός,[cxxxiii] ὁ ἐκκόπτων τοὺς ἀπίστους τῆς τῶν πατριαρχῶν τιμῆς, οἵ εἰσι | **14r** ῥίζα ἥτις μενεῖ κἂν οἱ κλάδοι κοπέντες πυρὶ παραδοθῶσι. Μένει γὰρ ἵνα ἐγκεντρισθῇ ἐν αὐτῇ τὰ ἔθνη.[cxxxiv]

8

14r (ΩΡΙΓΕΝΟΥΣ) Τὸ *γεννήματα ἐχιδνῶν*[153] δηλώσει τὴν ἕξιν τῆς κακίας. Φασὶ γὰρ τὴν ἔχιδναν ἐν τῷ συλλαμβάνειν ἀναιρεῖν τὸν ἐξ οὗ συλλαμβάνει ἄρρενα, οὗ ἡ σπορὰ αὐξάνουσα τὴν συλλαμβάνουσαν ἀναιρεῖ καὶ οὕτως ἐξέρχεται. Πατρολῷον οὖν καὶ μητρολῷον τῆς ἐχίδνης τὸ γέννημα.

> τὸ *γεννήματα ἐχιδνῶν* δηλώσει τὴν ἕξιν τῆς κακίας.[cxxxv]
>
> φασὶ γὰρ τὴν ἔχιδναν ἐν τῷ συλλαμβάνειν ἀναιρεῖν τὸν ἐξ οὗ συλλαμβάνει ἄρρενα, οὗ ἡ σπορὰ αὐξάνουσα τὴν συλλαβοῦσαν ἀναιρεῖ καὶ οὕτως ἀπεξέρχεται. πατρολῷαν οὖν καὶ μητρολῷαν[cxxxvi] τῆς ἐχίδνης τὸ γέννημα. [τοιοῦτοι καὶ οἱ Ἰουδαῖοι τοὺς πνευματικοὺς πατέρας καὶ διδασκάλους διαφθείροντες χερσίν].[cxxxvii]
>
> Φασὶ δὲ τὴν ἔχιδναν ἐν τῷ συλλαμβάνειν ἀναιρεῖν τὸν ἐξ οὗ συλλαμβάνει ἄρρενα, οὗ ἡ σπορὰ αὐξάνουσα, τὴν συλλαβοῦσαν ἀναιρεῖ καὶ οὕτως εἰς φῶς ἐξέρχεται, διαρρήξασα τῆς μητρὸς τὴν γαστέρα, ποινὴν ὥσπερ τοῦ διαφθαρέντος πατρός .... Τοιοῦτοι καὶ οἱ Ἰουδαῖοι, τοὺς πνευματικοὺς αὐτῶν πατέρας καὶ διδασκάλους διαφθείροντες χερσίν. Εἴρηται περὶ τούτων ἐν τῷ Ματθαίῳ πλατύτερον.[cxxxviii]

9

14r (ΩΡΙΓΕΝΟΥΣ) Εἰ *ἐκ τῶν λίθων* δίδονται *τέκνα τῷ Ἀβραάμ*,[154] οὐ τῇ ἕξει τῆς σαρκός ἐστι πατήρ, ἀλλὰ τῇ ἕξει τῆς ἀρετῆς,[cxxxix] | **14v** τοῦ Θεοῦ ὁ λαὸς χρηματίζει *πατέρα* ἔχων *τὸν Ἀβραάμ*.[155] Καὶ πῶς ἢ διὰ τί, ζήτει.
Οἱ λίθοι λαμβάνονται εἰς στεῖραν[156][cxl] καὶ εἰς τὴν εἰδωλολατρίαν τῶν ἐθνῶν.[157]

> Οἱ λίθοι λαμβάνονται εἰς στεῖραν καὶ εἰς τὴν εἰδωλολατρίαν τῶν ἐθνῶν. πρὸς τούτοις θεώρει καὶ τὴν πεπηγυῖαν ὡς λίθον καρδίαν τοῦ δράκοντος.[cxli]
>
> He calls the pagans stones because of their hardness of heart.[cxlii]

---

153 Matt. 3:7.
154 Matt. 3:9.
155 Matt.3:9; Luke, 3:8; cf. Rom. 4:17.
156 Cf. Gal. 4:27 (quoting Is. 51:1).
157 Cf. Deut. 4:28; 13:7; 28:36; 29:17.

Πρὸς τούτοις, θεώρει καὶ τὴν πεπηγυῖαν ὡς λίθον καρδίαν τοῦ δράκοντος.[158][cxliii]

Ἤδη δὲ καὶ ἡ ἀξίνη.[159] Ἀξίνην φησὶν τὸν Χριστὸν τὸν τομώτερον μαχαίρας διστόμου,[160] μέλλοντα ἐκκόπτειν τοὺς ἀπίστους Ἰουδαίους καὶ ἀλλοτριοῦνια ἀπὸ τῆς τῶν πατριαρχῶν τιμῆς καὶ κοινωνίας, οὓς *ρίζαν* εἶπεν, οἳ καὶ ἔμειναν οἱ πάλαι Θεῷ ἀρέσαντες πατέρες οἱ περὶ Ἀβραὰμ καὶ ὅσοι πρῴην ἅγιοι. Οἱ γὰρ ἐξ αὐτῶν ἄπιστοι ἐξεκόπησαν ὡς ἄκαρποι κλάδοι, ἡ δὲ ρίζα ἔμεινεν, ἐφ' ἧς οἱ *ἐξ ἐθνῶν*[161] ἐνεκεντρίσθησαν. Εἰρηναῖος δὲ ἀξίνην φησι τὸν λόγον τοῦ Θεοῦ, καθὰ καὶ Ἱερεμίας, ὁ λόγος Κυρίου *ὡς πέλυξ κόπτων πέτραν.*[162]

> Εἰ *ἐκ τῶν λίθων* δίδονται *τέκνα τῷ Ἀβραάμ*, οὐ τῇ ἕξει τῆς σαρκός ἐστι πατήρ, ἀλλὰ τῇ ἕξει τῆς ἀρετῆς ὁ λαὸς τοῦ θεοῦ χρηματίζει *πατέρα* ἔχων τὸν *Ἀβραάμ*. καὶ πῶς ἢ διὰ τί, ζήτει.[cxliv]

> Ἀξίνην φησὶν τὸν Χριστὸν τὸν τομώτερον μαχαίρας διστόμου τὸν μέλλοντα ἐκκόπτειν τοὺς ἀπίστους Ἰουδαίους καὶ ἀλλοτριοῦν ἀπὸ τῆς τῶν πατριαρχῶν τιμῆς καὶ κοινωνίας, οὓς καὶ ρίζαν εἶπεν, οἳ καὶ ἔμειναν οἱ πάλαι θεῷ ἀρέσαντες πατέρες οἱ περὶ Ἀβραὰμ καὶ ὅσοι πρῴην ἅγιοι. οἱ γὰρ ἐξ αὐτῶν ἄπιστοι ἐξεκόπησαν ὡς ἄκαρποι κλάδοι, ἡ δὲ ρίζα ἔμεινεν, ἐφ' ἧς οἱ ἐξ ἐθνῶν ἐνεκεντρίσθησαν. Εἰρηναῖος δὲ ἀξίνην φησὶν τὸν λόγον τοῦ θεοῦ, καθὰ καὶ Ἱερεμίας. ὁ λόγος κυρίου ὡς πέλυξ κόπτων πέτρα. τί γὰρ λέγω, φησίν, ὅτι ἐκπίπτειν μέλλετε.[cxlv] διά τοι τοῦτο οὐδὲ ἀφειστήκει τῆς ρίζης.[cxlvi]

> The proclamation of the word of the gospel, which is sharp and two-edged sword, is called an axe according to Jeremiah the prophet. He compares the word of God with an axe that can cur rock.

Τί γὰρ λέγω, φησί, ὅτι ἐκπίπτειν μέλλετε τῆς πρὸς τὸν πατριάρχην συγγενείας καὶ τοὺς ἀπὸ λίθων ὁρᾶν εἰς τὴν ὑμετέραν εἰσαγομένους προεδρίαν; Οὐ γὰρ μέχρι τούτου τὰ τῆς τιμωρίας ὑμῖν, ἀλλὰ καὶ περαιτέρω προβήσεται τὰ τῆς κολάσεως. Οὐκέτι γὰρ *δρέπανον πετόμενον*,[163] οὐδὲ φραγμοῦ καθαίρεσις,[164] οὐδὲ τὸ καταπατεῖσθαι τὸν ἀμπελῶνα,[165] ἀλλ' *ἀξίνη* σφόδρα ἀκμάζουσα καὶ ἤδη πρὸς τὴν *ρίζαν* κειμένη. Μὴ τοίνυν συνήθως ἀπιστοῦντες εἴπητε ὡς τοῖς προφήταις, ποῦ ἐστιν *ἡ ἡμέρα Κυρίου*,[166] *ἐλθέτω ἡ βουλὴ τοῦ ἁγίου Ἰσραὴλ ἵνα γνῶμεν.*[167] Ἀνίατα γὰρ πείσεσθε τοιούτοις ἐπιμένοντες | **15r** λογισμοῖς. Οὐ γὰρ δοῦλος ἐστιν ὁ παραγενόμενος, ὡς πρότερον, ἀλλ' αὐτὸς ὁ τῶν ὅλων δεσπότης. Ἂν τοίνυν μεταβάλησθε καὶ γένησθε βελτίους,

158 Cf. Job, 41:15.
159 Luke, 3:9. Matt. 3:10: ἤδη δὲ ἡ ἀξίνη.
160 Cf. Heb. 4:12.
161 Cf. Rom. 9:24; Acts, 15:23.
162 Jer. 23:29.
163 Zach. 5:1-2.
164 Cf. Ecclesiastes, 10:8.
165 Cf. Is. 16:10.
166 Cf. Sophonias, 1:14; Is. 13:6.
167 Is. 5:19.

ἀπελεύσεται ἡ *ἀξίνη* μηδὲν ἐργασαμένη. Ἂν δὲ τοῖς αὐτοῖς ἐπιμείνητε, πρόρριζον ἀνασπάσει τὸ δένδρον. Διά τοι τοῦτο, οὐδὲ ἀφειστήκει τῆς ῥίζης.[cxlvii]

ἐγὼ μὲν βαπτίζω ὑμᾶς.[168] Τὸ Ἰουδαϊκὸν βάπτισμα μόνα τὰ ἀπὸ τῶν φυσικῶν ῥύπων καὶ τὰ κρυπτὰ ἁμαρτήματα ἐκάθαιρε (τὰ γὰρ φανερὰ ἐτιμώρει ὁ νόμος, τὰ δὲ Ἰωάννης καὶ συνειδήσεως κακῆς καὶ ἁμαρτιῶν τῶν φανερῶν ἠλευθέρου), οὐ μόνον εἰς μετάνοιαν καλοῦν ἀλλὰ καὶ ἑτοιμάζον εἰς ἁγιασμοῦ ὑποδοχήν. Τὸ δὲ τὸ Χριστοῦ καὶ πάσας ἀφανίζει ἁμαρτίας καὶ *Πνεύματος Ἁγίου* δίδωσι *δωρεάν*,[169] τοῦ Πνεύματος δίκην πυρὸς ἀφανίζοντος τὸν ἰὸν τῆς ἁμαρτίας. Οὐ γὰρ ἐν *πυρὶ* πάντως βαπτίζει ὁ Χριστός.[170] Ἵνα γὰρ μὴ μόνον *ἄφεσιν ἁμαρτιῶν*[171] δῷ ἀλλὰ καὶ παντελῆ ἀνάλωσιν αὐτῶν, βαπτίζει ἐν *πυρί*, συνόντος τοῦ Πνεύματος τῷ βαπτιζομένῳ ἐν *ὕδατι* καὶ *πυρί*. Ἢ ὅτι καὶ ἐν *τῷ μέλλοντι αἰῶνι*[172] πᾶς *πυρὶ* ἁλισθήσεται καὶ ὅτι ἡ ἀγάπη πῦρ ὀνομάζεται.

> Τὸ πῦρ καθαρίζει, φωτίζει καὶ ἄλλα πολλὰ ἐνεργεῖ. φασὶ δὲ καὶ ὅτι ἡ ἀγάπη πῦρ ὀνομάζεται. καὶ τοῦτο θεώρει, μεθ' οὗ συνεργεῖ.[cxlviii]

Εἰ γὰρ καὶ τῷ *ὕδατι* μόνῳ προσέχομεν, ἀλλὰ τοῖς τῆς πίστεως ὀφθαλμοῖς ὁρῶμεν καὶ τὸ Πνεῦμα καὶ τὸ πῦρ. Δεικνὺς δὲ τὸ ὑπερέχον τῆς ἀξίας τοῦ Χριστοῦ καὶ τὸ αὐτοῦ εὐτελές, διὰ μέσου ἐπάγει λέγων, *οὗ οὐκ εἰμὶ ἱκανὸς τὰ ὑποδήματα βαστάσαι*·[173] τουτέστιν, οὔτε εὐτελὲς δούλου ἀξίωμα ἔχω ἵνα βαστάσω ἢ λύσω αὐτοῦ *τὰ ὑποδήματα*. | **15v** Ἢ τὴν ἔνσαρκον αὐτοῦ οἰκονομίαν αἰνίττεται. Εἶτα δείκνυσιν αὐτὸν καὶ κριτὴν εἶναι δίκαιον, καί φησι ὅτι οὐ μόνον χωρίζει τοὺς καθαροὺς ἀπὸ τῶν ἀδίκων καὶ ῥυπαρῶν, ἀλλὰ καὶ ἀκατάπαυστον ἐπάγει τὴν τιμωρίαν.[cxlix] Οἱ μὲν γὰρ ἄπιστοι πάντες εἰς πῦρ βάλλονται, οἱ δὲ πιστοὶ μετὰ διακρίσεως ἀφορίζονται ἀπὸ τῶν ἀπίστων καὶ ἀναλόγως τῶν πράξεων λαμβάνουσι τὰς ἀμοιβάς.[cl]

9a

(ΘΕΟΔΩΡΟΥ ΗΡΑΚΛΕΙΑΣ).[174] Ὥστε ὅταν ἀκούσῃς, *ὅτι Ἰσχυρότερός μου ἐστί*, μὴ νομίσῃς κατὰ σύγκρισίν τοῦτο εἰρηκέναι. Οὐδὲ γὰρ εἰς δούλου ἄξιός εἰμι τάττε-

168 Matt. 3:11: ἐγὼ μὲν ὑμᾶς βαπτίζω ἐν ὕδατι. Mark, 1:8: ἐγὼ ἐβάπτισα ὑμᾶς ὕδατι. Luke, 3:16: Ἐγὼ μὲν ὕδατι βαπτίζω ὑμᾶς. John, 1:26: Ἐγὼ βαπτίζω ἐν ὕδατι.

169 Acts, 2:38; cf. 10:45; Heb. 6:4.

170 Cf. Matt. 3:11; Luke, 3:16.

171 Mark, 1:4; Luke, 3:3; cf. Luke, 24:47; Acts, 2:38; 5:31; 10:43; 10:38; 24:18; Col. 1:14.

172 Cf. Matt. 12:32.

173 Matt. 3:11.

174 In this codex, the supposed-to-be fragments by Theodore of Heraclea are normally both preceded and followed by ones attributed to Origen. This happens with this one, too.

σθαι ἐκείνου, οὐδὲ εἰς δούλους τάσσεσθαι ἄξιός εἰμι, οὐδὲ τὸ εὐτελὲς τῆς διακονίας ἀναδέξασθαι μέρος. Διὰ τοῦτο οὐχ ἁπλῶς εἶπε, *τὰ ὑποδήματα*, ἀλλὰ *τὸν ἱμάντα*,[175] ὅπερ ἔσχατον πάντων ἐδόκει εἶναι.

> Ὥστε ὅταν ἀκούσῃς, *ὅτι Ἰσχυρότερός μου ἐστί*, μὴ νομίσῃς κατὰ σύγκρισίν με τοῦτο εἰρηκέναι. Οὐδὲ γὰρ εἰς δούλους ἄξιός εἰμι τάττεσθαι ἐκείνου, οὐδὲ εἰς δούλους ἐσχάτους, οὐδὲ τὸ εὐτελὲς τῆς διακονίας ἀναδέξασθαι μέρος. Διὰ τοῦτο οὐχ ἁπλῶς εἶπε, *τὰ ὑποδήματα*, ἀλλ' *οὐδὲ τὸν ἱμάντα*, ὅπερ ἔσχατον πάντων ἐδόκει εἶναι.[cli]

9b

(ΤΟΥ ΑΥΤΟΥ)[clii] *Ἐν πνεύματι ἁγίῳ καὶ πυρί.*[176] *Ἐν πυρὶ* λέγονται αἱ τῶν ἁγίων ψυχαὶ βαπτίζεσθαι εἰλικρινῶς ὡς *τὸ τῆς εὐσεβείας* παραδεχόμεναι *μυστήριον*[177] διὰ τὸ ἐν πυρίναις γλώσσαις κατεληλυθέναι τὸ πρῶτον ἐπὶ τοὺς μαθητὰς τὸ πνεῦμα,[178] δι' οὗ ἐβαπτίσθησαν τελειωθέντες τὰς ψυχάς. Ἢ ὅτι ἐν τῷ μέλλοντι αἰῶνι πάντες πυρὶ μέλλουσι βαπτισθῆναι· *πᾶς*[179] *γὰρ πυρὶ ἁλισθήσεται*,[180] ἵνα *ἑκάστου τὸ ἔργον, ὁποῖόν ἐστιν, τὸ πῦρ δοκιμάσῃ*.[181]

> This may mean that the Holy Spirit is a fire, as the Acts of the Apostles teach, when he descended and sat as a fire upon the tongues of the faithful,[182] and the word of the Lord was fulfilled who said, *I came to throw fire on the earth. I wish it were already kindled.*[183] Or it could mean that at present we are baptised with the Spirit and in the future with fire. The apostle's saying also conforms with the meaning of *And the fire itself will test what sort of work each man's work is.*[cliii]

Δεῖ γὰρ ἡμῖν καὶ ἀρετῆς καὶ πολλῆς τῆς φιλοσοφίας.

However, it turns out throughout this manuscript that passages by Origen were copied to the letter by John Chrysostom whose allegiance to Origen's text has been discussed in the Introduction, whereas he could have hardly copied from Theodore of Heraclea. This passage is identical with Chrysostom's one, anyway.

175 Luke, 3:16; John, 1:26.

176 Matt. 3:11.

177 1 Tim. 3:16.

178 Cf. Acts, 2:3.

179 Reuss: πᾶν.

180 Mark, 9:49.

181 1 Cor. 3:13.

182 Jerome essayed to adorn Origen's comments, which he copied, but at this point he made a mistake: 'the tongues like fire' were 'distributed to each one of' the disciples, not 'of the faithful'.

183 Luke, 12:47.

δεῖ γὰρ ἡμῖν καὶ ἀρετῆς καὶ πολλῆς τῆς φιλοσοφίας.[cliv]

Καὶ μηδεὶς γινέσθω ἄχυρον, μηδεὶς εὐρίπιστος ἔστω, μηδὲ ταῖς πονηραῖς ἐπιθυμίαις προκείσθω, πανταχοῦ ῥᾳδίως ὑπ᾽ αὐτῶν ἀναρριπιζόμενος.

Μηδεὶς τοίνυν γινέσθω ἄχυρον, μηδεὶς εὐρίπιστος ἔστω, μηδὲ ταῖς πονηραῖς ἐπιθυμίαις προκείσθω, πανταχοῦ ῥᾳδίως ὑπ᾽ αὐτῶν ἀναρριπιζόμενος.[clv]

10

| **16r** (ΩΡΙΓΕΝΟΥΣ) *Οὗ τὸ πτύον ἐν τῇ χειρὶ αὐτοῦ.*[184] Πτύον ἐστὶ διάκρισις ἀγαθῶν ἀπὸ κακῶν· πῶς δέ ἐστιν ἐν *χειρί*, ζήτει.

Πτύον δὲ διάκρισις ἀγαθῶν ἀπὸ κακῶν, πῶς δέ ἐστιν ἐν χειρί, ζήτει.[clvi]

11

(ΤΟΥ ΑΥΤΟΥ) *Καὶ συνάξει τὸν σῖτον.*[185] Σῖτος ἐστὶ δικαίων ψυχαί, ἀποθῆκαι δὲ τούτων οἱ οὐράνιοι τόποι. Τὸ δὲ *ἄχυρον* βασανίσεις.

σῖτος δὲ τῶν δικαίων αἱ ψυχαί, ἀποθῆκαι δὲ τούτων οἱ οὐράνιοι τόποι, τὸ δὲ *ἄχυρον* βασανίσεις.[clvii]

11a

16r (ΑΝΕΠ)[clviii] *ἐγὼ χρείαν ἔχω ὑπὸ σοῦ.*[186] Ὡς ἄνθρωπος τελῶν *πᾶσαν δικαιοσύνην*[187] βαπτίζεται ὑπὸ Ἰωάννου *ὁ Ἰησοῦς*,[188] ἵνα τε μαρτυρηθῇ ὑπὸ Ἰωάννου καὶ γνω | **16v** ρισθῇ τῆς Ἁγίας Τριάδος ἡ οὐσία ἐν τρισὶν ὑποστάσεσιν ἀμερίστως[clix] βαπτιζομένου. Τί οὖν ὁ Ἰωάννης ἐπιγνοὺς τὴν τοῦ Χριστοῦ δύναμιν; *Ἐγὼ χρείαν ἔχω*, φησί, *ὑπὸ σοῦ βαπτισθῆναι· καὶ σὺ ἔρχῃ πρός με;*[189] Πρὸς γὰρ τοῖς ἄλλοις κατεπλάγη καὶ τὸ βάπτισμα Ἰησοῦ ὁ Ἰωάννης χρήζων *βαπτισθῆναι ὑπὸ* τοῦ ἀμνοῦ τοῦ Θεοῦ τοῦ αἴροντος

184 Matt. 3:12; Luke, 3:16.
185 Matt. 3:12; cf. Luke, 3:16.
186 Matt. 3:14.
187 Matt. 3:15.
188 Matt. 3:16.
189 Matt. 3:14.

τὴν ἁμαρτίαν τοῦ κόσμου.[190] Ὁ δὲ Ἰησοῦς, *ἄφες ἄρτι*[191] φησὶ τῷ Ἰωάννῃ. Τοῦτο δὲ λέγει κωλύων τὸ μέγεθος τῆς αὐτοῦ θεότητος ἐκκαλύπτεσθαι. *Οὕτω* γὰρ *πρέπον ἐστί.* Τουτέστιν, ἀκόλουθον ὡς ἄνθρωπον εἰς πάντα ὑποταγῆναι καὶ *ὑπὸ σοῦ βαπτισθῆναι* καὶ *πᾶσαν* τὴν κατὰ νόμον *πληρῶσαι δικαιοσύνην.* Ἤτοι *πᾶσαν δικαιοσύνην* τὴν τελείωσιν τοῦ ἡμετέρου βαπτίσματός[clx] φησι. Ἦλθε γὰρ ἐπὶ τὸ βάπτισμα ἵνα πληρωθῇ πᾶσα δικαιοσύνη. Τὸ γὰρ *ἡμῖν*, ἀντὶ τοῦ ἐμοὶ καὶ σοί φησι. Ταῦτα ἀκούσας ὁ Ἰωάννης εὐθέως ὑπήκουσεν.

Τὸ *βάπτισμα Ἰωάννου μετανοίας*[192] ἦν καὶ ὁδὸς πρὸς τὸ τοῦ Χριστοῦ τέλειον βάπτισμα, οὐ μὴν *ἄφεσιν ἁμαρτιῶν*[193] εἶχεν. ἐλθόντος δὲ τοῦ Χριστοῦ πρὸς τὸ τοῦ Ἰωάννου βάπτισμα ἐταράσσοντο πολλοί, νομίζοντες αὐτὸν μετανοίας ἕνεκεν βαπτίζεσθαι. καὶ τούτου χάριν ὁ πρόδρομος ἐκώλυεν αὐτὸν βαπτίζεσθαι ὑπ᾽ αὐτοῦ, καὶ διὰ τοῦτό φησιν· *ἐγὼ* τῆς τοιαύτης καθάρσεως τυγχάνω δεόμενος, ἀλλ᾽ οὐχὶ *σύ.* ὁ γὰρ *ἀμνὸς τοῦ θεοῦ ὁ τὴν ἁμαρτίαν αἴρων κόσμου*[194] πῶς ἂν εἴη τῆς τοιαύτης καθάρσεως δεόμενος;[clxi]

Ὁ κατὰ νόμον τέλειος τὸ Ἰωάννου βάπτισμα βαπτιζόμενος εἰς τὸ τοῦ νόμου τέλος ἔφθασεν. διὸ καὶ ὁ Χριστὸς ὡς τέλειος ἐν νόμῳ ἐβαπτίσθη τὸ Ἰωάννου βάπτισμα. ὅθεν ἔλεγεν· *οὕτως γὰρ πρέπον ἐστὶν ἡμῖν πληρῶσαι πᾶσαν δικαιοσύνην.*[195][clxii]

Εἰ τοίνυν τὸ τῷ Θεῷ πείθεσθαι δικαιοσύνη, ὁ δὲ Θεὸς ἔπεμψε τὸν Ἰωάννην, ὥστε βαπτισθῆναι τὸν λαόν, μετὰ τῶν ἄλλων ἁπάντων τῶν νομικῶν καὶ τοῦτο ἐπλήρωσεν ὁ Χριστός. ἀλλὰ καὶ διὰ τὸ ἁγιάσαι τὰ ὕδατα ἡμῖν ἐβαπτίσθη. ἐν *εἴδει περιστερᾶς τὸ πνεῦμα* κάτεισιν, ἐπειδήπερ ὅπου καταλλαγὴ Θεοῦ, περιστερά, ὡς ἐπὶ τῆς κιβωτοῦ Νῶε. καὶ νῦν ἐν εἴδει περιστερᾶς, *τὸ πνεῦμα* ἔρχεται, τὸν ἔλεον τοῦ θεοῦ καταγγέλλον τῇ οἰκουμένῃ, ἅμα δὲ καὶ δηλοῦν ὅτι τὸν πνευματικὸν ἄνδρα ἀπόνηρον εἶναι χρὴ καὶ πρᾶον, ἁπλοῦν τε καὶ ἄδολον.[clxiii]

12

16v (ΩΡΙΓΕΝΟΥΣ) *Ἄφες ἄρτι.*[196] Καλῶς καὶ τὸ *ἄρτι* προσέθηκεν.

Now was suitably spoken.[clxiv]

Οὐ γὰρ διηνεκῶς ταῦτα ἔσται, φησί. Ἔσται γὰρ καιρὸς καθ᾽ ὃν δυνατὸν διὰ πάντων φανῆναί μου τὴν πρὸς σὲ ὑπεροχήν. Εἶτα καὶ δείκνυσι πῶς *πρέπον*, ὅτι τὸν νόμον

190 John, 1:29.
191 Matt. 3:15.
192 Cf. Mark, 1:4-6; Acts, 13:24; 19:3-4.
193 Cf. Mark, 1:4-6.
194 John, 1:29.
195 Matt. 3:15.
196 Matt. 3:15.

πληροῦμεν ἅπαντα. Ἐπεὶ οὖν πάσας τὰς ἄλλας ἐντολὰς ἠνύσαμεν, φησί, τοῦτο δὲ ὑπολέλειπται μόνον, δεῖ προσθεῖναι καὶ τοῦτο. Καὶ γὰρ ἦλθον λῦσαι τὴν ἀρὰν τὴν ἐπὶ τῇ παραβάσει τοῦ νόμου κειμένην.

οὕτω γὰρ πρέπον ἐστὶν ἡμῖν.[197] Τὸ *ἡμῖν*, ἀντὶ τοῦ ἐμοὶ καὶ σοί. Τουτέστι, παραχώρει τῇ σοφίᾳ τῆς οἰκονομίας καὶ ὑπούργει μόνον, τὸ ἀπρόσιτον τῆς ἐμῆς θεότητος | **17r** μὴ πτοούμενος, ἐπειδὴ προσιτός σοι γέγονα διὰ σαρκώσεως.

> [Καλῶς καὶ τὸ *ἄρτι* προσέθηκεν. οὐ γὰρ διηνεκῶς ταῦτα ἔσται φησίν. ἔσται γὰρ καιρὸς καθ᾽ ὃν δυνατὸν διὰ πάντων φανῆναί μου τὴν πρὸς σὲ ὑπεροχήν. εἶτα καὶ δείκνυσι πῶς *πρέπον*, ὅτι τὸν νόμον πληροῦμεν ἅπαντα. ἐπεὶ οὖν πάσας τὰς ἄλλας ἐντολὰς ἠνύσαμεν, φησί, τοῦτο δὲ ὑπολέλειπται μόνον, δεῖ προσθεῖναι καὶ τοῦτο. καὶ γὰρ ἦλθον λῦσαι τὴν ἀρὰν τὴν ἐπὶ τῇ παραβάσει τοῦ νόμου κειμένην.] *οὕτω γὰρ πρέπον ἐστὶν ἡμῖν*[198] (τὸ *ἡμῖν*, ἀντὶ τοῦ ἐμοὶ καὶ σοί). τουτέστι, παραχώρει τῇ σοφίᾳ τῆς οἰκονομίας καὶ ὑπούργει μόνον τὸ ἀπρόσιτον τῆς ἐμῆς θεότητος μὴ πτοούμενος, ἐπειδὴ προσιτός σοι γέγονα διὰ σαρκώσεως.[clxv]

> Καὶ οὐχ ἁπλῶς εἶπεν, *Ἄφες*. ἀλλὰ τὸ *ἄρτι*, προσέθηκεν. Οὐ γὰρ διηνεκῶς ταῦτα ἔσται, φησίν, ἀλλ᾽ ὄψει με ἐν τούτοις οἷς ἐπιθυμεῖς· ἄρτι μέντοι ὑπόμεινον τοῦτο. Εἶτα καὶ δείκνυσι πῶς τοῦτο πρέπον. Πῶς οὖν πρέπον ἐστίν; Ὅτι τὸν νόμον πληροῦμεν ἅπαντα· ὅπερ οὖν δηλῶν ἔλεγε, *Πᾶσαν δικαιοσύνην*. Δικαιοσύνη γάρ ἐστιν ἡ τῶν ἐντολῶν ἐκπλήρωσις. Ἐπεὶ οὖν πάσας τὰς ἄλλας ἐντολὰς ἠνύσαμεν, φησί, τοῦτο δὲ ὑπολέλειπται μόνον, δεῖ προστεθῆναι καὶ τοῦτο. Καὶ γὰρ ἦλθον λῦσαι τὴν ἀρὰν τὴν ἐπὶ τῇ παραβάσει τοῦ νόμου κειμένην.[clxvi]

Πληρῶσαι πᾶσαν δικαιοσύνην.[199] Τί ἐστὶ *πᾶσαν δικαιοσύνην*; Ἔμελλε παύειν τὴν νομικὴν λατρείαν, οὐ καταλύων αὐτὴν οὐδὲ τἀναντία νομοθετῶν, ἀλλ᾽ ἐπικαλύπτων διὰ τῆς τῶν εὐαγγελικῶν ἐνταλμάτων λαμπρότητος. Τοῦ γὰρ νόμου λέγοντος *οὐ φονεύσεις*,[200] αὐτὸς μηδὲ ὀργισθῆναι προσέταττεν. Ὥστε τῆς ὀργῆς προαναιρουμένης ἐξ ἧς ὁ φόνος, περιττὸν εἶναι τὸν νόμον λοιπὸν τὸν τὸν φόνον ἐπέχοντα. Οὕτω καὶ τὸ *οὐ μοιχεύσεις*[201] τῷ κωλύματι τοῦ μετ᾽ ἐπιθυμίας ἐμβλέψαι προανακόπτεται.[clxvii] Ἐπεὶ οὖν ἔμελλε διὰ τῆς τελειοτέρας καὶ εὐαγγελικῆς νομοθεσίας καταπαύειν τὸν νόμον, ἵνα μή τις εἴπῃ ὅτι ὡς ἀδυνατῶν αὐτὸν πληρῶσαι διὰ τοῦτο κατέπαυσε, πληροῖ πάντα τὰ αὐτοῦ δικαιώματα καὶ περιτομὴν διατεταγμένην ἐν αὐτῷ καταδέχεται, καὶ προσάγει *ζεῦγος τρυγόνων ἢ δύο νεοσσοὺς περιστερῶν*,[202] καὶ τὰ ἄλλα νόμιμα διεξέρχεται.

197 Matt. 3:15.
198 Matt. 3:15.
199 Matt. 3:15.
200 Ex. 20:15; Deut. 5:18.
201 Ex. 20:13; Deut. 5:17; Matt. 5:27; cf. 19:18.
202 Luke, 2:24, quoting Lev. 5:11.

Καὶ *βαπτισθεὶς ὁ Ἰησοῦς* μέσος ἔστη *τοῦ ὕδατος*.[203] *Ὁ στεγάζων ἐν ὕδασι τὰ ὑπερῷα αὐτοῦ*[204] καὶ τρέμουσαν καὶ ἀναδυομένην τὴν δεξιὰν ἐφ᾽ ἑαυτὸν ἕλκει τοῦ βαπτιστοῦ τῷ εἰπεῖν *ἄφες ἄρτι*. Θάρσος πρὸς τὴν διακονίαν ἐντιθεὶς καὶ τὴν κεφαλὴν ἐγκρύπτει τῷ ῥείθρῳ[clxviii] (μικροῦ δὲ κἀγὼ τρέμειν ἄρχομαι τὸ τῆς συγκαταβάσεως ἄπειρον ἐννοῶν) καὶ ἐπικλάζεται καὶ κάτω γίνεται ὁ στήσας *τὸ ὕδωρ* τὸ *ὑπεράνω*[205] | **17v** *τῶν οὐρανῶν*[206] καὶ ἐπέχων προστάγματι[207] μόνῳ τὸ κατωφερὲς[clxix] καὶ φύσει ῥευστόν.[clxx] Ζητεῖται παρὰ πολλοῖς, τί ποτε ἄρα ἦν *τὸ βάπτισμα*[208] ὅπερ ὁ Κύριος ἐβαπτίσθη; Τί οὖν ἐστιν ὁ Κύριος ἡμῶν καὶ Σωτὴρ Ἰησοῦς Χριστός, ὑπὲρ τῆς ἁπάντων σωτηρίας γενόμενος ἄνθρωπος καὶ δὴ βίου τινὸς παραδόξου μέλλων ἑαυτὸν ἀποφαίνειν ἀρχήν, καθὸ καὶ *Ἀδὰμ*[209] καλεῖται, ὥστε δι᾽ αὐτοῦ καὶ τῶν λοιπῶν ἀναστάντων ἀνθρώπων ἀρχὴν αὐτὸν τῆς ἀϊδίου γενέσθαι ζωῆς ἐκείνοις; Ὃν τρόπον ταύτης δὴ τῆς προσκαίρου καὶ θνητῆς ζωῆς ἀρχηγὸν τὸν Ἀδὰμ γενέσθαι συνέβη, ἅπαντα τὰ καθ᾽ ἡμᾶς ἐπ᾽ αὐτοῦ προετύπωσεν. Ὥσπερ γὰρ *ἀπέθανέ* τε *καὶ ἀνέστη*,[210] ἐπειδὴ ἐμέλλομεν καὶ ἡμεῖς, οὕτως, ἐπειδὴ τυπικῶς διὰ τοῦ βαπτίσματος ἀπὸ τοῦ παρόντος βίου μετοικιζόμενοι εἰς τὴν μέλλουσαν καθίστασθαι ζωὴν ἀναγκαίως ἐμέλλομεν, ἐφρόντισε τοῦτο πρότερον ἐπ᾽ αὐτοῦ πληρωθῆναι. Καὶ τοῦτο δὴ τὸ τῆς *υἱοθεσίας*[211] βάπτισμα οἰκονομικῶς τὸ δι᾽ *ὕδατος καὶ πνεύματος*[212] πρῶτος ἀναδεξάμενος, μέγα μὲν καὶ τίμιον ἀληθῶς ἔδειξε *τὸ βάπτισμα*[213] ἐφ᾽ ἑαυτοῦ πρῶτος καταδεξάμενος. Ἐπολιτεύσατο δὲ καὶ αὐτὸς τὴν ἔξω τοῦ νόμου τῆς χάριτος πολιτείαν, ἣν καὶ ἡμᾶς πολιτεύεσθαι ἔδει. Πρέπον οὖν ἦν τὸν Κύριον ταπεινοφρονοῦντα ὡς ἄνθρωπον ἕνα ἐκ τοῦ λαοῦ, τῷ προφήτῃ καὶ βαπτιστῇ ὑποταγῆναι εἰς *τὸ βάπτισμα* ἵνα ἁγιάσῃ τὰ ὕδατα καὶ τὴν *διὰ λουτροῦ* ἡμῖν παλιγγενεσίαν[214] καὶ *υἱοθεσίαν*[215] | **18r** καὶ ἁμαρτημάτων *ἄφεσιν*,[216] καὶ ὅσα ἄλλα ἐκ τοῦ βαπτίσματος ἡμῖν ἀγαθὰ ἐδωρήσατο ὡς ἐν ἑαυτῷ προτυπώσῃ, αὐτὸς μηδενὸς τούτων ἐπιδεόμενος ὡς Θεὸς καὶ *τὴν ἁμαρτίαν αἴρων τοῦ κόσμου*.[217] Διὰ τοῦτο ἐβαπτίσθη ὁ Χριστὸς παρὰ Ἰωάννου. Οὐχ ὡς ἁμαρτίας ἔνοχος,

203 Matt. 3:16: βαπτισθεὶς δὲ ὁ Ἰησοῦς εὐθὺς ἀνέβη ἀπὸ τοῦ ὕδατος.
204 Psalm 103:3.
205 Cod. ὑπὲρ ἄνω.
206 Psalm 48:4.
207 Cf. Psalm 148:4-6.
208 Cf. Matt. 3:7; 21:25; Mark, 1:4; 11:30; Luke, 3:3; 7:29; 20:4; Acts, 13:24; 18:25; 19:3-4.
209 1 Cor. 15:45.
210 1 Thess. 4:12.
211 Cf. Rom. 8:15&23; Gal. 4:5; Eph. 1:5.
212 John, 3:5.
213 Cf. Matt. 3:7; 21:25; Mark, 1:4; 11:30; Luke, 3:3; 7:29; 20:4; Acts, 13:24; 18:25; 19:3-4.
214 Tit. 3:5.
215 Cf. Rom. 8:15&23; Gal. 4:5; Eph. 1:5.
216 Cf. Mark, 1:4; Luke, 3:3; 24:47; Acts, 2:38; 5:31; 10:43; 10:38; 24:18; Col. 1:14.
217 John, 1:29.

ἀλλ᾽ ἵνα ὡς ἄνθρωπος πληρώσῃ *πᾶσαν δικαιοσύνην*.[218] Δεύτερον, ἵνα μαρτυρήσῃ τῷ Ἰωάννῃ ὅτι *παρὰ Θεοῦ*[219] ἀπέσταλτο πρὸς τὸ βαπτίζειν. Τρίτον, ἵνα διὰ τῆς καθόδου τοῦ Ἁγίου Πνεύματος ἁγιάσῃ τὰ τοῦ Ἰορδάνου ὕδατα καὶ πάντες οἱ βαπτιζόμενοι ἐν αὐτῷ ἁγιασθῶσιν. Ἀνοίγονται δὲ *οἱ οὐρανοὶ* καὶ *τὸ Πνεῦμα* κάτεισι βαπτισθέντος αὐτοῦ, καὶ *φωνὴ* ἔρχεται,[220] ἵνα μὴ μείζονα αὐτοῦ τὸν Ἰωάννην ὑπολαμβάνῃ τις.[clxxi] Οὐ κρείσσων δὲ πάντως ὁ βαπτίζων τοῦ βαπτιζομένου. Οὐδὲ γὰρ Ἀνανίας Παύλου.[clxxii]

Ἀνέβη εὐθὺς ἀπὸ τοῦ ὕδατος.[221] Αὐτὸς ὁ Ἰησοῦς βαπτισθεὶς *ἀνέβη*. Οὐ μὴν ὥς φασι Μανιχαῖοι ὁ μὲν βαπτισθεὶς κάτω ἔμεινε, τὸ δὲ ὕδωρ ἄλλον ἐν δοκήσει τοῦ ὄντος ἀντέδωκε. Διὸ καὶ τὸ *εὐθὺς* πρόσκειται καὶ τὸ *Ἰησοῦς*. Ἀνοίγονται δὲ *οἱ οὐρανοί*, οὓς ὁ Ἀδὰμ ἔκλεισεν ἑαυτῷ τε καὶ τοῖς μετ᾽ αὐτόν. Αὕτη δὲ σχίσις καὶ ἄνοιξις οὐρανῶν ἡ περὶ τῆς Τριάδος καὶ τῶν οὐρανίων ἐγγινομένη γνῶσις καὶ φανέρωσις.

Καὶ εἶδε τὸ Πνεῦμα τοῦ Θεοῦ καταβαῖνον.[222] Ἐπὶ τὸν Ἰησοῦν ἦλθε τὸ Πνεῦμα, ἕλκον ἐπ᾽ αὐτὸν τὴν μαρτυρίαν. Δέχεται δὲ δι᾽ οἰκονομίαν τὸ Πνεῦμα ὁ Ἰησοῦς, ἵνα δείξῃ ὅτι καὶ ἐπὶ πάντας τοὺς πιστοὺς μέλλει ἐπιφοιτᾶν βαπτιζομένους. *Ὡσ‹ε›ὶ*[223] περιστερὰ δὲ | **18v** δείκνυται διὰ τὸ φιλόστοργον καὶ ἀκέραιον. Ὥσπερ γὰρ ἡ περιστερὰ οὐκ ἀφίσταται τῶν συνήθων κἂν ἀδικῶσι τινὲς τὰ ἔγγονα αὐτῆς ἀποσπῶντες, οὕτω καὶ ὁ Θεός, καὶ ἀθετούμενος παρ᾽ ἡμῶν οὐκ ἀφίσταται διὰ τὴν οἰκείαν ἀγαθότητα καὶ τὸ περὶ ἡμᾶς φιλόστοργον τοῦ εὐεργετεῖν ἡμᾶς.

> Διὰ τοῦτο περιστερᾷ ὡμοιώθη τὸ πνεῦμα τὸ ἅγιον, διὰ τὸ φιλόστοργον, ὃ ἔχει περὶ ἡμᾶς, ὅτι ἀθετούμενος παρὰ τῶν ἀνθρώπων ὁ θεὸς οὐδὲν ἧττον πάλιν διὰ τὴν οἰκείαν ἀγαθότητα πλησιάζει τοῖς ἀνθρώποις. οὕτω γὰρ καὶ ἡ περιστερὰ οὐκ ἀφίσταται τῶν συνήθων, κἂν ἀδικῶσιν αὐτὴν ἐκεῖνοι τὰ ἔκγονα αὐτῆς ἀποσπῶντες ἐξ αὐτῆς.[clxxiii]

Ἡ δὲ *φωνὴ ἐκ τῶν οὐρανῶν*[224] ὁμολογεῖ τὸν δεικνύμενον υἱὸν εἶναι τοῦ λέγοντος. Καὶ φησί· *οὗτός ἐστιν ὁ υἱός μου*, ὁ φαινόμενος, ὡς εἷς ὢν μετὰ τῆς σαρκός, οὐχ ὁ κρυπτόμενος. Δεικνὺς δὲ τὸ ὁμοούσιον τὸ πρὸς τὸν πατέρα τῷ *ἐστὶ* προσρήματι κέχρηται.

Ὡσεὶ περιστεράν.[225] Κατακλυσμοῦ λύσιν καὶ παλιγγενεσίαν τοῦ κάτω κόσμου φαίνεται ἡ περιστερὰ δηλοῦσα ὡς ἡ ποτέ.[226] Τῶν δευτέρων γὰρ εἰκόνα φέρει τὰ πρῶτα.

---

218 Matt. 3:15.
219 John, 1:6.
220 Matt. 3:16-17; Mark, 1:11; Luke, 3:21-22.
221 Matt. 3:17: εὐθὺς ἀνέβη ἀπὸ τοῦ ὕδατος.
222 Matt. 3:16.
223 Cod. ὡσὶ.
224 Matt. 3:17; cf. Mark, 1:10; Luke, 3:22.
225 Matt. 3:16; cf. Mark, 1:10; Luke, 3:22; John, 1:32.
226 Cf. Gen. 8:8-12.

Κατακλυσμοῦ λύσιν καὶ παλιγγενεσίαν τοῦ κάτω κόσμου φαίνεται ἡ περιστερὰ δηλοῦσα, ὡς ἡ ποτέ. τῶν δευτέρων γὰρ εἰκόνα φέρει τὰ πρῶτα.[clxxiv]

13

(ΩΡΙΓΕΝΟΥΣ) Εἷς[clxxv] τῆς Τριάδος ἐβαπτίσθη· εἷς ἐν εἴδει[227] περιστερᾶς ὤφθη· εἷς ἄνωθεν ἐπεφώνει. Τρεῖς οὖν ὑποστάσεις, μία δὲ οὐσία τῶν τριῶν.

Εἷς τῆς Τριάδος ἐβαπτίσθη, εἷς ἐν *εἴδει* περιστερᾶς ὤφθη, εἷς ἄνωθεν ἐπεφώνει. τρεῖς οὖν ὑποστάσεις, μία δὲ οὐσία τῶν τριῶν.[clxxvi]

Καὶ ἰδοὺ φωνὴ ἐκ τῶν οὐρανῶν.[228] Διὰ τῆς τοῦ Πατρὸς μαρτυρίας καὶ τῆς τοῦ Πνεύματος καθόδου, δείκνυνται τῆς Ἁγίας Τριάδος αἱ ὑποστάσεις. Ἐμαρτύρησε γὰρ ἄνωθεν ὁ Πατὴρ ὅτι ὁ μὲν βαπτιζόμενος Θεὸς ἦν, ὁ δὲ βαπτίζων ἄνθρωπος. Τοῦτο δέ, ἵνα μή τις νομίσῃ ὅτι Ἰωάννης μείζων ἦν τοῦ Χριστοῦ ὡς βαπτίζων αὐτόν. Καὶ ἦν ὁ μὲν μαρτυρῶν, ὁ Πατήρ· ὁ δὲ Υἱός, ὁ μαρτυρούμενος· τὸ δὲ Πνεῦμα τὸ Ἅγιον, τὸ ὑποδεικνῦον τὸν μαρτυρούμενον.

Διὰ τῆς τοῦ πατρὸς μαρτυρίας καὶ τῆς τοῦ πνεύματος καθόδου δείκνυνται τῆς ἁγίας τριάδος αἱ ὑποστάσεις. ἐμαρτύρησε γὰρ ἄνωθεν ὁ πατήρ, ὅτι ὁ μὲν βαπτιζόμενος θεὸς ἦν, ὁ δὲ βαπτίζων ἄνθρωπος. τοῦτο δέ, ἵνα μή τις ὑποπτεύσῃ, ὅτι Ἰωάννης μείζων ἦν τοῦ Χριστοῦ ὡς βαπτίζων αὐτόν. καὶ ἦν ὁ μὲν μαρτυρῶν ὁ πατήρ, ὁ δὲ υἱὸς ὁ μαρτυρούμενος, τὸ δὲ πνεῦμα τὸ ἅγιον τὸ ὑποδεικνύον τὸν μαρτυρούμενον.[clxxvii]

Ἐν τῷ Ἰορδάνῃ ποταμῷ[229] πεφανέρωται τοῖς ἀνθρώποις ἡ τριάς. εἰ γὰρ ὁ πατὴρ ἐμαρτύρησε καὶ ὁ υἱὸς ἦν ὁ μαρτυρούμενος καὶ ὑποδεικνύον τὸ πνεῦμα τὸ ἅγιον, πῶς οὐ τριὰς ἡ θεότης;[clxxviii]

The mystery of the Trinity is manifested in the baptism. The Lord is baptised, the Spirit descends in the form of a dove, the voice of the Father testifying to the Son is heard.[clxxix]

Τότε ἀνήχθη ὁ Ἰησοῦς.[230] Ἤγετο *ὑπὸ τοῦ Πνεύματος* τοῦ Ἁγίου ὑποφωνοῦντος καὶ παρορμῶντος αὐτὸν τὴν τοῦ διαβόλου | **19r** πεῖραν ὑπενεγκεῖν καὶ καθελεῖν ἤδη τὴν μεγαλαυχίαν αὐτοῦ.

Τὸ πνεῦμα τὸ ἅγιον ὑποφωνοῦν ἀνήγαγεν αὐτὸν *εἰς τὴν ἔρημον*, παρορμῶν αὐτὸν ἤδη καθελεῖν τοῦ διαβόλου τὴν μεγαλαυχίαν.[clxxx]

---

227 Cf. Matt. 3:16; Mark, 1:10; Luke, 3:22; John, 1:32.
228 Matt. 3:17; cf. Mark, 1:11. Luke, 3:22.
229 Cf. Matt. 3:6; Mark, 1:5.
230 Matt. 4:1. Τότε ὁ Ἰησοῦς ἀνήχθη. Cf. Mark, 1:12.

Τί φής;[clxxxi] Ἄκων ἤγετο *ὑπὸ τοῦ Πνεύματος*; Καὶ ἡμεῖς μὲν αὐτεξουσίῳ βουλήματι τὴν ἑαυτῶν διοικοῦμεν ζωὴν καὶ αὐθαιρέτῳ πρὸς τοὺς τῆς ἀρετῆς ἐρχόμεθα πόνους καὶ τὴν ὑπὲρ αὐτῶν ὑπομένομεν πεῖραν. Αὐτὸς δὲ ἀβουλήτως εἵλκετο ἐπὶ τοῦτο; Καὶ πῶς οὐκ ἄτοπον τὸ τοιοῦτον καὶ λογίσασθαι μόνον; Ἀλλὰ τὸ *ἀνήχθη ὑπὸ τοῦ Πνεύματος* ταύτην ἔχει τὴν ἔννοιαν· ὥσπερ ἀνηγμένην τινὰ καὶ πνευματικὴν ἦλθε διαγωγήν, ἵνα καὶ χώραν δῷ τῷ πειράζοντι, καὶ τοῦτο δὲ τοῖς τῆς ἑκουσίου κενώσεως αὐτοῦ μέτροις ἁρμόδιον.

He is not led unwillingly or as a captive, but with the intent to wage a battle.[clxxxii]

Ὡς γὰρ εἵλετο ἀτρέπτως ἄνθρωπος γενέσθαι, οὕτω πάντα ὑπὲρ ἡμῶν τὰ ἀνθρώπινα διεξέρχεται, δεικνὺς ὡς προσήκει ἡμᾶς μετὰ τὸ βάπτισμα, τὴν τῆς υἱοθεσίας χάριν[231] πλουτήσαντας,[232] χωρεῖν πρὸς ἀνηγμένην ζωὴν καὶ ὑπὸ τοῦ Πνεύματος ἄγεσθαι καὶ μὴ ὑπὸ τοῦ βουλήματος τῆς σαρκός, καθὸ δὴ καὶ Παῦλος Ῥωμαίοις ἐπιστέλλων ἔλεγεν· *ὅσοι γὰρ Πνεύματι Θεοῦ ἄγονται, οὗτοί εἰσιν υἱοὶ Θεοῦ.*[233] Ὁ γὰρ ὁμοούσιον ἔχων τὸ Πνεῦμα τὸ Ἅγιον, καθὸ Θεὸς ἦν καὶ ὁμοούσιος τῷ Πατρί, πῶς ἔμελλε πνευματικῆς δεῖσθαι καὶ ἀνηγμένης ζωῆς; Οἱ μὲν φασὶ ὅτι ὑπὸ τοῦ διαβόλου ἤγετο κατὰ συγχώρησιν. Ἄλλοι δέ, ὅτι τὸ Πνεῦμα προετρέπετο αὐτὸν ἐπὶ τὸν κατὰ τοῦ διαβόλου ἀγῶνα. Ἤ, ὡς ἄλλοι, ὑπὸ τῆς ἰδίας θεότητος ἤτοι ἐν δυνάμει Πνεύματος ἀνέβη ἐπὶ τὴν ἔρημον ἢ πνευματικῶς ἔ‹στ›η[234] ἐν τῇ κατὰ τὴν ἔρημον διαγωγῇ μηδεμίαν[235] τῆς σαρκὸς ποιούμενος | **19v** πρόνοιαν, ἵνα καὶ χώραν δῷ τῷ πειράζοντι. Τοῦτο δὲ ἐποίησεν οἰκονομικῶς.

Οὐ γὰρ ἄκων εἵλκετο, ἀλλὰ πρὸς ἡμῶν ὑποτύπωσιν, ἵνα, μετὰ τὸ βάπτισμα, μηκέτι[236] ἑαυτοὺς ἄγωμεν, ἀλλ᾽ ἐκδῶμεν τοῖς νόμοις τοῦ Πνεύματος.

(Σευήρου) Οὐκ ἄκων εἵλκετο. Ταῦτα γὰρ πρὸς ἡμῶν ὑποτύπωσιν γέγονεν, ἵνα μετὰ τὸ βάπτισμα, μηκέτι αὐτοὺς ἄγωμεν, ἀλλ᾽ ἐκδῶμεν ἑαυτοὺς τοῖς νόμοις τοῦ Πνεύματος, καὶ ἀπ᾽ αὐτοῦ ἀγόμεθα ἐπὶ πνευματικὴν ζωὴν καὶ κατὰ τῶν τοῦ διαβόλου ἀγώνων.[clxxxiii]

14

(ΩΡΙΓΕΝΟΥΣ)[clxxxiv] *καὶ νηστεύσας ἡμέρας μ̄.*[237] Ὁ τῶν *τεσσαράκοντα* ἡμερῶν ἀριθμός, ἐκ τεσσάρων δεκάδων συγκείμενος, συγγενής ἐστι καὶ ταῖς τέσσαρσι μονάσι,

231 Cf. Eph. 1:5-6.
232 Cf. 1 Cor. 4:8; 2 Cor. 8:9.
233 Rom. 8:14.
234 Cod. ἔξη.
235 Cod. μὴ δὲ μίαν.
236 Cod. μὴ κέτι.
237 Matt. 4:2.

τάχα διὰ τὸ ἐκ τεσσάρων στοιχείων συνεστάναι τὸν αἰσθητὸν κόσμον ἢ καὶ διὰ τὸ ἐν τεσσαράκοντα ἡμέραις ἐν τῇ νηδύι μορφοῦσθαι τὸν ἄνθρωπον.

> Ὁ τῶν *τεσσαράκοντα* ἡμερῶν ἀριθμὸς ἐκ τεσσάρων δεκάδων συγκείμενος συγγενής ἐστι καὶ ταῖς τέσσαρσι μονάσι, τάχα διὰ τὸ ἐκ τεσσάρων στοιχείων συνεστάναι τὸν αἰσθητὸν κόσμον ἢ καὶ διὰ τὸ ἐν τεσσαράκοντα ἡμέραις ἐν τῇ νηδύι μορφοῦσθαι τὸν ἄνθρωπον.[clxxxv]

Καὶ ἵνα μὴ περαιτέρω νηστεύσας δῷ τινι ἔννοιαν ὅτι οὐκ ἀνέλαβε σάρκα κατὰ τὸ ἀληθές, *ὕστερον ἐπείνασεν.*[238] Ὁ δὲ *κατὰ πάντα* κοινωνήσας ἡμῖν *χωρὶς ἁμαρτίας*[239] καὶ συμμετασχὼν ἡμῖν τῶν αὐτῶν παθημάτων,[240]

> καὶ ἵνα μὴ περαιτέρω νηστεύσας δῷ τινι ἔννοιαν ὅτι οὐκ ἀνέλαβε σάρκα κατὰ τὸ ἀληθές, πεινᾷ *ὕστερον* κατὰ πάντα κοινωνήσας ἡμῖν πλὴν *ἁμαρτίας*[241] καὶ συμμετασχὼν ἡμῖν τῷ αὐτῷ παθήματι.[clxxxvi]

τὴν πεῖναν οὐκ ἔκρινεν ἁμαρτίαν, οὐδὲ ἀπώσατο τῆς ἑαυτοῦ πείρας τὸ κατ' αὐτὴν πάθος, ἀλλ' ἐδέξατο τὴν ὀρεκτικὴν τῆς φύσεως ὁρμὴν τὴν ἐπὶ τῇ τροφῇ γενομένην. Ἀπόσιτος γὰρ τεσσαράκοντα ἡμέρας διαμείνας, *ὕστερον ἐπείνασεν.* Ἔδωκε γὰρ ὅτε ἐβούλετο τῇ φύσει καιρὸν τὰ ἑαυτῆς ἐνεργῆσαι.

> Ὁ κατὰ πάντα κοινωνήσας ἡμῖν χωρὶς ἁμαρτίας, καὶ συμμετασχὼν ἡμῖν τῶν αὐτῶν παθημάτων, τὴν πεῖναν οὐκ ἔκρινεν ἁμαρτίαν, οὐδὲ ἀπώσατο τῆς ἑαυτοῦ πείρας τὸ κατ' αὐτὴν πάθος, ἀλλ' ἐδέξατο τὴν ὀρεκτικὴν ὁρμὴν τῆς φύσεως τὴν ἐπὶ τῇ τροφῇ γινομένην. Ἀπόσιτος γὰρ τεσσαράκοντα ἡμερῶν διαμείνας, ὕστερον ἐπείνασεν· ἔδωκε γὰρ ὅτε ἐβούλετο τῇ φύσει καιρὸν τὰ ἑαυτῆς ἐνεργῆσαι.[clxxxvii]

Νηστεύσας τοίνυν ὁ Χριστός,
οὐχ ὑπερέβη τὸ τῶν τεσσαράκοντα ἡμερῶν τῆς νηστείας μῆκος, ὃ ἐνήστευσε Μωσῆς καὶ Ἠλίας,

> Through the number forty, a mystery is being shown to us. Both Moses, on Mount Sinai, and Elias, near Mount Horeb,[242] fasted as many days' as this number.[clxxxviii]

ἵνα δῷ χώραν τῷ πειράζοντι προσβαλεῖν ὡς ἀνθρώπῳ[clxxxix]

> The body is permitted to hunger so that an opportunity might be granted to the devil to tempt him.[cxc]

238 Matt. 4:2.
239 Heb. 4:15.
240 Cf. Gal. 5:24; Phil. 3:10; Heb. 2:9.
241 Heb. 4:15.
242 Cf. Exodus, 24:18; 1 Kings, 19:8.

οὐχ ὑπερέβη δὲ ὁ Χριστὸς τὸ τῶν ἡμερῶν τῆς νηστείας μῆκος, ὃ ἐνήστευσε Μωϋσῆς καὶ Ἠλίας, ἵνα δῷ χώραν τῷ πειράζοντι προσβαλεῖν ὡς ἀνθρώπῳ καὶ πεσεῖν.[cxci]

‹καὶ› ἵνα μὴ περαιτέρω νηστεύσας δόξῃ μὴ ἀνειληφέναι σάρκα κατὰ τὸ ἀληθές. Νη | **20r** στεύει δὲ ὁ Χριστὸς ὑπὲρ ὅλου *τοῦ κόσμου αἴρων αὐτοῦ τὴν ἁμαρτίαν*[243] καὶ ἱλασκόμενος ὑπὲρ αὐτοῦ[244] καὶ τύπον ἡμῖν διδοὺς ‹τοῦ› νηστεύειν, καὶ *τὸ φρόνημα τῆς σαρκὸς*[245] ταῖς οἰκείαις μὴ τρέφειν τροφαῖς, τῷ δὲ Πνεύματι τὴν ψυχήν. Ἀκούσας τοίνυν ὁ διάβολος τῆς λεγούσης περὶ Ἰησοῦ φωνῆς, *οὗτος ἐστὶν ὁ υἱός μου ὁ ἀγαπητὸς ἐν ᾧ εὐδόκησα,*[246] ἀπιστῶν τῷ εἰπόντι, διστακτικὰς λέγει φωνάς. Φησὶ γάρ· *εἰ υἱὸς εἶ τοῦ Θεοῦ, εἰπὲ ἵνα οἱ λίθοι οὗτοι ἄρτοι γένωνται.*[247] Ἄλλο δὲ ἐρωτᾷ ἵνα ἄλλο μάθῃ. Ἐπειδὴ γὰρ ἑώρα τὸ μὲν σχῆμα τῆς φύσεως εὐτελές, τὴν δὲ πνευματικὴν μαρτυρίαν ὑπερβάλλουσαν, ἐταράττετο τῇ τῶν ξενιζόντων πείρᾳ, δυοῖν θάτερον λαβεῖν ἐλπίσας, ἢ νίκην κατὰ τοῦ παρόντος ἢ γνῶσιν ἀκριβῆ καὶ ἀναμφίβολον τοῦ νικῶτος. Ὁρῶν γὰρ αὐτὸν πεινῶντα, ἀμφιβόλως εἶχε, πῆ μὲν ὡς διασύρων αὐτόν, πῆ δὲ ὡς θέλων μαθεῖν τὸ ἀπόρρητον.

Εἰ υἱὸς εἶ τοῦ Θεοῦ.[248] Ταῦτα ἔλεγεν οἰηθεὶς ἀπατῆσαι αὐτόν. Ὤετο γὰρ πείσειν ἢ διὰ τὴν κατεπείγουσαν ἀνάγκην ἢ διὰ κενοδοξίαν. Τί οὖν ὁ Σωτήρ, διδάσκων ἐν μηδενὶ πείθεσθαι τῷ ἐχθρῷ κἂν δοκῇ μὴ ἄτοπα ἐπιτάττειν, δι᾽ ἀνεξικακίας αὐτοῦ περιεκράτησεν εἰπών; Ὅτι *οὐκ ἐπ᾽ ἄρτῳ μόνῳ ζήσεται ἄνθρωπος,*[249] καὶ τὰ ἑξῆς. Ὅπερ ἐστὶ δεῖγμα τῆς μελλούσης καταστάσεως, ὅπερ ἤρξατο ἐν Χριστῷ. Μέλλουσι γὰρ καὶ δίχα τροφῆς ζῆν οἱ ἄνθρωποι μετὰ τὴν ἀνάστασιν, ἄφθαρτοι διαμένοντες, διὰ λόγου Θεοῦ τρεφόμενοι.

Ἵνα οἱ λίθοι οὗτοι ἄρτοι γένωνται·[250] Ταῦτα λέγει μέχρι τοῦ νῦν | **20v** τοῖς ὑπὸ τῆς ἰδίας πειραζομένοις ὀρέξεως. Καὶ λέγων, ὡς ἐπὶ τὸ πολὺ πείθει ἐκ λίθων σιτοποιεῖσθαι τοὺς πρὸς αὐτὸν βλέποντας. Ὅταν γὰρ ἐκβαίνῃ τοὺς ἀναγκαίους ὅρους τῆς χρείας ἡ ὄρεξις, τί ἄλλο καὶ οὐχὶ διαβόλου ἐστὶ συμβουλή, τοῦ τὴν ἐκ σπέρματος παραγραφομένου τροφήν;

Γέγραπται, οὐκ ἐπ᾽ ἄρτῳ μόνῳ.[251] Εἰ ὡς Θεὸς ὁ Ἰησοῦς κατηγωνίσατο τὸν διάβολον, οὐδὲν μέγα ἐποίει νικήσας τὸν ὑπ᾽ αὐτοῦ πλασθέντα ἄγγελον ἀποστάτην, οὐδὲ νίκη ἐπεγράφετο τῇ ἀνθρωπότητι· ἀλλ᾽ ὡς ἄνθρωπος τῇ ἀνεξικακίᾳ περιεγένετο αὐτοῦ,

243 John, 1:29.
244 Cf. 1 John, 2:2; 4:10.
245 Rom. 8:6-7.
246 Matt. 3:17; cf. Mark, 1:11. Luke, 3:22.
247 Matt. 4:3; cf. Luke, 4:3.
248 Matt. 4:3; cf. Luke, 4:3.
249 Matt. 4:3; Luke, 4:4; Deut. 8:3.
250 Matt. 4:3; cf. Luke, 4:3.
251 Matt. 4:4; Luke, 4:3.

παιδεύων ἡμᾶς ὅτι τοῦ διαβόλου οὐ διὰ σημείων ἀλλὰ δι᾽ ἀνεξικακίας καὶ μακροθυμίας περιγίνεσθαι χρὴ καὶ μηδὲν εἰς ἐπίδειξιν ποιεῖν καὶ φιλοτιμίαν ἁπλῶς.

> The reason why the Lord replies in this way was that he decided to conquer the devil by humility, not by force.[cxcii]

Οὐ τρέφεται *ἄρτῳ* ἡ ἀρετή, οὐδὲ διὰ κρεῶν καὶ τῶν ἄλλων τῆς σαρκὸς ἐδωδίμων ἡ τῆς ψυχῆς δύναμις εὐεκτεῖ. Ἄρτος δὲ πνευματικός ἐστι καὶ ζωὴ τοῦ κατὰ ἀλήθειαν ἀνθρώπου, ἡ ἀρετή, σωφροσύνη, σοφία, δικαιοσύνη, ἀπάθεια.

> Οὐ τρέφεται *ἄρτῳ* ἡ ἀρετή, οὐ διὰ κρεῶν καὶ τῶν ἄλλων τῆς σαρκὸς ἐδωδίμων ἡ τῆς ψυχῆς δύναμις εὐεκτεῖ. ἄρτος δὲ πνευματικός ἐστι καὶ ζωὴ τοῦ κατὰ ἀλήθειαν ἀνθρώπου ἡ ἀρετή, σωφροσύνη, σοφία, δικαιοσύνη, ἀπάθεια.[cxciii]
>
> Therefore, if one is not fed by the word of God, he does not live.[cxciv]

τότε παραλαμβάνει αὐτὸν ὁ διάβολος εἰς τὴν ἁγίαν πόλιν.[252] Ὁ Χριστὸς Θεὸς ὤν, ἐδίδου τῶ διαβόλῳ ἑκουσίως ὡς ἄνθρωπον ἄγειν αὐτὸν εἰς τοὺς πειρασμούς, οἷς ἐπειρᾶτο αὐτὸν ἐκλῦσαι.

> The 'taking' spoken of here did not take place because of Lord's helplessness, but from the superciliousness of the enemy, who regards the willingness of the Saviour as duress.[cxcv]

Διὸ καὶ εἰς τὴν ἔρημον καὶ *εἰς τὴν ἁγίαν πόλιν*[253] ἀπῄει

> From this passage the meaning of another passage, which reads, *They went away into the holy city and they appeared to many*, is disclosed.[cxcvi]

καὶ εἰς *τὸ πτερύγιον* ἀνῄει *τοῦ ἱεροῦ*, ἐκ τῶν τόπων ἐρεθίζων αὐτὸν τοὺς ἁρμοδίους πειρασμοὺς ἐπάγειν, ἵνα πᾶσαν αὐτοῦ τὴν μηχανὴν ἐκχύσας ἐν ἑαυτῷ καὶ ἀποτυχών, ἀσθενὴς γένηται καὶ εὐάλωτος τοῖς ἀνθρώποις.

> (Σευήρου) Τὸ δὲ *παραλαμβάνει αὐτὸν ὁ διάβολος*, ὡς Θεὸς ἑκουσίως ἐδίδου τῷ διαβόλῳ ἄγειν αὐτὸν εἰς τοὺς πειρασμούς, οὓς ἐπειρᾶτο αὐτὸν ἑλκῦσαι ὁ διάβολος. διὸ καὶ εἰς τὴν ἔρημον ἀπῄει, καὶ *εἰς τὴν ἁγίαν πόλιν* καὶ *εἰς τὸ πτερύγιον τοῦ ἱεροῦ*, ἐκ τῶν τόπων ἐρεθίζων αὐτὸν τοὺς ἁρμοδίους πειρασμοὺς ἐπάγειν, ἵνα τὴν μανίαν αὐτοῦ ἐκχύσας, καὶ ἀποτυχών, ἀσθενὴς γένηται, καὶ εὐάλωτος τοῖς ἀνθρώποις.[cxcvii]

Τὸ δὲ ἐν τῷ ἐνενηκοστῷ ψαλμῷ[cxcviii] οὐ λέγεται περὶ Χριστοῦ, | **21r** ἀλλὰ περὶ δικαίων.

---

252 Matt. 4:5; cf. Luke, 4:9.

253 Cf. Matt. 27:53.

We read this in the ninetieth Psalm. However, the prophecy therein is not about Christ but about a holy man.[cxcix]

Οὐ γὰρ ὁ Χριστὸς φοβεῖται δαιμόνιον μεσημβρινόν, οὐδὲ νυκτερινόν,[254] οὐδὲ δεῖται βοηθείας ἀγγελικῆς. Εἰ δὲ καὶ περὶ Χριστοῦ λέγοιτο, πανούργως παρῆκε τὰ μεταξύ. Ταῦτα γὰρ αὐτὸς ἦν. Ἦν δὲ ἁρμόδιον τὸ εἰρημένον· ὁ εἰρηκὼς ὅτι *τοῖς ἀγγέλοις αὐτοῦ ἐντελεῖται,*[255] εἶπεν ἑαυτοὺς κατακρημνίζειν. Τοῦτο δὲ ἔλεγεν ὁ διάβολος, ἢ ἵνα ποιήσας τοῦτο καὶ διασωθεὶς (ὡς ᾤετο) εἰς κενοδοξίαν πέσῃ, ἢ ἵνα κατακρημνισθείς, ἀποθάνῃ. Καὶ νίκην κατὰ τοῦ παρόντος ἑνὸς ἐκ τῶν δύο ἐπιτυχών, ἄρηται καὶ παύσηται τῆς ἀμφιβολίας, ἐπιγνοὺς αὐτὸν ἄνθρωπον εἶναι καὶ οὐ Θεόν. Διὸ καὶ δυνάμενος τοῦτο ποιῆσαι καὶ διασωθῆναι, ὁ Κύριος οὐ ποιεῖ, διδάσκων μὴ ἐκπειράζειν *Θεόν,*[256] ἀλλ᾽ ἐν ἀνάγκαις αἰτεῖν ῥυσθῆναι *τοῦ πονηροῦ.*[257]

Γέγραπται γὰρ ὅτι τοῖς ἀγγέλοις αὐτοῦ ἐντελεῖται.[258] Ἐπειδὴ εἰκὸς τινές, πιστεύοντ‹ε›ς[259] τῷ διαβόλῳ ὡς καλῶς ἐξειληφότι τὴν προφητείαν οὐκ εἰς ἄλλον τινὰ ἢ εἰς τὸν Χριστὸν προφητευομένην, ἀπειθοῦσι τοῖς εἰρημένοις, γινωσκέτωσαν ὅτι πάντα τὰ κατὰ τὸν ψαλμὸν εἰς ἀνθρώπου φύσιν ἀναφέρεται, δεομένου πολλῆς βοηθείας καὶ σκέπης Θεοῦ καὶ τῆς ἀπ᾽ αὐτοῦ ἀντιλήψεως, ἵνα ῥυσθῇ ἀπὸ πάσης τῆς τῶν θηρευόντων *παγίδος* καὶ ἀπὸ παντὸς *ταραχώδους* καὶ ψευδοῦς *λόγου.*[260] Προφητείας μνημονεύει ὁ δόλιος καὶ ὁ ἀληθὴς προφητείας μέμνηται, τοῦ *οὐκ ἐκπειράσεις Κύριον τὸν Θεόν σου,*[261] ἐμὲ τὸν λαλοῦντά σοι.

> Ἐπειδὴ εἰκὸς τινὲς πιστεύοντες τῷ διαβόλῳ ὡς καλῶς ἐξειληφότι τὴν προφητείαν οὐκ εἰς ἄλλον τινὰ ἢ εἰς τὸν Χριστὸν προφητευομένην ἀπειθοῦσι τοῖς εἰρημένοις, γινωσκέτωσαν ὅτι πάντα τὰ κατὰ τὸν Ψαλμὸν εἰς ἀνθρώπου φύσιν ἀναφέρεται δεομένου πολλῆς βοηθείας καὶ σκέπης θεοῦ καὶ τῆς παρ᾽ αὐτοῦ ἀντιλήψεως, ἵνα ρυσθῇ ἀπὸ πάσης τῆς τῶν θηρευόντων *παγίδος* καὶ ἀπὸ παντὸς *ταραχώδους* καὶ ψευδοῦς *λόγου.* προφητείας μνημονεύει ὁ δόλιος, καὶ ὁ ἀληθὴς προφητείας μέμνηται. *οὐκ ἐκπειράσεις Κύριον τὸν Θεόν σου,*[262] ἐμὲ τὸν λαλοῦντά σοι.[cc]

Πάλιν παραλαμβάνει αὐτὸν εἰς ὄρος ὑψηλόν.[263] Ὅσα ἐνεθυμεῖτο | **21v** ὁ διάβολος μηχανήματα πρὸς ὑποσκελισμὸν τοῦ φαινομένου Ἀδάμ, αὐτὸς τὰς λαβὰς ἐδίδου. Οἷον ἔλεγεν ἐν ἑαυτῷ ὁ διάβολος· τὸν πρῶτον ἄνθρωπον διὰ βρώσεως ἠπάτησα·

254 Cf. Psalm 90:6.
255 Matt. 4:6. Psalm 90:11.
256 Matt. 4:9; Luke, 4:12; Deut. 6:16.
257 Cf. Matt. 6:3.
258 Matt. 4:6. Psalm 90:11. Luke, 4:16.
259 Cod. πιστεύοντας.
260 Psalm 90:3.
261 Matt. 4:9; Luke, 4:12; Deut. 6:16.
262 Matt. 4:9; Luke, 4:12; Deut. 6:16.
263 Matt. 4:8.

οὗτος οὐ πεινᾷ ἵνα αὐτὸν ἀπατήσω διὰ βρώσεως ‹ὃς› ἐνέδωκε τῇ πείνῃ;[264] Πάλιν ἔλεγεν ἐν ἑαυτῷ ὁ διάβολος· εἰ ἦν *εἰς ὑψηλὸν ὄρος*, ἐδείκνυον ‹ἂν› αὐτῷ σχήματα καὶ ἐπηγγελλόμην αὐτῷ καὶ πολλάκις ἠπάτων αὐτόν. Ἀνῆλθεν ὁ Σωτὴρ *εἰς τὸ ὄρος* καὶ ἔδωκεν αὐτῷ λαβήν. Οὕτω καὶ ἐν τῷ Ἰὼβ νόει· τὰς βουλὰς τοῦ διαβόλου συγχωρεῖ ὁ Θεὸς ἐνεργεῖν, ἐν οἷς τὸ δίκαιον τοῦ Θεοῦ φανεροῦται καὶ τὸ ἀνόσιον τῆς κακίας.

> Ὅσα ἐνεθυμεῖτο ὁ διάβολος μηχανήματα πρὸς ὑποσκελισμὸν τοῦ φαινομένου Ἀδάμ, αὐτὸς ἐδίδου τὰς λαβάς. Οἷον ἔλεγεν ἐν ἑαυτῷ ὁ διάβολος, τὸν πρῶτον ἄνθρωπον διὰ βρώσεως ἠπάτησα, οὗτος οὐ πεινᾷ ἵνα αὐτὸν ἀπατήσω διὰ βρώσεως; ἐνέδωκε τῇ πείνῃ. Πάλιν ἔλεγεν ἐν ἑαυτῷ ὁ διάβολος· εἰ ἦν *εἰς ὄρος ὑψηλόν*, ἐδείκνυον αὐτῷ σχήματα καὶ ἐπηγγελλόμην αὐτῷ καὶ πολλάκις ἠπάτων αὐτόν - ἀνῆλθεν ὁ σωτὴρ *εἰς τὸ ὄρος* καὶ ἔδωκεν αὐτῷ λαβήν. Οὕτω καὶ ἐν τῷ Ἰὼβ νόει· τὰς βουλὰς τοῦ διαβόλου συγχωρεῖ ὁ θεὸς ἐνεργεῖν, ἐν οἷς τὸ δίκαιον τοῦ Θεοῦ φανεροῦται καὶ τὸ ἀνόσιον τῆς κακίας.[cci]

Καὶ δείκνυσιν αὐτῷ πάσας τὰς βασιλείας.[265] Οἱ προλαβόντες δύο γενικοὶ πειρασμοί, ὁ μὲν τῆς γαστριμαργίας ὁ δὲ τῆς κενοδοξίας ἦν. Οὗτος δὲ τῆς φιλαργυρίας ἐστίν, ἥτις κορυφή ἐστι τῶν πειρασμῶν. Διὸ καὶ *εἰς ὄρος λίαν* ἀνηνέχθαι *ὑψηλὸν* λέγει τὸν Κύριον. Ἄλογον γὰρ τὸ αἰσθητῶς ἀκούειν τὸ *ὄρος* καὶ τὴν ἀνάβασιν καὶ *τὰς βασιλείας*. Μήποτ' οὖν ἀνήγαγεν αὐτὸν ἐπὶ τὸ ὕψος τῶν θεωρημάτων[ccii] καὶ τὰς διαφόρους δόξας τὰς περὶ εὐσεβείας· ἔδειξε δὲ καὶ *βασιλείας*, περὶ ὧν ἔφη· *ἔστησεν ὅρια ἐθνῶν κατὰ ἀριθμὸν ἀγγέλ‹ω›ν*[266] *Θεοῦ*.[267]

> Ἄλογον γὰρ τὸ αἰσθητῶς ἀκούειν τὸ *ὄρος* καὶ τὴν ἀνάβασιν καὶ *τὰς βασιλείας*. Μήποτ' οὖν ἀνήγαγεν αὐτὸν ἐπὶ τὸ ὕψος τῶν θεωρητῶν καὶ τὰς διαφόρους δόξας τὰς περὶ εὐσεβείας, ἔδειξε δὲ καὶ *βασιλείας*, τὰς *ὅτε διεμέριζεν ὁ ὕψιστος ἔθνη, οὓς δὲ ἔσπειρεν υἱοὺς Ἀδάμ, στήσας ὅρια ἐθνῶν κατὰ ἀριθμὸν ἀγγέλων θεοῦ*.[cciii]

Τινές δέ φασι ὅτι αὐτοπροσώπως καὶ αὐτοῖς ῥήμασιν ἐλάλησεν αὐτῷ ταῦτα ὁ διάβολος καὶ οὐ κατὰ διάνοιαν ὥσπερ καὶ ἡμῖν, ἐνιεὶς τοὺς ἐμπαθεῖς λογισμούς.[cciv] Οὔτε γὰρ δυνατὸν ἦν ἐν λογισμοῖς | **22r** διανοηθῆναι ἄτοπόν τι τὸν ἀκήρατον ἐκείνου νοῦν.[ccv] Ἐπειδὴ δὲ ὡς ἴδια ἔλεγε τὰ κτίσματα τοῦ Θεοῦ ὡς δημιουργὸς ὢν αὐτῶν, ἐπιτιμᾷ αὐτῷ ὡς ψεύστῃ. Καὶ ὁ μὲν Κύριος, ὡς πλούσιος ὢν καὶ ἀνενδεὴς Θεός, πᾶσαν τὴν ἀνθρωπίνην δόξαν καὶ ὅλον τὸν χρυσὸν προτεθέντα αὐτῷ ἐκ τοῦ Ἀντικειμένου ὑπεροορᾷ, ἡμᾶς δὲ οὐκ ἀφῆκεν ἀπατηθῆναι τοιούτοις ὁπηνίκα τὰς τοιαύτας φαντασίας ποιοῦντι ἐπιτιμῶν εἴρηκε, *γέγραπται, Κύριον τὸν Θεόν σου προσκυνήσεις, καὶ αὐτῷ μόνῳ λατρεύσεις*.[268] Ἐπειδὴ δὲ τὸ *ὕπαγε σατανᾶ*[269] μετὰ δυνάμεως εἴρητο (πρότερον γὰρ

264 Cf. Matt. 4:2.
265 Matt. 4:8; cf. Luke, 4:5.
266 Cod. ἄγγελον.
267 Deut. 32:8.
268 Matt. 4:10; Luke, 4:8; cf. Deut. 6:13; 10:20.
269 Matt. 4:10.

πράως ἀπεκρίνατο), *ἀφίησιν αὐτὸν ὁ διάβολος*,[270] *συντελέσας πάντα πειρασμόν*,[271] ὡς ὁ Λουκᾶς φησι. Τὰ γὰρ τρία ταῦτα πάντων κεφαλαιωδέστερα εἰσὶ τῶν πειρασμῶν.

Ὕπαγε ὀπίσω μου σατανᾶ.[272] Σατανᾶς ἑρμηνεύεται τῇ Ἑβραΐδι φωνῇ ὁ Ἀντικείμενος, ἡ δὲ γραφικὴ ῥῆσις ἐν ‹τῷ› Δευτερονομίῳ κεῖται. Παράπληκτος ὁ διάβολος τῷ θεῷ λόγῳ ἐπαγγελλόμενος διδόναι ἅπερ αὐτὸς ἐποίησεν. Ἐπιπληκτικῶς δὲ ὁ Κύριος τῷ διαβόλῳ λαλεῖ, λέγων ὅτι μόνῳ Θεῷ ἐδιδάχθημεν προσκυνεῖν, οὐχ ἑτέρῳ.[273] *Πάντες* γὰρ αὐτοῦ *εἰσὶ λειτουργικὰ πνεύματα εἰς διακονίαν ἀποστελλόμενα, διὰ τοὺς μέλλοντας κληρονομεῖν σωτηρίαν*.[274]

> Σατανᾶς ἑρμηνεύεται τῇ Ἑβραΐδι φωνῇ ὁ Ἀντικείμενος, ἡ δὲ γραφικὴ ῥῆσις ἐν τῷ Δευτερονομίῳ κεῖται. παράπληκτος ὁ διάβολος τῷ θεῷ λόγῳ ἐπαγγελλόμενος διδόναι ἅπερ αὐτὸς ἐποίησεν. Ἐπιπληκτικῶς δὲ ὁ κύριος τῷ διαβόλῳ λαλεῖ λέγων ὅτι μόνῳ Θεῷ ἐδιδάχθημεν προσκυνεῖν, οὐχ ἑτέρῳ. *πάντες* γὰρ αὐτοῦ *εἰσὶ λειτουργικὰ πνεύματα εἰς διακονίαν ἀποστελλόμενα, διὰ τοὺς μέλλοντας κληρονομεῖν σωτηρίαν*.[ccvi]

Καὶ ἰδοὺ ἄγγελοι προσῆλθον καὶ διηκόνουν.[275] Τίς δὲ ἦν αὕτη ἡ διακονία ἣν *διηκόνουν* οἱ *ἄγγελοι* τῷ Ἰησοῦ τότε, ἢ ὅτι ἕκαστος αὐτῶν ἐνεχει | **22v** ρίζετό[ccvii] τινας τῶν εἰς τὸν Ἰησοῦν πιστευόντων, ἵνα ἔχῃ ἕκαστος ἄγγελον *διὰ παντὸς βλέποντα τὸ πρόσωπον τοῦ ἐν οὐρανοῖς Πατρός*;[276] Οἵους δὲ εἰκὸς λόγους ὑπὸ Ἰησοῦ λελέχθαι τοῖς διακονουμένοις τὴν τῶν ἀνθρώπων σωτηρίαν ἀγγέλοις[277] καὶ οἵας αὐτοῖς ὑποθήκας ὑπέθετο, παρατιθέμενος αὐτοῖς τοὺς ἐν τῇ ἐκκλησίᾳ μικρούς,[278] ἵνα παρεμβάλλωσιν ἄγγελοι *κύκλῳ τῶν φοβουμένων αὐτὸν* καὶ ῥύωνται *αὐτούς*.[279]

> Τίς δὲ ἦν αὕτη ἡ διακονία ἣν *διηκόνουν* οἱ *ἄγγελοι* τῷ Ἰησοῦ τότε, ἢ ὅτι ἕκαστος αὐτῶν ἐνεχειρίζετό τινας τῶν εἰς τὸν Ἰησοῦν πιστευόντων, ἵνα ἔχῃ ἕκαστος ἄγγελον *διὰ παντὸς* βλέποντα *τὸ πρόσωπον τοῦ ἐν οὐρανοῖς Πατρός*;[280] Οἵους δὲ εἰκὸς λόγους ὑπὸ Ἰησοῦ λελέχθαι τοῖς διακονουμένοις τὴν τῶν ἀνθρώπων σωτηρίαν ἀγγέλοις καὶ οἵας αὐτοῖς ὑποθήκας ὑπέθετο, παρατιθέμενος αὐτοῖς τοὺς ἐν τῇ ἐκκλησίᾳ μικρούς, ἵνα παρεμβάλλωσιν ἄγγελοι *κύκλῳ τῶν φοβουμένων αὐτὸν* καὶ ῥύωνται *αὐτούς*.[ccviii]

> δῆλον δὲ ὅτι ‹καὶ› κατὰ τὸν εὐαγγελιστὴν Ἰωάννην οὗτος ἦν ὁ καιρὸς αὐτῷ τοῦ κεκλεῖσθαι εἰς φυλακήν. λέλεκται γὰρ παρ' αὐτῷ τὸ *ἦν δὲ καὶ Ἰωάννης βαπτίζων ἐν Αἰνὼν ἐγγὺς Σαλείμ. οὔπω γὰρ ἦν Ἰωάννης βεβλημένος εἰς φυλακήν*. κατὰ τοὺς τέσσαρας τοίνυν

270 Matt. 4:11.
271 Luke, 4:13.
272 Matt. 4:10.
273 Exodus, 34:14; Joshua, 23:8; Daniel, 3:95; cf. Psalms 80:10; 98:5&9.
274 Heb. 1:14.
275 Matt. 4:11; cf. Mark, 1:13.
276 Matt. 18:10.
277 Cf. Tobit, 5:17; 2 Macc. 4:6.
278 Cf. Matt. 10:42; 18:6&10&14. Mark, 9:42; Luke, 17:2.
279 Psalm 33:8.
280 Matt. 18:10.

εὐαγγελιστὰς οὔτε πρὶν βαπτίσασθαι Ἰησοῦν ἀπήντα τι κώλυμα βαπτίζοντι Ἰωάννῃ οὔτε μετὰ ταῦτα ‹ἔτι ἐβάπτισεν›, ἀλλ' ἔδει καταλῆξαι τὰ Ἰωάννου ἐν ἀρχῇ τοῦ οἰκονομεῖσθαι τὸ εὐαγγέλιον ὑπὸ τοῦ Ἰησοῦ. τάχα δὲ ἡ φρουροῦσα δύναμις Ἰωάννην,[ccix] ἕως ἐν Ἰησοῦ τελειώσῃ τὴν τοῦ βαπτίσματος οἰκονομίαν, κατέλιπεν αὐτὸν τῷ τε ἐν φυλακῇ πειρασμῷ καὶ τῷ ἀποκεφαλισμῷ.[ccx]

Ἔοικεν Ἰωάννης πληρώσας ἐν τῷ Ἰησοῦ τὴν τοῦ βαπτίσματος διακονίαν εἰς αὐτὸν καταλήξασαν μετὰ τοῦτο παραδεδόσθαι καὶ ἐν φυλακῇ κατακεκλεῖσθαι. μετὰ γὰρ τὸ βαπτίσασθαι τὸν Ἰησοῦν οὐδὲν εὕρομεν ἀναγεγραμμένον περὶ Ἰωάννου ἢ ὅτι μετὰ τὸν πρὸς τὸν διάβολον πειρασμὸν εὐθέως καὶ ἅμα τῷ βαπτίσματι ὑπὸ τοῦ πνεύματος ἐκβληθεὶς εἰς τὴν ἔρημον, ὡς ὁ Μᾶρκος ἔγραψεν, *ἀκούσας* Ἰησοῦς, *ὅτι Ἰωάννης παρεδόθη ἀνεχώρησεν εἰς τὴν Γαλιλαίαν*. ἀλλὰ καὶ ὁ Λουκᾶς τῇ περὶ τοῦ βαπτίζειν τὸν Ἰωάννην διηγήσει συνάπτει τὰ περὶ τοῦ κεκλεῖσθαι αὐτὸν ὑπὸ Ἡρῴδου. δῆλον δὲ ὅτι ‹καὶ› κατὰ τὸν εὐαγγελιστὴν Ἰωάννην οὗτος ἦν ὁ καιρὸς αὐτῷ τοῦ κεκλεῖσθαι εἰς φυλακήν. λέλεκται γὰρ παρ' αὐτῷ τὸ *ἦν δὲ καὶ Ἰωάννης βαπτίζων ἐν Αἰνὼν ἐγγὺς Σαλείμ. οὔπω γὰρ ἦν Ἰωάννης βεβλημένος εἰς φυλακήν*. κατὰ τοὺς τέσσαρας τοίνυν εὐαγγελιστὰς οὔτε πρὶν βαπτίσασθαι Ἰησοῦν ἀπήντα τι κώλυμα βαπτίζοντι Ἰωάννῃ οὔτε μετὰ ταῦτα ‹ἔτι ἐβάπτισεν›, ἀλλ' ἔδει καταλῆξαι τὰ Ἰωάννου ἐν ἀρχῇ τοῦ οἰκονομεῖσθαι τὸ εὐαγγέλιον ὑπὸ τοῦ Ἰησοῦ. τάχα δὲ ἡ φρουροῦσα δύναμις Ἰωάννην, ἕως ἐν Ἰησοῦ τελειώσῃ τὴν τοῦ βαπτίσματος οἰκονομίαν, κατέλιπεν αὐτὸν τῷ τε ἐν φυλακῇ πειρασμῷ καὶ τῷ ἀποκεφαλισμῷ.[ccxi]

Ἀκούσας δὲ ὁ Ἰησοῦς ὅτι Ἰωάννης παρεδόθη.[281] Πῶς *ἀκούσας ἀνεχώρησε* καὶ πρὶν ἀκοῦσαι οὐκ ᾔδει ὁ εἰδὼς *τί ἦν ἐν τῷ ἀνθρώπῳ*;[282] Ἀλλ' οὐδὲν λυπεῖ εἰδότα ἀκηκοέναι καὶ ἀκηκοότα ἀνακεχωρηκέναι, ἢ ἀκηκοέναι κατὰ τὴν οἰκονομίαν, καθ' ἣν καὶ ἐπειράσθη. Ἀλλὰ καὶ τὸ *αὐτὸς ἐγίνωσκε τί ἦν ἐν τῷ ἀνθρώπῳ*[283] παρὰ Ἰωάννῃ λέγεται τῷ μὴ γενεαλογήσαντι αὐτόν, ἀλλὰ θεολογήσαντι.

Ζητήσειεν δ' ἄν τις πρὸς τὸ *ἀκούσας ὅτι Ἰωάννης παρεδόθη ἀνεχώρησεν*, εἰ καὶ καὶ πρὶν ἀκοῦσαι οὐκ ᾔδει ὁ εἰδὼς *τί ἦν ἐν τῷ ἀνθρώπῳ*;[284] ἀλλ' οὐδὲν λυπεῖ εἰδότα ἀκηκοέναι καὶ ἀκηκοότα ἀνακεχωρηκέναι ἢ ἀκηκοέναι κατὰ τὴν οἰκονομίαν, καθ' ἣν καὶ ἐπειράσθη. ἀλλὰ καὶ τὸ *αὐτὸς ἐγίνωσκε τί ἦν ἐν τῷ ἀνθρώπῳ*[285] παρὰ Ἰωάννῃ λέγεται τῷ μὴ γενεαλογήσαντι αὐτόν, ἀλλὰ θεολογήσαντι.[ccxii]

Ἀνεχώρησεν εἰς τὴν Γαλιλαίαν.[286] Ἀναχωρεῖ νῦν ὁ Ἰησοῦς τηρῶν ἑαυτὸν ταῖς πρὸς τοῦ παθεῖν διδασκαλίαις καὶ ἰάσεσι καὶ διδάσκων ὅτι δεῖ φεύγειν τὸν ἀπὸ τῶν ἐπιβουλῶν κίνδυνον. Γαλιλαία δέ, ἡ μὲν τῆς Ἰουδαίας ἡ δὲ τῶν ἐθνῶν ἑρμηνεύονται κατακυλιστή,[ccxiii]

281 Matt. 4:12.
282 John, 2:25.
283 John, 2:25.
284 John, 2:25.
285 John, 2:25.
286 Matt. 4:12.

> νῦν δὲ ἡ καταλιποῦσα τὴν ΚΑΤΑΚΥΛΙΣΤΙΚΗΝ καὶ ΑΣΤΑΤΟΝ Γαλιλαίαν ψυχὴ καὶ ἑπομένη τῷ λόγῳ καὶ ποιοῦσα τὰ προσταττόμενα.[ccxiv]

> Γαλιλαία γὰρ ἡ κατακυλιστὴ τῇ Ἑλλάδι γλώσσῃ ἑρμηνεύεται.[ccxv]

> οἱ πρὶν ἐν Γαλιλαίᾳ ὄντες, ἥτις κατακυλιστὴ ἑρμηνεύεται.[ccxvi]

τύπος οὖσαι τῶν εἴτε ἐν Ἰουδαίοις, εἴτε ἐν ἔθνεσιν οὐχ ἑστηκότων, οὓς ἐλθὼν ἱδρύει ὁ Ἰησοῦς. Ἔρχεται δὲ *εἰς Καπερναούμ*, ἑρμηνευόμενον χωρίον παρακλήσεως,

> Καπερναούμ· χωρίον παρακλήσεως.[ccxvii]

> ἡ Καπερναούμ, χωρίον ἑρμηνεύεται παρακλήσεως.[ccxviii]

ἵν‹α›[287] ἔργῳ παρακαλέσῃ τοὺς ἐκεῖ ὄντας παραθαλασσίους προσκλυζομένους | **23r** ὑπὸ τῆς τῶν πειρασμῶν θαλάσσης. Καταλείπει γὰρ τὴν Ἰουδαίαν καὶ ἔρχεται εἰς τὸν παρακληθέντα ἀγρόν, τὰ ἔθνη, *ἐν ὁρίοις Ζαβουλών*[288] (ὅ ἐστι ῥύσις νυκτερείας,[ccxix] σημαίνων τοὺς ἀπὸ Ἰσραὴλ πιστεύσαντας, οἷς ἡ νὺξ πρὸ Χριστοῦ ῥεύσασα οὐκέτι ἦν) *καὶ Νεφθαλείμ*, ὅ ἐστι πλατυσμός,

> Ἑρμηνεύεται μὲν γὰρ ... Νεφθαλεὶμ δέ, *πλατυσμός*.[ccxx]

σύμβολον τῶν ἐθνῶν πλατυνθέντων ἐν εὐσεβείᾳ. Εἰ δὲ *Ζαβουλών* μέν ἐστιν *ὁ λαὸς ὁ καθήμενος ἐν σκότει καὶ ἐν σκιᾷ θανάτου*[289] διὰ τὸ τοῦ νόμου καὶ τῶν προφητῶν ἀκούειν περιαιρεθέντος διὰ Χριστοῦ τοῦ ἐν τῇ παλαιᾷ καλύμματος,[290] οὐ *φῶς* ὁρᾷ λύχνου, ἀλλὰ *μέγα*, τὸ ἀληθινόν. Ὁ δὲ καθήμενος *ἐν σκιᾷ* τοῦ *θανάτου*[291] τῆς εἰδωλολατρίας καὶ τῶν ἁμαρτιῶν *λαός*, οὗ ὁ *Νεφθαλείμ* τύπος, ὁρᾷ *φῶς* τοῦ εἰπόντος *ἐγώ εἰμι τὸ φῶς τοῦ κόσμου*.[292] Μόνοι γὰρ οἱ ἐν τῇ Ἰουδαίᾳ εἶχον τὸν νόμον ὡς λύχνον· ἐν δὲ σκότει ἦσαν οἱ ἐθνικοὶ ὡς μηδὲ αὐτὸ ἔχοντες τὸ λυχνιαῖον *φῶς*, οἷς ἐπέλαμψεν ὁ Χριστὸς διὰ τοῦ εὐαγγελίου, *φῶς μέγα* ὤν. *Φῶς* γάρ ἐστι *τοῦ κόσμου*.[293]
Οὐ διὰ δειλίαν ὑπεχώρησεν, ἀλλ' ἡμᾶς δι' ὧν ἐποίει διδάσκων ὑποχωρεῖν τοῖς διώκουσιν. Ἀναχωρεῖ δὲ ἐκ τῆς Ἰουδαίας ἐπὶ τὰ ἔθνη, δεικνὺς ὅτι οὐ μόνον ὅταν εἰς αὐτὸν τὸν Θεὸν ἐνυβρίσωσιν Ἰουδαῖοι ἀφίσταται αὐτῶν, ἀλλὰ καὶ ὅτε εἰς τοὺς ἁγίους προφήτας ἁμαρτάνουσι. *Φῶς* δὲ *μέγα*[294] ἐστὶ Χριστὸς ὁ Κύριος ἡμῶν καὶ ἡ φαιδρότης

287 Cod. ἵν'.
288 Matt. 4:13.
289 Is. 9:1, quoted in Matt. 4:16.
290 Cf. 2 Cor. 3:16.
291 Cf. Matt. 4:16; Luke, 1:17.
292 John, 8:12.
293 John, 8:12.
294 Is. 9:1, quoted in Matt. 4:16.

τοῦ εὐαγγελικοῦ κηρύγματος, οὐ | **23v** μὴν ὁ νόμος, ὃς λύχνῳ ἦν ἀπεικασθείς.[295] Διὸ ἀεὶ ἐν τῇ σκηνῇ *λύχνος* ἐκαίετο, διὰ τὸ βραχὺ[ccxxi] τῆς τοῦ νόμου αὐγῆς ἄχρι μόνων τῶν Ἰουδαϊκῶν ὅρων ἰσχύων ἐκπέμψαι τὸ ἴδιον φῶς. Οὐκοῦν[296] οἱ ἐθνικοὶ *ἐν σκότει* ἦσαν ὡς μηδὲ τὸ λυχνιαῖον ἔχοντες *φῶς*.

> [οὐ διὰ δειλίαν δὲ ὑπεχώρησεν, ἀλλ' ἡμᾶς δι' ὧν ποιεῖ διδάσκει ὑποχωρεῖν τοῖς διώκουσιν. ἀναχωρεῖ δὲ ἐκ τῆς Ἰουδαίας ἐπὶ τὰ ἔθνη, δεικνὺς ὅτι οὐ μόνον ὅταν εἰς αὐτὸν τὸν θεὸν ἐνυβρίσωσιν Ἰουδαῖοι ἀφίσταται αὐτῶν, ἀλλὰ καὶ ὅταν εἰς τοὺς ἁγίους προφήτας ἁμαρτάνωσι. *φῶς* δὲ *μέγα*[297] ἐστὶν ὁ Χριστὸς καὶ ἡ φαιδρότης τοῦ εὐαγγελίου οὐκέτι ὁ νόμος, ὃς λύχνῳ ἦν ἀπεικασθείς, διὸ καὶ ἀεὶ λύχνος ἐν τῇ σκηνῇ ἐκαίετο διὰ τῆς τοῦ νόμου αὐγῆς ἄχρι μόνων τῶν Ἰουδαϊκῶν ὅρων ἰσχύων ἐκπέμψαι τὸ ἴδιον φῶς. οὐκοῦν οἱ ἐθνικοὶ ἐν σκότει ἦσαν ὡς μηδὲ τὸ λυχνιαῖον ἔχοντες *φῶς*.][ccxxii]

> Οὐ διὰ δειλίαν δὲ ὑπεχώρησεν, ἀλλ' ἡμᾶς δι' ὧν ἐποίει διδάσκων ὑποχωρεῖν τοῖς διώκουσιν. *ἀναχωρεῖ* δὲ ἐκ τῆς Ἰουδαίας ἐπὶ τὰ ἔθνη, δεικνὺς ὅτι οὐ μόνον ὅταν εἰς αὐτὸν τὸν θεὸν ἐνυβρίσωσιν Ἰουδαῖοι ἀφίσταται αὐτῶν, ἀλλὰ καὶ ὅτε εἰς τοὺς ἁγίους προφήτας ἁμαρτάνουσιν. *φῶς* δὲ *μέγα* ἐστὶ Χριστὸς ὁ κύριος ἡμῶν καὶ ἡ φαιδρότης τοῦ εὐαγγελικοῦ κηρύγματος, οὐ μὴν ὁ νόμος, ὃς λύχνῳ ἦν ἀπεικασθείς. διὸ ἀεὶ ἐν τῇ σκηνῇ λύχνος ἐκαίετο διὰ τὸ βραχὺ τῆς τοῦ νόμου αὐγῆς ἄχρι μόνων τῶν Ἰουδαϊκῶν ὅρων ἰσχύων ἐκπέμψαι τὸ ἴδιον φῶς. οὐκοῦν οἱ ἐθνικοὶ *ἐν σκότει* ἦσαν ὡς μηδὲ τὸ λυχνιαῖον ἔχοντες *φῶς*.[ccxxiii]

Διδασκαλίας ἐστὶ τὸ ἀναχωρεῖν τὸν Ἰησοῦν. Σαφῶς ὁ λόγος διδάσκει ὅτι οὐ χρή τινα ἐπὶ τὸ διδασκαλεῖον ἐλθεῖν εἰ μὴ πρότερον βαπτισθῇ καὶ τύχῃ Πνεύματος Ἁγίου καὶ νηστεύσῃ ὁλοκλήρως καὶ νικήσῃ πᾶν εἶδος πειρασμοῦ, ὡς ὁ τύπος τῆς ἀληθείας ἐν Χριστῷ ἤρξατο καὶ διὰ Χριστοῦ γίνεται.

> Διδασκαλίας ἐστὶ τὸ ἀναχωρεῖν τὸν Ἰησοῦν. σαφῶς ὁ λόγος διδάσκει, ὅτι οὐ χρή τινα ἐπὶ τὸ διδασκαλεῖον ἐλθεῖν, εἰ μὴ πρότερον βαπτισθῇ καὶ τύχῃ πνεύματος ἁγίου καὶ νηστεύσῃ ὁλοκλήρως καὶ νικήσῃ πᾶν εἶδος πειρασμοῦ ὡς ὁ τύπος τῆς ἀληθείας ἐν Χριστῷ ἤρξατο καὶ διὰ Χριστοῦ γίνεται.[ccxxiv]

Ὁ λαὸς ὁ καθήμενος ἐν σκότει.[298] Σκότος ἐνταῦθα οὐ τὸ αἰσθητὸν καλεῖ, ἀλλὰ τὴν πλάνην καὶ τὴν ἀσέβειαν·[ccxxv]

> Οὐ σκότος αἰσθητὸν ἐνταῦθα καλεῖ, ἀλλὰ τὴν πλάνην καὶ τὴν ἀσέβειαν·[ccxxvi]

---

295 Cf. Ex. 27:20-21. Lev. 24:2-3.
296 Cod. οὐκ οὖν.
297 Is. 9:1, quoted in Matt. 4:16.
298 Is. 9:1, quoted in Matt. 4:16.

διὸ καὶ ἐπήγαγε· *τοῖς καθημένοις ἐν χώρᾳ καὶ σκιᾷ θανάτου φῶς* ἔλαμψεν αὐτοῖς. Εἶτα δεικνὺς ὅτι οὐκ αὐτοὶ ζητήσαντες εὗρον, ἀλλ᾽ ὁ Θεὸς αὐτοῖς ἄνωθεν ἐφάνη, φησί· αὐτὸ τὸ *φῶς ἀνέτειλε* καὶ ἔλαμψεν, οὐκ αὐτοὶ πρότερον τῷ φωτὶ προσέδραμον.[ccxxvii]

> Σκιὰν *θανάτου* εἴρηκε καὶ οὐ θάνατον διὰ τὸ μὴ δύνασθαι τὴν ἁμαρτίαν εἰς τὸ παντελὲς φθείρειν τὴν ψυχήν, ὥσπερ θάνατος τὰ σώματα, ἀλλὰ σκιὰν φέρειν αὐτῇ *θανάτου*. καὶ τὸ *ἀνέτειλε φῶς* σημαίνει ὅτι οὐχ ἡμῖν ζητοῦσιν *ἀνέτειλεν*, ἀλλ᾽ ἐν ἀμελείᾳ κειμένοις ἔλαμψεν.[ccxxviii]

Καὶ γὰρ *ἐν σκότει* τὰ ἀνθρώπινα ἦν πρὸ τῆς τοῦ Χριστοῦ παρουσίας.
Οὐδὲ γὰρ ἐβάδιζον *ἐν σκότει*, ἀλλ᾽ ἐκάθηντο, ὅπερ σημεῖον ἦν τοῦ μὴ ἐλπίζειν αὐτοὺς ἀπαλλάττεσθαι.

> ὁμοίως δὲ καὶ *φῶς* νοητὸν τὴν ἐπίγνωσιν τῆς ἀληθείας λέγει. οὐκ εἶπε δὲ ὅτι ἐβάδιζον ἐν σκότει, ἀλλ᾽ ἐκάθηντο. ὅπερ σημεῖον ἦν τοῦ μηδὲ ἐλπίζειν αὐτοὺς ἀπαλλάττεσθαι. ὥσπερ γὰρ οὐδὲ εἰδότες ποῦ δεῖ προβῆναι, οὕτω καταληφθέντες ὑπὸ τοῦ σκότους ἐκαθέσθησαν, μὴ δυνάμενοι μηδὲ στῆναι λοιπόν.[ccxxix]
>
> οὐκ εἶπε δὲ ὅτι ἐβάδιζον ἐν σκότει, ἀλλ᾽ ἐκάθηντο, ὅπερ σημεῖον ἦν, τοῦ μηδὲ ἐλπίζειν αὐτοὺς ἀπαλλάττεσθαι. ὥσπερ γὰρ οὐδὲ εἰδότες ποῦ δεῖ προβῆναι, οὕτω καταλειφθέντες ὑπὸ τοῦ σκότους ἐκαθέσθησαν, μὴ δυνάμενοι μηδὲ στῆναι λοιπόν.[ccxxx]

Ἀπὸ τότε ἤρξατο ὁ Ἰησοῦς κηρύσσειν.[299] Ὅτε ἐπαύσατο ὁ Ἰωάννης κηρύσσειν αὐτὸν μαρτυρῶν τὰ περὶ αὐτοῦ, τότε *ἤρξατο* αὐτὸς *κηρύσσειν* ὅτι αὐτὸς ἐστιν ὁ Χριστός. Εἰ δὲ τὰ αὐτὰ τῷ Ἰωάννῃ ὁ Σωτὴρ λέγει, οὐδὲν θαυμαστόν· εἷς γὰρ ὁ πέμψας ἀμφοτέρους Θεός.

> When John was driven away, Jesus begins to preach forthwith. The effect of the Law terminating is that the Gospel arises. But if the Saviour preaches the same things as those John the Baptist had previously said, he evinces that he is the Son of the same God whose [John] is a prophet.[ccxxxi]

Εἰ δὲ καὶ ὡς ἔν τισιν οὔτε τὸ *μετανοεῖτε* οὔτε τὸ *γὰρ* κεῖται, τάχα Ἰωάννης μὲν ὡς ἑτοιμάσων Κυρίῳ *λαὸν κατεσκευασμένον*[300] πρῶτος | **24r** λέγει τὸ *μετανοεῖτε*. Ἰησοῦς δὲ τὰ ἡτοιμασμένα παραλαβὼν μηκέτι δεόμενα μετανοίας, οὐδὲν λέγει πρὸ τοῦ *ἤγγικεν ἡ βασιλεία*.[301] Ἡ δὲ *βασιλεία τῶν οὐρανῶν* οὔτε χρόνῳ ἐγγίζει οὔτε ἐν τόπῳ ἐστίν, ἐν δὲ διαθέσει. Οὔτε γὰρ μετὰ παρατηρήσεως ἔρχεται, *ἐντός* τε *ἡμῶν ἐστιν*,[302]

---

299 Matt. 4:17.
300 Cf. Luke 1:17.
301 Matt. 3:2; 4:17; 10:7; Mark, 1:15; Luke, 10:9&11.
302 Cf. Luke, 17:21.

> Ἔν τισιν τὸ *μετανοεῖτε* οὐ κεῖται. εἰ δὲ τὰ αὐτὰ ὁ σωτὴρ Ἰωάννῃ λέγει, εἷς ὁ ἀμφοτέρους πέμψας Θεός. καὶ τάχα Ἰωάννης μὲν ὡς ἑτοιμάζων θεῷ *λαὸν κατεσκευασμένον* πρῶτος λέγει *μετανοεῖτε*, Ἰησοῦς δὲ ἡτοιμασμένα παραλαβὼν μηκέτι δεόμενα μετανοίας οὐ λέγει *μετανοεῖτε*. οὐκ ἀντικηρύσσων δὲ νόμῳ καὶ προφήταις, πληρώσαντι δὲ Ἰωάννῃ τὴν παλαιὰν *κηρύσσειν ἤρξατο* τὴν νέαν, αὐτὸς ἀρχὴ γενόμενος αὐτῆς. διὸ ἐπὶ Ἰωάννου οὐ γέγραπται τὸ *ἤρξατο*. πέρας γὰρ ἦν. καὶ ἔτι ὁ μὲν ἐν ἐρήμῳ κηρύσσει, ὁ δὲ ἐν λαῷ. ἡ δὲ *βασιλεία τῶν οὐρανῶν* οὐκ ἐν τόπῳ ἐστίν, ἐν δὲ διαθέσει. *ἐντὸς* γὰρ *ἡμῶν ἐστιν*. ὅρα δὲ εἰ Ἰωάννης μὲν κηρύσσει ἐγγίζουσαν βασιλείαν οὐρανῶν, βασιλεὺς Χριστὸς ἣν παραδώσει *τῷ θεῷ*[303] *καὶ πατρί*.[ccxxxii]

> Ἔν τισιν τὸ *μετανοεῖτε* οὐ κεῖται. εἰ δὲ τὰ αὐτὰ ὁ σωτὴρ Ἰωάννῃ λέγει, εἷς ὁ ἀμφοτέρους πέμψας Θεός. καὶ τάχα Ἰωάννης μὲν ὡς ἑτοιμάζων θεῷ *κατεσκευασμένον* πρῶτος λέγει *μετανοεῖτε*, Ἰησοῦς δὲ ἡτοιμασμένα παραλαβὼν μηκέτι δεόμενα μετανοίας οὐ λέγει *μετανοεῖτε*. οὐκ ἀντικηρύσσων δὲ νόμῳ καὶ προφήταις, πληρώσαντι δὲ Ἰωάννῃ τὴν παλαιὰν *κηρύσσειν ἤρξατο* τὴν νέαν, αὐτὸς ἀρχὴ γενόμενος αὐτῆς. διὸ ἐπὶ Ἰωάννου οὐ γέγραπται τὸ *ἤρξατο*. πέρας γὰρ ἦν. καὶ ὅτι ὁ μὲν ἐν ἐρήμῳ κηρύσσει, ὁ δὲ ἐν λαῷ. ἡ δὲ *βασιλεία τῶν οὐρανῶν* οὐκ ἐν τόπῳ ἐστίν, ἐν δὲ διαθέσει. *ἐντὸς* γὰρ *ἡμῶν ἐστιν*. ὅρα δὲ εἰ Ἰωάννης μὲν κηρύσσει ἐγγίζουσαν *βασιλείαν οὐρανῶν*, βασιλεὺς Χριστὸς ἣν παραδώσει *τῷ θεῷ καὶ πατρί*.[ccxxxiii]

ἴσχει δ᾽ αὐτὴν ὁ ἀποθέμενος *τὴν εἰκόνα τοῦ χοϊκοῦ* καὶ ἀναλαβὼν *τοῦ ἐπουρανίου*.[304] Τοῦτο γάρ ἐστι *βασιλεία οὐρανῶν*, τὸ ζῆν θεαρέστως καὶ ἀναμαρτήτως.

(ΩΡΙΓΕΝΟΥΣ, added on the margin). Βασιλεία οὐρανῶν ἢ τὰ μετὰ τὴν ἀνάστασιν ἀγαθὰ ἢ τὸ κήρυγμα.

> *Βασιλεία οὐρανῶν* ἢ τὰ μετὰ τὴν ἀνάστασιν ἀγαθὰ ἢ τὸ κήρυγμα.[ccxxxiv]

> λέγεται *βασιλεία* ἡ ἀνάστασις καθώς φησιν· *ἕως ἂν αὐτὸ πίνω καινὸν ἐν τῇ βασιλείᾳ*. λέγεται βασιλεία καὶ αὐτὸ τὸ κήρυγμα ὡς τῆς βασιλείας πρόξενον καθώς φησιν. ὁμοιώθη *ἡ βασιλεία τῶν οὐρανῶν κόκκῳ σινάπεως* καὶ *ὁμοία ἐστὶν ἡ βασιλεία τῶν οὐρανῶν ζύμῃ*. δι᾽ ἑκατέρας γὰρ παραβολῆς τὸ κήρυγμα ὑπαινίττεται.[ccxxxv]

(ΩΡΙΓΕΝΟΥΣ, main text. cont.) *εἶδεν*[ccxxxvi] *δύο ἀδελφούς, Σίμωνα τὸν λεγόμενον*.[305] Δευτέρα ἐστὶν ἡ κλῆσις αὕτη Ἀνδρέου καὶ Πέτρου. Ὁ γὰρ εὐαγγελιστὴς Ἰωάννης φησὶ ὅτι οὔπω βληθέντος ἐν τῇ φυλακῇ τοῦ Προδρόμου, προσῆλθον οὗτοι. Οὗτος δὲ ἐνταῦθα, μετὰ τὸ βληθῆναι. Κἀκεῖ μὲν ὁ Ἀνδρέας καλεῖ τὸν Πέτρον· ἐνταῦθα δὲ ἀμφοτέρους ὁ Κύριος.[306] Μετὰ γὰρ τὴν πρώτην κλῆσιν, διδαχθέντες ὑπὸ Χριστοῦ, πάλιν ὑπέστρεψαν εἰς τὸν Ἰωάννην. Μετὰ δὲ τὸ εἰς δεσμωτήριον εἰσελθεῖν τὸν Ἰωάννην, εἰς τὴν οἰκείαν τέχνην πάλιν ἐπανῆλθον.

---

303 Cf. 1 Cor. 15:24.

304 1 Cor. 15:49.

305 Matt. 4:18.

306 Matt. 4:18-20. John, 1:37-42.

> *Περιπατῶν δὲ παρὰ τὴν θάλασσαν τῆς Γαλιλαίας.* Χρὴ δὲ τοῦτο γινώσκειν ὅτι δευτέρα ἦν ἡ κλῆσις Πέτρου καὶ Ἀνδρέου,[ccxxxvii] ἣν ὁ Ματθαῖος λέγει. ὁ μὲν γὰρ Εὐαγγελιστὴς Ἰωάννης φησίν, ὅτι οὔπω βληθέντος ἐν τῇ φυλακῇ τοῦ προδρόμου προσῆλθον. ἐνταῦθα δὲ μετὰ τὸ ἐμβληθῆναι αὐτόν. κἀκεῖ μὲν ὁ Ἀνδρέας καλεῖ τὸν Πέτρον. ἐνταῦθα δὲ ἀμφοτέρους ὁ Κύριος Ἰησοῦς. καὶ ἐξ ἑτέρων δέ ἐστι τοῦτο συνιδεῖν. μετὰ δὲ τὴν πρώτην κλῆσιν, διὰ τοῦτο πάλιν εἰς τὴν οἰκείαν τέχνην ἐπανῆλθον, διὰ τὸ εἰς δεσμωτήριον εἰσελθεῖν τὸν Ἰωάννην.[ccxxxviii]

Ὁρῶν τοίνυν τὸ εὐφυὲς αὐτῶν ὁ Κύριος, ἔρχεται πάλιν αὐτοὺς ἀνακτησόμενος καὶ κελεύει ἀκολουθεῖν, ἵνα, ἀνθ' ὧν εἶχον δικτύων, λαβόντες τὴν ἀπὸ λόγου ἀληθείας πλακεῖσαν σαγήνην καὶ βαλόντες εἰς τὴν τοῦ βίου θάλασσαν, περιλάβωσιν ὅσους ἐὰν εὕρωσι, *παντὸς γένους*[307] πληροῦντες ἀνθρώπων.[308]

Καὶ προβὰς ἐκεῖθεν, εἶδεν ἄλλους δύο[309] *ἀδελφούς.*[310] Καὶ οὗτοι ἐν ἀγνοίᾳ καὶ *σκότῳ* καθήμενοι,[311] ἐκ τοῦ ἀκροᾶσθαι τοῦ κηρύγματος ἑωράκεισαν *φῶς μέγα.*[312] Διὸ καὶ καλοῦνται.
Εἰκὸς δὲ Ζεβεδαῖον μὴ παραδεδέχθαι τὸ κήρυγμα, διὸ εὐλόγως ἀφίεται.

> Εἰκὸς Ζεβεδαῖον μὴ παραδέχεσθαι τὸ κήρυγμα. διὸ εἰκότως ἀφίεται ὑπὸ τῶν ἐξελθόντων ἐκ τῆς συγγενείας καὶ τοῦ οἴκου τοῦ πατρός.[ccxxxix]

Ὅρα δὲ εἰ *οἱ μὲν ἐν σαρκὶ ὄντες ἐν* | **24v** *πλοίῳ*[313] *εἰσίν*, οἳ καὶ *Θεῷ ἀρέσαι οὐ δύνανται,*[314] οἱ δὲ μὴ *κατὰ σάρκα* στρατευόμενοι[315] γενόμενοι *ἐν πνεύματι*[316] ἀφιᾶσι τὸ πλοῖον. Τήρει δὲ ὅτι ἡ μήτηρ αὐτῶν ἐπείσθη τῷ κηρύγματι ἐκ τοῦ κατακολουθεῖν τῷ Ἰησοῦ πολλαχοῦ[317] καὶ πιστῶς αἰτεῖν ἵνα τῶν υἱῶν αὐτῆς ὁ μὲν *ἐκ δεξιῶν* ὁ δὲ ἐξ ἀριστερῶν καθεσθῶσι τοῦ Ἰησοῦ, *ἐν τῇ βασιλείᾳ* αὐτοῦ.[318]

Διδάσκων ἐν ταῖς συναγωγαῖς αὐτῶν καὶ κηρύσσων.[319] Εἰ καὶ προηγεῖται τὸ κηρύσσειν τοῦ διδάσκειν, ἀλλ' ἐπεὶ μὴ πάντων ἦν τὸ διδάσκεσθαι, πάλιν ἐπιφέρει τὸ κηρύσσειν. Ἐδίδασκε δὲ σαφηνίζων τὰ τοῖς συναγομένοις μὴ νοούμενα. *Ἐν δὲ*

---

307 Matt. 13:47.
308 Matt. 4:19.
309 Cod. β̅ for δύο.
310 Matt. 4:21.
311 Cf. Matt. 4:16; cf. Isaiah, 9:2; 42:7; Psalm 106:10. Luke, 1:79.
312 Cf. Is. 9:1; Matt. 4:16.
313 Matt. 4:21.
314 Rom. 8:8.
315 2 Cor. 10:3.
316 Cf. Matt. 3:11; 22:43; John, 4:23-24; Rom. 2:29; 8:9.
317 Cf. Matt. 27:56.
318 Matt. 20:20-21.
319 Matt. 4:23.

ταῖς συναγωγαῖς ἐδίδασκε καὶ ἐθαυματούργει, δεικνὺς δι᾽ ἀμφοτέρων ὅτι οὐκ ἦν *πλάνος*[320] οὐδὲ ἀντίθεος προτρεπόμενος εἰς πίστιν τῆς αὐτοῦ δυνάμεως. Ἀδιαφόρως δὲ ὁ εὐαγγελιστὴς τοὺς δαιμονιζομένους σεληνιαζομένους ἐκάλεσε, οὐκ ἐπειδὴ ἡ σελήνη πάθους ἐστὶ ποιητική, ἀλλ᾽ ἐπεὶ ὁ δαίμων κατά τινας αὐτῆς περιόδους ἐπιτίθεται τισίν, ἵνα ἐπὶ τὸν αὐτῆς δημιουργὸν ὡς κακῶν ποιητὴν ἡ βλασφημία ἔλθῃ.

> Εἰκὸς δὲ ὅτι, ὥσπερ τοῦτο τὸ ἐνεργοῦν τὸν καλούμενον σεληνιασμὸν πνεῦμα ἀκάθαρτον ἐπιτηρεῖ τοὺς τῆς σελήνης σχηματισμούς, ἵνα ἐνεργήσῃ εἰς τὸν διά τινας αἰτίας παραδιδόμενον αὐτῷ καὶ μὴ ποιήσαντα ἑαυτὸν ἄξιον φρουρᾶς ἀγγελικῆς, οὕτως καὶ ἄλλα πνεύματα καὶ δαιμόνια πρός τινας σχηματισμοὺς τῶν ἄλλων ἀστέρων, ἵνα μὴ μόνον σελήνη ἀλλὰ καὶ οἱ λοιποὶ λοιδορηθῶσιν ἀστέρες ὑπὸ τῶν *ἀδικίαν εἰς τὸ ὕψος*.[321] λαλούντων.[ccxl]

> He is speaking not of those who were truly lunatics, but of those who were thought to be lunatics, due to the deception by daemons. By observing the lunar periods, daemons crave besmirching the creation in order that blasphemies redound on the Creator.[ccxli]

Τοιαῦτα δὲ πάθη καὶ ψυχὴν ἐνοχλεῖ, ὡς θυμὸς καὶ ἐπιθυμία καὶ ἕτερα τινὰ ἐκκωφοῦντα ψυχὴν πρὸς τὸν σωτήριον καὶ εὐαγγελικὸν λόγον, *ποικίλαις νόσοις καὶ βασάνοις* συνεχομέν‹ην›.[322]
Τὸ ποικίλον τῶν κακιῶν ὄψει ἐν ἀσωτίᾳ ἢ φιλαργυρίᾳ ἢ ἀγροικίᾳ ἢ ἀκολασίᾳ καὶ εὐηθείᾳ καὶ πανουργίᾳ καὶ θρασύτητι καὶ δειλίᾳ καὶ πᾶσι φαύλοις ἐναντίοις. Βάσανοι δὲ ψυχῇ, χρήματα, δόξα, πενία, ἀδοξία. Καὶ ὑπὸ δαιμόνων ἀδικοῦνται μὲν σώματα, ἐνεργοῦνται δὲ ψυχαὶ εἰς τὸ ἁμαρτάνειν καὶ μαίνεσθαι. Ὁ δὲ σεληνια | **25r** ζόμενος ἔχει τὸ *ἄλαλον καὶ κωφὸν*[323] δαιμόνιον. Τοιαῦτα δὲ πάθη ἐκ διαλειμμάτων ἐνοχλεῖ ψυχῇ, ἐκκωφοῦντα πρὸς τὸν σωτήριον λόγον, ὡς θυμὸς παράλυσίς ἐστι ψυχῶν,[ccxlii] ὧν ὁ ἐπιβάλλων τόνος[ccxliii] παρίεται καὶ τὸ πρακτικὸν καὶ πορευτικόν. *Μαλακίαν*[324] δὲ ψυχῆς γενικῶς μὲν λέγουσιν Ἕλληνες τὴν ἀπὸ κακίας νόσον, ‹ε›ἰδικῶς δὲ τὴν ἐναντίαν τῇ καρτερίᾳ, ἔνδοσιν οὖσαν πρὸς ὑπομονὴν καὶ πόνους καὶ ἀλγηδόνας.[ccxliv]

> Τὸ ποικίλον τῶν κακιῶν ὄψει ἐν ἀσωτίᾳ ἢ φιλαργυρίᾳ ἢ ἀγροικίᾳ ἢ ἀκολασίᾳ καὶ εὐηθείᾳ καὶ πανουργίᾳ καὶ θρασύτητι καὶ δειλίᾳ καὶ πᾶσι φαύλοις ἐναντίοις, βάσανοι δὲ ψυχῆς χρήματα, δόξα, πενία, ἀδοξία. καὶ ὑπὸ δαιμόνων ἀδικοῦνται μὲν σώματα, ἐνεργοῦνται δὲ ψυχαὶ εἰς τὸ ἁμαρτάνειν καὶ μαίνεσθαι. ὁ δὲ σεληνιαζόμενος ἔχει τὸ *ἄλαλον καὶ κωφὸν* δαιμόνιον. τοιαῦτα δὲ πάθη ἐκ διαλειμμάτων ἐνοχλεῖ ψυχῇ, ἐκκωφοῦντα πρὸς τὸν σωτήριον λόγον, ὡς θυμὸς παράλυσίς ἐστι ψυχῶν, ὧν ὁ ἐπιβάλλων τόνος παρίεται καὶ τὸ πρακτικὸν καὶ πορευτικόν. *Μαλακίαν* δὲ ψυχῆς γενικῶς μὲν λέγουσιν

---

320 Cf. Matt. 27:63.
321 Cf. Psalms 72:8; 74:6.
322 Cod. συνεχομένους. Cf. Matt. 4:24.
323 Mark, 9:25.
324 Matt. 4:23; 9:35; 10:1.

Ἕλληνες τὴν ἀπὸ κακίας νόσον, εἰδικῶς δὲ τὴν ἐναντίαν τῇ καρτερίᾳ, ἔνδοσιν οὖσαν πρὸς ὑπομονὴν καὶ πόνους καὶ ἀλγηδόνας.[ccxlv]

Καὶ σεληνιαζομένους.[325] Δαίμων ὁ σεληνιακὸς τὴν τοῦ Θεοῦ διαβαλεῖν πειρώμενος κτίσιν τῇ κινήσει τῆς σελήνης ἐπὶ λύμῃ χωρεῖ. Καὶ ἄλλην δὲ αἰτίαν ἴσως εὑρήσεις καὶ τοῦτο ‹ε›ἰδικῶς· τὴν δὲ εἰκόνα θεωρῶν ὄψει.[ccxlvi]

Δαίμων ὁ σεληνιακὸς τὴν τοῦ Θεοῦ διαβαλεῖν πειρώμενος κτίσιν τῇ κινήσει τῆς σελήνης ἐπὶ λύμῃ χωρεῖ. Καὶ ἄλλην δὲ αἰτίαν ἴσως εὑρήσεις καὶ τοῦτο ‹ε›ἰδικῶς. τὴν δὲ εἰκόνα θεωρῶν ὄψει.[ccxlvii]

καὶ ἠκολούθησαν αὐτῷ ὄχλοι πολλοὶ ἀπὸ τῆς Γαλιλαίας.[326] Ἀκολουθοῦσι τῷ Ἰησοῦ ὄντι λόγῳ καὶ σοφίᾳ[ccxlviii] οἱ ἀπὸ τῶν εἰρημένων πόλεων πρὸς τὸ ῥητόν
καὶ οἱ ἀπὸ ἀστάτων προσερχόμενοι πραγμάτων, ὡς ἀπὸ τῆς κατακυλιστῆς[ccxlix] *Γαλιλαίας καὶ* οἱ *ἀπὸ τῆς Δεκαπόλεως* (τῆς ἐναντίας ἐκείναις περὶ ὧν λέγεται· *ἴσθι ἐπάνω δέκα πόλεων*[327]) καὶ οἱ ἀπὸ *Ἱερουσαλήμ*, τῆς ἀποκτεννούσης *τοὺς προφήτας*[328] *καὶ* ἀπὸ *Ἰουδαίας*, μερίδος Θεοῦ[329] ἡμαρτηκυίας[ccl] καὶ οἱ ἀπὸ τῶν πόρρω τοῦ ποταμοῦ,

Οἱ μὲν γὰρ ἀπὸ ἀστάτων πραγμάτων καὶ τροχηδὸν ἐγκαλινδουμένων, ὡς ἀπό τινος Γαλιλαίας προσέδραμον τῷ κηρύγματι. Γαλιλαία γὰρ κατακυλιστὴ ἑρμηνεύεται. οἱ δὲ ὡς ἀπὸ Δεκαπόλεως ὅσοι τῆς Ἰσραηλιτικῆς εὐγενείας ἐπρέσβευον τὴν τοῦ νόμου Δεκάλογον, εἶτα τοῖς εὐαγγελικοῖς δικτύοις ἐσαγηνεύθησαν. Ἀλλὰ καὶ οἱ ἀπὸ τῆς Ἱερουσαλὴμ ἐκείνης τῆς ἀποκτεννούσης τὸν προφητικὸν λόγον, τῷ μὴ τὰς προρρήσεις τῶν προφητῶν παραδέχεσθαι, καὶ οὗτοι ἐντὸς τῆς πίστεως γίνονται. Καὶ οἱ τῆς τῶν ἁμαρτωλῶν μερίδος ὑπάρχοντες, πόρνοι καὶ τελῶναι, ὡς ἐξ Ἰουδαίας τινὸς δι᾽ ἐξομολογήσεως εἴσω τῶν τῆς Ἐκκλησίας περιβόλων εἰσήχθησαν. Ἰουδαία γὰρ ἑρμηνεύεται *μερὶς ἡμαρτηκυῖα Θεῷ*, δηλοῖ δὲ καὶ τὴν ἐξομολόγησιν. Καὶ μὴν καὶ οἱ πέραν τοῦ Ἰορδάνου, οἱ μακρὰν δηλαδὴ τοῦ βαπτίσματος, τὴν ἐκ τῆς κολυμβήθρας ἀναγέννησιν δέχονται.[ccli]

ἐν ᾧ βαπτισθεὶς Ἰησοῦς πληροῖ *πᾶσαν δικαιοσύνην.*[330] Πλήν, τοὺς ὁποθενοῦν προσιόντας προσίεται.
Φεύγων δὲ τὸ φιλόκομπον[cclii] εἰς τὸ ὄρος ἄνεισιν, ἵνα ἐκτὸς ὄχλου καθ᾽ ἡσυχίαν διδάξῃ.

325 Matt. 4:24.
326 Matt. 4:25.
327 Luke, 19:17.
328 Matt. 23:37; Luke, 13:34.
329 Cf. Deut. 32:8-9; Psalms of Solomon, 14:5.
330 Matt. 3:15.

> Τίνος χάριν ὁ Κύριος καὶ Θεὸς ἡμῶν Ἰησοῦς Χριστὸς ἰδὼν τοὺς ὄχλους, ἀνέβη εἰς τὸ ὄρος; διὰ τὸ ἀφιλότιμον καὶ ἀκόμπαστον. ... καὶ τῶν ἐν μέσῳ θορύβων ἀπαλλάττεσθαι.[ccliii]

δεῖ δὲ καὶ τοὺς τῷ Χριστῷ προσκολλωμένους[331] μὴ ἐπὶ γῆς *τὸ φρόνημα*[332] ἔχειν, ἀλλ' ἀναβαίνειν ἐπὶ τὴν τῆς διανοίας κατάστασιν.

Ἰδὼν δὲ τοὺς ὄχλους, ἀνέβη εἰς τὸ ὄρος.[333] Ἀναδράμωμεν καὶ ἡμεῖς πρὸς | **25v** τὴν ἄνοδον, ἵνα μετὰ τοῦ Ἰησοῦ κατὰ τὴν ἀκρώρειαν τῆς ἐλπίδος γενόμενοι ἴδωμεν ἐκ περιωπῆς τὰ ἀγαθὰ ἐκεῖνα, ὅσα τοῖς ἀκολουθήσασιν ἐπὶ τὸ ὕψος ὁ λόγος δείκνυσι. Μὴ γὰρ δὴ τοῖς μαθηταῖς ἐκείνοις νόμιζε διαλέγεσθαι μόνον, ἀλλὰ καὶ δι' ἐκείνων ἅπασιν. Ἐν γὰρ τῇ πρὸς ἐκείνους διαλέξει καὶ τοῖς λοιποῖς ἅπασι τοῖς σφόδρα ἀποδέουσι τῶν λεγομένων ἀνεπαχθῆ παρασκευάζει τῆς φιλοσοφίας τὴν διδασκαλίαν.

> Ἀναδράμωμεν καὶ ἡμεῖς πρὸς τὴν ἄνοδον, ἵνα μετὰ τοῦ Ἰησοῦ κατὰ τὴν ἀκρώρειαν τῆς ἐλπίδος γενόμενοι ἴδωμεν ἐκ περιωπῆς τὰ ἀγαθὰ ἐκεῖνα, ὅσα τοῖς ἀκολουθήσασιν ἐπὶ τὸ ὕψος ὁ λόγος δείκνυσι. [μὴ γὰρ δὴ τοῖς μαθηταῖς ἐκείνοις νόμιζε διαλέγεσθαι μόνον, ἀλλὰ καὶ δι' ἐκείνων ἅπασιν. ἐν γὰρ τῇ πρὸς ἐκείνους διαλέξει καὶ τοῖς λοιποῖς ἅπασι τοῖς σφόδρα ἀποδέουσι τῶν λεγομένων ἀνεπαχθῆ παρασκευάζει τῆς φιλοσοφίας τὴν διδασκαλίαν.][ccliv]

> Οὐκοῦν δράμωμεν καὶ ἡμεῖς πρὸς τὴν ἄνοδον, ἵνα μετὰ Ἡσαΐου κατὰ τὴν ἀκρώρειαν τῆς ἐλπίδος γενόμενοι, ἴδωμεν ἐκ περιωπῆς τὰ ἀγαθὰ ἐκεῖνα, ὅσα τοῖς ἀκολουθήσασιν ἐπὶ τὸ ὕψος ὁ Λόγος δείκνυσιν. Ἀλλ' ἀνοιξάτω καὶ ἡμῖν ὁ Θεὸς Λόγος τὸ στόμα, καὶ διδαξάτω ἡμᾶς ἐκεῖνα, ὧν ἡ ἀκρόασις μακαριότης ἐστίν. γενέσθω δὲ ἡμῶν ἀρχὴ τῆς θεωρίας, ἡ τῶν εἰρημένων τῆς διδασκαλίας ἀρχή.[cclv]

Καὶ ἀνοίξας τὸ στόμα αὐτοῦ, ἐδίδασκεν.[334] Στόμα Θεοῦ ἀνοιγόμενον *οἱ θησαυροὶ τῆς σοφίας*[335] καὶ γνώσεώς εἰσίν, οὓς προφέρει διὰ τῆς διδασκαλίας, ἀρχόμενος πρεπόντως ἀπὸ μακαρισμῶν.

> Στόμα Χριστοῦ ἀνοιγόμενον *οἱ θησαυροὶ τῆς σοφίας* εἰσίν, οὓς προφέρει διὰ τῆς διδασκαλίας, ἀρχόμενος πρεπόντως αὐτῷ ἀπὸ μακαρισμῶν.[cclvi]

Καὶ πρῶτον μὲν οὐ τοὺς ἐν χρήμασι πτωχούς, ἀλλὰ τοὺς ἐν διανοίᾳ μακαρίζει λέγων· *μακάριοι οἱ πτωχοὶ τῷ πνεύματι, ὅτι αὐτῶν ἐστιν ἡ βασιλεία τῶν οὐρανῶν.*[336] Πτωχὸς γάρ ἐστι πνεύματι ὁ μὴ ὑπερόπτης ἀλλὰ ταπεινὸς αὐθαιρέτως διὰ θεοσέβειαν γενόμενος. Ἤτοι *πτωχοὶ τῷ πνεύματι* μακαριζόμενοι οἱ διὰ τὴν τοῦ Πνεύματος ἐντολὴν πάντα

331 Cf. 1 Cor. 6:17.
332 Cf. Rom. 8:6-7.
333 Matt. 5:1.
334 Matt. 5:2.
335 Col. 2:3.
336 Matt. 5:3.

ἀφέντες τὰ τῆς γῆς καὶ ἀκολουθήσαντες Χριστῷ,[337] ὧν τὸ ἔπαθλον *βασιλεία οὐρανῶν*. Οὐρανοὶ δέ,[cclvii] ἤτοι αἱ τῶν πλανωμένων σφαῖραι καὶ ἀπλανῶν ἢ περὶ τῶν μὴ παρερχομένων μὴ δὲ ἀπολλυμένων φησί.[338] Ἐπεὶ δὲ καὶ ὁ Χριστὸς *βασιλεία οὐρανῶν*,[cclviii] τὸ ἔπαθλον ἴσον τῷ αὐτῶν ἐστιν ὁ Χριστός. Διατί πρὸ πάντων μακαρίζει τοὺς πτωχοὺς τῷ πνεύματι, τουτέστιν τοὺς ταπεινούς; Ἐπειδὴ τὰ μέγιστα τῶν κακῶν ἐξ ἀπονοίας εἰσῆλθεν. Ὅ τε γὰρ διάβολος, οὐκ ὢν πρὸ τούτου τοιοῦτος, οὕτω διάβολος γέγονεν, ὅτε ὁ πρῶτος ἄνθρωπος, | **26r** ἰσοθεΐαν[cclix] φαντασθεὶς καὶ τοιαύταις ἐλπίσι παρὰ τοῦ διαβόλου φυσηθείς, ἐξετραχηλίσθη[339]
καὶ ἐπεὶ ἐμπέφυκέ πως τὸ κατὰ τὴν ἔπαρσιν πάθος παντὶ ἀνθρώπῳ.

> Ἐπεὶ οὖν ἐμπέφυκέ πως τὸ κατὰ τὴν ἔπαρσιν πάθος παντὶ σχεδὸν τῷ κοινωνοῦντι τῆς ἀνθρωπίνης φύσεως.[cclx]

Ἢ καὶ οὕτως· ὁ πάντων τῶν κατὰ κακίαν νοουμένων ἑκουσίως πτωχεύων, εἴη ἂν οὗτος ἐν τῇ τῶν μακαριζομένων πτωχείᾳ.

Μακάριοι οἱ πενθοῦντες.[340] Πενθοῦντας τοὺς μετὰ τὴν ἐπὶ τοῖς ἰδίοις παραπτώμασι μετάνοιαν πενθοῦντας καὶ ἐπὶ τοῖς τῶν πέλας διὰ τὸ συμπαθὲς μετ᾽ εὐλαβείας καὶ φροντίδος τῆς περὶ αὐτῶν φησι. Ἤτοι πενθοῦντας, τοὺς μὴ τρυφῶντας, ἀλλ᾽ ἐγκρατευομένους κατὰ τῶν τῆς σαρκὸς κινημάτων. Παρακαλοῦνται δὲ οὗτοι καὶ ὧδε κἀκεῖ ὑπὸ τῆς Ἁγίας Τριάδος.

14a

(ΣΕΥΗΡΟΥ)[cclxi] Πένθος ἐκάλεσε τὴν ἐποχὴν καὶ τὸν ἐξ ἐγκρατείας χαλινὸν τῆς τῶν ἐγκοσμίων ἡδονῶν διαχύσεως καὶ τὴν μονήρη ζωήν. Καθ᾽ ἣν ἔννοιαν καὶ ὁ Ἐκκλησιαστὴς ἔφησεν· *ἀγαθὸν πορευθῆναι εἰς οἶκον πένθους, ἢ ‹ὅτι πορευθῆναι› εἰς οἶκον πότου*.[341]

Μακάριοι οἱ πραεῖς.[342] Πραεῖς οὐ τοὺς ἠλιθίους ἐκ φύσεως, οἳ οὔτε στεφάνων ἀξιοῦνται, ἀλλὰ τοὺς ἐν καιρῷ ὀργῆς περιγινομένους τοῦ πάθους διὰ Θεόν φησι, οὐ μὴν ἀλλὰ καὶ πᾶσαν κακίαν ἐπέχοντας.
Πραότης[cclxii] ἐστὶν ἡσυχιότης[cclxiii] πρὸς τοὺς ἁμαρτάνοντας μετὰ ἀοργησίας· ἢ ἕξις καθ᾽ ἣν μετριαστικοί ἐσμεν περὶ τὰς κολάσεις· ἢ ἕξις εὐάγωγος[cclxiv] πρὸς τὸ ποιεῖν μὲν τὰ ἐπιβάλλοντα ἐν πᾶσι, μὴ ἐκφέρεσθαι δὲ εἰς ὀργὴν ἐν μηδενί· ἢ κρᾶσις ψυχῆς σύμμετρος· ἢ ῥαθυμία θυμοῦ ἐν τοῖς δοκοῦσι δεινοῖς· | **26v** ἡ ἐγκράτεια ὀργῆς, ὡς

337 Cf. Matt. 19:21.
338 Cf. Matt. 24:35; Mark, 13:31; Luke, 21:22.
339 Cf. Job, 15:25.
340 Matt. 5:4.
341 Ecclesiastes, 7:2.
342 Matt. 5:5.

ἀρχὴν μηδὲ[343] ἐγγ‹ί›νεσθαι· ἢ εὐκολία ψυχῆς ἀτάραχος· ἢ ἕξις καθ' ἣν ὁμιλοῦμεν κατ' αὐτάς, ποῖος μὲν πρᾶος, π‹οῖο›ς δὲ ‹οὐ› πρᾶος. Οὐ χαλεπὸν δὲ ἐφαρμόσαι τοὺς ὅρους Μωσεῖ, ὃς γέγραπται *πρᾶος παρὰ πάντας ἀνθρώπους τοὺς ἐπὶ τῆς γῆς.*[344] Καὶ ἔτι Δαυΐδ, περὶ οὗ εἴρηται· *μνήσθητι, Κύριε, τοῦ Δαυίδ καὶ πάσης τῆς πραότητος αὐτοῦ.*[345] Περὶ γὰρ τοῦ Σωτῆρος τί ἂν καὶ λέγοιμεν, ὃς διὰ πραότητα λέγεται ὅτι *ὡς πρόβατον ἐπὶ σφαγὴν ἤχθη,*[346] καὶ τὰ ἑξῆς; Ὃς καί φησι· *μάθετε ἀπ' ἐμοῦ ὅτι πρᾶός εἰμὶ καὶ ταπεινὸς τῇ καρδίᾳ.*[347]

Πραότης ἐστὶν ἡσυχιότης πρὸς τοὺς ἁμαρτάνοντας μετὰ ἀοργησίας, ἢ ἕξις καθ' ἣν μετριαστικοί ἐσμεν περὶ τὰς κολάσεις, ἢ ἕξις εὐάγωγος πρὸς τὸ ποιεῖν μὲν τὰ ἐπιβάλλοντα ἐν πᾶσι μὴ ἐκφέρεσθαι δὲ εἰς ὀργὴν ἐν μηδενί, ἢ κρᾶσις ψυχῆς σύμμετρος, ἢ ῥαθυμία θυμοῦ ἐν τοῖς δοκοῦσι δεινοῖς, ἢ ἐγκράτεια ὀργῆς ὡς ἀρχὴν μηδὲ ἐγγίνεσθαι, ἢ εὐκολία ψυχῆς ἀτάραχος, ἢ ἕξις καθ' ἣν ὁμιλοῦμεν κατ' αὐτάς, ποῖος μὲν πρᾶος, ποῖος δ' οὐ πρᾶος. οὐ χαλεπὸν δὲ ἐφαρμόσαι τοὺς ὅρους Μωσεῖ, ὃς γέγραπται *πρᾶος παρὰ πάντας ἀνθρώπους τοὺς ἐπὶ τῆς γῆς*, καὶ ἔτι Δαβίδ, περὶ οὗ εἴρηται. *μνήσθητι, Κύριε, τοῦ Δαβίδ καὶ πάσης τῆς πραότητος αὐτοῦ*. περὶ γὰρ τοῦ σωτῆρος τί ἂν καὶ λέγοιμεν, ὃς διὰ πραότητα λέγεται. *ὡς πρόβατον ἐπὶ σφαγὴν ἤχθη*, καὶ τὰ ἑξῆς, ὃς δέ φησι. *μάθετε ἀπ' ἐμοῦ ὅτι πρᾶός εἰμὶ καὶ ταπεινός*[348] *τῇ καρδίᾳ*.[cclxv]

(ΣΕΥΗΡΟΥ, cont.) Ἢ ἐπειδὴ πλεονάζει κατὰ τὴν φύσιν ἡ πρὸς τὰ κακὰ ταχυτής, καλῶς τὸ ἐν τοῖς τοιούτοις ἠρεμοῦν μακάριον.

Ἢ ἐπειδὴ πλεονάζει κατὰ τὴν φύσιν ἡ πρὸς τὰ κακὰ ταχυτής, καλῶς τὸ ἐν τοῖς τοιούτοις ἠρεμοῦν μακάριον.[cclxvi]

Ὅτι αὐτοὶ κληρονομήσουσι τὴν γῆν.[349] (ΣΕΥΗΡΟΥ, cont.) Γῆν δέ τινα καλοῦμεν ἀγαθὴν ῥέουσαν *λογικὸν ἄδολον γάλα*[350] καὶ μυστικὸν *μέλι*,[351] ἧς σκιὰ ἡ ἐν τῷ νόμῳ ὀνομασθεῖσα τοῖς *κατὰ σάρκα* Ἰουδαίοις.[352]

Γῆ ἐστι κληρονομίας ἡ ὑψηλὴ τῶν *ζώντων* καὶ τὰ ἴδια σώματα ἔνδοξα καὶ ἄφθαρτα κληρονομούντων.[cclxvii]

---

343 Cod. μὴ δὲ.

344 Num. 12:3: καὶ ὁ ἄνθρωπος Μωϋσῆς πραῢς σφόδρα παρὰ πάντας τοὺς ἀνθρώπους τοὺς ὄντας ἐπὶ τῆς γῆς.

345 Psalm, 131:1: πραΰτητος.

346 Is. 53:7, quoted in Acts, 8:32.

347 Matt. 11:29: πραΰς.

348 Matt. 11:29: πραΰς.

349 Matt. 5:4.

350 1 Peter, 2:2.

351 Cf. Ex. 3:8&17; 13:5; 33:3; Lev. 20:24; Num. 13:27; 14:8; 16:13-14; Deut. 6:3; 11:9-10; 26:9-10&15; 27:3; 31:20; Joshua, 5:6; Ecclesiasticus, 46:8; Jer. 11:5; 39:22; Baruch, 1:20; Ez. 20:6&15.

352 Cf. Rom. 8:4-5; 8:12-13; 9:3; 1 Cor. 18:18.

(ΣΕΥΗΡΟΥ, cont.)[cclxviii] Ἀλλ᾽ ἴσως ἐρεῖ ὁ ἀκούων, ἀδύνατον εἶναι μετὰ *τὴν τῶν οὐρανῶν βασιλείαν* τῆς γῆς τὴν κληρονομίαν καταλαμβάνεσθαι.[cclxix] Ἀλλ᾽ ἐνταῦθα *γῆν* τὴν ὑπερουράνιόν φησι. Εἰ δὲ τῇ προσηγορίᾳ τῆς γῆς ἡ ὑπερουράνιος λῆξις[cclxx] κατονομάζεται, μὴ θαυμάσῃς· τῷ γὰρ ταπεινῷ τῆς ἡμετέρας ἀκοῆς συγκαταβαίνει ὁ λόγος. Ὥσπερ γὰρ ἐπειδὴ μέγα τι καὶ ὑπὲρ πάντα τὰ τοῖς ἀνθρώποις περισπούδαστα τὸ τῆς βασιλείας κατὰ τὸν βίον ἐστί, διὰ τοῦτο συνεχρήσατο τῷ ὀνόματι τούτῳ πρὸς τὴν τῶν ὑπερκειμένων ἀγαθῶν δήλωσιν.

> Τὸν γὰρ τῷ πρώτῳ διὰ τῆς διανοίας ἐπιβεβηκότα μακαρισμῷ, δι᾽ ἀναγκαίας τινὸς τῆς τῶν νοημάτων ἀκολουθίας, ὁ μετ᾽ ἐκεῖνον ἐκδέχεται, κἂν ὑποξενίζειν δοκῇ παρὰ τὴν πρώτην ὁ λόγος. Μὴ γὰρ εἶναι δυνατὸν ἴσως ὁ ἀκούων ἐρεῖ, καθάπερ ἐν βαθμῶν διαθέσει, μετὰ τὴν τῶν οὐρανῶν βασιλείαν, τῆς γῆς τὴν κληρονομίαν καταλαμβάνεσθαι. ἀλλ᾽ εἴπερ ἔδει τῇ φύσει τῶν ὄντων τὸν λόγον ἕπεσθαι, τοῦ οὐρανοῦ τὴν γῆν ἀκολουθότερον ἦν προτετάχθαι, ὡς ἐντεῦθεν ἡμῖν ἐπ᾽ ἐκεῖνον ἐσομένης τῆς ἀναβάσεως. Ἀλλ᾽ εἰ πτερωθείημέν πως τῷ λόγῳ, καὶ ὑπὲρ τὰ νῶτα τῆς οὐρανίας ἀψῖδος σταίημεν, εὑρήσομεν ἐκεῖ τὴν ὑπερουράνιον γῆν, τὴν εἰς κληρονομίαν τοῖς κατ᾽ ἀρετὴν βεβιωκόσιν ἀποκειμένην, ... Εἰ δὲ τῇ προσηγορίᾳ τῆς γῆς ἡ ὑπερκειμένη κατονομάζεται λῆξις, θαυμάσεις μηδέν. τῷ γὰρ ταπεινῷ τῆς ἡμετέρας ἀκοῆς συγκαταβαίνει ὁ Λόγος, ὁ διὰ τοῦτο πρὸς ἡμᾶς καταβάς, ἐπειδὴ ἡμεῖς πρὸς αὐτὸν ἀνυψωθῆναι οὐχ οἷοί τε ἦμεν. Διὰ τοίνυν τῶν ἡμῖν γνωρίμων ῥημάτων τε καὶ ὀνομάτων παραδίδωσι τὰ θεῖα μυστήρια, ταύταις ταῖς φωναῖς κεχρημένος, ἃς ἡ συνήθεια τοῦ ἀνθρωπίνου περιέχει βίου. Καὶ γὰρ τῇ πρὸ ταύτης ἐπαγγελίᾳ τὸν ἄφραστον ἐκεῖνον ἐν τοῖς οὐρανοῖς μακαρισμόν, βασιλείαν ὠνόμασεν.[cclxxi]

(ΣΕΥΗΡΟΥ, cont.) Οὕτω καὶ *γῆν* ἔφησε τὴν ἄ | **27r** νω λῆξιν, περὶ ἧς καὶ Δαυίδ,[cclxxii] *πιστεύω τοῦ ἰδεῖν τὰ ἀγαθὰ Κυρίου ἐν γῇ ζώντων*,[353] ἐν ᾗ *τὸ ὕδωρ τῆς ἀναπαύσεως καὶ ὁ τῆς χλόης τόπος*[354] καὶ ἡ τετραχῇ μεριζομένη πηγή,[355] ἐφ᾽ ἧς *ἡ πόλις τοῦ βασιλέως τοῦ μεγάλου*,[356] περὶ ἧς τὰ *δεδοξασμένα ἐλαλήθη*.[357]

(ΣΕΥΗΡΟΥ, cont.) *Μακάριοι οἱ πεινῶντες καὶ διψῶντες*.[358] Πεινῶντας καὶ διψῶντας *τὴν δικαιοσύνην* τοὺς μετὰ πάσης σπουδῆς τὸ δίκαιον μεταδιώκοντας καὶ μὴ ἐξ ἀδικίας κερδᾶναί τι θέλοντάς φησί. Ἤτοι τοὺς ἀκορέστως ἔχοντας περὶ τὴν ἀγαθοεργίαν καὶ μὴ μετατρεπομένους. Δικαιοσύνη δέ, ἤτοι συνεκδοχικῶς πᾶσα ἀρετὴ ἢ κατ᾽ εἶδος μία ἀρετή, ὡς καὶ περὶ τῶν λοιπῶν λέγειν, *μακάριοι οἱ πεινῶντες* σωφροσύνην καὶ τὰς λοιπὰς ἀρετάς, αἵ εἰσι Χριστός,[cclxxiii]

> ὁ Χριστὸς γὰρ ἡ πᾶσα ἀρετή.[cclxxiv]

353 Psalm 26:13.
354 Cf. Psalm 22:2.
355 Cf. Gen. 2:10-14.
356 Psalm 47:3, quoted in Matt. 5:35.
357 Psalm 86:3.
358 Matt. 5:6.

(ΣΕΥΗΡΟΥ, cont.) γενόμενος[cclxxv] *ἡμῖν ἀπὸ Θεοῦ σοφία δικαιοσύνη τε καὶ ἁγιασμὸς καὶ ἀπολύτρωσις.*[359]

Εἰ δὲ χρὴ καί τινος τολμηροῦ καθάψασθαι λόγου, τάχα μοι δοκεῖ διὰ τοῦ κατ᾽ ἀρετὴν καὶ *δικαιοσύνην* λόγου ἑαυτὸν προτιθέναι τῇ ὀρέξει τῶν ἀκουόντων ὁ κύριος, *ὅς ἐγενήθη ἡμῖν σοφία ἀπὸ θεοῦ καὶ δικαιοσύνη καὶ ἁγιασμὸς καὶ ἀπολύτρωσις,* ἀλλὰ καὶ *ἄρτος ἐξ οὐρανοῦ καταβαίνων*[360] καὶ *ὕδωρ ζῶν*[361] οὗ διψῆν ὁμολογήσας ὁ μέγας Δαυὶδ ἔν τινι ψαλμῳδίᾳ φησίν· *ἐδίψησέν ἡ ψυχή μου πρὸς τὸν θεὸν τὸν ζῶντα. πότε ἥξω καὶ ὀφθήσομαι τῷ προσώπῳ ‹τοῦ θεοῦ*[362] *... ἐγὼ δὲ ἐν δικαιοσύνῃ σου ὀφθήσομαι τῷ προσώπῳ› σου, χορτασθήσομαι ἐν τῷ ὀφθῆναι τὴν δόξαν σου.*[363] αὕτη γοῦν ἐστιν (κατά γε τὸν ἐμὸν λόγον) ἡ ἀληθὴς ἀρετή, τὸ ἀμιγὲς τοῦ χείρονος ἀγαθόν, αὐτὸς ὁ θεός, ἡ τοὺς *οὐρανοὺς καλύψασα ἀρετή*, καθὼς ὁ ᾿Αμβακοὺμ διεξέρχεται.[cclxxvi]

Εἰ δὲ χρή τινος καὶ τολμηροῦ καθάψασθαι λόγου, δοκεῖ τάχα μοι διὰ τοῦ κατὰ τὴν ἀρετήν τε καὶ δικαιοσύνην λόγου ἑαυτὸν προτιθέναι τῇ ὀρέξει τῶν ἀκουόντων ὁ Κύριος, ὃς ἐγενήθη ἡμῖν σοφία ἀπὸ Θεοῦ, δικαιοσύνη τε καὶ ἁγιασμός, καὶ ἀπολύτρωσις, ἀλλὰ καὶ ἄρτος ἐξ οὐρανοῦ καταβαίνων, καὶ ὕδωρ ζῶν. οὗ διψῆν ὁμολογεῖ Δαβὶδ ἔν τινι ψαλμῳδίᾳ, τὸ μακαριστὸν τοῦτο τῆς ψυχῆς πάθος τῷ Θεῷ προσφέρων, ἐν οἷς φησιν· *᾿Εδίψησεν ἡ ψυχή μου πρὸς τὸν Θεὸν τὸν ἰσχυρόν, τὸν ζῶντα. πότε ἥξω καὶ ὀφθήσομαι τῷ προσώπῳ τοῦ Θεοῦ;* Ὅς μοι δοκεῖ τῇ δυνάμει τοῦ Πνεύματος προπαιδευθεὶς τὰ μεγαλοφυῆ ταῦτα τοῦ Κυρίου διδάγματα, καὶ τὴν πλησμονὴν τῆς τοιαύτης ὀρέξεως ἑαυτῷ προσειπεῖν. *᾿Εγὼ* γάρ, φησίν, *ἐν δικαιοσύνῃ ὀφθήσομαι τῷ προσώπῳ σου, χορτασθήσομαι ἐν τῷ ὀφθῆναί μοι τὴν δόξαν σου.* Αὕτη οὖν ἐστι κατά γε τὸν ἐμὸν λόγον ἡ ἀληθὴς ἀρετή, τὸ ἀμιγὲς τοῦ χείρονος ἀγαθόν, περὶ ὃ πᾶν νόημα τῶν πρὸς τὸ κρεῖττον νοουμένων καταλαμβάνεται αὐτὸς ὁ Θεὸς Λόγος, ἡ τοὺς οὐρανοὺς καλύψασα ἀρετή, καθὼς ὁ ᾿Αμβακοὺμ διεξέρχεται, καὶ καλῶς οἱ ταύτην τοῦ Θεοῦ τὴν δικαιοσύνην πεινῶντες, ἐμακαρίσθησαν.[cclxxvii]

(ΣΕΥΗΡΟΥ, cont.) Παρὰ τῷ Λουκᾷ μνημονεύονται μακαριζόμενοι ἁπλῶς *οἱ πεινῶντες.*[364] Νῦν δὲ ὁ Ματθαῖος διορίζει τοὺς ἑκόντας καὶ διὰ τὸν τοῦ καλοῦ πόθον τῶν κατὰ σάρκα ἡδέων ἀπεχομένους. Ὁμοίως οὖν ἀμφοτέρων ἀκουσόμεθα.

Παρὰ τῷ Λουκᾷ μνημονεύονται μακαριζόμενοι ἁπλῶς *οἱ πεινῶντες*, νῦν δὲ ὁ Ματθαῖος διορίζει τοὺς ἑκόντας καὶ διὰ τὸν τοῦ καλοῦ πόθον τῶν κατὰ σάρκα ἡδέων ἀπεχομένους. ὁμοίως οὖν ἀμφοτέρων ἀκουσόμεθα.[cclxxviii]

(ΣΕΥΗΡΟΥ, cont.) Ὁ *τὴν δικαιοσύνην* τοῦ Θεοῦ ποθήσας εὗρε τὸ ἀληθῶς ὀρεκτόν,[cclxxix] οὗ τὴν ἐπιθυμίαν οὐχ ἑνὶ τρόπῳ τῷ κατὰ τὴν ὄρεξιν ἐνεργουμένῳ ἐπλήρωσεν. Οὐ γὰρ μόνον ὡς βρῶσιν τὴν τοῦ δικαίου μετουσίαν[cclxxx] ἐπόθησεν·

---

359 1 Cor. 1:30.
360 John, 6:50.
361 Cf. John, 4:7.
362 Psalm 41:3.
363 Psalm 16:15.
364 Luke, 6:21.

ἡμιτελὴς γὰρ ἂν ἦν. Νῦν δὲ καὶ πότιμον τὸ ἀγαθὸν τοῦτο ἐποίησεν, ἵνα τὸ ἔνθερμόν τε καὶ διακαὲς τῆς ἐπιθυμίας τὸ πάθος τῆς δίψης ἐνδείξηται.

> Ὁ γὰρ τὴν δικαιοσύνην τοῦ Θεοῦ ποθήσας, εὗρεν τὸ ἀληθῶς ὀρεκτόν, οὗ τὴν ἐπιθυμίαν οὐχ ἑνὶ τρόπῳ τῶν κατὰ τὴν ὄρεξιν ἐνεργουμένων ἐπλήρωσεν· οὐ γὰρ μόνον ὡς βρῶσιν τὴν τοῦ δικαίου μετουσίαν ἐπόθησεν. Ἡμιτελὴς γὰρ ἂν ἦν ἐπὶ ταύτης μόνης τῆς διαθέσεως στᾶσα ἡ ὄρεξις· νυνὶ δὲ καὶ πότιμον τὸ ἀγαθὸν τοῦτο ἐποίησεν, ἵνα τὸ ἔνθερμόν τε καὶ διακαὲς τῆς ἐπιθυμίας τῷ πάθει τῆς δίψης ἐνδείξηται.[cclxxxi]

> ὁ τὴν *δικαιοσύνην* τοῦ θεοῦ ποθήσας εὗρε τὸ ἀληθῶς ὀρεκτόν, οὗ τὴν ἐπιθυμίαν οὐχ ἑνὶ τρόπῳ τῷ κατὰ τὴν ὄρεξιν ἐνεργουμένῳ ἐπλήρωσεν. οὐ γὰρ μόνον ὡς βρῶσιν τὴν τοῦ δικαίου μετουσίαν ἐπόθησεν. ἡμιτελὴς γὰρ ἦν. νῦν δὲ καὶ πότιμον τὸ ἀγαθὸν τοῦτο ἐποίησεν, ἵνα τὸ ἔνθερμόν τε καὶ διακαὲς τῆς ἐπιθυμίας τὸ πάθος τῆς δίψης ἐνδείξηται.[cclxxxii]

(ΣΕΥΗΡΟΥ, cont.) Ὁ τοιοῦτος, φησί, ἐμπλησθήσεται. ἡ δὲ πλησμονὴ οὐκ ἀποστροφήν, | **27v** ἀλλ᾽ ἐπίτασιν ποιεῖ τῆς ὀρέξεως.

> ὁ τοιοῦτός φησιν ἐμπλησθήσεται. ἡ δὲ πλησμονὴ οὐκ ἀποστροφήν, ἀλλ᾽ ἐπίτασιν ποιεῖ τῆς ὀρέξεως.[cclxxxiii]

(ΣΕΥΗΡΟΥ, cont.) *Μακάριοι οἱ ἐλεήμονες.*[365] Οὐ μόνον οἱ συμπαθητικῇ ψυχῇ[cclxxxiv] τοὺς ἐν ἐνδείᾳ χρημάτων εὐεργετοῦντες λέγονται *ἐλεήμονες*, ἀλλὰ καὶ οἱ θέλοντες, κἂν μὴ δύνωνται. Ἔστι γὰρ οὐ μόνον διὰ χρημάτων, ἀλλὰ καὶ διὰ πραγμάτων[cclxxxv] ἔλεος· ποικίλος γὰρ ὁ τῆς ἐλεημοσύνης τρόπος. Καὶ γὰρ καὶ αὐτοὶ μιμοῦνται κατὰ τὸ δυνατὸν τὸν Θεὸν ἐν καιρῷ κρίσεως ἐλεοῦντα τοὺς ἐλεήμονας, αἰτοῦντας ἀνθ᾽ ὧν καὶ αὐτοὶ εἰς τοὺς ἀδελφοὺς εὖ εἰργάσαντο. Δεόμενοι γὰρ ἀεὶ ἐλέους Θεοῦ, ἐλεοῦντες ἐλεηθήσονται.[366]

(ΣΕΥΗΡΟΥ, cont.) Ἔστιν ἔλεος ψεκτός, ὡς ἐπὶ τοῦ Σαοὺλ ἐπὶ *Ἄγαγ* τὸν ἀλλόφυλον.[367] Τὸ γὰρ ἀνωφελὲς οὐκ ἔλεος οὐδὲ ἐπιστημονικῶς. Καὶ διὰ τοῦτό φησι ὁ Θεὸς διὰ τοῦ προφήτου περὶ τῶν ἁμαρτωλῶν· *οὐκ οἰκτειρήσω καὶ οὐκ ἐλεήσω.*[368] Καὶ Παῦλος· *ἴδε οὖν χρηστότητα καὶ ἀποτομίαν Θεοῦ· ἐπὶ μὲν τοὺς πεσόντας ἀποτομία, ἐπὶ δὲ σὲ χρηστότης.*[369]

> Ἔστιν ἔλεος ψεκτὸς ὡς ἐπὶ τοῦ Σαοὺλ ἐπὶ Ἀγὰγ τὸν ἀλλόφυλον. τὸ γὰρ ἀνωφελὲς οὐκ ἔλεος οὐδὲ ἐπιστημονικῶς. καὶ διὰ τοῦτο φησὶν ὁ Θεὸς διὰ τοῦ προφήτου περὶ τῶν ἁμαρτωλῶν. *οὐκ οἰκτειρήσω καὶ οὐκ ἐλεήσω,*[370] καὶ Παῦλος. *ἴδε οὖν χρηστότητα καὶ ἀποτομίαν Θεοῦ. ἐπὶ μὲν τοὺς πεσόντας ἀποτομία, ἐπὶ δὲ σὲ χρηστότης.*[cclxxxvi]

---

365 Matt. 5:7.
366 Cf. Matt. 5:7.
367 Cf. 1 Kings, 15:8-9.
368 Cf. Jer. 13:14; 21:7.
369 Rom. 11:22.
370 Cf. Jer. 13:14; 21:7.

(ΣΕΥΗΡΟΥ, cont.)[371] *Μακάριοι οἱ καθαροὶ τῇ καρδίᾳ.*[372] Τούτους βούλεται καθαροὺς εἶναι τῇ καρδίᾳ τοὺς τὴν ἠθικὴν καὶ πνευματικὴν κατορθώσαντας ἀρετὴν καὶ ὀρθὰς ἔχοντας περὶ Θεοῦ δόξας· τουτέστι τοὺς εἰς ἐπίγνωσιν Θεοῦ ἀγομένους καὶ πᾶσαν ἀσκήσαντας ἀρετὴν σώματος καὶ ψυχῆς κατὰ ἁγίους διαλογισμούς, ὡς μὴ ἐπισκοτοῦντας τῷ ἡγεμονικῷ πρὸς τὸ ἰδεῖν τὸν Θεὸν τοῖς τῆς γνώσεως ὀφθαλμοῖς. Ἤτοι τούτους φησί, τοὺς διὰ τῆς πρακτικῆς ἀρετῆς[cclxxxvii] διὰ τοῦ τῆς καρδίας καθαροῦ γνωρίζοντας τὰ ἐν ταῖς θείαις γραφαῖς λαλούμενα. Τοῦ | **28r** το γάρ ἐστι τὸ χωρῆσαι ἰδεῖν Θεὸν ἐμπαρέχοντα ἑαυτὸν[cclxxxviii] βλέπεσθαι. Ἡ γὰρ ἀσκητικὴ[cclxxxix] καὶ πρακτικὴ πολιτεία γεωργοῦσα τὸ μακάριον πένθος, τὴν ἐν ταῖς θείαις ἡμῖν γραφαῖς γνῶσιν καὶ θεωρίαν χαρίζεται καὶ πρὸς τὴν καθαρότητα τῆς καρδίας ἀναβιβάζει, δι᾽ ἧς τοῖς τῆς γνώσεως ὀφθαλμοῖς ὁρῶμεν Θεὸν καὶ τοῦ μακαρισμοῦ τοῦ Σωτῆρος τυγχάνομεν, φήσαντος· *μακάριοι οἱ καθαροὶ τῇ καρδίᾳ, ὅτι αὐτοὶ τὸν Θεόν ὄψονται.* Πρακτικὴ γὰρ ἐργασία χηρεύουσα γνώσεως βάναυσός τις ἐστὶ καὶ ἄλογος καὶ ὁμοία τοῖς μετιοῦσι τεκτονικὴν ἢ χαλευκτικὴν καὶ οὐδὲν διανοουμένοις οὐράνιον.
Οὐκ ἔστι *Θεόν* ἰδεῖν μὴ καθαρθέντα *τῇ καρδίᾳ.* Ἡ οὖν καρδία ὀφθαλμός ἐστιν, ὁ δὲ ὀφθαλμὸς ἡ φύσις τοῦ νοός. Ὥσπερ οὖν ὁ ὀφθαλμὸς θεωρῶν τὸ φῶς κατὰ φύσιν ἐστὶν (εἰ δὲ οὐ, θεωρεῖ παρὰ φύσιν) οὕτω καὶ τὸ νοερόν. Τὸ οὖν κατὰ φύσιν ὁρᾶν, τὸ καθαρόν ἐστι.

> Οὐκ ἔστι *Θεόν* ἰδεῖν μὴ καθαρθέντα *τῇ καρδίᾳ.* Ἡ γὰρ καρδία ὀφθαλμός ἐστιν, ὁ δὲ ὀφθαλμὸς ἡ φύσις τοῦ νοός. ὥσπερ οὖν ὁ ὀφθαλμὸς θεωρῶν τὸ φῶς κατὰ φύσιν ἐστίν, εἰ δὲ οὐ θεωρεῖ παρὰ φύσιν, οὕτως καὶ τὸ νοερόν. τὸ γὰρ κατὰ φύσιν ὁρᾶν, τὸ καθαρόν ἐστιν.[ccxc]

Καρδία[ccxci] *Θεὸν* ὁρᾷ· ἀσωμάτῳ γὰρ τὸ ἀσώματον καταληπτόν. Τελειωθεῖσα δὲ ἡ καρδία τὴν ἐνδεχομένην τελείωσιν, οὕτως ὄψεται τὸ τέλειον. Τοῦτο δὲ αὐτῇ γίνεται ἐκ καθάρσεως τῶν ἐμποδιζόντων, ὥσπερ καὶ ὀφθαλμὸς ἐκκαθαιρόμενος ἐκ τῶν ἐμποδίων τῆς ὁράσεως ὁρᾷ τὸ φῶς.

> Καρδία θεὸν ὁρᾷ. ἀσωμάτῳ γὰρ τὸ ἀσώματον καταληπτόν. τελειωθεῖσα δὲ ἡ καρδία τὴν ἐνδεχομένην τελείωσιν οὕτως ὄψεται τὸ τέλειον. τοῦτο δὲ αὐτῇ γίνεται ἐκ καθάρσεως τῶν ἐμποδιζόντων, ὥσπερ καὶ ὁ ὀφθαλμὸς ἐκκαθαιρόμενος ἐκ τῶν ἐμποδίων τῆς ὁράσεως ὁρᾷ τὸ φῶς.[ccxcii]

(ΣΕΥΗΡΟΥ, cont.)[ccxciii] Καθαροὺς ἐνταῦθα φησὶ ἤτοι τοὺς καθολικὴν ἀρετὴν κεκτημένους καὶ μηδὲν ἑαυτοῖς συνειδότας πονηρόν, ἢ τοὺς ἐν σωφροσύνῃ διάγοντας. Οὐδενὸς γὰρ ἡμῖν οὕτως δεῖ πρὸς τὸ τὸν Θεὸν ἰδεῖν, ὡς τῆς ἀρετῆς ταύτης· διὸ καὶ Παῦλος ἔλεγεν· *εἰρήνην* | **28v** *διώκετε μετὰ πάντων, καὶ τὸν ἁγιασμόν, οὗ χωρὶς οὐδεὶς*

---

371 However, this text points to Origen, let alone that it contains Origen's known fragment 86 (Klostermann), which is known from at least five other codices. See endnotes next.

372 Matt. 5:8.

ὄψεται τὸν Κύριον.[373] Ὄψιν δὲ ἐνταῦθα φησὶ ἣν τοῖς ἀνθρώποις ἰδεῖν δυνατόν. Ἐπειδὴ γὰρ πολλοὶ ἐλεοῦσι μὲν καὶ οὐχ ἁρπάζουσιν οὐδὲ πλεονεκτοῦσι, πορνεύουσι δὲ καὶ ἀσελγαίνουσι, δεικνὺς ὅτι οὐκ ἀρκεῖ τὸ πρότερον καὶ τοῦτο προσέθηκεν,[ccxciv] *ὅτι αὐτοὶ τὸν Θεὸν ὄψονται.* Πῶς οὖν φησι, *Θεὸν οὐδεὶς ἑώρακε πώποτε;*[374]

> πῶς οὖν ἡ θεία φησὶ γραφή, ὅτι θεὸν οὐδεὶς ἑώρακεν πώποτε[375] καὶ οὐδεὶς ὄψεται τὸ πρόσωπόν μου καὶ ζήσεται[376] καὶ ὃν εἶδεν οὐδεὶς ἀνθρώπων οὐδὲ ἰδεῖν δύναται;[377][ccxcv]

(ΣΕΥΗΡΟΥ, cont.)[ccxcvi] Λέγομεν ὅτι λόγῳ ὁρᾶται καὶ καταλαμβάνεται. Ἢ ἐκ τῆς θείας γραφῆς τοῖς τῆς γνώσεως ὀφθαλμοῖς ὁρῶμεν Θεὸν ἢ ἐκ τῆς ἐμφαινομένης τῷ παντὶ σοφίας ἔστι τὸν πεποιηκότα στοχαστικῶς ἰδεῖν, καθάπερ καὶ ἐπὶ τῶν ἀνθρωπίνων δημιουργημάτων. Ὁρᾶται τρόπον τινὰ τῇ διανοίᾳ ὁ δημιουργὸς τοῦ προκειμένου ἔργου, ὁρᾶται δὲ οὐχ ἡ φύσις τοῦ τεχνιτεύσαντος, ἀλλὰ μόνη ἡ τεχνικὴ ἐπιστήμη. Οὕτω καὶ ὁ ἐν τῇ κτίσει βλέπων τὸν Θεόν,[378] οὐ τὴν οὐσίαν,[ccxcvii] ἀλλὰ τὴν σοφίαν τοῦ τὰ *πάντα* πεποιηκότος[379] ἀνατυποῦται. Οὐκοῦν[380] καὶ ὁ Κύριος ἀληθεύει ὀφθήσεσθαι τὸν Θεὸν τοῖς καθαροῖς *τῇ καρδίᾳ* ἐπαγγειλάμενος καὶ ἡ γραφὴ οὐ ψεύδεται μήτε ἑωρακέναι τινὰ τὸν *Θεόν,*[381] μήτε ἰδεῖν δύνασθαι.

> *ὅτι αὐτοὶ τὸν θεὸν ὄψονται.* πῶς οὖν φησιν, ὅτι τὸν *θεὸν οὐδεὶς ἑώρακε πώποτε;* λέγομεν, ὅτι λόγῳ ὁρᾶται καὶ καταλαμβάνεται. ἢ ἐκ τῆς θείας γραφῆς τοῖς τῆς γνώσεως ὀφθαλμοῖς ὁρῶμεν θεὸν ἢ ἐκ τῆς ἐμφαινομένης τῷ παντὶ σοφίας ἔστι τὸν πεποιηκότα στοχαστικῶς ἰδεῖν, καθάπερ καὶ ἐπὶ τῶν ἀνθρωπίνων δημιουργημάτων ὁρᾶται τρόπον τινὰ τῇ διανοίᾳ ὁ δημιουργὸς τοῦ προκειμένου ἔργου. ὁρᾶται δὲ οὐχ ἡ φύσις τοῦ τεχνιτεύσαντος, ἀλλὰ μόνη ἡ τεχνικὴ ἐπιστήμη. οὕτως καὶ ὁ ἐν τῇ κτίσει βλέπων τὸν θεὸν οὐ τὴν οὐσίαν, ἀλλὰ τὴν σοφίαν τοῦ τὰ πάντα πεποιηκότος ἀνατυποῦται. οὐκοῦν καὶ ὁ κύριος ἀληθεύει ὀφθήσεσθαι τὸν θεὸν τοῖς καθαροῖς τῇ καρδίᾳ, ἐπαγγειλάμενος καὶ ἡ γραφὴ οὐ ψεύδεται μήτε ἑωρακέναι τινὰ τὸν θεὸν μήτε ἰδεῖν δύνασθαι.[ccxcviii]

(ΣΕΥΗΡΟΥ, cont.) *μακάριοι οἱ εἰρηνοποιοί.*[382] Εἰρηνοποιοὶ δὲ οὐ μόνον οἱ φιλοποιοῦντες τοὺς ἐχθρούς, ἀλλὰ καὶ οἱ τὸν θυμὸν καὶ τὴν κακὴν ἐπιθυμίαν ἐξημεροῦντες, βιοῦντές τε ὀρθῶς ἔργῳ καὶ λόγῳ διὰ πίστεως ἀπταίστου. Πλὴν καὶ οἱ μεταδιδάσκοντες τοὺς ἀπίστους καὶ ἄγοντες πρὸς τὴν πίστιν, ὡς τοὺς ἐχθροὺς τοῦ Θεοῦ φιλοποι |

373 Heb. 12:14.
374 John, 1:18.
375 John, 1:18.
376 Cf. Ex. 33:20.
377 Cf. Ex. 33:20.
378 Matt. 5:8.
379 Cf. Psalm 103:24.
380 Cod. οὐκ οὖν.
381 Cf. John, 1:18.
382 Matt. 5:9.

29r οῦντες αὐτῷ, *μακάριοι* οἱ τοιοῦτοι, ὡς μιμησάμενοι τὸν Υἱὸν τοῦ Θεοῦ. *Υἱοὶ* γὰρ *Θεοῦ κληθήσονται*, ἀθανασίας μετασχόντες, ἤτοι συμβασιλεύσουσι[383] τῷ Χριστῷ ἐν τῇ δευτέρα αὐτοῦ παρουσίᾳ.

Εἰρηνοποιοὶ δὲ οὐ μόνον οἱ φιλοποιοῦντες τοὺς ἐχθρούς, ἀλλὰ καὶ οἱ τὸν θυμὸν καὶ τὴν κακὴν ἐπιθυμίαν ἐξημεροῦντες, βιοῦντές τε ὀρθῶς ἔργῳ καὶ λόγῳ διὰ πίστεως ἀπταίστου, πλὴν καὶ οἱ μεταδιδάσκοντες τοὺς ἀπίστους καὶ ἄγοντες πρὸς τὴν πίστιν ὡς τοὺς ἐχθροὺς τοῦ θεοῦ φιλοποιοῦντες αὐτῷ. *μακάριοι* οἱ τοιοῦτοι ὡς μιμησάμενοι τὸν υἱὸν τοῦ θεοῦ. *υἱοὶ* γὰρ κληθήσονται ἀθανασίας μετασχόντες ἤτοι συμβασιλεύσουσι τῷ Χριστῷ ἐν τῇ δευτέρᾳ αὐτοῦ παρουσίᾳ.[ccxcix]

(ΣΕΥΗΡΟΥ, cont.) Διώκονται δὲ *ἕνεκεν δικαιοσύνης*,[384] οὐ μόνον οἱ μάρτυρες καὶ ὀρθοὶ διδάσκαλοι, ἀλλὰ καὶ οἱ ἀσκηταὶ οἱ ἀπὸ τῶν βιωτικῶν ἀναχωροῦντες, οἳ *ἕνεκεν δικαιοσύνης* διώκονται. Πρόφασις γάρ ἐστιν μαρτυρίου πᾶς πειρασμός.

ἀλλὰ κἀκεῖνο γινώσκοντες πρόφασιν εἶναι μαρτυρίου τὸν ὁτινοῦν πειρασμόν.[ccc]

(ΣΕΥΗΡΟΥ, cont.) τότε δὲ οὗτοι *μακάριοι* ὅτ᾽ ἂν οὐ μισήσωσι τοὺς διώκοντας *ἕνεκεν δικαιοσύνης*.[385] Ἢ τῆς κοινῆς ἀρετῆς ἢ τῆς ἰδίως,[ccci] ὡς ἔ‹στ›ιν[386] λέγειν, *ἕνεκεν δικαιοσύνης*, *σωφροσύνης*, καὶ τῶν λοιπῶν· τὸ δὲ ἆθλον, *βασιλεία οὐρανῶν*.[cccii] Εἰρηνοποιός ἐστιν ὁ τὴν ἄλλοις φαινομένην μάχην τῶν γραφῶν ἀποδεικνὺς συμφωνίαν παλαιῶν πρὸς καινάς, νομικῶν πρὸς προφητικάς, εὐαγγελικῶν πρὸς εὐαγγελικάς, δι᾽ ἃ μιμησάμενος τὸν υἱὸν τοῦ Θεοῦ, υἱὸς *Θεοῦ* κληθήσεται, ἔργῳ τὸ τῆς *υἱοθεσίας πνεῦμα*[387] λαβών.

Τρίτος εἰρηνοποιός ἐστιν ὁ τὴν ἄλλοις φαινομένην μάχην τῶν γραφῶν ἀποδεικνὺς συμφωνίαν παλαιῶν πρὸς καινάς, νομικῶν πρὸς προφητικάς, εὐαγγελικῶν πρὸς εὐαγγελικάς. δι᾽ ἃ μιμησάμενος τὸν υἱὸν τοῦ θεοῦ *υἱὸς* κληθήσεται ἔργῳ τὸ *πνεῦμα* τῆς *υἱοθεσίας*[388] λαβών.[ccciii]

Εἰρηνοποιός ἐστιν ὁ τὴν ἄλλοις φαινομένην μάχην τῶν γραφῶν ἀποδεικνὺς συμφωνίαν, παλαιῶν πρὸς καινάς, νομικῶν πρὸς προφητικάς, εὐαγγελικῶν πρὸς εὐαγγελικάς. διὸ μιμησάμενος τὸν υἱὸν τοῦ θεοῦ *υἱὸς* κληθήσεται ἔργῳ τὸ *πνεῦμα* τῆς *υἱοθεσίας* λαβών.[ccciv]

(ΣΕΥΗΡΟΥ, cont.) Οἶμαι δὲ κυρίως εἰρηνοποιὸν χρηματίζειν τὸν τὴν ἐν ἑαυτῷ στάσιν τῆς σαρκὸς καὶ τοῦ πνεύματος καὶ τὸν ἐμφύλιον τῆς φύσεως πόλεμον εἰς

383 Cf. 1 Cor. 4:8; 2 Tim. 2:12.
384 Matt. 5:10.
385 Matt. 5:10.
386 Cod. ἔχειν.
387 Rom. 8:15.
388 Rom. 8:15.

εἰρηνικὴν συμφωνίαν ἄγοντα, ὅταν μηκέτι ἡ *σὰρξ* ἐπιθυμῇ *κατὰ τοῦ πνεύματος*,[389] ἀλλ' ἡ τοῦ πνεύματος χάρις ἐπικρατήσῃ τῶν σωματικῶν παθημάτων ὅταν μηκέτι ἐνεργῇ ὁ τοῦ σώματος νόμος ὁ ἀντιστρατευόμενος τῷ νοΐ,[390] ἀλλ' ὑποζευχθεὶς τῇ κρείττονι βασιλείᾳ ὑπηρέτης γένηται τῶν θείων ἐπιταγμάτων.

> ἀλλ' οἶμαι κυρίως εἰρηνοποιὸν χρηματίζειν, τὸν τὴν ἐν ἑαυτῷ στάσιν τῆς σαρκὸς καὶ τοῦ πνεύματος, καὶ τὸν ἐμφύλιον τῆς φύσεως πόλεμον εἰς εἰρηνικὴν συμφωνίαν ἄγοντα, ὅταν μηκέτι ἐνεργὸς ᾖ ὁ τοῦ σώματος νόμος, ὁ ἀντιστρατευόμενος τῷ νόμῳ τοῦ νοός, ἀλλ' ὑποζευχθεὶς τῇ κρείττονι βασιλείᾳ ὑπηρέτης γίνεται τῶν θείων ἐπιταγμάτων.[cccv]

(ΣΕΥΗΡΟΥ, cont.) *μακάριοι ἐστὲ* ὅταν *ὀνειδίσωσιν ὑμᾶς*.[391] | **29v** Οὐ κατὰ ἀπόφασιν· πρὸς παρόντας δὲ λέγει παρακλητικῶς διωκομένους διὰ Χριστόν, ὄντα δικαιοσύνην

> Δικαιοσύνη ἐστὶν ὁ Χριστὸς ὁ υἱὸς τοῦ θεοῦ.[cccvi]

(ΣΕΥΗΡΟΥ, cont.) καὶ πᾶσαν ἀρετήν,[cccvii]

> ὁ Χριστὸς γάρ, ἡ πᾶσα ἀρετή.[cccviii]

ὀνειδιζομένους διὰ τὴν εἰς αὐτὸν πίστιν καὶ διωκομένους ὑπὸ τῶν νομιζόντων *μωρὰ*[392] εἶναι *τὰ τοῦ πνεύματος τοῦ Θεοῦ*,[393] ἀκούοντας ψευδεῖς καὶ ἀθέσμους μίξεις[394] καὶ τροφὰς οὐρανίους[cccix] καὶ τὰ ὅμοια ἃ προεφήτευε λεχθησόμενα ἐπὶ ἀνατροπῇ τῶν πιστῶν. Χαίρειν δὲ δεῖ φησι τοὺς τοιούτους καρποφοροῦντας χαράν, καρπὸν *πνεύματος*,[395] ὅτι *μισθὸς* ἔσται αὐτοῖς *πολὺς ἐν οὐρανοῖς* παρὰ Κυρίου.

(ΣΕΥΗΡΟΥ, cont.) *Οὕτω*[396] *γὰρ ἐδίωξαν τοὺς προφήτας τοὺς πρὸ ὑμῶν*.[397] Ἐντεῦθεν αὐτοῖς παρέχεται τὴν παραμυθίαν ἀπὸ τῆς κοινωνίας τῶν πρὸ αὐτῶν πεπονθότων κακῶς. Ὥστε καὶ ἀπ' ἐκείνων εἰδέναι προσῆκεν ἡμᾶς ὅτι τοὺς ἀρετῆς ἐφιεμένους[cccx] ἔξω καθεστάναι τῶν λυπηρῶν οὐ δυνατόν.

> Ἐντεῦθεν αὐτοῖς παρέχεται τὴν παραμυθίαν ἀπὸ τῆς κοινωνίας τῶν πρὸ αὐτῶν πεπονθότων κακῶς, ὥστε καὶ ἀπ' ἐκείνων εἰδέναι προσῆκεν ἡμᾶς, ὅτι τοὺς ἀρετῆς ἐφιεμένους ἔξω καθεστάναι τῶν λυπηρῶν οὐ δυνατόν.[cccxi]

---

389 Gal. 5:17.
390 Cf. Rom. 7:23.
391 Matt. 5:11.
392 Cf. 1 Cor. 1:27.
393 1 Cor. 2:14.
394 Cf. 2 Peter, 2:7; Gen. 19:6-8.
395 Cf. Gal. 5:22.
396 Cod. οὕτως.
397 Matt. 5:12.

(ΣΕΥΗΡΟΥ, cont.) *Ὑμεῖς ἐστε τὸ ἅλας τῆς γῆς.*[398] Ἅλας καλεῖ τὴν φρόνησιν, δι᾽ ἧς πέπασται ὁ ἀποστολικὸς λόγος, ὁ σπαρεὶς ἐν ταῖς ἡμετέραις ψυχαῖς.

Εἰς ὅσα μὲν τῷ βίῳ τῶν ἀνθρώπων οἱ ἅλες εἰσὶ χρήσιμοι, τί δεῖ καὶ λέγειν; ἄξιον νυνὶ δὲ φάναι, κατὰ τί οἱ Ἰησοῦ μαθηταὶ ἁλσὶ παραβάλλονται. δοκεῖ τοίνυν μοι ὅτι, ὥσπερ οἱ ἅλες τὰ τοίαδε συνέχουσι ‹σώματα› πρὸς τὸ μὴ μεταβάλλειν εἰς σκώληκας ἀπὸ δυσωδίας καὶ ποιοῦσι χρήσιμα ἐπὶ πλεῖον εἶναι, ‹οὐκ ἂν διαμείναντα χρόνον, χρειώδη τοῖς ἀνθρώποις τυγχάνοντα, χωρὶς τῶν ἁλῶν›, οὕτως καὶ οἱ τοῦ Χριστοῦ μαθηταὶ πάντα τὸν περίγειον τοῦτον τόπον διακρατοῦσιν καὶ συνέχουσιν ἐνιστάμενοι τῇ ἐξ εἰδωλολατρείας καὶ πορνείας ἁμαρτιῶν δυσωδίᾳ. δοκεῖ μοι οὖν ὁ Ματθαῖος διὰ τοῦτο ἀναγεγραφέναι τοὺς μαθητὰς τοῦ Ἰησοῦ *ἅλας*. ὁ δὲ Λουκᾶς οὐ σαφῶς τοῦτο δηλοῖ, διόπερ ἀμφίβολος αὐτοῦ ἡ λέξις ἐστίν, δυναμένη καὶ κατὰ τὸν Μᾶρκον νοεῖσθαι ὅτι ἕκαστος ἡμῶν οὐκ ὢν *ἅλας* ἐν αὐτῷ ἔχειν ὀφείλει τοὺς ἅλας. καὶ τάχα τόσον τις ἔχει ἁλῶν ὅσον κεχώρηκε τῶν τοῦ Χριστοῦ χαρίτων κατὰ τὸ *χάρις ὑμῖν πληθυνθείη* ‹καί. ὅστις *εὗρε χάριν ἔναντι κυρίου τοῦ θεοῦ*, ὡς Νῶε καὶ Ἀβραὰμ καὶ Μωσῆς, καὶ εἴ τις ἄλλος ἀναγέγραπται εὑρηκέναι χάριν ἐνώπιον τοῦ θεοῦ›. συνήγαγεν δὲ ἐπὶ τὸ αὐτὸ τὴν χάριν καὶ τὸ ἅλας ὁ Παῦλος εἰπών, *ὁ λόγος ὑμῶν πάντοτε ἐν χάριτι, ἅλατι ἠρτυμένος*. εἴ τις οὖν χάριτος ἀξιωθεὶς κενὴν ταύτην ποιήσει, οὗτος ἂν εἴη ἐν ᾧ οἱ ἅλες ἐμωράνθησαν.[cccxii]

Ἅλας καλεῖ τὴν φρόνησιν.[cccxiii]

Ἅλας καλεῖ τὴν φρόνησιν, ἧς ἔμπλεός ἐστιν ὁ ἀποστολικὸς λόγος, ὃς σπαρεὶς ἐν ταῖς ἡμετέραις ψυχαῖς τὸν τῆς σοφίας ἡμῖν ἐνοικίζει λόγον, ὃς διὰ τὸ νόστιμον καὶ χαρίεν τούτῳ παρείκασται. ὅνπερ γὰρ τρόπον ἄνευ ἁλὸς οὔτε ἄρτος οὔτε ὄψον ἐδώδιμον, οὕτως ἄνευ τῆς ἀποστολικῆς συνέσεως καὶ διδασκαλίας πᾶσα ψυχὴ καὶ μωρὰ καὶ ἄνοστος καὶ οὐχ ἡδεῖά ἐστι παρὰ τῷ θεῷ.[cccxiv]

(ΣΕΥΗΡΟΥ, cont.) Εἰ οὖν τὸ ψυχικὸν ἄρτυμά ἐστι *τὸ ἅλας τῆς γῆς, ὑμεῖς ἐστε τὸ ἅλας* φησί, ὡς πᾶσαν τὴν γῆν μωρανθεῖσαν μέλλοντες ἐπιστύφειν διὰ τῶν ἐλέγχων καὶ ἐπιτιμήσεων. Ἐὰν δὲ παύσησθε τοῦ ἐλέγχειν καὶ ἐκνεύσητε πρὸς ἃ μὴ δεῖ μὴ ὄντος ἄλλου τινὸς τοῦ δυναμένου διορθώσασθαι ὑμᾶς, μέλλετε καταφρονεῖσθαι καὶ καταπατεῖσθαι *ὑπὸ τῶν ἀνθρώπων*.

ἅλας τῆς γῆς ἐστὶ τὸ τὸ ψυχικὸν ἄρτυμα.[cccxv]

(ΣΕΥΗΡΟΥ, cont.) Οἱ μὲν γὰρ ἄλλοι πίπτοντες δύνανται μυριάκις συγγνώμης τυχεῖν. ὁ δὲ διδάσκαλος ἐὰν τοῦτο πάθῃ, πάσης ἀπεστέρηται ἀπολογίας καὶ τὴν ἐ |
30r σχάτην δίδωσι τιμωρίαν.

Οἱ μὲν γὰρ ἄλλοι πίπτοντες δύνανται μυριάκις συγγνώμης τυχεῖν. ὁ δὲ διδάσκαλος ἐὰν τοῦτο πάθῃ, πάσης ἀπεστέρηται ἀπολογίας καὶ τὴν ἐσχάτην δίδωσι τιμωρίαν.[cccxvi]

398 Matt. 5:13.

Διό φησιν. *Ἂν δὲ τὸ ἅλας μωρανθῇ, ἐν τίνι ἁλισθήσεται;* Εἰς οὐδὲν ἰσχύει ἔτι, εἰ μὴ βληθῆναι ἔξω καὶ καταπατεῖσθαι ὑπὸ τῶν ἀνθρώπων. Οἱ μὲν γὰρ ἄλλοι μυριάκις πίπτοντες, δύνανται τυχεῖν συγγνώμης· ὁ δὲ διδάσκαλος, ἐὰν τοῦτο πάθῃ, πάσης ἀπεστέρηται ἀπολογίας, καὶ τὴν ἐσχάτην δώσει τιμωρίαν.[cccxvii]

(ΣΕΥΗΡΟΥ, cont.) *Ὑμεῖς ἐστε τὸ φῶς τοῦ κόσμου.*[399] Φῶς ἀληθινὸν ὁ Χριστός, ὡς φύσει Θεός· φῶς καὶ οἱ μαθηταὶ κατὰ χάριν καὶ μετοχὴν φωτίζοντες τοὺς ἀνθρώπους.

Φῶς ἐστιν ἀληθινὸν τὸ *τοῦ κόσμου* λέξοντος, *ἐσημειώθη ἐφ᾽ ἡμᾶς τὸ φῶς σου.*[400] *φῶς* δὲ καὶ αὐτοὶ κατὰ μετοχὴν γενόμενοι.[cccxviii]

(ΣΕΥΗΡΟΥ, cont.)[cccxix] Ὥσπερ γὰρ διὰ τοῦ φωτὸς ὁρᾷ τις τὰ ὁρώμενα,[cccxx] οὕτως καὶ οἱ πειθόμενοι αὐτοῖς διὰ τῆς αὐτῶν διδασκαλίας ὁρῶσι τὰ τῆς ἀρετῆς ἔργα· κόσμος δέ, ἡ ἐκκλησία.

λεγέσθω τοίνυν ἡ ἐκκλησία κόσμος.[cccxxi]

(ΣΕΥΗΡΟΥ, cont.) Οὐ λέγει δέ, *ὑμεῖς ἐστε* φῶτα, ἀλλὰ *φῶς*, ὡς ἅμα ὄντες *σῶμα Χριστοῦ*,[401] ὅς *φῶς* ἐστι *τοῦ κόσμου.*[402]

οὐ γὰρ εἶπεν *ὑμεῖς ἐστε τὰ φῶτα, ἀλλὰ τὸ φῶς*. ἑνότητα γὰρ πάντες πρὸς ἑαυτοὺς ἔχοντες οὕτω φῶς ἕν εἰσι, ἐκκλησία ὄντες.[cccxxii]

Λέγει τοίνυν ὅτι οἱ ἐπὶ τῇ πίστει ἱδρυμένοι,[cccxxiii] ὡς ἐπ᾽ ὄρους ὑψηλοῦ, οὐκ ὀφείλουσι κρύπτεσθαι, ἀλλὰ μετὰ παρρησίας τῆς ἀληθείας κηρύσσειν τὸν λόγον.

Τὸ δὲ *οὐ δύναται πόλις*, οἱ ἐπὶ τῇ πίστει ἱδρύμενοι, ὡς ἐπ᾽ ὄρους ὑψηλοῦ, οὐκ ὀφείλουσι λαθραίως ἢ μετὰ δειλίας λαλεῖν τὸν λόγον.[cccxxiv]

Καίουσι δὲ *λύχνον*[403] οἱ φωτίζοντες ἑαυτοῖς φῶς γνώσεως, ὃν οὐ *τιθέασιν ὑπὸ μόδιον*, τὴν κακίαν,

Καίουσι λύχνον οἱ φωτίζοντες ἑαυτοῖς φῶς γνώσεως, ὃν οὐ *τιθέασιν ὑπὸ μόδιον*, ἀλλὰ τῶν πιστῶν οἰκονόμων διδόντων *τὸ σιτομέτριον ἐν καιρῷ.*[404][cccxxv]

399 Matt. 5:14.
400 Psalm 4:7.
401 1 Cor. 12:27; cf. 10:17.
402 John, 8:12.
403 Matt. 5:15.
404 Luke, 12:42.

ἀλλ᾽ ἐπὶ τὴν λυχνίαν, τὴν λογικὴν ἕξιν, ἵνα *πᾶσι τοῖς ἐν τῇ οἰκίᾳ* λάμπῃ, τουτέστι τοῖς ἐκκλησιαστικοῖς κατὰ τὸ κοινωνικόν.

> *Ἐπὶ δὲ λυχνίαν* ψυχὴν ἢ λογικὴν ἕξιν, ἧς τύπος παρὰ Μωσεῖ λυχνία χρυσῆ,[405] ἵνα *πᾶσι τοῖς ἐν τῇ οἰκίᾳ* λάμπῃ, τουτέστιν τοῖς ἐκκλησιαστικοῖς κατὰ τὸ κοινωνικόν.[cccxxvi]

Λύχνος ἐπὶ λυχνίᾳ τιθέμενος, τὸ τῆς γνώσεώς φησι ὅτε διὰ φωνῆς ἀπαγγέλλεται καὶ φωτίζει τὸν νοῦν τῶν ἀκροατῶν. Οὐ δεῖ τοίνυν χωννύειν τὴν ἀρετήν, ἀλλ᾽ ἀνυποστόλως ταύτην ἐργάζεσθαι, ἥτις οὐ δύναται λαθεῖν κἂν βουληθῇ τις ταύτην δι᾽ ὑπερβάλλουσαν ταπείνωσιν ἐπισκιάσαι. Διδάσκει δὲ ὁ λόγος οὐ φιλοδοξεῖν, ἀλλ᾽ ἀνυποστόλως ἐργάζεσθαι τὸ ἀγαθόν, ὅπως δι᾽ ὧν τις ἐργάζεται ἀγαθῶν δοξάζηται ὁ Θεός.

Τὸ φῶς τοῦ κόσμου.[406] Πάλιν *τοῦ κόσμου* ‹εἰπὼν› οὐκ ἔθνους ἑνός, οὐδὲ εἴκοσι πόλεων, ἀλλὰ τῆς οἰκουμένης ἁπάσης· ‹καὶ ὥσπερ ἅλας πνευματικόν, οὕτω› καὶ *φῶς* νοητὸν καὶ τῆς ἀκτῖνος τῆς ἡλιακῆς πολὺ βέλτιον. *Ὥσπερ οὖν καὶ ἅλας* πνευματικόν, | 30v καὶ πρότερον *ἅλας* καὶ τότε *φῶς*, ἵνα μάθῃς ἡλίκον τῶν καταστυφόντων τὸ κέρδος καὶ τῆς σεμνῆς διδασκαλίας τὸ ὄφελος. Καὶ γὰρ στύφει καὶ οὐκ ἀφίησι διαρρεῦσαι καὶ διαβλέψαι ποιεῖ πρὸς ἀρετὴν χειραγωγοῦσα.

> *Ὑμεῖς ἐστε τὸ φῶς τοῦ κόσμου.* Πάλιν τοῦ κόσμου, οὐκ ἔθνους ἑνός, οὐδὲ εἴκοσι πόλεων, ἀλλὰ τῆς οἰκουμένης ἁπάσης. καὶ φῶς, νοητόν, καὶ τῆς ἀκτῖνος ταύτης πολὺ βέλτιον, ὥσπερ οὖν καὶ ἅλας πνευματικόν. Καὶ πρότερον ἅλας, καὶ τότε φῶς. ἵνα μάθῃς ἡλίκον τῶν κατεστυμμένων ῥημάτων τὸ κέρδος, καὶ τῆς σεμνῆς διδασκαλίας τὸ ὄφελος. Καὶ γὰρ σφίγγει, καὶ οὐκ ἀφίησι διαρρεῦσαι, καὶ διαβλέψαι ποιεῖ πρὸς ἀρετὴν χειραγωγοῦσα.[cccxxvii]

(ΣΕΥΗΡΟΥ, cont.) *Οὐ δύναται πόλις κρυβῆναι.*[407] *Πόλις* ἐστὶν *ἐπάνω ὄρους κειμένη* ἡ ἐν θεοσεβείᾳ ἐνάρετος πολιτεία.

> *Πόλις* ἐστὶν *ἐπάνω ὄρους κειμένη* ἡ ἐν θεοσεβείᾳ ἐνάρετος πολιτεία.[cccxxviii]

(ΣΕΥΗΡΟΥ, cont.) *Οὐδὲ καίουσι λύχνον.*[408] Οὐ χρὴ τὸν *λύχνον ὑπὸ τὸν μόδιον* εἶναι, *τὸ σιτομέτριον.*[409] Μοδίῳ μὲν γὰρ σιτομετρείσθωσαν ὑπὸ τοῦ πιστοῦ καὶ φρονίμου οἰκονόμου οἱ σύνδουλοι. Βλεπέτωσαν δὲ τὰς αὐγὰς τοῦ λύχνου ἐπικειμένου τῇ λυχνίᾳ καὶ εἰς φανερὸν διὰ λόγου προαγομένου *ἐν τῇ οἰκίᾳ* πάντες, τῇ ἐκκλησίᾳ. Ἀλλ᾽ οὐδὲ

405 Ex. 25:31; 38:13; Num. 8:4.
406 Matt. 5:14.
407 Matt. 5:14.
408 Matt. 5:15.
409 Mark, 4:21; Luke, 12:42.

ὑπὸ τὴν κλίνην[410] τιθέασι *τὸν λύχνον*, ἔνθα τις ἀναπαύεται, οὐδὲ ἄλλου τινὸς σκεύους ὑποκάτω. Τοῦτο γὰρ ὁ ποιῶν οὐ προνοεῖται τῶν εἰσπορευομένων[411] εἰς τὴν οἰκίαν.

> Οὐ χρὴ τὸν *λύχνον ὑπὸ τὸν μόδιον* εἶναι, *τὸ σιτομέτριον*. μοδίῳ μὲν γὰρ σιτομετρείσθωσαν ὑπὸ τοῦ πιστοῦ καὶ φρονίμου οἰκονόμου οἱ σύνδουλοι, βλεπέτωσαν δὲ τὰς αὐγὰς τοῦ λύχνου ἐπικειμένου τῇ λυχνίᾳ καὶ εἰς φανερὸν διὰ λόγου προαγομένου *ἐν τῇ οἰκίᾳ πάντων* τῇ ἐκκλησίᾳ. Ἀλλ᾽ οὐδὲ *ὑπὸ τὴν κλίνην* τιθέασι *τὸν λύχνον* ἔνθα τις ἀναπαύεται, οὐδὲ ἄλλου τινὸς σκεύους ὑποκάτω. Τοῦτο γὰρ ὁ ποιῶν οὐ προνοεῖται τῶν εἰσπορευομένων εἰς τὴν οἰκίαν.[cccxxix]

(ΣΕΥΗΡΟΥ, cont.) Οἱ καίοντες τὸν *λύχνον* καὶ τιθέντες *ἐπὶ τὴν λυχνίαν* ἵνα λάμπῃ *πᾶσι τοῖς ἐν τῇ οἰκίᾳ* προτρέψονται καὶ τοὺς *ἐν τῇ οἰκίᾳ* βλέποντας τὴν τοῦ λύχνου λαμπρότητα καὶ αὐτοὺς καίειν τὸν ἑαυτῶν *λύχνον*. Σπουδάζειν γὰρ χρὴ τὴν δοθεῖσαν ἡμῖν λαμπρότητα φυλάττειν ἐν ὑψηλῷ καὶ μὴ συγκαλύπτειν ἀργίᾳ, ἧς σύμβολον ἡ κλίνη, ἀναπαύουσα τὸ σῶμα ταῖς σαρκικαῖς ἡδοναῖς. Οὐ γὰρ φυσικὸν ἡμῖν ἀλλ᾽ ἐκ δόσεως τὸ καλόν. Τὸ δὲ τοιοῦτον ἀμελούμενον ἀφίσταται. Ἀπάγει δὲ ἡμᾶς τῆς ἰδίας φιλοδοξίας, τὴν τοῦ Θεοῦ δόξαν τέλος τῶν ἔργων προτιθείς.

> Οἱ καίοντες τὸν *λύχνον* καὶ τιθέντες *ἐπὶ τὴν λυχνίαν* ἵνα λάμπῃ *πᾶσι τοῖς ἐν τῇ οἰκίᾳ* προτρέπονται καὶ τοὺς *ἐν τῇ οἰκίᾳ* βλέποντας τὴν τοῦ λύχνου λαμπρότητα καὶ αὐτοὺς καίειν τὸν ἑαυτῶν *λύχνον*. [σπουδάζειν γὰρ χρὴ τὴν δοθεῖσαν ἡμῖν λαμπρότητα φυλάττειν ἐν ὑψηλῷ καὶ μὴ συγκαλύπτειν ἀργίᾳ, ἧς σύμβολον ἡ κλίνη ἀναπαύουσα τὸ σῶμα ταῖς σαρκικαῖς ἡδοναῖς. οὐ γὰρ φυσικῶς ἡμῖν ἀλλ᾽ ἐκ δόσεως τὸ καλόν. τὸ δὲ τοιοῦτον ἀμελούμενον ἀφίσταται. ἀπάγει δὲ ἡμᾶς τῆς ἰδίας φιλοδοξίας, τὴν τοῦ Θεοῦ δόξαν τέλος τῶν ἔργων προτιθείς.][cccxxx]

> Σπουδάζειν γὰρ χρὴ τὴν δοθεῖσαν ἡμῖν λαμπρότητα φυλάττειν ἐν ὑψηλῷ καὶ μὴ συγκαλύπτειν ἀργίᾳ, ἧς σύμβολον ἡ κλίνη ἀναπαύουσα τὸ σῶμα ταῖς σαρκικαῖς ἡδοναῖς. οὐ γὰρ φυσικῶς ἡμῖν, ἀλλ᾽ ἐκ δόσεως τὸ καλόν. τὸ δὲ τοιοῦτον ἀμελούμενον ἀφίσταται. ἀπάγει δὲ ἡμᾶς τῆς ἰδίας φιλοδοξίας τὴν τοῦ θεοῦ δόξαν τέλος τῶν ἔργων προτιθείς.[cccxxxi]

(ΣΕΥΗΡΟΥ, cont.) *Οὕτως λαμψάτω* | **31r** *τὸ φῶς ὑμῶν*.[412] Φῶς ἐστιν ἡ ἐνάρετος πολιτεία. Οὐ λέγει *λαμψάτω τὸ φῶς ὑμῶν ἔμπροσθεν* τοῦ Θεοῦ· οὐδὲ γὰρ λύχνων *φῶς* λάμπει *ἔμπροσθεν* ἡλίου. Οὐ δεῖ ἐν κρυφῇ λαλεῖν τὸν εὐαγγελικὸν λόγον, ἀλλὰ παρρησίᾳ, ἵνα οἱ ἐπὶ γῆς ἄνθρωποι φωτισθῶσιν.

> Φῶς ἐστιν, ἡ ἐνάρετος πολιτεία.[cccxxxii] Οὐ λέγει *λαμψάτω τὸ φῶς ὑμῶν ἔμπροσθεν* τοῦ Θεοῦ. οὐδὲ γὰρ λύχνων *φῶς* λάμπει *ἔμπροσθεν* ἡλίου.[cccxxxiii]

---

410 Mark, 4:21.
411 Cf. Luke, 8:16.
412 Matt. 5:16.

Καὶ ὅρα εἰ κατὰ τοῦτο καὶ τὸ ἐν τῷ εὐαγγελίῳ νοητέον. *Λαμψάτω τὸ φῶς ὑμῶν ἔμπροσθεν τῶν ἀνθρώπων.* Οὐ γάρ ‹φησιν› *Λαμψάτω τὸ φῶς ὑμῶν ἔμπροσθεν τοῦ θεοῦ.* τοῦτο γὰρ εἰ ἐνετέλλετο, ἀδύνατον ἂν ἐδίδου ἐντολήν, ὡς εἰ καὶ τοῖς λύχνοις ἐμψύχοις οὖσιν ἐντολὴν ἐδίδου τοῦ λάμψαι τὸ φῶς αὐτῶν ἔμπροσθεν τοῦ ἡλίου.[cccxxxiv]

(ΣΕΥΗΡΟΥ, cont.) *Μὴ νομίσητε ὅτι ἦλθον καταλῦσαι.*[413] Οὐχ ὡς ἀτελῆ φησι τὰ ἐν τῷ νόμῳ καὶ προφήταις καταλῦσαι *ἦλθον*, ἀλλ᾽ εἰς τέλος ἀγαγεῖν τὰ δι᾽ αὐτῶν λαλούμενα. Καὶ γὰρ ἐνανθρωπήσας διὰ τῆς ἑαυτοῦ παρουσίας πεπλήρωκε τὰ εἰρημένα νόμῳ καὶ προφήταις. Εἶτα πιστούμενος τὸν λόγον, ὥσπερ ὅρκον[cccxxxv] προφέρει τὸ *ἀμὴν*
καί φησι ὅτι οὐδὲν ἀτέλεστον ἔσται τῶν ἐν τῷ νόμῳ, ἀλλὰ καὶ τὸ βραχύτατον αὐτοῦ τελεσθῆναι δεῖ.

Τὸ δὲ *ἰῶτα ἕν*, καὶ τὰ ἑξῆς, τοῦτο δηλοῖ ὅτι ἀμήχανόν ἐστιν, ἀτέλεστόν τι μεῖναι τοῦ νόμου. ἀλλὰ καὶ τὸ βραχύτατον αὐτοῦ πληρωθῆναι δεῖ. ὅπερ καὶ αὐτὸς ἐποίησε μετὰ ἀκριβείας πάσης αὐτὸν ἀπαρτίσας.[cccxxxvi]

(ΣΕΥΗΡΟΥ, cont.) Κἂν γὰρ ἡμᾶς διαφεύγῃ ἡ ἀναλογία, ἀλλ᾽ *ἡ σοφία τοῦ Θεοῦ*[414] ἐπὶ πᾶσαν ἔφθασε θεόπνευστον γραφὴν[415] καὶ μέχρι τοῦ τυχόντος γράμματος.[cccxxxvii] Ἄλλως τε δέ· ἡ κατὰ κάθετον γραμμὴ ἡ ἄνωθεν ἐπὶ τὸ βάθος καθήκουσα, *ἰῶτα* λέγεται· ἡ δὲ ἐγκάρσιος ἀγομένη διὰ πλαγί‹ου›,[416] *κεραία* ὀνομάζεται.[cccxxxviii] Νόμος τοίνυν καὶ *ἰῶτα ἓν ἢ μία κεραία*[417] οὐ παρέρχ‹ον›ται,[418] παρέρχεται δὲ *τὸ σχῆμα τοῦ κόσμου τούτου.*[419] Οἱ γὰρ ἐν τῷ νόμῳ *λόγοι* μενοῦσι καὶ *οὐ παρελεύσονται.*[420] Τάχα γὰρ ἅπερ σαρκικῶς ἐποίουν οἱ Ἰουδαῖοι, ταῦτα καὶ νῦν πνευματικῶς ἡμεῖς ποιοῦμεν.

(ΣΕΥΗΡΟΥ, cont.) *Οὐκ ἦλθον καταλῦσαι ἀλλὰ πληρῶσαι.*[421] Ἀντὶ τῆς σαρκικῆς λατρείας, εἰσήγαγεν ὁ Κύριος τὴν *ἐν πνεύματι καὶ ἀληθείᾳ.*[422] Καὶ τάχα ἅπερ οὔτε σαρκικῶς ἐποίουν οἱ Ἰουδαῖοι, ταῦτα| **31v** νῦν πνευματικῶς οἱ Χριστοῦ μαθηταὶ ποιοῦσι. Διό φησι, *ἰῶτα ἓν ἢ μία κεραία οὐ μὴ παρέλθῃ ἐκ τοῦ νόμου ἕως ἂν πάντα γένηται.*[423] Δῆλον οὖν ὅτι οὐ πάντα ἐποίησαν οἱ Ἰουδαῖοι· ἤ, κἂν ἐποίησαν, ἐπαύσαντο τοῦ ποιεῖν μηκέτι συγχωρούμενοι ποιῆσαι αὐτά, πῇ μὲν διὰ τὸν φόβον τῶν βασιλέων, πῇ δὲ καὶ τὸ καταλελῦσθαι τὸν ναόν, ἐν ᾧ μόνῳ ἔδει τὰς θυσίας ἐπιτελεῖσθαι.

---

413 Matt. 5:17.
414 Eph. 3:10; cf. Luke, 11:49; 1 Cor. 1:21. Also, 2 Esdras, 7:25.
415 Cf. 2 Tim. 3:16.
416 Cod. πλαγί‹ου›ως.
417 Matt. 5:18.
418 Cod. παρέρχεται.
419 1 Cor. 7:31.
420 Matt. 24:35; Mark, 13:31; Luke, 21:33.
421 Matt. 5:17.
422 John, 4:23-24.
423 Matt. 5:18.

Ἀντὶ τῆς σαρκικῆς λατρείας, εἰσήγαγεν ὁ Κύριος τὴν *ἐν πνεύματι καὶ ἀληθείᾳ*. καὶ τάχα ἅπερ οὔτε σαρκικῶς ἐποίουν οἱ Ἰουδαῖοι, ταῦτα καὶ νῦν πνευματικῶς οἱ Χριστοῦ μαθηταὶ ποιοῦσιν. διό φησιν *ἰῶτα ἓν ἢ μία κεραία οὐ μὴ παρέλθῃ ἐκ τοῦ νόμου ἕως ἂν πάντα γένηται*. δηλονότι οὐ πάντα ἐποίησαν οἱ Ἰουδαῖοι, ἢ κἂν ἐποίησαν, ἐπαύσαντο τοῦ ποιεῖν μηκέτι συγχωρούμενοι ποιῆσαι αὐτά, πῇ μὲν διὰ τὸν φόβον τῶν βασιλέων, πῇ δὲ καὶ τὸ καταλελῦσθαι τὸν ναόν, ἐν ᾧ μόνῳ ἔδει τὰς θυσίας ἐπιτελεῖσθαι.[cccxxxix]

Τοῦτο εἶπεν οὐχ ἵνα Ἰουδαίων ἐμφράξῃ τὰ στόματα μόνον, ἀλλὰ καὶ τῶν αἱρετικῶν τῶν ἐκ τοῦ διαβόλου λεγόντων εἶναι τὴν παλαιάν.[cccxl]

Τοῦτο δὲ οὐκ Ἰουδαίων ἐμφράττει τὴν ἀναισχυντίαν μόνον, ἀλλὰ καὶ τῶν αἱρετικῶν ἀπορράπτει τὰ στόματα, τῶν ἐκ τοῦ διαβόλου λεγόντων εἶναι τὴν παλαιάν.[cccxli]

15

(ΩΡΙΓΕΝΟΥΣ) Ὥσπερ τὸ νήπιον, οὐ λυομένων τῶν σχημάτων ἢ τῶν μελῶν ἀνὴρ γίνεται ἀλλ᾽ αὐξανομένων, οὕτως καὶ τοῦτο ἀκούσῃ.

Ὥσπερ τὸ νήπιον οὐ λυομένων τῶν σχημάτων ἢ τῶν μελῶν ἀνὴρ γίνεται ἀλλ᾽ αὐξανομένων, οὕτως καὶ τοῦτο ἀκούσῃ.[cccxlii]

Ὥσπερ ἐπὶ τῶν νεογνῶν παιδίων ἔστιν ἰδεῖν (προκόπτουσι γὰρ ἐπὶ τὸ ἀνδρῶδες οὐ τῆς μορφώσεως αὐτῶν καταλυομένης, ἀλλ᾽ αὐξανομένης μᾶλλον καὶ ἔτι μορφουμένης κρειττόνως), οὕτως γέγονε καὶ ἐπὶ τοῦ νόμου. οὐ λυομένου [μᾶλλον] ἡ νέα παραγέγονε διαθήκη ἀλλὰ μεμορφωμένου ‹μᾶλλον› καὶ τετελειωμένου ἀκριβέστερον. καὶ τοῦτό ἐστιν ἡ ἐν χάριτι διαθήκη, ἡ παλαιὰ ἀνακαινισθεῖσά τε καὶ μορφωθεῖσα.[cccxliii]

Ἐὰν δέ, πῶς οὖν, ἐὰν μὴ ἀπόλλυται τὸ πᾶν, οἱ ἐξ ἐναντίας εἴπωσιν, ὁ μὲν κύριος τὸν οὐρανὸν παρελεύσεσθαι ἔφη καὶ τὴν γῆν, ὁ δὲ προφήτης ἀπολεῖσθαι μὲν τὸν οὐρανὸν ὡς καπνόν, τὴν δὲ γῆν ὡς ἱμάτιον παλαιωθήσεσθαι;[cccxliv] ἐπειδήπερ ἔθος ταῖς γραφαῖς, λέξομεν, τὴν εἰς τὸ κρεῖττον καὶ ἐνδοξότερον ἀπὸ ταύτης τῆς καταστάσεως τοῦ κόσμου μεταβολὴν[cccxlv] ἀπώλειαν λέγειν, οἷον τοῦ πρόσθεν σχήματος ἀπολλυμένου κατὰ τὴν εἰς τὸ φαιδρότερον ἁπάντων ἐξαλλαγήν. ὅτι μηδεμία ὑπεναντίωσις ἢ ἀτοπία ἐν τοῖς θείοις λόγοις. *παράγει* γὰρ *τὸ σχῆμα τοῦ κόσμου τούτου* καὶ οὐχ ὁ κόσμος εἴρηται. οὕτως ἔθος ἀπώλειαν καλεῖν τὰς γραφὰς τὴν πρὸς τὸ ἄμεινον ἔσθ᾽ ὅτε καὶ εὐμορφότερον τροπὴν τοῦ πρόσθεν σχήματος, οἷον ὥσπερ ὁπόταν τις ἀπώλειαν λέγοι τοῦ κατὰ τὸ νήπιον σχήματος τὴν εἰς τὸν ἄνδρα τὸν τέλειον μεταλλαγήν, τρεπομένης εἰς μέγεθος καὶ κάλλος τῆς ἡλικίας τοῦ νηπίου.[cccxlvi]

Οἱ *λόγοι* τοῦ νόμου *οὐ παρελεύσονται*·[424] καὶ γὰρ αὐτοὶ οὐ βλεπόμενοι καὶ αἰώνιοί[425] εἰσιν. Οὐ καταλύει δὲ *τὸν νόμον*, οὐδὲ ἐν σαββάτῳ λέγων *ἆρον τὸν κράββατόν σου*.[426]

424 Cf. Mark, 13:31; Luke, 21:33.
425 Cf. 2 Cor. 4:18.
426 Mark, 2:9; John, 5:8&11.

Καταλύειν δὲ δοκεῖ τὸ *γράμμα*, ἵνα τὸ *πνεῦμα*[427] στήσῃ ναοῦ, θυσιαστηρίου, θυσιῶν, καθαρισμῶν, ἀρχιερέων, *ἡμέρας ἱλασμοῦ*,[428] *σαββατισμοῦ γῆς*,[429] καὶ τῶν λοιπῶν. Δόξει δὲ καὶ τὸ *ὁ νόμος καὶ οἱ προφῆται ἕως Ἰωάννου*[430] καταλελῦσθαι· πληροῦται δὲ μᾶλλον καὶ τότε.

> Εἰ[cccxlvii] μέντοι ἐν τῷ νόμῳ *λόγοι* (ἔφη τις) μενοῦσι καὶ *οὐ παρελεύσονται*.[431] Καὶ γὰρ αὐτοὶ οὐ βλεπόμενοι καὶ αἰώνιοί[432] εἰσιν. οὐ καταλύει δὲ *τὸν νόμον* οὐδὲ ἐν σαββάτῳ λέγων. *ἆρον τὸν κράββατόν σου καὶ περιπάτει*.[433] καταλύειν δὲ δοκεῖ τὸ γράμμα, ἵνα τὸ πνεῦμα στήσῃ ναοῦ, θυσιαστηρίου, θυσιῶν, καθαρισμῶν, ἀρχιερέων, ἡμέρας ἱλασμοῦ, σαββατισμοῦ γῆς, καὶ λοιπῶν. δόξει δὲ καὶ τὸ *ὁ νόμος καὶ οἱ προφῆται ἕως Ἰωάννου* καταλελῦσθαι, πληροῦται δὲ μᾶλλον καὶ τότε.[cccxlviii]

Μία κεραία, οὐ παρ᾽ Ἕλλησι μόνον ἐστι τὸ *ἰῶτα*, ἀλλὰ καὶ παρ᾽ Ἑβραίοις, τὸ παρ᾽ αὐτοῖς καλούμενον ἰώθ. Δύναται δὲ τὸ *ἰῶτα ἓν ἢ μία κεραία* συμβολικῶς λέγεσθαι ὁ Ἰησοῦς, ἐπείπερ ἡ ἀρχὴ τοῦ ὀνόματος αὐτοῦ, οὐ παρ᾽ Ἕλλησι μόνοις ἀλλὰ καὶ παρ᾽ Ἑβραίοις, ἀπὸ τοῦ ἰῶτα ἄρχεται. Καὶ ἔσται ἡ *μία κεραία* ὁ Ἰησοῦς, *ὁ λόγος τοῦ Θεοῦ*[434] *ἐν τῷ νόμῳ*,[435] οὐ παρερχόμενος αὐτὸν *ἕως πάντα* | **32r** *γένηται*.[436] *Ἰῶτα* δ᾽ ἂν εἴη (ὡς ὁ αὐτός φησι) καὶ αἱ δέκα ἐντολαὶ τοῦ νόμου. Πάντα γὰρ παρέρχονται καὶ αὗται οὐ παρέρχονται.[437] Ἀλλ᾽ οὐδὲ Ἰησοῦς παρέρχεται. Κἂν πέσῃ *ἐπὶ τὴν γῆν*, ἑκουσίως πίπτει ἵνα *καρπὸν πολὺν* φέρῃ.[438] Τὸ δὲ *ἰῶτα ἓν ἢ μία κεραία* πάλιν τὰ ἄνω καὶ τὰ κάτω περικρατεῖ.

> *Μία* δὲ *κεραία* οὐ παρ᾽ Ἕλλησι μόνον ἐστι τὸ *ἰῶτα*, ἀλλὰ καὶ παρ᾽ Ἑβραίοις τὸ παρ᾽ αὐτοῖς καλούμενον ἰῶθ. Δύναται δὲ τὸ *ἰῶτα ἓν ἢ μία κεραία* συμβολικῶς λέγεσθαι ὁ Ἰησοῦς, ἐπείπερ ἡ ἀρχὴ τοῦ ὀνόματος αὐτοῦ οὐ παρ᾽ Ἕλλησι μόνοις ἀλλὰ καὶ παρ᾽ Ἑβραίοις, ἀπὸ τοῦ ἰῶτα ἄρχεται, καὶ ἔσται ἡ *μία κεραία* ὁ Ἰησοῦς, ὁ λόγος τοῦ Θεοῦ ἐν τῷ νόμῳ οὐ παρερχόμενος αὐτὸν ἕως *πάντα γένηται*.[439] *ἰῶτα* δ᾽ ἂν εἴη (ὡς ὁ αὐτός φησι) καὶ αἱ δέκα ἐντολαὶ τοῦ νόμου. πάντα γὰρ παρέρχονται καὶ αὗται οὐ παρέρχονται.[440] ἀλλ᾽ οὐδὲ Ἰησοῦς παρέρχεται. κἂν πέσῃ *ἐπὶ τὴν γῆν*, ἑκουσίως πίπτει ἵνα *καρπὸν πολὺν* φέρῃ.[441] Τὸ δὲ *ἰῶτα ἓν ἢ μία κεραία* πάλιν τὰ ἄνω καὶ τὰ κάτω περικρατεῖ.[cccxlix]

---

427 Cf. 2 Cor. 3:6; also, Rom. 2:29; 7:6.
428 Cf. Lev. 23:27-28; 25:9.
429 Cf. Heb. 4:9.
430 Matt. 11:13; cf. Luke, 16:16.
431 Matt. 24:35; Mark, 13:31; Luke, 21:33.
432 Cf. 2 Cor. 4:18.
433 John, 5:11.
434 Cf. Luke, 8:11; John, 10:35; Rom. 9:6; Heb. 4:12.
435 Cf. Luke, 24:44; John, 1:45; 15:25.
436 Matt. 5:18.
437 Cf. Mark, 13:31; Luke, 21:33.
438 Cf. John, 12:24.
439 Matt. 5:18.
440 Cf. Mark, 13:31; Luke, 21:33.
441 Cf. John, 12:24.

> Μία *κεραία* οὐ παρ᾽ Ἕλλησι μόνον ἐστὶ τὸ *ἰῶτα*, ἀλλὰ καὶ παρ᾽ Ἑβραίοις τὸ παρ᾽ αὐτοῖς καλούμενον ἰώθ. δύναται δὲ τὸ *ἰῶτα ἓν ἢ μία κεραία* συμβολικῶς λέγεσθαι ὁ Ἰησοῦς, ἐπείπερ ἡ ἀρχὴ τοῦ ὀνόματος αὐτοῦ οὐ παρ᾽ Ἕλλησι μόνον, ἀλλὰ καὶ παρ᾽ Ἑβραίοις ἀπὸ τοῦ ἰὼθ γράφεται. καὶ ἔστιν οὕτως τὸ *ἰῶτα ἓν ἢ μία κεραία* ὁ Ἰησοῦς, ὁ λόγος τοῦ θεοῦ ἐν τῷ νόμῳ, οὐ παρερχόμενος αὐτόν, *ἕως ἂν πάντα γένηται.*[cccl]

Ὃς ἐὰν οὖν λύσῃ μίαν τῶν ἐντολῶν.[442] Ὁ ἀθετῶν *μίαν τῶν* τοῦ νόμου *ἐντολῶν* ἀθετεῖται παρὰ τοῦ Θεοῦ ὡς θεομάχος καὶ ἀντινομοθετῶν τῷ Θεῷ. Καὶ νῦν ἐκ τοῦ εὐαγγελικοῦ νόμου δέχεται τὴν τιμωρίαν, ἣν ὁ νόμος πάλαι οὐκ ἦν ὁρίσας. Διὸ καὶ ἀκολούθως λέγει ὁ Χριστός ὅτι *οὐκ ἦλθον καταλῦσαι τὸν νόμον, ἀλλὰ πληρῶσαι.*[443] Ὃ γὰρ ἐκεῖ ἔλε‹ιπ›εν[444] ὧδε ἀνεπληρώθη, οἷον ἐν τῷ νόμῳ ἐλέχθη *ἀπὸ προσώπου πολιοῦ ἐξαναστήσῃ,*[445] καὶ *ἐὰν ἴδῃς τὸ ὑποζύγιον τοῦ ἐχθροῦ σου ἐπιπεπτωκὸς ὑπὸ τὸν γόμον, συνέγειρον αὐτὸ μετ᾽ αὐτοῦ.*[446] Ταῦτα εἰ παρέβη τις, οὐκ ἦν τιμωρία ὁρισθεῖσα ὑπὸ τοῦ νόμου, ἣν ἀποπληρῶν ὁ Χριστός φησι ὅτι *ἐν τῇ βασιλείᾳ* τοῦ Θεοῦ ὁ τοιοῦτος ἐξουθενηθήσεται. Ταύτην οὖν καλεῖ ἐλαχίστην ἐντολήν, ἐφ᾽ ἣν οὐκ ἦν ἐκεῖ παραβάσεως ἐπαγομένη κόλασις.

> Ὁ ἀθετῶν μίαν τῶν τοῦ νόμου ἐντολῶν ἀθετεῖται παρὰ τοῦ θεοῦ ὡς θεομάχος καὶ ἀντινομοθετῶν τῷ θεῷ. καὶ νῦν ἐκ τοῦ εὐαγγελικοῦ νόμου δέχεται τὴν τιμωρίαν, ἣν νόμος πάλαι οὐκ ἦν ὁρίσας. διὸ καὶ ἀκολούθως λέγει ὁ Χριστός, *ὅτι οὐκ ἦλθον καταλῦσαι τὸν νόμον, ἀλλὰ πληρῶσαι.* ὃ γὰρ ἐκεῖ ἔλειπε, ὧδε ἀνεπλήρωσεν, οἷον ἐν τῷ νόμῳ ἐλέχθη. *ἀπὸ προσώπου πολιοῦ ἐξαναστήσῃ* καὶ *ἐὰν ἴδῃς τὸ ὑποζύγιον τοῦ ἐχθροῦ σου ὑποπεπτωκὸς ὑπὸ τὸν γόμον, συνέγειρον αὐτὸ μετ᾽ αὐτοῦ.* ταῦτα εἰ παρέβη τις, οὐκ ἦν τιμωρία ὁρισθεῖσα ὑπὸ τοῦ νόμου. ἣν ἀποπληρῶν ὁ Χριστός φησιν, ὅτι ἐν τῇ βασιλείᾳ τοῦ θεοῦ ὁ τοιοῦτος ἐξουθενηθήσεται. ταύτην οὖν καλεῖ ἐλαχίστην ἐντολήν, ἐφ᾽ ἣν οὐκ ἦν ἐκ παραβάσεως ἐπαγομένη κόλασις.[cccli]

(ΩΡΙΓΕΝΟΥΣ cont.) Ὁ ἀθετῶν φησι *μίαν τῶν νομικῶν ἐντολῶν*, ἐφ᾽ ὧν ὁ νόμος οὐχ ὥρισε τιμωρίαν διὰ τὸ ἐλαχίστας εἶναι, οὗτος ἐκ τῆς νέας διαθήκης τιμωρηθήσεται. Ἢ τοῦτό φησι περὶ ὧν μέλλει λέγειν νῦν, ἃς καὶ ἐλαχίστας καλεῖ μετριοπαθῶν ὡς ἐξ αὐτοῦ λεχθείσας. Ἤτοι ἐλάχιστον τὸ κατὰ διάνοιαν ἁμάρτημα φησι· καὶ γὰρ καὶ αὐτὸ τιμωρίαν ἐπάγει.

---

442 Matt. 5:19.
443 Matt. 5:18.
444 Cod. ἔλεγεν.
445 Lev. 19:32.
446 Ex. 23:5.

16

35r (ΩΡΙΓΕΝΟΥΣ) *Ἴσθι εὐνοῶν τῷ ἀντιδίκῳ σου.*[447] Ἀντίδικός ἐστιν ὁ τῆς σωτηρίας ἡμῶν ἐναντίος καὶ ὁ τοῖς θελήμασιν ἐναντίος καὶ ὁ πλησίον ἐν τοῖς λυπηροῖς. Καὶ ὁ μὲν πρῶτος, ὁ διάβολος· ὁ δὲ δεύτερος, ἡ ἐντολή,[ccclii] καὶ ὁ τρίτος εἴρηται. Πῶς δὲ εὐνοοῦμεν ἑκάστῳ, ζήτει.[cccliii]

> Ἀντίδικός ἐστιν ὁ τῆς σωτηρίας ἡμῶν ἐναντίος καὶ ὁ τοῖς θελήμασιν ἐναντίος καὶ ὁ πλησίον ἐν τοῖς λυπηροῖς. Καὶ ὁ μὲν πρῶτος ὁ διάβολος. ὁ δὲ δεύτερος ἡ ἐντολή. καὶ ὁ τρίτος, ‹ὡς› εἴρηται. Πῶς δὲ εὐνοοῦμεν ἑκάστῳ, ζήτει.[cccliv]
>
> Διχῶς νοητέον τὸν ἀντίδικον. ὁτὲ μὲν τὸν διάβολον, ὁτὲ δὲ τὸν τοῖς θελήμασιν ἡμῶν ἀντικείμενον ‹νόμον›. καὶ ὁ μὲν διάβολος πρῶτός ἐστιν ἀντίδικος, δεύτερος δὲ ἡ ἐντολή. οὐκοῦν παραινεῖ ὁ Χριστὸς πρὸς ἀμφοτέρους διαλλαγῆναι, τουτέστι πρὸς μὲν τὸν διάβολον ὡς μὴ ἔχοντάς τι ἐν τῇ κρίσει τῶν ἐκείνῳ φίλων, πρὸς δὲ τὴν ἐντολὴν ὡς πάντα τελέσαντας τὰ παρ' αὐτοῦ ἐντεταλμένα. εἰ μὴ γὰρ οὕτω πρὸς τὴν κρίσιν ἔλθῃς, *τὸν ἔσχατον κοδράντην* ἀποδώσεις.[ccclv]
>
> Certain ones explain[ccclvi] it with an even more deduced exegesis, referring the words to baptism, namely, that each one forms a concord with the devil, and says: I renounce you, devil, and your showiness and your vices and your world, which has been under evil. Therefore, if we preserve this pact, we are being benevolent and conform with our adversary, and on no occasion shall we be shut up in prison. In truth, however, so far as we have transgressed in those things that we had promised to the devil, we will be handed over to the judge and to the officer, and we will be thrown into prison, and we shall not come out from it until we pay back the last farthing. The farthing is a kind of coin which is worth two mites. This explains why in one gospel that poor woman is said to have put a mite into the treasury, whereas, in another, [it is written] two mites.[ccclvii] The case is not that the gospels are incongruent, but that one farthing has the worth of two mites. Therefore, this is what he says: you will not come out from prison until you pay in full for even the last sins.[ccclviii]

Ὁδὸς γάρ ἐστιν οὗτος ὁ βίος.[ccclix]

> Ὁδὸς γάρ ἐστιν οὗτος ὁ βίος.[ccclx]

Ἀντίδικον εἶναι τοῦ ἀνθρώπου τὴν ἐκ τοῦ συνειδότος ὑπόμνησιν.[ccclxi] Τοῦτο οὖν ἔφησεν ὁ Κύριος· ἡνίκα ἂν ἁμάρτῃς ἢ ἁμαρτῆσαι προέλῃ, εὐνόει *τῷ ἀντιδίκῳ σου*· τουτέστι προσδέχου τοὺς ἐκ τοῦ συνειδότος ἐλέγχους, ἡνίκα ἂν ὑπομιμνήσκῃ σε καὶ ἐπιλαμβάνηταί σου ὡς ἁμαρτήσαντος ἢ ἁμαρτήσεσθαι μέλλοντος. Εἰ δὲ παρακρούσῃ τὴν ὑπόμνησιν καὶ μὴ ἐπίσχῃς σαυτὸν μηδὲ ὑπακούσῃς, οὐκ εὐνόησας, ἀλλὰ

447 Matt. 5:25.

κατεδυνάστευσας τὸν ἀντίδικον. | **35v** Νοεῖν δεῖ ἀντίδικον καὶ ὁδὸν καὶ ἄρχοντα προεστῶτα τοῦ ἀντιδίκου ἡμῶν. Τούτῳ τῷ τρόπῳ ὁδός ἐστιν ὁ βίος ἡμῶν. *Ἀντίδικος*, ἡ ἀντιπαλαίουσα ἡμῖν δύναμις παρεπομένη τῷ βίῳ· ἄρχων, *ὁ τοῦ κόσμου τούτου ἄρχων*,[448] *τουτέστιν ὁ διάβολος*.[449] Ὁ δὲ κριτής ἐστιν ὁ Χριστός, ᾧ *πᾶσαν τὴν κρίσιν ἔδωκεν ὁ Πατήρ*,[450] ὃς παρὰ τοῦ ἐχθροῦ καὶ ἐκδικητοῦ ἐλεγχθέντα ἐπὶ πολλοῖς ἐγκλήμασι *παραδώσει τῷ πράκτορι*,[451] τῷ ἐπὶ τῶν κολάσεων τεταγμένῳ ἀγγέλῳ,[cclxii] ὃς καλεῖ *εἰς τὴν φυλακήν*, τουτέστιν εἰς τὸν τόπον τῆς κολάσεως, δι᾽ ἐπιπόνων μαστίγων ἀπαιτῶν μέχρι καὶ τῶν μικροτάτων ἁμαρτημάτων.

Ἕως εἶ φησι κατὰ τὸν βίον τοῦτον (ὁδὸς γὰρ ὁ βίος ὑπὸ πάντων ἀνθρώπων παροδευόμενος) προσδέχου καὶ μὴ παραλογίζου τὴν ἐκ τοῦ συνειδότος ὑπόμνησιν. Εἰ δὲ παραλογίσῃ καὶ παραδράμῃς τὸν βίον, αὐτὸ τὸ συνειδὸς ἀντιδίκου τάξιν ἐπέχον ἐπὶ τοῦ κριτοῦ κατηγορήσει καὶ ὑπὸ τὴν ψῆφον ποιήσει σε τοῦ δικάζοντος καὶ παραδοθήσῃ ταῖς ἀνηκέστοις κολάσεσιν.[cclxiii] ἃ οὐκ ἂν ἔπαθες, εἴ γε κατὰ τὴν ὁδὸν εὔνοιαν ἐκτήσω πρὸς τὸν ἀντίδικον, τοὺς ἐλέγχους ὡς μετ᾽ εὐνοίας προσφερομένους καταδεχόμενος. Τοῦτο γὰρ καὶ ὁ θεσπέσιος εὐαγγελιστὴς Ἰωάννης ἐπιστέλλων φησι· *ἐὰν ἡ συνείδησις μὴ καταγινώσκῃ ἡμῶν, παρρησίαν ἔχομεν πρὸς τὸν Θεόν*.[452]

> Ἕως εἶ φησι κατὰ τὸν βίον τοῦτον (ὁδὸς γὰρ ὁ βίος ὑπὸ πάντων ἀνθρώπων παροδευόμενος) προσδέχου καὶ μὴ παραλογίζου τὴν ἐκ τοῦ συνειδότος ὑπόμνησιν. Εἰ δὲ παραλογίσῃ καὶ παραδράμῃς τὸν βίον, αὐτὸ τὸ συνειδὸς ἀντιδίκου τάξιν ἐπέχον ἐπὶ τοῦ κριτοῦ κατηγορήσει καὶ ὑπὸ τὴν ψῆφον ποιήσει σε τοῦ δικάζοντος καὶ παραδοθήσῃ ταῖς ἀνηκέστοις κολάσεσιν. ἃ οὐκ ἂν ἔπαθες, εἴ γε κατὰ τὴν ὁδὸν εὔνοιαν ἐκτήσω πρὸς τὸν ἀντίδικον, τοὺς ἐλέγχους ὡς μετ᾽ εὐνοίας προσφερομένους καταδεχόμενος. Τοῦτο γὰρ καὶ ὁ θεσπέσιος εὐαγγελιστὴς Ἰωάννης ἐπιστέλλων φησι· *ἐὰν ἡ συνείδησις μὴ καταγινώσκῃ ἡμῶν, παρρησίαν ἔχομεν πρὸς τὸν Θεόν*.[cclxiv]

> *Ἀγαπητοί, ἐὰν ἡ καρδία ἡμῶν μὴ καταγινώσκῃ ἡμῶν, παῤῥησίαν ἔχομεν πρὸς τὸν Θεόν*.[453] (Κυρίλλου.) Ἕως εἶ κατὰ τὸν βίον τοῦτον, ὁδὸς γὰρ ὁ βίος ὑπὸ πάντων ἀνθρώπων παροδευόμενος, προσδέχου καὶ μὴ παραλογίζου τὴν ἐκ τοῦ συνειδότος ὑπόμνησιν. εἰ δὲ παραλογίσῃ καὶ παραδράμῃς τὸν βίον, αὐτὸ τὸ συνειδὸς ἀντιδίκου τάξιν ἐπέχον ἐπὶ τοῦ κριτοῦ κατηγορήσει, καὶ ὑπὸ τὴν ψῆφον ποιήσει σε τοῦ δικάζοντος, καὶ παραδοθήσῃ ταῖς ἀνηκέστοις κολάσεσιν. Ἃ οὐκ ἂν ἔπαθες, εἴ γε κατὰ τὴν ὁδὸν εὔνοιαν ἐκτήσω πρὸς τὸν ἀντίδικον, τοὺς ἐλέγχους ὡς μετ᾽ εὐνοίας προσφερομένους καταδεχόμενος. Τοῦτο γὰρ καὶ ὁ θεσπέσιος εὐαγγελιστὴς Ἰωάννης ἐπιστέλλων φησίν. *Ἐὰν ἡ συνείδησις ἡμῶν μὴ καταγινώσκῃ ἡμῶν, παῤῥησίαν ἔχομεν πρὸς τὸν Θεόν*.[cclxv]

---

448 John, 12:31; 16:11; cf. Eph. 2:2.
449 Heb. 2:14.
450 John, 5:22.
451 Luke, 12:58: καὶ ὁ κριτής σε παραδώσει τῷ πράκτορι, καὶ ὁ πράκτωρ σε βαλεῖ εἰς φυλακήν.
452 1 John, 3:21.
453 1 John, 3:21.

῞Ο λέγει, τοιοῦτόν ἐστιν.[454] Πρὸ δίκης εὐγνωμόνει· ἐπεὶ ἐὰν αἰτιαθῇς καὶ φυλακισθῇς, οὐκ ἀπολύῃ ἕως οὗ ἀποτίσῃς ἕως ὀβολοῦ. Τοῦτο γὰρ ὁ κοδράντης δη | **36r** λοῖ.

> ῞Ο λέγει, τοιοῦτόν ἐστιν. πρὸ δίκης εὐγνωμόνει. ἐπεὶ καὶ ἐὰν ἐγκληθῇς καὶ φυλακισθῇς, οὐκ ἀπολύῃ ἕως οὗ ἀποτίσῃς ἕως ὀβολοῦ. τοῦτο γὰρ ὁ κοδράντης δηλοῖ.[ccclxvi]

῎Εστι τὸ ὑπόδειγμα χρήσιμον καὶ πρὸς ὃ παραλαμβάνεται χρησιμώτερον. Οἱ γὰρ πρὸ δίκης διαλυόμενοι φρονιμώτεροι εἰσὶ μὴ ἀναγκαζόμενοι.

> *῾Ως γὰρ ὑπάγεις μετὰ τοῦ ἀντιδίκου σου ἐπ᾽ ἄρχοντα,*[455] κ.τ.λ. Πάνυ χρήσιμον τὸ παράδειγμα πρὸς ὃ λαμβάνεται. Οἱ γὰρ πρὸ δίκης διαλυόμενοι, φρονιμώτεροί εἰσιν, ἀφ᾽ ἑαυτῶν τὸ δίκαιον ὁρῶντες.[ccclxvii]

Οἱ γὰρ ἀφ᾽ ἑαυτῶν τὸ δίκαιον ὁρῶντες, οὗτοι ἑαυτοῖς δικασταὶ γινόμενοι ἀποφέρονται τὴν ψῆφον τῆς δικαιοσύνης. ῞Οπερ δὲ καλὸν ἐνταῦθα ποιεῖν, τοῦτο καλόν ἐστιν ἐκεῖ ποιῆσαι. ᾽Εγκαλεῖ σοι φησιν ὅ τι ἥμαρτες καὶ ἔχεις συνειδὸς ἁμαρτημάτων· διάλυσαι πρὸς τὸν ἀντίδικόν σου· ἡ γὰρ ὀργὴ καὶ ἡ ἐπιθυμία καὶ τὰ λοιπὰ τῆς ἀτιμίας πάθη ἀντίδικοι ἡμῶν ὑπάρχουσιν. Οὐδεὶς γὰρ ἡμῶν ἕτερος ἀντίδικος, ἐὰν μὴ ἡμεῖς ἑαυτῶν διὰ τούτων γενώμεθα ἀντίδικοι. ῎Αγε τοίνυν ἀδελφέ. ᾽Εὰν αἴσθῃ ἐπιθυμίας σωματικῆς ἢ ὀργῆς ἢ ἑτέρου πάθους, διάλυσαι πρὸς ἐκεῖνο. κατάργησον αὐτοῦ τὰ σκιρτήματα. κατάπαυσον αὐτὸ κακῶς κινούμενον, ἵνα μὴ ἔλθῃς *πρὸς τὸν κριτὴν καὶ ὁ κριτής σε παραδῷ τῷ πράκτορι* (τοῖς ἀγγέλοις τοῖς διακονουμένοις πρὸς τὴν κρίσιν) *καὶ ὁ πράκτωρ σε βάλῃ εἰς τὴν φυλακὴν ἕως ἂν καὶ τὸ ἔσχατον λεπτὸν ἀποδῷς.*[456] Βλέπε φιλανθρωπίαν κριτοῦ. Προλέγει, ἵνα μὴ ἐμπέσωμεν.

῾Υποκείσθω τις, φησί, ἐφ᾽ ἑνὸς τῶν τεταγμένων εἰς ἀρχὴν αἰτιάματά τινα ποιησάμενος κατὰ σοῦ. Εἶτα, τοῖς ἀπάγουσιν ἐπὶ τὸ δικαστήριον ὑποδείξας, ἀποφέρεσθαι ποιεῖ. *῞Εως* τοίνυν, φησί, μετ᾽ αὐτοῦ *εἶ ἐν τῇ ὁδῷ* (τουτέστιν πρὶν ἀφικέσθαι πρὸς τὸν κριτήν), *δὸς ἐργασίαν*, ἀντὶ τοῦ πᾶσαν θέσθαι μὴ ὀκνήσῃς σπουδήν, ἵνα ἀπαλλαγῇς ἀπ᾽ αὐτοῦ. | **36v** Εἰ δὲ μὴ τοῦτο γένηται, παραδώσει σε *τῷ κριτῇ*. Εἶτα, ὅταν ἔνοχος τοῖς ὀφλήμασιν εὑρεθῇς, παραδοθήσῃ *τῷ πράκτορι* (τουτέστι, τοῖς ἀπαιτηταῖς) κἀκεῖνοι σε κατακλείσαντες ἀπαιτήσουσι καὶ *τὸ*[457] *ἔσχατον λεπτόν.* Οὐκοῦν ἔνοχοι μὲν πλημμελήμασιν ἐσμὲν ἅπαντες οἱ ὄντες *ἐπὶ τῆς γῆς*,[458] ἑκάστου γε μὴν ἀντίδικος καὶ κατήγορος, ὁ Σατανᾶς· ἐχθρὸς γάρ ἐστι καὶ ἐκδικητής. *῞Εως* τοίνυν ἐσμὲν *ἐν τῇ ὁδῷ*, τουτέστιν ἕως οὔπω πρὸς τὸ τῆς ἐνθάδε ζωῆς κατηντήσαμεν τέλος, ἀπαλλαγῶμεν αὐτοῦ· λύσωμεν τὰς αἰτίας τὰς καθ᾽ ἑαυτῶν· τὴν διὰ *Χριστοῦ χάριν*[459] ἁρπάσωμεν,

---

454 On Matt. 5:25.
455 Luke, 12:58.
456 Luke, 12:59.
457 Cod. τὸν.
458 Cf. Matt. 9:6.
459 Cf. Rom. 1:4-5; 2 Cor. 8:9; 2 Thess. 1:12; cf. John, 1:17.

ἐλευθεροῦσαν ἡμᾶς παντὸς ὀφλήματός τε καὶ δίκης, ἔξω τιθεῖσαν κολάσεώς τε καὶ φόβου. Μὴ ἄρα πως ἀναπόνιπτον ἐσχηκότες τὸν μολυσμὸν ἀπενεχθῶμεν πρὸς τὸν κριτὴν καὶ παραδοθῶμεν τοῖς πράκτορσιν, ἤτοι τοῖς κολασταῖς, ὧν οὐκ ἄν τις διαφύγ‹οι›[460] τὸ ἀπηνές, ἀπαιτηθήσεται δὲ μᾶλλον τὰς ἐπὶ παντὶ πλημμελήματι δίκας, μικρῷ ‹τε› καὶ μεγάλῳ. Τούτων ἔσονται μακρὰν οἱ τὸν τῆς *Χριστοῦ* παρουσίας καιρὸν[461] δοκιμάζοντες καὶ τὸ ἐπ᾽ αὐτῷ μυστήριον οὐκ ἠγνοηκότες.

> Ὑποκείσθω τις, φησί, ἐφ᾽ ἑνὸς τῶν τεταγμένων εἰς ἀρχήν, αἰτίασίν τινα ποιησάμενος κατὰ σοῦ, εἶτα τοῖς ἀπάγουσιν ἐπὶ τὸ δικαστήριον ὑποδείξας, ἀποφέρεσθαι ποιεῖ. Ἕως τοίνυν μετ᾽ αὐτοῦ εἶ ἐν τῇ ὁδῷ, τουτέστι πρὶν ἀφικέσθαι πρὸς τὸν κριτήν, δὸς ἐργασίαν, ἀντὶ τοῦ πᾶσαν θέσθαι μὴ ὀκνήσῃς σπουδήν, ἵνα ἀπαλλαγῇς αὐτοῦ. εἰ δὲ μὴ τοῦτο γένοιτο, παραδώσει σε τῷ κριτῇ. Εἶτα, ὅταν ἔνοχος τοῖς ὀφλήμασιν εὑρεθῇς, παραδοθήσῃ τῷ πράκτορι, τουτέστι τοῖς ἀπαιτηταῖς. κἀκεῖνοί σε κατακλείσαντες, ἀπαιτήσουσι καὶ τὸ ἔσχατον λεπτόν. Οὐκοῦν ἔνοχοι μὲν πλημμελήμασί ἐσμεν ἅπαντες οἱ ὄντες ἐπὶ τῆς γῆς. Ἑκάστου γε μὴν ἀντίδικος καὶ κατήγορος, ὁ Σατανᾶς. ἐχθρὸς γάρ ἐστι καὶ ἐκδικητής. Ἕως τοίνυν ἐσμὲν ἐν τῇ ὁδῷ, τουτέστιν ἕως οὔπω πρὸς τὸ τῆς ἐνθάδε ζωῆς κατηντήσαμεν τέλος, ἀπαλλαγῶμεν αὐτοῦ. λύσωμεν τὰς καθ᾽ ἑαυτῶν αἰτίας. τὴν διὰ Χριστοῦ χάριν ἁρπάσωμεν, ἐλευθεροῦσαν ἡμᾶς παντὸς ὀφλήματος, καὶ δίκης ἔξω τιθεῖσαν, κολάσεώς τε καὶ φόβου. Μὴ ἄρα πως ἀναπόνιπτον ἐσχηκότες τὸν μολυσμόν, ἀπενεχθῶμεν πρὸς τὸν κριτήν, καὶ παραδοθῶμεν τοῖς πράκτορσιν, ἤτοι τοῖς κολασταῖς, ὧν οὐκ ἄν τις διαφύγοι τὸ ἀπηνές, ἀπαιτηθήσεται δὲ μᾶλλον τὰς ἐπὶ παντὶ πλημμελήματι δίκας μικρῷ καὶ μεγάλῳ. Τούτων ἔσονται μακρὰν οἱ τὸν τῆς Χριστοῦ παρουσίας καιρὸν δοκιμάζοντες, καὶ τὸ ἐπ᾽ αὐτῷ μυστήριον οὐκ ἠγνοηκότες.[cclxviii]

(ΩΡΙΓΕΝΟΥΣ, cont.) *Καὶ τὸν ἔσχατον κοδράντην.*[462] Ὁ κοδράντης σημαίνει τὸ τέταρτον τοῦ ἶν μέτρου.

(ΩΡΙΓΕΝΟΥΣ, added on the margin) κατὰ τὴν Ἑβραίων φωνὴν ὁ κοδράντης δύο ἐστὶν ὀβολοί, ὅπερ ὁ Λουκᾶς σαφηνίσας λεπτὸν ὠνόμασεν.

> Ὁ μέντοι κοδράντης σημαίνει τὸ τέταρτον τοῦ ἶν μέτρου. οὗτος κατὰ τὴν Ἑβραίων φωνὴν δύο ἐστὶν ὀβολοί, ὅπερ ὁ Λουκᾶς σαφηνίσας λεπτὸν ὠνόμασεν. ἡμεῖς δὲ ἀπαλλαγῶμεν καὶ τοῦ ἐχθροῦ καὶ ἐκδικητοῦ, ἤγουν τοῦ διαβόλου, ἕως ἐσμὲν *ἐν τῇ ὁδῷ* ταύτῃ, καὶ τῶν τῆς ἀτιμίας παθῶν, ἅτινα *ἀντίδικοι* ἡμῶν εἰσιν. οὐδεὶς γὰρ ἡμῶν ἕτερος *ἀντίδικος*, ἐὰν μὴ ἡμεῖς ἑαυτῶν διὰ τούτων γενώμεθα *ἀντίδικοι* καὶ μὴ ἡ συνείδησις καταγινώσκῃ ἡμῶν ὡς καταφρονούντων τῆς ὑπομνήσεως αὐτῆς,[cclxix] μήποτε παραδοθῶμεν *τῷ κριτῇ* πάντων θεῷ ὑπὸ τῆς συνειδήσεως ἐλεγχθέντες. ὁ δὲ παραδώσει τοῖς πράκτορσιν, ἤγουν τοῖς κολασταῖς ἀγγέλοις,[cclxx] καὶ ἀπαιτηθησόμεθα τὰς ἐπὶ παντὶ πλημμελήματι δίκας, μικρῷ τε καὶ μεγάλῳ.[cclxxi]

460 Cod. διαφύγῃ.

461 Cf. 1 Cor. 15:23; 1 Thess. 5:23.

462 Matt. 5:26.

(ΩΡΙΓΕΝΟΥΣ, main text cont.) *ὅτι πᾶς ὁ βλέπων γυναῖκα πρὸς τὸ ἐπιθυμῆσαι.*[463] Οὐ τὸν ἐπιθυμήσαντα κατά τινα συντυχίαν κατάκριτον εἶναι λέγει, ἀλλὰ τὸν ἐκ πονηρίας τὸ πάθος ἐπισπασάμενον. Τὸ μὲν γὰρ ἐγγενέσθαί ποτε τοιαύτην ὁρμήν, ἡ συγκεκραμένη | **37r** τῇ φύσει πολλάκις ἀσθένεια καὶ παρὰ τὴν γνώμην παρασκευάζει· τὸ δὲ μὴ παρενεχθῆναι τῇ τοῦ πάθους ὁρμῇ, ἀλλ᾽ ἀνδρικῶς πρὸς τὴν τοιαύτην διάθεσιν στῆναι καὶ τοῖς λογισμοῖς τὸ πάθος ἀπώσασθαι, τοῦτο τῆς ἀρετῆς ἔργον ἐστί.

> Νυνὶ δέ φησιν οὐ τὸν ἐπιθυμήσαντα κατά τινα συντυχίαν εἶναι κατάκριτον, ἀλλὰ τὸν ἐκ προνοίας τὸ πάθος ἐπισπασάμενον. Τὸ μὲν γὰρ ἐγγενέσθαι ποτὲ τοιαύτην ὁρμήν, ἡ συγκεκραμένη τῇ φύσει πολλάκις ἀσθένεια καὶ παρὰ γνώμην παρασκευάζει. τὸ δὲ μὴ χειμάρρου δίκην παρενεχθῆναι τῇ τοῦ πάθους ὁρμῇ, ἀλλ᾽ ἀνδρικῶς πρὸς τὴν τοιαύτην διάθεσιν στῆναι, καὶ τοῖς λογισμοῖς τὸ πάθος ἀπώσασθαι, τοῦτο τῆς ἀρετῆς ἔργον ἐστίν.[ccclxxii]

Τὸ δὲ περιεργάζεσθαι ὁρῶντα καὶ ἐκ τοῦ πολὺ κατανοεῖν εἰς ἐπιθυμίας ἕλκεσθαι αἰσχρὰς ὁ τοιοῦτος, εἰ καιροῦ λάβηται καὶ ἐπὶ τὸ πάθος ἔρχεται, διὸ τὸν τοιοῦτόν φησι μοιχεύειν *ἐν τῇ καρδίᾳ αὐτοῦ*. Πῶς οὖν *ἐλαφρὸν τὸ φορτίον* τοῦ Χριστοῦ καὶ *ὁ ζυγὸς χρηστός*,[464] ὁ καὶ ἐκ μόνης ἐπιθυμίας ἐπάγων κόλασιν τοῦ νόμου οὐχ οὕτως ἔχοντος; Ὅτι *ὁ νόμος* τοῖς ἀσθενέσιν ἐδόθη,[465] ἡ δὲ Χριστοῦ διδαχὴ τοῖς ἰσχυροτέροις.
Ὁ γὰρ θεῖος λόγος γεγονὼς ἄνθρωπος καὶ ἑνώσας ἑαυτῷ τὴν φύσιν ἰσχυροποίησεν αὐτὴν κατὰ τῶν παθῶν καὶ ἐποίησε διαβῆναι τὴν χάριν ἐπὶ τοὺς κοινωνοῦντας αὐτῷ. Διὸ ὡς ἀνδρείοις διαλέγεται. Εἰ γὰρ καὶ τοῖς πρὸ Χριστοῦ ἀδύνατον ἦν, ἢ ἐγγὺς ἀδυνάτου, ἀλλὰ σήμερον τοῖς πιστοῖς εὐκατόρθωτον.

> Τάχα εἰσί τινες τοιοῦτον λαβόντες χάρισμα ὥστε μὴ ἐπιθυμεῖν. πλὴν ὁ Χριστὸς ὡς ἰσχυροποιήσας τὴν ἀνθρώπων φύσιν καὶ τὰ ὑπὲρ νόμον ἐπιτάσσει ὡς νῦν ἐγχωροῦντα. εἰ γὰρ καὶ τοῖς πρὸ τοῦ Χριστοῦ ἀδύνατον ἦν τοῦτο, ἀλλὰ τοῖς πιστοῖς εὐκατόρθωτον τὸ τὰς ἐπιθυμίας ἐκκόπτειν.[cccلxxiii]

Εἰ δὲ ὁ ὀφθαλμός σου ὁ δεξιὸς σκανδαλίζει.[466] Ὀφθαλμὸν δέ φησι δεξιὸν καὶ χεῖρα δεξιὰν[467] τὸν λογισμὸν τῆς ἐπιθυμίας, ὃν λέγει ἐκκόπτεσθαι.

> (Κύριλλος. Ἰωάννης [Chrysostom]. Ἰσίδωρος [of Pelusium]. Θεόδωρος Ἡρακλείας) Εἰπών, *ἐὰν ὁ ὀφθαλμός σου σκανδαλίζῃ σε, καὶ τὰ ἑξῆς*. ὀφθαλμὸν λέγει, τὸν λογισμὸν τῆς ἐπιθυμίας, ὃν λέγει ἐκκόπτεσθαι.[cccxxiv]

463 Matt. 5:28.
464 Matt. 11:30.
465 Cf. Heb. 7:28.
466 Matt. 5:29.
467 Matt. 5:30.

> Once he spoke above of lust for a woman, he has now rightly named 'eye' the roving thought and feeling. The right [hand] and the other parts of the body bespeak the beginnings of inclination and of emotion, so that we would fulfil in deed what we conceive in mind.[ccclxxv]

Ἤτοι τοῦτό φησι· ἐὰν ὦσι τινές σοι συγγενεῖς ἢ φίλοι καὶ τοσοῦτον εἰσὶ χρήσιμοι ὥστε ἴσον ὀφθαλμοῦ καὶ χειρὸς δεξιᾶς αὐτοὺς παραβάλλεσθαι, σκανδαλίζωσι δέ σε, ἔκκοψον ἀπ᾿ αὐτῶν. Λέγει δὲ τοὺς εἰς πορνείαν καὶ μοιχείαν[468] διὰ τῆς αὐτῶν συνηθείας καὶ φιλίας τινὰς ἐρεθίζοντας, ὧν θέλει ἐκκόπτεσθαι ὡς λοιμῶν μεταδιδόντων καὶ ἄλλοις τῆς νόσου. | **37v** Οὐχ ὅτι τῷ ὄντι καὶ ἐκκόψαι δεῖ τὰ μέλη, ἀλλ᾿ οἱονεὶ νεκρῶσαι καὶ ἀργὰ καταστῆσαι πρὸς ἁμαρτίαν, ὡς ὁ ἀπόστολος εἴρηκε,[469] καὶ μὴ φείσασθαι μηδὲ τῶν ἀναγκαιοτάτων, εἰ δι᾿ αὐτῶν τινὲς ἐνέργειᾳ φαύλῃ κινδυνεύοιεν. Τοῦτο περὶ τῶν φίλων τῶν ἐν τάξει χειρὸς καὶ ὀφθαλμῶν τεταγμένων νομοθετεῖ καὶ οὐχ ἡμᾶς αὐτοὺς κατὰ τῶν οἰκείων ὁπλίζει μελῶν.[ccclxxvi] Εἰ γὰρ μὴ διακόψ‹ῃ›ς[470] τὴν μοχθηρὰν φιλίαν, καὶ ἑαυτὸν προσαπολέσεις κἀκεῖνον οὐ σώσεις.

> Εἰπὼν δὲ ὅτι *ἐὰν ἡ χείρ σου ἢ ὁ ποῦς σου, ἢ ὁ ὀφθαλμός σου σκανδαλίζησεν* [sic] καὶ τὰ ἑξῆς. οὐ περὶ τῶν τοῦ σώματος μελῶν ταῦτα λέγει. ἄπαγε, ἀλλὰ περὶ φίλων καὶ προσηκόντων. οὓς ἂν ἐν τάξει μελῶν ἀναγκαίων ἔχομεν.[ccclxxvii]

> Here is another explanation: the right eye and right hand indicate affection for brothers, wife, children, neighbours, and close kinship.[471] If we see them as impediment hindering us from contemplating the true light, we ought to cut such parts off, lest, while we want to procure others, we ourselves should perish for ever.[ccclxxviii]

Ἐγὼ δὲ λέγω ὑμῖν ὅτι ὃς ἂν ἀπολύσῃ τὴν γυναῖκα αὐτοῦ.[472] Ἵνα μὴ ὡς κάκιστοι οἱ Ἰουδαῖοι μισοῦντες τὰς γυναῖκας ἀποκτείνωσι, δέδωκεν ὁ νόμος ἄδειαν τῷ βουλομένῳ ρεπουδιατεύειν τὴν γυναῖκα, τουτέστι διαζεύγνυσθαι καὶ χωρίζεσθαι αὐτῆς. *Βιβλίον*[473] δὲ ἐδίδοτο, ἵνα μὴ ἐξὸν ᾖ τῇ γυναικὶ ἐπαναλύειν πρὸς τὸν ἄνδρα ἄλλῃ συνοικοῦντα καὶ φανερῶς γίνονται αἱ μοιχεῖαι. Ὁ δὲ Κύριος, ὑπὸ ἔγκλημα φησι τὸν τὴν σώφρονα ἐκβάλλοντα. Δίδωσι γὰρ αὐτῇ ἄδειαν ἄλλῳ γαμηθῆναι, ὅπερ ἐστὶν εἶδος μοιχείας, ὡσανεὶ μὴ λυθείσης τῆς συζυγίας. Οὐ γὰρ τὸ ρεπούδιον παρὰ Θεῷ λύει[474] τὸν γάμον, ἀλλ᾿ ἡ ἄτοπος πρᾶξις.

---

468 Cf. Matt. 15:19; Mark, 7:21; 1 Cor. 6:9; Heb. 13:4.
469 Cf. Rom. 6:13; Col. 3:5.
470 Cod. διακόψεις.
471 Cf. Luke, 18:29-30.
472 Matt. 5:32.
473 Cf. Deut. 24:1&3; Is. 50:1; Jer. 3:8. Matt. 19:7; Mark, 10:4.
474 Cod. λύειν.

> Ὁ τὴν σώφρονα ἐκβάλλων δίδωσιν αὐτῇ ἄδειαν ἄλλῳ γαμηθῆναι, ὅπερ ἐστὶν εἶδος μοιχείας ὡσανεὶ μὴ λυθείσης συζυγίας. οὐ γὰρ τὰ ρεπούδια παρὰ θεῷ λύει τὸν γάμον, ἀλλ' ἡ ἄτοπος πρᾶξις.[cccl xxix]

> Διδάσκει σαφῶς διὰ τούτων, ὅτι οὐ τὸ ἄλογον ρεπούδιον λύει τὸν γάμον παρὰ θεῷ, ἀλλ' ἡ ἄτοπος πρᾶξις κἂν μὴ λυθῇ νόμῳ. ὅλη γὰρ ἡ Χριστοῦ διδασκαλία τὰ κατὰ διάθεσιν κρίνει.[ccclxxx]

Οὗτος οὖν ὑπὸ ἔγκλημά ἐστιν, ὡς ἀφορμὴν διδοὺς τῇ γυναικὶ συνευρεθῆναι ἄλλῳ καὶ μοιχευθῆναι καὶ ὁ λαβὼν αὐτὴν μοιχός ἐστι. Καὶ αὐτὴν δὲ τὴν γυναῖκα κωλύει ἄλλῳ συνευρεθῆναι, διὰ φιλίας ἐπιτρέπων ἀνακάμψαι πρὸς τὸν ἄνδρα. Καὶ ὁ ἀπολύων τοίνυν *τὴν γυναῖκα μοιχᾶται αὐτήν*, τουτέστιν ἀναγκάζει | **38r** μοιχευθῆναι. Καὶ ὁ δεχόμενος αὐτὴν *μοιχᾶται αὐτήν*, ἀφορμὴν παρέχων τοῦ ἁμαρτῆσαι τὴν γυναῖκα. Εἰ γὰρ μὴ δέχοιτο, ἐπανακάμψει‹εν ἂν›[475] πρὸς τὸν ἄνδρα.

Ἐρρέθη τοῖς ἀρχαίοις, οὐκ ἐπιορκήσεις.[476] Τίνος ἕνεκεν οὐκ ἦλθεν ἐπὶ τὴν κλοπὴν εὐθέως, ἀλλ' ἐπὶ τὴν ψευδομαρτυρίαν, ὑπερβὰς ἐκείνην τὴν ἐντολήν; Ὅτι ὁ μὲν κλέπτων ἔστιν ὅτε καὶ ὀμεῖται· ὁ δὲ μὴ ὀμνύναι μηδὲ ψεύδεσθαι εἰδὼς πολλῷ μᾶλλον οὐχ αἱρήσεται κλέπτειν. Ὥστε διὰ ταύτης κἀκείνην ἀνέτρεψε. Τὸ γὰρ ψεῦδος ἀπὸ τοῦ κλέπτειν.

Ἐγὼ δὲ λέγω ὑμῖν, μὴ ὀμόσαι ὅλως.[477] Τὸ εὐορκεῖν ὁ παλαιὸς νόμος εἶχεν· ὁ δὲ Κύριος οὐδόλως[478] ὀμνύειν βούλεται. Ἐπειδὴ δὲ Ἰουδαῖοι τοῦ Θεοῦ λέγοντος ἤκουον διὰ τοῦ προφήτου, *ὁ οὐρανός μοι θρόνος ἡ δὲ γῆ ὑποπόδιον τῶν ποδῶν μου*,[479] ὅρκιον ἐποιοῦντο τὸν οὐρανόν, θεῖον αὐτὸν ὀνομάζοντες θρόνον, ὁμοίως δὲ καὶ τὴν γῆν ὑπὸ πόδας Θεοῦ κειμένην, καὶ μετὰ τὴν *Ἱερουσαλήμ. Πόλις* γὰρ ἔφασκον ἐστὶ τοῦ πάντων κρατοῦντος Θεοῦ,[480] καίτοι τῶν ἀρχαιοτέρων ἁγίων τὸ *ζῇ Κύριος*[481] ἐν ὅρκου χρείᾳ πεποιημένων. Διὸ τὴν ἠλιθιωτάτην αὐτῶν ἔννοιαν κατακιβδηλεύων ὁ Σωτήρ, μὴ δεῖν ἀπόμνυσθαι λέγει, *μήτε ἐν τῷ οὐρανῷ ὅτι θρόνος ἐστὶ τοῦ Θεοῦ, μήτε ἐν τῇ γῇ ὅτι ὑποπόδιόν ἐστι τῶν ποδῶν αὐτοῦ, μήτε εἰς Ἱεροσόλυμα ὅτι πόλις ἐστι τοῦ μεγάλου βασιλέως.*[482] Ἃ γὰρ ἐκεῖνοι ληροῦντες ἔφασκον, ταῦτα χρησίμως διεστέλλετο ὁ Σωτήρ, πανταχοῦ ἐπίπλαστον καὶ οὐκ οἶδ' ὅθεν ἐξευρημένον, ἐλέγχων αὐτῶν τὸ ἐν τούτοις εὐλαβές. | **38v** Οἰχέσθω δὴ οὖν καὶ ἡ ἐπὶ τόδε πλάνησις. Ὁ γὰρ κατὰ τῶν κτισμάτων ὀμνύων τὸν

475 Cod. ἐπανακάμψει.
476 Matt. 5:33.
477 Matt. 5:34.
478 cod. οὐδ' ὅλως.
479 Is. 66:1, quoted in Acts, 7:49.
480 Psalm 47:3, quoted in Matt. 5:35.
481 Judices, 8:19; Ruth, 3:13; 1 Kings, 14:45; 19:6; 20:21; 26:10&16; 28:10; 29:6; 2 Kings, 2:27; 12:5; 15:21; 3 Kings, 1:29; 17:1&12; 18:10&15; 22:14; 4 Kings, 2:2-6; 3:14; 4:30; 5:16&20; Michah, 18:13; Jer. 4:2; 5:2; 12:16; 16:14-15; 45:16; 51:26.
482 Matt. 5:34-35.

Θεὸν τὸν πληροῦντα αὐτά[483] ὀμνύει. Οὐ δι᾿ ἑαυτὰ γὰρ τιμᾶται τὰ στοιχεῖα, ἀλλὰ διὰ τὸν ποιήσαντα. Κωλύει δὲ καὶ ἄλλως κατ᾿ αὐτῶν ὀμνύειν, ἵνα μὴ δῶμεν *τῇ κτίσει* τὸ ὑπὲρ τὴν κτίσιν ἀξίωμα θεοποιοῦντες αὐτά.[484] *Θρόνος* δὲ λέγεται Θεοῦ *ὁ οὐρανὸς* καὶ *ὑποπόδιον ἡ γῆ*, οὐχ ὅτι περιέχεται ὑπ᾿ αὐτῶν, ἀλλ᾿ ἐπειδὴ ἐπαναπαύεται τερπόμενος τῇ δημιουργίᾳ αὐτῶν.
᾿Απαγορεύει δὲ τὸν κατὰ τῆς ῾Ιερουσαλὴμ ὅρκον, ὅτι τύπος ἐστὶ τῆς ἄνω ῾Ιερουσαλήμ,

> ἀπαγορεύει δὲ καὶ τὸν κατὰ τῆς *῾Ιερουσαλὴμ* ὅρκον, ἐπειδὴ ἡ ἐπίγειος *῾Ιερουσαλὴμ* τῆς *ἄνω ῾Ιερουσαλὴμ* τύπος ἐστί.[ccclxxxi]

τῆς τῶν *πρωτοτόκων* ἐκκλησίας.[485] Οὔτε δὲ κατὰ τῆς κεφαλῆς ὀμνύειν κελεύει.[486] Οὔτε γὰρ τῆς κεφαλῆς αὐτοῦ κύριος ὁ ἄνθρωπος, ἑτέρου ὢν ποίημα, ὃς οὐδὲ *τρίχα* ἑαυτοῦ μεταποιῆσαι δύναται. Οὐδὲ γὰρ ὡς εὐτελοῦς οὔσης αὐτῆς ὀμνύειν δεῖ κατ᾿ αὐτῆς· τιμία γάρ ἐστιν οὕτως, ὡς καὶ *αἱ τρίχες* αὐτῆς ἠρίθμηνται παρὰ Θεῷ,[487] αἵτινες δοκοῦσιν εἶναι παρά τισι περιτταί.[ccclxxxii]
Μόνος δὲ ὁ Θεὸς ὀμνύει καθ᾿ ἑαυτοῦ,[488] τουτέστι κατὰ τῆς ἰδίας δόξης, ὡς μόνος ἐλεύθερος.[ccclxxxiii] Διὸ ὡς ὑπερβαινούσης ἡμᾶς τῆς ὁμοιότητος, οὐκ ὀφείλομεν καθ᾿ ἑαυτῶν ὀμνύειν,

> καὶ καθ᾿ ἑαυτοῦ μόνου ὀμνύει ὁ θεός, ὅ ἐστι τῆς ἰδίας δόξης. διὸ ὡς ὑπερβαινούσης ἡμᾶς τῆς ὁμοιότητος οὐκ ὀφείλομεν καθ᾿ ἑαυτῶν ἤτοι τῆς ἑαυτῶν ὀμνύειν δόξης. οὐ γὰρ ἐλεύθεροί ἐσμεν ὡς ὁ θεός, ἀλλ᾿ ὑπὸ τὴν τοῦ θεοῦ ἐσμεν ἐξουσίαν.[ccclxxxiv]

ἀλλὰ τὸ *ναί* καὶ τὸ *οὔ*[489] ἀντὶ τοῦ ὅρκου κεχρῆσθαι. Διὰ γὰρ τὸ ἀξιόπιστον τῶν πιστῶν, τὸ *ναί* ἀντὶ τοῦ ὅρκου ἐστί· *τὸ δὲ περισσὸν τούτων*, τουτέστι τὸ ὅλως κατά τινος ὀμνύναι, διαβολικόν ἐστι. Διὰ δὲ τὰς τῶν παλαιῶν ἀσθενείας τοῦτο συνεχωρήθη, ὡς καὶ αἱ δι᾿ αἱμάτων θυσίαι[ccclxxxv] καὶ ὅσα ὅμοια.

Μήτε ἐν τῷ οὐρανῷ, ὅτι θρόνος.[490] ᾿Επαίρει τὰ στοιχεῖα, | **39r** οὐκ ἀπὸ τῆς οἰκείας φύσεως, ἀλλ᾿ ἀπὸ τῆς τοῦ Θεοῦ περὶ αὐτὰ σχέσεως. ᾿Επειδὴ γὰρ πολλὴ ἡ τῆς εἰδωλολατρίας τυραννὶς ἦν, ἵνα μὴ δόξῃ τὰ στοιχεῖα δι᾿ ἑαυτὰ εἶναι τίμια, ταύτην τέθεικε τὴν αἰτίαν, ἥτις εἰς τὴν *τοῦ Θεοῦ δόξαν*[491] διέβαινεν. Οὐ γὰρ εἶπεν ἐπειδὴ καλὸς καὶ

---

483 Cf. Jer. 23:24.
484 Cf. Rom. 1:25.
485 Cf. Heb. 12:23.
486 Matt. 5:36.
487 Matt. 10:30; Luke, 12:7.
488 Cf. Ex. 13:11; Num. 32:10; Psalms 109:4 (quoted in Heb. 7:21); 131:11; Amos, 6:8; Is. 62:8; Jer. 28:14; Deut. 1:34; 6:10&18&23; *et passim.*
489 Matt. 5:37.
490 Matt. 5:34.
491 Cf. John, 11:40; 12:43.

μέγας ὁ οὐρανός, ἀλλ᾽ ἐπειδὴ τοῦ Θεοῦ ὁ μέν ἐστι *θρόνος*, ἡ δὲ *ὑποπόδιον*. Ὑποπόδιον δέ φησι τὴν γῆν, ὅτι ὑπὸ τὴν ἐξουσίαν εἰ καὶ μὴ τῆς ἁγιότητος αὐτοῦ δεκτικὴ νῦν διὰ τὰς ἁμαρτίας. Τὰ δὲ *Ἱεροσόλυμα* πόλιν *τοῦ μεγάλου βασιλέως*, πρὸς τὴν ὑπόληψιν τῶν Ἰουδαίων φησι. Ἔτι δὲ καὶ
διὰ τοῦτο κωλύει κατὰ τοῦ οὐρανοῦ καὶ τῆς γῆς ὀμνύειν, ἵνα μὴ δῶμεν τῇ κτίσει τὸ ὑπὲρ τὴν κτίσιν ἀξίωμα θεοποιοῦντες αὐτήν. Οἱ γὰρ ὀμνύοντες, φησὶ ὁ ἀπόστολος, *κατὰ τοῦ μείζονος ὀμνύουσιν*,[492]

> Κωλύει δὲ καὶ ἄλλως κατ᾽ αὐτῶν ὀμνύειν, ἵνα μὴ δῶμεν τῇ κτίσει τὸ ὑπὲρ τὴν κτίσιν ἀξίωμα θεοποιοῦντες αὐτά. οἱ γὰρ ὀμνύντες, φησίν, *κατὰ τοῦ μείζονος ὀμνύουσιν* ὡς ὁ ἀπόστολος ἔφη.[ccclxxxvi]

> Διὰ τοῦτο κωλύει ἡμᾶς ὀμνύναι κατὰ τοῦ οὐρανοῦ καὶ τῆς γῆς, ἵνα μὴ δῶμεν τῇ κτίσει τὸ ὑπὲρ κτίσιν ἀξίωμα, θεοποιοῦντες αὐτά. οἱ γὰρ ὀμνύντες, φησί, κατὰ τοῦ μείζονος ὀμνύουσιν, ὡς ὁ Ἀπόστολος φησί.[ccclxxxvii]

τὸ δὲ περισσὸν τοῦ *ναὶ* καὶ τοῦ *οὔ*, ὁ ὅρκος ἐστίν, οὐ τὸ ἐπιορκεῖν. Ἐκεῖνο γὰρ οὐδεὶς δεῖται μαθεῖν ὅτι *ἐκ τοῦ πονηροῦ ἐστι*.[493] Διὰ τοῦτο δὲ τὸ παλαιὸν ὁ ὅρκος νενομοθέτητο, ἵνα μὴ κατὰ τῶν εἰδώλων ὀμνύωσι. Καὶ ὁ εἰς τὴν κεφαλὴν δὲ αὐτοῦ ὀμνὺς τὸν αὐτῆς δημιουργὸν διασύρει ὡς εὐτελῶν ποιητήν.

ἔστω δὲ ὁ λόγος ὑμῶν.[494] Εὐορκῶν μὲν γάρ τις τυχὸν παρασφάλλεται, μὴ ὀμνὺς δὲ οὐκ ἄν τις ποτὲ ἐπιορκήσειεν. Ὅρκον δὲ εὑρήσεις τὴν *ἀμετάθετον* ἑκάστου *βεβαίωσιν*,[495][ccclxxxviii] ὡς ἐν τῷ *ὤμοσα καὶ ἔστησα*[496] καὶ *ὤμοσε Κύριος καὶ οὐ μεταμεληθήσεται*.[497]

> Εὐορκῶν μὲν γάρ τις τυχὸν παρασφάλλεται, μὴ ὀμνὺς δὲ οὐκ ἄν τις ποτὲ ἐπιορκήσειεν. Ὅρκον δὲ εὑρήσεις τὴν ἀμετάθετον ἑκάστου *βεβαίωσιν*, ὡς ἐν τῷ *ὤμοσα καὶ ἔστησα* καὶ *ὤμοσε Κύριος καὶ οὐ μεταμεληθήσεται*.[ccclxxxix]

Ἔστω ἡ τοῦ βίου ὑμῶν μαρτυρία | **39v** βεβαιοτέρα ὅρκου. Εἰ δέ τις ἀναιδὴς μὴ δυσωπούμενος ὑμῶν τῷ βίῳ τολμᾷ ὑμῖν ἐπαγαγεῖν ὅρκον, *ἔστω ὑμῶν τὸ ναὶ ναί, καὶ τὸ οὒ οὒ* ἀντὶ ὅρκου.

> Ἔστω ἡ τοῦ βίου ἡμῶν μαρτυρία βεβαιοτέρα ὅρκου. εἰ δέ τις ἀναιδὴς μὴ δυσωπούμενος ὑμῶν τῷ βίῳ τολμᾷ ὑμῖν ἐπαγαγεῖν ὅρκον. ἔστω *ὑμῶν τὸ ναὶ ναὶ καὶ τὸ οὒ οὒ* ἀντὶ τοῦ ὅρκου.[cccxc]

---

492 Heb. 6:16.
493 Matt. 5:37.
494 Matt. 5:37.
495 Cf. Heb. 6:16-17.
496 Psalm, 118:106: ὀμώμοκα καὶ ἔστησα.
497 Psalm 109:4, quoted in Heb. 7:21.

Ἔστω ἡ τοῦ βίου ἡμῶν μαρτυρία βεβαιοτέρα ὅρκου. εἰ δέ τις ἀναιδὴς μὴ δυσωπούμενος ὑμῶν τῷ βίῳ τολμᾷ ὑμῖν ἐπαγαγεῖν ὅρκον. ἔστω ὑμῖν τὸ ναί, ναί, καὶ τὸ οὔ, οὔ, ἀντὶ τοῦ ὅρκου.[cccxci]

ἠκούσατε ὅτι ἐρρέθη ὀφθαλμὸν ἀντὶ ὀφθαλμοῦ.[498] Ὁ νόμος συγκαταβαίνων συγχωρεῖ τὴν ταυτοπάθειαν, ἵνα, δέει τοῦ παθεῖν, μὴ ἀδικῇ τις. Ὁ δὲ Κύριος δι᾽ ἀνεξικακίας ἀμέτρου δυσωπεῖ τὸν ἀδικήσαντα μὴ ἐπὶ πλεῖον ἀδικῆσαι, ἀλλὰ πρὸς μετάνοιαν ἐλθεῖν, διδοὺς καὶ τῷ ἀδικηθέντι μισθὸν ἀτελεύτητον. Οὐκ ἔστι δὲ τοῦτο ἐναντίον τῷ νόμῳ, τὸ μὴ ἀμύνασθαι τὸν ἀδικήσαντα, ἀλλ᾽ ὑπὲρ νόμον ἐστί. Πονηρὸν δὲ πρωτοτύπως τὸν διάβολον φησι, ᾧ οὐ δεῖ *ἀντιστῆναι*, ὡς διὰ τοῦ ἀνθρώπου ἀδικοῦντι. Οὕτ‹ω›ς[499] δὲ οὐ μόνον ἀνθίσταται, ἀλλὰ καὶ νικᾷ αὐτὸν ὁ ἀνεξίκακος. Εἶτα τῷ θέλοντι δικάσασθαι πλείονα κελεύει διδόναι ὧν αἰτεῖ,[500] διὰ τῆς φιλοσοφίας τὸν πλεονέκτην ἱστῶν, διδάσκων διὰ τούτου μὴ μόνον ἀπροσπαθεῖς εἶναι πρὸς τὴν κτῆσιν, ἀλλὰ καὶ ἵνα μὴ διὰ τοῦ ἀντιποιεῖσθαι τούτων ἐξαγριαίνωμεν τοὺς ἐπιδικαζομένους. Κἂν γὰρ περὶ τῶν σῶν τις φιλονεικῇ καὶ ψεῦδος κατηγορῇ σου, καταφρόνησον, εἰ καὶ δεήσει γυμνόν σε περιπατεῖν, ἵνα μὴ εἰς δικαστήριον ἔλθῃς. Εἶτα, οὐ μόνον τὰ χρήματα κοινοποιεῖ, ἀλλὰ καὶ τὰ σώματα πρὸς ὑπηρεσίαν ἑτέρων ἐμπαρέχειν πλειόνως ὧν βούλονται κελεύει, διὰ τούτου δυσωπῶν τὸν ἀδικῆσαι προελόμενον. Ἐφεξῆς δὲ καὶ πάντας ἀδιακρίτως εὐεργετεῖν, εἴτε διὰ χρημάτων εἴτε διὰ λόγων βούλεται, κἂν φίλος ἐστιν, κἂν | **40r** ἐχθρός, κἂν πιστὸς ἢ ἄπιστος ἢ ἀλλόφυλος. Ὁ γὰρ μὴ φθάνων τὸ ἄκρον τῆς ἀρετῆς,[cccxcii] τὴν ἑκούσιον πενίαν,[cccxciii] τὸν ἀδίκως συναχθέντα πλοῦτον καλῶς διοικείτῳ.

ἀλλ᾽ ἐάν τις σε ῥαπίσῃ ἐπὶ τὴν δεξιάν.[501] Οὐ περὶ ἀνεξικακίας μόνον λέγει, προσθεὶς τῇ σιαγόνι τῇ δεξιᾷ *καὶ τὴν ἄλλην*. Παρὰ φύσιν γὰρ καὶ ἐνυβρίζων ταύτην τύπτει. Ὁ οὖν ἕτοιμος *πρὸς ἀπολογίαν παντὶ*[502] περὶ τῆς ἐν αὐτῷ πίστεως περιπεσὼν κακοήθει οὐκ ἀντιστήσεται. Τύπτοντι δὲ δεξιά, τὰ θεολογικὰ δόγματα, παραθήσει καὶ τὰ ἠθικά, δυσωπῶν παύσασθαι τῆς κατηγορίας καὶ τῆς προσκοπῆς[503] τῆς ἐπὶ τοῖς θειοτέροις σκανδαλιζούσης τοὺς μὴ βλέποντας αὐτὸν τὸν λόγον.

Οὐ περὶ ἀνεξικακίας μόνον λέγει, προστιθεὶς τῇ σιαγόνι τῇ δεξιᾷ *καὶ τὴν ἄλλην*. παρὰ φύσιν γὰρ καὶ ἐνυβρίζων ταύτην τύπτει. ὁ οὖν ἕτοιμος *πρὸς ἀπολογίαν παντὶ*[504] περιπεσὼν κακοήθει περὶ τῆς ἐν αὐτῷ πίστεως οὐκ ἀντιστήσεται, τύπτοντι δὲ δεξιὰ τὰ λογικὰ δόγματα, παραθήσει καὶ τὰ ἠθικά, δυσωπῶν παύσασθαι τῆς κατηγορίας. ‹καὶ› τῆς προκοπῆς τῆς ἐπὶ τοῖς θειοτέροις σκανδαλιζούσης τοὺς μὴ βλέποντας αὐτὸν τὸν λόγον.[cccxciv]

---

498 Matt. 5:38.
499 Cod. οὗτος.
500 Cf. Matt. 5:40.
501 Cf. Matt. 5:39: ἀλλ᾽ ὅστις σε ῥαπίζει εἰς τὴν δεξιὰν σιαγόνα.
502 Cf. 1 Peter, 3:15.
503 Cod. προσκοπῆς vs. Klostermann's erroneous προκοπῆς.
504 Cf. 1 Peter, 3:15.

> If a heretic strikes us in a controversy and has a yen for wounding right doctrines, another testimony from the scriptures should controvert him.[cccxcv]

Καὶ τῷ θέλοντι σοι κριθῆναι, καὶ τὸν χιτῶνα.[505] Οὐκ εἶπε τῷ θέλοντί σου λαβεῖν τὸ ἱμάτιον δὸς καὶ τὸ ἕτερον, ἀλλὰ *τῷ θέλοντί σοι κριθῆναι*, δεικνὺς ὅτι τὴν πρὸς τοὺς ἐναντίους φιλονεικίαν φεύγειν προσήκει ὅταν ὑπὲρ τῆς εὐσεβείας ταύτην ἡμῖν ἐπάγωσι, καὶ πάθη καὶ ζημίαν ὑπομένοντας ἡδέως, ὥστε τὴν εὐσέβειαν μὴ παριδεῖν. Τοῦτο δὲ φυλακτέον ἂν πρὸς ἀρετὴν βλέπειν ἑλοίμεθα.

Τῷ αἰτοῦντι σε δίδου.[506] Οὐκ ἐπὶ ψιλῆς τῆς λέξεως ἐξέθετο τὰ νόμιμα ἡμῖν παρέχων τὸν σκοπὸν αὐτῶν ἐξετάζειν ἀκριβῶς. Οὔτε γὰρ πάντως *αἰτοῦντι* διδόναι κελεύει κἂν μὴ ἔχῃ τις· ἀδύνατον γάρ. Οὔτε μὴν εἰ ἔχοι, αἰτοίη δέ τις κακῶς. Χείρων γὰρ ἡ δόσις ὅταν ὁ μὲν πρὸς ἀσέλγειαν αἰτοίη καὶ ἀκολασίαν καὶ μὴ πρὸς τὴν χρείαν, ὁ δὲ παράσχῃ ὕλην τῆς τοιαύτης ἀκολασίας διδούς. | **40v** Ἐπεί πως ἐπὶ τῶν ἀποστόλων κεῖται· διεδίδοτο δὲ ἑκάστῳ καθότι ἄν τις χρείαν εἶχεν.

Καὶ τὸν θέλοντα ἀπὸ σοῦ δανείσασθαι.[507] Κἂν τοίνυν φίλος ἐστι κἂν ἐχθρός, κἂν πιστὸς κἂν ἀλλόφυλος, ἀδιακρίτως εὐεργέτει τὸν δεόμενον.

> Δίδου, φησίν, ἀεὶ καὶ μὴ ἀναίνου, κἂν φίλος, κἂν ἐχθρός, κἂν πιστός, κἂν ἄπιστος τυγχάνῃ ὁ αἰτῶν καὶ εὐεργέτει διηνεκῶς τὸν δεόμενόν σου τῆς ἀντιλήψεως.[cccxcvi]

Ἐγὼ δὲ λέγω ὑμῖν, ἀγαπᾶτε τοὺς ἐχθροὺς ὑμῶν.[508] Εἰ καὶ ὑπὲρ φύσιν καὶ νόμον τὰ τοῦ Χριστοῦ, ἀλλ᾽ οὐκ ἀδύνατα, εἰ καὶ σπανίως γίνεται.
Ἀγαπῶμεν τοίνυν τοὺς ἐχθρούς, οὐ καθὸ μοιχοί εἰσιν ἢ φονεῖς, ἀλλὰ καθὸ ἄνθρωποι. Τὸ γὰρ ἁμαρτάνειν ἐνεργείας ἐστὶν οὐκ οὐσίας.

> τὸ δὲ ἀγαπᾶν τοὺς ἐχθροὺς οὐκ ἀγαπᾶν τὸ κακὸν λέγει οὐδὲ ἀσέβειαν ἢ μοιχείαν ἢ κλοπήν, ἀλλὰ τὸν κλέπτην καὶ τὸν ἀσεβῆ καὶ τὸν μοιχόν, οὐ καθὸ ἁμαρτάνει καὶ τῇ ποιᾷ ἐνεργείᾳ μολύνει τὴν ἀνθρώπου προσηγορίαν, καθὸ δὲ ἄνθρωπός ἐστι καὶ ἔργον θεοῦ. ἀμέλει τὸ ἁμαρτάνειν ‹ἐν› ἐνεργείᾳ κεῖται, οὐκ οὐσίᾳ. διὸ οὐδὲ ἔργον θεοῦ.[cccxcvii]

> Ἀγαπῶμεν τοὺς ἐχθροὺς οὐ καθὸ μοιχοί εἰσιν ἢ φονεῖς, ἀλλὰ καθὸ ἄνθρωποι. τὸ γὰρ ἁμαρτάνειν ἐνεργείας ἐστίν, οὐκ οὐσίας. διὸ οὐδὲ ἔργον θεοῦ ἡ ἁμαρτία.[cccxcviii]

Ὁ δὲ ἀγαπῶν οὐ μέχρι ψιλοῦ ῥήματος ὀφείλει θέλειν τινὶ καλῶς, ἀλλὰ καὶ συνεργεῖν πρὸς τὸ γενέσθαι τὰ δέοντα. Τὸ δὲ *εὐλογεῖτε τοὺς καταρωμένους ὑμᾶς* καὶ *προσεύχεσθε ὑπὲρ τῶν ἐπηρεαζόντων καὶ διωκόντων ὑμᾶς*[509] ἐν ἄλλοις οὐ κεῖται.

---

505 Matt. 5:40.
506 Matt. 5:42.
507 Matt. 5:42.
508 Matt. 5:44.
509 Matt. 5:44; cf. Luke, 6:28.

Ὑπερεύχου τοίνυν τῶν ἐχθρῶν, ἐν τούτῳ αὐτοὺς ἀμυνόμενος, ἐν τῷ μὴ συνεῖναι αὐτοῖς ἐμμένουσι τῇ πονηρίᾳ.

Ὑπερεύχου τῶν ἐχθρῶν, ἐν τούτῳ αὐτοὺς ἀμυνόμενος, ἐν τῷ μὴ συνεῖναι αὐτοῖς ἐμμένουσι τῇ πονηρίᾳ.[cccxcix]

Τοῦτο δέ ἐστι τὸ εἶδος τῆς εὐχῆς, τὸ μὴ αἰτεῖν τὸν Θεὸν τιμωρηθῆναι τοὺς ἐχθροὺς ὑπὲρ ὧν εἰς ἡμᾶς ἁμαρτάνουσιν, ἀλλὰ συγχωρηθῆναι. Τοῦτο δὲ ποιοῦντες, ἐξομοιούμεθα κατὰ τὸ δυνατὸν τῷ Θεῷ,[cd] ὃς οὐ μόνον οὐ βλάπτει τοὺς ἰδίους ἐχθροὺς ἀλλὰ καὶ ἀνέχεται αὐτῶν.
Δεῖ τοίνυν τοὺς θέλοντας υἱοθεσίας τυχεῖν κατὰ τὸ δυνατὸν μιμεῖσθαι Θεὸν[cdi] ἐν τῷ ἀδιακρίτως εὐεργετεῖν.

Πάντας τοὺς θέλοντας υἱοθεσίας ἀξιωθῆναι δεῖ κατὰ τὸ δυνατὸν μιμεῖσθαι θεὸν ἐν τῷ ἀδιακρίτως εὐεργετεῖν.[cdii]

Εἰ δὲ τὸ μὲν κατόρθωμα ἴσον ποιεῖ Θεῷ, ἡ δὲ ἀποτυχία ἴσον τελώνῃ, τὸ τέλειον ἀγαθὸν ἐν τῷ ἀγαπᾶν τὸν ἐχθρόν οὐ μὴν τοὺς φίλους, ὅπερ ἔθος ποιεῖν τελώναις καὶ ἁμαρτωλοῖς.
Τέλειος γάρ ἐστιν | **41r** ὁ πάσας ἔχων τὰς ἀρετάς.

Τέλειος γάρ ἐστιν, ὁ πάσας ἔχων τὰς ἀρετάς ἢ ὁ εἰς τέλος ἀγαθός.[cdiii]

Ἴσως φήσειέν τις· πῶς ὁ μακάριος Παῦλος Ἀλέξανδρον ἀρᾶται τὸν χαλκέα; Πρὸς ὅν φαμεν ὅτι οὐχ ὡς ἴδιον ἐχθρόν, ἀλλ᾽ ὡς ἐχθρὸν τοῦ εὐαγγελίου, διδάσκων ὅτι τοῖς τοῦ Θεοῦ ἐχθροῖς ἀεὶ χρὴ πολεμεῖν.

Ἴσως φήσειέ τις, πῶς ὁ μακάριος Παῦλος Ἀλέξανδρον ἀρᾶται τὸν χαλκέα; πρὸς ὅν φαμεν οὐχ ὡς ἴδιον ἐχθρόν, ἀλλ᾽ ὡς ἐχθρὸν τοῦ εὐαγγελίου κατηράσατο αὐτὸν διδάσκων, ὅτι τοῖς τοῦ θεοῦ ἐχθροῖς ἀεὶ χρὴ πολεμεῖν.[cdiv]

Ἔσεσθε οὖν ὑμεῖς *τέλειοι.*[510] Τέλειός ἐστιν ἄνθρωπος ὁ ἐν μιμήσει τοῦ Θεοῦ ἐν τοῖς ἰδίοις μέτροις.

Τέλειός ἐστιν ἄνθρωπος ὁ ἐν μιμήσει θεοῦ ἐν τοῖς ἰδίοις μέτροις.[cdv]

(ΩΡΙΓΕΝΟΥΣ, added on the margin) *Ὅτι τὸν ἥλιον ἀνατέλλει.*[511] Ὁ μιμητὴς τοῦ Θεοῦ καὶ Χριστοῦ, τὸν ἐν αὐτῷ λόγον *ἥλιον* καὶ τὴν ἐν αὐτῷ λάμπουσαν

510 Matt. 5:48.
511 Matt. 5:45.

δικαιοσύνην *ἀνατέλλει ἐπὶ πονηροὺς καὶ ἀγαθοὺς* καὶ τὸν διὰ στόματος λόγου αὐτοῦ *ὑετὸν* οἰκονομικῶς *βρέχει ἐπὶ δικαίους καὶ* ἁμαρτωλούς.[cdvi]

> Ὁ μιμητὴς τοῦ Θεοῦ καὶ Χριστοῦ τὸν ἐν αὐτῷ λόγον *ἥλιον* καὶ τὴν ἐν αὐτῷ λάμπουσαν δικαιοσύνην *ἀνατέλλει ἐπὶ πονηροὺς καὶ ἀγαθοὺς* καὶ τὸν διὰ στόματος λόγου αὐτοῦ *ὑετὸν* οἰκονομικῶς *βρέχει ἐπὶ δικαίους καὶ ἀδίκους*, τουτέστιν ἁμαρτωλούς.[cdvii]

(ΩΡΙΓΕΝΟΥΣ, main text cont.) *Προσέχετε τὴν ἐλεημοσύνην ὑμῶν.*[512] Ὁ ποιῶν ἐλεημοσύνην μὴ προαιρέσει τοῦ ὀφθῆναί τισι, κἂν ἐκ περιστάσεως ὀφθῇ, οὐδὲν ἐκλάβ‹ει›·[513] ὁ δὲ φιλοκομπίαν ποιῶν, κἂν μηδεὶς ἴδῃ, οὐδὲν κερδαίνει. Ἐπειδὴ δὲ ἔθος ἦν Ἰουδαίοις διὰ σαλπίγγων καλεῖν τοὺς ἐνδεεῖς ἐπὶ ἐλεημοσύνην, τοῦτο κωλύων ὁ Σωτήρ, *ὅταν ποιῇς ἐλεημοσύνην*, φησί, *μὴ σαλπίσῃς ἔμπροσθέν σου, ὥσπερ οἱ ὑποκριταὶ ποιοῦσιν,*[514]
ἤτοι σάλπιγγα τὴν ἐπίδειξιν καλεῖ.

> καὶ ἄλλως σάλπιγγα τὴν ἐπίδειξιν λέγει.[cdviii]

Σοῦ δὲ ποιοῦντος ἐλεημοσύνην, φησί, *μὴ γνώτω ἡ ἀριστερά σου, τί ποιεῖ ἡ δεξιά σου.*[515] Τουτέστιν, εἰ οἷόν τε ἐστί, καὶ τοὺς ἐγγυτάτω λαθεῖν. Ὑπερβολικὸν γάρ ἐστι τὸ ῥῆμα, ἵνα εἰ δυνατὸν καὶ ἑαυτὸν σπουδάσῃς λαθεῖν,
ὅπως ὁ Θεὸς μόνος γινώσκῃ τοῦτο ὁ καὶ τῶν κρυπτῶν γνώστης.[516] Οὔτε γὰρ αὐτὸς ὁ ἐλεῶν ὀφείλει γινώσκειν, ἐπεὶ συμβαίνει διὰ τούτου ποτὲ μὲν ἐλεεῖν ποτὲ δὲ οὔ.

> Τοῦτό φησιν, ἵνα ὁ Θεὸς μόνος γινώσκῃ. οὔτε γὰρ αὐτὸς ὁ ἐλεῶν ὀφείλει γινώσκειν. ἐπεὶ συμβαίνει διὰ τούτου, ποτὲ μὲν ἐλεᾶν, ποτὲ δὲ οὔ.[cdix]
>
> ἐὰν ποιήσῃς, φησίν, ἐλεημοσύνην, μηδεὶς γινωσκέτω. καὶ ἐὰν νηστεύσῃς, ἄλειψαι, ἵνα ὁ θεὸς μόνος γινώσκῃ, ἀνθρώπων δὲ οὐδὲ εἷς, ἀλλ' οὐδὲ αὐτὸς ὁ ἐλεῶν ὅτι ἐλεεῖ, γινώσκειν ὀφείλει. ἔσται γὰρ οὕτω ποτὲ μὲν οἰκτίρμων, ἄλλοτε δὲ οὔ.[cdx]

Ὁ δὲ λεληθότως ποιῶν τὸ καλὸν καὶ μὴ δημοσιεύων αὐτό, ἀλλὰ ζητῶν λαθεῖν καὶ αὐτὸν τὸν εὐεργετούμενον,

> Ὁ λεληθότως ποιῶν τὸ καλὸν καὶ μὴ δημοσιεύων αὐτό, ἀλλὰ ζητῶν λαθεῖν καὶ αὐτὸν τὸν εὐεργετούμενον, οὗτός ἐστι περὶ οὗ φησιν ὁ Κύριος, *μὴ γνώτω ἡ ἀριστερά σου, τί ποιεῖ ἡ δεξιά σου.*[cdxi]

---

512 Matt. 6:1.
513 Cod. ἐκλάβη.
514 Matt. 6:2.
515 Matt. 6:3.
516 Cf. Matt. 6:4.

ὡς *ἐν κρυπτῷ* ποιῶν, λαμβάνει τὴν ἀντιμισθίαν παρὰ Θεοῦ. Εἰ γὰρ καὶ πάντας λάθοι, ἀλλά γε τὸν Θεὸν οὐ λανθάνει, ὃς ἐν καιρῷ κρίσεως κατάδηλον πάσῃ τῇ κτίσει ποιήσει. Ἄλλως τε.
τότε τὸ δεξιὸν καὶ καθῆ | **41v** κον ἔργον γινώσκει[517] *ἡ ἀριστερά*, ὅτε ὑπὸ φιλοδοξίας οὐ μολύνεται.

> Τότε τὸ δεξιὸν καὶ καθῆκον ἔργον γινώσκει *ἡ ἀριστερά*, ὅτε ὑπὸ φιλοδοξίας οὐ μολύνεται.[cdxii]

> (Ὠριγένους) Τὸ δεξιὸν καὶ καθῆκον ἔργον γινώσκει ἡ ἀριστερά, ὅτε μολύνεται [sic] ὑπὸ φιλοδοξίας.[cdxiii]

Τάχα δὲ ἡ μὲν *ἀριστερὰ* ἡμῶν ἔξω τοῦ κρυπτοῦ ἐστιν, ἐφ᾽ ὃ οὐ φθάνει ὁ τοῦ Πατρὸς ὀφθαλμὸς ὁ βλέπων *ἐν* μόνω *κρυπτῷ* ἅπερ ἐστὶ δεξιά· ὅπερ κρυπτὸν *τῆς καρδίας* ἄνθρωπον ὁ Παῦλός φησι,[cdxiv] ἐφ᾽ ὃ φθάνει ὁ ἀποδιδοὺς ἐκείνῳ ἔνθα βλέπει. Ἐπεὶ τοίνυν τὰ φιλοῦντα μετὰ φιλοδοξίας ἔσθ᾽ ὅτε γίνεσθαι, ἐλεημοσύνη ἐστὶ καὶ εὐχὴ καὶ νηστεία.[cdxv] Ἀπὸ τούτων παρίστησι τὴν κενοδοξίαν νοεῖν.
Ἐν ἄλλοις ἀντιγράφοις, *τὴν δικαιοσύνην* φησί.[518] Σκοπὸν δὲ τῆς ἐλεημοσύνης προτίθησιν ἡμῖν τὴν *παρὰ* Θεῷ δόξαν, οὐ τὴν παρὰ ἀνθρώποις. Οἷς γάρ τις ἀρέσκειν βούλεται, παρὰ τούτων *μισθὸν* ἔχει τὸν ἔπαινον. Οὐ μὴν ὁ θεαθεὶς ἤδη *πρὸς τὸ θεαθῆναι* πεποίηκεν, ἀλλ᾽ ὁ θεωρεῖσθαι βουλόμενος καὶ τοῦτο ποιῶν.

> Ἐν ἄλλοις ἀντιγράφοις *τὴν δικαιοσύνην* φησί. σκοπὸν δὲ τῆς ἐλεημοσύνης προτίθησιν ἡμῖν τὴν *παρὰ* Θεῷ δόξαν, οὐ τὴν παρὰ ἀνθρώποις. οἷς γάρ τις ἀρέσκειν βούλεται, παρὰ τούτων *μισθὸν* ἔχει τὸν ἔπαινον. οὐ μὴν ὁ θεαθεὶς ἤδη *πρὸς τὸ θεαθῆναι* πεποίηκεν, ἀλλ᾽ ὁ θεωρεῖσθαι βουλόμενος καὶ τοῦτο ποιῶν.[cdxvi]

> Ἐν ἄλλοις ἀντιγράφοις *τὴν δικαιοσύνην* φησί. σκοπὸν δὲ τῆς ἐλεημοσύνης προτίθησιν ἡμῖν τὴν *παρὰ* Θεῷ δόξαν, οὐ τὴν παρὰ ἀνθρώποις. οἷς γάρ τις ἀρέσκειν βούλεται, παρὰ τούτων *μισθὸν* ἔχει τὸν ἔπαινον. οὐ μὴν ὁ θεαθεὶς ἤδη *πρὸς τὸ θεαθῆναι* πεποίηκεν, ἀλλ᾽ ὁ θεωρεῖσθαι βουλόμενος καὶ τοῦτο ποιῶν.[cdxvii]

Μὴ γνώτω ἡ ἀριστερά σου.[519] Πάλιν ἐνταῦθα οὐ χεῖρας αἰνίττεται, ἀλλ᾽ ὑπερβολικῶς αὐτὸ τίθεται. Εἰ γὰρ οἷόν τε ἐστί φησι σεαυτὸν ἀγνοῆσαι, περισπούδαστον ἔστω σοι τοῦτο, κἂν αὐτὰς δυνατὸν ᾖ τὰς διακονουμένας χεῖρας λαθεῖν.

> Πάλιν ἐνταῦθα οὐ χεῖρας αἰνίττεται, ἀλλ᾽ ὑπερβολικῶς αὐτὸ τέθεικεν. Εἰ γὰρ οἷόν τέ ἐστι, φησί, σεαυτὸν ἀγνοῆσαι, περισπούδαστον ἔστω σοι τοῦτο, κἂν αὐτὰς δυνατὸν ᾖ τὰς διακονουμένας χεῖρας λαθεῖν.[cdxviii]

---

517 Cod. οὐ γινώσκει.
518 Ref. to Matt. 6:1-2.
519 Matt. 6:3.

Καὶ ὅταν προσεύχῃ, οὐκ ἔσῃ ὥσπερ οἱ ὑποκριταί.[520] Τοὺς εὐχομένους ἐπὶ τῷ ὀφθῆναι ἀνθρώποις ὑποκριτὰς καλεῖ ὡς προφασιζομένους μὲν αἰτεῖν Θεόν, διὰ δὲ τοὺς ἀνθρώπους ποιοῦντας οὕτως, ὅπερ εἶδος ἐστὶν ἀνθρωπαρεσκίας.[521] Οὗτοι λαμβάνουσι *τὸν μισθὸν* παρὰ τῶν ἀνθρώπων, παρ' ὧν καὶ θέλουσιν, ἡ δὲ τιμωρία τοῦ μὴ ὡς δεῖ εὐχομένου ἐν τῷ ἀμίσθῳ ἐστίν· *ἀπέχουσι* γάρ φησι *τὸν μισθὸν αὐτῶν.*[522] Πλὴν καὶ τὸ ἐν συναγωγαῖς εὔχε | **42r** σθαι ἀπὸ μόνης ἔρχεται τῆς τῶν εὐχομένων γνώμης. Εἰ μὲν γὰρ εὔχεται ἐπὶ τῷ ὀφθῆναι πᾶσι, κεναῖς ἀπέρχεται ταῖς χερσίν. Εἰ δὲ ἀκενοδόξως[cdxix] γίνεται ἡ εὐχὴ καὶ οὐκ ἐπὶ τῷ ὀφθῆναι τισί, κἂν ἐν ἐκκλησίᾳ γίνηται, λήψεται τὸ ζητούμενον. Οὐ γὰρ κωλύει τὸ προσεύχεσθαι ἐν συναγωγαῖς, ἀλλὰ τὸ φανητιᾶν κατὰ σχῆμα, κατὰ βλέμμα, κατὰ λόγον αὐτοὺς ἐν ταῖς συναγωγαῖς.
Φαῦλον δὲ καὶ τὸ μὴ ἐπ' εὐθείας εὔχεσθαι, ἀλλ' *ἐν γωνίαις*, αἵ εἰσιν εὐθεῖαι κεκλασμέναι, καὶ ἐν πλατείαις, ὧν αἱ ὁδοὶ ἀπάγουσιν *εἰς τὴν ἀπώλειαν.*[523] Εἶτα διαβαλὼν τοὺς οὐ προσηκόντως χρωμένους τῇ εὐχῇ καὶ ἀπὸ τοῦ τόπου καὶ ἀπὸ τῆς διαθέσεως, εἰσάγει τὸν ἄριστον τῆς προσευχῆς τρόπον καί φησι· *σὺ δὲ ὅταν*[524] *προσεύχῃ, εἴσελθε εἰς τὸ ταμεῖον σου,*[525] καὶ ἑξῆς.

> Φαῦλον δὲ καὶ τὸ μὴ ἐπ' εὐθείας εὔχεσθαι, ἀλλ' *ἐν γωνίαις*, αἵ εἰσιν εὐθεῖαι κεκλασμέναι, καὶ ἐν πλατείαις, ὧν αἱ ὁδοὶ ἀπάγουσιν *εἰς τὴν ἀπώλειαν.* [εἶτα διαβαλὼν τοὺς οὐ προσηκόντως χρωμένους τῇ εὐχῇ καὶ ἀπὸ τοῦ τόπου καὶ ἀπὸ τῆς διαθέσεως εἰσάγει τὸν ἄριστον τῆς προσευχῆς τρόπον καί φησι. *σὺ δὲ ὅτ' ἂν προσεύχῃ, εἴσελθε.*][cdxx]

> Διαβαλὼν τοίνυν τοὺς οὐ προσηκόντως τῷ πράγματι χρωμένους, καὶ ἀπὸ τοῦ τόπου, καὶ ἀπὸ τῆς διαθέσεως, καὶ δείξας σφόδρα καταγελάστους ὄντας, εἰσάγει τὸν ἄριστον τῆς προσευχῆς τρόπον, καὶ πάλιν τὸν μισθὸν δίδωσιν, εἰπών. *Εἴσελθε εἰς τὸ ταμιεῖόν σου.*[cdxxi]

Καλῶς δὲ προσεύχεται ὁ εἰσελθὼν *εἰς τὸ ταμ‹ι›εῖον* τῆς ψυχῆς τῷ νῷ *κλείσας* τὴν τοῦ στόματος *θύραν.*[526] Οὐ γὰρ τὸ ἐν ἐκκλησίαις προσεύχεσθαι κωλύει, ἀλλ' ἐν ἡσυχίᾳ καὶ ἄνευ θορύβου βέλτιον, οὐ πρὸς ἀρέσκειαν ἀνθρώπων ἀποβλέποντας, ἐπεί, κἂν *εἰς τὸ ταμιεῖον* εἰσέλθῃς καὶ ἀποκλείσας, πρὸς ἐπίδειξιν ἐργάσῃ αὐτό, οὐδέν σοι τῶν θυρῶν ὄφελος. Ὥστε πρὸ τῆς τῶν θυρῶν ἀποκλείσεως, κατορθῶσαι σε βούλεται τὰς τῆς διανοίας ἀποκλείειν θύρας. Εἰ γὰρ καὶ τοῦ σώματος κρυπτομένου διὰ τῆς φωνῆς πᾶσιν ἑαυτοὺς καταδήλους ποιοῦμεν συρφετωδῶς βοῶντες, τί τὸ ὄφελος τῆς τῶν θυρῶν κλείσεως;

---

520 Matt. 6:5.
521 An acceptable alternative to ἀνθρωπαρεσκείας.
522 Matt. 6:5.
523 Cf. Matt. 7:13.
524 Cod. ὅτ' ἂν.
525 Matt. 6:6.
526 Cf. Matt. 6:6.

Ὁ γὰρ Θεὸς ἀόρατος ὢν ἀποδέχεται τὴν ἀόρατον τῶν ἀνθρώπων εὐχήν.

> Ἐπειδὴ γὰρ αὐτὸς ἐστιν ἀόρατος, καὶ τὴν εὐχήν σου τοιαύτην εἶναι βούλεται.[527]

ἥτις, κἂν ἐν ἐκκλησίᾳ γίνηται μόνον‹,› | **42v** ἐν ἡσυχίᾳ καὶ ἐν πρέποντι σχήματι ‹γενομένη›, εὐπρόσδεκτός ἐστι τῷ Θεῷ τῷ πανταχοῦ παρόντι καὶ *πρὸ*[528] τῆς φωνῆς ἀκούοντι καὶ τὰ ἀπόρρητα τῆς διανοίας ἐπισταμένῳ. Ἂν οὕτω προσεύχῃ, πολὺν ἀπολήψῃ τὸν *μισθόν*.

> Τί οὖν; ἐν ἐκκλησίᾳ, φησίν, οὐ δεῖ προσεύχεσθαι; Καὶ σφόδρα μέν, ἀλλὰ μετὰ γνώμης τοιαύτης. Πανταχοῦ γὰρ ὁ Θεὸς τὸν σκοπὸν ζητεῖ τῶν γινομένων. Ἐπεὶ κἂν εἰς τὸ ταμιεῖον εἰσέλθῃς, καὶ ἀποκλείσας, πρὸς ἐπίδειξιν αὐτὸ ἐργάσῃ, οὐδέν σοι τῶν θυρῶν ὄφελος. ... Ὥστε κἂν τὰς θύρας ἀποκλείσῃς, τοῦτο πρὸ τῆς τῶν θυρῶν ἀποκλείσεως κατορθῶσαί σε βούλεται, καὶ τὰς τῆς διανοίας ἀποκλείειν θύρας. ... Ἀλλ' ὅμως εἰσί τινες, ... ὡς καὶ τοῦ σώματος κρυπτομένου, διὰ τῆς φωνῆς πᾶσιν ἑαυτοὺς καταδήλους ποιεῖν, συρφετωδῶς βοῶντες, καὶ τῷ σχήματι καὶ τῇ φωνῇ καταγελάστους ποιοῦντες ἑαυτούς.[cdxxii]

Προσευχόμενοι δὲ μὴ βαττολογήσητε.[529] Ἐπειδὴ οἶδε τὸν νοῦν εὐπαράφορον τῶν ἀνθρώπων καὶ διὰ ἐννοιῶν καὶ φροντίδων ἀποπλανώμενον, μάλιστα ἐν καιρῷ προσευχῆς,[cdxxiii] διὰ συντόμου λέγει τὰς εὐχὰς γίνεσθαι, μὴ πάντα ὅσα θέλει τις ἀναγγέλλοντα, ἀλλ' ὅσα δεῖ, μάλιστα τὰ ψυχωφελῆ. Βαττολογία γάρ ἐστι πολυλογία καὶ φλυαρία καὶ τὸ αἰτεῖν ἃ μὴ δεῖ, τουτέστι δόξαν ἢ πλοῦτον ἢ νίκας κατ' ἐχθρῶν, ὅπερ *οἱ ἐθνικοὶ* ποιοῦσι,[530] παρὰ τῶν νομιζομένων θεῶν πᾶν ὅ, τι οὖν ἀδιακρίτως αἰτοῦντες. Δεῖ τοίνυν μὴ μακροὺς ἀναλίσκειν λόγο‹υ›ς,[531] ἀλλὰ τοῖς αὐτοῖς κεχρῆσθαι ῥήμασι συχνῶς, μηδὲ μακρὰς ποιεῖσθαι τὰς εὐχάς, οὐχὶ τῷ χρόνῳ, ἀλλὰ τῷ μήκει καὶ πλήθει τῶν λεγομένων. Παραμένειν μὲν γὰρ χρὴ τὰ αὐτὰ αἰτοῦντας, οὐχὶ τῷ πλήθει δὲ τῶν αἰτημάτων ἀδιαφόρως αἰτοῦντας δόξαν ἢ πλοῦτον καὶ τὰ ἑξῆς, ἀλλὰ μόνα τὰ ψυχωφελῆ. Εἰ δὲ καὶ οἶδεν ὁ ἄξια κρίνων τῆς ἑαυτοῦ γνώσεως ὧν χρήζομεν, ἀλλὰ πρὸς τοῖς μείζοσι δίδωσι καὶ τὰ ἀναγκαῖα, διατροφὰς λέγω καὶ σκεπάσματα. Οὐχ ἵνα τοίνυν διδάξωμεν αἰτοῦμεν, ἀλλ' ἵνα οἰκειωθῶμεν αὐτῷ[532] τῇ συνεχείᾳ τῆς ἐντεύξεως καὶ γνῶμεν ὅτι δι' αὐτοῦ *πᾶσα δόσις ἀγαθὴ καὶ πᾶν δώρημα τέλειον ἄνωθέν ἐστι.*[533]

Τινὲς ᾠήθησαν τὸν | **43r** Κύριον ἐν τούτοις ἀπαγορεύειν τῆς προσευχῆς τὸ πλῆθος, σφόδρα ἀποσφαλέντες τῆς ἀληθοῦς διανοίας τῶν ῥητῶν. Ποῦ γὰρ ἔχει χώραν τὸ τοῦ ἀποστόλου παράγγελμα *ἀδιαλείπτως προσεύχεσθε;*[534] Ὁ δέ γε Κύριος οὐ πλῆθος

527 John Chrysostom, *In Matthaeum*, PG.57.277.51-52.
528 Matt. 6:8.
529 Matt. 6:7.
530 Matt. 6:7.
531 Cod. λόγος.
532 Cf. Eph. 2:19.
533 James, 1:17.
534 1 Thess. 5:17.

ἐνταῦθα ἀναιρεῖ προσευχῶν, ἀλλ᾽ ἀτοπίαν αἰτήσεως. Βαττολογία γὰρ οὐχ ἡ πολυλογία λέγεται ἂν ἄριστα ᾖ τὰ λεγόμενα, ἀλλ᾽ ἡ ἄκαιρος φλυαρία.

> Τινὲς ᾠήθησαν τὸν κύριον ἐν τούτοις ἀπαγορεύειν τῆς προσευχῆς τὸ πλῆθος, σφόδρα ἀποσφαλέντες τῆς ἀληθοῦς διανοίας τῶν ῥητῶν. ποῦ γὰρ ἔχει χώραν τοῦ ἀποστόλου τὸ παράγγελμα *ἀδιαλείπτως προσεύχεσθε*; Ὁ δέ γε κύριος οὐ πλῆθος ἐνταῦθα ἀναιρεῖ προσευχῆς, ἀλλ᾽ ἀτοπίαν αἰτήσεως. βαττολογία γὰρ οὐχ ἡ πολυλογία λέγεται ἐὰν ἄριστα ᾖ τὰ λεγόμενα, ἀλλ᾽ ἡ ἄκαιρος φλυαρία.[cdxxiv]

Διὰ τοῦτο ὁ Χριστὸς παρακελεύεται διὰ συντόμου τὰς προσευχὰς ποιεῖσθαι, ἐπειδήπερ οἶδε τὸν νοῦν εὐπαράφορον ὄντα καὶ δι᾽ ἐννοιῶν καὶ φροντίδων ματαίων ἀποπλανώμενον, μάλιστα ἐν τῷ τῆς προσευχῆς καιρῷ. Καὶ παραγγέλλει νηφαλίως καὶ ταχέως αἰτεῖν τὸν Θεὸν ἃ ζητεῖ, μὴ πάντα ὅσα θέλει ἀναγγέλλοντα· τοῦτο γὰρ τῆς ἄκρας ἐστὶ φρενοβλαβείας. Οἶδε γὰρ ὁ Θεὸς καὶ πρὸ τοῦ ἡμᾶς αἰτῆσαι τίνων χρῄζομεν. Βαττολογία δὲ ἐκλήθη ἡ πολυλογία ἀπὸ Βάττου τινὸς Ἕλληνος μακροὺς καὶ πολυστίχους ὕμνους ποιήσαντος εἰς τὰ εἴδωλα καὶ ταυτολογίαν ἔχοντ‹α›ς.[535] Βαττολογία ἐστὶ τὸ ἔξω τοῦ καλοῦ.[cdxxv]

> Διὰ τοῦτο ὁ Χριστὸς παρακελεύεται διὰ συντόμου τὰς προσευχὰς ποιεῖσθαι, ἐπειδήπερ οἶδε τὸν νοῦν εὐπαράφορον ὄντα καὶ δι᾽ ἐννοιῶν καὶ φροντίδων ματαιῶν [sic] ἀποπλανώμενον, μάλιστα ἐν τῷ τῆς προσευχῆς καιρῷ. καὶ παραγγέλλει νηφαλέως [sic] καὶ ταχέως αἰτεῖν τὸν θεὸν ἃ ζητεῖ μὴ πάντα ὅσα θέλει ἀναγγέλλοντα. τοῦτο γὰρ τῆς ἄκρας ἐστὶ φρενοβλαβείας. οἶδε γὰρ ὁ θεὸς καὶ πρὸ τοῦ ἡμᾶς αἰτῆσαι τίνων χρῄζομεν. βαττολογία δὲ λέγεται ἡ πολυλογία ἀπὸ Βάττου τινὸς Ἕλληνος μακροὺς καὶ πολυστίχους ὕμνους ποιήσαντος εἰς τὰ εἴδωλα καὶ ταυτολογίαν ἔχοντας. βαττολογία ἐστὶ τὸ ἔξω τοῦ καλοῦ.[cdxxvi]

Πάτερ ἡμῶν ὁ ἐν τοῖς οὐρανοῖς.[536] Τότε πατὴρ *ἡμῶν* ὁ Θεὸς χρηματίζει ὅτε διὰ τῆς τοῦ Πνεύματος ἐπιφοιτήσεως τῆς *υἱοθεσίας Χριστοῦ*[537] ἀξιωθῶμεν. Ὁ γὰρ πατέρα καλῶν τὸν Θεὸν ὀφείλει καθαρὸς εἶναι ἀπὸ ἁμαρτιῶν καὶ κληρονόμος τῆς βασιλείας τῶν οὐρανῶν.[538] Θρασὺς δὲ ὁ μορφωθεὶς πρὸς τὸν διάβολον λέγων πατέρα τὸν Θεὸν ὃν οὐ δοξάζει. Εἰπὼν δὲ τὸ *ἡμῶν*, ἕνα τοὺς πολλοὺς δείκνυσιν, ὡς ἑνὸς σώματος, μιᾶς ἁπάντων οὔσης κεφαλῆς τοῦ Θεοῦ. Ὑπεμφαίνει δὲ καὶ | **43v** τὸ ὑπὲρ ἀλλήλων εὔχεσθαι, ὡς ὅτι *πάντες ἀδελφοί*[539] ἐσμεν. Τὸ δὲ *ἐν τοῖς οὐρανοῖς* ὅταν εἴπῃ οὐκ ἐκεῖ τὸν Θεὸν συγκλείων τοῦτο φησί, ἀλλὰ τῆς γῆς ἀπάγων τὸν εὐχόμενον καὶ τοῖς ὑψηλοῖς προσηλῶν.

---

535 Cod. ἔχοντος.
536 Matt. 6:9.
537 Cf. Eph. 1:5.
538 Cf. Matt. 25:34; James, 2:5; (*a contrario*) 1 Cor. 6:9-10; 15:50; 5:21; Eph. 5:5.
539 Matt. 23:8; cf. 1 Cor. 12:1-27.

Ἁγιασθήτω τὸ ὄνομά σου.[540] Ἅγιος γὰρ ὤν, *ἐν ἁγίοις κατοικεῖ.*[541] *ἔσεσθε γὰρ ἅγιοι,* φησί, *ὅτι ἐγὼ ἅγιός εἰμι.*[542] Οὐδεὶς δὲ οἶμαι βέβηλος καὶ ἀκάθαρτος καὶ πόρνος[cdxxvii] δύναται ἁγιάζειν *τὸ ὄνομα* τοῦ Θεοῦ. Ὧ γὰρ ἡγίασται, τούτῳ συμβέβηκεν αὐτῷ ἁγίῳ γεγονέναι. Καὶ τότε εὔχεται ἐλθεῖν τὴν βασιλείαν, λέγων *ἐλθέτω ἡ βασιλεία σου,* ὅταν μὴ βασιλεύῃ θάνατος ἐν αὐτῷ οὐδὲ ἡ βασιλεύουσα *ἁμαρτία*[543] ἐν τοῖς ἀνθρώποις. Θεὸς γὰρ ὤν, βασιλεύει πάσης λογικῆς ψυχῆς,[cdxxviii] ὅπου μηδεὶς ἄλλος βασιλεύει. Τὸ ‹δὲ› *ἁγιασθήτω* οὐ προ‹σ›τακτικῶς, εὐκτικῶς δέ, οἷον ἁγιασθείη.[cdxxix] Οὐχ ἵνα ἐκ βεβήλου ἁγιασθῇ, ἀλλ᾽ ἵνα ἡμῖν ἀποκαλυφθείσης τῆς ἁγιότητος αὐτοῦ ἀξίως αὐτοῦ διδῶμεν ἁγιότητα ὀνομάζοντες Θεόν.

> *ἁγιασθήτω τὸ ὄνομά σου.*[544] Ἅγιος γὰρ ὢν, ἐν ἁγίοις κατοικεῖ. *ἔσεσθε* γάρ φησι, *ἅγιοι, ὅτι ἐγὼ ἅγιός εἰμι.*[545] οὐδεὶς δὲ (οἶμαι) βέβηλος καὶ ἀκάθαρτος καὶ πόρνος δύναται ἁγιάζειν *τὸ ὄνομα* τοῦ Θεοῦ. ᾧ γὰρ ἡγίασται τοῦτο, συμβέβηκεν αὐτῷ ἁγίῳ γεγονέναι, καὶ τότε εὔχεται ἐλθεῖν τὴν βασιλείαν λέγων. *ἐλθέτω ἡ βασιλεία σου,* ὅταν μὴ βασιλεύῃ θάνατος ἐν αὐτῷ, οὐδὲ ἡ βασιλεύουσα *ἁμαρτία* ἐν τοῖς ἀνθρώποις. Θεὸς γὰρ ὢν βασιλεύει πάσης λογικῆς ψυχῆς, ὅπου μηδεὶς ἄλλος βασιλεύει.[cdxxx]
>
> Τὸ δὲ *ἁγιασθήτω* οὐ προστακτικῶς εὐκτικῶς δέ, οἷον ἁγιασθείη. οὐχ ἵνα ἐκ βεβήλου ἁγιασθῇ, ἀλλ᾽ ἵνα ἡμῖν ἀποκαλυφθείσης τῆς ἁγιότητος αὐτοῦ ἀξίως αὐτοῦ διδῶμεν ἁγιότητα ὀνομάζοντες θεόν.[cdxxxi]

Βασιλείαν δὲ Θεοῦ, ἢ τὴν μέλλουσαν τῶν ἀγαθῶν ἀπόλαυσιν φησι ἢ τὴν δευτέραν αὐτοῦ παρουσίαν.[cdxxxii]

> λέγεται δὲ βασιλεία οὐρανῶν οὐ μόνον τὸ ζῆν θεαρέστως, ἀλλὰ καὶ ἡ πρώτη καὶ δευτέρα Χριστοῦ παρουσία καὶ ἡ ἀπόλαυσις τῶν μελλόντων ἀγαθῶν.[cdxxxiii]

Ἐπειδὴ δὲ φύσει Θεὸς ὢν ὁ Χριστός, οἰκονομικῶς καλεῖται βασιλεὺς ὡς ἄνθρωπος, ἐπεύχονται οἱ πιστοὶ τοῦτο καὶ ἐπὶ τοὺς ἀπίστους ἐλθεῖν, ἵνα, εἰς Χριστὸν πιστεύσαντες, βασιλέα ἴδιον ἐπιγράψωνται αὐτόν.

> Οἰκονομικῶς ὡς ἄνθρωπος ὁ Χριστὸς βασιλεὺς καλεῖται καίπερ ὢν φύσει θεός. ἐπεύχονται τοίνυν οἱ πιστοὶ ἐνυπάρξαι καὶ τοῖς ἀπίστοις, ἵνα εἰς τὸν Χριστὸν πιστεύσαντες ἴδιον ἐπικαλῶνται, δι᾽ οὗ μεθέξουσι τῶν τελείων ἀγαθῶν νῦν μόνον ἔχοντες τὸν ἀρραβῶνα καὶ τὸ ἐκ μέρους ἀγαθόν. οὐ γὰρ ἂν ἐνεργῇ τότε τὰ πάθη τῆς ἀπαθείας παρούσης, φροῦδος ὁ θάνατος, ἀφανὴς ἡ φθορά, ὅταν ἐν ἡμῖν ἡ ζωὴ βασιλεύσῃ καὶ ἀφθαρσία τὸ κράτος ἔχῃ.[cdxxxiv]

---

540 Matt. 6:9.
541 Cf. Is. 57:15.
542 Lev. 19:2, quoted in 1 Peter, 1:16; cf. Lev. 20:26.
543 Cf. Rom. 5:21; 6:12.
544 Matt. 6:9.
545 Lev. 19:2, quoted in 1 Peter, 1:16; cf. Lev. 20:26.

Φύσει θεὸς ὁ Χριστὸς ὑπάρχων καὶ φύσει ἄνθρωπος οἰκονομικῶς λέγεται βασιλεύς, τοῦτ᾽ ἔστιν ὡς ἄνθρωπος. διὰ τοῦτο οἱ δίκαιοι ἐπεύχονται ἑαυτοῖς τοῦτο ὑπάρξειν, ἔτι δὲ καὶ τοῖς ἀπίστοις, ἵνα ὁρῶντες καὶ πιστεύοντες εἰς αὐτὸν οἰκεῖον ἑαυτῶν ἕξωσι βασιλέα.[cdxxxv]

Τὸ δὲ *γενηθήτω τὸ θέλημά σου ὡς ἐν οὐρανῷ καὶ ἐπὶ τῆς γῆς*,[546] τοῦτο δηλοῖ. Ὥσπερ *ἐν οὐρανῷ* καθαρῶς καὶ ἀμέμπτως οἱ ἄγγελοι πολιτεύονται, οὕτω καὶ τοὺς ἀνθρώπους ἐν τῇ γῇ ποίησον.
Ἢ οὕτως· *ὥσπερ οἱ ἄγγελοι ἐν οὐρανοῖς*[547] εἰσιν, οὕτω καὶ ἡμᾶς ἀξίωσον *ἐν τῇ ἀναστάσει*[548] | **44r** τοῦ πνευματικοῦ[cdxxxvi] καὶ καθαροῦ σώματος.[cdxxxvii] *Ἐπιούσιον* δὲ *ἄρτον*, ἢ τὸν συνιστῶντα τὸ σῶμα ἡμῶν φησί, τουτέστι τὸν ἐφήμερον, ἤτοι τὸν ἐπιόντα καὶ προσδοκώμενον τοῦ Πνεύματος ζωοποιὸν ἄρτον, τουτέστι τὸν μέλλοντα. Ὠνοματοπεποίηται[cdxxxviii] τοίνυν τὸ *ἐπιούσιον*, ἵν᾽ ᾖ τὸν μὴ τοῦ ἐνεστῶτος οἰκεῖον, ἀλλὰ τὸν ἀποδοθησόμενον ἐν τῷ μέλλοντι τοῖς ἁγίοις.

Οὕτω καὶ φασί τινες τὸ *ἐπιούσιον* παρὰ τὸ ἐπιέναι καὶ ἐπέρχεσθαι, ἵν᾽ ᾖ τοιοῦτον τὸ λεγόμενον. *τὸν* μὴ τοῦ ἐνεστῶτος αἰῶνος οἰκεῖον *ἄρτον*, ἀλλὰ τοῦ μέλλοντος καὶ μετὰ ταῦτα ἀποδοθησόμενον ὑπό σοῦ τοῖς ἀξίοις λαβεῖν ἤδη *δὸς ἡμῖν σήμερον καὶ καθ᾽ ἡμέραν*.[549] ἐπείπερ ἡ οὐσία ἡ ἑστῶσα βέβαιος (οἵα οὐδεμία σωματικὴ γινομένη ῥευστῶς καὶ ἀπογινομένη), ἣν τρέφει *θεὸς ὢν ὁ λόγος* ζῶν ἄρτος,[cdxxxix] ἀφ᾽ οὗ νηστεύουσιν ‹ὅτε› ἀφῄρηται ὁ νυμφίος[550] ὁ τὴν ἀόρατον ψυχὴν ἀοράτως τρέφων (διό φησιν ὁ Σωτήρ· *ὁ τρώγων τὸν ἄρτον τοῦτον ζήσεται εἰς τὸν αἰῶνα*)[551] - ἐπεὶ οὖν οὐ δεῖ νηστεύειν (φασίν) ἀπὸ τοῦ ἄρτου τούτου, λέγομεν *τὸν ἄρτον ἡμῶν τὸν ἐπιούσιον* καὶ τὰ ἑξῆς.[cdxl]

ταπεινοὶ δὲ οἱ νομίζοντες περὶ σωματικοῦ ἄρτου λέγειν τὸν διδάσκοντα μὴ μεριμνᾶν *περὶ τῆς αὔριον*, μάλιστα εἰ *τὸν ἐπιούσιον* ἀντὶ τοῦ *τὸν ἐπιόντα* καὶ *ἐπερχόμενον* λαμβάνουσιν. τοῦτο δὲ δῆλον ἐκ τοῦ εἰπεῖν, *οὐ γὰρ οἶδας, τί τέξεται ἡ ἐπιοῦσα*, τοῦτ᾽ ἔστιν ἡ αὔριον ἡ ἐπερχομένη.[cdxli]

Ὡς τρέφεται εἰς ζωὴν ὁ ἄνθρωπος, οὕτω καὶ φασί τινες τὸ *ἐπιούσιον* παρὰ τὸ ἐπιέναι[cdxlii] καὶ ἐπέρχεσθαι, ἵν᾽ ᾖ τοιοῦτον τὸ λεγόμενον· *τὸν* μὴ τοῦ ἐνεστῶτος αἰῶνος οἰκεῖον *ἄρτον*, ἀλλὰ τοῦ μέλλοντος καὶ μετὰ ταῦτα ἀποδοθησόμενον ὑπό σου τοῖς ἀξίοις λαβεῖν ἤδη *δὸς ἡμῖν σήμερον καὶ καθ᾽ ἡμέραν*.[cdxliii]

546 Matt. 6:10.
547 Cf. Matt. 18:10; 12:25.
548 Matt. 22:28; Mark, 12:23; Luke, 14:14; 20:33; John, 11:24; Rev. 20:6.
549 Cf. Luke, 11:3.
550 Cf. Matt. 9:14-15.
551 John, 6:58.

Δός ἡμῖν ἤδη ἢ ἐπείπερ οὐσία κυρίως ἐστὶν ἡ ἑστῶσα καὶ βέβαιος,[cdxliv] οἵα ἡ τῆς ψυχῆς ἡμῶν φύσις φοροῦσα τὸ *κατ' εἰκόνα*[552] *τοῦ ἀοράτου Θεοῦ.*[553][cdxlv] Κατὰ τοῦτο λέγοιτ' ἂν ὁ τῇ κυρίως οὐσίᾳ[cdxlvi] ὁμιλῶν ἄρτος *ἐπιούσιος*,
Θεὸς ὢν λόγος, ζῶν ἄρτος.

Θεὸς ὢν λόγος, ζῶν ἄρτος.[cdxlvii]

Εἶτα δυσωπῶν ὁ λόγος ἀμνησικακεῖν συνειδότας ἑαυτοῖς ἁμαρτίας, μετριάζειν διδάσκει τῷ τῶν ἴσων θέλειν τυχεῖν. Φησὶ γάρ· *καὶ ἄφες ἡμῖν τὰ ὀφειλήματα ἡμῶν, ὡς καὶ ἡμεῖς ἀφίεμεν τοῖς ὀφειλέταις ἡμῶν.*[554] Πᾶν δὲ ἁμάρτημα ὀφείλημά ἐστιν. Εἰ γὰρ μὴ ἐνδύσεταί τις τὴν τῆς ἀμνησικακίας ἀρετήν, οὐ δύναται τυχεῖν ἀφέσεως. Εἶτα διδάσκει μὴ παραιτεῖσθαι τοὺς ἀγῶνας· πλήν, μὴ ἐπιρρίπτειν ἑαυτούς. Εἰ δὲ ἀνάγκη καλέσοι, δεῖ εὔχεσθαι τοῦ ῥυσθῆναι καὶ μὴ ἡττηθῆναι. Ὁ γὰρ ἐν τῇ πάλῃ νικῶν καὶ μὴ ἐγκαταλειπόμενος οὐκ εἰσέρχεται *εἰς πειρασμόν.*[cdxlviii]

Εἰ *πειρατήριον ὁ βίος*,[555] οὐκ ἔστι μὴ πειρασθῆναι, ἀλλὰ μὴ ἡττηθῆναι ἐν πειρασμῷ. ὁ γὰρ κατ' ἀξίαν παραδιδόμενος *εἰς πάθη ἀτιμίας*[556] ἢ *ἀδόκιμον νοῦν*[557] *εἰς πειρασμὸν* εἰσέρχεται, ὁ δὲ ἐν πάλῃ νικῶν οὔτε ὑπὲρ ὃ δύναται[cdxlix] *** πειραζόμενος καὶ μὴ ἐγκαταλειπόμενος ‹οὐκ εἰσέρχεται *εἰς πειρασμόν*›.[cdl]

Πειρασμὸς γάρ ἐστιν ἡ ἧττα καὶ ἡ ἀπὸ τοῦ διαβόλου πλάνη. Ὁ δὲ μὴ εἰσελθὼν εἰς δίκτυα πειρασμοῦ, ἐρρύσθη *ἀπὸ τοῦ πονηροῦ.* Πονηρὸς δέ ἐστιν ὁ διάβολος, οὐ φύσει, ἀλλὰ προαιρέσει κακίας.[cdli] Τὸ δὲ *ὅτι σοῦ ἐστιν ἡ βασιλεία καὶ ἡ δύναμις καὶ ἡ δόξα*[558] ἔν τισιν | **44v** οὐ κεῖται μέχρι τοῦ *ἀμήν.*

Ἐὰν ἀφῆτε τοῖς ἀνθρώποις.[559] Πάλιν ἐπαναλαμβάνει τὸν τῆς φιλαδελφίας σκοπὸν καὶ διδάσκει ἀμνησικακεῖν. Τῇ γὰρ συμπαθείᾳ ἣν ἔχομέν φησι περὶ τὸν πλησίον ὁρίζεται καὶ ἡ περὶ ἡμᾶς τοῦ Θεοῦ φιλανθρωπία.

Ἀφήσει καὶ ὑμῖν ὁ πατὴρ ὑμῶν.[560] Καὶ αὐτὸς μὲν ὁ Ἰησοῦς ὡς Θεὸς δύναται ἀφιέναι ἁμαρτίας, ἀλλ' ὡς ἔτι ἀτελέσι τοῖς μαθηταῖς οὔπω τὸν περὶ τῆς ἰδίας θεότητος παρέδωκε λόγον.

552 Cf. Gen. 1:26-27; 5:1; Ecclesiasticus, 17:3; Col. 3:10.
553 Cf. Col. 1:15.
554 Matt. 6:12.
555 Job, 7:1.
556 Rom. 1:26.
557 Rom. 1:28.
558 Matt. 6:13.
559 Matt. 6:14.
560 Matt. 6:14.

> Δύναται καὶ ὁ Ἰησοῦς ὡς θεὸς ἀφιέναι ἁμαρτίας, ἀλλ᾽ ὡς ἔτι ἀτελέσι τοῖς μαθηταῖς οὔπω τὸν περὶ τῆς ἰδίας θεότητος παρέδωκε λόγον καθαρῶς.[cdlii]

Ἀφανίζουσι γὰρ τὰ πρόσωπα.[561] Περὶ γὰρ τὴν κεφαλὴν καὶ τὸ πρόσωπον αἱ πλείους τῶν αἰσθήσεων καθίδρυνται (ἀκοή, γεῦσις, ὅρασις, ὄσφρησις), δι᾽ ὧν ὡς θεραπαινίδων ὁ νοῦς ἐνεργεῖ[cdliii] πρὸς τὰ πρακτέα, διακονουμένων αὐτῷ, καὶ ἢ κακίαν συνεργαζομένων ἢ ἀρετήν. Ταύτας οὖν ὁ Κύριος νίπτειν καὶ καθαίρειν κελεύει τῇ ἀποχῇ τῶν κακῶν, ἀλείφειν δὲ καὶ φαιδρύ | **45r** νειν τῇ ἐνεργείᾳ τῶν ἀγαθῶν, οἷς ἡ χάρις ἐπιλάμπει τοῦ Πνεύματος.
Λέγει δὲ περὶ τοῦ διδασκάλου τῆς ἐκκλησίας, *μὴ θησαυρίζετε ὑμῖν θησαυροὺς ἐπὶ τῆς γῆς.*[562]

> Τινὲς δὲ τὸ *ὁ λύχνος τοῦ σώματός ἐστιν ‹ὁ› ὀφθαλμὸς* περὶ τοῦ διδασκάλου τῆς ἐκκλησίας εἰρῆσθαι ἔφασαν. ἀλλά μοι δοκοῦσιν οὐκ ἐπεσκέφθαι πᾶσαν τῶν εἰρημένων τὴν ἀκολουθίαν ἄνωθεν. ἤρξατο γὰρ *μὴ θησαυρίζετε*, εἶτα παρενθεὶς τὸ *ὁ λύχνος τοῦ σώματος* καὶ τὸ *οὐδεὶς δύναται δυσὶ κυρίοις δουλεύειν* ἐπήγαγεν. *οὐ δύνασθε θεῷ δουλεύειν καὶ μαμωνᾷ*, δι᾽ ὅλου δεικνύων, ὅτι σκοπὸς ἦν αὐτῷ τοὺς ἀκούοντας ἀποστῆσαι τῆς περὶ τὰ παρόντα σπουδῆς.[cdliv]

> Τινὲς δὲ τὸ *ὁ λύχνος τοῦ σώματός ἐστιν ὀφθαλμὸς* περὶ τοῦ διδασκάλου τῆς ἐκκλησίας εἰρῆσθαι ἔφασαν, ἀλλά μοι δοκοῦσιν οὐκ ἐπεσκέφθαι πᾶσαν τῶν εἰρημένων τὴν ἀκολουθίαν ἄνωθεν. ἤρξατο γὰρ *μὴ θησαυρίζετε*, εἶτα παρενθεὶς τὸ *ὁ λύχνος τοῦ σώματος* καὶ τὸ *οὐδεὶς δύναται δυσὶ κυρίοις δουλεύειν* ἐπήγαγεν. *οὐ δύνασθε θεῷ δουλεύειν καὶ μαμωνᾷ*, δι᾽ ὅλου δεικνύων, ὅτι σκοπὸς ἦν αὐτῷ τοὺς ἀκούοντας ἀποστῆσαι τῆς περὶ τὰ παρόντα σπουδῆς.[cdlv]

Δοκεῖ μὲν μόνον προτρέπειν ἐπὶ δόσιν καὶ κοινωνίαν. Ἤδη δὲ καὶ *ὁ μὲν σπείρων εἰς τὴν σάρκα* θησαυρίζει *ἐπὶ τῆς γῆς, ὅπου* τὰ ἀφανίζοντα καὶ βλ‹ά›πτοντα[563] τὰ ἐν τῇ ψυχῇ ὑπολείμματα τῶν καλῶν διορύσσοντα τὴν προαίρεσιν *ἀφανίζει*. Ὁ δὲ *σπείρων εἰς τὸ Πνεῦμα*,[564] φορῶν *τὴν εἰκόνα τοῦ ἐπουρανίου*[565] καὶ τὸ *πολίτευμα* ἔχων ἐκεῖ, *ἐν οὐρανοῖς*[566] θησαυρίζει. *Σὴς* μὲν γάρ ἐστι κατὰ τὰ πάθη ἔρωτες καὶ φαῦλοι διαλογισμοί, ἃ διορύττουσι τὴν ψυχήν· *κλέπται* δέ, περὶ ὧν λέγει ὁ Κύριος, *πάντες ὅσοι ἦλθον, κλέπται εἰσὶ καὶ λῃσταί.*[567]

Θησαυρίζετε δὲ ὑμῖν θησαυροὺς ἐν οὐρανῷ.[568] Τῷ ὄντι θησαυρὸς *ἐν οὐρανῷ* ἐστιν, ἔνθα δεῖ ἡμᾶς καὶ τὸ τῆς καρδίας ἔχειν σπούδασμα.

561 Matt. 6:15.
562 Matt. 6:19.
563 Cod. βλέπτοντα.
564 Gal. 6:8.
565 1 Cor. 15:49.
566 Phil. 3:20.
567 John, 10:8.
568 Matt. 6:20.

Ὁ λύχνος τοῦ σώματός ἐστιν ὁ ὀφθαλμός.[569] Λύχνος τοῦ σώματος, ὁ νοῦς,[cdlvi] οὗ καθαρεύοντος ὡς διὰ φωτὸς ὁδεύουσα ἡ ψυχὴ ὁδηγεῖται. Τοῦ δὲ νοῦ βλαβέντος τὰ πολλὰ τῆς ψυχῆς μέρη ἀνενέργητα μένει, οὐχ ὁρῶντα πῶς ἢ ποῦ βαδίζει.

> *Ἁπλοῦς ὀφθαλμός* ἐστιν ὁ ὡς ἔχει τὰ πράγματα βλέπων καὶ οὔτε δύο τὸ ἓν οὔτε μεῖζον τὸ μικρότερον οὔτε ψευδόμενον τὸ χρῶμα, ὁ δὲ μὴ ἁπλοῦς *πονηρός.*[cdlvii]

Ὡς δὲ ἰδίᾳ *ὀφθαλμὸς πονηρός* ἐστιν ὅτε οὐκ ἐνεργεῖ κατὰ ὀφθαλμοῦ ἀρετήν, οὕτως καὶ ἕκαστον μέλος τῆς ψυχῆς ὅλον τε τὸ σῶμα τῆς ψυχῆς σκοτεινὸν μὲν ἀναφανὲν πονηρίᾳ ὑπὸ τοῦ πονηροῦ, φωτεινὸν δὲ ἀπὸ τῆς διαυγοῦς ἁπλότητος.

> ὡς δὲ ἰδίᾳ *ὀφθαλμὸς πονηρός* ἐστιν, ὅτε οὐκ ἐνεργεῖ κατὰ ὀφθαλμοῦ ἀρετήν, οὕτως καὶ ἕκαστον μέλος τῆς ψυχῆς ‹ὅλον τε τὸ σῶμα τῆς ψυχῆς› σκοτεινὸν ‹μὲν ἀναφανὲν πονηρίᾳ ὑπὸ τοῦ πονηροῦ, φωτεινὸν› δὲ ἀπὸ τῆς διαυγοῦς ἁπλότητος. Εἰ δ᾽ οὖν ἐστι μέση ἕξις[cdlviii] σπουδαίου καὶ φαύλου ὁ πολλὰ κατορθῶν τῶν περί τι, πῶς *ὅλον τὸ σῶμα* τῆς ψυχῆς[cdlix] ἕξει *φωτεινόν*; μήποτε ὡς λύχνος ἀμαυρὸς ἢ φανότερος οὕτως καὶ ἐπὶ νοῦ λεγομένου λύχνου τῆς πεφυκυίας εἰς τὸν νοῦν οὐσίας, οὐ τῆς εἰς τὸ νοεῖν ἐπιμελείας, ὅτε λέγομεν. ὅδε νοῦν ἔχει. οὐ δύο δὲ σημαινόμενα νοῦ οἶδε τὸ εὐαγγέλιον.[cdlx]

Ὅτε οὖν ὁ νοῦς ἡμῶν ὕλῃ ἐστὶ φίλος, τὸ ἐν ἡμῖν *φῶς σκότος ἐστίν*. Εἰ τοίνυν τὸ πεφυκὸς | **45v** φωτίζειν, *ἐν σοὶ* γενόμενον ἐν ἀγνοίᾳ, *σκότος ἐστί*, σκότους ἐπέκεινα *τὸ φρόνημα τῆς σαρκὸς* καὶ ἡ ἐπιθυμοῦσα *κατὰ τοῦ Πνεύματος σάρξ.*[570]

> Ὅτε οὖν ὁ νοῦς ἡμῶν ὕλῃ ἐστὶ φίλος, τὸ ἐν ἡμῖν *φῶς σκότος ἐστίν*. Εἰ τὸ πεφυκὸς φωτίζειν *ἐν σοὶ* γενόμενον ἐν ἀγνοίᾳ *σκότος ἐστίν*, σκότους ἐπέκεινα *τὸ φρόνημα τῆς σαρκὸς* καὶ ἡ ἐπιθυμοῦσα *κατὰ τοῦ Πνεύματος σάρξ.*[cdlxi]

Ἐὰν οὖν ὁ ὀφθαλμός σου ἁπλοῦς ᾖ.[571] *Ἁπλοῦς ὀφθαλμὸς ἡ ἀνυπόκριτός* ἐστιν *ἀγάπη*,[572] δι᾽ ἧς ἅπαν *τὸ σῶμα* φωτίζεται, τὰ αὐτὰ τοῖς ἔσωθεν νοουμένοις καὶ διὰ τῶν ἔξωθεν μερῶν προφέρουσα. Ὁ δὲ πονηρὸς *ὀφθαλμός* ἐστὶν ἡ προσποίητος ἀγάπη (ἥτις καὶ ὑπόκρισις καλεῖται), δι᾽ ἧς ἅπαν *τὸ σῶμα* τοῦ ἀνθρώπου σκοτίζεται. Ἄξια μὲν σκότους πράγματα ἐννοούμενον[573] ἔσωθεν, διὰ δὲ τῶν ἔξωθεν μερῶν φωτὸς εἶναι δοκοῦντα προφέρον[574] ῥήματα. *Λύκοι* γάρ εἰσιν ὡς ἀληθῶς *προβάτων*[575] περιβεβλημένοι δορὰς οἱ *τὸ ἔξωθεν τοῦ ποτηρίου καὶ τῆς παροψίδος*[576] μόνον πλύνοντες καὶ οὐκ εἰδότες ὅτι

569 Matt. 6:22.
570 Gal. 5:17.
571 Matt. 6:22.
572 Cf. Rom. 12:9; 2 Cor. 6:6.
573 Cod. ἐννοούμενον πράγματα.
574 Cod. προφέροντα.
575 Cf. Matt. 7:15.
576 Matt. 23:25.

ἐὰν μὴ τὸ *ἔσωθεν* τούτου καθαρθῇ, οὐδὲ τὸ *ἔξωθεν* καθαρὸν δύναται γενέσθαι. Διόπερ τούτους σαφῶς ἐλέγχων φησὶ ὁ Σωτήρ· *εἰ οὖν τὸ φῶς τὸ ἐν σοὶ σκότος, τὸ σκότος πόσον;*[577] Εἰ γὰρ ἡ δοκοῦσα σου ἀγάπη, ὅ ἐστι *φῶς* διὰ τὴν *ἐν σοὶ* κεκρυμμένην ὑπόκρισιν, σκότους ἄξιόν ἐστιν ἔργον, τί τὰ προφανῆ σου παραπτώματα;

> Ἁπλοῦς ὀφθαλμός, ἡ ἀνυπόκριτός ἐστιν ἀγάπη, δι᾽ ἧς ὅταν τὸ σῶμα φωτίζηται, τὰ αὐτὰ τοῖς ἔσωθεν νοούμενοις, καὶ διὰ τῶν ἔξωθεν μερῶν προφέρουσα; ὁ δὲ πονηρὸς ὀφθαλμός ἐστιν ἡ προσποίητος ἀγάπη, ἥτις καὶ ὑπόκρισις καλεῖται. δι᾽ ἧς ἅπαν τὸ σῶμα σκοτίζεται τοῦ ἀνθρώπου. Ἄξια μὲν σκότους πράγματα ἐννοούμενον ἔσωθεν, διὰ δὲ τῶν ἔξωθεν μερῶν, φωτὸς εἶναι δοκοῦντα προφέρον ῥήματα. λύκοι γάρ εἰσιν ὡς ἀληθῶς, προβάτων περιβεβλημένοι δοράς. οἱ τὸ ἔξωθεν τοῦ ποτηρίου καὶ τῆς παροψίδος μόνον πλύνοντες, καὶ οὐκ εἰδότες, ὅτι ἐὰν μὴ τὸ ἔσωθεν τούτων καθαρισθῇ, οὐδὲ τὸ ἔξωθεν καθαρὸν δύναται γενέσθαι. Διόπερ τούτους σαφῶς ἐλέγχων, φησὶν ὁ Σωτήρ, ὅτι. *Εἰ τὸ φῶς τὸ ἐν σοί, σκότος, τὸ σκότος πόσον;* Τουτέστιν. εἰ ἡ δοκοῦσά σοι ἀγάπη εἶναι φῶς, διὰ τὴν ἐν σοὶ κεκρυμμένην ὑπόκρισιν σκότους ἄξιόν ἐστιν ἔργον, τί τὰ προφανῆ σου παραπτώματα;[cdlxii]

Ὁ αἰσθητὸς *ὀφθαλμὸς* πάντα τὰ παρεμπίπτοντα ὁρᾶ, ὁ δὲ νοῦς ὁ *ἁπλοῦς* διακριτικῶς τὰ μὲν ἀγαθὰ ὁρᾷ τὰ δὲ φαῦλα ἀποστρέφεται, μύων τρόπον τινὰ τοῦ μὴ ἰδεῖν ἢ ψηλαφῆσαι αὐτά. Τὸ γὰρ φαῦλον, σκότει πονηρίας σκοτίζεται καὶ φῶς νοητὸν φωτὶ ἀληθείας[cdlxiii] φωτίζεται.

> Ὁ αἰσθητὸς ὀφθαλμὸς πάντα τὰ παρεμπίπτοντα ὁρᾷ, ὁ δὲ νοῦς ὁ ἁπλοῦς διακριτικῶς τὰ μὲν ἀγαθὰ ὁρᾷ, τὰ δὲ πονηρὰ ἀποστρέφεται, μύων τρόπον τινὰ τοῦ μὴ ἰδεῖν ἢ ψηλαφῆσαι αὐτά. τὸ γὰρ φαῦλον σκότει πονηρίας σκοτίζεται καὶ φῶς νοητὸν φωτὶ ἀληθείας φωτίζεται.[cdlxiv]

Οὐδεὶς δύναται | **46r** *δυσὶ κυρίοις δουλεύειν.*[578] Ἀγαθὸς δεσπότης, ὁ *ἀφιλάργυρος τρόπος,*[579] φαῦλος δὲ ὁ ἐρῶν χρημάτων. Διὸ τῷ ἑνὶ προσθετέον· οὐ γὰρ δυνατὸν τοῖς δύο ἀρέσαι, διαφόρου καὶ ἐναντίας οὖσιν ἕξεως.

> Ἀγαθὸς δεσπότης ὁ ἀφιλάργυρος τρόπος, φαῦλος δὲ ὁ ἐρῶν χρημάτων. διὸ τῷ ἑνὶ προσθετέον. οὐ γὰρ δυνατὸν τοῖς δυσὶν ἀρέσαι διαφόρου καὶ ἐναντίας οὖσιν ἕξεως.[cdlxv]

Δύο κυρίους[580] τοὺς τὰ ἐναντία ἐπιτάττοντας λέγει ἐνταῦθα, ἐπεὶ εἰ μὴ τοῦτο εἴη, οὐδὲ *δύο* ἂν εἶεν. Ὅτε γὰρ διαφόρου φρονήματός εἰσιν, οὐ δυνατὸν τοῖς *δύο* ἀρέσαι. Εἰ δὲ κύριον καλεῖ καὶ τὸν Μαμωνᾶν, οὐκ ἀπὸ τῆς ἰδίας φύσεως τοῦτο ἐστίν, ἀλλ᾽ ἀπὸ τῆς

577 Matt. 6:23.
578 Matt. 6:24; Luke, 16:13.
579 Heb. 13:5.
580 Matt. 6:24; Luke, 16:13.

τῶν ὑποκειμένων αὐτῷ ταλαιπωρίας. *Κύριος* μὲν γὰρ *ἀληθῶς, ὁ Θεός*,[581] Μαμωνᾶς δὲ ὁ κύριος ἀναγορευόμενος ὑπὸ τῶν φιλαργύρων.
Ὁ οὖν φαῦλος οὐ μισεῖ Θεόν, καταφρονεῖ δὲ αὐτοῦ· καὶ οὐκ ἀγαπᾷ Μαμωνᾶν, ἀντέχεται δὲ αὐτοῦ. Ὁ δὲ δίκαιος οὐκ ἀντέχεται Θεοῦ ἀλλ᾽ ἀγαπᾷ, οὐδὲ καταφρονεῖ τῶν φαύλων ὅσον μισεῖ.

> Ἰστέον δὲ ὡς ὁ φαῦλος οὐ μισεῖ θεὸν καταφρονεῖ δὲ αὐτοῦ, καὶ οὐκ ἀγαπᾷ μαμωνᾶν ἀντέχεται δὲ αὐτοῦ. ὁ δὲ δίκαιος οὐκ ἀντέχεται Θεοῦ ἀλλὰ ἀγαπᾷ, οὐδὲ καταφρονεῖ τῶν φαύλων ὅσον μισεῖ, δι᾽ ὅλου δεικνὺς ὅτι σκοπὸς ἦν αὐτῷ τοὺς ἀκούσαντας ἀποστῆσαι τῆς ἐπὶ τὰ παρόντα σπουδῆς.[cdlxvi]

Πᾶν τὸ ἔξω Θεοῦ, Μαμωνᾶ ἐστιν, ὅστις καὶ *τῆς ἀδικίας*[582] ὠνομάσθη. Τὸ δὲ Μαμωνᾶς, χρήματα ἑρμηνεύεται.[cdlxvii]

> Πᾶν τὸ ἔξω Θεοῦ μαμωνᾶς ἐστιν, ὅστις καὶ *τῆς ἀδικίας* ὠνομάσθη. τὸ δὲ μαμωνᾶς, χρήματα ἑρμηνεύεται.[cdlxviii]
>
> In the Syriac language, riches are called *mammon*.[cdlxix]

Μὴ μεριμνᾶτε τῇ ψυχῇ ὑμῶν.[583] Εἰ τὸ περὶ μιᾶς ἡμέρας φροντίζειν βαρὺ καὶ κακωτικόν, πῶς τὸ περισσὸν οὐκ ἀφόρητον;
Ἄρ᾽ οὖν κακώσεως καὶ μόχθου καὶ ταλαιπωρίας καὶ πόνου ἡ παροῦσα ἡμέρα,

> Ἄρ᾽ οὖν κακώσεως καὶ μόχθου καὶ ταλαιπωρίας καὶ πόνου ἡ παροῦσα ἡμέρα.[cdlxx]

ὅπερ πολλοὶ ποιοῦσι. Κἂν ἴδωσι μοναχὸν ἱμάτιον περιττὸν ἔχοντα, τὸν νόμον αὐτῷ προβάλλονται τὸν δεσποτικὸν αὐτοὶ καθ᾽ ἑκάστην πλεονεκτοῦντες τὴν ἡμέραν. Κἂν ἴδωσι δαψιλεστέρας τροφῆς ἀπολαύοντα, πικροὶ γίνονται κατήγοροι καθ᾽ ἡμέραν αὐτοὶ μεθύοντες, οὐκ εἰδότες ὅτι μετὰ τῶν οἰκείων ἁμαρτημάτων μεῖ | **46v** ζον ἐντεῦθεν ἑαυτοῖς συνάγουσι *τὸ πῦρ*[584] καὶ πάσης ἑαυτοὺς ἀποστεροῦσιν ἀπολογίας.

> διὸ καὶ ἔλεγε. *τί βλέπεις τὸ κάρφος τὸ ἐν τῷ ὀφθαλμῷ τοῦ ἀδελφοῦ σου;*[585] καὶ γὰρ πολλοὶ νῦν τοῦτο ποιοῦσι. κἂν ἴδωσι μοναχὸν περιττὸν ἱμάτιον ἔχοντα, τὸν νόμον αὐτῷ προβάλλονται τὸν δεσποτικόν, αὐτοὶ μυρία ἁρπάζοντες καὶ καθ᾽ ἑκάστην πλεονεκτοῦντες τὴν ἡμέραν. κἂν ἴδωσι δαψιλεστέρας τροφῆς ἀπολαύοντα, πικροὶ γίνονται κατήγοροι καθ᾽ ἡμέραν αὐτοὶ μεθύοντες καὶ κραιπαλῶντες, οὐκ εἰδότες ὅτι μετὰ τῶν οἰκείων

581 3 Kings (1 Kings in Masoretic text), 18:39.
582 Luke, 16:9.
583 Matt. 6:25; Luke, 12:22.
584 Cf. John, 15:6; Matt. 3:12; Luke, 3:17.
585 Matt. 7:3-4.

> ἁμαρτημάτων μεῖζον ἑαυτοῖς ἐντεῦθεν συνάγουσι τὸ πῦρ, καὶ πάσης ἑαυτοὺς ἀποστεροῦσιν ἀπολογίας.[cdlxxi]

Τί φάγητε καὶ τί πίητε.[586] Ἐπεὶ τὸ τρεφόμενον ἐν τῷ σώματι ἡ ψυχή, οὐχ οὕτως ἡδομένη ἐστὶ τῷ σκέπτεσθαι.[cdlxxii] Διὰ τοῦτο *τῇ* μὲν *ψυχῇ* εἶπε τὸ *τί φάγητε* ἢ *τί πίητε*· τῷ δὲ σώματι, τὸ *τί ἐνδύσ‹η›σθε.*[587]

> Ἐπεὶ τὸ ἡδόμενον ἐν τῷ τρέφεσθαι ἡ ψυχή, οὐχ οὕτως ἡδομένη ἐπὶ τῷ σκέπεσθαι, διὰ τοῦτο *τῇ* μὲν *ψυχῇ* εἶπε τὸ *τί φάγητε* ἢ *τί πίητε*, τῷ δὲ σώματι, τὸ *τί ἐνδύσησθε.*[cdlxxiii]

Ἐνταῦθα τὸ *τί* μόριον τὴν ποικιλίαν τῆς τροφῆς ἐκβέβληκε, *μὴ μεριμνᾶτε* λέγον ποῖα *φάγητε* ἢ ποῖα *πίητε*. Πλεονεξία γὰρ καὶ τρυφὴ μεριμνᾶν ταῦτα. Τὸ δὲ φαγεῖν μόνον ψιλῶς νοούμενον ἀνάγκης ἐστὶ τεκμήριον, τὸ πλήρωμα τῆς ἐνδείας. Τὸ δὲ *τί* τὸ ἐκ περισσοῦ δηλοῖ. Σαφηνίζει δὲ τὴν διάνοιαν ἡ ἐπιφερομένη λέξις. Μετὰ γὰρ τὸ εἰπεῖν *μὴ ζητεῖτε τί φάγητε ἢ τί πίητε*, ἐπήγαγε παρ' ἄλλῳ εὐαγγελιστῇ, καὶ *μὴ μετεωρίζεσθε.*[588] Μετεώρους δὲ ἀπὸ τῆς ἀληθείας ἀλαζονεία καὶ τρυφὴ ποιεῖ καὶ ἡ εἰς τὰ περιττὰ ἀπασχολοῦσα ἡδυπάθεια. Διὸ ἐπάγει· *ταῦτα γὰρ πάντα τὰ ἔθνη τοῦ κόσμου ἐπιζητεῖ.*[589] Τουτέστιν οἱ ἄτακτοι καὶ ἀνόητοι. Τίνα δὲ λέγει ταῦτα; Τὴν τρυφὴν καὶ τὴν ἡδυπάθειαν. Ταῦτά ἐστι τὸ *τί*. Περὶ δὲ τῆς ψιλῆς τροφῆς, τῆς τε ξηρᾶς καὶ τῆς ὑγρᾶς, ὡς ἀναγκαίων οὐσῶν, *οἶδε*, φησίν, *ὁ πατὴρ ὑμῶν ὅτι χρήζετε τούτων.*[590]

> Ἐνταῦθα τὸ *τί* μόριον τὴν ποικιλίαν τῆς τροφῆς ἐκβέβληκε, σημαίνεται γὰρ ἐκ τῆς γραφῆς τοῦτο. *μὴ μεριμνᾶτε ποῖα φάγητε ἢ ποῖα πίητε.* πλεονεξία γὰρ καὶ τρυφὴ μεριμνᾶν ταῦτα. τὸ δὲ φαγεῖν μόνον ψιλῶς νοούμενον ἀνάγκης ἐστὶ τεκμήριον, τὸ πλήρωμα, ὡς ἔφαμεν, τῆς ἐνδείας. τὸ δὲ *τί* ἐκ περισσοῦ, τὸ δὲ περιττὸν ἐκ τοῦ διαβόλου μεμήνυκεν ἡ γραφή. Σαφηνίζει δὲ τὴν διάνοιαν ἡ ἐπιφερομένη λέξις. *Μὴ* γὰρ *ζητεῖτε τί φάγητε ἢ τί πίητε* εἰπών, ἐπήγαγεν. *καὶ ‹μὴ› μετεωρίζεσθε.* μετεώρους δὲ ἀπὸ τῆς ἀληθείας ἀλαζονεία καὶ τρυφὴ ποιεῖ, καὶ ἡ εἰς τὰ περιττὰ ἀπασχολοῦσα ἡδυπάθεια ἀπάγει τῆς ἀληθείας. διὸ καί φησι παγκάλως. *Ταῦτα δὲ πάντα τὰ ἔθνη τοῦ κόσμου ζητεῖ.* Οἱ ἄτακτοι καὶ ἀνόητοι τὰ ἔθνη εἰσίν. Τίνα δὲ λέγει *ταῦτα*; τὴν τρυφήν, τὴν ἡδυπάθειαν, τὴν καρυκείαν, τὴν ὀψοφαγίαν, τὴν λαιμαργίαν. ταῦτά ἐστι τὸ *τί*. Περὶ δὲ ψιλῆς τῆς τροφῆς, τῆς τε ξηρᾶς καὶ τῆς ὑγρᾶς, ὡς ἀναγκαίων οὐσῶν, *οἶδε*, φησίν, *ὁ πατὴρ ὑμῶν ὅτι χρῄζετε.*[cdlxxiv]

Τὸ δὲ *μὴ οὖν μεριμνήσητε εἰς τὴν αὔριον,*[591] ἤτοι ὑπερβολικῶς ἢ προτρεπτικῶς τοῦ μὴ ἐκκρέμασθαι τῶν κοσμικῶν.

---

586 Matt. 6:25.
587 Cod. ἐνδύσεσθε.
588 Luke, 12:29.
589 Cf. Luke, 12:29: ἐπιζητοῦσιν.
590 Luke, 12:30.
591 Matt. 6:34.

> Ὑπερβολικῶς ἀποκόπτειν ἡμᾶς θέλων ὁ σωτὴρ ἀπὸ τῶν βιωτικῶν πραγμάτων μηδὲ *τὴν αὔριον* μεριμνᾶν ἐδίδασκεν.[cdlxxv]

Ἑκάστης γὰρ ἡμέρας ἐχούσης τὸν ἴδιον κόπον (*κακία* γὰρ τῆς ἡμέρας *ὁ κόπος*[592] καὶ ἡ φροντὶς ἡ καθημερινή), οὐ δεῖ κακοπαθεῖν καὶ περιτ‹τ›ῆς[593] μήπω ἐλθούσης καὶ ἀδήλου οὔσης, εἰ ἥξει. *Ἡμέραν* οὖν | **47r** λέγει τὰ πρὸς τὴν χρείαν, ἅπερ τις καὶ αὐτὰ ἐπὶ μόχθῳ συνάγει. Ἡ δὲ *αὔριον*, τὰ ὑπὲρ τὴν χρείαν ἐστί, τὸ φροντίζειν περὶ τῶν μελλόντων. Οὐχὶ ἡ ψυχὴ πλεῖον ἐστὶ τῆς τροφῆς; Οὐχ ἡ ψυχὴ ἐσθίει, ἀλλὰ διὰ τροφῆς συνίσταται τὸ σῶμα ἐν ᾧ ἡ ψυχὴ διακρατεῖται. Δοκεῖ γὰρ μὴ ἀνέχεσθαι εἶναι ἐν τῷ σώματι ἡ ψυχή, εἰ μὴ τρέφοιτο ἡ σάρξ.[cdlxxvi] Ἐπειδὴ δὲ τὰ χρήματα ἀλλοτριοῖ Θεοῦ[cdlxxvii] καὶ ἡ περὶ ταῦτα μέριμνα, δεῖ μὴ μόνον χρημάτων,[cdlxxviii] ἀλλὰ καὶ αὐτῆς τῆς ἐφημέρου καταφρονεῖν τροφῆς ἵνα μὴ στερηθῶμεν Θεοῦ.
Ψυχῆς τοίνυν καὶ σώματος ἐπιμελητέον ἡμῖν, τῶν δὲ ἐλαττόνων καταφρονητέον, τροφῆς λέγω καὶ ἐνδύματος.

> Ἐπειδήπερ ἡ ψυχὴ καὶ τὸ σῶμα τιμιώτερά ἐστιν τῶν τροφῶν καὶ τῶν ἐνδυμάτων, καὶ τῶν ἐλαττόνων καταφρονητέον, ἐπιμελητέον δὲ καὶ τῶν τιμιωτέρων, ψυχῆς λέγω καὶ σώματος.[cdlxxix]

Ὁ γὰρ τὰ μείζω δούς, δίδωσι καὶ τὰ ἐλάττονα.

17

50v *Μὴ δῶτε τὸ ἅγιον τοῖς κυσί.*[594] **51r** (ΩΡΙΓΕΝΟΥΣ) Τὰ ἀνθρώπινα ἤθη κατά τινας τῶν ἁμαρτιῶν ἐξομοιοῦνται τοῖς ἀλόγοις ζώοις, διόπερ ὀνόμασι κέχρηται ὁ σωτὴρ τούτοις οἷς καὶ οἱ προφῆται. Τοὺς μὲν γὰρ δι᾽ ἀκολασίαν *ἵππους* ἐκάλεσαν *θηλ‹υ›μανεῖς*.[595] Καὶ ἄλλος φησί· *μὴ γίνεσθε ὡς ἵππος καὶ ἡμίονος, οἷς οὐκ ἔστι σύνεσις*.[596] Ἡρώδης δὲ διὰ τὴν πανουργίαν ἀλώπηξ ὠνομάσθη,[597] ἀλλὰ καὶ διὰ τὸ θανατηφόρον τοῖς ἀκούουσιν *ἰὸς ἀσπίδων ὑπὸ τὰ χείλη αὐτῶν*.[598] Ἀλλὰ καὶ *γεννήματα ἐχιδνῶν*[599] ἐλέγχθη ἄλλοις. Ἵνα γὰρ δείξῃ τὴν διαφορὰν τῆς ἐν ἀνθρώποις ἐνεργούσης ἁμαρ | **51v** τίας, ἑρπετῶν καὶ πετεινῶν καὶ τετραπόδων ὀνόμασιν ὠνόμασε. Πλὴν καὶ ἐξ αὐτῶν εἰς

592 Cf. Matt. 6:34.
593 Cod. περιτῆς.
594 Cf. Matt. 7:6.
595 Jer. 5:8. cod. θηλιμανεῖς.
596 Psalm 31:9.
597 Luke, 13.31-32.
598 Psalms 13:3 (quoted by Paul in Rom. 3:13); 139:4.
599 Matt. 3:7; 12:34; 23:33; Luke, 3:7.

μετάνοιαν ἐκάλεσε κατὰ τὸ *ὅραμα* Πέτρου τὸ ἐν ταῖς Πράξεσι λεγόμενον.[600] *Κύνας*[601] οὖν ἐκάλεσε διὰ τὴν ἀναίδειαν τοὺς πρὸς τὰς ὕβρεις εὐκαταφόρους καὶ ἐν λοιδορίαις ὑλακτικοὺς καὶ εἰς τὸ κολακεύειν ἑτοίμους γαστρὸς ἕνεκεν, καὶ διὰ τὸ ἀναιδὲς ἀνερυθριάστους. Χοίρους[602] δὲ τοὺς ἀπλήστους καὶ ἀκαθάρτους ἐν βορβόρῳ καὶ τοῖς ἀφοδεύμασι καταχρωμένους βρώσει. Διόπερ οὐ χρὴ τούτο‹ι›ς[603] κοινωνεῖν καὶ μεταδιδόναι, ἀφ᾽ ὧν ζώων οὐδὲ ἀντάλλαγμα προσφέρειν δεῖ *εἰς τὸν οἶκον τοῦ Θεοῦ.*[604] Πάντῃ γὰρ ἀλλότριον ἁγιασμοῦ τὸ ζῷον.

> Τὰ ἀνθρώπινα ἤθη κατά τινας τῶν ἁμαρτιῶν ἐξομοιοῦνται τοῖς ἀλόγοις ζώοις, διόπερ ὀνόμασι κέχρηται ὁ σωτὴρ τούτοις, οἷς καὶ οἱ προφῆται. τοὺς μὲν γὰρ δι᾽ ἀκολασίαν *ἵππους ἐκάλεσαν θηλυμανεῖς.* καὶ ἄλλος φησι. *μὴ γίνεσθε ὡς ἵππος καὶ ἡμίονος, οἷς οὐκ ἔστι σύνεσις.* Ἡρώδης δὲ διὰ τὴν πανουργίαν ἀλώπηξ ὠνομάσθη, ἀλλὰ καὶ διὰ τὸ θανατηφόρον τοῖς ἀκούουσιν *ἰὸς ἀσπίδων ὑπὸ τὰ χείλη αὐτῶν,*[605] ἀλλὰ καὶ *γεννήματα ἐχιδνῶν*[606] ἐλέγχθη ἄλλοις. ἵνα γὰρ δείξῃ τὴν διαφορὰν τῆς ἐν ἀνθρώποις ἐνεργουμένης ἁμαρτίας, ἑρπετῶν καὶ πετεινῶν καὶ τετραπόδων ὀνόμασιν ὠνόμασεν. πλὴν καὶ ἐξ αὐτῶν εἰς μετάνοιαν ἐκάλεσε κατὰ τὸ *ὅραμα* Πέτρου τὸ ἐν ταῖς Πράξεσι λεγόμενον. *Κύνας* οὖν ἐκάλεσε διὰ τὴν ἀναίδειαν τοὺς πρὸς τὰς ὕβρεις εὐκαταφόρους καὶ ἐν λοιδορίαις ὑλακτικοὺς καὶ εἰς τὸ κολακεύειν ἑτοίμους γαστρὸς ἕνεκεν[cdlxxx] καὶ διὰ τὸ ἀναιδὲς ἀνερυθριάστους. χοίρους δὲ τοὺς ἀπλήστους καὶ ἀκαθάρτους ἐν βορβόρῳ καὶ τοῖς ἀφοδεύμασι καταχρωμένους βρώσει. διόπερ οὐ χρὴ τούτοις κοινωνεῖν καὶ μεταδιδόναι, ἀφ᾽ ὧν ζώων οὐδὲ ἀντάλλαγμα προσφέρειν δεῖ *εἰς τὸν οἶκον τοῦ Θεοῦ.* Πάντῃ γὰρ ἀλλότριον ἁγιασμοῦ τὸ ζῷον.[cdlxxxi]

Αἰτεῖτε, καὶ δοθήσεται ὑμῖν.[607] Ἵνα μὴ ἀγνοῶσιν οἱ μαθηταὶ τίνες εἰσὶ κύνες ἢ χοῖροι ἐν τοῖς ἀκροαταῖς, ἐπιμόνως ζητήσατε (φησί) ἐκ Θεοῦ καὶ ἀποκαλύπτει ὑμῖν ταῦτα. Ἀρχὴ μὲν γὰρ ἀρετῆς τὸ δι᾽ εὐχῆς γνῶναι τὸ ἀγαθόν· εἶτα, τὸ εἰδέναι πῶς δεῖ ὁδεῦσαι τὴν ἀρετήν· τρίτον, τὸ διὰ τῶν ἔργων κρούειν ἀνοιγῆναι αὐτῷ τὴν θύραν· τοῦτο γὰρ σημαίνει ἡ διὰ τῶν χειρῶν κροῦσις. Τρισσῶς γὰρ ἡ τῶν σωτηρίων δογμάτων ἀλήθεια λαμβάνεται, ἐπιμελεῖ εὐχῇ καὶ τοῦ ἡγεμονικοῦ ἐν τῷ ζητεῖν τὰ ‹θεῖα› πράγματα καταστάσει[cdlxxxii] καὶ περὶ τοῦ εὑρεῖν σὺν αἰσθήσει τῆς τῶν κεκρυμμένων γραφῶν ἀσαφείας τὸ βάθος ἀκριβεῖ πολυπραγμοσύνῃ. Οὕτω γὰρ ἀνοίγεσθαί φησι τὰς γραφάς.

> Ἵνα μὴ ἀγνοῶσιν οἱ μαθηταὶ τίνες εἰσὶ κύνες ἢ χοῖροι ἐν τοῖς ἀκροαταῖς, ἐπιμόνως ζητήσατε (φησί) ἐκ Θεοῦ καὶ ἀποκαλύπτεται ὑμῖν ταῦτα. ἀρχὴ μὲν γὰρ ἀρετῆς τὸ δι᾽ εὐχῆς γνῶναι τὸ ἀγαθόν, εἶτα, τὸ εἰδέναι πῶς δεῖ ὁδεῦσαι τὴν ἀρετήν, τρίτον, τὸ διὰ

600 Acts, 10:12; 11:6.
601 Cf. Phil. 3:2; Rev. 22:15.
602 Cf. Matt. 7:6.
603 Cod. τούτους.
604 Cf. Deut. 23:19.
605 Psalms 13:3 (quoted by Paul in Rom. 3:13); 139:4.
606 Matt. 3:7; 12:34; 23:33; Luke, 3:7.
607 Matt. 7:7; Luke, 11:9.

τῶν ἔργων κρούειν ἀνοιγῆναι αὐτῷ τὴν θύραν. τοῦτο γὰρ σημαίνει ἡ διὰ τῶν χειρῶν κροῦσις. τρισσῶς γὰρ ἡ τῶν σωτηρίων δογμάτων ἀλήθεια λαμβάνεται, ἐπιμελεῖ εὐχῇ καὶ τοῦ ἡγεμονικοῦ ἐν τῷ ζητεῖν τὰ θεῖα καταστάσει καὶ περὶ τοῦ εὑρεῖν συναισθήτως τῆς τῶν κεκρυμμένων γραφῶν ἀσαφείας τὸ βάθος ἀκριβεῖ πολυπραγμοσύνῃ. οὕτω γὰρ ἀνοίγεσθαί φησι τὰς γραφάς.[cdlxxxiii]

Ἵνα μὴ ἀγνοῶσιν οἱ μαθηταί, τίνες εἰσὶν κύνες, ἢ χοῖροι ἐν τοῖς ἀκροαταῖς, ἐπιμόνως ζητήσατε, φησίν, ἐκ Θεοῦ, καὶ ἀποκαλύπτεται ὑμῖν πάντα. Ἀρχὴ μὲν γὰρ ἀρετῆς τὸ δι᾽ εὐχῆς γνῶναι τὸ ἀγαθόν. εἶτα τὸ εἰδέναι πῶς δεῖ ὁδεῦσαι τὴν ἀρετήν. τρίτον τὸ διὰ τῶν ἔργων κρούειν ἀνοιγῆναι αὐτῷ τὴν θύραν. Τοῦτο γὰρ σημαίνει ἡ διὰ τῶν χειρῶν κροῦσις. Τρισσῶς γὰρ ἡ τῶν σωτηρίων δογμάτων ἀλήθεια λαμβάνεται, ἐπιμελεῖ εὐχῇ, καὶ τοῦ ἡγεμονικοῦ ἐν τῷ ζητεῖν τὰ θεῖα καταστάσει, καὶ περὶ τοῦ εὑρεῖν συναισθήτως τῆς τῶν κεκρυμμένων Γραφῶν ἀσφαλείας τὸ βάθος, ἀκριβεῖ πολυπραγμοσύνῃ. οὕτω γὰρ ἀνοίγεσθαί φησι τὰς Γραφάς.[cdlxxxiv]

Αἰτεῖν ἐστι τὸ προσεύχεσθαι, ζητεῖν δὲ τὸ καὶ διὰ τῶν ἀγαθῶν ἔργων σύμφωνα πράττειν τῇ προσευχῇ. Καὶ οὐ μόνον ζητεῖν, ἀλλὰ καὶ κρούειν τὴν θύραν. | **52r** Τὸ δὲ κρούειν δηλοῖ τὸ τῇ μακροθυμίᾳ τοῦ Θεοῦ συμπαρεκτείνειν[cdlxxxv] ἡμᾶς τὰς δεήσεις καὶ ἐπιμένειν καὶ μὴ ἀποναρκᾶν[cdlxxxvi] καὶ ὀλιγωρεῖν.

Ζητεῖν ἐπιμελῶς δεῖ τὴν ἀλήθειαν τῶν δογμάτων. Δεύτερον δὲ τὸν Θεὸν αἰτεῖν ἵνα ἀποκαλυφθῇ ἡμῖν τὰ μυστήρια τῆς σοφίας[cdlxxxvii] τὰ ἀποκεκρυμμένα[608] *ἀπὸ τ‹ῶν› αἰ‹ώ›ν‹ων›*[609] *καὶ ἀπὸ τῶν γενεῶν τούτων.*[610] Τρίτον, ἵνα κρούσῃ καὶ εἰσελθὼν διὰ τῶν τῆς δικαιοσύνης θυρῶν[611] ἐξομολογήσηται. Ἐὰν οὖν ἑνὸς τούτων ἐλλίπῃς, οὐδενὸς τυγχάνεις. Ἔστιν οὖν ἐπιζητεῖν τὸ Πνεῦμα τὸ Ἅγιον, ἵνα δι᾽ αὐτοῦ αἰτήσωμεν τὸν Υἱόν,[612] καὶ ἀνο‹ί›ξα‹ν›[613] τὰς τῆς γραφῆς θύρας τὰ περὶ τοῦ Πατρὸς γνωρίσῃ ἡμῖν. Αὐτὸς γάρ ἐστιν *ἡ θύρα.*[614] Πῶς δέ τις λαμβάνει ἐὰν μὴ πρῶτον αἰτήσῃ; Πῶς δὲ εὑρίσκει, ἐὰν μὴ ζητήσῃ; Πῶς δὲ εἰσέρχεται, ἐὰν μὴ κρούσῃ;[615] Ὁ συνετὸς οὖν αἰτεῖ *ἵνα δοθῇ* αὐτῷ *λόγος ἐν ἀνοίξει τοῦ στόματος*[616] αὐτοῦ. Αἰτεῖν ἐκέλευσε καὶ τὴν δόσιν ἐν‹η›γγυήσατο.[617] Πλὴν οὐχ ἁπλῶς αἰτεῖν ἐκέλευσεν, ἀλλὰ μετὰ προσεδρείας πολλῆς καὶ εὐτονίας. Τοῦτο γάρ ἐστι τὸ *ζητεῖτε.* Καὶ γὰρ ὁ ζητῶν πάντα ἐκβαλὼν τῆς διανοίας πρὸς ἐκεῖνο τείνεται μόνον τὸ ζητούμενον καὶ οὐδένα τῶν παρόντων ἐννοεῖ. Καὶ γὰρ ἴσασι τοῦτο ὃ λέγω ὅσοι οἰκέτας ἢ χρυσίον ἀπολέσαντες ἐπιζητοῦσιν. Ἀπὸ δὲ τοῦ κρούειν τὸ μετὰ σφοδρότητος προσιέναι καὶ θερμῆς διανοίας ἐδήλωσεν.

---

608 Cf. 1 Cor. 2:7.
609 Cod. τοῦ αἰῶνος.
610 Cf. Col. 1:26.
611 Cf. Psalm 117:20; John, 10:7.
612 Cf. 1 Cor. 12:3.
613 Cod. ἀνοίξας.
614 Cf. John, 10:7; 10.9.
615 Cf. Matt. 7:7-8; Luke, 11:9-10.
616 Eph. 6:19.
617 Cod. ἐνεγγυήσατο.

Ζητεῖν ἐπιμελῶς δεῖ τὴν ἀλήθειαν τῶν δογμάτων, δεύτερον δὲ τὸν Θεὸν αἰτεῖν ἵνα ἀποκαλυφθῇ ἡμῖν τὰ μυστήρια τῆς σοφίας τὰ ἀποκεκρυμμένα[618] *ἀπὸ τῶν αἰώνων καὶ ἀπὸ τῶν γενεῶν* τούτων, τρίτον, ἵνα κρούσῃ καὶ εἰσελθὼν διὰ τῶν τῆς δικαιοσύνης θυρῶν ἐξομολογήσηται. ἐὰν οὖν ἑνὸς τούτων ἐλλίπῃ, οὐδενὸς τυγχάνει. Ἔστιν οὖν ἐπιζητεῖν τὸ Πνεῦμα τὸ Ἅγιον, ἵνα δι' αὐτοῦ αἰτήσωμεν τὸν Υἱόν, καὶ ἀνοίξας τὰς τῆς γραφῆς θύρας τὰ περὶ τοῦ Πατρὸς γνωρίσῃ ἡμῖν. αὐτὸς γάρ ἐστιν *ἡ θύρα*. πῶς δέ τις λαμβάνει ἐὰν μὴ πρῶτον αἰτήσῃ; πῶς δὲ εὑρίσκει, ἐὰν μὴ ζητήσῃ; πῶς δὲ εἰσέρχεται, ἐὰν μὴ κρούσῃ;[619] ὁ συνετὸς οὖν αἰτεῖ *ἵνα δοθῇ αὐτῷ λόγος ἐν ἀνοίξει τοῦ στόματος* αὐτοῦ. [αἰτεῖν ἐκέλευσε καὶ τὴν δόσιν ἐνηγγυήσατο. πλὴν οὐχ ἁπλῶς αἰτεῖν ἐκέλευσεν, ἀλλὰ μετὰ προσεδρείας πολλῆς καὶ εὐτονίας. τοῦτο γάρ ἐστι τὸ *ζητεῖτε*. καὶ γὰρ ὁ ζητῶν πάντα ἐκβαλὼν τῆς διανοίας πρὸς ἐκεῖνο τείνεται μόνον τὸ ζητούμενον καὶ οὐδένα τῶν παρόντων ἐννοεῖ. καὶ γὰρ ἴσασι τοῦτο ὃ λέγω ὅσοι οἰκέτας ἢ χρυσίον ἀπολέσαντες ἐπιζητοῦσιν. ἀπὸ δὲ τοῦ κρούειν τὸ μετὰ σφοδρότητος προσιέναι καὶ θερμῆς διανοίας ἐδήλωσεν.][cdlxxxviii]

Διὰ τοῦτο καὶ αἰτεῖν ἐκέλευσε, καὶ τὴν δόσιν ἐνηγγυήσατο. Πλὴν οὐχ ἁπλῶς αἰτεῖν ἐκέλευσεν, ἀλλὰ μετὰ προσεδρείας πολλῆς καὶ εὐτονίας. Τοῦτο γάρ ἐστι τό, *Ζητεῖτε*. Καὶ γὰρ ὁ ζητῶν, πάντα ἐκβαλὼν τῆς διανοίας, πρὸς ἐκεῖνο γίνεται μόνον τὸ ζητούμενον, καὶ οὐδένα τῶν παρόντων ἐννοεῖ. Καὶ ἴσασι τοῦτο ὃ λέγω, ὅσοι ἢ χρυσίον ἢ οἰκέτας ἀπολέσαντες ἐπιζητοῦσιν. Ἀπὸ μὲν οὖν τοῦ ζητεῖν, τοῦτο. ἀπὸ δὲ τοῦ κρούειν, τὸ μετὰ σφοδρότητος προσιέναι καὶ θερμῆς διανοίας ἐδήλωσε.[cdlxxxix]

So, let us knock the door of Christ of which it is said, *This is the gate of the Lord, the just shall enter through it.*[620] When we have entered in this way, may *the hidden and concealed treasures* in Christ Jesus, in which is all *knowledge*,[621] be opened to us.[cdxc]

Ἀρχὴ ἀρετῆς τὸ εὔχεσθαι γνωρισθῆναί τινι τὴν *ὁδὸν* τῆς *δικαιοσύνης*.[622] Δεύτερος βαθμός, τὸ ζητεῖν πῶς δεῖ ὁδεῦσαι τὴν ὁδόν. Τρίτος, τὸ‹ν›[623] ἁψάμενον τῆς ἀρετῆς κρούειν | **52v** τῷ Χριστῷ, ἵνα ἀνοίξῃ αὐτῷ τὴν θύραν καὶ ἀπαλλαγῇ τῆς στενῆς ὁδοῦ καὶ τεθλιμμένης[624] καὶ εἰσαγάγῃ αὐτὸν εἰς τὴν εὐρύχωρον γνωστικὴν ἐργασίαν. Ἅπερ πάντα διὰ τῆς ἐκ Θεοῦ καὶ πρὸς Θεὸν δεήσεως λαμβάνει τις. Ἴσως δὲ καὶ τὸ μετὰ πράξεως αἰτεῖν ᾐνίξατο διὰ τοῦ εἰπεῖν· *κρούετε*. Κρούει γάρ τις τῇ δεξιᾷ χειρί, ἀγαθῆς δὲ πράξεως σύμβολον ἡ δεξιὰ χείρ. Εἰ δὲ μὴ εὐθέως λάβῃς, μηδὲ οὕτως ἀπογνῷς. Διὰ γὰρ τοῦτο εἶπε *κρούετε*· ὅτι κἂν εὐθέως μὴ ἀνοίξῃ τὴν θύραν, παραμένειν δεῖ. Εἰ δὲ ἀπιστεῖς μου τῇ ἀποφάσει, φησί, κἀν τῷ ὑποδείγματι πίστευσον.

618 Cf. 1 Cor. 2:7.
619 Cf. Matt. 7:7-8; Luke, 11:9-10.
620 Psalm, 117:20.
621 Cf. Col. 2:3.
622 Cf. Job, 24:13; 2 Peter, 2:21.
623 Cod. τὸ.
624 Cf. Matt. 7:14.

> Ἀρχὴ ἀρετῆς τὸ εὔχεσθαι γνωρισθῆναί τινι τὴν ὁδὸν τῆς δικαιοσύνης, δεύτερος βαθμὸς τὸ ζητεῖν πῶς δεῖ ὁδεῦσαι τὴν ὁδόν, τρίτος τὸ ἁψάμενον τῆς ἀρετῆς κρούειν τῷ Χριστῷ, ἵνα ἀνοίξῃ αὐτῷ τὴν θύραν καὶ ἀπαλλάξῃ τῆς στενῆς ὁδοῦ καὶ τεθλιμμένης καὶ εἰσαγάγῃ αὐτὸν εἰς τὴν εὐρύχωρον γνωστικὴν ἐργασίαν, ἅπερ πάντα διὰ τῆς ἐκ Θεοῦ καὶ πρὸς Θεὸν δεήσεως λαμβάνει τις. ἴσως δὲ καὶ τὸ μετὰ πράξεως αἰτεῖν καὶ πρὸς Θεὸν αὐτῷ ᾐνίξατο διὰ τοῦ εἰπεῖν. *κρούσατε*. κρούει γάρ τις τῇ δεξιᾷ χειρί, ἀγαθῆς δὲ πράξεως σύμβολον ἡ δεξιὰ χείρ. [εἰ δὲ μὴ εὐθέως λαμβάνεις, μηδὲ οὕτως ἀπογνῷς. διὰ γὰρ τοῦτο εἶπεν *κρούετε*, ὅτι κἂν μὴ εὐθέως ἀνοίξῃ τὴν θύραν, παραμένειν δεῖ. εἰ δὲ ἀπιστεῖς μου τῇ ἀποφάσει κἂν τῷ ὑποδείγματι πίστευσον.][cdxci]

> Ἀρχὴ τῆς ἀρετῆς τὸ εὔχεσθαι γνωρισθῆναί τινι τὴν ὁδὸν τῆς ἀληθείας. δεύτερος βαθμὸς τὸ ζητεῖν πῶς δεῖ ὁδεῦσαι τὴν ὁδόν. τρίτος τὸ ἁψάμενον τῆς ἀρετῆς κρούειν τῷ Χριστῷ, ἵνα ἀνοίξῃ αὐτῷ τὴν θύραν καὶ ἀπαλλαγῇ τῆς στενῆς ὁδοῦ καὶ τεθλιμμένης καὶ εἰσαγάγῃ αὐτὸν εἰς τὴν εὐρύχωρον γνωστικὴν ἐργασίαν, ἅπερ πάντα διὰ τῆς ἐκ θεοῦ καὶ πρὸς θεὸν δεήσεως λαμβάνει τις. ἴσως δὲ καὶ τὸ μετὰ πράξεως αἰτεῖν ᾐνίξατο διὰ τοῦ εἰπεῖν. *κρούετε*. κρούει γάρ τις τῇ δεξιᾷ χειρί. ἀγαθῆς δὲ πράξεως σύμβολον ἡ δεξιὰ χείρ. εἰ δὲ μὴ εὐθέως λαμβάνεις, μηδὲ οὕτως ἀπογνῷς. διὰ γὰρ τοῦτο εἶπεν *κρούετε*.[cdxcii]

Τίς γάρ ἐστιν ἐξ ὑμῶν ἄνθρωπος, ὃν ἐὰν αἰτήσῃ ὁ υἱός αὐτοῦ ἄρτον μὴ λίθον ἐπιδώσει αὐτῷ;[625] Δύο εἰσάγει ἐνταῦθα· τὸ αἰτεῖν σφοδρῶς καὶ τὸ αἰτεῖν ἃ χρή. Οἱ γὰρ μὴ νηφαλίως καὶ ἃ χρὴ αἰτοῦντες οὐ πάντως λαμβάνουσι. Καὶ γὰρ καὶ ὑμεῖς πατέρες ὄντες, φησί, μένετε αἰτῆσαι τοὺς υἱούς. Κἂν ἀσύμφορόν τι παρ᾽ ὑμῶν αἰτήσωσι, κωλύετε τὴν δόσιν, ὥσπερ ἐὰν συμφέρον, ἐπινεύετε καὶ παρέχετε.

> Δύο τοίνυν εἶναι χρὴ τῷ εὐχομένῳ, καὶ τὸ αἰτεῖν σφοδρῶς, καὶ τὸ ἃ χρὴ αἰτεῖν. ἐπεὶ καὶ ὑμεῖς, φησί, κἂν πατέρες ἦτε, μένετε αἰτῆσαι τοὺς υἱούς. κἂν ἀσύμφορόν τι παρ᾽ ὑμῶν αἰτήσωσι, κωλύετε τὴν δόσιν. ὥσπερ οὖν ἐὰν συμφέρον, ἐπινεύετε καὶ παρέχετε.[cdxciii]

Οὕτω καὶ ὁ Θεός, ἐὰν μηδὲν αἰτήσωμεν κοσμικὸν ἀλλὰ πνευματικόν, ἐπινεύει καὶ παρέχει. Φιλοστοργότερος γὰρ ὁ Θεός ἐστι περὶ ἡμᾶς, ὑπὲρ τοὺς παραγαγόντας ἡμᾶς πατέρας. Ὅσον γὰρ πρὸς σύγκρισιν τῆς τοῦ Θεοῦ ἀγαθότητος καὶ ἡ ἀπὸ τῶν πατέρων πρὸς τοὺς παῖδας φιλοστοργία[cdxciv] πονηρία εἶναι δοκεῖ. Ἐὰν τοιαῦτα αἰτῇς οἷα καὶ τῷ αἰτουμένῳ δοῦναι πρέπει καὶ σοὶ τῷ αἰτοῦντι συμφέρει λαβεῖν, λήψῃ πάντως.[cdxcv]

Ὅρα δὲ καὶ εἰ ἄρτος μὲν | **53r** ἡ ἀναγκαία τῆς ψυχῆς ἐστιν ἐν γνώσει τροφή,[cdxcvi] ἧς ἄνευ οὐκ ἔστι σώζεσθαι, οἷον ὁ περὶ τοῦ πῶς βιωτέον[cdxcvii] ἀκριβὴς λόγος. Ἰχθὺς δὲ ἡ οἷον ὄψον φιλομάθεια *τοῦ εἰδέναι σύστασιν κόσμου, ἐνέργειαν στοιχείων, ἀρχὴν καὶ τέλος καὶ μεσότητα ‹χρόνων›*[626] καὶ ὅσα ἑξῆς ἡ Σοφία καταλέγει. Οὔτε οὖν ἀντὶ ἄρτου *λίθον*[627] δίδωσιν ὁ Θεὸς (ὃν ὁ διάβολος ἐβούλετο ὑπὸ Ἰησοῦ ἐσθίεσθαι) οὔτε ἀντὶ ἰχθύος *ὄφιν*, ὃν ἐσθίουσιν οἱ ἀνάξιοι τοῦ ἰχθῦν ἐσθίειν Αἰθίοπες.

---

625 Matt. 7:9.
626 Wisdom of Solomon, 7:18-19.
627 Cf. Matt. 4:3; 7:9.

Ταῦτα τῷ *αἰτεῖτε* ἐπιφέρεται προτρεπόμενα θαρρεῖν ἐν τῷ εὔχεσθαι. ὅρα δὲ εἰ ἄρτος μὲν ἡ ἀναγκαία τῆς ψυχῆς ἐν γνώσει τροφή, ἧς ἄνευ οὐκ ἔστι σώζεσθαι, οἷον ὁ περὶ τοῦ πῶς βιωτέον ἀκριβὴς λόγος. ἰχθῦς δὲ ἡ οἷον ὄψον φιλομάθεια, οἷον τὸ *εἰδέναι σύστασιν κόσμου, ἐνέργειαν στοιχείων, ἀρχὴν καὶ τέλος καὶ μεσότητα χρόνων* καὶ ὅσα ἑξῆς ἡ Σοφία καταλέγει. οὔτε οὖν ἀντὶ ἄρτου *λίθον* δίδωσιν ὁ Θεός, (ὃν ὁ διάβολος ἐσθίεσθαι ὑπὸ Ἰησοῦ ἐβούλετο), οὔτε ἀντὶ ἰχθύος *ὄφιν*, ὃν ἐσθίουσιν οἱ ἀνάξιοι τοῦ ἰχθῦν ἐσθίειν Αἰθίοπες. *ἐκεῖ* (γάρ φησιν ο Ψαλμός) *συνέθλασας τὰς κεφαλὰς τοῦ δράκοντος, ἔδωκας αὐτὸν βρῶμα λαοῖς τοῖς Αἰθίοψιν.*[cdxcviii]

Σὺ δὲ ὅρα, εἰ *ἄρτος* μὲν ἡ ἀναγκαία τῆς ψυχῆς ἐν γνώσει τροφή, ἧς ἄνευ οὐκ ἔστι σώζεσθαι. οἷον ὁ περὶ τοῦ, πῶς βιωτέον ἀκριβὴς λόγος. ἰχθὺς δὲ ἢ οἷον ὄψον φιλομάθεια. οἷον *τὸ εἰδέναι σύστασιν κόσμου, ἐνέργειαν στοιχείων, ἀρχὴν καὶ τέλος καὶ μεσότητα χρόνων*, καὶ ὅσα ἑξῆς ἡ σοφία καταλέγει. Οὕτως οὖν *ἀντὶ ἄρτου λίθον* οὐ δίδωσιν ὁ Θεός, ὃν ὁ διάβολος ἐβούλετο ὑπὸ Ἰησοῦ ἐσθίεσθαι. οὔτε ἀντὶ ἰχθύος ὄφιν, ὃν ἐσθίουσιν οἱ ἀνάξιοι τοῦ ἰχθύας ἐσθίειν Αἰθίοπες. *Ἐκεῖ* γάρ, φησὶν ὁ Ψαλμῳδός, *σὺ συνέθλασας τὴν κεφαλὴν τοῦ δράκοντος ἐπὶ τοῦ ὕδατος, ἔδωκας αὐτὸν βρῶμα λαοῖς τοῖς Αἰθίοψιν.* οὔτε ἁπλῶς ἀντὶ τροφίμου καὶ ὠφελοῦντος τὰ ἄβρωτα καὶ βλάπτοντα.[cdxcix]

Εἰ οὖν ὑμεῖς πονηροὶ ὄντες.[628] Ταῦτα ἔλεγεν, οὐ διαβάλλων τὴν ἀνθρωπίνην φύσιν οὐδὲ κακίζων τὸ γένος, ἀλλὰ πρὸς ἀντιδιαστολὴν τῆς ἀγαθότητος αὐτοῦ τὴν πνευματικὴν φιλοστοργίαν[d] πονηρίαν καλῶν. Τοσαύτη αὐτοῦ τῆς φιλανθρωπίας ἡ ὑπερβολή.

Ταῦτα ἔλεγεν, οὐ διαβάλλων τὴν ἀνθρωπίνην φύσιν, οὐδὲ κακίζων τὸ γένος, ἀλλὰ πρὸς ἀντιδιαστολὴν τῆς ἀγαθότητος τῆς αὐτοῦ, τὴν φιλοστοργίαν τὴν πατρικὴν πονηρίαν καλῶν. Τοσαύτη αὐτοῦ τῆς φιλανθρωπίας ἡ ὑπερβολή.[di]

Δώσει ἀγαθὰ τοῖς αἰτοῦσιν[629] (added on the margin).[dii] Ὅρα πῶς τοὺς μαθητὰς πονηροὺς ἐκάλεσεν; Εἰ γὰρ καὶ ἠκολούθησαν ἐκ προαιρέσεως, ἀλλ᾽ εἶχον τὸ τρεπτὸν τοῦ ἀνθρωπίνου νοῦ. Μόνος δὲ ἄτρεπτος ἦν καὶ θεότητι καὶ ἀνθρωπότητι ὁ τοῦ Θεοῦ Υἱός.

Πῶς δὲ τοὺς μαθητὰς πονηροὺς ἐκάλεσεν; εἰ γὰρ καὶ ἠκολούθησαν αὐτῷ, ἀλλ᾽ εἶχον τὸ τρεπτὸν τοῦ ἀνθρωπίνου νοῦ.[diii]

Πῶς δὲ τοὺς μαθητὰς πονηροὺς ἐκάλεσεν; Εἰ γὰρ καὶ ἠκολούθουν ἐκ προαιρέσεως, ἀλλ᾽ εἶχον τὸ τρεπτὸν τοῦ ἀνθρωπίνου. Μόνον δὲ ἄτρεπτος ἦν καὶ θεότητι καὶ ἀνθρωπότητι ὁ τοῦ Θεοῦ Υἱός.[div]

It should be noticed that he called the apostles 'evil'. It is possible, however, that in the persons of the apostles he is reprehending the entire human race, whose *heart from his youth is intently bent upon evil*[630] in comparison with the divine mercy.[dv]

628 Matt. 7:11.
629 Matt. 7:11.
630 Cf. Gen. 8:21 and 6:5.

(ΩΡΙΓΕΝΟΥΣ main text cont.) *Δόματα ἀγαθά*[631] καλεῖ τὰς πνευματικὰς δωρεάς. Ὁ δὲ Λουκᾶς *Πνεῦμα Ἅγιον* εἶπεν,[632] ἀντὶ τοῦ εἰπεῖν *ἀγαθά*. Καὶ οὐδὲν τὸ διάφορον. Τὸ Ἅγιον Πνεῦμα αὐτό ἐστι τὸ φύσει ἀγαθόν, διὸ καὶ τοῖς μετόχοις αὐτοῦ δίδωσιν *ἀγαθά*. Τοῖς δὲ ἄγαν πονηροῖς διὰ τὸ ἀνενδότως ἁμαρτάνειν, τρόπον τινὰ φύσις αὐτοῖς ἡ κακία γίνεται, οἷός ἐστιν ὁ Σατανᾶς καὶ οἱ δαίμονες. Δυνατὸν γὰρ καὶ τούτους φύσει κακοὺς εἰπεῖν, καίπερ μὴ φύσει κακοὺς δημιουργηθέντας, ἀλλ᾽ ἐξ αὐτοπροαιρέτου κακίας[dvi] ἀπεσκληκότας.

> Δόματα δὲ ἀγαθὰ καλεῖ τὰς πνευματικὰς δωρεάς. Ὁ δὲ Λουκᾶς Πνεῦμα ἅγιον εἶπεν, ἀντὶ τοῦ εἰπεῖν ἀγαθά. Καὶ οὐδὲν τὸ διάφορον. Τὸ γὰρ ἅγιον Πνεῦμα αὐτό ἐστι τὸ φῶς ἀγαθόν. διὸ καὶ τοῖς μετόχοις αὐτοῦ δίδωσιν ἀγαθά. Τοῖς δὲ ἄγαν πονηροῖς, διὰ τὸ ἀνενδότως ἁμαρτάνειν τρόπον τινὰ φύσις αὐτοῖς ἡ κακία γίνεται. οἷός ἐστιν ὁ Σατανᾶς καὶ οἱ δαίμονες. Δύναται γάρ τις καὶ τούτους φύσει κακοὺς εἰπεῖν, καίπερ μὴ φύσει κακοὺς δημιουργηθέντας, ἀλλ᾽ ἐξ αὐτοπροαιρέτου κακίας ἀπεσκληκότας.[dvii]

> [*δόματα* δὲ *ἀγαθὰ* καλεῖ τὰς πνευματικὰς δωρεάς, ὁ δὲ Λουκᾶς *πνεῦμα ἅγιον* εἶπεν, ἀντὶ τοῦ εἰπεῖν *ἀγαθά*. καὶ οὐδὲν τὸ διάφορον. τὸ γὰρ ἅγιον πνεῦμα αὐτό ἐστι τὸ φύσει ἀγαθόν, διὸ καὶ τοῖς μετόχοις αὐτοῦ δίδωσιν *ἀγαθά*. τοῖς δὲ ἄγαν πονηροῖς διὰ τὸ ἀνενδότως ἁμαρτάνειν τρόπον τινὰ φύσις αὐτοῖς ἡ κακία γίνεται, οἷός ἐστιν ὁ σατανᾶς καὶ οἱ δαίμονες. δύναται γὰρ καὶ τούτους φύσει κακοὺς εἰπεῖν, καίπερ μὴ φύσει κακοὺς δημιουργηθέντας, ἀλλ᾽ ἐξ αὐτοπροαιρέτου κακίας ἀπεσκληκότας.][dviii]

> *Δόματα* δὲ *ἀγαθὰ* καλεῖ τὰς πνευματικὰς δωρεάς, ὁ δὲ Λουκᾶς *πνεῦμα ἅγιον* εἶπεν ἀντὶ τοῦ εἰπεῖν *ἀγαθά*. καὶ οὐδὲν τὸ διάφορον. τὸ γὰρ *ἅγιον πνεῦμα* αὐτό ἐστι τὸ φύσει ἀγαθόν. διὸ καὶ τοῖς μετόχοις δίδωσιν *ἀγαθά*. τοῖς δὲ ἄγαν πονηροῖς διὰ τὸ ἀνενδότως ἁμαρτάνειν τρόπον τινὰ φύσις αὐτοῖς ἡ κακία γίνεται, οἷός ἐστιν ὁ σατανᾶς καὶ οἱ δαίμονες. δύναται γάρ τις καὶ τούτους φύσει κακοὺς εἰπεῖν, καίπερ μὴ φύσει κακοὺς δημιουργηθέντας, ἀλλ᾽ ἐξ αὐτοπροαιρέτου κακίας ἀπεσκληκότας.[dix]

18

54v *Οὐ δύναται δένδρον ἀγαθὸν καρποὺς πονηροὺς ποιεῖν.*[633] **55r** (ΩΡΙΓΕΝΟΥΣ) Ἐν ᾧ καλὸν τὸ *δένδρον* καὶ ὁ καρπός· ἐν ᾧ *σαπρὸν* τὸ *δένδρον* καὶ ὁ καρπός. Καρποὶ δέ εἰσι λογικῶν δένδρων λογικαὶ πράξεις.

> Ἐν ᾧ καλὸν τὸ *δένδρον* καὶ ὁ καρπός. ἐν ᾧ *σαπρὸν* τὸ *δένδρον* καὶ ὁ καρπός. Καρποὶ δέ εἰσι λογικῶν δένδρων λογικαὶ πράξεις.[dx]

631 Matt. 7:11.
632 Luke, 11:3.
633 Matt. 7:18.

Οὐ πᾶς ὁ λέγων μοι Κύριε Κύριε εἰσελεύσεται.[634] Ὁ μὴ τῇ ἕξει ποιωθεὶς τῆς βασιλείας οὐκ *εἰσελεύσεται* ἐν αὐτῇ. Ἕξιν δὲ κτήσασθαι λόγῳ οὐκ ἔστιν, ἀλλ᾽ ἢ πράξει.

> Ὁ μὴ τῇ ἕξει ποιωθεὶς τῆς βασιλείας οὐκ *εἰσελεύσεται* ἐν αὐτῇ. Ἕξιν δὲ κτήσασθαι λόγῳ οὐκ ἔστιν ἀλλ᾽ ἢ πράξει.[dxi]

Τὸ εἰπεῖν *Κύριε* τῷ Χριστῷ πίστεώς ἐστι μόνης τεκμήριον. Οὐ μόνη δὲ πίστις ἄνευ ἔργων εἰσάγει εἰς *βασιλείαν οὐρανῶν*, ὥσπερ οὐδὲ ἔργα δίχα πίστεως.
Καὶ μὴν οὐδεὶς δύναται εἰπεῖν *Κύριο‹ς› Ἰησοῦ‹ς›*,[635] *εἰ μὴ ἐν Πνεύματι Ἁγίῳ.*[636] Τοῦτο δέ φημι τὸ ἐν ἔργοις λέγειν Κύριον.

> Οὐδεὶς δύναται εἰπεῖν *κύριε κύριε εἰ μὴ ἐν Πνεύματι Ἁγίῳ.* ἀλλὰ τὸ τοιοῦτον ἐν ἔργοις ἐστίν, οὐ μὴν ἐν λόγοις, ὥς τινες ὑπολαμβάνουσι.[dxii]
>
> For both [sc. words and deeds] are necessary to God's servants, so that the deeds are attested by words, and one's confirmed are proven by their deeds. However, this might appear to be controverted by [the passage], *No one can say 'Jesus is Lord', but by the Holy Spirit.*[dxiii]

Ἀλλ᾽ ὁ ποιῶν τὸ θέλημα τοῦ πατρός μου.[637] | **55v** Οὗτος τῆς βασιλείας ἀπολαύει *τῶν οὐρανῶν*, ὅστις ἂν ἐπὶ τῶν ἔργων δείξῃ τὴν οἰκειότητα, ταῦτα διδάσκων τε καὶ *ποιῶν* ἃ καὶ παρὼν αὐτὸς παρέδωκα τοῖς ἀνθρώποις.

> Οὗτος τῆς βασιλείας ἀπολαύει τῶν οὐρανῶν, ὅστις ἂν ἐπὶ τῶν ἔργων δείξῃ τὴν οἰκειότητα, ταῦτα διδάσκων τε καὶ ποιῶν ἃ καὶ παρὼν αὐτὸς παρέδωκα τοῖς ἀνθρώποις.[dxiv]
>
> Οὗτος γὰρ *τῆς βασιλείας* ἀπολαύει *τῶν οὐρανῶν*, ὅστις ἂν ἐπὶ τῶν ἔργων δείξῃ τὴν οἰκειότητα ταῦτα διδάσκων τε καὶ ποιῶν, ἃ καὶ παρὼν αὐτὸς παρέδωκε τοῖς ἀνθρώποις.[dxv]

Οὐκ εἶπε δὲ *ὁ ποιῶν τὸ θέλημα* μου, ἀλλὰ *τοῦ πατρός μου*, ἵνα μὴ δόξῃ φιλοδοξεῖν. Ἄλλως τε δὲ καὶ τοῦτο δι᾽ ἐκείνου ᾐνίξατο.
Οὐδὲ γάρ ἐστιν ἕτερον θέλημα τοῦ Υἱοῦ παρὰ τὸ τοῦ Πατρός.

> Μετὰ δὲ τούτων κἀκεῖνό ἐστιν εἰπεῖν, ὅτι οὐδέ ἐστιν ἕτερον θέλημα τοῦ Υἱοῦ παρὰ τὸ τοῦ Πατρός.[dxvi]

---

634 Matt. 7:21.
635 Cod. $\overline{Κν}$ $\overline{Ιν}$.
636 1 Cor. 12:3.
637 Matt. 7:21.

Πολλοί ἐροῦσι μοι ἐν ἐκείνῃ τῇ ἡμέρα· Κύριε, οὐ τῷ σῷ ὀνόματι.[638] Τοῦτο λέγεται πρὸς αὐτοὺς τοὺς ψευδοπροφήτας. Εἰσὶ δὲ οἱ τὸ ὄνομα μὲν ἔχοντες, τοῖς δὲ ἔργοις ἀρνούμενοι. Διὸ ἀρνεῖται αὐτούς, ἐπεὶ ἠρνήσατο αὐτὸν πᾶσα αἵρεσις, καὶ οὐχ ὁμολογεῖ αὐτούς, ἀλλὰ λέγει· *ἀποχωρεῖτε ἀπ᾽ ἐμοῦ οἱ ἐργαζόμενοι τὴν ἀνομίαν.*[639] *Τοῖς* γὰρ *χείλεσί με* ἐτιμήσατε, *ἡ δὲ καρδία* ὑμῶν *πόρρω ἀπέχει ἀπ᾽ ἐμοῦ. Μάτην δὲ* ‹ἐ›σέβεσθέ *με, διδάσκοντες διδασκαλίας ἀνθρώπων.*[640]

> Τοῦτο λέγεται πρὸς αὐτοὺς τοὺς ψευδοπροφήτας, εἰσὶ δὲ οἱ τὸ ὄνομα μὲν ἔχοντες, τοῖς δὲ ἔργοις ἀρνούμενοι. διὸ ἀρνεῖται αὐτούς, ἐπεὶ ἠρνήσατο αὐτὸν πᾶσα αἵρεσις, καὶ οὐχ ὁμολογεῖ αὐτούς, ἀλλὰ λέγει. *ἀποχωρεῖτε ἀπ᾽ ἐμοῦ οἱ ἐργαζόμενοι τὴν ἀνομίαν. Τοῖς* γὰρ *χείλεσί με* ἐτιμήσατε, *ἡ δὲ καρδία* ὑμῶν, *πόρρω ἀπέχει ἀπ᾽ ἐμοῦ. μάτην δὲ ἐσέβεσθέ με, διδάσκοντες διδασκαλίας ἀνθρώπων.*[dxvii]

Ὁ λόγος κατὰ τῶν ἐν ἀρχῇ πιστευσάντων ὀρθῶς καὶ σημεῖα πεποιηκότων καὶ ὕστερον τραπέντων, οὓς καὶ ἐν ἴσῳ τοῖς οὐδὲ ὅλως ἐγνωσμένοις τίθησι. Διό φησι τὸ *οὐκ οἶδα ὑμᾶς.*[641] Τινὲς δέ φασι ὅτι ψευδόμενοι τοῦτο εἶπον, διόπερ οὐδὲ ἐσώθησαν. Ὅτι δὲ οὐκ ἔστι τοῦτο, αὐτὴ ἡ ἀπόκρισις καὶ τὸ κατ᾽ ἐρώτησιν λέγειν δείκνυσιν αὐτοὺς πεποιηκότας ταῦτα. Πολλοὶ γὰρ τῶν πιστευσάντων ἔλαβον χαρίσματα πονηροὶ ὄντες, οἷος ἦν ὁ τὰ δαιμόνια ἐκβάλλων καὶ οὐκ ὢν μετ᾽ αὐτοῦ, καὶ οἷος ἦν ὁ Ἰούδας. Καὶ ἐν τῇ παλαιᾷ δὲ εὕροι τις ἂν καὶ εἰς ἀναξίους τὴν χάριν ἐνεργήσασαν πολλάκις δι᾽ ὠφέλειαν | **56r** ἑτέρων. Πολλοὶ γὰρ ἄπιστοι τότε προεφήτευσαν, οἷον ὁ Βαλαὰμ καὶ Φαραὼ καὶ Ναβουχοδουνόσορ.[642] Ἐπειδὴ γὰρ μετὰ τὴν οἰκονομίαν οὐ πάντες ἐπιτηδείως εἶχον πρὸς πάντα, ἀλλ᾽ οἱ μὲν ἦσαν βίου καθαροῦ, πίστιν δὲ οὐ τοσαύτην εἶχον, οἱ δὲ τοὐναντίον, κἀκείνους διὰ τούτων προτρέπει ὥστε πολλὴν ἐνδείξασθαι πίστιν καὶ τούτους διὰ ταύτης τῆς δωρεᾶς ὥστε γενέσθαι βελτίους. Οὐ γὰρ δὴ μόνον ὁ πίστιν ἔχων τοῦ βίου ἠμελημένου τῆς *τῶν οὐρανῶν* ἐκβάλλεται *βασιλείας*· ἀλλὰ κἂν μετὰ τῆς πίστεως καὶ σημεῖα πεποιηκὼς ἢ οὐδὲν ἀγαθὸν ἐργασάμενος, ὡσαύτως ἐκβάλλεται. Τὸ γὰρ προφητεῦσαι καὶ σημεῖα ποιῆσαι θείας ἐστὶ χάριτος καὶ οὐδὲν ὠφελεῖ τὸν μὴ ἄλλην τινὰ ἐνάρετον ἔχοντα πολιτείαν ταῦτα, ἀλλὰ μᾶλλον εἰς κατάκρισιν πλείονα ἄγει. Ὅτι περὶ τὸν οὕτω τιμήσαντα ὥστε καὶ ἀναξίοις δοῦναι τὴν χάριν, ἀγνώμονες γεγόνασιν ‹καὶ›

---

638 Matt. 7:22.

639 Matt. 7:23.

640 Matt. 15:8-9; Mark, 7:6. Is. 29:13.

641 Matt. 25:12.

642 Cf. Balaam: Num. 23:5; 23:12; 23:16; 24:2-3; 24:15-17. Nebuchadnezzar: Daniel, 2:31-45. Pharaoh: Gen. 41.

τῷ ὀνόματι Κυρίου τινὲς προεφήτευσαν ‹ὄντες ἀνάξιοι›, Βαλαὰμ καὶ Σαοὺλ[643] *καὶ* Καϊάφας,[644] *καὶ δαιμόνια* ἐξέβαλον, ὡς Ἰούδας[645] καὶ υἱοὶ Σκευᾶ.[646]

> τινὲς προεφήτευσαν ἐν τῷ ὀνόματι τοῦ Χριστοῦ ὄντες ἀνάξιοι, Βαλαὰμ καὶ Σαοὺλ καὶ Καϊάφας, καὶ *δαιμόνια* ἐξέβαλον ὡς Ἰούδας καὶ υἱοὶ Σκευᾶ.[dxviii]

> There are occasions when to prophesy and to work miracles and to expel daemons does not stem from the merit of him who does them; instead, it is either the invocation of the name of Christ that does it, or it is granted because of the condemnation of those who invoke his name, or for the benefit of those who see and hear him. Therefore, although men may be seeing those who are doing the miracles, nevertheless, they should glorify God, at whose invocation such great wonders are being done. For Saul and Balaam and Caiaphas prophesied without knowing what they were saying. Pharaoh and Nebuchadnezzar knew the future owing to dreams; and in the Acts of the Apostles the sons of Sceva appeared to expel daemons. It is also narrated that the apostle Judas, with the heart of a traitor, did many miracles along with the other apostles.[dxix]

Καὶ τότε ὁμολογήσω αὐτοῖς.[647] Τότε, πότε; Ὅτε ἐκεῖνοι τὰ δοκοῦντα πράξουσι δίκαια· τὸ προφητεῦσαι, τὸ δαιμόνια πολλὰ ἐκβαλεῖν, τὸ δυνάμεις πολλὰς ἐπιτελέσαι. Ἐκ γὰρ τῶν τοιούτων δικαιωμάτων μᾶλλον ἕλκουσιν ἑαυτοῖς τὴν καταδίκην. Οἵ γὰρ οὓς ἐχρῆν τοσούτων ἀπολαύσαντας χαρισμάτων βίον κατάλληλον σπουδάζειν κτήσασθαι, ἵνα καὶ τὸν δεδωκότα διὰ τῶν ἔργων δοξάσωσι καὶ αὐτοὺς ἀξίους τῆς δωρεᾶς | **56v** ἐπιδείξωσιν. Οἱ δὲ τἀναντία δεδρακότες καὶ βλασφημεῖσθαι μὲν τῷ ὀνόματι *τοῦ Θεοῦ*[648] αἴτιοι γεγονότες ἀναξίους δὲ τῶν εὐεργεσιῶν ἑαυτοὺς ἀποφήναντες, οὗτοι δέον ἐγκαλύπτεσθαι καὶ σκυθρωπάζειν ὅτι τὴν δεσποτικὴν ἐνύβρισαν δωρεάν. ‹Ε›ἰ[649] δὲ καὶ ἐπ' αὐτῇ μέγα φρονοῦσι καὶ ἀξιοῦσι προάγειν αὐτὴν εἰς δικαίωμα, πῶς οὐ μυρίων κακῶν ἐνόχους ἑαυτοὺς δεικνύουσι; Διὸ καὶ ὁ δεσπότης ἀποτόμως φησὶ πρὸς αὐτούς· *οὐδέποτε ἔγνων ὑμᾶς.*[650] Οὐ γὰρ νῦν ὑμᾶς φησι ἀποστρέφομαι, ἀλλ' οὐδὲ κατὰ τὸν καιρὸν ἐκεῖνον ἔστεργον ὑμᾶς, καθ' ὃν τοῦ χαρίσματος ἀπολαύοντες διὰ τῆς τοῦ βίου μοχθηρίας ἀχαριστίᾳ με ἠμείβεσθε. Ἀλλ' οὖν εἰς τὸν παρόντα καιρὸν τὴν τιμωρίαν ἀνεβαλόμην, τὴν ἐπιστροφὴν ὑμῶν ἐκδεχόμενος. Ἐπεὶ δὲ οὐ μετεμελήθητε παρ' ὅλον τὸν τῆς ζωῆς ὑμῶν χρόνον, νῦν *ἀποχωρεῖτε ἐξ ἐμοῦ.*[651]

---

643 Cf. 1 Kings, 10:11.
644 Cf. John, 11:50-51.
645 Cf. Matt. 10:4-8; Mark, 3:19.
646 Acts, 19:14-16.
647 Matt. 7:23.
648 Cf. Rom. 2:24.
649 Cod. οἱ.
650 Matt. 7:23.
651 Matt. 7:23.

Τότε, πότε; ὅτε ἐκεῖνοι τὰ δοκοῦντα προάξουσι δίκαια, τὸ προφητεῦσαι, τὸ δαιμόνια πολλὰ ἐκβαλεῖν, τὸ δυνάμεις πολλὰς ἐπιτελέσαι. ἐκ γὰρ τῶν αὐτοῖς δικαιωμάτων μᾶλλον ἕλκουσιν ἑαυτοῖς τὴν καταδίκην. οἱ γὰρ οὓς ἐχρῆν τοσούτων ἀπολαύσαντας χαρισμάτων βίον κατάλληλον σπουδάζειν κεκτῆσθαι, ἵνα καὶ τὸν δεδωκότα διὰ τῶν ἔργων δοξάσωσιν καὶ αὐτοὺς ἀξίους τῆς δωρεᾶς ἐπιδείξωσιν, οἱ δὲ τἀναντία δεδρακότες καὶ βλασφημεῖσθαι μὲν τὸ ὄνομα τοῦ θεοῦ αἴτιοι γεγονότες (ἵνα τί γὰρ *τὸ ὄνομα τοῦ θεοῦ δι᾽ ὑμᾶς βλασφημεῖται ἐν τοῖς ἔθνεσιν*[652]), ἀναξίους δὲ τῶν εὐεργεσιῶν ἑαυτοὺς ἀποφήναντες, οὗτοι δέον αὐτοὺς ἐγκαλύπτεσθαι καὶ σκυθρωπάζειν, ὅτι τὴν δεσποτικὴν ἐνύβρισαν δωρεάν, οἱ δὲ καὶ ἐπ᾽ αὐτῇ μέγα φρονοῦσι καὶ ἀξιοῦσιν προάγειν αὐτὰ εἰς δικαίωμα, πῶς οὐ μυρίων κακῶν ἐνόχους ‹ἑαυτοὺς› δεικνύουσιν; διὸ καὶ ὁ δεσπότης ἀποτόμως φησὶν πρὸς αὐτούς. *οὐδέποτε ἔγνων ὑμᾶς. ἀποχωρεῖτε ἀπ᾽ ἐμοῦ οἱ ἐργαζόμενοι τὴν ἀνομίαν.* οὐ γὰρ νῦν, φησίν, ὑμᾶς ἀποστρέφομαι καὶ βδελύσσομαι, ἀλλ᾽ οὐδὲ κατὰ τὸν καιρὸν ἐκεῖνον ἔστεργον ὑμᾶς, καθ᾽ ὃν τοῦ χαρίσματος ἀπολαύοντες διὰ τῆς τοῦ βίου μοχθηρίας ἀχαριστίᾳ με ἠμείβεσθε. ἀλλ᾽ οὖν εἰς τὸν παρόντα καιρὸν τὴν τιμωρίαν ἀνεβαλόμην τὴν ἐπιστροφὴν ὑμῶν ἐκδεχόμενος. ἐπεὶ δὲ οὐ μετεμελήθητε παρ᾽ ὅλον τὸν τῆς ζωῆς ὑμῶν χρόνον, νῦν *ἀποχωρεῖτε ἐξ ἐμοῦ.*[dxx]

(ΤΟΥ ΑΥΤΟΥ [ΩΡΙΓΕΝΟΥΣ]) *πᾶς οὖν ὅστις ἀκούει μου τοὺς λόγους τούτους.*[653] Σημείωσαι ὅτι τὸ μὲν γενέσθαι φρόνιμον οὐκ ἔστιν ἄνευ τῆς τοῦ Θεοῦ συνεργίας καὶ ἐπιπνοίας. Διό φησι, ὁμοιώσω αὐτὸν *ἀνδρὶ φρονίμῳ*,[654] ἀντὶ τοῦ συναντιλήψομαι καὶ συνεργήσω εἰς τὸ τὰ παρ᾽ αὐτοῦ οἰκοδομηθέντα μὴ διαπεσεῖν μηδὲ διαφθαρῆναι. Ἐπὶ δὲ τοῦ μωροῦ, οὐκέτι *ὁμοιώσω*,[655] ἀλλ᾽ *ὁμοιωθήσεται*,[656] οἷον αὐτὸς ἑαυτῷ αἴτιος ἔσται τῆς θρασύτητος καὶ τῆς μωρίας. Ὅτι δέον ἀρετὴν διώκοντα τῆς τοῦ Θεοῦ βασιλείας ἐπιτυχεῖν, αὐτὸς δὲ κακίαν μετιὼν ἐντὸς ἑαυτὸν ποιεῖ τῆς κολάσεως. Οὕτως ἡ μὲν τῶν ἀρετῶν κτῆσις | **57r** ἡμετέρᾳ σπουδῇ καὶ τῇ τοῦ Θεοῦ κατορθοῦται χάριτι, ἡ δὲ τῆς κακίας πρᾶξις γνώμης μοχθηρίᾳ καὶ προαιρέσεως παρατροπῇ ἐπιγίνεται.

Σημειωτέον ὅτι τὸ μὲν γενέσθαι *φρόνιμον οὐκ* ἔστιν ἄνευ τῆς τοῦ θεοῦ συνεργίας καὶ ἐπιπνοίας. διό φησιν. *ὁμοιώσω αὐτὸν ἀνδρὶ φρονίμῳ* ἀντὶ τοῦ συναντιλήψομαι καὶ συνεργήσω εἰς τὸ τὰ παρ᾽ αὐτοῦ οἰκοδομηθέντα μὴ διαπεσεῖν μηδὲ διαφθαρῆναι. ἐπὶ δὲ *τοῦ μωροῦ* οὐκέτι ὁμοιώσω, ἀλλ᾽ *ὁμοιωθήσεται*, οἷον αὐτὸς ἑαυτῷ αἴτιος ἔσται τῆς ἀφροσύνης καὶ τιμωρίας, ὅτι δὲ τὸν ἀρετὴν διώκοντα τῆς παρὰ τοῦ θεοῦ δεδομένης αὐτῷ τυχεῖν βασιλείας ‹ἀγανακτῶν›, αὐτὸς διὰ κακίαν μετιὼν ἐντὸς ἑαυτὸν ποιεῖ τῆς κολάσεως. οὕτως οὖν ἡ μὲν τῶν ἀρετῶν κτῆσις ἡμετέρᾳ τε σπουδῇ καὶ τῇ τοῦ θεοῦ κατορθοῦται χάριτι, ἡ δὲ τῆς κακίας πρᾶξις γνώμης μοχθηρίᾳ καὶ προαιρέσεως παρατροπῇ ἐπιγίνεται.[dxxi]

Δεῖ τὸν ἀκούοντα συνιέναι τῶν λεγομένων· ἡ γὰρ σύνεσις φρόνησιν παρέχει καὶ ταύτῃ τὸ ἔργον ἀκολουθεῖ, καὶ οἰκοδομεῖ λίθους ἐκλεκτοὺς ἐπὶ τὸν τῶν *προφητῶν καὶ*

652 Is. 52:5, quoted in Rom. 2:24.
653 Matt. 7:24.
654 Matt. 7:24.
655 Matt. 7:24.
656 Matt. 7:26.

ἀποστόλων θεμέλιον,[657] περὶ οὗ λέγει· *ἐὰν μὴ Κύριος οἰκοδομήσῃ οἶκον, εἰς μάτην ἐκοπίασαν οἱ οἰκοδομοῦντες αὐτόν*.[658] *Δόξα καὶ πλοῦτος ἔσται ἐν τῷ οἴκῳ*[659] τούτῳ. Αὐτὸς δὲ ὁ οἶκος ἐκ τῶν ἐντολῶν τοῦ Θεοῦ οἰκοδομούμενος οἰκητήριον γίνεται τοῦ Θεοῦ· *ἐνοικήσω* γὰρ *ἐν αὐτοῖς καὶ ἐμπεριπατήσω*.[660] Οὗτος *ἐπὶ τὴν πέτραν* ᾠκοδόμηται,[661] *ἡ δὲ πέτρα ἦν ὁ Χριστός*.[662] *Θεμέλιον γὰρ ἄλλον οὐδεὶς δύναται θεῖναι παρὰ τὸν κείμενον, ὅς ἐστι ‹Ἰησοῦς› Χριστός*,[663] τόδε ἀκούων καὶ ποιῶν·[664] *πάντα* γὰρ ὅσα ἐὰν *ποιῆτε*[665] εἴτε διὰ λόγων εἴτε δι᾽ ἔργων, *ἐν ὀνόματι Ἰησοῦ*[666] Χριστοῦ ποιεῖτε.[667] Ἐὰν γὰρ ᾖ ὁ θεμέλιος κείμενος *ἐπὶ τὴν πέτραν*,[668] οὔτε ἄνεμος οὔτε *βροχὴ* οὔτε *ποταμοὶ* δύνανται βλάψαι τὴν οἰκίαν ἐκείνην. Χειμῶνος γίνονται *ποταμοί, ἄνεμοι* καὶ βροχαί.[669] Διὸ εὔχεσθε μὴ γενέσθαι *χειμῶνος* τὴν φυγὴν *ὑμῶν*.[670] Τοῖς γὰρ δικαίοις ὁ αἰὼν οὗτος χειμών ἐστι.[dxxii]

> Δεῖ τὸν ἀκούοντα συνιέναι τῶν λεγομένων. ἡ γὰρ σύνεσις φρόνησιν παρέχει καὶ ταύτῃ τὸ ἔργον ἀκολουθεῖ. καὶ οἰκοδομεῖ λίθους ἐκλεκτοὺς ἐπὶ τὸν τῶν *προφητῶν καὶ ἀποστόλων θεμέλιον*, περὶ οὗ λέγει τό. *ἐὰν μὴ κύριος οἰκοδομήσῃ οἶκον, εἰς μάτην ἐκοπίασαν οἱ οἰκοδομοῦντες αὐτόν. δόξα καὶ πλοῦτος ἔσται ἐν τῷ οἴκω* τούτῳ. αὐτὸς δὲ ὁ οἶκος ἐκ τῶν ἐντολῶν τοῦ θεοῦ οἰκοδομούμενος οἰκητήριον τοῦ θεοῦ γίνεται. *ἐνοικήσω* γὰρ *ἐν αὐτοῖς καὶ ἐμπεριπατήσω*. οὗτος *ἐπὶ τὴν πέτραν* ᾠκοδόμηται, *ἡ δὲ πέτρα, ἦν ὁ Χριστός. θεμέλιον γὰρ ἄλλον οὐδεὶς δύναται θεῖναι παρὰ τὸν κείμενον, ὅς ἐστι Ἰησοῦς Χριστός*. τὸ δὲ ἀκούων καὶ ποιῶν. *πάντα* γὰρ ὅσα ἐὰν *ποιῆτε* εἴτε διὰ λόγου εἴτε δι᾽ ἔργων *ἐν ὀνόματι Ἰησοῦ* Χριστοῦ ποιεῖτε. ἐὰν γὰρ ᾖ ὁ θεμέλιος κείμενος *ἐπὶ τὴν πέτραν*, οὔτε ἄνεμος οὔτε *βροχὴ* οὔτε *ποταμοὶ* δύνανται βλάψαι τὴν οἰκίαν ἐκείνην. χειμῶνος γίνονται *ποταμοί, ἄνεμοι* καὶ *βροχαί*. διὸ εὔχεσθε μὴ *χειμῶνος* γενέσθαι τὴν φυγὴν *ὑμῶν*. τοῖς γὰρ δικαίοις ὁ αἰὼν οὗτος χειμών ἐστιν.[dxxiii]

Ὅστις ᾠκοδόμησε τὴν οἰκίαν αὐτοῦ ἐπὶ τὴν πέτραν.[671] Οἶκον οἰκοδομηθέντα ἀσφαλῶς λέγει τὸν ἐν ἔργῳ καὶ λόγῳ μένοντα ἀκατάλυτον καὶ ἄπτωτον. Ἤτοι οἰκία ἐστὶ τῆς ἀρετῆς ἡ ἐργασία, πέτρα δὲ ἡ πίστις καὶ ἡ ἀσφάλεια τῶν τοῦ Χριστοῦ χαρισμάτων.

---

657 Cf. Eph. 2:20.
658 Psalm 126:1.
659 Psalm 111:3.
660 2 Cor. 6:16, *apud* Lev. 26:12.
661 Cf. Matt. 16:18; 7:24.
662 1 Cor. 10:4.
663 1 Cor. 3:10.
664 Cf. Matt. 7:24.
665 Cod. ποιήσητε.
666 Cf. Col. 3:17.
667 Cf. Col. 3:17.
668 Matt. 7:24.
669 Cf. Matt. 7:27.
670 Matt. 24:20.
671 Matt. 7:24.

Λαμβάνει γὰρ ἐν τῷ νῦν αἰῶνι ὁ ἐνάρετος καὶ πιστὸς | **57v** χάρισμα τὸ ἑδραῖος ἑστάναι καὶ μὴ νικηθῆναι ἐκ πειρασμοῦ. *Ἄνεμοι* δὲ καὶ *ποταμοὶ* καὶ βροχαὶ αἱ τῶν πειρασμῶν περιστάσεις,[dxxiv] τουτέστι πᾶν εἶδος πειρασμοῦ.

Καὶ κατέβη ἡ βροχή.[672] *Βροχή*, ὁ διάβολος· *ποταμοί, οἱ ἀντίχριστοι·*[673] *ἄνεμοι,*[674] *τὰ πνευματικὰ τῆς πονηρίας.*[675]

> Βροχή, ὁ διάβολος, ποταμοί, οἱ ἀντίχριστοι. ἄνεμοι, τὰ πνευματικὰ τῆς πονηρίας.[dxxv]
>
> This rain that tries to undermine the house is the devil; the rivers are all the antichrists who mull over in opposition to Christ; the winds are the spiritual hosts of wickedness in the heavenly places.[dxxvi]

(ΩΡΙΓΕΝΟΥΣ, added on the margin) λέγονται ποταμοὶ καὶ οἱ ἐναντίοι λογισμοί.[dxxvii]

(ΩΡΙΓΕΝΟΥΣ, main text cont.) Μωρὸς ἐπὶ ψάμμου οἰκοδομῶν ἐστι πάντες οἱ ποιοῦντες τὰ ἄνομα. Καὶ γὰρ οὐδὲ αὐτοὶ ἄνευ κόπου ποιοῦσιν. *Ἄμμος* δέ, ἡ κακία. Μεγάλην δὲ λέγει τὴν πτῶσιν τῶν πιστῶν καὶ μετατραπέντων ὡς ἀπὸ ὑψηλοτάτου πύργου πεσόντων. Οἱ γὰρ ἄπιστοι οὐ πίπτουσιν, ἀλλ᾽ ἀεὶ χαμαί εἰσιν.

> Μωρὸς ἐπὶ ψάμμου οἰκοδομῶν ἐστι πάντες οἱ ποιοῦντες τὰ ἄνομα. Καὶ γὰρ οὐδὲ αὐτοὶ ἄνευ κόπου ποιοῦσιν. *Ἄμμος* δέ, ἡ κακία. Μεγάλην δὲ λέγει τὴν πτῶσιν τῶν πιστῶν καὶ μετατραπέντων ὡς ἀπὸ ὑψηλοτάτου πύργου πεσόντων. Οἱ γὰρ ἄπιστοι οὐ πίπτουσιν, ἀλλ᾽ ἀεὶ χαμαί εἰσιν.[dxxviii]

Ὁ γὰρ ἀκροατὴς τῶν λόγων γεγονὼς καὶ οὐ ποιητής, οὗτος ἐν τῇ συντελείᾳ καταπίπτει καὶ χώννυται ἐπὶ τὴν ψάμμον ὡς ὁ *τὸ τάλαντον χώσας*,[676] ὅ ἐστι τὸ τοῦ πνεύματος χάρισμα ἢ τὸ Ἅγιον Πνεῦμα, οὗ στερεῖται ἐν καιρῷ κρίσεως. Οὐ γὰρ οἷόν τε σὺν τῷ πνεύματι παραπεμφθῆναι τινὰ εἰς κόλασιν.

Ὅστις ᾠκοδόμησε τὴν οἰκίαν αὐτοῦ ἐπὶ τὴν ψάμμον.[677] Καλῶς δὲ *μωρὸν* ἐκάλεσε τοῦτον. Τί γὰρ ἂν γένοιτο ἀνοητότερον τοῦ οἰκίαν οἰκοδομοῦντος ἐπὶ ψάμμου, καὶ τὸν μὲν πόνον ὑπομένοντος τοῦ δὲ καρποῦ καὶ τῆς ἀναπαύσεως ἀποστερουμένου, καὶ ἀντὶ τούτου κόλασιν ὑπομένοντος; Ὅτι γὰρ καὶ οἱ κακίαν μετιόντες κάμνουσι παντί που δῆλόν ἐστι, ἀλλ᾽ οὐδὲν ἀπὸ τῶν πόνων τούτων καρποῦνται κέρδος, ἀλλὰ καὶ πολλὴν ὑπομένουσι τὴν ζημίαν. Ὡς γὰρ ὁ Παῦλός φησι, *ὁ σπείρων ἐν τῇ σαρκὶ αὐτοῦ, ἐκ τῆς σαρκὸς θερίσει φθοράν.*[678]

---

672 Matt. 7:25.
673 1 John, 2:18.
674 Matt. 7:24.
675 Eph. 6:12.
676 Matt. 25:25.
677 Matt. 7:26 (ἄμμον).
678 Gal. 6:8.

Καλῶς δὲ μωρὸν ἐκάλεσε τοῦτον. Τί γὰρ ἂν γένοιτο ἀνοητότερον τοῦ οἰκίαν οἰκοδομοῦντος ἐπὶ τῆς ψάμμου, καὶ τὸν μὲν πόνον ὑπομένοντος, τοῦ δὲ καρποῦ καὶ τῆς ἀναπαύσεως ἀποστερουμένου, καὶ ἀντὶ τούτου κόλασιν ὑπομένοντος; Ὅτι γὰρ καὶ οἱ κακίαν μετιόντες κάμνουσι, παντί που δῆλόν ἐστι. καὶ γὰρ καὶ ὁ ἅρπαξ, καὶ ὁ μοιχός, καὶ ὁ συκοφάντης πολλὰ πονοῦσι καὶ ταλαιπωροῦνται, ὥστε τὴν αὐτῶν κακίαν εἰς τέλος ἀγαγεῖν. ἀλλ᾽ οὐ μόνον οὐδὲν ἀπὸ τῶν πόνων τούτων καρποῦνται τὸ κέρδος, ἀλλὰ καὶ πολλὴν ὑπομένουσι τὴν ζημίαν. Ἐπεὶ καὶ ὁ Παῦλος τοῦτο αἰνιττόμενος ἔλεγεν. *Ὁ σπείρων εἰς τὴν σάρκα αὐτοῦ, ἐκ τῆς σαρκὸς αὐτοῦ θερίσει φθοράν.*[dxxix]

Καὶ ἦν ἡ πτῶσις αὐτῆς μεγάλη.[679] Οὐχ ἁπλῶς, | **58r** *ἀλλὰ μεγάλη.* Ὅτι οὐχ ὑπὲρ τῶν τυχόντων ὁ κίνδυνος, ἀλλ᾽ ὑπὲρ ψυχῆς, ὑπὲρ ἐκπτώσεως ‹ἐκ› τῶν οὐρανῶν.

Οὐδὲ γὰρ ὑπὲρ τῶν τυχόντων ὁ κίνδυνος, ἀλλ᾽ ὑπὲρ ψυχῆς, ὑπὲρ ἐκπτώσεως οὐρανῶν καὶ τῶν ἀθανάτων ἐκείνων ἀγαθῶν.[dxxx]

Καὶ ἐγένετο ὅτε συνετέλεσεν ὁ Ἰησοῦς τοὺς λόγους.[680] Μόνος ἐτέλεσεν ὁ Ἰησοῦς *τοὺς λόγους*, ὁ τέλος ἐπιθεὶς τοῖς πράγμασι καὶ πληρώσας τὸ ἐνδεὲς τοῦ νόμου.[dxxxi]

καὶ ἐγένετο ὅτε συνετέλεσεν ὁ Ἰησοῦς τοὺς λόγους τούτους … μόνος ἐτέλεσε τοὺς λόγους ὁ Ἰησοῦς, ὁ ἐλθὼν τέλος ἐπιθεῖναι τοῖς πράγμασι καὶ πληρῶσαι τὸ ἐνδεὲς τοῦ νόμου διὰ τοῦ *ἐρρέθη τοῖς ἀρχαίοις*[681] καὶ τὰ ἑξῆς.[dxxxii]

Ἐξεπλήσσοντο δὲ ἐπὶ τῇ διδαχῇ αὐτοῦ οἱ ὄχλοι.[682] Οὐχ ὅτι φράσεως ὄγκῳ ἔπειθεν, οὐδ᾽ ὅτι οὐδὲν ἦν αὐτοῖς σκοτεινὸν ἢ αἰνιγματῶδες, ἀλλ᾽ ὅτι ἐν ἐξουσίᾳ ἐλάλει.[683]

Εἰκότως *ἐξεπλήσσοντο*. ἀρρήτῳ γὰρ δυνάμει τοὺς ἀκούοντας ἔπειθεν καὶ οὐ φράσεως ὄγκῳ *ἐξεπλήσσοντο*. οὐδὲ γὰρ ἦν ἐν αὐτοῖς περισκελὲς ἢ αἰνιγματῶδες ἢ σκοτεινόν.[dxxxiii]

Αὐθεντικῶς γὰρ ἐδίδασκεν ὡς Θεὸς καὶ οὐχ ὡς οἱ προφῆται ὡς ἀλλότρια ἐξηγοῦντο τὰ τοῦ Θεοῦ, *τάδε λέγει Κύριος*[684] λέγοντες. Οὐδὲν γὰρ τῶν τοῦ Μωσέως ἐτόλμων ἀφελεῖν ἢ προσθεῖναι. Ὁ δὲ *νόμου καὶ προφητῶν*[685] Κύριος ὡς Θεὸς ἰδίᾳ ἐξουσίᾳ ἐδίδασκε καὶ ἐν οἷς ἐδόκει αὐτῷ προσετίθει μετ᾽ ἐξουσίας μεταμορφῶν εἰς ἀλήθειαν τοὺς τύπους.

---

679 Matt. 7:27.

680 Matt. 7:28.

681 Matt. 5:21; 5:33.

682 Matt. 7:28; cf. 22:33.

683 Cf. Matt. 7:29.

684 Amos, 1:6; 1:9; *et passim*; Michac, 2:3; 3:5; Abdias, 1; Nahum, 1:2; 1:5; 1:7; 1:9; 2:6; 2:11; Zach. 1:3; 1:4; *et passim*; Malachi, 1:4; Is. 3:16; 7:7; *et passim*; Jer. 2:2; 2:5; *et passim*; Ez. 2:4; 3:11; *et passim*.

685 Cf. Acts, 28:23; Rom. 3:21.

The scribes were teaching the people what was written in Moses and the prophets. However, Jesus, being the God and Lord of Moses himself, by the freedom of his own intent, was either adding to the Law with reference to whatever seemed to be deficient, or he reformed it as he preached to the people. This is what we read above as well: *It was said to the ancient ones; but I tell you.*[686]

(ΩΡΙΓΕΝΟΥΣ added on the margin) *Καταβάντι δὲ αὐτῷ.*[687] Ὅταν ὁ εὐαγγελιστὴς Ματθαῖος καταβάντος αὐτοῦ *‹ἀπὸ› το‹ῦ› ὄρο‹υ›ς*[688] αὐτίκα τὸν λεπρὸν προσελθεῖν αὐτῷ κάτωθεν λέγ‹η›[689] *τοῦ ὄρους*, Λουκᾶς δὲ τοῦτον *ἐν μιᾷ τῶν πόλεων*[690] λέγ‹ει›,[691] οὐ μάχης τὸ εἰρημένον.[dxxxiv] Ἀμφότεροι γὰρ τἀληθὲς εἶπον. Ὁ μὲν Ματθαῖος εἰπὼν *καταβάντι δὲ*[692] *ἐκ τοῦ ὄρους ἠκολούθησεν αὐτῷ ὄχλος πολύς*,[693] τὴν εἰς τὴν πόλιν αὐτοῦ πορείαν ἐσήμανεν, ἣν ὁ Λουκᾶς ἀπομνημονεύσας ἀνεγράψατο ἐν τῇ θείᾳ αὐτοῦ βίβλῳ.

(ΩΡΙΓΕΝΟΥΣ main text cont.) *Καὶ ἰδοὺ λεπρὸς ἐλθών.*[694] Πολλὴ ἡ σύνεσις καὶ ἡ πίστις τοῦ προσελθόντος λεπροῦ. Οὐδὲ γὰρ εἶπεν ἐὰν εὔξῃ, *ἀλλ' ἐὰν θέλῃς δύνασαί με καθαρίσαι.*[695] Διὰ τοῦτο οὐδὲ εἶπεν αὐτῷ ἁπλῶς, *καθαρίσθητι, ἀλλὰ θέλω, καθαρίσθητι*,[696] τουτέστιν ἐπὶ τῷ σῷ ῥήματι τὴν κάθαρσίν σοι χαρίζομαι. Τῆς γὰρ ψυχῆς θέρμην καὶ καθαρὰν τὴν πίστιν ἐδήλωσε. *Θέλω καθαρίσθητι.*[697] Ἡ σὴ φωνὴ τὴν παρ' ἐμοῦ σοι τῆς ἰάσεως πηγὴν ἀνεστόμωσε. *Θέλω καθαρίσθητι·* ἔχεις πρόχειρον τὴν θεραπείαν, ὅτι βεβαίαν ἔχων προσελήλυθας τὴν γνώμην.

> πολλὴ δὲ ἡ σύνεσις τοῦ λεπροῦ. οὐδὲ γὰρ εἶπεν, ἐὰν εὔξῃ, *ἀλλ' ἐὰν θέλῃς*. διὰ τοῦτο οὐδὲ εἶπεν ἁπλῶς καθαρίσθητι, *ἀλλὰ θέλω, καθαρίσθητι*. τοῦτ' ἔστιν ἐπὶ τῷ σῷ ῥήματι τὴν κάθαρσίν σοι χαρίζομαι. τῆς γὰρ ψυχῆς θερμὴν καὶ καθαρὰν τὴν πίστιν ἐδήλωσεν ἡ σὴ φωνή, ἣ τὴν παρ' ἐμοῦ σοι τῆς ἰάσεως πηγὴν ἀνεστόμωσε. *θέλω, καθαρίσθητι*, ἔχεις πρόχειρον τὴν θεραπείαν, ὅτι βεβαίαν ἔχων προσελήλυθας τὴν γνώμην.[dxxxv]

Καὶ ἐκτείνας τὴν χεῖρα διὰ τῆς ἐπαφῆς ἐποιήσατο τὴν κάθαρσιν, δηλῶν ὅτι καὶ ἡ ἁγία αὐτοῦ σάρξ χρειώδης ἐστὶ πρὸς ἁγιασμόν. Τὸ μὲν γὰρ Πνεῦμα καθαίρει, ἡ δὲ | **58v** τοῦ σώματος ‹αὐτοῦ› κοινωνία ἐμποιεῖ τὸν ἁγιασμόν.

---

686 Matt. 5:21-22.
687 Matt. 8:1.
688 Cod. τὸ ὄρος.
689 Cod. λέγ.
690 Luke, 5:12.
691 Cod. λέγη.
692 Cod. εἰπὼν δὲ καταβάντι.
693 Cf. Matt. 8:1.
694 Matt. 8:2.
695 *Loc. cit.*
696 Matt. 8:3.
697 Matt. 8:3.

> Διὰ τῆς ἐπαφῆς ἐποιήσατο τὴν κάθαρσιν, δηλῶν ὅτι καὶ ἡ ἁγία αὐτοῦ σὰρξ χρειώδης ἐστὶ πρὸς ἁγιασμόν. τὸ μὲν γὰρ πνεῦμα καθαίρει, ἡ δὲ τοῦ σώματος κοινωνία ἐμποιεῖ τὸν ἁγιασμόν.[dxxxvi]

Καὶ εὐθέως, ἐκαθαρίσθη αὐτοῦ ἡ λέπρα.[698] Πρῶτος οὗτος ὡρισμένως τεθεραπεῦσθαι δηλοῦται λεπρός.
Καὶ νῦν μὲν *ἐκτείνας τὴν χεῖρα* ὁ Ἰησοῦς ἐκαθάρισε τὸν λεπρόν. Πολὺ δὲ πρὸ τῆς αἰσθητῆς ἥψατο αὐτοῦ διὰ τῆς ἀληθῶς θείας αὐτοῦ ἀφῆς, διχῶς ἀπαλλάττων αὐτόν, τῆς αἰσθητῆς λέπρας καὶ τῆς ἑτέρας.

> Παραπλησίως δὲ τούτοις καὶ νοητῶς μᾶλλον ἢ αἰσθητῶς Ἰησοῦς *ἥψατο* τοῦ λεπροῦ, ἵν᾽ αὐτὸν καθαρίσῃ, ὡς ἐγὼ οἶμαι, διχῶς, ἀπαλλάττων αὐτὸν οὐ μόνον, ὡς οἱ πολλοὶ ἀκούουσι, λέπρας αἰσθητῆς δι᾽ αἰσθητῆς ἀφῆς ἀλλὰ καὶ τῆς ἄλλης διὰ τῆς ὡς ἀληθῶς θείας αὐτοῦ ἀφῆς.[dxxxvii]

Καὶ ὁ μὲν Ἐλισσαῖος ὡς ὑπὸ νόμον ὢν οὐκ ἐτόλμησε τὸν Νεεμὰν ἰδεῖν ἢ ἅψασθαι αὐτοῦ.[699] Ὁ δὲ Κύριος ὡς ἐπάνω ὢν τοῦ νόμου καὶ ἅπτεται αὐτοῦ, ἵνα διδάξῃ μὴ ἀκαθάρτους νομίζειν τοὺς τοιούτους. Τί γὰρ ἐβλάπτετό τις τὴν ψυχὴν ἢ τὸ σῶμα ἀπτόμενος λεπροῦ; Διὰ τοῦτο δὲ εἶπε τὸ μετ᾽ ἐξουσίας τοῦτο ῥῆμα, *θέλω καθαρίσθητι*,[700] ὅπερ οὐδαμοῦ φαίνεται εἰρηκώς.

> Διὰ δὴ τοῦτο Ἐλισσαῖος μὲν οὐδὲ ἑώρα τὸν Νεεμάν, ἀλλὰ καὶ σκανδαλισθέντα ἰδών, ἐπειδὴ μὴ ἐξῆλθε καὶ ἥψατο, τηρῶν τοῦ νόμου τὴν ἀκρίβειαν, οἴκοι μένει, καὶ πέμπει πρὸς τὸν Ἰορδάνην αὐτὸν λουσόμενον. Ὁ δὲ Δεσπότης, δεικνὺς ὅτι οὐχ ὡς δοῦλος, ἀλλ᾽ ὡς κύριος θεραπεύει, καὶ ἅπτεται. Οὐ γὰρ ἡ χεὶρ ἀπὸ τῆς λέπρας ἐγένετο ἀκάθαρτος, ἀλλὰ τὸ σῶμα τὸ λεπρὸν ἀπὸ τῆς χειρὸς τῆς ἁγίας καθίστατο καθαρόν.[dxxxviii]

Ἐπειδὴ *ὡς ἐξουσίαν ἔχων*[701] ἐδίδασκεν, ἵνα μὴ νομισθῇ κόμπος εἶναι καὶ αὐθαδιασμὸς οὗτος τῆς διδασκαλίας ὁ τρόπος, διὰ τοῦτο καὶ ἐν τοῖς ἔργοις τὸ αὐτὸ ποιεῖ. *Ὡς ἐξουσίαν ἔχων* θεραπεύει.

> Ἐπειδὴ γὰρ ὡς ἐξουσίαν ἔχων ἐδίδασκεν, ἵνα μὴ νομισθῇ κόμπος εἶναι καὶ αὐθαδιασμὸς οὗτος τῆς διδασκαλίας ὁ τρόπος, καὶ ἐν τοῖς ἔργοις τὸ αὐτὸ τοῦτο ποιεῖ, ὡς ἐξουσίαν ἔχων θεραπεύειν.[dxxxix]

Καὶ ἵνα τὴν ὑπόνοιαν κυρώσῃ τοῦ τε δήμου παντὸς καὶ τοῦ λεπροῦ περὶ τῆς ἐξουσίας, ὃς μετὰ πολλῆς αὐτῷ προσέρχεται τῆς θερμότητος καὶ πρὸ τῶν γονάτων αὐτὸν

---

698 Matt. 8:3.
699 Cf. 4 Kings (2 Kings in Masoretic text), 5:9-11.
700 Matt. 8:3; Mark, 1:41; Luke, 5:13.
701 Matt. 7:29.

παρεκάλει ὡς ‹καὶ› ἕτερος φησι εὐαγγελιστής.[dxl] Καὶ οὐκ εἶπεν ἂν ἀξιώσῃς τὸν Θεὸν οὐδὲ ἂν εὔξῃ, ἀλλ᾽ *ἐὰν θέλῃς*.

> Ἐνταῦθα μέντοι ὥστε κυρῶσαι τὴν ὑπόνοιαν καὶ τοῦ δήμου παντὸς καὶ τοῦ λεπροῦ τὴν περὶ τῆς ἐξουσίας, διὰ τοῦτο προσέθηκε, *Θέλω*.[dxli] Καὶ οὐχ ἁπλῶς, ἀλλὰ μετὰ πολλῆς τῆς θερμότητος, καὶ πρὸ τῶν γονάτων αὐτὸν παρακαλεῖ, ὡς ἕτερός φησιν εὐαγγελιστής, καὶ μετὰ γνησίας τῆς πίστεως, καὶ τῆς προσηκούσης περὶ αὐτοῦ δόξης. Οὐδὲ γὰρ εἶπεν, Ἐὰν ἀξιώσῃς τὸν Θεόν, οὐδέ, Ἐὰν εὔξῃ· ἀλλ᾽, *Ἐὰν θέλῃς, δύνασαί με καθαρίσαι*.[dxlii]

Φεύγων δὲ τὸ φιλόκομπον[dxliii] καὶ θέλων ἐν ὅλῃ τῇ οἰκονομίᾳ λαθεῖν τὸν διάβολον, εἶπε *μηδενὶ εἰπεῖν τὸ γεγονός*,[702][dxliv] ἵνα μὴ γνωσθῇ· ἀλλ᾽ *ὕπαγε, σεαυτὸν δεῖξον τῷ ἱερεῖ*.[703] Οὐ λόγῳ ἤθελε τὸ πρᾶγμα, ἀλλ᾽ ὄψει κηρύττεσθαι. Πρὸς κατάκρι | **59r** σιν δὲ τῶν ἱερέων δεικνὺς τὴν αὐτοῦ δύναμιν, εἶπε τοῖς ἱερεῦσι δεῖξαι ἑαυτὸν *εἰς μαρτύριον*[704] ὡς μὴ πιστεύσασιν εἰς αὐτόν.

> ἀλλὰ μηδενὶ εἰπεῖν κελεύει, διδάσκων τὸ ἀκόμπαστον καὶ ἀφιλότιμον.[dxlv] Τί δέ ἐστιν, *εἰς μαρτύριον αὐτοῖς*; Εἰς ἔλεγχον, εἰς ἀπόδειξιν, εἰς κατηγορίαν, ἐὰν ἀγνωμονῶσιν. Ἐπειδὴ γὰρ ἔλεγον, Ὡς πλάνον καὶ ἀπατεῶνα διώκομεν, ὡς ἀντίθεον καὶ παράνομον. σύ μοι μαρτυρήσεις, φησί, κατ᾽ ἐκεῖνον τὸν καιρόν, ὅτι οὐ παράνομος ἐγώ.[dxlvi]

Ἔθος γὰρ εἶχον οἱ ἱερεῖς δυνάμει Θεοῦ λεπροὺς ἰᾶσθαι τακταῖς ἡμέραις. Τοῦτον δὲ τὸν λεπρὸν πολλῷ χρόνῳ μὴ δυνηθέντες ἰάσασθαι, ἔλεγον ὅτι οὐδεὶς δύναται τοῦτον ἰάσασθαι ἢ μόνος ὁ Χριστὸς ὅταν ἔλθῃ. Πολλὰ τοίνυν δεηθέντος τοῦ λεπροῦ, ὁ Σωτὴρ ἰασάμενος αὐτὸν εἶπεν ἀπελθεῖν καὶ δεῖξαι ἑαυτὸν τοῖς ἱερεῦσιν *εἰς μαρτύριον*, ὅτι τεθεράπευται οὗτος ἐφ᾽ οὗ εἰρήκατε ὅτι οὐδεὶς ἀλλ᾽ ἢ ὁ Χριστὸς μόνος αὐτὸν ἰάσεται. Ἦλθεν ὁ Χριστὸς καὶ πιστεύσατε αὐτῷ.

Σεαυτὸν δεῖξον τῷ ἱερεῖ.[705] Ἐπειδὴ οὐκ ἄλλως ὁ καθαρισθεὶς συνανεμίγνυτο τοῖς λοιποῖς, εἰ μὴ ἑωρακὼς αὐτὸν ὁ ἱερεὺς ἔκρινεν εἶναι καθαρόν ἵνα μὴ δόξῃ τὰ δίκαια τῶν ἱερέων ὑφαρπάζειν πέμπει αὐτὸν τοῖς ἱερεῦσιν.

> Καὶ τί τοῦτο, φησί, πρὸς τὴν τοῦ νόμου συντελεῖ φυλακήν, τὸ εἰπεῖν, *Δεῖξον σεαυτὸν τῷ ἱερεῖ*; Οὐ τὸ τυχόν. Καὶ γὰρ νόμος ἦν παλαιός, τὸν λεπρὸν καθαρθέντα μὴ ἑαυτῷ τὴν δοκιμασίαν ἐπιτρέπειν τοῦ καθαρισμοῦ, ἀλλὰ φαίνεσθαι τῷ ἱερεῖ, καὶ τοῖς ὀφθαλμοῖς τοῖς ἐκείνου παρέχειν τὴν ἀπόδειξιν, καὶ ἀπὸ τῆς ψήφου ταύτης ἐγκρίνεσθαι τοῖς καθαροῖς. Εἰ γὰρ μὴ εἶπεν ὁ ἱερεύς, ὅτι κεκάθαρται ὁ λεπρός, ἔτι μετὰ τῶν ἀκαθάρτων ἔμενεν ἔξω τῆς παρεμβολῆς.... Ἵνα γὰρ μὴ λέγωσιν, ὅτι τῶν ἱερέων τὴν δόξαν ἥρπασε, τὸ μὲν ἔργον αὐτὸς ἐπλήρωσε, τὴν δὲ δοκιμασίαν ἐκείνοις ἐπέτρεψε, καὶ κριτὰς αὐτοὺς ἐκάθισε τῶν οἰκείων θαυμάτων.[dxlvii]

---

702 Matt. 8:4: Ὅρα μηδενὶ εἴπῃς. Cf. 9:30. Mark, 1:44: Ὅρα μηδενὶ μηδὲν εἴπῃς.

703 Matt. 8:4; cf. Mark, 1:40; Luke, 5:14.

704 Matt. 8:4.

705 Matt. 8:4.

Οὐκ ἀναγκαίως τοίνυν ἀλλ᾽ οἰκονομικῶς τοῦτο ἐπέταξε, διὰ τοὺς φιλεγκλήμονας[dxlviii] Ἰουδαίους λέγοντας ὅτι λύει τὸν νόμον καὶ διασύροντας αὐτὸν ὡς παράνομον.[706]

> A concurrent reason [why Jesus sent the leper to the priests] is that he would not seem to be breaking the Law. This was a blame which very frequently they imputed to him.[dxlix]

Διὸ καὶ κελεύει ὧδε φυλαχθῆναι τὸν νόμον. Οὐ γὰρ ἀθετεῖ αὐτὸν ὡς ἐκ Θεοῦ ὄντα, εἰ καὶ τὰ ὑπὲρ νόμον διδάσκει ὡς τοῦ νόμου κύριος.

Εἰσελθόντι δὲ αὐτῷ εἰς Καπερναοὺμ προσῆλθεν αὐτῷ ἑκατόνταρχος.[707] Ἵνα μὴ ἐμποδίσωσι τῇ διδασκαλίᾳ, οὐ προσήνεγκαν αὐτῷ τοὺς ἀρρώστους ἐν τῷ ὄρει, ἀλλὰ μετὰ τὸ κατελθεῖν. Οὗτος δὲ ὁ *ἑκατόνταρχος* ὁ αὐτός ἐστι τῷ παρὰ τῷ Λουκᾷ,[708] ὁ δὲ παρὰ τῷ Ἰωάννῃ ἕτερος.[709][dl] Καὶ ὁ μὲν Ματθαῖος αὐτοψεὶ τὸν ἑκατόνταρχον | **59v** τῷ Κυρίῳ προσλαλοῦντα εἰσάγει. Λουκᾶς δὲ μηδ᾽ ὅλως τοῦτον ὀφθέντα εἶπεν, ἀλλὰ δι᾽ ἑτέρων τὴν ὑπὲρ τοῦ οἰκέτου αἴτησιν ποιεῖσθαι.[710] Τοῦτο δὲ οὐκ ἔστι διαφωνία. Καὶ γὰρ οἱ ἀποστελλόμενοι εἰς πρόσωπον τοῦ ἀποστείλαντος πάρεισιν ἐκείνου τὴν αἴτησιν ὡς παρόντος ποιούμενοι. Καὶ τινὲς μὲν λέγουσιν ὅτι διὰ τοῦτο οὐκ ἤνεγκαν τὸν παῖδα, ἐπειδὴ ἐν ἐσχάτῃ ἦν ἀναπνοῇ, ἵνα μὴ κατὰ τὴν ὁδὸν ἀποθάνῃ. Ἀλλ᾽ οὐκ ἔστι τοῦτο, ἀλλ᾽ ἐπειδὴ ᾔδει ὅτι καὶ ἀπὼν ὡς Θεὸς ἐδύνατο αὐτὸν θεραπεῦσαι. Διὸ καὶ ἔλεγεν· *εἰπὲ λόγω, καὶ ἰαθήσεται.*[711] Ὅτι δὲ οὐ κολακεύων αὐτὸν εἶπε τοῦτο, ἀλλ᾽ οὕτω πιστεύων, ἔδειξεν ὁ Χριστός, εἰπὼν *γενηθήτω σοι ὡς θέλεις.*[712][dli]

> Παῖδα νῦν οἰκέτην λέγει, καὶ σαφῶς τοῦτο δηλοῖ ὁ Λουκᾶς δοῦλον αὐτὸν ὀνομάζων. συνέσεως δὲ (φησίν) ἦν τὸ ἀπὸ τῶν καθ᾽ ἑαυτὸν εἰκότι λογισμῷ τοιαῦτα αὐτὸν πιστεῦσαι περὶ τοῦ Χριστοῦ. *ἄνθρωπος* γὰρ (φησί), κἀγώ, ἀλλ᾽ ὅμως ὢν ἔλαβον *τὴν ἐξουσίαν*, τούτων κύριός εἰμι. ὥστε οὐδὲ ἀπεικὸς καὶ σὲ ταύτην εἰληφότα παρὰ θεοῦ τὴν ἐξουσίαν *λόγῳ* μόνῳ κελεύοντα ἀπελαύνειν τὰ πάθη. οὐδὲ γὰρ ὡς υἱῷ θεοῦ καὶ πάσης ὄντι κυρίῳ τῆς κτίσεως προσῆλθεν ὁ *ἑκατόνταρχος* (τοῦτο γὰρ οὐδὲ τῶν μαθητῶν τότε ἦν εἰδέναι πρὸ τοῦ σταυροῦ), ἀλλ᾽ ὡς ἀνθρώπῳ δι᾽ ἀρετὴν εἰληφότι παρὰ τοῦ θεοῦ μείζονα ἢ κατὰ ἄνθρωπον ἐξουσίαν. ὅθεν οὕτω φησί. *καὶ γὰρ ἐγὼ ἄνθρωπός εἰμι.* ἐπειδὴ γὰρ εἶπε πρὸς αὐτὸν *εἰπὲ λόγῳ*, τοῦτο δὲ θεοῦ μόνου εἶναι ἐδόκει, καλῶς ἐπήγαγε τὸ *καὶ γὰρ ἐγὼ ἄνθρωπός εἰμι*, ἀντὶ τοῦ. οὐδὲν θαυμαστόν, εἰ τοῦτο δύνῃ ἄνθρωπος ὤν, λαβὼν παρὰ τοῦ θεοῦ, ἐπεὶ κἀγὼ τοῦτο ὢν λαμβάνω ὑπηκόους ὑπερέχων τῷ κελεύειν ὡς βούλομαι.[dlii]

Παῖδα νῦν οἰκέτην λέγει, καὶ σαφῶς τοῦτο δηλοῖ ὁ Λουκᾶς δοῦλον αὐτὸν ὀνομάζων. συνέσεως δέ, φησίν, ἦν τὸ ἀπὸ τῶν καθ᾽ ἑαυτὸν εἰκότων λογισμῶν τοιαῦτα αὐτὸν

706 Cf. Luke, 13:14.
707 Matt. 8:5.
708 Matt. 8:5; Luke, 7:2.
709 Cf. John, 4:46-49.
710 Luke, 7:3.
711 Matt. 8:8.
712 Cf. Matt. 8:17: ὡς ἐπίστευσας γενηθήτω σοι.

> πιστεῦσαι περὶ τοῦ Χριστοῦ. *ἄνθρωπος γάρ*, φησίν, *κἀγώ*, ἀλλ' ὅμως ὧν ἔλαβον τὴν *ἐξουσίαν*, τούτων κύριός εἰμι. ὥστε οὐδὲ ἀπεικὸς καὶ σὲ ταύτην εἰληφότα παρὰ θεοῦ τὴν ἐξουσίαν *λόγῳ* μόνῳ κελεύοντα ἀπελαύνειν τὰ πάθη. οὐδὲ γὰρ ὡς υἱῷ θεοῦ καὶ πάσης ὄντι κυρίῳ τῆς κτίσεως προσῆλθεν *ὁ ἑκατόνταρχος* (τοῦτο γὰρ οὐδὲ τῶν μαθητῶν τότε ἦν εἰδέναι πρὸ τοῦ σταυροῦ), ἀλλ' ὡς ἀνθρώπῳ δι' ἀρετὴν εἰληφότι παρὰ τοῦ θεοῦ μείζονα ἢ κατὰ ἄνθρωπον ἐξουσίαν. ὅθεν οὕτω φησίν. *καὶ γὰρ ἐγὼ ἄνθρωπός εἰμι*. ἐπειδὴ γὰρ εἶπε πρὸς αὐτὸν εἰπὲ λόγῳ, τοῦτο δὲ θεοῦ μόνου εἶναι ἐδόκει, καλῶς ἐπήγαγε τὸ καὶ γὰρ ἐγὼ ἄνθρωπός εἰμι, ἀντὶ τοῦ. οὐδὲν θαυμαστόν, εἰ τοῦτο δύνῃ ἄνθρωπος ὤν, λαβὼν παρὰ τοῦ θεοῦ, ἐπεὶ κἀγὼ τοῦτο ὢν λαμβάνω ὑπηκόους ὑπερέχων τῷ κελεύειν ὡς βούλομαι.[dliii]

Διὸ *καὶ ἰάθη ὁ παῖς* αὐτοῦ εὐθέως. Θεοπρεπῆ γὰρ ἔχων περὶ αὐτοῦ ἔννοιαν[dliv] λόγῳ μόνῳ ἐπίστευε τὴν ἴασιν γενέσθαι, ‹εἰ› καὶ ὁ ἰατρὸς ἀπῆν τοῦ κάμνοντος. Διὸ καὶ εἰδὼς ὁ Κύριος ὃ ἔμελλεν εἰπεῖν *ὁ ἑκατόνταρχος* ἐπηγγείλατο ἐλθεῖν, ἵνα εἰπόντος ἐκείνου, *εἰπὲ λόγῳ καὶ ἰαθήσεται*, κατάδηλος πᾶσι γένηται ἡ αὐτοῦ πίστις καὶ θαυμαστωθῇ, ὅτι οὐδὲν χαμαιπετὲς ἐλογίσατο περὶ αὐτοῦ. Φησὶ γάρ· ἐγὼ ὑπὸ βασιλεῖ ὢν ἄρχω στρατοπέδου καὶ ὡς θέλω ἐπιτάσσω.[713] Οὐ πολὺ μᾶλλον σὺ ὁ αὐτεξούσιος καὶ μὴ ὢν ὑπό τινι, ἀλλ' ὡς Θεός, ἢ διὰ σαυτοῦ ἢ διὰ τῶν σῶν ἀγγέλων ποιεῖς τὰς θεοσημείας; Ὥσπερ γὰρ ἐγὼ τῷ μὲν λέγω *ὕπαγε* τῷ δὲ *ἔρχου*[714] καὶ ὑπακούει, οὕτω καὶ σύ, ὡς δούλῳ τῷ θανάτῳ ἐπιτάττεις ὑπάγειν καὶ ἔρχεσθαι καθ' οὗ ἂν θέλῃς.

Ἀκού | **60r** *σας δὲ ὁ Ἰησοῦς, ἐθαύμασε.*[715] Τί οὖν ὁ Ἰησοῦς τούτων ἀκούσας ἐθαύμασεν;

Ἐπειδὴ οὐ μόνον πιστῶς ἀλλὰ καὶ ἀληθῶς εἴρηκεν. Εἰκὸς γὰρ ὅτι ἦσάν τινες ἐνέργειαι τὴν παράλυσιν καὶ τὰς βασάνους ἐμποιοῦσαι τῷ παιδὶ τοῦ ἑκατοντάρχου, ἃς ἐχρῆν κελεύσαντος Ἰησοῦ ἀπελαθῆναι ἀπὸ τοῦ παιδὸς ἢ προστάξαντος τοῖς διακονοῦσιν αὐτῷ ἀγγέλοις[716] ἀπελάσαι καὶ ἐκβαλεῖν τὰ τὴν παράλυσιν καὶ τὰς βασάνους ἐνεργοῦντα.

> Τάχα ἐπεὶ οὐ μόνον πιστῶς ἀλλὰ καὶ ἀληθῶς εἶπεν ὁ ἑκατοντάρχης ἐθαύμασεν ὁ Ἰησοῦς. Εἰκὸς γὰρ ὅτι ἦσάν τινες ἐνέργειαι τὴν παράλυσιν καὶ τὰς βασάνους ἐμποιοῦσαι τῷ παιδί, ἃς ἐχρῆν κελεύσαντος Ἰησοῦ ἀπελαθῆναι ἀπὸ τοῦ παιδὸς ἢ προστάξαντος τοῖς διακονοῦσιν αὐτῷ ἀγγέλοις ἀπελαθῆναι ἀπὸ τοῦ παιδὸς καὶ ἐκβαλεῖν τὰ τὴν παράλυσιν καὶ τὰς βασάνους ἐνεργοῦντα.[dlv]

> He marveled because he saw that the centurion comprehended his majesty. For the physical ailment, or rather the adverse powers that had produced the infirmity, powers which man is often subjected to, had to be expelled. This was brought about by both the Lord's word and the ministries of angels.[dlvi]

---

713 Cf. Matt. 8:9; Luke, 7:8.
714 Cf. Rev. 6: 1; 3; 5; 7; 22:17.
715 Matt. 8:10.
716 Cf. Matt. 4:11; Mark, 1:13.

τῷ παιδὶ τοῦ ἑκατοντάρχου. Διὸ καὶ εἰκότως ἀκούει ὑπὲρ πάντα τὸν Ἰσραὴλ μόνον αὐτὸν ἀξίως πεπιστευκέναι
Κύριον ζωῆς καὶ θανάτου εἶχεν ὁ *ἑκατόνταρχος* τὸν Ἰησοῦν.[717] Διὸ καὶ ἐθαυμάσθη. Οὐδένα γὰρ *ἐν τῷ Ἰσραὴλ* εὑρίσκομεν καταθαρρήσαντα τοῦ θανάτου.

Καὶ ζωῆς καὶ θανάτου εἶχεν ὁ *ἑκατόνταρχος* τὸν Ἰησοῦν ἐξουσιαστήν. διὸ καὶ ἐθαυμάσθη. οὐδένα ἐν τῇ Ἱερουσαλὴμ εὑρίσκομεν καταθαρρήσαντα τοῦ θανάτου.[dlvii]

Κύριον ζωῆς καὶ θανάτου εἶχεν ὁ *ἑκατόνταρχος* τὸν Ἰησοῦν. διὸ καὶ ἐθαυμάσθη. οὐδένα γὰρ *ἐν τῷ Ἰσραὴλ* εὑρίσκομεν καταθαρρήσαντα τοῦ θανάτου.[dlviii]

19

(ΩΡΙΓΕΝΟΥΣ) *Ὅτι πολλοὶ ἀπὸ ἀνατολῶν καὶ δυσμῶν.*[718] Εἰ *στενὴ καὶ τεθλιμμένη ἐστὶν ἡ ὁδός, καὶ ὀλίγοι οἱ εὑρίσκοντες αὐτήν*, διὰ ποίας *οἱ πολλοὶ*[719] εἰσελεύσονται; Περὶ γὰρ τῆς πλατείας καὶ εὐρυχώρου λέγει ὅτι *πολλοὶ δι᾽ αὐτῆς* εἰσέρχονται.[720] Ὁ μὲν τοῦ Σωτῆρος λόγος εἴρηται ἐπειδὴ ὀλίγοι ἀπὸ τοῦ Ἰσραὴλ ἐσῴζοντο. Οὐ *πολλοὶ* γὰρ ἐπίστευσαν εἰς αὐτόν. Διὸ καὶ ἔλεγε· *μὴ φοβοῦ τὸ μικρὸν ποίμνιον, ὅτι εὐδόκησεν* ὁ Θεὸς ἐν σοί.[721] Προφητικῶς δὲ ἐλέχθη τὸ *πολλοὶ ἥξουσιν*,[722] ὡς περὶ τῶν μελλόντων πιστεύειν ἀπὸ τῶν ἐθνῶν. *Πολλοί* φησι, ὡς πρὸς τοὺς Ἰσραηλίτας τοὺς μετὰ τὴν παρουσίαν μὴ πιστεύσαντας, οἱ ἀπὸ τῶν ἐθνῶν ἀνακλιθησόμενοι *μετὰ Ἀβραὰμ καὶ Ἰσαὰκ καὶ Ἰακὼβ ἐν τῇ βασιλείᾳ τῶν οὐρανῶν*.[723] Καὶ τῷ ἀριθμῷ δὲ πολλαπλασίους οὗτοι τῶν ἀπὸ Ἰσραὴλ καὶ τὸν Ἰησοῦν Χριστὸν ὁμολογούντων.

Εἰ *στενὴ καὶ τεθλιμμένη ἐστὶν ἡ ὁδός, καὶ ὀλίγοι οἱ εὑρίσκοντες αὐτήν*, διὰ ποίας *οἱ πολλοὶ* εἰσελεύσονται (περὶ γὰρ τῆς πλατείας καὶ εὐρυχώρου λέγει ὅτι *πολλοὶ δι᾽ αὐτῆς* εἰσέρχονται);[724] καί φαμεν μὲν τοῦ σωτῆρος λόγος εἴρηται, ἐπειδὴ ὀλίγοι ἀπὸ τοῦ Ἰσραὴλ διεσώζοντο. οὐ *πολλοὶ* γὰρ ἐπίστευσαν εἰς αὐτὸν ἀλλ᾽ ὀλίγοι, διὸ καὶ ἔλεγε· *μὴ φοβοῦ τὸ μικρὸν ποίμνιον, ὅτι εὐδόκησεν* ὁ Θεὸς ἐν σοί. προφητικῶς δὲ ἐλέχθη τὸ *πολλοὶ ἥξουσιν* ὡς περὶ τῶν μελλόντων πιστεύειν εἰς αὐτὸν ἀπὸ τῶν ἐθνῶν. [*ἀπὸ ἀνατολῶν* καὶ ἐκβαλλομένους *εἰς τὸ σκότος τὸ ἐξώτερον*.] *πολλοί* (φησίν), ὡς πρὸς τοὺς Ἰσραηλίτας τοὺς μετὰ τὴν παρουσίαν μὴ πιστεύσαντας, οἱ ἀπὸ τῶν ἐθνῶν ἀνακλιθησόμενοι *μετὰ Ἀβραὰμ καὶ τῶν ἐξ αὐτοῦ ἐν τῇ βασιλείᾳ τῶν οὐρανῶν*.[725] καὶ τῷ ἀριθμῷ δὲ πολλαπλασίους οὗτοι τῶν ἀπὸ Ἰσραὴλ καὶ τὸν Ἰησοῦν Χριστὸν ὁμολογούντων.[dlix]

---

717 Cf. Matt. 8:10.
718 Matt. 8:11. Cf. Luke, 13:29; Psalm 106:3; Psalms of Solomon, 11:2.
719 Matt. 7:13-14.
720 Matt. 7:13.
721 Cf. Luke, 12:32.
722 Matt. 8:11.
723 Cf. Matt. 8:11.
724 Matt. 7:13.
725 Cf. Matt. 8:11.

Δεικνὺς δὲ ὅτι οὐ μάχεται τῇ παλαιᾷ πολιτείᾳ τοῦ *Ἀβραὰμ* ἐ | **60v** μνήσθη, ἐπεὶ καὶ οἱ *ἐξ ἐθνῶν*[726] πιστοὶ τὸν *Ἀβραὰμ* πατέρα ἐπιγράφονται.[727] Εἰπὼν τοίνυν ὅτι πλείους τῶν Ἰουδαίων οἱ *ἐξ ἐθνῶν* πιστοὶ μέλλουσιν εἶναι *ἐν τῇ βασιλείᾳ* οἱ ἐξομοιωθέντες τῷ *Ἀβραὰμ* κατὰ πίστιν κοινωνοῦντες αὐτῷ τῶν τιμῶν, δείκνυσιν ὅτι καὶ οἱ Ἰουδαῖοι, δοκοῦντες εἶναι *υἱοί*, ἀπιστήσαντες μέλλουσιν ἐκπεσεῖν τῆς *τῶν οὐρανῶν* βασιλείας καὶ τοῦ συνεῖναι τοῖς πατριάρχαις. Εἰπὼν γὰρ τὰ ἐσόμενα ἀγαθά τοῖς πιστοῖς, εἶπε καὶ τὰ μέλλοντα ἀπαντῆσαι δεινὰ τοῖς ἀπίστοις.
Υἱοὶ δὲ βασιλείας ὠνομάσθησαν οἱ Ἰουδαῖοι διὰ τὸ *υἱός πρωτότοκός μου Ἰσραήλ*[728] καὶ διὰ τὰς ἐπαγγελίας καὶ τοὺς πατέρας καὶ ὅτι ἐξ αὐτῶν ἦν *ὁ Χριστὸς τὸ κατὰ σάρκα*.[729]

By *sons of the kingdom* he bespeaks the Jews in whom God previously reigned.[dlx]

Ἐξ ὧν δὲ ‹εἶπεν ὅτε› ἰάσατο λόγῳ τὸν παῖδα, ἔδειξεν ὅτι καὶ ἃ περὶ τῶν μελλόντων λέγει ἀληθεύει. Καὶ οἱ μὲν μὴ πιστεύσαντες Ἰουδαῖοι μέλλουσιν ἐκπεσεῖν *τῆς βασιλείας*. Οἱ δὲ ἐθνικοὶ πιστεύσαντες συμβασιλεῦσαι Χριστῷ[730] μετὰ καὶ τοῦ συνεῖναι τοῖς πατριάρχαις.

Εἶδε τὴν πενθερὰν αὐτοῦ βεβλημένην.[731] Ὁ Μᾶρκος καὶ τὸ *εὐθέως* προσέθηκε,[732] βουλόμενος καὶ τὸν χρόνον δηλῶσαι. Οὗτος δὲ μόνον τὸ σημεῖον τέθεικε, τὸν χρόνον οὐκ ἐπισημηνάμενος. Οὐ γὰρ ἦν προκείμενον τῷ Ματθαίῳ τὴν τάξιν τηρῆσαι, ἀλλ' ὅτι καὶ τόδε τὸ παράδοξον ἐποίησεν ὁ Ἰησοῦς. Τοῖς δὲ δυσὶ καὶ τὸ τὴν τάξιν τηρῆσαι ἐξεγένετο. Καὶ οἱ μὲν ἄλλοι φασὶ[733] ὅτι καὶ παρεκάλεσ‹α›ν αὐτ‹ῷ› περὶ τ›ῆ‹ς› κατακειμένη‹ς›.[734] Οὗτος δὲ καὶ τοῦτο ἐσίγησε. Τοῦτο δὲ οὐκ ἔστι διαφωνίας, ἀλλὰ τὸ μὲν συντομίας, τὸ δὲ ἀκριβοῦς ἐξηγήσεως. *Εἰς* | **61r** *τὴν οἰκίαν* δὲ *Πέτρου* εἰσῆλθε, δηλονότι τροφῆς μεταληψόμενος. Τοῦτο γὰρ ἐδήλωσεν εἰπὼν ὅτι *ἀνέστη καὶ διηκόνει αὐτῷ*.[735] Ἀψάμενος τοίνυν *τῆς χειρὸς αὐτῆς*, οὐχὶ τὸν πυρετὸν ἔσβεσε μόνον, ἀλλὰ καὶ καθαρὰν τὴν ὑγείαν ἀπέδωκεν. Ἐπειδὴ γὰρ τὸ νόσημα εὐτελὲς ἦν, τῷ τρόπῳ τῆς ἰάσεως τὴν δύναμιν ἐπεδείκνυτο. Ἐν ἀκαριαίῳ γὰρ χρόνῳ πάντα εἰργάσατο, τήν τε ὑγείαν καὶ τὸ ἀναλαβεῖν τὰς πρώτας δυνάμεις ὡς καὶ ἰσχῦσαι διακονεῖν. Καὶ γὰρ μετὰ τὴν ἀπαλλαγὴν τῶν πυρετῶν πολλοῦ δεῖ χρόνου τοῖς κάμνουσιν ὥστε εἰς τὴν προτέραν ὑγείαν ἐπανελθεῖν.

---

726 Cf. Rom. 9:24; Acts, 15:23.
727 Cf. Matt. 3:9; Luke, 3:8.
728 Ex. 4:22.
729 Cf. John, 7:42; Rom. 1:3; 2 Tim. 2:8.
730 Cf. 1 Cor. 4:8; 2 Tim. 2:12.
731 Matt. 8:14.
732 Mark, 1:30.
733 Mark, 1:31; Luke, 4:39.
734 Cod. παρεκάλεσεν αὐτὸν ἡ κατακειμένη.
735 Matt. 8:14: ἠγέρθη καὶ διηκόνει αὐτῷ.

Ὀψίας δὲ γενομένης, προσήνεγκαν αὐτῷ.[736] Διὰ τὸ θερμὸν τῆς πίστεως καὶ παρὰ καιρὸν προσῆγον αὐτῷ τοὺς ἀρρώστους· αὐτὸς δὲ φιλάνθρωπος ὢν πάντας ἐθεράπευσε, διαφόροις νοσήμασι κατεχομένους. Εἶτα, ἵνα μὴ τὸ μέγεθος τοῦ θαύματος εἰς ἀπιστίαν ἐμβάλῃ τινάς, εἴ γε τοσαῦτα νοσήματα ἐν μιᾷ καιροῦ ῥοπῇ λόγῳ ἔλυσεν, ἐπάγει τὸν προφήτην μαρτυροῦντα τοῖς γινομένοις. Οὐκ εἶπε δὲ *αὐτὸς τὰς ἀσθενείας ἡμῶν* ἔλυσεν, ἀλλ᾽ ὅτι ἔλαβε καὶ *ἐβάστασεν*,[737] ὃ περὶ ἁμαρτιῶν μᾶλλον εἰρῆσθαι δοκεῖ τῷ προφήτῃ. Ἐνταῦθα δὲ περὶ νοσημάτων αὐτὸ τίθησιν ὁ εὐαγγελιστής. Καὶ γὰρ τὰ πολλὰ τῶν νοσημάτων ἐξ ἁμαρτιῶν γίνεται ψυχικῶν.
Διατί δὲ ἡμέρας οὐ προσήνεγκαν; Εὐλαβούμενοι τοὺς γραμματεῖς καὶ Φαρισαίους ἢ αἰσχυνόμενοι ἐπὶ ταῖς ἀσθένειαις αὐτῶν, ὡς Νικόδημος, ἢ διὰ τὸ μὴ ἔχειν τοὺς ἀσθενοῦντας τινὰς προσαγαγεῖν αὐτοὺς τῷ Ἰησοῦ.

> Διὰ τί δὲ ἡμέρας οὐ προσήνεγκαν; πότερον εὐλαβούμενοι τοὺς γραμματεῖς καὶ Φαρισαίους ἢ ἂν πάλιν αἰσχυνόμενοι ἐπὶ ταῖς ἀσθενείαις αὐτῶν ὡς Νικόδημος ἢ ἂν διὰ τὸ μὴ ἔχειν τοὺς ἀσθενοῦντάς τινας προσαγαγεῖν αὐτοὺς τῷ Ἰησοῦ.[dlxi]

| **61v** *Αὐτὸς τὰς ἀσθενείας ἡμῶν ἔλαβε.*[738] Πῶς Ἡσαΐου εἰς τὸν σταυρὸν ἀνενέγκαντος τὸ ῥητὸν ὁ εὐαγγελιστὴς εἰς τὰς ἰάσεις ἀνάγει; Ὅτι καὶ τὸ πάθος αὐτοῦ ἴασις ἦν ἀνθρώπων καὶ οὐδὲν μᾶλλον ἔπασχεν ὁ Κύριος ἤπερ ἐνήργει διὰ τῶν εἰς αὐτὸν ἀτιμιῶν, καὶ διὰ τοῦ ἰδίου θανάτου τὴν τῶν ἀνθρώπων ζωὴν κατασκευάζων καὶ καταπολεμῶν τοὺς κακῶς αὐτοὺς διατιθέντας.
Ἰδὼν δὲ ὁ Ἰησοῦς πολλοὺς ὄχλους περὶ αὐτόν, ἐκέλευσεν ἀπελθεῖν εἰς τὸ πέραν.[739] Ὑπεχώρει ὁ Χριστὸς ἀπὸ τῶν ὄχλων ἵνα μὴ δόξῃ τις φιλόκομπος εἶναι, χαίρων τοῖς παρὰ τῶν πολλῶν ἐπαίνοις καὶ ἵνα μὴ ὀργίζωνται κατ᾽ αὐτοῦ οἱ Φαρισαῖοι (ἐλύπει γὰρ αὐτοὺς σφόδρα τὸ ἀκολουθεῖν αὐτῷ πολλούς) καὶ ἵνα ταῖς πλησίον πόλεσιν ἐπιλάμψῃ τὸ οἰκεῖον καὶ σωτήριον φῶς.

> Ἀπεχώρει δὲ ὁ Χριστὸς ἀπὸ τῶν ὄχλων, ἵνα μὴ δόξῃ τις φιλόκομπος εἶναι χαίρων τοῖς παρὰ τῶν πολλῶν ἐπαίνοις καὶ ἵνα μὴ ὀργίζωνται κατ᾽ αὐτοῦ οἱ Φαρισαῖοι. ἐλύπει γὰρ αὐτοὺς σφόδρα τὸ ἀκολουθεῖν αὐτῷ πολλούς. καὶ ἵνα ταῖς πλησίον πόλεσιν ἐπιλάμψῃ τὸ οἰκεῖον καὶ σωτήριον φῶς.[dlxii]

Κελεύει δὲ μόνοις τοῖς μαθηταῖς *ὁ Ἰησοῦς ἀπελθεῖν εἰς τὸ πέραν*, ἵνα μὴ δοκῇ ἐμποδίζεσθαι ὑπὸ τῶν θλιβόντων αὐτὸν ὄχλων ἀκούειν τοὺς μαθητὰς τῶν ἁρμοζόντων αὐτοῖς μαθημάτων ‹καὶ› γνησιωτέρως μελλόντων αὐτοῖς ἀποκαλύπτεσθαι τῶν τοῦ Θεοῦ μυστηρίων τῶν *ἐν παραβολαῖς τοῖς ὄχλοις*[740] λαλουμένων. Ὅτι καὶ αὐτοὶ πάντα

---

736 Matt. 8:16.
737 Matt. 8:17, *apud* Is. 53:4: οὗτος τὰς ἁμαρτίας ἡμῶν φέρει καὶ περὶ ἡμῶν ὀδυνᾶται.
738 Matt. 8:17, *apud* Is. 53:4.
739 Matt. 8:18.
740 Matt. 13:34.

τὰ ἐν χερσὶ καταλείψαντες μόνοι αὐτῷ ἠκολούθησαν ἕνεκεν φιλομαθείας. Κελεύει δὲ διαπερᾶν ἀπὸ τῶν προσκαίρων εἰς τὰ αἰώνια,[741] ἀπὸ τῶν ἐπιγείων ἐπὶ τὰ ἐπουράνια,[742] ἀπὸ τῶν σαρκικῶν εἰς τὰ πνευματικά.[743]

> Κελεύει δὲ μόνοις τοῖς μαθηταῖς ὁ *Ἰησοῦς ἀπελθεῖν εἰς τὸ πέραν*, ἵνα μὴ δοκῇ ἐμποδίζεσθαι ὑπὸ τῶν θλιβόντων αὐτὸν ὄχλων ἀκούειν τοὺς μαθητὰς τῶν ἁρμοζόντων αὐτοῖς μαθημάτων καὶ γνησιωτέρως μελλόντων αὐτοῖς ἀποκαλύπτεσθαι τῶν τοῦ Θεοῦ μυστηρίων τῶν *ἐν παραβολαῖς τοῖς ὄχλοις* λαλουμένων. ἐπεὶ πάντα τὰ ἐν χερσὶ καταλείψαντες μόνοι αὐτῷ ἠκολούθησαν ἕνεκεν φιλομαθίας. Κελεύει δὲ διαπερᾶν ἀπὸ τῶν προσκαίρων εἰς τὰ αἰώνια,[744] ἀπὸ τῶν ἐπιγείων ἐπὶ τὰ ἐπουράνια,[745] ἀπὸ τῶν σαρκικῶν εἰς τὰ πνευματικά.[dlxiii]

> Κελεύει δὲ μόνοις τοῖς μαθηταῖς ὁ *Ἰησοῦς ἀπελθεῖν εἰς τὸ πέραν*, ἵνα μὴ δοκῇ ἐμποδίζεσθαι ὑπὸ τῶν θλιβόντων αὐτὸν ὄχλων ἀκούειν τοὺς μαθητὰς τῶν ἁρμοζόντων αὐτοῖς μαθημάτων καὶ γνησιωτέρως μελλόντων αὐτοῖς ἀποκαλύπτεσθαι τῶν τοῦ θεοῦ μυστηρίων, τῶν *ἐν παραβολαῖς τοῖς ὄχλοις* λαλουμένων. ἐπεὶ πάντα τὰ ἐν χερσὶ καταλείψαντες μόνοι αὐτῷ ἠκολούθησαν ἕνεκεν φιλομαθίας, κελεύει δὲ διαπερᾶν ἀπὸ τῶν προσκαίρων ἐπὶ τὰ αἰώνια, ἀπὸ τῶν ἐπιγείων ἐπὶ τὰ ἐπουράνια, ἀπὸ τῶν σαρκικῶν ἐπὶ τὰ πνευματικά.[dlxiv]

Καὶ προσελθὼν εἷς γραμματεύς.[746] Αὐτὸς γραμματέα τὸν νομικὸν λέγει, τὸν τοῦ νόμου τὸ γράμμα ἐπιστάμενον.[dlxv]

Οὗτος προσελθὼν καὶ ἰδὼν πολλὰ σημεία προσεδόκησε χρηματίζεσθαι ἐκ | **62r** τῶν τοιούτων θαυμάτων τὸν Σωτῆρα. Διόπερ φιλοχρήματος ὢν ἀκολουθῆσαι ἔσπευδε. Τί οὖν ὁ Χριστός, οὐ πρὸς τὴν ἐρώτησιν τῶν ῥημάτων, ἀλλὰ πρὸς τὴν γνώμην τῆς διανοίας ἀπαντῶν μόνον, μονονουχὶ τοῦτο φησί· χρήματα προσδοκᾷς ἀκολουθῶν ἐμοὶ συλλέγειν; Εἶτα οὐχ ὁρᾷς ὅτι οὐδὲ καταγώγιόν μοι ἐστὶ τοσοῦτον ὅσον ταῖς ὄρνισιν ἢ ταῖς ἀλώπεξιν; Ἐπειδὴ γὰρ ὡς φιλόπλουτος ᾐτεῖτο αὐτῷ συνεῖναι, διὰ τῆς ἀποκρίσεως ἐλέγχων αὐτοῦ τὸν νοῦν ἐδημοσίευσεν εἰπὼν ὅτι *αἱ ἀλώπεκες καὶ τὰ πετεινὰ*[747] πλείω ἔχουσιν ἡμῶν ἀνάπαυσιν· ἀκτήμων γάρ εἰμι καὶ ἄοικος, καὶ οὕτως ὀφείλει εἶναι καὶ ὁ κατακολουθῶν ἐμοί. Ὃ καὶ ἀκούσας ἔμεινε καθ᾽ ἑαυτόν.

> Οὗτος γὰρ ἰδὼν τὰ πολλὰ σημεῖα, καὶ πολλοὺς ἐπισυρομένους, προσεδόκησε χρηματίζεσθαι ἐκ τῶν τοιούτων θαυμάτων. διόπερ καὶ ἀκολουθῆσαι ἔσπευδε. Καὶ πόθεν τοῦτο δῆλον; Ἀπὸ τῆς ἀποκρίσεως, ἧς ὁ Χριστὸς ποιεῖται, οὐ πρὸς τὴν ἐρώτησιν τῶν ρημάτων, ἀλλὰ πρὸς τὴν γνώμην τῆς διανοίας ἀπαντῶν. Τί γάρ; φησί. χρήματα προσδοκᾷς ἀκολουθῶν ἐμοὶ συλλέγειν; εἶτα οὐχ ὁρᾷς ὅτι οὔτε καταγώγιόν μοί ἐστιν, οὐδὲ τοσοῦτον

741 2 Cor. 4:18.
742 Cf. John, 3:12; 1 Cor. 15:40; 2 Cor. 4:18; 5:1; Phil. 2:10; 3:19-20.
743 Cf. Rom. 15:27; 1 Cor. 9:11.
744 2 Cor. 4:18.
745 Cf. John, 3:12; 1 Cor. 15:40; 2 Cor. 4:18; 5:1; Phil. 2:10; 3:19-20.
746 Matt. 8:19.
747 Matt. 8:20.

ὅσον τοῖς ὄρνισιν; *Αἱ γὰρ ἀλώπεκες*, φησί, *φωλεοὺς ἔχουσι, καὶ τὰ πετεινὰ τοῦ οὐρανοῦ κατασκηνώσεις. ὁ δὲ Υἱὸς τοῦ ἀνθρώπου οὐκ ἔχει ποῦ τὴν κεφαλὴν κλίνῃ*. Ταῦτα δὲ οὐκ ἦν ἀποτρεπομένου, ἀλλ᾽ ἐλέγχοντος μὲν τὴν πονηρὰν γνώμην, παρέχοντος δέ, εἰ βούλοιτο, μετὰ τῆς τοιαύτης προσδοκίας ἀκολουθεῖν. Καὶ ἵνα μάθῃς αὐτοῦ τὴν πονηρίαν, ἀκούσας ταῦτα καὶ ἐλεγχθεὶς οὐκ εἶπεν, Ἕτοιμός εἰμι ἀκολουθῆσαι.[dlxvi]

Διὰ τί τῷ εἰπόντι αὐτῷ *διδάσκαλε, ἀκολουθήσω σοι* καὶ τὰ ἑξῆς, *αἱ ἀλώπεκες φωλεοὺς ἔχουσιν*, ἀνταπεκρίθη; ἐπειδὴ χρημάτων δοῦλος ὑπάρχων ἐκεῖνος, καὶ ἰδὼν πολλὰ σημεῖα ποιοῦντα αὐτόν, καὶ πολλοὺς ἀκολουθοῦντας αὐτῷ, προσεδόκησεν χρηματίζεσθαι ἐκ τῶν τοιούτων θαυμάτων. διὸ γινώσκων αὐτὸς τὰ ἐν τῷ συνειδότι αὐτοῦ, καὶ τὴν πολλὴν ἀπόνοιαν καὶ φιλαργυρίαν, ταῦτα φησίν. ὡσανεὶ ἔλεγεν αὐτῷ, ὅτι σὺ μὲν χρήματα προσδοκᾷς ἀκολουθῶν ἐμοὶ συλλέγειν. σκόπει δὲ ὅτι οὔτε καταγώγιόν μοι ἐστίν, οὐδὲ τοσοῦτον, ὅσον ταῖς ἀλώπηξι καὶ τοῖς ὀρνέοις. ταῦτα δὲ τὰ ῥήματα οὐκ ἦν ἀποτρεπομένου, ἀλλ᾽ ἐλέγχοντος μὲν τὴν πονηρὰν γνώμην, παρέχοντος δὲ εἰ βούλοιτο, μετὰ τῆς τοιαύτης προσδοκίας ἀκολουθεῖν. ἐκεῖνος δὲ ταῦτα ἀκούσας καὶ ἐλεγχθείς, οὐκ εἶπεν, ἕτοιμός εἰμι ἀκολουθῆσαι, ἀλλ᾽ ἔδειξε τὴν ἑαυτοῦ πονηρίαν, εὐθέως ἐπαναχωρήσας.[dlxvii]

Therefore, such a faith [sc. as the scribe's] is appropriately condemned by the Lord's pronouncement to him, which goes thus: Why do you crave following me for the sake of wealth and wordly profit, when I am one of such great poverty that I do not even have a little shelter and I do not even use my roof?[dlxviii]

Αἱ ἀλώπεκες φωλεοὺς ἔχουσι.[748] *Ἀλώπεκες*, πονηροὶ ἄνθρωποι· *πετεινὰ δὲ οὐρανοῦ*, γόητες. Ἤτοι *ἀλώπεκες* καὶ *πετεινὰ οὐρανοῦ* οἱ ταῖς δολεραῖς ἀλώπεξι καὶ πτηνοῖς ἀπεικαζόμενοι δαίμονες.
Ἐπεὶ τοίνυν οἱ δαίμονες ἐν σοὶ ἐπαναπαύονται,[dlxix] ἐγὼ ἐν σοὶ ἀνάπαυσιν οὐ δύναμαι εὑρεῖν ὡς Θεός. Ὁ γὰρ Θεὸς *ἅγιος* ὢν *ἐν ἁγίοις* ἐπαναπαύεται,[749]

Ἐν ἁγίοις ὁ Χριστὸς *ἅγιος* ὢν ἐπαναπαύεται. διὸ καί φησι πρὸς αὐτόν. ἐν σοὶ δαίμονες ἀναπαύονται, τουτέστιν *αἱ ἀλώπεκες*. ἐγὼ δὲ οὐκ ἐν σοὶ ἀλλ᾽ *ἐν ἁγίοις* ἀναπαυθήσομαι.[dlxx]

Εἰ μὲν οὖν ἕτοιμος εἶ αὐτὸς ὁμοίως ἐμοὶ οὐκ ἔχοντι ποῦ τὴν κεφαλὴν κλῖναι, αἱρήσῃ διὰ τὴν ἐμὴν διδασκαλίαν τὸ ἀκατάστατον ἐνταῦθα ἐλπίδι τῆς τῶν οὐρανῶν βασιλείας, ἐπ᾽ οὐδενὶ τὴν ἀνάπαυσιν ἐνταῦθα μὴ προσδοκῶν, ἀλλ᾽ ἐν τῷ μέλλοντι. Οἱ γὰρ ἐμοὶ μαθηταί, δικαιοσύνην ἀσκοῦντες, ἐν τῷ κόσμῳ τούτῳ θλίψιν ἕξουσι. πονηροὶ δὲ καὶ γόητες, ἀλώπεξι καὶ πετεινοῖς οὐρανοῦ παραβαλλόμενοι, ἐν τῷ βίῳ τούτῳ προκόψουσι πλανῶντες καὶ πλανώμενοι.[dlxxi]

ὡς δὲ ὁ Θεὸς τοῖς ἀνθρώποις οἰκονομῶν ἐν παραβολῇ ἄνθρωπος λέγεται, τάχα δέ πως καὶ γίνεται οὕτω καὶ ὁ Σωτήρ, προηγουμένως Υἱὸς ὢν Θεοῦ καὶ Θεός, οὐ μένει ἐν ᾧ ἐστι, γίνεται δὲ κατ᾽ οἰκονομίαν τοῦ ἐν παραβολῇ *ἀνθρώπου* (ὄντος δὲ Θεοῦ)

748 Matt. 8:20.
749 Is. 57:15.

υἱός μιμούμενος κἀν τούτῳ τὸν Πατέρα. Ἕτερος δέ τις οὐκ αὐτομόλως ἀκολουθῆσαι προτραπείς, καθὼς ὁ Λουκᾶς φησι, ᾔτει *θάψαι τὸν πατέρα.*[750]

Ἄφες τοὺς νεκροὺς θάψαι τοὺς ἑαυτῶν.[751] Τί οὖν ὁ Σωτὴρ ἐκώλυσεν αὐτὸν τοῦ βουλήματος; Οὐ γὰρ ἔδει ἐπὶ τὰ γήϊνα σπεύδειν | **62v** τὸν τῶν οὐρανίων ἐφιέμενον. Ἦσαν γὰρ οἱ ἐκεῖνο πληρώσοντες καὶ οὐκ ἔμελλεν ἄταφος μένειν, καὶ οὐκ ἐχρῆν τοῦτον τῶν ἀναγκαιοτέρων ἀπάγεσθαι. Ἤτοι τοῦτο φησί, ὅτι ἄπιστος ἦν ὁ τετελευτηκώς. Τοῦτο δὲ δῆλον ἐκ τοῦ εἰπεῖν *τοὺς ἑαυτῶν νεκρούς*, διδάσκων αὐτὸν ὅτι οὐκ ἔστιν αὐτοῦ νεκρός. Διὸ καὶ κωλυθεὶς ἔμεινε.

> *Ἄφες τοὺς νεκροὺς θάψαι τοὺς ἑαυτῶν νεκρούς, σὺ δέ μοι ἀκολούθει.* Πανταχοῦ γὰρ τῇ γνώμῃ προσεῖχε. Καὶ τίνος ἕνεκεν οὐκ ἐπέτρεψε; φησίν. Ὅτι καὶ οἱ ἐκεῖνο πληρώσοντες ἦσαν, καὶ οὐκ ἔμελλεν ἄταφος μένειν. καὶ τοῦτον τῶν ἀναγκαιοτέρων ἀπάγεσθαι οὐκ ἐχρῆν. Εἰπὼν δέ, *τοὺς ἑαυτῶν νεκρούς*, δείκνυσιν ὅτι οὗτος οὐκ ἔστιν αὐτοῦ νεκρός. Καὶ γὰρ τῶν ἀπίστων, ὡς ἔγωγε οἶμαι, ἦν ὁ τετελευτηκώς. Εἰ δὲ θαυμάζεις τὸν νεανίσκον, ὅτι ὑπὲρ πράγματος οὕτως ἀναγκαίου τὸν Ἰησοῦν ἠρώτησε, καὶ οὐκ αὐτομάτως ἀπῆλθε· πολλῷ μᾶλλον θαύμασον, ὅτι καὶ κωλυθεὶς ἔμεινεν.[dlxxii]

Δεῖ μὲν γὰρ τιμᾶν γονεῖς· ἐπὰν δὲ θεῖον πρόκειται πρόσταγμα, δεῖ τὸν Θεὸν καὶ γονέων προτιμᾶσθαι,[dlxxiii] μάλιστα εἰ οἱ γονεῖς ἐμποδίζουσι θεοσεβεῖ προστάγματι τοῖς μεταβαλοῦσιν ἀπὸ κακίας πρὸς ἀρετήν. Τέθνηκεν ὁ διάβολος, παρὰ τῷ ἁμαρτάνοντι ζῶν. Καὶ ᾧ μὲν ἔτι ζῇ, οὐ λέγει ὁ Ἰησοῦς τὸ ἕπου *μοι*,[752] ᾧ δὲ τέθνηκε, διδάσκων ὅτι ᾧ μεν τέθνηκεν ὁ πονηρὸς πατήρ, οὗτος οὐ νεκρὸς ἀλλὰ ζῶν, καὶ ζήσας ἐκ τοῦ τεθνηκέναι αὐτῷ *τὸν πατέρα*. Ὁ δὲ νεκρὸς γενόμενος πατὴρ οὐκ ἔστι τοῦ ζῶντος νεκρός. Νεκρῶν δὲ ‹πατήρ ἐστι› οἷς *τοὺς ἑαυτῶν* καθῄκει θάπτειν *νεκρούς*.

Τὸ δὲ *ἄφες τοὺς νεκροὺς θάψαι τοὺς ἑαυτῶν νεκροὺς* τὸ μηκέτι σχολάζειν περὶ τὰ νενεκρωμένα πράγματα. *Νεκρώσατε* γὰρ ὑμῶν *τὰ μέλη τὰ ἐπὶ τῆς γῆς, ἅτινα ἐστι πορνεία* καὶ τὰ ἑξῆς.[753] Ταῦτα οὖν νεκρά ἐστιν. Ἀπόβαλε ἀπὸ σοῦ, ἀπόκοψον ὡς νενεκρωμένην σάρκα μιαίνουσαν ὅλον τὸ σῶμα, ἵνα μὴ ῥηθῇ *ἄφες τοὺς νεκροὺς* τοὺς ἔχοντας ἐν ἑαυτοῖς τὴν νεκροῦσαν ἁμαρτίαν[dlxxiv] *θάψαι τοὺς ἑαυτῶν νεκρούς*. Ἄτοπόν δε φαίνεταί τισι καὶ ἐναντίον τὸ μὴ ἐπιτρέπειν τὸν Σωτῆρα θάπτειν τὸν μαθητὴν *τὸν πατέρα*· ἀπανθρωπίας γὰρ ἦν τὸ ἔργον. Οὐ μέντοι ἐ | **63r** κώλυσεν ὁ Ἰησοῦς θάπτειν[754] τὸν νεκρόν, ἀλλὰ τὸν *ζῆν* ποιοῦντα τοὺς ἀνθρώπους[755] προκρῖναι, τῷ *κηρύσσειν τὴν βασιλείαν*[756] *τῶν οὐρανῶν.*[757] Περὶ γὰρ τὸ θάπτειν τὸ σῶμα ἦσαν πολλοί.

---

750 Matt. 8:21; Luke, 9:59.
751 Matt. 8:22; Luke, 9:60.
752 Cf. Matt. 8:22; Luke, 9:59.
753 Col. 3:5.
754 Cod. μὴ θάπτειν.
755 Cf. Deut. 32:39; 4 Macc. 18:19 (Odae, 2:9); Daniel, 4:37a.
756 Cf. Luke, 9:60.
757 Cf. Matt. 3:1; 4:17; 10:7.

Τὸ δὲ *ἄφες τοὺς νεκροὺς θάψαι τοὺς ἑαυτῶν νεκροὺς* τὸ μηκέτι σχολάζειν περὶ τὰ νενεκρωμένα πράγματα. *νεκρώσατε* γὰρ ὑμῶν *τὰ μέλη τὰ ἐπὶ τῆς γῆς*, ἅτινά ἐστι πορνεία καὶ τὰ ἑξῆς.[758] ταῦτα οὖν νεκρά ἐστιν, ἀπόβαλε ἀπὸ σοῦ, ἀπόκοψον ὡς νενεκρωμένην σάρκα μιαίνουσαν ὅλον τὸ σῶμα, ἵνα μὴ ρηθῇ. *ἄφες τοὺς νεκροὺς* τοὺς ἔχοντας ἐν ἑαυτοῖς τὴν νεκροῦσαν ἁμαρτίαν *θάψαι τοὺς ἑαυτῶν νεκρούς*. ἄτοπον δὲ φαίνεταί τισι καὶ ἐναντίον τὸ μὴ ἐπιτρέπειν τὸν σωτῆρα θάπτειν τὸν μαθητὴν *τὸν πατέρα*. ἀπανθρωπίας γὰρ τὸ ἔργον. οὐ μέντοι ἐκώλυσεν ὁ Ἰησοῦς μὴ θάπτειν τὸν νεκρόν, ἀλλὰ τὸν *ζῆν* ποιοῦντα τοὺς ἀνθρώπους προκρίνει, τῷ *κηρύσσειν τὴν βασιλείαν τῶν οὐρανῶν*. περὶ γὰρ τὸ θάπτειν τὸ σῶμα ἦσαν πολλοί.[dlxxv]

Ὑψηλότερον δέ. ὅτε ἐτεθνήκει τῷ νεανίσκῳ ὁ πατὴρ καὶ ἦν νεκρός, τότε ὑπὸ τοῦ σωτῆρος ἐκλήθη. νομίζω δὲ ὅτι, ὥσπερ ὁ κόσμος Παύλῳ ἐσταύρωτο καὶ νεκρὸς ἦν, ἐπεὶ τέθνηκεν αὐτῷ τὰ τοῦ κόσμου πράγματα, μηκέτι αὐτὰ σκοποῦντι ὡς *βλεπόμενα καὶ πρόσκαιρα*, οὕτως ἑκάστῳ δικαίῳ τέθνηκεν ὁ διάβολος, ὅστις αὐτῷ ἔζη ἁμαρτάνοντι. πᾶς γὰρ *ὁ ποιῶν τὴν ἁμαρτίαν ἐκ τοῦ διαβόλου γεγένηται*, παντὶ δὲ ἁμαρτάνοντι καὶ σκοποῦντι τὰ τῇδε ζῇ ὁ πονηρὸς πατήρ. παντὶ δέ, ᾧ τέθνηκεν ὁ πονηρός, λέγοιτ᾽ ἂν ὑπὸ τοῦ σωτῆρος τό. *ἀκολούθει μοι*. καὶ τάχα τοιοῦτόν ἐστι μυστικῶς νοούμενον τὸ δεῖν μισεῖσθαι ὑφ᾽ ἡμῶν τὸν πατέρα, εἰ μέλλοιμεν ἄξιοι ἔσεσθαι τοῦ Ἰησοῦ. τὸ δέ. *τοὺς νεκροὺς θάψαι* τοὺς ἑαυτῶν νεκροὺς ἀλληγορεῖται μόνον. θάπτουσι γάρ πως νεκροὶ *τοὺς ἑαυτῶν νεκροὺς* ἐν ἑαυτοῖς, τάφοι καὶ μνημεῖα αὐτῶν γενόμενοι. τέλεον δὲ καταλείπει τὸν νεκρὸν καὶ οὐδαμῶς ἔτι αὐτοῦ ἅπτεται ὁ πειθόμενος τῷ Ἰησοῦ. οἶδε γὰρ ὅτι ὁ ἁπτόμενος νεκροῦ μολύνεται.[dlxxvi]

Εἰ νεκροὶ εἰώθασι θάπτειν *τοὺς ἑαυτῶν νεκρούς*, ψυχὴ ἐν κακίᾳ οὖσα νεκρά ἐστι. Καὶ εἰ ὁ αἰσθητὸς θάνατος διὰ τὴν ἁμαρτίαν, καλῶς *ἡ ἁμαρτία θάνατος* λέγεται[759] καὶ ὁ ἐν αὐτῇ ὢν νεκρός ἐστιν. Εἰδὼς δὲ ὁ Χριστὸς τὴν ἐπιτηδειότητα τῆς τούτου ψυχῆς ἐπὶ τὰ καλὰ καὶ ἄκοντα ἀκολουθεῖν ἐκέλευσεν.

Εἰ νεκροὶ εἰώθασι θάπτειν *τοὺς ἑαυτῶν νεκρούς*, ψυχὴ ἐν κακίᾳ οὖσα νεκρά ἐστι. καὶ εἰ ὁ αἰσθητὸς θάνατος διὰ τὴν ἁμαρτίαν, καλῶς *ἡ ἁμαρτία θάνατος* λέγεται[760] καὶ ὁ ἐν αὐτῇ ὢν νεκρός ἐστιν. εἰδὼς δὲ ὁ Χριστὸς τὴν ἐπιτηδειότητα τῆς τούτου ψυχῆς ἐπὶ τὰ καλὰ καὶ ἄκοντα ἀκολουθεῖν ἐκέλευσεν.[dlxxvii]

Καὶ ἰδοὺ σεισμὸς μέγας ἐγένετο.[761] Ἵνα μὴ μέγα φρονῶσιν ἐπὶ τούτῳ ὅτι τοὺς ἄλλους πέμψας αὐτοὺς κατέσχε μόνους, ἀφίησιν αὐτοὺς κλυδωνισθῆναι καὶ ἵνα διὰ τοῦ σημείου ἐμποιήσῃ αὐτοῖς τὴν περὶ αὐτοῦ πίστιν. Διὰ τοῦτο δὲ καθεύδει, γυμνάζων αὐτοὺς τοὺς πειρασμοὺς φέρειν γενναίως. Εἰ γὰρ ἐγρηγορότος ἐγένετο ὁ χειμών, ἢ οὐκ ἂν ἐφοβήθησαν ἢ οὐκ ἂν παρεκάλεσαν ἢ οὐδ᾽ ἂν αὐτὸν ἐνόμισαν δύνασθαι τοιοῦτόν τι ποιεῖν. Καθεύδει τοίνυν διδοὺς καιρὸν τῇ δειλίᾳ καὶ ὡς ἄνθρωπος διδοὺς τῷ σώματι τὸ οἰκεῖον.

758 Col. 3:5.
759 Cf. Rom. 5:12; 6:16; 6:21&23; 7:10-11&13; 8:2; 1 Cor. 15:56; James, 1:15.
760 Cf. Rom. 5:12; 6:16; 6:21&23; 7:10-11&13; 8:2; 1 Cor. 15:56; James, 1:15.
761 Matt. 8:24.

> Διὰ τοῦτο ἀφίησι τοὺς μαθητὰς κλυδωνισθῆναι, ἵνα μὴ μέγα φρονῶσιν, ὅτι τοὺς ἄλλους ἐκπέμψας, αὐτοὺς κατέσχε μεθ' ἑαυτοῦ. ἅμα δὲ καὶ γυμνάζων αὐτοὺς πειρασμοὺς φέρειν γενναίως, μέλλοντας τῆς οἰκουμένης ἀθλητὰς γενέσθαι. τὸ δὲ *τί δειλοί ἐστε ὀλιγόπιστοι;* διὰ τούτου παιδεύων αὐτούς, ὅτι τὸν φόβον οὐχ ἡ τῶν πειρασμῶν ἐργάζεται ἐπαγωγή, ἀλλὰ τὸ τῆς διανοίας ἀσθενές.[dlxxviii] διὰ τοῦτο δὲ καὶ καθεύδει, διδοὺς καιρὸν τῇ δειλίᾳ, ἵνα δι' αὐτῆς αἰσθόμενοι σωτηρίας, καὶ αὐτοὶ εὐεργεθηθῶσιν. διὰ τοῦτο δὲ ἄνθρωπον οἱ ὄχλοι ὠνόμαζον, οὐχ ὡς Θεὸν ἐλογίσαντο τοιαῦτα θαυματουργήσαντα. *ποταπός,* γάρ φησιν, *ἔστιν ὁ ἄνθρωπος οὗτος,* καὶ τὰ ἑξῆς. ἀπό τε τῆς ὄψεως, ἀπό τε τοῦ ὕπνου καὶ τοῦ πλοίῳ κεχρῆσθαι.[dlxxix]

> Ἵνα γὰρ μὴ μέγα φρονῶσιν, ὅτι τοὺς ἄλλους ἐκπέμψας αὐτοὺς κατέσχεν, ἀφίησι κλυδωνισθῆναι, τοῦτό τε κατορθῶν, καὶ γυμνάζων πειρασμοὺς φέρειν γενναίως.[dlxxx]

Εἶτα, *προσελθόντες ἤγειραν αὐτὸν*[762] οἱ μαθηταὶ γνόντες τὴν ἰδίαν ἀσθένειαν καὶ δειλιάσαντες. Ὡς ἔτι γὰρ ἀτελεῖς ὄντες[dlxxxi] ὑπώπτευσαν ὅτι καθεύδων οὐκ ἐδύνατο αὐτοὺς σῶσαι.
Τὸ γὰρ εἰπεῖν *Κύριε σῶσον* ἡμᾶς ἔπαινον ἔχει πίστεως· τὸ δὲ εἰπεῖν *ἀπολλύμεθα* ὀλιγοπιστίας. Ὀλιγοπιστίας γὰρ ἔγκλημα τὸ κίνδυνον αὐτοὺς ὑποπτεύειν συμπλέοντος αὐτοῖς τοῦ Χριστοῦ,

> Τὸ εἰπεῖν *σῶσον* ἔπαινον ἔχει πίστεως, τὸ δὲ εἰπεῖν *ἀπολλύμεθα* ἔγκλημα ὀλιγοπιστίας τοῖς κίνδυνον ἐλπίζουσι συμπλέοντος Χριστοῦ. οὐκ ἄπιστοι δὲ ὁλοτελῶς, ἀλλ' ὀλιγόπιστοι οἱ μὴ καταθαρσήσαντες κινδύνων συνόντος Χριστοῦ.[dlxxxii]

διὸ καὶ ἤλεγξεν αὐτοὺς εἰπών, *τί δειλοί ἐστε ὀλιγόπιστοι;*

Τότε ἐγερθεὶς ἐπετίμησε τοῖς ἀνέμοις.[763] Μετὰ τὸ παῦσαι | **63v** τὸν χειμῶνα τῆς ψυχῆς αὐτῶν, λύει καὶ τὸν τῆς θαλάσσης κλύδωνα, δεικνὺς ὅτι τὸν φόβον οὐχ ἡ τῶν πειρασμῶν ἐργάζεται ἐπαγωγὴ ἀλλὰ τὸ τῆς διανοίας ἀσθενές.[dlxxxiii] Ἀτελεῖς γὰρ ὄντες ἔτι, ἠγνόουν ὅτι Θεὸς ἦν ὁ συμπλέων αὐτοῖς. Διὸ καὶ ἐθαύμαζον λέγοντες, *ποταπός ἐστι οὗτος, ὅτι καὶ οἱ ἄνεμοι καὶ ἡ θάλασσα ὑπακούουσιν αὐτῷ;*[764]

Ὑπήντησαν αὐτῷ δύο δαιμονιζόμενοι.[765] Ἐπειδὴ οὗτος μὲν *δύο* δαιμονιζομένους εἶπε τοὺς ἀπὸ *τῶν μνημείων* ἐξελθόντας, ὁ δὲ Λουκᾶς καὶ ὁ Μᾶρκος ἕνα,[766] σκέψαι μήποτε τῶν *δύο* τῶν παρὰ τῷ Ματθαίῳ εἷς ἦν ὁ τὸν λεγεῶνα ἔχων, περὶ οὗ τὸν λόγον ἐποιήσατο ὅ τε Λουκᾶς καὶ ὁ Μᾶρκος,[767] ἱστοροῦντες τὰ κατ' αὐτὸν μόνον διὰ τὸ ἐπισημότερον εἶναι ‹καὶ πλείονα περὶ αὐτὸν γεγονέναι›. Ὅθεν, τὰ μὲν ὁμοίως ὁ Ματθαῖος γενικῶς περὶ τῶν δύο δαιμονιζομένων ἀνέγραψε καὶ οὗτοι περὶ τοῦ ἑνὸς

---

762 Matt. 8:25.
763 Matt. 8:26.
764 Matt. 8:27.
765 Matt. 8:28.
766 Mark, 5:1-15; Luke, 8:26-39.
767 Mark, 5:9&15; Luke, 8:30.

ἐμνημόνευσαν, τὰ δὲ ἰδίως καὶ ἀφωρισμένως περὶ τοῦ τὸν λεγεῶνα ἐσχηκότος, διὰ τὸ σεσιωπῆσθαι τῷ Ματθαίῳ τὴν κατὰ μέρος περὶ αὐτοῦ διήγησιν.

(ΩΡΙΓΕΝΟΥΣ, added on the margin) Εἰ μὲν γὰρ εἶπον ὅτι εἷς μόνος ἦν ἕτερος δὲ οὐκ ἦν, ἐδόκουν ἀμφιβάλλειν τῷ Ματθαίῳ. Εἰ δὲ ὁ μὲν περὶ τοῦ ἑνὸς ὁ δὲ περὶ τῶν δύο διελέχθη, οὐ μάχης τὸ εἰρημένον ἀλλὰ διαφόρου διηγήσεως.

> Ἐπειδὴ ὁ Ματθαῖος μὲν *δύο* δαιμονιζομένους εἶπε τοὺς ἀπὸ *τῶν μνημείων* ἐξελθόντας, ὁ δὲ Λουκᾶς καὶ ὁ Μᾶρκος ἕνα, σκέψαι μήποτε τῶν *δύο* τῶν παρὰ τῷ Ματθαίῳ εἷς ἦν ὁ τὸν λεγεῶνα ἔχων, περὶ οὗ τὸν λόγον ἐποιήσατο ὅ τε Μᾶρκος καὶ ὁ Λουκᾶς, ἱστοροῦντες τὰ κατ᾽ αὐτὸν μόνον διὰ τὸ ἐπισημότερον εἶναι. καὶ πλείονα περὶ αὐτὸν γεγονέναι. ὅθεν τὰ μὲν ὁμοίως ὁ Ματθαῖος γενικῶς περὶ τῶν δύο δαιμονιζομένων ἀνέγραψε καὶ οὗτοι περὶ τοῦ ἑνὸς ἐμνημόνευσαν, τὰ δὲ ἰδίως καὶ ἀφωρισμένως περὶ τοῦ τὸν λεγεῶνα ἐσχηκότος, διὰ τὸ παρασεσιωπῆσθαι παρὰ τῷ Ματθαίῳ τὴν κατὰ μέρος περὶ αὐτοῦ διήγησιν.[dlxxxiv]

> Ἰστέον δὲ ὡς Μᾶρκος μὲν καὶ Λουκᾶς ἕνα φασὶν εἶναι τὸν δαιμονιζόμενον, Ματθαῖος δὲ δύο. τοῦτο δὲ οὐ διαφωνίαν ἐμφαίνει. εἰ μὲν γὰρ εἶπον ὅτι εἷς μόνος ἦν [sic], ἐδόκουν ἀμφιβάλλειν τῷ Ματθαίῳ. εἰ μὲν δὲ οἱ μὲν περὶ τοῦ ἑνός, ὁ δὲ περὶ τῶν δύο διελέχθη, οὐ μάχης τὸ εἰρημένον, ἀλλὰ διαφόρου διηγήσεως.[dlxxxv]

(ΩΡΙΓΕΝΟΥΣ, added on the margin) Οἱ Γεργεσηνοὶ ἐκ τοῦ γένους ἦσαν τοῦ Χαναάν.[dlxxxvi]

(ΩΡΙΓΕΝΟΥΣ, main text cont.) Ἐπειδὴ δὲ οὕτως φοβεροὶ ἦσαν οἱ δαιμονιζόμενοι καὶ οὐδεὶς αὐτοὺς προσαγαγεῖν ἐτόλμα τῷ Χριστῷ, οὗτος ἀφ᾽ ἑαυτοῦ ἀπῆλθεν ἐκεῖ. Ἐν τοῖς τάφοις δὲ ἐμφιλοχωροῦσιν οἱ δαίμονες,[dlxxxvii] ὀλέθριον δόγμα τοῖς πολλοῖς ἐνθεῖναι βουλόμενοι, ὅτι αἱ ‹φαῦλαι› ψυχαὶ μετὰ θάνατον δαίμονες γίνονται.[dlxxxviii]

> τίνος δὲ χάριν αὐτὸς ἀπῆλθε πρὸς αὐτούς; ἐπειδὴ οὐδεὶς αὐτοὺς προσενεγκεῖν ἐτόλμα τοῖς πολλοῖς ἐνθεῖναι βουλόμενοι, οἷον ὅτι αἱ ψυχαὶ τῶν ἀπελθόντων δαίμονες γίνονται. ὃ μὴ γένοιτό ποτε, κἂν μέχρις ἐννοίας λαβεῖν.[dlxxxix]

Ἐπειδὴ δὲ ὑπὸ τῆς ἀφάτου δυνάμεως αὐτοῦ ἐφλογίζοντο, ἀνέκραξαν λέγοντες· *τί ἡμῖν καὶ σοί Ἰησοῦ υἱὲ τοῦ Θεοῦ; ἦλθες ὧδε πρὸ καιροῦ βασανίσαι ἡμᾶς;*[768] Καὶ υἱὸν μὲν τοῦ Θεοῦ λέγουσι, | **64r** πῇ μὲν νικώμενοι ὑπὸ τῆς δυνάμεως αὐτοῦ, πῇ δὲ περιηχούμενοι ἀπὸ τῆς παρ᾽ αὐτοῦ ὡς Υἱοῦ Θεοῦ διδασκαλίας.[dxc]

> *υἱὲ* δὲ λέγουσι *Θεοῦ* οἱ δαίμονες πῇ μὲν νικώμενοι ὑπὸ τῆς δυνάμεως αὐτοῦ, πῇ δὲ περιηχούμενοι ἀπὸ τῆς παρ᾽ αὐτοῦ ὡς υἱοῦ Θεοῦ διδασκαλίας.[dxci]

> Τί δήποτε καὶ τοῖς τάφοις ἐμφιλοχωροῦσιν οἱ δαίμονες; ὀλέθριον δόγμα τοῖς πολλοῖς ἐνθεῖναι βουλόμενοι, οἷον ὅτι αἱ ψυχαὶ τῶν ἀπελθόντων δαίμονες γίνονται. ὃ μηδέποτε γένοιτο μηδὲ μέχρις ἐννοίας λαβεῖν.[dxcii]

---

768 Matt. 8:29; Luke, 8:28.

Τὸ δὲ *ἦλθες πρὸ καιροῦ βασανίσαι ἡμᾶς* νομίσαντες ἤδη τὴν κόλασιν ἐφεστάναι, λέγουσιν. Ἔδεισαν γὰρ ὡς εἰς τιμωρίαν ἐμπεσούμενοι καὶ πρὸ τῆς κρίσεως, ἐπειδὴ ἐνόμισαν αὐτὸν δι᾽ ὑπερβολὴν τῶν γινομένων οὐκ ἀναμενεῖν τὸν καιρὸν τῆς κρίσεως. Ἄλλως τε δέ, ᾔδεισαν ἀπὸ τῶν προφητῶν ὅτι ἔμελλεν ἥξειν ὁ Χριστὸς καὶ ὅτι αὐτὸς μέλλει κρίνειν αὐτούς. Φασὶ δὲ τὸ *πρὸ καιροῦ* ὡς διαβάλλοντες τὸν τῆς ἐνανθρωπήσεως καιρὸν γεγονότα. Πονηροὶ γὰρ ὄντες τολμῶσι λέγειν τοιαῦτα. Βάσανον γὰρ ἡγοῦνται μὴ συγχωρούμενοι ἀδικεῖν τοὺς ἀνθρώπους ἕως τοῦ καιροῦ *τῆς κρίσεως.*[769] ‹Μήποτε δὲ τὰ δαιμόνια οὐδέπω ἄξια ἐκρίθη τοῦ παθεῖν τι ἀπ᾽ ὀργῆς Θεοῦ τῆς παιδευούσης τοὺς μὴ θέλοντας λόγῳ εἶξαι.› Καὶ γὰρ ἡ μακροθυμία τοῦ Σωτῆρος συγχωρεῖ τὸν μεταξὺ τῆς συντελείας χρόνον διὰ τοὺς ἔτι ἀθλοῦντας καὶ δυναμένους κατὰ τῆς λεγεῶνος στῆναι τῶν δαιμόνων καὶ διὰ τοῦτο στεφανωθῆναι. ‹Ὡς οὖν καιρὸν ἔχοντες ἃ βούλονται ποιεῖν ἐν τῷ μέσῳ περὶ τοὺς ἀνθρώπους, οὕτω κατεβόων τοῦ Κυρίου, ὡς ἂν πρὸ τοῦ προσήκοντος καιροῦ μάτην αὐτοὺς βιαζομένου καὶ τιμωρίαις ὑπάγοντος.›

> Μήποτε δὲ τὰ δαιμόνια οὐδέπω ἄξια ἐκρίθη τοῦ παθεῖν τι ἀπ᾽ ὀργῆς θεοῦ τῆς παιδευούσης τοὺς μὴ θέλοντας λόγῳ εἶξαι. ἀλλ᾽ ἡ μακροθυμία τοῦ σωτῆρος συγχωρεῖ τὸν μεταξὺ τῆς συντελείας χρόνον διὰ ἐπαθλοῦντας καὶ δυναμένους κατὰ τῆς λεγεῶνος τῶν δαιμόνων στεφανωθῆναι. ὡς οὖν καιρὸν ἔχοντες ἃ βούλονται ποιεῖν ἐν τῷ μέσῳ περὶ τοὺς ἀνθρώπους, οὕτω κατεβόων τοῦ Κυρίου, ὡς ἂν πρὸ τοῦ προσήκοντος καιροῦ μάτην αὐτοὺς βιαζομένου καὶ τιμωρίαις ὑπάγοντος.[dxciii]

> ἄλλως δέ, φησιν, εἰ καὶ ἄγαν εἰσὶ μοχθηροὶ τὸν τρόπον οἱ δαίμονες, ἀλλ᾽ οὖν γε ἴσασιν ὅτι πάντως αὐτοὺς ὑπὲρ τῶν ἁμαρτημάτων μένει τις κόλασις ὕστερον. ὅτι δὲ οὐχ ὁ καιρὸς ἐπέστη τῆς κολάσεως, ῥᾳδίως ἠδύναντο γνῶναι, ἐξ ὧν οὐ τιμωρίᾳ παρεδίδοντο νῦν, ἀλλ᾽ ὥστε ἀναχωρῆσαι μόνον τῶν ἀνθρώπων συνώθει αὐτούς. ἔλεγε γὰρ ὁ Σωτήρ, *ἔξελθε τὸ πνεῦμα τὸ ἀκάθαρτον ἐκ τοῦ ἀνθρώπου.* ὡς οὖν καιρὸν ἔχοντες ἃ βούλονται ποιεῖν ἐν τῷ μέσῳ περὶ τοὺς ἀνθρώπους, οὕτω κατεβόων τοῦ Κυρίου, ὡς ἂν πρὸ τοῦ προσήκοντος καιροῦ μάτην αὐτοὺς βιαζομένου καὶ τιμωρίαις ὑπάγοντος.[dxciv]

Ζήτει εἰ κατὰ γνῶσιν λέγουσιν ἢ οὔ, ἢ κατ᾽ ἐκείνους τοὺς λέγοντας, *τὸ αἷμα αὐτοῦ ἐφ᾽ ἡμᾶς καὶ ἐπὶ τὰ τέκνα ἡμῶν.*[770] Ὅλην δὲ τὴν ἐξήγησιν κατὰ λέξιν ἐρεύνα νοερῶς. Οἱ δαίμονες τῶν ἐπουρανίων ἀποστάται γενόμενοι τὸν περίγειον τόπον κατέσχον, οὐκ ἀποκληρωτικῶς, ἀλλὰ λόγῳ τινὶ ἀπορρήτῳ.[dxcv] Ὅθεν καὶ φοβεροὶ ἦσαν ἔχοντες οἰκητήριον ἐνθάδε, ὅθεν καὶ τοῦτον ἤμειψαν κατὰ κρίσιν τοῦ Θεοῦ. Διὰ τοῦτο οὖν ἐβόων, *ἦλθες ὧδε.* Διὸ οὐδεὶς ἐδύνατο ὁδεύειν. Τὸ δὲ *πέραν* ζήτει· ἤτοι τοῦτον τὸν κόσμον ἐκ τοῦ κρείττονος ἢ τὰ ἔθνη ἐκ τοῦ Ἰσραήλ.

> Ζήτει εἰ κατὰ γνῶσιν λέγουσιν ἢ οὔ, ἢ κατ᾽ ἐκείνους τοὺς λέγοντας *τὸ αἷμα αὐτοῦ ἐφ᾽ ἡμᾶς καὶ ἐπὶ τὰ τέκνα ἡμῶν.* ὅλην δὲ τὴν ἐξήγησιν κατὰ λέξιν ἐρεύνα νοερῶς. οἱ δαίμονες

---

769 Cf. Esther, 10:3h; Ecclesiastes, 8:5-6.

770 Matt. 27:25.

τῶν ἐπουρανίων ἀποστάται γενόμενοι τὸν περίγειον τόπον κατέσχον, οὐκ ἀποκληρωτικῶς, ἀλλὰ λόγῳ τινὶ ἀπορρήτῳ, ὅθεν καὶ φοβεροὶ ἦσαν ἔχοντες οἰκητήριον ἐνθάδε, ὅθεν καὶ τοῦτον ἤμειψαν κατὰ κρίσιν τοῦ Θεοῦ. διὰ τοῦτο οὖν ἐβόων, *ἦλθες ὧδε*, διὸ οὐδεὶς ἠδύνατο ὁδεύειν. τὸ δὲ *πέραν* ζήτει ἤτοι τοῦτον τὸν κόσμον ἐκ τοῦ κρείττονος ἢ τὰ ἔθνη ἐκ τοῦ Ἰσραήλ.[dxcvi]

| **64v** *Ἦν δὲ μακρὰν ἀπ' αὐτῶν ἀγέλη χοίρων.*[771] Ὡς ἀσθενεῖς παρὰ μείζονος αἰτοῦσι δοῦναι αὐτοῖς κατὰ τῶν *χοίρων* τὴν ἐξουσίαν. Σκοπὸς γὰρ αὐτοῖς πονηροῖς οὖσιν οὐ μόνον ἀνθρώπους βλάπτειν ἀλλὰ καὶ ἄλογα.[dxcvii]
Τοῦτο δὲ συγχωρεῖ ὁ Σωτήρ, οὐ πειθόμενος τοῖς δαίμοσιν, ἀλλ' ἵνα δείξῃ τὸ πλῆθος τῆς λεγεῶνος τῶν δαιμόνων καὶ ὅτι οὐδὲ χοίρων κατατολμῶσι

Διὰ τί δέ, ὅπερ παρεκάλεσαν οἱ δαίμονες, ἐποίησεν ὁ δεσπότης τῶν ὅλων Χριστός, εἰς τὴν ἀγέλην τῶν χοίρων ἐπιτρέψας αὐτοῖς ἀπελθεῖν; οὐκ ἐκείνοις πειθόμενος τοῦτο ἐποίησεν, ἀλλ' ἵνα μάθωσιν ἅπαντες, ὅτι οὔτε χοίρων κατατολμῶσιν, εἰ μὴ αὐτὸς συγχωρήσειεν,[dxcviii]

καὶ ἵνα δείξῃ ποίας ὁ Χριστὸς ἀπήλλαξε τοὺς ἀνθρώπους τυραννίδος. Ἦ γὰρ ἂν καὶ χείρω τῶν χοίρων διεχρῶντο τοὺς ἀνθρώπους, εἰ τῆς ἐξουσίας αὐτῶν τὸ ὅλον ἦν. Ἀνεῖλον δὲ τοὺς χοίρους ἵνα λυπήσωσι τοὺς δεσπότας αὐτῶν, ἵνα μὴ παραδέξωνται τὴν τοῦ Χριστοῦ διδασκαλίαν.

διὰ τοῦτο δὲ τοὺς χοίρους ἀνεῖλον οἱ δαίμονες, ἵνα τοὺς ἀνθρώπους εἰς ἀθυμίαν ἐμβάλωσι. πανταχοῦ γὰρ χαίρουσιν ἐπὶ ταῖς συμφοραῖς ἡμῶν.[dxcix]

(ΩΡΙΓΕΝΟΥΣ, cont.) Εἰ μὴ οἱ χοῖροι *κατὰ τοῦ κρημνοῦ εἰς τὴν θάλασσαν* ὥρμησαν καὶ ἀπεπνίγησαν *ἐν τοῖς ὕδασιν*, οὐκ ἂν *οἱ βόσκοντες* τοὺς χοίρους *ἔφυγον* τοῦ βόσκειν χοίρους καὶ κήρυκες τῶν θαυμάτων τῆς ἀληθείας ἐγίνοντο.

Εἰ μὴ οἱ χοῖροι *κατὰ τοῦ κρημνοῦ εἰς τὴν θάλασσαν* ὥρμησαν καὶ ἀπεπνίγησαν *ἐν τοῖς ὕδασιν*, οὐκ ἂν *οἱ βόσκοντες* τοὺς χοίρους *ἔφυγον* τοῦ βόσκειν χοίρους καὶ κήρυκες τῶν θαυμάτων τῆς ἀληθείας ἐγίνοντο.[dc]

(Ὠριγένους.) Εἰ μὴ οἱ χοῖροι κατὰ τοῦ κρημνοῦ εἰς τὴν θάλασσαν ὥρμησαν καὶ ἀπεπνίγησαν ἐν τοῖς ὕδασιν, οὐκ ἂν οἱ βόσκοντες τοὺς χοίρους ἔφυγον τοῦ βόσκειν χοίρους, καὶ κήρυκες τῶν θαυμάτων τῆς ἀληθείας ἐγένοντο.[dci]

Διατὶ δὲ *εἰς τοὺς χοίρους* ἀξιοῦσιν εἰσελθεῖν; Ὅταν κατὰ ἀνθρώπων οὐ δύνωνται, κατὰ ἀλόγων βούλονται τῶν διὰ ἄνθρωπον ὄντων·[772] ἢ γὰρ αὐτὸν ἢ τὰ αὐτοῦ κακοῦσιν οἱ μισάνθρωποι.

771 Matt. 8:30; Luke 8:32. Cf. Mark, 5:11. Luke, 5:17-20.

772 Animals have been created for the sake of man. Cf. *Cels*, IV.74; *Philocalia*, 20.1-2.

Διατὶ δὲ *εἰς τοὺς χοίρους* ἀξιοῦσιν εἰσελθεῖν; ὅταν κατὰ ἀνθρώπων οὐ δύνωνται, κατὰ ἀλόγων βούλονται τῶν διὰ ἄνθρωπον ὄντων. ἢ γὰρ αὐτὸν ἢ τὰ αὐτοῦ κακοῦσιν οἱ μισάνθρωποι.[dcii]

Καὶ ἰδόντες αὐτὸν παρεκάλεσαν ὅπως μεταβῇ.[773] Ὡς ἀναίσθητοι τοῦτο εἶπον καὶ ἄγαν ἄπιστοι.[dciii]

Ὡς ἀναίσθητοι τοῦτο εἶπον καὶ ἄγαν ἄπιστοι.[dciv]

Διατὶ δὲ *εἰς τοὺς χοίρους* ἀξιοῦσιν εἰσελθεῖν; ὅταν κατὰ ἀνθρώπων οὐ δύνωνται, κατὰ ἀλόγων βούλονται τῶν διὰ ἄνθρωπον ὄντων. ἢ γὰρ αὐτὸν ἢ τὰ αὐτοῦ κακοῦσιν οἱ μισάνθρωποι. *ἰδόντες* δὲ τηλικοῦτον σημεῖον οἱ Γεργεσηνοὶ *παρακαλοῦσιν* τὸν Ἰησοῦν μεταβῆναι *ἀπὸ τῶν ὁρίων αὐτῶν*, ἐπειδὴ πόθον οὐκ εἶχον τοῦ ἀγαθοῦ. καὶ γὰρ οὐχ ὡς ἀναξίους ἑαυτοὺς κρίνοντες τοῦτ' εἶπον, ἀλλ' ὡς ἀναίσθητοι καὶ ἄγαν ἄπιστοι.[dcv]

Ἰδόντες δὲ οἱ Γεργεσ‹η›νοὶ[774] *παρεκάλεσαν* αὐτὸν μεταβῆναι *ἀπὸ τῶν ὁρίων αὐτῶν*, οὐκ ἀπωθούμενοι, ἀλλὰ ταπεινοφρονοῦντες, ὡς οὐκ ἄξιοι ὄντες τοσοῦτον ἀγαθὸν ἐπὶ τῆς οἰκείας χώρας ἔχειν, δείσαντες μήπου τι καὶ μεῖζον πάθωσιν ἀπὸ τῆς αὐτοῦ δυνάμεως τῶν οἰκείων ἁμαρτιῶν ἕνεκεν.

Καὶ ἰδόντες οἱ Γεργεσινοὶ *παρεκάλεσαν* αὐτὸν μεταβῆναι *ἀπὸ τῶν ὁρίων αὐτῶν*, οὐκ ἀπωθούμενοι, ἀλλὰ ταπεινοφρονοῦντες, ὡς οὐκ ἄξιοι ὄντες ἐπὶ τῆς οἰκείας χώρας ἔχειν τοσοῦτον ἀγαθόν, δείσαντες μήπου τι καὶ μεῖζον πάθωσιν ἀπὸ τῆς αὐτοῦ δυνάμεως τῶν οἰκείων ἁμαρτιῶν ἕνεκα.[dcvi]

(Ὠριγένους.) Οὐκ ἀπωθούμενοι, ἀλλὰ ταπεινοφρονοῦντες[dcvii]

Those who ask him to move out of their borders do this not out of pride (as some think[dcviii]), but out of humbleness. They evaluate themselves undeserving the presence of the Lord, just as Peter did also at the catch of the fish, when he fell down at his knees of the Saviour and said: 'Depart from me, for I am a sinful man, Lord'.[775][dcix]

Διεπέρασε καὶ ἦλθεν εἰς τὴν ἰδίαν πόλιν.[776] Ἰδίαν αὐτοῦ πόλιν | **65r** ἐνταῦθα τὴν Καπερναοὺμ λέγει· ἐκεῖ γὰρ διηνεκῶς ᾤκει. Ἤτοι τὴν Ναζαρέτ, ἐπειδὴ κἀκεῖ ἦν τραφείς. Ἡ ἡ μὲν γὰρ Βηθλεὲμ ἤνεγκεν αὐτόν, ἡ δὲ Ναζαρὲτ ἔθρεψεν,[dcx] ἡ δὲ Καπερναοὺμ εἶχεν οἰκοῦντα διηνεκῶς.

---

773 Matt. 8:34: καὶ ἰδόντες αὐτὸν παρεκάλεσαν ὅπως μεταβῇ ἀπὸ τῶν ὁρίων αὐτῶν.

774 Cod. Γεργεσινοί.

775 Luke, 5:8.

776 Matt. 9:1: Καὶ ἐμβὰς εἰς πλοῖον διεπέρασεν καὶ ἦλθεν εἰς τὴν ἰδίαν πόλιν.

Καὶ ἰδοὺ προσέφερον αὐτῷ παραλυτικόν.[777] Οὗτος ὁ παραλυτικὸς ἕτερός ἐστι παρὰ τὸν ἐν τῷ Ἰωάννῃ κείμενον.[778] Ὁ μὲν γὰρ ἐν τῇ κολυμβήθρᾳ κατέκειτο, οὗτος δὲ ἐν τῇ Καπερναούμ. Τοῦτο δέ φημὶ ἵνα μή τις διαφωνίαν εἶναι νομίσῃ ἕνα καὶ τὸν αὐτὸν ὑποπτεύσας παραλυτικὸν παρὰ πᾶσι τοῖς εὐαγγελισταῖς εἰρῆσθαι.

> Ὁ μέντοι παραλυτικὸς ἕτερος οὗτός ἐστι παρὰ τὸν ἐν τῷ Ἰωάννῃ κείμενον. Ὁ μὲν γὰρ ἐν τῇ κολυμβήθρᾳ κατέκειτο, οὗτος δὲ ἐν τῇ Καπερναοὺμ .... Ταῦτα δέ μοι οὐχ ἁπλῶς εἴρηται, ἀλλ᾽ ἵνα μή τις διαφωνίαν εἶναι νομίσῃ, ἕνα καὶ τὸν αὐτὸν ὑποπτεύσας παραλυτικόν.[dcxi]

Ὅτι μὲν γὰρ ὁ κατὰ Ἰωάννην παραλυτικὸς ἕτερός ἐστι τῶν ἐν τοῖς τρισὶν εἰρημένων, πολλὰ μὲν καὶ ἄλλα γνωρίσματα, μάλιστα δὲ τὸ τὸν μὲν ἐν ἐρημίᾳ εἶναι τῶν προστησομένων, τὸν δὲ ἔχειν τοὺς ἐπιμελουμένους, οἳ καὶ βαστάζοντες αὐτὸν ἔφερον. Μήποτε δὲ καὶ ἡ κατὰ πολλὰ ὁμοιότης παρὰ τοῖς τρισὶ περὶ τοῦ θεραπευθέντος παραλυτικοῦ εὑρεθ‹εί›η[779] ἄν[dcxii] τῷ ἐξετάζοντι, ὅτι
τρεῖς εἰσι παρὰ τοῖς τρισίν. Οὐδὲν γὰρ ἄτοπον τρεῖς παραλυτικοὺς διαφόρως προσενεχθῆναι αὐτῷ καὶ ὅμοια τινὰ τοῖς ἐφ᾽ ἑνὸς ἐπὶ τῶν ἄλλων δύο εἰρῆσθαι.

> Τρεῖς εἶναί φησι τοὺς παραλυτικούς, ἀλλ᾽ ἐν διαφόροις καιροῖς προσενηνέχθαι αὐτῷ, καὶ ὁμοιότητά τινα ἔχειν τοῖς ἐφ᾽ ἑνὸς ἐπὶ τῶν ἄλλων δύο.[dcxiii]

Ὁ μὲν γὰρ Ματθαῖος φησὶ ὅτι προσέφερον αὐτὸν μόνον, οἱ δὲ ἄλλοι καὶ ὅτι τὴν στέγην διατεμόντες καθῆκαν αὐτὸν καὶ προὔθηκαν τῷ Χριστῷ.[780] Δεύτερον δὲ παραλυτικὸν τοῦτον ὁ Ματθαῖός φησι· πρῶτος γὰρ ἦν ὁ τοῦ ἑκατοντάρχου παῖς.[781]

Ἰδὼν δὲ τὴν πίστιν αὐτῶν[782] ὁ Σωτήρ, τουτέστι τῶν προσενεγκόντων καὶ τοῦ παραλύτου ἢ τῶν προσενεγκόντων μόνον. Οὐ | **65v** γὰρ πανταχοῦ παρὰ τῶν καμνόντων ζητεῖ τὴν πίστιν, μάλιστα ὅταν ὑπὸ τοῦ νοσήματος ὦσιν ἐξεστηκότες. Λέγει τῷ παραλυτικῷ, *θάρσει τέκνον, ἀφέωνταί σοι αἱ ἁμαρτίαι σου.*[783] Αἰτίας γὰρ οὔσας τὰς ἁμαρτίας τῆς νόσου λύει αὐτὰς ὡς Θεός. Εἶτα, ἐπειδή *τινες τῶν γραμματέων* ἀκούσαντες τοῦτο, βλασφημίας ὑπώπτευσαν λέγειν αὐτόν, *εἰδὼς αὐτῶν τὰς ἐνθυμήσεις* ὡς Θεὸς φανεροῖ τὰς βουλὰς αὐτῶν καί φησι· *ἵνα τί ὑμεῖς ἐνθυμεῖσθε πονηρά,*[784] καὶ τὰ ἑξῆς.

777 Matt. 9:2; Mark, 2:3-12.
778 John, 5:7-8.
779 Cod. εὑρεθῇ.
780 Mark, 2:4.
781 Matt. 8:6.
782 Matt. 9:2.
783 Matt. 9:2.
784 Matt. 9:3-4.

Ἐπειδὴ δὲ οὐκ εἶχ‹ον›[785] παρὰ πόδας τὸν ἔλεγχον[dcxiv] τὸν ἀόρατον, καὶ ὁρατὴν ὑπισχνεῖται θεραπείαν. Δύο γὰρ ὑπέσχετο ποιεῖν εὐεργεσίας, μίαν ἀφανῆ καὶ μίαν ὁρατήν. Καὶ διὰ τῆς ὁρατῆς πιστοῦται καὶ τὴν ἀόρατον. Ἀμφότερα γὰρ ἰᾶται, ψυχὴν διὰ τῆς ἀφέσεως καὶ σῶμα διὰ τῆς ὑγείας. Διὰ οὖν τοῦ ἥττονος τὸ μεῖζον πιστοῦται.

> ἢ καὶ ἄλλως ἔστιν εἰπεῖν καὶ ἐπιλύσασθαι, ὡς ἑκάτερον μὲν τῆς αὐτῆς ἐστιν ἰσχύος. ἄμφω γὰρ τῆς θείας ἐστὶ καὶ ὑπὲρ ἀνθρώπους δυνάμεως. πλὴν ἐπειδὴ τὸ μὲν παρὰ πόδας ἔχει τὸν ἔλεγχον ἤτοι ἡ θεραπεία τοῦ σώματος, τὸ δὲ ἄδηλον ἔχει τῆς ἐπαγγελίας τὴν ἀπόδειξιν, εἰκότως *εὐκοπώτερον* ἐρρήθη ἡ τῆς ψυχῆς ἢ ἡ τοῦ σώματος ἴασις.[dcxv]

> Therefore, there is a bodily miracle that evinces the truth of the spiritual miracle. Nevertheless, the same power is needed to forgive the faults of both the body and the soul.[dcxvi]

Οἰκονομικῶς δὲ ἑαυτὸν υἱὸν *ἀνθρώπου*[786] φησί, δεικνὺς ὅτι καὶ ἄνθρωπος γεγονὼς καὶ Θεὸς ὀφθεὶς ἐπὶ γῆς ἀμφότερα θείᾳ δυνάμει ποιεῖ. Ἤτοι υἱὸν *ἀνθρώπου* τὴν κοινὴν τῶν ἀνθρώπων φύσιν καλεῖ, ἐπείπερ ἀρχὴν ἔλαβεν ὡς ἀπὸ ἀνθρώπου ἀναμαρτήτου τοῦ Χριστοῦ, διέβη δὲ καὶ ἐπὶ τοὺς πιστοὺς διὰ Πνεύματος Ἁγίου τὸ ἀφιέναι τὰς τινῶν ἁμαρτίας.

Ἀφέωνταί σοι αἱ ἁμαρτίαι σου.[787] Ἄλλο ζητῶ, καὶ ἄλλο χαρίζ‹ει›.[788] Ναί φησι, ἡ ψυχὴ νοσεῖ πρὸ τοῦ σώματος. Τὸ τοίνυν αἴτιον θεραπεύω τῆς νόσου καὶ συναναιρεῖται τὸ πάθος. Εἰσὶ γὰρ πολλοὶ καὶ δι᾽ ἁμαρτίας πάσχοντες.

Τί γάρ ἐστιν εὐκοπώτερον, εἰπεῖν ἀφέωνταί σοι αἱ ἁμαρτίαι;[789] Ὃ λέγει τοιοῦτόν ἐστι. Βλάσφημόν με νομίζετε ὡς ἐπαγγελλόμενον ἃ μὴ δύ | **66r** ναμαι, ἤγουν τῶν *ἁμαρτημάτων τὴν ἄφεσιν.*[790] Οὐκοῦν[791] εἰ μεγαλαυχίας τὴν φωνὴν ὑπολαμβάνετε εἶναι, τί νενόμισται ὑμῖν εὐκολώτερον ἐπαγγείλασθαι, τῶν ἁμαρτημάτων τὴν συγχώρησιν ἢ τῆς παραλύσεως τὴν θεραπείαν; Ἀλλὰ μὴν τοῦτο χαλεπώτερον εἰπεῖν τῷ μὴ δυναμένῳ τῶν ἀκουόντων ἐγγύθεν λαβεῖν τὸν ἔλεγχον τῆς ἀσθενείας αὐτοῦ δυναμένων ἅτε ὑπ᾽ ὄψεσιν οὔσης τῆς θεραπείας. Ὥστε δὲ μὴ νομίζειν ὑμᾶς ὅτι ὑπισχνοῦμαι τὸ ἀθέατον τοῖς ἀνθρώποις, ὃ καὶ μὴ παρέχοντα λαθεῖν δυνατόν, ὃ δύσκολον ἐπαγγείλασθαι τῷ μὴ δυναμένῳ, τοῦτο λέγω τε καὶ ποιῶ, ὥστε ἐντεῦθεν ὑμᾶς λαβεῖν τὴν ἀπόδειξιν τῆς δυνάμεως τῆς ἐμῆς.

> Ὃ δὲ λέγει, τοιοῦτόν ἐστιν. βλάσφημόν με νομίζετε ὡς ἐπαγγελλόμενον ἃ μὴ δύναμαι ἤγουν τῶν ἁμαρτημάτων τὴν ἄφεσιν. οὐκοῦν εἰ μεγαλαύχου [col. 1: μεγαλαυχίας]

785 Cod. εἶχε.
786 Matt. 9:5.
787 Luke, 5:20. Cf. Matt. 9:2: ἀφίενταί σου αἱ ἁμαρτίαι. Mark, 2:5: ἀφίενταί σοι αἱ ἁμαρτίαι σου.
788 Cod. χαρίζῃ.
789 Matt. 9:5.
790 Cf. Mark, 1:4; Luke, 3:3; Luke, 24:47; Acts, 2:38; 5:31; 10:43; 10:38; 24:18; Col. 1:14.
791 Cod. οὐκ οὖν.

τὴν φωνὴν ὑπολαμβάνετε εἶναι, τί νενόμισται ὑμῖν εὐκολώτερον ἐπαγγείλασθαι τῶν ἁμαρτημάτων τὴν συγχώρησιν ἢ τῆς παραλύσεως τὴν θεραπείαν; ἀλλὰ μὴν τοῦτο χαλεπώτερον εἰπεῖν τῷ μὴ δυναμένῳ, τῶν ἀκουόντων ἐγγύθεν λαβεῖν τὸν ἔλεγχον τῆς ἀσθενείας αὐτοῦ δυναμένων, ἅτε ὑπ' ὄψεσι οὔσης τῆς θεραπείας. ὥστε δὲ μὴ νομίζειν ὑμᾶς, ὅτι ὑπισχνοῦμαι τὸ ἀθέατον τοῖς ἀνθρώποις, ὃ καὶ μὴ παρέχοντα λαθεῖν δυνατόν, ὃ δύσκολον ἐπαγγείλασθαι τῷ μὴ δυναμένῳ, τοῦτο λέγω τε καὶ ποιῶ, ὥστε ἐντεῦθεν ὑμᾶς λαβεῖν τὴν ἀπόδειξιν δυνάμεως τῆς ἐμῆς.[dcxvii]

Τὴν μεθ' ἑαυτοῦ διατριβὴν[792] λέγει πάσης ὀδύνης ἀπαλλακτικὴν εἶναι. ὀδυνᾶται μὲν γὰρ ὁ μὴ παρὸν ἔχων τὸ ἀγαθόν, διὰ δὲ τὴν στέρησιν αὐτοῦ πενθεῖ ποθῶν τὴν ἀπόλαυσιν. ὁ δὲ παρόντος ἀπολαύων εἰκότως εὐφραίνεται καὶ οὐκ ὀδυνᾶται. νυμφίος δὲ τῆς ἀνθρωπίνης φύσεως ὁ ταύτης ἡγεμὼν λόγος, ὁ τὸ σπέρμα διδοὺς τῆς ζωῆς. *ὅταν* οὖν *ἀρθῇ ἀπ' αὐτῶν ὁ νυμφίος*, ποθοῦντες τὴν παρουσίαν αὐτοῦ *νηστεύσουσιν*, ἵνα συνῶσιν αὐτῷ κατὰ πνεῦμα, καθαιρόμενοι ἀπὸ σωματικῶν ἡδονῶν.[dcxviii]

Τὴν μεθ' ἑαυτοῦ διατριβὴν λέγει πάσης ὀδύνης ἀπαλλακτικὴν εἶναι. ὀδυνᾶται μὲν γὰρ ὁ μὴ παρὸν ἔχων τὸ ἀγαθόν. διὰ δὲ τὴν στέρησιν αὐτοῦ πενθεῖ ποθῶν τὴν ἀπόλαυσιν. ὁ δὲ παρόντος ἀπολαύων, εἰκότως εὐφραίνεται, καὶ οὐκ ὀδυνᾶται. νυμφίος δὲ τῆς ἀνθρωπίνης φύσεως ὁ ταύτης ἡγεμὼν Λόγος, ὁ τὸ σπέρμα διδοὺς τῆς ζωῆς. ὅταν οὖν ἀπαρθῇ ἀπ' αὐτῶν, ποθοῦντες τὴν παρουσίαν αὐτοῦ νηστεύσουσιν. ἵνα συνῶσιν αὐτῷ κατὰ πνεῦμα, καθαιρόμενοι ἀπὸ σωματικῶν ἡδονῶν.[dcxix]

20

69r (ΩΡΙΓΕΝΟΥΣ) *οὐδεὶς ἐπιβάλλει ἐπίβλημα ῥάκους ἀγνάφου.*[793] **69v** Ἀσκοὶ παλαιοί,[794] οἱ τῇ νομικῇ πολιτείᾳ[dcxx] πεποιωμένοι· οἶνος νέος, ἡ διὰ Χριστοῦ χάρις· ἀσκοὶ νέοι, οἱ ἐν ταύτῃ ποιωθέντες. Κατὰ τοῦτο *τὸ παλαιὸν ἱμάτιον* καὶ τὸ ἄγναφον ῥάκος. Διατί δὲ ἢ πῶς ῥάκος, ζήτει. Ὅπερ αἶρον τὸ πλήρωμα ἐκ *τοῦ παλαιοῦ χεῖρον σχίσμα γίνεται.*[795]

Ἀσκοὶ παλαιοί, οἱ τῇ νομικῇ πολιτείᾳ πεποιωμένοι. οἶνος νέος ἡ διὰ Χριστοῦ χάρις, ἀσκοὶ νέοι *οἱ ἐν ταύτῃ ποιωθέντες*. κατὰ τοῦτο τὸ *παλαιὸν ἱμάτιον* καὶ τὸ ἄγναφον ῥάκος. διατί δὲ ἢ πῶς ῥάκος, ζήτει, ὅπερ αἶρον *τὸ πλήρωμα* ἐκ *τοῦ παλαιοῦ χεῖρον σχίσμα γίνεται.*[dcxxi]

(Ὠριγένους.) Ἀσκοὶ παλαιοί εἰσιν οἱ τῇ νομικῇ πολιτείᾳ πεποιωμένοι. οἶνος δὲ νέος ἡ διὰ Χριστοῦ χάρις.[dcxxii]

792 Cf. Matt. 9:15.
793 Matt. 9:16.
794 Cf. Matt. 16:16-17.
795 Matt. 9:16; cf. Mark, 2:21-22.

21

70v (ΩΡΙΓΕΝΟΥΣ) *Ἰδοὺ ἄρχων εἷς ἐλθὼν προσεκύνει αὐτῷ λέγων.*[796] **71r** (ΩΡΙΓΕΝΟΥΣ) Πολλῶν ὄντων τῶν ἀρχισυναγώγων, οἱ μὲν λοιποὶ κατὰ τοῦ Σωτῆρος ἦσαν, σπάνιος δέ τις ἦν καὶ εἷς οὗτος, ὡς Νικόδημος καὶ εἴ τις τοιοῦτος. Καὶ τοῦτον ἡ χρεία κατηνάγκασεν ἐλθεῖν πρὸς τὸν Ἰησοῦν. Διὸ ἔλεγεν· *ἐὰν μὴ σημεῖα καὶ τέρατα ἴδητε οὐ μὴ πιστεύσητε.*[797] *Ἰάειρος δὲ οὗτος*[798] ἦν, ὃς οὐκ εἶχεν ὁμοίαν πίστιν τῷ ἑκατοντάρχῳ. ‹Εἰ›[799] γὰρ ἂν εἶπεν καὶ οὗτος, *οὐκ εἰμὶ ἱκανὸς ἵνα μου ὑπὸ τὴν στέγην εἰσέλθῃς,*[800] ἀλλ᾽ ὅμως ὁ Κύριος ἠπ‹ί›ως[801] ἠκολούθει.

> Πολλῶν ὄντων τῶν ἀρχισυναγώγων οἱ μὲν λοιποὶ κατὰ τοῦ σωτῆρος ἦσαν. σπάνιος δέ τις ἦν καὶ εἷς οὗτος, ὡς Νικόδημος. καὶ εἴ τις τοιοῦτος, καὶ τοῦτον ἡ χρεία κατηνάγκασεν ἐλθεῖν πρὸς τὸν Ἰησοῦν, διὸ ἔλεγεν. *ἐὰν μὴ σημεῖα καὶ τέρατα ἴδητε οὐ μὴ πιστεύσητε.* *Ἰάειρος δὲ οὗτος* ἦν, ὃς οὐκ εἶχεν ὁμοίαν πίστιν τοῦ ἑκατοντάρχου. ἢ γὰρ ἂν εἶπεν καὶ οὗτος, *οὐκ εἰμὶ ἱκανὸς ἵνα μου ὑπὸ τὴν στέγην εἰσέλθῃς,* ἀλλ᾽ ὅμως ὁ Κύριος ἠπίως ἠκολούθει.[dcxxiii]

Καὶ ἐγερθεὶς ὁ Ἰησοῦς ἠκολούθησεν αὐτῷ.[802] Οὐκ ἐποίησε δὲ ἀπὼν λόγῳ τὸ θαῦμα, ἵνα πᾶσι γένηται κατάδηλον τὸ πρᾶγμα. Ὡς τελείους δὲ τοὺς περὶ Πέτρον ἔλαβε μόνους μεθ᾽ ἑαυτοῦ, ἵνα παροξύνῃ καὶ τοὺς ἄλλους γενέσθαι τοιούτους.

> Οὐκ ἐποίησε δὲ ἀπὼν λόγῳ τὸ θαῦμα, ἵνα πᾶσι γένηται κατάδηλον τὸ πρᾶγμα. ὡς τελείους δὲ τοὺς περὶ Πέτρον ἔλαβε μόνους μεθ᾽ ἑαυτοῦ, ἵνα παροξύνῃ καὶ τοὺς ἄλλους γενέσθαι τοιούτους.[dcxxiv]

22

71r (ΩΡΙΓΕΝΟΥΣ) *Καὶ ἰδοὺ γυνὴ αἱμορροοῦσα.*[803] Μάστιξ ἦν ἡ αἱμόρροια τὸ πάθος. Οὕτως ἐρεῖς καὶ τὰ τοιαῦτα πάθη σωματικὰς μάστιγας εἶναι τοῦ Θεοῦ, διὰ τοιούτων τοὺς ἀξίους τῆς ἑαυτοῦ παιδείας μαστίζοντος. *Μαστιγοῖ,* γάρ φησι, πάντα *υἱὸν ὃν παραδέχεται.*[804] Διὸ ἔλεγε τῷ παραλυτικῷ καὶ αὐτὸν μάστιγος ἀπολύσας· *ἴδε ὑγιὴς*

---

796 Matt. 9:18.
797 John, 4:48.
798 Luke, 8:41; Mark, 5:22.
799 Cod. ἤ.
800 Matt. 8:8.
801 Cod. ἠπήως.
802 Matt. 9:19.
803 Matt. 9:20.
804 Prov. 3:12.

γέγονας, μηκέτι ἁμάρτανε, ἵνα μὴ χεῖρον τί σοι γένηται.[805] Καὶ οἱ μὲν μαθηταὶ αὐτοῦ ἥψαντο καὶ ἐψηλάφησαν αὐτόν, ἡ δὲ αἱμορροοῦσα, *τῶν ἱματίων αὐτοῦ*,[806][dcxxv] οἱ δὲ ὄχλοι οὐδὲ τῶν ἱματίων αὐτοῦ. Ὁμοίως δὲ τῇ αἱμορροούσῃ πιστεύοντες ἥπτοντο αὐτοῦ, διὸ συνθλίβειν αὐτὸν λέγονται,[807] | **71v** κατὰ δὲ τὸν Λουκᾶν, συνέχειν καὶ ἀποθλίβειν αὐτόν.[808] Οὐχὶ δὲ τὰ ἱμάτια αὐτοῦ ἔσῳζον τὴν γυναῖκα (ἐπεὶ καὶ οἱ ἐχθροὶ *διεμερίσαντο τὰ ἱμάτια αὐτοῦ*),[809] ἀλλ᾽ ὁ αὐτῆς λογισμός, εἰπούσης ὅτι κἂν *τοῦ ἱματίου αὐτοῦ ἅψωμαι, σωθήσομαι.*[810]

> Μάστιξ ἦν ἡ αἱμόρροια τὸ πάθος. οὕτως ἐρεῖς καὶ τὰ τοιαῦτα πάθη σωματικὰς μάστιγας εἶναι τοῦ θεοῦ. διὸ ἔλεγε τῷ παραλυτικῷ καὶ αὐτὸν μάστιγος ἀπολύσας. *ἴδε ὑγιὴς γέγονας, μηκέτι ἁμάρτανε, ἵνα μὴ χεῖρον τί σοι γένηται.* καὶ οἱ μὲν μαθηταὶ αὐτοῦ ἥψαντο καὶ ἐψηλάφησαν αὐτόν, ἡ δὲ αἱμορροοῦσα *τῶν ἱματίων αὐτοῦ*. ὁμοίως δὲ τῇ αἱμορροούσῃ πιστεύοντες ἥπτοντο αὐτοῦ, διὸ συνθλίβειν αὐτὸν λέγονται κατὰ δὲ τὸν Λουκᾶν συνέχειν καὶ ἀποθλίβειν αὐτόν. οὐχὶ δὲ τὰ ἱμάτια αὐτοῦ ἔσῳζον τὴν γυναῖκα (ἐπεὶ καὶ οἱ ἐχθροὶ *διεμερίσαντο τὰ ἱμάτια αὐτοῦ*), ἀλλ᾽ ὁ αὐτῆς λογισμὸς εἰπούσης ὅτι κἂν *τοῦ ἱματίου αὐτοῦ ἅψωμαι, σωθήσομαι.*[dcxxvi]

> Μάστιξ γὰρ ἦν ἡ αἱμόρροια. οὕτως ἐρεῖς καὶ τὰ ἄλλα πάθη τὰ σωματικὰ μάστιγας εἶναι θεοῦ, διὰ τῶν τοιούτων τοὺς ἀξίους τῆς ἑαυτοῦ παιδείας μαστιγοῦντος. *μαστιγοῖ δὲ πάντα υἱόν, ὃν παραδέχεται.* διὸ ἔλεγε τῷ παραλυτικῷ, καὶ αὐτὸν μάστιγος ἀπολύσας. *ἴδε ὑγιὴς γέγονας, μηκέτι ἁμάρτανε, ἵνα μὴ χεῖρόν τί σοι γένηται.*[dcxxvii]

Προσελθοῦσα ὄπισθεν, ἥψατο τοῦ κρασπέδου.[811] Ὡς ἀκάθαρτος οὖσα διὰ τὸ πάθος, οὐ προσῆλθε φανερῶς ἡ γυνή, μήπως κωλυθῇ ὑπὸ τῶν Ἰουδαίων· ἤτοι ὡς εὐτελὴς ἐνόμισε λανθάνειν.[dcxxviii] Πλὴν ἀνενδοιάστως ἤλπισεν ὑγιαίνειν *ἐὰν μόνον* ἅψηται τοῦ ἄκρου *τοῦ ἱματίου*·[dcxxix] τοῦτο γάρ ἐστι τὸ *κράσπεδον*. Τί οὖν ὁ Σωτήρ; Ἐδημοσίευσεν αὐτὴν οὐχ ὡς δόξης ἐρῶν, ἀλλ᾽ ἵνα δέους ἀπαλλάξῃ ὑπὸ τῆς συνειδήσεως κεντουμένην ὡς κεκλοφυῖαν τὴν δωρεάν, καὶ ἵνα μὴ νομίσῃ ὅτι ἔλαθε, καὶ ἵνα τὴν πίστιν αὐτῆς δημοσιεύσῃ πρὸς ὠφέλειαν ἡμῶν, καὶ ὅπως ὁ ἀρχισυνάγωγος εἰς πίστιν βεβαιωθῇ.[dcxxx] Ἵνα δὲ δείξῃ ὅτι οὐδεὶς ἔχων ἀκούσιον πάθος ἀκάθαρτος παρὰ Θεῷ, προσκαλεῖται αὐτήν, ἵνα τὸν τυπικὸν νόμον[dcxxxi] εἰς πνευματικὴν μεταγάγ‹ῃ›[812] θεωρίαν. Θυγατέρα δὲ αὐτὴν καλεῖ ὡς τῇ πίστει γεγονυῖαν. Διὸ καὶ ἰάθη ἀκούσασα ὅτι *ἡ πίστις σου σέσωκέ σε.*[813] Οὕτως οὔτε τόπος οὔτε λόγος οὔτε τι ἕτερον τῶν ἔξω σῴζει, ἀλλ᾽ ἕκαστον *ἡ πίστις* αὐτοῦ.

---

805 John, 5:14.
806 Cf. Mark, 5:28.
807 Cf. Mark, 5:31.
808 Cf. Luke, 8:45.
809 Psalm 21:19; Matt. 27:35; John, 19:24-25.
810 Matt. 9:21.
811 Matt. 9:20.
812 Cod. μεταγάγοι.
813 Matt. 9:22.

[῾Ως ἀκάθαρτος οὖσα διὰ τὸ πάθος οὐ προσῆλθε φανερῶς ἡ γυνή, μήπως κωλυθῇ ὑπὸ τῶν ᾿Ιουδαίων, ἤτοι ὡς εὐτελὴς ἐνόμισε λανθάνειν. πλὴν ἀνενδοιάστως ἤλπισεν ὑγιαίνειν, *ἐὰν μόνον* ἅψηται *τοῦ ἱματίου* τοῦ ἄκρου. τοῦτο γάρ ἐστι τὸ *κράσπεδον*. τί οὖν ὁ Σωτήρ; ἐδημοσίευσεν αὐτήν; Οὐχ ὡς δόξης ἐρῶν, ἀλλ᾽ ἵνα δέους ἀπαλλάξῃ ὑπὸ τῆς συνειδήσεως κεντουμένην ὡς κεκλοφυῖαν τὴν δωρεάν, καὶ ἵνα μὴ νομίσῃ ὅτι ἔλαθε, καὶ ἵνα τὴν πίστιν αὐτῆς δημοσιεύσῃ πρὸς ὠφέλειαν ἡμῶν, καὶ ὅπως ὁ ἀρχισυνάγωγος εἰς πίστιν βεβαιωθῇ. ἵνα δὲ δείξῃ ὅτι οὐδεὶς ἔχων ἀκούσιον πάθος ἀκάθαρτος παρὰ θεῷ, προσκαλεῖται αὐτήν, ἵνα τὸν τυπικὸν νόμον εἰς πνευματικὴν μεταγάγῃ θεωρίαν. θυγατέρα δὲ αὐτὴν καλεῖ ὡς τῇ πίστει γεγονυῖαν, διὸ καὶ ἰάθη ἀκούσασα ὅτι *ἡ πίστις σου σέσωκέν σε*. ὅτι δὲ μὴ τὰ ἱμάτια αὐτοῦ σέσωκεν αὐτήν, φησὶν *ἡ πίστις σου σέσωκεν*. οὕτως οὔτε τόπος οὔτε λόγος οὔτέ τι ἕτερον τῶν ἔξω σῴζει, ἀλλ᾽ ἕκαστον *ἡ πίστις* αὐτοῦ.][dcxxxii]

Δείκνυσιν, ὅτι παρὰ θεῷ οὐδεὶς ἔχων ἀκούσιον νόσον ἀκάθαρτος. διὸ καὶ προσκαλεῖται τὴν αἱμορροοῦσαν ὁ κύριος, ἵνα τὸν τυπικὸν νόμον εἰς πνευματικὴν μεταγάγῃ θεωρίαν.[dcxxxiii]

῎Εθος γὰρ ἦν τὰς ἀγάμους κόρας, ἡνίκα εἰσὶ πρὸς ὥραν γάμου τελευτώσας, θρηνεῖν διὰ τῶν συμβόλων τοῦ γάμου. Διὸ καὶ αὐληταὶ ἦσαν ἔσω, εἰ καὶ παρὰ τὸ πρόσταγμα τὸ Μωσαϊκὸν ‹τότε› ἐποίουν τοῦτο οἱ ᾿Ιουδαῖοι.

[῎Εθος ἦν τὰς ἀγάμους κόρας, ἡνίκα εἰσὶ πρὸς ὥραν γάμου τελευτώσας, θρηνεῖν διὰ τῶν συμβόλων τοῦ γάμου. διὸ καὶ αὐληταὶ ἦσαν εἴσω, εἰ καὶ παρὰ τὸ πρόσταγμα τὸ Μωσαϊκὸν τότε ἐποίουν τοῦτο οἱ ᾿Ιουδαῖοι.][dcxxxiv]

῎Εθος τοῖς ἀνθρώποις τὰς ἀγάμους κόρας, ἡνίκα εἰσὶ πρὸς ὥραν γάμου, τελευτώσας θρηνεῖν διὰ τῶν συμβολικῶν γάμων. διὸ καὶ αὐληταὶ ἦσαν ἔσω, εἰ καὶ παρὰ τὸ πρόσταγμα τὸ ᾿Ιουδαϊκὸν τότε ἐποίουν τοῦτο οἱ ᾿Ιουδαῖοι.[dcxxxv]

Up to today a girl lies dead in the ruler's house, and those who apparently are teachers they are the flute-players playing a funeral song. Besides, the crowd of Jews is one not of faithful, but of those making a clamour.[dcxxxvi]

Εἶτα, *ἐλθὼν εἰς τὴν οἰκίαν τοῦ ἄρχοντος ὁ ᾿Ιησοῦς*, εἶδε *τοὺς αὐλητὰς καὶ τὸν ὄχλον θορυβούμενον*[814] περὶ τὴν τεθνηκυῖαν. Πανταχοῦ δὲ | **72r** φεύγων τὸ φιλόκομπον[dcxxxvii] ἵνα μὴ δόξῃ τι μέγα πεποιηκέναι προστάσσει τῷ ὄχλῳ ἀναχωρεῖν, φάσκων μὴ τεθνηκέναι τὴν κόρην ἀλλὰ καθεύδειν.[815] Τοῦτο δὲ καὶ ἵνα καταγελάσωσιν αὐτοῦ οἱ ᾿Ιουδαῖοι ἔλεγεν ὡς τὴν νεκρὰν λέγοντος καθεύδειν καὶ ὁμολογήσωσιν ὅτι νεκρὰν ἀνέστησε καὶ ἵνα δείξῃ ὅτι εὔκοπον ἦν αὐτῷ ἐγεῖραι νεκρὸν ὑπὲρ τὸ ἐξ ὕπνου ἐγεῖραι ἄνθρωπον τὸν καθεύδοντα. ῾Ως γὰρ ζώσης παρ᾽ αὐτῷ εἶπε μὴ τεθνηκέναι αὐτὴν (*πάντες γὰρ ‹ἐν› αὐτῷ ζῶσι*)[816]

The girl is not dead but sleeps, because all things are alive to God.[dcxxxviii]

---

814 Matt. 9:23.

815 Cf. Matt. 9:23-24.

816 Cf. Luke, 20:38.

διὰ τὸ νεύματι μόνῳ δύνασθαι ὡς Θεόν ἐγεῖραι νεκρούς. Μετὰ γὰρ τὴν τοῦ *Χριστοῦ παρουσίαν*[817] οὐ δεῖ δεδιέναι τὸν θάνατον, ὡς ἐξ ὕπνου ἐγείροντος αὐτοῦ τοὺς νεκρούς. Πῶς εἶπεν *οὐκ ἀπέθανε* καίτοι ἀποθανούσης; Ὅτι οἱ ἐλπίδα ἔχοντες τῆς ἐν Χριστῷ ἀναστάσεως, οὐκ ἀπέθανον ἀλλὰ καθεύδουσι. Διὸ καὶ ὁ ἀπόστολος, *οὐ θέλω δὲ ὑμᾶς ἀγνοεῖν, ‹ἀδελφοί›, περὶ τῶν κεκοιμημένων, ἵνα μὴ λυπῆσθε καθὼς καὶ οἱ λοιποί οἱ μὴ ἔχοντες ἐλπίδα.*[818] Ἅμα δὲ καὶ σμικρύνων τὸ ἔργον ὃ ἔμελλε ποιεῖν, μᾶλλον δὲ κρύπτων αὐτό, ἔλεγεν ὅτι *καθεύδει·* διὸ καὶ ἑξῆς παρήνει *μηδενὶ λέγειν.*[819] Ἢ ἐπίτηδες ἔλεγεν ὅτι *καθεύδει*, ἵνα, εἰπόντων ἐκείνων ὅτι *ἀπέθανεν*, ὅτ᾽ ἂν ἀναστῇ μὴ δυνηθῶσιν ἀρνήσασθαι τὸ γεγονός.

> Πῶς εἶπεν *οὐκ ἀπέθανε* καίτοι ἀποθανούσης; ὅτι οἱ ἐλπίδα ἔχοντες τῆς ἐν Χριστῷ ἀναστάσεως, οὐκ ἀπέθανον ἀλλὰ καθεύδουσιν. διό φησιν καὶ ὁ ἀπόστολος, *οὐ θέλω δὲ ὑμᾶς ἀγνοεῖν, ‹ἀδελφοί›, περὶ τῶν κεκοιμημένων, ἵνα μὴ λυπῆσθε καθὼς καὶ οἱ λοιποί οἱ μὴ ἔχοντες ἐλπίδα*[820] ἅμα δὲ σμικρύνων τὸ ἔργον ὃ ἔμελλε ποιεῖν, μᾶλλον δὲ κρύπτων αὐτό, ἔλεγεν ὅτι *καθεύδει.* διὸ καὶ ἑξῆς παρήνει *μηδενὶ λέγειν.*[821] Ἢ ἐπίτηδες ἔλεγεν ὅτι *καθεύδει.* ἵνα, εἰπόντων ἐκείνων ὅτι *ἀπέθανεν*, ὅτ᾽ ἂν ἀναστῇ μὴ δυνηθῶσιν ἀρνήσασθαι τὸ γεγονός.[dcxxxix]

> (Ὠριγένους.) Οἱ ἐλπίδα ἔχοντες τῆς ἐν Χριστῷ ἀναστάσεως οὐκ ἀπέθανον, ἀλλὰ καθεύδουσι. διὸ φησὶν ὁ Ἀπόστολος. *οὐ θέλω δὲ ὑμᾶς ἀγνοεῖν, περὶ τῶν κεκοιμημένων, ἵνα μὴ λυπεῖσθε, ὡς καὶ οἱ λοιποὶ οἱ μὴ ἔχοντες ἐλπίδα.* ἅμα δὲ καὶ σμικρύνων τὸ ἔργον, ὃ ἤμελλε ποιεῖν, μᾶλλον δὲ κρύπτων αὐτό, ἔλεγεν ὅτι καθεύδει. διὸ καὶ ἑξῆς παρήνει μηδενὶ λέγειν.[dcxl]

Ἐκράτησε τῆς χειρὸς αὐτῆς.[822] Ἡ μὲν τοῦ Ἰησοῦ χεὶρ ζωτικὴ οὖσα τὸν νεκρὸν ἐζωοποίει. Τοῦτο γὰρ καὶ ὁ πατὴρ ἐπεζήτησεν εἰπὼν *ἐπίθες τὴν χεῖρα σου ἐπ᾽ αὐτὴν καὶ ζήσεται,*[823] ὁ δὲ λόγος καὶ διαναστῆναι αὐτὴν καὶ βαδίζειν ἐποίησε. Διὰ τοῦτο καὶ χειρὶ καὶ λόγῳ αὐτὴν ἀνέστησεν.

Ἠκολούθησαν αὐτῷ δύο τυφλοί.[824] Οἱ τυφλοὶ ὡς μὲν Θεῷ ἔλεγον τὸ *ἐλέησον,* | **72v** ὡς δὲ ἀνθρώπῳ τὸ *υἱός Δαυίδ*, διὰ πολλὴν τιμὴν φιλοτιμούμενοι αὐτῷ. Ἐθρυλεῖτο γὰρ παρὰ τοῖς Ἰουδαίοις ὅτι ὁ Με‹σ›σίας *ἐκ σπέρματος Δαυίδ* μέλλει εἶναι *τὸ κατὰ σάρκα*[825] καὶ διὰ τὴν ὀρθὴν αὐτῶν πίστιν ἔτυχον τῆς ἰάσεως. Διὰ δὲ τὸ ἀφιλόκομπον[dcxli] κατ᾽ ἰδίαν ἐν τῇ οἰκίᾳ θεραπεύει αὐτούς. Ἀνεβάλλετο δὲ πρὸς ὀλίγον τὴν ἴασιν, ἵνα τοὺς ὁρῶντας καὶ ἀπιστοῦντας Ἰουδαίους τὰς θεοσημείας κατακρίνῃ διὰ τῆς τῶν τυφλῶν

817 Cf. 2 Thess. 2:1; 2 Peter, 1:16.
818 Cf. 1 Thess. 4:13.
819 Luke 9:21; cf. Luke, 5:14; 8:56.
820 Cf. 1 Thess. 4:13.
821 Luke 9:21; cf. Luke, 5:14; 8:56.
822 Matt. 9:25; Luke, 8:54.
823 Matt. 9:18.
824 Matt. 9:27.
825 Cf. John, 7:42; Rom. 1:3; 2 Tim. 2:8.

ἀνεξικάκου ὑπομονῆς. Εἶτα φανερὰν ὁμολογίαν παρὰ τῶν τυφλῶν ἀπαιτεῖ,[826] ἵνα δείξῃ τὴν ἴασιν τῆς πίστεως οὖσαν καρπόν.
Οὐ γάρ ἐστι φιλοδοξίας τὸ ἀπαιτεῖν αὐτοὺς ὁμολογεῖν τὴν εἰς αὐτὸν πίστιν,

> Πολλαχοῦ γὰρ ἐσπούδακεν ἱκετευόμενος ἰᾶσθαι, ἵνα μή τις νομίσῃ διὰ φιλοτιμίαν αὐτὸν τοῖς θαύμασι τούτοις ἐπιπηδᾶν.[dcxlii]

ἀλλ' ἀνῆγεν αὐτοὺς ἐπὶ τὸ ὑψηλότερον.

> ἀλλ' ἐπειδὴ εἶπον υἱὸν Δαυίδ, ἀνάγων αὐτοὺς ἐπὶ τὸ ὑψηλότερον.[dcxliii]

Διὸ καὶ ἐπιγνόντες, Κύριον αὐτὸν ἐκάλουν ὡς Θεόν.
Πρῶτον γὰρ τὴν πίστιν ἀπαιτεῖ, καὶ ὅτε ἴδῃ ἔχοντα πίστιν, τότε ὡς φιλάνθρωπος θεραπεύει. Οὐ θεραπεύει δὲ καὶ τοὺς μὴ παρακαλοῦντας, ἵνα μὴ δόξῃ διὰ φιλοτιμίαν τοῖς θαύμασιν ἐπιπηδᾶν.

> [ἀπαιτεῖ δὲ καὶ τὴν πίστιν, καὶ ὅτε ἴδῃ ἔχοντα πίστιν, τότε ὡς φιλάνθρωπος θεραπεύει. Οὐ θεραπεύει δὲ καὶ τοὺς μὴ παρακαλοῦντας, ἵνα μὴ δόξῃ διὰ φιλοτιμίαν τοῖς θαύμασιν ἐπιπηδᾶν.][dcxliv]

> Unless they confess and say, 'Have pity on us, son of David', they will not receive the original light. And when Jesus asks them, 'Do you believe that I can do this?', they have to respond to him, 'Yes Lord'.[dcxlv]

Διὰ δὲ τὸ ἄτυφον[dcxlvi] παρήγγειλεν αὐτοῖς μηδενὶ εἰπεῖν.[827]

> The Lord has commanded this on account of his humility.[dcxlvii]

Οὐ γὰρ ἐβούλετο λέγειν τὴν γεγενημένην ἴασιν αὐτοῖς, ἀλλ' ὁρᾶσθαι ὑπὸ πάντων. Ἐκεῖνοι δὲ οὐχ ὡς ἀπειθοῦντες ἀλλ' εὐχαριστοῦντες τῷ ἰατρῷ *διεφήμισαν* τὸν λόγον, κἂν αὐτὸς οὐκ ἐπέτρεπεν. Εἰ δὲ ἀλλαχοῦ φαίνεται λέγων τῷ ἰαθέντι, *ἄπελθε διηγοῦ τὴν δόξαν τοῦ Θεοῦ*, οὐδὲν ἐναντίον. Θέλει γὰρ ἡμᾶς περὶ αὐτοῦ μηδὲν λέγειν τοὺς δὲ εὐεργετηθέντας μὴ σιωπᾶν, εἰ εἰς δόξαν Θεοῦ ἀνατρέχει ὁ λόγος.

> ἐκεῖνοι δὲ οὐκ ἠνέσχοντο, ἀλλ' ἐγένοντο κήρυκες καὶ εὐαγγελισταί. εἰ δὲ ἀλλαχοῦ φαίνεται λέγων, *ἄπελθε καὶ διηγοῦ τὴν δόξαν τοῦ Θεοῦ*, οὐκ ἔστιν ἐναντίον ἐκείνου τοῦτο, ἀλλὰ καὶ σφόδρα συμβαῖνον. ὅπου μὲν γὰρ εἰς τὸν Θεὸν ἡ δόξα ἀναφέρεται, οὐ μόνον οὐ κωλύει, ἀλλὰ καὶ ἐπιτάττει τοῦτο ποιεῖν. ὅπου δὲ παιδεύει ἡμᾶς ταπεινοφρονεῖν, ἐκεῖ καὶ κελεύει μηδενὶ λέγειν, ἀλλὰ καὶ τοὺς βουλομένους ἡμᾶς ἐγκωμιάζειν κωλύει.[dcxlviii]

---

826 Matt. 9:28; cf. John, 9:35-38.
827 Cf. Matt. 8:4; 9:30; Mark, 1:44; Luke, 5:14; 8:56.

Ἐλέησον ἡμᾶς υἱὲ Δαυίδ.[828] Οἱ βλέποντες οὐκ ἔγνωσαν τὸν υἱὸν τοῦ *Δαυίδ* οἱ δὲ τυ |
73r *φλοὶ* ἐπέγνωσαν, ἵνα πληρωθῇ τὸ ὑπ᾽ αὐτοῦ εἰρημένον (τὸ *ἐγὼ εἰς κρίσιν τοῦ κόσμου ἐλήλυθα, ἵνα οἱ μὴ βλέποντες βλέπωσιν καὶ οἱ βλέποντες τυφλοὶ γένωνται*).[829] Πῶς δὲ ἐπέγνωσαν, εἰ μὴ πάντως εἶχον τὸν ὁδηγοῦντα αὐτοὺς νοῦν ἀκολουθεῖν *τῷ καλῷ ποιμένι*;[830]

> Οἱ βλέποντες οὐκ ἔγνωσαν τὸν υἱὸν *Δαυίδ*, οἱ δὲ *τυφλοὶ* ἐπέγνωσαν, ἵνα πληρωθῇ τὸ ὑπ᾽ αὐτοῦ εἰρημένον (τὸ *ἐγὼ εἰς κρίσιν τοῦ κόσμου ἐλήλυθα, ἵνα οἱ μὴ βλέποντες βλέπωσιν*) *καὶ οἱ* τυφλοὶ ἀναβλέψωσι. πῶς ἐπέγνωσαν, εἰ μὴ πάντως εἶχον τὸν ὁδηγοῦντα αὐτοὺς νοῦν ἀκολουθεῖν *τῷ καλῷ ποιμένι*;[dcxlix]

Υἱὸς *Δαυὶδ* λέγεται ὁ Χριστός διὰ τὴν ἐξ ἐκείνου σάρκα. Οἱ οὖν βοῶντες υἱὸν *Δαυὶδ* Χριστὸν μὲν αὐτὸν ἔχουσι, *κατὰ σάρκα* δὲ γινώσκουσι *νήπιοι* ὄντες ἔτι.[831]

> Υἱὸς *Δαυὶδ* λέγεται ὁ Χριστὸς διὰ τὴν ἐξ ἐκείνου σάρκα. οἱ οὖν βοῶντες υἱὸν *Δαυὶδ* Χριστὸν μὲν αὐτὸν ἔχουσιν, *κατὰ σάρκα* δὲ γινώσκουσι νήπιοι ὄντες ἔτι. παρήγγειλε δὲ αὐτοῖς μηδενὶ λέγειν. οὐ γὰρ ἐβούλετο αὐτοὺς τὴν γεγενημένην ἴασιν λέγειν, ἀλλ᾽ ὁρᾶσθαι ὑπὸ πάντων τὸ γενόμενον.[dcl]

Πιστεύετε ὅτι δύναμαι τοῦτο ποιῆσαι;[832] Κόμπος οὐδεὶς ἐὰν ἡ *δύναμις*[833] λέγῃ περὶ ἑαυτῆς τὸ δύνασθαι. Κόμπος δ᾽ ἂν ἦν τῷ μὴ φύσει τὸ δύνασθαι ἔχοντι ἀλλὰ διὰ χάριτος λαμβάνοντι λέγειν ὅτι *δύναμαι*. Παρήγγειλε δὲ ὁ Σωτὴρ τοῖς τυφλοῖς τὸ μηδενὶ ἐξειπεῖν τὸ γενόμενον,[834] τὸ μὴ δεῖν ἐπιδείκνυσθαι διδάσκων ἡμᾶς. Οὐ γὰρ Θεῷ κόμπος ἦν τὸ τὴν ἀλήθειαν λέγεσθαι περὶ αὐτοῦ. Ἡ δὲ τῶν ἰαθέντων ὁμολογία τῆς ἰάσεως, οὐκ ἔγκλημα αὐτοῖς ἤνεγκεν, ἀλλ᾽ εὐγνωμοσύνην ἐμαρτύρησεν.

> Κόμπος οὐδεὶς ἐὰν ἡ *δύναμις* λέγῃ περὶ ἑαυτῆς τὸ δύνασθαι. κόμπος δ᾽ ἂν ἦν τῷ μὴ φύσει τὸ δύνασθαι ἔχοντι ἀλλὰ διὰ χάριτος λαμβάνοντι λέγειν ὅτι *δύναμαι*. παρήγγειλε δὲ ὁ σωτὴρ τοῖς τυφλοῖς τὸ μηδενὶ ἐξειπεῖν τὸ γενόμενον, τὸ μὴ δεῖν ἐπιδείκνυσθαι διδάσκων ἡμᾶς (οὐ γὰρ Θεῷ κόμπος ἦν τὸ τὴν ἀλήθειαν λέγεσθαι περὶ αὐτοῦ). ἡ δὲ τῶν ἰαθέντων ὁμολογία τῆς ἰάσεως οὐκ ἔγκλημα αὐτοῖς ἤνεγκεν, ἀλλ᾽ εὐγνωμοσύνην ἐμαρτύρησεν.][dcli]

> Κόμπος οὐδείς, ἐὰν ἡ δύναμις λέγῃ περὶ ἑαυτῆς τὸ δύνασθαι. κόμπος δ᾽ ἂν ἦν τῷ μὴ φύσει τὸ δύνασθαι ἔχοντι, ἀλλὰ διὰ χάριτος λαμβάνοντι λέγειν ὅτι *δύναμαι*. παρήγγειλε δὲ ὁ σωτὴρ τοῖς τυφλοῖς τὸ μηδενὶ ἐξειπεῖν τὸ γενόμενον, τὸ μὴ δεῖν ἐπιδείκνυσθαι

828 Matt. 9:27.
829 Cf. John, 9:39: Εἰς κρίμα ἐγὼ εἰς τὸν κόσμον τοῦτον ἦλθον.
830 Cf. John, 10:11&14.
831 1 Cor. 3:1; cf. Heb. 5:13-14.
832 Matt. 9:28.
833 Cf. 1 Cor. 1:24.
834 Matt. 9:30.

διδάσκων ἡμᾶς. οὐ γὰρ θεῷ κόμπος ἦν τὸ τὴν ἀλήθειαν λέγεσθαι περὶ αὐτοῦ. ἡ δὲ τῶν ἰαθέντων ὁμολογία περὶ τῆς ἰάσεως οὐκ ἔγκλημα ἤνεγκεν, ἀλλ' εὐγνωμοσύνην ἐμαρτύρησεν.[dclii]

Προσήνεγκαν αὐτῷ ἄνθρωπον κωφὸν δαιμονιζόμενον.[835] Οὐ τῆς φύσεως τὸ πάθος ἦν ἀλλὰ τοῦ δαίμονος ἡ ἐπιβουλή. Διὸ καὶ ἑτέρων δεῖται τῶν προσαγόντων. Οὐδὲ γὰρ δι' ἑαυτοῦ παρακαλέσαι ἐδύνατο ἄφωνος ὤν, τοῦ δαίμονος δήσαντος τὴν γλῶτταν. Διὸ οὐδὲ ἀπαιτεῖ παρ' αὐτοῦ πίστιν ὁ Χριστός, ἀλλ' εὐθέως διορθοῦται τὸ νόσημα. Ἤδει γάρ, ὅτι ὁ δαίμων ἦν ὁ κωλύων αὐτὸν λαλεῖν· *ἐκβληθέντος*, γάρ φησι, *τοῦ δαιμονίου ἐλάλησεν ὁ κωφός*. Τότε ὁ δῆμος ἐθαύμασε, φησί, λέγοντες ὅτι *οὐδέποτε οὕτως ἐφάνη ἐν τῷ Ἰσραήλ.*[836] Αἰνίττεται δὲ ὁ λόγος ὅτι καὶ προφήτας καὶ πατριάρχας παρέδραμεν ἐν ταῖς ἰάσεσιν ὁ Χριστός. Οὐδεὶς γὰρ οὕτω μετ' ἐξουσίας τοιαῦτα | **73v** καὶ τοσαῦτα νοσήματα καὶ ἀνιάτως ἔχοντα, οὕτω ῥᾳδίως ἐθεράπευσε. Καὶ ὁ μὲν δῆμος οὕτως· ἐλύπει δὲ τοὺς Φαρισαίους τὸ ἀποθαυμάζειν τοὺς ὄχλους, διὸ καὶ ἔλεγον· *ἐν τῷ ἄρχοντι τῶν δαιμονίων ἐκβάλλει τὰ δαιμόνια.*[837] Ἄκρας δὲ φρενοβλαβείας ἦν τὸ λέγειν ἔργα δαιμόνων τὰ μόνῃ τῇ θείᾳ πρέποντα φύσει. Οὐδεὶς γὰρ δαιμόνων δαιμόνια ἐκβάλλει.[dcliii] Τὰ γὰρ ἑαυτοῦ συγκροτεῖν εἴωθεν, οὐ καταλύειν. Ὅπουγε, οὐ μόνον δαίμονας ἐξέβαλλεν ἀλλὰ καὶ ἕτερα ποικίλα νοσήματα ἐθεράπευε. Καὶ οὐ μόνον τοῦτο, ἀλλὰ καὶ ἁμαρτήματα ἔλυε καὶ βασιλείαν ἐκήρυσσε καὶ τῷ Θεῷ καὶ Πατρὶ προσῆγεν. Ἅπερ οὔτ' ἂν ἕλοιτο ποτὲ δαίμων, οὔτ' ἂν δυνηθείη ἐργάσασθαι.

> Χρὴ γινώσκειν ὅτι ἡ κώφωσις ἣν εἶχεν ὁ δαιμονιζόμενος οὗτος, οὐ φύσεως ἦν τὸ πάθος, ἀλλὰ τοῦ δαίμονος ἦν ἡ ἐπιβουλή. διὸ καὶ ἑτέρων ἐδεήθη τῶν προσαγόντων. οὔτε γὰρ δι' ἑαυτοῦ προσκαλέσαι ἠδύνατο ἄφωνος ὢν, οὔτε ἑτέρους ἱκετεῦσαι, τοῦ δαίμονος δήσαντος τὴν γλῶτταν, καὶ τὴν ψυχὴν μετὰ τῆς γλώττης πεδήσαντος. διὰ τοῦτο οὐδὲ ἀπαιτεῖ πίστιν αὐτόν, ἀλλ' εὐθέως διορθοῦται τὸ νόσημα. *ἐκβληθέντος* γάρ, φησι, *τοῦ δαιμονίου, ἐλάλησεν ὁ κωφός. οἱ δὲ ὄχλοι ἐθαύμαζον*, καὶ τὰ ἑξῆς. ὃ δὴ μάλιστα ἠνία τοὺς Φαρισαίους, ὅτι πάντων αὐτὸν προὐτίθεσαν, οὐ τῶν τότε ὄντων, ἀλλὰ καὶ τῶν πώποτε γεγενημένων. προὐτίθεσαν δὲ οὐχ ὅτι ἐθεράπευσεν, ἀλλ' ὅτι ῥᾴως καὶ ταχέως. καὶ ὅτι ἄπειρα νοσήματα, καὶ ἀνιάτως ἔχοντα. καὶ ὁ μὲν ὄχλος οὕτως. οἱ δὲ Φαρισαῖοι τοὐναντίον ἅπαν. τοιοῦτον γὰρ ἡ πονηρία. τί γὰρ φησιν; *ἐν τῷ ἄρχοντι τῶν δαιμονίων, ἐκβάλλει τὰ δαιμόνια.* οὗ τί ἂν γένοιτο ἀνοητότερον; μάλιστα μὲν γάρ, ὃ καὶ προϊὼν φησίν, ἀμήχανον δαίμονα ἐκβάλλειν δαίμονα. τὰ γὰρ ἑαυτοῦ συγκροτεῖν εἴωθεν, οὐ καταλύειν ἐκεῖνος. αὐτὸς δὲ οὐχὶ δαίμονας ἐξέβαλε μόνον, ἀλλὰ καὶ λεπροὺς ἐκάθηρεν, καὶ νεκροὺς ἤγειρεν, καὶ θάλατταν ἐχαλίνου, καὶ ἁμαρτήματα ἔλυεν, καὶ βασιλείαν ἐκήρυττεν, καὶ τῷ Πατρὶ προσῆγεν. ἅπερ οὔτ' ἂν ἕλοιτό ποτε, οὔτ' ἂν δυνηθείη ποτὲ ἐργάσασθαι.[dcliv]

835 Matt. 9:32.
836 Matt. 9:33.
837 Matt. 9:34.

Μᾶλλον γὰρ οὗτοι καὶ νοσήματα ποιοῦσι καὶ Θεοῦ ἀπάγουσιν, εἰδώλοις προσάγοντες τοὺς ἀνθρώπους καὶ ἕτερα κακὰ ἐργάζονται, ἀπεναντίας πράττοντες τῷ φύσει ἀγαθῷ Θεῷ.

Καὶ περιῆγεν ὁ Ἰησοῦς τὰς πόλεις πάσας καὶ τὰς κώμας.[838] Κώμας καὶ πόλεις περιήει ὁ Σωτὴρ ὡς ὁλοτελῶς ποιῶν τὸ ἀγαθόν, εὐεργετῶν καὶ ἰώμενος καὶ τοὺς λοιδοροῦντας, ἵνα μή τις εἴπῃ ὅτι δόξης ἕνεκα τοῦτο ἐποίει καὶ ἵνα μή τις *ἐν ἡμέρᾳ κρίσεως*[839] εἴπῃ ὅτι οὐδεὶς ἡμᾶς ἐδίδαξεν. Οὐ μόνον γὰρ ἐδίδασκεν ὁ Σωτήρ, ἀλλὰ καὶ διὰ τῶν σημείων εἷλκε. Διὰ γὰρ τὸ δυσήκοον τῶν Ἰουδαίων καὶ *λόγῳ καὶ ἔργῳ*[840] διήλεγχεν αὐτῶν τὴν *σκληροκαρδίαν.*[841] Οὐδὲ γὰρ λεληθότως ἐκήρυττεν, ἀλλὰ πανταχοῦ περινοστῶν,[dclv] *διδάσκων ἐν ταῖς συναγωγαῖς.*[842] Ἐδίδασκε μὲν ἑρμηνεύων τὰς τῶν ἁγίων γραφῶν ἐπιλύσεις καὶ ζητήματα καὶ τὰς | **74r** περὶ αὐτοῦ μαρτυρίας·[843] τοῖς δὲ ἤδη προκόψασι καὶ δυναμένοις δέξασθαι *τὰ μυστήρια ‹τῆς βασιλείας› τῶν οὐρανῶν*[844] ἐκήρυσσε, τοὺς δὲ θεραπείας δεομένους *ἐθεράπευεν.*[845]

Καὶ κηρύσσων τὸ εὐαγγέλιον.[846] *Εὐαγγέλιον τῆς βασιλείας*[847] κηρύσσειν φησί. Τοῦτο δὴ τὸ πᾶσιν εὐαγγελίζεσθαι τῆς βασιλείας τῶν οὐρανῶν τὴν ἐγγύτητα.[848] Ὅταν γὰρ ἀναστῶμεν ἀπὸ τῶν νεκρῶν καὶ τῆς τοῦ Ἁγίου Πνεύματος μετάσχωμεν χάριτος, ἄτρεπτοι μένομεν τὰς ψυχὰς καὶ ἄφθαρτοι τὸ σῶμα ἐν οὐρανοῖς διαιτώμενοι. Ἠγγικέναι δὲ πανταχοῦ λέγει τὴν *βασιλείαν τῶν οὐρανῶν*[849] ὡς δὴ διὰ τῆς αὐτοῦ παρουσίας καὶ τὴν ἀληθῆ τοῦ πράγματος κομισαμένων ὑπόσχεσιν καὶ ὡς ἐν τύπῳ γενομένων ἤδη καὶ *τὴν ἀπαρχὴν* κομίζεσθαι *τοῦ Πνεύματος.*[850]

> Εὐαγγέλιον τῆς βασιλείας κηρύσσειν φησὶν τοῦτο δή, τὸ πᾶσιν εὐαγγελίζεσθαι τῆς βασιλείας τῶν οὐρανῶν τὴν ἐγγύτητα. ὅταν γὰρ ἀναστῶμεν ἀπὸ τῶν νεκρῶν καὶ τῆς τοῦ ἁγίου πνεύματος μετάσχωμεν χάριτος, ἄτρεπτοι μένομεν τὰς ψυχὰς καὶ ἄφθαρτοι τὸ σῶμα ἐν οὐρανοῖς διαιτώμενοι. ἠγγικέναι δὲ πανταχοῦ λέγει *τὴν βασιλείαν τῶν οὐρανῶν* ὡς δὴ διὰ τῆς αὐτοῦ παρουσίας καὶ τὴν ἀληθῆ τοῦ πράγματος κομισαμένων ὑπόσχεσιν καὶ ὡς ἐν τύπῳ γενομένων ἤδη καὶ *τὴν ἀπαρχὴν* κομίζεσθαι *τοῦ πνεύματος.*[dclvi]

838 Matt. 9:35; cf. 12:22-30.
839 Cf. Matt. 10:15; 11:22&24; 12:36; 2 Peter, 2:9; 3:7; 1 John, 4:17.
840 Rom. 15:18.
841 Cf. Deut. 10:16; Jer. 4:4; Matt. 19:8; Mark, 10:5.
842 Matt. 4:23; 9:35. Cf. Mark, 6:2; Luke, 6:6; 13:10; John, 6:59.
843 Cf. Luke, 22:37; 24:44; John, 5:31-32; 5:36-39; 5:46; 8:13-18; 8:58; 1 John, 5:9-10.
844 Matt. 13:11.
845 Cf. Luke, 4:10.
846 Matt. 9:35.
847 Matt. 4:23; 9:35; 24:14. Cf. Mark, 1:35; Luke, 4:43; 8:1; 16:16.
848 Cf. Matt. 3:2; 4:17; 10:7.
849 Matt. 4:17.
850 Rom. 8:23.

ὁ μὲν θερισμὸς πολύς, οἱ δὲ ἐργάται ὀλίγοι.[851] Οἱ ὄχλοι ὡς μόνῳ διδασκάλῳ προσέρχονται τῷ Χριστῷ. Τότε οὖν τοῖς ἑαυτοῦ μαθηταῖς φησι ὁ Σωτήρ· *ὁ μὲν θερισμὸς πολύς, οἱ δὲ ἐργάται ὀλίγοι.* Καὶ θερισμὸν μέν φησι τοὺς δεομένους τῆς διδασκαλίας· ὀλίγους, τοὺς πιστούς· ἐργάτας δέ, τοὺς διδασκάλους. Ὀλίγους δὲ εἶπεν ὡς οὐδενὸς ὄντος, ἤτοι

ἐργάτας λέγει τοὺς μαθητάς, οὓς ὀλίγους ὄντας ἔπεμψεν εἰς ὅλην τὴν *ὑπ᾽ οὐρανόν*,[852] ὡς ἐπὶ τὸν ἑαυτοῦ σπόρον, τουτέστι τὰ *διὰ τῶν προφητῶν*,[853] ὡς προφητῶν καὶ ἀποστόλων[854] Κύριος.

Τοὺς μαθητὰς λέγει ἐργάτας, οὓς ὀλίγους ὄντας ἔπεμψεν εἰς πᾶσαν τὴν ὑπ᾽ οὐρανόν.[dclvii]

Θερισμὸν λέγει τὸν ὄχλον τῶν ἐπιτηδείως ἐχόντων πρὸς θεοσέβειαν. *ἐργάται* θερισμοῦ εἰσιν οἱ κατὰ τὸ εὐαγγέλιον διδάσκαλοι. ἔστι δὲ καὶ ἕτερος θερισμός, *ἡ συντέλεια* τοῦ αἰῶνος, κατὰ τὸ *ἄφετε* τὰ ζιζάνια,[855] *καὶ ἐν καιρῷ τοῦ θερισμοῦ ἐρῶ τοῖς θερισταῖς.*[dclviii]

(Ὠριγένους.) Θερισμὸν λέγει τῶν ὄχλων τῶν ἐπιτηδείως ἐχόντων πρὸς θεοσέβειαν. ἐργάται θερισμοῦ εἰσιν οἱ κατὰ τὸ εὐαγγέλιον διδάσκαλοι. ἔστι δὲ καὶ ἕτερος θερισμός, ἡ *συντέλεια* τοῦ αἰῶνος, κατὰ τὸ *ἄφετε τὰ ζιζάνια, καὶ ἐν καιρῷ τοῦ θερισμοῦ, ἐρῶ τοῖς θερισταῖς.*[dclix]

The plentiful harvest is the entire crowd of the faithful; the few labourers are the apostles and their imitators who are sent to the harvest.[dclx]

Εἰπὼν γὰρ *δεήθητε τοῦ κυρίου τοῦ θερισμοῦ ὅπως ἐκβάλῃ ἐργάτας*,[856] ὡς αὐτὸς Κύριος ὢν τοῦ θερισμοῦ καὶ δίχα τοῦ αἰτῆσαι καίπερ τοῦτο ἐπιτάξας, προεχειρίσατο τοὺς *δώδεκα*, δηλῶν ὡς αὐτὸς ἦν ὁ γεωργός. Ὁ δὲ *θερισμός*, οἱ ὄχλοι· οἱ δὲ πρῶτοι *ἐργάται*, οἱ τῶν νομικῶν διδάσκαλοι, ὧν ἐπιλειψάντων ἀντεισήχθη τῶν ἀποστόλων ὁ χορός, οἵτινες *ὀλίγοι* ἦ | **74v** σαν ὡς πρὸς τὸ τῆς ἁπάσης οἰκουμένης *κήρυγμα*.

Οἱ δὲ θερισταί, ἄγγελοί εἰσι.[857] Καὶ νῦν τοῖς ἀγγέλοις τῶν ἀποστόλων λέγεται ταῦτα. *Θερισμός* ἐστι τῶν ἐπὶ *τὴν καλὴν γῆν*[858] ἑαυτῶν βαλόντων σπόρον τὸν λόγον. *Θερισταὶ* δὲ *ὀλίγοι*. Οὐ γὰρ πολλοὶ οἱ ἀνεπαισχύντως *ὀρθοτομοῦντες τὸν λόγον τῆς ἀληθείας.*[859]

851 Matt. 9:37; Luke, 10:2.
852 Cf. Esther. 4:17c; Proverbia, 8:26&28; Job, 1:7; *et passim*; Psalms of Salomon, 2:32; Baruch; 5:3; Luke, 17:24.
853 Cf. Matt. 2:23; Luke, 18:31; Rom. 1:2.
854 Cf. Luke, 11:49; 1 Cor. 12:49; 12:29; Eph. 2:20; 3:5; 4:11; 2 Peter 3:2; Rev. 18:20.
855 Matt. 13:30.
856 Matt. 9:38.
857 Matt. 13:39.
858 Cf. Matt. 13:8; 13:23; Mark, 4:8; 4:20; Luke, 8:8.
859 Cf. 2 Tim. 2:15.

> Εἰ *οἱ θερισταὶ ἄγγελοί εἰσι*, καὶ νῦν τοῖς ἀγγέλοις τῶν ἀποστόλων λέγεται ταῦτα. θερισμὸν δὲ τῶν *ἐπὶ τὴν καλὴν γῆν* ἑαυτῶν λαβόντων σπόρον τὸν λόγον. θερισταὶ δὲ *ὀλίγοι*, οὐ γὰρ πολλοὶ οἱ ἀνεπαισχύντως ὀρθοτομοῦντες τὸν λόγον τῆς ἀληθείας.[dclxi]

> (᾿Ωριγένους.) Εἰ οἱ *θερισταὶ* *῎Αγγελοι εἰσί*, καὶ νῦν τοῖς ἀγγέλοις τῶν ᾿Αποστόλων λέγεται ταῦτα. *θερισμὸν* δὲ τῶν ἐπὶ τὴν καλὴν γῆν ἑαυτῶν λαβόντων σπόρον τὸν λόγον. θερισταὶ δὲ ὀλίγοι, οὐ γὰρ πολλοὶ οἱ ἀνεπαισθήτως[dclxii] ὀρθοτομοῦντες τὸν λόγον τῆς ἀληθείας.[dclxiii]

Εἰ δὲ τὰ ἐνθάδε ἔξω ἐστίν, ἔσω ἡ τῶν μακαρίων ἐργατῶν χώρα. ᾿Εκβάλλονται δὲ *ἐργάται* εἰς τὸν θερισμὸν ὅταν ὁμολογήσωσιν οἱ *ὀλίγοι ἐργάται* δεῖσθαι θεριστῶν.

Δεήθητε οὖν τοῦ Κυρίου τοῦ θερισμοῦ.[860] ῾Ορᾶτε, φησί‹ν›, ὅση μὲν τῶν πιστευόντων ἡ ἐπίδοσις, ὅπως δὲ οὔκ εἰσιν οἱ τὰ προσήκοντα διδάξοντες αὐτούς, ὡς ἐντεῦθεν αὐτοὺς ἀναγκάζεσθαι ἐμοὶ κατακολουθοῦντας τοσοῦτον κάματον ὑπομένειν. Τὸ γὰρ *ὀλίγοι ἐργάται* ἐνταῦθα ἀντὶ τοῦ οὐκ εἰσὶ λέγει, τὴν ὀλιγότητα ἀντὶ τοῦ οὐκ εἶναι τεθεικώς,

> The plentiful harvest signifies the multitude of peoples; the few labourers indicate the lack of teachers. He commands that they ask the Lord of the harvest to send out workers into his harvest.[dclxiv]

ὡς καὶ παρὰ τῷ Δαυὶδ τὸ *ὠλιγώθησαν αἱ ἀλήθειαι ἀπὸ τῶν υἱῶν τῶν ἀνθρώπων.*[861] Θεριστὰς δὲ τοὺς ἀποστόλους ἐκάλεσε, δεικνὺς ὅτι καὶ τὰ *διὰ τῶν προφητῶν*[862] γεγονότα διὰ τῆς αὐτοῦ δυνάμεως καὶ ἐπιχορηγίας ἐγένετο, καὶ ὅτι καὶ *προφητῶν καὶ ἀποστόλων*[863] αὐτὸς κύριος καὶ πάντων ἀνθρώπων ὡς δημιουργός, καὶ ἐπὶ τὸν ἑαυτοῦ σπόρον, οὐκ ἐπ᾿ ἀλλότριον, ἀποστέλλει τοὺς μαθητάς.

> ῾Ορᾶτε, φησίν, ὅση μὲν τῶν πιστευόντων ἡ ἐπίδοσις, ὅπως δὲ οὔκ εἰσιν οἱ τὰ προσήκοντα διδάξοντες αὐτούς, ὡς ἐντεῦθεν αὐτοὺς ἀναγκάζεσθαι ἐμοὶ κατακολουθοῦντας τοσοῦτον κάματον ὑπομένειν. τὸ γὰρ *ὀλίγοι ἐργάται* ἐνταῦθα ἀντὶ τοῦ οὔκ εἰσι λέγει, τὴν ὀλιγότητα ἀντὶ τοῦ οὐκ εἶναι τεθεικώς, ὡς καὶ παρὰ τῷ Δαυὶδ τὸ *ὠλιγώθησαν αἱ ἀλήθειαι ἀπὸ τῶν υἱῶν τῶν ἀνθρώπων.*[864] θεριστὰς δὲ τοὺς ἀποστόλους ἐκάλεσε, δεικνὺς ὅτι καὶ τὰ *διὰ τῶν προφητῶν* γεγονότα διὰ τῆς αὐτοῦ δυνάμεως καὶ ἐπιχορηγίας ἐγένετο, καὶ ὅτι καὶ *προφητῶν καὶ ἀποστόλων* αὐτὸς κύριος καὶ πάντων ἀνθρώπων ὡς δημιουργός, καὶ ἐπὶ τὸν ἑαυτοῦ σπόρον οὐκ ἐπ᾿ ἀλλότριον ἀποστέλλει τοὺς μαθητάς.[dclxv]

Καὶ προσκαλεσάμενος ὁ ᾿Ιησοῦς τοὺς δώδεκα μαθητὰς αὐτοῦ.[865] Εἶτα προχειρίζεται εἰς τὸν θερισμὸν ἐργάτας *τοὺς δώδεκα μαθητάς*, δοὺς *αὐτοῖς ἐξουσίαν πνευμάτων*

860 Matt. 9:38.
861 Psalm 11:2.
862 Cf. Matt. 2:23; Luke, 18:31; Rom. 1:2.
863 Cf. Luke, 11:49; 1 Cor. 12:49; 12:29; Eph. 2:20; 3:5; 4:11; 2 Peter 3:2; Rev. 18:20.
864 Psalm 11:2.
865 Matt. 10:1.

ἀκαθάρτων καὶ νόσους *θεραπεύειν* ὡς Θεός, ἵνα διὰ τούτου καταπτήσσοντας τοὺς ἀνθρώπους, πειθηνίους ἔχωσι τοὺς ἀκροατὰς εἰς τὸ κήρυγμα.

> Εἶτα προχειρίζεται εἰς τὸν θερισμὸν ἐργάτας *τοὺς δώδεκα μαθητάς*, δοὺς *αὐτοῖς ἐξουσίαν πνευμάτων ἀκαθάρτων* καὶ νόσους *θεραπεύειν* ὡς θεός, ἵνα διὰ τούτου καταπτήσσοντας τοὺς ἀνθρώπους, ‹καὶ› πειθηνίους ἔχωσι τοὺς ἀκροατὰς εἰς τὸ κήρυγμα.[dclxvi]

Καὶ θεραπεύειν πᾶσαν νόσον καὶ πᾶσαν μαλακίαν.[866] | **75r** Εἰ καὶ μηδέπω ἦν Πνεῦμα Ἅγιον δοθέν, ἀλλ᾽ ὅμως ἀπὸ μόνης ἐπιταγῆς τοῦ Χριστοῦ τὴν τοιαύτην ἔλαβον *ἐξουσίαν*, οὐ μόνον σωματικὴν ἀλλὰ καὶ ψυχικὴν πληγὴν *θεραπεύειν*, ἵνα τὰ συναμφότερα συμφωνήσαντα ἐπὶ τὸ αὐτὸ (ψυχὴ λέγω καὶ σῶμα)[dclxvii] δοξάσωσι καὶ εὐλογήσωσι τὸν Θεὸν τὸν ἑνώσαντα αὐτ‹ά›.[867]

> [Εἰ καὶ μηδέπω ἦν πνεῦμα ἅγιον δοθέν, ἀλλ᾽ ὅμως ἀπὸ μόνης ἐπιταγῆς τοῦ Χριστοῦ τὴν τοιαύτην ἔλαβον *ἐξουσίαν*] οὐ μόνον σωματικὴν ἀλλὰ καὶ ψυχικὴν πληγὴν *θεραπεύειν*.[dclxviii]

> Ὡς καλὸς διδάσκαλος[868] ἀφθόνως τοῖς τελείοις τὰ τέλεια μαθήματα παραδίδωσι καὶ ὡς ἐπιστήμων ἀρχίατρος τοῖς φιλοπόνοις μαθηταῖς τὴν ἐπιστημονικὴν ἰατρικήν, οὐ μόνον σωματικὴν ἀλλὰ καὶ ψυχικὴν πληγὴν *θεραπεύειν*. διὰ γὰρ τῆς παρακοῆς τοῦ Ἀδὰμ περιέπεσεν ὁ ἄνθρωπος ποικίλαις νόσοις ψυχικαῖς τε καὶ σωματικαῖς. καὶ *ἐξουσίαν αὐτοῖς ἔδωκεν* καὶ *πνευμάτων ἀκαθάρτων* τῶν τὰς τοιαύτας νόσους ἀόρτως ἐνεργούντων, ὥστε *ἐκβάλλειν* αὐτάς, ἵνα τὰ συναμφότερα συμφωνήσαντα ἐπὶ τὸ αὐτό, λέγω ψυχή τε καὶ σῶμα, ἐπὶ τὸ αὐτὸ δοξάσωσι καὶ εὐλογήσωσι τὸν Θεὸν τὸν ἑνώσαντα αὐτά.[dclxix]

> The kind and clement Lord and teacher does not enviously refuse to grant his miraculous powers to his servants and disciples. On the contrary, just as he had healed every kind of disease and sickness, so too he gave to his disciples the power to heal every kind of disease and sickness.[dclxx]

Τῶν δὲ δώδεκα ἀποστόλων τὰ ὀνόματα.[869] Διὰ τοὺς ψευδαποστόλους ἐσημειώσατο τὰ ὀνόματα τῶν ἀποστόλων.

> ἐσημειώσατο δὲ ἐπιτηδείως τῶν ἀποστόλων τὰ ὀνόματα, ἵνα μηδενὶ πεισθῶμεν ἑτέρῳ παρὰ τοὺς εἰρημένους. ᾔδει γὰρ ὅτι ἔμελλόν τινες ψευδαπόστολοι ἐπιφημίσαι τὸ τοιοῦτον ἀξίωμα.[dclxxi]

> The catalogue of the apostles is recorded, so that those false apostles that might appear in the future should be excluded.[dclxxii]

---

866 *Loc. cit.*
867 Cod. αὐτούς.
868 Cf. Matt. 23:8; 26:18; Mark, 14:14; Luke, 22:11; John, 3:2; 13:13-14.
869 Matt. 10:2.

Καὶ γὰρ ὁ Μάνης ἀπόστολον ἑαυτὸν ὠνόμαζε, καὶ ἄλλοι τινές. Προτιμᾷ τοίνυν Πέτρον καὶ Ἀνδρέαν τῶν ἄλλων. Τὸν μὲν ἀπὸ τῆς ἀρετῆς, τὸν δὲ ἀπὸ τῆς εὐγενείας τῆς κατὰ τὸν τρόπον καὶ διὰ τὸ πρώτους τῶν ἄλλων τούτους κληθῆναι. Εἶτα κατὰ συζυγίαν τάσσει συμφώνως Μάρκῳ καὶ Λουκᾷ Ἰάκωβον τὸν τοῦ Ζεβεδαίου καὶ Ἰωάννην τὸν ἀδελφὸν αὐτοῦ,
οὐ κατὰ προτίμησιν ἐν βαθμοῖς τὰς ὀνομασίας τιθείς. Καὶ γὰρ ὁ Ἰωάννης οὐ μόνον τοῦ ἰδίου ἀδελφοῦ μείζων ἦν ἀλλὰ καὶ Ἀνδρέου.

> οὐ κατὰ προτίμησιν δὲ ποιεῖται τὰς ὀνομασίας.... καὶ ὁ Ἰωάννης οὐ μόνον τοῦ ἀδελφοῦ ἀλλὰ καὶ τῶν ἄλλων μείζων ἦν.[dclxxiii]

Εἶτα εἰπὼν *Φίλιππος καὶ Βαρθολομαῖος*, ἐπήγαγε· *Θωμᾶς καὶ Ματθαῖος ὁ τελώνης*, καίτοι γε
ὁ Ματθαῖος μείζων ἦν τοῦ Θωμᾶ.

> ὁ γὰρ Θωμᾶς καταδεέστερος ἦν τοῦ Ματθαίου.[dclxxiv]

Καὶ γὰρ ὁ Λουκᾶς οὐχ οὕτως, ἀλλ' ἀντιστρόφως τίθησι καὶ προτίθησιν αὐτὸν τοῦ Θωμᾶ.[870] Ἵνα δὲ δείξῃ τὴν χάριν τοῦ καλέσαντος καὶ τελώνην ἑαυτὸν καλεῖ. Εἶτα εἰπὼν *Ἰάκωβος ὁ τοῦ Ἀλφαίου* (ἦν γὰρ καὶ ὁ Ζεβεδαίου), ἐπήγαγε, *καὶ Λεββαῖος ὁ ἐπικληθεὶς Θαδδαῖος*. Εἶτα εἰπὼν Σίμωνα τὸν ζηλωτήν, ὃν καὶ Κανανίτην καλεῖ, ἐπὶ τὸν προδότην ἔρχεται Ἰούδαν, ἀπὸ τῆς πόλεως αὐτὸν καλῶν Ἰσκαριώτην. Ἦν δὲ καὶ ἕτερος Ἰούδας ὁ ἐπικληθεὶς *Θαδδαῖος*, ὁ καὶ *Λεββαῖος*, ὃν καὶ *Ἰα* | **75v** *κώβου* ὁ Λουκᾶς εἶναι λέγει.[871] Διὰ τοῦτο δὲ καὶ προδότην αὐτὸν ὠνόμασεν, ἀπὸ τοῦ ἐπονειδίστου δηλῶν ὅτι τοιούτων ἀξιωθεὶς χαρισμάτων προδέδωκε τὸν διδάσκαλον.
Δύο τοίνυν Ἰοῦδαι εἰσίν· εἷς, ὁ Θαδδαῖος ὁ καὶ Λεββαῖος, ὃς καὶ Ἰακώβου ἐκαλεῖτο, καὶ ὁ προδότης. Καὶ δύο Ἰάκωβοι, εἷς ὁ τοῦ Ζεβεδαίου καὶ ἕτερος ὁ τοῦ Ἀλφαίου. Καὶ δύο Σίμωνες, εἷς ὁ καὶ Πέτρος καὶ ἄλλος ὁ καὶ Κανανίτης.

> δύο Ἰοῦδαι, ‹εἷς ὁ Ἰακώβου καὶ ἄλλος› ὁ προδότης. καὶ ὁ καλούμενος Ἰσκαριώτης δὲ ἀπὸ τῆς πόλεως αὐτοῦ καλεῖται, ὃν καὶ προδότην καλεῖ.[dclxxv]

> δύο δὲ ἦσαν Σίμωνες, εἷς ὁ καὶ Πέτρος καὶ ἕτερος ὁ Κανανίτης. δύο Ἰάκωβοι, εἷς ὁ τοῦ Ζεβεδαίου καὶ ἄλλος ὁ τοῦ Ἀλφαίου.[dclxxvi]

Ἰστέον δὲ ὅτι καὶ ὁ Ἰσκαριώτης Ἰούδας Σίμων ἐκαλεῖτο, καὶ ὁ Θωμᾶς Ἰούδας.

---

870 Luke, 6:15.
871 Luke, 6:16.

23

(ΩΡΙΓΕΝΟΥΣ)[872] Ἢ ὤφειλε *καὶ τὰ ὀνόματα* ἐνδείξασθαι τῶν ἤδη γεγραμμένων *ἐν βίβλῳ ζώντων*[873] *ἐν οὐρανοῖς*. *Δώδεκα δέ*, κατὰ ἀριθμὸν τῶν δώδεκα φυλῶν τοῦ Ἰσραήλ[874] *καὶ* τῶν δώδεκα λεγεώνων ‹τῶν ἀγγέλων›,[875] *καὶ* τῶν δώδεκα μηνῶν τοῦ ἐνιαυτοῦ (*ἐνιαυτὸν* γὰρ ἔφη τις *Κύριου δεκτόν*),[876] *καὶ* τῶν δώδεκα ὡρῶν τῆς ἡμέρας, *ἣν ἐποίησεν ὁ Κύριος*.[877]

> Ἢ ὤφειλε *καὶ τὰ ὀνόματα* ἐνδείξασθαι τῶν ἤδη γεγραμμένων ἐν βίβλῳ ζώντων ἐν οὐρανοῖς. *δώδεκα* δὲ κατὰ ἀριθμὸν τῶν δώδεκα φυλῶν τοῦ Ἰσραήλ *καὶ* τῶν δώδεκα λεγεώνων ‹τῶν ἀγγέλων› *καὶ* τῶν δώδεκα μηνῶν τοῦ ἐνιαυτοῦ (*ἐνιαυτὸν* γὰρ ἔφη τις *Κύριου δεκτόν*) *καὶ* τῶν δώδεκα ὡρῶν τῆς ἡμέρας, *ἣν ἐποίησεν ὁ Κύριος*.[dclxxvii]

> Δώδεκα μαθητὰς ὁ σωτὴρ ἐξελέξατο κατὰ ἀριθμὸν τῶν δώδεκα λεγεώνων ἀγγέλων, ἢ καὶ τῶν δώδεκα ὡρῶν τῆς ἡμέρας. τέλειος γάρ ἐστιν ὁ ἓξ ἀριθμός.[dclxxviii] τοῦτον δὲ τὸν ἀριθμὸν διπλασιάσας ἰσαρίθμους τοὺς μαθητὰς ἐποίησεν.[dclxxix]

Εἰς ὁδὸν ἐθνῶν μὴ ἀπέλθητε.[878] Πρωτοτύπως ἔδει κηρυχθῆναι τοῖς Ἰουδαίοις τὸ εὐαγγέλιον, ἐπειδὴ πρὸς αὐτοὺς ἦσαν αἱ ἐπαγγελίαι καὶ ἐξ αὐτῶν ὁ *Χριστὸς τὸ κατὰ σάρκα*.[879]

> Ὅτι δεῖ πρῶτον τοῖς Ἰουδαίοις κηρύττειν. πρὸς αὐτοὺς γὰρ ἦσαν γεγονυῖαι αἱ ἐπαγγελίαι, ὅτι ἐξ αὐτῶν ἤμελλεν ὁ Χριστὸς τὸ κατὰ σάρκα ὀφθῆναι καὶ ὅταν ἠπείθησαν, τότε εἰς τὰ ἔθνη χωρῆσαι.[dclxxx]

Περικόπτων οὖν πᾶσαν πρόφασιν αὐτῶν, ταῦτα ἐνετέλλετο

> Περικόπτων οὖν πᾶσαν πρόφασιν αὐτῶν, ταῦτα ἐνετέλλετο.[dclxxxi]

ἵνα μὴ ἔχωσιν ἀπολογίαν λέγοντες ὅτι διὰ τοῦτο οὐκ ἐδεξάμεθα τοὺς ἀποστόλους. Ἐπειδὴ ἐπίσης ἡμῖν καὶ τοῖς ἐθνικοῖς καὶ τοῖς Σαμαρείταις, οὓς ἔδει φεύγειν,[880] ἐκήρυττον.

---

872 Cod. reaffirming attribution.
873 Psalm 68:29. Cf. Phil. 4:3; Rev. 3:5; 13:8; 17.8.
874 Cf. In OT, Ex. 24:4; 36:21; Josua, 4:5; Ezekiel 47:13; *et passim*. In NT, Matt. 19:28; Luke, 22:20; James, 1:1; Rev. 7:5-8; 21:12.
875 Cf. Matt. 26:53.
876 Is. 61:2, quoted in Luke, 4:19.
877 Psalm 117:24.
878 Matt. 10:5.
879 Cf. John, 7:42; Rom. 1:3; 2 Tim. 2:8.
880 Cf. Matt. 10:5.

οὔπω γὰρ ἦσαν παραιτησάμενοι τὴν διδασκαλίαν οἱ Ἰουδαῖοι. Ὅτε δὲ ἀπώσαντο τὸν λόγον, ἤκουσαν τὸ *ἰδοὺ ἡμεῖς στρεφόμεθα εἰς τὰ ἔθνη.*[881]

> οὔπω γὰρ ἦσαν παραιτησάμενοι τὴν διδασκαλίαν οἱ Ἰουδαῖοι … . ὅτε δὲ ἀπώσαντο τὸν λόγον, ἤκουσαν τό. *ἰδοὺ ἡμεῖς στρεφόμεθα εἰς τὰ ἔθνη.*[dclxxxii]

Τοὺς Σαμαρείτας δὲ συνάπτει τοῖς ἐθνικοῖς ἐπειδὴ καὶ *ἐξ ἐθνῶν*[882] ἦσαν, κατὰ γένος Βαβυλώνιοι ὄντες καὶ οἰκήσαντες τὴν Ἰουδαίαν.

> Σαμαρείτας δὲ συνάπτει τοῖς ἐξ *ἐθνῶν*, ἐπειδὴ καὶ ἐξ *ἐθνῶν* ἦσαν κατὰ γένος Βαβυλώνιοι ὄντες καὶ οἰκήσαντες τὴν Ἰουδαίαν.[dclxxxiii]

Ἐπειδὴ δὲ ἐν μέσῳ τῆς Ἰουδαί | **76r** ας ἦσαν αἱ πόλεις τῶν Σαμαρειτῶν δι᾿ ὧν ἔδει διελθεῖν, ἐπ᾿ αὐτῶν μὲν τὸ *μὴ εἰσέλθητε* εἶπε καὶ τὸ *εἰς πόλιν*, ἀλλ᾿ ἔξωθεν διαβαίνετε· ἐπὶ δὲ τῶν ἐθνικῶν ὡς ἔξω ὄντων τέθεικε τὸ εἰς *ὁδὸν ἐθνῶν μὴ ἀπέλθητε.*[883] *Πρόβατα* δὲ εἶπεν *ἀπολωλότα* τοὺς ἐξ *Ἰσραήλ.*[884] Ἀπωλώλεισαν γὰρ τὸν δοθέντα αὐτοῖς νόμον οὐ φυλάξαντες. *Πορευόμενοι* δὲ κελεύονται κηρύττειν τὴν βασιλείαν *τῶν οὐρανῶν.* Βασιλεία δὲ *οὐρανῶν* ἐστιν οὐρανοπολίτας[dclxxxiv] ποιοῦσα τοὺς πιστοὺς ἡ *διὰ πίστεως* χάρις[885] καὶ ἡ διὰ πνεύματος υἱοθεσία.[886] Τὸ δὲ *ἤγγικέ* φησι ἐπειδὴ διὰ τῆς σαρκώσεως ἦν ἐγγίσασα ἤδη.

> Βασιλείαν δὲ *οὐρανῶν* λέγει τὴν διὰ πίστεως χάριν, τὴν διὰ πνεύματος υἱοθεσίαν τὴν ἑνοῦσαν θεῷ τὸν ἄνθρωπον. ἠγγικέναι δὲ λέγει οὐχ ὡς ἐπίπαν (ἦν γὰρ ἐγγίσασα κυρίου σαρκωθέντος), ἀλλ᾿ ὅσον πρὸς τοὺς μήπω πιστεύσαντας δοκεῖ ὁ Χριστὸς ἀπεῖναι αὐτῶν.[dclxxxv]

> Βασιλείαν δὲ οὐρανῶν λέγει τὴν διὰ πίστεως χάριν, τὴν διὰ πνεύματος υἱοθεσίαν τὴν ἑνοῦσαν θεῷ τὸν ἄνθρωπον.[dclxxxvi]

> ἠγγικέναι δὲ λέγει οὐχ ὡς ἀποῦσαν. ἦν γὰρ ἐγγίσασα τοῦ κυρίου σαρκωθέντος, ἀλλ᾿ ὅσον πρὸς τοὺς μήπω πιστεύσαντας δοκεῖ ὁ Χριστὸς ἀπεῖναι αὐτῶν.[dclxxxvii]

Εἶτα δεικνὺς ὅτι καταθύμια ἦν τῷ Θεῷ τὰ κηρυττόμενα, κατεκόσμησεν αὐτοὺς ταῖς θεοσημείαις, ἵνα καὶ διὰ τούτων δυσωπήσωσι τοὺς ἀκροατάς. Ἐπειδὴ δέ φησι χάριτι ἐσχήκατε τὸ δῶρον, κἀγὼ ὑμῖν ἄνευ χρημάτων δέδωκα τὰ τηλικαῦτα, ἀδωροδοκήτως

---

881 Acts, 13:46.
882 Cf. Rom. 9:24; Acts, 15:23.
883 Matt. 10:5.
884 Matt. 10:6.
885 Cf. Eph. 2:8.
886 Cf. Rom. 8:15-16; 8:23.

καὶ ὑμεῖς ταῦτα διακονήσατε. Εἶτα παραινεῖ μὴ δεῖν τροφῆς φροντίζειν αὐτούς, ὡς αὐτοῦ προνοουμένου.[887]

Θέλει γὰρ τοὺς μαθητὰς κρείττονας χρημάτων εἶναι καὶ ἐλευθέρους τοῦ πάθους τῆς φιλοχρηματίας ὡς ἐμποδίζοντος τῇ κατὰ θεοσέβειαν ἀρετῇ. Ὑπερβολικὸς δέ ἐστιν ὁ λόγος. Ταῦτα γὰρ οὐ τὸν καθόλου βίον αὐτοῖς ρυθμίζει οὐδὲ τὴν χρείαν ἀπαγορεύει, ἀλλὰ τὰ περιττά.

> Καθ' ὑπερβολὴν ὁ λόγος πᾶσαν ἀπαγορεύει κτῆσιν ἀπὸ χρυσοῦ ἕως ράβδου ὡς μέγιστον οὖσαν κώλυμα πρὸς ἀρετὴν καὶ θεοσέβειαν. τὴν δ' ἀναγκαίαν τροφὴν οὐκ ἀπαγορεύει, ὥστε εἰ ἦν δυνατὸν καὶ χωρὶς τροφῆς ζῆν ἡμῖν καὶ ταύτην ἂν ἀπηγόρευσεν.[dclxxxviii]

Ὁρῶμεν γὰρ τὸν μακάριον Παῦλον οὐ δεξάμενον μόνον παρὰ Φιλιππησίων, ἀλλὰ καὶ εἰληφέναι ὁμολογοῦντα καὶ θαυμάζοντα τῆς προθυμίας αὐτούς.[888] Ἐπεὶ οὐδὲ Πέτρον τὸν ἀπόστολον ὑποδήματα ἔχειν ἐχρῆν,[889] οὔτε Παῦλον βίβλους τε καὶ φαιλόνην.[890] Δῆλον οὖν ὅτι τὰ τῆς χρείας ἔχειν | **76v** οὐ κωλυόμεθα. Ἐν ἐκείνῳ δὲ μόνῳ τῷ καιρῷ ἐπέταξε χρήσασθαι τῇ διαγωγῇ ταύτῃ καθ' ὃν ἐπὶ τῆς Ἰουδαίας ἀπεστέλλοντο κηρύττειν πρὸς ἐκείνους, τοὺς ὑπὸ τῷ νόμῳ πεπαιδευμένους παρ' οἷς ἐκράτει τοῦτο, ὅτι Μωσῆς ἐξήγαγεν αὐτοὺς εἰς τὴν ἔρημον οὐδὲν ἐπιφερομένους ἐπὶ πολλοῖς διαθρέψας αὐτοὺς τοῖς ἔτεσι. Τὸ δὲ *ἄξιος ὁ ἐργάτης τῆς τροφῆς αὐτοῦ*[891] φησὶ ἢ ὅτι ἀνάλογος αὐτοῖς μισθὸς ἐν οὐρανῷ ἀπόκειται ἢ ἵνα τρέφωνται ἐκ τῶν μαθητῶν καὶ μὴ ἐπαίρωνται ὡς μηδὲν λαμβάνοντες ὅπερ ἂν ποιῶσιν, οὐ παραβαίνουσι τὸν λόγον τὸν κωλύοντα αὐτοὺς λαμβάνειν δῶρα.

Οὐ τελείως ἀπέκοψε τοὺς ἀπὸ τῶν *ἐθνῶν* μέλλοντας πιστεύειν, οὔτε τοὺς Σαμαρείτας ὁ *πάντας ἀνθρώπους* θέλων *σωθῆναι καὶ εἰς ἐπίγνωσιν ἀληθείας ἐλθεῖν*.[892] Ἀλλ' ἔδει πρῶτον ἐπὶ τὰ *πρόβατα τὰ ἀπολωλότα οἴκου Ἰσραὴλ* πορεύεσθαι,[893] καθὰ καὶ αὐτὸς πρὸς τὴν Χαναναίαν φησί· *οὐκ ἀπεστάλην εἰ μὴ εἰς τὰ πρόβατα τὰ ἀπολωλότα οἴκου Ἰσραήλ*,[894] ἅπερ ὁ Θεὸς ζητήσειν ἐπηγγείλατο διὰ Ἰεζεκιὴλ τοῦ προφήτου.[895]

> Οὐ τελείως ἀπέκοψεν τοὺς ἀπὸ τῶν *ἐθνῶν* μέλλοντας πιστεύειν οὔτε τοὺς Σαμαρείτας ὁ *πάντας ἀνθρώπους* θέλων *σωθῆναι* καὶ εἰς ἐπίγνωσιν ἀληθείας ἐλθεῖν. ἀλλ' ἔδει πρῶτον ἐπὶ τὰ *πρόβατα τὰ ἀπολωλότα οἴκου Ἰσραὴλ* πορεύεσθαι, καθὰ καὶ αὐτὸς πρὸς τὴν Χαναναίαν φησίν. *οὐκ ἀπεστάλην εἰ μὴ πρὸς τὰ πρόβατα τὰ ἀπολωλότα.*[dclxxxix]

---

887 Cf. Matt. 10:9-10.
888 Cf. Phil. 4:10-19.
889 Cf. Acts, 12:7.
890 Cf. 2 Tim. 4:13.
891 Matt. 10:10.
892 1 Tim. 2:4.
893 Matt. 10:6; cf. 15:24.
894 Matt. 15:24.
895 Cf. Ez. 34:5-16.

> Οὐ τελείως ἀπέκοψεν τοὺς ἀπὸ τῶν *ἐθνῶν* μέλλοντας πιστεύειν οὔτε τοὺς Σαμαρείτας *ὁ πάντας ἀνθρώπους* θέλων *σωθῆναι καὶ* εἰς ἐπίγνωσιν ἀληθείας ἐλθεῖν, ἀλλ' ἔδει πρῶτον ἐπὶ *τὰ πρόβατα τὰ ἀπολωλότα οἴκου Ἰσραὴλ* πορεύεσθαι, καθὰ καὶ αὐτὸς πρὸς τὴν Χαναναίαν φησίν. *οὐκ ἀπεστάλην εἰ μὴ πρὸς τὰ πρόβατα τὰ ἀπολωλότα οἴκου Ἰσραήλ*, ἅπερ ὁ θεὸς ζητήσειν ἐπηγγείλατο διὰ Ἰεζεκιὴλ τοῦ προφήτου. ἀπωλώλεσαν δὲ τὸν δοθέντα αὐτοῖς νόμον οὐ φυλάξαντες.[dcxc]

Μήτε *δύο χιτῶνας*,[896] ἀλλὰ τὸν *ἄραφον καὶ ἄνωθεν ὑφαντὸν*[897][dcxci] Χριστὸν Ἰησοῦν. *Ὅσοι* γὰρ *εἰς Χριστὸν ἐβαπτίσθητε, Χριστὸν ἐνεδύσασθε.*[898][dcxcii] *Τὸν* γὰρ *παλαιὸν ἄνθρωπον* ἀποδύσασθαι δεῖ, *σὺν ταῖς πράξεσι* καὶ ταῖς ἐπιθυμίαις *αὐτοῦ.*[899][dcxciii] Τοῦτον καταλείψας Ἰωσὴφ *ἐν ταῖς χερσὶ* τῆς Αἰγυπτίας Μαρίας, γυμνὸς ἐξῆλθεν.[900]

> Μήτε δύο χιτῶνας, ἀλλὰ τὸν ἄραφον καὶ ἄνωθεν ὑφαντὸν Χριστὸν Ἰησοῦν. Ὅσοι γὰρ εἰς Χριστὸν ἐβαπτίσθητε, Χριστὸν ἐνεδύσασθε. Τὸν γὰρ παλαιὸν ἄνθρωπον ἀποδύσασθαι δεῖ, σὺν ταῖς πράξεσι καὶ ταῖς ἐπιθυμίαις αὐτοῦ. τοῦτον καταλείψας Ἰωσὴφ ἐν ταῖς χερσὶ τῆς Αἰγυπτίας Μαρίας, γυμνὸς ἐξῆλθεν.[dcxciv]

Μηδὲ ὑποδήματα.[901] Ἀποστόλῳ πρέπ‹ο›ν[902] ἐν ταῖς πορείαις μὴ ἔχειν νέκρωσιν, ζῶσι δὲ ποσὶν ὁδεύειν ‹πρὸς› τὸν εἰπόντα *ἐγώ εἰμι ἡ ὁδός*,[903] καὶ ἐπιβαίνειν ἁγίας γῆς,[904] μηδὲν ὑφορώμενον χαλεπόν. | **77r** Οὐ γάρ εἰσι ὁδοὶ *ὄφεως ἐπὶ πέτρας*,[905][dcxcv] τάχα δὲ οὐδὲ ἄλλου θηρίου.[dcxcvi]

> *μηδὲ ὑποδήματα.* ἀποστόλῳ πρέπον ἐν ταῖς πορείαις μὴ ἔχειν νέκρωσιν, ζῶσι δὲ ποσὶν ὁδεύειν ‹πρὸς› τὸν εἰπόντα *ἐγώ εἰμι ἡ ὁδός*, καὶ ἐκβαίνειν *ἁγίας γῆς*, μηδὲν ὑφορώμενον χαλεπόν. οὐ γάρ εἰσιν *ὁδοὶ ὄφεως ἐπὶ πέτρας*, τάχα δὲ οὐδὲ ἄλλου θηρίου.[dcxcvii]

Μηδὲ ὑποδήματα. Ὅσον γὰρ ἔχεις τὸν Σωτῆρα φωτίζοντα τὸ σκότος σου[906] καὶ φυλάσσοντα *τὴν εἴσοδόν σου καὶ τὴν ἔξοδόν σου*,[907] οὐκ ἔχεις χρείαν ὑποδημάτων.

> Ὅσον γὰρ ἔχεις τὸν σωτῆρα φωτίζοντα τὸ σκότος σου καὶ φυλάσσοντα τὴν εἴσοδόν σου καὶ τὴν ἔξοδόν σου, οὐκ ἔχεις χρείαν ὑποδημάτων.[dcxcviii]

---

896 Cf. Matt. 10:10.
897 John, 19:23.
898 Gal. 3:27.
899 Cf. Eph. 4:22; Col. 3:9.
900 Gen. 39:12.
901 Matt. 10:10.
902 Cod. πρέπων.
903 John, 14:6.
904 Cf. Ex. 35 (quoted in Acts, 7:33).
905 Cf. Prov. 30:19.
906 Cf. John, 8:12; 12:35.
907 Cf. Prov. 8:34-35.

μηδὲ ῥάβδον.[908] Ὅπου οὐκ ἔστιν ἀταξία ἀλλ' ἡμερότης, οὐ χρεία ῥάβδου, ἵνα μὴ ἐν ἀρχῇ δόξῃ ἐκφοβεῖν διὰ τῆς ῥάβδου. Τὰ γὰρ καλὰ *πρόβατα*[909] διὰ μόνης φωνῆς ἐπιστρέφουσι τοῦ ποιμένος.[910] Ὥστε, εἰ ἔχεις τὸ πρᾶον, μὴ φοβοῦ τὴν ῥάβδον ἣν Κορινθίοις ἐπανατείνεται ὁ Παῦλος.[911]

Ὅπου οὐκ ἔστιν ἀταξία, ἀλλ' ἡμερότης, οὐ χρεία ῥάβδου, ἵνα μὴ ἐν ἀρχῇ δόξῃ ἐκφοβεῖν διὰ τῆς ῥάβδου. τὰ γὰρ καλὰ πρόβατα διὰ μόνης φωνῆς ἐπιστρέφουσι τοῦ ποιμένος, ὥστε εἰ ἔχεις τὸ πρᾶον, μὴ φοβοῦ τὴν ῥάβδον, ἣν Κορινθίοις ἐπανατείνεται ὁ Παῦλος.[dcxcix]

24

(ΩΡΙΓΕΝΟΥΣ) *εἰς ἣν δ' ἂν οἰκίαν εἰσέλθητε*, ἐν ταύτῃ μένετε,[912]
διὰ τὸ βέβαιον καὶ ἀμετάστατον. Τοῖς μὲν γὰρ ἐμπορευομένοις μετιέναι ἐξ ἑτέρων εἰς ἑτέρους ἁρμόσει, τοῖς δὲ ἀδωροδοκήτοις οὐκέτι. Δικαίαν δὲ ἔδειξε τὴν τῶν ἀναγκαίων ἀπόλαυσιν· *τροφὴν*[913] δὲ εἰπὼν τὴν τρυφὴν ἀπήλασεν.

Διὰ τὸ βέβαιον καὶ ἀμετάστατον. τοῖς μὲν γὰρ ἐμπορευομένοις μετιέναι ἐξ ἑτέρων εἰς ἑτέρους ἁρμόσει, τοῖς δὲ ἀδωροδοκήτοις οὐκέτι. δικαίαν δὲ ἔδειξε τὴν τῶν ἀναγκαίων ἀπόλαυσιν, ‹παρὰ τῶν διδασκομένων, τῶν ἐργαζομένων οὖσαν μισθόν›. *τροφὴν*[914] δὲ εἰπὼν τὴν τρυφὴν ἀπεκώλυσεν.[dcc]

(Ὠριγένους.) Διὰ τὸ βέβαιον καὶ ἀμετάστατον. τοῖς μὲν γὰρ ἐμπορευομένοις μετιέναι ἐξ ἑτέρων εἰς ἑτέρους ἁρμόσει. τοῖς δὲ δωροδοκήτοις οὐκέτι. δικαίαν δὲ ἔδειξεν εἶναι τὴν τῶν ἀναγκαίων ἀπόλαυσιν παρὰ τῶν διδασκομένων, τῶν ἐργαζομένων οὖσαν μισθόν. τροφὴν δὲ εἰπών, τὴν τρυφὴν ἀπεκώλυσεν.[dcci]

Ἐξετάσατε τίς ἐν αὐτῇ ἄξιός ἐστιν εἰ καὶ αὐτὸς ὁ Χριστὸς ἐκολλᾶτο τοῖς ἀναξίοις. Ἀλλ' οὖν δίκαιον ἡγήσατο προτιμᾶσθαι τοὺς ἀγαθοὺς τῶν φαύλων. Εἰ δὲ προσίασιν οἱ φαῦλοι ὠφεληθησόμενοι, οὐ δεῖ αὐτοὺς ἀπωθεῖσθαι.
Λέγει γοῦν μετὰ πολλῆς διακρίσεως πρὸς τοὺς ἐναρέτους αὐτοὺς μένειν μὴ μεταβαίνοντας *ἐξ οἰκίας εἰς οἰκίαν*,[915] ἵνα μὴ δόξωσι τοὺς πρώτους ὑβρίζειν ἢ τὰς ἐκ τῶν πλειόνων θηρᾶσθαι τιμὰς καὶ δόξωσι γαστρίμαργοι εἶναι καὶ εὐχερεῖς.

908 Matt. 10:10.
909 Cf. Matt. 10:16.
910 Cf. John, 10:11&14.
911 1 Cor. 4:21.
912 Cf. Matt. 10:11.
913 Matt. 10:10.
914 Matt. 10:10.
915 Luke, 10:3.

> Οὐ θέλει τόπον ἐκ τόπου καὶ οἰκίαν ἐξ οἰκίας ἀμείβειν αὐτούς, ἵνα μὴ λύπη γένηται τῷ πρώτῳ ὑποδεξαμένῳ μηδὲ ὑπόνοιαν δέξωνται γαστριμαργίας καὶ εὐχερείας.[dccii]

Θέλει δὲ γίνεσθαι τὸν ἀσπασμὸν[916] οὐκ ἐν ψιλοῖς ῥήμασιν, ἀλλ᾽ ἐν ἀγάπῃ πληρεστάτῃ. Λέγει δὲ πρῶτον τὸν ἀσπασμὸν γίνεσθαι διὰ ταπείνωσιν ἀδιακρίτως καὶ πάντας τοὺς ἐν τῷ *οἴκῳ* εὐλογεῖσθαι. Καὶ ἐὰν μὲν ᾖ ἡ οἰκία ἀξία (τουτέστιν οἱ ἐν *τῷ οἴκῳ*), παραμένειν αὐτοῖς τὴν εὐλογίαν. Εἰ δὲ μή γε, ἐπαναστρέφειν ἐξ αὐτῶν τὴν | 77v εὐλογίαν. Εἰ γὰρ καὶ ὡς ἄνθρωποι ἠγνόησαν ἢ ἐψεύσαντο οἱ εἰπόντες καλοὺς εἶναι τοὺς φαύλους, ἀλλ᾽ ὥσπερ ἐχαρίσατο τὸ ἀφεῖναι τινῶν *ἁμαρτίας*[917] καὶ μή, οὕτω καὶ τοῦτο, τὸ διὰ τῆς αὐτῶν ἐνεργείας παραμένειν τοῖς ἀξίοις τὴν ἐξ αὐτῶν εὐλογίαν τοῖς δὲ ἀναξίοις οὔ. Σωματικώτερον δὲ εἶπε τὸ ἐπαναστρέφειν ἐκ τῶν ἀναξίων τὴν εὐλογίαν, ἥτις δοκεῖ μηδὲ[918] ἁρμόσαι τοῖς τοιούτοις ὅλως.

Ἐκτινάξατε τὸν κονιορτόν.[919] Οὐδὲ *κονιορτὸν* θέλει ἔχειν αὐτοὺς ἐπὶ *τῶν ποδῶν* ἐκ τῆς τῶν ἀνοσίων ἀνθρώπων γῆς, δεικνύντας ὅτι οὐδὲν ἐκομίσαντο ἀπὸ τῶν ἀπειθῶν. Δεῖγμά δέ ἐστι καὶ ὁ κονιορτὸς τοῦ κόπου, ὃν ὑπέμειναν δι᾽ αὐτόν. Λέγει δὲ ὅτι καὶ χείρονα τῶν Σοδομιτῶν πείσονται,[920] ὅτι ἐκεῖνοι μὲν ἀγγέλους ἠτίμασαν, οὗτοι δὲ τοὺς ἀποστόλους τοὺς ἐν τάξει ἀγγέλων ὄντας,[dcciii] μᾶλλον δὲ τὸν ἀποστείλαντα αὐτοὺς καὶ τὸν ἐκείνου Πατέρα. Καὶ οἱ μὲν ἐπὶ ξενίαν ἐληλυθέναι δοκοῦντας,[921] οἱ δὲ ἐπὶ βασιλείαν καλοῦντας.

> Οὐδὲ *κονιορτὸν* θέλει ἔχειν αὐτοὺς ἐπὶ *τῶν ποδῶν* ἐκ τῆς τῶν ἀνοσίων ἀνθρώπων γῆς, δεικνύντας ὅτι οὐδὲν ἐκομίσαντο ἀπὸ τῶν ἀπειθῶν. δεῖγμα δέ ἐστι καὶ ὁ κονιορτὸς τοῦ κόπου, ὃν ὑπέμειναν δι᾽ αὐτούς. λέγει δὲ ὅτι καὶ χείρονα τῶν Σοδομιτῶν πείσονται, ὅτι ἐκεῖνοι μὲν ἀγγέλους ἠτίμασαν, οὗτοι δὲ τοὺς ἀποστόλους τοὺς ἐν τάξει ἀγγέλων ὄντας, μᾶλλον δὲ τὸν ἀποστείλαντα αὐτοὺς καὶ τὸν ἐκείνου πατέρα, καὶ οἱ μὲν ἐπὶ ξενίαν ἐληλυθέναι δοκοῦντας, οἱ δὲ ἐπὶ βασιλείαν καλοῦντας.[dcciv]

> Ταῦτά φησιν ὥστε μὴ εὐκόλου καὶ προχείρου γνώμης ἀποφέρεσθαι δόξαν παρὰ τοῖς τὴν *πόλιν* οἰκοῦσιν. ἰσόρροπον δὲ τοῖς Σοδομίταις τὴν τιμωρίαν τοῖς μὴ δεξαμένοις ἐπάγει, ἐπειδήπερ οἱ μὲν ἐπὶ ξενίαν ἐληλυθέναι δοκοῦντας τοὺς ἀγγέλους ἐνύβρισαν, οἱ δὲ ἐπὶ βασιλείαν καλοῦντας παρῃτοῦντο.[dccv]

> Ταῦτά φησιν ὥστε μὴ εὐκόλου καὶ προχείρου γνώμης ἀποφέρεσθαι δόξαν παρὰ τοῖς τὴν *πόλιν* οἰκοῦσιν.[dccvi] ἰσόρροπον δὲ τοῖς Σοδομίταις τὴν τιμωρίαν τοῖς μὴ δεξαμένοις ἐπάγει,[dccvii] ἐπειδήπερ οἱ μὲν ἐπὶ ξενίαν ἐληλυθέναι δοκοῦντας τοὺς ἀγγέλους ἐνύβρισαν, οἱ δὲ ἐπὶ βασιλείαν καλοῦντας παρῃτοῦντο.[dccviii]

---

916 Matt. 10:12-15.
917 John, 20:22.
918 Cod. μὴ δὲ.
919 Matt. 10:14.
920 Matt. 11:15.
921 Cf. Gen. 18.

Ἐκέλευσε δὲ καὶ εἰς οἰκίαν μένειν μὴ μεθισταμένους, ὥστε μὴ εὐκόλου καὶ προχείρου γνώμης ἀποφέρεσθαι δόξαν παρὰ τοῖς τὴν πόλιν οἰκοῦσι. ἐκέλευσε δὲ τοῖς μὴ πειθομένοις αὐτῶν μηδὲ ὑποδεχομένοις, καὶ τὸν κονιορτὸν ἐκτινάσσειν τῶν ποδῶν, σύμβολον ὄντα τῆς ὁδοιπορίας ἣν ὑπέμενον ὑπὲρ αὐτῶν,[dccix] ἤτοι ὡς τῶν ἁμαρτιῶν αὐτῶν ὁ κονιορτὸς εἰς αὐτοὺς ἐπανέλθοι.[dccx]

Οὐ θέλει τόπον ἐκ τόπου καὶ οἰκίαν ἐξ οἰκίας ἀμείβειν αὐτούς, ἵνα μὴ λύπη γένηται τῷ πρώτῳ ὑποδεξαμένῳ μηδὲ ὑπόνοιαν δέξωνται γαστριμαργίας καὶ εὐχερείας. ὁ δὲ κονιορτὸς ἐκτινασσόμενος ἀπὸ τῶν ποδῶν αὐτῶν δεῖγμά ἐστι τῆς ἀνονήτου πρὸς αὐτοὺς ὁδοιπορίας καὶ τῶν κόπων, ὧν ὑπέμειναν δι᾿ αὐτούς. ἴσα δὲ τοῖς Σοδομίταις τιμωρηθήσονται εἴπερ ἐκεῖνοι μὲν ἠτίμασαν τοὺς ἀγγέλους, οὗτοι δὲ τοὺς ἀποστόλους.[dccxi]

Ἰδοὺ ἐγὼ ἀποστέλλω ὑμᾶς ὡς πρόβατα ἐν μέσῳ ‹λύκων›.[922] *Πρόβατα* καλεῖ τοὺς μαθητὰς διὰ τὸ ἐπιεικές, λύκους δὲ τοὺς Ἰουδαίους διὰ τὸ κατ᾿ αὐτῶν φονικόν. Τοῦτό δέ φησι ἑτοιμάζων αὐτοὺς πρὸς τὸ παθεῖν.

Πρόβατα τοὺς μαθητὰς λέγει, λύκους τοὺς τῶν Ἰουδαίων μαθητὰς διὰ τὸ κατ᾿ αὐτῶν φονικόν. φρονίμους δὲ αὐτοὺς εἶναι βούλεται διὰ τὸ μὴ ἀγνοεῖν τὰς τῶν φαύλων κακουργίας, ἀκεραίους δὲ πρὸς τὸ ἑτοίμως φέρειν τοὺς ἀδικοῦντας καὶ μὴ ἀμύνεσθαι καὶ ἵνα μὴ ὀργίζωνται κατὰ τῶν ἀπειθούντων.[dccxii]

Ὡς ἀδύνατον γὰρ μεταξὺ λύκων μὴ παθεῖν πρόβατον, οὕτω καὶ ὑμᾶς μεταξὺ ἀδίκων. Ἵνα γὰρ μὴ ὀργίζωνται κατὰ τῶν ἀπειθούντων, κελεύει αὐτοὺς μᾶλλον πάσχειν ἢ δρᾶν.
Εἶτα θέλει αὐτοὺς καὶ φρονίμους εἶναι πρὸς τὸ μὴ ἀγνοεῖν τὰς τῶν φαύλων κακουργίας.

Φρονίμους εἶναι βούλεται αὐτούς, ἵνα διδάσκωσι μὲν τὰ τῆς εὐσεβείας δόγματα ἀπαρακαλύπτως καὶ διὰ τὸ μὴ ἀγνοεῖν τὰς τῶν φαύλων κακουργίας.[dccxiii]

Διό φησι· *γίνεσθε οὖν φρόνιμοι ὡς οἱ ὄφεις.*[923] Ἐκεῖνος φρονίμως πορεύεται· ὑμεῖς φρονίμως τὰς τῶν ἐπιβουλευόντων εἰς ψυ | **78r** χὴν βλάβας ἀποτρίψατε.
Ὃν τρόπον γὰρ ὁ ὄφις ἄτρωτον τὴν ἑαυτοῦ κεφαλὴν ἐν ταῖς μάχαις διατηρεῖ καὶ πάντα προΐεται ὥστε τὴν κεφαλὴν διατηρῆσαι, οὕτω καὶ ἡμᾶς βούλεται πλὴν τῆς πίστεως πάντα ἐκδοῦναι. Κεφαλὴ γάρ ἐστιν ἡ πίστις, ἣν δεῖ φυλάττειν ὑπὲρ πάντα ὡς ὁ ὄφις τὴν κεφαλήν. Εἰ δέ τινες ἐπέρχονται ἀντιμαχοῦντες, θέλει ἡμᾶς ὀξεῖς εἶναι πρὸς φυγὴν ἵνα μή τι πάθωμεν περὶ τὴν πίστιν. Τάχα δὲ καὶ διὰ τὸ φρονίμως ἀποξύεσθαι τὸ γῆρας,[dccxiv] φησὶ τοῦτο. Καὶ γὰρ ἐπειδὰν ἀποδύεσθαι δέῃ τὴν λεβηρίδα, στενῷ τόπῳ καὶ ἀκριβῶς περισφίγγοντι τὸ σῶμα ἐπιδοὺς ἑαυτόν, οὕτω διείρων ἑαυτὸν ἀποδύεται

922 Matt. 10:16.
923 Matt. 10:16.

τὸ γῆρας. Τάχα οὖν καὶ ἡμᾶς βούλεται ὁ λόγος, διὰ τῆς στενῆς καὶ τεθλιμμένης ὁδοῦ[924] πορευομένους ἀποδύεσθαι μὲν *τὸν παλαιὸν ἄνθρωπον* ἐνδύεσθαι δὲ *τὸν νέον.*[925][dccxv]

Φρονίμους εἶναι ἡμᾶς κατὰ τὸν ὄφιν κελεύει ἐν παντὶ πειρασμῷ συντηροῦντας τὴν κεφαλὴν ἡμῶν, ἥτις ἐστὶν ἡ πίστις ἡμῶν. ὅσαις γὰρ ἂν πληγαῖς ὁ ὄφις συνέχηται, τὴν ἑαυτοῦ φυλάττει κεφαλὴν ἀβλαβῆ καὶ πάλιν σοφισμῷ τὴν παλαίωσιν ἀποτίθεται, ἐν στενωπῇ τινι παρεισδύσει θλιβόμενος καὶ τὸ γῆρας ἀποτιθέμενος.[dccxvi] βούλεται τοίνυν καὶ ἡμᾶς διὰ τῆς στενῆς ὁδοῦ καὶ κακώσεως *τὸν παλαιὸν* ἀπεκδύσασθαι *ἄνθρωπον* καὶ τὸν νέον ἀνταμφιέννυσθαι.[dccxvii]

(Ἰσιδώρου Πηλουσιώτου) Φρονίμους εἶναι ἡμᾶς κατὰ τὸν ὄφιν κελεύει, ἐν παντὶ πειρασμῷ συντηροῦντας τὴν κεφαλὴν ἡμῶν, ἥτις ἐστὶν ἡ πίστις ἡμῶν.[dccxviii]

εἰ δέ τινες ἐπέλθοιεν μὴ ἀντιστατεῖν, ἀπελθεῖν δὲ ἐξ αὐτῶν καὶ μὴ ἀπερισκέπτως ἐπιστρέφειν πρὸς τὸ παθεῖν. ὄφεσιν δὲ παρεικάζει διδάσκων, ὅτι δεῖ αὐτοὺς ὀξεῖς εἶναι πρὸς φυγὴν εἴ γέ τινες ἐπέλθοιεν θανατῶσαι θέλοντες.[dccxix]

Ἵνα δὲ μὴ ἀμυντικοί τινες ὦμεν ἀλλὰ φέρωμεν ἀνεξικάκως τοὺς ἀδικοῦντας, θέλει ἡμᾶς εἶναι ὡς τὰς *περιστεράς*, αἳ πρὸς τοὺς συνήθεις ἀεὶ ἐπανακάμπτουσι κἂν ἀδικῶνται παρ' αὐτῶν ἀφαιρούμεναι τῶν νεοττῶν. Διδάσκει δὲ ὁ λόγος μιμεῖσθαι τὴν περιστερὰν ὅταν οἱ διώκοντες παύσωνται καὶ μὴ δεῖν αὐτῶν ὁλοτελῶς ἀποφοιτᾶν, ἀλλ' ἐνδόντας πρὸς βραχὺ πάλιν ἐπὶ τὸ νουθετεῖν αὐτοὺς τὰ χρήσιμα ἔρχεσθαι.

περιστεραῖς δέ, ἐπειδὴ ἀμνησίκακον τὸ στρουθίον καὶ ἐμφιλοχωροῦν ἀεὶ πρὸς οἷς εἴθισεν τόποις καὶ ἐπανακάμπτον ἐπὶ τὸ αὐτό, ὅταν ὁ ἐκδιώκων παύσηται. διδάσκει οὖν ὁ λόγος, ὅτι οὐ δεῖ ὁλοτελῶς τῶν διωκόντων ἀποφοιτᾶν, ἀλλ' ἐνδόντας πρὸς βραχὺ πάλιν ἐπὶ τὸ νουθετεῖν αὐτοὺς ἐπανέρχεσθαι, ὅταν τὰ τῆς ὀργῆς παύσηται. οὕτως καὶ αὐτοῖς ὁ Χριστὸς ἐποίησεν διωκόμενος μὲν καὶ ὑποχωρῶν ἀπὸ τῆς Ἰουδαίας καὶ πάλιν ἐπανερχόμενος.[dccxx]

25

(ΩΡΙΓΕΝΟΥΣ) Τῆς πάλαι φρονήσεως τοῦ ὄφεως ὑπομιμνήσκει ὁ Ἰησοῦς τοὺς μαθητάς. Ἐκεῖνος βουληθεὶς τὴν ἰδίαν διδασκαλίαν παραδοῦναι, καὶ τόπον καὶ καιρὸν καὶ πρόσωπον εὐπειθὲς ἐστοχάσατο. Διὸ καὶ ἐπέτυχε τοῦ ἰδίου θελήματος. Οὕτως, φησί, καὶ ὑμεῖς. Ὁ ὄφις ὅλον τὸ σῶμα προδίδωσι φυλάσσων | **78v** πάσῃ δυνάμει τὴν ἰδίαν κεφαλήν. Ὁ ὄφις πίνων ὕδωρ ἀποτίθησι τὸν ἰόν.[dccxxi] Ὁ ὄφις ὑποχωρεῖ τοῖς διώκουσι καὶ κατακρύπτει ἑαυτόν. Καὶ πολλὰ ζητῶν εὑρήσεις ἐν αὐτῷ. Ἐν δὲ

924 Matt. 7:14.
925 Col. 3:9-10.

τῇ περιστερᾷ τὸ καθαρὸν καὶ ἡσύχιον καὶ φιλάνθρωπον καὶ ἀμνησίκακον ἐδήλωσε. Ὑπέμνησε δὲ τῆς πάλαι τοῦ Νῶε[926] περιστερᾶς.[dccxxii]

Τῆς πάλαι φρονήσεως τοῦ ὄφεως ὑπομιμνήσκει ὁ κύριος τοὺς μαθητάς. ἐκεῖνος γὰρ βουληθεὶς τὴν οἰκείαν διδασκαλίαν παραδοῦναι καὶ τόπον καὶ καιρὸν καὶ πρόσωπον εὐπειθὲς ἐστοχάσατο, διὸ καὶ ἐπέτυχε τοῦ ἰδίου θελήματος. οὕτω (φησὶ) καὶ ὑμεῖς. Ὁ ὄφις ὅλον τὸ σῶμα προδίδωσι φυλάσσων πάσῃ δυνάμει τὴν ἰδίαν κεφαλήν. ὁ ὄφις πίνων ὕδωρ ἀποτίθησι τὸν ἰόν. ὁ ὄφις ὑποχωρεῖ τοῖς διώκουσι καὶ κατακρύπτει ἑαυτόν. καὶ πολλὰ ζητῶν εὑρήσεις ἐν αὐτῷ, ἐν δὲ τῇ περιστερᾷ τὸ καθαρὸν καὶ ἡσύχιον καὶ ἀκέραιον καὶ φιλάνθρωπον καὶ ἀμνησίκακον ἐδήλωσε. ὑπέμνησε δὲ τῆς πάλαι τοῦ Νῶε περιστερᾶς.[dccxxiii]

(Ἰσιδώρου Πηλουσιώτου) ὅσαις γὰρ ἂν πληγαῖς ὁ ὄφις συνέχεται, τὴν ἑαυτοῦ φυλάττει κεφαλὴν ἀβλαβῆ. καὶ πάλιν σοφισμῷ τὴν παλαίωσιν ἀποτίθεται ἐν στενωπῇ τινὶ παρεισδύσει θλιβόμενος, καὶ τὸ γῆρας ἀποτιθέμενος. βούλεται τοίνυν καὶ ἡμᾶς διὰ τῆς στενῆς ὁδοῦ καὶ κακώσεως τὸν παλαιὸν ἀπεκδύσασθαι ἄνθρωπον, καὶ τὸν νέον ἀνταμφιέννυσθαι… . ἵνα τὴν μὲν φρόνησιν τοῦ ὄφεως ἔχωσιν εἰς τὸ τηρεῖν τὴν κεφαλήν. τουτέστι τὴν πίστιν. τὸ δὲ ἀκέραιον τῆς περιστερᾶς, τὴν ἀκακίαν εἰς τὸ μὴ ἀμύνασθαι τοὺς ἀδικοῦντας.[dccxxiv]

The dexterity of a serpent is an example: for by using the whole body, it hides its head and protects that part in which life dwells. Likewise, we should shield our head, who is Christ,[927] by risking our bodies. The simplicity of doves is demonstrated in the outward form of the Holy Spirit.[dccxxv]

Προσέχετε δὲ ἀπὸ τῶν ἀνθρώπων.[928] Προσέχειν αὐτοὺς φησι *ἀπὸ τῶν ἀνθρώπων* καὶ ‹τὰ› ἑξῆς. Καὶ διδάσκει ὁ λόγος ὅτι οὐ μόνον τοῖς Ἰουδαίοις ἔμελλεν αὐτοὺς πέμπειν, ἀλλὰ καὶ *πᾶσι τοῖς ἔθνεσι,*[929] τουτέστιν εἰς ἔλεγχον τῶν μὴ πιστευόντων.

[Προσέχειν αὐτοὺς φησιν ἀπὸ τῶν ἀνθρώπων καὶ τὰ ἑξῆς. καὶ διδάσκει ὁ λόγος ὅτι οὐ μόνον τοῖς Ἰουδαίοις ἔμελλεν αὐτοὺς πέμπειν, ἀλλὰ καὶ πᾶσι τοῖς ἔθνεσι, διὸ καὶ ἐπήγαγεν *εἰς μαρτύριον αὐτοῖς καὶ τοῖς ἔθνεσιν*, τουτέστιν εἰς ἔλεγχον τῶν μὴ πιστευόντων.][dccxxvi]

Τί δέ ἐστιν, *Εἰς μαρτύριον πᾶσι τοῖς ἔθνεσιν*; Ἐπειδὴ ἐκηρύχθη μὲν πανταχοῦ, οὐκ ἐπιστεύθη δὲ πανταχοῦ, *Εἰς μαρτύριον*, φησί, τοῖς ἀπιστήσασι. τουτέστιν, εἰς ἔλεγχον, εἰς κατηγορίαν, εἰς μαρτυρίαν. οἱ γὰρ πιστεύσαντες καταμαρτυρήσουσι τῶν μὴ πιστευσάντων, καὶ κατακρινοῦσιν αὐτούς.[dccxxvii]

---

926 Gen. 8:8-9.

927 Cf. Eph. 1:22; Col. 1:18.

928 Matt. 10:19.

929 Cf. Amos, 9:9; Is. 25:6; Epistle of Jeremiah, 50.

Μὴ μεριμνήσητε πῶς ἢ τί λαλήσετε.[930] Ἵνα μὴ λέγωσιν οἱ μαθηταί, ʽπῶς πεῖσαι δυνησόμεθα τοιούτων γινομένων πραγμάτων;ʼ ἄγαν *ἰδιῶται* ὄντες[931] μετὰ σοφῶν καὶ δυνατῶν[932] λαλοῦντες. Καὶ περὶ τῆς ἀπολογίας κελεύει θαρρεῖν, *μὴ μεριμνήσητε* λέγων *πῶς ἢ τί λαλήσετε*, καὶ τὰ ἑξῆς. Ὅταν μὲν γὰρ μεταξὺ φίλων μέλλῃ γίνεσθαι διάλεξις, δεῖ ἡμᾶς καὶ προμεριμνᾶν πρὸς τὸ ἑτοίμους εἶναι *πρὸς ἀπολογίαν.*[933] Ἔνθα δὲ μεταξὺ ὄχλου καὶ βασιλέων, ὅπου φόβος πολὺς καὶ δῆμοι μαινόμενοι καὶ δικαστήριον φοβερὸν καὶ πολλὴ ἡ ἐξέτασις γίνεται, ἐκεῖ τὴν ἑαυτοῦ σοφίαν ὑπισχνεῖται δώσειν ἵνα μὴ δειλιάσωμεν. Τὸ μὲν γὰρ ὁμολογεῖν, ἐφ ἡμῖν· τὸ δὲ ἀπολογεῖσθαι, οὐκ ἐφ᾽ ἡμῖν διὰ τὰς προειρημένας αἰτίας.

Ἀλλ᾽ *ἐν ἐκείνῃ τῇ ὥρᾳ* διὰ τῆς τοῦ Πνεύματος χάριτος δίδοται δύναμις διαλέξεως,[934] ἵνα μή τις εἴπῃ ὅτι διὰ φύσεως ἐπιτηδειότητα[dccxxviii] ἔσχον τὸ διαλεκτικόν. Εἶτα προλέγει καὶ τὰ συμβησόμενα αὐτοῖς δεινά, ἵνα μὴ θορυ | **79r** βηθῶσιν ὅταν συμβῇ ταῦτα ὡς ὅτι δι᾽ ἀσθένειαν ταῦτα πάσχουσι. Τοσαύτη γάρ φησι ἔσται αὐτῶν ἡ μανία, τηλικαύτη δὲ καὶ ἡ τοῦ κηρύγματος δύναμις, ὡς καὶ φύσιν καὶ συγγένειαν νικῆσαι.[dccxxix] *Παραδώσει* γάρ φησι *ἀδελφὸς ἀδελφὸν εἰς θάνατον καὶ πατὴρ τέκνον*, καὶ τὰ ἑξῆς.[935] Τὸ δὲ *ἔσεσθε μισούμενοι ὑπὸ πάντων*,[936] ἀντὶ τοῦ ὑπὸ πολλῶν φησι. Πολλοὶ γὰρ οἱ παραδεξάμενοι τὸν λόγον τῆς πίστεως οἳ καὶ ἠγάπων αὐτούς.

> Ἐν δὲ αὐτῇ τῇ ὥρᾳ κατεπηγγείλατο τὴν διαλεκτικὴν διδόναι χάριν, ἵνα δειχθῇ τὸ τοῦ πνεύματος χάρισμα. εἰ γὰρ πρὸ καιροῦ δεδώκει τῇ πείρᾳ, ἐνομίζετο εἶναι τὸ πρᾶγμα φύσεως ἀνθρωπίνης καὶ δεξιότητος, οὐ *παρὰ πάντων* δὲ ἔμελλον μισεῖσθαι, ἀλλὰ παρὰ πολλῶν μάλιστα κατ᾽ ἐκεῖνο καιροῦ. διὸ ἀπὸ τοῦ πλείονος εἶπεν τὸ *παρὰ πάντων*, ἐπεὶ οἱ δεξάμενοι τὸν λόγον ἠγάπων αὐτούς.[dccxxx]

Εἶτα δεικνὺς ὅτι ὁ μὴ ἴσον ἔχων τῆς ἐν ἀρχῇ θεοσεβείας τὸ τέλος οὐδὲν ὠφελεῖται, πάλιν ἐπάγει. *ὁ δὲ ὑπομείνας εἰς τέλος, οὗτος σωθήσεται*,[937] τουτέστι τῆς αἰωνίου μεθέξει ζωῆς καὶ τὴν τῶν ἐσομένων καλῶν λήψεται σωτηρίαν.

Ὅταν δὲ διώκωσιν ὑμᾶς ἐν τῇ πόλει ταύτῃ, φεύγετε.[938] Φειδοῖ τῶν ἀδίκων φονευτῶν ἐπιτάττει τοῖς ἁγίοις φεύγειν.

> (Κλήμεντος.) Φειδοῖ τῶν ἀδίκως φονευόντων ἐπιτάττει τοῖς ἁγίοις φεύγειν. διὸ ὁ μὴ φεύγων, ὡς ῥιψοκίνδυνος παρακούων τῆς κυριακῆς φωνῆς μεμπταῖος.[dccxxxi]

---

930 Matt. 10:19.
931 Acts, 4:13.
932 Cf. 1 Cor. 1:26.
933 1 Peter, 3:15.
934 Matt. 10:19-20.
935 Matt. 10:21.
936 Matt. 10:22.
937 Matt. 10:22.
938 Matt. 10:23.

Οὐ γὰρ δειλιᾶν αὐτοὺς προτρέπει, ἀλλὰ τὸ ἐναντίον, μὴ πόθῳ τῶν ἐλπιζομένων ἑτοίμως ἑαυτοὺς παραδιδόναι εἰς θάνατον καὶ ζημιοῦν τοὺς μέλλοντας ὠφεληθῆναι διὰ τοῦ κηρύγματος.

> Οὐ γὰρ δειλιᾶν αὐτοὺς θέλει, ἀλλὰ τὸ ἐναντίον, μὴ πόθῳ τῶν ἐλπιζομένων ἑτοίμους παραδιδόναι ἑαυτοὺς εἰς θάνατον καὶ ζημιοῦν τοὺς μέλλοντας ἐκ τοῦ κηρύγματος ὠφεληθῆναι.[dcccxxxii]

> Παρακελεύεται τοῖς μαθηταῖς ἀπὸ τῆσδε φεύγειν τῆς πόλεως εἰς τὴν ἄλλην καὶ ἐξ ἐκείνης εἰς ἑτέραν. τοῦτο δὲ λέγει οὐ διδάσκων αὐτοὺς δειλιᾶν, ἀλλὰ μὴ ῥίπτειν ἑαυτοὺς εἰς κινδύνους καὶ ἀποθνῄσκειν ῥᾳδίως καὶ ζημιοῦν τοὺς μέλλοντας ὠφεληθῆναι διὰ τοῦ κηρύγματος.[dcccxxxiii]

Τὸ δὲ *οὐ μὴ τελέσητε τὰς πόλεις τοῦ Ἰσραὴλ ἕως ἂν ἔλθῃ ὁ υἱὸς τοῦ ἀνθρώπου*,[939] οὐ τὴν δευτέραν αὐτοῦ ἄφιξιν αἰνίττεται, ἀλλὰ τὴν κατὰ διαφόρους καιροὺς πρὸ τοῦ σταυροῦ ἐπιφοίτησιν, δι᾽ ἧς ὀπτανόμενος τὴν παρ᾽ αὐτοῦ βοήθειαν καὶ ψυχαγωγίαν παρεῖχεν εὐθαρσεῖς αὐτοὺς ποιῶν διὰ τὸ διώκεσθαι.

> Παρουσίαν λέγει οὐ τὴν ἐπιφανῆ καὶ ἐπίδοξον, τὴν καθόλου συντέλειαν, ἀλλὰ τὴν κατὰ διαφόρους καιροὺς ἐπιφοίτησιν, δι᾽ ἧς ὀπτανόμενος, τὴν παρ᾽ αὐτοῦ βοήθειαν παρέξει εὐθαρσεῖς αὐτοὺς ποιῶν, διὰ τὸ διώκεσθαι, καὶ πάλιν εἰς τὸ αὐτό. Ὡς ἐπηγγείλατο ὅτι *ἐλευσόμεθα* ἐγὼ καὶ ὁ πατήρ μου *πρὸς αὐτὸν καὶ μονὴν παρ᾽ αὐτῷ ποιησόμεθα*.[dcccxxxiv]

> Ἄφιξιν ἑαυτοῦ λέγει οὐ τὴν ἐπιφανῆ καὶ ἐν τέλει τοῦ βίου ἐσομένην, ἀλλὰ τὴν κατὰ καιροὺς τοῖς διὰ θεὸν θλιβομένοις γινομένην παρ᾽ αὐτοῦ ψυχαγωγίαν τε καὶ βοήθειαν.[dcccxxxv]

> Οὐ τὴν δευτέραν αὐτοῦ λέγει ἄφιξιν, ἀλλὰ τὴν κατὰ καιρὸν ἐσομένην δι᾽ αὐτοῦ τοῖς ἁγίοις ψυχαγωγίαν.[dcccxxxvi]

Ἐγὼ γάρ, φησί, ἐπικαταλαμβάνω ὑμᾶς καὶ βεβαιῶ διὰ τῆς ἐμῆς διδασκαλίας. Ἤτοι πόλεις τοῦ Ἰσραὴλ φησι τῶν πιστῶν τὰ συστήματα, ἅτινα *ἕως συντελείας* εἰσὶ *τοῦ αἰῶνος*,[940] καὶ οὐ παύονται οἱ διδάσκοντες καὶ διδασκόμενοι, ἕως τῆς | **79v** δευτέρας τοῦ Κυρίου παρουσίας. Καὶ δοκοῦσι ζῆν ἕως τότε οἱ μαθηταὶ ἐπείπερ ἐκ τῶν συγγραμμάτων αὐτῶν ἅπαντες διδάσκουσι.

> Πόλεις δὲ τοῦ Ἰσραὴλ φησι καὶ τῶν πιστῶν τὰ συστήματα, ἅτινα ἕως τῆς συντελείας τοῦ αἰῶνός εἰσιν καὶ οὐ παύονται οἱ διδάσκοντες καὶ οἱ διδασκόμενοι ἕως τῆς δευτέρας ἐπιφανείας τοῦ κυρίου. καὶ δοκοῦσι ζῆν ἕως τότε οἱ μαθηταὶ καὶ εὐαγγελισταὶ ἐπείπερ ἐκ τῶν συγγραμμάτων αὐτῶν ἅπαντες διδάσκουσιν.[dcccxxxvii]

---

939 Matt. 10:23.
940 Cf. Matt. 24:3; 28:20.

26

80r (ΩΡΙΓΕΝΟΥΣ) *οὐδὲν γάρ ἐστι κεκαλυμμένον, ὃ οὐκ ἀποκαλυφθήσεται.*[941] Τάχα περὶ τοῦ καιροῦ ἐκείνου λέγει, *ὅτε κρινεῖ ὁ Θεὸς τὰ κρυπτὰ τῶν ἀνθρώπων*[942] καὶ *φωτίσει τὰ κρυπτὰ τοῦ σκότους καὶ φανερώσει τὰς βουλὰς τῶν καρδιῶν.*[943] | **80v** Ἢ καὶ οὕτως· ὅσῳ πειρᾶταί τις καλύπτειν τὰ καλὰ τῇ κακηγορίᾳ, κατὰ φύσιν τὸ καλὸν ἀκάλυπτόν ἐστιν. Οὕτω καὶ ἐπὶ τοῦ κακοῦ.

> Τάχα περὶ τοῦ καιροῦ ἐκείνου λέγει, ὅτε κρινεῖ ὁ θεὸς τὰ κρυπτὰ τῶν ἀνθρώπων καὶ φωτίσει τὰ κρυπτὰ τοῦ σκότους καὶ φανερώσει τὰς βουλὰς τῶν καρδιῶν.
> ἢ οὕτως.
> ὅσῳ πειρᾶταί τις καλύπτειν τὰ καλὰ τῇ κακηγορίᾳ, κατὰ φύσιν τὸ καλὸν ἀκάλυπτόν ἐστιν. οὕτω καὶ ἐπὶ τοῦ κακοῦ.[dcccxxxviii]

> Ἢ τοίνυν περὶ τοῦ καιροῦ ἐκείνου τοῦτο λέγει, ὅτε κρινεῖ ὁ θεὸς τὰ κρυπτὰ τῶν ἀνθρώπων καὶ φωτιεῖ τὰ κρυπτὰ τοῦ σκότους καὶ φανερώσει τὰς βουλὰς τῶν καρδιῶν.[dcccxxxix] ἢ ἐκεῖνό φησιν ὅτι, ὅσῳ πειρᾶταί τις καλύπτειν τὰ καλὰ τῇ κατηγορίᾳ, κατὰ φύσιν τὸ καλὸν ἀκάλυπτόν ἐστιν.[dcccxl]

> However, this has been written about the future time, when God will judge the secrets of men,[944] will shed light on the hidden places of darkness, and will manifest the council of hearts.[945]

Ὃ λέγω ὑμῖν ἐν τῇ σκοτίᾳ.[946] Μεθ᾽ ὑπερβολῆς κέχρηται τῷ λόγῳ. Ἐπειδὴ γὰρ μόνοις αὐτοῖς διελέγετο καὶ ἐν μικρᾷ γωνίᾳ τῆς Παλαιστίνης, διὰ τοῦτο εἶπεν *ἐν τῇ σκοτίᾳ* καὶ *εἰς τὸ οὖς* πρὸς τὴν μετὰ ταῦτα παρρησίαν ἐσομένην, ἣν ἔμελλεν αὐτοῖς διδόναι.

> Καίτοιγε οὐκ ἦν σκότος, ἡνίκα ταῦτα ἔλεγεν, οὐδὲ εἰς τὸ οὖς αὐτοῖς διελέγετο. ἀλλὰ μεθ᾽ ὑπερβολῆς κέχρηται τῷ λόγῳ. Ἐπειδὴ γὰρ μόνοις αὐτοῖς διελέγετο, καὶ ἐν μικρᾷ γωνίᾳ τῆς Παλαιστίνης, διὰ τοῦτο εἶπεν, *Ἐν τῇ σκοτίᾳ*, καί, *Εἰς τὸ οὖς*, πρὸς τὴν μετὰ ταῦτα παρρησίαν ἐσομένην. ἣν ἔμελλεν αὐτοῖς διδόναι, τὸν τρόπον τῆς διαλέξεως ἀντιδιαστέλλων ἐκείνης.[dcccxli]

Ἅπερ τοίνυν *ὑμῖν κατ᾽* ἰδίαν καὶ κατὰ μόνας ἐλάλησα, ἀφόβως καὶ μετὰ παρρησίας πάντας διδάξατέ φησι.

---

941 Matt. 10:26; cf. Luke, 12:2.
942 Rom. 2:16.
943 1 Cor. 4:5.
944 Cf. Rom. 2:16.
945 Cf. 1 Cor. 4:5.
946 Matt. 10:27.

> What I have instructed you in the little location of Judaea, proclaim audaciously in all cities and in the entire world.[dccxlii]

καὶ ἃ νῦν οὐκ ἐν ἐπηκόῳ πολλῶν διαλέγομαι, ταῦτα καθ' ὑπερβολὴν *ἐπὶ τῶν δωμάτων κηρύξατε* μετὰ παρρησίας πάσης ταῦτα λέγοντες.

> Ὅπερ νῦν (φησὶ) κατ' ἰδίαν *ὑμῖν λέγω*, μετὰ παρρησίας διδάξατε. καὶ ἃ νῦν οὐκ ἐν ἐπηκόῳ πολλῶν διαλέγομαι, ταῦτα καθ' ὑπερβολὴν *ἐπὶ τῶν δωμάτων κηρύξατε*, μὴ φοβούμενοι τοὺς ἀποκτιννύντας *σῶμα καὶ μὴ ψυχήν*.[dccxliii]

Τοῦτο γὰρ σημαίνει *τὸ ἐν φωτὶ καὶ ἐπὶ τῶν δωμάτων*.
Διδάσκει δὲ καὶ θανάτου καταφρονεῖν. Καὶ γὰρ θανάτου οὐδὲν παρὰ ἀνθρώποις φοβερώτερον, ἀλλ' ἔστι τούτου δεινότερον ἡ ἐν γεέννῃ κόλασις.[947] Ὁ μὲν γὰρ ἐνταῦθα μόνης σαρκὸς ποιεῖται φθοράν, ἡ δὲ μετὰ τὴν ἀνάστασιν[dccxliv] ἀμφότερα τιμωρεῖται, μηκέτι χωριζομένης τῆς ψυχῆς ἐκ τοῦ σώματος.[dccxlv] Συγκρίσει δὲ ὧν ἐξέθετο δύο φόβων, τὸν ἕτερον μᾶλλον διδάσκει φοβεῖσθαι.

> Διδάσκει τοίνυν θανάτου καταφρονεῖν, καὶ ὅτι ἀσώματος ἡ ψυχή, καὶ ὅτι ἄνευ σώματος οὐ κολάζεται, καὶ ὅτι τὸ ἀποκτιννύμενον οὐχ ὁ σύνθετος ἄνθρωπος οὐδὲ ἡ ψυχὴ ἀλλὰ τὸ σῶμα ἐξ αἰσθανομένου εἰς ἀναίσθητον μεταβάλλον καὶ ἀποθνῄσκον τὸν κοινὸν θάνατον, ὅτε καὶ ἡ ἔννοια τοῦ θανάτου τηρεῖται οὖσα ζωῆς στέρησις. οὔτε γὰρ τὸ σύνθετον στερεῖται ζωῆς οὔτε ἡ ψυχή, ἤτοι *ἐν κόλποις οὖσα Ἀβραὰμ* ἢ ὡς *ὁ πλούσιος* ἐν τῷ ἄντικρυς.[948] ἀπαράδεκτος δὲ οὖσα τοῦ μέσου θανάτου[dccxlvi] ἑτέρου ἐκ κακίας ἐγγινομένου δεκτική ἐστιν. *ψυχὴ* γοῦν *ἡ ἁμαρτάνουσα αὕτη ἀποθανεῖται*.[949] ὡς γὰρ στερήσει φωτὸς ὑφίσταται σκότος καὶ στερήσει ἀρετῆς κακία, οὕτως στερήσει τοῦ εἰπόντος *ἐγώ εἰμι ἡ ζωή*[950][dccxlvii] θάνατος ὁ ἐχθρὸς αὐτῇ. συγκρίσει τοίνυν ὧν ἐξέθετο δύο φόβων τὸν ἕτερον μᾶλλον φοβεῖσθαι διδάσκει.[dccxlviii]

Ἀπόλλυσιν οὖν ψυχὴν καὶ σῶμα *ἐν γεέννῃ*,[951] ἀπορρίπτων *ἀπὸ προσώπου τῶν ὀφθαλμῶν*[952] αὐτοῦ τὸν διὰ κακίαν ἀνάξιον ἀπολαύειν Θεοῦ.
Ἐν γεέννῃ δὲ εἰπὼν ἐσήμανε τὸ διηνεκὲς τῆς κολάσεως· διὰ ‹γὰρ τὴν ἀπὸ› γεννήσεως ἐπίδοσιν ἀεὶ δεχομένης τῆς τιμωρίας.[dccxlix]

> Διὰ δὲ τῆς γεέννης τὸ διηνεκὲς τῆς κολάσεως ἐδήλωσεν, γέενναν εἰπὼν ὡς ἀναμένουσαν δίκην τῶν διὰ γεννήσεως τὴν ἀπόδοσιν δεχομένων. καὶ τοῖς ὀνόμασι δὲ πολλὴν ἔδειξε τοῦ τρόπου τὴν διαφοράν, ἐνταῦθα μὲν *ἀποκτεννόντων* εἰπών, ἐκεῖ δὲ ἀπολλυμένων οὐδέ ἐστιν ἔτι ‹σωτηρία›.[dccl]

---

947 Matt. 5:22; 5:29-30; 10:28; 18:9; 23:15; 23:33; Mark, 9:43; 9:45; 9:47; Luke, 12:5; James, 3:6.
948 Cf. Luke, 16:22-23.
949 Ez. 18:4&20.
950 John 11:25; 14:6.
951 Matt. 10:28.
952 Cf. Psalm 30:23.

Καὶ μὴ φοβεῖσθε ἀπὸ τῶν ἀποκτεννόντων.[953] Εἰ γὰρ δεδοίκατέ φησι θάνατον δι᾽ αὐτὸ μὲν οὖν τοῦτο κηρύξατε· τοῦτο γὰρ ὑμᾶς ἐξαιρή | **81r** σεται τοῦ ὄντως θανάτου. Εἰ γὰρ καὶ μέλλουσιν ἀναιρεῖν ὑμᾶς, ἀλλὰ τοῦ κρείττονος οὐ περιέσονται κἂν μυρία φιλονεικήσωσι. Διὰ τοῦτο οὐκ εἶπε 'τὴν δὲ ψυχὴν μὴ ἀποκτεννόντων', ἀλλ᾽ *ἀποκτεῖναι μὴ δυναμένων.*

Τί γάρ; Δεδοίκατε, φησί, θάνατον, καὶ διὰ τοῦτο ὀκνεῖτε κηρύσσειν; Δι᾽ αὐτὸ μὲν οὖν τοῦτο κηρύξατε, ἐπειδὴ δεδοίκατε θάνατον. Τοῦτο γὰρ ὑμᾶς ἐξαιρήσεται τοῦ ὄντως θανάτου. Εἰ γὰρ καὶ μέλλουσιν ὑμᾶς ἀναιρεῖν, ἀλλὰ τοῦ κρείττονος οὐ περιέσονται, κἂν μυρία φιλονεικήσωσι. Διὰ τοῦτο οὐκ εἶπε, Τὴν δὲ ψυχὴν μὴ ἀποκτενόντων, ἀλλά, *Μὴ δυναμένων ἀποκτεῖναι.* Κἂν γὰρ θελήσωσιν, οὐ περιέσονται.[dccli]

27

(ΩΡΙΓΕΝΟΥΣ) Ἐν τούτοις τὴν μὲν ἀθανασίαν τῆς ψυχῆς ἐδίδαξε καὶ τὴν τοῦ σώματος ἀνάστασιν. Ἐν δὲ τοῖς καθεξῆς καὶ τὴν κρίσιν ἐδήλωσε. Πῶς δὲ ἀπόλλυσι *καὶ ψυχὴν καὶ σῶμα ἐν γεέννῃ*, ζήτει.

Ἐν τούτοις τὴν μὲν ἀθανασίαν τῆς ψυχῆς ἐδίδαξε καὶ τὴν τοῦ σώματος ἀνάστασιν, ἐν δὲ τοῖς καθεξῆς καὶ τὴν κρίσιν ἐδήλωσε. πῶς δὲ ἀπόλλυσι *καὶ ψυχὴν καὶ σῶμα ἐν γεέννῃ*, ζήτει.[dcclii]

Φοβήθητε δὲ μᾶλλον.[954] Τήρει τὸ *μᾶλλον* προσκείμενον τῷ *φοβήθητε*, καὶ ὅτι ὡς διαφέροντος τοῦ ἀποκτέννυσθαι παρὰ τὸ ἀπόλλυσθαι. Περὶ μὲν ἀνθρώπων λέγει τὸ ἀποκτιννύναι, περὶ δὲ Θεοῦ, οὐ τὸ *ἀποκτεῖναι*, ἀλλὰ τὸ *ἀπολέσαι ἐν γεέννῃ*. Καὶ ὅτι ἐπὶ μὲν ἀνθρώπων γέγραπται, οὐ τὸ *δυναμένων ἀποκτεῖναι*, ἀλλὰ τὸ *ἀποκτεννόντων*, ἐπὶ δὲ Θεοῦ, οὐ τὸ *ἀπολέσαι*, ἀλλὰ τὸ δύνασθαι *ἀπολέσαι*. Ὅτι δὲ τὸ *ἀπολέσαι* ἕτερον τοῦ *ἀποκτεῖναι*, δηλοῖ τὸ τὸν Σωτῆρα ἐληλυθέναι *ζητῆσαι καὶ σῶσαι τὸ ἀπολωλός.*[955]

Τήρει τὸ *μᾶλλον* προσκείμενον τῷ *φοβήθητε*, καὶ ὅτι ὡς διαφέροντος τοῦ ἀποκτίννυσθαι[dccliii] παρὰ τὸ ἀπόλλυσθαι περὶ μὲν ἀνθρώπων λέγει τὸ ἀποκτιννύναι, περὶ δὲ θεοῦ οὐ τὸ *ἀποκτεῖναι*, ἀλλὰ τὸ *ἀπολέσαι ἐν γεέννῃ*. καὶ ὅτι ἐπὶ μὲν ἀνθρώπων γέγραπται, οὐ τὸ *δυναμένων ἀποκτεῖναι*, ἀλλὰ τὸ *ἀποκτεννόντων*, ἐπὶ δὲ Θεοῦ, οὐ τὸ *ἀπολέσαι*, ἀλλὰ τὸ δύνασθαι *ἀπολέσαι*. ὅτι δὲ τὸ *ἀπολέσαι* ἕτερον τοῦ *ἀποκτεῖναι*, δηλοῖ τὸ τὸν σωτῆρα ἐληλυθέναι *ζητῆσαι καὶ σῶσαι τὸ ἀπολωλός.*[dccliv]

---

953 Cf. Matt. 10:28.
954 Matt. 10:28.
955 Luke, 19:20.

Οὐχὶ δύο στρουθία ἀσσαρίου πωλεῖται;[956] Διὰ τούτου δείκνυσι τὴν πολλὴν περὶ τοὺς ἀνθρώπους διάγνωσιν καὶ πρόνοιαν.[dcclv] Εἰ γὰρ στρουθίου φησὶ θάνατος οὐ λανθάνει Θεόν, πολλῷ μᾶλλον ὁ τῶν ἁγίων. Οὐ γὰρ τοῦτο φησί, ὅτι ἐνεργοῦντος αὐτοῦ πίπτει στρουθίον, ἀλλ' ὅτι οὐδὲ ἐκεῖνα ἁλώσεται ἀγνοοῦντος τοῦ Θεοῦ καὶ ὅτι οὐδὲν αὐτὸν λανθάνει τῶν γινομένων, οὐδὲ τῶν εὐτελεστάτων. Εἰ τοίνυν οὐδὲν τῶν τυχόντων ἀγνοεῖ, ὑμᾶς δὲ οὕτω φιλεῖ ὡς καὶ τὰς τρίχας ἠριθμηκέναι[957] οὐ χρὴ δεδοικέναι. Τοῦτο δὲ λέγει οὐχ ὅτι τρίχας ἀριθμεῖ, ἀλ | **81v** λ' ἵνα τὴν ἀκριβῆ γνῶσιν καὶ πρόνοιαν τὴν περὶ αὐτοὺς ἐνδείξηται.

> διὰ τοῦ εἰπεῖν, *οὐχὶ δύο στρουθία*, καὶ τὰ ἑξῆς, τοῦ περὶ προνοίας τοῦ Θεοῦ εἰσάγει λόγον. τί γὰρ ἐκείνων, φησίν, εὐτελέστερον; ἀλλ' ὅμως, οὐδὲ ἐκεῖνα κρατηθήσονται, ἀγνοοῦντος τοῦ Θεοῦ. οὐ γὰρ τοῦτο, φησίν, ὅτι ἐνεργοῦντος αὐτοῦ πίπτουσιν εἰς παγίδα. τοῦτο γὰρ ἀνάξιον Θεοῦ, ἀλλ' ὅτι οὐδὲν αὐτὸν λανθάνει τῶν γινομένων. εἰ οὖν ἀγνοεῖ οὐδὲν τῶν συμβαινόντων, ὑμᾶς δὲ φιλεῖ, παντὸς πατρὸς γνησιώτερον, καὶ οὕτως φιλεῖ, ὡς καὶ τὰς τρίχας ἠριθμηκέναι, οὐ χρὴ λοιπὸν δεδοικέναι. τοῦτο δὲ ἔλεγεν, οὐχ ὅτι τὰς τρίχας ὁ Θεὸς ἀριθμεῖ, ἀλλ' ἵνα τὴν ἀκριβῆ γνῶσιν καὶ τὴν πολλὴν πρόνοιαν, τὴν περὶ αὐτούς, ἐνδείξηται.[dcclvi]

τουτέστιν οὐδὲ μέχρι τριχὸς περιορᾷ ὑμᾶς ὁ Θεός, ἀλλὰ καὶ τὰ ἄχρηστα νομιζόμενα ἠξίωνται προνοίας Θεοῦ.[dcclvii]

> Διδάσκει ὅτι καὶ τὰ ἄχρηστα νομιζόμενα προνοίᾳ θεοῦ διοικεῖται.[dcclviii]

Ἄνευ τοῦ πατρὸς ὑμῶν.[958] Τὴν πρόνοιαν ἐν τούτῳ δείκνυσι τῶν πάντων. Τὸ δὲ *ἄνευ* οὐ τὴν βουλὴν δείκνυσιν, ἀλλὰ τὴν πρόγνωσιν. Τῶν γὰρ γινομένων ἃ μὲν κατὰ βούλησιν γίνεται, ἃ δὲ κατ' εὐδοκίαν καὶ συγχώρησιν. Καὶ ῥητῶς μὲν τὸ λεπτομερὲς τῆς προνοίας καὶ ἡ μέχρι τῶν τυχόντων γνῶσις δηλοῦται. Νοητῶς δὲ *πίπτει ἐπὶ τῆς γῆς* στρουθίον ἐπὰν (δέον ἄνω φέρεσθαι ‹ἢ›[959] ἀναπαύσεως χάριν ἐπὶ ὄρη καὶ βουνοὺς ἢ δώματα καθίπτασθαι) τὰ κάτω ζητοῦν *ἐπὶ γῆς* πίπτῃ τοῖς τῆς σαρκὸς ἐνεχόμενον κακοῖς, παραδοθὲν *εἰς πάθη ἀτιμίας*,[960] καὶ τὸ ἐλεύθερον μετὰ τοῦ τιμίου ἀπολωλεκός. Τοιοῦτος δὲ ὁ ὑπὸ λόγου μετεωρισθεὶς καὶ τὰ γήινα φρονήσας.

> Τὴν πρόνοιαν ἐν τούτῳ δείκνυσι τῶν πάντων. τὸ δὲ *ἄνευ* οὐ τὴν βουλὴν δείκνυσιν, ἀλλὰ τὴν πρόγνωσιν. Τῶν γὰρ γινομένων ἃ μὲν κατὰ βούλησιν γίνεται, ἃ δὲ κατ' εὐδοκίαν καὶ συγχώρησιν. καὶ ῥητῶς μὲν τὸ λεπτομερὲς τῆς προνοίας καὶ ἡ μέχρι τῶν τυχόντων γνῶσις δηλοῦται. νοητῶς δὲ *πίπτει ἐπὶ τῆς γῆς* στρουθίον, ἐπὰν (δέον ἄνω φέρεσθαι ἢ ἀναπαύσεως χάριν ἐπὶ ὄρη καὶ βουνοὺς ἢ δώματα καθίπτασθαι) τὰ κάτω ζητοῦν *ἐπὶ*

956 Matt. 10:29.
957 Matt. 10:30; Luke, 12:7.
958 Matt. 10:29.
959 cod. καὶ.
960 Rom. 1:26.

> *τῆς γῆς* πίπτῃ τοῖς τῆς σαρκὸς ἐνεχόμενον κακοῖς, παραδοθὲν *εἰς πάθη ἀτιμίας*, καὶ τὸ ἐλεύθερον μετὰ τοῦ τιμίου ἀπολωλεκός. τοιοῦτος δὲ ὁ ὑπὸ λόγου μετεωρισθεὶς καὶ τὰ γήινα φρονήσας.[dcclix]

> ῥητῶς μὲν οὖν τὸ λεπτομερὲς τῆς προνοίας καὶ ἡ μέχρι τῶν λεπτῶν γνῶσις ἐν τούτοις δηλοῦται, νοητῶς δὲ πίπτει ἐπὶ τῆς γῆς οἷα στρουθία τὸ φρόνημα,[961] ἐπὰν δέον ἄνω φέρεσθαι,[962] τὰ κάτω ζητῇ[963] τοῖς τῆς σαρκὸς ἐνεχομένον[964] κακοῖς, παραδοθὲν εἰς πάθη ἀτιμίας[965] καὶ τὸ ἐλεύθερον μετὰ τοῦ τιμίου ἀπολωλεκός. τοιοῦτος δὲ ὁ ὑπὸ τοῦ λόγου μετεωρισθεὶς καὶ τὰ γήϊνα φρονήσας. κατὰ δὲ τὸ ῥητὸν πάλιν, τό· οὐ πεσεῖται ἐπὶ τὴν γῆν ἄνευ τοῦ πατρὸς ὑμῶν οὐ τὴν βούλησιν δείκνυσιν, ἀλλὰ τὴν πρόγνωσιν. τῶν γὰρ γινομένων ἃ μὲν κατὰ βούλησιν γίνεται, ἃ δὲ κατ' εὐδοκίαν, ἃ δὲ κατὰ συγχώρησιν.[dcclx]

> Here then is the meaning of this: if small and insignificant animals do not die apart from God, and there is providence in eveything, and among all things those that are going to decease do not perish apart from the will of God, then you who are eternal should not fear that you would live without the providence of God.[dcclxi]

Πᾶς οὖν ὅστις ὁμολογήσει ἐν ἐμοί.[966] Αὐτόθεν εἰς μαρτύριον προτρέπει τὰ ῥητὰ καὶ ἀποτρέπει ἀρνήσεως. Ὅρα δέ, εἰ μὴ τὸ πλεονέκτημα τοῦ ἐν αὐτῷ ὁμολογοῦντος ἤδη ὄντος ἐν Χριστῷ δηλοῦται ἐκ τοῦ *κἀγὼ ἐν αὐτῷ ὁμολογήσω*, τὸ δὲ κακὸν τοῦ ἀρνουμένου ἐκ τοῦ μὴ συνῆφθαι τῇ ἀρνήσει, τὸ *ἐν ἐμοὶ* ἢ τὸ *ἐν αὐτῷ*.

> Αὐτόθεν εἰς μαρτύριον προτρέπει τὰ ῥητὰ καὶ ἀποτρέπει ἀρνήσεως. ὅρα δέ, εἰ μὴ τὸ πλεονέκτημα τοῦ ἐν αὐτῷ ὁμολογοῦντος ἤδη ὄντος ἐν Χριστῷ δηλοῦται ἐκ τοῦ *κἀγὼ ἐν αὐτῷ ὁμολογήσω*, τὸ δὲ κακὸν τοῦ ἀρνουμένου ἐκ τοῦ μὴ συνῆφθαι τῇ ἀρνήσει τὸ *ἐν ἐμοὶ* ἢ τὸ *ἐν αὐτῷ*.[dcclxii]

> (Ὠριγένους.) Αὐτόθεν μέν, εἰς μαρτύριον προτρέπει τὰ ῥήματα, καὶ ἀποτρέπει ἀρνήσεως. ὅρα δέ, εἰ μὴ τὸ πλεονέκτημα τοῦ ἐν αὐτῷ ὁμολογοῦντος, ἤδη ὄντως ἐν Χριστῷ δηλοῦται, ἐκ τοῦ, *κἀγὼ ἐν αὐτῷ* ὁμολογεῖν. τὸ δὲ κακὸν τοῦ ἀρνουμένου, ἐκ τοῦ μὴ συνῆφθαι τῇ ἀρνήσει τὸ *ἐν ἐμοὶ* ἢ τὸ *ἐν αὐτῷ*.[dcclxiii]

Οὐ γὰρ εἶπεν *ὅστις ὁμολογήσει* ἐμέ, *ἀλλ' ἐν ἐμοί*, δεικνὺς ὅτι οὐκ οἰκείᾳ δυνάμει ἀλλὰ τῇ ἄνωθεν βοηθούμενος χάριτι ὁμολογεῖ ὁ ὁμολογῶν. Περὶ δὲ τοῦ ἀρνουμένου οὐκ εἶπεν ἐν ἐμοί, *ἀλλ' ἐμέ*,[967] δεικνὺς ὡς μὴ ἔχων τὴν ἄνωθεν ἐπικουρίαν ἀρνεῖται. Πλὴν ἐπειδὴ αὐτὸς ἑαυτῷ γίνεται αἴτιος | **82r** τούτου, διὰ τοῦτο ἐγκαλεῖται ὡς μὴ θελήσας

---

961 *schLuc*: τὸ φρόνιμον.
962 *schLuc*: φέρεσθε.
963 *schLuc*: ζητεῖ.
964 *schLuc*: ἐνεχομένοις.
965 *schLuc*: πάθος ἀτιμίας.
966 Matt. 10:32.
967 Matt. 10:33.

σχεῖν τὸν Θεὸν βοηθόν. Οὐκ ἀρκεῖται δὲ μόνῃ τῇ κατὰ διάθεσιν πίστει, ἀλλὰ καὶ ῥήμασιν ἀπαιτεῖ τὴν ὁμολογίαν.
Πᾶς οὖν ὁ ὁμολογῶν ὅτι Θεός ἐστιν ὁ Χριστός μέλλει σχεῖν τὸν Χριστὸν ὁμολογοῦντα περὶ αὐτοῦ τῷ Πατρὶ ὅτι γνήσιός ἐστιν δοῦλος.

> Ὁ ὁμολογῶν, ὅτι θεός ἐστιν ὁ Χριστός, ταπεινώσας ἑαυτὸν μέλλει σχεῖν τὸν Χριστὸν ὁμολογοῦντα περὶ αὐτοῦ τῷ πατρί, ὅτι γνήσιός ἐστι δοῦλος.[dcclxiv]

ὁ δὲ ἀρνούμενος, ἀκούσεται τὸ *οὐκ οἶδα ὑμᾶς.*[968] ‹Τὸ δὲ› *ὁμολογήσω κἀγὼ ἐν αὐτῷ* ὑπερέχει ὡς παρὰ Θεοῦ τὸ ἔπαθλον. Οὐδὲ γὰρ ἴσον ἐπ᾽ ἀνθρώπων ὁμολογήσαντας ἐπὶ Θεοῦ ὁμολογηθῆναι. Ἐξ ἀντιστρόφου δὲ ὁ φόβος τοῖς ἀρνουμένοις. Μέγα γὰρ καὶ φοβερὸν τὸ ἐπὶ *τοῦ Πατρὸς* τὸν Κύριον ἀρνήσασθαι τοὺς δόξαντας εἶναι δούλους ὡς μάτην ἐπιγραψαμένους τοὔνομα. Δεῖ δὲ τὸν πιστεύοντα καρδίᾳ καὶ στόματι ὁμολογεῖν. *Καρδίᾳ γὰρ πιστεύεται εἰς δικαιοσύνην, στόματι δὲ ὁμολογεῖται εἰς σωτηρίαν.*[969]

> Ὑπερέχει ὡς παρὰ θεοῦ τὸ ἔπαθλον. οὐδὲ γὰρ ἴσον ἐπ᾽ ἀνθρώπων ὁμολογήσαντας ἐπὶ θεοῦ ὁμολογηθῆναι. ἐξ ἀντιστρόφου δὲ ὁ φόβος τοῖς ἀρνουμένοις. μέγα γὰρ καὶ φοβερὸν τὸ ἐπὶ τοῦ πατρὸς τὸν κύριον ἀρνήσασθαι τοὺς δόξαντας εἶναι δούλους ὡς μάτην ἐπιγραψαμένους τὸ ὄνομα. δεῖ δὲ τὸν πιστεύοντα καρδίᾳ καὶ στόματι ὁμολογεῖν. *καρδίᾳ γὰρ πιστεύεται εἰς δικαιοσύνην, στόματι δὲ ὁμολογεῖται εἰς σωτηρίαν.*[dcclxv]
>
> *Εἰρήνην*[970] οὐ τὴν τοῦ κόσμου τὴν δὲ ἑαυτοῦ δίδωσι τοῖς μαθηταῖς ὁ σωτήρ, ἣν οὐ βάλλει ἐπὶ τοὺς τὰ αἰσθητὰ καὶ γήινα φρονοῦντας. *μάχαιραν* δὲ τὸν διακόπτοντα λόγον τὴν ἐπιβλαβῆ φιλίαν ψυχῆς καὶ σώματός φησιν, ἵνα ἡ ψυχὴ ἐπιδοῦσα ἑαυτὴν τῷ στρατευομένῳ *κατὰ τῆς σαρκὸς*[971] πνεύματι φιλιωθῇ θεῷ διχάζοντι τοὺς ἀπὸ φαύλης ἑνώσεως πιστοὺς ἀπὸ ἀπίστων καὶ κοσμικῶν.[dcclxvi]
>
> Κατὰ μὲν τὸ αἰσθητόν, *μάχαιραν*[972] εἶπεν. οὐ τὴν φύσιν τοῦ πράγματος, ἀλλὰ τὴν προαίρεσιν τῶν ἀνθρώπων.[dcclxvii]
>
> (Ὠριγένους.) Κατὰ μὲν τὸ αἰσθητόν, *μάχαιραν* εἶπεν. οὐ τὴν φύσιν τοῦ πράγματος, ἀλλὰ τὴν προαίρεσιν τῶν ἀνθρώπων.[dcclxviii]
>
> Μάχαιρα μὲν οὖν ὀξεῖά ἐστι τὸ στόμα τοῦ υἱοῦ τοῦ θεοῦ, ἐπεὶ *ζῶν* τυγχάνει *ὁ λόγος τοῦ θεοῦ καὶ ἐνεργὴς καὶ τομώτερος ὑπὲρ πᾶσαν μάχαιραν δίστομον καὶ διϊκνούμενος ἄχρι μερισμοῦ ψυχῆς καὶ πνεύματος, ἁρμῶν τε καὶ μυελῶν, καὶ κριτικὸς ἐνθυμήσεων καὶ ἐννοιῶν καρδίας.* ἄλλως τε καὶ ἐλθὼν *οὐκ εἰρήνην* ἐπὶ τὴν γῆν, τουτ᾽ ἔστιν ἐπὶ τὰ σωματικὰ καὶ αἰσθητά, *βαλεῖν ἀλλὰ μάχαιραν*, καὶ διακόπτων τήν, ἵν᾽ οὕτως εἴπω, ἐπιβλαβῆ φιλίαν

---

968 Matt. 25:12; Luke, 13:25&27.
969 Rom. 10:10.
970 Matt. 10:34.
971 Cf. Gal. 5:17.
972 Matt. 10:34.

ψυχῆς καὶ σώματος, ἵν' ἡ ψυχὴ ἐπιδιδοῦσα αὐτὴν τῷ στρατευομένῳ κατὰ τῆς σαρκὸς πνεύματι φιλιωθῇ τῷ θεῷ.[dcclxix]

28

84r *Σὺ εἶ ὁ ἐρχόμενος;*[973] **84v** (ΩΡΙΓΕΝΟΥΣ) Ὅτι μὲν γὰρ αὐτός ἐστιν ᾔδει ὁ Ἰωάννης. Διδάσκων δὲ τοὺς ἰδίους μαθητὰς οὐκ ἔπειθεν, ἀλλ' ἐδόκουν ταπεινοφρονεῖν αὐτόν. Διὰ τοῦτο δύο μόνους ἀπέστειλεν, οὓς ᾔδει εὐπειθεστέρους, ἵνα μαρτυρήσαντες καὶ τοὺς ἄλλους πείσωσιν.[974]

[Ὅτι μὲν γὰρ αὐτός ἦν, ᾔδει ὁ Ἰωάννης, διδάσκων δὲ τοὺς ἰδίους μαθητὰς οὐκ ἔπειθεν, ἀλλ' ἐδόκουν ταπεινοφρονεῖν αὐτόν. διὰ τοῦτο δύο μόνους ἀπέστειλεν, οὓς ᾔδει εὐπειθεστέρους, ἵνα μαρτυρήσαντες καὶ τοὺς ἄλλους πείσωσιν.][dcclxx]

(Ὠριγένους.) Ἡ τοῦ Ἰωάννου ἐρώτησις, οὐκ αὐτοῦ μόνου ἦν χάριν, ἀλλὰ καὶ τῶν ἀποσταλέντων. οἱ μὲν γὰρ ἀποσταλέντες ἔχρῃζον μαθεῖν, εἰ αὐτὸς ἦν ὁ ἐλθών. τοῦτο δὲ ὁ Ἰωάννης ἐγίνωσκε, καὶ διδάσκων τοὺς ἰδίους μαθητὰς ἴσως οὐκ ἔπειθεν. ἐδόκουν δὲ ταπεινοφρονεῖν αὐτόν. περὶ δὲ τοῦ, εἰ αὐτὸς μέλλει ἔρχεσθαι, ἔχρῃζεν ὁ Ἰωάννης μαθεῖν. ἔρχεσθαι δὲ ἐν τοῖς κάτω, ἔνθα ηὐτρέπιστο πορεύεσθαι ὁ Ἰωάννης.[dcclxxi]

(ΩΡΙΓΕΝΟΥΣ, added on the margin) *Τούτων δὲ πορευομένων.*[975] Τοὺς μαθητάς φησι τοὺς ἐκπεμφθέντας εἰς τὸ τῆς ἀληθείας κήρυγμα ἐν ταῖς πόλεσι τοῦ Ἰσραήλ.

(ΩΡΙΓΕΝΟΥΣ, main text cont.) *Ἀπαγγείλατε Ἰωάννῃ ἃ ἀκούετε καὶ βλέπετε.*[976] Τί οὖν ὁ Σωτὴρ εἰδὼς ὡς Θεὸς τὸν τοῦ Ἰωάννου νοῦν καὶ μὴ θέλων αὐτὸς μαρτυρῆσαι ὑπὲρ ἑαυτοῦ πλουσίως ποιεῖ τὰς θεοσημείας; Ἵνα πεισθῶσιν ὅτι αὐτός ἐστιν ὁ ὑπὸ τῶν προφητῶν κηρυχθείς. Καί φησι· δι' ὧν ποιῶ καὶ λέγω παρασκευάζω ὑμᾶς ἀπελθεῖν καὶ εἰπεῖν *Ἰωάννῃ ἃ* ἑωράκατε *καὶ ἠκούσατε*, κἀκεῖνος ὑμᾶς διδάξει πάντα. Πτωχοὺς δὲ εὐαγγελίζεσθαι τοὺς μαθητάς φησι τοὺς διὰ πτωχείαν ἀγραμμάτους ὄντας. Εἶτα μειζόνως αὐτοὺς θέλων ἐπισπάσασθαι, μακαρίζει τοὺς πιστεύοντας εἰς αὐτόν,[977] ἐπειδὴ πολλοὶ ὁ | **85r** ρῶντες αὐτὸν ἐδίσταζον ὅτι αὐτός ἐστιν ὁ Χριστός. Τοῦτο δὲ καὶ ὡς πρὸς τοὺς μαθητὰς Ἰωάννου ὁρᾷ.

Τί ἐξήλθετε εἰς τὴν ἔρημον θεάσασθαι;[978] Εἰκὸς ἦν τοὺς ὄχλους διαλογίζεσθαι εἰς ἑαυτοὺς ἀκούσαντας τῆς τῶν Ἰωάννου μαθητῶν φωνῆς, μὴ εἰδότας τὴν γνώμην μεθ'

---

973 Matt. 11:2; cf. Luke, 7:19.
974 Matt. 11:2-3.
975 Matt. 11:7.
976 Matt. 11:4.
977 Matt. 11:6.
978 Matt. 11:7.

ἧς ἔπεμψεν αὐτοὺς καὶ πολλὰ ἄτοπα ὑπονοεῖν καὶ λέγειν ἐν ἑαυτοῖς. Ἆρα ὁ τοσαῦτα μαρτυρήσας μετεπείσθη νῦν καὶ ἀμφιβάλλει εἴτε οὗτος εἴτε ἕτερος εἴη *ὁ ἐρχόμενος*;[979] Ἀναιρῶν τοίνυν αὐτῶν τὴν ὑποψίαν καὶ δεικνὺς ὅτι ᾔδει τὰ ἀπόρρητα πάντων ὡς Θεός, διορθοῦται αὐτῶν τὴν ἀσθένειαν καὶ ἀπολογεῖται ὑπὲρ Ἰωάννου καὶ δείκνυσιν ὅτι οὐ μετέπεσε τῆς προτέρας δόξης οὐδὲ μεταβέβληται. Οὐ γάρ ἐστιν εὐρίπιστος[dcclxxii] ἄνθρωπος εἰ μὴ γὰρ τοιοῦτος ἦν.

Ἐπεὶ οὖν πολλὰ τοιαῦτα εἰκὸς ἦν αὐτοὺς ὑποπτεύειν, ὅρα πῶς αὐτῶν διορθοῦται τὴν ἀσθένειαν, καὶ ταύτας ἀναιρεῖ τὰς ὑποψίας… . Διὰ τοῦτο οὐδὲ ἐπιπληκτικῶς αὐτοῖς διαλέγεται, ἀλλὰ διορθοῦται αὐτῶν μόνον τὴν διάνοιαν, καὶ ἀπολογεῖται ὑπὲρ Ἰωάννου. καὶ δείκνυσιν ὅτι οὐ μετέπεσε τῆς προτέρας δόξης, οὐδὲ μεταβέβληται. Οὐδὲ γάρ ἐστιν εὔκολος ἄνθρωπος καὶ εὐρίπιστος, ἀλλὰ πεπηγὼς καὶ βέβαιος, καὶ οὐ τοιοῦτος, ὡς καὶ προδοῦναι τὰ ἐμπεπιστευμένα.[dcclxxiii]

Ἐπειδὴ γὰρ εἰκὸς ἦν αὐτοὺς ὡς περὶ εὐκόλου καὶ εὐριπίστου τινὸς διάκεισθαι τοῦ Ἰωάννου, ταύτην διορθούμενος τὴν ὑποψίαν, φησί. *Τί ἐξήλθετε εἰς τὴν ἔρημον ἰδεῖν; κάλαμον ὑπὸ ἀνέμου σαλευόμενον; ἢ ἄνθρωπον ἐν μαλακοῖς ἱματίοις ἠμφιεσμένον*; δι᾽ ἀμφοτέρων δηλῶν, ὅτι οὔτε οἴκοθέν ἐστιν εὐρίπιστος, οὔτε ἀπὸ τρυφῆς τινος μαλακισθήσεται. Οὕτω τοίνυν καὶ ἐνταῦθα πρὸς τὴν γνώμην τὴν ἀπόκρισιν ποιεῖται.[dcclxxiv]

Ἀλλὰ τί ἐξήλθετε ἰδεῖν; ἄνθρωπον ἐν μαλακοῖς ἱματίοις ἠμφιεσμένον; Ἰδοὺ οἱ τὰ μαλακὰ φοροῦντες, ἐν τοῖς οἴκοις τῶν βασιλέων εἰσίν. Ὃ δὲ λέγει τοιοῦτόν ἐστιν, ὅτι οἴκοθεν οὐκ ἦν εὐρίπιστος. καὶ τοῦτο ἐδηλώσατε διὰ τῆς σπουδῆς ὑμεῖς. Οὐ μὴν οὐδὲ ἐκεῖνο ἔχοι τις ἂν εἰπεῖν, ὡς στερρὸς μὲν ἦν, τρυφῇ δὲ δουλεύσας ὕστερον χαῦνος γέγονε. Τῶν γὰρ ἀνθρώπων οἱ μὲν οἴκοθέν εἰσι τοιοῦτοι, οἱ δὲ γίνονται.[dcclxxv]

(ΩΡΙΓΕΝΟΥΣ, cont.)[dcclxxvi] *Τί ἐξήλθετε, φησί, εἰς τὴν ἔρημον* ἰδεῖν; Οὐ γὰρ δὴ *κάλαμον* ἐξήλθετε ἰδεῖν *ὑπὸ ἀνέμου σαλευόμενον.*[980] Οἱ γὰρ ἐπὶ μηδενὸς ἑστῶτες, ἀλλὰ νῦν μὲν ταῦτα νῦν δὲ ἐκεῖνα λέγοντες καλάμῳ ἐοίκασι τῇδε κἀκεῖσε σαλευόμενοι. Κάλαμός ἐστιν εὐμετάβολος καὶ τρεπτὸς ἄνθρωπος, πάσῃ κινήσει περιφερόμενος. *Ἐν μαλακοῖς* ἱματίοις[981] ἠμφίεσται ὁ τὸν τρυφερὸν καὶ ἔκλυτον καὶ πρὸς ἀρετὴν ἀνεπιτήδειον βίον ἔχων. Ἐν τούτοις ὁ Ἰησοῦς τοὺς ἀκούσαντας τῆς περὶ αὐτοῦ πρῴην μαρτυρίας Ἰωάννου καὶ τῆς νῦν ἀποκρίσεως διδάσκει, μὴ κατὰ τροπὴν τὸν Ἰωάννην ἐρωτῶντα, ἀλλὰ διδασκαλίαν οἰκονομῶν.

Κάλαμός ἐστιν ‹ὁ› εὐμετάβολος καὶ τρεπτὸς ἄνθρωπος πάσῃ κινήσει περιφερόμενος. ἐν *μαλακοῖς* ἱματίοις ἠμφίεσται ὁ τὸν τρυφερὸν καὶ ἔκλυτον καὶ πρὸς ἀρετὴν ἀνεπιτήδειον βίον ἔχων. ἐν τούτοις ὁ Ἰησοῦς τοὺς ἀκούσαντας τῆς περὶ αὐτοῦ πρῴην μαρτυρίας Ἰωάννου καὶ τῆς νῦν ἀποκρίσεως διδάσκει, μὴ κατὰ τροπὴν τὸν Ἰωάννην ἐρωτῶντα, ἀλλὰ διδασκαλίαν οἰκονομοῦντα.[dcclxxvii]

---

979 Matt. 11:3.
980 Matt. 11:7-9.
981 Matt. 11:8.

29

89r (ΩΡΙΓΕΝΟΥΣ) Αὐλός ἐστιν ἡ χαρὰ τῆς ἡδύτητος τῆς βασιλείας τῶν οὐρανῶν. θρῆνός ἐστὶ τὰ ἠπειλημένα καὶ ἐπώδυνα τῆς γεέννης.[982]

> Αὐλός ἐστιν ἡ χαρὰ τῆς ἡδύτητος τῆς βασιλείας τῶν οὐρανῶν. θρῆνός ἐστὶ τὰ ἠπειλημένα καὶ ἐπώδυνα τῆς γεέννης.[dcclxxviii]

> αὐλὸς γάρ ἐστιν ἡ τῆς βασιλείας τῶν οὐρανῶν ἡδύτης, θρῆνος δὲ τὰ γεέννης ἐπώδυνα.[dcclxxix]

> Τουτέστιν εὐφροσύνης καὶ βασιλείας οὐρανῶν μαθήματα παραδεδώκαμεν καὶ οὐ μετὰ χαρᾶς προσεδέξασθε, καὶ πάλιν ἠπειλήσαμεν ὑμῖν τὰ σκυθρωπὰ καὶ τὴν κόλασιν καὶ ἐπὶ ταῖς ἰδίαις ἁμαρτίαις οὐκ ἐμετανοήσατε.[dcclxxx]

> (Ὠριγένους) Τουτέστιν εὐφροσύνης καὶ βασιλείας οὐρανῶν μαθήματα παραδεδώκαμεν, καὶ οὐ μετὰ χαρᾶς προσεδέξασθε, καὶ πάλιν ἠπειλήσαμεν ὑμῖν τὰ σκυθρωπὰ καὶ τὴν κόλασιν, καὶ ἐπὶ ταῖς ἰδίαις ἁμαρτίαις οὐκ ἐμετανοήσατε.[dcclxxxi]

Ἦλθε γὰρ ὁ Ἰωάννης μήτε ἐσθίων μήτε πίνων.[983] Ἦλθε τοίνυν ὁ Ἰωάννης τὸν σκληρὸν εἰσάγων βίον, ἐγὼ ‹δὲ› τὸν ἀνειμένον, καὶ οὐδενὶ ἐπείσθητε.

> τοιοῦτόν τι πεπόνθασιν Ἰουδαῖοι οὐδὲ τὸ στυγνὸν τοῦ Ἰωάννου οὔτε τὸ ἀνειμένον τοῦ Χριστοῦ ἀποδεξάμενοι οὐδὲ δι᾽ ἑνὸς τρόπου ὠφεληθέντες.[dcclxxxii]

Ἀλλὰ τὸν μὲν διὰ τὴν ἄκραν ἄσκησιν δαιμονῶντα ἐκαλέσατε, ἐμὲ δὲ διὰ τὴν τῶν πολλῶν ὠφέλειαν ἐσθίοντα ὀνειδίζετε ὡς τρυφητήν. Διὸ *καὶ ἐδικαιώθη ἡ σοφία ἀπὸ τῶν τέκνων*[984] *αὐτῆς*, ἤτοι ἐπὶ τοῖς | **89v** ἔργοις ἐξ ὧν εἰργάσατο ἐν Ἰωάννῃ καὶ ἐν ἑαυτῷ αὐτὸς ὢν ἡ ὑφεστῶσα σοφία[dcclxxxiii] ἐκρίθη δίκαιος ὑπὸ τῶν εἰς αὐτὸν πιστευόντων.

> Αὐτὸς ὢν ὁ Χριστὸς ἡ ζῶσα καὶ ὑφεστῶσα σοφία ὑπὸ τῶν εἰς αὐτὸν πιστευόντων ἐκρίθη δίκαιος πάντα οἰκονομήσας.[dcclxxxiv]

30

89v (ΩΡΙΓΕΝΟΥΣ, cont.) Μετάμελον γὰρ καὶ θρῆνον ἐδίδασκεν ἐπὶ τὸν βίον, ὃν κακῶς προέθεντο. Ὁ δὲ Κύριος *ἦλθεν ἐσθίων καὶ πίνων.*[985] Χαρᾶς γὰρ ἦν πάροχος, λύων τὰς ἁμαρτίας καὶ εἰς ζωὴν αἰώνιον μετατιθεὶς τοὺς ἀκούοντας.

---

982 Commenting on Matt. 11:17: *Ηὐλήσαμεν ὑμῖν καὶ οὐκ ὠρχήσασθε. ἐθρηνήσαμεν καὶ οὐκ ἐκόψασθε.* Cf. Luke, 7:32.

983 Matt. 11:18.

984 Luke, 7:35; cf. Matt. 11:19: ἀπὸ τῶν ἔργων αὐτῆς.

985 Matt. 11:19; Luke, 7:34.

> Μετάμελον γὰρ καὶ θρῆνον ἐδίδασκεν ἐπὶ τὸν βίον, ὃν κακῶς προέθεντο. ὁ δὲ κύριος *ἦλθεν ἐσθίων καὶ πίνων*. χαρᾶς γὰρ ἦν πάροχος, λύων τὰς ἁμαρτίας, καὶ εἰς ζωὴν αἰώνιον μετατιθεὶς τοὺς ἀκούοντας.[dcclxxxv]

Ὅτι τῷ μὲν Ἰωάννῃ ὡς οἰκέτῃ ἔπρεπε διὰ τῆς σκληραγωγίας νεκρῶσαι τὰ τῆς σαρκὸς πάθη, τῷ δὲ Χριστῷ ὡς τῇ δυνάμει τῆς θεότητος τὸν ἔμφυτον τῆς σαρκὸς νόμον κατέχοντι οὐ χρεία ἦν ἀσκήσεως. Ἔτι ὁ μὲν *Ἰωάννης βάπτισμα μετανοίας κηρύσσων*[986] τύπον ἑαυτὸν παρεῖχε διὰ τοῦ σκυθρωποῦ τοῖς ὀφείλουσι πενθεῖν, ὁ δὲ Κύριος *βασιλείαν οὐρανῶν* κηρύσσων εἰκότως τὸ ἀνειμένον καὶ φαιδρὸν ἐπεδείκνυτο.

> Ὅτι τῷ μὲν Ἰωάννῃ ὡς οἰκέτῃ ἔπρεπε διὰ τῆς σκληραγωγίας νεκρῶσαι τὰ τῆς σαρκὸς πάθη, τῷ δὲ Χριστῷ ὡς τῇ δυνάμει τῆς θεότητος τὸν ἔμφυτον τῆς σαρκὸς νόμον κατέχοντι οὐ χρεία ἦν ἀσκήσεως. ἔτι ὁ μὲν *Ἰωάννης βάπτισμα μετανοίας κηρύσσων* τύπον ἑαυτὸν παρεῖχε διὰ τοῦ σκυθρωποῦ τοῖς ὀφείλουσι πενθεῖν, ὁ δὲ Κύριος βασιλείαν οὐρανῶν κηρύσσων εἰκότως τὸ ἀνειμένον καὶ φαιδρὸν ἐπεδείκνυτο.[dcclxxxvi]

> Ἔπρεπεν Ἰωάννῃ ὡς οἰκέτῃ διὰ τῆς ἄγαν σκληραγωγίας κατανεκρῶσαι τὰ τῆς σαρκὸς πάθη, τῷ δὲ Χριστῷ ὡς ἐλευθέρῳ δυνάμει τῆς θεότητος ἐξουσιαστικῶς τὰ τῆς σαρκὸς νεκροῦν κινήματα καὶ τὸν ἔμφυτον τῆς σαρκὸς νόμον, οὐ μὴν δι᾽ ἀσκητικῶν πόνων εἰς τοῦτο βοηθεῖσθαι. ὅμως Ἰωάννης *βάπτισμα κηρύσσων μετανοίας* τύπον ἑαυτὸν πάρεσχε τοῖς ὀφείλουσι πενθεῖν, ὁ δὲ κύριος *βασιλείαν οὐρανῶν κηρύσσων* εἰκότως τὸ ἀνειμένον καὶ φαιδρὸν ἐν ἑαυτῷ ἐπεδείκνυτο, δι᾽ οὗ τοῖς πιστοῖς ὑπέγραφεν τὴν ἀνέκφραστον χαρὰν καὶ τὴν ἄπονον ζωήν. αὐλὸς γάρ ἐστιν ἡ τῆς βασιλείας τῶν οὐρανῶν ἡδύτης, θρῆνος δὲ τὰ γεέννης ἐπώδυνα.[dcclxxxvii]

(ΩΡΙΓΕΝΟΥΣ cont.) *Καὶ ἐδικαιώθη ἡ σοφία.*[987] Ἀντὶ τοῦ ἀπεφάνθη πάντα δικαίως γεγενημένα. Ἀφ᾽ ὧν γὰρ ἤνεσαν τινὲς ἐδείκνυτο οὐκ ἀργῶς οὐδὲ εἰκῇ καὶ μάτην πεπληρῶσθαι τὰ γεγενημένα. Τοῦτο γὰρ τὸ δικαιῶσαι τὴν σοφίαν τὸ τοὺς οἰκείους αὐτῆς καθάπερ παῖδας ἀποδέχεσθαι τὴν παρουσίαν αὐτῆς.

> [Τοῦτό ἐστιν. εἰ καὶ ὑμεῖς οὐκ ἐπείσθητε, ἀλλ᾽ ἐμοὶ λοιπὸν ἐγκαλεῖν οὐκ ἔχετε. Ὃ περὶ τοῦ πατρός φησιν. *ὅπως δικαιωθῇς τοῖς λόγοις σου.*[988] ὁ γὰρ θεός, κἂν μηδὲν ἀνύῃ πλέον ἀπὸ τῆς περὶ ἡμᾶς κηδεμονίας, τὰ ἑαυτοῦ πάντα πληροῖ, ὥστε τοῖς ἀναισχυντεῖν βουλομένοις μηδὲ σκιὰν καταλιπεῖν ἀγνώμονος ἀμφιβολίας. εἰ δὲ τὰ παραδείγματα εὐτελῆ καὶ κακέμφατα,[dcclxxxviii] μὴ θαυμάσῃς. πρὸς γὰρ τὴν ἀσθένειαν τῶν ἀκουόντων διελέγετο. Ὁ δὲ Λουκᾶς καὶ ἕτερόν φησιν. *οἱ* γὰρ *τελῶναι ἐδικαίωσαν τὸν θεόν,*[989] δεξάμενοι *τὸ βάπτισμα Ἰωάννου.*] ὅθεν τινὲς[dcclxxxix] τὸ *ἐδικαιώθη ἡ σοφία ἀπὸ τῶν τέκνων αὐτῆς* οὕτως ἐνόησαν. *ἐδικαιώθη* ἀπ᾽ αὐτῶν ἀντὶ τοῦ ἀπεφάνθη πάντα δικαίως γεγενημένα. ἀφ᾽ ὧν γὰρ ἤνεσάν τινες, ἐδείκνυτο οὐκ ἀργῶς οὐδὲ μάτην πεπληρῶσθαι

---

986 Mark, 1:4.
987 Matt. 11:19; cf. Luke, 7:35.
988 Psalm 50:6.
989 Luke, 7:29.

τὰ γεγενημένα. τοῦτο γὰρ τὸ δικαιῶσαι τὴν σοφίαν ‹τὸ› τοὺς οἰκείους αὐτῆς καθάπερ παῖδας ἀποδεδέχθαι τὴν παρουσίαν αὐτῆς.[dccxc]

(ΩΡΙΓΕΝΟΥΣ) Δικαιοῦται δὲ καὶ ἀπὸ *ἔργων σοφία* κατὰ σοφίαν ἐπιτελουμένη ἢ ἀπὸ λόγων.

Ἀπὸ *ἔργων* κατὰ σοφίαν ἐπιτελουμένων δικαιοῦται μᾶλλον ἢ *σοφία* ἀπὸ λόγων.[dccxci]

31

(ΩΡΙΓΕΝΟΥΣ, cont.) Καὶ ἐν τῇ σωτηρίᾳ τῶν σωζομένων καὶ ἐν τῇ ἀπωλείᾳ τῶν ἀπολλυμένων ἡ *σοφία Χριστός* ἐστιν.[990]

Καὶ ἐν τῇ σωτηρίᾳ τῶν σωζομένων καὶ ἐν τῇ ἀπωλείᾳ τῶν ἀπολλυμένων ἡ *σοφία Χριστός* ἐστιν.[dccxcii]

Καὶ ἐδικαιώθη ἡ σοφία ἀπὸ τῶν τέκνων αὐτῆς. τουτέστιν, Εἰ καὶ ὑμεῖς οὐκ ἐπείσθητε, ἀλλ᾽ ἐμοὶ λοιπὸν ἐγκαλεῖν οὐκ ἔχετε. Ὃ περὶ τοῦ Πατρός φησιν ὁ προφήτης. *Ὅπως ἂν δικαιωθῇς ἐν τοῖς λόγοις σου*. Ὁ γὰρ Θεός, κἂν μηδὲν ἀνύῃ πλέον ἀπὸ τῆς περὶ ἡμᾶς κηδεμονίας, τὰ παρ᾽ ἑαυτοῦ πάντα πληροῖ, ὥστε τοῖς ἀναισχυντεῖν βουλομένοις μηδὲ σκιὰν καταλιπεῖν ἀγνώμονος ἀμφιβολίας. Εἰ δὲ τὰ παραδείγματα εὐτελῆ καὶ κακέμφατα, μὴ θαυμάσῃς. πρὸς γὰρ τὴν ἀσθένειαν τῶν ἀκουόντων διελέγετο. Ἐπεὶ καὶ ὁ Ἰεζεκιὴλ πολλὰ λέγει παραδείγματα αὐτοῖς πρόσφορα, καὶ τῆς τοῦ Θεοῦ μεγαλωσύνης ἀνάξια. Ἀλλὰ καὶ τοῦτο μάλιστα ἄξιον αὐτοῦ τῆς κηδεμονίας. Σκόπει δὲ αὐτοὺς καὶ ἑτέρωθεν εἰς ἐναντίας περιενεχθέντας δόξας. Εἰπόντες γὰρ περὶ Ἰωάννου, ὅτι δαιμόνιον ἔχει, οὐκ ἔστησαν μέχρι τούτου, ἀλλὰ καὶ περὶ αὐτοῦ τὰ ἐναντία αἱρουμένου τὸ αὐτὸ τοῦτο εἶπον πάλιν. οὕτως εἰς μαχομένας ἀεὶ περιεφέροντο δόξας. Ὁ δὲ Λουκᾶς μετὰ τούτων καὶ ἑτέραν μείζονα τίθησιν αὐτῶν κατηγορίαν, εἰπών. *Οἱ γὰρ τελῶναι ἐδικαίωσαν τὸν Θεόν, δεξάμενοι τὸ βάπτισμα Ἰωάννου.*[dccxciii]

Οἱ πρὸς τὸ ἀληθὲς ὁρῶντες, φησί, ἀπεδέξαντο τὴν Ἰωάννου καὶ Χριστοῦ ἀγωγήν, ὡς μετὰ σοφίας τῆς τῶν βίων ἐναλλαγῆς οἰκονομηθείσης πρὸς ὠφέλειαν τῶν ὁρώντων. Αὐτὸ γὰρ τοῦτο σοφίαν καλεῖ, τὰ σοφῶς γεγονότα.

(ΩΡΙΓΕΝΟΥΣ, added on the margin; comm. on Matt. 11:19)[dccxciv] καὶ γὰρ εἰ καὶ μὴ Ἰουδαῖοι ἐπίστευσαν εἰς τὸν Χριστόν, μήτε διὰ τῆς Ἰωάννου νηστείας καὶ τοῦ ἐρημικοῦ βίου, μήτε διὰ τῆς συγκαταβατικῆς διαίτης καὶ οἰκονομικῆς πολιτείας αὐτοῦ τοῦ δεσπότου Χριστοῦ, ἀλλ᾽ οὖν αὐτὸς ὁ πάντα σοφῶς ἐκτελῶν τῷ μηδὲν παραλιπεῖν τῶν συντελούντων εἰς ὄνησιν καὶ σωτηρίαν αὐτῶν *ἐδικαιώθη* ἀπ᾽ αὐτῶν καὶ οὐκέτι λοιπὸν ἔχουσιν αὐτῷ ἐγκαλεῖν. Πάντα γὰρ ἐξεπλήρωσε τὰ αὐτοῦ μηδὲ σκιὰν αὐτοῖς ἢ ἀγνωμοσύνης ἢ ἀχαριστίας καταλιπών.

990 Cf. 1 Cor. 1:24.

Οἱ πρὸς τὸ ἀληθὲς ὁρῶντες, φησίν, ἀπεδέξαντο τὴν Ἰωάννου καὶ Χριστοῦ ἀγωγὴν ὡς μετὰ σοφίας τῆς τῶν βίων ἐναλλαγῆς οἰκονομηθείσης πρὸς ὠφέλειαν τῶν ὁρώντων. αὐτὸ γὰρ τοῦτο σοφίαν καλεῖ, τὰ σοφῶς γεγονότα. καὶ γὰρ εἰ καὶ μὴ Ἰουδαῖοι ἐπίστευσαν εἰς τὸν Χριστόν, μήτε διὰ τῆς Ἰωάννου νηστείας καὶ τοῦ ἐρημικοῦ βίου, μήτε διὰ τῆς συγκαταβατικῆς διαίτης καὶ οἰκονομικῆς πολιτείας αὐτοῦ τοῦ δεσπότου Χριστοῦ, ἀλλ᾽ οὖν αὐτὸς ὁ πάντα σοφῶς ἐκτελῶν τῷ μηδὲν παραλιπεῖν τῶν συντελούντων εἰς ὄνησιν καὶ σωτηρίαν αὐτῶν *ἐδικαιώθη* ἀπ᾽ αὐτῶν. καὶ οὐκέτι λοιπὸν ἔχουσιν αὐτῷ ἐγκαλεῖν. πάντα γὰρ ἐξεπλήρωσε τὰ αὐτοῦ μηδὲ σκιὰν αὐτοῖς ἢ ἀγνωμοσύνης ἢ ἀχαριστίας καταλιπών.[dccxcv]

(ΩΡΙΓΕΝΟΥΣ, main text cont.) Ἀπὸ *τότε ἤρξατο ὀνειδίζειν τὰς πόλεις*,[991] ὅτε οὔτε διὰ τῶν σημείων | **90r** οὔτε διὰ τῆς διὰ τῆς διδασκαλίας ὠφελήθησαν.

Ὀνειδισμὸς δέ ἐστιν πληγὴ λογικὴ ὑπομινήσκουσα ἁμαρτίας, μάλιστα τὸν ἀχάριστον καὶ ἀμνήμονα εὐποιίας.[dccxcvi]

A censure of the cities of Chorazin and Besthaida and Capernaum is expanded on the title this chapter. The reason he reprimandeded them was that they did not repent following the and many signs that had taken place.[dccxcvii]

Τότε ὀνειδίζει καὶ ἀπειλεῖ ἵνα κἂν οὕτως ἐντραπῶσιν. Εἰκότως δὲ τοὺς Τυρίους καὶ Σιδωνίους παρήγαγεν ὡς εἰδωλολατροῦντας[992] Σοδομήτας[dccxcviii] δὲ ὡς ἡδυπαθεῖς, ἵνα δείξῃ τούτων Ἰουδαίους χείρονας. Κατακρίνει δὲ Ἰουδαίους πλείω τῶν ἐθνικῶν.[993] Οὐδὲ γὰρ οὕτως εἰσὶν ἀσύγγνωστοι οἱ μὴ ἑωρακότες ὡς οἱ ἑωρακότες, καὶ ὅτι Τύριοι μὲν καὶ Σιδώνιοι τὸν φυσικὸν μόνον παρέβησαν νόμον,[dccxcix] Ἰουδαῖοι δὲ καὶ τὸν Μωσέως καὶ τοῖς διὰ Χριστοῦ σημείοις ἠπίστησαν.

καὶ οἱ Τύριοι δὲ καὶ οἱ Σιδώνιοι τὸν φυσικὸν μόνον παρέβησαν νόμον, Ἰουδαῖοι δὲ ἀπειθήσαντες τῷ Χριστῷ καὶ τὸν Μωσέως νόμον καὶ τοὺς προφήτας.[dccc]

Διὸ καὶ πικρότερον οὗτοι ἐκείνων τιμωρηθήσονται.

Καὶ σὺ Καπερναούμ.[994] Ἐπειδὴ δὲ ἐν Καπερναοὺμ πολλὰ ἦν ποιήσας σημεῖα, εἶπε πρὸς αὐτὴν τὸ μὴ ἐπαρθῇς. Εἰ γὰρ καὶ δι᾽ ὑπεροψίαν οἴει ἕως τοῦ ὕψους φθάνειν τοῦ οὐρανοῦ, ἀλλ᾽ εἰς ᾅδην *καταβιβασθήσῃ*. Καὶ γὰρ διὰ τὴν ἀπιστίαν ἔπεσεν *ἐξαίσιον πτῶμα*.[995] Οὐκ ἐγένοντο δὲ σημεῖα *ἐν Σοδόμοις*, ὅτι ἑκάστῳ καιρῷ τὸ πρόσφορον ᾠκονόμηται. Ὅτε γὰρ ἔδει, ἐσαρκώθη καὶ ἐποίησε τὰ σημεῖα.

---

991 Matt. 11:20.
992 Matt. 11:21.
993 Matt. 11:23.
994 Matt. 11:23; Luke, 10:15.
995 Cf. Job, 18:12; 20:5; 37:16.

(Χρυσοστόμου. Θεοδώρου Ἡρακλείας)[dcccci] Ἐπειδὴ πολλὰ σημεῖα ἐποίησεν ὁ Χριστὸς ἐν Καπερναούμ, ἐδόκει ἕως οὐρανοῦ ὑψοῦσθαι, ἥτις διὰ τὴν ἀπιστίαν πτῶμα πεσοῦσα ἐξαίσιον, ἕως ᾄδου ἔφθασεν. εἰ δέ τις εἴποι καὶ διατί οὐ γέγονε τὰ σημεῖα ἐν Σοδόμοις; ἐροῦμεν, ὅτι ἑκάστῳ καιρῷ, πρόσφορον ὁ Χριστὸς ᾠκονόμησεν. ὅτε ἔδει, ἐσαρκώθη ὁ Λόγος, καὶ ἐποίησε τὰ σημεῖα, πλὴν ἑκάστῃ γενεᾷ κατὰ ἀναλογίαν δίδωσι τὰς εὐθύνας.[dccccii]

Ἐπειδὴ δὲ πολλὰ σημεῖα ἐποίησεν ὁ Χριστὸς ἐν Καπερναούμ, ἐδόκει ἕως *οὐρανοῦ ὑψοῦσθαι*, ἥτις διὰ ἀπιστίαν πτῶμα πεσοῦσα ἐξαίσιον *ἕως ᾄδου* ἔφθασεν. εἰ δέ τις εἴποι. καὶ διὰ τί οὐ γέγονε τὰ σημεῖα ἐν *Σοδόμοις*, ἐροῦμεν, ὅτι ἑκάστῳ καιρῷ πρόσφορον ὁ Χριστὸς ᾠκονόμησεν. ὅτε ἔδει, ἐσαρκώθη ὁ λόγος καὶ ἐποίησε τὰ σημεῖα, πλὴν ἑκάστῃ γενεᾷ κατὰ ἀναλογίαν δίδωσι τὰς εὐθύνας. καὶ οἱ Τύριοι δὲ καὶ οἱ Σιδώνιοι τὸν φυσικὸν μόνον παρέβησαν νόμον, Ἰουδαῖοι δὲ ἀπειθήσαντες τῷ Χριστῷ καὶ τὸν Μωσέως νόμον καὶ τοὺς προφήτας. λέγει δὲ αὐτὰ ἴσως καὶ ἐπιτατικώτερον, ὡς ἐν παραθέσει μείζονα τὴν κακίαν αὐτῶν δεῖξαι βουλόμενος. ἢ γὰρ ἂν καὶ ἐγένετο ἐν *Τύρῳ καὶ Σιδῶνι, Σοδόμοις τε καὶ Γομόρροις*, εἰ καὶ μὴ ταῦτα, ἀλλ᾽ οὖν γε ἕτερα, εἴπερ δὴ μεταβολὴν ὁ τόπος ἐδέχετο. ἀλλ᾽ ὅπερ ἔφην, ἐπιτείνει τὴν σύγκρισιν εἰς μείζονα ἔνδειξιν τῆς τούτων κακίας.[dccciii]

Εἰ δὲ τότε ἦν σαρκωθεὶς καὶ ταῦτα τὰ σημεῖα ἦν πεποιηκὼς ἐκεῖ οὐκ ἂν κατεστράφη Σόδομα. Τὸ δὲ *ἀνεκτότερον ἔσται*[996] σημαίνει τὸ δύνασθαι ἀνέχεσθαι· διδάσκει δὲ διαφορὰς εἶναι κολάσεων.[dccciv]

ἐξομολογοῦμαί σοι πάτερ.[997] Τὸ *ἐξομολογοῦμαι σοι* ἀντὶ τοῦ εὐχαριστῶ σοι φημί.[dcccv]

τὸ γὰρ *ἐξομολογοῦμαι* ἴσον ἐστὶ τῷ εὐχαριστῶ.[dcccvi]

Confession does not always signify penance but also thanksgiving, as we read often in the Psalms.[dcccvii]

Εὐχαριστεῖ γὰρ ὁ Χριστὸς ὑπὲρ τῶν πιστῶν *ὡς ἀρχιερεὺς*[998] τὰς ὑπὲρ ἡμῶν προσφέρων εὐχαριστίας ἐν τάξει θυσίας πνευματικῆς. Εὐχαριστεῖ δὲ τῷ Πατρί καίτοι γε αὐτὸς ποιήσας ἅπερ εὔχεται τὴν πολλὴν ἀγάπην τὴν περὶ ἡμᾶς ἐνδεικνύμενος | 90v καὶ δεικνὺς ὅτι οὐ παρ᾽ αὐτοῦ ἐξελέγημεν μόνον ἀλλὰ καὶ παρὰ τοῦ Πατρός.

σοφοὺς δὲ καὶ *συνετοὺς* ἐνταῦθα τοὺς Ἰουδαίους ἢ τοὺς γραμματεῖς καὶ Φαρισαίους λέγει ἢ ὅτι ἐπιστεύθησαν τὰ λόγια τοῦ Θεοῦ ὡς τὸν ἕνα καὶ μόνον πιστεύοντες Θεὸν καὶ τοῖς Μωσέως ἐντραφέντες λόγοις. Ἢ *σοφοὺς* αὐτούς φησι οὐχ ὡς τὴν ὄντως οὖσαν ἔχοντας σοφίαν ἀλλὰ τὴν δοκοῦσαν ἀπὸ δεινότητος. Σοφοὶ γὰρ ἦσαν εἰς τὸ κακοποιῆσαι. Νηπίους δὲ τοὺς ἀφελεῖς ἐν κακίᾳ, οὐ μὴν μωρούς, τοὺς ἁλιεῖς καὶ ἀγραμμάτους φησι.

---

996 Matt. 11:24.

997 Matt. 11:25; Luke, 12:21.

998 Cf. Heb. 3:1; 4:14-15; 5:5; 8:1.

> *Σοφούς* ὧδε τοὺς Ἰουδαίους καλεῖ ἢ ὅτι ἐμπιστευθέντες ἦσαν τὰ τοῦ θεοῦ λόγια ἢ ὅτι κακοῦργοι ἦσαν καὶ σοφοὶ τοῦ κακοποιῆσαι, *νηπίους* δὲ τοὺς ἀποστόλους. ἢ *σοφοὺς* μὲν τοὺς γραμματεῖς καὶ Φαρισαίους οὐ τὴν ὄντως σοφίαν ἔχοντας, ἀλλὰ τὴν δοκοῦσαν ἀπὸ δεινότητος λόγων, *νηπίους* δὲ τοὺς ἁλιεῖς τοὺς ἀφελεῖς ἐν κακίᾳ.[dcccviii]

> Ἐκ *σοφῶν* κρύπτεται, τῶν τὴν δευτέραν σοφίαν ἐχόντων. *ναὶ ὁ πατὴρ* ἀντὶ τοῦ· καλῶς *ὁ πατήρ.*[dcccix]

> (Ὠριγένους.) Ἐκ σοφῶν κρύπτεται, τῶν τὴν δευτέραν σοφίαν ἐχόντων· *ναὶ ὁ πατήρ.* ἀντὶ τοῦ καλῶς *ὁ πατήρ.*[dcccx]

Ἤτοι νηπίους τοὺς ἐθνικοὺς φησι ὡς ἐξ ἀπείρου ἀπαιδευσίας πλανηθέντας. Ὃ οὖν λέγει τοιοῦτον ἐστίν· *εὐχαριστῶ σοι πάτερ,*[999] ὅτι οἱ δοκοῦντες ἔμπειροι εἶναι τῶν γραφῶν καὶ διδασκάλων ἔχοντες τάξιν ἠπείθησαν, οἱ δὲ δοκοῦντες ἄπειροι εἶναι τῶν νομικῶν ἐπείσθησαν. Οὐκ *ἐπ᾽ ἀπωλείᾳ* δὲ τούτων χαίρει[dcccxi] καὶ τῷ μὴ μαθεῖν ἐκείνους ταῦτα εὐχαριστεῖ, ἀλλ᾽ ὅτι ἃ σοφοὶ οὐκ ἔγνωσαν διαπτύοντες καὶ μὴ βουλόμενοι ἔγνωσαν οὗτοι.
Οὐχ ὡς χαίρων δὲ τοῦτο λέγει, ἀλλ᾽ ὅτι μέγα καλὸν τὸ μὴ γνῶναι τοὺς πονηροὺς τῶν θείων τὴν δύναμιν, ἵνα μὴ μετὰ τὸ γνῶναι διαπτύσαντες εἰς πλείονα ἐμπέσωσι κόλασιν.

> πλὴν οὐχ ὡς χαίρων τοῦτο λέγει ὁ Χριστός, ἀλλ᾽ ὅτι ὁδὸς ἀρίστη ἐστὶν τὸ μὴ γνῶναι τῶν θείων λόγων τὴν δύναμιν τοὺς πονηρούς, ἵνα μὴ μετὰ τὴν γνῶσιν διαπτύσαντες εἰς μείζονα ἐμπέσωσιν κόλασιν.[dcccxii]

Εἶτα δείκνυσιν ὅτι καὶ αὐτὸ προηγούμενον *θέλημα τοῦ πατρός.*[1000] Αὐτοῦ μὲν γὰρ τὸ εὐχαριστεῖν καὶ χαίρειν ἐπὶ τῷ γενομένῳ, τοῦ Πατρὸς δὲ τὸ δεικνύναι ὅτι οὐδὲ ἐκεῖνος παρακληθεὶς τοῦτο ἐποίησεν, ἀλλ᾽ ὅτι αὐτὸς οἴκοθεν ὁρμηθείς. Οὕτω γάρ φησι *εὐδοκία ἐγένετο ἔμπροσθέν σου,*[1001] τουτέστιν, οὕτως σοι ἤρεσεν. Εἰπὼν | **91r** γὰρ *εὐδοκία*, ἔδειξεν ὅτι προεγινώσκετο τῷ Πατρὶ τὸ ἐπὶ Χριστὸν *μυστήριον.*[1002]

32

91r (ΩΡΙΓΕΝΟΥΣ) Τὴν *ἐπὶ τὰ ἔθνη*[1003] μετάβασιν τοῦ λόγου προορῶν διὰ τὴν τοῦ Ἰσραὴλ ἀπείθειαν,[1004] ὑπὲρ ἡμῶν τῶν εὐεργετηθησομένων ὑμνεῖ καὶ δοξάζει

999 Cf. Matt. 11:25.
1000 Matt. 7:21; 12:50; 21:31; John, 6:40.
1001 Matt. 11:26.
1002 Cf. Col. 4:3; 1:27; 2:2; Rom. 16:25; Eph. 3:4&8-9.
1003 Cf Psalms 46:9; 56:7; Zach. 3:12; Acts, 10:45.
1004 Cf. Rom. 11:30.

τὸν Πατέρα. Εὐχαριστεῖ δὲ τῷ Πατρὶ μὲν ἑαυτοῦ, κυρίῳ δὲ *οὐρανοῦ καὶ γῆς*[1005] συσχηματιζόμενος τοῖς δούλοις καὶ τὰς ὑπὲρ δούλων πρὸς δεσπότην ἀναφέρων εὐχαριστίας. Λέγει δὴ κατὰ τὴν τοῦ Πατρὸς εὐαρέστησιν κεκρύφθαι μὲν ἀπὸ Ἰσραὴλ τοῦ σοφοῦ ἔθνους τὸ κατ᾽ αὐτὸν μυστήριον, τοῖς δὲ πρότερον ἀσυνέτοις ἔθνεσιν ἀποκαλυφθήσεσθαι.

> Τὴν ἐπὶ τὰ ἔθνη μετάβασιν τοῦ λόγου προορῶν διὰ τὴν τοῦ Ἰσραὴλ ἀπείθειαν ὑπὲρ ἡμῶν τῶν εὐεργετηθησομένων ὑμνεῖ καὶ δοξάζει τὸν πατέρα. Εὐχαριστεῖ δὲ τῷ πατρὶ μὲν ἑαυτοῦ, κυρίῳ δὲ *οὐρανοῦ καὶ γῆς* συσχηματιζόμενος τοῖς δούλοις ὁ κύριος καὶ τὰς ὑπὲρ δούλων πρὸς δεσπότην ἀναφέρων εὐχαριστίας. λέγει δὴ κατὰ τὴν τοῦ πατρὸς εὐαρέστησιν κεκρύφθαι μὲν ἀπὸ Ἰσραὴλ τοῦ σοφοῦ ἔθνους τὸ κατ᾽ αὐτὸν μυστήριον, τοῖς δὲ πρότερον ἀσυνέτοις ἔθνεσιν ἀποκαλυφθήσεσθαι. δι᾽ ὧν ἀποδεικνύεται, ὡς οὐ διέλαθεν θεὸν τὸ ἐσόμενον οὐδὲ ἀπέτυχε ἡ Χριστοῦ παρουσία τοῦ προκειμένου σκοποῦ, ἀλλὰ προειδότος θεοῦ ταῦτα ἐγένετο καὶ προτεταχότος τὴν τῆς χάριτος μετάνοιαν. τὸ δὲ δίκαιον τῆς εὐδοκίας ἐνταῦθα παρασιωπᾶται, ἑτέρως δὲ δείκνυται. οὐ γὰρ ἄλογος[dccxiii] *εὐδοκία θεοῦ*, οὐδ᾽ ἑτέρως ἢ δι᾽ ἑαυτοὺς ἀποτυγχάνουσι γνώσεως καὶ σοφίας ἄνθρωποι.[dcccxiv]

πάντα μοι παρεδόθη ὑπὸ τοῦ πατρός μου.[1006] *Παρεδόθη* αὐτῷ τὰ *πάντα* καθ‹ὼς› καὶ αὐτὸς[1007] παρεδόθη *ὑπὲρ πάντων.*[1008] Δῆλον δέ, ὅτι κατὰ τὸν τῆς οἰκονομίας λόγον.[dcccxv]

> However, the *all things* that have been handed over to himself should not be understood of heaven and earth and the elements and the other things which he himself made and created. Instead, it should be understood of those who have access to the Father through the Son, and who formerly were rebels, but subsequently they began to understand God.[dcccxvi]

Καὶ ὥσπερ ὁ Πατὴρ λέγεται πεποιηκέναι τὰ πάντα, καίπερ διὰ τοῦ Υἱοῦ πάντα ποιῶν,[dcccxvii] οὕτως καὶ λέγεται παραδιδόναι τῷ Υἱῷ *πάντα*, αὐτὸν ἔχων δύναμιν καὶ δι᾽ αὐτοῦ κατάρχων τῶν ὅλων καὶ συνὼν αὐτῷ. Σημαίνει τὴν ὑπακοὴν τοῦ παντὸς κόσμου, ὅπερ καὶ διὰ τοῦ *νηπίοις* ἀποκεκαλύφθαι τὸ μυστήριον προεδήλου. Ἵνα γὰρ μή τις ὑπονοήσῃ ὅτι αὐτὸς ὡς μὴ δυνάμενος τοῦτο ποιῆσαι εὐχαριστεῖ ἐπὶ τῷ συμβάντι, τὸ *πάντα μοι παρεδόθη* φησί. Διὰ τοῦτο δὲ εἶπεν *ὑπὸ τοῦ πατρός μου*, ἵνα μὴ δύο θεοὺς ἀγεννήτους νομίσῃς.[dcccxviii]

> *Παρεδόθη* αὐτῷ τὰ *πάντα* καθὼς καὶ αὐτὸς παρεδόθη *ὑπὲρ πάντων*, δῆλον δὲ ὅτι κατὰ τὸν τῆς οἰκονομίας λόγον. καὶ ὥσπερ ὁ πατὴρ λέγεται πεποιηκέναι τὰ πάντα, καίπερ διὰ τοῦ υἱοῦ πάντα ποιῶν, οὕτως καὶ λέγεται παραδιδόναι τῷ υἱῷ *πάντα*, αὐτὸν ἔχων δύναμιν καὶ δι᾽ αὐτοῦ κατάρχων τῶν ὅλων καὶ συνὼν αὐτῷ. [σημαίνει τὴν ὑπακοὴν τοῦ

1005 Matt. 11:25.
1006 Matt. 11:27.
1007 Cod. καθὸ.
1008 Cf. 2 Cor. 5:14-15; 1 Tim. 2:6.

παντὸς κόσμου. ὅπερ καὶ διὰ τοῦ *νηπίοις ἀπεκαλύφθη* τὸ μυστήριον προεδήλου. ἵνα γὰρ μή τις ὑπονοήσῃ ὅτι αὐτὸς ὡς μὴ δυνάμενος τοῦτο ποιῆσαι εὐχαριστεῖ ἐπὶ τῷ συμβάντι, τὸ *πάντα μοι παρεδόθη* φησί. διὰ τοῦτο δὲ εἶπεν *ὑπὸ τοῦ πατρός μου*, ἵνα μὴ δύο θεοὺς ἀγεννήτους νομίσῃς.][dcccxix]

Ὥσπερ οὖν ὁ πατὴρ λέγεται πεποιηκέναι τὰ πάντα, καίπερ διὰ τοῦ υἱοῦ πάντα ποιῶν, οὕτω καὶ λέγεται τῷ υἱῷ πάντα παραδιδόναι αὐτὸν ἔχων δύναμιν καὶ δι' αὐτοῦ κατάρχων τῶν ὅλων καὶ συνὼν αὐτῷ.[dcccxx]

Κατὰ διαφόρους ἐπινοίας ἡ θεοῦ γνῶσις. κτίστου, ᾗ ἔκτισεν, κριτοῦ ‹***› ἀποκαλύψῃ οὐχ ἑτέρως ὄντι υἱῷ θεοῦ, ὃς λαβὼν ἐξουσίαν τέκνον γενέσθαι ὅτε μὲν [ἔχει] οὐκ ἔγνω, οὐκ ἔχει τὸν πατέρα, ὅτε δὲ γίνεται ἀποκαλύψαντος Ἰησοῦ ὡς ἀδελφῷ γνώσεται.[dcccxxi]

Κατὰ διαφόρους ἐπινοίας ἡ θεοῦ γνῶσις. κτίστου, ᾗ ἔκτισεν, κριτοῦ ‹ᾗ ἔκρινε καὶ τὰ ἄλλα. ταῦτα δὲ πάντα φανερά, ᾧ ἂν ὁ υἱὸς› ἀποκαλύψῃ, οὐχ ἑτέρως ὄντι υἱῷ θεοῦ. ‹τοιγαροῦν› ὃς λαβὼν ἐξουσίαν τέκνον γενέσθαι ὅτε μὲν ἔχει οὐκ ἔγνω, οὐκ ἔχει τὸν πατέρα. ὅτε δὲ γίνεται ἀποκαλύψαντος Ἰησοῦ ὡς ἀδελφῷ γνώσεται.[dcccxxii]

Τὸ *πάντα* εἰπὼν ἔδειξεν ὅτι οὐ μόνον Ἰουδαίων, ἀλλὰ καὶ πάντων τῶν ἐθνῶν ἐχρημάτισε Θεός. Ὅταν δὲ λέγῃ τὸ *παρεδόθη*, οὐ δεῖ ἀνθρώπινόν τι νοεῖν ἀλλ' οἰκονομικῶς ὡς ἄνθρωπος λέγεται λαβεῖν *πάντα*, ὡς Θεὸς δεσπόζων πάντων. Ἐπειδὴ δὲ ἔδειξεν ὅ | **91v** τι πάντων ἐστὶ δεσπότης, δείκνυσι καὶ ἕτερον μεῖζον, τὸ εἰδέναι τὸν πατέρα καὶ τῆς αὐτῆς οὐσίας εἶναι. Καὶ γὰρ τοῦτο λανθανόντως δείκνυσιν ἐκ τοῦ μόνος αὐτὸν οὗτος εἰδέναι. Ὅταν γὰρ εἴπῃ ὅτι *οὐδεὶς γινώσκει τὸν πατέρα εἰ μὴ ὁ υἱός*, οὐ τοῦτό φησι ὅτι πάντες αὐτὸν ἠγνόησαν, ἀλλ' ὅτι τὴν γνῶσιν ἣν αὐτὸς αὐτὸν οἶδεν οὐδεὶς αὐτῶν ἐπίσταται. Οὐδὲ γὰρ περὶ ἀγνώστου Θεοῦ καὶ μηδενὶ γενομένου γνωρίμου τοῦτό φησί, ἀλλὰ τὴν ἀκριβῆ γνῶσιν ἐνταῦθα αἰνισσόμενος, ἐπεὶ οὐδὲ *τὸν υἱόν* ἴσμεν ὡς χρὴ εἰδέναι. Τὴν γὰρ ἀκριβῆ γνῶσιν ἣν ἔχει περὶ ἑαυτῆς ἡ Τριὰς *οὐδεὶς* οἶδεν. Ἐπειδὴ δὲ ἄνω ἐπὶ τοῦ Πατρὸς ἔταξε τὸ τῆς ἀποκαλύψεως, νῦν τῷ Υἱῷ αὐτὸ προσάπτει, ἵνα γνῶμεν ὅτι κοινὰ τὰ τῆς θεότητος. Διὰ γὰρ τούτου καὶ τοῦ ἀκαταλήπτου[dcccxxiii] δηλοῦνται αὐτῶν αἱ ἰσότητες. Ἕκαστος τοίνυν τῶν ἁγίων, διὰ τοῦ ἐπιγνῶναι *τὸν υἱόν* δέχεται τοῦ Πατρὸς τὴν γνῶσιν, καὶ τὸ ἀνάπαλιν.

(Τὸ *πάντα* εἰπὼν) ἔδειξεν ὅτι οὐ μόνον Ἰουδαίων, ἀλλὰ καὶ πάντων τῶν ἐθνῶν ἐχρημάτισε θεός. [ὅταν δὲ λέγῃ τὸ *παρεδόθη*, οὐ δεῖ ἀνθρώπινόν τι νοεῖν ἀλλ' οἰκονομικῶς ὡς ἄνθρωπος λέγεται λαβεῖν *πάντα*, ὡς θεὸς δεσπόζων πάντων. ἐπειδὴ δὲ ἔδειξεν ὅτι πάντων ἐστὶ δεσπότης, δείκνυσι καὶ ἕτερον μεῖζον, τὸ εἰδέναι τὸν πατέρα καὶ τῆς αὐτῆς οὐσίας εἶναι. καὶ γὰρ τοῦτο λανθανόντως δείκνυσιν ἐκ τοῦ μόνος αὐτὸν οὗτος εἰδέναι. ὅταν γὰρ εἴπῃ ὅτι *οὐδεὶς γινώσκει τὸν πατέρα εἰ μὴ ὁ υἱός*, οὐ τοῦτό φησι ὅτι πάντες αὐτὸν ἠγνόησαν, ἀλλ' ὅτι τὴν γνῶσιν ἣν αὐτὸς αὐτὸν οἶδεν οὐδεὶς αὐτῶν ἐπίσταται. οὐδὲ γὰρ περὶ ἀγνώστου Θεοῦ καὶ μηδενὶ γνωρίμου τοῦτό φησίν, ἀλλὰ τὴν ἀκριβῆ γνῶσιν ἐνταῦθα αἰνισσόμενος, ἐπεὶ οὐδὲ *τὸν υἱόν* ἴσμεν ὡς χρὴ εἰδέναι. τὴν γὰρ ἀκριβῆ γνῶσιν ἣν ἔχει περὶ ἑαυτῆς ἡ τριάς, *οὐδεὶς* οἶδεν. ἐπειδὴ δὲ ἄνω ἐπὶ τοῦ πατρὸς ἔταξε τὸ τῆς ἀποκαλύψεως, νῦν τῷ υἱῷ αὐτὸ προσάπτει, ἵνα γνῶμεν ὅτι κοινὰ τὰ τῆς θεότητος. διὰ γὰρ τούτου καὶ τοῦ ἀκαταλήπτου δηλοῦνται αὐτῶν αἱ ἰσότητες. ἕκαστος τοίνυν τῶν ἁγίων, διὰ τοῦ ἐπιγνῶναι *τὸν υἱόν* δέχεται τοῦ πατρὸς τὴν γνῶσιν, καὶ τὸ ἀνάπαλιν.][dcccxxiv]

> Καὶ τί θαυμαστόν, φησίν, εἰ πάντων εἰμὶ Δεσπότης, ὅπου γε καὶ ἕτερόν τι μεῖζον ἔχω, τὸ εἰδέναι τὸν Πατέρα, καὶ τῆς αὐτῆς οὐσίας εἶναι;[dcccxxv]

Καὶ ᾧ ἐὰν βούληται ὁ υἱός ἀποκαλύψαι.[1009] Ὁ ὁρῶν τὸν Υἱὸν τὴν τοῦ Πατρὸς εἰκόνα[1010] ἔχοντα ἐν ἑαυτῷ αὐτὸν ὁρᾷ τὸν Πατέρα. Ἀποκαλύπτει δὲ τὸν Πατέρα ὡς ἐν πρωτοτύπῳ αὐτὸς τῷ Πατρὶ φαινόμενος, ὑποφαίνων δὲ αὖ πάλιν ἐν ἰδίᾳ μορφῇ τὸ ἀρχέτυπον. Ταῦτα δὲ θεοπρεπῶς[dcccxxvi] νοητέον. Ἐπειδὴ δὲ εἶπε *πάντα μοι παρεδόθη*, ἵνα μὴ δόξῃ ἑτέρας φυλῆς εἶναι καὶ παρὰ τὸν Πατέρα ἥττων, ἐπήγαγε τοῦτο, ἵνα δείξῃ τὴν ἑαυτοῦ φύσιν ἀπόρρητον καὶ ἀκατάληπτον οὖσαν ὡς τὴν τοῦ Πατρός. Μόνη γὰρ ἡ θεία φύσις τῆς Τριάδος ἑαυτὴν ἐπιγινώσκει. Μόνος ὁ Πατὴρ οἶδε τὸν Υἱὸν τὸν ἴδιον, τὸν τῆς ἑαυτοῦ φύσεως καρπόν. Μόνον τὸ θεῖον γέν | **92r** νημα ἐπιγινώσκει τὸν ἐξ οὗ ἐτέχθη. Μόνον τὸ Ἅγιον *Πνεῦμα* οἶδε *τὰ βάθη τοῦ Θεοῦ*,[1011] ὅ ἐστι, τὰς ἐννοίας τοῦ Πατρὸς καὶ τοῦ Υἱοῦ.[dcccxxvii]

> Ὁ ὁρῶν τὸν υἱὸν τὴν τοῦ πατρὸς εἰκόνα ἔχοντα ἐν ἑαυτῷ αὐτὸν ὁρᾷ τὸν πατέρα. ἀποκαλύπτει δὲ τὸν πατέρα ὡς ἐν πρωτοτύπῳ αὐτὸς τῷ πατρὶ φαινόμενος, ὑποφαίνων δὲ ἂν πάλιν ἐν ἰδίᾳ μορφῇ τὸ ἀρχέτυπον. ταῦτα δὲ θεοπρεπῶς νοητέον. ἐπειδὴ δὲ εἶπε *πάντα μοι παρεδόθη*, ἵνα μὴ δόξῃ ἑτέρας φυλῆς εἶναι καὶ παρὰ τὸν πατέρα ἥττων, ἐπήγαγε τοῦτο, ἵνα δείξῃ τὴν ἑαυτοῦ φύσιν ἀπόρρητον καὶ ἀκατάληπτον οὖσαν ὡς τὴν τοῦ πατρός. μόνη γὰρ ἡ θεία φύσις τῆς τριάδος ἑαυτὴν ἐπιγινώσκει. μόνος ὁ πατὴρ οἶδεν τὸν υἱὸν τὸν ἴδιον τὸν τῆς ἑαυτοῦ φύσεως καρπόν, μόνον τὸ θεῖον γέννημα ἐπιγινώσκει τὸν ἐξ οὗ ἐτέχθη μόνον τὸ ἅγιον πνεῦμα οἶδεν *τὰ βάθη τοῦ θεοῦ*, ὅ ἐστι τὰς ἐννοίας τοῦ πατρὸς καὶ τοῦ υἱοῦ.[dcccxxviii]

> Let Eunomius blush, who presumes to have himself as much knowledge of the Father and the Son as they have among themselves. However, if he becomes combative and consoles his insanity by the following words: "And him to whom the Son will to reveal", [he should realise that] it is one thing to know what he knows by the equality of nature, but it is something else to know by the status of one who reveals.[dcccxxix]

Δεῦτε πρός με πάντες.[1012] Τὸ *δεῦτε*, οὐχ ὡς δεόμενος τῆς δόξης αὐτῶν φησι, ἀλλὰ δεόμενος αὐτῶν τῆς σωτηρίας.
Πάντας δὲ προσκαλεῖται. Οὐ γὰρ ὡς ὁ νόμος μόνους καλεῖ τοὺς ἐξ Ἰσραήλ, ἀλλ᾽ ὡς πάντων Κύριος. Πάντας κοπιῶντας δέ φησι ἤτοι τοὺς Ἰουδαίους τοὺς μὴ ἰσχύσαντας βαστάσαι τὸν νομικὸν *ζυγόν*,[1013] ἢ τοὺς τὸ ἄχθος τῶν ἁμαρτιῶν φέροντας. Πεφορτισμένους δέ, τοὺς εἰδωλολάτρας, τοὺς πλήθει τῶν ἁμαρτιῶν καταπεφορτισμένους ὑπὸ τοῦ διαβόλου.

1009 Matt. 11:27.
1010 Cf. 2 Cor. 4:4; Col. 1:15.
1011 1 Cor. 2:10.
1012 Matt. 11:28.
1013 Matt. 11:29.

> *πάντας* δὲ καλεῖ καὶ οὐ μόνους τοὺς ἐξ Ἰσραὴλ ὡς πάντων δημιουργὸς καὶ κύριος *καὶ κοπιῶντας* μὲν λέγει τοὺς Ἰουδαίους τοὺς μὴ ἰσχύοντας βαστάσαι τὸν νομικὸν ζυγόν, πεφορτισμένους τοὺς εἰδωλολάτρας τοὺς διὰ τοῦ διαβόλου καταφορτισθέντας καὶ τῷ πλήθει τῶν ἁμαρτιῶν καταβαρυνομένους.[dcccxxx]

Ζυγὸν δὲ ἑαυτοῦ, τὸν ἐνάρετον βίον λέγει, δι᾽ οὗ πρὸς μίμησιν τῆς ἑαυτοῦ πραότητος καὶ ταπεινοφροσύνης ἐνάγει.

> Κοπιῶντας λέγει τοὺς τὸ ἄχθος τῶν ἁμαρτημάτων ἔχοντας ἐν τῇ ψυχῇ.[dcccxxxi] ζυγὸν δέ, τὸν ἐνάρετον λέγει βίον, δι᾽ οὗ τις μιμεῖται Χριστόν, ἐν πραότητι καὶ ταπεινοφροσύνῃ.[dcccxxxii]

Ὡς ἡνίοχος τοίνυν διδάσκει ἡμᾶς τὸν ἑαυτοῦ *ζυγὸν* ὑπεισελθεῖν, ἵνα ἐπιβῇ ἐφ᾽ ἡμᾶς καὶ μάθωμεν τῇ πείρᾳ τὴν πραότητα. Βέλτιον οὖν Ἰουδαίῳ μὲν εἶναι ὑπὸ τὸν τοῦ Χριστοῦ *ζυγὸν* ἢ τὸν τοῦ νόμου. Ὁμοίως καὶ Ἕλληνι βέλτιον εἶναι ὑπὸ τὸν πρᾶον τοῦ Χριστοῦ ζυγὸν ἢ ὑπὸ τὸν διαβολικὸν ζυγόν.

Ὁ γὰρ ζυγός μου χρηστός.[1014][dcccxxxiii] Χρηστός ἐστιν διὰ τὴν συγχώρησιν, ἣν ὁ νόμος οὐ δίδωσιν· ἐλαφρὸς δέ, ὅτι οὐκ ἔχει τὰς σωματικὰς τοῦ νόμου παρατηρήσεις. Εἰ γὰρ καὶ *στενὴ ἡ ὁδὸς*[1015] τοῖς ῥαθύμοις, ἀλλὰ τοῖς σπουδαίοις ἐλαφρά. Καὶ εἰ πρὸς ὀλίγον ἔχει σωματικὸν πόνον, διὰ γοῦν τὴν ἐλπίδα τῆς ἀναπαύσεως ἐλαφρῶς τις φέρει τὰ ἐπιτάγματα τοῦ Χριστοῦ, αὐτοῦ ποιοῦντος αὐτὰ ἐλαφρά.

Χρηστὸς ὁ ζυγός, ἐπεὶ μὴ ἔστι κολαστὴς ὡς ὁ νόμος· *ἐλαφρὸν* δὲ *τὸ φορτίον*, ἐπειδὴ καὶ ἐν ἁπλοῖς ἐγχειρήμασι καὶ εὐκόλοις ὁ τῆς | **92v** μετανοίας ὑπογραμμός.

> *Χρηστὸς ὁ ζυγός*, ἐπεὶ μὴ ἔστι κολαστὴς ὡς ὁ νόμος. *ἐλαφρὸν* δὲ *τὸ φορτίον*, ἐπειδὴ καὶ ἐν ἁπλοῖς ἐπιχειρήμασι καὶ εὐκόλοις ὁ τῆς μετανοίας ὑπογραμμός.[dcccxxxiv]

> *Χρηστὸς ὁ ζυγός*, ἐπεὶ μὴ ἔστι κολαστὴς ὡς ὁ νόμος. *ἐλαφρὸν* δὲ *τὸ φορτίον*, ἐπειδὴ καὶ ἐν ἁπλοῖς ἐγχειρήμασι καὶ εὐκόλοις ὁ τῆς μετανοίας ὑπογραμμός.[dcccxxxv]

33

(ΩΡΙΓΕΝΟΥΣ) Ἐλαφρὸς ὁ ὑπὲρ εὐσεβείας ἀγὼν μεγίστην ἔχων ἀντίληψιν.

> Κόπος καὶ μέγιστον *φορτίον*[1016] ἡ ἁμαρτία, ὅτι παρὰ φύσιν. ἐλαφρὸς ὁ ὑπὲρ εὐσεβείας ἀγών, μεγίστην ἔχων ἀντίληψιν.[dcccxxxvi]

> (Ὠριγένους) Κόπος καὶ μέγιστον *φορτίον* ἡ ἁμαρτία, ὅτι παρὰ φύσιν. ἐλαφρὸς ὁ ὑπὲρ εὐσεβείας ἀγών, μεγίστην ἔχων ἀντίληψιν.[dcccxxxvii]

1014 Matt. 11:30.
1015 Matt. 7:14.
1016 Matt. 11:28-30.

[Εἰδὼς ὁ δεσπότης Χριστὸς ὡς προγνώστης, τὸ τί ἔμελλον ποιεῖν *οἱ μαθηταί*, τούτου χάριν ἤγαγεν αὐτοὺς *διὰ τῶν σπορίμων*.[1017] καὶ ἐπειδὴ ἐβούλετο λυθῆναι τὸ σάββατον, δι' αἰτίας τοῦτο ποιεῖ. καὶ οὐδέποτε χωρὶς αἰτίας αὐτὸ λύει, ἀλλὰ διδοὺς προφάσεις εὐλόγους, ἵνα καὶ τὸν νόμον ἀναπαύσῃ, καὶ τοὺς Ἰουδαίους μὴ πλήξῃ, εἴγε συνιέναι ἤθελον. ὃ δὴ καὶ ἐνταῦθα κατασκευάζει, τὴν τῆς φύσεως ἀνάγκην προβαλλόμενος, τὴν πεῖναν. χρὴ δὲ θαυμάζειν καὶ τῶν μαθητῶν τὴν ὑπομονήν, μηδένα τῶν σωματικῶν ποιουμένους λόγον, ἀλλὰ πάρεργον τιθεμένους τὴν τῆς σαρκὸς τράπεζαν καὶ λιμῷ μαχομένους διηνεκεῖ, καὶ οὐδὲ οὕτως ἀφισταμένους. εἰ μὴ γὰρ ἠνάγκαζεν αὐτοὺς σφόδρα τὸ πεινᾷν, ‹οὐκ ἂν› οὐδὲ τοῦτο ἐποίουν. διατί; ὅτε μὲν ἔτιλλον τοὺς *στάχυας* οἱ ἀπόστολοι, οὐ πάνυ σφοδρῶς οἱ Φαρισαῖοι παρωξύνθησαν. καίτοι μᾶλλον πρὸς τὴν γνώμην αὐτῶν τὴν σκληρὰν ἀκόλουθον ἦν. ὅτε δὲ τὴν *χεῖρα* τὴν *ξηρὰν*[1018] ἰάσατο, τότε οὕτως ἐξεθηριώθησαν, ὥστε καὶ ἐπὶ σφαγῆς αὐτοὺς βουλεύεσθαι καὶ ἀναιρέσεως.[1019] ἐπειδὴ ἐκεῖ μὲν οὐδὲν γέγονε μέγα καὶ γενναῖον, καὶ διὰ τοῦτο σφοδρῶς ἐταράχθησαν. ἐνταῦθα δὲ ἐπειδὴ εἶδόν τινας διὰ τὸ θαῦμα σωζομένους, διὰ τοῦτο ἀγριαίνονται καὶ ταράττονται. παράγει δὲ τὸν *Δαβὶδ* εἰς τὸ μέσον, ἐπειδὴ πολλὴ τοῦ προφήτου ἦν ἡ δόξα. *Λέγω δὲ ὑμῖν ὅτι τοῦ ἱεροῦ μείζων ἐστὶν ὧδε.*][dcccxxxviii]

Εἰ ὑπὲρ τὴν ἐντολὴν ἐδείκνυτο τὸ ἱερόν, ἆρα ὑπὲρ τὸν νόμον ἦν ὁ Χριστός.[dcccxxxix]

(Ὠριγένους.) Εἰδὼς ὁ δεσπότης Χριστὸς ὡς προγνώστης, τὸ τί ἔμελλον ποιεῖν οἱ μαθηταί, τούτου χάριν ἤγαγεν αὐτοὺς διὰ τῶν σπορίμων, καὶ ἐπειδὴ ἐβούλετο λυθῆναι τὸ σάββατον, δι' αἰτίας τοῦτο ποιεῖ. καὶ οὐδέποτε χωρὶς αἰτίας αὐτὸ λύει, ἀλλὰ διδοὺς προφάσεις εὐλόγους, ἵνα καὶ τὸν νόμον ἀναπαύσῃ, καὶ τοὺς Ἰουδαίους μὴ πλήξῃ, εἴγε συνιέναι ἤθελον. ὃ δὴ καὶ ἐνταῦθα κατασκευάζει, τὴν τῆς φύσεως ἀνάγκην προβαλλόμενος τὴν πεῖναν. χρὴ δὲ θαυμάζειν καὶ τῶν μαθητῶν τὴν ὑπομονήν, μηδένα τῶν σωματικῶν ποιουμένους λόγον, ἀλλὰ πάρεργον τιθεμένους τὴν τῆς σαρκὸς τράπεζαν, καὶ λιμῷ μαχομένους διηνεκεῖ, καὶ οὐδὲ οὕτως ἀφισταμένους. εἰ μὴ γὰρ ἠνάγκαζεν αὐτοὺς σφόδρα τὸ πεινᾷν, οὐδὲ τοῦτο ἐποίουν. διατί ὅτε μὲν ἔτιλλον τοὺς στάχυας οἱ Ἀπόστολοι, οὐ πάνυ σφοδρῶς οἱ Φαρισαῖοι ἐπαρωξύνθησαν. καίτοι μᾶλλον πρὸς τὴν γνώμην αὐτῶν τὴν σκληρὰν ἀκόλουθον ἦν. ὅτε δὲ τὴν χεῖρα τὴν ξηρὰν ἰάσατο, τότε οὕτως ἐξεθηριώθησαν, ὥστε καὶ ἐπὶ σφαγῆς αὐτοὺς βουλεύεσθαι καὶ ἀναιρέσεως; ἐπειδὴ ἐκεῖ μὲν οὐδὲν γέγονε μέγα καὶ γενναῖον, καὶ διὰ τοῦτο σφοδρῶς ἐταράχθησαν. ἐνταῦθα δὲ ἐπειδὴ εἶδον τινὰς διὰ τὸ θαῦμα σωζομένους, διὰ τοῦτο ἀγριαίνονται καὶ ταράττονται. παράγει δὲ τὸν Δαβὶδ εἰς τὸ μέσον, ἐπειδὴ πολλὴ τοῦ προφήτου ἦν ἡ δόξα. *Λέγω δὲ ὑμῖν ὅτι τοῦ ἱεροῦ μείζων ἐστὶν ὧδε.*[dcccxl]

(Ὠριγένους.) Εἰ ὑπὲρ τὴν ἐντολὴν ἐδείκνυτο τὸ ἱερόν, ἆρα ὑπὲρ τὸν νόμον ἦν ὁ Χριστός.[dcccxli]

Ἐπορεύθη ὁ Ἰησοῦς τοῖς σάββασι διὰ τῶν σπορίμων.[1020] Λύων τὰς νομικὰς παρατηρήσεις ἤγαγε τοὺς μαθητὰς ἐν σαββάτῳ *διὰ τῶν σπορίμων* ἵνα τίλαντες φάγωσι καὶ λύσωσιν ἐν τούτῳ τὸ σάββατον. Συνόντες γὰρ τῷ Χριστῷ, ὅς ἐστιν *ἡ ἀλήθεια*,[1021] πεινῶντες

1017 Matt. 12:1-3.
1018 Matt. 12:10.
1019 Matt. 12:14.
1020 Matt. 12:1.
1021 John, 14:6.

τῶν σαββατικῶν κατεφρόνησαν τύπων καὶ ἤσθιον ἁπλῆν τροφὴν διὰ τὴν τῆς φύσεως ἀνάγκην. Τί οὖν οἱ Φαρισαῖοι ὡς ἀδίκημα μέγα ποιησάντων τῶν μαθητῶν κατηγοροῦσιν αὐτῶν ὡς παραβαινόντων τὸν νόμον; Τί οὖν ὁ Σωτήρ, ἵνα μὴ δόξῃ ἀντίθεος εἶναι λύων τὰ παλαιὰ ἐκ παλαιᾶς ἱστορίας, τὰ ὅμοια συμβάντα παρήγαγεν; Ἐπεισάγει γὰρ τὸν *Δαυὶδ* τὰ ὅμοια ποιήσαντα[1022] διὰ τὸ ἐπίδοξον τοῦ ἀνδρὸς δυσωπῶν τοὺς κατηγόρους. Εἰ τοίνυν τὸν *Δαυὶδ* οὐ κατεκρίνατε διὰ τὴν φυσικὴν ἀνάγκην τὰ ὅμοια ποιήσαντα, οὐδὲ τοὺς μαθητὰς ὀφείλετε κατακρίνειν. Εἶτα καὶ ἕτερον κυριώτερον τούτου ἐπάγει, λέγων τὸ ὑπὸ τῶν ἱερέων γινόμενον (καὶ τὸ δὴ μεῖζον) τὸ μηδὲ ἔγκλημα εἶναι· *ἀναίτιοι* γάρ φησι *εἰσίν*.[1023] Εἰ οὖν οἱ ἐπίδοξοι ἱερεῖς λύουσι *τὸ σάββατον* οὐκ ἐν οἱῳδήποτε τόπῳ, ἀλλ᾽ *ἐν τῷ ἱερῷ*, καὶ οὐδὲ δι᾽ ἀνάγκην φύσεως ἀλλὰ νομικῇ ἐξουσίᾳ, καὶ *ἀναίτιοί εἰσι*, πολλῷ μᾶλλον οὗτοι. *Βεβηλοῦσι* δὲ εἶπε καὶ οὐ λύουσι, ὅπερ ἐστὶ φορτικώτερον.

(ΩΡΙΓΕΝΟΥΣ, added on the margin) Ἐν γὰρ τῷ σαββάτῳ παντὸς ἔργου χειροκμήτου κεκλυμένου, αὐτοὶ ἐν τῷ ἱερῷ ἐξυλοκόπουν, καὶ πῦρ ἧπτον καὶ ἐκρεανόμουν.

(ΩΡΙΓΕΝΟΥΣ, text cont.) *Λέγω δὲ ὑμῖν ὅτι τοῦ ἱεροῦ μεῖζον ἐστὶν ὧδε*.[1024] Εἰ λέγοι τις ὅτι οὐκ εἰσὶν ἱερεῖς οἱ μαθηταί, *λέγω ὑμῖν ὅτι τοῦ ἱεροῦ μεῖζόν ἐστιν ὧδε*.[1025] Μεί | **93r** ζων γὰρ τοῦ ναοῦ ὁ Κύριος τοῦ ναοῦ. Εἶτα καὶ ἐκ προφητικῆς ῥήσεως ἐλευθεροῖ τοῦ ἐγκλήματος τοὺς μαθητὰς καὶ ἐλέγχει αὐτοὺς *μὴ* εἰδότας *τὰς γραφάς*. *Εἰ γὰρ ἔγνωτε*, φησί, *τί ἐστιν ἔλεον θέλω καὶ οὐ θυσίαν*,[1026] *οὐκ ἂν κατεδικάσατε τοὺς ἀναιτίους*.[1027] Εἰ γὰρ διὰ θυσίαν λύετε τὸ σάββατον, ἡ δὲ φιλανθρωπία μείζων ἐστὶ τῆς θυσίας παρὰ Θεῷ, δότε τοῖς φαγοῦσι διὰ τὴν ἀνάγκην συγγνώμην.
Εἶτα δείκνυσιν ὅτι καὶ *κύριος ἐστὶν ὁ υἱὸς τοῦ ἀνθρώπου καὶ τοῦ σαββάτου*,[1028] περὶ ἑαυτοῦ τοῦτο λέγων ἢ περὶ τῆς κοινῆς φύσεως, ἐπειδὴ διὰ τὸν ἄνθρωπον τὸ σάββατον συνέστη καὶ πᾶσα ἡμέρα.

> Εἰ *κύριός* ἐστι *τοῦ σαββάτου ὁ υἱὸς τοῦ ἀνθρώπου* ἑαυτὸν λέγων καὶ βασιλεύς, ἔξεστι τῷ βασιλεῖ, πότε μὲν περὶ σαββάτου νομοθετεῖν, πότε δὲ καὶ παύειν τὸ σάββατον μετὰ τῶν θυσιῶν καὶ ὁλοκαυτωμάτων καὶ τῆς λοιπῆς λειτουργίας τοῦ ἱεροῦ, καινὴν διαθήκην νομοθετοῦντι. [διὰ τοῦ παραδείγματος τούτου συλλογιζόμενος αὐτούς, ὅπως μὴ ἔχωσι πρόφασιν ἀναισχυντίας, εἰς τὸ πάλιν ἐγκαλεῖν αὐτῷ διὰ τὴν θεραπείαν. καὶ τότε εἰπὼν τῷ ἀνθρώπῳ *ἔκτεινον τὴν χεῖρά σου*, καὶ *ἐξέτεινε*, καὶ *ἀπεκατεστάθη* ἡ χεὶρ αὐτοῦ *ὑγιὴς ὡς ἡ ἄλλη*. ἐκεῖνοι δὲ οὐδὲ ἀδικηθέντες ἐξέρχονται καὶ βουλεύονται ἵνα *ἀνέλωσιν αὐτόν*. τοσοῦτον ἡ βασκανία κακόν. ὁ δὲ ἥμερος καὶ πρᾶος *ἀνεχώρησε* ταῦτα μαθών. *ἠκολούθησαν* δὲ αὐτῷ *ὄχλοι πολλοί*, διατί; θαυμάζοντες αὐτόν, ἐκεῖνοι δὲ τῆς πονηρᾶς οὐκ ἀφίσταντο γνώμης.][dcccxlii]

1022 Matt. 12:3; cf. 1 Kings, 21:1-6.
1023 Matt. 12:5.
1024 Matt. 12:6.
1025 Matt. 12:6.
1026 Hosea, 6:6, quoted in Matt. 9:13.
1027 Matt. 9:13.
1028 Matt. 12:8.

> (᾿Ωριγένους) Εἰ Κύριός ἐστι τοῦ σαββάτου ὁ υἱὸς τοῦ ἀνθρώπου ἑαυτὸν λέγων καὶ βασιλεύς, ἔξεστι τῷ βασιλεῖ, πότε μὲν περὶ σαββάτου νομοθετεῖν, πότε δὲ καὶ παύειν τὸ σάββατον μετὰ τῶν θυσιῶν καὶ ὁλοκαυτωμάτων, καὶ τῆς λοιπῆς λειτουργίας τοῦ ἱεροῦ, καινὴν διαθήκην νομοθετῶν. διὰ τοῦ παραδείγματος τούτου συλλογιζόμενος αὐτούς, ὅπως μὴ ἔχωσι πρόφασιν ἀναισχυντίας, εἰς τὸ πάλιν ἐγκαλεῖν αὐτῶν διὰ τὴν θεραπείαν. καὶ τότε εἰπὼν τῷ ἀνθρώπῳ *ἔκτεινον τὴν χεῖρά σου, καὶ ἐξέτεινε, καὶ ἀπεκατεστάθη ἡ χεὶρ αὐτοῦ ὑγιὴς ὡς ἡ ἄλλη*. ἐκεῖνοι δὲ οὐδὲ ἀδικηθέντες ἐξέρχονται, καὶ βουλεύονται ἵνα ἀνέλωσιν αὐτόν. τοσοῦτον ἡ βασκανία κακόν. ὁ δὲ ἥμερος καὶ πρᾶος ἀνεχώρησε ταῦτα μαθών. ἠκολούθησαν δὲ αὐτῷ ὄχλοι πολλοί, διατί; θαυμάζοντες αὐτόν, ἐκεῖνοι δὲ τῆς πονηρᾶς οὐκ ἀφίσταντο γνώμης.[dccc xliii]

Καὶ ἐπηρώτησαν αὐτὸν λέγοντες, εἰ ἔξεστι τοῖς σάββασι θεραπεύειν;[1029] ᾿Ηρώτων αὐτὸν οὐχ ἵνα μάθωσιν, ἀλλ᾿ ἵνα σχῶσι κατ᾿ αὐτοῦ κατηγορίας ἀφορμήν. ῞Ινα γὰρ εἴπῃ ὅτι *ἔξεστι τοῖς σάββασι θεραπεύειν* καὶ μῖσος κατ᾿ αὐτοῦ ἐμποιήσωσι τοῖς πολλοῖς ἠρώτων αὐτὸν περὶ τούτου. Τί οὖν πρὸς τοῦτο φησι ὁ Σωτήρ; Διὰ συλλογισμοῦ δείκνυσι τούτους οὐ διὰ φιλανθρωπίαν, ἀλλὰ διὰ φιλοχρηματίαν λύοντας τὸ σάββατον. Εἰ γὰρ οὐ δεῖ φησι ἀπολέσθαι *πρόβατον* ἐμπεσὸν *εἰς βόθυνον*[1030] ἐν σαββάτῳ, διὰ τὴν τοῦ σαββάτου ἀργίαν δεῖ καὶ τοὺς ἀνθρώπους οἰκτείρειν ὑπὲρ τὰ ἄλογα καὶ ἐν σαββάτῳ. Συνελαύνει γὰρ αὐτοὺς ἢ καταγνωσθῆναι ὡς παρανόμους τοῦ νόμου κατηγοροῦντας ἢ δειχθῆναι ὠμοὺς καὶ ἀφιλοικτίρμονας καὶ διαφθονουμένους τῆς εἰς ἀνθρώπους σωτηρίας. Παράδοξον γάρ φησι, εἰ προβάτου φειδόμενοι τῆς τῶν ἀνθρώπων ὑπεροράτε σωτηρίας. Εἶτα ἐπάγει τὸ συμπέρασμα. Εἰ γὰρ ὁ Θεὸς διὰ τοῦτο ἔδωκε |
93v τὸν νόμον, φησί, ἵνα ἀγαθοεργῆτε (ὡς ἀγάπης εἰσηγητής), ἀπὸ τοῦ σκοποῦ τοῦ νόμου δῆλόν ἐστιν ὅτι *ἔξεστιν* ἀγαθοποιεῖν ἐν *σαββάτῳ*. Ταῦτα ἔλεγε, καὶ λόγῳ τὴν θεραπείαν ὡς Θεὸς τῷ κάμνοντι ἐδωρήσατο.

Τότε λέγει τῷ ἀνθρώπῳ τῷ ξηρὰ‹ν›[1031] ἔχοντι *τὴν χεῖρα*.[1032] Καὶ τοῦτον *αὐτῷ προσήνεγκαν*,[1033] δυνάμει κωλύοντες αὐτὸν θεραπευθῆναι, ἢ ὡς τοῦ Σωτῆρος ὑποστελλομένου διὰ τὸ σάββατον θεραπεῦσαι αὐτὸν καὶ ἀπιστῆσαι ποιήσωσί τινας, ὡς μὴ δυνηθέντος αὐτὸν *θεραπεῦσαι*, ἤ, εἰ ἐθεράπευσεν, ἵνα αὐτοῦ *κατηγορήσωσιν*.[1034] Εἰδὼς οὖν ὁ ᾿Ιησοῦς *αὐτῶν τὰς ἐνθυμήσεις*[1035] (αὐτὸς γὰρ μόνος ᾔδει τὰ ἐν τῷ ἀνθρώπῳ), λέγει *αὐτοῖς* τὸ περὶ τῶν ἄλλων ζῴων πρόβλημα.

> Τὸ θαυμαστὸν δὲ τοῦ σωτῆρος ἐδείκνυτο, ὅτι τὸ ἀπηγορευμένον καὶ νεκρὸν ἐζῳοποίησε. καὶ πάλιν *αὐτῷ προσήνεγκαν* δυνάμει κωλύοντες αὐτὸν *θεραπεῦσαι* αὐτόν, ἵνα ἀπιστῆσαι ποιήσωσι τινάς, ὡς μὴ δυνηθέντος αὐτὸν θεραπεῦσαι. ἤ, εἰ ἐθεράπευσεν, ἵνα

1029 Matt. 12:10.
1030 Matt. 12:11.
1031 Cod. ἐξηρα.
1032 Matt. 12:10-13; Mark, 3:1-5; Luke, 6:6-10.
1033 Matt. 12:22 (variant in certain codices).
1034 Matt. 12:10.
1035 Matt. 12:25; cf. Matt. 9:4; Luke, 6:8.

> αὐτοῦ *κατηγορήσωσιν*. εἰδὼς δὲ ὁ Ἰησοῦς *αὐτῶν τὰς ἐνθυμήσεις* λέγει *αὐτοῖς* τὸ περὶ τῶν ἄλλων ζῴων πρόβλημα.[dcccxliv]

Καὶ σὺ τοίνυν ἐὰν ἔχῃς τὴν *χεῖρα ξηράν*, ἀκούσας παρὰ τοῦ Σωτῆρος, *ἔκτεινον τὴν χεῖρα σου* ἐπὶ ἔργοις ἀγαθοῖς ἐνεργοῦντος τοῦ Ἰησοῦ, καὶ ἀποκατασταθήσεται *ὑγιὴς ὡς ἡ ἄλλη*.[1036]

> Καὶ σὺ ἄνθρωπε, ἐὰν ἔχῃς χεῖρα ξηράν, ἀκούσας παρὰ τοῦ Σωτῆρος, *ἔκτεινον τὴν χεῖρα σου* ἐπὶ ἔργοις ἀγαθοῖς, ἐνεργοῦντος τοῦ Ἰησοῦ, ἀποκατασταθήσεται ὑγιὴς ὡς ἡ ἄλλη.[dcccxlv]

Τὸ γὰρ *ξηρὰν* ἔχειν *χεῖρα* τὴν ἀκαρπίαν ἔδειξε, τὸ δὲ ξηρὸν ἐγγὺς ἐκριζώσεως.

> τὸ γὰρ *ξηρὰν* ἔχειν τὴν *χεῖρα* τὴν ἀκαρπίαν ἔδειξε.[dcccxlvi]

Καὶ μεταβὰς ἐκεῖθεν, ἦλθεν εἰς τὴν συναγωγήν.[1037] Ὅτε διατίθησι διαθήκην καινὴν καὶ τὸ σάββατον δυνάμει παύει, τότε μεταβαίνει ὅθεν αὐτοῦ καὶ τῶν μαθητῶν κατηγοροῦσιν, οὐκ ἔξω, ἀλλ' *εἰς τὴν συναγωγήν*, ἵνα τελείως αὐτῶν πληρωθῶσιν αἱ ἁμαρτίαι. Τὴν ἀκαρπίαν δὲ τῶν χειρῶν προσήνεγκαν τῷ Σωτῆρι. Τὸ γὰρ *ξηρὰν* ἔχειν τὴν *χεῖρα* τὴν ἀκαρπίαν ἔδειξε.

> Τὸ *μεταβὰς ἐκεῖθεν* τοῦτο δηλοῖ. ὅτε διατίθησι διαθήκην καινὴν καὶ τὸ σάββατον δυνάμει παύει, τότε μεταβαίνει, ὅθεν αὐτοῦ καὶ τῶν μαθητῶν κατηγοροῦσιν, οὐκ ἔξω ἀλλ' *εἰς τὴν συναγωγήν*, ἵνα τελείως αὐτῶν πληρωθῶσιν αἱ ἁμαρτίαι. τὴν ἀκαρπίαν δὲ τῶν χειρῶν προσήνεγκαν τῷ σωτῆρι. τὸ γὰρ *ξηρὰν* ἔχειν τὴν *χεῖρα* τὴν ἀκαρπίαν ἔδειξε. τὸ δὲ ξηρὸν ἐγγὺς ἐκριζώσεώς ἐστιν.[dcccxlvii]

Ἐξελθόντες δὲ οἱ Φαρισαῖοι, συμβούλιον.[1038] Ὅσῳ τις ἐγγίζει τῷ Ἰησοῦ *συμβούλιον* οὐ λαμβάνει. Οὐ γὰρ ἐγγίζει τῷ Ἰησοῦ ὁ σύμβουλος τῶν κακῶν. Ὅτε δέ τις τοῦ Ἰησοῦ ἔρχεται ἔξω, *συμβούλιον* λαμβάνει τοῦ ἀπολέσαι | **94r** τὸν Ἰησοῦν, *τὸ φῶς*,[1039] τὴν *ὁδὸν τὴν ἀγαθήν*,[1040] τὴν *ζωήν*,[1041] τὸν *θησαυρόν*,[1042] τὸν *μαργαρίτην*,[1043] τὴν *ἀγάπην*,[1044] τὴν *εἰρήνην*.[1045] Τοῦτον ἄν τις ἀπολέσῃ, *υἱὸς ἀπωλείας*[1046] καλεῖται.

1036 Matt. 12:10-13.
1037 Matt. 12:9.
1038 Mat. 12:14.
1039 John, 8:12.
1040 Cf. 1 Kings, 12:23; 3 Kings, 8:36 (& 2 Paralipomenon, 6:27).
1041 John, 14:6.
1042 2 Cor. 4:7.
1043 Matt. 13:46.
1044 1 John, 4:8-9; 4:12; 4:16.
1045 John, 14:27; 16:33; Phil. 4:9; 1 Thess. 5:23.
1046 Cf. John 17:12; 2 Thess. 2:3.

Ὁ δὲ Ἰησοῦς γνοὺς ἀνεχώρησεν.[1047] Οὐκ ἔδει γὰρ αὐτὸν μένειν μετὰ τῶν *υἱῶν τῆς ἀπωλείας.*[1048] Ἐκεῖνοι ἀπώλεσαν, ἡμεῖς μὴ ζητήσαντες εὕρομεν. *Εὑρέθην γὰρ τοῖς ἐμὲ μὴ ζητοῦσιν, ἐμφανὴς ἐγενόμην τοῖς ἐμὲ μὴ ἐπερωτῶσιν.*[1049] Αὐτὸς γὰρ ἦλθεν ἐπὶ *τὰ πρόβατα τὰ ἀπολωλότα οἴκου Ἰσραήλ,*[1050] αὐτοὶ δὲ ἐπελάθοντο τοῦ ἰδίου ποιμένος.[1051] Καὶ ἀναχωρεῖ οὐ δεδιὼς τὴν ἐπιβουλήν, ἀλλὰ τὴν κακίαν ἀναστέλλων. Καὶ ἵνα μή τις οἰηθείῃ διὰ δειλίαν αὐτὸν ἀποκεχωρηκέναι, *πάντας ἐθεράπευσε* τὴν παναλκῆ αὐτοῦ ἐνδεικνύμενος δύναμιν. Πλὴν ὑποστέλλει μὴ δημοσιεύεσθαι, ὡς ἐπιεικὴς καὶ ἀκενόδοξος.

Ὅσῳ τις ἐγγίζει τῷ Ἰησοῦ *συμβούλιον* οὐ λαμβάνει. οὐ γὰρ ἐγγίζει τῷ Ἰησοῦ ὁ σύμβουλος τῶν κακῶν. ἀλλ' ὅτε τις τοῦ Ἰησοῦ ἔρχεται ἔξω, *συμβούλιον* λαμβάνει τοῦ ἀπολέσαι τὸν Ἰησοῦν, *τὸ φῶς*, τὴν *ὁδὸν τὴν ἀγαθήν*, τὴν *ζωήν*, τὸν *θησαυρόν*, τὸν *μαργαρίτην*, τὴν *ἀγάπην*, τὴν *εἰρήνην*. τοῦτον ἄν τις ἀπολέσῃ, *υἱὸς ἀπωλείας* καλεῖται.
ὁ δὲ Ἰησοῦς γνοὺς ἀνεχώρησεν. οὐκ ἔδει γὰρ αὐτὸν μένειν μετὰ τῶν *υἱῶν τῆς ἀπωλείας*. ἐκεῖνοι ἀπώλεσαν, ἡμεῖς μὴ ζητήσαντες εὕρομεν. *εὑρέθην* γὰρ *τοῖς ἐμὲ μὴ ζητοῦσιν. ἐμφανὴς ἐγενόμην, τοῖς ἐμὲ μὴ ἐπερωτῶσιν*. αὐτὸς γὰρ ἦλθεν ἐπὶ *τὰ πρόβατα τὰ ἀπολωλότα οἴκου Ἰσραήλ*, αὐτοὶ δὲ ἐπελάθοντο τοῦ ἰδίου ποιμένος. καὶ ἀναχωρεῖ οὐ δεδιὼς τὴν ἐπιβουλήν, ἀλλὰ τὴν κακίαν ἀναστέλλων. καὶ ἵνα μή τις οἰηθείῃ διὰ δειλίαν αὐτὸν ἀνακεχωρηκέναι, *πάντας ἐθεράπευσε* τὴν παναλκῆ αὐτοῦ ἐνδεικνύμενος δύναμιν, πλὴν ὑποστέλλει μὴ δημοσιεύεσθαι, ὡς ἐπιεικὴς καὶ ἀκενόδοξος.[dcccxlviii]

Ὅσῳ τις ἐγγίζει τῷ Ἰησοῦ συμβούλιον οὐ λαμβάνει. Οὐ γὰρ ἐγγίζει τῷ Ἰησοῦ ἡ συμβουλὴ τῶν κακῶν. Ὅτε δέ τις τοῦ Ἰησοῦ ἔρχεται ἔξω, συμβούλιον λαμβάνει τοῦ ἀπολέσαι τὸ φῶς, τὴν ὁδὸν τὴν ἀγαθήν, τὴν ζωήν, τὸν θησαυρόν, τὸν μαργαρίτην, τὴν ἀγάπην, τὴν εἰρήνην. Τοῦτον ἄν τις ἀπολέσῃ, υἱὸς ἀπωλείας καλεῖται.
Ὁ δὲ Ἰησοῦς, γνοὺς ἀπεχώρησεν. Οὐκ ἔδει γὰρ αὐτὸν μένειν μετὰ *τῶν υἱῶν τῆς ἀπωλείας*. Ἐκεῖνοι ἀπώλεσαν, ἡμεῖς, μὴ ζητήσαντες, εὕρομεν. *Εὑρέθην γάρ*, φησί, *τοῖς ἐμὲ μὴ ζητοῦσιν. ἐμφανὴς ἐγενόμην τοῖς ἐμὲ μὴ ἐπερωτῶσιν*. Αὐτὸς γὰρ ἦλθεν *ἐπὶ τὰ πρόβατα τὰ ἀπολωλότα*. αὐτοὶ δὲ ἐπελάθοντο τοῦ ἰδίου ποιμένος. Ἀναχωρεῖ, οὐ δεδιὼς τὴν ἐπιβουλήν, ἀλλὰ τὴν κακίαν ἀναστέλλων. καὶ ἵνα μή τις οἰηθῇ διὰ δειλίαν αὐτὸν ἀποκεχωρηκέναι, πάντας οὖν ἐθεράπευσε, τὴν παναλκῆ αὐτοῦ ἐνδεικνύμενος δύναμιν. Πλὴν ὑποστέλλει μὴ δημοσιεύεσθαι, ὡς ἐπιεικὴς καὶ ἀκενόδοξος.[dcccxlix]

Καὶ ἠκολούθησαν αὐτῷ ὄχλοι πολλοί.[1052] Εὑρέθησαν οἱ ἀσθενοῦντες ὁλόκληροι καὶ οἱ δοκοῦντες ὁλόκληροι ἠσθένησαν. Ἀπώλεσαν γὰρ αὐτῶν τὸν ἰατρόν. Διὸ λέγει. *ἄφετε αὐτοὺς τυφλοί εἰσιν.*[1053] Ὅθεν Ἡσαΐας ἐβόα λέγων· *οἱ τυφλοὶ ἀναβλέψατε καὶ οἱ κωφοὶ ἀκούσατε.*[1054]

1047 Matt. 12:15.
1048 Cf. Abdias, 12; John, 17:12; 2 Thess. 2:3.
1049 Is. 65:1, quoted in Rom. 10:20.
1050 Matt. 10:6; 15:24; Luke, 15:6; cf. Psalm 118:176; Jer. 27:6; Ez. 34:4-5.
1051 Cf. John, 10:11&14.
1052 Mat. 12:15 (adding ὄχλοι); cf. Matt. 4:25; 8:1; 14:13; 19:12; Luke, 9:11.
1053 Matt. 15:14.
1054 Is. 42:18.

Εὑρέθησαν οἱ ἀσθενοῦντες ὁλόκληροι καὶ οἱ δοκοῦντες ὁλόκληροι ἠσθένησαν. ἀπώλεσαν γὰρ αὐτῶν τὸν ἰατρόν. διὸ λέγει. *ἄφετε αὐτοὺς τυφλοί εἰσιν.* ὅθεν Ἡσαΐας ἐβόα λέγων. *οἱ τυφλοὶ ἀναβλέψατε καὶ οἱ κωφοὶ ἀκούσατε.*[dcccl]

Ἐπεὶ δὲ οὔτε διὰ τοῦ θαύματος ἐδυσωποῦντο, ὑπερβολὴν ἔχων ἀνεξικακίας ὑποκρύπτων τε τὸ τῆς θεότητος μέγεθος, ὑπαναχωρεῖ τῶν Ἰουδαίων οἰκονομικῶς ὡς ἄνθρωπος, οὐ τὸν θάνατον δεδιώς, ἀλλ᾽ ἐκείνων φειδόμενος ἵνα μὴ κακοποιήσωσι καὶ ἡμᾶς διδάσκων χωρίζεσθαι τῶν ἐπιβουλευόντων. Ἀφιλόθεον γὰρ τὸ ριψοκίνδυνον.[dcccli] Δείκνυσι δὲ ὅτι οὐ διὰ δειλίαν ἀνεχώρησεν[dccclii] ἐξ ὧν αὖθις ἐποίει τὰς ἰάσεις. Παρήγγειλε δὲ τοῖς θερα | **94v** πευθεῖσι παραμυθούμενος τὸν τῶν Ἰουδαίων φθόνον, ἵνα μὴ φανερὸν αὐτὸν ποιήσωσιν. Οὐ γὰρ ἤθελε πρὸ τοῦ πάθους δοξασθῆναι ὡς Θεός.

Οὐκ ἐφιλονείκει πρὸς τὴν τῶν ἀρχόντων ἀπόνοιαν οὐδὲ κράζων ἐξηρέθιζεν καθ᾽ ἑαυτοῦ, ἀλλὰ μετὰ πραότητος ὑπανεχώρει, ἵνα μὴ ὄντας αὐτοὺς ἀσθενεῖς τῇ ψυχῇ ὡς *κάλαμον συντετριμμένον ἢ ὡς λίνον* καπνιζόμενον ἐγγὺς ὂν τοῦ σβεσθῆναι ἀπολέσαι ποιήσῃ διὰ τοῦ ἀντιλέγειν αὐτοῖς. ἀλλ᾽ ἔφερεν ἀνεξικάκως, ὅπως μὴ εἰς παντελῆ ἀπώλειαν ἑάλωσιν διὰ τὴν ἰδίαν ἀσθένειαν, ἕως ἂν πληρώσῃ τὸν τῆς οἰκονομίας σκοπόν, ὅπερ ἐστὶν ἐκβάλλειν εἰς τέλος *τὴν κρίσιν*, μεθ᾽ ἣν οἰκονομίαν πάντα *τὰ ἔθνη* ἐπίστευσαν.[dcccliii]

Οὐκ ἐφιλονείκει πρὸς τὴν τῶν ἀρχόντων ἀπόνοιαν οὐδὲ κράζων ἐξηρέθιζεν καθ᾽ ἑαυτοῦ, ἀλλὰ μετὰ πραότητος ὑπανεχώρει, ἵνα μὴ ὄντας αὐτοὺς ἀσθενεῖς τῇ ψυχῇ ὡς *κάλαμον συντετριμμένον ἢ ὡς λίνον* καπνιζόμενον ἐγγὺς ὂν τοῦ σβεσθῆναι ἀπολέσαι ποιήσῃ διὰ τοῦ ἀντιλέγειν αὐτοῖς. ἀλλ᾽ ἔφερεν ἀνεξικάκως, ὅπως μὴ εἰς παντελῆ ἀπώλειαν ἐλάσωσιν διὰ τὴν ἰδίαν ἀσθένειαν, ἕως ἂν πληρώσῃ τὸν τῆς οἰκονομίας σκοπόν, ὅπερ ἐστὶν ἐκβάλλειν εἰς τέλος *τὴν κρίσιν*, μεθ᾽ ἣν οἰκονομίαν πάντα *τὰ ἔθνη* ἐπίστευσαν.[dcccliv]

Εἶτα εἰσάγει λοιπὸν καὶ τὸν προφήτην τὸ πρᾶον αὐτοῦ καὶ ἀνεξίκακον προαναφωνοῦντα καὶ τὴν γνώμην μεθ᾽ ἧς ταῦτα ἐποίει. *Ἰδοὺ* γάρ φησιν *ὁ παῖς μου ὃν ᾑρέτισα.*[1055] Εἰ τοίνυν ὁ Πατὴρ αὐτὸν ᾑρέτισεν, οὐκ ἐναντιούμενος τῷ νομοθέτῃ λύει τὸν νόμον, ἀλλ᾽ ὡς ὁμογνώμων.[dccclv]

Τὴν πραότητα αὐτοῦ καὶ τὴν δύναμιν τὴν ἄφατον ἀνυμνεῖ, καὶ θύραν τοῖς ἔθνεσιν ἀνοίγνυσι μεγάλην καὶ ἐνεργῆ, καὶ τὰ καταληψόμενα τοὺς Ἰουδαίους προλέγει κακά, καὶ δείκνυσιν αὐτοῦ τὴν ὁμόνοιαν τὴν πρὸς τὸν Πατέρα. *Ἰδοὺ γάρ,* φησίν, *ὁ Παῖς μου, ὃν ᾑρέτισα, ὁ ἀγαπητός μου, εἰς ὃν εὐδόκησεν ἡ ψυχή μου.* Εἰ δὲ *ᾑρέτισεν*, οὐχ ὡς ἐναντιούμενος λύει τὸν νόμον, οὐδὲ ὡς ἐχθρὸς ὢν τοῦ Νομοθέτου, ἀλλ᾽ ὡς ὁμογνώμων καὶ τὰ αὐτὰ πράττων.[dccclvi]

1055 Matt. 12:18, paraphrasing Is. 42:1-4. Cf. Matt. 3:17; 17:3; Mark, 9:7; Luke, 3:22; 2 Peter, 1:17.

Εἶτα, *θήσω τὸ Πνεῦμά μου φησι ἐπ' αὐτόν,*[1056] τὸ *ὡσεὶ περιστερὰ καταβαίνον καὶ μένον ἐπ' αὐτόν.*[1057]

> Θήσω τὸ Πνεῦμα μου ἐπ' αὐτόν, τὸ ὡσεὶ περιστερὰ καταβαίνον καὶ μένον ἐπ' αὐτόν.[dccclvii]

Ὅπερ γὰρ ὡς Θεὸς εἶχε Πνεῦμα, τοῦτο οἰκονομικῶς ὑπὲρ πάντων χριόμενος ἐλέγετο εἶναι Χριστός. Εἶτα, *καὶ κρίσιν* φησὶ *τοῖς ἔθνεσιν ἀπαγγελεῖ.*[1058] Αὐτὸς γάρ ἐστιν ὁ εἰς τὴν *ὁδὸν τῆς ἀληθείας*[1059] τὰ *ἔθνη* ἐπιστρέψας.[1060]

οὐκ ἐρίσει οὐδὲ κραυγάσει.[1061] Ἐκείνην τὴν κραυγήν φησι, ἥτις ἔριδος ἔχεται καὶ πικρίας.

οὐδὲ ἀκούσει τις ἐν ταῖς πλατείαις τὴν φωνὴν αὐτοῦ.[1062] Οὐ γὰρ ἐν μέσῳ ἀγορᾶς (ὃ ποιοῦσιν οἱ κενῆς ἐφιέμενοι δόξης[dccclviii]) ἐδίδασκεν, ἀλλ' *ἐν τῷ ἱερῷ καὶ ἐν* ταῖς *συναγωγαῖς*[1063] τῶν Ἰουδαίων, καὶ ἐν *ἐρημίαις καὶ ὄρεσι*[1064] καὶ αἰγιαλοῖς.[dccclix]

Εἶτα, *κάλαμον συντετριμμένον οὐ κατεάξει,* φησί, *καὶ λῖνον τυφόμενον οὐ σβέσει,*[1065] τὴν Ἰουδαίων ἀσθένειαν διὰ τούτων αἰνιττόμενος
ὡς *κάλαμον* εὔθλαστον καὶ *λῖνον* καιόμενον δυνάμενον εὐχερῶς σβεσθῆναι. Οὓς καίτοι ὡς *κάλαμον* εὔθλαστον δυνάμενος συγκλάσαι καὶ ὡς *λῖνον* ὑφαφθὲν σβέσαι αὐτῶν τὸν θυμόν, οὐκ ἐποίησεν οὕτως διὰ τὸ ἄγαν ἐπιεικὲς ἕως | **95r** οὗ πληρώσῃ τὸν τῆς οἰκονομίας σκοπόν. Τοῦτο γάρ ἐστι τὸ *εἰς νῖκος* ἐκβαλεῖν *τὴν κρίσιν,*[1066]

> [Ἠδύνατό φησιν τοὺς Ἰουδαίους ὡς *κάλαμον συντετριμμένον* κατακλάσαι καὶ τὸν θυμὸν αὐτῶν ὡς *λῖνον τυφόμενον* ἤτοι καιόμενον σβέσαι. ἀλλ' οὐκ ἠθέλησεν *ἕως οὗ* πληρώσῃ τὴν οἰκονομίαν καὶ νικήσῃ διὰ πάντων αὐτούς. τοῦτό γαρ σημαίνει τὸ ἐπιλεγόμενον.][dccclx]

καὶ μηδεμίαν αὐτοῖς εἰς ἀπολογίαν καταλεῖψαι πρόφασιν. Τοῦτ' ἔστιν ἠνέσχετο ἕως ἀπέθανεν, ἵνα καὶ *ὁ θάνατος καὶ ἡ ἁμαρτία*[1067] *διὰ τοῦ θανάτου*[1068] αὐτοῦ καταδικασθῇ

1056 Matt. 12:18.
1057 Cf. Matt. 3:16; Mark, 1:10; Luke, 3:22; and John, 1:32, to which Origen's expression stands closest.
1058 Matt. 12:18; cf. Is. 42:1.
1059 Cf. Psalm 118:30; Wisdom of Solomon, 5:6; 2 Peter, 2:2.
1060 Cf. Tobit, 14:6.
1061 Matt. 12:19.
1062 Matt. 12:19. Cf. Psalm 143:14.
1063 Cf. John, 18:20.
1064 Heb. 11:38.
1065 Matt. 12:20.
1066 Matt. 12:20.
1067 Cf. Rom. 5:12.
1068 Cf. Rom. 5:10; Col. 1:22; Heb. 2:14.

εἰς τέλος,[1069] ἤτοι εἰς ἀποκίνησιν. Τοῦτο γὰρ σημαίνει τὸ *εἰς νῖκος.* Διὸ καὶ σεσώσμεθα ἀναστάντος αὐτοῦ ὅτι καὶ ἐπίστευσαν εἰς αὐτὸν *πάντα τὰ ἔθνη.*[1070]

καὶ κρίσιν τοῖς ἔθνεσι.[1071] Οὐ τῷ Ἰσραὴλ ἀπηγορευμένῳ, ἀλλὰ *τοῖς ἔθνεσι* τοῖς ἤδη πρὸ ὀφθαλμῶν ἔχουσι τὴν κρίσιν καὶ πιστεύσασιν εἰς τὸν κριτὴν *ζώντων καὶ νεκρῶν.*[1072]

> Οὐ τῷ Ἰσραὴλ ἀπηγορευμένῳ, ἀλλὰ *τοῖς ἔθνεσι* τοῖς ἤδη πρὸ ὀφθαλμῶν ἔχουσι τὴν *κρίσιν* καὶ πιστεύσασιν εἰς τὸν κριτὴν *ζώντων καὶ νεκρῶν.*[dccclxi]

Θήσω τὸ Πνεῦμα μου ἐπ᾽ αὐτόν.[1073] Ὁ Πατὴρ λέγει τῷ Υἱῷ τὸ *Πνεῦμα* καταπέμπειν. Οὐκοῦν προσκυνοῦμεν Τριάδα ὁμοούσιον. Θεὸν τὸν Πατέρα, Θεὸν τὸν Υἱόν, Θεὸν τὸ Πνεῦμα τὸ Ἅγιον. Μίαν φύσιν ἐν τρισὶν ἰδιότησι νοεραῖς, τελείαις, καθ᾽ ἑαυτὰς ὑφεστώσαις, ἀριθμῷ διαιρεταῖς καὶ οὐ διαιρεταῖς θεότητι.[dccclxii]

> Ὁ πατὴρ λέγει τῷ υἱῷ τὸ *πνεῦμα* καταπέμπειν. οὐκοῦν προσκυνοῦμεν τριάδα ὁμοούσιον καὶ ὁμολογοῦμεν θεὸν τὸν πατέρα, θεὸν τὸν υἱόν, θεὸν τὸ πνεῦμα τὸ ἅγιον. μίαν φύσιν ἐν τρισὶν ἰδιότησι νοεραῖς, τελείαις, καθ᾽ ἑαυτὰς ὑφεστώσαις, ἀριθμῷ διαιρεταῖς καὶ οὐ διαιρεταῖς θεότητι.[dccclxiii]

34

(ΩΡΙΓΕΝΟΥΣ) *Οὐδὲ ἀκούσει τίς ἐν ταῖς πλατείαις.*[1074] *Ἐν πλατείαις* οὐκ ἀκούεται ἡ *φωνὴ αὐτοῦ,* ἀλλ᾽ ἐν στενοῖς καὶ τεθλιμμένοις· *πλατεῖα* γὰρ *ἡ ὁδὸς ἡ ἀπάγουσα εἰς τὴν ἀπώλειαν.*[1075] Καὶ ἐπεὶ συνήθεια ἦν τοῖς Ἰουδαίοις περὶ τὰς ἀγορὰς καὶ πλατείας περιέρχεσθαι καὶ πωλεῖν οὐδὲν χρήσιμον ἀνδράσι πρὸς ἐργασίαν, ἀλλὰ γυναιξὶν ἐργαλεῖα καὶ μύρα πρὸς ἐμπλέγματα γυναικῶν, τῷ δὲ Σωτῆρι οὐδὲν τοιοῦτον ὑπῆρχε, διὰ τοῦτο *οὐδὲ τῆς φωνῆς αὐτοῦ* ἤκουσέ *τις ἐν ταῖς πλατείαις,* ἀλλ᾽ ἐν συναγωγαῖς[1076] διδάσκοντός τε καὶ θεραπεύοντος.

> Ἐν *πλατείαις* οὐκ ἀκούεται ἡ *φωνὴ αὐτοῦ,* ἀλλ᾽ ἐν στενοῖς καὶ τεθλιμμένοις. *πλατεῖα* γὰρ *ἡ ὁδὸς ἡ ἀπάγουσα εἰς τὴν ἀπώλειαν.*[1077] καὶ ἐπεὶ συνήθεια ἦν τοῖς Ἰουδαίοις περὶ τὰς ἀγορὰς καὶ πλατείας περιέρχεσθαι καὶ πωλεῖν οὐδὲν χρήσιμον ἀνδράσι πρὸς

1069 Cf. 1 Thess. 2:16.
1070 Cf. Matt. 25:32; 28:19; Mark, 13:10; Luke, 24:47; Acts, 15:17 (quoting Amos, 9:12); Psalm, 116:1 (quoted in Rom. 15:11).
1071 Matt. 12:18, quoting a paraphrase of Isaiah, 42:1-4.
1072 Acts, 10:42.
1073 Matt. 12:18, quoting a paraphrase of Isaiah, 42:1-4.
1074 Matt. 12:19.
1075 Matt. 7:13.
1076 Cf. John, 6:59; 18:20.
1077 Cf. Matt. 13-14.

> ἐργασίαν, ἀλλὰ γυναιξὶν ἐργαλεῖα καὶ μύρια πρὸς ἐμπλέγματα γυναικῶν, τῷ δὲ σωτῆρι οὐδὲν ὑπῆρχεν τοιοῦτον, διὰ τοῦτο *οὐδὲ τῆς φωνῆς αὐτοῦ ἤκουσέ τις ἐν ταῖς πλατείαις*, ἀλλ᾽ ἐν συναγωγαῖς διδάσκοντός τε καὶ θεραπεύοντος.[dccclxiv]
>
> *Neither will anyone hear his voice in the streets.* For *for wide is the gate and broad is the way that leads to destruction, and many are those who enter in by it.* Who are the *many?* Those who do not hear the voice of the Saviour, since they are not on te narrow road, but are on the spacious one.[dccclxv]

Κρίσιν δὲ | **95v** τὴν δικαιοσύνην οἶδε λέγειν *κάλαμον συντετριμμένον*.[1078] Κάλαμος συντετριμμένος ἐστὶ ψυχὴ ἐν ἁμαρτίαις συντετριμμένη. Λίνος δὲ τυφόμενος, οἱ κατεπαιρόμενοι τῆς ἀληθείας.[dccclxvi]

> Κάλαμος συντετριμμένος ἐστὶ ψυχὴ ἐν ἁμαρτίαις συντετριμμένη, λίνος δὲ τυφόμενος οἱ κατεπαιρόμενοι τῆς ἀληθείας.[dccclxvii]
>
> *Κάλαμον* λέγει τὸν διὰ προστάγματος Πιλάτου γράψαντα ἐν ἐμπαιγμῷ, τὸ *οὗτός ἐστιν ὁ βασιλεὺς τῶν Ἰουδαίων*,[1079] ὃν καὶ ἀορασία ὡς εὐκόλως δυνάμενον κατεάξαι, οὐ συνέτριψεν, ἀλλ᾽ ἠνέσχετο πάσχειν καὶ φέρειν τὴν ἐπιγραφήν. *λίνον* δέ φησι *τυφόμενον* τὸν τῶν κατεπαιρομένων βασιλέων τῦφον. λέγει δὲ Πιλάτου καὶ Ἡρώδου πεφυσιωμένων ἐπί τε τῇ ἀρχικῇ φαντασίᾳ καὶ ἀνεχομένων παρίστασθαι ὡς κριτὸν τὸν κριτὴν τῶν κριτῶν. ὃν καὶ οὐκ ἔσβεσε τέως ὁ κύριος Ἰησοῦς Χριστός, διὰ τοῦ οἰκείου πάθους τὴν τῶν ἀνθρώπων σωτηρίαν πραγματευόμενος.[dccclxviii]
>
> *Κάλαμον* λέγει, τὸν διὰ προστάγματος Πιλάτου γράψαντα ἐν ἐμπαιγμῷ, τὸ *οὗτός ἐστιν ὁ βασιλεὺς τῶν Ἰουδαίων*, ὃν καὶ ἀορασία ὡς εὐκόλως δυνάμενον κατεάξαι, οὐ συνέτριψεν, ἀλλ᾽ ἠνέσχετο πάσχειν καὶ φέρειν τὴν ἐπιγραφήν. *λίνον* δέ φησι, *τυφόμενον* τὸν τῶν κατεπαιρομένων βασιλέων τύφον. λέγει δὲ Πιλάτου καὶ Ἡρώδου πεφυσιωμένων ἐπί τε τῇ ἀρχῇ καὶ τῇ φαντασίᾳ, καὶ ἀνεχομένων παρίστασθαι ὡς κριτὸν τὸν κριτὴν τῶν κριτῶν. ὃν καὶ οὐκ ἔσβεσε τέως ὁ Κύριος Ἰησοῦς Χριστός, διὰ τοῦ οἰκείου πάθους τὴν τῶν ἀνθρώπων σωτηρίαν πραγματευόμενος.[dccclxix]

Τότε προσηνέχθη αὐτῷ δαιμονιζόμενος.[1080] Ἀπὸ τῆς τοῦ δαίμονος κακίας ταῦτα ὑπέστη ὁ ἄνθρωπος. Διὸ καὶ ὁ Κύριος ἅμα τῷ ἀπελάσαι τὸν δαίμονα ἀμφότερα ἀνέῳξε, καὶ ὄψιν καὶ ἀκοήν. Τοῦτο δὲ ἐποίησεν ὁ δαίμων πανταχόθεν αὐτὸν ἀποκλείων τοῦ δυνηθῆναι πιστεῦσαι τῷ Χριστῷ. Εἶτα, *οἱ ὄχλοι*, ἐπειδὴ τὰ σημεῖα ὑπερέβαινε καὶ τοὺς προφήτας ὡς μόνου τοῦ Χριστοῦ δυναμένου ταῦτα ποιεῖν ἔλεγον πρὸς ἀλλήλους· *μή τι οὗτός ἐστιν ὁ Χριστὸς ὁ υἱός Δαυίδ;*[1081] Τοῦτο δὲ ἔλεγον ὡς τῆς γραφῆς *ἐκ σπέρματος Δαυὶδ* λεγούσης *τὸ κατὰ σάρκα* εἶναι τὸν Χριστόν.[1082] *Οἱ δὲ Φαρισαῖοι*, εἰ καὶ οὐδὲν

1078 Matt. 12:20.
1079 Matt. 27:37; Mark, 15:26; Luke, 23:38; John, 19:19-21.
1080 Matt. 12:22; Luke, 11:14-15.
1081 Matt. 12:23.
1082 Rom. 1:3; cf. John, 7:42; 2 Tim. 2:8.

μέγα περὶ αὐτοῦ ἔλεγον, ὅμως ἐδάκνοντο ταῦτα ἀκούοντες περὶ αὐτοῦ καὶ τὰ τῆς θείας φύσεως ἔργα *τῷ Βεελζεβοὺλ* ἐχαρίζοντο καὶ δαιμονῶντα αὐτὸν ἔλεγον.[1083]

> Οὐκ ἦν ὁ *Βεελζεβοὺλ* μετὰ τοῦ Ἰησοῦ. ἀγαθὸς ὁ τὴν κακίαν ἐξορίζων, ὁ δὲ ἀγαθὸν τῷ κακῷ ἐπιγράφων πονηρός, ὁ καὶ τὴν πρᾶξιν κατηγορῶν καὶ τὸν ποιοῦντα.[dccclxx]

Πᾶσα βασιλεία μερισθεῖσα.[1084] Διὰ τοῦτο δημοσιεύει *τὰς ἐνθυμήσεις αὐτῶν*[dccclxxi] δ‹ε›ικνὺς[1085] ὅτι Θεὸς ἦν. Καὶ γὰρ διὰ τὸ ἄγαν ἀναίσχυντον οὐ φανερῶς ἔλεγον ἅπερ ἔλεγον. Τί οὖν ὁ Σωτὴρ οὐκ ἀπολογεῖται αὐτοῖς ἀπὸ τῆς γραφῆς, ἀλλ᾽ ἀπὸ τῶν κοινῇ συμβαινόντων καὶ δείκνυσι διὰ τῶν παραδειγμάτων ὅτι οὐ δυνατὸν γενέσθαι ἅπερ ἐκεῖνοι φασί; Ἡνίκα, γάρ φησι, ἐμφύλιοι γίνονται πόλεμοι, αὐτοὶ ὑφ᾽ ἑαυτῶν καταλύονται οἱ πολεμοῦντες καὶ οἱ πολεμούμενοι. Σατανᾶ‹ς›[1086] δὲ καλεῖ τοὺς δαίμονας, ἐπειδὴ πολλὴ συμφωνία πρὸς ἀλλήλους. Εἰ τοίνυν δοκεῖ τὸ κράτος τῶν | **96r** δαιμόνων κατὰ τῶν ἀνθρώπων εἶναι, νῦν δὲ καὶ καθ᾽ ὑμᾶς *ὁ σατανᾶς τὸν σατανᾶν ἐκβάλλει*,[1087] οὐκοῦν[1088] τέλος εἴληφε πορθῶν καὶ πορθούμενος. Εἶτα, ἐξ ἑτέρου παραδείγματος ἐπιεικῶς ἀποκρινόμενος, πείθει αὐτοὺς καὶ ἐπιστομίζει λέγοντας ὅτι πρὸς ἀπάτην τῶν ἀνθρώπων καὶ δαίμων ἐκβάλλει δαιμόνια. Ἔστω, γάρ φησι, καθ᾽ ὑμᾶς ὅτι ἐγὼ *ἐν Βεελζεβοὺλ* ἐκβάλλω *τὰ δαιμόνια. Οἱ υἱοὶ ὑμῶν*, ἢ οἱ νῦν ἢ οἱ ἐσόμενοι, *ἐν τίνι ἐκβάλλουσιν αὐτά;*[1089] Οὐκ εἶπε δὲ οἱ ἐμοὶ μαθηταί, ἀλλ᾽ *οἱ υἱοὶ ὑμῶν*, περὶ αὐτῶν λέγων ἵνα δῷ συνῳδὰ ἐκείνοις φρονεῖν. Εἴπατε τοίνυν· ἢ τῷ αὐτῷ τρόπῳ ἐκβάλλειν αὐτοὺς τὰ δαιμόνια ἢ θείᾳ δυνάμει· εἰ δὲ θείᾳ δυνάμει τοῦτο ποιοῦσιν *ἐν τῷ ὀνόματί μου*[1090] τοῦτο ποιοῦντες, αὐτοὶ ὑμᾶς μέλλουσι κατακρίνειν ὡς θεομάχους καὶ ὑβριστάς.

Διὰ τοῦτο αὐτοὶ ὑμῶν ἔσονται κριταί.[1091] Αὐτοὶ τοίνυν *ἔσονται ὑμῶν κριταί*, οὐ περὶ τῶν βεβιωμένων[dccclxxii] (μόνου γὰρ Θεοῦ ἐστι τοῦτο), ἀλλὰ περὶ τῆς εἰς Χριστὸν πίστεως, ἐπειδὴ οὐ τὰ αὐτὰ αὐτοῖς φρονεῖτε. Μέλλουσι γὰρ ὑμᾶς ἐλέγξαι ὡς βλασφήμους *ἐν ἡμέρᾳ κρίσεως.*[1092] Υἱοὺς δὲ τῶν Φαρισαίων καλεῖ τοὺς μαθητὰς ἐπειδὴ οἱ ἡγούμενοι τὸ πρόσωπον ἐπέχουσι τῆς τῶν Ἰουδαίων συναγωγῆς, ἐξ ἧς εἰσιν οἱ μαθηταὶ κατὰ σάρκα.

1083 Matt. 12:24; cf. 9:34; Mark, 3:22-27; Luke, 11:15-20.
1084 Matt. 12:25.
1085 cod. δικνὺς.
1086 Cod. σατανᾶν.
1087 Matt. 12:26.
1088 Cod. οὐκ οὖν.
1089 Matt. 12:27.
1090 Mark, 16:17; cf. Matt. 10:8; Luke, 9:49; John, 9:38; 14:13-14.
1091 Matt. 12:27.
1092 Cf. Matt. 10:15; 11:22; 11:24; 11:36; 2 Peter, 2:9; 3:7; 1 John, 4:17. In the OT, Esther, 10:3h; Judith, 16:17; Prov. 6:34; Psalms of Solomon, 15:12; Is. 34:8.

> By 'sons' of the Jews he uses by a traditional expression denoting either the exorcists of that nation or the apostles… . if this has been said about the apostles, which is also a way we should explain this [passage], the purport is that they will be judges of them, because they *will sit on the twelve thrones, judging the twelve tribes of Israel.*[1093]

Εἶτα δεικνὺς ὅτι μεγίστης δυνάμεως ἔργον τὸ δαίμονας ἀπελαύνειν καὶ οὐ τῆς τυχούσης χάριτος, ἐπάγει λέγων· *εἰ δὲ ἐγὼ ἐν Πνεύματι Θεοῦ ἐκβάλλω τὰ δαιμόνια*, οὐκοῦν[1094] *ἔφθασεν ἡ βασιλεία τοῦ Θεοῦ ἐφ' ὑμᾶς.*[1095] Βασιλείαν δὲ Θεοῦ τὴν ἑαυτοῦ παρουσίαν λέγει.[1096][dccclxxiii] Βούλεται γὰρ ἀπὸ τούτων συλλογίσασθαι καὶ εἰπεῖν ὅτι, εἰ δὲ τοῦτο ἐστίν, ἄρα | **96v** *ὁ υἱός τοῦ ἀνθρώπου*[1097] παρεγέγονεν. Ἀλλὰ τοῦτο μὲν οὐ λέγει, συνεσκιασμένως[dccclxxiv] δὲ αἰνίττεται αὐτὸ διὰ τὸ ἀνεπαχθὲς αὐτῶν.

> Ὁ μὲν οὖν Ματθαῖός φησιν. *Εἰ δὲ ἐγὼ ἐν Πνεύματι Θεοῦ ἐκβάλλω.* ὁ δὲ Λουκᾶς, *Εἰ δὲ ἐγὼ ἐν δακτύλῳ Θεοῦ ἐκβάλλω τὰ δαιμόνια*, δεικνὺς ὅτι μεγίστης δυνάμεως ἔργον ἐστὶ τὸ δαίμονας ἐκβάλλειν, καὶ οὐ τῆς τυχούσης χάριτος. Καὶ βούλεται μὲν ἀπὸ τούτων συλλογίσασθαι καὶ εἰπεῖν, ὅτι Εἰ δὲ τοῦτό ἐστιν, ἄρα ὁ Υἱὸς τοῦ Θεοῦ παραγέγονεν. Ἀλλὰ τοῦτο μὲν οὐ λέγει, συνεσκιασμένως δέ, καὶ ὡς ἐκείνοις ἀνεπαχθὲς ἦν, αἰνίττεται αὐτῷ λέγων. *Ἄρα ἔφθασεν ἐφ' ὑμᾶς ἡ βασιλεία τοῦ Θεοῦ.*[dccclxxv]

> Εἰπὼν δὲ *ἄρα ἔφθασεν ἐφ' ὑμᾶς ἡ βασιλεία τοῦ Θεοῦ* περὶ τῆς ἑαυτοῦ πρώτης παρουσίας λέγει, δεικνὺς αὐτοῖς ὅτι ὤφελον σκιρτᾷν καὶ χαίρειν ὅτι τὰ μεγάλα καὶ ἀπόρρητα ἐκεῖνα παραγέγονεν ἀγαθά, τὰ πάλαι παρὰ τῶν προφητῶν ᾀδόμενα. αὐτοὶ δὲ τουναντίον ἐποίουν. οὐ μόνον δεχόμενοι αὐτά, ἀλλὰ καὶ διαβάλλοντες, καὶ συντιθέντες οὐκ οὔσας αἰτίας. ὅτι *ἐγὼ μέν*, φησιν, *ἐν Πνεύματι Θεοῦ ἐκβάλλω τὰ δαιμόνια*, ὅπερ ἐστὶ μεγίστης δυνάμεως ἔργον, καὶ οὐ τῆς τυχούσης χάριτος.[dccclxxvi]

Ἤτοι *βασιλείαν Θεοῦ* τὴν τοῦ Πνεύματος μετάδοσίν φησι, δι' ἧς εἰς βασιλείαν εἰσάγονται οἱ πιστοί, καὶ τούτου μετασχόντες οἱ ἄνθρωποι καὶ δαίμονας ἐκβάλλουσιν.

Ἄρα ἔφθασεν ἐφ' ὑμᾶς ἡ βασιλεία τοῦ Θεοῦ.[1098] Ἐπειδὴ τῆς τοῦ Θεοῦ βασιλείας, ἤτοι τῆς δευτέρας παρουσίας[dccclxxvii] καταλαβούσης ἥ τε ἀμοιβὴ τῶν ἀγαθῶν καὶ ἡ τιμωρία καὶ ἡ κόλασις τῶν φαύλως πολιτευσαμένων ἐπιτελεῖται, εἰς ἐκεῖνον τὸν καιρὸν τὴν ἀντιμισθίαν τῶν ἑκάστῳ πεπραγμένων ταμιευομένου τοῦ Θεοῦ, δεικνὺς τὸ ἄτοπον αὐτῶν καὶ σφοδρὸν τῆς ἁμαρτίας, φησί· *ἔφθασεν ἐφ' ὑμᾶς ἡ βασιλεία τοῦ Θεοῦ.* ἀντὶ τοῦ, ὅσον ἐπὶ τῇ ὑπερβολῇ τῆς ἀπονοίας ὑμῶν καὶ μωρίας προεκκαλεῖσθε καὶ προφθάσαι βιάζεσθε τὸν τῆς τιμωρίας καὶ κολάσεως καιρόν, ὃς κατὰ τὴν δευτέραν ἀφώρισται παρουσίαν. Διὸ καὶ ἀποτόμως ἀποφαινόμενός φησι· *ἄρα ἔφθασεν ἐφ'*

1093 Matt. 19:28; Luke, 23:30. Jerome, *commMatt*, 12.27.
1094 Cod. οὐκ οὖν.
1095 Matt. 12:27.
1096 Matt. 12:26-28.
1097 Cf. Matt. 8:20; 9:6; 10:23; 11:9; 12:8; *et passim*.
1098 Matt. 12:28.

ὑμᾶς ἡ βασιλεία τοῦ Θεοῦ, ἤτοι ὁ τῆς κρίσεως καὶ ἀνταποδόσεως καιρός.[dccclxxviii] Πῶς γὰρ οὐκ ἂν αὐτοὶ ἐφ' ἑαυτοὺς τὴν τιμωρίαν καὶ πρὸ καιροῦ ἐκκαλεῖσθαι εἶεν αἴτιοι, οἵ γε τοῦ δεσπότου θαυματουργοῦντος καὶ τὰς νόσους ἰωμένου καὶ τοὺς δαιμονῶντας καθαίροντος ἐτόλμησαν εἰπεῖν ὅτι *ἐν τῷ ἄρχοντι τῶν δαιμονίων ἐκβάλλει τὰ δαιμόνια;*[dccclxxix] Πόσης γὰρ οὐ γέμει τοῦτο θεομαχίας; Πόσης ἀπονοίας; Πόσης δυσσεβείας καὶ παρανοίας; Ὕβριζον τὸ Πνεῦμα, ἐν ᾧ ἐξέβαλλε τὰ δαιμόνια καὶ (ἠλίκη ὕβρι‹ς›!)[1099] | **97r** εὐεργέτην τῶν ἀνθρώπων τὸν φθορέα καὶ λυμεῶνα τὸν Βεελζεβοὺλ εἰσῆγον, αὐτὸν καθ' ἑαυτοῦ μάχεσθαι τὸν σατανᾶν ἐφαντασιοῦντο. Οὕ‹τως›[1100] ἦσαν τῷ φθόνῳ καὶ τῇ βασκανίᾳ μεμηνότες καὶ βεβακχευμένοι, καὶ μηδὲν ὧν λέγουσι, πλὴν τοῦ βλασφημεῖν καὶ θεομαχεῖν ἐπιστάμενοι.

Ἐπειδὴ τῆς τοῦ θεοῦ βασιλείας ἤτοι τῆς δευτέρας παρουσίας καταλαβούσης ἥ τε ἀμοιβὴ τῶν ἀγαθῶν καὶ ἡ τιμωρία καὶ ἡ κόλασις τῶν φαύλως πολιτευσαμένων ἐπιτελεῖται, εἰς ἐκεῖνον τὸν καιρὸν τὴν ἀντιμισθίαν τῶν ἑκάστῳ πεπραγμένων ταμιευομένου τοῦ θεοῦ δεικνὺς τὸ ἄτοπον αὐτῶν καὶ σφοδρὸν τῆς ἁμαρτίας φησίν. *ἔφθασεν ἐφ' ὑμᾶς ἡ βασιλεία τοῦ θεοῦ* ἀντὶ τοῦ. ὅσον ἐπὶ τῇ ὑπερβολῇ τῆς ἀπονοίας ὑμῶν καὶ μανίας προεκκαλεῖσθε προφθάσαι καὶ βιάζεσθε τὸν τῆς τιμωρίας καὶ κολάσεως καιρόν, ὃς κατὰ τὴν δευτέραν ἀφώρισται παρουσίαν. διὸ καὶ ἀποτόμως ἀποφαινόμενός φησιν. ἄρα *ἔφθασεν ἐφ' ὑμᾶς ἡ βασιλεία τοῦ θεοῦ* ἤτοι ὁ τῆς κρίσεως καὶ ἀνταποδόσεως καιρός. πῶς γὰρ οὐκ ἂν αὐτοὶ ‹τοῦ› ἐφ' ἑαυτοὺς τὴν τιμωρίαν καὶ πρὸ καιροῦ ἐκκαλεῖσθαι εἶεν αἴτιοι, οἵ γε τοῦ δεσπότου θαυματουργοῦντος καὶ τὰς νόσους ἰωμένου καὶ τοὺς δαιμονῶντας καθαίροντος καὶ τοὺς δαίμονας ἀπελαύνοντος ἐτόλμησαν εἰπεῖν, ὅτι *ἐν τῷ ἄρχοντι τῶν δαιμονίων ἐκβάλλει τὰ δαιμόνια*. πόσης γὰρ οὐ γέμει τοῦτο θεομαχίας, πόσης ἀπονοίας, πόσης δυσσεβείας καὶ παροινίας. ὕβριζον τὸ πνεῦμα, ᾧ ἐξέβαλλεν τὰ δαιμόνια, καὶ ἡλίκην ὕβριν. εὐεργέτην τῶν ἀνθρώπων τὸν φθορέα καὶ λυμεῶνα τὸν Βεελζεβοὺλ εἰσῆγον. αὐτὸν καθ' ἑαυτοῦ μάχεσθαι τὸν σατανᾶν ἐφαντασιοῦντο, οὕτως ἦσαν τῷ φθόνῳ καὶ τῇ βασκανίᾳ μεμηνότες καὶ βεβακχευμένοι καὶ μηδὲν ὧν λέγουσιν πλὴν τοῦ βλασφημεῖν ἐπιστάμενοι.[dccclxxx]

(ΩΡΙΓΕΝΟΥΣ, added on the margin) Βασιλεία τοῦ Θεοῦ οὐχ ἡ δευτέρα, ἀλλ' ἡ πρώτη· ἐφ' ᾗ ‹εἰ καὶ› χαίρειν δέον καὶ ἀνυμνεῖν, ἀλλ' ὑμεῖς ὀργίζεσθε καὶ διαβάλλετε.

(ΩΡΙΓΕΝΟΥΣ, cont.) *Ἢ πῶς δύναταί τις εἰσελθεῖν εἰς τὴν οἰκίαν;*[1101] Δείκνυσιν ὅτι οὐδὲ ἄλλως δυνατὸν ἐκβαλεῖν δαίμονα, ἐὰν μὴ πρότερον ἐκείνου περιγένηται,

ὅτι οὐ μόνον ὁ Σατανᾶς τὸν Σατανᾶν οὐκ ἐκβάλλει, ἀλλ' οὐδὲ ἄλλῳ τινὶ δυνατὸν ἐκβάλλειν, ἐὰν μὴ πρότερον ἐκείνου περιγένηται. τοσοῦτον γὰρ ἀπέχω, φησί, συμμάχῳ χρήσασθαι τῷ διαβόλῳ, ὅτι καὶ πολεμῶ αὐτῷ καὶ δεσμῶ αὐτόν. καὶ τούτου τεκμήριον, τὸ τὰ σκεύη αὐτοῦ διαρπάσαι με. τουτέστι τοὺς δαίμονας ἀπελαύνειν με, καὶ τὴν οἰκουμένην ἅπασαν τῆς πλάνης ἐλευθερῶσαι με, καὶ τὰς μαγγανείας αὐτοῦ καταλῦσαί με, καὶ πάντα ἄχρηστα ποιῆσαί με τὰ ἐκείνου. *ἰσχυρὸν* δὲ αὐτὸν καλεῖ. οὐκ ἐπειδὴ τῇ φύσει

1099 Cod. ἡλίκην ὕβριν.

1100 Cod. οὗ.

1101 Matt. 12:29.

τοιοῦτός ἐστι, μὴ γένοιτο, ἀλλὰ τὴν ἔμπροσθεν σημαίνων τυραννίδα, τὴν ἐκ τῆς ῥαθυμίας[dccclxxxi] τῆς ἡμετέρας γεγενημένην.[dccclxxxii]

λέγων· *ἢ πῶς δύναταί τις εἰσελθεῖν εἰς τὴν οἰκίαν τοῦ ἰσχυροῦ;* καὶ τὰ ἑξῆς. Καὶ οἰκίαν μὲν λέγει τὴν γῆν,

Ἡ οἰκία *τοῦ ἰσχυροῦ*, ὁ περίγειος τόπος. ἰσχυρὸς δὲ ὁ διάβολος. *σκεύη* δὲ τοῦ ἰσχυροῦ, οἱ ὑπαγόμενοι τοῖς θελήμασιν αὐτοῦ.[dccclxxxiii]

Ἡ οἰκία τοῦ ἰσχυροῦ, ὁ περίγειος τόπος. ἰσχυρὸς δὲ ὁ διάβολος. σκεύη δὲ τοῦ ἰσχυροῦ, οἱ ὑπαγόμενοι τοῖς θελήμασιν αὐτοῦ.[dccclxxxiv]

ἰσχυρὸν δὲ τὸν διάβολον, οὐκ ἐπειδὴ τοιοῦτός ἐστι τῇ φύσει, ἀλλὰ τὴν ἐκ ῥαθυμίας ἡμῶν ἔμπροσθεν δηλῶν τυραννίδα σκεύη δὲ αὐτοῦ οὐ μόνον τοὺς δαίμονας, ἀλλὰ καὶ τοὺς τοῖς ἐκείνου θελήμασιν ὑπαγομένους ἀνθρώπους φησί.

(Ὠριγένους.) Ἰσχυρός ἐστιν ἡ ἁμαρτία. οἶκος δὲ τούτου, τὸ σῶμα, ὁ παλαιὸς ἄνθρωπος.[dccclxxxv]

Ἰσχυρός ἐστιν ἡ ἁμαρτία. οἶκος δὲ τούτου, τὸ σῶμα, ὁ παλαιὸς ἄνθρωπος.[dccclxxxvi]

(Τοῦ αὐτοῦ.) *Ἐὰν μὴ* περάσῃ καὶ *δήσῃ*, φησίν, τὸν εὐσεβῆ καὶ ἰσχυρὸν λογισμὸν τοῦ νοός, ἡ ἀντικειμένη τοῦ ἰσχυροῦ, λέγω δὴ τοῦ διαβόλου ἡ δύναμις, οὐ δύναται τὰς τῆς ψυχῆς ἀρετὰς λυμήνασθαι. καὶ τὴν οἰκείαν αὐτῆς σύζυγον, λέγω δὴ τὸ σῶμα, σὺν αὐτῇ ἐξαφανίσαι.[dccclxxxvii]

Ἐὰν μὴ περάσῃ καὶ *δήσῃ* (φησίν) τὸν εὐσεβῆ καὶ ἰσχυρὸν λογισμὸν τοῦ νοός, ἡ ἀντικειμένη *τοῦ ἰσχυροῦ* (λέγω δὴ τοῦ διαβόλου) δύναμις οὐ δύναται τὰς τῆς ψυχῆς ἀρετὰς λυμήνασθαι. καὶ *τὴν οἰκείαν* αὐτῆς σύζυγον (λέγω δὴ τὸ σῶμα) σὺν αὐτῇ ἐξαφανίσαι.[dccclxxxviii]

Ἰσχυρὸν δὲ καλεῖ τὸν διάβολον οὐχ ὡς φύσει τοῦτο ὄντα, ἀλλὰ τὴν αὐτοῦ τυραννίδα δηλοῖ, ἣν ἐκ τῆς ἡμετέρας ῥαθυμίας ἐκτήσατο. *διαρπάζω* δὲ αὐτόν, οὐκ ἐῶν ἔχειν προσκυνητὰς τοὺς ἀνθρώπους, ἀλλ᾽ εἰς ἐπίγνωσιν τοῦ θεοῦ μεταπείθων ἐλθεῖν. πῶς οὖν σύμμαχός μοι γενήσεται καθ᾽ ἑαυτοῦ;[dccclxxxix]

Εἰ τοίνυν ὁ Σατανᾶς πλεονεκτεῖται[1102] ὑπὸ τοῦ Πνεύματος, οὐ μὴν πρὸς ἐπικουρίαν ἐλήφθη ὥστε διώκειν δαίμονας, δηλονότι ἰσχυρότερος τοῦ φεύγοντος ὁ διώκων, καὶ τοσοῦτον, ὡς καὶ ἀπολέσαι ἐκεῖνον πάντα ὅσα εἶχεν ἐκ τυραννίδος. Εἶτα, καὶ τετάρτη λύσις. Πῶς οἷόν τέ ἐστι συμφωνῆσαι με τῷ Σατανᾷ, εἰ ἐγὼ μὲν πάντας θέλω σῶσαι καὶ οἰκειῶσαι Θεῷ[1103] οὗτος δὲ *σκορπίσαι;*[1104] Ἐνταῦθα δέ μοι δοκεῖ καὶ Ἰουδαίους

1102 Cf. 2 Cor. 2:11.
1103 Cf. Eph. 2:19; Rom. 8:9; 1 Cor. 3:16.
1104 Cf. Matt. 12:30; Luke, 11:23; John, 10:12.

αἰνίττεσθαι μετὰ τοῦ διαβόλου. Καὶ γὰρ οἱ Φαρισαῖοι βουλόμενοι διαστρέφειν τὸν ὄχλον, σκορπίζειν ἤθελον διὰ συκοφαντιῶν ἀπὸ τοῦ Χριστοῦ τοὺς πιστούς.

35

99v (ΩΡΙΓΕΝΟΥΣ) *Μοιχαλίς*[1105] ἐστιν ἡ τὸν κατὰ φύσιν ἄνδρα, τὸν Λόγον, λιποῦσα καὶ τῷ παρὰ φύσιν ἀνδρὶ κολληθεῖσα τῷ ἐναντίῳ. Ἢ *ὁ ἐν τοῖς μέλεσιν* ἡμῶν *νόμος ἀντιστρατευόμενος τῷ νόμῳ τοῦ νοός*[1106] μοιχός ἐστι ψυχῆς. Ἤδη δὲ καὶ πᾶσα δύναμις ἀντικειμένη μοιχεύει τὴν ἔχουσαν νυμφίον τὸν ὑπὸ Θεοῦ δοθέντα αὐτῇ λόγον[dccccxc] ψυχὴν μιγνυμένη αὐτῇ.[dccccxci]

> *Μοιχαλίς* ἐστιν ἡ τὸν κατὰ φύσιν ἄνδρα, τὸν Λόγον, λιποῦσα. καὶ τῷ παρὰ φύσει ἀνδρὶ κολληθεῖσα τῷ ἐναντίῳ, ἢ ὁ *ἐν τοῖς μέλεσιν* ἡμῶν νόμος *ἀντιστρατευόμενος τῷ νόμῳ τοῦ νοός* μοιχός ἐστι ψυχῆς. ἤδη δὲ καὶ πᾶσα δύναμις ἀντικειμένη μοιχεύει τὴν ἔχουσαν νυμφίον τὸν ὑπὸ Θεοῦ δοθέντα αὐτῇ λόγον ψυχὴν μιγνυμένη αὐτῇ.[dccccxcii]

> Γενικῶς μὲν οὖν ὁ ἐν τοῖς μέλεσιν νόμος ὁ ἀντιστρατευόμενος *τῷ νόμῳ τοῦ νοός* ὡς μοιχὸς ἀνὴρ ἐστι ψυχῆς. ἤδη δὲ καὶ πᾶσα δύναμις ἀντικειμένη, ἐπικρατοῦσα ἀνθρωπίνης ψυχῆς και ἀναμιγνυμένη αὐτῇ, μοιχός ἐστιν αὐτῆς, νυμφίον ἐχούσης ὑπὸ τοῦ θεοῦ αὐτῇ δοθέντα τὸν λόγον.[dccccxciii]

> Καὶ πονηρὰν μὲν εἶπεν αὐτοὺς γενεὰν διὰ τὴν ἀπὸ τοῦ πονηροῦ ποιότητα εἰς αὐτοὺς ἐγγενομένην (ἔστι δὲ ἡ πονηρία ἑκούσιος κακοποιία),[dccccxciv] μοιχαλίδα δὲ διὰ τοῦτο, ἐπεὶ τὸν τροπικῶς λεγόμενον ἄνδρα, τῆς ἀληθείας λόγον ἢ νόμον, καταλιπόντες οἱ *Φαρισαῖοι καὶ Σαδδουκαῖοι* ἐμοιχεύθησαν ὑπὸ τοῦ ψεύδους καὶ τοῦ νόμου *τῆς ἁμαρτίας*. εἰ γὰρ δύο εἰσὶ νόμοι, ὅ τε *ἐν τοῖς μέλεσιν* ἡμῶν ἀντιστρατευόμενος *τῷ νόμῳ τοῦ νοός* καὶ ὁ *τοῦ νοός*, λεκτέον ὅτι ὁ μὲν *τοῦ νοός* (τουτέστιν ὁ *πνευματικὸς*) ἀνήρ ἐστι, πρὸς ὃν ἡρμόσθη ἀπὸ θεοῦ γυνὴ (ἡ ψυχὴ) ἀνδρὶ (*τῷ νόμῳ*) κατὰ τὸ γεγραμμένον *παρὰ δὲ θεοῦ ἁρμόζεται ἀνδρὶ γυνή*, ὁ δὲ ἄλλος μοιχός ἐστι τῆς ὑποτασσομένης αὐτῷ ψυχῆς καὶ δι' αὐτὸν μοιχαλίδος χρηματιζούσης. ὅτι δὲ ὁ νόμος ἀνὴρ τῆς ψυχῆς ἐστι, σαφῶς ἐν τῇ πρὸς Ῥωμαίους ὁ Παῦλος παριστᾷ λέγων ὅτι *ὁ νόμος κυριεύει τοῦ ἀνθρώπου ἐφ' ὅσον χρόνον ζῇ. ἡ γὰρ ὕπανδρος γυνὴ τῷ ζῶντι ἀνδρὶ δέδεται νόμῳ* καὶ τὰ ἑξῆς ... ἤδη δὲ καὶ πᾶσα δύναμις ἀντικειμένη, ἐπικρατοῦσα τῆς ἀνθρωπίνης ψυχῆς καὶ ἀναμιγνυμένη αὐτῇ, μοιχός ἐστιν αὐτῆς, νυμφίον ἐχούσης ὑπὸ τοῦ θεοῦ αὐτῇ δοθέντα τὸν λόγον. μετὰ ταῦτα γέγραπται ὅτι καταλιπὼν αὐτοὺς ἀπῆλθεν. πῶς γὰρ οὐκ ἔμελλεν ὁ νυμφίος λόγος καταλιπεῖν τὴν μοιχαλίδα γενεὰν καὶ ἀπιέναι ἀπ' αὐτῆς; εἴποις δ' ἂν ὅτι τὴν Ἰουδαίων συναγωγὴν ὡς μοιχαλίδα καταλιπὼν ὁ τοῦ θεοῦ λόγος ἀπελήλυθεν ἀπ' αὐτῆς, καὶ ἔλαβε *γυναῖκα πορνείας* τοὺς ἀπὸ τῶν ἐθνῶν.[dccccxcv]

> *Πονηρὰ* διὰ τὴν ἀπὸ τοῦ πονηροῦ ποιότητα, *μοιχαλίς*, ὅτι καταλιποῦσα τὸν τροπικῶς αὐτῆς ἄνδρα λόγον ἀληθείας ἢ νόμον ἐγένετο τῷ ψευδεῖ. γενικῶς μὲν οὖν ὁ *ἐν τοῖς μέλεσιν* τῆς σαρκὸς ἡμῶν νόμος *ἀντιστρατευόμενος τῷ νόμῳ τοῦ νοός* μοιχός ἐστι ψυχῆς. ἤδη

1105 Matt. 12:39.
1106 Cf. Rom. 7:23.

> δὲ καὶ πᾶσα δύναμις ἀντικειμένη μοιχεύει τὴν ἔχουσαν νυμφίον τὸν ὑπὸ Θεοῦ δοθέντα αὐτῇ λόγον ψυχὴν μιγνυμένη αὐτῇ.[dcccxcvi]

Καὶ σημεῖον οὐ δοθήσεται αὐτῇ.[1107] Ἐπειδὴ ὡς πειράζοντες ᾔτουν σημεῖον εἶπε *καὶ σημεῖον οὐ δοθήσεται αὐτῇ. Σημεῖον* δὲ *Ἰωνᾶ* τὴν εἰς Ἅδου κάθοδον αὐτοῦ καὶ τὴν ἐκ νεκρῶν τριήμερον ἀνάστασιν αἰνιττόμενός φησι. *Καρδίαν* δὲ *γῆς*[1108] λέγει τὸν κατώτατον τῆς γῆς μυχόν, ἤτοι τὸν Ἅδην, διὰ τὸ ἐν τοῖς ἐσωτάτοις διακεῖσθαι τόποις. Τὴν δὲ τριήμερον ἀπὸ μέρους νοητέον, ἐπείπερ καὶ τὸ ἡμερονύκτιον μίαν καλοῦμεν ἡμέραν. Ἡ οὖν παρασκευὴ ἔχει τὴν ἑαυτῆς νύκτα, τὴν παρελθοῦσαν· καὶ τὸ σάββατον τὴν ἀπ᾽ ἀρχῆς νυκτὸς ἕως τέλους· καὶ ἡ ἑπομένη νὺξ τὴν κυριακήν.[dcccxcvii]

> Τῆς μετὰ τὸ σάββατον ἑσπέρας ἐπιστάσης ὁ κύριος ἀνέστη τὴν προειρημένην ὑπ᾽ αὐτοῦ τριήμερον ὑποτέμνων τῷ ληγούσης μὲν τῆς πρώτης ἡμέρας πεπονθέναι, εὐθὺς δὲ ἀρχομένης τῆς τρίτης ἀνίστασθαι.[dcccxcviii]

Διατί εἶπεν *εἰ μὴ τὸ σημεῖον Ἰωνᾶ;* Τὸ πάθος τὸ ἑαυτοῦ φησι δοθήσεσθαι αὐτοῖς, ἐπειδὴ διὰ τούτου μάλιστα γνωρίζεται Χριστός, παρατιθεμένων τῶν ἄνωθεν προφητειῶν, αἳ *παθητὸν*[1109] αὐτὸν | **100r** καταγγέλλουσιν, ὡς καὶ Παῦλος ἐπὶ Ἀγρίππα διορίζεται. Ἐδήλωσε δὲ τὸ πάθος τῇ κατὰ τὸν Ἰωνᾶν παραβολῇ. Τούτου γὰρ καὶ ἔχρῃζον οἱ αἰτήσαντες. Οὐρανίου γὰρ σημείου οὐκ ἦσαν ἄξιοι, οὔτε ἦν αὐτοῖς ποιητὸν εἰ μὴ τὸ τοῦ σταυροῦ σημεῖον, δι᾽ οὗ κατηργήθη αὐτῶν ἡ ἀσθένεια.[1110] Ζῶν ἦν Ἰωνᾶς *ἐν τῇ κοιλίᾳ τοῦ κήτους.*[1111] Καὶ Χριστὸς *ἐν θανάτῳ* γενόμενος *ἐλεύθερος*[1112] ἦν τούτου.

> Διατί εἶπεν *εἰ μὴ τὸ σημεῖον Ἰωνᾶ;* Τὸ πάθος τὸ ἑαυτοῦ φησι δοθήσεσθαι αὐτοῖς, ἐπειδὴ διὰ τούτου μάλιστα γνωρίζεται Χριστός, παρατιθεμένων τῶν ἄνωθεν προφητειῶν, αἳ παθητὸν αὐτὸν καταγγέλλουσιν, ὡς καὶ Παῦλος ἐπὶ Ἀγρίππα διορίζεται. ἐδήλωσε δὲ τὸ πάθος τῇ κατὰ τὸν Ἰωνᾶν παραβολῇ. τούτου γὰρ καὶ ἔχρῃζον οἱ αἰτήσαντες. οὐρανίου γὰρ σημείου οὐκ ἦσαν ἄξιοι, οὔτε ἦν αὐτοῖς ποιητὸν εἰ μὴ τὸ τοῦ σταυροῦ σημεῖον, δι᾽ οὗ κατηργήθη αὐτῶν ἡ ἀσθένεια.[dcccxcix]

> Ζῶν ἦν Ἰωνᾶς *ἐν τῇ κοιλίᾳ τοῦ κήτους*, καὶ Χριστὸς ἐν θανάτῳ γενόμενος ἐλεύθερος ἦν τούτου.[cm]

Ὥσπερ γὰρ ἦν Ἰωνᾶς ἐν τῇ κοιλίᾳ τοῦ κήτους τρεῖς ἡμέρας.[1113] Τρεῖς ἡμέρας καὶ τρεῖς νύκτας ὑπὸ γῆν διατρίψειν φησι. Τὴν μὲν παρασκευὴν ἀπὸ τέλους· τὸ δὲ σάββατον

1107 Matt. 12:39; 16:4; cf. Mark, 8:12; Luke, 11:29.
1108 Matt. 12:40.
1109 Cf. Acts, 26:23.
1110 Cf. Matt. 8:17, rendering Is. 53:4: οὗτος τὰς ἁμαρτίας ἡμῶν φέρει καὶ περὶ ἡμῶν ὀδυνᾶται.
1111 Matt. 12:40.
1112 Psalm 87:5.
1113 Matt. 12:40.

ὅλον· τὴν δὲ κυριακὴν ἀπὸ τῆς ἀρχῆς, κατὰ τὴν ὑπόληψιν τῶν ἀνθρώπων.[cmi] Ἐπεὶ καὶ ἡμεῖς τὴν τριταίαν τῶν τελευτησάντων ἡμέραν ἐπιτελοῦμεν, οὐκ ἐπειδ' ἂν ἴσῳ τῷ μέτρῳ πληρωθῆναι συμβαίη τὰς τρεῖς ἡμέρας καὶ τὰς τρεῖς νύκτας, ἀλλ' ἡμέραν μὲν μόνην καὶ τελείαν λογιζόμενοι ἐκείνην ἣν ἐν οἱῳδήποτε καιρῷ τετελεύτηκεν, ἡμέραν δὲ καὶ τὴν ἑτέραν, ἧς ἐν τοῖς προοιμίοις παρὰ τοὺς τάφους τῶν τετελευτηκότων ἄπιμεν. Κατὰ τὴν αὐτὴν τοίνυν ἀκολουθίαν καὶ ὁ Κύριος τρεῖς νύκτας καὶ ἡμέρας τοσαύτας ποιήσειν ἐπὶ τῆς γῆς ἐπηγγείλατο. Καὶ τούτου δεῖγμα σαφὲς τὸ καὶ τὰς γυναῖκας κατ' ἐκεῖνον ἐλθεῖν τὸν καιρὸν ὥστε τὰ νενομισμένα τῆς τριταίας ἡμέρας ἐπὶ νεκρῷ πληρῶσαι.

Τρεῖς ἡμέρας καὶ τρεῖς νύκτας ὑπὸ γῆν διατρίψειν φησίν, τὴν μὲν παρασκευὴν ἀπὸ τέλους, τὸ δὲ σάββατον ὅλον, τὴν δὲ κυριακὴν ἀπὸ τῆς ἀρχῆς κατὰ τὴν ὑπόληψιν τῶν ἀνθρώπων. ἐπεὶ καὶ ἡμεῖς τὴν τριταίαν τῶν τελευτησάντων ἡμέραν ἐπιτελοῦμεν, οὐκ ἐπειδὰν ἴσον τῷ μέτρῳ πληρωθῆναι συμβαίνῃ τὰς τρεῖς ἡμέρας καὶ τὰς τρεῖς νύκτας, ἀλλ' ἡμέραν μὲν μόνην καὶ τελείαν λογιζόμενοι ἐκείνην, ἣν ἐν οἵῳ δήποτε καιρῷ τετελεύτηκεν, ἡμέραν δὲ καὶ τὴν ἑτέραν, ἧς ἐν τοῖς προοιμίοις παρὰ τοὺς τάφους τῶν τετελευτηκότων ἄπειμεν. κατὰ τὴν αὐτὴν τοίνυν ἀκολουθίαν καὶ ὁ κύριος τρεῖς νύκτας καὶ ἡμέρας τοσαύτας ποιήσειν ὑπὸ τῆς γῆς ἐπηγγείλατο. καὶ τούτου δεῖγμα σαφὲς τὸ καὶ τὰς γυναῖκας κατ' ἐκεῖνον ἐλθεῖν τὸν καιρόν, ὥστε τὰ νενομισμένα τῆς τριταίας ἡμέρας ἐπὶ νεκρῷ πληρῶσαι.[cmii]

(Θεοδωρήτου.) *Σημεῖον Ἰωνᾶ* λέγει, τὸ τῆς θαλάσσης, ἐπειδὴ τριημέρευσεν ἐν τῷ κήτει. ὅθεν καὶ ὁ Κύριος ἡμῶν Ἰησοῦς Χριστός, τρεῖς ἡμέρας καὶ τρεῖς νύκτας ὑπὸ γῆς διέτριψεν, τὴν μὲν παρασκευήν, ἀπὸ τοῦ τέλους. τὸ δὲ σάββατον, ὅλον. τὴν δὲ κυριακήν, ἀπὸ τῆς ἀρχῆς, κατὰ τὴν ὑπόληψιν τῶν ἀνθρώπων. ἐπεὶ δὲ ἡμεῖς τὴν τριταίαν τῶν τελευτησάντων ἡμέραν ἐπιτελοῦμεν, οὐκ ἐπειδ' ἂν ἴσον τῷ μέτρῳ πληρωθῆναι συμβαίη τὰς τρεῖς ἡμέρας καὶ τὰς τρεῖς νύκτας, ἀλλ' ἡμέραν μὲν μόνην καὶ τελείαν λογιζόμενοι ἐκείνην, ἣν ἐν οἱῳδήποτε καιρῷ τελεύτηκεν. ἡμέραν δὲ καὶ τὴν ἑτέραν, ἧς ἐν τοῖς προοιμίοις παρὰ τοὺς τάφους τῶν τετελευτηκότων ἄπειμεν. κατὰ τὴν αὐτὴν τοίνυν ἀκολουθίαν, καὶ ὁ Κύριος τρεῖς νύκτας τε καὶ ἡμέρας ποιήσειν ἐπὶ τῆς γῆς. καὶ τούτου δεῖγμα σαφές, τὸ καὶ τὰς γυναῖκας κατ' ἐκεῖνον ἐλθεῖν τὸν καιρόν, ὥστε δὲ τὰ νενομισμένα τῆς τριταίας ἡμέρας ἐπὶ νεκρῷ πληρῶσαι.[cmiii]

36

| **101v** (ΩΡΙΓΕΝΟΥΣ) *Ὅτ‹α›ν*[1114] *δὲ τὸ ἀκάθαρτον πνεῦμα ἐξέλθῃ.*[1115] Ἡ παραβολὴ τοῦ ἀκαθάρτου πνεύματος περὶ τῶν ἐξ ἐπιστροφῆς εἰς ἀπροσεξίαν ἐρχομένων ἢ ἐξ ἰάσεως εἰς ῥαθυμίαν, δι' ἧς ἐπὶ τὸ χεῖρον ἕλκονται.

1114 Cod. ὅτ' ἄν.

1115 Matt. 12:43; cf. Zach. 13:2; Is. 34:14. Matt. 10:1; Mark, 1:23; 1:26-27; 3:11; 3:30; 5:2; 5:8; 5:13; 7:25; 9:25; Luke, 4:33; 4:36; 6:18; 8:29; 9:42; 11:24; Acts, 5:16; 8:7; 16:13; Rev. 18:2.

Ἡ παραβολὴ τοῦ ἀκαθάρτου πνεύματος περὶ τῶν ἐξ ἐπιστροφῆς εἰς ἀπροσεξίαν ἐρχομένων ἢ ἐξ ἰάσεως εἰς ῥᾳθυμίαν, δι᾽ ἧς ἐπὶ τὸ χεῖρον ἕλκονται.[cmiv]

(Ὠριγένους.) Ἡ παραβολὴ τοῦ ἀκαθάρτου πνεύματος, περὶ τῶν ἐξ ἐπιστροφῆς εἰς ἀπροσεξίαν ἐρχομένων, ἢ ἐξ ἰάσεως εἰς ῥᾳθυμίαν, δι᾽ ἧς ἐπὶ τὸ χεῖρον ἕλκονται.[cmv]

Ἐκ τούτου μανθάνομεν ὅτι ἀνεπίβατος[cmvi] τῷ δαίμονι ὁ τὰ καλλίω προαιρούμενος, ἔμφραγμα τῆς εἰσόδου τὴν ἀρετὴν προϊσχόμενος καὶ τόπον ἑαυτοῦ μηδένα | **102r** ἀφιείς, ὡς ὁ Ἐκκλησιαστὴς παραινεῖ.[1116] Τουναντίον δὲ ὁ ῥᾴθυμος ‹περὶ τὸ ἀγαθὸν› ἱππήλατός ‹ἐστι› τῷ πονηρῷ ‹πνεύματι›, καὶ ὅτι καὶ παραμυθίαν τινὰ τὴν εἰς τοὺς ἐπιτηδείους αὐτοῖς ἐνοίκησιν οἱ δαίμονες ἴσχουσιν, ὥσπερ ἐκ τῶν ἐναντίων καὶ ὁ Θεὸς *ἐν ἁγίοις ἀναπαυόμενος*.[1117]

Ἐκ τούτου μανθάνομεν ὅτι ἀνεπίβατος τῷ δαίμονι ὁ τὰ καλλίω προαιρούμενος, ἔμφραγμα τῆς εἰσόδου τὴν ἀρετὴν προϊσχόμενος καὶ τόπον ἑαυτοῦ μηδένα ἀφιείς, ὡς ὁ Ἐκκλησιαστὴς παραινεῖ. τοὐναντίον δὲ ὁ ῥᾴθυμος περὶ τὸ ἀγαθὸν ἱππήλατός ἐστιν τῷ πονηρῷ πατρί. μανθάνομεν δὲ ὅτι καὶ παραμυθίαν τινὰ τὴν εἰς τοὺς ἐπιτηδείους αὐτοῖς ἐνοίκησιν οἱ δαίμονες ἴσχουσιν, ὥσπερ ἐκ τῶν ἐναντίων καὶ ὁ Θεὸς *ἐν ἁγίοις ἀναπαυόμενος*.[cmvii]

Ἐκ τούτου μανθάνομεν, ὅτι μὴ κρατήσει δαίμων ἀνθρώπου τὰ καλλίω προαιρουμένου, ἀλλ᾽ ἀνεπίβατος ὁ τοιοῦτος ἔσται αὐτῷ ἔμφραγμα τῆς εἰσόδου τὴν ἀρετὴν προϊσχόμενος καὶ τόπον αὐτοῦ μηδένα ἀφιείς, ὡς ὁ Ἐκκλησιαστὴς παραινεῖ. τοὐναντίον δὲ ὁ κακὸς καὶ ῥάθυμος περὶ τὸ ἀγαθὸν ἱππήλατός ἐστι τῷ πονηρῷ πνεύματι. Μανθάνομεν δέ, ὅτι καὶ παραμυθίαν τινὰ τὴν εἰς τοὺς ἑαυτοῖς ἐπιτηδείους ἐνοίκησιν οἱ δαίμονες ἴσχουσιν, εἴ γε ὅτε μὴ δύνανται τοῦτο ποιεῖν οὐκ ἀναπαύονται, ὥσπερ ἐκ τῶν ἐναντίων λέγεται καὶ τοῦ θείου πνεύματος ἀνάπαυσις ἡ πρὸς αὐτὸ τῶν ἀνθρώπων ἐπιτηδειότης. *ἅγιος* γὰρ *ἐν ἁγίοις ἀναπαυόμενος* ὁ θεός. τὸ δὲ μετὰ πλειόνων ἐπεισιέναι τὸ ἅπαξ ἐξελθὸν αἰτίαν ἔχει τὴν τοῦ ἀνθρώπου ἀμετάβλητον πονηρίαν.[cmviii]

Ὃ ‹οὖν› λέγει τοιοῦτόν ἐστιν. *Ὅταν* ἔκ τινος *τὸ πνεῦμα ἐξέλθῃ* τῶν δαιμονώντων, περινοστεῖ[cmix] ταῖς τῶν ἁγίων ψυχαῖς, καὶ μὴ εὑρὸν ἀνάπαυσιν, ὥσπερ ὁ *δι᾽ ἀνύδρων* πορευόμενος *τόπων* (ἄνυδροι δέ εἰσι τόποι αἱ τῶν ἁγίων ἀφιλήδονοι[cmx] ψυχαί) ἐπανέρχεται ἐπ᾽ ἐκεῖνον ὅθεν ἐξῆλθε. Καὶ ἐὰν εὕρῃ αὐτὸν καθαρὸν *σχολάζοντα καὶ σεσαρωμένον*, τουτέστι κενὸν πράξεων ἀγαθῶν καὶ γυμνὸν θείας χάριτος, ὡς μὴ ὄντος ἔσω τοῦ δυναμένου αὐτὸν κωλῦσαι, ἐπιπηδᾷ αὐτῷ· πλὴν δειλιῶν οὐ μόνος τοῦτο ποιεῖ, ἀλλὰ συλλαμβάνει μεθ᾽ ἑαυτοῦ καὶ ἄλλους πολλοὺς πρὸς ἐπικουρίαν δαίμονας. Λέγει τοίνυν ὅτι ὥσπερ οἱ δαιμονῶντες ἐὰν ἀπαλλαγῶσι τῆς νόσου καὶ ῥαθυμότεροι γένωνται, χαλεπωτέραν καθ᾽ ἑαυτῶν ἐπισπῶνται τὴν νόσον, οὕτω καὶ ὑμεῖς. Ἐπειδὴ ἐν Αἰγύπτῳ δαίμοσι λατρεύοντες εἴχετε ἐν ἑαυτοῖς οἰκοῦν τὸ πνεῦμα τὸ πονηρόν·[cmxi] ὅτε ‹δὲ› θύσαντες τὸν ἀμνὸν διὰ τοῦ νόμου ἐπιστεύσατε εἰς Θεόν,

---

1116 Ecclesiastes, 10:4.

1117 Is. 57:15.

ἀπελήλατο ἐξ ὑμῶν. Ἀλλ᾽ ἐπειδὴ οὐ μόνον τοὺς προφήτας ἀλλὰ καὶ αὐτὸν τὸν τῶν προφητῶν Κύριον οὐκ ἐδέξασθε, πάλιν εἰσεπήδησε μετὰ πλείονος τῆς παρασκευῆς. Διὸ καὶ χείρονα τῶν πρώτων ὧν ὑπέμειναν οἱ πατέρες αὐτῶν ὑπὸ Βαβυλωνίων καὶ Αἰγύπτιων καὶ Ἀντιόχου ὑποστήσεσθαι αὐτοὺς ὑπὸ Ῥωμαίων φησὶ δεινά.[1118] | 102v Πάσης γὰρ στερηθέντες πνευματικῆς χάριτος, ταῖς τῶν δαιμόνων ἐπηρείαις εὐεπιχείρητοι[cmxii] γεγόνασιν· οἳ καὶ μανέντες ἐστασίασαν καθ᾽ ἑαυτοὺς καὶ ἐμφυλίου αἵματος ἔπλησαν τὴν Ἱερουσαλήμ. Διὸ καὶ τὴν ὑπὸ Ῥωμαίων ὑπέμειναν σφαγήν.

σεσαρωμένον καὶ κεκοσμημένον.[1119] Οἶκος σεσαρωμένος, εἰς ὃν δαιμόνια εἰσέρχονται, ψυχαί εἰσι τῶν δοκούντων βιοῦν κατὰ πρόθεσιν λόγων ὡς ἀληθῶν τῶν ἐν ψευδωνύμῳ γνώσει.[1120] Ὁ δ᾽ αὐτός ἐστι καὶ κεκοσμημένος ὡς ὁμοίωμα ναοῦ οὐκ ὢν ναός.

> Οἶκος σεσαρωμένος, εἰς ὃν δαιμόνια εἰσέρχονται, ψυχαί εἰσι τῶν δοκούντων βιοῦν κατὰ πρόθεσιν λόγων ὡς ἀληθῶν τῶν ἐν ψευδωνύμῳ γνώσει. Ὁ δ᾽ αὐτός ἐστι καὶ κεκοσμημένος ὡς ὁμοίωμα ναοῦ οὐκ ὢν ναός.[cmxiii]

Ἑπτά ἕτερα πνεύματα.[1121] Ἑπτὰ πνεύματα λογιστέον τὰ πολλά.[cmxiv] Καὶ γὰρ ἡ μὲν ἐν τοῖς ἔθνεσιν ὥσπερ ἐν ἀνύδροις τισὶ τόποις κατοίκησις ἐγίνετο τῷ πονηρῷ χαλεπή τε καὶ δύσβατος Θεὸν ὑποδεξαμένων τῶν ἐθνῶν. Ἡ δὲ εἰς τὸν Ἰσραὴλ ἐπάνοδος ῥᾴων ἢ πρότερον.

> *ἑπτὰ* δὲ *πνεύματα* λογιστέον τὰ πολλά. ἐπὶ γὰρ πλήθους πολλάκις τὰ *ἑπτὰ* παρὰ τῇ θείᾳ γραφῇ. κατ᾽ ἀρχὴν μὲν ἐν τοῖς Ἰουδαίοις ἐνῴκησε τὸ πνεῦμα τὸ πονηρόν, ὅτε κατ᾽ Αἴγυπτον εἰδωλολάτρουν, ἐξῆλθε δὲ ὅτε προσεκλήθησαν ὑπὸ θεοῦ. μετὰ ταῦτα δὲ ὅτε ἐξήμαρτον εἰς τὸν προσκαλεσάμενον, τότε μετέβαινεν ἡ χάρις ἐπὶ τὰ ἔθνη, οἱ δὲ ἐξεδίδοντο. καὶ ἡ μὲν ἐν τοῖς ἔθνεσιν ὥσπερ ἐν ἀνύδροις τισὶ τόποις κατοίκησις ἐγένετο τῶν πονηρῶν χαλεπή τε καὶ δύσβατος θεὸν ὑποδεξαμένων τῶν ἐθνῶν. ἡ δὲ εἰς τὸν Ἰσραὴλ ἐπάνοδος ῥᾷον ἢ πρότερον καὶ μετὰ πολλοῦ πλήθους τῆς ἐφόδου. διὸ κάκιον νῦν διάγουσιν ἢ ἐν Αἰγύπτῳ παραταττόμενοι μὲν εἰς τὰς κατὰ Χριστοῦ βλασφημίας ἀεί, τὴν δὲ πρὸς Ἀβραὰμ διαθήκην οὐκ ἔχοντες κατὰ τὸ δίκαιον προσδοκᾶν κἂν ὥσπερ τότε, ἀλλὰ ἀποκοπτόμενοι τῆς ἐλπίδος, ὅτι τὸν πληρωτὴν ταύτης ἠθετήκασιν. δεδήλωκεν οὖν ἐν τοῖς πρὸς αὐτοὺς λόγοις ὁ κύριος καὶ τὴν ἐσομένην ἀποβολὴν αὐτῶν καὶ τὴν ἐπικρίσεως τῆς μελλούσης αἰσχύνην καὶ τὴν ἤδη κράτησιν ὑπὸ τοῦ πονηροῦ.[cmxv]

Ἰδοὺ ἡ μήτηρ καὶ οἱ ἀδελφοί[1122] αὐτοῦ. Ἐπειδὴ ἐκ περιττῆς φιλοτιμίας τεθαρρηκότες λοιπὸν ὅτι ὑπακούει, ἐκάλεσαν αὐτὸν ἔτι λαλοῦντα ἔξω. Δοκεῖ πως αὐτοῖς ἐπιτιμᾶν ὡς σαρκικόν τι ἐνθυμουμένοις καὶ ἐνυβρίζει τὸ κενόδοξον. Ἐβούλετο γὰρ ἐνδείξασθαι ἡ μήτηρ τῷ δήμῳ ὅτι κρατεῖ καὶ αὐθεντεῖ τοῦ παιδός, οὐδὲν περὶ αὐτοῦ

1118 Cf. Matt. 12:45.
1119 Matt. 12:44.
1120 Cf. 1 Tim. 6:20.
1121 Matt. 12:44.
1122 Matt. 12:47.

μέγα φανταζομένη. Διὸ καὶ ὁ Κύριος οὐχ ὡς ἀτιμάζων τὴν κατὰ σάρκα συγγένειαν, οὐδ᾽ αἰσχυνόμενος τὴν ἐνανθρώπησιν, ἀλλὰ διορθούμενος ὅτι ὡς ἐπὶ ψιλῷ ἀνθρώπῳ ἐνεκαυχῶντο, εἶπε τὴν κατὰ Θεὸν συγγένειαν βελτίονα εἶναι τῆς κατὰ σάρκα. Οὐ γὰρ εἶπεν, οὐκ ἔστι μου μήτηρ· ἀλλὰ δι᾽ ὧν εἶπεν ἐδίδαξεν ὅτι οὐδὲν ὠφελεῖταί | **103r** τις ἐκ τῆς κατὰ σάρκα συγγενείας ἀρετῆς ἀμελῶν. Πάσης γὰρ συγγενείας προτιμᾷ ὁ Χριστός τοὺς κατὰ πίστιν οἰκείους καὶ ἀκούοντας καὶ ποιοῦντας *τὸ θέλημα τοῦ ἐν οὐρανοῖς πατρός.*[1123]

Ἰδοὺ ἡ μήτηρ σου καὶ οἱ ἀδελφοί σου ἔξω ἑστήκασι ζητοῦντες.[1124] Οἱ μὴ γινώσκοντες τὸ κατὰ τὴν παρθένον μυστήριον λέγουσιν *οἱ ἀδελφοί σου* τῷ Ἰησοῦ. Εἰ γὰρ ἐγίνωσκον, ἐπίστευον ‹ἂν› εἰς αὐτόν. Ἐκ δὲ τοῦ ποιεῖν *τὸ θέλημα τοῦ ἐν οὐρανοῖς πατρός, ἀδελφὸς ἢ ἀδελφὴ ἢ μήτηρ* τοῦ Ἰησοῦ τις γίνεται. Εἰ δ᾽ οὐδὲ τοῦτο, οὐ φύσει ἐστί τις *ἀδελφὸς* ἤ τι τῶν λοιπῶν. Ἔτι πᾶσα παρθένος καὶ ἀδιάφθορος ψυχὴ ἐξ Ἁγίου Πνεύματος συλλαβοῦσα, ἵνα γεννήσῃ τὸ πατρικὸν *θέλημα, μήτηρ* ἐστὶ τοῦ Ἰησοῦ.[cmxvi]

> Οἱ μὴ γινώσκοντες τὸ κατὰ τὴν παρθένον μυστήριον λέγουσιν *οἱ ἀδελφοί σου* τῷ Ἰησοῦ. εἰ γὰρ ἐγίνωσκον, ἐπίστευον εἰς αὐτόν. ἐκ δὲ τοῦ ποιεῖν *τὸ θέλημα τοῦ ἐν οὐρανοῖς πατρός, ἀδελφὸς ἢ ἀδελφὴ ἢ μήτηρ* τοῦ Ἰησοῦ τις γίνεται. εἰ δὲ οὐδὲ τοῦτο, οὐ φύσει ἐστί τις *ἀδελφὸς* ἤ τι τῶν λοιπῶν. ἔτι πᾶσα παρθένος καὶ ἀδιάφθορος ψυχὴ ἐξ ἁγίου πνεύματος συλλαβοῦσα, ἵνα γεννήσῃ τὸ πατρικὸν *θέλημα, μήτηρ* ἐστὶ τοῦ Ἰησοῦ.[cmxvii]

> Οἱ μὴ γινώσκοντες τὸ κατὰ τὴν παρθένον μυστήριον λέγουσιν *ἀδελφοί σου* τῷ Ἰησοῦ, εἰ γὰρ ἐγίνωσκον ἐπίστευον εἰς αὐτόν. ἐκ δὲ τοῦ ποιεῖν τὸ θέλημα τοῦ ἐν οὐρανοῖς πατρός, ἀδελφὸς ἢ ἀδελφὴ ἢ μήτηρ τοῦ Ἰησοῦ τις γίνεται. εἰ δὲ τοῦτο οὐ φύσει ἐστί τις *ἀδελφός*, ἤ τι τῶν λοιπῶν. Ἔτι πᾶσα παρθένος, καὶ ἀδιάφθορος ψυχὴ ἐξ Ἁγίου Πνεύματος συλλαβοῦσα, ἵνα γεννήσῃ τὸ πατρικὸν *θέλημα, μήτηρ* ἐστὶ τοῦ Ἰησοῦ.[cmxviii]

Τίς ἐστιν ἡ μήτηρ μου καὶ τίνες εἰσὶν οἱ ἀδελφοί μου;[1125] Ταῦτα εἶπεν οὐκ ἀποδοκιμάζων τὴν μητέρα καὶ τοὺς ἀδελφούς, ἀλλὰ δεικνὺς ὅτι πάσης σωματικῆς συγγενείας προτιμᾷ τῆς ψυχῆς τὴν οἰκειότητα. Πρὸς γὰρ τὸν οἰόμενον ὡς ἐπί τι σπουδαιότερον αὐτὸν καλεῖν τῶν οἰκείων τὴν ὁμιλίαν ἀναγκαῖον ἦν τοῦτο εἰπεῖν, ὁμοῦ καὶ εἰς διδασκαλίαν τῶν παρόντων. Ὡς γὰρ αὐτὸς εἶπεν τοῖς μαθηταῖς, *ὁ φιλῶν πατέρα ἢ μητέρα ὑπὲρ ἐμὲ οὐκ ἔστι μου ἄξιος,*[1126] οὕτως νόει μοι[cmxix] τὸν Ἰησοῦν προκρίνοντα τοὺς μαθητὰς ὑπὲρ *μητέρα καὶ ἀδελφούς.*

> Ταῦτα εἶπεν οὐκ ἀποδοκιμάζων *τὴν μητέρα καὶ τοὺς ἀδελφούς*, ἀλλὰ δεικνύς, ὅτι πάσης σωματικῆς συγγενείας προτιμᾷ τῆς ψυχῆς τὴν οἰκειότητα. πρὸς γὰρ τὸν οἰόμενον ὡς ἐπί τι σπουδαιότερον αὐτὸν καλεῖν τῶν οἰκείων τὴν ὁμιλίαν ἀναγκαῖον ἦν τοῦτο εἰπεῖν, ὁμοῦ καὶ εἰς διδασκαλίαν τῶν παρόντων. ὡς γὰρ αὐτὸς εἶπεν τοῖς μαθηταῖς. *ὁ φιλῶν*

1123 Matt. 12:50.
1124 Matt. 12:47.
1125 Matt. 12:48.
1126 Matt. 10:37.

πατέρα ἢ μητέρα ὑπὲρ ἐμὲ οὐκ ἔστι μου ἄξιος, οὕτως νόει μοι τὸν Ἰησοῦν προκρίνοντα τοὺς μαθητὰς ὑπὲρ *μητέρα καὶ ἀδελφούς*.[cmxx]

(Θεοδωρήτου.) Ταῦτα δὲ ἔφη, οὐκ ἀποδοκιμάζων πάντως τὴν μητέρα καὶ τοὺς ἀδελφούς, ἀλλὰ δεικνὺς ὅτι πάσης σωματικῆς συγγενείας προτιμᾷ τῆς ψυχῆς τὴν οἰκειότητα. διὰ τοῦτο κἀκείνους στέργων, εἰ ταῦτα ἐπάγοιντο. πρὸς γὰρ τὸν οἰόμενον ὡς ἐπί τι σπουδαιότερον καλεῖν αὐτὸν τῶν οἰκείων τὴν ὁμιλίαν, ἀναγκαῖον ἦν τοῦτο εἰπεῖν. ὃ μὲν καὶ εἰς διδασκαλίαν τῶν παρόντων. ὡς γὰρ αὐτὸς εἶπε τοῖς μαθηταῖς *ὁ φιλῶν πατέρα ἢ μητέρα* καὶ τὰ ἑξῆς. οὕτω μοι νόει τὸν Ἰησοῦν προκρίναντα τοὺς μαθητάς, ὑπὲρ μητέρα καὶ ἀδελφούς.[cmxxi]

Προκριτέα ἡ κατὰ Θεὸν συγγένεια τῆς κατὰ σάρκα, αὕτη γὰρ καὶ προηγουμένη καὶ μένουσα.[cmxxii]

(Ὠριγένους) Προκριτέα ἡ κατὰ Θεὸν συγγένεια τῆς κατὰ σάρκα, αὕτη γὰρ καὶ προηγουμένη καὶ μένουσα.[cmxxiii]

Therefore, every affection is cut off, all affinity is removed… . And so let no brother, wife, children, friends, or any affection that can exclude us from the kingdom of heaven be put before our love for the Lord.[cmxxiv]

37

106v (ΩΡΙΓΕΝΟΥΣ) *ὁ δὲ ἀποκριθεὶς εἶπεν αὐτοῖς ὅτι ὑμῖν δέδοται γνῶναι.*[1127] Τί οὖν ὁ Σωτὴρ πρὸς τοῦτό φησιν; *Ὑμῖν δέδοται* ἡ γνῶσις. Εἰπὼν *δέδοται* ἐσήμανεν ὅτι δωρεά ἐστι τὸ πρᾶγμα. Ὅμως οὐκ ἀναιρεῖ τὸ αὐτεξούσιον. Οὐ γὰρ παρὰ τοῦ δίδοντος αἰτίαν, ἀλλὰ παρὰ τὴν τῶν ἀκουόντων προαίρεσιν δίδοται ἢ οὐ δίδοται ἡ τῶν λεγομένων ἡ γνῶσις. Μόνοις δὲ τοῖς σπουδαίοις καὶ οὐ τοῖς ἀναξίοις ἀποκαλύπτεται τὰ θεῖα μυστήρια.
Τὸ ‹ὑμῖν› *δέδοται*, ἀντὶ τοῦ ‹τοῖς› ἀξίοις· ἡ γὰρ γνῶσις μισθός ἐστιν ἀγαθοῦ βίου, ὅν δίδωσιν ὁ Θεὸς ἐκείνοις, ‹οὓ›ς[1128] προγινώσκει ἐπιτηδείως ἔχοντας τοῦ λαβεῖν. Ἀγαθὸς οὖν ὁ θεὸς μὴ διδοὺς τὰ ἀνεπιτήδευτα τοῖς ἀνεπιτηδείοις, ἵνα μὴ κατακριθῶσιν.

Τὸ *‹ὑμῖν› δέδοται*, ἀντὶ τοῦ τοῖς ἀξίοις. ἡ γὰρ γνῶσις μισθός ἐστιν ἀγαθοῦ βίου, ὅν δίδωσιν ὁ Θεὸς ἐκείνοις, οὓς προγινώσκει ἐπιτηδείως ἔχοντας τοῦ λαβεῖν. ἀγαθὸς οὖν ὁ θεὸς μὴ διδοὺς τὰ ἀνεπιτήδευτα τοῖς ἀνεπιτηδεύτοις, ἵνα μὴ κατακριθῶσιν.[cmxxv]

τὸ δὲ *ὑμῖν δέδοται γνῶναι τὰ μυστήρια τῆς βασιλείας, ἐκείνοις δὲ οὐ δέδοται*, εἶπε, διὰ τὸ πάντων αἰτίους τῶν κακῶν ἑαυτοὺς ποιεῖν, ἐκείνους ἑκουσίως πεισθῆναι μὴ βουλομένους. οἱ γὰρ Ἀπόστολοι αὐθαιρέτως ἐπείσθησαν. οὐδὲ γὰρ ἀνάγκην εἰσάγω, φησίν,

1127 Matt. 13:11.
1128 Cod. οἷς.

> οὐδὲ ἀποκλήρωσίν[cmxxvi] τινα ἁπλῶς καὶ ὡς ἔτυχε γενομένην. οὐδὲ γὰρ τὸ αὐτεξούσιον ἀναιρῶ.[cmxxvii]

> *Ὅτι ὑμῖν δέδοται, φησί, …* ὅτι δωρεὰ τὸ πρᾶγμά ἐστι, καὶ χάρις ἄνωθεν δεδομένη. Οὐ μὴν ἐπειδὴ δωρεά, διὰ τοῦτο τὸ αὐτεξούσιον ἀνῄρηται.[cmxxviii]

38

107r (ΩΡΙΓΕΝΟΥΣ) *ὅστις γὰρ ἔχει, δοθήσεται αὐτῷ καὶ περισσευθήσεται.*[1129] Τουτέστιν, ὁ ἔχων κατορθώματα λαμβάνει καὶ τὴν τῶν θείων μαθημάτων γνῶσιν· τῷ δὲ μὴ ἔχοντι οὐ δίδοται, ἀλλὰ καὶ ὃ δοκεῖ ἔχειν ἀπόλλυται. Τῶν γὰρ κἂν σπινθῆρα μόν‹ον›[1130] τοῦ φωτὸς ἐσχηκότων καὶ εἰς ἀσύνετον τραπέντων νοῦν, καὶ αὐτὸς σβεσθήσεται.

> Τοῖς ἐπιεικέσι καὶ φιλομαθέσιν ἔχουσι γνῶσιν ἐνοικισθήσεται τὸ θεῖον φῶς πλουσιώτερον ἢ πάλαι, τοῖς δὲ ἐσχηκόσι σπινθῆρα φωτὸς νοητοῦ, εἰς ἀσύνετον δὲ τραπεῖσι γνῶσιν σβεσθήσεται καὶ αὐτὸ τὸ μικρὸν ὃ ἔχουσι σέλας.[cmxxix]

Οἱ γὰρ μὴ ἔχοντες ὑγιὲς φρόνημα οὔτε τὰ εὐχερῆ νοοῦσιν.
Ἐν τῷ παρόντι πιστεύσασιν ἡμῖν ἐδόθη ἡ χάρις διαφόρως, ἔχει δὲ αὐτὴν ὁ κατ᾽ αὐτὴν πεποιωμένος. *Δοθήσεται* οὖν τούτῳ ἡ βασιλεία. Εἰσὶν οὖν οἱ λαβόντες χάριν καὶ διὰ τὸ μὴ ἐργάζεσθαι αὐτὴν οὐκ ἔχουσιν αὐτήν. Ἐν τῷ οὖν μέλλοντι αἰῶνι *ἀρθήσεται* ἐξ αὐτῶν διὰ τὸ μὴ καλῶς αὐτῇ κεχρῆσθαι· περὶ οὗ λόγον τίσουσιν.

> Ἐν τῷ παρόντι πιστεύσασιν ἡμῖν ἐδόθη ἡ χάρις διαφόρως, ἔχει δὲ αὐτὴν ὁ κατ᾽ αὐτὴν πεποιωμένος. *δοθήσεται* οὖν τούτῳ ἡ βασιλεία. εἰσὶν οὖν οἱ λαβόντες χάριν καὶ διὰ τὸ μὴ ἐργάζεσθαι αὐτὴν οὐκ ἔχουσιν αὐτήν. ἐν τῷ οὖν μέλλοντι αἰῶνι *ἀρθήσεται* ἐξ αὐτῶν διὰ τὸ μὴ καλῶς αὐτῇ κεχρῆσθαι. περὶ οὗ λόγον τίσουσιν.[cmxxx]

Διὰ τοῦτο ἐν παραβολαῖς αὐτοῖς λαλῶ.[1131] *Διὰ τοῦτο* δέ φησι *ἐν παραβολαῖς λαλῶ* διὰ τοὺς ἑκοντὶ ἀβλεπτοῦντας. Εἰ γὰρ ἐκ φύσεως ἦν ἡ πήρωσις καὶ μὴ ἐκ διαθέσεως τρόπων ἔδει τὸν Χριστὸν ἀνοῖξαι αὐτῶν τοὺς τῆς διανοίας ὀφθαλμούς. Διὸ συμφερόντως | **107v** ἐσκότισεν αὐτῶν τὸν νοῦν[cmxxxi] εἰς τὸ μὴ νοεῖν, οὐ τοῦ Χριστοῦ αἴροντος ἀπ᾽ αὐτῶν τὴν νόησιν, ἀλλὰ μὴ ἀξιοῦντος αὐτοὺς τῶν ἑαυτοῦ πρὸς τὸ μὴ πλείονα δοῦναι δίκην. Ἵνα δὲ μὴ εἴπωσιν ὅτι ὡς ἐχθροῖς ταῦτα λέγει, παράγει καὶ προφητικὴν ῥῆσιν τὰ αὐτὰ λέγουσαν καὶ ἐλέγχει αὐτοὺς ὅτι καὶ ἀκούουσι καὶ βλέπουσι, καὶ αὐτοὶ βύουσι τὰ ὦτα τοῦ μὴ ἀκοῦσαι καὶ τοὺς ὀφθαλμοὺς μύουσι τοῦ μὴ ἰδεῖν.

1129 Matt. 13:12; cf. Matt. 25:29: τῷ γὰρ ἔχοντι παντὶ δοθήσεται καὶ περισσευθήσεται.

1130 Cod. μον.

1131 Matt. 13:13.

ἀκοῇ ἀκούσετε καὶ οὐ μὴ συνῆτε.[1132] Διότι ἔμελλον *βλέποντες* ἑκουσίως μὴ βλέπειν καὶ *ἀκούοντες* ἑκουσίως μὴ ἀκούειν, προεφήτευσεν Ἡσαΐας, *ἀκοῇ ἀκούσετε,*[1133] καὶ τὰ ἑξῆς. Ἵνα γὰρ μή τις νομίσῃ κατὰ ἀποκλήρωσιν Θεοῦ καὶ ἐπιλογὴν τοῖς μὲν δεδόσθαι, τοῖς δὲ μὴ δεδόσθαι, μᾶλλον δὲ (ὅπερ ἐστὶν ἀληθές) παρὰ τὴν ἀρετὴν τῶν λαβόντων καὶ τὴν κακίαν τῶν μὴ λαβόντων τοῦτο γεγενῆσθαι,[cmxxxii] ἐπιφέρει τὴν προφητείαν *Ἡσαΐου* αἰτιωμένην τῆς τῶν μὴ λαβόντων καρδίας τὸ παχὺ καὶ τυφλόν.

> Διότι ἔμελλον *βλέποντες* ἑκουσίως μὴ βλέπειν καὶ *ἀκούοντες* ἑκουσίως μὴ ἀκούειν, προεφήτευσεν Ἡσαΐας, *ἀκοῇ ἀκούσετε,* καὶ τὰ ἑξῆς. ἵνα γὰρ μή τις νομίσῃ κατὰ ἀποκλήρωσιν Θεοῦ καὶ ἐπιλογὴν τοῖς μὲν δεδόσθαι, τοῖς δὲ μὴ δεδόσθαι, μᾶλλον δὲ (ὅπερ ἐστὶν ἀληθές) παρὰ τὴν ἀρετὴν τῶν λαβόντων καὶ τὴν κακίαν τῶν μὴ λαβόντων τοῦτο γεγενῆσθαι, ἐπιφέρει τὴν προφητείαν *Ἡσαΐου* αἰτιωμένην τῆς τῶν μὴ λαβόντων καρδίας τὸ παχὺ καὶ τυφλόν.[cmxxxiii]

Ἐπαχύνθη γὰρ ἡ καρδία τοῦ λαοῦ.[1134] Εἶτα ἐπιτεταμένην αὐτῶν ἀπέχθειαν δεικνὺς ἣν εἶχον κατὰ τοῦ Χριστοῦ, ἐπάγει· *ἐπαχύνθη γὰρ ἡ καρδία τοῦ λαοῦ τούτου,* καὶ ἑξῆς. Τοῦτο δὲ ἐποίησαν, φησί, μήποτε *ἐπιστρέψωσι καὶ ἰάσομαι αὐτούς,*[1135] τὴν ἐπιτεταμένην αὐτῶν λέγων πονηρίαν καὶ τὴν μετὰ σπουδῆς ἀποστροφήν.

> ἐποίησαν δὲ τοῦτο, φησί, Μήποτε ἐπιστρέψωσι, καὶ ἰάσωμαι αὐτούς. τὴν ἐπιτεταμένην αὐτῶν λέγων πονηρίαν, καὶ τὴν μετὰ σπουδῆς ἀποστροφήν.[cmxxxiv]

Ὑμῶν δὲ μακάριοι οἱ ὀφθαλμοί.[1136] Μακαρίζει τοὺς μαθητὰς ὁ Σωτήρ, ἐπειδὴ ἐξ ἰδίας προαιρέσεως ἐπεδείξαντο τὴν εἰς αὐτὸν πίστιν, δι᾽ ἧς καὶ ἐδόθη αὐτοῖς ἡ γνῶσις ὡς ἀξιωθεῖσι τῆς θείας ἀκροάσεως.

> Τὰ ὑποδεχόμενα μακαρισμῶν καὶ περὶ παντὸς δὲ τοῦ βλέποντος τὰ θεῖα ὀφθαλμοῦ, καὶ ἀκούοντος τῶν πνευματικῶν ὤτων, ταῦτα ἂν λέγοιτο. περὶ τούτου φησὶν ὁ προφήτης *προσέθηκέ μοι Κύριος ὠτίον τοῦ ἀκούειν,*[1137] ἀντὶ τοῦ συνιεῖν τοῖς ἔνδοθεν ὠσὶν τὰς καρδίας *κατὰ τὸν ἔσω ἄνθρωπον.* ὁ γὰρ ἀπερίτμητος τῇ καρδίᾳ λαὸς ἐκωφώθη τοῖς ἔνδοθεν ὠσί.
>
> Καὶ μετ᾽ ὀλίγα.
>
> Διὸ καὶ αὐτὴν τὴν ἀκοήν, ἣν ἐδόκουν ἔχειν τοῦ νόμου καὶ τῶν προφητῶν, ἤρθη καὶ ἐδόθη τοῖς ἔχουσι τὴν καινὴν διαθήκην, ἵνα πληρωθῇ τὸ εἰρημένον ὑπὸ τοῦ Σωτῆρος. *ὑμῶν δὲ μακάρια τὰ ὦτα, ὅτι ἀκούουσι, καὶ οἱ ὀφθαλμοὶ ὅτι βλέπουσι.*[cmxxxv]

1132 Matt. 13:14, quoting Is. 6:9; so in Acts, 28:26.

1133 Is. 6:9.

1134 Matt. 13:15, quoting Is. 6:10.

1135 Matt. 13:15.

1136 Matt. 13:16.

1137 Is. 50:4-5.

Οἱ ἐπιθυμοῦντες *ἰδεῖν δίκαιοι* τὰ καταθύμια γνῶσιν ἔλαβον, ὧν ἐπεθύμουν. ἐπεθύμουν δὲ *ἰδεῖν*, καὶ ἀκοῦσαι ἃ οἱ Ἀπόστολοι ἔβλεπον, θεὸν ἐνανθρωπήσαντα, *καὶ ἀκοῦσαι* φωνὴν θεοῦ ἑνωθέντος σαρκὶ καθ' ὑπόστασιν.[cmxxxvi]

(Ὠριγένους.) Τὰ ὑποδεχόμενα μακαρισμῶν καὶ περὶ παντὸς δὲ τοῦ βλέποντος τὰ θεῖα ὀφθαλμοῦ, καὶ ἀκούοντος τῶν πνευματικῶν ὤτων, ταῦτα ἂν λέγοιτο. περὶ τούτου φησὶν ὁ προφήτης *προσέθηκέ μοι Κύριος ὠτίον τοῦ ἀκούειν*,[1138] ἀντὶ τοῦ συνιεῖν τοῖς ἔνδοθεν ὠσὶν τὰς καρδίας *κατὰ τὸν ἔσω ἄνθρωπον*.[1139] ὁ γὰρ ἀπερίτμητος τῇ καρδίᾳ[1140] λαὸς ἐκωφώθη τοῖς ἔνδοθεν ὠσί.

Καὶ μετ' ὀλίγον.

Διὸ καὶ αὐτὴν τὴν ἀκοήν, ἣν ἐδόκουν ἔχειν τοῦ νόμου καὶ τῶν προφητῶν, ἤρθη καὶ ἐδόθη τοῖς ἔχουσι τὴν καινὴν διαθήκην, ἵνα πληρωθῇ τὸ εἰρημένον ὑπὸ τοῦ Σωτῆρος. *ὑμῶν δὲ μακάρια τὰ ὦτα, ὅτι ἀκούουσι, καὶ οἱ ὀφθαλμοί, ὅτι*[1141] *βλέπουσι*.[cmxxxvii]

(Τοῦ αὐτοῦ.) Οἱ ἐπιθυμοῦντες *ἰδεῖν δίκαιοι*[1142] τὰ καταθύμια, γνῶσιν ἔλαβον ὧν ἐπεθύμουν. ἐπεθύμουν δὲ *ἰδεῖν* καὶ ἀκοῦσαι ἃ οἱ Ἀπόστολοι ἔβλεπον, Θεὸν ἐνανθρωπήσαντα, *καὶ ἀκοῦσαι* φωνῆς ἑνωθέντος σαρκὶ καθ' ὑπόστασιν.[cmxxxviii]

Μακαρίζει τοὺς μαθητὰς ὁ σωτήρ, ἐπειδὴ ἐξ ἰδίας προαιρέσεως ἐπεδείξαντο τὴν εἰς αὐτὸν πίστιν, δι' ἧς καὶ ἐδόθη αὐτοῖς ἡ γνῶσις ὡς ἀξιωθεῖσι θείας ἀκροάσεως.[cmxxxix]

Had we not read above that the listeners were challenged to understand when the Saviour said, *He who has ears to hear, let him he hear*,[1143] we would have thought that now the eyes and ears that receive the blessing should be understood as the bodily eyes. Instead, however, they seem to me to be those blessed eyes that can recognise the mysteries of Christ and that Jesus commanded to be lifted up on high to see the *white fields*,[1144] and the blessed ears are those of which Isaiah talks, *The Lord has given me an ear*.[cmxl]

Ματθαῖος ἔγραψε *πονηρός*, Μᾶρκος *σατανᾶς*, Λουκᾶς *ὁ διάβολος*. οὐ ταυτόν ἐστι *παρὰ τὴν ὁδὸν* καὶ ἐν τῇ ὁδῷ. δεόμεθα δὲ τῆς διαφορᾶς διὰ τὸ *ἐγώ εἰμι ἡ ὁδός*. πλὴν οἱ τρεῖς ἔγραψαν *παρὰ τὴν ὁδόν*. χαριέστατα δὲ Ματθαῖος καὶ Μᾶρκος *ἐπὶ τὰ πετρώδη*, οὐκ ἐπὶ *πέτραν* ἐσπάρθαι φασὶν τὸν λόγον. ἐπὶ μὲν σύμπαντος τοῦ *παρὰ τὴν ὁδὸν* εἴρηται τὸ *μὴ συνιέντος*, ἐπὶ δὲ τῆς καλῆς γῆς, *οὗτός ἐστιν ὁ τὸν λόγον ἀκούων καὶ συνιείς*. μήποτ' οὖν *ἐπὶ τὰ πετρώδη* καὶ οἱ εἰς *τὰς ἀκάνθας* μεταξύ εἰσιν ἀσυνετούντων καὶ συνιέντων. προτρεπτικὸν δὲ εἰς τὸ συνέσεως ἐπιμελεῖσθαι. εἰ γὰρ τοῦ *μὴ συνίεντος* ἁρπάζεται ὁ σπόρος, σύνεσιν ἀναληπτέον καὶ καλυπτέον τὸν σπόρον ἐν τῇ γῇ, τῇ μνήμῃ, ἵνα ῥιζοβολήσῃ καὶ μὴ γυμνὸν εὑρισκόμενον, ἁρπαγῇ ὑπὸ τῶν τῆς πονηρίας πνευμάτων.[cmxli]

(Τοῦ αὐτοῦ [Ὠριγένους]) Ματθαῖος ἔγραψε *πονηρός*, Μᾶρκος δὲ Σατανᾶς, Λουκᾶς *διάβολος*. οὐ ταυτόν ἐστι παρὰ τῇ ὁδῷ, καὶ ἐν τῇ ὁδῷ. δεόμεθα δὲ τῆς διαφορᾶς, διὰ

1138 Is. 50:4-5.
1139 Rom. 7:22.
1140 Acts, 7:51.
1141 Matt. 21:43.
1142 Matt. 13:17.
1143 Matt. 13:9.
1144 Cf. John, 4:35.

τὸ *ἐγώ εἰμι ἡ ὁδός*. πλὴν οἱ τρεῖς ἔγραψαν *παρὰ τὴν ὁδόν*. χαριέστατα δέ, Ματθαῖος καὶ Μᾶρκος *ἐπὶ τὰ πετρώδη*.[1145] οὐκ ἐπὶ *πέτραν* φησὶν ἐσπάρθαι τὸν λόγον. ἐπὶ μὲν σύμπαντος τοῦ *παρὰ τὴν ὁδὸν* εἴρηται τὸ *μὴ συνιέντος*. ἐπὶ δὲ τῆς καλῆς γῆς, *οὗτός ἐστιν ὁ τὸν λόγον ἀκούων καὶ συνιείς*. μήποτ᾽ οὖν *ἐπὶ τὰ πετρώδη* καὶ οἱ εἰς τὴν ἄκανθαν μεταξύ εἰσιν ἀσυνετούντων καὶ συνιέντων. προτρεπτικὸν δέ, εἰς τὸ συνέσεως ἐπιμελεῖσθαι. εἰ γὰρ τοῦ μὴ συνίεντος ἁρπάζεται ὁ σπόρος, σύνεσιν ἀναληπτέον καὶ καλυπτέον τὸν σπόρον ἐν τῇ γῇ τῇ μνήμῃ, ἵνα ῥιζοβολήσῃ, καὶ μὴ γυμνὸν εὑρισκόμενον, ἁρπαγῇ ὑπὸ τῶν τῆς πονηρίας πνευμάτων.[cmxlii]

Θλίψεως μὲν οἷον ὑπὸ τῶν γονέων ἢ συγγενῶν ἢ συνεργῶν ἢ δοκούντων φίλων συμβαινόντων. διωγμοῦ δέ, ὅτι *ἐπὶ ἡγεμόνας καὶ βασιλεῖς*[1146] φέρονταί τινες διὰ τὸν λόγον. γενικῶς δὲ ταῦτα ἀμφότερα πειρασμὸν[1147] ὠνόμασεν ὁ Λουκᾶς.[cmxliii]

(᾿Ωριγένους.) Θλίψεως ὑπὸ τῶν γονέων ἢ συγγενῶν, ἢ συνεργῶν, ἢ δοκούντων φίλων συμβαινόντων. διωγμοῦ δέ, ὅτι ἐπὶ ἡγεμόνας καὶ βασιλεῖς φέρονταί τινες διὰ τὸν λόγον. γενικῶς δὲ ταῦτα ἀμφότερα πειρασμῶν ὠνόμασεν ὁ Λουκᾶς.[cmxliv]

Ἡ ἀπάτη τοῦ πλούτου συμπνίγει καὶ ὁ τῶν ἑτεροδόξων λόγος. πλούσιοι γάρ εἰσι ψεῦσται, ὧν *κρείσσων πτωχὸς δίκαιος*,[1148] πτωχὸς μὲν *λόγῳ καὶ γνώσει*,[1149] βίῳ δὲ δίκαιος. ἡ δὲ παρὰ τῷ ἀποστόλῳ *μέριμνα πασῶν τῶν ἐκκλησιῶν*, οὐκ ἔστι *μέριμνα τοῦ αἰῶνος τούτου*,[1150] ἀλλ᾽ αἱ βιωτικαὶ μέριμναι. ταῦτα δὲ πάσχει ὁ μὴ νεώσας τὴν ἑαυτοῦ γῆν, ἀλλὰ ἀμελῶς τὸν λόγον δεχόμενος καὶ ἀναφύων ἀκάνθας, δι᾽ ἃς κατηράθη ἡ γῆ διὰ τῆς παρακοῆς ᾿Αδάμ, καὶ ἤκουσεν. *ἀκάνθας καὶ τριβόλους ἀνατελεῖ σοι*,[1151] ὧν *τὸ τέλος εἰς καῦσιν*.[1152] αὗται γὰρ οὐ σπείρονται, ἀλλ᾽ αὐτοφυεῖς εἰσιν ἐν τῷ ἀνθρώπῳ πνίγουσαι *τὸν λόγον* τοῦ θεοῦ διὰ προαίρεσιν μοχθηράν.[cmxlv]

(Τοῦ αὐτοῦ [᾿Ωριγένους]) *Ἡ ἀπάτη τοῦ πλούτου συμπνίγει*[1153] καὶ ὁ τῶν ἑτεροδόξων λόγος. πλούσιοι γάρ εἰσι ψεῦσται. ὧν κρεῖσσον ἀληθὴς πτωχὸς καὶ εὐσεβής. πτωχὸς μὲν λόγῳ καὶ γνώσει, βίῳ δὲ δίκαιος. ἡ δὲ παρὰ τῷ ᾿Αποστόλῳ *μέριμνα πασῶν τῶν ἐκκλησιῶν*,[1154] οὐκ ἔστι *μέριμνα τοῦ αἰῶνος τούτου*, ἀλλ᾽ αἱ βιωτικαὶ μέριμναι. ταῦτα δὲ ὑπομένει, ὁ μὴ νεώσας τὴν ἑαυτοῦ γῆν, ἀλλὰ ἀμελῶς τὸν λόγον δεχόμενος.[cmxlvi]

῾Ο ἀληθῶς γνωστικὸς καὶ συνίησι καὶ *καρποφορεῖ*. εἰ δέ τις δοκεῖ συνιέναι μὴ καρποφορῶν, οὐ συνίησιν, καὶ εἰ δοκεῖ καρποφορεῖν μὴ συνιείς, οὐ *καρποφορεῖ*. ὁ μέντοι εἰς *ἑξήκοντα* καὶ *τριάκοντα* καὶ *ἑκατὸν* ἐδήλωσεν τῆς ἀρετῆς τὸ ποικίλον, ἐπεὶ μὴ πάντες ἴσην ἐπιδείκνυνται τῆς ἀρετῆς τὴν ἀκρίβειαν, ἀλλ᾽ οἱ μὲν ἧττον, οἱ δὲ μᾶλλον αὐτῆς ἐπιμελόμενοι, ὥστε δεῖξαι ὅτι προσίεται καὶ τούτους κατὰ τὴν οἰκείαν ἀναλογίαν.[cmxlvii]

1145 Matt. 13:20; Mark, 4:16.
1146 Matt. 10:18.
1147 Cf. Luke, 8:13.
1148 Prov. 19:22.
1149 Cf. 1 Cor. 1:5.
1150 Matt. 13:22.
1151 Gen. 3:18.
1152 Heb. 6:8.
1153 Matt. 13:22.
1154 2 Cor. 11:28.

(Τοῦ αὐτοῦ.) Ἀληθῶς, γνωστικῶς συνιείς, καὶ εἰ δοκεῖ καρποφορῶν. εἰ δέ τις δοκεῖ συνίεναι μὴ καρποφορῶν, οὐ συνίησιν. καὶ εἰ δοκεῖ καρποφορεῖν, μὴ συνιεὶς ὃ καρποφορεῖ. ὁ μέντοι εἰς ἑξήκοντα καὶ τριάκοντα καὶ ἑκατόν, ἐδήλωσεν τῆς ἀρετῆς τὸ ποικίλον. ἐπεὶ μὴ πάντες ἴσην ἐπιδείκνυνται τῆς ἀρετῆς τὴν ἀκρίβειαν. ἀλλ᾽ οἱ μὲν ἧττον, οἱ δὲ μᾶλλον αὐτῆς ἐπιμελόμενοι. ὥστε δεῖξαι ὅτι προσίεται καὶ τούτους κατὰ τὴν οἰκείαν ἀναλογίαν.[cmxlviii]

Ὡμοιώθη, φησίν, *ἡ βασιλεία τῶν οὐρανῶν, σπείροντι καλὸν σπέρμα*, καὶ τὰ ἑξῆς. ἐν δὲ τῷ εἰπεῖν ὅτι *ἔσπειρε ζιζάνια*, τὰ τῶν αἱρετικῶν συστήματα καλεῖ. ἐπειδὴ ὥσπερ τὸ ζιζάνιον ἔοικεν τῷ σίτῳ, οὕτως καὶ ἡ πλάνη. πολλὰ τῇ ἀληθείᾳ ἐπιχρωννύει τὰ ὁμοιώματα. εἰπὼν δὲ ὅτι *ἐν τῷ καθεύδειν τοὺς ἀνθρώπους*, οὐ μικρὸν τοῖς ἱερεῦσιν ἐντεῦθεν ἐπικρεμνᾷ τὸν κίνδυνον. οὐ τοῖς ἱερεῦσι δὲ μόνοις, ἀλλὰ καὶ τῷ λαῷ. δείκνυσι δὲ καὶ τὴν πλάνην, μετὰ τὴν ἀλήθειαν οὖσαν. ὥσπερ γὰρ μετὰ τὸ σπαρῆναι τὸν σῖτον, ἐσπάρη τὰ ζιζάνια, οὕτως μετὰ τοὺς προφήτας, οἱ ψευδοπροφῆται. καὶ μετὰ τοὺς Ἀποστόλους, οἱ ψευδαπόστολοι. καὶ μετὰ τὸν Χριστόν, ὁ Ἀντίχριστος. ἂν γὰρ ἴδῃ τί μιμήσηται ὁ διάβολος, ἢ τίσιν ἐπιβουλεύσει, οὔτε ἐπιχειρεῖ, οὔτε οἶδεν. καὶ τί διαφέρουσιν οἱ καθεύδοντες, φησί, τῶν εἰς τὴν ὁδὸν σπαρέντων; πολύ. ὅτι ἐκεῖ εὐθέως ἥρπασεν. οὐδὲ γὰρ ριζωθῆναι ἀφῆκεν. ἐνταῦθα δέ, πλείονος ἐδεήθη τῆς μηχανῆς. ταῦτα δὲ εἶπεν ὁ Χριστός, παιδεύων ἡμᾶς διὰ παντὸς ἐγρηγορέναι καὶ νήφειν. κἂν γὰρ ἐκείνας διαφύγῃς τὰς βλάβας, φησίν, ἔστι καὶ ἑτέρα βλάβη. ὥσπερ γὰρ ἐκεῖ διὰ τῆς ὁδοῦ καὶ τῆς πέτρας καὶ τῶν ἀκανθῶν, οὕτως καὶ ἐνταῦθα διὰ τοῦ ὕπνου ἡ ἀπώλεια γίνεται. ὥστε διηνεκοῦς φυλακῆς δεῖ. διὸ καὶ ἔλεγεν. *ὁ δὲ ὑπομείνας εἰς τέλος, οὗτος σωθήσεται. ὅτε δὲ ἐβλάστησέν*, φησιν, *ὁ χόρτος, τότε ἐφάνη καὶ τὰ ζιζάνια*. παρὰ μὲν γὰρ τὴν ἀρχήν, συσκευάζουσιν ἑαυτοῖς οἱ αἱρετικοί. ἐπειδὰν δὲ πολλὴν λάβωσι παρρησίαν, καὶ λόγου τίς αὐτοῖς μεταδῷ, τότε τὸν ἰὸν ἐκχέουσιν.[cmxlix]

39

(ΩΡΙΓΕΝΟΥΣ) **110v** *Ἀνθρώπῳ σπείραντι καλὸν σπέρμα.*[1155] Ὅσα μὲν ἐν ἀνθρώπου ψυχῇ φύεται καλά, ὡς αἱ φυσικαὶ ἔννοιαι,[cml] ὑπὸ τοῦ λόγου σπείρεται, γεννήματα ὄντα τῆς τοῦ Θεοῦ βασιλείας, ὡς εἶναι τοὺς περὶ ἑκάστου ὑγιεῖς λόγους τοὺς *υἱοὺς τῆς βασιλείας.*[1156][cmli] Τὰ δὲ ὑπὸ τοῦ ἐχθροῦ ἐπισπειρόμενα[cmlii] εἶναι κακίαν καὶ τὰ μοχθηρὰ πράγματα, καθὸ *ἀγρὸς* ὅλος *ὁ κόσμος*[1157] καὶ οὐ μόνη ἡ ἐκκλησία. Ἔσται δὲ ἐπὶ τέλει τῶν πραγμάτων,[cmliii] ὃ καλεῖται συντέλεια,[1158] *θερισμός*,[1159] ἵνα ἀναλέξαντες οἱ ἅγιοι τὰ ἐν ψυχῇ φαῦλα νοήματα, παραδῶσιν εἰς ἀνάλωσιν τῷ φλεγομένῳ πυρί.[cmliv] Διδάσκει ὁ λόγος ὅτι οὐ λανθάνει τὰ τῶν αἱρετικῶν ἀναφυῆναι μέλλοντα συστήματα,[cmlv] οἳ ἔχουσι μὲν ὄνομα Χριστιανῶν,[cmlvi] ὡς καὶ τὰ ζιζάνια ἐμφέρειαν τινὰ πρὸς τὸν σῖτον, εἰ καὶ διεφθαρμέ | **111r** νην.

1155 Matt. 13:24.
1156 Matt. 13:37-38 (against 8:12).
1157 Matt. 13:38.
1158 Matt. 13: 39; 40; 49; 24:3; 28:20.
1159 Matt. 13:30.

Ὅσα ἐν τῇ ἀνθρωπίνῃ φύεται ψυχῇ καλά, ταῦτα ὑπὸ τοῦ *ἐν ἀρχῇ πρὸς τὸν θεὸν* λόγου θεοῦ ‹σπείρεται› γεννήματα τυγχάνοντα τῆς τοῦ θεοῦ βασιλείας, ὡς εἶναι τοὺς περὶ ἑκάστου ὑγιεῖς λόγους τοὺς υἱοὺς *τῆς βασιλείας*... ὁ διάβολος ἐπιτηρῶν ἐπισπείρει τὰ καλούμενα ζιζάνια, τὰ μοχθηρὰ δόγματα, ταῖς καλουμέναις ὑπό τινων φυσικαῖς ἐννοίαις καὶ σπέρμασι καλοῖς τοῖς ἀπὸ τοῦ λόγου. Κατὰ δὲ τοῦτο ἀγρὸς καὶ ὁ κόσμος πᾶς λέγοιτο ἂν καὶ οὐ μόνον ἡ ἐκκλησία τοῦ θεοῦ. ἐν γὰρ παντὶ κόσμῳ ὁ μὲν *υἱὸς τοῦ ἀνθρώπου* ἔσπειρε *τὸ καλὸν σπέρμα*, ὁ δὲ πονηρὸς τὰ ζιζάνια, ἅπερ εἰσὶν οἱ μοχθηροὶ λόγοι, οἱ ἀπὸ κακίας υἱοὶ τοῦ πονηροῦ. Δεήσει δὲ γενέσθαι ἐπὶ τέλει τῶν πραγμάτων ὃ καλεῖται *συντέλεια τοῦ αἰῶνος* θερισμόν, ἵν᾿ οἱ ἐπὶ τούτῳ τεταγμένοι ἄγγελοι τοῦ θεοῦ ἀναλέξωνται τὰ προσπεφυκότα τῇ ψυχῇ φαῦλα δόγματα καὶ παραδῶσιν αὐτὰ εἰς ἀνάλωσιν, τῷ λεγομένῳ καίειν πυρὶ ἀνατρέποντες αὐτά.[cmlvii]

ἐν δὲ τῷ εἰπεῖν ὅτι *ἔσπειρε ζιζάνια*, τὰ τῶν αἱρετικῶν συστήματα καλεῖ. ἐπειδὴ ὥσπερ τὸ ζιζάνιον ἔοικεν τῷ σίτῳ, οὕτως καὶ ἡ πλάνη. πολλὰ τῇ ἀληθείᾳ ἐπιχρωννύει τὰ ὁμοιώματα.[cmlviii]

Τοῖς οὖν οἰομένοις νοεῖν τὴν παραβολήν, ἐπαπορητέον ταῦτα. Τίς ὁ *ἄνθρωπος* ὁ τὸ *καλὸν σπέρμα* σπείρας; Καὶ τί τὸ *καλὸν σπέρμα*; Καὶ τίς *ὁ ἀγρός*; Τίνες οἱ καθεύδοντες ἄνθρωποι; Καὶ τίς ὁ ἐχθρὸς ὁ σπείρας *τὰ ζιζάνια ἀναμέσον τοῦ σίτου*; Καὶ διατί *ἄνθρωπος* λέγεται *ὁ ἐχθρός*; Καὶ τίνες *οἱ δοῦλοι τοῦ οἰκοδεσπότου*;

Τοῖς οἰομένοις νοεῖν τὴν παραβολήν, ἐπαπορητέον ταῦτα. τίνες οἱ καθεύδοντες ἄνθρωποι, καὶ τίνες *οἱ δοῦλοι τοῦ οἰκοδεσπότου*, καὶ διὰ τί *ἄνθρωπος* λέγεται *ὁ ἐχθρός*;[cmlix]

Δόξειε δ᾿ ἂν εἶναι σαφῆ[1160] εἰ *ἀγρός ἐστιν ὁ κόσμος, ὁ σπείρας*, ὁ υἱὸς τοῦ ἀνθρώπου, *τὸ καλὸν σπέρμα, οἱ υἱοὶ τῆς βασιλείας, τὰ ζιζάνια, οἱ υἱοὶ* τοῦ *πονηροῦ, ὁ σπείρας* αὐτὰ *ὁ διάβολος*. Οἱ δὲ καθεύδοντες ἄνθρωποι, ὁ μὴ προσέχων μηδὲ[1161] ἐγρηγορὼς τῶν ἀνθρώπων νοῦς, ἀλλ᾿ ὕπνῳ ἀμελείας κεκαρωμένος. Οἱ δὲ δοῦλοι, *ἄγγελοί εἰσιν*, οὓς ἐπέσχεν *ὁ υἱὸς τοῦ ἀνθρώπου* ἀνασπάσαι *τὰ ζιζάνια* διδοὺς καιρὸν μετανοίας,[cmlx] εἰδὼς ὅτι ἐκ μεταβολῆς τὸ ζιζάνιον δύναται γενέσθαι σῖτος. Οὐκ ἐν ἀρχῇ δὲ τοῦ Εὐαγγελίου ἐφάνησαν αἱ αἱρέσεις, αἵ εἰσι ζιζάνια, *ἀλλ᾿ ὅτε ἐβλάστησεν ὁ χόρτος καὶ καρπὸν ἐποίησε*·[1162] τουτέστιν, ὅτε τοῦ Εὐαγγελίου ὁ λόγος *εἰς πᾶσαν τὴν γῆν*[1163] ἐπλατύνθη. Ἀρχὴ γὰρ τοῦ φαίνεσθαι τὰ ζιζάνια ὅτε καρπὸν ποιεῖ βλαστήσας ὁ ἀπὸ τοῦ καλοῦ σπέρματος χόρτος. Οὐ θέλει δὲ ἐκτιλῆναι τὰ ζιζάνια παρ᾿ ἑτέρων. Ἔξεστι γὰρ καὶ τὰς ἐπιγινομένας ἀκάνθας καὶ τὰ σπαρέντα ζιζάνια ἡμᾶς ἐξαλείφειν, πλὴν παρ᾿ ἡμῶν καὶ οὐ παρ᾿ ἑτέρων ἐκτίλλεσθαι ταῦτα προσήκει, ἐπεὶ καὶ παρὰ τὴν ἡμῶν αἰτίαν ἐπιβέβληνται ταῦτα.

1160 Cf. Matt. 12:36-43.
1161 Cod. μὴ δὲ.
1162 Matt. 13:26.
1163 Cf. Psalm 18:5 (quoted in Rom. 10:18); Psalms of Solomon, 1:4; Ez. 11:16; Rev. 5:6.

Τρεῖς ‹δὲ› τάξεις εἰσὶν ἐν τοῖς πιστοῖς· ὁ τὰ *τριάκοντα*, ὁ τὰ *ἑξήκοντα*, ὁ τὰ *ἑκατὸν* ‹καρποφορῶν›.[1164] | **111v** Οἶμαι δὲ ὅτι καὶ ἐν τοῖς χειρίστοις οὕτως εὑρίσκονται.

> Τρεῖς τάξεις εἰσὶν ἐν τοῖς πιστοῖς. ὁ τὰ *τριάκοντα*, ὁ τὰ *ἑξήκοντα*, ὁ τὰ *ἑκατόν*. οἶμαι δὲ ὅτι καὶ ἐν τοῖς χειρίστοις οὕτως εὑρίσκεται.[cmlxi]
>
> There is a threefold diversity of the good earth: fruit of one hundredfold, sixtyfold, and thirtyfold.[cmlxii]

Προσελθόντες δὲ οἱ δοῦλοι.[1165] Ὄντως οἱ ἴδιοι τοῦ Κυρίου ταράττονται ὅταν ἐπιγνῶσι τοὺς αἱρετικούς, ἀνάγουσι δὲ ἐπὶ τὸν Κύριον τὴν περὶ τοῦ πράγματος φροντίδα. Ἢ ὅτι τοῦτο λυπήσει, *φησί*, καὶ τὰς ἀοράτους δυνάμεις εὐνοίᾳ τῇ πρὸς ἐμέ, ὡς ἐθελῆσαι καὶ ἀφανίσαι τοὺς εὑρετάς. Ἤτοι, τοὺς πειθομένους αὐτοῖς, ἀλλ᾽ ἐφέξω τοῦτο γενέσθαι.

> [Ἐχθρὸν δὲ ἄνθρωπον τὸν διάβολον καλεῖ διὰ τὴν εἰς ἀνθρώπους βλάβην. ἡ μὲν γὰρ ἐπήρεια καθ᾽ ἡμῶν, ἡ δὲ ἀρχὴ τῆς ἐπηρείας οὐκ ἀπὸ τῆς εἰς ἡμᾶς ἐπηρείας, ἀλλ᾽ ἀπὸ τῆς εἰς Θεὸν ἔχθρας ἐγένετο. ὅθεν δῆλον ὅτι ὁ θεὸς μᾶλλον ἡμᾶς φιλεῖ ἢ ἡμεῖς ἑαυτούς. διὰ τί δὲ μὴ πρὸ τούτου *ἔσπειρε τὰ ζιζάνια*, ἀλλ᾽ ὅτε ἦν ἅπαντα πεπληρωμένα; ἵνα τῇ σπουδῇ λυμήνηται τοῦ γεωργοῦ. οὕτως πρὸς τὸν θεὸν ἐχθρωδῶς ἔχων πάντα ἐποίει. τίνος ἕνεκεν εἰσάγει τοὺς δούλους λέγοντας ‹τὸ› γεγενημένον καὶ κατεπείγοντας ἤδη τὰ ζιζάνια ἀνασπάσαι, εἰ καὶ μὴ διεσκεμμένως λαλοῦσι; δεικνύων τὴν μέριμναν αὐτῶν τὴν ὑπὲρ τοῦ σπόρου, καὶ ἵνα τὸ νόσημα τέως ἐξέλωσιν. οὐχ ἑαυτοῖς δὲ ἐπιτρέπουσιν, ἀλλὰ τοῦ δεσπότου τὴν γνώμην ἀναμένουσιν. ὁ δὲ δεσπότης κωλύει. οὐδὲ γὰρ δεῖ φονεύειν αἱρετικὸν (τοῦτο γὰρ δηλοῖ, τὸ *θέλεις ἀπελθόντες συλλέξωμεν αὐτά*). καὶ γὰρ φονευομένων τῶν αἱρετικῶν, πόλεμον ἄσπονδον εἰς τὴν οἰκουμένην εἰσάγετε. τί δέ ἐστι *μήποτε ἐκλέγοντες τὰ ζιζάνια ἐκριζώσητε ἅμα σὺν αὐτοῖς τὸν σῖτον*; ἢ τοῦτό φησιν. ὅτι εἰ μέλλοιτε κινεῖν ὅπλα καὶ κατασφάττειν τοὺς αἱρετικούς, ἀνάγκη πολλοὺς καὶ τῶν ἁγίων συγκαταβάλλεσθαι.[cmlxiii] ἢ ὅτι καὶ ἀπ᾽ αὐτῶν τῶν ζιζανίων εἰκὸς πολλοὺς μεταβάλλεσθαι, καὶ γίνεσθαι *σῖτον*. ἂν τοίνυν προλαβόντες *ἐκριζώσητε* αὐτούς, λυμαίνεσθε τῷ μέλλοντι γίνεσθαι σίτῳ. οὐ τοίνυν ἐπιστομίζειν καὶ ἐκκόπτειν τὴν παρρησίαν τῶν αἱρετικῶν κωλύει, ἀλλὰ τὸ κατασφάττειν αὐτούς.[cmlxiv] τίνος χάριν *ἐρῶ*, φησι, *τοῖς θερισταῖς. συλλέξατε πρῶτον τὰ ζιζάνια*; ἵνα μὴ φοβήθωσιν οὗτοι (ἤγουν οἱ θερισταὶ) ὡς συναπαγομένου αὐτοῖς τοῦ σίτου. χρὴ δὲ σκοπεῖν καὶ τοῦ δεσπότου τὴν ἡμερότητα, ὅτι ἀναμένει τῶν ζιζανίων τὴν ἐπιστροφήν, ἴσως γίνεται σῖτος. ἂν δὲ μέχρι τέλους μένωσι *ζιζάνια, τότε* φησίν, *ἐρῶ τοῖς θερισταῖς. συλλέξατε καὶ δήσατε εἰς δεσμὰς πρὸς τὸ κατακαῦσαι αὐτά*. ὅπερ δηλοῖ, τὴν αἰώνιον αὐτῶν καταδίκην. θεριστὰς δὲ τοὺς ἀγγέλους[cmlxv] λέγει.][cmlxvi]
>
> (Ὠριγένους.) Ἐχθρὸν δὲ ἄνθρωπον, τὸν διάβολον καλεῖ, διὰ τὴν εἰς ἀνθρώπους βλάβην. ἡμᾶς γὰρ ἐπήρεια, καθ᾽ ἡμῶν. ἡ δὲ ἀρχὴ τῆς ἐπηρείας, οὐκ ἀπὸ τῆς εἰς ἡμᾶς ἐπηρείας, ἀλλ᾽ ἀπὸ τῆς εἰς Θεὸν ἔχθρας ἐγένετο. ὅθεν δῆλον, ὅτι ὁ Θεὸς μᾶλλον ἡμᾶς φιλεῖ, ἢ ἡμεῖς ἑαυτούς. διὰ τί δὲ μὴ πρὸ τούτου ἔσπειρε τὰ ζιζάνια, ἀλλ᾽ ὅτε ἦν ἅπαντα πεπληρωμένα;

1164 Matt. 13:23; Mark, 4:20.

1165 Matt. 13:27.

ἵνα τῇ σπουδῇ λυμήνηται τοῦ γεωργοῦ. οὕτως πρὸς τὸν Θεὸν ἐχθρωδῶς ἔχων, πάντα ἐποίει. τίνος ἕνεκεν εἰσάγει τοὺς δούλους λέγοντας γεγενημένον, καὶ κατεπείγοντας ἤδη τὰ ζιζάνια ἀνασπάσαι, εἰ καὶ μὴ διεσκεμμένως λαλοῦσι; δεικνύων τὴν μέριμναν αὐτῶν, τὴν ὑπὲρ τοῦ σπόρου, καὶ ἵνα τὸ νόσημα τέως ἐξέλωσιν. οὐχ ἑαυτοῖς δὲ ἐπιτρέπουσιν, ἀλλὰ τοῦ δεσπότου τὴν γνώμην ἀναμένουσιν. ὁ δὲ δεσπότης κωλύει. οὐδὲ γὰρ δεῖ φονεύειν αἱρετικόν. τοῦτο γὰρ δηλοῖ, τὸ *θέλεις ἀπελθόντες συλλέξωμεν αὐτά*. καὶ γὰρ φονευομένων τῶν αἱρετικῶν, πόλεμον ἄσπονδον εἰς τὴν οἰκουμένην εἰσάγετε. τί δέ ἐστι *μήποτε ἐκλέγοντες τὰ ζιζάνια, ἐκριζώσητε ἅμα σὺν αὐτοῖς τὸν σῖτον*; ἢ τοῦτό φησιν. ὅτι εἰ μέλλοιτε κινεῖν ὅπλα καὶ κατασφάττειν τοὺς αἱρετικούς, ἀνάγκη πολλοὺς καὶ τῶν ἁγίων συγκαταβάλλεσθαι. ἢ ὅτι καὶ ἀπ᾽ αὐτῶν τῶν ζιζανίων εἰκὸς πολλοὺς μεταβάλλεσθαι, καὶ γίνεσθαι σῖτον. ἂν τοίνυν προλαβόντες ἐκριζώσητε αὐτούς, λυμαίνεσθε τῷ μέλλοντι γίνεσθαι σίτῳ. οὐ τοίνυν ἐπιστομίζειν καὶ ἐκκόπτειν τὴν παρρησίαν τῶν αἱρετικῶν κωλύει, ἀλλὰ τὸ κατασφάττειν αὐτούς. τίνος χάριν *ἐρῶ*, φησι, *τοῖς θερισταῖς. συλλέξατε πρῶτον τὰ ζιζάνια*; ἵνα μὴ φοβήθωσιν οὗτοι. ἤγουν οἱ θερισταί, ὡς συναπαγομένου αὐτοῖς τοῦ σίτου. χρὴ δὲ σκοπεῖν, καὶ τοῦ δεσπότου τὴν ἡμερότητα. ὅτι ἀναμένει τῶν ζιζανίων τὴν ἐπιστροφήν. ἴσως γίνεται σῖτος. ἂν δὲ μέχρι τέλους μένωσι ζιζάνια, *τότε φησίν, ἐρῶ τοῖς θερισταῖς, συλλέξατε καὶ δήσατε εἰς δεσμάς, πρὸς τὸ κατακαῦσαι αὐτά*. ὅπερ δηλοῖ, τὴν αἰώνιον αὐτῶν καταδίκην. θεριστὰς δέ, τοὺς Ἀγγέλους λέγει.[cmlxvii]

Ὁ δὲ ἔφη, οὔ, μήποτε συλλέγοντες τὰ ζιζάνια.[1166] Θέλουσι τοίνυν οἱ δοῦλοι ἀπολέσαι τὰ ζιζάνια φειδοῖ τοῦ σίτου· οὓς κωλύει ὁ Χριστὸς φυλάττεσθαι, τούτους παρακελευόμενος, τιμωρηθησομένους καιρῷ τῷ προσήκοντι ὡς μηδὲν βλαπτομένου τοῦ σίτου μήπως καὶ οἱ ἅγιοι ἀναιρεθῶσιν ἐν τῷ γίνεσθαι κατὰ τῶν αἱρετικῶν πολέμους.[cmlxviii] *Θερισμὸν* δὲ νῦν τὴν συντέλειαν λέγει καὶ *θεριστάς*, τοὺς ἀγγέλους. Κωλύει δὲ ἀναιρεῖσθαι τοὺς αἱρετικούς, οὐ μέντοι γε περικόπτεσθαι αὐτῶν τὴν παρρησίαν καὶ τὰς συνόδους.[cmlxix] Πρῶτον δὲ τὰ ζιζάνια κελεύει συλλέξαι καὶ καῦσαι, ἵνα μὴ φοβηθῶσιν οἱ ὄντες πιστοὶ καὶ τῷ σίτῳ παρεικαζόμενοι ὡς οὐ συναγόμενοι. *Εἰς δέσμας* δὲ εἶπεν, ὡς ἅμα πάντων μοιχῶν ἐκβαλλομένων καὶ ἅμα τῶν φονέων,[1167] ὡς ἐν μιᾷ τάξει εἶναι τοὺς ἁμαρτωλούς, εἰ καὶ διάφοροι αἱ πράξεις διὰ τὸ τὴν τῶν ἕξεων ποιότητα μίαν εἶναι.

Ὡς φιλάνθρωπος δὲ ὁ Θεὸς[1168] δι᾽ ἑαυτοῦ μὲν σπείρει, δι᾽ ἑτέρων δὲ κολάζει.

[Ὡς φιλάνθρωπος δὲ ὁ Θεός δι᾽ ἑαυτοῦ μὲν σπείρει, δι᾽ ἑτέρων δὲ κολάζει.][cmlxx]

Χρὴ δὲ σκοπεῖν καὶ τὴν φιλανθρωπίαν τὴν ἄφατον, καὶ τὸ πρὸς κόλασιν ἠλλοτριωμένον. ὅτε μὲν γὰρ σπείρει, δι᾽ ἑαυτοῦ σπείρει. ὅτε δὲ κολάζει, δι᾽ ἑτέρων.[cmlxxi]

1166 Matt. 13:29.

1167 Cf. Ex. 20:13&16; Deut. 5:17&18; Jer. 7:9; Matt. 19:18; Mark, 10:19; Luke, 18:20; Rom. 13:9; James, 2:11.

1168 Cf. Tit. 3:4.

Ἀποθήκην[1169] δὲ λέγει τὴν ἄνω *Ἱερουσαλήμ*,[1170] ἤγουν τὰς οὐρανίους μονάς,[1171] ἐν αἷς οἱ ἅγιοι ὡς σῖτος ἀποτίθενται εἰς τὸ ἀναλόγως ἕκαστον κομίσα | **112r** σθαι τὴν παρὰ Θεοῦ διδομένην αὐτοῖς χάριν.[cmlxxii]

> *Ἀποθήκην* δὲ νοητέον τὴν *ἄνω Ἱερουσαλὴμ* ἤγουν τὰς οὐρανίους μονάς, ἐν αἷς οἱ ἅγιοι ὡς σῖτος ἀποτίθενται εἰς τὸ ἀναλόγως ἕκαστον κομίσασθαι τὴν παρὰ Θεοῦ διδομένην αὐτοῖς χάριν.[cmlxxiii]

Ὁμοία ἐστὶν ἡ βασιλεία τῶν οὐρανῶν, κόκκῳ σινάπεως.[1172] *Κόκκῳ σινάπεως* παρείκασε τὸν τοῦ Εὐαγγελίου λόγον, ὃς εἰ καὶ ἁπλοῦς εἶναι δοκεῖ διὰ τὸ ἁπλοῦν καὶ εὐτελὲς τῶν λέξεων,[cmlxxiv] δριμεῖαν ἔχει ἐνέργειαν περιεκτικὴν τῶν καθαρῶν δογμάτων, ὡς δένδρον δὲ ὑπερφυὲς γίνεται τὰ ὑπὲρ τὴν φύσιν διδάσκων μυστήρια. Ἤτοι τοῦτο φησί, ὡς ὀλίγου ὄντος τὸ κατ᾽ ἀρχὰς τοῦ κηρύγματος, ὕστερον δὲ πλατυνθέντος.

> Τὸ ἡμέτερον κήρυγμα σμικρότατον ἦν κατ᾽ ἀρχὰς καὶ εὐτελὲς διά τε τὸν σταυρὸν καὶ τὸν θάνατον καὶ τὸ τῆς λέξεως ἁπλοῦν τε καὶ ἀπερίεργον.[cmlxxv] οὐδὲ γὰρ ὥσπερ Ἕλληνες ἐν ταῖς λέξεσιν ἐκόμπαζον περὶ ματαίων διαλεγόμενοι, οὕτω καὶ οἱ ἀπόστολοι ἐποίουν. ἀλλὰ τῆς μὲν ποικιλίας τῶν λέξεων οὐδένα λόγον ἐτίθεντο, τῆς δὲ ἀληθείας ἐπεμελοῦντο, τὰ θαύματα ἐνεργοῦντες καὶ τοὺς ἀνθρώπους ἐκ τῆς πλάνης ἐλευθεροῦντες.[cmlxxvi]

Ἄλλως τε, ὁ τοῦ Χριστοῦ περὶ τῆς βασιλείας τοῦ Θεοῦ λόγος, μικρὸς κατ᾽ ἀρχὰς καὶ εὐτελὴς φαινόμενος πάντων τῶν πώποτε ἐν ἀνθρώποις σπαρέντων λόγων μείζω καὶ πλείω δεδύνηται τοσοῦτον, ὡς καὶ τὰς ἐπουρανίους δυνάμεις[1173] εὐκαίρως *πετεινὰ οὐρανοῦ*[1174][cmlxxvii] ὀνομασθείσας, ἀπαντώσας παρὰ τοῖς καρποφοροῦσιν ἐν αὐτῷ, ἀναπαύεσθαι. *Μεγάλους* δὲ οἶμαι *κλάδους* λέγεσθαι τοὺς ἐν τῷ λόγῳ τοῦ Θεοῦ μεγάλους.

> Ὁ περὶ τῆς βασιλείας τοῦ Θεοῦ λόγος, μικρὸς κατ᾽ ἀρχὰς καὶ εὐτελὴς φαινόμενος διὰ τὸν σταυρὸν καὶ τὸν θάνατον καὶ τὸ ἐν λέξει μικροπρεπές, οὕτως ηὐξημένος *πάντων τῶν πώποτε ἐν ἀνθρώποις σπαρέντων λόγων μεῖζον* καὶ πνεῖον δεδύνηται, ἐπὶ τοσοῦτον ὡς καὶ τὰς ἐπουρανίους δυνάμεις ὑπ᾽ αὐτῷ παρὰ τοῖς καρποφορήσασιν ἐν αὐτῷ ἀναπαύσασθαι. *μεγάλους* δὲ οἶμαι *κλάδους* λέγεσθαι τοὺς ἐν τῷ λόγῳ τοῦ θεοῦ μεγάλους.[cmlxxviii]

1169 Matt. 13:30.
1170 Gal. 4:26.
1171 Cf. John, 14:2.
1172 Matt. 13:31.
1173 Cf. Matt. 24:29; Mark, 13:25; Luke, 21:26; cf. 2 Paralipomenon (Chronicon 2), 18:18; Odae, 12:15.
1174 Matt. 13:32; Mark, 4:32; Luke, 13:19.

> Τὸ ἡμέτερον κήρυγμα σμικρότατον ἦν κατ' ἀρχὰς καὶ εὐτελὲς διά τε τὸν σταυρὸν καὶ τὸν θάνατον καὶ τὸ τῆς λέξεως ἁπλοῦν καὶ ἀπερίεργον. οὐδὲ γὰρ ὥσπερ οἱ Ἕλληνες ἐν ταῖς λέξεσιν ἐκόμπαζον περὶ ματαίων διαλεγόμενοι, οὕτω καὶ οἱ ἀπόστολοι ἐποίουν. ἀλλὰ τῆς μὲν ποικιλίας τῶν λέξεων οὐδένα λόγον ἐτίθεντο, τῆς δὲ ἀληθείας ἐπεμελοῦντο, τὰ θαύματα ἐνεργοῦντες καὶ τοὺς ἀνθρώπους ἐκ τῆς πλάνης ἐλευθεροῦντες.[cmlxxix]

> Compare teaching of this kind with the doctrines of philosophers, with their books and with the magnificence and fluency and the structure of their preaching. Then you will see how much the sowing of the Gospel is less than the other seeds. But when those seeds grow, they demonstrate no bite, no vigour, no vitality. They are entirely flaccid and flabby and they sprout to vegetable plants and herbs which quickly wane and fall. But this preaching, which seems insignificant in the beginning, once it has been sown, either into the soul of the believer or into the whole world, does not rise up into a vegetable plant, but it grows into a tree, so that the birds of the sky, which we ought to understand either as the souls of the believers or their strength of mind submitted to the service of God, come and dwell in its branches. I think the branches of the Gospel-tree which grows from the grain of mustard are the diverse doctrines in which each of the above-mentioned birds finds rest.[cmlxxx]

(ΩΡΙΓΕΝΟΥΣ,[cmlxxxi] added on the margin)[cmlxxxii] Πετεινὰ οὖν οὐ καλεῖ τοὺς ὑψηλοτέρους τῷ φρονήματι, καὶ παντὸς γεώδους ἀνωτέρους, τοὺς ἔχοντας τὴν τοῦ Θεοῦ σκέπην διὰ τῆς τοῦ Εὐαγγελίου διδαχῆς, παντὸς αὐτοὺς καύσωνος ἀπαλλάττουσαν διαβολικοῦ.[cmlxxxiii] Ἤτοι πετεινὰ λέγει τοὺς τῶν Ἑλλήνων σοφοὺς καὶ ὑψηλόφρονας, οἳ τὸ μὲν τῶν λόγων εὐφραδὲς ἴσασι, νενεύκασι δὲ ἐπὶ τὸ δοκοῦν μικρόν, τὴν πίστιν παραδεξάμενοι.[cmlxxxiv]

(ΩΡΙΓΕΝΟΥΣ, main text cont.) Εἰ δὲ περὶ *βασιλείας* οὐρανῶν διαλεγόμενος, κόκκου *σινάπεως* καὶ ζύμης μέμνηται, μὴ θαυμάσῃς. Ἰδιῶται γὰρ ἦσαν, μόλις καὶ διὰ τοιούτων παραδειγμάτων δυνάμενοι νοῆσαι.

> (Ὠριγένους) Μηδεὶς δὲ θαυμαζέτω, εἰ περὶ βασιλείας οὐρανῶν διαλεγόμενος, κόκκου σινάπεως καὶ ζύμης ἐμνήσθη. ἀνθρώποις γὰρ διελέγετο ἀπείροις καὶ ἰδιώταις, καὶ δεομένοις ἀπὸ τούτων ἐνάγεσθαι. οὕτω γὰρ ἦσαν ἀφελεῖς, ὡς καὶ μετὰ ταῦτα δεηθῆναι ἑρμηνείας πολλῆς.[cmlxxxv]

Ὁμοία ἐστὶν ἡ βασιλεία τῶν οὐρανῶν ζύμῃ.[1175] *Ζύμη μὲν τῶν Φαρισαίων,*[1176] ἡ διδαχή ἐστι, Χριστοῦ δέ, ἡ περὶ τῆς βασιλείας *τῶν οὐρανῶν*, ἥνπερ *λαβοῦσα γυνή*, ἡ ἐκκλησία, εἰς τὰ κρυπτὰ τοῦ ἀνθρωπίνου πνεύματος καὶ τοῦ ἐν τῇ ψυχῇ νοῦ καὶ τοῦ σώματος *ἔκρυψεν*, ἵνα ὅλος ζυμωθῇ ὁ ἄνθρωπος ἑνούμενος τῇ τοῦ Χριστοῦ διδασκαλίᾳ.

> *Ζύμη* μὲν τῶν Φαρισαίων, ἡ διδαχή ἐστιν, Χριστοῦ δὲ ἡ περὶ τῆς βασιλείας *τῶν οὐρανῶν*, ἥνπερ *λαβοῦσα γυνή*, ἡ ἐκκλησία, εἰς τὰ κρυπτὰ τοῦ ἀνθρωπίνου πνεύματος καὶ τοῦ ἐν

1175 Matt. 13:33.
1176 Cf. Matt. 16:11.

τῇ ψυχῇ νοῦ καὶ τοῦ σώματος *ἔκρυψεν*, ἵνα ὅλος ζυμωθῇ ὁ ἄνθρωπος ἑνούμενος τῇ τοῦ Χριστοῦ διδασκαλίᾳ.[cmlxxxvi]

Ὃ δὲ λέγει τοιοῦτόν ἐστιν. Ὡς ἡ ζύμη ὀλίγη οὖσα τὸ πολὺ τοῦ ἀλεύρου μεθίστησιν εἰς τὴν ἑαυτῆς ἰσχύν, | **112v** οὕτω καὶ ὑμεῖς, ὀλίγοι ὄντες τὴν πᾶσαν εἰς ἑαυτοὺς οἰκουμένην μεταστήσετε.

ὥσπερ τὸ πολὺ ἄλευρον μεθίστησιν ἡ ζύμη μικρὰ οὖσα εἰς τὴν ἑαυτῆς ἰσχύν, οὕτω, φησίν, καὶ ὑμεῖς οἱ μαθηταί μου, τὸν πάντα κόσμον μεταστήσετε,[cmlxxxvii]

Καθάπερ γὰρ αὕτη τὸ πολὺ ἄλευρον μεθίστησιν εἰς τὴν ἑαυτῆς ἰσχὺν, οὕτω καὶ ὑμεῖς τὸν πάντα κόσμον μεταστήσετε.[cmlxxxviii]

ὀλίγοι ὄντες, εἰς τὴν τῆς ἀληθείας ἐπίγνωσιν. καὶ ὥσπερ ἡ ζύμη τὸ φύραμα ζυμοῖ, ὅτ᾽ ἂν μίγῃ τὸ ἄλευρον, τοῦτο γὰρ δηλοῖ τὸ *ἔκρυψεν*, οὕτω καὶ ὑμεῖς, ὅτ᾽ ἂν κολληθῆτε καὶ ἑνωθῆτε τοῖς πολεμοῦσιν ὑμῖν, τότε αὐτῶν περιέσεσθε. καὶ καθάπερ ἐκεῖ καταχώννυται μὲν τῷ ἀλεύρῳ, οὐκ ἀφανίζεται δέ, ἀλλὰ καὶ μᾶλλον πρὸς τὴν ἑαυτῆς ἕξιν μεταποιεῖ πάντα. τὸν αὐτὸν τρόπον, καὶ ἐπὶ τοῦ κηρύγματος τούτου συμβήσεται.[cmlxxxix]

Τὰ *τρία* δὲ ὧδε τὰ πολλὰ σημαίνει.[cmxc]

τρία δὲ σάτα εἰπών, τὰ πολλὰ εἴρηκεν. οἶδε γὰρ τὸν ἀριθμὸν τούτων, ἐπὶ πλήθους λαμβάνειν.[cmxci]

τρία δὲ σάτα εἰπών, τὰ πολλὰ εἴρηκεν. οἶδε γὰρ τὸν ἀριθμὸν τούτων, ἐπὶ πλήθους λαμβάνειν.[cmxcii]

Ἤτοι *ζύμη* ἐστὶ τὸ Ἅγιον Πνεῦμα τὸ μεταποιοῦν τὸν ἄνθρωπον διὰ τῆς ἀναγεννήσεως[1177] ἀπὸ σαρκικοῦ φρονήματος εἰς πνευματικὴν ἕξιν. *Ζύμη* οὖν, τὸ Πνεῦμα· *γυνή*, ἡ σοφία, ‹ἥ›[1178] ἐστι Χριστός.[cmxciii]

Ἑτέρως ἔστι λαβεῖν τὴν μὲν γυναῖκα εἰς τὴν ἐκκλησίαν, τὴν δὲ ζύμην εἰς τὸ πνεῦμα τὸ ἅγιον, σάτα δὲ τρία σῶμα, πνεῦμα, ψυχήν. ἁγιάζεται δὲ ταῦτα τῇ ζύμῃ τοῦ ἁγίου πνεύματος, ὥστε γενέσθαι πρὸς τὸ ἅγιον πνεῦμα ἓν φύραμα, ἵν᾽ *ὁλόκληρον ἡμῶν τὸ σῶμα καὶ τὸ πνεῦμα καὶ ἡ ψυχὴ ἀμέμπτως τηρηθείῃ ἐν τῇ ἡμέρᾳ τοῦ κυρίου ἡμῶν Ἰησοῦ Χριστοῦ*,[1179] ὥς φησιν ὁ θεσπέσιος Παῦλος.[cmxciv]

This woman who took the yeast and buried it in three measures of meal until it was all leavened appears to me to refer either to the apostolic preaching or to the Church, which has been congregated from various nations. She takes the leaven, that is, the knowledge and understanding of the scriptures, and she buries it in three measures of flour, so that the spirit, soul, and body, having been coalesced

1177 Cf. John, 3:5-8; 1 Peter, 1:3.

1178 Cod. ὅς.

1179 1 Thess. 5:23.

into one, might not have discord among themselves, but would agree with two and three and would obtain from the Father whatever they ask for.[1180][cmxcv] ...

Γυνὴ δὲ ταύτην, ἡ σοφία τοῦ Θεοῦ, εἰς ἀλεύρου σάτα τρία ἐγκρύπτει. Τοῖς γοῦν πορισαμένοις ἐκ πολλῆς ἐπιμελείας καὶ τῆς τοῦ σπόρου γεωργίας ἀλεύρου σάτα τρία, δόγματα, θείαν γνῶσιν τὴν περὶ Πατρὸς καὶ Υἱοῦ καὶ ῾Αγίου Πνεύματος, ἡ τοῦ Θεοῦ σοφία τὸ ἅγιον Πνεῦμα χορηγεῖ. ῾Η δ᾽ αὐτή, καθ᾽ ἑτέραν διάνοιαν, πάντα τὸν ἐκ Θεοῦ ἄνθρωπον ἐκ σώματος καὶ ψυχῆς καὶ πνεύματος συνεστῶτα, τῇ ἐπιχορηγίᾳ τῆς θείας ἐμπνεύσεως, ζύμην ἐγκρύπτουσα, τὴν ἐξ αὐτῆς ὠφέλειαν, εἰς ἀλεύρου σάτα τρία τὰ νενοημένα, ἕως οὗ ζυμωθῇ ὅλον.[cmxcvi]

... I should also speak of a third consideration by some people,[cmxcvii] so that a curious reader might be able to pick out from the many ones that which pleases him.[cmxcviii] They interpret this woman as the Church, which has mixed the faith of a man into three measures of wheat by means of belief in the Father, in the Son, and in the Holy Spirit. And once the Church has been fermented into one, this leads us not to a threefold God, but to the knowledge of the one divinity.[cmxcix] This is how they interpret the three measures of wheat: while there is no different nature [of each person of the Trinity] they tend towards a unity of substance.[m]

Ἀλεύρου σάτα τρία, ὁ ἄνθρωπος ὁ ἔχων ἐν ἑαυτῷ τὰ τρία ταῦτα, ψυχὴν καὶ σῶμα καὶ πνεῦμα.[1181][mi]

ἀλεύρου σάτα τρία, ὁ ἄνθρωπός ἐστιν ὁ ἔχων ἐν ἑαυτῷ τὰ τρία ταῦτα, ψυχὴν καὶ σῶμα καὶ πνεῦμα.[mii]

᾽Ωριγένης τὴν μὲν γυναῖκα λαμβάνει εἰς τὴν ἐκκλησίαν, τὴν δὲ ζύμην εἰς τὸ Πνεῦμα τὸ ῞Αγιον, σάτα δὲ τρία, σῶμα, πνεῦμα, ψυχήν, ἁγιάζεται δὲ ταῦτα τῇ ζύμῃ τοῦ ῾Αγίου Πνεύματος, ὡς γενέσθαι πρὸς τὸ ῞Αγιον Πνεῦμα ἓν φύραμα.[miii]

῞Ητοι *τρία σάτα* φησὶ ῞Ελληνας, ᾽Ιουδαίους, Σαμαρείτας, ὡς μελλόντων τούτους εἰς ἑαυτοὺς ἑλκύσαι τῶν μαθητῶν ὥστε ἴσους αὐτοὺς ἑαυτῶν ποιῆσαι κατὰ τὴν πίστιν· ἐν γὰρ Χριστῷ ᾽Ιησοῦ, φησὶ ὁ ἀπόστολος, *οὐκ ἔνι ᾽Ιουδαῖος οὐδὲ ῞Ελλην.*[1182]

᾽Αλεύρου σάτα τρία ῞Ελληνας καὶ ᾽Ιουδαίους, καὶ Σαμαρείτας ὀνομάζει. τούτοις τοῖς τρισὶν ἐμβληθεῖσα ἡ ζύμη ἓν φύραμα τὴν φύσιν πάντων εἰργάσατο.[miv]

῍Η καὶ οὕτως· *γυνή* ἐστιν ἡ ᾽Εκκλησία,

῾Ετέρως ἐστι λαβεῖν τὴν μὲν γυναῖκα εἰς τὴν ἐκκλησίαν.[mv]

1180 Cf. Matt. 18:19.
1181 Cf. 1 Thess. 5:23.
1182 Gal. 3:28; Col. 3:11.

Ἑτέρως ἐστι λαβεῖν τὴν μὲν γυναῖκα εἰς τὴν Ἐκκλησίαν, τὴν δὲ ζύμη εἰς τὸ Πνεῦμα τὸ Ἅγιον. *Σάτα δὲ τρία, σῶμα, πνεῦμα, ψυχήν.*[mvi]

ζύμη, ἡ διδασκαλία, *ἀλεύρου σάτα τρία*, τὸ ἐκ τῶν ἐθνῶν σύστημα διὰ τὸ *εἰς πᾶσαν τὴν γῆν*[1183] ἐξεληλυθέναι τὸ εὐαγγελικὸν κήρυγμα.
τρία δὲ *σάτα* ὀνομάζει τὰ ἔθνη, ἐπειδὴ ἐκ τῶν τριῶν τοῦ Νῶε παίδων συνέστη.

ἀλεύρου δὲ *σάτα τρία* τοὺς τρεῖς τοῦ Νῶε παῖδας, τὸν *Σήμ*, τὸν *Χάμ*, τὸν *Ἰάφεθ*, ἐξ ὧν μόνων μετὰ τὸν κατακλυσμὸν πάντα προῆλθε τὰ ἔθνη τὰ νῦν ἐν τῇ ἐκκλησίᾳ συναγειρόμενα.[mvii]

Καὶ χωρὶς παραβολῆς οὐ‹δὲν›[1184] *ἐλάλει αὐτοῖς.*[1185] Ἐν παραβολαῖς ἐλάλει, φησί, ἵνα πληρώσῃ τὴν προφητείαν. Οὐ τοῦτό δέ φησι, ὅτι διὰ τοῦτο οὕτως ἐλάλει ἵνα πάντως ἀποπληρώσῃ τὰ προφητικά, ἀλλ' ἵνα φανῇ ὁ τῶν προφητῶν λόγος ἀληθής, ὡς ἐν γνώσει λαλησάντων τὰ πάντως ἐσόμενα.[mviii] Τὸ γὰρ *ὅπως*[1186] ἐνταῦθα οὐκ αἰτιολογίας ἐστίν, ἀλλ' ἐκβάσεως.[mix]
Διὰ δὲ τοὺς Ἰουδαίους ἐλάλει ἀσαφέστερον, ἵνα ἐρωτήσαντες μάθωσι τὴν λύσιν καὶ ὠφεληθῶσιν.

ἐλάλει δὲ ἐν παραβολαῖς, εἰς ἐρώτησιν τοὺς ὄχλους προτρεπόμενος.[mx]

Ἤτοι οὕτως λαλεῖ διὰ τοὺς ἀναμεμιγμένους ἀπίστους πρὸς τὸ μὴ ἐπιγνῶναι αὐτοὺς τοὺς μυστικοὺς λόγους. Εἶτα δει | **113r** κνὺς ἑαυτὸν μὴ καινοτομοῦντα, εἰσάγει τὸν προφήτην καὶ τοῦτον προαναφωνοῦντα τῆς διδασκαλίας τον τρόπον.

τότε ἀφεὶς τοὺς ὄχλους ἦλθεν εἰς τὴν οἰκίαν,[1187] ἵνα οἱ ὄχλοι ἄνεσιν[mxi] λάβωσιν. Οἴκαδε ἀναχωρεῖ[mxii] ὁ Σωτήρ. Οἱ δὲ μαθηταὶ ἐν τῇ οἰκίᾳ γενόμενοι, καίπερ δειλιῶντες,[mxiii] ἐθάρρησαν ἐρωτῆσαι τὴν *τῶν ζιζανίων παραβολήν*. Μόνην δὲ ταύτην ἠρώτησαν ὡς τῶν ἄλλων σαφεστέρων οὐσῶν καὶ ἵνα μάθωσι μήπως τινὲς τῶν ἀνθρώπων εἰσὶ φαῦλοι φύσει πρὸς οὓς οὐ δεῖ κηρῦξαι. Δεικνὺς τοίνυν ὅτι οὐκ ἔστι φύσεως τὸ ἁμαρτάνειν ἢ τὸ ἀγαθοποιεῖν,[mxiv] τοῖς μὲν κόλασιν ἀπειλεῖ, τοὺς δὲ τιμᾷ. Εἰ μὲν γὰρ φύσεως ἦν τοῦτο, οὔτε τούτους ἐκόλαζεν οὔτε τούτους ἐτίμα ‹ἂν› μηδὲν ἐκ προαιρέσεως πράξαντας.[mxv] Φησὶ γὰρ πρὸς τὸ τέλος τῆς παραβολῆς· *ἀποστελεῖ ὁ υἱὸς τοῦ ἀνθρώπου τοὺς ἀγγέλους αὐτοῦ, καὶ συλλέξουσιν ἐκ τῆς βασιλείας αὐτοῦ πάντα τὰ σκάνδαλα καὶ τοὺς ποιοῦντας τὴν ἀνομίαν καὶ βαλοῦσιν αὐτοὺς εἰς τὴν κάμινον τοῦ πυρός· ἐκεῖ ἔσται ὁ κλαυθμὸς καὶ ὁ βρυγμὸς τῶν ὀδόντων.*[1188] Εἶτα καὶ τὴν τῶν δικαίων ἐπάγει

1183 Psalm 18:5, quoted in Rom. 10:18.
1184 Cod. οὐκ.
1185 Matt. 13:34.
1186 Matt. 13:35.
1187 Matt.13:36.
1188 Matt. 13:41-42.

ἀπόλαυσιν λέγων· *τότε οἱ δίκαιοι ἐκλάμψουσιν ὡς ὁ ἥλιος ἐν τῇ βασιλείᾳ τοῦ πατρὸς αὐτῶν*·[1189] τουτέστι διὰ τῆς ἀφθαρσίας λάμψουσι δοξαζόμενοι ὑπὸ Κυρίου. Ἐπειδὴ δὲ φωτεινότερον οὐκ ἴσμεν ἄστρον τοῦ ἡλίου, πρὸς αὐτὸ ποιεῖται τὴν σύγκρισιν ἐπεὶ τούτου πολὺ λαμπρότεροι ἔσονται οἱ ἅγιοι.

Ὁ σπείρων τὸ καλὸν σπέρμα ἐστίν.[1190] Ὁ μὲν Κύριος ἐν τῷ ἰδίῳ ἀγρῷ *καλὸν* ἔσπειρε *σπέρμα, ἀγρὸς δέ ἐστιν ὁ κόσμος.*[1191]

| **113v** *Ἐν δὲ τῷ καθεύδειν τοὺς ἀνθρώπους ἦλθε καὶ ἔσπειρε ζιζάνια μέσον τοῦ σίτου ὁ ἐχθρὸς καὶ ἀπῆλθεν.*[1192] Ἔκτοτε γὰρ ἀποστάτης ὁ ἄγγελος οὗτος καὶ *ἐχθρὸς* ἀφότε[mxvi] ἐζήλωσε τὸ πλάσμα τοῦ Θεοῦ καὶ ἐχθροποιῆσαι ἑαυτὸν πρὸς τὸν Θεὸν ἐπεχείρησε. Διὸ καὶ ὁ Θεὸς τὸν μὲν παρ' αὐτοῦ τὸ ζιζάνιον λάθρᾳ ἐπισπείραντα (τουτέστι τὴν παράβασιν εἰσενεγκόντα) ἀφώρισε τῆς ἰδίας μετουσίας, τὸν δὲ ἀμελῶς μὲν ἀλλ' ἀκάκως παραδεξάμενον τὴν παρακοὴν ἄνθρωπον ἠλέησε καὶ ἀντέστρεψε τὴν *ἔχθραν* ἣν ἐχθροποιῆσαι πρὸς αὐτὸν ἠθέλησε τὸν ἐχθροποιοῦντα, ἀπωσάμενος μὲν ἀφ' ἑαυτοῦ τὴν πρὸς τὸν ἄνθρωπον *ἔχθραν*, ἀνακ‹λά›σας[1193] δὲ αὐτὴν καὶ ἀντιπέμψας πρὸς τὸν ὄφιν, καθὼς ἡ γραφή φησι εἰρηκέναι τῷ ὄφει τὸν Θεόν· *καὶ ἔχθραν θήσ‹ω›*[1194] *ἀνὰ μέσον σοῦ, καὶ ἀνὰ μέσον τῆς γυναικός.*[1195]

> (Εἰρηναίου ἐπισκόπου.) Ὁ μὲν Κύριος ἐν τῷ ἰδίῳ ἀγρῷ, καλὸν ἔσπειρε σπέρμα. ἀγρὸς δέ ἐστιν ὁ κόσμος. ἐν δὲ τῷ καθεύδειν τοὺς ἀνθρώπους, ἦλθεν ὁ ἐχθρός, καὶ ἔσπειρε ζιζάνια μέσον τοῦ σίτου, καὶ ἀπῆλθεν. ἔκτοτε γὰρ ἀποστάτης ὁ ἄγγελος οὗτος καὶ ἐχθρός, ἀφ' ὅτε ἐζήλωσεν τὸ πλάσμα τοῦ Θεοῦ, καὶ ἐχθροποιῆσαι αὐτὸν πρὸς τὸν Θεὸν ἐπεχείρησεν. διὸ καὶ ὁ Θεός, τὸν μὲν παρ' αὐτοῦ τὸ ζιζάνιον λάθρᾳ ἐπισπείραντα, τουτέστι τὴν παράβασιν εἰσενέγκοντα, ἀφώρισεν τῆς ἰδίας μετουσίας. τὸν δὲ ἀμελῶς καὶ κακῶς[mxvii] μὲν παραδεξάμενον τὴν παρακοὴν ἄνθρωπον ἠλέησεν. καὶ ἀντέστρεψε τὴν ἔχθραν, ἣν ἐχθροποίησεν πρὸς τὸν αὐτόν. ἀπωσάμενος μὲν ἀφ' ἑαυτοῦ τὴν πρὸς τὸν ἄνθρωπον ἔχθραν, ἀνακλάσας δὲ αὐτὴν καὶ ἀντιπέμψας πρὸς τὸν ὄφιν. καθὼς ἡ γραφὴ φησίν, εἰρηκέναι τῷ ὄφει τὸν Θεόν, *καὶ ἔχθραν θήσω ἀνὰ μέσον σοῦ, καὶ ἀνὰ μέσον τῆς γυναικός*, καὶ τὰ ἑξῆς.[mxviii]

Ὁ δὲ θερισμός, ἡ συντέλεια τοῦ αἰῶνος.[1196] Ἔσται δέ φησι ἐπὶ τέλει τῶν πραγμάτων[mxix] *θερισμός*, ὃ καλεῖται *συντέλεια*, ἵνα ἀναλέξαντες οἱ ἅγιοι τὰ ἐν τῇ ψυχῇ φαῦλα νοήματα[mxx] παραδῶσιν εἰς ἀνάλωσιν τῷ λεγομένῳ *πυρὶ* ἀνατρέποντες αὐτά, τουτέστι πάντας τοὺς τὴν ἀνομίαν ποιοῦντας λογισμοὺς ἀναλώσουσιν ὡς οὐ συναισθηθέντες

1189 Matt. 13:43.
1190 Matt. 13:37.
1191 Matt. 13:38.
1192 Matt. 13:25.
1193 Cod. ἀνακαλέσας.
1194 Cod. θήσομαι.
1195 Gen. 3:15: ἔχθραν θήσω. Cf. Origen, *commMatt*, 14.19; *homJer*, homily 20.7.
1196 Matt. 13:39.

ἑαυτῶν, διὰ τὸ κοιμᾶσθαι σπέρμα πονηροῦ λαβόντες καὶ ὡς περὶ ἑαυτοὺς θυμωθήσονται. Ὁ γὰρ *βρυγμὸς τῶν ὀδόντων*[1197] καὶ οὕτως νοεῖσθαι δύναται.

Ἔστι δὲ καὶ ἄλλως τοῦτο ἀκοῦσαι. Νῦν κόσμον φησὶ οὐ τὸ ἐξ οὐρανοῦ καὶ γῆς σύστημα,[mxxi] ἀλλὰ τὸν περὶ γῆν τόπον, ἐν ᾧ ὁ Σωτὴρ ἔσπειρε *τὸ καλὸν σπέρμα*. Ἀμελούν | **114r** των δὲ τῶν ἐγκεχειρισμένων τὰ τῆς ἐκκλησίας σπέρματα, ἐσπάρησαν οἱ ἑτερόδοξοι καὶ τὰ φαῦλα δόγματα, μέχρις ὄψεως τὸν σῖτον μιμούμενοι, οἳ συλλεγήσονται καὶ *βληθήσονται εἰς τὴν κάμινον τοῦ πυρός· ἔσται δὲ ἐκεῖ ὁ κλαυθμὸς καὶ ὁ βρυγμὸς τῶν ὀδόντων*.[1198]

> Understand the men who are asleep as the teachers of the Church… . In light of this, those who have been placed as chiefs in the Church must not fall asleep. Otherwise, while they are showing such negligence, the enemy will introduce the sowing of ryegrass, that is, doctrines of the heretics.[mxxii]

Ἡ γὰρ ψυχὴ ἡ μασητικὴ[mxxiii] καὶ λεαντικὴ τῶν ἰδίων τροφῶν ἐν καιρῷ ἐλέγχου δογμάτων ὑπ᾽ αὐτῆς πεφρονημένων συγκρουομένων τῇ ἀληθείᾳ βρύξει τοὺς ὀδόντας, ἥτ‹ις›[1199] τοιοῦτον παθοῦσα ἑαυτῆς καταγινώσκουσα βασανίζεται.

> Ἡ ψυχὴ ἡ μασητικὴ καὶ λεαντικὴ τῶν ἰδίων τροφῶν καὶ τῶν ἐν καιρῷ ἐλέγχου δογμάτων ὑπ᾽ αὐτῆς πεφρονημένων συγκρουομένων τῇ ἀληθείᾳ βρύξει τοὺς ὀδόντας ἢ τοιοῦτόν τι παθοῦσα ἑαυτῆς καταγινώσκουσα βασανίζεται.[mxxiv]

Προσθεὶς δὲ *ὁ ἔχων ὦτα ἀκούειν ἀκουέτω*,[1200] δηλοῖ ὅτι ἡ διήγησις τῆς παραβολῆς δεῖται σαφηνείας.

Πάλιν ὁμοία ἐστὶν ἡ βασιλεία τῶν οὐρανῶν θησαυρῷ κεκρυμμένῳ.[1201] Ἀγρός ἐστιν ἡ Γραφή, ποικίλην ἔχουσα ἐν τῷ ῥητῷ φυτείαν· θησαυρὸς δέ, τὰ ὑποκείμενα αὐτῇ τῆς σοφίας νοήματα, ἐν ᾗ κέκρυπται ὡς θησαυρὸς καὶ ἡ τοῦ Σωτῆρος γνῶσις. Κεκρύφθαι δὲ αὐτὸν λέγει ἐπειδὴ οὐ πᾶσιν ἐστὶ κατάδηλος ὁ περὶ τῆς σαρκώσεως τοῦ Μονογενοῦς λόγος, ὃν ἐάν τις γνῷ πάντων τῶν ὑπαρχόντων καταφρονεῖ ἵνα κτήσηται τὸν θεῖον τῆς γνώσεως θησαυρόν.

> This treasure, *in which there are hidden all the treasures of wisdom and knowledge*,[1202] is either the Logos of God, who is seen to be concealed in the flesh of Christ,[1203] or it is the Holy Scriptures, in which the knowledge of the Saviour is

1197 Matt. 13:42.
1198 Matt. 13:42.
1199 Cod. ἤτοι.
1200 Matt. 13:43.
1201 Matt. 13:44.
1202 Col. 2:3, quoted by Origen forthwith.
1203 Cf. John, 1:14.

stored. When anyone finds him hidden in them, he should despise all the gains of this world[1204] so that he should be able to possess the one he found.[mxxv]

Καθ᾽ ἑτέραν δὲ ἐκδοχὴν εἴη δ᾽ ἂν ἀγρὸς μὲν ἡ Γραφή, πολλοῖς καταπεφυτευμένη ρητοῖς νομικοῖς τε καὶ γραφικοῖς, καὶ ἱστορικοῖς. θησαυρὸς δὲ τὰ τούτοις ποικίλα ἐνόντα φανερά τε καὶ κεκρυμμένα νοήματα.[mxxvi]

Δοκεῖ δή μοι κατὰ ταῦτα ἀγρὸς μὲν εἶναι ἡ γραφὴ καταφυτευθεῖσα τοῖς φανεροῖς τῶν ρητῶν τῆς ἱστορίας καὶ τοῦ νόμου καὶ τῶν προφητῶν καὶ τῶν λοιπῶν νοημάτων (πολλὴ γὰρ φυτεία καὶ ποικίλη ἐστὶ καὶ ἡ τῶν ρητῶν τῆς ὅλης γραφῆς). ὁ δὲ *‹ἐν› τῷ ἀγρῷ* κεκρυμμένος θησαυρὸς τὰ ἀποκεκρυμμένα καὶ ὑποκείμενα τοῖς φανεροῖς νοήματα τῆς σοφίας *ἐν μυστηρίῳ* ἀποκεκρυμμένης καὶ τῷ Χριστῷ, *ἐν ᾧ εἰσιν οἱ θησαυροὶ τῆς σοφίας καὶ γνώσεως ἀπόκρυφοι.*[mxxvii]

Πολλοὶ γοῦν ἀπροσδοκήτως πιστεύσαντες εἰς Χριστόν, πάντων τῶν παλαιῶν καταφρονήσαντες εἰς μόνην εἶδον τὴν ἀλήθειαν, ἥ ἐστιν ἡ εἰς Χριστὸν πίστις.
Ἢ ἀγρόν φησι τὸν Χριστόν, ἐν ᾧ εἰσὶν *οἱ θησαυροὶ τῆς σοφίας καὶ τῆς γνώσεως ἀπόκρυφοι.*[1205] Θησαυρόν, τὴν τοῦ Χριστοῦ θεότητα τὴν οἱονεὶ σκεπομένην τῇ τῆς σαρκώσεως παραβολῇ.

καὶ Χριστὸς ὁ τίμιος τῆς Γραφῆς θησαυρός. Ἢ ἀγρὸς ὁ Χριστός, ἐν ᾧ Παῦλος λέγει ἐγκεκρύφθαι τοὺς ἀποκρύφους θησαυροὺς τῆς σοφίας καὶ τῆς γνώσεως τοῦ Θεοῦ.[mxxviii]

ὁ δὲ *‹ἐν› τῷ ἀγρῷ* κεκρυμμένος θησαυρὸς τὰ ἀποκεκρυμμένα καὶ ὑποκείμενα τοῖς φανεροῖς νοήματα τῆς σοφίας *ἐν μυστηρίῳ* ἀποκεκρυμμένης καὶ τῷ Χριστῷ, *ἐν ᾧ εἰσιν οἱ θησαυροὶ τῆς σοφίας καὶ γνώσεως ἀπόκρυφοι.* Ἄλλος δ᾽ ἂν λέγοι ἀγρὸν μὲν εἶναι τὸν ἀληθῶς πλήρη, ὃν εὐλόγησε κύριος, τὸν Χριστὸν τοῦ θεοῦ, τὸν δ᾽ ἐν αὐτῷ κεκρυμμένον θησαυρὸν τὰ εἰρημένα παρὰ τῷ Παύλῳ κεκρύφθαι ἐν Χριστῷ, λέγοντι περὶ Χριστοῦ τὸ *ἐν ᾧ εἰσιν οἱ θησαυροὶ τῆς σοφίας καὶ τῆς γνώσεως ἀπόκρυφοι.*[mxxix]

Κρύπτει δὲ ὁ τὰ τῶν γραφῶν ἀπόρρητα καὶ τοὺς ἐν Χριστῷ θησαυ | **114v** ροὺς μὴ ἐκφαίνων τοῖς τυχοῦσι.[mxxx] Πωλεῖ δὲ πάντα ὅσα ἔχει, ἀποθέμενος τὰ ἀπὸ κακίας καὶ ἰδιοποιεῖται ἢ ἃ πρῶτοι οἱ Ἰουδαῖοι *ἐπιστεύθησαν λόγια*[1206] ἢ ὃν προσεδόκων Χριστόν.

Εὑρὼν οὖν τις τὸν ἐν ταῖς Γραφαῖς θησαυρὸν τοῦτον, κρύπτει, μὴ ἀκίνδυνον εἰδὼς τῶν ἀπορρήτων τοῖς τυχοῦσι μεταδιδόναι. Ἄπεισι δὲ κρύψας, ἀγοράσων τὸν ἀγρὸν ὁπόσου ἂν βούλοιτο. ὃν Ἑβραῖοι πρὶν ἐπιστεύθησαν, παρ᾽ ὧν τοῦτον λαβὼν ὅστις κατ᾽ ἄλλην παραβολὴν ἀμπελών ἐστιν, ἴδιον κτῆμα τοῦτον ποιεῖ, πάντα πεπρακὼς αὐτοῦ τὰ ὑπάρχοντα.[mxxxi]

καὶ εὑρὼν κρύπτει, οὐκ ἀκίνδυνον εἶναι νομίζων τὰ τῶν γραφῶν ἀπόρρητα νοήματα ἢ τοὺς ἐν Χριστῷ θησαυροὺς *σοφίας καὶ γνώσεως*[1207] ἐκφαίνειν τοῖς τυχοῦσι, καὶ κρύψας

1204 Cf. Phil. 3:7.
1205 Col. 2:3.
1206 Rom. 3:2.
1207 Rom. 11:33.

> ἄπεισι πραγματευόμενος πῶς ἀγοράσει τὸν ἀγρὸν ἤτοι τὰς γραφάς, ἵνα ἴδιον κτῆμα αὐτὰς ποιήσῃ, λαβὼν ἀπὸ τῶν τοῦ θεοῦ τὰ λόγια τοῦ θεοῦ,[1208] ἃ πρῶτον Ἰουδαῖοι ἐπιστεύθησαν.[mxxxii]

Ἄλλως τε δέ, *βασιλείαν* νῦν τὴν πίστιν καλεῖ θησαυρῷ ἐοικυῖαν, ἣν ἐὰν οἱ ἐθνικοὶ εὕρωσι θυμηδίας ἐμπλησθέντες ὡς ἐξ ἀγροῦ ἀποδύονται τὴν ψευδῆ δόκησιν[mxxxiii] καὶ τὴν τῆς ἀληθείας γνῶσιν ὡς πλοῦτον ἁρπάζουσιν. *Βασιλείαν* δὲ *τῶν οὐρανῶν*, πῇ μὲν τὴν τοῦ Πνεύματος χάριν φησὶ ὡς ἐπὶ τῆς *ζύμης*, πῇ δὲ τὴν διδασκαλίαν, ὡς ἐπὶ τοῦ *σπόρου*, πῇ δὲ τὴν πίστιν, ὡς ἐνταῦθα. Οἱ δὲ πολλοὺς πωλοῦντες *μαργαρίτας* καὶ *ἕνα* κτώμενοι[1209] εἰσὶν οἱ ἐξ Ἰουδαίων, οἳ πολλοὺς ἔχουσι *μαργαρίτας* κατεσκιασμένους (τὴν παλαιὰν γραφήν), *ἕνα* δέ, τὸν διαφανῆ καὶ *πολύτιμον*, ὃν ἐὰν εὕρωσιν ἐκείνων καταφρονοῦσι καὶ μόνου τούτου ἀντέχονται. Δυνατὸν δὲ καὶ τοὺς καταφρονήσαντας τοῦ ἀνειμένου βίου καὶ μετατραπέντας ἐπὶ τὸ ποιῆσαι τὰ θεάρεστα νοῆσαι τοὺς εὑρόντας τὸν πολὺν πλοῦτον τὸν τῆς ἀρετῆς θησαυρὸν καὶ πωλήσαντας τὰ ἐν τῷ κόσμῳ τίμια ὡς λίθους εὐτελεῖς ἵνα κτήσωνται ἀξιάγαστον *μαργαρίτην*, τὴν τοῦ Θεοῦ *βασιλείαν*.[mxxxiv] Διδάσκει οὖν ὁ λόγος διὰ τῶν δύο παραβολῶν ὅτι δεῖ τὸ εὐαγγελικὸν κήρυγμα πάντων προτιμᾶν τῶν τιμίων ὡς *μαργαρίτην*, καὶ πολλὴν παρέχον εὐπορίαν, ὡς θησαυρόν.

Μαργαρῖται ἦσαν, ὁ δὲ μόνος πολυτίμητος μαργαρίτης, Χριστός.

> Ὁ δὲ ἀγελάρχης τῶν μαργαριτῶν, ᾧ εὑρισκομένῳ καὶ οἱ λοιποὶ συνευρίσκονται, ὁ πολυτίμητος μαργαρίτης, ὁ Χριστὸς τοῦ θεοῦ, ὁ ὑπὲρ τὰ τίμια γράμματα καὶ νοήματα τοῦ νόμου καὶ τῶν προφητῶν λόγος, οὗ εὑρεθέντος καὶ τἆλλα πάντα εὐμαρῶς παραλαμβάνονται.[mxxxv]

Τοῦ | **115r** τον δεῖ ἐμβληθῆναι ἵνα κοσμήσῃ ἡμῶν τὴν ἀκοὴν τῆς ψυχῆς ὡς τῆς Ῥεβέκκας. Μὴ ἐξέλωμεν αὐτὸν καὶ βάλωμεν *ἔμπροσθεν τῶν χοίρων*,[1210] ὡς ὁ λαὸς Ἰσραὴλ ἐν τῇ ἐρήμῳ τὰ ἐνώτια δόντες τῷ Ἀαρὼν ἐπὶ τῇ μοσχοποιΐᾳ.[1211] Ἐλευθέρας οὖν καὶ σώφρονος γυναικὸς τὸ κοσμεῖν ἑαυτὴν τούτῳ τῷ μαργαρίτῃ. Εἰ δὲ καὶ πόρναι γυναῖκες τούτῳ ἑαυτὰς κοσμοῦσι (τουτέστιν αἱ αἱρέσεις), ἀλλὰ πόρναι εἰσί, παγιδεύουσαι τὰς τῶν ἀνθρώπων ψυχάς. Ἀλλ᾽ οὐδὲ τῷ πολυτίμῳ μαργαρίτῃ ἑαυτὰς ἐκόσμησαν, ἀλλὰ μαργαριτῶν ψευδωνύμων. Ἔστιν οὖν οὗτος ὁ μαργαρίτης βασιλικός, ἀποστολιμαῖος,[mxxxvi] ἐν τῷ *θεμελίῳ* τῶν ἁγίων οἰκοδομούμενος.[1212]

Πάλιν ὁμοία ἐστὶν ἡ βασιλεία τῶν οὐρανῶν σαγήνῃ βληθείσῃ.[1213] Σαγήνης πλοκὴ νοητῆς ἡ ἐκ ποικίλων νοημάτων παλαιὰ καὶ καινὴ γραφή· *θάλασσα*, ὁ κυματούμενος τῶν ἀνθρώπων βίος, τὸ *πᾶν γένος* τὸ ποικίλον τῶν ἐν ἀνθρώποις προαιρέσεων, ἡ

1208 Rom. 3:2.
1209 Matt. 13:45-46.
1210 Matt. 7:6.
1211 Cf. Ex. 32:1-6.
1212 Cf. Eph. 2:20.
1213 Matt. 13:47.

παντοίων ἐθνῶν κλῆσις· ἐργάται σαγήνης, ὁ Κύριος καὶ οἱ προσελθόντες ἄγγελοι διακονεῖν αὐτῷ·[1214] *ἀγγεῖα*, αἱ διάφοροι *μοναί*.[1215] Οὐκ ἀνάγεται δὲ ἡ σαγήνη, ἕως *τὸ πλήρωμα τῶν ἐθνῶν εἰσέλθη*.[1216]

Σαγήνης πλοκὴ νοητὴ ἡ ἐκ ποικίλων νοημάτων παλαιὰ καὶ καινὴ Γραφή. *Θάλασσα*, ὁ κυματούμενος τῶν ἀνθρώπων βίος. *Τὸ πᾶν γένος* τὸ ποικίλον τῶν ἐν ἀνθρώποις προαιρέσεων, ἡ παντοίων ἐθνῶν κλῆσις. *Ἐργάται σαγήνης*, ὁ Κύριος καὶ οἱ προσελθόντες ἄγγελοι διακονεῖν αὐτῷ. *Ἀγγεῖα αἱ* διάφοροι μοναί. Οὐκ ἀνάγεται δὲ ἡ σαγήνη, *ἕως οὗ τὸ πλήρωμα τῶν ἐθνῶν εἰσέλθῃ*.[mxxxvii]

40

(ΩΡΙΓΕΝΟΥΣ, cont.) Ἤτοι *σαγήνη*[mxxxviii] ἡ ἀποστολικὴ διδασκαλία ἐστίν, ἡ ἀδιακρίτως συλλαμβανομένη Ἰουδαίους καὶ Ἕλληνας, βαρβάρους, Σκύθας, δούλους, ἐλευθέρους,[1217] πονηρούς τε καὶ ἀγαθούς· *θάλασσα*, ὁ τῶν ἀνθρώπων βίος· *αἰγιαλός*, τὸ τέρμα τούτου. Κατὰ τὸν νοῦν τοῦτον τὸ ὅλον ὄψει. *Ἐν δὲ τῇ συντελείᾳ*,[1218] ὅτε ἀνασπᾶται ἡ σαγήνη, ἀφορίζονται ἀπὸ τῶν φαύλων οἱ ἀγαθοί, οἱ μὲν τιμώμενοι, οἱ δὲ κολαζόμενοι. | **115v** Οὐ γὰρ πάντων τῶν πιστῶν ὅμοιος ὁ τρόπος. Ἵνα δὲ μὴ νομίσῃ τις ὅτι ἔξω μόνον βάλλονται οἱ κακοί, ἐσήμανεν ὅτι εἰς διηνεκῆ κόλασιν[mxxxix] παραπέμπονται εἰπών· *καὶ βαλοῦσιν αὐτοὺς εἰς τὴν κάμινον τοῦ πυρός· ἐκεῖ ἔσται ὁ κλαυθμός, καὶ ὁ βρυγμὸς τῶν ὀδόντων*.[1219]

Ἢ οὕτως. *Σαγήνη* ἐστὶν ἡ ἀποστολικὴ διδασκαλία, ἡ ἀδιακρίτως συλλαμβανομένη Ἰουδαίους καὶ Ἕλληνας, βαρβάρους, Σκύθας, δούλους, ἐλευθέρους, πονηροὺς καὶ ἀγαθούς. *Θάλασσα*, ὁ τῶν ἀνθρώπων βίος. *Αἰγιαλός*, τὸ τέρμα τούτου. Ἐν δὲ τῇ συντελείᾳ, ὅτε ἀνασπᾶται ἡ σαγήνη, ἀφορίζονται ἀπὸ τῶν φαύλων οἱ ἀγαθοί, οἱ μὲν τιμώμενοι, οἱ δὲ κολαζόμενοι. Οὐ γὰρ πάντων τῶν πιστῶν ὅμοιος ὁ τρόπος. Ἵνα δὲ μὴ νομίσῃ τις, ὅτι ἔξω μόνον βάλλονται οἱ ἄπιστοι καὶ πονηροί, ἐσήμανεν, ὅτι εἰς διηνεκῆ κόλασιν παραπέμπονται. *Καὶ βαλοῦσιν αὐτοὺς εἰς τὴν κάμινον τοῦ πυρός*, καὶ τὰ ἑξῆς.[mxl]

(ΩΡΙΓΕΝΟΥΣ, cont.) *Συνήκατε ταῦτα πάντα;*[1220] Καίτοι ἀποφαντικῶς εἰπόντι τῷ Σωτῆρι, οἱ μαθηταὶ συμμαρτυροῦσιν εἰπόντες τὸ *ναί*.
Ἢ ἐρωτᾷ οὐκ ἀγνοῶν.[mxli] Ἅπαξ γὰρ ἀναλαβὼν τὸν ἄνθρωπον, καὶ τοῖς ἀνθρωπίνοις χρῆται πᾶσι καὶ τῷ ἐρωτᾶν ἀπαιτεῖ τοίνυν αὐτοὺς μὴ μόνον τοῖς ῥήμασι προσέχειν,

1214 Matt. 4:11; Mark, 1:13.
1215 John, 14:2.
1216 Rom. 11:25.
1217 Col. 3:11.
1218 Matt. 13:49.
1219 Matt. 13:50.
1220 Matt. 13:51.

ἀλλὰ καὶ νοεῖν τὰ λεγόμενα. Οὗτοι δὲ ὡς νοήσαντες οὐκ ἠρώτησαν. Διὸ καὶ ἐρωτηθέντες εἰ ἐνόησαν εἶπον *ναί.*

> *Συνήκατε ταῦτα πάντα; Λέγουσι ναί.* Ὁ γινώσκων τὰ ἐν ταῖς καρδίαις τῶν ἀνθρώπων Χριστὸς Ἰησοῦς, ὡς καὶ περὶ τούτου ἐδίδαξεν ἐν τῷ εὐαγγελίῳ ὁ Ἰωάννης,[1221] οὐκ ἀγνοῶν ἐρωτᾷ, ἀλλ᾽ ἅπαξ ἀναλαβὼν ἄνθρωπον χρῆται καὶ τοῖς αὐτοῦ πᾶσιν, ὧν ἓν καὶ τὸ ἐρωτᾶν.[mxlii]

Ὁ δὲ εἶπεν αὐτοῖς· διὰ τοῦτο πᾶς γραμματεύς.[1222] Τί οὖν ὁ Χριστὸς εἰπόντων αὐτῶν ὅτι συνήκαμεν ἐπαινεῖ καὶ παρεικάζει αὐτοὺς *ἀνθρώπῳ οἰκοδεσπότῃ* ὡς ἔκ τινος θησαυροῦ τὰ τῆς νέας καὶ παλαιᾶς διδάγματα ἐκβάλλοντας; *Γραμματέα* δὲ λέγει τὸν ἔμπειρον τῆς γραφῆς καὶ παιδευθέντα ‹περὶ›[1223] τὰ εὐαγγελικά, ὃν καὶ μακαρίζει ὡς καὶ τὴν ἐν τύποις ἀρχαίαν πλουτήσαντα γραφὴν καὶ τὴν *ἐν ἀληθείᾳ*[1224] νέαν οὐ ζημιωθέντα διδαχὴν τοῦ Χριστοῦ· ὃν καὶ ἀπεικάζει πλουσίῳ ἄγαν ἀνθρώπῳ, ὃς εἰς ἐπίδειξιν τοῦ ἰδίου πλούτου προτίθησι καὶ ἃ εἶχε καὶ ἃ ἐπεκτήσατο.

41

(ΩΡΙΓΕΝΟΥΣ) *Γραμματεῖς* λέγει τοὺς μαθητάς. Διὸ καὶ ἀλλαχοῦ φησι, *ἀποστέλλω ὑμῖν σοφοὺς καὶ γραμματεῖς,*[1225] καθὸ πᾶς μαθητευθεὶς τῷ γράμματι τοῦ νόμου γραμματεὺς λέγεται.

Ἁπλῶς μὲν οὖν *‹γραμματεὺς› μαθητεύ* | **116r** *εται τῇ βασιλείᾳ*[1226] ἀπὸ Ἰουδαϊσμοῦ λαβὼν τὴν Χριστοῦ διδαχήν, βαθύτερον δέ, ὁ ἀπὸ τῆς τοῦ γράμματος εἰσαγωγῆς[mxliii] ἀναβὰς ἐπὶ τὰ πνευματικά.[mxliv] Ὁ οὖν πιστεύων τῇ ἀψευδεῖ γνώσει γίνεται ἐν οὐρανοῖς. *Καινὰ δὲ καὶ παλαιά,*[1227] ἡ εὐαγγελικὴ καὶ νομικὴ διαθήκη· τὸ δὲ *ἐκβάλλειν*, τοῦ φύειν καὶ βλαστάνειν ἔχει νοῦν.

> Μαθητεύεται δὲ *τῇ βασιλείᾳ τῶν οὐρανῶν γραμματεὺς* κατὰ μὲν τὸ ἁπλούστερον, ὅτε ἀπὸ Ἰουδαϊσμοῦ ἀναλαμβάνει τις τὴν Ἰησοῦ Χριστοῦ ἐκκλησιαστικὴν διδασκαλίαν. κατὰ δὲ τὸ βαθύτερον, ὅτε τὰς διὰ τοῦ γράμματος τῶν γραφῶν εἰσαγωγὰς παραλαβών τις ἀναβαίνει ἐπὶ τὰ πνευματικὰ ὀνομαζόμενα βασιλείαν *οὐρανῶν.*[mxlv]

1221 Cf. Rev. 2:23.
1222 Matt. 13:52.
1223 Cod. καὶ.
1224 Matt. 22:16; John, 4:23-24; 17:19; Eph. 6:14; Col. 1:6.
1225 Matt. 23:34.
1226 Cf. Matt. 13:52.
1227 Matt. 13:52.

Ὅτε ἐτέλεσεν ὁ Ἰησοῦς τὰς παραβολὰς ταύτας.[1228] *Ταύτας* εἶπεν ἐπειδὴ καὶ ἄλλας ἔμελλεν ἐρεῖν παραβολάς, ἃς μετ᾽ ὀλίγον ἐρεῖ. Ὡς ἄνθρωπος δὲ μεταβαίνει ὁ πανταχοῦ παρὼν ὡς Θεός, *πανταχοῦ*[1229] θέλων σπεῖραι τὸν λόγον πρὸς τὸ καὶ ἄλλους ὠφελῆσαι τῇ παρουσίᾳ αὐτοῦ.

Καὶ ἐλθὼν εἰς τὴν πατρίδα αὐτοῦ ἐδίδασκεν αὐτοὺς ἐν τῇ συναγωγῇ αὐτῶν.[1230] Ἐν ταῖς συναγωγαῖς δὲ ἐδίδασκεν ἵνα μὴ διαβάλωσιν αὐτὸν ὡς τὰς ἐρήμους διώκων διδάσκει τὰ παράνομα. Ἐξεπλήσσοντο δὲ πάντες ἐπὶ τῇ διδαχῇ αὐτοῦ, σοφὸν ὁρῶντες ὡς ἐκ πτωχῶν γονέων ὄντα οἰόμενοι αὐτὸν ψιλὸν εἶναι ἄνθρωπον, μὴ ἐννοοῦντες ὅτι Θεὸς ἦν φύσει καὶ αὐτὸς ἦν ἡ τοῦ *Θεοῦ σοφία,*[1231] ἀλλ᾽ ὑποπτεύοντες αὐτὸν παρ᾽ ἑτέρου σεσοφίσθαι. Μείζω γὰρ τῶν συνήθων ἀκούοντες, δυνάμεις τε ὁρῶντες μείζους ἢ κατὰ Μωσέα καὶ τοὺς παλαιούς, εἰκότως ἐθαύμαζον. Εἰς μόνην δὲ ἀφορῶντες τὴν σάρκα ᾤοντο αὐτὸν υἱὸν ἀνθρώπου ἐκ τῶν νομιζομένων ἀδελφῶν καὶ τοῦ πατρός. Ἐξερεθιζόμενοί τε ὑπὸ τοῦ φθόνου ἔλεγον· *πόθεν τούτῳ ἡ σοφία αὕτη καὶ αἱ δυνάμεις;*[1232] Ἡ *σοφία* ἐσόφιζε τοὺς σοφούς, αἱ δὲ *δυνάμεις* ἔπειθον τοὺς ἰδιώτας. Καὶ τὸν μὲν ἄνδρα ἐθεώρουν ὡς ψιλὸν ὄντα, | **116v** ἐπὶ δὲ τῇ σοφίᾳ καὶ τοῖς ἔργοις ἐξίσταντο (συνήργει γὰρ ἡ σοφία ταῖς δυνάμεσιν, αἱ δὲ δυνάμεις τῇ σοφίᾳ), μὴ νοοῦντες ὅτι αὐτὸς ὁ Λόγος ἐστὶ *σοφία Θεοῦ καὶ δύναμις.*[1233]

> Ἡ *σοφία* ἐσόφιζε τοὺς σοφούς, αἱ δὲ *δυνάμεις* ἔπειθον τοὺς ἰδιώτας. καὶ τὸν μὲν ἄνδρα ἐθεώρουν ὡς ψιλὸν ὄντα, ἐπὶ δὲ τῇ σοφίᾳ καὶ τοῖς ἔργοις ἐξίσταντο (συνήργει γὰρ ἡ σοφία ταῖς δυνάμεσιν, αἱ δὲ δυνάμεις τῇ σοφίᾳ), μὴ νοοῦντες ὅτι αὐτὸς ὁ λόγος ἐστὶ *σοφία Θεοῦ καὶ δύναμις.*[mxlvi]

Ὁ δὲ Ἰησοῦς εἶπεν αὐτοῖς· οὐκ ἔστι προφήτης ἄτιμος.[1234] Τί οὖν ὁ Σωτὴρ πρὸς αὐτούς, *οὐκ ἔστι* φησὶ *προφήτης ἄτιμος, εἰ μὴ ἐν τῇ πατρίδι αὐτοῦ καὶ ἐν τῇ οἰκίᾳ αὐτοῦ;*[1235] Εἰώθασι γὰρ τῶν ἐν συνηθείᾳ καταφρονεῖν οἱ ἄνθρωποι, τῶν δὲ δυσευρέτων ἐπιθυμοῦσιν. Ἵνα δὲ μὴ καὶ μετὰ τὰ σημεῖα μείναντες ἄπιστοι πλείονι ὑποβληθῶσι κολάσει, φειδόμενος αὐτῶν *οὐκ ἐποίησε* σημεῖα.[1236] Οὐ γὰρ πρὸς ἐπίδειξιν ἐποίει, ἀλλὰ διὰ τὴν τῶν ὁρώντων ὠφέλειαν. Διὰ τοῦτο δὲ ὅλως, κἂν ὀλίγα ἐποίησεν, ἵνα μὴ εἴπωσιν ὅτι εἰ ἐποίησε σημεῖα ἐπιστεύσαμεν ἄν.

1228 Matt. 13:53.
1229 Cf. Mark, 16:20; Luke, 9:6; 1 Cor. 4:17.
1230 Matt. 13:54.
1231 1 Cor. 1:24; 1:30.
1232 Matt. 13:54.
1233 Cf. 1 Cor. 1:24.
1234 Matt. 13:57.
1235 Matt. 13:57.
1236 Matt. 13:58.

Ἐν ἐκείνῳ τῷ καιρῷ ἤκουεν Ἡρῴδης ὁ τετράρχης.[1237] Ἕτερος ἦν *Ἡρῴδης*[mxlvii] ὁ βασιλεύς, ἕτερος δὲ *ὁ τετράρχης* υἱὸς ὢν ἐκείνου. Ἐπ᾽ ἐννέα γὰρ τοῖς ἔτεσιν μετὰ τὸν Ἡρώδου θάνατον κατεσχηκότος Ἀρχελάου τὴν ἀρχήν, εἶτα ἀτίμως τῆς βασιλείας ἐκπεσόντος, εἰς τετραρχίας διεῖλον οἱ Ῥωμαῖοι τὴν Ἡρώδου βασιλείαν εἰς τέσσαρα μερισθεῖσαν καὶ τετράρχης ἕκαστος αὐτῶν ὠνομάζετο ὡς τοῦ τετάρτου μέρους τὴν ἀρχὴν ἔχων. Συνέβη δὲ καὶ Ἡρώδην τὸν τοῦ Ἡρώδου υἱὸν ἕνα τούτων γενέσθαι μέρους τινὸς ἄρχοντα καὶ αὐτόν, ὃς καὶ ἀποκεφαλίσας τὸν Ἰωάννην δίκας ἔδωκεν οὐκ εἰς μακράν, ὡς ἀκριβῶς τὸν βουλόμενον μαθεῖν ἀπὸ τῆς Ἰωσήπου γραφῆς δυνατόν. Οὐκ ἐψεύσατο τοίνυν | **117r** ὁ εὐαγγελιστής, οὔτε ἐκείνου τὴν τελευτὴν τοῦ Ἡρώδου εἰπὼν οὔτε περὶ τούτου διηγησάμενος. Ἀλλὰ γὰρ καὶ τετράρχην εἰπὼν σαφῶς ἕτερον ὄντα παρ᾽ ἐκεῖνον ἐδήλωσεν, καίτοιγέ τινων καὶ βασιλέα καλούντων αὐτὸν εἴτε ἀπὸ τῆς τοῦ πράγματος συνηθείας, εἴτε καὶ ἀδεέστερον ἔτι τῇ φωνῇ κεχρημένων. Ὅθεν καὶ Μᾶρκος ἀδιαφόρως βασιλέα αὐτὸν ἐκάλεσε[1238] τοῦ Λουκᾶ ὁμοίως τῷ Ματθαίῳ ἀπὸ τῆς ἀξίας τετράρχην αὐτὸν ὀνομάσαντος[1239] ὡς παρὰ τοῦ Ἰωσήπου σαφέστερόν ἐστι μαθεῖν,[mxlviii] οὐ τὸν ἄνδρα λέγοντος μόνον ἀλλὰ καὶ τὴν πρᾶξιν αὐτοῦ διηγουμένου ταύτην καὶ προστιθέντος ἔτι καὶ τὴν τιμωρίαν, ἣν ἔδωκεν ὑπὲρ τούτου. Ἀκούων τοίνυν τοῦ Κυρίου τὰ θαύματα καὶ σφόδρα εἰδὼς ὅτι δίκαιον ὄντα μάτην ἀνεῖλε τὸν Ἰωάννην, ὑπέλαβεν αὐτὸν ἐγηγερμένον ἐκ νεκρῶν ταῦτα ποιεῖν.

42

| **117r** (ΩΡΙΓΕΝΟΥΣ) Κατὰ αἵρεσιν μετεμψυχώσεως[mxlix] ὁ Ἡρῴδης ἔφη τὸν Ἰωάννην ἀναστῆναι.[1240] Ἐδεδίει δὲ τὸν Ἰωάννην μὴ πλείονι κατ᾽ αὐτοῦ χρήσαιτο τῇ ἐλεγκτικῇ παρρησίᾳ ἅτε δυνατώτερος γεγονὼς τῷ ἀναστῆναι ἐκ νεκρῶν. Δεινὸν δὲ ἦν αὐτῷ τὸ ἀποστερηθῆναι τῆς αἰσχρουργίας.[ml]

Αὐτὸς ἠγέρθη ἀπὸ τῶν νεκρῶν.[1241] Τοῦτο τοίνυν ἔλεγεν, ἤτοι τινῶν λεγόντων περὶ τοῦ Χριστοῦ | **117v** ὅτι Ἱερεμίας ἐστίν, ἄλλων δὲ ὅτι Ἠλίας, ἄλλων ὅτι Ἰωάννης.[1242] Ὁ Ἡρῴδης δὲ ἔλεγεν ὅτι οὐκ ἔστιν ὁ Ἰωάννης· ἐγὼ γὰρ αὐτὸν ἀπεκεφάλισα. Ὃ τοίνυν ἄλλοις ἔλεγεν εἰκὸς ὅτι μετατραπεὶς γέγονε τῆς ἐκείνων δόξης καὶ οἰηθεὶς ἐκ νεκρῶν ἀνεστηκέναι αὐτὸν ἤρξατο αὐτὸν δειλιᾶν ὡς δυνατώτερον γεγονότα μήπως αὐτοῦ ἐπὶ πλεῖον ἐλέγξῃ τὴν αἰσχρουργίαν.[mli]

1237 Matt. 14:1.
1238 Mark, 6:14; cf. Luke, 1:5; Matt. 2:1; 2:3.
1239 Matt. 4:1; Luke, 3:1; 3:19; 9:7.
1240 Matt. 14:1-2.
1241 Matt. 14:2.
1242 Matt. 16:14.

> Οἰηθεὶς ἐκ νεκρῶν ἀνεστηκέναι τὸν βαπτιστήν, ἤρξατο αὐτὸν δειλιᾷν, ὡς δυνατώτερον γεγονότα. καὶ ἐδεδίει μὴ πλείονι κατ' αὐτοῦ χρήσοιτο τῇ ἐλεγκτικῇ παρρησίᾳ. ὅπερ ἦν αὐτῷ δεινόν, ἀποστερηθῆναι τῆς αἰσχρουργίας.[mlii]

Ἐπειδὴ δὲ ὅτε ἔζη ὁ *Ἰωάννης σημεῖον οὐκ ἐποίησεν*,[1243] ᾠήθη ὁ Ἡρώδης ὅτι ἀναστὰς προσέλαβε καὶ τοῦτο τὸ χάρισμα ἀπὸ Θεοῦ, τὸ ποιεῖν τερατουργίας. Ὁ γὰρ Ἰωάννης μὴ φέρων καθορᾶν τὸν θεῖον ἀθετούμενον νόμον, ἤλεγξε τὸν Ἡρώδην ἐπὶ τῇ παρανόμῳ μίξει τῇ γενομένῃ ἐπὶ τῇ γυναικὶ *Φιλίππου τοῦ ἀδελφοῦ αὐτοῦ*.[1244] Καὶ ἔλεγεν αὐτῷ ὅτι *οὐκ ἔξεστί σοι ἔχειν αὐτήν*.[1245]
Ζῶντος γὰρ ἔτι Φιλίππου ἀφήρητο αὐτοῦ καὶ τὴν γυναῖκα καὶ τὴν τετραρχίαν.[mliii]

> Οὐδέποτε τεθνήκει Φίλιππος, ἔτι δὲ ζῶν γὰρ Φιλίππου ἀφήρητο καὶ τὴν τετραρχίαν καὶ *τὴν γυναῖκα*. διὸ οὐ νομικὸς ἁμαρτωλὸς δὲ ὁ γάμος καὶ παρρησίας προφητικῆς χρῄζων.[mliv]

Ὁ οὖν Ἡρώδης μὴ φέρων τὸν ἔλεγχον ἤθελεν *αὐτὸν* φονεῦσαι. Φοβηθεὶς δὲ *τὸν ὄχλον*, ἐπειδὴ *ὡς προφήτην αὐτὸν εἶχον*,[1246] τέως ἐπέσχε τὸν φόνον, *διὰ δὲ τοὺς ὅρκους*[1247] ἀποκεφαλίζεται ὁ προφήτης.
Ἰστέον δὲ ὅτι ἔστιν ὅπου ἐπιορκεῖν μᾶλλον ἢ εὐορκεῖν χρή. Οὐ γὰρ ταὐτὸν ἔγκλημα ἐκ προπετείας ὅρκων ἐπιορκία καὶ ἀναίρεσις προφητικὴ δι' εὐορκίας. Χρήσῃ τῷ ρητῷ πρὸς τοὺς θέλοντας ἐμπεδοῦν προπετεῖς καὶ παρανόμους ὅρκους. Οὐ γὰρ πᾶσα χρῆσις ὅρκων καθήκουσα.

> Καὶ ἀποκεφαλίζεται ὁ προφήτης *δι' ὅρκους*, ἐφ' οἷς μᾶλλον ἐπιορκεῖν ἢ εὐορκεῖν ἔδει. οὐ ταὐτὸν γὰρ ἦν ἔγκλημα προπετείας ὅρκων καὶ τῆς διὰ τὴν προπέτειαν ἐπιορκίας ‹καὶ τὸ δι' εὐορκίας› ἔγκλημα ἀναιρέσεως προφητικῆς... . Χρήσῃ δέ ποτε χαριέντως τῷ ρητῷ πρὸς τοὺς προπετῶς ὀμνύοντας καὶ θέλοντας ἐμπεδοῦν ὅρκους ἐπὶ παρανομίᾳ παραληφθέντας, λέγων ὅτι οὐ πᾶσα τήρησις ὅρκων ἐστὶ καθήκουσα, ὡς οὐδὲ ἡ τοῦ Ἡρώδου.[mlv]

Καὶ πέμψας ἀπεκεφάλισε.[1248] Μετ' οὐ πολὺ δέ, ἐν τῇ τῶν γενεθλίων αὐτοῦ ἑορτῇ, *ἀπεκεφάλισεν* αὐτὸν *ἐν τῇ φυλακῇ· καὶ ἠνέχθη ἡ κεφαλὴ αὐτοῦ ἐπὶ πίνακι καὶ* | **118r**
ἐδόθη[1249] τῇ ὀρχησαμένῃ κόρῃ δῶρον τῆς ἀσέμνου ὀρχήσεως.[mlvi]

1243 John, 10:41.
1244 Matt. 14:3. Mark, 6:7.
1245 Matt. 14:3; cf. Mark, 6:8.
1246 Matt. 14:5.
1247 Matt. 14:9.
1248 Matt. 14:10.
1249 Matt. 14:10-11.

> Ἡ δὲ τοῦ βασιλέως τῆς Τραχωνίτιδος γυνή, πονηρά τις οὖσα δόξα καὶ μοχθηρὰ διδασκαλία, θυγατέρα ἐγέννησεν ὁμώνυμον, ἧς τὰ δοκοῦντα εὔρυθμα κινήματα ἀρέσαντα τῷ *Ἡρώδῃ* τὰ γενέσεως ἀγαπῶντι πράγματα, αἴτια γεγένηται τοῦ μηκέτι εἶναι ἐν τῷ λαῷ κεφαλὴν προφητικήν.[mlvii]

> Ἡ δὲ τοῦ βασιλέως τῆς Τραχωνίτιδος γυνή, πονηρά τις οὖσα δόξα καὶ μοχθηρὰ διδασκαλία, θυγατέρα ἐγέννησεν ὁμώνυμον, ἧς τὰ δοκοῦντα εὔρυθμα κινήματα ἀρέσαντα τῷ *Ἡρώδῃ* τὰ γενέσεως ἀγαπῶντι πράγματα, αἴτια γεγένηται τοῦ μηκέτι εἶναι ἐν τῷ λαῷ κεφαλὴν προφητικήν.[mlviii]

> Ἀλλ᾽ ἡ *Ἡρωδιάδος* ὄρχησις ἐναντία ἦν ὀρχήσει ἁγίᾳ, ἣν οἱ μὴ ὀρχησάμενοι ὀνειδισθήσονται ἀκούοντες, *Ηὐλήσαμεν ὑμῖν καὶ οὐκ ὠρχήσασθε.* Καὶ ἐν γενεθλίοις δὲ παρανόμου βασιλεύοντος αὐτῶν λόγου ὀρχοῦνται, ὡς ἀρέσκειν ἐκείνῳ τῷ λόγῳ τὰς κινήσεις αὐτῶν. Ἐτήρησε μὲν οὖν τις τῶν πρὸ ἡμῶν τὴν ἀναγεγραμμένην ἐν Γενέσει τοῦ Φαραὼ γενέθλιον καὶ διηγήσατο ὅτι[mlix]

> ὁ φαῦλος τὰ γενέσεως ἀγαπῶν πράγματα ἑορτάζει γενέθλιον. Ἡμεῖς δὲ ἀπ᾽ ἐκείνου ταύτην εὑρόντες ἀφορμὴν ἐπ᾽ οὐδεμιᾶς γραφῆς εὕρομεν ὑπὸ δικαίου γενέθλιον ἀγομένην.[mlx]

> Ὁ φαῦλος τὰ γενέσεως ἀγαπῶν ἑορτάζει γενέθλιον ὡς Φαραώ, ἅγιος δὲ οὐδεὶς εὑρίσκεται γενέθλιον ἄγων.[mlxi]

Παρ᾽ οἷς δὲ καθαρὰ καὶ ἀκάθαρτα ἐξετάζεται καταφρονεῖται προφητικὴ *κεφαλὴ ἐπὶ πίνακι*[1250] ἀντὶ ὄψου προσαγομένη.

> Ἔτι δὲ ὅρα τὸν λαὸν παρ᾽ ᾧ καθαρὰ μὲν καὶ ἀκάθαρτα ἐξετάζεται βρώματα, καταφρονεῖται δὲ προφητεία[mlxii] *ἐπὶ πίνακι* ἀντὶ ὄψου προσαγομένη.[mlxiii]

Καὶ νῦν δὲ οἱ Ἰουδαῖοι οὐ παρρησίᾳ, οἱονεὶ δὲ *ἐν φυλακῇ* ἀναιροῦσι τὰς προφητείας καὶ κρύφα. Ἔχουσι γὰρ αὐτὰς νεκρὰς καὶ ἀποτετμημένας, μὴ ἔχοντες τὸ κεφάλαιον Ἰησοῦν Χριστόν,[1251] ὃν ἡμεῖς ὁλόκληρον ἔχομεν. *Ὀστοῦν γὰρ αὐτοῦ* φησι *οὐ συντριβήσεται.*[1252]

> Καὶ νῦν δὲ οἱ Ἰουδαῖοι οὐ παρρησίᾳ οἱονεὶ δὲ *ἐν φυλακῇ* ἀναιροῦσι τὰς προφητείας καὶ κρύφα. ἔχουσι γὰρ αὐτὰς νεκρὰς καὶ ἀποτετμημένας, μὴ ἔχοντες τὸ κεφάλαιον Ἰησοῦν Χριστόν. ὃν ἡμεῖς ὁλόκληρον ἔχομεν, *ὀστοῦν* (γάρ φησιν) *οὐ συντριβήσεται ἀπ᾽ αὐτοῦ.*[mlxiv]

> *Τὴν* δὲ *κεφαλὴν* τῆς προφητείας Ἰουδαῖοι οὐκ ἔχουσι, τὸ κεφάλαιον πάσης προφητείας Χριστὸν Ἰησοῦν ἀρνούμενοι.[mlxv]

1250 Matt. 14:11.
1251 Cf. Eph. 1:10.
1252 John, 19:36; cf. Ex. 12:10&46; Numbers, 33:12; Psalm 33:21.

Τέθαπται δὲ τὸ σῶμα τοῦ βαπτιστοῦ,[1253] ἐν πόλει σεβαστῇ, ἡ δὲ τιμία κεφαλὴ αὐτοῦ ἀπετέθη εἰς Ἔμεσαν.[mlxvi] Οὐκ ἐμνήσθη δὲ ἐν τοῖς προλαβοῦσι τοῦ κατὰ Ἰωάννην διηγήματος ὁ Ματθαῖος ἐπειδὴ σκοπὸς ἦν αὐτῷ μόνα τὰ περὶ τοῦ Χριστοῦ εἰπεῖν. Καὶ νῦν διέρραψε τὸν λόγον[mlxvii] τοῦτον ἐπειδὴ καὶ οὗτος εἰς τὸν Χριστὸν ἑώρα. Περὶ γὰρ τοῦ Χριστοῦ ἀκούσας ὁ Ἡρώδης ἔλεγεν ὅτι ἀνέστη *ὁ Ἰωάννης*[1254] καὶ οὗτός ἐστιν *ὁ λεγόμενος Χριστός*.[1255]

Καὶ *ἀκούσας ὁ Ἰησοῦς ἀνεχώρησεν ἐκεῖθεν*.[1256] Οὐ δέει τοῦ Ἡρώδου ἀναχωρεῖ, ἀλλ᾽ οἰκονομικῶς φεύγει ὡς ἄνθρωπος, καιρῷ τῷ δέοντι φυλάττων τὴν τῆς θεότητος φανέρωσιν. Πρὸ δὲ τοῦ ἀκοῦσαι, καίπερ εἰδώς, οὐκ ἀνεχώρησε, δεικνὺς τῆς οἰκονομίας τὴν ἀλήθειαν. Ἤτοι ἀναχωρεῖ νῦν φεύγων τὴν Ἡρώδου μιαιφονίαν καὶ εἰς τὸν τοῦ Πάσχα καιρὸν ἑαυτὸν τηρῶν καὶ διδάσκων ὅτι δεῖ πολλάκις καὶ τὸν ἐχθρὸν διαλαθεῖν, ἵνα μὴ ὁρώμενος αὐτῷ ἐπὶ πλεῖον αὐτὸν ἀγριαίνῃ.

> They announce the death of the Baptist to the Saviour. Once he hears about it, he departs to a desert location. He did so not because he was scared of death, as some think, but in order to spare his enemies from adding one murder to another, or in order to put off his own death to the day of the Passover.[mlxviii] ... Or he departed in order to offer to us an example of eschewing the rushness of those who hand themselves in their own accord.[mlxix]

Ἢ καὶ διὰ τὴν τῶν ὄχλων δοκιμασίαν ἀναχωρεῖ· ὅθεν καὶ ἠκολούθησαν αὐτῷ μισθὸν τοῦ συνεῖναι αὐτῷ δεξάμενοι τὰς τῶν | **118v** ἀρρώστων ἰάσεις. Διὸ οὐκ ἀπαιτεῖ αὐτοὺς ἐνταῦθα πίστιν. Δῆλοι γὰρ ἦσαν πιστοί, ὄντες ἐξ ὧν ἐν ἐρήμῳ αὐτῷ ἠκολούθουν δίχα τροφῆς.

Ἄλλως τε δέ· μετὰ τὴν τῶν προφητῶν ἀναίρεσιν, ὁ λόγος ἀναχωρεῖ εἰς τὰ ἀκολουθοῦντα αὐτῷ ἔθνη ἐν ἐρήμῳ ὄντα χάριτος Θεοῦ, ἐφ᾽ ἃ καὶ σπλαγχνίζεται καὶ ἰᾶται τοὺς ἀρρώστους αὐτῶν.[1257] Ἅμα δὲ ὑποδείκνυσιν ὅπως ἐν ταῖς τῶν δικαίων διώξεσι προσήκει ποιεῖν. Οὐ ‹γὰρ› θρασύνεσθαι κατὰ τῶν διωκόντων οὐδὲ ὁμόσε χωρεῖν τοῖς δεινοῖς ἐντεῦθεν δῆλον.[mlxx] Ὅτι καὶ οἱ μαθηταὶ Ἰωάννου προσῳκειώθησαν τῷ Χριστῷ. Μετὰ γὰρ τὸ ἀναγγεῖλαι αὐτῷ τὸν τοῦ διδασκάλου θάνατον, ἠκολούθησαν αὐτῷ,[1258] πῇ μὲν ἀπὸ τῆς συμφορᾶς, πῇ δὲ καὶ διὰ τῶν λόγων τῆς ἀποκρίσεως ὠφεληθέντες.

Ὀψίας δὲ γενομένης προσῆλθον αὐτῷ οἱ μαθηταὶ ‹αὐτοῦ› λέγοντες· ἔρημός ἐστιν ὁ τόπος.[1259] Ἐλεήσαντες τοίνυν οἱ μαθηταὶ τοὺς ὄχλους νήστεις ἐν ἐρήμῳ ἐπὶ πολὺ

1253 Matt. 14:12.
1254 Matt. 14:1.
1255 Cf. Matt. 1:16; 27:17&22; John, 4:25.
1256 Matt. 14:13.
1257 Matt. 14:14.
1258 Cf. Matt. 9:14; Mark, 2:18.
1259 Matt. 14:15.

συνόντας, ἔλεγον τῷ Σωτῆρι ἀπολῦσαι αὐτοὺς πρίασθαι ἄρτους. Τί οὖν ὁ Σωτὴρ ἵνα μὴ ὡς ἀνθρώπῳ αὐτῷ διαλέγωνται εἶπε; *Δότε αὐτοῖς ὑμεῖς φαγεῖν.*[1260] Οἱ δὲ οὐκέτι συνῆκαν πρὸς τί εἶπε τοῦτο, διὸ καί φασι ὅτι *οὐκ ἔχομεν*. Ἵνα γὰρ μὴ δόξῃ φιλοκοκομπεῖν, οὐκ εἶπεν ἐγὼ τρέφω αὐτούς, ἀλλὰ *δότε αὐτοῖς ὑμεῖς*, διεγείρων αὐτοὺς εἰς πίστιν, ἵνα εἰπόντων αὐτῶν *οὐκ ἔχομεν*, δόξῃ δι᾽ ἀνάγκην ἔρχεσθαι ἐπὶ τὸ σημεῖον. Καὶ γὰρ ὁ τόπος καὶ ἡ ὥρα καὶ τὸ μηδὲν ἐννοεῖν ὑπὲρ τὴν ἀνθρώπου φύσιν ἐν Χριστῷ ἐνεποίει αὐτοῖς τὴν δειλίαν. Μό | **119r** λις γὰρ πέντε ἀνθρώποις ἀρκοῦσαν τροφὴν ἐπεφέροντο. Τί οὖν ὁ Σωτὴρ *φέρετέ μοι* τοὺς ἄρτους *ὧδε* φησί;
Διὰ τούτου διδάσκων αὐτοὺς ὅτι ὁ τὴν οἰκουμένην τρέφων μὴ ὑποκείμενος ὥρᾳ παρῆν εὐθὺς πάντα κατεργαζόμενος.

> *Φέρετέ μοι αὐτοὺς ὧδε.* Εἰ γὰρ καὶ ἔρημος ὁ τόπος, ἀλλ᾽ ὁ τρέφων τὴν οἰκουμένην πάρεστιν. εἰ δὲ *καὶ ἡ ὥρα παρῆλθεν*, ἀλλ᾽ ὁ μὴ ὑποκείμενος ὥρᾳ ὑμῖν διαλέγεται.[mlxxi]

> *φέρετέ μοι αὐτοὺς ὧδε.* εἰ γὰρ καὶ ἔρημος ὁ τόπος, ἀλλ᾽ ὁ τρέφων τὴν οἰκουμένην πάρειμι. *καὶ ἡ ὥρα παρῆλθεν.* ἀλλ᾽ ὁ μὴ ὑποκείμενος αὐταῖς ὑμῖν διαλέγεται.[mlxxii]

Οἱ δὲ μαθηταὶ καίπερ τούτους μόνους ἔχοντες ἑτοίμως δεδώκασι. Διδάσκει δὲ ὁ λόγος διὰ τούτου ὅτι δεῖ τοὺς φιλοξενεῖν θέλοντας ἑτοίμως παρατιθέναι ἃ ἔχουσι, κἂν ὀλίγα ὦσιν. Εἶτα, *κελεύσας τοὺς ὄχλους*, φησὶ ὁ Σωτὴρ *ἀνακλιθῆναι ἐπὶ τοὺς χόρτους*,[1261] ‹καὶ› διέθρεψεν αὐτοὺς ὡς Θεὸς *ὁ διδοὺς τροφὴν πάσῃ σαρκί.*[1262] Μετὰ πολλῆς δὲ τῆς ταπεινότητος τοῦτο ποιεῖ διὰ τοῦ τῆς εὐχῆς σχήματος.
Ἀναβλέψας γὰρ *εἰς τὸν οὐρανὸν εὐλόγησεν*[1263] αὐτούς, πάντα εἰς τὸν Πατέρα ἀναφέρων,

> Τὸν αὐτοῦ πατέρα ὑποδεικνύων ἡμῖν ὁ σωτὴρ αἴρει τοὺς ὀφθαλμοὺς πρὸς *τὸν οὐρανόν*. τοῦτο δὲ ἐποίει, ἵν᾽ ἡμεῖς ἐκ μὲν τῶν θαυμάτων πιστεύσωμεν αὐτῷ ὡς θεῷ, ἐκ δὲ τοῦ εὐχαριστεῖν καὶ βλέπειν πρὸς *τὸν οὐρανὸν* ἄνθρωπον εἶναι αὐτὸν ὁμολογήσωμεν.[mlxxiii]

καίπερ ἐπὶ τῶν ἄλλων σημείων αὐθεντικῶς ποιῶν ὡς ἴσος ὢν τῷ πατρί, ἵνα πείσῃ τοὺς ὄχλους ὅτι ἐκ τοῦ πατρὸς ἦν.[mlxxiv]
Ἐκ τούτου δὲ διδασκόμεθα ὅτι δεῖ πρῶτον εὐχαριστεῖν καὶ οὕτως ἐσθίειν.

> τότε ἀναβλέπει *εἰς τὸν οὐρανόν*. ὁμοῦ μὲν ταῦτα κατασκευάζων, ἅπερ εἶπον, ὁμοῦ δὲ παιδεύων ἡμᾶς, μὴ πρότερον ἅπτεσθαι τραπέζης, ἕως ἂν εὐχαριστήσωμεν τῷ τὴν τροφὴν ἡμῖν ταύτην παρέχοντι.[mlxxv]

1260 Matt. 14:16.
1261 Matt. 14:19.
1262 Psalm 135:25.
1263 Matt. 14:19.

> Χάριν δὲ τίνος ἕνεκεν *ἀνέβλεψεν εἰς τὸν οὐρανὸν καὶ εὐλόγησεν*; ἵνα δείξῃ, ὅτι ἀπὸ τοῦ πνεύματος ἐστίν. ὁμοῦ δὲ καὶ ἡμᾶς παιδεύων, μὴ πρότερον ἅπτεσθαι τραπέζης, ἕως ἂν εὐχαριστήσωμεν τῷ τὴν τροφὴν ἡμῖν παρέχοντι.[mlxxvi]

Ἄλλως τε· ἀναβλέπει εἰς τὸν οὐρανὸν ἐκεῖ ἕλκων τοὺς ὁρῶντας αὐτόν· ἢ ἐπειδὴ κατὰ τὴν ἔρημον τοῦ Θεοῦ τὸ μάννα παρέχοντος αὐτοῖς οἱ Ἰσραηλῖται ἐτόλμησαν εἰπεῖν περὶ αὐτοῦ, *μὴ καὶ ἄρτον δύναται δοῦναι*;[1264] Ἵνα ‹δὲ› μὴ δόξῃ ἐπὶ τοῦτο χωρεῖν αὐτοὺς ὡς ἂν μείζονα τοῦ Θεοῦ ποιῶν ἑαυτόν, σφόδρα τῶν Ἰουδαίων πολλὰς κατ᾽ αὐτοῦ πλέκειν ἀφορμὰς ἐπιχειρούντων, πρὸ τοῦ ποιῆσαι εἰς τὸν Πατέρα ἀνήνεγκε τὸ γινόμενον. Ἐκ τῶν *πέντε* δὲ ἄρτων παρήγαγε τοὺς ἄλλους καὶ ἀπὸ τῶν ὀλίγων ἰχθύων ‹πολλούς›, ἵνα δείξῃ ὅτι αὐτός ἐστιν ὁ γῆς καὶ θαλάσσης δημιουργός.

> Οὐ ποιεῖ δὲ ἐκ μὴ ὄντων, ἀλλ᾽ ἐκ τῶν ὑποκειμένων, ἐμφράττων τὸ Μαρκίωνος καὶ Μανιχαίου στόμα, τῶν τὴν κτίσιν ἀλλοτριούντων αὐτοῦ. ἅμα δὲ καὶ δεικνύς, ὅτι καὶ τὰ ὁρώμενα αὐτοῦ ἔργα καὶ κτίσματα εἰσί.[mlxxvii]

ἔ | **119v** *δωκε τοῖς μαθηταῖς τοὺς ἄρτους*.[1265] Διὰ τῶν χειρῶν τῶν μαθητῶν προσάγει τὰς τροφάς, δεικνὺς διὰ τούτου ὅτι ἐγγύς εἰσιν *οἱ ἅγιοι* τοῦ *Θεοῦ*,[mlxxviii] οἱ δὲ μὴ τοιοῦτοι ἔξω ἑστήκασι τοῦ Θεοῦ.

The crowds receive nourishment from the Lord through the apostles.[mlxxix]

Διὰ τοῦτο ἐν ταῖς τῶν μαθητῶν χερσὶ περιττεύειν αὐτοὺς ἐποίει. Ἵνα δὲ μὴ φαντασίᾳ τις τοῦτο εἴπῃ γεγενῆσθαι, διὰ τῶν περισσευσάντων πείθει καὶ τοὺς ἀπόντας ὁρῶντας τοὺς *δώδεκα κοφίνους*[1266] τῶν κλασμάτων. Εἰκὸς δὲ διὰ τοῦτο εἴασε πεινᾶσαι καὶ ἐκόρεσεν, ἵνα μὴ φαντασίαν τις εἴπῃ τὸ γεγονός.
Διὰ τοῦτο δὲ καὶ *δώδεκα κοφίνους* περισσεῦσαι ἐποίησεν, ἵνα, ἕκαστος τῶν μαθητῶν βαστάζων, ἐκ τοῦ ὄγκου πλείονα λάβῃ τοῦ θαύματος αἴσθησιν.

> περισσεῦσαι δὲ ἐποίησεν, οὐχὶ ἄρτους, ἀλλὰ καὶ κλάσματα. ἵνα δείξῃ ὅτι τῶν πέντε ἄρτων εἰσὶ ταῦτα τὰ κλάσματα, καὶ ὥστε τοὺς ἀπόντας μαθεῖν τὸ γεγενημένον. καὶ ἵνα μήτις φαντασίαν εἶναι νομίσῃ τὸ γεγονός, δώδεκα κοφίνους εἰς μέσον παρήγαγεν. ἵνα καὶ Ἰούδας βαστάσῃ.[mlxxx]

Ὅτι γὰρ καὶ αὐτοὶ ἀμφίβολον ἔτι περὶ τοῦ γενομένου τὴν γνώμην εἶχον οἱ μαθηταὶ διὰ τὸ ἄγαν παράδοξον, δηλοῖ Μάρκος σαφῶς εἰπών· *οὐ γὰρ συνῆκαν ἐπὶ τοῖς ἄρτοις. ἦν γὰρ αὐτῶν ἡ καρδία πεπωρωμένη*.[1267] Ὡς δὲ ὁ Ἰωάννης φησὶ ὅτι οἱ ἄρτοι κρίθινοι

1264 Psalm 77:19-20.
1265 Matt. 14:19.
1266 Matt. 14:20.
1267 Mark, 6:52.

ἦσαν,[1268] σημαίνει ὁ λόγος δι᾽ αἰνιγμάτων τὴν κτηνώδη καὶ παχεῖαν τροφὴν τὴν διὰ Μωσέως ἐν Πεντατεύχῳ δοθεῖσαν. Οἱ δὲ *δύο* ἰχθύες, ἡ εὐαγγελικὴ καὶ ἰσχνὴ[mlxxxi] καὶ πνευματική ἐστι τροφή, δι᾽ ἧς δηλοῦται ἡ τῶν ἁλιέων συγγραφὴ ἀποστολική τε καὶ εὐαγγελική.

Ἠνάγκασεν ὁ Ἰησοῦς τοὺς μαθητὰς ἐμβῆναι εἰς τὸ πλοῖον.[1269] Ἠνάγκασεν αὐτοὺς ἐπειδὴ οὐκ ἤθελον ἀποστῆναι ἀπ᾽ αὐτοῦ· *εἰς τὸ ὄρος* δὲ ἀναβαίνει *κατ᾽ ἰδίαν προσεύξασθαι,*[1270] παιδεύων ἡμᾶς ὅτι καλὸν ἡ ἐρημία καὶ ἡ μόνωσις ὅταν ἐντυγχάνειν δέῃ Θεῷ. *Μόνος* δὲ ηὔχετο διὰ τὸ συνιέναι καὶ νοεῖν.
Εἰ γὰρ καὶ ὡς Θεὸς οὐ δεῖται εὐχῆς, ἀλλ᾽ ὡς *ἀρχιερεὺς*[1271] ὑπὲρ ἡμῶν | **120r** ποιεῖται τὰς ἱκεσίας καὶ ἕως ἑσπέρας εὔχεται, διδάσκων ἡμᾶς μὴ ἀψικόρως[mlxxxii] τοῦτο ποιεῖν. Πλὴν πρῶτον ἐδίδαξεν ἐν ᾧ χρεία ἐστὶ δεῖν πρῶτον τὰ κοινωφελῆ διδάξαι καὶ μετὰ τοῦτο χωρεῖν εἰς προσευχήν.

> Εὔχεται δέ, οὐχ ὡς δεόμενος, ἀλλ᾽ ὡς ἀρχιερεὺς τὰς ὑπὲρ ἡμῶν ἱκεσίας ποιούμενος. Καὶ μετ᾽ ὀλίγον. Ἕως ἑσπέρας. ἵνα δείξῃ, ὅτι οὐ δεῖ ἀψικόρως ἔχειν περὶ τούτου, ἀλλ᾽ ὑπομονὴν καὶ προθυμίαν. διδάσκει δὲ καὶ τοῦτο. ὥστε ἐν ᾧ χρεία, ὀφείλομεν τὰ κοινωφελῆ λαλεῖν τοῖς ἐντυγχάνουσιν, καὶ μετὰ τὴν τοιαύτην διάλεξιν καὶ διδασκαλίαν, ἐπὶ τὴν προσευχὴν χωρεῖν.[mlxxxiii]

> Προσεύχεται οὐχ ὡς δεόμενός τινος ὁ θεός, ἀλλ᾽ ὡς ἀρχιερεὺς τὰς ὑπὲρ ἡμῶν ἱκεσίας ποιούμενος, καίτοι καθ᾽ ὃ νοεῖται καί ἐστι θεὸς φύσει αὐτὸς χορηγῶν τοῖς ἁγίοις τὰ αἰτήματα. εὔχεται δὲ ἕως ἑσπέρας, ἵνα δείξῃ, ὅτι οὐ χρὴ ἀψικόρως ἔχειν περὶ αὐτοῦ, ἀλλ᾽ ὑπομονὴν καὶ μακροθυμίαν ἐνδείκνυσθαι. ὁ μὲν οὖν ἀνέβαινεν ἐκεῖσε καὶ προσηύχετο.[mlxxxiv]

Τὸ δὲ πλοῖον ἤδη μέσον τῆς θαλάσσης ἦν, βασανιζόμενον.[1272] Εἶτα τούτου προσευχομένου, κλυδωνίζονται οἱ μαθηταὶ μέσον τῆς θαλάσσης διαπερῶντες ἐν τῷ πλοίῳ, ἵνα μάθωσι γενναίως φέρειν τὰ παρεμπίπτοντα. Οὐκ εὐθέως δὲ αὐτοῖς ἐπέστη λύων τὸν χειμῶνα, παιδεύων αὐτοὺς μὴ ταχέως λύσιν ἐπιζητεῖν τῶν συνεχουσῶν συμφορῶν, ἀλλὰ φέρειν τὰ προσπίπτοντα γενναίως.

Περὶ τετάρτην γὰρ φυλακὴν τῆς νυκτὸς ἦλθε πρὸς αὐτοὺς περιπατῶν ἐπὶ τῆς θαλάσσης.[1273] Τετάρτην δὲ φυλακὴν τὴν τριωρίαν λέγει τὴν μετὰ τὴν ἐνάτην ὥραν. Περὶ γὰρ τὸ τέλος ἦλθε τῆς νυκτὸς χειμαζομένων αὐτῶν. Ὡς Θεῷ δὲ καθυπεστρώθη[mlxxxv] αὐτῷ ἡ θάλασσα καὶ περιεπάτει ἐπάνω τοῦ ὕδατος. Οἱ δὲ μαθηταὶ διὰ τὴν

1268 John, 6:9&13.
1269 Matt. 14:22.
1270 Matt. 14:23.
1271 Heb. 2:17; 3:1; 4:14-15; 5:5-6 (quoting Psalm 109:4); 5:10; 6:20 (quoting Psalm 109:4); 7:17 (quoting Psalm 109:4); 7:26-27; 8:1-3; 9:11&25; 13:11-12.
1272 Matt. 14:24.
1273 Mark, 6:48; cf. Matt. 14:25.

παραλλαγὴν τῆς συνηθείας οἰήθη‹σαν›[1274] *φάντασμα* εἶναι. Ἔδοξαν γὰρ ἀέριον εἶναι πνεῦμα[mlxxxvi] ἐπιλαθόμενοι τοῦ φόβου τοῦ χειμῶνος.

Ἐπὶ πλεῖον *ἐταράχθησαν*.[1275] Ἐπειδὴ δὲ ἀπὸ τῆς ὄψεως οὐκ ἐπέγνωσαν αὐτόν, διὰ τῆς φωνῆς ἑαυτὸν ἐφανέρωσεν εἰπών, *θαρσεῖτε, ἐγώ εἰμι· μὴ φοβεῖσθε*,[1276] καὶ διὰ τοῦ ῥήματος τούτου ἔλυσεν αὐτῶν τὴν ἀγωνίαν. Εἰπὼν γὰρ τὸ *θαρσεῖτε*, τὴν πίστιν ἀπαιτεῖ, δι' ἧς ὁ εἰς Χριστὸν πιστεύων σώζεται. Μὴ ἀγωνιᾶτε τοίνυν φησί· *ἐγώ εἰμι* ὁ πάντα δυνάμενος ποιῆσαι καὶ μετασκευάσαι ὡς Θεός.

Κύριε εἰ σὺ εἶ, κέλευσόν | **120v** *με πρός σὲ ἐλθεῖν*.[1277] Τοῦτο εἶπεν ὁ Πέτρος ἵνα λυθῇ αὐτῷ ἡ ἀμφιβολία· ᾔδει γὰρ ὅτι οὐ μόνον ὁ Χριστὸς δύναται περιπατῆσαι ἐπὶ τῶν ὑδάτων ἀλλὰ καὶ ἑτέρους εἰς τοῦτο ἀγαγεῖν. Ἐναργὲς δὲ σημεῖον τοῦ μὴ εἶναι φάντασμα ᾔτει τοῦτο ὡς Θεόν· διὸ καὶ τὸ *κέλευσόν* φησι. Καὶ δεικνὺς ὅτι οὐ δι' ἐπίδειξιν ζητεῖ τοῦτο, οὐκ εἶπε *κέλευσόν* μοι περιπατῆσαι ἐπὶ τῶν ὑδάτων, *ἀλλ' ἐλθεῖν πρός σέ*. Εἰδὼς γὰρ τὸ τῆς ἐξουσίας ὑπερφερὲς πρὸς πληροφορίαν αἰτεῖ ἵνα γνῷ ὅτι αὐτός ἐστιν ὁ Ἰησοῦς. Διὸ καὶ ἐπιτρέψας αὐτῷ ἐλθεῖν ὑπέστρωσεν αὐτοῖς τὴν θάλασσαν δεικνὺς αὐτῷ τὴν θεοπρεπῆ αὐτοῦ δύναμιν.

Καὶ καταβὰς ἀπὸ τοῦ πλοίου ὁ Πέτρος.[1278] *Καταβὰς* τοίνυν *ἀπὸ τοῦ πλοίου* θαρρήσας ᾔει πρὸς αὐτόν, οὐχ οὕτως τῷ περιπατεῖν ἐπὶ τῶν ὑδάτων, ὡς τῷ πρὸς αὐτὸν ἔρχεσθαι χαίρων. Καὶ τοῦ μείζονος περιγενόμενος τοῦ περιπατεῖν *ἐπὶ* τῶν ὑδάτων, τὸ ἧττον ἐφοβήθη ὡς ἄνθρωπος τὸν ἄνεμον. Καὶ ὅτε μὲν πρὸς τὸν Ἰησοῦν ἔβλεπε, περιεπάτει *ἐπὶ* τῶν ὑδάτων· ὅτε δὲ ἀπεῖδεν ἐπὶ *τὸν ἄνεμον*, ἐδειλίασε καὶ ἐβαπτίσθη, πλὴν καὶ παρεμυθήσατο τοὺς μαθητὰς τὸ βυθισθῆναι αὐτόν. Ἔτι γὰρ εἶχον ζῆλον κατ' ἀλλήλων μήπω τοῦ Πνεύματος ἀξιωθέντες.
Τοῦτο δὲ καὶ τὸ μέσον ἐνδείκνυται τοῦ διδασκάλου καὶ τοῦ μαθητοῦ.

Τοῦτο δὲ καὶ τὸ μέσον ἐδείκνυ τοῦ διδασκάλου καὶ τοῦ μαθητοῦ.[mlxxxvii]

(ΩΡΙΓΕΝΟΥΣ, added on the margin) Ἐκ τούτου δῆλόν ἐστι ὅτι ‹ὡ›ς[1279] ὁ Πέτρος περιεπάτησεν ἐπὶ τῶν ὑδάτων ἐλθεῖν πρὸς τὸν Ἰησοῦν, πάλιν τὴν αὐτὴν πορείαν ποιήσεται σὺν τῷ Ιησοῦ ὁ ὁδηγούμενος ὑπ' αὐτοῦ ἕως ἔλθωσιν εἰς τὸ πλοῖον.

(ΩΡΙΓΕΝΟΥΣ, main text cont.) Εἶτα δεικνὺς ὅτι ἀπὸ μικροψυχίας ἐκινδύνευεν οὐκέτι τῆς θαλάσσης ἀνεχομένης φέρειν τὸν διψυχήσαντα, οὐκέτι τῷ ἀνέμῳ ἐπετίμησεν, ἀλλὰ τῷ Πέτρῳ ὠνείδισε διὰ τὴν ἀπιστίαν. Διὸ καὶ ἀνενεγκὼν αὐτὸν ἔστησεν ἐπὶ τοῦ | **121r** ὕδατος ἐάσας τὸν ἄνεμον πνεῖν, ἵνα δείξῃ ὅτι οὐχ ὁ ἄνεμος ἀλλ' ἡ ἀπιστία αὐτοῦ ἐβύθισεν αὐτόν. Εἶτα σώσας, καὶ ὀνειδίσας τὴν ἀπιστίαν, μείζονα

1274 Cod. οἰηθέντες.
1275 Matt. 14:26; cf. Mark, 6:50.
1276 Matt. 14:27.
1277 Matt. 14:28.
1278 Matt. 14:29.
1279 Cod. ὅς.

ἐποίησεν αὐτῷ χάριν ἔχειν ὑπὲρ τοῦ σωθῆναι. Οἱ δὲ ἐν τῷ πλοίῳ ἐκ πάντων τῶν γεγονότων ἐναργεῖς λαβόντες τὰς ἀποδείξεις[mlxxxviii] καὶ ἀπὸ τοῦ ὑποτάσσεσθαι αὐτῷ τὸν ἄνεμον συνεώρων ὅτι Θεὸς ἦν καὶ προσκυνοῦσιν αὐτὸν ὡς Θεὸν καὶ Υἱὸν Θεοῦ ὁμολογοῦσιν.[1280] Ἀνακτέον δὲ καὶ εἰς θεωρίαν τὸν λόγον. Ἔοικε σκάφει ἡ γῆ, ἐφ ἧς οἱ ἄνθρωποι ἐχειμάζοντο ὑπὸ τῶν πονηρῶν πνευμάτων ἐπὶ τὰς κοσμικὰς ἡδονὰς διεγειρόντων αὐτούς. Ἐκλυδωνίζοντο οὖν, σκότους ἀγνωσίας Θεοῦ κατέχοντος αὐτούς. Ἀλλ᾽ ἐν ἐσχάτοις καιροῖς[1281] ἐπιφανεὶς ὁ τῶν ὅλων Σωτὴρ καὶ συνεισελθὼν τοῖς ἀνθρώποις εἰς τὸ σκάφος ἔσωσε. Καὶ οὕτως ἐπιγνωσθεὶς προσεκυνήθη ὡς Θεός.

Καὶ ἐπιγνόντες αὐτὸν οἱ ἄνδρες τοῦ τόπου ἐκείνου.[1282] Εἶτα, ἐπειδὴ διὰ πολλοῦ χρόνου ἐπεδήμησε τῇ Γεννησαρέτ, *ἐπιγνόντες αὐτὸν οἱ ἄνδρες τοῦ τόπου ἐκείνου* οὐ μόνον ἐκ τῆς ὄψεως ἀλλὰ καὶ ἀπὸ τῶν σημείων, ἤνεγκαν *πάντας τοὺς* ἐκ τῆς χώρας ἀρρώστους, οἳ καὶ μετὰ πίστεως ἁπτόμενοι αὐτοῦ ἐθεραπεύοντο.[1283] Συνεχώρει γὰρ τοῦτο ποιεῖν καὶ διὰ τῆς ἁφῆς ἐδωρεῖτο αὐτοῖς τὴν ἴασιν.

Οἱ ἀπὸ Ἱεροσολύμων γραμματεῖς.[1284] Εἰ καὶ πᾶσαι αἱ φυλαὶ εἶχον γραμματεῖς καὶ Φαρισαίους, ἀλλ᾽ οἱ ἐντιμότεροι ἦσαν ἐν Ἱερουσαλήμ· διὸ καὶ ἤχθοντο τοῦ Χριστοῦ εὐδοκιμοῦντος ὑπὲρ αὐτούς, ὡς ἐξουθενοῦντος δὲ τοὺς πρεσβυτέρους διέσυρον τοὺς |
121v μαθητάς. Οὐδὲ γὰρ ἐφρόντιζον τῶν τοιούτων παραδόσεων ὡς περιττῶν. Τί οὖν ὁ Σωτὴρ οὐδὲν πρὸς τοῦτο ἀπελογήσατο, ἀλλ᾽ ἀντεγκαλεῖ αὐτοῖς λέγων ὅτι ὁ τὰ μεγάλα ἁμαρτάνων οὐκ ὀφείλει περὶ εὐτελῶν ἄλλοις ἐγκαλεῖν, καὶ ἐλέγχει αὐτοὺς ὡς τὰς ἀγράφους παραδόσεις πλείω τῶν ἐγγράφων τετιμηκότας νόμων καὶ τῶν Φαρισαίων τὴν ἐντολὴν τῶν πρεσβυτέρων ἀπαιτούντων; Αὐτὸς εἰσάγει τὴν τῶν πρεσβυτέρων ἐντολὴν μαχομένην τῇ τοῦ Θεοῦ ἐντολῇ. Καθάπτεται τοίνυν τῶν ταῦτα νομοθετησάντων καί φησὶ τοῦ Θεοῦ καὶ ἀπὸ ψιλῆς ῥημάτων ἀτιμίας θάνατον ὁρίσαντος τὸ ἐπιτίμιον ἐπὶ τῇ εἰς τοὺς γονεῖς ἀπὸ τῶν παίδων ὕβρει γενομένῃ. *Ὑμεῖς* φατὲ ὅτι ἐν ἐξουσίᾳ κεῖται τοῖς παισὶ τὸ τιμῆσαι τοὺς γονεῖς ἢ μή; Καὶ οὐδὲν ἄτοπον. Λέγουσι γὰρ λέγειν τοῖς παισὶ πρὸς τοὺς πατέρας *ὃ ἐὰν* λάβῃς παρ᾽ *ἐμοῦ*, τοῦτο ὡς *δῶρον* κομίζ‹ω›[1285] καὶ χάριν ὀφείλεις μοι ἔχειν, ὀφείλεται δέ σοι τιμὴ παρ᾽ ἐμοὶ οὐδεμία[1286] πληροῦν οὐ βουλομένῳ. Καὶ οὐκ ἀφίετε, φησί, τιμᾶν τοὺς γονεῖς, εἰ μήπου οἱ παῖδες ἐκ φιλοτιμίας τοῦτο θελήσουσι ποιῆσαι, διὰ τούτου ἀθετοῦντες *τὴν ἐντολὴν τοῦ Θεοῦ* τὴν κελεύουσαν τιμᾶν τοὺς γονεῖς.

Ἄλλως τε δέ, ἐπειδὴ νόμος ἀπῄτει τοὺς παῖδας τιμᾶν τοὺς γονεῖς καὶ τὰ τῶν παίδων τῶν πατέρων ἐλέγετο εἶναι, οἱ τῶν Ἰουδαίων πρεσβύτεροι παρεσκεύαζον τοὺς παῖδας λέγειν τοῖς γονεῦσιν ὅτι τὰς οὐσίας ἡμῶν ἀφιερώσαμεν τῷ Θεῷ, ἵνα |

1280 Matt. 14:33.
1281 Cf. 2 Tim. 3:1; 1 Peter, 1:5.
1282 Matt. 14:34.
1283 Matt. 14:36.
1284 Matt. 15:1.
1285 Cod. κομίζῃ.
1286 Matt. 15:2-5.

122r μὴ τολμῶσιν αὐτῶν ἅψασθαι οἱ γονεῖς. Εἶτα προσφέροντες αὐτὰ τοῖς πρεσβυτέροις συνεμερίζοντο αὐτὰ μετ' αὐτῶν, διὸ καὶ τὴν κατὰ τῶν γονέων ἀδικίαν εἰσηγοῦντο, διδάσκοντες λέγειν τοὺς νέους, πᾶν ὃ ἐὰν αἰτῶσιν οἱ γονεῖς διὰ πενίαν παρ' ὑμῶν ἀποκρίνεσθε πρὸς αὐτοὺς λέγοντες ὅτι *ὃ ἐὰν ἐξ ἐμοῦ ὠφεληθῇς*,[1287] τουτέστι λάβῃς.[mlxxxix]

Οὐ ‹μὴ› τιμήσει πατέρα ἢ μητέρα.[1288] Καὶ πῶς *οὐ μὴ τιμήσῃ*; Δῶρον γάρ ἐστι, φησί, εἰς τὸ προσενεχθῆναι Θεῷ καὶ ἐπιβλαβὲς τῷ πατρὶ ἢ τῇ μητρὶ δίδοσθαι αὐτό. Τοίνυν διὰ τούτου ἐλέγχει αὐτοὺς ὁ Κύριος ὡς τὰ οἰκεῖα ἐντάλματα τῶν ἐντολῶν τοῦ Θεοῦ ἰσχυρότερα εἶναι ἐτίθεντο καὶ διὰ φιλαργυρίαν ἔχοντες τὰς ψυχὰς ἐρρυπωμένας, τὰς ἔξωθεν χεῖρας νίπτοντες διὰ τὸ φαίνεσθαι τοῖς ἀνθρώποις καθαροί, τοὺς καθαροὺς *τῇ καρδίᾳ*[1289] μαθητὰς κατέκρινον μὴ ποιοῦντας τοῦτο. Καὶ[mxc] τί κοινωνεῖ τῷ τῶν Φαρισαίων ἐγκλήματι τῷ αἰτιωμένῳ τὸ ἄνιπτον τῶν χειρῶν ἡ τιμᾶσθαι δεῖν παρακελεύουσα τοὺς γονεῖς ἐντολή; Φιλαργυρίᾳ[1290] νοσοῦντες[mxci] οἱ πρεσβύτεροι καὶ οἱ Φαρισαῖοι καὶ οἱ γραμματεῖς ἔχαιρον τῷ περιέργῳ τῶν παραδόσεων· καὶ ὁρῶντες λυμαινομένην αὐτοῖς τὴν τιμᾶν τοὺς γονεῖς κελεύουσαν ἐντολὴν καὶ τὸν ἐσπουδασμένον αὐτοῖς πόρον ἐγκόπτουσαν, τί μηχανῶνται; Ἐπιτειχίζουσιν αὐτῇ τὴν πασῶν μείζονα ἐντολήν, τὴν *ἀγαπήσεις Κύριον τὸν Θεόν σου ἐξ ὅλης τῆς καρδίας σου*,[1291] καὶ τὰ ἑξῆς. Οἱ γὰρ παῖδες οὐδὲν τῶν οἰκείων πόνων καὶ πόρων ἐνόμιζον ἴδιον εἶναι, ἀλλὰ πάντα τοῖς | **122v** πατράσι προσεπόριζον, δεδιότες μὴ προσκρούσωσι τῷ τιμᾶν τοὺς γονεῖς βουλομένῳ νόμῳ. Ἐπέτρεψαν οὖν οἱ πρεσβύτεροι τοῖς παισὶ τοιαῦτα κηρύττειν καὶ προδιαμαρτύρεσθαι τῷ πατρὶ ἢ τῇ μητρί, καὶ λέγειν· πᾶν ὃ *ἂν ὠφεληθῇς* (τουτέστι κερδάνῃς) ἐξ ἐμοῦ καὶ πρὸς σῆς ὠφελείας εἶναι λογίσαιο, τοῦτο δῶρόν ἐστιν ἀφιερωθὲν ἤδη Θεῷ παρ' ἐμοῦ. Καὶ λοιπὸν οἱ γονεῖς εὑρίσκοντο κρείττονι μαχόμενοι νόμῳ τῷ βουλομένῳ πάντων προτιμᾶσθαι Θεόν καὶ ἀναγκαίως παρεχώρουν, μηδὲ ἐφάψασθαι τολμῶντες τῶν προεπηγγελμένων καὶ ἀνατεθέντων ὡς ἱερῶν. Καὶ ταύτῃ τῇ μηχανῇ τοὺς γονεῖς ἀποστεροῦντες τῆς ὀφειλομένης τιμῆς, τῶν ἀνοσίων λημμάτων τοῖς πρεσβυτέροις ἐκοινώνουν οἱ παῖδες. Ὁ δὲ Μᾶρκος σαφέστερον τὸ δῶρον *κορβᾶν*[1292] εἶπεν, ὅπερ τῇ Ἑβραίων γλώττῃ σημαίνει τὴν προσφορὰν καὶ τὸ δῶρον τὸ ἀφιερωθὲν τῷ Θεῷ. Ἦσαν γάρ τινες οἳ καθιεροῦν ἑαυτοὺς ἐσπούδαζον τῷ Θεῷ, σπάνει δὲ χρημάτων ἀνακοπτόμενοι, τὴν εἰς τοὺς γονέας αἰδῶ παραπόδισμα ἔχειν προετείνοντο. Μόλις γὰρ σφίσι τε αὐτοῖς κἀκείνοις τὰ ζωαρκῆ πορίζεσθαι δύνασθαι. Οἱ δὲ πρεσβύτεροι ἀνέπειθον παρ' οὐδὲν ἡγεῖσθαι τὸ χρῆμα διὰ Θεόν, κἂν εἰ προσίοιεν οἱ γεγεννηκότες τὴν συνήθη παρ' αὐτῶν ζητοῦντες ἐπικουρίαν, χρῆναι λέγειν ἐδίδασκον ὅτι ὅπερ *ἂν ἐξ ἐμοῦ* λάβοις, τὸ θεῖον ἴσθι τοι παραβλάπτων ἀνά | **123r** θημα

1287 Matt. 15:5.

1288 Matt. 15:5.

1289 Cf. Matt. 5:8.

1290 Cod. φιλαργυρίαν.

1291 Deut. 6:5; Mark, 12:30; Luke, 10:27.

1292 Mark, 7:11.

καὶ χρήμασιν ἱεροῖς τὰς χεῖρας ἐπάγων. Ἀνατέθεικα γὰρ ἐμαυτὸν καὶ ὡς δῶρον ἐπήγγελμαι τῷ Θεῷ. Οἱ δὲ τὰ ἐκ τῆς ἱεροσυλίας δεδιότες βλάβη διεκαρτέρουν οἰμώζοντες καὶ τὴν εἰς Θεὸν εὐσέβειαν πρόφασιν λιμοῦ ἔχοντες. Διατί τοίνυν *ἠκυρώσατε τὴν ἐντολήν;*[1293] Οὔτε γὰρ τῶν τῷ Θεῷ πρεπόντων ἀμελητέον διὰ τὰ ἀνθρώπινα, οὔτε μὴν εἰς ἅπαν τῶν ἀνθρωπίνων καταρρᾳθυμητέον.

Καὶ τί κοινωνεῖ τῷ τῶν Φαρισαίων ἐγκλήματι τῷ αἰτιωμένῳ τὸ ἄνιπτον τῶν χειρῶν ἡ τιμᾶσθαι δεῖν παρακελεύουσα τοὺς γονεῖς ἐντολή; Φιλαργυρίαν νοσοῦντες οἱ πρεσβύτεροι καὶ οἱ Φαρισαῖοι καὶ οἱ γραμματεῖς ἔχαιρον τῷ περιέργῳ τῶν παραδόσεων καὶ ὁρῶντες λυμαινομένην αὐτοῖς τὴν τιμᾶν τοὺς γονεῖς κελεύουσαν ἐντολὴν καὶ τὸν ἐσπουδασμένον αὐτοῖς πόρον ἐγκόπτουσαν τί μηχανῶνται; ἐπιτειχίζουσιν αὐτῇ τὴν πασῶν μείζονα ἐντολῶν τὴν *ἀγαπήσεις κύριον τὸν θεόν σου ἐξ ὅλης τῆς καρδίας σου* καὶ τὰ ἑξῆς. οἱ γὰρ παῖδες οὐδὲν τῶν οἰκείων πόνων καὶ πόρων ἐνόμιζον ἴδιον εἶναι, ἀλλὰ πάντα τοῖς πατράσι προσεπόριζον δεδιότες μὴ προσκρούσωσιν τῷ τιμᾶν τοὺς γονεῖς βουλομένῳ νόμῳ. ἐπέτρεψαν οὖν οἱ πρεσβύτεροι τοῖς παισὶ τοιαῦτα κηρύττειν καὶ προδιαμαρτύρεσθαι τῷ πατρὶ ἢ τῇ μητρὶ καὶ λέγειν πᾶν, ὃ ἐὰν ὠφεληθῇς, τοῦτ᾽ ἔστιν κερδαίνῃς, ἐξ ἐμοῦ καὶ πρὸς σῆς ὠφελείας εἶναι λογίσαιο, τοῦτο δῶρόν ἐστιν ἀφιερωθὲν ἤδη θεῷ παρ᾽ ἐμοῦ. καὶ λοιπὸν οἱ γονεῖς εὑρίσκοντο κρείττονι μαχόμενοι νόμῳ τῷ βουλομένῳ πάντων προτιμᾶσθαι θεὸν καὶ ἀναγκαίως παρεχώρουν μηδὲ ἐφάψασθαι τολμῶντες τῶν προεπηγγελμένων καὶ ἀνατεθέντων ὡς ἱερῶν. καὶ ταύτῃ τῇ μηχανῇ τοὺς γονεῖς ἀποστεροῦντες τῆς ὀφειλομένης τιμῆς τῶν ἀνοσίων λημμάτων τοῖς πρεσβυτέροις ἐκοινώνουν οἱ παῖδες. ὁ δὲ Μᾶρκος σαφέστερον τὸ δῶρον *κορβᾶν* εἶπεν, ὅπερ τῇ τῶν Ἑβραίων γλώττῃ σημαίνει τὴν προσφορὰν καὶ τὸ δῶρον τὸ ἀφιερωθὲν τῷ θεῷ. ἦσαν γάρ τινες, οἳ καθιεροῦν ἑαυτοὺς ἐσπούδαζον τῷ θεῷ. σπάνει δὲ χρημάτων ἀνακοπτόμενοι τὴν εἰς τοὺς γονεῖς αἰδῶ παραπόδισμα ἔχειν προετείνοντο. μόλις γὰρ σφίσι τε αὐτοῖς κἀκείνοις τὰ ζωαρκῆ πορίζεσθαι δύνασθαι. οἱ δὲ πρεσβύτεροι ἀνέπειθον παρ᾽ οὐδὲν ἡγεῖσθαι τὸ χρῆμα διὰ θεόν. κἂν εἰ προσίοιεν οἱ γεγεννηκότες τὴν συνήθη παρ᾽ αὐτῶν ζητοῦντες ἐπικουρίαν, χρῆναι λέγειν ἐδίδασκον, ὅτι ὅπερ ἂν ἐξ ἐμοῦ λάβοις τὸ θεῖον ἴσθι σοι παραβλάπτων ἀνάθημα καὶ χρήμασιν ἱεροῖς τὰς χεῖρας ἐπάγων. ἀνατέθεικα γὰρ ἐμαυτὸν καὶ ὡς δῶρον ἐπήγγελμαι τῷ θεῷ. οἱ δὲ τὰ ἐκ τῆς ἱεροσυλίας δεδιότες βλάβη διεκαρτέρουν οἰμώζοντες καὶ τὴν εἰς θεὸν εὐσέβειαν πρόφασιν λιμοῦ ἔχοντες. διὰ τί τοίνυν ἠκυρώσατε τὴν ἐντολήν; οὔτε γὰρ τῶν τῷ θεῷ πρεπόντων ἀμελητέον διὰ τὰ ἀνθρώπινα οὔτε μὴν εἰς ἅπαν τῶν ἀνθρωπίνων καταρρᾳθυμητέον.[mxcii]

Καλῶς προεφήτευσεν περὶ ὑμῶν Ἡσαΐας.[1294] Δείκνυσι καὶ διὰ τῆς Ἡσαΐου φωνῆς καὶ περὶ τῶν Πατέρα τοιούτους ὄντας. Συμφώνους γὰρ δείκνυσι τοὺς τοῦ Ἡσαΐου λόγους[1295] τοῖς νῦν πράγμασι. Πονηροὶ γὰρ ὄντες καὶ διὰ τῶν ἀσεβῶν ἔργων μακρύνοντες ἑαυτοὺς τοῦ Θεοῦ, στόματι[1296] μόνῳ ἐλάλουν τὰ *τοῦ Θεοῦ λόγια.*[1297] Εἶτα, αὐξήσας τὴν κατηγορίαν ἀπὸ τῆς τῶν προφητῶν φωνῆς, ἐκείνοις μὲν οὐδὲν

1293 Matt. 15:6.
1294 Matt. 15:7; Mark, 7:6.
1295 Cf. Is. 29:13; cf. Ez. 33:31.
1296 Cf. Matt. 15:8.
1297 Cf. Psalm 106:11; Num. 24:4; 24.16; Rom. 3:2.

διαλέγεται ἀδιορθώτως ἔχουσι λοιπόν, τὸν δὲ λόγον τρέπει πρὸς τοὺς ὄχλους ὥστε τὸ δόγμα ὑπερενεγκεῖν. Καὶ λαβὼν ἀφορμὴν καὶ τὴν τῶν βρωμάτων παρατήρησιν ἐκβάλλει, δι᾽ ὧν δὲ προσκαλεῖται τὸν ὄχλον εὐπαράδεκτον ποιεῖ τὸν λόγον καί φησι, *ἀκούετέ* μου τῶν λόγων *καὶ συνίετε.*[1298] Τοῦτο δέ φησι διανιστῶν τὸν ἀκροατήν, ἐπειδὴ καὶ τὰ Μωσέως ἀκούοντες οὐ συνίεσαν τῶν λεγομένων τὴν δύναμιν. Τίς γὰρ τῶν νοῦν ἐχόντων[mxciii] εἴποι τι τῶν βρωμάτων κοινὸν ἢ ἀκάθαρτον ἐκτισμέν‹ο›ν[1299] ‹εἶναι› ὑπὸ Θεοῦ;

Οὐ τὸ εἰσερχόμενον εἰς τὸ στόμα.[1300] Εἰπὼν τοίνυν *εἰσερχόμενον εἰς τὸ στόμα* |**123v** καὶ μὴ εἰπὼν τὰ βρώματα, συνεσκιασμένως[mxciv] τοῦτό φησι διὰ τὸ ἀσθενὲς τῶν ἀκροατῶν, ὅπερ εἰκὸς ἦν καὶ περὶ τῶν ἀνίπτων χειρῶν ὑποπτεύειν. Αὐτὸς μὲν γὰρ περὶ βρωμάτων εἶπεν· ἐνοήθη δ᾽ ἂν καὶ περὶ τούτου,

> Διὰ τοῦτο οὐδὲ εἶπε, Τὰ βρώματα, ἀλλ᾽, *Οὐ τὰ εἰσερχόμενα κοινοῖ τὸν ἄνθρωπον·* ὅπερ εἰκὸς ἦν καὶ περὶ τῶν ἀνίπτων χειρῶν ὑποπτεύειν. Αὐτὸς μὲν γὰρ περὶ βρωμάτων ἔλεγεν, ἐνοήθη δ᾽ ἂν καὶ περὶ τούτων.[mxcv]

διὸ σημαίνει ὅτι οὔτε *τὸ ἀνίπτοις χερσὶν* ἐσθίειν *κοινοῖ τὸν ἄνθρωπον,*[1301] τουτέστι, ρυποῖ. Τοίνυν τῶν Φαρισαίων αἰτιωμένων τοὺς μαθητὰς ὡς *ἀνίπτοις χερσὶν* ἐσθίοντας, ὁ Κύριος τὸν περὶ βρωμάτων ποιεῖται λόγον, δεικνὺς ὡς ὅτι οὐ βρῶμα ρυποῖ *τὸν ἄνθρωπον, ἀλλ᾽ οἱ πονηροὶ* λογισμοί. Διὰ γὰρ *τὰ ἐκπορευόμενα*[1302] καὶ τῶν εἰσπορευομένων βρωμάτων συμβολικῶς ἐγένετο ἡ ἀπαγόρευσις. Πταίσμασι γὰρ ἐνόχους ποιεῖ τοὺς ἀνθρώπους, οὐ τὸ μὴ νίπτεσθαι τὰς χεῖρας, ἀλλὰ τὸ ἃ μὴ προσήκει λαλεῖν καὶ τὰ τῷ νόμῳ ὑπεναντία ποιεῖν.

Διετάξατο ὁ νόμος τίνα μὲν ἐσθίειν δεῖ, τίνων δὲ ἀπέχεσθαι.[1303] Οὐχ ὅτι τὰ βρώματα τῆς κατὰ διάνοιαν καθαρότητος ἢ ἀκαθαρσίας ὑπῆρχε ποιητικά, ἀλλ᾽ ἵνα μὴ κατὰ τὰ θηρία πρὸς πάντα ἀχαλίνῳ φερόμεθα στόματι,[mxcvi] μήτε τὴν ἡδονὴν τῆς βρώσεως ποιώμεθα. Διὸ καὶ ἔλεγε, *πᾶν στέαρ καὶ πᾶν αἷμα οὐκ ἔδεσθε,*[1304] τὸ μὲν ὡς λιπαῖνον τὸ σῶμα καὶ πρὸς ἀκολασίαν ἐξάγον, τὸ δὲ ὡς θηριῶδες καὶ ἄγριον. Μὴ θαυμάσωμεν δὲ εἰ τοῦ νόμου ταῦτα ἀπαγορεύοντος ὁ Κύριος δοκεῖ τοὐναντίον εἰσηγεῖσθαι ὡς οὐδεμιᾶς ἀκαθαρσίας οὔσης σωματικῆς. Τὰ μὲν γὰρ τοῦ νόμου πρὸς τὸν ἔξω μᾶλλον ἄνθρωπον ἀφεώρα, τὰ δὲ τοῦ Κυρίου πρὸς τὸν ἔνδον.

> Διετάξατο ὁ νόμος, τίνα μὲν ἐσθίειν δεῖ, τίνων δὲ ἀπέχεσθαι. οὐχ ὅτι τὰ βρώματα τῆς κατὰ διάνοιαν καθαρότητος ἢ ἀκαθαρσίας ὑπῆρχε ποιητικά. ἀλλ᾽ ἵνα μὴ κατὰ τὰ θηρία

1298 Matt. 15:10.
1299 Cod. ἐκτισμένων.
1300 Matt. 15:11.
1301 Matt.15:20.
1302 Matt. 15:18.
1303 Cf. Lev. 11; Deut. 14.
1304 Lev. 3:17.

> πρὸς πάντα ἀχαλίνῳ φερόμεθα στόματι, μήτε τὴν ἡδονὴν τῆς βρώσεως ποιώμεθα. διὸ καὶ ἔλεγε. *πᾶν στέαρ καὶ πᾶν αἷμα οὐκ ἔδεσθε.* τὸ μὲν ὡς λιπαῖνον τὸ σῶμα καὶ πρὸς ἀκολασίαν ἐξάγον, τὸ δὲ ὡς θηριῶδες καὶ ἄγριον. [μὴ θαυμάσωμεν δὲ εἰ τοῦ νόμου ταῦτα ἀπαγορεύοντος ὁ κύριος δοκεῖ τοὐναντίον εἰσηγεῖσθαι ὡς οὐδεμιᾶς ἀκαθαρσίας οὔσης σωματικῆς. τὰ μὲν γὰρ τοῦ νόμου πρὸς τὸν ἔξω μᾶλλον ἄνθρωπον ἀφεώρα, τὰ δὲ τοῦ κυρίου πρὸς τὸν ἔνδον.][mxcvii]

> μὴ θαυμάσωμεν δὲ εἰ τοῦ νόμου σωματικὰς ἀκαθαρσίας εἰδότος καὶ ταύτας ἀπαγορεύοντος, ὁ Κύριος δοκεῖ τοὐναντίον εἰσηγεῖσθαι, ὡς οὐδεμιᾶς ἀκαθαρσίας οὔσης σωματικῆς ἐν ἀνθρώπῳ. τὰ μὲν γὰρ τοῦ νόμου πρὸς τὸν ἔξω μᾶλλον ἄνθρωπον ἀφεώρα. τὰ δὲ τοῦ Κυρίου πρὸς τὸν ἔνδον.[mxcviii]

| **124r** *Τότε προσελθόντες οἱ μαθηταί.*[1305] *Σκληρὸς ὁ λόγος*[1306] ἐδόκει τὸ παρὰ συνήθειαν ἐσθίειν τὰ ἀπὸ τοῦ νόμου λεγόμενα κοινοῦν *τὸν ἄνθρωπον.*

> *Σκληρὸς ὁ λόγος* ἐδόκει τὸ παρὰ συνήθειαν ἐσθίειν τὰ ἀπὸ τοῦ νόμου λεγόμενα κοινοῦν *τὸν ἄνθρωπον.*[mxcix]

Οἶδας ὅτι οἱ Φαρισαῖοι ἀκούσαντες.[1307] Οἱ μὲν μαθηταὶ διὰ αὐτοὺς ‹τοὺς› Φαρισαίους λέγουσι, πλὴν καὶ αὐτοὶ ἐθορυβήθησαν περὶ τοῦ λόγου. Διὸ καὶ ὁ Πέτρος θέλων τοῦτο ἀκριβῶς γνῶναι, εἶπε· *φράσον ἡμῖν τὴν παραβολήν.*[1308] Καὶ ἐπετίμησεν αὐτοῖς καὶ ἀκούσας ὅτι *ἐσκανδαλίσθησαν*[1309] κατεφρόνησεν αὐτῶν. Ἐσκανδαλίσθησαν δὲ ὡς παράνομον αὐτοῦ εἰρηκότος μὴ νοήσαντες τὸ ἀληθές.
Τὶ οὖν ὁ Σωτὴρ *πᾶσαν φυτείαν* τὴν μὴ *ἐκ τοῦ πατρὸς* οὖσαν *ἐκριζωθήσεσθαι* φησι;[1310] Τὰς τῶν πρεσβυτέρων παραδόσεις λέγων καὶ οὐ τὰ τοῦ νόμου ἐντάλματα ὡς Μανιχαῖοί φασι.

> *Φυτεία* ἐστὶν εἰ μὴ ἐκ θεοῦ πᾶν τὸ ἔξω θεοῦ, ὅπερ καὶ *ἐκριζωθήσεται.* ὁ ταύτῃ ποιούμενος *τυφλὸς* ἐστιν.[mc]

> [Μανιχαῖοι δὲ βουλόμενοι δεικνῦναι τὸν νόμον οὐκ εἶναι τοῦ Πατρὸς τοῦ Χριστοῦ, ταύτῃ κέχρηνται τῇ μαρτυρίᾳ. πλεῖστον ὅσον τῆς ἀληθείας ἀποσφαλέντος. οὐ γὰρ περὶ τῆς κατὰ νόμον λέγει διαγωγῆς, ἀλλὰ τῆς τῶν Φαρισαίων αἱρέσεως, οἳ ταῖς οἰκείαις ἐπινοίαις, πλεῖστα ἐναντία τοὺς πειθομένους αὐτοῖς ἐξεπαίδευον. καθὼς καὶ αὐτὸς ὁ Κύριος ἀνωτέρω φαίνεται σαφῶς ἐλέγχων αὐτούς.][mci]

> (Κυρίλλου Ἀλεξανδρείας. Ὠριγένους.) Φυτεία ἐστὶν εἰ [sic] μὴ ἐκ Θεοῦ, πᾶν τὸ ἔξω Θεοῦ. ὅπερ καὶ ἐκριζωθήσεται. ὁ ταύτῃ ποιούμενος τυφλὸς ἦν.[mcii]

1305 Matt. 15:12.
1306 John, 6:60.
1307 Matt. 15:12.
1308 Matt. 15:15.
1309 Matt. 15:12.
1310 Matt. 15:13.

(Θεοδώρου Μομψουεστίας.) Μανιχαῖοι δὲ βουλόμενοι δεικνῦναι τὸν νόμον οὐκ εἶναι τοῦ Πατρὸς τοῦ Χριστοῦ, ταύτῃ κέχρηνται τῇ μαρτυρίᾳ. πλεῖστον ὅσον τῆς ἀληθείας ἀποσφαλέντος. οὐ γὰρ περὶ τῆς κατὰ νόμον λέγει διαγωγῆς, ἀλλὰ τῆς τῶν Φαρισαίων αἱρέσεως, οἳ ταῖς οἰκείαις ἐπινοίαις, πλεῖστα ἐναντία τοὺς πειθομένους αὐτοῖς ἐξεπαίδευον. καθὼς καὶ αὐτὸς ὁ Κύριος ἀνωτέρω φαίνεται σαφῶς ἐλέγχων αὐτούς.[mciii]

Μετὰ ταῦτα ἄξιον ἰδεῖν λέξιν συκοφαντουμένην ὑπὸ τῶν φασκόντων οὐ τὸν αὐτὸν εἶναι νόμου καὶ εὐαγγελίου Ἰησοῦ Χριστοῦ θεόν. οἵτινές φασιν ὅτι οὐκ ἔστιν ὁ Ἰησοῦ Χριστοῦ οὐράνιος πατὴρ γεωργὸς τῶν κατὰ τὸν Μωσέως νόμον οἰομένων θεὸν εὐσεβεῖν. Αὐτὸς εἶπεν ὁ Ἰησοῦς τοὺς Φαρισαίους, οἳ ἦσαν λατρεύοντες τῷ κτίσαντι τὸν κόσμον καὶ τὸν νόμον θεῷ, εἶναι φυτείαν ἣν *οὐκ ἐφύτευσεν ὁ οὐράνιος* αὐτοῦ πατήρ, καὶ διὰ τοῦτο αὐτὴν ἐκριζοῦσθαι. Εἴποιεν δ' ἂν καὶ ταῦτα ὅτι οὐκ ἄν, εἴπερ πατὴρ ἦν τοῦ Ἰησοῦ ὁ *εἰσαγαγὼν* καὶ φυτεύσας τὸν ἀπὸ Αἰγύπτου ἐξελθόντα λαὸν *εἰς ὄρος κληρονομίας* ἑαυτοῦ, *εἰς ἕτοιμον κατοικητήριον* ἑαυτοῦ, εἶπεν ἂν ὁ Ἰησοῦς ἐπὶ τοῖς Φαρισαίοις ὅτι *πᾶσα φυτεία ἣν οὐκ ἐφύτευσεν ὁ πατήρ μου ὁ οὐράνιος ἐκριζωθήσεται*. Πρὸς ταῦτα δὲ φήσομεν ὅτι ὅσοι διὰ τὴν μοχθηρὰν περὶ τῶν κατὰ τὸν νόμον ἐκδοχὴν οὐκ ἦσαν *φυτεία τοῦ* ἐν οὐρανοῖς *πατρός*, οὗτοι τετύφλωντο *τὰ νοήματα*, ὡς *μὴ πιστεύοντες τῇ ἀληθείᾳ ἀλλὰ εὐδοκοῦντες τῇ ἀδικίᾳ* ὑπὸ τοῦ θεοποιηθέντος ἀπὸ τῶν υἱῶν τοῦ αἰῶνος τούτου καὶ διὰ τοῦτο λεγομένου παρὰ τῷ Παύλῳ θεοῦ *τοῦ αἰῶνος τούτου*.[mciv]

43

(ΩΡΙΓΕΝΟΥΣ) Καὶ τί φήσομεν[mcv] πρὸς τὸ *ἐγὼ ἐφύτευσα, Ἀπολλὼς ἐπότισεν;*[1311] Ὅρα δὲ εἰ λύεται τῷ *ὁ δὲ Θεὸς ηὔξησε*[1312] καὶ τῷ *Θεῷ ἐσμεν συνεργοί*.[1313] Συνεργοὶ γὰρ Θεοῦ τοῦ συμφυτεύοντος καὶ συνεργοῦντος.

Καὶ τί φήσομεν πρὸς τὸ *ἐγὼ ἐφύτευσα, Ἀπολλὼς ἐπότισεν*; ὅρα δὲ εἰ λύεται τῷ *ὁ δὲ Θεὸς ηὔξανε* καὶ τῷ *θεοῦ ἐσμεν συνεργοί*. συνεργοὶ γὰρ θεοῦ τοῦ συμφυτεύοντος καὶ συνεργοῦντος.[mcvi]

Every plant, he says, *which my heavenly Father didn't plant will be uprooted*.[1314] Consequently, that plant will be uprooted about which the apostle says, *I planted, Apollos watered*. However, the problem is resolved by virtue of what follows: *But God gave the growth*.[1315] And he himself says, *You are God's farming, God's building*.[1316] And in another place, *We are God's fellow-workers*. But if we are fellow-workers, then while Paul plants and Apollos waters, God is planting and watering along his workers.[mcvii]

1311 1 Cor. 3:6.
1312 1 Cor. 3:6: ὁ θεὸς ηὔξανεν.
1313 1 Cor. 3:6: θεοῦ γάρ ἐσμεν συνεργοί. Cf. 3 John, 8.
1314 Matt. 15:13.
1315 1 Cor. 3:7.
1316 1 Cor. 3:9.

Ἄφετε αὐτούς.[1317] Δεικνὺς ὅτι οὐ ποιεῖται τῶν Φαρισαίων λόγον τινά, εἶπεν *ἄφετε αὐτούς*. Ἤτοι ὡς ἀπεγνωσμένους ὄντας καὶ ὡς μὲν πεπορωμένους τὴν καρδίαν *τυφλοὺς* αὐτοὺς εἶπεν. Ὡς δὲ καὶ ἄλλους ἐπιχειροῦντας ἀγνο‹οῦν›τας[1318] τῆς ἀληθείας διδάσκειν, *ὁδηγοὺς* εἶπε *τυφλῶν*, δι᾽ οὗ συμβαίνει τούς τε διδάσκοντας καὶ τοὺς διδασκομένους ἐν ταὐτῷ κινδυνεύειν. Τοῦτο δὲ εἶπεν ἀποσχίσαι ἐξ αὐτῶν βουλόμενος τοὺς πειθομένους αὐτοῖς. Ὡς μὲν γὰρ μὴ ἀκολουθοῦντες τῇ διὰ Μωσέως ἀρχαίᾳ ἐντολῇ, *τυφλοί* εἰσιν. Ὡσαύτως καὶ | **124v** οἱ πειθόμενοι αὐτοῖς, ὡς ἀμαθεῖς τοὺς ἀμαθεστέρους ἐμβάλλοντας εἰς ἃ μὴ δεῖ. Διὰ γὰρ τοῦ *βοθύνου* διδάσκει ὅτι καὶ κίνδυνος ἦν τὸ πείθεσθαι αὐτοῖς.

ἀποκριθεὶς δὲ ὁ Πέτρος, εἶπεν αὐτῷ· φράσον ἡμῖν τὴν παραβολήν.[1319] Τί οὖν οἱ μαθηταί ἐπειδὴ ᾔδεισαν ὅτι ὁ νόμος ἐκέλευσε μὴ πάντα ἀδεῶς ἐσθίειν εἰκότως ἐρωτῶσι διὰ τοῦ Πέτρου; Παραβολὴν δὲ τὸν ἀσαφῆ λόγον ὀνομάζουσιν.[mcviii] Ἀσαφὲς δὲ ἦν αὐτοῖς πῶς οὐ μολύνει *τὸν ἄνθρωπον* βρῶμα ἀκάθαρτον *εἰς τὸ στόμα* χωροῦν.
Ἀσυνέτους[1320] δὲ αὐτοὺς ὁ Κύριος ἔφη περὶ τὸ σῶμα στρεφομένους ὥσπερ οἱ Φαρισαῖοι καὶ μὴ διαβαίνοντας ἐπὶ τὸν *ἔσω ἄνθρωπον.*[1321][mcix]

> Καὶ αὐτοὺς ἀσυνέτους ὁ κύριός φησι περὶ τὸ σῶμα στρεφομένους, ὥσπερ οἱ Φαρισαῖοι, καὶ μηδέπω διαβαίνοντας ἐπὶ τὸν ἔσω ἄνθρωπον. βρώματα οὖν, φησίν, σώματος ἔχει πλήρωσιν, καρδίας δὲ οὐκ ἐφάπτεται. τὸ δὲ καρδίας μὴ ἐφαπτόμενον οὐ δύναται κοινῶσαι τὸν ἄνθρωπον τὸν ἀληθινὸν ἢ μὴ καθαρὸν ἀπεργάσασθαι.[mcx]

Εἰ δέ τις εἴποι· εἰ οὖν τὰ πορευόμενα *εἰς τὸ στόμα* μὴ *κοινοῖ τὸν ἄνθρωπον*,[1322] ἐχρῆν καὶ τοὺς μάρτυρας τῶν ἑλληνικῶν θυσιῶν ἀπογεύεσθαι, λέληθεν ἑαυτὸν[mcxi] ὁ τοιο‹ύ›το‹υ›[1323] βρώματος μνησθείς, οὐ μονοειδοῦς ἀλλὰ βλασφημίᾳ συμπεπλεγμένου καὶ κοινοῦντος. Οὐχ ὅτι βρῶμα ὑπῆρχεν, ἀλλ᾽ ὅτι βλάσφημον καὶ ἀνίερον. Τὴν δὲ βλασφημίαν *ἐκ τῆς καρδίας*[1324] ἐξέρχεσθαι πρόδηλον.

Ἀκμὴν καὶ ὑμεῖς ἀσύνετοι ἐστέ,[1325] ὡς ἔτι οὖσιν ἀτελέσει καὶ αὐτοῖς καὶ σκανδαλισθεῖσιν ὡς παρανόμου ὄντος τοῦ λόγου. Ἢ ὡς τὸ σαφὲς ἐρωτῶσιν ἐπιτιμᾷ, ἵνα τὴν περὶ βρωμάτων πρόληψιν ἀνέλῃ· διὸ καὶ ἀπὸ τῆς κοινῆς φύσεως τὸν ἑαυτοῦ συνίστησι λόγον. Φησὶ γὰρ ὅτι *οὔπω νοεῖτε ὅτι πᾶν τὸ εἰς τὸ στόμα εἰσιὸν εἰς τὴν κοιλίαν χωρεῖ καὶ εἰς ἀφεδρῶνα ἐκβάλλεται,*[1326] καὶ τὰ ἑξῆς. Καὶ γὰρ αἱ τροφαὶ οὐ μένουσιν

1317 Matt. 15:14.
1318 Cod. ἀγνῶντας.
1319 Matt. 15:15.
1320 Matt. 15:16; Mark, 7:18.
1321 Rom. 7:22; Eph. 3:16.
1322 Matt. 15:11; cf. 15:18&20; Mark, 7:23.
1323 Cod. τοιοῦτος.
1324 Matt. 15:18.
1325 Matt. 15:16.
1326 Matt. 15:17.

ἔσω, φησί, | **125r** ἀλλ' *εἰς τὴν κοιλίαν*, κἀκεῖθεν ἐκβάλλονται ἐκκρινόμεναι. Τὰ δὲ *τῆς καρδίας* ἔνδον μένει, καὶ οὐ μόνον μένοντα ἀλλὰ καὶ ἐξελθόντα *κοινοῖ*. Οἱ γὰρ λογισμοὶ ἔσωθεν γεννώμενοι ἐπὶ ἀσεβεῖς πράξεις παρορμῶσι τὸν ἄνθρωπον, τὸ δὲ ἐσθίειν τὰ ἀπηγορευμένα τῷ νόμῳ *οὐ κοινοῖ*. Τοῦτο δὲ οὐκ εἶπεν, ἀλλὰ τὸ *ἀνίπτοις χερσὶ φαγεῖν οὐ κοινοῖ τὸν ἄνθρωπον*.[1327] Τοῦτο δὲ ὡς πρὸς τὴν φαρισαϊκὴν κατηγορίαν ἐνέφηνεν. Οὐδὲ γὰρ ἠνείχοντο οὕτως αὐτὸ σαφῶς ἀκοῦσαι, *ὁ λελουμένος, οὐκ ἔχει χρείαν* χεῖρας *νίψασθαι*,[1328] ὡς ἐδιδάχθη ὁ εἰπὼν *μὴ τοὺς πόδας μου μόνον*.[1329] Διὸ οὐκ ἐνίπτοντο τὰς χεῖρας οἱ μαθηταὶ ἐσθίοντες ἄρτον.

44

(ΩΡΙΓΕΝΟΥΣ) Οἱ δὲ *Φαρισαῖοι* μὴ εἰδότες τὴν δύναμιν τοῦ λόγου *ἐσκανδαλίσθησαν*.[1330] Σκανδαλίζεται δὲ ὁ *ἐν σκότει* πορευόμενος,[1331] ἤτοι *ὁ τυφλὸς* καὶ μὴ ἔχων ὁδηγόν. Καὶ γὰρ ἀληθῶς καταλείψαντες *τὸ ἀληθινὸν φῶς*[1332] καὶ τὸν ἑτοιμάσαντα καὶ προομαλίσαντα τὴν καλὴν ὁδὸν καὶ τὸν ὁδηγήσαντα αὐτοὺς *ἐν τῇ ἐρήμῳ*[1333] ἐπορεύθησαν *ἐν σκότει*.[1334] Διὸ ὁ Σωτὴρ λέγει· *ἄφετε αὐτούς, τυφλοί εἰσιν*.[1335]

> *Ὁ λελουμένος, οὐκ ἔχει χρείαν* χεῖρας νίψασθαι, ὡς ἐδιδάχθη ὁ εἰπὼν *μὴ τοὺς πόδας μου μόνον*. διὸ οὐκ ἐνίπτοντο τὰς χεῖρας οἱ μαθηταὶ ἐσθίοντες ἄρτον. Οἱ δὲ *Φαρισαῖοι* μὴ εἰδότες τὴν δύναμιν τοῦ λόγου *ἐσκανδαλίσθησαν*. σκανδαλίζεται δὲ ὁ ἐν σκότει πορευόμενος, ἤτοι *ὁ τυφλὸς* καὶ μὴ ἔχων ὁδηγόν. καὶ γὰρ ἀληθῶς καταλείψαντες *τὸ ἀληθινὸν φῶς* καὶ τὸν προετοιμάσαντα καὶ προομαλίσαντα τὴν καλὴν ὁδὸν καὶ τὸν ὁδηγήσαντα αὐτοὺς ἐν τῇ ἐρήμῳ ἐπορεύθησαν ἐν σκότει. διὸ ὁ σωτὴρ λέγει. *ἄφετε αὐτούς, τυφλοί εἰσιν*.[mcxii]

Καὶ ἐξελθὼν ἐκεῖθεν.[1336] Ὅτε εἶδεν ὁ Σωτὴρ ἀπειθοῦντας τοὺς Ἰουδαίους ἐπὶ τῷ λόγῳ τῷ περὶ τῶν βρωμάτων, μετέβη *ἐπὶ τὰ ἔθνη*.[1337] Εἰδὼς οὖν τὸ μέλλον ἔσεσθαι, ἦλθεν ἐπὶ τὴν γῆν τῶν Χαναναίων[mcxiii] ἵνα τὴν τῶν Ἰουδαίων ἀπιστίαν ἐν τούτῳ κατακρίνῃ.

1327 Matt. 15:20.
1328 John, 13:9-10.
1329 John, 13:9.
1330 Matt. 15:12.
1331 Cf. Psalm 81:5; Ecclesiastes, 2:14; 6:4; Job, 29:3; Is. 9:1; 50:10; 42:7; Matt. 4:16 & Luke, 1:79 (Is. 9:1); Rom. 2:19; 1 Thess. 5:4.
1332 John, 1:9; 1 John, 2:8.
1333 Jer. 2:6.
1334 Psalms 81:5; 90:6; Prov. 2:13; 4:18; Ecclesiastes, 2:14; 6:4; Job, 29:3; Is. 9:1; 50:10.
1335 Matt. 15:14.
1336 Matt. 15:21.
1337 Cf. Psalms 46:9; 65:7; Psalms of Solomon, 17:3; Zach. 1:15; 2:12; Jer. 25:14; Ez. 29:15; 36:7. Acts, 10:45.

Καὶ ἰδοὺ γυνὴ Χαναναία.[1338] Ὅρα δὲ ἡ *Χαναναία* εἰς τὴν *ἐξ ἐθνῶν*[1339] ἐκκλησίαν,[mcxiv] ἥτις διὰ τῶν ρημάτων τούτων τὴν τῆς πίστεως ἀκρίβειαν | **125v** ἐπεδείξατο. *Κύριον* μὲν γὰρ αὐτὸν εἶπεν ὡς Θεόν, *υἱὸν δὲ Δαυίδ* διὰ τὸ ἀνθρώπινον σχῆμα τὸν ἐξ αὐτοῦ αἰτοῦσα ἔλεον, *ἐλέησόν με* λέγουσα ὅτι *ἡ θυγάτηρ μου κακῶς δαιμονίζεται.*[1340] Οὐδὲ γὰρ εἰς ὄψιν αὐτοῦ ἀγαγεῖν ἐτόλμησε, διὰ δὲ τὸ Ἰουδαίων ὠμὸν οὐδὲ εἰς Ἱερουσαλὴμ ἦλθεν. Ὁ μέντοι Ἰησοῦς *οὐκ ἀπεκρίθη αὐτῇ λόγον,*[1341] οὐχ ὡς ὑπερόπτης, ἀλλ᾽ ἵνα δημοσιεύσῃ αὐτῆς τὴν πίστιν. Δείκνυσι δὲ καὶ ὡς ἐκ τύπου[mcxv] ὅτι οὐκ εἰσακούει τῆς τῶν ἐθνῶν αἰτήσεως, ἀλλὰ παρασιωπᾷ. Καὶ διὰ τούτου ἐλέγχει τῶν μὲν Ἰουδαίων τὴν ἀπιστίαν μὴ ἀνεχομένων δέξασθαι τὰς παρ᾽ αὐτοῦ διδομένας αὐτοῖς ἑτοίμως θεραπείας, τῶν δὲ ἐθνικῶν τὸ ἐπίμονον μετὰ ἱκεσίας. Εἶτα ἐλεήσαντες αὐτὴν οἱ μαθηταὶ (ἢ καὶ βαρυνόμενοι τῇ ἐκβοήσει) ἔλεγον· *ἀπόλυσον αὐτήν,*[1342] διὰ τῆς λέξεως τὴν αὐτοῦ δύναμιν αἰνιττόμενοι, τὴν καταλύουσαν εὐκόλως ὅσα βούλεται. Τοῦτο γὰρ δηλοῖ τὸ *ἀπόλυσον.* Τί οὖν ὁ Σωτήρ; Κατακρίνει τοὺς Ἰουδαίους πρὸς μόνους αὐτοὺς ἀπεστάλθαι λέγων. *Ἀπολωλότα* δὲ εἰπὼν *πρόβατα*[1343] αἰνίττεται τὴν ἀπώλειαν αὐτῶν γεγενῆσθαι ἐκ τῶν ἱερέων καὶ ὅτι αὐτός ἐστιν ὁ ἀρχιποίμην. Διὰ τούτου δὲ τοῦ λόγου καὶ τὴν τῆς γυναικὸς ἐπὶ πλεῖον δημοσιεύει πίστιν. Εἰ γὰρ καὶ πρὸς πάντας ἦλθεν ὡς ἅπαν μέλλων σῴζειν τὸ ἀνθρώπινον, ἀλλὰ πρωτοτύπως πρὸς Ἰουδαίους κηρῦξαι τὸν λόγον ἐβούλετο.[1344] Οὐδὲν δὲ ἄτοπον καὶ ἀπίστους προστρέχοντας θεραπεῦσαι. | **126r** Καὶ γὰρ καὶ ὁ νόμος ἐδέχετο τοὺς προσηλύτους.[mcxvi]

Ἐκ τῶν ὁρίων ἐκείνων ἐξελθοῦσα.[1345] Πόθεν ἐξῆλθεν ἡ Χαναναῖτις; Ἀπὸ τῆς εἰδωλολατρίας Τύρου καὶ Σιδόνος,[mcxvii] ἀπὸ τοῦ λαοῦ αὐτῆς καὶ ἀπὸ *τοῦ οἴκου τοῦ πατρός*[1346] αὐτῆς. Ποῦ ἐξῆλθεν; Εἰς *ὀσμὴν μύρων*[1347] τοῦ Σωτῆρος. Τύπον γὰρ ἐπέχει τῆς *ἐξ ἐθνῶν*[1348] ἐκκλησίας. Ἀλλὰ καὶ ὁ Σωτὴρ ἐξῆλθεν *ἐκ τῆς συγγενείας* τοῦ Ἰσραὴλ καὶ τοῦ *οἴκου τοῦ πατρός* αὐτοῦ,[1349] τῆς Ἱερουσαλήμ. Καὶ ὑποδέχεται αὐτὸν ἡ Χαναναῖτις ἡ καὶ τὸν Ἠλίαν δεξαμένη χήρα.[1350] Τί δὲ ἐβόα κράζουσα *Κύριε υἱὲ Δαυίδ*; Πόθεν ᾔδει οὕτω καλεῖν μήτε νόμον μήτε προφήτας μελετήσασα; *Κύριον* μὲν κατὰ τὴν θεότητα· *υἱὸν* δὲ *Δαυὶδ* κατὰ τὴν σάρκα. Νόει μοι τὸν τῆς χήρας υἱὸν νεκρὸν ὄντα[1351] (τουτέστι

1338 Matt. 15:22.
1339 Cf. Rom. 9:24; Acts, 15:23.
1340 Matt. 15:22.
1341 Matt. 15:23.
1342 Matt. 15:23.
1343 Matt. 15:24; cf. 10:6; Jer. 27:6.
1344 Cf. Matt. 10:6; 15:24.
1345 Matt. 15:22.
1346 Cf. Gen. 12:1; 20:13; 24:7&40; Psalm 44:11.
1347 Cf. Song of Songs, 1:3-4.
1348 Cf. Rom. 9:24; Acts, 15:23.
1349 Cf. Gen. 12:1.
1350 Luke, 4:26.
1351 Luke, 7:12.

τὸ νενεκρωμένον σῶμα), τὴν δὲ ψυχὴν καθαρθεῖσαν τοῦ δαιμονίου. Ἀποκατέστησε τὰ ἀμφότερα σῶα.

> Πόθεν ἐξῆλθεν ἡ Χαναντῖτις; ἀπὸ τῆς εἰδωλολατρίας *Τύρου καὶ Σιδῶνος*, ἀπὸ τοῦ λαοῦ αὐτῆς καὶ ἀπὸ *τοῦ οἴκου τοῦ πατρὸς* αὐτῆς. ποῖ ἐξῆλθεν; εἰς ὀσμὴν μύρου τοῦ σωτῆρος. τύπον γὰρ ἐπέχει τῆς ἐξ ἐθνῶν ἐκκλησίας. ἀλλὰ καὶ ὁ σωτὴρ ἐξῆλθεν *ἐκ τῆς συγγενείας* τοῦ Ἰσραὴλ *καὶ τοῦ οἴκου τοῦ πατρὸς* αὐτοῦ, τῆς Ἰερουσαλήμ. καὶ ὑποδέχεται αὐτὸν ἡ Χαναντῖτις, ἡ καὶ τὸν Ἡλίαν δεξαμένη χήρα. τί δὲ ἐβόα κράζουσα. κύριε, υἱὲ Δαβίδ; πόθεν ᾔδει οὕτως καλεῖν, μήτε νόμον μήτε προφήτας μελετήσασα; κύριον μὲν κατὰ τὴν θεότητα, υἱὸν δὲ Δαβὶδ κατὰ τὴν σάρκα. νόει μοι τὸν τῆς χήρας υἱὸν νεκρὸν ὄντα, τοῦτ' ἔστιν τὸ νενεκρωμένον σῶμα, τὴν δὲ ψυχὴν καθαρισθεῖσαν τοῦ δαιμονίου. ἀπεκατέστησε τὰ ἀμφότερα σῶα.[mcxviii]

Ὁ δὲ οὐκ ἀπεκρίθη αὐτῇ λόγον.[1352] Οὐκ ἀποκρίνεται ὁ Ἰησοῦς τῇ Χαναναίᾳ, τὸν νόμον πληρῶν καὶ τὴν περὶ τὴν ἀλήθειαν ῥῶσιν τῆς γυναικὸς δεικνύς, ᾗ θεωρεῖται εἰς τὴν *ἐξ ἐθνῶν*[1353] ἐκκλησίαν. Ἄρτος ἐστὶν ἡ διδασκαλία· τέκνα οἱ ἐξ Ἰσραήλ· κύνες τὰ ἔθνη διὰ τὰ εἰδωλόθυτα καὶ τὸ ἀκάθαρτον τοῦ βίου. Ἐξ ἧς προτάσεως πλέκει τὴν συνηγορίαν ἑαυτῆς ἡ γυνὴ λέγουσα· κύων μέν εἰμι, πλὴν οὐκ ἀλλοτρία, ἀλλὰ σή· καὶ δεῖ με, εἰ καὶ μὴ τῶν ἄρτων, ἀλλ' οὖν *τῶν ψιχίων* μετασχεῖν. Τὸ δὲ οἰηθῆναι ὅτι καὶ τὸ βραχύτατον αὐτοῦ τῆς δυνάμεως (τοῦτο γὰρ *ψιχίων* ὀνομάζει)[mcxix] ἱκανὸν τῆς θυγατρὸς αὐτῇ παρασχεῖν τὴν ἴασιν, πίστε‹ως›[1354] | **126v** ὑπερεχούσης.[mcxx] Δείκνυται γὰρ *ἡ Χαναναία* πολλῆς γνώσεως μεστὴ καὶ ταπεινοφροσύνης καὶ πίστεως.

> Οὐκ ἀποκρίνεται ὁ Ἰησοῦς τῇ Χαναναίᾳ τὸν νόμον πληρῶν καὶ τὴν περὶ τὴν ἀλήθειαν ῥῶσιν τῆς γυναικὸς δεικνύς, ᾗ θεωρεῖται εἰς τὴν ἐξ ἐθνῶν ἐκκλησίαν. ἄρτος ἐστὶν ἡ διδασκαλία, τέκνα οἱ ἐξ Ἰσραήλ. κύνες, τὰ ἔθνη διὰ τὰ εἰδωλόθυτα καὶ τὸ ἀκάθαρτον τοῦ βίου. ἐξ ἧς προτάσεως πλέκει τὴν συνηγορίαν ἑαυτῆς ἡ γυνὴ λέγουσα. κύων μέν εἰμι, ἀλλ' οὐκ ἀλλοτρία, ἀλλὰ σή, καὶ δεῖ με, εἰ καὶ μὴ τοῦ ἄρτου ἀλλ' οὖν *τῶν ψιχίων* μεταλαβεῖν. τὸ δὲ οἰηθῆναι ὅτι καὶ τὸ βραχύτατον αὐτοῦ τῆς δυνάμεως (τοῦτο γὰρ *ψιχίον* ὀνομάζει) ἱκανὸν τῇ θυγατρὶ αὐτῆς παρασχεῖν τὴν ἴασιν, πίστεως ὑπερεχούσης. δείκνυται γὰρ *ἡ Χαναναία* πολλῆς γνώσεως μεστὴ καὶ ταπεινοφροσύνης καὶ πίστεως.[mcxxi]

Ἡ δὲ ἐλθοῦσα, προσεκύνησεν αὐτῷ.[1355] Ὅτε εἶδε τοὺς συνηγόρους ἑαυτῆς ἀποτυχόντας ἡ γυνή, τότε πάλιν δι' ἑαυτῆς αἰτεῖ καὶ οὐκ ἀπέστη,[1356] ἀλλ' ὡς Κυρίῳ λέγει· *βοήθει μοι*, οὐ μὴν δεήθητι ὑπὲρ ἐμοῦ. Εἶτα πάλιν φησὶ ὁ Σωτήρ· *οὐκ ἔστι καλὸν λαβεῖν τὸν ἄρτον τῶν τέκνων καὶ βαλεῖν τοῖς κυναρίοις.*[1357] Καὶ κύνα μὲν καλεῖ τὴν ἐθνικὴν διὰ τὸ τῆς ζωῆς ἀκάθαρτον καὶ τὴν περὶ εἰδωλολατρίας λιχνείαν·

1352 Matt. 15:23.
1353 Cf. Rom. 9:24; Acts, 15:23.
1354 Cod. πίστε.
1355 Matt. 15:25.
1356 Cod. ἀπτέστη.
1357 Matt. 15:26.

Pagans are called dogs because of their idolatry.mcxxii

τέκνα δὲ τοὺς Ἰουδαίους διὰ τὸ δοκεῖν ἀνακεῖσθαι Θεῷ·mcxxiii *ἄρτον* δὲ καλεῖ οὐ μόνον τὴν διὰ λόγων διδασκαλίαν, ἀλλὰ καὶ τὴν διὰ σημείων τρέφουσαν τοὺς πιστούς. Πρὸς κατάκριμα δὲ τῶν Ἰουδαίων προῆλθεν ὁ λόγος, ἐπείπερ δοθείσης αὐτοῖς τῆς ἐν Κυρίῳ ζωῆς ὡς ἄρτου οὐ προσήκαντο. Εἶτα, οὔτε ὑβριζομένη ἀγανακτεῖ ἡ γυνή. Τί οὖν ὁ Σωτήρ; Ἐφανέρωσε τὸ ἐξ ἀρχῆς οἰκονομούμενον τῆς ἀποκρίσεως. Διὰ τοῦτο γὰρ ἀνεβάλλετο, ἵνα τοῦτο ἀναβοήσῃ τὸ ῥῆμα ἡ γυνὴ καὶ δείξῃ αὐτὴν μυρίων οὖσαν στεφάνων ἀξίαν. Οὐ γὰρ ὡς μὴ βουλόμενος δοῦναι αὐτῇ τὴν χάριν ὑπερετίθετο, ἀλλ᾽ ἐκκαλύψαι αὐτῆς τὴν πίστιν προμηθούμενος. Τιμᾷ δὲ τοῖς ἐπαίνοις αὐτήν, τύπον ἔχουσαν τῆς *ἐξ ἐθνῶν* ἐκκλησίας. Οὐκ εἶπε δὲ *ἰαθήτω ἡ παῖς*[1358] σου, ἀλλὰ *γενηθήτω σοι ὡς θέλεις*,[1359] ἵνα δείξῃ ὅτι ἡ δύναμις τῆς πίστεως αὐτῆς ἐξεβιάσατο τὴν θεραπείαν. | **127r** Εἰ δὲ καὶ πλειόνων ἀξία ἦν, ἀλλ᾽ ὃ ἤθελε τοῦτο ἐδόθη αὐτῇ.

> Ὅτε εἶδεν τοὺς συνηγόρους ἑαυτῆς ἀποτυχόντας ἡ γυνή, τότε πάλιν δι᾽ ἑαυτῆς αἰτεῖ καὶ οὐκ ἀπέστη, ἀλλ᾽ ὡς κυρίῳ λέγει *βοήθει μοι*, οὐ μὴν δεήθητι ὑπὲρ ἐμοῦ. εἶτα πάλιν φησὶν ὁ σωτήρ. *οὐκ ἔστι καλὸν λαβεῖν τὸν ἄρτον τῶν τέκνων καὶ βαλεῖν τοῖς κυναρίοις*. καὶ κύνα μὲν καλεῖ τὴν ἐθνικὴν διὰ τὸ τῆς ζωῆς ἀκάθαρτον καὶ τὴν περὶ εἰδωλολατρίας λιχνείαν, τέκνα δὲ τοὺς Ἰουδαίους διὰ τὸ δοκεῖν ἀνακεῖσθαι θεῷ, *ἄρτον* δὲ καλεῖ οὐ μόνον τὴν διὰ λόγων διδασκαλίαν, ἀλλὰ καὶ τὴν διὰ σημείων τρέφουσαν τοὺς πιστούς. πρὸς κατάκριμα δὲ τῶν Ἰουδαίων προῆλθεν ὁ λόγος, ἐπείπερ δοθείσης αὐτοῖς τῆς ἐν κυρίῳ ζωῆς ὡς ἄρτου οὐ προσήκαντο. εἶτα οὐδὲ ὑβριζομένη ἀγανακτεῖ ἡ γυνή. τί οὖν ὁ σωτήρ; ἐφανέρωσε τὸ ἐξ ἀρχῆς οἰκονομούμενον τῆς ἀποκρίσεως. διὰ τοῦτο γὰρ ἀνεβάλλετο, ἵνα τοῦτο ἀναβοήσῃ τὸ ῥῆμα ἡ γυνὴ καὶ ἐπιδείξῃ αὐτὴν μυρίων οὖσαν στεφάνων ἀξίαν. οὐ γὰρ ὡς μὴ βουλόμενος δοῦναι αὐτῇ τὴν χάριν ὑπερετίθετο, ἀλλ᾽ ἐκκαλύψαι αὐτῆς τὴν πίστιν προμηθούμενος. τιμᾷ δὲ τοῖς ἐπαίνοις αὐτὴν τύπον ἐπέχουσαν τῆς ἐξ ἐθνῶν ἐκ κλησίας. οὐκ εἶπε δέ. ἰαθήτω ἡ παῖς σου, ἀλλά. *γενηθήτω σοι ὡς θέλεις*, ἵνα δείξῃ, ὅτι ἡ δύναμις τῆς πίστεως αὐτῆς ἐξεβιάσατο τὴν θεραπείαν. εἰ δὲ καὶ πλειόνων ἀξία ἦν, ἀλλ᾽ ὃ ἤθελε τοῦτο ἐδόθη αὐτῇ.mcxxiv

Τὸ μὲν γὰρ ἑλέσθαι καὶ ἐν κυνὸς τάξει καταλογισθῆναι τῷ Κυρίῳ εὐλαβείας ἦν· τὸ δὲ οἰηθῆναι ὅτι καὶ τὸ βραχύτατον αὐτοῦ τῆς δυνάμεως (τοῦτο γὰρ *ψιχίων* ὀνομάζει) ἱκανὸν τῆς θυγατρὸς αὐτῇ παρασχεῖν τὴν ἴασιν, πίστεως ὑπερβαλλούσης.mcxxv Τὸ δὲ ἀπὸ τῆς λοιδορίας ἁρπάσαι τὴν οἰκείωσιν καὶ ποιήσασθαι ἀπόκρισιν οὕτω θαυμαστὴν συνέσεως εἶχε γνώρισμα. Τί γάρ φησι; Ὅτι χάριν ἔχω καὶ ἐν κυνὸς εἶναί σοι τάξει. Τέως γὰρ οὐκ ἀλλοτρία ἀλλά τις οἰκεία *ἀπὸ τῆς τραπέζης* ἐσθίουσα τῆς δεσποτικῆς, εἰ καὶ μὴ ἄρτου ἀλλὰ τῶν ψιχίων. Τοσοῦτός δέ σου τῆς τραπέζης ὁ πλοῦτος, ὥστε ἀρκεῖν μοι καὶ *ψιχίων* πρὸς ἀπόλαυσιν τῶν σπουδαζομένων.

1358 Cf. Luke, 7:7.
1359 Matt. 15:28.

> τὸ μὲν γὰρ ἑλέσθαι καὶ ἐν κυνὸς τάξει καταλογισθῆναι τῷ Κυρίῳ, εὐλαβείας ἦν. τὸ δὲ οἰηθῆναι ὅτι καὶ τὸ βραχύτατον αὐτοῦ τῆς δυνάμεως (τοῦτο γὰρ ψίχια ὀνομάζει) ἱκανὸν τῆς θυγατρὸς αὐτῆς παρασχεῖν τὴν ἴασιν, πίστεως ὑπερβαλλούσης. τὸ δὲ ἀπὸ τῆς λοιδορίας ἁρπάσαι τὴν οἰκείωσιν καὶ ποιήσασθαι ἀπόκρισιν οὕτω θαυμαστήν, συνέσεως εἶχε γνώρισμα. τί γάρ φησιν; ὅτι χάριν ἔχω καὶ ἐν κυνὸς εἶναί σοι τάξει. τέως γὰρ οὐκ ἀλλοτρία, ἀλλὰ τῆς οἰκείας ἀπὸ τῆς τραπέζης ἐσθίουσα τῆς δεσποτικῆς, εἰ καὶ μὴ τοῦ ἄρτου, ἀλλὰ τῶν γοῦν ψιχίων. τοσοῦτος δεσπότου τῆς τραπέζης ὁ πλοῦτος, ὥστε ἀρκεῖν μοι καὶ ψίχιον πρὸς ἀπόλαυσιν τῶν σπουδαζομένων.[mcxxvi]

> τὸ μὲν γὰρ ἑλέσθαι καὶ ἐν κυνὸς τάξει καταλογισθῆναι τῷ κυρίῳ εὐλαβείας ἦν. τὸ δὲ οἰηθῆναι, ὅτι καὶ τὸ βραχύτατον αὐτοῦ τῆς δυνάμεως τοῦτο γὰρ ψιχίον ὀνομάζει ἱκανὸν τῆς θυγατρὸς αὐτῆς παρασχεῖν τὴν ἴασιν πίστεως ὑπερβαλλούσης. τὸ δὲ ἀπὸ τῆς λοιδορίας ἁρπάσαι τὴν οἰκείωσιν κα ποιήσασθαι ἀπόκρισιν συνέσεως εἶχε γνώρισμα. τί γάρ φησιν; ὅτι χάριν ἔχω καὶ ἐν κυνὸς εἶναί σοι τάξει. τέως γὰρ οὐκ ἀλλοτρία, ἀλλά τις οἰκεία ἀπὸ τραπέζης ἐσθίουσα τῆς δεσποτικῆς, εἰ καὶ μὴ τοῦ ἄρτου, ἀλλὰ τῶν γοῦν ψιχίων. τοσοῦτος δέ σου τῆς τραπέζης ὁ πλοῦτος, ὥστε ἀρκεῖν μοι καὶ ψιχία πρὸς ἀπόλαυσιν τῶν σπουδαζομένων.[mcxxvii]

Εἰπὼν δὲ *γενηθήτω σοι ὡς θέλεις*, βασιλικῶς ἐφθέγξατο, οὐ δι᾽ εὐχῆς τὸ πρᾶγμα ἀνύσας, ἀλλὰ διὰ τῆς θεοπρεποῦς αὐτοῦ ἐξουσίας.

> (Κυρίλλου Ἀλεξανδρείας.) Εἰπὼν δὲ *γενηθήτω*, βασιλικῶς ἐφθέγξατο. οὐ δι᾽ εὐχῆς τὸ ὅραμα ἀνύσας, ἀλλὰ διὰ τῆς θεοπρεποῦς ἐξουσίας.[mcxxviii]

Καὶ ἰάθη ἡ θυγάτηρ αὐτῆς.[1360] Ῥηθέντος τοῦ λόγου, τὸ ἔργον οὐ χρονίζει. Θεὸς γὰρ ὁ λέγων καὶ τὸ ῥῆμα ἐνεργὸν καὶ ἡ δύναμις πανταχοῦ.

> Ῥηθέντος τοῦ λόγου, τὸ ἔργον οὐ χρονίζει. θεὸς γὰρ ὁ λέγων καὶ τὸ ῥῆμα ἐνεργὸν καὶ ἡ δύναμις πανταχοῦ.[mcxxix]

> ῥηθέντος τοῦ λόγου, τὸ ἔργον οὐ χρονίζει. Θεὸς γὰρ ὁ λέγων, καὶ τὸ ῥῆμα ἐνεργοῦν, καὶ ἡ δύναμις πανταχοῦ.[mcxxx]

Καὶ μεταβὰς ἐκεῖθεν ὁ Ἰησοῦς ἦλθε παρὰ τὴν θάλασσαν τῆς Γαλιλαίας.[1361] Παρῃτεῖτο τοὺς τῶν Ἰουδαίων τόπους ὁ Σωτὴρ διὰ τὴν πολλὴν αὐτῶν ἀπιστίαν, *εἰς τὸ ὄρος* δὲ ἄνεισι συνεχῶς τῆς θείας αὐτοῦ φύσεως τὸ ὑπερφερὲς δι᾽ αἰνιγμάτων δεικνύς. Τοσαύτη δὲ ἦν ἡ πίστις τῶν προσιόντων, ὡς καὶ *χωλοὺς* καὶ *τυφλοὺς* ἀναβαίνειν εἰς τὸ ὄρος καὶ μόνον προσπίπτοντας θεραπεύεσθαι.[1362] Ὡς γὰρ Θεὸς ὢν καὶ τοῦ παντὸς ἀνθρώπου δημιουργὸς καὶ τὸ λεῖπον ἀνεπλήρου τοῦ σώματος. Διὸ καὶ ἐδό | **127v** ξαζον *τὸν*

1360 Matt. 15:28.
1361 Matt. 15:29.
1362 Matt. 15:30.

Θεόν[1363] ἐπὶ τούτοις. Τὸ γὰρ πλῆθος τῶν θεραπευομένων καὶ τὸ εὔκολον τῆς θεραπείας ἐποίει αὐτοὺς θαυμάζειν. Διὸ καὶ ἐγίνετο ἡ θεραπεία, διὰ τὴν τῶν ὁρώντων ὠφέλειαν. Εἰ δὲ καὶ τὸν Θεὸν ἐδόξαζον ἐπὶ τούτῳ, ὁ Υἱὸς ἦν ἐν Πατρὶ δοξαζόμενος.

Καὶ ἐδόξασαν τὸν Θεὸν Ἰσραήλ.[1364] Οὔπω τὸ τοῦ Κυρίου ἡμῶν Ἰησοῦ Χριστοῦ κατέμαθον ἀξίωμα, ὅτι τὰς ἰάσεις αὐτοδυνάμως παρέχεται ὡς ἂν αὐτὸς ὢν δι᾽ οὗ τὰ πάντα ἐργάζεται ὁ Πατήρ,[mcxxxi] ἀλλ᾽ ἄνθρωπον ἐνόμιζον ἐνεργοῦντα ὑπὲρ ἄνθρωπον καὶ Θεῷ τὴν δόξαν ἀνάγουσι. Καὶ ἐνταῦθα ἐπληροῦτο τὸ λεγόμενον ὑπὸ τοῦ Κυρίου πρὸς τὸν Πατέρα, *ἐγώ σε ἐδόξασα ἐπὶ τῆς γῆς.*[1365] Ἄνθρωπος μὲν γὰρ ἐνεργῶν τι θαυμάσιον οὐκ αὐτὸς δοξάζει Θεόν, ἀλλ᾽ ὑπὸ τοῦ Θεοῦ δοξάζεται τῆς θαυματουργοῦ μεταλαμβάνων δυνάμεως. Χριστὸς δὲ αὐτός ἐστιν ὁ τὰ *θαυμάσια*[1366] κατεργαζόμενος. Αὐτὸς τὸν Πατέρα δοξάζει καθιστὰς ἐμφανῆ τὴν δύναμιν αὐτοῦ, ἥτις ἐστιν αὐτός.[1367] *Θεὸν* δὲ οὐχ ἕτερον, ἀλλὰ τὸν τοῦ *Ἰσραὴλ* δοξάζουσιν. Οὐδὲ γάρ ἐστιν ἕτερος κατὰ τὴν Μαρκίωνος ἄνοιαν, ἀλλ᾽ αὐτὸς μόνος.

> Οὔπω τὸ τοῦ κυρίου ἡμῶν Ἰησοῦ Χριστοῦ κατέμαθον ἀξίωμα, ὅτι τὰς ἰάσεις αὐτοδυνάμως παρέχεται, ὡς ἂν αὐτὸς ὢν δι᾽ οὗ τὰ πάντα ἐργάζεται ὁ πατήρ, ἀλλ᾽ ἄνθρωπον ἐνόμιζον ἐνεργοῦντα ὑπὲρ ἄνθρωπον καὶ θεῷ τὴν δόξαν ἀνάγουσι. καὶ ἐνταῦθα ἐπληροῦτο τὸ λεγόμενον ὑπὸ τοῦ κυρίου πρὸς τὸν πατέρα. *ἐγώ σε ἐδόξασα ἐπὶ τῆς γῆς*. ἄνθρωπος μὲν γὰρ ἐνεργῶν τι θαυμάσιον οὐκ αὐτὸς δοξάζει θεόν, ἀλλ᾽ ὑπὸ θεοῦ δοξάζεται τῆς θαυματουργοῦ μεταλαμβάνων δυνάμεως. Χριστὸς δὲ αὐτός ἐστιν ὁ τὰ θαυμάσια κατεργαζόμενος, αὐτὸς τὸν πατέρα δοξάζει καθιστὰς ἐμφανῆ τὴν δύναμιν αὐτοῦ, ἥτις ἐστιν αὐτός. *θεὸν* δὲ οὐχ ἕτερον, ἀλλὰ τὸν τοῦ *Ἰσραὴλ* δοξάζουσιν. οὐδὲ γάρ ἐστιν ἕτερος κατὰ τὴν Μαρκίωνος ἄνοιαν, ἀλλ᾽ αὐτὸς μόνος.[mcxxxii]

> Οὔπω τὸ τοῦ κυρίου κατέμαθον ἀξίωμα, ὅτι θεός ἐστιν, ἀλλ᾽ ἄνθρωπον ἐνόμιζον αὐτὸν ψιλόν. διὸ καὶ τῷ θεῷ Ἰσραὴλ τὴν δόξαν ἀνέπεμπον.[mcxxxiii]

Ὁ δὲ Ἰησοῦς προσκαλεσάμενος τοὺς μαθητὰς αὐτοῦ εἶπε· σπλαγχνίζομαι ἐπὶ τὸν ὄχλον.[1368] Δυνάμενος καὶ δίχα τοῦ ἐρωτῆσαι τοὺς μαθητὰς ὁ Σωτὴρ ποιῆσαι τὸ σημεῖον, ἐπίτηδες ἐρωτᾷ ἵνα προσεκτικωτέρους αὐτοὺς ποιήσῃ καὶ γυμνάσῃ αὐτῶν τὴν πίστιν εἰ λέγουσι, ποίησον ἄρτους ἵνα φάγωσιν· οἱ δὲ οὐ συνῆκαν. Εἰ δὲ καὶ ἀσθενείᾳ λογισμοῦ εἶπον ἃ εἶπον, ἀλλ᾽ ἀνύποπτον. | **128r** Διατί δὲ καὶ νῦν,[mcxxxiv] ὡς ἐπὶ τῶν πέντε ἄρτων, οὐκ ‹ε›ἶπ‹ο›ν[1369] οἱ ἀπόστολοι ‹ὅτι› *καὶ τί ταῦτα ἐπ᾽ αὐτούς;*[mcxxxv] ‹Ἐπειδὴ› εἴ καὶ

1363 Matt. 15:31.
1364 Matt. 15:31.
1365 John, 17:5.
1366 Cf. Psalms 71:18; 76:15; 85:10.
1367 Cf. 1 Cor. 1:24.
1368 Matt. 15:32.
1369 cod. οίπων.

μὴ τελ‹ε›ίως[1370] ὑψ‹η›λοὶ[1371] ἐγένοντο, ἀλλ᾽ ὅμως ᾔδ‹ε›σαν[1372] τὴν αὐτοῦ δύναμιν. Διατὶ ἐπὶ μὲν τῶν πέντε ἄρτων πεντακισχιλίων ὄντων *δώδεκα κόφινοι* ἐπερίσσευσαν,[1373] ἐνταῦθα δὲ τετρακισχιλίων ὄντων *ἑπτὰ* σπυρίδες μόνον ἐπερισσεύσαν; Καὶ τοῦτο ἐστὶν ὅτι ‹αἱ› σπυρίδες[1374] τῶν κοφίνων μείζους ἦσαν. Ἢ ἵνα πάλιν μὴ ἡ ἰσότης τοῦ σημ‹ε›ίου[1375] εἰς λ‹ή›θην[1376] αὐτοὺς ἀγάγ‹ῃ›[1377] τοῦ θαύματος.

(Θεοδώρου Μοναχοῦ.) τίνος δὲ ἕνεκεν, εἰ οὐκ ἤθελεν ἀπολῦσαι αὐτοὺς νήστεις, οὐ ποιεῖ τὸ σημεῖον, ἀλλ᾽ ἐρωτᾷ; ἵνα ἐν τῇ ἐρωτήσει ταύτῃ καὶ τῇ ἀποκρίσει, προσεκτικωτέρους ποιήσει τοὺς μαθητάς, καὶ τὴν αὐτῶν πίστιν ἐπιδείξωνται ἐκ τοῦ προτέρου θαύματος τῶν πέντε ἄρτων, προσερχόμενοι καὶ λέγοντες. Κύριε, ποίησον ἄρτους. ἀλλ᾽ οὐδὲ οὕτως συνῆκαν τῆς ἐρωτήσεως τὴν αἰτίαν.

καὶ οἱ μὲν ἀσθενεῖ λογισμῷ τοῦτο ἔλεγον. τὸ δὲ σημεῖον καὶ ἐντεῦθεν ἀνύποπτον ἐγίνετο, ἵνα μὴ λέγῃ τίς, ὅπερ καὶ ἤδη εἶπον, ὅτι ἀπὸ πλησίον κώμης τινὸς οὔσης τοὺς ἄρτους ἔλαβον.

Διὰ τί καὶ νῦν ἐπὶ τῶν ἑπτὰ ἄρτων, οὐκ εἶπον οἱ Ἀπόστολοι, ὥσπερ ἔμπροσθεν ἐπὶ τῶν πέντε, ὅτι *καὶ τί ταῦτά ἐστιν εἰς τοσούτους*;[1378] ἐπειδὴ εἰ καὶ τελείως ὑψηλοὶ οὐ γεγόνασιν, ἀλλ᾽ ὅμως ἐπὶ τὸ κρεῖττον κατὰ μικρὸν προέκοπτον… . τί δήποτε ἐπὶ μὲν τῶν πέντε ἄρτων, καίτοιγε πεντακισχιλίων ὄντων, χωρὶς γυναικῶν καὶ παιδίων, δώδεκα κόφινοι περίσσευσαν, ἐνταῦθα δὲ τετρακισχιλίων ὑπαρχόντων, καὶ ἑπτὰ ἄρτων, ἑπτὰ σπυρίδες; ἢ τοίνυν τοῦτό ἐστιν εἰπεῖν, ὅτι αἱ σπυρίδες τῶν κοφίνων μείζους ἦσαν. ἢ εἰ μὴ τοῦτο, ἵνα μὴ πάλιν ἡ ἰσότης τοῦ σημείου εἰς λήθην αὐτοὺς ἐμβάλῃ τοῦ ἑνός. διὰ τοῦτο τῇ διαφορᾷ τὴν μνήμην αὐτῶν διεγείρει. ἵνα ἐκ τοῦ παρηλλαγμένου μνησθῶσι. κἀκείνου καὶ τούτου.[mcxxxvi]

Διὰ τοῦτό φησιν, *Ἵνα μὴ ἐκλυθῶσιν ἐν τῇ ὁδῷ*. δεικνὺς ὅτι καὶ πόρρωθεν ἀφεστήκεσαν, καὶ οὐδὲν αὐτοῖς ὑπολελειμμένον ἦν. Καὶ εἰ μὴ θέλεις ἀπολῦσαι νήστεις, τίνος ἕνεκεν οὐ ποιεῖς τὸ σημεῖον; Ἵνα ἐν τῇ ἐρωτήσει ταύτῃ καὶ τῇ ἀποκρίσει προσεκτικωτέρους ποιήσῃ τοὺς μαθητάς, καὶ τὴν πίστιν αὐτῶν ἐπιδείξωνται, προσιόντες καὶ λέγοντες. Ποίησον ἄρτους. Ἀλλ᾽ οὐδὲ οὕτω συνῆκαν τῆς ἐρωτήσεως τὴν αἰτίαν.[mcxxxvii]

Ἀλλὰ διατί τότε μὲν πεντακισχιλίων ὄντων, δώδεκα κόφινοι ἐπερίσσευσαν, ἐνταῦθα δὲ τετρακισχιλίων, ἑπτὰ σπυρίδες; τίνος οὖν ἕνεκεν καὶ διατί ἐλάττονα ἦν τὰ λείψανα, καίτοι οὐ τοσούτων ὄντων τῶν ἑστιωμένων; Ἢ τοίνυν τοῦτο ἔστιν εἰπεῖν, ὅτι αἱ σπυρίδες τῶν κοφίνων μείζους ἦσαν. ἢ εἰ μὴ τοῦτο, ἵνα μὴ πάλιν ἡ ἰσότης τοῦ σημείου εἰς λήθην αὐτοὺς ἐμβάλῃ, τῇ διαφορᾷ τὴν μνήμην αὐτῶν διεγείρει, ἵνα ἐκ τοῦ παρηλλαγμένου ἀναμνησθῶσι κἀκείνου καὶ τούτου.[mcxxxviii]

1370 cod. τελίως.
1371 Cod. ὑψιλοί.
1372 Cod. εἴδησαν.
1373 Matt. 14:20.
1374 Cod. εσπυρίδες.
1375 Cod. σημίου.
1376 Cod. λίθην.
1377 Cod. ἀγάγει.
1378 Cf. John, 6:9.

Ποῖον *σημεῖον* ζητοῦσιν *οἱ Φαρισαῖοι* δειχθῆναι αὐτοῖς;[1379] Ἢ ἵνα στήσῃ τὸν ἥλιον καὶ τὴν σελ‹ή›νην[1380] ‹ἢ›[1381] κεραυνοὺς ἵνα κατενέγκ‹ῃ›;[1382] Ἵνα τὸν ἀέρα μεταβάλ‹ῃ›,[1383] ἢ ἄλλο τ‹ο›ι‹ῦ›τον[1384] ποιήσῃ;[1385] Ὅπερ δὲ εἶπεν (*τὸ πρόσωπον τοῦ οὐρανοῦ καὶ τῆς γῆς γίνωσκετ‹ε›*[1386] δοκιμάζειν, τὸν δὲ καιρὸν τοῦτον οὐ γινώσκετε;)[1387] τοῦτο δηλοῖ· ὅτι ‹ὥ›σπερ[1388] ἐπὶ *τοῦ οὐρανοῦ* ἄλλο μὲν τὸ *σημεῖον* τοῦ χειμ‹ῶ›νος[1389] ‹ἄλλο δὲ τῆς εὐδίας, καὶ οὐκ ἄν τις τὸ σημεῖον› ἰδὼν τοῦ χειμῶνος› γαλ‹ή›νην[1390] ζητεῖ, ‹ἢ›[1391] ἐρόντι ἀπὸ ταύτης ὄντ‹ω›ς[1392] καὶ ἐπ᾽ ἐμοῦ λογίζεσθαι χρ‹ή›.[1393] Ἄλλος γὰρ οὗτος ὁ τῆς ἐμῆς παρουσίας κ‹αι›ρὸς[1394] καὶ ἄλλος ὁ τότε. Νῦν γὰρ χρεία τῶν σημείων τούτων τῶν ἐν τῇ γῇ, τὰ δὲ ἐν τῷ οὐρανῷ ἐκείνῳ τεταμιεύετ‹αι›[1395] τῷ κ‹αι›ρῷ.[1396] Νῦν ὡς ἰατρὸς ἦλθον, τότε ὡς δικαστὴς ἐλεύσ‹ο›μ‹αι›.[1397][mcxxxix] Ὑποκριτὰς δὲ αὐτοὺς καλεῖ ὅτι ‹ἕ›τερα[1398] μὲν ἔλεγ‹ον,[1399] ἕτερα δὲ ἐφρόνουν.[1400] Οὐ γὰρ διὰ τὸ πιστεῦσαι ἐζήτουν τὰ *σημεῖα*, ἐπ‹ε›ὶ[1401] ἔδωκεν ἄν, ἀλλ᾽ ὥστε ἐπιλαβέσθαι αὐτοῦ.

Ποῖον σημεῖον οἱ Φαρισαῖοι καὶ οἱ Σαδδουκαῖοι νῦν ἐπιζήτουσιν, ἐκ τοῦ οὐρανοῦ ἐπιδειχθῆναι αὐτοῖς; ἢ ἵνα στήσῃ τὸν ἥλιον, ἢ τὴν σελήνην χαλινώσῃ. ἢ κεραυνοὺς κατενέγκῃ, ἢ τὸν ἀέρα μεταβάλῃ. ἢ ἄλλο τι τοιοῦτον ποιήσῃ. ὅπερ δὲ καὶ αὐτὸς εἶπεν αὐτοῖς. ὅτι *τὸ πρόσωπον τοῦ οὐρανοῦ γινώσκετε. τὰ δὲ σημεῖα τῶν καιρῶν, οὐ γινώσκετε*, τοῦτο δηλοῖ, ὅτι ὥσπερ, φησίν, ἐπὶ τοῦ οὐρανοῦ, ἄλλο μὲν σημεῖον τοῦ χειμῶνος, ἄλλο δὲ τῆς εὐδίας, καὶ οὐκ ἄν τις τὸ σημεῖον ἰδὼν τοῦ χειμῶνος, γαλήνην ζητήσειεν. οὐδὲ ἐν γαλήνῃ χειμῶνα, οὕτως καὶ ἐπ᾽ ἐμοῦ λογίζεσθαι χρή. ἄλλος γὰρ οὗτος ὁ τῆς ἐμῆς παρουσίας καιρός, καὶ ἄλλος ὁ μέλλων. νῦν χρεία τούτων τῶν σημείων τῶν ἐν τῇ γῇ. τὰ δὲ ἐν τῷ οὐρανῷ,

1379 Matt. 16:1.
1380 Cod. σελίνην.
1381 Cod. εἶ.
1382 Cod. κατενέγκει.
1383 Cod. μεταβάλει.
1384 Cod. τι οὗτον.
1385 Cod. ποιήσει.
1386 Cod. γίνωσκεται.
1387 Matt. 16:3; cf. Luke, 12:56.
1388 Cod. ὅσπερ
1389 Cod. χειμόνος.
1390 Cod. γαλίνην.
1391 Cod. ἤ.
1392 Cod. ὄντος.
1393 Cod. ἔχρω.
1394 Cod. κερὸς.
1395 Cod. τεταμιεύετε.
1396 Cod. κερῶ.
1397 Cod. ἐλεύσωμε.
1398 Cod. ἕτερα.
1399 Cod. ἐλεγων.
1400 Cod. εὐφρόνουν.
1401 Cod. ἐπὶ.

> ἐκείνῳ τεταμίευται τῷ καιρῷ. νῦν, ὡς ἰατρὸς ἦλθον. τότε, ὡς δικαστὴς ἐλεύσομαι. ὑποκριτὰς δὲ αὐτοὺς καλεῖ καὶ νῦν, ὅτι καὶ ἕτερα μὲν ἔλεγον, ἕτερα δὲ ἐφρόνουν. οὐ γὰρ διὰ τὸ πιστεῦσαι ἐζήτουν τὰ σημεῖα, ἀλλ' ὥστε ἐπιλαβέσθαι, ἐπεὶ ἔδωκεν ἄν. ὁ γὰρ τῇ γυναικὶ εἰπών, *οὐκ ἔστι καλὸν δοῦναι*, καὶ μετὰ ταῦτα δούς, πολλῷ μᾶλλον ἂν τούτοις παρέσχεν. καὶ ὁ τὰ μείζονα δούς, τουτέστιν ἁμαρτήματα λύσας, καὶ δαίμονας ἀπελάσας, καὶ τὰ ἄλλα πάντα, καὶ ἐν τούτοις μὴ πείσας, πῶς ἂν ἐν τοῖς μικροτέροις πείθειν ἔμελλεν; μικρότερα γὰρ πρὸς ταῦτα, τὸ τὸν ἥλιον ἀποκρύψαι, καὶ σελήνην χαλινῶσαι, καὶ κεραυνοὺς κατενεγκεῖν. χρὴ δὲ σκοπῆσαι τὴν πώρωσιν αὐτῶν. ὅτι περ εἰπόντος τοῦ δεσπότου Χριστοῦ πρὸς αὐτούς, ὅτι *οὐ δοθήσεται αὐτοῖς σημεῖον, εἰ μὴ τοῦ Ἰωνᾶ*, οὐκ ἐρώτωσι τί ποτε ἦν τὸ λεγόμενον. ἐπειδή, ὥσπερ ἔφην, οὐκ ἐπιθυμίᾳ ταῦτα ἐποίουν. διὰ δὴ τοῦτο καὶ αὐτὸς ἀφεὶς αὐτούς, ἀπῆλθεν.[mcxl]

> Τί δὲ σημεῖον ἐκ τοῦ οὐρανοῦ ᾔτουν; Ἢ τὸν ἥλιον στῆσαι, ἢ τὴν σελήνην χαλινῶσαι, ἢ κεραυνοὺς κατενεγκεῖν, ἢ τὸν ἀέρα μεταβαλεῖν, ἢ ἄλλο τι τοιοῦτον. Τί οὖν πρὸς ταῦτα αὐτός; *Τὸ μὲν πρόσωπον τοῦ οὐρανοῦ γινώσκετε διακρίνειν, τὰ δὲ σημεῖα τῶν καιρῶν οὐ δύνασθε*; ... Ὥσπερ ἐπὶ τοῦ οὐρανοῦ, φησίν, ἄλλο μὲν σημεῖον τοῦ χειμῶνος, ἄλλο δὲ τῆς εὐδίας, καὶ οὐκ ἄν τις τὸ σημεῖον ἰδὼν τοῦ χειμῶνος γαλήνην ζητήσειεν, οὐδὲ ἐν γαλήνῃ εὐδινῇ χειμῶνα. οὕτω καὶ ἐπ' ἐμοῦ λογίζεσθαι χρή. Ἄλλος γὰρ οὗτος τῆς παρουσίας ὁ καιρός, ἄλλος δὲ ὁ μέλλων. Νῦν χρεία τούτων τῶν σημείων τῶν ἐν τῇ γῇ. τὰ δὲ ἐν τῷ οὐρανῷ ἐκείνῳ τεταμίευται τῷ καιρῷ. Νῦν ὡς ἰατρὸς ἦλθον, τότε ὡς δικαστὴς παρέσομαι.[mcxli]

> Ἀλλ' ἐπειδὴ οὐ πιστεῦσαι ἐζήτουν, διὰ τοῦτο καὶ ὑποκριτὰς ἑτέρωθι καλεῖ, ὅτι ἕτερα μὲν ἔλεγον, ἕτερα δὲ ἐφρόνουν. Εἰ γὰρ ἐπίστευον, οὐδ' ἂν ᾔτησαν.[mcxlii]

> Ὁ γὰρ τῇ γυναικὶ εἰπών, *Οὐκ ἔστι καλόν*, καὶ μετὰ ταῦτα δούς, πολλῷ μᾶλλον ἂν τούτοις παρέσχεν.[mcxliii]

> Ἢ τὸν ἥλιον στῆσαι, ἢ τὴν σελήνην χαλινῶσαι, ἢ κεραυνοὺς κατενεγκεῖν, ἢ τὸν ἀέρα μεταβαλεῖν, ἢ ἄλλο τι τοιοῦτον.[mcxliv]

Διὰ τί εἶπεν ὁ Κύριος τοῖς ἀποστόλοις, *προ‹σέ›χετ‹ε›*[1402] *ἀπὸ τῆς ζύμης τῶν Φαρισ‹αί›ων*[1403] *καὶ Σαδδουκαίων*[1404] καὶ οὐχὶ ἀπὸ τῆς διδαχῆς; ‹Ὅτι› ἐβούλετο ἀναμνῆσ‹α›ι αὐτοὺς τ‹ῶ›ν ἄρτ‹ω›ν[1405] τῶν *ἑπτὰ* καὶ τῶν *πέντε* τὰ σημεῖα. Ἤδει γὰρ αὐτοὺς ἐπιλελησμένους. Διὸ ‹καὶ›[1406] ἔλεγον ὅτι *ἄρτους οὐκ ἐλάβ‹ο›μεν*.[1407] Ἔτι γὰρ περὶ τὰ | **128v** καθ‹άρ›σια[1408] τὰ Ἰουδαϊκὰ ἦσαν ἐπτοημένοι καὶ περὶ τὰς τῶν βρωμάτων παρατηρήσεις. Διὸ καὶ σφοδρότερον αὐτοῖς ἐπιτ‹ί›θεται[1409] λέγων· *τί*

1402 Cod. πρὸς ἔχεται.
1403 Cod. Φαρισέων.
1404 Matt. 16:12.
1405 Cod. τὸν ἄρτον.
1406 Cod. τὲ.
1407 Matt. 16:7. Cod. ελάβωμεν.
1408 Cod. καθασία.
1409 Cod. ἐπιτήθεται.

διαλογ‹ί›ζεσθ‹ε›[1410] *ὀλιγόπιστοι ὅτι ἄρτους οὐκ* ἔχετε; *Οὔπω νοεῖτε οὐδὲ μνημονεύετε*[1411] τῶν πέντε ἄρτων καὶ πάλιν τῶν ἑπτά; Ὅρα ὅτι οὐ πανταχοῦ ἡ πραότης καλόν. Διὸ καὶ ὁ Χριστὸς πολλάκις ἐπιτ‹ι›μ‹ᾷ›[1412] τοὺς μαθητάς. Βλέπε δὲ πόσον ἴσχυσεν ἡ ἐπιτ‹ί›μησ‹ι›ς.[1413] Τοῦτο γὰρ μόνον προσθέντος (ὅτι *οὔπω νοεῖτε* ὅτι *οὐ περὶ ἄρτων ε‹ἶ›π‹ο›ν*[1414] *ὑμῖν;*),[1415] εὐθέως συνῆκαν ὅτι περὶ *τῆς διδαχῆς τῶν Φαρισαίων καὶ Σαδδουκαίων* εἶπεν, καίτοι[1416] τοῦτο αὐτοῦ μὴ ἑρμηνεύσαντος.

Διὰ τί εἶπεν ὁ Κύριος τοῖς Ἀποστόλοις, *προσέχετε ἀπὸ τῆς ζύμης τῶν Φαρισαίων*, καὶ οὐκ εἶπεν, ἀπὸ τῆς διδασκαλίας αὐτῶν; ἐπειδὴ ἐβούλετο ἀναμνῆσαι αὐτοὺς τῶν γενομένων σημείων. ἐγίνωσκε γὰρ αὐτοὺς ἐπιλελησμένους. καίπερ διπλοῦ τοῦ θαύματος γενομένου. λέγω δὴ τοῦ πλεονασμοῦ *τῶν πέντε ἄρτων καὶ τῶν ἑπτά*. καὶ τὸ μὲν ἁπλῶς ἐγκαλέσαι αὐτοῖς, οὐκ ἐδόκει λόγον ἔχειν. τὸ δὲ ἀφορμὴν παρ᾿ αὐτῶν λαβόντα οὕτως ἐπιτιμῆσαι, εὐπαράδεκτον ἐποίει τὸ ἔγκλημα, καὶ τὸ εἰς μέσον ἐνεγκεῖν τοὺς διαλογισμοὺς αὐτῶν τί διελογίζοντο, *ὅτι ἄρτους οὐκ ἐλάβομεν*. ἔτι γὰρ ἐπὶ τὰ καθάρσια τὰ Ἰουδαϊκὰ ἦσαν ἐπτοημένοι, καὶ περὶ τὰς τῶν βρωμάτων παρατηρήσεις. διὸ πάντων ἕνεκεν, καὶ σφοδρότερον αὐτοῖς ἐπιτίθεται λέγων. *τὶ διαλογίζεσθε ἐν ἑαυτοῖς ὀλιγόπιστοι, ὅτι ἄρτους οὐκ ἔχετε; οὔπω νοεῖτε, οὐδὲ μνημονεύετε*, καὶ τὰ ἑξῆς. εἶδες ἀγανάκτησιν ἐπιτεταμένην, οὐδὲ γὰρ ἀλλαχοῦ φαίνεται αὐτοῖς οὕτως ἐπιτιμήσας·

τοῦτο δὲ ὅλον πεποίηκεν, ὥστε πάλιν τὴν τῶν βρωμάτων ὑπόληψιν ἐκβαλεῖν. οὐ γὰρ πανταχοῦ ἡ πραότης καλόν. ὥσπερ γὰρ μετεδίδου παρρησίας αὐτοῖς, οὕτως καὶ ἐπιτιμᾷ. δι᾿ ἀμφοτέρων τὴν σωτηρίαν αὐτῶν οἰκονομῶν. χρὴ δὲ σκοπῆσαι καὶ τὴν μετὰ τὴν ἐπιτίμησιν πολλὴν αὐτοῦ ἐπιείκειαν. ὡς γὰρ ἀπολογούμενος αὐτοῖς ὑπὲρ τῆς ἐπιτιμήσεως, τῶν πέντε ἄρτων καὶ τῶν ἑπτὰ ἀνέμνησεν. διὰ τοῦτο δὲ τὸν ἀριθμὸν τίθησιν, καὶ τῶν τραφέντων, καὶ τῶν λειψάνων τῶν ἄρτων. ὁμοῦ τὲ εἰς ἀνάμνησιν αὐτοὺς ἄγων τῶν παρελθόντων, καὶ εἰς τὸ μέλλον προσεκτικωτέρους ποιῶν. τοσοῦτον δὲ ἴσχυσεν ἡ ἐπιτίμησις, καὶ ἤγειρε καθεύδουσαν τὴν αὐτῶν διάνοιαν, ὅτι μετὰ τὴν ἐπιτίμησιν τοῦτο μόνον προσθέντος, ὅτι *οὐ περὶ ἄρτων εἶπον ὑμῖν*, εὐθέως συνῆκαν, ὅτι περὶ τῆς διδασκαλίας τῶν Φαρισαίων καὶ τῶν Σαδδουκαίων εἶπεν. καίτοι τοῦτο αὐτοῦ μὴ ἑρμηνεύσαντος. ὅθεν δέον ἡμᾶς γινώσκειν πόσα ἀγαθὰ ἡ ἐπιτίμησις αὕτη εἰργάσατο. πρῶτον μέν, τῶν Ἰουδαϊκῶν αὐτοὺς ἀπήγαγε παρατηρήσεως. ἔπειτα ῥαθύμους ὄντας, προσεκτικωτέρους ἐποίησεν, καὶ τῆς ὀλιγοπιστίας ἀπήλλαξεν, ὥστε μὴ φοβεῖσθαι, εἴποτε ἄρτους φαίνοιντο ὀλίγους ἔχοντες. μηδὲ ὑπὲρ λιμοῦ φροντίζειν, ἀλλ᾿ ὑπερορᾶν τούτων ἁπάντων.[mcxlv]

Ὁ δὲ Ἰησοῦς εἶπεν αὐτοῖς. *Ὁρᾶτε καὶ προσέχετε ἀπὸ τῆς ζύμης τῶν Φρισαίων καὶ Σαδδουκαίων*. Καὶ διατί μὴ εἶπε, Προσέχετε ἀπὸ τῆς διδασκαλίας, σαφῶς; Βούλεται αὐτοὺς ἀναμνῆσαι τῶν γενομένων. καὶ γὰρ ᾔδει ἐπιλελησμένους… . ἃ γὰρ διελογίζοντο, ταῦτα εἰς μέσον φέρει. Τί δὲ διελογίζοντο; *Ὅτι ἄρτους*, φησίν, *οὐκ ἐλάβομεν*… . Ἔτι γὰρ περὶ τὰ καθάρσια ἦσαν τὰ Ἰουδαϊκὰ ἐπτοημένοι, καὶ τὰς τῶν βρωμάτων παρατηρήσεις.

1410 Cod. διαλογήζεσθαι.
1411 Matt. 16:8-9.
1412 Cof. ἐπιτημὰ.
1413 Cod. ἐπιτήμησης.
1414 Cod. εἴπων.
1415 Cf. Matt. 16:9-12.
1416 Cod. καί τι.

Διὸ ἁπάντων ἕνεκεν καὶ σφοδρότερον αὐτοῖς ἐπιτίθεται, λέγων. *Τί διαλογίζεσθε ἐν ἑαυτοῖς, ὀλιγόπιστοι, ὅτι ἄρτους οὐκ ἐλάβετε; Οὔπω νοεῖτε*, οὐδὲ συνίετε;

Εἶδες ἀγανάκτησιν ἐπιτεταμένην; Οὐδὲ γὰρ ἀλλαχοῦ φαίνεται οὕτως αὐτοῖς ἐπιτιμήσας... . Οὐ γὰρ πανταχοῦ ἡ προσήνεια καλόν. Ὥσπερ γὰρ μετεδίδου παρρησίας αὐτοῖς, οὕτω καὶ ἐπιτιμᾷ, τῇ ποικιλίᾳ ταύτῃ τὴν σωτηρίαν αὐτῶν οἰκονομῶν... . Οὐδὲν γὰρ πλέον εἰπόντος τοῦ Ἰησοῦ, ἀλλ᾽ ἐπιτιμήσαντος, καὶ τοῦτο προσθέντος μόνον, *Πῶς οὐ νοεῖτε, ὅτι οὐ περὶ ἄρτων εἶπον ὑμῖν προσέχειν, ἀλλ᾽ ἀπὸ τῆς ζύμης τῶν Φαρισαίων καὶ Σαδδουκαίων*; ἐπήγαγε λέγων. *Τότε συνῆκαν, ὅτι οὐκ εἶπε προσέχειν ἀπὸ τῆς ζύμης τοῦ ἄρτου, ἀλλ᾽ ἀπὸ τῆς διδασκαλίας τῶν Φαρισαίων καὶ Σαδδουκαίων*. καίτοι αὐτοῦ τοῦτο μὴ ἑρμηνεύσαντος. Ὅρα πόσα ἀγαθὰ ἡ ἐπιτίμησις εἰργάσατο.[mcxlvi]

Δι‹ὰ›[1417] τί ἀπελθὼν εἰς Καισάρειαν *τῆς Φιλ‹ί›ππου*;[1418] Ἔστι γὰρ καὶ ἑτέρα, ἡ Στράτωνος.

Διὰ τί ἀπελθὼν εἰς Καισάρειαν τῆς Φιλίππον; ἔστι γὰρ καὶ ἑτέρα ἡ Στράτωνος, ἐν ἐκείνῃ, καὶ οὐκ ἐν ταύτῃ, ὁ Χριστὸς ἠρώτα τοὺς μαθητὰς αὐτοῦ λέγων. *τίνα με λέγουσιν οἱ ἄνθρωποι εἶναι*, τὸν υἱὸν τοῦ ἀνθρώπου; πόρρω τῶν Ἰουδαίων ἀπάγων αὐτούς, ὡς πάσης ἀπαλλαγέντας ἀγωνίας, μετὰ παρρησίας εἰπεῖν τὰ κατὰ διάνοιαν ἅπαντα. διὰ τοῦτο ἐν ἐκείνῃ, καὶ οὐκ ἐν ταύτῃ ἐπηρώτησεν αὐτούς. οὐκ ἐρωτᾷ δὲ τὴν αὐτῶν γνώμην εὐθέως, ἀλλὰ τὴν τῶν πολλῶν. ἵνα περ εἰπόντας τὴν ἐκείνων, εἶτα ἐρωτηθέντες, εἰς μείζονα ἀναχθῶσιν ἔννοιαν, καὶ μὴ εἰς τὴν αὐτὴν ταπεινότητα τοῖς πολλοῖς συμπέσωσι. διὰ δὴ τοῦτο, οὐδὲ ἐν ἀρχῇ τοῦ κηρύγματος αὐτῶν πυνθάνεται. ἀλλ᾽ ὅτε σημεῖα πολλὰ ἐποίησεν, καὶ περὶ πολλῶν αὐτοῖς διηλέχθη, καὶ ὑψηλῶν δογμάτων, καὶ τῆς αὐτοῦ θεότητος, καὶ τῆς πρὸς τὸν Πατέρα ὁμονοίας, πολλὰς παρέσχε τὰς ἀποδείξεις. τότε τὴν πεῦσιν προσάγει ταύτην. καὶ οὐκ εἶπεν τίνα με λέγουσιν οἱ γραμματεῖς, καὶ οἱ Φαρισαῖοι εἶναι. καίτοι γε οὗτοι αὐτῷ πολλάκις προσῄεσαν καὶ διελέγοντο. ἀλλὰ *τίνα με λέγουσιν οἱ ἄνθρωποι εἶναι*. τὴν τοῦ πλήθους γνώμην τὴν ἀδέκαστον ἐξετάζων. εἰ γὰρ καὶ πολλῷ ταπεινότερα τοῦ δέοντος ἦν, ἀλλὰ πονηρίας ἀπήλλακτο. ἐκείνη δὲ πολλῆς ἔγεμε τῆς κακίας. *υἱὸν δὲ ἀνθρώπου* αὐτὸν εἶπεν, σφόδρα βουλόμενος τὴν οἰκονομίαν ὁμολογεῖσθαι, καθὼς καὶ ἀλλαχοῦ πολλαχῶς τοῦτο ποιεῖ.[mcxlvii]

Οὐ μάτην δὲ τοῦ τοποκτίστου ὁ εὐαγγελιστὴς ἐμνημόνευσεν οὕτως εἰπών. *Ἐλθὼν ὁ Ἰησοῦς εἰς τὰ μέρη Καισαρείας τῆς Φιλίππου*. ἀλλ᾽ ἐπειδὴ ἔστι καὶ ἄλλη Καισάρεια, ἡ λεγομένη τοῦ Στράτωνος, ἵνα μή τις πλάνη ἐκ τῆς ὁμωνυμίας γένηται τοῖς ἀκροαταῖς, ἀναγκαίως τὴν ὁμωνυμίαν διέστειλε.[mcxlviii]

Ἐν ταύτῃ καὶ οὐκ ἐν ἐκείνῃ ἐρωτᾷ τοὺς μαθητάς, *τίνα με λέγουσιν οἱ ἄνθρωποί εἶναι*;[1419] Πόρρω τῶν Ἰουδαίων ἀπάγει αὐτούς, ‹ὡ›ς[1420] πάσης ἀπαλλαγέντας ἀγωνίας μετὰ παρρησίας εἰπεῖν τὰ κατὰ διάνοιαν ἅπαντα. ‹Διὰ τοῦτο ἐν ἐκείνῃ, καὶ οὐκ ἐν ταύτῃ ἐπηρώτησεν αὐτούς.› Οὐκ ἐρωτᾷ δὲ τὴν αὐτῶν γνώμην εὐθέως, ἀλλὰ τὴν τῶν πολλῶν, ἵνα εἰς μείζονα ἀναχθῶσιν ἔννοιαν. Διὰ τοῦτο γὰρ οὐδὲ ἐν ἀρχῇ

1417 Cod. δὶ.
1418 Cod. Φιλήππου.
1419 Matt. 16:13.
1420 Cod. ὡς.

τοῦ κηρύγματος ἠρώτησεν, ἀλλ' ὅτε *σημεῖα πολλὰ ἐποίησεν*,[1421] ‹ἃ›[1422] τῆς αὐτοῦ θε‹ό›τ‹η›τος[1423] καὶ τῆς πρὸς τὸν Πατέρα ὁμονοίας πολλὰς παρέσχε τὰς ἀποδείξεις ‹τότε τὴν πεῦσιν προσάγει ταύτην›. Καὶ οὐ λέγει *τίνα με λέγουσιν οἱ* γραμματ‹εῖ›ς[1424] καὶ οἱ Φαρισαῖοι ‹εἶναι›, ἀλλ' *οἱ ἄνθρωποι*, καίτοι οὗτοι[1425] αὐτῷ διελέγοντο, ἀλλὰ τὴν ἀδέκαστον γνώμην τοῦ πλήθους ἐξετάζων. ‹Εἰ›[1426] γὰρ καὶ πολλῷ ταπεινότερα τοῦ δέοντος ‹αὕτη ἦ›ν,[1427] ἀλλὰ πάσης | **129r** πονηρίας ἀπήλλακτ‹ο›,[1428] ἐκεῖνοι δὲ ἔγεμον πάσης πονηρίας.[1429] *Υἱὸν* δὲ *ἀνθρώπου* ἑαυτὸν ε‹ἶ›πεν[1430] σφόδρα βουλόμενος τὴν οἰκονομίαν ὁμολογεῖσθαι.

Εἶτα εὐθέ‹ω›ς[1431] προπηδᾷ ὁ ἐν ἅπασι θερμώτατος *Πέτρος* κα‹ὶ› φ‹η›σι·[1432] *σὺ ‹εἶ› ὁ Χριστὸς ὁ Υἱὸς τοῦ Θεοῦ τοῦ ζῶντος*.[1433] Διὰ τοῦτο δὲ αὐτὸν μακαρίζει ὁ Χριστός, ὅτι οὐχ ὡς οἱ ἐ‹ν› τῷ πλοίῳ,[1434] οὐδὲ ὡς ὁ Ναθαναὴλ *υἱὸν Θεοῦ*[1435] εἶπεν ‹ὡς ἕνα τῶν πολλῶν›, ἀλλὰ γνήσιον Υἱὸν τοῦ Πατρός. Διὰ τοῦτο δὲ καὶ τὸν ἀποκαλ‹ύ›ψαντα[1436] αὐτὸν Πατέρα δείκνυσιν ὁ Χριστός, ἵνα μή τις, διὰ τὸ εἶναι τὸν Πέτρον θερμὸν ἐραστὴν αὐτοῦ, φιλίας καὶ κολακείας ὑπολάβ‹ῃ›[1437] τὰ ῥήματα ἀλλὰ μὴ ἀποκαλύψεως τοῦ Πατρός.

> Μετὰ οὖν τὸ εἰπεῖν αὐτοὺς τὴν πεπλανημένην δόξαν τοῦ πλήθους, τότε καὶ αὐτοὺς ἐρωτᾷ, καὶ εὐθέως πρὸ πάντων ὁ Πέτρος, τὸ στόμα τῶν Ἀποστόλων, ὁ πανταχοῦ θερμός, ὁ τοῦ χοροῦ τῶν μαθητῶν κορυφαῖος, προπηδᾷ καὶ προλαμβάνει, καὶ φησίν, *σὺ εἶ ὁ Χριστός, ὁ Υἱὸς τοῦ Θεοῦ τοῦ ζῶντος*. διὰ τοῦτο δὲ αὐτὸν ὁ Χριστὸς μακαρίζει, ὅτι οὐχ ὡς οἱ ἐν τῷ πλοίῳ, οὐδὲ ὡς ὁ Ναθαναὴλ εἶπεν αὐτὸν υἱὸν Θεοῦ, ὡς ἕνα τῶν πολλῶν, ἀλλὰ γνήσιον Υἱὸν ὄντα τοῦ Πατρός, κατὰ ἀλήθειαν αὐτὸν ὡμολόγησεν, ὡς ἐκ τῆς αὐτοῦ προσελθόντα οὐσίας. διὰ τοῦτο δὲ καὶ τὸν ἀποκαλύψαντα αὐτῷ Πατέρα δείκνυσιν ὁ Χριστός, ἵνα μήτις διὰ τὸ εἶναι τὸν Πέτρον θερμὸν ἐραστὴν αὐτοῦ, φιλίας καὶ κολακείας ὑποπτεύσῃ τυγχάνειν τὰ ῥήματα, ἀλλὰ μᾶλλον δόγμα θεῖον τὰ εἰρημένα εἶναι πιστεύσῃ.[mcxlix]

1421 John, 20:30.
1422 Cod. ὃ.
1423 Cod. θεὅτιτος.
1424 Cod. γραμματοῖς.
1425 Cod. οὖτοι.
1426 Cod. ἡ.
1427 Cod. ἦν.
1428 Cod. πονηρείας ἀπήλλακτω.
1429 Cod. πονηρείας.
1430 Cod. εἰπεῖν.
1431 Cod. εὐθέος.
1432 Cod. καὶ φυσί.
1433 Matt. 16:16.
1434 Cf. Matt. 14:24-31.
1435 Cf. John, 1:48-50.
1436 Cod. ἀποκαλήψαντα.
1437 Cod. ὑπολάβει.

Διὰ τοῦτο καὶ ὁ Χριστός φ‹η›σι[1438] ὅτι ὥσπερ σὺ τοῦ *Ἰωνᾶ* υἱός, οὕτ‹ω›ς[1439] ἐγὼ τοῦ Πατρὸς τοῦ ἐμοῦ.

Διὰ τί δὲ εἶπεν, *ἐγὼ δέ σ‹οί› δ‹ώ›σω*[1440] *τὰς κλεῖς τῆς βασιλείας τῶν οὐρανῶν;* ‹Ὡς› δεικνύ‹ω›ν[1441] τὸ ὁμότ‹ι›μον[1442] καὶ ὁμοδύναμον τὸ πρὸς τὸν Πατέρα. Ὅτι *ὁ μὲν Πατήρ*, φ‹η›σί,[1443] ἔδωκέν σοι τὸ ἐμὲ γνῶναι, ἐγὼ δέ *σοι τὰς κλεῖς τῶν οὐρανῶν δ‹ώ›σω.*[1444]

Τίνος ἕνεκεν οὐκ αὐτὸς ἀποφαίνεται, οὐδὲ λέγει, ἐγώ εἰμι ὁ Χριστός, ἀλλὰ διὰ τῆς ἐρωτησέως τοῦτο κατασκευάζει, καὶ αὐτοὺς εἰσάγει ὁμολογοῦντας; ἐπειδὴ οὕτως καὶ αὐτῷ πρεπωδέστερον ἦν καὶ ἀναγκαῖον, καὶ ἐκείνους μᾶλλον ἐφείλκετο πρὸς τὴν πίστιν τῶν λεγομένων. διὰ τοῦτο καὶ ὁ Χριστὸς φησὶ πρὸς αὐτόν. ἐπειδήπερ ἐκήρυξάς μου τὸν Πατέρα, καὶ ἐγὼ τὸν γεγενηκότα σε ὀνομάζω, καὶ ὥσπερ σὺ τοῦ Ἰωνᾶ παῖς, οὕτως καὶ ἐγὼ τοῦ ἐμοῦ Πατρός, καὶ τῆς αὐτῆς οὐσίας τῷ γεγεννηκότι. τὸ δὲ *ἐπὶ τῇ πέτρᾳ ταύτῃ*, τὸν ἐπὶ τῇ πίστει, καὶ τῇ ὁμολογίᾳ δηλοῖ. καὶ ὅτιπερ πολλοὶ μέλλουσι πιστεύειν. ἀνίστησι δὲ αὐτοῦ τὸ φρόνημα, καὶ ποιμένα αὐτὸν ποιεῖ. καὶ *ὅτι πύλαι ᾅδου οὐ κατισχύσουσιν αὐτῆς*. εἰ δὲ ἐκείνης οὐ κατισχύσουσί, φησι, πολλῷ μᾶλλον ἐμοῦ. διὰ τί εἶπεν, *καὶ ἐγὼ δώσω σοι*; ὅτι ὁ μὲν Πατὴρ φησίν, ἔδωκέ σοι τὸ ἐμὲ γνῶναι, καὶ ἐγὼ δέ σοι τὰς κλεῖς τῶν οὐρανῶν δώσω. καὶ διὰ τούτου δεικνὺς τὸ ὁμότιμον καὶ ὁμοδύναμον τὸ πρὸς τὸν Πατέρα.[mcl]

Τὸ δὲ *ἐπὶ τὴν πέτραν ταύτην*,[1445] ἐπὶ τὴν πίστ‹ι›ν[1446] λέγει καὶ τὴν ὁμολογίαν.

Πέτραν δὲ καλεῖ τὴν εὐσεβῆ πίστιν, τὴν ἀληθῆ ὁμολογίαν.[mcli]

Ἀπὸ τότε ἤρξατο ὁ Ἰησοῦς δεικνύ‹ε›ιν[1447] *τοῖς μαθηταῖς ὅτι δεῖ αὐτὸν εἰς Ἱεροσόλυμα ἀπελθεῖν καὶ πολλὰ παθεῖν.*[1448] Ὅτε ἔπ‹η›ξεν[1449] ἐν αὐτοῖς τὸ δόγμα, ὅτε τὴν ἀρχὴν τῶν ἐθνῶν εἰσήγαγεν. Ἀλλ᾽ οὐδὲ ο‹ὕ›τως[1450] συν‹ῆ›καν,[1451] ἀλλὰ πολλῷ βέλτιον

1438 Cod. φυσὶ.
1439 Cod. οὗτος.
1440 Cod. σὺ δόσω.
1441 Cod. δεικνύον.
1442 Cod. ὁμότημον.
1443 Cod. φυσὶ.
1444 Cod. δόσω.
1445 Matt. 16:18-19.
1446 Cod. πίστην.
1447 Cod. δείκνυσιν.
1448 Matt. 16:21.
1449 Cod. ἔπιξεν.
1450 Cod. οὗτως.
1451 Cf. Luke, 9:45. Cod. σινῆκαν.

ἐνόμιζ‹ο›ν[1452] εἶναι τὸ ‹μὴ› παθεῖν αὐτόν. Διὰ τοῦτο πάλιν ὁ Πέτρος θερμὸς ὢν ἐρωτᾷ κατ' ‹ἰ›δίαν[1453] καί φ‹η›σιν·[1454] *ἵλε‹ώ›ς*[1455] *σοι Κύριε· οὐ μὴ ἔστ‹αι›*[1456] *σοι τοῦτο.*[1457]

> *Ἀπὸ τότε*, φησίν, *ἤρξατο ὁ Ἰησοῦς δεικνύειν τοῖς μαθηταῖς, ὅτι δεῖ αὐτὸν εἰς Ἱεροσόλυμα ἀπελθεῖν*, καὶ τὰ ἑξῆς. *ἀπὸ τότε*, ὅτε ἔπηξεν αὐτοῖς τὸ δόγμα. ὅτε τὴν ἀρχὴν τῶν ἐθνῶν εἰσήγαγεν. ἀλλ' οὐδὲ οὕτως συνίεσαν, καὶ πολλῷ βέλτιον ἐνόμιζον εἶναι τὸ μὴ ἀποθανεῖν αὐτόν. διὰ τοῦτο τῶν ἄλλων θορυβουμένων καὶ ἀπορούντων, πάλιν ὁ Πέτρος θερμὸς ὤν, μόνος τολμᾷ περὶ τούτων διαλεχθῆναι, καὶ οὐδὲ παρρησίᾳ, ἀλλὰ κατ' ἰδίαν λαβών. τουτέστιν τῶν λοιπῶν ἀποχωρίσας μαθητῶν, καὶ φησίν. *ἵλεώς σοι, Κύριε. οὐ μὴ ἔσται σοι τοῦτο.*[mclii]

Διατί δὲ ὁ ἀποκαλύψεως ἀξιωθεὶς σφάλλεται; Ὅτι περὶ τούτου οὐκ ἀπεκαλύφθη, ἀλλὰ καὶ τὸ πρῶτον οὐκ ‹ο›ἴκοθεν[1458] ἐφθέγξατο, ἀλλ' ἐκ τοῦ Πατρός. Ἵνα δ‹ε›ιχθῇ[1459] οὖν τοῦτο, διὰ τοῦτο καὶ κατέπεσεν.

> διὰ τί ὁ ἀποκαλύψεως τυχὼν καὶ μακαρισθείς, οὕτως ταχέως ἔπεσεν, καὶ ἐσφάλη, ὡς φοβηθῆναι αὐτοῦ τὸ πάθος; ἐπειδὴ οὐκ ἐδέξατο καὶ τὴν περὶ τούτου ἀποκάλυψιν. ὅθεν καὶ ἐκ τούτου μανθανόμενος, ὅτι οὐδὲ ἐκεῖνα οἴκοθεν ἐφθέγξατο, ἀλλ' ἐκ τῆς τοῦ Πατρὸς ἀποκαλύψεως.[mcliii]

| **129v** Τὸ δὲ *οὐ φρονεῖς τὰ τοῦ Θεοῦ ἀλλὰ τὰ τῶν ἀνθρώπων*,[1460] τοῦτο δηλοῖ. Τὸ πρᾶγμα ἐξετάζων οἷς ἠβούλ‹ε›το[1461] τὸ πάθος ἀκοῦσαι, οὐκ ᾔδει ὅτι ‹τοῦτο› ὑπὲρ τοῦ κόσμου ἐστὶ καὶ *εὐδοκία*[1462] τοῦ Πατρός ἐστι.

> τὸ δὲ *οὐ φρονεῖς τὰ τοῦ Θεοῦ, ἀλλὰ τὰ τῶν ἀνθρώπων*, τοῦτο δηλοῖ, ὅτι ἀνθρωπίνῳ λογισμῷ καὶ γηΐνῳ τὸ πρᾶγμα ἐξετάζων, ἐνόμιζεν αἰσχρὸν εἶναι αὐτῷ τὸ παθεῖν. καθαπτόμενος δὲ αὐτοῦ ὁ Χριστός, δείκνυσιν ὅτι οὐ τὸ παθεῖν τῆς τοῦ διαβόλου γνώμης ὑπάρχει.[mcliv]

1452 Cod. ἐνόμιζων.
1453 Cod. κατιδείαν.
1454 Cod. φυσίν.
1455 Cod. ἵλεός.
1456 *Cod.* ἔστε.
1457 Matt. 16:22.
1458 Cod. ικοθεν.
1459 Cod. διχθῇ.
1460 Matt. 16:23.
1461 Cod. ἠβούλητο.
1462 Cf. Matt. 3:17; 11:26; 12:18 (cf. Is. 42:1); 17:5; Mark, 1:11; Luke, 3:22; 10:21; 12:32; 2 Peter, 1:17.

Τότε ὁ Ἰησοῦς εἶπεν τοῖς μαθηταῖς.[1463] *Τότε*, πότε; Μετὰ τὸ ἐπιτιμηθῆναι τὸν Πέτρον. *Εἴ τις θέλει ὀπίσω μου ἐλθεῖν, ἀπαρνησά‹σθω›*[1464] ἑαυτὸν[1465] *καὶ ἀράτω τὸν σταυρὸν αὐτοῦ καὶ ἀκολουθήτω μοι.*[1466] Ὃ δὲ λέγει τοιοῦτόν[1467] ἐστιν. Σὺ Πέτρε λέγεις ὅτι *ἵλε‹ώ›ς*[1468] *σοι Κύριε, οὐ μὴ ἔσται σοι τοῦτο.*[1469] Ἐγὼ δέ σοι λέγω ὅτι οὐ μόνον ἐμὲ κ‹ω›λύειν[1470] ἐπιβλαβές σοι ἐστίν, ἀλλ᾽ οὐδὲ αὐτὸς σωθῆναι δυνήσῃ ἐάν μ‹ή›[1471] πρὸς τὸ ἀποθανεῖν ὑπάρχεις παρασκευασμένος. Τὸ δὲ *‹εἴ›*[1472] *τις θέλει* δηλ‹οῖ›[1473] ὅτι οὐ βι‹α›ζ‹ό›με‹νος›[1474] οὐδὲ ἀναγκάζων.

> μετὰ δὲ τὸ ἐπιτιμηθῆναι τὸν Πέτρον, βουλόμενος ὁ Εὐαγγελιστὴς δεῖξαι, τήν τε παρὰ τοῦ Πέτρου εἰρημένην ἀτοπίαν, καὶ τὸ κέρδος τὸ ἀπὸ τοῦ πάθους, οὐχ ἁπλῶς φησιν ὅτι εἶπεν ὁ Ἰησοῦς, ἀλλὰ προσέθηκε τὸ *τότε*, οὕτως λέγων. ὅτι *τότε ὁ Ἰησοῦς, εἶπεν τοῖς μαθηταῖς αὐτοῦ. εἴτις θέλει ὀπίσω μου ἐλθεῖν, ἀπαρνησάσθω ἑαυτόν*, καὶ τὰ ἑξῆς. ὃ δὲ λέγει τοιοῦτόν ἐστι. σύ μοι, ὦ Πέτρε, εἶπας, φησίν, ὅτι *ἵλεώς σοι Κύριε. οὐ μὴ ἔσται σοι τοῦτο.* ἐγὼ δέ σοι λέγω. ὅτι οὐ μόνον τὸ ἐμὲ κωλύειν καὶ τῷ ἐμῷ πάθει δυσχεραίνειν, ἐπιβλαβές σοι καὶ ὀλέθριον, ἀλλ᾽ ὅτι οὐδὲ σὺ αὐτὸς σωθῆναι δυνήσῃ, ἐὰν μὴ πρὸς τὸ ἀποθανεῖν παρεσκευασμένος ὑπάρχεις ἀεί. τὸ δὲ *εἴ τις θέλει*, δηλοῖ ὅτι οὐ βιαζόμενος οὐδὲ ἀναγκάζων, ἀλλ᾽ ἕκαστον κύριον τῆς ἑαυτοῦ προαιρέσεως ποιῶ.[mclv]

Τί δὲ ἐστὶ τὸ ἀπαρνήσασθαι; Ὥσπερ ἐάν τις ἀπαρνησάμενός τ‹ι›να[1475] κἂν μαστιζόμενον ἴδῃ, κἂν ἐπὶ θάνατον ἀγ‹ό›μενον[1476], οὐ βοηθεῖ οὐκ ἐπικλᾶτ‹αι›[1477], οὕτως βούλεται ἡμᾶς τοῦ σώματος καταφρονεῖν τοῦ ἑαυτῶν. Τὸ δὲ *ἀράτω τὸν σταυρὸν αὐτοῦ* δ‹η›λοῖ[1478] ὅτι οὐ μέχρι‹ς›[1479] ὕβρεων καὶ πληγῶν δεῖ ἀπαρνεῖσθαι ἑαυτόν, ἀλλὰ *μέχρι θανάτου,*[1480] καὶ το‹ύ›το‹υ›[1481] ἐπονειδίστου. Τοῦτο γὰρ ὁ *σταυρὸς* σημαίνει.

1463 Matt. 16:24.
1464 Cod. ἀπαρνησάτο.
1465 Cod. ἑ ἀυτον.
1466 Matt. 16:24.
1467 Cod. τοι οὗτον.
1468 Cod. ἤλεός.
1469 Matt. 16:22.
1470 Cod. κολύειν.
1471 Cod. μοι.
1472 Cod. ἤ.
1473 Cod. δειλῶν.
1474 Cod. βιἄζομε.
1475 Cod. τηνά.
1476 Cod. ἀγώμενον.
1477 Cod. ἐπίκλατε.
1478 Cod. δειλοὶ.
1479 Cod. μέχροι.
1480 Cf. Phil 2:8; 2:30.
1481 Cod. τοῦτο.

> τί δέ ἐστιν *ἀπαρνησάσθω ἑαυτόν*; ὅμοιον, ἐάν τις ἀπαρνησάμενος ὅν τινα οὖν, κἄν μαστιζόμενον ἴδῃ, κἄν δεσμούμενον καὶ ἐπὶ θάνατον ἀπαγόμενον, οὐ παρίσταται, οὐ βοηθεῖ, οὐκ ἐπικλᾶται, ... τὸ δὲ *ἀράτω τὸν σταῦρον* [sic] *αὐτοῦ*, δηλοῖ τὸ μέχρι πόσου ἀπαρνήσασθαι χρὴ ἑαυτόν. ἵνα γὰρ μὴ νομίσωμεν, ὅτι μέχρις ὕβρεως καὶ πληγῶν δεῖ ἀπαρνεῖσθαι ἑαυτόν, λέγει ὅτι μέχρι θανάτου, καὶ θανάτου τοῦ ἐπονειδίστου. τοῦτο γὰρ ὁ σταῦρος [sic] σημαίνει.[mclvi]

Τὸ δὲ *ἀκολουθήτω μοι*, τὴν σ‹ω›φροσύνην,[1482] τὴν ἐπιείκειαν καὶ πᾶσαν φιλοσοφίαν ἣν εἶχεν ὁ Χριστὸς ἀσπάζεσθαι παρακελεύεται. Ἔτι δὲ καὶ τοῦτο, ἵνα δι᾽ αὐτὸν πάσχωμεν.[1483]

> τὸ δὲ *ἀκολουθείτω μοι*, ἐμφαίνει, ὅτι ἐπειδὴ ἔστι πάσχοντά τινα μὴ ἀκολουθεῖν αὐτῷ, ὅτ᾽ ἂν μὴ δι᾽ αὐτὸν πάθῃ τίς. καὶ γὰρ λησταὶ καὶ λοιποὶ κακοῦργοι πολλὰ χαλεπὰ πάσχουσιν, προστίθησι τὴν ὑπόθεσιν, ἵνα δι᾽ αὐτὸν ὑπομένωμεν. ἔτι δὲ καὶ τοῦτο δηλοῖ τὸ ἀκολουθεῖν τῷ Χριστῷ, μὴ μόνον τὴν ἐν τοῖς διωγμοῖς ἔχειν ἀνδρίαν, ἀλλὰ καὶ σωφροσύνην καὶ ἐπιείκειαν, καὶ πᾶσαν ἐπιδείκνυσθαι φιλοσοφίαν.[mclvii]

> Καὶ γὰρ καὶ τοῦτο δηλοῖ τό, *Ἀκολουθείτω μοι*. ὥστε μὴ μόνον ἀνδρείαν τὴν ἐν τοῖς δεινοῖς, ἀλλὰ καὶ σωφροσύνην, καὶ ἐπιείκειαν, καὶ πᾶσαν ἐπιδείκνυσθαι φιλοσοφίαν. Τοῦτο γάρ ἐστιν ἀκολουθεῖν ὡς χρή, τὸ καὶ τῆς ἄλλης ἀρετῆς ἐπιμελεῖσθαι, καὶ τὸ δι᾽ αὐτὸν πάντα πάσχειν.[mclviii]

Ἔστι γὰρ καὶ δι᾽ ἄλλας προφάσεις πάσχειν τινά, ἀλλ᾽ οὐ τοῦτο θέλει. Τί δέ ἐστιν ‹τὸ *ὅ*›*ς*[1484] *ἐὰν θέλ‹ῃ›*[1485] *τὴν ψυχὴν αὐτοῦ σ‹ῶ›σαι*,[1486] *ἀπολέσει αὐτήν*;[1487] Τουτέστιν, ὅστις ἂν θελήσ‹η›[1488] διαφυλάξαι αὐτὴν ἐκ τῶν ὑπὲρ τῆς εὐ | **130r** σεβείας κινδύνων, οὗτος *ἀπολέσει αὐτὴν* ἐν τῇ μελλούσ‹ῃ›[1489] κολάσει.

> Τί ἐστιν *ὃς γὰρ ἂν θέλῃ τὴν ψυχὴν αὐτοῦ σῶσαι, ἀπολέσῃ αὐτήν*; περὶ τῆς παρὰ τὸ δέον σωτηρίας λέγει, τὴν ἐκ τῶν κινδύνων διαφυγήν ταύτην ἀπώλειαν ἐκάλεσεν, ὥσπερ οὖν καὶ τὴν ἐν τοῖς ὑπὲρ αὐτοῦ κινδύνοις γινομένην ἀπώλειαν σωτηρίαν ὠνόμασεν. *οὗτος γάρ*, φησιν, *εὑρήσει αὐτήν*, εἰς ζωὴν αἰώνιον. ἐκεῖνος δὲ *ἀπολέσει αὐτήν*, εἰς κόλασιν αἰώνιον.[mclix]

1482 Cod. σοφροσύνην.
1483 Cf. 1 Peter, 2:14.
1484 Cod. ὡς.
1485 Cod. θέλει.
1486 cod. σώσαι.
1487 Matt. 16:25.
1488 Cod. θελήσει.
1489 Cod. μελλούσει.

Ἢ τὸ ἔμπαλιν· *ὅστις*, φησ‹ί›,[1490] *θέλει τὴν ψυχὴν αὐτοῦ σῶσαι ἐν τῇ ἡμέρᾳ τῆς κρίσεως*,[1491] οὗτος ἀπολεσάτω αὐτὴν ἐν τῷ νῦν αἰῶνι, ἐν κόποις καὶ τοῖς ὑπὲρ αὐτοῦ κινδύνοις, ἵνα τις τοσοῦτον ἑαυτὸν βι‹ά›σ‹η›ται[1492] ἕως ἀπ‹ό›ληται[1493] ἐξ αὐτοῦ καὶ ἐξέλθ‹ῃ›[1494] ἀπ᾿ αὐτοῦ. *Ὅστις*, γάρ φησι, *ἀπολέσει* οὕτως ἐνταῦθα *τὴν ψυχὴν αὐτοῦ*, οὗτος *εἰς ζωὴν αἰώνιον* φυλάξει αὐτήν, ἤτ‹ο›ι εὑρ‹ή›σει.[1495]

Ὃς γὰρ ἂν θέλῃ τὴν ψυχήν. τὸ θέλον σῴζεσθαι καὶ ἀπόλλυσθαι πέφυκεν ἡ ψυχή. ἔστιν ἀμφίβολος ἡ λέξις. καὶ ὁ μὲν καταφρονήσας τῶν λόγων αὐτοῦ[mclx] ἀπόλλυσι *τὴν ψυχὴν* ἐκτὸς τῆς μακαριότητος. ὁ δὲ καταφρονῶν αὐτῆς καὶ ἕως θανάτου διὰ τὸν κατ᾿ εὐσέβειαν λόγον σώσει *αὐτήν*.[mclxi]

Ὃς γὰρ ἂν θέλῃ τὴν ψυχὴν αὐτοῦ σῶσαι, ἀπολέσει αὐτήν. Ἀμφίβολος ἡ πρώτη λέξις. ἔστι γὰρ ἀπ᾿ αὐτῆς καθ᾿ ἕνα μὲν τρόπον ταῦτα νοῆσαι. εἴ τις ὡς φιλόζωος καὶ οἰόμενος τὴν ἐνεστηκυῖαν εἶναι ζωὴν ἀγαθόν, περιέπει *τὴν* ἑαυτοῦ *ψυχὴν* πρὸς τὸ ἐν σαρκὶ ζῆν, φοβούμενος ἀποθανεῖν ὡς διὰ ‹τούτου› τοῦ θανάτου ἀπολέσων αὐτήν, οὗτος ἐν αὐτῷ τῷ θέλειν τὸν τρόπον τοῦτον σώζειν *τὴν ψυχὴν* ἑαυτοῦ *ἀπολέσει αὐτήν*, ἔξω ποιῶν αὐτὴν τῶν ὅρων τῆς μακαριότητος. εἰ δέ τις καταφρονῶν τοῦ ἐνεστηκότος ζῆν διὰ τὸν ἐμὸν λόγον πείσαντα περὶ αἰωνίου ζωῆς μέχρι θανάτου ἀγωνίζεσθαι ὑπὲρ ἀληθείας, ἀπόλλυσι *τὴν ἑαυτοῦ ψυχὴν* *** παραδιδοὺς αὐτὴν ὑπὲρ εὐσεβείας τῷ κοινότερον ὀνομαζομένῳ θανάτῳ, οὗτος, ὡς δι᾿ ἐμὲ ἀπολέσας *τὴν ψυχήν*, σώσει *αὐτὴν* μᾶλλον καὶ περιποιήσεται ***. καὶ καθ᾿ ἕτερον δὲ τρόπον οὕτως ἂν ἐκδεχοίμεθα τὸ ρητόν. εἴ τις νοήσας, ὅ τί ποτέ ἐστιν ἡ σωτηρία, βούλεται κομίσασθαι τὴν σωτηρίαν τῆς ἑαυτοῦ ψυχῆς, οὗτος ἀποταξάμενος τούτῳ τῷ βίῳ καὶ ἀρνησάμενος αὐτὸν καὶ ἄρας *τὸν σταυρὸν αὐτοῦ καὶ* ἀκολουθῶν *μοι* ἀπολλύτω τῷ κόσμῳ *τὴν ψυχὴν ἑαυτοῦ*. ἐμοῦ γὰρ ἕνεκεν καὶ πάσης μου τῆς διδασκαλίας ἀπολλὺς αὐτήν, τέλος τῆς τοιαύτης ἀπωλείας *** κομίσεται τὴν σωτηρίαν.[mclxii]

Μέλλει γὰρ ὁ υἱός του ἀνθρώπου ἔρχεσθαι ἐν τῇ δόξ‹ῃ τοῦ πατρὸς›[1496] αὐτοῦ, *καὶ τότε ἀποδώσει ἑκάστῳ* κατὰ τὰ ἔργα αὐτοῦ.[1497] Δόξαν αὐτοῦ λέγει τὴν ἐν τῇ μελλούσ‹ῃ›[1498] κρίσει, ἔπειτα δὲ καὶ τὴν ἐν τῇ μεταμορφώσει, ‹ἥ›τις[1499] καὶ τύπος ἦν τῆς μελλούσης ἐκείνης καὶ φοβερᾶς.

1490 Cod. φισί.
1491 2 Peter, 2:9; 3:7; cf. Matt. 10:15; 11:22&24; 12:36; 1 John:4:17.
1492 Cod. βιάσειτε.
1493 Cod. ἀπώληται.
1494 Cod. ἐξέλθει.
1495 Cod. ἤ τι εὑρίσει.
1496 Cod. δόξει.
1497 Matt. 16:27.
1498 Cod. μελλούσει.
1499 Cod. ἥ τις.

Καὶ μεθ᾽ ἡμέρας ἓξ παραλαμβάνει[1500] *ὁ Ἰησοῦς τὸν Πέτρον καὶ Ἰάκωβον καὶ Ἰωάννην, καὶ ἀναφέρει αὐτοὺς εἰς ὄρος ὑψηλὸν κατ᾽ ἰδίαν.*[1501] Ὁ Λουκᾶς δὲ μετὰ *ὀκτ‹ὼ›*[1502] λέγει ἀριθμὸν ἀριθμῶν καὶ τὰς ἄκρας (‹ᾗ›[1503] γοῦν καθ᾽‹ἣ›ν[1504] ἐφθέγξατο καὶ καθ᾽‹ἣ›ν[1505] αὐτοὺς ‹ἤ›γαγεν[1506] εἰς τὸ ὄρος), ὁ δὲ τὰς μεταξύ.

> Ἐγένετο δὲ μετὰ τοὺς λόγους τούτους ὡσεὶ ἡμέραι ὀκτώ. Ματθαῖος μὲν *ἓξ* λέγει μήτε τὴν ἡμέραν ἐν ᾗ ἐλέχθη μήτε τὴν ἐν ᾗ μετεβλήθη ψηφίσας, ἀλλὰ μόνας τὰς ἓξ τὰς μέσας. οὗτος δὲ ὅλας συνῆψεν. Ζητήσωμεν πῶς ὁ μὲν Λουκᾶς φησιν. *ἐγένοντο δὲ μετὰ τοὺς λόγους τούτους ὡσεὶ ἡμέραι ὀκτώ*, ὁ δὲ Μᾶρκος. *ὡσεὶ μεθ᾽ ἡμέρας ἕξ*. ὅσον ἐπὶ τῷ ρητῷ τῷ *ἐγένοντο ὡσεὶ ἡμέραι ὀκτώ*, ὁ Λουκᾶς μετρεῖ καὶ ταύτην τὴν ἡμέραν, [καὶ] ἐν ᾗ γίνεται, Μᾶρκος δὲ μετρεῖ τὰς μέσας μόνας, καὶ οὐκ ἔστι διαφωνία πρὸς τὸ ρητόν.[mclxiii]

> ἄλλος δὲ Εὐαγγελιστής, *μετὰ ὀκτὼ* λέγει. οὐκ ἐναντιούμενοι δὲ ἀλλήλοις τοῦτο εἶπον, ἀλλὰ καὶ σφόδρα συνᾴδοντες. ὁ μὲν γάρ, καὶ αὐτὴν τὴν ἡμέραν, καθ᾽ ἣν ἐφθέγξατο. κἀκείνην καθ᾽ ἣν ἀνήγαγεν εἶπεν. ὁ δέ, τὰς μεταξὺ τούτων εἶπεν μόνον.[mclxiv]

> Now it is asked how it can be that after *six* days he takes them and leads them *onto a mountain by themeselves*. For the evangelist Luke records the number *six*.[mclxv] But the answer is easy: here only the days in between are recorded, whereas there the first and last days are recorded.[mclxvi]

Διατί δὲ τούτους τοὺς τρεῖς λαμβάνει μόνους; Ὅτι τῶν ἄλλων ἦσαν ὑπερέχοντες·[1507] ὁ μὲν Πέτρος ἐκ τοῦ σφόδρα φιλεῖν, ὁ δὲ Ἰωάννης ἐκ τοῦ σφόδρα ‹ἀ›γα‹πᾶν›, ὁ δὲ Ἰάκωβος διὰ τὸ αὐτὸν εἶναι σφοδρὸν τοῖς Ἰουδαίοις καὶ θερμότερον τῶν λοιπῶν.

> διὰ τί δὲ τούτους τοὺς τρεῖς λαμβάνει; ἐπειδὴ οὗτοι τῶν ἄλλων ἦσαν ὑπερέχοντες. καὶ ὁ μὲν Πέτρος, ἐκ τοῦ σφόδρα φιλεῖν τὸν Χριστὸν ἐδήλου τὴν ὑπεροχήν, ὁ δὲ Ἰωάννης, ἐκ τοῦ σφόδρα φιλεῖσθαι. καὶ Ἰάκωβος δέ, ἀπὸ τῆς ἀποκρίσεως, ἧς ἀπεκρίθη μετὰ τοῦ ἀδελφοῦ λέγων, δυνάμεθα πιεῖν τὸ ποτήριον. οὐκ ἀπὸ τῆς φωνῆς δὲ μόνον, ἀλλὰ δὲ ἀπὸ τῶν ἔργων, τῶν τε ἄλλων, καὶ ἀφ᾽ ὧν ἐπλήρωσαν ἅπερ εἶπεν. οὕτω γὰρ ἦν σφοδρὸς καὶ βαρὺς τοῖς Ἰουδαίοις, ὡς καὶ τὸν Ἡρώδην ἐν τούτῳ νομίσαι χαρίζεσθαι τοῖς Ἰουδαίοις, εἰ ἐκεῖνον ἀνέλοι.[mclxvii]

1500 Cod. παραλαμβάννει.
1501 Matt. 17:1.
1502 Luke, 9:28. Cod. ὀκτῶ.
1503 Cod. ἢ.
1504 Cod. καθεῖν.
1505 Cod. καθεῖν.
1506 Cod. ἤγαγεν.
1507 Cod. ὑπερ ἔχοντες.

Οὐ‹κ›[1508] ἀναφέρει δὲ πάντας | **130v** ἵνα μὴ ἔχ‹ῃ›[1509] ὁ Ἰούδας εὔλογον ἀφορμήν. Οὐ γὰρ ‹ἦ›ν[1510] ἄξιος τῆς θέας ἐκείνης. Δι᾽αὐτὸν γὰρ καὶ τοὺς λοιποὺς ἀφ‹ῆ›κε.[1511]
Διὰ τί δὲ *μετὰ ἓξ ἡμέρας*; Ἵνα ἐν τῷ ἀριθμῷ τῶν ἡμερῶν ἐν ἐπιθυμίᾳ γέν‹ω›νται[1512] τῆς θέας ταύτης καὶ νήφωσιν. Ἀορίστως δὲ ἐλάλησεν ὁ Χριστός, ὅτι *εἰσί τινες*,[1513] ἵνα μὴ οἱ λοιποὶ ὡς παροφθέντες ἀγανακτ‹ή›σωσι.[1514]

> οὐκ ἀνάγει δὲ αὐτοὺς ὁ Χριστός, ἀλλὰ μετὰ ἓξ ἡμέρας. οὐδὲ τὰ ὀνόματα τῶν μελλόντων ἀνέρχεσθαι λέγει, ἀλλὰ μόνον ἀορίστως. ὅτι *εἰσὶ τινὲς τῶν ὧδε ἑστώτων, οἵτινες οὐ μὴ γεύσωνται θανάτου*, καὶ τὰ ἑξῆς. ἵνα μὴ ἀγανακτήσωσιν οἱ λοιποί, ὡς παροφθέντες. διὰ τοῦτο δὲ προλέγει, ἵνα ἐν τῷ ἀριθμῷ τῶν ἡμέρων τῆς ἐπιθυμίας ἐμπλησθέντες, οὕτως νηφούσῃ καὶ μεμεριμνημένῃ διανοίᾳ παραγένωνται.[mclxviii]

Τὸ ‹δὲ› *οὐ μὴ γεύσ‹ω›νται*[1515] *θανάτου ἕως ἂν ἴδωσι τὴν βασιλείαν τοῦ Θεοῦ*,[1516] διὰ[1517] τὴν μεταμόρφωσιν λέγει.

> Τὸ δὲ *οὐ μὴ γεύσονται θανάτου* εἴρηται μὲν καὶ περὶ τῶν ἀποστόλων, ὅτι *οὐ μὴ γεύσονται* τοῦ φυσικοῦ *θανάτου ἕως ἂν ἴδωσιν* διὰ τῆς μεταμορφώσεως τὴν εἰκόνα τῆς μελλούσης ἔσεσθαι τοῖς ἁγίοις λαμπρότητος.[mclxix]

Εἰ μὲν γὰρ εἶπεν *οὐκ ἐγεύσ‹α›ντ‹›*[1518] *θανάτου*, ἴσως περὶ Ἰωάννου ἐνομ‹ί›σαμεν[1519] ‹ἂν› τοῦτο λεχθῆναι, ὅτι μένει *ἕως τῆς συντελείας* ἵνα ἴδῃ τὴν δόξαν τῆς παρουσίας. Ἀλλ᾽ οὐκ ἔστι τοῦτο.
Διὰ τὶ Μωσ‹ῆ›ν[1520] καὶ Ἠλίαν εἰς μέσον ἄγει; Ὅτι ἔλεγον οἱ ὄχλοι, οἱ μὲν *ὅτι Ἠλίας ἐστίν*, οἱ δὲ ὅτι Ἰερεμίας ἐστίν.[1521] Διὰ τοῦτο ‹ἤ›γαγεν[1522] τὸν Ἠλίαν, δε‹ῖ›ξαι[1523] θέλων ὡς οὐκ ἔστιν Ἠλίας, ἀλλ᾽ ὁ Θεὸς τοῦ Ἠλία. Πάλιν, ἐπ‹ε›ιδ‹ὴ›[1524] παράνομον

1508 Cod. οὖς.
1509 Cod. ἔχει.
1510 Cod. ἦν.
1511 Cod. ἀφίκε.
1512 Cod. γένονται.
1513 Matt. 16:28; Mark, 9:1; Luke, 9:27.
1514 Cod. ἀγανακτίσωσι.
1515 Cod. γεύσονται.
1516 Matt. 16:28; Mark, 9:1; Luke, 9:27.
1517 Cod. διὰ δὲ.
1518 Cod. ἐγεύσονται.
1519 Cod. ἐνομήσαμεν.
1520 Cod. Μωσὶν.
1521 Matt. 16:14.
1522 Cod. ἤγαγεν.
1523 Cod. δείξαι.
1524 Cod. ἐπιδεῖ.

αὐτὸν ἐκάλουν, ἤγαγεν τὸν Μωσ‹ῆ›ν[1525] συ‹μ›μαρτυροῦντα,[1526] τὸν δὲ ᾿Ηλίαν καὶ ὡς ζηλωτήν. Δείκνυσι ὅτι ‹εἰ›[1527] ζηλωτής ἐστιν, ο‹ὐκ›[1528] ἂν ἦλθεν εἰ παρέβαινε Χριστὸς τὸν νόμον

> Τίνος ἕνεκεν Μωϋσῆν καὶ ῾Ηλίαν εἰς μέσον ἄγει; πρῶτον μέν, ἐπειδὴ ἔλεγον οἱ ὄχλοι, οἱ μὲν ῾Ηλίαν, οἱ δέ, ῾Ιερεμίαν, οἱ δέ, ἕνα τῶν προφητῶν αὐτὸν εἶναι. διὰ τοῦτο τοὺς κορυφαίους τῶν ᾿Αποστόλων ἄγει, ἵνα τὸ μέσον καὶ ἐντεῦθεν ἴδωσι τῶν δούλων καὶ τοῦ δεσπότου. δεύτερον δέ, ἐπειδὴ συνεχῶς ἐνεκάλουν τῷ Χριστῷ, ὡς παραβαίνοντι τὸν νόμον. ἵνα δείξῃ, εἴπερ ἤθελον λογίσασθαι οἱ ᾿Ιουδαῖοι, ὅτι, οὐδ᾿ ἂν Μωϋσῆς μέν, ὁ τὸν νόμον δεδωκώς, περιεῖδε πατούμενον αὐτὸν ὑπ᾿ αὐτοῦ, ὡς ἐνόμιζον ἐκεῖνον. καὶ οὐδ᾿ ἂν παρέστη αὐτῷ, ἢ ὑπήκουσεν. καὶ ῾Ηλίας δὲ ὑπὲρ τῆς δόξης τοῦ Θεοῦ ἐζήλωσεν. καὶ οὐκ ἄν, εἰ ἦν ἀντίθεος, Θεὸν σαυτὸν λέγων, μὴ ὢν ὅπερ ἔλεγεν, ἐθεράπευσεν ἂν αὐτὸν παραγενόμενος.[mclxx]

καὶ ἵνα μάθωσιν ὅτι *ἐξουσίαν ἔχει ζωῆς καὶ τοῦ θανάτου,*[1529] καὶ ἵνα δείξ‹ῃ›[1530] τοῦ σταυροῦ τὴν δόξαν καὶ παραμυθήσηται τοὺς μαθητὰς δεδοικότας τὸ πάθος καὶ ἀναστήσει αὐτῶν τὰ φρονήματα. Καὶ γὰρ ἐλάλουν, φησί,[1531] τὴν δόξαν[mclxxi] *αὐτοῦ ἣν ἔμελλε* τελεῖν εἰς *῾Ιερουσαλὴμ*[1532] (τουτέστι τὸ πάθος τοῦ σταυροῦ)· *συνελάλουν*[1533] δὲ τῷ Χριστῷ[1534] περὶ τῆς ἐ | **131r** ξόδου αὐτοῦ.

> τρίτην δέ, ἵνα μάθωσιν, ὅτι καὶ θανάτου καὶ ζωῆς τὴν ἐξουσίαν ἔχει, καὶ τῶν ἄνω καὶ κάτω κρατεῖ.[mclxxii] τέταρτον δέ, ἵνα δείξῃ τοῦ σταυροῦ τὴν δόξαν, καὶ παραμυθήσηται τὸν Πέτρον καὶ ἐκείνους, δεδοικότας τὸ πάθος, καὶ ἀναστήσει αὐτῶν τὰ φρονήματα. καὶ γὰρ *ἐλάλουν* φησί, *Μωϋσῆς καὶ ῾Ηλίας τὴν δόξαν ἣν ἔμελλε πληροῦν εἰς ῾Ιερουσαλήμ.* τουτέστι τὸ πάθος καὶ τὸν σταυρόν. οὕτω γὰρ αὐτὰ καλοῦσιν, τουτέστι δόξαν ἀεί.[mclxxiii]

Καὶ ὁ μὲν Μωσῆς ἔλεγεν· *ἄκουε* ᾿Ιερουσαλὴμ[1535] νοητῶς (αἰσθητῶς γὰρ ἀκούειν οὐ δύναται[1536]) οὗτός ἐστιν ἡ τῶν ἀνθρώπων ζωή, ὃν ἐγὼ εἶπον *ὄψεσθ‹ε›*[1537] *τὴν ζωὴν ἡμῶν κρεμαμένην*[1538] *ἀπέναντι τῶν ὀφθαλμῶν ὑμῶν*·[1539] καὶ πάλιν, *προφήτην ὑμῖν*

1525 Cod. Μωσὶν.
1526 Cod. συνμαρτυροῦντα.
1527 Cod. ἢ.
1528 Cod. οὖσ.
1529 Wisdom of Solomon, 16:13.
1530 Cod. δείξει.
1531 Cod. φησίν.
1532 Cf. Luke, 9:31.
1533 Luke, 9:30.
1534 Matt. 17:2.
1535 Cf. Deut. 4:1; 5:1; 6:4; 9:1; 12:28; 20:3; 27:9. Actually, the expression is, ἄκουε, Ισραήλ.
1536 Cod. δύνατε.
1537 Cod. ὄψεσθαι.
1538 Cod. κρεμμαμένην.
1539 Cf. Deut. 28:66: καὶ ἔσται ἡ ζωή σου κρεμαμένη ἀπέναντι τῶν ὀφθαλμῶν σου.

ἀναστήσει Κύριος ὁ Θεὸς ἐκ τῶν ἀδελφῶν ὑμῶν,[1540] καὶ Ἠλίας οὗτός ἐστιν ὃν ἐγὼ ἐν αὔρᾳ λεπτῇ ἐθεασάμην.[1541] Καὶ ἕτερ‹α›[1542] πλείονα εἰκὸς λέγειν αὐτούς.
Διὰ τί εἶπεν ὁ Πέτρος *καλὸν ἡμᾶς ‹ὧ›δε*[1543] *εἶναι;*[1544] Ἐπειδὴ ἤκουσε ‹ὅτι› *δεῖ αὐτὸν εἰς Ἱερουσαλὴμ ἀπελθεῖν καὶ πολλὰ παθεῖν*[1545] καὶ ἐπεὶ ε‹ἶ›δεν[1546] τὸ ὄρος καὶ τὴν ἐρημίαν, ὑπὸ φόβου κρατούμενος, ἐβούλετο αὐτὸν ἐκεῖ εἶναι διηνεκῶς. Ἔτι δὲ καὶ τὸν Ἠλίαν καὶ τὸν Μωσ‹ῆ›ν[1547] ἰδὼν ἐθάρ‹ρη›σεν·[1548] ὅτι ὁ μὲν *πῦρ κατήγαγεν ἐκ τοῦ οὐρανοῦ,*[1549] ὁ δὲ *εἰς τὸν γνόφον* εἰσελθὼν Θεῷ διελέγετο,[1550] καὶ ‹διὰ τοῦτο› οὐ φοβηθησόμεθα ‹ἐνταῦθα ὄντες›.

> Διὰ τί εἶπεν ὁ Πέτρος, *καλόν ἐστιν ἡμᾶς ὧδε εἶναι;* ἐπειδήπερ ἤκουσεν, ὅτι δεῖ εἰς τὰ Ἱεροσόλυμα αὐτὸν ἀπελθεῖν καὶ παθεῖν. φοβούμενός τι καὶ τρέμων ὑπὲρ αὐτοῦ. εἶδεν δὲ ὄρος, καὶ πολλὴν τὴν ἀναχώρησιν καὶ τὴν ἐρημίαν. διὰ τοῦτο βούλεται αὐτὸν ἐκεῖ εἶναι διηνεκῶς. διό, καὶ σκηνῶν μέμνηται. ἔτι δὲ καὶ τοῦτο λογισάμενος, ὅτι Μωϋσῆς πάρεστι καὶ Ἠλίας. Μωϋσῆς ὁ εἰς τὸν γνόφον ἐλθών, καὶ τῷ Θεῷ διαλεχθείς. ἡμῖν δὲ ὁ ἐπὶ τοῦ ὄρους πῦρ κατενεγκών, καὶ διὰ τοῦτο οὐ φοβηθησόμεθα ἐνταῦθα ὄντες. τοῦτο δὲ ἔλεγεν, ὡς θερμὸς ἐραστὴς τοῦ Χριστοῦ. εἰ γὰρ καὶ μὴ ἐξητασμένος ὁ τρόπος ἦν τῶν ῥημάτων, ἀλλ' ὅμως πολλῆς θερμότητος γέμοντος. οὕτως καὶ περιεκαίετο τοῦ Χριστοῦ. εἰ δὲ *μὴ ᾔδει τί ἐλάλει*, καθὼς ὁ Λουκᾶς φησί.[mclxxiv]

Τὸ δὲ *‹β›ε‹β›αρημέν‹οι› ‹ἦ›σαν ‹ὕ›πνῳ*[1551] τοῦτο δηλοῖ· ὅτι καθάπερ ὀφθαλμοὶ ἐξ ὑπερβαλλούσης σκοτοῦνται λαμπηδόνος, οὕτω καὶ οὗτοι ἔπαθον. Οὐ γὰρ δὴ νὺξ ἦν, ἀλλ' ἡμέρα. Τῆς γὰρ θεϊκῆς αὐγῆς τὸ ὑπερόγκον θεασάμενοι ἐβαρήθησαν τὴν τῶν ὀφθαλμῶν ἀσθενείᾳ.

> [Ὕπνον ἐνταῦθά φησι τὸν πολὺν κάρον τὸν ἀπὸ τῆς ὄψεως. καθάπερ γὰρ ὀφθαλμοὶ ἐξ ὑπερβαλλούσης σκοτοῦνται λαμπηδόνος, οὕτω καὶ οὗτοι τότε ἔπαθον. οὐ γὰρ δὴ νὺξ ἀλλ' ἡμέρα, καὶ τὸ τῆς ‹αὐγῆς› τῆς θεϊκῆς ὑπέρογκον ἐβάρει τὴν τῶν ὀφθαλμῶν ἀσθένειαν.][mclxxv]

> τὸ δὲ *βεβαρημένοι ἦσαν ὕπνῳ*, τοῦτο δηλοῖ, ὅτι πολλῷ κατείχοντο κάρῳ τῷ ἀπὸ τῆς ὄψεως αὐτοῖς ἐκείνοις γεγενημένῳ. καθάπερ γὰρ ὀφθαλμοὶ ἐξ ὑπερβαλλούσης

1540 Cf. Deut. 18:5: προφήτην ἐκ τῶν ἀδελφῶν σου ὡς ἐμὲ ἀναστήσει σοι κύριος ὁ θεός σου.
1541 3 Kings (1 Kings in Masoretic text), 19:12: καὶ μετὰ τὸ πῦρ φωνὴ αὔρας λεπτῆς, κακεῖ κύριος.
1542 Cod. ἕτερον.
1543 Cod. ὅδε.
1544 Matt. 17:4; Mark, 9:5; Luke, 9:33.
1545 Matt. 16:21; cf. 17:12. Cf. Mark, 8:31; Luke, 9:22; 17:25.
1546 Cod. εἴδεν.
1547 Cod. Μωσῖν.
1548 Cod. ἐθάρισεν.
1549 3 Kings (1 Kings in Masoretic text), 18:38; 4 Kings (1 Kings in Masoretic text), 1:12.
1550 Ex. 20:21; Ecclesiasticus, 45:5.
1551 Luke, 9:32.

> σκοτοῦνται λαμπηδόνος, οὕτως καὶ οὗτοι τότε ἔπαθον. οὐ γὰρ δὴ νύξ, ἀλλ' ἡμέρα καὶ τὸ τῆς αὐγῆς τῆς θεϊκῆς ὑπέρογκον, ἐβάρει τὴν τῶν ὀφθαλμῶν ἀσθένειαν.[mclxxvi]

Διὰ τί δὲ ἐκ τῆς νεφέλης φωνὴν ἀφίησιν ὁ Πατήρ; Ὅτι ο‹ὕ›τ‹ω›ς[1552] εἴωθε φαίνεσθαι ὁ Θεός. *Νεφέλ‹η›*,[1553] γάρ φ‹η›σ‹ι›,[1554] *καὶ γνόφος κύκλῳ αὐτοῦ.*[1555] Καὶ πάλιν· *ὁ τιθεὶς νέφ‹η›*[1556] *τὴν ἐπίβασιν αὐτοῦ.*[1557] ‹Ἵ›ν‹α›[1558] οὖν πιστεύωσιν ὅτι | **131v** ἀπὸ τοῦ Πατρὸς ἡ *φωνή*, διὰ τοῦτο ἀπὸ τῆς νεφέλης ‹ἠ›νέχθη.[1559] *Νεφέλη δὲ φωτειν‹ή›*[1560] ἦν ὅτι οὐκ ἐβούλετο φοβ‹ῆ›σαι[1561] ἀλλὰ διδάξαι.[1562] Ὅπου γὰρ *ἀπ‹ει›λή, σκοτειν‹ή›*[1563] ἐστιν, ὥσπερ ἐν τῷ ὄρει Σιν‹ᾷ›.[1564] Διὰ τοῦτο δὲ ἡ φων‹ὴ›[1565] ἠνέχθη μετὰ τὸ ἀφανεῖς ‹γενέσθαι› Μωϋσῆν καὶ Ἠλίαν, ἵνα φανῇ ὅτι οὐ περὶ ἑνὸς τῶν δύο λέγει, ἀλλὰ περὶ τοῦ Χριστοῦ μόνο‹υ›.[1566] Οὐ τὸν Χριστὸν δὲ μόνον ὑπέλαβεν ‹ἡ› *νεφέλ‹η›*,[1567] ‹ἀλλὰ πάντας,› ἵνα μὴ νομ‹ι›σθῇ[1568] ὅτι ὁ Χριστὸς τὴν φωνὴν ἐκείνην ἀφ‹ῆ›κεν.[1569] Ἀγαπητὸν δὲ αὐτὸν υἱὸν καλεῖ καὶ διὰ τὸ φύσει ἀγαπητὸν αὐτὸν[1570] εἶναι τῷ Πατρί καὶ διὰ τὸν Πέτρον. Ὅτι κἂν μυριάκις αὐτὸν ἀγαπᾷς, οὐ φιλεῖς αὐτὸν ἴσον ἐμο‹ί›.[1571] ‹Εἰ› ο‹ὖ›ν[1572] φιλεῖται παρ' ἐμοῦ, μὴ φοβοῦ τὸ πάθος· ἴσος γάρ μου ἐστί.[mclxxvii]

Τὸ δὲ *ἐν ᾧ ηὐδόκησα*, τουτέστιν ἐν ᾧ ἠθέλησα, τὴν σωτηρίαν τοῦ κόσμου γενέσθαι ‹δηλοῖ›. Ὥστε κἂν σταυρωθ‹ῆ›ναι[1573] θέλει, μὴ κωλ‹ύ›σῃς·[1574] ἐγὼ ‹γὰρ› ἠθέλησα.

1552 Cod. οὗτος.
1553 Cod. νεφέλει.
1554 Cod. φυσί.
1555 Psalm 96:2.
1556 cod. νέφει.
1557 Psalm 103:3.
1558 Cod. ἦν.
1559 Cod. ἠνέχθη.
1560 Cod. φωτεινί.
1561 Cod. φοβήσαι.
1562 Cf Ex. 13:21-22; 14:19&24; 16:10; 19:16; 24:15; etc.
1563 Cod. ἀπηλή. σκοτηνί.
1564 Cod. σινὰ.
1565 Cod. φωνί.
1566 Cod. μόνον.
1567 Cod. εἴ νεφέλει.
1568 Cod. νομησθῇ.
1569 Cod. ἀφήκεν.
1570 Cod. αὐτὸν αὐτὸν.
1571 Cod. ἐμοῦ.
1572 Cod. Ιοὺν.
1573 Cod. σταυρωθήναι.
1574 Cod. κωλήσης.

Διατὶ εἰς μὲν τὸν Ἰορδάνην τῆς φωνῆς γενομένης ἔλεγον βροντὴν γεγονέναι[1575] καὶ ὄχλου τοσοῦτου ὄντος οὐδεὶς κατέπεσεν *ἐπὶ πρόσωπον*,[1576] νῦν δὲ ἐν τῷ ὄρει καταπλαγέντες τοῦτο ἔπαθον; Ἐπ‹ε›ιδ‹ὴ›[1577] καὶ ἔρημος καὶ ὕψος καὶ καὶ ἡσυχία ‹ἦ›ν[1578] πολλή, καὶ μεταμόρφωσις φρίκης γέμουσα, καὶ φῶς ἄκρατον καὶ *νεφέλη* ἐκ | **132r** τεταμένη.[1579] ἅπερ ἅπαντα εἰς πολλὴν αὐτοὺς ἀγωνίαν ‹ἐ›νέβαλεν,[1580] ὡς καταπεσόντας προσκυνῆσαι. Διὰ τοῦτο δὲ αὐτ‹οῖς›[1581] ἐνετείλατ‹ο›[1582] *μηδενὶ* τοῦτο ‹εἰ›πεῖν[1583] *ἕως* ἂν *ἐκ νεκρῶν ἀναστῇ*.[1584] Ἐπ‹ε›ιδ‹ὴ›[1585] ὅσῳ περὶ αὐτοῦ ἐλέγετο μ‹εί›ζονα[1586] τοσούτῳ δ‹υ›σπαραδεκτοτέρα ‹ἦ›ν[1587] τοῖς πολλοῖς.

[φθέγγεται μὲν οὖν ὁ πατὴρ ἐκ τῆς νεφέλης. οὕτω γὰρ ἀεὶ φαίνεται ὁ θεός. νεφέλη γὰρ καὶ γνόφος κύκλῳ αὐτοῦ, καὶ κάθηται ἐπὶ νεφέλης κούφης,[1588] καὶ ‹πάλιν› ὁ τιθεὶς νέφει νέφη τὴν ἐπίβασιν αὐτοῦ καὶ νεφέλη ὑπέλαβεν αὐτὸν[1589] καὶ ὡς υἱὸς ἀνθρώπου ἐρχόμενος ἐπὶ τῶν νεφελῶν.[1590] Ἵν' οὖν πιστεύωσιν ὅτι ἀπὸ θεοῦ φωνὴ φέρεται ἐκεῖ, ἔρχεται καὶ νεφέλη νῦν φωτεινή. ὅταν μὲν γὰρ ἀπειλῇ, καὶ σκοτεινὴν δείκνυσιν ὥσπερ ἐπὶ τῷ Σινᾷ, ἐνταῦθα δέ, ἐπειδὴ οὐ φοβῆσαι ἐβούλετο ἀλλὰ διδάξαι, νεφέλη φωτεινή. εἶτα ἵνα δειχθῇ ὅτι περὶ ἑνὸς τῶν τριῶν ἐγένετο, ἐκποδὼν ἐγένοντο οἱ τοιοῦτοι. καὶ τί φησιν ἡ φωνή; οὗτός ἐστιν ὁ υἱός μου ὁ ἀγαπητός, ἐν ᾧ ηὐδόκησα.[1591] εἰ δὲ ἀγαπητός, μὴ φοβοῦ Πέτρε. οὐδεὶς ὃν ἀγαπᾷ προΐεται. εἰ δυνατὸς ὁ θεός, δῆλον ὅτι καὶ ὁ υἱός, ἐν ᾧ ηὐδόκησα. οὐ γὰρ ἐπειδὴ ἐγέννησε μόνον φιλεῖ, ἀλλ' ἐπειδὴ ἴσος αὐτῷ καὶ ὁμογνώμων κατὰ πάντα. ὥστε διπλοῦν τὸ φίλτρον αὐτοῦ ἀκούετε, κἂν σταυρωθῆναι (φησὶ) βουληθῇ, μὴ ἀντιπέσητε. ταῦτα ἀκούσαντες κατεπλάγησαν. καίτοι πρὸ τούτου ἠνέχθη ἡ φωνὴ ἐπὶ τοῦ Ἰορδάνου καὶ ὄχλος παρῆν,[1592] καὶ οὐδεὶς τοιοῦτον ἔπαθεν, ἀλλ' ἐκεῖ θόρυβος ἦν πολύς. καὶ μετὰ ταῦτα πάλιν, ὅτε καὶ βροντὴν ἔλεγον γεγονέναι,[1593] οὐδὲ τότε τοιοῦτον οὐδὲν ὑπέμειναν.

πῶς οὖν ἐν τῷ ὄρει ἔπεσον;

1575 Cf. Matt. 3:16-17; Mark, 1:10-11; Luke, 3:21-22.
1576 Matt. 17:6.
1577 Cod. ἐπὶ δεὶ.
1578 Cod. ἡσυχεία ἣν.
1579 Cod. ἐκτεταγμένη.
1580 Cod. ἀνέβαλεν.
1581 Cod. αὐτὰ.
1582 Cod. ἐνετείλατω.
1583 Cod. ἠπεῖν.
1584 Matt. 17:9.
1585 Cod. ἐπὶ δεῖ.
1586 Cod. μήζονα.
1587 Cod. δῆς παράδεκτότερα ἣν.
1588 Is. 19:1.
1589 Acts, 1:9.
1590 Matt. 24:30; 26:64; cf. Daniel, 7:13.
1591 Matt. 17:5; cf. 2 Peter 1:17.
1592 Cf. Luke, 3:21 ff.
1593 Cf. John, 12:29.

ὅτι καὶ ἐρημία καὶ ὕψος καὶ ἡσυχία καὶ μεταμόρφωσις φρίκης γέμουσα καὶ φῶς ἄκρατον καὶ νεφέλη ἐκτεταμένη ‹ἃ› καὶ εἰς πολλὴν ἀγωνίαν ἐνέβαλεν. καὶ πανταχόθεν ἔκπληξις συνήγετο, καὶ ἔπεσον φοβηθέντες ὁμοῦ καὶ προσκυνοῦντες. ὥστε δὲ μὴ ἐπὶ πολὺ τὸ δέος μεῖναν ἐκβάλοι αὐτῶν τὴν μνήμην, εὐθέως ἔλυσεν αὐτῶν τὴν ἀγωνίαν καὶ ἐντέλλεται αὐτοῖς μηδενὶ τοῦτο εἰπεῖν, ἕως ἂν ἐκ νεκρῶν ἀναστῇ.

ὅσῳ γὰρ μείζονα ἐλέγετο περὶ αὐτοῦ, τοσούτῳ δυσπαραδεκτότερα ἦσαν τοῖς τότε, καὶ τὸ σκάνδαλον δὲ τὸ ἀπὸ τοῦ σταυροῦ[mclxxviii] ἐπετείνετο μᾶλλον ἐντεῦθεν.[mclxxix] τί οὖν; μετὰ ταῦτα οὐκ ἔμελλον σκανδαλίζεσθαι; οὐδαμῶς. τὸ γὰρ ζητούμενον ὁ πρὸ τοῦ σταυροῦ καιρὸς ἦν. μετὰ γὰρ ταῦτα καὶ πνεύματος ἁγίου κατηξιώθησαν καὶ τὴν ἀπὸ τῶν σημείων φωνὴν εἶχον συνηγοροῦσαν αὐτοῖς, καὶ πάντα ὅσα ἔλεγον λοιπὸν εὐπαράδεκτα ἦν, σάλπιγγος λαμπρότερον ‹τῶν πραγμάτων› ἀνακηρυττόντων αὐτοῦ τὴν ἰσχύν.][mclxxx]

πότε οὖν *ἀπήγγειλαν*; μετὰ τὴν ἀνάληψιν, μετὰ τὴν τοῦ πνεύματος παρουσίαν. τότε γὰρ ἐπλήσθησαν παρρησίας καὶ πνεύματος κατηξιώθησαν καὶ τὴν ἀπὸ τῶν σημείων εἶχον φωνὴν συνηγοροῦσαν αὐτοῖς, καὶ πάντα ὅσα ἔλεγον λοιπὸν εὐπαράδεκτα ἦν.[mclxxxi]

Τίνος ἕνεκεν ἐκ τῆς νεφέλης φωνὴν ἀφίησιν ὁ Πατήρ; ἐπειδὴ οὕτως ἀεὶ φαίνεται ὁ Θεός. *νεφέλη γάρ*, φησι, *καὶ γνόφος, κύκλῳ αὐτοῦ*. καὶ πάλιν. ὅτι *θεὶς νέφη τὴν ἐπίβασιν αὐτοῦ*. καὶ *νεφέλη ὑπέλαβεν αὐτόν, ἀπὸ τῶν ὀφθαλμῶν αὐτῶν*, καὶ *ὡς υἱὸς ἀνθρώπου ἐρχόμενος ἐπὶ τῶν νεφελῶν*. ἵνα οὖν πιστεύσωσιν, ὅτι παρὰ τοῦ Θεοῦ ἡ φωνὴ φέρεται. διὰ τοῦτο ἀπὸ τῆς νεφέλης ἠνέχθη. νεφέλη δὲ φωτεινή, ἐπειδὴ φοβῆσαι οὐκ ἐβούλετο, ἀλλὰ διδάξαι. ὅπου γὰρ ἀπειλήν, σκοτεινὴν δείκνυσιν, ὥσπερ ἐν τῷ Σινᾶ. διὰ τοῦτο δὲ ἡ φωνὴ ἠνέχθη, μετὰ τὸ ἀφανεῖς γενέσθαι Μωϋσῆν καὶ Ἠλίαν, ἵνα δειχθῇ ὅτι οὐ περὶ ἑνὸς τῶν δύο ἐλέχθη, ἀλλὰ περὶ τοῦ Χριστοῦ μόνον. οὐ τὸν Χριστὸν δὲ μόνον ὑπέλαβεν ἡ νεφέλη, ἀλλὰ πάντας. ἵνα μὴ νομισθῇ ὅτι ὁ Χριστὸς ἀφῆκε τὴν φωνὴν ἐκείνην. *ἀγαπητὸν δὲ υἱὸν* αὐτὸν εἶπεν, διὰ τὸν Πέτρον. ὃ δὲ λέγει, τοιοῦτόν ἐστιν. ὅτι κἂν μυριάκις αὐτὸν φιλεῖς, οὐ φιλεῖς αὐτὸν τοῦ γεγεννηκότος ἶσον. εἰ οὖν φιλεῖται παρ᾽ ἐμοῦ, φησίν, μὴ φοβοῦ τὸ πάθος. καὶ γὰρ ἴσος μου ἐστὶ κατὰ πάντα, καὶ ἰσογνώμων. τὸ δὲ *ἐν ᾧ εὐδόκησα*, δηλοῖ, ἐφ᾽ ᾧ ἀναπαυόμενος, ᾧ ἀρέσκομαι, διὰ τὸ κατὰ πάντα ἐξισῶσθαι αὐτὸν πρός με μετὰ ἀκριβείας. τὸ δὲ *αὐτοῦ ἀκούετε*, σημαίνει, ὅτι κἂν σταυρωθῆναι βουληθῇ, μὴ ἀντιπέσῃς. Διὰ τί εἰς μὲν τὸν Ἰορδάνην ἐνεχθείσης τῆς φωνῆς, καὶ ὄχλου τοσούτου παρόντος, καὶ μετὰ ταῦτα πάλιν, ὅτε βροντὴν ἔλεγον γεγονέναι, οὐδεὶς κατέπεσεν ἐπὶ πρόσωπον. νῦν δὲ ἐν τῷ ὄρει καταπλαγέντες, τοῦτο ἔπαθον; ἐπειδὴ καὶ ἔρημος καὶ ὑψηλός, καὶ ἡσυχία ἦν πολλή, καὶ μεταμόρφωσις φρίκης γέμουσα, καὶ φῶς ὅρατον, καὶ νεφέλη ἐκτεταμένη. ἅπερ ἅπαντα, εἰς πολλὴν αὐτοὺς ἀγωνίαν ἐνέβαλεν, ὥστε καταπεσόντας, προσκυνῆσαι. διὰ τοῦτο δὲ ἐνετείλατο αὐτοῖς, μὴ εἰπεῖν τοῦτο τινί, ἕως οὗ ἐκ νεκρῶν ἀναστῇ. ἐπειδὴ ὅσῳ μείζονα διελέγετο περὶ αὐτοῦ, τοσούτῳ δυσπαραδεκτοτέρα ἦν τοῖς πολλοῖς τότε.[mclxxxii]

Μετὰ δὲ τὴν ἀνάστασιν, ὡς ἰδὼν ὁ Χριστὸς ὅτι πιστεῦσαι ἔχουσιν,[mclxxxiii] προστάσσει εἰπεῖν.

Καὶ ἐπ‹η›ρώτ‹η›σαν[1594] *αὐτόν· τί οὖν οἱ γραμματ‹ε›ῖς*[1595] *λέγουσι‹ν› ὅτι Ἠλίαν δεῖ ἐλθεῖν πρῶτον;*[1596] Αἱ γραφαὶ δύο λέγουσι ‹προδρόμους› τοῦ Χριστοῦ παρουσίας· εἷς μὲν

1594 Cod. ἐπιρωτισαν.
1595 Cod. γραμματοῖς.
1596 Matt. 17:10.

τῆς δευτέρας, πρόδρομον λέγουσιν τὸν Ἠλίαν, τῆς δὲ προτέρας τὸν Ἰωάννην, ὃν καὶ Ἠλίαν[1597] ὁ Χριστὸς καλεῖ.[mclxxxiv] Οὐχ ὅτι Ἠλίας ἦν, ἀλλ᾽ ὅτι τὴν διακονίαν ἀνεπλήρωσεν τοῦ Ἠλία. Καὶ οἱ γραμματ‹ε›ῖς[1598] ταῦτα συγχ‹έ›οντες[1599] καὶ διαστρέψαντες, τῆς δευτέρας ἐμνημόνευσ‹αν›[1600] μόνης καὶ πρὸς τὸν δῆμον ἔλεγον· ‹εἰ›[1601] ο‹ὗ›τος[1602] ἐστὶν ὁ Χριστός, ἔδει τὸν Ἠλίαν ἐλθεῖν, ἤγουν προλαβεῖν. Αὐτὸς δὲ πρὸς τοὺς μαθητάς· *Ἠλίας μὲν ἔρχετ‹αι›,*[1603] *καὶ ἀπο* | **132v** *καταστήσει πάντα.*[1604] Πο‹ῖα›;[1605] Ἅπερ ὁ προφήτης Μαλαχίας λέγει· *ἀποστελῶ* γάρ φησι *Ἠλίαν τὸν Θεσβ‹ί›την,*[1606] *ὃς ἀποκαταστήσει καρδίαν πατρὸς πρὸς υἱόν.*[1607] Ἐπ‹ε›ιδ‹ὴ›[1608] γὰρ πατέρες τῶν ἀποστόλων ‹ἦσαν οἱ› Ἰουδαῖοι, λέγει ὅτι κατὰ τῶν ἀποστόλων τὴν πίστ‹ι›ν[1609] μεταποιήσει τὰς καρδίας αὐτῶν εἰς τὸ πιστεῦσαι τ‹ῷ› Χριστ‹ῷ›,[1610] ἵνα μὴ ἀπόλ‹ω›νται[1611] ἄρδην ἅπαντες παραγενομένου ἐν τ‹ῇ›[1612] δευτέρᾳ αὐτοῦ παρουσίᾳ.

> αἱ μὲν γὰρ γραφαί, δύο λέγουσι τοῦ Χριστοῦ παρουσίας... . καὶ οἱ προφῆται δέ, ἑκατέρας μέμνηνται. τῆς μέντοι δευτέρας πρόδρομον λέγουσι τὸν Ἠλίαν ἔσεσθαι. τῆς δὲ προτέρας, Ἰωάννης ἐγένετο. ὃν καὶ Ἠλίαν ὁ Χριστὸς καλεῖ.[mclxxxv] οὐκ ἐπειδὴ Ἠλίας ἦν, ἀλλ᾽ ἐπειδὴ τὴν διακονίαν ἐπλήρωσεν τοῦ Ἠλία. οἱ γραμματεῖς οὖν ταύτας συγχέοντες καὶ διαστρέφοντες, τῆς δευτέρας ἐμνημόνευον μόνον πρὸς τὸν δῆμον, καὶ ἔλεγον, εἰ οὗτός ἐστιν ὁ Χριστός, ἔδει τὸν Ἠλίαν προλαβεῖν. αὐτὸς δέ φησι πρὸς τοὺς μαθητάς. *Ἠλίας μὲν ἔρχεται, καὶ ἀποκαταστήσει πάντα.* ποῖα πάντα; ἅπερ ὁ προφήτης λέγει Μαλαχίας. *ἀποστελῶ γὰρ ὑμῖν Ἠλίαν τὸν Θεσβίτην. ὃς ἀποκαταστήσει καρδίαν πατρὸς πρὸς υἱόν.* ἐπειδὴ γὰρ πατέρες τῶν Ἀποστόλων ἦσαν οἱ Ἰουδαῖοι, λέγει ὅτι ἀποκαταστήσει τοῖς δόγμασι τῶν υἱῶν αὐτῶν, τουτέστι τῶν Ἀποστόλων, τὰς καρδίας τῶν πατέρων, τουτέστι τοῦ γένους τῶν Ἰουδαίων. τὴν διάνοιαν δέ, εἰς τὸ πιστεῦσαι τῷ Χριστῷ, ἵνα μὴ πάντες ἄρδην ἀπόλωνται, παραγενομένου εἰς τὴν δευτέραν αὐτοῦ παρουσίαν. *λέγω δὲ ὑμῖν,* φησὶν ὁ Χριστός, *ὅτι Ἠλίας ἤδη ἦλθεν, καὶ οὐκ ἐπέγνωσαν αὐτόν. ἀλλ᾽ ἐποίησαν ἐν αὐτῷ, ὅσα ἠθέλησαν. τότε συνῆκαν οἱ μαθηταί, ὅτι περὶ Ἰωάννου τοῦ βαπτιστοῦ, εἶπεν αὐτοῖς.*[mclxxxvi]
>
> καὶ γὰρ λοιπὸν ὀξύτεροι εἰς τὸ νοεῖν ἐγένοντο, καὶ προσεκτικώτεροι πρὸς τὰ λεγόμενα. Πόθεν δὲ ἔγνωσαν τοῦτο οἱ μαθηταί; ἐκ τοῦ ἤδη προειρηκέναι αὐτοῖς, ὅτι αὐτὸς

1597 Matt. 11:14.
1598 Cod. γραμματοῖς.
1599 Cod. συγχαίωντες.
1600 Cod. ἐμνημονευσες.
1601 Cod. ἢ.
1602 Cod. οὔτος.
1603 Cod. ἔρχιτε.
1604 Matt. 17:11.
1605 Cod. ποιᾶ.
1606 Cod. θεσβήτην.
1607 Cf. Malachi, 3:22-23.
1608 Cod. ἐπιδεὶ.
1609 Cod. πίστην.
1610 Cod. τὸν Χριστόν.
1611 Cod. ἀπόλλονται.
1612 Cod. τὴ.

ἐστιν Ἠλίας ὁ μέλλων ἔρχεσθαι. ἀλλὰ μηδεὶς θορυβηθῇ, μὴ δὲ πεπλανῆσθαι νομίσῃ τὸν λόγον. εἰ ποτὲ μὲν αὐτὸν ἥξειν, ποτὲ δὲ ἐληλυθέναι ἔφη. πάντα γὰρ ἀληθῆ εἶπεν. ὅτε μὲν γάρ φησιν ὅτι Ἠλίας ἔρχεται, καὶ ἀποκαταστήσει πάντα. αὐτὸν τὸν Ἠλίαν λέγει, καὶ τὴν τῶν Ἰουδαίων τότε ἐπιστροφὴν ἐσομένην. ὅτ' ἂν δὲ εἴπῃ ὁ μέλλων ἔρχεσθαι, τὰ κατὰ τὸν τρόπον τῆς διακονίας, τὸν Ἰωάννην Ἠλίαν καλεῖ. διὸ καὶ ἐπήγαγεν. *ὅτι ἦλθεν, καὶ οὐκ ἐπέγνωσαν αὐτόν, ἀλλ' ἐποίησαν εἰς αὐτόν, πάντα ὅσα ἠθέλησαν.*[mclxxxvii]

A tradition among the Pharisees had it that, in accordance with the prophet Malachi, Elias would come before the advent of the Saviour. He would lead back the hearts of the fathers and would restore all things in their previous state.[mclxxxviii]

Λέγω δὲ ὑμ‹ῖ›ν[1613] *ὅτι Ἠλίας ἤδη ‹ἦ›λθεν,*[1614] *καὶ οὐκ ‹ἐ›πέγνωσαν*[1615]*αὐτόν, ἀλλ' ἐποίησαν ἐν αὐτῷ ‹ὅ›σα*[1616] *ἠθέλησαν.*[1617] *Τότε ἔγνωσαν ὅτι περὶ Ἰωάννου τοῦ βαπτιστοῦ λέγει.*[1618] Πο‹ῖα›[1619] δὲ ἐποίησαν αὐτῷ;[1620]; Ὅτι ἐνέβαλον αὐτὸν εἰς φυλακήν, ὅτι ‹ὕ›βρισαν,[1621] ὅτι ἀπέκτ‹ει›ναν[1622] αὐτόν, ὅτι ἤνεγκαν τὴν κεφαλ‹ή›ν[1623] αὐτοῦ ἐπὶ πίνακι.

ποῖα ταῦτα; ὅτι ἐνέβαλον εἰς δεσμωτήριον. ὅτι ὕβρισαν. ὅτι ἀπέκτειναν. ὅτι ἤνεγκαν τὴν κεφαλὴν αὐτοῦ ἐπὶ πίνακος.[mclxxxix]

Εὐκαίρως δὲ αὐτοὺς ἀναμιμνήσκει λοιπόν, καὶ περὶ τοῦ ἰδίου πάθους ἀπὸ τοῦ πάθους Ἰωάννου, πολλὴν αὐτοῖς προξενῶν τὴν παραμυθίαν. φησὶ γὰρ αὐτοῖς, καὶ ὁ υἱὸς τοῦ ἀνθρώπου μέλλει πάσχειν ὑπ' αὐτῶν. οὐκ ἐκ τούτου δὲ μόνον, ἀλλὰ καὶ ἐκ τοῦ θαύματα εὐθέως ἐργάσασθαι μέγαλα. καὶ γὰρ πολλαχοῦ παρατηρήσαντες τοῦτό ἐστι εὑρεῖν, ὅτι καὶ πρὸ τοῦ εἰπεῖν περὶ τοῦ πάθους, καὶ μετὰ τὸ εἰπεῖν, εὐθέως θαυματουργεῖ τούτου ἕνεκεν.[mcxc]

| 133r Ὁ δὲ Λουκᾶς[mcxci] καὶ τὴν πρὸ τῆς πρώτης ἀριθμεῖ ἐν ᾗ εἶπε τοῦτο καὶ τὴν μετὰ τὴν ἕκτην ἐν ᾗ ἀνῆλθε. Τὰ γὰρ τῷ λόγῳ προδηλούμενα καὶ ἔργῳ προθεωρεῖσθαι δίδωσιν ὁ Θεὸς καὶ τὴν προθεωρίαν ὡς αὐτὴν δεικνύει τὴν ἀλήθειαν, ὥσπερ καὶ τῆς οὐσίας αὐτοῦ τῆς ἀοράτου τύπον ἐδείκνυ τὸ παλαιὸν καὶ ὁ τύπος ὡς αὐτὸς ὁ Θεὸς ἑωρᾶτο, ὥστε λέγεσθαι περὶ τοῦ τῷ Μωυσῇ φανέντος ἀγγέλου ὅτι *εὐλαβεῖτο κατεμβλέψαι κατενώπιον τοῦ Θεοῦ.*[1624] Προλέγων τοίνυν τὴν βασιλείαν ἐν ᾗ παρέσται μετὰ δόξης

1613 Cod. ὑμήν.
1614 Cod. ἤλθεν.
1615 Cod. αιπέγνωσαν.
1616 Cod. ὄσα.
1617 Matt. 17:12.
1618 Matt. 17:13.
1619 Cod. πόι.
1620 Cod. ἐναυτῶ.
1621 Cod. ἤβρισαν.
1622 Cod. ἀπέκτηναν.
1623 Cod. κεφαλὶν.
1624 Ex. 3:6.

καὶ δεῖξαι ταύτην ὡς οἷόν τε τοῖς μαθηταῖς ἐβουλήθη. Καὶ τὸν μὲν Πέτρον ἔλαβεν ὡς σφόδρα ἀγαπῶντα αὐτόν· τὸν δὲ Ἰωάννην ὡς πάνυ ἀγαπώμενον ὑπ᾽ αὐτοῦ· Ἰάκωβον δὲ ὡς ἄγαν κατὰ τῶν Ἰουδαίων ἐρχόμενον, ὃν πρὸς χάριν καὶ Ἡρώδης ἀνεῖλε. Τοὺς γνησιωτέρους τοίνυν παραλαβὼν ἔδειξεν ὅτι οἱ μᾶλλον ἐνάρετοι πλεῖον τῶν ἄλλων τιμῶνται παρὰ Θεῷ καὶ θεωρίας ἐνθέου ἀξιοῦνται.
Εἰς τὸ ὄρος δὲ ἄνεισιν ὡς ἔθος ἔχων ἐν ἀποκρύφῳ ποιεῖν τὰς θαυματουργίας καὶ διδάσκων ὅτι ὁ χθαμαλὸς νοῦς οὐκ ἂν γένοιτο πρὸς θεωρίαν ἐπιτήδειος.

> *Εἰς τὸ ὄρος* ἄνεισι δεικνύς, ὅτι ὁ χθαμαλὸς νοῦς οὐκ ἂν γένοιτο πρὸς θεωρίαν ἐπιτήδειος, ἀλλ᾽ ὁ κατ᾽ ἰδίαν γεγονὼς καὶ ἔξω φροντίδων βιωτικῶν ἐν ἡσυχίᾳ.[mcxcii]

Ἡ δὲ μεταμόρφωσις τοῦτο δηλοῖ· ὅτι μείναντος τοῦ σώματος ἐπὶ σχήματος, ἐπὶ τὸ ἐνδοξότερον[mcxciii] οἱ χαρακτῆρες διὰ φωτοειδοῦς χρώματος ἔλαμπον.[mcxciv]

> Πεπρᾶχθαι δέ φαμεν τὴν μεταμόρφωσιν οὐχὶ δήπου τὸ σχῆμα τὸ ἀνθρώπινον μεταβαλόντος τοῦ σώματος, ἀλλὰ δόξης τινὸς φωτοειδοῦς περιστελλούσης αὐτό. μείναντος γὰρ τοῦ σώματος ἐπὶ τοῦ σχήματος ἐπὶ τὸ ἐνδοξότερον οἱ χαρακτῆρες διὰ φωτοειδοῦς χρώματος διεχρώννυντο.[mcxcv]

Διὰ οὖν τῆς μεταμορφώσεως τοῦ τε προσώπου καὶ τῶν ἱματίων τὰ ἐσόμενα αὐτοῖς ὡς ἐν σκιᾷ διαγράφει. Ὅσον οὖν ἐχώρουν ὀφθαλμοφανῶς ἰδεῖν τὴν βασιλείαν, ἔδειξεν αὐτοῖς· ἐξ ὧν δὲ | **133v** μετεβλήθη ἔδειξεν αὐτοῖς οἷος ἦν κατὰ φύσιν. Ἐξ ὧν δὲ παρίστανται αὐτῷ Μωσῆς καὶ Ἠλίας ἔδειξεν ὅτι καὶ νεκρῶν καὶ ζώντων κύριος ἦν· οὐ μόνον δέ, ἀλλὰ καὶ νόμου καὶ προφητῶν. Συλλαλοῦσι δὲ αὐτῷ· σύμφωνοι γὰρ αὐτῷ νόμος καὶ προφῆται. Διὰ δὲ τοῦ δεῖξαι αὐτοὺς ἐν δόξῃ ἔδειξεν ὅτι οἱ ἅγιοι πάντες οὕτως ἔχουσιν ὀφθῆναι ἐν δόξῃ ἀνεικάστῳ[mcxcvi] καὶ ὡς κριτῇ πάντες οἱ ζῶντες καὶ νεκροὶ παραστῆναι. Καὶ ἵνα λύσῃ τὴν ὑπόνοιαν τῶν λεγόντων αὐτὸν Ἠλίαν ἢ ἄλλον προφήτην, καὶ δείξῃ τὸ διάφορον ἑαυτοῦ καὶ τῶν δούλων, καὶ ὅτι ὁ Πέτρος καλῶς αὐτὸν ὡμολόγησεν υἱὸν Θεοῦ.

> *This is my beloved Son*: it is for this one that a tabernacle must be made, it is for this one that obedience must be given. This is my Son, they are servants.[mcxcvii]

Τὸ δὲ συμπαρεῖναι Μωσῆν καὶ Ἠλίαν τοῖς μαθηταῖς, ἄκραν συμφωνίαν τοῦ νόμου καὶ τῶν προφητῶν πρὸς τὸ εὐαγγέλιον σημαίνει.

καὶ ἰδοὺ ὤφθησαν αὐτοῖς Μωσῆς καὶ Ἠλίας.[1625] Ὁ μὲν ὡς τοῦ νόμου λειτουργὸς καὶ ὡς πρῶτος διδάσκαλος τοῦ λόγου τῆς εὐσεβείας. Ἠλίας δὲ ὡς πρόδρομος τῆς ἐνδόξου δευτέρας παρουσίας. Ἐκάλεσα Μωσέα νεκρὸν ἵνα, ὅταν ταφῶ, μὴ ἀμφιβάλῃς ὅτι ἐγείρομαι. Εἰ δὲ ψυχῇ ὤφθη ἢ σώματι ὀκνοῦμεν θάτερόν τι τῶν εἰρημένον

1625 Matt. 17:3.

ἰσχυρίσασθαι καὶ εἰπεῖν. Ἀλλὰ κατὰ τὸ Παύλῳ τῷ σοφωτάτῳ λελεγμένον, ἀσφαλὲς ἡγούμεθα λέγειν ὅτι *εἴτε ἐν σώματι εἴτε ἐκτὸς τοῦ σώματος, οὐκ οἶδα. ὁ Θεὸς οἶδεν.*[1626] Ὅτι δὲ τῶν ἐνδεχομένων ἐστὶ καὶ ψυχὴν εἰς σώματος τύπον μεταμορφωθεῖσαν ἐπιφανῆναι,[mcxcviii] δηλοῦσι καὶ ἀγγελικαὶ δυνάμεις ἐν εἴδεσιν ἀν | **134r** δρῶν ἤτοι μορφαῖς τοῖς ἁγίοις προφήταις ἐπιφανεῖσαι, καὶ σώμασιν ἐκ ποικίλων μεμορφωμένοις ὑλῶν, χρυσοῦ καὶ χαλκοῦ καὶ τῶν τούτοις παραπλησίων, ὡς αἱ ὁράσεις αἱ φοβεραὶ δηλοῦσι τοῦ Δανιήλ.[1627]

Καλόν ἐστιν ἡμᾶς ὧδε εἶναι.[1628] Τοῦτο εἶπεν ὁ Πέτρος οἰηθεὶς ὅτι ἡ ἐν τῷ ὄρει διατριβὴ ποιεῖ αὐτοὺς βλέπειν τὴν δόξαν ἐκείνην, ἤτοι πραγματευόμενος τὸ μὴ καταβῆναι τὸν Χριστὸν μὴ βουλόμενος αὐτὸν ἀποθανεῖν.

Εἰ θέλεις, ποιήσωμεν ὧδε τρεῖς σκηνάς.[1629] Διὸ καὶ σκηνὰς εἶπε ποιῆσαι ἐκεῖ ἔνθα οὐδεὶς γινώσκει, οἰόμενος ὅτι καὶ ἐάν τις ἔλθῃ ἐκεῖ θέλων αὐτὸν ἀποκτεῖναι ἔχει σὺν αὐτῷ Μωσῆν καὶ Ἠλίαν, τὸν μὲν σκέποντα αὐτὸν ὑπὸ *τὸν γνόφον*,[1630] τὸν δὲ κατάγοντα πῦρ καὶ ἀναιροῦντα τοὺς ἐπεμβαίνοντας αὐτῷ.[1631] Ταῦτα δὲ ἐκ πολλοῦ φόβου δεδιὼς ἐλάλει,[mcxcix] μὴ εἰδὼς ἃ ἐλάλει, ὡς ὁ ‹Μᾶρκό›ς[1632] φησι.[1633] Εἰκὸς γὰρ ἦν αὐτὸν ἐκ τῆς ἀσυνήθους θέας καὶ τὸ νηφάλιον ἀπολέσαι. *Οὐ γὰρ ᾔδει τί λαλήσει*·[1634] μήπω γὰρ τοῦ Χριστοῦ παθόντος καὶ ἀναστάντος καὶ μήπω τῆς φθορᾶς τοῦ σώματος ἡμῶν καταλυθείσης οὐχ οἷόν τε συνεῖναι Χριστῷ καὶ τῶν σκηνῶν ἐφίεσθαι τῶν εἰς οὐρανόν, ἅπερ μετὰ τὴν τοῦ κόσμου κατάλυσιν γίνεται. Ὅρα δὲ καὶ τὸν σκοπὸν τοῦ εἰπόντος *καλόν ἐστιν ἡμᾶς ὧδε εἶναι*,[1635] δεδιότος τὰ κάτω καὶ ποθοῦντος τὰ ἄνω.

καὶ *ἰδοὺ νεφέλη φωτεινὴ ἐπεσκίασεν αὐτοῖς.*[1636] Φωτεινὴ νεφέλη τὸ περίεργον διακόπτουσα τὸ ὑπὲρ τὴν ἑαυτοῦ δύναμιν ζητεῖν τι καὶ μὴ φέροντας. Διὰ οὖν τῆς φωτοειδοῦς νεφέλης | **134v** ὁ Πατὴρ τὴν ἑαυτοῦ δόξαν ἐνδείκνυται καὶ πρὸς μεῖζον θαῦμα ἐκ τῆς νεφέλης μαρτυρεῖ τῷ Υἱῷ καὶ αὐτοῦ παραγγέλλει ἀκούειν.[1637] Δείκνυται δὲ ἀντὶ τῆς σκηνῆς *φωτεινὴ νεφέλη* ἐπισκιάζουσα αὐτοῖς λαλοῦντος ἐν αὐτῇ τοῦ Θεοῦ. Εἰς γὰρ τὰς αὐτὰς σκηνὰς ἀνάγουσι νόμος καὶ προφῆται καὶ εὐαγγέλιον. Τρεῖς μὲν ἀριθμούμεναι, ἓν δὲ οὖσαι διὰ τὸ πρὸς ἓν τέλος ὁρᾶν πάντας.

1626 2 Cor. 12:3.
1627 Cf. Daniel, 2:31-38 &45; (translatio Graeca), 10:6.
1628 Matt. 17:4.
1629 Matt. 17:4: ποιήσω.
1630 Cf. Ex. 20:21; Ecclesiasticus, 45:5.
1631 Cf. 3 Kings, 18:36-38; 4 Kings, 1:10-14.
1632 Cod. Λουκᾶς.
1633 Mark, 9:6.
1634 Mark, 9:6.
1635 Matt. 17:4; Mark, 9:5; Luke, 9:33.
1636 Matt. 17:5.
1637 Luke, 9:35.

> *ταῦτα δὲ αὐτοῦ λέγοντος νεφέλη ἐπεσκίασεν αὐτούς*, τὸ περίεργον διακόπτουσα τοῦ ὑπὲρ δύναμιν τὴν ἑαυτῶν ζητεῖν τι, καὶ διὰ τούτου προδιατυπῶν, ὅτι μέλλουσι πάντες οἱ ἅγιοι οἱ πρὸ τῆς ἐπιδημίας καὶ οἱ μετὰ τὴν ἐπιδημίαν ἅμα γενέσθαι, καὶ ὅτι εἰς τὰς αὐτὰς σκηνὰς ἀνάγουσι νόμος καὶ προφῆται καὶ εὐαγγέλιον, τρεῖς μὲν ἀριθμούμεναι, πρὸς ἓν δὲ τέλος ὁρῶσαι, καὶ ὅτι ἐν τῇ ἀναστάσει μέλλουσιν *ἁρπαγῆναι ἐν νεφέλαις* οἱ ἅγιοι *εἰς ἀπάντησιν τοῦ κυρίου καὶ σὺν αὐτῷ εἶναι* διηνεκῶς.[mcc]

Διδάσκει δὲ ἡ φωνὴ ὅτι *οὗτός ἐστιν* ὁ ὁρώμενος ἄνθρωπος διὰ τὸ σεσαρκῶσθαι, ὁ ἀρρήτως ἐξ ἐμοῦ τεχθεὶς πρὸ τῶν αἰώνων. Τὸ γὰρ *ἔστι* ῥῆμα τῷ Θεῷ ἁρμόζει, τὸ δὲ ἦν καὶ ἔσται τῇ κτίσει. Ἀγαπητὸν δὲ εἶπε τὸν υἱὸν ὡς τὴν εἰς ἡμᾶς ἀγάπην, ἐν τῷ Ἐμμανουὴλ πρῶτον θεμελιῶν καὶ μετάγων εἰς ἡμᾶς τοὺς βδελυκτούς, οὓς οὐκ ἔκ τινος αἰτίας ἠλέησεν, ἀλλ᾽ ὅτι καλῶς ἔχειν τοῦτο αὐτῷ ἐφάνη. Εὐδοκία γάρ ἐστι κυρίως τὸ πρῶτον θέλημα[mcci] τὸ δι᾽ αὐτὸ τὸ καλὸν καὶ μὴ δι᾽ ἄλλο τι γινόμενον.[mccii]
Τὸ γὰρ *ἐν ᾧ εὐδόκησα* δηλοῖ τὸ ἐν ᾧ ἐπαναπαύομαι.

> Τί δέ ἐστιν, *Ἐν ᾧ εὐδόκησα*; Ὡσανεὶ ἔλεγεν, Ἐν ᾧ ἀναπαύομαι, ᾧ ἀρέσκομαι.[mcciii]

Διδάσκει δὲ ἡ φωνὴ καὶ ὅτι δεῖ τῇ διδαχῇ τοῦ Χριστοῦ πειθαρχεῖν μᾶλλον ἢ τοῖς νομικοῖς γράμμασιν· ἤτοι οὐ δεῖ ἀντιλέγειν αὐτῷ, κἂν σταυρωθῆναι ἐθέλῃ. Μὴ ἐνεγκόντες τοίνυν τὴν λαμπηδόνα τοῦ νέφους οἱ μαθηταί, μήτε τὴν ἀκοὴν φέροντες τῆς φωνῆς, ὑπὸ τοῦ δέους *ἔπεσον* χαμαί.[1638] Ἵνα δὲ μὴ μείνῃ ἐπὶ πολὺ τὸ δέος καὶ διώξῃ ἀπ᾽ αὐτῶν τὴν μνήμην τῶν ὁραθέντων, ἐγείρει αὐτοὺς καὶ λύει τὴν ἀγωνίαν, αὐτὸς μόνος ὁραθεὶς σὺν αὐτοῖς, | **135r** ἵνα μή τις ἀμφιβολία γένηται περὶ τίνος εἶπεν ὁ Πατὴρ *οὗτός ἐστιν ὁ υἱός μου*, καὶ τὰ ἑξῆς.
Οἱ μαθηταὶ *ἔπεσον ἐπὶ πρόσωπον*[1639] τάχα νοήσαντες τὸν Υἱὸν τοῦ Θεοῦ Μωσεῖ κεχρηματικέναι καὶ αὐτὸν εἰρηκέναι τὸ *οὐδεὶς ὄψεται τὸ πρόσωπόν μου καὶ ζήσεται*,[1640] καὶ διὰ τοῦτο ἔκρυψαν τὰς ὄψεις. Τῇ δὲ ἐπαφῇ τοῦ Ἰησοῦ εὐεργετηθέντες ἐπάρσει ὀφθαλμῶν εἶδον Ἰησοῦν μόνον, εὐαγγέλιον, νόμον, προφήτας γενόμενα ἕν.[mcciv] Ταῦτα μὲν μυστικῶς. Ψιλῶς γὰρ τάχα Μωσῆς καὶ Ἠλίας ἀπῆλθον ὅθεν ἐληλύθεισαν μεταδώσοντες ὧν ἤκουσαν τοῖς ὅσον οὔπω εὐεργετηθησομένοις ἐν τῷ τοῦ πάθους καιρῷ, ὅτε ἔμελλον *πολλὰ σώματα ἁγίων*[1641] ἀνίστασθαι.

> Οἱ μαθηταὶ *ἔπεσον ἐπὶ πρόσωπον* τάχα νοήσαντες τὸν υἱὸν τοῦ θεοῦ Μωσεῖ κεχρηματικέναι καὶ αὐτὸν εἰρηκέναι τὸ οὐδεὶς ὄψεται *τὸ πρόσωπόν μου καὶ ζήσεται*, καὶ διὰ τοῦτο ἔκρυψαν τὰς ὄψεις. Τῇ δὲ ἐπαφῇ τοῦ Ἰησοῦ εὐεργετηθέντες ἐπάρσει τῶν ὀφθαλμῶν εἶδον Ἰησοῦν μόνον, εὐαγγέλιον, νόμον, προφήτας γενόμενα ἕν. Ταῦτα μὲν μυστικῶς. ψιλῶς γὰρ τάχα Μωσῆς καὶ Ἠλίας ἀπῆλθον ὅθεν καὶ ἐληλύθεισαν μεταδώσοντες ὧν

1638 Cf. Matt. 17:6.
1639 Matt. 17:6.
1640 Cf. Ex. 33:20: οὐ γὰρ μὴ ἴδῃ ἄνθρωπος τὸ πρόσωπόν μου καὶ ζήσεται.
1641 Matt. 27:52.

ἤκουσαν τοῖς ὅσον οὔπω εὐεργετηθησομένοις ἐν τῷ τοῦ πάθους καιρῷ, ὅτε ἔμελλον *πολλὰ σώματα ἁγίων* ἀνίστασθαι.[mccv]

Ἧς ἀκούσαντες, καὶ ταύτην τὴν δόξαν μὴ φέροντες, *ἔπεσον ἐπὶ πρόσωπον* ταπεινωθέντες ὑπὸ τὴν κραταιὰν χεῖρα τοῦ Θεοῦ, σφόδρα φοβηθέντες, εἰδότες τὸ λεχθὲν πρὸς Μωϋσῆν. *Οὐ γὰρ ὄψεται ἄνθρωπος τὸ πρόσωπόν μου, καὶ ζήσεται. Ἐπάραντες δὲ τοὺς ὀφθαλμούς, μόνον εἶδον τὸν Ἰησοῦν.* Ἓν γάρ, οἶμαι, γέγονε Μωσῆς ὁ νόμος, καὶ Ἡλίας ἡ προφητεία, Ἰησοῦ τῷ Εὐαγγελίῳ. Καὶ οὐχ ὥσπερ ἦσαν πρότερον τρεῖς μεμενήκασι. Ταῦτα δέ μοι νόει μυστικώτερον. Πρὸς γὰρ τὸ ὑψηλὸν τοῦ γράμματος βούλημα, Μωϋσῆς καὶ Ἠλίας ὀφθέντες ἐν δόξῃ, καὶ συλλαλήσαντες τῷ Ἰησοῦ, ἀπεληλύθασιν ὅθεν ἐληλύθεισαν. Οὐδὲ γὰρ βλέπεται ὁ Ἰησοῦς λεχθῆναι τὰ τῆς δόξης αὐτοῦ. ἐβλάβησαν γὰρ ἂν οἱ ἀκούοντες, καὶ μάλιστα οἱ ὄχλοι, τὸν οὕτω δεδοξασμένον θεωροῦντες σταυρούμενον. Οὐ τοίνυν φθονήσαντες ἔκρυψαν, ἀλλ᾽ ὡς φοβηθέντες μὴ ἀπιστηθῶσι.[mccvi]

Καὶ καταβαινόντων αὐτῶν ἐκ τοῦ ὄρους.[1642] Διὰ ταπεινοφροσύνην παρήγγειλε τοῖς μαθηταῖς μὴ εἰπεῖν τὰ ὁραθέντα, ἤτοι ἵνα μὴ μετὰ τὸ ἀκοῦσαι ταῦτα ἐὰν ἴδωσι τὸ ἐπὶ τῷ σταυρῷ πάθος σκανδαλισθῶσιν ὡς ἄνθρωποι, ἤθελε δὲ λαθεῖν τὸν διάβολον.

Οὐδὲ βούλεται Ἰησοῦς λεχθῆναι τὰ τῆς δόξης αὐτοῦ πρὸ τῆς μετὰ τὸ πάθος δόξης αὐτοῦ. ἐβλάβησαν γὰρ ἂν οἱ ἀκούοντες καὶ μάλιστα οἱ ὄχλοι τὸν οὕτω δεδοξασμένον θεωροῦντες σταυρούμενον.[mccvii]

Τί οὖν οἱ γραμματεῖς λέγουσιν;[1643] Ἀπατῶντες τὸν λαὸν *οἱ γραμματεῖς* ἐξ ἀμαθίας ἔλεγον ὅτι οὐκ ἦν αὐτὸς ὁ Χριστὸς (εἰ γὰρ ἦν, Ἠλίας ἤρχετο πρῶτον), οὐκ εἰδότες ὅτι τῆς δευτέρας τοῦ Χριστοῦ παρουσίας ὁ Ἠλίας πρόδρομος, οὐ τῆς πρώτης.

Οἱ δὲ γραμματεῖς ἀπατῶντες τὸν λαὸν ἔλεγον, ὅτι πρὸ τῆς τοῦ Χριστοῦ παρουσίας ἔρχεται *Ἠλίας*. καὶ περιεφέρετο ὁ λόγος οὗτος καὶ ἐν τῷ ἀπείρῳ δήμῳ, ὃ καὶ ἐρωτῶσιν νῦν οἱ μαθηταί. πῶς οὖν αὐτὸ λύει;[mccviii]

Τινές δέ φασι ὅτι οἱ μαθηταὶ ἀγνοοῦντες τὴν ἀκρίβειαν τῆς γραφῆς, ἑωρακότες τὴν ἐν τῷ ὄρει φαντασίαν ἐνόμισαν ὅτι ἦλθεν ἡ συντέλεια. Διὸ καὶ τὰ περὶ τοῦ Ἠλία ἠρώτων. Ἤτοι τοῦτό φασι, ὅτι ἅμα ἀναστῇ ὁ Χριστός, τὸ κοινὸν ἥξει τέλος. Εἰ γὰρ ἅμα τῇ ἀναστάσει Χριστοῦ τὸ κοινὸν ἥξει τέλος, οὔτε ἡμεῖς κηρύξομεν τὸν λόγον. | **135v** Λυομένου τοῦ κόσμου οὔτε Ἠλίας ἥξει καὶ ψευδὴς εὑρεθήσεται ὁ περὶ τούτου λόγος. Τί οὖν ὁ Χριστός;
Εἰπὼν ὅτι Ἠλίας μὲν ἔρχεται ἔδειξεν ὅτι οὔπω ἦλθεν, ἀλλὰ τῆς δευτέρας ἔσται συντελείας πρόδρομος, πρὸ τῆς συντελείας ἐρχόμενος καὶ ἀποκαθιστῶν πρὸς *ἐπίγνωσιν ἀληθείας*[1644] πάντα τὸν πειθόμενον.

1642 Matt. 17:9.
1643 Matt. 17:10.
1644 1 Tim. 2:4.

> Οὐκοῦν τῆς δευτέρας αὐτοῦ παρουσίας ἔσται πρόδρομος περὶ τὸν τῆς συντελείας καιρόν, ὅτε καὶ *ἀποκαταστήσει πάντα* πρὸς ἐπίγνωσιν ἀληθῆ, πάντα τὸν πειθόμενον αὐτῷ ἀποκαθιστάς.[mccix]

Ἀποκαταστήσει γὰρ καὶ διορθώσεται τοὺς Ἰουδαίους καὶ πείσει δέξασθαι τὸ ἐπὶ *Χριστὸν μυστήριον.*[1645] Εἶτά φησιν ὅτι λέγω ὑμῖν ὅτι *Ἠλίας ἤδη ἦλθε, καὶ οὐκ ἐπέγνωσαν αὐτόν,*[1646] Ἠλίαν τὸν Ἰωάννην λέγων, ὡς *ἐν πνεύματι καὶ δυνάμει Ἠλίου*[1647] ἐλθόντα, ὃς ἦλθε προετοιμάζων τὰς τῶν ἀνθρώπων ψυχὰς εἰς τὸ πεισθῆναι Χριστῷ. Πλὴν οὔτε τὸν Ἰωάννην ἐδέξαντό φησι ἀγνοήσαντες τὰς γραφάς, ἀλλὰ καὶ ἀνεῖλον μὴ εἰδότες ὅτι πρόδρομός ἐστιν. Οὕτω κἀμὲ μέλλουσιν ἀνελεῖν, μὴ εἰδότες ὅτι ἐγώ εἰμι ὁ Χριστός. Τότε οὖν ὡς ὀξύτεροι γεγονότες οἱ μαθηταὶ ἔγνωσαν ὅτι Ἠλίαν καλεῖ τὸν Ἰωάννην[1648] διὰ τὸ κοινὸν τῆς διακονίας. Πόθεν δὲ τοῦτο ἔγνωσαν; Ἦν ἤδη προειρηκὼς *αὐτός ἐστιν Ἠλίας ὁ μέλλων ἔρχεσθαι.*[1649]
Τὸ βούλημα τῆς ἐπερωτήσεως τῶν μαθητῶν τοιοῦτον εἶναί μοι φαίνεται. Ἡμεῖς μὲν τὸν Ἠλίαν νῦν σὺν σοὶ ‹ε›ἴδ‹ο›μεν,[1650] πρότερον αὐτοῦ σὲ ἑωρακότες, *οἱ δὲ γραμματεῖς Ἠλίαν πρῶτόν*[1651] σου ἔρχεσθαί φασι καὶ πυνθανόμεθα εἰ ψεύδονται.[mccx]

> Τὸ βούλημα τῆς ἐρωτήσεως τῶν μαθητῶν τοιοῦτόν τι εἶναί μοι φαίνεται. ἡμεῖς μὲν τὸν Ἠλίαν νῦν σὺν σοὶ εἴδομεν, πρότερον αὐτοῦ σὲ ἑωρακότες, *οἱ δὲ γραμματεῖς Ἠλίαν πρῶτόν* σου ἔρχεσθαι φασι. καὶ πυνθανόμεθα, εἰ ψεύδονται.[mccxi]

Προσῆλθεν αὐτῷ ἄνθρωπος γονυπετῶν.[1652] Οὗτος ὁ ἄνθρωπος ἄπιστος ἦν σφόδρα, τοῦτο δὲ δῆλον ἐξ ὧν εἶπεν ὁ Χριστός· *ὦ γενεὰ ἄπιστος,*[1653] καὶ *πάντα δυνατὰ τῷ πιστεύοντι.*[1654] Καίτοι δὲ πολλὰ τοιαῦτα ἰασαμένων τῶν ἀποστό | **136r** λων καὶ χαιρόντων ὅτι *τὰ δαιμόνια* αὐτοῖς ὑπετάσσετο,[1655] ἐνταῦθα κατ᾽ οἰκονομίαν ἐπεσχέθη τὰ τῆς θεραπείας ἐπὶ τοῦ σεληνιαζομένου παιδός. Καὶ γὰρ ἔχρηζεν ὁ πατὴρ αὐτοῦ ἐπιτιμήσεως καὶ ἐλέγχου παιδευτικοῦ. Κοινωνούντων δὲ τῆς ἀπιστίας καὶ τῶν περιεστηκότων ὄχλων, κοινὴν ποιεῖται τὴν ἐπιτίμησιν. Καὶ γὰρ καὶ τῶν ἄλλων δαιμονώντων θεραπευθέντων, ἔλεγον *ἐν Βεελζεβοὺλ ἄρχοντι τῶν δαιμόνων,*[1656] καὶ τὰ ἑξῆς. Καὶ νῦν μικρᾶς ἀναβολῆς γενομένης γελᾶν ἐδόκουν τὸ ἀσθενές. Τοσοῦτον δὲ ὠφέλησε τὸν

1645 Cf. Eph. 5:32; Rom. 16:25; Eph. 3:4; Col. 1:27; 2:2; 4:3.
1646 Matt. 17:11.
1647 Luke, 1:17.
1648 Matt. 17:13.
1649 Matt. 11:14.
1650 Cod. οἴδομεν.
1651 Matt. 17:10; Mark, 9:11.
1652 Matt. 17:14.
1653 Matt. 17:17.
1654 Mark, 9:23.
1655 Cf. Luke, 17:10.
1656 Matt. 12:24; Mark, 3:22; Luke, 11:15.

πατέρα ἡ ἐπιτίμησις ὅτι καὶ ἐβόα λέγων (ὡς ὁ Μᾶρκός φησι), *πιστεύω* Κύριε· *βοήθει μου τῇ ἀπιστίᾳ.*[1657] Διὰ τοῦτο δὲ ἐνεκάλεσε τοῖς μαθηταῖς, ἐπειδὴ καὶ δίχα τῆς τῶν προσενεγκόντων πίστεως πολλάκις ἐνήργησεν ἡ τῶν ἁγίων θεραπεία.
Οὐκέτι δὲ πάθος σεληνιασμοῦ, ἀλλ᾽ ὁ δαίμων ἐπιτηρεῖ τινὰς τῆς σελήνης συνόδους καὶ ἐπιτίθεται τῷ κάμνοντι, ἵνα βλασφημῆται ὁ ποιήσας αὐτήν.

> Εἰκὸς δὲ ὅτι, ὥσπερ τοῦτο τὸ ἐνεργοῦν τὸν καλούμενον σεληνιασμὸν πνεῦμα ἀκάθαρτον ἐπιτηρεῖ τοὺς τῆς σελήνης σχηματισμούς, ἵνα ἐνεργήσῃ εἰς τὸν διά τινας αἰτίας παραδιδόμενον αὐτῷ καὶ μὴ ποιήσαντα ἑαυτὸν ἄξιον φρουρᾶς ἀγγελικῆς, οὕτως καὶ ἄλλα πνεύματα καὶ δαιμόνια πρός τινας σχηματισμοὺς τῶν ἄλλων ἀστέρων, ἵνα μὴ μόνον σελήνη ἀλλὰ καὶ οἱ λοιποὶ λοιδορηθῶσιν ἀστέρες ὑπὸ τῶν *ἀδικίαν εἰς τὸ ὕψος* λαλούντων. ἔστι γοῦν ἀκοῦσαι τῶν γενεθλιαλόγων, τὴν αἰτίαν πάσης μανίας καὶ παντὸς δαιμονιασμοῦ ἀναφερόντων ἐπὶ τοὺς τῆς σελήνης σχηματισμούς.[mccxii]

> What is the reason why a daemon observes the course of the moon, seizes men, and strives to defame the Creatore through the creatures, this we have explained above.[mccxiii]

Ὁ οὖν πατὴρ αὐτοῦ πλανώμενος εἶπεν ὅτι *σεληνιάζεται.*[1658] Κατ᾽ οἰκονομίαν δέ, ὡς εἴρηται, οὐκ ἰάθη ὑπὸ τῶν μαθητῶν ὁ δαιμονῶν διὰ τὴν ἀπιστίαν τοῦ πατρὸς αὐτοῦ. Οὗτος δὲ τὸ ἑαυτοῦ πταῖσμα τῆς ἀπιστίας τῶν μαθητῶν κατηγόρει ὡς ἠσθενηκότων περὶ τὴν ἴασιν. Διὸ καὶ ὁ Κύριος, ἐπειδὴ ἐπὶ τοῦ ὄχλου οὗτος διέσυρε τοὺς μαθητάς, ἐπὶ αὐτῶν αὐτοῦ δημοσιεύει τὴν ἀπιστίαν εἰπών *ὦ γενεὰ ἄπιστος καὶ διεστραμμένη,*[1659] κοινῇ πάντας ὀνειδίσας, ὡς οὐ μόνον τοῦ πατρὸς τοῦ σεληνιαζομένου, ἀλλὰ καὶ τοῦ περιεστῶτος ὄχλου ἀπιστοῦντος. Εἰπὼν δὲ τὸ | **136v** *ἕως πότε ἔσομαι μεθ᾽ ὑμῶν*, δείκνυσιν ὅτι ἐπιποθεῖ τὸ ἐπὶ τῷ σταυρῷ πάθος καὶ τὴν ἐκ τοῦ σώματος ἐκδημίαν. *Ἕως πότε*, φησί, συνδιαιτῶμαι ὑμῖν τοῖς οὕτως ὑβρίζουσι καὶ ἀπίστοις; Ἐπειδὴ δὲ ‹οὐ›[1660] γέγραπται ὅτι ἐπετίμησε τῷ δαιμονίῳ, ἀλλ᾽ αὐτῷ τῷ σεληνιαζομένῳ, δείκνυται ὅτι δι᾽ ἁμαρτίας τούτῳ πάσχοντι ἐπιτιμᾷ, ἵνα παραδεξάμενος τὴν ἐπιτίμησιν συνεργήσῃ τῷ ἐξελθεῖν τὸ δαιμόνιον.

τότε προσελθόντες οἱ μαθηταὶ τῷ Ἰησοῦ κατ᾽ ἰδίαν.[1661] Οὐκ αἰσχυνόμενοι *ἰδίᾳ* ἠρώτων οἱ δημοσίᾳ ἐλεγχθέντες διὰ τοῦ πράγματος, ἀλλ᾽ ἐπειδὴ περὶ μεγάλου καὶ ἀπορρήτου ἠρώτων. Ἐδεδίεσαν γὰρ μὴ ἀπολέσαντες ἦσαν τὴν δοθεῖσαν αὐτοῖς χάριν κατὰ δαιμόνων. Ὁ δὲ Κύριος ὡς ἀτελεστέροις ὀνειδίζων τὴν αἰτίαν φησὶ δι᾽ ἣν οὐκ ἴσχυσαν ἐκβαλεῖν *τὸ δαιμόνιον*, ἐπειδὴ οὐκ ἦσαν τέλειοι περὶ τὴν πίστιν, ὅπως αἰσχυνθέντες συντείνωσιν ἑαυτοὺς εἰς τελειότητα πίστεως. Οὐ γὰρ ὁλοτελῆ ἀπιστίαν αὐτοῖς

1657 Mark, 9:24.
1658 Matt. 17:15.
1659 Matt. 17:17.
1660 Cod. μή.
1661 Matt. 17:19.

ἐγκαλεῖ, ἀλλ᾽ *ὀλιγοπιστίαν.*[1662] *'Εάν*, γάρ φησι, θερμὴν καὶ ζέουσαν *ἔχητε πίστιν*, τὴν διὰ τὸ μικροπρεπὲς τοῦ λόγου εὐτελῆ καὶ ὡς *κόκκῳ σινάπεως* ἀπεικασθεῖσαν ἢ διὰ τὸ σφοδρὸν καὶ θερμὸν τῆς δυνάμεως, πάντα εὐκόλως ἐργάσεσθε καὶ τὰ δυσχερῆ. Δείκνυσι δὲ ὅτι καὶ τὸ ἐλάχιστον τῆς γνησίας πίστεως μεγάλα δύναται ποιῆσαι. 'Εδύναντο γάρ, εἰ ἤθελον, καὶ *ὄρη* μετακινῆσαι·[1663] ὅπερ, εἰ καὶ ἐγένετο, οὐκ ἐγράφη ἢ ὅτι αὐτοὶ οὐκ ἠθέλησαν ποιῆσαι.[mccxiv]
Τινὲς δέ φασι ὅτι ὑπερβολικῷ ἐχρήσατο ρήματι λέγων ὅτι ἡ εἰλικρινὴς πίστις, εἰ χρεία καλέσοι, καὶ ὄρη |**137r** μετακινεῖ.

'Υπερβολικῶς μὲν οὖν [*** κ]ἂν ἔχω πᾶσαν τὴν πίστιν ὥστε ὄρη μεθιστάναι.[mccxv]

Διατί εἶπε τοῖς μαθηταῖς *διὰ τὴν ἀπιστίαν ὑμῶν;*[1664] Συστέλλων αὐτοὺς πρὸς τὸ ταπεινὸν καὶ τὸ ἀεὶ νομίζειν ἐνδεῶς ἔχειν πρὸς ἅπαν καλόν καὶ τὸ ἑαυτοὺς αἰτιᾶσθαι ἀεί, τῆς παρ᾽ αὐτοῦ χάριτος αὐτομολούσης[1665] ἐνίοτε κατά τινα λόγον ἀπόρρητον. Εἶτα, ἵνα μὴ πάλιν οἰηθῶσι πίστεως μόνης εἶναι τὸ πᾶν, πράξεων δὲ μὴ δεῖν, προσεπάγει λέγων, καθὰ φησι ὁ εὐαγγελιστὴς Μᾶρκος,[mccxvi] *τοῦτο δὲ τὸ γένος οὐκ ἐκπορεύεται, εἰ μὴ ἐν προσευχῇ καὶ νηστείᾳ.*[1666][mccxvii] Τούτου δὲ χάριν οὐκ εἶπεν ἐὰν μὴ νηστεύσητε ὑμεῖς ἢ ἐκεῖνοι οἱ θεραπευόμενοι, ἵνα κοινὸν ᾖ καὶ θεραπευόντων καὶ θεραπείας δεομένων τὸ τῆς προσευχῆς καὶ νηστείας γυμνάσιον. *Τοῦτο δὲ τὸ γένος* εἰς νηστείαν προτρεπόμενος, τούς τε ποιοῦντας καὶ τοὺς πάσχοντας.

τοῦτο δὲ τὸ γένος, καὶ τὰ ἑξῆς.[1667] Εἰπὼν δὲ *τὸ γένος*, ἐδήλωσεν ὅτι πᾶν τὸ τῶν δαιμόνων λέγει σύστημα·[mccxviii] ἢ γὰρ ἂν εἶδος εἶπε καὶ οὐ γένος.

Καὶ ὃς ἐὰν δέξηται παιδίον τοιοῦτον ἓν ἐπὶ τῷ ὀνόματί μου, ἐμὲ δέχεται.[1668] Παραινεῖ δέχεσθαι τοὺς πιστοὺς ἐπὶ τῷ ὀνόματι αὐτοῦ ἓν παιδίον τοιοῦτο, ἢ ἓν τῶν τοιούτων παιδίων τῶν πνευματικῶν καὶ μεμορφωμένων [τὸν Χριστὸν], κατὰ τὸ ταπεινῶσαν ἑαυτὸ πνεῦμα. κατὰ δὲ τὸν Λουκᾶν τὸ δεικνύμενον ὑπὸ τοῦ σωτῆρος παιδίον δέχεσθαι δεῖ ἐν τῷ ὀνόματι αὐτοῦ, ἵνα ἐν αὐτῷ δέξηται τὸν Χριστὸν ὄντα καὶ ἐν τῷ Πνεύματι. ἢ ἓν τοιοῦτο, ἐπεὶ ἕν εἰσι πάντες οἱ πνευματικοί. προτρέπει δὲ ὁ λόγος καὶ τὸ δέχεσθαι τῶν ἁπλῶν καὶ πραέων τῇ καρδίᾳ ἐν τῷ λόγῳ Χριστοῦ, ἀνακόπτων τὸ φιλόνεικον τῶν μαθητῶν. ἐπεὶ δὲ ὅτε οἱ διδάσκαλοι μάχονται, σχίσματα γίνονται πολλῶν σκανδαλιζομένων, βουλομένων τῶν σκανδαλιζομένων ἐπισπᾶσθαι εἰς αὐτοὺς τοὺς ἀκροατάς, προλέγει τὴν κατ᾽ αὐτῶν τιμωρίαν. τοῦτο δὲ ἐπιτεταγμένως ἐλέχθη, τουτέστιν κἂν εὐτελῆ ἄνθρωπον τῶν πιστῶν σκανδαλίσητε, βαρεῖα ἔσται καθ᾽ ὑμῶν ἡ τιμωρία. [τὴν γὰρ ἀφόρητον τιμωρίαν διὰ τοῦ μύλου καὶ καταποντισμοῦ σημαίνει,] τὴν ἐσομένην κατὰ τῶν

1662 Matt. 17:20 (alt.): διὰ τὴν ὀλιγοπιστίαν ὑμῶν.
1663 Cf. 1 Cor. 13:2.
1664 An alternative to Matt. 17:20.
1665 Cod. οὐκ αὐτομολούσης.
1666 Matt. 17:21.
1667 Matt. 17:21.
1668 Matt. 18:3.

τοὺς τοιούτους ὑβριζόντων. [σκάνδαλον γὰρ ἐνταῦθα τὴν ὕβριν καλεῖ.] ταῦτα δέ φησι, ἐπειδὴ οἱ μικροὶ εὐσκανδάλιστοί εἰσιν, ἵνα μὴ καταφρονῶμεν αὐτῶν. ὁ γὰρ μέγας καὶ τέλειος ἐν ἀρετῇ παντὸς σκανδάλου καταφρονεῖ. ἐξ ὧν δὲ προλέγει καὶ θρηνεῖ τοὺς τοιούτους, δίδωσιν αὐτοῖς καιρὸν μετανοίας. [εἰπὼν δὲ ἀνάγκη οὐκ ἀναιρεῖ τὸ αὐτεξούσιον, ἀλλὰ τὸ προγνωστικὸν τοῦ πάντως ἐσομένου δηλοῖ.] διὸ καὶ τὸ οὐαὶ αὐτοῖς ἐπιφωνεῖ, ὡς ἑκουσίως πταίουσι. κόσμον δὲ λέγει τοὺς ἀσέμνους ζῶντας ἀνθρώπους.[mccxix]

Παραινεῖ δέχεσθαι τοὺς πιστοὺς *ἐπὶ τῷ ὀνόματι* αὐτοῦ ἓν *παιδίον τοιοῦτον*, ἢ ἓν τοιούτων τῶν πνευματικῶν καὶ μεμορφωμένων τὸν Χριστόν, κατὰ τὸ ταπεινῶσαι τὸ ἑαυτοῦ πνεῦμα. Κατὰ δὲ τὸν Λουκᾶν, τὸ δεικνύμενον ὑπὸ τοῦ Σωτῆρος παιδίον δέχεσθαι δεῖ *ἐν τῷ ὀνόματι* αὐτοῦ, ἵνα ἐν αὐτῷ δέξηται τὸν Χριστὸν ὄντα καὶ ἐν τῷ Πνεύματι. Ἢ *ἓν τοιοῦτον*, ἐπεὶ ἕν εἰσι πάντες οἱ πνευματικοί. Προτρέπει δὲ ὁ λόγος καὶ τὸ δέχεσθαι τῶν ἁπλῶν καὶ πραέων τῇ καρδίᾳ ἐν τῷ λόγῳ Χριστοῦ. Ἀνακόπτων τὸ φιλόνικον τῶν μαθητῶν (ἐπειδὴ ὅτε οἱ διδάσκαλοι μάχονται, σχίσματα γίνονται πολλῶν σκανδαλιζομένων, βουλομένων τῶν σκανδαλιζομένων ἐπισπᾶσθαι εἰς αὐτοὺς τοὺς ἀκροατάς), προλέγει τὴν μετ᾽ αὐτῶν τιμωρίαν. Τοῦτο δὲ ἐπιτεταγμένως ἐλέχθη. Τουτέστιν κἂν εὐτελῆ ἄνθρωπον τῶν πιστῶν σκανδαλίσητε, βαρεῖα ἔσται καθ᾽ ὑμῶν ἡ τιμωρία. Τὴν γὰρ ἀφόρητον τιμωρίαν διὰ τοῦ μύλου καὶ καταποντισμοῦ σημαίνει, τὴν ἐσομένην μετὰ τῶν τοὺς τοιούτους ὑβριζόντων. Σκάνδαλον γὰρ ἐνταῦθα τὴν ὕβριν καλεῖ. Ταῦτα δέ φημι, ἐπειδὴ οἱ μικροὶ εὐσκανδάλιστοί εἰσιν, ἵνα μὴ καταφρονῶμεν αὐτῶν. Ὁ γὰρ μέγας καὶ τέλειος ἐν ἀρετῇ παντὸς σκανδάλου καταφρονεῖ. Ἐξ ὧν δὲ προλέγει καὶ θρηνεῖ τοὺς τοιούτους, δίδωσιν αὐτοῖς καιρὸν μετανοίας. Εἰπὼν δέ, *Ἀνάγκη*, οὐκ ἀναιρεῖ τὸ αὐτεξούσιον, ἀλλὰ τὸ προγνωστικὸν τοῦ πάντως ἐσομένου δηλοῖ.[mccxx] Διὸ καὶ τὸ *οὐαὶ* αὐτοῖς ἐπιφωνεῖ, ὡς ἑκουσίως πταίουσι. Κόλασιν δὲ λέγει τοὺς ἀσέμνους ζῶντας ἀνθρώπους.[mccxxi]

45

143v (ΩΡΙΓΕΝΟΥΣ) *Ὅτι οἱ ἄγγελοι αὐτῶν ἐν οὐρανοῖς.*[1669] Αἱ διάνοιαι τῶν ἁγίων δίκην ἀγγέλων *βλέπουσι τὸ πρόσωπον Πατρὸς* τὸν Θεὸν φανταζόμεναι. Εἰσὶ μέντοι καὶ *ἄγγελοι* κατὰ τὴν πρόνοιαν προϊστάμενοι τῶν πιστῶν, καθὼς καὶ Παῦλός φησι, *οὐχὶ πάντες εἰσὶ λειτουργικὰ πνεύματα;*[1670] καὶ τὰ ἑξῆς.

Αἱ διάνοιαι τῶν ἁγίων δίκην ἀγγέλων *βλέπουσι τὸ πρόσωπον πατρὸς* τὸν θεὸν φανταζόμεναι. εἰσὶ μέντοι καὶ *ἄγγελοι* κατὰ τὴν πρόνοιαν προϊστάμενοι τῶν ἐπὶ γῆς πιστῶν, καθὼς καὶ Παῦλός φησι. *οὐχὶ πάντες εἰσὶ λειτουργικὰ Πνεύματα*; καὶ τὰ ἑξῆς.

Βλέπουσι τὸ πρόσωπον.[1671] Οὐ | **144r** χ ὅτι Θεοῦ τις ὁρᾷ πρόσωπον. Ποῖον γὰρ ἕξει πρόσωπον ὁ ἀσχημάτιστος[mccxxii] καὶ ἀσώματος; Ἢ πῶς ὁραθείη ὁ ἀθέατος; Ἀλλὰ *πρόσωπον* ἔθος τῇ θείᾳ γραφῇ τὴν ἐφ᾽ ἡμᾶς ἐπισκοπὴν καλεῖν τοῦ Θεοῦ,[mccxxiii] κατὰ τὸ

1669 Matt. 18:10.
1670 Heb. 1:14.
1671 Matt. 18:10.

εἰρημένον τῷ ψαλμῳδῷ· *μὴ ἀποστρέψῃς τὸ πρόσωπόν σου ἀπ᾽ ἐμοῦ*,[1672] *καὶ ἐπίφανον τὸ πρόσωπόν σου ἐπὶ τὸν δοῦλον σου*.[1673] *Βλέπουσιν* οὖν *οἱ ἄγγελοι* (τουτέστι κατανοοῦσι) πηλίκη τις ἐπισκοπὴ καὶ πρόνοια περὶ τὰ νήπια τοῦ Θεοῦ[1674] καὶ φυλάττουσιν αὐτὰ μετ᾽ ἐπιμελοῦς καὶ ἀγρύπνου τῆς φυλακῆς.

ἐὰν γένηταί τινι ἀνθρώπῳ.[1675] Τινὶ ἀνθρώπῳ τῷ Χριστῷ φησι τῷ πρότερον *ἐν μορφῇ Θεοῦ* ὑπάρχοντι.[1676] Πᾶσα δὲ ἡ λογικὴ κτίσις ἀγγέλων καὶ ἀνθρώπων τὰ *ἑκατόν* εἰσι *πρόβατα*. Ὁ οὖν Χριστός, ὡς μὴ ὢν κτίσμα, *ποιμὴν*[1677] ἐστι καὶ οὐ πρόβατον. Οὗτος *ἀφῆκε τὰ ἐνενηκονταεννέα ἐπὶ τὰ ὄρη* μορφὴν δούλου λαβών, ἦλθε δὲ τὸ ἓν πρόβατον, ὅπερ ἐστὶν ἡ ἀνθρωπότης, *ζητῆσαι καὶ σῶσαι τὸ ἀπολωλός*,[1678]

> Some think that this shepherd is he *who while existing in the form of God, did not consider it robbery to be equal with God, but emptied himself, taking the form of a servant, having become obedient to the Father, to the point of death, indeed the death of the cross.*[1679] And thereupon, the reason he came down to the earthly [region] was to save the one little ship that had gone astray, that is, the human genus.[mccxxiv]

ἵνα μὴ λίπῃ τῇ λογικῇ κτίσει πρὸς τὴν εἰς Θεὸν δοξολογίαν, καὶ *χαίρει ἐπὶ τούτῳ*[1680] ἢ ἐπὶ τῇ τῶν ἀγγέλων στερρότητι. Ὅπου γὰρ οὐκ ἔστι φροντὶς ἀπωλείας, οὔτε αἴσθησίς ἐστι τῆς ἐκ τούτου λύπης. Ὁ σκοπὸς τοίνυν τῆς παραβολῆς τοιοῦτον ἔχει τὸν νοῦν. Ὥσπερ ὁ ποιμὴν *χαίρει* ἐπὶ τῇ εὑρέσει τοῦ ἀπολωλότος, οὕτω καὶ ὁ Θεὸς ἐπιμελεῖται τῆς ἐπιστροφῆς τῶν ἁμαρτωλῶν ἢ *χαίρει* ἐπὶ τοῖς ἐπίμονον ἔχουσι τὴν ἀρετήν.[mccxxv]

Καὶ ἐὰν γένηται εὑρεῖν αὐτό.[1681] Κατὰ τοῦτο εἰκότως καὶ τὴν εἰς κόσμον αὐτοῦ παρουσίαν τῇ προκειμένῃ παραβολῇ προσαρμόζει, ὡς ἐπὶ *τὸ ἀπολωλὸς* | **144v** γεγονυῖαν *πρόβατον*,[1682] τουτέστι τὸν ἄνθρωπον, ἀπὸ τῶν προβάτων ὄντα τῶν *ἑκατόν*, ἀπὸ τοῦ πλήθους τῶν οὐρανίων δυνάμεων ὁμοιογενῆ αὐτοῖς ὄντα καθὸ λογικός, καθὸ πρόβατον ἐν προβάτοις ἀριθμούμενον, ἐλάχιστον δὲ ὡς πρὸς τὸ πολὺ πλῆθος, καὶ διὰ τοῦτο ἐν προβάτοις *ἑκατόν*. Πλάνη δὲ αὐτοῦ τὸ πταῖσμα τὸ ἐν Ἀδάμ. Ζητεῖται δὲ εἰκότως, ὅτι καὶ ὁμοιογενὴς τοῖς παρὰ Θεῷ μείνασι καὶ πρὸς ἀναπλήρωσιν αὐτῶν ἀναγκαῖον, ἵνα μὴ ἐνδεὴς εἴη ποιμὴν καὶ κολοβὸς εἴη,[mccxxvi] καθὸ καὶ ἀνακεφαλαίωσιν

1672 Psalms 26:9; 121:3 142:7; Tobit, 3:6.
1673 Psalm 30:17.
1674 Cf. Matt. 11:25; 21:16; Luke, 10:21; 1 Cor. 3:1.
1675 Matt. 18:12.
1676 Phil. 2:6.
1677 John, 10:11&14.
1678 Luke, 19:10.
1679 Phil. 2:6-8.
1680 Matt. 18:11-13; Luke, 15:4-6.
1681 Matt. 18:13.
1682 Luke, 15:6; cf. Psalm 118:176; Jer. 27:6; Ez. 34:2-6; Matt. 10:6; 15:24.

τῶν πάντων εἶπεν ὁ Παῦλος *ἐν Χριστῷ*,[1683] τὴν τοῦ περιρρυέντος μέρους ἐπανάληψιν οὐκ ἐντελοῦς οὔσης τῆς τῶν ὅλων *ἐν Χριστῷ* συστάσεως διὰ τὸ ἐκλεῖπον καὶ ἐλλεῖπον.

> Κατὰ τοῦτο εἰκότως καὶ τὴν εἰς κόσμον αὐτοῦ παρουσίαν τῇ προκειμένῃ παραβολῇ προσαρμόζει ὡς ἐπὶ τὸ ἀπολωλὸς γεγονυῖαν *πρόβατον*, τοῦτ᾽ ἔστιν τὸν ἄνθρωπον ἀπὸ τῶν προβάτων ὄντα τῶν *ἑκατόν*, ἀπὸ τοῦ πλήθους τῶν οὐρανίων δυνάμεων, ὁμοιογενῆ αὐτοῖς ὄντα καθὸ λογικός, καθὸ πρόβατον ἐν προβάτοις ἀριθμούμενον, ἐλάχιστον δὲ ὡς πρὸς τὸ πολὺ πλῆθος καὶ διὰ τοῦτο ἐν προβάτοις *ἑκατόν*. πλάνη δὲ αὐτοῦ τὸ πταῖσμα τοῦ Ἀδάμ. *ζητεῖται* δὲ εἰκότως, ὅτι καὶ ὁμοιογενὴς τοῖς παρὰ θεῷ μείνασι καὶ πρὸς ἀναπλήρωσιν αὐτῶν ἀναγκαῖον, ἵνα μὴ ἐνδεὴς εἴη ποιμὴν καὶ κολοβὸς εἴη, καθὸ καὶ ἀνακεφαλαίωσιν τῶν πάντων εἶπεν ὁ Παῦλος *ἐν Χριστῷ* τὴν τοῦ περιρρυέντος μέρους ἐπανάληψιν οὐκ ἐντελοῦς οὔσης τῆς τῶν ὅλων ἐν Χριστῷ συστάσεως διὰ τὸ ἐκλεῖπον καὶ ἐλλεῖπον.[mccxxvii]

Ἐὰν δὲ ἁμάρτῃ εἰς σὲ ὁ ἀδελφός σου.[1684] Διὰ τούτου προτρέπεται τοὺς ἀδικηθέντας εἰς τὸ μὴ μνησικακεῖν· ἰδίᾳ δὲ θέλει τοὺς ἁμαρτήσαντας πρῶτον ἐλεχθῆναι, ἵνα μὴ ἐπὶ πλειόνων ἐλεγχθέντες ἰταμώτεροι γένωνται. Ἐὰν δὲ καὶ ἐπὶ δύο ἐλεγχθεὶς μὴ δυσωπηθῇ, τότε λέγει ἐπὶ τῶν *τῆς ἐκκλησίας*[1685] προέδρων δημοσιεύεσθαι τὸ πταῖσμα. Ἔνθα μὲν γὰρ ἀλλότριος ὁ τύπτων, *στρέψον αὐτῷ καὶ τὴν* ἑτέραν[1686] φησί. Ἐὰν δὲ *ἀδελφὸς ᾖ*, πάντα ποίει τοῦ ἀνακόψαι αὐτὸν τοῦ ἁμαρτεῖν. Τοὺς τοίνυν παρακούοντας *τῆς ἐκκλησίας* ἐκβάλλεσθαι λέγει, οὐ μίσει τῷ πρὸς αὐτούς, ἀλλ᾽ ἵνα μὴ τῆς ἰδίας διδασκαλίας μεταδῶσιν ἄλλοις. Παρεικάζει δὲ τοῖς ἀπίστοις τοὺς τελώνας, διὰ τὸ ἄπληστον τῆς πλεονεξίας.

Ὅσα ἂν δήσητε ἐπὶ τῆς γῆς.[1687] Ὡς Θεὸς τὸ θεοπρεπὲς ἀξίωμα[mccxxviii] παραπέμπει τοῖς μαθηταῖς, | **145r** καί φησι ὅτι τὰ ὧδε δεθέντα ἢ λυθέντα, *δεδεμένα* ἢ *λελυμένα* μένει ἐν τοῖς οὐρανοῖς. Ὅσοι γὰρ ἀπειθοῦντες ἐκβάλλονται ὑπὸ τῶν διδασκάλων τῆς ἐκκλησίας δεσμούμενοι ταῖς σειραῖς τῶν ἰδίων ἁμαρτιῶν, συγκαταδεσμοῦνται ὑπὸ Χριστοῦ *ἐν* τοῖς οὐρανοῖς. Καὶ πάλιν, συλλύονται οἱ λυθέντες ἐξ αὐτῶν μετανοήσαντος, τοῦ ἡμαρτηκότος δηλονότι. Ὁ δὲ ἐμμένων τῇ ἁμαρτίᾳ πρὸς τῇ ἐνταῦθα τιμωρίᾳ καὶ τῇ ἐκεῖθεν κολάσει ὑπόκειται. Ἐξ ὧν δὲ οἱ ἡγούμενοι δύνανται λῦσαι τὸν μετανοοῦντα, δίδωσι μετανοίας καιρὸν[mccxxix] τῷ ἀφορισθέντι.

> Τότε προσελθὼν αὐτῷ ὁ Πέτρος, εἶπε. *Κύριε, ποσάκις ἁμαρτήσει εἰς ἐμὲ ὁ ἀδελφός μου, καὶ ἀφήσω αὐτῷ; ἕως ἑπτάκις;*[1688] *Δύο* συνηγμένοι ἐπὶ τῷ τοῦ Χριστοῦ ὀνόματι σῶμα καὶ πνεῦμα μὴ ἀντιστρατευόμενα, ὑποταγέντος μὲν τοῦ σώματος, τοῦ δὲ πνεύματος μεταδιδόντος αὐτῷ θείας ζωῆς. τρεῖς δὲ ὅτε ὁλόκληρον πνεῦμα, ψυχή, σῶμα τηρεῖται ἐν

1683 Eph. 1:10.
1684 Matt. 18:15: Ἐὰν δὲ ἁμάρτήσῃ. Cf. Luke, 17:3-4; Lev. 19:17.
1685 Matt. 18:17.
1686 Matt. 5:39.
1687 Matt. 18:18.
1688 Matt. 18:21.

τῇ παρουσίᾳ Χριστοῦ.[1689] ἔτι αἱ δύο διαθῆκαι, ὅταν ὁ συναγωγεὺς αὐτῶν τὸ πνεῦμα τὸ ἅγιον ἐν αὐταῖς ᾖ, τρεῖς δέ, νόμον, προφήτας, εὐαγγέλιον. [ἢ ‹ἄνδρα καὶ γυναῖκα καὶ τέκνον, ἢ› θυμὸν καὶ ἐπιθυμίαν καὶ λογισμόν, ἢ τὴν κλῆσιν καὶ ἐκλογὴν καὶ τὸ εἰς πρώτην τιμὴν τασσόμενον γένος μεθ' ἡμῶν.¨ τήρει δὲ ὅτι οὐκ εἶπεν. ἔσομαι, ἀλλ' εἰμί. ὡς θεὸς γὰρ πανταχοῦ ὢν, ἐν μέσῳ ἐστὶ τῶν δι' εὐσεβείας συναπτομένων. ἡ γὰρ πανεπίσκοπος τοῦ θεοῦ δύναμις ἀμερίστως μεριστὴ γίνεται τοῖς ἀξίοις.][mccxxx]

Δύο συνημμένοι [sic] ἐπὶ τῷ τοῦ Χριστοῦ ὀνόματι, σῶμα καὶ πνεῦμα, μὴ ἀντιστρατευόμενα. ὑποταγέντος μὲν τοῦ σώματος, τοῦ δὲ πνεύματος μεταδιδόντος αὐτῷ θείας ζωῆς. *τρεῖς* δέ τε ὁλόκληρον, πνεῦμα, ψυχή, σῶμα, τηρεῖ τῇ παρουσίᾳ Χριστοῦ. Ἢ αἱ δύο διαθῆκαι, ὅταν ὁ συναγωγεὺς αὐτῶν τὸ Πνεῦμα τὸ ἅγιον ἐν αὐταῖς ᾖ. *τρεῖς* δέ, νόμον, προφήτας, Εὐαγγέλιον. ἢ θυμὸν καὶ ἐπιθυμίαν, καὶ λογισμόν. ἢ τὴν κλῆσιν καὶ ἐκλογήν, καὶ τὸ εἰς πρώτην τιμὴν τασσόμενον γένος μεθ' ἡμῶν. Τήρει δέ, ὅτι οὐκ εἶπεν ἔσομαι, ἀλλ' *εἰμί*. Ὡς Θεὸς γὰρ πανταχοῦ ὢν, ἐν μέσῳ ἐστὶ τῶν δι' εὐσεβείας συναπτομένων. Ἡ γὰρ πανεπίσκοπος τοῦ Θεοῦ δύναμις ἀμέριστος [sic] μεριστὴ γίνεται τοῖς ἀξίοις.[mccxxxi]

46

146v (ΩΡΙΓΕΝΟΥΣ) *Οὐ λέγω σοι ἕως ἑπτάκις.*[1690] Ὅρα εἰ δύναται· ἐπεὶ ὁ μὲν ἓξ ἀριθμὸς ἐργατικὸς καὶ ἐν γενέσει κόσμου, ὁ δὲ ἑπτὰ ἀναπαύσεως. Ὁ μὲν τὰ τοῦ κόσμου καὶ ὑλικὰ ἀγαπῶν ἐξαμαρτάνων, τέλος ἔχει τὴν ἑβδομάδα· ὅ | **147r** περ νοήσας *ὁ Πέτρος* συγχωρεῖν θέλει ἐν τῷ ἑπτά. Ὁ δὲ Κύριος ἐπιτείνει τοῦτο ἐν τῷ αὐτῷ τρόπῳ. Ἀναλογία γὰρ μονάδων πρὸς δεκάδας καὶ ἑκατοντάδας, ὡς τὸν ὑπερβάντα τὰ κοσμικά, κἂν τελειότερα ᾖ τὰ ἁμαρτήματα, μηκέτι ἔχειν *ἄφεσιν.*[1691] Ἡ γὰρ ἄφεσις ἐπὶ τὰ τῇδε, εἴτε βράδιον εἴτε τάχιον.

Ὅρα εἰ δύναται. ἐπεὶ ὁ μὲν ἓξ ἀριθμὸς ἐργατικὸς καὶ ἐν γενέσει κόσμου, ὁ δὲ ἑπτὰ ἀναπαύσεως, ὁ μὲν τὰ τοῦ κόσμου καὶ ὑλικὰ ἀγαπῶν ἓξ ἁμαρτάνων τέλος ἔχει τὴν ἑβδομάδα. ὅπερ νοήσας *ὁ Πέτρος* συγχωρεῖν θέλει ἐν τῷ ἑπτά. ὁ δὲ κύριος ἐπιτείνει τοῦτο ἐν τῷ αὐτῷ τρόπῳ, ἀναλογία γὰρ μονάδος πρὸς δεκάδας καὶ ἑκατοντάδας, ὡς τὸν ὑπερβάντα τὰ κοσμικά, κἂν [τε]λειότερα ᾖ τὰ ἁμαρτήματα, μηκέτι ἔχειν ἄφεσιν. ἡ γὰρ ἄφεσις ἐπὶ τὰ τῇδε εἴτε βράδιον εἴτε τάχιον.[mccxxxii]

Ὅρα δὲ εἰ δύναται. Ἐπεὶ ὁ μὲν ἓξ ἀριθμὸς ἐργατικὸς καὶ ἐν γενέσει κόσμου, ὁ δὲ ἑπτὰ ἀναπαύσεως. ὁ μὲν τὰ τοῦ κόσμου καὶ ὑλικὰ ἀγαπῶν, ἐξαμαρτάνων τέλος ἔχει τὴν ἑβδομάδα. ὅπερ νοήσας ὁ Πέτρος, συγχωρεῖν θέλει ἐν τῷ ἑπτά. Ὁ δὲ Κύριος ἐπιτείνει τοῦτο ἐν τῷ αὐτῷ τρόπῳ, ἀναλόγως γὰρ μονάδος πρὸς δεκάδας καὶ ἑκατοντάδας, ὡς τὸν ὑπερβάντα τὰ κοσμικὰ μηκέτι ἔχειν ἄφεσιν τῶν ἁμαρτημάτων. ἡ γὰρ ἄφεσις ἐπὶ τὰ τῇδε εἴτε βραδύ, εἴτε τάχιον.[mccxxxiii]

1689 1 Thess. 5:23.

1690 Matt. 18:22.

1691 Cf. Mark, 1:4; Luke, 3:3; 24:47; Acts, 2:38; 5:31; 10:43; 10:38; 24:18; Col. 1:14.

Διὰ τοῦτο ὡμοιώθη ἡ βασιλεία τῶν ‹οὐρανῶν›.[1692] Ἡ ἡ μὲν περίνοια τῆς παραβολῆς διδάσκει συγχωρεῖν τὰ εἰς ἡμᾶς ἁμαρτανόμενα, μάλιστα τῷ δεηθέντι, ἀλλὰ καὶ ὅτι τῶν ἀφεθέντων εἴσπραξις γίνεται, εἰ μὴ καὶ αὐτοὶ ἀφῶμεν τὰ εἰς ἡμᾶς.

> Ἡ μὲν περίνοια τῆς παραβολῆς διδάσκειν βούλεται συγχωρητικοὺς εἶναι τῶν εἰς ἡμᾶς ἡμαρτημένων τοῖς ἀδικήσασιν ἡμᾶς, καὶ μάλιστα εἰ μετὰ τὸ ἀδικῆσαι δέοιτο τοῦ ἠδικημένου ὁ ἀδικήσας, συγχωρηθῆναι ἀξιῶν αὐτῷ τὰ προημαρτημένα. καὶ ταῦτα διδάσκειν ἡμᾶς βούλεται ἡ παραβολὴ παριστᾶσα ὅτι καὶ τῶν ἤδη συγχωρηθέντων ἡμῖν ὑπὸ τοῦ θεοῦ ἁμαρτημάτων, ἐφ᾽ οἷς ἄφεσιν εἰλήφαμεν, ἔκπραξις γένοιτ᾽ ἂν καὶ μετὰ τὴν ἄφεσιν, εἰ μὴ ἀφίοιμεν τοῖς ἡμᾶς ἠδικηκόσι τὰ ἁμαρτήματα αὐτῶν, ὡς μηδὲ τὴν τυχοῦσαν μνήμην ἔτι ἐν ἡμῖν καταλείπεσθαι τοῦ ἠδικῆσθαι. ἀλλ᾽ ὅλῃ καρδίᾳ ὑπὸ ἀμνησικακίας ὠφελημένῃ (οὐ τῆς τυχούσης ἀρετῆς) συγχωροῖμεν τῷ ἡμᾶς ἀδικήσαντι τὰ κακῶς εἴς τινα ἡμῶν ἀπ᾽ αὐτοῦ καὶ ἐπιβουλευτικῶς πεπραγμένα.[mccxxxiv]

Τὰ δὲ κατὰ μέρος συνεῖναι τοῦ *πνεῦμα Χριστοῦ*[1693] ἔχοντός ἐστι. *Βασιλεία* μὲν γὰρ *οὐρανῶν* ὁ Χριστὸς[1694][mccxxxv] *ἐν ὁμοιώματι σαρκὸς ἁμαρτίας*[1695] γενόμενος καὶ *ὑπὲρ ἡμῶν* ἁμαρτία.[1696] Ὁ θεῖος λόγος καὶ αὐτοσοφία[mccxxxvi] ὡμοίωται *βασιλεῖ.*[1697] Δοῦλοι δὲ νῦν οἱ τοῦ νόμου οἰκονόμοι καὶ πραγματευταί. Συναίρει δὲ *λόγον,*[1698] ὅτε τοὺς *πάντας* ἡμᾶς *δεῖ* παραστῆναι τῷ βήματι τοῦ Χριστοῦ, *ἵνα κομίσηται ἕκαστος πρὸς ἃ ἔπραξε.*[1699] *Μυρίων* δὲ *ταλάντων*[1700] ἡμᾶς χρεωφειλέτας ὁ λόγος παρίστησιν, ἐπειδὴ πολλὰ καλὰ ἔχοντες ἐξ αὐτοῦ καὶ πολὺ ὀφείλοντες αὐτὸν ἀγαπᾶν καὶ ἁμαρτάνομεν εἰς αὐτόν. Τὸ γὰρ φυλάσσειν *τὰς ἐντολὰς*[1701] δοκεῖ τις ἀμοιβὴ γίνεσθαι τῶν εἰς ἡμᾶς γεγονότων. Ὁ δὲ μηδὲν ποιήσας ἀγαθόν, ἄπορος. Τὸ δὲ πιπράσκεσθαι αὐτὸν σὺν τοῖς αὐτοῦ[1702] δηλοῖ τὴν ἀφαίρεσιν τῶν ἀγαθῶν καὶ τὴν ἀπὸ Θεοῦ ἀλλοτρίωσιν,[mccxxxvii] ὅπερ ἐστὶ δεῖγμα τῆς ἐσχάτης κολάσεως, τῆς μελλούσης ἐπάγεσθαι τοῖς ἡμαρτηκόσιν.

| **147v** *Ἐκέλευσεν ὁ Κύριος αὐτοῦ πραθῆναι καὶ τὴν γυναῖκα.*[1703] Ἴδιον τῆς παραβολῆς τὸ κελεῦσαι *πραθῆναι τὴν γυναῖκα καὶ τὰ τέκνα καὶ πάντα ὅσα ἔχει καὶ ἀποδοθῆναι.* Ἐπὶ μὲν γὰρ τῶν ἀνθρωπίνων πραγμάτων τοῦτο δυνατόν· ἐπὶ δὲ τῆς παρὰ Χριστῷ κρίσεως οὐκ οἰκείων πιπρασκομένων οὐδὲ χρημάτων ἡ ἀπόδοσις ἂν γένοιτο τῶν

1692 Matt. 18:23.
1693 Rom. 8:9; 1 Peter, 1:11.
1694 Cf. Matt. 3:2; 4:17; 10:7.
1695 Rom. 8:3.
1696 2 Cor. 5:21.
1697 Matt. 18:23.
1698 Matt. 18:23.
1699 2 Cor. 5:10.
1700 Matt. 18:24.
1701 Lev. 22:31; 26:3; Deut. 4:2; 5:29; 6:17&25; 7:9&11; *et passim*; Psalms 88:32; 118: 4; 60; 63; 134; Ecclesiastes, 12:13; Ez. 18:21; Daniel, 9:4.
1702 Matt. 18:25.
1703 Matt. 18:25.

ὀφειλομένων, ἀλλ' ὑποδείκνυται ἡ πάντων ἀφαίρεσις ὧν τις ἔχει τερπνῶν καὶ καθ' ἡδονὴν καὶ ἡ διὰ τῶν παθημάτων ἀπόδοσις. Ἐπὶ δὲ τῶν ἐναντίων, τὸ ἐναντίον λύεται.[mccxxxviii] Τὰς οὖν ἡδονὰς οἱ πόνοι λύουσι. Διὸ καὶ ὁ Σωτὴρ ἀποδοῦναι *τὰς ἁμαρτίας τοῦ κόσμου*[1704] βουληθεὶς πέπονθεν ὑπὲρ ἡμῶν.[1705]

καὶ τὸ δάνειον ἀφῆκεν αὐτῷ.[1706] Διὰ τοῦ ἀφεῖναι δηλοῖ τὴν μετάνοιαν καὶ τὴν ἄφατον τοῦ Θεοῦ φιλανθρωπίαν συγχωροῦσαν τὰ προγεγονότα πταίσματα ὅτε καὶ ἡμεῖς συγχωροῦμεν, καὶ ὅτι λύει τὴν ἁμαρτίαν ἡ μετάνοια πρὸ τῆς κολάσεως, καὶ ὅτι ὁ Θεὸς δίδωσι καὶ τὰ ὑπὲρ αἴτησιν. Οὐχ ὡς θέλων δὲ πωλῆσαι αὐτὸν εἴρηκε τοῦτο, ἀλλ' ὡς θέλων αὐτὸν ποιῆσαι ὥστε παρακαλέσαι ἵνα συγχωρήσῃ αὐτῷ, ἐπεὶ οὐκ ἂν οὔτε μετὰ ταῦτα παρεχώρει. Μετὰ δὲ τὸ λογοθέσιον τοῦτο ποιεῖ, διδάσκων ἡμᾶς ὅσα ἐχρεώστει καὶ ὅσων ἠλευθερώθη καὶ ὅτι τοσούτων τυχὼν οὐκ ἐπαιδεύθη εἰς ἀρετήν, ἀλλ' ὠμὸς γέγονε περὶ τὸν σύνδουλον. Καὶ ὅτι ὀλίγην αἰτήσαντος προθεσμίαν, ὁ Κύριος δι' ὑπερβολὴν εὐσπλαγχνίας τὸ πᾶν συνεχώρησεν, ὅπερ καὶ πρὸ τοῦ αἰτηθῆναι ἤθελε ποιῆσαι, ἀλλ' ἐβου | **148r** λήθη κἀκείνου εἶναί τι, ἵνα μὴ αἰσχυνθῇ ὡς οὐδὲν αὐτὸς ποιήσας, καὶ ἵνα δι' ὧν ἤτησε μάθῃ συγγινώσκειν τοῖς αἰτοῦσι. Συνδούλους δὲ ἡμῶν τοὺς ἀγγέλους λέγει.

ἰδόντες δὲ οἱ σύνδουλοι αὐτοῦ.[1707] *Οἱ σύνδουλοι* οἱ καὶ μηνύοντες τὸν ἀπηνῶς χρησάμενον τῷ συνδούλῳ ἄγγελοί τέ εἰσι καὶ ἄνθρωποι τὴν οἰκονομίαν ἐγκεχειρισμένοι,[mccxxxix] ὁποῖος ἦν Παῦλος, ὁ *τῷ διαβόλῳ* παραδοὺς τὸν αἴσχιστα ἠδικηκότα.[1708] Καὶ ὥσπερ ὁ τὸ χρέος ἐκτίσας ἐλεύθερος γίνεται, οὕτως ὁ παθὼν ὑπὲρ ὧν ἠδίκησεν ἐλευθεροῦται πρὸς σωτηρίαν. Προσεκτέον δὲ κἀκείνῳ, ὅτι περὶ τοῦ δεῖν συγχωρεῖν ἀλλήλοις τοὺς ἀνθρώπους διαλεγόμενος, καὶ πρὸς τοῦτο τῇ παραβολῇ κεχρημένος, οὕτως ἤρξατο, *διὰ τοῦτο ὡμοιώθη ἡ βασιλεία τῶν οὐρανῶν.*[1709]

Καὶ ἐλθόντες διεσάφησαν.[1710] Οὐ φέροντες γὰρ τὴν πονηρίαν ἡμῶν οἱ ὁμόδουλοι ἡμῶν ἄγγελοι κατηγοροῦσιν ἡμῶν ἐπὶ Θεοῦ, οὐχ ὡς ἀγνοοῦντος, ἀλλ' ὡς ἀγανακτοῦντες κατὰ τῶν τοὺς τῆς φιλανθρωπίας πατούντων νόμους. *Βασανιστὰς*[1711] δὲ τοὺς ἐπὶ τῶν κολάσεων τεταγμένους ἀγγέλους[mccxl] λέγει. Τὸ δὲ *ἕως οὗ ἀποδῷ πᾶν τὸ ὀφειλόμενον,*[1712] τουτέστι διηνεκῶς[mccxli] αὐτὸν παρέδωκεν εἰς τὸ βασανίζεσθαι· οὐ γὰρ ἐδύνατο ἀποδοῦναί ποτε.[mccxlii] Ἐνταῦθα μὲν γὰρ ἐπιστρέφων τὸν ἄνθρωπον ὁ Θεὸς πειρασμοῖς καὶ νόσοις καὶ βασάνοις ἑτέραις παραδίδωσιν, ἐν δὲ τῷ μέλλοντι, ἀκαταπαύστως βασανίζεσθαι εἰς τὸ διηνεκές. Οὐκ εἶπε δέ, *οὕτως καὶ ὁ πατὴρ* ὑμῶν *ποιήσει*

1704 Odae (LXX), 14:9.
1705 Cf. 2 Cor. 5:21; Gal. 2:13; Col. 2:14; Rom. 5:8; 8:32; Tit. 2:14.
1706 Matt. 18:27.
1707 Matt. 18:31.
1708 1 Tim. 1:20.
1709 Matt. 18:23.
1710 Matt. 18:31.
1711 Matt. 18:34.
1712 Matt. 18:34.

ὑμῖν, ἀλλ᾽ ὁ πατήρ μου.[1713] Ἀνάξιοι γὰρ οἱ τοιοῦτοι ὀνομάζεσθαι υἱοὶ Θεοῦ. Διαγρά |
148v φει τοίνυν ὡς ἐν συντόμῳ ὁ λόγος τὴν ἄφατον τοῦ Θεοῦ φιλανθρωπίαν,[mccxliii] ἣν ὁ μὴ μιμησάμενος κατὰ τὸ δυνατὸν ἀπότομον ὑποστήσεται τιμωρίαν[mccxliv] παρὰ τοῦ δικαίου κριτοῦ. Εἰ δὲ καὶ εἴρηται *ἀμεταμέλητα τὰ χαρίσματα τοῦ Θεοῦ,*[1714] ἀλλὰ τοσοῦτον ἴσχυσεν ἡ κακία ὡς τοῦτον ἀνατρέψαι τὸν λόγον. Δύο οὖν ἡμᾶς ἀπαιτεῖ ὁ λόγος· καὶ μεμνῆσθαί τινα τῶν ἑαυτοῦ ἁμαρτημάτων καὶ ἀμνησικακεῖν τῷ πταίοντι.

> Οὐ φέροντες γὰρ τὴν πονηρίαν ἡμῶν οἱ ὁμόδουλοι ἡμῶν ἄγγελοι κατηγοροῦσιν ἡμῶν ἐπὶ θεῷ, οὐχ ὡς ἀγνοοῦντι, ἀλλ᾽ ὡς ἀγανακτοῦντες κατὰ τῶν τοὺς φιλανθρωπίας πατούντων νόμους. *βασανιστὰς* δὲ τοὺς ἐπὶ τῶν κολάσεων τεταγμένους ἀγγέλους λέγει. τὸ δὲ *ἕως οὗ ἀποδῷ πᾶν τὸ ὀφειλόμενον*, τοῦτ᾽ ἔστιν διηνεκῶς αὐτὸν παρέδωκεν εἰς τὸ βασανίζεσθαι. οὐ γὰρ ἠδύνατο ἀποδοῦναί ποτε. ἐνταῦθα μὲν γὰρ ἐπιστρέφων τὸν ἄνθρωπον ὁ θεὸς πειρασμοῖς καὶ νόσοις καὶ βασάνοις ἑτέραις παραδίδωσιν, ἐν δὲ τῷ μέλλοντι ἀκαταπαύστως βασανίζεσθαι εἰς τὸ διηνεκές. οὐκ εἶπε δὲ *οὕτως καὶ ὁ πατὴρ* ὑμῶν *ποιήσει ὑμῖν, ἀλλ᾽ ὁ πατήρ μου.* ἀνάξιοι γὰρ οἱ τοιοῦτοι ὀνομάζεσθαι υἱοὶ θεοῦ. διαγράφει τοίνυν ὡς ἐν συντόμῳ ὁ λόγος τὴν ἄφατον τοῦ θεοῦ φιλανθρωπίαν, ἣν ὁ μὴ μιμησάμενος κατὰ τὸ δυνατὸν ἀπότομον ὑποστήσεται τιμωρίαν παρὰ τοῦ δικαίου κριτοῦ. εἰ δὲ καὶ εἴρηται. *ἀμεταμέλητα τὰ χαρίσματα* τοῦ θεοῦ, ἀλλὰ τοσοῦτον ἴσχυσεν ἡ κακία ὡς τοῦτον ἀνατρέψαι τὸν λόγον. δύο οὖν ἡμᾶς ἀπαιτεῖ ὁ λόγος καὶ μεμνῆσθαί τινα τῶν ἑαυτοῦ ἁμαρτημάτων καὶ ἀμνησικακεῖν τῷ πταίοντι.[mccxlv]

> Ποιεῖ τοῦτο ἐκείνους εὐεργετῶν, καὶ δι᾽ ἐκείνων πολλοὺς ἑτέρους.[mccxlvi]

> ἡ γὰρ τῆς τούτων ἀσθενείας διόρθωσις, ἑτέροις ὑπόθεσις θεογνωσίας ἐγένετο.[mccxlvii]

> ἤ, ὡς Ματθαῖός φησιν, ἐθεράπευσεν αὐτούς, διττὴν αὐτοῖς προσάγων τὴν ἴασιν, τήν τε κατὰ ψυχὴν (τοιαύτη γὰρ ἡ διδασκαλία) καὶ τὴν κατὰ σῶμα. ἡ γὰρ τῆς τούτων ἀσθενείας διόρθωσις, οὐ μόνον αὐτοῖς, ἀλλὰ καὶ ἑτέροις ὑπόθεσις θεογνωσίας ἐγένετο.[mccxlviii]

> Ἐθεράπευε δὲ ὁ Χριστός, ἐκείνους τε εὐεργετῶν, καὶ δι᾽ ἐκείνων πολλοὺς ἑτέρους. Ἡ γὰρ τῆς τούτων ἀσθενείας διόρθωσις ἑτέροις ὑπόθεσις θεογνωσίας ἐγίνετο.[mccxlix]

Καὶ προσῆλθον αὐτῷ οἱ Φαρισαῖοι.[1715] Πονηρῶς ἐρωτῶσι τὸν Σωτῆρα, ἵνα ἐὰν εἴπῃ ἔξεστιν, εἴπωσιν αὐτῷ· πῶς οὖν εἶπας ὥστε μὴ ἐξεῖναί τινι ἀπολύειν *γυναῖκα παρεκτὸς λόγου πορνείας;*[1716] Ἐὰν δὲ εἴπῃ οὐκ ἔξεστι, διαβάλωσιν αὐτὸν ὡς ἀντινομοθετοῦντα Μωσῇ. Οἴονται γὰρ ἐγκαλέσειν αὐτῷ καθ᾽ ἑκάτερον, ἢ ὡς ἐπὶ τοῖς τυχοῦσι διαλύοντι τοὺς γάμους ἢ ὡς μετὰ ἁμαρτημάτων ἐπιτρέποντι συνοικεῖν.

> Here is why the sect of Pharisees and scribes asks him whether it is lawful for a man to divorce his wife for any reason. They want to trap him in the horns of a dilemma, as the saying has it. No matter what he replies, it will expose him

---

1713 Matt. 18:35.
1714 Rom. 11:29.
1715 Matt. 19:3.
1716 Matt. 5:32; cf. 19:9.

to a prevarication. If he says that a wife should to be divorced for any reason and another can be married, this preacher of chastity would appear as teaching contrary things. But if he replies that for no cause should she be divorced, he will be held guilty of blasphemy and as contravening the doctrine of Moses, and, through Moses, that of God.[mccl]

Τί οὖν πρὸς τοῦτό φησιν ὁ Χριστός; Δείκνυσιν ὅτι οὐ μόνον αὐτοῦ ἀλλὰ καὶ τοῦ Πατρὸς ἔργον ἐστὶ τοῦτο, τὸ τῆς μονογαμίας δηλονότι. Ὁ γὰρ ποιήσας ἐξ ἀρχῆς ἕνα ἄρσενα καὶ μίαν θήλειαν[1717] (οὐ μὴν πολλὰς θηλείας) ἐδίδαξεν ὅτι οὐ δεῖ ἕνα πολλαῖς συνοικεῖν, ἀλλ᾽ οὔτε μίαν πολλοῖς. Οἰκονομικῶς δὲ οὐκ εἶπεν ἐγὼ ὁ κτίσας τὸν ἄνθρωπον, ἀλλ᾽ *ὁ ποιήσας ἀπ᾽ ἀρχῆς*,[1718] πρὸς τὸ μὴ ταράξαι ἀτελεῖς ὄντας τοὺς Ἰουδαίους. Τήρει δὲ ὅτι τούτων καὶ τῶν ἑξῆς ἐν τῇ Γενέσει ὑπὸ τοῦ Ἀδὰμ νομιζομένων λέγεσθαι, ὁ Σωτὴρ ὑπὸ Θεοῦ αὐτὰ εἰρῆσθαί φησι, οἱονεὶ νομοθετοῦντος.[1719] Οὕτω γὰρ περισπούδαστόν ἐστι τὸ τῆς ἑνώσεως ταύτης τῷ Θεῷ, | **149r** ὅτι καὶ γονεῖς ἀφεῖναι ἐκέλευσε καὶ προσκολληθῆναι ἑαυτοῖς, δι᾽ οὗ δηλοῖ τὸ ἀδιάσπαστον. Διὰ γὰρ τῆς φυσικῆς στοργῆς τὰς ψυχὰς ἑνούμενοι *εἰς μίαν* ἐκτελοῦνται *σάρκα, καὶ οὐκέτι εἰσὶ δύο*.[1720] Οὐ δεῖ οὖν τὰ ἐκ Θεοῦ ζευχθέντα δι᾽ ἀνθρώπου λύεσθαι. Καὶ γὰρ πρὸ Μωσέως οὕτω νενομοθέτηται ὑπὸ Θεοῦ. Οὐκ εἶπε δὲ *μὴ χωριζέτω* ὁ Μωϋσῆς, ἀλλ᾽ *ἄνθρωπος*,[1721] τουτέστιν ἡ εἰς ἄνθρωπον τιμὴ μὴ ἀντιπραττέτῳ τῇ τοῦ Θεοῦ.

Διὰ οὖν τῆς σοφῆς ἀποκρίσεως ταύτης περιήγεν ὁ Κύριος τοὺς Ἰουδαίους μὴ αὐτῷ ἐγκαλεῖν ἀλλὰ τῷ Μωϋσεῖ, ἐπείπερ ἀμφότερα εἰρηκὼς ἐδόκει ἐναντία ἑαυτῷ λέγειν. Διὸ καὶ ἀναγκασθέντες, εἰς μέσον ἄγουσι τὸν Μωϋσῆν ὡς ἀντινομοθετοῦντα, καί φασι· πῶς *οὖν Μωυσῆς ἐνετείλατο δοῦναι βιβλίον ἀποστασίου καὶ ἀπολύειν*;[1722] Λέγει αὐτοῖς ὅτι *Μωσῆς πρὸς τὴν σκληροκαρδίαν ὑμῶν*.[1723] Τότε ὁ Κύριος περιτρέπων τὸ πᾶν τῆς κατηγορίας εἰς τοὺς Ἰουδαίους, ὑπὲρ Μωσέως ἀπολογεῖται καί φησι οὐκ ἐναντία τῷ Θεῷ νομοθετῶν Μωσῆς τοῦτο διέταξεν, ἀλλὰ τῇ τῶν τρόπων ὑμῶν μοχθηρίᾳ μετρῶν τὸ πρᾶγμα τὴν ἀντινομίαν εἰσήγαγεν, ἵνα μὴ δι᾽ ἀκολασίαν ἑτέραις συνεῖναι βουλόμενοι ἀνέλητε τὰς πρώτας. Ταύτην οὖν τὴν ἀτελῆ διορθούμενος νομοθεσίαν, ἐπὶ τὴν ἀρχαίαν αὐτοὺς ἀνάγει νομοθεσίαν, μὴ διδοὺς ἄδειαν λύειν τὸν γάμον, εἰ μὴ μόνῳ τῷ καταλαβόντι πορνευομένην τὴν γυναῖκα διὰ τὸ τὴν γνησίαν γονὴν νοθεύειν. Ἵν᾽ οὖν μή τις εἴπῃ πόθεν δῆλον ὅτι διὰ *τὴν σκληροκαρδίαν ἡμῶν* εἶπε τοῦτο Μωσῆς, ἐπιστομίζει αὐτοὺς δι᾽ ὧν λέγει, ‹ὅτι› πρὸ Μωσέως | **149v** οὐκ ἦν οὕτως. Εἰ γὰρ συνέφερεν ὁ Μωσέως, οὐκ ἂν ἄλλος ἐδόθη ἐξ ἀρχῆς ὅτε ἐπλάσθη ὁ ἄνθρωπος, ὅτε τὰς πρώτας αὐτῷ διαταγὰς δέδωκεν ὁ Θεός. Μετὰ οὖν τὸ ἐπιστομίσαι αὐτούς, λοιπὸν

1717 Gen. 1:27; Matt. 19:4.
1718 Matt. 19:4.
1719 Cf. Matt. 9:5-6; Gen. 2:24.
1720 Gen. 2:24; Matt. 19:5-6; Mark, 10:8. Cf. 1 Cor. 6:16; Eph. 5:31.
1721 Cf. Gen. 2:24; Matt. 19:6; Mark, 10:9.
1722 Matt. 19:7.
1723 Matt. 19:8.

ἐπάγει καὶ τὸ δοκοῦν αὐτῷ. Τὴν γὰρ πορνευθεῖσαν ἐκβάλλει ὡς τὸν γαμικὸν διαλύουσαν δεσμόν, μοιχείᾳ ὑποβαλὼν τοὺς ἄνευ τούτου τολμῶντας τοῦτο ποιεῖν. Ὡς γὰρ ἄτοπον ἐκβάλλειν τὴν σώφρονα, οὕτως ἀσεβὲς τὸ κατασχεῖν μοιχαλίδα. Οὐ γὰρ πολυγαμίαν ἔτι συγχωρεῖ ὁ Θεὸς (τότε γὰρ ἀπῄτει ὁ καιρὸς ὅτε αὐξάνεσθαι καὶ πληθύνεσθαι[1724] ἐχρῆν), ἀλλὰ μονογαμίαν νομοθετεῖ διὰ τῶν εἰρημένων.

Καὶ ὁ ἀπολελυμένην γαμήσας μοιχᾶται.[1725] Μοιχεία φησὶ τὸ τῇ μὴ ἰδίᾳ συνεῖναι, οὐκ ἰδίᾳ δὲ σύνεστιν ὁ τὴν ἰδίαν ἀπολιπών. Διὰ τοῦτο *μοιχᾶται ἐπ᾽* αὐτήν, τουτέστιν ἐπὶ τὴν δευτέραν, ἣν ἐπεισάγει τῇ κατὰ φύσιν αὐτῷ συνημμένῃ, ἐὰν τὸν ἴδιον καταλίπῃ. Πῶς οὖν ὁ νόμος οὐ συνεχώρει λέγων *οὐ μοιχεύσεις*;[1726] Ἐροῦμεν ὅτι ὁ μὲν νόμος τὴν προφανῆ μοιχείαν ἀπεκώλυεν, ὅτε τὴν συνοικοῦσαν ἑτέρῳ τις διαφθείροι. Ὁ δὲ Σωτὴρ καὶ τὴν οὐχ ὁμολογουμένην παρὰ πᾶσιν ‹οὐδὲ γινωσκομένην τῇ φύσει οὐδὲ διελεγχομένην› ὅτι μοιχεία ἐστί. Τῆς μέντοι πόρνης ἂν ἀποστῇς, συγχωρεῖ ὁ Χριστός, ὅτι δὴ διέλυσεν αὐτὴ τὴν φυσικὴν σύζευξιν.[mccli]

> Μοιχείαν δέ φησι τὸ τῇ ἰδίᾳ μὴ συνεῖναι. οὐκ ἰδίᾳ δὲ σύνεστιν ὁ τὴν ἰδίαν ἀπολιπών. διὰ τοῦτο *μοιχᾶται ἐπ᾽ αὐτήν*, τοῦτ᾽ ἔστιν ἐπὶ τὴν δευτέραν, ἣν ἐπεισάγει τῇ κατὰ φύσιν αὐτῷ συνημμένῃ, ἐὰν τὸν ἴδιον καταλίπῃ. πῶς οὖν ὁ νόμος οὐ συνεχώρει ὁ τὸ *οὐ μοιχεύσεις* λέγων; ἐροῦμεν, ὅτι ὁ μὲν νόμος τὴν προφανῆ μοιχείαν ἀπεκώλυσεν, ὅτε τὴν συνοικοῦσαν ἕτερός τις διαφθείροι. ὁ δὲ σωτὴρ καὶ τὴν οὐχ ὁμολογουμένην παρὰ πᾶσιν οὐδὲ γινωσκομένην τῇ φύσει οὐδὲ διελεγχομένην, ὅτι μοιχεία ἐστίν, τὴν μέντοι πορνεύσασαν ἀποστῆσαι συγχωρεῖ Χριστός, ὅτι δὴ διέλυσεν αὕτη τὴν φυσικὴν σύζευξιν καὶ οὐκέτι ὑπὸ τοῦ ἀνδρὸς τοῦτο γίνεται.[mcclii]

Λέγουσιν αὐτῷ οἱ μαθηταὶ αὐτοῦ.[1727] Ὅτε ἐξ ἀρχῆς ἐλέχθη ὁ λόγος, οὐκ ἐνόησαν αὐτὸν οἱ μαθηταί. Νῦν δὲ σαφέστερον αὐτὸν γνόντες, θορυβοῦνται καὶ φασὶ εἰ διὰ τοῦτο συνήφθησαν, ἵνα ἓν ὦσι καὶ ἀδιάσπαστοι μένωσι παρ᾽ ὅ | **150r** λον τὸν βίον, κἂν μοχθηρὰ λίαν καὶ θηριώδης ᾖ ἡ γυνή, οὐ συμφέρει γαμῆσαι. Βέλτιον γὰρ ἄνθρωπον μὴ γαμεῖν καὶ πρὸς τὴν φυσικὴν ἐπιθυμίαν παλαίειν ἢ πρὸς γυναῖκα πονηράν. Αἰτίαν γὰρ ἀνθρώπου μετὰ τῆς γυναικὸς τὴν ἀδιάσπαστον ἕνωσιν λέγει. Ἤτοι οὕτω φησί· εἰ αἰτίαν λήψεται καὶ παρανομίαν ὁ ἀνὴρ ἐπὶ τούτοις ἐκβάλλων τὴν γυναῖκα, *οὐ συμφέρει γαμῆσαι.*[1728] Κουφότερον γὰρ πρὸς ἐπιθυμίαν μάχεσθαι καὶ πρὸς ἑαυτὸν ἢ πρὸς γυναῖκα πονηράν. Τί οὖν ὁ Κύριος ἐπαίρει τὸ πρᾶγμα, μέγα λέγων τὸ τῆς παρθενίας εἶναι κατόρθωμα καὶ δυσκόλως κατορθούμενον οἷς καὶ ὁ Θεὸς συνεργεῖ; Τοῖς γὰρ φυσικοῖς κινήμασιν οὐκ ἐξαρκεῖ ἡ φυσικὴ προαίρεσις μάχεσθαι εἰ μὴ καὶ ἡ θεία προσεπικουρήσει δύναμις. Δι᾽ ὧν δὲ αὐτοὶ μὲν εἶπον κοῦφον τὸ τῆς παρθενίας αὐτὸς δὲ μέγα, ἐφέλκεται αὐτοὺς ὡς εἰς εὐχερές.

1724 Gen. 1:22&28; 8:17; 9:1&7.
1725 Matt. 19:9.
1726 Ex. 20:13; Deut. 5:17.
1727 Matt. 19:10.
1728 Matt. 19:10.

Ὁ δὲ εἶπεν αὐτοῖς· οὐ πάντες χωροῦσι τὸν λόγον.[1729] Πάρεστιν ἀπὸ τῆς τοῦ Κυρίου διαιρέσεως, τοῖς μὲν κάτω βαδίζουσιν ὑπομένειν τὸ ἐν κόσμῳ λυπηρὸν μᾶλλον ἢ τοῦ δικαίου καταφρονεῖν. Τοῖς δὲ δυναμένοις ὑπερβαίνειν τὸν κόσμον, οἷον ὑπὸ πτέρυγος[1730] φέρεσθαι πρὸς τὴν ἄνω δικαιοσύνην, ἀλύπους τε ὄντας καὶ ἐλευθέρους ἀπὸ τῶν ἐν κόσμῳ λυπηρῶν. Οὐκ ἐπιβάλλων οὖν *βρόχον*,[1731] εἶπεν· *οὐ πάντες χωροῦσι τὸν λόγον, ἀλλ' οἷς δέδοται.*[1732] Τὸ δὲ *οἷς δέδοται*, χαρισμάτων φυσικῶν ἐστι δηλωτικόν, ὅπερ ἄν τις καὶ φύσεως ἐπιτηδειότητα[mccliii] λέγοι καὶ τὴν ἀπὸ γεννήσεως εὐφυΐαν εἰς τὸ τῆς σωφροσύνης κατόρθωμα.[mccliv] | **150v** *Εἰσὶ γάρ* τινες καὶ ἐκ φύσεως διαφοραὶ πρὸς ἑκάστην ἀρετήν, τῶν μὲν μᾶλλον τῶν δὲ ἧττον πρὸς αὐτὴν πεφυκότων. Εἰ καὶ ὅτι μάλιστα μὴ ἐντελῆ τὰ φυσικά, μηδ' αὖ ἀμετακίνητα καὶ ἀκατόρθωτα παντελῶς, ἀλλὰ καὶ τὸ ἐπιτήδειον εἰς ἀγαθὸν ἀσκήσει τελειοῦται καὶ τὸ μὴ ἐπιτήδειον ἀγῶνι πολλῷ θεραπεύεται.

> Πάρεστιν ἀπὸ τῆς τοῦ κυρίου διαιρέσεως τοῖς μὲν ἐν ‹τῷ› κάτω βαδίζουσιν ὑπομένειν τὸ ἐν κόσμῳ λυπηρὸν μᾶλλον ἢ τοῦ δικαίου καταφρονεῖν, τοῖς δὲ δυναμένοις ὑπερβαίνειν τὸν κόσμον οἷον ὑπὸ πτέρυγος φέρεσθαι πρὸς τὴν ἄνω δικαιοσύνην, ἀλύπους δὲ ὄντας καὶ ἐλευθέρους ἀπὸ τῶν ἐν κόσμῳ λυπηρῶν. οὐκ ἐπιβάλλων οὖν βρόχον εἶπεν. *οὐ πάντες χωροῦσι τὸν λόγον, ἀλλ' οἷς δέδοται.* τὸ δὲ οἷς δέδοται χαρισμάτων φυσικῶν ἐστι δηλωτικόν, ὅπερ ἄν τις καὶ φύσεως ἐπιτηδειότητα λέγοι καὶ τὴν ἀπὸ γεννήσεως εὐφυίαν εἰς τὸ τῆς σωφροσύνης κατόρθωμα. *εἰσὶ γάρ* τινες καὶ ἐκ φύσεως διαφοραὶ πρὸς ἑκάστην ἀρετήν, τῶν μὲν μᾶλλον, τῶν δὲ ἧττον πρὸς αὐτὴν πεφυκότων. εἰ καὶ ὅτι μάλιστα μὴ ἐντελῆ τὰ φυσικά, μηδ' ἂν ἀμετακίνητα καὶ ἀκατόρθωτα παντελῶς, ἀλλὰ καὶ τὸ ἐπιτήδειον εἰς ἀγαθὸν ἀσκήσει τελειοῦται καὶ τὸ μὴ ἐπιτήδειον ἀγῶνι πολλῷ θεραπεύεται.[mcclv]

Εἰπὼν δὲ *ἀλλ' οἷς δέδοται*, ἔδειξε καὶ τῆς ἄνωθεν ἐπικουρίας[mcclvi] χρῄζειν. Ὀλίγων ἐστί φησι τὸ κατόρθωμα ὡς ὑπὲρ φύσιν ὂν καὶ τῆς τοῦ Θεοῦ ἐπικουρίας χρεία, δυνατὸν αὐτοῖς ποιοῦντος τοῦτο. Τρία δὲ εἴδη εἰρηκὼς εὐνούχων,[1733] μόνους ἐκείνους λέγει τυγχάνειν τῆς ἐν οὐρανοῖς τιμῆς τοὺς δι' ἀρετὴν πολεμοῦντας τοῖς τῆς σαρκὸς πάθεσι καὶ αἱρουμένους τὴν ἰσάγγελον πολιτείαν.[mcclvii] Οἱ γὰρ ἐκ φύσεως ἔχοντες τὴν σωφροσύνην ἄμισθοί εἰσιν. Ὁμοίως δὲ καὶ οἱ δι' ἀνθρωπίνην ἀρέσκειαν σωφρονεῖν νομιζόμενοι καὶ μὴ δι' αὐτὸ τὸ καλὸν[1734] (οἳ καὶ λέγονται εὐνουχίζεσθαι *ὑπὸ τῶν ἀνθρώπων*) καὶ αὐτοὶ ἄμισθοί εἰσιν. Εἰπὼν δὲ *ὁ δυνάμενος χωρεῖν χωρείτω*[1735] ἔδειξεν ὅτι οὐ νομοθετεῖ τὴν ἀγαμίαν, ἀλλὰ προαιρέσεως θέλει εἶναι τὸ πρᾶγμα.

1729 Matt. 19:11.
1730 Cod. ὑποπτερύγους.
1731 1 Cor. 7:35.
1732 Matt. 19:11.
1733 Matt. 19:12.
1734 Cf. *supra*, folio 134v: τὸ δι' αὐτὸ τὸ καλὸν καὶ μὴ δι' ἄλλο τι γινόμενον.
1735 Matt. 19:12.

47

(ΩΡΙΓΕΝΟΥΣ) Εὐνοῦχος ‹γάρ› ἐστιν ὁ τὴν εὔνοιαν φυλάττων τῷ ἰδίῳ δεσπότῃ καὶ βασιλεύων τῶν ἰδίων παθῶν.

> Εὐνοῦχός ἐστιν ὁ τὴν εὔνοιαν φυλάττων τῷ ἰδίῳ δεσπότῃ καὶ βασιλεύων τῶν ἰδίων παθῶν.[mcclviii]

Τότε προσηνέχθη αὐτῷ παιδία.[1736] Ἐπειδὴ ἀκόσμως καὶ μετὰ θορύβου προσῆγον αἱ μητέρες τὰ βρέφη, ἵνα μὴ ὀχλῆται ἐκώλυον οἱ μαθηταί, ἢ ὡς τιμὴν παρέχοντες τῷ Σωτῆρι. Αὐτὸς δὲ ἀνακόπει αὐτούς, διδάσκων ἐκ τούτου μηδενὸς *τῶν μικρῶν*[1737] καταφρονεῖν.
Ἤτοι ὡς ἐξευτελιζο | **151r** μένου τοῦ ἀξιώματος αὐτοῦ ἀπεσ‹ό›βουν[1738] τὰ παιδία. Ὁ δὲ Κύριος προσλαμβάνεται αὐτά διδάσκων ἡμᾶς κοσμικὸν τῦφον ἀποβάλλεσθαι.

> Διὰ τί οἱ μαθηταὶ ἀπεσόβουν τὰ παιδία, ἅπερ αὐτῷ προσηνέχθη ἐπὶ τὸ προσεύξασθαι αὐτοῖς; τύφου ἕνεκεν. αὐτὸς δὲ διδάσκων αὐτοὺς μετριάζειν, καὶ τύφον καταπατεῖν κοσμικόν, καὶ λαμβάνει καὶ εὐαγκαλίζεται, καὶ τοῖς τοιούτοις τὴν βασιλείαν κατεπήγγελται.[mcclix]

> Καὶ τίνος ἕνεκεν οἱ μαθηταὶ ἀπεσόβουν τὰ παιδία; Ἀξιώματος ἕνεκεν. Τί οὖν αὐτός; Διδάσκων αὐτοὺς μετριάζειν, καὶ τύφον καταπατεῖν κοσμικόν, καὶ λαμβάνει καὶ ἐναγκαλίζεται, καὶ τοῖς τοιούτοις τὴν βασιλείαν ἐπαγγέλλεται.[mcclx]

Μὴ κωλύετε αὐτά.[1739] Μόνη γὰρ κακία καὶ διαφθορὰ τῆς δημιουργίας κωλύει προσελθεῖν τῷ Δημιουργῷ, τὸ δὲ τῆς φρονήσεως ἐνδεὲς οὐ κωλυτικόν. Διὸ καὶ ἀκριβὴς ἡ λέξις. Οὐ γὰρ εἶπε, τούτων *ἐστὶν ἡ βασιλεία τῶν οὐρανῶν, ἀλλὰ τῶν τοιούτων.* Ἐπειδὴ γὰρ πρόσεστι τοῖς παιδίοις καὶ τὸ τῆς φρονήσεως ἐνδεές, οὗ ἀποτρέπων ὁ ἀπόστολος ἔλεγε, *μὴ παιδία γίνεσθε ταῖς φρεσίν.*[1740] Ὁ δὲ Μᾶρκος καὶ τὴν αἰτίαν ἐπεξῆλθεν, οἷον ἑρμηνεύων τὸ *τῶν τοιούτων ἐστὶν ἡ βασιλεία τῶν οὐρανῶν. Ἀμὴν λέγω ὑμῖν, ὃς ἂν μὴ δέξηται τὴν βασιλείαν τοῦ Θεοῦ ὡς παιδίον, οὐ μὴ εἰσέλθῃ εἰς αὐτήν.*[1741] Ἃ ἐκεῖνα τῇ φύσει ἔχει, ταῦτα ἡμᾶς ὁ Θεὸς θέλει ἔχειν τῇ προαιρέσει· τὴν ἁπλότητα, τὴν ἀμνησικακίαν, τὸ ἀγαπᾶν τὴν μητέρα κἂν τύπτωνται ὑπ' αὐτῆς, τὸ μὴ ζητεῖν πλείω τῶν εἰς κόρον.

1736 Matt. 19:13.
1737 Cf. Matt. 10:42; 18:6&10&14; Mark, 9:42; Luke, 17:2.
1738 Cod. ἀπεσώβουν.
1739 Matt. 19:14.
1740 1 Cor. 14:20.
1741 Mark, 10:15.

> Μόνη κακία καὶ διαφθορὰ τῆς δημιουργίας ἀποκωλύει προσελθεῖν τῷ δημιουργῷ, τὸ δὲ τῆς φρονήσεως ἐνδεὲς οὐ κωλυτικὸν τῆς προσόδου. πλήρωσιν γὰρ ἐπιζητεῖ, ταύτῃ δὲ ἡ πρόσοδος χαρίζεται. διὸ καὶ ἀκριβὴς ἡ λέξις *τῶν τοιούτων ἐστὶν ἡ βασιλεία τῶν οὐρανῶν*. οὐ γὰρ τούτων εἶπεν, ἀλλὰ *τῶν τοιούτων*, ἐπειδὴ πρόσεστιν καὶ τὸ τῆς φρονήσεως ἐνδεὲς τοῖς παισὶν οὗπερ ἀποτρέπων ὁ ἀπόστολος ἔλεγεν. *μὴ παιδία γίνεσθε ταῖς φρεσίν, ἀλλὰ τῇ κακίᾳ νηπιάζετε*. ὁ δὲ Μᾶρκος καὶ ἐπεξῆλθε τὴν αἰτίαν λέγων καὶ οἷον ἑρμηνεύων. *τῶν τοιούτων ἐστὶν ἡ βασιλεία* τῶν οὐρανῶν. *ἀμὴν λέγω ὑμῖν, ὃς ἂν μὴ δέξηται τὴν βασιλείαν τοῦ θεοῦ ὡς παιδίον, οὐ μὴ εἰσέλθῃ εἰς αὐτήν*. τὸ δὲ αὐτὸ καὶ ὁ Λουκᾶς καὶ ἀνωτέρω δὲ ἔλεγεν ὁ Ματθαῖος. *ὅστις οὖν ταπεινώσει ἑαυτὸν ὡς τὸ παιδίον τοῦτο, οὗτός ἐστιν ὁ μείζων ἐν τῇ βασιλείᾳ τῶν οὐρανῶν*. ἅπερ γὰρ ἐκεῖνα ἔχει τῇ φύσει, ταῦτα ἡμᾶς ὁ θεὸς θέλει ἔχειν τῇ προαιρέσει, τὴν ἁπλότητα, τὴν ἀμνησικακίαν, τὸ ἀγαπᾶν τοὺς γονέας, κἂν τύπτηται ὑπ᾽ αὐτῶν. ἐπετίθη δὲ τὰς χεῖρας τοῖς παιδίοις τῆς ἐπιθέσεως τῶν χειρῶν διδασκούσης τὴν τῆς θείας δυνάμεως ὅπλισιν.[mcclxi]

> ᾿Ιδίον [sic] τοῦ δημιουργοῦ τὸ τοῖς ἑαυτοῦ ποιήμασι χαίρειν, καὶ τὴν πρόσοδον αὐτῶν τὴν πρὸς ἑαυτὸν μὴ ἀποκωλύειν, καὶ μάλιστα τοῦ κωλύοντος οὐκ ὄντος. μόνη γὰρ κακία καὶ διαφθορὰ τῆς δημιουργίας ἀποκωλύει προσελθεῖν τῷ δημιουργῷ. τὸ δὲ τῆς φρονήσεως ἐνδεὲς οὐ κωλυτικὸν τῆς προσόδου. πλήρωσιν γὰρ ἐπιζητεῖ. ταύτην δὲ πρόσοδος χαρίζεται. διὸ καὶ ἀκριβὴς ἡ λέξις, *τῶν τοιούτων ἐστιν ἡ βασιλεία τῶν οὐρανῶν*. οὐ γὰρ τούτων εἶπεν, ἀλλὰ τῶν τοιούτων. ἐπειδὴ πρόσεστι καὶ τὸ τῆς φρονήσεως ἐνδεὲς τοῖς παισίν. οὗπερ ἀποτρέπων ὁ ᾿Απόστολος ἔλεγε, *μὴ παιδία γίνεσθε ταῖς φρεσίν*. ἐπεξῆλθε δὲ ὁ παρὼν Εὐαγγελιστὴς τὴν αἰτίαν λέγων, καὶ οἷον ἑρμηνεύων, *τὸ τῶν τοιούτων γὰρ ἐστὶν ἡ βασιλεία*.[mcclxii]

Τῶν γὰρ τοιούτων ἐστὶν ἡ βασιλεία.[1742] Οὐκ εἶπε δὲ τούτων *ἐστὶν ἡ βασιλεία* ἀλλὰ τῶν *τοιούτων*, ἵνα μὴ τοὺς λοιποὺς ἀποκλείσῃ, τουτέστι, τῶν κατὰ τοὺς παῖδας ἀμνησικάκων.

> He has meaningfully said, *of such*, not *of these*, in order to show that it is not the age but moral quality that is the supreme thing. To those who have a similar innocence and simplicity, a reward is promised.[mcclxiii]

Θέλει γὰρ ἡμᾶς ὁ Κύριος τὴν ἀκεραιότητα καὶ τὴν ἀτυφίαν τῶν παίδων ἔχειν,

> *τῶν τοιούτων ἐστὶν ἡ βασιλεία*, ἵνα τῇ προαιρέσει ταῦτα ἐργαζώμεθα, ἃ τῇ φύσει τὰ παιδία ἔχει.[mcclxiv]

οὐ μὴν τὸ ἀδιάκριτον, τουτέστιν ἀφελεῖς εἶναι καὶ μὴ ἐπαίρεσθαι ὡς οἱ Φαρισαῖοι.

Ἐπιθεὶς δὲ *αὐτοῖς τὰς χεῖρας*.[1743] Τύπον ταῖς ἐκκλησίαις ἐν τούτῳ κατέλειψε τῆς ἐπιθέσεως τῶν χειρῶν, διδασκούσης τὴν τῆς θείας δυνάμεως ἐπίθεσιν.

1742 Matt. 19:14; Mark, 10:14.

1743 Matt. 19:15.

ἐπετίθει δὲ τὰς χεῖρας τοῖς παιδίοις, τῆς ἐπιθέσεως τῶν χειρῶν διδασκούσης τὴν τῆς θείας δυνάμεως ἐπίθεσιν, ᾗ τὸ ἔργον τὸ ἑαυτῆς τελειοῖ.[mcclxv]

Καὶ ἰδοὺ εἷς προσελθὼν εἶπεν αὐτῷ· διδάσκαλε ἀγαθέ.[1744] Ὁ Μᾶρκος[mcclxvi] ἕνα | **151v** λέγει τοῦτον τῶν παρὰ Ἰουδαίοις διδασκάλων. Δεδιὼς δὲ οὗτος μὴ ἀποβάληται αὐτὸν ὁ Κύριος ὡς καὶ τοὺς Φαρισαίους καὶ οὐ τύχῃ ἀποκρίσεως, προσποιεῖται μὴ εἶναι ἐκείνων. Διὸ φιλοφρόνως αὐτῷ διαλέγεται. Ἀλλ᾽ ὁ Κύριος φανεροποιῶν αὐτοῦ τὴν ἀπάτην, ἀπηνέστερον αὐτῷ διαλέγεται. Τινές δέ φασι μὴ εἶναι αὐτὸν τοιοῦτον. Οὐδὲ γὰρ ἂν ἀπῆλθε λυπούμενος εἰ ἐπείραζεν. Ἐπεὶ δὲ ὡς ἀνθρώπῳ προσῆλθε τῷ Χριστῷ καὶ διδάσκαλον αὐτὸν ἀγαθὸν προσηγόρευσεν, ὡς ἄνθρωπος αὐτῷ καὶ αὐτὸς διαλέγεται, καί φησιν ὅτι *οὐδείς ἐστιν ἀγαθὸς* ὅσον πρὸς ἀντιδιαστολὴν τῆς τοῦ Θεοῦ ἀγαθότητος. Διὸ ἐπήγαγεν, *εἰ μὴ εἷς ὁ Θεός*. Τὸ γὰρ *εἷς* εἶπεν ἀπαλλάττων αὐτὸν τῶν ἐπὶ γῆς, ὅπως εἰς τὸν ἕνα πιστεύῃ Θεόν. Τὸ δὲ εἰπεῖν οὐκ *ἀγαθός* εἰμι ὡς ἄνθρωπος, οὐ τοῦτο λέγει ὅτι πονηρός εἰμι, ἀλλ᾽ ὅτι μὴ κατὰ φύσιν μηδὲ ἀτρέπτως ἀγαθὸς ὁ ἄνθρωπος. Ἑαυτὸν γὰρ μετὰ τῶν ἀνθρώπων συναριθμήσας κατὰ τὴν σάρκα τοῦτο εἶπε καὶ πρὸς τὸν νοῦν τοῦ προσελθόντος. Ἢ τοῦτό φησι, οὐκ ἀγαθὸς ἀκούσας μόνον ἀλλὰ διδάσκαλος ἀγαθός, ὡς πρὸς πειράζοντα οὖν ἀπεκρίνατο καὶ ἀγνοοῦντα ὅτι Θεὸς *ἀγαθός* ἐστιν καὶ οὐχ ἁπλῶς διδάσκαλος ἀγαθός. Ἤ, ἐπεὶ ὡς φιλόδοξος οὗτος προσῆλθε κολακικῶς αὐτῷ οἰόμενος ὅτι τῶν ὁμοίων τεύξεται καὶ αὐτός, τραχύτερον αὐτῷ ἀπεκρίνατο ὁ Κύριος διαβάλλων αὐτὸν ὡς οὐκ ἀγαθόν. Πλὴν ἐπὶ τὰς τοῦ νόμου ἐντολὰς ἀπάγων αὐτόν, ἐπήγαγεν· *εἰ δὲ θέλεις εἰσελθεῖν εἰς τὴν ζωήν, τήρει τὰς ἐντολάς.*[1745]

Τί με λέγεις ἀγαθόν;[1746] | **152r** Πρὸς τὸν σκοπὸν τοῦ εἰπόντος *διδάσκαλε ἀγαθέ*, ἀπεκρίθη *ὁ Ἰησοῦς*. Οὐδὲ γὰρ ὡς Θεὸν ἐκάλεσεν ἀγαθὸν οὐδὲ εἶπεν, ὦ Θεὲ *ἀγαθὲ* (τοῦτο γὰρ πάντας ὁμοῦ τότε τοὺς ἀνθρώπους ὑπερέβαινεν), ἀλλὰ *διδάσκαλε ἀγαθέ*. Εἰ δὲ τὸ *εἷς ὁ Θεὸς ἀγαθὸς* ἐκβάλλει τοῦ εἶναι τὸν Κύριον ἀγαθόν, ἄρα καὶ τὸ *εἷς Κύριος Ἰησοῦς Χριστός*[1747] ἐκβάλλει τὸν Πατέρα τῆς κυριότητος Ὅτι δὲ οὐκ ἀναιρῶν τὸ αὐτὸς *ἀγαθὸς* εἶναι ταῦτα ἔφη, οἶμαι δῆλον τῷ γε νοῦν ἔχοντι.[mcclxvii] Τοῦτο γὰρ ἦν σαφῶς διδάξαι μηδένα δεῖν πείθεσθαι τοῖς παρ᾽ αὐτοῦ λεγομένοις. Ἐπεὶ γὰρ ὁ οὐκ ὢν *ἀγαθὸς* οὔτε φθέγγεται ποτέ τι καλόν, οὐδαμῶς πείθεσθαι τῷ τοιούτῳ λέγοντι προσῆκον. Πῶς δὲ οὐκ ἄτοπον οἰηθῆναι τὸν Κύριον οὐκ ἐπιτρέπειν αὐτὸν καλεῖσθαι ἀγαθόν, ὅς γε καὶ περὶ ἀνθρώπων οὐκ ὀκνεῖ τοῦτο λέγειν, ὅταν[1748] δὴ νεύειν αὐτοὺς πρὸς τὸ κρεῖττον συμβαίνῃ, οὕτω σαφῶς εἰρηκώς· *Ὁ ἀγαθὸς ἄνθρωπος ἐκ τοῦ ἀγαθοῦ θησαυροῦ ἐκβάλλει τὰ ἀγαθά.*[1749] Ἐνταῦθα γὰρ οὐ τὸν ἄνθρωπον μόνον προσεῖπεν ἀγαθόν, ἀλλὰ γὰρ καὶ τὴν πρόθεσιν αὐτοῦ καὶ τὰ ῥήματα.

1744 Matt. 19:16; Mark, 10:17; Luke, 18:18.
1745 Matt. 19:17: τήρησον.
1746 Matt. 19:17; Mark, 10:18; Luke, 18:19.
1747 1 Cor. 8:6.
1748 Cod. ὅτ᾽ ἄν.
1749 Matt. 12:35; cf. Luke, 6:45.

> Πρὸς τὸν σκοπὸν τοῦ εἰπόντος *διδάσκαλε ἀγαθὲ* ἀπεκρίθη *ὁ Ἰησοῦς*. οὐδὲ γὰρ ὡς Θεὸν ἐκάλεσεν ἀγαθὸν οὐδὲ εἶπεν ὦ Θεὲ *ἀγαθέ* (τοῦτο γὰρ πάντας ὁμοῦ τότε τοὺς ἀνθρώπους ὑπερέβαινεν), *ἀλλὰ διδάσκαλε ἀγαθέ*. εἰ δὲ τὸ *εἷς* ὁ θεὸς *ἀγαθὸς* ἐκβάλλει τοῦ εἶναι τὸν κύριον ἀγαθόν, ἄρα καὶ τὸ *εἷς κύριος Ἰησοῦς Χριστὸς* ἐκβάλλει τὸν Πατέρα τῆς κυριότητος ὅτι δὲ οὐκ ἀναιρῶν τὸ αὐτὸς *ἀγαθὸς* εἶναι ταῦτα ἔφη, οἶμαι δῆλον τῷ γε νοῦν ἔχοντι. τοῦτο γὰρ ἦν σαφῶς διδάξαι μηδένα δεῖν πείθεσθαι τοῖς παρ᾽ αὐτοῦ λεγομένοις. ἐπεὶ γὰρ ὁ οὐκ ὢν *ἀγαθὸς* οὐδὲ φθέγγεται ποτέ τι καλόν, οὐδαμῶς πείθεσθαι τῷ τοιούτῳ λέγοντι προσῆκον. πῶς δὲ οὐκ ἄτοπον οἰηθῆναι τὸν κύριον οὐκ ἐπιτρέπειν αὐτὸν καλεῖσθαι *ἀγαθόν*, ὅσγε καὶ περὶ ἀνθρώπων οὐκ ὀκνεῖ τοῦτο λέγειν, ὅταν δὴ νεύειν αὐτοὺς πρὸς τὸ κρεῖττον συμβαίνῃ, οὕτω σαφῶς εἰρηκώς. *ὁ ἀγαθὸς ἄνθρωπος ἐκ τοῦ ἀγαθοῦ θησαυροῦ ἐκβάλλει τὰ ἀγαθά*; ἐνταῦθα γὰρ οὐ τὸν ἄνθρωπον μόνον προσεῖπεν ἀγαθόν, ἀλλὰ γὰρ καὶ τὴν πρόθεσιν αὐτοῦ καὶ τὰ ῥήματα.[mcclxviii]

Λέγει αὐτῷ. ποίας;[1750] Ὁ δὲ προσδοκῶν ἀκοῦσαι ξένας τινὰς παρὰ τὰς νομικὰς (ἤτοι τὰς εὐαγγελικὰς) ἐντολὰς εἶπε, *ποίας*; Ἤτοι, ὡς ἐπιθυμητικῶς ἔχων ὠφεληθῆναι. Ὁ δὲ Κύριος ἵνα μὴ εἴπωσιν οἱ Ἰουδαῖοι ὅτι τὰ παλαιὰ ἀθετεῖ, τὸ καιριώτατον τῶν ἐντολῶν ἐπισημηνάμενος ἐδίδαξεν, ὅτι ἡ τούτων φυλακὴ εἰσάγει εἰς τὴν *αἰώνιον ζωήν*. Ὁ δὲ θηρώμενος τὸν ἀπὸ τοῦ Χριστοῦ ἔπαινον οὐκ ἀρκεῖται τοῖς εἰρημένοις πρὸς τὸ τυχεῖν ὧν ἐπιθυμεῖ. Διὸ ἐπήγαγε· *τί ἔτι ὑστερῶ;*[1751] Ἢ ὅτι κατὰ ἀλή | **152v** θειαν ἦν ποιήσας ταῦτα ἢ καθ᾽ ὑπόθεσιν, φησί· νόμισον ὅτι κατώρθωταί μοι πάντα ὅσα εἶπας· οὐδὲν *ἔτι ὑστερῶ*. Ἐψεύσατο γὰρ εἰ *πάντα* εἶπε πεπληρωκέναι. Οὐδὲ γὰρ πεπλήρωκε τὸ *ἀγαπήσεις τὸν πλησίον σου ὡς σεαυτὸν* εὐαγγελικῶς ἐργαζόμενος τὸ τῆς εὐποιΐας ἔργον, οὐ μὴν στενῶς, τουτέστιν ἰουδαϊκῶς. Ἐξ ὧν δὲ ἑαυτῷ μαρτυρεῖ, δείκνυται φιλόδοξος, οὐ μὴν ἐνάρετος. Τί οὖν φησι πρὸς αὐτὸν ὁ Κύριος; Δείκνυσι τὸν ἐν νόμῳ τέλειον ἀτελῆ ὄντα καὶ μόλις ἥκοντα εἰς ἀρχὰς τοῦ εὐαγγελικοῦ νόμου. Διὸ κελεύει τῷ πλούτῳ ἀποτάξασθαι καὶ αὐτῷ ἀκολουθεῖν τῷ ἄγοντι εἰς τελειότητα. Τί οὖν φησι ὁ νεανίσκος, ὁ τέλειον λέγων ἑαυτὸν ἐν νόμῳ; Οὐδὲ ἓν πρόσταγμα τοῦ Κυρίου ὑπήνεγκεν, ἀλλ᾽ *ἀπῆλθε λυπούμενος*[1752] τὴν αὐθαίρετον ἀκούσας πενίαν[mcclxix] ὡς ἀπολέσας τὰ χρήματα, αἱρησόμενος τῶν φαινομένων τὴν κτῆσιν καὶ οὐ πιστεύσας τοῖς ἐπαγγελθεῖσιν ἀγαθοῖς.

Εἰπὼν δὲ ὁ Μᾶρκος ὅτι *ἐμβλέψας αὐτῷ ὁ Ἰησοῦς ἠγάπησεν αὐτόν*,[1753] ζήτησιν κινεῖ. Πῶς ἠγαπήθη ὁ μὴ μέλλων ἐπὶ *τὴν ζωὴν*[1754] ἀκολουθεῖν; Ἔστι δὲ ἐπὶ μὲν τοῖς προτέροις ἀγάπης ἄξιος ὁ τὰ τοῦ νόμου φυλάξας, καὶ ταῦτα *ἐκ νεότητος*.[1755] Τῇ δὲ περὶ τὸ τέλειον ὀλιγωρίᾳ τὴν ἐπὶ τοῖς πρόσθεν ἀγάπην τελείαν οὐκ εἴασε γενέσθαι, ὥσπερ οὐδὲ τὴν τελειότητα ἐδέξατο.

1750 Matt. 19:18.

1751 Matt. 19:20.

1752 Matt. 19:22.

1753 Mark, 10:21.

1754 Matt. 19:17; cf. Matt. 7:14; 18:8-9; 19:17; Mark, 9:43-45; John, 5:24; 11:25; 14:6; 1 John, 1:2; 5:12.

1755 Matt. 19:20; Mark, 10:20; Luke, 18:21.

φησὶ γὰρ ὁ Μᾶρκος ὅτι *ἐμβλέψας αὐτῷ* ὁ Ἰησοῦς *ἠγάπησεν αὐτόν*. οὐκ ἂν δὲ ἐπὶ τῇ τοῦ ἀλλοτρίου πληρώσει ἠγάπησεν τὸν περὶ ταύτης παρρησιασάμενον. ζήτησιν δὲ κινεῖ, πῶς ἠγαπήθη ὁ μὴ θέλων ἀκολουθεῖν ἐπὶ *τὴν ζωήν*. ἔστι δὲ ἐπὶ μὲν τοῖς προτέροις ἀγάπης ἄξιος ὁ τὸ τοῦ νόμου φυλάξας, τῇ δὲ περὶ τὸ τέλειον ὀλιγωρίᾳ τὴν ἐπὶ τοῖς πρόσθεν ἀγάπην τελείαν οὐκ εἴασε γενέσθαι τελείαν.[mcclxx]

Διόπερ ὁ Παῦλος ἀτελὲς ἅπαν τὸ ἐν νόμῳ καταλαβὼν ἐπὶ τὴν τελειότητα ἔσπευσεν. Ἐξελέγχεται δὲ ἐν τῷ λόγῳ Μαρκιωνιστῶν τε παράνοια καὶ Μανιχαίων, οἳ τὸν νόμον ἀλλότριον εἶναι φασὶ Χριστοῦ. Οὐ γὰρ ἐπὶ τῇ τοῦ | **153r** ἀλλοτρίου πληρώσει *ἠγάπησεν* ἂν ὁ Χριστὸς τὸν περὶ ταύτης παρρησιασάμενον.

Ἐξελέγχεται δὲ ἐν τῷ λόγῳ Μαρκιωνιστῶν [τε] παράνοια [καὶ Μανιχαίων], οἳ τὸν νόμον ἀλλότριον εἶναι φασὶ Χριστοῦ… . οὐκ ἂν δὲ ἐπὶ τῇ τοῦ ἀλλοτρίου πληρώσει ἠγάπησε τὸν περὶ ταύτης παρρησιασάμενον.[mcclxxi]

48

154v (ΩΡΙΓΕΝΟΥΣ) *Κάμηλον,*[1756] οἱ μὲν τὸ σχοινίον τῆς μηχανῆς, οἱ δὲ τὸ ζῷον. Τὸ πρῶτον δὲ τοῦ δευτέρου βεβαιότερον κατ᾽ αἴσθησιν. Κατὰ δὲ νοῦν, νόει.

κάμηλον[1757] οἱ μὲν τὸ σχοινίον τῆς μηχανῆς, οἱ δὲ τὸ ζῷον. τὸ πρῶτον δὲ τοῦ δευτέρου βεβαιότερον κατ᾽ αἴσθησιν. κατὰ δὲ νοῦν νόει.[mcclxxii]

49

(ΤΟΥ ΑΥΤΟΥ) *παρὰ ἀνθρώποις* τοῦτο *ἀδύνατον.*[1758] Παρὰ ἀνθρωπίνης καταστάσεως[mcclxxiii] *ἀδύνατον*, παρὰ δὲ χάριτος Θεοῦ, δυνατόν.

Παρὰ μὲν ἀνθρωπίνης καταστάσεως *ἀδύνατον*, παρὰ δὲ χάριτος Θεοῦ, δυνατόν.[mcclxxiv]

Ἰδοὺ ἡμεῖς ἀφήκαμεν πάντα.[1759] Κοινωφελὴς ἡ ἐρώτησις, εἰ ἆρα οὐ μόνοι πλούσιοι σῴζονται, ἀλλὰ καὶ οἱ κατὰ τὸν Πέτρον πτωχοί, οἳ διὰ τὸ ἀφεῖναι πάντα εὐκόλως ἠκολούθησαν τῷ Χριστῷ. Τὸ γὰρ *πάντα* ὧδε οὐκ ἐπὶ χρημάτων νοεῖται μόνον, ἀλλὰ καὶ ἐπὶ πάσης κοσμικῆς ἡδυπαθείας καὶ τῆς πρὸς τοὺς συγγενεῖς φιλοσαρκίας, ἅπερ οὐ μόνον κατὰ πλουσίων ἀλλὰ καὶ κατὰ πενήτων ἐπιστρατεύεται.

1756 Matt. 19:24; Mark, 10:25; Luke, 18:25.
1757 Matt. 19:24; Mark, 10:25; Luke, 18:25.
1758 Matt. 19:26; Mark, 10:27; Luke, 18:27.
1759 Matt. 19:27; Mark, 10:28; Luke, 18:28.

50

(ΩΡΙΓΕΝΟΥΣ) Τῇ προθέσει κρίνεται τὰ πράγματα. Ταύτῃ πάντα κατέλιπον οἱ ἀπόστολοι,

> Τῇ προθέσει κρίνεται τὰ πράγματα, ταύτῃ πάντα κατέλιπον οἱ ἀπόστολοι.[mcclxxv]

οὐχ ὡς μεγάλα τινὰ καταλελοιπότες, ἀλλ' αὐτῶν ὧν εἶχον ἐκστάντες καὶ τὴν προαίρεσιν ἐπιδείξαντες, τὴν ἁπάντων προτιμῶσαν Χριστόν.[mcclxxvi]

51

156r (ΩΡΙΓΕΝΟΥΣ) *Πολλοὶ δὲ ἔσονται πρῶτοι ἔσχατοι.*[1760] Πρῶτοι οἱ Ἰουδαῖοι, ἔσχατοι τὰ ἔθνη,

> Πρῶτοι οἱ Ἰουδαῖοι, ἔσχατοι τὰ ἔθνη.[mcclxxvii]

εἰ καὶ ἐπὶ πολλῶν ἁρμόζει ἀορίστως λεχθὲν τὸ *πολλοὶ ἔσονται πρῶτοι ἔσχατοι καὶ ἔσχατοι πρῶτοι.* Ἀλλὰ | **156v** καὶ ἐπὶ τῶν Φαρισαίων δύναται τοῦτο νοεῖσθαι, οἳ πρῶτοι ὄντες τῇ τάξει, δι' ἀπιστίαν ἐξεβλήθησαν καὶ εἰς τὴν ἐκείνων τάξιν εἰσῆλθον οἱ πιστοί. Ἵνα δὲ διδάξῃ τοῦ λόγου τὴν δύναμιν, συνάπτει τὴν ἐσομένην παραβολὴν τοῦ ἀμπελῶνος.

ὁμοία γάρ ἐστιν ἡ βασιλεία τῶν οὐρανῶν ἀνθρώπῳ οἰκοδεσπότῃ.[1761] Πολλαχοῦ μὲν τῆς γραφῆς ἄνθρωπος ὁ Θεὸς λέγεται, καθὸ τροποφορῶν[mcclxxviii] ἡμᾶς τὸν ἀνθρώπου τρόπον ἀναλαμβάνει. Ἐπεὶ δὲ πολλαὶ ἐπίνοιαι Θεοῦ, νῦν *οἰκοδεσπότης*[1762] λέγεται τῷ ἔχειν *ἀμπελῶνα*, ἐπιτρόπους μισθοῦσθαι, γεωργούς.

> Πολλαχοῦ μὲν τῆς γραφῆς ἄνθρωπος ὁ θεὸς λέγεται, καθὸ τροποφορῶν ἡμᾶς τὸν ἀνθρώπου τρόπον ἀναλαμβάνει. ἐπεὶ δὲ πολλαὶ ἐπίνοιαι τοῦ θεοῦ, νῦν οἰκοδεσπότης λέγεται τῷ ἔχειν *ἀμπελῶνα*, ἐπιτρόπους, μισθωτούς, γεωργούς.[mcclxxix]

Ἀ*μπελῶνα* δὲ λέγει τὸ τῆς εὐσεβείας πολίτευμα[mcclxxx]

> οἰκοδεσπότην δὲ τὸν θεὸν λέγει, ἀμπελῶνα δὲ τὸ τῆς εὐσεβείας πολίτευμα.[mcclxxxi]

ἢ τὰ τοῦ Θεοῦ προστάγματα. Ὁ δὲ τῆς ἐργασίας χρόνος, ὁ παρὼν βίος.

1760 Matt. 19:30; Mark, 10:31.
1761 Matt. 20:1.
1762 Cf. Matt. 21:33; 24:43; Luke, 12:39; 13:25; 14:21.

Οἰκοδεσπότης ἐστὶν ὁ Χριστός· οἶκος, τὸ ὅλον τῆς χωρητικῆς φύσεως.[mcclxxxii] (ΩΡΙΓΕΝΟΥΣ) Ὁ ἐξελθὼν *ἅμα πρωΐ*, αὐτός ἐστιν ὁ λόγος, *ἐξῆλθε* δὲ ἐκ τῶν οὐρανῶν ἐπὶ τὴν γῆν.[mcclxxxiii] Τὸ δὲ *πρωΐ*, ζήτει· ἤτοι τὸ προηγούμενον πρωῒ ἢ ἡ ἀρχὴ τούτου· ‹ἐργάται› εἰσὶν ἅγιοι ἄγγελοι ἐργαζόμενοι τὸ θέλημα αὐτοῦ ἐν τῷ ἀμπελῶνι *αὐτοῦ*. *Ἐξῆλθε* δὲ τοὺς ἔξω καλέσαι. Ἀμπελών ἐστι τὰ θεῖα θελήματα· τρίοδός ἐστιν ἡ πάντων ὁδός· ὀψία[1763] ἐστὶ τέλος τῆς ἡμέρας, σύμβολον συντελείας τοῦ αἰῶνος.[mcclxxxiv]

> *Οἰκοδεσπότης* ἐστὶν ὁ Χριστός, οἶκος, τὸ ὅλον τῆς χωρητικῆς φύσεως. ὁ ἐξελθὼν *ἅμα πρωΐ*, αὐτός ἐστιν ὁ λόγος. *ἐξῆλθε* δὲ ἐκ τῶν οὐρανῶν ἐπὶ τὴν γῆν. τὸ δὲ *πρωΐ*, ζήτει, ἤτοι τὸ προηγούμενον πρωῒ ἢ ἡ ἀρχὴ τούτου. ‹ἐργάται› εἰσὶν ἅγιοι ἄγγελοι ἐργαζόμενοι τὸ θέλημα αὐτοῦ ἐν τῷ ἀμπελῶνι *αὐτοῦ*. *ἐξῆλθε* δὲ τοὺς ἔξω καλέσαι. ἀμπελών ἐστι τὰ θεῖα θελήματα, τρίοδός ἐστιν ἡ πάντων ὁδός. ὀψία ἐστὶ τέλος τῆς ἡμέρας, σύμβολον συντελείας τοῦ αἰῶνος.[mcclxxxv]
>
> *λέγει αὐτοῖς, Τὸ μὲν ποτήριόν μου πίεσθε, τὸ δὲ καθίσαι ἐκ δεξιῶν μου καὶ ἐξ εὐωνύμων οὐκ ἔστιν ἐμὸν τοῦτο δοῦναι, ἀλλ' οἷς ἡτοίμασται ὑπὸ τοῦ πατρός μου.*[mcclxxxvi] Ὅταν ἐν τῇ τριάδι βαθμοὺς ἀκούσῃς, τῆς καταστάσεως ἡμῶν λήψῃ τὸν νοῦν. πατρὸς μεγαλωσύνην καὶ υἱοῦ σμικρότητα ἀκούων οὐ φύσεως καὶ ὑποστάσεως δέξῃ ὑπόνοιαν, ἀλλ' ἡμετέρας καταστάσεως.[mcclxxxvii]

52

166v (ΩΡΙΓΕΝΟΥΣ) Ὁ καταρτίσας τὸν *αἶνον ἐκ στόματος νηπίων*,[1764] ὁ Χριστός ἐστιν, οὗ *τῶν δακτύλων ἔργα*[1765] εἰσὶν οἱ οὐρανοί.

> Ὁ καταρτίσας τὸν *αἶνον ἐκ στόματος νηπίων*, ὁ Χριστός ἐστιν, οὗ *τῶν δακτύλων ἔργα* εἰσὶν οἱ οὐρανοί.[mcclxxxviii]

Καὶ καταλιπὼν αὐτούς, ἐξῆλθεν.[1766] Τὸ *καταλιπὼν* τὴν ὡς ἀπὸ ἀναξίων ἀναχώρησιν δηλοῖ. Ἥκει γὰρ ἐπὶ τὸ πάθος, δι' αὐτοῦ τὴν βασιλείαν ἀφαιρησόμενος τῆς Ἱερουσαλὴμ καὶ *ἐφ' ἡμᾶς* μετοίσων τὴν χάριν,[1767] καθὰ προελέγετο διὰ τῶν προφητῶν, ὡς ὁ Ἱερεμίας προφητεύει, *ἐγκαταλέλοιπα τὸν οἶκον μου· ἀφῆκα τὴν κληρονομίαν μου*,[1768] καὶ τὰ ἑξῆς. Ἦλθεν οὖν ὡς ἐπὶ *κληρονομίαν* ἰδίαν,[1769] καταλιμπάνει δὲ αὐτοὺς ὡς ἀλλοτρίους, ὥστε τὸ ἀναχωρεῖν *εἰς* τὴν *Βηθανίαν* εἰς τύπον τῆς μελλούσης

1763 Matt. 20:8.
1764 Matt. 21:16, quoting Psalm 8:3.
1765 Psalm 8:4.
1766 Matt. 21:17; Mark, 11:11.
1767 Cf. Eph. 2:7-8.
1768 Jer. 12:7.
1769 Cf. Matt. 21:38; Acts, 20:32.

ἀναχωρήσεως ἐποίει. Καὶ ταῦτα ἔπραττε | **167r** μετὰ τοῦ καὶ οἰκτείρειν τὴν πόλιν. Κατὰ τοῦτό φησι Λουκᾶς· *καὶ ὡς ἤγγισεν ἰδὼν τὴν πόλιν ἔκλαυσεν ἐπ᾽ αὐτήν*,[1770] καὶ τὰ ἑξῆς.

Πρωΐας δὲ ἐπανάγων εἰς τὴν πόλιν ἐπείνασε· καὶ ἰδὼν συκῆν.[1771] Ἔρχεται ἐπὶ τὴν *συκῆν* ὁ Κύριος οὐ τροφῆς δεόμενος (ἠπίστατο γὰρ τῆς ἀκαρπίας τὸν καιρόν), ἀλλ᾽ ἀράσασθαι αὐτῇ μόνῃ τῇ συκῇ τῇ ὁμοφυεῖ ἐκείνῃ τῇ ἐν παραδείσῳ ὅθεν λαβόμενοι οἱ γηγενεῖς ἐκεῖνοι *ἔρραψαν ἑαυτοῖς περιζώματα*[1772] πρὸς τὸ στῆναι καὶ δυσωπῆσαι Θεόν. Ἵν᾽ οὖν ὑποδείξῃ ὅτι αὐτὸς ἦν ὁ τότε προσλαλήσας αὐτοῖς ἐν παραδείσῳ,[mcclxxxix] ταύτῃ ὥσπερ αἰτίᾳ τῆς ἁμαρτίας γεγονυίᾳ ἀρᾶται. Ἔδει δὲ καὶ μὴ καιροῦ ὄντος *σύκων*[1773] αὐτῷ φέρειν πεινῶντι καρπόν. Δούλη γὰρ αὐτοῦ πᾶσα ἡ κτίσις,[1774] τὸ δὲ μὴ δουλεῦον τῷ θελήματι αὐτοῦ ἀφανίζεται.[mccxc] Διὸ καὶ *ἡ συκῆ* ἠφανίσθη, ὅτι πεινῶντι τῷ Ἰησοῦ καὶ μέχρις αὐτῆς ἐλθόντι καὶ βουληθέντι καὶ παρὰ καιρὸν ἐξ αὐτῆς λαβεῖν καρπὸν οὐχ ὑπήκουσε. Τύπος δὲ *ἡ συκῆ* καὶ τῆς τῶν Ἰουδαίων συναγωγῆς καὶ τῆς ἐν νόμῳ σκιᾶς[1775] καρπὸν οὐκ ἐχούσης βρώσιμον καὶ ἀρεστὸν τῷ Θεῷ. Οὐ γὰρ ἀγαπᾷ τὰ ἐν τύποις. Καὶ μὴ εὑρὼν καρπόν, μόνον δὲ φαντασίαν ζωτικὴν ἐν αὐτῇ, λέγει τὸ ἀποβαῖνον. Διὸ οὐκέτι[1776] αἱ *κατὰ νόμον* θυσίαι[1777] ὠφελῆσαι δύνανται τοὺς Ἰουδαίους.

Ἄλλως τε. Ὑποδείγματι κέχρηται τῷ ἀλόγῳ δένδρῳ εἰς σωφρονισμὸν ἀνθρώπων τῶν μὴ παρεχόντων αὐτῷ πεινῶντι καρποὺς οἵους βούλεται. Πεινᾷ δὲ ὁ θεῖος λόγος τὴν ἡμετέραν σωτηρίαν.[mccxci] Ἄλλος δέ φησι· εἰ μὲν οὖν *ἦν καιρὸς* | **167v** *σύκων*,[1778] ἡ δὲ *καρπὸν οὐκ* εἶχε[1779] καὶ ἐπικατηράθη. Ἐνομίσθη ἂν τῷ τύπῳ ἠγανακτηκέναι, ὅπερ ἄτοπον. Οὐδεὶς γὰρ ἀγανακτεῖ ἀλόγῳ δένδρῳ.[mccxcii] Εἰ δὲ ἔχοντι καρπὸν κατηράσατο, ἀτοπώτερον ἦν τὸ καταράσασθαι καὶ ξηράναι καρπῶν ἔμπλεων δένδρον.

> Διαγράψωμεν οὖν καὶ ὡς ἐν συντόμῳ τὸν λόγον. συκῆ ἤτοι ἡ πόλις Ἱερουσαλὴμ ἢ ἡ τῶν Ἰουδαίων συναγωγὴ ἢ ἡ ἀνθρωπότης πᾶσα. οἰκοδεσπότης, οὗ τινος καὶ ἡ συκῆ ἦν, ὁ θεὸς καὶ πατὴρ ἤτοι αὐτὸς ὁ σωτήρ. ὁ δὲ ἀμπελουργὸς ὁ υἱὸς τοῦ θεοῦ. τρίτον δὲ λέγει ἐληλυθέναι αὐτόν, τοῦτ᾽ ἔστι διὰ Μωϋσέως, διὰ τῶν προφητῶν, δι᾽ ἑαυτοῦ. ἤτοι πρῶτον ἔτος, καθ᾽ ὃ πρῶτον τῷ Ἀδὰμ ἐνετείλατο λέγων. *ἀπὸ παντὸς ξύλου τοῦ ἐν τῷ παραδείσῳ βρώσει φάγῃ* καὶ τὰ ἑξῆς. δεύτερον, καθ᾽ ὃ ἐν τῷ νόμῳ διὰ Μωϋσέως τῷ Ἰσραὴλ δέδωκεν ἐντολάς. τρίτον, καθ᾽ ὃ αὐτὸς δι᾽ ἑαυτοῦ ἐν τῷ εὐαγγελίῳ τὸν τέλειον δέδωκε νόμον.[mccxciii]

1770 Luke, 19:41.
1771 Matt. 21:18-19; Mark, 11:13.
1772 Gen. 3:7.
1773 Cf. Mark, 11:13.
1774 Cf. Psalm, 118:91; Judith, 16:14.
1775 Cf. Col. 2:17; Heb. 8:5; 10:1; cf. Luke, 13:6-7.
1776 Cod. οὐκ ἔτι.
1777 Cf. 1 Macc. 4:53.
1778 Mark, 11:13.
1779 Cf. Luke, 13:7.

> Οὐκοῦν εἰς εἰκόνα δέχεται τῆς ᾿ Ιουδαίων Συναγωγῆς, ὡς ἔφην, ἤγουν τῶν ἐξ ᾿Ισραήλ, τὴν ἐν τῇ παραβολῇ λεγομένην συκῆν. ῏Ηλθε δέ, φησί, ζητῶν καρπόν, καὶ οὐχ εὗρε. Τοῦτο τρίτον ἦλθε. τὸ πρῶτον, διὰ Μωϋσέως καὶ ᾿Ααρών. δεύτερον, καθ᾿ ὃν ἦν ᾿Ιησοῦς ὁ τοῦ Ναυῆ, καὶ μετ᾿ αὐτὸν οἱ κριταί. τρίτον δὲ μετὰ τούτους, καθ᾿ ὃν γεγόνασιν οἱ μακάριοι προφῆται μέχρις ᾿Ιωάννου τοῦ Βαπτιστοῦ. ᾿Εν τούτοις γέγονε τοῖς καιροῖς ἄκαρπος ὁ ᾿Ισραήλ. ῞Οσον γὰρ ἧκεν εἰς τὸ ἀγαθὸν θέλημα τοῦ Θεοῦ καὶ Πατρός, δῆλον δὲ ὅτι καὶ τοῦ Υἱοῦ, ἀπαράδεκτος ἦν ὡς ἐν σκιαῖς καὶ τύποις λατρεία, ἄκαρπος παντελῶς τό γε ἧκον εἰς πνευματικὴν εὐοσμίαν.[mccxciv]

Νυνὶ δὲ βουλόμενος δεῖξαι τοῖς ἑαυτοῦ μαθηταῖς ὅτι δυνατός ἐστι καὶ ἀνθρώπους κολάζειν, εἰς οὐδένα μὲν ἀνθρώπων τοῦτο εἰργάσατο, ἐπὶ δὲ τῆς συκῆς ἔδειξε τὴν κολαστικὴν αὐτοῦ δύναμιν,[mccxcv] παριστὰς ὅτι καὶ εἰς ἀνθρώπους ἐδύνατο μέν, οὐκ ἐβούλετο δέ τινα τιμωρήσασθαι. Καὶ δείκνυσι διὰ τούτου ὅτι οὐ μόνον εἰς τὸ εὐεργετεῖν, ἀλλὰ καὶ εἰς τὸ τιμωρεῖσθαι ἔχει δύναμιν.

> Πῶς πρωΐας πεινᾷ ὁ ᾿Ιησοῦς; ὅτε συνεχώρησε τῇ σαρκὶ τοῦτο παθεῖν. διὰ τί δὲ κατηράθη ἡ συκῆ; τῶν μαθητῶν ἕνεκεν, ἵνα θαρρῶσιν. ἐπειδὴ πανταχοῦ μὲν εὐεργέτει, οὐδένα δὲ ἐκόλασεν. ἔδει δὲ τῆς τιμωρητικῆς αὐτοῦ δυνάμεως ἀπόδειξιν παρασχεῖν.[mccxcvi] ἵνα μάθωσιν οἱ μαθηταί, ἔτι δὲ καὶ ᾿Ιουδαῖοι, ὅτι δυνάμενος ξηράναι τοὺς σταυροῦντας αὐτόν, τοῦτο οὐκ ἐβούλετο εἰς ἀνθρώπους ἐνδείξασθαι. διὰ τοῦτο εἰς τὸ φυτὸν τῆς ἐνεργείας αὐτοῦ τῆς τιμωρητικῆς τὴν ἀπόδειξιν ταύτην παρέσχετο.[mccxcvii] ὅτ᾿ ἂν δὲ εἰς τόπους, ἢ εἰς φυτόν, ἢ εἰς ἄλογα γένηταί τι τοιοῦτον, μὴ ἀκριβολογοῦ, μὴ δὲ λέγε, πῶς οὖν δικαίως ἐξηράνθη ἡ συκῆ, εἰ καιρὸς οὐκ ἦν; τὸ γὰρ λέγειν τοῦτο, ἐσχάτης ληρωδίας ἐστί. μόνον δὲ τὸ θαῦμα διόρα, καὶ θαύμαζε τὸν θαυματουργόν. ἐπεὶ καὶ ἐπὶ τῶν χοίρων τῶν καταποντισθέντων, πολλοὶ τοῦτο εἰρήκασι, τὸν τοῦ δικαίου γυμνάζοντες λόγον. ἀλλ᾿ οὐδὲ ἐνταῦθα προσεκτέον αὐτοῖς. καὶ γὰρ καὶ ταῦτα ἄλογα,[1780] ὥσπερ ἐκεῖνο φυτὸν ἄψυχον.[mccxcviii]

Πεῖνα μὲν οὐκ ἦν, πρόσχημα[1781] δὲ ἦν πείνης, τὴν ἰδίαν ἐνδεικνυμένου δύναμιν, εἰς τὸ μὴ οἴεσθαι αὐτοὺς ἀτονίᾳ τὸ πάθος ἀναδέχεσθαι.

> Πεῖνα [sic][mccxcix] μὲν οὐκ ἦν, πρόσχημα δὲ ἦν πείνης τὴν ἰδίαν ἐνδεικνυμένου δύναμιν εἰς τὸ μὴ οἴεσθαι αὐτοὺς ἀτονίᾳ τὸ πάθος ἀναδέχεσθαι.[mccc]

μηκέτι[1782] *ἐκ σοῦ καρπὸς γένηται.*[1783] Τὴν μέλλουσαν κατὰ τῆς ῾Ιερουσαλὴμ κρίσιν ἐπὶ τῆς συκῆς ἔδειξεν, ὥσπερ καὶ ἡ ἐν τῷ Λουκᾷ παραβολῇ δηλοῖ· *συκῆν εἶχέ τις ἐν τῷ ἀμπελῶνι αὐτοῦ πεφυτευμένην, καὶ ἦλθε ζητῶν καρπὸν ἐν αὐτῇ καὶ οὐχ εὗρεν.*[1784] ῞Οπερ οὖν ἐκεῖ λόγῳ διεξῆλθε, τοῦτο ἐνταῦθα ἔργῳ δέδειχεν, ὥσπερ καὶ ἄλλα πεποίηκε

1780 Cf. *supra*, folio 167v, Origen: οὐδεὶς γὰρ ἀγανακτεῖ ἀλόγῳ δένδρῳ.
1781 Cod. πρόσσχημα.
1782 Cod. μὴ κἔ τι.
1783 Matt. 21:19.
1784 Luke, 13:6.

συμβολικά, καὶ δι᾽ ἑαυτοῦ καὶ πάλαι διὰ τῶν προφητῶν. Ὅτι μᾶλλον ἀκοῆς ὅρασις καθάπτεται καὶ ἐν μνήμῃ σώζεται. Ἡ μὲν οὖν παραβολὴ τὴν ἀκαρπίαν ἐλέγχει τῆς Ἱερουσαλὴμ

> Ἄλλως[mccci] δέ φησι τὴν μέλλουσαν κατὰ τὴν Ἱερουσαλὴμ κρίσιν ἐπὶ τῆς συκῆς ἔδειξεν, ὥσπερ καὶ ἡ παραβολὴ δηλοῖ. ἣν καὶ ὁ Λουκᾶς ἀπεμνημόνευσε λέγων, *συκὴν εἶχέν τις πεφυτευμένην ἐν τῷ ἀμπελῶνι αὐτοῦ, καὶ ἦλθεν ζητῶν καρπὸν ἐν αὐτῇ καὶ οὐχ εὗρεν. εἶπεν δὲ πρὸς τὸν ἀμπελουργόν. ἰδοὺ τρία ἔτη ἀφ᾽ οὗ ἔρχομαι ζητῶν καρπὸν ἐν τῇ συκῇ ταύτῃ καὶ οὐχ εὑρίσκω. ἔκκοψον αὐτήν. ἵνα τί καὶ τὴν γῆν καταργῇ; ὁ δὲ ἀποκριθεὶς αὐτῷ λέγει. Κύριε, ἄφες αὐτὴν καὶ τοῦτο τὸ ἔτος, ἕως οὗ σκάψω περὶ αὐτὴν καὶ βάλλω κόπρια. κἂν μὲν ποιήσῃ καρπόν, εἰ δὲ μήγε εἰς τὸ μέλλον ἐκκόψεις αὐτήν.*[1785] ὅπερ οὖν λόγῳ διεξῆλθεν, τοῦτο καὶ ἔργῳ δέδειχεν. ὥσπερ καὶ ἄλλα ἐποίησε συμβολικά, καθὼς ἐν τῇ παρουσίᾳ καὶ διὰ τῶν προφητῶν. ὅτι μᾶλλον ἀκοῆς ὅρασις ψυχῆς καθάπτεται, καὶ ἐν μνήμῃ σώζεται. ἡ μὲν παραβολὴ τὴν ἀκαρπίαν ἐλέγχει τῆς Ἱερουσαλήμ.[mccccii]

ἄχρι τρίτου ἔτους,[mcccciii] δεύτερον μὲν ἀπαιτηθείσης διὰ | **168r** τῶν προφητῶν, τρίτον δὲ ὑπὸ τοῦ Θεοῦ.[mccciv] *Φύλλα* δὲ εἶχε μόνον *ἡ συκῆ* ὡς καὶ τῆς Ἱερουσαλὴμ καρπὸν μὲν μὴ ἐχούσης, φύλλων δὲ *μόνον σκιάν*, τουτέστι τὴν οἰκοδομὴν καὶ τὸν ναόν καὶ τοὺς ἱερεῖς καὶ τὸ θυσιαστήριον. Τὸ δὲ *μηκέτι καρπὸς ἐκ σοῦ γένηται*[1786] οὐκ ἀποκλείει τοὺς ἐξ Ἰουδαίων μετὰ ταῦτα πιστεύσαντας. Οὐ γὰρ ἐξ αὐτῆς ὁ καρπὸς ἐκεῖνος, ἀλλ᾽ ἐκ τῆς νέας, ὃν ἡ δοθησομένη αὐτοῖς Χριστοῦ γνῶσις παρέξει.

Τὸ δὲ *ἦλθεν* εἰ ἄρα εὕροι καρπὸν *ἐν αὐτῇ*,[1787] τῆς ὑπονοίας τῶν μαθητῶν ἦν. Οὐ γὰρ διὰ τοῦτο ἦλθε. Μὴ γὰρ αὐτὸς ἠγνόει ὅτι *καιρὸς οὐκ ἦν σύκων*;[1788] Καὶ γὰρ καὶ τὰς ὑπονοίας γράφουσιν. Ὥσπερ οὖν τοῦτο τῆς ὑπονοίας αὐτῶν, οὕτω καὶ τὸ νομίζειν διὰ τοῦτο αὐτὴν κατηρᾶσθαι. Τὸ δὲ ὅλον διὰ τοῦτο ἦλθεν, ἵνα τῆς τιμωρητικῆς αὐτοῦ δυνάμεως ἀπόδειξιν παράσχῃ.

> Ὅθεν δῆλον, ὅτι τῆς ὑπονοίας τῶν μαθητῶν ἦν τοῦτο, ἀτελέστερον ἔτι διακειμένων. Καὶ γὰρ τὰς ὑπονοίας τῶν μαθητῶν πολλαχοῦ γράφουσιν οἱ εὐαγγελισταί. Ὥσπερ οὖν τοῦτο τῆς ὑπονοίας αὐτῶν ἦν, οὕτω καὶ τὸ νομίζειν διὰ τοῦτο αὐτὴν κατηρᾶσθαι, διὰ τὸ μὴ ἔχειν καρπόν. Τίνος οὖν ἕνεκεν κατηράθη; Τῶν μαθητῶν ἕνεκεν, ἵνα θαρρῶσιν. Ἐπειδὴ γὰρ πανταχοῦ μὲν εὐηργέτει, οὐδένα δὲ ἐκόλασεν. ἔδει δὲ καὶ τῆς τιμωρητικῆς αὐτοῦ δυνάμεως ἀπόδειξιν παρασχεῖν, ἵνα μάθωσι καὶ οἱ μαθηταὶ καὶ οἱ Ἰουδαῖοι, ὅτι δυνάμενος ξηρᾶναι τοὺς σταυροῦντας αὐτόν, ἑκὼν συγχωρεῖ, καὶ οὐ ξηραίνει. οὐκ ἐβούλετο δὲ τοῦτο εἰς ἀνθρώπους ἐνδείξασθαι. εἰς τὸ φυτὸν τῆς ἐνεργείας αὐτοῦ τῆς τιμωρητικῆς τὴν ἀπόδειξιν παρέσχετο.[mcccv]

1785 Mark, 13:7-9.
1786 Matt. 21:19.
1787 Mark, 11:13; Luke, 13:6.
1788 Mark, 11:13.

καὶ ἐξηράνθη παραχρῆμα ἡ συκῆ.[1789] Συκῆν νοητέον ὧδε τὴν τῶν Ἰουδαίων συναγωγὴν[mccccvi] καὶ τὴν ἐν τύποις καὶ σκιαῖς λατρείαν[1790] καρπὸν οὐκ ἔχουσαν βρώσιμον καὶ ἀρέσκοντα τῷ Θεῷ, τὴν *ἐν πνεύματι* λατρείαν.[1791] Διὸ ὡς μὴ ποιοῦσαν καρπὸν γλυκὺν ἐξήρανεν ὁ Κύριος Ἰησοῦς, τρόπον τινὰ πεινῶν καὶ τὸν ἐκ τῆς ἀνθρωπότητος ζητῶν καρπόν. Οὐκοῦν ἐξ ὧν εἶπεν ὅτι οὐ μὴ *ἐκ σοῦ καρπὸς γένηται,*[1792] διδάσκει ὅτι οὐκέτι[1793] αἱ κατὰ νόμον λατρεῖαι ὠφελῆσαι δύνανται τοὺς Ἰουδαίους.

> *Συκῆν* δὲ νοητέον ὧδε τὴν τῶν Ἰουδαίων συναγωγὴν καὶ τὴν ἐν τύποις καὶ σκιαῖς λατρείαν καρπὸν οὐκ ἔχουσαν βρώσιμον καὶ ἀρέσκοντα τῷ θεῷ, τὴν ἐν πνεύματι λατρείαν. διὸ ὡς μὴ ποιοῦσαν καρπὸν γλυκὺν ἐξήρανεν αὐτὴν ὁ κύριος Ἰησοῦς τρόπον τινὰ πεινῶν καὶ τὸν ἐκ τῆς ἀνθρωπότητος ζητῶν καρπόν. οὐκοῦν ἐξ ὧν εἶπεν, ὅτι *οὐ μὴ ἐκ σοῦ καρπὸς γένηται,* διδάσκει, ὅτι οὐκέτι αἱ κατὰ νόμον λατρεῖαι ὠφελῆσαι δύνανται τοὺς Ἰουδαίους.[mccccvii]

Τινὲς τὴν ξηρανθεῖσαν συκῆν εἰς τὴν παλαιὰν Ἱερουσαλὴμ ἐξέλαβον.[mccccviii] Ἔχει δὲ καὶ ἕτερον νοῦν, ἐὰν συνῇς *‹συκῆν›* τὴν ἐξ ἧς μετὰ τὴν παράβασιν *ῥάψαντες ἑαυτοῖς φύλλα, ἐποίησαν* | **168v** *περιζώματα.*[1794] Καὶ τοῦτο νοήσεις ἐκ τοῦ συνάψαι τὴν συκῆν ταύτην *τῷ ὄρει.*[1795] Τὸ δὲ ὄρος τοῦτο εἰς τὸν διάβολον ἐκλαμβάνεται.[mccccix]

> Τινὲς τὴν ξηρανθεῖσαν συκῆν εἰς τὴν παλαιὰν Ἱερουσαλὴμ ἐξέλαβον. ἔχει δὲ καὶ ἕτερον νοῦν, ἐὰν συνῇς *‹συκῆν›* τὴν ἐξ ἧς μετὰ τὴν παράβασιν *ῥάψαντες ἑαυτοῖς φύλλα, ἐποίησαν περιζώματα.* καὶ τοῦτο νοήσεις ἐκ τοῦ συνάψαι τὴν συκῆν ταύτην *τῷ ὄρει,* τὸ δὲ ὄρος τοῦτο εἰς τὸν διάβολον ἐκλαμβάνεται.[mccccx]

Ἐὰν ἔχητε πίστιν καὶ μὴ διακριθῆτε.[1796] Ἐπαγγέλλεται ὁ Κύριος τὴν τῶν ὁμοίων ποίησιν τοῖς μαθηταῖς ἐὰν μὴ μετὰ ἐνδοιασμοῦ καὶ ἀμφιβολίας αἰτήσωσι, κἂν μὴ φέρηται δὲ ἐν τῇ γραφῇ ὅτι τοῦτο πεποιήκασιν οἱ μαθηταὶ ἢ ‹ὅτι› καὶ ὄρη μετήγαγον, οὐδὲν ἐκ τούτου. Ἢ γὰρ οὐκ ἐποίησαν διὰ τὸ ἀκενόδοξον[mccccxi] ἢ οὐκ ἐγράφη.[mccccxii] Τοῦτο δὲ οὐχ ἡ πίστις ποιεῖ, ἀλλ' ἡ τοῦ Θεοῦ παντοδύναμος ἐνέργεια χαρίζεται τοῖς πιστοῖς διὰ τὴν ὠφέλειαν τῶν ὁρώντων.

ἐν ποίᾳ ἐξουσίᾳ ταῦτα ποιεῖς;[1797] Κακοήθως ἐρωτῶσιν οὗτοι, ἵνα, εἰ μὲν εἴπῃ ὅτι ἐν τῇ τοῦ Θεοῦ, ἀποστήσωσιν αὐτοῦ τὸν ὄχλον τὸν ὑμνοῦντα αὐτὸν ὡς Θεόν· εἰ δὲ εἴπῃ, ἐν τῇ ἐμῇ, ὡς περίαυτον[mccccxiii] διαβάλωσι καὶ αὐθάδη. Τοῦτο δὲ ἐποίουν αἰτιώμενοι

1789 Matt. 21:19.
1790 Cf. Heb. 8:5.
1791 John, 4:23-24.
1792 Matt. 21:19.
1793 Cod. οὐκ ἔτι.
1794 Cf. Gen. 3:7.
1795 Matt. 21:21.
1796 Matt. 21:21.
1797 Matt. 21:23.

ὡς ὑφαρπάζοντα τὴν ἱερατικὴν ἀξίαν καὶ διατυποῦντα τὸ ἱερὸν ὡς τὴν ἀξίαν ὠνησάμενον παρὰ Ῥωμαίων[mcccxiv] καὶ ποιοῦντα πρᾶγμα παράνομον.[mcccxv]

> Ἐπειδήπερ Ἰουδαῖοι ὑπὸ Ῥωμαίους γεγονότες ἠγόραζον παρὰ τὸν νόμον τὴν ἱερατείαν καὶ τὰς κατὰ Ἰουδαίων ἀρχάς, θέλοντες δεῖξαι αὐτὸν παράνομον ὑπαινίττονται αὐτὸν διὰ τοῦ ἐγκαλεῖν τὸ τοιοῦτον ἄσεμνον πρᾶγμα. ἐρωτῶσιν δὲ ἵνα, εἰ μὲν εἴπῃ ἐν τῇ τοῦ Θεοῦ *ἐξουσίᾳ ταῦτα ποιῶ*, ἀποστήσωσιν αὐτοῦ τὸν ὄχλον τὸν ὑμνολογοῦντα αὐτὸν τοῖς ὑπὲρ ἄνθρωπον ἐπαίνοις, εἰ δὲ εἴπῃ. ἐν τῇ ἐμῇ, ὡς περίαυτον διαβάλωσι καὶ αὐθάδη.[mcccxvi]

Ἐπειρῶντο γὰρ δεῖξαι ὅτι ἐν ἄλλῃ *ἐξουσίᾳ* καὶ οὐχ ὡς Θεὸς αὐτὸ ἐποίει, ἅπερ μόνῳ ποιεῖν ἔπρεπε Θεῷ, ὡς ἀντίθεος ὑφαρπάζων εἰς ἑαυτὸν τὴν τοῦ Θεοῦ τιμήν. Μονονουχὶ γὰρ τοῦτο ἔλεγον πρὸς αὐτόν· σὺ ὡς τίς ἐκβάλλεις τοὺς πωλοῦντας μήτε ἱερατικὴν ἀρχὴν ἔχων μήτε τὸν διδασκαλικὸν λαχὼν θρόνον; Ἢ τὸ ἐν *ποίᾳ ἐξουσίᾳ* ἐνόμισαν ὥς τινες ἐξ αὐτῶν ἐν περιεργίαις καὶ ἑτέραις δυνάμεσι φαντασίαν ἐμποιούσαις[mcccxvii] πολ | **169r** λοὺς ἐπλάνων. Νόει γάρ μοι τὸ ὑπ᾽ αὐτῶν λεγόμενον *ὅτι ἐν Βεελζεβοὺλ ἄρχοντι τῶν δαιμονίων ἐκβάλλει τὰ δαιμόνια.*[1798] Πόθεν γὰρ ἂν ἐπῄει αὐτοῖς τοῦτο λέγειν, εἰ μὴ ἐγίνετο ὑπό τινων ἐν αὐτοῖς;

> Τινὲς ἐξ αὐτῶν ἐν περιέργοις καὶ ἑτέραις δυνάμεσι φαντασίαν ἐμποιούμενοι πολλοὺς ἀνθρώπους ἐπλάνων. νόει γάρ μοι τὸ ὑπ᾽ αὐτῶν λεγόμενον τῷ σωτῆρι τὸ *οὗτος ἐν Βεελζεβοὺλ τῷ ἄρχοντι τῶν δαιμονίων ἐκβάλλει τὰ δαιμόνια.* πόθεν γὰρ ἦν αὐτοῖς τοῦτο λέγειν, εἰ μὴ ἐγένετο ὑπό τινων ἐν αὐτοῖς; θεώρει γάρ μοι τὸν Σίμωνα μαγείας τέχνῃ χρησάμενον καὶ πολλοὺς πλανήσαντα ἐν τῷ λαῷ.[1799] καὶ πάλιν. ᾔδεισαν τοὺς φαρμακοὺς ἐν Αἰγύπτῳ[1800] ἀντιστάντας ταῖς μαγείαις τῷ Μωϋσεῖ ἐν ἀλλοτρίᾳ δυνάμει. πλὴν νόει μοι τὴν τοῦ θεοῦ δύναμιν τὴν κατακυριεύουσαν τῶν ἀλλοτρίων δυνάμεων, τῆς μὲν συνεργούσης τῷ Μωϋσεῖ περιγινομένης τῶν Αἰγύπτου φαρμακῶν,[1801] τῆς δ᾽ ἐν τοῖς ἀποστόλοις τῆς τοῦ Σίμωνος.[1802] τὸ δὲ *τίς σοι ἔδωκε τὴν ἐξουσίαν ταύτην* ἀκουέτωσαν αὐτοῦ λέγοντος *ἐγὼ ἀπ᾽ ἐμαυτοῦ οὐδὲν ποιῶ, ἀλλὰ καθὼς βλέπω τὸν πατέρα ποιοῦντα οὕτως ἐγὼ ποιῶ.*[1803] εἰ γὰρ ἠπίστασθε, φησίν, ὅτι *τὸ φῶς* εἰμι *τὸ ἀληθινόν*,[1804] καὶ ὅτι ἐκεῖνος *ἦλθεν εἰς μαρτυρίαν, ἵνα περὶ τοῦ φωτὸς μαρτυρήσῃ*,[1805] ἔγνωτε τοῦτο ἄν, ὅτι εἰκότως ἀφαιρῶ τὸν σκότον ἀπὸ τοῦ ἱεροῦ. σκότος γὰρ φιλοκέρδεια καὶ αἰσχροκέρδεια, τὸ καλὸν ἰδεῖν οὐκ ἐῶσα.[mcccxviii]

Τί οὖν ὁ Σωτὴρ ἐρωτᾷ αὐτοὺς περὶ τοῦ βαπτίσματος Ἰωάννου ὁμοιοτρόπως;[mcccxix] Ἢ ἵνα εἴπωσιν *ἐξ οὐρανοῦ* καὶ εὑρεθῶσι θεομάχοι, ἢ ἀτιμάζοντες τὸν βαπτιστὴν

1798 Matt. 12:24; Mark, 3:22; Luke, 11:15.
1799 Cf. Acts, 8:9 ff.
1800 Cf. Ex. 7:17.
1801 Cf. Ex. 7:12; 8:14; 9:11.
1802 Cf. Acts, 8:18 ff.
1803 John, 5:30.
1804 John, 1:9.
1805 John, 1:7.

κινδυνεύσωσιν ὑπὸ Ἰουδαίων τῶν ὑπ᾽ αὐτοῦ βαπτισθέντων. Πανούργως δὲ εἰπόντων ἀγνοεῖν, οὐδὲ αὐτὸς ἀπεκρίνατο, διδάσκων ὅτι τοῖς ἐκ κακουργίας ψευδομένοις οὐδὲν τῶν χρησίμων ἀποκαλύπτει ὁ Χριστός. Ἤτοι διλήμματον[mccccxx] οὖσαν τὴν πεῦσιν, ἀγνοεῖν προεφασίσαντο.

Οὐδὲ ἐγὼ λέγω ὑμῖν.[1806] Διὸ καὶ ὁ Σωτὴρ τὴν πρόφασιν λαβὼν ἐξ αὐτῶν τοῦ μὴ ἀποκρίνασθαι, ἐσιώπησε. Τοῦτο δὲ ποιεῖ οὐκ ἀπορῶν λῦσαι τὴν ἐρώτησιν, ἀλλὰ δεικνὺς αὐτοὺς ἀσυνέτους καὶ φθονερούς. Καὶ φεύγων τὸ ἑαυτὸν ἐγκωμιάζειν, εἰ τοίνυν ἐπίστευσαν Ἰωάννῃ περὶ ὧν εἶπε περὶ αὐτοῦ, καὶ ὅτι αὐτός ἐστιν *ὁ αἴρων τὴν ἁμαρτίαν τοῦ κόσμου*,[1807] οὐκ ἂν ἠρώτων ἐν *ποίᾳ ἐξουσίᾳ ταῦτα ποιεῖς*.[1808] Εἰ δὲ ἠγνόουν, ἔδει διδαχθῆναι αὐτούς. Πλὴν οὔτε *ἐξ ἀνθρώπων* ἐτόλμησαν εἰπεῖν διὰ τὸν ὄχλον οὔτε *ἐξ οὐρανοῦ*.[1809] Διὸ καὶ αὐτῷ μαρτυροῦντι περὶ τοῦ Χριστοῦ οὐκ ἐπίστευσαν, ἀλλ᾽ οὐδὲ αὐτῷ τῷ Χριστῷ.

Ἄνθρωπος εἶχε τέκνα δύο.[1810] Δύο τάγματα εἰσάγει ἀπειθοῦντα ἐξ ἀρχῆς. Καὶ τὸ μὲν ἓν λέγει μετεγνωκὸς καὶ βαπτισθὲν *τὸ βάπτισμα Ἰωάννου*,[1811] τὰς *πόρνας* καὶ *τελώνας*·[1812] τὸ δὲ ἕτερον, τὸ τῶν Φαρισαίων τῶν λεγόντων πείθεσθαι τοῖς | **169v** τοῦ Θεοῦ λόγοις καὶ μήτε τὸ *Ἰωάννου* δεξαμέν‹ων›[1813] *βάπτισμα*, μήτε μετανοησάντ‹ων›,[1814] οὓς καὶ ἀλλοτρίους λέγει τῆς βασιλείας τοῦ Θεοῦ.[mccccxxi]
Ἢ *τέκνα δύο* τοῦ ὡς ἀνθρώπου τροποφ‹ο›ρ‹ο›ῦντος[1815] τὸν Υἱὸν τοῦ Θεοῦ, ὁ παλαιὸς λαὸς καὶ ὁ πιστεύσας *ἐξ ἐθνῶν*,[1816] ὃς πρῶτος ὢν τῷ προωρίσθαι καὶ προεγνῶσθαι καὶ προεκτίσθαι, ἀκούσας *ὕπαγε ἐργάζου*,[1817] ὑπερέθετο φεύγων τοὺς πόνους, ἐπὶ δὲ συντελείᾳ *μεταμεληθεὶς ἐποίησε τὸ θέλημα τοῦ πατρός*. Δευτέρου δὲ ἀκούσαντος τοῦ *κατὰ σάρκα Ἰσραὴλ*[1818] καὶ ψευσαμένου τοῖς ἔργοις τὴν ὑπόσχεσιν.

> *Τέκνα δύο* τοῦ ὡς ἀνθρώπου τροποφοροῦντος τὸν υἱὸν τοῦ θεοῦ ὁ παλαιὸς λαὸς καὶ ὁ πιστεύσας ἐξ ἐθνῶν, ὃς πρῶτος ὢν τῷ προωρίσθαι καὶ προεγνῶσθαι καὶ προεκτίσθαι *ἀκούσας ὕπαγε ἐργάζου* ὑπερέθετο φεύγων τοὺς πόνους, ἐπὶ δὲ συντελείᾳ *μεταμεληθεὶς ἐποίησε τὸ θέλημα τοῦ πατρός*, δευτέρου μὲν ἀκούσαντος τοῦ κατὰ σάρκα Ἰσραὴλ διαψευσαμένου τοῖς ἔργοις τὴν ὑπόσχεσιν. Χρήσῃ τῇ παραβολῇ ἐπὶ τοῖς ἢ μηδὲν

1806 Matt. 21:27.
1807 John, 1:29.
1808 Matt. 21:23.
1809 Matt. 21:25-26.
1810 Matt. 21:28.
1811 Matt. 21:25.
1812 Matt. 21:31-32.
1813 Cod. δεξαμένους.
1814 Cod. μετανοήσαντας.
1815 Cod. τροποφρονοῦντος.
1816 Cf. Rom. 9:24; Acts, 15:23.
1817 Matt. 21:28.
1818 1 Cor. 10:18; cf. Rom. 9:3-4.

> ἔργον ἐπαγγελομένοις χρηστὸν ἢ ἐλάττονα, ἔργῳ δὲ ποιοῦσι, καὶ ἐπὶ τοῖς ἐν μεγάλαις ἐπαγγελίαις μηδὲν ἀνύουσιν.[mcccxxii]

> (Ὠριγένους.) Τέκνα δύο ὡς ἄνθρωπον τροποφοροῦντα τὸν Υἱὸν τοῦ Θεοῦ, ὁ παλαιὸς λαός, καὶ ὁ πιστεύσας ἐξ ἐθνῶν, ὃς πρῶτος ὢν τὸ προωρεῖσθαι καὶ προεγνῶσθαι καὶ προεκτίσθαι. ἀκούσας ὕπαγε, ἐργάζου. ὑπερέθετο, φεύγων τοὺς πόνους. ἐπὶ δὲ συντελείᾳ μεταμεληθείς, ἐποίησε τὸ θέλημα τοῦ πατρός. δευτέρου μὲν ἀκούσαντος τοῦ κατὰ σάρκα Ἰσραήλ, διαψευσαμένου δὲ τοῖς ἔργοις τὴν ὑπόσχεσιν. χρήσῃ τῇ παραβολῇ, ἐπὶ τοῖς ἢ μηδὲν ἐπαγγελλομένοις χρηστόν, ἢ ἐλάττονα, ἔργῳ δὲ ποιοῦσι. καὶ ἐπὶ τοῖς ἐν μεγάλαις ἐπαγγελίαις, οὐδὲν ἀνύουσιν.[mcccxxiii]

Οἱ μὲν γὰρ ἐθνικοὶ μηδέπω ἀκούσαντες τῶν τοῦ Κυρίου λόγων, ἐπίστευσαν διὰ τῶν ἔργων τὴν ὑπακοὴν ἐνδειξάμενοι. Οἱ δὲ Ἰουδαῖοι εἰπόντες *πάντα ὅσα ἂν εἴπῃ ὁ Θεὸς ποιήσομεν καὶ ἀκουσόμεθα,*[1819] ἔργῳ παρήκουσαν. Τὸ οὖν *οἱ τελῶναι καὶ αἱ πόρναι*[1820] περὶ τῶν *ἐξ ἐθνῶν*[1821] λέγεται· τὸ δὲ *ὑμᾶς* περὶ τοῦ *κατὰ σάρκα Ἰσραὴλ* οὐκ ἀποκλεισμένου τοῖς προάγουσι. Τίς γὰρ προάγει τὸν οὐκ ἐσόμενον ἐν ᾧ προάγει τόπῳ;

> Πολλοὶ καὶ μέχρι τοῦ νῦν ὑπισχνοῦνται μὲν τῷ θεῷ καὶ πατρὶ μοναχοὶ τυχὸν ἔσεσθαι ἢ ἱερεῖς, μετὰ δὲ τὴν ὑπόσχεσιν ῥαθυμοῦσιν. ἕτεροι δὲ μοναχικὴν μὲν ἢ ἱερατικὴν διαγωγὴν οὐκ ἐπηγγείλαντο, μοναχικῶς δὲ καὶ ἱερατικῶς διάγουσιν. ὥστε οὗτοι τέκνα εὐπειθῆ οἱ πράττοντες κἂν μηδὲν ὑπέσχοντο.[mcccxxiv]

Ἐμφαίνεται δὲ τῷ ῥητῷ τὸ ὅταν *εἰσέλθῃ τὸ πλήρωμα τῶν ἐθνῶν, τότε πᾶς Ἱερουσαλὴμ σωθήσεται.*[1822] Διὰ οὖν τῆς παραβολῆς διδασκόμεθα ὅτι οὐκ ἐν λόγοις τις πληροῖ τὸν νόμον, ἀλλ᾽ ἔργοις.

Ἄνθρωπός τις εἶχε δύο υἱούς.[1823] Ὁ μὲν πρῶτος ἐστὶ τὰ ἔθνη, οὓς ὁ Θεὸς ὁ κοινὸς πατὴρ πρώτους ἐκάλεσε. Τὸν γὰρ διδακτὸν καὶ φυσικὸν νόμον ταῖς διανοίαις ἐγκατασπείρας, ἔδωκε κήρυκας τὰ ὁρώμενα,[mcccxxv] *ἀλλ᾽ ἡ* τῆς ψυχῆς αὐτῶν εὐταξία,[mcccxxvi] συνεχύθη ἐπὶ ξύλα καὶ λίθους· *εἶπ‹αν›*[1824] γὰρ *τῷ ξύλῳ,* | **170r** *πατήρ μου εἶ σύ.*[1825] Διὸ οὐκ ἠνέσχοντο καλούμενοι. Εἶπον γάρ· οὐκ οἴδαμεν τὸν Κύριον. Οὗτοι οὖν μεταμεληθέντες, *ὕστερον* ἀπῆλθον εἰς τὸν ἀμπελῶνα.

Καὶ προσελθὼν τῷ ἑτέρῳ εἶπεν.[1826] Τοῦ πρώτου παραιτησαμένου προσῆλθεν ὁ πατὴρ τῷ δευτέρῳ, τουτέστι τῷ Ἰσραήλ, ὅστις καλούμενος διὰ Μωϋσέως εἶπε· *πάντα ὅσα ἐλάλησεν ὁ Θεός, ποιήσομεν καὶ ἀκουσόμεθα.*[1827] Οἵτινες οὔτε ἐποίησαν

1819 Ex. 19:8: πάντα ὅσα ἂν εἶπεν. Cf. 24:3&7; Deut. 5:27.
1820 Matt. 21:31-32.
1821 Cf. Rom. 9:24; Acts, 15:23.
1822 Rom. 11:26.
1823 Matt. 21:28.
1824 Cod. εἶπε.
1825 Jer. 2:27.
1826 Matt. 21:30.
1827 Ex. 19:8.

οὔτε ἤκουσαν οὔτε μετεμελήθησαν ὕστερον. Οὓς κατέκριναν *αἱ πόρναι καὶ οἱ τελῶναι*, τουτέστιν[1828] τὰ ἔθνη.

> *Ἄνθρωπός τις εἶχεν δύο* υἱοὺς καὶ ὁ μὲν πρῶτός ἐστιν τὰ ἔθνη, οὓς ὁ θεὸς ὁ κοινὸς πατὴρ πρώτους ἐκάλεσεν. τὸν γὰρ διδακτὸν καὶ φυσικὸν νόμον ταῖς διανοίαις ἐγκατασπείρας ἔδωκε κήρυκας τὰ ὁρώμενα, ἀλλ᾿ ἡ τῆς ψυχῆς αὐτῶν εὐταξία συνεχύθη ἐπὶ ξύλα καὶ λίθους. εἶπαν, γὰρ *τῷ ξύλῳ. πατήρ μου εἶ σύ.* διὸ οὐκ ἠνέσχοντο κωλυόμενοι. εἶπον γὰρ οὐκ οἴδαμεν τὸν κύριον. οὗτοι οὖν μεταμεληθέντες *ὕστερον* ἀπῆλθον εἰς τὸν ἀμπελῶνα. τοῦ δὲ πρώτου παραιτησαμένου προσῆλθεν ὁ πατὴρ *τῷ δευτέρῳ*, τουτ᾿ ἔστιν τῷ Ἰσραήλ, ὅστις καλούμενος διὰ Μωυσέως εἶπεν. *πάντα ὅσα ἐλάλησεν* ὁ θεὸς καὶ *ποιήσομεν καὶ ἀκουσόμεθα*. οἵτινες οὔτε ἐποίησαν οὔτε ἤκουσαν οὔτε μετεμελήθησαν ὕστερον. οὓς κατέκριναν αἱ πόρναι καὶ οἱ τελῶναι, τοῦτ᾿ ἔστιν τὰ ἔθνη.[mcccxxvii]

Ὅτι οἱ τελῶναι καὶ αἱ πόρναι προάγουσιν.[1829] Τοῦτο βούλεται εἰπεῖν ἡ παραβολή, ὅτι *οἱ* μὲν *τελῶναι καὶ αἱ πόρναι* μετανοήσαντες καὶ τὰ ἀρεστὰ τῷ Θεῷ ποιήσαντες δικαιοῦνται Ἰωάννῃ πεισθέντες, εἰ καὶ κατ᾿ ἀρχὰς ἠπείθουν τῷ νόμῳ, μᾶλλον δὲ τῷ Θεῷ. Οἱ δὲ λέγοντες τηρεῖν τὸν νόμον Φαρισαῖοι ἐν μόνοις ῥήμασι ψιλοῖς ἀπόβλητοί εἰσι παρὰ Θεῷ. Οὐ γὰρ ἐν λόγοις ἡ βασιλεία τῶν οὐρανῶν, ἀλλ᾿ ἐν ἔργοις.[mcccxxviii] *Οὐ γὰρ ὁ ἀκροατὴς τοῦ* νόμου, *ἀλλ᾿ ὁ ποιητὴς* δίκαιος[1830] καὶ οἱ λοιποὶ *παρὰ τῷ Θεῷ.*[1831] Οὗτοι ὅμοιοί εἰσι τοῖς ὑποσχομένοις ἀπελθεῖν *εἰς τὸν ἀμπελῶνα*[1832] ἐπὶ τῷ ἐργάσασθαι καὶ μὴ ἀπελθοῦσιν.

> Τοῦτο βούλεται εἰπεῖν ἡ *παραβολή*. ὅτι *οἱ* μὲν *τελῶναι καὶ αἱ πόρναι* μετανοήσαντες καὶ τὰ ἀρεστὰ τῷ Θεῷ ποιήσαντες δικαιοῦνται Ἰωάννῃ πεισθέντες, εἰ καὶ κατ᾿ ἀρχὰς ἠπείθουν τῷ νόμω, μᾶλλον δὲ τῷ θεῷ. οἱ δὲ λέγοντες τηρεῖν τὸν νόμον Φαρισαῖοι ἐν μόνοις ῥήμασιν ψιλοῖς ἀπόβλητοί εἰσιν παρὰ θεῷ. *οὐ γὰρ ἐν λόγοις ἡ βασιλεία τῶν οὐρανῶν, ἀλλ᾿ ἐν ἔργοις. οὐ γὰρ ὁ ἀκροατὴς τοῦ νόμου, ἀλλ᾿ ὁ ποιητὴς δίκαιος.* καὶ οἱ λοιποὶ παρὰ τῷ Θεῷ οὗτοι ὅμοιοι εἰσὶ τοῖς ὑποσχομένοις ἀπελθεῖν εἰς τὸν ἀμπελῶνα ἐπὶ τῷ ἐργάσασθαι. καὶ μὴ ἀπελθοῦσιν.[mcccxxix]

> (Ἐξ ἀνεπιγράφου.) Τοῦτο βούλεται εἰπεῖν ἡ παραβολή, ὅτι οἱ μὲν τελῶναι, καὶ αἱ πόρναι μετανοήσαντες, καὶ τὰ ἀρεστὰ τῷ Θεῷ ποιήσαντες, δικαιοῦνται. εἰ καὶ κατὰ τὴν ἀρχὴν ἠπείθουν τῷ νόμῳ, μᾶλλον δὲ τῷ Θεῷ, Ἰωάννῃ πεισθέντες. οἱ δὲ λέγοντες τηρεῖν τὸν νόμον Φαρισαῖοι, ἐν μόνοις ῥήμασι ψιλοῖς, ἀπόβλητοί εἰσι παρὰ τῷ Θεῷ. οὐ γὰρ ἐν λόγοις ἡ βασιλείᾳ τῶν οὐρανῶν, ἀλλ᾿ ἐν ἔργοις. *οὐ γὰρ ὁ ἀκροατὴς νόμου, ἀλλ᾿ ὁ ποιητής, δίκαιος παρὰ τῷ Θεῷ.* οὗτοι ὅμοιοι εἰσὶ τοῖς ὑποσχομένοις ἀπελθεῖν εἰς τὸν ἀμπελῶνα, ἐπὶ τὸ ἐργάσασθαι, καὶ μὴ ἀπελθοῦσιν.[mcccxxx]

1828 Cod. τουτ᾿ ἔστιν.
1829 Matt. 21:31.
1830 Cf. James, 1:22-23 & 25.
1831 Cf. Rom. 2:13.
1832 Matt. 20:1-7.

Ἄνθρωπός τις ἦν οἰκοδεσπότης, ὅστις ἐφύτευσεν ἀμπελῶνα.[1833] Ἡ παραβολὴ οἰκοδεσπότην λέγει τὸν Θεὸν καὶ Πατέρα, τὸν πολλὴν πρόνοιαν ἐξ ἀρχῆς εἰς τοὺς Ἰουδαίους ἐνδειξάμενον. *Ἀμπελὼν* δὲ ἁπλῶς μὲν ὁ πρῶτος λαός, τουτέστιν ὁ Ἰσραήλ, φυτευθεὶς ὑπὸ τοῦ Θεοῦ ἐν τῇ *γῇ τῆς ἐπαγγελίας*·[1834] *φραγμός*, ὁ νόμος οὐκ ἐῶν αὐτοὺς ἐπιμιγῆναι τοῖς ἔθνεσι·[1835] ληνός, τὸ θυσιαστή | **170v** ριον, ἤτοι ὁ τόπος τῶν σπονδῶν· πύργος, ἡ Σιὼν ἢ ναός· *γεωργοί*, οἱ πρεσβύτεροι τοῦ λαοῦ καὶ οἱ σοφοὶ καὶ οἱ διδάσκαλοι· ἀποδημία οἰκοδεσπότου, ὅτε οὐκέτι ἡμέρας *ἐν στύλῳ νεφέλης* καὶ νυκτὸς *ἐν στύλῳ πυρὸς*[1836] αὐτοῖς ἐπιφαίνεται ἢ *ἡ τοῦ Θεοῦ μακροθυμία*,[1837] ἡ μὴ παραπόδας[mcccxxxi] ἀπαιτοῦσα τοὺς Ἰουδαίους τὴν τῶν πταισμάτων τιμωρίαν· ἀπόδοσις *καρπῶν*, ὁ ἐν νόμῳ βίος· *καιρὸς* αὐτῶν, ἡ προφητικὴ ἀπαίτησις· *δοῦλοι* πρῶτοι καὶ δεύτεροι παθόντες ἄτοπα, οἱ κατὰ διαφόρους καιροὺς ἀποσταλέντες προφῆται, ‹ὧν›[1838] τὸν *μὲν ἔδειραν*,[1839] ὡς Μιχαίαν[mcccxxxii] παταξάντος *ἐπὶ σιαγόνα* Σεδεκίου,[1840] τὸν δὲ *ἀπέκτειναν*, ὡς Ζαχαρίαν *μεταξὺ τοῦ ναοῦ καὶ τοῦ θυσιαστηρίου*,[1841] ‹τ›όν[1842] *δὲ ἐλιθοβόλησαν*, ὡς ‹Ἀζ›αρίαν[1843] *υἱὸν Ἰωδαὲ τὸν ἱερέα*.[1844] Τάχα δὲ *ἀμπελὼν* νῦν ἡ βασιλεία τοῦ Θεοῦ καὶ τὰ μυστήρια αὐτῆς *ἐν νόμῳ καὶ προφήταις*[1845] καὶ τῇ ἄλλῃ φυσιολογίᾳ.[mcccxxxiii] Καρποὶ δὲ ὁ ἐνάρετος ἐν ἤθει βίος· φραγμός, ὁ λογικὸς τόπος καὶ τὸ γράμμα, ὡς μὴ κατοπτεύοιτο τοῖς ἔξω τὰ ἐν κρυπτῷ· *ληνός*, τὸ βάθος τῆς δεχομένης τοὺς καρποὺς τούτους ψυχῆς πᾶν ἐπιπόλαιον ἀποβαλλούσης· *πύργος*, ὁ διῃρμένος περὶ Θεοῦ λόγος, ναὸς ὢν τοῦ ἐν αὐτῷ θείου νοῦ· *γεωργοί*, οἱ πρῶτοι πιστευθέντες *τὰ λόγια τοῦ Θεοῦ*,[1846] οἷς ἀποδημεῖ εἰς τὴν ἑαυτοῦ περιωπήν,[mcccxxxiv] δοὺς ἀφορμὰς ἐξ ὧν αὐτὸς *ἐφύτευσε φραγμὸν* ‹τε› *περιέθηκεν, ὤρυξεν, ᾠκοδόμησε*, τοῦ φέρειν καρπούς· *καιρὸς καρπῶν*[1847] ὃν οἶδεν ὁ *οἰκοδεσπότης*, τάχα δὲ οὐχ ὁ τοῦ ἐκφύειν φύλλα | **171r** ἢ κυπρίζειν ἢ ὀμφακίζειν ἢ τρυγᾶσθαι· οἷον ὁ τῆς νηπιότητος ἢ ὁ τῆς συμπληρώσεως τοῦ λόγου[1848] ἢ ὁ τῆς ἐναρέτου ἀρχῆς ἢ

1833 Matt. 21:33.
1834 Heb. 11:9; cf. Is. 60:21; 61:3. Jer. 39:41; 49:10.
1835 Cf. Jesus Nave, 23:12; 1 Esdras, 8:67; 8:64; Psalm 105:35.
1836 Ex. 13:21-22; cf. 14:19; 14:24; 19:9; 33:9-10; Num. 12:5; 14:14; Deut. 31:15; 2 Esdras, 19:12; Psalm 98:7; Ecclesiasticus, 24:4.
1837 1 Peter, 3:20; cf. Rom. 2:4.
1838 Cod. οἷς.
1839 Matt. 21:35.
1840 3 Kings, 22:24; 2 Paralipomenon (2 Chronicon), 18:23.
1841 Matt. 23:35.
1842 Cod. ὅν.
1843 Cod. Ζαχαρίαν.
1844 2 Paralipomenon (2 Chronicon), 24:20-22.
1845 Cf. Luke, 24:44.
1846 Rom. 3:2; cf. Heb. 5:12.
1847 Matt. 21:34.
1848 Origen's favourite Stoic notion of 'completion of reason'.

προκοπῆς, ὁ δὲ τῆς ἀγάπης καὶ χαρᾶς καὶ εἰρήνης καὶ τῶν λοιπῶν·[1849] *δοῦλοι*, οἱ προφῆται τὰ πνευματικὰ καρπώματα ἀπαιτοῦντες προσάγειν ὡς *ἱερεῖς τῷ Θεῷ*.[1850][mccccxxxv]

Ἡ παραβολὴ *οἰκοδεσπότην* λέγει τὸν Θεὸν καὶ πατέρα, τὸν πολλὴν πρόνοιαν ἐξ ἀρχῆς εἰς τοὺς Ἰουδαίους ἐνδειξάμενον. *ἀμπελὼν* δὲ ἁπλῶς μὲν ὁ πρῶτος λαὸς τουτέστιν ὁ Ἰσραὴλ φυτευθεὶς ὑπὸ τοῦ θεοῦ ἐν τῇ γῇ τῆς ἐπαγγελίας, *φραγμός*, ὁ νόμος, οὐκ ἐῶν αὐτοὺς μιγῆναι τοῖς ἔθνεσι, ληνὸς τὸ θυσιαστήριον ἤτοι ὁ τόπος τῶν σπονδῶν, πύργος, ἡ Σιὼν ἢ ναός. *γεωργοὶ* οἱ πρεσβύτεροι τοῦ λαοῦ καὶ οἱ σοφοὶ καὶ οἱ κατὰ καιροὺς διδάσκαλοι. ἀποδημία οἰκοδεσπότου, ὅτε οὐκέτι ἡμέραις *ἐν στύλῳ νεφέλης* καὶ νυκτὸς *ἐν στύλῳ πυρὸς* αὐτοῖς ἐπιφαίνεται ἢ ἡ τοῦ Θεοῦ μακροθυμία, ἡ μὴ παρὰ πόδας ἀπαιτοῦσα τοὺς Ἰουδαίους τὴν τῶν πταισμάτων τιμωρίαν. ἀπαίτησις δὲ *καρπῶν*, ὁ ἔννομος βίος, *καιρὸς* αὐτῶν ἡ προφητικὴ ἀπαίτησις, *δοῦλοι* πρῶτοι καὶ δεύτεροι παθόντες ἄτοπον οἱ κατὰ διαφόρους καιροὺς ἀποσταλέντες προφῆται. ὧν *τὸν μὲν ἔδειραν*, ὡς Μιχαίαν παταξάντος *ἐπὶ σιαγόνα* Σεδεκίου, *τὸν δὲ ἀπέκτειναν* ὡς Ζαχαρίαν *μεταξὺ τοῦ ναοῦ καὶ τοῦ θυσιαστηρίου, τὸν δὲ ἐλιθοβόλησαν*, ὡς *Ἀζαρίαν υἱὸν Ἰωδαὲ τὸν ἱερέα*. τάχα δὲ *ἀμπελὼν* νῦν ἡ βασιλεία τοῦ θεοῦ καὶ τὰ μυστήρια αὐτῆς ἐν νόμῳ καὶ προφήταις καὶ τῇ ἄλλῃ φυσιολογίᾳ, καρποὶ δὲ ὁ ἐνάρετος ἐν ἤθεσι βίος, φραγμός, ὁ λογικὸς τόπος καὶ τὸ γράμμα ὡς μὴ κατοπτεύοιτο τοῖς ἔξω τὰ κεκρυμμένα μυστήρια, ληνὸς τὸ βάθος τῆς δεχομένης τοὺς καρποὺς τούτους ψυχῆς πᾶν ἐπιπόλαιον ἀποβαλλούσης, *πύργος*, ὁ διηρμένος περὶ θεοῦ λόγος, ναὸς ὢν τοῦ ἐν αὐτῷ θείου νοῦ. *γεωργοί*, οἱ πρῶτοι πιστευθέντες *τὰ λόγια τοῦ Θεοῦ*, οἷς ἀποδημεῖ εἰς τὴν αὐτοῦ περιωπὴν δοὺς ἀφορμὴν (ἐξ ὧν αὐτὸς ἐφύτευσε, *φραγμόν τε ἔθηκεν, ὤρυξεν, ᾠκοδόμησε*) τοῦ φέρειν καρπόν, *καιρὸς καρπῶν* ὃν οἶδεν ὁ οἰκοδεσπότης τάχα δὲ οὐχ ὁ τοῦ ἐκφύειν φύλλα ἢ κυπρίζειν ἢ ὀμφακίζειν ἢ τρυγᾶσθαι, οἷον ‹δὲ› οἱ τῆς νηπιότητος ἢ οἱ τῆς συμπληρώσεως τοῦ λόγου ἢ ὁ τῆς ἐν ἀρετῇ προκοπῆς ἢ ἀρχῆς, οἱ δὲ τῆς ἀγάπης καὶ χαρᾶς καὶ εἰρήνης καὶ τῶν λοιπῶν. δοῦλοι οἱ προφῆται τὰ πνευματικὰ καρπώματα ἀπαιτοῦντες προσάγειν ὡς ἱερεῖς τῷ θεῷ.[mccccxxxvi]

Ἡ παραβολὴ *οἰκοδεσπότην* λέγει τὸν Θεὸν καὶ πατέρα, τὸν πολλὴν πρόνοιαν ἐξ ἀρχῆς εἰς τοὺς Ἰουδαίους ἐπιδειξάμενον. *Ἀμπελὼν* δὲ ἁπλῶς μὲν ὁ πρῶτος λαός, τουτέστιν ὁ Ἰσραήλ, φυτευθεὶς ὑπὸ τοῦ Θεοῦ ἐν τῇ γῇ τῆς ἐπαγγελίας. *Φραγμὸς* δὲ ὁ νόμος, οὐκ ἐῶν αὐτοὺς μιγῆναι τοῖς ἔθνεσι. *Ληνὸς* τὸ θυσιαστήριον, ἤτοι ὁ τόπος τῶν σπονδῶν. *Πύργος* ἡ Σιών, ἢ ὁ οὐρανός. *Γεωργοὶ* οἱ πρεσβύτεροι τοῦ λαοῦ καὶ οἱ σοφοί, καὶ οἱ κατὰ καιροὺς διδάσκαλοι. *Ἀπεδήμησε* δὲ ὁ οἰκοδεσπότης, ὅτε οὐκέτι ἡμέρᾳ ἐν στύλῳ νεφέλης καὶ νυκτὸς αὐτοῖς ἐν στύλῳ πυρὸς ἐπιφαίνεται. Ἢ ἡ τοῦ Θεοῦ μακροθυμία, ἡ μὴ παρὰ πόδας ἀπαιτοῦσα τοὺς Ἰουδαίους τὴν τῶν πταισμάτων τιμωρίαν. Ἀπαίτησις δὲ *καρπῶν* ὁ ἔννομος βίος. *Καιρὸς αὐτῶν* ἡ προφητικὴ ἀπαίτησις. *Δοῦλοι* πρῶτοι καὶ δεύτεροι παθόντες ἄτοπον, οἱ κατὰ διαφόρους καιροὺς ἀποσταλέντες προφῆται, οἷς τὸν μὲν ἔδηραν, ὡς Μιχαίαν, πατάξαντος ἐπὶ σιαγόνα Σεδεκίου. τὸν δὲ ἀπέκτειναν, ὡς Ζαχαρίαν, μεταξὺ τοῦ ναοῦ καὶ τοῦ θυσιαστηρίου. τὸν δὲ ἐλιθοβόλησαν, ὡς Ζαριοῦ υἱὸν Ἰωδαὲ τὸν ἱερέα. Τάχα δὲ *ἀμπελών*, ἢ ἡ βασιλεία τοῦ Θεοῦ, καὶ τὰ μυστήρια αὐτοῦ ἐν νόμῳ καὶ προφήταις, καὶ τῇ ἄλλῃ φυσιολογίᾳ. *Καρποὶ* δὲ ὁ ἐνάρετος ἐν ἤθεσι βίος. *Φραγμὸς* ὁ λογικὸς τόπος, καὶ τὸ γράμμα, ὡς μὴ κατοπτεύοιτο τοῖς ἔξω τὰ κεκρυμμένα

1849 Cf. Gal. 5:22; Rom. 14:17; 15:13.
1850 Cf. Ex. 19:22. Rev. 1:6; 5:10.

μυστήρια. *Ληνὸς* τὸ βάθος τῆς δεχομένης τοὺς καρποὺς τοὺς τῆς ψυχῆς, πᾶν ἐπὶ πόλεμον ἐπιβαλλούσης. *Πύργος* καὶ διῃρημένος περὶ Θεοῦ λόγος. Ναὸς μὲν ἡ τοῦ ἐν αὐτῷ θείου ναοῦ. *Γεωργοὶ* οἱ πρῶτοι πιστευθέντες τὰ λόγια τοῦ Θεοῦ. οἷς ἀποδημεῖ εἰς τὴν αὐτοῦ περιοπεῖν,[1851] δοὺς ἀφορμήν, ἐξ ὧν αὐτὸς ἐφύτευσε, φραγμόν τε ἔθηκεν, ὤρυξεν, ᾠκοδόμησε, τοῦ φέρειν καρπόν. *Καιρὸς καρπῶν*, ὃν οἶδεν οἰκοδεσπότης, τάχα οὐχ ὅτι ἐκφύειν φύλλα, ἢ κυπρίζειν, ἢ ὀμφακίζειν, ἢ τρυγᾶσθαι. οἷον οἱ τῆς νηπιότητος, ἢ τῆς συμπληρώσεως τοῦ λόγου, ἢ οἱ τῆς ἐν ἀρετῇ προκοπῆς, ἢ ἀρχῆς. οἱ δὲ τῆς ἀγάπης, καὶ χαρᾶς, καὶ εἰρήνης, καὶ τῶν λοιπῶν. *Δοῦλοι* οἱ προφῆται τὰ πνευματικὰ καρπώματα ἀπαιτοῦντες προσάγειν ὡς ἱερεῖς τῷ Θεῷ.[mccccxxxvii]

Οἰκοδεσπότην λέγει τὸν Θεόν, *ἀμπελῶνα*, τὸν διὰ τῆς εὐσεβείας κατασκευασθέντα λαόν, τὸν Ἰσραήλ, *φραγμόν*, τὴν ὑπὸ τῆς τοῦ Θεοῦ βοηθείας ἀσφάλειαν ‹παρασχεθεῖσαν αὐτῷ›, καθ᾽ ἣν τῆς ἐπιβουλῆς τῶν πολεμίων ἀπαλλαγεὶς ἔμεινεν ἐπὶ τῆς οἰκείας γῆς, ἣν νέμεσθαι αὐτοῖς ἐδεδώκει τῶν ἀλλοτρίων ἀφελόμενος ὁ δεσπότης· *πύργον*, τὸν ναόν, ἐν ᾧ συνιόντας ἐχρῆν τοὺς τῆς εὐσεβείας καρποὺς τῷ Θεῷ προσκομίζειν, ἅπαν πληροῦντας ἐκεῖ τὸ κατὰ νόμον τῇ τοῦ Θεοῦ θρησκείᾳ ὀφειλόμενον παρ᾽ αὐτῶν. Ἀλλὰ μὴν καὶ *ληνὸν* τὸν βωμόν, ἐφ᾽ οὗ τῶν θυσιῶν ἐξεχεῖτο τὸ αἷμα, *γεωργοὺς* δὲ τὸ ἱερατικὸν τάγμα[mccccxxxviii] καὶ ἅπαντας τοὺς τοῦτο ἐγκεχειρισμένους ὥστε παρασκευάζειν τὸν λαὸν τὴν ἀπὸ τῆς τοῦ νόμου διδασκαλίας ἐπικαρπίαν τῷ Θεῷ προσάγειν δι᾽ *ἀγαθῆς συνειδήσεως*.[1852] Ἀποσταλέντας δὲ *δούλους*, τοὺς κατὰ καιρὸν λέγει προφήτας, οἳ ἀπεστέλλοντο ‹πρὸς τὸ› εὐγνώμονα γενέσθαι τὸν λαὸν ποιήσοντες περὶ τὰ ὀφειλόμενα τῷ Θεῷ (εἴτε καὶ τοὺς ἱερέας· συνεχὴς γὰρ αὐτοῖς ὁ ἔλεγχος κατ᾽ ἐκείνων μάλιστα ἐγίνετο ὡς καὶ τοῖς λοιποῖς αἰτίων τῆς βλάβης). Παθόντες δὲ μυρία ὅσα παρὰ τῶν Ἰουδαίων κακά, καὶ μάλιστα παρὰ τῶν ἡγεῖσθαι δοκούντων ἐν αὐτοῖς, | **171v** διετέλεσαν ἀνύοντες πλέον οὐδέν.

Οἰκοδεσπότην λέγει, τὸν τῶν ὅλων θεόν, *ἀμπελῶνα* τὸν διὰ τῆς εὐσεβείας κατασκευασθέντα λαὸν τὸν Ἰσραήλ, καὶ *φραγμὸν* τὴν ὑπὸ τῆς τοῦ Θεοῦ βοηθείας ἀσφάλειαν παρασχεθεῖσαν αὐτῷ καθ᾽ ἣν τῆς ἐπιβουλῆς τῶν πολεμίων ἀπαλλαγεὶς ἔμεινεν ἐπὶ τῆς οἰκείας γῆς, ἣν νέμεσθαι αὐτοῖς ἐδεδώκει τῶν ἀλλοτρίων ἀφελόμενος ὁ δεσπότης, *πύργον*, τὸν ναὸν ἐν ᾧ συνιόντας ἐχρῆν τοὺς τῆς εὐσεβείας καρποὺς τῷ θεῷ προσκομίζειν ἅπαν πληροῦντας ἐκεῖ τὸ κατὰ νόμον τῇ τοῦ θεοῦ θρησκείᾳ ὀφειλόμενον παρ᾽ αὐτῶν. ἀλλὰ μὴν καὶ *ληνὸν* τὸν βωμόν, ἐφ᾽ οὗ τῶν θυσιῶν ἐξεχεῖτο τὸ αἷμα, *γεωργοὺς* δὲ τὸ ἱερατικὸν τάγμα καὶ ἅπαντας τοὺς τοῦτο ἐγκεχειρισμένους ὥστε παρασκευάζειν τὸν λαὸν τὴν ἀπὸ τῆς τοῦ νόμου διδασκαλίας ἐπικαρπίαν τῷ θεῷ προσάγειν δι᾽ *ἀγαθῆς συνειδήσεως*, ἀποσταλέντας δὲ *δούλους* τοὺς κατὰ καιρὸν λέγει προφήτας οἳ ἀπεστέλλοντο πρὸς τὸ εὐγνώμονα γενέσθαι τὸν λαὸν ποιήσοντες περὶ τὰ ὀφειλόμενα τῷ θεῷ (εἴτε καὶ τοὺς ἱερέας, συνεχὴς γὰρ αὐτοῖς ὁ ἔλεγχος κατ᾽ ἐκείνων μάλιστα ἐγίνετο ὡς καὶ τοῖς λοιποῖς αἰτίων τῆς βλάβης), παθόντες δὲ μυρία ὅσα παρὰ τῶν Ἰουδαίων κακ καὶ μάλιστα παρὰ τῶν ἡγεῖσθαι δοκούντων ἐν αὐτοῖς διετέλεσαν ἀνύοντες πλέον οὐδέν.[mccccxxxix]

1851 Sic.

1852 Cf. 1 Tim. 1:5&19; 1 Peter, 3:16&21; Acts, 23:1.

Οἰκοδεσπότην μὲν λέγει τὸν τῶν ὅλων δεσπότην θεόν, *ἀμπελῶνα* δὲ τὸν διὰ τῆς εὐσεβείας κατασκευασθέντα λαὸν Ἰσραήλ, λέγων καὶ *φραγμὸν* τὴν ὑπὸ τῆς τοῦ θεοῦ βοηθείας ἀσφάλειαν παρασχεθεῖσαν αὐτῷ, καθ' ἣν τῶν ἀλλοτρίων ἀπαλλαγεὶς τῆς ἐπιβουλῆς ἔμεινεν ἐπὶ τῆς οἰκείας γῆς. *πύργον* δὲ τὸν ναόν, ἐν ᾧ συνιόντας ἐχρῆν τοὺς τῆς εὐσεβείας καρποὺς προσκομίζειν τῷ θεῷ, ἅπαντα πληροῦντας ἐκεῖ τὰ κατὰ νόμον. ἀλλὰ μὴν καὶ ληνὸν τὸν βωμόν, ἐφ' οὗ τὸ τῶν θυσιῶν ἐξεχεῖτο τὸ αἷμα, *γεωργοὺς* δὲ τὸ ἱερατικὸν τάγμα καὶ ἅπαντας τοὺς τοῦτο ἐγκεχειρισμένους, ὥστε σκευάζειν τὸν λαὸν τὴν ἀπὸ τῆς τοῦ νόμου διδασκαλίας ἐπικαρπίαν τῷ θεῷ δι' *ἀγαθῆς* προσάγειν *συνειδήσεως*. ἀποσταλέντας *δούλους* τοὺς κατὰ καιρὸν λέγει προφήτας, οἳ ἀπεστέλλοντο πρὸς τὸ εὐγνώμονα γενέσθαι τὸν λαὸν περὶ τὰ ὀφειλόμενα τῷ θεῷ ἢ καὶ τοὺς ἱερέας. συνεχὴς γὰρ αὐτοῖς ὁ ἔλεγχος κατ' ἐκείνων μάλιστα ἐγίνετο ὡς καὶ τοῖς λοιποῖς αἰτίων τῆς βλάβης. παθόντες δὲ ὅσα μυρία παρὰ τῶν Ἰουδαίων κακὰ καὶ μάλιστα παρὰ τῶν ἡγεῖσθαι δοκούντων ἐν αὐτοῖς διετέλεσαν ἀνύοντες πλέον οὐδέν.[mcccxl]

[Ὅτε γὰρ ἐξ Αἰγύπτου ἐξῆλθον, καὶ νόμον ἔδωκεν καὶ πόλιν ἀνέστησεν καὶ ναὸν *ᾠκοδόμησεν* καὶ θυσιαστήριον κατεσκεύασεν καὶ χρόνον πολὺν ἔμεινεν. τὴν γὰρ ἀποδημίαν τοῦτο αἰνίττεται, τὴν πολλὴν μακροθυμίαν *καὶ ἀπέστειλεν τοὺς δούλους αὐτοῦ*, τουτέστιν τοὺς προφήτας, *τοὺς καρποὺς λαβεῖν*, τουτέστιν τὴν ὑπακοὴν τὴν διὰ τῶν ἔργων ἐπίδειξιν.][mcccxli]

Ὅτε γὰρ ἐξ Αἰγύπτου ἐξῆλθον, καὶ νόμον ἔδωκε, καὶ πόλιν ἀνέστησε, καὶ ναὸν ᾠκοδόμησε, καὶ θυσιαστήριον κατεσκεύασε. *Καὶ ἀπεδήμησε*. τουτέστιν, ἐμακροθύμησεν, οὐκ ἀεὶ τοῖς ἁμαρτήμασι παραπόδας ἐπάγων τὰς τιμωρίας. τὴν γὰρ ἀποδημίαν τὴν πολλὴν αὐτοῦ μακροθυμίαν φησί. *Καὶ ἀπέστειλε τοὺς δούλους αὐτοῦ*, τουτέστι, τοὺς προφήτας, *τὸν καρπὸν λαβεῖν*, τουτέστι, τὴν ὑπακοήν, τὴν διὰ τῶν ἔργων ἐπίδειξιν.[mcccxlii]

ἐντραπήσονται τὸν υἱόν μου.[1853] Υἱός, ὁ Χριστὸς παθὼν ὑπ' αὐτῶν ἀναστάς τε καὶ κακῶς ἀπολλὺς αὐτοὺς ἐξάρσει τῆς πόλεως, τοῦ ναοῦ, τῶν ἄλλων κακῶν ἃ πεπόνθασιν ὑπὸ Ῥωμαίων *ἔξω* ἑαυτοὺς ποιήσαντες *τοῦ Θεοῦ*.[1854]
Τὸ δὲ *ἴσως τοῦτον ἰδόντες ἐντραπήσονται*,[1855] φησὶ οὐκ ἀγνοῶν ὅτι ἔμελλον αὐτὸν ἀποκτεῖναι, ἀλλὰ τὸ ὀφειλόμενον γενέσθαι σημάνας.

What he added, *they will respect my son*, does not suggest ingnorance. For what would the householder not know, since in this passage stands for God the Father?[mcccxliii]

Ἔδει γάρ φησι εἰ καὶ τοὺς δούλους ἀπέκτειναν, ἀλλὰ τοῦ Υἱοῦ ἐντραπῆναι τὸ ἀξίωμα. Οὕτω δὲ λέγει ὡς ἀγνοῶν, ἵνα μή τινες εἴπωσιν ὅτι τὸ προγνωστικὸν τοῦ Θεοῦ ἠνάγκασεν αὐτοὺς παρακοῦσαι.[mcccxliv]
Ἄφιξιν λέγει τοῦ υἱοῦ, τὴν αὐτοῦ παρουσίαν.

1853 Matt. 21:37.
1854 Rev. 3:12.
1855 Cf. Matt. 21:37; Mark, 12:6.

> Ἄφιξιν δὲ λέγει τοῦ υἱοῦ τὴν αὐτοῦ παρουσίαν.[mccccxlv]

> ἄφιξιν δὲ λέγει τοῦ υἱοῦ τὴν αὐτοῦ παρουσίαν παθόντος ὑπ᾽ αὐτῶν καὶ ἀναστάντος καὶ κακῶς ἀπολέσαντος αὐτούς.[mccccxlvi]

Ἄλλοι γεωργοί, οἱ ἀπόστολοι καὶ οἱ τῶν πιστῶν εὐγνώμονες, οἳ καὶ ἀποδεδώκασι *τοὺς καρποὺς* ἐν θεοσεβείᾳ ζήσαντες· οἷς καὶ ἐξεδόθη ὁ ἀμπελὼν ἐπιμελουμένοις αὐτοῦ, ἐπειδὴ ἐν Ἡσαΐᾳ καὶ ἐν Ἰερεμίᾳ ὁ ἀμπελών, λαὸς οὐ φέρων καρποὺς ἀλλ᾽ *ἀκάνθας*[1856] καὶ πικρίας[1857] μεστός. Νῦν δὲ ὁ μὲν ἀμπελὼν φροντίζεται ὑπὸ τοῦ δεσπότου. Οὐ γὰρ ἐξεκόπη ὁ ἀμπελών, ἀλλ᾽ *ἄλ‹λ›οις*[1858] ἐδόθη *γεωργοῖς*.[1859] Ὑπαίτιοι δέ, οἱ πρῶτοι γεωργοί.

> Ἄλλοι γεωργοὶ οἱ ἀπόστολοι καὶ οἱ τῶν πιστῶν εὐγνώμονες, οἳ καὶ ἀποδεδώκασι *τοὺς καρποὺς* ἐν θεοσεβείᾳ ζήσαντες. οἷς καὶ ἐξεδόθη ὁ ἀμπελὼν ἐπιμελουμένοις αὐτοῦ, ἐπειδὴ ἐν Ἡσαΐᾳ καὶ ἐν Ἰερεμίᾳ ὁ ἀμπελών, λαὸς οὐ φέρων καρποὺς ἀλλ᾽ *ἀκάνθας* καὶ πικρίας μεστός. νῦν δὲ ὁ μὲν ἀμπελὼν φροντίζεται ὑπὸ τοῦ δεσπότου. οὐ γὰρ ἐξεκόπη ὁ ἀμπελών, ἀλλ᾽ *ἄλλοις* ἐδόθη *γεωργοῖς*. ὑπαίτιοι δὲ οἱ πρῶτοι γεωργοί.[mccccxlvii]

καὶ ἡμῶν ἔσται ἡ κληρονομία.[1860] Τοῦτο ἐστὶν ὅπερ καὶ ὁ εὐαγγελιστὴς ἔλεγεν· *ἐὰν ἀφῶμεν αὐτόν, ἔρχονται οἱ Ῥωμαῖοι καὶ ἀροῦσιν ἡμῶν καὶ τὴν πόλιν καὶ τὸ ἔθνος.*[1861]
λέγει αὐτοῖς· οὐδέποτε ἀνέγνωτε ἐν ταῖς γραφαῖς, λίθον ὃν ἀπεδοκίμασαν.[1862] *Λίθον* ἑαυτὸν καλεῖ· οἰκοδόμους δέ, τοὺς διδασκάλους τῶν Ἰουδαίων, οἳ ὡς ἀχρεῖον μὲν αὐτὸν *ἀπεδοκίμασαν*, τουτέστιν ἀπώσαντο.

> Οἰκοδόμοι εἰσὶν οἱ τὸν ζωοποιὸν *λίθον* ἀποδοκιμάσαντες, τὴν ἀλήθειαν, οἱ τῷ ψεύδει τῇ διδασκαλίᾳ ***[mccccxlviii]

> (Ὠριγένους.) Οἰκοδόμοι εἰσίν, οἱ τὸν ζωοποιὸν *λίθον* ἀποδοκιμάσαντες, τὴν ἀλήθειαν, οἱ τῷ ψεύδει τῇ διδασκαλίᾳ **[mccccxlix]

Ἐκ νε | **172r** κρῶν δὲ ἀναστὰς συνῆψε τοὺς δύο λαούς, τουτέστιν Ἰουδαίους καὶ τοὺς *ἐξ ἐθνῶν*,[1863] εἰς μίαν πίστιν ἑνώσας αὐτούς. Τοῦτο γὰρ εἶπε σημαίνων ὅτι μέλλει

1856 Cf. Is. 5:2-7; Jer. 4:3; 12:13.
1857 Jer. 2:21.
1858 Cod. ἄλοις.
1859 Matt. 21:41.
1860 Mark, 12:7; cf. Matt. 21:38.
1861 John, 11:48.
1862 Matt. 21:42.
1863 Cf. Rom. 9:24; Acts, 15:23.

διαβῆναι ἡ χάρις καὶ ἐπὶ τὰ ἔθνη,[1864] ὃ καὶ ἡ τοῦ Πνεύματος χάρις[1865] ἔκπαλαι προανεφώνησε καὶ ὁ Πατὴρ ἐψηφίσατο. Αἴρεται τοίνυν ἀπὸ μὲν Ἰουδαίων *ἡ βασιλεία τοῦ Θεοῦ*[1866] (τουτέστιν ἔξω γίνονται τῶν αὐτοῦ ἀγαθῶν οἳ καὶ τῆς οἰκείας ἐξεώθησαν γῆς) οἰκειοῦνται δὲ τῷ Θεῷ[1867] οἱ πιστεύοντες εἰς Χριστόν. *Λίθον* δὲ ἑαυτὸν εἰπών, ἔδειξεν ὅτι οὐ μόνον νῦν, ἀλλὰ καὶ ἐν τῇ δευτέρᾳ αὐτοῦ παρουσίᾳ ἐπιπίπτων (τουτέστι κατακρίνων) *λικμήσει*[1868] αὐτοὺς (ὅ ἐστι σκορπίσει) πέμπων εἰς σκότος, εἰς *γεένναν*.[1869] Δύο γὰρ λέγει αὐτῶ‹ν›[1870] ἀπωλείας. Μίαν μὲν τὴν ἀπὸ τῆς ἁλώσεως, ἑτέραν δὲ τὴν ἀπὸ τῆς ἐν τῇ δευτέρᾳ αὐτοῦ παρουσίᾳ κατακρίσεως.

εἰς κεφαλὴν γωνίας.[1871] Γωνία ἐστὶ συγκρότησις δύο τοίχων. Τὸ ἐξ Ἰσραὴλ *λεῖμμα*[1872] *καὶ τῶν ἐθνῶν τὸ πλήρωμα*,[1873] εἰς ἓν συγκροτῶν ὁ λίθος, ὁ Χριστός, *ἡ ἀλήθεια*,[1874] τὴν γωνίαν ποιεῖ, καθὸ γέγραπται· *παρὰ Κυρίου ἐγένετο αὕτη*.[1875]

> Γωνία ἐστὶ συγκρότησις δύο τοίχων. τὸ ἐξ Ἰσραὴλ *λεῖμμα καὶ τῶν ἐθνῶν τὸ πλήρωμα*, εἰς ἓν συγκροτῶν ὁ λίθος ὁ Χριστός, ἡ ἀλήθεια, τὴν γωνίαν ποιεῖ, καθὼς γέγραπται. *παρὰ Κυρίου ἐγένετο αὕτη*.[mcccl]

> Γωνία ἐστὶ συγκρότησις δύο τοίχων, τὸ ἐξ Ἰσραὴλ λῆμμα, καὶ τῶν ἐθνῶν τὸ πλήρωμα, εἰς ἓν συγκροτῶν ὁ λίθος Χριστός, ἡ ἀλήθεια, τὴν γωνίαν ποιήσας, καθὼς γέγραπται, *παρὰ Κυρίου ἐγένετο αὕτη*.[mcccli]

53

172r (ΩΡΙΓΕΝΟΥΣ) *Καὶ ὁ πεσὼν ἐπὶ τὸν λίθον τοῦτον*.[1876] Πᾶσα πτῶσις ἐν τῷ πνευματικῷ λίθῳ λυσιτελὴς καὶ ἐπίπονος.[mccclii] Οὐκ ἔστι γὰρ πτώσεως, ἀλλ' οἰκοδομῆς.

> Πᾶσα πτῶσις ἐν τῷ πνευματικῷ λίθῳ λυσιτελὴς καὶ ἐπίπονος. οὐκ ἔστι γὰρ πτώσεως, ἀλλ' οἰκοδομῆς. πῶς δὲ συνθλᾷ καὶ λικμᾷ καὶ τὰ αἴτια τούτων ζήτει.[mcccliii]

1864 Cf. Matt. 21:43.
1865 Cf. Rom. 1:4; Heb. 10:29; James, 4:5.
1866 Matt. 21:43.
1867 Cf. Eph. 2:19.
1868 Matt. 21:44.
1869 Matt. 5:22 & 29-30; 18:9; Mark, 9:43-47; Luke, 12:5.
1870 Cod. αὐτῷ.
1871 Matt. 21:42.
1872 Rom. 11:5.
1873 Rom. 11:8 & 25.
1874 John, 14:6.
1875 Psalm, 117:23, quoted in Matt. 21:42 and Mark, 12:11.
1876 Matt. 21:44.

Πᾶσα πτῶσις ἐν τῷ πνευματικῷ λίθῳ ἀλυσιτελὴς καὶ ἐπίπονος. οὐκ ἔστι γὰρ πτώσεως, ἀλλ᾽ οἰκοδομῆς, πῶς δὲ συνθλᾷ καὶ λικμᾷ καὶ τὰ αἴτια τούτων ζητεῖ.[mccliv]

54

(ΩΡΙΓΕΝΟΥΣ)[mccclv] *Ὡμοιώθη ἡ βασιλεία τῶν οὐρανῶν ἀνθρώπῳ βασιλεῖ.*[1877] Νῦν οὐκ *οἰ* | **172v** *κοδεσπότῃ* ὡμοίωται *ἡ βασιλεία τῶν οὐρανῶν*, ἀλλὰ (τὸ μεῖζον) *βασιλεῖ.* Τάχα δὲ ἄνθρωπος μὲν βασιλεὺς ἀνθρώποις οὖσιν ἡμῖν, οἷς καὶ ὀργίζεται, θεοῖς δὲ ὢν *ἐν μέσῳ* ἐστὶ διακρίνων,[1878] Θεὸς βασιλεύς.[mccclvi]

Νῦν μὲν οὐκ οἰκοδεσπότῃ ὁμοιοῦται, ἀλλὰ βασιλεῖ τῷ μείζονι. πέμπει γὰρ *στρατεύματα*, λέγει ἐν ἐξουσίᾳ δῆσαι *ποδῶν καὶ χειρῶν*, ἐμβαλεῖν *εἰς τὸ σκότος.* τάχα ἄνθρωπος βασιλεὺς ἡμῖν οἷς καὶ ὀργίζεται, θεὸς δὲ ὢν *ἐν μέσῳ* ἔστη διακρίνων θεούς.[mccclvii]

Ὅρα δὲ εἰ παυομένων ἡμῶν τοῦ *κατὰ ἄνθρωπον* περιπατεῖν,[1879] διὸ *ὡς ἄνθρωποι* ἀποθνήσκομεν,[1880] καὶ ἀξιωθέντων ἀκοῦσαι *θεοί ἐστε*[1881] παύεται *ἀνθρώπῳ βασιλεῖ* ὁμοιουμένη *ἡ βασιλεία* τοῦ θεοῦ.

καὶ τότε παύσεται ὁμοιουμένη *ἡ βασιλεία τῶν οὐρανῶν ἀνθρώπῳ*, ὅταν παυσαμένου ζήλου καὶ ἔριδος καὶ τῶν λοιπῶν παθῶν καὶ ἁμαρτημάτων καὶ τοῦ *κατὰ ἄνθρωπον* περιπατεῖν, ἄξιοι γενώμεθα ἀκοῦσαι ἀπὸ τοῦ θεοῦ. *ἐγὼ εἶπα. θεοί ἐστε καὶ υἱοὶ ὑψίστου πάντες*, ἢ τοῦ Χριστοῦ αὐτοῦ, μηκέτι πράττοντες τοιαῦτα ἐφ᾽ οἷς λέγοιτ᾽ ἂν ‹ἡμῖν›. *ὑμεῖς δὲ ὡς ἄνθρωποι ἀποθνήσκετε.* ἐγὼ δ᾽ οἶμαι ὅτι οὐ μόνον τὸ *ἀνθρώπῳ βασιλεῖ* ὁμοιοῦσθαι τὴν βασιλείαν *τῶν οὐρανῶν* παύσεται, ἀλλὰ καὶ ἄλλα μυρία ὧν χρῄζει ἁμαρτωλὸς ἄνθρωπος.[mccclviii]

Γάμον μὲν οὖν λέγει τὴν ἁρμονίαν καὶ συνάφειαν τοῦ Υἱοῦ τὴν γενομένην πρὸς τὴν ἐκκλησίαν,[mccclix]

(Θεοδώρου Ἡρακλείας.) Γάμον λέγει τὴν ἁρμονίαν καὶ συνάφειαν τοῦ Υἱοῦ τὴν γενομένην πρὸς τὴν Ἐκκλησίαν. τοὺς δὲ ἀποστελλομένους καλέσαι τοὺς κεκλημένους, τοὺς μαθητάς, μεθ᾽ οὓς ἔπεμψε τοὺς ἑβδομήκοντα.[mccclx]

(Κυρίλλου Ἀλεξανδρείας.) Γάμον λέγει τὴν πρὸς τὸν Υἱὸν τῶν πιστῶν συνάφειαν, καλῶν εἰς τοῦτον τοὺς Ἰουδαίους, πάλαι μὲν διὰ τῶν προφητῶν, ὕστερον δὲ διὰ τῶν μαθητῶν, πρὸ τοῦ πάθους καὶ τῆς ἀναστάσεως.[mccclxi]

1877 Matt. 22:2.
1878 Cf. Psalm 81:1.
1879 Cf. 1 Cor. 3:3.
1880 Cf. Psalm 81:7.
1881 Cf. Psalm 81:6.

συνάπτει ‹δὲ› Θεῷ τὸν ἄνθρωπον καὶ οἰκεῖον[1882] αὐτὸν ποιεῖ καὶ θείας φύσεως κοινωνόν. Γάμον δὲ καλεῖ τὸ πρᾶγμα διὰ τὴν φαιδρότητα καὶ τὸν πόθον ὃν ἔχει πρὸς ἡμᾶς ὁ Θεός.

> *Γάμους* ὁ πατὴρ ποιεῖ, τὴν εὐφροσύνην τῇ ἀποκαταστάσει τῆς ἐκκλησίας πρὸς Χριστὸν καὶ τὴν πνευματικὴν κοινωνίαν λόγου καὶ νύμφης ψυχῆς λαμβανούσης καὶ γεννώσης λογικὰ γεννήματα. κοινῶς μὲν *δοῦλοι* καλοῦνται διδάσκαλοι καὶ πάντες οἱ διάκονοι τοῦ λόγου, νῦν δὲ πατριάρχαι. *κλητοὶ* ὁ πρῶτος λαὸς καὶ τὸ τῶν εὐγενῶν Ἰσραηλιτικῶν ψυχῶν γένος. τοὺς γὰρ πρὸς σύνεσιν εὐφυεῖς καὶ τῇ κατασκευῇ διορατικωτέρους[mccclxii] θέλει ἥκειν εἰς τὴν μακαρίαν ἑστίαν ὁ θεός.[mccclxiii]

> οἱ δὲ γάμοι τοῦ υἱοῦ τοῦ βασιλέως ἡ ἀποκατάστασις τῆς νύμφης ἐκκλησίας Χριστοῦ πρὸς Χριστὸν τὸν νυμφίον αὐτῆς. οἱ δὲ ἀποστελλόμενοι δοῦλοι *καλέσαι τοὺς κεκλημένους εἰς τοὺς γάμους* οἱ κατὰ καιρόν εἰσι προφῆται[mccclxiv] ἐπιστρέφοντες τοὺς ἀπὸ τοῦ λαοῦ διὰ τῶν προφητειῶν ἐπὶ τὴν εὐφροσύνην ἀγομένην ἐπὶ τῇ ἀποκαταστάσει τῆς ἐκκλησίας πρὸς Χριστόν.[mccclxv]

> ἐν πνευματικοῖς δὲ γάμοις κοινωνίαν νόει λόγου νυμφίου ‹ὑποδοχήν,› τόκον δὲ καλῶς ποιούμενα νύμφης ψυχῆς, γαμουμένης λόγῳ καὶ μὴ φθειρομένης ὑπ᾿ αὐτοῦ, ἀλλὰ καὶ καθ᾿ ἑκάστην τὴν πρὸς αὐτὸν κοινωνίαν ἀφθαρσίας μεταλαμβανούσης καὶ γεννώσης, ὁποῖα γένοιτο ἐκ τοιούτων γάμων λογικὰ γεννήματα.[mccclxvi]

55

(ΩΡΙΓΕΝΟΥΣ) Συνάψας ἑαυτῷ *τὸ πλάσμα*[1883] τῶν χειρῶν αὐτοῦ, *γάμους*[1884] ὠνόμασε τὴν παρὰ τῶν εὐσεβῶν ἐπὶ τῶν θείων μελῶν περιπλοκήν. Νοῦς πρὸς νοῦν συνάπτεται, εἰ καὶ διὰ μέσης σαρκός.[mccclxvii] Ἐπὶ ταύτῃ οὖν δεδέμεθα, καθ᾿ οὓς οἶδε λόγους. Πρῶτοι δὲ καὶ δεύτεροι ‹οἱ› καλοῦντες. Πρῶτοι μέν εἰσι καὶ οἱ κατὰ τὴν τοῦ Κυρίου παρουσίαν προδραμόντες ἀπόστολοι,[1885] δεύτεροι δὲ οἱ μετὰ τὴν ἀνάληψιν ἀπόστολοί τε καὶ ἀποστόλων συνεργοὶ καὶ διάδοχοι.[mccclxviii]

> Συνάψας ἑαυτῷ τὸ πλάσμα τῶν χειρῶν αὐτοῦ *γάμους* ὠνόμασε τὴν παρὰ τῶν εὐσεβῶν ἐπὶ τῶν θείων μελῶν περιπλοκήν. νοῦς πρὸς νοῦν συνάπτεται, εἰ καὶ διὰ μέσης σαρκός. ἐπὶ ταύτῃ οὖν δεδέμεθα, καθ᾿ οὓς οἶδε λόγους. πρῶτοι δὲ καὶ δεύτεροι καλοῦντες καλοῦνται. πρῶτοι μέν εἰσι, καὶ οἱ κατὰ τὴν τοῦ Κυρίου παρουσίαν προδραμόντες ἀπόστολοι, δεύτεροι δὲ οἱ μετὰ τὴν ἀνάληψιν ἀπόστολοί τε καὶ ἀποστόλων συνεργοὶ καὶ διάδοχοι.[mccclxix]

1882 Cf. Eph. 2:19.
1883 Cf. Psalm, 102:14; Habacuc, 2:18; Is. 29:16 (quoted in Rom. 9:20).
1884 Matt. 22:1-4.
1885 Cf. 1 Cor. 12:28.

56

(ΤΟΥ ΑΥΤΟΥ) Οὗτος ὁ αἰὼν κλῆσις,[mccclxx] οὗτος παρασκευή· ἐκεῖνος, σάββατον[mccclxxi] καὶ ὀγδοάς.[mccclxxii]

Οὗτος ὁ αἰὼν κλῆσις, οὗτος παρασκευή. ἐκεῖνος, σάββατον καὶ ὀγδοάς.[mccclxxiii]

Καὶ ἀπέστειλε τοὺς δούλους.[1886] *Δοῦλοι* καλοῦντες, ‹οἱ› προφῆται, κοινῶς μὲν ‹οἱ› διδάσκαλοι καὶ πάντες οἱ διάκονοι τοῦ λόγου. Νῦν δέ, οἱ πατριάρχαι. *Κλητοί,*[1887] ὁ πρῶτος λαὸς ὁ ἐξ Ἰσραήλ. Τοὺς γὰρ πρὸς σύνεσιν εὐφυεῖς καὶ τῇ κατασκευῇ διορατικωτέρους θέλει ἥκειν | **173r** εἰς τὴν μακαρίαν ἑστίαν ὁ Θεός. Ἄλλοι *δοῦλοι,* Μωσῆς καὶ οἱ προφῆται. Ἢ *τοὺς* μὲν πρώτους λέγει *δούλους* τοὺς περὶ Μωσέα καὶ προφήτας, οἳ οὐκ ἔπεισαν τὸν λαὸν εἰς ἄκραν ἐλθεῖν πίστιν, μεθ' οὓς Ἰωάννης καὶ οἱ μαθηταί, οἳ καὶ ἔλεγον ἡτοιμάσθαι τοῖς πιστοῖς τὴν πλουσίαν παράθεσιν τῆς τῶν ἀγαθῶν τρυφῆς. Ἡ γὰρ παρασκευὴ τοῦ *γάμου*[mccclxxiv] γίνεται διὰ τῆς τῶν πλουσίων χαρισμάτων δόσεως, ἅπερ εἰκάζεται ταύροις καὶ σιτιστοῖς,[1888] τοῖς ἐν εὐωχίᾳ πλουσίᾳ παρασκευαζομένοις. *Ἐν παντὶ* γὰρ πεπλουτίσθαι ἡμᾶς *ἐν Χριστῷ* ὁ Παῦλός φησιν *ἐν λόγῳ καὶ γνώσει.*[1889] Ἤτοι *ταῦροι* μὲν ἡ λογικὴ καὶ ὡς ἐν καθαροῖς μείζων τροφή. *Σιτιστὰ* δέ, τὸ πνευματικῶς ἡδὺ τῆς θεωρίας καὶ οὐκ ἀσθενές.[mccclxxv] Θύσις, ἡ διαίρεσις[mccclxxvi] καὶ τροπολογία τῶν προβλημάτων. *Πάντα,* οἱ περὶ τῶν ὄντων ποικίλοι λόγοι καὶ θεωρίαι.[mccclxxvii] Τὸ δὲ *ἕτοιμα,* προτρέπει.

Δοῦλοι καλοῦνται προφῆται, κοινῶς μὲν οἱ διδάσκαλοι καὶ πάντες οἱ διάκονοι τοῦ λόγου. νῦν δὲ οἱ πατριάρχαι. *κλητοί,* ὁ πρῶτος λαὸς ὁ ἐξ Ἰσραήλ. τοὺς γὰρ πρὸς σύνεσιν εὐφυεῖς καὶ τῇ κατασκευῇ διορατικωτέρους θέλει ἥκειν εἰς τὴν μακαρίαν ἑστίαν ὁ Θεός. ἄλλοι *δοῦλοι,* Μωσῆς καὶ οἱ προφῆται. Ἢ *τοὺς* μὲν πρώτους λέγει *δούλους* τοὺς περὶ Μωσέα καὶ προφήτας, οἳ οὐκ ἔπεισαν τὸν λαὸν εἰς ἄκραν ἐλθεῖν πίστιν, μεθ' οὓς Ἰωάννης καὶ οἱ μαθηταί, οἳ καὶ ἔλεγον ἡτοιμάσθαι τοῖς πιστοῖς τὴν πλουσίαν παράθεσιν τῆς τῶν ἀγαθῶν τρυφῆς. ἡ γὰρ παρασκευὴ τοῦ *γάμου* γίνεται διὰ τῆς τῶν πλουσίων χαρισμάτων δόσεως, ἅπερ εἰκάζεται ταύροις καὶ σιτιστοῖς τοῖς ἐν εὐωχίᾳ πλουσίᾳ παρασκευαζομένοις (*ἐν παντὶ* γὰρ πεπλουτίσθαι ἡμᾶς *ἐν Χριστῷ* ὁ Παῦλος φησίν, *ἐν λόγω καὶ γνώσει*).[mccclxxviii]

Δοῦλοι οἱ πατριάρχαι, δηλονότι ἢ Μωσῆς καὶ οἱ προφῆται. ἄριστον ὑπὸ τῆς λεγούσης ἡτοιμακέναι *τὴν ἑαυτῆς τράπεζαν* Σοφίας ἡτοίμασται πνευματικὴ στάσις, οἰνοχόων καὶ λειτουργῶν ἄλλων, ἐπιστήμῃ καὶ καιρῷ διακονούντων ὡς παρὰ τῷ Σολομῶντι τῷ εἰρηνικῷ,[mccclxxix] καθὰ ἐν Βασιλείοις γέγραπται περὶ αὐτοῦ.[1890] *ταῦροι* δὲ ἡ λογικὴ καὶ ὡς ἐν καθαροῖς μείζων τροφή. *σιστιστὰ* τὸ πνευματικῶς ἡδὺ τῆς θεωρίας καὶ οὐκ ἀσθενές.

1886 Matt. 22:3.
1887 Matt. 22:14.
1888 Matt. 22:4.
1889 1 Cor. 1:4-5.
1890 Cf. 3 Kings, 10:5.

> θύσις ἡ διαίρεσις καὶ τροπολογία τῶν προβλημάτων. *πάντα* οἱ περὶ τῶν ὄντων ποικίλοι λόγοι καὶ θεωρίαι. τὸ δὲ *ἕτοιμα*, προτρέπει.[mccclxxx]

οἱ δὲ ἀμελήσαντες.[1891] Ἀμέλεια κωλύει τοὺς κεκλημένους· οἱ γὰρ *κατὰ σάρκα* περιπατοῦντες[1892] οὐχ ἕπονται κλήσει θείᾳ τῇ κατὰ Χριστόν.

> ἀμέλεια δὲ κωλύει τοὺς καλουμένους. οἱ γὰρ *κατὰ σάρκα περιπατοῦντες* οὐχ ἕπονται κλήσει θείᾳ τῇ κατὰ Χριστόν.[mccclxxxi]

Εἰς ἀγρὸν δὲ καὶ ἐμπορίαν ἠσχολῆσθαι φησὶν τοὺς Ἰουδαίους ὡς ὑπὸ τῶν σωματικῶν ἡδονῶν κατεχομένους, οἳ πρῶτον μὲν τοῖς προφήταις ἀπετάξαντο, ἀπωσάμενοι τὸν νόμον καὶ εἰδ‹ω›λολατρήσαντες.[1893] Κληθέντες δὲ ὑπὸ τῶν ἀποστόλων, ἀπετάξαντο διὰ φιλοχρηματίαν καὶ φιλοσαρκίαν ταῦτα τῆς πρὸς Θεὸν οἰκειότητος[1894] καὶ τῆς αἰωνίου τρυφῆς προτιμήσαντες· οἳ πρὸς τῷ μὴ ἐλθεῖν καὶ τοὺς καλοῦντας *ἀπέκτειναν*,[1895] καίτοι *εἰς γάμους* καλούμενοι τοῦ ἀναιρεθέντος παρ᾽ αὐτῶν Υἱοῦ. Οἱ δὲ καλοῦντες, ὡς ἀπὸ Πατρὸς πεμφθέντες ἐκάλουν. Οἱ δὲ πρὸς τῷ ὑβρίσαι καὶ *ἀπέκτειναν*· ἀνεῖλον γὰρ Στέφανον καὶ Ἰά | **173v** κωβον καὶ ἑτέρους πολλούς.

Καὶ *ἀκούσας ὁ βασιλεὺς ἐκεῖνος ὠργίσθη.*[1896] Μετὰ οὖν τὸ μὴ πεισθῆναι, κατέλαβεν αὐτοὺς μετὰ τεσσαράκοντα ἔτη τὰ ἐπὶ Οὐεσπασιανοῦ[1897] κακά, τουτέστιν ἡ ὑπὸ τῶν Ῥωμαίων τῆς πόλεως αὐτῶν καὶ ἑαυτῶν ἀπώλεια.

Στρατεύματα[1898] γὰρ λέγονται τοῦ Θεοῦ καὶ οἱ ἐμπρήσαντες τὰ Ἱεροσόλυμα καὶ ἀνελόντες τοὺς ἐν τῇ πόλει Ῥωμαῖοι καὶ ἡ οὐράνιος στρατιὰ καὶ οἱ ἐπὶ τῶν κολάσεων ἄγγελοι.[mccclxxxii] *Δοῦλοι*, οἱ ἀπόστολοι καὶ οἱ ἐπιτεταγμένοι τῇ κλήσει τῶν ἐθνῶν ἄγγελοι.

> Τίνας *ὕβρισαν*; τοὺς πατριάρχας. *στρατεύματα* δέ εἰσιν οἱ ἐμπρήσαντες τὰ Ἱεροσόλυμα, καὶ ἀνελόντες τοὺς ἐν τῇ πόλει Ῥωμαῖοι καὶ ἡ οὐράνιος στρατιὰ καὶ οἱ ἐπὶ τῶν κολάσεων ἄγγελοι καὶ οἱ ἀναιροῦντες Ἰουδαϊκὴν διδασκαλίαν καὶ ψευδώνυμον γνῶσιν.[1899] *δοῦλοι* οἱ ἀπόστολοι, καὶ οἱ ἐπιτεταγμένοι τῇ κλήσει τῶν ἐθνῶν ἄγγελοι. *οὐκ ἦσαν ἄξιοι.*[1900] ὡς οὐκ ἀξίοις λέγουσιν οἱ ἀπόστολοι. *ὑμῖν ἀναγκαῖον ἦν ἀναγγεῖλαι τὸν λόγον τοῦ Θεοῦ. ἐπεὶ δὲ ἀναξίους ἑαυτοὺς ἐκρίνατε*, πορευόμεθα *εἰς τὰ ἔθνη.*[1901] διέξοδοι

1891 Matt. 22:5.
1892 Rom. 8:4; 1 Cor. 3:3; 2 Cor. 10:2-3; Gal. 5:16.
1893 Cod. εἰδολολατρήσαντες.
1894 Cf. Eph. 2:9.
1895 Matt. 21:35.
1896 Matt. 22:7.
1897 Cod. οὐ ἐσπασιανοῦ.
1898 Matt. 22:7.
1899 Cf. 1 Tim. 6:20.
1900 Matt. 22:8.
1901 Acts, 13:46.

> *ὁδῶν*[1902] εἰσι τὰ ἔξω τοῦ Ἰσραὴλ δόγματα.[mccclxxxiii] ἀδιακρίτως συνάγουσι, *πονηροὺς* μέν, ἵνα ἀποθέμενοι τοῦτο τὸ *ἔνδυμα γάμου* καὶ ἑστίαν θεοῦ ἔχωσιν. *ἀγαθοὺς* δὲ ἁπλούστερον τοὺς μετριωτέρους[mccclxxxiv] (*ἔθνη γὰρ τὰ μὴ νόμον ἔχοντα*,[1903] καὶ τὰ ἑξῆς). βίος καὶ πράξεις ἀγαθαί εἰσι τὸ *ἔνδυμα*, ἅπερ ὁ μὴ ἔχων ἐξ ἰδίας σπουδῆς οὐκ ἔχει *ἔνδυμα*. ἡ γὰρ κλῆσις ἡ διδοῦσα ἀναμαρτησίαν καὶ πνεύματος ἁγίου μετοχὴν κατὰ χάριν ἐστίν.[mccclxxxv]

> (Ὠριγένους.) Τίνας *ὕβρισαν*; τοὺς πατριάρχας. *στρατεύματα* δέ εἰσιν οἱ ἐμπρήσαντες τὰ Ἱεροσόλυμα, καὶ ἀνελόντες τοὺς ἐν τῇ πόλει Ῥωμαῖοι, καὶ ἡ οὐράνιος στρατιά, καὶ οἱ ἐπὶ τῶν κολάσεων Ἄγγελοι, καὶ οἱ ἀναιροῦντες Ἰουδαϊκὴν διδασκαλίαν καὶ ψευδώνυμον γνῶσιν. *δοῦλοι* οἱ Ἀπόστολοι, καὶ οἱ ἐπιτεταγμένοι τῇ κλήσει τῶν ἐθνῶν Ἄγγελοι. *οὐκ ἦσαν ἄξιοι*, ὡς οὐκ ἀξίοις λέγουσιν οἱ Ἀπόστολοι *ὑμῖν ἀναγκαῖον ἦν ἀναγγεῖλαι τὸν λόγον τοῦ Θεοῦ. ἐπεὶ δὲ ἀναξίους ἑαυτοὺς ἐκρίνατε*, πορευόμεθα *εἰς τὰ ἔθνη*. διέξοδοι *ὁδῶν* εἰσι τὰ ἔξω τοῦ Ἰσραὴλ δόγματα. ἀδιακρίτως συνάγουσι, *πονηροὺς* μέν, ἵνα ἐπιθέμενοι τὸ *ἔνδυμα γάμου*, καὶ ἑστίαν Θεοῦ ἔχωσιν. *ἀγαθοὺς* δέ, ἁπλούστερον τοὺς μετριωτέρους. *ἔθνη γὰρ τὰ μὴ νόμον ἔχοντα*, καὶ τὰ ἑξῆς. βίος καὶ πράξεις ἀγαθαί εἰσι τὸ *ἔνδυμα*, ἅπερ ὁ μὴ ἔχων ἐξ ἰδίας σπουδῆς, οὐκ ἔχει ἔνδυμα. ἡ γὰρ κλῆσις ἡ διδοῦσα ἀναμαρτησίαν καὶ Πνεύματος Ἁγίου μετοχήν, κατὰ χάριν ἐστίν.[mccclxxxvi]

Μετὰ οὖν τὸ παραιτήσασθαι τοὺς Ἰουδαίους, λοιπὸν ἡ κλῆσις τῶν ἐθνῶν. Τοῦτο γὰρ λέγει, *συνήγαγον πάντας ὅσους εὗρον*,[1904] καὶ οὐκέτι διάκρισις γένους. Οὐδὲ τῷ Ἰσραὴλ τὰ προνόμια, ἀλλὰ καὶ τοῖς ἠμελημένοις καὶ ἀπερριμμένοις ἡ χάρις ἐδόθη, *σοφοῖς τε καὶ ἀνοήτοις*,[1905] πονηροῖς τε καὶ ἀγαθοῖς,

> εἶτα λοιπὸν ἡ κλῆσις τῶν ἐθνῶν καὶ οὐκέτι διάκρισις γένους οὐδὲ τῷ Ἰσραὴλ ἡ προνομία, ἀλλὰ καὶ τοῖς ἠμελημένοις καὶ τοῖς ἀπερριμμένοις ἡ χάρις, *σοφοῖς τε καὶ ἀνοήτοις* ὡς ὁ Παῦλός φησιν, πονηροῖς τε καὶ ἀγαθοῖς ὡς ἡ παραβολὴ λέγει.[mccclxxxvii]

ὅτι καὶ οἱ ἀγαθοὶ τῆς ὄντως ἀγαθότητος δέονται.
Ἀγαθοὺς γὰρ ἁπλούστερον τοὺς μετριωτέρους λέγει, ἤτοι τοὺς ποσῶς ἑαυτῶν ἐπιμεληθέντας συγκρίσει τῶν ἐξ ‹ὅ›λου[1906] φαύλων.

> Ἀδιακρίτως συνάγουσι.[1907] *πονηροὺς* μέν, ἵνα ἀποθέμενοι τοῦτο ‹τὸ ἔνδυμα› ἔνδυμα *γάμου* καὶ ἑστίαν θεοῦ ἔχωσιν, *ἀγαθοὺς* δὲ ἁπλούστερον τοὺς μετριωτέρους. *ἔθνη* γὰρ *τὰ μὴ νόμον ἔχοντα φύσει τὰ τοῦ νόμου ποιοῦσι*.[1908] τοὺς γὰρ τοὺς ποσῶς ἑαυτῶν ἐπιμεληθέντας συγκρίσει τῶν ἐξ ὅλου φαύλων ἐνταῦθά φησιν. *πάντες γὰρ*

1902 Matt. 22:9.
1903 Cf. Rom. 2:14.
1904 Matt. 22:10.
1905 Rom. 1:14.
1906 Cod. ἐξόλου.
1907 Cf. Matt. 22:10.
1908 Cf. Rom. 2:14.

ἥμαρτον καὶ ὑστεροῦνται τῆς δόξης τοῦ θεοῦ.[1909] οὕτως ἐδικαιώθη Σόδομα[1910] ὑπὲρ Ἱερουσαλήμ.[mccclxxxviii]

ἀδιακρίτως συνάγουσι, πονηροὺς μέν, ἵνα ἐπιθέμενοι τὸ ἔνδυμα γάμου, καὶ ἑστίαν Θεοῦ ἔχωσιν. ἀγαθοὺς δέ, ἁπλούστερον τοὺς μετριωτέρους. *ἔθνη* γὰρ *τὰ μὴ νόμον ἔχοντα*, καὶ τὰ ἑξῆς.[mccclxxxix] τοὺς γὰρ ποσωσοῦν ἑαυτῶν ἐπιμεληθέντας συγκρίσει τῶν ἐξ ὅλου φαύλων οὕτως καλεῖ.[mccccxc]

Καὶ ἕως σήμερον ἔρχονται πονηροί τε καὶ ἀγαθοί οἱ ἐν ταῖς *ὁδοῖς* καὶ διεξόδοις[1911] ὄντες τοῦ Ἰσραήλ, τουτέστιν εἰδωλολάτραι ἄοικοι καὶ εὐτελεῖς. Δέον δὲ ἦν τοῖς πειθομένοις ἔθνεσι πρῶτον κηρῦξαι. Οὐκ ἐποίησε δέ, ἵνα μὴ σχῶσιν ἀφορμήν, ἐπειδὴ πρὸς Ἰουδαίους ἦσαν γεγενημέναι αἱ ἐπαγγελίαι. Ἐπεὶ δὲ ἑτοιμασθέντων αὐτοῖς τῶν ἀγαθῶν ἠπίστησαν, οὐκ ἀφῆκεν ὁ Θεὸς τὰ τηλικαῦτα ἀγαθὰ εἰς τὸ μηδὲν χωρῆσαι, ἀλλὰ καλεῖ τοὺς *ἐν ταῖς ὁδοῖς*, τουτέστι τὰ ἔθνη. Διδάσκει δὲ ἡ παραβολὴ ὅτι ὀφείλουσιν οἱ σύμβουλοι πάντα κηρῦξαι τὰ χρήσιμα, κἂν οὐ πείθωνται οἱ ἀκούοντες.

Πορεύεσθε ἐπὶ τὰς διεξόδους.[1912] | **174r** Διέξοδοι *τῶν ὁδῶν*, τὰ ἔξω τοῦ Σωτῆρος δόγματα καὶ τοῖς τυχοῦσι καὶ τοῖς ἀπερριμμένοις. Ἐπειδὴ γὰρ ἄνω καὶ κάτω ἔλεγεν ὅτι *πόρναι καὶ τελῶναι*[1913] κληρονομήσουσι καὶ *‹ἔσονται› οἱ πρῶτοι ἔσχατοι καὶ οἱ ἔσχατοι πρῶτοι*,[1914] δείκνυσιν ὅτι δικαίως ταῦτα γίνεται, ὃ μάλιστα πάντων ἔδακνεν Ἰουδαίους.

Διέξοδοι *τῶν ὁδῶν*, τὰ ἔξω τοῦ Ἰσραὴλ δόγματα[mccccxci] καὶ τοῖς τυχοῦσι καὶ τοῖς ἀπερριμμένοις. [ἐπειδὴ γὰρ ἄνω καὶ κάτω ἔλεγεν ὅτι *πόρναι καὶ τελῶναι* κληρονομήσουσι καὶ *ἔσονται οἱ πρῶτοι ἔσχατοι καὶ οἱ ἔσχατοι πρῶτοι*, δείκνυσιν ὅτι δικαίως ταῦτα γίνεται, ὃ μάλιστα πάντων ἔδακνεν Ἰουδαίους.[mccccxcii]

Εἶτα, ἵνα μὴ θαρρῶσιν οὗτοι ‹οἱ ἀπὸ τῶν διεξόδων κληθέντες› τῇ πίστει μόνῃ, καὶ περὶ τῆς ‹π›ίσ‹τ›εως[1915] αὐτοῖς διαλέγεται, τοῖς μὲν μηδέπω πεπιστευκόσι περὶ τοῦ προσελθεῖν τῇ πίστει, τοῖς δὲ πεπιστευκόσι περὶ τῆς κατὰ τὸν βίον ἐπιμελείας. Ἔνδυμα γὰρ βίος ἐστὶ καὶ πρᾶξις.

τοῦ αὐτοῦ.
ἵνα μὴ θαρρῶσιν οὗτοι τῇ πίστει μόνῃ, καὶ περὶ τῆς πίστεως αὐτοῖς διαλέγεται, τοῖς μὲν μηδέπω πεπιστευκόσιν περὶ τοῦ προσελθεῖν τῇ πίστει, τοῖς δὲ πεπιστευκόσι περὶ τῆς κατὰ τὸν βίον ἐπιμελείας.][mccccxciii]

1909 Rom. 3:23.
1910 Cf. Ez. 16:51-52.
1911 Cf. Matt. 22:9.
1912 Matt. 22:9.
1913 Matt. 21:31-32.
1914 Matt. 19:30; 20:16; Mark, 10:31.
1915 Cod. κρίσεως.

> βίος καὶ πράξεις ἀγαθαί εἰσι τὸ ἔνδυμα, ἅπερ ὁ μὴ ἔχων ἐξ ἰδίας σπουδῆς, οὐκ ἔχει ἔνδυμα.[mcccxciv]

> Ἐπεὶ οὖν οὐκ ἦσαν ἄξιοι, *Πορεύεσθε*, φησίν, *εἰς τὰς τριόδους, καὶ ὅσους ἐὰν εὕρητε, καλέσατε.* καὶ τοὺς τυχόντας καὶ τοὺς ἀπερριμμένους. Ἐπειδὴ γὰρ ἄνω καὶ κάτω ἔλεγεν, ὅτι *Πόρναι καὶ τελῶναι κληρονομήσουσι τὸν οὐρανόν*· καί, *Οἱ πρῶτοι ἔσχατοι ἔσονται, καὶ οἱ ἔσχατοι πρῶτοι.* δείκνυσιν ὅτι δικαίως ταῦτα γίνεται. ὃ μάλιστα πάντων ἔδακνεν Ἰουδαίους, καὶ τῆς κατασκαφῆς χαλεπώτερον μᾶλλον ἔκνιζε, τὸ εἰς τὰ ἐκείνων, καὶ πολλῷ μείζω τῶν ἐκείνων, τοὺς ἐξ ἐθνῶν ὁρᾷν εἰσαγομένους. Εἶτα ἵνα μηδὲ οὗτοι τῇ πίστει θαρρήσωσι μόνῃ, καὶ περὶ τῆς κρίσεως αὐτοῖς διαλέγεται τῆς ἐπὶ ταῖς πονηραῖς πράξεσι, τοῖς μὲν οὐδέπω πεπιστευκόσι περὶ τοῦ προσελθεῖν τῇ πίστει, τοῖς δὲ πεπιστευκόσι περὶ τῆς κατὰ τὸν βίον ἐπιμελείας. Ἔνδυμα γὰρ βίος ἐστὶ καὶ πρᾶξις.[mcccxcv]

Εἰσελθὼν δὲ ὁ βασιλεύς.[1916] Ἡ εἴσοδος τοῦ βασιλέως εἰς τὸν νυμφῶνα, τὴν μέλλουσαν παρουσίαν λέγει. Ὁ δὲ *ἔνδυμα γάμου μὴ ἔχων*, οἱ μετὰ *τὸ βάπτισμα*[1917] καὶ τὴν γνῶσιν ἀσεβήσαντες.
Καὶ μὴν χάριτος ἦν ἡ κλῆσις. Τίνος οὖν ἕνεκεν ἀκριβολογεῖται ὅτι τὸ μὲν κληθῆναι χάριτος ἦν, τὸ δὲ κληθέντα καὶ καθαρὰ ἐνδυσάμενον μεῖναι τοιαῦτα διατηροῦντα τῆς τῶν κληθέντων σπουδῆς;

> Καὶ μὴν χάριτος ἦν ἡ κλῆσις. τίνος οὖν ἕνεκεν ἀκριβολογεῖται; Ὅτι τὸ μὲν κληθῆναι καὶ καθαρθῆναι, χάριτος ἦν. τὸ δὲ κληθέντα καὶ καθαρὰ ἐνδυσάμενον μεῖναι τοιαῦτα διατηροῦντα, τῆς τῶν κληθέντων σπουδῆς.[mcccxcvi]

Πῶς εἰσῆλθες ὧδε;[1918] Ἐλέγχεται διὰ τούτου καὶ τὴν εἴσοδον μὴ ἀληθῆ πεποιημένος. Ὅρα δέ· καίτοι τοῦ πράγματος ὄντος καταδήλου, οὐ πρότερον κολάζει ἕως ἂν αὐτὸς τὴν ψῆφον ἐξενέγκῃ. Ἡ μὲν εἴσοδος ἀδιάκριτος γίνεται, ἡ δὲ τῶν εἰσελθόντων μετὰ ταῦτα ζωὴ οὐκ ἀζήτητος ἔσται. Ἀλλὰ καὶ πάνυ ἀκριβῶς αὐτὴν ἐξετάζει ὁ βασιλεύς, δι᾽ ἑαυτοῦ εἰσερχόμενος καὶ ἕκαστον θεωρῶν ὡς ἔχει σχήματος καὶ εἰ μὴ ἔχοι βίον καθαρὸν ἀποδυσάμενος *τὸν παλαιὸν ἄνθρωπον.*[1919] Ὁ δὲ τοιοῦτος ὡς μὴ ἔχων *ἔνδυμα γάμου* | **174v** οὐ μόνον ἐκ τοῦ νυμφῶνος ἐκβάλλεται, ἀλλὰ καὶ εἰς πῦρ πέμπεται.
Μὴ μεταθέμενος γὰρ καὶ μεταμφιασάμενος τὸ ἦθος καὶ ἐνδυσάμενος τὸ ὕφασμα τῆς ἀρετῆς, Χριστόν, *σπλάγχνα* τε *οἰκτιρμοῦ* καὶ τὰ ὅμοια,[mcccxcvii]

> Μὴ μεταθέμενον ἢ μεταμφιασάμενον τὸ ἦθος, και ἐνδυσάμενον τὸ ὕφασμα τῆς ἀρετῆς, Χριστόν, σπλάγχνα τε οἰκτιρμῶν καὶ τὰ ὅμοια. κατὰ δὲ τὸ *ἐνεδύσατο κατάραν ὡς ἱμάτιον.*[mcccxcviii]

1916 Matt. 22:11.
1917 Cf. Matt. 3:7; 21:25; Mark, 1:4; 11:30; Luke, 3:3; 7:29; 20:4; Acts, 13:24; 18:25; 19:3-4.
1918 Matt. 22:12.
1919 Col. 3:9; cf. Eph. 4:22.

> Εἶτ' ἐπεὶ *πονηροὺς καὶ ἀγαθοὺς* καλεῖσθαι ‹μὲν ἔ›δει, οὐ μὴν ὥστε τοὺς *πονηροὺς* μένειν πονηρούς, ἀλλὰ μεταμφιασαμένους καὶ ἀποθεμένους τὰ ἀλλότρια τοῦ γάμου ἐνδύματα ἐνδύσασθαι τὰ τοῦ *γάμου, σπλάγχνα οἰκτιρμοῦ, χρηστότητα, ταπεινοφροσύνην, πραότητα, μακροθυμίαν* (ταῦτα γάρ ἐστι τὰ τοῦ *γάμου* ἐνδύματα).[mcccxcix]

οὐκ εἴσεισί τις εἰς τὸν νυμφῶνα τὸν ἐν οὐρανῷ.

Ἐπειδὴ δὲ ἔν τισι κεῖται τὸ *ἑταῖρε*, ῥητέον ὅτι ἐν τῇ Καινῇ οἱ φαῦλοι ἑταῖροι ἀκούουσιν[1920] ‹τοῦτο›, ὡς ὁ Ἰούδας[1921] καὶ ὁ ἀγανακτῶν ἐπὶ τῇ τοῦ δηναρίου ‹κοινῇ› δόσει[1922] ‹ἐπὶ τῶν τοῦ ἀμπελῶνος ἐργατῶν›.

> Ἐπειδὴ ἔν τισι πρόσκειται τὸ *ἑταῖρε*, ῥητέον ὅτι ‹ἐν τῇ› καινῇ οἱ φαῦλοι ἀκούουσι τοῦτο, ὡς Ἰούδας καὶ ὁ ἀγανακτῶν ἐπὶ τῇ τοῦ δηναρίου κοινῇ δόσει[1923] ἐπὶ τῶν τοῦ ἀμπελῶνος ἐργατῶν.[mcd]

Ἐξ ὧν δὲ φιμοῦται[1924] (τουτέστι σιωπᾷ μὴ ἔχων ἀπολογίαν) κληθείς, εἰσελθών, ἀναπεσών, κατακρίνει ἑαυτόν. Πρὸ τοῦ δείπνου δὲ εἴσεισιν ἵνα κρίσει ὁ ἄξιος εὐωχηθῇ. Ζητῆσαι δέ ἐστι πότερον ἐπὶ τῆς ἐνταῦθα ἐκκλησίας ἢ ἐπὶ τῆς ἀποκαταστάσεως τῶν ἁγίων. Εἰ γὰρ ἐνθάδε, πῶς ἀνάκεινται οἱ ὀφείλοντες ἐργάζεσθαι; Εἰ δὲ ἐκεῖ, πῶς λαθών τις κατατάττεται τοῖς ἁγίοις; Διάκονοι δὲ οἱ ἐκβάλλοντες τοὺς τοιούτους ἄγγελοί εἰσι.

> Ζητήσεις πότερον ἐπὶ ταύτης τῆς ἐκκλησίας ἢ ἐπὶ τῆς ἀποκαταστάσεως τῶν ἁγίων. εἰ γὰρ ἐνθάδε, πῶς ἀνάκεινται οἱ ὀφείλοντες ἐργάζεσθαι; εἰ δὲ ἐκεῖ, πῶς λαθών τις κατατάσσεται τοῖς ἁγίοις; συνανάκεινται δὲ οἱ προσαναπαυόμενοι ἐν πίστει καὶ θεοσεβείᾳ. οἱ δὲ διάκονοι οἱ δεσμοῦντες νῦν ἄγγελοί εἰσιν οἱ ἐπὶ τῶν κολάσεων τεταγμένοι.[mcdi]

Ποδῶν δὲ καὶ χειρῶν δέσις, ἡ πάσ‹η›ς[1925] ἐνεργείας ἐποχή, τῷ μηδὲν λοιπὸν δύνασθαι χρηστὸν ποιῆσαι.

> *ποδῶν* δὲ *καὶ χειρῶν* δέσις ἡ πάσης ἐνεργείας ἐποχή. οὐ γὰρ ἔτι πρᾶξις οὐδεμία τοῖς πονηροῖς ἐνδίδοται πεπληρωμένου τοῦ καιροῦ τῶν ξένων ἐν ᾧ πεπράχασιν οὐδὲν ἀγαθόν.[mcdii]

Ἡ γὰρ τοῦ καλοῦ ἐργασία μέχρι τοῦ παρόντος αἰῶνος ἐκτείνεται. Οὐ μόνον δὲ τὴν κίνησιν καὶ τὴν πρᾶξιν διὰ τῶν ποδῶν καὶ τῶν χειρῶν ἐσήμανεν, ἀλλὰ καὶ τὴν ὁρατικήν,

---

1920 Cod. ἀκούουσι.
1921 Matt. 26:50.
1922 Matt. 20:13.
1923 Matt. 20:13.
1924 Cf. Matt. 12:12.
1925 Cod. πάσις.

τῷ εἰπεῖν ἐν σκότῳ ἐξωτέρῳ ἐκβάλλεσθαι. *Σκότος δὲ ἐξώτερον* λέγων, τὰ πορρωτάτω λέγει τῆς θείας ἀρετῆς τε καὶ δόξης.

> *σκότος δὲ ἐξώτερον* λέγων τὰ πορρωτάτω λέγει τῆς θείας ἀρετῆς τε καὶ δόξης.[mcdiii]

> Καὶ οὐκ ἀρκεῖ γε τὸ ἐκβληθῆναι τοῦ γάμου τὸν ἀτιμάσαντα τὴν κλῆσιν. δεῖ γὰρ αὐτὸν ὑπὸ τῶν διακόνων τοῦ βασιλέως τῶν πρὸς τοῖς δεσμοῖς τεταγμένων, δεθέντα τὴν πορείαν ᾗ οὐκ εἰς δέον ἐχρήσατο καὶ τὴν δραστήριον δύναμιν ἐν ᾗ πρᾶξιν ἀγαθὴν οὐκ ἐτέλεσεν, οὐ μόνον ἀπὸ τοῦ γάμου ἐκβληθῆναι, ἀλλ᾽ ὥστε καὶ εἰς τὸν ἀλλότριον φωτὸς ‹παντὸς› καταδικασθῆναι τόπον, ἔνθα σκότος ἦν τὸ ὡς ἐν σκότεσι βαθύτερον καὶ καλούμενον *σκότος ἐξώτερον*. καὶ εἴ τίς γε ἡμῶν ἐπὶ τὴν κλῆσιν ἐλθὼν τοῦ βασιλέως *εἰς τοὺς γάμους* τοῦ υἱοῦ αὐτοῦ, δοκεῖ μὲν ὑπακούειν καὶ ἔρχεσθαι μετὰ τῶν κεκλημένων, οὐ μὴν ἐνδέδυται τὸ προειρημένον *ἔνδυμα γάμου*, ταῦτα πείσεται καὶ δεθεὶς *ποδῶν καὶ χειρῶν ἐκβληθήσεται εἰς τὸ σκότος τὸ ἐξώτερον*, ἔνθα κατὰ τὸ *οὐαί, οἱ γελῶντες νῦν, ὅτι κλαύσετε*[1926] *ὁ κλαυθμὸς* τοῖς τὰ τοῦ κλαυθμοῦ καὶ θρήνου ἄξια ἁμαρτήσασι. κλαύσονται δὲ θρηνοῦντες τὰς ἰδίας ταλαιπωρίας. εἶθ᾽ ἵνα παραστήσῃ ὁ λόγος τὸν φόβον καὶ τὸν τρόμον καὶ τὰ σκυθρωπὰ πράγματα καὶ τοὺς πόνους ἐν οἷς ἔσονται οἱ μὴ ἐνδεδυμένοι *ἔνδυμα γάμου*, εἶπε τὸ ἐκεῖ ἔσται ὁ κλαυθμὸς καὶ οὐ μόνον *ὁ κλαυθμός*, ἀλλὰ καὶ *ὁ βρυγμὸς τῶν ὀδόντων*.[mcdiv]

> Δεσμεύουσιν Ἄγγελοι, *πόδας*, πορείαν, *χεῖρας*, τὴν δραστικὴν τῶν ἔργων δύναμιν.[mcdv]

Ἐκβάλλουσι δὲ εἰς τὸν ἀλλότριον καὶ ἀμιγῆ φωτὸς τόπον | **175r** ἵν᾽ ἐν σκυθρωποῖς καὶ ἐπιπόνοις[mcdvi] γινόμενοι κλαύσωσι καὶ βρύξωσι τοὺς ὀδόντας,

> ὅστις ὡς ἄξιος κολάσεως καὶ κρίσεως καταδικάζεται ὑπὸ τοῦ εἰπόντος *τοῖς διακόνοις* (ἄλλοις παρὰ τὰ ἄνω *στρατεύματα*), ἵνα *δήσαντες αὐτοῦ πόδας καὶ χεῖρας* οἷς οὐκ εἰς δέον ἐχρήσατο (οὔτε γὰρ ἣν ἔδει πορείαν περιεπάτησεν οὔτε ἃς ἐχρῆν πράξεις ἐπετέλεσεν), ἐκβάλωσιν *αὐτὸν* οὐ μόνον ἔξω τῆς ἑστίας τοῦ γάμου ἀλλὰ καὶ εἰ‹σβάλωσιν εἰ›ς *τὸ ἐξώτερον σκότος* καὶ πάντη φωτὸς ἀμιγές, ἵνα διψήσας φωτὸς μετὰ τὸ γεγονέναι ἐν σκότῳ τῷ ἐξωτέρῳ κλαύσῃ πρὸς τὸν δυνάμενον αὐτὸν εὐεργετῆσαι κἀκεῖθεν ῥύσασθαι θεόν, καὶ τοὺς ὀδόντας βρύξῃ τοὺς διὰ τὴν κακίαν φαγόντας τὸν ὄμφακα καὶ διὰ τοῦτο αἱμωδιάσαντας.[mcdvii]

ὅπερ σημαίνει τὴν τότε γινομένην ἀνονήτως μεταμέλειαν[mcdviii] ἐφ᾽ οἷς ἐν τῷ νῦν αἰῶνι οὐκ ἔπραξαν τὰ σωτηρίας ἐχόμενα ἔργα.

> Δηλοῖ τῶν ὀδόντων ὁ βρυγμὸς καὶ ὁ κλαυθμὸς τὴν ὑστεροβουλίαν, καὶ τὴν τότε γινομένην ἀνονήτως μεταμέλειαν, ἐφ᾽ οἷς ἐν τῷ νῦν αἰῶνι οὐκ ἐπράξαμεν τὰ σωτηρίας ἔργα.[mcdix]

1926 Luke, 6:25.

Τὸ δὲ *πολλοὶ γάρ εἰσι κλητοί, ὀλίγοι δὲ ἐκλεκτοί*,[1927] δύναται εἰρῆσθαι διὰ τὸ πολλῶν κληθέντων, ὀλίγους ἐληλυθέναι. Γένοιντο δ᾽ ἂν *κλητοὶ* μὲν παρὰ τὸν κεκληκότα, *ἐκλεκτοὶ* δὲ παρ᾽ ἑαυτοὺς κατὰ τὸ αὐτεξούσιον.

Τότε προσελθόντες οἱ Φαρισαῖοι συμβούλιον ἔλαβον.[1928] Μετὰ τῶν ἰδίων μαθητῶν πέμπουσιν οἱ Φαρισαῖοι τοὺς Ἡρωδιανούς, τοὺς μὲν ἀπαιτοῦντας τὸ δίδραχμον,[1929] τοὺς δὲ φόρους. Ἐρωτῶσι δὲ εἰ ἔξεστιν αὐτοῖς τελεῖν, ἢ οὔ, ἵνα, ἢ τοῦτο εἰπόντος ἢ ἐκεῖνο, ἐπιλάβωνται αὐτοῦ. Εἰ μὲν γὰρ εἶπε χρῆναι τὸ τέλος εἰσφέρειν, πάντως ἂν οἱ Φαρισαῖοι πρὸς τοὺς πειθομένους αὐτοῖς διέβαλλον αὐτὸν λέγοντες ὡς παρὰ τὸν νόμον Μωσέως ἀφίστησι μὲν τῆς δουλείας τοῦ Θεοῦ, πρὸς ξένην δὲ ἡμᾶς ἀρχὴν ἕλκει καὶ οὐχ ὁμόφυλον. Εἰ δὲ οὐκ ἐπένευσε δίδοσθαι τὸν φόρον, δημοσίων αὐτὸν ἐγκλημάτων ποιήσειν ὑπεύθυνον ἔσπευδον καὶ παραχρῆμα ἂν ἐπ᾽ αὐτὸν οἱ Ἡρωδιανοὶ τὰς χεῖρας ἐπέβαλλον ὡς τῇ ἐξουσίᾳ Ῥωμαίων οὐχ ὑποκύπτοντα. Ἔλεγον γὰρ οἱ Ἰουδαῖοι ὅτι οὐ δεῖ ἡμᾶς καὶ Θεῷ διδόναι τὸ δίδραχμον καὶ δεκάτας θυσίας καὶ Καίσαρι φόρον τελεῖν ἀλλοφύλῳ ὄντι. Διὰ οὖν τῶν ἐπαίνων δῆθεν ἐφέλκονται αὐτὸν θέλοντες τυχεῖν τῆς παρ᾽ αὐτοῦ ἀποκρίσεως. Διὸ καὶ ὡς ἀνυπόκριτον ὄντα κολακεύουσι, διὰ τὸ εἰπεῖν τι κατὰ Ἡρώδου· ᾤοντο γὰρ | **175v** αὐτὸν διαβαλεῖν τὸν Ἡρώδην ὡς ἐναντιούμενον τοῖς Μωσέως νόμοις. Τοῦτο γὰρ ἔλεγον, ὀφειλόμενον ἀνθρώποις τελεῖν φόρον καὶ μὴ Θεῷ ἢ τὸ ἐναντίον, οἰόμενοι ὅτι εἰς τὴν παλαιὰν αὐτοὺς ἀνάγων αὐτονομίαν εἴποι ἂν μὴ *δοῦναι* αὐτοῖς φόρον *Καίσαρι*, ὅπερ οἱ Ῥωμαῖοι *κῆνσον* ἐκάλουν. Φόρος δὲ ἀπὸ τοῦ *φαρὲς* ἑρμηνεύεται, ὅ ἐστι διακοπὴ ἢ διαίρεσις.[mcdx]

Ἡρωδιανοὶ δὲ ἐλέγοντο οἱ στρατιῶται Ἡρώδου ἢ ὅσοι πειθόμενοι τῷ Ἡρώδῃ παρεῖχον αὐτῷ φόρον.

> Ἡρωδιανούς φασιν εἶναι τοὺς Ἡρώδου στρατιώτας ἢ τοὺς ἀπαιτητὰς τῶν τελῶν τῶν ἐπιβληθέντων τοῖς Ἰουδαίοις ὑπὸ Ῥωμαίων.[mcdxi]

Τῶν γὰρ Φαρισαίων λεγόντων μὴ δεῖν φόρους τελεῖν βασιλεῖ ἐπιγείῳ ἀλλὰ μόνῳ Θεῷ, τοῦ δὲ Ἡρώδου συμβουλεύοντος δοῦναι, ὅσοι πειθόμενοι τῷ Ἡρώδῃ παρεῖχον ἐκαλοῦντο Ἡρωδιανοί.[mcdxii]

Τινὲς δὲ τούτους λέγουσιν Ἡρωδιανοὺς ὅσοι τὸν Ἡρώδην ἐνόμιζον εἶναι τὸν Χριστὸν

> Ἡρωδιανοὶ κατ᾽ ἐκείνους τοὺς χρόνους ἦσαν οἱ τὸν Ἡρώδην Χριστὸν εἶναι λέγοντες, ὡς ἱστορεῖται. ἄλλοι δὲ Ἡρωδιανούς φασι τοὺς Ἡρώδου στρατιώτας.[mcdxiii]

> Some Latins ridiculously think that the Herodians believed that Herod was the Christ, which we have never read at all.[mcdxiv]

1927 Matt. 22:14.

1928 Matt. 22:15: πορευθέντες οἱ Φαρισαῖοι.

1929 Cf. Matt. 17:24.

τὸν ἐν τοῖς προφήταις διηγορευμένον διὰ τὸ ἐν τῇ βασιλείᾳ αὐτοῦ ἀρχὴν λαβεῖν τοὺς Ἰουδαίους ἄρχεσθαι ἐξ ἀλλογενῶν ὡς ἐκλείψαντος ἄρχοντος ἐξ Ἰούδα.[mcdxv]

τίνος ἡ εἰκὼν αὕτη καὶ ἡ ἐπιγραφή;[1930] Τί οὖν πρὸς αὐτοὺς ὁ Κύριος; Δημοσιεύει αὐτῶν τὸν ἐπίπλαστον δόλον, δεικνὺς ὅτι ὡς Θεὸς οἶδεν αὐτῶν τὰ ἀπόρρητα. Καὶ ἐρωτᾷ, *τίνος ἡ εἰκὼν καὶ ἡ ἐπιγραφή*, οὐχ ‹ὡς› πνεύματος ἀγνοῶν, ἀλλὰ διὰ τῆς αὐτῶν φωνῆς ἐκφέρων τὴν κατ᾽ αὐτῶν ψῆφον.

> Those who think that the Saviour's question indicates ignorance, and not dispensation, learn from the present point that Jesus assuredly whose image was on the coin; and yet, he asks the question in order to give them a fitting response.[mcdxvi]

Ὃ δὲ λέγει τοιοῦτόν ἐστιν. Εἰ τὸ νόμισμα *Καίσαρος* ὑπάρχει, δότε αὐτῷ τὸ αὐτοῦ. Οὐδὲν γὰρ τοῦτο ἐμποδίζει τῷ λατρεύειν Θεῷ. Τὸ γὰρ ὑποφόρους ὑμᾶς γενέσθαι Καίσαρος ταῖς ὑμετέραις ἁμαρτίαις ἐπιγραπτέον καὶ οὐ τῷ Θεῷ.

καὶ ἀφέντες αὐτὸν ἀπῆλθον.[1931] Ὅρα δὲ ὅτι οἱ παγιδευταὶ τοῦ λόγου οὐ μένουσι μετ᾽ αὐτοῦ ὡς οἱ | **176r** μαθηταί, ἀλλ᾽ ἀφιᾶσιν αὐτόν. Οἱ γὰρ ἅγιοι λέγουσιν ὡς ἡ νύμφη,[mcdxvii] *ἐκράτησα αὐτὸν καὶ οὐκ ἀφήσω αὐτόν.*[1932]

57

(ΩΡΙΓΕΝΟΥΣ) *ἐν ἐκείνῃ τῇ ἡμέρᾳ προσῆλθον αὐτῷ Σαδδουκαῖοι.*[1933] Σαδδουκαῖοι αἵρεσίς ἐστιν Ἰουδαίων ἑτέρα παρὰ Φαρισαίους, οἵτινες καὶ τὴν ἐν τῇ συνηθείᾳ ἀνάστασιν καὶ ψυχῆς ἀθανασίαν ἢ ἐπιμονὴν ἀθετοῦσιν. Οἳ λόγον τινὰ πλάττουσι καὶ πρᾶγμα συντιθέασιν οὔπω γεγενημένον, οἰόμενοι εἰς ἀπορίαν τὸν Κύριον ἐμβαλεῖν καὶ θέλοντες ἀμφότερα ἀνατρέψαι. Καὶ τὸ ἀνάστασιν εἶναι, καὶ τὸ τοιαύτην ἀνάστασιν, καὶ μετ᾽ ἐπιεικείας δῆθεν τὸ πρόβλημα τιθέασι, λέγοντες καὶ Μωσέα τῷ πλάσματι αὐτῶν συνηγορεῖν. *Ἑπτὰ*[1934] γάρ φασι μιᾷ χρήσασθαι γυναικὶ εἰς γάμον ἀδελφούς. *Ἑπτὰ* δὲ εἶπον ἵνα ἐπὶ πολὺ κωμῳδήσωσι τὸ τῆς ἀναστάσεως μυστήριον. Εἶτα, *τῶν ἑπτὰ* κατὰ διαφόρους καιροὺς διῃρημένως αὐτὴν ἐσχηκότων καὶ πάντων ἰδιαιτέρως ἀποθανόντων, ἔσχατον καὶ αὐτὴν τὴν γυναῖκα φασὶ τετελευτηκέναι. Ἐν τῇ οὖν ἀναστάσει *τῶν ἑπτὰ* ἀντιποιουμένων αὐτῆς *τίνος* αὐτῶν *ἔσται γυνή*, φησί· *πλανᾶσθε μὴ εἰδότες τὰς γραφάς.*[1935] Τί οὖν ὁ Σωτὴρ πρὸς ἀμφότερα ἀπεκρίνατο οὐ πρὸς τὰ ῥήματα ἀλλὰ πρὸς τὴν γνώμην ἱστάμενος καὶ πανταχοῦ τὰ ἀπόρρητα αὐτῶν ἐκκαλύπτων;

1930 Matt. 22:20.
1931 Matt. 22:22.
1932 Song of Songs, 3:4.
1933 Matt. 22:23.
1934 Matt. 22:28.
1935 Matt. 22:29.

᾿Αμφότερα γὰρ δείκνυσι, καὶ ὅτι ἀνάστασις ἔσται καὶ ὅτι ‹οὐ› τοιαύτη ‹ἡ› ἀνάστασις οἵαν ὑποπτεύουσι. Τί γάρ φησι; *Πλανᾶσθε μὴ εἰδότες τὰς γραφὰς μηδὲ τὴν δύναμιν τοῦ Θεοῦ.* Ἤτοι τὸν θεῖον ἐν ταῖς γραφαῖς νοῦν ἢ *Χριστὸν* ὄντα *Θεοῦ δύναμιν*[1936] καὶ ὅτι τῷ *Θεῷ πάντα δυνατά.*[1937] Καὶ πρῶτον μὲν δείκνυ | **176v** σι τὸ αἴτιον τοῦ μὴ νομίζειν ἀνάστασιν τὸ νομίζειν τοιαύτην εἶναι τὴν τῶν πραγμάτων κατάστασιν. Εἶτα δείκνυσι τῆς ἀναστάσεως τὸν τρόπον. *᾿Εν γὰρ τῇ ἀναστάσει,* φησί, *οὔτε γαμοῦσιν, οὔτε ἐκγαμίζονται, ἀλλ᾿ ὡς ἄγγελοι Θεοῦ ἐν οὐρανῷ εἰσι.*[1938] Τουτέστιν, ἐν τῷ μέλλοντι αἰῶνι μὴ ὄντος θανάτου, οὔτε παιδοποιΐας χρεία, οὔτε γὰρ ἐπιθυμίᾳ τις ὑπόκειται, σαρκὸς ἀφθάρτων γεγονότων τῶν σωμάτων. Πῶς γάρ φησι γάμους λέγετε γίνεσθαι ἐν τῇ ἀναστάσει μηδὲν τῆς γραφῆς εἰπούσης; Οἱ γὰρ ἀνιστάμενοι οὔτε μείωσιν οὔτε προσθήκην δέχονται, ἀλλὰ πάσης φθορᾶς καὶ σαρκικῆς ἐπιθυμίας ἐλευθεροῦνται *ὡς ἄγγελοι* ὄντες *ἐν οὐρανῷ.* Καὶ διὰ μὲν τούτου ἐδήλωσεν ἡλίκη ἡ ἀνάστασις. Ὅτι δὲ καὶ ἀνάστασίς ἐστι, δείκνυσι. Καὶ πάλιν ἀπὸ τοῦ Μωσέως ἐπιστομίζει αὐτοὺς (ἐπειδὴ κἀκεῖνοι ἐξ ἀρχῆς Μωσέα προεβάλοντο μάρτυρα) καὶ φησί· *περὶ δὲ τῆς ἀναστάσεως τῶν νεκρῶν οὐκ ἀνέγνωτε τὸ ῥηθὲν ὑπὸ τοῦ Θεοῦ λέγοντος, ἐγώ εἰμι ὁ Θεὸς ᾿Αβραὰμ καὶ ὁ Θεὸς ᾿Ισαὰκ καὶ ὁ Θεὸς ᾿Ιακώβ; οὐκ ἔστιν ὁ Θεός, Θεὸς νεκρῶν, ἀλλὰ ζώντων.*[1939] Ὃ δὲ λέγει τοιοῦτόν ἐστιν. Ὁ Θεὸς τῶν ὑφισταμένων ἐστίν, οὐ τῶν μὴ ὄντων. Οὐ γὰρ εἶπεν *ἐγὼ ἤμην, ἀλλ᾿ εἰμί.*

Τίνες εἰσὶν οἱ Σαδδουκαῖοι; αἵρεσις ᾿Ιουδαίων ἑτέρα λέγουσα μὴ εἶναι ἀνάστασιν, μήτε Ἄγγελον, μήτε πνεῦμα. καὶ ἐντεῦθεν μὲν οὐδὲν αὐτῷ περὶ ἀναστάσεως λέγουσι. πλάττουσι δέ τινα λόγον, καὶ πρᾶγμα συντιθέασιν ὡς ἐπίπαν μὴ γεγενημένον, οἰόμενοι εἰς ἀπορίαν αὐτὸν ἐκβαλεῖν, καὶ τὸ ἀνάστασιν εἶναι ἀνατρέψαι. καὶ τίνος ἕνεκεν οὐκ ἔπλασαν δύο ἢ τρεῖς, ἀλλ᾿ ἑπτά; ὥστε ἐκ περιουσίας κωμῳδῆσαι τὴν ἀνάστασιν. διὸ καὶ λέγουσι, πάντες ἔσχον αὐτήν. τί οὖν ὁ Χριστός; πρὸς ἀμφότερα ἀποκρίνεται, οὐ πρὸς τὰ ῥήματα, ἀλλὰ πρὸς τὴν γνώμην, ἱστάμενος καὶ ὅτι ἀνάστασις ἔσται, καὶ οὐ τοιαύτη ἀνάστασις οἵαν, ὥς φασί τινες, τοὺς Φαρισαίους ὑπολαμβάνειν. τί γάρ φησι; *πλανᾶσθε μὴ εἰδότες τὰς γραφὰς μηδὲ τὴν δύναμιν τοῦ Θεοῦ.* ἐπεὶ γὰρ ὡς εἰδότες, Μωσέα προεβάλλοντο καὶ τὸν νόμον, δείκνυσιν αὐτοὺς τὰς γραφὰς ἀγνοοῦντας, ἐκ δὲ τούτου καὶ τὴν δύναμιν τοῦ Θεοῦ. καὶ ἐπειδὴ αἴτιον ἦν τοῦ μὴ νομίζειν ἀνάστασιν, τὸ τοιαύτην ὑποπτεύειν γενήσεσθαι πραγμάτων κατάστασιν, τὸ αἴτιον θεραπεύει, εἶτα καὶ τὸ σύμπτωμα. *ἐν γὰρ τῇ ἀναστάσει,* φησίν, *οὔτε γαμοῦσιν, οὔτε γαμίσκονται.* ψεῦδος οὖν ὑποτίθεσθε ἀγνοοῦντες τὴν περὶ τῆς ἀναστάσεως γραφήν, καὶ *τὴν δύναμιν τοῦ Θεοῦ*, τὴν ἐκ μὴ ὄντων τῷ λόγῳ τὰ πάντα συστησαμένην. ἥτις καὶ τὰ διεφθαρμένα εἰς ἀνάστασιν ἄγει. καὶ ἐπειδὴ μενοῦσιν ὡσαύτως ἄνθρωποι μηκέτι αὐξανόμενοι εἰς πλῆθος, καθάπερ καὶ οἱ Ἄγγελοι. διὰ τοῦτο κοινωνία γάμων ἀναιρεθήσεται. τοῦτο γὰρ *τὸ ὡς Ἄγγελοι τοῦ Θεοῦ ἐν τοῖς οὐρανοῖς.* ὥσπερ γὰρ τὸ ἀγγελικὸν πλῆθος πολὺ μὲν ὄν, οὐ μὴν ἐκ γενέσεως αὐξηθέν, ἀλλ᾿ ἐκ δημιουργίας ὑπάρχον. οὕτω δὴ καὶ τὸ ἀνιστάμενον πλῆθος. ὅτι δὲ γενήσεται ἀνάστασις, καὶ οὐκ ἀδύνατον τὸ πρᾶγμα τοῦτο, ἐξ ἐπαγγελίας τοῦ Θεοῦ

1936 1 Cor. 1:24.
1937 Matt. 19:26; Mark, 10:27; Luke, 18:27.
1938 Matt. 22:30.
1939 Matt. 22:31-32.

συνίστησι, καὶ οὐκ ἐκ φυσιολογίας. οὐχὶ γὰρ τῶν οὐκ ὄντων, φησίν, ἅγιος Θεὸς ὁ Θεός, οὐ γὰρ εἶπεν ἤμην, ἀλλ᾽ *εἰμὶ* τῶν ζώντων καὶ τῶν ὄντων.[mcdxviii]

Εἰ γὰρ καὶ ἐτελεύτησαν, ἀλλ᾽ ἔζων τῇ ἐλπίδι τῆς ὑποσχεθείσης ἀναστάσεως. Εἰπὼν δὲ *οὐκ ἔστιν ὁ Θεὸς νεκρῶν, ἀλλὰ ζώντων,*[1940] οὐκ ἐναντιοῦται τῷ εἰρημένῳ, *ἵνα καὶ νεκρῶν καὶ ζώντων κυριεύσῃ.*[1941] Νεκροὺς γὰρ ἐκεῖ τοὺς μέλλοντας ζήσεσθαι λέγει. Διὸ οὐ δύναται *ὁ Θεὸς νεκρῶν* εἶναι, *ἀλλὰ ζώντων.* Ζωογονεῖ γὰρ πάντας εἰς τὸ εἶναι διηνεκῶς. Οἱ δὲ μὴ τυχόντες τῆς αὐτοῦ δόξης εἰ καὶ διηνεκῶς ζῶσιν | **177r** ἀλλὰ κολασθησόμενοι αἰωνίως, ὅπερ οὐ ζωή, ἀλλ᾽ αἰώνιος θάνατός ἐστιν.

(ΩΡΙΓΕΝΟΥΣ, cont.) Ἴσμεν δὲ ὅτι καὶ πρὸς τὴν λέξιν αὐτὴν οἱ ἀπὸ Οὐαλεντίνου καὶ Μαρκίωνος ἔτι διαμάχονται, ἐπὶ ψυχὰς ἀνάγοντες τὸν λόγον. Ταύτας γὰρ ζῆν καὶ περὶ τούτων εἰρηκέναι τὸν Κύριον, ὡς τούτων ὄντος Θεοῦ τοῦ Θεοῦ. Οὐ δήπου δὲ Σαδδουκαίοις περὶ ψυχῶν ἦν ἡ ἀντιλογία, ἀλλὰ περὶ σωμάτων, ὥστε περὶ τούτων ἡ ἀπόκρισις. Λέγεται δὲ τότε ἀνίστασθαι ὁ νεκρὸς ὅτε μετὰ σώματος ἡ ψυχή, οὐχ ὡς ἐν τῶ μεταξὺ τῆς ψυχῆς διαλελυμένης ἀλλ᾽ ὡς ἀπράκτου οὔσης καὶ τὰ τῆς ζωῆς ἴδια ὅσα μετὰ σώματος οὐκ ἐχούσης. Ἕν γάρ τι τὸ συναμφοτερόν ἐστιν ἄνθρωπος καὶ ἡ ζωὴ κοινή, καὶ ἑκατέρων δεῖ πρὸς τὸ τὴν ἐκ θανάτου ζωὴν πάλιν συστῆναι.

> Ἴσμεν δέ, ὅτι καὶ πρὸς τὴν λέξιν ταύτην οἱ ἀπὸ Μαρκίωνος καὶ Οὐαλεντίνου ἔτι διαμάχονται εἰς ψυχὰς ἀνάγοντες τὸν λόγον. ταύτας γὰρ ζῆν καὶ περὶ τούτων εἰρηκέναι τὸν κύριον ὡς τούτων ὄντος θεοῦ τοῦ θεοῦ. οὐδέπω δὲ Σαδδουκαίοις περὶ ψυχῶν ἦν ἡ ἀντιλογία, ἀλλὰ περὶ σωμάτων, ὥστε περὶ τούτων ἡ ἀπόκρισις. λέγεται δὲ τότε ἀνίστασθαι ὁ νεκρός, ὅτε μετὰ σώματος ἡ ψυχή, οὐχ ὡς ἐν τῷ μεταξὺ τῆς ψυχῆς διαλελυμένης, ἀλλ᾽ ὡς ἀπρακτούσης καὶ τὰ τῆς ζωῆς ἴδια, ὅσα μετὰ σώματος, οὐκ ἐχούσης. ἕν γάρ τι τὸ συναμφοτερόν ἐστιν, ἄνθρωπος καὶ ἡ ζωὴ κοινή, καὶ ἑκατέρων δεῖ πρὸς τὸ τὴν ἐκ θανάτου ζωὴν πάλιν συστῆναι.[mcdxix]

> Ἴσμεν δέ, ὅτι καὶ πρὸς τὴν λέξιν ταύτην οἱ ἀπὸ Οὐαλεντίνου καὶ Μαρκίωνος[mcdxx] ἔτι διαμάχονται ἐπὶ ψυχὰς ἀνάγοντες τὸν λόγον. ταύτας γὰρ ζῆν καὶ περὶ τούτων εἰρηκέναι τὸν κύριον ὡς τούτων ὄντος θεοῦ τοῦ θεοῦ. οὐ δήπου δὲ Σαδδουκαίοις περὶ ψυχῶν ἦν ἡ ἀντιλογία, ἀλλὰ περὶ σωμάτων, ὥστε περὶ τούτων ἡ ἀπόκρισις. λέγεται δὲ τότε ἀνίστασθαι ὁ νεκρός, ὅτε μετὰ σώματος ἡ ψυχή, οὐχ ὡς ἐν τῷ μεταξὺ τῆς ψυχῆς διαλελυμένης, ἀλλ᾽ ὡς ἀπράκτου οὔσης καὶ τὰ τῆς ζωῆς ἴδια ὅσα μετὰ σώματος οὐκ ἐχούσης. ἓν γάρ τι τὸ συναμφοτερόν ἐστιν ἄνθρωπος καὶ ἡ ζωὴ κοινὴ καὶ ἑκατέρων δεῖ πρὸς τὸ τὴν ἐκ θανάτου ζωὴν πάλιν συστῆναι.[mcdxxi]

> ἴσμεν δὲ ὅτι καὶ πρὸς τὴν λέξιν ταύτην οἱ ἀπὸ τοῦ Οὐαλεντίνου καὶ Μαρκίωνος ἔτι διαμάχονται, ἐπὶ ψυχὰς ἀνάγοντες τὸν λόγον.ταύτας γὰρ ζῆν, καὶ περὶ τούτων εἰρηκέναι τὸν Κύριον ὡς τούτων ὄντος Θεοῦ τοῦ Θεοῦ. οὐ δήπου δὲ Σαδδουκαίοις περὶ ψυχῶν ἦν ἡ αἰτιολογία, ἀλλὰ περὶ σωμάτων. ὥστε περὶ τούτων ἡ ἀπόκρισις. λέγεται δὲ τότε ἀνίστασθαι ὁ νεκρός, ὅτε μετὰ σώματος ἡ ψυχή. οὐκ ὡς ἐν τῷ μεταξὺ τῆς ψυχῆς διαλελυμένης,

1940 Matt. 22:32.
1941 Rom. 14:9.

> ἀλλ᾽ ὡς ἀπρακτούσης, καὶ τὰ τῆς ψυχῆς ἴδια ὅσα μετὰ σώματος ἔσχεν οὐκ ἐχούσης. ἕν γάρ τι τὸ συναμφότερόν ἐστιν ἐν ἀνθρώποις, καὶ ἡ ζωὴ κοινή, καὶ ἑκατέρων δεῖ πρὸς τὸ τὴν ἐκ θανάτου ζωὴν πάλιν συστῆναι.[mcdxxii]

καὶ ἐπηρώτησεν εἷς ἐξ αὐτῶν νομικός.[1942] Ἐξ ἀμέτρου ἀναιδείας διαφθονούμενοι οἱ Φαρισαῖοι ἐπειδὴ καταισχυνθέντων τῶν Σαδδουκαίων ἐπηνεῖτο ὑπὸ τῶν ὄχλων, μεθ᾽ ὑποκρίσεως πάλιν ἐρωτῶσι πειράζοντες αὐτὸν εἰ προστίθησι τῇ ἐντολῇ τῇ πρώτῃ ὡς διορθούμενος τὸν νόμον, ἵνα εὕρωσι κατ᾽ αὐτοῦ λαβήν. Καὶ ὁ μὲν Ματθαῖος καὶ Λουκᾶς νομικὸν ἔλεγον εἶναι τὸν ἐρωτήσαντα,[1943] Μᾶρκος δὲ γραμματέα.[1944] Οὐκ ἔστι δὲ τοῦτο διαφωνία. Οἱ μὲν γὰρ νομομαθῆ τοῦτον ἀποδεικνύουσιν, ὁ δὲ γραμματοεισαγωγέα,[1945] ὅπερ ἐστὶ τοῦ νόμου ἑρμηνεὺς τῷ λαῷ. Ὁ δὲ Κύριος δημοσιεύει αὐτῶν τὴν κακίαν, ὅτι οὐ διὰ τοῦτο ἦλθον ἐρωτῆσαι ὥστε ὠφεληθῆναι, ἀλλ᾽ ἀπὸ τοῦ μὴ ἔχειν ἀγάπην, | **177v** καὶ ἀπὸ τοῦ φθονεῖν. Καὶ διδάσκει ὅτι οὐ δεῖ ἐν μέρει μὲν ἀγαπᾶν τὸν Θεόν, ἐν μέρει δὲ τοῖς γηΐνοις προσκεῖσθαι. Δι᾽ ὧν δὲ ὁ Κύριος εἶπε (ταύτην τὴν ἐντολὴν πασῶν κεφαλαιωδεστέραν οὖσαν) ἔδοξεν ὁ νομικὸς ἐμβ‹ά›λλε‹ι›ν[1946] αὐτὸν εἰς κίνδυνον, ὡς θεοποιοῦντα ἑαυτόν. Ὅθεν καὶ μὴ εἰπόντα τοῦτο ἐπῄνεσεν ὁ νομικὸς ὡς ὁ Μᾶρκός φησιν.[1947] Ἡ μὲν οὖν *πρώτη ἐντολὴ* πᾶν εἶδος εὐσεβείας διδάσκει· ἡ δὲ δευτέρα τὰ πρὸς ἀνθρώπους δίκαια περιέχει. Καὶ ἡ μὲν ὁδοποιεῖ τῇ δευτέρᾳ, ἡ δὲ ἐκ ταύτης συγκροτεῖται. Ὁ γὰρ ἀγαπῶν *τὸν Θεόν*, ἀγαπᾷ καὶ *τὸν πλησίον·* καὶ ὁ ἀγαπῶν *τὸν πλησίον πάσας τὰς ἐντολὰς*[mcdxxiii] τηρεῖ.

> Ἐξ ἀμέτρου ἀναιδείας διαφθονούμενοι οἱ Φαρισαῖοι, ἐπειδὴ καταισχυνθέντων τῶν Σαδδουκαίων ἐπηνεῖτο ὑπὸ τῶν ὄχλων, μεθ᾽ ὑποκρίσεως πάλιν ἐρωτῶσι πειράζοντες αὐτόν, εἰ καὶ προστίθησι πάλιν τῇ ἐντολῇ τῇ πρώτῃ ὡς διορθούμενος τὸν νόμον, ἵνα εὕρωσι κατ᾽ αὐτοῦ λαβήν. καὶ ὁ μὲν Ματθαῖος καὶ Λουκᾶς νομικὸν εἶναι ἔλεγεν τὸν ἐρωτήσαντα, Μᾶρκος δὲ γραμματέα. οὐκ ἔστι δὲ τοῦτο διαφωνία. οἱ μὲν γὰρ νομομαθῆ τοῦτον ἀποδεικνύουσιν, οἱ δὲ γραμματεισαγωγέα, ὅπερ ἐστὶ τοῦ νόμου ἑρμηνεὺς τῷ λαῷ. ὁ δὲ κύριος δημοσιεύει αὐτῶν τὴν κακίαν, ὅτι οὐ διὰ τοῦτο ἦλθον ἐρωτῆσαι, ὥστε ὠφεληθῆναι, ἀλλ᾽ ἀπὸ τοῦ μὴ ἔχειν [missing ἀγάπην] καὶ τῷ φθόνῳ κατέχεσθαι, καὶ διδάσκει, ὅτι οὐ δεῖ ἐν μέρει μὲν ἀγαπᾶν τὸν θεόν, ἐν μέρει δὲ τοῖς γηΐνοις προσκεῖσθαι. δι᾽ ὧν δὲ ὁ κύριος εἶπεν ταύτην τὴν ἐντολὴν κεφαλαιωδεστέραν οὖσαν πασῶν, ἔδοξεν ὁ νομικὸς ἐμβάλλειν αὐτὸν εἰς κίνδυνον ὡς θεοποιοῦντα ἑαυτόν. ὅθεν καὶ μὴ εἰπόντα τοῦτο ἐπῄνεσεν ὁ νομικὸς ὡς ὁ Μᾶρκος φησίν. ἡ μὲν οὖν *πρώτη ἐντολὴ* πᾶν εἶδος εὐσεβείας διδάσκει. τὸ γὰρ ἐξ *ὅλης καρδίας τὸν θεὸν* ἀγαπᾶν αἴτιόν ἐστιν παντὸς ἀγαθοῦ, ἡ δὲ δευτέρα τὰ πρὸς ἀνθρώπους δίκαια περιέχει. καὶ ἡ μὲν ὁδοποιεῖ τῇ δευτέρᾳ, ἡ δὲ ἐκ ταύτης συγκροτεῖται. ὁ γὰρ τὴν πρὸς θεὸν ἀγάπην κατορθώσας δηλονότι καὶ τὴν πρὸς

1942 Matt. 22:35.
1943 Luke, 10:25.
1944 Mark, 12:28.
1945 Cf. Deut. 1:15; 16:18; 29:9; 31:28.
1946 Cod. ἐμβαλεῖν.
1947 Mark, 12:32.

> *τὸν πλησίον* εἰς πάντα *ὡς ἑαυτὸν ἀγαπᾷ*. πασῶν τῶν ἐντολῶν ὁ τοιοῦτος ἐκπληρωτὴς τυγχάνει.[mcdxxiv]

τί ὑμῖν δοκεῖ περὶ τοῦ Χριστοῦ;[1948] Ἐπειδὴ ψιλὸν ἄνθρωπον ᾤοντο εἶναι τὸν Χριστόν, ἀνατρέπει αὐτῶν τὴν δόξαν καὶ διδάσκει τὸ ἀληθὲς διὰ τῆς *τοῦ Δαυὶδ* προφητείας ὅτι καὶ *Κύριός* ἐστι τὴν θεότητα αὐτοῦ ἀνακηρύττοντος. Εἰπόντων γὰρ τῶν Φαρισαίων ὅτι *υἱός* ἐστι *τοῦ Δαυὶδ* ὁ Χριστός, ψιλὸς ἄνθρωπος, ὡς μὴ ἀκολούθως ἀποκριθέντων φησὶ *πῶς οὖν Δαυὶδ Κύριον αὐτὸν καλῶν*[1949] ἀληθεύει εἰ *υἱός* αὐτοῦ ἐστι καὶ ψιλὸς ἄνθρωπος; Οὐκ ἀναιρεῖ δὲ οὐδὲ ἀρνεῖται *υἱός* εἶναι *Δαυίδ*, ἀλλὰ δείκνυσιν ὅτι οὐ ψιλός ἐστιν ἄνθρωπος, ἀλλὰ καὶ Θεός.

> Ἐρωτήσας γὰρ αὐτοὺς πρότερος, ἐπειδὴ οὐκ ἀπεκρίναντο τἀληθῆ περὶ αὐτοῦ (ἄνθρωπον γὰρ αὐτὸν ἔφησαν εἶναι ψιλόν), ἀνατρέπων τὴν πεπλανημένην αὐτῶν δόξαν, οὕτως εἰσάγει τὸν Δαυῒδ, ἀνακηρύττοντα αὐτοῦ τὴν θεότητα. Ἐκεῖνοι μὲν γὰρ ἐνόμιζον, ὅτι ψιλὸς ἄνθρωπος ἦν, διὸ καὶ ἔλεγον, Τοῦ Δαυίδ. αὐτὸς δὲ τοῦτο διορθούμενος παράγει τὸν προφήτην, καὶ τὴν κυριότητα αὐτοῦ, καὶ τὸ γνήσιον τῆς υἱότητος, καὶ τὸ ὁμότιμον τὸ πρὸς τὸν Πατέρα μαρτυροῦντα.[mcdxxv]

Εἰπὼν δὲ ὅτι *ἐν Πνεύματι* αὐτὸν καλεῖ, δείκνυσιν ὅτι οὐ πρὸς χάριν τοῦτο εἶπεν, ἀλλ᾽ *ἐν Πνεύματι* Ἁγίῳ ἐφθέγξατο. Ὡς περὶ ἑτέρου δὲ λαλεῖ, ἵνα μὴ δόξῃ βαρὺς εἶναι ἐπὶ τοῦ ἰδίου προσώπου γυμνάζων ταῦτα.
Εἰκότως δὲ ταῦτα ἰδικῶς | **178r** προσέθηκεν ἐκ τοῦ Πατρὸς εἰρηκέναι ἵνα φοβήσῃ αὐτούς.

> Καὶ οὐδὲ μέχρι τούτου ἵσταται. ἀλλ᾽ ὥστε καὶ φοβῆσαι καὶ τὸ ἑξῆς ἐπάγει λέγων.[mcdxxvi]

Καὶ ἀναγκάζει αὐτοὺς ὁμολογῆσαι ἀπὸ τῶν ἰδίων στομάτων ὅτι Κύριός ἐστιν ὁ Χριστός, τοῦτο συνιστῶν ἀπὸ τῆς προφητείας. Ἐρωτᾷ δὲ ἵνα, ἢ εἰπόντες οὐκ ἴσμεν ἐρωτήσωσι καὶ μάθωσιν, ἢ τὸ ἀληθὲς εἰπόντες πιστεύσωσιν, ἢ μηδὲν εἰπεῖν δυνηθέντες αἰσχυνθῶσιν. Ὅπερ καὶ ἔπαθον μετ᾽ αἰσχύνης ἀναχωρήσαντες καὶ μηκέτι τολμήσαντες τοῦ λοιποῦ ἐρωτῆσαι αὐτόν.[1950]

ἐπὶ τῆς Μωσέως καθέδρας ἐκάθισαν.[1951] Διὰ τούτων διδάσκει ὁ Κύριος ὅτι οὐκ ἐναντιοῦται τῷ νόμῳ καὶ θέλει τοὺς ἀκροατὰς μὴ καταφρονεῖν τῶν λεγομένων, κἂν οἱ διδάσκοντες οὐκ ἐπαινετοί. *Ὅσα*, γάρ φησι, *λέγουσιν* οὐκ εἰσὶν αὐτῶν ἀλλὰ τοῦ Μωσέως, μᾶλλον δὲ τοῦ Θεοῦ. Διὸ χρὴ τιμᾶν τοὺς ἱερεῖς ὡς ἐπὶ τῆς *Μωσέως καθέδρας*

1948 Matt. 22:42.
1949 Matt. 22:43.
1950 Matt. 22:46.
1951 Matt. 23:2.

καθεζομένους, εἰ καὶ μὴ ἔχουσιν ἐξ οἰκείας ἀρετῆς καυχᾶσθαι (οὐ γὰρ καθ‹αι›ρεῖ[1952] αὐτοὺς τῆς ἀξίας) καὶ δεῖ σέβειν αὐτοὺς καὶ τὴν ὀρθὴν αὐτῶν δέχεσθαι διδασκαλίαν. Πᾶς δὲ ὁ διδάσκων τὰ ἀπὸ τῆς θείας γραφῆς τὴν *Μωσέως* ἔχει *καθέδραν* (πρῶτος γὰρ ἐκεῖνος ἤρξατο τούτου), νῦν δὲ καὶ τὴν τοῦ Χριστοῦ.

> Νῦν δὲ οὐκ ἔστιν εἰπεῖν. ᾿Επὶ τῆς Μωϋσέως καθέδρας ἐκάθισαν οἱ ἱερεῖς, ἀλλ᾿, ᾿Επὶ τῆς τοῦ Χριστοῦ. Τὴν γὰρ ἐκείνου διεδέξαντο διδασκαλίαν.[mcdxxvii]

πάντα οὖν ὅσα ἐὰν εἴπωσιν ὑμῖν.[1953] ᾿Επεὶ δὲ λοιπὸν εἰς ἀθεΐαν ἐτράπησαν οἱ τῶν ᾿Ιουδαίων διδάσκαλοι καὶ τὸν ὄντως Κύριον ᾿Ιησοῦν τὸν Χριστὸν ὡς Θεὸν οὐκ εδέξαντο, οὐ χρὴ τοῦ λοιποῦ δέχεσθαι ἔτι ποιοῦντάς τι ἢ διδάσκοντας. ᾿Ελέγχει τοίνυν αὐτῶν *τὰ ἔργα* πρὸς τὸ μὴ ἀπαιτεῖσθαι τοὺς ὄχλους μιμεῖσθαι αὐτούς, ἀλλὰ μόνοις προσέχειν τοῖς ἐκείνων λόγοις. Καὶ | **178v** δείκνυσι διὰ τούτου ὅτι οὐχ οἱ τὰ ὀρθὰ διδάσκοντες μόνον ἐπαινετοί, ἀλλ᾿ οἱ ἐνάρετοι πρὸς τῷ διδάξαι.

δεσμεύουσι γὰρ φορτία βαρέα.[1954] Αἰνίττεται διὰ τούτου ὅτι τὰ μὴ κείμενα ἐν τῷ νόμῳ ἐπέταττον καὶ βαρέως ἐπέκειντο τοῖς μὴ ποιοῦσιν αὐτά, τιμωρούμενοι ἀσύγγνωστα τοὺς παραβαίνοντας. Τὸ δὲ μὴ προσψαῦσαι *τῷ δακτύλῳ*[1955] δηλοῖ τὸ μὴ συγγινώσκειν μηδὲ θέλειν ἐπικουφίσαι τῶν παραβαινόντων τὰς τιμωρίας. Ἢ ἐπειδὴ βαρὺς ὁ νόμος διὰ τὰς λεπτολογίας τῶν ἐθνῶν καὶ διότι οἱ Φαρισαῖοι ἀπήτουν εὐθύνας τοὺς παραβαίνοντας ἐντολήν, αὐτοὶ μηδὲ[1956] ἁπτόμενοι τῶν τοιούτων ἔργων. Τοῦτο γὰρ σημαίνει τὸ μηδὲ ἅψασθαι *τῷ δακτύλῳ* ‹καὶ› τὸ *δεσμεύουσι φορτία βαρέα καὶ δυσβάστακτα.*

Οὐχ ἁπλῶς φησὶ ὁ δεσπότης ὅτι *βαρέα* τυγχάνει *καὶ δυσβάστακτα*, ἀλλὰ τῇ αὐτῶν ἐκείνων τῶν ἱερέων κρίσει *βαρέα* φανέντα *καὶ δυσβάστακτα*. Ἃ γὰρ αὐτοὶ οὐδὲ *τῷ δακτύλῳ* κινοῦσι, τουτέστιν οὐδὲ ἀπάρχονται πράττειν, πῶς οὐχὶ *βαρέα καὶ δυσβάστακτα* νομίζεσθαι πεποιήκασιν; ᾿Αλλ᾿ οὗτοι *βαρέα καὶ δυσβάστακτα* δι᾿ ὧν οὐ πράττουσιν ἐπιδείξαντες, ὅμως ἐπιτιθέασιν αὐτὰ τοῖς ἄλλοις, πράττειν ἀπαραιτήτως ἐκβιαζόμενοι. Διὸ πράττειν μὲν ὁ δεσπότης τὰ παρ᾿ αὐτῶν προστατόμενα τοῖς ὄχλοις ἐπιτρέπει, καὶ ταῦτα δὲ οὐχ ἁπλῶς, ἀλλ᾿ ὅσα τῆς Μωσαϊκῆς *καθέδρας* ἄξια. Διὰ τοῦτο γὰρ καὶ ταύτην προέταξεν εἰπὼν *ἐπὶ τῆς Μωσέως καθέδρας*[1957] καὶ ἑξῆς. Οὐ γὰρ ὅσα αὐτοῖς ἐπινε | **179r** νόηται ταῦτα ποιεῖν κελεύει (ταῦτα γὰρ προδιήλεγξε *παραδόσεις ἀνθρώπων*[1958][mcdxxviii] εἰπὼν ἐπὶ παραλύσει τῶν ἐντολῶν τοῦ Θεοῦ) οὐδὲ τὰ μικροπρεπῆ ταῦτα καὶ παιδαγωγικὰ καὶ ἀνάξια πολιτείας τελείας καὶ ὑψηλῆς, οἷα

1952 Cod. καδερεῖ.
1953 Matt. 23:3.
1954 Matt. 23:4.
1955 Matt. 23:4; cf. Luke, 11:46.
1956 Cod. μὴ δὲ.
1957 Matt. 23:2.
1958 Cf. Mark, 7:8-9, quoting Is. 29:13; cf. Col. 2:8.

τὰ περὶ βρωμάτων καὶ σαββάτων παρατηρήσεως καὶ τὰ ὅμοια. Καὶ γὰρ καὶ ταῦτα προεξέβαλε· τούτων γὰρ ἐργάται ἀκριβεῖς ὑπῆρχον οἱ ἱερεῖς. Ποῖα οὖν προστασσόντων τῶν γραμματέων ὁ δεσπότης κελεύει τὸν ὄχλον ποιεῖν; Ἐκεῖνα, ὡς ἔφημεν, ὅσα τῆς Μωσαϊκῆς *καθέδρας* ἄξια, τουτέστιν ὅσα δύναται ψυχὴν σαλευομένην καὶ ὀκλάζουσαν ὑποστηρίζειν καὶ ἐνδυναμοῦν. Ταῦτά δέ ἐστιν ἡ πρὸς Θεὸν ἀγάπη εἰλικρινής, ἡ πρὸς τὸν πλησίον, καὶ ἁπλῶς ὅσα συνᾴδει τῇ νομοθεσίᾳ τῆς χάριτος.[mcdxxix] Ἅπερ οὐ μόνον οὐκ ἐξέβαλεν ὁ δεσπότης, ἀλλὰ καὶ βεβαίως φυλάττεσθαι παρέδωκεν, ἅτινα οὐδὲ *τῷ δακτύλῳ* φησὶ θέλειν τοὺς ἱερέας κινεῖν, ἐξ ὧν αὐτὰ *βαρέα καὶ δυσβάστακτα* καὶ τοῖς ἄλλοις νομίζεσθαι πεποιήκασιν. Ταῦτα *πάντα*, φησίν, ἂν λέγωσιν *ὑμῖν* οἱ ἱερεῖς ποιεῖν, *ποιεῖτε*, μὴ ἔχοντες πρόφασιν ἀναβολῆς ὅτι ἐκεῖνοι οὐ ποιοῦσι. Καὶ γὰρ οὐδὲ *κατὰ τὰ ἔργα αὐτῶν* καὶ ὑμᾶς ποιεῖν ἐπιτάσσω· τουναντίον δὲ καὶ ἀποτρέπω. *Κατὰ τὰ ἔργα αὐτῶν*, φησί, *μὴ ποιεῖτε*. Πῶς οὖν ἃ λέγουσι ποιεῖν κελεύει;[1959] Ἀκολούθως λίαν· ὅτι αὐτοὶ ἃ *λέγουσιν οὐ ποιοῦσιν*, ἐν τούτῳ μόνῳ δοκοῦντες εὐδοκιμεῖν, ἐν τῷ *τὰς ἐντολὰς τοῦ Θεοῦ*[1960] ἄλλοις ἀναγγέλλειν. Εἰ δὲ καὶ ἔπραττον ἃ ἔλεγον, καὶ ἃ πράττουσι προσέταττον | **179v** ἂν μιμεῖσθαι. Διὰ τοῦτο δὲ ταλανίζει αὐτοὺς ὁ δεσπότης, ὅτι ᾔδεισαν αὐτοὶ τὰς ἐντολάς ‹πλὴν› ὅτι οὐκ ἔπραττον εἰδότες. Ὅτι βαρὺ αὐτὰς καὶ δυσβάστακτον δι᾽ ὧν οὐκ ἔπραττον ἐποίουν φορτίον. Ὅτι καὶ ἃ ἔπραττον εὐτέλειαν ἔχοντα καὶ ταπεινότητα ἰουδαϊκὴν καὶ αὐτὰ οὐχ ὡς ἐντολὴν ἐποίουν, ἀλλ᾽ ὥστε τοῖς ὁρῶσιν ἀρέσαι.

> Τὸ *δεσμεύουσιν φορτία βαρέα καὶ δυσβάστακτα* οὐχ ἁπλῶς φησιν ὁ δεσπότης, ὅτι *βαρέα* τυγχάνει *καὶ δυσβάστακτα*, ἀλλὰ τὰ τῇ αὐτῶν ἐκείνων τῶν ἱερέων κρίσει *βαρέα* φανέντα *καὶ δυσβάστακτα*. ἃ γὰρ *αὐτοὶ* οὐδὲ *τῷ δακτύλῳ* κινοῦσιν, τοῦτ᾽ ἔστιν οὐδὲ ἀπάρχονται πράττειν, πῶς οὐχὶ *βαρέα καὶ δυσβάστακτα* νομίζεσθαι πεποιήκασιν; ἀλλ᾽ οὗτοι *βαρέα καὶ δυσβάστακτα* δι᾽ ὧν οὐ πράττουσιν ἐπιδείξαντες ὅμως ἐπιτιθέασιν αὐτὰ τοῖς ἄλλοις πράττειν ἀπαραιτήτως βιαζόμενοι. διὸ πράττειν μὲν ὁ δεσπότης τὰ παρ᾽ αὐτῶν προσταττόμενα τοῖς ὄχλοις ἐπιτρέπει καὶ ταῦτα δὲ οὐχ ἁπλῶς, ἀλλ᾽ ὅσα τῆς Μωσαϊκῆς *καθέδρας* ἄξια. διὰ τοῦτο γὰρ καὶ ταύτην προέταξεν εἰπών. *ἐπὶ τῆς καθέδρας Μωυσέως* καὶ ἑξῆς. οὐ γὰρ ὅσα αὐτοῖς ἐπινενόηται ταῦτα ποιεῖν κελεύει (ταῦτα γὰρ προδιήλεγξεν παραδόσεις ἀνθρώπων εἰπὼν ἐπὶ παραλύσει τῶν ἐντολῶν τοῦ θεοῦ) οὐδὲ τὰ μικροπρεπῆ ταῦτα καὶ παιδαγωγικὰ καὶ ἀνάξια πολιτείας τελείας καὶ ὑψηλῆς, οἷα τὰ περὶ βρωμάτων καὶ σαββάτων παρατηρήσεως καὶ τὰ ὅμοια. καὶ γὰρ καὶ ταῦτα προεξέβαλεν. τούτων γὰρ ἐργάται ἀκριβεῖς ὑπῆρχον οἱ ἱερεῖς. ποῖα οὖν προστασσόντων τῶν γραμματέων ὁ δεσπότης κελεύει τὸν ὄχλον ποιεῖν; ἐκεῖνα, ὡς ἔφαμεν, ὅσα τῆς Μωσαϊκῆς *καθέδρας* ἄξια, τοῦτ᾽ ἔστιν ὅσα δύναται ψυχὴν σαλευομένην καὶ ὀκλάζουσαν ὑποστηρίζειν καὶ ἐνδυναμοῦν. ταῦτα δέ ἐστιν ἡ πρὸς θεὸν ἀγάπη εἰλικρινής, ἡ πρὸς τὸν πλησίον καὶ ἁπλῶς ὅσα συνᾴδει τῇ νομοθεσίᾳ τῆς χάριτος. ἅπερ οὐ μόνον οὐκ ἐξέβαλλεν ὁ δεσπότης, ἀλλὰ καὶ βεβαίως φυλάττεσθαι παρέδωκεν, ἅτινα οὐδὲ *τῷ δακτύλῳ* φησὶν θέλειν τοὺς ἱερέας κινεῖν, ἐξ ὧν αὐτὰ καὶ *βαρέα καὶ δυσβάστακτα* καὶ τοῖς ἄλλοις νομίζεσθαι πεποιήκασιν. ταῦτα πάντα, φησίν, ἂν λέγωσιν ὑμῖν οἱ ἱερεῖς ποιεῖν, ποιεῖτε μὴ ἔχοντες προφάσεως ἀναβολήν, ὅτι ἐκεῖνοι οὐ ποιοῦσιν. καὶ γὰρ οὐδὲ *κατὰ τὰ ἔργα αὐτῶν* καὶ ὑμᾶς ποιεῖν

1959 Cod. κελεύεις.

1960 Cf. Psalm 118:115; Deut. 4:2; 6:17; *et passim*. Rev. 12:17.

> ἐπιτάσσω. τοὐναντίον δὲ καὶ ἀποτρέπω. *κατὰ τὰ ἔργα αὐτῶν*, φησίν, *μὴ ποιεῖτε*. πῶς οὖν ἃ *λέγουσιν* ποιεῖν κελεύεις; ἀκολούθως λίαν, ὅτι αὐτοὶ ἃ *λέγουσιν οὐ ποιοῦσιν*, ἐν τούτῳ μόνῳ δοκοῦντες εὐδοκιμεῖν, ἐν τῷ τὰς ἐντολὰς τοῦ θεοῦ ἄλλοις ἀναγγέλλειν. εἰ δὲ καὶ ἔπραττον, ἃ ἔλεγον, καὶ ἃ πράττουσιν προσέταττεν ἂν μιμεῖσθαι. διὰ τοῦτο δὲ ταλανίζει αὐτοὺς ὁ δεσπότης, ὅτι ᾔδεσαν αὐτοὶ τὰς ἐντολάς, ὅτι οὐκ ἔπραττον εἰδότες, ὅτι βαρὺ αὐτοῖς καὶ δυσβάστακτον, δι᾽ ὧν οὐκ ἔπραττον, ἐποίουν φορτίον, ὅτι καὶ ἃ ἔπραττον εὐτέλειαν ἔχοντα καὶ ταπεινότητα ἰουδαϊκὴν καὶ αὐτὰ οὐχ ὡς ἐντολὴν ἐποίουν, ἀλλ᾽ ὥστε τοῖς ὁρῶσιν ἀρέσαι.[mcdxxx]

πλατύνουσι δὲ τὰ φυλακτήρια.[1961] Πρὸς τούτοις δὲ καὶ ἐν πᾶσιν ἐσχηματίζοντο πρὸς τὸ ὁρᾶσθαι τοῖς ἀνθρώποις περίβλεπτοι καὶ διὰ σχηματισμοῦ ψεύδους ὑπεπλάττοντο εὐσέβειαν, πλατύνοντες *τὰ φυλακτήρια* καὶ *τὰ κράσπεδα* μεγαλύνοντες.
᾿Ακούσαντες γὰρ γεγραμμένου ἐν τῷ νόμῳ περὶ τῶν θείων ρημάτων ὅτι *ἀφάψατε αὐτὰ ἐπὶ τῆς χειρὸς ὑμῶν καὶ ἔσται ἀσάλευτα πρὸ ὀφθαλμῶν ὑμῶν*,[1962] οἱ τὰ ἔργα αὐτῶν ποιοῦντες *πρὸς τὸ θεαθῆναι τοῖς ἀνθρώποις*,[1963] γράψαντές τινα τοῦ νόμου ρητὰ εἰς περικομμάτια διφθερῶν δύο καὶ περιδήσαντες, τὸ μὲν ἕτερον φοροῦσιν ὡς στέφανον ἐπὶ τῆς κεφαλῆς τιθέντες κατὰ τοῦ μετώπου τὸ γεγραμμένον·

> The Pharisees, interpreting this[mcdxxxi] faultily, wrote on small parcments the Decalogue of Moses (that is, the ten words of the Law), and folded them up, they even bound them to their forehand and made a sort of on their head, so that they would always be moving before their eyes… . They called those little representations of the Law *phylacteries*, because whoever had them had his own protection and defense, as it were.[mcdxxxii]

τὸ δὲ ἕτερον, κατὰ τοῦ βραχίονος τῆς ἑτέρας τῶν χειρῶν. Καὶ καλοῦσι ταῦτα *φυλακτήρια*. Οὕτω δὴ καὶ περὶ κρασπέδου τι εὑρόντες ἐν τῷ Δευτερονομίῳ,[1964] οἴονται τηρεῖν τὸν νόμον, κράσπεδόν τι ποιήσαντες ἐπί τινος κλώσματος, ὃ φοροῦσιν ἐπὶ τοῖς ἐνδύμασι. *Κράσπεδα* δὲ καλοῦνται τὰ περὶ τὴν ᾤαν τὴν περὶ τοὺς πόδας ραπτόμενα ὑακίνθινα κλώσματα ἢ καὶ κόκ | **180r** κινα. Ταῦτα δὲ ἐποίουν ἵνα ὁρῶντες αὐτὰ μὴ ἐπιλάθωνται τῶν τοῦ Θεοῦ ἐντολῶν. Τὸ μὲν γὰρ ἔχειν ἐπὶ τῆς χειρὸς τὸ φυλακτήριον σημαίνει[1965] ἐργάζεσθαι τὰς ἐντολάς, τὸ δὲ κράσπεδον δηλοῖ τὴν τοῦ Θεοῦ οἰκονομίαν, σώζουσαν δι᾽ αἵματος τοὺς ἀντεχομένους αὐτῆς. Μεγάλα δὲ ἐποίουν *τὰ κράσπεδα*, ἵνα διὰ τούτων δόξωσι νομοφύλακες εἶναι, ὡς σύμβολον ὄντα τῆς τῶν νόμων τηρήσεως,

1961 Matt. 23:5: πλατύνουσι γὰρ τὰ φυλακτήρια.
1962 Deut. 11:18: καὶ ἀφάψετε αὐτὰ εἰς σημεῖον ἐπὶ τῆς χειρὸς ὑμῶν, καὶ ἔσται ἀσάλευτον πρὸ ὀφθαλμῶν ὑμῶν. *Op. cit.* 6:8: καὶ ἀφάψεις αὐτὰ εἰς σημεῖον ἐπὶ τῆς χειρός σου, καὶ ἔσται ἀσάλευτον πρὸ ὀφθαλμῶν σου.
1963 Matt. 23:5.
1964 Cf. Deut. 22:12.
1965 Cod. σημαίνει ὥστε.

ἐν δὲ τοῖς φυλακτηρίοις εἶχον γεγραμμένην τὴν δεκάλογον ἐξηρτημένην ἐν τοῖς τραχήλοις.

> (ἀκούσαντες γὰρ) γεγραμμένου ἐν τῷ νόμῳ περὶ τῶν θείων ρημάτων ὅτι *ἀφάψατε αὐτὰ ἐπὶ τῆς χειρὸς ὑμῶν, καὶ ἔσται ἀσάλευτα πρὸ ὀφθαλμῶν ὑμῶν* οἱ τὰ ἔργα αὐτῶν ποιοῦντες πρὸς τὸ θεαθῆναι τοῖς ἀνθρώποις, γράψαντές τινα τοῦ νόμου ρητὰ εἰς περικομμάτια διφθερίων δύο καὶ περιδήσαντες τὸ μὲν ἕτερον φοροῦσιν ὡς στέφανον ἐπὶ τῆς κεφαλῆς τιθέντες κατὰ τοῦ μετώπου τὸ γεγραμμένον, τὸ δὲ ἕτερον κατὰ τοῦ βραχίονος τῆς ἑτέρας τῶν χειρῶν. καὶ καλοῦσι ταῦτα φυλακτήρια. οὕτω δὲ καὶ περὶ κρασπέδου τι εὑρόντες ἐν τῷ Δευτερονομίῳ οἴονται τηρεῖν τὸν νόμον κράσπεδόν τι ποιήσαντες ἐπί τινος κλώσματος ὃ φοροῦσιν ἐπὶ τοῖς ἐνδύμασι.[mcdxxxiii]

> Τοῦτο τοιοῦτον ἦν. ἐν τῷ νόμῳ ἔκειτο. *ἀφάψατε αὐτὰ ἐπὶ τῆς χειρὸς ὑμῶν καὶ ἔσται ἀσάλευτα πρὸ ὀφθαλμῶν ὑμῶν*. ἔγραψαν οὖν ἐπὶ δύο διφθερίων τουτέστι χαρτίων τὰς δέκα τοῦ νόμου ἐντολὰς καὶ ἐτίθεσαν τὸν μὲν ἓν ἐπὶ τοῦ μετώπου αὐτῶν τὸ δὲ ἕτερον ἐκρέμων ἐπὶ τῆς δεξιᾶς. *τὰ* δὲ *κράσπεδα* ἐποίουν ἐπὶ τῶν ἄκρων τῶν ἱματίων, ὑακίνθινά τινα ἢ κόκκινα κλώσματα οἷον κρόσσους (καὶ τοῦτο δὲ ἐν τῷ νόμῳ κείμενον εὗρον),[1966] ἵνα ὁρῶντες αὐτὰ μὴ ἐπιλανθάνωνται τῶν ἐντολῶν τοῦ θεοῦ. ὁ δὲ θεὸς οὐ τοῦτο ἐβούλετο, ἀλλὰ τὸ μὲν ἔχειν *ἐπὶ τῆς χειρὸς*[1967] τὸ φυλακτήριον ἐσήμαινε τὸ δεῖν ἐργάζεσθαι τὰς ἐντολάς, τὸ δὲ κόκκινα εἶναι τὰ κράσπεδα ἐδήλου ὅτι δεῖ ἡμᾶς τῷ αἵματι τοῦ κυρίου σημειοῦσθαι. ἐκεῖνοι οὖν *τὰ φυλακτήρια* μεγάλα καὶ *τὰ κράσπεδα*, ἵνα δόξωσι νομοφύλακες εἶναι τοῖς ὁρῶσι ταῦτα.[mcdxxxiv]

φιλοῦσι ‹τ›ε[1968] *τὴν πρωτοκλισίαν.*[1969] Ταῦτα δὲ ἐσχηματίζοντο φησι διὰ τὸ τιμᾶσθαι μὲν ἐν τοῖς ἀσπασμοῖς,[1970] φιλεῖν τε τὴν πρωτοκαθεδρίαν *ἐν ταῖς συναγωγαῖς* καὶ τὰς πρωτοκλισίας ἐν τοῖς δείπνοις, φιλεῖν τε *καλεῖσθαι ὑπὸ τῶν ἀνθρώπων* διδάσκαλοι.

ὑμεῖς δὲ μὴ κληθῆτε ραββί.[1971] Οὐ τοῦτο φησὶν διὰ τὸ μὴ θέλειν καλεῖσθαι τινὰ διδάσκαλον, ἀλλὰ τὸ μὴ ἐμπαθῶς θέλειν ἀκούειν διδάσκαλον ἑαυτόν τινα. Τὸ γὰρ διδασκαλικὸν ἀξίωμα μόνῳ μέτεστι τῷ Θεῷ.

> Καὶ ὁ μακάριος Παῦλος *ἐν τῇ ἐκκλησίᾳ* τάττων *διδασκάλους*[1972] καταχρηστικοὺς καὶ οὐ ἀκριβεῖς καλεῖ. *εἷς γὰρ*[1973] μόνος ὁ κυρίως *διδάσκαλος.*[mcdxxxv]

Ἤτοι ἐπεὶ ποιητὴς τοῦ λογικοῦ μόνος ὁ Υἱός, μόνος καλεῖται διδάσκαλος. *Πάντες* δὲ ἡμεῖς *ἀδελφοί* ἐσμεν, ὡς ἕνα ἔχοντες τῆς φύσεως ὅρον ἢ ὡς μόνον πάντων ποιητὴν

1966 Cf. Deut. 22:11-12.
1967 Deut. 11:18.
1968 Cod. δὲ.
1969 Matt. 23:6.
1970 Matt. 23:7.
1971 Matt. 23:8.
1972 Cf. 1 Cor. 12:28.
1973 Matt. 23:8.

καὶ πατέρα[mcdxxxvi] τὸν Θεὸν ἔχοντες. Οὐ γὰρ ὁ σπείρας ἡμᾶς αἴτιός ἐστι τοῦ εἶναι ἡμᾶς, ἀλλὰ συναίτιος, μᾶλλον δὲ διάκονος γεννήσεως.[mcdxxxvii] Διὰ οὖν φιλοκομπίαν κωλύει καὶ τοῦτο, ἐπεὶ θέλει ἡμᾶς τιμᾶν τοὺς γονεῖς καὶ μάλιστα τοὺς πνευματικοὺς πατέρας.

Εἶτα εἰπών, *μηδὲ κληθῆτε καθηγηταί*, ἐπήγαγεν· *εἷς γάρ ἐστιν ὑμῶν ὁ καθηγητής, ὁ Χριστός.*[1974] Εἰπὼν δὲ *εἷς*, οὐκ ἐκβάλλει τὸν Πατέρα. Τὸ γὰρ *εἷς* πρὸς ἀντιδιαστολὴν τῶν ἀνθρώπων | **18ον** λέγεται. Ἤτοι καθὸ ἄνθρωπος γέγονεν ὁ Υἱός, καλεῖται *καθηγητὴς* καὶ πρωτεύει πάντων τῶν ἀδελφῶν. *Εἷς* καὶ μόνος ὢν *καθηγητής*, καθὸ δὲ φύσει Θεός ἐστι πάντων ὑπερέχει καὶ τῶν ἀοράτων. Εἶτα, διδάσκων μετριοπαθεῖν, ἐπήγαγεν· *ὁ δὲ μείζων ὑμῶν ἔσται ὑμῶν διάκονος.*[1975] Τὸ γὰρ θέλειν ὑπηρετεῖν καταστέλλει τὸ τῆς ὑπεροψίας νόσημα.

Μὴ διδασκάλους ἑαυτοὺς καινῶν δογμάτων χειροτονήσητε. Πάντων γὰρ τῶν καλῶν καὶ θείων μαθημάτων ἐγώ εἰμι *καθηγητὴς* ὑμῖν, *ὁ Χριστός*, καὶ διδάσκαλος, *ὑμεῖς δὲ ἀδελφοί*[1976] καὶ τὰ αὐτὰ παρειλήφατε δόγματα. Καὶ *ἀδελφοὶ* διὰ τοῦτο χρηματίζετε, πατέρα κοινὸν τὸν ἐν οὐρανοῖς Πατέρα κτησάμενοι. Ὥσπερ οὖν ὁ πατέρα ἄλλον παρὰ τὸν *ἐν οὐρανοῖς*[1977] ἐπιζητῶν καὶ καλῶν ἐκπίπτει τῆς θαυμασίας ἐκείνης συγγενείας τῶν ἀδελφῶν, ἀφαιρούμενος δηλονότι καὶ τὴν τῶν δογμάτων ἀδελφότητα, οὕτως καὶ ὁ καθηγητὴν ἑαυτὸν προστησάμενος ἐξοστρακίζει ἑαυτὸν τῆς τῶν δογμάτων ἀδελφότητος καὶ τῆς συγγενείας τῶν ἀδελφῶν, ὧν *ἐν οὐρανοῖς πατὴρ* κοινὸς ὑπάρχει πατήρ. Δείκνυσι δὲ διὰ τούτων ὅτι, εἰ καὶ αὐτός ἐστιν ὁ διδάσκαλος, ἀλλ᾽ οὖν τὰ διδάγματα αὐτοῦ *εἰς υἱοθεσίαν*[1978] ἄγει τοὺς ἀνθρώπους τοῦ Θεοῦ καὶ Πατρός. Καὶ εἰ ἐκεῖνος υἱοποιεῖται τοὺς ἀνθρώπους, ἀλλ᾽ οὖν οὐκ ἄνευ τῆς διδασκαλίας καὶ προσενέξεως τοῦ Υἱοῦ, πανταχοῦ τὸ σύμφωνον καὶ ὁμόγνωμον καὶ ἰσότιμον αὐτοῦ τε καὶ τοῦ Πατρὸς ἀναδεικνύς.

> Οὐχ ἁπλῶς λέγει *μὴ* καλεῖσθε διδάσκαλοι. ἀλλὰ πονηρῶν δογμάτων *μὴ* εἴητε διδάσκαλοι. πάντων γὰρ τῶν καλῶν καὶ θείων μαθημάτων ἐγώ εἰμι *καθηγητής. ὑμεῖς δὲ ἀδελφοὶ* καὶ τὰ αὐτὰ παρειλήφατε δόγματα κοινὸν τὸν ἐν οὐρανοῖς πατέρα κτησάμενοι.[mcdxxxviii]

> Μὴ διδασκάλους ἑαυτοὺς καινῶν δογμάτων χειροτονήσητε. πάντων γὰρ τῶν καλῶν καὶ θείων μαθημάτων ἐγὼ ὑμῖν *ὁ Χριστός* εἰμι *καθηγητὴς* καὶ διδάσκαλος, *ὑμεῖς δὲ ἀδελφοὶ* καὶ τὰ αὐτὰ παρειλήφατε δόγματα καὶ *ἀδελφοὶ* διὰ τοῦτο χρηματίζετε *πατέρα* κοινὸν τὸν *ἐν οὐρανοῖς πατέρα* κτησάμενοι. ὥσπερ οὖν ὁ *πατέρα* ἄλλον παρὰ τὸν *ἐν οὐρανοῖς* ἐπιζητῶν καὶ καλῶν ἐκπίπτει τῆς θαυμασίας ἐκείνης συγγενείας τῶν ἀδελφῶν ἀφαιρούμενος δηλονότι καὶ τὴν τῶν δογμάτων ἀδελφότητα, οὕτως καὶ ὁ τὸν κοινὸν καθηγητὴν παρωσάμενος καὶ ἐκφύλων μαθημάτων καθηγητὴν ἑαυτὸν προστησάμενος

1974 Matt. 23:10.
1975 Matt. 23:11.
1976 Matt. 23:8.
1977 Matt. 23:9.
1978 Eph. 1:5; cf. Rom. 8:15&23; Gal. 4:5.

> ἐξοστρακίζει ἑαυτὸν τῆς τῶν δογμάτων ἀδελφότητος καὶ τῆς συγγενείας τῶν ἀδελφῶν, ὧν ὁ ἐν οὐρανοῖς πατὴρ κοινὸς ὑπάρχει πατήρ. δείκνυσιν δὲ διὰ τούτων, ὅτι, εἰ καὶ αὐτός ἐστιν ὁ διδάσκαλος, ἀλλ' οὖν τὰ διδάγματα αὐτοῦ εἰς υἱοθεσίαν ἄγει τοὺς ἀνθρώπους τοῦ θεοῦ καὶ πατρός. καὶ εἰ ἐκεῖνος υἱοποιεῖται τοὺς ἀνθρώπους, ἀλλ' οὖν οὐκ ἄνευ τῆς διδασκαλίας καὶ προσενέξεως τοῦ υἱοῦ, πανταχοῦ τὸ σύμφωνον καὶ ὁμόγνωμον καὶ ἰσότιμον αὐτοῦ τε καὶ τοῦ πατρὸς ἀναδεικνύς.[mcdxxxix]

Εἷς γάρ ἐστιν ὁ πατὴρ ὑμῶν.[1979] Ἔστι τις | **181r** καὶ ἕτερος μυστικώτερος λόγος. Τοὺς γὰρ τῆς θείας γεννήσεως ἀξιουμένους καὶ *τέκνα Θεοῦ* χρηματίζοντας οὐ χρὴ ἔτι *τέκνα σαρκὸς*[1980] ἀλλ' υἱοὺς Θεοῦ ὀνομάζεσθαι.[mcdxl]

Ὁ δὲ μείζων ὑμῶν ἔσται ὑμῶν διάκονος.[1981] Ἐπειδὴ τοὺς εἰς καινότητα δογμάτων ἐκφερομένους ἔστιν ὡς ἐπίπ‹α›ν[1982] ἰδεῖν κενοδοξίας καὶ ἀλαζονείας πάθ‹ε›ι[1983] ‹εἰς› τοῦτον τὸν ὄλεθρον συμποδιζομένους, ἐπικόπτει λοιπὸν καὶ τὴν ἀρχὴν καὶ ῥίζαν τῆς κενοδοξίας ἀμφιστόμῳ καὶ ἠκονημένῃ μαχαίρᾳ.[1984] Καὶ γὰρ εἰ δόξης πρωτείων ἐρᾷς, τὴν τῶν διακόνων καὶ ὑστέρων τάξιν ἐπιζήτει, τουτέστι ταπεινοφροσύνην ἄσκει. Διὰ ταύτης γὰρ ἔστι τυχεῖν τῶν ὡς ἀληθῶς πρωτείων καὶ τῆς ἀνεκφράστου δόξης. Εἰ δ' οὐδ' οὕτως πείθεσθε καταφρονεῖν δόξης καὶ πρωτείων, γινώσκετε ὅτι εἰς τοὐναντίον τὰ τῆς σπουδῆς ὑμῖν περιτραπήσεται. Ταπεινωθήσεσθε γάρ. Καὶ γὰρ *ὁ ὑψῶν ἑαυτὸν ταπεινωθήσεται.*[1985] Οἱ δὲ τὰς ἐντολάς μου φυλάξαντες καὶ ταπεινωθέντες, ὑψωθήσονται. Πῶς γὰρ *ὁ ταπεινῶν ἑαυτὸν ὑψωθήσεται;*[1986] Ἡ γὰρ ταπείνωσις σύμβολον τῆς τῶν δογμάτων φυλακῆς, ἡ δὲ φυλακὴ σύνδεσμος τῆς συγγενείας τῶν ἀδελφῶν, ἡ δὲ τὸν οὐράνιον πατέρα δείκνυσιν.

> Ἐπειδὴ τοὺς εἰς καινότητα δογμάτων ἐκφερομένους ἔστιν ὡς ἐπίπαν ἰδεῖν κενοδοξίας καὶ ἀλαζονείας ἔρωτι εἰς τοῦτον τὸν ὄλεθρον συμποδιζομένους, ἐκκόπτει λοιπὸν καὶ τὴν ἀρχὴν καὶ ῥίζαν τῆς κενοδοξίας ἀμφιστόμῳ καὶ ἠκονημένῃ μαχαίρᾳ. καὶ γὰρ εἰ δόξης καὶ πρωτείων ἐρᾷς, τὴν τῶν διακόνων καὶ ὑστέρων τάξιν ἐπιζήτει, τοῦτ' ἔστιν ταπεινοφροσύνην ἄσκει. διὰ ταύτης γάρ ἐστιν τυχεῖν τῶν ὡς ἀληθῶς πρωτείων καὶ τῆς ἀνεκφράστου δόξης. εἰ ἐρῶμεν δόξης τυχεῖν καὶ πρωτείων, μισήσωμεν δόξαν καὶ πρωτεῖα. εἰ δὲ οὐδὲ οὕτως πείθεσθε καταφρονεῖν δόξης καὶ πρωτείων, γινώσκετε ὅτι εἰς τοὐναντίον τὰ τῆς σπουδῆς ὑμῖν περιτραπήσεται. ταπεινωθήσεσθε γάρ. καὶ γὰρ ὁ ὑψῶν *ἑαυτὸν ταπεινωθήσεται.* οἱ δὲ τὰς ἐντολάς μου φυλάξαντες καὶ ταπεινωθέντες ὑψωθήσονται. πᾶς γὰρ ὁ ταπεινῶν ἑαυτὸν *ὑψωθήσεται.* ἡ γοῦν ταπείνωσις σύμβολον τῆς τῶν δογμάτων φυλακῆς, ἡ φυλακὴ δὲ σύνδεσμος τῆς συγγενείας τῶν ἀδελφῶν, ἡ δὲ τὸν οὐράνιον πατέρα δείκνυσιν. ἀγαπήσωμεν ἐκ καρδίας τὴν ταπεινοφροσύνην.[mcdxli]

1979 Matt. 23:9.
1980 Rom. 9:8.
1981 Matt. 23:11.
1982 Cod. ἐπίποθῶν.
1983 Cod. πάθοι.
1984 Cf. Heb. 4:12.
1985 Luke, 14:11; 18:14; cf. Matt. 23:11.
1986 Luke, 14:11; 18:14; cf. Matt. 23:12.

Οὐαὶ δὲ ὑμῖν γραμματεῖς καὶ Φαρισαῖοι ὑποκριταί.[1987] Ὑποκριτὰς αὐτοὺς καλεῖ ὡς ἐπαγγελλομένους μὲν εὐλάβειαν, μηδὲν ποιοῦντας τῆς ἐπαγγελίας, ἀλλὰ προφάσει τοῦ προσεύχεσθαι *μακρά*, πλείονα παρὰ *τῶν χηρῶν* ἀπαιτοῦντες. Διὸ ὡς δὴ παίζοντες τοὺς παρόντας καὶ ψευδῶς προσιόντες τῷ Θεῷ, πλεῖον *κρῖμα* λήψονται. | **181v** Εἰ γὰρ πᾶς ὁ ποιῶν κακὸν ἄξιος ἐστὶ τιμωρίας, ὁ ἐν προσχήματι[1988] εὐλαβείας τοῦτο ποιῶν χαλεπωτέρας ἐστὶ τιμωρίας ὑπεύθυνος. Διασύρει δὲ αὐτοὺς καὶ ὡς γαστριμάργους καὶ ἀπηνεῖς, οἳ οὐ τοὺς πλουσίους ἀλλὰ τὰς χήρας σφοδρῶς ἐζημίουν (διό φησι τὸ *κατεσθίετε*), αἷς ἔδει καὶ ἐπιχορηγεῖν. Ἢ τὸ *κατεσθίετε τὰς οἰκίας τῶν χηρῶν*, ἀντὶ τοῦ καρποῦσθε τοὺς οἴκους, ἃ ταῖς χήραις καὶ τοῖς ἀσθενέσιν ἔδει δίδοσθαι κομιζόμενοι.

> Τάχα οὐ τοῖς παροῦσι μόνοις γραμματεῦσι λέγει τὸ *οὐαί*, παντὶ δὲ πλὴν τοῦ γράμματος μηδὲν εἰδότι. ζήτει δέ, εἰ ὥς ἐστι γραμματεύς νομικός, οὕτως ἐστὶ καὶ εὐαγγελικός.[mcdxlii]

> Οὕτως δέ τις διηγήσεται καὶ τὸ *οὐαὶ ὑμῖν, γραμματεῖς καὶ Φαρισαῖοι ὑποκριταί*, ὡς παντὶ εἰρημένον τῷ πλὴν τοῦ γράμματος μηδὲν ἐπισταμένῳ. Ἔνθα ζητήσεις εἰ ὥσπερ νομικὸς γραμματεὺς οὕτως ἐστὶ καὶ εὐαγγελικός, καὶ ὥσπερ τὸν νόμον ἀναγινώσκων καὶ ἀκούων καὶ λέγων *ἅτινά ἐστιν ἀλληγορούμενα*,[1989] οὕτω καὶ τὸ εὐαγγέλιον, ὡς εἰδέναι τηρουμένης τῆς κατὰ τὰ γενόμενα ἱστορίας τὴν ἐπὶ τὰ πνευματικὰ ἄπταιστον ἀναγωγήν, ἵνα μὴ ᾖ μαθήματα *πνευματικὰ πονηρίας*,[1990] ἀλλ᾽ ἐναντίως ἔχοντα πνευματικοῖς πονηρίας πνευματικὰ ἀγαθότητος.[mcdxliii]

ὅτι κλείετε τὴν βασιλείαν.[1991] Οἱ *γραμματεῖς καὶ οἱ Φαρισαῖοι*[1992] εἶχον *τὰς κλεῖς* τῶν θυρῶν *τῆς βασιλείας τοῦ Θεοῦ*,[1993] τουτέστι τὰς θείας γραφάς.

> Οἱ γραμματεῖς καὶ οἱ Φαρισαῖοι εἶχον τὰς κλεῖς τῶν θυρῶν τῆς βασιλείας τοῦ Θεοῦ, τουτέστι τὰς θείας γραφάς.[mcdxliv]

Τοῦτο φησὶ ἐπειδὴ ἐκακοποίουν ἐν προσχήματι[1994] εὐλαβείας. Ὡς γὰρ διδάσκαλοι ὀφείλοντες σῴζειν, οὐ μόνον ἑαυτοὺς ἀπώλλυον ἀπιστοῦντες τῷ Χριστῷ, ἀλλὰ καὶ τοὺς θέλοντας πιστεύειν ἀνέτρεπον, ἔξω τοίνυν μένοντες αὐτοὶ τῆς βασιλείας διὰ τὸ μηδὲν τῶν δεόντων πράττειν καὶ μὴ πιστεύειν εἰς Χριστόν. Διὰ τῆς μοχθηρᾶς αὐτῶν διδασκαλίας κωλύουσιν ἀπατῶντες καὶ τοὺς βουλομένους *εἰσελθεῖν*.

1987 Matt. 23:13; cf. Mark, 12:40; Luke, 20:47.
1988 Cod. προσσχήματι.
1989 Gal. 4:24.
1990 Eph. 6:12.
1991 Matt. 23:14.
1992 Cf. Matt. 23:2.
1993 Cf. Matt. 16:19: τὰς κλεῖδας. Cf. Luke, 11:52.
1994 Cod. προσσχήματι.

Χαλεπὸς ὁ κατὰ τούτων ἔλεγχος, οἳ οὐ μόνον ἔσπευδον τὰς οἰκείας ἀπ‹ο›λλύειν[1995] ψυχάς, ἀλλὰ καὶ τὰς τῶν ὑποχειρίων, μήτε πιστεύοντες εἰς τὸν Χριστὸν δι᾽ οὗ εἰς *βασιλείαν οὐρανῶν* εἰσήεσαν, μήτε ἄλλους συγχωροῦντες πιστεύειν ὡς διδάσκαλοι οἷς εἴωθεν ὁ ὑπήκοος ἀκολουθεῖν λαός. Οὐ μόνον δὲ τοὺς ἀγνοοῦντας οὐκ ἐδίδασκον, ἀλλὰ καὶ τοὺς θέλοντας πιστεύειν ἀπέτρεπον, ὑβρίζοντες τὸν Χριστὸν καὶ δαιμονῶντα καλοῦντες[1996] καὶ τοῖς ὄχλοις παραγγέλλοντες μὴ ἀκούειν αὐτοῦ, | **182r** καὶ ἀποσυναγώγους ποιοῦντες τοὺς ὀνομάζοντας αὐτὸν Χριστόν.[1997]

> Χαλεπὸς ὁ κατὰ τούτων ἔλεγχος, οἳ οὐ μόνον ἔσπευδον τὰς οἰκείας ἀπολλύειν ψυχὰς ἀλλὰ καὶ τὰς τῶν ὑποχειρίων, μήτε πιστεύοντες εἰς τὸν Χριστὸν δι᾽ οὗ εἰς *βασιλείαν οὐρανῶν* εἰσήεσαν μήτε ἄλλους συγχωροῦντες πιστεύειν ὡς διδάσκαλοι οἷς εἴωθεν ὁ ὑπήκοος ἀκολουθεῖν λαός. οὐ μόνον δὲ τοὺς ἀγνοοῦντας οὐκ ἐδίδασκον, ἀλλὰ καὶ τοὺς θέλοντας πιστεύειν ἀπέτρεπον, ὑβρίζοντες τὸν Χριστὸν καὶ δαιμονῶντα καλοῦντες καὶ τοῖς ὄχλοις παραγγέλλοντες μὴ ἀκούειν αὐτοῦ καὶ ἀποσυναγώγους ποιοῦντες τοὺς ὀνομάζοντας αὐτὸν Χριστόν.[mcdxlv]

ὅτι περιάγετε τὴν θάλασσαν καὶ τὴν ξηράν.[1998] Πάλιν *οὐαὶ ὑμῖν*, ὅτι καὶ οὓς μετὰ κόπου κέκτησθε οὐκ ἀγαπᾶτε οὐδὲ φυλάσσετε, ἀλλὰ καὶ χείρους ποιεῖτε. Πέφυκε γὰρ ὁ μαθητής, εἰ φαῦλον κέκτηται τὸν διδάσκαλον, ὑπεραναβαίνειν αὐτοῦ διὰ τὴν ἐπὶ τὸ χεῖρον εὐχέρειαν. Ὅταν, γάρ φησι, ὑμῖν τις πεισθεὶς τὸν βίον ζηλώσῃ, κινδυνεύει. Ἤτοι, ὅταν ἐξ εἰδωλολατρίας δυνηθῆτε μεταρρυθμίσαι τινά, οὐκ ἐᾶτε τοὺς πιστεύσαντας ἀκολουθεῖν τῷ νόμῳ, ἀλλὰ ταῖς ἀνθρωπίναις διδασκαλίαις. Τὸ οὖν δοκοῦν αὐτῶν εἶναι καλόν, ἄχρηστον ἀποφαίνει.
Υἱὸν δὲ γεέννης φησί, ἀντὶ τοῦ αὐτογέενναν ποιεῖτε αὐτόν·

> *Υἱὸν* δὲ *γεέννης* φησί, τουτέστιν, αὐτογέενναν.[mcdxlvi]

ἤτοι υἱὸς *γεέννης* λέγεται τις διὰ τὸ οἰκειότητα τινὰ λαβεῖν πρὸς τὸ τῆς *γεέννης* πῦρ.

> *Υἱὸν γεέννης* φησὶ τὸν ἀπολλύμενον ἐξ εὐπειθείας ὡς δυσσεβείας εἰς τοῦτο κατολισθεῖν.[mcdxlvii]

Διπλότερον δὲ αὐτῶν εἶπεν, ἵνα ἀμφοτέρους φοβήσῃ,

> *Εἶπε δέ, Διπλότερον ὑμῶν*, ἵνα καὶ ἐκείνους φοβήσῃ.[mcdxlviii]

τούς τε διδασκάλους καὶ τοὺς ἀκροατάς.

1995 Cod. ἀπωλλύειν.
1996 Matt. 9:34; 12:24; Mark, 3:22; Luke, 11:15; John, 10:20.
1997 Cf. John, 9:22; 12:42.
1998 Matt. 23:15.

Τοῦτο τοίνυν φησί. Πολλὴν μὲν ἐπιδείκνυσθε σπουδὴν ὥστε τινὰ τῶν ἀλλοτρίων δῆθεν τοῦ Ἰσραὴλ ἐπὶ τὴν εὐσέβειαν ἀγαγεῖν καὶ *ποιῆσαι προσήλυτον*. Ἐπειδ‹ὰ›ν[1999] δὲ οἰκεῖον τοῦ νόμου αὐτὸν καὶ τῆς εὐσεβείας εἶναι δόξητε ποιεῖν, τότε αὐτὸν ἐργάζεσθε *υἱὸν γεέννης*, ὡς μηδὲ λόγον τινὰ ποιεῖσθαι τῆς τῶν προσηκόντων διδασκαλίας. Ὥστε μάτην μέγα φρονεῖτε ἐπὶ τῷ διδάσκειν ἑτέρους.

> Τοῦτο τοίνυν φησί. πολλὴν μὲν ἐπιδείκνυσθε σπουδήν, ὥστε τινὰ τῶν ἀλλοτρίων δῆθεν τοῦ Ἰσραὴλ ἐπὶ τὴν εὐσέβειαν ἀναγαγεῖν καὶ *ποιῆσαι προσήλυτον*. ἐπειδὰν δὲ οἰκεῖον τοῦ νόμου αὐτὸν καὶ τῆς εὐσεβείας εἶναι δόξητε ποιεῖν, τότε αὐτὸν ἐργάζεσθε *υἱὸν γεέννης*, ὡς μηδὲ λόγον τινὰ ποιεῖσθαι τῆς τῶν προσηκόντων διδασκαλίας. ὥστε μάτην μέγα φρονεῖτε ἐπὶ τῷ διδάσκειν ἑτέρους.[mcdxlix]

Τὸν *υἱὸν γεέννης* ἀντὶ τοῦ οὕτως ἔχειν οἰκείως δι' ὧν ἁμαρτάνει πρὸς τὴν γέενναν παρασκευάζετε.[mcdl]

58

182v (ΩΡΙΓΕΝΟΥΣ) *Οὐαὶ ὑμῖν ὁδηγοὶ τυφλοί*.[2000] Τυφλοὺς αὐτοὺς καλεῖ ὡς μὴ θέλοντας τὰ πρέποντα διδάσκειν. Λέγει δὲ καὶ τὰ σφάλματα αὐτῶν τῷ λέγειν ἀδιακρίτως ὃ ἐδόκει αὐτοῖς, ὡς τῶν ἀξιαγάστων μὲν καταφρονοῦντας τῶν δὲ ἐλαχιστοτέρων λόγον ποιουμένους καὶ οὐ τὰ αἴτια τοῦ ἁγιασμοῦ τιμῶντας, ἀλλὰ τὰ δι' ἐκείνων ἁγιασθέντα.

Τὰ γὰρ χρυσᾶ σκεύη, οἷον τὰ *χερουβίμ*, τὴν *στάμνον*, καὶ τὰ ὅμοια,[2001] πρ‹ο›τιμότερα[2002] ᾤοντο τοῦ ναοῦ. Διὸ διασύρει αὐτοὺς ὁ Κύριος, ὅτι οὐ μόνον συνεχώρουν τινὰς ὀμνύειν, ἀλλ' ὅτι καὶ ἔλεγον *οὐδέν ἐστι* τὸ κατὰ τοῦ ναοῦ ὀμνύειν.[2003]

> (Θεοδώρου Ἡρακλείας.) Τὸν *ἐν τῷ ναῷ χρυσόν*, λέγει, τὰ εἰς δόξαν Θεοῦ χρυσᾶ σκεύη ἀνατιθέμενα ἐν τῷ ἱερῷ, ἤτοι τὰ χρυσᾶ Χερουβίμ, ἢ τὴν χρυσῆν στάμνον, τὴν ἔχουσαν τὸ μάννα, ἅπερ προτιμότερα εἶναι ὑπελάμβανον Ἰουδαῖοι τοῦ ναοῦ·[mcdli]

Οὔτε γὰρ ὅρκον ἡγεῖσθε, φησί, τὸ ὀμόσαι *ἐν τῷ ναῷ*, ἀλλὰ τὸ εἰς τὸν χρυσὸν τὸν *ἐν τῷ ναῷ* περικείμενον, ὃς διὰ τοῦτο ἦν αἰδέσιμος, ὅτι εἰσῆλθεν *ἐν τῷ ναῷ*. Καὶ γὰρ τὰ ἐπὶ τοῦ θυσιαστηρίου τιθέμενα ἁγιάζεται ἐπιτιθέμενα αὐτῷ· ἐπὶ δὲ ἡμῶν, τὸ ἐναντίον ἐστί. Τὰ γὰρ ἐπὶ τοῦ λογικοῦ ἡμῶν θυσιαστηρίου[mcdlii] ἐπιτελούμενα καὶ τελούμενα ἁγιάζει καὶ τὴν | **183r** τράπεζαν καὶ τὰ ἐν αὐτῇ σκεύη. Ἀντίτυπα[mcdliii] γάρ εἰσι τοῦ

1999 Cod. ἐπειδ' ἄν.
2000 Matt. 23:16.
2001 Cf. Ex. 16:33; 25:18; Heb. 9:4-5.
2002 Cod. πρωτιμότερα.
2003 Matt. 23:16.

δεσποτικοῦ σώματος. Ἐὰν οὖν τις εὑρέθη ὀμόσας κατὰ τοῦ χρυσοῦ σκεύους ἢ βοὸς προσαχθέντος εἰς θυσίαν, ἐπιορκήσας κατεδικάζετο τὰ ἴσα ἀποτίσαι καθ᾽ ὧν καὶ ὤμοσεν. Εἰ δὲ κατὰ τοῦ ναοῦ ὤμοσεν, ἐπείπερ οὐχ οἷόν τε ἦν ποιῆσαι τὸν ψευσάμενον ἕτερον ναὸν ἢ θυσιαστήριον, ἀπελύετο. Οὗτοι δὲ οἱ ὅρκοι τῶν Φαρισαίων ἦσαν εὑρέματα, οὐ τῆς γραφῆς. Αὕτη γὰρ κατὰ μόνου τοῦ Θεοῦ λέγει ὀμνύειν.

μωροὶ καὶ τυφλοί· τίς γὰρ μείζων ἐστί;[2004] Ἐπειδὴ γὰρ χρυσὸν ἐθαύμαζον τὸν *ἐν τῷ ναῷ* ὑπὲρ τὸν ναόν, διὰ τοῦτο χρυσὸν ὑπὲρ τὸν ναὸν ἐτίμων. Δέον μὴ τὴν ὕλην τιμᾶν, ἀλλὰ τὸ ὄνομα τοῦ Θεοῦ, ὅτι Θεοῦ ὀνόματι *ὁ ναὸς* ἀνέκειτο καὶ *ὁ χρυσὸς* διὰ τὸ ὄνομα τοῦ ναοῦ τίμιος ἀπεδείκνυτο. Καὶ ἐπειδὴ τῶν θυσιῶν ὠρέγοντο διὰ τὰ ἐξ αὐτῶν κέρδη, τὸ δῶρον τοῦ θυσιαστηρίου μᾶλλον ἐδόξαζον, ὃ πρὶν μὲν ἐπιτεθῆναι τῷ θυσιαστηρίῳ πρόβατον ἦν ἢ μόσχος, ἤ τι τοιοῦτον. Διὰ δὲ τὴν ἐπὶ τὸ θυσιαστήριον ἐπίθεσιν, θῦμα ἤδη Θεοῦ καὶ ἦν καὶ ὠνομάζετο καὶ ἅγιον ἐπεδείκνυτο. Καὶ γὰρ τὸ μὲν θυσιαστήριον ἐχρίετο τῷ ἁγιάζοντι χρίσματι, *τὸ* δὲ *δῶρον* δι᾽ ἐκείνου μετελάμβανεν ἁγιασμοῦ. Οὐ μὴν ἐπί γε τῶν πνευματικῶν οὕτως. *Χρυσὸς* γὰρ ἐν *τῷ* νῦν Θεοῦ *ναῷ* τῷ πνευματικῷ, τὸ Πνεῦμα ἐστὶν αὐτό, καὶ *δῶρον* ἐπὶ τοῦ πνευματικοῦ θυσιαστηρίου τὸ σῶμα τοῦ Χριστοῦ. Διόπερ τὰ ἐνόντα μείζονα νῦν ἢ τὰ δεχόμενα. Ταῦτα μὲν γὰρ ἁγιάζει, ἐκεῖνα δὲ ἁγιάζεται.

> (Ἀπολιναρίου.) Ἐπειδὴ γὰρ χρυσὸν ἐθαύμαζον, τὸν ἐν τῷ ναῷ χρυσὸν ὑπὲρ τὸν ναὸν ἐτίμων. δέον μὴ τὴν ὕλην τιμᾷν, ἀλλὰ τὸ ὄνομα, ὅτι Θεοῦ ὀνόματι ὁ ναὸς ἀνέκειτο. καὶ ὁ χρυσὸς δὲ τὸ ὄνομα τοῦ ναοῦ, τίμιος ἀπεδείκνυτο. καὶ ἐπειδὴ τῶν θυσιῶν ὀρέγοντο [sic] διὰ τὰ ἐξ αὐτῶν κέρδη, τὸ δῶρον τοῦ θυσιαστηρίου μᾶλλον ἐδόξαζον, ὃ πρὶν μὲν ἐπιτεθῆναι τῷ θυσιαστηρίῳ, πρόβατον ἦν, ἢ μόσχος, ἢ τί τοιοῦτον. διὰ δὲ τὴν ἐπὶ τὸ θυσιαστήριον ἐπίθεσιν, θυμὸν[mcdliv] ἤδη Θεοῦ ἦν καὶ ὠνομάζετο, καὶ ἅγιον ἐπεδείκνυτο. καὶ γὰρ τὸ μὲν θυσιαστήριον ἐχρίετο τῷ ἁγιάζοντι χρίσματι, τὸ δὲ δῶρον δι᾽ ἐκείνου μετελάμβανεν ἁγιασμοῦ, οὐ μὴν ἐπῆγε τῶν πνευματικῶν οὕτως. χρυσὸς γὰρ ἐν τῷ νῦν ναῷ Θεοῦ τῷ πνευματικῷ, τὸ πνεῦμα ἦν αὐτό, καὶ δῶρον ἐπὶ τοῦ πνευματικοῦ θυσιαστηρίου τὸ σῶμα τοῦ Χριστοῦ. διόπερ τὰ ἐνόντα μείζονα νῦν ἢ τὰ δεχόμενα. ταῦτα μὲν γὰρ ἁγιάζει, ἐκεῖνα δὲ ἁγιάζεται.[mcdlv]

Κατεγινώσκοντο δὲ ὑπὸ τοῦ Κυρίου ὅτι λέγοντες *οὐδέν ἐστι* τὸ κατὰ τοῦ ναοῦ ὀμόσαι εἴθιζον τὸν λαὸν ἀδιαφόρως ἐπιορκεῖν.

> διὸ καὶ κατεγνώσκοντο ὑπὸ τοῦ Κυρίου, ὅτι οὐ μόνον παρεώρουν [sic] τοὺς ὀμνύοντας, καὶ συνεχώρουν αὐτοὺς ὀμνύειν, ἀλλ᾽ ὅτι ἔλεγον οὐδέν ἐστι τὸ κατὰ τοῦ ναοῦ ὀμόσαι, καὶ εἴθιζον τὸν λαὸν ἀδιαφόρως ἐπιορκεῖν κατὰ τοῦτο.[mcdlvi]

| **183v** Ἔχει δέ τι ὁ λόγος καὶ αἴνιγμα κατ᾽ αὐτῶν, ἀνθ᾽ ὧν τὸν Χριστὸν οὐ δεχόμενοι, τὴν ἀλήθειαν,[2005] τὸν Μωϋσέα καὶ τοὺς δι᾽ αὐτοῦ τύπους τιμιωτέρους ἔκρινον,

---

2004 Matt. 23:17.
2005 Cf. John, 14:6.

τὸν μὲν Χριστὸν τὸν ἁγιάζοντα Μωϋσέα ἀθετοῦντες, ἐπαινοῦντες δὲ τὸν νόμον, ὅσπερ ἐπαινετὸς οὐχ ὅτι ἔχει τὰς *σκιὰς*[2006] ‹καὶ› τοὺς τύπους,[mcdlvii] ἀλλ᾽ ὅτι προ‹α›νατυποῖ[2007] τῆς ἐν Χριστῷ λατρείας τὸ ἀληθὲς μυστήριον, ὡς καλὸς *ὁ χρυσὸς* διὰ τὸν ἁγιάζοντα αὐτὸν ναὸν καὶ καλὸς ὁ οὐρανὸς διὰ τὸν ἁγιάζοντα αὐτὸν Θεὸν καὶ ἐνοικοῦντα *ἐν αὐτῷ*.[2008]

> ἔχει δὲ ὁ λόγος αἴνιγμα κατ᾽ αὐτῶν, ἀνθ᾽ ὧν τὸν Χριστὸν οὐ δεχόμενοι τὴν ἀλήθειαν, τὸν Μωϋσέα καὶ τοὺς δι᾽ αὐτοῦ τύπους, τιμιωτέρους ἔκρινον τοῦ Χριστοῦ. τὸν μὲν Χριστὸν[mcdlviii] τὸν ἁγιάζοντα Μωσέα ἀθετοῦντες, ἐπαινοῦντες δὲ τὸν νόμον, ὥσπερ ἦν καὶ ἐπαινετός. οὐχ ὅτι ἔχει τὰς σκιὰς τοὺς τύπους, ἀλλ᾽ ὅτι προανατυποῖ τῆς ἐν Χριστῷ λατρείας τὸ ἀληθὲς μυστήριον. ὡς καλὸς ὁ χρυσός, διὰ τὸν ἁγιάζοντα αὐτὸν ναόν, καὶ καλὸς ὁ οὐρανός, διὰ τὸν ἁγιάζοντα αὐτὸν Θεόν, καὶ ἐνοικοῦντα ἐν αὐτῷ.[mcdlix]

Ὅτι ἀποδεκατοῦτε τὸ ἡδύοσμον.[2009] Πάλιν σκώπτει αὐτοὺς ὡς ἀνοήτους, τῶν μὲν μειζόνων ἐντολῶν μὴ ποιουμένους λόγον, ἐν δὲ τοῖς μικροῖς ζητοῦντας τὴν ἀκρίβειαν. Οὔτε γὰρ τοῦ κυμίνου τῆς δεκάτης παραχωροῦντες, ὡς τοῦ νόμου κελεύοντος, διὰ φιλοκέρδειαν τῆς τοῦ δικαίου ἐπιμελείας οὐδένα ἐποιοῦντο λόγον οὐ κρίνοντες τὸ ὀρθόν, οὐδὲ συμπαθοῦντες, οὐδὲ πίστιν ἔχοντες εἰς Θεὸν γνησίαν.

> Ἀκριβεῖς μέν ἐστε, φησίν, τὰς δεκάτας ἀπαιτεῖν ὡς μηδὲ *τοῦ ἡδυόσμου ἢ τοῦ κυμίνου* τῆς δεκάτης παραχωρεῖν, τῆς δὲ τοῦ δικαίου ἐπιμελείας οὐδένα ποιεῖσθε λόγον καὶ τῆς περὶ τὸν πλησίον ἀγάπης καὶ τοῦ βεβαίαν ἔχειν περὶ τὸ θεῖον τὴν *πίστιν*, ἅπερ δεῖ ποιεῖν καὶ οὕτως, εἰ ἄρα, τὰ μικρά.[mcdlx]

ταῦτα ἔδει ποιῆσαι.[2010] Εἰπὼν δέ, *ταῦτα ἔδει ποιῆσαι κἀκεῖνα μὴ ἀφιέναι*, οὐχ ὡς προτρεπόμενος ἡμᾶς ἐπὶ τὴν νομικὴν σμικρολογίαν ταῦτά φησι, ἀλλ᾽ ἐκ τῶν σωματικῶν ἐπὶ τὰς ψυχικὰς ἀρετὰς ἀνάγων. Διὸ καὶ ἐλέους καὶ κρίσεως ἐμνήσθη, ἅπερ ἐστὶ συνεκτικὰ τῆς ζωῆς ἡμῶν. Διὰ μὲν γὰρ τοῦ ἐλεεῖν καὶ ἡμεῖς ἐλεούμεθα· διὰ δὲ τῆς κρίσεως βοηθεῖν διδασκόμεθα τοῖς ἐπηρεαζομένοις· διὰ δὲ τῆς πίστεως, μὴ εἶναι ἀπατεῶνες. Ὡς δὲ ἄγαν χαλεποὺς καὶ μηδὲν εἰδότας τῶν δεόντων, καλεῖ αὐτοὺς *ὁδηγοὺς τυφλούς*,[2011] μὴ ἀνεχομένους διορθωθῆναι, ἀλλὰ καὶ ἄλ | **184r** λους ἐπιχειροῦντας διδάσκειν καὶ οἰομένους πάντα εἰδέναι.[mcdlxi]
Τὸ τοίνυν παρατρέχειν τὰ μεγάλα καταπίνειν *τὴν κάμηλόν* ἐστιν. Τὸ δὲ ζητεῖν τὰ λεπτὰ καὶ εὐτελῆ καὶ περὶ ταῦτα ‹ἀ›σχολ‹εῖ›σθαι[2012] ἄγαν διυλίζειν ἐστὶ *τὸν κώνωπα*.[2013]

2006 Cf. Col. 2:17; Heb. 8:5; 10:1.
2007 Cod. προ ἀνατυποι.
2008 Cf. Matt. 23:20.
2009 Matt. 23:23.
2010 Matt. 23:23.
2011 Matt. 23:24; cf. Matt. 15:14; 23:16; Luke, 6:39; Rom. 2:19.
2012 Cod. ἠσχολῆσθαι.
2013 Matt. 23:24.

> νῦν δὲ τοὐναντίον. περὶ μὲν τὰ εὐτελῆ τοῦ νόμου ἄγαν ἀσχολεῖσθε ὡς φιλοκερδεῖς, ὅπερ ἐστὶ *διυλίζειν τὸν κώνωπα*, τὰ δὲ μεγάλα παραπέμπεσθε, ὅ ἐστι *τὴν κάμηλον καταπίνειν.*[mcdlxii]

Τὰ οὖν μικρὰ διὰ τὰ μεγάλα νενομοθέτηται. διὸ ἐκείνων ἀμελουμένων οὐδὲ τὰ μικρὰ οὐδὲν ὠφελεῖ.

Ὅτι καθαρίζετε τὸ ἔξωθεν τοῦ ποτηρίου.[2014] Τοῦτό φησι ἐπειδὴ δι᾽ ἀνθρωπίνας παραδόσεις ἔπλυνον *τὰ ποτήρια καὶ τὰς παροψίδας* (ἤτοι τοὺς πίνακας), ἐμόλυνον δὲ αὐτὰ διὰ τῶν *ἔσωθεν* ἐπιβαλλομένων αὐτοῖς, *οἶνον ἐκ συκοφαντιῶν* πίνοντες[mcdlxiii] καὶ *ἐξ ἁρπαγῆς* ἐσθίοντες. Μὴ κτήσῃ οὖν οἶνον ἐξ ἀδικίας καὶ γίνεται ὁ πινόμενος οἶνος ὁ *ἔσωθεν τοῦ ποτηρίου* καθαρός.

> Ἀνθρωπίναις δὲ παραδόσεσιν ἀκολουθοῦντες ἔπλυνον *τὰ ποτήρια καὶ τὰς παροψίδας*, ἐμόλυνον δὲ αὐτὰ διὰ τῶν *ἔσωθεν* ἐπιβαλλομένων, ἐν αὐτοῖς οἶνον ἐκ συκοφαντιῶν πίνοντες καὶ *ἐξ ἁρπαγῆς* ἐσθίοντες. διὸ ἀπέχεσθαι τούτων παραγγέλλει, *ἵνα* δι᾽ ὧν [sic][mcdlxiv] καθαρῶν πίνουσιν οἶνον οὐκ *ἐξ ἀδικίας* πορισθέντα καθαρὸν *γένηται καὶ τὸ* πινόμενον, ὅπερ *ἔσωθέν* ἐστι *τοῦ ποτηρίου.*[mcdlxv]

> Οἱ τὴν σωματικὴν ἀρετὴν περιποιούμενοι εἰς τὸ ἐμφανῆ, τὴν δὲ τοῦ ἔσω ἔχοντες ἀκάθαρτον, ὅμοιοι εἰσὶ τῶν πλυνόντων *τὸ ἔξωθεν τοῦ ποτηρίου*, καὶ *διϋλίζοντες τὸν κώνωπα.*[mcdlxvi]

> (Ὠριγένους.) Οἱ τὴν σωματικὴν ἀρετὴν περιποιούμενοι εἰς τὸ ἐμφανῆ, τὴν δὲ τοῦ ἔσω ἔχοντες ἀκάθαρτον, ὅμοιοι εἰσὶ τῶν πλυνόντων *τὸ ἔξωθεν τοῦ ποτηρίου*, καὶ *διυλίζοντες τὸν κώνωπα.*[mcdlxvii]

Ὡς γὰρ ὀφείλει, φησί, τὰ ποτήρια καὶ οἱ πίνακες *ἔσωθεν* καὶ *ἔξωθεν* εἶναι καθαρά, καὶ ὑμεῖς οὐ μόνον σχήματι ὀφείλετε φαίνεσθαι θεοσεβεῖς, ἀλλὰ καὶ *ἔσωθεν* ἐν *καρδίᾳ*[2015] εἶναι καθαροί. Οὐδεμία γὰρ βλάβη γίνεται ἐκ τοῦ τῶν σωματικῶν καταφρονεῖν ἀκαθαρσιῶν, φροντίζειν δὲ δεῖ τῶν τῆς ψυχῆς καθάρσεων. Οὐδὲ γὰρ περὶ *ποτηρίου* λέγει, ἀλλὰ τὸ μὲν *ἔξωθεν* λέγει, τὸ σῶμα, τὸ δὲ ἔσω, τὴν ψυχήν. Ὃ οὖν λέγει, τοιοῦτόν ἐστι. Μόνον σπουδάζετε τοῖς ἀνθρώποις δίκαιοι φαίνεσθαι οὐδὲν τῶν τῆς ψυχῆς ἐπιμελούμενοι, ὡς οἱ *τὸ ἔξωθεν τῆς παροψίδος καὶ τοῦ ποτηρίου* πλύνοντες, ρυπαρὰ δὲ βρώματα τιθέντες.

Καθάρισον πρῶτον.[2016] Πολὺ γὰρ κάλλιον καθαίρει τὸ σκεῦος ἡ δικαιοσύνη παρὰ τὸ ὕδωρ, ὥσπερ καὶ ἐπ᾽ αὐτῶν τῶν ἀνθρώπων εἶχε. Καθαροὶ τὰ σώματα ἦσαν οἱ δίκαιοι | **184v** παρὰ ‹τοὺς› τοῖς ὕδασι καθαιρομένους, ὥς φησι ὁ Δαυίδ· *νίψομαι ἐν ἀθώοις τὰς χεῖράς μου.*[2017][mcdlxviii] Ὥστε σύμφωνα τοῖς τοῦ νόμου καὶ τὰ τοῦ Κυρίου.

2014 Matt. 23:25.
2015 Cf. Matt. 5:8.
2016 Matt. 23:26.
2017 Psalm 25:6.

> Πολὺ γὰρ κάλλιον καθαίρει τὸ σκεῦος ἡ δικαιοσύνη παρὰ τὸ ὕδωρ, ὥσπερ καὶ ἐπ᾽ αὐτῶν τῶν ἀνθρώπων εἶχε. καθαροὶ τὰ σώματα ἦσαν οἱ δίκαιοι παρὰ τοὺς τοῖς ὕδασι καθαιρομένους, ὥς φησιν ὁ Δαβίδ. *νίψομαι ἐν ἀθῴοις τὰς χεῖράς μου*, ὥστε σύμφωνα τοῖς τοῦ νόμου καὶ τὰ τοῦ κυρίου.[mcdlxix]

Διὰ συμβόλων ὁ νόμος ἐδίδασκε τὴν ἐν τῶ νόμῳ καθαρότητα. Καὶ ἡ κατὰ Ἰουδαίους συνήθεια τοιαύτη τις ἦν ἐκ τῶν αὐτῶν παραδόσεων, ἀποκλύζειν τὰ ποτήρια καὶ τὸ τοῦ ὄψου σκεῦος, ἵνα καθαρὸν ἐκ τῆς τῶν ἁμαρτωλῶν ἐπαφῆς τοῦτο κατέχοιεν καὶ οὕτως τὴν τῶν ἁμαρτωλῶν φεύγοιεν κοινωνίαν, ὡς μηδὲ ὧν ἐφήψαντο σκευῶν ἐφάπτεσθαι. Πολλῷ δὲ μᾶλλον παρεσκευάζοντο διὰ τῶν τοιούτων ἐθῶν φεύγειν τὴν ἁμαρτίαν. Οἱ δὲ τὰ μὲν ἔθη αὐτὰ ἐφύλαττον ἐπιμελῶς, αὐτοὶ δὲ ἁρπάζοντες καὶ βιαίως κερδαίνοντες βδελυροὶ διὰ τῶν ἔργων ἐγίνοντο.

> Διὰ συμβόλων ὁ νόμος ἐδίδασκεν τὴν ἐν τῷ βίῳ καθαρότητα. καὶ ἡ κατὰ Ἰουδαίους συνήθεια τοιαύτη τις ἦν, ἐκ τῶν ἀρχαίων παραδόσεων ἀποκλύζειν τὰ ποτήρια καὶ τὸ τοῦ ὄψου σκεῦος, ἵνα καθαρὸν ἐκ τῆς τῶν ἁμαρτωλῶν ἐπαφῆς τοῦτο κατέχοιεν καὶ οὕτως τὴν τῶν ἁμαρτωλῶν φεύγοιεν κοινωνίαν, ὡς μηδὲ ὧν ἐφήψαντο σκευῶν ἐφάπτεσθαι. πολλῷ δὲ μᾶλλον παρεσκευάζοντο διὰ τῶν τοιούτων ἐθῶν αὐτὴν φεύγειν τὴν ἁμαρτίαν. οἱ δὲ τὰ μὲν ἔθη ταῦτα ἐφύλαττον ἐπιμελῶς, αὐτοὶ δὲ ἁρπάζοντες καὶ βιαίως κερδαίνοντες βδελυροὶ διὰ τῶν ἔργων ἐγίνοντο. ταύτην οὖν, φησίν, ἀπόφυγε τὴν ἀδικίαν, ὦ *Φαρισαῖε τυφλέ*[2018] καὶ μηδὲ ἃ πράττεις ὁρῶν. καὶ καθαρά ἐστί σοι τὰ ἐν τῷ ποτηρίῳ καὶ ἐν τῇ παροψίδι μὴ ἐξ ἀδικίας λαμβανόμενα. πολὺ κάλλιον καθαίρει τὸ σκεῦος ἡ δικαιοσύνη παρὰ τὸ ὕδωρ.[mcdlxx]

ὅτι παρομοιάζετε τάφοις.[2019] Καὶ αὕτη ἡ παραβολὴ ὁμοία τῇ προλαβούσῃ τὸ δυσῶδες αὐτῶν διαγράφουσα. *ἔξωθεν* μὲν γὰρ ἐσχηματίζοντο εὐλάβειαν, *ἔσωθεν* δὲ ἔγεμον ἀσεβείας, ὅπερ ἐστὶν ὑποκριτῶν. Ταλανίζει τοίνυν αὐτοὺς ὡς κενοδόξους καὶ ἐλέγχει αὐτοὺς *ἀκαθαρσίας* γέμειν διὰ τὴν προσοῦσαν αὐτοῖς ὑπόκρισιν,[mcdlxxi] σπουδάζοντας μὲν εὐπρεπεῖς φανῆναι τοῖς ἀνθρώποις, μὴ φροντίζοντας δὲ ἀρετῆς.

> Καὶ αὕτη ἡ παραβολὴ ὁμοία τῇ προλαβούσῃ τὸ δυσῶδες αὐτῶν διεγράψατο. *ἔξωθεν* μὲν γὰρ ἐσχηματίζοντο εὐλάβειαν, *ἔσωθεν* δὲ ἔγεμον ἀσεβείας. ὅπερ ἐστὶν ὑποκριτῶν. Ταλανίζει τοίνυν αὐτοὺς ὡς κενοδόξους καὶ ἐλέγχει αὐτοὺς *ἀκαθαρσίας* γέμειν διὰ τὴν προσοῦσαν αὐτοῖς ὑπόκρισιν, σπουδάζοντας μὲν εὐπρεπεῖς φανῆναι τοῖς ἀνθρώποις, μὴ φροντίζοντας δὲ ἀρετῆς.[mcdlxxii]

Εἰς κενοδοξίαν αὐτοὺς σκώπτει τάφους κεκονιαμένους καλῶν. Διὰ τοῦτο πᾶσιν ἐπιλέγει, *ὑποκριταί*, ὅπερ ἐστὶν αἴτιον πάντων τῶν κακῶν καὶ ἀπωλείας αὐτοῖς ὑπόθεσις. Οὐχ ἁπλῶς δὲ τάφους κεκονιαμένους ἐκάλεσεν, ἀλλὰ καὶ *ἀκαθαρσίας* γέμοντας καὶ ὑποκρίσεως, δεικνὺς τὴν αἰτίαν δι᾽ ἣν οὐκ ἐπίστευσαν. Τάχα δὲ οὐχ ὁ Κύρι | **185r** ος

2018 Matt. 23:26.
2019 Matt. 23:27.

μόνον, ἀλλὰ καὶ οἱ προφῆται συνεχῶς ἐγκαλοῦσιν, ὅτι *μεστοὶ* ἦσαν *ὑποκρίσεως καὶ ἀνομίας*,[2020] ὅτι ἁρπάζουσιν, ὅτι οὐ κρίνουσιν οἱ ἄρχοντες αὐτῶν κατὰ τὸν τοῦ δικαίου λόγον. Καὶ πανταχοῦ εὕροις ἂν τὰς μὲν θυσίας ἐκβαλλομένας, ταῦτα δὲ ἐπιζητούμενα. Ὥστε οὐδὲν ξένον, οὐδὲ καινόν, οὔτε τὸ τῆς νομοθεσίας, οὔτε τὸ τῆς κατηγορίας. Ἀλλαχοῦ γὰρ ὁ προφήτης καὶ ἐπέτεινε τοῦτο εἰρημένον, οὐχ ἁπλῶς τάφον καλέσας, ἀλλὰ τάφον ἀνεῳγμένον[2021] τὸν λάρυγγα αὐτῶν.[mcdlxxiii]

Εἰς κενοδοξίαν αὐτοὺς σκώπτει τάφους κεκονιαμένους καλῶν. διὰ τοῦτο πᾶσιν ἐπιλέγει, *ὑποκριταί*, ὅπερ ἐστὶν αἴτιον πάντων τῶν κακῶν καὶ ἀπωλείας αὐτοῖς ὑπόθεσις. οὐχ ἁπλῶς δὲ τάφους κεκονιαμένους ἐκάλεσεν, ἀλλὰ καὶ *ἀκαθαρσίας* γέμοντας καὶ ὑποκρίσεως, δεικνὺς τὴν αἰτίαν δι᾽ ἣν οὐκ ἐπίστευσαν. τάχα δὲ οὐχ ὁ κύριος μόνον ἀλλὰ καὶ οἱ προφῆται συνεχῶς ἐγκαλοῦσιν ὅτι *μεστοὶ* ἦσαν *ὑποκρίσεως καὶ ἀνομίας*, ὅτι ἁρπάζουσιν, ὅτι οὐ κρίνουσιν οἱ ἄρχοντες αὐτῶν κατὰ τὸν τοῦ δικαίου λόγον, καὶ πανταχοῦ εὕροις ἂν τὰς μὲν θυσίας ἐκβαλλομένας, ταῦτα δὲ ἐπιζητούμενα. ὥστε οὐδὲν ξένον οὐδὲ καινόν, οὔτε τὸ τῆς νομοθεσίας, οὔτε τὸ τῆς κατηγορία. ἀλλαχοῦ γὰρ ὁ προφήτης καὶ ἐπέτεινε τοῦτο ‹τὸ› εἰσηγμένον οὐχ ἁπλῶς τάφον καλέσαι, ἀλλὰ τάφον ἀνεῳγμένον τὸν λάρυγγα αὐτῶν.[mcdlxxiv]

Εἶτα πάλιν εἰς κενοδοξίαν αὐτοὺς σκώπτει, τάφους κεκονιαμένους καλῶν, καὶ πᾶσιν ἐπιλέγων, *Ὑποκριταί*. ὃ πάντων αἴτιόν ἐστι τῶν κακῶν, καὶ ἀπωλείας αὐτοῖς ὑπόθεσις. Οὐχ ἁπλῶς δὲ τάφους κεκονιαμένους ἐκάλεσεν, ἀλλὰ καὶ *ἀκαθαρσίας* γέμειν καὶ ὑποκρίσεως ἔφησε. Ταῦτα δὲ ἔλεγε, δεικνὺς τὴν αἰτίαν, δι᾽ ἣν οὐκ ἐπίστευσαν, ὅτι μεστοὶ ἦσαν ὑποκρίσεως καὶ ἀνομίας. Ταῦτα δὲ οὐχ ὁ Χριστὸς μόνον, ἀλλὰ καὶ οἱ προφῆται συνεχῶς ἐγκαλοῦσιν, ὅτι ἁρπάζουσιν, ὅτι οὐ κρίνουσιν οἱ ἄρχοντες αὐτῶν κατὰ τὸν τοῦ δικαίου λόγον. καὶ πανταχοῦ εὕροις ἂν τὰς μὲν θυσίας ἐκβαλλομένας, ταῦτα δὲ ἐπιζητούμενα. Ὥστε οὐδὲν ξένον, οὐδὲ καινόν, οὔτε τῆς νομοθεσίας, οὔτε τῆς κατηγορίας. ἀλλ᾽ οὐδὲ τὸ τῆς εἰκόνος τοῦ τάφου. Μέμνηται γὰρ αὐτῆς ὁ προφήτης, οὐδὲ αὐτὸς ἁπλῶς τάφον καλέσας, ἀλλὰ *Τάφον ἀνεῳγμένον τὸν λάρυγγα αὐτῶν*.[mcdlxxv]

59

185r (ΩΡΙΓΕΝΟΥΣ) Ὀστέα ἐστὶ νεκρὰ[2022] δύναμις τῆς ἁμαρτίας, ἔργα ἁμαρτιῶν.

Ὀστέα εἰσὶ νεκρὰ δύναμις τῆς ἁμαρτίας, ἔργα ἁμαρτιῶν.[mcdlxxvi]

(Ὠριγένους.) Ὀστέα εἰσὶ νεκρά, δύναμις τῆς ἁμαρτίας, ἔργα ἁμαρτιῶν. Τίνος ἕνεκεν καταγινώσκει τῶν φονευσάντων τοὺς προφήτας; ποῖον γὰρ ἔγκλημα υἱὸν εἶναι αὐτῶν ὡς υἱῶν ὄντων ἀνδροφόνου; ἂν μὴ κοινωνῇ τῇ γνώμῃ τοῦ πατρός, οὐδέν. ὅθεν διὰ τὴν αἰτίαν ταύτην, ἐκ τούτου τὴν κατὰ συγγένειαν κακίαν αἰνιττόμενος. διὰ τοῦτο γὰρ καὶ ἐπήγαγεν, *ὄφεις, γεννήματα ἐχιδνῶν*, ὡσανεὶ ἔλεγεν, ὅτι ὥσπερ ἐκεῖνα ἔοικε τοῖς γονεῦσι

2020 Matt. 23:28.
2021 Psalms 5:10; 13:3, quoted in Rom. 3:13.
2022 Matt. 23:27.

κατὰ τὴν ἰοῦ λύμην, οὕτω καὶ ὑμεῖς τοῖς πατράσι κατὰ τὸ φονικόν, πονηροὶ παῖδες, πονηρῶν πατέρων ὄντες. τὸ δὲ *καὶ ὑμεῖς πληρώσατε τὸ μέτρον τῶν πατέρων ὑμῶν*, οὐκ ἐπιτάττων τοῦτο φησίν, ἀλλὰ προαναφωνῶν τὸ ἐσόμενον, τουτέστι τὴν ἑαυτοῦ σφαγήν. καὶ δεικνὺς μείζονα τολμῶντας. οἱ μὲν γὰρ τοὺς προφήτας ἀπέκτειναν, οὗτοι δὲ τὸν δεσπότην τῶν προφητῶν. διὸ καὶ ἐπάγει. *πῶς φύγητε ἀπὸ τῆς κρίσεως τῆς γεέννης*, ἐκείνους μιμούμενοι τοὺς τὰ τοιαῦτα τετολμηκότας. εἶπε δὲ τοῦτο, φόβον πολὺν αὐτοῖς ἐντιθών.[mcdlxxvii]

Ὅτι οἰκοδομεῖτε τοὺς τάφους τῶν προφητῶν.[2023] Πάλιν ταλανίζει αὐτούς, οὐχ ὅτι οἰκοδομοῦσι *τοὺς τάφους τῶν προφητῶν*, οὐδ᾽ ὅτι καταγινώσκουσι *τῶν πατέρων* ἑαυτῶν,[2024] ἀλλ᾽ ὅτι, προσποιούμενοι ταῦτα, χείρονα ἐκείνων ἐποίουν. *Κοσμεῖτε*, οὖν φησι, *τῶν προφητῶν* τοὺς τάφους, οὐ τιμῶντες αὐτούς, ἀλλὰ τὴν τῶν φονευσάντων αὐτοὺς ἐκπομπεύοντες τόλμαν καὶ ὁμολογοῦντες ἑαυτοὺς υἱοὺς εἶναι τῶν φονευτῶν,[2025] ἵνα μὴ σβεσθῇ τὰ τολμηθέντα ἐκείνοις ἀφανισθέντων τῶν τάφων τῶν ἀναιρεθέντων ἐξ αὐτῶν καὶ ‹ἵνα φανῇ ὅτι› οὐκ ἦν ‹ὑμῖν› αὐτοῖς τοῦτο ἔγκλημα εἰ μὴ καὶ αὐτοὶ τῆς ἐκείνων ἦσαν προαιρέσεως.

(Ὠριγένους.) Τάφους δὲ κεκονιαμένους καλῶν, περὶ τῆς αὐτῆς αὐτοὺς σκώπτεσθαι δοξομανίας, ἔτι δὲ καὶ τὸ πάντων αἴτιον τῶν κακῶν ἐπιλέγει αὐτοῖς. *ὑποκριταί*, ὅπερ ἐστὶν ἀπωλείας ὑπόθεσις. οὐχ ἁπλῶς δὲ τάφους κεκονιαμένους αὐτοὺς ἐκάλεσεν, ἀλλὰ καὶ μεστοὺς ὑποκρίσεως καὶ ἀνομίας, ὅπερ δηλοῖ, ἔξωθεν μὲν αὐτοὺς καλλωπίζεσθαι, πάσης δὲ ἁμαρτίας ἔνδον ὑπάρχειν πεπληρωμένους. καθὼς καὶ νῦν εἰσὶ πολλοί, τῶν μὲν ἔξωθεν καθαρισμῶν πολλὴν τὴν φροντίδα ποιούμενοι, τῶν δὲ κατὰ ψυχὴν μηδεμίαν, ἀλλὰ σκωλήκων καὶ ἰχώρων καὶ δυσωδίας ἀφάτου. ἐπιθυμιῶν ἀτόπων, λέγω, καὶ πονηρῶν τὴν ψυχὴν ἐμπιπλῶντες. εἰπὼν δὲ ὅτι *οἰκοδομεῖτε τοὺς τάφους τῶν προφητῶν*, καὶ τὰ ἑξῆς, οὐχὶ ὡς αὐτῶν τῶν πραγμάτων οἰκοδομούντων τοῦτο εἶπεν, ἀλλὰ τὴν γνώμην αὐτῶν ἐνδιαβάλλων, ὅτι περ καὶ δι᾽ ὧν λέγουσι καταγνώσκειν τῶν πατέρων αὐτῶν, *ὅτι εἰ ἦμεν ἐν ταῖς ἡμέραις αὐτῶν, οὐκ ἂν ἦμεν αὐτῶν κοινωνοὶ ἐν τῷ αἵματι τῶν προφητῶν*, χείρονα πράττοντες αὐτοί. ἐποίουν δὲ τοῦτο οὐ διὰ τιμὴν τῶν σφαγέντων προφητῶν καὶ δικαίων, ἀλλὰ μᾶλλον ἐκπομπεύοντες ταῖς σφαγαῖς, μήποτε μαρανθῇ τῆς τοσαύτης μνήμης ἡ τόλμη.[mcdlxxviii]

Τὴν κατὰ πονηρίαν συγγένειαν αἰνίττεται.[mcdlxxix]

(Ὠριγένους) *Υἱοὶ τῶν φονευσάντων*, τὴν κατὰ πονηρίαν συγγένειαν αἰνίττεται.[mcdlxxx]

Ἐπειδὴ γὰρ εἶπεν, Ὥστε μαρτυρεῖτε ἑαυτοῖς, ὅτι υἱοί ἐστε τῶν φονευσάντων τοὺς προφήτας, δηλῶν ὅτι τὴν κατὰ πονηρίαν συγγένειαν λέγει.[mcdlxxxi]

Οὐ προστάττων τοῦ ποιῆσαι λέγει τὸ *πληρώσατε*, ἀλλὰ σύμβολον αἰνίττεται.[mcdlxxxii]

2023 Matt. 23:29.
2024 Matt. 23:30.
2025 Matt. 23:31.

> (᾽Ωριγένους) Οὐ προστάττων τοῦ ποιῆσαι λέγει τὸ *πληρώσατε*, ἀλλὰ σύμβολον αἰνίττεται.[mcdlxxxiii]

> *Καὶ ὑμεῖς πληρώσατε τὸ μέτρον τῶν πατέρων ὑμῶν.* οὐκ ἐπιτάττων, ἀλλὰ προαναφωνῶν τὸ ἐσόμενον. τουτέστι, τὴν ἑαυτοῦ σφαγήν.[mcdlxxxiv]

60

186v (ΩΡΙΓΕΝΟΥΣ) *Ἀπὸ τοῦ αἵματος Ἄβελ τοῦ δικαίου.*[2026] Εὐκαίρως ὧδε τοῦ Ἄβελ μέμνηται, ἐπειδὴ καὶ ἐκεῖνος διὰ φθόνον ἀνῃρέθη.

> εὐκαίρως δὲ αὐτοὺς καὶ τοῦ Ἄβελ ἀνέμνησεν, ὅτι περ διὰ φθόνον καὶ ὁ εἰς αὐτὸν φόνος γέγονε.[mcdlxxxv]

Ζαχαρίαν δὲ τὸν Ἰωδαὲ λέγει·[mcdlxxxvi] διώνυμος γὰρ ἦν. Εὑρίσκομεν δὲ καὶ Ἀζαρίαν ἐν τοῖς Παραλειπομένοις, ἱερέα φονευθέντα μεταξὺ τοῦ ναοῦ καὶ τοῦ θυσιαστηρίου ὑπὸ Ἰωὰς βασιλέως,[2027]

> Τίς δὲ ἐστὶν οὗτος ὁ Ζαχαρίας, περὶ οὗ εἶπεν *ἕως τοῦ αἵματος Ζαχαρίου υἱοῦ Βαραχίου*; οἱ μὲν τὸν Ἰωάννου πατέρα φασίν, οἱ δὲ τὸν προφήτην, οἱ δὲ ἕτερον τινὰ διώνυμον ἱερέα, ὃν καὶ Ἰωδαὲ φησὶν ἡ Γραφή.[mcdlxxxvii]

ὃν Ἰώσηππος Ζαχαρίαν καλεῖ ἐξελληνίζων τὸ ὄνομα.[mcdlxxxviii]

61

186v (ΩΡΙΓΕΝΟΥΣ) Τινὲς δὲ Ζαχαρίαν υἱὸν τοῦ Βαραχίου οὐ τὸν ἐν τοῖς δώδεκα τεταγμένον φασὶ ἐνταῦθα εἰρῆσθαι, ἀλλὰ τὸν πατέρα Ἰωάννου τοῦ βαπτιστοῦ. Οὐ δύνανται γὰρ τὸν ἐν τοῖς δώδεκα τεταγμένον Ζαχαρίαν ἀνῃρηκέναι οἱ νῦν ὑπὸ τοῦ Σωτῆρος ὀνειδιζόμενοι· ἀλλ᾽ εἰκός, καθώς φησι‹ν›[2028] Ἰώσηππος, Ζαχαρίαν νῦν λέγεσθαι τὸν Ἰωάννου πατέρα. Περὶ οὗ ἀπὸ μὲν γραφῆς δεῖξαι οὐκ ἔχομεν, οὐδ᾽ ὅτι υἱὸς *Βαραχίου* ἦν, οὐδ᾽ ὅτι οἱ γραμματεῖς καὶ οἱ Φαρισαῖοι ἐφόνευσαν αὐτὸν *μεταξὺ τοῦ ναοῦ καὶ τοῦ θυσιαστηρίου*. Ἀλλ᾽ ἐκ παραδόσεως ἐστὶν εἰπεῖν, ὡς ἄρα ὄντος τινὸς περὶ τὸν ναὸν τόπου ἔνθα ἐξῆν τὰς μὲν παρθένους εἰσιέναι καὶ προσκυνεῖν τῷ Θεῷ, τὰς δὲ ἤδη πεπειραμένας κοίτης ἀνδρὸς | **187r** οὐκ ἐπέτρεπον ἐν ἐκείνῳ. Ἡ οὖν Μαρία μετὰ τὸ γεννῆσαι τὸν Σωτῆρα ἡμῶν, ἐλθοῦσα προσκυνῆσαι ἔστη ἐν τῷ τόπῳ τῶν

2026 Matt. 23:35.

2027 2 Paralipomenon (2 Chronicon), 24:20-22.

2028 Cod. φησί.

παρθένων ὡς ἔτι παρθένος οὖσα καὶ μὴ κωλύσαντα αὐτὴν τὸν Ζαχαρίαν, ὡς σαφῶς παρανομοῦντα καὶ εἰς τὸν τόπον τῶν παρθένων ἐπιτρέποντα γυναῖκα γίνεσθαι, *ἀπέκτειναν μεταξὺ τοῦ ναοῦ καὶ τοῦ θυσιαστηρίου*. Οἱ τῆς γενεᾶς οὖν ἐκείνης ὀνειδίζονται παρὰ τοῦ Σωτῆρος, οὐχ ὡς *υἱοὶ* τῶν *τοὺς προφήτας* ἀποκτεινάντων[2029] καὶ τὸν Ζαχαρίαν μετὰ τῶν προφητῶν, ἀλλ᾽ ὡς αὐτοὶ φονεύσαντες. *Γενεὰν δὲ ταύτην*,[2030] ὡς ἅπαν τὸ τῶν φονευτῶν γένος λέγει. Οὐ θαυμαστὸν δὲ εἰ ἔτυχεν ὥσπερ ὁμωνύμους εἶναι τὸν πατέρα Ἰωάννου Ζαχαρίαν τοῦ ἐν τοῖς δώδεκα, οὕτω καὶ τὸν πατέρα τοῦ πατρός.

> Τινὲς δὲ Ζαχαρίαν υἱὸν τοῦ Βαραχίου οὐ τὸν ἐν τοῖς δώδεκα τεταγμένον φασὶ ἐνταῦθα εἰρῆσθαι, ἀλλὰ τὸν πατέρα Ἰωάννου τοῦ βαπτιστοῦ. οὐ δύνανται γὰρ τὸν ἐν τοῖς δώδεκα τεταγμένον Ζαχαρίαν ἀνηρηκέναι οἱ νῦν ὑπὸ τοῦ σωτῆρος ὀνειδιζόμενοι. ἀλλ᾽ εἰκός, καθὼς φησι‹ν› Ἰώσηπος, Ζαχαρίαν νῦν λέγεσθαι τὸν Ἰωάννου πατέρα. περὶ οὗ ἀπὸ μὲν γραφῆς δεῖξαι οὐκ ἔχομεν, οὐδ᾽ ὅτι υἱὸς *Βαραχίου* ἦν, οὐδ᾽ ὅτι οἱ γραμματεῖς καὶ οἱ Φαρισαῖοι ἐφόνευσαν αὐτὸν *μεταξὺ τοῦ ναοῦ καὶ τοῦ θυσιαστηρίου*. Ἀλλ᾽ ἐκ παραδόσεως ἐστὶν εἰπεῖν, ὡς ἄρα ὄντος τινὸς περὶ τὸν ναὸν τόπου ἔνθα ἐξῆν τὰς μὲν παρθένους εἰσιέναι καὶ προσκυνεῖν τῷ θεῷ, τὰς δὲ ἤδη πεπειραμένας κοίτης ἀνδρὸς οὐκ ἐπέτρεπον ἐν ἐκείνῳ. Ἡ οὖν Μαρία μετὰ τὸ γεννῆσαι τὸν σωτῆρα ἡμῶν, ἐλθοῦσα προσκυνῆσαι ἔστη ἐν τῷ τόπῳ τῶν παρθένων ὡς ἔτι παρθένος οὖσα καὶ μὴ κωλύσαντα αὐτὴν τὸν Ζαχαρίαν ὡς σαφῶς παρανομοῦντα καὶ εἰς τὸν τόπον τῶν παρθένων ἐπιτρέποντα γυναῖκα γίνεσθαι *ἀπέκτειναν μεταξὺ τοῦ ναοῦ καὶ τοῦ θυσιαστηρίου*. οἱ τῆς γενεᾶς οὖν ἐκείνης ὀνειδίζονται παρὰ τοῦ σωτῆρος, οὐχ ὡς υἱοὶ τῶν τοὺς προφήτας ἀποκτεινάντων καὶ τὸν Ζαχαρίαν μετὰ τῶν προφητῶν, ἀλλ᾽ ὡς αὐτοὶ φονεύσαντες. *γενεὰν δὲ ταύτην*, ὡς ἅπαν τὸ τῶν φονευτῶν γένος λέγει. οὐ θαυμαστὸν δὲ εἰ ἔτυχεν ὥσπερ ὁμωνύμους εἶναι τὸν πατέρα Ἰωάννου Ζαχαρίαν τοῦ ἐν τοῖς δώδεκα, οὕτω καὶ τὸν πατέρα τοῦ πατρός.[mcdlxxxix]

> Οὐ δύνανται γὰρ τὸν ἐν τοῖς δώδεκα τεταγμένον Ζαχαρίαν υἱὸν Βαραχίου ἀνηρηκέναι οἱ νῦν ὑπὸ τοῦ σωτῆρος ὀνειδιζόμενοι. ἀλλ᾽ εἰκὸς [καθὼς φησιν Ἰώσηππος] Ζαχαρίαν νῦν λέγεσθαι τὸν Ἰωάννου πατέρα, περὶ οὗ ἀπὸ μὲν γραφῶν δεῖξαι οὐκ ἔχομεν οὔτε ὅτι υἱὸς ἦν Βαραχίου, οὔτε ὅτι οἱ γραμματεῖς καὶ οἱ Φαρισαῖοι ἐφόνευσαν αὐτὸν μεταξὺ τοῦ ναοῦ καὶ τοῦ θυσιαστηρίου. ἀλλ᾽ ἦλθεν εἰς ἡμᾶς τοιαύτη τις παράδοσις, ὡς ἄρα ὄντος τινὸς περὶ τὸν ναὸν τόπου, ἔνθα ἐξῆν τὰς μὲν παρθένους εἰσιέναι καὶ προσκυνεῖν τῷ θεῷ, τὰς δὲ ἤδη πεπειραμένας κοίτην ἀνδρὸς οὐκ ἐπέτρεπον ἐν ἐκείνῳ. ἡ οὖν Μαρία μετὰ τὸ γεννῆσαι τὸν σωτῆρα [ἡμῶν] ἐλθοῦσα προσκυνῆσαι ἔστη ἐν τῷ τόπῳ τῶν παρθένων. καὶ κωλυόντων τῶν εἰδότων αὐτὴν γεννήσασαν ὁ Ζαχαρίας ἔλεγε τοῖς κωλύουσιν ἀξίαν αὐτὴν εἶναι τοῦ τόπου τῶν παρθένων ἔτι παρθένον οὖσαν. ὡς οὖν σαφῶς παρανομοῦντα καὶ εἰς τὸν τόπον τῶν παρθένων ἐπιτρέποντα γυναῖκα γίνεσθαι ἀπέκτειναν μεταξὺ τοῦ ναοῦ καὶ τοῦ θυσιαστηρίου οἱ τῆς γενεᾶς ἐκείνης. ὀνειδίζονται γοῦν ὑπὸ τοῦ σωτῆρος οὐχ ὡς υἱοὶ τῶν τοὺς προφήτας ἀποκτεινάντων καὶ τὸν Ζαχαρίαν μετὰ τῶν προφητῶν, ἀλλ᾽ ὡς αὐτοὶ φονεύσαντες. οὐ θαυμαστὸν δέ, εἰ ἔτυχεν ὥσπερ ὁμωνύμους εἶναι τὸν πατέρα Ἰωάννου Ζαχαρίαν τοῦ ἐν τοῖς δώδεκα. οὕτω καὶ τὸν πατέρα τοῦ πατρός.[mcdxc]

2029 Matt. 23:31.
2030 Matt. 23:36.

Ἱερουσαλὴμ Ἱερουσαλὴμ ἡ ἀποκτείνουσα.[2031] Τί βούλεται ὁ διπλασιασμός; Ἐλεοῦντος αὐτὴν καὶ ταλανίζοντος τοῦτο τὸ σχῆμα καὶ σφόδρα φιλοῦντος. Ὡς γὰρ πρὸς ἐρωμένην τινὰ φιληθεῖσαν μὲν διὰ παντός, καταφρονήσασαν δὲ τοῦ ἐραστοῦ, ἀπολογεῖται λοιπὸν ὑπὲρ οὗ ἔμελλε πληγὰς αὐτῇ ἐπαγαγεῖν, διὰ τὸ εἶναι αὐτὴν μιαιφόνον. Αἰτιᾶται τοίνυν αὐτὴν ὡς φονικήν. *Ἡ ἀποκτείνουσα*, γάρ φησι, *τοὺς προφήτας καὶ λιθοβολοῦσα τοὺς ἀπεσταλμένους πρὸς αὐτήν*, καὶ ὅτι πολλάκις δυναμένη τυχεῖν ἐλέους οὐκ ἠθέλησε. Τὸ γὰρ *ποσάκις* πολλοὺς ἔδειξε χρόνους καὶ πολλὰς γενεάς, ὅτε τὸν λαὸν ἐξ αἰχμαλωσίας ἐπανήγαγεν·[mcdxci] οἱ δὲ ἐσκόρπιζον ἑαυτοὺς διὰ τῶν ἁμαρτιῶν. Εἰπὼν δὲ *πτέρυγας* καὶ *σκέπην*, διδάσκει τὸ θεοπρεπὲς αὐτοῦ καὶ ἐν ἀνθρωπίνῃ μορφῇ, οἷον τὸ ὑπὸ Μωσέως εἰς Θεὸν εἰρημένον,[mcdxcii] *διεὶς τὰς πτέρυγας αὐτοῦ ἐδέξατο αὐτούς·*[2032] | **187v** καὶ ὁ Δαυίδ· *οἱ δὲ υἱοὶ τῶν ἀνθρώπων ἐν σκέπῃ τῶν πτερύγων σου ἐλπιοῦσιν.*[2033] Ἐπειδὴ γὰρ ὁ Σατανᾶς διεσκόρπιζεν αὐτούς, πῇ μὲν εἰς εἰδωλολατρίαν, πῇ δὲ εἰς φιληδονίας, ἀπέστειλε προφήτας. Εἶτα καὶ δι᾽ ἑαυτοῦ ἦλθεν, ὥστε συναγαγεῖν αὐτοὺς *εἰς ἕν.*[2034] Οἱ δὲ οὐκ ἠνέσχοντο ὑπὸ τὴν *σκέπην*[2035] αὐτοῦ εἶναι. Ἐγὼ μὲν γάρ φησι, ὡς ὄρνις φιλόστοργος ἀεί σε ἤθελον προσεπισπᾶσθαι πρὸς ἐμαυτόν· σὺ δὲ οὐκ ἤθελες, ἀλλ᾽ ἐσκόρπιζες ἑαυτὴν διὰ τοῦ ἁμαρτάνειν, ἔξω ποιοῦσα ἑαυτὴν τοῦ Θεοῦ. Ἡ δὲ *ὄρνις*[mcdxciii] πολύτεκνος καὶ θερμὴ περὶ τὴν ἀγάπην καὶ κηδομένη τῶν τέκνων καὶ ἑαυτὴν παραδιδοῦσα ὑπὲρ αὐτῶν.[mcdxciv]

> Τί βούλεται ὁ διπλασιασμός; Ἐλεοῦντος αὐτὴν καὶ ταλανίζοντος τοῦτο τὸ σχῆμα, καὶ σφόδρα φιλοῦντος. Ὥσπερ γὰρ πρὸς ἐρωμένην, φιληθεῖσαν μὲν διαπαντός, καταφρονήσασαν δὲ τοῦ ἐραστοῦ, καὶ διὰ τοῦτο κολάζεσθαι μέλλουσαν, ἀπολογεῖται λοιπὸν μέλλων ἐπάγειν τὴν κόλασιν. Ὃ καὶ ἐν τοῖς προφήταις ποιεῖ λέγων. *Εἶπον, Ἀνάστρεψον πρός με, καὶ οὐκ ἀνέστρεψεν.*[2036] Εἶτα καλέσας αὐτήν, λέγει καὶ τὰς μιαιφονίας αὐτῆς. *Ἡ ἀποκτέννουσα τοὺς προφήτας, καὶ λιθοβολοῦσα τοὺς ἀπεσταλμένους πρὸς αὐτήν, ποσάκις ἠθέλησα συναγαγεῖν τὰ τέκνα σου, καὶ οὐκ ἠθελήσατε*; καὶ ταύτῃ ὑπὲρ τῶν καθ᾽ ἑαυτὸν ἀπολογούμενος, ὅτι Οὐδὲ τούτοις με ἀπέστρεψας, οὐδὲ ἀπέστησας τῆς περὶ σὲ πολλῆς εὐνοίας, ἀλλ᾽ ἠθέλησα καὶ οὕτως, καὶ οὐχ ἅπαξ καὶ δίς, ἀλλὰ πολλάκις σε ἐπισπάσασθαι. *Ποσάκις* γάρ, φησίν, *ἠθέλησα ἐπισυναγαγεῖν τὰ τέκνα ὑμῶν, ὥσπερ ὄρνις τὰ νοσσία ἑαυτῆς, καὶ οὐκ ἠθελήσατε*; Τοῦτο δὲ λέγει, δηλῶν ὅτι ἀεὶ ἑαυτοὺς ἐσκόρπιζον διὰ τῶν ἁμαρτημάτων. Καὶ τὸ φιλόστοργον ἀπὸ τῆς εἰκόνος ἐνδείκνυται. καὶ γὰρ θερμὸν τὸ ζῶον περὶ τὰ ἔκγονα.[mcdxcv]

> Ὑπὲρ οὗ ἔμελλε πληγὰς αὐτῇ ἐπαγαγεῖν διὰ τὸ εἶναι αὐτὴν μιαιφόνον. αἰτιᾶται τοίνυν αὐτὴν ὡς φονικήν. *ἡ ἀποκτείνουσα* γάρ, φησίν, *τοὺς προφήτας καὶ λιθοβολοῦσα τοὺς ἀπεσταλμένους πρὸς αὐτὴν* καὶ ὅτι πολλάκις δυναμένη τυχεῖν ἐλέους οὐκ ἠθέλησεν. τὸ γὰρ ποσάκις πολλοὺς ἔδειξε χρόνους καὶ πολλὰς γενεάς, ὅτε τὸν λαὸν ἐξ αἰχμαλωσίας

2031 Matt. 23:37; Luke, 13:34-35.
2032 Deut. 32:11.
2033 Psalm 35:8.
2034 Cf. John, 11:52.
2035 Cf. Psalm 104:39; Wisdom of Solomon, 10:17; Hosea, 14:8; Is. 49:2.
2036 Jer. 3:7.

> ἐπανήγαγεν. οἱ δὲ ἐσκόρπιζον ἑαυτοὺς διὰ τῶν ἁμαρτιῶν. εἰπὼν δὲ *πτέρυγας* καὶ *σκέπην* διδάσκει τὸ θεοπρεπὲς αὐτοῦ καὶ ἐν ἀνθρωπίνῃ μορφῇ οἷον τὸ ὑπὸ Μωυσέως εἰς θεὸν εἰρημένον. *διεὶς τὰς πτέρυγας αὐτοῦ ἐδέξατο αὐτούς*.[2037] καὶ ὁ Δαβίδ. *οἱ δὲ υἱοὶ τῶν ἀνθρώπων ἐν σκέπῃ τῶν πτερύγων σου ἐλπιοῦσιν*.[2038] ἐπειδὴ γὰρ ὁ σατανᾶς διεσκόρπιζεν αὐτοὺς πῇ μὲν εἰς εἰδωλολατρίαν, πῇ δὲ εἰς φιληδονίας, ἀπέστειλε προφήτας, εἶτα καὶ δι᾽ ἑαυτοῦ ἦλθεν ὥστε *συναγαγεῖν* αὐτοὺς *εἰς ἕν*. οἱ δὲ οὐκ ἠνέσχοντο ὑπὸ τὴν σκέπην αὐτοῦ εἶναι. ἐγὼ μὲν γάρ, φησίν, ὡς ὄρνις φιλόστοργος ἀεί σε εἶχον προσεπισπᾶσθαι πρὸς ἐμαυτόν, σὺ δὲ οὐκ ἤθελες, ἀλλ᾽ ἐσκόρπιζες ἑαυτὴν διὰ τοῦ ἁμαρτάνειν ἔξω ποιοῦσα ἑαυτὴν τοῦ θεοῦ. ἡ δὲ ὄρνις πολύτεκνος καὶ θερμὴ περὶ τὴν ἀγάπην καὶ κηδομένη τῶν τέκνων καὶ ἑαυτὴν παραδιδοῦσα ὑπὲρ αὐτῶν.[mcdxcvi]

> Εἰ μηδὲν πρὸ τῆς ἐνσωματώσεως πεποιήκει ὁ κύριος ὑπὲρ τῆς σωτηρίας Ἱερουσαλήμ, πῶς ἔλεγεν. *ποσάκις ἠθέλησα ἐπισυναγαγεῖν τὰ τέκνα σου;*[2039] χρήσῃ οὖν τῷ ῥητῷ τούτῳ πρός τους τὴν θεότητα τῆς σαρκὸς καὶ τὴν καινὴν τῆς παλαιᾶς διαθήκης διαιροῦντας.[mcdxcvii]

Ἰδοὺ ἀφίεται ὁ οἶκος ὑμῶν ἔρημος.[2040] Διὰ τοῦτο τοίνυν ἀφιστῶ ἐμαυτὸν τοῦ ναοῦ καὶ οὐκέτι ἐνοικεῖ ἐν αὐτῷ ἡ ἁγιάζουσα δόξα μου. Ἤτοι τὸ γενέσθαι τὸν οἶκον ἔρημον τῆς παρ᾽ αὐτοῦ δηλαδὴ βοηθείας ἀνατροπὴν σημαίνει τῆς πάσης αὐτῶν πολιτείας. Ἄρα αὐτὸς ἦν ὁ καὶ ἔμπροσθεν αὐτῶν προϊστάμενος.

> Ἄρα αὐτὸς ἦν ὁ καὶ ἔμπροσθεν αὐτῶν προϊστάμενος, καὶ συνέχων καὶ διακρατῶν.[mcdxcviii]

Εἶτα, τὴν δευτέραν αὐτοῦ ἄφιξιν προαναφωνεῖ. Τὸ γὰρ *ἀπάρτι*[2041] δηλοῖ τὸν χρόνον τὸν ἕως τοῦ σταυροῦ,[mcdxcix]

> τὴν γὰρ μέλλουσαν ἡμέραν τῆς δευτέρας αὐτοῦ παρουσίας ἐνταῦθα λέγει. Τί οὖν; οὐκ εἶδον αὐτὸν ἔκτοτε; Ἀλλ᾽ οὐχὶ τὴν ὥραν ἐκείνην δηλοῖ λέγων, *Ἀπάρτι*, ἀλλὰ τὸν καιρὸν τὸν μέχρι τοῦ σταυροῦ.[md]

μεθ᾽ ὃν αὐτὸν οὐκέτι εἶδον. Εἰ γὰρ καὶ ὤφθη τισὶν ἁγίοις μετὰ τὴν ἀνάστασιν, ἀλλ᾽ οὐχὶ τοῖς ἀπίστοις Ἰουδαίοις. Δείκνυσι δὲ διὰ τούτου καὶ ὅτι μέλλει ἀναστῆναι καὶ ἐλθεῖν ἐν καιρῷ κρίσεως, καὶ ὅτι ἄκοντες Ἰουδαῖοι ὑποταγήσονται αὐτῷ, οἱ δὲ πιστοὶ καὶ ἅγιοι καὶ τὸν ὕμνον ἐροῦσι περιχαρῶς διὰ τὰ ἐλπιζόμενα ἀγαθά.

Ἕως ἂν εἴπητε, εὐλογημένος ὁ ἐρχόμενος.[2042] Τὸ εἰρημένον νοητὴν ἔχει τὴν διὰ πίστεως θέαν. Ὅταν γὰρ *εἰσέλθῃ τὸ πλήρωμα τῶν ἐθνῶν*[2043] καὶ πιστεύ | **188r** σωσι

2037 Deut. 32:11.
2038 Psalm 35:8.
2039 Matt. 23:37.
2040 Matt. 23:38; Luke, 13:35.
2041 Matt. 23:39.
2042 Matt. 23:39.
2043 Rom. 11:25.

τῷ Χριστῷ, τότε οἱ μετὰ ταῦτα πιστεύσαντες Ἰουδαῖοι ὁρῶσι τὸ τῆς θεότητος κάλλος τοῦ Χριστοῦ, ἐν Υἱῷ θεωροῦντες τὸν Πατέρα καὶ αὐτὸν εἶναι λέγοντες τὸν λυτρωτὴν τὸν διὰ τῶν προφητῶν κηρυχθέντα, περὶ οὗ προμεμήνυκεν ὁ προφήτης ὡς ἐρχομένου *ἐν ὀνόματι Κυρίου.*[2044] Οἱ γὰρ ἄλλοι προφῆται οὐκ *ἐν ὀνόματι Κυρίου* ἦλθον. Ἔλεγον γάρ· *τάδε λέγει Κύριος,*[2045] καὶ *δοῦλος Κυρίου ἐγώ εἰμι καὶ τὸν Θεὸν τοῦ οὐρανοῦ ἐγὼ σέβομαι.*[2046]

> Τὸ εἰρημένον νοητὴν ἔχει τὴν διὰ πίστεως θέαν. ὅταν γὰρ *εἰσέλθῃ τὸ πλήρωμα τῶν ἐθνῶν* καὶ πιστεύσωσι τῷ Χριστῷ, τότε οἱ μετὰ ταῦτα πιστεύσαντες Ἰουδαῖοι ὁρῶσι τὸ τῆς θεότητος κάλλος τοῦ Χριστοῦ ἐν υἱῷ θεωροῦντες τὸν πατέρα καὶ αὐτὸν εἶναι λέγοντες τὸν λυτρωτὴν τὸν διὰ τῶν προφητῶν κηρυχθέντα, περὶ οὗ προμεμήνυκεν ὁ προφήτης ὡς ἐρχομένου *ἐν ὀνόματι Κυρίου.* Οἱ γὰρ ἄλλοι προφῆται οὐκ *ἐν ὀνόματι Κυρίου* ἦλθον. Ἔλεγον γάρ· *τάδε λέγει Κύριος, καί· δοῦλος Κυρίου ἐγώ εἰμι καὶ τὸν Θεὸν τοῦ οὐρανοῦ ἐγὼ σέβομαι.*[mdi]

> Τὸ εἰρημένον νοητὴν ἔχει τὴν διὰ πίστεως θέαν. ὅταν γὰρ *εἰσέλθῃ τὸ πλήρωμα τῶν ἐθνῶν* καὶ πιστεύσωσι τῷ Χριστῷ, τότε οἱ μετὰ ταῦτα πιστεύσαντες Ἰουδαῖοι ὁρῶσι τὸ τῆς θεότητος κάλλος τοῦ Χριστοῦ ἐν υἱῷ θεωροῦντες εἶναι τὸν πατέρα καὶ αὐτὸν λέγοντες εἶναι τὸν λυτρωτὴν τὸν διὰ τῶν προφητῶν κηρυχθέντα, περὶ οὗ προμεμήνυκεν ὁ προφήτης ὡς *ἐρχόμενον ἐν ὀνόματι κυρίου.* οἱ γὰρ ἄλλοι προφῆται οὐκ *ἐν ὀνόματι κυρίου* ἦλθον· ἔλεγον γάρ· *τάδε κύριος* καὶ *δοῦλος κυρίου ἐγώ εἰμι, καὶ τὸν θεὸν τοῦ οὐρανοῦ ἐγὼ σέβομαι.*[mdii]

Καὶ ἐξελθὼν ὁ Ἰησοῦς.[2047] Εἰπὼν *ἀφίεται ὑμῖν ὁ οἶκος ὑμῶν*, ἀκόλουθον τοῦτο ποιεῖ *ἐξελθὼν* ἐκ *τοῦ ἱεροῦ* καὶ πορευόμενος. *Ἐξελθὼν* δὲ ἐκ *τοῦ ἱεροῦ* ὁ Κύριος ἔδειξε καὶ τὴν ἀπὸ τοῦ γένους τῶν Ἰουδαίων μετάστασιν τῆς χάριτος ἐπὶ τὰ ἔθνη,

> Εἰπὼν *ἀφίεται ὑμῖν ὁ οἶκος ὑμῶν* ἀκόλουθον τοῦτο ποιεῖ *ἐξελθὼν* ἀπὸ *τοῦ ἱεροῦ* καὶ πορευόμενος καὶ διὰ τοῦτο δεικνὺς τὴν ἐκ τοῦ γένους τῶν Ἰουδαίων ἀπόστασιν τῆς θείας χάριτος.[mdiii]

> Εἰπὼν *ἀφίεται ὑμῖν ὁ οἶκος ὑμῶν* ἀκόλουθον τοῦτο ποιεῖ *ἐξελθὼν ἀπὸ τοῦ ἱεροῦ* καὶ πορευόμενος καὶ διὰ τοῦτο δεικνὺς τὴν ἐκ τοῦ γένους τῶν Ἰουδαίων ἀπόστασιν τῆς θείας χάριτος, ἐφ᾽ ἑτέρους μεταχωρούσης. ὑπερβολικῶς δὲ ἐχρήσατο τούτοις, ὅμως καὶ ἔργῳ ἐξέβη ἐριπωθὲν τελείως τὸ τέμενος.[mdiv]

καὶ λέγει[mdv] τὴν κατάλυσιν τοῦ ναοῦ, ἀπάγων αὐτοὺς μὴ ἐφήδεσθαι τοῖς ἐπιγείοις ἀλλ᾽ ἐπὶ τὴν ἄνω *Ἱερουσαλὴμ* μετάγειν τὸν νοῦν. Ἐπειδὴ γὰρ ἐπεδείκνυον αὐτῷ οἱ

2044 Psalm 117:26, quoted in Matt. 21:9; 23:39; Mark, 11:9; Luke, 13:35; John, 12:13.

2045 Amos, 1:6; 1:9; *et passim*; Michac, 2:3; 3:5; Abdias, 1; Nahum, 1:2; 1:5; 1:7; 1:9; 2:6; 2:11; Zach. 1:3; 1:4; *et passim*; Malachi, 1:4; Is. 3:16; 7:7; *et passim*; Jer. 2:2; 2:5; *et passim*; Ez. 2:4; 3:11; *et passim*.

2046 Jonas, 1:9.

2047 Matt. 24:1.

μαθηταὶ *τὰς οἰκοδομὰς τοῦ ἱεροῦ*[2048] καὶ ἐθαύμαζον εἰ μέλλοι *ἔρημος* γενέσθαι ὁ περικαλλὴς οὗτος ναός, καὶ περὶ ὁλοτελοῦς αὐτοῦ ἀπωλείας προλέγει.[2049]

Καθημένου δὲ αὐτοῦ ἐπὶ τοῦ ὄρους τῶν ἐλαιῶν.[2050] Ὡς περὶ τοιούτων μέλλοντες ἐρωτᾶν, ἰδίᾳ ἐποιήσαντο τὴν ἐρώτησιν.
Δύο δὲ ἐρωτῶσι, περί τε τῆς τοῦ ναοῦ κατασκαφῆς καὶ περὶ τῆς αὐτοῦ παρουσίας. Τί οὖν ὁ Σωτήρ; Πολλοί φησι ἥξουσι κηρύσσοντες τὴν ἐμὴν ἄφιξιν καὶ ἕτερον ἀντ᾽ ἐμοῦ τοῖς ἀνθρώποις ἀποδεικνύοντες ἑαυτοὺς Χριστόν. Δοσίθεος γὰρ Σαμαρείτης ὢν εἶπεν ἑαυτὸν τὸν ὑπὸ Μωσέως ἀνακηρυχθέντα προφήτην. Ὁμοίως καὶ Σίμων ὁ μάγος Σαμαρείτης ὢν ἔλεγεν ἑαυτὸν τὴν μεγάλην τοῦ Θεοῦ δύναμιν. Μοντανὸς | **188v** εἶπεν, ἐγώ εἰμι ὁ λόγος, ὁ νυμφίος, ὁ παράκλητος, ὁ παντοκράτωρ· ἐγὼ τὰ πάντα.[mdvi]

> διὸ καὶ δύο συντελείας προαναφωνεῖ. μίαν μὲν τὴν τῶν Ἱεροσολύμων, δευτέραν δὲ τὴν τῆς οἰκουμένης πάσης. καὶ τίνες ἦλθον *ἐπὶ τῷ ὀνόματι* αὐτοῦ; Σίμων ὁ μάγος λέγων ἑαυτὸν εἶναι τὴν δύναμιν τὴν μεγάλην, ἦλθεν Μανιχαῖος, ἦλθεν Δοσίθεός τις Σαμαρείτης τὸν ὑπὸ Μωσέως ἀνακηρυχθέντα προφήτην λέγων ἑαυτόν. Μοντανὸς εἶπεν ἐν οἰκείοις συγγράμμασιν. ἐγώ εἰμι ὁ λόγος, ὁ νυμφίος, ὁ παράκλητος, ὁ παντοκράτωρ, ἐγὼ τὰ πάντα.[mdvii]

> One of these is Simon the Samaritan of whom we read in the Acts of Apostles, who claimed to be the great power of God (Dei virtutem).[2051] Among other things, he left the following written statement in his books: "I am the Word of God (sermo Dei), I am the Beautiful (speciosus), I am the Paraclete (paracletus), I am the Omnipotent (omnipotens), I am God's All (omnia Dei)."[mdviii]

Εἰκὸς δὲ καὶ ἄλλους ἐληλυθέναι οὓς οὐκ ἴσμεν. Ἥξει δὲ καὶ ὁ Ἀντίχριστος ὕστερον. Πλὴν ὅτε συνεχεῖς γίνονταί φησι *κατὰ* πᾶσαν τὴν οἰκουμένην *πόλεμοι καὶ σεισμοὶ καὶ λιμοὶ καὶ λοιμοί,*[2052] ἐγγύς ἐστι λοιπὸν ὁ *τῆς συντελείας* καιρός. *Ὁρᾶτε* γάρ φησι καὶ *μὴ θροεῖσθε.*[2053] Οὐ γὰρ διασπασθήσεται τὸ κήρυγμα ἀπὸ τῶν συμβησομένων δεινῶν. *Δεῖ γὰρ ταῦτα γενέσθαι,* ἀλλ᾽ οὐ διακόπτεταί τι τῶν εἰρημένων παρ᾽ ἐμοῦ. *Ἔθνος* δὲ *ἐπὶ ἔθνος καὶ* βασιλείας *ἐπὶ βασιλείαν* ἐξεγερθησόμενας[2054] φησὶ διὰ τὰ ἐσόμενα τοῖς Ἰουδαίοις κακά, ἅπερ εἰσὶν *ἀρχὴ ὠδίνων.*[2055] Ὥσπερ γὰρ αἱ ὠδῖνες γίνονται τῇ τικτούσῃ καὶ οὕτω τίκτεται ἄνθρωπος, οὕτως ὁ παρὼν αἰὼν διὰ συγχύσεως καὶ πολέμων γεννήσει τὸν μέλλοντα.

2048 Matt. 24:1.
2049 Matt. 24:2.
2050 Matt. 24:3.
2051 Cf. Acts, 8:10.
2052 Matt. 24:7.
2053 Matt. 24:6.
2054 Matt. 24:7; cf. Mark, 13:8; Luke, 21:10.
2055 Matt. 24:8.

Καὶ τότε σκανδαλισθήσονται πολλοί.[2056] Τῇ προγνώσει παραθαρρύνει τοὺς ἁγίους εἰς τὰ συμβησόμενα δεινὰ κατὰ τὸν τῆς παρουσίας τοῦ Ἀντιχρίστου καιρόν. Τότε δὲ πολλὰ μέλλουσι γίνεσθαι δεινὰ παρὰ τοῖς ἀνθρώποις· φθόνοι, ἔχθραι, σκανδαλισμοί, ἀναδείξεις ψευδοπροφητῶν ἀποπλανώντων πολλοὺς ἀπὸ τῆς θεογνωσίας. Πρόδρομοι δέ εἰσιν οἱ *ψευδοπροφῆται* τοῦ Ἀντιχρίστου. Διὰ γὰρ τῆς ἐξ αὐτῶν γινομένης ἀπάτης λαμβάνει χώραν καὶ ἡ εἰς τὸν *Ἀντίχριστον*[2057] ἀπάτη. Καὶ διὰ τὴν πολλὴν *ἀνομίαν ἀναιρεῖται ἡ ἀγάπη*[2058] καὶ πάντες ἐπέρχονται τοῖς ἁγίοις ὡς μηδὲ τὴν ἀπὸ τῶν οἰκείων ἔτι σῴζεσθαι συμπάθειαν. *Ὁ δὲ* ὑπομένων ταῦτα, φησὶ (οὐχ ὁ πρὸς ὀλίγον πειρασθεὶς καὶ | **189r** ἀποστάς, ἀλλ᾽ ὁ μέχρι τέλους μείνας[2059] εἰς τὴν παράταξιν), οὗτος δόκιμος ἀνακηρυχθήσεται στρατιώτης καὶ κηρυχθήσεται τὸ εὐαγγέλιον τοῦτο. Ὡς Θεὸς προεῖπε τὸ ἐσόμενον. Ἐκηρύχθη γὰρ πανταχοῦ *τὸ εὐαγγέλιον*, ἵνα μή τις ἄγνοιαν προβάληται ἐν καιρῷ κρίσεως. Οὐ πάντα δὲ τὰ ἔθνη ἐπίστευσαν, ἀλλ᾽ ὅσῳ λείπει τῆς οἰκουμένης ἔθνη παρ᾽ οἷς οὐκ ἐκήρυκται τὸ εὐαγγέλιον τοσούτῳ λείπει εἰς τὸ ἥκειν *τὸ τέλος*. Μετὰ δὲ τὸ κηρυχθῆναι πανταχοῦ *τὸ εὐαγγέλιον, τότε ἥξει τὸ τέλος*,[2060] ἤτοι τοῦ παρόντος αἰῶνος ἢ τῶν Ἱεροσολύμων. Ἄλλως τε δέ, δι᾽ ὧν πολεμοῦνται οἱ τοῦ Χριστοῦ διὰ τοῦτο ἐξάκουστον γίνεται πᾶσι *τὸ εὐαγγέλιον*, ἵνα ἐν τῇ κρίσει μὴ ἔχωσιν ἀπολογίαν ἀγνοίας οἱ ἀπιστήσαντες. Ὅτε οὖν πάντες γνῶσι, *τότε* ἔσται *τὸ τέλος*, ὡς τῆς εἰς ἀνθρώπους τοῦ Θεοῦ οἰκονομίας καὶ ἀγάπης πάσης συμπεπερασμένης. Εἰ δὲ καὶ πρὸς τοὺς μαθητὰς ἐλέχθη ὁ λόγος, ἀλλ᾽ ἐπὶ τοὺς ἅπαντας ἕλκεται οὓς καὶ μέλλει καταλαβεῖν τὰ εἰρημένα.

Ὅταν οὖν ἴδητε τὸ βδέλυγμα τῆς ἐρημώσεως.[2061] *Βδέλυγμα ἐρημώσεως* καθολικῆς ὁ Ἀντίχριστος λέγων *ἑαυτὸν* εἶναι τὸν Χριστὸν καὶ ἀπατῶν τοὺς ἀνθρώπους ὡς Θεῷ προσκυνεῖν αὐτῷ. Γέγονε δὲ *βδέλυγμα ἐρημώσεως* τῆς Ἱερουσαλὴμ ἡ εἰκὼν Καίσαρος ἣν ἀνέστησε Πιλάτος ἐν τῷ ναῷ, δι᾽ ἣν καὶ στασιάσαντες οἱ Ἰουδαῖοι ἐπορθήθησαν. *Ἐρημώσεως* δὲ αὐτὸ λέγει διὰ τὴν τῆς πόλεως ἐρήμωσιν καὶ τοῦ ναοῦ.[mdix]

> *Βδέλυγμα ἐρημώσεως* καθολικῶς ὁ Ἀντίχριστος λέγων *ἑαυτὸν* εἶναι τὸν Χριστὸν καὶ ἀπατῶν τοὺς ἀνθρώπους ὡς θεῷ προσκυνεῖν αὐτῷ. Γέγονε δὲ *βδέλυγμα ἐρημώσεως* τῆς Ἱερουσαλὴμ ἡ εἰκὼν Καίσαρος ἣν ἀνέστησε Πιλάτος ἐν τῷ ναῷ, δι᾽ ἣν καὶ στασιάσαντες οἱ Ἰουδαῖοι ἐπορθήθησαν. [*ἐρημώσεως* δὲ αὐτὸ λέγει διὰ τὴν τῆς πόλεως ἐρήμωσιν καὶ τοῦ ναοῦ.][mdx]

> (Θεοδώρου Ἡρακλείας.) *Βδέλυγμα ἐρημώσεως* καθολικῶς ὁ Ἀντίχριστος, γέγονε δὲ καὶ βδέλυγμα τῆς ἐρημώσεως Ἱερουσαλὴμ ἡ εἰκὼν Καίσαρος, ἣν ἀνέστησε Πιλάτος ἐν τῷ ναῷ.[mdxi]

2056 Matt. 24:10.
2057 1 John, 2:18&22; 4:3; 2 John, 7.
2058 Matt. 24:12.
2059 Cf. Matt. 24:13; 10:22; Mark, 13:13.
2060 Matt. 24:14.
2061 Matt. 24:15; Mark, 13:14; cf. Daniel, 9:27.

Nevertheless, this [abomination of desolation] can be accepted either simply as the Antichrist, or the image of Caesar that Pilate placed in the Temple, or the equestrian statue of Hadrian, which stands to the present day in the location itself of the holy of holies.[mdxii]

Βδέλυγμα τῆς ἐρημώσεως Ἰουδαῖοι οἴονται τὸ τελευταῖον Ῥωμαίων μηχάνημα, ‹ἢ› τὴν εἰσπεμφθεῖσαν εἰς τὸν ναὸν χοιρείαν κεφαλήν, ἢ τὰς ὑπὸ Πιλάτου εἰς τὸ ἱερὸν εἰσαχθείσας σημαίας.

> *Βδέλυγμα τῆς ἐρημώσεως* Ἰουδαῖοι οἴονται τὸ τελευταῖον Ῥωμαίων μηχάνημα ἢ εἰσπεμφθεῖσαν εἰς τὸν ναὸν χοιρείαν κεφαλὴν εἶναι τὸ βδέλυγμα ἢ τὰς ὑπὸ Πιλάτου εἰς τὸ ἱερὸν εἰσαχθείσας σημείας.[mdxiii]

Βδέλυ | **189v** *γμα ἐρημώσεως* κατὰ ἀναγωγὴν ἑτερόδοξος λόγος καὶ ἀσεβὲς δόγμα εἰσαγόμενον ἀπὸ τῶν ῥητῶν τῆς γραφῆς, οἷς χρῶνται οἱ ἑτερόδοξοι. Τὸ δὲ *ἑστὼς* δηλοῖ ὅτι κατασκευαῖς βεβαιοῦν θέλει τὰ ἑαυτοῦ δόγματα ὁ ἀντίχριστος λόγος. Ἀεὶ μὲν οὖν τὸν ἀναγινώσκοντα μάλιστα δε‹ῖ›[2062] σπεύδειν νοεῖν δεῖ τὰς γραφάς, ὅτε δόγμα φανερὸν εἰς ἐρήμωσιν τῆς ψυχῆς πρόκειται.[mdxiv]

> Ἐπεὶ δὲ καὶ ἀναγωγῆς δεῖται τὸ ρητόν, *βδέλυγμα ἐρημώσεως* κατὰ ἀναγωγὴν ἑτερόδοξος λόγος καὶ ἀσεβὲς δόγμα εἰσαγόμενον ἀπὸ τῶν ρητῶν τῆς γραφῆς, οἷς χρῶνται οἱ ἑτερόδοξοι. τὸ δὲ *ἑστός* δηλοῖ ὅτι κατασκευαῖς βεβαιοῦν θέλει τὰ ἑαυτοῦ δόγματα ὁ Ἀντίχριστος λόγος. ἀεὶ μὲν οὖν τὸν ἀναγινώσκοντα [μάλιστα] δεῖ σπεύδειν νοεῖν τὰς γραφάς, ‹μάλιστα Kl› ὅτε δόγμα φανερὸν εἰς ἐρήμωσιν τῆς ψυχῆς πρόκειται.[mdxv]

Τότε οἱ ἐν τῇ Ἰουδαίᾳ.[2063] Οἱ ἐν εὐσεβείᾳ ἐρηρεισμένοι (τοῦτο γὰρ *Ἰουδαία* ἑρμηνεύεται)[mdxvi] ἐπὶ τὴν ὑψηλὴν καταφυγὴν ἀφοράτωσαν ὑπὸ τῆς οἰκείας ὁμολογίας φρουρούμενοι.

> Οἱ ἐν εὐσεβείᾳ *ΕΡΗΡΕΙΣΜΕΝΟΙ* (τοῦτο γὰρ *Ἰουδαία* ἑρμηνεύεται) ἐπὶ τὴν ὑψηλὴν καταφυγὴν ἀφοράτωσαν ὑπὸ τῆς οἰκείας ὁμολογίας φρουρούμενοι.[mdxvii]
>
> Οἱ ἐν εὐσεβείᾳ ἐρηρεισμένοι (τοῦτο γὰρ Ἰουδαία ἑρμηνεύεται) ἐπὶ τὴν ὑψηλὴν καταφυγὴν ἀφοράτωσαν ὑπὸ τῆς οἰκείας ὁμολογίας φρουρούμενοι.[mdxviii]
>
> εἰ δὲ καὶ κατ' ἀναγωγὴν πρὸς τὰ ἡμέτερα μεθαρμοσθῆναι τὸν λόγον εἰκότως βούλεσθε. *οἱ ἐν τῇ Ἰουδαίᾳ φευγέτωσαν εἰς τὰ ὄρη*, οἱ ἐν εὐσεβείᾳ ἑδραῖοι (τοῦτο γὰρ Ἰουδαία ἑρμηνεύεται) ἐπὶ τὴν ὑψηλὴν καταφυγὴν Χριστὸν ἀφοράτωσαν ὑπὸ τῆς σφῶν ὁμολογίας φρουρούμενοι.[mdxix]

2062 Cod. δὲ.
2063 Matt. 24:16; Mark, 13:14; Luke, 21:20.

φευγέτωσαν εἰς τὰ ὄρη.[2064] Φανέντος τοῦ σημείου *τῆς ἐρημώσεως* χρὴ φεύγειν τὸν προσδοκώμενον θάνατον μηδένα τῶν τῆς οἰκίας σκευῶν ποιησαμένους λόγον. Ἐν δὲ τῇ παρουσίᾳ τοῦ Ἀντιχρίστου λέγει φεύγειν τοὺς πιστοὺς ἐν τοῖς ὄρεσιν, ὅ ἐστιν, ἐπὶ τὰς ὑψηλὰς ἀρετὰς καὶ ἀπὸ τῶν ἀγρῶν ἀναχωρεῖν, ἐκ τῆς τῶν γηΐνων εἰδ‹ωλ›οποιΐας,[2065]
ἀποθεμένους *τὸν παλαιὸν ἄνθρωπον*[2066] (τοῦτο γάρ φησι τὸ *ἱμάτιον*).

> ἀποτιθεμένους τὸν παλαιὸν ἄνθρωπον (τοῦτο γάρ φησι τὸ ἱμάτιον).[mdxx]

Προδιαγράφει Χριστὸς τὰ ἐσόμενα κακὰ ἐν τῇ τοῦ Ἀντιχρίστου παρουσίᾳ τοῖς ἁγίοις τοῖς τὴν νοητὴν Ἰουδαίαν οἰκοῦσι, τὴν τοῦ Χριστοῦ ἐκκλησίαν, ἐν ᾗ μετὰ τὸ Χριστοῦ ὄνομα καὶ ἡ ἐν Πνεύματι περιτομή. Ἐν ὄρεσι δὲ λέγει καταφεύγειν, ἀντὶ τοῦ ἐπὶ τὴν ὑψηλὴν καταφυγήν, τὸν Θεόν· ἢ εἰς τὰς ὑψηλὰς ἀρετὰς ἐν καιρῷ πειρασμῶν τοὺς τοῦ Χριστοῦ δούλους καὶ ἀπὸ τῶν ἀγρῶν ἀναχωρεῖν,[2067] ἀντὶ τοῦ ἐκ τῆς τῶν ἐπιγείων ματαιοπονίας. *Ἐν γαστρὶ* ἐχούσας[2068] λέγει ψυχὰς ἐχούσας ἐν αὐταῖς τὴν φαυλότητα, μήπω δὲ ποιούσας τὰ δεινά, ἀλ | **190r** λ᾽ ἑτοίμους οὔσας εἰς τὸ δρᾶσαι καὶ τεκεῖν τὴν ἁμαρτίαν. Θηλαζούσας δὲ νοητέον τὰς φανερῶς ποιούσας τὸ κακόν, αἳ καὶ οἱονεὶ μητέρες εὑρίσκονται τῆς ἁμαρτίας καὶ τροφοί.

> Προδιαγράφει Χριστὸς τὰ ἐσόμενα κακὰ ἐν τῇ τοῦ Ἀντιχρίστου παρουσίᾳ τοῖς ἁγίοις τοῖς Ἰουδαίαν τὴν νοητὴν οἰκοῦσι, τὴν τοῦ Χριστοῦ ἐκκλησίαν, ἐν ᾗ μετὰ τὸ Χριστοῦ ὄνομα καὶ ἡ ἐν πνεύματι περιτομή. ἐν ὄρεσι δὲ λέγει καταφεύγειν ἀντὶ τοῦ ἐπὶ τὴν ὑψηλὴν καταφυγήν, τὸν θεόν, ἢ εἰς τὰς ὑψηλὰς ἀρετὰς ἐν καιρῷ πειρασμῶν τοὺς τοῦ Χριστοῦ δούλους καὶ ἀπὸ τῶν ἀγρῶν ἀναχωρεῖν, ἀντὶ τοῦ ἐκ τῆς τῶν ἐπιγείων ματαιοπονίας. *ἐν γαστρὶ* δὲ ἐχούσας λέγει ψυχὰς ἐχούσας ἐν αὐταῖς τὴν φαυλότητα μήπω δὲ ποιούσας τὰ δεινά, ἀλλ᾽ ἑτοίμους οὔσας εἰς τὸ δρᾶσαι καὶ τεκεῖν τὴν ἁμαρτίαν. θηλαζούσας δὲ νοητέον τὰς φανερῶς ποιούσας τὸ κακόν, αἳ καὶ οἱονεὶ μητέρες εὑρίσκονται τῆς ἁμαρτίας καὶ τροφοί.[mdxxi]

ὁ ἐπὶ τοῦ δώματος μὴ καταβαινέτω.[2069] Ὁ τῆς παρούσης καταφρονήσας σκιᾶς[mdxxii] καὶ πᾶσαν τὴν ἐντεῦθεν καταπατήσας σκηνὴν[mdxxiii] καὶ ὑψηλὸς τῷ βίῳ γενόμενος καὶ τὰ ἔνοικα πάθη[mdxxiv] ἀποπεμψάμενος μηδὲν ἐξ αὐτῶν ἐπισπάσθω· μὴ δειλίαν, μὴ ἀθυμίαν, μὴ δόξαν κενήν, μὴ ὄρεξιν πλούτου, ἅπερ ἀφ᾽ ὕψους ἐστὶ κατάβασις.

> [Ὁ τῆς παρούσης καταφρονήσας οἰκίας καὶ πᾶσαν τὴν ἐντεῦθεν καταπατήσας σκηνὴν καὶ ὑψηλὸς τῷ βίῳ γενόμενος καὶ τὰ ἔνοικα πάθη ἀποπεμψάμενος μηδὲν ἐξ αὐτῶν

2064 Matt. 24:16; Mark, 13:14.
2065 Abbreviated in cod.
2066 Cf. Col. 3:9.
2067 Matt. 24:18; Mark, 13:16.
2068 Matt. 24:19; Mark, 13:17.
2069 Matt. 24:19; cf. Mark, 13:15.

> ἐπισπάσθῳ, μὴ δειλίαν, μὴ ἐπιθυμίαν, μὴ δόξαν κενήν, μὴ ὄρεξιν πλούτου. ἅπερ ἀφ' ὕψους ἐστὶ κατάβασις.][mdxxv]

> Ὁ τῆς παρούσης περιφρονήσας οἰκίας καὶ πᾶσαν τὴν ἐνταῦθα καταπατήσας σκηνὴν καὶ ὑψηλὸς τῷ βίῳ γενόμενος καὶ τὰ ἔνοικα πάθη ἀποπεμψάμενος, μηδὲν ἐξ αὐτῶν ἐπισπάσθῳ, μὴ δειλίαν, μὴ ῥαθυμίαν, μὴ δόξαν κενήν, μὴ ὄρεξιν πλούτου, ἅπερ ἀφ' ὕψους ἐστὶ κατάβασις.[mdxxvi]

> ὁ τῆς παρούσης περιφρονήσας σκιώδους ζωῆς καὶ πᾶσαν τὴν ἐνταῦθα καταπατήσας σκηνὴν καὶ ὑψηλὸς τῷ βίῳ γενόμενος καὶ τὰ ἔνοικα πάθη ἀποπεμψάμενος μηδὲν ἐξ αὐτῶν ἐπισπάσθω, μὴ δέος, μὴ ἀθυμίαν, μὴ δόξαν κενήν, μὴ ὄρεξιν πλούτου, ἅπερ ἀφ' ὕψους ὑπάρχει κατάβασις.[mdxxvii]

Ὁ ἐν τῷ ἀγρῷ μὴ ἐπιστρεψάτω.[2070] Ὁ *τὸν παλαιὸν* ἀπεκδυσάμενος *ἄνθρωπον* καὶ τοῖς σαρκικοῖς ἀποταξάμενος *τὸν νέον* φορείτω, ὃς αὐτὸν *εἰς ἐπίγνωσιν*[2071] Θεοῦ ἀνεκαίνισε καὶ τῆς ἰλύος ἐκάθηρεν. Ἐν τούτοις γὰρ ἕξει τὸ πρὸς ἐκείνην τὴν μεγάλην κάκωσιν ἀνεπίβουλον.

> Ὁ *τὸν παλαιὸν* ἀπεκδυσάμενος *ἄνθρωπον* καὶ τοῖς σαρκικοῖς ἀποταξάμενος *τὸν νέον* φορείτω, ὃς αὐτὸν *εἰς ἐπίγνωσιν* Θεοῦ ἀνεκαίνισε καὶ τῆς ἰλύος ἐκάθηρεν. ἐν τούτοις γὰρ ἕξει τὸ πρὸς ἐκείνην τὴν μεγάλην κάκωσιν ἀνεπίβουλον.[mdxxviii]

> Ὁ *τὸν παλαιὸν* ἀπεκδυσάμενος *ἄνθρωπον* καὶ τοῖς σαρκίνοις ἀποταξάμενος *τὸν νέον* φορείτω, ὃς αὐτὸν *εἰς ἐπίγνωσιν* Θεοῦ ἀνεκαίνισε καὶ τῆς ἰλύος ἐκάθηρεν. Ἐν τούτοις γὰρ ἕξει τὸ πρὸς ἐκείνην τὴν μεγάλην κάκωσιν ἀνεπίβουλον.[mdxxix]

> ὁ ἐν τῷ ἀγρῷ μὴ ἐπιστρεψάτω ἆραι τὸ ἱμάτιον αὐτοῦ, ὁ τὸν παλαιὸν ἀπεκδυσάμενος ἄνθρωπον καὶ τοῖς σαρκίνοις ἀποταξάμενος τὸν νέον φορείτω, ὃς αὐτὸν εἰς ἐπίγνωσιν θεοῦ ἀνεκαίνισεν καὶ τῆς ἰλύος ἐκάθαρεν. ἐν τούτῳ γὰρ ἕξει τὸ πρὸς πᾶσαν ἐπιβουλὴν ἀχείρωτον.[mdxxx]

οὐαὶ δὲ ταῖς ἐν γαστρί.[2072] Ταλανίζει ὁ λόγος τὰς ἐν γαστρὶ ἐχούσας καὶ θηλαζούσας τότε. Τὰς μὲν διὰ τὸ μὴ δύνασθαι δραμεῖν *ἐπὶ τὰ ὄρη*[2073] καὶ ἀμβλώσας· τὰς δὲ διὰ τὸν δεσμὸν τῆς πρὸς τὰ ἑαυτῶν τέκνα συμπαθείας μήτε ἐᾶσαι αὐτὰ δυναμένας μήτε βαστάσαι αὐτὰ καὶ σὺν αὐτοῖς σωθῆναι. Καὶ οὕτως εἰς τοσαύτην φησὶ οἱ πολέμιοι τραπήσονται ὠμότητα, ὥστε οὐδὲ τὰς ἐγκύους καὶ τὰ βρέφη ἐλεῆσαι. Καὶ γὰρ καὶ ἱστορικῶς τοῦτο κατὰ πᾶσαν τὴν Ἰουδαίων ἐγένετο, τῆς Ῥωμαίων αὐτοὺς καταπολεμησάσης χειρός, ὡς καὶ τὰς *ἐν γαστρὶ* ἐχούσας καὶ τὰς θηλαζούσας αὐτοῖς ἐγγόνοις ἀναιρεθῆναι πικρῶς ἢ κατὰ γαστρὸς ἔτι φερομένοις ἢ ὑπὸ μαστῷ.

2070 Matt. 24:18; cf. Mark, 13:16.
2071 Col. 3:9-10.
2072 Matt. 24:19; Mark, 13:17.
2073 Matt. 24:16.

Καὶ ἀνηγμένως δέ, κατὰ τὴν τῆς συντελείας ἡμέραν ἄξιαι θρήνων αἱ ψυχαὶ λογισθήσονται | **190v** αἱ τὴν τῆς ἀρετῆς ἐργασίαν ἐν νῷ λαβοῦσαι, καὶ ὥσπερ *ἐν γαστρὶ* φέρουσαι καὶ ἐναρξάμεναι τὸ σπέρμα τοῦ τῆς εὐσεβείας λόγου, μόλις ποτὲ κύειν ἐν ἑαυταῖς, ἢ προαγαγοῦσαι μὲν εἰς φῶς καὶ ὥσπερ τεκοῦσαι λίαν δὲ ἀτελὲς τὸ ἔργον φέρουσαι κατὰ τὰς μὴ ἰσχυσάσας εἰς τέλος ἐκθρέψαι τα ἔκγονα. Δεῖ γὰρ τοὺς ἐργαζομένους τὴν ἀρετὴν κατὰ τὴν ἐν τῷ εὐαγγελίῳ παραβολὴν ἢ τέλειον φέρειν τὸ *μέτρον*,[2074] ὡς εἰς τὸν τῶν ἑκατὸν ἀριθμὸν ἀναβαίνειν ἢ ἐν *ἑξήκοντα* μέτροις καρποφορεῖν ἢ τὸ ἐλάχιστον ἐν *τριάκοντα*.[2075] Τὸ γὰρ ἧττον τούτου, καθάπερ ἀτελὲς βρέφος καὶ ἄτροφον, ἀντ᾽ οὐδενὸς λογισθήσεται.
Ἢ *ἐν γαστρὶ* μὲν ἔχουσαι ψυχαί εἰσιν, αἵτινες τὴν μὲν θείαν πίστιν ἔνδον ἐγκυμονοῦσιν, οὐ θαρροῦσι δὲ παρρησιάσασθαι τὴν ὁμολογίαν.

> Ταῖς ἐγκυμονούσαις δηλονότι τὸν θεῖον ἔρωτα ψυχαῖς καὶ οὐ θαρρούσαις παρρησιάσασθαι καὶ τεκεῖν τὴν περὶ θεοῦ ὁμολογίαν καὶ ἔνστασιν.[mdxxxi]

> Ταῖς ἐγκυμονούσαις δηλονότι τὸν θεῖον ἔρωτα ψυχαῖς καὶ οὐ θαρρούσαις παρρησιάσασθαι καὶ τεκεῖν τὴν περὶ θεοῦ ὁμολογίαν καὶ ἔνστασιν.[mdxxxii]

Αἱ δὲ θηλάζουσαι, αἳ τὴν θείαν ὁμολογίαν ἀτελῆ κατέχουσιν, αἳ ἔτεκον μὲν καὶ ὡμολόγησαν τὴν εἰς Θεὸν πίστιν, διὰ δέ τινα δειλίαν ἢ ἀσθένειαν ἢ ἀφροσύνην προέδωκαν τὴν εὐσέβειαν.

Προσεύχεσθε δὲ ἵνα μὴ γένηται ἡ φυγὴ ὑμῶν χειμῶνος.[2076] Ὡς πρὸς Ἰουδαίους φησὶ τοῦτο, τὸ τοῦ σαββάτου διακρινομένους εἰ δεῖ μεῖναι καὶ ἀναιρεθῆναι ἢ φυγεῖν καὶ τῆς μωσαϊκῆς ἐντολῆς καταφρονῆσαι. Δεῖ οὖν εὔχεσθαι *ἵνα μὴ* ἐν τοιούτῳ καιρῷ ἐπέλθωσι ταῦτα, ὅτε φυγῆς χρεία καὶ οὐκ ἐᾷ φυγεῖν τοὺς Ἰουδαίους ὁ τοῦ νόμου φόβος.
Ἤτοι αἴνιγμα ἔχει ὁ λόγος, ὥστε εὔχεσθαι ἡμᾶς μὴ γενέσθαι ἐν ἐκδημίᾳ τοῦ σώματος, ἀντὶ τοῦ μὴ ἀποθανεῖν, μήτε ἐν ἀργίᾳ ὄντας ἔργου χρηστοῦ (ὃ ὑποσημαίνει τὸ σάββατον) μήτε ἐν ἀκαρπίᾳ ὄντας ἔργων | **191r** ἀγαθῶν (ὃ δηλοῖ ὁ χειμών).

> Ἴσως καὶ αἴνιγμα ἔχει ὁ λόγος, ὥστε εὔχεσθαι ἡμᾶς μὴ ἐκδημῆσαι ἀπὸ τοῦ σώματος μήτε ἐν ἀργίᾳ ὄντας ἔργου ἀγαθοῦ, ὃ ὑποσημαίνει τὸ σάββατον, μήτε *ἐν ἀκαρπίᾳ, ὃ δηλοῖ χειμών. σημειωτέον* γὰρ ὅτι χειμῶνα κακῶν ὁ θεὸς οὐκ ἐποίησεν, ἐν χειμῶνι δὲ ἐσμεν, ὅταν τὰ πάθη τῆς σαρκὸς δυναστεύῃ ἐν ἡμῖν.[mdxxxiii]

Ἔσται δὲ τότε θλῖψις ἀφόρητος,[2077] ἤτοι ἐν τῇ συντελείᾳ ἢ ἐν τῇ τῶν Ἱεροσολύμων καταστροφῇ. Τοῦτο γὰρ ἦσαν οἱ τῶν Ῥωμαίων στρατιῶται κελευσθέντες, ὥστε μηδένα Ἰουδαίων ἐᾶσαι ζῆσαι. Ἀλλ᾽ ὁ Θεὸς *διὰ τοὺς ἐκλεκτοὺς* μαθητὰς οὐκ ἀφῆκεν

2074 Cf. Mark, 4:20.
2075 Cf. Matt. 13:8&23; Mark, 4:8&20.
2076 Matt. 24:20; Mark, 13:18.
2077 Matt. 24:21; cf. Mark, 13:19.

ἄρδην ἀναιρεθῆναι τὸ τῶν Ἰουδαίων γένος. Ἢ τοῦτό φησι· εἰ μὴ τάχιον ἐλήφθη ἡ Ἱερουσαλήμ, πάντες εἶχον οἱ ἔσω ὑπὸ λιμοῦ διαφθαρῆναι. Κολοβοῦσθαι[2078] δὲ λέγει οὐ τὸ δωδεκάωρον τοῦ χρόνου, ἀλλὰ τὸν ἀριθμὸν τῶν θλίψεων *διὰ τοὺς ἐκλεκτούς*· ἤτοι τὸν τῆς τοῦ Ἀντιχρίστου βασιλείας χρόνον *ἐν τῇ συντελείᾳ*,[2079] καθὼς Δανιὴλ φησι, *καιρὸν καὶ καιροὺς καὶ ἥμισυ καιροῦ*.[2080] Τοῦτο διπλῆν ἔχει τὴν ἔννοιαν. Γίνωσκε καὶ ἱστορικῶς μὲν ἤδη συμβεβηκέναι τοῖς Ἰουδαίοις, προσδοκᾶσθαι δὲ καὶ ἀνηγμένως, ἐπὶ τῆς τοῦ παντὸς κόσμου συντελείας γενήσεσθαι. Καὶ γὰρ μετὰ τὴν τόλμαν τὴν ἐπὶ τῷ σταυρῷ τὰς τῆς θεοκτονίας[mdxxxiv] ἀπαιτούμενοι δίκας, Ῥωμαίων ἐπιστρατευσάντων αὐτοῖς καὶ προσκαθημένων καὶ τὴν Ἰουδαίαν ἅπασαν καὶ τὴν περιοικίδα χώραν ἐκπολιορκούντων ἐπὶ ἐνιαυτοῖς ὁλοκλήροις καὶ κατὰ τὰς χειμερίους ὥρας ὑφίσταντο τὰ ἐκ τοῦ πολέμου κακά. Καὶ ταῦτα ὡς ἐπὶ τὸ πλεῖστον ἐν τῷ χειμῶνι πολεμούντων, οὐ μὴν ἀλλὰ καὶ ἐν σαββάτῳ κατεσφάττοντο, μὴ δυνάμενοι διὰ τὴν σαββατικὴν ἀργίαν χεῖρας κινεῖν καὶ τοὺς πολεμοῦντας ἀμύνασθαι. Ἐπὶ δὲ τῆς συντελείας καὶ τῶν τοῦ Ἀντιχρίστου καιρῶν τὰ τῆς προρρήσεως ταύτης τοῦ Σωτῆρος ἀναγόμενα ῥήματα παρασκευάζει τοὺς πιστοὺς ἀεὶ τῶν τῆς ἀρετῆς πόνων ἀντέχεσθαι | **191v** καὶ ἐπείγεσθαι, μήτε ἐν χειμῶνι καταληφθῆναι μήτε ἐν *σαββάτῳ* κατὰ τὸν τελευταῖον χρόνον ἐκεῖνον. Ἢ καὶ τὴν ἔξοδον τῆς ἑκάστου ψυχῆς καὶ τὸν ἀπὸ τοῦ σώματος χωρισμόν, τοῦ μὲν *χειμῶνος* δηλοῦντος τὴν ἀκαρπίαν, ἢ ὥς τινες τὴν πολυπαθῆ τῶν ἀνθρώπων τύρβην, τοῦ δὲ σαββάτου τὴν ἀργίαν τῆς ἀρετῆς. Ἴσμεν γὰρ ὡς ὁ χειμὼν πρὸς καρπῶν ἐστι γένεσιν ἄγονος καὶ ὅτι τὸ σάββατον ἀργίαν ὑποδηλοῖ.

Τότε ἐάν τις ὑμῖν εἴπῃ, ἰδοὺ ὧδε.[2081] Ἐπειδὴ δύο ἐρωτήσεις προσήνεγκαν οἱ μαθηταὶ τῷ Χριστῷ, περί τε τῆς τῶν Ἱεροσολύμων συντελείας καὶ περὶ τῆς τοῦ κόσμου, εἰπὼν περὶ τῆς τῶν Ἱεροσολύμων τά τε προάγοντα σημεῖα καὶ τὰ ἐν αὐτῇ πάθη καὶ τὴν ὑπερβολὴν τοῦ πάθους καὶ τὴν ἐπὶ τῇ κολοβώσει τῶν ἡμερῶν ἐκείνων φιλανθρωπίαν τοῦ Θεοῦ, νῦν μεταβαίνει καὶ ἐπὶ τὴν τοῦ κόσμου συντέλειαν. Τὸ δὲ *τότε* οὐκ ἔστιν ἐμφαντικὸν τοῦ μετὰ τοῦτο εὐθέως, ἀλλὰ τοῦ καιροῦ μόνον παραστατικόν ἐστιν ἐκείνου καθ' ὃν τὰ ῥηθησόμενα μέλλει γίνεσθαι. Οὐ γὰρ τὸν μετὰ τὴν ἅλωσιν Ἱερουσαλὴμ σημαίνει χρόνον, ἀλλὰ τὸν πρὸ τῆς συντελείας. *Τότε* τοίνυν, πρὸ τῆς τοῦ Ἀντιχρίστου παρουσίας, ἔσονται αὐτοῦ πρόδρομοί τινες *ψευδόχριστοι καὶ ψευδοπροφῆται, σημεῖα* ποιοῦντες ἐκ φαντασίας δαιμόνων, διαπαίζοντες τοὺς τῶν ὁρώντων ὀφθαλμοὺς πρὸς τὸ ἀπατῆσαι τινάς, ὥστε, εἰ μὴ νήψωσι, καὶ οἱ δίκαιοι ἀπατ‹ηθ›ῶ‹σι›ν.[2082]

Οἱ κατὰ θεωρίαν ἐκλαμβάνοντες τὰ εἰρημένα, φασί· *τὸ βδέλυγμα* ἔστηκε· πῶς ἐστιν ὧδε ἢ ὧδε; Καὶ ὁ μὲν ἔξω τῆς πίστεως καὶ τοῦ | **192r** τῆς ἐκκλησίας κανόνος καὶ τῆς γραφῆς, λέγει· *ἰδοὺ ἐν τῇ ἐρήμῳ*. Διὸ ἐπιφέρεται, *μὴ ἐξέλθητε*. Ὁ γὰρ σοφίᾳ κοσμικῇ

2078 Matt. 24:22; Mark, 13:20.
2079 Matt. 13:40&49.
2080 Daniel, 12:7, quoted in Rev. 12:14.
2081 Matt. 24:23; Mark, 13:21.
2082 Abbreviated in cod.

πιστεύσας, ἐξῆλθε καὶ γέγονεν ἐθνικός. Ὁ δὲ ἀπόκρυφα ἐπαγγελλόμενος ἐρεῖ· *ἰδοὺ ἐν τοῖς ταμείοις*. Διὸ ἐπιφέρεται, *μὴ πιστεύσητε*.[2083] Καὶ γενικῶς μὲν εἷς Ἀντίχριστος, ὡς τὸ ψεῦδος ἕν· ‹ε›ἰδικῶς δὲ πολλοὶ καὶ πολλὰ ψευδῆ δόγματα. Ὡς δὲ Χριστοῦ, ἀληθοῦς λόγου, προφῆται, καὶ Ἀντιχρίστου ὄντος ψευδοῦς λόγου ψευδοπροφῆται.

> οἱ κατὰ θεωρίαν ἐκλαμβάνοντες τὰ εἰρημένα φασί τὸ βδέλυγμα ἕστηκε, πῶς ἔστιν ὧδε ἢ ὧδε; καὶ ὁ μὲν ἔξω τῆς πίστεως καὶ τοῦ τῆς ἐκκλησίας κανόνος καὶ τῆς γραφῆς λέγει. ἰδοὺ ἐν τῇ ἐρήμῳ. διὸ ἐπιφέρεται. *μὴ ἐξέλθητε*. ὁ γὰρ σοφίᾳ κοσμικῇ πιστεύσας ἐξῆλθε καὶ γέγονεν ἐθνικός. ὁ δὲ ἀπόκρυφα ἐπαγγελλόμενος ἐρεῖ. ἰδοὺ ἐν τοῖς ταμείοις, διὸ ἐπιφέρεται. *μὴ πιστεύσητε*.[mdxxxv]

> Καὶ γενικῶς μὲν εἷς Ἀντίχριστος, ὡς τὸ ψεῦδος ἕν. ‹ε›ἰδικῶς δὲ πολλοὶ καὶ πολλὰ ψευδῆ διδάγματα καὶ δόγματα. ὡς δὲ Χριστοῦ, ἀληθοῦς λόγου, προφῆται, καὶ Ἀντιχρίστου, ὄντος ψευδοῦς λόγου, ψευδοπροφῆται.[mdxxxvi]

Ἰδοὺ ἐν τῇ ἐρήμῳ.[2084] Ὃ δὲ λέγει τοιοῦτόν ἐστιν· ἐὰν ἔλθωσιν οἱ ἀπατεῶνες λέγοντες ὅτι ἦλθεν ὁ Χριστός, ἀλλ᾽ *ἐν τῇ ἐρήμῳ* ἐστὶ κρυπτόμενος ἢ ἐν οἰκίᾳ, μὴ ἀπατηθῆτε. Ὥσπερ γὰρ πᾶσι κατάδηλός ἐστιν *ἡ ἀστραπὴ*[2085] καὶ οὐ χρήζει τοῦ κατασημαίνοντος, οὕτως καὶ ἡ τοῦ Χριστοῦ παρουσία.

Τὴν ἔρημον λέγει διὰ τὸ τὸν Ἰωάννην ἐν ἐρήμῳ τηνικαῦτα διάγειν. Ἐν δὲ *τοῖς ταμείοις*, διὰ τὸ τὸν Χριστὸν ἐν τῇ πρώτῃ παρουσίᾳ ἐν σπηλαίῳ καὶ οἰκίσκῳ μικρῷ γεγεννῆσθαι.

> Τὴν ἔρημον λέγει διὰ τὸ τὸν Ἰωάννην ἐν ἐρήμῳ τηνικαῦτα διάγειν, ἐν δὲ *τοῖς ταμείοις* διὰ τὸ τὸν Χριστὸν ἐν τῇ πρώτῃ παρουσίᾳ ἐν σπηλαίῳ καὶ οἰκίσκῳ μικρῷ γεγεννῆσθαι.[mdxxxvii]

> τὴν ἔρημον λέγει διὰ τὸ τὸν Ἰωάννην ἐν ἐρήμῳ τηνικαῦτα διάγειν, ἐν δὲ *τοῖς ταμείοις* διὰ τὸ τὸν Χριστὸν ἐν τῇ πρώτῃ παρουσίᾳ ἐν σπηλαίῳ καὶ οἰκίσκῳ μικρῷ γεγεννῆσθαι.[mdxxxviii]

Ὥσπερ γὰρ ἡ ἀστραπή.[2086] Τροπικῶς ἡ τῆς ἀληθείας *ἀστραπή*, ᾗ ἔοικεν *ἡ παρουσία τοῦ υἱοῦ τοῦ ἀνθρώπου*, ἐν πάσῃ ἐξομαλίζεται νομικῇ, προφητικῇ, εὐαγγελικῇ, ἀποστολικῇ γραφῇ. Καὶ ἐξελθοῦσα *ἀπὸ ἀνατολῶν*, τῶν ἀρχῶν τοῦ Θεοῦ, φαίνεται *ἕως* τῶν κατὰ τὴν οἰκονομίαν τοῦ πάθους *δυσμῶν*. Ὅρα δέ, εἰ μία ἀνατολὴ ὁ νόμος, μία δύσις τὸ πέρας τοῦ νόμου. Ἄλλη ἀνατολὴ ἕως δύσεως, Ἰησοῦς Χριστὸς ἕως Παύλου, ᾧ ἐσχάτῳ *πάντων ὡσπερεὶ ἐκτρώματι ἐφάνη*.[2087]

2083 Matt. 24:26.
2084 Matt. 24:26.
2085 Cf. Matt. 24:27; Luke, 17:24.
2086 Matt. 24:27; Luke, 17:24.
2087 1 Cor. 15:8.

> τροπικῶς ἡ τῆς ἀληθείας ἀστραπή, ᾗ ἔοικεν ἡ παρουσία τοῦ υἱοῦ τοῦ ἀνθρώπου, ἐν πάσῃ ἐξομαλίζεται νομικῇ, προφητικῇ, εὐαγγελικῇ, ἀποστολικῇ γραφῇ. καὶ ἐξελθοῦσα ἀπὸ ἀνατολῶν, τῶν ἀρχῶν τοῦ Χριστοῦ, φαίνεται ἕως τῶν κατὰ τὴν οἰκονομίαν τοῦ πάθους δυσμῶν. ὅρα δὲ εἰ μία ἀνατολὴ ὁ νόμος, μία δύσις τὸ πέρας τοῦ νόμου. ἄλλη ἀνατολὴ ἕως δύσεως Ἰησοῦς Χριστὸς ἕως Παύλου, ᾧ ἐσχάτῳ *πάντων ὡσπερεὶ ἐκτρώματι ἐφάνη*.[mdxxxix]

Ὅπου γὰρ ἐὰν ᾖ τὸ πτῶμα.[2088] Ὥσπερ ἐπὶ νεκρῷ ζώῳ *οἱ ἀετοὶ* καταρράσσουσιν ἵνα τραφῶσιν, οὕτως καὶ τοῦ Χριστοῦ ὀφθέντος συνενεχθήσονται αὐτῷ οἱ ἅγιοι. | **192v** Οὐ γὰρ (ὥσπερ ἐπὶ τῇ πρώτῃ παρουσίᾳ) ἀπὸ τόπου εἰς τόπον ἐποιεῖτο τὴν μετάβασιν διὰ τὴν σάρκα οὕτω καὶ ἐπὶ τῆς δευτέρας ἔσται· ἀλλ᾽ *ἐν ῥιπῇ ὀφθαλμοῦ*[2089] πᾶσι κατάδηλος ἔσται ἡ παρουσία αὐτοῦ, ὡς *ἀστραπὴ* μὴ δεομένη τοῦ μηνύοντος. Καὶ εὐθέως πρὸς αὐτὸν συνάγονται πάντες οἱ ἅγιοι, πτεροφυήσαντες ὡς ἀετοί.

> Ὥσπερ γὰρ ἐπὶ νεκρῷ ζῴῳ *οἱ ἀετοὶ* καταρράσσουσιν, ἵνα τραφῶσιν, οὕτω καὶ τοῦ Χριστοῦ ὀφθέντος συνενεχθήσονται αὐτῷ οἱ ἅγιοι. οὐ γὰρ ὥσπερ ἐπὶ τῇ πρώτῃ παρουσίᾳ ἀπὸ τόπου εἰς τόπον ἐποιεῖτο τὴν μετάβασιν διὰ τὴν σάρκα, οὕτω καὶ ἐπὶ τῆς δευτέρας ἔσται, ἀλλ᾽ *ἐν ῥιπῇ ὀφθαλμοῦ* πᾶσι κατάδηλος ἔσται ἡ παρουσία αὐτοῦ, ὡς ἀστραπὴ μὴ δεομένη τοῦ μηνύοντος. καὶ εὐθέως πρὸς αὐτὸν συνάγονται πάντες οἱ ἅγιοι πτεροφυήσαντες ὡς ἀετοί.[mdxl]

Ὅπου γὰρ *τὸ* κατὰ τὴν οἰκονομίαν τοῦ πάθους *πτῶμα* πεσόντος Ἰησοῦ ἵνα τοὺς πεσόντας στήσῃ, *συναχθήσονται* οὐχ οἱ τυχόντες, ἀλλ᾽ οἱ πτεροφυοῦντες μαθηταὶ καὶ κατὰ τὸν Σολομῶνα κατασκευάσαντες πτέρυγας ὡς ἀετοί,[2090] μεγαλοφυῶς καὶ βασιλικῶς πρὸς τὸ πάθος Χριστοῦ πεπιστευκότες. Διὸ οὐ γῦπες, οὐ κόρακες, ἀλλὰ τὸ μὴ νεκροβόρον ζῷον.

> *ὅπου* γὰρ τὸ κατὰ τὴν οἰκονομίαν τοῦ πάθους *πτῶμα* πεσόντος τοῦ Ἰησοῦ, ἵνα τοὺς πεσόντας στήσῃ, *συναχθήσονται* οὐχ οἱ τυχόντες, ἀλλ᾽ οἱ πτεροφυοῦντες μαθηταὶ καὶ κατὰ τὸν Σολομῶνα κατασκευάσαντες πτέρυγας ὡς ἀετοὶ μεγαλοφυῶς καὶ βασιλικῶς, πρὸς τὸ πάθος Χριστοῦ πεπιστευκότες. διὸ οὐ γῦπες, οὐ κόρακες, ἀλλὰ τὸ μὴ νεκροβόρον ζῷον.[mdxli]

> Ὅπου γὰρ ἂν ᾖ τὸ πτῶμα (φησί) ἐκεῖ συναχθήσονται οἱ ἀετοί. ὅπου γὰρ τὸ κατὰ τὴν οἰκονομίαν πτῶμα πεσόντος τοῦ Ἰησοῦ, ἵνα τοὺς πεσόντας στήσῃ, συναχθήσονται οὐχ οἱ τυχόντες, ἀλλ᾽ οἱ πτεροφυήσαντες μαθηταὶ καὶ κατὰ τὸν Σολομῶντα κατασκευάσαντες πτέρυγας ὡς ἀετοί, μεγαλοφυῶς καὶ βασιλικῶς πρὸς τὸ πάθος Χριστοῦ πεπιστευκότες. διὸ οὐ γῦπες, οὐ κόρακες, ἀλλὰ τὸ μὴ νεκροβόρον ζῷον.[mdxlii]

2088 Matt. 24:28.
2089 1 Cor. 15:52.
2090 Prov. 23:5.

> ὅπου γὰρ τὸ κατὰ τὴν οἰκονομίαν τοῦ πάθους πτῶμα πεσόντος Ἰησοῦ, ἵνα τοὺς πεσόντας στήσῃ, συναχθήσονται οὐχ οἱ τυχόντες, ἀλλ' οἱ πτεροφυοῦντες μαθηταὶ καὶ κατὰ τὸν Σολομῶνα κατασκευάσαντες πτέρυγας.[mdxliii]

Οὐδὲ γάρ, ὥς φασι οἱ ἱστοροῦντες περὶ αὐτοῦ, ἕτοιμον θήραν ἀξιοῖ λαβεῖν, ἐὰν μὴ ἀγωνίσηται περὶ τῆς τροφῆς.

> Οὐδὲ γὰρ (ὥς φασιν οἱ ἱστοροῦντες περὶ αὐτοῦ) ἕτοιμον θήραν ἀξιοῖ λαβεῖν, ἐὰν μὴ ἀγωνίσηται περὶ τῆς τροφῆς.[mdxliv]

Ὅτι δὲ οὐκ ἄλογον *πτῶμα* ἐπὶ Χριστοῦ λαβεῖν Συμεὼν λέγει· *οὗτος κεῖται εἰς πτῶσιν καὶ ἀνάστασιν πολλῶν.*[2091] Καὶ ἐπὶ Θεοῦ Παῦλος *τὸ μωρὸν τοῦ Θεοῦ* λέγει *καὶ τὸ ἀσθενὲς τοῦ Θεοῦ.*[2092] Ὅρα δὲ εἰ *πτῶμα* ἡ νεκρωθεῖσα σὰρξ ὑπὸ Κυρίου, ὃ οἱ μιμούμενοι συνάγονται ὡς *ἀετοί.*
Καθ' ὁμοίωσίν[mdxlv] τινα καὶ παραβολὴν εἴρηται καὶ παράδειγμα. Ὥσπερ γὰρ ὅταν *πτῶμα* καὶ σῶμα νεκρὸν εὑρεθείη που κείμενον, ἀπὸ τῶν ὑψηλοτάτων τόπων δι' ἀέρος φερόμενοι καὶ *ἀετοὶ* καὶ ἄλλα τῶν σαρκοφάγων ὀρνίθων ἐκ τοῦ ἀφανοῦς ἀδοκήτως ἐφίστανται τραφησόμενοι, τὸν αὐτὸν τρόπον, φησί, *ἔσται καὶ ἡ παρουσία τοῦ υἱοῦ τοῦ ἀνθρώπου.* Φαινομένου γὰρ αὐτοῦ πάλιν ἐπὶ τῆς γῆς κατὰ τὴν δευτέραν καὶ ἔνδοξον παρουσίαν ἐπὶ τῷ κρῖναι τὴν οἰκουμένην, καὶ ἀγγέλων τάγμα | **193r** τα δορυφοροῦντα φανήσεται· καὶ πάντες οἱ ἅγιοι διαναστάντες *ἐν ἀτόμῳ, ἐν ῥιπῇ ὀφθαλμοῦ* κατὰ τὴν σάλπιγγα τὴν ἐσχάτην,[2093] ὥς φησι ὁ ἀπόστολος, καθάπερ *ἀετοί* τινες πτηνοὶ καὶ ὀξεῖς τὴν κίνησιν ἐκ τοῦ ἀφανοῦς θᾶττον ἐπιφανήσονται, μάλα εἰκότως ἀετοῖς παρεικασθέντες διὰ τὸ φρονεῖν τὰ ὑψηλὰ καὶ οὐράνια καὶ ἀξίως τῆς βασιλείας τῶν οὐρανῶν πολιτεύεσθαι. Τινὲς δὲ τὸ ῥητὸν τοῦτο οὕτως ἐπειράθησαν ἐξηγήσασθαι, καὶ ἔφασαν ὡς ἐν *τῇ παρουσίᾳ* τῇ *δευτέρᾳ* τοῦ Κυρίου πάντες οἱ δικαίως πολιτευσάμενοι καὶ κατὰ τοὺς ἀετοὺς ὑψηλοὶ καὶ οὐράνιοι τῷ φρονήματι τὸν παράδεισον ἀπολήψονται καὶ κατ' ἐκεῖνον *συναχθήσονται* τὸν τόπον ὅπου *τὸ πτῶμα* γέγονε τοῦ Ἀδὰμ καὶ τῆς ἐντολῆς ἡ παράβασις,[2094] δι' ἧς εἰς ἁμαρτίαν κατέπεσεν.

> Καθ' ὁμοίωσίν τινα καὶ παραβολὴν εἴρηται καὶ παράδειγμα. ὥσπερ γάρ, ὅταν *πτῶμα* καὶ σῶμα νεκρὸν εὑρεθείη παρακείμενον, ἀπὸ τῶν ὑψηλοτάτων τόπων δι' ἀέρος φερόμενοι καὶ *ἀετοὶ* καὶ ἄλλοι σαρκοφάγοι ὀρνίθων ἐκ τοῦ ἀφανοῦς ἀδοκήτως ὑφίστανται τραφησόμενοι, τὸν αὐτὸν τρόπον, φησίν, ἔσται καὶ ἡ παρουσία *τοῦ υἱοῦ τοῦ ἀνθρώπου.* φαινομένου γὰρ αὐτοῦ πάλιν ἐπὶ τῆς γῆς κατὰ τὴν δευτέραν καὶ ἔνδοξον παρουσίαν ἐπὶ τῷ κρῖναι τὴν οἰκουμένην καὶ ἀγγέλων τάγματα δορυφοροῦντα φανήσεται καὶ πάντες οἱ ἅγιοι διαναστάντες *ἐν ἀτόμῳ, ἐν ῥιπῇ ὀφθαλμοῦ* κατὰ τὴν σάλπιγγα τὴν ἐσχάτην, ὡς

2091 Luke, 2:34. Origen, *commJohn*, XXVIII.22.188.
2092 1 Cor. 1:25.
2093 1 Cor. 15:52.
2094 Cf. 4 Macc. 13:15; 16:24; Matt. 15:3.

φησιν ὁ ἀπόστολος, καθάπερ *ἀετοί* τινες πτηνοὶ καὶ ὀξεῖς τὴν κίνησιν ἐκ τοῦ ἀφανοῦς θᾶττον ἐπιφανήσονται, μάλα εἰκότως *ἀετοῖς* παρεικασθέντες διὰ τὸ φρονεῖν τὰ ὑψηλὰ καὶ οὐράνια καὶ ἀξίως τῆς βασιλείας τῶν οὐρανῶν πολιτεύεσθαι. τινὲς δὲ τὸ ῥητὸν τοῦτο οὕτως ἐπειράθησαν ἐπεξηγήσασθαι καὶ ἔφασαν ὡς ἐν τῇ παρουσίᾳ τῇ δευτέρᾳ τοῦ κυρίου πάντες οἱ δικαίως πολιτευσάμενοι καὶ κατὰ τοὺς *ἀετοὺς* ὑψηλοὶ καὶ οὐράνιοι τῷ φρονήματι τὸν παράδεισον ἀπολείψονται [sic] καὶ κατ᾽ ἐκεῖνον *συναχθήσονται* τὸν τόπον, ὅπου τὸ πτῶμα γέγονε τοῦ Ἀδὰμ καὶ τῆς ἐντολῆς ἡ παράβασις, δι᾽ ἧς εἰς ἁμαρτίαν κατέπεσεν.[mdxlvi]

Ἀλλαχοῦ, ‹*πτῶμα*› τὸ σῶμα λέγει.[2095] Τὸ δὲ σῶμα ἐστὶν ἡ βρῶσις τῶν ἀετῶν. Ἐν μὲν τῷ πτώματι νόει τὸν παράδεισον, ἔνθα καὶ ἡ πτῶσις ἐγένετο· ἢ τὸν Ἅδην, ἔνθα ἡ πτῶσις τῶν πεπτωκότων. Ἐν δὲ τῷ σώματι, νόει τοῦ Χριστοῦ τὴν βασιλείαν.

Ἀλλαχοῦ, τὸ σῶμα λέγει. τὸ δὲ σῶμα ἐστὶν ἡ βρῶσις τῶν ἀετῶν. ἐν μὲν τῷ πτώματι νόει τὸν παράδεισον, ἔνθα καὶ ἡ πτῶσις ἐγένετο, ἢ τὸν ᾄδην, ἔνθα ἡ πτῶσις τῶν πεπτωκότων. ἐν δὲ τῷ σώματι, νόει τὴν τοῦ Χριστοῦ βασιλείαν.[mdxlvii]

Εὐθέως δὲ μετὰ τὴν θλῖψιν.[2096] Μετὰ τὴν πολλὴν ταραχὴν τῶν ἡμερῶν τοῦ Ἀντιχρίστου καὶ τῶν ψευδοπροφητῶν (φησί) *ὁ ἥλιος* ἀμαυρωθήσεται, οὐκ ἀφανισθήσεται. Τίς γὰρ ἔτι τοῦ ἡλίου ἢ τῶν ἀστέρων χρεία τοῦ ἡλίου τῆς *δικαιοσύνης*[2097] ὀφθέντος; Οὐδὲ γὰρ ἔτι τῶν ἀστέρων ἢ τῆς σελήνης χρεία νυκτὸς οὐκ οὔσης.

Τότε *καὶ αἱ δυνάμεις τῶν οὐρανῶν σαλευθήσονται.*[2098] Τῆς γὰρ κτίσεως πρὸς τὸ δοκοῦν τῷ Θεῷ ἀνακαινιζομένης ὁρῶντες οἱ ἄγγελοι τὸν μετασχηματισμὸν καὶ τοὺς ἀπὸ Ἀδὰμ μέχρι τότε λόγον ἀπαιτουμένους | **193v** ὧν ἔπραξαν, φρίξουσι καὶ *σαλευθήσονται*, τουτέστι θορυβηθήσονται. Τότε δὲ καὶ *τὸ σημεῖον τοῦ υἱοῦ τοῦ ἀνθρώπου φανήσεται ἐν τῷ οὐρανῷ*,[2099] τουτέστιν ὁ σταυρὸς λάμπων ὑπὲρ τὸν ἥλιον. Δείκνυσι δὲ καὶ τὰ τοῦ ἰδίου σώματος τραύματα πρὸς ἔλεγχον τῶν Ἰουδαίων.

Καὶ τότε κόψονται πᾶσαι αἱ φυλαί.[2100] Καὶ τότε θρηνήσουσι καὶ *κόψονται*[2101] *πᾶσαι αἱ φυλαί*, ὡς μὴ χρείας οὔσης κατηγορίας. Ἑαυτοὺς γὰρ ἐλέγξουσι καὶ θρηνήσουσι τῆς ἑαυτῶν δυσσεβείας τὴν τόλμαν. Ἥξει δὲ μετὰ τοῦ σταυροῦ, τὴν γνῶσιν τῆς μετὰ σαρκὸς οἰκονομίας πᾶσι τοῖς ἐπὶ γῆς ἀποκαλύπτων, ἵνα μὴ μόνον Ἰουδαῖοι ἀλλὰ καὶ οἱ ὀνομαζόμενοι μὲν Χριστιανοί, μὴ ὁμολογοῦντες δὲ Θεὸν τὸν ἐσταυρωμένον, θρηνήσωσι καὶ κόψωνται μεταμελόμενοι. Εἰ δὲ καὶ μετὰ τοῦ σταυροῦ ἔρχεται, ἀλλὰ *μετὰ δυνάμεως καὶ δόξης ἐπὶ τῶν νεφελῶν*, ὥσπερ καὶ ἀνελήφθη. Ἀποστελεῖ δὲ τοὺς ἀγγέλους

2095 Cf. Luke, 17:37.
2096 Matt. 24:29; cf. Mark, 13:24.
2097 Cf. Malachi, 3:20; Wisdom of Solomon, 5:6.
2098 Matt. 24:29; cf. Mark, 13:25.
2099 Matt. 24:30.
2100 Matt. 24:30.
2101 Cf. Micah, 1:8.

αὐτοῦ ἐπισυνάξαι τοὺς ἁγίους καὶ τοὺς ἐκ νεκρῶν ἀναστάντας, ὥστε ὑπαντῆσαι αὐτῷ ἐν νεφέλαις, ἵνα τιμήσῃ αὐτούς.

Καὶ ἀποστελεῖ τοὺς ἀγγέλους.[2102] *Ἀποστελεῖ* λέγων *τοὺς ἀγγέλους αὐτοῦ* ὁ υἱὸς τοῦ ἀνθρώπου, Θεὸν ἔδειξε τὸν υἱὸν τοῦ ἀνθρώπου. Θεοῦ γάρ εἰσιν οἱ ἄγγελοι καὶ τὸ ἀποστέλλειν αὐτοὺς ἴδιον Θεοῦ.

> *Ἀποστελεῖ* λέγων *τοὺς ἀγγέλους αὐτοῦ* ὁ υἱὸς τοῦ ἀνθρώπου, Θεὸν ἔδειξε τὸν υἱὸν τοῦ ἀνθρώπου. Θεοῦ γάρ εἰσιν οἱ ἄγγελοι καὶ τὸ ἀποστέλλειν αὐτοὺς ἴδιον Θεοῦ.[mdxlviii]

Τὸ δὲ *ἀπ' ἄκρων οὐρανῶν ἕως ἄκρων αὐτῶν*[2103] διδάσκει ἡμᾶς τὰ αὐτὰ εἶναι καὶ γῆς καὶ οὐρανῶν ἄκρα. Ὥστε Χριστῷ πιστεύειν δεῖ καὶ μὴ ἀπατᾶσθαι, ὡς ἐλαχίστου μορίου τῆς γῆς οὔσης ἐν μέσῳ τοῦ οὐρανοῦ ἀπείροις μεγέθεσιν ὑπερβάλλοντος αὐτήν.

> Τὸ δὲ *ἀπ' ἄκρων οὐρανῶν ἕως ἄκρων αὐτῶν* διδάσκει ἡμᾶς ταὐτὰ εἶναι καὶ γῆς καὶ οὐρανῶν ἄκρα, ὥστε Χριστῷ πιστεύειν δεῖ καὶ μὴ ἀπατᾶσθαι ὡς ἐλαχίστου μορίου τῆς γῆς οὔσης ἐν μέσῳ τοῦ οὐρανοῦ ἀπείροις μεγέθεσιν ὑπερβάλλοντος αὐτήν.[mdxlix]

> Τὸ δὲ *ἀπ' ἄκρων οὐρανῶν ἕως ἄκρων αὐτῶν* διδάσκει ἡμᾶς τὰ αὐτὰ εἶναι καὶ γῆς καὶ οὐρανῶν ἄκρα, ὥστε Χριστῷ πιστεύειν δεῖ καὶ μὴ ἀπατᾶσθαι, ὡς ἐλαχίστου μορίου τῆς γῆς οὔσης ἐν μέσῳ τοῦ οὐρανοῦ ἀπείροις μεγέθεσιν ὑπερβάλλοντος αὐτήν.[mdl]

Ἀπὸ δὲ τῆς συκῆς μάθετε.[2104] Ὁ νοῦς *τῆς συκῆς* καὶ τοῦ ἀμυγδάλου εἷς ἐστι.[mdli] Ταῦτα γὰρ τοῦ | **194r** παρελθόντος χειμῶνος δηλοῦσι τὴν ὥραν καὶ τῶν σωμάτων τὴν ἀνάστ‹ασ›ιν.[mdlii] Διὰ τῆς παραβολῆς *τῆς συκῆς* διδάσκει ὅτι οὐκ εὐθὺς ἐρχομένων τῶν σημείων ἔσται ἡ συντέλεια, ἀλλ' ἔστι καὶ χρόνος τις μεταξὺ τούτων, ὡς ἐπὶ τῆς ὀλύνθου *τῆς συκῆς* καὶ τοῦ θέρους. Ὅταν οὖν *ταῦτα* γένηται, φησί, οὐ πολὺ τὸ μέσον τῆς συντελείας καὶ τῆς παρουσίας τῆς ἐμῆς. *Θέρος* γάρ ἐστι πνευματικὸν ὁ μέλλων αἰὼν διὰ τὴν γαλήνην τὴν μετὰ τὸν νῦν αἰῶνα, ὅς ἐστι χειμών.[mdliii] Ὅτι δὲ πάντα ἔσται τὰ ἐσόμενα καὶ ὅτι ὄψεται πάντα *ἡ γενεὰ αὕτη* πρὸς βεβαίωσιν ἐπήγαγε τὸ *ἀμήν.*[2105] Γενεὰν δὲ ταύτην τοὺς πιστοὺς λέγει τοὺς ἀρξαμένους ἀπὸ τοῦ καιροῦ τῆς ἐπιδημίας καὶ διαμένοντας *ἕως τῆς συντελείας.*[2106] Ἵνα γὰρ μή τις εἴπῃ ὅτι σημείων καὶ τεράτων ὑπὸ τοῦ Ἀντιχρίστου ἐπιδεικνυμένων πρὸς ἀπάτην τῶν πολλῶν πάντες κατ' ἐκεῖνο καιροῦ ἀπατηθήσονται, ἐπήγαγεν· *ὅτι οὐ μὴ παρέλθῃ ἡ γενεὰ αὕτη.*[2107] Τουτέστι, πολλοὶ πιστοὶ καὶ ἀνεξαπάτητοι διαμενοῦσι καὶ ἐπ' αὐτῆς τῆς συντελείας. Ἢ γενεὰν λέγει τὴν τῶν πονηρῶν συναγωγὴν ἀπ' ἀρχῆς ἕως τέλους ἢ τὸ ἀνθρώπινον γένος.

2102 Matt. 24:31.
2103 Matt. 24:31.
2104 Matt. 24:32.
2105 Matt. 24:34.
2106 Matt. 28:20.
2107 Matt. 24:34.

Τουτέστι, πάντα ἃ εἶπον ἐκβήσεται πάντως καὶ ὄψεται αὐτὰ τὸ ἀνθρώπινον. Τινὲς δὲ τοὺς τότε πιστούς φασι λέγειν τοὺς ἐπὶ τῆς ἐν σαρκὶ παρουσίας αὐτοῦ ὄντας. Οὗτοι γὰρ οὐ μὴ ἀπόλωνταί φησὶ *ἕως ἂν* ἴδωσι τὰ μέλλοντα κακὰ τὴν Ἰουδαίαν καταλαβεῖν. Ἅπερ, ἐὰν *ἴδητε*, μὴ ἀμφιβάλητε ὅτι καὶ τὰ ἄλλα ἔσται ἃ εἶπον.

62

(ΩΡΙΓΕΝΟΥΣ) *Ὁ οὐρανὸς καὶ ἡ γῆ παρελεύσονται.*[2108] Οἱ γὰρ τοῦ Σωτῆρος λόγοι ἀεὶ τὰ οἰκεῖα ἐνεργήσουσιν, ὡς τέλειοι καὶ οὐκ ἐπιδεχόμενοι βελτίους | **194v** γενέσθαι παρελθόντες. Ἀλλ᾽ *οὐρανὸς* μὲν *καὶ ἡ γῆ παρελεύσονται, οἱ δὲ λόγοι* αὐτῶν μενοῦσι, λόγοι ὄντες τοῦ δι᾽ οὗ τὰ *πάντα ἐγένετο.*[2109][mdliv] Ὁ γὰρ λόγος τῶν γεγονότων οὐ παρέρχεται, εἰ καὶ αὐτὰ παρέρχεται.

> οἱ γὰρ τοῦ σωτῆρος λόγοι ἀεὶ τὰ οἰκεῖα ἐνεργήσουσιν ὡς τέλειοι καὶ οὐκ ἐπιδεχόμενοι βελτίους γενέσθαι παρελθόντες ὅ εἰσιν. ἀλλ᾽ *ὁ οὐρανὸς* μὲν *καὶ ἡ γῆ παρελεύσονται, οἱ δὲ λόγοι* αὐτοῦ μενοῦσι λόγοι ὄντες τοῦ δι᾽ οὗ τὰ πάντα ἐγένετο. ὁ γὰρ λόγος τῶν γεγονότων οὐ παρέρχεται, εἰ καὶ αὐτὰ παρέρχεται.[mdlv]

Περὶ δὲ τῆς ἡμέρας ἐκείνης καὶ ὥρας.[2110] Διδάσκει διὰ τούτου τοὺς μαθητὰς μὴ ζητεῖν πάντα μανθάνειν, ἅπερ τὴν ἀνθρωπίνην ὑπεραναβαίνει γνῶσιν. Εἰπὼν γὰρ *οὔτε οἱ ἄγγελοι*, ἐπεστόμισεν αὐτοὺς μαθεῖν ὅπερ ἐκεῖνοι ἀγνοοῦσι. Μόνῳ δὲ τῷ Πατρὶ ἀνατίθησι τὸ πρᾶγμα, φοβερὸν αὐτὸ διὰ τούτου κατασκευάζων. Ἄλλως τε δέ, δείκνυσι διὰ τούτου ἡμῖν ἐννοεῖν ὅτι τοῦ Πατρὸς εἰδότος καὶ αὐτὸς οἶδεν (οὐδὲ γὰρ εἶπεν ὅτι ὁ Υἱὸς ‹οὐ› γινώσκει ἀλλὰ μόνος *ὁ Πατήρ*), τουτέστιν ἡ αἰτία τοῦ εἰδέναι τὸν Υἱὸν παρὰ Πατρός ‹ἐστιν›. Εἴπερ γάρ ἐστι καὶ ὁμοούσιος, καὶ τὸ γινώσκειν ἔχει. Πολλὰ δὲ καὶ ἀπὸ τοῦ ἀνθρωπίνου μέρους ὁ Κύριος διαλέγεται. Εἰ γὰρ καὶ γινώσκει ὡς Θεός, ἀλλ᾽ ὡς ἄνθρωπος ἀγνοεῖ ὅταν τὸ φαινόμενον χωρίσῃ τοῦ νοουμένου. Εἰ δὲ λέγοιεν τινὲς ἀγνοεῖν τὸν Υἱόν, λεκτέον ὅτι πῶς οἷόν τε ἐστιν ἀγνοεῖν τὴν ἡμέραν, ᾧ τὰ πρὸ ὀλίγου ἐσόμενα εὔγνωστα ‹ἦν› καὶ ‹αὐτός ἐστιν› ὁ τῶν χρόνων ποιητής;[mdlvi] Πῶς ‹δὲ› μέρος ἐλάχιστον τοῦ χρόνου ἀγνοεῖ, πᾶσιν οὖν εὔδηλον· ὅτι γινώσκει μὲν ὡς Θεός, ἀγνοεῖ δὲ ὡς ἄνθρωπος. Ἤτοι διὰ τὸ αἰφνιδίως καὶ ἀπροόπτως ὀφθῆναι αὐτὸν μέλλειν, εἶπε τοῦτο. Τί τοίνυν ἐστὶν ἐν τούτοις ἐπισημήνασθαι ἄξιον; Ὅτι ὁ μὲν Ματθαῖος οὐδὲν εἶπε περὶ τῆς τοῦ Υἱοῦ ἀγνωσίας. Δοκεῖ δὲ τῷ Μάρκῳ ἐμφέρεσθαι καὶ τούτου τὴν ἔννοιαν ἐκ τοῦ φᾶναι *εἰ μὴ ὁ πατὴρ μόνος.*[2111] Ἡμεῖς δὲ ἡγούμεθα τὸ *μόνος* πρὸς τὴν τῶν | **195r** ἀγγέλων διαστολὴν εἰρῆσθαι, τὸν δὲ Υἱὸν μὴ συμπαραλαμβάνεσθαι τοῖς ἑαυτοῦ δούλοις

2108 Matt. 24:35.
2109 John, 1:3.
2110 Matt. 24:36; cf. Mark, 13:32.
2111 Mark, 13:32.

κατὰ τὴν ἄγνοιαν. Ἀψευδὴς γὰρ ὁ εἰπὼν ὅτι *πάντα ὅσα ἔχει ὁ πατὴρ ἐμά ἐστιν.*[2112] Ἓν δὲ ὧν ἔχει καὶ ἡ γνῶσις ἐστὶ τῆς ἡμέρας ἐκείνης καὶ τῆς ὥρας. Παρασιωπήσας τοίνυν ὡς ὁμολογούμενον τὸ ἑαυτοῦ πρόσωπον ἐν τῇ λέξει τοῦ Ματθαίου ὁ Κύριος, τοὺς ἀγγέλους εἶπεν ἀγνοεῖν, εἰδέναι δὲ τὸν Υἱὸν μόνον τὴν τοῦ Πατρὸς γνῶσιν κατὰ τὸ σιωπώμενον καὶ ἑαυτοῦ εἶναι λέγων διὰ τὸ καὶ ἐν ἄλλοις εἰρηκέναι, *καθὼς γινώσκει με ὁ πατὴρ κἀγὼ γινώσκω τὸν πατέρα.*[2113][mdlvii] Εἰ δὲ γινώσκει ὁ Πατὴρ τὸν Υἱὸν ὅλον διόλου, ὥστε καὶ τὴν ἐναποκειμένην αὐτῷ σοφίαν πᾶσαν ἐπίστασθαι, κατὰ τὸ ἴσον μέτρον καὶ ἐπιγνωσθήσεται παρὰ τοῦ Υἱοῦ, δηλονότι μετὰ πάσης τῆς ἐνυπαρχούσης αὐτῷ σοφίας καὶ τῆς προγνώσεως τῶν μελλόντων. Ταύτης μὲν οὖν ἀξιοῦμεν τῆς παραμυθίας τὸ παρὰ τῷ Ματθαίῳ κείμενον, *εἰ μὴ ὁ πατὴρ μόνος*. Τὸ δὲ Μάρκου, ἐπειδὴ φανερῶς δοκεῖ καὶ τὸν Υἱὸν ἀπομερίζειν τῆς γνώσεως, οὕτω νοοῦμεν· ὅτι *οὐδεὶς οἶδεν* οὔτε οἱ ἄγγελοι τοῦ Θεοῦ, ἀλλ᾽ οὐδ᾽ ἂν ὁ Υἱὸς ἔγνω *εἰ μὴ ὁ Πατήρ.*[2114] Τουτέστιν ἡ αἰτία τοῦ εἰδέναι τὸν Υἱὸν παρὰ τοῦ Πατρός ‹ἐστιν›. Καὶ ἀβίαστός ἐστι τῷ εὐγνωμόνως ἀκούοντι ἡ ἐξήγησις αὕτη, ἐπειδὴ οὐ πρόσκειται τὸ *μόνος* ὡς καὶ παρὰ τῷ Ματθαίῳ. Ἔστιν οὖν ὁ νοῦς ὁ παρὰ τῷ Μάρκῳ τοιοῦτος· *περὶ δὲ τῆς ἡμέρας ἢ ὥρας οὐδεὶς οἶδεν,* οὔτε οἱ ἄγγελοι τοῦ Θεοῦ ἀλλ᾽ οὐδ᾽ ἂν ὁ Υἱὸς ἔγνω, *εἰ μὴ ὁ Πατήρ.*[2115] Ἐκ γὰρ τοῦ Πατρὸς αὐτοῦ ὑπῆρχε δεδομένη ἡ γνῶσις. Τοῦτο δὲ εὐφημότατόν ἐστι καὶ θεοπρεπὲς περὶ τοῦ Υἱοῦ λέγειν, | **195v** ὅτι οὗπερ ἐστὶν ὁμοούσιος ἐξ αὐτοῦ καὶ τὸ γινώσκειν ἔχει καὶ τὸ ἐν πάσῃ σοφίᾳ καὶ δόξῃ τῇ πρεπούσῃ αὐτοῦ τῇ θεότητι θεωρεῖσθαι.

Arius and Eunomius revel, as if ignorance of the master is the glory of the disciples, and they say: He who knows and he who does not know cannot be equal. Against them, the following things need to be said briefly. Jesus, that is, the Logos of God, made all time (for *all things were made through him, and without him nothing was made*[2116]), therefore, the day of judgment is included in all things. How then could he be ignorant of a part of which he knows the whole? Moreover, this should be said: What is greater, knowledge of the Father or of the judgment? If he knows the greater, how is he ignorant of the lesser? We read the saying, *all things that are the Father's have been given to me.*[2117] If all things of the Father are the Son's, by what reason has he reserved for himself the knowledge of a single day and refused to communicate it to the Son? Nevertheless, the following should be added, too: If he is ignorant of the last day of time, he is ingorant also of the penultimate day, and of all days in back of it. For it is not possible that one who is ignorant of the first would know what is the second. Therefore, since we have shown that the Son is not ignorant of the day of consummation, why he is said not to know calls for explanation. The apostle writes

2112 John, 16:15.
2113 John, 10:15.
2114 Mark, 13:32.
2115 Mark, 13:32.
2116 John, 1:3.
2117 Matt. 11:27; Luke, 10:22.

of the Saviour: *In whom are hidden all the treasures of wisdom and knowledge.*[2118] Consequently, all the treasures of wisdom and knowledge are in Christ, yet they are hidden. Why are they hidden? After his resurrection, when he was asked by the apostles about the day, he answered plainly: *It is not for you to know times or kairoi which the Father has set within His own authority.*[2119] When he says, *It is not for you to know,* he shows that he himself knows, but it is not expedient for the apostles to know, so that they should be always uncertain about the coming of the Judge: they will live every day in such a way as though they will be judged on another day.[mdlviii]

63

196v (ΩΡΙΓΕΝΟΥΣ) Ἀπέκρυψεν ὁ Υἱὸς εἰπὼν μὴ γινώσκειν εἰς τὸ συμφέρον τῶν μαθητῶν.[mdlix]

> ἀπέκρυψεν ὁ υἱὸς εἰπὼν μὴ γινώσκειν εἰς τὸ συμφέρον τῶν μαθητῶν.[mdlx] Πατρὶ οὐχ ὡς ἂν ὑποτάκτου[mdlxi] ποτὲ ὄντος, ἀλλ' ὡς μηδέπω τῶν μελῶν αὐτοῦ πάντων τελειωθέντων. οὕτως ὅσον τὸ σῶμα τοῦ Χριστοῦ οὐκ *οἶδεν* τὴν ἡμέραν ἐκείνην ἢ τὴν ὥραν, *οὐδὲ* αὐτὸς λέγει εἰδέναι. καὶ κατὰ τὴν γραφὴν δὲ περὶ τοῦ εἰδέναι συνήθεια, ὡς καὶ *ὁ φυλάσσων ἐντολὰς οὐ γνώσεται πρᾶγμα πονηρόν*[2120] (ἀντὶ τοῦ. οὐ πεσεῖται. καὶ *τὸν μὴ γνόντα ἁμαρτίαν ἁμαρτίαν ὑπὲρ ἡμῶν ἐποίησεν*[2121] (ἀντὶ τοῦ μὴ ἁμαρτόντα) καὶ *Ἀδὰμ ἔγνω Εὔαν*[2122] *τὴν γυναῖκα αὐτοῦ.*[mdlxii]
>
> ἀπέκρυψεν ὁ υἱὸς εἰπὼν μὴ γινώσκειν εἰς τὸ συμφέρον τῶν μαθητῶν. ἕτερος δέ φησιν, ὅτι ὥσπερ ὁ Παῦλός φησι *τότε καὶ ὁ υἱὸς ὑποταγήσεται τῷ πατρί,*[2123] οὐχ ὡς ἂν ὑποτάκτου [Diehl: ἀνυποτάκτου] ποτὲ ὄντος, ἀλλ' ὡς μηδέπω τῶν μελῶν αὐτοῦ πάντων τελειωθέντων. Οὕτως ἐπεὶ τὸ σῶμα τοῦ Χριστοῦ οὐκ οἶδε τὴν ἡμέραν ἐκείνην ἢ τὴν ὥραν, οὐδὲ αὐτὸς λέγει εἰδέναι ... καὶ κατὰ τὴν τῆς γραφῆς περὶ τοῦ εἰδέναι συνήθειαν καὶ *ὁ φυλάσσων ἐντολὰς οὐ γνώσεται πταῖσμα,* ἀντὶ τοῦ οὐ πείσεται. καὶ *τὸν μὴ γνόντα ἁμαρτίαν ἁμαρτίαν ὑπὲρ ἡμῶν ἐποίησε.* τοιοῦτόν τι σημαίνει καὶ τὸ *οὐδὲ ὁ υἱός*, καὶ κατὰ τὸ *ἔγνω Ἀδὰμ Εὔαν τὴν γυναῖκα αὐτοῦ.*[mdlxiii]

Ὥσπερ δὲ αἱ ἡμέραι τοῦ Νῶε.[2124] Πρὸς σύστασιν τῶν ἀψευδῶν αὐτοῦ λόγων κέχρηται τοῖς ἤδη γεγονόσιν, ἀσφαλιζόμενος τὸν ἀκροατὴν διὰ τὸ ἀπροσδοκήτως μέλλειν ἐπελθεῖν τὴν τοῦ Κυρίου παρουσίαν. *Ὥσπερ* γὰρ τῷ *Νῶε* ἠπίστουν σημαίνοντι τὸν κατακλυσμόν, οὕτω καὶ νῦν χλεύην ἡγοῦνται τοὺς εὐαγγελικοὺς λόγους ἕως ἔλθῃ

2118 Col. 2:3.
2119 Acts, 1:7.
2120 Ecclesiastes, 8:5.
2121 2 Cor. 5:21.
2122 Gen. 4:1.
2123 1 Cor. 15:28.
2124 Matt. 24:37; cf. Luke, 17:26-27.

τῶν πραγμάτων ὁ καιρός. Σημαίνει δὲ ὅτι καὶ εἰς *τὸ τέλος*[2125] οὐδὲν ἧττον οἱ ἄνθρωποι ἐξ ἀναισθησίας[mdlxiv] ἀφορήτου τρυφῶσι κατὰ τὴν ὁμοιότητα τῶν ἡμερῶν *Νῶε*. Ἕως γὰρ τοῦ φανῆναι τὸν κριτὴν οὐκ ἀποστήσονται οἱ ἄνθρωποι τῆς φιληδονίας, ἐξ αὐτῶν | **197r** τῶν ἔργων ἐξαρπάζοντα[mdlxv] αὐτούς.

Ἐνταῦθα ὁ Κύριος[mdlxvi] τῇ τρυφῇ τῇ ἐπὶ *τοῦ Νῶε* παραβάλλει τὸν καιρὸν τῆς παρουσίας αὐτοῦ. Εἰ τοίνυν τρυφὴ καὶ *εἰρήνη καὶ ἀσφάλεια*,[2126] καθὼς καὶ ὁ Παῦλος φησί, πῶς λέγει *μετὰ τὴν θλῖψιν τῶν ἡμερῶν ἐκείνων*;[2127] Εἰ τρυφή, πῶς θλῖψις; Τρυφὴ μέν, τοῖς ἀναισθήτως διακειμένοις· θλῖψις δὲ τοῖς δικαίοις. Δεικνύει γὰρ ὅτι τοῦ Ἀντιχρίστου ἐλθόντος ἡ ‹τ›ομή[2128] πλείων ἔσται τοῖς παρανόμοις, ἅτε τῆς οἰκείας ἀπεγνωκόσι σωτηρίας. Τότε γαστριμαργία καὶ κῶμοι, τότε μέθαι. Διὸ μάλιστα καὶ ὑπόδειγμα τίθησιν ἁρμόζον. Καθάπερ γὰρ τῆς κιβωτοῦ γινομένης οὐκ ἐπίστευον, ἀλλὰ προέκειτο μὲν ἐν μέσῳ τὰ μέλλοντα προκηρύττουσα κακά, ἐκεῖνοι δὲ ὁρῶντες αὐτὴν ὡς οὐδενὸς ἐσομένου οὕτως ἐτρύφων, οὕτω καὶ νῦν φαίνεται μὲν ὁ Ἀντίχριστος προμηνύων τὰ εἰρημένα, οἱ δὲ τῇ μέθῃ τῆς κακίας[mdlxvii] κατεχόμενοι οὔτε αἰσθάνονται τῶν παρόντων. Διὸ καὶ ὁ Παῦλός φησι· *ὥσπερ ἡ ὠδὶν τῇ ἐν γαστρὶ ἐχούσῃ*,[2129] οὕτως αὐτοῖς πάρεστιν.

> Ταῦτα δὲ εἶπε, δηλῶν ὡς ἀθρόον ἥξει, καὶ ἀπροσδοκήτως, καὶ τῶν πλειόνων τρυφώντων.... Εἰ γὰρ τρυφὴ τότε, καὶ εἰρήνη, καὶ ἀσφάλεια, καθὼς ὁ Παῦλός φησι, πῶς λέγει, *μετὰ τὴν θλῖψιν τῶν ἡμερῶν ἐκείνων*; Εἰ τρυφή, πῶς θλῖψις; Τρυφὴ τοῖς ἀναισθήτως διακειμένοις, καὶ εἰρήνη.... Ἐντεῦθεν δείκνυσιν, ὅτι τοῦ ἀντιχρίστου ἐλθόντος, τὰ τῶν ἀτόπων ἡδονῶν ἐπιταθήσεται ἐν τοῖς παρανόμοις καὶ τῆς οἰκείας ἀπεγνωκόσι σωτηρίας. Τότε γαστριμαργίαι, κῶμοι, τότε καὶ μέθαι. Διὸ καὶ μάλιστα ὑπόδειγμα τίθησιν ἁρμόζον τῷ πράγματι. Καθάπερ γὰρ τῆς κιβωτοῦ γινομένης οὐκ ἐπίστευον, φησίν, ἀλλὰ προέκειτο μὲν ἐν μέσῳ τὰ μέλλοντα προανακηρύττουσα κακά, ἐκεῖνοι δὲ ὁρῶντες αὐτήν, ὡς οὐδενὸς ἐσομένου δεινοῦ, οὕτως ἐτρύφων. οὕτω καὶ νῦν, φανεῖται μὲν ὁ ἀντίχριστος, ... οἱ δὲ τῇ μέθῃ τῆς κακίας κατεχόμενοι οὐδὲ αἰσθήσονται τοῦ φόβου τῶν ἐσομένων. Διὸ καὶ Παῦλός φησιν. *Ὥσπερ ἡ ὠδὶν τῇ ἐν γαστρὶ ἐχούσῃ*, οὕτως αὐτοῖς παραστήσεται τὰ φοβερὰ ἐκεῖνα καὶ ἀνήκεστα.[mdlxviii]

τότε δύο ἔσονται ἐν τῷ ἀγρῷ.[2130] Τότε (φησί)
ἀμερίμνων ὄντων πάντων

> οὕτως ἀμερίμνων αὐτῶν ὄντων, ἐπελεύσεται.[mdlxix]

2125 Cf. Matt. 24:6&14; Mark, 13:7; Luke, 21:9.
2126 1 Thess. 5:3.
2127 Matt. 24:29.
2128 Cod. δομή.
2129 1 Thess. 5:3.
2130 Matt. 24:40.

καὶ ἐργαζομένων (*εἴτε δοῦλοι* εἰσὶν *εἴτε ἐλεύθεροι*,[2131] εἴτε ἄρρενες εἴτε θήλειαι)[2132] οἱ μὲν δίκαιοι ἁρπάζονται εἰς ὑπάντησιν τοῦ Κυρίου, οἱ δὲ ἀσεβεῖς ἐῶνται.
Ἤτοι ἀγρὸν λέγει τὸν κόσμον, ἔνθα *ὁ μὲν εἰς τὸ Πνεῦμα σπείρων*, θερίζει *ζωήν*, *ὁ δὲ εἰς τὴν σάρκα, φθοράν*.[2133]

> Κατὰ δὲ τοῦτο ἀγρὸς καὶ *ὁ κόσμος* πᾶς λέγοιτο ἂν καὶ οὐ μόνον ἡ ἐκκλησία τοῦ θεοῦ. ἐν γὰρ παντὶ κόσμῳ ὁ μὲν *υἱὸς τοῦ ἀνθρώπου* ἔσπειρε *τὸ καλὸν σπέρμα*, ὁ δὲ πονηρὸς *τὰ ζιζάνια*, ἅπερ εἰσὶν οἱ μοχθηροὶ λόγοι, οἱ ἀπὸ κακίας υἱοὶ τοῦ πονηροῦ.[mdlxx]

ἀληθούσας[2134] δέ, τοὺς διδασκάλους τοὺς ἀπολεπτύνοντας τὰς γραφάς.
Ἢ *δύο ἐν τῷ ἀγρῷ*, τῷ ἡγεμονικῷ, ὅ τε τοῦ σπουδαίου νοῦς καὶ ὁ τοῦ φαύλου καὶ τῶν ἀληθουσῶν ἐν τῷ βαρεῖ *μυλῶνι* τοῦ κόσμου ψυχῶν (ἐν αὐτῷ γὰρ καθάπερ ἐν μύλῃ περιστρεφόμεθα ἐν κακοπαθείᾳ καὶ μόχθῳ τὸν ἄρτον ἐσθίοντες)[mdlxxi] ἔνθα ἡ μὲν καλὴ καὶ ἀγαθὴ *παραλαμβάνεται*[2135] (τουτέστιν οἱ πονοῦντες[2136] ἐπωφελῶς, | **197v** ἐν τοῖς τῆς δικαιοσύνης ἔργοις[2137]), ἡ δὲ φαύλη, ὡς ἀναξία *ἀφίεται*, ἤγουν οἱ ἐν τοῖς ματαίοις τὴν σπουδὴν ἔχοντες, μυλῶνι, πτωχεία, κλίνῃ, πλούτῳ.

> Νῦν δὲ *ἐν τῷ ἀγρῷ*, τῷ ἡγεμονικῷ, ‹γενικῶς› *δύο*, ‹ὅ› μέν ἐστι τοῦ σπουδαίου νοῦς ὡς Νῶε *γεωργὸς γῆς*[2138] ὁ δὲ τοῦ φαύλου ὡς Κάϊν *γῆς ἐργάτης*.[2139] καὶ τῶν ἀληθουσῶν δὲ ἐν τῷ βαρεῖ *μυλῶνι* ψυχῶν τοῦ κόσμου ἡ μὲν καλὴ καὶ ἀγαθὴ *παραλαμβάνεται*, ἡ δὲ φαύλη ὡς ἀναξία *ἀφίεται*.[mdlxxii]
>
> δύναται δὲ σημαίνεσθαι καὶ τὰ δύο ἐπὶ μιᾶς ὕλης σώματα, ὧν τὸ μὲν τοῦ δικαίου ὁ ἕτερός ἐστι τῶν ἐπὶ τῆς μιᾶς κλίνης ὁ παραλαμβανόμενος, τὸ δὲ τοῦ ἀδίκου ὁ ἕτερος καὶ ἀφιέμενος. καὶ τὸ μὲν σῶμα ὡς ἀσθενὲς ἐπὶ κλίνης ἐστὶν κἂν παραλαμβάνηται, ἡ δὲ ψυχὴ διὰ πολλῶν, ‹ὧν Kl› ἀνέχεται ἐν τῷ βίῳ, ἀλήθει ἐν τῷ μυλῶνι τοῦ κόσμου.[mdlxxiii]
>
> Μυλῶνι, πτωχεία, κλίνῃ πλούτῳ.[mdlxxiv]
>
> ἢ δύο ἐν τῷ ἀγρῷ τῷ ἡγεμονικῷ, ὅ τε τοῦ σπουδαίου νοῦς καὶ ὁ τοῦ φαύλου, καὶ τῶν ἀληθουσῶν ἐν τῷ βαρεῖ μυλῶνι τοῦ κόσμου ψυχῶν ἔνθα ἡ μὲν καλὴ καὶ ἀγαθὴ παραλαμβάνεται, ἡ δὲ φαύλη ὡς ἀναξία ἀφίεται. δύναται δὲ σημαίνεσθαι καὶ τὰ δύο ἐπὶ μιᾶς ὕλης σώματα, ὧν τὸ μὲν τοῦ δικαίου ὁ ἕτερός ἐστι τῶν ἐπὶ τῆς μιᾶς κλίνης ὁ παραλαμβανόμενος, τὸ δὲ τοῦ ἀδίκου ὁ ἕτερος καὶ ἀφιέμενος. καὶ τὸ μὲν σῶμα ὡς ἀσθενὲς ἐπὶ κλίνης ἐστὶν κἂν παραλαμβάνηται, ἡ δὲ ψυχὴ διὰ πολλῶν, ‹ὧν Kl› ἀνέχεται ἐν τῷ βίῳ, ἀλήθει ἐν τῷ μυλῶνι τοῦ κόσμου.[mdlxxv]

2131 1 Cor. 12:13; cf. Gal. 3:28; Eph. 3:28; Col. 3:11.
2132 Cf. Gal. 3:28.
2133 Cf. Gal. 6:8.
2134 Matt. 24:42.
2135 Matt. 24:4; Luke, 17:34-35.
2136 Cod. πονοοῦντες.
2137 Cf. Is. 32:17; Psalms of Solomon, 18:8.
2138 Cf. Gen. 9:20.
2139 Cf. Gen. 4:2.

Ὅπερ δέ φησι ὁ Λουκᾶς ὅτι καὶ *δύο ἔσονται ἐν τῇ κλίνῃ*,[2140] δηλοῖ ὅτι ἐν νυκτὶ ἔσται ἡ παρουσία.[mdlxxvi]

Γρηγορεῖτε οὖν.[2141] Ἀγρυπνεῖν ἐπιτάττει πρὸς ἐργασίαν ἀρετῆς διὰ τὸ ἄδηλον τῆς παρουσίας τοῦ κριτοῦ. Καὶ γὰρ καὶ οἱ τοὺς λῃστάς φησι τηροῦντες τὴν πᾶσαν ἀγρυπνοῦσι νύκτα. Ἀπὸ δὲ τῆς παραβολῆς διδάσκει ὅτι εἰ ᾔδεισαν οἱ πολλοὶ πότε ἀποθανοῦνται, εἶχον ἂν κατ' ἐκείνην τὴν ἡμέραν σπουδάσαι μόνον. Διὰ τοῦτο ἐν ἀδήλῳ τέθεικε καὶ τὴν ἰδικὴν ἡμέραν τῆς ἑκάστου ἡμῶν τελευτῆς καὶ τὴν κοινήν, ὥστε ἡμᾶς ἀεὶ πρὸς τὴν τοῦ βίου συντέλειαν παρασκευάζεσθαι φυλάσσοντας ἑαυτοὺς ὡς οἱ τοὺς λῃστὰς τηροῦντες.[mdlxxvii]

Διὰ τοῦτο καὶ ὑμεῖς γίνεσθε ἕτοιμοι.[2142] Τὸ ἕτοιμόν ἐστι τὸ τὰ τῆς ἀρετῆς ἔργα ἔχειν τεθησαυρισμένα οὐκ *ἐπὶ γῆς, ἀλλ' ἐν οὐρανοῖς*.[2143] Οἰκοδεσπότου γάρ ἐστι θησαυρίζειν καὶ ἑτοιμάζειν ἑαυτῷ εἰς καιρὸν θλίψεως.

> Τὸ ἕτοιμόν ἐστι τὸ τὰ τῆς ἀρετῆς ἔργα ἔχειν τεθησαυρισμένα οὐκ *ἐπὶ γῆς*, ἀλλ' ἐν οὐρανοῖς. οἰκοδεσπότου γάρ ἐστι θησαυρίζειν καὶ ἑτοιμάζειν ἑαυτῷ εἰς καιρὸν θλίψεως.[mdlxxviii]

Τίς ἄρα ἐστὶν ὁ πιστὸς δοῦλος καὶ φρόνιμος;[2144] Τάχα παροξύνων εἰς τὸ ζητῆσαι ἕνα τινὰ σπάνιον (τῇ γὰρ τοῦ *ἄρα* ἀμφιβολίᾳ τὸ σπάνιον ἔδειξε[mdlxxix] καὶ δυσεύρετον τοῦ τοιούτου οἰκονόμου) καὶ οὐκ ἄλλον αὐτοῦ τὸν πιστὸν καὶ φρόνιμον οἰκονόμον εἰδὼς κατασταθησόμενον ἐπὶ τοῖς τοῦ Πατρός, ὡς περὶ ἑτέρου ἑαυτοῦ λέγει τὸ *τίς ἄρα ἐστί.* Μήποτε δὲ δοῦλος ὁ Σωτήρ, ὡς *μορφὴν δούλου λαβών.*[2145]

> Τάχα παροξύνων εἰς τὸ ζητῆσαι ἕνα τινὰ σπάνιον (τῇ γὰρ τοῦ *ἄρα* ἀμφιβολίᾳ τὸ σπάνιον ἔδειξε καὶ δυσεύρετον τοῦ τοιούτου οἰκονόμου) καὶ οὐκ ἄλλον αὐτοῦ τὸν πιστὸν καὶ φρόνιμον οἰκονόμον εἰδὼς κατασταθμισόμενον ἐπὶ τοῖς τοῦ πατρός ἔργοις, λέγω δὴ ἐπὶ τῇ ἀνθρωπότητι. ὡς γὰρ περὶ ἑτέρου λέγει ἐπισκιάζων αὐτὸ τῇ ὑπερβολῇ τῆς σοφίας. δοῦλον δὲ ἑαυτὸν εἶπε διὰ τὸ *μορφὴν δούλου* λαβεῖν.[mdlxxx]

> Τάχα παροξύνων εἰς τὸ ζητῆσαι ἕνα τινὰ σπάνιον. Τῇ γὰρ τοῦ ἄρα ἀμφιβολίᾳ τὸ σπάνιον ἔδειξε τοῦ τοιούτου οἰκονόμου, καὶ οὐκ ἄλλον αὐτοῦ τὸν πιστὸν καὶ φρόνιμον οἰκονόμον εἰδώς, κατασταθμαζόμενον ἐπὶ τοῖς τοῦ Πατρὸς ἔργοις, λέγω δὲ ἐπὶ τῇ ἀνθρωπότητι. Ὡς γὰρ περὶ ἑτέρου λέγει, ἐπισκιάζων αὐτὸ τῇ ὑπερβολῇ τῆς σοφίας. Δοῦλον δὲ ἑαυτὸν εἶπε διὰ τὸ μορφὴν δούλου λαβεῖν.[mdlxxxi]

Ὅρα δὲ εἰ μὴ καὶ τοὺς τοιαῦτα ἐγχειρισθέντας ἐπισκόπους καὶ διδασκάλους δυσωπεῖ ὁ λόγος, φρονίμως ἑκάστῳ κατ' ἀξίαν χρῆσθαι καὶ ἐπιστήμῃ τὰς πνευματικὰς

2140 Luke, 17:34.
2141 Matt. 24:42; likewise, 25:13; 26:38&41; Mark, 13:35&37; 14:34&38.
2142 Matt. 24:44; cf. Luke, 12:40.
2143 Cf. Matt. 6:19-20.
2144 Matt. 24:45.
2145 Phil. 2:7.

διατάσσειν τροφὰς *καιρῷ*, ποσότητι, ποιότητι. Τὸ δὲ *τίς ἄρα* εἶπεν οὐχ ὡς ἀγνοῶν, ἀλλ' ἵνα μὴ περιεργάσωνται. Ἁρμόζει δὲ ὁ λόγος, | **198r** καὶ κατὰ παντὸς τοῦ ἐμπιστευθέντος τι παρὰ Θεοῦ, εἴτε χρήματα εἴτε ἀρχὴν εἴτε λόγον εἴτε δυναστείαν ἄλλην τινά. Δύο δὲ ἀπαιτεῖται ὁ οἰκονόμος, πίστιν καὶ φρόνησιν, ἵνα μήτε κλέψῃ τὰ δεσποτικά, ἀλλὰ καὶ δεόντως αὐτὰ δαπανᾷ. Ἤτοι πιστὸν λέγει τὸν ἔχοντα πρὸς Θεὸν ὀρθὴν συνείδησιν καὶ μὴ ἀφιστάμενόν τινος τῶν δεόντων καὶ τὸν ὀρθῶς διδάσκοντα. Φρόνιμον δὲ τὸν μὴ παραφερόμενον ταῖς τῶν αἱρετικῶν μωρολογίαις, ἀλλὰ διακρίνοντα τὸ ἀκριβὲς τοῦ λόγου. Ἤτοι τὸν μὴ περιπειρόμενον ἁμαρτίαις, καὶ διὰ τὸ ποικίλον καὶ πολύτροπον τῶν ἀνθρώπων εἰδότα πότε μὲν διδάξαι δεῖ, πότε δὲ ἐλέγξαι· καὶ πότε μὲν ἐπιτιμῆσαι, πότε δὲ παρακαλέσαι·[2146] καὶ τίνας μὲν δεῖ ποτίσαι *γάλα* ὡς νηπίους,[2147] τίσι δὲ μεταδοῦναι τῆς *στερεᾶς τροφῆς*.[2148]

> ὅρα δὲ εἰ μὴ καὶ τοὺς τοιαῦτα ἐγχειρισθέντας ἐπισκόπους καὶ διδασκάλους δυσωπεῖ ὁ λόγος, φρονίμως ἑκάστῳ κατ' ἀξίαν χρῆσθαι καὶ ἐπιστημόνως τὰς πνευματικὰς διατάσσειν τροφὰς *καιρῷ*, ποσότητος, ποιότητος. τὸ δὲ *τίς ἄρα* εἶπεν οὐχ ὡς ἀγνοῶν, ἀλλ' ἵνα μὴ περιεργάσωνται. ἁρμόζει δὲ ὁ λόγος καὶ κατὰ παντὸς τοῦ ἐμπιστευθέντος τι παρὰ τοῦ θεοῦ, εἴτε χρήματα εἴτε ἀρχὴν εἴτε λόγον εἴτε δυναστείαν ἄλλην τινά. δύο δὲ ἀπαιτεῖται ὁ οἰκονόμος, πίστιν καὶ φρόνησιν, ἵνα μήτε κλέψῃ τὰ δεσποτικά, ἀλλὰ καὶ δεόντως αὐτὰ οἰκονομήσῃ, ἢ τὸν ἔχοντα πρὸς *θεὸν ἀγαθὴν συνείδησιν*[2149] καὶ μὴ ἀφιστάμενόν τινος τῶν δεόντων καὶ τὸν ὀρθῶς διδάσκοντα λέγειν πιστόν. φρόνιμον δὲ τὸν μὴ παραφερόμενον ταῖς τῶν αἱρετικῶν μωρολογίαις ἀλλὰ διακρίνοντα τὸ ἀκριβὲς τοῦ λόγου ἢ τὸν μὴ πειρώμενον ἁμαρτίαις, καὶ διὰ τὸ ποικίλον καὶ πολύτροπον τῶν ἀνθρώπων, τὸν εἰδότα πότε δεῖ ἐλέγξαι ἢ ἐπιτιμῆσαι ἢ παρακαλέσαι ἢ διδάξαι καὶ τίνας μὲν ποτίσαι δεῖ *γάλα*, τίσι δὲ μεταδοῦναι τῆς *στερεᾶς τροφῆς*.[mdlxxxii]

> Ὅρα δὲ εἰ μὴ τοιαῦτα ἐγχειρισθέντας ἐπισκόπους καὶ διδασκάλους δυσωπεῖ ὁ λόγος φρονίμως ἑκάστῳ τὰ κατ' ἀξίαν χρῆσθαι, καὶ ἐπιστημόνως τὰς πνευματικὰς διατάσσειν τροφὰς καιρῷ ποσότητος, ποιότητος. Τὸ δέ, *Τίς ἄρα*, εἶπεν, οὐχ ὡς ἀγνοῶν, ἀλλ' ἵνα μὴ περιεργάζωνται. Ἁρμόζει δὲ ὁ λόγος καὶ κατὰ παντὸς τοῦ ἐμπιστευθέντος τι παρὰ τοῦ Θεοῦ, εἴτε χρήματα, εἴτε ἀρχήν, εἴτε δυναστείαν ἄλλην τινά. Δεύτερον δὲ ἀπαιτεῖται ὁ οἰκονόμος πίστιν καὶ φρόνησιν, ἵνα μήτε κλέψῃ τὰ δεσποτικά, ἀλλὰ καὶ δεόντως αὐτὰ οἰκονομήσῃ. Ἢ τὸν ἔχοντα πρὸς Θεὸν ἀγαθὴν συνείδησιν, καὶ μὴ ἀφιστάμενόν τινος τῶν δεόντων. Καὶ τὸν ὀρθῶς διδάσκοντα λέγει πιστόν. Φρόνιμον δὲ τὸν μὴ παραφερόμενον ταῖς τῶν αἱρετικῶν μωρολογίαις, ἀλλὰ διακρίνοντα τὸ ἀκριβὲς τοῦ λόγου, ἢ τὸν μὴ πειρόμενον [sic] ἁμαρτίαις, διὰ τὸ μὴ ποικίλον καὶ πολύτροπον τῶν ἀνθρώπων. Τὸν εἰδότα πότε δεῖ ἐλέγξαι, ἢ ἐπιτιμῆσαι, ἢ παρακαλέσαι, ἢ διδάξαι. καὶ τίνας μὲν ποτίσαι δεῖ γάλα, τίσι δὲ μεταδοῦναι τῆς στερεᾶς τροφῆς.[mdlxxxiii]

2146 Cf. 2 Tim. 4:2.
2147 Cf. 1 Cor. 3:1-2; Heb. 5:12-13.
2148 Heb. 5:12-14.
2149 Cf. 1 Peter, 3:21.

μακάριος ὁ δοῦλος ἐκεῖνος.[2150] Ἐπαγγέλλεται ὁ λόγος τῷ πιστῷ καὶ φρονίμῳ οἰκονόμῳ[2151] τὴν τελείαν ἀπόλαυσιν. Ἐπὶ πάντων γὰρ τῶν ὑπαρχόντων αὐτοῦ καθιστᾷ αὐτὸν *ὁ τῶν οὐρανῶν βασιλεὺς*[2152] *ἐν τῇ βασιλείᾳ*[2153] αὐτοῦ. *Συγκληρονόμοι* γὰρ γινόμεθα *Χριστοῦ*[2154] ἐν τῇ *βασιλείᾳ τῶν οὐρανῶν.*[2155]

Ἐὰν δὲ εἴπῃ ὁ κακὸς δοῦλος.[2156] *Ὅτι* ὁ λόγος κατὰ τῶν ἡγουμένων τῶν ἐν τρυφαῖς σχολαζόντων. Κακὸν γὰρ καὶ πονηρὸν δοῦλον ὀνομάζει τὸν ἀμελῆ διδάσκαλον, ὃς διὰ τὸ ἀπεῖναι τὸν κριτὴν καὶ μὴ ὁρᾶσθαι διὰ τὸ ἀνεξίκακον, τύπτει πικρῶς τοὺς ὑπὸ χεῖρα καὶ συναναμίγνυται τοῖς φιλοσάρκοις. Οἱ γὰρ ἁμαρτάνοντες ὡς μὴ παρόντος τοῦ κριτοῦ ἁμαρτάνουσιν, ὡς μηδὲ λογιζόμενοι κρίσιν, διὰ δὲ τοῦ τύπτεσθαι[2157] τινὰς ἐξ αὐτ‹ῶν›,[2158] δείκνυσι τοὺς κατὰ ψυχὴν βλαπτομένους ἐκ τῆς τῶν ἡγουμένων τρυφῆς,[2159] ὡς καὶ ὁ ἀπόστολος φησι, *οὕτως δὲ ἁμαρτάνοντες εἰς τοὺς ἀδελφοὺς καὶ τύπτοντες αὐτῶν τὴν συνείδησιν.*[2160] | **198v** Ἐπαπειλεῖ οὖν τοῖς τρυφῶσι τὰ ἔσχατα ὑποστῆναι. Ἀποσχίζει γὰρ αὐτὸν καὶ διαιρεῖ ἀπ᾽ αὐτοῦ μετ᾽ ἀλγηδόνων τῷ ζῶντι ἑαυτοῦ λόγῳ[2161] τοῦ ἑνωθέντος αὐτῷ *ἐν τῷ νῦν αἰῶνι*[2162] *Πνεύματος.*[2163] Οἱ γὰρ ὑποκρινόμενοι τὰ ὀρθὰ φρονεῖν, μὴ φρονοῦντες δὲ ὡς δεῖ, διχῇ τμηθήσονται κατὰ τὴν φοβερὰν *ἡμέραν τῆς κρίσεως.*[2164]

> Ὅτι δὲ ὁ λόγος κατὰ τῶν ἡγουμένων τῶν ἐν τρυφαῖς σχολαζόντων. κακὸν γὰρ καὶ πονηρὸν δοῦλον ὠνόμασε τὸν ἀμελῆ διδάσκαλον, ὃς διὰ τὸ ἀπεῖναι τὸν κριτὴν καὶ μὴ ὁρᾶσθαι διὰ τὸ ἀνεξίκακον τύπτει πικρῶς τοὺς ὑπὸ χεῖρα καὶ συναναμίγνυται τοῖς φιλοσάρκοις. οἱ γὰρ ἁμαρτάνοντες ὡς μὴ παρόντος τοῦ κριτοῦ ἁμαρτάνουσιν καὶ ὡς μὴ λογιζόμενοι κρίσιν. διὰ δὲ τοῦ τύπτεσθαί τινας ἐξ αὐτῶν δείκνυσι τοὺς κατὰ ψυχὴν βλαπτομένους ἐκ τῆς τῶν ἡγουμένων τρυφῆς, καθὼς φησιν ὁ ἀπόστολος. οὕτως δὲ ἁμαρτάνοντες εἰς τοὺς ἀδελφοὺς καὶ τύπτοντες αὐτῶν τὴν συνείδησιν ἀσθενοῦσαν. ἐπαπειλεῖ οὖν τοῖς τρυφῶσι τὰ ἔσχατα ὑποστῆναι. ἀποσχίζει γὰρ αὐτὸν καὶ διαιρεῖ ἀπ᾽ αὐτοῦ μετ᾽ ἀλγηδόνων τῷ ζῶντι ἑαυτοῦ λόγῳ τοῦ ἑνωθέντος αὐτῷ ἐν τῷ αἰῶνι πνεύματος ἤγουν τοῦ θείου χαρίσματος. οἱ ὑποκρινόμενοι γὰρ τὰ ὀρθὰ φρονεῖν μὴ φρονοῦντες δὲ ὡς δεῖ, ἀλλὰ

2150 Matt. 24:46.
2151 Cf. Luke, 12:42; Matt. 24:45.
2152 Cf. 3 Macc. 2:2; Psalms of Solomon, 2:30; Matt. 18:23; 22:2.
2153 Matt. 13:43; 16:28; 20:21; 26:29; Mark, 14:25; Luke, 7:28; 13:28-29; 14:15; 22:16; 22:30; 23:42; Eph. 5:5.
2154 Rom. 8:17; Heb. 11:9; 1 Peter, 3:7.
2155 Matt. 5:3&10&19; 8:11; 11:11; 18:1&4; 19:14; 22:2; 25:1.
2156 Matt. 24:48.
2157 Cf. Matt. 24:49.
2158 Cod. αὐτοῦ.
2159 Cf. 2 Peter, 2:13.
2160 1 Cor. 8:12.
2161 Cf. Heb. 4:12.
2162 1 Tim. 6:17; Tit. 2:12.
2163 Cf. 2 Tim. 1:14; James, 4:5; 1 John, 3:24; 4:13.
2164 2 Peter, 2:9; 3:7; cf. Matt. 10:15; 11:22&24; 12:36; 1 John:4:17.

> τὴν ἀρετὴν μὲν ἔξωθεν σχήματι μόνῳ περικείμενοι διχῇ τμηθήσονται κατὰ τὴν φοβερὰν ἡμέραν τῆς κρίσεως·[mdlxxxiv]

Διχοτομία δέ ἐστιν ἡ ἀπὸ τοῦ Πνεύματος εἰς τὸ διηνεκὲς τῆς ψυχῆς ἀλλοτρίωσις.[mdlxxxv] Νῦν μὲν γάρ, εἰ καὶ μὴ ἀνακέκραται τοῖς ἀναξίοις, ἀλλ' οὖν παρεῖναι δοκεῖ πως τοῖς ἅπαξ ἐσφραγισμένοις,[2165] τὴν ἐκ τῆς ἐπιστροφῆς αὐτῶν σωτηρίαν ἀναμένον. Τότε δέ, ἐξ' ὅλης τῆς βεβηλωσάσης αὐτοῦ τὴν χάριν ψυχῆς ἀποτμηθήσεται.

> Ἀλλὰ διχοτομία, ὥσπερ ἔφην, ἡ ἀπὸ τοῦ Πνεύματος εἰς τὸ διηνεκὲς τῆς ψυχῆς ἀλλοτρίωσις. Νῦν μὲν γάρ, εἰ καὶ μὴ ἀνακέκραται τοῖς ἀναξίοις, ἀλλ' οὖν παρεῖναι δοκεῖ πως τοῖς ἅπαξ ἐσφραγισμένοις. τὴν ἐκ τῆς ἐπιστροφῆς σωτηρίαν αὐτῶν ἀναμένον. τότε δὲ ἐξ ὅλου τῆς βεβηλωσάσης αὐτοῦ τὴν χάριν ψυχῆς ἀποτμηθήσεται.[mdlxxxvi]

> ἥ ἐστιν ἀπὸ τοῦ πνεύματος εἰς τὸ διηνεκὲς ἀλλοτρίωσις. νῦν μὲν γὰρ εἰ καὶ μὴ ἀνακέκραται τοῖς ἀναξίοις, ἀλλ' οὖν παρεῖναί πως δοκεῖ τοῖς ἅπαξ ἐσφραγισμένοις τὴν ἐκ τῆς ἐπιστροφῆς αὐτῶν σωτηρίαν ἀναμένων. τότε δὲ ἐξ ὅλης τῆς βεβηλωσάσης αὐτοῦ τὴν χάριν ψυχῆς ἀποτμηθήσεται.[mdlxxxvii]

καὶ μετὰ τῶν ὑποκριτῶν τὸ μέρος αὐτοῦ τεθήσεται.[2166] Ὑποκριτοῦ γὰρ τὸ προσποιεῖσθαι μὲν ὀρθὰ διδάσκειν ἑτέρους, δι' ὧν δὲ ποιεῖ καταβλάπτειν πλείω τοὺς μαθητευομένους. Ἐπὶ τοίνυν, φησί, τῶν οὐ κατὰ τὸ δέον χρησαμένων ἐν τῷ παρόντι βίῳ τῇ κατὰ τὴν γενομένην αὐτοῖς χάριν τοῦ Πνεύματος ἐγχειρισθείσῃ λειτουργίᾳ, οὐ μόνον οὐ προσθήσει ἑτέραν ὁ κριτὴς ἀλλὰ καὶ τὴν ἤδη μετουσίαν αὐτοῖς ἐγγενομένην τοῦ Πνεύματος (οὗ ἔτυχον πρὸς ἐκκλησιαστικὴν λειτουργίαν προχειρισθέντες) ἀφελόμενος, οὕτως αὐτοὺς παραδώσει τῇ κολάσει. Οὐ γὰρ οἷόν τε σὺν τῷ Πνεύματι δοθῆναι τινὰ εἰς κόλασιν· οὐ γὰρ σωματικὴν ὑποφαίνει τομήν, ἀλλὰ τὴν τῆς υἱοθεσίας *τοῦ Πνεύματος*[2167] γύμνωσιν.

> καὶ *μετὰ τῶν ὑποκριτῶν τὸ μέρος αὐτοῦ* τεθήσεται. ὑποκριτὰς δέ φησι τοὺς τὰ ὀρθὰ μὲν διδάσκειν πειρωμένους, δι' ὧν δὲ ποιοῦσιν καταβλάπτοντας πλείω τοὺς μαθητευομένους. ἐπὶ τοίνυν, φησίν, τῶν οὐ κατὰ τὸ δέον χρησομένων ἐν τῷ παρόντι βίῳ τῇ ἐγχειρισθείσῃ αὐτοῖς λειτουργίᾳ παρὰ κυρίου οὐ μόνον οὐ προσθήσει ἑτέραν, ἀλλὰ καὶ τὴν ἤδη μετουσίαν αὐτοῖς ἐγγενομένην τοῦ πνεύματος, οὗ ἔτυχον πρὸς ἐκκλησιαστικὴν λειτουργίαν προχειρισθέντες, ἀφελόμενος, οὕτως αὐτοὺς παραδώσει τῇ κολάσει. οὐ γὰρ οἷόν τε σὺν τῷ πνεύματι παραδοθῆναί τινα εἰς κόλασιν. οὐ γὰρ σωματικὴν ὑποφαίνει τομήν, ἀλλὰ τὴν τῆς υἱοθεσίας τοῦ πνεύματος γύμνωσιν.[mdlxxxviii]

Κλαίουσι τοίνυν, ἀνθ' ὧν ἐγέλων. Βρύξουσι δὲ τοὺς ὀδόντας, λογιζόμενοι τὸ τέλος τοῦ πόνου καὶ τὴν ὑπερβολὴν τῆς κολάσεως,

---

2165 Cf. Rev. 7:3-4.
2166 Matt. 24:51.
2167 Cf. Rom. 8:15.

> κλαίουσι τοίνυν ἀνθ᾽ ὧν ἐγέλων, βρύξουσι δὲ τοὺς ὀδόντας λογιζόμενοι τὸ τέλος τοῦ πόνου καὶ τὴν ὑπερβολὴν τῆς κολάσεως[mdlxxxix]

> κολάζονται τοίνυν ἀνθ᾽ ὧν ἐγέλων, βρύξουσι δὲ *τοὺς ὀδόντας* λογιζόμενοι τὸ τέλος τοῦ πόνου καὶ τὴν ὑπερβολὴν τῆς κολάσεως.[mdxc]

οἱονεὶ θέλοντες αὐτὰ γενναίως φέρειν.

> οἱονεὶ θέλοντες αὐτὰ γενναίως φέρειν.[mdxci]

τότε ὁμοιώθη *ἡ βασιλεία τῶν οὐρανῶν δέκα παρθένοις.*[2168] Παρθένοις παρεικάζει τοὺς τῶν λαῶν ἡγουμένους. Δεῖ γὰρ ἄσπιλον εἶναι τὸν ἱερέα ψυχῇ καὶ σώματι. *Δέκα* δὲ καλεῖ παρθένους τὸν πάντα βίον, ἐν ᾧ ἑκάστῳ ἀπονέμει | **199r** καὶ ὁσίας καὶ μωρὰς ψυχάς.
Ἐν ᾧ δὲ πᾶσαι *ἐξῆλθον* σὺν ταῖς λαμπάσι, δείκνυσιν ὅτι πᾶσαι αἱ ψυχαὶ κατεφωτίσθησαν ὑπὸ τοῦ Θεοῦ φυσικοῖς[mdxcii] τε καὶ ἐμφύτοις[mdxciii] νόμοις καὶ τοῖς διὰ Μωσέως γραπτοῖς, καὶ π‹ᾶσαι›[2169] προέθεντο *ἀρέσαι Θεῷ*[2170] (τοῦτο γὰρ ἡ ἀπάντησις[mdxciv]) καὶ συναφθῆναι τῷ νυμφίῳ πνευματικῶς. Πλὴν ἀδιακρίτως τινὲς οὐκ ἠνέσχοντο ἐπιεικῶς ζῆσαι, καίπερ ἔχουσαι ἐκ Θεοῦ τὸν φωτισμόν· ὅπερ ἐποίησαν αἱ φρόνιμοι.

> ἐν ᾧ δὲ πᾶσαι ἐξῆλθον σὺν ταῖς λαμπάσι, δείκνυσιν, ὅτι πᾶσαι αἱ ψυχαὶ κατεφωτίσθησαν ὑπὸ τοῦ θεοῦ φυσικοῖς τε καὶ ἐμφύτοις νόμοις, ἀλλὰ μὴν καὶ τοῖς διὰ Μωσέως γραπτοῖς νόμοις. καὶ πάντες *ἐξῆλθον* εἰς συνάντησιν τῷ νυμφίῳ ἀντὶ τοῦ πάντες προέθεντο ἀρέσαι τῷ θεῷ καὶ συναφθῆναι πνευματικῶς τῷ νυμφίῳ τῷ ἐνσπείροντι ἐν ταῖς καρδίαις τῶν πιστῶν πᾶν εἶδος ἀρετῆς, διὸ καὶ νυμφίος καλεῖται. πλὴν ἀδιακρίτως τινὲς καίπερ ἔχοντες τὸν ἐκ θεοῦ φωτισμὸν οὐκ ἠνέσχοντο ἐπιεικῶς ζῆσαι, ὅπερ ἐποίησαν αἱ συνεταὶ ψυχαί, ...[mdxcv]

Ἔλαιον οὖν νοητέον τὴν ἀγαθὴν φιλεργίαν ἢ τὴν πρὸς τοὺς δεομένους φιλανθρωπίαν, ὃ οὐκ ἔχουσιν οἱ ἀργοὶ πάσης ἀγαθοεργίας καὶ οὐκ ἐκλάμπει ἐν αὐτοῖς θεῖος φωτισμός.

> ἔλαιον νοητέον τὴν φιλεργίαν τὴν ἀγαθήν, ὃ οὐκ ἔχουσιν οἱ ἀργοί, οὗ μὴ ὄντος ἐπὶ τὸ ἀκαλλέστερον μεταβαίνει ὁ ἐν ἡμῖν θεῖος φωτισμός.[mdxcvi]

Λαμπάδας δέ, τὴν παρθενίαν. *Αἱ* οὖν *φρόνιμοι* πρὸς τῇ παρθενίᾳ αὐτῶν καὶ πίστει εἶχον καὶ ἔργα ἐνάρετα, ἅπερ οὐκ εἶχον *αἱ μωραί.* Ἤτοι πᾶσα ψυχὴ πιστῶν παρθένος συναφθεῖσα Χριστῷ. Λαμπὰς δέ, ἡ διὰ τῶν πρακτικῶν πόνων καὶ τῆς ἐνεργοῦς μελέτης τοῦ θείου νόμου τῶν ἀρετῶν πλεκομένη σειρὰ καὶ τῷ ἄνωθεν φωτὶ λαμπομένη τοῦ οὐρανίου πυρός, μάλιστα δέ, ἡ ἐλεημοσύνη. Αἱ δὲ μὴ ἔχουσαι βίον ὀρθόν, κἂν

2168 Matt. 25:1: ὁμοιωθήσεται.
2169 Cod. πάντες.
2170 Rom. 8:8; cf. 1 Thess. 2:4; 2:15; 4:1.

πίστιν ἔχωσιν, οὐ δύνανται αὗται κυρίως κληθῆναι *παρθένοι*. Αἳ καὶ *μωραὶ* λέγονται διὰ τὸ μὴ ἔχειν πρὸς ταῖς λαμπάσι καὶ *ἔλαιον*, ἤτοι διὰ τὸ μὴ ἔχειν συμπάθειαν ἀλλὰ κολάζειν ἀπηνῶς, προφάσει θεοσεβείας ποιοῦσαι τὰ μὴ Θεῷ ἀρεστά.

Ἄλλως τε δέ. Τέλειος ὁ τῶν δέκα ἀριθμός·[mdxcvii] διὸ κἂν μυρίοι προστιθῶνται πιστοί, μία ἐστὶν ἡ ἐκκλησία καὶ τελεία ὅσον ἐπὶ τῇ κλήσει τοῦ κεκληκότος. Αἱ πέντε τοίνυν αἰσθήσεις, ἐὰν ὀρθῶς πολιτεύωνται, ἔχουσι τὸν ἄνωθεν φωτισμόν. Ἐὰν δὲ ἔχωσι καὶ τὸ *ἔλαιον*, ἀντὶ πέντε, δέκα τῷ νυμφίῳ νομίζονται. Ἐὰν δὲ χηρεύσωσι τούτου, *μωραὶ* κρίνονται τὸν περὶ τὰ ἄλλα πόνον ματαίως ἐπιδειξάμεναι. Καὶ *λαμπάδας* μὲν ἔχουσι | **199v** διὰ τὴν λοιπὴν ἄσκησιν, ξηρὰς δὲ καὶ οὐ δυναμένας ἀναφθῆναι παρὰ τοῦ ἄνωθεν φωτός. Νυμφὼν οὖν ἐστιν *ἡ βασιλεία τῶν οὐρανῶν*, διὰ τὸ λαμπρὸν καὶ εὐφροσύνης μεστός, *νυμφίος* δὲ ὁ Κύριος ἡμῶν Ἰησοῦς Χριστός. Χρονίζειν δὲ λέγει τὸν νυμφίον, ἐπειδὴ πολύ ἐστι τὸ διάστημα τὸ μεταξὺ τῆς πρώτης καὶ δευτέρας παρουσίας τοῦ Χριστοῦ·
ὕπνος δέ ἐστιν ὁ θάνατος, ὃς ἐξ ἀνάγκης ἐπέρχεται φρονίμοις τὲ καὶ ἀσυνέτοις.

> ὕπνῳ δὲ παρεικάζει καὶ νυσταγμὸν ἀποκαλεῖ τὸν τῆς σαρκὸς θάνατον ὃς ἐξ ἀνάγκης προεπέρχεται φρονίμοις τε καὶ ἀσυνέτοις.[mdxcviii]

Πάντες οὖν οἱ κεκοιμημένοι ἀναμένουσι τὴν ἄφιξιν τοῦ Κυρίου, ἣν καὶ τάχα στοχαστέον γίνεσθαι ἐν νυκτί.[mdxcix] Γίνονται δὲ τότε φωναὶ καὶ σάλπιγγες φωνῇ ἀρχαγγέλων λεγόντων, *ὁ νυμφίος ἔρχεται*.[2171] Τότε *αἱ* μὲν *φρόνιμοι* λαμπρότερον ἐποίησαν τὸ τῆς παρθενίας κάλλος πρὸς τῷ ἐλαίῳ καὶ τὴν ἀρετὴν ἐπιφερόμεναι·
οἱ δὲ θατέρου λειπόμενοι, στυγνοί εἰσιν. Εὐτρεπίζει δὲ ἕκαστος τὸν ἴδιον ἀναλογιζόμενος βίον, πρὸς ἀπολογίαν τῷ κριτῇ, ὅ ἐστι κόσμος λαμπάδων.

> ὅπερ ἐστὶν διακοσμῆσαι τὰς λαμπάδας ἑκάστου τὸν ἴδιον ἀναλογιζομένου βίον. τῶν δὲ φαύλων μηδὲν ἐπιφερομένων ἄρχεται στυγνάζειν ἡ ψυχὴ[mdc]

Αἱ οὖν μὴ δυνάμεναι ψυχαὶ ἐξ ἰδίων ἀρετῶν κοσμῆσαι ἑαυτάς, αἰτοῦσι λαβεῖν τὰς ἐχούσας δοῦναι αὐταῖς ἐκ τῆς προσούσης αὐταῖς ἐπιζητοῦσαι ἀρετῆς καὶ οὐ τυγχάνουσιν. Ἐκεῖ γὰρ οὐ δύναταί τις προσθεῖναι τινὶ τῶν μὴ ἐχόντων ἔργον. Μόναις γὰρ ἐκείναις συμβάλλεται, ταῖς ἐχούσαις αὐτὸ δι᾽ οἰκείων ἱδρώτων·
διὸ ἤκουσαν *μήποτε οὐκ ἀρκέσ‹ει›*[2172] πρὸς σωτηρίαν ψυχῆς ἡ ἑκάστου ἀρετὴ διὰ τὸ πολλὰ πταίειν καὶ τοὺς ἄγαν ἐπιεικεῖς.

> μόλις γὰρ ἀρκέσει πρὸς σωτηρίαν ψυχῆς ἡ ἑκάστου ἀρετὴ διὰ τὸ πολλὰ πταίειν καὶ τοὺς ἄγαν ἐπιεικεῖς.[mdci]

2171 Matt. 25:6; cf. 1 Peter, 3:15.
2172 Matt. 25:9. Cod. ἀρκέσῃ.

Πέμπουσιν οὖν αὐτὰς *πρὸς τοὺς πωλοῦντας*,[2173] οἵ εἰσιν οἱ πένητες,

> εἰσὶ δὲ οἱ πωλοῦντες τὸν ἔλαιον, οἱ πένητες.[mdcii]

ἐν τῷ νῦν αἰῶνι εὑρισκόμενοι, οὐκ ἐν τῷ μέλλοντι.
Ἑτοίμως οὖν ἐχουσῶν τούτων ἀπελθεῖν, οὐ συνεχώρησεν ὁ καιρὸς τῶν βεβιωμένων ποιούμενος τὴν ἐξέτασιν·

> ὠνήσασθαι δὲ ἤτοι διδαχθῆναι ὁ καιρὸς οὐκ εἴασεν τῶν βεβιωμένων ποιούμενος ἐξέτασιν.[mdciii]

κἂν γὰρ φιλάνθρωποι γινώμεθα μετὰ τὸ ἀπελθεῖν, οὐδὲν κερδήσομεν. Διὸ καὶ πρὸ τοῦ ὅλως κτήσασθαί τι, αἱ μὲν *φρόνιμοι* συνεισῆλθον, αἱ δὲ *μωραὶ* ἔξωθεν ἔμειναν διὰ τὸ μὴ ἔχειν | **200r** αὐτὰς τῆς ἐνθέου πολιτείας[mdciv] τὸ περιφανές.

καὶ ἐκλείσθη ἡ θύρα.[2174] Μηδεὶς νομιζέτω περὶ τῶν γάμου κοινωνίαν ἀρνησαμένων μόνων ἐνταῦθα τὸ εὐαγγέλιον διαλέγεσθαι, ἀλλὰ περὶ πάσης ψυχῆς διὰ τῆς *τοῦ λουτροῦ παλιγγενεσίας*[2175] κατεγγυηθείσης Χριστῷ καὶ λαμπάδα πάντως ἀπαιτουμένης ἔχειν τῶν ἀρετῶν τὴν παρασκευήν. Ἵν' ὅταν ἐξ οὐρανῶν κατίῃ τὸ δεύτερον *μετὰ δόξης*,[2176] ἑκάστη ψυχὴ τὸν τῶν οἰκείων ἔργων ἀνατείνῃ πυρσόν, τῷ εἰς τοὺς πένητας ἐλέῳ προαποτεθέντι καταρδόμενον καὶ διὰ τῆς φαιδρότητος τοῦ νυμφίου τὸ πρόσωπον ἐφελκόμενον.

64

200r (ΩΡΙΓΕΝΟΥΣ) *Δέκα* παρθένους εἶναι, φησί, τὰς ἐν ἑκάστῃ ψυχῇ αἰσθήσεις ἀποστάσας εἰδωλολατρίας τῷ παραδέξασθαι *εἴτε προφάσει εἴτε ἀληθείᾳ*[2177] τὸν τοῦ Θεοῦ καθαρὸν λόγον καὶ παρθενοποιηθείσας. Εἰσὶ δὲ αἵ τε κοινῶς νοούμεναι καὶ ἐν Παροιμίαις κείμεναι, αἳ καὶ ἀντακολουθοῦσιν, ὡς αἱ ἀρεταὶ τῇ ὑποστάσει ὁ Χριστός.[mdcv] Διὸ καὶ ἐν τῇ πεντάδι οὐχ αἱ μὲν *μωραὶ αἱ δὲ φρόνιμοι*, ἀλλ' εἰ μία, καὶ πᾶσαι. Ἐξῆλθον δὲ *εἰς ἀπάντησιν* αἱ παραδεξάμεναι τὸ περὶ Χριστοῦ καὶ ἐκκλησίας μυστήριον. Ἐξίασι γὰρ ἀπὸ τῆς τοῦ κόσμου πλάνης, σπεύδουσαι πρὸς τὸν ἑτοίμως ὁρμῶντα πρὸς αὐτάς.[mdcvi]

2173 Matt. 25:9.
2174 Matt. 25:11.
2175 Tit. 3:5.
2176 2 Tim. 2:10.
2177 Phil. 1:18.

δέκα παρθένους εἶναί φησι τὰς ἐν ἑκάστῃ ψυχῇ αἰσθήσεις ἀποστάσας τῆς εἰδωλολατρείας τῷ παραδέξασθαι *εἴτε προφάσει εἴτε ἀληθείᾳ* τὸν τοῦ θεοῦ καθαρὸν λόγον καὶ παρθενοποιηθείσας ... αἵ καὶ ἀντανακολουθοῦσαι ὡς αἱ ἀρεταὶ τῇ ὑποστάσει τοῦ Χριστοῦ (var. lect. ὁ Χριστός). εἰσὶ δὲ αἵ τε κοινῶς νοούμεναι καὶ αἱ ἐν Παροιμίαις κείμεναι, διὸ καὶ ἐν τῇ πεντάδι οὐχ *αἵ μὲν μωραὶ αἵ δὲ φρόνιμοι*, ἀλλ᾽ εἰ μία καὶ πᾶσαι.... λαμπάδες δὲ τὰ ὄργανα τοῦ καλῶς καὶ κατὰ λόγον βιοῦντος ἢ ἐναντίως. ἐξῆλθον δὲ εἰς ἀπάντησιν αἱ παραδεξάμεναι τὸ περὶ Χριστοῦ καὶ ἐκκλησίας μυστήριον. ἐξίασι γὰρ ἀπὸ τῆς τοῦ κόσμου πλάνης πρὸς τὸν ἑτοίμως ὁρμῶντα πρὸς αὐτάς.[mdcvii]

Πέντε δὲ ἦσαν ἐξ αὐτῶν φρόνιμοι.[2178] Μωρὰς καλεῖ κατ᾽ ἐκεῖνον τὸν οἰκοδόμον·[2179] *λαμπάδας* φησὶ ἐνταῦθα αὐτὸ τὸ τῆς παρθενίας χάρισμα, τὸ καθαρὸν τῆς ἁγιωσύνης· *ἔλαιον* δέ, τὴν φιλανθρωπίαν καὶ τὴν περὶ τοὺς δεομένους θεραπείαν.[mdcviii]

Μωρὰς καλεῖ κατ᾽ ἐκεῖνον τὸν οἰκοδόμον. [*λαμπάδας* φησι ἐνταῦθα αὐτὸ τὸ τῆς παρθενίας χάρισμα, τὸ καθαρὸν τῆς ἁγιωσύνης. ἔλαιον δέ, τὴν φιλανθρωπίαν καὶ τὴν περὶ τοὺς δεομένους θεραπείαν.][mdcix]

Λαμπάδας δὲ ἐνταῦθά φησιν αὐτὸ τὸ τῆς παρθενίας χάρισμα, τὸ καθαρὸν τῆς ἁγιωσύνης. ἔλαιον δέ, τὴν φιλανθρωπίαν, τὴν ἐλεημοσύνην, τὴν περὶ τοὺς δεομένους βοήθειαν.[mdcx]

Πολλοὶ γάρ εἰσιν οἵ αὐτάρκη μὲν πρὸς τὴν χρῆσιν τῆς πολιτείας ἔχουσι λόγον, οὐ μὴν ὥστε καὶ ἑτέρους διδάξαι.

πολλοὶ γάρ εἰσιν, οἵ αὐτάρκη μὲν πρὸς τὴν χρῆσιν τῆς πολιτείας ἔχουσι λόγον, οὐ μὴν ὥστε καὶ ἑτέρους διδάξαι.[mdcxi]

ὁ δὲ μὴ ἐν καιρῷ τὸ λογικὸν ἔλαιον κτώμενος ἀπόλλυσιν ὄντως τὸ συνεισελθεῖν εἰς τοὺς γάμους τῷ νυμφίῳ. ὁποῖοί εἰσιν οἱ πρὸς τὴν ἔξοδον μανθάνειν ἀρξάμενοι.[mdcxii]

ὁ δὲ μὴ ἐν καιρῷ τὸ λογικὸν ἔλαιον κτώμενος ἀπόλλυσιν ὄντως τὸ συνεισελθεῖν εἰς τοὺς γάμους τῷ νυμφίῳ. ὁποῖοί εἰσιν οἱ πρὸς τὴν ἔξοδον μανθάνειν ἀρξάμενοι.[mdcxiii]

65

200r (ΩΡΙΓΕΝΟΥΣ) Ἕτερον ἡ παρθενία παρὰ τὴν ἐλεημοσύνην καὶ ἕτερος ὁ νοῦς παρὰ τὸ σῶμα. Καὶ τοῦτο λήψῃ εἰς τὰς *δέκα* παρθένους.

Ἕτερον ἡ παρθενία παρὰ τὴν ἐλεημοσύνην καὶ ἕτερος ὁ νοῦς παρὰ τὸ σῶμα. Καὶ τοῦτο λήψῃ εἰς τὰς *δέκα* παρθένους.[mdcxiv]

2178 Matt. 25:2.
2179 Cf. Matt. 7:26; Luke, 6:49.

66

200r (ΩΡΙΓΕΝΟΥΣ) *Φρόνιμοι* μὲν οὖν αἱ τοῦ κατὰ λόγον βιοῦντος αἰσθήσεις· *μωραὶ* δέ, τοῦ ἐναντίως βιοῦντος, εἰ καὶ παρθένοι. *ἔλαιον* ὁ ἐπιχεόμενος λόγος. Καθεύδουσιν | **200v** οἱ ἀπανιστάμενοι τοῦ ζωτικοῦ τόνου.[mdcxv] Οὐκ ἀπολλύουσι γοῦν *τὰς λαμπάδας, αἱ δὲ φρόνιμοι* οὐδὲ ἀπροσεκτοῦσι περὶ τὴν τήρησιν τοῦ ἐλαίου. Ἐμβοῶσιν ‹γὰρ› οἱ ἄγγελοι ταῖς κοιμωμέναις αἰσθήσεσι διεγείροντες αὐτάς, τὰ *λειτουργικὰ πνεύματα εἰς διακονίαν ἀποστελλόμενα διὰ τοὺς μέλλοντας κληρονομεῖν σωτηρίαν.*[2180]

> *Φρόνιμοι* μὲν οὖν αἱ τοῦ κατὰ λόγον βιοῦντος αἰσθήσεις. *μωραὶ* δὲ αἱ τοῦ ἐναντίως καὶ παρὰ τὸν ὀρθὸν λόγον πολιτευομένου. *Λαμπάδες* ἡ πανάρετος πρᾶξις. ἔλαιον δὲ ὁ ἐπιχεόμενος λόγος τοῦ ψυχικοῦ, τοῦ τὴν ἀγαθὴν πρᾶξιν ἐργαζομένου. *Καθεύδουσιν* οἱ ἀπανιστάμενοι τοῦ ζωτικοῦ τόνου. Οὐκ ἀπολλύουσιν οὖν τὰς λαμπάδας αἱ φρόνιμοι, οὐδὲ ἀπροσεκτοῦσι περὶ τὴν τήρησιν τοῦ ἐλαίου. Ἐμβοῶσιν οἱ ἄγγελοι ταῖς κοιμωμέναις αἰσθήσεσι, διεγείροντες αὐτάς. τουτέστι *τὰ λειτουργικὰ πνεύματα εἰς διακονίαν ἀποστελλόμενα διὰ τοὺς μέλλοντας κληρονομεῖν σωτηρίαν.*[mdcxvi]

Κόσμος λαμπάδων, ἡ κατὰ τὰς αἰσθήσεις εὐαγγελικὴ χρῆσις ὀφθαλμῶν (ἐπὶ τῷ θαυμάζειν τὸν πεποιηκότα καὶ μύειν ἵνα μὴ ἴδωσιν ἀδικίαν), ἀκοῆς (μὴ παραδεχομένης μάταιον μηδὲ κρίσιν αἵματος, τοῦ δὲ Ἰησοῦ λόγου), γεύσεως (ἐσθλούσης χρηστὸν Κύριον), ὀσφρήσεως (*Χριστοῦ εὐωδίας*[2181] ἀπολαυούσης καὶ τοῦ ἐκκενωθέντος μύρου[2182]), ἁφῆς (ἁπτομένης τοῦ λόγου, ὡς Ἰωάννης λέγει, *αἱ χεῖρες ἡμῶν ἐψηλάφησαν περὶ τοῦ λόγου τῆς ζωῆς*).[2183]

> κόσμος λαμπάδων ἡ κατὰ τὰς αἰσθήσεις εὐαγγελικὴ χρῆσις, ὀφθαλμῶν ἐπὶ τῷ θαυμάζειν τὸν πεποιηκότα καὶ μύειν *ἵνα μὴ ἴδωσιν ἀδικίαν,*[2184] ἀκοῆς μὴ παραδεχομένης μάταιον μηδὲ *κρίσιν αἵματος,*[2185] τοῦ δὲ Ἰησοῦ λόγους, γεύσεως ἐσθιούσης Χριστὸν κύριον, ὀσφρήσεως *Χριστοῦ εὐωδίας*[2186] ἀπολαυούσης καὶ τοῦ ἐκκενωθέντος μύρου[2187], ἁφῆς ἁπτομένης τοῦ λόγου ὡς Ἰωάννης λέγει *αἱ χεῖρες ἡμῶν ἐψηλάφησαν περὶ τοῦ λόγου τῆς ζωῆς*[2188] συμπέρασμα δὲ τοῦ λόγου, παντὶ καιρῷ παρεσκευάσθαι πρὸς τὴν ἔξοδον.[mdcxvii]

We can interpret the virgins (both the wise and the foolish) as standing for the *five* senses: some of them hasten to heavenly things and desire the things above;[2189]

2180 Heb. 1:14.
2181 2 Cor. 2:15.
2182 Song of Songs, 1:3.
2183 1 John, 1:1.
2184 Is. 33:15.
2185 Is. 33:15; cf. Ez. 44:24.
2186 2 Cor. 2:15.
2187 Cf. Song of Songs, 1:3.
2188 1 John 1:1.
2189 Cf. Col. 3:2.

others cast longing eyes at earthly corruption and do not have the solace of the truth by which they may illuminate their hearts. For sight, sound, and touch are spoken of in a spiritual sense.[mdcxviii]

Μέσης δὲ νυκτὸς κραυγὴ γέγονεν.[2190] Μεσονυκτίου γίνεται φωνή· ἐκείνῃ τῇ ὥρᾳ ᾗ ἐξῆλθον οἱ υἱοὶ Ἰσραὴλ ἐξ Αἰγύπτου,[2191] ἐν ᾗ καὶ ὁ Χριστὸς ἀνέστη ἐκ νεκρῶν. Φωνή ἐστιν ἡ σάλπιγξ, ἡ τοὺς νεκροὺς ἐγείρουσα καὶ ἐξάγουσα ἐκ τῶν τάφων.[2192] Ἔχει δὲ καὶ μυστικὸν νοῦν τὸ *ἐξέλθετε*. *Λαμπάδες* τῶν παρθένων ὁ τῆς *γνώσεως*[2193] φωτισμός· *ἔλαιον* δὲ εἰς τὰς λαμπάδας, ἡ ἐν ἐπιγνώσει σπουδή. Αὕτη γὰρ τὸ ἐν ἡμῖν διαφυλάσσει φῶς ἁπλοῦν τὸν ὀφθαλμὸν διατηροῦσα, ὥστε φωτίζεσθαι πᾶν *τὸ σῶμα*[2194] κατὰ τὸν λόγον τοῦ Κυρίου.

Μεσονυκτίου δὲ γίνεται ἡ φωνή, ἐκείνῃ τῇ ὥρᾳ ᾗ ἐξῆλθον οἱ υἱοὶ Ἰσραὴλ ἐξ Αἰγύπτου, ἐν ᾗ καὶ ὁ Χριστὸς ἀνέστη ἐκ νεκρῶν. φωνή ἐστιν ἡ σάλπιγξ, ἡ τοὺς νεκροὺς ἐγείρουσα καὶ ἐξάγουσα ἐκ τῶν τάφων. ἔχει δὲ καὶ μυστικὸν νοῦν τὸ *ἐξέλθετε*. ἐὰν γὰρ μὴ ἐξέλθωμεν, τὸν νυμφίον ἀπαντῆσαι οὐ δυνάμεθα. *λαμπάδες* παρθένων ὁ *τῆς γνώσεως* φωτισμός. *ἔλαιον* δὲ εἰς τὰς λαμπάδας ἡ ἐν ἐπιγνώσει σπουδὴ καὶ ‹ἡ› τῶν ἐντολῶν ἐργασία. αὕτη γὰρ τὸ ἐν ἡμῖν διαφυλάττει φῶς ἁπλοῦν τὸν ὀφθαλμὸν διατηροῦσα, ὥστε φωτίζεσθαι *ὅλον* ἡμῶν *τὸ σῶμα* κατὰ τὸν τοῦ κυρίου λόγον. αἱ μὲν οὖν *λαβοῦσαι* τὴν ἐπιμελῆ σπουδὴν πρὸς τὴν τῶν ἐντολῶν ἐργασίαν *φρόνιμοι*. αἱ δὲ ἀμελεῖς *μωραί*, τὸν προσήκοντα καιρὸν ἀναλώσασαι εἰς τὴν τῶν ματαίων σπουδήν. τὸ δὲ *ἐκάθευδον* τὴν κοίμησιν τοῦ θανάτου λέγει. τὸ μεσονύκτιον δὲ τὸ αἰφνίδιον δηλοῖ καὶ τὸ ἀπροσδόκητον, ἅμα καὶ τὸ φοβερόν. καὶ ταῖς μὲν ἐξαναστάσαις πάρεστιν ἃ ἐπόνεσαν. τῶν δὲ ῥᾳθύμων, περὶ τὴν εὐσέβειαν μηδὲν ἐπιφερομένων, ἄρχεται στυγνάζειν ἡ ψυχὴ καὶ οἱονεὶ κατασβέννυσθαι καὶ εἰς παραφροσύνην χωρεῖν, ὥστε οἰηθῆναι ἐλεηθῆναι αὐτοὺς διὰ τῆς ἑτέρων ἀρετῆς. διὸ ἀποδοκιμάζονται λεγόντων ἐκείνων. *μήποτε οὐκ ἀρκέσει ἡμῖν καὶ ὑμῖν.* πωλοῦσι δὲ τὸ ἔλαιον οἱ διδάσκοντες μισθοῦ, προσεδρίας, προσοχῆς, φιλομαθίας, σπουδῆς, φιλοπονίας.
ἢ *πωλοῦντές* εἰσι προφῆται, ἀπόστολοι, εὐαγγελισταί, δι᾽ ὧν τις μαθητευθεὶς τὴν ἀρετὴν ἐργάζεται.[mdcxix]

Μεσονύκτιον δὲ γίνεται ἡ *φωνή*. ἐκείνῃ τῇ ὥρᾳ, ᾗ ἐξῆλθον οἱ υἱοὶ Ἰσραὴλ ἐξ Αἰγύπτου, ἐν ᾗ καὶ ὁ Χριστὸς ἀνέστη ἐκ τῶν νεκρῶν. *Φωνὴ* ἐστιν ἡ σάλπιγξ, ἡ τοὺς νεκροὺς ἐγείρουσα, καὶ ἐξάγουσα ἐκ τῶν τάφων. Ἔχει δὲ καὶ μυστικὸν νοῦν τὸ *ἐξέλθετε*. Ἐὰν γὰρ μὴ ἐξέλθωμεν, τὸν νυμφίον ἀπαντῆσαι οὐ δυνάμεθα. *Λαμπάδα* τῆς παρθενίας ὁ τῆς γνώσεως φωτισμός. ἔλαιον δὲ εἰς τὰς λαμπάδας ἡ ἐν ἐπιγνώσει σπουδή, καὶ τῶν ἐντολῶν ἐργασία. Αὕτη γὰρ τὸ ἐν ἡμῖν διαφυλάττει φῶς, ἁπλοῦν τὸν ὀφθαλμὸν διατηροῦσα, ὥστε φωτίζεσθαι ὅλον ἡμῶν τὸ σῶμα, κατὰ τὸν τοῦ Κυρίου λόγον. Αἱ μὲν οὖν λαβοῦσαι τὴν ἐπιμελῆ σπουδὴν πρὸς τὴν τῶν ἐντολῶν ἐργασίαν *φρόνιμοι*. αἱ δὲ ἀμελεῖς *μωραί*, τὸν προσήκοντα καιρὸν ἀναλώσασαι εἰς τὴν τῶν ματαίων σπουδήν. Τὸ

2190 Matt. 25:6.
2191 Cf. Ex. 12:29 ff.
2192 Cf. 1 Kor. 15:52.
2193 Cf. 2 Kor. 4:6.
2194 Cf. Matt. 6:22.

δέ, *ἐκάθευδον*, τὴν κοίμησιν τοῦ θανάτου λέγει. τὸ μεσονύκτιον δέ, τὸ αἰφνίδιον δηλοῖ καὶ τὸ ἀπροσδόκητον, ἅμα καὶ τὸ φοβερόν. Καὶ *ταῖς μὲν ἐξαναστάσαις πάρεστιν* ἃ ἐπόνεσαν. τὴν δὲ ῥᾳθυμίαν περὶ τὴν εὐσέβειαν μηδὲν ἐπιφερομένων ἄρχεται στυγνάζειν ἡ ψυχή, καὶ οἱονεὶ κατασβέννυσθαι, καὶ εἰς παραφροσύνην χωρεῖν, ὥστε οἰηθῆναι αὐτὰς διὰ τῆς ἑτέρων ἀρετῆς. Διὸ ἀποδοκιμάζονται, λεγόντων ἐκείνων, *Μήποτε οὐκ ἀρκέσει ἡμῖν καὶ ὑμῖν*. Πωλοῦσι δὲ τὸ ἔλαιον οἱ διδάσκοντες μισθοῦ προσεδρείᾳ, προσοχῆς, φιλομαθίας, φιλοπονίας.[mdcxx]

Ἢ *πωλοῦντές* εἰσι προφῆται, ἀπόστολοι, εὐαγγελισταί, δι᾽ ὧν τις μαθητευθεὶς τὴν ἀρετὴν ἐργάζεται.[mdcxxi]

Αἱ μὲν οὖν *λα‹β›οῦσαι*[2195] τὴν ἐπιμελῆ σπουδήν, *φρόνιμοι*, αἱ δὲ ἀμελεῖς *μωραί*. Τὸ δὲ *ἐκάθευδον*, τὴν κοίμησιν τοῦ θανάτου λέγει· τὸ μεσονύκτιον δὲ τὸ αἰφνίδιον δηλοῖ καὶ τὸ ἀπροσδόκητον, ἅμα καὶ τὸ φοβερόν. Καὶ ταῖς μὲν ἐξαναστάσαις πάρεστιν ἃ ἐπόνεσαν· τῶν δὲ φαύλων μηδὲν ἐπιφερομένων, ἄρχεται στυγνάζειν ἡ ψυχὴ καὶ οἱονεὶ κατασβέννυσθαι καὶ εἰς παραφροσύνην χωρεῖν, ὥστε οἰηθῆναι ἐλεηθῆναι αὐτοὺς διὰ τῆς ἑτέρων ἀρετῆς. Διὸ ἀποδοκιμάζονται | **201r** λεγόντων ἐκείνων, *μήποτε οὐκ ἀρκέσει ἡμῖν καὶ ὑμῖν· πορεύεσθε δὲ μᾶλλον πρὸς τοὺς πωλοῦντας*.[2196]

67

201r (ΩΡΙΓΕΝΟΥΣ) Πωλοῦσι τὸ ἔλαιον οἱ διδάσκοντες μισθοῦ, προσεδρείας, προσοχῆς, φιλομαθίας, σπουδῆς, φιλοπονίας.

68

204r *Ὅτ᾽ ἂν δὲ ἔλθῃ ὁ υἱός τοῦ ἀνθρώπου*.[2197] (ΩΡΙΓΕΝΟΥΣ) Τὸ *ἀπὸ*[2198] ἢ *πρὸ*[2199] *καταβολῆς κόσμου* τὸ ὡρισμένον ἐν προγνώσει δηλοῖ. Ἔχει δὲ καὶ μυστικόν τι, ὅπερ ζήτει.[mdcxxii]

Τὸ ἀπὸ ἢ πρὸ καταβολῆς κόσμου τὸ ὡρισμένον ἐν προγνώσει δηλοῖ. ἔχει δὲ καὶ μυστικόν τι, ὅπερ ζήτει.[mdcxxiii]

2195 Cod. λαχοῦσαι.
2196 Matt. 25:9.
2197 Matt. 25:31.
2198 Matt. 13:35; 25:34; Luke, 11:50; Heb. 4:3; 9:26; Rev. 13:8.
2199 John, 17:24; Eph. 1:4; 1 Peter, 1:20.

Καὶ ἀφοριεῖ αὐτούς.[2200] Νῦν γὰρ ἀναμεμιγμένοι εἰσὶν ἅ | **204v** παντες· ἡ δὲ διαίρεσις τότε ἔσται μετὰ ἀκριβείας ἁπάσης καὶ τότε ἀπὸ τῆς στάσεως αὐτοὺς διαιρεῖ καὶ ποιεῖ δήλους. Εἶτα καὶ ἀπὸ τῶν ὀνομάτων τὸν ἑκάστου τρόπον ἐνδείκνυται, τοὺς μὲν *ἐρίφια* καλῶν, τοὺς δὲ *πρόβατα,*[2201] ἵνα τῶν μὲν τὸ ἄκαρπον δείξῃ (οὐδεὶς γὰρ ἀπ᾽ ἐρίφου καρπὸς γένοιτ᾽ ἄν) τῶν δὲ τὴν πολλὴν πρόσοδ‹ο›ν.[2202] Καὶ γὰρ πολλὴ τῶν προβάτων ἡ πρόσοδος, ἀπό τε τοῦ ἐρίου, ‹ἀπό τε γάλακτος› ἀπό τε τῶν τικτομένων, ὧν ἁπάντων ἔρημον ἔριφος.

> [Νῦν γὰρ ἀναμεμιγμένοι εἰσὶν ἅπαντες. ἡ δὲ διαίρεσις, τότε ἔσται μετὰ ἀκριβείας ἁπάσης. καὶ τότε ἀπὸ τῆς στάσεως αὐτοὺς διαιρεῖ καὶ ποιεῖ δήλους. εἶτα καὶ ἀπὸ τῶν ὀνομάτων τὸν ἑκάστου τρόπον ἐνδείκνυται, τοὺς μὲν ἐρίφια καλῶν, τοὺς δὲ *πρόβατα*, ἵνα τῶν μὲν τὸ ἄκαρπον δείξῃ (οὐδεὶς γὰρ ἀπ᾽ ἐρίφου καρπὸς γένοιτ᾽ ἄν) τῶν δὲ τὴν πολλὴν πρόσοδον (καὶ γὰρ πολλὴ τῶν προβάτων ἡ πρόσοδος, ἀπό τε τοῦ ἐρίου, τοῦ γάλακτος, ἀπό τε τῶν τικτομένων, ὧν ἁπάντων ἔριφος ἔρημος.][mdcxxiv]

> Νῦν μὲν γὰρ οὐκ εἰσὶν ἀφωρισμένοι, ἀλλὰ ἀναμὶξ ἅπαντες. ἡ δὲ διαίρεσις τότε ἔσται μετὰ ἀκριβείας ἁπάσης. Καὶ τέως ἀπὸ τῆς στάσεως αὐτοὺς διαιρεῖ καὶ ποιεῖ δήλους. εἶτα καὶ ἀπὸ τῶν ὀνομάτων τὸν ἑκάστου τρόπον ἐνδείκνυται, τοὺς μὲν ἐρίφια καλῶν, τοὺς δὲ πρόβατα, ἵνα τῶν μὲν τὸ ἄκαρπον δείξῃ. οὐδεὶς γὰρ ἀπὸ ἐρίφων καρπὸς γένοιτ᾽ ἄν. τῶν δὲ τὴν πολλὴν πρόσοδον. καὶ γὰρ πολλὴ τῶν προβάτων ἡ πρόσοδος, ἀπό τε ἐρίου, ἀπό τε γάλακτος, ἀπό τε τῶν τικτομένων, ὧν ἁπάντων ἔρημον ἔριφος.[mdcxxv]

Πάντα δὲ τὰ ἔθνη,[2203] τουτέστι πᾶσα ἡ τῶν ἀνθρώπων φύσις.

> *Πάντα δὲ τὰ ἔθνη*, τουτέστι πᾶσα ἡ τῶν ἀνθρώπων φύσις.[mdcxxvi]

> Εἶτα, *Συναχθήσεται*, φησί, *πάντα τὰ ἔθνη*, τουτέστι, *πᾶσα ἡ τῶν ἀνθρώπων φύσις*.[mdcxxvii]

Πρόβατόν ἐστιν ἕξις ἀγαθή· ἔριφος, ἕξις κακή. Ζητητέον δὲ εἰ τοὺς δικαίους *ἐκ δεξιῶν*[2204] ἔστησε, π‹ῶς›[2205] πάλιν λέγει· *δεῦτε* εἰς τὴν τῶν οὐρανῶν *βασιλείαν.*[2206]

> Πρόβατον δέ ἐστιν ἕξις ἀγαθή, ἔριφος ἕξις κακή. ζητητέον δὲ εἰ τοὺς δικαίους *ἐκ δεξιῶν* ἔστησε, πῶς πάλιν λέγει. *δεῦτε* εἰς τὴν τῶν οὐρανῶν *βασιλείαν.*[mdcxxviii]

2200 Matt. 25:32.
2201 Matt. 25:33.
2202 Cod. πρόσοδων.
2203 Matt. 25:32.
2204 Matt. 25:33-34.
2205 Cod. ποῦ.
2206 Matt. 25:34.

Καὶ εἰ ἡτοίμαστό φησι ἡ βασιλεία, ποία χάρις αὐτοῖς τὰ ἡτοιμασμένα κληρονομεῖν; Διότι οὐχ ὅτι ἡτοίμαστο κληρονομοῦσιν, ἀλλ᾽ ὅτι κληρονομεῖν ἔμελλον, διὰ τοῦτο ἡτοίμαστο.[mdcxxix]

> Καὶ εἰ ἡτοίμαστο (φησίν) ἡ βασιλεία, ποία χάρις αὐτοῖς τὰ ἡτοιμασμένα κληρονομεῖν; διότι οὐχ ὅτι ἡτοίμαστο κληρονομοῦσι, ἀλλ᾽ ὅτι κληρονομεῖν ἔμελλον διὰ τοῦτο ἡτοίμαστο.[mdcxxx]

Δεῦτε οἱ εὐλογημένοι.[2207] Πρώτους δὲ δικαίους καλεῖ, ἵνα κατὰ πρόσωπον πληγῶσιν οἱ ἄδικοι.

> Πρώτους δὲ δικαίους καλεῖ, ἵνα κατὰ πρόσωπον πληγῶσιν οἱ ἄδικοι.[mdcxxxi]

Ἐπείνασα γάρ, καὶ ἐδώκατε.[2208] Τοῦτο δὲ ποιεῖ ἀνθ᾽ ὧν εὖ ἐποίησαν τοὺς μαθητάς, οὓς καὶ ἀδελφοὺς[2209] καλεῖ οἰκειοποιούμενος τὰς εἰς αὐτοὺς εὐποιίας. *Ἐπείνασα γάρ*, φησί, καὶ ἐθρέψατέ με. Ἤτοι τὰς εἰς πάντας ἀνθρώπους γινομένας εὐποιίας ἢ συμπαθείας οἰκειοποιεῖται καὶ τούτους καλεῖ ἀδελφούς, ὡς ὁμοιωθέντας τῇ αὐτοῦ ἐπιεικείᾳ.

Ἄλλως τε δέ. Ἐξ τῆς ἀγάπης (ἧς οὐδὲν τῶν καλῶν ἐστιν ἰσοστάσιον[mdcxxxii]) ἀπαριθμεῖται τὰ εἴδη, ἐφ᾽ οἷς ἑαυτῷ ἀναδέχεται τὴν εἰς τοὺς δεομένους φιλανθρωπίαν.[mdcxxxiii] Τοῖς γὰρ ἐλεήμοσιν ἀντιταλαντεύων τῷ ἐλέῳ τὸν ἔλεον καὶ τὰ γέρα νέμων τῆς ἐκεῖθεν μακαριότητος, τὰ τοιάδε φησὶ τοῖς ἀξίοις. Τέλος δὲ τῆς ἀγάπης εἶναι φασὶ τὸ ἀγαθόν, ὅπερ ἐστὶν αὐτὸς ὁ Θεός,[2210] ἡ τῶν ἐφετῶν ἀκρότης.[mdcxxxiv] Ἡ γὰρ ἀγάπη | **205r** διὰ τῆς ἑξάδος τῶν οἰκείων μερῶν κατορθωθεῖσα[mdcxxxv] διαφερόντως Θεῷ συνάπτει τὸν ἄνθρωπον τῆς θεολογίας τὸ πῦρ ἀναφλέγουσα. Ὁ οὖν ταύτην κτησάμενος θρέψει μὲν καὶ ποτίσει Χριστὸν *πεινῶντα* καὶ *διψῶντα*[2211] τὴν πάντων σωτηρίαν,[mdcxxxvi] τὸν πᾶσιν εἰσοικισθέντα διὰ τῶν δεομένων τοῖς λαβοῦσιν αὐτὸν διὰ πίστεως. Συναγάγ‹ει›[2212] δὲ ξενιτεύοντα, ἐνδύσει δὲ γυμνητεύοντα, θεραπεύσει ἀσθενοῦντα καὶ *ἐν φυλακῇ* καθειργμένον. Οὐ παρόψεται πόθῳ τοῦ εὐεργετεῖν σφοδρῶς ἐπειγόμενος καὶ διὰ τὴν ἐπαινετὴν τῶν καλῶν ἀπληστίαν. Οὐ μέχρι τῶν φαινομένων στήσεται, οὐδὲ τῇ περὶ τὰ ἔξω φιλοφροσύνῃ περιορίσει τὴν εἰς τὸν δεσπότην φιλανθρωπίαν, ἀλλὰ καὶ ἐνδοτέρω χωρήσει τοῦ φαινομένου καὶ τῶν ψυχικῶν παθημάτων φροντίδα ποιήσεται καὶ ἰατρείαν ἐπινοήσει τὴν πρέπουσαν καὶ κατασκηνώσει μὲν εἰς *τόπον χλόης*[2213] θρέμματα λογικά, ἀρτιπαγῇ πρὸς εὐσέβειαν, *ἐπὶ* δὲ ὕδατος

2207 Matt. 25:34.
2208 Matt. 25:35.
2209 Cf. Matt. 25:40.
2210 1 John, 4:8&16; cf. Rom. 8:5; 2 Cor. 13:11; Eph. 2:4; 2 Thess. 1:7; 1 John, 4:12.
2211 Matt. 25:37.
2212 Cod. συναγάγοι.
2213 Cf. Psalm 22:2.

ἀναπαύσεως αὐτὰ διαθρέψει.[2214] Καὶ τὸν μὲν ἐκδημήσαντα τῆς οἰκείας πατρίδος καὶ ἐπὶ ξένης γῆς διατρίβοντα ἐπὶ τὴν ἰδίαν ἑστίαν, ἥτις ποτέ ἐστιν, ἀσμένως χορηγήσειεν. Ἀλλὰ καὶ ἄλλον ἀπογυμνωθέντα τῆς πατρικῆς οὐσίας θεώμενος, τῆς τε κατὰ προαίρεσιν ἀφθαρσίας τὴν στολὴν ἐκδυσάμενον, ἐλεήσας τῆς γυμνώσεως ἐνδύσει πάλιν, τὸν κατὰ Θεὸν καὶ μακάριον εἰσηγούμενος βίον. Τὸν δὲ ἀσθενοῦντα τῇ πίστει καὶ περὶ τὴν διάκρισιν τῶν πρακτέων νηπιάζουσαν ἔτι τὴν διανοίαν φέροντα, οὐ παραδραμεῖται, ἀλλ᾽ ἐπὶ τὴν ποθουμένην ὑγείαν καὶ τὸ οἰκεῖον τέλος ἀνακαλέσεται τῷ λόγῳ τῆς ἀληθείας. Ἐπὶ τούτοις, καὶ τὸν καθειργμένον τῷ ζόφῳ τῆς ἀγνοίας ἰδεῖν δὲ τὸ φῶς τῆς γνώσεως κωλυόμενον, τῷ σκοτεινῷ χωρίῳ κατὰ πρόνοιαν ἐπιστάς, ὥσπερ διά τινος ἀγγέλου τοῦ φωτίζοντος τὴν διάνοιαν λόγου, | **205v** τὰ τῆς ἀγνοίας διαρρήξας δεσμά, ἐπὶ τὸ φῶς προαγάγ‹ει›[2215] τῆς κατὰ Χριστὸν ἐλευθερίας καὶ πολιτείας. Πάντα ταῦτα καὶ τὰ τοιαῦτα κατὰ τὸν εἰκότα λόγον καὶ τρόπον ὁ ὑπὸ τῆς ἀγάπης τὴν ψυχὴν φρυκτωρούμενος διττῶς ἐπιδείξεται. Καὶ γὰρ διπλῶν ὄντων ἡμῶν ἐκ ψυχῆς καὶ σώματος, διπλοῦν καὶ τῆς ἐπιμελείας τὸ εἶδος, ἧς καὶ αὐτοὶ χρήζομεν πάντες. Διὸ φιλανθρώπως ἀλλήλοις χρηστέον, ἵνα καὶ ἄλλως μᾶλλον ἑαυτοὺς εὐεργετῶμεν. Τὸ γὰρ εὐεργέτημα μεῖζον ἑαυτῷ παρὰ τῷ εὖ παθόντι γενόμενον, ἐπὶ τὸν εὐεργέτην διαφιλέστερον ἀντεπάνεισι, καὶ οὕτως εἰς τὸ εὐεργετεῖσθαι τὸ εὐεργετεῖν ἀντιπεριΐσταται. Ὁ τοίνυν διὰ τῆς αὐτοτελοῦς ἑξάδος[mdcxxxvii] τῶν ἐντολῶν ἑαυτὸν ἀνακαθάρας, ὡς οἷόν τε, καὶ ἐν τῇ ἀγάπῃ τελειωθείς, ἆθλον ἀρετῆς κομιεῖται διὰ τῆς ἐν Πνεύματι φυσικῆς θεωρίας τὴν ἄπταιστον γνῶσιν τῶν ὑπὸ χρόνον καὶ φύσιν καὶ τὸν ἓξ ἡμέραις ὑποστάντα κόσμον[mdcxxxviii] (τὸν ὑλικὸν καὶ ὁρώμενον, τύπον εἰδὼς τοῦ ἀναβεβηκότος τὴν αἴσθησιν) ὄψεται καλῶς διὰ τοῦ ὁρωμένου τὸν μὴ ὁρώμενον,[mdcxxxix] καὶ οὕτω τὴν κτίσιν, ἐπὶ τὸν ἑαυτῆς αἴτιον ἕξει χειραγωγοῦσαν αὐτοῦ τὴν διάνοιαν. Οἱ δέ γε μὴ οὕτω πολιτευσάμενοι, ἀξίως τῇ κολάσει ὑποβληθήσονται, κατάλληλα τῆς ἑαυτῶν ὠμότητος κομιούμενοι τὰ τέλη καὶ τῷ αἰωνίῳ παραδοθήσονται πυρὶ τῷ ἡτοιμασμένῳ *τῷ διαβόλῳ καὶ τοῖς ἀγγέλοις αὐτοῦ*,[2216] αἰωνίως κολασθησόμενοι.

τότε ἀπεκριθήσονται αὐτῷ οἱ δίκαιοι.[2217] Διὸ καὶ ὡς εὐγνώμονες, μηδὲν ἑαυτοῖς συνειδότες εἰς τὸν Κύριον πεπραχέναι, εἶπον μηδὲν τοιοῦτον πεπρᾶχθαι τούτοις ποτέ. Εἶτα, τοὺς ἐξ εὐωνύμων ὡς φαύλους μὴ ποιήσαντας τὰ αὐτὰ τοῖς ἀγαθοῖς τῇ αὐτῇ κολάσει τῷ διαβόλῳ ὑποβάλλει ὡς συνδραμόντας τῷ διαβόλῳ. | **206r** Καλεῖ δὲ αὐτοὺς κατηραμένους[2218] οὐκ ἀπὸ τοῦ Πατρός. Τὰ γὰρ ἴδια αὐτῶν ἔργα ποιεῖ αὐτοὺς ἐπικαραράτους. Πᾶσι μὲν γὰρ ἡτοίμασε τὴν βασιλείαν, τῷ δὲ διαβόλῳ *πῦρ ἄσβεστον*.[2219] Οὗτοι δὲ ἐάσαντες τὴν βασιλείαν, ἐπὶ τὸ *ἡτοιμασμένον τῷ διαβόλῳ πῦρ*

2214 Cf. Psalm 22:2.
2215 Cod. προαγάγοι.
2216 Matt. 25:41.
2217 Matt. 25:37.
2218 Matt. 25:41.
2219 Mark, 9:43; cf. Matt. 3:12; Luke, 3:17.

ἑκοντὶ ἀπῆλθον, ἐπείπερ οὐ συνεπάθησαν κατά τι τοῖς ἐνδεέσιν, οὓς καὶ ἐλαχίστους[2220] καλεῖ διὰ τὴν πενίαν.
Ἄρα δὲ οἱ ἁμαρτωλοὶ μόνην τὴν ἐλεημοσύνην ἀπαιτηθήσονται, ἢ καὶ τὴν εὐσέβειαν. Πρῶτα μὲν τὴν εὐσέβειαν, ἔπειτα δὲ καὶ τὸ εἰς ἀλλήλους φιλάνθρωπον.

> Ἄρα δὲ οἱ ἁμαρτωλοὶ μόνην τὴν ἐλεημοσύνην ἀπαιτηθήσονται, ἢ καὶ τὴν εὐσέβειαν. πρῶτα μὲν τὴν εὐσέβειαν, ἔπειτα δὲ καὶ τὸ εἰς ἀλλήλοις φιλάνθρωπον.[mdcxl]

Τριχῶς γάρ ἐστιν ἡ ἐλεημοσύνη· διά τε ψυχῆς, διά τε σώματος καὶ τῶν ἐκτὸς ἐπιτελουμένη.

> Τριχῶς γάρ ἐστιν ἡ ἐλεημοσύνη. διά τε ψυχῆς διά τε σώματος καὶ τῶν ἐκτὸς ἐπιτελουμένη.[mdcxli]

Ἐφ᾽ ὅσον οὐκ ἐποιήσατε ἑνὶ τούτων τῶν ἐλαχίστων.[2221] Ἄνω μὲν ἀδελφοὺς καλεῖ,[2222] ἐπειδὴ ἀδελφοὺς ἐργάζεται τὸ βάπτισμα καὶ ἡ τῶν μυστηρίων κοινωνία. Ἤτοι ἀδελφοὺς ἐλαχίστους[2223] ἄνω καλεῖ τοὺς ἀποσταλέντας πρὸς αὐτοὺς καθὰ προείρηται. Οὐχ ὅτι εὐτελεῖς ἦσαν οἱ τῆς βασιλείας ἄξιοι, ἀλλ᾽ ὅτι ἐν τῇ ζωῇ αὐτῶν ὑπενοήθησαν πᾶσιν ἄσημοί τινες εἶναι καὶ εὐτελεῖς. Ὧδε δέ, *ἐλαχίστων* μόνον εἰπών, ἔδειξεν ὅτι τοὺς πτωχοὺς καὶ εὐτελεῖς καλεῖ, οὓς καὶ οἰκειοποιεῖται διὰ τὸ καὶ τῆς αὐτῶν φύσεως μετασχεῖν. Κρίνει γὰρ τοὺς ἁμαρτάνοντας οὐ μόνον ἐξ ὧν ἥμαρτον, ἀλλὰ καὶ ἐξ ὧν οὐκ ἐποίησαν καλῶν. Εἰ δὲ καὶ μετὰ ἐπιεικείας φθέγγονται καὶ οἱ ἄδικοι μηδὲν αὐτοῖς πεπρᾶχθαι τοιοῦτον, ἀλλ᾽ οὐδὲν ὄφελος, ἐπείπερ οὐκ ἐποίησαν εὐχερὲς ὂν τὸ ἐπίταγμα τῆς εὐποιΐας. Διὸ οἱ τοιοῦτοι ἀπέρχονται *εἰς αἰώνιον κόλασιν*, οἱ δὲ δίκαιοι *εἰς ζωὴν αἰώνιον.*[2224] Ὥσπερ γὰρ αἱ τῶν δικαίων τιμαὶ ἀκατάλυτοι, οὕτω καὶ αἱ τῶν ἀδίκων τιμωρίαι ἄπαυστοι.

Οἴδατε ὅτι μετὰ δύο ἡμέρας τὸ πάσχα.[2225] | **206v** Μετὰ τὸ προσλαλῆσαι τὸν σωτῆρα Χριστὸν πάντα τὰ μέλλοντα γίνεσθαι ἐν τῷ Ὄρει τῶν Ἐλαιῶν πρὸ δύο ἡμερῶν τοῦ *πάσχα*, ἅτινα ἐπιμνησθέντες ἐν ὑστεροπρώτοις[mdcxlii] ἀνεγράψαντο οἱ τῆς ἀληθείας ἀκροαταὶ γενόμενοι, αὐτίκα καὶ τοῦ σωτηριώδους πάθους τὴν ἀπόδειξιν ποιεῖται αὐτοῖς ἐν αὐτῷ τῷ ὄρει. Ὅθεν λαθραίως τὸν Ἰούδαν καταβάντα πεπληρωμένον τῆς τοῦ διαβόλου ἐνεργείας[2226] οἰχέσθαι πρὸς τοὺς ἡγουμένους τῶν Ἰουδαίων καὶ τῆς φιλαργυρίας τὸν ἰὸν ἀπεμέσας συντάττεται *πρὸ τῆς τοῦ πάσχα ἑορτῆς*[2227] παραδώσειν

2220 Matt. 25:45.
2221 Matt. 25:45.
2222 Matt. 23:8; cf. 28:10.
2223 Matt. 25:40.
2224 Matt. 25:46.
2225 Matt. 26:2.
2226 Cf. John, 6:70; 13:2.
2227 John, 13:1.

αὐτόν. Ὅθεν αὐτοῦ ἐπαναστρέψαντος ἐδόκει λανθάνειν τὸν γινώσκοντα *τί ἦν ἐν τῷ ἀνθρώπῳ*.[2228] Ἀλλ᾽ οὐ μὴν ὡς εἰδὼς παραυτα καὶ ταχὺ τῆς προδοσίας τὸν ἔλεγχον πεποίηκεν ὁ Μονογενής· ἀλλὰ κρύψας τοῖς λοιποῖς μαθηταῖς, ἐᾷ τοῦτο πάλιν ἐν αὐτοῖς εἶναι, μεθ᾽ ὧν ὁ προδότης καὶ δολιόγλω‹σ›σος[2229] ἔφασκεν· *ποῦ θέλεις ἀπελθόντες ἑτοιμάσ‹ω›μέν*[2230] *σοι φαγεῖν τὸ πάσχα;*[2231]
Πρὸ δύο ἡμερῶν τοῦ πάσχα ἡ βούλησις. Διὸ καὶ τὴν τετάρτην ἐν τῇ ἑβδομάδι νηστεύομεν, ὡς τοῦ πάθους ἀρχὴν τοῦ κατὰ τὴν ἕκτην ἐπιτελεσθέντος. Ἔδει δὲ καὶ τὴν προφητείαν πληρωθῆναι τὴν ἐν τῇ νομικῇ διατυπώσει, ἐν ᾗ τὸ πάσχα ἐθύετο μηνὶ πρώτῳ τεσσαρεσκαιδεκάτῃ ἡμέρᾳ.[mdcxliii] Ἐν τούτῳ γὰρ τῷ μηνὶ καὶ ἐν ταύτῃ τῇ ἡμέρᾳ καὶ τὸ ἀληθινὸν πάσχα ἔδει τυθῆναι.[2232]

> Πρὸ δύο ἡμερῶν τοῦ *πάσχα* ἡ βουλή, διὸ καὶ τὴν τετάρτην ἐν τῇ ἑβδομάδι νηστεύομεν ὡς τοῦ πάθους ἀρχὴν τοῦ κατὰ τὴν ἕκτην ἐπιτελεσθέντος. ἔδει δὲ καὶ τὴν προφητείαν πληρωθῆναι τὴν ἐν τῇ νομικῇ διατυπώσει, ἐν ᾗ τὸ πάσχα ἐθύετο μηνὶ πρώτῳ τεσσαρεσκαιδεκάτῃ ἡμέρᾳ· ἐν τούτῳ γὰρ τῷ μηνὶ καὶ ἐν ταύτῃ τῇ ἡμέρᾳ καὶ τὸ ἀληθινὸν πάσχα ἔδει τυθῆναι.[mdcxliv]

> Πρὸ δύο ἡμέρας τοῦ πάθους ἡ βουλή. διὸ δὲ τὴν τετάρτην ἐν τῇ ἑβδομάδι νηστείαν ἄγομεν, ὡς τοῦ πάθους ἀρχὴν τοῦ κατὰ τὴν ἕκτην ἐπιτελεσθέντος. δόλον δὲ μηχανῶνται διὰ τὸν λαὸν τὸν ἀκολουθοῦντα καὶ περιεστῶτα ἀεί. καὶ τὴν μὲν ἑορτὴν ὑπερθέσθαι βούλονται. οὐ συγχωροῦνται δέ, ἐπειδὴ τὴν προφητείαν ἔδει πληροῦσθαι τὴν ἐν τῇ νομικῇ διατυπώσει, ἐν ᾗ τὸ Πάσχα ἐθύετο, μηνὶ πρώτῳ, τεσσαρεσκαιδεκάτῃ ἡμέρᾳ. ἐν τούτῳ γὰρ τῷ μηνὶ καὶ ἐν ταύτῃ τῇ ἡμέρᾳ τὸ ἀληθινὸν Πάσχα ἔδει τυθῆναι.[mdcxlv]

Τότε συνήχθησαν οἱ ἀρχιερεῖς.[2233] Τοῦ νόμου κελεύοντος ἕνα ἀρχιερέα εἶναι,[mdcxlvi] πολλοὺς ἐποίουν αὐτοί. Καλῶς δὲ εἶπε *τοῦ λαοῦ* αὐτοὺς εἶναι *ἀρχιερεῖς* καὶ οὐχὶ τοῦ Θεοῦ, μεθ᾽ ὧν καὶ περὶ ἀδίκου φόνου ἐβουλεύοντο. Οὐ διὰ τὴν ἑορτὴν δὲ ἤθελον αὐτὸν μετὰ τὴν ἑορτὴν φονεῦσαι, *ἵνα μὴ μιανθῶσιν*,[2234] ἀλλὰ διὰ τὸν ὄχλον. | **207r** Ἐδεδίεσαν γὰρ μήποτε μισοπονήρως φερόμενοι διὰ τὸν ἀνόσιον φόνον ἀνέλωσιν αὐτούς. Ἢ ὅτι οὐ μὴ προσαγάγωσι τὰς κατὰ νόμον θυσίας ἰδόντες τῶν ἱερέων τὸ μιαιφόνον περὶ τὸν Ἰησοῦν, ὃν ἡγοῦντο μέγαν εἶναι, εἰ καὶ μὴ ἐπίστευον ὅτι Θεὸς ἦν, καὶ ἵνα μὴ ἐν ἐπισήμῳ ἡμέρᾳ γεγονότος τοῦ πάθους φανερὸν γένηται πᾶσι. Πλὴν καὶ *πρὸ τῆς ἑορτῆς*[2235] κατασχόντες αὐτὸν ἐπειδὴ εὗρον τὴν τοῦ Ἰούδα εὐκαιρίαν, οὐκ εὐθὺς αὐτὸν ἀνεῖλον, ἀλλὰ τῇ ἑξῆς, ὅτε ὁ Κύριος οἰκονομικῶς συνεχώρει αὐτοῖς.

2228 John, 2:25.
2229 Cod. δολιόγλωσος.
2230 Cod. ἑτοιμάσομέν.
2231 Matt. 26:17.
2232 Cf. 1 Cor. 5:7.
2233 Matt. 26:3.
2234 John, 18:28.
2235 John, 13:1.

Πολλάκις γὰρ θελήσαντες αὐτὸν συσχεῖν, οὐκ ἠδυνήθησαν. Ἐπειδὴ δὲ καὶ ἔδοξεν αὐτῷ παθεῖν, συνέσχον αὐτόν, καίπερ συνθέμενοι ἀναβαλέσθαι τότε, διὰ τὸ μὴ ποιῆσαι θόρυβον τῷ ὄχλῳ.[2236] Ἐβουλεύσαντο οὖν *πρὸ τῆς ἑορτῆς*[2237] φονεῦσαι αὐτόν. Ὁ δὲ Κύριος *ἐν τῇ ἑορτῇ*[2238] παθὼν ἔδειξε κἀκείνους ψεύστας καὶ ὅτι, εἰ μὴ ᾗ ὥρισεν ἡμέρᾳ, οὐκ ἔπαθε. Διὸ καὶ προλέγει, δεικνὺς ὅτι εἰδὼς ἔπαθεν ὅτε ἤθελεν.

> πρὸς δὲ τούτοις δείκνυται καὶ ὡς ἑκοντὶ ἑαυτὸν ἐξέδωκε, τὸ ὑπὲρ ἡμῶν καταδέξασθαι, ὅτι βουλόμενοι μὲν κατασχεῖν αὐτόν, πολλάκις οὐκ ἴσχυσαν. ὅτε δὲ μὴ συλλαβέσθαι αὐτὸν ἐβούλοντο, τότε ἑαυτὸν ἐκδοὺς παρὰ πᾶσαν ἐλπίδα τὸ σπουδαζόμενον αὐτοῖς εἰς πέρας ἐξελθεῖν παρεσκεύασε.[mdcxlvii]

Τοῦ δὲ Ἰησοῦ γενομένου ἐν Βηθανίᾳ ἐν οἰκίᾳ Σίμωνος τοῦ λεπροῦ.[2239] Ὁ λεπρὸς θεωρεῖται ὡς ἐν ἀναγωγῇ εἰς τὰ ἔθνη, παρ᾿ οἷς καθαρισθεῖσι καταλύει Χριστός· *γυνὴ* δέ ἐστιν ἡ ἐκκλησία· τὸ μύρον δέ, ἡ κατ᾿ εὐσέβειαν ἀρετή, ὅπερ ἐπὶ τὸν Χριστὸν ἐκχέει, ὅς ἐστιν *ἡ κεφαλὴ*[2240] ἣν διεκόσμησεν, ὁμοίως δὲ καὶ Θεὸν φύσει καὶ Θεοῦ Υἱὸν κατὰ φύσιν ὁμολογοῦσα τὸν Χριστόν. Καὶ ὡς *ὀσμὴν εὐωδίας*[2241] πανταχοῦ ταύτην περιάγουσα τὴν ὁμολογίαν, δοκεῖ *μύρον ἐπὶ τῆς κεφαλῆς*[2242] καταχέειν. Ταύτῃ ἐπιτιμᾷ ὁ Ἰούδας, ὡς Ἰωάννης φησί,[2243] τύπον ἔχων τῶν Ἰουδαίων τῶν διὰ φιλοχρηματίαν μὴ ὁμολογούντων Θεὸν τὸν Χριστόν, ἀλλὰ διωκόντων *τὴν ἐκκλησίαν.*[2244] Οἷς ἐπιτιμᾷ ὁ Χριστὸς ὡς ἀνοσίως ἐγκαλοῦσι τῇ ὀρθῇ τῆς ἐκκλησίας πίστει καὶ ἀποδείξῃ | 207v αὐτῆς τὴν πίστιν.[2245] Προαναφωνεῖ δὲ καὶ τὴν εἰς τὰ ἔθνη ἔξοδον τῶν μαθητῶν, τῶν κηρυξάντων πανταχοῦ ὃ ἐποίησεν ἡ γυνὴ *ἐν τῇ οἰκίᾳ τοῦ λεπροῦ,*[2246] ὅπερ θείᾳ δυνάμει ἐξηχήθη πανταχοῦ.

> Καίτοι οὐδὲ τὸ πρόσωπον ἐπίσημον ἦν, οὔτε μάρτυρας ἔχον πολλούς, οὔτε ἐν θεάτρῳ τὸ γεγενημένον, ἀλλ᾿ ἐν οἰκίᾳ, καὶ ἐν οἰκίᾳ λεπροῦ τινος, τῶν μαθητῶν μόνων παρόντων. Τίς οὖν αὐτὸ ἐξήχησε καὶ διαδοθῆναι ἐποίησεν; Ἡ τοῦ ταῦτα λέγοντος δύναμις.[mdcxlviii]

2236 Matt. 26:5; Mark, 14:2.
2237 Cf. John, 13:1; Matt. 25:5; Mark, 14:2.
2238 Cf. Matt. 26:5; Mark, 14:2; John, 7:11; 12:20.
2239 Matt. 26:6.
2240 Matt. 26:7; cf. 1 Cor. 11:3; Eph. 4:15; 5:23.
2241 Cf. Gen. 8:21; Ex. 29:18; *et passim* in OT. Also, cf. Eph. 5:2.
2242 Matt. 26:7; Mark, 14:3; cf. Psalm, 132:2.
2243 John, 12:1-5.
2244 Cf. Acts, 8:1.
2245 Matt. 26:10-12.
2246 Mark, 14:3; Matt. 26:6.

Προσῆλθεν αὐτῷ γυνή.[2247] Ἁπλούστερον μὲν οὗτος ἔγραψε, μὴ εἰπὼν τὸ ὄνομα τῆς γυναικός· ἦν δὲ Μαρία ἡ ἀδελφὴ Λαζάρου.[2248] Αἱ γὰρ ὡς Ἰωσήφ[2249] ἀλείψασαι τὸν Κύριον μύρον γυναῖκες τρεῖς εἰσί· μία ἡ ἀδελφὴ Λαζάρου ἐν Βηθανίᾳ ἐν τῷ οἴκῳ αὐτῆς,[2250] *πρὸ ἓξ ἡμερῶν τοῦ πάσχα*[2251] (*κατὰ* δὲ τὸν Ματθαῖον *καὶ* Μᾶρκον,[2252] πρὸ δύο ἡμερῶν τοῦ *πάσχα, ἐν οἰκίᾳ Σίμωνος τοῦ λεπροῦ*) *κατέχεε* τὸ μύρον *ἐπὶ τῆς κεφαλῆς αὐτοῦ.*[2253] Ἤτοι, δύο μὲν αὐτὰς λέγομεν· μίαν μέν, τὴν τοῦ Λαζάρου, τὴν δὲ ἑτέραν, ἁμαρτωλὸν γυναῖκα, τὴν πρὸ τοῦ πάθους αὐτὸν ἀλείψασαν, ὕστερον δὲ ἐνάρετον γενομένην. Καὶ πάλιν ἄλλο ἅπαξ πρὸ *δύο* ἡμερῶν τοῦ *πάσχα* ἀλείψασαν *τοὺς πόδας αὐτοῦ.* Ὁ δὲ Λουκᾶς, πρὸ πολλῶν ἡμερῶν τοῦ *πάσχα* ἐν οἰκίᾳ Σίμωνος *τοῦ Φαρισαίου*, γυναῖκα λέγει ἁμαρτωλὸν εἰσελθοῦσαν ἀλεῖψαι *τοὺς* τοῦ Κυρίου *πόδας.*[2254] Ὅταν οὖν ὁ Ματθαῖος καὶ ὁ Μᾶρκος *ἐν οἰκίᾳ Σίμωνος τοῦ λεπροῦ* λέγωσι τὸν Κύριον ἑστιάσασθαι, Λουκᾶς δὲ *ἐν οἰκίᾳ τοῦ Φαρισαίου*, οὐ τοῦτο διαφωνίαν ἔχει. Οἱ μὲν γὰρ τοῦ ὀνόματος τὴν προσηγορίαν τηλαυγῶς ἀνεγράψαντο, ὁ δὲ τῆς τοῦ ἔθνους τῶν Ἰουδαίων αἱρέσεως ἐπεμνήσθη. Φαρισαῖος γὰρ ἦν ὁ Σίμων ὁ λεπρὸς ὁ καὶ τοῦ Λαζάρου πατήρ. Οὗτος οὐ νῦν λεπρὸς ἦν, ἀλλὰ ποτέ, ἐθεράπευσε δὲ αὐτὸν καθαρίσας ὁ Κύριος. Ὃς καὶ τοὺς μαθητὰς ἀποδεξάμενος ἐν τῷ οἴκῳ καὶ δείξας τὸ ἀνώγαιον ἐστρωμένον, ἠρώτα ὅπως παρ' αὐτῷ εἰσελθὼν ὁ Κύριος ποιήσει *τὸ πάσχα.*[2255]

69

(ΩΡΙΓΕΝΟΥΣ) Οἱ οὖν τρεῖς εὐαγγελισταὶ μίαν δοκοῦσι σημαίνειν γυναῖκα· ὁ δὲ Ἰωάννης ἄλλην τινὰ θαυμαστήν, ἣν καὶ Μα | **208r** ρία‹ν› καλεῖ καὶ τοῦ Λαζάρου ἀδελφή‹ν›.[2256]

Τάχα μὲν εἴποι τις τέσσαρας εἶναι τὰς γυναῖκας περὶ ὧν ἀνέγραψαν οἱ εὐαγγελισταί· ἐγὼ δὲ μᾶλλον προτίθημι τὸ τρεῖς αὐτὰς εἶναι. Καὶ μία μὲν περὶ ἧς ἀνέγραψαν Ματθαῖος καὶ Μᾶρκος, ἐν πολλοῖς ἄλλοις συνᾴδοντες τῆς εὐαγγελικῆς γραφῆς· ἑτέραν δὲ περὶ ἧς ὁ Λουκᾶς, διαφέρουσαν δέ τινα τῶν προειρημένων, περὶ ἧς ὁ Ἰωάννης. Εἰ γὰρ καὶ *ἐν Βηθανίᾳ* ἀνέγραψαν τὰ κατὰ τὴν γυναῖκα γενόμενα Ματθαῖος καὶ Μᾶρκος,[2257] *ἐν οἰκίᾳ Σίμωνος τοῦ λεπροῦ* διηγήσαντο τὰ περὶ τούτων ἀπηντηκέναι.

2247 Matt. 26:7; cf. Mark, 14:3.
2248 Cf. John, 11:2; 12:3.
2249 Cf. John, 19:38-40. Cod. ὡς Ἰωσήφ, αἱ γάρ.
2250 John, 11:1-2.
2251 John, 12:1.
2252 Matt. 26:2; Mark, 14:1.
2253 Matt. 26:2&6-7; Mark, 14:3.
2254 Luke, 7:36-39.
2255 Matt. 26:17-18.
2256 Cf. John, 11:2; 12:3.
2257 Matt. 26:6; Mark, 14:3.

Ἰωάννης δέ φησι ὅτι *πρὸ ἓξ ἡμερῶν τοῦ πάσχα ἦλθεν εἰς Βηθανίαν, ὅπου ἦν Λάζαρος ὃν ἤγειρεν ἐκ νεκρῶν,*[2258] καὶ ἑξῆς.

> Τάχα μὲν εἴποι … ὁ Ἰωάννης οὐ μόνον τὸ κατὰ τόπον μύρον ἀνέγραψεν ἀλλ᾽ ὅτι καὶ *ἠγάπα ὁ Ἰησοῦς τὴν Μαρίαν καὶ τὴν Μάρθαν,*[2259] εἰ καὶ *ἐν Βηθανίᾳ* ἔγραψε τὰ κατὰ τὴν γυναῖκα γενόμενα, ‹ὡς› Ματθαῖος καὶ Μᾶρκος, καὶ Ἰωάννης. ἀλλὰ πρόσχες ὅτι Ματθαῖος καὶ Μᾶρκος, *ἐν οἰκίᾳ Σίμωνος τοῦ λεπροῦ* διηγήσαντο τὰ περὶ τούτων ἀπηντηκέναι, Ἰωάννης δέ φησιν ὅτι *Ἰησοῦς πρὸ ἓξ ἡμερῶν τοῦ πάσχα ἦλθεν εἰς Βηθανίαν, ὅπου ἦν Λάζαρος ὃν ἤγειρεν ἐκ νεκρῶν, και ἐποίησαν αὐτῷ δεῖπνον*[2260] καὶ τὰ ἑξῆς.[mdcxlix]

70

212v (ΩΡΙΓΕΝΟΥΣ) *Ὀψίας γενομένης.*[2261] *Ὀψίας γενομένης*, ὡς εἶπον οἱ θεσπέσιοι μαθηταί, κάτεισιν ἐξ Ἱερουσαλὴμ ὁ Κύριος εἰς τὴν Βηθανίαν, ὅπως ἐκεῖ τοῦ ἀληθινοῦ πάσχα γεύσηται, ἐάσας τὸ τυπικόν, τουτέστιν τὸ σφαγιαζόμενον *πρόβατον*, ὅπερ αὐτὸς ὁ ἐνανθρωπήσας διετύπωσεν ἐν Αἰγύπτῳ τῷ γένει Ἰσραὴλ διὰ Μωσέως τελεῖν, τὸ πάσχα Κυρίου,[2262] αἰνιττόμενος αὐτοῖς τὸ πάθος τῆς ἰδίας σαρκὸς αὐτοῦ διὰ τῆς σφαγῆς τοῦ ἀμνοῦ.[2263] Τούτου οὖν τοῦ τυπικοῦ μὴ γευσάμενος, ὡς εἴπομεν, ὅρα οἷον ἀληθινὸν πάσχα *μετὰ τὸ δειπνῆσαι*[2264] διατίθεται.

> *Ὀψίας γενομένης*, ὡς εἶπον οἱ θεσπέσιοι μαθηταί, κάτεισιν ἐξ Ἱερουσαλὴμ ὁ κύριος εἰς τὴν Βηθανίαν, ὅπως ἐκεῖ τοῦ ἀληθινοῦ πάσχα γεύσηται ἐάσας τὸ τυπικὸν τουτέστιν τὸ σφαγιαζόμενον *πρόβατον*, ὅπερ αὐτὸς ὁ ἐνανθρωπήσας διετύπωσεν ἐν Αἰγύπτῳ τῷ γένει Ἰσραὴλ διὰ Μωϋσέως τελεῖν, τὸ πάσχα κυρίου, αἰνιττόμενος αὐτοῖς τὸ πάθος τῆς ἰδίας σαρκὸς αὐτοῦ διὰ τῆς σφαγῆς τοῦ ἀμνοῦ. τούτου οὖν τοῦ τυπικοῦ μὴ γευσάμενος, ὡς εἴπομεν, ὅρα οἷον ἀληθινὸν πάσχα *μετὰ τὸ δειπνῆσαι* διατίθεται.[mdcl]

71

212v (ΤΟΥ ΑΥΤΟΥ) Ἡ ἑσπέρα σύμβολον ἔχει. Τοῦ μὲν παλαιοῦ πάσχα τὸ τέλος, | **213r** τοῦ δὲ νέου ἡ ἀρχή. Ἡ ἑορτὴ γὰρ ἦν τῶν νέων.[mdcli]

2258 John, 12:1.
2259 John, 11:5.
2260 John, 12:1 ff.
2261 Matt. 26:20.
2262 Ex. 12:5-11&27&48; Lev. 23:5; Num. 9:4-14; 28:16; Deut. 16:1-6.
2263 Is. 53:7, quoted in Acts, 8:32.
2264 Luke, 22:20; cf. 1 Cor. 11:25.

Ἡ ἑσπέρα σύμβολον ἔχει. τοῦ μὲν παλαιοῦ πάσχα τὸ τέλος, τοῦ δὲ νέου ἡ ἀρχή, ἡ ἑορτὴ γὰρ ἦν τῶν νέων.[mdclii]

Ἀνέκειτο μετὰ τῶν δώδεκα.[2265] Ἡ μὲν ἑτοιμασία γέγονε τοῦ *πάσχα*. Δεῖπνον δέ ἐστι καὶ οὔπω τοῦ *πάσχα* βρῶσις. Οὐδὲ γὰρ ἦν σχῆμα τῶν *τὸ πάσχα* ἐσθιόντων, ἀλλ' ἀνέκειντο δειπνοῦντες. Καὶ ὁ Ἰωάννης δὲ δεῖπνον[2266] εἴρηκεν, οὐδεμίαν μνήμην τοῦ πάσχα ποιησάμενος λέγων· *πρὸ δὲ τῆς ἑορτῆς τοῦ πάσχα εἰδὼς ὁ Ἰησοῦς ὅτι ἦλθεν αὐτοῦ ἡ ὥρα ἵνα μεταβῇ ἐκ τοῦ κόσμου τούτου πρὸς τὸν πατέρα ἀγαπήσας τοὺς ἰδίους τοὺς ἐν τῷ κόσμῳ, εἰς τέλος ἠγάπησεν αὐτούς*, καὶ τὰ ἑξῆς. *Πρὸ τῆς ἑορτῆς τοῦ πάσχα* λέγει,[2267] οὐκ ἐν τῇ ἑορτῇ τοῦ πάσχα, ὥς τε καὶ τὴν πρώτην *τῶν ἀζύμων*[2268] οἰκείως ἐδεξάμεθα, τὴν πρὸ τῶν ἀζύμων νοήσαντες. Ἐκ τούτου φασί τινες[mdcliii] ὅτι ἐν τῷ ἐνιαυτῷ ἐκείνῳ οὐκ ἔφαγε τὸν ἀμνὸν ὁ Κύριος· οὐδὲ γὰρ ἐξῆν αὐτοῖς φαγεῖν εἰ μὴ ἱσταμένοις. Εἰκὸς δὲ αὐτοὺς μετὰ τὸ φαγεῖν τὸ Ἰουδαϊκὸν πάσχα ἀνακλιθῆναι. Ἐσθιόντων οὖν αὐτῶν, φειδόμενος τοῦ προδότου ὁ Κύριος καὶ διδοὺς αὐτῷ μετανοίας ἀφορμήν, οὐκ εἶπεν ὁ δεῖνα με παραδώσει. Ἠρήσατο[mdcliv] γὰρ πάντας φοβῆσαι ἵνα ἀσφαλεστέρους ποιήσῃ καὶ οὐκ ἤλεγξε τὸν Ἰούδαν. Προαναγγέλλει τοίνυν τὰ περὶ τοῦ Ἰούδα, ἵνα γνῶμεν ὅτι ἑκὼν ἔπαθε καὶ ἵνα γνῷ ὁ Ἰούδας ὅτι ᾔδει ὡς Θεὸς ὃ ἔμελλε ποιεῖν. Οἱ δὲ λοιποὶ μαθηταὶ καθαρὸν[2269] εἶχον τὸ συνειδός, ἀλλ' οὖν ἐκείνῳ μᾶλλον ἢ ἑαυτοῖς πιστεύσαντες ἠγωνίων. Ἤδεισαν γὰρ ὅτι ἀδύνατον ἦν ψεύσασθαι τὸν Χριστόν, διὸ καὶ ἠρώτων. Τί οὖν ὁ Χριστὸς λύων πάντων τὸν φόβον καὶ διορθούμενος τὸν Ἰούδαν, πρῶτον μὲν διὰ συμβόλων μηνύει τὸν προδότην; Ἐπειδὴ δὲ ἀδιορίστως ἐλεγχόμενος οὐκ ἔφερεν ἐπαχθῶς, ἐλέγχει αὐτὸν φανερῶς εἰς ἕνα περιτρέπων τὴν αἰτίαν, | **213v** εἰπὼν *ὁ ἐμβάψας μετ' ἐμοῦ*,[2270] εἴ πως μεταβληθῇ. Εἶτά φησι· *ὁ μὲν υἱὸς τοῦ ἀνθρώπου ὑπάγει καθὼς γέγραπται*. Τουτέστιν, εἰ καὶ προώριστο παθεῖν τὸν Χριστὸν καθὼς εἶπον αἱ γραφαί, πλὴν *οὐαὶ τῷ ἀνθρώπῳ ἐκείνῳ δι' οὗ ὁ υἱὸς τοῦ ἀνθρώπου παραδίδοται.*[2271] Οὐ γὰρ συνεργῶν τῇ τοῦ Θεοῦ βουλῇ τοῦτο ἔπραξε. Διὸ καὶ ταλανίζει αὐτόν, ἵνα μή τις οἰηθῇ ἀνέγκλητον αὐτὸν εἶναι. Ἐξ ὧν δὲ ἀπειλεῖ κακῶν τῷ προδότῃ, δείκνυσιν ἀθέλητον αὐτῷ τὸ πάθος ὑπάρχειν, εἰ καὶ θελητὸν αὐτὸ ἐποιήσατο διὰ τὰ ἐκ τοῦ πάθους ἀγαθά. *Καλὸν* γάρ φησι αὐτῷ *εἰ οὐκ ἐγεννήθη.*[2272] Πολὺ γὰρ συμφέρει ἡ ἀνυπαρξία μᾶλλον τοῦ γεγονότα τινὰ ἐργάσασθαι κακὰ καὶ διὰ τοῦτο ἐμβληθῆναι *εἰς γέενναν.*[2273]

2265 Matt. 26:20; Mark, 14:17-18.
2266 John, 13:2.
2267 John, 13:1.
2268 Matt. 26:17; Mark, 14:12.
2269 Cod. εἰς καθαρόν.
2270 Matt. 26:23.
2271 Matt. 26:24.
2272 Matt. 26:24.
2273 Cf. Luke, 12:5; Matt. 5:29-30.

> Ἀλλὰ *τοῦτό*[2274] φησι δεικτικῶς, ἵνα πιστεύσωμεν δι᾽ ἐνεργείας τοῦ πάντα ἰσχύοντος θεοῦ μεταποιεῖσθαι κατὰ τὸ ἀληθὲς εἰς *σῶμα* καὶ *αἷμα* Χριστοῦ τὰ παρενηνεγμένα, οὕτως τε δεχόμενοι τὴν ζῳοποιὸν αὐτοῦ καὶ ἁγιαστικὴν δύναμιν ἔχωμεν ἐν ἑαυτοῖς.[mdclv]

72

| **218r** (ΩΡΙΓΕΝΟΥΣ) *Παρελθέτω ἀπ᾽ ἐμοῦ τὸ ποτήριον τοῦτο· πλὴν οὐχ ὡς ἐγὼ θέλω, ἀλλ᾽ ὡς σύ.*[2275] Φασὶν οἱ πατέρες ὅτι ἐν τούτοις καὶ τῇ προσευχῇ ἐδελέαζε τὸν διάβολον. Τὸ δὲ *εἰ δυνατὸν* διδάσκει ἡμᾶς ὅτι χρειωδῶς ὁ Χριστὸς ἀπέθανε, καὶ εἰ μὴ *θανάτου* ἐγεύσατο *ὑπὲρ ἡμῶν*,[2276] οὐκ ἂν ἐρρύσθημεν.

> Φασὶν οἱ πατέρες ὅτι ἐν τούτοις καὶ τῇ προσευχῇ ἐδελέαζε τὸν διάβολον. τὸ δὲ *εἰ δυνατὸν* διδάσκει ἡμᾶς ὅτι χρειωδῶς ὁ Χριστὸς ἀπέθανε, καὶ εἰ μὴ *θανάτου* ἐγεύσατο *ὑπὲρ* ἡμῶν, οὐκ ἂν ἐρρύσθημεν.[mdclvi]

Εἰ δυνατόν.[2277] | **218v** Οἰκονομικῶς εἶπε τοῦτο,[mdclvii] ὡς τῆς ἡμῶν φύσεως κοινωνήσας τῆς δειλιώσης τὸν θάνατον, ἑκὼν ὑποστὰς τὸ τῆς δειλίας πάθος ἵνα δείξῃ ὅτι παρὰ φύσιν ἐνέσκηψε τοῖς ἀνθρώποις ὁ θάνατος[mdclviii] καὶ πρὸς τὸ ἀπατηθῆναι τὸν διάβολον καὶ ὡς ψιλῷ ἀνθρώπῳ ἐπιπηδῆσαι αὐτῷ καὶ καταλυθῆναι σὺν τῷ θανάτῳ, καὶ ἵνα μὴ δῷ Ἰουδαίοις ἀπολογίαν λέγειν ὅτι οὐχ ἡμάρτομεν ἀποκτείναντες τὸν ἐπιδραμόντα τῷ πάθει καὶ ἑκουσίως τοῦτο ἁρπάσαντα, καὶ ἵνα ἡμῖν γένηται τύπος, μὴ ἐπιρρίπτειν ἑαυτοὺς εἰς τὸ παθεῖν, ἀλλ᾽ εὔχεσθαι μὲν μὴ παθεῖν, ἐπελθὸν δὲ τοῦτο γενναίως προσδέχεσθαι. Προβὰς δὲ ὀλίγον εὔχεται, ἵνα τῶν λεγομένων ἀκούσαντες ἐπὶ τῶν ὁμοίων τὰ ὅμοια ποιήσωσι. Διὰ τοῦτο δὲ εὔχεται ἵνα μὴ δόξῃ ὑπόκρισις εἶναι τὸ πρᾶγμα. Ὅθεν καὶ εἶπε τὸ *εἰ δυνατόν*, ἵνα δείξῃ τὸ ἀνθρώπινον καὶ ὅτι οὐ καθ᾽ ἡδονὴν αὐτῷ ὁ θάνατος. Τῷ δὲ εἰπεῖν *πλὴν οὐχ ὡς ἐγὼ θέλω, ἀλλ᾽ ὡς σύ*,[2278] ἔδειξεν ὅτι εἰ καὶ ἀθέλητον δοκεῖ τὸ πάθος, ἀλλ᾽ οὖν διὰ τὴν τοῦ Πατρὸς εὐδοκίαν[2279] καταδέχεται τὸν θάνατον ἑκοντί, ἵνα διὰ τῆς οἰκονομίας τῆς ὑπακοῆς δείξῃ ἑαυτὸν ἐν πᾶσι συμφωνοῦντα τῷ Πατρὶ καὶ ὅτι οὐκ ἀγνοεῖ τὸ τοῦ Πατρὸς θέλημα, καὶ ἡμᾶς διδάσκων ὅτι κἂν ἡ φύσις ἀνθέλκῃ, δεῖ πείθεσθαι τῷ Θεῷ. *Ποτήριον* δὲ καλεῖ τὸν θάνατον, διὰ τὴν εἰς ὕπνον κάρωσιν καὶ μέθην. Ἄλλως τε, παραβιβασθῆναι μὲν θέλει *τὸ ποτήριον*, διὰ τὴν ἐπακολουθήσουσαν ἐκδίκησιν τῷ αἵματι αὐτοῦ ἐπὶ καθαιρέσει τοῦ λαοῦ καὶ τοῦ ναοῦ καὶ τῆς περὶ τὸ ἁγίασμα λατρείας. Πάλιν δὲ οὐ τὸ ἴδιον, ἀλλὰ τὸ πατρικὸν προκρίνει

2274 Matt. 26:26-28.
2275 Matt. 26:39; cf. Matt. 14:36; Luke, 22:42.
2276 Cf. Heb. 2:9.
2277 Matt. 26:39.
2278 Matt. 26:39.
2279 Cf. Matt. 3:17; 17:5.

θέλημα, συγκλείων εἰς ἀπείθειαν τὰ πάντα, ἵνα ἀνὰ μέρος πάντων ἀπειθησάντων ἀνὰ μέρος πάντες ἐλεηθῶσι καὶ τῷ ἐκείνων παραπτώματι ἡ σωτηρία τοῖς ἔθνεσι γένηται.

Εἶτα, μετὰ τὸ προσεύξασθαι *ἔρχ‹ε›ται*[2280] *πρὸς τοὺς μαθητὰς εὑρίσκει αὐτοὺς καθεύδοντας.*[2281] | **219r** Ἐπειδὴ δὲ ὁ Πέτρος θρασύτερον ἐλάλησε, πρὸς αὐτὸν διαλέγεται καὶ αὐτοῦ καὶ τῶν ἄλλων ἐλέγχει τὴν ἀσθένειαν, καὶ ὡς προπετῶν καταβοᾷ τῶν ὑποσχομένων μὲν ὑπὲρ αὐτοῦ ἀποθανεῖν, μὴ ἰσχυσάντων δὲ σὺν αὐτῷ ἀγρυπνῆσαι καὶ συναλγῆσαι ἀθυμοῦντι. Διδάσκει δὲ διὰ προσευχῆς αἰτεῖν μὴ λαβεῖν τῶν κακῶν πεῖραν διὰ τὴν φυσικὴν τοῦ σώματος ἀσθένειαν. Οὐ γὰρ δεῖ πρὸς μόνην τὴν προθυμίαν ὁρᾶν, ἀλλὰ καὶ τῆς σαρκὸς λογίζεσθαι τὴν ἀσθένειαν.

Πάλιν ἐκ δευτέρου ἀπελθὼν[2282] πάλιν εἰς πτῶσιν τῶν Ἰουδαίων αἰτεῖ μὴ γενέσθαι αὐτῷ τὸν θάνατον. Δεύτερον δὲ καὶ τρίτον ηὔξατο, δεικνὺς ὅτι ἀληθῶς ἄνθρωπος γέγονε καὶ διδάσκων τοὺς ἀνθρώπους συνεχῶς εὔχεσθαι, μάλιστα ἐν καιρῷ πειρασμῶν.

Ἐλθὼν δὲ πάλιν πρὸς τοὺς μαθητὰς καὶ εὑρὼν αὐτοὺς *καθεύδοντας*, οὐ διήλεγξε γινώσκων αὐτῶν τὴν ἀσθένειαν, ἵνα μὴ λυπήσῃ αὐτούς, ἀλλ᾽ ἀφεὶς αὐτούς, *ἀπελθὼν πάλιν προσηύξατο ἐκ τρίτου.*[2283] Εἶτα ἐλθὼν πάλιν *πρὸς* αὐτούς, δεικνὺς ὅτι ἤδη μέλλει παραδίδοσθαι, καὶ οὐ χρείαν ἔχει τῆς αὐτῶν ἐπικουρίας, *καθεύδετε τὸ λοιπόν*, φησι, *καὶ ἀναπαύεσθε.*[2284] Τουτέστιν, εἰ δοκεῖ ὑμῖν εὔκαιρον εἶναι καθεύδειν ὅτε μέλλω παραδίδοσθαι, *καθεύδετε.*

> Τὸ *καθεύδετε λοιπὸν καὶ ἀναπαύεσθε*[2285] οὐχ ὡς ἐπιτρέπων ἔλεγεν, ἀλλ᾽ ὡς ὀνειδίζων, τουτέστιν. ἰδοὺ ὁ *παραδιδούς με ἤγγικε*, καὶ ὑμεῖς *καθεύδετε λοιπόν*; πῶς ἀποθνήσκειν ὑπὲρ ἐμοῦ ὑπέσχεσθε;[mdclix]

Συγχωρεῖ μὲν γὰρ νυστάζουσι διὰ τὴν φύσιν, οὐ μὴν ἐπαινεῖ. Ἤτοι τοῦτό φησι· ἐπειδὴ ὁ καιρὸς οὐκ ἀπαιτεῖ ὑμᾶς πρὸς ἀγῶνας ἐλθεῖν, *ἀναπαύεσθε τὸ λοιπόν*, καὶ ὕστερον ἀγωνίζεσθε. Δεικνὺς δὲ ὅτι καὶ ᾔδει τὰ ἐσόμενα μετὰ ἀκριβείας, ἐπάγει· *ἰδοὺ ἤγγικεν ἡ ὥρα καὶ ὁ παραδιδούς με ἤγγικεν· ἐγείρεσθε ἄγωμεν.*[2286]

Ἰδοὺ Ἰούδας εἷς τῶν δώδεκα.[2287] Θαυμάζων ὁ εὐαγγελιστὴς ὅτι *τῶν δώδεκα εἷς* ὢν προέδωκε τὸν διδάσκαλον, εἶπε τοῦτο. Θαρρῶν δὲ τῇ τοῦ διδασκάλου ἐπιεικείᾳ *ὁ Ἰούδας* κατεφίλει *αὐτόν.*[2288] Ὁ δὲ Κύριος ἀνέχεται ἵνα κἂν οὕτως αἰδεσθῇ, ὅτι ἕως ἐσχάτης ὥρας διετήρει τὴν πρὸς αὐτὸν ἀγάπην.

2280 Cod. ἔρχηται.
2281 Matt. 26:40.
2282 Matt. 26:42.
2283 Matt. 26:44.
2284 Matt. 26:45.
2285 Matt. 26:45.
2286 Matt. 26:45-46.
2287 Matt. 26:47.
2288 Matt. 26:48.

Θαυμάζων ὁ εὐαγγελιστὴς ὅτι *τῶν δώδεκα εἷς* ὢν παρέδωκε τὸν διδάσκαλον εἶπεν τοῦτο. [θαρρῶν δὲ τῇ τοῦ διδασκάλου ἐπιεικείᾳ][mdclx] *ὁ Ἰούδας κατεφίλει αὐτόν*. ὁ δὲ κύριος ἀνέχεται, ἵνα κἂν οὕτως αἰδεσθῇ, ὅτι ἕως ἐσχάτης ὥρας διετήρει τὴν πρὸς αὐτὸν ἀγάπην.[mdclxi]

73

219r (ΩΡΙΓΕΝΟΥΣ) Εἰώθει ‹δὲ› ἀσπάζεσθαι ὁ προδότης τὸν διδάσκαλον, ὡς πάντες οἱ μαθηταὶ ὅτε μακρόθεν ἤρχοντο.

Εἰώθει δὲ ἀσπάζεσθαι ὁ προδότης τὸν διδάσκαλον ὡς πάντες οἱ μαθηταί, ὅτε μακρόθεν ἤρχοντο.[mdclxii]

| **219v** *Ὁ δὲ Ἰησοῦς εἶπεν αὐτῷ· ἑταῖρε ἐφ᾿ ᾧ πάρει;*[2289] Ὅτε δὲ οὐδὲ οὕτως ἐδυσωπήθη, τότε ἑαυτὸν ἐξέδωκεν εἰπών· *ἑταῖρε ἐφ᾿ ᾧ πάρει;* Δηλοῖ δὲ τοῦτο ὅτι οὐ χρεία τοῦ προσχήματος τούτου δι᾿ οὗ θέλεις ὀφθῆναι φίλος. Ποίει ὃ βούλει· ἀνέχομαι γάρ, ἐπειδήπερ ἐμαυτὸν ἑκὼν ἐκδέδωκα. Οὐ γὰρ ἵνα με ἀσπάσῃ ἦλθες, ἀλλ᾿ ἵνα παραδῷς.
Φασί δέ τινες ὅτι εἶχε τι αἰδοῦς πρὸς τὸν διδάσκαλον ὁ Ἰούδας.

φασὶ δέ τινες ὅτι εἶχε τι αἰδοῦς πρὸς τὸν διδάσκαλον ὁ Ἰούδας.[mdclxiii]

Μαχομέναις γὰρ κρίσεσιν ἐχρῆτο περὶ τοῦ διδασκάλου. Διὸ οὔτε ὅλῃ ψυχῇ ἐτήρησε τὴν αἰδῶ.

Ἑταῖρε.[2290] Τούτῳ τῷ ὀνόματι οὐδένα οἴδαμεν τῶν ἀστείων καλούμενον. Καὶ γὰρ καὶ ὁ μὴ ἔχων *ἔνδυμα γάμου*, οὕτως ἐκλήθη· *ἑταῖρε πῶς εἰσῆλθες ὧδε;*[2291] Καὶ πρὸς τὸν γογγύσαντα ἐργάτην λέγεται *ἑταῖρε οὐκ ἀδικῶ σε.*[2292]

Τούτῳ τῷ ὀνόματι οὐδένα οἴδαμεν τῶν ἀστείων καλούμενον. Καὶ γὰρ καὶ ὁ μὴ ἔχων *ἔνδυμα γάμου*, οὕτως ἐκλήθη. *ἑταῖρε πῶς εἰσῆλθες ὧδε;* Καὶ πρὸς τὸν γογγύσαντα ἐργάτην λέγεται *ἑταῖρε οὐκ ἀδικῶ σε.*[mdclxiv]

τούτῳ τῷ ὀνόματι οὐδένα οἴδαμεν τῶν ἀστείων καλούμενον. καὶ γὰρ καὶ ὁ μὴ ἔχων ἔνδυμα γάμου οὕτω ἐκλήθη. *ἑταῖρε, πῶς εἰσῆλθες ὧδε;* καὶ πρὸς τὸν γογγύσαντα ἐργάτην λέλεκται. *ἑταῖρε, οὐκ ἀδικῶ σε.*[mdclxv]

2289 Matt. 26:50.
2290 Matt. 26:50.
2291 Matt. 22:11-12.
2292 Matt. 20:13.

Καὶ ἰδοὺ εἷς τῶν μετὰ Ἰησοῦ ἐκτείνας τὴν χεῖρα ἀπέσπασε τὴν μάχαιραν.[2293] Πέτρος ἦν οὗτος,[2294] εἶχε δὲ *μάχαιραν*, ὡς ἐν αὐτῇ θύσας τὸ ἀρνίον καὶ ὡς νομικῷ προστάγματι ἀκολουθῶν, τοὺς ξιφήρεις διὰ μαχαίρας ἀμύνεται. Ὁ δὲ Κύριος μεταρρυθμίζων αὐτὸν εἰς εὐαγγελικὴν πολιτείαν[mdclxvi] διδάσκει μὴ χρῆσθαι μαχαίρᾳ κἂν ὑπὲρ Θεοῦ δοκῇ τις ἀγανακτεῖν ὡς ὑβριζομένου. Εἶτα τὴν κατὰ τῶν φονέων ἀπειλὴν λέγει καὶ τὸν νόμον τὸν τιμωρούμενον τοὺς χρωμένους μαχαίρᾳ. *Πάντες* γάρ φησι *οἱ λαβόντες μάχαιραν*,[2295] καὶ ἑξῆς.
Ὑπεξ‹αι›ρ‹εῖ›σθαι[2296] δὲ χρὴ τοῦ λόγου τούτου τοὺς ἐν στρατείᾳ ζῶντας.

Ὑπεξαιρεῖσθαι δὲ χρὴ τοῦ λόγου τούτου τοὺς ἐν στρατείᾳ ζῶντας.[mdclxvii]

Εἶτα, ὅτι δύναται ἐὰν θέλῃ ἐπαμῦναι ἑαυτῷ καὶ ὅτι ταῖς γραφαῖς τοῦτο δοκεῖ καὶ κατὰ Θεοῦ γίνεται γνώμην. Ταῦτα δὲ εἶπεν ἵνα μὴ οἰηθῶσιν ὅτι ἄκων ἔπαθεν. Οὐκ εἶπε δὲ ὅτι ἐγὼ δύναμαι ποιῆσαι τοῦτο, ἀλλὰ *παρακαλέσαι τὸν πατέρα μου*, οἰκονομικῶς ὡς ἄνθρωπος διὰ τὴν αὐτῶν ἀσθένειαν. Πολλὰ γὰρ ἦν τότε ἐπιδείξας ἀνθρώπινα καὶ πρὸς τὸν φόβον αὐτῶν σχηματίζεται τοὺς *δώδεκα λεγεῶνας τῶν ἀγγέλων*,[2297] ὅπου γε | **220r** εἷς ἐξαρκεῖ πολλοὺς ἀνελεῖν ἀνθρώπους. Εἰ γὰρ ἤθελε, φησί, παρίσταντο ἂν αὐτῷ ἀντὶ τῶν δώδεκα μαθητῶν, ‹δώ›δεκα[2298] λεγεῶνες ἀγγέλων. Καὶ διδάσκει ὅτι ταῦτα πάντα εἴρηται περὶ αὐτοῦ ἐν ταῖς γραφαῖς καὶ ὅτι αὐτός ἐστιν ὁ Χριστὸς καὶ ὅτι δεῖ ταῦτα ἐξ ἀνάγκης γενέσθαι.

74

227r (ΩΡΙΓΕΝΟΥΣ) *ἀπὸ δὲ ἕκτης ὥρας σκότος ἐγένετο.*[2299] Περὶ ταύτης τῆς ἐκλείψεως[mdclxviii] προεφήτευσε Ζαχαρίας εἰπών· *ἐν ἐκείνῃ τῇ ἡμέρα οὐκ ἔσται φῶς καὶ ψῦχος καὶ πάγος ἔσται* | **227v** *μίαν ἡμέραν, καὶ ἡ ἡμέρα ἐκείνη γνωστὴ τῷ Κυρίῳ, καὶ οὐχ ἡμέρα καὶ οὐ νύξ, καὶ πρὸς ἑσπέραν ἔσται φῶς.*[2300]

Περὶ ταύτης τῆς ἐκλείψεως προεφήτευσε Ζαχαρίας εἰπών. *ἐν ἐκείνῃ τῇ ἡμέρα οὐκ ἔσται φῶς καὶ ψῦχος καὶ πάγος ἔσται μίαν ἡμέραν, καὶ ἡ ἡμέρα ἐκείνη γνωστὴ τῷ κυρίῳ, καὶ οὐχ ἡμέρα καὶ οὐ νύξ, καὶ πρὸς ἑσπέραν ἔσται φῶς.*[2301][mdclxix]

2293 Matt. 26:51.
2294 John, 18:10.
2295 Matt. 26:52.
2296 Cod. ὑπεξηρῆσθαι.
2297 Matt. 26:53.
2298 Cod. δέκα.
2299 Matt. 27:45.
2300 Zach. 14:6-7.
2301 Zach. 14:6-7.

> Περὶ ταύτης τῆς ἐκλείψεως καὶ ὁ προφήτης Ζαχαρίας εἰπών. *Ἐν ἐκείνῃ τῇ ἡμέρᾳ,* φησίν, *οὐκ ἔσται φῶς. Καὶ ψῦχος καὶ πάγος ἔσται μίαν ἡμέραν. Καὶ ἡ ἡμέρα ἐκείνη γνωστὴ τῷ Κυρίῳ. Καὶ οὐχ ἡμέρα, καὶ οὐ νύξ. καὶ πρὸς ἑσπέραν ἔσται φῶς.*[mdclxx]

Εἰκὼν δὲ τὸ *σκότος* τοῦ ἐσκοτίσθαι τοὺς ἐπιβαλόντας χεῖρα τῷ φωτί.[2302] Ὡς γὰρ Αἰγυπτίοις *σκότος καὶ τοῖς υἱοῖς Ἰσραὴλ φῶς,*[2303] οὕτως καὶ νῦν, τῇ μὲν ἐκκλησίᾳ φῶς, τοῖς Ἰουδαίοις δὲ σκότος τριῶν ὡρῶν, φωτὸς πατρικοῦ, ἀπαυγάσματος Χριστοῦ, ἐκλάμψεως Ἁγίου Πνεύματος.[mdclxxi] Καὶ ἐπεὶ ἐν τῇ ἕκτῃ ἡμέρᾳ γεγένηται ὁ ἄνθρωπος, καὶ εἰκὸς τὸν ἄνθρωπον τῇ ἕκτῃ ὥρᾳ ἐσφάλθαι, τάχα διὰ τοῦτο ὁ ὑπὲρ σωτηρίας ἀνθρώπων πάσχων ὥρᾳ ἕκτῃ ἐκρεμάσθη.[mdclxxii]

> Εἰκὼν δὲ τὸ *σκότος* τοῦ ἐσκοτίσθαι τοὺς ἐπιβαλόντας χεῖρα τῷ φωτί. ὡς γὰρ Αἰγυπτίοις *σκότος καὶ τοῖς υἱοῖς Ἰσραὴλ φῶς,* οὕτως καὶ νῦν, τῇ μὲν ἐκκλησίᾳ φῶς, τοῖς Ἰουδαίοις δὲ σκότος τριῶν ὡρῶν, φωτὸς πατρικοῦ. ἀπαυγάσματος Χριστοῦ, ἐκλάμψεως Ἁγίου Πνεύματος. καὶ ἐπεὶ ἐν τῇ ἕκτῃ ἡμέρᾳ γεγένηται ὁ ἄνθρωπος, καὶ εἰκὸς τὸν ἄνθρωπον τῇ ἕκτῃ ὥρᾳ ἐσφάλθαι, τάχα διὰ τοῦτο ὁ ὑπὲρ σωτηρίας ἀνθρώπων πάσχων ὥρᾳ ἕκτῃ ἐκρεμάσθη.[mdclxxiii]

Τοῦτό ἐστιν τὸ *σημεῖον,*[mdclxxiv] ὅπερ ἔμπροσθεν αἰτοῦσιν ὑπέσχετο δώσειν, λέγων· *γενεὰ πονηρὰ καὶ μοιχαλὶς σημεῖον ἐπιζητεῖ· καὶ σημεῖον οὐ δοθήσεται αὐτῇ εἰ μὴ τὸ σημεῖον Ἰωνᾶ.*[2304] Καὶ *ὅταν ὑψώσητε τὸν υἱὸν τοῦ ἀνθρώπου, τότε γνώσεσθε ὅτι ἐγώ εἰμι.*[2305] Καὶ γὰρ πολλῷ θαυμαστότερον ἐπὶ τοῦ σταυροῦ προσηλωμένου ταῦτα γενέσθαι ἢ βαδίζοντος ἐπὶ τῆς γῆς. Οὐ ταύτῃ δὲ μόνον τὸ παράδοξον ἦν, ἀλλ᾽ ὅτι καὶ ἐκ τοῦ οὐρανοῦ γέγονεν, ὅπερ ἐζήτουν *καὶ ἐπὶ πᾶσαν τὴν* οἰκουμένην, ὅπερ οὐδὲ πρότερον συνέβη ἀλλ᾽ ἐν Αἰγύπτῳ μόνον, ὅτε τὸ πάσχα ἐτελεῖτο. Καὶ γὰρ ἐκεῖνα τούτων τύπος ἦν. Καὶ σκόπει, πῶς ἀκριβῶς γίνεται. Ἵνα γὰρ μὴ εἴπωσιν ἔκλειψιν εἶναι τὸ γεγενημένον, διὰ τοῦτο τῇ τεσσαρεσκαιδεκάτῃ γίνεται, ὅτε ἔκλειψιν συμβῆναι ἀμήχανον· ἐν μέσῃ δὲ ἡμέρᾳ, ἵνα πάντες οἱ *τὴν γῆν* οἰκοῦντες μάθωσιν ὅτι πανταχοῦ τῆς οἰκουμένης ἡμέρα ἦν. Καὶ Φλέγων[mdclxxv] δέ τις παρ᾽ Ἕλλησι φιλόσοφος μέμνηται τούτου τοῦ σκότους ὡς παραδόξως γεγονότος ἐν τῇ τεσσαρεσκαιδεκάτῃ τῆς σελήνης, ὅτε οὐ πέφυκεν | **228r** ἔκλειψις γίνεσθαι, ὅτε ἀπέχει πολὺ ‹τὸ› τοῦ ἡλίου διάστημα, ὅσον ἀπὸ ἀρχῆς τοῦ οὐρανοῦ ἕως τέλους. Τότε γὰρ γίνονται ἐκλείψεις, ὅταν πλησιάσωσιν ἀλλήλοις οἱ δύο οὗτοι φωστῆρες. Γίνεται γὰρ ἔκλειψις ἡλίου συνόδῳ ὑποδραμούσης αὐτὸν σελήνης, οὐ πανσελήνῳ, ὅτε διάμετρός ἐστι τῇ σελήνῃ.[mdclxxvi] Τοῦτο δὲ γέγονεν ὡς πενθούσης τῆς κτίσεως ἐπὶ τῷ γεγονότι καὶ διὰ τούτου δηλούσης ὅτι τῆς παροινίας ταύτης πραχθείσης ἐξ Ἰουδαίων ἐσκοτίσθη αὐτῶν ὁ νοῦς[mdclxxvii] καὶ ἀπέστη ἀπ᾽ αὐτῶν ὁ νοητὸς

2302 Cf. John, 8:12.

2303 Ex. 10:21-23.

2304 Matt. 12:39; Mark, 16:4; cf. Mark, 8:12; Luke, 11:29-30.

2305 John, 8:28.

ἥλιος.[2306] Εἴτε γὰρ *αὐτὸν* ἐνόμιζον τοῦτο πεποιηκέναι, ἔδει πιστεῦσαι καὶ φοβηθῆναι. Εἴτε οὐκ αὐτόν, ἀλλὰ τὸν Πατέρα, καὶ ἐκ τούτου ἔδει κατανυγῆναι. Ὀργιζομένου γὰρ ἦν τὸ *σκότος* ἐκεῖνο καὶ δεῖγμα τοῦ μέλλοντος λαβεῖν τοὺς μιαιφόνους. Διὰ τοῦτο γὰρ μετὰ πάντα τὰ τῆς παροινίας τοῦτο γίνεται. Ὅτε γὰρ κόρον ἔλαβον τῶν σκωμμάτων καὶ πάντες ἐφθέγξατο ὅσα ἠθέλησαν.[mdclxxviii]

[Τοῦτό ἐστιν τὸ *σημεῖον*, ὅπερ ἔμπροσθεν αἰτοῦσιν ὑπέσχετο δώσειν, λέγων. *γενεὰ πονηρὰ καὶ μοιχαλὶς σημεῖον ἐπιζητεῖ.* καὶ ἑξῆς καί. *ὅταν ὑψώσητε τὸν υἱὸν τοῦ ἀνθρώπου, τότε γνώσεσθε ὅτι ἐγώ εἰμι.* καὶ γὰρ πολλῷ θαυμαστότερον ἐπὶ τοῦ σταυροῦ προσηλουμένου ταῦτα γενέσθαι ἢ ἐπὶ τῆς γῆς βαδίζοντος. οὐ ταύτῃ δὲ μόνον τὸ παράδοξον ἦν, ἀλλ᾽ ὅτι καὶ ἐκ τοῦ οὐρανοῦ γέγονεν, ὅπερ ἐζήτουν καὶ *ἐπὶ πᾶσαν* τὴν οἰκουμένην, ὅπερ οὐδὲ πρότερον συνέβη ἀλλ᾽ ἐν Αἰγύπτῳ μόνον, ὅτε τὸ πάσχα ἐτελεῖτο. καὶ γὰρ ἐκεῖνα ἦν τύπος τούτων. καὶ σκόπει, πῶς ἀκριβῶς γίνεται. ἵνα γὰρ μὴ εἴπωσιν ἔκλειψιν εἶναι τὸ γεγενημένον, διὰ τοῦτο τῇ τεσσαρεσκαιδεκάτῃ γίνεται, ὅτε ἔκλειψιν συμβῆναι ἀμήχανον. ἐν μέσῃ δὲ ἡμέρᾳ, ἵνα πάντες οἱ τὴν γῆν οἰκοῦντες μάθωσιν ὅτι πανταχοῦ τῆς οἰκουμένης ἡμέρα ἦν.] Καὶ Φλέγων δέ τις παρ᾽ Ἕλλησιν φιλόσοφος μέμνηται τούτου τοῦ σκότους, ὡς παραδόξως γεγενημένου ἐν τῇ τεσσαρεσκαιδεκάτῃ τῆς σελήνης, ὅτε οὐ πέφυκεν ἔκλειψις γίνεσθαι, ὅτε πολὺ ἀπέχει τὸ τοῦ ἡλίου διάστημα, ὅσον ἀπὸ ἀρχῆς τοῦ οὐρανοῦ ἕως τέλους. τότε γὰρ γίνονται ἐκλείψεις, ὅταν πλησιάσωσιν ἀλλήλοις οἱ δύο οὗτοι φωστῆρες. γίνεται γὰρ ἔκλειψις ἡλίου συνόδῳ ὑποδραμούσης αὐτὸν σελήνης, οὐ πανσελήνῳ, ὅτε διάμετρός ἐστι τῇ σελήνῃ. τοῦτο δὲ γέγονεν ὡς πενθούσης τῆς κτίσεως ἐπὶ τῷ γεγονότι καὶ διὰ τούτου δηλούσης ὅτι τῆς παροινίας ταύτης πραχθείσης ἐκ Ἰουδαίων, ἐσκοτίσθη αὐτῶν ὁ νοῦς καὶ ἀπέστη ἀπ᾽ αὐτῶν ὁ νοητὸς ἥλιος. [εἴτε γὰρ αὐτὸν ἐνόμιζον τοῦτο πεποιηκέναι, ἔδει πιστεῦσαι καὶ φοβηθῆναι, εἴτε οὐκ αὐτόν, ἀλλὰ τὸν πατέρα, καὶ ἐκ τούτου ἔδει κατανυγῆναι. ὀργιζομένου γὰρ ἦν τὸ *σκότος* ἐκεῖνο καὶ δεῖγμα τοῦ μέλλοντος λαβεῖν τοὺς θεομάχους τε καὶ μιαιφόνους. διὰ τοῦτο γὰρ μετὰ πάντα τὰ τῆς παροινίας τοῦτο γίνεται, ὅτε κόρον ἔλαβον τῶν σκωμμάτων καὶ πάντα ἐφθέγξατο ὅσα ἠθέλησαν.][mdclxxix]

Εἰπὼν δὲ *τὸ σκότος* τὸ ἐσκοτίσθαι τοὺς βάλλοντας χεῖρας τῷ φωτί. Ὡς γὰρ Αἰγυπτίοις σκότος, καὶ τοῖς υἱοῖς Ἰσραὴλ φῶς. οὕτως καὶ νῦν τῇ μὲν Ἐκκλησίᾳ φῶς, τοῖς δὲ Ἰουδαίοις σκότος τριῶν ἡμερῶν, φωτὸς πατρικοῦ, ἀπαυγάσματος Χριστοῦ, ἐκλάμψεως ἁγίου Πνεύματος. Καὶ ἐπεὶ ἐν τῇ ἕκτῃ ἡμέρᾳ γεγένηται ὁ ἄνθρωπος, εἰκὸς δὲ αὐτὸν ἐν τῇ ἕκτῃ ὥρᾳ ἐσφάλθαι. τάχα διὰ τοῦτο ὁ ὑπὲρ σωτηρίας ἀνθρώπων πάσχων ὥρᾳ ἕκτῃ ἐκρεμάσθη. Τοῦτό ἐστι τὸ σημεῖον, ὅπερ ἔμπροσθεν αἰτοῦσιν ὑπέσχετο δώσειν, λέγων. *Γενεὰ πονηρὰ καὶ μοιχαλὶς σημεῖον ἐπιζητεῖ*, καὶ ἑξῆς. καί, *Ὅταν ὑψώσητε τὸν Υἱὸν τοῦ ἀνθρώπου τότε γνώσεσθε, ὅτι ἐγώ εἰμι.* Καὶ γὰρ πολλῷ θαυμαστότερον ἐπὶ τοῦ σταυροῦ προσηλουμένου ταῦτα γενέσθαι ἢ ἐπὶ γῆς βαδίζοντος. Οὐ ταύτῃ δὲ μόνον τὸ παράδοξον ἦν, ἀλλ᾽ ὅτι καὶ ἐκ τοῦ οὐρανοῦ γέγονεν ὅπερ ἐζήτουν, *καὶ ἐπὶ πᾶσαν τὴν οἰκουμένην*, ὅπερ οὐδὲ πρότερον συνέβη, ἀλλ᾽ ἐν Αἰγύπτῳ μόνον, ὅτε καὶ τὸ Πάσχα ἐτελεῖτο. καὶ γὰρ ἐκεῖνα τύπος ἦν τούτων. Ἵνα γὰρ μὴ εἴπωσιν ἔκλειψιν εἶναι τὸ γεγενημένον, διὰ τοῦτο τῇ ιδ′ γίνεται, ὅτε ἔκλειψιν συμβῆναι ἀμήχανον. Ἐν μέσῃ δὲ ἡμέρᾳ, ἵνα πάντες οἱ τὴν γῆν οἰκοῦντες μάθωσιν, ὅτι πανταχοῦ τῆς οἰκουμένης ἡμέρα ἦν. Καὶ Φλέγων[mdclxxx] δέ τις παρ᾽ Ἕλλησι φιλόσοφος μέμνηται τούτου τοῦ σκότους, ὡς παραδόξως γεγενημένου ἐν τῇ ιδ′ τῆς σελήνης. ὅτε οὐ πέφυκεν ἔκλειψις γίνεσθαι, ὅτε πολὺ ἀπέχει τὸ τοῦ ἡλίου

2306 Cf. Malachi, 3:20; Wisdom of Solomon, 5:6.

διάστημα, ὅσον ἀπ' ἀρχῆς τοῦ οὐρανοῦ ἕως τέλους. Τότε γὰρ γίνονται ἐκλείψεις, ὅταν πλησιάσωσιν ἀλλήλοις οἱ δύο οὗτοι φωστῆρες. Γίνεται γὰρ ἔκλειψις ἡλίου συνοδικῶς ὑποδραμούσης αὐτὸν σελήνης, οὐ πανσελήνῳ, ὅτε διάμετρός ἐστι τῇ σελήνῃ. Τοῦτο δὲ γέγονεν, ὡς πενθούσης τῆς κτίσεως ἐπὶ τῷ γεγονότι, καὶ διὰ τοῦτο δηλούσης, ὅτι, τῆς παροινίας ταύτης πραχθείσης ἐξ Ἰουδαίων, ἐσκοτίσθη αὐτῶν ὁ νοῦς, καὶ ἀπέστη ἀπ' αὐτῶν ὁ νοητὸς ἥλιος. Εἴτε γὰρ αὐτὸν ἐνόμιζον τοῦτο πεποιηκέναι, ἔδει πιστεῦσαι καὶ φοβηθῆναι. εἴτε οὐκ αὐτόν, ἀλλὰ τὸν Πατέρα, καὶ ἐκ τούτου ἔδει κατανυγῆναι. Ὀργιζομένου γὰρ ἦν τὸ σκότος ἐκεῖνο, καὶ δεῖγμα τοῦ μέλλοντος λαβεῖν τοὺς θεομάχους τε καὶ μιαιφόνους. Διὰ τοῦτο γὰρ μετὰ πάντων τῆς παροινίας τοῦτο γίνεται, ὅτε κόρος ἔλαβε τῶν σκωμμάτων, καὶ πάντων ἐφθέγξαντο ὅσα ἠθέλησαν.[mdclxxxi]

Περὶ δὲ τὴν ἐνάτην ὥραν ἀνεβόησεν ὁ Ἰησοῦς φωνῇ.[2307] Ταύτην τὴν βοὴν ὁ ἀπόστολος ἰσχυρὰν κραυγὴν ἀπεκάλεσε,[2308] μεθ' ἧς ἱκετεύσας ἐδάκρυσεν, ἡμῖν χρήσας τὰ δάκρυα καθάπερ καὶ τὴν φωνήν. Ἰσχυρὰ γὰρ ὡς ἀληθῶς ἡ ἰσχύσασα διὰ τοσούτου χρόνου πρὸς ἡμᾶς ἐπικλῖναι τὴν ἀκοὴν τοῦ Πατρός, ἣν ἀπέστρεψεν ἡ παράβασις τοῦ Ἀδάμ. Πῶς γὰρ ἔμελλεν *ἰσχυρᾶς κραυγῆς*[2309] χρῄζειν ὑπὲρ ἑαυτοῦ δεόμενος ὁ Υἱός, τελώνου[2310] καὶ πόρνης[2311] στεναζόντων ἡσυχῇ καὶ ἀκουομένων;

Ἠλί· ἠλί.[2312] Ἑβραΐδι διαλέκτῳ εἶπε τὸ προφητικόν, ἵνα δείξῃ ὅτι οὐ μάχεται τῇ παλαιᾷ γραφῇ καὶ ὅτι τιμᾷ τὸν Πατέρα καὶ ὅτι οὐκ ἔστιν ἀντίθεος.

Ἐν εἰκοστῷ πρώτῳ Ψαλμῷ γέγραπται. *ὁ θεός, ὁ θεός μου, ἵνα τί με ἐγκατέλιπες*[2313] (τὸ γὰρ *πρόσχες μοι*, οὐ κεῖται ἐν τῷ Ἑβραϊκῷ).[mdclxxxii] τὸ δὲ *ἵνα τί με ἐγκατέλιπες*, ἵν' ὁ μετὰ τοὺς προφήτας ἁμαρτὼν εἰς ἐμὲ τοσαῦτα λαὸς ἀξίως στερηθῇ τοῦ φωτὸς καὶ γένηται ἐν σκότει. ἢ τὸ *ἵνα τί* ἀντὶ τοῦ. τί τηλικοῦτο τοῖς ἔθνεσι κατώρθωται, ἵνα τὸ τίμιόν μου αἷμα περὶ αὐτῶν ἐκχυθῇ,[2314] *τῷ* δὲ Ἰουδαίων *παραπτώματι ἡ σωτηρία*[2315] αὐτοῖς γένηται; τὸ δὲ θεὸς παρ' Ἑβραίοις Ἐλωὶμ ὀνομάζεται, φέρονταί γε μὴν ἐπὶ τῆς θείας προσηγορίας καὶ ἕτεραί τινες ἐκφωνήσεις, ὥσπερ οὖν τὸ Σαδδαὶ καὶ τὸ Ἰὰ καὶ τὸ Ἦλ καὶ ἄλλα τούτοις παραπλήσια. ὁ δὴ οὖν Ψαλμὸς ἀπὸ τοῦ Ἦλ τὸ ΗΛΙ ΛΕΜΑ ΣΑΒΑΧΘΑΝΙ περιέχει, ᾧ κέχρηται καὶ ὁ κύριος Ἰησοῦς Χριστός, ἵνα μάθωσιν ὅτι μέχρι τῆς ἐσχάτης ἀναπνοῆς ‹***›[mdclxxxiii] καὶ οὐκ ἔστιν ἀντίθεος.[mdclxxxiv]

καὶ λέγει, *Ἐλωΐ, Ἐλωΐ, λαμμᾶ σαβαχθανί*, ἵνα μάθωσιν ὅτι μέχρις ἐσχάτης ἀναπνοῆς τιμᾷ τὸν πατέρα καὶ οὐκ ἔστιν ἀντίθεος. διὸ καὶ προφητικὴν ἀφῆκε φωνήν, ὥστε αὐτὸν γενέσθαι κατάδηλον, διὰ πάντων δεικνὺς αὐτοῦ τὴν ὁμόνοιαν τὴν πρὸς τὸν γεγενηκότα.[mdclxxxv]

2307 Matt. 27:46.
2308 Cf. Heb. 5:7.
2309 Heb. 5:7.
2310 Luke, 18:10-14.
2311 Luke, 7:37-38; cf. Matt. 21:31-32.
2312 Matt. 27:46.
2313 Psalm 21:2.
2314 Cf. 1 Peter, 1:19.
2315 Cf. Rom. 11:11.

Οὐχ ὡς ἀσθενὴς δὲ ἢ δεόμενος τῆς ἄλλου ἐπικουρίας εἶπε τοῦτο, ἀλλ᾽ οἰκο | **228v** νομικῶς ὡς ἄνθρωπος ἐκ προσώπου τῆς ἀνθρωπότητος καὶ ἕλκων εἰς ἡμᾶς τὸν ἄνωθεν ἔλεον. Οὐ γὰρ ἁρμόζει ὡς ἀπὸ Χριστοῦ λεχθῆναι τὸ ῥῆμα ὡς ἐγκαταλελειμμένου τοῦ ἀναμαρτήτου. Οὐδέποτε γὰρ ὁ Υἱὸς ἐγκατελείφθη ὑπὸ τοῦ Πατρός, ἀλλ᾽ ὑπὲρ ἡμῶν ταῦτα ἔλεγεν ὁ Σωτὴρ παρὰ τῷ σταυρῷ. Καὶ ἦν ἐνταῦθα τὸ σημαινόμενον ὅτι, παρὰ τὸν καιρὸν τοῦ θανάτου, ἣν ἔχει τὸ σῶμα ἔμφυτον ὄρεξιν περὶ τὴν ἑαυτοῦ ζωήν, ταύτην ἐξεῖπεν ὁ Σωτήρ, ἵνα καὶ οὕτως δείξῃ μὴ φαντάσματι ἀλλ᾽ ὄντως ἀληθείᾳ τῇ πρὸς ἡμᾶς ὁμοιώσει συνῆφθαι αὐτόν. Ὁμοῦ δέ, καὶ ἵνα κατορθώσῃ τῇ ἡμετέρα τῶν ἀνθρώπων φύσει, τὸ μετὰ παρρησίας λέγειν πρὸς τὸν Θεόν, *ἵνα τί με ἐγκατέλιπες;*[2316] Μόνοις γὰρ τοῖς καθαροῖς καὶ ἁμαρτίας ἐκτὸς ἔστιν ἀδεὲς τὸ τοιοῦτο βοᾶν, ὅπερ πάλιν οἰκονομικῶς ἤρξατο ἀπὸ τοῦ Χριστοῦ, ὡς ἁμαρτίαν μὴ πεποιηκότος μὴ δὲ ἔχοντος δόλον *ἐν τῷ στόματι αὐτοῦ.*[2317] Λέγων δὲ *Θεέ μου* πρὸς τὸν Πατέρα ὅταν ὡς ἄνθρωπος λέγῃ τὰ τῇ ἀνθρωπότητι πρέποντα, οὐδὲν ὑπομένει βλάβος περὶ τὴν οἰκείαν θεότητα καὶ δόξαν, Θεὸς ὢν φύσει. Τοῦ γὰρ ἑνωθέντος αὐτῷ σώματος καθ᾽ ὑπόστασιν τῷ ξύλῳ προσηλωμένου, αὐτός ἐστιν ὁ ὡς Θεὸς ἀπαθὴς μείνας ἐν τοῖς πάθεσιν ὁ ταῦτα εἰπών. Ἐπείπερ καὶ ἡμεῖς ὅταν καλῶμεν τὸν Θεὸν πατέρα, οὐ παρὰ τοῦτο ἀπεβαλόμεθα τὸ εἶναι ἄνθρωποι φύσει καὶ κτίσματα Θεοῦ, εἰ καὶ κατὰ χάριν ἡμᾶς ὁ Θεὸς εἰς υἱότητα ἀνήγαγε διὰ τὴν εἰς Χριστὸν πίστιν καὶ τὴν τῆς σαρκὸς αὐτοῦ καὶ τοῦ αἵματος κοινωνίαν καὶ τὴν διὰ μετουσίας τοῦ Ἁγίου Πνεύματος ἀναστοιχείωσιν.[mdclxxxvi]

75

(ΩΡΙΓΕΝΟΥΣ) Τὸ *ἠλὶ ἠλί, λιμὰ σαβαχθανὶ* ζήτει, πότερον ὀλοφυρτικὸν τοῦτο ἢ ἀπορητικὸν ἢ ἐρωτηματικόν. Καὶ εἰ μὲν τὰ τρία, ζήτει τὴν ἑκάστου δύναμιν. | **229r** Εἰ δὲ μή, ὄψει ὑπὲρ ἡμῶν ἡ φωνή.

> Τὸ *ἠλὶ ἠλὶ λιμὰ σαβαχθανὶ* ζήτει. πότερον ὀλοφυρτικὸν τοῦτο ἢ ἀπορητικὸν ἢ ἐρωτηματικόν. καὶ εἰ μὲν τὰ τρία, ζήτει τὴν ἑκάστου δύναμιν. εἰ δὲ μή, ὄψει ὑπὲρ ἡμῶν ἡ φωνή.[mdclxxxvii]

(ΩΡΙΓΕΝΟΥΣ, on the margin) **228v** Ἐντεῦθεν σοι πάλιν ἡ γνῶσις ἔστιν τοῦ ἀληθινοῦ προβάτου.[mdclxxxviii] Σφαγιάζεται γὰρ τὸ πρὸς ὀψὲ τὸ ζωοποιὸν σῶμα τοῦ Χριστοῦ[mdclxxxix] κατὰ τὸν τῶν ἐθνῶν διδάσκαλον Παῦλον τὸν λέγοντα· *καὶ γὰρ τὸ πάσχα ἡμῶν ὑπὲρ ἡμῶν* ἐτύθ‹η›[2318] *Χριστός.*[2319] Τούτου οὖν τετελειωμένου λοιπὸν

2316 Matt. 27:47.
2317 Is. 53:9, quoted in 1 Peter, 2:22.
2318 Cod. ἐτύθι.
2319 1 Cor. 5:7.

τὸ *κατὰ νόμον*[2320] ἐτελεῖτο πάσχα ὑπὸ τῶν θεοκτόνων Ἰουδαίων, τοῦ δεσποτικοῦ ἀμνοῦ ὑπὸ γῆν τεθαμμένου. Ὅτι οὖν ὁ Ματθαῖος πρὸ τελευτῆς αὐτοῦ σφαζόμενον | **229r** ὑπὸ τοῦ στρατιώτου τῇ *λόγχῃ* εἰς *τὴν πλευρὰν* ‹οὐκ› ἐδήλωσεν εἰθούτως[mdcxc] νυχθέντ‹α›[2321] τελευτῆσαι, ὁ δέ γε θεσπέσιος Ἰωάννης τοῦτον ἔφησε τῇ λόγχῃ νυχθῆναι μετὰ τὸ τελειωθῆναι,[2322] οὐ μάχης τὸ εἰρημένον. Ἀμφότεροι γὰρ τὸ ἀληθὲς ἐμήνυον. Ὁ μὲν γὰρ Ματθαῖος, ὡς πλειστάκις τὸν λόγον ποιούμενος, ταχέως τῆς ἀναγραφῆς ἐπιμνησθεὶς καὶ τῆς σφαγῆς τῆς μετὰ τὸν θάνατον, ἀναμὶξ τὴν γραφὴν πεποίηται.[2323] Ὁ δὲ θεολόγος Ἰωάννης τὴν τούτου ἀκριβῆ γνῶσιν ἐμηνύσεν μετὰ τὸν θάνατον καὶ τὴν σφαγὴν ὑποδέξασθαι τὸ σῶμα.[mdcxci]

(ΩΡΙΓΕΝΟΥΣ, main text cont.) *Ὁ δὲ Ἰησοῦς πάλιν κράξας.* Διὰ τοῦτο *κράξας φωνῇ μεγάλῃ ἀφῆκε τὸ πνεῦμα,*[2324] ἵνα γνῶμεν ὅτι ὅτε θέλει κατ' ἐξουσίαν ἀφίησι *τὴν ψυχήν.*[2325] Ἡ δὲ φωνὴ ἐστὶν αὕτη· *Πάτερ εἰς χεῖρας σου παρατίθημι τὸ πνεῦμα μου·*[2326] δι' οὗ διδάσκει ὅτι οὐ βεβιασμένως, ἀλλ' ἑκοντὶ ἀφῆκε τὸ πνεῦμα. Τοῦτο γὰρ σημαίνει τὸ *παρατίθημι.* Πλὴν καὶ τοῦτο ἡμῖν ὁ Σωτὴρ κατώρθωσεν, ὥστε τὰς τῶν πιστῶν ψυχὰς ἐξιούσας ἁγιασμοῦ τυγχάνειν καὶ εἰς τὰς τοῦ Θεοῦ *χεῖρας* ἀπιέναι καὶ μηκέτι ἐν τοῖς τοῦ ᾅδου μυχοῖς. Καλῶς δὲ *μεγάλῃ* χρώμενον μετὰ παρρησίας πρὸς Θεὸν *φωνῇ*, ἀφιέναι τὸ *ζωτικὸν πνεῦμα*[mdcxcii] φησί, ἵνα τὸ *πνεῦμα ἡμῶν ἐπιστρέψῃ πρὸς τὸν Θεόν, ὃς ἔδωκεν αὐτό,*[2327] εἴτε ἑπομένης τῆς ψυχῆς, εἴτε προοικονομουμένης.

> Συμβολικῶς δηλοῖ τὰ κρυπτὰ τοῦ νόμου ἐν Χριστῷ διὰ τοῦ πάθους αὐτοῦ ἀποκαλύπτεσθαι. δύο δὲ ὄντων καταπετασμάτων τοῦ τε ἔνδον καὶ τοῦ ἔξω ζητήσεις πότερον *ἐσχίσθη.* ἄλλος φησίν, ὅτι φωνὴ ἣν ἔκραζεν ὁ Χριστὸς ἐν τῷ σταυρῷ καθώς φησιν Ἰωάννης.[2328] *πάτερ, εἰς χεῖρας σου παρατίθημι τὸ πνεῦμα μου.* τοῦτο δὲ καὶ ὁ Λουκᾶς φησιν διδάσκων,[mdcxciii] ὅτι αἱ τῶν ἁγίων ψυχαὶ οὐκέτι εἰς ᾅδου κατακλείονται ἀλλὰ παρὰ τῷ Θεῷ εἰσι, τούτου γεγονότος ὡς ἐν ἀπαρχῇ τῷ Χριστῷ.[mdcxciv]

> Ἔοικε δέ τι καὶ ἕτερον ὑπεμφαίνειν ἡμῖν τὸ γεγενημένον, τὸ τὰ κρυπτὰ τοῦ νόμου ἐν Χριστῷ διὰ τοῦ πάθους αὐτοῦ ἀποκαλύπτεσθαι. τὸ γὰρ *καταπέτασμα* κατακρύπτον ἔσω *τὰ ἅγια τῶν ἁγίων*[2329] ἐνστάντος καιροῦ, καθ' ὃν ἔδει συστέλλεσθαι τὴν τοῦ νόμου σκιάν, περιρρηγνύμενον ἀνεῳχθῆναι δηλοῖ *τὰ ἅγια τῶν ἁγίων* τοῖς διὰ πίστεως τῆς εἰς Χριστὸν δεδικαιωμένοις δεικνύντος ὥσπερ αὐτὰ τοῦ θεοῦ τοῖς ἀξίοις, ἵνα λοιπὸν εἴργοντος οὐδενὸς εἰς τὴν ἐσωτέραν τρέχωμεν σκηνήν. δύο δὲ ὄντων καταπετασμάτων τοῦ τε ἔνδον καὶ τοῦ ἔξω ζητήσεις πότερον *ἐσχίσθη.*[mdcxcv]

2320 Cf. Num. 6:21; Phil. 3:5; Heb. 7:6; 8:4; 10:8.
2321 Cod. νυχθέντι.
2322 John, 19:34.
2323 Matt. 27:35-50.
2324 Matt. 27:50.
2325 Cf. John, 10:17-18.
2326 Luke, 23:36.
2327 Ecclesiastes, 12:7.
2328 Which should be Λουκᾶς.
2329 Cf. Lev. 21:22-23.

> Αὕτη ἡ φωνή, ἣν ἔκραξεν ἐπὶ τῷ σταυρῷ. *εἰς χεῖράς σου παρατίθημι τὸ πνεῦμά μου*, διδάσκει, ὅτι αἱ τῶν ἁγίων ψυχαὶ οὐκέτι εἰς ᾅδου κατακλείονται, καθὰ καὶ πρῴην, ἀλλὰ παρὰ τῷ θεῷ εἰσιν, τούτου γεγονότος ὡς ἐν ἀπαρχῇ ἐν Χριστῷ. κάτω γὰρ ἦν ἡ χώρησις καὶ ἡ κατοχὴ τῶν ψυχῶν, ἀλλὰ ταύτην τὴν κάτω πορείαν ὁ κύριος εἰς τὰ ἄνω μετέστησε δι᾽ ἑαυτοῦ. [ἐπειδὴ γὰρ ἐν αὐτῷ τὸ ἀπλημμελὲς ἡ ἀνθρώπου φύσις εὑρέθη πλουτήσασα, κεκαινοτόμηκεν ἡμῖν τὸ πέμπεσθαι *εἰς χεῖρας θεοῦ ζῶντος* τὰς σωμάτων ἀπαλλασσομένας ψυχάς, καὶ τοῦτο εἰδὼς ὁ ἅγιος ἔφη Στέφανος. *κύριε Ἰησοῦ, δέξαι τὸ πνεῦμά μου.*] τὸ δὲ *παρατίθημι* τὸ ἑκούσιον διδάσκει τοῦ πάθους καὶ δείκνυσιν, ὅτι οὐκ ἀπόλλυται.[mdcxcvi]

Τὸ δὲ *εἰς χεῖρας σου παρατίθημι τὸ πνεῦμα μου*,[2330] ἀρχὴ γέγονε τῆς τῶν ψυχῶν εἰς τὰ οὐράνια μεταθέσεως. καὶ δηλοῖ ὅτι αἱ τῶν *δικαίων ψυχαὶ* οὐκέτι εἰς Ἅδου κατακλείονται,[2331] ἀλλὰ παρὰ τῷ Θεῷ εἰσιν,[mdcxcvii]

> Τοῦτο δὲ καὶ ἀρχὴ τῆς τῶν ψυχῶν εἰς τὰ οὐράνια μεταθέσεως. ὅσαι δὲ ἀκολουθοῦσι Χριστῷ, μεθίστανται, ὅπερ ἐνεφάνισε Στέφανος εἰπών. *κύριε Ἰησοῦ Χριστέ, δέξαι τὸ πνεῦμά μου* καὶ ὁ Παῦλος. *κρεῖσσον τὸ ἀναλῦσαι καὶ σὺν Χριστῷ εἶναι.* τοὐναντίον δὲ ἐπὶ τῶν παλαιῶν ἐλέγετο τὸ προστίθεσθαι τῶν ἀποθνῃσκόντων ἕκαστον *πρὸς τὸν λαὸν αὐτοῦ.* κάτω γὰρ ἦν ἡ χώρησις καὶ ἡ κατοχὴ τῶν ψυχῶν καὶ ταύτην τὴν κάτω πορείαν ὁ κύριος εἰς τὰ ἄνω μεθίστησι δι᾽ ἑαυτοῦ.[mdcxcviii]

> δι᾽ ὧν δὲ λέγει ὅτι *παρατίθημι* τὸ ἑκούσιον διδάσκει τοῦ πάθους.[mdcxcix]

ὅσαι δὴ ἀκολουθοῦσι Χριστῷ τούτου γεγονότος, ὡς ἐν ἀπαρχῇ ἐν τῷ Χριστῷ.[2332] Ὅπερ ἐνεφάνισε Στέφανος εἰπών· *Κύριε Ἰησοῦ Χριστὲ δέξαι τὸ πνεῦμα μου.*[2333] Καὶ ὁ Παῦλος· κρεῖσσον *τὸ ἀναλῦσαι καὶ σὺν Χριστῷ εἶναι.*[2334] Τοὐναντίον δὲ ἐπὶ τῶν παλαιῶν ἐλέγετο τὸ προστίθεσθαι τῶν ἀποθνῃσκόντων ἕκαστον *πρὸς τὸν λαὸν αὐτοῦ.*[2335]
κάτω γὰρ ἦν ἡ χώρησις καὶ ἡ κατοχὴ τῶν ψυχῶν. Καὶ ταύτην τὴν κάτω πορείαν ὁ Κύριος εἰς *τὰ ἄνω*[2336] μετέστησε δι᾽ ἑαυτοῦ.

> κάτω γὰρ ἦν ἡ χώρησις καὶ ἡ κατοχὴ τῶν ψυχῶν, ἀλλὰ ταύτην τὴν κάτω πορείαν ὁ κύριος εἰς τὰ ἄνω μετέστησε δι᾽ ἑαυτοῦ.[mdcc]

> κάτω γὰρ ἦν ἡ χώρησις καὶ ἡ κατοχὴ τῶν ψυχῶν καὶ ταύτην τὴν κάτω πορείαν ὁ κύριος εἰς τὰ ἄνω μεθίστησι δι᾽ ἑαυτοῦ.[mdcci]

2330 Luke, 23:46.
2331 Cf. Psalm 15:10, quoted in Acts, 2:27.
2332 Cf. 1 Cor. 15:20-23.
2333 Acts, 7:59.
2334 Phil. 1:23.
2335 Cf. Gen. 25:8; 49:33; Num. 20:24; Deut. 32:50; Judith, 16:22.
2336 Cf. Col. 3:1-2.

Παρέδωκε τὸ πνεῦμα,[2337] καθὼς ἔφη· *τίθημι τὴν ψυχήν μου ὑπὲρ*[2338] τῶν παραδοθέντων καὶ ἀφεθέντων.[2339]

> *Παρέδωκε τὸ πνεῦμα*, καθὼς ἔφη. *τίθημι τὴν ψυχήν μου* ὑπὲρ τῶν παραδοθέντων καὶ ἀφεθέντων.[mdccii]

Λουκᾶς φησι, *εἰς χεῖρας σου παρατίθημι τὸ πνεῦμα μου·*[2340] ὃ δὴ καὶ ἀκοῦσαι τοὺς παρόντας ἀναγκαῖον ἦν τὴν ἔξοδον τῆς ψυχῆς, ἐπὶ τίσιν ἐγένετο. Ἐδήλου γὰρ τὸ *παραθήσομαι*[mdcciii] ὅτι *πάλιν* λήψεται αὐτήν.[2341]

> Λουκᾶς φησιν. *εἰς χεῖρας σου παρατίθημι τὸ πνεῦμα μου.* ὃ δὴ καὶ ἀκοῦσαι τοὺς παρόντας ἀναγκαῖον ἦν τὴν ἔξοδον τῆς ψυχῆς, ἐπὶ τίσιν ἐγένετο. ἐδήλου γὰρ τὸ παραθήσομαι, ὅτι πάλιν λήψεται αὐτήν.[mdcciv]

> ἐδήλου γὰρ τὸ *παραθήσομαι*, ὅτι πάλιν αὐτὴν ἀπολήψεται.[mdccv]

Καὶ ἰδοὺ τὸ καταπέτασμα τοῦ ναοῦ ἐσχίσθη.[2342] Ἐπὶ ταῖς τῶν Ἰου | **229v** δαίων δυσσεβείας ταῖς εἰς Χριστὸν δηλονότι γεγενημέναις καὶ αὐτὴ τῶν στοιχείων ἡ φύσις παρωξύνθη ὑβρισμένον ὁρῶσα τὸν ἑαυτῆς δεσπότην. Καὶ τὸ μὲν *καταπέτασμα τοῦ ναοῦ ἐσχίσθη ἄνωθεν ἕως κάτω*, ἥλιος δὲ τὴν οἰκείαν ἀκτῖνα συνέστελλε καὶ *σκότος* ἐποίει *ἀπὸ ἕκτης ὥρας ἕως ἐνάτης.*[2343] Ἐσχίζοντο δὲ *καὶ αἱ πέτραι.* Τάχα δὲ καὶ περὶ τὸν τῆς σελήνης κύκλον ἐπράττετό τι τῶν ἀσυνήθων, ὡς δοκεῖν εἰς αἷμα μεταπεποιῆσθαι αὐτήν. Σεσίγηται μὲν οὖν τὸ τοιόνδε παρὰ τοῖς εὐαγγελισταῖς, ἀξιόχρεώς γε μὴν ἡ πίστις ἐκ τῆς προφητείας.[2344]
Τὸ ἐν τῷ ναῷ *καταπέτασμα*[2345] ὀθόνη τις ἦν καθιεμένη διαμπὰξ εἰς αὐτὸν τοῦ οἴκου τὸ μεσαίτατον συσκιάζουσά πως τὰ ἐσώτερα, καὶ βάσιμον ὥσπερ τιθεῖσα τῷ ἀρχιερεῖ τὴν ἐνδοτέρω σκηνήν.

> Τὸ ἐν τῷ ναῷ καταπέτασμα ὀθόνη τις ἦν καθιεμένη διαμπὰξ εἰς αὐτὸ τοῦ οἴκου τὸ μεσαίτατον, καὶ συσκιάζουσά πως τὰ ἐσωτέρω, καὶ βάσιμον ὥσπερ μόνῳ τιθεῖσα τῷ ἀρχιερεῖ τὴν ἐνδοτέρω σκηνήν.[mdccvi]

2337 John, 19:30.
2338 John, 10:15; cf. 10:17.
2339 Cf. John, 10:15.
2340 Luke, 23:36.
2341 Cf. John, 10:17-18.
2342 Matt. 27:51.
2343 Matt. 27:45.
2344 Cf. Joel, 3:4, quoted in Acts, 2:20.
2345 Ex. 26:31-37; 27:21; 30:6; Lev. 21:23; Num. 4:5.

Σχίζεται τοίνυν *τοῦ ναοῦ τὸ καταπέτασμα ἀπὸ ἄνωθεν ἕως κάτω,*[2346] *τὰ ἅγια τῶν ἁγίων*[2347] ἀνακαλύπτοντος ὥσπερ ἤδη τοῦ Θεοῦ καὶ βατὴν τοῖς πιστεύουσιν εἰς Χριστὸν τὴν ἔσω λοιπὸν τιθέντος σκηνήν.
Πρόκειται γὰρ ἤδη τῶν θείων μυστηρίων ἡ γνῶσις, οὐκέτι παχύτητι τοῦ νομικοῦ[mdccvii] γράμματος[mdccviii] καθάπερ τινὶ καταπετάσματι κατημφιεσμένη,[2348] ἀλλ' ἐν ἁπλότητι πίστεως καὶ ἐν ὀλίγοις ῥήμασιν.

> πρόκειται γὰρ ἤδη τῶν θείων ἡμῖν μυστηρίων ἡ γνῶσις, οὐκέτι τῇ παχύτητι τοῦ νομικοῦ γράμματος καθάπερ τινὶ καταπετάσματι κατημφιεσμένη, οὐδὲ τὸ ἐκ τῆς ἱστορίας ἔχουσα κατακάλυμμα, ἤγουν τὸ ἐν τύποις ἀφανὲς τοῖς τῆς διανοίας ἡμῶν ὄμμασιν ἀνατειχίζουσα, ἀλλ' ἐν ἁπλότητι πίστεως καὶ ἐν ὀλίγοις κομιδῇ τοῖς ῥήμασιν.[mdccix]

'Αλλ' ἕως μὲν οὔπω τῆς ἡμετέρας ὑπεραθλήσας ζωῆς τὸν τῆς σαρκὸς θάνατον ὑπέμεινεν ὁ Χριστός, ἥπλωτό πως ἔτι *τὸ καταπέτασμα.* 'Εκράτει γὰρ ἔτι τῆς κατὰ νόμον ἐντολῆς ἡ δύναμις. 'Επεὶ δὲ πάντα *τετέλεσται*[2349] τὰ ἐπὶ Χριστῷ τολμήματα παρὰ τῶν 'Ιουδαίων καὶ λοιπὸν *ἐξέπνευσε*[2350] δι' ἡμᾶς, καιρὸς ἦν ἤδη λοιπὸν περιρρήγνυσθαι τὸ ἀρχαῖον ἐκεῖνο καὶ πλατὺ *καταπέτασμα* (τουτέστι τὴν τοῦ νομικοῦ γράμματος ἀσάφειαν) καὶ ἀπογυμνοῦσθαι τοῖς *διὰ τῆς πίστεως*[2351] *ἡγιασμένοις ἐν Χριστῷ*[2352] τῆς ἀληθείας τὸ κάλλος. Σχίζεται δὲ δι' ὅλου.[2353] Οὐ γὰρ μερικὴν ἔχει τὴν ἀπο | **230r**
κάλυψιν τὸ σωτήριον κήρυγμα.

"Αλλως τε δέ· ἔθος ἦν παρὰ τοῖς 'Ιουδαίοις ἐπὶ ταῖς κατὰ Θεοῦ βλασφημίαις τὴν ἐσθῆτα περιρρηγνύναι, τὸ τοῖς πενθοῦσι πρέπον διαπραττομένοις σχῆμα. Τούτω τοίνυν τῷ ἔθει καὶ ὁ θεῖος ὥσπερ ἐχρήσατο ναός, διαρρήξας ὡς ἱμάτιον τὸ ἴδιον *καταπέτασμα* τοῦ Σωτῆρος ἡμῶν εὐθὺς ἀποπνεύσαντος. "Ητοι τοῦτο γέγονε τὴν ἐρήμωσιν δηλοῦντο τοῦ πράγματος τὴν μέλλουσαν ἐπικαταλαβεῖν τὸν ναόν. "Ητοι ὡς ἐπὶ θανάτου καὶ πένθους κοινοῦ περιεσχίσθη ὁ ναός, δηλῶν ὅτι ἡ ἐν αὐτῷ θεία δύναμις ὑπανεχώρει ὡς ἀναξίους ἀποφαίνουσα τοὺς 'Ιουδαίους τῆς ἐν τῷ ναῷ χάριτος·
ἢ ἵνα οἱ *ἐξ ἐθνῶν*[2354] ἴδωσι τὰ ἅγια, ἅπερ οὐχ ἑώρων τῇ τοῦ γράμματος παχύτητι ἐμποδιζόμενοι. ἢ καὶ ὡς ἐπὶ θανάτου καὶ πένθους, ὅπου περισχίζονται οἱ ἄνθρωποι τὰς ἐσθῆτας.[mdccx]

2346 Matt. 27:51; Mark, 15:38.
2347 Ex. 30:29; Lev. 2:10; 21:22; 24:9; Num. 4:19; 3 Kings, 8:6; Ez. 42:13; 44:13; 45:3.
2348 Cf. Heb. 10:20.
2349 John, 19:28&30.
2350 Mark, 15:37; Luke, 23:46.
2351 Gal. 3:14&26; Eph. 3:12.
2352 1 Cor. 1:2.
2353 Cod. διόλου.
2354 Cf. Rom. 9:24; Acts, 15:23.

> *ἐσχίσθη* δὲ *τὸ καταπέτασμα* ὅλον ἵνα οἱ ἐξ ἐθνῶν ἴδωσι τὰ ἅγια ἅπερ οὐχ ἑώρων τῇ τοῦ γράμματος παχύτητι ἐμποδιζόμενοι. ἢ καὶ ὡς ἐπὶ θανάτου καὶ πένθους, ὅπου περισχίζονται οἱ ἄνθρωποι τὰς ἐσθῆτας.[mdccxi]

Ἐποίησε δὲ τοῦτο οὐκ ἐνυβρίζων εἰς τὸν ναὸν (οὐδὲ γὰρ ὁ Πατὴρ αὐτοῦ ὅτε παρέδωκεν αὐτὸν τοῖς Βαβυλωνίοις), ἀλλ᾽ ἀναξίους αὐτοὺς ἀποφαίνων τῆς ἐκεῖ διατριβῆς.[2355] Καὶ τὰ στοιχεῖα δὲ φρίττοντα τὸ γεγονὸς ἐτρόμασαν καὶ τὴν εἰς τοὺς Ἰουδαίους ὀργὴν ἐνεδείκνυντο. Δείκνυσι δὲ διὰ τούτων ὅτι καὶ *οὐρανοῦ καὶ γῆς Κύριος* καὶ δημιουργός.[2356]

Ἄλλως τε δέ· *ἐσείσθη ἡ γῆ* τὴν τῶν πραγμάτων μετάθεσιν ἐπὶ τὸ κρεῖττον σημαίνουσα. *Αἱ* δὲ *πέτραι ἐσχίσθησαν*,[2357] σημεῖον οὖσαι τοῦ *τὴν λιθίνην καρδίαν*[2358] τῶν ἐθνῶν ἀνοιχθῆναι πρὸς ὑποδοχὴν τοῦ εὐαγγελικοῦ σπόρου, ὥστε ποιῆσαι καρπὸν φιλοθέου πολιτείας. Ἐπεὶ δὲ καὶ *πέτρα ὁ Χριστός*,[2359] καὶ οἱ *μιμηταὶ*[2360] αὐτοῦ ἀπόστολοι καὶ προφῆται πέτραι ὀνομάζονται, οὕτω διανοίγονται, ἵνα τὰ τοῖς ἐν βάθεσι τῶν λογίων τοῦ *Θεοῦ*[2361] θεασώμεθα *ἐποικοδομηθέντες ἐπὶ τῷ θεμελίῳ τῶν ἀποστόλων καὶ προφητῶν, ὄντος ἀκρογωνιαίου Ἰησοῦ Χριστοῦ*.[2362] Ἡ δὲ τῶν νεκρῶν ἔγερσις,[2363] τὴν ἐν τῷ Ἅδῃ τῶν ψυχῶν ἐλευθερίαν ἐδήλου, ἃς παρέπεμψεν ἐν τῷ παραδείσῳ. Δεῖγμα δὲ καὶ τῆς καθόλου | **230v** ἀναστάσεως ἦν, ἥτις πολλοῖς ὤφθη[2364] ἵνα μὴ δόξῃ φάντασμα εἶναι. Οὐ πρόωρον τοίνυν ἔλαβον μόνοι ἐκεῖνοι τὸ τῆς ἀναστάσεως χάρισμα, ἀλλ᾽ εἰς σημεῖον γέγονεν ὅτι κατηργήθη *ὁ θάνατος διὰ τοῦ θανάτου Χριστοῦ*.[2365] Ταφέντος γὰρ τοῦ *τῆς ζωῆς*[2366] σώματος, τὰ *σώματα τῶν ἁγίων*[2367] ζωτικῆς ᾐσθάνθησαν δυνάμεως.[mdccxii] Καὶ τῆς ψυχῆς τοῦ Χριστοῦ καταβάσης εἰς Ἅδου, ἀπελύθησαν αἱ ψυχαὶ *τῶν ἁγίων*, καὶ ἦλθον ἐν τοῖς ἰδίοις σώμασι καὶ ἀνέστησαν καὶ ὤφθησαν *πολλοῖς*.[2368] Καὶ γὰρ ἔδει πάντως ἅμα πως τῷ καταβῆναι εἰς Ἅδου τὸν καταργοῦντα *τὸν θάνατον*[2369] ἀνοιγῆναι τοῦ *Ἅδου* τὰς πύλας[2370] καὶ τοῦτο γενέσθαι γνωστὸν ἅπασι διὰ τῆς τῶν μνημείων ἀνοίξεως. Ὅτε γὰρ *ἀνέστη*[2371] ἐξελθὼν ἐκ τοῦ

2355 Cf. 1 Esdras, 6:17; 2 Esdras, 5:12-14; 6:5.
2356 Acts, 17:24.
2357 Matt. 27:51.
2358 Cf. Ez. 11:19; 36:26.
2359 1 Cor. 10:4.
2360 1 Cor. 11:1; Eph. 5:1.
2361 Cf. Rom. 11:33.
2362 Eph. 2:20.
2363 Matt. 27:52.
2364 Matt. 27:53.
2365 Cf. 1 Cor. 15:26; 2 Tim. 1:10; Heb. 2:14.
2366 Cf. John, 6:35&48; 8:12; Acts, 3:15; 2 Cor. 5:4; 1 John, 1:1.
2367 Matt. 27:52.
2368 Matt. 27:52-53.
2369 Cf. 1 Cor. 15:26; 2 Tim. 1:10; Heb. 2:14.
2370 Cf. Matt. 16:18.
2371 Cf. 1 Thess. 4:14.

τάφου ὁ Χριστός, τότε καὶ αὐτοὶ ἐξελθόντες τῶν τάφων εἰσῆλθον ἐν τῇ πόλει ἀπάντων ἡμῖν ἀπαρχομένου τῶν ἀγαθῶν τοῦ Χριστοῦ. Διὸ καὶ εἰσελθὼν πρῶτος εἰς τὸν παράδεισον εἰσήγαγε καὶ τὸν λῃστήν.[2372]

Καὶ πολλὰ σώματα τῶν κεκοιμημένων.[2373] Τὸ τὰ *σώματα τῶν ἁγίων* ἀνίστασθαι ἐδήλου τὸν θάνατον τοῦ Χριστοῦ ζωῆς αἴτιον ὄντα. Οὐ μὴν ἐνεφανίσθησαν πρότερον, πρὶν τὸν Κύριον ἀναστῆναι, ἐπειδὴ πρώτην ἔδει τὴν τοῦ Σωτῆρος γνωσθῆναι ἀνάστασιν καὶ τότε τοὺς δι' αὐτοῦ ἀναστάντας ὀφθῆναι. Δῆλον δὲ ὅτι καὶ τεθνήκασι πάλιν, σημείου χάριν ἀναστάντες καὶ πάλιν ἀποθέμενοι τὰ *σώματα* πρὸς τοὺς οἰκείους ἀπεχώρησαν τόπους τὴν κοινὴν καὶ ἐλπιζομένην πᾶσιν ἀνάστασιν ἀναμένοντες.[2374] Οὐδὲ γὰρ ἐνεδέχετο πρωτοτόκους τῶν νεκρῶν ἐπὶ τῇ αἰωνίῳ ζωῇ τινὰς ἐγερθῆναι, ἀλλ' οὕτως ὥσπερ οἱ λοιποί.

> Τὸ τὰ σώματα τῶν ἁγίων ἀνίστασθαι ἐδήλου τὸν θάνατον τοῦ Χριστοῦ ζωῆς αἴτιον ὄντα. οὐ μὴν ἐνεφανίσθησαν πρότερον πρὶν τὸν κύριον ἀναστῆναι, ἐπειδὴ πρώτην ἔδει τὴν τοῦ σωτῆρος γνωσθῆναι ἀνάστασιν καὶ τότε τοὺς δι' αὐτοῦ ἀναστάντας ὀφθῆναι. δῆλον δέ, ὅτι καὶ τεθνήκασι πάλιν σημείου χάριν ἀναστάντες. οὐδὲ γὰρ ἐνεδέχετο πρωτοτόκους τῶν νεκρῶν ἐπὶ τῇ αἰωνίῳ ζωῇ τινας ἐγερθῆναι, ἀλλ' οὕτως ὥσπερ οἱ λοιποί. λέγει δὲ ὁ Λουκᾶς τοὺς ὄχλους τοὺς παραγενομένους *τύπτοντας τὰ στήθη ὑποστρέφειν*. οὕτως οὐδὲ Ἰουδαίους ἔλαθεν καὶ ἐν αὐτῷ τῷ πάθει καὶ τῇ ἀδοξίᾳ τοῦ σωτῆρος ἡ θεία ὑπερβολή, ἀλλ' ἡ συνήθης τοῖς ἀνθρώποις λήθη κατέσχεν αὐτοὺς καὶ ἡ τῶν διδασκάλων ἀπάτη παρῆγεν πολλούς.[mdccxiii]

Περιττὸν οὖν τὸ λέγειν ὡς ἀπέστειλεν ὁ Χριστὸς τοὺς ἀναστάντας εἰς τὸν παράδεισον.[mdccxiv]

> Ἐγένετο μετὰ *τὴν ἐννάτην ὥραν*[2375] ἐν ᾗ τέθνηκεν ὁ Χριστὸς ὑπόλοιπον τῆς παρασκευῆς ἡμέρα μία, τοῦ δὲ σαββάτου νυχθήμερον ὁλόκληρον δευτέρα, *ὀψὲ* δὲ *σαββάτων*[2376] ὡς ὁ Ματθαῖος εἶπεν τῆς ἐπικειμένης αὐτῇ τὴν νύκτα φωτίζεσθαι (ἀλλ' οὐχὶ τὴν ἡμέραν ὑπὸ τῆς νυκτὸς καταλαμβανούσης αὐτὴν σκοτοῦσθαι ὑπὸ τῆς νυκτὸς ἄκρας) τρίτη γέγονεν ἡμέρα, ἐν ᾗ κατὰ τὴν πρόρρησιν αὐτοῦ ὁ κύριος ἡμῶν ἀνέστη. ὁ δὲ λέγων. διὰ τοῦτο ‹τὸ› *ἀπὸ ϛ' ὥρας μέχρι θ' σκότος*[2377] εἰς νύκτα καταλαμβανόμενον τρεῖς ἡμέραι καὶ τρεῖς νύκτες γέγονεν,[2378] μέρη μὲν κἀκεῖνος ἡμερῶν εἰς τελείας ἡμέρας καταλέγει. τὴν γὰρ παρασκευὴν διαιρῶν τὸ μὲν μέχρις ἕκτης ὥρας ὡς ὁλοτελῆ μίαν ἡμέραν ἐκτίθεται, τὸ δὲ ἀπὸ θ' ὥρας ὡς δευτέραν. καὶ ὁπότερον τούτων ἐστὶν παρασκευὴ καὶ ποῖον τὸ σάββατον; οὐ γὰρ δὴ δύο ἐφεξῆς ἡμέραι γίνονται παρασκευαὶ ἢ δύο σάββατα, καὶ μίαν ἀληθῆ νύκτα οἶδεν ἑτέραν δὲ οὐκ οὖσαν. πάθος γάρ τι τεράστιον καὶ πένθος ὥσπερ τῆς ἡμέρας ἐκεῖνο γέγονε σκότος, μόνον οὐκ ἐγκαλυψάμενου και μελανειμονήσαντος ἐπὶ

2372 Luke, 23:43.
2373 Matt. 27:52.
2374 Cf. 1 Peter, 1:3.
2375 Cf. Matt. 27:46; Mark, 15:33; Luke, 23:44-46.
2376 Matt. 28:1.
2377 Matt. 27:45; Mark, 15:33; Luke, 23:44.
2378 Cf. Matt. 27:40.

τοῖς γενομένοις τοῦ ἡλίου. νὺξ δὲ οὐκ ἦν ἐναρίθμιος, εἰ δὲ καί ξένη καὶ περιττὴ λέγοιτο νὺξ ἀσέληνος καὶ ἄναστρος, καὶ διὰ τοῦτο ταῖς ἄλλαις νυξὶ οὐ συγκατεψήφισται. εἰ δὲ *μετὰ τὴν παρασκευὴν*[2379] ἦν τὸ σάββατον καὶ μετὰ τοῦτο *μία σαββάτων*, πεπλήρωτο μὲν δηλονότι μέχρι τῆς ϛʹ ὥρας τότε ἡ παρασκευὴ ἀπὸ δὲ τῆς θʹ ἦλθε τὸ σάββατον καὶ μία *σαββάτων* γέγονε ὕστερον [uncertain codex reading; Kl.]. εἰ δὲ μία *σαββάτων* εἰς δευτέραν ὑπερετάθη, [uncertain codex reading; Kl.] καὶ πῶς ἔτι κυριακὴν αὐτὴν ἑορτάζομεν; καὶ συνεχύθη δηλονότι τῶν ἡμερῶν ὁ ἀριθμὸς καὶ ἡ τάξις, παραπεμπούσης τῆς ἐμβολίμου ἡμέρας, ὡς προεφήτευσεν Ζαχαρίας. *ἐν ἐκείνῃ τῇ ἡμέρᾳ οὐκ ἔσται φῶς καὶ ψῦχος καὶ πάγος ἔσται μίαν ἡμέραν, καὶ ἡ ἡμέρα ἐκείνη γνωστὴ τῷ κυρίῳ, καὶ οὐχὶ ἡμέρα καὶ οὐ νύξ, καὶ πρὸς ἑσπέραν ἔσται φῶς.*[mdccxv]

76

236v (ΩΡΙΓΕΝΟΥΣ) *Ἄγγελος γὰρ Κυρίου καταβὰς ἐξ οὐρανοῦ.*[2380] Ὁ λίθος σύμβολον *κακίας*[mdccxvi] καὶ *ἀπιστίας*·[mdccxvii] ὃν *ἀπεκύλισεν ἐξ οὐρανοῦ καταβὰς*[2381] ταῖς ζητούσαις ψυχαῖς τὴν ζωήν, τοῖς μὲν ἐναντίοις φοβερὸς ὢν καὶ νεκρότητος αἴτιος, τοῖς δὲ ἰδίοις φαιδρὸς καὶ προσηνής.

Ὁ λίθος σύμβολον κακίας καὶ ἀπιστίας. ὃν *ἀπεκύλισεν ὁ ἐξ οὐρανοῦ καταβὰς* ταῖς ζητούσαις ψυχαῖς τὴν ζωήν, τοῖς μὲν ἐναντίοις φοβερὸς ὢν καὶ νεκρότητος αἴτιος, τοῖς δὲ ἰδίοις φαιδρὸς καὶ προσηνής.[mdccxviii]

Δεῦτε ἴδετε τὸν τόπον.[2382] Τοῖς περιέργοις καὶ ὀλισθηροῖς εἰς ἀπάτην ὀφθαλμοῖς τῆς γυναικὸς τοῖς φιληδόνως θεασαμένοις ἐν παραδείσῳ τὸ ξύλον,[2383] οὗ μετέχειν τῆς βρώσεως ὁ θεῖος νόμος ἐκώλυεν,[2384] ἔλεγεν ὁ *ἄγγελος* ὁ ἐπὶ τοῦ ζωοποιοῦ τάφου καθήμενος· *δεῦτε ἴδετε τὸν τόπον ὅπου ἔκειτο ὁ Κύριος.*[2385] Ταῖς προξενησάσαις τὴν πτῶσιν ἡμῖν, αὐταῖς ἐκέλευεν εὐαγγελίζεσθαι τὴν ἀνάστασιν, αἳ τὸ σπέρμα τῆς λύπης τῷ βίῳ καταβαλλόμεναι ἤκουον πρῶται παρὰ τοῦ ἀναστάντος *χαίρετε.*[2386]
Ἄλλως, ἐπειδὴ γυνὴ τῆς λύπης ἡμῖν πρόξενος γέγονεν ἐκ τοῦ ἀπηγορευμένου *καρποῦ τοῦ ξύλου*[2387] φαγεῖν τὸν Ἀδὰμ ἀναπείσασα, αὕτη πρώτη μετὰ τοὺς ἀγγέλους τὴν σὴν ἀνάστασιν εὐηγγελίζετο Χριστὲ ὁ Θεός.

διὰ γυναικὸς γὰρ ἔδει τὸ ἀγαθὸν γνωσθῆναί τε καὶ ἀγγελθῆναι, ὥστε τὴν κακῶς γενομένην διὰ γυναικὸς γνῶσιν λυθῆναι διὰ τῆς ἀγαθῆς γνώσεως, ἣν ἐκόμισεν ἡ γυνή.[mdccxix]

2379 Cf. Matt. 27:62.
2380 Matt. 28:2.
2381 Matt. 28:2.
2382 Matt. 28:6.
2383 Gen. 3:6.
2384 Gen. 2:16-17.
2385 Matt. 28:6.
2386 Matt. 28:9.
2387 Gen. 3:6.

Σὺ γὰρ διὰ πάντων ἔλυσας τὴν κατὰ τοῦ γένους ἡμῶν ἀρὰν καὶ κατήφειαν καὶ ἐπλήρωσας χαρᾶς τὸν οὐρανὸν καὶ τὴν γῆν, μίαν ποιήσας χορείαν πνευματικὴν ἐξ ἡμῶν καὶ τῶν ἄνω δυνάμεων, εἰς τὸ ὑμνεῖν σὲ τὸν μόνον ἀγαθὸν καὶ φιλάνθρωπον.

Καὶ ἰδοὺ Ἰησοῦς ἀπήντησεν αὐταῖς λέγων, Χαίρετε.[2388] Προσφωνεῖ ταῖς γυναιξὶ τὸ *χαίρετε* ὁ Σωτὴρ λύων τῆς ἀρᾶς ἅπαν τὸ τῶν γυναικῶν γένος, τὸ πρῶτον τῆς ἀρᾶς μετασχὸν διὰ τῆς Εὔας·

> Thus, the curse of the woman Eve was driven out among women.[mdccxx]

ἤτοι εὐλογῶν αὐτὸ διὰ τοῦ *χαίρετε* | **237r** ἢ ἐπειδὴ ἔχαιρον ἑωρακυῖαι αὐτὸν *ἐκ νεκρῶν ἀναστάντα*[2389] προσεῖπεν αὐταῖς τὸ *χαίρετε.* Αἱ δὲ καὶ διὰ τῆς ἀφῆς τεκμήριον λαβοῦσαι τῆς ἀναστάσεως αὐτοῦ ἐναργές, προσκυνοῦσιν αὐτῷ ὡς Θεῷ. Ὁ δὲ Κύριος λύσας αὐτῶν τὸν φόβον ὃν εἶχον ἑωρακυῖαι τὸ παράδοξον τῆς ἀναστάσεως καὶ ἀμειβόμενος αὐτάς, πέμπει αὐτὰς εὐαγγελίσασθαι *τοῖς μαθηταῖς* τὸ ἀσθενὲς ἰασάμενος γένος. Ἀδελφοὺς[2390] δὲ καλεῖ τοὺς μαθητάς, εἰ καὶ θεϊκώτερον αὐτοῖς τότε ἐφαίνετο διὰ τὸ κεκλῆσθαι αὐτοὺς εἰς ἀδελφότητα διὰ τοῦ ἁγιασμοῦ. Ἄλλος δέ φησι ὅτι διὰ μὲν τοῦ εἰπεῖν *χαίρετε* ἐνεποίησε ταῖς γυναιξὶ πνεῦμα χαρᾶς, διὰ δὲ τοῦ *μὴ φοβεῖσθε, πνεῦμα δυνάμεως.*[2391] Διὸ θαρσαλέως περιδραξάμεναι τῶν τελευταίων τοῦ ὅλου σώματος Ἰησοῦ, προσκυνοῦσιν αὐτῷ.

Ἐπίτηδες γὰρ *αὐτοῦ τοὺς πόδας ἐκράτησαν,*[2392] ἵνα ὑπονοίας ἀπαλλαγῶσι τῆς περὶ τοῦ πνεῦμα αὐτὸν εἶναι.

> [Διὰ τῆς ἀφῆς τεκμήριον λαμβάνουσι τῆς ἀναστάσεως.][mdccxxi] καὶ γὰρ ἐπίτηδες (ὡς οἶμαι) *ἐκράτησαν αὐτοῦ τοὺς πόδας,* ἵνα ὑπονοίας ἀπαλλαγῶσι τῆς περὶ τοῦ πνεῦμα αὐτὸν εἶναι.[mdccxxii]

Ὁ δὲ Κύριος ἀποστέλλει αὐτὰς εὐαγγελίσασθαι τοῖς μαθηταῖς, *ἀδελφοὺς* αὐτοὺς προσειπὼν καὶ τιμῶν τῷ τῆς ἀδελφότητος ὀνόματι. Καὶ κυροῖ τοὺς τοῦ ἀγγέλου λόγους, τὰ αὐτὰ αὐταῖς προσφθεγξάμενος. Τάχα δὲ καὶ ὁ θέλων ἰδεῖν τὴν δόξαν αὐτοῦ τῆς ἀναστάσεως, ἐν τῇ Γαλιλαίᾳ ὁρᾷ,[2393] ἵνα μᾶλλον *ὁ λαὸς ὁ καθήμενος ἐν σκότει ἴδῃ φῶς μέγα*[2394] *καὶ τοῖς πορευομένοις ἐν σκότει καὶ σκιᾷ θανάτου φῶς* ἀναλάμψῃ.[2395]

2388 Matt. 28:9.
2389 Cf. John, 21:14; Rom. 4:24; *et passim.*
2390 Matt. 28:10.
2391 Cf. Wisdom of Solomon, 5:23; 2 Tim. 1:7.
2392 Matt. 28:9.
2393 Matt. 28:10.
2394 Matt. 4:16; cf. Luke, 1:79; John, 1:9; Is. 9:1; 42:7; 58:10.
2395 Is. 9:1.

Ὁ Σωτὴρ τὴν μὲν προσκύνησιν οὐκ ἀποκωλύει, τὴν δὲ ἐπαφὴν ἀπεκώλυσεν, ὡς Ἰωάννης γράφει.[2396] Τὸ γὰρ ὁμοίως ἀναμίγνυσθαι αὐτῷ καθὰ καὶ πρότερον, οὐκ‹έ›τι[2397] δυνατὸν ἦν πρὸ τῆς ἀνακαινώσεως τῶν ἀνθρώπων. Καινοῖς γὰρ καινοῦ ἅπτεσθαι προσήκει.

> Ὁ σωτὴρ τὴν μὲν προσκύνησιν οὐκ ἀποκωλύει, τὴν δὲ ἐπαφὴν ἀπεκώλυσεν, ὡς Ἰωάννης γράφει. τὸ γὰρ ὁμοίως ἀναμίγνυσθαι αὐτῷ καθὰ καὶ πρότερον οὐκέτι δυνατὸν ἦν πρὸ τῆς ἀνακαινώσεως τῶν ἀνθρώπων. καινοῖς γὰρ καινοῦ ἅπτεσθαι προσήκει.[mdccxxiii]

Καὶ ἰδού τινες τῆς κουστωδίας.[2398] Οἱ μὲν οὖν ἀπὸ *τῆς κουστωδίας* εἰς μαρτύριον τοῖς ἀρχιερεῦσιν ἀπαγγέλουσιν ὅτι ἠσφάλιστο λίθῳ καὶ σφρα | **237v** γῖσιν ὁ τάφος· ὅτι γυναικῶν ἐλθουσῶν ἐκεῖ ἐγένετο σεισμός· ὅτι *ἄγγελος καταβὰς ἐξ οὐρανοῦ ἀπεκύλισε τὸν λίθον*, φοβερὸς ὄψει καὶ ἐνδύσει, *καὶ ἐκάθητο ἐπάνω αὐτοῦ*·[2399] ὅτι αὐτοὶ μὲν φοβηθέντες, *ἐγένοντο ὡς νεκροί*.[2400] Ὃ δ' ἔλεγε ταῖς γυναιξίν, ἀνεστάναι αὐτόν, καὶ προσέταττε λέγειν *τοῖς μαθηταῖς αὐτοῦ* ἀπιέναι *εἰς τὴν Γαλιλαίαν* ὀψομένους αὐτόν,[2401] τάχα δὲ καὶ τὰ συνυπακουόμενα πάντα,[2402] τὸ πεφάνθαι ταῖς γυναιξὶ καὶ τὸ προσκυνηθέντα τὸν Ἰησοῦν εἰρηκέναι ἃ εἶπεν. Οἱ δὲ σκληροκάρδιοι Ἰουδαῖοι[mdccxxiv] οὔτε τὰ ἐπὶ τῷ πάθει γενόμενα οὔτε τὰ λεχθέντα δυσωπηθέντες, τῷ ἰδίῳ πάθει τῇ φιλαργυρίᾳ νοθεύουσι τοὺς στρατιώτας, τὸ πάντων ἀσεβέστατον φθέγξασθαι. Εἰρήκασι γὰρ ψευδόμενοι ὅτι ἐκλάπη ὑπὸ τῶν μαθητῶν.
Οὐ γὰρ ἂν κλέψαντες τὸ σῶμα οὕτω γνησίως τῇ διδασκαλίᾳ αὐτοῦ ἠγωνίζοντο, ὡς καὶ ἀδοξεῖν καὶ ἀποθνῄσκειν δι' αὐτόν.

> Οὐ γὰρ ἂν κλέψαντες τὸ σῶμα οἱ μαθηταὶ ὡς αὐτοὶ διεφήμισαν οὕτω γνησίως αὐτοῦ τῇ διδασκαλίᾳ συνηγωνίζοντο ὡς καὶ ἀδοξεῖν καὶ ἀποθνῄσκειν δι' αὐτήν.[mdccxxv]

Διαφημίζουσι τοίνυν *μέχρις* οὗ τὸ *σήμερον* λέγει.[2403] Οἱ μὲν ἐκ περιτομῆς τὸ ψεῦδος ταῖς ἀλήθειαν ἀποστρεφομέναις ψυχαῖς, οἱ δὲ μαθηταὶ Ἰησοῦ τὸ ἀληθὲς τοῖς ἀξίοις. Καὶ ἡ τῶν ἐκ περιτομῆς ἀπιστία τὴν πίστιν τοῦ Θεοῦ καταργῆσαι οὐ δύναται, ἀλλ' ὅσῳ ἐκεῖνοι κατὰ Χριστοῦ τοσούτῳ Χριστιανοὶ πλείους γίνονται καὶ ὁσημέραι εἰς πλῆθος ἐπιδιδόασιν.[mdccxxvi]

2396 John, 20:17.
2397 cod. οὐκ ἔτι.
2398 Matt. 28:11.
2399 Matt. 28:2.
2400 Matt. 28:4.
2401 Matt. 28:7.
2402 Cod. τῷ πάντα.
2403 Matt. 28:15.

77

237v (ΩΡΙΓΕΝΟΥΣ) *Ἀργύρια ἱκανὰ ἔδωκαν τοῖς στρατιώταις.*[2404] Καὶ Ἰούδας μὲν ἀργυρίου προδίδωσι τὸν Ἰησοῦν, ἐπιλαθόμενος ὧν εἶδε σημείων. Οἱ δὲ στρατιῶται *ἀργύρια ἱκανὰ λαβόντες*, ἃ μὲν ἰδόντες *προαπήγγειλαν τοῖς ἀρχιερεῦσι*[2405] τεράστια ἐσιώπησαν, εἰρήκασι δὲ τὰ μὴ γενόμενα.

> Καὶ Ἰούδας μὲν ἀργυρίου προδίδωσι τὸν Ἰησοῦν, ἐπιλαθόμενος ὧν εἶδε σημείων. οἱ δὲ στρατιῶται *ἀργύρια ἱκανὰ λαβόντες* ἃ μὲν ἰδόντες *προαπήγγειλαν τοῖς ἀρχιερεῦσι* τεράστια, ἐσιώπησαν, εἰρήκασι δὲ τὰ μὴ γενόμενα.[mdccxxvii]

> Καὶ Ἰούδας μὲν ἀργυρίων προδίδωσι τὸν Ἰησοῦν ἐπιλαθόμενος ὧν εἶδεν σημείων, οἱ δὲ στρατιῶται ἀργύρια ἱκανὰ λαβόντες ἃ μὲν ἰδόντες προαπήγγειλαν τοῖς ἀρχιερεῦσι τεράστια ἐσιώπησαν, εἰρήκασι δὲ τὰ μὴ γενόμενα.[mdccxxviii]

Οἱ δὲ ἕνδεκα μαθηταὶ ἐπορεύθησαν.[2406] Κατὰ τὸν Ἰωάννην, τρίτον ὤφθη τοῖς μαθηταῖς ὁ Ἰησοῦς. Τὸ μὲν πρῶτον, κατ᾽ αὐτὴν τὴν ἡμέραν τῆς ἀναστάσεως·[2407] δεύτερον δέ, | **238r** *μεθ᾽ ἡμέρας ὀκτώ*,[2408] ἔνθα τὸν Θωμᾶν τῆς ἀπιστίας θεραπεύει.[2409] Ἐπειδὴ δὲ κεκελευσμένοι ἦσαν ἅμα πάντες οἱ μαθηταὶ ἐπὶ *τὴν Γαλιλαίαν* ἀπαντᾶν, ἔπραττον δὲ καὶ *οἱ ἕνδεκα* μετὰ τῶν λοιπῶν τὸ κελευσθὲν καὶ ὁ καθ᾽ εἷς αὐτῶν ἐπισυνήγετο μήπω τῶν *ἕνδεκα* ἠθροισμένων, ἀλλ᾽ ἔτι μελλόντων τὸ τρίτον παρὰ τὴν θάλασσαν τῆς Γαλιλαίας, οὐ τοῖς *ἕνδεκα* φαίνεται, ἀλλὰ μόνοις ἑπτά.[2410] Μετὰ γοῦν τὸ ὀφθῆναι αὐτὸν τρίτον τοῦτο τοῖς εἰρημένοις ἑπτά, τετάρτην ὀπτασίαν οὐκ ἂν ἁμάρτοις τὴν παρὰ τῷ Ματθαίῳ φήσας εἶναι. Οὐκ ἀπεικὸς δὲ μετὰ ταῦτα καὶ πέμπτον καὶ ἄλλοτε πολλάκις ὦφθαι αὐτόν, ὁμοῦ συνηγμένοις τοῖς *ἕνδεκα* καὶ τοῖς ἑβδομήκοντα. Ὁ δὲ ἀπόστολος καὶ ἔτι τούτων πλείοσιν ἱστορεῖ ἑωρᾶσθαι τὸν Σωτῆρα μετὰ τὴν ἀνάστασιν· *ὤφθη* γάρ φησι *Κηφᾷ· εἶτα τοῖς ι‹β›*·[2411] *ἔπειτα ἐπάνω πεντακοσίοις ἀδελφοῖς ἐφ᾽ ἅπαξ.*[2412] Οἱ οὖν ἕνδεκα μαθηταὶ σὺν τοῖς λοιποῖς, ὡς εἰκός, *ἰδόντες αὐτόν, προσεκύνησαν*, εἰ δὲ καί τινες *ἐδίστασαν.*[2413] Ἀλλὰ καὶ οὗτοι διὰ τῆς ὄψεως ἐβεβαιώθησαν.

Οἱ τοίνυν μὴ προσκυνήσαντες καὶ *ἐδίστασαν*, εἴτε δὲ Θωμᾶς ἐστιν ὁ διστάσας εἴτε Φίλιππος, ζητητέον. Οὔπω γὰρ ἦν ἐν αὐτοῖς ἡ τοῦ Πνεύματος χάρις. Ἤτοι ἐπεὶ

2404 Matt. 28:12.
2405 Matt. 28:11.
2406 Matt. 28:16.
2407 John, 20:19.
2408 John, 20:26.
2409 John, 20:27-29.
2410 John, 21:1-23.
2411 Cod. ια.
2412 1 Cor. 15:5-6.
2413 Matt. 28:17.

μεμνημένοι ἦσαν τοῦ *πολλοὶ ἐλεύσονται ἐπὶ τῷ ὀνόματί μου λέγοντες ὅτι ἐγώ εἰμί*[2414] *ὁ Χριστός*,[2415] ἢ τῶν ὁμοίως, ἴσως *ἐδίστασαν*. Διὸ μὴ μεμψάμενος, συγγνώμην δὲ ἀπονείμας, τ‹αῦ›τ‹α›[2416] ἐντέλλεται.

> *Προσεκύνησαν*, οὐ προσηύξαντο,[mdccxxix] *οἱ δὲ* μὴ προσκυνήσαντες *καὶ ἐδίστασαν*, εἴτε Θωμᾶς εἴτε Φίλιππος (ἐβάπτιζε γὰρ καὶ οὐκ ἐδίδου πνεῦμα ἅγιον), ὥστε προσεπιμεμνημένοι τοῦ *πολλοὶ ἐλεύσονται ἐν τῷ ὀνόματί μου λέγοντες. ἐγώ εἰμὶ ὁ Χριστός*, ἢ τῶν ὁμοίως, *ἐδίστασαν*. ‹διὸ› μὴ μεμψάμενος συγγνώμην δὲ ἀπονείμας ταῦτα ἐντέλλεται.[mdccxxx]

Τινὲς δὲ τὸ εἶδος τοῦ δισταγμοῦ, ὡς τῷ Ματθαίῳ παραλειφθέν, παρὰ Ἰωάννῃ εἰρῆσθαι φασί, ἐν οἷς καὶ ὅτι διστάσας Θωμᾶς ἦν εἰρήκει. Ἀλλὰ *μεθ᾽ ἡμέρας ὀκτὼ*[2417] πληροφορηθεὶς ὄψει τε καὶ ἁφῇ, ἑδραίως ἐπίστευσεν.[2418]

78

239v (ΩΡΙΓΕΝΟΥΣ) Τὸ *ἐδόθη μοι πᾶσα ἐξουσία ἐν οὐρανῷ καὶ ἐπὶ γῆς*[2419] εἰς τὴν ἐνανθρώπησιν νόει. Καὶ εἰ εἰς τὴν θεότητα χωρήσεις θεωρεῖν, οὕτω λήψῃ τὸ *ἐδόθη μοι ἐξουσία*, ἀντὶ τοῦ ἐχωρήθη, ἐδόθη, ἠνέχθη μοι παρὰ τοῦ αὐτεξουσίου, ἐπιστεύθη. Χώραν ἔσχεν ἡ ζωὴ πρῶτον ἐν τοῖς ἄνω, εἶτα καὶ νῦν καὶ ἐν τοῖς κάτω. Οὓς θαρροῦντες βαπτίσατε *εἰς τὸ ὄνομα τοῦ Πατρὸς καὶ τοῦ Υἱοῦ καὶ τοῦ Ἁγίου Πνεύματος*. Εἷς ὁ σώζων,[2420] μία ἡ σωτηρία. Εἷς ὁ ζῶν, Πατὴρ καὶ Υἱὸς καὶ Ἅγιον Πνεῦμα. Εἷς ἐστιν, οὐ συναλ‹ο›ιφῇ[2421][mdccxxxi] τῶν τριῶν, ἀλλ᾽ οὐσίᾳ μιᾷ. Τρεῖς δὲ ὑποστάσεις τέλειαι ἐν πᾶσι καὶ κατάλληλοι. Κατὰ φύσιν ἐγέν‹ν›ησεν[2422] ὁ Θεός. Διόπερ ὁμοούσιος ὁ γεννηθείς. Οὐ σῶμα ὁ Θεός, καὶ οὐ κατὰ ῥεῦσιν ἢ κίνησιν ἤ τι τῶν τοιούτων ἃ ἐν τοῖς σώμασι θεωρεῖται. Ὁ Θεὸς ὁ ἀσώματος ἐγέννησεν. Ἐνυπόστατος ‹ἡ› γέννησις. Ἀπετέχθη ἐκ τῆς οὐσίας τοῦ Πατρὸς ὁ Υἱός.[mdccxxxii]

2414 Matt. 24:5; 13:6.

2415 Matt. 24:5; cf. Mark, 13:5-6. Luke, 21:8.

2416 Cod. τὰ αὐτά.

2417 John, 20:26.

2418 John, 20:24-29.

2419 Matt. 28:18.

2420 Cf. Jerome, *commMatt*, 13.33: "They interpret this woman as the Church, which has mixed the faith of a man into three measures of wheat by means of belief in the Father, in the Son, and in the Holy Spirit. And once the Church has been fermented into one, this leads us not to a threefold God, but to the knowledge of the one divinity."

2421 Cod. συναλιφῇ.

2422 Cod. ἐγένησεν.

[Τὸ *ἐδόθη μοι πᾶσα ἐξουσίᾳ ἐν οὐρανῷ καὶ ἐπὶ γῆς*[2423] εἰς τὴν ἐνανθρώπησιν νόει. εἰ δὲ καὶ εἰς τὴν θεότητα χωρήσεις θεωρεῖν, καὶ οὕτω λήψῃ τὸ *ἐδόθη μοι ἐξουσία*, ἀντὶ τοῦ ἐχωρήθη, ἐδόθη, ἠνέχθη μοι, παρὰ τοῦ αὐτεξουσίου. ἐπιστεύθη. χώραν ἔσχεν ἡ ζωὴ πρῶτον ἐν τοῖς ἄνω, εἶτα νῦν καὶ ἐν τοῖς κάτω. οὓς θαρροῦντες βαπτίσατε *εἰς τὸ ὄνομα τοῦ πατρὸς καὶ τοῦ υἱοῦ καὶ τοῦ ἁγίου πνεύματος*. εἷς ὁ σώζων, μία ἡ σωτηρία. εἷς ὁ ζῶν, πατὴρ καὶ υἱὸς καὶ ἅγιον πνεῦμα. εἷς ἐστιν οὐ συναλοιφῇ τῶν τριῶν, ἀλλ᾽ οὐσία μία, τρεῖς δὲ ὑποστάσεις τέλειαι ἐν πᾶσι καὶ κατάλληλοι. κατὰ φύσιν ἐγέννησεν ὁ πατήρ, διόπερ ὁμοούσιος ὁ γεννηθείς. οὐ σῶμα ὁ θεός, διὰ τοῦτο οὐ κατὰ ῥεῦσιν ἢ κίνησιν ἤ τι τῶν τοιούτων ἃ ἐν τοῖς σώμασι θεωρεῖται. Ὁ θεὸς ὁ ἀσώματος ἐγέννησεν. ἐνυπόστατος ἡ γέννησις, ἀπετέχθη ἐκ τῆς οὐσίας τοῦ πατρὸς ὁ υἱός.][mdcccxxxiii]

Τό, *Ἐδόθη μοι πᾶσα ἐξουσία*, καὶ ἑξῆς, εἰς τὴν ἐνανθρώπησιν νόει. Εἰ δὲ καὶ εἰς τὴν θεότητα … θεωρεῖν, καὶ οὕτω λήψῃ τὸ *Ἐδόθη μοι ἐξουσία*, ἀντὶ τοῦ *Ἐχωρήθη*. *Ἐδόθη*, ἠνέχθη μοι, περὶ τοῦ αὐτεξουσίου ἐπιστεύθην. Χώραν ἔσχεν ἡ ζωὴ πρῶτον μὲν ἐν τοῖς ἄνω, εἶτα νῦν καὶ ἐν τοῖς κάτω. οὓς θαρροῦντες βαπτίσατε εἰς τὸ ὄνομα τοῦ Πατρός, καὶ τοῦ Υἱοῦ, καὶ τοῦ ἁγίου Πνεύματος. Εἷς ὁ σώζων, μία ἡ σωτηρία. Εἷς ὁ ζῶν Πατήρ, ὁ Υἱός, καὶ τὸ ἅγιον Πνεῦμα. Εἷς ἐστιν οὐ συναλοιφῇ τῶν τριῶν, ἀλλ᾽ οὐσίᾳ μιᾷ. τρεῖς δὲ ὑποστάσεις τέλειαι ἐν πᾶσι, καὶ κατάλληλοι. Κατὰ φύσιν ἐγέννησεν ὁ Πατήρ. διόπερ ὁμοούσιος ἐγεννήθη. Οὐ σῶμα ὁ Θεός. διὰ τοῦτο οὐκ ἀσταρεῦσιν ἢ κίνησιν, ἤ τι τῶν τοιούτων, ἃ ἐν τοῖς σώμασι θεωρεῖται, ὁ Θεὸς ὁ ἀσώματος ἐγέννησεν. Ἐνυπόστατος ἡ γέννησις. ἀπετέχθη ἐκ τῆς οὐσίας τοῦ Πατρὸς ὁ Υἱός.[mdcccxxxiv]

αὐτὸν εἶναι κυρίως καὶ μόνον ἀληθῶς Υἱὸν, οὐ νόθον οὐδὲ ψευδώνυμον, ἀλλ᾽ ἐκ τῆς οὐσίας τοῦ Θεοῦ καὶ Πατρὸς οὐ κατὰ ἀποκοπὴν, ἢ ῥεῦσιν, ἢ μερισμὸν, ἢ τομὴν … καὶ ἐξ αὐτοῦ προελθόντα ἀμερίστως καὶ ἀδιαστάτως, ἐπεὶ μηδὲ κατὰ σῶμα τὸ θεῖον.[mdcccxxxv]

They are baptised in the name of the Father, and of the Son, and of the Holy Spirit. Thus, there one bestowal from those whose divinity is one. And the name of Trinity is one God.[mdcccxxxvi]

Βαπτίζοντες αὐτούς.[2424] Ἀρχὴν τῆς διδασκαλίας τῶν ἐθνῶν τὸ βάπτισμα δίδωσιν. Ὅτι πρότερον μέν ἐστι τὸ καθαρθῆναι, δεύτερον δὲ τὸ πλη | **240r** ρωθῆναι τῶν ἀγαθῶν. Τῷ δὲ βαπτίσματι συνῆψε τὴν τῆς Τριάδος[2425] θεολογίαν, τὴν καινὴν εἰσάγων χάριν. Ὅτι βάπτισμα ἦν δι᾽ ὕδατος ἐν νόμῳ. Καὶ παρὰ Ἰωάννῃ γε τὸ δι᾽ ὕδατος ἔτι μετὰ τῆς πρὸς Θεὸν συναφείας καὶ οὐκ ἦν βάπτισμα πώποτε. Νῦν δὲ ἡ συνάφεια πρῶτον, ὅτε νέος ἀπὸ τοῦ βαπτίσματος ἄνθρωπος, ὡσπερεὶ ζῶν ἐκ νεκρῶν πληρούμενος *Ἁγίου Πνεύματος*, ὅπερ ἐστὶν δῶρον Χριστοῦ, οὗ ἡ ἀρχὴ ὁ Πατήρ. Διόπερ ἀναγκαία τῆς Τριάδος ἡ ὀνομασία. Καὶ ὅπερ ἂν ὑπεξαιρῇ τις ὄνομα, κολοβὸν ποιεῖ τὸ τῆς θεολογίας. Ἀτελὲς μέν, ἐὰν τὸ Πνεῦμα περιαιρῇ· διεστῶσαν δὲ τοῦ τέλους τὴν ἀρχὴν ἐὰν τὸ μέσον ἐξαιρῇ, τὸν Υἱόν. Ἀδύνατον δὲ τὸν κατὰ μίαν ἐνέργειαν γινόμενον

2423 Matt. 28:18.
2424 Matt. 28:19.
2425 Cod. $\overline{\text{τρι}}$Δος.

ἁγιασμὸν ἐκ διαφόρων καὶ ἀσυναρτήτων οὐσιῶν ἐπιτελεῖσθαι. Ἀσεβὲς γὰρ τὸ τὰ ἑτεροφυῆ καὶ ἀσύναπτα μιᾷ τῇ ἐνεργείᾳ περιλαβεῖν.

> Of the existence of the Holy Spirit, however, we are taught in many passages of scripture… . From all of which we learn that the person of the Holy Spirit is of so great authority and dignity that saving baptism is not complete except when performed with the authority of the whole most excellent Trinity, that is, by the naming of Father, Son and Holy Spirit; and that the name of the Holy Spirit must be joined to that of the unbegotten God the Father and his only-begotten Son.[mdccxxxvii]

> He who is *born again through God*[2426] to salvation has need of both Father and Son and Holy Spirit and will not obtain salvation apart from the entire Trinity, and … is it impossible to become partaker of the Father and the Son without the Holy Spirit.[mdccxxxviii]

> The power of the Trinity is one and the same… . there is no separation in the Trinity, but that which is called the *gift of the Spirit*[2427] is ministered through the Son and worked by God the Father… . This then is the testimony we bear to the unity of Father, Son, and Holy Spirit.[mdccxxxix] … This blessed and ruling power, therefore, that is, the power that exercises control of all things, we call the Trinity.[mdccxl]

Τριάδα τοίνυν τοῖς μαθηταῖς ὁμοούσιον τοῖς βαπτιζομένοις διδόναι παρεγγυᾷ, οὐχ ἕτερος ὢν αὐτῆς, ἀλλ' ἑαυτὸν Υἱὸν ἀορίστως προσονομάζων, ἅτε δὴ καὶ γνήσιος ὢν καὶ ἀληθινὸς καὶ μόνος κυρίως *τοῦ Πατρὸς* Υἱός. Ὥσπερ δὴ καὶ τὸν Πατέρα ἀορίστως Πατέρα φησί, ἅτε δὴ πατέρα ἀληθῶς ὑπάρχοντα καὶ οὐχ ἑτέρου υἱοῦ, ἀλλὰ μόνον κυρίως Πατέρα τοῦ ἀληθινοῦ *Υἱοῦ*. Καὶ τὸ Πνεῦμα δὲ Ἅγιόν φησι πρὸς ἀντιδιαστολὴν τῶν βεβήλων καὶ τῶν μὴ ἁγίων κατὰ φύσιν πνευμάτων.

> Ἀρχὴν τῆς διδασκαλίας τῶν ἐθνῶν τὸ βάπτισμα δίδωσιν, ὅτι πρότερον μέν ἐστι τὸ καθαρθῆναι, δεύτερον δὲ τὸ πληρωθῆναι τῶν ἀγαθῶν. τῷ δὲ βαπτίσματι συνῆψε τὴν τῆς τριάδος θεολογίαν τὴν καινὴν εἰσάγων χάριν, ὅτι ἦν βαπτίσματα δι' ὕδατος ἐν νόμῳ καὶ παρὰ Ἰωάννῃ γε τὸ δι' ὕδατος ἔτι. μετὰ δὲ τῆς πρὸς θεὸν συναφείας οὐκ ἦν βάπτισμα πώποτε. νῦν δὲ ἡ συνάφεια πρῶτον, ὅτε νέος ἀπὸ τοῦ βαπτίσματος ἄνθρωπος ὡσπερεὶ ζῶν ἐκ νεκρῶν πληρούμενος ἁγίου πνεύματος, ὅπερ ἐστὶ δῶρον Χριστοῦ, οὗ ἡ ἀρχὴ ὁ πατήρ. διόπερ ἀναγκαία τῆς τριάδος ἡ ὀνομασία. καὶ ὅπου ἂν ὑπεξαιρῇ τις ὄνομα, κολοβὸν ποιεῖ τὸ τῆς θεολογίας. ἀτελὲς μέν, ἐὰν τὸ πνεῦμα περιαιρῇ. διεστῶσαι δὲ τοῦ τέλους τὴν ἀρχήν, ἐὰν τὸ μέσον ἐξαιρῇ, τὸν υἱόν. ἀδύνατον δὲ τὸν κατὰ μίαν ἐνέργειαν γινόμενον ἁγιασμὸν ἐκ διαφόρων καὶ ἀσυναρτήτων οὐσιῶν ἐπιτελεῖσθαι. ἀσεβὲς γὰρ τὸ τὰ ἑτεροφυῆ καὶ ἀσύναπτα μιᾷ τῇ ἐνεργείᾳ περιλαβεῖν. τριάδα τοίνυν τοῖς μαθηταῖς ὁμοούσιον τοῖς βαπτιζομένοις παρεγγυᾷ παραδιδόναι οὐχ ἕτερος ὢν αὐτός, ἀλλ' ἑαυτὸν υἱὸν ἀορίστως προσονομάζων ἅτε δὴ καὶ γνήσιος ὢν καὶ ἀληθινὸς καὶ μόνος κυρίως τοῦ

2426 1 Peter, 1:3.

2427 Cf. 1 Cor. 12:4-11.

> πατρὸς υἱός. ὥσπερ δὴ καὶ τὸν πατέρα ἀορίστως πατέρα φησίν, ἅτε δὴ πατέρα ἀληθῶς ὑπάρχοντα καὶ οὐχ ἑτέρου υἱοῦ, ἀλλὰ μόνον κυρίως πατέρα τοῦ ἀληθινοῦ υἱοῦ, καὶ τὸ πνεῦμα δὲ τὸ ἅγιόν φησι πρὸς ἀντιδιαστολὴν τῶν βεβήλων καὶ τῶν μὴ ἁγίων κατὰ φύσιν πνευμάτων.[mdccxli]

Τοῦ πατρὸς καὶ τοῦ υἱοῦ.[2428] Τὸν Θεὸν γεννῶντα καὶ γεννώμενον οὐκ ἔστιν ὑποβάλλειν χρόνῳ. Θεὸς γὰρ οὐχ ὑποπίπτει χρόνῳ. Οὐκ ἔστιν ἀσεβὲς λέγειν ὅτι ὁ Θεὸς ἐγέννησεν. Μηδεὶς δεδιέτω. Οὐκ ἔστι γὰρ ἐναντίον ἢ αἴτιον κακῆς ἐννοίας τοῦτο, ἐὰν θεοπρεπῶς ὑποληφθείῃ. Εἷς ὁ Πατὴρ ἑνὸς *Υἱοῦ*. Εἷς ἀγέννητος Πατήρ. Εἷς γεννητὸς Θεός, ὁ Υἱός. Καὶ ὥσπερ οὐκ ἔστιν | **240v** συναγέννητος ἕτερος Ἰησοῦς, οὕτω οὐδὲ συγγεγενημένος ἕτερος Θεός, Υἱός. Οὐκ ἔστιν Υἱὸς τὸ Πνεῦμα τὸ Ἅγιον. Ἔχει ὁ Πατὴρ ὑπόστασιν *Πατρός*. Ἔχει ὁ Υἱὸς ὑπόστασιν Υἱοῦ. Ἔχει τὸ Πνεῦμα ὑπόστασιν *Ἁγίου Πνεύματος.*[mdccxlii] Ἀσώματος καὶ νοερὰ καὶ λογικὴ καὶ ἐν πᾶσι τελεία ἡ ὑπόστασις *τοῦ Πατρός*, τουτέστιν ὁ Πατήρ. Ὅμοιος ὁ Υἱὸς τῷ Πατρὶ ἐν πᾶσι καὶ πλήρης κατ' αὐτόν, ἐκτὸς τοῦ εἶναι Πατήρ. Υἱὸς γάρ ἐστιν καθ' ὑπόστασιν. Τέλειον τὸ Πνεῦμα τὸ Ἅγιον καὶ πλῆρες ἐν πᾶσι. Καθὼς ὁ Πατὴρ τέλειος καὶ ὁ Υἱὸς τέλειος καὶ τὸ Πνεῦμα τὸ Ἅγιον τέλειον ὁμοίως τ‹ῷ› Πατρ‹ὶ› καὶ τ‹ῷ› Υἱ‹ῷ›,[2429] πάρεξ τοῦ εἶναι Πατὴρ ἢ Υἱός. Ἔστι γὰρ καθ' ὑπόστασιν ἰδίαν Πνεῦμα Ἅγιον, ὁμοούσιον τ‹ῷ› Πατρ‹ὶ› καὶ τ‹ῷ› Υἱ‹ῷ›,[2430] ἐκ τοῦ Πατρὸς ἐκπορευόμενον, δι' Υἱοῦ πεφηνός, ἀχώριστον τοῦ Πατρὸς καὶ τοῦ Υἱοῦ, ὡς ἴδιον. Τρεῖς οὖν τετελειωμέναι ὑποστάσεις *Πατρὸς καὶ Υἱοῦ καὶ Ἁγίου Πνεύματος*, μία δὲ οὐσία.

> Τὸν θεὸν γεννῶντα καὶ γεννώμενον οὐκ ἔστιν ὑπὸ χρόνῳ βαλεῖν. θεὸς γὰρ οὐχ ὑποπίπτει χρόνῳ. οὐκ ἔστιν ἀσεβὲς λέγειν, ὅτι ὁ θεὸς ἐγέννησεν. μηδεὶς δεδιέτω. οὐκ ἔστιν γὰρ ἐναντίον ἢ αἴτιον κακῆς ἐννοίας τοῦτο, ἐὰν θεοπρεπῶς ὑποληφθείη. εἷς ὁ πατὴρ ἑνὸς υἱοῦ, εἷς ἀγέννητος πατήρ, εἷς γεννητὸς θεὸς ὁ υἱὸς καὶ ὥσπερ οὐκ ἔστιν συναγέννητος ἕτερος θεός, οὕτως οὐδὲ συγγεγεννημένος ἕτερος θεὸς ὁ υἱός. οὐκ ἔστιν υἱὸς τὸ πνεῦμα τὸ ἅγιον. ἔχει ὁ πατὴρ ὑπόστασιν πατρός, ἔχει ὁ υἱὸς ὑπόστασιν υἱοῦ, ἔχει τὸ πνεῦμα ὑπόστασιν ἁγίου πνεύματος. ἀσώματος καὶ νοερὰ καὶ λογικὴ καὶ ἐν πᾶσι τελεία ἡ ὑπόστασις τοῦ πατρός, τοῦτ' ἔστιν ὁ πατήρ. ὅμοιος ὁ υἱὸς τῷ πατρὶ ἐν πᾶσι καὶ πλήρης κατ' αὐτὸν ἐκτὸς τοῦ εἶναι πατήρ. υἱὸς γάρ ἐστι καθ' ὑπόστασιν. τέλειον τὸ πνεῦμα τὸ ἅγιον καὶ πλῆρες ἐν πᾶσι. καθὼς ὁ πατὴρ τέλειος καὶ ὁ υἱὸς τέλειος, οὕτω καὶ τὸ πνεῦμα τὸ ἅγιον τέλειον ὁμοίως τοῦ πατρὸς καὶ τοῦ υἱοῦ πάρεξ τοῦ εἶναι πατὴρ ἢ υἱός. ἔστι γὰρ καθ' ὑπόστασιν ἰδίαν πνεῦμα ἐγέννησεν. μηδεὶς δεδιέτω. οὐκ ἔστιν γὰρ ἐναντίον ἢ αἴτιον κακῆς ἐννοίας τοῦτο, ἐὰν θεοπρεπῶς ὑποληφθείη. εἷς ὁ πατὴρ ἑνὸς υἱοῦ, εἷς ἀγέννητος πατήρ, εἷς γεννητὸς θεὸς ὁ υἱὸς καὶ ὥσπερ οὐκ ἔστιν συναγέννητος ἕτερος θεός, οὕτως οὐδὲ συγγεγεννημένος ἕτερος θεὸς ὁ υἱός. οὐκ ἔστιν υἱὸς τὸ πνεῦμα τὸ ἅγιον. ἔχει ὁ πατὴρ ὑπόστασιν πατρός, ἔχει ὁ υἱὸς ὑπόστασιν υἱοῦ, ἔχει τὸ πνεῦμα ὑπόστασιν ἁγίου πνεύματος. ἀσώματος καὶ νοερὰ καὶ λογικὴ καὶ ἐν πᾶσι τελεία ἡ ὑπόστασις τοῦ πατρός, τοῦτ' ἔστιν ὁ πατήρ. ὅμοιος ὁ υἱὸς τῷ πατρὶ ἐν πᾶσι καὶ πλήρης κατ' αὐτὸν ἐκτὸς τοῦ

2428 Matt. 28:19.
2429 Cod. τοῦ πατρὸς καὶ τοῦ υἱοῦ.
2430 Cod. τοῦ πατρὸς καὶ τοῦ υἱοῦ.

> εἶναι πατήρ. υἱὸς γάρ ἐστι καθ' ὑπόστασιν. τέλειον τὸ πνεῦμα τὸ ἅγιον καὶ πλῆρες ἐν πᾶσι. καθὼς ὁ πατὴρ τέλειος καὶ ὁ υἱὸς τέλειος, οὕτω καὶ τὸ πνεῦμα τὸ ἅγιον τέλειον ὁμοίως τοῦ πατρὸς καὶ τοῦ υἱοῦ πάρεξ τοῦ εἶναι πατὴρ ἢ υἱός. ἔστι γὰρ καθ' ὑπόστασιν ἰδίαν πνεῦμα ἅγιον ὁμοούσιον τοῦ πατρὸς καὶ τοῦ υἱοῦ ἐκ τοῦ πατρὸς ἐκπορευόμενον, δι' υἱοῦ πεφηνός, ἀχώριστον τοῦ πατρὸς καὶ τοῦ υἱοῦ ὡς ἴδιον. τρεῖς οὖν τετελειωμέναι ὑποστάσεις, *πατρός, υἱοῦ καὶ ἁγίου πνεύματος*, μία δὲ οὐσία.[mdccxliii]

Διδάσκοντες αὐτοὺς τηρεῖν.[2431] Τὸ μὲν [sc. *διδάσκοντες*] περὶ δογμάτων, τὸ δὲ [sc. *τηρεῖν*] περὶ ἐντολῶν. Καὶ Ἰουδαίων μὲν οὐδὲ μέμνηται, οὐδὲ εἰς μέσον φέρει τὰ γεγενημένα, οὐδὲ ὀνειδίζει Πέτρῳ τὴν ἄρνησιν, οὐδὲ τῶν ἄλλων οὐδενὶ τὴν φυγήν. Κελεύει δὲ εἰς τὴν οἰκουμένην ἐκχυθῆναι πᾶσαν, σύντομον διδασκαλίαν ἐγχειρίσας, τὴν διὰ τοῦ βαπτίσματος.

> *Πορευθέντες μαθητεύσατε πάντα τὰ ἔθνη, βαπτίζοντες αὐτοὺς εἰς τὸ ὄνομα τοῦ Πατρός, καὶ τοῦ Υἱοῦ, καὶ τοῦ ἁγίου Πνεύματος, διδάσκοντες αὐτοὺς τηρεῖν πάντα ὅσα ἐνετειλάμην ὑμῖν.* τὸ μὲν περὶ δογμάτων, τὸ δὲ περὶ ἐντολῶν παραγγέλλων. Καὶ Ἰουδαίων μὲν οὐδὲν μέμνηται, οὐδὲ εἰς μέσον φέρει τὰ γεγενημένα, οὐδὲ ὀνειδίζει Πέτρῳ τὴν ἄρνησιν, οὐδὲ τῶν ἄλλων οὐδενὶ τὴν φυγήν. κελεύει δὲ εἰς τὴν οἰκουμένην ἐκχυθῆναι πᾶσαν, σύντομον διδασκαλίαν ἐγχειρίσας, τὴν διὰ τοῦ βαπτίσματος.[mdccxliv]

> τὸ δὲ *πορευθέντες μαθητεύσατε πάντα τὰ ἔθνη*, καὶ τὰ ἑξῆς, δηλοῖ, ὅτι τὸ μὲν περὶ δογμάτων, τὸ δὲ περὶ ἐντολῶν αὐτοῖς παραγγέλλει. καὶ Ἰουδαίων μὲν οὐδὲν μέμνηται. οὐδὲ εἰς μέσον φέρει τὸ γεγενημένον. οὐδὲ ὀνειδίζει Πέτρῳ τὴν ἄρνησιν. οὐδὲ τῶν ἄλλων οὐδενὶ τὴν φυγήν. κελεύει δὲ τὴν οἰκουμένην ἐκχυθῆναι πᾶσαν, σύντομον διδασκαλίαν ἐγχειρίσας, τὴν διὰ τοῦ βαπτίσματος, καὶ ὥστε παραγγέλλειν πᾶσι τηρεῖν, οὐ τὰ μέν, καὶ τὰ δέ, ἀλλὰ πάντα ὅσα ἐνετείλατο.[mdccxlv]

Καὶ ἰδοὺ ἐγὼ μεθ' ὑμῶν εἰμι πάσας τὰς ἡμέρας ἕως τῆς συντελείας.[2432] Εἰπὼν δὲ *ἕως τῆς συντελείας* συνεῖναι τοῖς ἁγίοις, οὐ τοῦτο λέγει ὅτι μετὰ τὴν συντέλειαν οὐκέτι αὐτὸν ὄψονται. Τότε γὰρ μάλιστα συνέσται τοῖς ἁγίοις, ὅτι οὐ *δι' ἐσόπ‹τ›ρ‹ου›*,[2433] οὔτε *δι'* αἰνιγμάτων ‹αὐ›τὸν ὁρῶσιν, ἀλλὰ *πρόσωπον πρὸς πρόσωπον*[2434] ἀεί.

> Ἆρα γὰρ εἰπὼν τοῦτο, *ἕως* μὲν *τῆς συντελείας τοῦ αἰῶνος* ἔμελλεν αὐτοῖς συνέσεσθαι, μετὰ δὲ τὴν συντέλειαν τοῦ αἰῶνος, ἐνισταμένου τοῦ ἑτέρου (τοῦ καλουμένου μέλλοντος) οὐκέτι συνέσεσθαι αὐτοῖς ἐπηγγέλλετο, ὡς κατὰ τοῦτο κρεῖττον εἶναι ἂν τοῖς μαθηταῖς τὸ *ἕως τῆς συντελείας τοῦ αἰῶνος* περὶ αὐτοῖς κατάστημα τοῦ μετὰ τὴν συντέλειαν τοῦ αἰῶνος; ἀλλ' οὐκ ἂν οἶμαί τινα τολμῆσαι λέγειν ὅτι μετὰ τὴν συντέλειαν τοῦ αἰῶνος οὐκέτι συνέσται τοῖς μαθηταῖς ὁ υἱὸς τοῦ θεοῦ, ἐπεὶ ἡ λέξις ἐπὶ τοσοῦτον ἔσεσθαι αὐτὸν μετ' αὐτῶν φησιν, ἕως ἡ συντέλεια τοῦ αἰῶνος ἐνστῇ. σαφὲς γὰρ ὅτι τὸ ζητούμενον ἦν, εἰ πρὸ τοῦ μέλλοντος αἰῶνος καὶ τῶν ἐλπιζομένων ἀμοιβαίων ἐπαγγελιῶν

2431 Matt. 28:20.
2432 Matt. 28:20.
2433 Cod. ἐσόπρω.
2434 1 Cor. 13:12.

τοῦ θεοῦ ἤδη συνέσεσθαι τοῖς μαθηταῖς ἔμελλεν ὁ υἱὸς τοῦ θεοῦ. ζητούμενον δ' ἂν ἦν, διδομένου τοῦ συνέσεσθαι τοῖς ***, μήποτε ὁτὲ μὲν συνῆν αὐτοῖς ὁτὲ δὲ οὐ συνῆν. διόπερ ἀπολύων ἡμᾶς τῆς περὶ τοῦ διστάζειν ὑπονοίας, ἀπεφήνατο ὅτι ἤδη καὶ ἐπὶ *πάσας τὰς ἡμέρας* συνεῖναι τοῖς μαθηταῖς ἤμελλεν, οὐ καταλείψων τοὺς μαθητευθέντας αὐτῷ *ἕως τῆς συντελείας τοῦ αἰῶνος.*[mdccxlvi]

Τὸ δὲ *ἕως*, ἐνταῦθα δηλοῖ τὸν κατεπείγοντα περὶ τοῦ δηλουμένου χρόνον, οὐ περιοριζόμενον, ὥστε γενέσθαι μετὰ τὸ *ἕως* τὸ ἐν αὐτῷ τῷ δηλουμένῳ, ὡς τό. *Καὶ ἰδοὺ ἐγὼ μεθ' ὑμῶν εἰμι ἕως τῆς συντελείας τοῦ αἰῶνος.*[mdccxlvii]

Endnotes

i Origen, *Fragmenta ex commentariis in evangelium Matthaei*, E. Benz - E. Klostermann, *Origenes Werke*, vol. 12, GCS 41.1, Leipzig, 1941 [hereinafter, *commMatt*, fr. ... (Klostermann)], fr. 1. Cf. Cyril of Alexandria (copying from Origen), *apud Catena in Matthaeum*, p. 5 & *frMatt*, fr. 1: (Κυρίλλου) Εὐαγγέλιον ἐστὶ λόγος περιέχων ἀγαθῶν ἀγγελίαν πραγμάτων κατὰ τὸ εὔλογον καὶ διὰ τὸ ὠφελεῖν εὐφρα...ων τὸ ...... πάντα ἐὰν παραδέξηται τὸ ἀπαγγελλόμενον. ἢ λόγος περιέχων ἀγαθῶν παρούσιαν [sic] ἢ ....τέλλων ἀγαθῶν, τὸ προσδοκώμενον.

ii Origen, *commJohn*, I.5.27. This was copied by the *Doctrina Patrum*, p. 257: Εὐαγγέλιόν ἐστιν ἀγαθοῦ τινος ἀγγελία. Εὐαγγέλιόν ἐστι λόγος περιέχων ἀγαθοῦ παρουσίαν, ἢ λόγος ἀπαγγέλλων παρεῖναι τὸ προσδοκώμενον ἀγαθόν. *Doctrina Patrum* is an extremely anti-Origenist document (e.g. pp. 1; 146; 179-82; 335), but its compiler(s) had no inkling of the fact that they were actually quoting Origen's words.

iii Origen, *op. cit.* I.5.28.

iv Origen, *commMatt*, fr. 2 (Klostermann). Cf. John Chrysostom, *In Matthaeum*, PG.57.27.4-13. Τίνος δὲ ἕνεκεν Βίβλον αὐτὴν γενέσεως καλεῖ Ἰησοῦ Χριστοῦ; καίτοιγε οὐ τοῦτο ἔχει μόνον τὴν γέννησιν, ἀλλὰ πᾶσαν τὴν οἰκονομίαν. Ὅτι πάσης τῆς οἰκονομίας τὸ κεφάλαιον τοῦτο, καὶ ἀρχὴ καὶ ῥίζα πάντων ἡμῖν τῶν ἀγαθῶν γίνεται. Ὥσπερ οὖν βιβλίον οὐρανοῦ καὶ γῆς καλεῖ Μωϋσῆς, καίτοιγε οὐ περὶ οὐρανοῦ καὶ γῆς διαλεχθεὶς μόνον, ἀλλὰ καὶ περὶ τῶν ἐν μέσῳ πάντων. οὕτω καὶ οὗτος ἀπὸ τοῦ κεφαλαίου τῶν κατορθωμάτων τὸ βιβλίον ἐκάλεσε.

v Origen, *commMatt*, fr. 3 (Klostermann); col. 2; see also col. 1. This is also Origen's text in *schMatt*, PG.17.289.34-37: Οὐκοῦν εἴη ἂν ἐπὶ Χριστοῦ γένεσις μέν, οὐκ ἐκ τοῦ μὴ ὄντος εἰς τὸ εἶναι πρόοδος, ἀλλ' ὁδὸς ἀπὸ τοῦ ἐν μορφῇ Θεοῦ ὑπάρχειν εἰς τὸ ἀναλαβεῖν τὴν τοῦ δούλου μορφήν.

vi ἑβραΐδι φωνῇ. Cf. Origen, *Cels*, III.6; *Epistula ad Africanum*, PG.11.61.16-17 & 30-31. Anastasius of Sinai (copying from Origen once again), *In Hexaemeron*, Book 8, lines 523-536: Πρῶτος ὁ Ματθαῖος ὁ λεγόμενος *Φεισών*, ὅπερ ἑρμηνεύεται *στόματος ἀλλοίωσις*. Ἑβραΐδι γὰρ διαλέκτῳ τοῦ Ματθαίου τὸ εὐαγγέλιον ἐκθεμένου ἠλλοιώθη καὶ μεθερμηνεύθη ὁ λόγος τοῦ στόματος αὐτοῦ ὑπὸ Λουκᾶ καὶ τοῦ Παύλου εἰς τὴν Ἑλλάδα φωνήν. See fuller quotation *infra*, endnote ix.

vii Origen, *commMatt*, fr. 1 (Klostermann), pp. 3-5, *apud* Eusebius, *HE*, 6.25.4-6; copied by Nicephorus Callistus Xanthopulus, *HE*, 5.16.

viii Origen is the sole author who averred that John the Baptist 'is the beginning of the Gospel and the last of prophets'. He did so in the commentary on John, and it now turns out that he wrote this also in this preamble to his commentary on Matthew. *commJohn*, I.4.22: καὶ Μᾶρκος, εἰδὼς ὃ γράφει, *ἀρχὴν* διηγεῖται *τοῦ εὐαγγελίου*, τάχα εὑρισκόντων ἡμῶν τὸ τέλος αὐτοῦ παρὰ τῷ Ἰωάννῃ [διηγουμένῳ] τὸν *ἐν ἀρχῇ* λόγον, θεὸν λόγον. *Op. cit.*, I.13.80-81: ἰστέον, ὅτι πρώτως τῆς κεφαλῆς τοῦ ὅλου τῶν σῳζομένων σώματος, Χριστοῦ Ἰησοῦ, ἐστὶ τὸ εὐαγγέλιον, ὥς φησιν ὁ Μᾶρκος. *Ἀρχὴ τοῦ εὐαγγελίου Χριστοῦ Ἰησοῦ.* ... Φησὶ γὰρ ὁ αὐτὸς Μᾶρκος. *Ἀρχὴ τοῦ εὐαγγελίου Ἰησοῦ Χριστοῦ, καθὼς γέγραπται ἐν Ἡσαΐᾳ τῷ προφήτῃ. Ἰδοὺ ἐγὼ ἀποστέλλω τὸν ἄγγελόν μου πρὸ προσώπου σου, ὃς κατασκευάσει τὴν ὁδόν σου. Φωνὴ βοῶντος ἐν τῇ ἐρήμῳ. Ἑτοιμάσατε τὴν ὁδὸν κυρίου, εὐθείας ποιεῖτε τὰς τρίβους αὐτοῦ.*

This unique exegesis was employed by the compiler of the catena on Mark, but by no other author. The catenist provides an interesting little story concerning Mark's biblical quotation upon the beginning of his gospel: in the first place, he endorses Origen's exegesis to the letter ('John is the last of prophets and the beginning of the Gospel'). Subsequently, however, he recounts Eusebius' remarks that Mark's quotation is not 'by

Isaiah', as the evangelist wrote, but by Malachi, which Eusebius pointed out 'in his exegesis addressed to Marinus' and argued that this is a scribal error (γραφέως ἐστὶ σφάλμα). In the extant text of Eusebius' treatise this remark does not appear; however, see Eusebius, *Supplementa Minora ad Queastiones ad Marinum*, PG.22.1008.37-41 (excerpted from this catena). Nevertheless, Mark's catenist proceeds with adducing Origen's analysis 'in the sixth volume of his commentary on John'. However, Origen did not consider this as a 'mistake', either scribal or otherwise. Instead, he argued that Mark made an abbreviated compilation (ἐπιτεμόμενος) of Isaiah, 40:3 and Malachi, 3:1, thus representing this combination as a saying by Isaiah (ἐπιτεμόμενος οὖν ὁ Εὐαγγελιστὴς ὡς ὑπὸ Ἡσαΐου εἰρημένας τὰς δύο χρήσεις παρέθηκεν). *Catena in Marcum*, p. 266-267. Furthermore, Origen adduced a similar example of such incision (he used the term ἐπιτεμόμενος ['one who abridges a text'] and its derivative, ἐπιτομή, *epitome*). The catenist copied this section to the letter from Origen's *commJohn*, VI.24.127-131, in which he argued that there is nothing wrong with Mark 'epitomising' and combining different prophetic saying, and adduced similar examples from the gospel of John.

ix Some Christian authors associated the four evangelists with four living creatures, which normally were, (1) a winged man, or angel; 2) a winged lion; (3) a winged ox or bull; (4) an eagle. However, specific correspondence between an evangelist and each of those animals varied in authors such as Irenaeus, Augustine, Pseudo-Athanasius, and Jerome. In any case, the imagery of those four animals originated with the text of Apocalypse 4:7. Cf. Pseudo-Athanasius, *Synopsis Scripturae Sacrae*, PG.28.432.44-50 (four evangelists / four animals); *op. cit.* PG.28.729.9-14 (Rev. 4:7 / gospels). Despite the appeal of such adumbrations, Origen did not employ either of those. Instead, according to his theory that 'Paradise' stands for spiritual truths rather than for an earthly location, he was fascinated by the passage of Genesis, 2:10-14. Accordingly, he saw 'the four rivers' in which 'a river that proceeds out of Eden' is 'divided' as standing for the four evangelists: river Geon represents Matthew; river Phison, Mark; river Tigris, Luke; river Euphrates, John.

None of Origen's known acolytes did ever consider this interconnection, which now comes to light for the first time. Actually, it was only a long time later that Anastasius of Sinai took up the passage and idea of the present *Codex Holy Cross 104*. Meantime, another anonymous author (almost certainly one not earlier than the sixth century) concealing himself under the signature 'Epiphanius of Salamis' briefly seized on Origen's same idea. No other author did ever pay attention to this idea of Origen's whatsoever.

Anastasius of Sinai, *In Hexaemeron*, Book 8, lines 523-6: Καὶ αὐτὴ δὲ ἡ τῶν τεσσάρων ποταμῶν ἀκόλουθος θέσις τὴν τῶν ἁγίων εὐαγγελιστῶν ἀπαράλλακτον προσημαίνει θέσιν καὶ τάξιν. Πρῶτος ὁ Ματθαῖος ὁ λεγόμενος Φεισών, ὅπερ ἑρμηνεύεται στόματος ἀλλοίωσις, Ἑβραΐδι γὰρ διαλέκτῳ τοῦ Ματθαίου τὸ εὐαγγέλιον ἐκθεμένου ἠλλοιώθη καὶ μεθερμηνεύθη ὁ λόγος τοῦ στόματος αὐτοῦ ὑπὸ Λουκᾶ καὶ τοῦ Παύλου εἰς τὴν Ἑλλάδα φωνήν. Δεύτερος προσφόρως ὁ Μᾶρκος ποταμὸς ὁ λεγόμενος Γεών, ἐπειδὴ καὶ τῇ Αἰγύπτῳ ὁ Μᾶρκος εὐαγγελισάμενος ἐκεῖ διὰ τοῦ Πνεύματος τὸν ποταμὸν ἐκ τῆς κοιλίας αὐτοῦ ἐξέβλυσεν ὕδατος ζῶντος τοῦ κηρύγματος. Τρίτος ὁ Λουκᾶς ὁ καλούμενος Τίγρις, ὃς πλατὺς ἑρμηνεύεται. Τί γὰρ ἐν εὐαγγελίοις πλατύτερον ἢ πλουσιώτερον τοῦ κατὰ Λουκᾶν εὐαγγελίου; Παύλῳ γὰρ τῇ πηγῇ τῶν δογμάτων μαθητεύσας ὑπὲρ τὰ ποτάμια ῥεῖθρα ἐκ τῶν τοῦ Παύλου κρουνῶν ἀνέβλυσε. Τέταρτος Ἰωάννης ἀγαπητὸς ἐπιστήθιος ὁ μέγας τοῦ ἡλίου τῆς δικαιοσύνης Εὐφράτης.

Pseudo-Epiphanius of Salamis, *Homilia in Festo Palmarum*, PG.43.432.7-10: ἐν ᾗ [ἑορτῇ τῶν βαΐων] οὐ Φυσών, Γεών, Τίγρις, Εὐφράτης, ἀλλὰ Ματθαῖος, Μᾶρκος, Λουκᾶς, καὶ Ἰωάννης, οἱ τοῦ Χριστοῦ τῆς Ἐκκλησίας ποτίζοντες παράδεισον.

The interpretation of river Phison (Φεισών) is perhaps the only case in which Origen deviated from Philo concerning translation of Hebrew names. Whereas the latter translated this 'mutation of mouth' (στόματος ἀλλοίωσις), Origen rendered it 'mouth of a girl' (στόμα κόρης).

Philo, *Legum Allegoriarum*, 1.74: Φεισὼν ἑρμηνεύεται *στόματος ἀλλοίωσις*. Origen, *selGen*, PG.12.100.11-12: διὸ καὶ τὸν ποταμὸν τὸν Φείσων, ἑρμηνεύεσθαι *στόμα κόρης*, ὡς ἐκ τοῦ Ἐδὲμ ἐκπορευομένου τοῦ ποταμοῦ τοῦ πρώτου.

More strange still, Eusebius who always treated Origen's translations from Hebrew as authoritative, followed neither Philo nor Origen: instead, he advised that Phison means 'multitude' (πληθύς). *Onomasticon*, p. 166.

Despite those renditions, Michael Psellus opted for a still different one, which is somehow a combination of those by Philo and Origen: *Phison* means 'mutation of the tongue' (ἀλλοίωσις γλώσσης). *Theologica*, opusculum 24, lines 12-13.

The only author who followed Origen's translation of *Phison* was the lexicographer Hesychius of Alexandria, (*Lexicon*, letter phi, entry 276), who also identified this with river Ganges: Φεισών. ποταμὸς παραδείσου, ὃ ἑρμηνεύεται στόμα κόρης. παρὰ δὲ Ἕλλησι Γάγγης. See this identification (without the translation of *Phison*) also in Hesychius, *op. cit.* letter gamma, entry 16.

By contrast, Anastasius of Sinai employed Philo's translation and appealed also to the similar locution of Psalm 76:11 (αὕτη ἡ ἀλλοίωσις τῆς δεξιᾶς τοῦ ὑψίστου). *In Hexaemeron*, Book 8, lines 162-3. More strange still is that he repeated this translation later in the same work, yet at a point where he copied Origen's comment that identified the names of the four evangelists with each of the four rivers of Genesis, 2:10-14.

As for *which* river this *Phison* actually was, Hippolytus simply and plainly identified Phison with river Indus. *Chronicon*, 237. Later authors, however, gave rise to confusion and mostly determined that this was but river Ganges. Eusebius, *Onomasticon*, pp. 80; 166. Hesychius of Alexandria, *Lexicon*, letter gamma entry 16; letter phi entry 276. Pseudo-Caesarius (Cassian the Sabaite), *Quaestiones et Responsiones*, chapter 163. Pseudo-Palladius of Helenopolis, *De Gentibus Indiae et Bragmanibus*, 1.1. Leo Diaconus, *Historia*, pp. 129-30. Neophytus Inclusus, *Decem Homiliae*, homily 9.24&33. Epiphanius of Salamis followed, *Ancoratus*, 58.2, but he identified Ganges with river Indus, and so did Pseudo-Caesarius (Cassian the Sabaite), *loc. cit.* and Cosmas Indicopleustes, *Topographia Christiana*, 2.81. The idiosyncratic John Tzetzes added to the confusion, arguing that the river that the Hebrews called Phison was the same as that the people of India called Ganges, the Ethiopians Indus, and the Greeks Danube (!). *Scholia et Glossemata in Chiliades*, chilias 2, lemma 65. Perhaps the most learned report was that of John of Damascus, who realised the mistake of Epiphanius of Salamis and explained that 'river Phison is but river Ganges in India' (τουτέστι Γάγγης ὁ Ἰνδικός). *Expositio Fidei*, 23.

x This appears as continuation from the preceding passage of *Codex Holy Cross 104*, Ἀπεικαστέον δὲ Γηών, etc ... It is pretty clear that Origen means that he had examined this point of 'four rivers' in his commentary on Genesis and had already identified each of those 'rivers' respectively with the four evangelists. The commentary on Genesis was one of his early works, which he wrote almost simultaneously with the first books of the commentary on John and the *First Principles*. See *Princ*, I.3.3. Besides, when he wrote the second book of *De Principiis*, II.3.6, he had already written a comment of Genesis, 1:1. See *Princ*, II.3.6.

xi Origen, *commMatt*, fr. 11 (Klostermann). This is also the text of Origen, *schMatt*, PG.17.289.7-292.2, with only a couple of slight editorial variations.

xii Origen, *commMatt*, fr. 10 (Klostermann).
xiii Jerome, *commMatt*, 2.2.
xiv Cf. below the ensuing quotation from the *schMatt*: Διαφέρει γένεσις καὶ γέννησις.
xv Origen, *schMatt*, PG.17.289.7-292.2.
xvi Origen, *commMatt*, fr. 12 (Klostermann), col. 1.
xvii Origen, *commMatt*, fr. 12 (Klostermann), col. 2.
xviii Cf. Origen, *commMatt*, (Klostermann), part of fr. 3, pp. 14-15: Ἀλλ᾽ ἐπειδὴ ἐκ μόνης τῆς παρθένου τὸ κατὰ σάρκα ὁ Χριστός, αὕτη δὲ ἐκ Δαβὶδ εἶχε τὸ γένος, εἰκότως ἐκ *Δαβίδ* αὐτὸν καὶ αὐτὸς γενεαλογεῖ. Cyril's copying from this is evident. Cyril of Alexandria, *apud Catena in Matthaeum*, p. 10: (Κυρίλλου Ἀρχιεπισκόπου Ἀλεξανδρείας) Μετὰ τὴν μνηστείαν συνέλαβεν, ἵνα δείξῃ ἐξ αὐτοῦ κεκυηκέναι. καὶ ἵνα ἐξ αὐτοῦ γενεαλογηθῇ, καὶ σχῇ καὶ κηδεμόνα ἐν ταῖς ἐπιβουλαῖς.
xix Theodore of Heraclea, *frMatt*, fr. 4, col. 2. Right from the start, it becomes all too evident that he copied from Origen (if indeed Theodore wrote a commentary on Matthew at all). This will appear as a recurring phenomenon during the edition of the present codex.
xx This text runs parallel to Origen's one in his homilies on Luke. Besides, Klostermann (fr. 13II) came upon this being attributed to Origen in one codex, and to Theodore of Heraclea in another one (*frMatt*, fr. 5, J. Reuss). J.A. Cramer found this attributed to Chrysostom (*Catena in Matthaeum*, p. 10). We will come upon texts of Origen being ascribed to Theodore of Heraclea at several points in this volume. The most extreme case is a staunchly Nicene Trinitarian statement of Origen's being ascribed to a such avowed enemy of Nicaea and of Athanasius personally, such as Theodore of Heraclea. See *infra*, folios 239v-240r.
xxi Cf. Origen, *homLuc*, homily 6.34: Τί δήποτε κρίνας ὁ θεὸς ἐκ παρθένου γεννῆσαι τὸν σωτῆρα οὐκ ἐπελέξατο παρθένον ἀμνήστευτον; Origen, *op. cit.* homily, 6.35: καὶ ἔλαθε τὸν ἄρχοντα τοῦ αἰῶνος τούτου ἡ παρθενία Μαρίας. ... Ἐβούλετο δὲ ὁ σωτὴρ καθ᾽ ὅλην τὴν οἰκονομίαν λανθάνειν τὸν διάβολον.
xxii Cf. Exodus, 22:15, and the only parallel to this appears in Theodotus of Ancyra (fourth-fifth century), *In Domini Nostri Jesu Christi Diem Natalem*, 3: διὰ τί οὐκ ἐξ ἀμνηστεύτου ἐτέχθη παρθένου.
xxiii The term συνεσκιασμένος is a Late Antique coinage introduced by Philo referring to 'veiled things' (συνεσκιασμένων πραγμάτων), which call for exegetical interpretation beyond the literal narrative. Cf. *De Ebrietate*, 6; 65&66 (συνεσκιασμένας δυνάμεις); *De Josepho*, 90 (τὰ συνεσκιασμένα τῶν πραγμάτων ἀνακαλύπτειν). Galen explained this term, but he did not actually employ this himself: *Linguarum seu Dictionum Exoletarum Hippocratis Explicatio*, p. 143 (συνηρεφές. ἐπικεκαλυμμένον, συνεσκιασμένον). During the same period, the learned and precious grammarian Julius Pollux (or Naucratites, or Poludeuces) explained this, and adduced a host of synonymous terms. *Onomasticon*, 6.209: ἄδηλον, ἀφανές, ἀσαφές, ἄγνωστον, ἀνέλεγκτον, ἀπόρρητον, ἀνέκπυστον, ἄφθεγκτον, σεσιγημένον, ἀνέκφορον, ἐπικεκρυμμένον, κρυπτόν κρυπτόμενον ἐπικρυπτόμενον διακρυπτόμενον, ἀγνοούμενον, λανθάνον, συνεσκιασμένον συγκεκαλυμμένον, παρακεκαλυμμένον ὑπὸ παραπετάσματι. Shortly later, Sextus Empiricus took this up. *Adversus Dogmaticos 1* (= *Adversus Logicos 1*), 7.26; *Adversus Dogmaticos 2* (= *Adversus Logicos 2*), 8.320. So did Alexander of Aphrodisias, *commTop*, p. 582. It is all but coincidence that Origen was a careful student of all of the foregoing authors. Then, his admirer Porphyry, *Introductio in Tetrabiblum Ptolemaei*, p. 190. After Origen, the term appears in his adherents. Eusebius, *Demonstratio Evangelica*, 7.1.82; *In Isaiam*, 2.50. Gregory of Nyssa, *Liber De Cognitione Dei* (= *Θεογνωσία*), PG.130.293.54. Basil of Caesarea, *De Spiritu Sancto*, 2.4. Pseudo-Basil of Caesarea (*forsan* Cassian

the Sabaite), *Enarratio in Prophetam Isaiam*, 9.231. All of those authors used this term occasionally, indeed rather hesitantly. However, as it happened, once John Chrysostom seized on that, he could not have enough of this, and used it at no less than four dozens of instances. Theodoret applied this moderately (at six points) and so did Nilus of Ancyra and Procopius of Gaza. It is characteristic that, with John of Damascus (*Sacra Parallela*, PG.96.124.17&452.50), use of this term faded and then was abandoned. Consequently, if Theodore of Heraclea did in fact ever use the term συνεσκιασμένος, this could have been but copying from Origen's commentary on Matthew. See also endnote dccclxxiv.

xxiv Cf. Origen, *commMatt*, fr. 13 II (Klostermann); see endnotes xiv-xviii and xxi. Συνυπῆρχε δὲ τῷ Ἰωσὴφ ἡ παρθένος, ἵν' ἡ τοῦ Χριστοῦ λάθῃ γέννησις τούς τε Ἰουδαίους καὶ τὸν διάβολον. See Theodore of Heraclea, *frMatt*, fr. 5. Συνῴκει δὲ ἡ Μαρία τῷ ἑαυτῆς μνηστῆρι διὰ τὸ συνεσκιασμένως γενέσθαι τὴν τοῦ Χριστοῦ γέννησιν, ἵνα καὶ τοὺς Ἰουδαίους λάθῃ καὶ τὸν διάβολον κυοφορούμενος καὶ τικτόμενος ὁ τοῦ θεοῦ λόγος, ὃς *σπέρματος Ἀβραὰμ* ἐπελάβετο [cf. Heb. 2:16] ἄνθρωπος γεγονώς, οὐ μὴν ἀγγέλοις ἑαυτὸν ἀπήκασε τοῖς δυναμένοις καὶ μετασχηματίζεσθαι καὶ ἄλλο ὁρᾶσθαι καὶ φαντάζειν τοὺς ὁρῶντας ἀνθρώπους. ἔμεινε δὲ ἡ παρθένος καὶ μετὰ τὸ τεκεῖν ἀμύητος σωματικῆς συμπλοκῆς καὶ οὐκ ἔγημεν. ὁ γὰρ εὐαγγελιστὴς ἐξηγήσατο τὸ γεγονός, ὃ τὴν τοῦ μὴ γεγονότος ἔμφασιν ἐξ ἀντιδιαστολῆς δηλοῖ. John Chrysostom copied from Origen, too: *Catena in Matthaeum*, p. 10: Συνῴκει δὲ τῷ μνηστῆρι ἡ Μαριὰμ διὰ τὸ συνεσκιασμένως γενέσθαι τὴν γέννησιν.

xxv Cf. Origen, *homLuc*, homily 6.34.

xxvi Origen, *op. cit.* homily, 6.35.

xxvii Jerome appeals to Justin. Origen would have employed this point from Ignatius, whom he commended for this particular exegesis which Origen himself endorsed (*homLuc*, homily 6, p. 34, quoted *infra*, endnote xxx). Thus, when Jerome cited Ignatius, in fact he copied from Origen having cited Ignatius. Besides, Origen used this exegesis in his own commentary on Matthew. See Origen, *commMatt*, fr. 13 I (Klostermann), quoted forthwith *infra*.

xxviii Jerome, *commMatt*, 1.18.

xxix This text keeps on being designated 'Unattributed' (ΑΝΕΠ[ΙΓΡΑΦΟΝ]). In fact, however, this is Origen's, subsequently copied by Eusebius.

xxx Origen, *commMatt*, fr. 13 I (Klostermann). Cf. Origen, *homLuc*, homily, 6, pp. 34-35: Δι' ὃ καλῶς ἐν μιᾷ τῶν μάρτυρός τινος ἐπιστολῶν γέγραπται (τὸν Ἰγνάτιον λέγω, τὸν μετὰ τὸν μακάριον Πέτρον τῆς Ἀντιοχείας δεύτερον ἐπίσκοπον, τὸν ἐν τῷ διωγμῷ ἐν Ῥώμῃ θηρίοις μαχησάμενον) *καὶ ἔλαθε τὸν ἄρχοντα τοῦ αἰῶνος τούτου ἡ παρθενία Μαρίας.* Cf. Ignatius of Antioch, *Epistulae*, epistle 1.19.1. Origen was the first to quote this. After him, the passage (with some wider context) was quoted by the following authors: Eusebius (citing 'a holy man named Ignatius'), *Ad Stephanum*, PG.22.881.28-36. Basil of Caesarea (citing, 'it has been said by someone of old'), *In Sanctam Christi Generationem*, PG.31.1464.34-37. Photius, *Bibliotheca*, Codex 222, p. 195b (citing Ignatius). Nicolas Hydruntinus, *Disputatio Contra Judaeos*, p. 193 (citing Ignatius).

xxxi Origen, *commMatt*, fr. 14 (Klostermann), col. 1.

xxxii Origen, *commMatt*, fr. 14 (Klostermann), col. 2.

xxxiii In view of the preceding Klostermann's fragment 15, this text of the present codex could be only Origen's.

xxxiv Origen, *commMatt*, fr. 15 (Klostermann, citing four codices in which the attribution is made jointly to both Origen and Eusebius). The editor put part of this text in brackets because this runs parallel to that of Eusebius (with slight differences; see Introduction, p. XLIII. Eusebius, *Ad Stephanum*, PG.22.884.30-36). But whom could have Eusebius taken up this from other than Origen? Besides, Cramer's *Catena in Matthaeum* ascribes this to both Origen and Eusebius, and the real source of this exegesis is all too clear. In the present Codex 232, under the designation 'by Eusebius and Cyril' we have virtually the same text being used by Eusebius, from whom in all probability Cyril copied. In another codex, Klostermann found this ascribed to 'the blessed Chrysostom, whom Theodore [of Mopsuestia] followed, too' (ταῦτα μὲν ὁ μακάριος Ἰωάννης, ἕπεται δὲ τῇ τούτου ἑρμηνείᾳ καὶ Θεόδωρος). Once again, we are upon the stunning extent to which Origen's ideas were seized upon by later authors. See discussion in Introduction.

xxxv This text is in effect the same as in the present codex. However, to the extent this is different, we have Origen's original one, and then Eusebius having paraphrased this (quoted below). Besides, no other author did ever consider the difference between the verbs δειγματίσαι and παραδειγματίσαι, which is an analysis very much like Origen.

xxxvi *Catena in Matthaeum*, p. 12. The same in Eusebius, *Ad Stephanum*, PG.22.884.18-53.

xxxvii Origen, *commMatt*, fr. 21 (Klostermann).

xxxviii The ensuing quotation from *Cels*, I.35 confirms that this *anepigraphon* is but Origen's text. He discussed this also in the preceding section, *Cels*, I.34. Authors much later to Origen took up his argument largely using his own words. Pseudo-Athanasius, *Dialogus Athanasii et Zacchaei*, 31-32. Anonymous, *Dialogus cum Judaeis* (e cod. Vatoped. 236), chapter 5, lines 228 ff. Anonymous, *Dialogus Timothei et Aquilae*, 34. Nicolas Hydruntinus, *Disputatio contra Judaeos*, pp. 132-133. See the next endnotes.

xxxix This passage on folios 4r-v is 'Unattributed' (ΑΝΕΠ[ΙΓΡΑΦΟΝ]). But the ensuing part of this should leave no doubt as to its real author.

xl This passage of Isaiah was so translated by Theodotion of Ephesus and Acylas of Pontus, 'both of whome were Jewish proselytes'; the Ebionites endorsed this, arguing that Jesus 'was born from Joseph'. Irenaeus, *Adversus Haereses*, 30, copied by Eusebius, *HE*, 5.8.10, and then by Nicephorus Callistus Xanthopulus, *HE*, 4.14. This was also the translation by 'the Ebionite Symmachus'. Eusebius, *Demonstratio Evangelica*, 7.1.33. Justin Martyr rebutted this in his *Dialogus cum Tryphone*, 43.8; 67.1; 71.3. The claim was rebutted also by Cyril of Alexandria, *In Isaiam*, PG.70.204. However, it was Origen alone who confuted this by reference to the Hebrew text itself, and showing that 'the word ἀαλμά, which the Seventy translated *virgin* whereas others rendered *girl*, in the Deuteronomium is applied to a virgin. Cf. Deut. 22:23: Ἐὰν δὲ γένηται παῖς παρθένος μεμνηστευμένη ἀνδρί. This argument was embraced by Basil of Caesarea, *In Sanctam Christi Generationem*, PG.31.1465.34-1468.12. Subsequently, this was expounded further in a commentary by 'Pseudo-Basil of Caesarea' (in all probability, the newly discovered moderate Origenist of the sixth century Cassian the Sabaite), *Enarratio in Prophetam Isaiam*, 7.202, who characteristically copied from the text of the present codex.

xli The term ἀπειρόγαμος (literally, 'unwedded') designating a virgin woman was introduced into Christian vocabulary by Origen, but in fact this was more ancient, and had been used by Eubulus (Athenian comic poet, fourth century BC). Origen read this in Athenaeus, *Deipnosophistae*, 7.56 (Eubulus, *Fragmenta*, fr. 35), who quoted this verse: νύμφα ἀπειρόγαμος τεύτλῳ περὶ σῶμα καλυπτὰ λευκόχρως παρέσται. This epithet meant a woman that never tested intercourse with a man and was used exclusively about Mary the mother of Jesus, being both a mother and virgin. This is why Greek authors did not care to use this word, except Nonnus in his *Dionysiaca* so styling goddess Athena. Nonnus of Panopolis (fifth century AD), *Dionysiaca*, book 47, lines 415-416: ἀντὶ γὰρ Ἥρης, ἣν Ζυγίην καλέουσιν, ἀπειρογάμοιο θεαίνης ὤμοσεν ἀχράντοιο γαμήλιον ὅρκον Ἀθήνης. Cf. *op. cit.* book 13, line 98.

Origen's adherents embraced this immediately. Eusebius, *Demonstratio Evangelica*, 4.10.20; 7.1.19; 7.1.96; *Ad Stephanum*, PG.22.881.39. Didymus, *commZacch*, 1.309; 2.364; 3.177; 5.125. Gregory of Nyssa, *In Canticum Canticorum*, p. 388; *De Virginitate*, 1.1; *Oratio in Diem Natalem Christi*, PG.46: 1136.19; 1137.45. Gregory of Nazianzus, *Carmina Dogmatica*, col. 460; *Carmina Moralia*, col. 533. Basil of Caesarea, *In Ebriosos*, PG.31.461.2; *Sermones De Moribus*, PG.32.1349.48. Pseudo-Epiphanius of Salamis, *Homilia In Laudes Mariae Deiparae*, PG.43: 488.18; 496.55. Pseudo-Athanasius, *Testimonia e Scriptura*, PG.28.64.36; *Homilia De Passione et Cruce Domini*, PG.28.197.33; *Sermo Contra Omnes Haereses*, PG.28: 505.28; 508.28; 509.2; 512.26; *et passim*. John Chrysostom, *Contra Eos Qui Subintroductas Habent Virgines*, 1; *De Virginitate*, 39; *et passim* (at about two dozens of instances). Theodoret, *Historia Religiosa*, Vita 9.12 (not in relation to Mary). Cyril of Alexandria, *Quod Unus Sit Christus*, p. 724; *Epistulae Paschales*, PG.77.980.10. Pseudo-Basil of Seleucia, *De Vita et Miraculis Sanctae Theclae*, 1.7. Procopius of Gaza, *Catena in Canticum Canticorum*, p. 1692. Justinian, *Contra Monophysitas*, 120. Oecumenius, *Commentarius in Apocalypsin*, p. 41. Pseudo-Basil of Caesarea (*forsan* Cassian the Sabaite), *Enarratio in Prophetam Isaiam*, 7.202. Cassian the Sabaite (Pseudo-Caesarius), *Quaestiones et Responsiones*, 36; 185; 218. John of Damascus, *Contra Nestorianos*, 2; *Oratio Prima in Dormitionem Sanctae Dei Genitricis Mariae*, 14; *Oratio Tertia in Dormitionem Sanctae Dei Genitricis Mariae*, 2; *Laudatio Sanctae Martyris Barbarae*, 4. This was also used abundantly in Byzantine ecclesiastical hymnography.

xlii Origen, *Cels*, I.35.

xliii Alluding to 'Emmanuel' meaning 'God is with us'. Matt. 1:23. Cf. Origen, *Princ*, IV.1.5 (*Philocalia*, I.5); *Cels*, I.34: I.35. Both the argument and the characteristic vocabulary are exactly the same as in Origen's *Cels*, I.35. This is natural, since Origen wrote *Contra Celsum* well before the commentary on Matthew. Eusebius followed Origen's analysis both in content and vocabulary. Cf. *In Isaiam*, 1.48: μὴ ἐξ ἀνδρὸς γὰρ καὶ γυναικός, ἀλλ' ἐξ ἀδιαφθόρου νεάνιδος καὶ ἐξ ἀπειρογάμου παρθένου τεχθήσεσθαι, σφόδρα ἀναγκαίως ἐν τούτοις αὐτὸς ὁ κύριος, οὐκέτι τῷ Ἄχαζ οὐδὲ τῷ οἴκῳ Ἰούδα, ἀλλ' αὐτῷ μόνῳ τῷ προφήτῃ τὸ μυστήριον ἀνακαλύπτει τῆς ἀπορρήτου γενέσεως τοῦ *Ἐμμανουὴλ καί πως ἡ παρθένος ἐν γαστρὶ λήψεται καὶ τέξεται υἱόν*. Cf. Pseudo-Basil of Caesarea (*forsan* Cassian the Sabaite), *Enarratio in Prophetam Isaiam*, 7.202. This author copied from Origen abundantly: Ἀνθίστανται οἱ Ἰουδαῖοι τῇ ἐκδόσει τῶν Ἑβδομήκοντα, λέγοντες μὴ κεῖσθαι παρὰ τῷ Ἑβραίῳ τὸ *Ἡ παρθένος*, ἀλλ' *Ἡ νεᾶνις*, ὡς δυναμένης νεάνιδος ὀνομάζεσθαι τῆς ἀκμαζούσης καθ' ἡλικίαν, οὐχὶ δὲ τῆς ἀπειρογάμου γυναικός. Πρὸς οὓς ῥᾳδία καὶ αὐτόθεν ἡ ἀπάντησις. Εἰ γὰρ σημεῖόν ἐστι τεραστίου τινὸς καὶ παρηλλαγμένου τὴν κοινὴν συνήθειαν τῶν ἀνθρώπων ἐπίδειξις, τί θαυμαστὸν ἦν, μίαν τῶν πολλῶν γυναῖκα, ἀνδρὶ συνοικοῦσαν, μητέρα γενέσθαι παιδίου; Πῶς δ' ἂν καὶ τὸ ἀπὸ θελήματος σαρκὸς γεννηθὲν Ἐμμανουὴλ προσηγορεύετο; Ὥστε, εἰ μὲν σημεῖόν ἐστι τὸ διδόμενον, παράδοξος ἔστω καὶ ἡ γέννησις. Εἰ δὲ κοινὸς ὁ τρόπος τῆς γεννήσεως τοῦ παιδίου, μήτε *σημεῖον* [Luke, 2:12] λεγέσθω, μήτε *Ἐμμανουὴλ* [Matt. 1:23; Isaiah, 7:14] προσαγορευέσθω. Ὥστε εἰ μὴ παρθένος ἡ τεκοῦσα, ποῖον τοῦτο σημεῖον; Καὶ εἰ μὴ θειοτέρα ἢ κατὰ τοὺς πολλοὺς ἡ γέννησις, πῶς ἡ τοῦ Ἐμμανουὴλ παρουσία; Ὅτι μέντοι ἡ νεᾶνις ἐπὶ παρθένων ἰδίως ὠνομάσθη, δῆλον ἐκ τῶν ἐν τῷ Δευτερονομίῳ οὕτως εἰρημένων· ...

xliv See endonote xlvii and Origen, *commMatt*, fr. 22 (Klostermann), quoted forthwith.

xlv See also Origen passages supporting his view from *commMatt*, 12.34, and *schLuc*, PG.17.341.25-29, which are quoted in endnote mdccxlvi (p. 558). The author of a polemic treatise argued for ἕως meaning 'always' by using exactly the same scriptural instances. Anonymous, *Dialogus cum Judaeis* (*e cod. Vatoped. 236*), chapter 11, lines 81-102.

xlvi However, LXX has it κόραξ, not περιστερά, and reads thus: καὶ ἀπέστειλεν τὸν κόρακα τοῦ ἰδεῖν εἰ κεκόπακεν τὸ ὕδωρ. καὶ ἐξελθὼν οὐχ ὑπέστρεψεν ἕως τοῦ ξηρανθῆναι τὸ ὕδωρ ἀπὸ τῆς γῆς ('And he sent forth a raven; and it went forth and returned not until the water was dried from off the earth'). Instead, Origen's quotation reads, 'the dove did not return to Noah until the water was dried out' (οὐκ ἀνέστρεψεν ἡ περιστερὰ πρὸς τὸν Νῶε, ἕως τοῦ ξηρανθῆναι τὸ ὕδωρ). Where Origen read this variant is impossible to determine (perhaps it was a paraphrased quotation from memory), but it is illuminative that this occurs in some authors making the same point, namely, 'until' (ἕως) does not signify a terminus. See *Catena in Matthaeum*, p. 13 (passage ascribed jointly to Origen, Eusebius, and Isidore of Pelusium); Photius, *Epistulae et Amphilochia*, epistle 30; *Suda*, letter epsilon, entry 1904. See Origen's exegesis of the conjunction 'until' (ἕως) also at the end of this commentary (folio 240v) in relation to Matt. 28:20 ('And behold, I am with you always, until the end of the age').

xlvii Origen, *commMatt*, fr. 22 (Klostermann). In the *Catena in Matthaeum*, p. 13, this text is jointly ascribed to 'Eusebius, Origen, Isidore of Pelusium' (see also, Isidore of Pelusium, *Epistulae De Interpretatione Divinae Scripturae*, Book 1, epistle 18). Likewise, in the same chain, p. 12, the attribution is made to 'Basil and Chrysostom': *Καὶ οὐκ ἐγίνωσκεν αὐτὴν ἕως οὗ ἔτεκε τὸν υἱόν αὐτῆς τὸν πρωτότοκον.* (Βασιλείου. Τοῦ Χρυσοστόμου) Τοῦτο ἀκούοντες μὴ ὑποπτεύσωμεν διὰ τὸ *ἕως*, ὅτι μετὰ ταῦτα αὐτὴν ἔγνω. τὸ γὰρ *ἕως* ἔθος ἐστὶ τῇ γραφῇ πολλάκις τιθέναι δὲ εἰς τὸ διηνεκές. οἷον, οὐχ ὑπέστρεψεν ὁ κόραξ, εἰς τὴν κιβωτόν, ἕως οὗ ἐξηράνθη ἡ γῆ. καίτοιγε οὐδὲ μετὰ ταῦτα ὑπέστρεψεν.

The point introduced by Origen (i.e. the scriptural use of the conjunction ἕως as idiomatic and not always meaning 'until such time as') was embraced by subsequent theologians. In fact, this came to be established as a standard exegesis appealing to the same scriptural passages as Origen himself did (namely, Psalm 109:1, also 1 Cor. 15:25 paraphrased; Isaiah, 46:4). Didymus, *apud Catena in Acta*, p. 66; *frPs*(*al*), fr. 1054. Theodoret, *Interpretatio in Psalmos*, PG.80.1768.47-1769.9: Τὸ δὲ *ἕως*, οὐ χρόνου σημαντικόν, ἀλλ' ἰδίωμα τῆς θείας Γραφῆς ... Οὐδὲ γὰρ ἐνταῦθα τὸ *ἄχρις οὗ* χρόνου δηλωτικόν. Likewise, *In Epistulas Sancti Pauli*, PG.82.356.26 ff. Theodore of Mopsuestia, *Expositio in Psalmos*, on Psalm 56:2d. Anonymous, *Dialogus cum Judaeis*, chapter 11, lines 80 ff. Severian of Gabala, *Fragmenta in Epistulam i ad Corinthios*, p. 274. John Chrysostom, *apud Catena in Epistulam i ad Corinthios*, p. 306. Pseudo-John Chrysostom, *Eclogae i-xlviii ex Diversis Homiliis*, PG.63.830.51-831.8. Once again, a point made by Origen became a lemma in the *Suda*, letter epsilon, entries 1904 & 1905. Nicolas of Methone (*Orationes*, oration 5, p. 304) claimed that 'ἕως does not always mean *until*', that is, 'it does not indicate a temporal terminus'. He appealed to this as being an exegesis that had been advanced 'by the holy fathers, especially the coryphaeus one, Basil the great' (τὸ δὲ *ἄχρις οὗ* καὶ τὸ *ἕως*, ὅτι μὴ πανταχοῦ χρονικοῦ πέρατός εἰσι παραστασικά, φθάνουσιν ἱκανῶς οἱ θεῖοι Πατέρες ἡρμηνευκότες, καὶ μάλιστα ὁ κορυφαῖος ἐν τούτοις ὁ μέγας Βασίλειος). Cf. Basil of Caesarea echoing Origen's exegesis. *In Sanctam Christi Generationem*, PG.31.1428.29-40 (quoted *infra*, folio 240v). Photius reviewing a book by Ephraem of Amida (Patriarch of Antioch, 526-44), noted that the author advanced the same exegesis and argued that this had been sustained by Gregory of Nazianzus and Leo of Rome. Naturally, Photius went along with that. *Bibliotheca*, Codex 229, p. 263b: Ἀλλ' ὁ μὲν ἱερὸς συγγραφεὺς [Ephraem of Amida] δείκνυσι τὸ ἐπίρρημα παρὰ τοῖς ἱεροῖς λογίοις οὐ χρονικὴν μόνον διάνοιαν ὑποσημαῖνον, ἀλλ' ἐν πολλοῖς πολλάκις καὶ τὸ ἀπέραντον. (i.e. *ἕως* means also limitless future time).

More importantly, Origen's interpretation of ἕως meaning indefinite time, not terminus, was upheld in relation to interpretation of Matt. 1:25 (Joseph 'knew' Mary 'not, until she had given birth to a son'). Cf. Photius, *Epistulae et Amphilochia*, epistle 30: καὶ *ἰδοὺ ἐγὼ μεθ' ὑμῶν εἰμι πάλιν ὁ σωτὴρ τοῖς μαθηταῖς φησιν, ἕως τῆς συντελείας τοῦ αἰῶνος.* καὶ δῆλον ὡς ἐνταῦθα τὸ ἕως οὐ χρονικόν τι μεθόριον καὶ πέρας παρεισάγει, μέγεθος δὲ θείων πραγμάτων ἡ λέξις συμπαραδηλοῦσα εἰς ἀπεριόριστον παράτασιν τὸν νοῦν τῶν ἐντυγχανόντων ἀναπέμπει. ... καὶ ἄλλα μυρία, δι' ὧν εὔδηλον καὶ τοῖς λίαν ἐθελοκωφοῦσιν καθίσταται ὡς ἀντὶ τοῦ *διηνεκῶς* καὶ [*εἰς*] *τὸν αἰῶνα* ἡ λέξις παραλαμβάνεται. ... τότε διαπορείτωσαν καὶ εἰ μετὰ τὸν ἄρρητον καὶ παρθένον τόκον ἀνδρὸς ὁμιλίαν ἡ παρθένος ἐμελέτησεν. Also, in relation to interpretation of Matt. 18:34 (see folio 148r: Τὸ δὲ *ἕως οὗ ἀποδῷ πᾶν τὸ ὀφειλόμενον*, τουτέστι διηνεκῶς αὐτὸν παρέδωκεν εἰς τὸ βασανίζεσθαι. οὐ γὰρ ἐδύνατο ἀποδοῦναί ποτε), Philagathus copied Origen's exegesis while blaming Origen by name for being a heretic (which was an irony that happened all too often with many authors, as I have argued several times). Cf. Philagathus (Philip Cerameus, twelfth century), *Homiliae*, homily 2.15: *Καὶ παραδίδωσιν αὐτὸν τοῖς βασανισταῖς, ἕως ἂν ἀποδῷ πᾶν τὸ ὀφειλόμενον.* Βασανισταὶ οἱ ἐπὶ τὸ κολάζειν τεταγμένοι ἀσυμπαθεῖς ἄγγελοι· τὸ μέντοι *ἕως ἀποδῷ πᾶν τὸ ὀφειλόμενον* οὐ χρονικὴν σημασίαν δηλοῖ, κατὰ τὴν μυθώδη Ὠριγένους ἀποκατάστασιν, ἀλλὰ τὸ ἀόριστον καὶ ἀτελεύτητον τῆς κολάσεως. ἐπειδὴ γὰρ ἀμήχανον πᾶν τὸ ὀφειλόμενον ἀποτῖσαι τὸν κολαζόμενον, ἀνάγκη τοῦτον ἀϊδίως κολάζεσθαι.

xlviii Origen, *schLuc*, PG.17.341.25-29, commenting on the particle *ἕως* (= until, till) as in Matt. 16:28; Mark, 9:1; Luke, 9:27, in apposition with Matt. 20:20.

xlix The term ὑποστικτέον means 'put a comma at this point', and no author other than Origen could have used this word in a Christian commentary. For this was introduced by Alexander of Aphrodisias, which is but only one of the numerous terms that Origen took up from his predecessor, as I have shown in both this and previous books of mine. The term ὑποστικτέον always remained characteristic of commentators who were exceptionally apt to recognise even the slightest nuances involved in a text, which is why only a couple of Christian authors but a vast multitude of anonymous commentators used this. Cf. Alexander of Aphrodisias, *commMetaph*, pp. 692; 696; 526; 745. Porphyry, *Quaestionum Homericarum ad Iliadem Pertinentium Reliquiae*, on *Ilias*, VI.150. Then, Simplicius, *commCael*, pp. 316; 389; *commPhys*, p. 368. John Philoponus, *commAnalPost*, pp. 161; 261; *commGenCorr*, p. 122; *commGenAnim*, pp. 22; 103; 173; 179; 204; 214; 225; *commAnim*, p. 59; *commPhys*, p. 75. Michael Psellus, *commPhys*, 1.24. Michael of Ephesus, *In Parva Naturalia Commentaria*, p. 51; *In Libros De Partibus Animalium Commentaria*, pp. 9; 36; *In Libros De Animalium Motione Commentarium*, p. 127; *In Librum De Animalium Incessu Commentarium*, p. 137; *In Aristotelis Sophisticos Elenchos Commentarius*, pp. 169; 184; 196 (this work also appeared spuriously under the name of Alexander of Aphrodisias; see Bibliography).

Naturally, Aristotle's commentators used the term after Alexander of Aphrodisias. However, this became also a coin of later anonymous commentators of other authors, such as Homer, Aeschylus, Euripides, Demosthenes, Plato, and Thucydides.

Despite this copious Greek usage, of Christians only a couple used it, namely, Didymus, *Fragmenta in Proverbia*, PG.39.1624.29; Theodoret, *Interpretatio in Psalmos*, PG.80: 892.14; 932.30; *In Epistulas Sancti Pauli*, PG.82: 173.12 (& *Catena in Epistulam ad Romanos*, p. 393); 400.38; 540.39.

l Jerome, *commMatt*, 1.24-25.

li Jerome, *commMatt*, 12.49. Origen mentioned 'some who, drawing on tradition, namely, the Gospel of Peter or the Book [sc. *Protevangelium*] of James, say that the brothers of Jesus were Joseph's sons by a previous wife.' Origen recognised that this meant to maintain 'the virginity of Mary to the end', but he did not express this as a view of his own. See *commMatt*, 10.17. Nevertheless, the text of *frJohn*, fr. 31, asserts that those were brothers by a deceased previous wife of Joseph.

lii The expression θεία σύλληψις ('divine conception') was introduced by Origen; *homLuc*, homily 6, p. 33; homily 17, p. 106. Up until the fifth century, only Basil of Caesarea apparently used this once, if indeed the text is really his own (which I doubt). *Epistulae*, epistle 260.9.

liii Cf. Origen, *frJohn*, fr. 32: καὶ μάλιστα ἐξηγριωμένων καὶ φονώντων κατ' αὐτοῦ. καὶ αὐτοὶ γοῦν οἱ Ἰουδαῖοι καταπλαγέντες ἐπὶ τῷ τολμηθέντι φασὶν ἐν τοῖς ἑξῆς πρὸς αὐτόν. Gregory of Nyssa, *De Opificio Hominis*, p. 220: ἐπὶ τῆς Ἰουδαίας ἐν μέσῳ τῶν φονώντων γενέσθαι. John Chrysostom, *In Joannem*, PG.59.273.25: φονώντων τῶν Ἰουδαίων. *In Epistulam ad Romanos*, PG.60.416.38: φονώντων Ἰουδαίων. *In Epistulam ad Galatas*, PG.61.640.24-25: φονώντων Ἰουδαίων καὶ μαινομένων. Theodoret, *Interpretatio in xiv Epistulas Sancti Pauli*, PG.82.169.23: φονῶντας Ἰουδαίους. Cyril of Alexandria, *In Joannem*, v. 1, p. 400: φονῶντας παραιτεῖται τοὺς Ἰουδαίους. *Op. cit.* v. 1, p. 656: φονῶσαν τὴν τῶν Ἰουδαίων διάνοιαν. *Op. cit.* v. 3, p. 110: τοῦ τῶν Ἰουδαίων θυμοῦ, καὶ φονώντων ἐκθύμως.

liv The turn, θεομάχοι μᾶλλον πρὸς μιαιφονίαν, belongs to Origen, who first introduced this. Cf. *schMatt*, PG.17.309.28-30: Ὀργιζομένου γὰρ ἦν τὸ σκότος ἐκεῖνο, καὶ δεῖγμα τοῦ μέλλοντος λαβεῖν τοὺς θεομάχους τε καὶ μιαιφόνους. As it normally happened, Gregory of Nyssa followed his creative flare. *Oratio Catechetica*, 29: οὐδὲ ἡ τῶν Αἰγυπτίων θεομαχία, οὐδὲ ἡ τῶν Ἀσσυρίων ὑπερηφανία, οὐδὲ ἡ τῶν Ἰουδαίων κατὰ τῶν ἁγίων τοῦ Θεοῦ μιαιφονία. Eusebius, *De Laudibus Constantini*, 5.2: τὰ λυμαντικὰ συνομαρτεῖ βλαστήματα, βίος ἄσωτος, πλεονεξίαι, μιαιφονίαι, θεομαχίαι, δυσσέβειαι. Cyril of Alexandria, *commProphXII*, v. 1, p. 665: θεομάχος τε γὰρ καὶ εἰδωλολάτρης, βδελυρός τε καὶ βέβηλος ἦν, καὶ τοῖς τῆς μιαιφονίας ἐγκλήμασιν οὐ μετρίως ἐνισχημένος. Then, Photius, *Bibliotheca*, Codex 277, p. 518b; *Homiliae*, homily 8, p. 83; *Epistulae et Amphilochia*, epistle 161, lines 107-108. George Cedrenus, *Compendium Historiarum*, v. 1, p. 374.

lv Origen used the term Θεοτόκος for Mary a good 180 years before this was sanctioned by the council of Ephesus (431). See *frLuc*, frs. 26; 41b; 80; *schLuc*, PG.17.321.8; *selDeut*, PG.12.813.8. The excerpted text in the *Catena in Lucam*, p. 26, is ascribed to Origen, too: καὶ ᾔδει μὲν ἡ παναγία Θεοτόκος μὴ τέκνον αὐτὸν εἶναι τοῦ Ἰωσήφ, ἀλλὰ διὰ τὴν ὑποψίαν τῶν Ἰουδαίων νομιζόντων ἐκ πορνείας αὐτὸν γεγενῆσθαι. And yet, Justinian accused him of positing Jesus as 'a bare man'. Justinian, *Edictum contra Origenem*, p. 110 & ACO, *Synodus Constantinopolitana et Hierosolymitana anno 536*, tome 3, p. 210: Ἐκ τοῦ δευτέρου λόγου τοῦ Περὶ ἀρχῶν βιβλίου, ὅτι ἄνθρωπον ψιλὸν λέγει τὸν κύριον. However, Origen's references beyond the present codex against this allegation abound. *frJohn*, fr. 33: τὸ γὰρ ἐκ πράξεων καὶ λόγων ἐπίστασθαί τινας καὶ ἀνθρώπῳ ψιλῷ δυνατόν. ἀλλ' Ἰησοῦς, οὐ ψιλὸς ἄνθρωπος ὤν, ἀλλὰ θεὸς γενόμενος ἄνθρωπος, πάντα οἶδεν, τὸ κρυπτὸν καταλαμβάνων τοῦ νοῦ. *homLuc*, homily 19, p. 115: πρὸ γὰρ ἐτῶν δώδεκα ψιλὸς ἄνθρωπος οὐ χωρεῖ πληρότητα σοφίας. *frLuc*, fr. 56: ἔτι ἡ μὲν Ἐλισάβετ *υἱὸν* γεννᾷ, ἡ δὲ Μαρία *τὸν υἱὸν* μετὰ τοῦ ἄρθρου, ἵνα ἐμφατικῶς ὁ λόγος διδάξῃ, ὅτι αὕτη μὲν ψιλὸν ἄνθρωπον υἱὸν ἐγέννησεν, ἐκείνη δὲ οὐ ψιλὸν μόνον, ἀλλὰ σαρκωθέντα τὸν υἱὸν τοῦ θεοῦ. *Op. cit.* fr. 98: *ἐδείκνυεν αὐτῷ τὰς βασιλείας τοῦ κόσμου*, ... ὅθεν ὡς ψιλὸν ἄνθρωπον προέτρεπεν ἐπὶ τοῦτο, βουλόμενος καὶ αὐτοῦ ὡς καὶ τῶν λοιπῶν περιγενέσθαι. *frPs*, on Psalm 109:1-6: καὶ Ἰουδαίων γὰρ ψιλὸν ἄνθρωπον αὐτὸν ὑπολαμβανόντων, ὡς ἐκ Δαυὶδ ἔδειξεν, αὐτὸς Κύριος ὢν διὰ τὴν θεότητα ἐν εὐαγγελίοις. Theodoret attested that this doctrine was urged by Ebion and then by Marcellus and his pupil Photinus. *Haereticarum Fabularum Compendium*, PG.83.337.41-47: Τὸ δὲ δεύτερον, τοὺς τἀναντία τούτοις ἐπιδείξει τεθρησκευκότας. οἵ μίαν μὲν ἀρχὴν εἶναι τῶν ὅλων συνωμολόγησαν, ψιλὸν δὲ ἄνθρωπον τὸν Κύριον προσηγόρευσαν. Ταύτης δὲ τῆς αἱρέσεως ἦρξε μὲν Ἐβίων, μέχρι δὲ Μαρκέλλου καὶ Φωτεινοῦ τὰς διαφόρους ἐπινοίας ἐδέξατο. Nevertheless, the doctrine of Jesus being 'a bare man' was identified with Paul of Samosata. Socrates Scholasticus wrote that Eusebius, in his book *Against Marcellus*, rebutted this doctrine, too. *HE*, 2.20. Several later authors laid the same heresy also at the door of Nestorius. However, Socrates Scholasticus disputed that this is what Nestorius really believed. *Op. cit.* 7.32.

lvi Cf. Origen, *homLuc*, homily 16, p. 96: Εἰς πατέρα δὲ τὸν Ἰωσὴφ θαυ‹μαστῶς τίθησι, οὐ πατέρα› κηρυκεύ‹ων τοῦτο εἰπ›ών, ἀλλ' ἐπ‹εὶ προ›φητεύει περὶ τοῦ παιδίου, εὐλογήσας τὸν πατέρα καὶ τὴν μητέρα. M. Rauer emended ἐπ‹εὶ προ›φητεύει to ἐπ‹ιπρο›φητεύει, which is not a Greek word and makes no sense at all.

lvii Cf. Origen, *frLuc*, fr. 74a: Ἤδει μὲν ἡ παρθένος μὴ τέκνον αὐτὸν εἶναι τοῦ Ἰωσήφ, ἀλλ' εἰς πατέρα τούτῳ τὸν ἑαυτῆς ἐγκρίνει μνηστῆρα διὰ τὴν τῶν Ἰουδαίων ὑποψίαν, οἰομένων αὐτὸν ἐκ πορνείας γεγεννῆσθαι. Cyril of Alexandria, *commLuc*, PG.72.508.51-509.2. Ἤδει μὲν γὰρ ἡ μήτηρ αὐτοῦ μὴ τέκνον εἶναι αὐτὸν τοῦ Ἰωσήφ. ἀλλὰ διὰ τὴν ὑποψίαν τῶν Ἰουδαίων τοῦτό φησι. He copied from Origen once again, since the selfsame passage (in the *Catena in Lucam*, p. 26) is ascribed to Origen: καὶ ᾔδει μὲν ἡ παναγία Θεοτόκος μὴ τέκνον αὐτὸν εἶναι τοῦ Ἰωσήφ, ἀλλὰ διὰ τὴν ὑποψίαν τῶν Ἰουδαίων νομιζόντων ἐκ πορνείας αὐτὸν γεγενῆσθαι.

lviii Eusebius, *Commentaria in Psalmos*, PG.23.769.20-22: Ὁρῶν δὲ πολλοὺς διαφθονουμένους τῇ κατὰ Θεὸν αὐτοῦ προκοπῇ καὶ βασκαίνοντας αὐτοῦ τῇ σωτηρίᾳ τῆς ψυχῆς.

lix See *supra*, folio 1v.

lx This passage of Ignatius of Antioch (*Epistulae*, 1.191) was quoted only by Eusebius, *Ad Stephanum*, PG.22.881.32-36. During the next millennium, the only author who did so was Nicolas Hydruntinus, *Disputatio Contra Judaeos*, p. 193.

lxi Although unattributed in the present codex, this has appeared as Theodore of Heraclea's *frMatt*, fr. 7 (Reuss). The rest of Reuss' text reads thus: Ὁ δὲ ἀστὴρ διὰ τοῦτο ἀπεκρύβη πρὸς καιρόν, ἵνα ἀναγκασθῶσιν οἱ μάγοι ἐρωτῆσαι *ποῦ ἐστιν ὁ τεχθεὶς βασιλεὺς τῶν Ἰουδαίων* καὶ γένηται τοῦτο πᾶσι κατάδηλον. But see discussion of this point in Introduction, about the notion of 'seventy weeks'; pp. XXXII-XXXIII.

lxii Jerome (*commMatt*, 14b) translated: "stella quam futuram Balaam (cuius successors errant) vaticinio noverant" (note by Klosterman, p. 26).

lxiii Origen, *commMatt*, fr. 24 (Klostermann).

lxiv Origen, *commMatt*, fr. 27 (Klostermann). This is the same idea expressed by Origen in his *selNum*, PG.12.577.36.-580.4: *Καὶ ἦλθεν ὁ Κύριος πρὸς αὐτόν* (cf. Num. 22:20). Κατὰ ἀλήθειαν θεία δύναμις παρεγένετο πρὸς Βαλαὰμ οὐ κληθεῖσα ὑπ' αὐτοῦ. Παρεγένετο οὖν, ἵνα ἀποτροπιασμὸν ποιήσῃ τῶν καλουμένων ὑπὸ τοῦ Βαλαὰμ δαιμόνων καὶ τὰς θείας προρρήσεις οἰκονομήσῃ.

lxv Jerome, *commMatt*, 2.2.

lxvi In the present codex this is 'Unattributed', but this text is a known one as Origen, *commMatt*, fr. 24 (Klostermann, quoted immediately below). Moreover, this runs parallel to Origen's tenor, vocabulary, and ideas (reference to Balaam as ancestors of those Magi) that are involved in this section, which did not enjoy much currency, thus making Origen's distinctive mark upon this. Origen, *adNum*, PG.17.21.38-24.5 (on Num. 24:17): *Καὶ ἀναστήσεται ἄνθρωπος ἐξ Ἰσραήλ.* Φασὶ τὸν Βαλαὰμ ἔχειν φοιτητὰς τῇ τέχνῃ, μαθητεύσαντας αὐτῷ τῇ μαγικῇ. καὶ δόξαν περὶ αὐτοῦ ἔχοντας, ἀναγράψασθαι τὰς προφητείας αὐτοῦ, καὶ καταλιπεῖν, ἐν αἷς καὶ τὸ *Ἀνατελεῖ ἄστρον.* Ἢ καὶ ἐκ τῆς πατρικῆς παραδόσεως τοῦτο καὶ διαδοχῆς παραλαβόντες οἱ Μάγοι, ἐπὶ τὴν Βηθλεὲμ παρεγένοντο. Cf. Pseudo-John Chrysostom, *In Natale Domini Nostri Jesu Christi*, PG.61.766.46-55: Οὗτοι οὖν οἱ μάγοι ἐκ τοῦ γένους τοῦ Βαλαὰμ τοῦ προφήτου ὁρμώμενοι, κατακολουθήσαντες αὐτοῦ ταῖς βίβλοις καὶ ταῖς προφητείαις, καὶ νοήσαντες ὅτι, ὅτε *ἀνατελεῖ ἄστρον*, τότε ἀναστήσεται καὶ ὁ ἄνθρωπος, δηλονότι ὁ Βασιλεὺς τῶν Ἰουδαίων, ὅστις οὐ μόνον τοὺς ἀρχηγοὺς Μωὰβ συντρίψει, ἀλλὰ καὶ πάσας τοῦ διαβόλου τὰς βασιλείας λεπτυνεῖ καὶ λικμήσει κατὰ τὸν Δανιήλ, παρετήρουν τὸν καιρόν. καὶ θεωρήσαντες τὸν ἀστέρα ξένον παρὰ τοὺς ἄλλους ἀνατείλαντα, ἔγνωσαν αὐτὸν εἶναι τὸν πάλαι προφητευθέντα. John of Damascus, *Homilia in Nativitatem Domini*, 6 (quoting also Num. 24:17): Ὅνπερ ἰδόντες οἱ μάγοι, Περσῶν βασιλεῖς ἀστρονόμοι, τοῦ Βαλαὰμ ἀπόγονοι, ἐκπλαγέντες τῇ τοῦ ἀστέρος σφοδροτάτῃ ἐκλάμψει, τὴν τοῦ Βαλαὰμ προφητείαν ἀναλαβόντες, τὸ *ἀνατελεῖ ἄστρον ἐξ Ἰακὼβ καὶ ἀναστήσεται ἄνθρωπος ἐξ Ἰσραὴλ καὶ θραύσει τοὺς ἀρχηγοὺς Μωάβ*, ὡς ἅτε βασιλέα μέγαν ὑπονοήσαντες τῇ τοῦ ἀσυνήθους ἀστέρος μεγαλοπρεπεστάτῃ ἐκλάμψει κυρίαν αὐτὸν κρατεῖν μεγάλην πάσης τῆς γῆς καὶ τῆς οἰκουμένης ἐθέσπισαν.

lxvii This short passage (in codex, eight lines, comm. on Matt. 2:2: εἴδομεν γὰρ αὐτοῦ τὸν ἀστέρα) is attributed to Theodore of Heraclea, designated as Theodore of Heraclea, *frMatt*, fr. 8 (Reuss). However, Klostermann's fragment 24, which I quote just below, reveals that the text is Origen's. Cf. the beginning of Theodore of Heraclea, *frMatt*, fr. 8 (Ὡς κομῆται δὲ καὶ τοιαῦτα περὶ τὸν αἰθέρα καινόν τι τῷ βίῳ σημαίνουσιν, οὕτω πολὺ πλέον παράδοξος ὁ ἀστὴρ ἐφαίνετο τοῦ μεγάλου βασιλέως Ἰησοῦ) which is the phrase in Origen's fragment 24, quoted forthwith. Besides, the idea that the star of Bethlehem was 'a comet' was one that Origen set forth at a later stage of his life (namely, in *Cels*, I.59), that is, before he wrote the commentary on Matthew. There is no point in wondering whether Theodore 'endorsed Origen's theory', or not: the passage is simply Origen's, as it happens with almost all (probably, *all*) the 'fragments attributed to Theodore of Heraclea. Just for the record: Origen dismissed astrology and argued that heavenly bodies are not causes of events in nature and human history. In *Cels* (VI.80), he wrote that 'the duplicitous art of astrology has devoured men' (ἡ ἀπατηλὸς γενεθλιαλογία νενέμηται τοὺς ἀνθρώπους). Nevertheless, he maintained that heavenly bodies are 'indicators' (σημαντικοί) of such events. *commGen*, PG.12: 61; 69; 73; (*Philocalia*, 23: 1; 6; 14; 16). This section of Origen's work was quoted also by Eusebius, *Praeparatio Evangelica*, 6.11. Didymus, the other ardent follower of Origen, endorsed the theory, too. *In Genesim*, cod. p. 75: Σημαντικοὶ οὖν εἰσιν οἱ ἀστέρες, οὐ ποιητικοί. Likewise, *op. cit.* cod. p. 24. A mild, if not detailed, criticism of this theory was developed by Diodore of Tarsus, in his book *Against Fate* (*Κατὰ Εἱμαρμένης*), which we learn from Photius who reviewed this treatise. Upon describing the ideas of 'those who maintained this theory', Diodore largely quoted from Origen's work, but he did not cite his name. Photius, *Bibliotheca*, Codex 223, p. 220a.

lxviii The epithet ἀλλόκοτος never appears in Theodore of Heraclea's alleged 'fragments'. By contrast, see Origen, *commMatt*, 15.3: καὶ ταραττούσας τὸ φανταστικὸν ἀλλόκοτα φαντασιούμενον ἀπὸ τῆς τοιᾶσδε ὕλης. *Cels*, V.61 (& *Philocalia*, 16.3): οἱ τὰ ἀλλόκοτα ἀναπλάσματα καὶ μὴ ἀρέσκοντα τοῖς τῆς ἀπὸ τοῦ Ἰησοῦ διαδοχῆς ἐπεισαγαγόντες εἶεν ἂν Χριστιανοί. *Op. cit.* VI.27: ἑαυτῷ τινα ἐκτίθεται ἀλλόκοτα. *Op. cit.* VIII.60: ἀλλοκότοις μελῳδίαις ἀγομένων. *Homiliae in Exodum*, p. 222: ἀλλοκότους γάρ τινας διαγράφουσι δαίμονας.

lxix See discussion of why the ensuing passage should be attributed to Origen. Introduction, pp. XXXVII-XXXIX.

lxx This argument was used also by Arethas, *Scripta Minora*, opus 33, p. 275: εἰ γάρ τις ἐπὶ τὸν Ζοροβάβελ ἀπευθύνει τὸν λόγον, πλανᾶται. οὐ γὰρ ἐν Βηθλεὲμ ἐγεννήθη, ἀλλ' ἐν Βαβυλῶνι, Βαβὲλ γὰρ ἡ Βαβυλὼν παρ' Ἑβραίοις καλεῖται, ὅθεν καὶ τὸ Ζοροβάβελ ὄνομα εἰς τὴν Ἑλλάδα γλῶσσαν ἀπὸ τῆς Ἑβραΐδος ἀναπτυσσόμενον δηλοῦν βούλεται τὸ *ἐγεννήθη ἐν Βαβυλῶνι*, καὶ ἵνα κατὰ μίαν ἐκφώνησιν αὐτὸ προάξωμεν, Βαβυλωγέννητος ἂν ῥηθείη. Gennadius Scholarius, *De Prophetiis Principalibus Jesu Christi*, p. 305: Οἱ δὲ πάλαι Ἰουδαῖοι ἄλλως ἐνόησαν. καίτοι γὰρ πολὺ μετὰ Ζοροβάβελ ἐρωτηθέντες ποῦ ὁ Χριστὸς γεννᾶται, τὴν τοῦ Μιχαίου περὶ τῆς Βηθλεὲμ μαρτυρίαν προσήγαγεν. Damascenus Studites, *Thesaurus*, oration 2, lines 187-190 (ref. to Micah, 5:1-3; quoted in Matt. 2:6): Ἀλλ' εἰς αὐτὸ τὸ ῥητὸν ἐναντιοῦνται οἱ φιλόνικοι Ἰουδαῖοι καὶ λέγουν ὅτι διὰ τὸν Ζοροβάβελ τὸ λέγει αὐτὸ ὁ Προφήτης καὶ ψεύδονται εἰς αὐτό.

διότι ἕνα μέν, ὅτι ὁ Ζοροβάβελ δὲν ἐγεννήθη εἰς τὴν Βηθλεέμ, ἀμὴ εἰς τὴν Βαβυλῶνα. Likewise, Anonymous, *Dissertatio contra Judaeos*, chapter 3, line 430-467.

lxxi This text coincides with both Klostermann's fr. 23 (quoted forthwith) from Origen's commentary on Matthew and with a passage attributed to 'Origen and Eusebius' in the *Catena in Matthaeum*, p. 15, which reads thus: (Εὐσεβίου. Ὠριγένους). Ὁ χρόνος, ὃν ἠκρίβωσεν ὁ Ἡρώδης παρὰ τῶν μάγων, διετὴς ἦν. μετὰ γὰρ τὸ γεννηθῆναι τὸν Σωτῆρα, διὰ δύο ἐτῶν ἦλθον ἀπὸ τῆς χώρας αὐτῶν. τὰ γοῦν ἀπὸ διετοῦς βρέφη ἀνεῖλε.

Καὶ μετ' ὀλίγον.

Ἐντεῦθεν σοι ἡ γνῶσίς ἐστιν, ὅτι οὐ παρ' αὐτὰ τοῦ Κυρίου γεννηθέντος, ἐν τῷ σπηλαίῳ προσεκύνησαν οἱ μάγοι τὸ βρέφος, τὸ ὑπὸ τοῦ μηνύοντος ἐν τῇ φάτνῃ. ἀλλ' ὅτι μὲν οἱ ποιμένες εὐθέως ἐν ἐκείνῃ τῇ νυκτὶ μετὰ τὴν τῶν Ἀγγέλων θέαν δρομαῖοι ἀπήεσαν ἰδεῖν τὸ ἀληθές, ἅτε γειτνιῶντος τοῦ σπηλαίου αὐτοῖς. οἱ δὲ μάγοι συμπεριλαβόντος ἔτους δευτέρου μετὰ τὸ εὐλογηθῆναι αὐτὸν ὑπὸ Συμεών. καταβάντων πάλιν ἐν τῇ Βηθλεέμ, τοῦ βρέφους φερομένου τὲ ἐν ἀγκάλαις τῆς τεκούσης, καὶ παροικῆσαν ἐν οἰκείᾳ ξενίας ἡμέρας πολλάς, εἰς οἶκον κατὰ μὲν τὸν αὐτὸν ἐλθόντες οἱ μάγοι ἐκ γῆς ἀνατολῆς, κἀκεῖ προσενέγκαντες αὐτῷ τὰ δῶρα, θεαταὶ γεγόνασι τοῦ αἰωνίου βασιλέως. φησὶ γὰρ ὁ Εὐαγγελιστὴς τὸν Ἡρώδην κελεύσαντα τοῖς δημίοις, ἀπὸ διετοῦς μόνον καὶ κατωτέρω κατακτεῖναι τὰ βρέφη *κατὰ τὸν χρόνον ὃν ἠκρίβωσε παρὰ τῶν μάγων*. φεύγει δὲ τὴν Ἡρώδου μανίαν μετὰ τῶν κατὰ σάρκα γονέων εἰς Αἴγυπτον ὢν ἐτῶν δύο, καὶ καταμένει ἐκεῖ σὺν αὐτοῖς ἕτερα ἔτη δύο, μέχρι τοῦ πρώτου ἔτους τῆς Ἀρχελάου βασιλείας, ἐν τῇ καλουμένῃ Πανός. εἶθ' οὕτως κακῶς τὸν βίον μετελθόντος Ἡρώδου, διὰ χρηματισμοῦ πάλιν ἄνεισιν ἐξ Αἰγύπτου ὁ Κύριος σὺν αὐτοῖς εἰς γὴν Ἰσραήλ, ὢν ἐτῶν τεσσάρων τὸ κατὰ σάρκα. ἔτους με' τῆς βασιλείας Αὐγούστου. μετὰ δὲ τὴν ἐξ Αἰγύπτου ἐπάνοδον, εὑρήσεις τὸν Λουκᾶν λέγοντά σοι τὰ καθεξῆς ἀκόλουθα.

lxxii This is the view that John Chrysostom embraced; see *infra*, endnote lxxxiii.

lxxiii On Jesus being styled 'the eternal king', see Origen, *frLuc*, fr. 25: Τὸ δὲ *ἔσται* καὶ *κληθήσεται* τῇ κατὰ σάρκα πρέπον οἰκονομίᾳ, καὶ τὸ *δώσει δὲ αὐτῷ κύριος* τῇ οἰκονομίᾳ ἁρμόττει. εἰ δὲ καὶ λαμβάνειν λέγεται διὰ ταύτην *τὸν θρόνον Δαβίδ*, ἀλλ' ἔστιν ὁ αὐτὸς καὶ βασιλεὺς αἰώνιος θεοπρεπῶς. Prior to Origen, Justin Martyr, *Dialogus cum Tryphone*, 118.2: οὗτος γὰρ ἐξαίρετος ἱερεὺς καὶ αἰώνιος βασιλεύς, ὁ Χριστός, ὡς υἱὸς θεοῦ. *Op. cit.* 135.1: οὐχὶ ἀληθῶς τὸν Χριστὸν τὸν αἰώνιον βασιλέα ἀκούσεσθε; Irenaeus, *Adversus Haereses*, 10 (quoted by Theodoret, *Eranistes*, p. 97): Εἰς τί δὲ καὶ τὸ *ἐν πόλει Δαυὶδ* προσέθηκαν, εἰ μὴ ἵνα τὴν ὑπὸ Θεοῦ γεγενημένην τῷ Δαυὶδ ὑπόσχεσιν, ὅτι ἐκ καρποῦ τῆς κοιλίας αὐτοῦ αἰώνιος ἔσται Βασιλεύς, πεπληρωμένην εὐαγγελίσωνται; *Op. cit.* 32 (quoted by Theodoret, *loc cit.*): Καὶ ἐν τῷ εἰπεῖν σημαίνοντος ἦν ὅτι ὃν ἐπηγγείλατο τῷ Δαυὶδ ὁ Θεὸς ἐκ καρποῦ τῆς κοιλίας αὐτοῦ αἰώνιον ἀναστήσειν Βασιλέα, οὗτός ἐστιν ὁ ἐκ τῆς δαυιτικῆς παρθένου γεννώμενος. After Origen, Eusebius, *Demonstratio Evangelica*, 4.16.4: δυνάστην τινὰ μέγαν καὶ βασιλέα αἰώνιον καὶ λυτρωτὴν ἑαυτῶν ἔσεσθαι τὸν ἥξοντα Χριστὸν προσδοκῶντες. Epiphanius of Salamis, *Ancoratus*, 3.3-4. ἐὰν γὰρ μή τις δέξηται πνεῦμα ἅγιον, οὐ λέγει τὸν Ἰησοῦν κύριον ὄντως καὶ θεὸν ὄντως καὶ υἱὸν θεοῦ ὄντως καὶ βασιλέα ὄντως αἰώνιον. Likewise, Athanasius, *Vita Antonii*, 81; *Oratio i Contra Arianos*, 47.7; 48.1. Didymus, *commZacch*, 4.145. Pseudo-Didymus (Cassian the Sabaite), *De Trinitate*, 32.21. The source of the expression presumably was Daniel, 7.27; also (in Theodotion's version) 4:3; 7:27. Cf. 2 Peter, 1:11.

lxxiv Origen, *commMatt*, fr. 23 (Klostermann).

lxxv This is Origen, *commMatt*, fr. 28 (Klostermann).

lxxvi Origen, *commMatt*, fr. 28 (Klostermann).

lxxvii This is Origen's as demonstrated by the ensuing fr. 23 (Klostermann), and the text ascribed to both 'Eusebius, and Origen' in the *Catena in Matthaeum*, p. 15.

lxxviii This the final part of Origen, *commMatt*, fr. 23 (Klostermann), which is fully quoted *supra*, folio 7v-8r.

lxxix Eusebius, Origen, *apud Catena in Matthaeum*, p. 15.

lxxx The codex text continues; hence, we now have the heretofore unknown sequel of Origen's text which complemens Klostermann's fragment.

lxxxi It could appear that this reference to 'the most superstitious Egyptians' originated with Eusebius, to whom the parallel text is attributed along with Origen. However, such ascriptions only mean what is obvious, namely, that Eusebius drew on Origen plainly and copiously. In earler works of mine, I have suggested that Origen had read Lucian of Samosata's work and it was from him that he took up some characteristic turns of phrase. This is the case at this point, too. Lucian of Samosata, *Pro Imaginibus*, 27: ἐῶ γὰρ τοὺς Αἰγυπτίους, οἵπερ καὶ δεισιδαιμονέστατοί εἰσιν πάντων. As it happened, once Origen used innovative and characteristic expressions, later authors hooked on and used them at scores of points, the most striking case being John Chrysostom and Cyril of Alexandria, as shown at numerous points of this volume. This was the case with Eusebius, who spoke at several points of 'the most superstitious Egyptians'. *Demonstratio Evangelica*, 2.3.34: οἱ πάντων δεισιδαιμονέστατοι Αἰγύπτιοι. *Op. cit.* 5.4.17: ἐπειδὴ γὰρ Αἰγύπτιοι ἐδόκουν πάντων τῶν ἐθνῶν δεισιδαιμονέστατοι τυγχάνειν. *In Isaiam*, 1.75: τῆς τοῦ κυρίου παρουσίας ἐξαιρέτως ἐδεῖτο ἡ Αἴγυπτος, ἐπειδὴ πάντων ἀνθρώπων δεισιδαιμονεστάτων γεγόνασιν. *Op. cit.* 1.76: Αἰγύπτιοι οἱ πάλαι δεισιδαιμονέστατοι. *Op. cit.* 2.24: τοὺς πάντων ἀνθρώπων δεισιδαιμονεστάτους Αἰγυπτίους. *De Laudibus Constantini*, 16.9: Αἰγυπτίους δὲ τοὺς πάντων δεισιδαιμονεστάτους. *Commentaria in Psalmos*, PG.23.717.4-5: Αἰγύπτιοι δὲ ἦσαν οἱ πάντων ἀνθρώπων καὶ πάντων ἐθνῶν δεισιδαιμονέστατοι. Cyril of Alexandria, *In Isaiam*, PG.70.336.45-47: Αἰγύπτιοι δὲ μάλιστα δεισιδαιμονέστατοι παρὰ τοὺς ἄλλους καὶ δεινοὶ πρὸς τοῦτο γεγόνασι. *Op. cit.* PG.70.453.27-30: μάλιστα δὲ τῶν ἄλλων τοὺς Αἰγυπτίους. Δεισιδαιμονέστατοι γὰρ γεγόνασι παρὰ τοὺς ἄλλους, καὶ τάχα που νικῶντες ἐν πλάνῃ Πέρσας τε καὶ Ἀσσυρίους. *Op. cit.* PG.70.469.34-36: Ὅρα τοίνυν ἐξ οἵων εἰς οἷα μεταπέπτωκε τὰ Αἰγυπτίων πράγματα. Οἱ γὰρ πάλαι τῶν ἄλλων ἁπάντων δεισιδαιμονέστεροι. *Op. cit.* PG.70.612.28-30: Δύο τέθεικε χώρας τὰς ὅτι μᾶλλον τῶν ἄλλων δεισιδαιμονεστέρας, τήν τε Ἀσσυρίων, φημί, καὶ τῶν Αἰγυπτίων. As for the 'Babylonians', Eusebius did not mention them in this context, but Cyril did, once again taking his cue from Origen. Cyril of Alexandria, *In Isaiam*, 70.885.38-41: Δεισιδαιμονέστεροι δὲ τῶν ἄλλων γεγόνασι Χαλδαῖοι, καὶ Φοίνικες, καὶ ὅσοι τὴν Αἰγυπτίων ἔχουσι γῆν, μέχρι Συήνης τε καὶ Αἰθιοπίας.

lxxxii See folios 116r; 118r; 207r; 228r.

lxxxiii At this point, I include a text which is both interesting in terms of scriptural exegesis and illuminating with respect to how Origen's thought was copied by 'Theodore' (of Heraclea) and subsequently suppressed by posterity. The issue is about the apparently discrepant accounts of Jesus' birth involving the Magi who 'prostrated and worshipped' the baby Jesus (an instance only in Matthew) and the 'manger' (φάτνη, mentioned by Luke only), both of which suggest that Matthew and Luke *wrote about different times* of the baby Jesus: whereas Luke wrote about the newly born Jesus, Matthew wrote about Jesus being two years old, which was the time when the Magi reached him and offered their pilgrimage and gifts (of which Luke wrote nothing, nor indeed anything about Magi whatsoever).

This was the reason why Herod 'killed all the male children who were in Bethlehem and in all the surrounding countryside, from two years old and under, according to the exact time which he had learned from the wise men' (Matt. 2:16). Besides, Matthew

(2:11) wrote that the Magi prostrated before Jesus 'in a house', whereas Luke (2:7-16) wrote that Mary laid the new-born Jesus in 'a feeding trough, because there was no room for them in the inn', and it was therein that the 'shepherds' saw 'the baby'.

On this question, there were two different exegeses throughout all of Christian literature. In the twelfth century, Michael Glycas pointed this out and advised that, on the one hand, Epiphanius of Salamis maintained that, when the Magi visited, prostrated and worshipped the newborn Messiah, Jesus was two years old, not a newly born baby, since it took them two years to reach Jesus from the time when they saw the star in heaven. On the other, John Chrysostom maintained that the Magi saw the star two years prior to Jesus' birth, and they were in place along with the shepherds right upon Jesus' birth. Glycas quoted from a relevant text of Chrysostom. However, although he added that this was also the opinion of both Athanasius and John of Damascus, he adduced no evidence for this. In any case, this is not correct: John of Damascus wrote that the Magi saw the star *upon* Jesus' birth (*Homilia in Nativitatem Domini*, 6), not two years prior to this so as to be in place upon that event, as Chrysostom would like to believe; and Athanasius did not really concern himself about this question; only at one point and in passing does he seem to allow that the Magi were present at the 'manger', but this was not his main point (*Epistula ad Maximum*, PG.26.1089.21-23). In fact, the text which Glycas quoted is not Chrysostom's: it is probably a paraphrase of his own, but the idea is in fact Chrysostom's and it appears in his *In Matthaeum* PG.57.76.21-34: Καὶ γὰρ πρὸ πολλοῦ χρόνου δοκεῖ μοι ὁ ἀστὴρ φανῆναι. Ἐπειδὴ γὰρ πολὺν κατὰ τὴν ὁδοιπορίαν ἔμελλον ἀναλίσκειν οἱ μάγοι χρόνον, ἵνα εὐθέως ἐπιστῶσι τῷ τεχθέντι. ἔδει γὰρ ἐν αὐτοῖς προσκυνηθῆναι τοῖς σπαργάνοις αὐτόν, ὥστε τὸ θαυμαστὸν καὶ παράδοξον φανῆναι τοῦ πράγματος, πρὸ πολλοῦ τοῦ χρόνου δείκνυσιν ἑαυτὸν ὁ ἀστήρ. Εἰ γὰρ ἡνίκα ἐτέχθη ἐν Παλαιστίνῃ, τότε αὐτοῖς ὤφθη ἐν τῇ ἀνατολῇ, πολὺν κατὰ τὴν ὁδοιπορίαν διατρίβοντες χρόνον, οὐκ ἂν ἐν σπαργάνοις εἶδον αὐτὸν παραγενόμενοι. Εἰ δὲ ἀπὸ διετοῦς ἀναιρεῖ καὶ κατωτέρω, μὴ θαυμάσωμεν. ὁ γὰρ θυμὸς καὶ τὸ δέος ὑπὲρ πλείονος ἀσφαλείας καὶ πλείονα προσετίθει χρόνον, ὥστε μηδένα διαφυγεῖν.

What Glycas did not say is that the discrepant accounts by Matthew and Luke were first considered by Origen and then by Eusebius. This is why at this point I quote the text of Eusebius, of which I have no doubt that this is Origen's account almost to the letter confirmed by Origen's fr. 23 by Klostermann. Besides, the parallel text 'by Theodore' (which J. Reuss ascribed tentatively to 'Theodore of Heraclea or Theodore of Mopsuestia') makes it all too evident that this is but a slightly abbreviated version, which is otherwise a *verbatim* copy of Eusebius' account. In the following, it will be demonstrated that almost all of the 'fragments' (and definitely all of the critical ones) that J. Reuss found being attributed to 'Theodore of Heraclea' are in fact passages from Origen's commentary on Matthew. In terms of methodology, it is precisely this fact that allows for the conjecture that the passage by 'Theodore of Heraclea' was in fact copied not from Eusebius, but from Origen's commentary on Matthew and possibly from his commentary on Luke, too. In any event, I certainly do not dispute that the present passage of Eusebius was written by Eusebius himself – only, as usual, he wrote by reproducing the writings of his master Origen, which he never cared to conceal, anyway.

Besides, it is irony that Origen's account of this question was followed faithfully by his most fanatic detractor, namely, Epiphanius of Salamis, *Panarion*, v. 1, pp. 372-373: μετὰ γὰρ δύο ἐτῶν χρόνον, ὡς ἔδειξαν τῷ Ἡρῴδῃ τὸν χρόνον τοῦ ἀστέρος *ἀπὸ διετοῦς καὶ κατωτέρω* ἐλθόντες εἰς Ἱερουσαλὴμ καὶ ἐρωτήσαντες οἱ αὐτοὶ μάγοι καὶ γνόντες ὅτι ἐν Βηθλεὲμ ὁ Χριστὸς γεννᾶται, ἐξῆλθον πάλιν τοῦ ἀστέρος ὁδηγοῦντος αὐτοὺς καὶ ἦλθον ἀπὸ Ἱεροσολύμων εἰς Βηθλεέμ. καὶ εἰσελθόντες εὗρον αὐτὸν μετὰ τῆς μητρὸς αὐτοῦ Μαρίας καὶ πεσόντες προσεκύνησαν αὐτῷ καὶ προσήνεγκαν τὰ δῶρα. *Op. cit.* v. 2, p. 287: τὰ ᾿Επιφάνεια καλῶς εἴρηται ἡ ἔνσαρκος γέννησις τοῦ σωτῆρος ἡ ἐν Βηθλεὲμ γενομένη, ὀγδόῃ ὥρᾳ γεννηθέντος αὐτοῦ καὶ ἐπιφανέντος τοῖς ποιμέσι καὶ τῷ κόσμῳ διὰ τῆς τῶν ἀγγέλων μαρτυρίας. ἐπεφάνη δὲ καὶ τῇ Μαρίᾳ καὶ τῷ ᾿Ιωσήφ. ἐν ἐκείνῃ δὲ τῇ ὥρᾳ καὶ ὁ ἀστὴρ ἐφάνη ἐν τῇ ἀνατολῇ τοῖς μάγοις πρὸ δύο ἐτῶν τῆς αὐτῶν εἰς ῾Ιερουσαλὴμ καὶ Βηθλεὲμ ἀφίξεως, ὅτε καὶ ἀκριβῶς ὁ ῾Ηρῴδης ἐπυνθάνετο ‹παρ'› αὐτῶν τῶν μάγων τὸν χρόνον τοῦ φανέντος ἀστέρος καὶ ἤκουσε παρ' αὐτῶν ὅτι ἀπὸ διετοῦς καὶ κατωτέρω, ὃ καὶ αὐτὸ τὸ ῥῆμα τῶν ᾿Επιφανείων ἐποιεῖτο τὴν ἐπωνυμίαν ἐκ τοῦ τὸν ῾Ηρῴδην λέγειν *τοῦ φανέντος ἀστέρος*.

Moreover, nearly two centuries after Michael Glycas (fl. c. 1120-1150), Nicephorus Callistus Xanthopulus (fl. c. 1320) embraced Eusebius' Origenian account entirely and wrote that 'it is more accurate' to maintain that the Magi reached Jesus when he was two years old. *HE*, 1.13: Καὶ δῆτα δύο ἐξῆς παρῳχηκότων ἐνιαυτῶν μετὰ τὴν ἄσπορον ἐκείνην κυοφορίαν, ἐν τῇ κατὰ τὴν Βηθλεὲμ οἰκίᾳ διατριβούσης, τῆς Θεομήτορος ὡς δ' ἕτεροι, πρὸ δύο μᾶλλον ἐνιαυτῶν τῆς θείας γεννήσεως τῶν οἴκοι ἀπάραντες, ἐν φάτνῃ καὶ σπαργάνοις ὄντι Χριστῷ, καὶ ἐν τῷ καταλύματι εἴτουν ἐν τῷ σπηλαίῳ ἔτι οὔσης τῆς Θεομήτορος, [οἱ Μάγοι ἀπὸ Ἀνατολῶν] παραγίνονται. ὃ δῆτα καὶ ἀκριβέστερον.

lxxxiv Eusebius, *Ad Stephanum*, PG.22.933.19-36.

lxxxv Theodore of Heraclea, *commMatt*, fr. 8. However, this is Origen's. Through the expression Ἕτεροι δέ φασιν Theodore (if indeed he wrote a commentary on Matthew; otherwise, the catenist) reveals the source of this passage, which is but a copy from Origen.

lxxxvi Matt. 2:11. Theodore of Heraclea or Theodore of Mopsuestia, *frMatt*, fr. 8.

lxxxvii Origen, *commMatt*, fr. 34 (Klostermann), col. 2.

lxxxviii Origen, *commMatt*, fr. 35 (Klostermann).

lxxxix Origen, *apud Catena in Matthaeum*, p. 18.

xc Origen, *loc. cit.*

xci Origen, *apud Catena in Matthaeum*, pp. 18-19.

xcii This is part of a text, of which the last part is Origen's *commMatt*, fr. 36 (Klostermann), which means that we now have a hitherto unknown wider context of this.

xciii The adjective ἐνύποπτος ('suspicious') is an extremely rare term and its usage can be traced in no more than four instances, to which the present one should be added. Given the keen interest that Origen had in medicine, it could be plausible to surmise that he took this up from his reading of the physician Soranus of Ephesus, who flourished in the turn of first to second century AD, he practiced in Alexandria and subsequently in Rome, and was one of the chief representatives of the Methodic school of medicine, which arose in reaction to both the Empiric and the Dogmatic schools. This means that its scientific spirit perfectly fitted Origen's mentality. Soranus, *Gynaeciorum*, 2.10.4-5: ἐνύποπτον ὡς διά τινα περίστασιν τοῦτο πάσχον. Later, Pseudo-Callisthenes, *Historia Alexandri Magni* (*recensio*), 1.9.1-2: ἐνυπόπτως ἡ ᾿Ολυμπιὰς ἠσπάσατο αὐτόν. In theology, this was used only once by Serapion of Thmuis (bishop, fourth century AD), *Contra Manichaeos*, 31: καὶ πότε γέγονεν ἐνύποπτος; It seems that the term was familiar to some schools of medicine, since Aëtius of Amida also used this in the sixth century. *Iatricorum Liber v*, 54: Γνωρίσματα τοῦ μὴ τελέως λελύσθαι τὸ νόσημα. γνωρίσομεν δὲ τοὺς ἐνυπόπτου εἰς ὑποστροφὴν ἐκ τοῦ λελύσθαι μὲν νομίζειν τὸ νόσημα, παραμένειν δὲ τὰ παραπλήσια. This was all Antiquity made of this term as far as extant literature goes. And yet this occurs in the present commentary on Matthew.

xciv See Origen's *commMatt*, fr. 36 (Klostermann) quoted forthwith.

xcv Origen, *commMatt*, fr. 36 (Klostermann).

xcvi Cyril of Alexandria clearly suggested that this exegesis came from a predecessor, whom though Cyril was not willing to cite by name (*κατά τινας*), which is what he normally did.

xcvii Song of Songs, 2:1. Cyril of Alexandria, *frMatt*, fr. 16. As it happened, posterity credited Cyril, not Origen, with the fatherhood of this idea. Anonymous, *Dialogus cum Judaeis*, chapter 6, lines 315-323: Προστίθησι δὲ τούτοις καί τινα εὔλογον αἰτίαν ὁ εὐαγγελιστής, εἰπὼν ὡς διατοῦτο κατῴκησεν Ἰησοῦς ἐν Ναζαρέτ, *ὅπως πληρωθῇ τὸ ῥηθὲν διὰ τῶν προφητῶν ὅτι Ναζωραῖος κληθήσεται.* Τοῦτο ζητεῖς ποῖος προφήτης προεῖπεν; Ἄκουε φανερῶς· ὁ Ναζωραῖος ἐκ τῆς Ἑβραΐδος γλώττης εἰς τὴν Ἑλλάδα μεταβαλλόμενος, ἄνθος ἑρμηνεύεται· ἄνθος τοίνυν ὁ σωτὴρ ἡμῶν καὶ παρὰ Σολομῶντος ἐν τῷ Ἄσματι τῶν Ἀσμάτων προείρηται, καὶ παρὰ τῷ Ἡσαΐᾳ γέγραπται. Pseudo-Zonaras, *Lexicon*, letter nu, p. 1383 (copying from Cyril, who cited 'certain ones', *κατά τινας*, i.e. Origen): Ναζωραῖος. ἅγιος ἑρμηνεύεται. ἢ κατά τινας ἄνθος. εὑρίσκεται τοῦτο παρὰ πολλοῖς τὸ ὄνομα.

xcviii Cf. the Greek: ἀλλ᾽ ὁ νοῦς.

xcix Jerome, *commMatt*, 2.23.

c The sequel of the text once again reveals Origen being the author of this.

ci Origen knew Hebrew well and was perfectly aware of his superiority over Celsus on that score. Cf. *Cels*, I.35: Ἵνα δὲ μὴ δοκῶμεν ἀπὸ λέξεως ἑβραϊκῆς τοῖς μὴ καταλαμβάνουσι, πότερον συγκαταθετέον αὐτῇ ἢ μή, φέρειν παραμυθίαν περὶ τοῦ προφήτην εἰρηκέναι ἐκ παρθένου τεχθήσεσθαι τοῦτον, ἐφ᾽ οὗ τῇ γενέσει λέλεκται τὸ *μεθ᾽ ἡμῶν ὁ θεός*, φέρε ἀπ᾽ αὐτῆς τῆς λέξεως παραμυθησώμεθα τὸ λεγόμενον. See also his interpretation of the name 'Jeremiah' derived from Ἰαὼ in Hebrew meaning 'the elevation of Iao'. *commJohn*, II.1.7: ὡσαύτως δὲ καὶ πρὸς Ἱερεμίαν θείῳ μετεωρισμῷ ἐπαρθέντα. ἑρμηνεύεται γὰρ *μετεωρισμὸς Ἰαώ.* In all probability, Origen knew this from the magical writings, in which the following explanation appears. *Papyri Magicae* (Christian fragments, Preisendanz), number 14, lines 27-36: Ἰησοῦς Ἰὼ σωτηρία φῶς μου θεοῦ ἰσχὺς θεοῦ Ἰάω πίστις Ἰὼ πατὴρ θεέ μου, θεέ μου, ἐς τί με ἐνκατέλιπες χάρις θεοῦ Ἰάω ἐξομολόγησις οἰκτιρμοῦ ... Ἰάω κράτος Ἰάω ἀνάστασις Ἰάω. It would be plausible to surmise that Origen was aware of this text, since he made it clear that he knew of the books on magic. *Cels*, IV.33: "In magical treatises it is often to be found that God is invoked by this formula [sc. 'the God of Abraham, the God of Isaac, the God of Jacob'] and that in spells against daemons His name is used in close connexion with the names of these men." Cf. *op. cit.* I.22; I.24; V.45. Besides, he made clear that he was aware of magical practices. In *Cels*, VI.31-32, he exhibits to his challenger his knowledge of those practices and of magical incantation. In *op. cit.* VI.41, he reveals that he had himself experienced attacks by 'magic and daemons' but was able to ward them off by means of his 'living according to the gospel and use of the appointed prayers'. Likewise, in *op. cit.* VIII.44, he reveals that he had averted daemons that attacked him. It would have been natural for him to study those practices since he believed that 'magic is not nonexistent as the followers of Epicurus and of Aristotle believe' (*Cels*, I.24). Consequently, he treated magic as something really existing and effecting certain outcomes. Cf. *Cels*, I.38; I.57; I.68; II.51 ('magic and sorcery really exists and is wrought by evil daemons'); VI.32 (ref. to those who 'have not any understanding of the art of magic'); VI.80; VIII.60; *selNum*, PG.12.584.18-19 (ἡ τῆς μαγείας κακοτεχνία). Cf. Hesychius of Alexandria, *Lexicon*, letter iota, entry 1212: Ἰωάννης. χάρις. John Tzetzes, *Chiliades*, chilias 7, history 126, lines 146-147: ΠΕΡΙ ΤΟΥ ΧΑΡΙΤΩΝΥΜΟΣ ΗΤΟΙ ΙΩΑΝΝΗΣ. Ἑβραϊκῶς τὸ ἰαὼ ἀόρατον σημαίνει, ὁ Ἰωνᾶς περιστεράν, ὁ δ᾽ Ἰωάννης χάριν. See also *supra*, folio 3r.

cii *Codex Sabaiticus 232*, folio 11r, tagged ΑΝΕΠ[ΙΓΡΑΦΟΝ]. It turns out that this is Origen's, too. See *infra*, folio 24r. Cf. Origen, *commMatt*, 10.5: Τὰ οὐράνια τοίνυν πράγματα καὶ *ἡ βασιλεία τῶν οὐρανῶν* ὥσπερ ἐν εἰκόνι γέγραπται ταῖς γραφαῖς αἵτινές εἰσιν *ἡ βασιλεία τῶν οὐρανῶν* ἢ αὐτός ἐστιν ὁ Χριστὸς ὁ βασιλεὺς τῶν αἰώνων *ἡ βασιλεία τῶν οὐρανῶν ὡμοιωμένη θησαυρῷ κεκρυμμένῳ ἐν τῷ ἀγρῷ*. *schMatt*, PG.17.296.7-11: Τὰ οὐράνια τοίνυν πράγματα, καὶ ἡ βασιλεία τῶν οὐρανῶν ὥσπερ ἐν εἰκόνι γέγραπται ταῖς Γραφαῖς, αἵτινές εἰσι βασιλεία τῶν οὐρανῶν. ἡ δέ ἐστιν αὐτὸς ὁ Χριστός, οὗ ἡ γνῶσις κατὰ δύναμιν ἐν ἡμῖν ἐστιν. *Op. cit.* PG.17.293.26-29: Ἡ δὲ *βασιλεία τῶν οὐρανῶν* αὐτός ἐστιν ὁ Χριστός, προτρεπόμενος πάντας εἰς μετάνοιαν, καὶ ἕλκων εἰς ἑαυτὸν διὰ τῆς χάριτος.

ciii Origen, *apud Catena in Matthaeum*, p. 20. This is also Origen, *commMatt*, fr. 38 II (Klostermann), col. 1 (quoted *infra*, p. 20).

civ Origen, *commMatt*, fr. 38 II (Klostermann), col. 1.

cv Jerome, *commMatt*, 3.2.

cvi But this is Origen's, which the ensuing quotation from the folio 24r of the present codex reveals.

cvii Origen, *infra*, folio 24r.

cviii This is Origen's, too; see *infra*, folio 24r.

cix This is Origen's, since it re-appears under the Origen's name *infra*, folio 24r: Τοῦτό γαρ ἐστι *βασιλεία οὐρανῶν*, τὸ ζῆν θεαρέστως καὶ ἀναμαρτήτως.

cx Cf. folio 96: τῆς τοῦ Θεοῦ βασιλείας, ἤτοι τῆς δευτέρας παρουσίας. Cf. Isidore Glabas copying from this; *Oratio ad Thessalonicenses ii*, p. 579: ἄλλως τε καὶ ἡ τῶν οὐρανῶν βασιλεία, πολύσημόν ἐστι. σημαίνει γὰρ αὐτὸν τὸν Χριστόν. καὶ τὴν πρώτην αὐτοῦ παρουσίαν. καὶ τὴν δευτέραν. καὶ τὰ μετὰ τὴν ἀνάστασιν ἀγαθά. καὶ αὐτὸ τὸ ζῆν θεαρέστως καὶ κατ᾽ ἐπιταγὴν τοῦ καινοῦ νόμου.

cxi On the 'enjoyment of future goods' (ἀπόλαυσις τῶν μελλόντων ἀγαθῶν), cf. Origen, *expProv*, PG.17.205.18-21: Ἢ τὴν ψυχὴν λέγει, ζωῆς καὶ θανάτου δεκτικήν, ἀφ᾽ ὧν τὸ αὐτεξούσιον δείκνυται τῶν νῦν τε καὶ τῶν μελλόντων τοὺς καρποὺς αὐτῆς ἀπολαῦσαι καλῶν τε ἢ κακῶν. Gregory of Nyssa followed suit; *De Sancto Theodoro*, PG.46.737.20-22: Καὶ τέως, εἰ δοκεῖ, τῆς ἀπολαύσεως τῶν μελλόντων ἀγαθῶν σχολαζούσης, ἣν ἐλπὶς ἀγαθὴ ταμιεύεται τοῖς δικαίοις. So did a vast number of subsequent authors, but this turn was introduced by Origen. Once again, a relevant passage was ascribed to Theodore of Heraclea, *frMatt*, fr. 75: Δευτέρα γέννησις ἡ τῆς ἀναστάσεως δι᾽ ἧς ἀναγεννώμεθα καὶ δι᾽ ἁγίου πνεύματος τυγχάνομεν ἀθανασίας οἱ μέλλοντες ἀπολαύειν τῶν ἀγαθῶν. καὶ ὁ πάνυ ἐλάχιστος ἐκεῖ ὑπεραναβαίνει τὸν Ἰωάννην, εἰ καὶ ἐκ μήτρας ἐτύγχανεν ἁγίου πνεύματος. However, in the *Catena in Matthaeum*, p. 85, this was ascribed jointly to Isidore of Pelusium, Cyril [of Alexandria], and Theodore of Heraclea. This is just one of the similar cases, in which Origen's words were attributed to those who copied from him.

cxii Origen, *commMatt*, fr. 75 (Klostermann).

cxiii Origen, *commMatt*, fr. 38 I (Klostermann) (partially). Quite evidently, the present *Codex Sabaiticus 232* renders Origen's text in far more accurate manner and impeccable Greek, which is faithfully consonant with a cardinal point of his theology.

cxiv Origen, *commMatt*, fr. 38 II (Klostermann), col. 2.

cxv Origen, *commMatt*, fr. 226 (Klostermann).

cxvi Photius, *commMatt*, fr. 61.

cxvii Cf. *infra*, folio 240r: καὶ παρὰ Ἰωάννῃ γε τὸ δι᾽ ὕδατος ἔτι. μετὰ ‹δὲ› τῆς πρὸς Θεὸν συναφείας καὶ οὐκ ἦν βάπτισμα πώποτε.

cxviii This is Origen's text from *commJohn*, VI.17.95, quoted forthwith.

cxix John 7:37. Origen, *commJohn*, VI.17.95.

cxx On the 'conceptions' of the Son, see *COT*, pp. 48-64.

cxxi Jerome, *commMatt*, 3.4. See Origen in the ensuing passage.

cxxii Cf. the expression 'doing something οὐ παρέργως' in Origen, *frPs*, on Psalm 118:10. He took up this expression from his usual sources. Philo, *Legum Allegoriarum*, 2.11; *De Posteritate Caini*, 78; *De Confusione Linguarum*, 1; *Quaestiones in Genesim* (*fragmenta*), Book 2, fr. 54d. Josephus, *De Bello Judaico*, 7.136. Galen, *De Theriaca ad Pisonem*, pp. 219; 238. Pseudo-Galen, *De Affectuum Renibus Insidentium Dignotione et Curatione*, p. 688. Lucian of Samosata, *De Morte Peregrini*, 12. Athenaeus, *Deipnosophistae*, 1.2; 5.17. Sextus Empiricus, *Adversus Mathematicos et Grammaticos*, 1.77; 1.96. Alexander of Aphrodisias, *commMetaph*, pp. 562; 666; 720. Then, Eusebius, *Praeparatio Evangelica*, 8.3.2; 11.7.3; *HE*, 3.6.6. Epiphanius of Salamis, *Ancoratus*, 94.8.

cxxiii This passage has been ascribed also to Theodore of Mopsuestia, *frMatt*, fr. 12 (Reuss), although its ideas and vocabulary clearly ring an Origenist bell. Now its real authorship is revealed. See discussion of this in Introduction, pp. XXXIV-XXXV. Moreover, cf. Origen, *frLuc*, fr. 58a: Ποιμέσι πρῶτον ἀποκαλύπτεται τὸ ὑπὸ τῶν ἀγγέλων ὑμνούμενον μυστήριον οἵτινες τύπον ἐπέχουσι τῶν τὰς ἐκκλησίας μελλόντων ποιμαίνειν. καὶ μάλα εἰκότως. *Op. cit.* fr. 60a: Ὢ τύπου μυστηρίου θεοπρεποῦς. Βηθλεὲμ γὰρ οἶκος ἄρτου μεθερμηνεύεται. *Fragmenta in Librum Primum Regnorum*, fr. 20: καὶ εὕρῃ πρὸς κεφαλῆς ἀπόρρητα μυστήρια, ὧν ὀλυρίτης ἐγκρυφίας τύπος ἦν. Here is how his admirers followed him suit. Gregory of Nyssa, *In Christi Resurrectionem Oratio i*, p. 275: τοῦ ἁγίου πνεύματος τὸ μέγα μυστήριον τυπικῶς ἀμφοτέροις ἐπιμερίσαντος. Gregory of Nazianzus, *Apologetica*, PG.35.505.11-12: καὶ τριημέρῳ ταφῇ, τύπον ἐχούσῃ μυστηρίου μείζονος. *Ad Gregorium Nyssenum*, PG.35.833.24-25: καὶ τύπῳ μυστηρίου μείζονος. Athanasius, *Expositiones in Psalmos*, PG.27.112.54: εὑρήκαμεν τὸ Χριστοῦ μυστήριον ἐν τύποις. Theodoret, *In Epistulas Sancti Pauli*, PG.82.244.47-48: δεῖξαι βουλόμενοι τῶν ἡμετέρων μυστηρίων τοὺς τύπους. *Eranistes*, p. 210: τῆς οἰκονομίας μυστηρίου τὸν τύπον. *Haereticarum Fabularum Compendium*, PG.83.549.13-14: οἱ παλαιοὶ τύπον εἶχον τῶν ἱερῶν μυστηρίων τὰ περιρραντήρια, καὶ τὰς θείας ἱερουργίας. Also, Theodoret in the *Catena in Epistulam i ad Corinthios*, p. 45: καὶ γὰρ δεῖξαι βουλόμενος τῶν ἡμετερῶν μυστηρίων τοὺς τύπους, τὸν ἀμνὸν εἰς μέσον φέρομεν. Consequently, both John Chrysostom and Cyril of Alexandria used it abundantly.

cxxiv The term φαύλια referring only to fruits means 'coarse'. Origen's knowledge is stunning, since this had been explained by Athenaeus reporting the view of a certain (otherwise unknown) agriculturist named Glaucides. Athenaeus, *Deipnosophistae*, 3.20: Γλαυκίδης δέ φησιν ἄριστα τῶν ἀκροδρύων εἶναι μῆλα κυδώνια, φαύλια, στρουθία. The same in *op. cit.* 20.42, and *Deipnosophistae* (*epitome*), v. 2.1, p. 7.

cxxv Only an erudite man who had a high command of Greek language could have used this word, which perhaps he coined himself, yet with reason. We know that Euripides had used the verb ἀκρίζειν (Euripides, *Fragmenta* [*Nauck*], fr. 570: ἀκρίζων), which was attested to by some authors, such as Hesychius of Alexandria, *Lexicon*, letter alpha, entry 2564. Their impression was that, by this verb, Euripides meant 'walking on tiptoe', but in fact they were unaware of the context since this was just an isolated word. Nevertheless, as Eustathius of Thessaloniki attests, 'to those of old, ἄκριες meant ἄκρα', namely, the 'extremities' (e.g. the peak of a mountain or a headland) and anyway 'the fathest' part of anything. *Commentarii ad Homeri Odysseam*, v. 1, pp. 352-353: Ἄκριες δὲ κατὰ τοὺς παλαιοὺς ἄκρα ὀρῶν. λόφοι. ἐσχατιαί. γωνίαι. καὶ ἀκρίζειν, τὸ τὰ ἄκρα ἐπιπορευέσθαι. ὃ καὶ ἐξακρίζειν Εὐριπίδης φησίν. ἕτερος δέ τις ἐπήκρισε φησὶν ἀντὶ τοῦ ἐπάκρον ἤγαγε καὶ τέλος ἐπέθηκεν. οἱ δὲ παλαιοὶ φασὶ καὶ οὕτως. ἄκριες, λόφοι ὀρῶν οἱ καὶ ἄμβωνες, ὧν πολλὴ ἡ χρῆσις. We know of no author ever having used the *noun* ἄκρισμα, which Origen does here. The meaning is 'the outermost part' of a fruit, which normally should be cut out. Hence, the *Suda* provided the right explanation ('cut out the outermost section' of something); letter alpha, entry 983: Ἀκρίζω. τὸ ἄκρον κόπτω.

cxxvi The verb μετεωροπορεῖν (adjective: μετεωροπόρος) rings a Platonic bell (instead of μετεωροπορεῖν, some authors wrote μετεωροπολεῖν, yet both terms mean 'being involved with sublime things'). Plato, *Phaedrus*, 246b-c: ψυχὴ ... τελέα μὲν οὖν οὖσα καὶ ἐπτερωμένη μετεωροπορεῖ τε καὶ πάντα τὸν κόσμον διοικεῖ (discussed by Plotinus, *Enneades*, IV.3.7; IV.8.2; V.8.7). Philo, *Legum Allegoriarum*, 3.71: ὅταν γὰρ ὁ νοῦς μετεωροπολῇ καὶ τὰ τοῦ κυρίου μυστήρια μυῆται, πονηρὸν καὶ δυσμενὲς κρίνει τὸ σῶμα. *Op. cit.* 3.83-84: ἑρμηνεύεται γὰρ Ἀβρὰμ *πατὴρ μετέωρος*, δι᾽ ἀμφοτέρων τῶν ὀνομάτων ἐπαινετός. ὁ γὰρ νοῦς, ... ἀποστὰς μετεωροπολῇ καὶ συνδιατρίβῃ θεωρήμασι τοῖς περὶ κόσμου καὶ τῶν μερῶν αὐτοῦ καὶ ἔτι μᾶλλον ἐπανιὼν ἐρευνᾷ τὸ θεῖον καὶ τὴν τούτου φύσιν δι᾽ ἔρωτα ἐπιστήμης ἄλεκτον. *Quod Deterius Potiori Insidiari Soleat*, 27: τὸν περίγειον καταλελοιπότες χῶρον μετεωροπολεῖν ἐγνώκασιν οὐδεμίαν τῶν σωματικῶν ἐφελκόμενοι κηρῶν. Also, *De Plantatione*, 145; *Quis Rerum Divinarum Heres Sit*, 128; *De Somniis*, 1.140; *et passim.* Likewise, Galen, *In Hippocratis Librum De Articulis et Galeni in Eum*, p. 720. Origen, *selEz*, PG.13.788.37-39: αἱ πτέρυγες τῆς γῆς οἱ διορατικώτατοί εἰσι καὶ μετεωροπόροι παρὰ πάντας τοὺς ἐπὶ τῆς γῆς. *homPs*, homily 9.10: Ἐὰν ἴδῃς ψυχὴν ἤδη μετεωροποροῦσαν, ἤδη φανταζομένην τὰ ἐπουράνια. *Op. cit.* homily 19.6: Κἂν μετεωροποροῦσι καὶ λέγουσι. *Loc. cit.* καὶ εἴτι ἄλλο ἐστὶν ἐκκλησιαστικὸν καὶ μετεωροπόρον. Gregory Thaumaturgus, *In Origenem Oratio Panegyrica*, 8: Τί δεῖ λέγειν τὰ τῶν ἱερῶν μαθημάτων, γεωμετρίαν μὲν τὴν πᾶσι φίλην καὶ ἀναμφισβήτητον καὶ ἀστρονομίαν τὴν μετεωροπόρον; Iamblichus, *De Mysteriis*, 5.15. Gregory of Nyssa, *Contra Eunomium*, 2.1.68; *De Virginitate*, 5.1; *et passim.*

cxxvii Cf. Origen's usual expression ἐξετάζειν τὸ βούλημα ('perusing the deeper meaning') of a scriptural text. *Cels*, III.53 (& *Philocalia*, 18.23): Ἀλλὰ σαφὲς τῷ ἐξετάζοντι ὅλον τὸ βούλημα τῶν ἡμετέρων γραμμάτων. *Op. cit.* VI.77 (& *Philocalia*, 15.20): τοῖς ἐχθροῖς τοῦ θείου λόγου καὶ μὴ φιλαλήθως τὰ χριστιανισμοῦ ἐξετάσασιν εἰδέναι τὸ βούλημα τῶν διαφόρων τοῦ Ἰησοῦ μορφῶν. *In Jeremiam*, homily 1.2: ἐὰν μὴ προσέχῃ τῇ ἀναγνώσει μηδὲ ἐξετάζῃ τὸ βούλημα τῶν γεγραμμένων ἀναγνωσμάτων. *Op. cit.* homily 3.1: Τίς οὖν γενόμενος ἐν τῷ τόπῳ οὐκ ἂν ζητήσαι ἐξετάζων τὸ βούλημα τοῦ γεγραμμένου; *Op. cit.* homily 14.3: ὅτε συνετοὶ ὄντες οἱ ἀκροαταὶ καὶ οὐχ ἁπαξαπλῶς παραδέχονται, ἀλλὰ ἀντιβασανίζουσι καὶ ἐρωτῶσι καὶ ἐξετάζουσι τὸ βούλημα τῶν λεγομένων.

cxxviii This analysis has a unique parallel occuring in the *Catena in Marcum*, which is in fact the continuation of Origen's exegesis expounded above about John the Baptist being considered as 'the last of prophets' (see p. XXXIV and endnote viii). The text evidently carries on with this analysis about the Baptist and, anyway, this is clearly the same exegesis, which the catenist of the gospel of Mark uses in relation to Mark, 1:6, and the catenist of codex *Sabaiticus 232* in relation to Matt. 3:4 – both scriptural instances are the same: 'John's food was locusts and wild honey'. All of the characteristic (and indeed very rare) terminology is present in both texts (see next quotation and compare: λόγῳ μετεωροπόρῳ, οὐ βεβηκότι ὑπὲρ τῶν πτερύγων, μέλι ἄγριον ... μὴ γεωργούμενον ... διά ... ζητήσεως). *Catena in Marcum* (*recensio ii*), p. 269: Ἡ δὲ τροφὴ αὐτοῦ, ὡς ἡγοῦμαι, σύμβολον ἦν τῆς λογικῆς τοῦ λαοῦ τότε τροφῆς, οὐκ ἐσθίοντός τι τῶν καθαρῶν πετεινῶν τοῦ οὐρανοῦ, τρεφομένου δὲ τῷ μὲν δοκοῦντι λόγῳ μετεωροπόρῳ, ἀλλ᾽ οὐ βεβηκότι ὑπὲρ τῶν πτερύγων, οὐδὲ δυναμένῳ ὑπεραναβῆναι τῆς γῆς, καὶ ἐπὶ τὰ ὑψηλὰ φθάναι αὐτῆς. Ὥσπερ ἦν καὶ μέλι ἄγριον γενόμενον μὲν ὑπὸ τῶν νοητῶν μελισσῶν τῶν προφητῶν, μὴ γεωργούμενον δὲ καὶ ἡμερούμενον διὰ τῆς ἐμμελοῦς νοήσεως καὶ ζητήσεως. In the beginning of this analysis, the *Catena in Marcum* cites Origen's name (p. 266; so it does on pp. 314 & 418), and the selfsame text that now occurs in the present codes makes it clear that, in that section, the catenist drew entirely on Origen's work.

cxxix It was Origen alone who could have written this, since he appears to have been the sole Christian author who arguably was aware to the last detail of how vipers act and react, as this appears in the ensuing passage attributed to him. Cf. Anonymous, *Scholia in Euripidis Orestem* (on *Orestes*, verse 479: ὁ μητροφόντης ὅδε πρὸ δωμάτων δράκων, 'Here is that matricide dragon before the house'): νῦν δὲ δράκων ἀντὶ τοῦ ἔχις [= viper]. οὗτοι γὰρ οὐκ ἐξ ὠῶν γεννῶνται, ἀλλὰ ζῳοτοκοῦνται, καὶ τικτόμενοι διαρρηγνύουσι τὰς τῶν μητέρων γαστέρας, ὥς φησι Νίκανδρος *γαστέρ' ἀναβρώσαντες ἀμήτορες ἐξεγένοντο*. διὸ ἔχιν αὐτὸν ὡς μητροκτόνον φησίν. The author quotes from Nicander of Colophon (second century B.C.), *Theriaca*, line 134 (a hexameter poem in 958 verses) on the nature of venomous animals and the wounds which they inflict. No matter whether Origen had read the work of Nicander, or not, definitely he had read of this function of vipers in Euripides, whom he admired and extolled for his philosophical inspiration, and certainly in Galen, *De Theriaca ad Pisonem*, p. 239 (quoting Nicander).

This information about vipers was not widely known, and it appears again in the fifth-century anonymous *Vita Sanctae Syncleticae*, lines 315-317: αἱ γὰρ ἔχιδναι γεννώμεναι λέγονται μὴ ἀναμένειν τὸν καιρὸν τῆς γεννήσεως, ἀλλὰ τὰς γαστέρας τῶν μητέρων ἀναρρηγνύναι πρῶτον. διαφθείρουσι ταύτας, καὶ οὕτως ἐξελθοῦσαι ὁπλίζονται κατὰ τῶν ἄλλων. As for Nicander, he was widely known in Late Antiquity: his name and works were cited by numerous authors, but by no Christian at all (except in Photius' *Lexicon*, letter tau, pp. 592; 603; 637, and *Bibliotheca*, Cod. 279, p. 532b, but these were in fact either excerpts from earlier lexica, or Photius had read them in the book he reviewed). References to Nicander by Eustathius of Thessaloniki actually do not count as *Christian* ones. Cf. *Commentarii ad Homeri Iliadem*, v. 2, pp. 374; 554). Here are some references to Nicander. Plutarch, *Quomodo Adolescens Poetas Audire Debeat*, p. 16C; *Fragmenta*, frs. 113-115. Herodian, *Περὶ Παθῶν*, p. 188; *et passim*. Julius Pollux (Naucratites), *Onomasticon*, 5.38. Athenaeus, *Deipnosophistae*, 2.73; 7.90; 7.95; 9.2; 14.61. Stephanus Byzantius, *Ethnica*, p. 375. Eutecnius, *Paraphrasis in Nicandri Theriaca*, p. 19. Oribasius, *Collectiones Medicae*, 12.9. *Etymologicum Genuinum*, letter alpha, entries 171; 672; 817; 1134; *et passim* (at more than 20 points). *Suda*, letter mu, entry 194 ('Marianus, a Roman lawyer, translated Nicander's *Theriaca* in Latin); letter nu, entry 374. *Etymologicum Magnum*, pp. 18; *et passim* (at more than fifty points).

cxxx See *infra*, folio 219v: Ὁ δὲ Κύριος μεταρρυθμίζων αὐτὸν εἰς εὐαγγελικὴν πολιτείαν.

cxxxi Cf. *infra*, folio 14v: Οἱ λίθοι λαμβάνονται εἰς στεῖραν καὶ εἰς τὴν εἰδωλολατρίαν τῶν ἐθνῶν.

cxxxii Cf. Origen, *homLuc*, homily 22, p. 138: Οὐ λίθους ἐδείκνυεν ἀψύχους, ἀλλ' ἀνθρώπους ἀναισθήτους ὄντας λίθους, ἐπειδήπερ λίθοις καὶ ξύλοις προσεκύνουν.

cxxxiii The same, also *infra*, folio 14v.

cxxxiv Continuing in present codex, folios 13v-14r.

cxxxv Origen, *commMatt*, fr. 44 (Klostermann), col. 2.

cxxxvi Once again, *Codex Sabaiticus 232* is more accurate: since both adjectives πατρολῷον and μητρολῷον qualify the neuter γέννημα, Klostermann's feminine adjectives πατρολῷαν and μητρολῷαν are incorrect. Cf. the same idea in the *Catena in Matthaeum*, p. 22 (attributed to Severian and John Chrysostom, who quite evidently drew on Origen): *Γεννήματα ἐχιδνῶν*. Εἶπεν δὲ αὐτοὺς γεννήματα ἐχιδνῶν, ὅτι οὐδὲν ἄμεινον διέκειντο αὗτοί τε καὶ οἱ γεγεννηκότες αὐτοὺς τοῦ θηρίου τούτου. καὶ γὰρ τοῦτο διαφθείρει τὴν ὠδίνουσαν, καὶ διατρώγων τὴν γαστέρα αὐτῆς, οὕτως ἐξέρχεται εἰς φῶς, ὅπερ καὶ οὗτοι ἐποίουν, πατραλοῖαι γινόμενοι, καὶ μητραλοῖαι, καὶ τοὺς διδασκάλους ταῖς ἑαυτῶν διαφθείροντες χερσί.

cxxxvii Origen, *commMatt*, fr. 44 (Klostermann), col. 1. Likewise, see the similar text in Klostermann, fr. 44, col. II, pp. 33-34. The editor placed the last passage in brackets, because he found a parallel in John Chrysostom. But this was a mistake only because Klostermann was not aware of Origen's selfsame statement in the commentary on Luke. Once again, Chrysostom simply copied from Origen, which he normally did, especially in respect of the exegesis of the gospel of Matthew. I quote Origen's text forthwith.

cxxxviii Origen, *schLuc*, PG.17.322.26-33. The same in Origen, *frLuc*, fr. 87. Here is how John Chrysostom copied from this. *In Matthaeum*, PG.57.193.65-194.5: Καλῶς δὲ αὐτοὺς καὶ *γεννήματα ἐχιδνῶν* ἐκάλεσε. Καὶ γὰρ ἐκεῖνο τὸ θηρίον διαφθεῖρον τὴν ὠδίνουσαν, καὶ διατρῶγον τὴν γαστέρα αὐτῆς, οὕτω λέγεται προϊέναι εἰς φῶς. ὅπερ καὶ οὗτοι ἐποίουν, πατραλοῖαι καὶ μητραλοῖαι γινόμενοι, καὶ τοὺς διδασκάλους ταῖς ἑαυτῶν διαφθείροντες χερσίν.

cxxxix Cf. Origen, *Cels*, IV.16: Εἰσὶ γὰρ διάφοροι οἱονεὶ τοῦ λόγου μορφαί, καθὼς ἑκάστῳ τῶν εἰς ἐπιστήμην ἀγομένων φαίνεται ὁ λόγος, ἀνάλογον τῇ ἕξει τοῦ εἰσαγομένου ἢ ἐπ' ὀλίγον προκόπτοντος ἢ ἐπὶ πλεῖον ἢ καὶ ἐγγὺς ἤδη γινομένου τῆς ἀρετῆς ἢ καὶ ἐν ἀρετῇ γεγενημένου. *frPs*, on Psalm 118:78: ὅτε δὲ εἰς ἄκρον φθάσει τελειότητος, ἐν ἕξει ἀρετῆς καταστᾶσα, ἔξω γενήσεται παντὸς φόβου. *selPs*, PG.12.1193.19-22: Εἰ οἱ προκόπτοντες κατὰ μείωσιν κακίας προκόπτουσι, δίκαιοι λέγονται οἱ τελείαν ἕξιν τῆς δικαιοσύνης κτησάμενοι, καὶ οἱ ἀνεμποδίστως προκόπτοντες. *Op. cit.* PG.12.1509.43-45: Τὴν μὲν διάθεσιν τῆς κακίας διὰ τῶν Αἰγυπτίων ᾐνίξατο. τὴν δὲ ἕξιν διὰ τῶν Αἰθιόπων δεδήλωκεν.

cxl Cf. Origen, *deOr*, 13.3: ἄγονοί τε γὰρ ἐπὶ πολὺ γεγενημέναι ψυχαί, ᾐσθημέναι τῆς στειρώσεως τῶν ἰδίων ἡγεμονικῶν καὶ τῆς ἀγονίας τοῦ νοῦ ἑαυτῶν, ἀπὸ τοῦ ἁγίου πνεύματος διὰ ἐπιμόνου εὐχῆς κυήσασαι σωτηρίους λόγους. *Op. cit.* 13.4: καὶ ἐν ἡμῖν γὰρ ἀσκητέον μὴ ἐγγενέσθαι ἄγονον ἢ στεῖραν, ἀκούουσι τοῦ πνευματικοῦ νόμου ὡσὶ πνευματικοῖς. ἵνα ἀποτιθέμενοι τὸ εἶναι ἄγονοι ἢ στεῖραι ἐπακουσθῶμεν ὡς Ἄννα καὶ Ἐζεκίας. *Op. cit.* 16.3: μᾶλλον οὖν κεκαρποφορήκει ἀπό τινος στειρώσεως μεταβαλοῦσα ἡ τῆς Ἄννης ψυχὴ ἤπερ τὸ σῶμα, κυῆσαν τὸν Σαμουήλ.

cxli Origen, *commMatt*, fr. 46 (Klostermann).

cxlii Jerome, *commMatt*, 3.9.

cxliii Origen, *homJob*, PG.17.105.10456-105.4; *homJob*, p. 388 (Pitra).

cxliv Origen, *commMatt*, fr. 45 (Klostermann).

cxlv This dash actually means a lacuna: in fact, Cyril omitted some of Origen's text while copying from this. See Origen's text continuing below: διά τοι τοῦτο, οὐδὲ ἀφειστήκει τῆς ῥίζης.

cxlvi Cyril of Alexandria, *frMatt*, fr. 24. See the last phrase, Διά τοι τοῦτο, οὐδὲ ἀφειστήκει τῆς ῥίζης, *infra*, folio 15r.

cxlvii διά τοι τοῦτο, οὐδὲ ἀφειστήκει τῆς ῥίζης: Cyril (*supra*, *frMatt*, fr. 24) copied this after he had omitted some of Origen's intervening text.

cxlviii Origen, *commMatt*, fr. 47 (Klostermann).

cxlix The notion of 'endless punishment' is a recurring motif. Cf. διηνεκὴς κόλασις.

cl This means that Origen maintained not only the idea of different degrees of punishment (see endnote dccciv), but also that of different rewards in accordance with one's deeds.

cli John Chrysostom, *In Matthaeum*, PG.57.196.56-62. Cf. *op. cit.* PG.57.421.40-41: Οὐδὲ γὰρ Ἰωάννης ὅταν λέγῃ, *Ἰσχυρότερός μού ἐστι*, συγκρίνων λέγει.

clii Part of this passage is known as Theodore of Heraclea, *frMatt*, fr. 18. Once again, this attribution is made between two Origen's texts. However, this coincides with Theodore of Heraclea's fragment only partially, that is, up to τὸ πῦρ δοκιμάσῃ. The rest of the present passage (although attributed to Theodore of Heraclea) is absent from Reuss' fragment, which goes on differently. The text at hand is in fact two portions from John Chrysostom, *In Matthaeum*, PG.57.198.51-52 & PG.57.199.1-4.

cliii 1 Cor. 3:13. Jerome, *commMatt*, 3.11.

cliv John Chrysostom, *In Matthaeum*, PG.57.198.51-52.

clv John Chrysostom, *op. cit.* PG.57.199.1-4.

clvi Origen, *commMatt*, fr. 51 (Klostermann), continued *infra*.

clvii Origen, *commMatt*, fr. 51 (Klostermann). There is unique parallel to this text of Origen's; this is by John Chrysostom, who continues to indicate that he wrote his works while reading Origen's commentary. *Expositiones in Psalmos*, PG.55.98.27-28: Τί τὸ πτύον; Ἡ διάκρισις. Cf. Theodoret, *De Incarnatione Domini*, PG.75.1464.53-54: οὐ πτύου δεομένην καὶ διακρίσεως.

clviii Once again, an 'unattributed' passage appears between two Origen's ones. However, there are characteristic points revealing Origen's thought in this. (1) the notion of 'pefection of our baptism' (τελείωσιν τοῦ ἡμετέρου βαπτίσματος) discussed in a moment (see endnote clx); (2) Origen's extensive text in the *Catena in Lucam*, which treats not only this idea (of 'pefection of our baptism') but also 'Jacob's prophecy' (Gen. 49:1-30), which Origen made a major point of discussion in relation to Hosea, 3:4, as discussed in the Introduction, p. XXXVII, note 81.

clix Cf. Origen, *commMatt*, fr. 382 (Klostermann) & Origen, *schMatt*, PG.17.297.53-300.13: ἡ γὰρ πανεπίσκοπος τοῦ θεοῦ δύναμις ἀμερίστως μεριστὴ γίνεται τοῖς ἀξίοις.

clx The notion of 'pefection of our baptism' (τελείωσιν τοῦ ἡμετέρου βαπτίσματος) was introduced by Origen. An extensive text in the *Catena in Lucam*, (pp. 26-30) makes this all too clear; p. 28: Ἐκήρυσσε δὲ βάπτισμα μετανοίας εἰς ἄφεσιν ἁμαρτιῶν. Τὸ μὲν γὰρ Θεῷ βάπτισμα τελείως ἔχει ἄφεσιν ἁμαρτιῶν ἐξ αὐτοῦ τοῦ βαπτίζεσθαι, τὸ δὲ Ἰωάννου εἰς αὐτὸ μὲν εἶχεν ἄφεσιν ἁμαρτιῶν, διὰ μετανοίας δέ, ἀτελὴς γὰρ ἦν, εἰ καὶ τῶν Ἰουδαϊκῶν βαπτισμάτων τελειότερον ὑπῆρχεν. This runs parallel to Origen's *Fragmenta in Lucam*, fr. 84: κηρύσσει δὲ *βάπτισμα εἰς ἄφεσιν ἁμαρτιῶν* τίνι ἢ τῷ μηκέτι ἁμαρτάνοντι; τὸ μὲν γὰρ Χριστοῦ βάπτισμα τελείως ἔχει ἄφεσιν ἁμαρτιῶν ἐξ αὐτοῦ τοῦ βαπτίζεσθαι. τὸ δὲ Ἰωάννου, εἰ καὶ εἶχεν ἄφεσιν ἁμαρτιῶν, ἀλλὰ διὰ μετανοίας. ἀτελὲς γὰρ ἦν, εἰ καὶ τῶν Ἰουδαϊκῶν βαπτισμάτων τελειότερον.

The idea was taken up by his usual followers. Cf. Gregory of Nyssa, *Adversus Macedonianos De Spiritu Sancto*, p. 106: τῇ ἐνεργείᾳ τοῦ πνεύματος τελειοῦσθαι τοῖς ἀξιουμένοις. εἰ οὖν ἡ ζωὴ διὰ τοῦ βαπτίσματος, τὸ δὲ βάπτισμα ἐν ὀνόματα πατρὸς καὶ υἱοῦ καὶ πνεύματος ἁγίου τὴν τελείωσιν ἔχει, τί λέγουσιν οἱ τὸ παρεκτικὸν τῆς ζωῆς ἀντ' οὐδενὸς λογιζόμενοι; Gregory of Nazianzus, *Supremum Vale*, PG.36.473.44-477.1 (quoted also by Justinian, *Contra Monophysitas*, 179): πιστεύομεν εἰς Πατέρα, καὶ Υἱόν, καὶ Πνεῦμα ἅγιον, ὁμοούσιά τε καὶ ὁμόδοξα. ἐν οἷς καὶ τὸ βάπτισμα τὴν τελείωσιν ἔχει, ἔν τε ὀνόμασι καὶ πράγμασιν (οἶδας ὁ μυηθείς). Athanasius, *Oratio II contra Arianos*, 41.2-5: διὰ τί καὶ ἐν τῇ τελειώσει τοῦ βαπτίσματος συγκατονομάζεται τῷ πατρὶ ὁ υἱός; ... εἰ γὰρ εἰς ὄνομα πατρὸς καὶ υἱοῦ δίδοται ἡ τελείωσις, οὐ λέγουσι δὲ πατέρα ἀληθινὸν διὰ τὸ ἀρνεῖσθαι τὸ ἐξ αὐτοῦ καὶ ὅμοιον τῆς οὐσίας, ἀρνοῦνται δὲ καὶ τὸν ἀληθινὸν υἱὸν καὶ ἄλλον ἑαυτοῖς ἐξ οὐκ ὄντων κτιστὸν ἀναπλάττοντες ὀνομάζουσι. ... ἵν' ἐκ τῆς μαθήσεως ἡ πίστις ὀρθὴ γένηται καὶ μετὰ πίστεως ἡ τοῦ βαπτίσματος τελείωσις προστεθῇ. Epiphanius of Salamis wrote that this notion involved a Gnostic tenor. *Panarion*, v. 2, p. 35 (ref. to Gnostics): τὸ μὲν γὰρ βάπτισμα τοῦ φαινομένου Ἰησοῦ ἀφέσεως ‹εἶναι› ἁμαρτιῶν, τὴν δὲ ἀπολύτρωσιν τοῦ ἐν αὐτῷ κατελθόντος Χριστοῦ εἰς τελείωσιν, καὶ τὸ μὲν ψυχικόν, τὴν δὲ πνευματικὴν εἶναι ὑφίστανται, καὶ τὸ μὲν βάπτισμα ὑπὸ Ἰωάννου κατηγγέλθαι εἰς μετάνοιαν, τὴν δὲ ἀπολύτρωσιν ὑπὸ Χριστοῦ κεκομίσθαι εἰς τελείωσιν.

clxi Origen, *commMatt*, fr. 53 (Klostermann). Cf. John Chrysostom, *In Matthaeum*, PG.57.202.56-203.12.

clxii Origen, *commMatt*, fr. 55 (Klostermann). The editor notes that he came upon other codices attributing this also to Theodore of Heraclea. This is the usual case which we come upon every now and then in the present codex.

clxiii Origen, *commMatt*, fr. 56 (Klostermann). A similar text appears in John Chrysostom, *De Baptismo Christi*, PG.49.369.23-26 & 31-47, and in the *Catena in Marcum*, p. 271. This fragment that Klosterman came upon being attributed to Origen is a combination of the above two ones, which probably suggests that this served as a prototype for both Chrysostom and the catenist on the gospel of Mark.

John of Damascus preserved the last phrase as a sort of proverb and this coincides with Origen's present fragment. *Sacra Parallela*, PG.95.1296.38-39: Τὸν πνευματικὸν ἀπόνηρον εἶναι χρὴ καὶ ἁπλοῦν καὶ ἄδολον. Cf. Origen, *homLuc*, homily 27, fr. 160: διὰ τὸ πρᾶον καὶ ἀκέραιον, ἵνα καὶ ἡμεῖς τὸ πρᾶον καὶ ἀκέραιον τῆς περιστερᾶς μιμησώμεθα καὶ τὸ πέτασθαι τῷ νῷ ὑπὲρ τὰ γήϊνα. *frLuc*, fr.152: καὶ ἀπόνηρον παιδίον. *frPs*, on Psalm 138:14-16: τὸ ἄκακον καὶ ἀπόνηρον καὶ ἀνεξέργαστόν μου ἔργον.

clxiv Jerome, *commMatt*, 3.15.

clxv Origen, *commMatt*, fr. 54 (Klostermann).

clxvi John Chrysostom copied from Origen's commentary once again. *In Matthaeum*, PG.57.203.36-46.

clxvii Origen reflects after Rom. 13:8-10.

clxviii Meaning, τὸ ῥεῖθρον τοῦ Ἰορδάνου.

clxix Cf. Origen, *frPs*, on Psalm 37:6: Φύσει δὲ τῆς κακίας κατωφεροῦς τε οὔσης καὶ βαρυτάτης, μόνος ὁ μετανοῶν τοῦ βάρους αὐτῆς ἐπαισθάνεται. The same in *frPs*(*al*), fr. 376, only to confirm once again that this collection largely contains Origen's characteristic terminology. Corpus Hermeticum, *Poimandres*, 14: καὶ ἔδειξε τῇ κατωφερεῖ φύσει τὴν καλὴν τοῦ θεοῦ μορφήν. Here is how Cyril of Alexandria copied; *Expositio in Psalmos*, PG.69.957.33-34: Φύσει δὲ τῆς κακίας κατωφεροῦς οὔσης καὶ βαρυτάτης ὡς ταλάντῳ μολίβδου παραβάλλεσθαι. John Philoponus, *commPhys*, p. 670: πόθεν δὲ καὶ κατωφερὲς τὸ ὕδωρ φύσει ὑπάρχον ἐπὶ τὸ ἄνω κινεῖται.

clxx The ensuing portion is part of Origen's text (which is otherwise continuous), Ζητεῖται παρὰ πολλοῖς, ... οὐδὲ γὰρ Ἀνανίας Παύλου, and has been ascribed also to Theodore of Mopsuestia, *frMatt*, fr. 14.

clxxi See *infra*, this being copied by Theodore of Mopsuestia.

clxxii This concludes the alleged ascription to Theodore of Mopsuestia.

clxxiii Theodore of Mopsuestia, *op. cit.* fr. 15, col. 1. He copied from Origen, and this idea about the dove's behavioural attributes is unique in literature. Likewise, Theodore of Mopsuestia, *op. cit.* (col. 2): Ἐν εἴδει περιστερᾶς ἐφάνη τὸ πνεῦμα τὸ ἅγιον ὡς φιλόστοργόν τε καὶ φιλάνθρωπον καὶ πολλάκις ὑφ' ὑμῶν ἀθετούμενον πάλιν ἔχεται ἡμῶν καὶ εὐεργετεῖ διὰ τὴν αὐτοῦ ἀγαθότητα. ἡ γὰρ περιστερὰ φιλόστοργον οὖσα καὶ φιλάνθρωπον ζῷον ὑπὸ τῶν ἀνθρώπων ἀδικουμένη τὰ ἐκείνης ἔκγονα ἀποσπώντων τε καὶ ἐσθιόντων οὐκ ἀφίσταται τῶν συνήθων, ἀλλ' ἔχεται παντοίως.

clxxiv Origen, *commMatt*, fr. 57 (Klostermann).

clxxv This passage follows immediately after the preceding one; but there is the indication 'by Origen' once again.

clxxvi Origen, *commMatt*, fr. 58 (Klostermann), col. 1.

clxxvii Theodore of Mopsuestia, *frMatt*, fr. 16.

clxxviii Origen, *commMatt*, fr. 58 (Klostermann), col. 2.

clxxix Jerome, *commMatt*, 3.16. Quoted also by Klostermann as footnote to his fr. 58: "mysterium trinitatis in baptismate de patris demonstratum: dominus baptisatur, spiritus descendit in specie columbae, patris vox testimonium filio praebentis auditur." Once again, Jerome's copying from Origen is all too evident.

clxxx Origen, *commMatt*, fr. 60 (Klostermann).

clxxxi The oratorical turn Τί φής; (with question mark) is a distinctively stylistic Greek one, which only a profoundly educated writer such as Origen could have used, especially once his knowledge of Plato and Euripides is considered. See Euripides, *Fragmenta* (*Nauck*), fr. 1008. Sophocles, *Electra*, verses 675; 855; *Oedipus Tyrannus*, verses 330; 654; 957; *et passim*. Aristophanes, *Equites*, verse 1345; *Nubes*, verse 1443; *Pax*, verse 872; *Aves*, verse 414; *Lysistrata*, verse 70; *et passim*. Plato, *Euthyphro*, 2b; 5d; *Philebus*, 12a; 23d; *Crito*, 47a; *Meno*, 71d; 79e; *Charmides*, 129a; *Theaetetus*, 187c; *Protagoras*, 309c; 349e; 359e; *Gorgias*, 516c; *et passim* (also in *Hippias minor*, *Respublica*, *Leges*). Then, Philo, *De Somniis*, 2.296; *De Virtutibus*, 59; *Legatio ad Gaium*, 347. Plutarch, *Quomodo Quis Suos In Virtute Sentiat Profectus*, p. 78A. Galen, *De Methodo Medendi*, pp. 144; 259. Lucian of Samosata, *Juppiter Confutatus*, 18; 35; 36; *Timon*, 7; *et passim* (abundantly). Athenaeus, *Deipnosophistae*, 2.87; 4.77; *et passim* (abundantly). After Origen (and not incidentally), this appears in admirers of his, such as Gregory of Nyssa, Eusebius, Gregory of Nazianzus, Athanasius, John Chrysostom, *et. al.* The fact that Aristotle did not use this expressive style should be noticed.

clxxxii Jerome, *commMatt*, 4.1.

clxxxiii Severus of Antioch, *apud Catena in Matthaeum*, p. 25.

clxxxiv The text of the codex continues without interruption, but the catenist added 'by Origen' once again.

clxxxv Origen, *commMatt*, fr. 61 (Klostermann), col. 1, continued *infra*.

clxxxvi Origen, *commMatt*, fr. 61 (Klostermann), col. 1; see also col. 2.

clxxxvii Gregory of Nyssa, *Orationes viii De Beatitudinibus*, PG.44.1236.59-1237.7. Also, Gregory of Nyssa, *apud Catena in Lucam*, p. 35. This is the same text, only instead of ἐδέξατο τὴν ὀρεκτικὴν ὁρμὴν τῆς φύσεως, it reads εἴξατο τὴν ὀρεκτικὴν τῆς φύσεως ὁρμήν.

clxxxviii Jerome, *commMatt*, 4.2.

clxxxix Cf. Epiphanius of Salamis, *apud Catena in Matthaeum*, p. 23: (Ἐπιφανίου) Ἐπείνασεν ἵνα δείξῃ τὴν ἀληθινὴν ἐνανθρώπησιν.

cxc Jerome, *commMatt*, 4.2.

cxci Severus of Antioch, *apud Catena in Matthaeum*, p. 25.

cxcii Jerome, *commMatt*, 4.4.

cxciii Origen, *commMatt*, fr. 64 (Klostermann).

cxciv Jerome, *commMatt*, 4.4.

cxcv Jerome, *commMatt*, 4.5.

cxcvi Jerome, *loc. cit.*

cxcvii Severus of Antioch, *apud Catena in Matthaeum*, pp. 25-26.

cxcviii Psalm 90:11, which is quoted in paraphrase in Matt. 4:6.

cxcix Jerome, *commMatt*, 4.6.

cc Origen, *commMatt*, fr. 65 (Klostermann), col. 1.

cci Origen, *commMatt*, fr. 62 (Klostermann).

ccii Cf. Origen, *commJohn*, I.30.208: τὰ δὲ εὐφραίνοντα καὶ ἐνθουσιᾶν ποιοῦντα ἀπόρρητα καὶ μυστικὰ θεωρήματα, τοῖς κατατρυφῶσι τοῦ κυρίου ἐγγινόμενα. *Op. cit.* I.34.244: Εἰ δέ τις οἷος τέ ἐστιν ἀσώματον ὑπόστασιν ποικίλων θεωρημάτων περιεχόντων τοὺς τῶν ὅλων λόγους ζῶσαν καὶ οἱονεὶ ἔμψυχον ἐπινοεῖν, εἴσεται τὴν ὑπὲρ πᾶσαν κτίσιν σοφίαν τοῦ θεοῦ. *Op. cit.* I.38.283: οὕτω τὰ τῆς ἀληθείας θεωρήματα οὐ συνέχων ὁ πατὴρ ἐρεύγεται καὶ ποιεῖ τὸν τύπον αὐτῶν ἐν τῷ λόγῳ. *Op. cit.* II.18.126: Ζητητέον δὲ εἰ συστήματος θεωρημάτων ὄντος ἐν αὐτῷ, καθ' ὃ *σοφία* ἐστίν, ἐστί τινα θεωρήματα ἀχώρητα τῇ λοιπῇ παρ' αὐτὸν γεννητῇ φύσει, ἅτινα οἶδεν ἑαυτῷ. *Op. cit.* II.28.172: Ἐὰν γάρ τις κατανοήσῃ τὸ πλῆθος τῶν περὶ θεοῦ θεωρημάτων καὶ γνώσεως ἄληπτον τυγχάνον ἀνθρωπίνῃ φύσει, τάχα δὲ καὶ ἑτέροις παρὰ

Χριστὸν καὶ τὸ ἅγιον πνεῦμα γενητοῖς. *Op. cit.* V.5.1 (& *Philocalia*, 5.4): Ὁ πᾶς δὴ τοῦ θεοῦ λόγος ὁ ἐν ἀρχῇ πρὸς τὸν θεὸν οὐ πολυλογία ἐστίν. οὐ γὰρ λόγοι. λόγος γὰρ εἷς συνεστὼς ἐκ πλείονων θεωρημάτων, ὧν ἕκαστον θεώρημα μέρος ἐστὶ τοῦ ὅλου λόγου. *Op. cit.* VI.1.1: ἡ τῶν τῆς ἀληθείας θεωρημάτων δεκτική, λογικὴ ὡς ἐν ἀπαγγελίᾳ καὶ γράμμασιν οἰκοδομή. *Op. cit.* X.17.102: ζητοῦντες καὶ τρεφόμενοι ἀπὸ τῶν εὑρισκομένων τῆς ἀληθείας θεωρημάτων. *Op. cit.* XIII.46.302: ἐπὶ πάσης τῆς ἐκ πλειόνων θεωρημάτων τέχνης καὶ ἐπιστήμης σπείρει μὲν ὁ τὰς ἀρχὰς εὑρίσκων. *Op. cit.* XXXII.15.172: Ὁ παραλαμβάνων σοφίας θεωρήματα ἔσθ᾽ ὅτε ἐπὶ προτέροις, δι᾽ ἃ ἤδη σοφός ἐστιν, ἀναλαμβάνει δεύτερα, ἐφ᾽ οἷς οὐ πρότερον ἦν σοφός, καὶ σοφώτερος ἔσται. *frJohn*, fr. 64: τῷ λογικῷ τῆς ἀληθείας ἀπεριστάτως πλουσίων θεωρημάτων. *Op. cit.* 87: ἀπολαμβάνοντας κατὰ τὴν ἀξίαν ἐν τῇ ἀναστάσει σῶμα δόξης ὑπερεχούσης καὶ διαφερούσης ἐν ἐκείνοις γίνεσθαι τοῖς χωρίοις ὡς ἐπιτηδειοτάτοις πρὸς τὴν σχολὴν τῶν θεωρημάτων τοῦ θεοῦ λόγου. *Op. cit.* 131: πορισμὸν τῆς Χριστοῦ ἀληθείας καὶ τῶν πλουσίων θεωρημάτων αὐτοῦ τὴν γνῶσιν προσαιτοῦντας. *Op. cit.* 139: τοὺς διαφέροντας τῇ λαμπρότητι ἀπολαμβάνοντας κατὰ τὴν ἀξίαν ἐν τῇ ἀναστάσει χωρίοις γίνεσθαι ὡς ἐπιτηδειοτάτοις πρὸς τὴν σχολὴν τῶν θεωρημάτων τοῦ θεοῦ λόγου. *deOr*, 13.3: ἀπὸ τοῦ ἁγίου πνεύματος διὰ ἐπιμόνου εὐχῆς κυήσασαι σωτηρίους λόγους θεωρημάτων ἀληθείας πεπληρωμένους, γεγεννήκασιν. *Op. cit.* 25.2: ἀεὶ μὲν πλείονα θεωρήματα *σοφίας* καὶ *γνώσεως* ἐν τῷ ἐπακούεσθαι ληψόμενος. *Op. cit.* 30.3: τῶν ἐνθέων καὶ σωτηρίων λογισμῶν, ἐντυπουμένων ἀπὸ τῶν τῆς ἀληθείας θεωρημάτων. *frLam*, fr. 7: τὸ μὲν πλῆθος τοῦ λαοῦ σημαίνοι ἂν τῆς μακαριζομένης Ἱερουσαλὴμ τὸν πλοῦτον τῶν θεωρημάτων. *Op. cit.* 20: τὰ ἐν τῇ ἐπιστημονικῇ ψυχῇ θεωρήματα ὁ λαός ἐστι τῆς Ἱερουσαλήμ. *Cels*, VI.19: Δαυῒδ τὴν βαθύτητα τοῦ πλήθους τῶν ἐν τοῖς ὑπεραναβεβηκόσι τὰ αἰσθητὰ ὑπαρχόντων περὶ θεοῦ θεωρημάτων πάλαι παρέστησεν. *Op. cit.* VI.20: ἀναλαβόντες κατὰ τὴν Ἰησοῦ διδασκαλίαν ποταμούς τε χωρήσαντες τῶν θεωρημάτων. *homLuc*, homily 1, p. 8 & *schLuc*, PG.17.313.29-30: τινῶν μὲν θεωρημάτων τὸ τέλος ἡ θεωρία ἐστίν, τινῶν δὲ θεωρημάτων τὸ τέλος ἡ πρᾶξις. *Libri x in Canticum Canticorum (fragmenta)*, p. 175 & *Scholia in Canticum Canticorum*, PG.17.260.38-40: *Σύσκιον* δέ φησι τὸν νυμφίον διὰ τὴν πυκνότητα τῶν ἐν τῷ λόγῳ καὶ τῇ σοφίᾳ θεωρημάτων. *Scholia in Canticum Canticorum*, PG.17.269.31-33: ἵνα καὶ μετὰ τὴν ἐντεῦθεν ἔξοδον, εἰσέλθοι αὐτῷ εἰς τὸν οἶκον τῆς ἄνω Ἱερουσαλήμ, ἔνθα εἰσάγῃ τὰ κοινότερα τῶν τοῦ λόγου θεωρημάτων. *Op. cit.* PG.17.272.9-10: καὶ ἡ νύμφη ἐν τῷ βάθει κρύπτει τὰ θεωρήματα. *Op. cit.* PG.17.285.40-41: ἐπ᾽ ἂν τρανώσῃ τὰ νοήματα καὶ προφητικὰ θεωρήματα. *commMatt*, 12.6: οὐ γὰρ διαρκῇ καὶ συμπαρεκτεινομένην μνήμην ἀναλαβεῖν δυνάμεθα τῷ πλήθει τῆς φύσεως τῶν θεωρημάτων. *Op. cit.* 17.3: οἱ ἐνταῦθα *ἀρχιερεῖς καὶ πρεσβύτεροι τοῦ λαοῦ* οὐδαμῶς ἄξιοι ἦσαν τοιούτων θεωρημάτων. *commEph*, fr. 9: τὸ *πνεῦμα* τῆς *σοφίας* ποσότητι τῶν θεωρημάτων τῆς σοφίας διαφόρως σοφοὺς ποιεῖ. *frPs*, on Psalm 4:4: ἐθαυμαστώθησαν ὑπὸ Θεοῦ οἱ ὅσιοι, θαύμασι προσαχθέντες τῶν ἀπορρήτων μυστηρίων καὶ τῶν ἁγίων θεωρημάτων. *selDeut*, PG.12.812.17: τὰ κεκρυμμένα τῶν θεωρημάτων. *selPs*, PG.12.1109.5-6: ἑαυτοὺς παρέχοντες ἀξίους τῆς χρηστότητος τῶν θεωρημάτων τοῦ λόγου. *Op. cit.* PG.12.1569.47-48: Ἡ σοφία τοῦ Θεοῦ, καθὸ μὲν ἀφθονίαν παρέχει θεωρημάτων, πλοῦτος καλεῖται. *expProv*, PG.17.229.25-28: πάντες οἱ πεπιστευκότες Χριστῷ, ἀπὸ τῶν ἁγίων προφητῶν καὶ ἀποστόλων λαμβάνοντες θεωρήματα, οὐ λέγονται κλέπται ἀλλοτρίων θεωρημάτων.

cciii Origen, *commMatt*, fr. 66 (Klostermann). Once again, Klostermann's text falls short of *Codex Sabaiticus 232*, which is far more accurate and written in correct Greek. Klostermann opted for οὓς δὲ ἔσπειρεν instead of the LXX ὡς διέσπειρεν, and for στήσας ὅρια instead of ἔστησεν ὅρια. More striking still is that he bypassed a cardinal theory of Origen, and wrote ὕψος τῶν θεωρητῶν instead of ὕψος τῶν θεωρημάτων. Cf. Origen, *expProv*, PG.17.252.48-49: Λόγον γὰρ ἔχουσι θεωρημάτων ἐπιστήμονα, μηδὲν ἔχοντες ὑψηλόν. Nilus of Ancyra, *Commentarii in Canticum Canticorum*, 39: εἰς ταπεινὰ καὶ ἀνάξια ὕψους θείων θεωρημάτων καταχρησάμενον τῇ δυνάμει. Cyril of Alexandria, *commProphXII*, v. 1, p. 331:

καρπόν, τὸν περὶ τῆς ἁγίας καὶ ὁμοουσίου Τριάδος, ἤγουν παιδεύσεως ἠθικῆς, τῆς ὡς ἐν ὕψει θεωρημάτων.

cciv Cf. ἐμπαθεῖς λογισμοί, Origen, *selPs*, PG.12: 1085.22; 1197.20; 1240.1; 1536.44; *expProv*, PG.17: 172.15; 180.20; 245.54; 248.3. Cf. *homJer*, homily 14.10: ψυχὴν ἐμπαθῆ καὶ ἁμαρτωλόν. *homLev*, p. 406: ψυχὴ ἐμπαθής.

ccv The expression ἀκήρατος νοῦς ('undefiled nous') comes from Plato, *Cratylus*, 396b, and the general Neoplatonic tendency was to identify this with Cronus. Cf. Plotinus, *Enneades*, V.1.4 (8); (the text was extensively quoted by Eusebius, *Praeparatio Evangelica*, 11.17.1). Proclus, *Theologia Platonica*, v. 5, pp. 21; 23; 51; 124-125. Cf. Anonymous, *Lexicon De Atticis Nominibus*, entry 37: Κρόνος. ὁ καθαρώτατος καὶ ἀκήρατος νοῦς. Gregory of Nyssa identified this with God; *De Beneficentia*, p. 103: τῆς πρώτης καὶ ἀκηράτου καὶ πάντα νοῦν ὑπερβαινούσης οὐσίας. Synesius of Cyrenia, *Dion*, 6: οὐ γάρ ἐσμεν ὁ ἀκήρατος νοῦς, ἀλλὰ νοῦς ἐν ζῴου ψυχῇ. Cyril of Alexandria took up the Anaxagorean notion of Nous and identified with God from Origen, and he could not have enough with entertaining this. Cyril of Alexandria, *commProphXII*, v. 1, p. 273: ὁ θεῖος τε καὶ ἀκήρατος νοῦς. *Op. cit.* v. 2, p. 69: τὸν ἀκήρατον νοῦν. *Op. cit.* v. 2, p. 105: ὁ θεῖος τε καὶ ἀκήρατος νοῦς. *Epistulae Paschales*, PG.77.721.1: ὁ θεῖος τε καὶ ἀκήρατος νοῦς. *Op. cit.* PG.77.740.41: ὁ ἀκήρατος νοῦς. *Op. cit.* PG.77.868.24: τὸν θεῖον καὶ ἀκήρατον νοῦν. *Op. cit.* PG.77.905.6: τὸν θεῖον τε καὶ ἀκήρατον νοῦν. *De Adoratione*, PG.68.524.29-30: ὁ θεῖος τε καὶ ἀκήρατος νοῦς. *Op. cit.* PG.68.845.22-23: καὶ οὐκ ἄν τι διαλάθοι νοῦν τὸν ἀκήρατον. *Glaphyra in Pentateuchum*, PG.69.45.49: τὸν θεῖον τε καὶ ἀκήρατον νοῦν. *In Isaiam*, PG.70.657.47: τὸν θεῖον τε καὶ ἀκήρατον νοῦν. *Contra Julianum*, 1.29: ὁ θεῖος τε καὶ ἀκήρατος νοῦς. Also, Isidore of Pelusium, *Epistulae*, epistle 1572: ὁ ἀκήρατος νοῦς. *Op. cit.* epistle 1574: ὁ θεῖος καὶ ἀκήρατος νοῦς. Michael Psellus, *Orationes Forenses et Acta*, oration 1, line 2837; *Opuscula i*, opusculum 44, lines 85; 108; *Theologica*, opusculum 8a, line 51; opusculum 10, lines 14; 43; opusculum 62, line 53; opusculum 64, line 93; opusculum 94, line 44. Nicephorus Callistus Xanthopulus, *HE*, 8.39.

ccvi Heb. 1:14. Origen, *commMatt*, fr. 67 (Klostermann).

ccvii Cf. Origen, *commJohn*, X.39.269: Τὴν δὲ περὶ τούτων οἰκονομίαν καὶ λειτουργίαν ἐγχειρισθήσονται ἅγιαι δυνάμεις, ἄγγελοι θεοῦ, αἱ μέν τινες οὖσαι κυριότητες, ἢ θρόνοι, ἢ ἀρχαί, ἢ ἐξουσίαι, αἱ δὲ τούτοις ὑποτεταγμέναι, ὧν τύποι οἱ τρισχίλιοι καὶ ἑξακόσιοι ἄρχοντες ἐπιστάται, ἄρχοντες κατεσταμένοι ἐπὶ τῶν ἔργων τῶν Σαλομών, καὶ ἑβδομήκοντα χιλιάδες τῶν αἰρόντων ἄρσιν, καὶ αἱ τῶν λατόμων ὀγδοήκοντα χιλιάδες ἐν τῷ ὄρει, οἱ ποιοῦντες τὰ ἔργα καὶ ἑτοιμάσαντες τοὺς λίθους καὶ τὰ ξύλα. *homLuc*, homily 12, p. 75: Οἷον ἐν Ἐφέσῳ εἰκός, ὅτι διὰ μὲν τοὺς ἁμαρτάνοντας ἄγγελός τις ἦν ἐγκεχειρισμένος τοὺς ἁμαρτάνοντας, διὰ δὲ τοὺς πιστεύοντας, ὅτι ἄγγελός τις ἦν τῆς Ἐφεσίων ἐκκλησίας, οὕτω δὴ καὶ πανταχοῦ καὶ πρὸ τῆς Χριστοῦ ἐπιδημίας. *Op. cit.* homily 13, p. 77: ἡ ἀγγελικὴ στρατιὰ ... κεκμήκει βοηθοῦσα τοῖς ἀνθρώποις καὶ ἑώρα, ὅτι οὐκ ἠδύνατο τελειῶσαι τὸ ἔργον, ὃ ἦν ἐγκεχειρισμένη, χωρὶς τοῦ σωτῆρος. *commMatt*, 10.13: Ταῦτα δέ φαμεν οὐκ ἀγνοοῦντες τινῶν ἀγγέλων τῶν μὴ τοιαύτην οἰκονομίαν ἐγκεχειρισμένων. *Op. cit.* 13.28: τὸν ἐγκεχειρισμένον ἅμα γενέσει ψυχήν τινα. *Cels*, VIII.57: Κἂν ἴδωμεν δὲ μὴ δαίμονάς τινας ἀγγέλους δὲ τεταγμένους ἐπὶ τῶν τῆς γῆς καρπῶν καὶ ἐπὶ τῆς τῶν ζῴων γενέσεως, εὐφημοῦμεν αὐτοὺς καὶ μακαρίζομεν, ἐγχειρισθέντας ὑπὸ τοῦ θεοῦ τὰ χρήσιμα τῷ γένει ἡμῶν.

ccviii Psalm 33:8. Origen, *commMatt*, fr. 68 (Klostermann).

ccix The notion of 'guardian power' (φρουροῦσα δύναμις) was introduced by Origen, and subsequently it was taken up by his ardent adherents, such as Eusebius and Didymus. As it normally happened, Cyril of Alexandria and Maximus Confessor followed by employing Origenian formulas. It was probably through Didymus that Proclus took up this one (see *RCR*, 'Christian Influence on Neoplatonism', pp. 333-377). Origen, *frLam*, fr. 59: ταῦτα, φησίν, ὑπάρχει αὐτοῖς, καὶ εἰ μὴ πάλιν τὴν λύπην σημαίνει τῆς πάλαι φρουρούσης δυνάμεως, ὑπερβολικῶς τοῦτο δηλῶν. Then, Eusebius, *Commentaria in Psalmos*, PG.23.425.52-56: Οἶμαι, ὅτι ταῖς τὴν Ἐκκλησίαν τοῦ Θεοῦ καὶ τὸ ἐν αὐτῇ θεοσεβὲς πολίτευμα φρουρούσαις θείαις δυνάμεσιν, ἀγγέλοις τε ἁγίοις. Τούτοις οὖν αὐτοῖς τὸ Πνεῦμα τὸ ἅγιον προσφωνεῖ λέγον. *Κυκλώσατε Σιών, καὶ περιλάβετε αὐτήν* [Psalm 47:13]. (Cf. the characteristic expression, τὸ ἐν αὐτῇ θεοσεβὲς πολίτευμα, also in Eusebius, *In Isaiam*, 1.86; 2.3). The same passage has been attributed to Athanasius, *Expositiones in Psalmos*, PG.27.221.34-39. See also Didymus, *Commentarii in Job* (*5.1-6.29*), cod. p. 163: ἡ φρουροῦσα τοὺς ἁγίους δύναμις. *frPs*(*al*), fr. 75 (I have repeatedly argued that numerous passages of this 'alternative' compilation were probably written by Origen rather than Didymus): αἱ δὲ ἐποπτικαὶ καὶ ἔφοροι τοῦ θεοῦ δυνάμεις ὀφθαλμοὶ αὐτοῦ καλούμεναι, πρὸς τὸν πένητα γινόμεναι φρουροῦσιν αὐτὸν ἀβλαβῆ τῶν περὶ αὐτὸν οἰκονομηθέντων. *Op. cit.* fr. 275: Ἐν ταῖς σκεπαζούσαις καὶ φρουρούσαις δυνάμεσι χερσίν σου χρηματιζούσαις οἱ κλῆροί μου τυγχάνουσιν. *Fragmenta in Epistulam ii ad Corinthios*, p. 42: ἡ φρουροῦσα τὸ ἡγεμονικὸν θεοῦ δύναμις πολλάκις οἰκονομεῖ τὸν φρουρούμενον ἔξω γενέσθαι τῆς ὑπ᾽ αὐτῆς σκέπης. Pseudo-Cyril of Alexandria, *Collectio Dictorum Veteris Testamenti*, PG.77.1276.42-45: Ὁ μὴ σωφρονισθεὶς τῷ πρώτῳ τῆς ὀργῆς, ὑποπίπτει τῷ δευτέρῳ, καὶ ἀφαιρεῖται τὴν τῶν χαρισμάτων ἐνέργειαν, καὶ γίνεται τῆς φρουρούσης δυνάμεως ἔρημος. This passage was employed by Maximus Confessor, who time and again drew on Origen's ideas and expressions. *Quaestiones ad Thalassium*, 52. Also, Maximus Confessor, *Expositio in Psalmum lix*, lines 275-278: ἀνάλωτος καὶ ἀπροσπέλαστος γίνεται τοῖς πολεμίοις διὰ τὴν φρουροῦσαν αὐτὸν τῶν ἁγίων δυνάμεων περιβολὴν ὅ γε ἀληθῶς θεοσεβὴς καὶ φιλόθεος.

What is fascinating about this construction is that we are upon one more influence of Origen's legacy upon Neoplatonism, especially on Proclus, for which I have argued in the past (see *RCR*, 'Christian Influence on Neoplatonism', pp. 333-377).

Perhaps, Proclus took up the expression 'guardian power', also from Iamblichus who referred to Plato's *Laws*, 796b (*De Mysteriis*, 3.10: ἐπεὶ τῶν μὲν Κορυβάντων φρουρητική πώς ἐστιν ἡ δύναμις καὶ ἐπιτελεστική), and Proclus himself used this in a reference to the same passage of Plato's (Proclus, *Theologia Platonica*, v. 5, p. 129: Τὸ δὲ *ἐνόπλιον* τῆς φρουρητικῆς ἐστι δυνάμεως σύνθημα, καθ᾽ ἣν τὰ ὅλα συνέχουσι καὶ φρουροῦσιν ἐξῃρημένα τῶν δευτέρων καὶ ἐν αὑτοῖς ἑστῶτα διαφυλάττουσι).

If it were remarked that 'guardian power' is rendered by both Iamblichus and Proclus φρουρητικὴ δύναμις whereas Origen's expression was φρουροῦσα δύναμις, my reply to this could be that the Neoplatonic usage was there already ever since Proclus couched Origen's idea, and there is every reason to assume that Origen himself qualified the noun δύναμις not only through the participle φρουροῦσα, but also through the synonymous epithet φρουρητική.

Anyway, Didymus used both expressions, namely, φρουροῦσα δύναμις (as above) and φρουρητικὴ δύναμις, as follows. Didymus, *Commentarii in Job* (*1-4*), cod. p. 22: τὴν σκεπαστικὴν καὶ φρουρητικὴν δύναμιν. *Commentarii in Job*, PG.39.1121.52-53: τὴν φρουρητικὴν καὶ σκεπαστικὴν δύναμιν. So did other Christian authors. Cyril of Jerusalem, *Catecheses ad Illuminandos*, 6.8: Τῆς γὰρ φρουρητικῆς αὐτοῦ δυνάμεως εἰς πτέρυγας λαμβανομένης. Cyril of Alexandria, *Expositio in Psalmos*, PG.69.816.48-52: ὁ Σωτὴρ ... αἰτεῖ παρὰ τοῦ Πατρὸς τὴν φρουρητικὴν δύναμιν. *Op. cit.* PG.69.1121.43-44: Τὴν φρουρητικὴν δύναμιν τοῦ Θεοῦ σημαίνει. Michael Psellus, *Opuscula*, p. 133: δυνάμεις οἱ Χαλδαῖοι ἐν τῷ κόσμῳ τίθενται ... τῷ μὲν ἀκαμπεῖ τῆς σταθερᾶς αὐτῶν δηλουμένης δυνάμεως, τῷ δὲ ἀνοχικῷ τῆς φρουρητικῆς. *De Omnifaria Doctrina*, 16: ὁ γὰρ θεὸς οὔτε πλῆθος ἐστίν, ἀλλὰ κυρίως ἕν· ... οὐ γὰρ πέρατι περιλαμβάνεται ἡ τούτου ἐνέργεια, ἀλλ᾽ ἥ τε γεννητικὴ αὐτοῦ δύναμις ἥ τε φρουρητικὴ ἥ τε ζωογόνος ἥ τε ἀναγωγικὴ καὶ ἁπλῶς πᾶσαι αἱ δυνάμεις αὐτοῦ ἄπειροι εἰσὶ καὶ ἀνέκλειπτοι.

Of Neoplatonists, it was only Syrianus (sparingly) and Proclus (abundantly) that entertained the same idea by means of the same expression. Syrianus, *commMetaph*, p. 59: ὥστε συνοχικὴν αὐτοῖς ταύτην ἐφίστησι καὶ φρουρητικὴν δύναμιν ἡ τοῦ πρὸ πάντων ἑνὸς ἀγαθότης. *Op. cit.* pp. 144-5: ἐκ δὲ τῆς δυάδος τῆς ἀορίστου τό τε ἀμερὲς καὶ τὸ ἐπὶ πάντα διῆκον ταῖς δημιουργίαις καὶ προνοίαις καὶ ταῖς φρουρητικαῖς δυνάμεσι. Proclus, *Theologia Platonica*, v. 1, p. 78: Παρ᾽ αὐτῶν γὰρ οἶμαι τῶν τὰ θεῖα σοφῶν *πατρικάς* τε *δυνάμεις* καὶ *φρουρητικὰς* καὶ *ἡγεμονικὰς* καὶ *παιωνείους* ὑμνημένας ἀκούομεν. *Op. cit.* v. 4, p. 52: ἡ φρουρητικὴ τῆς τριάδος ταύτης δύναμις ἡ ἀναπόδραστος. *Op. cit.* v. 5, p. 130: ἡ πανοπλία τῆς μεριστῆς τῶν φρουρητικῶν δυνάμεων διανομῆς προϋφέστηκε. *Op. cit.* v. 6, p. 67: Καὶ μὴν καὶ ὁ ἀριθμὸς οὗτος, ἡ τριάς, προσήκει ταῖς φρουρητικαῖς ταύταις δυνάμεσιν ὡς τέλειος. ... Καὶ τί οὕτω προσήκει ταῖς γονίμοις συντετάχθαι δυνάμεσιν ὡς τὸ φρουρητικὸν τῶν θεῶν γένος. *commCrat*, 110: πολλῶν δ᾽ οὐσῶν ἐν τῷ Οὐρανῷ δυνάμεων, οἷον συνεκτικῶν φρουρητικῶν ἐπιστρεπτικῶν. *commTim*, v. 1, p. 38: τῶν τῆς τάξεως φρουρητικῶν δυνάμεων τῆς ἀνανταγωνίστου ῥώμης. *Op. cit.* v. 1, p. 125: τὰς συνεκτικὰς δυνάμεις καὶ φρουρητικάς. *Op. cit.* v. 2, p. 106: ταῖς μὲν γὰρ φρουρητικαῖς δυνάμεσι συνέχει τὸ κέντρον. *Op. cit.* v. 2, p. 107: ἀλλά τινα δύναμιν αὐτῆς φρουρητικὴν τῆς ὅλης τάξεως. *Op. cit.* v. 2, p. 292: καὶ τὸ πᾶν τῷ τε μέσῳ φρουρητικὰς ἐπιστήσασα δυνάμεις. *Op. cit.* v. 3, p. 139: τὴν μίαν ταύτην δύναμιν τὴν φρουρητικὴν τῆς ἀνακυκλήσεως τῶν ὅλων. *Op. cit.* v. 3, p. 208: ἐκείνοις τε γὰρ ἐνδίδωσι φρουρητικὴν αὐτῶν καὶ σωστικὴν δύναμιν καὶ αὐτὸς ἐξῃρημένως συνέχει τὴν οὐσίαν αὐτῶν. *Op. cit.* v. 3, p. 312: καὶ μὴν καὶ ἡ ἀρχὴ τὴν προνοητικὴν τῶν θεῶν ἐπιστασίαν καὶ τὴν συνεκτικὴν δύναμιν καὶ τὰς φρουρητικὰς ἀνεγείρει περιοχάς. Finally, it was natural for Pseudo-Dionysius the Areopagite to echo Proclus once again. *De Caelesti Hierarchia*, p. 51: τῶν οἰκείων οὔσας φρουρητικὰς δυνάμεων. *Op. cit.* p. 55: τὰς δὲ ζώνας τὸ τῶν γονίμων αὐτῶν δυνάμεων φρουρητικὸν καὶ τὸ τὴν συναγωγὸν αὐτῶν ἕξιν εἰς ἑαυτὴν ἑνιαίως συνεστράφθαι.

ccx Origen, *commMatt*, fr. 69 (Klostermann). The editor (*op. cit.* p. 43) found this text in an eleventh-century codex at Mount Athos (C[a]), the attribution being to ΙΩ, ΘΕ, and Origen. The former presumably points to Chrysostom, the latter to 'Theodore', which might be either the one of Heraclea or that of Mopsuestia. This is why J. Reuss tentatively attributed a number of passages that indicated ΘΕ[ΟΔΩΡΟΥ] to 'either Theodore of Heraclea or Theodore of Mopsuestia'. J. Reuss, *Matthäus-Kommentare aus der griechischen Kirche* [*Texte und Untersuchungen* 61. Berlin, 1957], pp. 136-150. However, beyond the fact that Origen is being attributed this passage, in the present volume it becomes recurrently and abundantly clear that both Theodores, as well as John Chrysostom, copied from Origen unabashedly.

ccxi Theodore of Heraclea or Theodore of Mopsuestia, *apud frMatt*, fr. 14.

ccxii Origen, *commMatt*, fr. 70 (Klostermann) (continued *infra*).

ccxiii Cf. Origen, *commSerMatt*, p. 293: νῦν δὲ ἡ καταλιποῦσα τὴν ΚΑΤΑΚΥΛΙΣΤΙΚΗΝ καὶ ΑΣΤΑΤΟΝ Γαλιλαίαν ψυχὴ καὶ ἑπομένη τῷ λόγῳ καὶ ποιοῦσα τὰ προσταττόμενα. Apollinaris, *frMatt*, fr. 151: Γαλιλαία γὰρ ἡ κατακυλιστὴ τῇ Ἑλλάδι γλώσσῃ ἑρμηνεύεται. There should be no doubt that this fragment actually belongs to Origen, just like so many other ones identified in the present volume. Then, Cyril of Alexandria, *frMatt*, fr. 37: οἱ πρὶν ἐν Γαλιλαίᾳ ὄντες, ἥτις κατακυλιστὴ ἑρμηνεύεται. Hesychius of Alexandria, *Lexicon*, letter gamma, entry 51: Γαλιλαία. κατακυλιστή. *Suda*, letter gamma, entry 36: Γαλιλαία. κατακυλιστὴ τῇ Ἑλλάδι γλώσσῃ. διὸ καὶ γελγὲλ ὁ τροχὸς ὀνομάζεται. *Op. cit.* letter gamma, entry 103: Γελγέλ. ὁ τροχὸς ὀνομάζεται. ... διὸ καὶ Γαλιλαία κατακυλιστὴ λέγεται τῇ Ἑλλάδι γλώσσῃ. The same in Pseudo-Zonaras, *Lexicon*, letter gamma, p. 419: Γαλιλαία. κατακυλιστὴ ἑρμηνεύεται τῇ ἑλλάδι γλώσσῃ. Michael Choniates, *Orationes*, v. 1, oration 12, p. 188: καὶ ἡ Γαλιλαία εἰς κατακυλιστὴν μεταγλωττίζεται. Philagathus (Philip Cerameus), *Homiliae*, homilies 5.4 & 20.5: Γαλιλαία γὰρ κατακυλιστὴ ἑρμηνεύεται. Germanus II of Constantinople, *Orationes et Homiliae*, homily 2, p. 218: εἰς κατακυλιστὴν δὲ ἡ Γαλιλαία μεταγλωττίζεται.

ccxiv Origen, *commSerMatt*, p. 293. The term was introduced by Origen, its use always remained exclusive to the interpretation of 'Galilee', and little wonder that this is absent from modern lexica such as that of L&S.

ccxv Apollinaris, *frMatt*, fr. 151.

ccxvi Cyril of Alexandria, *frMatt*, fr. 37.

ccxvii Hesychius of Alexandria, *Lexicon*, letter kappa, entry 741.

ccxviii Isidore Glabas, *Oratio ad Thessalonicenses ii*, p. 573.

ccxix Origen probably received this from Philo, *De Somniis*, 2.34: Ζαβουλὼν δὲ φωτός, ἐπειδὴ ρύσις νυκτερίας ὀνομάζεται. Cf. Nilus of Ancyra, *Epistulae*, book 1, epistle 90: Ζαβουλών, ρύσις νυκτερίας. Hesychius of Jerusalem, *Commentarius Brevis*, on Psalm 67:28: Ζαβουλὼν γὰρ ρύσις νυκτὸς ἑρμηνεύεται, Νεφθαλεὶμ δὲ πλατυσμός. Hesychius of Alexandria, *Lexicon*, letter zeta, entry 13: Ζαβουλών. ρύσις νυκτερινή, τουτέστι χύσις σκότους. Isidore Glabas, *Oratio ad Thessalonicenses ii*, p. 573: ἡ δὲ Ζαβουλών, παρά τισι μέν, ρύσις νυκτερείας ἢ κατοικητήριον δαιμόνων. παρ' ἑτέροις δὲ εὐωδία καὶ εὐλογία. τὴν δὲ Νεφθαλείμ, εἰσίν, οἵ φασι σημαίνειν τὸν πλατυσμόν. ἄλλοι δέ, στέλεχος ἀνειμένον, ἢ προσευχήν.

ccxx Cyril of Alexandria, *Glaphyra in Pentateuchum*, PG.69.216.19&49-50. Likewise, *op. cit.*, PG.69. 216.47-49: Γεγόνασι τοίνυν ἐκ Βάλλας Δάν τε καὶ Νεφθαλείμ, ὅ ἐστι *κρίσις* καὶ *πλατυσμός*. So Hesychius of Jerusalem, *Commentarius Brevis*, on Psalm 67:28 (quoted in the previous note). Hesychius of Alexandria, *Lexicon*, letter nu, entry 384: Νεφθαλείμ. πλατυσμός. Isidore Glabas, *Oratio ad Thessalonicenses ii*, p. 573 (quoted in the previous note).

ccxxi Adding διὰ τὸ βραχὺ is an important gloss showing the superiorty of Codex 232. The texts of both Klostermann and of Cyril of Alexandria fall short of making sense on this point in the absence of διὰ τὸ βραχύ.

ccxxii Origen, *commMatt*, fr. 70 (Klostermann) (continued from above).

ccxxiii Cyril of Alexandria, *frMatt*, fr. 34.

ccxxiv Cyril of Alexandria, *op. cit.* fr. 33.

ccxxv Copied by John Chrysostom, *apud Catena in Matthaeum*, p. 28: εἰπὼν δὲ *ὁ λαὸς ὁ καθήμενος ἐν σκότει*, οὐ σκότος αἰσθητὸν ἐνταῦθα καλεῖ, ἀλλὰ τὴν πλάνην καὶ τὴν ἀσέβειαν. ὁμοίως δὲ καὶ φῶς νοητόν, τὴν ἐπίγνωσιν τῆς ἀληθείας λέγει.

ccxxvi Origen, *commMatt*, fr. 72 (Klostermann).

ccxxvii Copied by John Chrysostom, *op. cit.* p. 28: εἶτα δεικνὺς ὅτι οὐκ αὐτοὶ ζητήσαντες εὗρον, ἀλλ' ὁ Θεὸς ἄνωθεν ἐπεφάνη, φησίν, ὅτι τὸ φῶς ἀνέτειλε καὶ ἔλαμψε. καὶ οὐκ αὐτοὶ πρότερον τῷ φωτὶ προσέδραμον. καὶ γὰρ ἐν ἐσχάτοις κακοῖς τὰ ἀνθρωπίνα ἦν, πρὸ τῆς Χριστοῦ παρουσίας.

ccxxviii Origen, *commMatt*, fr. 73 (Klostermann, partially).

ccxxix Origen, *commMatt*, fr. 72 (Klostermann, continued).

ccxxx John Chrysostom, *In Matthaeum*, p. 28.

ccxxxi Jerome, *commMatt*, 4.17. See also Origen, *commMatt*, fr. 74 (Klostermann), quoted *infra*.

ccxxxii Origen, *commMatt*, fr. 74 (Klostermann).

ccxxxiii Cyril of Alexandria copied from Origen once again. *frMatt*, fr. 36.

ccxxxiv Origen, *commMatt*, fr. 75 (Klostermann).

ccxxxv Photius, *commMatt*, fr. 61.

ccxxxvi Now the main text attributed to Origen continues.

ccxxxvii Also, *Supplementum et Varietas Lectionis ad Commentarium Chrysostomi in Evangelium Sancti Matthaei*, p. 450: κα'. Περὶ τῆς κλήσεως Πέτρου καὶ Ἀνδρέα, ὅτι οὐ πρώτη ἦν αὕτη ἀλλὰ δευτέρα.

ccxxxviii John Chrysostom, *apud Catena in Matthaeum*, pp. 28-29.

ccxxxix Copied by John Chrysostom, *apud op. cit.* p. 30.

ccxl Cf. Origen, *commMatt*, 13.6.

ccxli Jerome, *commMatt*, 4.24.

ccxlii Origen's Stoic background and mentality is implicitly present once again. To Cleanthes, 'sorrow is paralysis of the soul'. Stobaeus, *Anthologium*, 4.44.59 (quoting from Sotion's *On Wrath*): ὁ δὲ Κλεάνθης ἔλεγε τὴν λύπην ψυχῆς παράλυσιν. ὁ δὲ φρόνιμος ἐρεῖ *τολμήεις μοι θυμός, ἐπεὶ μάλα πολλὰ πέπονθα, μετὰ καὶ τόδε τοῖσι γενέσθω.* Sotion of Alexandria (fl. c. 200-170 BC) was a Greek doxographer and biographer, and an important source for Diogenes Laertius. Cf. Origen's favourite author Polybius, *Historiae*, 30.32.10 (later copied by Constantine Porphyrogenitus, *De Legationibus*, p. 336): περὶ τοὺς ἀνακεκλημένους ἐγένετό τις ὁλοσχερὴς ἀθυμία καὶ παράλυσις τῆς ψυχῆς.

ccxliii Τόνος (tension', vital force, in nature and human being) was a technical Stoic term. See Cleanthes, frs. 514; 563. Chrysippus, *Fragmenta Logica et Physica*, 450; 457; 546; 785; 877; *Fragmenta Moralia*, fr. 473. Galen, *De Placitis Hippocratis et Platonis*, 4.6.5; 5.2.26; 7.3.2; *De Semine*, p. 572; *De Usu Pulsuum*, p. 172; *De Locis Affectis*, pp. 301-302; *et passim.* Origen, *deOr*, 27.8. Also, *commSerMatt*, p. 148 & *schMatt*, PG.17.304.31-32: καθεύδουσιν οἱ ἀπανιστάμενοι τοῦ ζωτικοῦ τόνου. The idea is that during 'sleep' (he refers to the parable of ten virgins, as in Matt. 25:1-13) the vital force of the *hegemonikon*, that is, the perceptive ability, is suspended. This was exactly the Stoic theory reported by Diogenes Laertius, *Vitae* (Life of Zeno), 7.158: τὸν δὲ ὕπνον γίνεσθαι ἐκλυομένου τοῦ αἰσθητικοῦ τόνου περὶ τὸ ἡγεμονικόν. Αἰτίας δὲ τῶν παθῶν ἀπολείπουσι τὰς περὶ τὸ πνεῦμα τροπάς.

ccxliv Cf. a similar analysis by Origen in *commMatt*, 13.4-5. Once again, his Greek background is present – only it needs to be made out. Cf. Pseudo-Plutarch, *Apophthegmata Laconica*, p. 234B, quoting an old Spartan apophtegm: κρεῖττον ταῖς ἀλγηδόσι μὴ ἐνδόντα τελευτᾶν ἢ περίφωρον γενόμενον διὰ μαλακίαν τὸ ζῆν αἰσχρῶς περιποιήσασθαι. This was anthologised in the fifttenth-century by the paroemiographer Michael Apostolius, *Collectio Paroemiarum*, 10.13. Cf. Aspasius, *commEthNicom*, pp. 132-133: ἡ γὰρ τρυφὴ μαλακία τὶς ἐστιν ... ὁμοίως δὲ ἔχειν φησὶν καὶ περὶ ἐγκράτειαν καὶ ἀκρασίαν ὡς ἔχει καὶ περὶ καρτερίαν καὶ μαλακίαν. πῶς δὲ ὁμοίως ἔχει, αὐτὸς δηλοῖ ἐπὶ τῆς ἀκρασίας μάλιστα καὶ τῆς μαλακίας. οὐ γὰρ εἴ τις ὑπερβαλλουσῶν ἀλγηδόνων ἡττᾶται ἢ λυπῶν θαυμάσιον ἀλλὰ συγγνώμης ἄξιον.

ccxlv Origen, *commMatt*, fr. 77 (Klostermann).

ccxlvi Cf. Origen, *commMatt*, 13.6, quoted *supra*, p. 47, and endnote ccxl.

ccxlvii Origen, *commMatt*, fr. 78 (Klostermann).

ccxlviii Cf. 1 Cor. 1:24. Origen, *commJohn*, II.7.56: Καὶ τί τὸ καταργούμενον τῇ ἐπιφανείᾳ τῆς παρουσίας Χριστοῦ, σοφίας καὶ λόγου νοουμένου; *frJohn*, fr. 17: ὡς γὰρ φωνὴ λόγου προτρέχει, οὕτω καὶ τοῦ Χριστοῦ, λόγου ὄντος, ὡς φωνὴ ὁ Ἰωάννης. *Op. cit.* fr. 23: ἔστι δὲ τὸ ἀκολουθεῖν τῷ Ἰησοῦ τὸ ἕπεσθαι λόγῳ, σοφίᾳ, δικαιοσύνῃ, πράττοντα καὶ φρονοῦντα ὀρθῶς. *homJer*, homily 14.12: τὸ ὅσον ἐπ᾽ αὐτοῖς ἀποκτεινάντων δικαιοσύνην, εἰ Χριστὸς δικαιοσύνη, ἀποκτεινάντων [τὴν] σοφίαν, εἰ Χριστὸς σοφία, ἀποκτεινάντων ἀλήθειαν, εἰ Χριστὸς ἀλήθεια. *commMatt*, 12.24: τὸ ὅσον ἐπ᾽ αὐτοῖς ἀποκτεινάντων δικαιοσύνην, εἰ Χριστὸς δικαιοσύνη, ἀποκτεινάντων [τὴν] σοφίαν, εἰ Χριστὸς σοφία, ἀποκτεινάντων ἀλήθειαν, εἰ Χριστὸς ἀλήθεια. *commSerMatt*, p. 118: τὸ ἰδεῖν τὴν Χριστοῦ λόγου ἔνδοξον ἐσομένην αὐτῷ καὶ τελείαν ἐπιδημίαν. *commEph*, fr. 14: πολλάκις δὲ εἴπομεν ὅτι ὁ πάντα λόγῳ ποιῶν *πεπίστευκεν* εἰς τὸν Χριστὸν Λόγον. *expProv*, PG.17.185.30-31: ὁ δὲ Χριστὸς σοφία ἐστί. *selPs*, PG.12.16.80.31-33: Υἱῶν δὲ Σιὼν βασιλεύει Χριστός, τουτέστι σοφία, λόγος, ἀλήθεια. *excPs*, PG.17.125.32-34:

Ὥσπερ δέ ἐστιν ὁ Σωτὴρ σοφία, Λόγος, εἰρήνη καὶ δικαιοσύνη, οὕτως καὶ ὑπομονή. *frPs*, on Psalm 68:23: Ἐπίστησον δὲ εἰ τράπεζα δύναται λέγεσθαι ὁ Χριστός, σοφία τυγχάνων.

ccxlix See *supra*, folio 22v and endnote ccxiii, Origen's explanation of 'Galilee' meaning 'being rolled over', i.e. 'erratic': Γαλιλαία δέ, ἡ μὲν τῆς Ἰουδαίας ἡ δὲ τῶν ἐθνῶν ἑρμηνεύονται κατακυλιστή.

ccl This implies an alternative translation of 'Judaea', meaning 'the province that sinned against God', which was reproduced only by Philagathus, whose portion is quoted beside. Normally, Origen rendered 'Judaea' 'one who confesses', which Philagathus mentions, too. Cf. Origen, *frJer*, fr. 11: καὶ τὴν τῶν οἰκητόρων ἀρίστην πολιτείαν ἥξουσιν οἱ δῶρα προσφέροντες, ἔκ τε τῶν πόλεων Ἰούδα [Jer. 17:26] τῶν Ἐξομολογουμένων τῷ θεῷ. *Op. cit.*, fr. 58 (on Jer. 38:23): τοῦτο δὲ ποιεῖ τις *ἐν Ἰουδαίᾳ* γενόμενος, ὃ ἑρμηνεύεται Ἐξομολογουμένη, τῷ θεῷ. *selPs*, PG.12.1572.43-45: Εἰ ἁγίασμα τοῦ Θεοῦ ἡ Ἰουδαία ἐστίν, ἡ δὲ Ἰουδαία ἐξομολογούμενος ἑρμηνεύεται, πᾶσα ἐξομολογουμένη ψυχὴ ἁγίασμα τοῦ Θεοῦ ἐστι. Cf. Clement of Alexandria, *Stromateis*, 7.16.105.3. Athanasius, *Expositiones in Psalmos*, PG.27.417.50-5. Didymus, *frPs*(*al*) (which is possibly Origen's work), frs. 502; 942; 1060. Cyril of Alexandria, *Expositio in Psalmos*, PG.69.1177.14. Hesychius of Jerusalem, *Commentarius Brevis*, on Psalms 47:12; 68:36; 75:2; 96:8. Pseudo-Basil of Caesarea (*forsan* Cassian the Sabaite), *Enarratio in Prophetam Isaiam*, 7.197. Maximus Confessor, *Quaestiones ad Thalassium*, section 55, lines 454-455. Michael Psellus, *Theologica*, opusculum 12 (implicitly).

ccli Philagathus (Philip Cerameus, twelfth century), *Homiliae*, homily 20.5.

cclii The term φιλοκόμπος and its cognates, although unknown to the Liddell and Scott lexicon, had been used prior to Origen. Cf. Aesopus, *Proverbia*, 8: Ὁ φιλοκόμπον ἦθος ἐλέγχων. Justin, *Apologia Secunda*, 3.1: τοῦ φιλοψόφου καὶ φιλοκόμπου (copied by Eusebius, *HE*, 4.16.3, and Nicephorus Callistus Xanthopulus, *HE*, 3.32). Cyril of Alexandria, *commProphXII*, v. 2, p. 78; *In Joannem*, v. 1, pp. 300; 433; 717*; et passim.* Photius, *Bibliotheca*, Codex 128, p. 96a. *Homiliae*, homily 2, p. 23; *Lexicon*, letter phi, p. 648. *Suda*, letter phi, entry 380. *Etymologicum Magnum*, p. 794.

ccliii John Chrysostom, *apud Catena in Matthaeum*, pp. 30-31.

ccliv Origen, *commMatt*, fr. 79 (Klostermann). The text in brackets has been attributed also to John Chrysostom, who evidently copied from Origen. Cf. his *In Matthaeum*, PG.57.223.38-46: Ὅταν δὲ ἀκούσῃς ὅτι *Ἐδίδασκεν αὐτούς*, μὴ τοῖς μαθηταῖς αὐτὸν διαλέγεσθαι νόμιζε μόνον, ἀλλὰ καὶ δι' ἐκείνων ἅπασιν. Ἐπειδὴ γὰρ τὸ πλῆθος δημῶδες ἦν, ἔτι δὲ καὶ τῶν χαμαὶ συρομένων, τῶν μαθητῶν τὸν χορὸν ὑποστησάμενος, πρὸς ἐκείνους ποιεῖται τοὺς λόγους, ἐν τῇ πρὸς αὐτοὺς διαλέξει καὶ τοῖς λοιποῖς ἅπασι, τοῖς σφόδρα ἀποδέουσι τῶν λεγομένων, ἀνεπαχθῆ γίνεσθαι παρασκευάζων τῆς φιλοσοφίας τὴν διδασκαλίαν. It is hardly a surpsise that three codices ascribed this to Gregory of Nyssa, against another two codices (plus the present one) which recognised this as one written by Origen, whereas John Chrysostom simply copied and then added paraphrased expatiations in his flowery prose. However, the case is quite simple: long before Chrysostom copied from Origen, Gregory of Nyssa employed the text of his creative flare, Origen, and wrote the text which I am quoting. In fact, throughout all literature (both Christian and Greek) there are only two authors who used the characteristic expression ἀκρώρεια ἐλπίδος ('the topmost summit of hope'): these are Origen in the present text, and Gregory of Nyssa. The instance of this usage is in fact unique, since Gregory copied the selfsame text from Origen, who anyway used the term ἀκρώρεια in this metaphorical sense at other points, too. Cf. *Cels*, VI.44: ἄξιοι φανέντες τῆς εἰς τὰ θεῖα ἀναβάσεως ἀνιμηθῶσιν ὑπὸ τοῦ λόγου ἐπὶ τὴν ἀνωτάτω πάντων μακαριότητα καί, ἵν' οὕτως ὀνομάσω, ἀκρώρειαν τῶν ἀγαθῶν. *selPs*, PG.12.1265.37-39: Καὶ ὄρος μέν φησι Κυρίου τὸ τελικὸν ἀγαθὸν καὶ τὸν Θεὸν

Λόγον. σπάνιος γὰρ ὁ πρὸς τὴν ἀκρώρειαν αὐτοῦ διὰ προκοπῆς ἀναβῆναι δυνάμενος. *Op. cit.* PG.12.1497.13-16: καὶ οἱ βουνοί, ἐφ' ὧν ἔθυον δαίμοσι, τοὺς εὐαγγελικὸν μετιόντας ὑποδέξονται βίον, περίβλεπτοι διὰ τούτους γενόμενοι. Καὶ νῦν δὲ ἅπαντες πρὸς τοὺς τὰς ἀκρωρείας κατειληφότας τρέχουσι. *excPs*, PG.17.113.37-39: *Τίς ἀναβήσεται εἰς τὸ ὄρος τοῦ Κυρίου; ἢ τίς στήσεται ἐν τόπῳ ἁγίῳ αὐτοῦ;* [Psalm 23:3] Καὶ ὄρος μέν φησι Κυρίου τὸ τελικὸν ἀγαθὸν καὶ τὸν Θεὸν Λόγον. σπάνιος γὰρ ὁ πρὸς τὴν ἀκρώρειαν αὐτοῦ διὰ προκοπῆς ἀναβῆναι δυνάμενος. Here is how Eusebius copied this to the letter. *Commentaria in Psalmos*, PG.23.221.30-36: *Τίς ἀναβήσεται εἰς τὸ ὄρος τοῦ Κυρίου; ἢ τίς στήσεται ἐν τόπῳ ἁγίῳ αὐτοῦ;* [Psalm 23:3] τὸ τελικὸν ἀγαθὸν καὶ τὸν Θεὸν Λόγον λεκτέον, ἐφ' ὃ ἀναβαίνει ὁ διὰ προκοπῆς ἐπὶ τὴν ἀκρώρειαν αὐτοῦ φθάσαι γλιχόμενος. Σπάνιος δὲ ὁ τοιοῦτος. διὸ εἴρηται. *Τίς ἀναβήσεται εἰς τὸ ὄρος τοῦ Κυρίου; ἢ τίς στήσεται ἐν τόπῳ ἁγίῳ αὐτοῦ;*

The term ἀκρώρεια appeared no earlier than the Late Antiquity, and some authors prior to Origen had used this in its literal sense. But it was Origen who first applied this in its metaphorical / ethical sense, indicating attainment of the highest standard of personal moral quality. Even Gregory of Nyssa, who employed the term abundantly in its literal sense, used it in this metaphorical one only once, namely, in the present instance, copying from Origen.

cclv Gregory of Nyssa, *Orationes viii De Beatitudinibus*, PG.44.1196.9-17, comm. on Isaiah 2:3, 'Let us ascend to the mountain of the Lord' (see the same, in Micah, 4:2). In the present volume, we will come several times upon this work of Gregory, since it turns out that it contains numerous passages copied from Origen.

cclvi Origen, *commMatt*, fr. 80 (Klostermann).

cclvii Since Jesus spoke of his *logoi* being indestructible, Origen interpreted this as meaning that the *logoi* (as generative, cohesive, and dissolving causes – according to his Anaxagorean Theory of Logoi) are indestructible, and 'kingdom of heavens' is but the totality of *logoi*. See *Anaxaghoras*, pp. 862; 1142; 1309; 1318-1326.

cclviii See *supra*, folios 11r-11v: Origen, *commMatt*, fr. 38 II (Klostermann), col. 2; folio 24r: Origen, *commMatt*, fr. 75 (Klostermann).

cclix Cod. ἰσοθείαν. This should be ἰσοθεῖαν. Cf. Didymus, *frPs*(*al*), fr. 68: τὴν πανοπλίαν τοῦ θεοῦ. ὅθεν τοὺς ὀφθαλμοὺς εἰς τὸν πένητα ἔχει πειθόμενος αὐτὸν ἔχειν ἁλωτόν, τὸν αὐτὸν ὄντα τῷ ἐμπυριζομένῳ πτωχῷ ἐπὶ τῇ τοῦ ἀσεβοῦς ὑπερηφανίᾳ. Ἐνεδρεύει ἐν ἀποκρύφῳ οἷα ἄγριος λέων ἐν τῇ μάνδρᾳ αὐτοῦ τοῦ ἁρπάσαι πτωχὸν διὰ λόγων ἀπατηλῶν (ἔστιν δ' ὅτε καὶ διὰ πράξεων), ὃν καὶ ἑλκύσει μετὰ τὸ ἁρπάσαι ἐν τῇ παγίδι αὐτοῦ ἐπὶ τῷ καταφαγεῖν. θὴρ γὰρ ἄγριός ἐστιν, μᾶλλον δὲ αὐτὸ τοῦτο λέων. πολλάκις γοῦν ἐνεδρεύων, περὶ οἰκονομίας δῆθεν ὁμιλῶν, ἐγκρύπτει τὸν περὶ φιλαργυρίας λόγον. ὡς αὖ περὶ σωφροσύνης φθεγγόμενος τρόπον ἀκολασίας ὑποβάλλει, οὕτως τὴν Εὔαν ἠπάτησεν ἐν τῷ παραδείσῳ διὰ τῆς παραβάσεως τῆς ἐντολῆς ἰσοθείαν ὑποβαλὼν καὶ τὸν Ἰούδαν διὰ φιλαργυρίας.

cclx Gregory of Nyssa, *Orationes viii De Beatitudinibus*, PG.44.1201.12-14. He keeps on copying from Origen. See the entire passage (PG.44.1201.1-21), which is an impressively striking paraphrase of Origen's present text.

cclxi From folio 26r to 31v, there is a text attributed to Severus of Antioch. However, in the Introduction (pp. XXXIX-XLI) I have been arguing that nothing 'by Severus' remains once the critical study of the parallel passages that are quoted below this text (in smaller fonts) are considered. Nevertheless, I maintain the attribution 'By Severus' as in the codex.

cclxii However, the ensuing text is Origen's *commMatt*, fr. 81 (Klostermann) quoted forthwith. Now we have the entire context of this on folios 26r-31v, which continues with attribution to Origen (31v).

cclxiii The term ἡσυχιότης appears only in the following authors. Plato, *Charmides*, 159b5; 159d10; 160b5; 160b7. (Perhaps) Chrysippus, *Fragmenta Moralia*, 632, *apud* Stobaeus, *Anthologium*, 2.7.11s. Lysias, *Περὶ τῆς Εὐάνδρου Δοκιμασίας*, 5. Clement of Alexandria, *Stromateis*, 7.3.18.2. Proclus, *In Platonis Alcibiadem i*, 198.

cclxiv The expression ἕξις εὐάγωγος was used only once by Pseudo-Plato, *Definitiones*, 412e: Φιλανθρωπία ἕξις εὐάγωγος ἤθους πρὸς ἀνθρώπου φιλίαν.

cclxv Origen, *commMatt*, fr. 81 (Klostermann).

cclxvi Origen, *loc. cit.* This is a note to the fragment by Klostermann, from *Codex Parisinus suppl. gr. 612* (ante 1164), in which this passage is 'unattributed' (Ἀνεπίγραφος). It can be shown that Gregory of Nyssa kept on copying and slightly paraphrasing from Origen, which Klostermann did not notice. See Gregory of Nyssa, *Orationes viii De Beatitudinibus*, PG.44.1213.41-43: Οὐκοῦν ἐπειδὴ πλεονάζει κατὰ τὴν φύσιν ἡμῶν ἡ πρὸς τὰ κακὰ ταχύτης, καλῶς τὸ ἐν τοῖς τοιούτοις ἠρεμοῦν μακαρίζεται.

cclxvii Origen, *commMatt*, fr. 82 (Klostermann). On the 'land of the living' (γῆ ζώντων), cf. Psalms, 26:13; 51:7; 141:6; 114:9. On 'glorious body' (σῶμα ἔνδοξον) after resurrection, see Origen, *selPs*, PG.12.1093.45-1096.3: Οὕτως μέλλοντας κληρονομεῖν βασιλείαν οὐρανῶν, καὶ ἐν τόποις διαφέρουσιν ἔσεσθαι, ἀναγκαῖον χρῆσθαι σώμασι πνευματικοῖς, οὐχὶ τοῦ εἴδους τοῦ προτέρου ἀφανιζομένου, κἂν ἐπὶ τὸ ἐνδοξότερον γένηται αὐτοῦ ἡ τροπή, ὥσπερ ἦν τὸ Ἰησοῦ εἶδος, καὶ Μωϋσέως, καὶ Ἠλίου, οὐχ ἕτερον ἐν τῇ μεταμορφώσει, παρ' ὃ ἦν. *frLuc*, fr. 140: Τότε δέ τις ὁρᾷ τὸν λόγον μεταμορφούμενον ἐνδόξως, ὅτε συνάνεισί τε αὐτῷ καὶ συνυψοῦται καὶ ὁρᾷ αὐτὸν ὡς αὐτολόγον καὶ ὡς ἀρχιερέα κοινολογούμενον καὶ εὐχόμενον τῷ πατρί. Ἐπειδὴ δὲ οὔπω τελείως τὸ σῶμα εἰς ἀφθαρσίαν ἀμετάθετον ἀγαγὼν ἦν, ὤφθη μετὰ τῶν φθαρτῶν ἱματίων λάμψας σὺν αὐτοῖς. *commJohn*, VI.5.29: τὴν παρὰ τοῖς πεπιστευκόσι κατηγγελμένην δευτέραν σωματικὴν Ἰησοῦ ἔνδοξον ἐπιδημίαν.

cclxviii Notice the striking similarities with Gregory of Nyssa's ensuing text. The question then is this: given that the allegedly Severus' text runs parallel to Origen's one, whom would Gregory have taken up this from?

cclxix Cf. Gregory of Nyssa, *Orationes viii De Beatitudinibus*, PG.44.1208.55-1209.1: Μὴ γὰρ εἶναι δυνατόν, ἴσως ὁ ἀκούων ἐρεῖ, καθάπερ ἐν βαθμῶν διαθέσει, μετὰ τὴν τῶν οὐρανῶν βασιλείαν, τῆς γῆς τὴν κληρονομίαν καταλαμβάνεσθαι.

cclxx Here is one more instance of Christian influence on Neoplatonism, which I have discussed in *COT*, pp. 333-377 (Proclus, Simplicius, Damascius). Plato had introduced the expression ὑπερουράνιος τόπος ('the place above the heavens, *Phaedrus*, 247c3) of which Origen declared himself aware and claimed that Plato 'learned these words from certain Jews' (*Cels*, VI.19). However, the expresion ὑπερουράνιος λῆξις was a different theme, which was taken up by Proclus, followed (as it often happened) by Pseudo-Dionysius the Areopagite. Proclus, *Theologia Platonica*, v. 6, p. 103: Καὶ γὰρ Διὸς καὶ Ἥρας καὶ Ἀπόλλωνος καὶ Ἀθηνᾶς μετὰ τὴν ὑπερουράνιον λῆξιν καὶ μετὰ τῶν ἐγκοσμίων θεῶν κοιναὶ πρόοδοι καὶ συντάξεις εἰσίν. Pseudo-Dionysius the Areopagite, *De Ecclesiastica Hierarchia*, p. 69: ἡ πρὸς τὴν τῆς ὑπερουρανίας λήξεως ἀναγωγὴν ἡμῶν ὁδοποίησις.

cclxxi Gregory of Nyssa, *Orationes viii De Beatitudinibus*, PG.44.1208.52-1209.27.

cclxxii Cf. Gregory of Nyssa, who kept on following Origen's analyses in the *Orationes viii De Beatitudinibus*, PG.44.1209.-1212.7-18: Ἐκείνην μοι πολυπραγμόνει τὴν γῆν, ἥτις οὐ πάντων ἐστὶ κληρονομία, πλὴν εἴ τινες διὰ τῆς τοῦ βίου πραότητος ἄξιοι τῆς ἐπαγγελίας ἐκείνης κρίνονται. ἥν μοι δοκεῖ καὶ ὁ μέγας Δαβίδ, ... εἰπὼν *Πιστεύω τοῦ ἰδεῖν τὰ ἀγαθὰ Κυρίου ἐν γῇ ζώντων*. ... ἐν ᾗ τὸ ὕδωρ τῆς ἀναπαύσεως, καὶ ὁ τῆς χλόης τόπος, καὶ ἡ τετραχῇ μεριζομένη πηγὴ καὶ ἡ παρὰ τοῦ Θεοῦ τῶν ὅλων γεωργουμένη ἄμπελος, καὶ ὅσα ἄλλα δι' αἰνιγμάτων παρὰ τῆς θεοπνεύστου διδασκαλίας ἀκούομεν. *In Sanctum et Salutare Pascha*, pp. 310-311: τότε διὰ τῆς παρακοῆς τοῦ παραδείσου ἐξῳκίσθημεν, νῦν διὰ πίστεως τοῦ παραδείσου εἴσω γινόμεθα. Πάλιν ὁ καρπὸς τῆς ζωῆς εἰς τρυφὴν πρόκειται κατ᾽ ἐξουσίαν ἡμῖν. πάλιν ἡ τοῦ παραδείσου πηγὴ ἡ τετραχῇ διὰ τῶν εὐαγγελικῶν ποταμῶν μεριζομένη ἅπαν ποτίζει τὸ πρόσωπον τῆς ἐκκλησίας. Ephraem Syrus, *De Locis Beatis*, pp. 299-300: Ὅπου τὸ ὕδωρ τῆς ἀναπαύσεως, ὁ τῆς χλόης τόπος, καὶ ἡ τετραχῇ μεριζομένη πηγή, καὶ ἡ παρὰ τοῦ Θεοῦ τῶν ὅλων γεωργουμένη ἄμπελος, εἰς ἐκείνην τὴν μακαρίαν γῆν.

cclxxiii Part of Klostermann's fr. 83 was attributed to Gregory of Nyssa in one codex only (see his note on p. 49). But Gregory of Nyssa continued following Origen in the same work *Orationes viii De Beatitudinibus*, PG.44.1245.56-1248.4: Αὕτη οὖν ἐστι κατά γε τὸν ἐμὸν λόγον ἡ ἀληθὴς ἀρετή, τὸ ἀμιγὲς τοῦ χείρονος ἀγαθόν, περὶ ὃ πᾶν νόημα τῶν πρὸς τὸ κρεῖττον νοουμένων καταλαμβάνεται αὐτὸς ὁ Θεὸς Λόγος, ἡ τοὺς οὐρανοὺς καλύψασα ἀρετή, καθὼς ὁ Ἀμβακοὺμ διεξέρχεται, καὶ καλῶς οἱ ταύτην τοῦ Θεοῦ τὴν δικαιοσύνην πεινῶντες, ἐμακαρίσθησαν. In Klostermann's text, the expression, Εἰ δὲ χρὴ καί τινος τολμηροῦ καθάψασθαι λόγου is probably Gregory's own. But see Origen *commJohn*, VI.56.291.

The expression ἀμιγὴς χείρονος rings an Anaxagorean bell (Origen was influenced by Anaxagoras, anyway). In fact, not only did Gregory of Nyssa use this, but also he entertained the selfsame idea that Origen expounds at this point, namely, that Jesus was referring to *every* virtue. Gregory of Nyssa, *op. cit.* PG.44.1244.1-7: Εἰ δὲ παντὸς τοῦ χείρονος ἀμιγὴς ὁ τῆς δικαιοσύνης λόγος ἐστίν, ἅπαν ἐν ἑαυτῷ πάντως τὸ ἀγαθὸν περιείληφεν. ἀγαθὸν δὲ πᾶν τὸ κατ᾽ ἀρετὴν θεωρούμενον. Οὐκοῦν πᾶσα ἀρετὴ τῷ ὀνόματι τῆς δικαιοσύνης ἐνταῦθα διασημαίνεται, ἧς τοὺς πεινῶντάς τε καὶ διψῶντας μακαρίζει ὁ Λόγος. *Op. cit.* PG.44.1245.56-57: Αὕτη οὖν ἐστι κατά γε τὸν ἐμὸν λόγον ἡ ἀληθὴς ἀρετή, τὸ ἀμιγὲς τοῦ χείρονος ἀγαθόν. *Dialogus De Anima et Resurrectione*, PG.46.81.28-30: Ἀλλ᾽ ἑκουσίως ὁ ἄνθρωπος ἐν τῷ αὐτεξουσίῳ κινήματι καταλιπὼν τὴν ἀμιγῆ τοῦ χείρονος μοῖραν.

Then, as it usually happened, once Cyril of Alexandria took up a phrase from Origen he could not have enough of it. Cf. *De Sancta Trinitate Dialogi*, p. 614: παρίστησιν ὥσπερ εἰλικρινῆ τὴν ἀρχὴν καὶ τοῦ χείρονος ἀμιγῆ παραδίδωσι τῷ Θεῷ καὶ Πατρὶ τὴν βασιλείαν ὁ Υἱός. *De Adoratione*, PG.68.644.7-8: ὁ περί γε τῶν θείων δογμάτων ὀρθός τε καὶ ἀληθὴς καὶ ἀμιγὴς τοῦ χείρονος λόγος. *Glaphyra in Pentateuchum*, PG.69.56.1-2: Ἕως μὲν οὖν τὸ ἱερὸν γένος αὐτὸ καθ᾽ ἑαυτὸ καὶ ἀμιγὲς τοῦ χείρονος διετέλει. *In Isaiam*, PG.70.53.6-8: καὶ ψυχρῶν καὶ ὑδαρεστέρων ἐννοιῶν παρεισκρίνοντες οὐκ ἀμιγεῖ τοῦ χείρονος.

Once Origen used this expression in this commentary, Gregory Thaumaturgus did so for himself in his *Panygeric* oration in honour of Origen. Not surprisingly, this occurs almost in the beginning of that speech, when Gregory spoke of God being the source of all goods and virtues (ἐκεῖθεν ἡμῖν πᾶσαι μὲν αἱ τῶν ἀγαθῶν ἀρχαί). *In Origenem Oratio Panegyrica*, 3: γυμνὸν δὲ αὐτὸν ὅτι καθαρώτατον λαμπρότατόν τε καὶ εἰλικρινέστατον καὶ ἀμιγῆ παντὸς χείρονος.

See Origen maintaining that 'Christ contains all of the virtues in himself'. *commMatt*, 12.14: τάχα δὲ καὶ ἑκάστη ἀρετὴ οὐρανοῦ ἐστι βασιλεία, καὶ πᾶσαι ἅμα βασιλεία τῶν οὐρανῶν· ... ὁ Χριστὸς γάρ, ἡ πᾶσα ἀρετή, ἐπιδεδήμηκε καὶ λαλεῖ. *commJohn*, VI.19.107: Ὁ γὰρ σωτήρ, εἰς ὃν πᾶσά ἐστιν ἀρετή, ταῖς ἐπινοίαις πολύς. *homJer*, homily 6.1: οὕτως ἐπὶ πάσας ἀρετὰς *ὀφθαλμοὶ κυρίου*. *homLuc*, homily 30, p. 173: Ἀλλ᾽ ὁ σωτὴρ βασιλεῦσαι μὲν θέλει καὶ ὑποτάξαι πάντα τὰ ἔθνη, ἵνα δοῦλα γένηται δικαιοσύνης καὶ ἀληθείας καὶ πάσης ἀρετῆς. *selPs*, PG.12.1297.50-1300.3: Νῦν δὲ τέθεικε τὴν δικαιοσύνην, ἐπειδὴ περιεκτική ἐστι πασῶν τῶν ἀρετῶν. Ἢ τάχα δικαιοσύνην λέγει τὸν Χριστόν. αὐτὸς γὰρ *ἐγενήθη ἡμῖν σοφία ἀπὸ Θεοῦ, δικαιοσύνη τε καὶ ἁγιασμὸς καὶ ἀπολύτρωσις*. *Cels*, III.81: καὶ ἀντιπαραθέτω τὸ καθ᾽ ἡμᾶς παρὰ θεῷ ἐν Χριστῷ, τουτέστι τῷ λόγῳ καὶ τῇ σοφίᾳ καὶ πάσῃ ἀρετῇ. *Op. cit.*

V.39: Κἂν δεύτερον οὖν λέγωμεν θεόν, ἴστωσαν ὅτι τὸν δεύτερον θεὸν οὐκ ἄλλο τι λέγομεν ἢ τὴν περιεκτικὴν πασῶν ἀρετῶν ἀρετήν. *frProv*, PG.13.28.27-30: Ὁ οὖν ἐπικαλούμενος τὸν Χριστόν, εἰ νοεῖ τίς ἐστιν, ἐπικαλεῖται σοφίαν, σύνεσιν, ἁγιασμόν, δικαιοσύνην, καὶ πᾶσαν ἀρετήν.

cclxxiv Origen, *commMatt*, 12.14. Cf. *commEph*, fr. 33: ἢ τὴν ἀρετὴν ἥτις ἐστὶν ὁ Χριστός.

cclxxv Cf. Origen, *commJohn*, I.10.60: πλῆθος ἀγαθῶν ἐστιν Ἰησοῦς. *Op. cit.* I.19.112: Καὶ οὐ θαυμαστὸν εἰ, ὡς προειρήκαμεν, πολλὰ ὧν ἀγαθὰ ὁ σωτὴρ ἐνεπινοούμενα ἔχει ἐν αὑτῷ πρῶτα καὶ δεύτερα καὶ τρίτα. *Op. cit.* I.20.119: Ὁ θεὸς μὲν οὖν πάντη ἕν ἐστι καὶ ἁπλοῦν. ὁ δὲ σωτὴρ ἡμῶν διὰ τὰ πολλά, ἐπεὶ *προέθετο αὐτὸν ὁ θεὸς ἱλαστήριον* καὶ ἀπαρχὴν πάσης τῆς κτίσεως, πολλὰ γίνεται ἢ καὶ τάχα πάντα ταῦτα, καθὰ χρῄζει αὐτοῦ ἡ ἐλευθεροῦσθαι δυναμένη πᾶσα κτίσις. *Commentary on the epistle to the Romans*, 7.7.7 (Latin): "Christ is indeed one in essence, but may be designated in many ways according to his virtues and operations; for example, he is understood to be Grace itself, as well as Righteousness, Peace, Life, Truth, Logos." Likewise, *Cels*, II.64; *Princ*, I.2.1; I.2.13; IV.4.1. Cf. *infra*, folio 200r: αἱ ἀρεταὶ τῇ ὑποστάσει ὁ Χριστός.

cclxxvi Cf. Habacuc, 3:3. Origen, *commMatt*, fr. 83 (Klostermann).

cclxxvii Gregory of Nyssa, *Orationes viii De Beatitudinibus*, PG.44.1245.40-1248.4. Klostermann found two codices ascribing this to Origen, whereas another one attributed to Gregory of Nyssa part of this (Εἰ δὲ χρὴ ... *τῷ προσώπῳ σου*). However, the text of the present codex continues in the same spirit, and the ensuing passage suggests that the case was that Gregory of Nyssa actually copied from Origen.

cclxxviii Apollinaris, *frMatt*, fr. 11, continued *infra*.

cclxxix The term ὀρεκτὸν ('object of desire') is a characteristic term introduced in philosophical considerations by Aristotle (*De Anima*, 433a-b; *et passim*), which enjoyed further consideration by the Stoics. This made its way into Christian vocabulary pretty early, actually since the times of Athenagoras and Clement of Alexandria.

cclxxx Once again, Proclus appears influenced by an expression used by a Christian scholar, and I have shown that Proclus' influences go back to Origen's writings (it could have been extremely unlikely that Proclus could have ever read any of Gregory of Nyssa's works). Cf. Proclus, *commTim*, v. 1, p. 238: ὅταν μὲν αὐτὸ καλὸν φῶμεν καὶ αὐτὸ δίκαιον, τὸ μὴ κατὰ μετοχὴν κάλλους μηδὲ κατὰ μετουσίαν δικαίου καλὸν ἢ δίκαιον ὁρῶμεν, ἀλλ᾽ αὐτὸ πρώτως καλὸν καὶ πρώτως δίκαιον ὑπάρχον. No other author did ever use the expression τὴν τοῦ δικαίου μετουσίαν.

cclxxxi Gregory of Nyssa, *Orationes viii De Beatitudinibus*, PG.44.1240.52-1241.3.

cclxxxii Apollinaris, *frMatt*, fr. 11, continued *infra*.

cclxxxiii Apollinaris, *loc. cit.*

cclxxxiv Cf. John Chrysostom, *In Acta Apostolorum*, PG.60.306.21-22: Οὐκοῦν ἔχωμεν ψυχὴν συμπαθητικήν.

cclxxxv This turn appears as characteristic of John Chrysostom and apparently it was taken up only once by Theodoret. Cf. John Chrysostom, *In Matthaeum*, PG.57.227.45-47: *Μακάριοι οἱ ἐλεήμονες.* Ἐνταῦθα οὐ τοὺς διὰ χρημάτων ἐλεοῦντας μόνον ἐμοὶ δοκεῖ λέγειν, ἀλλὰ καὶ τοὺς διὰ πραγμάτων. *Op. cit.* PG.57.236.13-15: Ταῦτ᾽ οὖν εἰδότες πολὺν ποιῶμεν τὸν ἔλεον, καὶ πολλὴν τὴν φιλανθρωπίαν ἐπιδειξώμεθα, καὶ διὰ χρημάτων, καὶ διὰ πραγμάτων. *In Epistulam ii ad Corinthios*, PG.61.427.14-15: τὸ ἐλεεῖν διὰ χρημάτων, διὰ πραγμάτων. *Homilia Dicta in Templo Sanctae Anastasiae*, PG.63.498.5-7: Παύλου ψυχὴ πεπλήρωτο μυρίων πειρασμῶν, καθημερινῶν κινδύνων, ἔξωθεν, ἔσωθεν, διὰ ῥημάτων, διὰ πραγμάτων, διὰ χρημάτων, διὰ δόλων. John Chrysostom, *apud Catena in Matthaeum*, p. 32: Τοὺς ἐλεήμονας δὲ μακαρίζει, οὐ τοὺς διὰ χρημάτων ἐλεοῦντας μόνον, ἀλλὰ καὶ τοὺς διὰ πραγμάτων. Theodoret, *Interpretatio in Psalmos*, PG.80.1133.14-16: τὰς παντοδαπὰς τοῦ δικαίου εὐεργεσίας δηλοῖ, τὰς διὰ χρημάτων, τὰς διὰ πραγμάτων, τὰς διὰ λόγων καὶ συμβουλῶν.

cclxxxvi Origen, *commMatt*, fr. 85 (Klostermann).

cclxxxvii The expression πρακτικὴ ἀρετὴ ('virtue' demonstrated and realised 'in action') belongs to the locution of the Aristotelian ethics (e.g. *Ethica Nicomachea*, 1177b; *Magna Moralia*, 1.34.29; cf. *Politica*, 1324a-1325b). Cf. Pseudo-Alexander of Aphrodisias, *De Anima Libri Mantissa*, p. 154; *'Ηθικὰ Προβλήματα*, pp. 143; 150. Plutarch, *An Seni Respublica Gerenda Sit*, p. 783F; *De Virtute Morali*, p. 433E. Stobaeus, *Anthologium*, 2.7.1; 2.31.120. However, it was the Stoic Panaetius of Rhodes (c. 185-c. 110 BC) who engaged in detailed consideration of 'theoretical' and 'active' virtues, a distinction which he himself introduced (Diogenes Laertius, *Vitae*, 7.92). Clement of Alexandria applied this Stoic distinction to Christian context (*Paedagogus*, 1.3.9.4: λόγος αὐτὸς ἐναργῶς σὰρξ γενόμενος τὴν αὐτὴν ἀρετὴν πρακτικὴν ἅμα καὶ θεωρητικὴν ἐπιδεικνύς). Origen followed along the same line. *Princ*, III.1.15 (*Philocalia*, 21.14); *selPs*, PG.12: 1277.35; 1429.34; 1545.41; 1556.15; 1581.52; 1652.10; 16.77.8; *expProv.* PG.17: 192.32; 196.9; 209.29; 224.30; 225.32; 232.18; *frJohn*, frs. 45; 125. So did Plotinus (*Enneades*, I.1.12; VI.3.16) and Iamblichus (*Protrepticus*, pp. 3; 21). Unlike what happened with other ideas and technical expressions, of Origen's followers it was Didymus who entertained this notion galore, and Evagrius more moderately, but neither Athanasius nor any of the Cappadocians did so at all. It is highly doubtful that John Chrysostom did so, whereas this appears occasionally in Cyril of Alexandria, but only at a few of points (*commProphXII*, v. 1, p. 733; *Expositio in Psalmos*, PG.77: 1197.44; 1213.20; 1277.46). However, Theodoret engaged in detailed consideration of this notion and applied this profusely. Cf. *Curatio*, 12.6; *et passim*. Therefore, the notion and terminology appeared only in the later of Origen's admirers (if not openly), such as Pseudo-Basil of Caesarea (*forsan* Cassian the Sabaite), *Enarratio in Prophetam Isaiam*, 8.211), Maximus Confessor (*Quaestiones ad Thalassium*, 3; 10; 16; 25; 27; *et passim*, at scores of points). Subsequent intellectuals, such as Michael Psellus, Eustratius of Nicaea, and Eustathius of Thessaloniki, entertained this idea conveniently, but the overall itinerary of this in Christian thought is pretty strange. For it is apparently hard to explain why was it that eminent theologians, who seized on so many Greek notions and terms, shunned this one, which after all made a considerable mark in hymnography. Cf. Analecta Hymnica Graeca, *Canones Septembris*, 1.2.5; *Canones Decembris*, 6.11.2; 29.56.2; *Canones Januarii*, 27.33(1).3; *Canones Februarii*, 7.7. Synaxarium; *Canones Aprilis*, 1.5.5; *Canones Maii*, 24.26.7; *Canones Augusti*, 7.8.3. Nevertheless, this is not impossible to account for: I have argued (*Scholia in Apocalypsin*, pp. 24-25;) that Christian hymnography was mainly an achievement of Antioch – and once Theodoret had written of πρακτικὴ ἀρετὴ so heavily, it was natural for this development to occur.

cclxxxviii Origen took up the turn ἐμπαρέχειν ἑαυτὸν from Philo, who was the first to use it, and from Plutarch. Philo, *De Vita Mosis*, 2.69. Plutarch, *Quomodo Adulator ab Amico Internoscatur*, p. 64E: γέλωτος ὄργανον ἐμπαρέχων ἑαυτόν. *De Pythiae Oraculis*, p. 407C: ὅθεν οὐχ ἥκιστα ποιητικὴ δοκοῦσα κοινὴν ἐμπαρέχειν ἑαυτὴν ἀπατεῶσι καὶ γόησιν ἀνθρώποις. *Quaestiones Convivales*, p. 722B: καὶ οὐσίαν ἐμπαρέχων ἑαυτόν. Origen was the first to introduce this in Christian literature. *commJohn*, I.36.7: μὴ ἐμπαρεσχηκόσιν ἑαυτοὺς τῇ ἀγάπῃ καὶ τῇ πραότητι τοῦ πατρός. *Op. cit.* VI.33.166: τῷ ἐμπαρέχοντι ἑαυτὸν τῇ θειότητι. *Op. cit.* VI.56.291: 'Εχρῆν γὰρ μᾶλλον ἑαυτὸν ἐμπαρέχειν τῇ ἁφῇ, ἅτε τὸ τέλειον βάπτισμα διὰ τοῦ μυστηρίου τοῦ πάθους εἰληφότα. *Op. cit.* X.1.2: κατὰ δύναμιν ἐμπαρέχειν ἑαυτοὺς τῷ δωρεῖσθαι τὰ κάλλιστα βουλομένῳ θεῷ. *Op. cit.* XXXII.6.67: παρὰ τὸ καθῆκον ἑαυτῶν τοὺς πόδας ἐμπαρεσχηκότων τῷ Ἰησοῦ. *Op. cit.* XXXII.12.137: τοῖς κατ' εὐλάβειαν μὴ ἐμπαρέχουσιν ἑαυτῶν τοὺς πόδας ἡμῖν ἵνα αὐτοὺς νίψωμεν. *Cels*, II.23: καὶ τῷ πατρὶ πειθόμενος ἐμπαρεῖχε ἑαυτόν. *Op. cit.* VI.4 (& *Philocalia*, 15.6): τοῖς δυναμένοις ἑαυτοὺς ἐμπαρέχειν παραπλησίους ἐκείνοις, οἷς ὤφθη ὁ θεός. *deOr*, 25.1: πᾶς ἁμαρτωλὸς τῷ ἐνεστῶτι αἰῶνι πονηρῷ ᾠκείωται, μὴ ἐμπαρέχων ἑαυτὸν τῷ δόντι *ἑαυτὸν περὶ τῶν ἁμαρτιῶν ἡμῶν*. [Gal. 1:4; P. Koetschau's editing, ... πονηρῷ. ᾠκείωται, μὴ ἐμπαρέχων ἑαυτὸν τῷ δόντι *ἑαυτὸν περὶ τῶν ἁμαρτωλῶν* ἡμῶν, is hopelessly erroneous]. *Op. cit.* 27.9: ἵνα ... μεταδῷ τῆς ἰδίας δυνάμεως τῷ ἐμπαρεσχηκότι ἑαυτὸν τῇ ἀπ' αὐτοῦ τροφῇ· ... ἕκαστον τῶν τρεφομένων κατὰ τὴν ἀναλογίαν, ἣν [P. Koetschau's ᾧ is wrong] ἐμπαρέσχεν ἑαυτὸν λόγῳ. *frLuc*, fr. 162: οὐκοῦν ὁ ταῦτα εἰπὼν ἐμπαρέσχεν ἑαυτὸν τῷ Ἀβραὰμ τότε. *selPs*, PG.12.1480.44-45: τοῦ αἰσθανομένου, καὶ ἐμπαρέχοντος ἑαυτὸν τῷ Θεῷ εἰς τὸ τελειωθῆναι. Then, Eusebius, *Commentaria in Psalmos*, PG.23.93.24-25. Gregory of Nyssa, *In Inscriptiones Psalmorum*, p. 55. Basil of Caesarea, *De Spiritu Sancto*, 26.62; 29.73; *Homiliae super Psalmos*, PG.29.380.36. Gregory of Nazianzus, *Apologeticus ad Patrem*, PG.35.821.11-12. Evagrius of Pontus, *Practicus*, 89. Maximus Confessor, *Quaestiones ad Thalassium*, 6 (& *Catena in Epistulam Joannis i*, p. 126). It turns out then that no author other than Origen did ever use this phrase so abundantly, and all of those few Christians who employed this were his ardent admirers. As for Greek authors after Plutarch, they made absolutely nothing of this.

cclxxxix Up until the sixth century, it was only Theodoret who took up the expression ἀσκητικὴ πολιτεία ('ascetic conduct' of life), which he made the title of the prologue to his treatise *Historia Religiosa* (*Φιλόθεος Ἱστορία*). The expression enjoyed some currency among some monastic communities only much later. Theodoret, *Historia Religiosa*, Prologue.10; 2.9; 4.12; 17.1; *HE*, pp. 154; 283; 324; 337. Then, Cyril of Scythopolis (sixth century), *Vita Euthymii*, p. 16.

ccxc Origen, *commMatt*, fr. 86 (Klostermann).

ccxci But the ensuing text is attributed also to Apollinaris who used to copy from Origen; see next endnote.

ccxcii Apollinaris, *Fragmenta in Matthaeum*, fr. 12; continued and concluded *infra*.

ccxciii However, this is Chrysostom's (see next note). The notion of 'universal virtue' (καθολικὴ ἀρετή) appears to be exclusive to Chrysostom; cf. *Expositiones in Psalmos*, PG.55.67.10; *In Matthaeum*, PG.57.227.57.58; *In Epistulam ad Ephesios*, PG.62.96.38 (& *Catena In Epistulam ad Ephesios*, p. 180).

ccxciv This is the selfsame text as John Chrysostom's *In Matthaeum*, PG.57.227.57-228.7. See the same text attributed to Chrysostom also in the *Catena in Matthaeum*, p. 32. Cf. Pseudo-Zonaras, *Lexicon*, letter kappa, p. 1141: Καθαροί. οἱ τὴν καθολικὴν ἀρετὴν κεκτημένοι, καὶ μηδὲν ἑαυτοῖς συνειδότες πονηρόν.

ccxcv This is the concluding phrase of Apollinaris, *Fragmenta in Matthaeum*, fr. 12. Origen explained the scriptural passages about God been invisible in *commJohn*, II.35.212; VI.3.14; *frJohn*, fr. 13; *Cels*, II.71; VII.27.

ccxcvi But this is Apollinaris, *Fragmenta in Matthaeum*, fr. 13.

ccxcvii From the point of view of creation, this is contemplation of God in his economic activity towards men, not of God in Himself (see *COT*, pp. 146 ff). Cf. Origen, *commMatt*, 17.19: νῦν μὲν γάρ, κἂν ἀξιωθῶμεν βλέπειν τὸν θεὸν τῷ νῷ καὶ τῇ καρδίᾳ, οὐ βλέπομεν *αὐτὸν καθώς ἐστιν* ἀλλὰ καθὼς διὰ τὴν ἡμετέραν οἰκονομίαν ἡμῖν γίνεται. ἐπὶ δὲ τέλει τῶν πραγμάτων καὶ τῆς *ἀποκαταστάσεως πάντων ὧν ἐλάλησε διὰ στόματος τῶν ἁγίων. ἐξ αἰῶνος προφητῶν αὐτοῦ*, ὀψόμεθα αὐτόν, οὐχ ὡς νῦν, ὅ οὐκ ἔστιν, ἀλλ' ὡς πρέπει τότε, ὅ ἐστιν. *schLuc*, PG.17.364.51-365.2: Εἰ γὰρ καὶ ἀξιωθῶμεν βλέψαι νῦν τὸν Θεὸν τῷ νῷ καὶ τῇ καρδίᾳ, οὐ βλέπομεν αὐτὸν *καθώς ἐστιν*, ἀλλὰ καθὼς διὰ τὴν ἡμετέραν οἰκονομίαν ἡμῶν γίνεται. ἐν δὲ τῇ *ἀποκαταστάσει πάντων, ὧν ἐλάλησε διὰ στόματος τῶν ἁγίων αὐτοῦ*, ὀψόμεθα οὐχ ὡς νῦν ὃ οὐκ ἔστιν, ἀλλ' ὡς πρέπει τότε, ὅ ἐστι. Παρ' ἡμῖν μὲν οὖν τοῖς ἀνθρώποις ἀνθρώπῳ ὡμοιώθη. παρὰ δὲ ἑαυτοὺς ἀποθεώσασι Θεῷ. *Ὁ Θεὸς γάρ ἐστι*, φησίν, *ἐν συναγωγῇ θεῶν*.

ccxcviii Apollinaris, *Fragmenta in Matthaeum*, fr. 13.

ccxcix Cyril of Alexandria, *frMatt*, fr. 39.

ccc Clement of Alexandria, *Stromateis*, 4.6.41.4.

ccci This consideration of 'righteousness' meaning 'virtue' classified as either 'universal' or 'particular' one is simple on the face of it. And yet what stands behind this is Origen's enormous Greek background. Although this distinction appeared in Plato speaking of 'virtue' which is 'common' to all animals (meaning, for example, an instinct of distributing food between themselves, *Critias*, 110c, quoted also by Stobaeus, *Anthologium*, 4.1.64). Cf. Aristotle in *Ethica Nicomachea*, 1102b, echoing his teacher's idea: ταύτης μὲν οὖν κοινή τις ἀρετὴ καὶ οὐκ ἀνθρωπίνη φαίνεται ('the excellence of this faculty therefore appears to be common to all animate things and not peculiar to man'). However, it was Aristotle who made this idea a specific point of his moral philosophy, speaking of either 'universal righteousness' or 'particular' one. *Ethica Nicomachea*, 1130b: μέρος γὰρ αὕτη ἡ ἀδικία τῆς ὅλης ἀδικίας, ὁμοίως δὲ καὶ ἡ δικαιοσύνη τῆς δικαιοσύνης. ὥστε καὶ περὶ τῆς ἐν μέρει δικαιοσύνης καὶ περὶ τῆς ἐν μέρει ἀδικίας λεκτέον, καὶ τοῦ δικαίου καὶ ἀδίκου ὡσαύτως. As I have demonstrated several times, Origen learned everything about Aristotle's throught from the commentaries of Alexander of Aphrodisias. *commTop*, p. 39: ὡς καὶ δικαιοσύνη ἡ κοινή τε καὶ ἡ ἐν μέρει. *Op. cit.* p. 114: ἀλλὰ καὶ ἡ δικαιοσύνη καὶ τὴν κοινὴν ἀρετὴν σημαίνουσα καὶ τὴν ἀντιδιαιρουμένην ταῖς ἄλλαις ἀρεταῖς ὁμώνυμος (quoted, slightly paraphrased, in *Suda*, letter delta, entry 1073, and by Pseudo-Zonaras, *Lexicon*, letter delta, p. 518). Cf. similar commentaries by later authors. Michael of Ephesus, *commEthNic*, p. 461: Ὅτι μὲν ἡ φιλία μόριόν ἐστιν οὐ τῆς ὅλης δικαιοσύνης, τῆς ὡς νομιμότητος, ἀλλὰ τῆς ἐν μέρει, ἥτις ἦν τοῦ ἴσου διανεμητική, οὐ παντάπασιν ἄδηλόν ἐστιν. Also, *op. cit.* p. 114; *In Librum Quintum Ethicorum Nicomacheorum Commentarium*, p. 13: οὕτως οὖν δείξας ὅτι ἔστι τις ἐν μέρει ἀδικία ἑτέρα τῆς καθόλου, ἔχων δὲ ἀπὸ ταύτης τῆς ἀποδείξεως ὅτι ἔστι καὶ δικαιοσύνη τις ἑτέρα τῆς καθόλου. Gennadius Scholarius, *epitSummae*, chapter 68: Εἰ γὰρ καὶ κοινὸν ἔχουσι τὸν τῆς ἀρετῆς λόγον (διὸ καὶ ἀρεταὶ πολλάκις καλοῦνται) ἀλλ' ἔχουσί τι ὑπεραναβεβηκός, καθόσον εἰσὶ αἵτινες ἀρεταὶ τελειοῦσαι τὸν ἄνθρωπον καθόσον ὑπὸ Θεοῦ κινεῖται, ὡς καὶ ὁ Φιλόσοφος [sc. Aristotle] τίθησιν ὑπὲρ τὴν κοινὴν ἀρετὴν ἡρωϊκήν τινα καὶ θείαν. καὶ οὕτω δῶρα καλοῦνται. Anonymous, *commEthNic*, p. 211: ὡς γὰρ ἀνάβασις καὶ κατάβασις ταὐτὸν ὄντα κατὰ τὸ ὑποκείμενον τὸ εἶναι οὐ ταὐτὸν ἔχουσιν, οὕτω καὶ ἡ ὅλη ἀρετὴ καὶ ἡ τοιαύτη δικαιοσύνη. ἐπεὶ τοίνυν ἡ μὲν τοιαύτη δικαιοσύνη ἐστὶν ὅλη ἀρετή, ἡμεῖς δὲ ζητοῦμεν τὴν ἐν μέρει λεγομένην (οὕτω γὰρ καὶ περὶ τῶν ἄλλων ἀρετῶν ἑκάστης καθ' ἑαυτὴν εἰρήκαμεν), δῆλον ὡς περὶ ἄλλης ἡμῖν δικαιοσύνης ὁ λόγος λεκτέος ἐστίν, ἀλλ' οὐ περὶ ταύτης. *Op. cit.* p. 214: δείξας ὅτι τις ἐν μέρει δικαιοσύνη ἀρετὴ καὶ ἐν μέρει ἀδικία κακία, περὶ τούτων, φησί. *Op. cit.* p. 222: Δύο εἴδη διδάξας τῆς δικαιοσύνης τῆς ἐν μέρει ἀρετῆς, ἀλλ' οὐ τῆς κοινῆς τῆς ὡς νομιμότητος λεγομένης τό τε διανεμητικὸν καὶ τὸ διορθωτικόν. Anonymous, *commEthNic*, p. 24: ἐν ταύτῃ μὲν οὖν τῇ δυνάμει [sc. τοῖς ζῴοις πᾶσιν] οὐκ ἔστιν εὑρεῖν ἰδίως ἀρετὴν ἀνθρωπίνην ἀλλὰ κοινὴν ἅπασιν. ἡ γὰρ τοιαύτη ἀρετὴ τὸ τρέφεσθαι καὶ αὐξάνεσθαι καὶ ὑπνώττουσιν ἐνεργεῖται καὶ μάλιστα τότε, ἡ δὲ ἀνθρωπίνη ἀρετὴ οὐδαμῶς.

By entertaining this idea of 'virtue' being either 'common' or 'particular', Origen meant an excelling virtue that has become an individual character by means of one's own free will. This is the idea that was embraced by admirers of Origen as different as Porphyry and the Christian Didymus, whose profound knowledge of Peripatetic philosophy I have discussed in the past (see my *NDGF*, pp. 456; 509; *Scholia in Apocalypsin*, pp. 63; 68; 89). Porphyry, *De Abstinentia*, 3.11: ἐξέχει γὰρ ἐν ἑκάστῳ ἰδία τις ἀρετή. Didymus, *Commentarii in Job*, fr. 393: ἔστιν γὰρ καὶ ἰδικὴ ἀδικία ἡ περὶ τὰ συναλλάγματα, ὥσπερ δικαιοσύνη ἡ ἰδικὴ καὶ ἡ πᾶσα ἀρετὴ πολλάκις καλεῖται. *frPs(al)*, fr. 1146: Αἱ διάφοροι ἐντολαί σου προστάξεις οὖσαι τῶν κατ' εἶδος ἀρετῶν ‹ἓν› πᾶσαι τυγχάνουσιν, ἡ καθόλου γενικὴ ἀρετὴ τῷ ἀντακολουθεῖν τὰς ἰδικὰς ἀρετάς, ὡς τὸν μίαν τελείως ἔχοντα πάσας ἔχειν. *Op. cit.* fr. 1261: Οὐδὲν δὲ διαφέρει πληθυντικῶς ἢ ἑνικῶς τὰ θελήματα ἢ τὸ θέλημα φάναι. θελήματα γὰρ αὐτοῦ αἱ κατ' εἶδος ἀρεταί, ἓν δὲ γενικὸν θέλημα αὐτοῦ ἡ καθόλου καὶ κοινὴ ἀρετή. Nevertheless, it should be added that, in reality, Plato did not feel strongly about the notion of 'many' kinds of 'virtue'. Actually, he believed that 'there is one form of virtue, whereas the forms of evil are infinite' (ἓν μὲν εἶναι εἶδος τῆς ἀρετῆς, ἄπειρα δὲ τῆς κακίας, *Respublica*, 445c), perhaps because he embraced the Pyrhagorean doctrine expressed through the verse ἐσθλοὶ μὲν γὰρ ἁπλῶς, παντοδαπῶς δὲ κακοί ('Goodness is simple, wickedness manifold'), from an unknown source, which Aristotle quoted in the *Ethica Nicomachea*, 1106b35. Likewise, Origen, *commJohn*, II.4.39-40.

cccii Cf. Origen's followers entertaining the notion of 'kingdom of heavens' being a 'prize'. Gregory of Nazianzus, *In Laudem Heronis Philosophi*, PG.35.1201.1-3: καὶ ὧν ἆθλον, οὐρανῶν βασιλεία. Basil of Ancyra, *De Virginitate*, PG.30.677.2: δῆλον ὡς βιαστῶν ἆθλον εἶναι τὴν τῶν οὐρανῶν βασιλείαν γινώσκουσα. Theodoret, *Historia Religiosa*, Vita 30.5: Μίαν δὲ καὶ βασιλείαν οὐρανῶν ὁ ἀγωνοθέτης τοῖς νικηφόροις προτέθηκεν, ἆθλον τοῦτο κοινὸν τοῖς ἀγῶσιν ὁρίσας. *De Incarnatione Domini*, PG.75.1448.18-19: συναθλοῦν, ἆθλον τῶν πόνων ἔχει τὴν τῶν οὐρανῶν βασιλείαν. *Op. cit.* PG.75.1456.41-42: Πόνων γὰρ ἆθλον ἡ τοιαύτη βασιλεία. *Interpretatio in xiv Epistulas Sancti Pauli*, PG.82:553.17-17: ἆθλον ἡμῖν πρόκειται τῆς παρατάξεως ἡ βασιλεία τῶν οὐρανῶν. *Op. cit.* PG.82.881.45-46: τοῦτο δέ ἐστιν ἡ τῶν οὐρανῶν βασιλεία. *Βραβεῖον* τὸ ἆθλον ἐκάλεσεν. Basil of Seleucia, *Sermones*, col. 125: καὶ φανεὶς ἀθλητὴς δοκιμώτατος, ἆθλον ἀρετῆς τὴν βασιλείαν κομίζεται.

ccciii Origen, *commMatt*, fr. 87 (Klostermann), col. 2.

ccciv Cyril of Alexandria, *frMatt*, fr. 38.

cccv Gregory of Nyssa, *Orationes viii De Beatitudinibus*, PG.44.1289.40-47. Cf. *De Perfectione Christiana ad Olympium Monachum*, p. 184: ὅταν οὖν ἐξαιρεθῇ τῆς φύσεως ἡμῶν ὁ ἐμφύλιος πόλεμος. We have seen that Pseudo-Zonaras oftentimes used Origen's portions in order to explain a lemma in his lexicon. This is what he did with the term εἰρηνοποιὸς ('peace-maker'), which is a copy from the present text. Pseudo-Zonaras, *Lexicon*, letter epsilon, pp. 627-628: κυρίως δὲ εἰρηνοποιὸς ὁ τὴν ἑαυτοῦ στάσιν τῆς σαρκὸς καὶ τοῦ πνεύματος καὶ τὸν ἐμφύλιον τῆς φύσεως πόλεμον εἰς εἰρηνικὴν ἄγων συμφωνίαν. ὅταν γὰρ ἡ σὰρξ μηκέτι ἐπιθυμεῖ κατὰ τοῦ πνεύματος, ἀλλ' ἡ τοῦ πνεύματος χάρις ἐπικρατήσῃ τῶν σωματικῶν παθῶν.

cccvi Origen, *commMatt*, fr. 88 (Klostermann), col. 2.

cccvii See *supra* endnote cclxxii.

cccviii Origen, *commMatt*, 12.14. Cf. *commEph*, fr. 33: ἢ τὴν ἀρετὴν ἥτις ἐστὶν ὁ Χριστός.

cccix Cf. Wisdom of Solomon, 16:20.

cccx The expression τῆς ἀρετῆς ἐφίεσθαι ('longing for virtue') was introduced in Christian literature by Origen, who possibly took this from Philo. Nevertheless, in my previous books I have shown that he had read all the other authors who preceded Philo on this, namely, Xenophon, Demosthenes, Sextus Empiricus, Josephus, Alexander of Aphrodisias. See Xenophon, *Memorabilia*, 4.2.11: ταύτης τῆς ἀρετῆς ἐφίεσαι. *Op. cit.* 4.8.11: οἱ ἀρετῆς ἐφιέμενοι. *Symposium.* 8.41-2: ἀγαθῶν γὰρ φύσει καὶ τῆς ἀρετῆς φιλοτίμως ἐφιεμένων. *Apologia Socratis*, 17 & 34: τῶν ἀρετῆς ἐφιεμένων. Pseudo-Demosthenes, *Eroticus*, 25: μετρίως ἀρετῆς ἐφιεμένοις. Philo, *Legum Allegoriarum*, 2.81: τὰ σώματα σωματικῆς ἐφίενται ἀρετῆς. *De Agricultura*, 125: τὸν οὖν ἐφιέμενον ἀρετῆς. *De Mutatione Nominum*, 75-77: βελτιοῦται τὸ ἦθος κτήσεως ὁμοῦ καὶ χρήσεως ἀρετῆς ἐφιέμενον. Josephus, *De Bello Judaico*, 6.36: μάλιστα προσήκει μάχεσθαι τοῖς δυσκόλοις τοὺς ἀρετῆς ἐφιεμένους. Sextus Empiricus, *Adversus Musicos*, 6.34: ἀνάπαλιν γὰρ ἀντικόπτει καὶ ἀντιβαίνει πρὸς τὸ τῆς ἀρετῆς ἐφίεσθαι. Pseudo-Alexander of Aphrodisias, *Ἠθικὰ Προβλήματα*, p. 142: ὁρίζεται δὲ ὁ σκοπὸς ὑπὸ τῆς ἠθικῆς ἀρετῆς (οὗ γὰρ ἐφιέμεθα, περὶ τούτου βουλευόμεθα, ἡ δὲ τῶν προσηκόντων ἔφεσις ἀπὸ τῆς ἠθικῆς ἀρετῆς, ὥσπερ εἶπεν Ἀριστοτέλης).

Subsequently, Origen bequeathed this to his Christian successors, starting with Evagrius of Pontus, *Practicus*, 52: τοῦ ἐφιεμένου τῆς ἀρετῆς (two centuries later, this was quoted by Dorotheus of Gaza, *Doctrinae Diversae*, 17.176). *Op. cit.* 86: Κατὰ φύσιν ἐνεργεῖ ψυχὴ λογικὴ ὅταν τὸ μὲν ἐπιθυμητικὸν αὐτῆς μέρος τῆς ἀρετῆς ἐφίεται. Diodore of Tarsus, *Fragmenta in Epistulam ad Romanos*, p. 106: τοῖς τῆς ἀρετῆς ἐφιεμένοις ἁρμόζει μάλιστα κοινωνεῖν ταῖς τῶν ἁγίων μνήμαις. John Chrysostom, *Expositiones in Psalmos*, PG.55.105.31: οὐδὲ μετὰ μισθοῦ τῆς ἀρετῆς ἐφίενται (four centuries later, this was quoted by George Monachus, *Chronicon*, p. 159 and *Chronicon Breve*, PG.110.209). *In Matthaeum*, PG.57.267.46-47: παιδευόμενος καταφρονεῖν μὲν κακίας, ἐφίεσθαι δὲ ἀρετῆς. *In Joannem*, PG.59.441.37-38: καὶ τῆς ἀρετῆς ἐφιέμενοι χλευαζώμεθα παρ' ἐκείνων. *In Acta Apostolorum*, PG.60.285.9: ἐφίεσθαι τῆς ἀρετῆς. Pseudo-John Chrysostom, *In Psalmum 118*, PG.55.675.58: καὶ τοὺς τῆς τελείας ἀρετῆς ἐφιεμένους. Theodoret, *Curatio*, 5.77: καὶ ἀρετῆς ἐφιέμεθα. *Interpretatio in Psalmos*, PG.80.1821.4-5: καὶ τοὺς τῆς τελείας ἀρετῆς ἐφιεμένους. *In Epistulas Sancti Pauli*, PG.82.124.24-26: Αὕτη ἡμῖν καὶ εἰς τὴν τῆς ἀρετῆς κατόρθωσιν συντελεῖ. Ὁ γὰρ μὴ ἐφιέμενος ταύτης, τῶν ὑπὲρ ταύτης οὐκ ἀνέχεται πόνων. Cyril of Alexandria, *commProphXII*, v. 2, p. 199: εἰ δὲ ἐποπτεύοι πάλιν ἐφιεμένους ἀρετῆς καὶ ζῆν ἐννόμως ἐθέλοντας. Sozomenus, *HE*, 8.9.2: τὸν κατὰ θεὸν τῆς ἄκρας ἀρετῆς ἐφιέμενον. Pseudo-Dionysius the Areopagite, *De Caelesti Hierarchia*, p. 45: ἐπιγνοῦσαι πρῶται θεὸν καὶ θείας ἀρετῆς ὑπερκειμένως ἐφιέμεναι. Maximus Confessor, *Quaestiones ad Thalassium*, 47: πρὸς ὠφέλειαν τῶν ἀρετῆς τε καὶ γνώσεως ἐφιεμένων. John Philoponus, *commPhys*, p. 509: ὁ τῆς ἀρετῆς ἐφιέμενος.

cccxi Theodore of Heraclea or Theodore of Mopsuestia, *frMatt*, fr. 17 (J. Reuss). However, it is clear that all those alleged fragments on the commentary on Matthew under the name 'Theodore' constantly turn out to be excerpts from Origen's commentary.

cccxii Origen, *commMatt*, fr. 91 (Klostermann, p. 52). The editor used also two other codices along with the text of Cramer's text of catenae (1840) of *Catena in Marcum*, p. 369 (on Mark, 9:50), which runs parallel to the present one, except for its initial few lines.

cccxiii Cyril of Alexandria, *apud Catena in Matthaeum*, p. 33.

cccxiv Cyril of Alexandria, *frMatt*, fr. 41.

cccxv Theodore of Heraclea, *frMatt*, fr. 23 (J.A. Crammer) & *Catena in Matthaeum*, p. 33 (J. Reuss). However, the ensuing turn of phrase demonstrates that once again we are upon Origen's words.

cccxvi Origen, *commMatt*, fr. 92 (Klostermann).

cccxvii John Chrysostom, *In Matthaeum*, PG.57.231.64-232.4. Not only did he copy from Origen to the letter, but also produced a paraphrased rendering of his own, in which he maintained Origen's vocabulary. See John Chrysostom, *apud Catena in Matthaeum*, p. 33: (Τοῦ Χρυσοστόμου.) Τί ἐστιν *ἐὰν δὲ τὸ ἅλας μωρανθῇ* καὶ τὰ ἑξῆς; ὅτι οἱ μὲν ἄλλοι, φησί, τοῦ λαοῦ ἀρετὰς κατορθοῦντες καὶ πίπτοντες δύνανται διὰ μετανοίας ταχέως τυγχάνειν συγγνώμης. ὁ δὲ διδάσκαλος ἐὰν τοῦτο πάθῃ, πάσης ἀπεστέρηται ἀπολογίας, καὶ τὴν ἐσχάτην δίδωσι τιμωρίαν· … ἐὰν γὰρ φοβηθῆτε ὀνειδισμοὺς καὶ διωγμούς, καταφρονηθήσεσθε, ὅπερ ἐστὶ καταπατηθῆναι.

cccxviii Origen, *commMatt*, fr. 93 (Klostermann).

cccxix However it is all too plausible to assume that since the text continues, we are upon the context of Origen's own words.

cccxx This is a proposition that could have been made only by an erudite Greek, since it was only with Aristotle that the notion of light being indispensable for sight to take place was set forth. Cf. Aristotle, *De Anima*, 419a: ὅτι τὸ μὲν ἐν φωτὶ ὁρώμενον χρῶμα. διὸ καὶ οὐχ ὁρᾶται ἄνευ φωτός. Alexander of Aphrodisias, *De Anima*, p. 46: ἥτις δὲ ἐν τῷ πυρὶ καὶ ἐν τοῖς ἄλλοις τοῖς φωτὸς ποιητικοῖς ἐνοῦσα δύναμις αὐτά τε μάλιστα ὁρατὰ ποιεῖ, καὶ τοῖς ἄλλοις χρώμασιν αἴτια τοῦ ὁρᾶσθαι, τῷ φωτὸς αὐτὰ εἶναι ποιητικά, δι' οὗ ὁρᾶται τὰ ὁρώμενα. *In Librum De Sensu Commentarium*, pp. 36-37: τὸ ἐντὸς πᾶν τὸ μέχρι τῆς ὁρατικῆς δυνάμεως ἐφωτίζετο ἀπὸ τοῦ ἐκτὸς φωτός. *Op. cit.* p. 57: καὶ γὰρ τότε ἀπορρεύσεται τὰ εἴδωλα καὶ δέξεται αὐτὰ ὁ ὀφθαλμός. ἢ διὰ τί φωτὸς χρεία πρὸς τὸ ὁρᾶν, δεχομένου τὸ ὁρώμενον τοῦ ὀφθαλμοῦ, γίνεται; *Op. cit.* p. 135: οὕτως δὲ γινομένου τοῦ φωτὸς ἀχρόνως εὐλόγως καὶ τὸ ὁρώμενον ἀχρόνως τῇ ὄψει προσβάλλει. Pseudo-Alexander of Aphrodisias, *De Anima Libri Mantissa*, p. 166: ἀλλ' ὅμως πρὸς τὸ εὖ ὁρᾶν καὶ φωτὸς δεόμεθα καὶ ἄλλων τινῶν. Besides, Origen knew both the text and the ideas of Aristotle from Alexander of Aphrodisias, which I have pointed out several times in the past. On Alexander of Aphrodisias and Origen, see, *Anaxagoras*, pp. 354; 397-398; 512; 522; 597; 658; 672; 676; 843; 869; 927 (God styled αὐτοζωή); 928-929; 978; 991-992; 996-997. *RCR*, pp. 173; 313; 368; 377; *PHE*, pp. 269; 404; *NDGF*, pp. 305-306; 352; 516; 581; *Scholia*, pp. 40; 147; 166; 199; 262; 265-268; 277; 279; 294; 300; 304; 330; 337; 345; 385; 397; 402-404. Eusebius expressed explicitly his respect for Alexander of Aphrodisias. *PE*, 6.8.39-6.9.32. In his commentaries, Alexander of Aphrodisias quoted from Aristotle lemma after lemma, and commented on them -a paradigm Origen himself used in his Christian commentaries.

cccxxi Origen, *commJohn*, VI.59.304; cf. *op. cit.* I.4.21: οὗ κόσμου τὴν ἁμαρτίαν ἦρεν ὁ Χριστός. περὶ γὰρ τοῦ κόσμου τῆς ἐκκλησίας ὁ λόγος ἐστὶν ὁ γεγραμμένος. *Op. cit.* VI.59.301: κόσμος δὲ τοῦ κόσμου ἡ ἐκκλησία, κόσμου αὐτῆς γενομένου Χριστοῦ.

cccxxii Origen's devotee Didymus, *In Genesim*, cod. p. 39.

cccxxiii Cf. Origen, *commJohn*, II.6.48: Καθέζεται δὲ ἐπὶ τὸν λευκὸν ἵππον ὁ καλούμενος *πιστός*, ἱδρυμένος βεβαιότερον (C. Blanc's βεβαιώτερον is wrong). This is one more instance of the usual phenomenon: once later stars of theology came upon a rhetorical turn that Origen used once in while, or indeed once, they seized on that and could not have enough of it. This time is not John Chrysostom: it is Cyril of Alexandria referring to those who 'hold fast to the faith', which appears at this point of Origen's commentary on Matthew. He used this at about a dozen of points, such as *commProphXII*, v. 2, p. 421; *In Joannem*, v. 2, p. 381; *op. cit.* v. 3, pp. 109; 110; *Epistulae Paschales*, PG.77: 680.18-19; 717.27; *De Adoratione*, PG.67.425.5-7; *et passim.* However, this should not obscure the fact that (once again) he copied from Origen's present commentary. Moreover, the expression that Origen introduced had been already used by his usual admirers, such as the following. Gregory of Nyssa, *De Instituto Christiano*, p. 42: ταύτην συνειδότες ὑμῖν τὴν εὐσεβῆ καὶ ἀδιαμάρτητον τῆς πίστεως ὁμολογίαν ἐν τῷ βάθει τῆς ψυχῆς ἀσφαλῶς ἱδρυμένην. Athanasius, *Epistula ad Monachos*, PG.26.1185.41-42: Τοῖς τὸν μονήρη βίον ἀσκοῦσι, καὶ ἐν πίστει Θεοῦ ἱδρυμένοις, ἀγαπητοῖς καὶ ποθεινοτάτοις ἀδελφοῖς. Didymus, *commZacch*, 1.232: οἱ βεβαίως κατὰ ἁγιότητα ἱδρύμενοι, στάσιν μόνιμον κατὰ πίστιν ἀπειληφότες. *frPs*(*al*), fr. 463: ἐν ἀρετῇ δὲ καὶ πίστει τὴν ἵδρυσιν ἔχουσα.

cccxxiv Cyril of Alexandria, *apud Catena in Matthaeum*, p. 34 & *frMatt*, fr. 43.

cccxxv Origen, *commMatt*, fr. 95 I (Klostermann), col. 1. Cf. Theodore of Mopsuestia, *frMatt*, fr. 26: *Μόδιον* τὴν κακίαν εἶπεν, *λύχνον* δὲ τὴν ἀρετήν. See the same idea ascribed to 'Theodore Monachus', *apud Catena in Matthaeum*, p. 34. This designation (Θεοδώρου Μονάχου, 'Theodore, monk') appears fifteen times in this catena. He should not be either Theodore of Mopsuestia or Theodore of Heraclea, since, on pp. 126-127, attribution is made to those two authors alongside 'Theodore'.

cccxxvi See also, Origen, *commMatt*, fr. 93, Klostermann, columns 2 (quoted *infra*) and 3.

cccxxvii John Chrysostom, *In Matthaeum*, PG.57.232.20-29. Likewise, John Chrysostom, *apud Catena in Matthaeum*, p. 34.

cccxxviii Origen, *commMatt*, fr. 94 (Klostermann).

cccxxix Origen, *commMatt*, fr. 95 I (Klostermann, col. 2).

cccxxx Origen, *commMatt*, fr. 95 II (Klostermann), in seven codices. In two of them, the text is in brackets and designated Ἀπολλιναρίου. In one codex, this is 'unattributed' (Ἀνεπιγράφου).

cccxxxi Apollinaris, *frMatt*, fr. 15.

cccxxxii Here is how Apollinaris copied this; *frMatt*, fr. 17: Φῶς ἐστιν, ἡ ἐνάρετος πολιτεία. Likewise, Theodore of Heraclea or Theodore of Mopsuestia, *frMatt*, fr. 19 (J. Reuss): *Φῶς* ἐστιν ἡ ἐνάρετος πολιτεία. οὐ δεῖ ἐν κρυφῇ λαλεῖν τὸν εὐαγγελικὸν λόγον, ἀλλὰ παρρησίᾳ, ἵνα οἱ ἐπὶ γῆς ἄνθρωποι φωτισθῶσιν.

cccxxxiii Origen, *commMatt*, fr. 96 (Klostermann).

cccxxxiv Origen, *commJohn*, II.17.121. Once again, it is evident that later authors copied from Origen abundantly. Theodore of Heraclea or Theodore of Mopsuestia, *frMatt*, fr. 18 (J. Reuss): Οὐ λέγει. *λαμψάτω τὸ φῶς ὑμῶν ἔμπροσθεν* τοῦ θεοῦ. οὐδὲ γὰρ λύχνων φῶς λάμπει ἔμπροσθεν ἡλίου.

cccxxxv Cf. Gregory of Nyssa, *In Canticum Canticorum*, p. 130: Ὅρκος ἐστὶ λόγος πιστούμενος δι' ἑαυτοῦ τὴν ἀλήθειαν. This proverbial phrase was copied by Procopius of Gaza, *Catena in Canticum Canticorum*, p. 1592, and by Matthaeus Blastares, *Collectio Alphabetica*, letter epsilon, chapter 32.

cccxxxvi John Chrysostom, *apud Catena in Matthaeum*, pp. 34-35. Likewise, John Chrysostom, *In Matthaeum*, PG.57.242.49-52: Ὃ δὲ λέγει, τοιοῦτόν ἐστιν. Ἀμήχανον ἀτέλεστον μεῖναι, ἀλλὰ καὶ τὸ βραχύτατον αὐτοῦ πληρωθῆναι δεῖ. Ὅπερ αὐτὸς ἐποίησε, μετὰ ἀκριβείας αὐτὸν ἁπάσης ἀπαρτίσας.

cccxxxvii Origen's conviction that 'even the minutest letter' of Scripture contains 'the wisdom of God' was the point of departure for him to apply textual philological analysis of this and bring to light the truths concealed therein.

cccxxxviii Cf. Gregory of Nyssa, *In Christi Resurrectionem Oratio i*, pp. 302-303: *Οὐρανὸς καὶ γῆ παρελεύσεται* καὶ ὅλου *τοῦ κόσμου παράγει τὸ σχῆμα*, τὸ δὲ *ἰῶτα* τὸ ἐκ τοῦ νόμου καὶ ἡ *κεραία* οὐ παρέρχεται. ἡ κάθετος γραμμὴ ἡ ἄνωθεν ἐπὶ τὸ βάθος καθήκουσα *ἰῶτα* λέγεται, ἡ δὲ ἐγκαρσίως ἀγομένη διὰ πλαγίου *κεραία* ὀνομάζεται, καθὼς ἔστι καὶ παρὰ τῶν ναυτιλλομένων τοῦτο μαθεῖν. τὸ γὰρ ξύλον τὸ διὰ πλαγίου τῷ ἱστίῳ ἐπικείμενον, οὗ καὶ τὴν ὀθόνην ἐξαπλοῦσι, κεραίαν λέγουσιν ἐκ τοῦ σχήματος ὀνομάζοντες. *De Vita Mosis*, 2.151: Ἀληθῶς γάρ, τοῖς καθορᾶν δυναμένοις, ἐν τῷ νόμῳ μάλιστα τὸ κατὰ τὸν σταυρὸν θεωρεῖται μυστήριον. Διό φησί που τὸ Εὐαγγέλιον ὅτι ἐκ τοῦ νόμου τὸ *ἰῶτα* καὶ ἡ *κεραία* οὐ παρέρχεται, σημαῖνον διὰ τῶν εἰρημένων τήν τε ἐκ πλαγίου γραμμὴν καὶ τὴν κάθετον, δι' ὧν τὸ σχῆμα τοῦ σταυροῦ καταγράφεται.

As it often happened, lexica took this up in pertinent lemmata. See Photius, *Lexicon*, letter iota, entry 239: ἱστὸς καὶ κεραία. ὁ μὲν ἱστὸς τὸ ἐπίμηκες ξύλον ἄνω τεταμένον. κεραία δὲ τὰ πλάγια, ὥστε γενέσθαι γράμμα τὸ ταῦ. διετείνετο δὲ πολλάκις ὁ τῆς Ἀθηνᾶς πέπλος εἰς τοιοῦτο σχῆμα ξύλων καὶ ἐπόμπευεν. *Suda*, letter kappa, entry 1393: *Κεραία*. τὸ πλάγιον τοῦ ἱστοῦ. Michael Psellus, *Poemata*, poem 6, line 352: κεραία δὲ τὸ πλάγιον πρὸς τὸ ἱστίον ξύλον. Pseudo-Zonaras, *Lexicon*, letter kappa, p. 1188: Κεραία. τὸ κερατάριον, τὸ διὰ πλαγίου ξύλον τῷ ἱστῷ ἐπικείμενον. οὗ καὶ τὴν ὀθόνην ἐξάπτουσι.

cccxxxix Cyril of Alexandria, *In Matthaeum*, fr. 46.

cccxl An assault on the Gnostics. A semicolon follows, and then the siglum ΩΡΙΓΕΝΟΥΣ appears.

cccxli John Chrysostom, *In Matthaeum*, PG.57.241.11-14. Likewise, in *op. cit.* PG.57.262.6-24.

cccxlii Origen, *commMatt*, fr. 97 (Klostermann), col. 1.

cccxliii Origen, *commMatt*, fr. 97 (Klostermann), col. 2.

cccxliv Cf. Psalm 101:26-27, quoted in Heb. 1:11. Origen, *Cels*, IV.56; *selPs*, PG.12: 1240.39-51; 1560.5-8.

cccxlv This is one more token of Epiphanius writing while having in mind Origen's words. Cf. Origen, *Philocalia*, 15.14: καὶ οὐ θαυμαστὸν τὴν φύσει τρεπτὴν καὶ ἀλλοιωτὴν καὶ εἰς πάντα ἃ βούλεται ὁ δημιουργὸς ὕλην μεταβλητήν, καὶ πάσης ποιότητος ἣν ὁ τεχνίτης βούλεται δεκτικήν, ὁτὲ μὲν ἔχειν ποιότητα καθ' ἣν λέγεται τὸ *Οὐκ εἶχεν εἶδος οὐδὲ κάλλος*. ὁτὲ δὲ οὕτως ἔνδοξον καὶ καταπληκτικὴν καὶ θαυμαστήν. *frLuc*, fr. 140: ὡς δὲ τὸ τούτων εἶδος οὐκ ἐγένετο ἕτερον παρὰ τὸ τῆς μεταμορφώσεως, οὕτως ἐν τῇ ἀναστάσει πολλῷ ἐνδοξότερον τὸ περὶ τοὺς ἁγίους εἶδος ἔσται, παρ' ὃ εἶχον ἐν τῷ βίῳ τούτῳ, οὐχ ἕτερον δέ. οἱ δὲ περὶ Ἰησοῦν ἐνδόξως ὤφθησαν τοῖς μαθηταῖς, Μωϋσῆς μὲν τοῦ νόμου τὸ πρόσωπον δηλῶν, Ἠλίας δὲ τῶν προφητῶν. *Dialogus cum Heraclide*, 3: *Ὁ γὰρ κολλώμενος τῷ Κυρίῳ ἓν πνεῦμά ἐστιν*. Οὐκ ἔστιν ὃς μὲν οὐσίας ὑποδεεστέρας ἢ καταβεβηκυίας καὶ ἐλάττονος, Χριστὸς δὲ θειοτέρας καὶ ἐνδοξοτέρας καὶ μακαριωτέρας; *commSerMatt*, p. 108: υἱὸν δὲ ἀνθρώπου ἑαυτόν φησιν ὡς ἐνσώματον ἐλευσόμενον, ὥσπερ δὲ ὅτε μετεμορφώθη παραλαβὼν τοὺς τρεῖς μαθητάς, νεφέλη φωτεινὴ ἐπεσκίασεν αὐτούς, οὕτως ἐν τῇ δευτέρᾳ παρουσίᾳ ἐνδοξότερον μεταμορφωθεὶς ἐπὶ πλειόνων ἥξει νεφελῶν, ὡς ἂν οὐ τρισὶν ἀλλὰ πλείοσιν ὁρώμενος. *selPs*, PG.12.1096.45-1096.3: οὕτως μέλλοντας κληρονομεῖν βασιλείαν οὐρανῶν, καὶ ἐν τόποις διαφέρουσιν ἔσεσθαι, ἀναγκαῖον χρῆσθαι σώμασι πνευματικοῖς, οὐχὶ τοῦ εἴδους τοῦ προτέρου ἀφανιζομένου, κἂν ἐπὶ τὸ ἐνδοξότερον γένηται αὐτοῦ ἡ τροπή. ὥσπερ ἦν τὸ Ἰησοῦ εἶδος, καὶ Μωϋσέως, καὶ Ἠλίου, οὐχ ἕτερον ἐν τῇ μεταμορφώσει, παρ' ὃ ἦν.

cccxlvi Epiphanius, *Panarion*, v. 2, pp. 462-463. He is the only one who reproduced Origen's exegesis of Matt. 5:17 faithfully. Otherwise, he declared himself Origen's avowed enemy, only to confirm that old habits die hard.

cccxlvii This should have been emended to Οἱ. Otherwise, the sentence makes no sense.

cccxlviii Origen, *commMatt*, fr. 98 (Klostermann).

cccxlix Origen, *commMatt*, fr. 99 (Klostermann).

cccl Origen, *frLuc*, fr. 221.

cccli Cyril of Alexandria, *frMatt*, fr. 48; also, *op. cit.* fr. 47: Θεομάχος, φησίν, κληθήσεται ὁ τὴν ἐλαχίστην τῶν ἐν τῷ νόμῳ ἐντολῶν ἀθετῶν. διὸ καὶ ἀθετεῖται παρὰ θεοῦ ὡς αὐτῷ ἀνθιστάμενος καὶ ἀντινομοθετῶν.

ccclii Origen has in mind scriptural passages such as the following. Rom 7:10: "I was alive apart from the law once, but when the commandment came, sin revived, and I died. The commandment, which was for life, this I found to be for death." 1 Cor. 15:56: "The sting of death is sin, and the power of sin is the law."

cccliii Here is one more proof that Chrysostom had read Origen's work. John Chrysostom (starting with 'some say', τινὲς ... φασι), *In Matthaeum*, PG.57.253.8-12: Τινὲς μὲν οὖν τὸν διάβολον αὐτὸν αἰνίττεσθαί φασι τῇ τοῦ ἀντιδίκου προσηγορίᾳ, καὶ κελεύειν μηδὲν ἔχειν τῶν ἐκείνου. τοῦτο γὰρ εἶναι τὸ εὐνοεῖν αὐτῷ. ὡς οὐκ ἐνὸν διαλύσασθαι μετὰ τὴν ἐντεῦθεν ἀπαλλαγήν, τῆς ἀπαραιτήτου λοιπὸν ἡμᾶς ἐκδεχομένης κολάσεως.

cccliv Origen, *commMatt*, fr. 102 I (Klostermann), col. 1.

ccclv Origen, *commMatt*, fr. 102 I (Klostermann), col. 2.

ccclvi The present codex now makes it clear that Jerome had in mind Origen's commentary.

ccclvii However, this had been already explained in Scripture. Cf. Mark, 12:42; Luke, 21:2. Origen explaining that these mean 'even the minutest sin', did not make much of the scholastic distinction between κοδράντης and λεπτὸν (*commMatt*, 14.8), although at another point he explained that κοδράντης betokens 'the multitude of sin' and λεπτὸν 'the minutest sin'. *homLuc*, homily 35, p. 203. See *infra*, folio 36v, Origen explaining that 'one κοδράντης compisises two obols'.

ccclviii Jerome, *commMatt*, 5:25-26.

ccclix See also *infra*, folio 35v: ὁδὸς γὰρ ὁ βίος ὑπὸ πάντων ἀνθρώπων παροδευόμενος. Cf. Origen, *frLuc*, fr. 214: Οὗτοι τὰ ἔθνη εἰσὶν ἐν πλατείαις μὲν ὡς τὴν εὐρύχωρον βαδίζοντες ὁδόν, βιοῦντες ἄνευ διδαχῆς καὶ δογμάτων. *selPs*, PG.12.1312.26-28: *Γενηθήτω ἡ ὁδὸς αὐτῶν σκότος*, κ. τ. ἑ. Ὁδὸν ἀσεβῶν τὸν μοχθηρὸν βίον ὀνομάζει, καθ' ὃν τὴν πορείαν ἐποιήσαντο. *Op. cit.* PG.12.1444.42-44: Ἡμέραν πονηράν, τὴν ἡμέραν λέγει τῆς κρίσεως. καὶ πτέρναν τὴν ὁδὸν καὶ τὸν βίον. *Op. cit.* PG.1473.45-48: Καὶ πλατείας αὐτῆς ἡγητέον εἶναι τὰς διὰ τὸ φιλήδονον πλατυνούσας ἑαυτάς, τῷ τὴν πλατεῖαν καὶ εὐρύχωρον ὁδεύειν ὁδόν, τουτέστι, τὸν ἡδονικὸν καὶ παθητικὸν βίον. *excPs*, PG.17.124.10-12: Ἀποκάλυψον πρὸς Κύριον τὴν ὁδόν σου, τουτέστι, δεῖξον αὐτῷ τὸν σὸν ἐπίμωμον βίον.

ccclx Origen, *commMatt*, fr. 102 I (Klostermann), col. 1. Cyril of Alexandria copied this from Origen. See *infra*, p. 68.

ccclxi See also the codex text *infra*, f. 35v: καὶ μὴ παραλογίζου τὴν ἐκ τοῦ συνειδότος ὑπόμνησιν.

ccclxii Cf. Origen, *homJer*, homily 19.14: *καὶ πεσοῦνται μαχαίρᾳ ἐχθρῶν αὐτῶν* [Jer. 20:4]. οἱ ἐπὶ τῶν κολάσεων τεταγμένοι, οὗτοί εἰσιν οἱ τὰς μαχαίρας ἔχοντες καὶ ποιοῦντες πίπτειν αὐτούς. *commMatt*, 14.10: τοῖς ἀγγέλοις τοῖς ἐπὶ τῶν κολάσεων τεταγμένοις. *Op. cit.* 14.13: τίνες δ' ἂν εἶεν οὗτοι ἢ οἱ ἐπὶ τῶν κολάσεων τεταγμένοι; *Op. cit.* 17.23: τοὺς τεταγμένους ἐπὶ τῶν κολάσεων ἀγγέλους. *Epistula ad Africanum*, PG.11.64.19-20: ἄγγελοι ἐπὶ τῶν κολάσεων τεταγμένοι τινὲς ταῦτα διαθήσουσι. Cyril of Alexandria, *frMatt*, fr. 52: ὁ δὲ παραδώσει τοῖς πράκτορσιν, ἤγουν τοῖς κολασταῖς ἀγγέλοις.

ccclxiii This characteristic expression referring to 'incurable punishments' (ἀνήκεστοι κολάσεις) was taken up by Eusebius and by later authors. Cf. Eusebius, *Vita Constantini*, 2.26. Basil of Caesarea, *In Quadraginta Martyres Sebastenses*, PG.31.513.4. John Chrysostom, *Quod Regulares Feminae Viris Cohabitare Non Debeant*, 3; *In Matthaeum*, PG.57: 317.38; 355.56; 450.9. Pseudo-John Chrysostom, *Eclogae i-xlviii ex Diversis Homiliis*, PG.63: 751.29; 893.22. Theodoret, *Curatio*, 11.21. Isidore of Pelusium, *Epistulae*, epistle 1489, lines 21-22. Maximus Confessor, *Quaestiones et Dubia*, section 1.5. John of Damascus, *Contra Manichaeos*, 71. Theodore Studites, *Sermo De Sancto Bartholomeo Apostolo*, p. 45. Nicephorus I of Constantinople, *Refutatio et Eversio Definitionis Synodalis anni 815*, chapter 24, line 38. George Monachus, *Chronicon*, p. 434; *Chronicon Breve*, PG.110.508.27. George Cedrenus, *Compendium Historiarum*, v. 1, p. 339. Nicephorus Gregoras, *Historia Romana*, v. 3, p. 547.

ccclxiv Origen, *commMatt*, fr. 102 II (Klostermann). In one codex this editor came upon the tag 'unattributed or by Severus' (Klostermann, p. 58). But see Severus' alleged passages *supra*, folios 24r-31v.

ccclxv Cyril of Alexandria, *Fragmenta in Acta Apostolorum et in Epistulas Catholicas*, PG.74.1021.45-1024.13 & *Catena in Epistulam Joannis i*, p. 129. Hence, Cyril's comment on 1 John, 3:21 ("My dear ones, if our hearts does not lay any charge on us, we have freedom of speech toward God") is a copy from Origen's analysis in the commentary on Matthew. However, 1 John, 3:21 has nothing to do the idea of *life* being likened to *road*, which is exactly Origen's context commenting on Matt. 5:25 ("Agree with your adversary quickly, while you are with him in the way; lest perhaps the prosecutor deliver you to the judge, and the judge deliver you to the officer, and you be cast into prison") for which this codex supplies not just a portion but the entire context, and the ensuing reference to 'incurable punishments' comes naturally as inherently related to the context of both Origen's analysis and that of the scriptural passage. At this point, we have Origen's fuller context from his commentary on the gospel of Matthew. Thus, on the one hand, there is an isolated phrase attributed to Cyril, which though is irrelevant to, and incoherent with, the scriptural instance it is supposed to explain. On the other, there is Origen's plain text of the commentary, which contains this passage coherently along with its widest context possible and stands in harmony not only with the scriptural clause of which this is an exegesis, but also with the frame of textual reference of the commentary itself both before and after this point.

ccclxvi Cyril of Alexandria, *frMatt*, fr. 54 (col. 1). Also, *op. cit.* (col. 2): Ὃ δὲ λέγει, τοιοῦτόν ἐστιν. παραινεῖ γὰρ εὐγνωμονεῖν καὶ μὴ τῇ κρίσει θαρρεῖν. εἰ γάρ τι συμβαίη παρ᾽ ἐλπίδα καὶ κατασχεθῇς ὑπὸ τοῦ κριτοῦ, οὐκ ἀπολυθήσῃ ἕως οὗ ἀποτίσῃς *τὸν ἔσχατον* ὀβολόν. τοῦτο γὰρ λέγεται κοδράντης. However, the expression παροδεύειν τὸν βίον (meaning 'living this life as a temporary state' in view of the eternal one) was introduced by Origen, and then taken up by his devotees, as well as by others. Cf. Eusebius, *Commentaria in Psalmos*, PG.23.1012.3-5: ἐν τούτοις τὸν ἀνθρώπινον ἔφαμεν δηλοῦσθαι βίον, ὃν ὁ μακαριζόμενος παροδεύων καὶ παρατρέχων. Athanasius, *Contra Gentes*, 30: εἰ καὶ μὴ πάντες αὐτὴν ὁδεύειν, ἀλλὰ παροδεύειν ἐκβαίνοντες θέλουσι διὰ τὰς ἔξωθεν αὐτοὺς ἑλκούσας ἡδονὰς τοῦ βίου. *Expositiones in Psalmos*, PG.27.100.13-15: Ἁγίου γὰρ ἀνδρὸς παροδεύειν τὸν βίον τοῦτον, ἐπάγεσθαι δὲ πρὸς ἑτέραν ζωήν.The same by Basil of Caesarea, *Homiliae super Psalmos*, PG.29.252.8-9. John Chrysostom, *De Sancta Droside Martyre*, PG.50.685.1-3: Ὁδὸς γὰρ ὁ παρὼν βίος ἐστὶ καὶ οὐδὲν στάσιμον ἔχει, ἀλλὰ καὶ τὰ λυπηρὰ αὐτοῦ καὶ τὰ χρηστὰ παροδεύομεν. *Epistulae ad Olympiadem*, epistle 5.1: τὰ χρηστὰ καὶ τὰ λυπηρὰ τοῦ παρόντος βίου παροδεύεται ἅπαντα. *Epistulae*, PG.52.634.26-28: καὶ γὰρ καὶ ἡ ἄνεσις καὶ ἡ θλῖψις ἡ τοῦ παρόντος παροδεύεται βίου, καὶ αὐτῷ τῷ βίῳ συγκαταλύεται. *Op. cit.* PG.52.642.15-17: Ἴστε γὰρ ὅτι ὁδὸς ὁ παρὼν βίος, καὶ τὰ χρηστὰ αὐτοῦ καὶ τὰ λυπηρὰ παροδεύεται. *Op. cit.* PG.52.664.37-39: Ὁδὸς γὰρ τὰ παρόντα, καὶ τὰ χρηστὰ καὶ τὰ λυπηρὰ τοῦ βίου τούτου, καὶ ἑκάτερα ὁμοίως παροδεύεται, καὶ οὐδὲν αὐτῶν πάγιον, οὐδὲ βεβηκός. *In Matthaeum*, PG.57.314.35-37: Τούτων δὲ οὐδὲν μόνιμον, ἀλλὰ πάντα παροδεύεται καὶ τὰ λυπηρὰ καὶ τὰ χρηστὰ τοῦ βίου. Eustathius of Antioch, *De Engastrimytho contra Origenem*, 12.9: ἐπειγόμενοι τὰ μὲν ἤδη παροδεύσαντα τοῦ βίου πράγματα.

ccclxvii Cyril of Alexandria, *commLuc*, PG.72.760.24-26. See the rest of the text quoted forthwith.

ccclxviii Cyril of Alexandria, *commLuc*, PG.72.760.27-55.

ccclxix Cf. *supra*, Origen, folio 35r: Ἀντίδικον εἶναι τοῦ ἀνθρώπου τὴν ἐκ τοῦ συνειδότος ὑπόμνησιν. ... προσδέχου τοὺς ἐκ τοῦ συνειδότος ἔλεγχος ἐλέγχους, ἡνίκα ἂν ὑπομιμνήσκῃ σε καὶ ἐπιλαμβάνηταί σου ὡς ἁμαρτήσαντος ἢ ἁμαρτήσεσθαι μέλλοντος. Also, folio 35v: προσδέχου καὶ μὴ παραλογίζου τὴν ἐκ τοῦ συνειδότος ὑπόμνησιν.

ccclxx Cf. Origen, *Cels*, VIII.25: Οὕτως δὲ καὶ οὐ πάντες ἄγγελοι *ἄγγελοι* λέγονται εἶναι *τοῦ θεοῦ* ἀλλὰ μόνοι οἱ μακάριοι, οἱ δ᾽ ἐκτραπέντες ἐπὶ τὴν κακίαν ἄγγελοι τοῦ διαβόλου ὀνομάζονται. *Op. cit.* VIII.33: τάχα δὲ ὡς ἄξιοι τῶν πονηρῶν ἐπιστάται καὶ κολασταὶ αὐτῶν ὑπὸ τοῦ διοικοῦντος τὰ ὅλα λόγου ἐτάχθησαν ἄρχειν τῶν ἑαυτοὺς ὑποταξάντων τῇ κακίᾳ καὶ οὐ τῷ θεῷ. *homEz*, p. 323: Οὐ γὰρ μόνα κολαστήρια ἔχει ὁ λόγος, ἀλλ᾽ ἔχει καὶ δι᾽ ὧν ἀναπαύει, κολάζει δὲ διὰ τῶν κάτω δυνάμεων. *homJer*, homily 20.9: οἱ μὲν οὖν κολασταὶ ἐτάζουσι πλευράς, ἐτάζουσι σώματα. κύριος δὲ μόνος καινὸν ἔχει τρόπον ἐτασμῶν. *selPs*, PG.12.1565.27-28: *Καὶ ἐπῆρε τὴν χεῖρα αὐτοῦ ἐπ᾽ αὐτούς*, κ. τ. ἑ. [Psalm 105:26]. Χεῖρα λέγει τὰς κολαστικὰς αὐτοῦ δυνάμεις. See *infra*, folio 111v: Ὡς φιλάνθρωπος δὲ ὁ Θεὸς δι᾽ ἑαυτοῦ μὲν σπείρει, δι᾽ ἑτέρων δὲ κολάζει. Also, Origen, *Cels*, VIII.31: ἀλλ᾽ εἰ χρὴ ἀποτολμήσαντα λέγειν τινά, εἰ μὴ ταῦτα, δαιμόνων ἐστὶν ἔργα, φήσομεν ὅτι λιμοὶ καὶ ἀφορίαι σταφυλῆς καὶ ἀκροδρύων καὶ αὐχμοὶ ἀλλὰ καὶ ἡ τοῦ ἀέρος διαφθορὰ ἐπὶ λύμῃ τῶν καρπῶν ἔσθ᾽ ὅτε δὲ καὶ τῷ τῶν ζῴων θανάτῳ καὶ τῷ κατὰ τῶν ἀνθρώπων λοιμῷ. While making the same point, Porphyry copied from Origen almost to the letter. *De Abstinentia*, 2.40: ἓν γὰρ δὴ καὶ τοῦτο τῆς μεγίστης βλάβης τῆς ἀπὸ τῶν κακοεργῶν δαιμόνων θετέον, ὅτι αὐτοὶ αἴτιοι γιγνόμενοι τῶν περὶ τὴν γῆν παθημάτων, οἷον λοιμῶν, ἀφοριῶν, σεισμῶν, αὐχμῶν καὶ τῶν ὁμοίων, ἀναπείθουσιν ἡμᾶς, ὡς ἄρα τούτων αἴτιοί εἰσιν οἵπερ καὶ τῶν ἐναντιωτάτων [τουτέστιν τῶν εὐφοριῶν], ἑαυτοὺς ἐξαιροῦντες τῆς αἰτίας καὶ αὐτὸ τοῦτο πραγματευόμενοι πρῶτον, τὸ λανθάνειν ἀδικοῦντες.

ccclxxi Cyril of Alexandria, *frMatt*, fr. 52. This is Origen's foregoing text on folio 36v.

ccclxxii Gregory of Nyssa, *Orationes viii De Beatitudinibus*, PG.44.1216.21-30. This is the work in which he copied symptomatic passages from Origen. See endnotes cclxxxi, cclxxvii, cclv, etc. The same passage, in *Catena in Matthaeum*, pp. 37-38.

ccclxxiii Cyril of Alexandria, *frMatt*, fr. 56; the same in the *Catena in Matthaeum*, p. 37.

ccclxxiv Cyril of Alexandria, John [Chrysostom], Isodore [of Pelusium], Theodore of Heraclera, *apud Catena in Matthaeum*, p. 39. Also, Cyril of Alexandria, *frMatt*, fr. 58: Εἰπὼν *ἐὰν ὁ ὀφθαλμός σου σκανδαλίζῃ σε* καὶ τὰ ἑξῆς, ὀφθαλμὸν λέγει τὸν λογισμὸν τῆς ἐπιθυμίας, ὃν λέγει ἐκκόπτεσθαι. All of them copied from Origen.

ccclxxv Jerome, *commMatt*, 5.29.

ccclxxvi This is a personal experience. In the same commentary on Matthew, Origen expressed his regret for having committed self-castration. See *commMatt*, 15.1.

ccclxxvii *Catena in Matthaeum*, pp. 144-145 (anonymous). Likewise, *Supplementum et Varietas Lectionis ad Commentarium Chrysostomi in Evangelium sancti Matthaei*, p. 471: Εἰπὼν δὲ ὅτι *ἐὰν ὁ ὀφθαλμός σου σκανδαλίζῃ σε, καὶ ἡ χείρ σου* καὶ τὰ ἑξῆς. οὐ περὶ μελῶν ἔλεγεν τοῦτό φησιν, ἄπαγε· ... τίνος οὖν ἕνεκεν τὸν δεξιὸν ἔθηκεν καὶ τὴν χεῖρα προσέθηκεν; ἵνα μάθωμεν ὅτι οὐ περὶ μελῶν ὁ λόγος, ἀλλὰ περὶ τῶν οἰκείως πρὸς ἡμᾶς ἐχόντων. Also, Cyril of Alexandria, John [Chrysostom], Isodore [of Pelusium], Theodore of Heraclera, *apud Catena in Matthaeum*, p. 39. ("Ἄλλως. Τῶν αὐτῶν.) Ὀφθαλμὸς καὶ χεὶρ νοεῖται ὁ φίλος. ἐὰν γάρ τινα οὕτως φιλῇς, ὡς ἐν τάξει ὀφθαλμοῦ δεξιοῦ, καὶ χρήσιμον αὐτὸν νομίζεις, ὡς ἐν τάξει δεξιᾶς χειρός, καὶ βλάπτει σου τὴν ψυχήν, ἀπότεμε τούτους ἀπὸ σοῦ, καὶ πόρρω χωρίσθητι ἀπ᾽ αὐτῶν. ὅτ᾽ ἂν γὰρ μὴ ἀλλήλους σώζητε, ἀλλὰ μᾶλλον ἀμφότεροι προσαπόλλυσθε ὄντες ὁμοῦ, συμφέρει χωρισθέντα, κἂν τὸν ἕνα σωθῆναι. So Cyril of Alexandria, *frMatt*, fr. 59.

ccclxxviii Jerome, *commMatt*, 5.29.

ccclxxix Cyril of Alexandria, *frMatt*, fr. 61.

ccclxxx Theodore of Heraclea, *op. cit.* fr. 34.

ccclxxxi Cyril of Alexandria, *op. cit.* fr. 63.

ccclxxxii Once again, we are upon Origen's stupendous erudition. The Stoic Chrysippus (whom Origen had studied diligently) maintained that whether one's number of hair is odd or even is 'indifferent' (ἀδιάφορον). *Fragmenta Moralia*, fr. 118 (*apud* Stobaeus, *Anthologium*, 2.7.7); fr. 119 (*apud* Diogenes Laertius, *Vitae*, 7.104 & *Suda*, letter alpha, entry 478); fr. 121 (*apud* Stobaeus, *op. cit* 2.82.5); fr. 122 (Sextus Empiricus, *Adversus Dogmaticos 5* [= *Adversus Ethicos*], 11.59-60). An anonymous scholiast averred that, save those animals which have 'well-wrought wool', hair in the rest of them is 'useless' (τῶν γὰρ ἄλλων ζῴων αἱ τρίχες περιτταί). *Scholia in Odysseam* (*scholia vetera*), on Odyssey, IX.425. To Aristotle, 'man's hair is due to that which remains after the digestion of food, which happens more so with man's hair rather than with sheep's wool' (*Problemata*, 893b); 'bones, sinews and hair are made out of residues' of the body (*De Generatione Animalium*, 744b-745a; 783a; 786b), by 'residues' meaning 'dung, phlegm, yellow and black bile', *Historia Animalium*, 511b). Cf. John Philoponus, *commGenAnim*, pp. 55; 115-116; 198.

In this volume, it becomes evident that several Christian authors copied from Origen's commentary. However, during the first millennium, none of them did ever comment on such a specialised point, obviously because no one could treat the issue or make out Origen's Greek sources. Two brilliant exceptions evincing awareness of this are the erudite Aristotelist Didymus, *Commentarii in Ecclesiasten* (*11-12*), cod. p. 325, *Commentarii in Ecclesiasten* (*3-4.12*), cod. p. 122, and Theodoret, *commCant*, PG.81.129.1-3.

In any event, I believe that Origen learned about this theory by combining his studies of Chrysippus and those on the following three authors, whom several times I have identified as his sources on many issues: Plutarch, *De Iside et Osiride*, p. 352D; *Quaestiones Convivales*, p. 651A. Galen, *De Temperamentis*, p. 641; *De Usu Partium*, p. 641; *De Sanitate Tuenda*, p. 67. Pseudo-Alexander of Aphrodisias, *Problemata*, 1.51; 2.19; 4.59; 4.62; 4.79; *et passim.*

ccclxxxiii Cf. Origen, *frPs*, on Psalm 131:1: Λέγει δὲ καὶ ὁ Ὠριγένης. Τὸ ἀψευδὲς τῆς ἐπαγγελίας, ὅρκον ὠνόμασεν. Ἄνθρωποι μὲν γὰρ κατὰ τοῦ μείζονος ὀμνύουσιν. ὁ δὲ Θεὸς κατ᾽ οὐδενὸς ἔχει ὀμόσαι.

ccclxxxiv Cyril of Alexandria, *frMatt*, fr. 63.

ccclxxxv Cf. Ex. 23:18; 24:6; *et passim;* Lev. 1:5; 1:11; *et passim;* etc.

ccclxxxvi Cyril of Alexandria, *op. cit.* fr. 63.

ccclxxxvii Cyril of Alexandria, *apud Catena in Epistulam Jacobi*, p. 36.

ccclxxxviii Cf. Origen, *selPs*, PG.12.1609.16-19. Basil of Caesarea, *homPs*, PG.29.260.26-47.

ccclxxxix Origen, *commMatt*, fr. 107 (Klostermann).

cccxc Origen, *commMatt*, fr. 106 (Klostermann), col. 1; see also columns 2 and 3.

cccxci Cyril of Alexandria, *apud Catena in Epistulam Jacobi*, p. 36. However, the usual confusion with Origen's words is here once again, since the same passage was attributed also to Theodore of Heraclea, *frMatt*, fr. 36. Likewise, Cyril of Alexandria, *frMatt*, fr. 62 & *Fragmenta in Acta Apostolorum et in Epistulas Catholicas*, PG.74.1012.40-43: Τὸ οὐκ ἐπιορκήσεις καὶ τὰ ἑξῆς. Ἐάν τις ἀναιδὴς ἐπάγῃ τοῖς ἁγίοις ὅρκον, ἀντὶ τοῦ ὅρκου ἔσται αὐτοῖς τὸ ναὶ καὶ τὸ οὔ. However, it was also recognised that Origen was the source of this. *Catena in Matthaeum*, pp. 39-40: (Ὠριγένους. Κυρίλλου.) Τὸ *οὐκ ἐπιορκήσεις* καὶ τὰ ἑξῆς. ἐάν τις ἀναιδὴς ἐπάγῃ τοῖς ἁγίοις ὅρκον, ἀντὶ τοῦ ὅρκου ἔσται αὐτοῖς τὸ ναὶ καὶ τὸ οὔ.

cccxcii Cf. ἄκρον ἀρετῆς ('peak of virtue') in Origen's usual philological source, Galen, *De Temperamentis*, p. 585: εἰς ἄκρον ἥκειν ἀρετῆς. *De Rebus Boni Malique Suci*, p. 809: εἰς ἄκρον ἥκοντο ἀρετῆς. *De Antidotis*, p. 25: τῶν εἰς ἄκρον ἀρετῆς ἡκόντων. *In Hippocratis Librum De Articulis et Galeni in Eum*, p. 337: εἰς ἄκρον ἀρετῆς ... ἥκει. Also, Lucian of Samosata, *Vitarum Auctio*, 23: πρὸς τὸ ἀκρότατον τῆς ἀρετῆς ἀφικόμενος. Dio Chrysostom, *Orationes*, 13.35: ὅταν δὲ ἐληλυθότες ἦτε ἐπ' ἄκρον ἀρετῆς. Then, Origen himself. *selNum*, PG.12.580.47-50: Δύο εἰσὶ κορυφαί, τουτέστιν ἀκροτάτης ἀρετῆς καὶ τῆς κακίας. καὶ ὁ μὲν Μωϋσῆς ἐπὶ τὸ ἄκρον τῆς ἀρετῆς ἀναβέβηκεν, ὁ δὲ Βαλαὰμ ἐπὶ τὸ ἄκρον τῆς κακίας. Origen's classmate, Plotinus, *Enneades*, III.2.14: Ὁ δὲ καθ' ἕκαστα, ᾗ τοῦτο, οὐκ ἀπαιτητέος τέλεος εἶναι εἰς ἀρετῆς ἄκρον. Subsequently, Origen's followers were the first to embrace this turn. Gregory of Nyssa, *Vita Sanctae Macrinae*, 1: διὰ σιωπῆς συγκαλυφθεῖσα ἡ πρὸς τὸν ἀκρότατον τῆς ἀνθρωπίνης ἀρετῆς ὅρον. *De Oratione Dominica*, p. 290: Ἦλθεν προϊὼν ὁ λόγος ἐπ' αὐτὸ τῆς ἀρετῆς τὸ ἀκρότατον. Eusebius, *Praeparatio Evangelica*, 5.17: περὶ τῆς εἰς ἄκρον ἀρετῆς. *De Ecclesiastica Theologia*, 3.18.4: κατὰ δὲ τελείωσιν τῆς εἰς ἄκρον ἀρετῆς. *Eclogae Propheticae*, p. 64: περὶ τοῦ ἀνεπιλήπτου βίου τοῦ Χριστοῦ. καὶ περὶ τῆς ἐπ' ἄκρον ἀρετῆς πολιτείας αὐτοῦ. *Et passim*. Gregory of Nazianzus, *Contra Julianum*, PG.35.633.21-29: ὁ πρὸς τὸ τῆς ἀρετῆς ἄκρον συγκλείων Χριστιανοὺς ... καὶ τοῦ ἄκρου τῆς ἀρετῆς ἐπιβαίνειν. Basil of Caesarea, *Adversus Eunomium*, PG.29.509.1-2: πρὸς αὐτὸ τὸ ἀκρότατον τῆς ἀρετῆς ἀνελθόντι. Didymus, *Commentarii in Job (1-4)*, cod. p. 5: εἰς ἄκρον ἀρετῆς φθάσαντα. *In Genesim*, cod. p. 29: τοῖς οὔπω ἐπὶ τὸ τέρμα τῆς ἄκρας ἀρετῆς ἐλθοῦσιν. *frPs(al)*, fr. 532: εἰς ἄκρον ἀρετῆς φθάσαντες. Pseudo-Basil of Caesarea, *Enarratio in Prophetam Isaiam* (*forsan* Cassian the Sabaite), 9.228: καὶ τὴν ἐπὶ τὸ ἀκρότατον τῆς ἀρετῆς τελείωσιν. *Epistulae ad Castorem*: πρὸς τὸ ἀκρότατον τῆς ἀρετῆς ἀνελθεῖν (See *NDGF*, folio 11r). Naturally, John Chrysostom took this up and used it at dozens of points, as indeed others did so (to lesser extent), namely, Theodoret, Cyril of Alexandria, and a long series of other Christian authors. Besides, since Plotinus had used this, Proclus followed suit (*Theologia Platonica*, v. 6, p. 53) and so did Asclepius of Tralles (*commMetaph*, p. 341), but Damascius and Simplicius paid no attention to it. In other words, this metaphor appealed mainly to Christian authors, but hardly did they know that Origen was their source.

cccxciii Cf. the expression 'willingly-chosen poverty' (ἑκούσιος πενία) in Origen, who was the first to use it. *Cels*, II.41: Ὅσος δὲ καὶ ἄλλος χορὸς πενήτων ἐστὶ παρ' Ἕλλησι φιλοσοφησάντων καὶ ἑκούσιον πενίαν ἀναδεξαμένων. Then, as always, John Chrysostom, *De Virginitate*, 4: Ὁ δὲ πενίαν μὲν ἑκούσιον ὑποστάς. *Op. cit.* 15: καὶ τὸν πλοῦτον δὲ οὕτως τῆς ἑκουσίου προτιμήσεις πενίας. *In Epistulam ad Hebraeos*, PG.63.93.16-17; *Fragmenta in Proverbia*, PG.64.673.15-16. Cyril of Alexandria, *Epistulae Paschales*, PG.77.644.36-37: καὶ πενίαν ἑκούσιον τῆς ἐκ πλούτου μερίμνης προτιθείς. *Expositio in Psalmos*, PG.69.765.53-54: Ἀντὶ γὰρ τῆς ἑκουσίου πενίας τούτῳ τὸν ἑαυτοῦ πλοῦτον ὁ Θεὸς χαρίζεται. Ephraem Syrus, *De Iudicio et Compunctione*, p. 395: ἑκούσιον πενίαν. Gennadius Scholarius used the expression as a title at two points. *epitSummae*, book 3, chapters 131-132: Περὶ τῶν τῆς ζωῆς τρόπων, οἷς ζῶσιν οἱ τὴν ἑκούσιον πενίαν αἱρούμενοι. *Op. cit.* book 3, chapter 133: Ὅτι ἡ ἑκούσιος πενία ἀγαθόν ἐστιν. Of non-Christian authors, see Libanius, *Epistulae*, epistle 1367, section 2: ὁ θεῖος οὗτος ἀνὴρ καὶ μισούμενος ὑπὸ Περσῶν μισθὸν τῆς ἑκουσίου πενίας σοὶ μὲν δοῦναι τὸ μετὰ τὴν βασιλείαν μέγιστον. Hierocles of Alexandria, *In Aureum Carmen*, 13.12: ἕνα καὶ τὸν ὑπὲρ ἀρετῆς λογιούμεθα λόγον, ἑκουσίαν πενίαν μετὰ τοῦ καλοῦ ἀνταλλαττόμενοι. In any event, all of the authors that employed this expression were posterior to Origen, whereas no author had used this prior to him.

cccxciv Origen, *commMatt*, fr. 108 (Klostermann).

cccxcv Jerome, *commMatt*, 5.38-40.

cccxcvi Theodore of Heraclea, *frMatt*, fr. 38, col. 2.

cccxcvii Clement of Alexandria, *Stromateis*, 4.13.93.-4.13.94.1. Quoted also by John of Damascus, *Sacra Parallela*, PG.95.1201.50-1204.3.

cccxcviii Cyril of Alexandria, *frMatt*, fr. 67 & *Catena in Matthaeum*, p. 41. But John of Damascus (see previous note) quoted this from Clement of Alexandria, not from Cyril.

cccxcix Theodore of Heraclea, *frMatt*, fr. 39 & *Catena in Matthaeum*, p. 41.

cd This is a famous and widely known Platonic expression. Plato, *Theaetetus*, 176b: φυγὴ δὲ ὁμοίωσις θεῷ κατὰ τὸ δυνατόν. *Phaedrus*, 253a-b: ἐπὶ τὴν τοῦ ἐρωμένου ψυχὴν ἐπαντλοῦντες ποιοῦσιν ὡς δυνατὸν ὁμοιότατον τῷ σφετέρῳ θεῷ. *Respublica*, 613a-b: ἐπιτηδεύων ἀρετὴν εἰς ὅσον δυνατὸν ἀνθρώπῳ ὁμοιοῦσθαι θεῷ.

cdi Although 'becoming like God as much as possible' was a distinctly Platonic expression (as above), 'imitating God' was an expression of quite different provenance. Actually, Origen took this up from Philo, and perhaps from a casual reference which he read in Alexander of Aphrodisias. See Philo, *De Specialibus Legibus*, 4.73-74: τί δ' ἂν εἴη κρεῖττον ἀγαθὸν ἢ μιμεῖσθαι θεὸν γενητοῖς τὸν ἀίδιον; *De Virtutibus*, 168: τῇ λογικῇ φύσει πρεπωδέστατον, μιμεῖσθαι θεὸν καθ' ὅσον οἷόν τε. Pseudo-Alexander of Aphrodisias, *Ἀπορίαι καὶ Λύσεις*, p. 63: καὶ τὴν αὐτοῦ [sc. τοῦ κόσμου] κίνησιν κινούμενον ἐφέσει μιμήσεως τοῦ πρώτου θεοῦ. Clement of Alexandria, *Protrepticus*, 11.117.1: οὐ γὰρ μιμεῖσθαί τις δυνήσεται τὸν θεὸν ἢ δι' ὧν ὁσίως θεραπεύσει. *Stromateis*, 4.26.171.4: θεὸν χρὴ μιμεῖσθαι εἰς ὅσον δύναμις τῷ γνωστικῷ. Origen, *commMatt*, 13.18: τὸ ταπεινῶσαι ἑαυτὸν ὑπὲρ θεοῦ καὶ τὸ μιμήσασθαι τὸ ὑπὲρ σωτηρίας ἀνθρώπων ταπεινῶσαν ἑαυτὸ πνεῦμα ἅγιον. *Op. cit.* 17.20: ἀλλὰ γίνεται κατ' οἰκονομίαν (τοῦ ἐν παραβολαῖς λεγομένου ἀνθρώπου ὄντος δὲ θεοῦ) υἱὸς ἀνθρώπου κατὰ τὸ μιμεῖσθαι, ὅταν ἀνθρώπους οἰκονομῇ, τὸν θεόν. *selPs*, PG.12.1105.6-8: ἀποκρίνεται πρὸς τοὺς ἀγγέλους ὁ Υἱὸς τοῦ Θεοῦ, προτρέπων αὐτοὺς ἐπὶ τὸ μιμήσασθαι αὐτόν. This expression became a conventional one in Christian literature. Eusebius, *Praeparatio Evangelica*, 12.30.4. Gregory of Nyssa, *De Oratione Dominica*, p. 294; *De Professione Christiana ad Harmonium*, pp. 136-137. Gregory of Nazianzus, *Carmina Moralia*, col. 909. Athanasius, *Oratio i Contra Arianos*, 23.4. Didymus, *In Genesim*, cod. pp. 57; 180. Epiphanius of Salamis, *Panarion*, v. 3, p. 236. Ephraem Syrus, *Sermo De Virtutibus et Vitiis*, 14; *In Sermonem, Quem Dixit Dominus, Quod: In Hoc Mundo Pressuram Habebitis, et De Perfectione Hominis*, pp. 354; 375.

Emperor Julian wrote that 'imitating God' was a Hebraic ideal. *Contra Galilaeos*, p. 192: τίς δὲ ἡ παρ' Ἑβραίοις ὑμνουμένη τοῦ θεοῦ μίμησις; However, this made its mark also in eminent Neoplatonists. Hermias of Alexandria, *schPhaedr*, p. 109. Proclus, *In Platonis Parmenidem*, p. 1022; *commTim*, v. 1, p. 69; *De Decem Dubitationibus circa Providentiam*, 65. There should be little doubt that Proclus took this up from Porphyry, and that the latter was inspired by Origen, as it happened on several other issues. Porphyry, *De Abstinentia*, 2.3: ἥ τε ἀποχὴ τῶν ἐμψύχων, καθάπερ κἀν τῷ πρώτῳ ἐλέγομεν, οὐχ ἁπλῶς πᾶσιν ἀνθρώποις παραγγέλλεται, ἀλλὰ τοῖς φιλοσόφοις, καὶ τούτων μᾶλλον τοῖς ἐκ τοῦ θεοῦ καὶ τῆς τούτου μιμήσεως τὴν σφῶν εὐδαιμονίαν ἀνάψασιν. In a forthcoming work, I will be arguing that this work of Porphyry was decisively influenced by Origen. Then, Iamblichus, *Protrepticus*, p. 121: μίμησιν θεοῦ κατὰ τὸ δυνατὸν (modifying Plato's ὁμοίωσις θεῷ κατὰ τὸ δυνατόν).

cdii Theodore of Heraclea, *frMatt*, fr. 43 & *Catena in Matthaeum*, p. 41.

cdiii Origen, *commMatt*, fr. 111 (Klostermann).

cdiv Cyril of Alexandria, *frMatt*, fr. 68, col. 1: Also, *apud Catena in Matthaeum*, p. 42, and likewise, *op. cit.* fr. 68, col. 2: Ἀλλ' ἴσως τις τὸν μακάριον Παῦλον ὡς καταρώμενον τὸν χαλκέα Ἀλέξανδρον προσάγων ἡμῖν πείσειε μὴ τοὺς ἐχθροὺς ἀγαπᾶν. πρὸς ὅν ἐστιν εἰπεῖν, ὅτι οὐχ ὡς ἴδιον ἐχθρόν, ἀλλ' ὡς τοῦ Χριστοῦ καὶ τοῦ εὐαγγελίου καταρᾶται ὁ Παῦλος διδάσκων ὡς ἀεὶ τοῖς τοιούτοις χρὴ πολεμεῖν. Cf. 2 Tim. 4:14.

cdv Origen, *commMatt*, fr. 112 (Klostermann).

cdvi J. Reuss found this being attributed to Theodore of Heraclea (*frMatt*, fr. 42). However, in J.A. Cramer's codices this is ascribed to Origen (*Catena in Matthaeum*, p. 42, quoted forthwith).

cdvii Origen, *commMatt*, fr. 109 (Klostermann). The same, Origen, *apud Catena in Matthaeum*, p. 42.

cdviii John Chrysostom, *Catena in Matthaeum*, p. 43.

cdix Clement of Alexandria, *apud Catena in Matthaeum*, p. 43.

cdx Clement of Alexandria, *Stromateis*, 4.22.138.2-3. Quite evidently, Origen took this up from Clement and slightly paraphrased it.

cdxi Severus of Antioch, *Catena in Matthaeum*, p. 43.

cdxii Origen, *commMatt*, fr. 115 (Klostermann).

cdxiii Origen, *apud Catena in Matthaeum*, p. 43; the missing οὐ is a mistake.

cdxiv Actually, this is from 1 Peter, 3:4: ὁ κρυπτὸς τῆς καρδίας ἄνθρωπος.

cdxv The idea is this: since it is not easy to escape notice when one practices charity, this activity should be coupled with prayer and fast, which could pass unnoticed more easily. Cf. Pseudo-Athanasius, *Quaestiones in Evangelia*, PG.28.701.53-57: Διὰ τί ἐπὶ μὲν τῆς ἐλεημοσύνης προσέθηκεν εἰπών, ἐπὶ δὲ τῆς προσευχῆς καὶ τῆς νηστείας οὐδαμῶς; Ἀπόκ[ρισις]. Ἐπειδὴ τὴν ἐλεημοσύνην μὲν ἀδύνατον πάντη λαθεῖν, εὐχὴν δὲ καὶ νηστείαν δυνατόν. Neophytus Inclusus, *Decem Homiliae*, homily 6.30: Εἰ δέ που μὴ δύναταί τις λαθεῖν τοῦ ποιῆσαι ἐλεημοσύνην ἢ προσεύξασθαι ἢ νηστεῦσαι διὰ πλῆθος ἴσως συναυλίας λαοῦ καὶ ἀπορίαν ταμείου, οὐ χρὴ διὰ ταῦτα εἴργεισθαι τοῦ ἀγαθοῦ, ἀλλὰ καὶ ἐλεημοσύνην καὶ εὐχὴν καὶ νηστείαν ἐπιτελεῖν, ὡς ἐνῆν, κἄν τινες τύχωσι καθορᾶν τὴν τοιαύτην εὐποιΐαν ἡμῶν.

cdxvi Origen, *commMatt*, fr. 113 (Klostermann).

cdxvii Apollinaris, *frMatt*, fr. 26.

cdxviii John Chrysostom, *In Matthaeum*, PG.57.275.23-27.

cdxix Cf. Origen, *schMatt*, PG.17.293.50-51: Πλὴν ὑποστέλλει μὴ δημοσιεύεσθαι, ὡς ἐπιεικὴς καὶ ἀκενόδοξος.

cdxx Origen, *commMatt*, fr. 117 (Klostermann). He put in brackets the text which runs parallel to that of Chrysostom. But the present codex evinces that the text is entirely Origen's.

cdxxi John Chrysostom, *In Matthaeum*, PG.57.276.40-45.

cdxxii John Chrysostom, *In Matthaeum*, PG.57.276.46-277.5. The same, John Chrysostom, *apud Catena in Matthaeum*, pp. 43-44.

cdxxiii The same *infra;* cf. Cyril of Alexandria, *frMatt*, fr. 71.

cdxxiv Origen, *commMatt*, fr. 117 (Klostermann); once again, the Greek of the present codex is better (e.g. Cod. πλῆθος προσευχῶν / Kl. πλῆθος προσευχῆς).

cdxxv As it happened, lexica of later times drew on Origen's work. See *Etymologicum Genuinum*, letter beta, entry 68: Βαττολογία. ἡ πολυλογία. ἀπὸ † Βάτου τινὸς Ἕλληνος μακροὺς καὶ † πολυμήκους στίχους ποιήσαντος εἰς τὰ εἴδωλα ταυτολογίαν ἔχοντας. *Suda*, letter beta, entry 183: Βαττολογία. ἡ πολυλογία. ἀπὸ Βάττου τινός, μακροὺς καὶ πολυστίχους ὕμνους ποιήσαντος, ταυτολογίας ἔχοντας. Likewise, *Etymologicum Magnum*, p. 191. *Etymologicum Symeonis*, p. 412. Pseudo-Zonaras, *Lexicon*, letter beta, p. 374. Cf. Gregory of Nyssa, who received the idea from Origen; *De Oratione Dominica*, p. 216: ἀλλὰ βαττολόγος, ὡς ἄν τις Ἑλληνικώτερον ἑρμηνεύων εἴποι τὸν νοῦν, φλυαρία, καὶ λῆρος, καὶ φλήναφος, καὶ εἴ τι ἄλλο τῆς τοιαύτης σημασίας ἐστίν.

cdxxvi Cyril of Alexandria, *frMatt*, fr. 71 (also, *op. cit.* fr. 71, col. 2). But here this is not a 'fragment': it is part from Origen's flowing text. This was taken up by lexica, with very slight occasional variations. *Suda*, letter beta, entry 183. *Etymologicum Symeonis*, p. 412. Pseudo-Zonaras, *Lexicon*, letter beta, p. 374. The only lexicon which provides some more information about Vattus is the *Etymologicum Magnum*, p. 191. This text appears as reproducing more context from the original source, which should have been Origen. The author of *Etymologicum Magnum* evidently knew of Origen's work (see p. 630; cf. pp. 166; 411), whereas he never mentioned Cyril.

cdxxvii Cf. 1 Cor. 5:9-11; 6:9; Eph. 5:5; 1 Tim. 1:9-10; Heb. 12:16; 13:4.

cdxxviii Origen, *commMatt*, 12.33: πᾶσα δὲ λογικὴ ψυχὴ ἤτοι ζῶντι τρέφεται ἄρτῳ ἢ νεκρῷ. *schLuc*, PG.17.341.10-11: Πᾶσα δὲ λογικὴ ψυχὴ θατέρῳ τούτων τρέφεται. *Cels*, IV.58: ψυχὴ μὲν θεοῦ ἔργον, σώματος δὲ ἄλλη φύσις ... οὐ γὰρ ἐσαφήνισε, πότερον πᾶσα ψυχὴ θεοῦ ἔργον ἢ μόνη ἡ λογική. *Op. cit.* VIII.72: ἡμεῖς δὲ τῆς λογικῆς φύσεώς φαμεν ὅλης κρατῆσαί ποτε τὸν λόγον καὶ μεταποιῆσαι πᾶσαν ψυχὴν εἰς τὴν ἑαυτοῦ τελειότητα.

Origen's reference to 'every rarional soul' rings a Stoic bell, which is why J. von Arnim excerpted this reference from *Cels*, III.69 (ἡμεῖς δὲ μίαν φύσιν ἐπιστάμενοι πάσης λογικῆς ψυχῆς etc.) as Chrysippus, *Fragmenta Moralia*, fr. 233. Nevertheless, in reality, Origen took up this handy expression from a work ascribed to Alexander of Aphrodisias, which was also written in Stoic tenor. Pseudo-Alexander of Aphrodisias, *Ἠθικὰ Προβλήματα*, p. 128: εἴη δ' ἂν ἐκείνη λόγος ἡ πάσης λογικῆς ψυχῆς ἕξις ἀρίστη.

Origen's reference did not enjoy currency among Christians (probably because this was deemed 'dangerous') save a casual reference by Eusebius, which could have been received as rather bold. *HE*, 10.4.22: ὁ μέγας τῶν ὅλων ἀρχιερεύς, ᾧ μόνῳ θέμις πάσης λογικῆς ψυχῆς τὰ ἀπόρρητα διερευνᾶσθαι. But this is exactly what makes Origen's seal on the present commentary a distinctive one.

On the other hand, Hermias of Alexandria used this confidently, but in any case this has always remained a scarce expression. *schPhaedr*, p. 47: θείας γὰρ τῷ ὄντι μοίρας μετέχει πᾶσα λογικὴ ψυχή. *Op. cit.* p. 102: προεῖπε δὴ αὐτὸς *δεῖν πρῶτον ψυχῆς φύσεως πέρι* διαλεχθῆναι *θείας τε καὶ ἀνθρωπίνης*, τουτέστι περὶ πάσης λογικῆς ψυχῆς. ὥστε περὶ τῆς λογικῆς ψυχῆς ἐστιν ὁ παρὼν λόγος. ... οὖν φάναι, περὶ πάσης λογικῆς ψυχῆς ὁ λόγος. John Philoponus, *commAnim*, p. 122: Τινές φασιν, ἐπειδὴ τὰ περὶ τῆς τοῦ παντὸς ψυχῆς λεγόμενα ἁρμόζει καὶ ἐπὶ πάσης λογικῆς ψυχῆς, τὸ μέν φασιν ἐκληπτέον ὡς ἐπὶ τῆς καθ' ἡμᾶς ψυχῆς.

cdxxix Origen, *deOr*, 24.5: ἔτι περὶ τοῦ *ἁγιασθήτω τὸ ὄνομά σου* καὶ τῶν ἑξῆς προστακτικῷ χαρακτῆρι εἰρημένων λεκτέον ὅτι συνεχῶς προστακτικοῖς ἀντὶ εὐκτικῶν ἐχρήσαντο καὶ οἱ ἑρμηνεύσαντες.

cdxxx Origen, *commMatt*, fr. 119 (Klostermann).

cdxxxi Origen, *commMatt*, fr. 121 (Klostermann).

cdxxxii Cf. Origen, *frLuc*, fr. 227: *Ἐπορεύθη εἰς χώραν μακρὰν λαβεῖν ἑαυτῷ βασιλείαν* ὁ Χριστὸς μετὰ τὴν ἀνάληψιν. ὑποστρέφει δὲ ἐν τῇ δευτέρᾳ παρουσίᾳ. Athanasius, *Expositiones in Psalmos*, PG.27.129.56-132.1: *Ὑψώθητι, Κύριε, ἐν τῇ δυνάμει σου.* Ὅμοιον τῷ. *Ἐλθέτω ἡ βασιλεία σου.* Τὴν δευτέραν δὲ σαφῶς παρουσίαν εὔχεται διὰ τοῦτο γενέσθαι. Pseudo-Athanasius, *Quaestiones in Scripturam Sacram*, PG.28.713.25-28: *Ὑψώθητι, Κύριε, ἐν τῇ δυνάμει σου.* Ὅμοιον τῷ. *Ἐλθέτω ἡ βασιλεία σου.* Τὴν δευτέραν δὲ σαφῶς παρουσίαν εὔχεται διὰ τοῦτο γενέσθαι. Oecumenius, *Commentarius in Apocalypsin*, p. 256: τὴν γὰρ τοῦ Κυρίου δευτέραν παρουσίαν ζητεῖν προστετάγμεθα, ἀλλὰ καὶ ἐν εὐχῇ τίθεσθαι. ὁ γάρ τοι λέγων *ἐλθέτω ἡ βασιλεία σου* πρὸς τὸν Θεὸν τὴν Χριστοῦ βασιλείαν ἐξαιτεῖ, ἥτις καὶ τοῦ Πατρὸς καὶ τοῦ Πνεύματός ἐστι βασιλεία. Germanus I of Constantinople, *Historia Mystica Ecclesiae Catholicae*, 42: *Ἐλθέτω η βασιλεία σου*, τουτέστιν, ἡ δευτέρα παρουσία (antholigised by Marcus Monachus, *Florilegium*, 35.3).

cdxxxiii See this also *supra*, folio 24r, in this codex (folio 11r: ΑΝΕΠ[ΙΓΡΑΦΟΝ]) running parallel to Origen's text.

cdxxxiv Cyril of Alexandria, *frMatt*, fr. 72 (col. 1).

cdxxxv Cyril of Alexandria, *loc. cit.* (col. 2).

cdxxxvi Cf. Origen, *Dialogus cum Heraclide*, 5: πάντῃ γὰρ τὸ πνευματικὸν νεκρωθῆναι οὐχ οἷόν τέ ἐστιν, ἢ ἀναίσθητον τὸ πνευματικὸν γενέσθαι οὐχ οἷόν τέ ἐστιν. εἰ γὰρ δύναται πνευματικὸν νεκρωθῆναι, φόβος ἐστὶν μὴ μετὰ τὴν ἀνάστασιν τῶν νεκρῶν, ὅταν ἐγερθῇ ἡμῶν τὸ σῶμα κατὰ τὸν ἀπόστολον λέγοντα *Σπείρεται ψυχικόν, ἐγείρεται πνευματικόν*, ἀποθνήσκωμεν *πάντες*. *selPs*, PG.12.1592.55-57: καὶ ἔσται ψυχὴ ἥτις κολληθεῖσα τῷ Κυρίῳ ἐν τῇ καθολικῇ ἀναστάσει γίνεται ἓν πνεῦμα, καὶ γίνεται τὸ σῶμα πνευματικόν. Didymus, *commZacch*, 5.175: ἐν τῷ προσδοκωμένῳ καιρῷ τῆς ἀναστάσεως, τοῦ φθαρτοῦ σώματος ἀφθάρτου ἐγειρομένου καὶ τοῦ ψυχικοῦ πνευματικοῦ σώματος ἐγειρομένου. *frPs(al)*, fr. 1113 (most of these fragments are probably Origen's): ἐν τῷ προσδοκωμένῳ καιρῷ τῆς ἀναστάσεως, τοῦ φθαρτοῦ σώματος ἀφθάρτου ἐγειρομένου καὶ τοῦ ψυχικοῦ πνευματικοῦ σώματος ἐγειρομένου. *Op. cit.* fr. 1290: ἡ ψυχὴ μετὰ τὴν ἀνάστασιν, ἀντὶ φθαρτοῦ καὶ ἀσθενοῦς καὶ ἀτίμου καὶ ψυχικοῦ σώματος ἄφθαρτον δυνατὸν ἔνδοξον πνευματικὸν ἀναλαβοῦσα τὸ σῶμα. *comm1Cor*, p. 10: νοητέον δὲ ὅτι τὸ τῶν ἐγειρομένων ἐκ νεκρῶν σῶμα ὁμοιοῦται τῷ τοῦ Χριστοῦ σώματι πνευματικῷ μετὰ τὴν ἀνάστασιν γεγονότι. *In Genesim*, cod. p. 104: Ἀναστὰς γὰρ ἐν πνευματικῷ σώματι οὐράνιον ἕξεις πολιτείαν ἐν τῇ *γῇ τῶν πραῶν* γινόμενος. *Apud Catena Palestinensis*, Biblical verse 81c: ὅταν δὲ ἀΰλου μεταλάβῃ ζωῆς καὶ ἄφθαρτον καὶ πνευματικὸν ἐξ ἀναστάσεως ἀναλάβῃ τὸ σῶμα. *Apud Catena in Acta*, p. 46: ὡς γὰρ ὁ ἐγειρόμενος νεκρὸς μετὰ ἀνάστασιν ζῶν καὶ οὐ νεκρός ἐστιν, οὕτως ἡ ἐγειρομένη σὰρξ μετὰ τὴν ἔγερσιν πνευματικὸν καὶ ἄφθαρτον σῶμά ἐστι. Photius, *Bibliotheca*, Codex 234, p. 299b (Methodius of Olympus rebutting Origen's 'resurrected spiritual body'). But Photius himself endorsed Origen's idea. *comm1Cor*, p. 580, *apud Catena in Epistulam i ad Corinthios*, p. 324: εἰ δὲ τοῦτο, δῆλον ὡς καὶ πνευματικὸν ἕξουσιν οὗτοι ἐν τῇ ἀναστάσει σῶμα, μηκέτι δυνάμενον εἰς ψυχικὸν τραπῆναι. Symeon the New Theologian, *Orationes Ethicae*, 10.1, lines 725-726: μετὰ δὲ τὴν ἀνάστασιν, καὶ αὐτὸ τὸ σῶμα πνευματικόν. *Op. cit.* lines 845-846: μετὰ τὴν ἀνάστασιν καὶ μετὰ τὸ ἀπολαβεῖν τὸ πνευματικὸν ἐκεῖνο καὶ ἄφθαρτον σῶμα. Michael Glycas, *Quaestiones in Sacram Scripturam*, chapter 7, p. 74, and chapter 92, p. 420, drawing on John of Damascus, *Expositio Fidei*, 100, endorsing Origen's theory.

cdxxxvii Cf. Origen, *Cels*, VII.5: ἐπὶ τοὺς τόπους τῶν καθαρωτέρων καὶ αἰθερίων σωμάτων. ... τὸ καθαρώτερον ἔξω σωμάτων ζῆν. *frJohn*, fr. 87: ὡς ἐν σωματικοῖς τόποις ἔστι τις τόπος τοῦ αἰθέρος ἐν τοῖς καθαρωτάτοις καὶ λεπτότητι φωτὸς διαυγεστέροις. *Op. cit.* 139. εἰ δὲ καὶ τόπον σωματικῶς τις ὑπολάβοι, καὶ οὗτος οὐκ ἂν ἁμάρτοι. ἐν γὰρ τοῖς καθαρωτάτοις τοῦ αἰθέρος καὶ λεπτότητι φωτὸς διαυγεστέροις τοὺς διαφέροντας τῇ λαμπρότητι ἀπολαμβάνοντας κατὰ τὴν ἀξίαν ἐν τῇ ἀναστάσει χωρίοις γίνεσθαι ὡς ἐπιτηδειοτάτοις πρὸς τὴν σχολὴν τῶν θεωρημάτων τοῦ θεοῦ λόγου.

cdxxxviii Origen maintained that the term ἐπιούσιος was coined in order to express the eschatological significance of the Dominical 'bread'. He felt comfortable with this, since Aristotle had written that 'in order to render rightly a correlation, if there is no word [in Greek], perhaps sometimes it is necessary to coin a [new] name'. *Categoriae*, 7a. Another case which he saw likewise was the term εὐδοκία (*commEph*, fr. 3). The verb ὀνοματοποιέω means 'coin a name'. However, the Present Perfect middle voice, especially in third person definitive (in impersonal sense – i.e. ὠνοματοπεποίηται) appeared with Galen (one of Origen's most favourite authors) explaining several neologisms introduced by Hippocrates. *Dictionum Exoletarum Hippocratis Explicatio*, pp. 96; 112; 114; 128; 134. Likewise, Nicomachus, *Harmonicum Enchiridion*, 3.1. Following them, this form appears in Origen as in the present codex, and then it disappeared to show again much later with Photius, *Lexicon*, letter kappa, entry 708, and other lexica of that period (ninth century, e.g. *Etymologicum Genuinum*, letter beta, entries 177; 184; 232; 251).

cdxxxix See *infra*, Origen: ἄρτος *ἐπιούσιος*, Θεὸς ὢν λόγος, ζῶν ἄρτος.

cdxl Origen, *commMatt*, fr. 122 (Klostermann).

cdxli Origen, *frLuc*, fr. 181. Origen confirmed the meaning of ἐπιούσιος by comparing to the ἐπιοῦσα [= 'forthcoming'] of Proverbs, 3:28 & 27:1. Hence, both etymologies (which in effect are one) of ἐπιούσιος (derived from τὸ ἐπιέναι and from ἐπέρχεσθαι) are Origen's, and they were hardly employed by other authors, except for this 'Theodore' who makes it clear that he copied from Origen's texts. See also next endnote.

cdxlii That is, Origen; see *deOr*, 27.13: ἐρεῖ δέ τις τὸ *ἐπιούσιον* παρὰ τὸ ἐπιέναι κατεσχηματίσθαι. Ostensibly, only two authors reproduced this etymology of '*epiousios* bread': (1) Theodore of Heraclea quoting Origen's words, which is one more point revealing false attributions to 'Theodore'; (2) Apollinaris, only to confirm that he copied from Origen's commentary on Matthew, if indeed he wrote one. We are upon the same phenomenon once again: those who pleaded themselves intractable enemies of Origen's copied from him extensively. As discussed in the Introduction (p. LIII), Apollinaris of Laodicea was one of the four Origen's detractors whom Theotimus styled 'the slanderous tetrad' (ἡ τῶν κακολόγων τετρακτύς) and demonstrated that their obloquy was both malicious and inconsistent.

cdxliii Theodore of Heraclea or Theodore of Mopsuestia (J. Reuss), *frMatt*, fr. 23.

cdxliv The expression οὐσία ἡ ἑστῶσα καὶ βέβαιος is exclusive to Origen. *Cels*, VI.64: ἡ κυρίως οὐσία ἡ ἑστῶσα καὶ ἀσώματος. *commSerMatt*, p. 83: τὸ δὲ *ἑστὸς* δηλοῖ ὅτι κατασκευαῖς βεβαιοῦν θέλει τὰ ἑαυτοῦ δόγματα ὁ Ἀντίχριστος λόγος. *commJohn*, VI.38.189: *Μέσος ἕστηκεν* ὁ αὐτὸς καὶ βέβαιος ὢν λόγος, ὑπὸ τοῦ πατρὸς ἐστηριγμένος πανταχοῦ. *fr1Cor*, fr. 90: *Στήκετε*. μὴ σαλεύεσθε ἀλλὰ βέβαιοι γίνεσθε. ὁ δίψυχος οὐχ ἕστηκεν ἐν τῇ πίστει ἢ ὁ ἀμφιβάλλων περὶ τῶν κατὰ τὴν πίστιν πραγμάτων. Cf. his influence on Neoplatonism. Proclus, *In Platonis Alcibiadem i*, 96: ταύτης γοῦν ἔτι τὴν ἠθικὴν ἀρετὴν εἴποις ἂν μᾶλλον ἔχειν τὸ βέβαιον καὶ τὸ ἑστώς. Simplicius, *commCateg*, p. 287: ἴσως δὲ ἐροῦσι τὴν ἀρετὴν ἐπιστήμην οὖσαν ἐξ ἑαυτῆς ἔχειν τὸ πάγιον. τῶν γὰρ οἰκείων λόγων οὖσα θεωρητικὴ καὶ στοχαζομένη ἀεὶ τοῦ καθ' ἑαυτὴν πάντα ποιεῖν ἐνεργεῖ βεβαίως ἑστῶσα ἐν τῷ ἀμεταπτώτῳ εἴδει τῆς ἐπιστήμης.

cdxlv Cf. Origen, *deOr*, 27.9: *ἐπιούσιος* τοίνυν *ἄρτος* ὁ τῇ φύσει τῇ λογικῇ καταλληλότατος καὶ τῇ οὐσίᾳ αὐτῇ συγγενής, ὑγείαν ἅμα καὶ εὐεξίαν καὶ ἰσχὺν περιποιῶν τῇ ψυχῇ καὶ τῆς ἰδίας ἀθανασίας (ἀθάνατος γὰρ ὁ λόγος τοῦ θεοῦ) μεταδιδοὺς τῷ ἐσθίοντι αὐτοῦ. *Princ*, III.1.13 (*Philocalia*, 21.12): ἄφθαρτον γὰρ φύσιν πεποίηκε τὴν νοερὰν καὶ αὐτῷ συγγενῆ, καὶ οὐκ ἀποκλείεται ὥσπερ ἐπὶ τῆς ἐνταῦθα ζωῆς ἡ λογικὴ ψυχὴ τῆς θεραπείας. *exhMar*, 47: Ἔτι δὲ καὶ φιλοζωεῖ ἄνθρωπος πεῖσμα λαβὼν περὶ οὐσίας λογικῆς ψυχῆς ὡς ἐχούσης τι συγγενὲς θεῷ. νοερὰ γὰρ ἑκάτερα καὶ ἀόρατα καί, ὡς ὁ ἐπικρατῶν ἀποδείκνυσι λόγος, ἀσώματα. *Cels*, III.40 (&. *Philocalia*, 19.3): Καὶ εὐθέως ὡσπερεὶ τὸ συγγενὲς ἐπιγνοῦσα ἡ λογικὴ ψυχὴ ἀπορρίπτει μὲν ἃ τέως ἐδόξαζεν εἶναι θεοὺς φίλτρον δ' ἀναλαμβάνει φυσικὸν τὸ πρὸς τὸν κτίσαντα. *Op. cit.* VI. 18: Ἡ οὖν ἀνθρωπίνη ψυχὴ περὶ αὐτὰ ὀρέγεται μαθεῖν, ποῖα ἄττα ἐστί, βλέπουσα εἰς τὰ αὐτῆς συγγενῆ, ὧν οὐδὲν ἱκανῶς ἔχει.

cdxlvi Cf. κυρίως οὐσία ('substance par excellence' or 'substance proper'), Origen, *deOr*, 27.9: ἡ μέντοι κυρίως οὐσία τοῖς μὲν προηγουμένην τὴν τῶν ἀσωμάτων ὑπόστασιν εἶναι φάσκουσι νενόμισται κατὰ τὰ ἀσώματα, τὸ εἶναι βεβαίως ἔχοντα καὶ οὔτε προσθήκην χωροῦντα οὔτε ἀφαίρεσιν πάσχοντα. *frLuc*, fr. 181: καὶ γὰρ ὁ ἔσω ἄνθρωπος, ὃς κυρίως οὐσία ‹ἐστίν›, μὴ τυχὼν ζῶντος ἄρτου ἐχθρῷ ζωῆς θανάτῳ γίνεται, ὡς τὸ σῶμα μὴ τρεφόμενον. *commJohn*, XX.18.158: Ακολουθεῖ δὲ αὐτοῖς καὶ σῶμα λέγειν τὸν πατέρα καὶ τὸν υἱὸν καὶ διῃρῆσθαι τὸν πατέρα, ἅπερ ἐστὶν δόγματα ἀνθρώπων μηδ᾽ ὄναρ φύσιν ἀόρατον καὶ ἀσώματον πεφαντασμένων, οὖσαν κυρίως οὐσίαν. *Cels*, VI.64: Πολὺς δ᾽ ὁ περὶ τῆς οὐσίας λόγος καὶ δυσθεώρητος καὶ μάλιστα, ἐὰν ἡ κυρίως οὐσία ἡ ἑστῶσα καὶ ἀσώματος ᾖ.

cdxlvii See this *supra*, in the full text of Origen, *commMatt*, fr. 122 (Klostermann).

cdxlviii Cf. Origen, *selPs*, PG.12.1236.16-22: Πεῖρά τις, οἶμαι, ὁ βίος ἐν τῷ Ἰώβ. Περιστάσεως δὲ οὐκ ἔνι ῥυσθῆναι πικρῶν ἢ τὸν ἐν Θεῷ γεγονότα. Γίνεται δέ τις ἐν Θεῷ, μετέχων αὐτοῦ, ὡς καὶ τῶν ἀγνοημάτων ῥύεταί τις ἐν ἐπιστήμῃ γενόμενος, ὅστις εἰς πειρασμὸν οὐκ εἰσέρχεται, οὐ τῷ μὴ πειρασθῆναι, ἀλλὰ τῷ μὴ ἁλῶναι ταῖς παγίσι τοῦ πειρασμοῦ. *deOr*, 29.11: χρὴ τοίνυν εὔχεσθαι οὐχ ἵνα μὴ πειρασθῶμεν (τοῦτο γὰρ ἀδύνατον) ἀλλ᾽ ἵνα μὴ ὑπὸ τοῦ πειρασμοῦ περιβληθῶμεν, ὅπερ πάσχουσιν οἱ ἐνεχόμενοι αὐτῷ καὶ νενικημένοι. ἐπεὶ οὖν ἔξω μὲν τῆς εὐχῆς γέγραπται μὴ εἰσελθεῖν εἰς πειρασμόν, ὅπερ ἐκ τῶν εἰρημένων δύναταί πως εἶναι σαφές, ἐν δὲ τῇ εὐχῇ λέγειν ἡμᾶς δεῖ. *μὴ εἰσενέγκῃς ἡμᾶς εἰς πειρασμὸν* τῷ πατρὶ θεῷ. ἄξιον ἰδεῖν, πῶς χρὴ νοεῖν τὸν θεὸν εἰσάγειν τὸν μὴ εὐξάμενον ἢ τὸν μὴ ἐπακουόμενον *εἰς* τὸν *πειρασμόν*. ἀπεμφαίνει γάρ, τοῦ νικωμένου εἰσερχομένου *εἰς* τὸν *πειρασμόν*, τὸν θεὸν νομίζειν εἰσάγειν τινὰ *εἰς πειρασμόν*, οἱονεὶ τῷ νικᾶσθαι αὐτὸν παραδόντα. ἡ δ᾽ αὐτὴ ἀπέμφασις περιμένει καὶ τὸν ὅπως ποτὲ ἐξηγούμενον τὸ εὔχεσθε μὴ εἰσελθεῖν *εἰς πειρασμόν*. εἰ γὰρ κακὸν τὸ ἐμπεσεῖν *εἰς πειρασμόν*, ὅπερ ἵνα μὴ πάθωμεν εὐχόμεθα, πῶς οὐκ ἄτοπον νοεῖν τὸν ἀγαθὸν θεόν, μὴ δυνάμενον *καρποὺς* φέρειν πονηρούς, περιβάλλειν τινὰ τοῖς κακοῖς.

cdxlix Cf. Origen, *deOr*, 29:2: ὅτι δὲ *πειρατήριον πᾶς ὁ ἐπὶ γῆς ἀνθρώπινος βίος* [Job, 7:1.] ἀπὸ τοῦ Ἰὼβ μεμαθήκαμεν διὰ τούτων. *πότερον οὐχὶ πειρατήριόν ἐστιν ὁ βίος τῶν ἀνθρώπων ἐπὶ γῆς;* καὶ ἀπὸ τοῦ ἑπτακαιδεκάτου ψαλμοῦ τὸ αὐτὸ δηλοῦται ἐν τῷ. *ἐν σοὶ ῥυσθήσομαι ἀπὸ πειρατηρίου* [Psalm 17:30]. Ἀλλὰ καὶ ὁ Παῦλος Κορινθίοις γράφων οὐχὶ τὸ μὴ πειράζεσθαι ἀλλὰ τὸ μὴ παρὰ δύναμιν πειράζεσθαί φησι χαρίζεσθαι τὸν θεόν, λέγων. *πειρασμὸς ὑμᾶς οὐκ εἴληφεν εἰ μὴ ἀνθρώπινος. πιστὸς δὲ ὁ θεός, ‹ὃς› οὐκ ἐάσει ὑμᾶς πειρασθῆναι ὑπὲρ ὃ δύνασθε, ἀλλὰ ποιήσει σὺν τῷ πειρασμῷ καὶ τὴν ἔκβασιν τοῦ δύνασθαι ὑπενεγκεῖν* [1 Cor. 10:13].

cdl Origen, *commMatt*, fr. 123 (Klostermann).

cdli 'Devil' does not suggest 'nature' but 'choice' (προαίρεσις); hence, devil *became* the prince of evil whereas in the beginning he was an angel. This is a fundamentally anti-Gnostic thesis, which Origen bequeathed to later Christian authors. Origen, *Princ*, III.1.10, *apud Philocalia*, 21.9: αἱ δὲ προαιρέσεις αἱ διάφοροι οἱονεὶ ἡ γεγεωργημένη γῆ ἐστι καὶ ἡ ἠμελημένη, μία τῇ φύσει ὡς γῆ τυγχάνουσα. *expProv*, PG.17.241.16-18: κατὰ γὰρ τὴν τῶν ἀγγέλων φύσιν πρὸ τῆς παραβάσεως καὶ πτώσεως ὁ διάβολος τῶν ἀγγέλων καὶ ἡμῶν ὑπῆρχε. *commJohn*, XX.23.198: Εἰς ταῦτα δὲ ὁ Ἡρακλέων φησί. πρὸς οὓς ὁ λόγος ἐκ τῆς οὐσίας τοῦ διαβόλου ἦσαν. ὡς ἑτέρας οὔσης τῆς τοῦ διαβόλου οὐσίας παρὰ τὴν τῶν ἁγίων λογικῶν οὐσίαν. *Cels*, IV.65: Καὶ οὐδεὶς μὴ διαλαβὼν τὰ περὶ τοῦ καλουμένου διαβόλου καὶ τῶν ἀγγέλων αὐτοῦ, τίς τε πρὸ τοῦ διάβολος γεγενῆσθαι οὗτος ἦν καὶ πῶς γεγένηται διάβολος καὶ τίς ἡ αἰτία τοῦ συναποστῆναι αὐτῷ τοὺς καλουμένους αὐτοῦ ἀγγέλους, οἷός τε ἔσται γνῶναι τὴν γένεσιν τῶν κακῶν. *Op. cit.* VIII.26: τὸν αὐτὸν τρόπον οἱ νοήσαντες δαιμόνων φύσιν καὶ προαίρεσιν καὶ κακίαν οὐκ ἄν ποτε βούλοιντο εὐμενεῖς ἔχειν τοὺς δαίμονας. *commMatt*, 10.11: οὐ γὰρ φύσις ἐν ἡμῖν αἰτία τῆς πονηρίας, ἀλλὰ προαίρεσις ἑκούσιος οὖσα κακοποιητική. Οὕτως δὲ οὐδὲ φύσις αἰτία δικαιοσύνης ὡς ἀνεπίδεκτος ἀδικίας, ἀλλὰ λόγος ὃν παρεδεξάμεθα ὁ κατασκευάζων δικαίους. Basil of Caesarea, *Quod Deus non est Auctor Malorum*, PG.31.348.10-12: Οὕτω πονηρὸς ὁ διάβολος, ἐκ προαιρέσεως ἔχων τὴν πονηρίαν, οὐ φύσις ἀντικειμένη τῷ ἀγαθῷ. Severian of Gabala, *In Job*, PG.56.572.80-573.2: Διάβολος γάρ, ἀδελφοί, οὐ φύσεως ὄνομα, ἀλλὰ προαιρέσεως. Διὰ τί διάβολος; Οὐ γὰρ διάβολος ἐγένετο ἀπ᾽ ἀρχῆς, ἀλλὰ ἄγγελος ἐκτίσθη. John Chrysostom, *De Diabolo Tentatore*, PG.49.259.40-42: Ἀφείσθω ὁ διάβολος ὁ σφόδρα πονηρὸς οὐ φύσει, ἀλλὰ προαιρέσει καὶ γνώμῃ. ὅτι γὰρ οὐκ ἔστι φύσει πονηρὸς ὁ διάβολος, ἀπ᾽ αὐτῶν τῶν ὀνομάτων μάνθανε. Basil of Seleucia, *Sermones*,

PG.85.249.35-37: Ἐπειδὴ γὰρ οὐ φύσεως πονηρᾶς ὁ διάβολος, ἀλλὰ προαιρέσεως μοχθηρᾶς ὑπάρξας. Pseudo-Caesarius (Cassian the Sabaite), *Quaestiones et Responsiones*, 122: Ἄπαγε φύσιν λέγειν τῶν κακῶν. ἁμαρτία δ᾽ ἐμοὶ δοκεῖ πᾶσα τοῦ κρείττονος ἀντίστασις καὶ ἀντιπαράταξις. ταύτην δέ φημι ὑπάρχειν τὸν διάβολον οὐ φύσει, ἀλλὰ προαιρέσει ἐπὶ τὸ χεῖρον τραπέντα.

cdlii Cyril of Alexandria, *frMatt*, fr. 73.

cdliii Cf. Origen, *expProv*, PG.17.249.53-252.3: βρῶμα δέ ἐστι ψυχῆς, ἡ μελέτη τῶν θείων λόγων. ἔργα δέ, αἱ ἀρεταί. θεραπαινίδες δέ, αἱ αἰσθήσεις. ταῦτ᾽ οὖν παρέχει ἡ τιμιωτέρα λίθων πολυτελῶν ψυχὴ τῷ σωματικῷ αὐτῆς οἴκῳ.

cdliv Origen, *commMatt*, fr. 126 (Klostermann). Origen's view is that Matt. 6:19, urging not to 'lay up treasures upon earth', is addressed to 'the teachers of the church', and that the term 'light' of Matt. 6:22 ('the light of the body is the eye') means 'the mind' (νοῦς) of *all* men. This fragment of Klostermann is in tune with parallel analyses of Origen at other points of his work, as well as with the ensuing Klostermann's fr. 127. Cf. Origen, *frLuc*, fr. 121a & *schLuc*, PG.17.336.3-8: Ὅ γε μὴν βουλόμενος τὸν λύχνον ἐφαρμόζειν τοῖς τελειωτάτοις τῶν τοῦ Ἰησοῦ μαθητῶν δυσωπήσει ἡμᾶς ἀπὸ τῶν περὶ Ἰωάννου εἰρημένων, ὅτι *ἐκεῖνος ἦν ὁ λύχνος ὁ καιόμενος καὶ φαίνων. ἀλλὰ καὶ ὁ λύχνος τοῦ σώματός ἐστιν ὁ ὀφθαλμὸς* ἀναφερόμενος ἐπὶ τὸν ἐν ἑκάστῳ νοῦν. *Op. cit.* 18: Δοκεῖ γάρ μοι ἐν τῷ *ὁ λύχνος τοῦ σώματός ἐστιν ὁ ὀφθαλμὸς* τοιοῦτόν τι ἀποφαίνεσθαι. τὸ διορατικὸν ἐν τῇ ὅλῃ ψυχῇ, ἐν τῷ ὅλῳ ἀνθρώπῳ ὁ νοῦς ἐστιν. ἵνα δὲ τούτου ἐπιμέλειαν ποιώμεθα, εἴρηται τό *ἔστωσαν ὑμῖν οἱ λύχνοι καιόμενοι· ...* καὶ μὴ θαυμάσῃς δέ, εἰ ἐν τῷ *ὁ λύχνος τοῦ σώματός ἐστιν ὁ ὀφθαλμὸς* τροπολογικῶς τὸ σῶμα ἐπὶ τῆς ψυχῆς λαμβάνομεν, καίτοι γε τῷ ἰδίῳ λόγῳ οὔσης ἀοράτου καὶ ἀσωμάτου. ...... διόπερ μὴ θαυμάσῃς, εἰ καὶ τὸ τοῦ *σώματος* ὄνομα ἀνάλογον τοῖς ὀνόμασι τῶν μερῶν τοῦ σώματος ἀναγομένοις ἐπὶ τὰς δυνάμεις τῆς ψυχῆς ἐπὶ ὅλην ἀναφέρεται τὴν ψυχὴν ἐν τῷ *ὁ λύχνος τοῦ σώματός ἐστιν ὁ ὀφθαλμός*. *frPs*, on Psalm 118:148: Μήποτε δὲ καὶ ὁ λύχνος τοῦ σώματος ἡμῶν ὁ νοῦς, λεγόμενος ὀφθαλμός. *selPs*, PG.12.1236.6-9: Ἡ λύχνος ψυχῆς ὁ νοῦς, ὡς δὴ φωτὸς δεκτικός. Σκότος δὲ ταύτης τό τε θυμικὸν καὶ ἐπιθυμητικόν, ἃ δὴ φωτίζεται ὑπὸ τοῦ νοῦ δεξαμένου τὰς θείας αὐγάς. *expProv*, PG.17.189.53-192.2: *Ὁ λύχνος, λέγων, τοῦ σώματός ἐστιν ὁ ὀφθαλμός*. λύχνον μὲν εἶπε τὸν νοῦν. αὐτὸς γάρ ἐστι γνώσεως δεκτικός. σῶμα δὲ τὸ θυμικὸν καὶ ἐπιθυμητικὸν μέρος τῆς ψυχῆς, ὅπερ τινὲς μέν, ἄλογον, τινὲς δέ, παθητικὸν μέρος καλοῦσιν.

cdlv Theodore of Heraclea or Theodore of Mopsuestia, *frMatt*, fr. 24 (J. Reuss). But this is only proof that this 'Theodore' wrote (if indeed he wrote) in his own commentary on Matthew while having Origen's work in front of him.

cdlvi See previous endnote (cdliv) on Origen, *commMatt*, fr. 126 (Klostermann).

cdlvii Origen, *commMatt*, fr. 128 (Klostermann); continued forthwith.

cdlviii The technical expression μέση ἕξις ('intermediary entrenched habit') was introduced by Aristotle, *Ethica Eudemia*, 1222a-b; 1231b22; *Ethica Nicomachea*, 1109b24; 1126b5; 1126b21; *Physiognomonica*, 811b11&25; 812a2; 812b19. By this, he meant his theory of 'middle' action being the best between two excessive limits, wherefore this 'middle' procures virtuous action (since 'virtue' itself is a certain 'middle', μέσον, *Ethica Nicomachea*, 1106b; 1107a; *Magna Moralia*, 1.22.2; *Politica*, 1295a). The Stoics took up both this idea and the expression, as indeed they did with the term ἕξις itself, which I have rendered in English not merely as 'habit' (which native speakers have done): for ἕξις is more than merely a 'habit' and less than one's 'nature'; it is an *entrenched* habit; and if this persists with the passage of time, it would become part of one's *nature*.

Origen is the distinguished former Greek philosopher who took this up, and the Christian author who confidently introduced this in his commentary on Matthew. The only other Christian who did so was Basil of Caesarea (*Homilia in Principium*

Proverbiorum, PG.31.409.40), who was a devout follower and anthologer of Origen, yet a mediocre student of philosophy. Since it is my firm conviction that Origen learned everything about Aristotle from Alexander of Aphrodisias, I assume that he came upon this in both in him and in Stoic writings (which should have been not only those of the old Stoics, but also those of the later Cornutus). See Pseudo-Alexander of Aphrodisias (but probably this is a genuine work by Alexander), *'Ηθικὰ Προβλήματα*, p. 121: Ὅτι δικαιοσύνης καὶ ἀδικίας καὶ ὅλως ἀρετῆς τε καὶ κακίας ἐστίν τις ἕξις μεταξύ, ἣν μέσην ἕξιν λέγομεν. Cf. *op. cit.* p. 122. Chrysippus, *Fragmenta Moralia*, fr. 238, *apud* Simplicius, *commCateg*, p. 402 (but Simplicius cited 'the Stoics' in general, not Chrysippus; however, as it happened, J. von Arnim made almost everything a wholsale attribution to Chrysippus, which is why the second volume of *SVF* is large). Also (the foregoing passage) Chrysippus, *Fragmenta* fr. 537, *apud* Pseudo-Alexander of Aphrodisias, *'Ηθικὰ Προβλήματα*, p. 121 (but Alexander did not mention any Stoic or 'Stoics' whatsoever). Besides, there should be no doubt that Origen received this notion also from Galen, to whom he owed a vast number of trenchant philosophical expressions and ideas. Cf. Galen, *Thrasybulus*, p. 816; *In Hippocratis Librum iii Epidemiarum*, p. 542; *In Hippocratis Librum De Fracturis*, p. 321.

The notion of μέση ἕξις was attested by Arius Didymus in the first century BC and subsequently was reported by Stobaeus six centuries later: *Anthologium*, 2.7: 20; 24-25. This appeared also in commentaries on Aristotle prior to Origen (such as that by Aspasius, *commEthNicom*, pp. 117; 122; 125), but Origen's dues were to Alexander of Aphrodisias and to Galen. Then, there is a leap to the fifth century, not only with Stobaeus but also with Hierocles of Alexandria (*In Aureum Carmen*, 11.22), Ammonius of Alexandria (*commDeInterpr*, pp. 164; 172-174; 184), and Proclus (*commCrat*, 116; *commTim*, v. 2, p. 137). Once Ammonius applied this locution, it was natural for this to appear in later philosophers of sixth and seventh centuries, if casually. Damascius, *In Parmenidem*, p. 210. Simplicius, *commCateg*, p. 402 (ref. to 'Stoics'); *commEpict*, p. 111. John Philoponus, *commAnim*, p. 535. Asclepius of Tralles, *commMetaph*, p. 344. Olympiodorus of Alexandria, *In Platonis Alcibiadem*, 129. Stephanus of Alexandria, *commDeInterpr*, pp. 41-42; 66.

cdlix See the endnote on Origen's *commMatt*, fr. 126 (Klostermann): he explains that, in the phrase 'light of the body' (Matt. 6:22), the term 'body' means 'the soul'.

cdlx Origen, *commMatt*, fr. 127 (Klostermann).

cdlxi Gal. 5:17. Origen, *commMatt*, fr. 128 (Klostermann).

cdlxii Gregory Thaumaturgus, *Fragmentum in Evangelium Matthaei 6.22-23*, PG.10.1189.25-41. This is the sole fragment on the gospel of Matthew attributed to Gregory, and evidently it was not he himself who wrote this: it was his hero Origen who did.

cdlxiii Cf. Origen, *Cels*, IV.29: καὶ οὐδεὶς τῷ λαμπρῷ φωτὶ τῆς ἀληθείας καταυγαζόμενος τὴν ψυχὴν νυκτερίδι ἂν εὐλόγως παραβάλλοιτο. *Op. cit.* V.13: εἴπωμεν τὰ ἀπὸ τοῦ τῆς ἀληθείας φωτὸς δοθησόμενα ἡμῖν. *commJohn*, XIII.42.284: ἵνα τὴν λευκότητα καὶ τὴν λαμπρότητα θεάσηταί τις τοῦ τῆς ἀληθείας πανταχοῦ φωτός. *adDeut*, PG.17.33.39-40: Τυφλοὺς γὰρ ὄντας αὐτοὺς καὶ μήπω τὸ φῶς τῆς ἀληθείας ἐσχηκότας καὶ θεογνωσίας.

cdlxiv Theodore of Heraclea, *frMatt*, fr. 47, col. 1.

cdlxv Cyril of Alexandria, *frMatt*, fr. 79.

cdlxvi Origen, *commMatt*, fr. 130 (Klostermann).

cdlxvii Here is one more phrase of Origen which became a lexicon lemma. Pseudo-Zonaras, *Lexicon*, letter mu, p. 1328: Μαμωνᾶς. τὰ χρήματα ἑρμηνεύεται. ἢ ὁ ἄδικος ὑπὲρ τὴν χρείαν συναγόμενος πλοῦτος.

cdlxviii Origen, *commMatt*, fr. 129 (Klostermann).

cdlxix Jeerome, *commMatt*, 6.24.

cdlxx Origen, *commMatt*, fr. 135 (Klostermann).

cdlxxi John Chrysostom, *In Matthaeum*, PG.57.309.34-44.

cdlxxii The idea involved in this portion is Aristotelian: Aristotle had argued that since food is indispensable for an animate being to be maintaind alive, it follows that food sustains both body and soul, not the body alone. For 'that which has a soul has its growth promoted by food ... because it preserves its substance and continues to exist so long as it is nourished.' *De Anima*, 416b (partially quoted in the *Suda*, letter tau, entry 930). Alexander of Aphrodisias explained this further in his own treatise on the soul (*De Anima*, p. 36), from which Origen presumably got familiar with the pertinent analysis. This point attracted the attention also of later commentators, such as Themistius (*paraphrAnim*, p. 53), Sophonias (*paraphrAnim*, p. 62), Gennadius Scholarius (*commAnim*, 2.9), and, best of them all, John Philoponus, who explained this in more detail, which could be summarised thus: once aliment is chararacteristic of animate beings only, and once life is given to them by their soul, it follows of necessity that an animate body is nourished *qua* an *animate* one (ἀνάγκη τὸ ἔμψυχον σῶμα εἶναι τὸ τρεφόμενον κατ᾽ αὐτὸ τοῦτο, καθὸ ἔμψυχόν ἐστι). For a body did not become animate just because it has been nourished, but it needs to be nourished because this is animate in the first place. Consequently, once that which is nourished is animate, food goes to the animate itself (εἰ δὲ τὸ τρεφόμενον ἔμψυχον, καὶ ἡ τροφὴ καθ᾽ αὑτὸ τοῦ ἐμψύχου ἐστίν). *commAnim*, pp. 285-287. This is the point that Origen makes here: granted, the soul takes pleasure once the body enjoys food; however, the pleasure that souls takes at theoretical reflection is of different kind.

cdlxxiii Origen, *commMatt*, fr. 131 (Klostermann).

cdlxxiv Clement of Alexandria, *Paedagogus*, 2.10bis.103.2-5. Quite evidently, Origen drew on Clement.

cdlxxv Origen, *commMatt*, fr. 133 (Klostermann).

cdlxxvi See *supra*, endnote cdlxxii.

cdlxxvii Although in the Old Testament references to 'alien gods' (ἀλλότριοι θεοὶ) abound (Gen. 35:2&4; Deut. 31:16-20; 32:12; etc.), the notion of a human being being 'alienated from God' (ἀλλότριον θεοῦ) or 'becoming alienated from God' (ἀλλοτριοῦσθαι θεοῦ) is a different matter: it appeared in literature with Philo referring to Aristotle. Philo, *De Aeternitate Mundi*, 40 (Aristotle, *Fragmenta Varia*, fr. 21, from his lost treatise *On Philosophy*): τὸ μὲν δὴ πρότερον ἀλλότριον θεοῦ. It was Origen who made this a heavily recurrent motif, and little wonder that both Plotinus and Porphyry did so, too, if only just. Plotinus, *Enneades*, I.6.7 (8-9): πᾶν ὅσον ἀλλότριον τοῦ θεοῦ. Porphyry, *In Platonis Parmenidem Commentaria* (*fragmenta*), fr. 1: πρᾶγμα ἀλλοτριώτατον τοῦ θεοῦ ἀκούσας τὸ ἕν. This has been attributed also to Speusippus, *Fragmenta*, fr. 49b.

Origen, *commJohn*, X.30.139: Οἱ ἀπὸ τῶν ἐθνῶν, οἳ ἦσαν ξένοι τῶν διαθηκῶν καὶ ἀλλότριοι τῆς ἐπαγγελίας τοῦ θεοῦ. *exhMar*, 36: νομιζόμενον παρὰ τοῖς ἀλλοτρίοις θεοῦ. *selGen*, PG.12.144.19-20: Τοῦτο δὲ νομιστέον ὑπὸ πάντων τῶν ἀλλοτρίων τοῦ Θεοῦ λέγεσθαι. *deOr*, 21.2: καὶ εἷς μὲν ὁ τοῦ θεοῦ λόγος, πολλοὶ δὲ οἱ ἀλλότριοι τοῦ θεοῦ. *Op. cit.* 25.3: τὰ ἀλλότρια τοῦ θεοῦ προκαλουμένης ἡμῶν τὴν ψυχήν. *fr1Cor*, fr. 35: ὁ γάμος οὐκ ἀλλότριός ἐστι θεοῦ. *commEph*, fr. 18: ματαιότης νοὸς καὶ σκότωσις διανοίας, τὰ ἀλλοτριοῦντα τῆς ζωῆς τοῦ Θεοῦ. *commMatt*, 13.1 & *Fragmenta in Evangelium Matthaei* (E. Benz - E. Klostermann), p. 4: ἵνα μὴ ἐμπίπτω εἰς τὸ ἀλλότριον τῆς ἐκκλησίας τοῦ θεοῦ περὶ τῆς μετενσωματώσεως δόγμα. *homLuc*, homily 35, pp. 201-202: οἰκεῖος μὲν γίνῃ τούτου, ἀλλότριος δὲ τοῦ θεοῦ.

Cels, VIII.5: ἀπὸ τῶν ἀλλοτρίων τῆς πολιτείας τοῦ θεοῦ καὶ ξένων τῶν διαθηκῶν αὐτοῦ. *Op. cit.* VIII.10: τίνες μέν εἰσι τοῦ θεοῦ καὶ ὅτι μόνοι οἱ σοφοί, τίνες δὲ οἱ ἀλλότριοι. *Op. cit.* VIII.33: ὁ τῆς θειότητος ἀλλότριος. *Op. cit.* VIII.43: τοὺς ξένους τῶν διαθηκῶν τοῦ θεοῦ καὶ ἀλλοτρίους τῶν ἐπαγγελιῶν. *frPs*, on Psalm 29:8: ἀσθένεια ψυχῆς ἐκ τῆς ἀπὸ Θεοῦ ἀλλοτριώσεως. *Op. cit.* Psalm 77:45: οἱ γὰρ ἀλλότριοι τοῦ Θεοῦ καὶ παρὰ τοῖς νομιζομένοις ἄποροί εἰσι. *Op. cit.* Psalm 87:9: ἀλλοτριουμένους Ἰησοῦ Χριστοῦ τοῦ Θεοῦ. *selPs*, PG.12.1236.30-31: Καὶ *πνεύματι δὲ ζέουσι*, καὶ ἀλλότριον Θεοῦ οὐ παραδέχονται πῦρ. *Op. cit.* PG.12. 1645.10-11: Οὐδεὶς ἀλλότριος τοῦ Θεοῦ τούτων τεύξεται.

Following this, the expression was confidently and conveniently taken up by Origen's devout admirers (Eusebius and the Cappadocians) and (as it happened) by detractors such as Epiphanius of Salamis. Gregory of Nyssa, *Contra Eunomium*, 2.1.521; *Refutatio Confessionis Eunomii*, 175; *De Oratione Dominica*, p. 222; *Dialogus De Anima et Resurrectione*, PG.46.52.12; *De Infantibus Praemature Abreptis*, p. 81; *Ad Simplicium De Fide*, p. 62; *Adversus Arium et Sabellium De Patre et Filio*, p. 80; *In Canticum Canticorum*, p. 11. Eusebius, *In Isaiam*, 1.73; 2.10; *Ad Stephanum*, PG.22.896.55; *Supplementa ad Quaestiones ad Stephanum*, PG.22.964.7; *Commentaria in Psalmos*, PG.23.420.20; *op. cit.* PG.23.1333.6.

There should be no doubt that Origen's devotees wrote following their creative flare: Gregory of Nyssa, *De Oratione Dominica*, pp. 221-222: Τίς δὲ ψυχῆς ἐπιβουλή, τίς ἄλλη, εἰ μὴ θεοῦ ἀλλοτρίωσις; Ἀλλοτριοῦται δὲ ἀπὸ θεοῦ ἀνθρωπίνη ψυχὴ οὐκ ἄλλως ἢ διὰ τῆς ἐμπαθοῦς διαθέσεως. Eusebius, *Commentaria in Psalmos*, PG.23.1293.32-34: ψυχῆς δὲ ἐπιβουλὴ Θεοῦ ἀλλοτρίωσις διὰ τῆς ἐμπαθοῦς γινομένης διαθέσεως. Gregory of Nazianzus, *Funebris Oratio in Laudem Basilii Magni*, 40.3: καὶ ἀλλοτρίωσιν ἀπὸ Θεοῦ νομίζειν τὴν ἀπ' ἐκείνου διάστασιν. *Comparatio Vitarum*, line 184 & *Carmina Moralia*, col. 662: Θεοῦ γὰρ ἀλλοτρίωσις ἡ ἁμαρτία. *Carmina Moralia*, col. 824: Ταῦτ' οὐκ ἀλλοτρίωσις ἐνδήλως Θεοῦ; *De Theologia*, 7: λύσις δὲ ἀλλότριον πάντῃ θεοῦ καὶ τῆς πρώτης φύσεως. *Ad Cives Nazianzenos*, PG.35.965.4-5; *In Aegyptiorum Adventum*, PG.36.249.22-23; *In Sanctum Baptisma*, PG.36: 388.30; 424.42. Basil of Caesarea, *Adversus Eunomium*, PG.29.536.19; *Homiliae super Psalmos*, PG.29: 248.21; 320.13; *et passim*. Athanasius, *Oratio iii Contra Arianos*, 41.2. Pseudo-Basil of Caesarea (*forsan* Cassian the Sabaite), *Enarratio in Prophetam Isaiam*, 5.159; 6.191; 13.268. As for Epiphanius of Salamis, he could not have enough of using both the notion and the locution. *Ancoratus*, 2.5-6: εἷς θεὸς τοίνυν ὁ πατὴρ καὶ μόνος ἀληθινὸς θεὸς καὶ θεὸς ὁ μονογενής. οὐκ ἄρα ἀλλότριος θεοῦ καὶ τῆς μονάδος. *Op. cit.* 6.9 & 10; 11.4; 12.4; 11.4; 14.5; 16.2; 52.2; 118.2; *Panarion*, v. 1, p. 220; *et passim* abundantly. In the subsequent centuries, Christian usage of the expression and idea thrived, but hardly were Christian authors aware of Origen having been the real source of this. Cf. *infra*, folio 147r: δηλοῖ τὴν ἀφαίρεσιν τῶν ἀγαθῶν καὶ τὴν ἀπὸ Θεοῦ ἀλλοτρίωσιν. Folio 169v: οὓς καὶ ἀλλοτρίους λέγει τῆς βασιλείας τοῦ Θεοῦ. Folio 198v: Διχοτομία δέ ἐστιν ἡ ἀπὸ τοῦ Πνεύματος εἰς τὸ διηνεκὲς τῆς ψυχῆς ἀλλοτρίωσις.

cdlxxviii Although apparently this is *en passant* phrase, in fact, Origen rejects an opinion of Demosthenes, which came to be one of the most famous and proverbial ones throughout all Antiquity. Demosthenes, *Olynthiaca 1*, 20: Δεῖ δὴ χρημάτων, καὶ ἄνευ τούτων οὐδὲν ἔστι γενέσθαι τῶν δεόντων ('We certainly need money, and without money nothing can be done of those that need to be done'). Rhetors, philologists, philosophers, lexicographers, indeed almost all sorts of intellectuals quoted this phrase during the subsequent two thousand years. Libanius, *Progymnasmata*, 4.3.1. Aphthonius, *Progymnasmata*, p. 7. John of Sardis, *Commentarium in Aphthonii Progymnasmata*, p. 58. Stobaeus, *Anthologium*, 4.31a.31. Syrianus, *Commentarium in Hermogenis Librum*

Περὶ Στάσεων, p. 189. Olympiodorus of Alexandria, *commPhaed*, 6.8. Anonymous, *Scholia ad Hermogenis Librum Περὶ Στάσεων*, p. 758. Anonymous (lexicographer), *Συναγωγὴ Λέξεων Χρησίμων*, letter delta, lemma 54. Photius, *Lexicon*, letter delta, entry 100. Theophanes Continuatus, *Chronographia*, p. 257. *Suda*, letter delta, entry 299. *Etymologicum Gudianum, Additamenta in Etymologicum Gudianum*, entry delta, p. 337. Anna Comnena, *Alexias*, 1.16.5. George Pachymeres, *Progymnasmata*, chapter 4 (title). Arsenius of Monembasia (paroemiographer), *Apophthegmata*, 5.90i. Anonymous (rhetor), *Progymnasmata*, p. 605. *Lexica Segueriana, Collectio Verborum Utilium e Differentibus Rhetoribus et Sapientibus Multis*, entry delta, p. 189.

cdlxxix Cyril of Alexandria, *frMatt*, fr. 80.

cdlxxx See also, Origen, *commMatt*, fr. 137 I (Klostermann): τοῖς οὖν ἀναιδῶς ἀνερυθριάστοις καὶ λοιδόροις ὑλακτικοῖς ἢ διὰ γαστέρα κόλαξιν, ὧν ἀντάλλαγμα οὐκ εἰσίει *εἰς οἶκον κυρίου*, μυστηρίων ἁγίων οὐ κοινωνητέον. οὐδὲ φιληδόνοις καὶ φαύλοις μεταδοτέον τῶν κοσμούντων τὴν νύμφην τοῦ λόγου μαργαριτῶν, μὴ τοῖς ἀκαθάρτοις καὶ βεβορβορωμένοις *ποσὶν καταπατήσωσιν* ‹αὐτούς›.

cdlxxxi Origen, *commMatt*, fr. 137 II (Klostermann).

cdlxxxii Cf. κατάστασις τοῦ ἡγεμονικοῦ in *Cels*, IV.65: ὡς ἐν καταστάσει δαιμόνων αὐτῶν ὑποστῆναι τὸ ἡγεμονικόν. *deOr*, 25.1: καὶ οἶμαι νοεῖσθαι θεοῦ μὲν βασιλείαν τὴν μακαρίαν τοῦ ἡγεμονικοῦ κατάστασιν.

cdlxxxiii Origen, *commMatt*, fr. 138 II (Klostermann), col. 1.

cdlxxxiv Origen, *schMatt*, PG.17.292.9-23: *Αἰτεῖτε, καὶ δοθήσεται ὑμῖν. ζητεῖτε, καὶ εὑρήσετε. κρούετε, καὶ ἀνοιγήσεται ὑμῖν.* In terms of Greek language, the text of the present codex is a much better version than Migne's.

cdlxxxv The term συμπαρεκτείνων ('stretched out alongside with', which I have discussed in my *COT*) was introduced into Christian literature by Origen, who deemed this demonstrative of his Stoic concept of Time as 'extension' (διάστημα) co-extended along with the structure of this world', namely, with 'space' proper.

In the *Metaphysics*, 1072b28-31, Aristotle described God's 'life' as 'a continuous eternal existence belonging to God': φαμὲν δὴ τὸν θεὸν εἶναι ζῷον ἀΐδιον ἄριστον, ὥστε ζωὴ καὶ αἰὼν συνεχὴς καὶ ἀΐδιος ὑπάρχει τῷ θεῷ. τοῦτο γὰρ ὁ θεός. This phrase clearly suggests that this 'life and unfailing eternity' are *in* God – they are not God himself. It was precicely this idea that Alexander of Aphrodisias rendered brilliantly by introducing the participle συμπαρεκτεινομένη for 'life', and proposing that αἰὼν is the 'life, which is stretched alongside with everyone's being' (αἰὼν γάρ ἐστιν ἡ ἑκάστῳ συμπαρεκτεινομένη ζωή, *commMetaph*, p. 699). Thus, he made divine life not timelessness but evelasting duration, which is a matter calling for discussion yet outside the present scope. The fact of the matter is that the verb συμπαρεκτείνειν / συμπαρεκτείνεσθαι did not exist in Aristotle's times, and it cropped up simultaneously with Galen and Alexander of Aphrodisias.

In Galen there is a single case of the term 'stretched out alongside with' being associated with 'time'. *De Difficultate Respirationis*, p. 915: ἐπεὶ γὰρ συμπαρεκτείνεται τῷ μήκει τοῦ χρόνου τῆς ἀναπνοῆς ὁ πόνος, ὁ θᾶττον ἂν ἐπισχὼν τὴν κίνησιν τῶν ἀναπνευστικῶν θᾶττον ὀδυνώμενος παύσεται. Otherwise, Galen used the term only in its literal sense. *De Anatomicis Administrationibus*, p. 370; *De Ossibus ad Tirones*, p. 777; *De Venarum Arteriarumque Dissectione*, p. 823; *De Usu Partium*, v. 3, p. 710; v. 4, pp. 59; 202; *De Locis Affectis*, p. 323. Cf. Marcus Aurelius, *Τὰ εἰς Ἑαυτόν*, 7.30.1: Συμπαρεκτείνειν τὴν νόησιν τοῖς λεγομένοις. Cleomedes, *Caelestia*, 2.1; 2.6.

Origen took this up from his favourite philological sources, namely, Galen and Alexander of Aphrodisias. He was an assiduous reader of Galen's works because he had a keen interest in medicine. At the same time, he perused Alexander because he wanted to study Aristotle's works glossed by Alexander. Those commentaries were particularly serviceable since they were composed in form of class-lessons: Aristotle's text was quoted is short passages followed by Alexander's comments on them. In general, Origen drew from those authors *terms* and expressions rather than *ideas*, which is why I have argued that, to him, those sources were 'philological'.

Subsequently, to Origen, συμπαρεκτείνων became a multi-purpose term used in various contexts. *commJohn*, I.29.204: οὐκ ἔνι γὰρ ἑσπέρα θεοῦ, ἐγὼ δὲ ἡγοῦμαι, ὅτι οὐδὲ πρωΐα, ἀλλὰ ὁ συμπαρεκτείνων τῇ ἀγενήτῳ καὶ ἀϊδίῳ αὐτοῦ ζωῇ, ἵν᾽ οὕτως εἴπω, χρόνος ἡμέρα ἐστὶν αὐτῷ *σήμερον*, ἐν ᾗ γεγέννηται ὁ υἱός. *Op. cit.* VI.30.154: δοξολογίαν περὶ τῆς προηγουμένης οὐσίας Χριστοῦ διηγεῖται, ὅτι δύναμιν τοσαύτην ἔχει ὡς καὶ ἀόρατος εἶναι τῇ θειότητι αὐτοῦ, παρὼν παντὶ ἀνθρώπῳ παντὶ δὲ καὶ ὅλῳ τῷ κόσμῳ συμπαρεκτεινόμενος. *commEph*, fr. 4, *apud Catena in Epistulam ad Ephesios*, p. 110: ἀντιφιλοτιμούμενον καὶ συμπαρεκτεινόμενον κατὰ τὸ δυνατὸν ἔχει τὸν τυγχάνοντα τῶν προειρημένων. *Op. cit.* fr. 9, *apud Catena in Epistulam ad Ephesios*, p. 135: ὁ μὲν οὖν τις ἁπλούστερον *αἰῶνα τοῦ κόσμου τούτου* ἡγήσεται τὸν συμπαρεκτεινόμενον χρόνον τῇ τούτου τοῦ κόσμου ἀπ᾽ ἀρχῆς μέχρι τέλους κατασκευῇ. *expProv*, PG.17.189.8-9: τὸ γὰρ συμπαρεκτεινόμενον τῇ συστάσει τῆς ζωῆς αὐτοῦ, αἰῶνα ὠνόμασεν. Cf. *commMatt*, 12.6: οὐ γὰρ διαρκῆ καὶ συμπαρεκτεινομένην μνήμην ἀναλαβεῖν δυνάμεθα τῷ πλήθει τῆς φύσεως τῶν θεωρημάτων.

Origen was the first Christian author to take this up, following those two pioneers, who happened to be those of his most favourite intellectuals. Perhaps he was aware that Posidonius' pupil Asclepiodotus had used this, too (*Tactica*, 6.2: συμπαρεκτείνεσθαι τῇ φάλαγγι τῶν ὁπλιτῶν). Origen's idea became a blueprint, which was employed by later Christian authors. Eusebius, *Commentaria in Psalmos*, PG.23.584.34-35: τῇ τοῦ Θεοῦ ζωῇ συμπαρεκτείνεσθαι ἀνθρώπου φύσις. *Op. cit.* PG.23: 817.15; 1105.18-19: ἀλλὰ ταῖς ἡμέραις τοῦ οὐρανοῦ συμπαρεκτείνεσθαι ποιήσω. *Vita Constantini*, 2.58.1. Gregory of Nazianzus, *In Theophania*, PG.36.320.14-18 & *In Sanctum Pascha*, PG.36.628.30-34: Αἰὼν γάρ, οὔτε χρόνος, οὔτε χρόνου τι μέρος. οὐδὲ γὰρ μετρητόν. ἀλλ᾽ ὅπερ ἡμῖν ὁ χρόνος, ἡλίου φορᾷ μετρούμενος, τοῦτο τοῖς ἀϊδίοις, αἰών, τὸ συμπαρεκτεινόμενον τοῖς οὖσιν, οἷόν τι χρονικὸν κίνημα καὶ διάστημα. *De Moderatione in Disputando*, PG.36.197.48-49. Gregory of Nyssa, *In Sextum Psalmum*, p. 188: τὸν συμπαρεκτεινόμενον τῇ κατασκευῇ τοῦ κόσμου χρόνον. *Contra Fatum*, p. 45: πάσῃ γὰρ κινήσει εἴτε ποταμῶν εἴτε ἀστέρων εἴτε ἀνθρώπων ὁ χρόνος συμπαρεκτείνεται. *Oratio Catechetica*, 32: ἴδιόν ἐστι τῆς θεότητος τὸ διὰ πάντων ἥκειν καὶ τῇ φύσει τῶν ὄντων κατὰ πᾶν μέρος συμπαρεκτείνεσθαι. *Contra Eunomium*, 1.1.424&425; 633; 2.1.70: αὕτη διαστηματικῇ τινι παρατάσει συμπαρεκτείνεται, καὶ χρόνῳ καὶ τόπῳ περιειργομένη. *Dialogus De Anima et Resurrectione*, PG.46.48.23. Basil of Caesarea, *Homiliae in Hexaemeron*, 6.9; *Epistulae*, epistle 204.1; *Adversus Eunomium*, PG.29.560.26-27 (copying from Origen): Χρόνος δέ ἐστι τὸ συμπαρεκτεινόμενον τῇ συστάσει τοῦ κόσμου διάστημα. *Op. cit.* PG.29.593.18-28: ὁ δὲ Θεὸς τῶν ὅλων ... τῇ ἑαυτοῦ ἀϊδιότητι συμπαρεκτεινομένην ἔχει τὴν (ἵν᾽ οὕτως ὀνομάσω) πατρότητα. *Op. cit.* PG.29.596.27-29: Εἰ γὰρ ἦν τι διάστημα πρεσβύτερον τοῦ Υἱοῦ, συμπαρεκτεινόμενον τῇ ζωῇ τοῦ Πατρός. *Op. cit.* PG.29.600.15-16: Συμπαρεκτείνεται δὲ καὶ τὸ *Ἦν* τῷ ἀνυπερθέτῳ τῆς ἀρχῆς ταύτης. *Homilia in Martyrem Julittam*, PG.31.244.11-12: καὶ πράξεσι ταῖς κατ᾽ ἀρετὴν παντὶ τῷ βίῳ συμπαρεκτεινομέναις. *In illud: In Principio Erat Verbum*, PG.31.480.26-27: πανταχοῦ συμπαρεκτεινομένην εὑρήσεις τοῦ Υἱοῦ τὴν ὑπόστασιν. *Asceticon Magnum* (probably not really Basil's work, but a sixth-century spurious one), PG.31.912.5-7: εὐχὴν ἐποιοῦντο πάσῃ τῇ αἰωνίᾳ ζωῇ συμπαρεκτείνεσθαι τὴν θεωρίαν τῆς τερπνότητος τοῦ Κυρίου. Evagrius of Pontus, *Practicus*, Prologue, 3: Βασιλεία Θεοῦ ἐστι γνῶσις τῆς ἁγίας

Τριάδος συμπαρεκτεινομένη τῇ συστάσει τοῦ νοός. *Expositio in Proverbia Salomonis*, p. 91 & *Scholia in Proverbia*, 123 (copying from Origen): καὶ ὁ Παῦλος *Οὐ μὴ φάγω, φησίν, κρέα εἰς τὸν αἰῶνα, ἵνα μὴ τὸν ἀδελφόν μου σκανδαλίσω*, αἰῶνα τὸ συμπαρεκτεινόμενον τῇ συστάσει τῆς ζωῆς αὐτοῦ διάστημα ὀνομάζων. *De Malignis Cogitationibus*, 36. Pseudo-Athanasius, *Contra Sabellianos*, PG.28.113.4-6: Οὐ συμπαρεκτεινόμενος τοῖς πᾶσι πεπλήρωκε τὰ πάντα ὁ Θεός. Nilus of Ancyra, *Epistulae*, book 3, epistle 33, line 373. John Chrysostom, *In Genesim*, PG.53.147.52-54: ὅτι διηνεκῆ καὶ τῷ παντὶ αἰῶνι συμπαρεκτεινομένην αὐτῷ τὴν τιμωρίαν ἐπήγαγε. *Op. cit.* PG.53.254.24: παντὶ τῷ αἰῶνι συμπαρεκτεινόμενον. *Op. cit.* PG.53.278.47: ἵνα παντὶ τῷ αἰῶνι συμπαρεκτείνηται. *Op. cit.* PG.53.279.16-17: ὥστε τὴν μνήμην παντὶ τῷ αἰῶνι συμπαρεκτείνεσθαι. *Op. cit.* PG.53.288.11: ὡς παντὶ τῷ αἰῶνι συμπαρεκτείνεσθαι αὐτήν. *Op. cit.* PG.54.386.26: ἅπασι τοῖς αἰῶσι συμπαρεκτεινόμενος. *Catecheses ad Illuminandos*, 7.14: τὰ τῷ διηνεκεῖ αἰῶνι συμπαρεκτεινόμενα. *In Sanctum Julianum Martyrem*, PG.50.668.4; *Expositiones in Psalmos*, PG.55.62.2. Pseudo-Basil of Caesarea (*forsan* Cassian the Sabaite), *Enarratio in Prophetam Isaiam*, 1.31: Τὴν ἡμέραν Κυρίου τὴν μεγάλην, ... τῷ αἰῶνι παντὶ συμπαρεκτεινομένη. *Op. cit.* p.227: ἡ δὲ παρὰ τοῦ Κυρίου εἰρήνη τῷ αἰῶνι παντὶ συμπαρεκτείνεται, ἀπεριόριστος οὖσα καὶ ἀτερμάτιστος. Olympiodorus, the deacon of Alexandria, *Commentarii in Ecclesiasten*, PG.93.488.14-17: Τῶν κτισμάτων τὰ μέν εἰσι μονογενῆ, καὶ ἀδιάδοχα, οἷον ἥλιος, καὶ σελήνη, καὶ τὰ τῷ αἰῶνι συμπαρεκτεινόμενα. John of Damascus, *Expositio Fidei*, 15 & *apud Catena in Epistulam ad Romanos*, p. 494: Λέγεται πάλιν αἰὼν οὐ χρόνος οὐδὲ χρόνου τι μέρος ἡλίου φορᾷ καὶ δρόμῳ μετρούμενον ἤγουν δι᾽ ἡμερῶν καὶ νυκτῶν συνιστάμενον, ἀλλὰ τὸ συμπαρεκτεινόμενον τοῖς ἀϊδίοις οἷόν τι χρονικὸν κίνημα καὶ διάστημα. ὅπερ γὰρ τοῖς ὑπὸ χρόνον ὁ χρόνος, τοῦτο τοῖς ἀϊδίοις ἐστὶν αἰών. *Expositio Fidei*, 51; *Sacra Parallela*, PG.96.364.12.

Greek philosophers also used the expression, presumably after Alexander of Aphrodisias. Iamblichus, *De Communi Mathematica Scientia*, 52; *In Nicomachi Arithmeticam Introductionem*, p. 45. Themistius, *paraphrPhys*, pp. 141; 145; 154: Ἐπειδὴ δέ ἐστιν ἡ κίνησις ἐν χρόνῳ τῷ καταμετρεῖσθαι τὸ εἶναι αὐτῆς ὑπὸ τοῦ χρόνου οὐ γὰρ ἄλλο τὸ εἶναι τῆς κινήσεως ἢ τὸ γίγνεσθαι ᾧ συμπαρεκτείνεται ὁ χρόνος καὶ ὃ καταμετρεῖ. *Op. cit.* p. 186: συμπαρεκτείνεται γὰρ ὁ τῆς κινήσεως χρόνος τῷ διαστήματι. Ammonius of Alexandria, *commDeInterpr*, pp. 54; 185; 165. Proclus, *commTim*, v. 1, p. 278: καὶ αὐτὴν τὴν ἀϊδιότητα τῷ ὅλῳ χρόνῳ συμπαρεκτεινομένην ἔχοντα. *Op. cit.* v. 3, p. 218: τὴν μετὰ χρόνου ζωὴν καὶ τὴν ἀπ᾽ ἄλλης αἰτίας πάροδον καὶ τὴν τῷ χρόνῳ παντὶ συμπαρεκτεινομένην. *commEucl*, pp. 62; 100. Simplicius, *commPhys*, pp. 530; 699; 741. John Philoponus, *commCateg*, p. 136; *commPhys*, p. 739: τῷ γὰρ ἀριθμεῖσθαι τὴν κίνησιν κατὰ τὸ πρότερον καὶ ὕστερον οὖσαν συνεχῆ συνεχὴς ἡ τοῦ χρόνου οὐσία ὑφέστηκε, συμπαρεκτεινομένη τῇ συνεχείᾳ τῆς κινήσεως. *Op. cit.* 760: διὰ τὸ συμπαρεκτείνεσθαι τῷ παντὶ χρόνῳ τὴν ἀνυπαρξίαν αὐτοῦ. Olympiodorus, the philosopher of Alexandria, *In Aristotelis Meteora Commentaria*, p. 10.

cdlxxxvi Cf. Origen, *deOr*, 5.6: χρήσιμα δέ, ὡς οἶμαι, ταῦτα πρὸς λύσιν τῶν ἀποναρκᾶν πρὸς τὸ εὔχεσθαι ποιούντων προδιαληπτέον.

cdlxxxvii Cf. τὰ μυστήρια τῆς σοφίας (*apud* 1 Cor. 2:7). Origen, *Cels*, III.61; *commJohn*, II.8.62; X.15.85; X.41.286; XIX.9.56; *Philocalia*, 15.19; *commMatt*, 10.5; 12.14; 13.3; 15.28; *selPs*, PG.12.1453.44-52 (& *Philocalia*, 1.29); *expProv*, PG.17.212.12-15; *schLuc*, PG.17.345.49-50.

cdlxxxviii Origen, *commMatt*, fr. 139 (Klostermann).

cdlxxxix John Chrysostom, *In Matthaeum*, PG.57.312.22-30. Also, John Chrysostom, *apud Catena in Matthaeum*, p. 52: διὰ τοῦτο οὖν αἰτεῖν ἐκέλευσε, καὶ τὴν δόσιν ἐγγυήσατο.

πλὴν οὐχ ἁπλῶς αἰτεῖν ἐκέλευσεν, ἀλλὰ μετὰ προσεδρίας πολλῆς καὶ εὐτονίας. τοῦτο γάρ ἐστι τὸ *ζητεῖτε*. καὶ γὰρ ὁ ζητῶν πάντα ἐμβαλὼν τῆς διανοίας, πρὸς ἐκεῖνο μόνον γίνεται τὸ ζητούμενον. καὶ πάλιν δὲ τὸ *κρούειν* σημαίνει τὸ μετὰ σφοδρότητος προσιέναι καὶ θερμῆς διανοίας, διὰ τῶν ἀνθρωπίνων ὑποδειγμάτων συγκαταβαίνων τῇ ἀσθενείᾳ ἡμῶν.

cdxc Jerome, *commMatt*, 7.7.

cdxci Origen, *commMatt*, fr. 138 II (Klostermann).

cdxcii Cyril of Alexandria, *frMatt*, fr. 85. But this was also ascribed to John Chrysostom, *In Matthaeum*, PG.57.312.37-43: Εἰ δὲ μὴ εὐθέως λαμβάνεις, μηδὲ οὕτως ἀπογνῷς. Διὰ γὰρ τοῦτο εἶπε, *κρούετε*, ἵνα δείξῃ ὅτι κἂν εὐθέως μὴ ἀνοίξῃ τὴν θύραν, παραμένειν δεῖ. Εἰ δὲ ἀπιστεῖς μου τῇ ἀποφάσει, κἂν τῷ ὑποδείγματι πίστευσον. *τίς γάρ ἐστιν ἐξ ὑμῶν ἄνθρωπος, ὃν ἐὰν αἰτήσῃ ὁ υἱὸς αὐτοῦ ἄρτον μὴ λίθον ἐπιδώσει αὐτῷ;* In other words, both Cyril of Alexandria and John Chrysostom copied from Origen.

cdxciii John Chrysostom, *In Matthaeum*, PG.57.313.5-10.

cdxciv The turn 'parental tender love (φιλοστοργία) for children' was abundantly used by John Chrysostom, Cyril of Alexandria, and moderately by Theodoret. All of this usage was but Origen's influence, who had received this from Philo, *De Specialibus Legibus*, 2.240: γονεῖς παῖδας ὑπερβαλλούσῃ χρώμενοι φιλοστοργίᾳ περιέπουσι καὶ πάντοθεν ἐκπορίζοντες αὐτοῖς τἀγαθὰ χαρίζονται μηδένα πόνον ἢ κίνδυνον ὑπερτιθέμενοι. Besides, this was used by Libanius (c. 314-392 or 393), who also could have been a source for his younger contemporary John Chrysostom (c. 349-407). Libanius, *Declamationes*, 40.2.1: πατέρες μὲν ὑμεῖς καὶ τὴν περὶ τοὺς παῖδας φιλοστοργίαν οὐκ ἀγνοεῖτε. *Op. cit.* 40.2.25: καὶ τοῦ πατρὸς περὶ τοὺς παῖδας φιλοστοργότερον καταιδέσαι δυνήσομαι. *Op. cit.* 40.2.28: πατέρες τέ εἰσι καὶ τὴν ἐντεῦθεν περὶ τοὺς παῖδας φιλοστοργίαν οὐκ ἀγνοοῦσι. *Op. cit.* 40.2.78: μὴ γίνου πατρὸς πρὸς τοὺς παῖδας φιλοστοργότερος. Cf. John Chrysostom, *De Lazaro*, PG.48.1023.12-14; *De Paenitentia*, PG.49.320.10-11; *et passim* (more than two dozens of points). Cyril of Alexandria, *commProphXII*, v. 1, p. 34; *frHeb*, p. 412; *Epistulae Paschales*, PG.77: 492.22; 832.43. Theodoret, *Quaestiones in Libros Regnorum et Paralipomenon*, PG.80.669.22-23; *Interpretatio in Psalmos*, PG.80.1689.29-30; *Interpretatio in Jeremiam*, PG.81.524.26; *In Epistulas Sancti Pauli*, PG.82.832.25-26.

cdxcv John Chrysostom, *In Matthaeum*, PG.57.313.19-20: Ἂν οὕτως αἰτῶμεν, ληψόμεθα.

cdxcvi Cf. Origen, *commMatt*, 12.33: πᾶσα δὲ λογικὴ ψυχὴ ἤτοι ζῶντι τρέφεται ἄρτῳ ἢ νεκρῷ, δι᾽ ὧν παραδέχεται ‹ἔργων ἢ› δογμάτων ἀστείων ἢ φαύλων. *excPs*, PG.17.145.1-7 & *frPs*, on Psalm 77:19-25: Περὶ ἧς τροφῆς καὶ σὺ ἐδιδάχθης εὔχεσθαι. Ἐὰν νοῇς τὸν ἐπιούσιον ἄρτον, τὸν μὴ ἐκχωροῦντα, τὸν μὴ ὑποκρινόμενον, τὸν ἀναδιδόμενον εἰς τὴν οὐσίαν τῆς ψυχῆς, ὅταν διαλαμβάνω περὶ Θεοῦ, περὶ τῆς θεότητος αὐτοῦ, περὶ τῆς ἐν ἀνθρωπίνῳ σώματι καὶ ψυχῇ αὐτοῦ ἐνοικήσεως, ἄρτον ἀγγέλων ἐσθίω, τὸ μάννα.

cdxcvii The turn πῶς βιωτέον ('how one ought to live') introducing considerations of what conduct of life should be, seems a simple one on the face of it. However, there only three authors ever to use this: Plato, Aristotle, and Origen. Plato, *Gorgias*, 492d: ἵνα τῷ ὄντι κατάδηλον γένηται πῶς βιωτέον. Aristotle, *Ethica Nicomachea*, 1162a29-31: τὸ δὲ πῶς βιωτέον ἀνδρὶ πρὸς γυναῖκα καὶ ὅλως φίλῳ πρὸς φίλον, οὐδὲν ἕτερον φαίνεται ζητεῖσθαι ἢ πῶς δίκαιον. Marcellus had accused Origen of using a phrase (in the opening of *De Principiis*) that rang a Platonic bell and that it had been taken up from *Gorgias*. Eusebius, *Contra Marcellum*, 1.4.25-26 (quoting from Marcellus): γέγραφεν γὰρ ἀρχόμενος οὕτως. *οἱ πεπιστευκότες καὶ πεπεισμένοι*, τοῦτο ‹τὸ› ῥητὸν οὕτως εἰρημένον εὕροις ἂν ἐν τῷ Γοργίᾳ Πλάτωνος. To this Eusebius' retort was, 'so what?'; indeed 'what has possibly Origen's *De Principiis* to do with Plato?' (ποία γὰρ πρὸς ταῦτα κοινωνία γένοιτ᾽ ἄν ποτε Πλάτωνι;), given that 'Origen propounded doctrines that were entirely different from those of Plato's'? *Op. cit.* 1.4.16-27.

cdxcviii Psalm 73:13-14. Origen, *commMatt*, fr. 140 (Klostermann).

cdxcix Origen, *schLuc*, PG.17.353.56-356.12.

d An expression which two authors took up. Theodoret (comm. on Phil. 1:8), *In Epistulas Sancti Pauli*, PG.82.561.32-34: *Σπλάγχνα* γὰρ *Ἰησοῦ Χριστοῦ* τὴν πνευματικὴν φιλοστοργίαν ἐκάλεσε. John Chrysostom, *Catecheses ad Illuminandos*, 4.4: διὰ τῆς παραινέσεως τῆς πνευματικῆς τὴν περὶ αὐτοὺς φιλοστοργίαν ἐπιδειξώμεθα.

di John Chrysostom, *In Matthaeum*, PG.57.313.33-37.

dii This is an enhanced rendering of Origen's words, which adds to Klostermann's fr. 141.

diii Origen, *commMatt*, fr. 141 (Klostermann); continued *infra*.

div Origen, *schMatt*, PG.17.292.36-39.

dv Jerome, *commMatt*, 7.11.

dvi The turn αὐτοπροαίρετος κακία ('self-chosen wickedness') was introduced by Origen and only a few authors seized on this. Eusebius, *HE*, 1.2.19: τά τε λογικὰ καὶ ἥμερα τῆς ἀνθρώπων ψυχῆς σπέρματα αὐτοπροαιρέτου κακίας ὑπερβολῇ διαφθείροντες. *Demonstratio Evangelica*, 9.4.3: οὔτε γὰρ ἐπισχεῖν τὸν Ἡρώδην τῆς αὐτοπροαιρέτου κακίας προσῆκον ἦν. Hierocles of Alexandria, *In Aureum Carmen*, 24.21: ὅτι πρὸς αὐτοπροαίρετον κακίαν εἱλκύσθησαν (cf. *op. cit.* 11.9: κατὰ τὸ αὐτοπροαίρετον ἡμῖν τὸν βίον διατίθεσθαι πάντα). Nicephorus Callistus Xanthopulus, *HE*, 1.3: κακίαν δὲ πᾶσαν ἐξ αὐτοπροαιρέτου γνώμης ἀναπλαττόμενοι. Cf. Origen, *exhMar*, 22: ὁ αὐτοπροαιρέτως τὸν θάνατον ὑπὲρ εὐσεβείας ἀναδεξάμενος. It appears that it was Origen who coined the term αὐτοπροαίρετος itself. As it happened, it was not only his followers or admirerst hat took notice of this (Gregory of Nyssa, Eusebius, Cassian the Sabaite [Pseudo-Didymus], *De Trinitate*, 6.3,2; PG.39.905.18; John Chrysostom, Theodore of Mopsuestia, Cyril of Alexandria, Cyril of Jerusalem), but also his detractor Epiphanius of Salamis (*Panarion*, v. 2, p. 444).

dvii Origen, *schMatt*, PG.17.292.39-49.

dviii Origen, *commMatt*, fr. 141 (Klostermann). See the same text in Origen, *schMatt*, PG.17.292.36-49. Once again, egregious copying from Origen without mentioning his name by Cyril of Alexandria is all too evident.

dix Cyril of Alexandria, *frMatt*, fr. 86.

dx Origen, *commMatt*, fr. 146 (Klostermann).

dxi Origen, *commMatt*, fr. 148 (Klostermann).

dxii Origen, part of fr. 150 (Klostermann). See the rest of this *infra*.

dxiii 1 Cor. 12:3. Jerome, *commMatt*, 7.21.

dxiv This is the last part of Origen, *commMatt*, fr. 149 (Klostermann); see also *infra*.

dxv Theodore of Heraclea or Theodore of Mopsuestia (J. Reuss), *frMatt*, fr. 25.

dxvi John Chrysostom, *In Matthaeum*, PG.57.321.8-10.

dxvii This is the first part of Origen, *commMatt*, fr. 149 (Klostermann).

dxviii Origen, part of *commMatt*, fr. 150 (Klostermann). See the first part of this *supra*. Cf. Origen, *commJohn*, XXVIII.13.98-100: Οὐχὶ εἴ τις προφητεύει, προφήτης ἐστὶν ἐκεῖνος. Ὁ γοῦν Καϊάφας, ἀρχιερεὺς ὢν τοῦ ἐνιαυτοῦ ἐκείνου, προεφήτευσεν μὲν ὅτι ἔμελλεν Ἰησοῦς ἀποθνήσκειν ὑπὲρ τοῦ ἔθνους, καὶ οὐχ ὑπὲρ τοῦ ἔθνους μόνον, ἀλλ' ἵνα καὶ τὰ τέκνα τοῦ θεοῦ τὰ διεσκορπισμένα συναγάγῃ εἰς ἕν, οὐ μὴν καὶ προφήτης ἦν. Εἰ δὲ καὶ Βαλαὰμ προεφήτευσεν τὰ ἐν τοῖς Ἀριθμοῖς ἀναγεγραμμένα φάσκων. *Τὸ ῥῆμα ὃ ἐὰν ἐμβάλῃ ὁ θεὸς εἰς τὸ στόμα μου, τοῦτο λαλήσω*, καὶ εἰπὼν τὰ ἀπὸ τοῦ *Ἐκ Μεσοποταμίας μετεπέμψατό με* καὶ τὰ ἑξῆς, σαφὲς ὅτι προφήτης οὐκ ἦν· μάντις γὰρ εἶναι ἀναγέγραπται. Εἴ τις μὲν οὖν προφήτης ἐστίν, πάντως προφητεύει· εἰ δέ τις προφητεύει, οὐ πάντως ἐστὶν προφήτης.

dxix Jerome, *commMatt*, 7:22-23. Baside the present codex text, Jerome's analysis about 'false-prophets' (such as Caiaphas, Saul, Balaam, Judas) is but Origen's ones, as in *commJohn*, XXVIII: 13.98-106; 15.129; 17.140-145; 20.175-177; *frJohn*, fr. 85; *commGen*, PG.12.60 (& *Philocalia*, 23.5).

dxx Photius, *frMatt*, fr. 33.

dxxi Photius, *op. cit.* fr. 34.

dxxii See *infra*, folio 194r: Θέρος γάρ ἐστι πνευματικὸν ὁ μέλλων αἰὼν διὰ τὴν γαλήνην τὴν μετὰ τὸν νῦν αἰῶνα, ὅς ἐστι χειμών.

dxxiii Origen, *commMatt*, fr. 152 (Klostermann).

dxxiv Cf. Origen, *commMatt*, 11.5: ὁ τῶν πειρασμῶν καὶ περιστάσεων ἀγών. *frPs*, on Psalm 118:50: τὸν καιρὸν τῶν περιστάσεων καὶ τῶν πειρασμῶν. *Op. cit.* on Psalm 118:71: Εὐαρεστούμενος τοῖς ἐπιπόνοις πειρασμοῖς καὶ περιστάσεσιν. *selPs*, PG.12.1672.42-43: Καὶ ἐν περιστάσεσι καὶ πειρασμοῖς ὧν εὐλογήσω σε.

dxxv Origen, *commMatt*, fr. 151 (Klostermann). Cf. Hermas, *Pastor*, 52.2.

dxxvi Jerome, *commMatt*, 7.25.

dxxvii Klostermann notes that he found this as 'unattributed' in only one codex (note to fr. 151, p. 75). However, this is now attributed to Origen, and anyway there is no parallel to it in any other author.

dxxviii Theodore of Mopsuestia, *frMatt*, fr. 39.

dxxix John Chrysostom, *In Matthaeum*, PG.57.325.33-46.

dxxx John Chrysostom, *op. cit.* PG.326.59-327.2.

dxxxi The phrase τὸ ἐνδεὲς τοῦ νόμου is a unique structure which no author other than Origen did ever use.

dxxxii Origen, *commMatt*, 14.14.

dxxxiii Theodore of Heraclea, *frMatt*, fr. 53.

dxxxiv The expression μάχης εἰρημένον (in effect, meaning 'incongruous statements') referring to two or more accounts or events mutually conflicting either logically or factually or otherwise, is an illuminating one, especially because its usage has always remained scarce. Origen bequeathed this to his usual followers and admirers, but this was one more turn of phrase that he himself had taken up from Galen. Cf. Galen, *In Hippocratis De Natura Hominis*, p. 168: ὥσπερ γὰρ ἐξ ὕπνου βαθέος ἐγερθέντες ᾔσθοντο τῆς πρὸς Ἱπποκράτην μάχης τοῦ κατὰ τὴν προκειμένην ῥῆσιν εἰρημένου. Basil of Caesarea, *Adversus Eunomium*, PG.29.512.13-15 (on the logical inconsistencies of Eunomius): Περὶ μὲν οὖν τῆς ἐν οἷς εἶπεν ἐναντιότητος καὶ τῆς ἀναισχύντου μάχης τῶν εἰρημένων πρὸς ἄλληλα μικρὸν ὕστερον ἐροῦμεν. John Chrysostom, *In Matthaeum*, PG.57.352.55-57 (on apparently conflicting reports by the evangelists): εἰ δέ, ὁ μὲν περὶ τοῦ ἑνός, ὁ δὲ περὶ τῶν δύο διελέχθη, οὐ μάχης τὸ εἰρημένον, ἀλλὰ διαφόρου διηγήσεως. Cyril of Alexandria, *frMatt*, fr. 228 (on apparently conflicting reports by the evangelists): ὅτι δὲ ὁ μὲν Ματθαῖος *ὄνον καὶ πῶλον* ἀγηοχέναι τῷ κυρίῳ λέγει, Λουκᾶς δὲ καὶ Μᾶρκος ἑνὸς μόνου ὑποζυγίου ἀπεμνημόνευσαν, οὐ μάχης τὸ εἰρημένον. *Catena in Marcum*, p. 315 (unattributed): τοῦτο δὲ οὐ διαφωνίαν ἐμφαίνει. ... εἰ μὲν δὲ οἱ μὲν περὶ τοῦ ἑνός, ὁ δὲ περὶ τῶν δύο διελέχθη, οὐ μάχης τὸ εἰρημένον.

dxxxv Photius, *frMatt*, fr. 35.

dxxxvi Cyril of Alexandria, *frMatt*, fr. 92.

dxxxvii Origen, *Cels*, I.48.

dxxxviii John Chrysostom, *In Matthaeum*, PG.57.329.13-21. The ensuing identical portions vividly and palpably demonstrate Chrysostom's method upon copying from Origen: the text which runs parallel to this codex that I am quoting belongs to adjacent points of Chrysostom's text, but he does not follow the exact sequence of Origen's one: as already pointed out, he seized on passages from Origen *literatim*, while at the same time adding his own elaborating remarks.

dxxxix John Chrysostom, *op. cit.* PG.57.328.19-22.

dxl The expression Ἐὰν θέλῃς δύνασαί με καθαρίσαι is the same in both Matt. 8:2 and Mark, 1:40.

dxli John Chrysostom, *op. cit.* PG.57.328.53-55.

dxlii John Chrysostom, *op. cit.* PG.57.328.29-35.

dxliii Φεύγων δὲ τὸ φιλόκομπον. Cf. endnote cclii. Origen, *commMatt*, fr. 187 III (Klostermann): Φεύγων δὲ τὸ φιλόκομπον ἄγει αὐτοὺς *εἰς τὴν οἰκίαν*.

dxliv In reference to this event, Origen uses the phrase μηδενὶ εἰπεῖν of Luke, 5:14, which is expanded to μηδενὶ εἰπεῖν τὸ γεγονὸς in the instance of Luke, 8:56.

dxlv John Chrysostom, *In Matthaeum*, PG.57.329.43-44.

dxlvi John Chrysostom, *op. cit.* PG.57.330.33-37.

dxlvii John Chrysostom, *op. cit.* PG.57.330.15-30.

dxlviii Cf. Origen, *commMatt*, 11.8: Πλὴν πάνυ φαίνονται *φιλεγκλήμονες* οἱ περὶ μὲν ἐντολῆς θεοῦ μηδὲν ἔχοντες ἐγκαλεῖν τοῖς Ἰησοῦ μαθηταῖς, μόνον δὲ περὶ πρεσβυτέρων παραδόσεως μιᾶς. Καὶ μάλιστα ἐμφαίνεται οὕτως τὸ *φιλέγκλημον*, ὅτι παρ' αὐτοῖς τοῖς ἰαθεῖσιν ἀπὸ τοῦ κακῶς ἔχειν προσάγουσι τὸ ἔγκλημα (italics are mine). The term φιλεγκλήμων ('litigious', 'querulous', 'one who is obsessively a detractor') was first used by Polybius (*Historiae*, 12.4.6), whom Origen certainly had read (see *Scholia*, pp. 270; 322-323); then, by Philo (*De Sacrificiis Abelis et Caini*, 32; *De Agricultura*, 64) and by Galen, who was a favourite inexhaustible source for Origen to draw on, as I have shown at many points of my works (Galen, *De Simplicium Medicamentorum Temperamentis ac Facultatibus*, p. 222; *De Compositione Medicamentorum Per Genera*, p. 485; *In Platonis Timaeum Commentarii Fragmenta*, 11). Also, Clement of Alexandria, *Paedagogus*, 1.6.25.1; *Stromateis*, 1.2.19.1; 1.20.99.1, and Eusebius, *Praeparatio Evangelica*, 4.6.1; 14.27.13. But then (as it happened with numerous similar cases, such as the term φιλόκομπος, above and below), Cyril of Alexandria came up with using this term profusely (*In Joannem*, v. 1, pp. 175; 277; 311; v. 2, pp. 38; 169; *Epistulae Paschales*, 13.1; *et passim*, at no less than sixteen points). Anyway, the word was rather rare (which is why this is absent from the vocabulary of conspicuous authors, such as the Cappadocians, and of other ones until John of Damascus), although the grammarian Julius Naucratites (or, Pollux) included this in his *Onomasticon* (3.139; 6.166) and occasional (indeed extremely scarce) usage in philosophical locution is there, too (Syrianus, *commMetaph*, p. 81; John Philoponus, *commAnim*, p. 446). In the present volume, comparative study evinces every now and then Cyril of Alexandria's practice of drawing on Origen without mentioning him, which is what he always did. As explained in the Introduction, presumably this had to do with the quarrel of his predecessor and uncle Theophilus with a band of Egyptian monks, concerning the anthropomorphism attributed to Cod.

dxlix Jerome, *commMatt*, 8.4.

dl Quite evidently, Chrysostom followed Origen on this, too. Here is a note that the catenist added in the *Catena in Lucam*, p. 51: Λέγει δὲ ὁ Χρυσόστομος εἰς τὸ κατὰ Ματθαῖον, ἑρμηνεύων τὰ περὶ τοῦ ἑκατοντάρχου, τὸν αὐτὸν εἶναι τὸν εἰς τὸν Λουκᾶν, τὸν δὲ εἰς τὸν Ἰωάννην ἕτερον.

dli The expression γενηθήτω σοι ὡς θέλεις, which Origen uses at this point, is from the instance of Matt. 15:28.

dlii Origen, *commMatt*, fr. 154 (Klosterman). As if the catenist wanted to take distances from Origen, he added that 'these are written by one who normally opposes the holy fathers': ταῦτα ὁ συνήθως τοῖς ἁγίοις πατράσιν ἐναντιούμενος, τοῖς δὲ ἐντυγχάνουσι συνιδεῖν καταλιμπάνω τῶν ἐξηγήσεων τὸ διάφορον, καὶ τίς ὁ μᾶλλον ἐφικνούμενος τῆς εὐαγγελικῆς καὶ ἀληθοῦς διανοίας. Kostermann came upon this remark in a catena-fragment attributed to Theodore of Mopsuestia (fr. 41a, J. Reuss), but he found the main text of the fragment ascribed to Origen also in the *Codex Vindobonensis 154* (tenth century).

dliii Theodore of Mopsuestia, *frMatt*, fr. 41a.

dliv Gregory of Nyssa took up expressions such as θεοπρεπὴς ἔννοια, θεοπρεπῶς νοεῖν, and similar ones, from his hero Origen who had advised that scriptural words should be understood in 'a manner befitting God'. So did his other admirers, namely, Eusebius and Basil of Caesarea. Cf. Gregory of Nyssa, *Contra Eunomium*, 2.1.234; 3.1.54; *De Vita Mosis*, 2.91; *Oratio Catechetica*, 9; *Ad Eustathium De Sancta Trinitate*, p. 8; *Adversus Macedonianos De Spiritu Sancto*, p. 92; *Ad Theophilum Adversus Apollinaristas*, p. 125; *De Perfectione Christiana ad Olympium Monachum*, p. 182; *In Ecclesiasten*, p. 391. Eusebius, *Contra Marcellum*, 1.1.18. Basil of Caesarea, *Adversus Eunomium*, PG.29.625.28; *Epistulae*, epistle 189.5. Then, John Chrysostom, *In illud: Filius ex Se nihil facit*, PG.56.256.29-30; *Expositiones in Psalmos*, PG.55: 97.51; 121.8; 220.43; 276.17; 418.61. Pseudo-John Chrysostom, *De Sancta Trinitate*, PG.48.1091.68. Macarius of Magnesia, *Apocriticus*, book 4, p. 188. Cyril of Alexandria, *In Joannem*, v. 1, p. 13. Nilus of Ancyra, *Commentarii in Canticum Canticorum*, 33. Photius, *Bibliotheca*, Codex 170, p. 117b; *Epistulae et Amphilochia*, epistles 180; 192; *Fragmenta in Epistulam ad Romanos*, p. 479. Symeon the New Theologian, *Orationes Theologicae*, oration 3, line 115; *Orationes Ethicae*, oration 1.6, lines 22 & 158; oration 13.1, line 53; *Catecheses*, oration 28, line 95; oration 33, lines 148 & 151. Gennadius Scholarius, *De Spiritu Sancto i*, Part 3, p. 102; Part 6, p. 245; *Tractatus Contra Fautores Acindyni ad Joannem Basilicum De Verbis Theodori Grapti Interrogantem*, p. 210; *De Unica Via ad Salutem Hominum*, 13. Analecta Hymnica Graeca, *Canones Januarii*, 27.34.3. Cf. Origen, *commJohn*, VI.4.19: ἐπεὶ ὁ ἑωρακὼς τὸν υἱὸν ἑώρακε τὸν πατέρα, ἀναγεγραμμένοι εἰσί, θεὸν νενοηκότες καὶ θεοῦ λόγων θεοπρεπῶς ἀκηκοότες. *deOr*, 2.1: ἓν τῶν ἀδυνάτων ὅσον ἐπὶ τῇ ἀσθενείᾳ ἡμῶν πείθομαι τυγχάνειν τρανῶσαι τὸν περὶ τῆς εὐχῆς ἀκριβῶς καὶ θεοπρεπῶς πάντα λόγον. *excPs*, PG.17.108.18-19: Ὅσα σωματικῶς ἀσωμάτου τυγχάνοντος λέγοιτο περὶ τοῦ Θεοῦ, θεοπρεπῶς ἀκουστέον.

dlv Origen, *commMatt*, fr. 156 (Klostermann).

dlvi Jerome, *commMatt*, 8.10.

dlvii Origen, *commMatt*, fr. 155 (Klostermann), col. 1.

dlviii Origen, *loc. cit.* col. 2.

dlix Origen, *commMatt*, fr. 157 (Klostermann).

dlx Jerome, *commMatt*, 8.12.

dlxi Cyril of Alexandria, *frMatt*, fr. 95 (on Matt. 8:16). Cf. John, 19:39: "Nicodemus, who at first came to Jesus by night, also came bringing a mixture of myrrh and aloes, about a hundred Roman pounds." He came by night because he was as feeble as to be afraid of the Jews. Once again, this is a point revealing how Christian 'literature' was composed and authorship of texts identified after the condemnation of Origen. At this point, the passage, Διατί δὲ ἡμέρας οὐ προσήνεγκαν, ... ἢ διὰ τὸ μὴ ἔχειν τοὺς ἀσθενοῦντας τινὰς προσαγαγεῖν αὐτοὺς τῷ Ἰησοῦ is an integral part of Origen's commentary. However, the anonymous catenist was quick to attribute this to Cyril of Alexandria as an isolated 'passage' and out of any context whatsoever.

As it happened with numerous ideas and terms of Origen, Cyril of Alexandria took up also this idea of Nicodemus' 'weakness' (*In Joannem*, v. 1, p. 216), which anyway no other theologian other than Chrysostom did ever care to comment upon.

However, there is more to it. Another catenist decided to make mention of Nicodemus' 'weakness' (due to which he 'came to Jesus by night'), and wrote a section entitled 'On Nicodemus' (Περὶ Νικοδήμου) attributing this to Cyril of Alexandria. However, this time the text belonged to John Chrysostom. See John Chrysostom, *In Joannem*, PG.59.144.29-42. Καὶ μετὰ τὸν σταυρὸν δὲ πολλὴν τὴν ἐπιμέλειαν τῆς ταφῆς τοῦ Δεσποτικοῦ σώματος πεποίηται. *Ἦλθε* γάρ, φησί, *καὶ Νικόδημος ὁ ἐλθὼν πρὸς τὸν Κύριον νυκτός, φέρων μίγμα μύρου καὶ ἀλόης ὡς λίτρας ἑκατόν* [John, 19:39]. Καὶ νῦν δὲ διέκειτο μὲν περὶ τὸν Χριστόν, οὐχ ὡς ἐχρῆν δέ, οὔτε μετὰ διανοίας τῆς προσηκούσης, ἀλλ' ἔτι ὑπὸ τῆς Ἰουδαϊκῆς κατείχετο ἀσθενείας. Διὰ τοῦτο καὶ νυκτὸς ἦλθε, δεδοικὼς ἐν ἡμέρᾳ τοῦτο ποιῆσαι. Ἀλλ' ὁ φιλάνθρωπος Θεὸς οὐδὲ οὕτως αὐτὸν ἀπώσατο, οὐδὲ διήλεγξεν, οὐδὲ τῆς αὐτοῦ διδασκαλίας ἀπεστέρησεν, ἀλλὰ καὶ μετὰ πολλῆς αὐτῷ τῆς ἐπιεικείας διαλέγεται, καὶ δόγματα αὐτῷ παρανοίγει τὰ σφόδρα ὑψηλά, αἰνιγματωδῶς μέν, παρανοίγει δὲ ὅμως. Likewise, in *op. cit.* PG.59.149.4-13. Cf. *De Consubstantiali* (*Contra Anomoeos, homilia 7*), PG.48.760.31-42. Now, the same text of Chrysostom (slightly yet insignificantly paraphrased at a couple of points) was attributed to Cyril. *Catena in Joannem*, p. 202: καὶ μετὰ τὸν σταυρὸν δὲ πολλὴν τὴν ἐπιμέλειαν τῆς τοῦ δεσποτικοῦ σώματος φαίνεται κηδείαν ποιούμενος. Διέκειτο μὲν οὖν περὶ τὸν Χριστόν, ἀλλ' οὐχ ὡς ἐχρῆν. ἔτι γὰρ τῆς Ἰουδαϊκῆς εἴχετο ἀσθενείας. διὰ τοῦτο καὶ νυκτὸς ἦλθε δεδοικὼς ἐν ἡμέρᾳ τοῦτο ποιῆσαι. Ἀλλ' ὁ φιλάνθρωπος Χριστὸς οὐδὲ οὕτως αὐτὸν ἀπώσατο, οὐδὲ εἰπόντι ὅτι ἀπὸ Θεοῦ ἐλήλυθε διδάσκαλος, διήλεγξεν αὐτὸν λέγων, τί οὖν νύκτωρ ἔρχῃ πρὸς τὸν τὰ τοῦ Θεοῦ λέγοντα, καὶ ἐκεῖθεν ἥκοντα;

This is one more characteristic case of catenists feeling 'safe' by ascribing texts of Origen to stars of Christian orthodoxy. However, it turns out that catenists did not manage always to be consistent in making their false attributions to authors who plundered Origen's texts while anxiously suppressing of his name.

dlxii Cyril of Alexandria, *frMatt*, fr. 96.

dlxiii Origen, *commMatt*, fr. 159 (Klostermann).

dlxiv Cyril of Alexandria, *frMatt*, fr. 97.

dlxv Cf. Origen, *commMatt*, 10.14: Οὕτως δέ τις διηγήσεται καὶ τὸ *οὐαὶ ὑμῖν, γραμματεῖς καὶ Φαρισαῖοι ὑποκριταί*, ὡς παντὶ εἰρημένον τῷ πλὴν τοῦ γράμματος μηδὲν ἐπισταμένῳ. Ἔνθα ζητήσεις εἰ ὥσπερ νομικὸς γραμματεὺς οὕτως ἐστὶ καὶ εὐαγγελικός.

dlxvi John Chrysostom, *In Matthaeum*, PG.57.346.49-347.3.

dlxvii John Chrysostom, *apud Catena in Matthaeum*, p. 62.

dlxviii Jerome, *commMatt*, 8:19-20.

dlxix Cf. Origen, *frLuc*, fr. 154: *πονηροὶ δὲ καὶ γόητες*, ἀλώπεξι καὶ πετεινοῖς οὐρανοῦ παραβαλλόμενοι ἐν τῷ βίῳ τούτῳ, *προκόψουσι πλανῶντες καὶ πλανώμενοι*. μάλιστα δὲ ἁρμόζει πρὸς τὸ *ὁ υἱὸς τοῦ ἀνθρώπου οὐκ ἔχει ποῦ τὴν κεφαλὴν κλῖναι* τὸ ἀστατοῦμεν ὑπὸ Παύλου, ἐν ᾧ Χριστὸς ἐλάλει, ῥηθέν. *Op. cit.* 155: Ὁ δὲ λέγει, τοιοῦτόν ἐστιν. εἰ μὴ τῶν πετεινῶν καὶ θηρίων ἤτοι τῶν δαιμόνων σαυτὸν ἀπαλλάξεις, οὐ δύναμαι ἐν σοὶ καταλῦσαι οὔτε σὺ τοιοῦτος ὢν δύνασαι τὸ ἀποστολικὸν ἀξίωμα λαβεῖν. *schLuc*, PG.17.349.37-41: Οἱ γὰρ ἐμοὶ μαθηταί, δικαιοσύνην ἀσκοῦντες, *ἐν τῷ κόσμῳ* τούτῳ *θλῖψιν* ἕξουσι. *πονηροὶ δὲ καὶ γόητες*, ἀλώπεξι καὶ πετεινοῖς οὐρανοῦ παραβαλλόμενοι, ἐν τῷ βίῳ τούτῳ *προκόψουσι πλανῶντες καὶ πλανώμενοι*. *expProv*, PG.17.216.9-12: Ἡ συναγωγὴ τῶν γιγάντων [Prov. 21:16] ἡ κακία καὶ ἡ ἀγνωσία ἐστίν. Γίγαντες δὲ οἱ δαίμονες. Τουτέστιν ἐν μεγάλαις ἁμαρτίαις ἀναπαύσεται ὁ πλανώμενος ἐξ ὁδοῦ δικαιοσύνης.

dlxx Origen, *commMatt*, fr. 160 (Klostermann).

dlxxi Origen, *schLuc*, PG.17.349.33-41. Likewise, *frLuc*, fr. 154.

dlxxii John Chrysostom, *In Matthaeum*, PG.57.347.48-348.2.

dlxxiii Loyalty to God should take precedence over loyalty to parents. This was an old Pythagorean thesis embraced by Christians, too. Diogenes Laertius, *Vitae*, 8.23 (so *Suda*, letter pi, entry 3124): καὶ θεοὺς μὲν δαιμόνων προτιμᾶν, ἥρωας δ᾽ ἀνθρώπων, ἀνθρώπων δὲ μάλιστα γονέας. So Menander, *Sententiae*, 1, lines 229-230: Θεὸν προτίμα, δεύτερον τοὺς σοὺς γονεῖς. Clement of Alexandria, *Stromateis*, 6.12.100.2-3: ὁ γνωστικὸς ... οὐ τὸ ζῆν, ἀλλὰ τὸ εὖ ζῆν περὶ πλείστου ποιήσεται, μήτ᾽ οὖν παῖδας μήτ᾽ αὖ γάμον ἢ τοὺς γονεῖς τῆς πρὸς τὸν θεὸν ἀγάπης καὶ τῆς ἐν βίῳ δικαιοσύνης προτιμῶν. Didymus, *Commentarii in Psalmos 22-26.10*, cod. p. 112: προκριτέα ἐστὶν πάντων ἡ τοῦ θεοῦ ἀγάπη. ἐὰν ἀνθέλκῃ γονεὺς ἢ γῆρας γονέως, προτίμησον τὸν θεόν. Cyril of Alexandria, *frMatt*, fr. 183: καὶ δεῖ μὲν τὸν θεὸν προτιμᾶσθαι τῶν γονέων, χρῆναι δὲ ‹λέγω› καὶ τὴν εἰς γονέας τιμὴν φυλάττεσθαι ἀπαιτεῖν. Symeon the New Theologian, *Capita Theologica*, 1.12: Οἱ τοὺς ἑαυτῶν γονεῖς ἔν τινι προτιμῶντες τῆς τοῦ Θεοῦ ἐντολῆς πίστιν οὐ κέκτηνται πρὸς Χριστόν. Also *infra*, note cmxxi.

dlxxiv Origen took up the expression 'mortifying sin' (νεκροῦσα ἡ ἁμαρτία) from the man who probably played a critical part in his conversion to Christianity, namely, Hippolytus, the first and only other author who used this pithy turn of phrase. Hippolytus, *Fragmenta in Proverbia*, fr. 47: διὰ τούτων τῶν πράξεων νεκροῦσα ἡ ἁμαρτία τὸν ἄνθρωπον.

dlxxv Origen, *commMatt*, fr. 161 (Klostermann).

dlxxvi Origen, *frLuc*, fr. 156.

dlxxvii Origen, *commMatt*, fr. 162 (Klostermann), col. 2; see col. 1, which is similar to Origen, *apud Catena in Matthaeum*, p. 63: (Ὠριγένους.) Οἱ νεκροὶ εἰώθασι *θάπτειν τοὺς ἑαυτῶν νεκρούς*. ψυχὴ ἐν κακίᾳ οὖσα νεκρά ἐστιν. ὁ αἰσθητὸς δὲ θάνατος διὰ τὴν ἁμαρτίαν. καλῶς οὖν *ἡ ἁμαρτία θάνατος* λέγεται, καὶ ὁ ἐν αὐτῇ ὢν νεκρός ἐστιν.

dlxxviii See this *infra*, f. 63v: ὅτι τὸν φόβον οὐχ ἡ τῶν πειρασμῶν ἐργάζεται ἐπαγωγὴ ἀλλὰ τὸ τῆς διανοίας ἀσθενές.

dlxxix Origen, *apud Catena in Matthaeum*, p. 63.

dlxxx John Chrysostom, *In Matthaeum*, PG.57.350.48-51. The same, in the *Catena in Marcum*, p. 31: τοὺς μὲν οὖν μαθητὰς μεθ᾽ ἑαυτοῦ ἔλαβεν, τοὺς ὄχλους ἀφείς, ἤγουν προπέμψας. παρέλαβε δὲ οὐ μάτην οὐδὲ εἰκῇ, ἀλλ᾽ ὥστε ποιῆσαι θεατὰς τοῦ μέλλοντος ἔσεσθαι θαύματος καὶ ἵνα μὴ μέγα φρονῶσιν, ὅτι τοὺς ἄλλους πέμψας, αὐτοὺς κατέσχεν, ἀφίησι κλυδωνισθῆναι. τοῦτό τε κατορθῶν καὶ πειρασμοὺς φέρειν γενναίως.

dlxxxi Cf. Origen, *commMatt*, 16.4: δεδόσθω δὲ ὅτι καὶ οἱ δύο ἀπόστολοι, ὡς ἄνθρωποι ἔτι ἀτελεῖς καὶ μηδὲν νοοῦντες βαθύτερον περὶ τῆς βασιλείας Χριστοῦ, τοιαῦτα ὑπελάμβανον περὶ τῶν συγκαθεζομένων τῷ Ἰησοῦ.

dlxxxii Cyril of Alexandria, *frMatt*, fr. 99.

dlxxxiii See this *supra*, (quoted in folio 63r) Origen, *apud Catena in Matthaeum*, p. 63: ὅτι τὸν φόβον οὐχ ἡ τῶν πειρασμῶν ἐργάζεται ἐπαγωγὴ ἀλλὰ τὸ τῆς διανοίας ἀσθενές.

dlxxxiv This is the first part of Origen, *commMatt*, fr. 164 (Klostermann). See *infra* the rest of this running parallel to the present text.

dlxxxv *Catena in Marcum*, pp. 314-315 (anonymous); the same in John Chrysostom, *homMatt*, PG.57.352.51-56.

dlxxxvi Cf. Gen. 10:15. Hippolytus, *Chronicon*, 122. Epiphanius of Salamis, *Ancoratus*, 114.6.

dlxxxvii Cf. Origen, *frJohn*, fr. 79: ἁμαρτωλοῖς γὰρ οἱ τάφοι οἰκίαι εἰσίν, ὅθεν καὶ οἱ δαιμονιζόμενοι ὡς ἐπὶ οἰκεῖον τόπον εἰς τὰ μνημεῖα καταφεύγουσιν. *frLuc*, fr. 124 & *schLuc*, PG.17.337.1-5 (on the same instance. i.e. Luke, 8:26-39): μή ποτε οὖν οἱ φιλήδονοι καὶ γαστρὶ καὶ τοῖς ὑπὸ γαστέρα φίλοι, ὅπου τὰ μνημεῖα καὶ πλησίον τοῦ λεγεῶνος τῶν δαιμόνων βόσκονται.

dlxxxviii Cf. Origen, *Cels*, VII.5.

dlxxxix Origen, *apud Catena in Matthaeum*, p. 63. See Origen's entire text in *op. cit.* pp. 63-64.

dxc See Introduction, pp. LXXX-LXXXII (Jerome's allegations).

dxci This is continuation of Origen, *commMatt*, fr. 164 (Klostermann).

dxcii *Catena in Marcum*, p. 316; but this is Origen's text itself.

dxciii Origen, *commMatt*, fr. 164 (Klostermann) carries on.

dxciv This is keeping up the text of *Catena in Marcum*, p. 316, quoted just above. The final part, ὡς οὖν καιρὸν ἔχοντες … καὶ τιμωρίαις ὑπάγοντος is the selfsame one as Klostermann's (fr. 164), which he found in two codices being attributed to Origen.

dxcv Cf. Origen, *Cels*, VIII.54 & 60 & 62; *exhMar*, 45: Ἐπεὶ δέ τινες μὴ θεωροῦντες τὸν περὶ τῶν δαιμόνων λόγον, καὶ ὡς ὑπὲρ τοῦ παραμένειν ἐν τῷ παχεῖ τούτῳ καὶ περιγείῳ ἀέρι δεόμενοι τροφῆς τῆς διὰ τῶν ἀναθυμιάσεων ἐπιτηροῦσιν ὅπῃ κνίσσα ἀεὶ καὶ αἵματα καὶ λιβανωτοί, ἐξευτελίζουσιν ὡς ἀδιάφορον τὸ θύειν. Cf. Pseudo-Basil of Caesarea (*forsan* Cassian the Sabaite), *Enarratio in Prophetam Isaiam*, 10.237: Τὰ γὰρ δαιμόνια τὰ προσδιατρίβοντα τῷ περιγείῳ τόπῳ σεισθήσεται φυγαδευόμενα καὶ εἰς τὸν οἰκεῖον τῆς ἀβύσσου ἀπελαθήσεται τόπον ἐν τῇ ἐπιδημίᾳ τοῦ Κυρίου.

dxcvi Origen, *commMatt*, fr. 166 (Klostermann).

dxcvii Cf. *Cels*, IV.65; VII.67; VIII.31.

dxcviii Origen, *apud Catena in Matthaeum*, p. 64.

dxcix Origen, *loc. cit.*

dc Origen, *commMatt*, fr. 168 (Klostermann).

dci Origen, *apud Catena in Matthaeum*, p. 64.

dcii Origen, *commMatt*, fr. 167 (Klostermann).

dciii The same, in Origen, *apud Catena in Matthaeum*, p. 65: (Ὠριγένους.) Ὡς ἀναίσθητοι τοῦτο εἶπον καὶ ἄγαν ἄπιστοι οἱ Γεργεσηνοί.

dciv Origen, *commMatt*, fr. 170 (Klostermann).

dcv Apollinaris, *apud frMatt*, fr. 39.

dcvi Origen, *commMatt*, fr. 171 (Klostermann). See also attributions of this to Theodore of Heraclea and Theodore of Mopsuestia and Apollinaris. *Catena in Matthaeum*, p. 65: (Θεοδώρου Ἡρακλείας.) Ὡς ἀναξίους ἑαυτοὺς κρίναντες τῆς τοῦ Κυρίου ἐπιδημίας, εἶπον τοῦτο οἱ Γεργεσηνοὶ τῷ Χριστῷ, ὡς καὶ ὁ Πέτρος ἐπὶ τῇ τῶν ἰχθύων ἄγρᾳ. (Θεοδώρου Μομψουεστίας.) Παρεκάλεσαν τοίνυν ἐφ' ἑτέρους μεταβῆναι τόπους, ὡς οὐκ ἄξιοι ὄντες τοσοῦτον ἀγαθὸν ἐπὶ τῆς οἰκείας ἔχειν χώρας, δείσαντες μήπου ἁμαρτημάτων ἕνεκεν. (Ἀπολιναρίου.) Ἐπειδὴ πόθον οὐκ εἶχον τοῦ ἀγαθοῦ, ἀλλ' ἀργῶς διέκειντο καὶ ὀκνηρῶς πρὸς τὴν τοῦ μεγάλου ἀγαθοῦ κατάληψιν.

dcvii Origen, *apud Catena in Matthaeum*, p. 65.

dcviii This is certainly not a reference to Origen; otherwise Jerome follows Origen's exegesis to the letter.

dcix Jerome, *commMatt*, 8.34.

dcx Cf. Origen, *commGen*, PG.12.60.37-39: Τί δὲ δεῖ λέγειν τὰς περὶ Χριστοῦ προφητείας, οἷον τόπον γενέσεως αὐτοῦ Βηθλεὲμ καὶ τόπον ἀνατροφῆς αὐτοῦ Ναζαρέτ;

dcxi John Chrysostom, *In Matthaeum*, PG.57.357.42-55.

dcxii This is Origen's characteristic style. Cf. *commJohn*, XXXII.22.291: ὁ μὲν οὖν περὶ τούτου ἀληθὴς λόγος παρὰ τοῖς ἐμοῦ εὑρεθείη ἂν πολλῷ σοφωτέροις. Origen, *apud Catena in Epistulam i ad Corinthios*, p. 57: ἐὰν ἄλλος τις ἔλθῃ ἐποικοδομούμενος, τιμιώτερος ἀργυρίου εὑρεθείη ἂν χρυσός.

dcxiii Origen, *commMatt*, fr. 172 (Klostermann).

dcxiv The expression παρὰ πόδας ἔλεγχος is an extremely rare colloquialism, which was used just a few times and only by higly educated intellectuals. This idiomatic turn παρὰ πόδας means 'immediately' or 'at hand'. Cf. Polybius (whose work Origen had read), *Historiae*, 1.7.5; 1.8.2; 1.35.3; 1.87.1-2; 2.60.6; 4.48.11; 5.13.3; 5.26.13-14; 5.38.4; 6.9.2-3; *et passim*, abunbdantly; also in OT, Esther, 8:12; 3 Macc. 4:8; 5:8. Besides, Philo, *De Confusione Linguarum*, 4. Galen, *De Placitis Hippocratis et Platonis*, 2.7.22; *De Differentia Pulsuum*, pp. 602; 607. Sextus Empiricus, *Adversus Musicos*, 6.26. Philostratus, *Vita Apollonii*, 1.6 (supposedly quoting from Aristotle, who used this expression also in the *Topica*, 164b19). Alexander of Aphrodisias, *commTop*, p. 590. Origen, *commJohn*, XX.30.273; *schMatt*, PG.17.300.56; *Cels*, II.23; II.70. Clement of Alexandria, *Paedagogus*, 1.6.30.1. Hippolytus, *Refutatio Omnium Haeresium*, 6.14.11.

Following this, παρὰ πόδας ἔλεγχος means one's ability to handle or control a certain situation immediately, or to check the validity of a certain proposition; anyway, this suggests one's unmitigated mastership over things either practical or intellectual. Once again, we are upon Origen having taken up an expression from Alexander of Aphrodisias, whereas I have shown in the past that Polybius and Lucian of Samosata served to Origen's own locution in terms of philology. During later Byzantine times, Photius took up not only Origen's expression but also the tenor of his specific comment of Matthew's passage, and naturally this was bequeathed to later Byzantine intellectuals, who presumably had no idea of Origen being the source of this. Cf. Lucian of Samosata, *Quomodo Historia Conscribenda Sit*, 13: τίς κομιδῇ ἀνόητος εἴη ὡς χαίρειν τὰ τοιαῦτα ἐπαινούμενος ὧν παρὰ πόδας οἱ ἔλεγχοι; Ptolemy, *Geographia*, 1.12.2: διὰ τὸ παρὰ πόδας εἶναι τὸν ἔλεγχον. Alexander of Aphrodisias, *De Fato*, p. 200: τοῦτό τοι καὶ οἵ μάντεις εἶναι λέγουσίν γε ὑφορώμενοι φεύγοντες τοὺς παρὰ πόδας ἐλέγχους. Simplicius, *commCateg*, p. 234: παρὰ πόδας γὰρ ἔχει ταῦτα τὸν ἔλεγχον. Photius (but I have argued that several of the epistles of this collection were probably written by Cassian the Sabaite, and perhaps by other intellectuals), *Epistulae et Amphilochia*, epistle 145: εἰ δὲ συνίεσαν, πῶς ἐθάρρησαν μέθην αἰτιάσασθαι, παρὰ πόδας τὸν ἔλεγχον ἔχοντες, αὐτῶν τῶν ἀκουόντων καὶ συνιέντων τὴν αἴσθησιν; Nicephorus Gregoras, *Historia Romana*, v. 2, p. 1024: τοῦ παρὰ πόδας ἐλέγχου κατὰ διάμετρον ἱσταμένου. Gennadius Scholarius, *De Spiritu Sancto i*, Part 4, p. 162: ὅτι παρὰ πόδας αὐτοῖς ὁ τῆς κακουργίας ἔλεγχος. *Contra Plethonis Ignorationem De Aristotele*, book 1, p. 9: ἅμα δὲ καὶ παρὰ πόδας ὑποστήσεται τοὺς ἐλέγχους.

dcxv Photius, *frMatt*, fr. 36.

dcxvi Jerome, *commMatt*, 9.5.

dcxvii Theodore of Mopsuestia, *frMatt*, fr. 45, col. 1; the text of col. 2 is similar.

dcxviii Origen, *commMatt*, fr. 177 (Klostermann).

dcxix *Catena in Marcum*, p. 290 (anonymous), comm. on Mark, 2:19 (cf. Matt. 9:15). In this catena, Origen is drawn to as an authority on pp. 266; 314; 418.

dcxx Here is one more expression introduced by Origen: νομικὴ πολιτεία (the 'State of Law') is contrasted with εὐαγγελικὴ πολιτεία (the 'State of the Gospel'). Both expressions were introduced by Origen himself, their impact was sweepingly stupendous once they were taken up by the most eminent of Christian authors. Cf. νομικὴ πολιτεία (the 'State of Law' = perception and conduct of life according to the Old Testament) after Origen. Cf. Didymus, *frPs(al)*, 343. John Chrysostom, *Adversus Judaeos*, PG.48.865.1; *In Matthaeum*, PG.57.35.30; *Fragmenta in Proverbia*, PG.64.681.4. Theodoret, *In Isaiam*, 2.334; 5.210; 291.22; 294.11; *Interpretatio in Psalmos*, PG.80: 1117.40; 1273.20; 1565.21; *commCant*, PG.81.145.48; *Interpretatio in Danielem*, PG.81.1265.33; *In Epistulas Sancti Pauli*, PG.82: 60.20; 116.39; 376.15; 433.33; 460.29; 496.41; 509.26; 581.38; 584.17; 593.31; 609.17; 737.3; 760.26; 768.2; 768.4; 789.8. Cyril of Alexandria, *commProphXII*, v. 1, pp. 232; 311; *et passim*; *In Joannem*, v. 1, pp. 229; 284; 297; 606; v. 2, pp. 394; 408; *et passim; De Adoratione*, PG.68: 137.13; 1121.16; *Glaphyra in Pentateuchum*, PG.69.452.51; *Expositio in Psalmos*, PG.69.941.38; *In Isaiam*, PG.70: 108.42; 820.30; *commLuc*, PG.72.865.45; *Thesaurus De Sancta Consubstantiali Trinitate*, PG.75.628.26; Pseudo-Cyril of Alexandria, *Collectio Dictorum Veteris Testamenti*, PG.77.1185.55. Pseudo-Dionysius the Areopagite, *De Ecclesiastica Hierarchia*, 83. Also, *Catena in Matthaeum*, pp. 6 (attr. to John Chrysostom); 69 (attr. to Origen, quoted above). *Catena in Acta*, p. 68 (attr. to Severus of Antioch). *Catena in Epistulam ad Hebraeos*, p. 584 (attr. to John Chrysostom). Pseudo-Caesarius (Cassian the Sabaite), *Quaestiones et Responsiones*, 195. Pseudo-John of Damascus, *Commentarii in Epistulas Pauli*, PG.95: 929.14; 936.25. George Syncellus, *Ecloga Chronographica*, p. 212. Photius, *Bibliotheca*, Codex 222, pp. 192a; 194b; *Epistulae et Amphilochia*, 248; *Epistula ad Arsenium De Manichaeis*, 17. Nicephorus Callistus Xanthopulus, *HE*, 3.13.

Cf. εὐαγγελικὴ πολιτεία (the 'State of the Gospel' = perception and conduct of life according to the Gospel). Origen, *frLuc*, fr. 185; *Libri x in Canticum Canticorum*, p. 98: Ὅρα δέ ὡς ἐπὶ μὲν τῆς εὐαγγελικῆς πολιτείας ὀσμὴν ἔφη. ἐπὶ τῆς νομικῆς λατρείας αὐτὰ τέθεικε τὰ ἀρώματα. *excPs*, PG.17.113.30. Eusebius, *HE*, 2.Pref.1.4; 7.32.30; 2.3.177; *In Isaiam*, 2.36; *Commentaria in Psalmos*, PG.23.816.53. Athanasius, *Expositiones in Psalmos*, PG.27: 305.26; 312.39; 377.20; 469.45. Basil of Caesarea, *De Spiritu Sancto*, 15.35; 29.74; *Epistulae*, epistles 43.1; 128.3; *Adversus Eunomium*, PG.29.509.7; *Homilia Exhortatoria ad Sanctum Baptisma*, PG.31.440.15. Didymus, *frPs(al)*, frs. 343; 486; 1268. Theodore of Heraclea, *Fragmenta in Joannem*, fr. 340. John Chrysostom, *In Principium Actorum*, PG.51.103.57; *Ad Eos Qui Scandalizati Sunt*, 13.12; *In Epistulam i ad Corinthios*, PG.61.34.49; 29. *In Epistulam ad Hebraeos*, PG.63.213.22; *Commentarius in Job*, p. 3. Theodoret, *Philotheus*, 4.3; 4.10; 10.1; 26.28; *Quaestiones in Octateuchum*, p. 156; *Interpretatio in Psalmos*, PG.80: 860.47; 1117.40; 1949.11; *Interpretatio in Ezechielem*, PG.81.1256.3; *In Epistulas Sancti Pauli*, PG.82: 53.19. 197.50; 612.53; 745.54. Pseudo-Theodoret (*forsan* Cassian the Sabaite), *Quaestiones et Responsiones ad Orthodoxos*, p. 48. Cyril of Alexandria, *commProphXII*, v. 1, pp. 349; 411; 525; v. 2, pp. 166; 537; 602; *In Joannem*, v. 1, pp. 229; 297; 606; v. 2, pp. 384; 408; 567; 581; 649; 651; 669; 710; v. 3, pp. 25; 98; 158; *De Incarnatione Unigeniti*, p. 690; *frMatt*, fr. 20; *Epistulae Paschales*, PG.77: 612.20; 692.37; 801.19; 837; 845.24; *De Adoratione*, PG.68: 236.25; 256; 629.5; 632.40; 657.4; 716.52; 820.54; 824.3; 944.54; 1013.31; 1020.26; 1032.48; 1049.47; 1089.38; 1097.56; *Glaphyra in Pentateuchum*, PG.69: 72.29&37; 241.50; 245.3; 329.31; 345.17; 452.50; *Expositio in Psalmos*, PG.69: 908.14; 1161.6; 1176.15; 1225.11; *In Isaiam*, PG: 70.44.23; 76.12; 232.30; 272.39; 312.56; 333.13; 557.56; 569.55; 572.52; 625.9; 633.9; 721.39; 753.46; 804.5; 857.34; 872.33; 912.17; 937.28; 1140.39; 1252.37; 1273.7; 1373.14; 1393.31; *commLuc*, PG.72: 513.20; 516.19; .576.29; .601.18; .773.11; 884.30; *Thesaurus De Sancta Consubstantiali Trinitate*, PG.75: 169.19; 628.25. Pseudo-Cyril of Alexandria, *Collectio Dictorum Veteris Testamenti*, PG.77.1185.55. Pseudo-Justin Martyr (*forsan* Cassian the Sabaite), *Quaestiones et Responsiones ad Orthodoxos*, p. 409. Gregory of Nyssa, *Epistulae*, epistle 2.1.9. Gennadius I of Constantinople, *Fragmenta in Epistulam ad Romanos*, 352.15. Nilus of Ancyra, *Εἰς τὸ τῶν Ἀσμάτων Ἆσμα*, 76. Procopius of Gaza, *Catena in Canticum Canticorum*, pp. 1549; 1737; 2397; 2477; 2657; 2700. Cyril of Scythopolis, *Vita Sabae*, p. 88. Pseudo-Basil of Caesarea (*forsan* Cassian the Sabaite), *Enarratio in Prophetam Isaiam*, 1.38. Cosmas Indicopleustes, *Topographia Christiana*, 5.193; 5.196; 5.200. Maximus Confessor, *Quaestiones et Dubia*, 36. Gregory of Acragas, *Commentarius in Ecclesiasten*, 6.3.46; 6.7.16. John of Damascus, *Sacra Parallela*, PG.96.277.33. Pseudo-John of Damascus, *Commentarii in Epistulas Pauli*, PG.95: 876.18; 929.13; 936.25; *Vita Barlaam et Joasaph*, p. 436. Theodore Studites, *Epitaphius in Matrem Suam*, section 1, line 660. Nicephorus I of Constantinople, *Adversus Iconomachos*, chapter 4; *Refutatio et Eversio Definitionis Synodalis anni 815*, chapters 161; 163. Photius, *Bibliotheca*, Codex 197, p. 161a; Codex 222, p. 183a. Nicetas David, *Encomium in Apostolum Petrum*, p. 44. Symeon the New Theologian, *Capita Theologica*, 1.48; *Catecheses*, oration 28. Michael Psellus, *Orationes Forenses et Acta*, oration 1, line 414; *Orationes Hagiographicae*, oration 1a, line 138; *Encomium in Matrem*, line 1219. Michael Glycas, *Quaestiones in Sacram Scripturam*, chapter 16, p. 185. Nicephorus Callistus Xanthopulus, *HE*, 2.40. Gennadius Scholarius, *Orationes et Panegyrici*, oration 11, sections 9; 10; 14. *De Spiritu Sancto ii*, Part 1, p. 286. Also, *Catena in Acta*, pp. 144; 349.

dcxxi Origen, *commMatt*, fr. 178 (Klostermann).

dcxxii Origen, *apud Catena in Matthaeum*, p. 69. This is also Origen, *commMatt*, fr. 172 (Klostermann), col. 1.

dcxxiii Origen, *commMatt*, fr. 179 (Klostermann).

dcxxiv Origen, *commMatt*, fr. 180 (Klostermann).

dcxxv Cf. Origen, *homJer*, 1.16; 10.5; *selEx*, PG.12.272.50-51 (& *Philocalia*, 27.6); *op. cit.* PG.12.293.58-59; *selPs*, PG.12: 1137.12-13; 1261.12 & 27; 1549.30-31; *excPs*, PG.17.113. 7-8 & 18-19.

dcxxvi Origen, *commMatt*, fr. 181 (Klostermann).

dcxxvii Origen, *frLuc*, fr. 127a.

dcxxviii Cf. John Chrysostom, *In Matthaeum*, PG.57.371.31-37: Ἠσχύνετο διὰ τὸ πάθος, ἀκάθαρτος εἶναι νομίζουσα. ... καὶ γὰρ πολλὴ παρὰ τῷ νόμῳ ἀκαθαρσία ἐνομίζετο εἶναι τὸ πάθος. Διὰ τοῦτο λανθάνει καὶ κρύπτεται.

dcxxix Cf. John Chrysostom, *op. cit.* PG.57.371.44-49: Οὐδὲ γὰρ ἀμφέβαλεν, οὐδὲ εἶπεν ἐν ἑαυτῇ· Ἆρα ἀπαλλαγήσομαι τοῦ νοσήματος; ἆρα οὐκ ἀπαλλαγήσομαι; ἀλλὰ θαρρήσασα περὶ τῆς ὑγιείας οὕτω προσῆλθεν. *Ἔλεγε γάρ, φησίν, ἐν ἑαυτῇ. Ἐὰν μόνον ἅψωμαι τοῦ ἱματίου αὐτοῦ, σωθήσομαι.*

dcxxx Cf. John Chrysostom, *op. cit.* PG.57.371.52-372.3: Τί οὖν ὁ Χριστός; Οὐκ ἀφῆκεν αὐτὴν λαθεῖν, ἀλλ' εἰς μέσον ἄγει καὶ δήλην καθίστησι, πολλῶν ἕνεκεν. Καίτοι γέ τινες τῶν ἀναισθήτων φασί, δόξης αὐτὸν ἐρῶντα τοῦτο ποιεῖν. Διατί γάρ, φησίν, οὐκ ἀφῆκεν αὐτὴν λαθεῖν; Τί λέγεις, ὦ μιαρὲ καὶ παμμίαρε; ὁ κελεύων σιγᾷν, ὁ μυρία παρατρέχων θαύματα, οὗτος δόξης ἐρᾷ; Τίνος οὖν ἕνεκεν εἰς μέσον ἄγει; Πρῶτον λύει τὸ δέος τῆς γυναικός, ἵνα μὴ ὑπὸ τοῦ συνειδότος κεντουμένη, καθάπερ κεκλοφυῖα τὴν δωρεάν, ἐν ἀγωνίᾳ διατρίβῃ. Δεύτερον, αὐτὴν διορθοῦται, ἐπειδὴ ἐνόμισε λανθάνειν. Τρίτον, πᾶσι τὴν πίστιν αὐτῆς ἐπιδείκνυται, ὥστε καὶ τοὺς ἄλλους ζηλῶσαι· ... Ἔπειτα, τὸν ἀρχισυνάγωγον μέλλοντα διαπιστεῖν καὶ ταύτῃ τὸ πᾶν διαφθείρειν κατορθοῖ διὰ τῆς γυναικός.

dcxxxi The expression τυπικὸς νόμος ('the formal Law') originated with Origen, which is fully consonant with his overall typological theory. Cf. 1 Cor. 10:11: ταῦτα δὲ τυπικῶς συνέβαινεν ἐκείνοις, ἐγράφη δὲ πρὸς νουθεσίαν ἡμῶν. Cf. Heb. 10:1. Origen, *frPs*, on Psalm 70:22: οὐ τύπους καὶ σύμβολα νομικά. *Op. cit.* Psalm 76:21: τοῦ νόμου τὴν βουλὴν ὡς τύπον τινὰ δηλοῦσαν. *De Pascha*, p. 110: τὸ γὰρ σκιὰν εἶναι τὸν νόμον καὶ τύπον. Gregory of Nyssa, *In Diem Luminum*, p. 233: ἔδει γὰρ εἶναι τυπικῶς τὸν νόμον ἐν κιβωτῷ. *In Canticum Canticorum*, p. 268: τὰ τυπικὰ πάντα τοῦ νόμου ἀρώματα. Pseudo-Gregory of Nyssa, *De Occursu Domini*, PG.46.1173.46-48: ὁ Ἰσραήλ, εἰ καὶ μετρίως, ὅμως γοῦν τῷ τυπικῷ ἐφωτίζετο νόμῳ. Eusebius, *Commentaria in Psalmos*, PG.23.77.13: τὸν σκιώδη καὶ τυπικὸν νόμον. Basil of Caesarea, *De Baptismo*, PG.31.1585.11-12: τυπικῶς ἐκ τοῦ νόμου μανθάνομεν. Pseudo-Macarius, *Sermones 64 (collectio B)*, 10.2.3. Cyril of Jerusalem, *Catecheses ad Illuminandos*, 17.29: τῶν νομικῶν καὶ τυπικῶν πραγμάτων. Socrates Scholasticus, *HE*, 5.22: τὰ ἀκριβῆ καὶ τυπικὰ τοῦ Μωσαϊκοῦ νόμου ἐπαύσατο. Pseudo-John Chrysostom,

De Occursu Domini, De Deipara et Symeone, PG.50.809.35: τυπικῶς κατὰ τὸν νόμον. *In Psalmos*, PG.55.643.25-6: τῶν τυπικῶν τοῦ νόμου καὶ τῆς σκιᾶς. *In Sanctum Pascha*, 2: διὰ περιτομῆς ἐπέδειξεν ἡμῖν ὁ νομοθέτης τυπικῶς. Anastasius of Sinai, *In Hexaemeron*, book 8, lines 395-396: τὸν φυσικὸν καὶ Μωσαϊκὸν καὶ προφητικὸν τυπικὸν νόμον. Michael Psellus, *Theologica*, opusculum 5: ὁ τυπικὸς νόμος.

dcxxxii Origen, *commMatt*, fr. 182 (Klostermann).

dcxxxiii Once again, a passage of Origen occurring in full context has been attributed to Cyril of Alexandria, *frMatt*, fr. 108 (on Matt. 9:20-22) & *Catena in Matthaeum*, p. 70.

dcxxxiv Origen, *commMatt*, fr. 184 (Klostermann).

dcxxxv This was considered a 'fragment' attributed to Cyril of Alexandria, *frMatt*, fr. 109 (on Matt. 9:23) & *Catena in Matthaeum*, p. 70. However, now we have all of Origen's surrounding text, not a 'fragment'.

dcxxxvi Jerome, *commMatt*, 9.23.

dcxxxvii Cf. Origen, (Klostermann), fr. 187 III.

dcxxxviii Jerome, *commMatt*, 9.24.

dcxxxix Origen, *commMatt*, fr. 185 (Klostermann); a combination of columns 1 and 2, which amounts to the present text.

dcxl Origen, *apud Catena in Matthaeum*, pp. 70-71.

dcxli See *supra*, folio 72r: φεύγων τὸ φιλόκομπον. See endnote cclii.

dcxlii John Chrysostom, *In Matthaeum*, PG.57.377.27-29. But see Origen *apud Catena in Matthaeum*, p. 71: δεύτεραν δὲ ἐρώτησιν προσάγει, σπουδάζων ἱκετεύεσθαι πολλάκις, καὶ τότε τὴν ἴασιν παρέχειν, ἵνα μή τις νομίσῃ διὰ φιλοτιμίαν αὐτὸν τοῖς θαύμασιν ἐπιπηδᾷν.

dcxliii John Chrysostom, *In Matthaeum*, PG.57.377.34-36. Again, this is Origen *apud Catena in Matthaeum*, p. 71: ὁμολογησάντων οὖν αὐτὸν οὐκ ἔτι υἱὸν Δαβίδ, ἀλλὰ τὸ ὑψηλότερον προσειπόντων Κύριον.

dcxliv This is part of Origen, *commMatt*, fr. 187 III (Klostermann). He put this in brackets, because he found the following parallel in John Chrysostom, *In Matthaeum*, PG.57.377.22-23: Υἱὸν δὲ Δαυῒδ ἐκάλουν, ἐπειδὴ τὸ ὄνομα τιμῆς ἐδόκει εἶναι. But this is Origen *apud Catena in Matthaeum*, p. 71: υἱὸν δὲ Δαβὶδ ἐκάλουν, ἐπειδὴ τὸ ὄνομα τιμῆς εἶναι ἐδόκει.

dcxlv Jerome, *commMatt*, 9.27-28.

dcxlvi Cf. Origen *apud Catena in Matthaeum*, p. 71: διὰ τὸ ἀκόμπαστον, κελεύει μετὰ πολλῆς τῆς σφοδρότητος μηδενὶ εἰπεῖν· ... Ἰησοῦς παραγγέλλων τοῖς ἰωμένοις μηδενὶ λέγειν τὰς εὐεργεσίας αὐτοῦ, ἡμᾶς διδάσκει φεύγειν τὸ ἐπιδεικτικὸν ὡς αἴτιον τῶν κακῶν. See also the last phrase of this in Origen, *commMatt*, fr. 187 III (Klostermann): Τοὺς τυφλοὺς ἐθεράπευσεν ὁ σωτὴρ καὶ οὐκ ἐβούλετο αὐτοὺς εἰπεῖν τίς ἐστιν ὁ θεραπεύων αὐτούς, ἡμᾶς διδάσκει φεύγειν τὸ ἐπιδεικτικὸν ὡς αἴτιον τῶν κακῶν. Likewise, Origen, *commMatt*, fr. 187 III (Klostermann): Φεύγων δὲ τὸ φιλόκομπον ἄγει αυτοὺς εἰς τὴν οἰκίαν κἀκεῖ αὐτοὺς ἰᾶται.

dcxlvii Jerome, *commMatt*, 9.30-31.

dcxlviii Origen, *apud Catena in Matthaeum*, p. 71 & Chrysostom, *In Matthaeum*, PG.57.378.10-15.

dcxlix Origen, *commMatt*, fr. 187 II (Klostermann).

dcl Origen, *commMatt*, fr. 187 I (Klostermann).

dcli Origen, *commMatt*, fr. 187 III (Klostermann), col. 2. He came upon this being attributed to Origen in six codices, yet he put it in brackets because one other codex ascribed this to Apollinaris.

dclii Apollinaris, *frMatt*, fr. 42.

dcliii Since passages of Origen have been attributed to Theodore of Heraclea (even to a degree of flagrant ludicrousness, see *infra*, folios 239v-240r), here is one more instance evincing that this is but a copy from Origen almost to the word. Theodore of Heraclea, *frMatt*, fr. 58: Ἄκρας ἀσεβείας δεῖγμα τὸ τὰς θείας δυνάμεις λέγειν δαιμόνων εἶναι. οὐδεὶς γάρ ποτε δαιμόνων δαίμονα ἐκβάλλει οὐδὲ τὰ ἑαυτοῦ καταλύει. οὐ μόνους δὲ δαίμονας ἐξέβαλεν, ἀλλὰ καὶ μυρία πάθη ἐθεράπευσεν. ὁ δαίμων πρὸς τὰ εἴδωλα σύρει, ὁ Χριστὸς τῷ πατρὶ προσῆγεν. ὁ δαίμων ὑβριζόμενος οὐκ εὐεργετεῖ, ὁ δὲ Χριστὸς τοὺς ὑβρίζοντας φέρων ἀνεξικάκως περιῄει θεραπεύων πάντας.

dcliv Origen *apud Catena in Matthaeum*, p. 71.

dclv Origen could have received the turn πανταχοῦ περινοστῶν ('stalking about everywhere') either from Nicander of Colophon (second century B.C.), who wrote the *Theriaca* (of which he was perhaps aware, see *supra*, endnote cxxix), or from Eutecnius, who wrote of paraphrase of this using the verb at four points, and possibly he was Origen's contemporary (although he could have lived later than Origen). Cf. Eutecnius, *Paraphrasis in Nicandri Theriaca*, p. 29: πανταχοῦ περινοστοῦσι τά τε δύσβατα τῶν χωρίων καὶ τὰς αἱμασιὰς οἱ ἔλαφοι. In any event, the verb περινοστῶ ('go about') was already there since the times of Aristophanes, who used this repeatedly (*Pax*, verse 762; *Thesmophoriazusae*, verse 796; *Plutus*, verse 121), and had been used by authors familiar to Origen, such as Diodore of Sicily, Dionysius of Halicarnassus, Philo, Athenaeus, and abundantly by Lucian of Samosata and Plutarch. Cf. Origen, *expProv*, PG.17.232.50; also, Porphyry, *Περὶ Ἀγαλμάτων*, 7: περινοστεῖν τὸν κόσμον.

dclvi Theodore of Heraclea, *frMatt*, fr. 59.

dclvii Cyril of Alexandria, *frMatt*, fr. 111. He copied from Origen once again.

dclviii This is the first part of Origen, *commMatt*, fr. 189 (Klostermann). See the rest of this quoted *infra*.

dclix Origen, *apud Catena in Matthaeum*, p. 73.

dclx Jerome, *commMatt*, 9.37.

dclxi Origen, *commMatt*, fr. 190 (Klostermann).

dclxii Writing ἀνεπαισθήτως instead of ἀνεπαισχύντως is a serious editorial mistake by J.A. Cramer.

dclxiii Origen, *apud Catena in Matthaeum*, p. 73.

dclxiv Jerome, *commMatt*, 9.37.

dclxv Origen, *commMatt*, fr. 191 (Klostermann).

dclxvi Origen, *commMatt*, fr. 192 (Klostermann).

dclxvii Cf. Origen, *frLuc*, 242: ἓν γάρ τι τὸ συναμφότερόν ἐστιν ἄνθρωπος καὶ ἡ ζωὴ κοινή, καὶ ἑκατέρων δεῖ πρὸς τὸ τὴν ἐκ θανάτου ζωὴν πάλιν συστῆναι. A man is characterised either by soul or body or both of these conjointly, but not also of spirit, which is more divine than these. The *spiritual man* receives this title in accordance with his predominate participation in the 'spirit'; *commJohn*, II.21.138: τοῦ ἀνθρώπου ἤτοι ἐν ψυχῇ ἢ ἐν σώματι ἢ ἐν συναμφοτέροις χαρακτηριζομένου, οὐχὶ δὲ καὶ ἐν τῷ τούτων θειοτέρῳ πνεύματι, οὗ κατὰ μετοχὴν ἐπικρατοῦσαν χρηματίζει ὁ πνευματικός. Cf. *Cels*, VI.63: εἰ δέ ἐστι ἐν τῷ συναμφοτέρῳ τὸ *κατ' εἰκόνα τοῦ θεοῦ*.

dclxviii Origen, *commMatt*, fr. 193 (Klostermann), col. 1.

dclxix Origen, *commMatt*, fr. 193 (Klostermann), col. 2.

dclxx Jerome, *commMatt*, 10.1.

dclxxi This is part of Origen, *commMatt*, fr. 194 (Klostermann).

dclxxii Jerome, *commMatt*, 10.2.

dclxxiii This is part of Origen, *commMatt*, fr. 194 (Klostermann).

dclxxiv This is part of Origen, *commMatt*, fr. 194 (Klostermann).

dclxxv This is part of Origen, *commMatt*, fr. 194 (Klostermann).

dclxxvi This is part of Origen, *commMatt*, fr. 194 (Klostermann).

dclxxvii Origen, *commMatt*, fr. 195 I (Klostermann), col. 1. See also fr. 195 II.

dclxxviii Cf. Origen, *commJohn*, XXVIII.1.1: Οἱ φύσεις ἀριθμῶν ἐρευνήσαντες πρῶτον μὲν τέλειον τὸν ἓξ εἰρήκασιν, τοῖς ἑαυτοῦ μέρεσιν ‹ἴσον› ἱστάμενον, ἔκ τε τῆς συνθέσεως τοῦ ἀπὸ μονάδος διπλασιαζομένου, ἑνὸς καὶ δύο, ὅ ἐστι τρία, ἀριθμὸς πρῶτος, καὶ τοῦ ἐφ᾽ ὃν ἔφθασεν ὁ διπλασιασμός, λέγω δὲ τοῦ δύο. γενόμενος γὰρ ὁ δύο ἐπὶ τὸν τρία πεποίηκεν τὸν ἕξ. *Op. cit.* X.39.270: οἱ δὲ ἐπιστάται, ‹τρισχίλιοι καὶ› ἑξακόσιοι τυγχάνοντες, τῷ τοῦ ἓξ τελείῳ ἀριθμῷ οἱονεὶ ἐφ᾽ ἑαυτὸν πολυπλασιαζομένῳ συνάπτονται. *Princ*, IV.2.5 (*Philocalia*, 1.12): *ἓξ* δὲ *ὑδρίαι* εὐλόγως εἰσὶ τοῖς ἐν κόσμῳ καθαριζομένοις, γεγενημένῳ ἐν ἓξ ἡμέραις, ἀριθμῷ τελείῳ. *commMatt*, 12.36: ἐν ἓξ ἡμέραις, τελείῳ ἀριθμῷ, ὁ σύμπας γεγένηται κόσμος, τὸ τέλειον τοῦτο δημιούργημα. *schLuc*, PG.17.344.28-29: ἐν ἓξ ἡμέραις τελείῳ ἀριθμῷ ὁ σύμπας κόσμος γεγένηται.

dclxxix Origen, *commMatt*, fr. 195 I (Klostermann), col. 2.

dclxxx This is the first part of Cyril of Alexandria, *frMatt*, fr. 113. *Catena in Matthaeum*, p. 75. See the rest of this *infra*. See also col. 2: Δίκαιον γάρ ἐστι πρὸς Ἰουδαίους πρῶτον κηρυχθῆναι τὸν λόγον, ἐπεὶ καὶ πρὸς ἐκείνους αἱ ἐπαγγελίαι πρῶτον, καὶ ὅτι ἐξ αὐτῶν ὁ Χριστὸς τὸ κατὰ σάρκα ἐφάνη. Ὅτε δὲ ἠπείθησαν, ἀναγκαῖον ἦν εἰς τὰ ἔθνη χωρῆσαι.

dclxxxi This is part of Origen, *commMatt*, fr. 197 (Klostermann); see columns 1 and 2.

dclxxxii This is part of Origen, *commMatt*, fr. 197 (Klostermann).

dclxxxiii This is the concluding part of Cyril of Alexandria, *frMatt*, fr. 113 (col. 1) (J. Reuss). Likewise, col. 2: συνάπτει δὲ τοῖς ἐξ ἐθνῶν τοὺς Σαμαρείτας ὡς ἐξ ἐθνῶν ὑπάρχοντας καὶ αὐτοὺς καὶ τὴν Ἰουδαίαν οἰκήσαντας.

dclxxxiv The term οὐρανοπολίτης ('citizen of heaven') appeared first in the second-century apocryphon, *Acta Joannis*, 16:1: καὶ πολλὰς θαυματουργίας κἀκεῖσε ἐπιτελέσας τῇ τοῦ ἁγίου πνεύματος χάριτι πολλοὺς καὶ τῶν ἐκεῖσε μαθητὰς τοῦ Χριστοῦ καὶ οὐρανοπολίτας εἰργάσατο. Then, Pseudo-Gregory Thaumaturgus, *Sermo in Omnes Sanctos*, PG.10.1201.25. Pseudo-Epiphanius of Salamis, *Homilia in Assumptionem Christi*, PG.43.485.33. Ephraem Syrus, *Paraenesis ad Ascetas*, p. 345; *Encomium in Magnum Basilium*, p. 353. Asterius of Amasea, *Homiliae*, 8.2.2. John Chrysostom, *De Paenitentia*, PG.49.290.60; *In Matthaeum*, PG.58.654.21. Cassian the Sabaite (Pseudo-Didymus), *De Trinitate*, PG.39.877.46. Oecumenius, *Commentarius in Apocalypsin*, p. 136. Cyril of Scythopolis, *Vita Euthymii*, pp. 8; 84; *Vita Theodosii*, p. 235. John Philoponus, *commAnim*, p. 563 (discussed by Michael Psellus, *Opuscula*, p. 69). Photius, *Bibliotheca*, Codex 193, p. 157b. Analecta Hymnica Graeca, *Canones Decembris*, 6.8.2; 29.59.3; *Canones Januarii*, 10.20.5; 11.22.9; 14.23.6; *Canones Junii*, 30.20.9.

dclxxxv This is the last part of Origen, *commMatt*, fr. 198 (Klostermann). See the parallel to the last part of the present text *infra*.

dclxxxvi Cyril of Alexandria, *frMatt*, fr. 114.

dclxxxvii Apollinaris, *frMatt*, fr. 45.

dclxxxviii Cyril of Alexandria, *frMatt*, fr. 115.

dclxxxix Origen, *commMatt*, fr. 196 (Klostermann).

dcxc Apollinaris, *frMatt*, fr. 43.

dcxci Cf. Origen, *commJohn*, VI.32.164: Τίς ὃς νοήσει τὸν ἐκ τῶν ἄνωθεν χιτῶνα ἄραφον διὰ τὸ δι᾽ὅλου ὑφαντὸν τυγχάνειν καταλαβεῖν ὃν ἔχει λόγον;

dcxcii Cf. Origen, *commSerMatt*, p. 86: ἀποτιθεμένους τὸν παλαιὸν ἄνθρωπον (τοῦτό γάρ φησι τὸ ἱμάτιον).

dcxciii Cf. Origen, *Cels*, VI.63; VIII.17; *frJohn*, fr. 35; *homJer*, homily 5.13; *Dialogus cum Heraclide*, 16.

dcxciv Apollinaris, *frMatt*, fr. 47.

dcxcv Cf. Origen, *commJohn*, I.27.184; *commMatt*, 12.11: οὔτε γὰρ τῆς πέτρας, ἐφ᾽ ἧς ὁ Χριστὸς οἰκοδομεῖ τὴν ἐκκλησίαν, οὔτε τῆς ἐκκλησίας πύλαι ᾅδου κατισχύσουσιν, ὡς οὐδὲ *ὁδὸς ὄφεως ἐπὶ πέτρας* (κατὰ τὸ ἐν Παροιμίαις γεγραμμένον) εὑρεθείη ἄν.

dcxcvi Cf. Origen, *commJohn*, I.27.183-184: ἡ ἐν σοφίᾳ πορεία ... παρίστησιν ἡμῖν νοεῖν πῶς αὐτός ἐστιν *ἡ ὁδός*, ἐφ᾽ ἣν ὁδὸν οὐδὲν αἴρειν δεῖ, οὔτε πήραν οὔτε ἱμάτιον, ἀλλ᾽ οὐδὲ ῥάβδον ἔχοντα ὁδεύειν χρή, οὐδὲ ὑποδήματα ὑποδεδέσθαι κατὰ τοὺς πόδας. Αὐτάρκης γὰρ ἀντὶ παντὸς ἐφοδίου αὐτὴ ἡ ὁδός, καὶ ἀνενδεὴς τυγχάνει πᾶς ὁ ταύτης ἐπιβαίνων, κεκοσμημένος ἐνδύματι ᾧ πρέπει κεκοσμῆσθαι τὸν ἐπὶ τὴν κλῆσιν τοῦ γάμου ἀπιόντα, οὐδενός τε χαλεποῦ δυναμένου ἀπαντῆσαι κατὰ ταύτην τὴν ὁδόν. *Op. cit.* VI.19.107: Ὁ γὰρ σωτήρ, ... ἐστιν ... ἔτι προκόπτοντι ὁδός ... Ταύτην τὴν ὁδὸν ‹ὁ› ὁδεύων διδάσκεται μηδὲν αἴρειν εἰς αὐτὴν ἔχουσαν ἄρτους καὶ τὰ πρὸς ζωήν, διὰ τὸ μηδὲν δύνασθαι τοὺς πολεμίους ἐν αὐτῇ οὐδὲ ῥάβδου χρήζων, καὶ ἐπεὶ ἁγία ἐστὶν οὐδ᾽ ὑποδημάτων. *commEph*, fr. 34: ὁ μὲν οὖν ὁδεύων ὑποδεδέσθω, ὁ δὲ φθάσας ἐπὶ τὴν ἁγίαν γῆν ὑπολυέσθω. *λῦσαι* γάρ φησι, *τὸ ὑπόδημα ἐκ τῶν ποδῶν σου. ὁ γὰρ τόπος, ἐν ᾧ σὺ ἕστηκας, γῆ ἁγία ἐστίν.* [Exodus, 3:5]. Also, *Princ*, IV.3.8 (*Philocalia*, 1.24); *commJohn*, VI.45.234&236; *frJohn*, frs. 32; 75; *deOr*, 27.14; *homJer*, homilies 4.2; 7.3; *Cels*, VII.28&30; *frLam*, fr. 93; *frPs*, on Psalm 77:38; *homEz*, p. 319; *selEz*, PG.13.824.46-47; *exhMar*, 17; *Homiliae in Jesu Nave*, p. 455.

dcxcvii Apollinaris, *frMatt*, fr. 48.

dcxcviii Apollinaris, *op. cit.* fr. 49.

dcxcix Apollinaris, *op. cit.* fr. 50.

dcc Origen, *commMatt*, fr. 199 (Klostermann).

dcci Origen, *apud Catena in Matthaeum*, p. 76.

dccii Cyril of Alexandria, *frMatt*, fr. 116. I quote the entire fragment shortly below (p. 144) which makes clear how Cyril and Apollinaris copied from Origen, sometimes paraphrasing him, but mostly *verbatim* (especially Apollinaris, who was all by shy about copying from Origen without caring for paraphrasing the latter's words).

dcciii Cf. Origen, *commMatt*, 17:23: εἶπε *τοῖς δούλοις αὐτοῦ ὁ βασιλεὺς* [Matt. 22:8] ἀποστόλοις Χριστοῦ ἢ ἀγγέλοις θεοῦ τεταγμένοις ἐπὶ τῆς κλήσεως τῶν ἐθνῶν. *Libri x in Canticum Canticorum (fragmenta)*, p. 184 & *Scholia in Canticum Canticorum*, PG.17.261.36-39: Ταῦτα πρὸς τοὺς φίλους τοῦ νυμφίου φησί, τοὺς ἁγίους ἀγγέλους ἢ ἀποστόλους τε καὶ προφήτας. *homJer*, 12:12: φωτεινὰ ὄρη οἱ ἅγιοι ἄγγελοι τοῦ θεοῦ, οἱ προφῆται, Μωσῆς ὁ θεράπων, οἱ ἀπόστολοι Ἰησοῦ Χριστοῦ.

dcciv Origen, *commMatt*, fr. 200 (Klostermann).

dccv Origen, *commMatt*, fr. 198 (Klostermann).

dccvi J.A. Cramer attributed the passage up to this point to Theodoret. *Catena in Matthaeum*, p. 76: (Θεοδωρήτου Ἐπισκόπου Κύρρου.) Ταῦτα φησίν, ὥστε μὴ εὐκόλου καὶ προχείρου γνώμης ἀποφέρεσθαι δόξαν παρὰ τοῖς τὴν πόλιν οἰκοῦσιν. However, this is in effect the same one attributed to Cyril of Alexandria (fr. 116) shortly below in an edition also by Cramer.

dccvii This is effectively the same text as that attributed to Cyril of Alexandria, *frMatt*, fr. 116, quoted below (p. 144).

dccviii This is Apollinaris, *frMatt*, fr. 51, as well as the first part of Origen, *commMatt*, fr. 198 (Klostermann); see the last part of this *supra:* Βασιλείαν δὲ *οὐρανῶν* λέγει τὴν διὰ πίστεως χάριν, etc.).

dccix Part of this passage has been attributed to Theodoret, *apud Catena in Matthaeum*, p. 76: (Θεοδωρήτου.) Τὸ ἐκτινάσσειν τὸν κονιορτὸν τῶν ποδῶν, κατὰ τῶν μὴ ὑποδεχομένων αὐτούς, σύμβολον τῆς ὁδοιπορίας, ἣν ὑπέμειναν ὑπὲρ αὐτῶν.

dccx *Catena in Marcum*, p. 323 (comm. on Mark, 6:10). The catenist(s) supposedly copied mainly from Cyril of Alexandria commentary on Mark (claiming that he was 'the only one who wrote a commentary on Mark', p. 263). However, in this collection, passages from Chrysostom's work abound. Besides, shortly before this parallel text (on p. 321) there is 'one more comment by someone else' (Σχόλιον Ἄλλο Ἔτι Τινός). It is not clear whether this additional 'comment by someone else' is part of the end of the chapter, or somehow it carries on in the next one.

dccxi Cyril of Alexandria, *frMatt*, fr. 116.

dccxii Here is one more proof of how Theodore of Heraclea copied from Origen's commentary. *frMatt*, fr. 65.

dccxiii Cyril of Alexandria, *frMatt*, fr. 117. See more of this fragment *infra*.

dccxiv The ensuing passage, including the characteristic expression ἀποξύεσθαι τὸ γῆρας, was copied by the sixth-century moderate Origenist Cassian the Sabaite, the recently discovered Greek father, about whom I have written three volumes (*NDGF*, *RCR*, and the *Scholia in Apocalypsin*). Cf. Pseudo-Basil of Caesarea (*forsan* Cassian the Sabaite), *Enarratio in Prophetam Isaiam*, Prologue, 1: *Γίνεσθε φρόνιμοι ὡς οἱ ὄφεις.* Τάχα διὰ τὸ φρονίμως καὶ συνετῶς ἀποξύεσθαι τὸ γῆρας. καὶ γὰρ ἐπειδὰν ἀποδύεσθαι δέῃ τὴν λεβηρίδα, στενῷ τόπῳ καὶ ἀκριβῶς προσφίγγοντι αὐτοῦ τὸ σῶμα ἐπιδοὺς ἑαυτόν, οὕτω διείρων ἑαυτόν, ἀποδύεται τὸ γῆρας. Τάχα οὖν καὶ ἡμᾶς βούλεται ὁ λόγος διὰ τῆς στενῆς καὶ τεθλιμμένης ὁδοῦ πορευομένους ἀποδύεσθαι μὲν τὸν παλαιὸν ἄνθρωπον, ἐνδύσασθαι δὲ τὸν νέον, ὥστε καὶ ἡμῶν αὐτῶν ἀνακαινισθῆναι, ὡς ἀετοῦ, τὴν νεότητα.

The expression ἀποξύεσθαι τὸ γῆρας comes from Homer, *Ilias*, IX.446: οὐδ' εἴ κέν μοι ὑποσταίη θεὸς αὐτὸς γῆρας ἀποξύσας θήσειν νέον ἡβώοντα ("nay, not though a god himself should pledge him to strip from me my old age and render me strong in youth") and became proverbial: Aristonicus, *De Signis Iliadis*, (on *Ilias*, IX.446), scholion 2. Apollonius (sophist), *Lexicon Homericum*, p. 115. Pseudo-Justin, *Cohortatio ad Gentiles*, pp. 17D; 22E. Libanius, *Epistulae*, epistle 938.4. Cyril of Alexandria, *Contra Julianum*, 1.37. Eudocia Augusta, *Homerocentones*, section 1, line 668. Eustathius of Thessaloniki, *Commentarii ad Homeri Iliadem*, v. 2, p. 754. Michael Choniates, *Orationes*, oration 5, p. 38. Anonymous, *Scholia in Euripides Andromacham*, scholiom 553. Anonymous, *Scholia in Iliadem* (*scholia vetera*) (on *Ilias*, IX.446), scholia 1 & 2. However, the example of snakes renewing their skin was introduced by Origen and taken up only by a couple of later authors, such as Theodore Prodromus, *Carmina Historica*, poem 24, line 18, and Michael Choniates, *Orationes*, v. 1, oration 14, p. 255. Didymus used the phrase in a context faithfully reproducing Origen's analysis at this point of the commentary. *Commentarii in Psalmos 40-44.4*, cod. p. 297: ἀποξύεται τὸ γῆρας τῆς κακίας, τὸν παλαιὸν ἄνθρωπον, καὶ τὸν νέον ἐνδιδύσκεται ἀντ' αὐτοῦ, κἂν παροιμιωδῶς [= 'proverbially', i.e. after Homer] κἂν ἐπὶ ρητοῦ αὐτὸ θέλῃς λαβεῖν.

dccxv Likewise *infra*, folios 78r-v, which is the same as Origen's fr. 202 (Klostermann).

dccxvi This is a paraphrase of Origen's foregoing expression ἀποξύεσθαι τὸ γῆρας.

dccxvii Theodore of Heraclea, *frMatt*, fr. 66. The passage ὅσαις γὰρ ἂν πληγαῖς ... καὶ τὸν νέον ἀνταμφιέννυσθαι is the selfsame one as that attributed to Isidore of Pelusium (*apud Catena in Matthaeum*, pp. 76-77) shortly below.

dccxviii Isidore of Pelusium, *apud Catena in Matthaeum*, p. 76. See the rest of the fragment *infra*.

dccxix Cyril of Alexandria, *frMatt*, fr. 117. See the rest of the fragment *infra*.

dccxx Cyril of Alexandria, *op. cit.*

dccxxi Cf. Origen, *commMatt*, fr. 202 (Klostermann), col. 2: Ὡς γὰρ ὁ ὄφις (φησὶ) πίνων ὕδωρ ἀποτίθησι τὸν ἰόν, οὕτω καὶ ὑμεῖς ἀποτίθεσθε τὴν κακίαν, δεξάμενοι τὸ εὐαγγέλιον.

dccxxii Cf. John Chrysostom, *In Matthaeum*, PG.57.390.20-24: τὴν μὲν φρόνησιν τοῦ ὄφεως εἰς τὸ μὴ πλήττεσθαι ἐν τοῖς καιρίοις παραλαβών· τὸ δὲ ἀκέραιον τῆς περιστερᾶς, εἰς τὸ μὴ ἀμύνεσθαι τοὺς ἀδικοῦντας, μηδὲ τιμωρεῖσθαι τοὺς ἐπιβουλεύοντας. *Op. cit.* PG.57.390.9-15: Ἀλλ' ἴδωμεν ποίαν φρόνησιν ἐνταῦθα ἀπαιτεῖ. Τὴν τοῦ ὄφεως, φησί. Καθάπερ γὰρ ἐκεῖνος τὰ πάντα προΐεται, κἂν αὐτὸ δέῃ τὸ σῶμα ἀποτμηθῆναι, οὐ σφόδρα ἀντέχεται αὐτοῦ, ὥστε τὴν κεφαλὴν διατηρῆσαι. οὕτω καὶ σύ, φησί, πλὴν τῆς πίστεως πάντα ἐκδίδου, κἂν χρήματα, κἂν τὸ σῶμα, κἂν αὐτὴν τὴν ψυχὴν ἐκδοῦναι δέῃ.

dccxxiii Origen, *commMatt*, fr. 202 (Klostermann), col. 1.

dccxxiv Isidore of Pelusium, *apud Catena in Matthaeum*, pp. 76-77. See the first part of the fragment *supra*. The passage ὅσαις γὰρ ἂν πληγαῖς … καὶ τὸν νέον ἀνταμφιέννυσθαι is the selfsame one as that just above which has been attributed to Theodore of Heraclea (*frMatt*, fr. 66).

dccxxv Jerome, *commMatt*, 10.16.

dccxxvi Origen, *commMatt*, fr. 203 (Klostermann).

dccxxvii John Chrysostom, *In Matthaeum*, PG.58.689.7-12.

dccxxviii The expression φύσεως ἐπιτηδειότης (meaning the specific capabilities of one's nature) is one more of those that Origen introduced and bequeathed to Porphyry, *Epistula ad Anebonem*, 2.18d (& Iamblichus, *De Mysteriis*, 10:3). The actual philological source is Plato' expression in *Respublica*, 374e: Ἆρ' οὖν οὐ καὶ φύσεως ἐπιτηδείας εἰς αὐτὸ τὸ ἐπιτήδευμα; ("Does it not also require a nature adapted to that very pursuit?"). It occurs also in the vocabulary of Galen, from whom Origen picked up several elegant technical phrases and adapted them to his own purposes. Cf. Pseudo-Galen, *Ad Gaurum Quomodo Animetur Fetus*, 16.2 (quoted also by Oribasius, *Collectiones Medicae*, 24.4.4): σωμασκεῖν μὲν εὐγονίᾳ φύσεως ἐπιτήδειον. Subsequently, both Christian and Greek authors took this up, if just casually. Dexippus, *commCateg*, p. 4. Simplicius, *commCateg*, p. 242. Gregory of Nazianzus, *In Dictum Evangelii: Cum Consummasset Jesus Hos Sermons*, PG.36.305.24: τὸ ἐκ φύσεως ἐπιτήδειον. Basil of Caesarea, *Epistulae*, epistle 116.1; *Homilia in Principium Proverbiorum*, PG.31.417.13. Cyril of Alexandria, *De Adoratione*, PG.68.892. 2 & 19; *commLuc*, PG.72.816.20-21; *In Joannem*, v. 1, p. 500. Michael Psellus, *Orationes Hagiographicae*, oration 7, line 120; *Theologica*, opusculum 70, line 94; *Encomium in Matrem*, line 1016. Eustratius of Nicaea, *commEthNic*, p. 403. Gennadius Scholarius, *Tractatus De Uno Deo*, p. 176.

dccxxix Cf. John Chrysostom, *In Matthaeum*, PG.57.392.27-31. Ταῦτα δὲ καὶ ἄλλως ἱκανὰ ἦν ἀνορθῶσαι αὐτῶν τὰ φρονήματα, εἴγε τοσαύτη τοῦ κηρύγματος ἔμελλεν ἀνάπτεσθαι δύναμις, ὡς φύσιν ἀτιμάζεσθαι, καὶ συγγένειαν ἐκβάλλεσθαι, καὶ προτιμᾶσθαι πάντων τὸν λόγον, κατὰ κράτος πάντα ἐλαύνοντα.

dccxxx Cyril of Alexandria, *frMatt*, fr. 119.

dccxxxi Clement of Alexandria, *apud Catena in Matthaeum*, p. 78 & Clement of Alexandria, *Fragmenta* (L. Früchtel, O. Stählin, U. Treu), fr. 56. It seems that Origen availed himself of his predecessor.

dccxxxii Cyril of Alexandria, *frMatt*, fr. 120, col. 1.

dccxxxiii Cyril of Alexandria, *op. cit.* col. 2.

dccxxxiv Origen, *commMatt*, fr. 204 (Klostermann), col. 1 (see also col. 2). This is the same as the passage of Origen, *apud Catena in Matthaeum*, p. 78.

dccxxxv Theodore of Heraclea, *frMatt*, fr. 68, col. 1 and *Catena in Matthaeum*, p. 78.

dccxxxvi Theodore of Heraclea, *loc. cit.*, col. 2.

dccxxxvii Cyril of Alexandria, *frMatt*, fr. 121.

dccxxxviii Origen, *commMatt*, fr. 206 (Klostermann), col. 1; see part of this also in col. 2.

dccxxxix Once again, an indisputable text of Origen's was ascribed to Theodore of Mopsuestia, *frMatt*, fr. 55: *Τάχα καὶ περὶ τοῦ καιροῦ ἐκείνου λέγει, ὅτε κρινεῖ ὁ θεὸς τὰ κρυπτὰ τῶν ἀνθρώπων καὶ φωτίσει τὰ κρυπτὰ τοῦ σκότους καὶ φανερώσει τὰς βουλὰς τῶν καρδιῶν.*

dccxl Origen, *frLuc*, fr. 191 (on Luke 12:2).

dccxli John Chrysostom, *In Matthaeum*, PG.57.399.56-400.1 (homily 34). However, styling the land of the Jews 'a corner of Palestine' (γωνία τῆς Παλαιστίνης) was a denigrating expression used for the first time by Celsus in his *True Discourse*, who spoke of the creation narrated in the Genesis in utter contempt, and styled this a story by 'uneducated people who distorted the story by Hesiod and by other divine men'. See Celsus, *apud* Origen, *Cels*, IV.36: Ἰουδαῖοι ἐν γωνίᾳ που τῆς Παλαιστίνης συγκύψαντες, παντελῶς ἀπαίδευτοι καὶ οὐ προακηκοότες πάλαι ταῦτα Ἡσιόδῳ καὶ ἄλλοις μυρίοις ἀνδράσιν ἐνθέοις ὑμνημένα, συνέθεσαν ἀπιθανώτατα καὶ ἀμουσότατα, ἄνθρωπόν τινα ὑπὸ χειρῶν θεοῦ πλασσόμενόν τε καὶ ἐμφυσώμενον καὶ γύναιον ἐκ τῆς πλευρᾶς ... etc. The expression 'a corner of Palestine' (γωνία τῆς Παλαιστίνης) did not win the day, except at an instance where Eusebius used this, evindently influenced by Origen's text (Eusebius, *In Isaiam*, 1.62, line 176), and at another one by an unknown author who obviously had read the present passage of Chrysostom's commentary on Matthew (which was a mere copy from Origen) and essayed to imitate Chrysostom's style (Pseudo-John Chrysostom, *In illud: Exiit Edictum*, PG.50.796.27-28). No other author did ever use this expression, which ultimately was Celsus' one.

dccxlii Jerome, *commMatt*, 10.27.

dccxliii This is the first part of Origen, *commMatt*, fr. 207 (Klostermann).

dccxliv On the idea of 'the state after the resurrection' (μετὰ τὴν ἀνάστασιν), see Origen arguing that the Scripture says certain things about this, yet not explicitly, but allegorically. *commMatt*, 17.34: Ἕκαστος μὲν οὖν τῶν ἐπιστησάντων τῇ ἐπαπορήσει ἡμῶν ζητείτω ἀπὸ τῶν γραφῶν παριστάμενα τὰ ὑπὸ τοῦ σωτῆρος εἰρημένα περὶ τῶν μετὰ τὴν ἀνάστασιν. Ἡμεῖς δὲ τοιαῦτα φήσομεν ὅτι περιέχουσι ταῦτα αἱ γραφαὶ οὐκ αὐτολεξεὶ οὐδ᾽ ὥστε τοῖς τυχοῦσι νοηθῆναι, ἀλλ᾽ ἐν τροπολογίᾳ.

dccxlv Cf. Origen, *commJohn*, XX.11.83: Ἀλλ᾽ εἰ τοιοῦτός τίς ἐστιν λόγος ὥστε καὶ τὸ σῶμα αὐτοῦ καὶ τὴν ψυχήν, τῷ ἄξια εἶναι ἀπωλείας, ἀπόλλυσθαι δύνασθαι, φοβητέον τὸν δυνάμενον θεὸν λόγον καὶ ψυχὴν καὶ σῶμα ἀπολέσαι καὶ ἐξαφανίσαι, εἴτε ἐν γεέννῃ εἴτε ὅπως βούλεται. *selPs*, PG.12.1097.9-14: Τὸ δέ, *Φοβήθητε τὸν δυνάμενον καὶ ψυχὴν καὶ τὸ σῶμα ἀπολέσαι ἐν γεέννῃ.* [Matt. 10:28] τάχα μὲν διδάσκει, ὅτι ἀσώματος ἡ ψυχή, τάχα δὲ δηλοῖ καὶ ὅτι χωρὶς σώματος οὐ κολασθήσεται. περὶ οὗ φυσιολογοῦντες τὰ περὶ τοῦ εἴδους καὶ τοῦ πρώτου ὑποκειμένου εἰρήκαμεν. *exhMar*, 34.

dccxlvi By speaking of μέσος θάνατος ('middle death', i.e. the physical one), Origen reflected in Stoic terms (which he did frequently), meaning the natural end of one's lifetime, which is morally indifferent (ἀδιάφορον), as indeed 'life' in its natural sense is morally 'indifferent', too. In the following passage, he speaks of both 'morally indifferent life' (ἀδιάφορος ζωή) and 'morally indifferent death' in their Stoic sense. *commJohn*, XX.25.224: Ἐπίστησον δὲ καὶ τῷ *Ἐν τῷ Ἀδὰμ πάντες ἀποθνήσκουσιν, καὶ ἐν τῷ Χριστῷ πάντες ζωοποιηθήσονται*, ἐν οἷς οὔτε ὁ μέσος θάνατος σημαίνεται κατὰ τὸ *Ἐν τῷ Ἀδὰμ πάντες ἀποθνήσκουσιν*, οὔτε ἡ ἀδιάφορος ζωὴ καὶ μήτε ἀγαθὸν οὖσα καθ᾽ αὑτὴν μήτε κακὸν κατὰ τὸ *Ἐν τῷ Χριστῷ πάντες ζωοποιηθήσονται*, καὶ ὄψει τὴν ζωὴν τοῦ κατ᾽ εἰκόνα ἀνθρώπου. *Op. cit.* XX.39.363-4: Ὥσπερ ἐστίν τις ζωὴ ἀδιάφορος, ἡ μήτε ἀγαθὸν μήτε κακὸν τυγχάνουσα, καθ᾽ ἣν λέγομεν ζῆν καὶ τοὺς ἀσεβεῖς καὶ τὰ ἄλογα ζῷα, καὶ ἑτέρα διάφορος ἀλλὰ ἀγαθόν, περὶ ἧς φησιν ὁ Παῦλος. *Ἡ ζωὴ † ἡμῶν κέκρυπται σὺν τῷ χριστῷ ἐν τῷ θεῷ·* καὶ αὐτὸς ὁ κύριος ἡμῶν περὶ ἑαυτοῦ· *Ἐγώ εἰμι ἡ ζωή*, οὕτως τὸν μὲν ἐναντίον τῇ ἀδιαφόρῳ ζωῇ θάνατον ἀδιάφορον ἐρεῖς, τὸν δὲ ἐχθρὸν τῷ εἰπόντι, *Ἐγώ εἰμι ἡ ζωὴ* πονηρόν τινα καὶ χαλεπὸν θάνατον, ὃν ὁ ἀποθνήσκων ἐστὶν ἐν τῷ θανάτῳ. περὶ οὗ γέγραπται. *Ἔσχατος ἐχθρὸς καταργεῖται ὁ θάνατος.* Origen maintained that daemons always conspire to do evil, yet God does not always allow them to do so, and sometimes divine judgment encumbers their doing evil. In *Cels*, VIII.32, he speaks of daemons who 'always will to hurt, but they cannot do always so, because they are prevented' from doing so: Εἰ δὲ καὶ ἄλλο τι παρὰ ταῦτα γίνεται ὅθ' οἱ δαίμονες ἐπιτρέπονται, ἀεὶ μὲν βουλόμενοι ταῦτα ποιεῖν οὐκ ἀεὶ δὲ δυνάμενοι διὰ τὸ κωλύεσθαι, ὁ δυνάμενος ἐξεταζέτω, τὴν θείαν κρίσιν κατὰ τὸ δυνατὸν ἀνθρωπίνῃ φύσει φανταζόμενος περὶ ἀθρόας πολλῶν ψυχῶν ἀπαλλαγῆς ἀπὸ σώματος, τοιαῖσδε ταῖς ἐπὶ τὸν μέσον θάνατον φερούσαις ὁδοῖς χρωμένων. Accordingly, when 'divine judgment' allows daemons to get involved in the process 'of separation of many souls from the body', this is 'death', yet a kind of death which is 'morally indifferent' (see *supra*, on 'punishing angels', endnote ccclxx, p. 429, quoting Origen, *homEz*, p. 323). In the dialogue with Heraclides, he distinguished three kinds of death (the indifferent natural one; dying to sin [cf. Rom. 6:2]; and death of the soul because of sin [cf. Ez. 18:4&20]). Once again, he set not too a great store by the 'indifferent' natural death (μέσον θάνατον). *Dialogus cum Heraclide*, 25-26: Κατὰ τὸν μέσον θάνατον πάντες ἄνθρωποι ἀποθνήσκομεν, ὃν διάλυσιν νομίζομεν εἶναι. ‹Τοῦτον› τὸν θάνατον οὐδεμία ψυχὴ ἀνθρώπου ἀποθνήσκει· εἰ γὰρ ἀπέθνησκεν, οὐκ ἂν ἐκολάζετο μετὰ τὸν θάνατον. *commRom* (*I.1-XII.21*), fr. 30: *θάνατος* λέγεται νῦν ὁ μέσος καὶ ἀδιάφορος. ... φήσει τοίνυν οὐδὲν θαυμαστὸν κατὰ τοῦτον τὸν χαρακτῆρα καὶ τὸν ἀπόστολον εἰρηκέναι, τὸ μὲν *ἀπεθάνομεν σὺν Χριστῷ* τάσσοντα οὐκ ἐπὶ τοῦ κοινοτέρου τὸ δὲ ὡς *θανάτου* νῦν τοῦ μέσου ὀνομαζομένου.

dccxlvii Cf. Origen, *selEz*, PG.13.816.42-44: *Ἡ ψυχὴ ἡ ἁμαρτάνουσα, αὐτὴ ἀποθανεῖται.* Θνῆσιν τῆς ἁμαρτίας, κατὰ στέρησιν τοῦ εἰπόντος, *Ἐγώ εἰμι ἡ ζωή.*

dccxlviii Origen, *commMatt*, fr. 209 (Klostermann).

dccxlix Cf. Origen, *schMatt*, PG.17.297.13-16: Ἵνα δὲ μὴ νομίσῃ τις ὅτι ἔξω μόνον βάλλονται οἱ ἄπιστοι καὶ πονηροί, ἐσήμανεν ὅτι εἰς διηνεκῆ κόλασιν παραπέμπονται. *Καὶ βαλοῦσιν αὐτοὺς εἰς τὴν κάμινον τοῦ πυρός*, καὶ τὰ ἑξῆς. Origen was the first who spoke of 'endless punishment' through the expression διηνεκὴς κόλασις. As it happened, Eusebius took this up (*Vita Constantini*, 2.54.1), but this turn of phrase remained idle until John Chrysostom took this up and used it abundantly. *In Genesim*, PG.53: 203.59; 246.46; *De Lazaro*, PG.48.1001.57-58; *Contra Eos Qui Subintroductas Habent Virgines*, 2; *Expositiones in Psalmos*, PG.55.238.44; *et passim*. Likewise, Theodoret, *Interpretatio in Psalmos*, PG.80.873.16. Cyril of Alexandria, *commLuc*, PG.72: 692.4; 732.1. Olympiodorus, the daecon of Alexandria, *Commentarii in Ecclesiasten*, PG.93.500.29; *Commentarii in Jeremiam*, PG.93.668.5-6. Photius, *Bibliotheca*, Codex 222, p. 201a; *Homiliae*, homily 2, p. 21; *Epistulae et Amphilochia*, epistle 13; *Fragmenta in Epistulam i ad Thessalonicenses*, p. 635. Michael Psellus, *Opuscula i*, opusculum 39.

dccl Theodore of Mopsuestia, *frMatt*, fr. 56.

dccli John Chrysostom, *In Matthaeum*, PG.57.400.40-48. One can see that he composed his homilies while having Origen's commentary in front of him, yet never mentioning his source. This is why Epiphanius of Salamis incriminated Chrysostom for 'Origenism'. See Introduction.

dcclii Origen, *commMatt*, fr. 208 (Klostermann).

dccliii This is Past Tense infinitive of the verb ἀποκτίννυμαι (Middle voice). The form ἀποκτέννυσθαι of the present codex is acceptable as a form of the verb ἀποκτέννυμαι (other variants: ἀποκτείνομαι, ἀποκτένομαι, ἀποκτίννυμαι, ἀποκτιννύομαι).

dccliv Origen, *commMatt*, fr. 210 (Klostermann).

dcclv The expression *διάγνωσιν καὶ πρόνοιαν* is a turn of phrase which no Christian took up from Origen, perhaps because to most of them this appeared incomprehensible, and certainly so to those who latched on his work, such as John Chrysostom, Cyril of Alexandria, Theodore of Heraclea, Appolinaris, and others. Cf. Galen, *De Sanitate Tuenda*, pp. 419-420 (explaining the three cases of 'anomalous structures of bodies', τὰς ἀνωμάλους κατασκευὰς τῶν σωμάτων): εὐκολωτέρα μὲν οὖν ἐστιν ἡ τρίτη λεγομένη καὶ *διαγνωσθῆναι* καὶ *προνοίας* τυχεῖν, δυσκολωτέρα δὲ ἡ δευτέρα, χαλεπωτάτη δὲ ἡ πρώτη. βέλτιον οὖν ἀπὸ τῆ τρίτης ἄρξασθαι ῥᾴονα τήν τε *διάγνωσιν* ἐχούσῃ *καὶ τὴν πρόνοιαν*. Italics are mine. Origen was enamoured of Galen's works because of his keen interest in medicine. A by-product of his readings was the vast variety of Galen's expressions that he employed. This is about terms and expressions, not ideas, but the way he put those expressions to use for his own purposes and in his own context is fascinating to study.

dcclvi Attributed to John Chrysostom, *apud Catena in Matthaeum*, pp. 79-80.

dcclvii John Chrysostom put Origen's statement to use by means of the same terms (see italics). *Expositiones in Psalmos*, PG.55.488.6-11: Τίνος ἕνεκεν οὕτω μεταχειρίζει τὸν λόγον; Ἐκ περιουσίας δεικνὺς τοῦ Θεοῦ *τὴν πρόνοιαν*. Εἰ γὰρ τὰ δοκοῦντα *ἄχρηστα* εἶναι, καὶ πολέμια τῷ γένει τῶν ἀνθρώπων, οὕτως ἐστὶ καλά, οὕτω χρήσιμα, ὡς καὶ αὐτὰ ὕμνον ἀναφέρειν τῷ Θεῷ καὶ δοξολογίαν διὰ τῆς οἰκείας δημιουργίας. *Commentarius in Job*, p. 194: τίνος δὲ ἕνεκεν οὐκ ἐμνήσθη βοὸς οὐδὲ προβάτων οὐδὲ τῶν ἄλλων τῶν τοιούτων οὐδενός, ἀλλὰ *τῶν ἀχρήστων* καὶ εἰκῇ δοκούντων εἶναι; Δεικνύς, ὅτι, εἰ ἐν ἐκείνοις σοφία τοσαύτη καὶ *πρόνοια* τοῖς οὐδὲν δοκοῦσι συντελεῖν, πολλῷ μᾶλλον ἐν τούτοις.

dcclviii This is the first phrase of Origen, *commMatt*, fr. 211 (Klostermann).

dcclix Origen, *commMatt*, fr. 212 (Klostermann).

dcclx Origen, *frLuc*, fr. 192 & *schLuc*, PG.17.357.10-22 (brackets indicate editorial variants in this work).

dcclxi Jerome, *commMatt*, 10.29.

dcclxii Origen, *commMatt*, fr. 213 (Klostermann).

dcclxiii Origen, *apud Catena in Matthaeum*, p. 80.

dcclxiv Cyril of Alexandria, *frMatt*, fr. 125.

dcclxv Apollinaris, *frMatt*, fr. 56. But now we have Origen's own text both preceding and following that phrase.

dcclxvi Origen, *commMatt*, fr. 214 (Klostermann).

dcclxvii Origen, *commMatt*, fr. 215 (Klostermann).

dcclxviii Origen, *apud Catena in Matthaeum*, p. 81.

dcclxix Origen, *commJohn*, I.32.229.

dcclxx Origen, *commMatt*, fr. 220 II (Klostermann), col. 1. The editor placed this fragment in brackets because he thought that this runs parallel to Chrysostom's thirty-sixth homily on Matthew. However, in this case Chrysostom did not copy from Origen and there is no parallel. The text is very much like Origen. Nevertheless, see John Chrysostom, *In Matthaeum*, PG.57.414.36-52: Ἕως μὲν οὖν ἦν Ἰωάννης μετ' αὐτῶν, παρεκάλει συνεχῶς καὶ ἐδίδασκε, καὶ οὐδὲ οὕτως ἔπειθεν· ... Ἀναμένει παρ' αὐτῶν ἀκοῦσαι, ὅτι θαύματα ἐργάζεται. καὶ οὐδὲ οὕτως αὐτοῖς παραινεῖ, οὐδὲ πάντας πέμπει, ἀλλὰ δύο τινὰς οὓς ᾔδει ἴσως τῶν ἄλλων εὐπειθεστέρους ὄντας.

dcclxxi Origen, *apud Catena in Matthaeum*, p. 83. Cf. Origen, *De Engastrimytho*, 7: τοιοῦτόν τινά μοι νόει καὶ τὸν Ἰωάννην. ... ἰδὼν τὴν τηλικαύτην δόξαν ἀμφέβαλλεν καὶ τάχα ἠπίστει, εἰ ὁ οὕτως ἔνδοξος καὶ μέχρις ᾅδου καὶ μέχρι τῆς ἀβύσσου κατελεύσεται. Διὰ τοῦτο ἔλεγεν· *σὺ εἶ ὁ ἐρχόμενος, ἢ ἄλλον προσδοκῶμεν;*

dcclxxii The term εὐρίπιστος (derived from ευ- [easily] + the verb ῥιπίζω [blow up or fan]) is a neologism introduced by Alexander of Aphrodisias, meaning 'changeable' in reference to blowing wind. *In Librum De Sensu Commentarium*, p. 26: εὐρίπιστος γὰρ ὁ ἀήρ. However, once Origen took this up (while no one else had done so prior to him), he used it in a metaphorical sense, in reference to a person being unstable, volatile, erratic – hence, 'easily swayed', frivolous, light-minded. Strange though it appears, the epithet was used by no Greek author at all, even though the source of this was the eminent Aristotelian commentator. Both Classical and Later Antique philosophers were content with the adjective κοῦφος, which has the same meaning.

Cf. Origen, *commJohn*, X.24.142: Σύμβολον δὲ τῶν ... τῶν κούφων καὶ εὐριπίστων λογισμῶν ἡ περιστερά. *frPs*, on Psalm 94:10-11: τὸ κοῦφον αὐτῶν καὶ εὐρίπιστον τῆς γνώμης. After Origen, this became part of the Christian locution, and remained entirely absent from Greek literature. Gregory of Nyssa, *Contra Eunomium*, 3.2.99. Eusebius, *Commentaria in Psalmos*, PG.23.224.56. Epiphanius of Salamis, *Panarion*, v. 2, p. 364. Athanasius, *Expositiones in Psalmos*, PG.27.368.13. Julian the Arian, *Commentarius in Job*, pp. 168; 293. Ephraem Syrus, *Sermo in Adventum Domini*, p. 118; *Encomium in Sanctos Quadraginta Martyres*, p. 148. Socrates Scholasticus, *HE*, 3.17. Theodoret, *Epistulae: Collectio Sirmondiana (epistulae 96-147)*, epistle 29; *Interpretatio in Psalmos*, PG.80: 1644.25; 1824.44-45; *Haereticarum Fabularum Compendium*, PG.83.532.3-4. Cyril of Alexandria, *Expositio in Psalmos*, PG.69.897.1213. Gelasius of Cyzicus, *HE*, 1.4.2. Olympiodorus, the deacon of Alexandria, *Commentarii in Job*, p. 244. Oecumenius, *Commentarius in Apocalypsin*, p. 14. Pseudo-Caesarius (Cassian the Sabaite), *Quaestiones et Responsiones*, 111. Cyril of Scythopolis, *Vita Sabae*, p. 146. John of Damascus, *Sacra Parallela*, PG.95.1132.35. Photius, *Bibliotheca*, Codex 222, p. 188a; Codex 258, p. 480a; *Epistulae et Amphilochia*, epistles 73; 135; 283.

It appears then that Christian usage of the epithet was rather sporadic and scarce, and definitely no instance of this prior to Origen can be traced. However, we are upon the usual exception, namely, John Chrysostom: as he normally did, once he took up a stirring term from Origen, he put it to recurrent use. Cf. *Ad Populum Antiochenum*, PG.49: 21.18; 42.42; *De Sanctis Martyribus*, PG.50.654.2; *et passim*. See this also in the texts running parallel to Origen's one at this point, which I am quoting. Theodore of Heraclea, who normally copied promiscuously from this work of Origen's, was rather baffled at the neologism εὐρίπιστος, hence, he only used the term εὐμετάφορος ('easily transferrable'), which is nearly synonymous in this context, if less accurate; *frMatt*, fr. 74 & *Catena in Matthaeum*, p. 84: Ἵνα μὴ νομίσωσί τινες ὅτι εὐμετάφορος ἦν Ἰωάννης, ὃν πρῴην ἐκήρυξε Χριστὸν νῦν ἀγνοῶν, εἶπε τοῦτο. Otherwise, he kept on copying from Origen's text even peculiar turns of phrase, as shown shortly below. See *infra*, folio 90r, Origen's use of the biblical expression ἐξαίσιον πτῶμα ('horrendous fall') and the same text in Theodore of Heraclea's alleged fragment 78.

dcclxxiii John Chrysostom, *In Matthaeum*, PG.57.419.28-46.

dcclxxiv John Chrysostom, *op. cit.* PG.57.347.26-34.

dcclxxv John Chrysostom, *op. cit.* PG.57.420.15-22.

dcclxxvi In what follows, we have Origen's continuous text against scattered fragments of this, which are quoted in smaller fonts at the proper points.

dcclxxvii Origen, *commMatt*, fr. 221 (Klostermann). But now we have the entire text which precedes this fragment.

dcclxxviii Origen, *commMatt*, fr. 232 (Klostermann), col. 2.

dcclxxix This is part of Cyril of Alexandria, *frMatt*, fr. 144, quoted *infra*.

dcclxxx Origen, *commMatt*, fr. 232 (Klostermann), col. 1.

dcclxxxi Origen, *apud Catena in Matthaeum*, p. 87.

dcclxxxii This is part of Cyril of Alexandria, *frMatt*, fr. 142, also in the *Catena in Matthaeum*, p. 87.

dcclxxxiii This Codex reveals that Gregory Thaumaturgus took up from his teacher Origen not only the idea, but also the expression about the Subsistent Wisdom (ὑφεστῶσα σοφία). Cf. Gregory Thaumaturgus *apud* Gregory of Nyssa, *De Vita Gregorii Thaumaturgi*, PG.46.912.47-48: Εἷς Θεὸς Πατὴρ Λόγου ζῶντος, σοφίας ὑφεστώσης καὶ δυνάμεως. This text of Gregory Thaumaturgus was quoted also by several subsequent authors, who cited his name, such as the following ones: Germanus I of Constantinople, *Narratio De Haeresibus et Synodis ad Anthimum Diaconum*, 11. John of Damascus, *De Sancta Trinitate* (*fragmentum*), PG.95.12.20 ff. John Beccus, *In Andronici Camateri Animadversiones*, p. 577. Theodore II Ducas Lascaris, *De Processione Spiritus Sancti*, lines 294 ff. Neophytus Prodromenus, *Contra Latinos*, 26. Marcus Eugenicus, *Testimonia Spiritum Sanctum ex Patre Procedere Probantia*, Testimonium 120. ACO, *Synodus Constantinopolitana et Hierosolymitana anno 536*, tome 3, p. 3. *Concilium Universale Constantinopolitanum Tertium* (*680-681*), Document 8, p. 218 (without citing Gregory). Also, *Doctrina Patrum*, p. 284.

Beyond this, Origen's expression and notion of ὑφεστῶσα σοφία ('Subsistent Wisdom') was naturally used *verbatim* by Eusebius, *De Ecclesiastica Theologia*, 3.2.3-4: ἀλλ᾽ ὑφεστῶσαν καὶ ζῶσαν σοφίαν, τὴν αὐτὴν οὖσαν τῷ υἱῷ τοῦ θεοῦ. Maximus Confessor, *Quaestiones ad Thalassium*, 13: τὴν κατ᾽ οὐσίαν ἔμφυτον αὐτοῦ σοφίαν ὑφεστῶσαν καὶ τῶν ὄντων συνεκτικὴν διδασκόμεθα. *Op. cit.* 39: Ὡς γὰρ ἡλίου χωρὶς ἡμέραν γενέσθαι παντελῶς ἀμήχανον, οὕτω δίχα τῆς οὐσιώδους καὶ ὑφεστώσης σοφίας νόμος εἶναι δικαιοσύνης οὐ δύναται.

Theodore of Heraclea simply copied from Origen's passage as this appears in the present codex. *frMatt*, fr. 77 (*Catena in Matthaeum*, p. 86), col. 1: Αὐτὸς ὢν ὁ Χριστὸς ἡ ζῶσα καὶ ὑφεστῶσα σοφία ὑπὸ τῶν εἰς αὐτὸν πιστευόντων ἐκρίθη δίκαιος πάντα οἰκονομήσας. Col 2: Ἡ ὑφεστῶσα σοφία ἐκρίθη δίκαιος ὑπὸ τῶν εἰς αὐτὸν πιστευότων.

Cf. Origen identifying the 'Subistent Wisdom' with the Son. *commJohn*, VI.38.188: περὶ τοῦ υἱοῦ τοῦ θεοῦ, τοῦ λόγου, δι᾽ οὗ τὰ πάντα γέγονεν, ὑφεστηκότος οὐσιωδῶς κατὰ τὸ ὑποκείμενον, τοῦ αὐτοῦ ὄντος τῇ σοφίᾳ. *expProv*, PG.17.185.1-7: Οὐσία οὖσα ἡ τοῦ Θεοῦ σοφία, πρὸ αἰώνων γεγένηται, καὶ πρὸ κτίσεως ἀΐδιος ἦν. ὅτε δὲ σχέσιν πρὸς τὰ γεννητὰ ἐδέξατο, τότε ἀρχὴ τῶν ὁδῶν τοῦ Θεοῦ γέγονε τῶν ποιητικῶν καὶ προνοητικῶν. σύζυγος οὖν ἡ ἀρχὴ τοῖς κτίσμασιν ὧν γέγονεν ἀρχή, τουτέστιν ἡ πρὸς τὰ γεννητὰ σχέσις. ἡ δὲ σοφία ἀΐδιος, οὐσιωδῶς πρὸ αἰώνων παρὰ τῷ Θεῷ ὑπάρχουσα.

dcclxxxiv Once again, Theodore of Heraclea copied from Origen's text.

dcclxxxv Origen, *commMatt*, fr. 233 (Klostermann). But now we have Origen's text both before and after this 'fragment'.

dcclxxxvi Origen, *commMatt*, fr. 235 (Klostermann).

dcclxxxvii Cyril of Alexandria, *frMatt*, fr. 144. The last period (αὐλός … καὶ ἐπώδυνα τῆς γεέννης) runs parallel to Origen's text (as well as to Origen, *commMatt*, fr. 232, Klostermann, col. 2, quoted also *supra*, folio 89r). Thus, Cyril copied from Origen to the letter by intermingling the latter's statements.

dcclxxxviii The term κακέμφατος ('ill-sounding') is another neologism which appeared for the first time in Herodian, *Περὶ Ῥημάτων*, pp. 800 & 801 (see also George Choeroboscus, *Prolegomena et Scholia in Theodosii Alexandrini Canones Isagogicos De Flexione*

Verborum, p. 143 (attribution of κακένφατος to the second-century BC philosopher Demetrius of Laconia is highly precarious). As a lemma to be explained it appears only in Hesychius of Alexandria's, *Lexicon*, letter kappa, entry 298 (opposite; ἀκακέμφατος, 'of no ill repute'; Hesychius, *op. cit.* etter alpha, entry 2236). Theodoret used this once (*Eranistes*, p. 263) whereas, earlier, Methodius of Olympus had used its opposite, that is, ἀκακέμφατος. As it happened with the term εὐρίπιστος that I have just discussed, John Chrysostom took this up and used at no less than five points (*In Matthaeum*, PG.57: 405.40; 424.27; *In Epistulam i ad Corinthios*, PG.61: 79.27; 543.53; *In Epistulam ad Hebraeos*, PG.63.32.53). He is the only author of whom we know having used this more than once after Herodian. Nevertheless, considering how abundantly he used terms that he had received from Origen, five instances are all but many, which allows for the conjecture that he used this term *after* he had read Origen's commentary on Matthew, from which he copied extensively. Besides, to believe that Chrysostom received this term from Herodian could be rather unlikely, whereas usage of the opposite term ἀκακέμφατος by Methodius of Olympus (which no one had ever used before, as far as extant literature goes) could hardly have been irrelevant to Methodius' obsessive reading of Origen's works.

dcclxxxix This is allusion to Origen and this is as far as Chrysostom went paying his dues to Origen, to whom he owed several points of his sermons on Matthew's gospel.

dccxc Origen, *commMatt*, fr. 234 (Klostermann).

dccxci Origen, *commMatt*, fr. 236 (Klostermann).

dccxcii Origen, *commMatt*, fr. 237 (Klostermann), col. 1.

dccxciii John Chrysostom, *In Matthaeum*, PG.57.424.19-39. The text preceding this point (verses 5-16) expounds Origen's ideas found in this commentary and it is couched in his own characteristic terms (e.g. τὸν σκυθρωπὸν καὶ ἀνειμένον ἄνθρωπον, τὸν ἀνειμένον βίον, τὰ γεγενημένα). In *Codex B 113* of the Great Laura of Mount Athos (eleventh century), this text is attributed jointly to Origen and John Chrysostom (Klostermann, *op. cit.* p. 110), which suggests the usual case of the latter having copied from the former.

dccxciv Both this and the preceding portion make up the ensuing fragment which has been attributed also to Theodore of Mopsuestia.

dccxcv Theodore of Mopsuestia, *frMatt*, fr. 62 (Reuss).

dccxcvi Origen, *commMatt*, fr. 238 (Klostermann). This is a laconic yet pithy definition which no author did ever care to reproduce.

dccxcvii Jerome, *commMatt*, 11.20.

dccxcviii The only author who wrote a derivative from Sodoma, namely, the adjective Σοδομητικὸς (-ή) with η, instead of ι (Σοδομιτικός), is Pseudo-Basil of Caesarea (*forsan* Cassian the Sabaite), *Enarratio in Prophetam Isaiam*, 1.22: Τοῦτο οὖν τὸ σπέρμα, τοὺς ὅσον ἐπὶ τῇ ἀξίᾳ τῶν βεβιωμένων ὀφείλοντας, παθεῖν τὰ Σοδόμων καὶ πυρὶ καὶ θείῳ ἐκτριβῆναι διὰ τὴν κακίαν φθάνουσαν εἰς τὸ Σοδομητικὸν μέτρον, τῇ παρ' ἑαυτοῦ παρουσίᾳ ἐκώλυσεν. ... Αὐταὶ δέ εἰσι τῆς Σοδομητικῆς πενταπόλεως. Besides, as it happened, his vocabulary is characteristically that of Origen. For example, Cassian's expression ἐπὶ τῇ ἀξίᾳ τῶν βεβιωμένων is one that Origen had received from two earlier authors whose work he had read, then he bequeathed this to his usual admirers, and then this was embraced more widely. Also, in my *Scholia in Apocalypsin* (compiled by Cassian the Sabaite), scholion XXXVII, p. 186: ἐπὶ τὸ λαβεῖν ἕκαστος ἐπαξίως τῶν βεβιωμένων. See also, pp. 399-400; 474. Cf. *infra*, folio, 96r: Αὐτοὶ τοίνυν ἔσονται ὑμῶν κριταί οὐ περὶ τῶν βεβιωμένων. Also, folio 199v: οὐ συνεχώρησεν ὁ καιρὸς τῶν βεβιωμένων. Lucian of Samosata, *Pseudologista*, 2: σοὶ δὲ μυρία συνειδὼς ἰάμβων ἄξια βεβιωμένα. Philostratus, *Vita Apollonii*, 6.21: ὡς οὐκ ἀξίᾳ τῶν ἑαυτῷ βεβιωμένων. Origen, *frPs*, on Psalm 74:8: Ὃν θέλει δηλαδὴ [sc. ὑψοῖ or ταπεινοῖ] κατὰ τὴν ἀξίαν τῶν βεβιωμένων ἑκάστῳ. Gregory of Nyssa, *In illud: Quatenus Uni ex His Fecistis Mihi Fecistis*, pp. 111-112: κατὰ τὴν ἀξίαν τῶν βεβιωμένων ἑκάστῳ τὴν κρίσιν ἐπάγοντα. *In Sanctum Pascha*, p. 264: ὡς ὑπ' ἐκείνῳ κριτῇ τὰς πρὸς ἀξίαν ἀμοιβὰς τῶν βεβιωμένων κομίσασθαι. *Contra Eunomium*, 3.3.36-37: ἀνάστασιν, ὁμόθρονός τε καὶ ὁμόδοξος ὢν τῷ ἰδίῳ πατρὶ κατ' ἀξίαν τῶν βεβιωμένων ἐν τῇ ἡμέρᾳ τῆς κρίσεως ἐποίσει τὴν ψῆφον τοῖς κρινομένοις. Gregory of Nazianzus, *Ad Julianum Tributorum Exaequatorem*, PG.35.1061.14-15: γεγράμμεθα κατ' ἀξίαν τῶν ἐνταῦθα βεβιωμένων ἕκαστος. Basil of Caesarea, *Homiliae in Hexaemeron*, 1.4: τὸν Θεὸν ἐννοῆσαι ποιητὴν τοῦ παντὸς καὶ κριτὴν δίκαιον, τὴν ἀξίαν ἀντίδοσιν τοῖς βεβιωμένοις ἐπάγοντα. *Quod Deus Non est Auctor Malorum*, PG.31.329.46-47: εἰ οὐκ ἔστιν ὁ ἀντιδιδοὺς ἑκάστῳ κατὰ τὴν ἀξίαν τῶν βεβιωμένων. Likewise, Ephraem Syrus, *Beati Ephraem Testamentum*, p. 411. John Chrysostom, *In Genesim*, PG.53.211.41; *In Epistulam ad Hebraeos*, PG.63.85.48. Theodoret, *Interpretatio in Ezechielem*, PG.81.1145.35. Pseudo-Caesarius (Cassian the Sabaite), *Quaestiones et Responsiones*, chapters 60; 204; 209. Maximus Confessor, *Mystagogia*, 14; *Ambigua ad Joannem*, 53.7. Photius, *Bibliotheca*, Cod. 251, p. 466a; *Epistulae et Amphilochia*, epistle 59. Gennadius Scholarius, *De Quo Debet Sapere et Docere Sacerdos*, 2; *Fragmentum Exhortationis ad Peccatorem*, p. 286.

dccxcix Cf. Origen, *frJohn*, fr. 50: νόμος γὰρ φυσικὸς τοῖς γεννῶσιν ἀγαπᾶν τὰ γεννώμενα. *Op. cit.* 127: Τὸ ἀγαπᾶν ἀνθρωπινώτερον πάλιν ἀκούομεν· νόμος δέ ἐστι φυσικός. *frLam*, fr. 101: οἱ μὲν τὸν φυσικὸν νόμον εἶχον μόνον, οἱ δὲ καὶ γραπτὸν καὶ προφήτας. *commRom* (*I.1-XII.21*), fr. 39: κἀνταῦθα δέ τις νόμον τὸν φυσικὸν ἀπέδωκεν οὕτω λέγων. *commRom*, p. 204: Φήσει γὰρ ὅτι οὗτος ὁ φυσικῶς ἡμῖν ἐγγεγραμμένος νόμος. *selPs*, Pd.12.1520.26: παράνομον [τὸν Σατανᾶν λέγει] δὲ διὰ τὸ παραβῆναι τὸν φυσικὸν νόμον αὐτοῦ.

dccc Theodore of Heraclea, *frMatt*, part of fr. 78, col. 1; otherwise, the text both before and after this phrase is different.

dccci In the following it becomes once again evident that, against alleged attributions of 'fragments' to other authors, now we have Origen's continuous text of which extant 'fragments' are only small portions.

dcccii *Catena in Matthaeum*, p. 78, attributed to both John Chrysostom and Theodore of Heraclea. Once again, it is evident that the text is Origen's.

dccciii Theodore of Heraclea, *frMatt*, fr. 78, col. 1. Likewise, *op. cit.* col. 2: Πολλὰ σημεῖα ἐποίησεν ὁ Χριστὸς ἐν τῇ πόλει Καπερναοὺμ καὶ διὰ τοῦτο ἐχρῆν μᾶλλον πιστεύειν τοὺς ἐν αὐτῇ οἰκοῦντας. Διὰ γοῦν τὰ θαύματα *ὑψοῦσθαί* φησι μέχρις *οὐρανοῦ* ταύτην, διὰ δὲ τὴν ἁμαρτίαν καὶ ἀπιστίαν τῶν ἐν αὐτῇ πτῶμα ἐξαίσιον γέγονεν *ἕως ᾅδου*.

dccciv The idea of 'different degrees of punishment' was introduced by Origen and subsequently it was taken up by later authors. In the commentary on John (XX.34.298-302), he argued thus: 'The paradox is this, that someone is more a son of God than another is son of God, and that someone is twice as much as son of God as another. We will demonstrate how this is proven from its opposite as follows. The second 'woe to the scribes and Pharisees' in the gospel according to Matthew is as follows. *Woe to you scribes and Pharisees, hypocrites, because you traverse sea and land to make one proselyte, and when he is made, you make him twice as much a son of hell as yourselves* [Matt. 23:15]. According to this, then, neither are some sons of hell by nature, nor are the sons of hell equally sons of hell, since one is twice as much a son of hell as another. But, if one is twice as much a son of hell as another, why not also of destruction, death, darkness, and the other things which those who sin in various degrees are sons? Now, if this is so in the case of these, why will not some also be twice as much sons of light as others, and sons of life, and sons of wisdom, and thus sons of God?." This was the argument positing 'different degrees of punishment' depending on degrees of sinning, which inherently involved Origen's cardinal doctrine of creaturely free will and opposition to the Gnostic doctrine about qualities of men being ones 'by nature'. *Op. cit.* XX.34.300: οὐκοῦν κατὰ τοῦτο οὔτε φύσει υἱοὶ γεέννης εἰσίν τινες, οὔτε ἐπ' ἴσης οἱ τῆς γεέννης υἱοὶ υἱοί εἰσιν αὐτῆς. Cf. Origen, *commMatt*, fr. 451 (Klostermann), comm. on Matt. 23:15: *Υἱὸν γεέννης* φησὶ τὸν ἀπολλύμενον ἐξ εὐπειθείας ὡς δυσσεβείας εἰς τοῦτο κατολισθεῖν.

Cf. Ephraem Syrus, *Sermo in Secundum Adventum Domini Nostri Jesu Christi*, p. 24: Διάφοροι τῶν κολάσεων τόποι εἰσίν, ὡς ἐν τῷ Εὐαγγελίῳ ἠκούσαμεν. ... Ὥσπερ δὲ ὧδέ εἰσι διαφοραὶ κολάσεων, οὕτω καὶ ἐν τῷ μέλλοντι αἰῶνι. *Sermo De Communi Resurrectione*, p. 68: εἰπὲ ἡμῖν καὶ τὴν διαφορὰν τῶν κολάσεων. *Sermo in Pretiosam et Vivificam Crucem*, p. 149: Δηλώσω δὲ ὑμῖν, ἀδελφοί μου, καὶ περὶ τῆς διαφορᾶς τῶν κολάσεων, καθὼς ἐν τῷ Εὐαγγελίῳ ἠκούσαμεν. *Loc. cit.* Καὶ ὥσπερ εἰσὶ διαφοραὶ ἁμαρτιῶν, οὕτως καὶ διαφοραὶ κολάσεων. Cyril of Alexandria, *Expositio in Psalmos*, PG.69.753.41-43: Ῥομφαίαν γε μὴν τόξον τε καὶ βέλη καὶ σκεύη θανάτου, ἢ τὰς διαφορὰς τῶν κολάσεών φαμεν ὑποδηλοῦν. Andreas of Caesarea, *Commentarii in Apocalypsin*, Logos 13.39.14.3b-5: καὶ πολλαὶ διαφοραὶ κολάσεων. Anastasius of Sinai, *Questiones et Responsiones*, 7.1: Ὥσπερ γὰρ ἐπὶ τῶν δικαίων πολλαὶ μοναὶ παρὰ τῷ Θεῷ, οὕτω καὶ ἐπὶ τῶν ἁμαρτωλῶν πολλαὶ κολάσεων διαφοραί. Gennadius Scholarius, *epitSummae*, book 3 chapter 141 (title of section): Περὶ τῆς τάξεως καὶ διαφορᾶς τῶν κολάσεων.

In monastic texts ascribed to Basil of Caesarea, 'different degrees of punishment' are based on Luke, 12:47-48 (but these texts could have been later ones having taken their cue from Basil's contemporary Ephraem Syrus): "That servant, who knew his lord's will and did not prepare nor do what he wanted, will be beaten with many stripes, but he who did not know, and did things worthy of stripes, will be beaten with few stripes." Also, on Proverbs, 14:12 &16:25 (on 'the bottom of Hades' – which is assumed to suggest other damned ones who live not 'in the bottom'), and the 'outer darkness' (Matt. 8:12; 22:13; 25:30 – which supposedly implies another 'darkness' which is not the 'outemost' one). Cf. Basil of Caesarea, *Asceticon Magnum*, PG.31.1265.14-47 (I doubt that this is really Basil's work): τὸ *Δαρήσεται πολλάς*, καὶ τὸ *Δαρήσεται ὀλίγας*, οὐχὶ τέλος, ἀλλὰ διαφορὰν κολάσεως δηλοῖ. ... δύναται εἶναι ... ἄξιος ... καὶ ἄλλος καὶ ἄλλος γεέννης διάφορα πάντως ἐχούσης τὰ κολαστήρια. ... Καὶ τὸ ἐξώτερον δὲ σκότος ὑποφαίνει πάντως εἶναί τι καὶ ἐσώτερον. Καὶ τό, *Εἰς πυθμένα ᾅδου*, ἐν Παροιμίαις εἰρημένον δηλοῖ, ὅτι εἰσί τινες ἐν τῷ ᾅδῃ μέν, οὐκ ἐν πυθμένι δὲ ᾅδου, κουφοτέραν ὑπομένοντες τὴν κόλασιν. ...... Ὥστε τό, *πολλὰς καὶ ὀλίγας δέρεσθαι* πάλιν λέγω, οὐκ ἐν τῇ τοῦ χρόνου παρατάσει ἢ συμπληρώσει, ἀλλ' ἐν τῇ διαφορᾷ τῆς κολάσεως γίνεται. This text is largely the same as the one in Basil of Caesarea (?), *Sermones De Moribus*, PG.32.1301. In the sixth century, the newly discovered moderate Origenist Cassian the Sabaite thought along the same lines, too. See Cassian the Sabaite, *First Contribution by Abba Serenus*, in P. Tzamalikos, *NDGF*, p. 276: δεύτερον δέ, ὅτι ἀπὸ τοῦ Θεοῦ αὐτοῖς ἐπιφέρονται τὰ δοκοῦντα λυπηρά, ὡς παρὰ ἀγαθοῦ πατρὸς καὶ φιλανθρώπου ἰατροῦ, πρὸς τὸ αὐτοῖς συμφέρον ἐπὶ τὸ παραδοθέντας παιδαγωγοῖς τισι καὶ σωφρονισταῖς ταπεινωθῆναι, ἵνα, ἐξερχόμενοι ἐκ τούτου τοῦ κόσμου, ἢ καθαροὶ πρὸς τὸν ἄλλον κόσμον μετενεχθῶσιν, ἢ τιμωρίαις ἐλαφροτέραις παραπεμφθῶσιν.

dcccv Cf. Origen, *deOr*, 14.5: εὐχαριστίας δὲ παράδειγμα ἡ τοῦ κυρίου ἡμῶν φωνή, λέγοντος. *ἐξομολογοῦμαί σοι, πάτερ, κύριε τοῦ οὐρανοῦ καὶ τῆς γῆς, ὅτι ἀπέκρυψας ταῦτα ἀπὸ σοφῶν καὶ συνετῶν καὶ ἀπεκάλυψας αὐτὰ νηπίοις.* τὸ γὰρ *ἐξομολογοῦμαι* ἴσον ἐστὶ τῷ *εὐχαριστῶ*. *commMatt*, 16.25: ἐφ' οἷς εὐχαριστῶν τῷ πατρὶ ὁ υἱὸς λέγει. *ἐξομολογοῦμαί σοι, πάτερ, κύριε τοῦ οὐρανοῦ καὶ τῆς γῆς, ὅτι ἀπέκρυψας ταῦτα ἀπὸ σοφῶν καὶ συνετῶν, καὶ ἀπεκάλυψας αὐτὰ νηπίοις. ναί, ὁ πατήρ, ὅτι οὕτως ἐγένετο*, καὶ τὰ ἑξῆς. So Cyril of Alexandria, *commLuc*, p. 106 (copied by Pseudo-Zonaras, *Lexicon*, letter epsilon, p. 782): Τὸ *Ἐξομολογοῦμαί* φησι κατὰ συνήθειαν ἀνθρωπίνην ἀντὶ τοῦ Χάριν ὁμολογῶ, ἤγουν Δοξάζω σε, *Εὐχαριστῶ* σοι. Theodore of Heraclea and Theodore Monachus, *apud Catena in Matthaeum*, p. 88: (Θεοδώρου Ἡρακλείας. Θεοδώρου Μονάχου) Τὸ *ἐξομολογοῦμαί σοι* ἐνταῦθα, ἀντὶ τοῦ *εὐχαριστῶ σοι* τέθεικεν. The ensuing text of the present codex is the same as the first part of this passage by 'Theodore of Heraclea and Theodore Monachus' (Reuss). Like Cyril, John Chrysostom drew on Origen once again. See, *In Matthaeum*, PG.57.429.3-4: Τὸ γὰρ *Ἐξομολογοῦμαί σοι*, ἐνταῦθα *Εὐχαριστῶ* ἐστιν. Εὐχαριστῶ, φησίν, *ὅτι ἀπέκρυψας ταῦτα ἀπὸ σοφῶν καὶ συνετῶν*. See continuation of this passage of Chrysostom in next endnote. Also, Pseudo-John Chrysostom, *Interpretatio in Danielem Prophetam*, PG.56.202.50-51: *Ἐξομολογοῦμαι*, φησί, εὐχαριστῶ, καὶ αἰνῶ.

dcccvi Origen, *deOr*, 14.5.

dcccvii Jerome, *commMatt*, 11.25.

dcccviii Theodore of Heraclea, *frMatt*, fr. 80 (see continuation of this *infra*). This is also Theodore of Heraclea, *apud Catena in Matthaeum*, p. 87. Besides, Theodore of Heraclea and Theodore Monachus, *apud Catena in Matthaeum*, p. 88: (Θεοδώρου Ἡρακλείας. Θεοδώρου Μονάχου) Σοφοὺς μεγίστους Ἰουδαίους, ὅτι ἐπιστεύθησαν τὰ λόγια τοῦ Θεοῦ, ἢ ὅτι σοφοὶ ἦσαν τοῦ κακοποιῆσαι, νηπίους δὲ τοὺς Ἀποστόλους.

dcccix Origen, *commMatt*, fr. 241 (Klostermann).

dcccx Origen, *apud Catena in Matthaeum*, p. 88.

dcccxi Origen wrote this having in mind the passage of Wisdom of Solomon, 1.13: "For God did not create death, nor does He rejoice at the destruction of the living onesς (ὅτι ὁ θεὸς θάνατον οὐκ ἐποίησεν οὐδὲ τέρπεται ἐπ' ἀπωλείᾳ ζώντων), which he quoted and discussed upon beginning his second homily on Jeremiah (2.1) and in his commentary on Genesis. See *selGen*, PG.12.100.40-41. Once again, John Chrysostom copied from Origen's present commentary. *In Matthaeum*, PG.57.429.5-6: Τί οὖν; ἐπ' ἀπωλείᾳ χαίρει καὶ τῷ μὴ μαθεῖν ἐκείνους ταῦτα; Οὐδαμῶς.

dcccxii Theodore of Heraclea, *frMatt*, fr. 80 (continuing from the point quoted *supra*).

dcccxiii Cf. Origen, *commJohn*, II.19.130: Ἀλλὰ λόγος μὲν *ἐν ἀρχῇ* οὐκ ἐγένετο· οὐκ ἦν γὰρ ὅτε ἡ ἀρχὴ ἄλογος ἦν, διὸ λέγεται. *Ἐν ἀρχῇ ἦν ὁ λόγος*.

dcccxiv Origen, *commMatt*, fr. 239 (Klostermann).

dcccxv Cf. Origen, *frLuc*, fr. 164: δικαιότατα δὲ *πάντα* παραδέδωκεν αὐτῷ ὁ πατήρ, ἐπεὶ καὶ αὐτὸς ὁ υἱὸς παρεδόθη *ὑπὲρ πάντων* [2 Cor. 5:14-15; 1 Tim. 2:6], *ὅς ἐστι σωτὴρ πάντων ἀνθρώπων, μάλιστα πιστῶν* [1 Tim. 4:10] καὶ *ἱλασμός ἐστι περὶ τῶν ἁμαρτιῶν ἡμῶν, οὐ περὶ τῶν ἡμετέρων δὲ μόνον, ἀλλὰ καὶ περὶ ὅλου τοῦ κόσμου* [1 John, 2:2]. Παρεδόθη δὲ καθ' ὃ γέγονεν ἄνθρωπος.

dcccxvi Jerome, *commMatt*, 11.27.

dcccxvii Cf. Origen, *Cels*, II.9: προσταχθέντα δὲ τὸν λόγον πεποιηκέναι πάντα, ὅσα ὁ πατὴρ αὐτῷ ἐνετείλατο. *Op. cit.* II.31: ὁ θεὸς ἐνετείλατο περὶ τῶν τοσούτων ἐν κόσμῳ, καὶ ἐκτίσθη, καὶ ὅτι ὁ τὴν ἐντολὴν λαβὼν ὁ θεὸς λόγος ἦν. *Cels*, VI.60: Δυνάμει δὲ εἴπομεν καὶ εἰς τὸ κελεύων, γενέσθω τόδε καὶ ἕτερον τόδε ἢ τόδε, ὅτε παρετιθέμεθα τὸ *Αὐτὸς εἶπε καὶ ἐγενήθησαν, αὐτὸς ἐνετείλατο καὶ ἐκτίσθησαν*, λέγοντες τὸν μὲν προσεχῶς δημιουργὸν εἶναι τὸν υἱὸν τοῦ Θεοῦ Λόγον, καὶ ὡσπερεὶ αὐτουργὸν τοῦ κόσμου, τὸ δὲ πατέρα του Λόγου τῷ προστεταχέναι τῷ υἱῷ αὐτοῦ Λόγῳ ποιῆσαι τὸν κόσμον καὶ πρώτως δημιουργόν.

dcccxviii John Chrysostom copied from Origen once again. *In Matthaeum*, PG.57.430.19-21: *Πάντα μοι παρεδόθη*. Ὅταν δὲ ἀκούσῃς, Παρεδόθη, μηδὲν ἀνθρώπινον ὑποπτεύσῃς. Ἵνα γὰρ μὴ δύο θεοὺς ἀγεννήτους νομίσῃς, ταύτην τὴν λέξιν τίθησιν. So did Theodore Monachus, *apud Catena in Matthaeum*, p. 88: (Θεοδώρου Μονάχου) Πάντων εἶπεν, ἵνα μὴ δύο Θεοὺς ἀγεννήτους νοήσῃς. Μηδὲν ἀνθρώπινον ὑποπτεύσωμεν. ἵνα γὰρ μὴ δύο Θεοὺς ἀγεννήτους νομίσωμεν, ταύτην τὴν λέξιν τέθεικεν.

dcccxix Origen, *commMatt*, fr. 242 (Klostermann).

dcccxx Cyril of Alexandria, *frMatt*, fr. 147; see the rest of fragment (two lines of text).

dcccxxi Origen, *commMatt*, fr. 243 (Klostermann).

dcccxxii Cyril of Alexandria, *frMatt*, fr. 146.

dcccxxiii That is, Matt. 11:27, 'no man knows the Son but the Father; neither knows any man the Father, but the Son, and he to whomsoever the Son will reveal him'.

dcccxxiv Origen, *commMatt*, fr. 244 (Klostermann).

dcccxxv John Chrysostom, *In Matthaeum*, PG.57.430.31-33. Cf. *In illud: Filius ex Se nihil facit*, PG.56.255.50-256.2: Εἰ γὰρ δύναται τὸν Πατέρα ὁρᾷν ἐργαζόμενον, καὶ εἰδέναι πῶς ἐργάζεται τῆς αὐτῆς ἐστιν οὐσίας.

dcccxxvi See *supra*, endnote dliv, discussion of θεοπρεπῶς νοεῖν.

dcccxxvii Cf. Origen, *commMatt*, 17.14: ὁποῖοί εἰσιν οἱ συγχέοντες πατρὸς καὶ υἱοῦ ἔννοιαν καὶ τῇ ὑποστάσει ἕνα διδόντες εἶναι τὸν πατέρα καὶ τὸν υἱόν, τῇ ἐπινοίᾳ μόνῃ καὶ τοῖς ὀνόμασι ‹μόνοις› διαιροῦντες τὸ ἓν ὑποκείμενον.

dcccxxviii Cyril of Alexandria, *frMatt*, fr. 148.

dcccxxix Jerome, *commMatt*, 11.27.

dcccxxx This is part of Cyril of Alexandria, *frMatt*, fr. 149. The rest of surrounding text is different, which means that Cyril paraphrased from Origen's commentary.

dcccxxxi See *supra*, Origen, *commMatt*, fr. 245 (Klostermann).

dcccxxxii Theodore of Heraclea, *apud Catena in Matthaeum*, p. 53.

dcccxxxiii Cf. Origen, *exhMar*, 32; *frLam*, frs. 31; 76; *selPs*, PG.12.105.16.

dcccxxxiv Origen, *commMatt*, fr. 246 (Klostermann).

dcccxxxv Theodore of Heraclea, *frMatt*, fr. 83. Likewise, Cyril of Alexandria, *frMatt*, fr. 150: ἐλαφρός ἐστιν ὁ ζυγὸς τοῦ Χριστοῦ, ἐπεὶ οὐ κολάζει ἡμᾶς καθάπερ ὁ νόμος, τὸ ἀναμάρτητον ἀπαιτῶν καὶ ἀπαθές, ἀλλ' ἐν ἁπλοῖς ῥήμασιν ἔχει τὴν ἐπαγγελίαν καὶ τὸν τῆς ἀρετῆς ὑπογραμμόν.

dcccxxxvi Origen, *commMatt*, fr. 245 (Klostermann).

dcccxxxvii Origen, *apud Catena in Matthaeum*, p. 89.

dcccxxxviii Origen, *commMatt*, fr. 247 (Klostermann); he placed this in brackets because in one codex he found this attributed to Chrysostom.

dcccxxxix Origen, *commMatt*, fr. 248 (Klostermann).

dcccxl Origen, *apud Catena in Matthaeum*, p. 89.

dcccxli Origen, *loc. cit.*

dcccxlii Origen, *commMatt*, fr. 250 (Klostermann).

dcccxliii Origen, *apud Catena in Matthaeum*, p. 90.

dcccxliv Origen, *commMatt*, fr. 251 (Klostermann).

dcccxlv Apollinaris, *frMatt*, fr. 69 & *Catena in Matthaeum*, p. 91.

dcccxlvi This is Origen's last phrase in fr. 249 (Klostermann), which is quoted forthwith.

dcccxlvii Origen, *commMatt*, fr. 249 (Klostermann).

dcccxlviii Origen, *commMatt*, fr. 252 (Klostermann).

dcccxlix Origen, *schMatt*, PG.17.296.33-51.

dcccl Origen, *commMatt*, fr. 253 (Klostermann).

dcccli This is one more autobiographical statement. Origen made much of Matt. 10:23 ('when they persecute you in this city, flee into the next'); also, of Matt. 4:3 ('when Jesus heard that John was delivered up, he withdrew into Galilee'), and of Matt. 14:12-13 ('when Jesus heard this [sc. of the death of John the Baptist], he withdrew from there in a boat'). This was implicitly taken as justifying Origen's leaving Alexandria, following his being blackmailed and offering inscence to the idols (Epiphanius of Salamis, *Panarion*, v. 2, p. 404). Cf. Origen, *Cels*, I.61: Οὐκ ἔστι δ' ἀγεννὲς τὸ μετ' οἰκονομίας περιϊστάμενον τοὺς κινδύνους μὴ ὁμόσε αὐτοῖς χωρεῖν, οὐ διὰ φόβον θανάτου ἀλλ' ὑπὲρ τοῦ χρησίμως αὐτὸν τῷ βίῳ ἐπιδημοῦντα ἑτέρους ὠφελεῖν, ἕως ἐπιστῇ ὁ ἐπιτήδειος καιρός. *Op. cit.* I.65 (& *Philocalia*, 18.11): καὶ διδάσκων παράδειγμα αὐτοῖς ἐγίνετο εὐσταθοῦς βίου, οἰκονομοῦντος μὴ εἰκῇ μηδ' ἀκαίρως καὶ ἀλόγως ὁμόσε χωρεῖν τοῖς κινδύνοις. *Op. cit.* I.66 (& *Philocalia*, 18.12): Καὶ ἐχρῆν τὸν προνοούμενον τῆς ὡς ἀνθρώπου ἑαυτοῦ εἰς τὸν βίον ἐπιδημίας μὴ ἀκαίρως ὁμόσε χωρεῖν τῷ ἕως θανάτου κινδύνῳ. *commMatt*, 16.1: φαμὲν γὰρ ὅτι οὔτε πάντοτε καθήκει ἐκκλίνειν τοὺς κινδύνους οὔτε ἀεὶ ὁμόσε χωρεῖν πρὸς αὐτούς. Σοφοῦ δέ τινος ἐν Χριστῷ χρεία εἰς τὸ δοκιμάζειν, ποῖος μὲν ἀπαιτεῖ καιρὸς ἀναχώρησιν, ποῖος δὲ τὴν εἰς τὸν ἀγῶνα προθυμίαν χωρὶς ἀναχωρήσεως καὶ πολλῷ πλέον χωρὶς φυγῆς. Once again, John Chrysostom seized on Origen's idea and couched this in the selfsame locution. *In Genesim*, PG.54.474.19-23: ἐκεῖνα συμβουλεύει τῷ παιδί, ἅπερ ὁ Χριστὸς παρῄνει τοῖς μαθηταῖς, συμβουλεύων μὴ ὁμόσε χωρεῖν τοῖς κινδύνοις, ἀλλὰ διὰ τῆς ἀναχωρήσεως παραμυθεῖσθαι τοῦ πάθους τὴν μανίαν. *In Epistulam ii ad Corinthios* PG.61.572.39-42: Ταῦτα ψυχῆς ἀποστολικῆς, τὸ πάσχειν τοσαῦτα, καὶ μηδαμοῦ περιτρέπεσθαι, ἀλλὰ φέρειν γενναίως τὰ ἐμπίπτοντα, καὶ μὴ ὁμόσε χωρεῖν τοῖς κινδύνοις μηδὲ ἐπιπηδᾷν. See further, *infra*, p. 210 & endnote mlxix.

dccclii Cf. Origen, *Cels*, VIII.44: Κἂν φεύγῃ δέ τις Χριστιανός, οὐ διὰ δειλίαν φεύγει, ἀλλὰ τηρῶν ἐντολὴν τοῦ διδασκάλου καὶ ἑαυτὸν φυλάττων καθαρὸν ἑτέρων ὠφεληθησομένων σωτηρίᾳ. Cyril of Alexandria, *frMatt*, fr. 34: Οὐ διὰ δειλίαν δὲ ὑπεχώρησε, ἀλλὰ ἡμᾶς δι' ὧν ἐποίει διδάσκων ὑποχωρεῖν τοῖς διώκουσι.

dcccliii Origen, *commMatt*, fr. 254 (Klostermann); cf. fr. 259. This time John Chrysostom copied the idea, though not Origen's very words. See John Chrysostom, *In Matthaeum*, PG.57.441.18-26.

dcccliv Theodore of Heraclea, *frMatt*, fr. 85, col. 2; see also col. 1.

dccclv Cf. Origen, *commMatt*, fr. 362 (Klostermann): οὐ γὰρ ἐπεὶ ἐγέννησε μόνον φιλεῖ, ἀλλ' ἐπειδὴ ἴσος αὐτῷ καὶ ὁμογνώμων κατὰ πάντα.

dccclvi John Chrysostom, *In Matthaeum*, PG.57.441.6-14.

dccclvii Origen, *commMatt*, fr. 255 (Klostermann).

dccclviii Subsequent authors took up the expression κενῆς ἐφίεσθαι δόξης (meaning 'pursuit of vain glory'), which ended up proverbial. Cf. John Chrysostom, *In Genesim*, PG.53.94.3-6: μήτε ὁ περὶ τὴν κενὴν ταύτην δόξαν ἐπτοημένος μάθῃ ταύτης ὑπερορᾷν καὶ τῆς ἀληθοῦς ἐφίεσθαι δόξης. *Op. cit.* PG.53.348.8-11: ὅταν μὴ τὴν δόξαν τὴν κενὴν τοῦ βίου τούτου ἐπιζητῶμεν, ἀλλὰ ταύτης ὑπερορῶντες, ἐκείνης ἐφίεσθαι σπουδάζωμεν τῆς ἀληθοῦς καὶ ἀεὶ μενούσης. Cyril of Alexandria, *In Joannem*, v. 1, p. 583: πολλῶν γάρ, ὡς εἰκός, λεληθότως θαυματουργουμένων παρὰ Χριστοῦ κατὰ τὴν Γαλιλαίαν, κενῆς ἐφίεσθαι δόξης αὐτὸν ἀναπείθουσι. Cyril of Scythopolis, *Vita Euthymii*, p. 12: οὔτε μὴν ἐφίετο κενῆς δόξης οὔτε ἤργει τὸ στόμα ἀπὸ δοξολογίας θεοῦ. Stephanus Diaconus, *Vita Stephani Iunioris*, 8: οὔτε κενῆς δόξης ἐφίετο οὔτε τὸ στόμα αὐτοῦ ἀπὸ δοξολογίας Θεοῦ ἤργει ποτέ. Neophytus Inclusus, *Liber Catechesium*, 2.54: δεύτερον δὲ ὡς κενῆς δόξης ἐφιέμενος τὰ ἑαυτοῦ ἐθριάμβευσε κατορθώματα. Andronicus Callistus, *Defensio*

Theodori Gazae adversus Michaelem Apostolium, 2.3: μηδενὶ ξυννῷ σαυτὸν εἰς τοιαύτας ἀγωνίας καθιέντι καὶ κενῆς τὰ μάλιστα δόξης ἐφιεμένῳ.

dccclix See text *infra*, along with Origen's fr. 258 (Klostermann) which is quoted, too.

dccclx Origen, *commMatt*, fr. 259 (Klostermann); cf. fr. 254 quoted *supra*.

dccclxi Origen, *commMatt*, fr. 256 (Klostermann).

dccclxii The Third Council of Constantinople (680-81) used Origen's words, deeming them a weapon and proof in order to defend orthodoxy. ACO, *Concilium Universale Constantinopolitanum Tertium* (*680-681*), Document 11, p. 424: ἀριθμεῖται γοῦν ἡ μακαρία τριὰς ... ὑποστάσεσι καὶ ἰδιότησι νοεραῖς τελείαις καθ' ἑαυτὰς ὑφεστώσαις, ἀριθμῷ διαιρεταῖς καὶ οὐ διαιρεταῖς τῇ θεότητι. Much later this was taken up by Neophytus Prodromenus (monk, Constantinople, Thessaloniki, Edessa, fourteenth century), *Contra Latinos*, section 9, lines 695-699: Αὐτοὶ δὲ προσκυνοῦσι τὸν Πατέρα καὶ τὸν Υἱὸν καὶ τὸ Πνεῦμα ... Θεὸν τὸν Πατέρα, Θεὸν τὸν Υἱόν, Θεόν, εἰ μὴ τραχύνῃ, τὸ Πνεῦμα τὸ ἅγιον. Μίαν φύσιν ἐν τρισὶν ἰδιότησι, νοεραῖς, τελείαις, καθ' ἑαυτὰς ὑφεστώσαις, ἀριθμῷ διαιρεταῖς καὶ οὐ διαιρεταῖς θεότητι. He copied this from Gregory of Nazianzus writing about the faith of orthodox Christians -but Gregory's passage is in fact a copy of Origen's words as in this point of the codex, which Klostermann also came upon in another five codices. See Gregory of Nazianzus, *Contra Arianos et De Seipso* (*orat. 33*), PG.36.236.3-11: Αὐτοὶ δὲ προσκυνοῦσι τὸν Πατέρα, καὶ τὸν Υἱόν, καὶ τὸ ἅγιον Πνεῦμα, μίαν θεότητα. Θεὸν τὸν Πατέρα, Θεὸν τὸν Υἱόν, Θεόν, εἰ μὴ τραχύνῃ, τὸ Πνεῦμα τὸ ἅγιον, μίαν φύσιν ἐν τρισὶν ἰδιότησι, νοεραῖς, τελείαις, καθ' ἑαυτὰς ὑφεστώσαις, ἀριθμῷ διαιρεταῖς, καὶ οὐ διαιρεταῖς θεότητι.

The irony about this Council is that the orthodox doctrine was expounded through a long letter by Sophronius addressing Sergius I, Patriarch of Constantinople. Sophronius (c. 560-638) was elected Patriarch of Jerusalem in 634 and was dead by the time of the Council, in which Jerusalem was represented by Byzantine appointees. The gist of the Trinitarian doctrine of this letter is in fact Origen's own words from the present point of his commentary on Matthew, which Sophronius probably knew, and anyway he was one more witness to the existence of two Origens, of whom 'Origen Adamantius' was later to the former Origen mentioned by Epiphanius.

The Third Council of Constantinople (680-81) repudiated monothelitism (a doctrine that won widespread support when formulated in 638), condemned monoenergism and monothelitism as heretical, and defined Jesus Christ as having two energies and two wills (divine and human), and its acts include also anathematisation of Theodoret's Twelve Chapters. Thus, on the one hand, this assembly expounded the orthodox Trinitarian doctrine by copying from Origen, while, on the other, it anathematised Origen by means of vilifying neologisms of remarkable inventiveness, such as μυθομέριμνος ('infatuated with myths'), which was coined and used *ad hoc*, but never again by any author. Here are the recurrent anathematisations of Origen, as well as of authors such as Didymus, Evagrius, Themistius, John Philoponus, and Theodoret's Refutation of Cyril' Twelve Chapters.

ACO, *op. cit.* Document 11, p. 462: ὡς 'Ωριγένης ὁ παράφορος βούλεται καὶ οἱ τούτου συμμύσται καὶ σύμφρονες Δίδυμος καὶ Εὐάγριος καὶ ὁ λοιπὸς αὐτῶν μυθομέριμνος ὅμιλος. Document 8, p. 228: 'Ωριγένην τε καὶ Δίδυμον καὶ Εὐάγριον καὶ τὰ μυθώδη τούτου ληρήματα. Document 11, p. 478: they anathematised two Origens: 'Ωριγένης, 'Ωριγένης ἕτερος ὁ καὶ Ἀδαμάντιος. Document 11, p. 480: Δίδυμος καὶ Εὐάγριος οἱ τῆς 'Ωριγενιανῆς τερθρείας μυστηριάρχαι παμμίαροι, 'Ιωάννης ὁ γραμματικός, ὁ τὴν ἐπωνυμίαν Φιλόπονος, μᾶλλον δὲ ματαιόπονος. In Document 21, p. 876, they anathematised Θεμίστιον, 'Ωριγένην τὸν καὶ Ἀδαμάντιον, Δίδυμον, καὶ Εὐάγριον, ὡσαύτως τὰ συγγράμματα Θεοδωρίτου τὰ κατὰ τῶν δεκαδύο κεφαλαίων τοῦ ἁγιωτάτου Κυρίλλου. Here is the synodical decision to destroy all of Origen's works. Document 11, p. 470: ἀναιρεῖ δὲ καὶ ἐκρίπτει πρὸς ὄλεθρον πρωτοτύπως μὲν Ὠριγένην τὸν ἄφρονα καὶ πάντα αὐτοῦ τὰ ὀνειρώδη κομψεύματα καὶ πολυειδοῦς ἀσεβείας πλήρη συγγράμματα, Εὐαγρίου τε σὺν αὐτῷ καὶ Διδύμου τὰ δόγματα καὶ πάντα αὐτῶν τὰ Ἑλληνικὰ καὶ τερατώδη, οὐ μὴν ἀλλὰ καὶ μυθώδη ληρήματα.

dccclxiii Origen, *commMatt*, fr. 257 (Klostermann). He found this in several codices, all of which attributed this passage to Origen.

dccclxiv Origen, *commMatt*, fr. 258 (Klostermann).

dccclxv Jerome, *commMatt*, 12.19.

dccclxvi This is also, Origen, *Catena in Matthaeum*, p. 92: (Ὠριγένους.) *Κάλαμός* ἐστι *συντετριμμένος*, ψυχὴ ἐν ἁμαρτίαις συντετριμμένη. *λίνος* ἐστὶ *τυφόμενος*, οἱ κατεπαιρόμενοι τῇ ἀληθείᾳ.

dccclxvii Origen, *commMatt*, fr. 260 (Klostermann).

dccclxviii Origen, *commMatt*, fr. 261 (Klostermann).

dccclxix Origen, *apud Catena in Matthaeum*, p. 92.

dccclxx Origen, *commMatt*, fr. 263 (Klostermann).

dccclxxi The expression δημοσιεύειν τὰς ἐνθυμήσεις ('to make one's considerations public') is peculiar to Origen and two subsequent authors took this up: one, the newly discovered Cassian the Sabaite, a sixth-century moderate Origenist, whose texts I have edited and published in 2012. See *NDGF*, p. 32: ἢ ἰδίᾳ κενοδοξίᾳ αἰσχυνομένους δημοσιεῦσαι τὰς ἑαυτῶν ἐνθυμήσεις. Secondly, Nilus of Ancyra, in his commentary on the Song of Songs. *Εἰς τὸ τῶν Ἀσμάτων Ἆσμα*, 49.5: οἱ γὰρ προερχόμενοι λόγοι, οἷοί περ ἂν ὦσιν, ἄγγελοι τῆς τεκούσης αὐτοὺς γίνονται διανοίας ἑρμηνεύοντες ἐν τῇ προφορᾷ τὴν διάθεσιν καὶ γλώσσῃ τὸ κρυπτὸν δημοσιεύοντες τῆς ἐνθυμήσεως.

dccclxxii Cf. Origen, *frPs*, on Psalm 74:8. Ὃν θέλει δηλαδὴ [ὁ Θεὸς κριτής ἐστι] κατὰ τὴν ἀξίαν τῶν βεβιωμένων ἑκάστῳ. Cf. *Scholia in Apocalypsin* (comm. on Rev. 11:18), scholion XXXVII: *Καὶ ἦλθεν ἡ ὀργή σου καὶ ὁ καιρὸς τῶν νεκρῶν* κατὰ τὸν τῆς συντελείας καιρὸν φανερωθέντων πάντων τῷ βήματι τοῦ Χριστοῦ ἐπὶ τὸ λαβεῖν ἕκαστον ἐπαξίως τῶν βεβιωμένων. I have maintained that this work is a compilation by Cassian the Sabaite (c. 465- 20 July, 546), the newly discovered Greek father and Abbot at the Laura of Sabas, who added some comments of his own. My conclusion was that this specific scholion originated in Origen. See P. Tzamalikos, *op. cit.* pp. 186-187; 339-340.

dccclxxiii Photius took this up in his *frMatt*, fr. 61: *Βασιλεία τῶν οὐρανῶν* καὶ βασιλεία τοῦ θεοῦ λέγεται μὲν ἡ πρώτη τοῦ δεσπότου Χριστοῦ παρουσία καθὼς λέγει, *εἰ δὲ ἐν πνεύματι θεοῦ ἐκβάλλω τὰ δαιμόνια, ἄρα ἔφθασεν ἐφ' ὑμᾶς ἡ βασιλεία.*

dccclxxiv This is a term that Origen took up from those predecessors to whom his locution owed a great deal. The term συνεσκιασμένος (Present Perfect Participle of the verb συσκιάζομαι) meaning 'obscure' or 'veiled' or 'disguised', entered philosophical locution with Philo. *De Ebrietate*, 6: ἀλήθεια ἡ τὰ τῶν συνεσκιασμένων πραγμάτων ἀνακαλυπτήρια ἄγουσα δύναμις. *Op. cit.* 65-6: τὰς δὲ ἀφανεῖς καὶ συνεσκιασμένας δυνάμεις οὐ κατανοοῦσιν. *De Josepho*, 90: βούλεται δὲ [σχ. θεός] τὰ συνεσκιασμένα τῶν πραγμάτων ἀνακαλύπτειν τοῖς ἀλήθειαν ποθοῦσιν. Then, Galen, *Linguarum seu Dictionum Exoletarum Hippocratis Explicatio*, p. 143: συνηρεφές. ἐπικεκαλυμμένον, συνεσκιασμένον. Julius Pollux (Naucratites), *Onomasticon*, 6.209: συνεσκιασμένον συγκεκαλυμμένον, παρακεκαλυμμένον ὑπὸ παραπετάσματι. Sextus Empiricus, *Adversus Dogmaticos 1* (= *Adversus Logicos 1*), 7.26: μήτε ἐν τοῖς προφανέσι μήτε ἐν τοῖς συνεσκιασμένοις εὑρισκομένου τινὸς ἀληθοῦς. *Op. cit.* 8.320: ἅπερ δεδυκυῖαν μὲν καὶ συνεσκιασμένην ἡμῖν ἔχει τὴν φύσιν. Alexander of Aphrodisias, *commTop*, p. 582:

ὁρᾷς ὅπως οὐ φανερῶς ἔλαβε τὰ ἀντικείμενα ἀλλὰ συνεσκιασμένως τῷ λαβεῖν τοιαῦτα ἰσοδύναμα. In turn, those who either admired Origen (such as Porphyry), or wrote under his spell, took this up. Here is one more instance of Porphyry having employed Origen's manner of writing. *Introductio in Tetrabiblum Ptolemaei*, p. 190: τὰ ἐξ αὐτῆς τετηρημένα τῶν ἀποτελεσμάτων εἴδη ὁλοσχερῶς ὁ Πτολεμαῖος διείληφε συνεσκιασμένην μέντοι καὶ ἀσυμφανῆ τῇ παλαιᾷ τῶν ὀνομάτων χρήσει τὴν φράσιν ἐκθέμενος. Likewise, Eusebius, *Praeparatio Evangelica*, 6.10.50; *Demonstratio Evangelica*, 7.1.82; *In Isaiam*, 2.50. Basil of Caesarea, *De Spiritu Sancto*, 2.4. Pseudo-Gregory of Nyssa, *Liber De Cognitione Dei*, PG.130.273.54-55. Pseudo-Athanasius, *De Sancta Trinitate*, PG.28.1200.41-42. Pseudo-Basil of Caesarea (*forsan* Cassian the Sabaite), *Enarratio in Prophetam Isaiam*, 9.231. Theodoret, *Haereticarum Fabularum Compendium*, PG.83.417.3031; *HE*, p. 166; *De Providentia*, PG.83.704.20-21; *Interpretatio in Ezechielem*, PG.81.964.46-47; *In Epistulas Sancti Pauli*, PG.82.208.16-17; *Eranistes*, p. 255. Nilus of Ancyra, *Commentarii in Canticum Canticorum*, 36; 57; *Epistulae*, epistle 1.70. Procopius of Gaza, *Catena in Canticum Canticorum*, p. 1600; *Commentarii in Isaiam*, p. 2021. Pseudo-Dionysius the Areopagite, *De Ecclesiastica Hierarchia*, p. 84. Oecumenius, *Commentarius in Apocalypsin*, p. 37. Photius, *Bibliotheca*, Codex 203, p. 164a; Codex 222, p. 197a; *Epistulae et Amphilochia*, epistles 64; 290. Michael Psellus, *Poemata*, poem 53, line 556. John Chrysostom used this formula profusely: *In Isaiam*, 2.1, *et passim* (nearly fifty instances). The ensuing phrase in the present commentary demonstrates that he knew of Origen's commentary on Matthew and employed points of this *verbatim*, in which the present passage is included. Quite remarkably, apart from Porphyry, no Greek author did ever use this term.

dccclxxv John Chrysostom, *In Matthaeum*, PG.57.447.26-35.

dccclxxvi Theodore of Heraclea, *apud Catena in Matthaeum*, p. 93.

dccclxxvii Cf. folio 11r: Λέγεται δὲ βασιλεία οὐρανῶν ... καὶ ἡ πρώτη καὶ δευτέρα Χριστοῦ παρουσία.

dccclxxviii The expression ἀνταποδόσεως καιρὸς (*kairos* of recompense) was introduced by Origen paraphrasing the scriptural *ἡμέρα ἀνταποδόσεως* (Hosea, 9:7; Isaiah, 61:2; 63:4) and *ἐνιαυτὸς ἀνταποδόσεως* (Isaiah, 34:8). Origen, *frLam*, fr. 34 (on Lam. 1:15): ὁ δὲ κληθεὶς εἰς τὸ συντριβῆναι καιρός ἐστιν ὁ τῆς ἀνταποδόσεως. *selPs*, PG.12.1456.34-36: καὶ ἐν καιρῷ τῆς ἀνταποδόσεως, ἐμὲ τὸν ἐκ μετανοίας ἐλεηθέντα εἰς μέσον παραγαγών. Then, Eusebius employed this, and after him a vast number of Christian authors adopted the expression while hardly having inkling of Origen being the source of it. Eusebius, *Demonstratio Evangelica*, 9.13.11&12; *In Isaiam*, 2.23; *Commentaria in Psalmos*, PG.23.1237.7-8. Basil of Caesarea, *De Baptismo*, PG.31.1528.7-8. Didymus, *In Genesim*, cod. p. 232. Ephraem Syrus, *Quomodo Latro Ante Resurrectionem in Paradisum Intrauit*, lines 21-22. John Chrysostom, *De Lazaro*, PG.48.1054.1. Pseudo-John Chrysostom, *In illud: Verumtamen Frustra Conturbatur*, PG.55.562.38; *Interpretatio in Danielem Prophetam*, PG.56.231.20-21. Theodoret, *commProphXII*, PG.81.1976.44. Cyril of Alexandria, *frMatt*, fr. 280, col. 2; *In Isaiam*, PG.70: 1356.35; 1385.7. Theodore of Mopsuestia, *Fragmenta in Epistulam ad Hebraeos*, pp. 210; 211. Nilus of Ancyra, *Εἰς τὸ τῶν Ἀσμάτων Ἆσμα*, 67.6; 74.14. Procopius of Gaza, *Catena in Canticum Canticorum*, p. 1721; *Commentarii in Isaiam*, pp. 2669; 2701. Ammonius of Alexandria (presbyter), *Fragmenta in Joannem*, 142. Pseudo-Basil of Caesarea (*forsan* Cassian the Sabaite), *Enarratio in Prophetam Isaiam*, 13.270. Photius, *Epistulae et Amphilochia*, epistle 62; *frMatt*, fr. 49. *Et. al.*

dccclxxix This was copied by Photius, who otherwise condemned Origen vehemently.

dccclxxx Photius, *frMatt*, fr. 49, col. 1. See also col. 2: Ἀποτόμως λέγει, ὅτι *ἔφθασεν ἐφ' ὑμᾶς ἡ βασιλεία τοῦ θεοῦ*, τοῦτ' ἔστιν ὅσον οὔπω λήψεσθε τὴν τῶν ἡμαρτημένων ὑμῖν ἀνταπόδοσιν.

dccclxxxi See *infra*, Origen: ἀλλὰ τὴν ἐκ ῥαθυμίας ἡμῶν ἔμπροσθεν δηλῶν τυραννίδα σκεύη δὲ αὐτοῦ οὐ μόνον τοὺς δαίμονας, ἀλλὰ καὶ τοὺς τοῖς ἐκείνου θελήμασιν ὑπαγομένους ἀνθρώπους φησί.

dccclxxxii Theodore of Heraclea, *apud Catena in Matthaeum*, pp. 93-94 (attribution is made amidst text of Origen both before and after this one).

dccclxxxiii Origen, *commMatt*, fr. 268 (Klostermann).

dccclxxxiv Origen, *apud Catena in Matthaeum*, p. 94.

dccclxxxv Origen, *loc. cit.*

dccclxxxvi Origen, *commMatt*, fr. 267 (Klostermann).

dccclxxxvii Origen, *loc. cit.*

dccclxxxviii Origen, *commMatt*, fr. 269 (Klostermann).

dccclxxxix Cyril of Alexandria, *frMatt*, fr. 155.

dcccxc Origen, *deOr*, 17.2: νυμφίος λόγος ὢν θεοῦ ἐρᾷ, ψυχῆς τυγχανούσης ἀνθούσης ὑπερουρανίῳ καὶ ὑπερκοσμίῳ κάλλει. *frLam*, fr. 7: Ἡ *πεπληθυμμένη λαοῦ μόνη καθέζεται* τῷ τὸν νυμφίον λόγον ἡ νύμφη ἀποβεβληκέναι *γινομένη ὡς χήρα* ἥ ποτε τοῖς προειρημένοις ἔθνεσι πλήθουσα. *Homiliae in Exodum*, p. 277: Οὕτως ἐπὶ ψυχῆς ἐχούσης ἕνα λόγον ἕνα νυμφίον. *Libri x in Canticum Canticorum* (*fragmenta*), p. 175 & *Scholia in Canticum Canticorum*, PG.17.260.33-35: Τάχα δὲ *κλίνην* κοινὴν ἑαυτῆς καὶ τοῦ νυμφίου τὸ σῶμα αἰνίττεται, ἐν ᾧ ἔτι οὖσα ἡ ψυχὴ ἀξιοῦται τῆς τοῦ λόγου κοινωνίας. *Scholia in Canticum Canticorum*, PG.17.273.41-46: ἐξέρχεται καὶ ἐκδημεῖ τοῦ σώματος ἡ ψυχὴ διὰ τὸν τοῦ νυμφίου λόγον ἔχουσα ἐν οὐρανῷ τὸ πολίτευμα. ... Συνεχῶς ἡ ψυχὴ τὸν νυμφίον λόγον ἐπιζητεῖ. *Op. cit.* PG.17.277.42-46: λόγος ἐστὶν ὁ νυμφίος, λογικὸν ζῷον ἡ νύμφη, ἐὰν νοήσῃ ψυχὴ καὶ λάβῃ ὁ νυμφίος τὴν νύμφην. ἀλλ' ἐπεί ἐστιν ὁ λόγος οὗτος, οὐ μιᾷ ψυχῇ κοινωνῶν, ἀλλὰ πλείοσι καὶ διαφόροις.

dcccxci This exegesis is exclusive to Origen. The text of both the present codex and Klostermann's is the same as the following one.

dcccxcii Origen, *commMatt*, fr. 274 (Klostermann), col. 2; see also col. 1, which follows immediately.

dcccxciii Origen, *commMatt*, 12.4.

dcccxciv This is a pithy definition of 'knavery' (πονηρία) which was paid no attention by posterity. See discussion in Introduction, pp. XLVI-XLVII.

dcccxcv Origen, *commMatt*, 12.4. Cf. *op. cit.* 17.21: ἐν πνευματικοῖς δὲ γάμοις κοινωνίαν νόει λόγου νυμφίου ‹ὑποδοχήν,› τόκον δὲ καλῶς ποιούμενα νύμφης ψυχῆς, γαμουμένης λόγῳ καὶ μὴ φθειρομένης ὑπ' αὐτοῦ, ἀλλὰ καὶ καθ' ἑκάστην τὴν πρὸς αὐτὸν κοινωνίαν ἀφθαρσίας μεταλαμβανούσης καὶ γεννώσης, ὁποῖα γένοιτο ἐκ τοιούτων γάμων λογικὰ γεννήματα. *frProv*, PG.13.33.27-30: Τοιαύτη καὶ πᾶσα γυνὴ μοιχαλίς, ἡ ἀλλοτριώσασα ἑαυτὴν τοῦ νυμφίου, καὶ ψυχὴ καταλιποῦσα τὸν ἄνδρα, καὶ ὀπίσω τῶν ἐραστῶν πορευομένη. Therefore, the following text is Origen's. *Catena in Marcum*, p. 351 (comm. on Mark, 8:38): μοιχαλὶς δὲ λέγεται ἡ γενομένη ἀνδρὶ ἑτέρῳ. καὶ ἡ τὸν Θεὸν τὸν ἀλήθινον νυμφίον καταλιποῦσα ψυχὴ καὶ μὴ τῇ αὐτοῦ διδασκαλίᾳ κατακολουθοῦσα, ἀλλ' ἑτέροις αὐτὴν ὑποστρώσασα, καὶ ἀσεβείας σπέρματα δεχομένη, μοιχαλὶς χρηματίζει δηλονότι καὶ ἁμαρτωλός.

dcccxcvi Origen, *commMatt*, fr. 274 (Klostermann), col. 1.

dcccxcvii See also *infra*, folio 100r, and Origen, *commMatt*, fr. 565 (Klostermann) quoted on pp. 371-372.

dcccxcviii This is the first phrase of the text ascribed to Apollinaris, *Fragmenta in Joannem*, fr. 148; see its concluding one *infra*, pp. 372-373. Origen's exegesis concerning the question of Jesus having been 'three days' in the grave was followed by Eusebius, *Ad Marinum*, PG.22.956.37-59; Didymus, *In Genesim*, cod. pp. 189-190; Michael Glycas, *Annales*, p. 416 (reporting the similar analysis by Isidore of Pelusium). It seems that Apollinaris employed this exegesis, too, which is not unexpected, given his extensive copying from Origen's present commentary.

dcccxcix Origen, *commMatt*, fr. 275 (Klostermann).

cm Origen, *commMatt*, fr. 276 (Klostermann).

cmi Cf. *infra*, folio 230v, quotation of Origen, *commMatt*, fr. 565 (Klostermann).

cmii Theodore of Heraclea, *frMatt*, fr. 90.

cmiii *Catena in Matthaeum*, p. 129 (anonymous). Michael Glycas wrote that he read this account of the 'three days about Jesus having remained in grave' in Isidore of Pelusium. *Annales*, pp. 415-416: πείθου δὲ μᾶλλον Ἰσιδώρῳ τῷ Πηλουσιώτῃ λέγοντι ὅτι καθάπερ ἐπὶ τῶν τελευτώντων ποιεῖν εἰώθαμεν, ὁποίᾳ δ' ἂν ὥρᾳ τελευτήσῃ τις, τὴν ἑξῆς μόνην ὑπερτιθέμεθα, τῇ δὲ ἑτέρᾳ ἕωθεν τριταίαν ἄγομεν ἡμέραν αὐτοῦ. Καὶ οὕτω καὶ ἐπὶ αὐτοῦ τοῦ Χριστοῦ διανοεῖσθαί σε χρή. We have come upon Isidore of Pelusium having availed himself of this commentary of Origen's on p. 71.

cmiv Origen, *commMatt*, fr. 278 (Klostermann).

cmv Origen, *apud Catena in Matthaeum*, p. 98.

cmvi Cf. Justinian, *Novellae*, p. 696, citing Gregory of Nazianzus and quoting from his 'Great Apologetius': ἀνεπιλήπτους ἐν ἅπασι καὶ ἀνεπιβάτους τοῖς πονηροῖς. Migne has it, ἀλήπτους ἐν πᾶσι καὶ ἀνεπάφους τοῖς πονηροῖς. Gregory of Nazianzus, *Apologetica*, PG.35.477.33-39. However, usage by Gregory of Nyssa shows that Justinian's text was the correct one. *Contra Eunomium*, 1.1.368: ἄληπτα καὶ ἀνεπίβατα λογισμοῖς. *Op. cit.* 2.1.141: ἄρρητον εἶναι καὶ λογισμοῖς ἀνεπίβατον. Likewise, *op. cit.* 3.1.107. For his part, Michael Glycas wrote, ἀνεπίβατός ἐστι δαίμοσιν ἡ οἰκία ἐκείνη ἐν ᾗ βίβλος ἀπόκειται ἱερά. *Quaestiones in Sacram Scripturam*, chapter 65, p. 194.

This term ἀνεπίβατος ('inaccessible', 'unapproachable') was coined by Late Antique authors, and Origen happened to have read most of those who used it prior to him, such as Clement of Alexandria, *Stromateis*, 1.5.29.1; Alexander of Aphrodisias, *commMetaph*, p. 540; Posidonius, *Fragmenta*, 194b, *apud* Diodore of Sicily, *Bibliotheca Historica*, 36.11.3; Josephus, *Antiquitates Judaicae*, 3.181; *De Bello Judaico*, 3.167; *Josephi Vita*, 152; Pseudo-Plutarch, *Apophthegmata Laconica*, pp. 216A; 228B. After Origen, this occurs in his adherents: Gregory of Nyssa, at no less than thirty points, e.g. *In Canticum Canticorum*, p. 275; *Encomium in Sanctum Stephanum Protomartyrem i*, p. 16; *De Vita Mosis*, 1.49; 2.172; 2.188; *De Oratione Dominica*, pp. 248; 250; *Orationes viii De Beatitudini*, PG.44.1268.32; *Dialogus De Anima et Resurrectione*, PG.46.133.5; *De Vita Gregorii Thaumaturgi*, PG.46.901.34. Eusebius, *In Isaiam*, 2.6. Epiphanius of Salamis, *Liturgia Praesanctificatorum*, 1. Gregory of Nazianzus, *In Laudem Cypriani*, PG.35.1180.9; *Contra Arianos et De Seipso*, PG.36.233.10. Cyril of Alexandria, *In Joannem*, v. 2, p. 344. Procopius of Gaza, *Commentarii in Isaiam*, p. 2304. Pseudo-Didymus (Cassian the Sabaite), *De Trinitate*, PG.39: 788.2; 916.30. Pseudo-Caesarius (Cassian the Sabaite), *Quaestiones et Responsiones*, chapters 166; 218. On Cassian the Sabaite's authorship, see *NDGF*, Appendices I & II.

cmvii Origen, *commMatt*, fr. 280 (Klostermann).

cmviii This is the first part of Apollinaris, *frMatt*, fr. 74 & *Catena in Matthaeum*, p. 98.

cmix This expression about daemons 'stalking about' (περινοστεῖν) is only one of the numerous philological constructions that Origen received from Plutarch reporting the philosophy of Chrysippus (a philosopher very familiar to Origen) about 'evil daemons' being used by gods as punishers. In this case, Origen had in mind Plutarch's report of Chrysippus' philosophy about 'evil daemons' being used by gods as public executioners (δήμιοι). Plutarch, *Aetia Romana et Graeca*, pp. 276F-277A: καθάπερ οἱ περὶ Χρύσιππον οἴονται φιλόσοφοι φαῦλα δαιμόνια περινοστεῖν, οἷς οἱ θεοὶ δημίοις χρῶνται ‹καὶ› κολασταῖς ἐπὶ τοὺς ἀνοσίους καὶ ἀδίκους ἀνθρώπους. Cf. *Cels*, VII.70: Like public executioners (ὡς οἱ δήμιοι), daemons are the proximate perpetrators of all those afflictions. In accordance with divine judgment, at certain times they receive power to commit those calamities, either for the correction of men who drifted towards profusion of evil or to the purpose of training rational beings. *Cels*, VIII.31. See also *op. cit.* IV.65: "We even expel them [sc. daemons] from human souls and from places where they have established themselves, and sometimes even from animals. For frequently the daemons act to the detriment of those, too."

I have remarked several times that J. von Arnim attributed to Chrysippus passages in which this Stoic name is not cited at all, and sometimes not even 'the Stoics' are mentioned. In this case, the practice was reversed: a testimony to Chrysippus by name is not included in his collection of 'fragments'. Nevertheless compare Origen having been influenced by this Stoic idea as reported by Plutarch: Origen, *Cels*, VIII.33: τάχα δὲ ὡς ἄξιοι τῶν πονηρῶν ἐπιστάται καὶ κολασταὶ αὐτῶν ὑπὸ τοῦ διοικοῦντος τὰ ὅλα λόγου ἐτάχθησαν ἄρχειν τῶν ἑαυτοὺς ὑποταξάντων τῇ κακίᾳ καὶ οὐ τῷ θεῷ. *homJer*, homily 20.9: οἱ μὲν οὖν κολασταὶ ἐτάζουσι πλευράς, ἐτάζουσι σώματα. *selPs*, PG.12.1565.28: Χεῖρα λέγει τὰς κολαστικὰς αὐτοῦ δυνάμεις.

cmx The adjective ἀφιλήδονος ('not fond of sensuality') is a neologism apparently introduced by Philo, *Quod Omnis Probus Liber Sit*, 84: τὸ ἀφιλήδονον is listed as one of the characteristics of someone 'who loves virtue' (τοῦ φιλαρέτου). Eusebius quoted extensively from this book, including this point. *Praeparatio Evangelica*, 8.12.12. Then, Marcus Aurelius, *Τὰ εἰς Ἑαυτόν*, 5.5.1 (τὸ ἀφιλήδονον, in a list likewise describing a virtuous man). Apart from these instances and the present one by Origen, this epithet shows only in a spurious text (Pseudo-John Chrysostom, *In Sanctum Pascha*, 17: ἡ σπουδὴ σύντονος ἀφιλήδονος), and, several centuries later, in Gregory Palamas, *Homiliae*, 15.3, which in fact he copied from Eusebius, who in turn had copied from Philo.

cmxi Cf. Apollinaris, on p. 184, *frMatt*, fr. 74: ὅτε κατ' Αἴγυπτον εἰδωλολάτρουν.

cmxii Once again, John Chrysostom paraphrased from Origen's commentary. *In Matthaeum*, PG.57.460.42-50 (homily 43, comm. on the same instance, namely, Matt. 12:43-45): διὰ τοῦτο χαλεπώτερα πείσεσθε τῶν προτέρων, τῶν κατὰ Βαβυλῶνα λέγω, καὶ κατ' Αἴγυπτον, καὶ κατὰ Ἀντίοχον τὸν πρῶτον. Τὰ γὰρ ἐπὶ Οὐεσπασιανοῦ καὶ Τίτου συμβάντα αὐτοῖς πολλῷ μᾶλλον τούτων χαλεπώτερα. Διὸ καὶ ἔλεγεν. *Ἔσται θλῖψις μεγάλη, οἵα οὐδέποτε γέγονεν, οὐδὲ μὴ ἔσται.* [Matt. 24:21]. Οὐ τοῦτο δὲ μόνον δηλοῖ τὸ ὑπόδειγμα, ἀλλ' ὅτι καὶ ἀρετῆς ἁπάσης ἔσονται ἔρημοι καθόλου, καὶ τῇ τῶν δαιμόνων ἐνεργείᾳ εὐεπιχείρητοι μᾶλλον ἢ τότε. Cf. *Op. cit.* PG.57.355.7-9: δεῖ δὲ εἰδέναι σαφῶς, ὡς οἱ χοιρώδεις τῶν ἀνθρώπων εὐεπιχείρητοι ταῖς τῶν δαιμόνων ἐνεργείαις εἰσί. Notice Chrysostom's usage of Origen's perculiar phrase about sinners who are 'easily attacked and manipulated by daemons (εὐεπιχείρητοι).

cmxiii Origen, *commMatt*, fr. 279 (Klostermann).

cmxiv Cf. *infra*, folio 112v: Τὰ τρία δὲ ὧδε τὰ πολλὰ σημαίνει.

cmxv This is the rest of the passage attributed to Apollinaris, which has been quoted *supra*, p. 183 *frMatt*, fr. 74 & *Catena in Matthaeum*, p. 98.

cmxvi Origen wrote this commentary by the end of his life, quite a long time after he had written his rebuttal of Celsus. I will be arguing that Porphyry was profoundly influenced by Origen's theory of daemons as expounded in the *Contra Celsum.* Origen's specific vocabulary in those works is outstandingly present in Porphyry's *De Abstinentia*, and to some extent in his letter to Marcella – but in no other work of his. At this point, the parallel is striking indeed: Porphyry uses the metaphor of a 'virgin soul' which 'begets' divine things. Porphyry, *Ad Marcellam*, 33-4: φεῦγε τῆς ψυχῆς πᾶν τὸ θηλυνόμενον, ὡς εἰ καὶ ἄρρενος εἶχες τὸ σῶμα περικείμενον. Ἐκ παρθένου γὰρ ψυχῆς καὶ ᾐθέου νοῦ τὰ τικτόμενα μακαριώτατα· ἐξ ἀδιαφθόρων γὰρ τὰ ἄφθορα· ἃ δὲ τίκτει τὸ σῶμα, μιαρὸν πᾶσι τοῖς θεοῖς ἐνομίσθη. Μεγάλη οὖν παιδεία ἄρχειν τοῦ σώματος.

cmxvii Origen, *commMatt*, fr. 281 (Klostermann), col. 2; see also col. 1.

cmxviii Origen, *apud Catena in Matthaeum*, p. 99.

cmxix The characteristic turn νόει μοι (which periprastically means 'do me the favour of understanding this') was introduced by Galen, and Origen took this up, as he usually did with similar ones to which he took a fancy. Galen, *De Usu Partium*, pp. 270; 741; *Synopsis Librorum Suorum De Pulsibus*, p. 468; *De Simplicium Medicamentorum Temperamentis ac Facultatibus*, p. 585; *De Septimestri Partu*, line 40; *De Tremore, Palpitatione, Convulsione et Rigore*, p. 640; *In Hippocratis Prorrheticum i*, p. 567; *In Hippocratis Librum De Articulis et Galeni in Eum*, p. 426; *In Platonis Timaeum Commentarii Fragmenta*, fr. 11. Maximus of Tyre, *Dissertationes*, 13.4. Origen, *commJohn*, XXXII.15.175; *homJer*, homilies 1.14; 4.2; 10.6; 12.2; 14.18; 18.6; *homGen*, p. 29; *commMatt*, 14.8; 15.25; 16.18; 17.32; *frPs*, on Psalm 22:5; *homJob*, PG.17.76.17; *frJer* fr. 2.2 (*Philocalia*, 10.2); *Homiliae in Jesu Nave*, p. 417. It was through Origen that this expression entered into Christian literature and was used by his adherents and detractors alike. Epiphanius of Salamis, *Ancoratus*, 101.7. Evagrius of Pontus, *Tractatus ad Eulogium*, PG.79: 1100.28-29; 1101.34; 1117.19. Methodius of Olympus, *Symposium*, 9.3. Gregory of Nyssa, *Adversus Arium et Sabellium De Patre et Filio*, p. 81; *De Vita Mosis*, 2.80; *De Infantibus Praemature Abreptis*, p. 89; *In Canticum Canticorum*, p. 238 (excerpted also by Procopius of Gaza, *Catena in Canticum Canticorum*, p. 1648). Eusebius, *In Isaiam*, 2.34. Gregory of Nazianzus, *Carmina De Se Ipso*, p. 1425. Basil of Caesarea, *Homiliae in Hexaemeron*, 3.7; *Homiliae super Psalmos*, PG.29.373.17&19; *Homilia Dicta in Lacisis*, PG.31.1440.42; *In Sanctam Christi Generationem*, PG.31.1473.15. Themistius, *paraphrPhys*, p. 42. Cyril of Alexandria, *In Isaiam*, PG.70.824.1. John Chrysostom, *In Genesim*, PG.53.328.30. Hesychius of Jerusalem, *Commentarius Brevis*, on Psalms 46:9; 50:9; 52:6; 74:8; 106:26. Nilus of Ancyra, *Epistulae*, epistles 1.242; 2.193. Pseudo-Caesarius (Cassian the Sabaite), *Quaestiones et Responsiones*, 218. Also, other Byzantine authors during and after the sixth century. It is remarkable that this characteristic turn appeared also in Proclus, of whom I have argued that he had been influenced by Christian literature, especially by Origen. *In Platonis Parmenidem*, p. 903. Later, Damascius used this, too, presumably after Proclus. *De Principiis*, pp. 174; 274. Also, John Philoponus, *commAnim*, p. 533.

cmxx Theodore of Mopsuestia, *frMatt*, fr. 71.

cmxxi Theodoret, *apud Catena in Matthaeum*, p. 100. The same passage appears in the *Catena in Marcum*, pp. 301-302: Δείκνυσιν ὅτι πάσης προτιμᾷ συγγενείας τοὺς κατὰ τὴν πίστιν οἰκείους. ταῦτα δὲ ἔφη οὐκ ἀποδοκιμάζων πάντως τὴν μητέρα καὶ τοὺς ἀδελφούς. ἀλλὰ δεικνὺς ὅτι πάσης σωματικῆς συγγενείας προτιμᾷ τῆς ψυχῆς τὴν οἰκειότητα. διὰ τούτου κἀκείνους στέργων ταῦτα ἐπάγοιντο. πρὸς γὰρ τὸν οἰόμενον ὡς ἐπὶ σπουδαιότερον καλεῖν αὐτὸν τῶν οἰκείων τὴν ὁμιλίαν, ἀναγκαῖον ἦν τοῦτο εἰπεῖν, ὁμοῦ καὶ εἰς διδασκαλίαν τῶν παρόντων. Thus, Origen's passage has been attributed to both Theodore of Mopsuestia and Theodoret, whereas it appears as unattributed also in the *Catena in Marcum*. See also *supra*, note dlxxiii, p. 451.

cmxxii Origen, *commMatt*, fr. 282 (Klostermann). See Origen's fuller analysis in *commMatt*, 13.25.

cmxxiii Origen, *apud Catena in Matthaeum*, p. 100. Cf. Eusebius, *Ad Stephanum*, PG.22.889.42-43: διὸ καὶ μάλιστα μιᾶς τῆς κατὰ Θεὸν συγγενείας μετεῖχον (ref. to Elisabeth and Mary).

cmxxiv Jerome, *commMatt*, 18.8-9.

cmxxv Origen, *commMatt*, fr. 284 (Klostermann).

cmxxvi See *infra*, folio 107v: Ἵνα γὰρ μή τις νομίσῃ κατὰ ἀποκλήρωσιν Θεοῦ καὶ ἐπιλογὴν τοῖς μὲν δεδόσθαι, τοῖς δὲ μὴ δεδόσθαι.

cmxxvii Origen, *apud Catena in Matthaeum*, pp. 101-102.

cmxxviii John Chrysostom, *In Matthaeum*, PG.58.471.26-34.

cmxxix Cyril of Alexandria, *frMatt*, fr. 165, col. 1. See also col. 2: Τοῖς εὐμαθέσιν ἀνθρώποις καὶ καλῶς διακειμένοις πρὸς παραδοχὴν θείων λόγων ἐνοικισθήσεται τὸ πνεῦμα τὸ ἅγιον αὐξάνον ἐν αὐτοῖς τὰ χαρίσματα, τοῖς δὲ σπινθῆρα φωτὸς κεκτημένοις καὶ τούτου ἀμελήσασι σβεσθήσεται πάντως καὶ ἀρθήσεται ἀπ᾽ αὐτῶν καὶ τὸ σμικρότατον, ὃ πρότερον εἶχον.

cmxxx Origen, *commMatt*, fr. 285 (Klostermann).

cmxxxi See *infra*, folio 228r: ἐσκοτίσθη αὐτῶν ὁ νοῦς, and endnote mdclxxvi.

cmxxxii Cf. Origen, *apud Catena in Matthaeum*, pp. 101-102: τὸ δὲ *ὑμῖν δέδοται γνῶναι τὰ μυστήρια τῆς βασιλείας, ἐκείνοις δὲ οὐ δέδοται*, εἶπε, διὰ τὸ πάντων αἰτίους τῶν κακῶν ἑαυτοὺς ποιεῖν, ἐκείνους ἑκουσίως πεισθῆναι μὴ βουλομένους. Οἱ γὰρ Ἀπόστολοι αὐθαιρέτως ἐπείσθησαν. Οὐδὲ γὰρ ἀνάγκην εἰσάγω, φησίν, οὐδὲ ἀποκλήρωσίν τινα ἁπλῶς καὶ ὡς ἔτυχε γενομένην· οὐδὲ γὰρ τὸ αὐτεξούσιον ἀναιρῶ. Εἰπὼν δὲ *ὅτι ὅστις ἔχει δοθήσεται αὐτῷ καὶ περισσευθήσεται, ὅστις δὲ οὐκ ἔχει, καὶ ὃ ἔχει ἀρθήσεται ἀπ᾽ αὐτοῦ*, ἐδήλωσε διὰ τούτου, ὅταν τις προθυμίαν ἔχῃ καὶ σπουδήν, δοθήσεται αὐτῷ καὶ παρὰ τοῦ Θεοῦ ἅπαντα. ὅταν δὲ τούτων κενὸς ᾖ, καὶ παρ᾽ ἑαυτοῦ μὴ εἰσφέρῃ, οὐδὲ τὰ παρὰ τοῦ Θεοῦ αἱροῦντος, ἀλλὰ καὶ ζητοῦντος καὶ ἀμελοῦντος, ἐκ πάντων ἀποπίπτει. Here is how John Chrysostom copied this. *In Matthaeum*, PG.58.471.26-34: Τί οὖν ὁ Χριστός; *Ὅτι ὑμῖν δέδοται, φησί, γνῶναι τὰ μυστήρια τῆς βασιλείας τῶν οὐρανῶν. ἐκείνοις δὲ οὐ δέδοται;* Τοῦτο δὲ εἶπεν, οὐκ ἀνάγκην εἰσάγων, οὐδὲ ἀποκλήρωσίν τινα ἁπλῶς καὶ ὡς ἔτυχε γινομένην. ἀλλὰ δεικνὺς αὐτοὺς ἁπάντων αἰτίους ὄντας τῶν κακῶν, καὶ παραστῆσαι θέλων, ὅτι δωρεὰ τὸ πρᾶγμά ἐστι, καὶ χάρις ἄνωθεν δεδομένη. Οὐ μὴν ἐπειδὴ δωρεά, διὰ τοῦτο τὸ αὐτεξούσιον ἀνήρηται. καὶ τοῦτο ἐκ τῶν ἑξῆς δῆλον.

cmxxxiii Origen, *commMatt*, fr. 286 (Klostermann). Cf. Jerome, *commMatt*, 15.15.

cmxxxiv John Chrysostom, *In Matthaeum*, PG.58.473.6-8 & *Catena in Matthaeum*, p. 102. It seems that he was so fascinated by Origen's expression, that he used this *verbatim* also in his commentary on the Acts. John Chrysostom, *apud Catena in Acta*, p. 419: ἐποίησαν δὲ τοῦτό, φησι, μήποτε ἐπιστρέψωσι, καὶ ἰάσομαι αὐτούς. ἐπιτεταμένην αὐτῶν πονηρίαν καὶ τὴν μετὰ σπουδῆς ἀποστροφήν.

cmxxxv Origen, *commMatt*, fr. 287 (Klostermann).

cmxxxvi Origen, *commMatt*, fr. 288 (Klostermann).

cmxxxvii Origen, *apud Catena in Matthaeum*, p. 103.

cmxxxviii Origen, *loc. cit.*

cmxxxix This was either copied by Photius (*frMatt*, fr. 58) or attributed to him by some catenist who wished to suppress the 'heretic' Origen.

cmxl Isaiah, 50:4. Jerome, *commMatt*, 13.16.

cmxli Origen, *commMatt*, fr. 291 (Klostermann).

cmxlii Origen, *apud Catena in Matthaeum*, p. 104.

cmxliii Origen, *commMatt*, fr. 292 (Klostermann).

cmxliv Origen, *loc. cit.*

cmxlv Origen, *commMatt*, fr. 294 (Klostermann).

cmxlvi Origen, *loc. cit.*

cmxlvii Origen, *commMatt*, fr. 295 (Klostermann).

cmxlviii Origen, *loc. cit.*

cmxlix Origen, *apud Catena in Matthaeum*, pp. 104-105.

cml Cf. Origen, *commSerMatt*, p. 134: ὁ δὲ κλέπτης ἀντικείμενος διορύσσων τὰς φυσικὰς ἐννοίας τῆς ψυχῆς, ἃς ᾠκοδόμησεν ὁ λόγος. *commMatt*, 10.2: ὁ διάβολος ἐπιτηρῶν ἐπισπείρει τὰ καλούμενα *ζιζάνια*, τὰ μοχθηρὰ δόγματα, ταῖς καλουμέναις ὑπό τινων φυσικαῖς ἐννοίαις καὶ σπέρμασι καλοῖς τοῖς ἀπὸ τοῦ λόγου. *Cels*, IV.14: Οὐδὲ γὰρ δεδύνηνται οὗτοι [sc. the Stoics] τρανῶσαι τὴν φυσικὴν τοῦ θεοῦ ἔννοιαν ὡς πάντῃ ἀφθάρτου καὶ ἁπλοῦ καὶ ἀσυνθέτου καὶ ἀδιαιρέτου. *commRom* (*I.1-XII.21*), fr. 10: δύναται δὲ νῦν *νόμος* νοεῖσθαι καὶ ὁ κατὰ τὰς φυσικὰς ἐννοίας. *commRom*, p. 204: οὗτος ὁ φυσικῶς ἡμῖν ἐγγεγραμμένος νόμος καὶ *ἐν πλαξὶν καρδίαις σαρκίναις* ὑπὸ τοῦ Θεοῦ ἐντετυπωμένος. *Loc. cit.:* Τὰ δὲ περὶ τοῦ Ἀβραὰμ φερόμενα ἐξ ἀποκρύφων ὡς ἄρα ἀπὸ φυσικῶν ἐννοιῶν κινηθεὶς ἐπίστευσεν τῷ Θεῷ ἀντιλέγεται. *selPs*, PG.12.1197.13-15: Καὶ ταῦτα δρῶσι, τὰς φυσικὰς καὶ κατὰ φύσιν ὀρθὰς καθελόντες ἐννοίας ἐξ ἑαυτῶν. *expProv*, PG.17.209.6-8: τὴν δὲ προσθήκην τῆς ψυχῆς, ἀφανισμὸν τῶν φυσικῶν περὶ Θεοῦ ἐννοιῶν, παντάπασιν αὐτῆς εἰς ἀλογίαν καταπεσούσης.

cmli Cf. Origen, *commMatt* 10.2: Καὶ πρόσχες γε εἰ δύνασαι *τὸ καλὸν σπέρμα* τοὺς υἱοὺς *τῆς βασιλείας* πρὸς τοῖς προαποδεδομένοις καὶ ἑτέρως λαβεῖν, ὅτι ὅσα ἐν τῇ ἀνθρωπίνῃ φύεται ψυχῇ καλά, ταῦτα ὑπὸ τοῦ *ἐν ἀρχῇ πρὸς τὸν θεὸν* λόγου θεοῦ σπείρεται γεννήματα τυγχάνοντα τῆς τοῦ θεοῦ βασιλείας, ὡς εἶναι τοὺς περὶ ἑκάστου ὑγιεῖς λόγους τοὺς υἱοὺς *τῆς βασιλείας*. *frPs*, on Psalm 44:9-10: υἱοὶ γὰρ ὄντες τῆς βασιλείας οἱ μαθηταί, εἰκότως ἂν καὶ βασιλεῖς ὀνομάζοιντο.

cmlii Use of the non-scriptural verb ἐπισπείρειν was introduced by Origen in the same scriptural context. The verb had been used by Greeks such as Pindar, Herodotus, Posidonius, Plutarch, heavily by Theophrastus, even by Christians such as Athenagoras, Irenaeus, and Clement of Alexandria. However, (1) Origen was the first to use it in relation to the parable of Matthew 13:24-30; (2) subsequent Christian authors used the verb mostly in this particular context. Strange though it may be, after Theophrastus, Greek intellectuals altogether set this verb aside. Cf. Origen, *homJer*, homily 1.14: ἄκουε ὅτι ὁ *ἐχθρὸς ἄνθρωπος τοῦτο ἐποίησεν*, ὁ ἐπισπείρας τὰ *ζιζάνια ‹ἀνὰ› μέσον τοῦ σίτου*. [Matt. 13:25-28] Ἐφέστηκεν οὖν ὁ θεὸς ἔχων τὰ σπέρματα, καὶ ὁ διάβολος, ἐὰν διδῶμεν *τόπον τῷ διαβόλῳ*, [Eph. 4:27] *ὁ ἐχθρὸς* [Matt. 13:25] ἐπισπείρει *φυτείαν, ἣν οὐκ ἐφύτευσεν ὁ πατὴρ ὁ οὐράνιος, πάντως ἐκριζωθησομένην*. [Matt. 15:13] ἐὰν μὴ διδῶμεν *τόπον τῷ διαβόλῳ*, ἀλλὰ διδῶμεν τόπον τῷ θεῷ, χαίρων ὁ θεὸς σπείρει τὰ σπέρματα αὐτοῦ ἐπὶ τὸ ἡγεμονικὸν ἡμῶν. Epiphanius of Salamis, *Ancoratus*, Prologue.1.1. Gregory of Nazianzus, *De Moderatione in Disputando*, PG.36.180.29-32 (quoted also by John of Damascus, *Sacra Parallela*, PG.96.329.35): μήποτε … ἐπισπείρῃ τὰ πονηρὰ σπέρματα ὁ ἐχθρός. *In Sanctum Baptisma*, PG.36.408.37-38: μὴ … κακῶς ἐπισπείρῃ ὁ ἐχθρὸς τὰ ζιζάνια. Basil of Caesarea, *Epistulae*, epistle 222.1: μήποτε ὁ κοινὸς ἐχθρὸς … ἐπισπεῖραι δυνηθῇ τὰ ἑαυτοῦ ζιζάνια. Didymus, *frPs*(*al*), 1073; *In Genesim*, cod. p. 164: καὶ περὶ τοῦ ἐπισπείροντος δὲ διαβόλου κακὰς ἐννοίας εἴρηται. *Ἐχθρὸς ἄνθρωπος τοῦτο ἐποίησεν* [Matt. 13:28]. Evagrius of Pontus, *De Malignis Cogitationibus*, 37: ἀλλὰ καὶ ὁ σωτὴρ ἐν τοῖς Εὐαγγελίοις ἐχθρὸν ἄνθρωπον εἶπε τὸν ἐπισπείραντα ἡμῖν τὰ τῆς κακίας ζιζάνια. [Matt. 13:28]. Ephraem Syrus, *Hypomnesticon*, p. 55: ὁ ἐχθρὸς …

μήπως ... ἐπισπείρῃ αὐτοῦ τὰ ζιζάνια. *Sermo Animae Utilis*, p. 109: μήπως εὕρῃ σου τὸν νοῦν σχολάζοντα ἀπὸ τῆς μελέτης τῶν ἐντολῶν τοῦ Θεοῦ, καὶ ἐπισπείρῃ αὐτοῦ τὰ ζιζάνια. Olympiodorus, the deacon of Alexandria, *Commentarii in Jeremiam*, p. 689. Andreas of Caesarea, *Commentarii in Apocalypsin*, Epilogue, 1.1. Cyril of Alexandria, quoted in ACO, *Concilium Universale Ephesenum anno 431*, 1.1.7, p. 173. Then, ACO, *Sententia Synodica Contra Theodorum Mopsuestenum*, 4.1, p. 239. Later, also John Chrysostom, Cyril of Alexandria, Theodoret, *et al.*

cmliii Cf. Origen, *commJohn*, II.8.62: Καὶ ὥσπερ *ἀπέδρα ὀδύνη καὶ λύπη καὶ στεναγμὸς* [Isaiah, 35:10] ἐπὶ τῷ τέλει τῶν πραγμάτων. *commGen*, PG.12.64.20-21 (*Philocalia*, 23.8): καὶ οὕτω μέχρι τέλους τῶν πραγμάτων ἐπιπορευθεὶς [sc. ὁ Θεὸς] οἶδεν ἃ ἔσται. Cf. *commMatt*, 10.2: ἐπὶ τέλει τῶν πραγμάτων ὃ καλεῖται *συντέλεια τοῦ αἰῶνος*. *Op. cit.* 14.19: ὁ γὰρ ἔσχατος ἀνὴρ ἐμίσησε τὴν γυναῖκα καὶ *γράψει αὐτῇ* ποτε ἐπὶ τέλει τῶν πραγμάτων *βιβλίον ἀποστασίου* [Deut. 24:1&3; Matt. 17:9], τοῦτο οἰκονομοῦντος τοῦ θεοῦ. *Op. cit.* 17.19: νῦν μὲν γάρ, κἂν ἀξιωθῶμεν βλέπειν τὸν θεὸν τῷ νῷ καὶ τῇ καρδίᾳ, οὐ βλέπομεν *αὐτὸν καθώς ἐστιν* [1 John, 3:2] ἀλλὰ καθὼς διὰ τὴν ἡμετέραν οἰκονομίαν ἡμῖν γίνεται· ἐπὶ δὲ τέλει τῶν πραγμάτων καὶ τῆς *ἀποκαταστάσεως πάντων ὧν ἐλάλησε διὰ στόματος τῶν ἁγίων ἐξ αἰῶνος προφητῶν* αὐτου [Acts 3:21], *ὀψόμεθα αὐτὸν* [1 John, 3:2], οὐχ ὡς νῦν, ὃ οὐκ ἔστιν, ἀλλ᾽ ὡς πρέπει τότε, ὅ *ἐστιν*. *Cels*, VIII.72: καὶ τὸ τέλος τῶν πραγμάτων ἀναιρεθῆναι ἐστὶ τὴν κακίαν.

cmliv Cf. Origen, *commMatt*, 10.2: Δεήσει δὲ γενέσθαι ἐπὶ τέλει τῶν πραγμάτων ὃ καλεῖται *συντέλεια τοῦ αἰῶνος* [Matt. 13: 39; 40; 49; 24:3; 28:20] θερισμόν, ἵν᾽ οἱ ἐπὶ τούτῳ τεταγμένοι ἄγγελοι τοῦ θεοῦ ἀναλέξωνται τὰ προσπεφυκότα τῇ ψυχῇ φαῦλα δόγματα καὶ παραδῶσιν αὐτὰ εἰς ἀνάλωσιν, τῷ λεγομένῳ καίειν πυρὶ ἀνατρέποντες αὐτά.

cmlv John Chrysostom copied from this once again. *In Matthaeum*, PG.58.475.39-41: Ἐκεῖ τοὺς μηδὲ ὅλως προσεσχηκότας αὐτῷ φησιν, ἀλλ᾽ ἀποπηδήσαντας καὶ τὸν σπόρον προεμένους· ἐνταῦθα δέ, τῶν αἱρετικῶν λέγει τὰ συστήματα.

cmlvi Cf. Theodoret (dubious; probably this is by Cassian the Sabaite), *Quaestiones et Responsiones ad Orthodoxos*, p. 132: οἱ δὲ τὸν ἀληθῆ Χριστὸν μὴ γινώσκοντες Χριστιανοὶ ἀληθῶς οὐ δύνανται εἶναι, κἂν Χριστιανοὶ ὀνομάζονται, οἷά ἐστι τῶν αἱρετικῶν τὰ συστήματα.

cmlvii Origen, *commMatt*, 10.2.

cmlviii Origen, *apud Catena in Matthaeum*, pp. 104-105.

cmlix Origen, *commMatt*, fr. 297 (Klostermann).

cmlx Cf. καιρὸν μετανοίας ('time of repentance'). Origen, *schMatt*, PG.17.297.43-44: Ἐξ ὧν δὲ προλέγει καὶ θρηνεῖ τοὺς τοιούτους, δίδωσιν αὐτοῖς καιρὸν μετανοίας. *selPs*, PG.12.1389.35-36: οὐχ ἔξω μετανοίας καιρόν.

cmlxi Origen, *commMatt*, fr. 296 (Klostermann); see the last phrase of this *supra*.

cmlxii Jerome, *commMatt*, 13.23.

cmlxiii See *infra*, folio 111v: μήπως καὶ οἱ ἅγιοι ἀναιρεθῶσιν ἐν τῷ γίνεσθαι κατὰ τῶν αἱρετικῶν πολέμους.

cmlxiv Cf. *infra*, folio 111v: Κωλύει δὲ ἀναιρεῖσθαι τοὺς αἱρετικούς, οὐ μέντοι γε περικόπτεσθαι αὐτῶν τὴν παρρησίαν καὶ τὰς συνόδους.

cmlxv Cf. Origen, *commJohn*, XIII.43.286 & 290; XIII.49.324.

cmlxvi Origen, *commMatt*, fr. 298 (Klostermann).

cmlxvii Origen, *apud Catena in Matthaeum*, pp. 105-106.

cmlxviii Cf. *supra*, Origen, *commMatt*, fr. 298 (Klostermann): ἢ τοῦτό φησιν· ὅτι εἰ μέλλοιτε κινεῖν ὅπλα καὶ κατασφάττειν τοὺς αἱρετικούς, ἀνάγκη πολλοὺς καὶ τῶν ἁγίων συγκαταβάλλεσθαι.

cmlxix See *supra*, Origen, *commMatt*, fr. 298 (Klostermann): οὐδὲ γὰρ δεῖ φονεύειν αἱρετικὸν ... οὐ τοίνυν ἐπιστομίζειν καὶ ἐκκόπτειν τὴν παρρησίαν τῶν αἱρετικῶν κωλύει, ἀλλὰ τὸ κατασφάττειν αὐτούς.

cmlxx This is the last phrase of Origen, *commMatt*, fr. 296 (Klostermann), but now we are upon the wider context of his analysis. Klostermann put this in brackets because he thought that this derived from a homily of Chrysostom. He did not quote this, but I am doing so now. John Chrysostom, *In Matthaeum*, PG.58.482.48-51: Σκόπει δὲ αὐτοῦ φιλανθρωπίαν ἄφατον, καὶ τὸ πρὸς εὐεργεσίαν ἐπιρρεπές, καὶ τὸ πρὸς κόλασιν ἠλλοτριωμένον. Ὅταν μὲν γὰρ σπείρῃ, δι᾿ ἑαυτοῦ σπείρει, ὅταν δὲ κολάζῃ, δι᾿ ἑτέρων, τουτέστι, τῶν ἀγγέλων. Beyond the fact that the present codex ascribes this to Origen, and so this appears also in the catena on Matthew, the notion of 'punishing powers' (κολαστικαὶ δυνάμεις, suggesting evil angels implementing divine punishment upon human wickedness) is a fundamental point of Origen's thought. See *supra*, endnote cmix: τὰς κολαστικὰς αὐτοῦ δυνάμεις.

cmlxxi Origen, *apud Catena in Matthaeum*, p. 108.

cmlxxii This is how Cyril of Alexandria paraphrased Origen. *De Adoratione*, PG.68.292.4-11: Ἅλω δὲ εἶναί φαμεν ὡς ἐξ ὁμοιώσεως καὶ εἰκόνος τὴν Ἐκκλησίαν, ἐφ᾿ ᾗ δραγμάτων, ἤγουν ἀσταχύων, συλλέγονται δίκην οἱ τῆς ἀπὸ κόσμου ζωῆς διὰ τοῦ λόγου τῶν ἁγίων κειρόμενοι θεριστῶν, τοῦτ᾿ ἔστιν, ἀποστόλων τε καὶ εὐαγγελιστῶν, ἵνα καὶ εἰς τὰς ἄνω συγκομισθεῖεν αὐλάς, καὶ καθάπερ εἰς ἀποθήκην δεσποτικήν, εἰς τὴν ἐπουράνιον Ἱερουσαλήμ.

cmlxxiii Origen, *commMatt*, fr. 300 (Klostermann).

cmlxxiv The following is a unique parallel to this point. Origen, *Cels*, VII.59 (& *Philocalia*, 15.8): Οὐδὲ πάλιν ὑπὸ τοῦ κάλλους τῆς ἑλληνικῆς φράσεως λεγόμενον τὸ αὐτὸ πάντως κρεῖττον εἶναι νομιστέον τοῦ εὐτελέστερον ἀπαγγελλομένου καὶ ἁπλουστέραις λέξεσι παρὰ Ἰουδαίοις ἢ Χριστιανοῖς.

cmlxxv The characteristic expression ἁπλοῦς καὶ ἀπερίεργος ('simple and unsophisticated') probably comes from Chrysippus, *Fragmenta Moralia*, fr. 630, *apud* Stobaeus, 2.7.11m (from Arius Didymus): τὸν δὲ σπουδαῖον ... καὶ ἀπερίεργον καὶ ἁπλοῦν καὶ ἄπλαστον. τὸν δὲ φαῦλον ἔνοχον πᾶσι τοῖς ἐναντίοις. Prior to Origen, this had been used by Clement of Alexandria, *Paedagogus*, 2.1.2.1. This became a Christian coin, but Greek authors made nothing of this. Cf. Pseudo-John Chrysostom, *In Lazarum*, PG.62.772.75-76. Cyril of Alexandria, *commProphXII*, v. 1; p. 404; *In Joannem*, v. 1, p. 682; v. 2, p. 412. Sozomenus, *HE*, 1.17.6; 5.17.6. Gelasius of Cyzicus, *HE*, 2.1.10. Olympiodorus, the deacon of Alexandria, *Commentarii in Jeremiam*, PG.93.689.38. John Philoponus deemed that the peculiarity of this expression was noteworthy and deserved to become a lexicographical lemma; *De Vocabulis Quae Diversum Significatum Exhibent Secundum Differentiam Accentus*, letter alpha, entry 5: ἁπλοῦς. ὁ ἀπερίεργος. However, most of other lexicographers did not feel likewise (presumably because this never became part of Greek technical locution), except Pseudo-Zonaras in the thirteenth century. *Lexicon*, letter alpha, p. 254: Ἁπλοῦν. ἀπερίεργον. καὶ ἁπλότης ἕξις ἀπερίεργος, τὸ πιστὸν ἑτοίμως ἔχουσα.

cmlxxvi Origen, *commMatt*, fr. 301 II (Klostermann).

cmlxxvii Cf. Origen, *selPs*, PG.12.1193.51-56: ἐν δὲ τοῖς κεκτημένοις γνῶσιν καὶ ἀρετὴν αἱ ἅγιαι δυνάμεις ἐπαναπαύονται, ὧν σύμβολά ἐστι τὰ πετεινὰ τοῦ οὐρανοῦ κατασκηνοῦντα ἐν τοῖς κλάδοις σινάπεως. ὃ σημαίνει τὴν ἐνυπάρχουσαν ἡμῖν κατὰ δύναμιν βασιλείαν οὐρανῶν. Anastasius of Sinai, *In Hexaemeron*, book 4, lines 536-537: Εἶτα δεύτερα λέγει τὰ πετεινὰ τοῦ οὐρανοῦ τὰς νοερὰς δυνάμεις, περὶ ὧν φησιν ὅτι *Ἔγνωκα πάντα τὰ πετεινὰ τοῦ οὐρανοῦ.*

cmlxxviii Origen, *commMatt*, fr. 301 I (Klostermann).

cmlxxix Origen, *commMatt*, fr. 301 II (Klostermann).

cmlxxx Jerome, *commMatt*, 13.31-32; cf. *op. cit.* 17.20. This exegesis has been received with admiration by some moderns scholars. See Introduction, p. LXXXII. They however did not realise that Klostermann (Origen, *commMatt*, fr. 301 I) pointed out Jerome's allegiances to Origen. Actually, Klostermann could have done so also with fragment 301 II, too.

cmlxxxi This passage advances two antithetical exegeses of 'birds which come and lodge'. This conforms with Origen maintaining two diametrically opposed conceptions of 'birds' – a positive and a negative one ('there are birds either clean or unclean'; cf. *selLev*, PG.12.401.24-25; *adnotDeut*, PG.17.25.21-23; *homPs*, homily 19.6). The present portion of Matt. 13:32 is couched in the same vocabulary as Psalm 103:12 ('the birds of the heaven come and lodge'), which Origen combined and explained in the same terms by using the vocabulary of Matt. 13:31-32 in his exegesis of Psalm 103:2. See *frPs*, on Psalm 103:12: "The birds of the heaven come and lodge because they have had faith like a grain of mustard seed". Likewise, *selPs*, PG.12.1193.49-56: the 'birds' stand for 'the holy powers which lodge on the branches of the mustard seed'. Similarly, *commMatt*, 13.5; *schLuc*, PG.17.348.44-46. Origen's negative references to 'birds' (standing for opposing powers) stemmed from pertinent biblical passages. Cf. *commMatt*, 16.27; *schLuc*, PG.17.349.39-41; *frLuc*, frs. 154; 155; *fr1Cor*, fr. 41; *commEph*, fr. 9; *selEz*, PG.13.813.51-53; *frPs*, on Psalm, 78:2.

cmlxxxii Jerome's foregoing exegesis draws on this passage of Origen, too.

cmlxxxiii Origen, *Scholia in Canticum Canticorum*, PG.17.272.37-38: ὅταν ὁ καύσων τοῦ παρόντος βίου παύσηται καὶ καιρὸς τῆς ἀναψύξεως ἐπιστῇ. Cf. Maximus Confessor, of whom at many points I have shown that he followed Origen. *Quaestiones et Dubia*, 11: ἐπειδὴ γὰρ ἠσθένησεν αὐτὴ διὰ τῆς παραβάσεως καὶ τῳ διαβολικῷ καύσωνι ἐθανατώθη. *Op. cit.* 94: ἀπὸ τοῦ διαβολικοῦ τῶν πειρασμῶν καύσωνος.

cmlxxxiv Cf. Origen, *Cels*, VII.14: Εἶτα μετὰ ταῦτα, [Celsus] βουλόμενος ἀνατρέπειν τὴν πίστιν τῶν διὰ τὸ πεπροφητεῦσθαι παραδεξαμένων τὰ τοῦ Ἰησοῦ, φησί.

cmlxxxv Origen, *apud Catena in Matthaeum*, p. 107.

cmlxxxvi Origen, *commMatt*, fr. 302 (Klostermann), col. 1. On 'woman' betokening the Church, see also *infra*, folio 112v.

cmlxxxvii Origen, *apud Catena in Matthaeum*, p. 107, continued forthwith.

cmlxxxviii John Chrysostom, *In Matthaeum*, PG.58.478.25-27. His copying one more specific portion from Origen is all too evident once again. Otherwise, his text both before and after that point is different. Cf. *De Diabolo Tentatore*, PG.49.266.50-53: καὶ γὰρ καὶ ἡ ζύμη μικρά, ἀλλ᾽ οὐδὲν ἡ μικρότης παραβλάπτει τὸ φύραμα, ἀλλ᾽ ἡ σμικρότης ἐκείνη ἅπαν τὸ ἄλευρον πρὸς ἑαυτὴν μεθίστησι διὰ τῆς ἐνούσης αὐτῇ δυνάμεως.

cmlxxxix Origen, *apud Catena in Matthaeum*, p. 107, continued forthwith.

cmxc See *supra*, folio 102v: Ἑπτὰ πνεύματα λογιστέον τὰ πολλά. Cf. John Chrysostom, *In Matthaeum*, PG.58.478.43-44: Τρία δὲ σάτα ἐνταῦθα τὰ πολλὰ εἴρηκεν.

cmxci Origen, *apud Catena in Matthaeum*, p. 107.

cmxcii John Chrysostom, *In Matthaeum*, PG.58.478.25-27. This is one more glaring evidence of how he copied from Origen. He used this phrase in an otherwise different text, but in the Catena on Matthew, this is part of a very extensive text all of which is ascribed to Origen. *Catena in Matthaeum*, p. 107 (J.A. Cramer).

cmxciii Cf. Origen, *commMatt*, fr. 302 (Klostermann), col. 3. The same in Origen, *schLuc*, PG.17.357.43-44: Γυνὴ δὲ ταύτην, ἡ σοφία τοῦ Θεοῦ, εἰ ἀλεύρου σάτα τρία ἐγκρύπτει. No surprise that the entire fragment (the selfsame text) was ascribed also to Eusebius, *Fragmenta in Lucam*, PG.24.565-568.

cmxciv Origen, *frLuc*, fr. 205.

cmxcv Jerome, *commMatt*, 13.33. Further, he expounds two more alternative exegeses. However, characteristically, he presented this as the one of his own, although he knew that this was Origen's.

cmxcvi Origen, *schLuc*, PG.17.357.42-53.

cmxcvii That is, Origen. See Origen, *schLuc*, PG.17.357.42-53, just quoted.

cmxcviii This is what Jerome himself did: he 'picked up' the foregoing exegesis from Origen and did not expound Origen's alternative one.

cmxcix Cf. Origen, *infra*, folio 239v & *schMatt*, PG.17.309.44-48: Εἷς ὁ σώζων, μία ἡ σωτηρία. Εἷς ὁ ζῶν, Πατὴρ καὶ Υἱὸς καὶ Ἅγιον Πνεῦμα. Εἷς ἐστιν, οὐ συναλ‹ο›ιφῇ τῶν τριῶν, ἀλλ' οὐσίᾳ μιᾷ. Τρεῖς δὲ ὑποστάσεις τέλειαι ἐν πᾶσι καὶ κατάλληλοι. Κατὰ φύσιν ἐγέν‹ν›ησεν ὁ Θεός, διόπερ ὁμοούσιος ὁ γεννηθείς. *selPs*, PG.12.1633.39-42: Δοῦλοι κυρίων Πατρὸς καὶ Υἱοῦ πνεῦμα καὶ σῶμα. παιδίσκη δὲ κυρίας τοῦ ἁγίου Πνεύματος ἡ ψυχή. Τὰ δὲ τρία Κύριος ὁ Θεὸς ἡμῶν ἐστιν· οἱ γὰρ τρεῖς τὸ ἕν εἰσιν. *Cels*, VIII.12: Ἕνα οὖν θεόν, ὡς ἀποδεδώκαμεν, τὸν πατέρα καὶ τὸν υἱὸν θεραπεύομεν.

m Jerome, *commMatt*, 13.33. This is Origen's theology, particularly expressed in the present manuscript.

mi The same in Origen, *schLuc*, PG.17.357.31-33, quoted forthwith.

mii Origen, *commMatt*, fr. 302 (Klostermann), col. 2.

miii Origen, *frLuc*, fr. 205, quoted in the *Catena in Lucam*, p. 108. Likewise, *schLuc*, PG.17.357.28-35.

miv Theodore of Mopsuestia, *frMatt*, fr. 72, col. 2.

mv Origen, *commMatt*, fr. 302 (Klostermann), col. 3.

mvi Origen, *schLuc*, PG.17.357.31-33. The same in *homPs*, homily 29.1.

mvii Pseudo-Caesarius (Cassian the Sabaite), *Quaestiones et Responsiones*, chapter 200. This newly discovered moderate Origenist is the sole one who reproduced this particular exegesis of Origen's.

mviii Cf. Origen, *deOr*, 5.3: οὕτως ἀνόητος ἂν εἴη ἄνθρωπος, ὅστις οἴεται διὰ τὴν ἑαυτοῦ εὐχὴν γίνεσθαι τὰ καὶ μὴ εὐξαμένου αὐτοῦ πάντως ἐσόμενα ἄν. *commGen*, PG.12.68.35-36 (*Philocalia*, 23.10): ὡς πάντως ἐσομένου τοῦ προειρημένου. *schMatt*, PG.17.297.44-45: οὐκ ἀναιρεῖ τὸ αὐτεξούσιον, ἀλλὰ τὸ προγνωστικὸν τοῦ πάντως ἐσομένου δηλοῖ.

mix See *supra*, folio 4r: Οὐκ ἐπειδὴ δὲ ἐρρέθη ἐγένετο (τὸ γὰρ τοιοῦτον οὐ προφητεία), ἀλλ' ἐπειδὴ ἔμελλε γίνεσθαι ἐρρέθη· καὶ τοῦτο ἡ προφητεία.

mx Origen, *apud Catena in Matthaeum*, p. 107.

mxi Cf. *Cels*, III.15: καὶ τῇ ἀνέσει ἑαυτοὺς ἐπιδιδόναι. *deOr*, 27.14: ἀνέσεώς τε ἀπὸ γεωργίας τῆς ἁγίας γῆς λαβεῖν. *Philocalia*, 27.5: περὶ τὸν τόπον τῆς ἀνέσεως. *frJer*, fr. 14: μετέστη πρὸς ἄνεσιν. *frPs*, on Psalm 38:14: ... ἐκ τῆς πρὸς σοῦ μοι γενομένης ἀνέσεως. Ἄνεσις δὲ Θεοῦ ἐστιν ἀπάθεια. *Op. cit.* on Psalm 138:11-12: τὴν ἐν θλίψεσιν ἄνεσιν, ὡς καὶ τοῖς ἐν ἀνέσει τυγχάνει ὅμοιον. *selPs*, PG.12.1125.42: ὕπνον δὲ ἄνεσιν ψυχῆς. *Op. cit.* PG.12.1664.50: εἰς ἄνεσιν οἱ δίκαιοι παραληφθήσονται. *homPs*, homily 8.3: καὶ ἄνεσιν γενομένην ἐν τῇ χρηστότητι αὐτοῦ. *Op. cit.* 19.1: τοὺς υἱοὺς Ἰσραὴλ πέμψαι πρὸς αὐτὸν αἰτοῦντας ἄνεσιν. *Op. cit.* 8.2; 14.5. Likewise, *selEx*, PG.12.272.13; *selPs*, PG.12.1252.47; 24.4.

mxii See term οἴκαδε in Origen's favourite author, Plutarch, *Aemilius Paullus*, 39.5; *Pelopidas*, 10.5; *Aratus*, 44.3. Cf. Pseudo-Plato, *Epistulae*, 317a. Dionysius of Halicarnassus, *Antiquitates Romanae*, 6.15.1. The phrase οἴκαδε ἀναχωρεῖν ('to return home') comes from Thucydides, *Historiae*, 2.68.3. Also, Plutarch, *De Genio Socratis*, p. 596E. Pausanias, *Graeciae Descriptio*, 2.8.6; 4.11.8; 4.19.4; 10.22.2. Cassius Dio, *Historiae Romanae*, 46.29.4; 51.23.5; 75.9.3. Then, Eusebius, *Commentaria in Psalmos*, PG.23.125.30. Gregory of

Nazianzus, *Contra Julianum Imperatorem 1* (*orat. 4*), PG.35.609.34. John Chrysostom, *De Lazaro*, PG.48.966.19; *et passim*, at scores of points.

mxiii Cf. Origen, *exhMar*, 29: ἐκείνου δὲ δειλιάσαντος, apropos of Psalm 26:1 (ἀπὸ τίνος δειλιάσω;), which he quotes and comments on also in *commJohn*, XXXII.23.296; *Cels*, VIII.27; *selPs*, PG.12.1276.26. Likewise, on Psalm 103:7 (ἀπὸ φωνῆς βροντῆς σου δειλιάσουσιν); *deOr*, 33.2; *frPs*, on Psalm 103:7-8. Cf. *homPs*, homily 25.2: καὶ διὰ τοῦτο μὴ δειλιᾶν. *Op. cit.* homily 25.2: οὐ δειλιάσεις (on Psalm 77:53: καὶ οὐκ ἐδειλίασαν). *Op. cit.* 13.4, quoting John 14:1 (μηδὲ δειλιάτω).

mxiv Against the Gnostics, once again.

mxv Cf. Origen, *Cels*, IV.3: ὅτι ἀρετῆς μὲν ἐὰν ἀνέλῃς τὸ ἑκούσιον, ἀνεῖλες αὐτῆς καὶ τὴν οὐσίαν.

mxvi An extremely rare word (which, instead of ἀφότου, could be also ἀφ᾽ ὅτε -both of them meaning 'since'), which Origen took up from Hermas and Hippolytus, the only authors that used it prior to himself. Hermas, *Pastor*, 72.6: βλέπεις δὲ ἐξ αὐτῶν πολλοὺς μετανενοηκότας ἀφότε ἐλάλησας αὐτοῖς τὰς ἐντολάς μου. Hippolytus, *Refutatio Omnium Haeresium*, 9.16.4: πληρουμένων τριῶν ἐτῶν Τραϊανοῦ Καίσαρος, ἀφότε ὑπέταξεν ἑαυτοῦ τῇ ἐξουσίᾳ τοὺς Πάρθους.

mxvii This is Cramer's editiorial mistake (it should be ἀκάκως), but the editors of Ireneus' fragments (L. Doutreleau, B. Hemmerdinger, B.C. Mercier, and A. Rousseau) emended to the correct ἀλλ᾽ ἀκάκως.

mxviii Irenaeus, *apud Catena in Matthaeum*, p. 109, which has been recorded as Irenaeus, *Adversus Haereses* (*liber 4*), fr. 28. However, this was written by Origen. Cf. *commRom*, p. 244 (on Rom. 5:1-2): οὐ γὰρ δυνατόν ἐστιν *εἰρήνην ἔχειν πρὸς τὸν Θεὸν* τὰ ἐναντία ἔργα τῇ ἀρετῇ πράττοντα ἅπερ ἐχθροποιεῖ Θεῷ τὸν κατεργαζόμενον. The text of the alleged fragment from Irenaeus' *Adversus Haereses* is slightly different from the catena-one, certainly corrected, and stands closer to that of Origen's. Irenaeus is not among the authors from who the anthologist of *Codex Sabaiticus 232* culled.

mxix See *supra*, folio 110v and endnote cmliii: ἐπὶ τέλει τῶν πραγμάτων.

mxx The expression φαῦλα νοήματα ψυχῆς ('evil thoughts of the soul') is characteristic of Origen. *selPs*, PG.12.1660.2-4: Ὅσοι κατὰ τὴν διδασκαλίαν τοῦ Χριστοῦ τὰ φαῦλα νοήματα διαφθείρουσι τῆς ψυχῆς. Cf. *op. cit.* PG.12.1664.34-36: Ἀλλὰ καὶ τὰ φαῦλα νοήματα πολλάκις οἱ δαίμονες οὐ γυμνὰ ἀποτίθενται ἡμῖν. *frPs*, on Psalm 73:13-14: τὰ κατὰ τὴν διάνοιαν συνιστάμενα φαῦλα νοήματα.

mxxi Cf. Origen, *commMatt*, 13.20: οὐ γὰρ ταὐτόν ἐστιν ἁπλῶς ὁ κόσμος καὶ ὁ κόσμος τοῦ οὐρανοῦ ἢ ὁ κόσμος τῆς Ἐσθήρ. Τὸ δὲ νῦν ἡμῖν ζητούμενον ἄλλο. Νομίζω οὖν ὅτι οὐ τὸ ἐξ οὐρανοῦ καὶ γῆς σύστημά ἐστι κατὰ τὰ θεῖα γράμματα ὁ κόσμος, ἀλλ᾽ ὁ περίγειος μόνος τόπος, καὶ οὗτος οὐ καθ᾽ ὅλην νοούμενος τὴν γῆν, ἀλλ᾽ ὁ κατὰ τὴν ἡμετέραν οἰκουμένην. *ἐν τῷ κόσμῳ* γὰρ *ἦν τὸ ἀληθινὸν φῶς*, τῷ περιγείῳ τόπῳ τῷ κατὰ τὴν ἡμετέραν ‹οἰκουμένην› νοουμένῳ, ... ἄτοπον γὰρ λέγειν τὸ ἐξ οὐρανοῦ καὶ γῆς καὶ τῶν ἐν αὐτοῖς σύστημα, ὥστ᾽ εἰπεῖν ἂν ὅτι ἥλιος καὶ σελήνη καὶ ὁ χορὸς τῶν ἀστέρων καὶ οἱ ἐν ὅλῳ τῷ κόσμῳ τούτῳ ἄγγελοι οὐκ ἔγνωσαν *τὸ ἀληθινὸν φῶς* καὶ ἀγνοοῦντες αὐτὸ ἐτήρησαν τὴν ἐπιτεταγμένην αὐτοῖς ἀπὸ θεοῦ τάξιν. Portraying the universe as 'system of heaven and earth and the natures within these' (σύστημα οὐρανοῦ καὶ γῆς καὶ τῶν ἐν αὐτοῖς φύσεων) is a characteristic Stoic definition. See Chrysippus, *Fragmenta Logica et Physica*, frs. 527; 528; 529; 638; Posidonius, *Fragmenta*, fr. 271c; 276. The definition in *De Mundo*, 391b, is made in a work that could have been much later than Aristotle himself. Likewise, see this definition in Cleomedes, *Caelestia*, 1.1. Philo, *De Aeternitate Mundi*, 4. Origen, *Cels*, VI.59; *commGen*, PG.12.89.21-23 (*Philocalia*, 14.2). This came to be a definition of cosmos: *Suda*, letter kappa, entry 2148.

mxxii Jerome, *commMatt*, 13.37.

mxxiii Cf. Origen, *selPs*, PG.12.1097.5-7: οὕτως ζητητέον τῶν κολαζομένων τὸν βρυγμὸν τῶν ὀδόντων, τῆς ψυχῆς δύναμιν μασητικὴν ἐχούσης. This is part of Origen's words in an epitome by Methodius of Olympus, which Epiphanius of Salamis quoted in the *Panarion*, v. 2, p. 426. The term μασητικὸς means 'able to chew' and was used by Origen in relation to 'gnashing of teeth' (βρυγμὸς ὀδόντων, Matt. 8:12, 13:42; 13:50; 22:13; 24:51; 25:30; Luke, 13:28). Didymus, always a devout follower of Origen, used this in his commentary on Psalm; 34:16, which contains the same expression (ἔβρυξαν ἐπ' ἐμὲ τοὺς ὀδόντας αὐτῶν, a similar one in Psalms 36:12; 111:10; Job 16:9; Lamentations, 2:16). *Commentarii in Psalmos 29-34*, cod. p. 220: οἱ ὀδόντες πολλάκις τῆς ψυχῆς λέγονται αἱ μασητικαὶ αὐτῆς δυνάμεις. In fact, the verbal adjective μασητικὸς was coined by Origen himself, and no author other than Didymus did ever use this, save the quotation of Origen's passage by Methodius and Epiphanius.

mxxiv Origen, *commMatt*, fr. 304 (Klostermann).

mxxv Jerome, *commMatt*, 13.44. This is in effect a *verbatim* translation of Origen's foregoing text.

mxxvi Origen, *schMatt*, PG.17.293.56-296.4.

mxxvii Origen, *commMatt*, 10.5.

mxxviii Origen, *schMatt*, PG.17. 296.2-7.

mxxix Origen, *commMatt*, 10.5.

mxxx Cf. Origen, *commJohn*, XIX.9.52: ἅπερ οὐ τοῖς τυχοῦσιν λέγει ἀλλ', ὥς φησιν ὁ Μᾶρκος, τοῖς μαθηταῖς αὐτοῦ. *Op. cit.* XXXII.13.143: οὐ γὰρ τὸ τηλικοῦτον ὄνομα τὸ μακάριον εὔλογον ἐπὶ τοῖς τυχοῦσιν φῆσαι παρεῖναι τισίν. *selEz*, PG.13.785.18-21: Ἅμα δὲ παραθετέον τὸ ῥητὸν [sc. Jer. 18:7] τοῖς ἀδιακρίτως διαλεγομένοις πᾶσι καὶ τοῖς τυχοῦσι καὶ περὶ τῶν μειζόνων τοῖς ἁπλουστέροις καὶ ἀκεραιοτάτοις ἀνακοινουμένοις.

mxxxi Origen, *schMatt*, PG.17.296.12-19.

mxxxii Origen, *commMatt*, 10.6.

mxxxiii Against the Docetists.

mxxxiv Cf. Origen recalling his former renown as a Greek philosopher of note, which he somewhat despised after he had converted to Christianity. *exhMar*, 43: εἰ δεῖ ἑαυτὸν συνιστάναι *διὰ τῶν ὅπλων τῆς δικαιοσύνης τῶν δεξιῶν καὶ τῶν ἀριστερῶν*, [2 Cor. 6:7] συστήσαντες ἑαυτοὺς *διὰ δόξης* [2 Cor. 6:8] καὶ μὴ χαυνωθέντες ἐπ' αὐτῇ νῦν καὶ τὴν ἀτιμίαν ὑπομείνωμεν. Ἀλλ' εἰ καὶ εὐφημίας ἀξίως ἐπολιτευσάμεθα καὶ εὐφημήθημεν, νῦν καὶ τῆς ἀπὸ τῶν δυσσεβῶν δυσφημίας ἀνασχώμεθα. Ἔτι δὲ εἰ ὡς ἀληθεῖς παρὰ τοῖς φιλαλήθεσιν ἐθαυμάσθημεν, νῦν ἐπὶ τῷ λέγεσθαι ἡμᾶς πλανᾶσθαι γελάσωμεν. Ἐπὶ πολλοῖς κινδύνοις, ἀφ' ὧν ἐρρύσθημεν, πολλοὶ εἶπον ἡμᾶς ἀπὸ θεοῦ ἐπιγινώσκεσθαι. Νῦν ὁ βουλόμενος λεγέτω ἡμᾶς ἀγνοεῖσθαι, ὅτε τάχα μᾶλλον ἐπιγινωσκόμεθα. Φέροντες γοῦν τὰ συμβαίνοντα παιδευόμεθα μέν, οὐ θανατούμεθα δέ, καὶ ὁμοιούμεθα λυπουμένοις οἱ χαίροντες.

mxxxv Origen, *commMatt*, 10.8.

mxxxvi Prior to Origen, the term ἀποστολιμαῖος ('apostolic') was used only literally ('sent off') by Achilles Tatius, *Leucippe et Clitophon*, 2.9.2. Later, Theophanes Confessor, *Chronographia*, p. 234. Michael Psellus, *Chronographia*, 6.79; *Encomium in Matrem*, line 1555. Eustathius of Thessaloniki, *Commentarii ad Homeri Iliadem*, v. 3, p. 20.

mxxxvii Origen, *schMatt*, PG.17.296.55-297.5. This is also Origen, *commMatt*, fr. 309 I (Klostermann).

mxxxviii Cf. Origen, *schMatt*, PG.17.297.5-16: Ἢ οὕτως. *Σαγήνη* ἐστὶν ἡ ἀποστολικὴ διδασκαλία, ἡ ἀδιακρίτως συλλαμβανομένη Ἰουδαίους καὶ Ἕλληνας, βαρβάρους, Σκύθας, δούλους, ἐλευθέρους, πονηροὺς καὶ ἀγαθούς. *Θάλασσα*, ὁ τῶν ἀνθρώπων βίος. *Αἰγιαλός*, τὸ τέρμα τούτου.

Ἐν δὲ τῇ συντελείᾳ, ὅτε ἀνασπᾶται ἡ σαγήνη, ἀφορίζονται ἀπὸ τῶν φαύλων οἱ ἀγαθοί, οἱ μὲν τιμώμενοι, οἱ δὲ κολαζόμενοι. Οὐ γὰρ πάντων τῶν πιστῶν ὅμοιος ὁ τρόπος. Ἵνα δὲ μὴ νομίσῃ τις ὅτι ἔξω μόνον βάλλονται οἱ ἄπιστοι καὶ πονηροί, ἐσήμανεν, ὅτι εἰς διηνεκῆ κόλασιν παραπέμπονται. *Καὶ βαλοῦσιν αὐτοὺς εἰς τὴν κάμινον τοῦ πυρός*, καὶ τὰ ἑξῆς.

mxxxix Cf. folio 80v: τὸ διηνεκὲς τῆς κολάσεως. Folio 80v: εἰς διηνεκῆ κόλασιν παραπέμπονται. Folio 148r: ἐν δὲ τῷ μέλλοντι, ἀκαταπαύστως βασανίζεσθαι εἰς τὸ διηνεκές. Folio 177v: ἀλλὰ κολασθησόμενοι αἰωνίως.

mxl Origen, *op. cit.* PG.17.297.5-16. This is also, Origen, *commMatt*, fr. 309 II (Klostermann).

mxli Cf. Origen, *commMatt*, fr. 344 (Klostermann): ἐρωτᾷ δὲ οὐκ ἀγνοῶν. So in *commMatt*, 10.14; *frLuc*, fr. 132.

mxlii Origen, *commMatt*, 10.14.

mxliii Cf. Origen, *Cels*, II.4: Ἀληθῶς μὲν γὰρ Χριστιανοῖς ἡ εἰσαγωγή ἐστιν ἀπὸ τῶν ἱερῶν Μωϋσέως καὶ τῶν προφητικῶν γραμμάτων. Καὶ μετὰ τὴν εἰσαγωγὴν ἐν τῇ διηγήσει καὶ σαφηνείᾳ αὐτῶν ἐστι τοῖς εἰσαγομένοις ἡ προκοπή.

mxliv Origen, *commMatt*, 10.14: Ἔνθα ζητήσεις εἰ ὥσπερ νομικὸς γραμματεὺς οὕτως ἐστὶ καὶ εὐαγγελικός, καὶ ὥσπερ τὸν νόμον ἀναγινώσκων καὶ ἀκούων καὶ λέγων *ἅτινά ἐστιν ἀλληγορούμενα* [Gal. 4:24], οὕτω καὶ τὸ εὐαγγέλιον, ὡς εἰδέναι τηρουμένης τῆς κατὰ τὰ γενόμενα ἱστορίας τὴν ἐπὶ τὰ πνευματικὰ ἄπταιστον ἀναγωγήν, ἵνα μὴ ᾖ μαθήματα *πνευματικὰ πονηρίας* [Eph. 6:12], ἀλλ᾽ ἐναντίως ἔχοντα πνευματικοῖς πονηρίας πνευματικὰ ἀγαθότητος. Μαθητεύεται δὲ τῇ βασιλείᾳ *τῶν οὐρανῶν γραμματεὺς* κατὰ μὲν τὸ ἁπλούστερον, ὅτε ἀπὸ Ἰουδαϊσμοῦ ἀναλαμβάνει τις τὴν Ἰησοῦ Χριστοῦ ἐκκλησιαστικὴν διδασκαλίαν. Κατὰ δὲ τὸ βαθύτερον, ὅτε τὰς διὰ τοῦ γράμματος τῶν γραφῶν εἰσαγωγὰς παραλαβών τις ἀναβαίνει ἐπὶ τὰ πνευματικὰ ὀνομαζόμενα βασιλείαν *οὐρανῶν*.

mxlv Origen, *commMatt*, 10.14. This is also Origen, *commMatt*, fr. 311 (Klostermann).

mxlvi Origen, *commMatt*, fr. 312 (Klostermann).

mxlvii From this point down to ἐγηγερμένον ἐκ νεκρῶν ταῦτα ποιεῖν this appears as Theodore of Mopsuestia, *frMatt*, fr. 76, col. 2 (J. Reuss). Cf. the initial part of this slightly paraphrased as fr. 77.

mxlviii Cf. Josephus, *Antiquitates Judaicae*, 14.382; 15.362; 18.Proem; 18.27; *et passim; De Bello Judaico*, 2: 167-168; 178; 182-183.

mxlix Once again, he dismisses 'the heresy of transmigration', see pp. LXXXVII-LXXXIX.

ml This is also Origen, *commMatt*, fr. 314 (Klostermann).

mli Cf. Origen, *commMatt*, 10.23: Λέγοι δ᾽ ἄν τις τὴν τῆς μετενσωματώσεως ψευδοδοξίαν γεγονέναι ἐν τῷ Ἡρώδῃ καί τισι τῶν ἀπὸ τοῦ λαοῦ, ἀφ᾽ ἧς ᾤοντο τόν ποτε Ἰωάννην ἐν γενέσει γενέσθαι καὶ ἐκ νεκρῶν ἐληλυθέναι εἰς τὸν βίον ὡς Ἰησοῦν. Ἀλλ᾽ οὐδὲ ταύτην τὴν ψευδοδοξίαν πιθανὴν ἐᾷ νομισθῆναι ὁ μεταξὺ χρόνος τῆς γενέσεως Ἰωάννου καὶ Ἰησοῦ, οὐ πλεῖον μηνῶν ἓξ τυγχάνων. Τάχα δὲ μᾶλλον τοιαύτη τις ὑπόληψις ἦν ἐν τῷ Ἡρώδῃ, ὅτι *αἱ* ἐνεργήσασαι *δυνάμεις* ἐν τῷ Ἰωάννῃ μετέστησαν ἐπὶ τὸν Ἰησοῦν, ἀφ᾽ ὧν ὁ Ἰωάννης βαπτιστὴς εἶναι πεπίστευτο ἐν τῷ λαῷ.

mlii Theodore of Heraclea, *frMatt*, fr. 93 & *Catena in Matthaeum*, pp. 113-114.

mliii Cf. Origen, *commMatt*, 10.21-22: Ἡμεῖς δέ, μηδαμῇ σαφῶς εὑρίσκοντες τεθνηκέναι τὸν Φίλιππον, μεῖζον ἔτι τὸ παρανόμημα τῷ Ἡρώδῃ λογιζόμεθα γεγονέναι, ὅτι καὶ ζῶντος ἀπέστησε *τοῦ ἀδελφοῦ τὴν γυναῖκα.*

mliv Origen, *commMatt*, fr. 315 (Klostermann).

mlv Origen, *commMatt*, 10.22.

mlvi The exquisite poetic expression ἄσεμνος ὄρχησις ('ignoble dancing', insinuating a 'pantomimic' one intending to be sexually enticing) did not become part of those whom we have seen having copied from Origen's work abundantly, such as Chrysostom, Cyril,

Apollinaris, *et. al.* Nevertheless, this turn of phrase inspired a couple of later humble Christians and hymnographers, who set out to write of the Baptist's death in poetical style. Cf. Chrysippus of Jerusalem (presbyter, fifth century), *Encomium in Joannem Baptistam*, p. 46: Ὦ Ἡρῴδη, οὐκ ἀνέξομαί σοι. ἆρα ποίους ὅρκους ἐδίδους ἔμπροσθεν τῶν δαιμόνων; Τὸ ἥμισυ τῆς βασιλείας σου ἐχαρίσω τοῖς δαίμοσιν. Οὕτως ἀναισχύντως σκορπίζεις τὰ τῆς βασιλείας; δι᾽ ὄρχησιν ἄσεμνον τὸ ἥμισυ τῆς βασιλείας σου δίδως; Also, Analecta Hymnica Graeca, *Canones Augusti*, 29.2.2: Ἄδικε, ἄνομε, τίς ὁ κινήσας σε ὅρκοις τάξασθαι τῇ Ἡρωδιάδι τὴν τιμίαν κεφαλὴν τοῦ κατὰ τὸν νόμον σε Μωσέως ἐλέγξαντος; Τὰ μέλη τὰ λελυμένα τῆς ἀσέμνως ἐπὶ σοὶ ὀρχησαμένης παιδός; *Op. cit.* 29.2.8: Γενεσίων Ἡρώδου ἀγομένων, τῆς ἀσέμνου παιδὸς ὀρχησαμένης.

mlvii Origen, *commMatt*, fr. 316 (Klostermann).

mlviii Origen, *commMatt*, 10.22 (cont.).

mlix Origen, *op. cit.* 10.22 (cont.).

mlx Origen, *commMatt*, 10.22.

mlxi Origen, *commMatt*, fr. 317 (Klostermann).

mlxii The word προφητεία is R. Girod's erroneous editorial reading. The present codex supplies the correct προφητικὴ κεφαλή.

mlxiii Origen, *commMatt*, 10.22.

mlxiv Origen, *commMatt*, fr. 318 (Klostermann).

mlxv Origen, *commMatt*, 10.22.

mlxvi This is the oldest source informing that the head of John the Baptist was stored in Emesa (present-day Homs) of Syria. Two centuries later, the presbyter Chrysippus of Jerusalem wrote that Herodias buried John's head next to her house out of fear that this could be re-united with the Baptist's body upon his resurrection, and that some years later, a certain faithful person transferred John's head to Emesa. It was at that site that the head performed numerous miracles. Chrysippus of Jerusalem, *Encomium in Joannem Baptistam*, pp. 46-47. Two centuries later (seventh century), the *Chronicon Paschale* (p. 591) recorded that Baptist's head was discovered in Emesa in c. 455, which was '425 years after his decapitation'. Other variants of the story are much later (cf. Nicephorus Callistus Xanthopulus, *HE*, 12.29).

mlxvii This is one more characteristic instance of Origen drawing sophisticated vocabulary from his usual sources, namely, Plutarch and Galen. The verb διαρράπτω is a very rare one: it means 'sew together' and was coined in the second century AD (although perhaps Strabo had used this a little earlier just once; *Geographica*, 15.1.67). In the first place, its connotation was medical, suggesting a fine thread or any other material used surgically to stitch a wound or to join tissues; in a more general sense, it referred to the process of seaming two surfaces or edges. Galen, *De Anatomicis Administrationibus*, pp. 511; 552; *De Compositione Medicamentorum Per Genera*, p. 601; *In Hippocratis Librum De Officina Medici*, p. 746; *De Musculorum Dissectione ad Tirones*, p. 996. Pseudo-Galen, *Introductio*, p. 791. Plutarch, *De Sollertia Animalium*, p. 798A; *Cato Minor*, 70.10. Phrynichus of Bithynia (or Arabius, sophist, second century AD), *Praeparatio Sophistica*, p. 110. Later (fourth century), Oribasius, *Collectiones Medicae*, 25.48.3; 45.3.7; 47.13.5. Then, John Chrysostom used this also in its literal sense. *In Matthaeum*, PG.58: 501.59-60; 502.14. It turns out, therefore, that the present usage by Origen is the only one in which the verb διαρράπτω is applied in a metaphorical sense: διέρραψε τὸν λόγον means 'he composed his narrative in such a way as'.

mlxviii Jerome, *commMatt*, 14.13.

mlxix Jerome, *commMatt*, 14.13 (then, he appeals to Matt. 12:23). Cf. Origen (also quoting Matt. 12:23), *commMatt*, 10.23; 16.1; *commJohn*, XXVIII.23.198; *exhMar*, 34; *Cels*, I.65 (& *Philocalia*, 18.11). See also Origen, forthwith *infra:* οὐδὲ ὁμόσε χωρεῖν τοῖς δεινοῖς ἐντεῦθεν δῆλον.

mlxx Cf. Origen, *commMatt*, 10.23: *Ἀκούσας δὲ ὁ Ἰησοῦς ἀνεχώρησεν ἐκεῖθεν ἐν πλοίῳ εἰς ἔρημον τόπον κατ᾽ ἰδίαν.* Τὸ μὲν ῥητὸν διδάσκει ἡμᾶς ὅση δύναμις ἀπὸ τῶν διωκόντων καὶ τῆς προσδοκίας τοῦ διὰ τὸν λόγον ἐπιβουλεύεσθαι ἀναχωρεῖν. τοῦτο μὲν γὰρ κατὰ τὸ εὐλόγιστον γένοιτ᾽ ἄν, τὸ δὲ δυνάμενον ἔξω εἶναι τῶν περιστατικῶν ὁμόσε χωρεῖν αὐτοῖς προπετές ἐστι καὶ θρασύ. Ἀμφιβάλοι ἄν περὶ τοῦ ἐκκλίνειν τὰ τοιαῦτα, τοῦ Ἰησοῦ οὐ μόνον ἐπὶ τοῖς κατὰ τὸν Ἰωάννην ἀναχωρήσαντος, ἀλλὰ καὶ διδάσκοντος καὶ λέγοντος. *Ἐὰν διώκωσιν ὑμᾶς ἐν τῇ πόλει ταύτῃ, φεύγετε εἰς τὴν ἑτέραν. Op. cit.* 16.1: Φαμὲν γὰρ ὅτι οὔτε πάντοτε καθήκει ἐκκλίνειν τοὺς κινδύνους οὔτε ἀεὶ ὁμόσε χωρεῖν πρὸς αὐτούς. Σοφοῦ δέ τινος ἐν Χριστῷ χρεία εἰς τὸ δοκιμάζειν, ποῖος μὲν ἀπαιτεῖ καιρὸς ἀναχώρησιν, ποῖος δὲ τὴν εἰς τὸν ἀγῶνα προθυμίαν χωρὶς ἀναχωρήσεως καὶ πολλῷ πλέον χωρὶς φυγῆς. *Cels*, I.65 (& *Philocalia*, 18.6): Καὶ διδάσκων παράδειγμα αὐτοῖς ἐγίνετο εὐσταθοῦς βίου, οἰκονομοῦντος μὴ εἰκῇ μηδ᾽ ἀκαίρως καὶ ἀλόγως ὁμόσε χωρεῖν τοῖς κινδύνοις. *Op. cit.* I.66 (& *Philocalia*, 18.12): Καὶ ἐχρῆν τὸν προνοούμενον τῆς ὡς ἀνθρώπου ἑαυτοῦ εἰς τὸν βίον ἐπιδημίας μὴ ἀκαίρως ὁμόσε χωρεῖν τῷ ἕως θανάτου κινδύνῳ.

mlxxi John Chrysostom, *In Matthaeum*, PG.58.497.50-53.

mlxxii *Catena in Matthaeum*, p. 115 (anonymous).

mlxxiii Origen, *commMatt*, fr. 321 (Klostermann).

mlxxiv Cf. *infra*, folio 131v: ‹Εἰ› ο‹ὖ›ν φιλεῖται παρ᾽ ἐμοῦ, μὴ φοβοῦ τὸ πάθος· ἴσος γάρ μου ἐστί.

mlxxv John Chrysostom, *In Matthaeum*, PG.58.498.28-32.

mlxxvi *Catena in Matthaeum*, p. 115 (anonymous).

mlxxvii *Catena in Matthaeum, loc. cit.* (anonymous).

mlxxviii Cf. οἱ ἅγιοι τοῦ Θεοῦ in Origen (evidently, after Psalm 33:10: φοβήθητε τὸν κύριον, οἱ ἅγιοι αὐτοῦ), *selGen*, PG.12.144.26; and then, Eusebius, *De Ecclesiastica Theologia*, 3.3.14; *In Isaiam*, 1.14; *Commentaria in Psalmos*, PG.23: 157.5; 181.10; 665.20.

mlxxix Jerome, *commMatt*, 14.19.

mlxxx *Catena in Matthaeum*, p. 116 (anonymous).

mlxxxi Cf. Cyril of Alexandria, *In Joannem*, v. 2, p. 649: καὶ *ἐζήτουν ἀποκτεῖναι* κατὰ τὸ γεγραμμένον, διὰ τὸ μεταρρυθμίζειν τῶν πιστευόντων τὸν νοῦν ἐκ νομικῆς καὶ παχείας ἐντολῆς εἰς τὴν τῆς εὐαγγελικῆς πολιτείας ἰσχνότητα. *Epistulae Paschales*, PG.77.756.23-25: Ὅτι τοίνυν ἀναγκαία πρὸς ὄνησιν ἡ τῶν εὐαγγελικῶν θεσπισμάτων ἀνάβλησις ἦν, ὑπεμφήνειεν ἄν, καὶ μάλα ἰσχνῶς. *In Isaiam*, PG.70.721.37-41: Διακέκραγε γὰρ ὁ Μωσέως νόμος τὸ τοῦ Χριστοῦ μυστήριον καὶ τῆς εὐαγγελικῆς πολιτείας τὴν δύναμιν ὡς ἐν σκιαῖς εὑρήσομεν, ἰσχνὸν ἐνιέντες τοῖς γεγραμμένοις τὸν νοῦν. Cf. Origen, *commJohn*, II.7.57: τὰ ὑλικώτερα καὶ παχύτερα τῶν νοημάτων. πάντα δὲ τὴν ἰσχνότητα καὶ λεπτότητα ἐκπέφευγε τῆς ἀληθείας τὰ ὁπωσποτοῦν ψευδόμενα. *Op. cit.* II.9.66: Ἀλλὰ καὶ τὸ *οὗτος* [John, 1:2] κατὰ δεῖξιν ἐκφερόμενον νομισθήσεται ἐπὶ τοῦ λόγου τετάχθαι ἢ ἐπὶ τοῦ θεοῦ ὑπὸ τοῦ μὴ ἰσχνότερον ἐρευνῶντος. *selEz*, PG.13.812.45-47: Τρίχαπτά ἐστιν, οἷον ὡσεὶ ἔλεγε, σφόδρα ἰσχνὰ νοήματα, βαθέα, ἢ ποικίλα δὲ διὰ τὰ διάφορα εἴδη τῆς ἀρετῆς. *frLuc*, fr. 125 & *schLuc*, PG.17.337.35-37: Πλὴν ἀλλὰ τοιαύτη μὲν ἡ τοῦ θαύματος ἱστορία, χρὴ δὲ ἴσως καὶ ἰσχνότερον αὐτὴν θεωρῆσαι καὶ ὑψηλότερον. Given these, who else other than Origen could Cyril taken his characteristic expression from?

mlxxxii Cf. *Catena in Lucam*, p. 90: ἵνα μὴ ἀψικόρως τὴν προσευχὴν ποιώμεθα. This is part of an extensive fragment attributed to Titus of Bostra (*op. cit.* pp. 86-92), whereas the previous one (p. 86) is ascribed to Origen. Quite plainly, Titus took up the charectistic phrasing μὴ ἀψικόρως εὔχεσθαι from Origen. Anyhow, there is a passage which is attributed jointly to both authors (*op. cit.* p. 6).

mlxxxiii Cyril of Alexandria, *frMatt*, fr. 180 & *Catena in Matthaeum*, p. 118 (on Matt. 14:23).

mlxxxiv Cyril of Alexandria, *frMatt*, fr. 180, col. 2.

mlxxxv This is an almost unique expression about the 'sea' made 'flat' by Jesus, which was used by Cyril of Jerusalem (fourth century), *Homilia in Paralyticum Juxta Piscinam Jacentem*, 8 (writing of Jesus): τὸν θαλάσσης ἡνίοχον, τὸν μὴ μόνον ἑαυτῷ κρηπῖδος δίκην ὑπεστρωμένην ἔχοντα τὴν θάλασσαν. Also, in a homily by Bishop Reginus of Constantia in Cyprus (an anti-Nestorian) at the Council of Ephesus. ACO, *Concilium Universale Ephesenum anno 431*, tome 1.1.2, p. 71: θάλασσα μὲν γὰρ τὸν δεσπότην ἰδοῦσα τὰ νῶτα ὑπέστρωσε. See also *infra*, folio 120v: ὑπέστρωσεν αὐτῶν τὴν θάλασσαν.

mlxxxvi I have discussed the notion of 'aerial spirit' (ἀέριον πνεῦμα) suggesting daemonic powers, in *RCR* (pp. 174-178), which was used by Cassian the Sabaite, the newly discovered moderate Origenist Greek father. Cassian the Sabaite, *First Contribution by Abba Serenus*, *NDGF*, p. 265. Cassian was the same person as Pseudo-Caesarius (see *NDGF*, Appendix II) and entertained this idea in his *Quaestiones et Responsiones*, 14; 102; 112 (Pseudo-Caesarius). Although this idea was thought to be Pythagorean, testimonies suggest that in fact this was of Chaldean origin. In the Platonic *Epinomis*, 984e, 'daemons' are styled 'an aerial race' (quoted by Eusebius, *Praeparatio Evangelica*, 13.18.3). Origen must have read this in apocrypha such as the *Testamenta XII Patriarcharum*, 12.3.4 (τοῦ ἀερίου πνεύματος τοῦ Βελιάρ), and in writings on magic, which definitely he had read. Cf. *Papyri Magicae* (Christian fragments, Preisendanz), number 1, lines 97; 179-80; number 4, line 1116. Authors who normally drew on Origen followed suit on applying this idea. Gregory of Nyssa, *In Ecclesiasten*, p. 291. Epiphanius of Salamis, *Panarion*, v. 3, p. 338. Basil of Caesarea, *De Spiritu Sancto*, 16.38; *Adversus Eunomium*, PG.29.728.45; *Epistulae*, epistle 46.2. Macarius of Magnesia, *Apocriticus*, book 3, p. 145. Theodore of Mopsuestia, *commProphXII*, Hosea, 4.19a; Amos, 4.12-13. Pseudo-Dionysius the Areopagite, *De Caelesti Hierarchia*, p. 55. John Philoponus, *De Opificio Mundi*, pp. 19-20; 277. Maximus Confessor, *Quaestiones et Dubia*, 188. Photius, *Epistulae et Amphilochia*, epistle 16 (if indeed this is not Cassian the Sabaite's, as I have maintained). Analecta Hymnica Graeca, *Canones Junii*, 14.6.6. Severian of Gabala associated ἀέριον πνεῦμα with Paul's evil 'prince of the powers of the air' (Eph. 2:2: κατὰ τὸν ἄρχοντα τῆς ἐξουσίας τοῦ ἀέρος τοῦ τοῦ πνεύματος τοῦ νῦν ἐνεργοῦντος ἐν τοῖς υἱοῖς τῆς ἀπειθείας). *Fragmenta in Epistulam ad Ephesios*, p. 308.

mlxxxvii John Chrysostom, *In Matthaeum*, PG.58.506.44-45.

mlxxxviii The notion of ἐναργὴς ἀπόδειξις (meaning 'demonstrably manifest proof', i.e. a palpable and strong one, hence, irrefutable) is one more point demonstrating Origen's stunning erudition. Cf. *Cels*, IV.89 (& *Philocalia*, 20.16): καὶ τὴν ἀπολογίαν μετὰ τοῦτ' ἐναργεστέρως ἀποδεῖξαι. *Op. cit.* VIII.59: ἐναργεστέρας ἀποδείξεις λήψεται τοῦ ταῦθ' οὕτως ἔχειν. *Philocalia*, 23.20 (*commGen*, PG.12.84.2-5): οὐ μὴν ἐναργῆ τὴν ἀπόδειξιν, ἀλλὰ πεπιστευμένην ὡς ἁρμόζουσαν τῷ ἀγενήτῳ νῷ καὶ ὑπὲρ πᾶσαν φύσιν τυγχάνοντι. *commMatt*, 14.11: καὶ πληροφοροῦντος δι' ἐναργῶν ἀποδείξεων. Prior to him, Clement of Alexandria, *Stromateis*, 7.16.102.1: ἡ τῆς ἐκ τῶν γραφῶν μαρτυρίας ἐναργὴς ἀπόδειξις. *Excerpta ex Theodoto*, 4.75.1-2: ἐναργὴς δὲ ἀπόδειξις καὶ ἡ τῶν μαθημάτων θεωρία. As it normally happened, Origen took this up from Galen and Philo, but in the past I have shown that he had read Demosthenes and Diodore of Sicily, too. Cf. Demosthenes, *De Corona*, 300: τίνες αἱ τούτων ἀποδείξεις; ἐναργεῖς καὶ φανεραί. Diodore of Sicily, *Bibliotheca Historica*, 3.3.2: ἐναργεστάτην ἔχειν ἀπόδειξιν. Philo, *De Vita Mosis*, 1.196: πεπιστευκέναι δ' αὐτῷ λαβόντες ἀποδείξεις ἐναργεστάτας. *Op. cit.* 2.262: ἀλλ' ὅ γε πατὴρ δυσὶν ἐναργεστάταις ἀποδείξεσι τὸ λόγιον τοῦ προφήτου διασυνέστησεν. Nevertheless, here is a definite source for him to have drawn on. Galen, *De Naturalibus Facultatibus*, p. 117: τὰ δ' ἤτοι χωρὶς ἀποδείξεως ὡς ἐναργῆ πρὸς αὐτῶν εἰρημένα. *De Usu Partium*, p. 169: ἀλλ' ἐναργέσιν ἀποδείξεσιν ἐκ τῶν ἀνατομῶν εὑρισκομέναις. *De Utilitate Respirationis*, pp. 508-509: λήμμασι τῶν ἀποδείξεων τοῖς ἐναργῶς γινωσκομένοις χρησαμένους. *De Animi Cuiuslibet Peccatorum Dignotione et Curatione*, p. 94: ὡμολόγηται μὲν ἡ ἀπὸ τῶν ἐναργεστάτων ἀρχὴ πάσης ἀποδείξεως. *De Placitis Hippocratis et Platonis*, 3.1.28: ἢ ἐξ ὧν εἴρηκεν ὁ Χρύσιππος νῦν ἐναργέστερον ἄν τις ἀποδείξειεν. *De Plenitudine*, p. 522: οὐκ ἐν τῷ καταφρονεῖν τῶν ἐναργῶν, ἃ πάσης ἀποδείξεώς εἰσιν ἀρχαί. *De Locis Affectis*, p. 159: περὶ γὰρ ἡγεμονικοῦ ψυχῆς ἀποδείξεων οὐσῶν ἐναργῶν. *De Diebus Decretoriis*, pp. 924-925: ἀπόδειξις δ' ἐναργεστάτη. *De Methodo Medendi*, p. 839: τοῦ δὲ ζωτικοῦ πνεύματος οὐχ ὁμοίως μὲν ἐναργῶς ἡ ἀπόδειξις ἦν. *De Simplicium Medicamentorum Temperamentis ac Facultatibus*, p. 14: οὔθ' εὕρηταί τι τοιοῦτον οὔτ' ἐναργῶς ἀποδεῖξαι δυνατόν. *Adversus Ea Quae a Juliano in Hippocratis Aphorismos Enuntiata Sunt Libellus*, p. 254: ἡμῖν δ' οὐκ ἐξέσται δι' ἀποδείξεων ἐναργῶν ἐξελέγχειν αὐτοῦ τὴν ἀπαιδευσίαν. *Alimentorum Facultatibus* (quoting from Diocles of Carystus), p. 454: ἐκ νοήσεως ἐναργοῦς ἀπόδειξίς τε καὶ πίστις ἄρχεται.

As always, his devout adherents seized on the expression, which subsequently became a recurrent motif in Christian ligterature. Eusebius, *Praeparatio Evangelica*, 1.1.11; 1.3.4; 1.3.6; *HE*, 2.17.18; 5.5.5; *Demonstratio Evangelica*, 1.1.15; 3.1.6; 3.2.78; 8.5.5; *Vita Constantini*, 2.42.1; *De Laudibus Constantini*, 11.7; 15.1; 16.11; 17.12; *Generalis Elementaria Introductio*, fr. 472; *Commentaria in Psalmos*, PG.23.1200.10-11. Gregory of Nyssa, *In Diem Luminum*, p. 238; *In Sanctum Pascha*, p. 257; *Contra Eunomium*, 2.1.190; 2.1.265; *Epistulae*, epistle 19.3; *Encomium in xl Martyres ii*, PG.46.784.25; *Contra Fatum*, p. 58. Gregory of Nazianzus, *In Laudem Cypriani*, PG.35.1184.11. Basil of Caesarea, *De Jejunio*, PG.31.189.46; *Sermones De Moribus*, PG.32.1248.46; *Epistulae*, epistles 189.8; 204.6; 223.6; 244.5. Athanasius, *De Incarnatione Verbi*, 33.2. As it happened, his detractor could not help Origen's influence: Epiphanius of Salamis, *Panarion*, v. 2, p. 180; and as always, Cyril of Alexandria made the most of Origen's locution without mentioning his name, not even just once: *In Joannem*, v. 1, pp. 515; 572; 609; 704; v. 2, pp. 35; 139; 589; 652; v. 3, pp. 21; 54; *Fragmenta in Sancti Pauli Epistulam ad Romanos*, pp. 181; *Fragmenta in Sancti Pauli Epistulam i ad Corinthios*, p. 255; *Fragmenta in Sancti Pauli Epistulam ad Hebraeos*, p. 381; *De Sancta Trinitate Dialogi*, pp. 412; 488; 501; 604; *Quod Unus Sit Christus*, p. 735; *Epistulae Paschales*, PG.77: 725.49; 729.11; 760.10; 916.50; *De Adoratione*, PG.68: 432.27; 601.10; 900.52; 948.42; *Glaphyra in Pentateuchum*, PG.69.140.25; *In Isaiam*, PG.70: 213.53; 469.20; 605.6; 764.18; 1261.15; 1388.44; *Thesaurus De Sancta Consubstantiali Trinitate*, PG.75: 176.26; 181.43; *Contra Julianum*, 2.1. Then, Gelasius of Cyzicus, *HE*, 2.17.9; 2.21.21; 2.37.30. Naturally, also Origen's sixth-century moderate follower Pseudo-Caesarius (Cassian the Sabaite), *Quaestiones et Responsiones*, 19; 44; 183; 218 (lies 212 & 526). Later, Photius, in the dubious *Epistulae et Amphilochia* (some of which probably were written by Cassian the Sabaite), epistles, 284; 290. Michael Psellus, *Theologica*, opusculum 15; *Epistulae*, epistle 16; *commPhys*, 7.3. Eustratius of Nicaea, *commEthNic*, p. 270.

Greek intellectuals used the expression, although not as heavily as Christian ones. Stobaeus, *Anthologium*, 2.31.125. Ammonius of Alexandria, *commDeInterpr*, pp. 146; 148; 177. Proclus, *commRep*, v. 1, p. 159; *Theologia Platonica*, v. 5, p. 4; v. 6, p. 3; *In Platonis Parmenidem*, p. 1238; *commEucl*, p. 426. Damascius, *In Parmenidem*,

p. 120. Simplicius, *commCael*, pp. 118; 217; 335; 460; 540; *commPhys*, pp. 272; 524; 668; 962. John Philoponus, *commAnim*, p. 216; *commPhys*, p. 828; *De Aeternitate Mundi*, pp. 200; 248; 396.

mlxxxix Cf. Origen, *commMatt*, 11.9-10.

mxc From this point onwards, Photius copied from Origen's text. See quotation forthwith.

mxci The notion of 'avarice' being a 'disease' was explicated only by the following authors, all of whom were dear to Origen. Philo, *De Specialibus Legibus*, 1.24. Longinus, *De Sublimitate*, 44.6. Plutarch, *Aemilius Paullus*, 8.11; *De Garrulitate*, p. 502E.

mxcii Photius, *frMatt*, fr. 65. Jerome slightly paraphrased this in the otherwise 'his own' commentary; *commMatt*, 15.2-10.

mxciii The elegant stylistic turn τίς τῶν νοῦν ἐχόντων, introducing a rhetorical question (and meaning, 'no sensible person could ever make such a claim'), was one of the exquisite moments of Greek oratory, indeed as old as Anaximenes of Lampsacus (rhetorician, historian, c. 380-320 BC), *Ars Rhetorica*, Proem, section 8: τίς γὰρ δὴ τοῦτ' ἀμφισβητήσειε τῶν νοῦν ἐχόντων; As it so often happened, it was Origen who introduced this in Christian literature, to be followed (as in most of such cases) by Gregory of Nyssa, Gregory of Nazianzus, and then (once again) by John Chrysostom, Cyril of Alexandria, and others. Origen's sources of this expressive style are the same as those we come upon time and again. Galen, *De Methodo Medendi*, p. 591; *In Hippocratis De Victu Acutorum*, p. 481. Pseudo-Apollonius of Tyana, *Apollonii Epistulae*, epistle 58. Dionysius of Halicarnassus, *Antiquitates Romanae*, 4.47.4. After Origen: Gregory of Nyssa, *De Mortuis Non Esse Dolendum*, p. 46; *Contra Eunomium*, 2.1.209; 2.1.38; 2.1.483; 3.2.2. Gregory of Nazianzus, *De Spiritu Sancto*, 19. John Chrysostom, *In Genesim*, PG.53: 34.16; 35.4; 135.22; *In Epistulam ad Colossenses*, PG.62.319.6. Cyril of Alexandria, *In Joannem*, v. 2, p. 421. Pseudo-John of Damascus, *Vita Barlaam et Joasaph*, p. 406. ACO, *Concilium Lateranense a. 649 Celebratum*, Act 5, p. 258 (quoting from Ambrose of Milan). As surprising as it is, a distinctively Greek oratorical turn of phrase did not appeal to Greek authors later to Origen, save the exception in Julian the emperor's *Encomium to Emperor Constantius*, section 2.

mxciv See *supra*, endnote xxiii and dccclxxiv. At this point, compare Chrysostom's parallel text copied from Origen. John Chrysostom, *In Matthaeum*, PG.58.513.52-514.1: Διά τοι τοῦτο καὶ αὐτὸς ἐξ ἀρχῆς οὐ φανερῶς εἶπε περὶ βρωμάτων, ἀλλά, *Τὰ εἰσερχόμενα εἰς τὸ στόμα.* Καὶ πάλιν, ὅτε σαφέστερον ἔδοξεν ὕστερον λέγειν, ἀπὸ τοῦ τέλους αὐτὸ συνεσκίασεν εἰπών. *Τὸ δὲ ἀνίπτοις χερσὶ φαγεῖν οὐ κοινοῖ τὸν ἄνθρωπον.*

mxcv John Chrysostom, *In Matthaeum*, PG.58.513.41-45.

mxcvi This is a proverbial phrase, meaning 'unbridled mouth', which comes from the Classical age. This had been used by Plato (*Leges*, 701c7: ἀχάλινον κεκτημένον τὸ στόμα) and Aristophanes (*Ranae*, verse 838: ἀχάλινον ἀκρατὲς ἀπύλωτον στόμα). However, it was Euripides' usage that remained proverbial. *Bacchae*, verses 836-838: ἀχαλίνων στομάτων ἀνόμου τ' ἀφροσύνας τὸ τέλος δυστυχία. ('Misfortune is the result of unbridled mouths and lawless folly'). Subsequently, this was quoted by the following authors. Stobaeus, *Anthologium*, 2.7.3a (*apud* Arius Didymus); also, Stobaeus, *op. cit.* 3.36.13. Lucian of Samosata, *Revivescentes*, 3. Andronicus Callistus, *Defensio Theodori Gazae Adversus Michaelem Apostolium*, 22.2. Michael Apostolius (paroemiographer), *Collectio Paroemiarum*, 3.54. Arsenius of Monembasia (paroemiographer), *Apophthegmata*, 4.63a. Bessarion, *In Calumniatorem Platonis*, 4.16.1.

Euripides used the same expression in his lost tragedy *Melanippe Fettered* (Μελανίππη Δεσμῶτις), which Athenaeus quoted in his *Deipnosophistae*, 14.2: ἐγὼ δέ πως μισῶ γελοίους, οἵτινες τήτει σοφῶν ἀχάλιν' ἔχουσι στόματα. Plato's expression was quoted by posterity, too: Timaeus (Neoplatonist sophist, grammarian), *Lexicon Platonicum*, letter alpha, p. 977b. *Suda*, letter alpha, entry 3459. Thus, the expression became part of the locution of several intellectuals. Philo, *Quis Rerum Divinarum Heres Sit*, 110; *De Somniis*, 2.132; 2.165; 2.275; *De Abrahamo*, 29; 191; *De Josepho*, 246; *De Vita Mosis*, 2.198; *De Specialibus Legibus*, 1.3 ('unbridled tongue'); 1.241; *Legatio ad Gaium*, 163. Lucian of Samosata, *Pseudologista*, 32. Julius Naucratites (or, Pollux), *Onomasticon*, 6.146. Eusebius, *frLuc*, PG.24.592.23. Basil of Caesarea, *Epistulae*, epistles 71.1; 207.2; *Homilia Adversus Eos Qui Irascuntur*, PG.31.356.3-4 (quoted also by John of Damascus, *Sacra Parallela* PG.96.268.29-30). Ephraem Syrus, *Adversus Improbas Mulieres*, p. 205. Theodoret, *De Providentia*, PG.83.561.41-42 ('unbridled tongue'). Cyril of Alexandria, *commProphXII*, v. 2, p. 200. Olympiodorus, the deacon of Alexandria, *Commentarii in Ecclesiasten*, PG.93.541.6-7. Michael Psellus, *Theologica*, opusculum 7, line 91; opusculum 59, line 64.

mxcvii Origen, *commMatt*, fr. 329 (Klostermann). The editor put the last passage in brackets while wondering whether this has been attributed to Photius. However, the present codex knows this as part of Origen's flowing text in wider context. Besides, the same passage has been inserted in the commentary on Mark, which I quote *infra.*

mxcviii *Catena in Marcum*, p. 335. This part of the text concludes with the phrase, Παραβολὴν δέ, τὸν ἀσαφῆ λόγον ὀνομάζουσιν, which appears in the present codex (folio 124v). This suggests that probably this part of the *Catena in Marcum* is largely a text of Origen's.

mxcix Origen, *commMatt*, fr. 331 (Klostermann).

mc Origen, *commMatt*, fr. 333 (Klostermann).

mci Origen, *commMatt*, fr. 334 (Klostermann).

mcii Cyril of Alexandria and Origen, *apud Catena in Matthaeum*, p. 122. Also, Cyril of Alexandria, *frMatt*, fr. 184.

mciii Theodore of Mopsuestia, *frMatt*, fr. 81 & *Catena in Matthaeum*, p. 122.

mciv Origen, *commMatt*, 11.14.

mcv Considering Matt. 15:13.

mcvi Origen, *commMatt*, fr. 332 (Klostermann).

mcvii Jerome, *commMatt*, 15.13.

mcviii Παραβολὴν δέ, τὸν ἀσαφῆ λόγον ὀνομάζουσιν. This appears unattributed in the *Catena in Marcum*, p. 321; see *op. cit.* p. 321: "Another comment by one more" author (Σχόλιον Ἄλλο Ἔτι Τινός): παραβολὴν τὸν ἀσαφῆ λόγον ὀνομάζοντες. A similar note appears on p. 359: (Σχόλιον).

mcix Cf. Origen, *apud Catena in Matthaeum*, p. 103: (Ὠριγένους.) Τὰ ὑποδεχόμενα μακαρισμῶν καὶ περὶ παντὸς δὲ τοῦ βλέποντος τὰ θεῖα ὀφθαλμοῦ, καὶ ἀκούοντος τῶν πνευματικῶν ὤτων, ταῦτα ἂν λέγοιτο. Περὶ τούτου φησὶν ὁ προφήτης *προσέθηκέ μοι Κύριος ὠτίον τοῦ ἀκούειν*, [Isaiah, 50:4] ἀντὶ τοῦ συνιεῖν τοῖς ἔνδοθεν ὠσὶν τὰς καρδίας κατὰ τὸν ἔσω ἄνθρωπον. Ὁ γὰρ ἀπερίτμητος τῇ καρδίᾳ λαὸς ἐκωφώθη τοῖς ἔνδοθεν ὠσί.

mcx Cyril of Alexandria, *frMatt*, fr. 185.

mcxi λέληθεν ἑαυτὸν (one who is 'out of one's mind') is a phrase that Origen probably took up from Plato; *Phaedrus*, 255d6; *Meno*, 92a4. Likewise (λανθάνειν ἑαυτόν), Demosthenes, *De Falsa Legatione*, 13. Aristotle, *Analytica Priora*, 65a; *Ethica Nicomachea*, 1156a. Then, authors favourite to Origen employed this, too. Philo, *De Confusione Linguarum*, 54; *De Fuga et Inventione*, 20; cf. *De Somniis*, 1.211; *De Decalogo*, 43. Posidonius, *Fragmenta*, fr. 184. Plutarch, *De Stoicorum Repugnantiis*, p. 1043A. Galen, *De Differentia Pulsuum*, p. 612. After Origen, Porphyry, *Ad Marcellam*, 18. Gregory of Nyssa, *Contra Eunomium*,

1.1.234; 2.1.618; 3.4.26; *Oratio Catechetica*, 39. John Philoponus, *commMeteor*, p. 41. Anastasius of Sinai, *Viae Dux*, 22.4. Photius, *Epistulae et Amphilochia*, epistle 284, lines 2267-2268; epistle 27, line 157; epistle 38, line 83; epistle 75, line 38.

mcxii Origen, *commMatt*, fr. 331 (Klostermann), col. 2; see col. 1, quoted *supra*, p. 219.

mcxiii Chanaan was the ancient name of the land of Judaea. Abraham along with his people moved from Babylon to Chanaan and named this Judaea. David expelled the Chananites from this land altogether. Josephus, *Antiquitates Judaicae*, 1.Prologue: ὅπως Ἄβραμος ὁ πρόγονος ἡμῶν ἐξελθὼν ἐκ τῆς Χαλδαίων γῆς κατέσχε τὴν τότε μὲν Χαναναίαν νῦν δὲ Ἰουδαίαν λεγομένην. *Op. cit.* 1.134: Χαναναῖος δὲ τέταρτος ὢν Χάμου παῖς τὴν νῦν Ἰουδαίαν καλουμένην οἰκίσας ἀπ᾽ αὐτοῦ Χαναναίαν προσηγόρευσεν. *Op. cit.* 1.160: Ἁβράμης ... σὺν τῷ σφετέρῳ λαῷ εἰς τὴν τότε μὲν Χαναναίαν λεγομένην νῦν δὲ Ἰουδαίαν μετῴκησε. *Op. cit.* Book 7 (table of contents): ὡς πολιορκήσας Ἱεροσόλυμα Δαυίδης καὶ λαβὼν τὴν πόλιν ἐξέβαλε μὲν ἐξ αὐτῆς τοὺς Χαναναίους, ἐνῴκισε δὲ εἰς αὐτὴν Ἰουδαίους. *De Bello Judaico*, 6.439: τὸν μὲν δὴ τῶν Χαναναίων λαὸν ἐκβαλὼν ὁ τῶν Ἰουδαίων βασιλεὺς Δαυίδης κατοικίζει τὸν ἴδιον. Theophilus of Antioch, Apologist, *Ad Autolycum*, 2.32: γῆν Χαναναίαν, καὶ Ἰουδαίαν καὶ Φοινίκην ἐπικληθεῖσαν. *Op. cit.* 3.9: ὁ θεὸς ... ἐξήγαγεν ἐκ τῆς Αἰγύπτου ... καὶ ἀπεκατέστησεν [Ἰουδαίους] εἰς τὴν Χαναναίαν γῆν, μετέπειτα δὲ Ἰουδαίαν ἐπικληθεῖσαν.

mcxiv Cf. Origen, *commMatt*, fr. 336 (Klostermann), and *commMatt*, 11:16-17.

mcxv This turn is illustrative of Origen's typological exegesis. It could be instructive to notice that it was Cyril who took this up, only to confirm that not only do his works show his knowledge of Christian writers (such as Eusebius, Origen, and Didymus), but also that he copied from them abundantly. Cf. Origen's expression ὡς ἐκ τύπου, which Cyril alone embraced although Origen's typological analyses were treated with suspicion. Cyril of Alexandria, *In Joannem*, v. 1, p. 400; *Fragmenta in Sancti Pauli Epistulam ad Hebraeos*, p. 363 (& *Catena in Epistulam ad Hebraeos*, p. 115); *De Adoratione*, PG.68: 701.27-28; 784.27-28; 820.3-4; *Glaphyra in Pentateuchum*, PG.69.104.6-7 (& *Catena in Epistulam ad Hebraeos*, p. 531). *Op. cit.* PG.69: 597.16-17; 640.15; *commLuc*, PG.72.553.31-32 (& *Catena in Lucam*, pp. 40 & 42).

mcxvi Cf. Exodus, 12:48-49; 20:10; 22:20; 23:9; *et passim* in OT.

mcxvii The Genitive Σιδόνος, instead of Σιδῶνος, was acceptable, especially by grammarians such as Aristonicus, *De Signis Iliadis*, on *Ilias*, VI.291 (ἤγαγε Σιδονίηθεν). Herodian, *Περὶ Κλίσεως Ὀνομάτων*, pp. 727-729. Theodosius of Alexandria (grammarian, fourth century AD), *Περὶ Κλίσεως τῶν εἰς ων Ὀξυτόνων*, p. 22. George Choeroboscus, *Prolegomena et Scholia in Theodosii Alexandrini Canones Isagogicos De Flexione Nominum*, pp. 274-275; 281. Also, Posidonius, *Fragmenta*, fr. 87. Anonymous, *Scholia in Iliadem*, commenting on *Ilias*, VI.291. Procopius of Gaza, *Commentarii in Isaiam*, p. 218. Cyril of Scyrhopolis (abbot of the Laura of Sabas, in which the present codex was probably scribed, too), *Vita Sabae*, p. 150.

mcxviii Apollinaris, *frMatt*, fr. 81.

mcxix So has it the *Catena in Marcum*, p. 337: Τέκνα οὖν τοὺς Ἰουδαίους φησί, κυνάρια δὲ τοὺς ἐθνικούς, ἄρτον τὰς τῶν θαυμάτων εὐεργεσίας, ψίχας (sic, instead of ψιχία) δὲ τὸ βραχύτατον τῆς δυνάμεως αὐτοῦ.

mcxx So *infra*, folio 127r: πίστεως ὑπερβαλλούσης. See this also in the *Catena in Marcum*, p. 337: τὸ δὲ οἰηθῆναι ὅτι καὶ τὸ βραχύτατον αὐτοῦ τῆς δυνάμεως (τοῦτο γὰρ ψιχία ὀνομάζει) ἱκανὸν τῆς θυγατρὸς αὐτῆς παρασχεῖν τὴν ἴασιν, πίστεως ὑπερβαλλούσης. However, the same passage has been attributed to Theodore of Mopsuestia, *frMatt*, fr. 82.

mcxxi Origen, *commMatt*, fr. 337 (Klostermann).

mcxxii Jerome, *commMatt*, 15.25.

mcxxiii The expression ἀνακεῖσθαι Θεῷ in effect means 'standing very close to God' or 'being dedicated to God'. It was introduced by Plato, who could have never imagined the extent to which this was destined to be current among Christian authors and almost shunned by Greek ones. For indeed, following Cornutus and Philo who took this up, this appeared almost inadvertently only in Plutarch, Athenaeus, and much later in Proclus. See Plato, *Symposium*, 197e: Οὗτος, ἔφη, ὁ παρ' ἐμοῦ λόγος, ὦ Φαῖδρε, τῷ θεῷ ἀνακείσθω ("Let this speech be my offer to God, o Phaedrus"). Then, Philo, *De Somniis*, 2.297; *De Specialibus Legibus*, 2.27. Cornutus, *De Natura Deorum*, p. 68. Plutarch, *De Genio Socratis*, p. 593A. Athenaeus, *Deipnosophistae*, 7.126. Proclus, *commCrat*, 170.

On the other hand, Christians used this expression copiously. Irenaeus, *Adversus Haereses*, 2.41.3. Clement of Alexandria, *Stromateis*, 5.4.19.4; 7.5.29.8. Origen, *Cels*, III: 3; 5; 73; IV: 26; 75; V: 43; 57; VIII: 31; 36; 61; *commJohn*, I.2.12; II.30.183; *deOr*, 13.5; 31.5; *homJer*, 8.2; *De Engastrimytho*, 3; *commMatt*, 11.3; 11.9; 16.19; 17.25; *frPs*, on Psalm 77:48-51; *selPs*, PG.12.1165.3-4. Methodius of Olympus, *Symposium*, 5.2. Gregory of Nyssa, *Contra Eunomium*, 2.1.51; *In Canticum Canticorum*, p. 272; *In Basilium Fratrem*, 11. Eusebius, *Praeparatio Evangelica*, 4.1; *Demonstratio Evangelica*, 1.10.38; 3.3.5; *In Isaiam*, 1.3; 1.58; 1.68; 1.81; 2.13; *et passim*. Didymus, *Commentarii in Ecclesiasten (1.1-8)*, cod. p. 6; *Commentarii in Psalmos 22-26.10*, cod. p. 99; *Commentarii in Psalmos 29-34*, cod. p. 189; *frPs(al)*, frs. 151; 558; *Fragmenta in Epistulam ii ad Corinthios*, p. 41; *Commentarii in Ecclesiasten (3-4.12)*, cod. p. 82. Cassian the Sabaite (Pseudo-Didymus), *De Trinitate*, PG.39.734.32. Cassian the Sabaite (Pseudo-Caesarius), *Quaestiones et Responsiones*, 1. Pseudo-Justin, *Quaestiones et Responsiones ad Orthodoxos*, 403A; 473B. I have pointed out strong indications that this work was written by Cassian the Sabaite, see *COT*, *NDGF*. Also, abundantly in John Chrysostom, Theodoret, Cyril of Alexandria, and occasionally in later Byzantine authors.

mcxxiv Theodore of Mopsuestia, *frMatt*, fr. 83.

mcxxv So *supra*, folio 126r-v: πίστεως ὑπερεχούσης. Cf. *supra*, Origen, *commMatt*, fr. 337 (Klostermann).

mcxxvi *Catena in Marcum*, p. 337 (anonymous).

mcxxvii Theodore of Mopsuestia, *frMatt*, fr. 82.

mcxxviii Cyril of Alexandria, *apud Catena in Matthaeum*, p. 125 & *frMatt*, fr. 186.

mcxxix Origen, *commMatt*, fr. 338 (Klostermann).

mcxxx Cyril of Alexandria, *apud Catena in Matthaeum*, p. 125 & *frMatt*, fr. 187.

mcxxxi Cf. Origen, *commJohn*, XIII.20.119: Εἰ ζητεῖ ὁ πατήρ, διὰ τοῦ υἱοῦ ζητεῖ τοῦ ἐληλυθότος ζητῆσαι καὶ σῶσαι τὸ ἀπολωλός. Athanasius, *Oratio ii Contra Arianos*, 41.6: ἃ ὁ πατὴρ ἐργάζεται, διὰ τοῦ υἱοῦ ἐργάζεται. *Epistulae Quattuor ad Serapionem*, 1.31.2: τὸ συνδοξαζόμενον πατρὶ καὶ υἱῷ καὶ θεολογούμενον μετὰ τοῦ λόγου ἐνεργοῦν τε ἅπερ ὁ πατὴρ διὰ τοῦ υἱοῦ ἐργάζεται, πῶς ὁ λέγων κτίσμα οὐκ ἄντικρυς εἰς αὐτὸν θεὸν ἀσεβεῖ;

mcxxxii Origen, *commMatt*, fr. 339 (Klostermann).

mcxxxiii Cyril of Alexandria, *frMatt*, fr. 188.

mcxxxiv At this point, another scribe takes over, whose education is glaringly far too inferior to the normal scribe's one and his knowledge of Greek is evidently less than elementary. His handwriting is rather primitive and urefined, his Greek untutored, and his lack of experience for carrying out such as job is all too evident. Consequently, the section he wrote (folios 128r-132v) is full of egregious grammatical mistakes. I surmise that scribing this section, while listenting to a senior monk reciting the text, was one day's job. Little wonder that, upon resuming his job, the normal scribe (dismayed as he was at the text his replacement wrote) decided that some points should be repeated (see folio 133r).

mcxxxv He refers to John, 6:9: ἀλλὰ ταῦτα τί ἐστιν εἰς τοσούτους;

mcxxxvi Theodore Monachus (who should be neither Theodore of Mopsuestia nor that of Heraclea, who are cited alongside this author), *apud Catena in Matthaeum*, pp. 126-127.

mcxxxvii John Chrysostom, *In Matthaeum*, PG.58.525.50-57 (homily 53, commenting on the same passage as Origen, namely, Matt. 15:32). Cf. John Chrysostom, *In Joannem*, PG.59.146.5-8: Διὰ τοῦτο γὰρ καὶ ἀσαφῶς πολλαχοῦ φθέγγεται ὁ Χριστὸς πρὸς τὴν ἐρώτησιν, τοὺς ἀκούοντας διαναστῆσαι βουλόμενος καὶ προσεκτικωτέρους ἐργάσασθαι. *Op. cit.* PG.59.259.51-53: Τὸ γὰρ ἀσαφὲς τῶν εἰρημένων ἀεὶ τὸν ἀκροατὴν διανίστησι καὶ προσεκτικώτερον ἐργάζεται. Proclus explained Socrates' method, who ostensibly asked his interlocutors questions upon practicing paedagogical dialectics. *In Platonis Alcibiadem i*, 170: οὗτος γὰρ ὁ τρόπος τῶν λόγων, ὁ διαλεκτικός, ἐρωτήσεσι καὶ ἀποκρίσεσι τελειούμενος, πρῶτον μὲν τὸν ἀκούοντα προσεκτικώτερον ποιεῖ, παρακολουθεῖν αὐτὸν ἀναγκάζων ταῖς ἐρωτήσεσιν, ἀλλ᾽ οὐκ ἀφέντα τὴν τοῦ λέγοντος ῥοπὴν αὐτὸν πρὸς ἄλλοις ἔχειν τὸν νοῦν.

mcxxxviii John Chrysostom, *In Matthaeum*, PG.527.38-47.

mcxxxix This was taken into account by John Chrysostom, *op. cit.* PG.58.528.41-46: Ἄλλος γὰρ οὗτος τῆς παρουσίας ὁ καιρός, ἄλλος δὲ ὁ μέλλων. Νῦν χρεία τούτων τῶν σημείων τῶν ἐν τῇ γῇ. τὰ δὲ ἐν τῷ οὐρανῷ ἐκείνῳ τεταμίευται τῷ καιρῷ. Νῦν ὡς ἰατρὸς ἦλθον, τότε ὡς δικαστὴς παρέσομαι. νῦν ὥστε ζητῆσαι τὸ πεπλανημένον, τότε ὥστε ἀπαιτῆσαι εὐθύνας. See the same text in the *Catena in Marcum*, p. 342, introduced by 'another one says' (Ἄλλος, φησίν), which perhaps suggests Chrysostom, but does not name him.

mcxl Theodore of Heraclea, *apud Catena in Matthaeum*, p. 128. It is quite obvious that this author, as well as Chrysostom, quoted from Origen without strictly following the sequence of his text. Nevertheless, all in all their passages are copied word for word.

mcxli John Chrysostom, *In Matthaeum*, PG.528.20-45.

mcxlii John Chrysostom, *op. cit.* PG.528.22-24.

mcxliii John Chrysostom, *op. cit.* PG.528.20-22.

mcxliv John Chrysostom, *op. cit.* PG.528.28-30.

mcxlv *Catena in Matthaeum*, pp. 129-130 (anonymous).

mcxlvi John Chrysostom, *In Matthaeum*, PG.529.9-530.4.

mcxlvii *Catena in Matthaeum*, pp. 130-132 (anonymous); but see the same text in John Chrysostom, *In Matthaeum*, PG.58.533.36-61.

mcxlviii Philagathus (Philip Cerameus), *Homiliae*, 27.5. Likewise, Damascenus Studites, *Thesaurus*, oration 11, lines 128-135: Ὁ Κύριος περιπατῶντας εἰς τὴν γῆν σωματικῶς, ὑπῆγε καὶ ὡς τὰ μέρη τῆς Καισαρείας τῆς Φιλίππου. Δύο Καισάρειαι εἶναι· μία εἶναι τῆς Ἀνατολῆς, ὁποῦ λέγεται τοῦ Στράτωνος Καισάρεια· ἄλλη δὲ εἶναι αὐτή, ὁποῦ ἀναφέρει τὸ Εὐαγγέλιον. αὐτὴν τὴν ἔκτισεν ὁ Φίλιππος ὁ Μακεδών, καὶ διὰ τοῦτο ὀνομάζεται τοῦ Φιλίππου. Εἰς αὐτῆς γοῦν τῆς Καισαρείας τὰ μέρη ἠρώτησεν ὁ Χριστὸς τοὺς Μαθητάς του, ὅτι. *Τίνα μὲ λέγουσιν οἱ ἄνθρωποι;*

mcxlix *Catena in Matthaeum, loc. cit.* Cf. John Chrysostom, *In Matthaeum*, PG.58.533.36-61.

mcl *Catena in Matthaeum*, pp. 130-132 (anonymous). The texts of two eminent theologians who copied from Origen's present commentary are remarkably the same, in terms not only of the ideas expounded but also of use of Origen's characteristic vocabulary at this point (e.g. Πέτρος προπηδᾷ, comparison with how the disciples addressed Jesus after the miracle 'with the ship' [Matt. 14:24-31] and with how Nathaniel addressed Jesus [John, 1:48-50]). The text of this catena runs parallel to that of Chrysostom's. Cf. Cyril of Alexandria, *commLuc*, PG.72.648.2532: Προπηδᾷ δὲ πάλιν τῶν ἄλλων ὁ Πέτρος, καὶ παντὸς τοῦ χοροῦ γίνεται στόμα καὶ τὰς φιλοθέους ἐρεύγεται φωνάς, ἀκριβῆ δὲ τῆς εἰς αὐτὸν πίστεως ὁμολογίαν ἐκφέρει, λέγων, Τὸν Χριστὸν τοῦ Θεοῦ. Ἀσφαλὴς ὁ μαθητής· οὐ γάρ τοι φησὶν ἁπλῶς Χριστὸν αὐτὸν εἶναι, τοῦ Θεοῦ τὸν Χριστὸν δὲ μᾶλλον. The same, somewhat paraphrased in the *Catena in Lucam*, p. 75: προπηδᾷ δὲ πάλιν τῶν ἄλλων ὁ Πέτρος καὶ παντὸς τοῦ χοροῦ γίνεται στόμα καὶ τοὺς φιλοθέους ἐρεύγεται φωνήν, ἀκριβῆ δὲ τῆς εἰς αὐτὸν πίστεως τὴν ὁμολογίαν ἐκφέρει λέγων *τὸν Χριστὸν τοῦ Θεοῦ* ἀσφαλὴς ὁ μαθητής. Οὐ γάρ τοι φησὶν ἁπλῶς Χριστὸν αὐτὸν εἶναι τοῦ Θεοῦ, τὸν Χριστὸν δὲ μᾶλλον.

mcli Theodoret, *commCant*, PG.81.108.4-5.

mclii *Catena in Matthaeum*, pp. 132-133 (anonymous). But compare this and the ensuing portions with John Chrysostom, *In Matthaeum*, PG.58.536.5-537.1.

mcliii *Catena in Matthaeum, loc. cit.* (anonymous).

mcliv *Catena in Matthaeum, loc. cit.* (anonymous).

mclv *Catena in Matthaeum*, p. 133 (anonymous).

mclvi *Catena in Matthaeum, loc. cit.* (anonymous).

mclvii *Catena in Matthaeum, loc. cit.* (anonymous).

mclviii John Chrysostom, *In Matthaeum*, PG.58.542.43-48.

mclix *Catena in Matthaeum*, pp. 133-134 (anonymous).

mclx Klostermann added [τὸ], which I omit since this is not necessary; as it stands, the text is plain: "whosoever despises [Jesus'] words, he loses his soul'."

mclxi Origen, *commMatt*, fr. 352 (Klostermann).

mclxii Origen, *commMatt*, 12.26.

mclxiii Origen, *frLuc*, frs. 138; 139.

mclxiv *Catena in Matthaeum*, p. 134 (anonymous). Likewise, Epiphanius of Salamis, *Panarion*, v. 3, pp. 227-228: *καὶ τῇ ὀγδόῃ ἡμέρᾳ*, ὡς λέγει τὸ εὐαγγέλιον, ἢ ὡς τὸ ἕτερον λέγει *μετὰ ἓξ ἡμέρας*, οὐ τῶν εὐαγγελιστῶν ἕτερα ἀνθ' ἑτέρων λεγόντων, ἀλλὰ μιᾶς οὔσης τῆς ἀκριβείας, ἀεί ποτε δὲ ἀσφαλιζομένης, ἵνα μὴ πρόφασις γένηται τὸ τοὺς ἀνθρώπους προσκόπτειν ἐν τοῖς ἀναγκαίοις, ἐπειδήπερ *ἔγκειται ἡ ἔννοια τοῦ ἀνθρώπου ἐπὶ τὰ πονηρὰ ἐκ νεότητος ἐπιμελῶς*. Διὰ τοῦτο εἷς εὐαγγελιστὴς τῇ ὀγδόῃ ἡμέρᾳ εἶπεν. Ἦν γὰρ μέρος τι τῆς ἡμέρας ὑπολειπόμενον, ὅτε τὸν λόγον ἔφη, καὶ συνηρίθμησεν ἀπ' ἐκείνης τῆς ἡμέρας καὶ τῆς ὥρας, εἰ ἦν ἡ ἡμέρα κεκλικυῖα περὶ ἐνάτην ὥραν ἢ δεκάτην. Καὶ πάλιν ἐν τῇ ὀγδόῃ ἡμέρᾳ περὶ τὴν τρίτην ἢ τετάρτην ὥραν τοῦ πράγματος γεγονότος, ὀγδόη αὕτη ἐκαλεῖτο. Ὁ δὲ ἄλλος εὐαγγελιστὴς ἀσφαλίζεται καὶ λέγει μετὰ ἓξ ἡμέρας· οὐκ ἠρίθμησε γὰρ ἐν ᾗ τὸν λόγον ἔφη τοῖς μαθηταῖς οὐδὲ ἐν ᾗ τὸ ἔργον ἐπετέλεσεν, ἀλλὰ τὰς μέσον ἓξ πληρεστάτας ἡμέρας. John Chrysostom, *In Matthaeum*, PG.58.549.38-43: *Καὶ μεθ' ἡμέρας ἓξ παραλαμβάνει Πέτρον καὶ Ἰάκωβον καὶ Ἰωάννην*. Ἕτερος δὲ μετὰ ὀκτὼ φησιν, οὐκ ἐναντιούμενος τούτῳ, ἀλλὰ καὶ σφόδρα συνᾴδων. Ὁ μὲν γὰρ καὶ αὐτὴν τὴν ἡμέραν καθ' ἣν ἐφθέγξατο, κἀκείνην καθ' ἣν ἀνήγαγεν εἶπεν, ὁ δὲ τὰς μεταξὺ τούτων μόνον.

mclxv Luke, 9:28.

mclxvi Jerome, *commMatt*, 17.1.

mclxvii *Catena in Matthaeum*, pp. 134-135 (anonymous). This text appears also in John Chrysostom, *In Matthaeum*, PG.58.549.55-550.16. Chrysostom's relation to, and availing of, Origen's writings has been discussed in the Introduction. This is probably why in this catena on Matthew this is anonymous. Besides, the same text obtains in the *Catena in Lucam*, p. 72, and once again the indication is 'Unattributed' (Ἐξ ἀνεπιγράφου). Moreover, this appears in the *Catena in Marcum*, p. 352, and no attribution is made there either. Much later (twelfth century), the same passage was used by Philagathus (Philip Cerameus) in one of his homilies, but he cited no source, in just like a manner Chrysostom used extensive portions from Origen's work without mentioning him. Philagathus (Philip Cerameus), *Homiliae*, homily 31.16.

mclxviii *Catena in Matthaeum*, p. 135 (anonymous).

mclxix Maximus Confessor, *Quaestiones et Dubia*, 190. In the fourteenth century, the Byzantine theologian Theodore Dexius appealed to John Chrysostom allegedly having explained that Jesus' words in Matt. 16:28 suggest his transfiguration. However, nowhere did Chrysostom say anything of the kind. This is indicative of how Origen's exegeses were ascribed to subsequent stars of theology. See Theodore Dexius, *Appelatio Adversus Iohannem Cantacuzenum*, 25: *Εἰσί φησιν ὁ σωτὴρ τινες τῶν ὧδε ἑστηκότων, οἳ οὐ μὴ γεύσωνται θανάτου, ἕως ἂν ἴδωσι τὴν βασιλείαν τοῦ Θεοῦ*, τὸ μυστήριον οὕτω δηλῶν τῆς θείας μεταμορφώσεως, ὡς ὁ θεῖος φησὶ Χρυσόστομος, καὶ τοὺς συνανελθόντας αὐτῷ ἐπὶ τοῦ ὄρους καὶ ταύτην ἰδόντας μαθητάς.

mclxx *Catena in Matthaeum*, p. 135 (anonymous); but cf. John Chrysostom, *In Matthaeum*, PG.58.550-27-53.

mclxxi John Chrysostom, *op. cit.* PG.58.551.7-8. Cyril of Alexandria, *commLuc*, PG.72.1013.20-21. Also, *Catena in Matthaeum*, p. 135. *Catena in Marcum*, p. 354.

mclxxii *Catena in Matthaeum*, p. 135 (anonymous).

mclxxiii *Catena in Matthaeum, loc. cit.* (anonymous).

mclxxiv *Catena in Matthaeum*, p. 136 (anonymous).

mclxxv Origen, *commMatt*, fr. 362 (Klostermann), continued forthwith. However, in the codex *Laura B 113* of Athos (eleventh century), Klostermann came upon this being attributed jointly to Origen and Chrysostom, whereas Cramer recorded this as an anonymous one (quoted next).

mclxxvi *Catena in Matthaeum*, p. 136 (anonymous).

mclxxvii Cf. *supra*, folio 119r: καίπερ ἐπὶ τῶν ἄλλων σημείων αὐθεντικῶς ποιῶν ὡς ἴσος ὢν τῷ πατρί, ἵνα πείσῃ τοὺς ὄχλους ὅτι ἐκ τοῦ πατρὸς ἦν.

mclxxviii Cf. Gal. 5:11.

mclxxix Cf. *Catena in Marcum*, pp. 356-357: Ὅσῳ γὰρ μείζονα ἐλέγετο περὶ αὐτοῦ, τοσοῦτον δυσπαραδεκτότερα ἦν τοῖς πολλοῖς τότε, καὶ τὸ σκάνδαλον τὸ ἀπὸ τοῦ σταυροῦ ἐπετείνετο μᾶλλον.

mclxxx Origen, *commMatt*, fr. 362 (Klostermann). The editor put this fragment in brackets for two reasons: (1) he saw similar ideas in John Chrysostom (citing homily 56); (2) Cramer's parallel text was anonymous. In reality though this text is Origen's for two reasons: (1) this is attributed to Origen in the present codex; (2) in a codex of Mount Athos (*Laura, B 113*, eleventh century), Klostermann found this text attributed jointly to Origen and to ΙΩ [that is, John, presumably Chrysostom]. To put it simply, this is one of the numerous cases of Chrysostom having copied from Origen, as shown in the present edition every now and then. Here is the citation from Chrysostom's homily 56, as in PG.58.553.14-554.38. As it normally happened, he paraphrased from Origen's commentary, adding his own prose. For instance, the exclamation 'Peter, do not be afraid!' is certainly Chrysostom's. However, the fundamental theological ideas in this passage are Origen's. I should have thought that the Athonite catenist was aware of this, which is probably why he attributed the text to both theologians. However, the compiler of the present codex (or that of an earlier codex, from which the present one copied) attributed this to Origen alone.

mclxxxi Origen, *frLuc*, fr. 148; likewise, *schLuc*, PG.17.345.24-28: Τότε οὖν ἀπήγγειλαν, μετὰ τὴν ἀνάληψιν, μετὰ τὴν τοῦ Πνεύματος παρουσίαν. Ὅτε γὰρ ἐπλήσθησαν παρρησίας, καὶ Πνεύματος ἠξιώθησαν, καὶ τὴν ἀπὸ τῶν σημείων εἶχον φωνὴν συνηγοροῦσαν αὐτοῖς, καὶ πάντα ὅσα ἔλεγον, εὐπαράδεκτα ἦν.

mclxxxii *Catena in Matthaeum*, pp. 136-137 (anonymous).

mclxxxiii Origen probably took up the rhetorical periphrasis πιστεῦσαι ἔχω ('I have come to believe') from Lucian of Samosata, *Dialogi Meretricii*, 8.1: οὕτως οἱ μεγάλοι ἔρωτες γίγνονται, καὶ εἰ πείθοιντο ἀμελεῖσθαι, εἰ δὲ πιστεῦσαι μόνος ἔχειν, ἀπομαραίνεταί πως ἡ ἐπιθυμία. This remained always a very rare usage that made a mark much later. Pseudo-Athanasius, *Dialogus Athanasii et Zacchaei*, 64: Καὶ ἔχω πιστεῦσαι τοῖς εὐαγγελίοις σου; John Chrysostom, *In Epistulam i ad Timotheum*, PG.62.551.54-55: Πόθεν οὖν ἔχουσι πιστεῦσαι; Ἀπὸ σημείων; Ἀλλ' οὐ γίνεται ταῦτα. Pseudo-John Chrysostom, *In illud: Si Qua in Christo Nova Creatura*, PG.64.29.69-70: "Οταν οὖν τὰ πάθη καὶ ξύλα θεοποιεῖς, πῶς ἔχεις ὀφθαλμούς; τὰ ὁρώμενα οὐ βλέπεις καὶ τὰ μὴ ὁρώμενά σοι ἔχω πιστεῦσαι; Gennadius Scholarius, *Epistulae Contra Unionem Florentinam*, epistle 3, p. 164: Ἐγὼ δὲ τῇ ἀληθείᾳ οὐδὲ πιστεῦσαι ἔχω. Also, in an anonymous scholion on Origen's favourite Euripides; *Scholia in Euripidem* (on *Hippolytus*, verse 1250: *οὐ δυνήσομαί ποτε*): οὐδαμῶς ἔχω πιστεῦσαι ὅτι κακὸς ἐφάνη ὁ ἐμὸς δεσπότης.

mclxxxiv Origen, *frLuc*, frs. 17a; 17b; 17c: Λέγεται δυνάμει Ἠλίας ὁ Ἰωάννης καὶ ὡς πρόδρομος γεγονὼς τῆς πρώτης τοῦ Χριστοῦ παρουσίας ὡς καὶ ὁ Θεσβίτης τῆς δευτέρας. Λέγεται *ἐν δυνάμει Ἠλίου* ὁ Ἰωάννης, ἀλλὰ καὶ ὡς ἀσκητὴς καὶ ὡς παρθένος καὶ ὡς ἐν ἐρήμοις τὰ πολλὰ διάγων καὶ ὡς πεπαρρησιασμένως ἐλέγχων τοὺς ἁμαρτάνοντας βασιλεῖς τε καὶ ἰδιώτας. Διὸ καὶ εἰκότως ἐκλήθη δυνάμει Ἠλίας. Οὐ γὰρ ἐναργεῖ πράγματι ἦν Ἠλίας ὁ Ἰωάννης, ὥς φασιν οἱ μετεμψύχωσιν δοξάζοντες, λέγοντες, ὅτι ἡ ψυχὴ Ἠλίου εἰς Ἰωάννην ἦλθεν. See a full analysis of this in the *commMatt*, 13.2; also, *homLuc*, homily 4.27. Earlier still, *commJohn*, VI.11.66-7; VI.20.114. Origen decisively dismissed the doctrine of transmigration of souls throughout his life.

mclxxxv Cf. Origen, *commMatt*, fr. 363 (Klostermann): Ὁ μὲν ὡς τοῦ νόμου λειτουργὸς καὶ ὡς πρῶτος διδάσκαλος τοῦ λόγου τῆς εὐσεβείας, *Ἠλίας* δὲ ὡς πρόδρομος τῆς ἐνδόξου δευτέρας παρουσίας.

mclxxxvi *Catena in Matthaeum*, pp. 137-138 (anonymous), continued *infra*. See the same analysis in similar phraseology (quoting the same biblical instances) also in John Chrysostom, *In Matthaeum*, PG.58.557.53-559.15.

mclxxxvii *Catena in Matthaeum*, pp. 137-138 (anonymous).

mclxxxviii Jerome, *commMatt*, 17.10. He draws heavily on Origen, *commMatt*, 13.1-2.

mclxxxix *Op. cit.* p. 138 (anonymous). The same, in John Chrysostom, *In Matthaeum*, PG.58.560.8-11.

mcxc *Op. cit.* pp. 137-138 (anonymous). Once again, Origen's text was copied, and this appears also in the *Catena in Marcum*, pp. 357-358. The catenist claimed that he based his anthology on 'the sole father who wrote a commentary' on this gospel, naming Cyril of Alexandria, while taking into account things that 'have been said sporadically by other teachers of the Church' (*op. cit.* p. 262). This explains why so many portions from Chrysostom are there, excerpted from his commentary on Matthew in relation to the same points occurring in the two gospels.

mcxci At this point, the initial scribe takes over again, and the text is discontinued; in fact, there is some repetition of content. This is not hard to explain: the scribe who had replaced him was nearly uneducated, and when the normal scribe took over again, he decided that some content should be written in correct Greek. See *supra*, endnote mcxxxiv.

mcxcii Cyril of Alexandria, *frMatt*, fr. 197.

mcxciii It was Origen who introduced the idiosyncratic turn about 'a more glorious body' assumed upon resurrection. Origen, *selPs*, PG.12.1093.45-1096.2 (*apud* Epiphanius of Salamis, *Panarion*, v. 2, p. 424): οὕτως μέλλοντας κληρονομεῖν βασιλείαν οὐρανῶν, καὶ ἐν τόποις διαφέρουσιν ἔσεσθαι, ἀναγκαῖον χρῆσθαι σώμασι πνευματικοῖς, οὐχὶ τοῦ εἴδους τοῦ προτέρου ἀφανιζομένου, κἂν ἐπὶ τὸ ἐνδοξότερον γένηται αὐτοῦ ἡ τροπή. ὥσπερ ἦν τὸ Ἰησοῦ εἶδος, καὶ Μωϋσέως, καὶ Ἡλίου, οὐχ ἕτερον ἐν τῇ μεταμορφώσει, παρ' ὃ ἦν. Likewise, Epiphanius, *op. cit.* v. 2, p. 428. Gregory of Nyssa, *De Vita Mosis*, 2.217: Καὶ οὕτω γίνεται τοῦ Μωϋσέως ἡ ἐπὶ τὸ ἐνδοξότερον μεταποίησις. John of Damascus, *Sacra Parallela*, PG.96.497.6-16. Also, Origen, *frLuc*, fr. 140; *commSerMatt*, p. 108.

mcxciv The quality of bodies of Moses and Elias upon Jesus' transfiguration was an instance that appeared to Origen as providing some clues as to how posthumous bodies are, and, ultimately, how the resurrected bodies will be. This is a reply to the circulating nonsense that Origen posited that, either posthumously or upon the resurrection, the bodies will be spherical. Continuing from the previous note, see also *De Resurrectione* (*fragmenta*), PG.11.96.12-16, *apud* Photius, *Bibliotheca*, Codex 234, p. 301a: Καὶ τάχα τὸ τῆς ψυχῆς ἅμα τῇ ἀπαλλαγῇ σχῆμα ὁμοειδὲς ὂν τῷ παχεῖ καὶ γηΐνῳ σώματι δύναται οὕτως λαμβάνεσθαι. Εἴ ποτε γοῦν ἱστόρηταί τις τῶν κεκοιμημένων φαινόμενος, ὅμοιος ἑώραται τῷ ὅτε τὴν σάρκα εἶχε σχήματι. *Op. cit.* p. 299b: Ὥσπερ ἐκεῖνοι [sc. Moses and Elias], φάμενος, μετὰ τὴν ἀπὸ τοῦ βίου ἔξοδον ὤφθησαν οὐχ ἕτερον παρ' ὃ εἶχον εἶδος ἐξ ἀρχῆς διασῴζοντες, κατὰ τὰ αὐτὰ καὶ ἡ πάντων ἔσται ἀνάστασις. This text from Methodius was quoted also by the presbyter Eustratius of Constantinople, who lived two centuries before Photius. *De Statu Animarum Post Mortem*, lines 1730-1732. Origen argued that both the resurrected body of Lazarus and that of Jesus 'had the same form (εἶδος)' as their physical ones. This is what Methodius criticised, accusing Origen of compromising the incorporeality of the soul, because, the resurrected body is supposed to 'have a tongue, fingures, and the rest'. Justinian argued reversely: if the body of the Lord was spheroid, how was it that he had 'hands and feet, and the wounds on his side'? *Edictum Contra Origenem*, p. 98; then, in the condemnation by the *Synodus Constantinopolitana et Hierosolymitana anno 536*, tome 3, p. 204. Also, ACO, *Canones xv* (*Contra Origenem sive Origenistas*), tome 4.1, p. 249.

However, things are quite simple: despite Origen's endorsing several Stoic doctrines duly transformed and adapted to his theology, he advanced a thesis which was diametrical to that of Chrysippus, who maintained that, following death, the body has a spherical shape. Instead, Origen endorsed the thesis of Antisthenes, who averred that the posthumus body has the same shape as the physical one. Antisthenes, *Fragmenta Varia*, fr. 57, *apud* Anonymous, *Scholia in Iliadem* (*scholia vetera*), comm. on *Ilias*, XXIII.65-67 (ἦλθε δ' ἐπὶ ψυχὴ Πατροκλῆος δειλοῖο, πάντ' αὐτῷ μέγεθός τε καὶ ὄμματα κάλ' ἐϊκυῖα καὶ φωνήν, καὶ τοῖα περὶ χροῒ εἵματα ἕστο. ['then there came to him the spirit of hapless Patroclus, in all things like his very self, in stature and fair eyes and in voice, and in like raiment was he clad withal']): ἐντεῦθεν Ἀντισθένης ὁμοσχήμονας φησὶ τὰς ψυχὰς τοῖς περιέχουσι σώμασιν εἶναι. Χρύσιππος (*SVF*, v. 2, fr. 815) δὲ μετὰ τὸν χωρισμὸν τοῦ σώματός φησιν αὐτὰς σφαιροειδεῖς γενέσθαι.

When Origen spoke of 'spiritual body', he meant an 'aetheral' one (αἰθέριον), but he never determined the precise nature of this, quite simply because he did not know its precise nature. See *Cels*, III.41-42 (& *Philocalia*, 19.4-5); IV.56; VIII.32; *commJohn*, I.26.173; XIII.40.267; *deOr*, 7.1. At best, he could say that this body is '*something* aetheral and superior' in terms of quality (αἰθέριόν τι καὶ κρεῖττον), and that the angelic bodies are 'aetheral and have the nature of light'. Origen, *commMatt*, 17.29: ἵνα γὰρ καθ' ὑπόθεσιν μὴ ᾖ ἀληθὴς ἡ πεπιστευμένη παρὰ τοῖς πολλοῖς ἀνάστασις, οὐκ *ἐν ταύτῃ τῇ ζωῇ* ἤλπικε *μόνον ἐν Χριστῷ* ὁ ἐκείνην ἀθετῶν ζώσης τῆς ψυχῆς, οὐκ ἐκεῖνο μὲν ἀπολαμβανούσης τὸ σῶμα ἐνδυομένης δὲ αἰθέριόν τι καὶ κρεῖττον. *Op. cit.* 17.30: ἐγὼ δ' οἶμαι διὰ τούτων δηλοῦσθαι ὅτι οὐ μόνον κατὰ τὸ μὴ γαμεῖν καὶ τὸ μὴ γαμεῖσθαι *ὡς οἱ ἐν τῷ οὐρανῷ ἄγγελοι* γίνονται οἱ καταξιούμενοι τῆς ἐκ νεκρῶν ἀναστάσεως, ἀλλὰ καὶ κατὰ τὸ μετασχηματιζόμενα αὐτῶν τὰ σώματα *τῆς ταπεινώσεως* γίνεσθαι τοιαῦτα, ὁποῖά ἐστι τὰ τῶν ἀγγέλων σώματα, αἰθέρια καὶ αὐγοειδὲς φῶς. This was simply Stoic terminology. Cf. Plutarch, *De Facie In Orbe Lunae*, p. 928C (Chrysippus, *Fragmenta Logica et Physica*, fr. 788); (of the soul), *De Sera Numinis Vindicta*, p. 365D, which Origen implicitly quotes in *Cels*, II.60: Τὰ μὲν οὖν γινόμενα περὶ μνημεῖα τεθνηκότων φαντάσματα ἀπό τινος ὑποκειμένου γίνεται, τοῦ κατὰ τὴν ὑφεστηκυῖαν ἐν τῷ καλουμένῳ αὐγοειδεῖ σώματι ψυχήν.

The resurrected body will be something *like* this. For example, Origen wrote (*Cels*, VII.32), καὶ ἀόρατος ψυχὴ ἐν παντὶ σωματικῷ τόπῳ τυγχάνουσα δέεται σώματος οἰκείου τῇ φύσει τῷ τόπῳ ἐκείνῳ. His ardent admirer Porphyry wrote (*Sententiae*, 29, *apud* Stobaeus, *Anthologium*, 1.49.55), [ἡ ψυχὴ] ὡς γὰρ ἂν διατεθῇ, εὑρίσκει σῶμα τάξει καὶ τόποις οἰκείοις διωρισμένον. Origen (*loc. cit.*) wrote, εἰς τοὺς καθαρωτέρους καὶ αἰθερίους καὶ οὐρανίους τόπους. Porphyry wrote (*loc. cit.*), διὸ καθαρώτερον μὲν διακειμένῃ σύμφυτον τὸ ἐγγὺς τοῦ ἀΰλου σῶμα, ὅπερ ἐστὶ τὸ αἰθέριον (a body being nearly immaterial, which is the aetheral one).

It is sheer irony that Methodius of Olympus (Origen's relentless detractor) accused him *not* of holding 'spherical resurrected bodies' (which was subsequently claimed by the inquisitors of sixth-century imperial orthodoxy), but of maintaining that those bodies will be 'consubstantial with the angelic ones' (τοῖς ἀγγελικοῖς ὁμοούσιον ὑπάρχον) and made of 'pure air and fire' (ἐκ καθαροῦ ἀέρος καὶ καθαροῦ πυρὸς συνιστάμενον σύγκριμα). This vague notion was epitomised through the expression 'spiritual body' (τοιοῦτον καὶ ἐκ τούτων τὸ ἀναστῆναι μέλλον σῶμα ἀνθρώπου ὁ Ὠριγένης ἐφαντάζετο, ὃ καὶ πνευματικὸν ἔφη). Likewise, the idea attributed to Origen was that resurrected bodies will have the same form (εἶδος) as the physical ones (βούλεται τοίνυν ὁ Ὠριγένης τὴν μὲν αὐτὴν σάρκα μὴ ἀποκαθίστασθαι τῇ ψυχῇ, τὴν δὲ ποιὰν ἑκάστου μορφήν, κατὰ τὸ εἶδος τὸ τὴν σάρκα καὶ νῦν χαρακτηρίζον, ἐν ἑτέρῳ πνευματικῷ ἐντετυπωμένην ἀναστήσεσθαι σώματι, ἵνα ἕκαστος πάλιν ὁ αὐτὸς φανῇ κατὰ τὴν μορφήν, καὶ τοῦτο εἶναι τὴν ἐπαγγελλομένην ἀνάστασιν). Photius, *Bibliotheca*, Codex 234, pp. 299a-b. Origen professed agnosticism concerning bodies of rational beings other that the human ones: he spoke of them as having 'bodies, or something else which is different from a body' (*commJohn*, XX.28.250). He opted for leaning this point moot (on which Gregory of Nyssa followed him, see *infra*): all he cared about was to secure his fundamental doctrine that there is no such thing as '*incorporeal* rational being', and that 'life without a body is exclusive to Trinity alone'. *Princ*, II.2.2 (cf. I.6.4; I.7.3); also *Princ* (Lat.), I.6.4; II.2.2; IV.3.15; *Homilies on Exodus* (Lat.), 6.5. Also, Gennadius Scholarius, *epitGent*, 2.91: τοῦ Ὠριγένους εἰπόντος μηδεμίαν οὐσίαν παρὰ τὴν θείαν Τριάδα ἄνευ σώματος ὑφεστάναι.

As always, it was Gregory of Nyssa who followed Origen suit and argued that the precise nature of resurrected bodies is beyond the human ken and will be known at the time when 'the mystery of resurrerction' will be realised: *Dialogus De Anima et Resurrectione*, PG.46.145.29-34: ὁ μὲν ἀληθὴς περὶ τούτων λόγος ἐν τοῖς ἀποκρύφοις σοφίας θησαυροῖς τεταμίευται, τότε εἰς τὸ ἐμφανὲς ἥξων, ὅταν ἔργῳ τὸ τῆς ἀναστάσεως διδαχθῶμεν μυστήριον, ὅτε οὐκέτι δεήσει ῥημάτων ἡμῖν πρὸς τὴν ἐλπιζομένων φανέρωσιν. To Gregory, 'Origen was the leader of Christian philosophy during his own times' (τῷ, κατὰ τὸν χρόνον ἐκεῖνον τῆς τῶν Χριστιανῶν φιλοσοφίας καθηγουμένῳ, Ὠριγένης δὲ οὗτος ἦν, οὗ πολὺς ἐπὶ τοῖς συγγράμμασι λόγος). *De Vita Gregorii Thaumaturgi*, PG.46.905.43-46.

mcxcv Cyril of Alexandria, *op. cit.* fr. 198.

mcxcvi The expression ἀνείκαστος δόξα, meaning the 'indescribable [divine] glory' (literally: 'unsusceptible of artistic representation') is one of those introduced by Origen, but this did not win the day. Once again, it was his detractor Epiphanius that took this up in like a manner he did so with numerous of Origen's innovative turns. *Panarion*, v. 3, p. 327: μόνη δὲ ἡ τριὰς ἐν ἀκαταληψίᾳ καὶ ἐν δόξῃ ἀνεικάστῳ καὶ ἀκαταλήπτῳ. Pseudo-Macarius, *Homiliae*, homily 52.7. Ephraem Syrus, *Reprehensio Sui Ipsius atque Confessio*, p. 83; *De Paenitentia*, p. 373; *Beautitudines*, chapter 55; *De Recta Vivendi Ratione*, chapter 77; *Sermo in Secundum Adventum Domini Nostri Jesu Christi*, pp. 13; 127; 141; *In Adventum Domini*, p. 198; *Sermo De Passione Saluatoris*, p. 41. Pseudo-John Chrysostom, PG.60.703.20. Pseudo-John of Damascus, *Vita Barlaam et Joasaph*, p. 478. Symeon the New Theologian, *Hymni*, hymn 20, line 190. Analecta Hymnica Graeca, *Canones Aprilis*, 1.4.8. Also, the recently discovered sixth-century moderate Origenist, Cassian the Sabaite (Pseudo-Didymus), *De Trinitate*, PG.39.661.41-42. Use of this expression has been always exclusive to Christian authors.

mcxcvii Jerome, *commMatt*, 12.5.

mcxcviii See *supra*, endnote mcxcix.

mcxcix Cf. *Catena in Marcum*, pp. 355-356 (anonymous): Παρέστη δὲ καὶ Μωϋσῆς ὁ εἰς τὸν γνόφον εἰσελθὼν καὶ τῷ Θεῷ διαλεχθείς, καὶ Ἠλίας ὁ ἐπὶ τοῦ ὄρους πῦρ κατενεγκών. *Οὐ γὰρ ᾔδει τι λαλήσει· ἦσαν γὰρ ἔκφοβοι.*

mcc Origen, *frLuc*, fr. 146. Cf. *commMatt*, 12.42: ἢ τὸ εὐαγγέλιον καὶ τὸν νόμον καὶ τοὺς προφήτας *νεφέλη* ἐπισκιάζει *φωτεινὴ* τῷ δυναμένῳ ἐνορᾶν τῷ φωτὶ αὐτῆς κατὰ τὸ εὐαγγέλιον καὶ τὸν νόμον καὶ τοὺς προφήτας.

mcci Origen pointed out that the term εὐδοκία was not current among the Greeks, 'and, I think, this was coined by those who interpreted the prophetic words' of the Scripture (τὸ τῆς *εὐδοκίας* ὄνομα οὐ πάνυ τι τετριμμένον ἐν τῇ τῶν Ἑλλήνων συνηθείᾳ νομίζω ὄν, ὠνοματοποιῆσθαι δὲ ὑπὸ τῶν ἑρμηνευσάντων). Upon explaining Eph. 1:9, he felt it necessary to point out the etymology of the noun: εὐδοκία is derived from εὖ and δοκεῖν (*commEph*, fr. 3). As always, he was philologically scrupulous: the *noun* was coined in relation to scriptural interpretation, since the *verb* εὐδοκῶ is abundantly used in the Septuagint. The 'good will' (εὐδοκία) of the Father has been expressed by means of His involving Himself with the world through 'Christ', who is the subsistent expression of this good will. *frLuc*, fr. 163: ταύτην οὖν καὶ εὐδοκίαν πατρὸς δηλοῖ Χριστός. *homJob* (*fragmenta in catenis, typus I+II*), p. 384: Εὐδοκίᾳ γὰρ τοῦ Πατρὸς ἐλθὼν ἐπὶ γῆς, συνῆψεν ἐν ἑαυτῷ τοὺς δύο λαούς, τῶν Ἰουδαίων τε καὶ ἐθνῶν. The Son is the 'image of the invisible God' (Col. 1:15), since Christ is the expression of the Father's 'first will' (πρῶτον θέλημα) and the manifestation of the True Deity. *commJohn*, XIII.36.234: Καὶ τάχα διὰ ταῦτα *εἰκών ἐστιν τοῦ θεοῦ τοῦ ἀοράτου*. καὶ γὰρ τὸ ἐν αὐτῷ θέλημα εἰκὼν τοῦ πρώτου θελήματος καὶ ἡ ἐν αὐτῷ θεότης εἰκὼν τῆς ἀληθινῆς θεότητος. Ontologically, the Son is co-eternal with the Father and equal with Him (see folio 119r: ὡς ἴσος ὢν τῶ πατρί); he *became* God's benevolent will (εὐδοκία θεοῦ γενόμενος) once God willed to *become* Creator. *frJohn*, fr. 1: λέγεται δὲ καὶ *σοφία* ὁ τοῦ θεοῦ υἱός, *ἀρχὴ ὁδῶν* τοῦ θεοῦ κτισθεῖσα κατὰ τὴν τῶν Παροιμιῶν γραφήν, ὅτι ἡ *τοῦ θεοῦ σοφία*, πρὸς τὸν οὗ ἐστι σοφία ὑπάρχουσα, οὐδεμίαν σχέσιν πρὸς ἕτερόν τινα εἶχεν, ἀλλ' εὐδοκία θεοῦ γενόμενος τὰ κτίσματα ὑπάρξαι ἠβουλήθη. See *COT*, pp. 48, 136. Accordingly, *Christ* (which indicates God's voluntary engagement with the world that he created) is the manifestation of the *first will* of the Father, which was the initial divine decision to create (this is what later misinformed and fanatic detractors twisted towards claiming that 'the Son *was born* from the Father's will'). Following this *first will*, God is constantly related to the world through a dialectical relation with rational creatures (see my *PHE*), but this involvement is *subsequent* to the original 'benevolent decision of God' to *become* Creator.

I made this analysis in order to demonstrate how closely did John Chrysostom follow Origen's thought and drew on this, for which Epiphanius of Salamis castigated him, as explained in the Introduction. Indeed, Chrysostom grasped Origen's correlation of the term εὐδοκία with 'first will' (πρῶτον θέλημα): he simply named it προηγούμενον θέλημα, which is the same, both literally and in terms of content. John Chrysostom, *In Epistulam ad Ephesios* (also explaining Eph. 1:9), PG.62.12-24: *Κατὰ τὴν εὐδοκίαν, φησί, τοῦ θελήματος αὐτοῦ.* Τουτέστιν, διὰ τὸ σφοδρῶς θελῆσαι. Ἡ ἐπιθυμία αὐτοῦ, ὡς ἂν τις εἴποι, αὕτη ἐστί· πανταχοῦ γὰρ εὐδοκία τὸ θέλημά ἐστι τὸ προηγούμενον. Ἔστι γὰρ καὶ ἄλλο θέλημα, οἷον, θέλημα πρῶτον, τὸ μὴ ἀπολέσθαι ἡμαρτηκότας· θέλημα δεύτερον, τὸ γενομένους κακοὺς ἀπολέσθαι. Οὐ γὰρ δὴ ἀνάγκῃ αὐτοὺς κολάζει, ἀλλὰ θέλημα. ... Εὐδοκίαν οὖν τὸ πρῶτον θέλημά φησι, τὸ σφοδρὸν θέλημα, τὸ μετὰ ἐπιθυμίας θέλημα, τὸ πεῖσμα. This was slightly paraphrased in the *Catena in Epistulam ad Ephesios*, p. 108: (Χρυσοστόμου.) Ὁ δὲ μακάριος Ἰωάννης οὕτω φησί· τουτέστι, διὰ τὸ σφοδρῶς θελῆσαι ἡ ἐπιθυμία αὐτοῦ, ὡς ἂν τις εἴποι, αὕτη ἐστί· πανταχοῦ γὰρ εὐδοκία τὸ θέλημά ἐστι τὸ προηγούμενον· ἔστι γὰρ καὶ ἄλλο θέλημα, οἷον θέλημα πρῶτον, τὸ μὴ ἀπολέσθαι ἡμαρτηκότας· θέλημα δὲ δεύτερον, τὸ γενομένους κακοὺς ἀπολέσθαι. Οὐ γὰρ δὴ ἀνάγκῃ αὐτοὺς κολάζει, ἀλλὰ θέλων· ... εὐδοκίαν οὖν, τὸ πρῶτον θέλημα φησί, τὸ σφοδρὸν θέλημα, τὸ μετ' ἐπιθυμίας θέλημα, ὃ ἐφ' ἡμῶν.

John of Damascus took up the idea, and explained the noun εὐδοκία by using both expressions at the same time (allowing the tautology for the sake of clarity), that is, Origen's πρῶτον θέλημα and Chrysostom's προηγούμενον θέλημα. *Expositio Fidei*, 43: Λέγεται οὖν τὸ μὲν πρῶτον προηγούμενον θέλημα καὶ εὐδοκία ἐξ αὐτοῦ ὄν, τὸ δὲ δεύτερον ἑπόμενον θέλημα καὶ παραχώρησις ἐξ ἡμετέρας αἰτίας. Καὶ αὕτη διττή· ἡ μὲν οἰκονομικὴ καὶ παιδευτικὴ πρὸς σωτηρίαν, ἡ δὲ ἀπογνωστικὴ πρὸς τελείαν κόλασιν, ὡς εἰρήκαμεν. Ταῦτα δὲ ἐπὶ τῶν οὐκ ἐφ' ἡμῖν.

So did an anonymous author of a spurious text (perhaps, a sixth-century one). Pseudo-Athanasius, *Dialogus Athanasii et Zacchaei*, 20: Ζακχαῖος εἶπεν. Εἰ ὁ θεὸς ὁ θεός, καὶ θεὸς ἡ εἰκών, δύο θεοί. Ἀθανάσιος εἶπε. Δύο θεοί εἰσιν ὅτ' ἂν ἄλλο θέλημα τὸ πρωτότυπον καὶ ἄλλο ἡ εἰκών. Ὅτ' ἂν δὲ τὸ αὐτὸ θέλημα, ἡ αὐτὴ γνῶσις, ἡ αὐτὴ γνώμη, ἡ αὐτὴ φύσις, εἷς θεός, διὰ τὸ ἀπαράλλακτον τῆς οὐσίας. I should remind that it is this author that employed Origen's extremely rare expression ἔχω πιστεῦσαι from the present commentary. Cf. *supra*, endnote mclxxxiii. Pseudo-Athanasius, *Dialogus Athanasii et Zacchaei*, 64: Καὶ ἔχω πιστεῦσαι τοῖς εὐαγγελίοις σου;

So did Damascene's predecessor Andreas of Caesarea, evidently having in mind Chrysostom's text. *Commentarii in Apocalypsin*, 20.59.19 (17b-18): Τὸ μὲν προηγούμενον τοῦ θεοῦ θέλημα, ὃ καὶ εὐδοκία λέγεται καὶ δεῖπνον αὐτῷ περιπόθητον. Andreas' much later descendant, namely, Arethas Archbishop of Caesarea, just copied from him while slightly paraphrasing. Arethas, *Commentarius in Apocalypsin*, col. 745: Δεῖπνον δὲ ὅλως εἴρηται τὸ προηγούμενον θέλημα τοῦ Θεοῦ, ὃ καὶ εὐδοκία λέγεται καὶ δεῖπνον τριπόθητον.

mccii Cf. *infra*, folio 150v: οἱ δι' ἀνθρωπίνην ἀρέσκειαν σωφρονεῖν νομιζόμενοι καὶ μὴ δι' αὐτὸ τὸ καλόν. Although Chrysostom took up Origen's consideration of the scriptural neologism εὐδοκία, perhaps he lacked the background which was indispensable for him to be able to follow Origen all the way through. Hence, the present consideration is exclusive to Origen alone and it brings his stupendous erudition to the fore. Over many years, I have demonstrated that Origen was a devout student of Alexander of Aphrodisias. It was not only critical terms that he received from Alexander and put them to use in his own context, which is a matter of philology after all: what is more, he owed all of his knowledge of Aristotle to Alexander, since the latter's commentaries had the merit of quoting Aristotle's work passage after passage and then considering and explaining each one of them. This is the present case, too. But let me first cast some light on Aristotle's idea on this: he considered things that are chosen for the sake of an ulterior goal (e.g. money for the sake of health, health for the sake of our work in everyday life, and so on), but eventually we must arrive at an ultimate 'good' (ἀγαθὸν) which we desire and pursue for its own sake, not as an agent for the sake of another goal.

Here is what Aristotle wrote in his *On the Soul*, 406b: "That which is good for itself is not good because of anything else, and that which is good for its own sake is not good for the sake of anything else (τὸ καθ' αὑτὸ ἀγαθὸν ἢ δι' αὑτό, τὸ μὲν δι' ἄλλο εἶναι, τὸ δ' ἑτέρου ἕνεκεν).ς Also, in *Ethica Nicomachea*, 1097a: "Now there do appear to be several ends at which our actions aim; but as we choose some of them (for instance wealth, or flutes, and instruments generally) as a means to something else, it is clear that not all of them are final ends, whereas the Supreme Good seems to be something final. Consequently if there be some one thing which alone is an ultimate end, this thing (or if there be several ultimate ends, the one among them which is the most ultimate) it will be the Good which we are seeking. In speaking of degrees of finality, we mean that a thing pursued as an end in itself is more final than one pursued as a means to something else, and that a thing never chosen as a means to anything else is more ultimate than things chosen both as ends in themselves and as means to that thing; and accordingly a thing chosen always as an end and never as a means we call absolutely ultimate." *Protrepticus*, fr. 25 (quoted by Iamblichus, *Protrepticus*, p. 34): "that which is pursued for the sake of itself is always superior to that which is [pursued] for the sake of something else" (κρεῖττον δὲ πανταχοῦ τὸ δι' αὑτὸ τοῦ δι' ἄλλο).

This is the idea that fascinated Origen: if pursuit of good for the sake of good alone is considered as characteristic of superior human quality, this disposition reaches its highest and more sublime peak in God himself, who *decided to become* Creator and to make the 'good creature' called 'world' for the sake of goodness alone. This is the step Origen took beyond the pertinent analyses of his Greek predecessor and commentator. Cf. Alexander of Aphrodisias, *commTop*, pp. 6; 230-231; 265; 350; 385; *commMeteor*, p. 78. In other words, goodness (therefore, virtue), is pursued not for the sake of anything else; rather, everything else should be pursued for the sake of goodness. Cf. *Suda*, letter kappa, entry 41: τὴν γὰρ ἀρετὴν δι' αὑτὸ ἐπιτηδεύομεν καὶ οὐκ ἄλλου τινὸς ἕνεκα. I hardly need to point out that Origen went well beyond both Aristotle and his commentator: for whereas he wrote having in mind Aristotle, he made this a cardinal theological topic, not simply an issue to be persused in the context of ethics.

Once we seek to explore who were the Christian authors that embraced this idea (like the legion of ideas they took up from Origen, whether being aware of this, or not), it will turn out that all of them are absent. Even Didymus the Blind, who was at the same time an erudite Aristotelist and a devout student of Origen, used Aristotle's locution not in relation to God himself (which Origen does at this point of the codex), but in relation to Abraham, who 'pursued virtue for the sake of the Good, not for the sake of anything else' (τοῦ νοῦ τὴν ἔντευξιν Θεῷ ποιουμένου, μὴ δι' ἄλλο τὰς ἀρετὰς ἐνεργοῦντος ἀλλὰ δι' αὐτὸ τὸ ἀγαθόν). Didymus, *In Genesim*, cod. p. 223.

mcciii John Chrysostom, *In Matthaeum*, PG.58.553.60-61. In the *Catena in Matthaeum*, p. 137, the same passage is anonymous. So it is in the *Catena in Marcum*, p. 356, yet the wider context of this is but the text attributed to John Chrysostom and has been quoted above (homily 56: PG.58.553.14-554.38), which is simply Origen's fr. 362 (Klostermann), only to confirm once again that Chrysostom copied from Origen, whose idea became a lexicon lemma, too. See Pseudo-Zonaras, *Lexicon*, letter epsilon, p. 919: *Εὐδόκησας.* σῆς ἠξίωσας οἰκειότητος. εὐδόκησα καὶ τὸ ἠθέλησα. εὐδόκησα καὶ τὸ ἀναπαύομαι καὶ τὸ ἀρέσκομαι, ὡς τὸ *ἐν ᾧ εὐδόκησα* ἐν τῷ εὐαγγελίῳ.

mcciv Cf. Origen, *commMatt*, 12.42: ἢ τὸ εὐαγγέλιον καὶ τὸν νόμον καὶ τοὺς προφήτας *νεφέλη* ἐπισκιάζει *φωτεινὴ* τῷ δυναμένῳ ἐνορᾶν τῷ φωτὶ αὐτῆς κατὰ τὸ εὐαγγέλιον καὶ τὸν νόμον καὶ τοὺς προφήτας. *frLuc*, fr. 146: Ὠριγένης εἰς τὸ *ἰδοὺ ἄνδρες δύο συνελάλουν* [Luke, 9:30] ... καὶ ὅτι εἰς τὰς αὐτὰς σκηνὰς ἀνάγουσι νόμος καὶ προφῆται καὶ εὐαγγέλιον, τρεῖς μὲν ἀριθμούμεναι, πρὸς ἓν δὲ τέλος ὁρῶσαι.

mccv Origen, *commMatt*, fr. 362 (Klostermann), col. 1.

mccvi Origen, *schLuc*, PG.17.345.8-24.

mccvii Origen, *frLuc*, fr. 148.

mccviii Theodore of Mopsuestia, *frMatt*, fr. 94 (second part; see the first part forthwith below).

mccix Theodore of Mopsuestia, *op. cit.* (first part). But now we have all of Origen's text and context.

mccx Cf. Origen, *commMatt*, 13.2.

mccxi Origen, *commMatt*, fr. 368 (Klostermann).

mccxii Origen, *commMatt*, 13.6. This is a unique seal by Origen, since no other author did ever come up with this exegesis.

mccxiii Jerome, *commMatt*, 17.15-16.

mccxiv Cf. *infra*, folio 168v: κἂν μὴ φέρηται δὲ ἐν τῇ γραφῇ ὅτι τοῦτο πεποιήκασιν οἱ μαθηταὶ ἢ ‹ὅτι› καὶ ὄρη μετήγαγον, οὐδὲν ἐκ τούτου. ἢ γὰρ οὐκ ἐποίησαν διὰ τὸ ἀκενόδοξον ἢ οὐκ ἐγράφη.

mccxv Origen, *commRom*, p. 182.

mccxvi Cf. Mark, 9:29: Τοῦτο τὸ γένος ἐν οὐδενὶ δύναται ἐξελθεῖν εἰ μὴ ἐν προσευχῇ. The ensuing phrase in this codex appears only in some manuscripts. The first who quoted this was Origen. Cf. *Catena in Matthaeum*, p. 141 (unattributed, but certainly Origen's, as shown above). Basil of Caesarea, *De Jejunio*, PG.31.180.43; *Asceticon Magnum* (almost certainly, spurious), PG.31.965.45. John Chrysostom, *De Paenitentia*, PG.49.307.9; *In Genesim*, PG.53.279.49; *In Psalmum 145*, PG.55.525.9; *In Matthaeum*, PG.58.563.18. Antiochus of Palestine (or Antiochus of Ancyra, seventh century), *Pandecta Scripturae Sacrae*, homily 7, line 78; homily 99, line 24. Anastasius of Sinai, *Viae Dux*, 8.1; *Questiones et Responsiones*, 26.3. John of Damascus, *Sacra Parallela*, PG.95.1437.40. Michael Glycas, *Annales*, p. 117; *Quaestiones in Sacram Scripturam*, chapter 31, p. 364; chapter 81, p. 329. Gennadius Scholarius, *Orationes et Panegyrici*, 4.9.

mccxvii Cf. Origen, *commMatt*, 13.7.

mccxviii Cf. Origen, *frLuc*, fr. 169 & *Catena in Lucam*, p. 87: λῃστὰς δὲ λέγει τὸ τῶν ἀγρίων δαιμόνων σύστημα.

mccxix Origen, *commMatt*, fr. 375 (Klostermann). The editor put some passages in brackets, since these apparently run parallel to Chrysostom. However, Chrysostom's usual practice of using Origen's phrase here and there as a sort of patchwork has been discussed in the Introduction.

mccxx Cf. Origen's characteristic expression τὰ πάντως ἐσόμενα (or, τὸ πάντως ἐσόμενον) about a certain inexorable eventuality following a sequence of events. *deOr*, 5.3: οὕτως ἀνόητος ἂν εἴη ἄνθρωπος, ὅστις οἴεται διὰ τὴν ἑαυτοῦ εὐχὴν γίνεσθαι τὰ καὶ μὴ εὐξαμένου αὐτοῦ πάντως ἐσόμενα ἄν. *commGen*, PG.12.68.34-36 (*apud Philocalia*, 23.10): ἵνα μὴ ... αἰτία γένηται ἡ πρόγνωσις ἐκλύσεως, οὐκ ἔτι εὐτόνως ἱσταμένοις κατὰ τῆς ἁμαρτίας, ὡς πάντως ἐσομένου τοῦ προειρημένου. As it happened with similar cases, this expression entered into Christian vocabulary through Origen drawing on his Greek readings. This time, he took this up from favourite authors of his, such as Chrysippus, Alexander of Aphrodisias, Plutarch, Galen, and the grammarian Apollonius Dyscolus. This expression was particularly used in considering the relation between freedom and fate (or, hemarmene), or freedom and prognostication: if a certain event has been foretold, what should be made of human freedom? Cf. Chrysippus, *Fragmenta Logica et Physica*, fr. 939, *apud* Eusebius, *Praeparatio Evangelica*, 4.3.10: εἰ γὰρ φήσει τις σωθήσεσθαι τὸ χρήσιμον τῆς μαντικῆς διὰ τὸ προλέγεσθαι τὸ πάντως ἐσόμενον δυσχερὲς εἰ μὴ φυλαξαίμεθα, οὐκέτι πάντα δείξει συμβησόμενα καθ' εἱμαρμένην, ἐφ' ἡμῖν ὄντος τοῦ φυλάξασθαί τε καὶ μὴ φυλάξασθαι. Plutarch, *De Pythiae Oraculis*, p. 399B: ἀλλὰ καὶ πῶς καὶ πότε καὶ μετὰ τί καὶ μετὰ τίνος, οὐκ ἔστιν εἰκασμὸς τῶν τάχα γενησομένων ἀλλὰ τῶν πάντως ἐσομένων προδήλωσις. Apollonius Dyscolus, *De Pronominibus*, 2.2.2, p. 10. Ptolemy of Alexandria, *Syntaxis Mathematica*, p. 499; *Apotelesmatica* (*Tetrabiblos*), 1.3.4: τῶν πάντῃ πάντως ἐσομένων ἡ πρόγνωσις περισσή. Artemidorus, *Onirocriticon*, 3.66; 4.2. Alexander of Aphrodisias, *De Fato*, p. 187. Pseudo-Galen, *De Historia Philosophica*, 106 (considering the views of Herophilus on dreams 'sent by gods' and their relation to human freedom).

Once Origen used this philological formula, his devout adherents followed suit once again. Gregory of Nyssa, *Oratio Catechetica*, 34. Eusebius, *Praeparatio Evangelica*, 4.3.7; 6.11.48. Didymus, *frPs(al)*, fr. 343; *Fragmenta in Epistulam ii ad Corinthios* (*in catenis*), p. 32. Then, once John Chrysostom took this up, as usually, he made it a recurrent usage. *In illud: Pater, Si Possibile Est, Transeat*, PG.51.33.5&11&30; *Expositiones in Psalmos*, PG.55.99.8; *et passim*, at more than a dozen of instances. Theodoret, *Interpretatio in Psalmos*, PG.80: 1120.6; 1333.46. Cyril of Alexandria, *commProphXII*, v. 1, p. 244; *In Joannem*, v. 2, pp. 327; 572; 592; *et passim*, at more points than Chrysostom. John of Damascus, *Expositio Fidei*, 94. Despite the secular provenance of this construction, later Greeks made nothing of it. See a just casual use by Simplicius, *commCael*, p. 431.

Origen argued extensively that divine foreknowledge does not compromise human freedom (*Philocalia*, 25.1). His reference at this point of the commentary on Matthew is simply made *en passant* as reiteration of his fundamental thesis. Therefore, Chrysostom's passage is but Origen's analysis, and Klostermann should have not put some lines of Origen's fragment in brackets only because they are reminiscent of Chrysostom's, *In Matthaeum*, PG.58.574.41-44, which reads thus: Ὅταν δὲ ἀνάγκην εἴπῃ, οὐ τὸ αὐθαίρετον τῆς ἐξουσίας ἀναιρῶν, οὐδὲ τὴν ἐλευθερίαν τῆς προαιρέσεως, οὐδὲ ἀνάγκῃ τινὶ πραγμάτων ὑποβάλλων τὸν βίον, φησὶ ταῦτα. ἀλλὰ τὸ πάντως ἐσόμενον προλέγει. On Chrysostom's expression ἐλευθερίαν τῆς προαιρέσεως, see Origen, *frJohn*, fr. 43: αὐτεξούσιοι ὄντες οἱ ἄνθρωποι, τῷ προαίρεσιν ἐλευθέραν ἔχειν. *selPs*, PG.12.1608.37-38: Ἐμφαίνει δὲ τὸ ἐλεύθερον τῆς προαιρέσεως. However, Origen used more often the technical Stoic expression τὸ ἐφ' ἡμῖν, in effect meaning 'human freedom', which is not impaired by the pronouncement of Biblical prophecies. *commRom* (*I.1-XII.21*), fr. 1; *commGen*, PG.12.52.9 ff (*apud Philocalia*, 23.7); PG.12.61.29 ff (*apud Philocalia*, 23.7). Cf. *Princ*, III.1 (with extensive Greek text from the *Philocalia*); *Cels*, 1.66.

mccxxi Origen, *schMatt*, PG.17.297.18-47.

mccxxii Origen was supposedly the first to have advanced the idea of God being 'formless' (ἀσχημάτιστος). However, Clement of Alexandria's excerpts from Theodotus (of the eastern school of the Gnostic Valentinians, but unknown otherwise) show that this was also the latter's view, who (unlike Origen) dismissed the notion of 'person' being attributed to God. Clement of Alexandria, *Excerpta ex Theodoto*, 1.11.2: Πρόσωπον δὲ τοῦ ἀσχηματίστου πῶς ἂν εἴη; Photius related that the Anthropomorphites (a sect of Christians in the fourth century) asked Patriarch Theophilus of Alexandria to condemn Origen for maintaining that God is 'formless' and Theophilus of Alexandria promised them to do so only in order to escape death. Photius, *Bibliotheca*, Codex 96, p. 82a: Τῶν δὲ καὶ Ὠριγένην, ὡς ἀσχημάτιστον τὸ θεῖον λέγοντα, ἀναθεματισθῆναι προσεπιζητούντων, ὑπέσχετο [sc. Theophilus of Alexandria] ποιήσειν καὶ τοῦτο, καὶ διέφυγε τὸν θάνατον. Nicephorus Callistus Xanthopulus, *HE*, 13.10: Ὅσοι μὲν οὖν Θεοφίλῳ προσέκειντο Ὠριγενειαστὰς τοὺς ἄλλους ἐκάλουν· ὅσοι δὲ ἀσώματον τὸ θεῖον ὡρίζοντο εἶναι καὶ ἀσχημάτιστον, Ἀνθρωπομορφιανοὺς τοὺς ἐρεθιζομένους ὑπὸ Θεοφίλου καὶ τἀναντία φρονοῦντας ὠνόμαζον. Καὶ μεταξὺ τῶν μοναχῶν πόλεμος ἄσπονδος ἀνερράγη, παρατριβῆς οὐ σμικρᾶς γινομένης. Cf. Origen, *frPs*, on Psalm 109:1-6: Εἴρηται δὲ τοῦτο, οὐχ ὅτι ὁ Θεὸς ἔχει δεξιὰ καὶ ἀριστερὰ [ref. to Mat. 20:23] ὁ ἀσχημάτιστος καὶ πάντα πληρῶν. However, to orthodox theologians, the notion of 'formless' God (including the 'person' of God) became a matter of course in the ensuing centuries. Cf. Gelasius of Cyzicus, *HE*, 2.21.27: ἀλλὰ πρόσωπον ἀκούοντες, μὴ ἀνθρωπόμορφον τὸ θεῖον ὑπολάβωμεν· ἀσύνθετον γὰρ καὶ ἀσχημάτιστον. Anonymous, *Adversus Haereses* (*e cod. Coisl. 299, saec. XI*), p. 281 (G. Bardy): ἕνα Θεὸν ἐν τρισὶν ἀσχηματίστοις προσώποις εὐσεβῶς κηρυττόμενον καὶ δοξαζόμενον. Anastasius of Sinai, *Viae Dux*, 2.3: Πρόσωπα δὲ καὶ χαρακτῆρας λέγομεν ἐπὶ θεοῦ ἀσώματα καὶ ἀπερίγραπτα καὶ ἀσχημάτιστα. Πρόσωπον ἤγουν ὑπόστασίς ἐστι κατὰ τοὺς ἁγίους πατέρας τὸ ἰδικὸν παρὰ τὸ κοινόν. *Op. cit.* 8.4: ὀπτανομένου αὐτοῖς ἐν ἀνθρωπίνῳ σχήματι τοῦ ἀοράτου καὶ ἀσχηματίστου θεοῦ. *Loc. cit.* ἀσώματον τὸ θεῖον καὶ ἀπρόσωπον καὶ ἀσχημάτιστον. Pseudo-Zonaras, *Lexicon*, letter upsilon, p. 1773: καὶ χαρακτῆρας λέγομεν ἐπὶ θεοῦ, ἀσώματα καὶ ἀσχημάτιστα. πρόσωπον ἤγουν ὑπόστασίς ἐστι κατὰ τοὺς ἁγίους πατέρας τὸ ἰδικὸν παρὰ τὸ κοινόν. Neophytus Prodromenus, *Contra Latinos*, 3: Πρόσωπα δὲ καὶ χαρακτῆρας λέγομεν ἐπὶ Θεοῦ, ἀσωμάτου καὶ ἀΰλου καὶ ἀπεριγράπτου, ἀσώματα καὶ ἀπερίγραπτα καὶ ἀσχημάτιστα. Πρόσωπον δέ, ἤτοι ὑπόστασίς ἐστι, κατὰ τοὺς ἁγίους Πατέρας, τὸ ἰδικὸν παρὰ τὸ κοινόν. If the following passage was in fact written by Apollinaris, this is one more influence by Origen (assuming that this was not indeed written by Origen himself, like so many other passages of Origen that have been attributed to Apollinaris, as we have seen). Apollinaris, *Fragmenta in Joannem*, fr. 115: πᾶς ὁ περὶ θεοῦ λόγος τοιοῦτος ἐσχημάτισται σχήματος ἀνθρωπίνου καὶ τῶν παθημάτων ὀνόμασι τῶν ἡμετέρων τὸν ἀσώματον καὶ ἀσχημάτιστον καὶ ἀπαθῆ θεὸν ἑρμηνεύων. However, the same text and its wider context was ascribed also to Ammonius, the presbyter of Alexandria, in the *Catena in Joannem*, p. 357.

mccxxiii Explaining God's 'face' as divine 'superintendence' is an exegesis introduced by Origen, which some of his ardent admirers embraced. Cf. Origen, *commJohn*, VI.19.104: διὰ τοῦτο ὁ ἐπισκοπούμενος ἀντιλαμβανόμενος τῆς ἀπὸ τῆς ἐπισκοπῆς ὠφελείας φησίν. *Ἐσημειώθη ἐφ' ἡμᾶς τὸ φῶς τοῦ προσώπου σου, Κύριε. deOr*, 23.4: τοιοῦτός τις καὶ ὁ ἐν τῷ παραδείσῳ, κρυπτομένου θεὸν καὶ φεύγοντος τὴν ἐπισκοπὴν αὐτοῦ ... οὕτω γὰρ καὶ *Κάϊν ἐξῆλθεν ἀπὸ προσώπου τοῦ θεοῦ καὶ ᾤκησεν ἐν γῇ Ναῒδ κατέναντι Ἐδέμ.* Eusebius, *Commentaria in Psalmos*, PG.23.1301.34-36: Πρόσωπον δὲ ἐνταῦθα τὴν ἐπιφάνειαν αὐτοῦ φησί, τὴν ἐπισκοπήν, τὴν πρόνοιαν, τὴν κηδεμονίαν, τὴν βοήθειαν, τὴν συμμαχίαν, τὴν ἔννοιαν τὴν περὶ αὐτόν. Gregory of Nazianzus, *De Spiritu Sancto*, 22: τὴν δὲ ἐπισκοπήν, πρόσωπον. Moreover, Severus of Antioch, *apud Catena in Acta*, p. 47: (Τοῦ ἁγίου Σευήρου Ἀντιοχείας.) Πρόσωπον Κυρίου νοητέον τὴν θεοπρεπεστάτην θεοφάνειαν καὶ τὴν ἡμετέραν ἐπισκοπήν, ἣν ἡμᾶς τότε τελειωτέρον ἐπισκέψεται. Compared with influence on posterity exerted by other contributions of Origen, the impact of this one was rather limited.

mccxxiv Jerome, *commMatt*, 18.12.

mccxxv The expression ἐπίμονος ἀρετὴ ('persevering virtue') is a peculiar one coined by Origen and taken up by Theodoret alone. *Interpretatio in Danielem*, PG.81.1393.10-12: Φύγωμεν τοίνυν, παρακαλῶ, τοῦ διαβόλου τὴν ἐξαπάτην, καὶ τὴν ἐπίμονον ἀρετὴν τῆς ἡδονῇ βραχείᾳ κεχρημένης προτιμήσωμεν ἁμαρτίας.

mccxxvi Rational nature is one of the constituents of the The Body of Logos. See *Anaxagoras*, pp. 867-964; 1348-1368.

mccxxvii Apollinaris, *frMatt*, fr. 89. But now we have Origen's context of this analysis.

mccxxviii Cf. Origen, *frLuc*, fr. 92: θεοπρεπὲς ἀξίωμα μεμαρτύρηκε τῷ Χριστῷ. He commented on Matt. 3:11 (Luke, 3:16). Cyril of Alexandria used this schema commenting on the same instance. *Quod Unus Sit Christus*, p. 748, which John of Damascus copied (*Contra Nestorianos*, 18) without mentioning Cyril.

mccxxix See the expression 'kairos of repentance' (καιρὸς μετανοίας) also *supra*, p. 192 & endnote cmlx in the passage from Origen, *schMatt*, PG.17.297.18-47, and its parallel fr. 375 (Klostermann). See also pp. 255; 257. Μετανοίας καιρὸς is an expression that Origen took up from Josephus and introduced it into Christian literature. Josephus, *De Bello Judaico*, 3.127: [ref. to Vespasian] ἐπιδεικνύμενος τὴν στρατιὰν εἰς κατάπληξιν τοῖς πολεμίοις καὶ μετανοίας καιρὸν διδούς. Also, Origen, *selPs*, PG.12.1389.35-36: Ἐὰν οὖν, φησί, μὴ ἀφῇς μοι τὴν ἁμαρτίαν, καὶ ἀναψύξω πρὶν ἀπελθεῖν ἐκεῖ, οὐχ ἕξω μετανοίας καιρόν, οὐδὲ ὑπάρξω ἐν τῇ παρὰ σοὶ ζωῇ. He was followed by his most eminent devotees, plus some other authors. Gregory of Nyssa, *De Virginitate*, 18.3. Eusebius, *Commentaria in Psalmos*, PG.23.352.28. Gregory of Nazianzus, *In Pentecosten*, PG.36.346.36. Athanasius, *Expositiones in Psalmos*, PG.27: 77.9; 156.49; 228.18; 236.49; 393.7 (but it should be borne in mind that several passages of this collection are actually Origen's). Basil of Caesarea, *Epistulae*, 8.6. Pseudo-Basil of Caesarea (*forsan* Cassian the Sabaite), *Enarratio in Prophetam Isaiam*, 4.138; Pseudo-Caesarius (Cassian the Sabaite). *Quaestiones et Responsiones*, 146; 218. Didymus, *Commentarii in Job* (*12.1-16.8a*), fr. 372; *frPs*(*al*), fr. 44; *In Genesim*, cod. p. 169. Also, John Chrysostom, Theodoret, but never Cyril of Alexandria.

mccxxx Origen, *commMatt*, fr. 382 (Klostermann).

mccxxxi Origen, *schMatt*, PG.17.297.53-300.13.

mccxxxii Origen, *commMatt*, fr. 383 (Klostermann).

mccxxxiii Origen, *schMatt*, PG.17.300.27-36.

mccxxxiv Origen, *commMatt*, 14.6.

mccxxxv Cf. *supra*, folio 10v: Πρῶτος δὲ Ἰωάννης κηρύσσει βασιλείαν οὐρανῶν, ἥτις ἦν ὁ Χριστός. Folio 11r: Λέγεται δὲ βασιλεία οὐρανῶν οὐ μόνον τὸ ζῆν θεαρέστως, ἀλλὰ καὶ ἡ πρώτη καὶ δευτέρα Χριστοῦ παρουσία. Folio 11v: Βασιλεία Θεοῦ αὐτὸς ἂν εἴη ὁ Χριστός. Folio 25v: Ἐπεὶ δὲ καὶ ὁ Χριστὸς βασιλεία οὐρανῶν.

mccxxxvi Cf. Origen, *commMatt*, 14.7: *Ὡμοιώθη* (φησίν) *ἡ βασιλεία τῶν οὐρανῶν* καὶ τὰ ἑξῆς. Εἰ δὲ *βασιλεῖ ὡμοιώθη* τοιῷδε καὶ τοιάδε πεποιηκότι, τίνα χρὴ λέγειν ἢ τὸν υἱὸν τοῦ θεοῦ; Αὐτὸς γάρ ἐστιν ὁ βασιλεὺς *τῶν οὐρανῶν*, καὶ ὥσπερ αὐτός ἐστιν ἡ αὐτοσοφία καὶ ἡ αὐτοδικαιοσύνη καὶ ἡ αὐτοαλήθεια, οὕτω μήποτε καὶ ἡ αὐτοβασιλεία. On the Logos being αὐτοσοφία, see *Cels*, III.41 (& *Philocalia*, 19.4): ὃν μὲν νομίζομεν καὶ πεπείσμεθα ἀρχῆθεν εἶναι θεὸν καὶ υἱὸν θεοῦ, οὗτος ὁ αὐτολόγος ἐστὶ καὶ ἡ αὐτοσοφία καὶ ἡ αὐτοαλήθεια. *Op. cit.* V.39: τοῦ αὐτολόγου καὶ τῆς αὐτοσοφίας καὶ τῆς αὐτοδικαιοσύνης. *Op. cit.* VI.47: τῷ αὐτολόγῳ καὶ αὐτοσοφίᾳ καὶ αὐτοαληθείᾳ καὶ αὐτοδικαιοσύνη ... καὶ ἡ αὐτοσοφία, *εἰκὼν οὖσα τῆς ἀγαθότητος αὐτοῦ*. *Op. cit.* VII.17: τῇ ἄκρᾳ μετοχῇ τοῦ αὐτολόγου καὶ τῆς αὐτοσοφίας. *commJohn*, XXXII.28.347; *commRom*, p. 146: ὥσπερ ὁ μονογενὴς τοῦ Θεοῦ ἐστιν αὐτολόγος καὶ αὐτοσοφία καὶ αὐτοαλήθεια, οὕτως καὶ αὐτονόμος. *Scholia in Canticum Canticorum*, PG.17.253.26-27: ἔστι γὰρ αὐτοσοφία καὶ δικαιοσύνη.

mccxxxvii Eph. 4:18: ἐσκοτωμένοι τῇ διανοίᾳ ὄντες, ἀπηλλοτριωμένοι τῆς ζωῆς τοῦ θεοῦ. Cf. Col. 1:21. Origen, *homLuc*, homily 35, pp. 201-202: οἰκεῖος μὲν γίνῃ τούτου, ἀλλότριος δὲ τοῦ θεοῦ, συνθήκην ποιούμενος μετὰ τοῦ ἀντιδίκου. *commEph*, fr. 18; *deOr*, 25.3: ἡ ἁμαρτία ... ἐπὶ *τὰ ἔργα τῆς σαρκὸς* καὶ τὰ ἀλλότρια τοῦ θεοῦ προκαλουμένης ἡμῶν τὴν ψυχήν. *frPs*, on Psalm 29:8: ἀσθένεια ψυχῆς ἐκ τῆς ἀπὸ Θεοῦ ἀλλοτριώσεως. *Op. cit.* on Psalm 77:45: οἱ γὰρ ἀλλότριοι τοῦ Θεοῦ καὶ παρὰ τοῖς νομιζομένοις ἄποροί εἰσι. *Op. cit.* on Psalm 87: 9: ὁρῶν δέ τις Ἰούδαν ἢ ἀλλοτριουμένους Ἰησοῦ Χριστοῦ τοῦ Θεοῦ. *selPs*, PG.12.1645.10-11: Οὐδεὶς ἀλλότριος τοῦ Θεοῦ τούτων τεύξεται. *selGen*, PG.12.144.19-20: Τοῦτο δὲ νομιστέον ὑπὸ πάντων τῶν ἀλλοτρίων τοῦ Θεοῦ λέγεσθαι. *Cels*, VIII.5 & 43. Cf. in the present codex, folio 47r: τὰ χρήματα ἀλλοτριοῖ Θεοῦ. Folio 169v: οὓς καὶ ἀλλοτρίους λέγει τῆς βασιλείας τοῦ Θεοῦ. Folio 169v: οὓς καὶ ἀλλοτρίους λέγει τῆς βασιλείας τοῦ Θεοῦ. Folio 198v: Διχοτομία δέ ἐστιν ἡ ἀπὸ τοῦ Πνεύματος εἰς τὸ διηνεκὲς τῆς ψυχῆς ἀλλοτρίωσις.

mccxxxviii Cf. Origen, *commJohn*, II.20.133: Πάλιν, ἐπεὶ ἔστι τὰ παραλελειμμένα τῶν ἐναντίων νοεῖσθαι ἐκ τῶν εἰρημένων περὶ τῶν ἐναντίων, λέγεται δὲ περὶ ζωῆς καὶ φωτὸς ἀνθρώπων, ἐναντίον δὲ τῇ ζωῇ θάνατος καὶ ἐναντίον φωτὶ ἀνθρώπων σκότος ἀνθρώπων, ἔστιν ἰδεῖν ὅτι ὁ ἐν σκότῳ τῶν ἀνθρώπων τυγχάνων ἐν θανάτῳ ἐστὶν καὶ ὁ τὰ τοῦ θανάτου πράττων οὐκ ἀλλαχόσε τοῦ σκότους ἐστίν.

mccxxxix Cf. Origen, *homLuc*, homily 12, p. 75: Οἷον ἐν Ἐφέσῳ εἰκός, ὅτι διὰ μὲν τοὺς ἁμαρτάνοντας ἄγγελός τις ἦν ἐγκεχειρισμένος τοὺς ἁμαρτάνοντας, διὰ δὲ τοὺς πιστεύοντας, ὅτι ἄγγελός τις ἦν τῆς Ἐφεσίων ἐκκλησίας. *Op. cit.* homily 13, p. 77: ἀγγελικὴ στρατιὰ ... οὐκ ἠδύνατο τελειῶσαι τὸ ἔργον, ὃ ἦν ἐγκεχειρισμένη, χωρὶς τοῦ σωτῆρος. *commMatt*, 10.13: Ταῦτα δέ φαμεν οὐκ ἀγνοοῦντες τινῶν ἀγγέλων τῶν μὴ τοιαύτην οἰκονομίαν ἐγκεχειρισμένων, ἀλλ᾽ οὐδὲ τούτων πάντων.

mccxl Origen, *commMatt*, 14.10 (on the same passage of Matthew, 18:23-25): τοῖς ἀγγέλοις τοῖς ἐπὶ τῶν κολάσεων τεταγμένοις. *Op. cit.* 14.13 (on the same passage): τίνες δ᾽ ἂν εἶεν οὗτοι ἢ οἱ ἐπὶ τῶν κολάσεων τεταγμένοι; *Op. cit.* 17.23: τοὺς τεταγμένους ἐπὶ τῶν κολάσεων ἀγγέλους. *homJer*, homily 19.14: οἱ ἐπὶ τῶν κολάσεων τεταγμένοι, οὗτοί εἰσιν οἱ τὰς μαχαίρας ἔχοντες. *Epistula ad Africanum*, PG.11.64.19-20: ἄγγελοι ἐπὶ τῶν κολάσεων τεταγμένοι τινὲς ταῦτα διαθήσουσι.

mccxli Cf. *supra*, p. 9, Origen, *commMatt*, fr. 22 (Klostermann): Τὸ *ἕως* ἐν τῇ γραφῇ πολλάκις ἐπὶ διηνεκοῦς εὑρίσκεται. Also, *commMatt*, 12.34; cf. *schLuc*, PG.17.341.25-29: Τὸ δέ, *ἕως*, ἐνταῦθα δηλοῖ τὸν κατεπείγοντα περὶ τοῦ δηλουμένου χρόνον, οὐ περιοριζόμενον, ὥστε γενέσθαι μετὰ τὸ ἕως τὸ ἐν αὐτῷ τῷ δηλουμένῳ. ὡς τό. *Καὶ ἰδοὺ ἐγὼ μεθ᾽ ὑμῶν εἰμι ἕως τῆς συντελείας τοῦ αἰῶνος.* The same, in *commMatt*, 12.34: παραστήσωμεν κατά τινα συνήθειαν τῆς γραφῆς τὸ *ἕως* δηλοῦν τὸν κατεπείγοντα περὶ τοῦ δηλουμένου χρόνον, οὐ περιοριζόμενον. See also *infra*, p. 381.

mccxlii John Chrysostom copied from Origen once again. *In Matthaeum*, PG.58.594.8-10: *Παρέδωκε γὰρ αὐτόν, ἕως οὗ ἀποδῷ τὸ ὀφειλόμενον.* τουτέστι, διηνεκῶς. οὔτε γὰρ ἀποδώσει ποτέ.

mccxliii Origen, *frPs*, on Psalm 134:12-14: Καὶ νῦν ὁ προφήτης ἐννοήσας τήντε καθόλου πρόνοιαν καὶ τὰ συμβάντα περὶ τὸν Ἰσραήλ, πυρωθεὶς ἀπὸ τῆς ἀφάτου φιλανθρωπίας, δοξολογεῖ τὸν Θεόν.

mccxliv ἀπότομος τιμωρία ('severe' or 'relentless' 'punishment') is one more expression from Origen's readings: he took this up from Diodore of Sicily and Josephus. Cf. Diodore of Sicily, *Bibliotheca Historica*, 1.65.4 (quoting from Hecataeus of Abdera, who is apparently the ultimate source of this): τοῖς μὲν κολαζομένοις τὸ τῆς τιμωρίας ἀπότομον ἠλαττωκέναι. Also, Josephus, *Antiquitates Judaicae*, 19.329: ἐκείνῳ γὰρ πονηρὸν ἦν ἦθος ἐπὶ τιμωρίαν ἀπότομον. Then, as usual, he was followed by Christian authors. John Chrysostom, *Epistulae ad Olympiadem*, epistle 8.3: τὰς ἀποτόμους τιμωρίας, τὴν κόλασιν τὴν οὐκ ἔχουσαν τέλος, τὸν ζόφον τὸν ἀφεγγῆ, τὸ σκότος τὸ ἐξώτερον. Theodoret, *Interpretatio in Ezechielem*, PG.81.929.34: ἵνα μὴ ἀποτομίαν νομίσῃ τὴν τιμωρίαν. Cyril of Alexandria, *De Exitu Animi*, PG.77.1072.34-35: Φοβοῦμαι τὰς ἀποτόμους τιμωρίας. Φοβοῦμαι τὴν κόλασιν τὴν οὐκ ἔχουσαν τέλος. Φοβοῦμαι τὸν ζόφον τὸν ἀφεγγῆ. Φοβοῦμαι τὸ σκότος τὸ ἐξώτερον (which is but John Chrysostom's passage just quoted). This is one of the numerous instances of 'plagiarism' that we come upon every now and then. Little wonder that the extensive passage of Origen surrounding this point was attributed to Apollinaris of Laodicea.

mccxlv Apollinaris, *frMatt*, fr. 92.

mccxlvi In Cramer's *Catena in Matthaeum*, p. 150, this is attributed to Origen alone. Klostermann (*frMatt*, fr. 384) noted that a joint attribution to Origen and John Chrysostom appears in *Codex Coislianus 195* (tenth century).

mccxlvii This is Origen, *commMatt*, fr. 384 (Klostermann) and Origen, *apud Catena in Matthaeum*, p. 150. Klostermann wrote that he found this in one codex, the joint ascription being to John Chrysostom and Origen.

mccxlviii *Catena in Marcum*, p. 371 (anonymous); cf. *op. cit.* pp. 266; 314; 418.

mccxlix John Chrysostom, *In Matthaeum*, PG.58.595.52-54.

mccl Jerome, *commMatt*, 19.3.

mccli Cf. Origen, *commMatt*, 14.24-25. *Catana in Marcum*, p. 374 (anonymous).

mcclii Apollinaris, *frMatt*, fr. 94.

mccliii See analysis of the notion φύσεως ἐπιτηδειότης, *supra*, folio 78v, endnote dccxxviii.

mccliv The Stoic tenor of the phrase τῆς σωφροσύνης κατόρθωμα is evident. The formula was taken up *verbatim* by Gregory of Nyssa, *In Canticum Canticorum*, p. 230; also, by Ephraem Syrus, *Sermo Paraeneticus*, p. 400; John Chrysostom, *Epistulae ad Olympiadem*, epistle 10.10; *Epistula ad Cyriacum*, line 447; Pseudo-John Chrysostom, *In Publicanum et Pharisaeum*, PG.59.596.58-59. So Theodore of Mopsuestia, *Fragmenta in epistulam i ad Corinthios*, p. 185. Cf. Apollinaris, *frMatt*, fr. 95, col. 2. *Οὐ πάντες φησὶν χωροῦσι τὸν λόγον, ἀλλ' οἷς δέδοται.* τὸ δὲ *οἷς δέδοται* χαρισμάτων φυσικῶν ἐστι δηλωτικὸν καὶ τῆς ἀπὸ γεννήσεως εὐφυίας εἰς τὸ τῆς σωφροσύνης κατόρθωμα.

mcclv Apollinaris, *frMatt*, fr. 95.

mcclvi The expression ἄνωθεν ἐπικουρία ('succour from on high') entered into literature through Origen and has always been used exclusively by Christian authors. Naturally, his devotees embraced this. Eusebius, *Commentaria in Psalmos*, PG.23.1301.28-31: παρὰ πάντα τὸν βίον τὴν ἄνωθεν ἐπικουρίαν προσήκει ζητεῖν. Athanasius, *Expositiones in Psalmos*, PG.27.481.3-5: τῆς ἄνωθεν ἐπικουρίας χωρὶς οὐ δυνατόν τινα φύλακα γενέσθαι τοῦ νόμου. Then, Theodoret, *Quaestiones in Octateuchum*, p. 294; *Interpretatio in Psalmos*, PG.80: 1609.18; 1612.11; 1709.37; 1813.33; *In Epistulas Sancti Pauli*, PG.82.845.24. Once again, once Cyril of Alexandria took up an expression from Origen, and he applied this a dozens of points. *commProphXII*, v. 1, pp. 52; 57; 133; 162; 242; and *passim*, in almost all of his works. Also, Basil of Seleucia, *Sermones*, PG.85.428.6. Nilus of Ancyra, *Epistulae*, book 3, epistle 228. Procopius of Gaza, *Commentarii in Isaiam*, pp. 1988; 2128. Procopius of Caesarea, *De Bellis*, 4.20.5; 8.14.20. John of Damascus, *Sacra Parallela*, PG.95: 1452.21; 1520.12; 1565.35. Photius, *Homiliae*, homily 1, p. 2; *Epistulae et Amphilochia*, epistle 191. Michael Psellus, *Orationes Hagiographicae*, 3.b.

mcclvii Cf. Luke, 20:36. Origen, *commJohn*, II.22.140: ὅταν προκόψωμεν, ἰσάγγελοι ἐσόμεθα. *Op. cit.* XIII.16.99: οἱ ἤδη τῇ διαθέσει τὸ ἰσάγγελοι εἶναι ἐσχηκότες οὐδὲ ἐν Ἱεροσολύμοις προσκυνήσουσιν τῷ πατρί. *Cels*, IV.29: ὥστε τοὺς ἀνθρώπους τελειωθέντας ἰσαγγέλους γίνεσθαι. John Chrysostom, *De Virginitate*, 21: ὁ τὴν ἰσάγγελον ταύτην διαβάλλων πολιτείαν πόσην ὀργὴν ἐπισπάσεται κατὰ τῆς ἑαυτοῦ κεφαλῆς; Pseudo-John Chrysostom, *In Parabolam Samaritani*, PG.62.755.42-43: ὁ Ἀδὰμ πρὸ τῆς παρακοῆς εἶχε τὸ ἐπουράνιον φρόνημα καὶ τὴν ἰσάγγελον πολιτείαν. Cyril of Alexandria, *Epistulae Paschales*, PG.77.412.55-413.1: Νηστεία, τῆς ἰσαγγέλου πολιτείας τὸ μίμημα. *Catena in Acta*, p. 127 (unattributed): οἷς ὁ νόμος δέδοται, διατάξεις ἔχων, αἵτινες ἰσάγγελον ἐποίουν πολιτείαν ἔχειν τοὺς τελοῦντας αὐτόν. Anonymous, *Scholia in Lucianum* (on Pseudo-Lucian of Samosata's, *Demosthenis Encomium*), 50: *ὀπαδός τις δαίμων* ... τὴν ἰσάγγελον πολιτείαν παρεισάγει ὁ ἀλιτήριος.

mcclviii Origen, *commMatt*, fr. 386 (Klostermann). Cf. fr. 378 (on Matt. 18:8-9): Οὐ τὰ μέλη ἐκκόπτειν διδασκόμεθα, ἀλλὰ τὰ πάθη τῶν μελῶν καὶ τοὺς εἰς τόπον μελῶν φίλους, εἰ καὶ ἐπιχειροῦσι τοῦ σκανδαλίζειν. It was in the commentary on Matthew that Origen expressed his regret for having committed self-castration following his reading a *sententia* by Sextus (*Sententae Sexti*, 13) and a passage in Philo (*Quod Deterius Potiori Insidiari Soleat*, 176), and urged his readers not to to so by mistaking Matt. 19:12. See *commMatt*, 15.25.

mcclix *Catena in Matthaeum*, p. 154, attributed to Apollinaris, but in fact this is a copy from Origen.

mcclx John Chrysostom, *In Matthaeum*, PG.58.600.54-58. See the same text slightly paraphrased, in the *Catena in Marcum*, p. 375 (no specific attribution to any author): Τίνος δὲ ἕνεκεν ἀπεσόβουν τὰ παιδία οἱ μαθηταί; ἀξιώματος ἕνεκεν. τί οὖν αὐτός; διδάσκει αὐτοὺς μετριάζειν καὶ τῦφον καταπατεῖν κοσμικόν. τὰ παιδία δὲ λαμβάνει καὶ ἐναγκαλίζεται καὶ τοῖς τοιούτοις ἐπαγγέλλεται τὴν βασιλείαν.

mcclxi Apollinaris, *frMatt*, fr. 96.

mcclxii *Catena in Marcum*, pp. 374-375 (anonymous), on Mark, 10:13-16. Then the text quoted above follows, Τίνος δὲ ἕνεκεν ἀπεσόβουν τὰ παιδία; ...

mcclxiii Jerome, *commMatt*, 19.14.

mcclxiv *Catena in Marcum*, p. 375 (anonymous).

mcclxv *Catena in Marcum, loc. cit.*

mcclxvi The name Mark is written instead of Luke. See Luke, 18:18: Καὶ ἐπηρώτησέν τις αὐτὸν ἄρχων λέγων. Mark (10:17) only wrote of 'someone who ran' towards Jesus (προσδραμών τις).

mcclxvii τῷ γε νοῦν ἔχοντι. See Plato, *Theaetetus*, 167d; *Timaeus*, 89b; Aristotle, *Ethica Nicomachaea*, 1115b; and then, Polybius, Plutarch, Galen. After Origen, Gregory of Nyssa, Gregory of Nazianzus, Epiphanius of Salamis, John Chrysostom. *Supra*, note mxciii (p. 493).

mcclxviii Origen, *commMatt*, fr. 387 (Klostermann).

mcclxix This expression about 'freely chosen poverty' (αὐθαίρετος πενία) comes from Origen's secular background, namely, from Philostratus, *Vita Apollonii*, 8.7: κατὰ ταὐτά σοι φιλοσοφεῖν ἤθελον, σφόδρα ἂν εὐδαιμόνως ἔπραττε φιλοσοφία τε καὶ πενία. Φιλοσοφία μὲν ἀδεκάστως ἔχουσα, πενία δὲ αὐθαιρέτως. ... φιλοσοφίας μὲν τὸ ἀδέκαστον, πενίας δὲ τὸ αὐθαίρετον. Unlike what happened with other expressions that he introduced into Christian locution, this one was taken up by Theodoret alone. *Epistulae: Collectio Sirmondiana* (*epistulae 96-147*), epistle 113, line 125: ἀλλὰ τὴν αὐθαίρετον ἠσπασάμην πενίαν. *In Epistulas Sancti Pauli*, PG.82.333.9-12: Ἐνταῦθα τοῖς μεγίστοις εἴδεσι τῆς ἀρετῆς, τῇ τῶν χρημάτων ὑπεροψίᾳ, καὶ αὐθαιρέτῳ πενίᾳ, καὶ τοῖς ὑπὲρ τῆς εὐσεβείας ἀγῶσι, τὴν ἀγάπην συγκρίνων. *Op. cit.* PG.82.425.27-29: Τὴν τελειότητα μὲν ὁ Δεσπότης ὁρίζεται τῇ παντελεῖ τῶν χρημάτων ὑπεροψίᾳ, καὶ τῇ αὐθαιρέτῳ πενίᾳ.

mcclxx This is the second part of Origen, *commMatt*, fr. 388 (Klostermann); the first part of this follows forthwith.

mcclxxi This is the first part of Origen, *commMatt*, fr. 388 (Klostermann); the phrase in between is the one quoted above: φησὶ γὰρ ὁ Μᾶρκος ὅτι *ἐμβλέψας αὐτῷ ὁ Ἰησοῦς ἠγάπησεν αὐτόν*.

mcclxxii Origen, *commMatt*, fr. 390 (Klostermann).

mcclxxiii 'Human condition' (ἀνθρωπίνη κατάστασις) is a distinctly Origenian expression, apparently introduced by Origen himself, which was taken up mostly by his followers, as well as by some others. Origen, *expProv*, PG.17.197.22; *frJohn*, fr. 35. Gregory of Nyssa, *Contra Eunomium*, 3.5.26 (quoting Eunomius). Didymus, *Commentarii in Job (1-4)*, cod. p. 65. Evagrius of Pontus, *Expositio in Proverbia Salomonis*, pp. 95; 117; *Scholia in Proverbia*, scholia 153; 340. Basil of Caesarea, *Sermones De Moribus*, PG.32.1241.31 (this is not actually Basil's work). Pseudo-Basil of Caesarea (*forsan* Cassian the Sabaite), *Enarratio in Prophetam Isaiam*, 1.35. Epiphanius of Salamis, *Panarion*, v. 3, p. 334. Cyril of Jerusalem, *Catecheses ad Illuminandos*, 4.18. Ephraem Syrus, *Sermo Adversus Haereticos*, p. 154. John Chrysostom, *Fragmenta in Job*, PG.64.512.8. Nilus of Ancyra, *Epistulae*, epistle 3.21. John of Damascus, *Laudatio Sanctae Martyris Barbarae*, 15. Photius, *Epistulae et Amphilochia*, 240. Gennadius Scholarius, *De Unica Via ad Salutem Hominum*, chapter 12 (bis). Bessarion, *In Calumniatorem Platonis*, 4.17.1. ACO, *Synodus Constantinopolitana et Hierosolymitana anno 536*, tome 3, p. 95.

mcclxxiv Origen, *commMatt*, fr. 390 (Klostermann), col. 1; see the similar passage in col. 2.

mcclxxv Origen, *commMatt*, fr. 392 (Klostermann); his footnote (on p. 167) informs that, in a certain codex, the foregoing text, Κοινωφελὴς ἡ ἐρώτησις ... κατὰ πενήτων ἐπιστρατεύεται, appears under the designation 'anonymous'. However, in the present codex this is attributed to Origen.

mcclxxvi Once again, we have the heretofore unknown context of Klostermann's fr. 392.

mcclxxvii Origen, *commMatt*, fr. 394 (Klostermann); likewise, its context comes to light for the first time.

mcclxxviii There is a story to be told concerning the verb τροποφορέω / ῶ. To begin with, Origen himself advises that this word was nonexistent in Greek and was coined by the Seventy, 'who did so with many other words, too' (καὶ ἐοίκασιν οἱ ἀπὸ ἑβραϊσμοῦ ἑρμηνεύσαντες, μὴ εὑρόντες τὴν λέξιν κειμένην παρ' Ἕλλησιν, ἀναπεπλακέναι ὡς ἐπ' ἄλλων πολλῶν καὶ ταύτην καὶ πεποιηκέναι). He wrote this in reference to his quoting Deut. 1:31, in which, however, the verb is τροφοφορῶ ('nourish'), in reference to God who sustained his people 'in the desert', although the alternative τροποφορῶ apparently appeared in another manuscript (ἐτροποφόρησέν σε κύριος ὁ θεός σου); see A. Ralphs – R. Hanhart, critical note on p. 286 of *Septuaginta, Editio altera*, Stuttgat, 2006. This is why Origen felt he should explain the meaning of this neologism as 'taking up the manners of' (τουτέστι τοὺς τρόπους σου ἐφόρεσεν). *homJer*, homily 18.6. As it happened, his remarks of this kind are highly authoritative and beyond dispute, yet in this case we have also the Acts, 13:18 (καὶ ὡς τεσσαρακονταετῆ χρόνον ἐτροποφόρησεν αὐτοὺς ἐν τῇ ἐρήμῳ), in which the meaning of Deut. 1:31 is reproduced by use of the verb attested by Origen, namely, τροποφορῶ.

Therefore, the term suggested God who spoke to men in a manner similar 'to that of an old man who speaks to a child in a childish manner', actually in a babyish manner (*loc. cit.* λέγοιτο ἂν τῷ γέροντι τῷ λαλοῦντι πρὸς τὸ παιδίον παιδικῶς). Henceforth, Origen used this neologism at different points of his work. *Loc. cit.*

(shortly after the previous point): τοιαῦτα γὰρ ἄλλα μυρία εὑρήσεις λεγόμενα περὶ τοῦ θεοῦ τροποφοροῦντος τὸν ἄνθρωπον. Accordingly, whenever he quoted Deut. 1:31, he used this verb. *Cels*, IV.71: *Ἐτροποφόρησέ σε κύριος ὁ θεός σου, ὡς εἴ τις τροποφορήσαι ἄνθρωπος τὸν υἱὸν αὐτοῦ.* Οἱονεὶ ἀνθρώπου τρόπους πρὸς τὸ ἀνθρώποις λυσιτελὲς φορῶν ὁ λόγος τοιαῦτα λέγει. *commMatt*, 10.14: Καὶ οὐ θαυμαστὸν εἰ ὁ σωτὴρ τοῦτο ποιεῖ, ὅπου γε καὶ ὁ τῶν ὅλων θεὸς τροποφορῶν τοὺς ἀνθρώπους *ὡς εἴ τις τροποφορήσαι ἄνθρωπος τὸν υἱὸν αὐτοῦ* πυνθάνεται. *Op. cit.* 17.4: οὗτοι γὰρ τὰ δύο τέκνα, ἃ εἶχεν ὁ *ὡς ἄνθρωπος τροποφορῶν τὸν υἱὸν αὐτοῦ* θεός. *Op. cit.* 17.6: *ἐτροποφόρησέ σε κύριος ὁ θεός σου ὡς εἴ τις τροποφορήσαι ἄνθρωπος τὸν υἱὸν αὐτοῦ.* Οὕτως γάρ, διὰ τὸ τροποφορεῖν καὶ φέρειν ἐν τῷ ἀνθρώπους ὠφελεῖν τρόπον ἀνθρώπινον τὸν ὠφελοῦντα ἀνθρώπους, ἔν τισι παραβολαῖς λέγεται εἶναι *ἄνθρωπος*.

Quite significantly, Origen reports that this is the verb Philo used in his *Allegories of the Holy Laws.* According to this testimony, Philo quoted and used this version of Deut. 1:31 in order to explain biblical instances about God behaving in anthropomorphic manner, whereas Philo also used Numbers, 23:19 (οὐχ ὡς ἄνθρωπος ὁ θεὸς διαρτηθῆναι) in order to argue that in God there is absolutely nothing resembling humans. This point is not found in Philo's extant edition of that work, although certainly he argued against any anthropomorphism being applied to God (*Legum Allegoriarum*, 1.38; 1.43; 1.88).

This is the background of Origen's *reasoned* use of this term, of which the translator of *Homilies on Jeremiah* was entirely unaware when he wrote that 'perhaps the copyist or Origen himself has mistakenly recalled Acts 13.18 or perhaps the copyist erred in the transmission of both texts', meaning Acts 13:18 and Origen's one. (See Origen, *Homilies on Jeremiah, homily 1 on Kings*, tr. by John Clark Smith, Washington, 1998, p. 198, note 70). However, the only one who 'erred' was this translator, and G.W.H. Lampe did not care to include this in his *Patristic Lexicon*, whereas Liddell and Scott explained this as 'bear with another's moods', which is only partially correct.

The fact is that verb τροποφορῶ in reference to Deuteronomium 1:31 was used by Didymus, *Commentarii in Psalmos 29-34*, cod. p. 152. Later writers of monastic texts felt at liberty to apply the verb to different contexts: Pseudo-Macarius, *Sermones 1-22, 24-27*, homilies 9.2 (which is Ephraem Syrus, *De Patientia*, p. 313); 27.7. Also, Hesychius of Jerusalem, *Commentarius Brevis*, on Psalms 43:2; 77:40; *Commentarius in Odas*, ode 2.18; (all of the instances are remarks on Deuteronomium 1:31). Theodore Studites, *Epistulae*, epistle 279; *Parva Catechesis*, catechesis 27, line 46; catechesis 80, line 22. Ignatius Diaconus (or, Ignatius Melodus, Nicaea, Constantinople, eighth / ninth century), *Vita Gregorii Decapolitae*, Proem.

Although writing a lexicon, Photius listed the term alone without providing any explanation of this. *Lexicon*, letter tau, p. 607. Finally, the author of *Suda* used the term, yet not out of his own: in a lemma for *σκύμνος* (lion's 'whelp'), he simply copied a passage from an anonymous commentator of Aristophanes' *Frogs.* See *Scholia in Ranas* (*scholia vetera*), on verse 1432 (ἦν δ᾽ ἐκτραφῇ τις, τοῖς τρόποις ὑπηρετεῖν). However, when the same author of *Suda* had to make the verb τροποφορεῖν a lemma (letter tau, entry 1057), he just listed this without any explanation, probably because Photius (on whom this author frequently drew) had done so, too.

mcclxxix Origen, *commMatt*, fr. 395 (Klostermann).

mcclxxx Klostermann footnotes that he found the text *Ἀμπελῶνα* δὲ λέγει ... ὁ παρὼν βίος being 'Unattributed' in two codices, and ascribed to Chrysostom in one codex. However, the expression 'the constitution of piousness' (τὸ τῆς εὐσεβείας πολίτευμα) showed for the first time in Eusebius' texts, and we have seen that he used to take up Origen's expressions. This expression, 'constitution of piousness', means conduct of life in accordance with Scripture. Cf. Eusebius, *Demonstratio Evangelica*, 1.2.10: καὶ τοῦτ' ἂν εἴη ὁ χριστιανισμός, οὔτε ἑλληνισμός τις ὢν οὔτε ἰουδαϊσμός, ἀλλὰ τὸ μεταξὺ τούτων παλαιότατον εὐσεβείας πολίτευμα, καὶ ἀρχαιοτάτη μέν τις φιλοσοφία πλὴν ἀλλὰ νεωστὶ πᾶσιν ἀνθρώποις τοῖς καθ' ὅλης τῆς οἰκουμένης νενομοθετημένη. *Op. cit.* 4.17.21: τροπωσάμενος τοὺς αἰχμαλώτους ἡμᾶς οἰκείους αὐτοῦ κατηρτίσατο, καὶ ἐξ ἡμῶν αὐτῶν, ὡς ἂν ἐκ λίθων ζώντων, τὸν οἶκον τοῦ θεοῦ καὶ τὸ τῆς εὐσεβείας πολίτευμα ἐστήσατο. *Op. cit.* 5.4.2: Τέως μὲν ταῦτα ὁ τῶν ὅλων ποιητὴς θεὸς περί τινος βασιλέως καὶ σωτῆρος μέλλοντος οἰκοδομεῖν τὸ τῆς εὐσεβείας πολίτευμα λυτρώσασθαί ‹τε› τὴν ἐπισυμβᾶσαν ἀνθρώποις ὑπὸ τῆς δαιμονικῆς πλάνης αἰχμαλωσίαν διὰ τοῦ προφήτου θεσπίζει. *Commentaria in Psalmos*, PG.23.1257.44-46: τὴν ἐν ἀνθρώποις Χριστοῦ ἐπιφάνειαν, αἰτίαν ἐσομένην τοῦ ἀνοικοδομηθῆναι τὴν Σιών, τουτέστι τοῦ ἀνεῳχθῆναι τὸ τῆς εὐσεβείας πολίτευμα. Moreover, the same expression shows in a series of comments on the Psalms, which has been attributed to Didymus alongside his own commentary on on the Psalms, but I have argued several times that internal evidence points to several of them having been composed either earlier by Origen himself, or later, by the moderate Origenist Cassian the Sabaite. Didymus, *frPs(al)*, fr. 969: τὰ περὶ τῆς Σιὼν ἐπηγγελμένα. ... ἔνθα δὴ γενόμενος, μή μοι τὴν ἐπὶ γῆς πόλιν ὑπολάμβανε μηδὲ τὴν ἐπίγειον Ἱερουσαλὴμ νόμιζε δηλοῦσθαι ἀλλὰ τοῦ τῆς εὐσεβείας πολιτεύματος τὴν ἀνανέωσιν. Little wonder that this comment was copied by someone who wished to represent himself as 'John Chrysostom', that is, the author who drew on Origen systematically and conveniently. Pseudo-John Chrysostom, *In Psalmos 101-107*, PG.55.638.31-37. In view of this, the passage attributed to Theodore of Heraclea is one more case of attributing Origen's texts to him, and, anyway, its Origenistic tenor and content is striking. In any event, this was all that literature made of Origen's expression 'the constitution of piousness', wherefore tracing this back to him is plausible and all but difficult.

mcclxxxi Theodore of Heraclea, *frMatt*, part of fr. 108. However, against this 'fragment' we now have Origen's text along with its context.

mcclxxxii See also, Οἰκοδεσπότης ἐστὶν ὁ Χριστός· οἶκος, τὸ ὅλον τῆς χωρητικῆς φύσεως also in footnote to Klostermann's fr. 395, p. 167; the same in fr. 400, p. 169. Cf. *commMatt*, 10.15; 15.32-34.

mcclxxxiii Cf. Origen, on John, 8:42, 'I came out and have come from God' (cf. 13:3; 16:47). *commJohn*, XX.18.153-155; XXXII.3.35.

mcclxxxiv Cf. Origen, *commMatt*, 11.1: *Ὀψίας δὲ γενομένης προσῆλθον αὐτῷ οἱ μαθηταὶ αὐτοῦ*, τουτέστιν ἐπὶ συντελείᾳ τοῦ αἰῶνος, καθ' ὃν ἔστιν εὐκαίρως εἰπεῖν τὸ *ἐσχάτη ὥρα ἐστίν*, ἐν τῇ Ἰωάννου ἐπιστολῇ κείμενον. *Op. cit.*, 15.35: Μετὰ ταῦτα *ὀψίας γενομένης*, τουτέστι τῆς συντελείας τῆς τοῦ αἰῶνος. *schLuc*, PG.17.361.20-21: Ὀψία δὲ ἡ συντέλεια τοῦ αἰῶνος, ὅτε οἱ ἐργάται *οἱ ἔσχατοι πρῶτοι* τὸν μισθὸν λαμβάνουσιν.

mcclxxxv Origen, *commMatt*, fr. 400 (Klostermann).

mcclxxxvi Matt. 20:23; cf. Mark, 10:40.

mcclxxxvii Origen, *commMatt*, fr. 404 (Klostermann).

mcclxxxviii Origen, *commMatt*, fr. 413 (Klostermann). Now the ensuing context of this 'fragment' comes to light.

mcclxxxix One of Origen's fundamental doctrines was that God who appeared and spoke in the Biblical history was God the Logos.

mccxc Cf. Origen, *frLuc*, fr. 204 (on Luke, 13:6): Διαγράψωμεν οὖν καὶ ὡς ἐν συντόμῳ τὸν λόγον. Συκῆ ἤτοι ἡ πόλις Ἱερουσαλὴμ ἢ ἡ τῶν Ἰουδαίων συναγωγὴ ἢ ἡ ἀνθρωπότης πᾶσα· οἰκοδεσπότης, οὗ τινος καὶ ἡ συκῆ ἦν, ὁ θεὸς καὶ πατὴρ ἤτοι αὐτὸς ὁ σωτήρ· ὁ δὲ ἀμπελουργὸς ὁ υἱὸς τοῦ θεοῦ.

mccxci This metaphor of Origen was taken up by Christian theologians of the next thousand years. Didymus, *frPs(al)*, fr. 526: Πεινᾷ ὁ σωτὴρ τὴν τινων σωτηρίαν. John Chrysostom, *In Epistulam ad Romanos*, PG.60.454.5-7: Ἐνταῦθα γὰρ διψῇ, ἐνταῦθα πεινᾷ. διψῇ δέ, ἐπειδὴ τὴν σὴν διψῇ σωτηρίαν. Maximus Confessor, *Quaestiones et Dubia*, 45: Πεινᾷ γὰρ ἀεὶ ὁ λόγος τὴν ἡμῶν σωτηρίαν μετὰ τῶν ἑπομένων αὐτῷ. Theodore Studites, *Epistulae*, epistle 483: πεινᾷ γὰρ τὴν ἑκάστου σωτηρίαν καὶ οἱονεὶ ἐπισκέπτεται τὴν συκῆν· κἂν μὲν εὕρῃ καρπὸν ἐν αὐτῇ θεόβλαστον, ταύτῃ τρέφεται, εἰ δ' οὖν, ἐπικεκατάραται, καθάπερ ἱστορεῖ τὸ εὐαγγέλιον. *Sermones Catecheseos Magnae*, catechesis 86, p. 40 (the same, in *Μεγάλη Κατήχησις*, catechesis 104, pp. 762-3): πεινᾷ ἡμῶν τὴν σωτηρίαν ὁ ἀγαθὸς δεσπότης. καὶ εἰ μὲν εὕροι, εὐφραίνεται ἀπογευόμενος τοῦ καρποῦ, εἰ δὲ μή γε, ὡς τὴν ἀκαρπίαν τῆς συκῆς ὑπὸ κατάραν ἵστησιν. Symeon the New Theologian, *Catecheses*, oration 9: Διψᾷ γὰρ ἀληθῶς τὴν σωτηρίαν ἑνὸς ἑκάστου ἡμῶν καὶ πεινᾷ. Eustathius of Thessaloniki, *Sermones*, oration 9, p. 158: πεινᾷ τὴν ἡμῶν σωτηρίαν ὁ πάντων τροφεύς.

mccxcii This is criticism of Docetists, which we learn from Hippolytus recounting their explanation of this parable. *Refutatio Omnium Haeresium*, 8.8.3-4: καρπὸν ζητούμενον, ἐφ' ὃν ἦλθεν ὁ ζητῶν, φησί, τρίς, καὶ οὐχ εὗρε· διὸ ‹καὶ› κατηράσατο, φησίν, τῇ συκῇ, ὅτι τὸν γλυκὺν ἐκεῖνον καρπὸν οὐχ εὗρεν ἐν αὐτῇ [καρπὸν ζητούμενον]. Τοιούτου δὲ ὄντος, ὡς εἰπεῖν τύπῳ, καὶ τηλικούτου, μικροῦ καὶ ‹παμ›μεγέθους, κατ' ἐκείνους τοῦ θεοῦ, γέγονεν ὁ κόσμος, ὡς ἐκείνοις δοκεῖ.

mccxciii Origen, *frLuc*, fr. 204.

mccxciv Cyril of Alexandria, *commLuc*, PG.72.764.40-52.

mccxcv 'Punishing power' (κολαστικὴ δύναμις) is one more expression introduced by Origen and taken up by his followers, and then by others. See Eusebius, *Demonstratio Evangelica*, 7.1.64; *In Isaiam*, 1.21; 1.59; 2.7; *Commentaria in Psalmos*, PG.23.1073.49. Basil of Caesarea, *Homiliae super Psalmos*, PG.29.248.2. Didymus, *Commentarii in Psalmos 40-44.4*, cod. p. 309; *In Genesim*, cod. p. 115. John Chrysostom, *De Lazaro*, PG.48.968.48. Also in *frPs(al)*, 284 (but numerous instances which are hardly coincidental suggest that part of this commentary was probably written by Cassian the Sabaite drawing on Origen; see my *Scholia in Apocalypsin*, pp. 10; 34-39; 80-81; 89). Theodoret, *commCant*, PG.81.92.26; *commProphXII*, PG.81.1865.16. Procopius of Gaza, *Commentarii in Isaiam*, pp. 1861; 1928; 2029. Pseudo-Basil of Caesarea (*forsan* Cassian the Sabaite), *Enarratio in Prophetam Isaiam*, 5.118; 9.230. Photius, *Fragmenta in Epistulam ii ad Corinthios*, p. 603. Michael Psellus, *Theologica*, opusculum 32, line 152. It is noteworthy that Plotinus considered different kinds of 'fall', such as 'flight from God' according to Empedocles and wandering, and 'sin upon which judgment comes' (ἡ ἁμαρτία, ἐφ' ᾗ ἡ δίκη), which he regarded as 'an eternal law of Nature' (ἀναγκαῖον ἀϊδίως φύσεως νόμῳ), and concluded that 'the word *judgment* indicates what happens by divine decree' and 'the boundless kind of wickedness is judged to deserve greater punishment under the dominion of chastising daemons' (ἐπιστασίᾳ τινυμένων δαιμόνων). *Enneades*, IV.8.5. Once again, we come upon a vocabulary common to him and Origen, who described divine judgment as 'eternal law'. *commJohn*, XX.39.375: καὶ νομιστέον γε τοῦτο δόγμα εἶναι καὶ νόμον αἰώνιον.

mccxcvi See Origen, *infra*, folio 168r: ἵνα τῆς τιμωρητικῆς αὐτοῦ δυνάμεως ἀπόδειξιν παράσχῃ.

mccxcvii See further in the same passage: διὰ τὸ ἐπιδεῖξαι, ὡς προέφην, τὴν τιμωρητικὴν αὐτοῦ δύναμιν· οὐδὲ γὰρ αὐτὸς ἠγνόει πότε ἦν ὁ καιρὸς τοῦ καρποῦ αὐτῆς.

mccxcviii *Catena in Matthaeum*, p. 170. This is unattributed (the style is very much like Chrysostom; cf. John Chrysostom, *In Matthaeum*, PG.58.633.46-634.4) and its author endorses Origen's idea that Jesus did this miracle in order to demonstrate his 'punishing power', but rejects the notion of fig tree standing for the 'unfaithful synagogue of the Jews'. This is certainly a text not by Cyril of Alexandria, since he did maintain that the fig tree betokened 'the unfaithful synagogue of the Jews'. Cf. *commProphXII*, v. 1, p. 203; v. 2, p. 346; *Fragmenta in Canticum Canticorum*, PG.69.1285.28-29; so his passage excerpted by Procopius of Gaza, *Catena in Canticum Canticorum*, p. 1616. The same exegesis was employed by Pseudo-Caesarius (Cassian the Sabaite), *Quaestiones et Responsiones*, chapter 203. Anastasius of Sinai, *In Hexaemeron*, book 11, lines 47-49; 65-67. Photius, *Homiliae*, homily 6, p. 65. Nicephorus Callistus Xanthopulus, *HE*, 1.27, lines 86-88.

mccxcix This is an editorial mistake; for πείνα is not the same word as πεῖνα ('hunger'): πείνα means 'pearl ear ring', which is irrelevant to this point.

mccc Origen, *commMatt*, fr. 414 (Klostermann). This passage is part of the text *Catena in Marcum*, pp. 390 ff and it is attributed to Origen in at least five other codices (Klostermann, p. 173), which means that the entire section in this *Catena in Marcum* is Origen's text.

mccci No doubt, this is an editorial mistake: this should be ἄλλος, meaning 'another one [explains]', namely, Origen.

mcccii *Catena in Marcum*, p. 392 (anonymous).

mccciii Cf. Nicolas V (1397-1455, Pope 1447-1455, born Tommaso Parentucelli), *Epistula ad Imperatorum Romanorum Constantinum Translata De Voce Latina in Vocem Graecam Theodoro Gazae*, pp. 60-61: Εὖ μὲν γὰρ πάντα συνίεμεν, ἀνεχόμεθα δὲ ἀποβλέποντες εἰς Ἰησοῦν τὸν ἀΐδιον ἀρχιερέα καὶ κύριον, ὃς τὴν ἄκαρπον ἐκείνην συκῆν διατηρῆσαι ἄχρι τρίτου ἔτους ἐκέλευσε τοῦ γεωργοῦ, ἀποκόπτειν ἤδη τὸ φυτὸν ἀξιοῦντος διὰ τὸ μηδένα φέρειν καρπόν.

mccciv Cf. Origen, *frLuc*, fr. 204 (on Luke, 13:6): τρίτον δὲ λέγει ἐληλυθέναι αὐτόν, τοῦτ' ἔστι διὰ Μωϋσέως, διὰ τῶν προφητῶν, δι' ἑαυτοῦ· ἤτοι πρῶτον ἔτος, καθ' ὃ πρῶτον τῷ Ἀδὰμ ἐνετείλατο λέγων *ἀπὸ παντὸς ξύλου τοῦ ἐν τῷ παραδείσῳ βρώσει φάγῃ* καὶ τὰ ἑξῆς· δεύτερον, καθ' ὃ ἐν τῷ νόμῳ διὰ Μωϋσέως τῷ Ἰσραὴλ δέδωκεν ἐντολάς· τρίτον, καθ' ὃ αὐτὸς δι' ἑαυτοῦ ἐν τῷ εὐαγγελίῳ τὸν τέλειον δέδωκε νόμον.

mccciv John Chrysostom, *In Matthaeum*, PG.58.633.41-55.

mcccvi Cyril of Alexandria endorsed Origen's idea that Jesus aimed at demonstrating 'his punitive power'.

mcccvii Apollinaris, *frMatt*, fr. 109.

mcccviii By this Origen suggests that the idea of 'old Jerusalem' identified with the 'fig tree' was maintained by someone prior to himself.

mcccix Cf. Origen, *commJohn*, XIII.16.95: εἰπὼν ὄρος μὲν τὸν διάβολον λέγεσθαι ἢ τὸν κόσμον αὐτοῦ, ἐπείπερ μέρος ἓν ὁ διάβολος ὅλης τῆς ὕλης, φησίν, ἦν, ὁ δὲ κόσμος τὸ σύμπαν τῆς κακίας ὄρος. *frJer*, fr. 41: ἀναγωγῆς δὲ λόγῳ καὶ ὁ διάβολος ὄρος ὠνόμασται, ὡς ἐν τῷ Ζαχαρίᾳ. *τίς εἶ σύ, τὸ ὄρος τὸ μέγα τὸ πρὸ προσώπου Ζοροβάβελ;* [Zachariah, 4:7] καὶ περὶ τοῦ ἔχοντος *κωφὸν καὶ ἄλαλον* δαιμόνιον ἔλεγεν ὁ σωτήρ. *ἐὰν ἔχητε πίστιν ὡς κόκκον σινάπεως, ἐρεῖτε τῷ ὄρει τούτῳ. μετάβηθι, καὶ μεταβήσεται.* Ὄρος οὖν ὁ διάβολος ἀπὸ τῆς ἰδίας διεφθαρμένον κακίας καὶ διαφθεῖρον τοὺς ὅσοι φρονοῦσι τὰ γήϊνα. *homJer*, homily 12.12: Ταῦτα πάντα ὄρη ἐστὶ φωτεινά, καὶ περὶ τούτων νομίζω λελέχθαι ἐν τοῖς Ψαλμοῖς. *οἱ θεμέλιοι αὐτοῦ ἐν τοῖς ὄρεσι τοῖς ἁγίοις* [Psalm 86:1]. Ποῖα δὲ ὄρη σκοτεινά; οἱ τὰ ὑψώματα ἐπαίροντες κατὰ τῆς γνώσεως τοῦ θεοῦ [2 Cor. 10:5]. Ὁ διάβολος ὄρος σκοτεινόν ἐστιν, οἱ ἄρχοντες τοῦ αἰῶνος τούτου οἱ καταργούμενοι [cf. 1 Cor. 2:6] ὄρη εἰσὶ σκοτεινά, καὶ τὸ δαιμόνιον ὁ σεληνιασμὸς ὄρος ἦν καὶ σκοτεινὸν ὄρος ἦν, περὶ οὗ ἔλεγεν ὁ σωτήρ. *ἐρεῖτε τῷ ὄρει τούτῳ* [Matt. 17:20].

mccccx Origen, *commMatt*, fr. 415 (Klostermann).

mccccxi The term ἀκενόδοξος (one 'without vain conceit', meaning one who does not seek vain glory) was a neologism introduced by Marcus Aurelius. This was hardly necessary, since the synonymous epithet ἄτυφος ('not puffed up') was already there: it had been used since Plato, and then by Cleanthes and later still by Plutarch. The second author who took up ἀκενόδοξος was Origen (who had read Marcus' *Meditations*) and used this in his commentary on Matthew. As it happened with similar instances that we have perused, despite the secular origin of the term, this was used exclusively by Christian authors, with one significant exception, namely, Origen's admirer, Porphyry. Marcus Aurelius, *Τὰ εἰς Ἑαυτόν*, 1.16.1: τὸ ἀκενόδοξον περὶ τὰς δοκούσας τιμάς. *Op. cit.* 6.30.2: τὸ μειλίχιον καὶ τὸ ἀκενόδοξον. *Op. cit.* 8.1.1: Καὶ τοῦτο πρὸς τὸ ἀκενόδοξον φέρει. Origen, *schMatt*, PG.17.293.49-51: πάντας οὖν ἐθεράπευσε, τὴν παναλκῆ αὑτοῦ ἐνδεικνύμενος δύναμιν. Πλὴν ὑποστέλλει μὴ δημοσιεύεσθαι, ὡς ἐπιεικὴς καὶ ἀκενόδοξος. Porphyry, *Quaestionum Homericarum ad Odysseam Pertinentium Reliquiae*, comm. on Odyssey, III.411: φασὶν οὖν ὅτι ἁπλοϊκῶς καὶ ἀκενοδόξως τότε διέκειντο καὶ οὐκ ἔχοντες ἔπαρσιν. Subsequently, a long series of Christian authors made much of this, and most of them did so in the context of Origen's point (it was out of modesty that Jesus bid his disciples not to make some of his miracles public). Athanasius, *Vita Antonii*, 30. Pseudo-Basil of Caesarea, *Sermo 11*, PG.31.632.25. Asterius of Antioch, *Commentarii in Psalmos*, 26.4. Pseudo-Macarius, *Sermones*, 7.4. Cyril of Jerusalem, *Homilia in Paralyticum Juxta Piscinam Jacentem*, 16. Pseudo-Amphilochius of Iconium, *Oratio in Mesopentecosten*, line 97. Evagrius of Pontus, *De Vitiis Quae Opposita Sunt Virtutibus*, PG.79: 1141.8; 1144.42. Ephraem Syrus, *De Virtute, Ad Novitium Monachum*, 1; *In illud: Attende Tibi Ipsi*, 2, line 32; *In Sermonem, Quem Dixit Dominus, Quod: In hoc Mundo Pressuram Habebitis, et De Perfectione Hominis*, pp. 349; 397; *De Abstinendo ab Omni Consuetudine Perniciosa, et De Continentia*, p. 234; *De Virtutibus et Passionibus*, p. 393; *Fragmenta Paraenetica*, 2. As it happened with other loans from Origen, John Chrysostom used this profusely, too. *In Matthaeum*, PG.57: 282.12; 329.51; 374.1; 379.25; *In Joannem*, PG.59.344; *In Acta Apostolorum*, PG.60: 179.48; 185.29; *et passim*. Cyril of Alexandria, *De Exitu Animi*, PG.77.1088.47. Diadochus of Photike, *Capita Centum De Perfectione Spirituali*, 9; 11; 69. Also in catenae, and naturally in the *Catena in Matthaeum*, pp. 57; 70; also, *Catena in Joannem*, p. 318; *Catena in Acta*, p. 238. Olympiodorus, the deacon of Alexandria, *Commentarii in Job*, p. 136; *Commentarii in Ecclesiasten*, PG.93.528.47. Maximus Confessor, *Quaestiones et Dubia*, 90. John Climacus, *Scala Paradisi*, (chapter / col.) 3.668; 4.725; 22.956; 26.1017; 29.1149. John of Damascus, *Dialectica*, 1; *Laudatio Sancti Johannis Chrysostomi*, 12.

mccccxii Cf. *supra*, folio 136v: Ἐδύναντο γάρ, εἰ ἤθελον, καὶ ὄρη μετακινῆσαι· ὅπερ, εἰ καὶ ἐγένετο, οὐκ ἐγράφη ἢ ὅτι αὐτοὶ οὐκ ἠθέλησαν ποιῆσαι.

mccccxiii See the rare adjective περίαυτος ('boastful', 'swollen-headed', 'egotistical') used by Origen's followers, and then by others. This word is not included in any lexicon of Greek, either ancient or modern. See this in Gregory of Nyssa, *Contra Eunomium*, 1.1.25. Didymus, *Commentarii in Job* (*7.20c-11*), cod. p. 260. Julian the Arian, *Commentarius in Job*, p. 2 (using the even more rare -and also unknown to lexica- adjective αὐτεπαίνετος, self-laudatory, boastful): οὐκ ἦν περίαυτος ὁ ἀνὴρ οὐδ᾽ αὐτεπαίνετος. *Op. cit.* p. 122. ταῦτα οὐχ ὡς περίαυτος λέγει. *Op. cit.* p. 197: ταῦτα πάντα ἀπαριθμεῖται ὁ ἅγιος οὐχ ὡς περίαυτός τις καὶ φανητιῶν ('exhibitionist', also unknown to L&S). Cyril of Alexandria, *commLuc*, PG.72.677.42.

mcccxiv With and after Herod, the Jewish archpriests were autocratically chosen by the Romans for a sum of money, and they remained in office for as long as the Romans wanted them to be there. Theodoret, *Interpretatio in Danielem*, PG.81.1477.40-49: Ἐν δὲ τούτῳ τῷ χρόνῳ, μετὰ τὴν Ὑρκανοῦ, φημί, ἀναίρεσιν, μέχρι τῆς τοῦ Σωτῆρος ἡμῶν ἐπιφανείας, παρανόμως λοιπὸν οἱ ἀρχιερεῖς ἐγίνοντο. Τοῦ γὰρ νόμου κελεύοντος διὰ βίου τοὺς ἀρχιερέας ἱερατεύειν, καὶ μετὰ τὴν τελευτὴν τοὺς διαδόχους λαμβάνειν, Ἡρώδης, καὶ οἱ μετ᾽ ἐκεῖνον Ῥωμαῖοι, ὠνητὰς τὰς ἀρχιερωσύνας ποιησάμενοι, συχνὰς αὐτῶν ἐποιοῦντο διαδοχάς. ἐνίους δὲ οὐδὲ ἐκ τοῦ ἱερατικοῦ γένους καταγομένους ἀρχιερέας προεχειρίζοντο. This was copied by Nicolas Hydruntinus, *Disputatio Contra Judaeos*, p. 106. Theodoret quoted some passages from Josephus (*Antiquitates Judaicae*, 18.26; 18.34; 20.247-9). See also, Ammonius, the presbyter of Alexandria, *Fragmenta in Joannem*, fr. 392: Ὅτε ἐγένοντο ὠνηταὶ αἱ ἱερωσύναι, οὐκέτι τὸν ἅπαντα χρόνον ἑαυτῶν οἱ ἱερεῖς ἱεράτευον οὔτε κατὰ γένος, ἀλλ᾽ οἷς ἐβούλοντο οἱ Ῥωμαῖοι ἐδίδουν αὐτὴν διαδεχόμενοι αὐτούς, ὅτε ἤθελον.

mcccxv This is in effect part of Klostermann's fragment quoted forthwith.

mcccxvi Origen, *commMatt*, fr. 416 (Klostermann).

mcccxvii The expression φαντασίαν ἐμποιεῖν (meaning, an image or impression made upon a man's perception, following sensation caused by an external stimulus) comes from Aristotle. Cf. *Metaphysica*, 1024b24; 1025a5; *Meteorologica*, 372b8; *Sophisticos Elenchos*, 165b25. This has always been conspicuously absent from the vast majority of Christian theologians, except for Origen and some later ones who wrote (or, essayed to write) in Origen's spirit. Pseudo-Gregory Thaumaturgus, *Ad Tatianum De Anima per Capita Disputatio*, PG.10: 1140.26; 1144.59. Basil of Caesarea, *Homiliae in Hexaemeron*, 6.4. Pseudo-Maximus Confessor, *Opusculum De Anima*, 1; 7. Nevertheless, use by Greeks was not frequent either. Polyaenus, *Strategemata*, 2.4.1. Cleomedes, *Caelestia*, 2.6.

My conjecture is that Origen would have taken this up not directly from Aristotle works, but from such authors as Galen, Ptolemay, and Sextus Empiricus, since he had read Aristotle's works through the commentaries of Alexander of Aphrodisias, in whose extant works Aristotle's expression does not appear. Cf. Galen, *De Victu Attenuante*, 17-18: κατὰ ταὐτὰ δὲ κἂν εὐωδίαν τινὰ κατὰ τὴν ὀσμὴν ἔχον ἀρώματος ἐμποιῇ τῇ γεύσει φαντασίαν, ἀνάγκη καὶ τοῦτο θερμὸν μὲν εἶναι τὴν δύναμιν, ἀλλ᾽ ἧττον τῶν δακνόντων τε καὶ διαβιβρωσκόντων καὶ θερμαινόντων ἐπιφανῶς. *De Methodo Medendi*, p. 992: οὗτος ὁ λόγος ἀεί σοι μνημονευέσθω, διαφέρων εἰς τὴν τῶν ὀνομάτων χρῆσιν, ἐξαπατῆσαι δυναμένων τοὺς ἀσκέπτους ἐμποιῆσαί τε διαφωνίας φαντασίαν. Ptolemy of Alexandria, *Harmonica*, 2.6: ὅθεν ἐκείνη μὲν οὐκ ἐμποιεῖ ταῖς αἰσθήσεσι φαντασίαν ἑτερότητος τῆς κατὰ τὴν δύναμιν, ὑφ᾽ ἧς κινεῖται τὸ ἦθος. Sextus Empiricus, *Adversus Rhetores*, 2.63: ὅπερ ἐναργῶς τε ἀληθές ἐστι καὶ ἀληθοῦς ἐμποιοῦν φαντασίαν ἐπισπᾶται ἡμᾶς εἰς συγκατάθεσιν. *Adversus Dogmaticos 2* (*Adversus Logicos 2*), 8.410: καὶ κατὰ τοῦτο ἐδύνατο φαντασίαν ἐμποιεῖν τῷ παιδί. Origen, *commJohn*, X.4.17: καὶ τὸν θεὸν ὑπολαμβάνοντι κατὰ περιγραφὴν εἶναι ἐν τόπῳ, μὴ δυνάμενον τῷ αὐτῷ πλείονας ἑαυτοῦ ἐμποιῆσαι φαντασίας πλείοσιν ἐν πλείοσιν τόποις καὶ πλείονα ἅμα λέγειν. *Philocalia*, 15.15: καὶ καταληπτικὴν ἐμποιῆσαι περὶ αὐτῆς φαντασίαν.

mcccxviii Origen, *commMatt*, fr. 417 (Klostermann). The editor included in brackets the first and last words from a passage which runs parallel to John Chrysostom, *In Matthaeum*, PG.58.634.49-635.17.

mcccxix Unlike what happened with the term ἀκενόδοξος that we just saw, the adverb ὁμοιοτρόπως ('in the same way', 'likewise') came from the Greek literature of old. Significantly though this was used by Origen and his most renowned followers, yet not by Chrysostom and Cyril of Alexandria, or by those who normally picked up Origen's terms and used them every now and then. Cf. Thucydides, *Historiae*, 6.20.3. Philolaus, *Testimonia*, fr. 21 (*apud* Pseudo-Plutarch, *Placita Philosophorum*, p. 896A, quoted also by Eusebius, *Praeparatio Evangelica*, 15.58.2). Aristotle, *Metaphysica*, 1003b4; 1008a10; *De Anima*, 404b21; *De Generatione Animalium*, 755b28; *De Insomniis*, 461a29; *De Interpretatione*, 21b26. Anaximenes of Lampsacus, *Ars Rhetorica*, 1.24; 2.13; 3.2; 3.5; 4.1; 5.4; 17.2; 18.5; 28.3; 32.7; 34.9; 35.10; 35.16; 36.30; 37.2. Xenocrates, *Testimonia, Doctrina et Fragmenta*, fr. 260 (*apud* Themistius, *paraphrAnim*, p. 11). Philo, *De Aeternitate Mundi*, 20. Nicomachus, *Introductio Arithmetica*, 2.6.6; 2.10.2. Cassius Dio, *Historiae Romanae*, 50.32.2. Alexander of Aphrodisias, *commMetaph*, p. 242. Pseudo-Alexander of Aphrodisias, *De Anima Libri Mantissa*, p. 142. Pseudo-Galen, *Prognostica De Decubitu ex Mathematica Scientia*, pp. 572; 573; 526. Origen, *frJohn*, fr. 20; *Selecta in Jesu Nave*, PG.12.820.37. Gregory of Nyssa, *In Christi Resurrectionem Oratio i*, p. 292; *In Inscriptiones Psalmorum*, p. 38; *Contra Eunomium*, 1.1.465; 2.1.73; 3.1.85; 3.7.55; *Refutatio Confessionis Eunomii*, 71; 155; *In Canticum Canticorum*, p. 304; *Dialogus De Anima et Resurrectione*, PG.46.76.9; *In illud: Tunc et Ipse Filius*, p. 11; *Oratio Catechetica*, Prologue and chapter 12. Pseudo-Basil of Caesarea (*forsan* Cassian the Sabaite), *Enarratio in Prophetam Isaiam*, 2.88. Cassian the Sabaite (Pseudo-Didymus), *De Trinitate*, PG.39: 628.15; 724.42. Procopius of Gaza, *Commentarii in Isaiam*, p. 1888. Anastasius of Sinai, *In Hexaemeron*, book 7, line 308. Photius, *Homiliae*, homily 9, p. 92. Later commentators took their cue from Aristotle. Ammonius of Alexandria, *commDeInterpr*, p. 220. Simplicius (or, whoever the author), *commAnim*, p. 29. John Philoponus, *commAnalPr*, p. 468; *commGenCorr*, p. 109; *commAnim*, pp. 79. Asclepius of Tralles, *commMetaph*, p. 229.

mcccxx This is one more neologism that Origen took up from Galen. By the term διλήμματος (masculine adjective) he bespeaks the possibility of a term or a propositional postulation being understood in a twofold sense, hence, an ambiguous or two-handled one. Galen, *Institutio Logica*, 6.5: συλλογισμοὶ δὲ ἀλλήλοις ἀντιστρέφουσιν οἱ διλήμματοι ὧν ἓν λῆμμα κοινόν, τὸ δὲ λοιπὸν καθ' ἕτερον ἀντίκειται τῷ τοῦ λοιποῦ συμπεράσματι. Then, Pseudo-Hermogenes considered this technical term in an *ad hoc* section entitled *Περὶ διλημμάτου*, in the treatise *Περὶ Εὑρέσεως*, 4.6 (using the term at eight points). Subsequently, Gregory of Nyssa took this term up from Origen. *Contra Eunomium*, 1.1.492; 2.1.376; 2.1.463; 3.7.16; *Refutatio Confessionis Eunomii*, 39; *Ad Ablabium Quod Non Sint Tres Dei*, p. 38. Olympiodorus of Alexandria, *commPhaed*, 6.10. Anonymous, *Scholia ad Hermogenis Librum Περὶ Στάσεων*, pp. 635-636. Subsequently, the term was included in lexica as a technical one used by orators. Anonymous, *Συναγωγὴ Λέξεων Χρησίμων* (*versio antiqua*), letter delta, lemma 296 & *Collectio Verborum Utilium e Differentibus Rhetoribus et Sapientibus Multis* (*recensio aucta e cod. Coislin. 345*), entry pi, p. 337: διλήμματον. διχῶς νοούμενον. ἔστι δὲ καὶ σχῆμα ῥητορικόν. Likewise, *op. cit.*, letter pi, lemma 337. Photius took up this definition to the letter, if partially. *Lexicon*, letter delta, entry 613: διλήμματον. διχῶς νοούμενον. The *Suda* (letter delta, entry 1121) copied this from Photius. Also, Photius, *op. cit.*, letter pi, pp. 416 & 657 (taken up from the foregoing lexicon and then copied also by *Suda*, letter pi, entry 1094, and by the *Etymologicum Magnum*, p. 699). This was also copied later by Pseudo-Zonaras, *Lexicon*, letter delta, p. 526. Moreover, Photius, *Bibliotheca*, Codex 247, p. 412a; *De Spiritu Sancti Mystagogiae*, 76. Michael Psellus, *Theologica*, opusculum 2 (lines 11 & 80); opusculum 53, lines 14 & 19; opusculum 54, line 2; opusculum 55, line 14; opusculum 57, lines 24 & 57; opusculum 58, line 33. Here is his poetic definition of the technical term: Τὸ δὲ διλήμματόν ἐστι σχῆμα δριμύ τι λόγου, ὅταν ἐρώτημα τεμὼν εἰς τμήματά πως δύο, ὧν ἕκαστον ἀμφίκρημνον, ἐχθρῶν τινων πυνθάνῃ. *Poemata*, poem 7, lines 307-309. Eustathius of Thessaloniki, *Commentarii ad Homeri Iliadem*, v. 1, p. 594; v. 2, p. 724. John Tzetzes, *Chiliades*, chilias 11, history 369, line 301. Therefore, it turns out that, up until the ninth century, the Christian authors that used this sophisticated rhetorical term were only Origen and Gregory of Nyssa.

mcccxxi Cf. folio 47r: τὰ χρήματα ἀλλοτριοῖ Θεοῦ. Folio 147r: δηλοῖ τὴν ἀφαίρεσιν τῶν ἀγαθῶν καὶ τὴν ἀπὸ Θεοῦ ἀλλοτρίωσιν. Folio 198v: Διχοτομία δέ ἐστιν ἡ ἀπὸ τοῦ Πνεύματος εἰς τὸ διηνεκὲς τῆς ψυχῆς ἀλλοτρίωσις. See pp. 440-441, endnote cdlxxvii.

mcccxxii Origen, *commMatt*, fr. 419 (Klostermann).

mcccxxiii Origen, *apud Catena in Matthaeum*, pp. 173-174.

mcccxxiv Origen, *commMatt*, fr. 418 (Klostermann). This is an autobiographical statement reflecting Origen's last part of life at Tyre in loneliness, being on bad terms with the local bishop, and excoriating the putrefaction of the clergy.

mcccxxv Anaxagoras taught (and Euripides followed suit) that 'phenomena are only the external manifestation of things that are concealed' (ὄψις τῶν ἀδήλων τὰ φαινόμενα) – and those 'things' were the Anaxagorean principles / logoi. See my analysis in *Anaxagoras*, pp. 503-504; 685-686. Cf. Sextus Empiricus, *Adversus Dogmaticos 1* (*Adversus Logicos 1*), 7.140, adding that Democritus praised Anaxagoras for having said this: ὄψις γὰρ τῶν ἀδήλων τὰ φαινόμενα, ὥς φησιν Ἀναξαγόρας, ὃν ἐπὶ τούτῳ Δημόκριτος ἐπαινεῖ. Cf. *Adversus Geometras*, 3.23; 3.58; *Pyrrhoniae Hypotyposes*, 1.138. Therefore, when he attributed this to Chrysippus, he knew that the origin was Anaxagoras. Cf. Chrysippus, *Fragmenta Logica et Physica*, fr. 56, *apud* Sextus Empiricus, *Adversus Dogmaticos 1* (*Adversus Logicos 1*), 372. The apologist Athenagoras of Athens (*Legatio*, 5.2) attributed this to Euripides. Oddly enough, although Christian authors cherished this proverbial phrase, Greeks did not pay attention to it. Cf. Justin Martyr, quoted in the *Catena in Marcum* (*recensio ii*), p. 265. Eusebius, *De Laudibus Constantini*, 16.11; *De Theophania* (*fragmenta*), fr. 6. Anonymous, *Vitae S. Alypii Stylitae* (*vita altera*) (sixth century), 11. Macarius Chrysocephalus (Metropolitan of Philadelphia, paroemiographer, fourteenth century), *Paroemiae*, 6.84. Also, *Appendix Proverbiorum*, 4.50. Theoctistus Studites (fourteenth century), *Vita Athanasii Archiepiscopi Constantinopolitani*, p. 50. Proclus took up the Anaxagorean axiom in his own terms. *commTim*, v. 3, p. 192: "Zeus brings into light those that are hidden" (φανερὰ δὲ ἐξ ἀφανῶν ὁ Ζεὺς ἀποτελεῖ). See *infra*, folio 205v: Ὁ τοίνυν διὰ τῆς αὐτοτελοῦς ἐξάδος τῶν ἐντολῶν ἑαυτὸν ἀνακαθάρας, ... ὄψεται καλῶς διὰ τοῦ ὁρωμένου τὸν μὴ ὁρώμενον.

mcccxxvi See the notion of ψυχῆς εὐταξία ('discipline of the soul', meaning harmony and moderation with respect to the 'parts of the soul') in Pseudo-Plato, *Definitiones*, 411d-e; 412b. Aristotle, *Divisiones Aristoteleae*, 54; 60. Chrysippus, *Fragmenta Moralia*, fr. 632 *apud* Arius Didymus, *Liber De Philosophorum Sectis*, epitome by Stobaeus, *Anthologium*, 2.7.11s. Origen, *comm1Cor*, fr. 21, *apud Catena in Epistulam i ad Corinthios*, p. 87: ἔτι δὲ καὶ τοῦτο κατανοητέον. Ἐὰν καὶ δεώμεθα παιδαγωγοῦ, πάντως ὁ πεπιστευμένος τοῦτο παραδεῖγμα τὸν λόγον, τὸν βίον, διδότω τῇ ἡμετέρᾳ εὐταξίᾳ. ἔστιν οὖν πατὴρ μὲν ὁ πρώτως σπείρας τὸν χριστιανισμὸν ἐν ψυχῇ. Παιδαγωγὸς δὲ ὁ μετὰ τοῦτον παραλαβὼν παῖδα καὶ ἄγων αὐτόν. Gregory of Nyssa, *In Canticum Canticorum*, p. 446. Ephraem Syrus, *Precationes ad Dei Matrem*, prayer 3, p. 360. John Chrysostom, *Ad Populum Antiochenum*, PG.49.111.35; *De Paenitentia*, PG.49.301.53&57; *In Sanctum Pascha*, PG.52.772.33-34; *In Matthaeum*, PG.57.19.4-5; *In Epistulam i ad Timotheum*,

PG.62.576.1; *De Inani Gloria et De Educandis Liberis*, lines 347-348. Theodoret, *Interpretatio in Danielem*, PG.81.1500.24-25. Theon of Alexandria, *Commentaria in Ptolemaei Syntaxin Mathematicam*, p. 324. Pseudo-Theodosius of Alexandria (grammarian), *Περὶ Γραμματικῆς*, p. 92. Syrianus, *commMetaph*, p. 177; *Commentarium in Hermogenis Librum Περὶ Στάσεων*, p. 177. Proclus, *In Platonis Alcibiadem i*, 325; *commTim*, v. 3, p. 289. John Philoponus, *commAnim*, p. 25.

mcccxxvii Theophilus of Alexandria, *frMatt*, fr. 2.

mcccxxviii Cf. *supra*, folio 169v: Διὰ οὖν τῆς παραβολῆς διδασκόμεθα ὅτι οὐκ ἐν λόγοις τις πληροῖ τὸν νόμον, ἀλλ' ἔργοις. In order for someone to attain to the kingdom of heavens it takes deeds, not words. This is a statement succinctly recapitulating various scriptural sayings, such as Matt. 5:19 ('Whoever, therefore, shall decipher one of these least commandments, and teach others to do so, shall be called least in the kingdom of heaven; but whoever shall do and teach them shall be called great in the kingdom of heaven'), or 1 Cor. 4:19 ('And I will know, not the word of those who are puffed up, but the power.'). However, there was some misunderstanding of Origen's statement: this was taken as being a scriptural quotation itself, which also holds for a similar statement by Eusebius, in the *frLuc*, PG.24.533.28-29: ὅτι οὐκ ἐν λόγῳ ἡ βασιλεία τοῦ Θεοῦ, ἀλλ' ἐν δυνάμει. Consequently, this form of statement was used as if a dictum by either Jesus of Paul. See Pseudo-Macarius, *Sermones 64*, homily 16.2: φησὶ γὰρ ἡ γραφή. *ἡ βασιλεία τῶν οὐρανῶν οὐκ ἔστιν ἐν λόγῳ, ἀλλ' ἐν ἔργῳ καὶ δυνάμει. Homiliae Spirituales*, homily 17, lines 144-5: *ἐν ἔργῳ καὶ δυνάμει φησὶ ἐστὶν ἡ βασιλεία τοῦ θεοῦ*, οὐκ ἐν λόγῳ, ἀλλ' ἐν ἔργῳ καὶ δυνάμει. *Sermo 28*, p. 160: κατ' αὐτὴν τὴν τοῦ δεσπότου ἀπόφασιν, ὅτι ἡ βασιλεία οὐκ *ἐν λόγῳ ἀλλ' ἐν ἔργῳ καὶ δυνάμει·* καὶ πάλιν, *ἡ βασιλεία ἐντὸς ὑμῶν ἐστιν.* Πάλιν ὁ ἀπόστολος λέγει· *ἡ βασιλεία τοῦ θεοῦ οὐκ ἔστιν ἐν λόγῳ, ἀλλ' ἐν δυνάμει.* Ephraem Syrus, *De Patientia et Compunctione*, p. 327: κατὰ τὸ γεγραμμένον· *οὐ γὰρ ἐν λόγῳ ἡ βασιλεία τῶν οὐρανῶν, ἀλλ' ἐν δυνάμει.*

As a matter of fact, John Chrysostom took Paul's statement in Rom. 15:18-19 ('For I will not dare to speak of any things except those which Christ worked through me, for the obedience of the Gentiles, by word and deed, in the power of signs and wonders') as suggesting teaching by means of deeds. John Chrysostom, *In Epistulam ad Romanos*, PG.60.20-24: Ὅταν γὰρ εἴπῃ, *Ἐν λόγῳ καὶ ἔργῳ, ἐν δυνάμει σημείων καὶ τεράτων*, τοῦτο λέγει, τὴν διδασκαλίαν, τὴν περὶ βασιλείας φιλοσοφίαν, τὴν τῶν ἔργων, καὶ τῆς πολιτείας ἐπίδειξιν. Photius took his cue from this remark by Chrysostom. *Fragmenta in Epistulam i ad Corinthios*, p. 552 (comm. on 1 Cor. 4:19) *Καὶ γνώσομαι οὐ τὸν λόγον.* Οὐ γὰρ λόγων, φησί, χρεία ἀλλὰ τοῦ ἔργον ποιεῖν πνευματικόν. Οὐκ ἂν γὰρ λόγοι χωρὶς ἔργων εἰσενέγκοιεν εἰς τὴν βασιλείαν τῶν οὐρανῶν, *δύναμιν γάρ* φησι τὴν τῶν ἔργων ἐπίδειξιν.

mcccxxix Theophilus of Alexandria, *frMatt*, fr. 3. J. Reuss attributed three passages to Theophilus of Alexandria (*Matthäus-Kommentare aus der griechischen Kirche* [*Texte und Untersuchungen* 61. Berlin, 1957], pp. 151-152). The first of them is just one line long, and it is now clear that frs. 2 and 3 are in fact Origen's. Reuss mistakenly included the phrase οὐ γὰρ ἐν λόγοις ἡ βασιλεία τῶν οὐρανῶν, ἀλλ' ἐν ἔργοις in quotation marks, as if this were a scriptural one. By contrast, J.A. Cramer, who designated the passage as 'Unattributed' ('Ἐξ ἀνεπιγράφου) treated this as just a remark by the anthologising commentator. *Catenae Graecorum Patrum in Novum Testamentum*, v. 1, Oxford, 1840 (repr. Hildesheim: Olms, 1967), p. 174.

mcccxxx *Catena in Matthaeum*, pp. 174, 'Unattributed' ('Ἐξ ἀνεπιγράφου).

mcccxxxi See *supra* endnote dcxiv on εἶχον παρὰ πόδας τὸν ἔλεγχον.

mcccxxxii See Origen's same text same in the *Catena in Matthaeum*, p. 176: (Ὠριγένους.) Ἔδειραν ὡς Μιχαίαν, πατάξαντες ἐπὶ σιαγόνα Σεδεκίου· ἀπέκτειναν Ζαχαρίαν, μεταξὺ τοῦ ναοῦ καὶ τοῦ θυσιαστηρίου· ἐλιθοβόλησαν, ὡς Ἀζαρίαν υἱὸν Ἰοδαέ, τὸν ἱερέα, ὡς ἐν τοῖς Βασιλείοις.

mcccxxxiii By φυσιολογία he means natural knowledge, which is deposited in the Ecclesiastes. Origen maintained that Scripture teaches all sorts of knowledge: the Proverbs contain moral teaching; the Ecclesiastes, natural science; the Song of Songs, the most sublime theological doctrines. *expProv*, PG.17.220.50-221.2: Ὁ πλατύνας διὰ τῆς καθαρότητος τὴν καρδίαν αὑτοῦ, νοήσει τοὺς τοῦ Θεοῦ λόγους, τούς τε πρακτικούς, καὶ τοὺς σοφιστικούς, καὶ τοὺς θεολογικούς. Πᾶσα γὰρ ἡ κατὰ τὴν Γραφὴν πραγματεία, τέμνεται τριχῶς, εἰς ἠθικὴν καὶ φυσικὴν καὶ θεολογικήν. Καὶ ἀκολουθεῖ τῇ μὲν πρώτῃ, αἱ Παροιμίαι· τῇ δὲ δευτέρᾳ, ὁ Ἐκκλησιαστής· τῇ δὲ τρίτῃ, ᾎσμα ᾈσμάτων· ἅπερ νοηθέντα διὰ καθαρότητος ἐναπογράφεται τῇ καρδίᾳ.

mcccxxxiv Origen uses Plato's expression in the *Statesman*, from the tale about the reversed motion of the universe and the relation of God to this. *Politicus*, 272e: τότε δὴ τοῦ παντὸς ὁ μὲν κυβερνήτης, οἷον πηδαλίων οἴακος ἀφέμενος, εἰς τὴν αὑτοῦ περιωπὴν ἀπέστη ('then the steersman of the universe dropped the tiller and withdrew to his supervising place'). Origen saw this as parallel to Gen. 2:2-3, about God who 'rested from all his work' of creation on the seventh day. Slight differences apart, this was also the view of Celsus. *Cels*, V.59. The phrase was deemed suitable to use in reference to God not only by Platonists, such as Numenius (*Fragmenta*, 1.12, *apud* Eusebius, *Praeparatio Evangelica*, 11.18.10; see also *op. cit.* 11.18.12; 11.34.1; *Commentaria in Psalmos*, PG.23.1168.26), but also by Clement of Alexandria, *Stromateis*, 7.2.5.5. Origen felt at liberty to make use of the Platonic expression, all the more so since Alexander of Aphrodisias had done so, too (*commMetaph*, p. 71). Cf. Origen, *commJohn*, XXXII.28.350. The text in the present codex can easily be confirmed by his *commMatt*, 17.7, which runs parallel to this. The Platonic phrase and idea was naturally used by later philosophers. Cf. Hermias of Alexandria, *schPhaedr*, pp. 62; 65. Proclus, *Theologia Platonica*, v. 4, pp. 18; 38; 71; 77; v. 5, pp. 26; 29-31; 33; 44; 65; 74; 92-3; 123; 138; v. 6, pp. 32; 41; 75; 94; *In Platonis Parmenidem*, pp. 959; 988; 1020; 1031; *commCrat*, 110; *commTim*, v. 3, pp. 199; 227; *commRep*, v. 1, pp. 136, 166; *In Platonis Alcibiadem i*, 19; 21; 83; *commEucl*, p. 27; *De Providentia et Fato et Eo Quod in Nobis ad Theodorum Mechanicum*, 18. Damascius, *De Principiis*, pp. 95; 252. Simplicius, *commCael*, p. 306. Also, by Christian authors: Didymus, *Commentarii in Psalmos 35-39*, cod. p. 234; *Fragmenta in Joannem*, 11; *frPs(al)*, frs. 704a; 1247. Theodoret, *Curatio*, 4.44. Olympiodorus, the deacon of Alexandria, *Commentarii in Job*, p. 56. John Philoponus, *De Aeternitate Mundi*, p. 624. Cassian the Sabaite (Pseudo-Didymus), *De Trinitate*, 28.1.

mcccxxxv It can be easily seen that ascription of the following fragment (couched in words and phrases identical with those of Origen's, and largely being the selfsame text) to Theodore of Heraclea is simply ridiculous. *Catena in Matthaeum*, p. 176: Ἡ παραβολὴ οἰκοδεσπότην λέγει τὸν Θεὸν καὶ Πατέρα, τὸν πολλὴν πρόνοιαν ἐξ ἀρχῆς εἰς τοὺς Ἰουδαίους ἐνδειξάμενον, καὶ τὸ ἄνωθεν μέχρι τέλους τῶν Ἰουδαίων φιλόνεικον περὶ τὸν Θεόν. Ἀμπελὼν δέ ἐστιν ὁ Ἰσραήλ, ὃν κατεφύτευσεν ἐν τῇ γῇ τῆς ἐπαγγελίας. φραγμὸς δὲ ὁ νόμος, οὐκ ἐῶν αὐτοὺς ἐπιμιγῆναι τοῖς ἔθνεσι· ληνὸς τὸ θυσιαστήριον. πύργος ἡ Σιών· γεωργοὶ οἱ διδάσκαλοι· δοῦλοι οἱ κατὰ διαφόρους καιροὺς ἀποσταλέντες προφῆται, οὓς ἀπέκτειναν· υἱὸς ὁ Ἰησοῦς, ὃν ἀπέκτειναν, καὶ τὰ δεινὰ ὑποστάντες ὑπὸ Ῥωμαίων, ἔξω αὐτοὺς ἐποίησαν τοῦ Θεοῦ, ἀντεισενεχθέντων εἰς τὸν τῶν Ἰουδαίων τόπον τῶν μαθητῶν καὶ Ἀποστόλων, οἳ καὶ ἀποδεδείκασι τοὺς καρποὺς ἐν θεοσεβείᾳ, ζήσαντες ἐναρέτως.

mcccxxxvi Origen, *commMatt*, fr. 421 (Klostermann).

mcccxxxvii Origen, *schMatt*, PG.17.300.41-301.28. See the text in Origen, *commMatt*, 17.7, which is nearly the same, yet not identical: Καὶ ὅρα εἰ δυνάμεθα τὴν μὲν κατὰ τὴν θείαν γραφὴν φυσιολογίαν τὸν *ἀμπελῶνα* εἰπεῖν, τὸν δὲ ἀκόλουθον τῇ ἀληθεῖ φυσιολογίᾳ βίον ἐν ἀρετῇ καὶ καλλίστοις ἤθεσι καρποφοροῦντα λέγειν εἶναι τὸν τοῦ ἀμπελῶνος καρπόν, τὸν δὲ λογικὸν τόπον καὶ πᾶν τὸ γράμμα τῆς γραφῆς τὸν *φραγμὸν* εἶναι τοῦ ἀμπελῶνος περικείμενον ἔξωθεν ὡς μὴ κατοπτεύεσθαι τοῖς ἔξωθεν τὸν *ἀμπελῶνα* καὶ τὸν ἐν κρυπτῷ μάλιστα καρπὸν αὐτοῦ, τὸ δὲ βάθος *** τῆς δεχομένης τοὺς καρποὺς τούτους ψυχῆς πᾶν ἐπιπόλαιον ἀποβαλούσης τὴν ὀρυχθεῖσαν εἶναι ἐν τῷ ἀμπελῶνι *ληνόν*. Ὁ δὲ οἰκοδομηθεὶς ἐν τῷ ἀμπελῶνι πύργος, ἀνάστημα ἔχων καὶ δίαρμα καὶ ὕψος ὑπὲρ τὸν *ἀμπελῶνα* καὶ τὸν *φραγμὸν* καὶ τὴν *ληνόν*, ὁ περὶ θεοῦ (οἶμαι) λόγος ἐστί, ναὸς ὢν τοῦ ἐν αὐτῷ θείου νοῦ. Καὶ περὶ τοιούτου νομίζω λελέχθαι πύργου ὑπὸ τοῦ σωτῆρος τὸ *τίς ἐξ ὑμῶν βουλόμενος πύργον οἰκοδομῆσαι οὐχὶ πρῶτον ψηφίζει* εἰ δύναται θεῖναι τὸν θεμέλιον καὶ ἐκτελέσαι, *ἵνα μὴ ἄρξωνται οἱ θεωροῦντες ἐμπαίζειν* τῷ μὴ τελειώσαντι; Διὰ γὰρ παραβολῆς κἀκεῖ δοκεῖ μοι λέγεσθαι ὅτι μέλλων θεολογεῖν σκόπησον, εἰ δύνασαι ἀρξάμενος πάντα ἃ ἀπαιτεῖ σε ὁ λόγος εἰς θεολογίαν τελειῶσαι, ἵνα μὴ ἀρξάμενος τῶν τῆς εὐσεβείας δογμάτων ἀτελῆ καταλίπῃς τὸν περὶ θεοῦ *πύργον* καὶ στεφάνην αὐτῷ μὴ ἐποικοδομήσῃς. Εἰ γὰρ στεφάνην οὐκ ἐποικοδομήσεις, πεσεῖταί τις ἀπὸ τῆς περὶ θεοῦ ἐννοίας καὶ ἀποθανεῖται. Τοῦτον δὴ τὸν (ὡς ἀποδεδώκαμεν) *ἀμπελῶνα ἐξέδοτο γεωργοῖς*, τῷ πρὸ ἡμῶν λαῷ, ὁ θεός, *καὶ* ἀπεδήμησεν *εἰς τὴν ἑαυτοῦ περιωπήν*, δοὺς ἀφορμὰς τοῖς *γεωργοῖς*, ἐξ ὧν αὐτὸς *ἐφύτευσε* καὶ *περιέθηκε* καὶ *ὤρυξε* καὶ *ᾠκοδόμησε*, τοῦ φέρειν *τοὺς καρποὺς ἐν τοῖς καιροῖς αὐτῶν*. Ἤγγισαν μὲν οὖν καθ᾽ ἕκαστον οἱ καιροὶ *τῶν καρπῶν*, οἶμαι δ᾽ ὅτι καὶ ‹γενικῶς› ὅλῳ τῷ λαῷ. Τὸ δὲ ἐγγίσαι τοὺς καιροὺς *τῶν καρπῶν* ἀκριβῶς μὲν διηγήσασθαι ἕξεως μείζονός ἐστιν ἢ καθ᾽ ἡμᾶς, καὶ καρδίας πολλῷ καθαρωτέρας καὶ διορατικ‹ωτέρ›ας παρ᾽ ἡμᾶς. Ὅμως δὲ κατὰ δύναμιν ἐπιβαλοῦμεν οὕτως τῷ τόπῳ, ἀρξάμενοι ἀπὸ τῶν καθένα.

mcccxxxviii The expression ἱερατικὸν τάγμα ('priestly order', literally, 'priestly legion') was introduced by Origen (perhaps having in mind the irrelevant context of 1 Cor. 15:23) and it is characteristic of his vocabulary, which he bequeathed to his posterity that used it only casually, although eminent admirers of his (e.g. Gregory of Nyssa, Evagrius) did not make anything of this. Origen used this expression upon setting on to write his Christian works. *commJohn*, I.1.1; then, *Homiliae in Jesu Nave*, p. 456. Eusebius, *Commentaria in Psalmos*, PG.24.20.49-50. Once again, Epiphanius of Salamis on the one hand condemned Origen, while, on the other, habitually took up the vocabulary of the man he inculpated. Cf. *Panarion*, v. 2 p. 327; v. 3, p. 477. Gregory of Nazianzus, *Epistulae*, epistle 11.11. Basil of Caesarea, *Epistulae*, epistle 54.1. I myself doubt the authenticity of both of those allegedly Cappadocean epistles. Didymus, *commZacch*, 4.80. Socrates Scholasticus, *HE*, 6.18. Theodoret, *HE*, pp. 153; 226; *Interpretatio in Psalmos*, PG.80.1196.20; *In Epistulas Sancti Pauli*, PG.82.788.16-17. Sozomenus, *HE*, 1.23.4. Nilus of Ancyra, *Narrationes Septem De Monachis in Sina*, 6.20. Pseudo-Dionysius the Areopagite, *De Ecclesiastica Hierarchia*, p. 110. Eustathius of Thessaloniki, *Sermones*, oration 6, p. 93. Nicephorus Callistus Xanthopulus, *HE*, 11.30. Synods took the expression up: ACO, *Concilium Universale Ephesenum anno 431*, tome 1.1.5, p. 120; *Concilium Universale Chalcedonense anno 451*, tome 2.2.1, p. 145; *Synodus Constantinopolitana et Hierosolymitana anno 536*, tome 3, p. 18. Once again, this use of an expression which is distinctly characteristic of Origen shows the absurdity of attributing this part of his commentary on Matthew to Apollinaris as a 'fragment'.

mcccxxxix Origen, *commMatt*, fr. 422 (Klostermann).
mcccxl Apollinaris, *frMatt*, fr. 110; see the last phrase of this *infra*.
mcccxli Origen, *commMatt*, fr. 420 (Klostermann).
mcccxlii John Chrysostom, *In Matthaeum*, PG.58.640.21-29. Cf. John Chrysostom, *In Epistulam ad Romanos*, PG.60.20-24: Ὅταν γὰρ εἴπῃ, *Ἐν λόγῳ καὶ ἔργῳ, ἐν δυνάμει σημείων καὶ τεράτων*, τοῦτο λέγει, τὴν διδασκαλίαν, τὴν περὶ βασιλείας φιλοσοφίαν, τὴν τῶν ἔργων, καὶ τῆς πολιτείας ἐπίδειξιν.
mcccxliii Jerome, *commMatt*, 21.37.
mcccxliv Cf. Origen, *Philocalia*, 21.20: ποιεῖ μὲν γὰρ ὁ δημιουργὸς σκεύη τιμῆς καὶ σκεύη ἀτιμίας οὐκ ἀρχῆθεν κατὰ τὴν πρόγνωσιν, ἐπεὶ μὴ κατ᾽ αὐτὴν προκατακρίνει ἢ προδικαιοῖ. *commRom* (*I.1-XII.21*), fr. 1 (& *Philocalia*, 25.2): οὐ νομιστέον τοίνυν εἶναι τῶν ἐσομένων αἰτίαν τὴν πρόγνωσιν τοῦ θεοῦ· ἀλλ᾽ ἐπεὶ ἔμελλεν γίνεσθαι κατ᾽ ἰδίας ὁρμὰς τοῦ ποιοῦντος, διὰ τοῦτο προέγνω, εἰδὼς τὰ πάντα πρὸ γενέσεως αὐτῶν. See also *supra*, endnote mccxx, discussion of Origen's characteristic expression τὰ πάντως ἐσόμενα.
mcccxlv Origen, *commMatt*, fr. 423 (Klostermann); but now we have several pages of Origen's text of which this fragment is just a tiny portion.
mcccxlvi This is the last phrase of Apollinaris, *frMatt*, fr. 110. Origen's context makes it all too clear who the source of this was.
mcccxlvii Origen, *commMatt*, fr. 425 (Klostermann).
mcccxlviii Origen, *commMatt*, fr. 426 (Klostermann).
mcccxlix Origen, *apud Catena in Matthaeum*, p. 176.
mcccl Origen, *commMatt*, fr. 428 (Klostermann).
mcccli Origen, *apud Catena in Matthaeum*, pp. 176-177.
mccclii Origen used this unique turn having in mind a phrase of Xenophon, *Memorabilia*, 1.7.2-3: ἀλλὰ καὶ ἄνθρωπος ἀλαζών. Καίτοι πολλὰ μὲν δαπανῶν, μηδὲν δ᾽ ὠφελούμενος, πρὸς δὲ τούτοις κακοδοξῶν, πῶς οὐκ ἐπιπόνως τε καὶ ἀλυσιτελῶς καὶ καταγελάστως βιώσεται.
mcccliii Origen, *commMatt*, fr. 427 (Klostermann).
mcccliv Origen, *apud Catena in Matthaeum*, p. 177.
mccclv The tag ΩΡΙΓΕΝΟΥΣ has been placed a little below this point. However, the text is arguably Origen's since the parallel to this is extant. Besides, at the point of folio 172v, where Origen's name is written, the text is not discontinued in relation to its either preceding or ensuing content.
mccclvi Cf. Origen, *commMatt*, 17.20: παρὰ δὲ τοῖς κατὰ τὰς γραφὰς λεγομένοις θεοῖς, ὧν *ἐν συναγωγῇ ἔστη ὁ θεός, ἐν μέσῳ θεοὺς* διακρίνων, *ἡ βασιλεία τῶν οὐρανῶν* ἐστιν ὁμοία θεῷ βασιλεῖ.
mccclvii Origen, *commMatt*, fr. 429 (Klostermann).
mccclviii Origen, *commMatt*, 17.19.
mccclix Here is how Apollinaris apparently copied from this. *frMatt*, fr. 111: *Γάμος* οὗτος ἐκκλησίας συναπτομένης τῷ λόγῳ.
mccclx Theodore of Heraclea, *apud Catena in Matthaeum*, p. 179 & Theodore of Heraclea, *frMatt*, fr. 113.
mccclxi Cyril of Alexandria, *apud Catena in Matthaeum*, p. 179. Both this and the foregoing passage are the same text. However, the present codex provides Origen's context of phrase, from which those two 'fragments' were excerpted.
mccclxii Origen maintained that to be 'more perceptive' or 'insightful' (διορατικώτερον) was a faculty bestowed by the Holy Spirit as a result of one's righteous conduct of life. Cf. *commJohn*, XX.33.288; *frJohn*, fr. 76; *Cels*, VII.3-4. He included himself among those 'more insightful' (οἱ διορατικώτεροι). *homLuc*, homily 38, p. 214: Ζητῶ, μήποτε

καὶ ἐνταῦθα ἐφ᾽ ἡμᾶς ὁ κλαυθμὸς τοῦ κυρίου φθάνῃ. Ἡμεῖς γάρ ἐσμεν ἡ Ἱερουσαλὴμ ἡ κλαιομένη, οἱ διορατικώτεροι. Ἐὰν μετὰ τὸ ἀποκαλυφθῆναι ἡμῖν τὰ μυστήρια τῆς ἀληθείας καὶ κηρυχθῆναι τὸν λόγον τῆς σωτηρίας ἁμαρτάνωμεν, κλαιόμεθα. Οὐδεὶς γὰρ ἐθνικὸς κλαίεται, κλαίεται δὲ ἡ τοιαύτη Ἱερουσαλήμ. Nevertheless, he was as modest as to believe that there were other Christian intellectuals who possessed 'a more pure and more perceptive heart' than his. *commMatt*, 17.7: τὸ δὲ ἐγγίσαι τοὺς καιροὺς *τῶν καρπῶν* ἀκριβῶς μὲν διηγήσασθαι ἕξεως μείζονός ἐστιν ἢ καθ᾽ ἡμᾶς καὶ καρδίας πολλῷ καθαρωτέρας καὶ διορατικ‹ωτέρ›ας παρ᾽ ἡμᾶς.

mccclxiii Origen, *commMatt*, fr. 430 (Klostermann).

mccclxiv Cf. Origen, *commMatt*, 17.9: εὐχερὲς μὲν οὖν εἰπεῖν ὅτι δούλους λέγει τοὺς προφήτας. *Op. cit.* 17.15: οἱ δὲ ἀποστελλόμενοι ἄλλοι δοῦλοι ἄλλο ἄθροισμα προφητῶν. *schMatt*, PG.17.301.3-5: Δοῦλοι πρῶτοι καὶ δεύτεροι παθόντες ἄτοπον, οἱ κατὰ διαφόρους καιροὺς ἀποσταλέντες προφῆται. *Op. cit.* PG.17.301.27-28: Δοῦλοι οἱ προφῆται τὰ πνευματικὰ καρπώματα ἀπαιτοῦντες προσάγειν ὡς ἱερεῖς τῷ Θεῷ. *expProv*, PG.17.185.32-34: ὡσαύτως καὶ ἐπὶ τῶν λοιπῶν ἀποστόλων καὶ προφητῶν τὸν λόγον συνάξομεν, δούλους τῆς σοφίας αὐτοῦ ἀποδείξαντες.

mccclxv Origen, *commMatt*, 17.15.

mccclxvi Origen, *op. cit.* 17.21. See text *infra*, folios 172v-173r.

mccclxvii Origen suggests his opinion about the Son / Logos being present (1) in the transcendent timelessness; (2) in the entire world, by permeating this; and (3) in each individual human being, 'in the midst of it' (as in John, 1:26), meaning the chest, which was normally considered as the seat of the *hegemonikon*. *commJohn*, II.35.215: Μετὰ δὲ ταῦτα ἄλλη μαρτυρία τοῦ αὐτοῦ βαπτιστοῦ περὶ Χριστοῦ ἐστι, τὴν προηγουμένην αὐτοῦ ὑπόστασιν ἔτι διδάσκουσα διήκουσαν ἐπὶ πάντα τὸν κόσμον κατὰ τὰς ψυχὰς τὰς λογικάς, ὅ τε φησί. *Μέσος ὑμῶν ἕστηκεν ὃν ὑμεῖς οὐκ οἴδατε, ὀπίσω μου ἐρχόμενος, οὗ οὐκ εἰμὶ ἄξιος ἐγὼ ἵνα λύσω αὐτοῦ τὸν ἱμάντα τοῦ ὑποδήματος* [John, 1:26-27]. Καὶ ἐπίσκεψαι, εἰ διὰ τὸ ἐν μέσῳ τοῦ παντὸς εἶναι σώματος τὴν καρδίαν, ἐν δὲ τῇ καρδίᾳ τὸ ἡγεμονικόν, κατὰ τὸν ἐν ἑκάστῳ λόγον δύναται νοεῖσθαι τὸ *μέσος ὑμῶν ἕστηκεν ὃν ὑμεῖς οὐκ οἴδατε*. *Op. cit.* VI.30.154: ὅτι δύναμιν τοσαύτην ἔχει [Χριστός] ὡς καὶ ἀόρατος εἶναι τῇ θειότητι αὐτοῦ, παρὼν παντὶ ἀνθρώπῳ παντὶ δὲ καὶ ὅλῳ τῷ κόσμῳ συμπαρεκτεινόμενος. ὅπερ δηλοῦται διὰ τοῦ *Μέσος ὑμῶν ἕστηκεν*.

mccclxviii Again, here is how Apollinaris copied from this. *frMatt*, fr. 111: πρῶτοι δὲ καὶ δεύτεροι δοῦλοι καλοῦνται, πρῶτοι μὲν οἱ κατὰ τὴν τοῦ κυρίου παρουσίαν προσδραμόντες ἀποστόλων συνεργοὶ καὶ διάδοχοι.

mccclxix Origen, *commMatt*, fr. 431 (Klostermann).

mccclxx Cf. Origen, *schLuc*, PG.17.360.51-54 (on Luke, 14:16-24 and Matt. 22:1-14): Εἴποι δ᾽ ἄν τις καὶ ἑτέρως ἐξηγούμενος ἐφαρμόττειν τὰ τῆς παραβολῆς δηλούμενα, τοῖς ἀνέκαθεν ἐκ πρώτης τοῦ βίου συστάσεως μέχρι συντελείας τοῦ αἰῶνος καταξιουμένοις τῆς ἐνθέου κλήσεως.

mccclxxi Cf. Origen, *excPs*, PG.17.144.40-42: Εἰ δὲ βούλει, ἅπερ ἐνταῦθα συλλέξομεν ἐν παρασκευῇ, ταῦτα ἐκεῖσε σαββατίσαντες εὑρήσομεν καὶ τραφησόμεθα. See *PHE*, chapters 9-11, and Conclusion.

mccclxxii Cf. Origen, *selEz*, PG.13.781.19-22: Οὐκ ἐχρῆν γὰρ τὸν οὕτως ἀκάθαρτον βρωθησόμενον ἄρτον ἐν ἁγίῳ παραλαμβάνεσθαι ἀριθμῷ, ὁποῖός ἐστιν ὁ τῆς δεκάδος, καὶ ἑβδομάδος, ἢ τριακάδος, ὀγδοάδος, ἤ τινος τῶν ὁμοίων ἀριθμῶν. *commJohn*, X.39.270: Παρατηρητέον δὲ ὅτι οἱ μὲν ἀναγεγραμμένοι αἴρειν ἄρσιν ἑβδομάδος εἰσὶν συγγενεῖς. Οἱ δὲ λατόμοι καὶ ἐκτυποῦντες τοὺς λίθους, πρὸς τὸ ἁρμονίους αὐτοὺς γενέσθαι τῷ ναῷ, ὀγδοάδι προσῳκείωνται. *Op. cit.* X.39.272: Ὀγδοάδι μέντοι γε ἐτῶν συντελεῖται ὁ οἶκος τῷ ὀγδόῳ μηνὶ τοῦ ὀγδόου ἔτους ἀπὸ τῆς θεμελιώσεως.

mccclxxiii Origen, *commMatt*, fr. 432 (Klostermann), comm. on Matt. 22:3. Cf. Origen, *schMatt*, PG.17.300.27-29: Ἐπεὶ ὁ μὲν ἓξ ἀριθμὸς ἐργατικὸς καὶ ἐν γενέσει κόσμου, ὁ δὲ ἑπτὰ ἀναπαύσεως. Ὁ μὲν τὰ τοῦ κόσμου καὶ ὑλικὰ ἀγαπῶν, ἐξαμαρτάνων τέλος ἔχει τὴν ἑβδομάδα (this is also part of Origen, *commMatt*, fr. 383, [Klostermann], quoted *supra*). Cf. Origen's idea running parallel to this point, in *selPs* (comm. on Psalm 118:164), PG.12.1624.29-32: Ὥσπερ ἡ ὀγδόη σύμβολόν ἐστι τοῦ μέλλοντος αἰῶνος, δύναμιν ἀναστάσεως περιέχουσα, οὕτω καὶ ἡ ἑβδόμη σύμβολόν ἐστι τοῦ κόσμου τούτου. *deOr*, 27.16: ταῦτα τοίνυν ὁ ἰδὼν καὶ τῇ διανοίᾳ αἰώνων ἑβδομάδα, ἵνα σαββατισμόν τινα ἅγιον θεωρήσῃ, … ἵνα τὸ ἕβδομον ἅγιον ἔτος καταλαμβάνῃ, … πῶς δύναται μικρολογῆσαι περὶ τοῦ ἐλαχίστου μορίου ὥρας τῆς τοῦ τηλικούτου αἰῶνος ἡμέρας καὶ οὐχὶ πάντα ποιήσει, ἵνα ἀπὸ τῆς ἐνταῦθα παρασκευῆς ἄξιος γενόμενος τοῦ τυχεῖν τοῦ ἐπιουσίου ἄρτου.

Origen is the source of a far-reaching tradition, which was upheld by his admirers and (unconsciously) by others, such as Anastasius of Sinai. Gregory of Nazianzus, *In Novam Dominicam*, PG.36.612.36-47 (comm. on Gen. 2:2): ἵν', ὥσπερ ἡ πρώτη κτίσις τὴν ἀρχὴν ἀπὸ Κυριακῆς λαμβάνει (δῆλον δέ· ἀπὸ γὰρ ταύτης ἑβδόμη τὸ Σάββατον γίνεται, κατάπαυσις οὖσα τῶν ἔργων), οὕτω καὶ ἡ δευτέρα πάλιν ἐκ τῆς αὐτῆς ἄρχηται, πρώτη οὖσα τῶν μετ' αὐτήν, καὶ ὀγδοὰς ἀπὸ τῶν πρὸ αὐτῆς, ὑψηλῆς ὑψηλοτέρα, καὶ θαυμασίας θαυμασιωτέρα. Likewise (comm. on the same point of Genesis) Olympiodorus, the deacon of Alexandria, *Commentarii in Ecclesiasten*, PG.93.605.46-50: Ἀρχὴ δὲ τοῦ μέλλοντος αἰῶνος ἡ ὀγδόη, ἧς σύμβολον ἡ Κυριακὴ ἀνάστασις. Didymus, *Commentarii in Psalmos 22-26.10* (on the inscription of Psalm 23:1), cod. p. 65: *μίαν σαββάτου*. ἡ ὀγδοὰς ἡ ἑπομένη. Αὕτη καὶ πρώτη σαββάτου ἐστίν. Εἶτ', ἐπεὶ ἀρχή ἐστιν δῆθεν κύκλου ἑβδομάδος, καλεῖται καὶ ὀγδοάς. *Op. cit.* cod. p. 70: ἐλάβομεν τὴν ἐπιγραφὴν τοῦ ψαλμοῦ *εἰς τὴν μίαν τῶν σαββάτων*, ἐλέγομεν δὲ τὴν ἀνάστασιν τοῦ σωτῆρος τὴν κυριακὴν καλουμένην ὁτὲ μὲν ὀγδοάδα ὁτὲ δὲ μίαν σαββάτου κατὰ διαφόρους ἐπινοίας. Gregory of Nyssa (on the same issue as Didymus), *In Inscriptiones Psalmorum*, p. 121: ὁ γὰρ τὴν κληρονομίαν γνωρίσας αὐτὸς καὶ τῆς Ὀγδόης μέμνηται, ἥτις πέρας τε τοῦ ἐνεστῶτος χρόνου γίνεται καὶ ἀρχὴ τοῦ μέλλοντος αἰῶνος. Ἴδιον δὲ τῆς Ὀγδόης τὸ μηκέτι καιρὸν εἰς παρασκευὴν ἀγαθῶν ἢ κακῶν ἐνδιδόναι τοῖς ἐν αὐτῇ γινομένοις, ἀλλ' ὧν ἄν τις ἑαυτῷ καταβάληται διὰ τῶν ἔργων τὰ σπέρματα, τούτων ἀντιπαρέχειν τὰ δράγματα. Anastasius of Sinai, *In Hexaemeron*, book 7, lines 444-447: Λοιπὸν ἀπόστηθι τῆς ἑβδόμης ἡμέρας σου καὶ φθάσον εἰς τὴν ὀγδόην καὶ πρώτην Χριστοῦ, ἵνα λάβῃς τὴν πνευματικὴν περιτομὴν ἐπὶ ταῖς αἰσθήσεσί σου τὴν Τριάδα τὴν ἁγίαν δεχόμενος καὶ γινόμενος καλὴ ὀγδοάς. I have discussed Origen's Eschatology, including this particular point, in *PHE*, chapters 9, 10, 11.

mccclxxiv Again, here is how Apollinaris copied from this. *frMatt*, fr. 111: καὶ παρασκευὴ τοῦ γάμου διὰ τῆς τῶν πλουσίων χαρισμάτων δόσεως, ἅπερ εἰκάζεται *ταύροις καὶ σιτιστοῖς* ἐν εὐωχίᾳ πλουσίᾳ παρασκευαζομένοις. *ἐν παντὶ* γὰρ *πεπλουτίσθαι* ἡμᾶς ἐν Χριστῷ ὁ Παῦλός φησιν, *ἐν λόγῳ καὶ γνώσει*.

mccclxxv Cf. Origen, *commMatt*, 17.15: τὸ δὲ ἡτοιμασμένον *ἄριστον*, ἐν ᾧ *οἱ ταῦροι* τοῦ βασιλέως καὶ *τὰ σιτευτὰ* αὐτοῦ τεθυμένα ἦν, αἱ στερεαὶ ἦσαν καὶ λογικαὶ τῶν μυστηρίων τοῦ θεοῦ τροφαί. οὕτω δὲ καὶ *πάντα ἕτοιμα*, οἱ περὶ πάντων τῶν ὄντων λόγοι ‹ἕτοιμοι›, οὓς *ὅταν ἔλθῃ τὸ τέλειον* [1 Cor. 13:10]) οἱ τῇ κλήσει ἀκολουθήσαντες φάγονται καὶ πίονται.

mccclxxvi Cf. Origen, *schMatt*, PG.17.301.16: Πύργος καὶ διῃρημένος περὶ Θεοῦ λόγος. *commJohn*, XIII.13.82: τὸ δὲ τῆς διαιρέσεως ἐπὶ τῆς εὐλογίας, τῶν σοφῶν τῇ διαιρέσει τεταγμένως χρωμένων ἐφ' ἑκάστου τῶν προβλημάτων, ἥτις ἐστὶν ἀναγκαία πρὸς τὴν τῆς ἀληθείας κατανόησιν.

mccclxxvii Origen, *commMatt*, 17.22: Δοκεῖ δή μοι εὐγενῶν τινων ψυχῶν Ἰσραηλιτικῶν γεγονέναι ἡ προηγουμένη κλῆσις *εἰς τοὺς γάμους*. Προηγουμένως γὰρ διὰ τῶν καλούντων τῷ τῆς διδασκαλίας λόγῳ βούλεται ὁ θεὸς ἥκειν εἰς τὴν μακαρίαν ταύτην ἑστίαν τοὺς πρὸς σύνεσιν εὐφυεστέρους. Καὶ ἔστιν ἰδεῖν ὅτι οὐ θέλουσιν οἱ τοιοῦτοι *ἐλθεῖν* εἰς τὴν κλῆσιν, καὶ διὰ τοῦτο ἀποστέλλονται ἄλλοι δοῦλοι προκαλούμενοι τοὺς μὴ θέλοντας *ἐλθεῖν* καὶ ἐπαγγελλόμενοι, εἰ ἔλθοιεν οἱ κεκλημένοι, μεταλήψεσθαι αὐτοὺς ἑτοιμασθέντος ὑπὸ τοῦ βασιλέως ἀρίστου, καὶ ταύρων τῶν ὡς ἐν καθαροῖς πάντων τῶν καθαρῶν μειζόνων, καὶ σεσιτευμένων τῇ ποικίλῃ καὶ πολλῇ ἀποδείξει τῶν εἰς ἕκαστον πρόβλημα νοημάτων. Οἱονεὶ γὰρ σιτιστὸν παρατίθησι λόγον ἢ διῃρημένον καὶ ἐν τροπολογίᾳ λεγόμενον τεθυμένον ὁ τὴν περὶ τοῦ προκειμένου προβλήματος ἀπόδειξιν πολλὴν φέρων καὶ πλήρη. Likewise, in *op. cit.* 17.15.

mcccIxxviii Origen, *commMatt*, fr. 433 (Klostermann), col. 2.

mcccIxxix Cf. Origen, *commJohn*, VI.1.5: Σολομὼν γὰρ ἑρμηνεύεται *εἰρηνικός*. *frProv*, PG.13.17.35-38: *Παροιμίαι Σολομῶντος υἱοῦ Δαυίδ.* Υἱὸς Δαυὶδ καὶ ὁ Σωτὴρ λέγεται. Οὗτος εἰρηνικὸς ἡμῶν Σωτὴρ *ὁ γενόμενος ἐκ σπέρματος Δαυΐδ, τὸ κατὰ σάρκα*, [Rom. 1:3] ἐβασίλευσεν ἐν Ἰσραήλ.

mcccIxxx Origen, *apud Catena in Matthaeum*, p. 179. This is the same text as Origen, *commMatt*, fr. 433 (Klostermann), col. 1.

mcccIxxxi Apollinaris (*frMatt*, fr. 111) keeps on copying from Origen, but now we have all of Origen's text that includes this portion, too.

mcccIxxxii Cf. Origen, *commMatt*, 14.10: τοῖς ἀγγέλοις τοῖς ἐπὶ τῶν κολάσεων τεταγμένοις. *Op. cit.* 17.23: Τὸ δὲ ἔργον τῆς ὀργῆς ἐστι πεμφθῆναι *τὸ στράτευμα* τοῦ βασιλέως, ἤτοι τὸ *πλῆθος τῆς οὐρανίου στρατιᾶς* ἢ τοὺς τεταγμένους ἐπὶ τῶν κολάσεων ἀγγέλους. *Epistula ad Africanum*, PG.11.64.19-20: ἄγγελοι ἐπὶ τῶν κολάσεων τεταγμένοι τινὲς ταῦτα διαθήσουσι.

mcccIxxxiii See the same in Origen, *commMatt*, fr. 435 II (Klostermann): διέξοδοι *ὁδῶν* εἰσι τὰ ἔξω τοῦ Ἰσραὴλ δόγματα καὶ τοῖς τυχοῦσι δεδομένα καὶ τοῖς ἀπερριμένοις.

mcccIxxxiv The same in Origen, *commMatt*, fr. 435 II (Klostermann): *ἀγαθοὺς* τοὺς μετριωτέρους λέγει ἤτοι τοὺς ποσὸν ἑαυτῶν ἐπιμεληθέντας συγκρίσει τῶν δι᾽ ὅλου φαύλων. See also this a fuller version of this *infra*, and Origen, *commMatt*, fr. 437 (Klostermann).

mcccIxxxv Origen, *commMatt*, fr. 435 I (Klostermann).

mcccIxxxvi Origen, *apud Catena in Matthaeum*, pp. 179-180.

mcccIxxxvii This is part of Apollinaris, *frMatt*, fr. 111.

mcccIxxxviii Origen, *commMatt*, fr. 437 (Klostermann), col. 1.

mcccIxxxix Origen, *apud Catena in Matthaeum*, p. 180.

mccccxc This is part of Apollinaris, *frMatt*, fr. 111. Once again, it is quite evident that Apollinaris copied from Origen. See this fragment further (*infra*, folio 174v) running parallel to that of the present codex.

mccccxci The same in Origen, *apud Catena in Matthaeum*, p. 180: *διέξοδοι ὁδῶν* εἰσι τὰ ἔξω τοῦ Ἰσραὴλ δόγματα.

mccccxcii Origen, *commMatt*, fr. 435 II (Klostermann); continued *infra*.

mccccxciii Origen, *commMatt*, fr. 435 II (Klostermann), concluded.

mccccxciv Origen, *apud Catena in Matthaeum*, p. 180.

mccccxcv John Chrysostom, *In Matthaeum*, PG.58.650.31-45.

mccccxcvi John Chrysostom, *op. cit.* PG.58.650.45-53 (homily 69, going on with the text quoted above).

mccccxcvii Cf. the idea of someone being in possession of 'a heart of compassion' (σπλάγχνα οἰκτιρμοῦ), Col. 3:12; cf. Phil. 2:1. Origen, *Scholia in Canticum Canticorum*, PG.17.272.51-53: ἱμάτια δὲ τῆς νύμφης, οἱ ἐνδεδυμένοι *Χριστὸν* Ἰησοῦν [Gal. 3:27], *σπλάγχνα οἰκτιρμῶν καὶ χρηστότητα καὶ ταπεινοφροσύνην* [Col. 3:12]; *excPs*, PG.17.120.56-121.3:

Καὶ ἔνδυμα. ὅθεν ὁ μὲν ἁμαρτωλὸς *ἐνεδύσατο κατάραν ὡς ἱμάτιον* [Psalm 108:18], ὁ δὲ δίκαιος *τὸν Κύριον Ἰησοῦν* [Gal. 3:27], καὶ *σπλάγχνα οἰκτιρμῶν*, καὶ *πανοπλίαν Θεοῦ* [Eph. 6:11&13]. Οὕτως ὁ μὲν τῶν αὐτοῦ μόνον ἀκούων λόγων προτρεπτικῶν τρέφεται. *frPs*, on Psalm 64:14: Ἐνεδύσαντο Χριστὸν καὶ σπλάγχνα οἰκτιρμῶν.

mcccxcviii Origen, *apud Catena in Matthaeum*, p. 180.

mcccxcix Origen, *commMatt*, 17.16.

mcd Origen, *commMatt*, fr. 440 (Klostermann), but here is the rest of Origen's context coming to light.

mcdi Origen, *commMatt*, fr. 439 (Klostermann).

mcdii This is part of Apollinaris, *frMatt*, fr. 111; continued *infra*.

mcdiii Apollinaris, *frMatt*, fr. 111. But this is only a portion of Origen's *text* in this point.

mcdiv Origen, *commMatt*, 17.16.

mcdv Origen, *commMatt*, fr. 441 (Klostermann). See the same text attributed to Origen in the *Catena in Matthaeum*, p. 180.

mcdvi An expression distinctly characteristic of Origen and of his followers. Cf. σκυθρωπὰ καὶ ἐπίπονα ('stern threats and painful punishments') in Origen, *Cels*, V.15: τὸ ἀπὸ τῶν σκυθρωπῶν καὶ ἐπιπόνων ἐπαγόμενον τοῖς ἀλγοῦσι τέλος. Basil of Caesarea, *Homilia Exhortatoria ad Sanctum Baptisma*, PG.31.440.32: τὸ τῆς γεέννης ἐπίπονον καὶ σκυθρωπόν. *Sermones De Moribus*, PG.32.1285.23-24: σιωπᾶν δὲ ἐπὶ τοῖς σκυθρωποτέροις καὶ ἐπιπόνοις πράγμασιν. Didymus, *commZacch*, 5.76: προσδοκίᾳ τῶν ἐλευσομένων σκυθρωπῶν τε καὶ ἐπιπόνων. *frPs(al)*, 178: ἐπιπόνων καὶ σκυθρωπῶν περιεστηκότων ἃ νὺξ ἀλληγορικῶς ἐστιν. Pseudo-Basil of Caesarea (*forsan* Cassian the Sabaite), *Enarratio in Prophetam Isaiam*, 4.135: διὰ τὸ σκυθρωπὸν καὶ ἐπίπονον τῶν ἐν ἁμαρτίαις εὑρισκομένων. Later, Germanus I of Constantinople, *Historia Mystica Ecclesiae Catholicae*, 19. John of Damascus, *Sacra Parallela*, PG.95: 1164.25-26; 1528.54. Nicephorus I of Constantinople, *Pseudo-Epiphanii sive Epiphaniis Confutatio*, 8; *Refutatio et Eversio Definitionis Synodalis anni 815*, chapter 68. George Monachus, *Chronicon*, p. 342; *Chronicon Breve*, PG.110.405.33-34.

mcdvii Origen, *commMatt*, 17.16.

mcdviii The expression ἀνόνητος μεταμέλεια ('profitless repentance') has always remained extremely rare and appears only in two of Origen's admirers. Gregory of Nyssa, *Contra Usurarios*, p. 204 (using this in the same context as Origen): καὶ ὀργισθεὶς ὁ κύριος παρέδωκεν αὐτὸν τοῖς βασανισταῖς, ἕως οὗ ἀποδῷ πᾶν τὸ ὀφειλόμενον αὐτῷ. Τότε σε καταλήψεται ἡ ἀνόνητος μεταμέλεια, στεναγμοὶ δὲ καταλήψονται βαρεῖς καὶ κόλασις ἀπαραίτητος. Gregory of Nazianzus, *Contra Julianum*, PG.35.665.20-22: καὶ τὰς ἐν αὐτοῖς τοῖς δεινοῖς ἐξαγορεύσεις καὶ ἀνονήτους μεταμελείας. Later, an instance occurs in Photius, who has been shown to be aware of Origen's present commentary. Photius, *Fragmenta in Epistulam i ad Corinthios*, p. 580 (*apud Catena in Epistulam i ad Corinthios*, p. 325): μᾶλλον μὲν οὖν καὶ πολλὴν μεταμέλειαν, εἰ καὶ ἀνόνητον ἐφ' οἷς ὑπηρετήσαντο, ἕξουσιν. Finally, this appears in the *Epistulae et Amphilochia*, but I have argued that this collection cannot be entirely attributed to Photius and that there are several 'epistles' for which there are stong indications that they were written by the sixth-century moderate Origenist Cassian the Sabaite. Anyway, see *Epistulae et Amphilochia*, epistle 284, lines 2384-2386: ἐκεῖθεν (οἴμοι) τῶν τολμημάτων τὴν συναίσθησιν ἕξουσιν, ἂν μὴ ἐνταῦθα, ὅτε καὶ ἡ μεταμέλεια τὸ ἀνόνητον καὶ ἡ τιμωρία τὸ ἀδυσώπητόν τε καὶ ἄφυκτον τοῖς τιμωρουμένοις ἐπάγει.

mcdix *Catena in Matthaeum*, p. 180. This is 'unattributed ('Εξ ἀνεπιγράφου) and the last of a series of fragments attributed to Origen. However, this is Origen's, too.

mcdx Cf. Origen, *frJohn*, fr. 34: *Φαρὲς* γὰρ παρ' Ἑβραίοις *Ὁ διῃρημένος*. He received this from Joesephus, and then bequeathed it to only a couple of authors, who normally drew on him. Cf. Josephus, *Antiquitates Judaicae*, 10.244: *φαρές·* καὶ τοῦτο κλάσμα δηλοῖ καθ' Ἑλλάδα γλῶτταν. Eusebius, *Ad Stephanum*, PG.22.909.27: ἑρμηνεύεται γοῦν *Φαρὲς μερισμός*. John Chrysostom, *In Genesim*, PG.54.534.68-70: *Καὶ ἐκάλεσε τὸ ὄνομα αὐτοῦ Φαρές*. Διακοπὴ γὰρ ἑρμηνεύεται τὸ ὄνομα, καὶ μερισμός, ὡς ἂν εἴποι τις. *In Matthaeum*, PG.57.35.9: τὸ γὰρ *Φαρὲς* διαίρεσίς ἐστι καὶ διακοπή. John Zonaras, *Epitome Historiarum*, v. 1, p. 188: τὸ δὲ *φαρὲς* διαίρεσιν ἑρμηνεύων ὁ προφήτης, τοῦτο γὰρ εἰς Ἕλληνα φωνὴν ἡ λέξις μεταγομένη δηλοῖ. Michael Psellus interpreted this as 'purity' on account of the Pharisees' self-segregation from the multitude. *Theologica*, opusculum 106: ὡς οἱ Φαρισσαῖοι καλούμενοι (τὸ γὰρ *φαρὲς* ὁ Ἑβραῖος καθαρὸν εἶναι βούλεται).

mcdxi Theodore of Heraclea or Theodore of Mopsuestia, *frMatt*, fr. 42.

mcdxii Cf. Origen, *commMatt*, 17.25-6; 17.28.

mcdxiii *Catena in Marcum*, p. 400 (anonymous).

mcdxiv Jerome, *commMatt*, 22.16. What he styled *ridiculous* pointed at authors such as Tertullian (*De Praescriptione Haereticorum*, 45), Pseudo-Tertullian (*Adversus Omnes Haereses*, 1.1), and Philaster of Brescia (*Diversarum Hereseon*, 28). It is quite characteristic of Jerome's character that he proposed the view he styled 'ridiculous' as one of his own in the *Dialogus adversus Luciferianos*, PL.13.178B. The present codex makes it evident that Origen, too, was aware of this hearsay. Consequently, so was Epiphanius of Salamis, *Panarion*, v. 1, p. 224. Likewise, *Catena in Marcum*, p. 400 (anonymous). It appears that Jerome perhaps placed the *ridicule* at the door of 'some Latins', subsequent to some of his discussions with Epiphanius.

mcdxv This report about the belief that Herod was Christ (supposedly after Gen. 49:10) appears with Origen for the first time, and was reproduced by a few authors only after the fifth century. Pseudo-Epiphanius, *Anacephalaeosis*, v. 1, p. 168: Ἡρῳδιανοί, οἳ Ἰουδαῖοι *μὲν ἦσαν κατὰ πάντα*, Ἡρῴδην δὲ Χριστὸν *προσεδόκων καὶ τούτῳ τὸ τοῦ Χριστοῦ ἀπεδίδοσαν γέρας καὶ ὄνομα*. *Catena in Marcum*, p. 400: Ἡρωδιανοὶ κατ' ἐκείνους τοὺς χρόνους ἦσαν οἱ τὸν Ἡρώδην Χριστὸν εἶναι λέγοντες, ὡς ἱστορεῖται. John of Damascus, *De Haeresibus*, 20: Ἡρωδιανοὶ Ἰουδαῖοι μὲν ἦσαν *κατὰ πάντα*, Ἡρώδην δὲ Χριστὸν προσεδόκουν καὶ αὐτῷ τὸ τοῦ Χριστοῦ γέρας ἀπεδίδουν καὶ ὄνομα. Pseudo-Zonaras, *Lexicon*, letter eta, p. 1003: *Ἡρωδιανοί*. οὗτοι τὸν Ἡρώδην Χριστὸν ἐνόμιζον καὶ ἐπ' αὐτῷ ἐσεμνύνοντο, ἐκ τοῦ ῥητοῦ συναρπασθέντες τοῦ λέγοντος, *οὐκ ἐκλείψει ἄρχων ἐξ Ἰούδα, ἕως ἂν ἔλθοι ὃ ἀπόκειται*. [Cf. Gen. 49:10] Ἐπειδὴ γὰρ ἐξέλιπον οἱ ἐκ τοῦ Ἰούδα ἄρχοντες, μετ' ἐκείνους δὲ ὁ Ἡρώδης ἐβασίλευσεν οὐκ ὢν ἀπὸ γένους τοῦ Ἰούδα, ἀλλ' ἀλλόφυλος, τούτῳ ἀπέκειτο τὸ εἶναι Χριστόν.

mcdxvi Jerome, *commMatt*, 22.20.

mcdxvii Cf. Origen, *commMatt*, 17.28: διὰ τοῦτο ἀκούσαντες τὰ δοκοῦντα αὐτῷ πρὸς τὸ πύσμα αὐτῶν καὶ θαυμάσαντες, ὅτι μὴ ἔδωκεν αὐτοῖς ἀφορμὰς τοῦ αὐτῷ ἐπιβουλεύειν οὐκ ἔμειναν μὲν παρ' αὐτῷ, ὡς οἱ μαθηταί, οὐδὲ ἁπλῶς *ἀπῆλθον*, ὡς περὶ ἄλλων γέγραπται, *ἀφέντες δὲ αὐτὸν ἀπῆλθον*. Καὶ τοιοῦτοί γέ εἰσιν οἱ ἀφιέντες τὸν λόγον καὶ ἀπιστοῦντες αὐτῷ καὶ ἀπιόντες ἀπ' αὐτοῦ μετὰ τὸ ἀκοῦσαι αὐτοῦ. Καὶ οὐχ ἁμαρτήσει λέγων περὶ τῶν μετὰ τὸ ἀκοῦσαι ἀποστάντων καὶ τοῦ ἀκούειν, ὅτι οἱ τοιοῦτοι *ἀφέντες* τὸν Ἰησοῦν *ἀπῆλθον*. Ἡμεῖς δὲ ἐροῦμεν τὸ τῆς νύμφης· *ἐκράτησα αὐτόν, καὶ οὐκ ἀφῆκα αὐτόν* (Song of Songs, 3:4).

mcdxviii *Catena in Marcum*, p. 402 (anonymous).

mcdxix Origen, *frLuc*, fr. 242.

mcdxx Whereas it could have been possible for Valentinians and Marcionites to controvert each other in Origen's times, it is highly unlikely that this could have happened during

Apollinaris' times, i.e. in the fourth century, when those sects were a remote story of the past. Thus, beyond the fact that this passage is indubitably Origen's, attributing this to Apollinaris would be absurd on historical grounds.

mcdxxi Apollinaris, *frMatt*, fr. 113 & *Catena in Matthaeum*, p. 183. But this is the selfsame text as Origen's *frLuc*, fr. 242.

mcdxxii *Catena in Marcum*, p. 402 (anonymous).

mcdxxiii Cf. Lev. 26:15; Num. 15:22; 15:40; Deut. 6:25; 8:1; 11:8; 11:13; 13:19; 11:22; 15:5; 17:19; 19:9; 26:13; 26:18; 27:1; 27:10; 28:1; 28:15; 30:10; 3 Kings, 8:58; 1 Paralipomenon, 28:8; 2 Esdras, 20:30; Psalms, 118:6; 118:128; 1. Ez. 18:21.

mcdxxiv Cyril of Alexandria, *frMatt*, fr. 251.

mcdxxv John Chrysostom, *In Matthaeum*, PG.58.663.22-31.

mcdxxvi John Chrysostom, *op. cit.* PG.58.663.31-32.

mcdxxvii John Chrysostom, *In Joannem*, PG.59.472.17-20.

mcdxxviii Only one author paraphrased this passage of Isaiah and formulated it παραδόσεις ἀνθρώπων, thus following Origen's phraseology and commenting on the same topic (namely, scriptural reference to the hypocricy of Jewish leaders). This author was Eusebius, who no doubt had read this part of Origen's commentary on Matthew. Eusebius, *In Isaiam*, 1.96: Ταῦτα δὲ περὶ αὐτοὺς ἔσεσθαί φησιν ὁ θεὸς μετὰ τοῦ καὶ τὴν αἰτίαν ἐπιλέγειν. Ἐπειδὴ γὰρ μέχρι στόματος καὶ χειλέων τιμᾶν τὸν θεὸν προσεποιοῦντο, ἡ δὲ διάνοια αὐτῶν παρελογίζετο τὴν ἐπαγγελίαν, σέβειν μὲν αὐτὸν προσποιουμένων, προτιμώντων δὲ τῶν αὐτοῦ λόγων διδασκαλίας τινὰς καὶ *παραδόσεις ἀνθρώπων*, ἃς περιποιοῦσι δευτερώσεις πρεσβυτέρων τινῶν κατέχειν σεμνυνόμενοι. *Op. cit.* 2:48: Ἐπειδὴ δὲ μετὰ τὴν τοσαύτην κακίαν ἐπαγγέλλονται μὲν τὰς ἀπὸ τῶν θείων γραφῶν διδασκαλίας, ἐκπίπτουσι δὲ εἰς γραώδεις μύθους καὶ εἰς *παραδόσεις ἀνθρώπων* οὐδὲν ὑγιὲς οὐδὲ ὠφέλιμον περιεχούσας. As for Photius, he did not really follow Origen on this: he just copied from Origen *verbatim* (assuming that attribution of a passage of Origen to Photius was not a manoeuvre by a subsequent scribe seeking to thwart the name of the 'heretic' Origen).

mcdxxix This is a characteristic phrase introduced by Origen and later taken up only by Theodoret, *In Epistulas Sancti Pauli*, PG.82.109.34-36: Διά τοι τοῦτο καὶ ἀκριβεστέρα τοῦ νόμου ἡ νομοθεσία τῆς χάριτος, ὡς τῆς ἐπικουρίας τὴν δυσκολίαν λυούσης. Photius did not really employ this: he just copied from Origen.

mcdxxx Photius, *frMatt*, fr. 84, col. 1; see also the first few lines of this also in col. 2.

mcdxxxi Meaning, Deut. 6:8.

mcdxxxii Jerome, *commMatt*, 23.6.

mcdxxxiii Origen, *commSerMatt*, pp. 21-22.

mcdxxxiv Origen, *commMatt*, fr. 445 (Klostermann).

mcdxxxv Origen, *commMatt*, fr. 446 (Klostermann).

mcdxxxvi This is reminiscent of Plato's proverbial phrase that was quoted by a vast number of authors throughout all Antiquity, including Origen. *Timaeus*, 28c4-29a3: "Now to discover the Maker and Father of this universe is a hard thing to do; and once one has discovered Him, it is impossible to communicate Him to all men" (τὸν μὲν οὖν ποιητὴν καὶ πατέρα τοῦδε τοῦ παντὸς εὑρεῖν τε ἔργον καὶ εὑρόντα εἰς πάντας ἀδύνατον λέγειν). Cf. Origen, *Princ*, I.1.6: "Our mind is of itself unable to behold God as he is, it understands the parent of the universe (parentem universitatis) from the beauty of his works and the comeliness of his creatures." *Op. cit.* I.2.1: "God ... the parent of the universe"; *op. cit.* II.1.2 & II.1.3: 'God ... the parent of all things'. Likewise, *Cels*, VII.42-43.

mcdxxxvii See *Anaxagoras*, pp. 521-522: Philostratus (*Vita Apollonii*, 1.13) argued that, since the cosmic principles determine what ostensibly appears as generation, it can be said that a child is born not *from* its parents, but *by means of* (or, through) its parents (ὁ γεννηθεὶς διὰ γονέων γεγέννηται, οὐχ ὑπὸ γονέων). It is impressive, yet not surprising, that Origen fully endorsed this notion: although parents provide the material for offspring to be formed, and thus 'we have parents as far as our bodies are concerned', otherwise 'there is neither mother nor father of any soul, since the latter is created by God alone' (οὐ γάρ ἐστι ψυχῆς μήτηρ ἢ πατήρ· ταύτης γὰρ ὁ Θεὸς μόνος ἐστὶ ποιητὴς καὶ πατήρ). This is what God means by saying 'all souls are mine', since 'every soul has an existence of its own', and none of them is produced from one another (i.e. transmigration is banned). Origen, *selEz*, PG.13.817.16-23: ἑκάστη ψυχὴ ἰδίαν ὑπόστασιν ἔχει, ἐν τῷ ἰδίῳ λόγῳ ἱσταμένη, καὶ οὐκ ἐν ἄλλῳ, commenting on Ezekiel, 18:4, 'all the souls are mine'. The expression ἐν τῷ ἰδίῳ λόγῳ means 'in itself'. A unique parallel appears in Pseudo-Alexander of Aphrodisias, *'Απορίαι καὶ Λύσεις*, p. 52: ὁπότερον γάρ, εἰ εἶχεν ἐν τῷ ἰδίῳ λόγῳ, οὐκ ἂν ἦν ἐν τῷ ἑτέρῳ γενόμενον. Once again, Origen availed himself of Alexander's formulas.

mcdxxxviii Origen, *commMatt*, fr. 447 (Klostermann).

mcdxxxix Photius, *frMatt*, fr. 85.

mcdxl Cf. Origen, *Princ*, IV.3.6 (*Philocalia*, 1.22); IV.3.8 (*Philocalia*, 1.24); *exhMar*, 38; *frLuc*, fr. 174.

mcdxli Photius, *frMatt*, fr. 86.

mcdxlii Origen, *commMatt*, fr. 450 (Klostermann).

mcdxliii Origen, *commMatt*, 10.14.

mcdxliv Origen, *commMatt*, fr. 449 (Klostermann).

mcdxlv Origen, *commMatt*, fr. 448 (Klostermann).

mcdxlvi Cf. John Chrysostom, *In Matthaeum*, PG.58.673.56: *Υἱὸν δὲ γεέννης* φησί, τουτέστιν, αὐτογέενναν. Likewise, (slightly paraphrased) *Catena in Matthaeum*, p. 189: τὸ δὲ *υἱὸν γεέννης* δηλοῖ αὐτογεένναν.

mcdxlvii Origen, *commMatt*, fr. 451 (Klostermann).

mcdxlviii John Chrysostom, *In Matthaeum*, PG.58.673.56-57 & (anonymously) *Catena in Matthaeum*, p. 189: *διπλότερον* δὲ εἶπεν, ἵνα καὶ ἐκείνους φοβήσῃ. But cf. *supra*, folio 178r: προσέθηκεν ἐκ τοῦ πατρὸς εἰρηκέναι ἵνα φοβήσῃ αὐτούς.

mcdxlix Origen, *commMatt*, fr. 452 (Klostermann).

mcdl Origen used this portion from Matthew in order to argue for his notion of 'difference of punishments'. *commJohn*, XX.34.298-302. See *supra*, endnote dccciv.

mcdli Theodore of Heraclea, *frMatt*, fr. 115 & *apud Catena in Matthaeum*, p. 189; to be continued *infra*.

mcdlii The notion of 'logical altar' (λογικὸν θυσιαστήριον, meaning human mind opting freely for righteousness and willingly dedicating to God 'sacrifice' of its own passions) is distinctly Origen's and so it has remained always. See *frLam*, fr. 49: ψυχῆς δὲ θυσιαστήριον τὸ ἐν ἡμῖν λογικόν, δι' οὗπερ ἱερουργεῖται τὰ πάθη νεκρούμενα. *selPs*, PG.12.1273.48-52: Λογικὸν θυσιαστήριον Θεοῦ ὁ νοῦς ἡμῶν ἐστιν, ἐφ' οὗ καίομεν τῷ παρὰ τοῦ Πατρὸς εἰς τὴν γῆν βληθέντι πυρὶ πάντα λογισμὸν ἄλογον ἀποσκιρτῶντα τῆς ἀγέλης τοῦ δεσπότου. During the first millennium, this idea was reproduced by Chrysostom alone. *In Epistulam ii ad Corinthios*, PG.61.540.19-30 ('altar' identified with one's own 'body' and 'action'). Centuries later the notion of 'rational man' being 'altar' of God was explicitly set forth and identified with human 'mind' in patently Origenian spirit and vocabulary by Callistus I of Constantinople (Patriarch, died 1363), *Capitula De Puritate Animae*, 30: οὕτω μοι νόει καὶ ἐπὶ τοῦ νοός. Αὐτοῦ γὰρ ἐκεῖθεν εἰσδύντος πρὸς τὸ τῆς ψυχῆς ταμεῖον, καθάπερ κέντρῳ τινὶ προσκολλᾶται μετὰ τοῦ Πνεύματος ἡ ψυχὴ καὶ εὐθὺς ἅμα μετὰ τοῦ ἀΰλου καὶ ἀκτίστου συμπλέκεται τῇ ἀγάπῃ Θεοῦ καὶ ὁλικῶς ἑνωθεῖσα ἐξομοιοῦται Θεῷ καθόσον ἐστὶν ἐφικτόν. Ἐνταῦθά γάρ ἐστι τὸ λογικὸν θυσιαστήριον τοῦ Θεοῦ. The expression μοι νόει, (see endnote cmxix; cf. dcclxxi) which Origen used abundantly after having received this from Galen, is also characteristic, and so is the expression τὸ λογικὸν θυσιαστήριον. Moreover, the tenor of this passage rings a bell of the Platonic idea of 'becoming like God as far as possible' (*Theaetetus*, 176b). Likewise, Callistus I, *op. cit.* 3: Ναὸς Θεοῦ καὶ θυσιαστήριον ἐστὶ κυρίως ὁ λογικὸς ἄνθρωπος· ἐν αὐτῷ γὰρ τελειοῦνται αἱ νοεραὶ θυσίαι καὶ λατρεῖαι μυστικῶς κατὰ τὸν ἔσω ἄνθρωπον.

mcdliii This is the first time of the bread and wine of the Holy Eucharist being styled 'material' existence of the Body of the Logos. This involves an interesting story, which is instructive as to how history of ideas has been formed.

The notion couched by means of this specific locution appeared as an echo only in later Byzantine scholars, who argued that, whereas prior to the mystery of Eucharist bread and wine are 'images' of the Lord's Body, subsequent to that, they are the Body *itself.* Nicephorus Blemmydes (scholar and theologian, clergyman, 1197-1272), *Fragmentum ex Typico* (*cap. 4*), lines 13-16: Ἀλλὰ τὸ μὲν θυμίαμα τύπος ὄν, μένει τύπος, ὁ δ' ἄρτος, ἱερουργούμενος μὲν ἔστι, καὶ ἀντὶ τοῦ δεσποτικοῦ σώματος τῷ θυσιαστηρίῳ προκείμενος, ἀντίτυπος ἐκείνου κατὰ τοῦτον τὸν λόγον εἴρηται, καὶ ὁ οἶνος, τοῦ αἵματος. Bessarion, *De Sacramento Eucharistiae*, 1 (appealing to James, Basil of Caesarea, and Chrysostom), 1: ἄρτον καὶ οἶνον τὰ προκείμενα δῶρα καλοῦσιν καὶ ἀντίτυπα τοῦ σώματος καὶ αἵματος. *Op. cit.* (appealing to James, Clement [of Rome], Basil of Caesarea, and Chrysostom, adding John of Damascus and Pseudo-Dionysius the Areopagite) 13.1: δευτέρα δὲ ἡ τοῦ θείου Δαμασκηνοῦ ῥῆσις, ἀντίτυπα λέγοντος τὸν μακάριον Βασίλειον τὰ δῶρα εἰπεῖν πρὸ τοῦ ἁγιασθῆναι, ἐκεῖνον δὲ αὐτὰ καλέσαι ἀντίτυπα πολλῷ μετὰ τὰ κυριακὰ ῥήματα. The claim was that John of Damascus attributed the idea to Basil of Caesarea, who wrote, 'even if *certain ones* styled bread and wine images of the Lord's body and blood (as the divinely inspired Basil of Caesarea said), they called them so not as really being such [i.e. *images* of the Body] *after* their sanctification; instead, they called them so [i.e. 'images'] considering the state of this offer as this was *prior to* its sanctification.' John of Damascus, *Expositio Fidei*, 86, lines 163-166: Εἰ δὲ καί τινες ἀντίτυπα τοῦ σώματος καὶ τοῦ αἵματος τοῦ κυρίου τὸν ἄρτον καὶ τὸν οἶνον ἐκάλεσαν, ὡς ὁ θεοφόρος ἔφη Βασίλειος, οὐ μετὰ τὸ ἁγιασθῆναι εἶπον, ἀλλὰ πρὶν ἁγιασθῆναι αὐτὴν τὴν προσφορὰν οὕτω καλέσαντες. This is confirmed as a saying by Basil by the following parallel: John of Damascus, *frMatt*, PG.96.1409.35-37: Οὐκ ἔστι τύπος ὁ ἄρτος καὶ οἶνος τοῦ σώματος καὶ αἵματος τοῦ Χριστοῦ, μὴ γένοιτο, ἀλλ' αὐτὸ τὸ σῶμα καὶ αὐτὸ τὸ αἷμα. *frMatt* (cont.) PG.96.1409.40 & *Expositio Fidei*, 86, lines 163-166: Εἰ δὲ καί τινες ἀντίτυπα τοῦ σώματος καὶ τοῦ αἵματος τοῦ Κυρίου τὸν ἄρτον καὶ τὸν οἶνον ἐκάλεσαν, ὡς ὁ θεοφόρος Βασίλειος, οὐ μετὰ τὸ ἁγιασθῆναι εἶπον, ἀλλὰ πρὶν ἁγιασθῆναι, τὴν προσφορὰν οὕτω καλέσαντες. Ἀντίτυπα δὲ τῶν μελλόντων λέγονται, οὐχ ὡς μὴ ὄντα ἀληθῶς σῶμα καὶ αἷμα Χριστοῦ, ἀλλ' ὅτι νῦν μὲν δι' αὐτῶν μετέχομεν τῆς Χριστοῦ θεότητος, τότε δὲ νοητῶς διὰ μόνης τῆς θέας. John of Damascus himself endorsed this doctrine. *Expositio Fidei*, 86, lines 180-182: Ἀντίτυπα δὲ τῶν μελλόντων λέγονται οὐχ ὡς μὴ ὄντα ἀληθῶς σῶμα καὶ αἷμα Χριστοῦ, ἀλλ' ὅτι νῦν μὲν δι' αὐτῶν μετέχομεν τῆς Χριστοῦ θεότητος, τότε δὲ νοητῶς διὰ μόνης τῆς θέας. Cf. *Orationes De Imaginibus Tres*, 1.27; 2.22.

In other words, Basil reported that the peculiar reference to bread and wine being material representation of the Lord's Body (ἀντίτυπα τοῦ σώματος καὶ αἵματος) was not

Basil's own, but it had been so couched by *certain earlier theologians* (τινὲς ἀντίτυπα τοῦ σώματος καὶ τοῦ αἵματος τοῦ κυρίου τὸν ἄρτον καὶ τὸν οἶνον ἐκάλεσαν). It could be easy to surmise that those 'certain ones' pointed to Basil's hero Origen, but now this can be definitely confirmed by the present codex, from which we learn that this was Origen's idea from start to finish: it is the holiness itself of the holy mystery that sanctifies bread and wine as material representation of the Body of the Lord. See also *infra*, Origen, *commMatt*, fr. 527 (Klostermann): the elementary natures of bread and wine are *really* transmuted into 'body and blood of Christ' (κατὰ τὸ ἀληθὲς εἰς σῶμα καὶ αἷμα Χριστοῦ), i.e. this is *transubstantiation*. This is percisely the idea that Gregory of Nyssa took up from Origen and argued that, during the mystery of the Holy Eucharist, bread and wine are *really* altered into ther real Body of the Logos. *Oratio Catechetica*, 37, line 90-103: Καλῶς οὖν καὶ νῦν τὸν τῷ Λόγῳ τοῦ Θεοῦ ἁγιαζόμενον ἄρτον εἰς σῶμα τοῦ Θεοῦ Λόγου μεταποιεῖσθαι πιαστεύομεν. … Οὐοῦν ὅθεν ὁ ἐ ἐκείνῳ τῷ σώματι μεταποιηθεὶς ἄρτος εἰς θείαν μετέστη δύναμιν, διὰ τοῦ αὐτοῦ καὶ νῦν τὸ ἴσον γίνεται. … οὐ διὰ βρώσεως προϊὼν εἰς τὸ σῶμα γενέσθαι τοῦ Λόγου, ἀλλ' εὐθὺς πρὸς τὸ σῶμα διὰ τοῦ Λόγου μεταποιούμενος, καθὼς εἴρηται διὰ τοῦ Λόγου, *Τοῦτο ἐστὶ τὸ σῶμα μου*. [Matt. 26:26; Mark, 14:22; Luke, 22:19]. This was copied by only two much later authors, both of whom cited Gregory and quoted a very extensive part of that section. Theorianus of Constantinople (twelfth century), *Disputatio Secunda cum Nersete Patriarcha Generali Armeniorum*, p. 261; and Bessarion, *De Sacramento Eucharistiae*, 10.7.

Nevertheless, when Bessarion composed his own treatise on the mystery of the Holy Eucharist and recalled how 'John of Damascus explained the term *image* (ἀντίτυπος)', he wrote that it was Basil of Caesarea *himself* who said that bread and wine are 'images of the Lord's body and blood', and that those words were found in the text of Basil's *Liturgy*. Bessarion, *De Sacramento Eucharistiae*, 14.1: πρὸς ἃ δὲ ὁ ἱερὸς Ἰωάννης ὁ Δαμασκηνὸς περὶ τῆς τοῦ ἀντιτύπου φωνῆς λέγει, ὡς διὰ τοῦτο τὸν μέγαν Βασίλειον εἰπεῖν τὰ ἱερὰ δῶρα ἀντίτυπα τοῦ σώματος καὶ αἵματος τοῦ κυρίου, διότι οὔπω ἡγίασται, κεῖσθαι δὲ ταῦτα τὰ ῥήματα ἐν τῇ τῆς ἱερᾶς τελετῆς συνθήκῃ τοῦ παμμάκαρος Βασιλείου πολλῷ μετὰ τὰ κυριακὰ ῥήματα. Also, *op. cit.* 14.3: τὰ ῥήματα ἐκεῖνα τὰ Βασιλείου, ἐν οἷς τὰ δῶρα ἀντίτυπα καλεῖ τοῦ σώματος. However, those words were not Basil's: they were Origen's, and Basil correctly reported that they were not his own – and yet Bessarion distorted historical truth, probably unconsciously, out of misunderstanding. Be that as it may, other theologians of that era wrote along the same line, arguing that those were Basil's words. Symeon of Thessaloniki, *Expositio De Divino Templo*, 66: αὐτοῖς τοῖς δώροις, ἀντιτύποις οὖσιν, ὡς ὁ μέγας φησὶ Βασίλειος. *Op. cit.* 83: ἀντίτυπα τὰ δῶρα φησὶν ὁ μέγας Βασίλειος. *Op. cit.* 65: τὰ θεῖα δῶρα … ἡτοιμασμένα εἰσί, καὶ ἀνάθημα Θεῷ καὶ ἀντίτυπα τοῦ δεσποτικοῦ σώματός τε καὶ αἵματος. Marcus Eugenicus, *Epistulae*, epistle 2.2: τύπον δὲ καὶ εἰκόνα λέγομεν καὶ ἡμεῖς ἀποσῴζειν τὰ θεῖα δῶρα πρὸ τοῦ τελειωθῆναι τοῦ Δεσποτικοῦ σώματος καὶ αἵματος. Ὅθεν καὶ ὁ μέγας Βασίλειος ἐν τῇ ἱερᾷ λειτουργίᾳ *ἀντίτυπα* ταῦτα καλεῖ. *Προθέντες γάρ φησι τὰ ἀντίτυπα τοῦ τιμίου σώματος καὶ αἵματος τοῦ Χριστοῦ σου*. In the *Libellus De Consecratione Eucharistica*, 4, Marcus Eugenicus quotes from what he believed to be Basil's *Liturgy*, this time in much wider context, part of which reads thus: θαρροῦντες προσεγγίζομεν τῷ ἁγίῳ σου θυσιαστηρίῳ, καὶ προθέντες τὰ ἀντίτυπα τοῦ ἁγίου σώματος καὶ αἵματος τοῦ Χριστοῦ σου.

How those words came to be attributed to Basil is a bit of mystery, since we find them also in earlier texts, such as the ninth-century anonymous text, *Epistula ad Theophilum Imperatorem De Imaginibus, Finis alter* (*e cod. Iviron 381*), 31: Καὶ ὁ ἅγιος Βασίλειος. *Ὅς ἐστιν εἰκὼν τῆς σῆς ἀγαθότητος, σφραγὶς ἰσότυπος, ἐν ἑαυτῷ δεικνὺς σὲ τὸν Πατέρα· πλάσας γὰρ τὸν ἄνθρωπον καὶ τῇ σῇ εἰκόνι τιμήσας αὐτόν*. Καὶ πάλιν φησί· *Καὶ προθέντες τὰ ἀντίτυπα τοῦ ἁγίου σώματος καὶ αἵματος τοῦ Χριστοῦ σου*. Much later (fourteenth century), the same passage was also attributed to Basil by Gregory Acindynus (*Refutatio Magna*, oration 3.56) and Manuel Calecas (*De Principiis Catholicae Fidei*, PG.152.541.24-28).

The first of those two quotations is more likely to be Athanasius' (*In illud: Omnia Mihi Tradita Sunt*, PG.25.217.30-31: Σφραγὶς γάρ ἐστιν ἰσότυπος ἐν αὐτῷ δεικνὺς τὸν Πατέρα). However, Basil used the expression σφραγὶς ἰσότυπος ('identical seal') in reference to the Son (*De Spiritu Sancto*, 26.64: διὰ δὲ τοῦ χαρακτῆρος, ἐπὶ τὸν οὗ ἐστιν ὁ χαρακτὴρ καὶ ἡ ἰσότυπος σφραγὶς ἀναγόμεθα). So did Cassian the Sabaite (Pseudo-Didymus), *De Trinitate*, 16.30: συνυφεστηκυίας δὲ δηλονότι τῆς σφραγίδος τῷ ἀρχετύπῳ καὶ ἰσοτύπου οὔσης. Cf. Pseudo-Basil of Caesarea, *Consolatoria ad Aegrotum*, PG.31.1721.36 (*apud* Proclus of Constantinople, *Homilia Consolatoria ad Aegrotum*, line 163; then, *Epistula ad Theophilum Imperatorem De Imaginibus*, 31, as above, and Gregory Acindynus, *Refutatio Magna*, 3.56, both of them considering this as Basil's genuine work).

Despite all those references attributing this notion and locution to Basil of Caesarea (although Basil himself ascribed this to 'certain ones' prior to him), we come upon this in the acts of oecumenical synods as vocabulary of Cyril of Alexandria. ACO, *Concilium Universale Ephesenum anno 431*, tome 1.1.6, pp. 11 & 87: βλέπε περὶ τοῦ σώματος αὐτῷ τοῦ δεσποτικοῦ τὸ προκείμενον ‹ὄν›· *ὁσάκις ἂν ἐσθίητε τὸν ἄρτον τοῦτον*, οὗ ἐστι τὸ σῶμα ἀντίτυπον. However, there is no text of Cyril's entertaining the notion of this 'body' in the sense of 'image' (at one point he uses the term ἀντίτυπος in the sense of a body resisting change of its shape, i.e. literally. *Expositio in Psalmos*, PG.69.1164.54).

Anyhow, in the fifteenth century, Gennadius Scholarius passionately argued for the *real* transubstantiation (μετουσίωσις) of bread and wine into the Lord's body. *Epitome Summae Contra Gentiles Thomae Aquinae*, 4.64; *Quaestiones Principales*, line 101; *Orationes et Panegyrici*, oration 7.6; *De Ingressis Sanctis et Contra Azymos*, pp. 198-202; in the last of those works (p. 200), he argued against those who preached that the Holy Communion is ἀντίτυπον of the Lord's body (οὔτε δὲ ἀντίτυπά εἰσιν); instead, he posited that this is 'really the body and blood' of Jesus. One century later, the Patriarch of Alexandria Meletius I Pegas (1549-601, in office since 1590) argued along this line (mentioning Gennadius) in equal fervour. *Epistulae*, epistle 258.

It is remarkable that John of Damascus' foregoing quotation from Basil (Οὐκ ἔστι τύπος ὁ ἄρτος καὶ οἶνος τοῦ σώματος καὶ αἵματος τοῦ Χριστοῦ, μὴ γένοιτο, ἀλλ᾽ αὐτὸ τὸ σῶμα καὶ αὐτὸ τὸ αἷμα) was treated as highly authoritative and was quoted by later authors, such as Euthymius Zigabenus, *Panoplia Dogmatica ad Alexium Comnenum*, chapter 25, column 1269; Bessarion, *De Sacramento Eucharistiae*, section 5.3 (citing 'Damascenus'); Dositheus II, Patriarch, *Δωδεκάβιβλος Δοσιθέου Ζ'-Η'*, Book 8, p. 393.

Let this analysis be one more case which is symptomatic of how Origen's original ideas and formulations were lost into a labyrinth of false references, misguided reports, misattributions, and distortions.

mcdliv This is a serious mistake, either scribal or editorial. But the *Catena in Matthaeum* has the correct word, namely, θῦμα.

mcdlv Apollinaris, *frMatt*, fr. 116 & *apud Catena in Matthaeum*, p. 189-190. But now we have more of Origen's flowing text.

mcdlvi This is the continuation of the passage attributed to Theodore of Heraclea, *frMatt*, fr. 115 & *apud Catena in Matthaeum*, p. 189; to be continued *infra*.

mcdlvii Cf. Origen, *commJohn*, II.6.49: καὶ ἀληθινὸς γὰρ πρὸς ἀντιδιαστολὴν σκιᾶς καὶ τύπου καὶ εἰκόνος … ὁ γὰρ ἐπὶ γῆς οὐ τοιοῦτος ὁποῖος ὁ ἐν οὐρανῷ, ἅτε γενόμενος σὰρξ καὶ διὰ σκιᾶς καὶ τύπων καὶ εἰκόνων λαλούμενος. *Op. cit.* XIII.24.146: καὶ ἐν ἀληθείᾳ σέβειν αὐτὸν καὶ μηκέτι τύποις μηδὲ σκιαῖς καὶ ὑποδείγμασιν. *frJohn,* fr. 12: καὶ τῆς ἀληθείας ὑπερβαινούσης τὰς σκιὰς καὶ τοὺς τύπους. *frLuc,* fr. 78: ὅτι θεοῦ ἦν ὁ ναὸς καὶ ἦν ἐν ἰδίοις ὁ Χριστός, ὁ καὶ πάλαι διὰ τοῦ νόμου γραφόμενος καὶ ὡς ἐν σκιαῖς καὶ τύποις μορφούμενος. *De Pascha,* p. 110: τὸ γὰρ σκιὰν εἶναι τὸν νόμον καὶ τύπον, δηλοῖ φάσκον τὸ λόγιον *Ὅρα ποιήσεις πάντα κατὰ τὸν τύπον τῆς σκηνῆς τὸν δειχθέντα σοι ἐν τῷ ὄρει* (Exodus, 25:40, quoted in Heb. 8:5; cf. Acts, 7:44).

mcdlviii The words, τὸν μὲν Χριστὸν occur in Theodore of Heraclea, *frMatt,* fr. 115 (Reuss), but not in Cramer's *Catena in Matthaeum.* Obviously, at this point Reuss' text is full and correct, and it is the same as that of the present codex.

mcdlix This is the rest of the passage attributed to Theodore of Heraclea (continued from above). *Catena in Matthaeum,* p. 189.

mcdlx Theodore of Mopsuestia, *frMatt,* fr. 100; to be continued *infra.*

mcdlxi The expression πάντα εἰδέναι (referring to 'those who believe that they know everything') was pretty favourite to Origen, especially during the later period of his life. *Cels,* I.54: Ἐπεὶ δὲ ὁ ἐπαγγελλόμενος εἰδέναι τὰ τοῦ λόγου πάντα Κέλσος. *Op. cit.* II.32: Οὐ γὰρ ᾔδει ὁ ὡς ἀληθῶς ἀλαζὼν Κέλσος καὶ ἐπαγγελλόμενος εἰδέναι πάντα τὰ Χριστιανῶν. *Philocalia,* 18.1: Πρὸς τοὺς Ἑλλήνων φιλοσόφους πάντα ἐπαγγελλομένους εἰδέναι. The cause for Origen to make this a recurrent theme was Celsus' allegation, 'for I know everything' (πάντα γὰρ οἶδα, *Cels,* I.12). The present codex shows that Origen maintained a memory of this when he wrote the commentary on Matthew, which he did quite a long time after he wrote the *Contra Celsum.*

mcdlxii This is the last part of the passage attributed to Theodore of Mopsuestia, *frMatt,* fr. 100.

mcdlxiii An implicit reference to Amos, 2:8: καὶ οἶνον ἐκ συκοφαντιῶν ἔπινον ἐν τῷ οἴκῳ τοῦ θεοῦ αὐτῶν. It was Theodoret alone who took up Origen's expression. *commProphXII,* PG.81.1673.51-52: τὸν ἐξ ἀδικίας πεπορισμένον ἔπινον οἶνον. Theodore of Heraclea (if indeed did he ever write a commentary on Matthew) simply copied from Origen once again.

mcdlxiv So Reuss in Theodore of Heraclea, *frMatt,* fr. 116. Cramer's *Catena in Matthaeum* has the correct δι' ὅν.

mcdlxv Theodore of Heraclea, *frMatt,* fr. 116 & Theodore of Heraclea, *apud Catena in Matthaeum,* p. 191.

mcdlxvi Origen, *commMatt,* fr. 453 (Klostermann).

mcdlxvii Origen, *apud Catena in Matthaeum,* p. 191.

mcdlxviii Commenting on this, Origen wrote about 'rational altar' (λογικὸν θυσιαστήριον), as above (endnote mcdlii). *selPs,* PG.1273.47-1276.7.

mcdlxix Following an ambiguous Θεοδώρου alone (so frequent in catenae) this has been attributed tentatively to 'either Theodore or Heraclea or Theodore of Mopsuestia', *frMatt,* fr. 43 (Reuss). In fact, however, this belonged to neither of them: it was written by Origen.

mcdlxx Apollinaris, *apud frMatt,* fr. 117.

mcdlxxi Cf. Origen, *frJohn,* fr. 3: ἐκ τῆς προσούσης ἀγνοίας. *homJob,* p. 366: ἡ ἐπὶ τοῖς προσοῦσιν ἄδεια. *selPs,* PG.12.1477.16-17: ἀπὸ τῆς προσούσης αὐτοῖς ἰσχύος. Gregory of Nyssa, *Epistulae,* epistle 19.6-7: διὰ τὴν προσοῦσαν ἐκ τοῦ βίου αὐτῇ πρὸς τὸν θεὸν παρρησίαν. Cassian the Sabaite (the newly discovered moderate Origenist of the sixth century), *Scholia in Apocalypsin,* scholion 31: σημαίνων τὴν προσοῦσαν αὐτοῖς δικαιοσύνην. *Epistula ad Castorem,* folio 13r διὰ τὴν προσοῦσαν αὐτῷ πολιτείαν (*NDGF,* p. 44). Porphyry, *Zetemata codicis Vaticani,* p. 295: διὰ τὴν προσοῦσαν στιλβηδόνα.

mcdlxxii Origen, *commMatt*, fr. 454 (Klostermann).

mcdlxxiii Cf. Origen, *commRom* (*I.1-XII.21*), fr. 13; *commRom* (*cod. Athon. Laura 184 B64*, O. Bauernfeind), 3.13; *frPs*, Psalms 5:10; 87:12-13; *selPs*, PG.12: 1172.34-45; 1681.12-18.

mcdlxxiv Origen, *commMatt*, fr. 455 (Klostermann). See also Origen's similar passage in the *Catena in Matthaeum*, pp. 191-192, which I quote anon; *infra*, p. 316.

mcdlxxv John Chrysostom, *In Matthaeum*, PG.58.675.42-58.

mcdlxxvi Origen, *commMatt*, fr. 456 (Klostermann).

mcdlxxvii Origen, *apud Catena in Matthaeum*, p. 192.

mcdlxxviii Origen, *apud op. cit.* pp. 191-192.

mcdlxxix Origen, *commMatt*, fr. 458 (Klostermann).

mcdlxxx Origen, *apud Catena in Matthaeum*, p. 192.

mcdlxxxi John Chrysostom, *In Matthaeum*, PG.58.679.53-56.

mcdlxxxii Origen, *commMatt*, fr. 459 (Klostermann).

mcdlxxxiii Origen, *loc. cit.*

mcdlxxxiv John Chrysostom, *op. cit.* PG.58.679.57-680.1.

mcdlxxxv In the present codex, this is attributed to Origen, but in the *Catena in Matthaeum*, p. 193, this is tagged as Chrysostom's. Cf. the latter's *In Matthaeum*, PG.58.681.30-31 (homily 74). Following discussion in the Introduction, it could be surmised that Chrysostom copied from Origen once again, only because he joined a long tradition which originated with Origen and went on during the ensuing millennium. Gregory of Nyssa, *Orationes viii De Beatitudinibus*, PG.44.1289.2-4: Τοιοῦτος ὁ Κάϊν, ὁ τῇ εὐδοκιμήσει τοῦ Ἄβελ ἐπιλυσσήσας. ὁ φθόνος μὲν ἔνδοθεν τὸν φόνον ἐνεκελεύετο. Pseudo-Athanasius, *Quaestiones in Scripturam Sacram*, PG.28.737.29-30: Τοῖς παρὰ τοῦ Κάϊν τετολμημένοις πρῶτον ἁμάρτημα φθόνος ἐπὶ τῇ προτιμήσει τοῦ Ἄβελ. This is a statement that was reduplicated invariably by a considerable number of subsequent authors, such as the following ones. Basil of Caesarea (?), *Epistulae*, epistle 260.3. Cyril of Alexandria, *Ad Optimum Episcopum*, PG.77.369.1-2. George Monachus, *Chronicon*, p. 9; the same in his *Chronicon Breve*, PG.110.52.3-5. *Suda*, letter kappa, entry 27. Likewise, John Zonaras, *Epitome Historiarum*, v. 1, pp. 17-18: καὶ προσέσχεν ὁ θεὸς τοῖς τοῦ Ἄβελ δώροις, τῇ δὲ τοῦ Κάϊν οὐ προσέσχε προσαγωγῇ. Ὁ δὲ φθονήσας ἐπὶ τῇ προτιμήσει κτείνει τὸν ἀδελφόν. Moreover, Severian of Gabala, *In Job*, PG.56.566.62-63: καὶ οὕτω διὰ τὴν τιμὴν τοῦ Ἄβελ φθονήσας ὁ Κάϊν, ἀναστὰς ἐφόνευσε τὸν ἀδελφόν. In view of this tradition, the statement by John Chrysostom was a late arrival reproducing Origen's blueprint in both spirit and letter, which is confirmed by the present codex. Cf. John Chrysostom, *De Paenitentia*, PG.49.285.32-35: Κάϊν ἀπέκτεινε τὸν ἀδελφὸν αὐτοῦ Ἄβελ τῷ φθόνῳ κατεχόμενος, ὡς τῷ φθόνῳ φόνον ἐπακολουθῆσαι. *In Genesim*, PG.53.172.19-21: ἀλλ᾽ οὗτος προλαβὼν διὰ τὸ μῖσος τὸν ἀδελφόν, καὶ τὸν φθόνον τὸν ἔνδοθεν αὐτὸν τήκοντα, ἐπὶ σφαγὴν ὥρμησε τοῦ Ἄβελ. *Op. cit.* PG.54.473.19-21: Ῥίζα γὰρ τοῦ φόνου ὁ φθόνος. Οὕτω καὶ ἐξ ἀρχῆς ἐπὶ τοῦ Κάϊν καὶ ἐπὶ τοῦ Ἄβελ γέγονεν. Pseudo-John Chrysostom, *In Psalmum 75*, PG.55.597.33-35: Οὔπω γὰρ ἦν θάνατος γευσάμενος ἄνθρωπον, εἰ μὴ Κάϊν διὰ τοῦ φθόνου τὸν φόνον ἐκύησε. Τί γάρ σε ἔβλαπτε, Κάϊν, ἡ τοῦ Ἄβελ ζωή; *Op. cit.* PG.55.598.14-15: Ὁ ὄφις διὰ φθόνον τὴν Εὔαν ἠπάτησε, καὶ Κάϊν τὸν Ἄβελ διὰ φθόνον ἐφόνευσε. Cyril of Alexandria, *In Joannem*, v. 2, p. 98: ἐπαίνων δὲ καὶ τιμῆς ἠξιοῦτο δικαίως ὁ Ἄβελ, ὃ δὴ καὶ τροφὴ φθόνου τῷ Κάϊν ἐγίνετο. Pseudo-Martyrius (Martyrius: a fifth-century Patriarch of Antioch), *Oratio Funebris in Laudem Iohannis Chrysostomi*, 3: παρακέκληται μὲν γὰρ Ἄβελ, ἕτερον Ἄβελ ὁρῶν εὐλαβείᾳ κομῶντα καὶ διὰ τοῦτο φθόνῳ βαλλόμενον καὶ καταβαλλόμενον ἀδελφικῇ δεξιᾷ. Basil of Seleucia, *Sermones*, PG.85.72.8-11: ἡ τοῦ θυμοῦ φλὸξ ἀναπτομένη τῷ φθόνῳ τὸν φόνον ἀπέτεκε. *Ἀνέστη*, φησίν, *Κάϊν ἐπὶ Ἄβελ τὸν ἀδελφὸν αὐτοῦ, καὶ ἀπέκτεινεν αὐτόν*. Nilus of Ancyra, *Narrationes Septem De Monachis in Sina*, 2.12: τὸν Ἄβελ ἐπ' εὐσεβείᾳ παρὰ τοῦ θεοῦ μεμαρτυρημένον φθονέσας ἀνεῖλεν ὁ Κάϊν. Cf. Pseudo-Caesarius (Cassian the Sabaite), *Quaestiones et Responsiones*, 31: φησὶν γὰρ τῷ πρωτοφόνῳ Κάϊν βασκανίᾳ τὸν ἀδελφὸν κτείναντι ἐπὶ τῇ προτιμήσει τῶν δώρων ἐνδομυχοῦντος τοῦ φθόνου καὶ θήγοντος τοῦ φόνου τὸ φάσγανον· *ποῦ Ἄβελ ὁ ἀδελφός σου;* Romanus Melodus, *Cantica*, hymn 36.5: φθόνῳ φόνος γὰρ ἕπεται· καὶ μάρτυς ὁ Ἄβελ ὑπὸ Κάϊν φθονηθείς, φονευθεὶς δὲ μετέπειτα. Cosmas Indicopleustes, *Topographia Christiana*, 5.75: Οὗτος [sc. Χριστὸς] ἐστὶν Ἄβελ, ὁ ὡς ἐν αἰνίγματι μιμητὴς τοῦ πάθους τοῦ Χριστοῦ ὑπάρχων, ὃς διὰ φθόνον ἀγαθῶν ἔργων ὑπὸ τοῦ ἀδελφοῦ ἀδίκως ἀπεκτάνθη. Maximus Confessor, *Quaestiones ad Thalassium*, 23: διὰ τῆς ἐκβολῆς τοῦ πρωτοτόκου καὶ ἀπίστου Ἰσραήλ, ἐπαναστάντος τῷ νοητῷ Ἄβελ διὰ φθόνον καὶ ἀποκτείναντος κατὰ τὸν Κάϊν. Theodore Studites, *Parva Catechesis*, catechesis 40: ὁ φθόνος, ὑφ' οὗ ἀναφθεὶς ὁ Κάϊν ἔκτεινε τὸν ἀδελφὸν αὐτοῦ Ἄβελ. Photius, *Epistulae et Amphilochia*, epistle 11: χείρων μὲν γὰρ οὗτος [sc. Κάϊν], ἀμείνων δ' ἦν Ἄβελ. Καὶ πῶς οἷόν τε ἦν τὸν καὶ δόλου καὶ φθόνου καὶ τῆς ἄλλης κακίας καθαρεύοντα μιαιφόνους ἐπαφεῖναι χεῖρας τῷ ἀδελφῷ; Symeon the New Theologian, *Catecheses*, oration 15: Οὕτω δὲ καὶ ὁ Κάϊν ὁ υἱὸς αὐτοῦ, εἰ μὴ πρῶτον εἰς μῖσος καὶ φθόνον ἐξεκαύθη κατὰ τοῦ ἀδελφοῦ αὐτοῦ Ἄβελ, οὐκ ἂν αὐτὸν ἀπέκτεινεν. Michael Glycas, *Annales*, p. 221: ὁ γὰρ Ἄβελ φονευθεὶς παρὰ τοῦ Κάϊν διὰ φθόνον. *Op. cit.* p. 225: Φθόνος μὲν οὖν, ὡς εἴρηται, τῇ τοῦ Κάϊν ἐγκαθιδρύσας ψυχῇ τὸν τοῦ Ἄβελ φόνον ἀπέτεκεν. *Versus in Carcere Scripti*, lines 430-431: Ἀνὴρ ὁ Ἄβελ δίκαιος, ἀλλὰ παρὰ τοῦ Κάιν οὕτω ματαίως φθονηθεὶς θανάτῳ παρεδόθη. *Quaestiones in Sacram Scripturam*, chapter 36, p. 406: Ὅρα γὰρ ὡς εἴγε μὴ τὸν Κάϊν εἰς φόνον ὁ φθόνος ἠρέθισεν, οὐκ ἂν ὁ Ἄβελ καὶ πρὸ ὥρας τὸ τοῦ βίου πέρας ἐδέξατο. *Op. cit.* chapter 37, p. 443: Εὔδηλον οὖν ὅτι καὶ εἰσέτι ζῆν ὁ Ἄβελ ἔμελλεν, εἰ μή γε φθονήσας ὁ Κάϊν φόνου πεποίηκεν ἔργον αὐτόν. *Op. cit.* chapter 37, p. 449: Λάβε μοι κατὰ νοῦν, εἰ βούλει, τὸν δίκαιον ἐκεῖνον Ἄβελ καὶ ἴδε πῶς ἐπαναστὰς αὐτῷ κατὰ φθόνον ὁ Κάϊν φόνου πεποίηκεν ἔργον αὐτόν. Also, *Chronicon Paschale*, p. 453.

This long and unbroken tradition of following Origen's proposition, which started with his devout admirer Gregory of Nyssa, demonstrates that the specific passage of the present codex is indeed Origen's, and John Chrysostom simply copied from him to the letter. This is why Epiphanius of Salamis denounced Chrysostom's unremitting reading Origen's works, which is glaring present in Chrysostom's homilies on the gospel of Matthew. However, despite Epiphanius's persistence, never did Chrysostom yield; instead, he defiantly went on with *verbatim* replicating Origen's statements.

mcdlxxxvi Cf. Origen, *commSerMatt*, pp. 42-43; *commMatt*, 10:18. Jerome (*commMatt*, 23.235-236) reproduced all of this by referring to different testimonies ('some say … others want this Zachariah to be understood as … others want this Zachariah to be …) as to who this Zachariah really was. In fact, however, all of this was but copying from Origen, even though Jerome assured that he had conducted independent research on this issue ('I have read diverse things in diverse sources').

mcdlxxxvii John Chrysostom kept on copying from Origen. See *Catena in Matthaeum*, p. 193.

mcdlxxxviii This appears in Josephus, *Antiquitates Judaicae*, 9.168-169; 9.171. Once again, the extent of Origen's readings and his memory is stupefying indeed. See his detailed citations of, and references to, Josephus in *Cels*, I.16; I.47; IV.11; *commMatt*, 10.17; *commSerMatt*, p. 42; *frJer*, fr. 14; *frLam*, frs. 105; 109; 115; *frPs*, on Psalm 73:5; *selPs*, PG.12.1529.46-47.

mcdlxxxix Origen, *commMatt*, fr. 457 I (Klostermann).

mcdxc Origen, *commSerMatt*, pp. 42-43.

mcdxci The phrase, Τὸ γὰρ *ποσάκις* πολλοὺς ἔδειξε χρόνους καὶ πολλὰς γενεάς, ὅτε τὸν λαὸν ἐξ αἰχμαλωσίας ἐπανήγαγεν, is part of Origen's *commMatt*, fr. 461 (Klostermann). The present codex provides the full context of this comment.

mcdxcii Here is how Cyril of Alexandria reduplicated Origen's text. *frMatt*, fr. 264: Εἰπὼν τοῦτο δείκνυσιν ἑαυτοῦ τὸ θεοπρεπὲς καὶ ἐν ἀνθρωπίνῃ μορφῇ ὤν. Καὶ γὰρ περὶ τοῦ θεοῦ εἶπεν Μωυσῆς· *διεὶς τὰς πτέρυγας αὐτοῦ ἐδέξατο αὐτούς* [Deut. 32:11]; καὶ πάλιν Δαβίδ· *οἱ δὲ υἱοὶ τῶν ἀνθρώπων ἐν σκέπῃ τῶν πτερύγων σου ἐλπιοῦσιν* [Psalm 35:8].

mcdxciii The phrase ἡ δὲ *ὄρνις* πολύτεκνος καὶ θερμὴ περὶ τὴν ἀγάπην καὶ κηδομένη τῶν τέκνων καὶ ἑαυτὴν παραδιδοῦσα ὑπὲρ αὐτῶν is part of Origen, *commMatt*, fr. 462 (Klostermann). Although the editor found this being attributed to Origen in four codices, he had some reservations only because this text runs parallel to a passage of John Chrysostom, *In Matthaeum*, PG.58.683.31-51 (homily 74). This is why he put this in brackets. However, beyond Chrysostom's carbon copy (which I am quoting), the last phrase of this passage is ascribed to Origen also in the *Catena in Matthaeum*, p. 194: (Ὠριγένους) Ὄρνις πολύτεκνος καὶ θερμὴ περὶ τὴν ἀγάπην κηδομένη τῶν τέκνων, καὶ ἑαυτὴν παραδιδοῦσα ὑπὲρ αὐτῶν.

mcdxciv Here is the replication by John Chrysostom, *apud Catena in Matthaeum*, pp. 193-194: διὰ τοῦτο τὸν διπλασιασμὸν ἐπήγαγεν, ἔτι δὲ καὶ σφόδρα φιλοῦντος· ὥσπερ γὰρ πρὸς ἐρωμένην φιληθεῖσαν μὲν διὰ παντός, καταφρονήσασαν δὲ τοῦ ἐραστοῦ, καὶ διὰ τοῦτο κολάζεσθαι μέλλουσαν ἀπολογεῖται λοιπόν, μέλλων ἐπάγειν τὴν κόλασιν. Μέμνηται δὲ καὶ τῶν μιαιφονιῶν αὐτῆς, δεῖξαι βουλόμενος ὅτι οὐδὲ οὕτως ἀπέστη τῆς πρὸς αὐτὴν εὐνοίας. Τοῦτο γὰρ δηλοῖ τὸ *ποσάκις ἠθέλησα ἐπισυναγαγεῖν τὰ τέκνα σου*, καὶ τὰ ἑξῆς. Καὶ γὰρ ἀεὶ ἑαυτοὺς ἐσκόρπιζον διὰ τῶν ἁμαρτημάτων. Ἐνδείκνυται δὲ καὶ τὸ φιλόστοργον διὰ τῆς εἰκόνος τῆς ὥσπερ ὄρνις· καὶ γὰρ τοῦτο τὸ ζῶον θερμόν ἐστι περὶ τὰ ἔγγονα.

mcdxcv John Chrysostom, *In Matthaeum*, PG.58.682.31-51.

mcdxcvi Apollinaris, *frMatt*, fr. 121.

mcdxcvii Origen, *commMatt*, fr. 460 (Klostermann). This is an attack on Gnostics by Origen reaffirming his cardinal doctrine that God who appeared in all instances of the Biblical history was God the Logos. Cf. *supra*, folio 187r: Τὸ γὰρ *ποσάκις* πολλοὺς ἔδειξε χρόνους καὶ πολλὰς γενεάς, ὅτε τὸν λαὸν ἐξ αἰχμαλωσίας ἐπανήγαγεν, which is also part of Origen, *commMatt*, fr. 461 (Klostermann).

mcdxcviii John Chrysostom, *In Matthaeum*, PG.58.682.56-58.

mcdxcix Origen's flowing continuous text demonstrates how Chrysostom copied from this.

md John Chrysostom, *op. cit.* PG.58.683.5-9. Once again, it is quite evident that Chrysostom wrote his own commentary having Origen' one in front of him.

mdi Origen, *commMatt*, fr. 464 (Klostermann).

mdii Cyril of Alexandria, *frMatt*, fr. 264.

mdiii Origen, *commMatt*, fr. 465 (Klostermann).

mdiv Cyril of Alexandria, *frMatt*, fr. 265.

mdv Origen's text flows – this is not a 'fragment', and it simply reveals how Cyril copied from him.

mdvi Cf. Origen (Dositheus), *Princ*, IV.3.2 (*Philocalia*, 1.18); *commJohn*, XIII.27.162; *Cels*, I.57; VI.11; (Simon Magus), *commJohn*, II.33.142; VI.33.167; *Cels*, I.57; VI.11; *homJer*, homily, 5.3; *adDeut*, PG.17.32-33.

mdvii Apollinaris, *frMatt*, fr. 122.

mdviii Jerome, *commMatt*, 24.5. See Epiphanius of Salamis, *Panarion*, v. 1, pp. 238-245; 311.

mdix Cf. Theodoret, *apud Catena in Matthaeum*, p. 197. (Θεοδωρήτου Ἐπισκόπου Κύρου.) Τὸ ῥητὸν τοῦτο πολλαχῶς ἐννοεῖται παρὰ τοῖς θείοις πατράσι. Καὶ πρῶτον μὲν εἰσενήνεκται τὸ *βδέλυγμα τῆς ἐρημώσεως* εἰς τὸν θεῖον νεών, ὅτε τὸν βωμὸν τῷ Διῒ ἀνέστησεν ὁ δυσσεβὴς βασιλεὺς Ἀντίοχος. Καὶ χοῖρον γὰρ ἐν αὐτῷ προσενήνοχεν εἰς θυσίαν καὶ προσωνόμασε Διὸς Ὀλυμπίου τὸν ἐν Ἱεροσολύμοις ναόν. Εἶτα, μετ' ἐκεῖνον πάλιν Πόντιος Πιλᾶτος ἡγεμονεύων ἐν Ἱεροσολύμοις νύκτωρ εἰς τὸν θεῖον ναὸν τὰς βασιλικὰς εἰσεκόμισεν εἰκόνας παρὰ τὸν θεῖον νόμον. Μετὰ τούτους δὲ ἐπὶ τῆς συντελείας τοῦτο γενήσεται. Τὸ γὰρ ἀληθινὸν *βδέλυγμα τῆς ἐρημώσεως* τοῦ κόσμου, ἤτοι *ὁ ἄνθρωπος τῆς ἀνομίας*, *ὁ υἱὸς τῆς ἀπωλείας*, λέγω δὴ ὁ Ἀντίχριστος, καθεσθήσεται εἰς τὸν ἐν Ἱεροσολύμοις ναὸν βλασφημῶν, καὶ ἀποδεικνύων ἑαυτὸν εἶναι Θεόν.

mdx Origen, *commMatt*, fr. 469 I (Klostermann).

mdxi Theodore of Heraclea, *frMatt*, fr. 122 & *Catena in Matthaeum*, p. 196. Origen's flowing text reveals once again that the fragments attributed to this 'Theodore' are either a misattribution or of flagrant copying by that author.

mdxii Jerome, *commMatt*, 24.15.

mdxiii Theodore of Heraclea, *frMatt*, fr. 121 col. 1; likewise col. 2, adding, ἢ ὅπερ αἰνίττεται ὁ Ἰώσηπος γεγενῆσθαι ἐν τῇ πολιορκίᾳ τῶν Ἱεροσολύμων. Καὶ γὰρ γυναῖκες θύσασαι τὰ ἑαυτῶν τέκνα ἔφαγον.

mdxiv This also Origen, *commMatt*, fr. 469 II (Klostermann).

mdxv Origen, *commSerMatt*, pp. 83-84.

mdxvi A unique translation of 'Judaea', which was never repeated by any author other than the newly discovered moderate Origenist of the sixth century Cassian the Sabaite; see *NDGF* and *RCR*.

mdxvii Origen, *commMatt*, fr. 472 (Klostermann).

mdxviii Isidore of Pelusium, *Epistulae De Interpretatione Divinae Scripturae*, book 1, epistle 210. He wrote this as a quotation by a third party, but he did not cite his source. Anyway, this short letter 'to Christodorus' evidently is a compendium of exegeses as to 'what is the meaning of *At that time let the Jews flee to the mountains* is' (cf. Matt. 23:16). What Isidore did not say is that the 'third party' was no other than Origen.

mdxix Pseudo-Caesarius (Cassian the Sabaite), *Quaestiones et Responsiones*, 216; see this continued *infra*.

mdxx Origen, *commSerMatt*, p. 86.

mdxxi Origen, *commMatt*, fr. 470 (Klostermann).

mdxxii Cf. *infra* the parallel text by Cassian the Sabaite: περιφρονήσας σκιώδους ζωῆς. Origen considered the present life as a 'shadow' in accordance with Job, 8:9 (σκιὰ γάρ ἐστιν ἡμῶν ἐπὶ τῆς γῆς ὁ βίος) and with Psalm 143:4 (αἱ ἡμέραι αὐτοῦ ὡσεὶ σκιὰ παράγουσιν). *homJob*, p. 364: Καὶ σκιᾶς δίκην, παρελθὼν τὸν βίον, οὐδὲ μνημόσυνόν τι τοῖς ζῶσιν ἀφίησιν. *frPs*, on Psalm 101:12: Σκιὰ γάρ ἐστιν ὁ βίος ἡμῶν ἐπὶ τῆς γῆς. *selPs*, PG.12.1389: Πάντες οἱ τῶν δικαίων ὡς δικαίων πατέρες, πάροικοί εἰσι καὶ παρεπίδημοι, σκιὰν ἡγούμενοι τὸν βίον τὸν ἐπὶ τῆς γῆς. *Op. cit.* PG.12.1552.2-3: *Σκιά γαρ ἡμῶν*, φησὶν Ἰώβ, *ἐστὶν ὁ βίος ἐπὶ τῆς γῆς*. *Libri x in Canticum Canticorum* (*fragmenta*), p. 183 & *Scholia in Canticum Canticorum*, PG.17.261.27-32: νῦν ἐσμεν ὑπὸ σκιὰν πολλῷ διαφέρουσαν ... Ἔστι γὰρ *ὁ βίος* ἡμῶν *ὡς σκιὰ καὶ ἐν σκιᾷ θανάτου*. *Scholia in Canticum Canticorum*, PG.17.268.13-15: καὶ μέχρι παρέλθωσιν αἱ σκιαὶ τοῦ βίου. Κατὰ τὸ *ὡς σκιαὶ ἡμέραι ἡμῶν παράγουσιν* [cf. Psalm 143:4]. *Op. cit.* PG.17.272.37-40: ὅταν ὁ καύσων τοῦ παρόντος βίου παύσηται, καὶ καιρὸς τῆς ἀναψύξεως ἐπιστῇ, λυομένης καὶ τῆς σκιᾶς. Σκιὰ γάρ ἐστιν ὁ παρὼν βίος.

mdxxiii Origen, *selEz*, PG.13.821.26-28: Ἐκ τῶν οὐρανῶν ἐρρίφη ὁ ριφεὶς ἐπὶ τὴν γῆν, ὧν τῷ *ὑποδείγματι καὶ τῇ σκιᾷ* ἐλάτρευον οἱ ἐν τῇ σκηνῇ λατρεύοντες. [Cf. Heb. 8:5]. Cf. *Princ*, IV.2.6 (*Philocalia*, 1.13); *commJohn*, I.6.34; VI.51.265-6; X.16.91; *Cels*, II.2; V.44; *commMatt*, 16.3; *selPs*, PG.12.1148.15-18.

mdxxiv The expression ἔνοικα πάθη ('indwelling passions') has always remained extremely scarce. It appears in two authors only, namely, in a epistle supposedly written by Basil of Caesarea and in Pseudo-Caesarius, who was no other than the newly discovered Cassian the Sabaite. I have suggested that some of the epistles ascribed to Basil were not really his own, but were written later, and probably Cassian the Sabaite was the author of some of them. No matter what the case, this section of Origen's commentary was in effect copied by Cassian the Sabaite. Cf. Basil of Caesarea, *Epistulae*, 2.1 (copied by John of Damascus, *Sacra Parallela*, PG.95.1212.15-17): Τὰ γὰρ ἔνοικα πάθη συμπεριφέροντες πανταχοῦ μετὰ τῶν ὁμοίων θορύβων ἐσμέν.

mdxxv Origen, *commMatt*, fr. 471 (Klostermann).

mdxxvi Isidore of Pelusium, *Epistulae De Interpretatione Divinae Scripturae*, book 1, epistle 210. The variations of expression suggest that he pararaphrased the text that had reached him.

mdxxvii Pseudo-Caesarius (Cassian the Sabaite), *Quaestiones et Responsiones*, 216, continued from *supra*.

mdxxviii Origen, *commMatt*, fr. 473 (Klostermann).

mdxxix Isidore of Pelusium, *Epistulae De Interpretatione Divinae Scripturae*, book 1, epistle 210.

mdxxx Pseudo-Caesarius (Cassian the Sabaite), *op. cit.* 216, continued from *supra*. In my *NDGF* and *RCR*, I have discussed a peculiar (if interpretable) sixth-century phenomenon: authors, on the one hand, damned Origen's name, while, on the other, they drew abundantly on his work. In any event, Origen's ideas and sixth-century 'Origenism' were two different things. Accordingly, Cassian the Sabaite ('Pseudo-Caesarius'), on the one hand castigated Origen's name (see *op. cit.* sections 166; 168; 170), whereas, on the other, he copied profusely and *literatim* from Origen's commentary on Matthew.

mdxxxi Origen, *commMatt*, fr. 474 (Klostermann).

mdxxxii Isidore of Pelusium, *Epistulae De Interpretatione Divinae Scripturae*, Book 1, epistle 211. Whereas Klostermann found this attributed to Origen in an eleventh-century codex, attribution to Isidoere appeared in a sixteen-century catena.

mdxxxiii Cyril of Alexandria, *frMatt*, fr. 269, col. 1. See the text of col. 2, which is similar.

mdxxxiv The term was taken up by John Chrysostom, *Adversus Judaeos*, PG.48.854.23, and by Pseudo-Caesarius (Cassian the Sabaite), *Quaestiones et Responsiones*, 189; 218. See also, Anonymous, *Dialogus cum Judaeis*, chapter 6, line 209; chapter 9, line 142. Scarce use of this re-appeared in the ninth century and later, amounting to no more than half-a dozen of instances in all.

mdxxxv Origen, *commSerMatt*, pp. 93-95. This is also Origen, *commMatt*, fr. 475 (Klostermann), continued *infra*.

mdxxxvi Origen, *commSerMatt*, pp. 96-97. This is also Origen, *commMatt*, fr. 475 (Klostermann), concluded.

mdxxxvii Origen, *commMatt*, fr. 476 (Klostermann).

mdxxxviii Apollinaris, *frMatt*, fr. 123.

mdxxxix Origen, *commSerMatt*, pp. 95-96. This is also Origen, *commMatt*, fr. 477 (Klostermann).

mdxl Apollinaris, *frMatt*, fr. 125, continued *infra*.

mdxli Origen, *commSerMatt*, p. 98.

mdxlii Origen, *commMatt*, fr. 478 (Klostermann).

mdxliii Apollinaris, *frMatt*, fr. 125.

mdxliv Although Klostermann (*op. cit.* fr. 478, p. 197) found this passage in an eleventh-century codex as part of Origen's text immediately following the preceding one (which is the case in this codex, too), in another codex (thirteenth-century) he came upon this portion being attributed to Theodore of Heraclea. I am afraid that the learned editor did not realise the extent of false attributions made to that protagonist of Arianism, which will appear also below. The extreme case of this phenomenon occurs at the end of the present volume, apropos of a passage by Origen in the present codex having been attributed to Theodore of Heraclea by Reuss (fr. 134), which represents the fanatic anti-Nicene Theodore (a persistent colluder against Athanasius) as an exponent of an impeccable Nicene doctrine and defender of the *homoousion*.

mdxlv See *infra* how Origen's ensuing flowing text was copied by Apollinaris.

mdxlvi Apollinaris, *frMatt*, fr. 126.

mdxlvii Origen, *commMatt*, fr. 479 (Klostermann).

mdxlviii Apollinaris, *frMatt*, fr. 127, continued *infra*.

mdxlix Origen, *commMatt*, fr. 480 (Klostermann).

mdl Apollinaris, *frMatt*, fr. 127, only because this passage appears under the siglum 'By Origen, and Apollinaris' in Codex *Great Laura B 113*, Athos (eleventh century).

mdli This is one more token of Origen's erudition. Lumping fig tree and almond-tree together was a remark made by Theophrastus, who had added palm-tree to them. What he saw as their common characteristic is that these are apt to throw off their fruits earlier than their maturation. Theophrastus, *De Causis Plantarum*, 2.9.3: Ἀποβλητικὰ δὲ μάλιστα τῶν καρπῶν πρὶν πεπᾶναι συκῆ καὶ φοῖνιξ καὶ ἀμυγδαλῆ.

mdlii Cf. Procopius of Gaza, *Commentarii in Isaiam*, pp. 2593-2596 (comm on Isaiah, 58:11): Δι᾽ ὧν ἔοικε δηλοῦν τὴν ἀνάστασιν τῶν σωμάτων, ἀνισταμένων οἷα τις πόα, νεκρὰ μὲν ἐν χειμῶνι, ἀναθήλασα δὲ πάλιν ἐν ἔαρι. Πῶς δὲ ἀνίσταται; τῇ ζωοποιῷ δηλονότι *πιαινόμενα*.

mdliii See *supra*, folio 57r: τοῖς γὰρ δικαίοις ὁ αἰὼν οὗτος χειμών ἐστι. Cf. Origen, *exhMar*, 31: καὶ ὑμεῖς ἔτι μέμνησθε ὅτι οὐκ ἄλλως ἔστιν ἀκοῦσαι τό, *ὁ χειμὼν παρῆλθεν*, [Song of Songs, 2:11] ἐὰν μὴ τὸν παρόντα χειμῶνα ἐρρωμένως καὶ εὐτόνως ἀγωνίσησθε.

mdliv See *Anaxagoras*, 'The Theory of Logoi', pp. 750-781.

mdlv Origen, *commSerMatt*, pp. 123-124. This is also Origen, *commMatt*, fr. 484 (Klostermann).

mdlvi The characteristic expression ὁ τῶν χρόνων ποιητὴς ('the Creator of times') was taken up by only a couple of later authors: Cyril of Alexandria, *Thesaurus De Sancta Consubstantiali Trinitate*, PG.75.97.34. John of Damascus, *Expositio Fidei*, 17 & *Catena in Epistulam ad Romanos*, p. 301. The relevant text of Pseudo-Athanasius, *Sermo De Descriptione Deiparae*, PG.28.956.11, actually is John of Damascus', *Homilia in Nativitatem Domini*, 5.

mdlvii Cf. Origen, *Princ*, II.4.3: "Nor indeed must anyone suppose that we have entertained any thought as impious as to assert that the Father is not visible even to the Son."

mdlviii Jerome, *commMatt*, 24.36. He repeats the same explanation in *op. cit.* 24.42.

mdlix The phrase of Basil of Caesarea in the same codex (folio 195v) is a plain influence by Origen: διὰ τὸ μὴ συμφέρειν τοῖς ἀνθρώποις ἀκοῦσαι, τὸν καιρὸν τῆς κρίσεως ἀπεσιώπησεν.

mdlx Origen, *commMatt*, fr. 486 (Klostermann).

mdlxi However, in Greek there are not such epithets as ὑποτάκτης or ὑπόταχτος, although there is the antonym ἀνυπόταχτος.

mdlxii Origen, *commMatt*, fr. 485 (Klostermann).

mdlxiii Origen, *commSerMatt*, pp. 126-127.

mdlxiv Cf. the non-scriptural term ἀναισθησία ('torpor') being pointed out as a sinful condition by Origen. *schLuc*, PG.17.328.24; *frLuc*, fr. 163; *commJohn*, VI.27.142; *Cels*, III.75; V.43; *commEph*, fr. 18; *frPs*, on Psalm 93:3-4 & 8-9; *selPs*, PG.12.1105.55. Cf. in this codex, *infra*, folio 197r: Τρυφὴ μέν, τοῖς ἀναισθήτως διακειμένοις.

mdlxv Cf. the verb ἐξαρπάζω ('snatch away from') being used by Origen, *expProv*, PG.17.189.32-34: ἐξαρπάζεται ὁ εὐσεβὴς ὑπὸ Θεοῦ, ὁ δὲ ἀσεβὴς ἐγκαταλειφθεὶς περιπίπτει. *Cels*, V.52: τῆς Μαρίας κυούσης πρὸς τὸν τέκτονα ἧκεν ἄγγελος καὶ ὑπὲρ τοῦ τὸ βρέφος ἐξαρπάσαντας φυγεῖν ἄλλος ἄγγελος. *Op. cit.* V.58: τῆς Μαρίας κυούσης ἐληλυθέναι πρὸς τὸν Ἰωσὴφ ἄγγελον καὶ πάλιν ὑπὲρ τοῦ τὸ βρέφος γεννηθὲν καὶ ἐπιβουλευόμενον ἐξαρπάσαντας φυγεῖν εἰς Αἴγυπτον.

mdlxvi Jerome's explanation is identical, the phraseology is paraphrased. He also uses Origen's appeal to 1 Thess. 5:3.

mdlxvii Origen took up this expression from Philo, *De Ebrietate ii*, fr. 6: ῥᾳθυμίᾳ καὶ μέθῃ κακίας συνεργάταις χρῆσθαι. Cf. Isaiah, 29:9; 51:21. Origen, *Cels*, III.76: Παραστησάτω γὰρ ἐκ τῶν γραμμάτων, φέρ' εἰπεῖν, Παύλου ὅτι ἐμέθυεν ὁ τοῦ Ἰησοῦ ἀπόστολος καὶ οὐκ ἦσαν οἱ λόγοι αὐτοῦ νήφοντες, ἢ ἐξ ὧν ἔγραψεν Ἰωάννης ὅτι οὐχὶ σωφρονοῦντος καὶ ἀπηλλαγμένου τῆς ἀπὸ κακίας μέθης πνεῖ αὐτοῦ τὰ νοήματα. *deOr*, 28.7: πλὴν καὶ ἐπὶ τῶν τοιούτων τὴν θεραπείαν παντὶ τρόπῳ ζητητέον ἐγγενέσθαι τῷ τὰ πάντα διαστραφέντι, ὡς μηδὲ συναισθέσθαι τῶν ἰδίων κακῶν μεθύειν δὲ μέθην ὀλεθριωτέραν τῆς *ἀπὸ οἴνου*, [Cf. Isaiah, 29:9; 51:21] τὴν ἀπὸ τοῦ σκοτισμοῦ τῆς κακίας.

mdlxviii John Chrysostom, *In Matthaeum*, PG.58.703.50-704.22.

mdlxix John Chrysostom, *op. cit.* PG.58.704.38-39.

mdlxx Origen, *commMatt*, 10.2.

mdlxxi Cf. Origen, *selPs*, PG.12.1540.40-43 (comm. on Psalm 76:19): *Φωνὴ τῆς βροντῆς σου ἐν τροχῷ*, κ. τ. ἑ. Ὁ τροχὸς ἢ τὸν αἰῶνα σημαίνει τοῦτον, ἢ τὸν κόσμον τὸν αἰσθητόν, ἢ τὴν καθαρὰν καὶ αἰώνιον ψυχήν, εἴπερ ἡ κακία παρὰ γωνίαν παρεδρεύει.

mdlxxii Origen, *commMatt*, fr. 488 (Klostermann).

mdlxxiii Origen, *commMatt*, fr. 489 (Klostermann).

mdlxxiv Origen, *commMatt*, fr. 490 (Klostermann).

mdlxxv Origen, *commSerMatt*, p. 132.

mdlxxvi Cf. folio 199v: Πάντες οὖν οἱ κεκοιμημένοι ἀναμένουσι τὴν ἄφιξιν τοῦ Κυρίου, ἣν καὶ τάχα στοχαστέον γίνεσθαι ἐν νυκτί.

mdlxxvii Cf. Jerome, *supra*.

mdlxxviii Origen, *commMatt*, fr. 491 (Klostermann).

mdlxxix This is also Origen, *commMatt*, fr. 492 (Klostermann): Τὸ *ἄρα* ἀντὶ τοῦ σπανίου.

mdlxxx Origen, *commMatt*, fr. 493 (Klostermann), continued *infra*.

mdlxxxi Origen, *schMatt*, PG.17.301.35304.4, continued *infra*.

mdlxxxii Origen, *commMatt*, fr. 493 (Klostermann).

mdlxxxiii Origen, *schMatt*, PG.17.301.35304.4.

mdlxxxiv Cyril of Alexandria, *frMatt*, fr. 277, continued *infra*.

mdlxxxv Cf. *supra*, folio 47r: τὰ χρήματα ἀλλοτριοῖ Θεοῦ. Folio 147r: δηλοῖ τὴν ἀφαίρεσιν τῶν ἀγαθῶν καὶ τὴν ἀπὸ Θεοῦ ἀλλοτρίωσιν. Folio 169v: οὓς καὶ ἀλλοτρίους λέγει τῆς βασιλείας τοῦ Θεοῦ. See endnote mccxxxvii.

mdlxxxvi Here is Origen's text copied by Basil of Caesarea, *De Spiritu Sancto*, 16.40.

mdlxxxvii Cyril of Alexandria, *frMatt*, fr. 277, continued *infra*.

mdlxxxviii Cyril of Alexandria, *loc. cit.*, continued *infra*.

mdlxxxix Origen, *commSerMatt*, p. 140, continued forthwith.

mdxc Cyril of Alexandria, *frMatt*, fr. 277, concluded.

mdxci Origen, *commSerMatt*, p. 140.

mdxcii Cf. Origen, *commRom (I.1-XII.21)*, fr. 39: κἀνταῦθα δέ τις νόμον τὸν φυσικὸν ἀπέδωκεν οὕτω. *commRom*, p. 204: οὗτος ὁ φυσικῶς ἡμῖν ἐγγεγραμμένος νόμος καὶ *ἐν πλαξὶν καρδίαις σαρκίναις* ὑπὸ τοῦ Θεοῦ ἐντετυπωμένος. *frJohn*, fr. 50: νόμος γὰρ φυσικὸς τοῖς γεννῶσιν ἀγαπᾶν τὰ γεννώμενα. *Op. cit.* 127: Τὸ ἀγαπᾶν ἀνθρωπινώτερον πάλιν ἀκούομεν· νόμος δέ ἐστι φυσικός. *frLam*, fr. 101: οἱ μὲν τὸν φυσικὸν νόμον εἶχον μόνον, οἱ δὲ καὶ γραπτὸν καὶ προφήτας ὅσα τε παραδόξως ὁ θεὸς ἠργάζετο ἐν αὐτοῖς. *selPs*, PG.12.1520.27-28: παράνομον δὲ διὰ τὸ παραβῆναι τὸν φυσικὸν νόμον αὐτοῦ. Likewise, φυσικὴ ἔννοια, which is the equivalent of Descartes' *ideae innatae*. Cf. Origen, *commRom* (*I.1-XII.21*), fr. 10: δύναται δὲ νῦν νόμος νοεῖσθαι καὶ ὁ κατὰ τὰς φυσικὰς ἐννοίας. *commRom*, p. 204: Τὰ δὲ περὶ τοῦ Ἀβραὰμ φερόμενα ἐξ ἀποκρύφων ὡς ἄρα ἀπὸ φυσικῶν ἐννοιῶν κινηθεὶς ἐπίστευσεν τῷ Θεῷ ἀντιλέγεται. *commSerMatt*, p. 134: ὁ δὲ κλέπτης ἀντικείμενος διορύσσων τὰς φυσικὰς ἐννοίας τῆς ψυχῆς. *commMatt*, 10.2: ὁ διάβολος ἐπιτηρῶν ἐπισπείρει τὰ καλούμενα ζιζάνια, τὰ μοχθηρὰ δόγματα, ταῖς καλουμέναις ὑπό τινων φυσικαῖς ἐννοίαις καὶ σπέρμασι καλοῖς τοῖς ἀπὸ τοῦ λόγου. *Cels*, IV.14: Οὐδὲ γὰρ δεδύνηνται οὗτοι τρανῶσαι τὴν φυσικὴν τοῦ θεοῦ ἔννοιαν ὡς πάντῃ ἀφθάρτου καὶ ἁπλοῦ καὶ ἀσυνθέτου καὶ ἀδιαιρέτου. *expProv*, PG.17.209.6-8, quoted *supra*, note cml.

mdxciii Cf. Origen, *frPs*, on Psalm 77:65: ἡ μέθη, ἐπείσακτον πάθος ἐστίν, οὐκ ἔμφυτον.

mdxciv Meaning Matt. 25:1: ἐξῆλθον εἰς ἀπάντησιν τοῦ νυμφίου (var. lect. ὑπάντησιν).

mdxcv Cyril of Alexandria, *frMatt*, fr. 280, continued *infra*.

mdxcvi Cyril of Alexandria, *frMatt*, fr. 280, to be continued.

mdxcvii Number ten was widely vested with reverence by several authors on different accounts. However, this number is not 'perfect' in the strict mathematical sense, namely, a number which is a positive integer that is equal to the sum of its proper positive divisors, that is, the sum of its positive divisors excluding the number itself (also known as its *aliquot sum*).

mdxcviii Cyril of Alexandria, *frMatt*, fr. 280.

mdxcix Cf. folio 197v: Ὅπερ δέ φησι ὁ Λουκᾶς ὅτι καὶ δύο ἔσονται ἐν τῇ κλίνῃ, δηλοῖ ὅτι ἐν νυκτὶ ἔσται ἡ παρουσία.

mdc Cyril of Alexandria, *frMatt*, fr. 280.

mdci Cyril of Alexandria, *loc. cit.*

mdcii *Catena in Matthaeum*, p. 207 (anonymous).

mdciii Cyril of Alexandria, *frMatt*, fr. 280, columns 1 & 2.

mdciv Cf. Origen, *adDeut*, PG.17.33.29-34: *Ἐπικατάρατος ὁ μετατιθεὶς ὅρια τοῦ πλησίον.* Ὅρια τοῦ πλησίον μετατίθησι καὶ ὁ ἀπὸ τῆς ἀληθοῦς θεογνωσίας, καὶ τῆς ἐνθέου πολιτείας παρασαλεύων τὸν ἐντὸς εὑρισκόμενον. Καὶ δηλοῖ τὰ ἐπαγόμενα. The expression 'godly conduct' of life (ἔνθεος πολιτεία) is one more innovation that Origen introduced in literature, and was followed by a considerable number of authors, incliuding his detractors, such as Eustathius of Antioch (*De Engastrimytho Contra Origenem*, 1.1). See Eusebius, *HE*, 4.7.13; *Ad Stephanum*, PG.22.912.11. Ephraem Syrus, *Hypomnesticon*, p. 51; *Consilium De Vita Spiritali, ad Monachum Novitium*, 58. Pseudo-John Chrysostom, *In Psalmos 101-107*, PG.55.671.2. Cyril of Alexandria, *In Joannem*, v. 2, p. 672; v. 3, p. 8. Basil of Seleucia, *Sermones*, PG.85.112.41. Pseudo-Dionysius the Areopagite, *De Ecclesiastica Hierarchia*, pp. 71; 91; *Epistulae*, epistle 9.5. Maximus Confessor, *Quaestiones ad Thalassium*, 15. Andreas of Caesarea, *Commentarii in Apocalypsin*, 16.48.16,7. Photius, *Bibliotheca*, p. 205b; *Fragmenta in Epistulam i ad Corinthios*, p. 581 (& *Catena in Epistulam i ad Corinthios*, p. 327). Now, there is one fragment attributed to Theodore of Heraclea using this expression, which partially reads thus: *Fragmenta in Joannem*, fr. 194: τοῖς δὲ μαθηταῖς κατ' ἴχνος αὐτοῦ τῆς ἀρετῆς καὶ τῆς ἐνθέου πολιτείας ἀκολουθοῦσιν αὐτόθεν ἐπαγγέλλεται κατ' οὐρανὸν οἴκησιν. I leave for readers to consider whether this is one more passage by Origen, or Theodore copied from Origen's work, just like Chrysostom and Cyril normally did.

mdcv Cf. *supra*, folio 27r: καὶ τὰς λοιπὰς ἀρετάς, αἵ εἰσι Χριστός. Cf. *schMatt*, PG.17.296.7-10: τὰ οὐράνια τοίνυν πράγματα καὶ ἡ βασιλεία τῶν οὐρανῶν ... ἐστὶν αὐτὸς ὁ Χριστός. Also, *commJohn*, I.15.86: καὶ γὰρ εἰ ὁ εὐαγγελιζόμενος *ἀγαθὰ εὐαγγελίζεται* [cf. Is. 52:7; Rom. 10:15], πάντες δὲ οἱ πρὸ τῆς σωματικῆς Χριστοῦ ἐπιδημίας Χριστὸν εὐαγγελίζονται ὄντα *τὰ ἀγαθά*, ὡς ἀπεδείξαμεν, πάντων πως εἰσὶν οἱ λόγοι τοῦ εὐαγγελίου μέρος. See also endnote cclxxv (πλῆθος ἀγαθῶν ἐστιν Ἰησοῦς).

mdcvi This is also Origen, *commMatt*, fr. 496 (Klostermann).

mdcvii Origen, *commSerMatt*, pp. 145-147.

mdcviii So in the *Catena in Matthaeum*, p. 207 (anonymous): Τί δὲ σημαίνουσιν αἱ λαμπάδες; αὐτὸ τῆς παρθένου τὸ χάρισμα, τὸ ἔλαιον δὲ τὴν φιλανθρωπίαν, τὴν ἐλεημοσύνην, τὴν περὶ τὴν ἁγιωσύνην τοῖς δεομένοις βοήθειαν.

mdcix Origen, *commMatt*, fr. 497 (Klostermann).

mdcx John Chrysostom, *In Matthaeum*, PG.58.711.54-57.

mdcxi Origen, *commSerMatt*, p. 149. This is also Origen, *commMatt*, fr. 502 (Klostermann).

mdcxii Origen, *commMatt*, fr. 501 (Klostermann).

mdcxiii Origen, *commSerMatt*, pp. 149-150.

mdcxiv Origen, *commMatt*, fr. 498 (Klostermann). The same, in Origen, *schMatt*, PG.17.304.24-26. See the full context of this in *op. cit.* PG.17.304-305.

mdcxv ζωτικὸς τόνος is one more term that Origen received from Galen, and he was one of the very few non-medical doctors that entertained this idea. Perhaps, this was Galen's technical elaboration on the Stoic τόνος, which was more or less the same notion. Cf. Chrysippus, *Fragmenta Logica et Physica*, fr. 876, *apud* Galen, *De Locis Affectis*, p. 301. However, the term was made a really scientific one only with Galen himself, despite his occasional pertinent references to doctors of old such as Erasistratus (Galen, *De Differentia Pulsuum*, p. 646). See Galen, *De Differentia Pulsuum*, pp. 546; 623; *De Semine*, p. 588; *De Sanitate Tuenda*, p. 321; *De Tremore, Palpitatione, Convulsione et Rigore*, p. 601; *De Pulsibus Libellus ad Tirones*, p. 374; *De Dignoscendis Pulsibus*, pp. 776; 802; 927; 929; 953; *De Causis Pulsuum*, p. 161; *De Praesagitione ex Pulsibus*, p. 252; *De Crisibus*, p. 745; *Ad Glauconem*, p. 50; *In Hippocratis Librum vi Epidemiarum*, p. 218. Subsequently, Origen, *commSerMatt*, p. 148 & *schMatt*, PG.17.304.32 (both citations are the same text, which occurs also in the present codex). Pseudo-Galen, *Definitiones Medicae*, p. 376. Oribasius, *Collectiones Medicae*, 9.22; *Libri ad Eunapium*, 1.11.3. Basil of Caesarea, *In Ebriosos*, PG.31.452.3; *Sermones De Moribus*, PG.32.1325.1-2 (I believe that this work is spurious).

mdcxvi Origen, *schMatt*, PG.17.304.26-37. This is largely the same as Origen's *commSerMatt*, pp. 147-148.

mdcxvii Origen, *schMatt*, PG.17.304.37-46. & *commSerMatt*, pp. 150-151. The entire text, *Φρόνιμοι* μὲν οὖν ... τῆς ζωῆς, is also Origen's: *commMatt*, fr. 499 (Klostermann).

mdcxviii Jerome, *commMatt*, 25.1-2.

mdcxix Origen, *commMatt*, fr. 500 (Klostermann).

mdcxx Cf. Origen, *commSerMatt*, p. 149: πωλοῦσι δὲ τὸ ἔλαιον οἱ διδάσκοντες μισθοῦ προσεδρίας, προσοχῆς, φιλομαθίας, σπουδῆς, φιλοπονίας.

mdcxxi Origen, *schMatt*, PG.17.304.46-305.18. Cyril of Alexandria once again copied from Origen to the letter. *frMatt*, part of fr. 280: ἀλλὰ *πορεύεσθε πρὸς τοὺς πωλοῦντας*, οἵτινές εἰσιν προφῆται, ἀπόστολοι, εὐαγγελισταί, δι' ὧν τις μανθάνει τὴν ἀρετὴν ἐργάζεσθαι, καὶ ὀρθοὶ διδάσκαλοι τῶν ὀρθῶν δογμάτων.

mdcxxii Cf. *commJohn*, XIX.22.149-150. *Anaxagoras*, pp. 639-641.

mdcxxiii Origen, *commMatt*, fr. 516 (Klostermann). The same, Origen, *apud Catena in Matthaeum*, p. 214.

mdcxxiv Origen, *commMatt*, fr. 512 (Klostermann).

mdcxxv John Chrysostom, *In Matthaeum*, PG.58.717.47-56. However, in the *Catena in Matthaeum*, p. 211, this is anonymous. I should repeat that this catena contains also several anonymous passages which are in fact excerpts from Chrysostom's homilies on Matthew.

mdcxxvi Origen, *commMatt*, fr. 513 (Klostermann).

mdcxxvii John Chrysostom, *op. cit.* PG.58.717.44-46. Likewise, anonymous in the *Catena in Matthaeum*, p. 211.

mdcxxviii Origen, *commMatt*, fr. 514 (Klostermann).

mdcxxix Cf. Origen, *commRom (I.1-XII.21)*, fr. 1 (& *Philocalia*, 25.2): Οὐ νομιστέον τοίνυν εἶναι τῶν ἐσομένων αἰτίαν τὴν πρόγνωσιν τοῦ θεοῦ· ἀλλ' ἐπεὶ ἔμελλεν γίνεσθαι κατ' ἰδίας ὁρμὰς τοῦ ποιοῦντος, διὰ τοῦτο προέγνω, *εἰδὼς τὰ πάντα πρὸ γενέσεως αὐτῶν*. *commGen*, PG.12.65.1-4: ἀλλὰ παραδοξότερον μέν, ἀληθὲς δὲ ἐροῦμεν, τὸ ἐσόμενον αἴτιον τοῦ τοιάνδε εἶναι τὴν περὶ αὐτοῦ πρόγνωσιν. Οὐ γὰρ ἐπεὶ ἔγνωσται, γίνεται, ἀλλ' ἐπεὶ γίνεσθαι ἔμελλεν, ἔγνωσται. *Adnotationes in Genesim*, PG.17.12.44-46: Ὁ δὲ Θεὸς οὕτως ὁρᾷ τὰ μετὰ πολλὰς ἐσόμενα γενεάς, ὡς ἤδη γεγενημένα. Ὡς προορῶν τοίνυν καὶ προγινώσκων, οὕτως ἅπαντα πρυτανεύει. John Chrysostom grasped Origen's idea and embraced this, just as he did with the rest of the commentary, although he deemed this particular point too intricate to elaborate on. *In Matthaeum*, PG.58.719.34-36: Πρὶν ἢ γὰρ ὑμᾶς γενέσθαι, φησί, ταῦτα ὑμῖν ἡτοίμαστο καὶ ηὐτρέπιστο, ἐπειδὴ ᾔδειν τοιούτους ἐσομένους ὑμᾶς.

mdcxxx Origen, *commMatt*, fr. 515 (Klostermann).

mdcxxxi Origen, *commMatt*, fr. 517 (Klostermann).

mdcxxxii Here is a unique parallel to this expression. Gregory of Nyssa, *Contra Eunomium*, 1.1.337: καὶ ἐνταῦθα τὸ ἰσοστάσιον τῆς ἀγάπης ὁ θεὸς λόγος νομοθετῶν οὕτω φησὶ δεῖν τιμᾶσθαι τὸν υἱόν, ὡς ὁ πατὴρ τιμᾶται. Cf. Origen, *Philocalia*, 23.10 (*commGen*, PG.12.68.25-26): ἀλλ' [ὁ θεός] οἱονεὶ τὸ ἰσοστάσιον τῶν δυνάμεων γενέσθαι δεικνύς. *Cels*, IV.64: κατὰ τοὺς ἄφθαρτον τὸν κόσμον τηροῦντας τὸ ἰσοστάσιον τῶν στοιχείων ἀπὸ τῆς προνοίας γίνεται.

mdcxxxiii Origen classifies 'six kinds of love' in accordance with Jesus' statement of love being exhibited to other people apropos of them being 'hungry; thirsty; strip-naked; strangers and unacquainted; ill; prisoners'). The only author who reproduced this 'classification of love' (indeed in relation to Jesus' words) is the anonymous scholiast of Maximus Confessor, on whom I have several times shown influence by Origen. Anonymous, *Scholia in Maximum Confessorem*, 40: καὶ ἡ καθόλου ἀγάπη εἰς ἓξ ἀρετῶν εἴδη μερίζεται. Πεῖναν γὰρ καὶ δίψαν καὶ γύμνωσιν καὶ ξενιτείαν καὶ ἀσθένειαν καὶ φυλακὴν τῶν τούτοις κατειλημμένων εἴτε σωματικῶς εἴτε πνευματικῶς ὁ παραμυθούμενος τὴν ἐκ τῶν ἓξ ἀρετῶν συνισταμένην πεπλήρωκεν πρός τε τὸν θεὸν καὶ τὸν πλησίον ἀγάπην, ὡς μόνῳ τῷ θεῷ πεποιωμένην, τῆς ψυχῆς διατηρήσας τὴν ἔφεσιν. See further *infra*, on number 'six', endnote mdcxxxv.

mdcxxxiv The expression τῶν ἐφετῶν ἀκρότης ('the highest pitch of desirable' things) being identified with Christ shows only in later Byzantine literature, actually during and after the eleventh century. Obviously, this is an echo from Aristotle, *Physica*, 192a17: ὄντος γάρ τινος θείου καὶ ἀγαθοῦ καὶ ἐφετοῦ. Then, Plutarch, *Non Posse Suaviter Vivi Secundum Epicurum*, p. 1091D. Albinus, *Epitome Doctrinae Platonicae*, 10.6. Alexander of Aphrodisias, *commTop*, pp. 93; 192. Plotinus, *Enneades*, I.6.7; V.5.6; VI.7.19-20&22; *et passim*. I should not exclude the possibility of this gloss in the present codex being an addition by scribes of a later period, all the more so since *Codex Sabaiticus 232* was written during the early eleventh century, too. Anyway, cf. John Mauropus, *Canones in Sanctum Nicolaum*, canon 8, ode 4: Θεῷ συνανεκράθης ὀρεκτῶν τῷ ἐσχάτῳ καὶ παντὸς ἐφετοῦ τῇ ἀκρότητι. Michael III of Anchialus (Patriarch of Constantinople, 1170-1178), *Epistula ad Alexandrum III Papam*, lines 15-16: εἰς ἓν καὶ μόνον ἀφορῶσι τὸ κατὰ ἀλήθειαν ἓν καὶ τῶν ἐφετῶν τὴν ἀκρότητα. Philotheus

Coccinus, *Orationes et Homiliae*, oration 9, lines 100-102: Εἶτα καὶ πρὸς ζωὴν τὴν ἀτελεύτητον ἀπελεύσεσθε ... ἥτις αὐτός ἐστιν ὁ Χριστός, τὸ τῶν ὀρεκτῶν ἔσχατον, ἡ ὑμνουμένη τῶν ἐφετῶν ἀκρότης. Manuel II Palaeologus, *Oratio in Dormitionem Deiparae*, p. 557: τὸν Υἱόν τε καὶ Θεόν, τῶν ἐφετῶν τὴν ἀκρότητα. Macarius Macres, *Monodia in David Hieromonachum*, lines 229-231: τὸν θειότατον δεσπότην Ἰησοῦν σὺν τῷ ἀνάρχῳ αὐτοῦ Πατρὶ καὶ τῷ ὁμοδόξῳ Πνεύματι, τὴν τῶν ἀγαθῶν πηγήν, τῶν ἐφετῶν τὴν ἀκρότητα.

mdcxxxv Origen pointed out that, in Matt. 24:35-36, Jesus mentioned six instances of practicing love (as classified above,). In effect, however, Origen's analysis involves a Pythagorean echo: number *six* is a 'perfect' one (see *supra*, endnote mdcxxxiii) and associated with the perfect love of God, actually, with the perfect love which *is* God. See a later intimation of this by Theodore II Ducas Lascaris (rhetor and theologian, Emperor of Nicaea from 1254 to 1258), *Epistula ad Georgium Acropolitam*, lines 192-203: εἰ δ᾽ ἴσως ἐν ἡμῖν εὑρεθῇ καὶ ἡ ἑξὰς τετρακτὺς *κατὰ τοὺς σπερματικοὺς λόγους* ἀριθμητικῶς καὶ γεωμετρικῶς, φανήσεται καὶ τοῦτο καινότερον. ... ἔχεις τοίνυν ἑξάδα, ‹διὰ› τὴν δὲ εἰς παγίωσιν ἡμῶν ἀγάπην τὴν ἀδιάρρηκτον, τετράδα καὶ στερεόν. Ἄρα γοῦν ἡ ἑξὰς ἐν ἡμῖν *κατὰ τοὺς σπερματικοὺς λόγους*, ὡς Πλάτων καὶ πρὸ τούτου Πυθαγόρας βοῶσιν, ἐτελείωσε τετρακτύν.

Throughout his life, Origen made pretty much of number *six* being a 'perfect' one. *Princ*, IV.2.5 (*Philocalia*, 1.12): ἐν κόσμῳ ... γεγενημένῳ ἐν ἓξ ἡμέραις, ἀριθμῷ τελείῳ. *commMatt*, 12.36: ἐν ἓξ ἡμέραις, τελείῳ ἀριθμῷ, ὁ σύμπας γεγένηται κόσμος, τὸ τέλειον τοῦτο δημιούργημα. *schLuc*, PG.17.344.28-29: ἐν ἓξ ἡμέραις τελείῳ ἀριθμῷ ὁ σύμπας κόσμος γεγένηται. *commJohn*, X.39.270-1: οἱ δὲ ἐπιστάται, ‹τρισχίλιοι καὶ› ἑξακόσιοι τυγχάνοντες, τῷ τοῦ ἓξ τελείῳ ἀριθμῷ οἱονεὶ ἐφ᾽ ἑαυτὸν πολυπλασιαζομένῳ συνάπτονται. *Op. cit.* XXVIII.1.1 (a full definition of 'perfect numbers'): Οἱ φύσεις ἀριθμῶν ἐρευνήσαντες πρῶτον μὲν τέλειον τὸν ἓξ εἰρήκασιν, τοῖς ἑαυτοῦ μέρεσιν ‹ἴσον› ἱστάμενον, ἔκ τε τῆς συνθέσεως τοῦ ἀπὸ μονάδος διπλασιαζομένου, ἑνὸς καὶ δύο, ὅ ἐστι τρία, ἀριθμὸς πρῶτος, καὶ τοῦ ἐφ᾽ ὃν ἔφθασεν ὁ διπλασιασμός, λέγω δὲ τοῦ δύο. Γενόμενος γὰρ ὁ δύο ἐπὶ τὸν τρία πεποίηκεν τὸν ἕξ. Δεύτερον δὲ τέλειόν φασιν εἶναι τὸν εἴκοσι καὶ ὀκτώ.

mdcxxxvi See *supra*, endnote mccxci, in relation to the phrase, Πεινᾷ δὲ ὁ θεῖος λόγος τὴν ἡμετέραν σωτηρίαν.

mdcxxxvii Once again, ἑξὰς betokens perfection.

mdcxxxviii See *supra*, note lx.

mdcxxxix One more echo of Origen's Anaxagorean background. See ὄψις τῶν ἀδήλων τὰ φαινόμενα, discussed in *Anaxagoras*, pp. 503-504; 685-686. See *supra*, folio 169v: ὁ Θεὸς ὁ κοινὸς πατὴρ ... τὸν γὰρ διδακτὸν καὶ φυσικὸν νόμον ταῖς διανοίαις ἐγκατασπείρας, ἔδωκε κήρυκας τὰ ὁρώμενα.

mdcxl Origen, *commMatt*, fr. 518 (Klostermann).

mdcxli Origen, *commMatt*, fr. 519 (Klostermann).

mdcxlii The term ὑστεροπρώτοις is used instead of πρωθυστέρως, which appeared in the fourth century (Cassian the Sabaite used πρωθύστερα parallel to ὑστεροπρώτως): Cassian the Sabaite (Pseudo-Didymus), *De Trinitate*, PG.39.884.3. Cf. Hippolytus, *Commentarium in Danielem*, 1.5.3: Ἔθος γὰρ ἦν τοῖς γραμματεῦσιν ὑστερόπρωτα πολλὰ ἐν ταῖς γραφαῖς τιθέναι. Εὑρίσκομεν γὰρ καὶ ἐν τοῖς προφήταις ὁράσεις τινὰς πρώτας γεγενημένας καὶ ἐπ᾽ ἐσχάτων πεπληρωμένας καὶ αὖ πάλιν ἐπ᾽ ἐσχάτων εἰρημένας καὶ πρώτας γεγενημένας. *Op. cit.* 1.32.28: Καὶ ἔτι· τὸν γὰρ ἠλαττωμένον βλέπομεν Ἰησοῦν διὰ τὸ πάθημα τοῦ θανάτου δόξῃ καὶ τιμῇ ἐστεφανωμένον. Ὑστεροπρώτως εἴρηται. Φησὶν γάρ. τὸν δοκοῦντά τισιν διὰ τὸ πάθημα τοῦ θανάτου ἠλαττῶσθαι Ἰησοῦν βλέπομεν δόξῃ καὶ τιμῇ ἐστεφανωμένον.

mdcxliii Cf. Exodus, 12:18; Lev. 23:5; Num. 9:2-5; 28:16; Jesus Nave, 5:10; 1 Esdras, 1:1; Ez. 45:21.

mdcxliv Origen, *commMatt*, fr. 520 (Klostermann).

mdcxlv *Catena in Marcum*, p. 417 (anonymous). A few lines following this point, the text expounds Origen's views of who and how many the women who 'poured' on Jesus' 'head very expensive ointment' were (Matt. 26:7; Mark, 14:3). *Op. cit.* p. 418: Ὠριγένης δὲ πάλιν ἄλλην μέν φησι τὴν παρὰ Ματθαίῳ καὶ Μάρκῳ ἐκχέουσαν *τῆς κεφαλῆς* τὸ μύρον ἐν οἰκίᾳ Σίμωνος τοῦ λεπροῦ, ἄλλην δὲ τὴν παρὰ τῷ Λουκᾷ γεγραμμένην ἁμαρτωλὸν κατεκχέσασαν τῶν ποδῶν αὐτοῦ τὸ μύρον *ἐν τῇ οἰκίᾳ τοῦ Φαρισαίου.* This is also Origen, *commMatt*, fr. 521 II (Klostermann). Cf. the name of Origen being cited in this catena: pp. 266 & 316 (at both points, citing 'the sixth book of his commentary on John').

mdcxlvi Cf. Lev. 4:3. Theodoret wrote that existence of two archpriests at the same time was 'unheard of'. *Interpretatio in Danielem*, PG.81.148.14-18: Ταῦτα διδάσκων καὶ ὁ μακάριος Λουκᾶς φησιν. *Ἔτους πεντεκαιδεκάτου Τιβερίου Καίσαρος, ἐπὶ ἀρχιερέων Ἄννα καὶ Καϊάφα* [Luke, 3:1-2]. Δύο δὲ κατὰ ταὐτὸν ἀρχιερέας κατὰ νόμον γεγενημένους οὐ μεμαθήκαμεν πώποτε. This is the context of his drawing on Josephus and quoting from his information about Herod having introduced this practice, also advising that archpriests maintained the office for no definite time, and office and bribery were involved in getting the job. See *supra*, endnote mcccxiv.

mdcxlvii *Catena in Marcum*, p. 417 (anonymous).

mdcxlviii John Chrysostom, *In Matthaeum*, PG.58.725.38-43.

mdcxlix Origen, *commMatt*, fr. 521 I (Klostermann).

mdcl Origen, *commMatt*, fr. 526 (Klostermann).

mdcli That is, month Νισάν, the seventh one of the Hebrew civic year and the first of the religious year. This is the month during which the Hebrew Pesah ('Passover') is celebrated (traditionally 8 days from Nissan 15) – the period from middle of March to middle of April (cf. Origen, *deOr*, 27.14). Origen called this 'month of the new [things]' (μὴν τῶν νέων), evidently translating from Hebrew, on which Didymus followed him (*commZacch*, 5.88) and later so did Sozomenus, also an admirer and advocate of Origen. Sozomenus wrote that 'the Samaritans, who were devout zealots of the Mosaic law', celebrated Passover only once the new fruits had appeared, since 'this is why the law calls this feats of the new ones'. To them, 'it was unlawful to celebrate prior to appearance of new fruits; hence, of necessity, this could not be celebrated until spring equinox occurred'. Sozomenus, *HE*, 7.18.9-10. Nicephorus Callistus Xanthopulus copied this while paraphrasing slightly. *HE*, 12.32. Origen was more specific, and explained that this was about the 'fruits of the vineyard', which 'in Judaea flourished at the time of the Passover' (*Scholia in Canticum Canticorum*, PG.17.280.14-17). However, what he saw in 'the feast of new things' (or, in the Hebrew 'feast of the unleavened [bread]', ἑορτὴ τῶν ἀζύμων) was the renewal of human nature following Jesus' passion and resurrection. Accordingly, he explained 'feast of new things' by quoting such portions as, 'The old things have passed away' (2 Cor. 5:17), 'you have put off the old man with his acts, and have put on the new man, being renewed in knowledge after the image of his Creator' (Col. 3:9-10), 'For indeed Christ, our Passover, has been sacrificed in our place. Therefore, let us keep the feast, not with old yeast, neither with the yeast of malice and wickedness, but with the unleavened bread of sincerity and truth.' (1 Cor. 5:7-8). Origen, *selEx*, PG.12: 285.5-9; 296.12-35. *selPs*, PG.12.1421.18-20. Cf. *commJohn*, X.16.91; *frICor*, fr. 25.

mdclii Origen, *commMatt*, fr. 525 (Klostermann).

mdcliii Origen pays his respects to Hippolytus, the man who in all probability convinced him to convert to Christianity and brokered his acquaintance with the wealthy sponsor Ambrose. The following are Hippolytus' words quoted in the *Chronicon Paschale*, p. 13: Ὁρῶ μὲν οὖν ὅτι φιλονεικίας τὸ ἔργον. Λέγει γὰρ οὕτως· ἐποίησε τὸ πάσχα ὁ Χριστὸς τότε τῇ ἡμέρᾳ καὶ ἔπαθεν· διὸ κἀμὲ δεῖ ὃν τρόπον ὁ κύριος ἐποίησεν, οὕτω ποιεῖν. Πεπλάνηται δὲ μὴ γινώσκων ὅτι ᾧ καιρῷ ἔπασχεν ὁ Χριστὸς οὐκ ἔφαγε τὸ κατὰ νόμον πάσχα. Οὗτος γὰρ ἦν τὸ πάσχα τὸ προκεκηρυγμένον καὶ τὸ τελειούμενον τῇ ὡρισμένῃ ἡμέρᾳ. Καὶ πάλιν ὁ αὐτὸς ἐν τῷ πρώτῳ λόγῳ τοῦ περὶ τοῦ ἁγίου πάσχα συγγράμματος εἴρηκεν οὕτως. Οὐδὲ ἐν τοῖς πρώτοις οὐδὲ ἐν τοῖς ἐσχάτοις ὡς οὐκ ἐψεύσατο πρόδηλον, ὅτι ὁ πάλαι προειπὼν ὅτι Οὐκέτι φάγομαι τὸ πάσχα εἰκότως τὸ μὲν δεῖπνον ἐδείπνησεν πρὸ τοῦ πάσχα, τὸ δὲ πάσχα οὐκ ἔφαγεν, ἀλλ' ἔπαθεν. Οὐδὲ γὰρ καιρὸς ἦν τῆς βρώσεως αὐτοῦ. Furthermore, the author of the *Chronicon Paschale* adduces similar views by Apollinaris of Laodicea and Clement of Alexandria (pp. 13-15).

mdcliv As it stands, the form ἠρήσατο makes no sense, since this means 'he made prayer' (derived from the verb ἀρῶ / ῶμαι, very frequent in Homer: see *Suda*, letter eta, entry 508; *Etymologicum Gudianum*, entry eta, p. 248). However, the meaning of the present text is 'he chose to'. At this point, this is a wrong word, which the author of the *Etymologicum Magnum* (p. 777) styled ἀνελλήνιστον ('not Grecian', in other words, a 'barbarism') 'since there is no Aorist ἤρησα, and this should be εἵλετο (Aorist of the verb αἱροῦμαι). See, *Epimerismi Homerici* (on *Ilias*, I.351), lemma: ἠρήσατο. The same, in Anonymous, *Scholia in Iliadem*, (on *Ilias*, I.351). See *Etymologicum Magnum*, p. 777: Ὑπεξαιρῆσαν. Ἀντὶ τοῦ ὑπεξελόν. ἀνελλήνιστόν ἐστι. τοῦ γὰρ ἀορίστου μὴ ὄντος, λέγω δὴ τοῦ ἤρησα, οὐδὲ ἡ μετοχὴ αἱρήσας, οὐδὲ οὐδέτερον τὸ αἱρῆσαν. However, use of this form ἠρήσατο instead of εἵλετο was a reality at the late Byzantine period (there should be no doubt that this was written by the scribe, not by Origen himself). For example, 'when a certain Theodore, an hermit from the Church of Alexandria, came to meet Pachomius and the other brothers at Thebais, *he chose to stay* therein for ever (ἠρήσατο γὰρ διὰ παντὸς συνεῖναι αὐτοῖς). *Sancti Pachomii Vita Tertia*, p. 350.

mdclv Origen, *commMatt*, fr. 527 (Klostermann). See *supra*, folio 182v.

mdclvi Origen, *commMatt*, fr. 531 (Klostermann).

mdclvii Ephraem Syrus, *De Panoplia, Ad Monachos*, p. 22: Βλέπετε δὲ καὶ τὸν Κύριον ἡμῶν Ἰησοῦν Χριστὸν οἰκονομικῶς εὐχόμενον καὶ λέγοντα. *Πάτερ, εἰ δυνατόν ἐστι, παρελθέτω ἀπ' ἐμοῦ τὸ ποτήριον τοῦτο. πλὴν οὐχ ὡς ἐγὼ θέλω, ἀλλ' ὡς σύ.*

mdclviii 'Death fell in against nature' means that death was not meant to be part of divine creation. Cf. Pseudo-Zonaras, *Lexicon*, letter pi, p. 1508 (lemma: 'against nature'): Παρὰ φύσιν. ὃ ὁ θεὸς οὐκ ἐποίησεν, οἷόν ἐστιν ἡ ἁμαρτία καὶ ὁ θάνατος. I should have thought that this statement derived from Origen. Be that as it may, it is remarkable that the next lemma (definition of 'proverb') is entirely Origen's own words and this was taken up by several subsequent authors. Origen, *expProv*, PG.17.161.20-21: Παροιμία ἐστὶ λόγος ἀπόκρυφος δι' ἑτέρου προδήλου σημαινόμενος. This was copied to the letter by the following authors: George Monachus, *Chronicon*, p. 151; *Chronicon Breve*, PG.110.201.5-6. *Suda*, letter pi, entry 733. *Etymologicum Gudianum*, entry pi, p. 454. George Cedrenus, *Compendium Historiarum*, v. 1, p. 97. Pseudo-Zonaras, *Lexicon*, letter pi, p. 1508.

mdclix Origen, *commMatt*, fr. 532 (Klostermann).

mdclx Klostermann having in mind Chrysostom put this in brackets. However, in reality Chrysostom copied from Origen. See John Chrysostom, *In Matthaeum*, PG.58.733.32-36: ὅτε δὲ αὐτὸν δῆλον ἐποίησεν, ἐτόλμησε πάλιν ἐρέσθαι, τῇ ἐπιεικείᾳ τοῦ Διδασκάλου θαρρῶν, ὡς οὐκ ἐλέγξοντος αὐτόν. *Op. cit.*, PG.58.747.56-57: *Ὃν ἂν φιλήσω*, φησίν. Ἐθάρρει τῇ ἐπιεικείᾳ τοῦ Διδασκάλου. See also the *Catena in Matthaeum*, p. 225 (anonymous):

τὸ δὲ σημεῖον δέδωκεν αὐτοῖς ὁ προδότης, ὅτι πολλάκις κατασχεθεὶς ὑπ᾽ αὐτῶν ὁ Χριστὸς διῆλθεν ἐκ μέσου αὐτῶν οὐκ ἐπεγνωκότων αὐτόν· φίλημα δὲ θαρρῶν τῇ ἐπιεικείᾳ τοῦ διδασκάλου. The pages from 214 up to this point (p. 225) are anonymous. The last attribution preceding this section is Origen's (p. 214).

mdclxi Origen, *commMatt*, fr. 533 (Klostermann).

mdclxii Origen, *commMatt*, fr. 534 (Klostermann).

mdclxiii Origen, *commSerMatt*, p. 219. See also, *Cels*, II.11.

mdclxiv Origen, *commMatt*, fr. 535 (Klostermann).

mdclxv Origen, *commSerMatt*, p. 220.

mdclxvi Cf. Cyril of Alexandria inspired by Origen's text. *In Joannem*, v. 2, p. 649: καὶ *ἐζήτουν ἀποκτεῖναι* κατὰ τὸ γεγραμμένον, διὰ τὸ μεταρρυθμίζειν τῶν πιστευόντων τὸν νοῦν ἐκ νομικῆς καὶ παχείας ἐντολῆς εἰς τὴν τῆς εὐαγγελικῆς πολιτείας ἰσχνότητα.

mdclxvii Origen, *commMatt*, fr. 537 (Klostermann).

mdclxviii Origen was always alert and investigative as to the *historicity* of events and places concerning Jesus' life and activity (*PHE*, chapters 10 & 11). Accordingly, he never disputed that this was a darkening of the sun, yet not a *natural* eclipse, since it was not in tune with the astronomical data of the moment of crucifixion, when the positions of sun and moon 'were diametrical' (hence, a *natural* eclipe was impossible to happen). Cf. *Cels*, II.33; *commSerMatt*, p. 274. Therefore, this was a miraculous event not caused by the intervening position of the moon. In *Cels*, II.36, he wrote that 'the eclipsed sun' (ὁ ἐκλιπὼν ἥλιος) was 'a certain sign from God' (θεοσημία τις), therefore, an inexplicable 'paradox from the heaven'. Julius Africanus endorsed Origen's argument and styled this 'darkness caused by God' (σκότος θεοποίητον). *Chronographiae*, fr. 50, *apud* George Syncellus, *Ecloga Chronographica*, p. 391. See immediately *infra*, Origen styling this phenomenon a manifestation of the Father's wrath; folio 228r: Ὀργιζομένου γὰρ ἦν τὸ *σκότος* ἐκεῖνο καὶ δεῖγμα τοῦ μέλλοντος λαβεῖν τοὺς μιαιφόνους.

mdclxix Origen, *commMatt*, fr. 554 (Klostermann).

mdclxx Origen, *schMatt*, PG.17.308.39-44.

mdclxxi Also Origen, *commSerMatt*, pp. 277-278: εἰκὼν δὲ τὸ σκότος τοῦ σκοτίζεσθαι τοὺς ἐπιβαλόντας χεῖρα τῷ φωτί. Ὡς γὰρ Αἰγυπτίοις σκότος καὶ τοῖς υἱοῖς Ἰσραὴλ φῶς, οὕτω καὶ νῦν τῇ μὲν ἐκκλησίᾳ φῶς, τοῖς δὲ Ἰουδαίοις σκότος τριῶν ὡρῶν, φωτὸς πατρικοῦ, ἀπαυγάσματος Χριστοῦ, ἐλλάμψεως ἁγίου πνεύματος.

mdclxxii Cf. Origen, *frLuc*, fr. 249: Περὶ ταύτης τῆς ἐκλείψεως expl. ἐκρεμάσθη τῆς ἕκτης ἡμέρας, ἵνα τὸν ἐν τῇ ἕκτῃ ἡμέρᾳ γεγονότα καὶ τῇ ἕκτῃ ὥρᾳ τοῦ παραδείσου ἐκπεσόντα πάλιν ἀνακαλέσηται. This is also Origen, *commMatt*, fr. 557 II (Klostermann). Likewise, Origen, *commMatt*, fr. 557 III (Klostermann): Ἔδει γὰρ τὸν ἐν τῇ ϛ′ ἡμέρᾳ τὸν ἄνθρωπον ποιήσαντα τῇ ϛ′ ἡμέρᾳ ὑποστῆναι τὸν ὑπὲρ αὐτοῦ θάνατον, ἵνα ἐξέληται αὐτὸν τῆς παρακοῆς.

mdclxxiii Origen, *commMatt*, fr. 557 I (Klostermann).

mdclxxiv The text following this point (Τοῦτό ἐστιν τὸ *σημεῖον*) down to οἱ τὴν γῆν οἰκοῦντες μάθωσιν, is exactly the same as the following one in the *Catena in Marcum*, p. 439: Ἕκτης ὥρας λοιπὸν γενομένης, γέγονεν ὅπερ ᾔτουν τὸν Ἰησοῦν ἐξ οὐρανοῦ σημεῖον, ὅπερ καὶ ὑπέσχετο δώσειν, λέγων, *γενεὰ πονηρὰ καὶ μοιχαλὶς σημεῖον ἐπιζητεῖ, καὶ σημεῖον οὐ δοθήσεται αὐτῇ εἰ μὴ τὸ σημεῖον Ἰωνᾶ*, καὶ *ὅταν ὑψώσητε τὸν υἱὸν τοῦ ἀνθρώπου, τότε γνώσεσθε ὅτι ἐγώ εἰμι*. Καὶ γὰρ πολλῷ θαυμαστότερον ἐπὶ τοῦ σταυροῦ προσηλωμένου ταῦτα γενέσθαι ἢ βαδίζοντος ἐπὶ τῆς γῆς. Καὶ ὅπερ οὐδέποτε πρότερον συνέβη, ἀλλ᾽ ἢ ἐν Αἰγύπτῳ μόνον ὅτε τὸ Πάσχα ἐτελεῖτο· καὶ γὰρ ἐκεῖνα τούτων τύπος ἦν. Καὶ ἵνα μὴ εἴπωσιν, ἔκλειψιν εἶναι τὸ γεγενημένον, διὰ τοῦτο καὶ τέσσαρες καὶ δέκατον γίνεται, ὅτε ἔκλειψιν συμβῆναι ἀμήχανον. Ἐν μέσῃ δὲ ἡμέρᾳ, ἵνα πάντες οἱ τὴν γῆν οἰκοῦντες μάθωσιν.

mdclxxv Phlegon was a native of Tralles and freedman of the emperor Hadrian or Antoninus Pius (*Suda*, letter phi, entry 527; cf. *Codex Palatinatus Graecus*, folio 234r). He lived in the second century AD and was contemporary with Plutarch (George Monachus, *Chronicon Breve*, PG.110.528.23-24). John Malalas (*Chronographia*, 10.14) styles him 'an Athenian', obviously considering a later stage of his life. His main work was the *Olympiads* (to others: *Chronicles*), a compendium of Olympiads and Olympic winners (Photius: ὀλυμπιονικῶν καὶ χρονικῶν συναγωγή) in sixteen books, from the first down to the two-hundred and twenty-ninth Olympiad (776 BC to AD 137). He is mentioned by several authors more or less quoting from his works. Herodian, *De Prosodia Catholica*, pp. 153; 325; p. 867; *et passim* (abundantly). Origen, *Cels*, II.14; II.33; II.59. *commSerMatt*, p. 273; *schMatt*, PG.17.309.13. Apollinaris, *frMatt*, fr. 142 (the passage is Origen's). Theodore of Heraclea, *frMatt*, fr. 131 (the passage is Origen's). Julius Africanus, *Chronographiae*, fr. 50. Eusebius, *Praeparatio Evangelica*, 10.10.4. Diogenes Laertius, *Vitae*, 1.111. *Chronicon Paschale*, pp. 412; 417. George Syncellus, *Ecloga Chronographica*, pp. 391 (quoting from Julius Africanus, see *infra*, note mdclxxvi); 394. George Cedrenus, *Compendium Historiarum*, p. 331. John Laurentius Lydus, *De Mensibus*, 1.21. Evagrius Scholasticus, *HE*, p. 29. John Philoponus, *De Opificio Mundi*, pp. 99-101; 129; 208. Stephanus Byzantius, *Ethnica* (*epitome*), pp. 145; 162; 177; 204; 233; 245; *et passim*. Photius, *Bibliotheca*, p. 83b. Constantine Porphyrogenitus, *De Thematibus*, Europe, chapter 12. Nicephorus Callistus Xanthopulus, *HE*, 14.50. Also in lexica: *Etymologicum Magnum*, p. 19; *Etymologicum Symeonis*, p. 74; *Suda*, letter theta, entry 17; letter phi, entry 527.

mdclxxvi This is exactly the same argument that Origen's pupil, namely, Julius Africanus, used and quite obviously he followed Origen also on this. He quoted from 'the third book of Thallus' *History*', in which Thallus (historian, first-second century AD) described this as an eclipse. Julius argued that this was an irrational claim (ἀλόγως), since, during the Jewish Pascha, the positions of the sun and moon were 'almost diametrical' (κατὰ διάμετρον σχεδόν). Julius Africanus, *Chronographiae*, fr. 50 (from the fifth book), quoted by George Syncellus, *Ecloga Chronographica*, p. 391. Later, George Cedrenus reproduced the same argument, and his text is a remarkable combination of the same expressions used by Origen and Julius Africanus alike. Moreover, Cedrenus wrote that 'it was Phlegon and Africanus who reported the darkness that took place during that day' (i.e. the day of Crucifixion). *Compendium Historiarum*, v. 1, pp. 331-332.

mdclxxvii Cf. *supra*, folio 107v: ἐσκότισεν αὐτῶν τὸν νοῦν. The idea involved is that of Eph. 4:17-18, referring to the 'darkened' and 'futile mind of the nations' (ἐν ματαιότητι τοῦ νοὸς αὐτῶν, ἐσκοτωμένοι τῇ διανοίᾳ ὄντες). Following this, Origen introduced the expression ἐσκοτισμένος νοῦς ('stupefied mind') which, although not strictly scriptural, conveys Paul's meaning. Origen, *commEph*, fr. 18; *selPs*, PG.12.1532.47; *expProv*, PG.17.165.40; *schMatt*, PG.17.309.25. It was this expression that subsequent authors made the most of. Athanasius, *Contra Gentes*, 9. Pseudo-Basil of Caesarea (*forsan* Cassian the Sabaite), *Enarratio in Prophetam Isaiam*, 16.103. Evagrius of Pontus, *De Octo Spiritibus Malitiae*, PG.79.1153.35. Pseudo-John Chrysostom, *De Pseudoprophetis*, PG.59.562.24. Cyril of Alexandria, *Encomium in Sanctam Mariam Deiparam*, PG.77.1040.3. Romanus Melodus, *Cantica*, hymn 15.7. *Et. al.*

mdclxxviii Origen's text has been copied so unbridledly that its real author was eventually eclipsed by those who used to loot and plunder his work while suppressing his name. For one, the portion, Καὶ Φλέγων δέ τις ... πάντα ἐφθέγξαντο ὅσα ἐθέλησαν is one which J. Reuss conveniently included in his collection attributing this to both Apollinaris (fr. 142) and Theodore of Heraclea (fr. 131), allegedly from their purported commentaries on Matthew. On the other hand, J.A. Cramer included the same text as part of a wider context, of which Origen's original is extant (*schMatt*, PG.17.308.44-309.33) and yet no less conveniently did he rest content with the catenist's 'Unattributed' (Ἐξ ἀνεπιγράφου). *Catena in Matthaeum*, pp. 236-238. However, simply and plainly the text is Origen's.

Furthermore, according to his habit, John Chrysostom copied passages selectively and included them in his own context. In this case, he copied the following words from Origen's commentary: John Chrysostom, *In Matthaeum*, PG.58.775.38-42: Μετὰ γὰρ πάντα τὰ τῆς παροινίας, καὶ τῆς παρανόμου κωμῳδίας, τοῦτο γίνεται, ὅτε τὸν θυμὸν εἴασαν, ὅτε ἀνεπαύσαντο γελῶντες, ὅτε κόρον ἔλαβον τῶν σκωμμάτων, καὶ πάντα ἐφθέγξαντο ἅπερ ἠθέλησαν.

Even Gennadius Scholarius in the fifteenth century did so, too. His replication is revealing, since it shows that Eusebius had copied the present words of Origen, which was natural for Eusebius to do, and, anyway, he never sought to suppress his hero's name. Gennadius quotes from Eusebius' explanation to Marinus about Jesus' 'three days' stay in Hades (see *Ad Marinum*, PG.22.956.37-59), which originated with Origen as the present codex evinces (which Klostermann's extensive fragment 565 also does). But Gennadius' text *quotes* from another edition of Eusebius' text that was available to him (... φασὶ γάρ, i.e. Eusebius) and this quotation from Eusebius is but Origen's own words (ὅτε γὰρ κόρον ἔλαβον τῶν παροινιῶν καὶ τῶν σκωμμάτων, τότε τὸ σκότος ἐδείχθη). Eusebius naturally drew on Origen's explanation of the 'three days', but Gennadius only wrote that 'many subsequent authors favoured this exegesis of Eusebius' (Οὕτω μὲν ἐπιλύει τὴν ἀπορίαν Μαρίνου ὁ Παμφίλου Εὐσέβιος, καὶ πολλοῖς τῶν ὑστέρων αὕτη μᾶλλον ἡ λύσις ἤρεσεν). Gennadius Scholarius, *Responsiones Aliquorum Quaestionum in Scripturam Sacram*, response 4, p. 327. The irony is that 'subsequent authors' quoted words that in fact were Origen's ones, but ancient catenists and modern editors alike did not care to conduct some research, hence, they attributed Origen's words to 'subsequent authors'. Little wonder then that Origen's explanation has been attributed to such authors as Isidore of Pelusium (Michael Glycas, *Annales*, p. 416), Apollinaris (*frMatt*, fr. 142), even to Theodore of Mopsuestia (John Philoponus, *De Opificio Mundi*, p. 102).

mdclxxix Origen, *commMatt*, fr. 556 (Klostermann).

mdclxxx The rest of this passage (Καὶ Φλέγων δέ τις ... ὅσα ἐθέλησαν) has been also attributed to Apollinaris (*frMatt*, fr. 142). This is one of the most telling of the instances evincing how misleading attributions took the best of some ancient catenists. For this passage is one of Origen's best documented ones, since this appears not only in catenae, but also in the extant text of his commentary on Matthew. However, there is more to this: the largest part of this text (Φλέγων γάρ τις ὀνόματι φιλόσοφος ... τοὺς μιαιφόνους, that is, all of this passage, except for the last period) has been attributed also to Theodore of Heraclea, *frMatt*, fr. 131. It appears then that, after all, this could have been ascribed to all of the authors who copied from Origen's commentary.

mdclxxxi Origen, *schMatt*, PG.17.308.44-309.33. This has been attributed also to Apollinaris (*frMatt*, fr. 143), which is glaring evidence of how Origen's texts have been treated.

mdclxxxii Origen's enthusiastic devotee Eusebius was the only one to reproduce this comment. *Commentaria in Psalmos*, PG.23.204.5-11: *Ὁ Θεὸς ὁ Θεός μου, πρόσχες μοι. ἵνα τί ἐγκατέλιπές με; μακρὰν ἀπὸ τῆς σωτηρίας μου οἱ λόγοι τῶν παραπτωμάτων μου.* Μὴ προκειμένου δὲ ἐν τῷ Ἑβραϊκῷ τοῦ, *πρόσχες μοι*, ὃ δὴ κατὰ μόνους τοὺς Ἑβδομήκοντα προσέκειτο τῷ πρώτῳ στίχῳ, ἀκριβῶς καὶ ὑπὸ τῆς φωνῆς τοῦ Σωτῆρος ἡμῶν παραλέλειπται.

mdclxxxiii Klostermann notes that in one codex (*P* [=Peter of Laodicea]) this lacuna has it, οὐ μάχεται τῇ παλαιᾷ γραφῇ καὶ ὅτι τιμᾷ τὸν πατέρα, which is precisely the text of the present codex.

mdclxxxiv Origen, *commMatt*, fr. 558 (Klostermann).

mdclxxxv *Catena in Marcum*, p. 439 (anonymous).

mdclxxxvi Cf. the newly discovered Cassian the Sabaite (a moderate Origenist of the sixth century) following Origen suit. Cassian the Sabaite (Pseudo-Didymus), *De Trinitate*, PG.39.801.45-48: Εἰ ἅμα τῷ Θεῷ Πατρὶ καὶ τῷ Υἱῷ αὐτοῦ τὸ ἅγιον Πνεῦμα διὰ τοῦ βαπτίσματος ἀναστοιχειοῖ ἡμᾶς εἰς εἰκόνα τὴν πρώτην, καὶ διὰ τῆς μετουσίας αἴτιον ἡμῖν υἱοθεσίας καὶ τοῦ γίνεσθαι θεούς ἐστιν.

mdclxxxvii Origen, *commMatt*, fr. 559 (Klostermann).

mdclxxxviii Origen introduced the turn ἀληθινὸς ἀμνὸς ('real lamb'), evidently after John, 1:29 & 36 (cf. Acts, 8:32, quoting Is. 53:7). See *frLuc*, fr. 100 (2): ὁ ἀμνὸς ὁ ἀληθινὸς ὑπὲρ τῆς ἁμαρτίας τοῦ κόσμου προσεφέρετο. *De Pascha*, p. 140: Ταῦτα τὸ ἀληθινὸν πρόβατον, ὁ ἀληθῶς *ἀμνὸς ὁ αἴρων τὴν ἁμαρτίαν τοῦ κόσμου*. As it happened, his devotees adopted this. Gregory of Nyssa, *De Vita Mosis*, 2.95: ἐνταῦθα ἡ πρώτη τῆς κακίας εἴσοδος καθ' ἡμῶν διὰ τοῦ ἀληθινοῦ ἀμνοῦ ἀποστρέφεται. Athanasius, *Expositiones in Psalmos*, PG.27.214.29-30: τὴν διὰ τοῦ αἵματος τοῦ ἀληθινοῦ Χριστοῦ ἀμνοῦ γενησομένην ἅπασιν ἀποκάθαρσιν. Didymus, *commZacch*, 5.196: Αὐτίκα γοῦν καὶ ὁ Σωτὴρ ἀληθινὸς ἀρχιερεὺς ὑπάρχων καὶ ἀμνὸς καὶ ποιμὴν προσαγορεύεται. Also, Amphilochius of Iconium, *Contra Haereticos*, line 974. John Chrysostom himself did not notice Origen's introduction of this expression; hence, this appears only in spuria under his name. Pseudo-John Chrysostom, *In Psalmum 118*, PG.55.680.26&29; *De Jejunio*, PG.60. 720.33; 721.2; PG.62.759.1; *Oratio De Hypapante*, p. 64. By contrast, Cyril of Alexandria made the most of this. *commProphXII*, v. 2, p. 250; *In Joannem*, v. 1, pp. 170; 639; v. 2, pp. 297; 688; *Homiliarum Incertarum Fragmenta*, p. 467; *Epistulae Paschales*, PG.77: 493.53; 824.39; 945.27; 957.28; *De Adoratione*, PG.68: 829.33; 1009.13; *Glaphyra in Pentateuchum*, PG.69: 296.29; 425.3; 433.57; 481.48; *In Isaiam*, PG.70: 937.40; 1173.56; 1192.19. Hesychius of Jerusalem, *Homilia i De Hypapante*, 3. Basil of Seleucia, *Homilia in Pentecosten*, PG.52.811.8. Photius, *Epistulae et Amphilochia*, epistle 295, line 2.

Accordingly, Origen articulated the same notion ('real lamb') also by using the synonymous expression ἀληθινὸν πρόβατον. However (unlike ἀληθινὸς ἀμνός), this did not win the day, but it is exactly this fact that makes Origen's seal on this passage all the more distinctive. See Origen, *selEx*, PG.12.284.37-40 & *De Pascha*, p. 116: Πρὸς ἑσπέραν δὲ κελευόμεθα σφάξαι τὸ πρόβατον, ἐπειδὴ καὶ ἐσχάτῃ ὥρᾳ τὸ ἀληθινὸν ἡμῶν πρόβατον εἰς τὸν κόσμον ἦλθεν, ὁ Σωτήρ. *De Pascha*, p. 108: ὁ τὸ ἀληθινὸν πρόβατον λαβών, τοῦτ' ἔστιν Χριστόν. ... τὸ ἀληθινὸν πρόβατον θῦσαι καὶ φαγεῖν. *Op. cit.* p. 120: Οὕτως οὖν καταλλήλου καθὸ δυνάμεθα μέρους μεταλαμβάνομεν τοῦ προβάτου τοῦ ἀληθινοῦ μεταλαμβάνοντες τοῦ λόγου τοῦ θεοῦ. Likewise, *op. cit.* pp. 124; 140; 148. Gregory of Nyssa, *Antirrheticus Adversus Apollinarium*, p. 131. Eusebius, *Eclogae Propheticae*, p. 145; *De Solemnitate Paschali*, PG.24.701.26. Pseudo-Basil of Caesarea (*forsan* Cassian the Sabaite), *Enarratio in Prophetam Isaiam*, 1.27. Hesychius of Jerusalem, *Homilia i De Hypapante*, 3.

mdclxxxix See the idea of 'life-giving body' (ζωοποιοῦν σῶμα) of Christ in Origen, *commEph*, fr. 9 & *apud Catena in Epistulam ad Ephesios*, p. 133 (comm. on Eph. 1:22-23): *σῶμα Χριστοῦ* εὑρίσκοντες λεγομένην τὴν ἐκκλησίαν, ζητοῦμεν πότερόν ποτε, ὡς παρὰ τὴν κεφαλὴν τὸ λοιπὸν σῶμα, ... ἐὰν μέντοιγε τὸ δεύτερον ᾖ, ἔσται τὸ μὲν ἀνθρωπικώτερον αὐτοῦ καὶ αὐτὸ μέρος τυγχάνον τοῦ ὅλου σώματος, τὸ δὲ θεῖον καὶ ζωοποιοῦν πᾶσαν τὴν ἐκκλησίαν ἡ ὡσπερεὶ ψυχοῦσα αὐτὴν δύναμις θεία. Then, Theodoret, *Eranistes*, p. 152: Οὕτως αὐτὸ καὶ ὁ κύριος προσηγόρευσε, καὶ αὐτὸ δὲ τὸ σῶμα θεῖον ὀνομάζομεν σῶμα, καὶ ζωοποιὸν καὶ δεσποτικὸν καὶ κυριακόν. *Op. cit.* p. 262: Οἱ ζωοποιὸν τοῦ κυρίου τὴν σάρκα προσαγορεύοντες. *In Isaiam*, 20: τὸ ζωοποιὸν σῶμα. *In Epistulas Sancti Pauli*, PG.82.781.53-54: Ἀντὶ δὲ τῆς κόνεως αὐτὸ τὸ ζωοποιὸν ἡμῖν γίνεται σῶμα. Cyril of Alexandria (τὸ ζωοποιὸν σῶμα of the Lord), *In Joannem*, v. 1, pp. 483; 514; 530; 551; 553; v. 2, p. 158; *commLuc*, PG.72.609.43-44.

mdcxc This is a late Byzantine form of εἶτα οὕτως.

mdcxci End of text on the margin.

mdcxcii Wisdom of Solomon, 15:11. Nevertheless, the notion of 'animating spirit' was a fundamental one maintained by the physician Erasistratus of Kea (c. 304-c. 250 BC): Ἐρασιστράτῳ τε καὶ τοῖς οἰομένοις ὄργανα τοῦ ζωτικοῦ πνεύματος ὑπάρχειν αὐτάς, *apud* Galen, *An In Arteriis Natura Sanguis Contineatur*, p. 714. Also, Ἐρασίστρατος οὖν οὐχ ἁπλῶς, ὥσπερ οὗτοι (sc. Hippocrates and Plato) τὸ ζητούμενον λαμβάνων, ἀλλὰ μετὰ κατασκευῆς λόγων οὐκ ὀλίγης, ἐκ μὲν κεφαλῆς φησι τὸ ψυχικόν, ἐκ δὲ τῆς καρδίας τὸ ζωτικὸν ὁρμᾶσθαι πνεῦμα, *apud* Galen, *De Placitis Hippocratis et Platonis*, 2.8.38. Galen himself entertained this idea abundantly. See *De Usu Partium*, v. 3, pp. 307; 701; v. 4, p. 183; *De Semine*, pp. 531; 588; *et passim.* Prior to Origen, see Justin Martyr, *Dialogus cum Tryphone*, 6.2. Although the notion could have claimed biblical origin (and so it was used once by Methodius of Olympus, *Symposium*, 2.7, and later by Anastasius of Sinai, *Viae Dux*, 1.2), this was scarcely used in both Christian and Greek literature, and mainly remained an idea treated by medical doctors. See, for example, Eusebius, *Praeparatio Evangelica*, 11.24.9. Pseudo-Gregory of Nyssa, *Ad Imaginem Dei et ad Similitudinem*, PG.44.1340.18. Pseudo-John Chrysostom, *In Ramos Palmarum*, PG.59.718.42; *In Lazarum*, PG.62.775.1- 2. Theodoret, *Interpretatio in Ezechielem*, PG.81.1192.4.

mdcxciii Cf. Luke, 23:46.

mdcxciv Origen, *commMatt*, fr. 560 (Klostermann); continued *infra.*

mdcxcv Origen, *frLuc*, fr. 251.

mdcxcvi Origen, *frLuc*, fr. 253; continued *infra.*

mdcxcvii Cf Wisdom of Solomon, 3:1: Δικαίων δὲ ψυχαὶ ἐν χειρὶ θεοῦ. Cf. Daniel, 3:86.

mdcxcviii Apollinaris, *frMatt*, fr. 143. Once again, copying from Origen is all too evident.

mdcxcix Origen, *commMatt*, fr. 560 (Klostermann); continued *infra.*

mdcc This is part of Origen's *frLuc*, fr. 253; see quotation of this on pp. 172; 367; 368.

mdcci Apollinaris, *frMatt*, fr. 143, quoted herein, p. 367.

mdccii Origen, *commMatt*, fr. 561 (Klostermann).

mdcciii After Psalm 30:6: εἰς χεῖράς σου παραθήσομαι τὸ πνεῦμά μου.

mdcciv Origen, *commMatt*, fr. 562 (Klostermann).

mdccv Origen, *frLuc*, fr. 253; concluded.

mdccvi Cyril of Alexandria, *In Joannem*, v. 3, p. 97. He copied from Origen once again.

mdccvii Cf. Origen, *Cels*, II.76: Καὶ περὶ αὐτοῦ δὲ τοῦ Μωϋσέως νόμου ἡμεῖς μᾶλλον δυνησόμεθα ἀπολογήσασθαι, ἅτε συνετώτερον διδαχθέντες ὑπὸ τοῦ Ἰησοῦ ἀκούειν τῶν νομικῶν γραμμάτων ἤπερ ὁ Ἰουδαῖος. *Op. cit.* VII.20: οὕτω καὶ ὁ Παῦλος, ὅπου μὲν τὸ τοῦ νομικοῦ γράμματος διαβαλεῖν θέλει, φησίν. *selPs*, PG.12.1501.47-48: Διδάσκει δὲ οὐ κατά, φησί, τὸ γράμμα τὸ νομικόν, ἀλλ' ὡς Νέας Διαθήκης κῆρυξ.

mdccviii Cf. *infra*, folio 230r: τῇ τοῦ γράμματος παχύτητι. Origen, *Libri x in Canticum Canticorum (fragmenta)*, p. 98: Ὅρα δέ, ὡς ἐπὶ μὲν τῆς εὐαγγελικῆς πολιτείας ὀσμὴν ἔφη· ἐπὶ τῆς νομικῆς λατρείας αὐτὰ τέθεικε τὰ ἀρώματα, δηλῶν ἐκείνης τὸ ὑπερέχον καὶ πνευματικόν, ταύτης δὲ τὸ παχύ.

mdccix Cyril of Alexandria, *In Joannem*, v. 3, p. 99. He copied sporadically from Origen in exactly the same way Chrysostom did. Origen's passages appear in the text of both authors somehow like a patchwork. This is what happens here, too: Cyril pasted the passage of Origen while treating an entirely different context.

mdccx The expression ἐσθῆτα περισχίσαι is a rare yet characteristic one, which Origen took up from Plutarch, who extolled Cicero's noble character in highly acclamatory terms. Plutarch, *Cicero*, 36.5: λέγεται δὲ μήτε ῥάβδοις αἰκίσασθαί τινα, μήτ' ἐσθῆτα περισχίσαι, μήτε βλασφημίαν ὑπ' ὀργῆς ἢ ζημίαν προσβαλεῖν μεθ' ὕβρεως. In my previous books, I have shown several times that Plutarch was one of the authors from whom Origen received distinctive expressions, the other two authors beings Galen and Alexander of Aphrodisias, and, sometimes, Sextus Empiricus. As a matter of fact, Plutarch and Origen are the only authors who used this expression up until the sixth century, whereas it is hard to find more than a couple of such instances in later authors.

mdccxi This is the concluding part of Origen, *commMatt*, fr. 560 (Klostermann), in which περιρχίζονται is a typo.

mdccxii See *supra*, endnote mdcxv.

mdccxiii Apollinaris, *frMatt*, fr. 144.

mdccxiv H. Crouzel's assertion that Origen seems to be the first to open Paradise up to the saints before the resurrection is an egregious error of fact. Origen's riposte to such allegations was clear: to believe that any 'alteration' (μεταβολή, *commJohn*, II.20.136; X.30.187, that is, translation to another order of being), may take place 'before the consummation of the aeon' (πρὸ *τῆς συντελείας τοῦ αἰῶνος*), is an opinion urged by those who 'have not grasped the meaning of the Scripture and desire things which are impossible' (μήτε τὴν γραφὴν νενοηκέναι καὶ ἀδυνάτων ἐπιθυμεῖν). H. Crouzel, "L'Hadès et la Géhenne selon Origène", *Gregorianum, Commentarii De Re Theologica et Philosophica*, Roma, 59, pp. 291-331, (1978), p. 330. Origen, *commMatt*, 10.13: Τούτων δὲ ἀναγεγραμμένων περὶ τῆς σαγήνης καὶ τῶν ὑπὸ τὴν σαγήνην, ὁ βουλόμενος, πρὸ *τῆς συντελείας τοῦ αἰῶνος* καὶ πρὸ τοῦ ἐξελθόντας τοὺς ἀγγέλους ἀφορίσαι *τοὺς πονηροὺς ἐκ μέσου τῶν δικαίων*, μὴ εἶναι καὶ *πονηροὺς* ὑπὸ τὴν σαγήνην *ἐκ παντὸς γένους* ἔοικε μήτε τὴν γραφὴν νενοηκέναι καὶ ἀδυνάτων ἐπιθυμεῖν. See *PHE*, pp. 230-231.

mdccxv Zachariah, 14:6-7. Origen, *commMatt*, fr. 565 (Klostermann). Cf. *supra*, folio 100r.

mdccxvi Cf. Origen, *Princ*, III.1.14-15 (*Philocalia*, 21.13-14) (comm. on Ezekiel's, 11.19 & 36.26: λιθίνη καρδία).

mdccxvii Cf. Origen, *commJohn*, VI.22.121 (ἄπιστοι λίθοι).

mdccxviii Origen, *commMatt*, fr. 566 (Klostermann).

mdccxix This is the concluding phrase of Apollinaris, *Fragmenta in Joannem*, fr. 148.

mdccxx Jerome, *commMatt*, 28.9.

mdccxxi In an eleventh-century codex of Mount Athos (*Great Laura B 113*) this is attributed to Origen (Klostermann). Cf. John Chrysostom, *In Matthaeum*, PG.58.78436-38: ἐλάμβανον καὶ διὰ τῆς ἀφῆς τεκμήριον καὶ πληροφορίαν τῆς ἀναστάσεως.

mdccxxii Origen, *commMatt*, fr. 568 (Klostermann).

mdccxxiii Apollinaris, *frMatt*, fr. 148.

mdccxxiv Cf. Deut. 10:16; Jer. 4:4; Matt. 19:8; Mark, 10:5; 16:14. This reference to the 'hard-hearted Jews' was employed by Clement of Alexandria, *Paedagogus*, 2.2.32.4: τὴν Ἰουδαίων ἐπονειδίζων σκληροκαρδίαν. Origen took this up and bequeathed it to his successors. Eusebius, *De Ecclesiastica Theologia*, 2.18.7; 2.20.1. Athanasius, *Expositiones in Psalmos*, PG.27.116.52. Pseudo-Athanasius, *Quaestiones ad Antiochum Ducem*, PG.28.700.20. Ephraem Syrus, *De Paenitentia*, p. 41; *Sermo in Pulcherrimum Ioseph*, p. 261. Nilus of Ancyra, *Epistulae*, epistle 1.78. John Chrysostom, *De Virginitate*, 41. Pseudo-John Chrysostom, *Synopsis Scripturae Sacrae*, PG.56.377.29. Theodoret, *In Epistulas Sancti Pauli*, PG.82.113.38. Cyril of Alexandria, *commProphXII*, v. 2, p. 485; *In Joannem*, v. 1, pp. 289; 479; v. 2, p. 158; *Fragmenta in Epistulam ii ad Corinthios*, p. 331; *Epistulae Paschales*, PG.77: 404.39-40; 521.44-45; *Expositio in Psalmos*, PG.69.1077.10-11; *In Isaiam*, PG.70.68.2-3; *commLuc*, PG.72.620.44. Hesychius of Jerusalem, *Commentarius Brevis*, Psalm 46 (prologue). Anonymous, *Dialogus Timothei et Aquilae*, 44.13; *Papisci et Philonis Iudaeorum Cum Monacho Colloquium*, p. 82. Andreas of Caesarea, *Commentarii in Apocalypsin*, 16.48.14 (4-6).

mdccxxv Apollinaris, *frMatt*, fr. 150.

mdccxxvi During Origen's times, Christians were no longer a marginal sect: they were numerous; and yet Origen complained that only a few of them observed the precepts of faith. *homJer*, homily 4.3: Καὶ ἀληθῶς ἐὰν κρίνωμεν τὰ πράγματα ἀληθείᾳ καὶ μὴ ὄχλοις, καὶ κρίνωμεν τὰ πράγματα προαιρέσει καὶ μὴ τῷ βλέπειν πολλοὺς συναγομένους, ὀψόμεθα νῦν ὡς οὐκ ἐσμὲν πιστοί. ἀλλὰ τότε ἦσαν πιστοί, ὅτε τὰ μαρτύρια τὰ γενναῖα ἐγίνοντο, ὅτε ἀπὸ τῶν κοιμητηρίων προπέμψαντες τοὺς μάρτυρας ἠρχόμεθα ἐπὶ τὰς συναγωγάς, καὶ ὅλη ἡ ἐκκλησία μὴ θλιβομένη παρεγίνετο, καὶ οἱ κατηχούμενοι ἐπὶ τοῖς μαρτυρίοις κατηχοῦντο καὶ ἐπὶ τοῖς θανάτοις τῶν ὁμολογούντων τὴν ἀλήθειαν *μέχρι θανάτου, μὴ πτυρόμενοι μηδὲ ταρασσόμενοι ἐπὶ τὸν ζῶντα θεόν*· Τότε οἴδαμεν καὶ σημεῖα ἑωρακότας παράδοξα καὶ τεράστια, τότε ἦσαν πιστοὶ ὀλίγοι μὲν πιστοὶ δὲ ἀληθῶς, *τὴν στενὴν καὶ τεθλιμμένην* ὁδεύοντες *ὁδὸν τὴν ἀπάγουσαν εἰς τὴν ζωήν*· νῦν δὲ ὅτε γεγόναμεν πολλοί, ἐπεὶ οὐ δυνατὸν εἶναι πολλοὺς ἐκλεκτοὺς (οὐ γὰρ ψεύδεται ὁ εἰπὼν Ἰησοῦς, *Πολλοὶ οἱ κλητοί, ὀλίγοι δὲ ἐκλεκτοί*). Ἐκ [γὰρ] τοῦ πλήθους τῶν ἐπαγγελλομένων θεοσέβειαν σφόδρα εἰσὶν ὀλίγοι οἱ καταντῶντες ἐπὶ τὴν ἐκλογὴν τοῦ θεοῦ καὶ τὴν μακαριότητα.

mdccxxvii Origen, *commMatt*, fr. 569 (Klostermann).

mdccxxviii Apollinaris, *frMatt*, fr.149.

mdccxxix See also, Origen, *apud Catena in Matthaeum*, p. 243 (comm. on Matt. 28:17): (Ὠριγένους.) *Προσεκύνησαν*, οὐ προσηύξαντο· *οἱ δὲ* μὴ προσκυνήσαντες καὶ *ἐδίστασαν*, εἴτε δὲ Θωμᾶς ἐστιν, εἴτε Φίλιππος.

mdccxxx Origen, *commMatt*, fr. 570 (Klostermann).

mdccxxxi These are Origen's statements against Sabellius. He used the latter's locution in order to dismiss the ideas involved. Cf. *Synodicon Orthodoxiae*, lines 590-593: ἤδη δὲ καὶ τὰ Σαβελλίου νοσοῦσι καὶ τὴν παλαιὰν ἐκείνου συναίρεσιν καὶ σύγχυσιν καὶ *συναλοιφὴν* ἐπὶ τῶν τριῶν τῆς θεότητος ὑποστάσεων νῦν ἐπὶ τῆς θείας οὐσίας καὶ ἐνεργείας ἀνακαινίζειν τολμῶσι καὶ ὁμοίως δυσσεβῶς αὐτὰς *συναλείφουσι*. Peter III (Patriarch of Antioch, tenth-eleventh century), *Epistulae Quattor*, epistle 3: Πιστεύω τοίνυν τῇ ἁγίᾳ καὶ ὁμοουσίῳ καὶ ἀδιαιρέτῳ καὶ ἀσυγχύτῳ τριάδι, οὐδεμίαν ἐν ταύτῃ συναλοιφὴν εἰδὼς τῶν τριῶν ὑποστάσεων οὐδὲ φυσικὴν δογματίζων διαίρεσιν, ἐν μονάδι φύσεως τριάδα προσώπων τιμῶν καὶ ἐν τοῖς τρισὶν ὑποστάσεσι μίαν θεότητα εἴτ οὖν φύσιν ὁμολογῶν. Theodore Dexius (fourteenth century), *Appelatio Adversus Iohannem Cantacuzenum*, 64: πῶς οὐ ταυτὸ φαίνῃ πεπονθὼς καὶ δεδρακὼς τῷ Λίβυϊ Σαβελλίῳ καὶ ἔτι Ἀρείῳ, ἵνα τοὺς ἄλλους ἐάσωμεν, ὧν ὁ μὲν ἐκ τοῦ *Ἐγὼ καὶ ὁ πατὴρ ἕν ἐσμέν*, μὴ συννενοηκὼς ὅπως εἴρηται, ὅτι διὰ τὴν ἰσοτιμίαν καὶ τὸ ταυτὸν τῆς φύσεως, φωνὰς βεβήλους καὶ καινὰς καὶ βδελυρὰς ἀπεφθέγξατο, τὴν *εἰς ἓν συναλοιφὴν τῶν τριῶν ὑποστάσεων* καὶ τὴν περιθρύλητον υἱοπατορίαν καὶ τὸ μονοπρόσωπον εἶναι τὸ θεῖον.

mdccxxxii Both the phraseology and the ideas that Origen uses became essential part of the later orthodoxy. Socrates Scholasticus wrote about the dissent of Eusebius and of others at Nicaea in respect of the term *homoousios*, of which they thought that *ipso facto* it bespoke corporeality and generation in material terms (one of the terms they used was 'generation κατὰ ρεῦσιν'). All of this rationale stemmed from their conception of *ousia* as suggesting material substance. Socrates Scholasticus, *HE*, 1.8.32: Ἐπεὶ γὰρ ἔφασαν ὁμοούσιον εἶναι ὃ ἔκ τινος ἐστὶν ἢ κατὰ μερισμὸν ἢ κατὰ ρεῦσιν ἢ κατὰ προβολὴν … κατ' οὐδὲν δὲ τούτων ἐστὶν ὁ υἱός. Nicephorus Callistus Xanthopulus slightly paraphrased Socrates' text, but to the names of those who denied to sign up to the resolution of Nicaea (Eusebius of Nicomedia, Theognis of Nicaea, Maris of Chalcedon, Theonas of Marmarike, Secundus of Ptolemais) he added those of Menophantus of Ephesus, Patrophilus of Scythia, and Narcissus of Neronias. *HE*, 8.18. Likewise, Pseudo-Caesarius (Cassian the Sabaite) once again reflected after Origen, *Quaestiones et Responsiones*, 3: Οὐχ ἴσα βροτοῖς κατὰ ρεῦσιν ἢ τομὴν ἢ διάστασιν ὁ υἱὸς καὶ τὸ πνεῦμα ἐκ τοῦ πατρὸς προῆλθον. Symeon of Thessaloniki, *Epistulae*, epistle 2, lines 324-325: Σῶμα γὰρ ὅμοιον γεννᾷ κατὰ ρεῦσίν τε καὶ τομήν, ὡς καὶ τὰ λοιπὰ ζῷα. Anonymous, *Scholia in Maximum Confessorem*, 61.10: Ἀρχὴν ἔσχεν μετὰ τὴν παράβασιν, φησίν, ἡ τῶν ἀνθρώπων φύσις τῆς ἰδίας γενέσεως τὴν καθ' ἡδονὴν ἐκ σπορᾶς σύλληψιν καὶ τὴν κατὰ ρεῦσιν γέννησιν, καὶ τέλος τὸν κατ' ὀδύνην διὰ φθορᾶς θάνατον. Eunomius used Origen's formulation οὐ κατὰ ρεῦσιν in order to argue for a notion which was diametrical to that of Origen's: he urged that the Son is a creature produced from the will of the Father. We know his words (in italics) from Gregory of Nyssa, *Contra Eunomium*, 3.2.28: Καὶ τοῦτο δείκνυσι περιφανῶς δι' ὧν τοῖς εἰρημένοις ἐπαγωνίζεται λέγων *γεγεννῆσθαι παρὰ τοῦ πατρὸς τοῦ υἱοῦ τὴν οὐσίαν, οὐ κατὰ ἔκτασιν προβληθεῖσαν, οὐ κατὰ ῥεῦσιν ἢ διαίρεσιν τῆς τοῦ γεννήσαντος συμφυΐας ἀποσπασθεῖσαν, οὐ κατὰ αὔξησιν τελειωθεῖσαν, οὐ κατὰ ἀλλοίωσιν μορφωθεῖσαν, μόνῃ δὲ τῇ βουλήσει τοῦ γεννήσαντος τὸ εἶναι λαχοῦσαν.*

Origen had given his own reply to this during very early times, when he wrote his commentary on John. *commJohn*, XX.18.157-9: Ἄλλοι δὲ τὸ *Ἐξῆλθον ἀπὸ τοῦ θεοῦ* [John, 8:42] διηγήσαντο ἀντὶ τοῦ 'γεγέννημαι ἀπὸ τοῦ θεοῦ'· οἷς ἀκολουθεῖ ἐκ τῆς οὐσίας φάσκειν τοῦ πατρὸς γεγεννῆσθαι τὸν υἱόν, οἱονεὶ μειουμένου καὶ λείποντος τῇ οὐσίᾳ ᾗ πρότερον εἶχεν τοῦ θεοῦ, ἐπὰν γεννήσῃ τὸν υἱόν, ὡσεὶ νοῆσαι τις τοῦτο καὶ ἐπὶ τῶν ἐγκυμόνων. Ἀκολουθεῖ δὲ αὐτοῖς καὶ σῶμα λέγειν τὸν πατέρα καὶ τὸν υἱὸν καὶ διῃρῆσθαι τὸν πατέρα, ἅπερ ἐστὶν δόγματα ἀνθρώπων μηδ' ὄναρ φύσιν ἀόρατον καὶ ἀσώματον πεφαντασμένων, οὖσαν κυρίως οὐσίαν. Οὗτοι δὲ δῆλον ὅτι ἐν σωματικῷ τόπῳ δώσουσιν τὸν πατέρα, καὶ τὸν υἱὸν τόπον ἐκ τόπου ἀμείψαντα σωματικῶς ἐπιδεδημηκέναι τῷ βίῳ, καὶ οὐχὶ κατάστασιν ἐκ καταστάσεως, ὥσπερ ἡμεῖς ἐξειλήφαμεν. This reply was aimed not only at those who claimed that God is a material body (such as Melito of Sardis, whom Origen rebutted by name for this), but also on those who were taking *ousia* as only meaning *matter*, and consequently interpreted the proposition 'from the essence of the Father' in corporeal terms.

mdccxxxiii Origen, *commMatt*, fr. 572 (Klostermann *apud* five codices).

mdccxxxiv Origen, *schMatt*, PG.17.309.37-53. Migne's nonsensical ἀσταρεῦσιν should be emended to κατὰ ρεῦσιν. The same goes for some erroneous acute accents to grave ones, which I have emended, too. Also, εἰς τὴν θεότητα ...... θεωρεῖν, should have been emended to εἰς τὴν θεότητα [βούλει] θεωρεῖν.

mdccxxxv Cyril of Alexandria, *Commentarii in Joannem*, v. 1, p. 190.

mdccxxxvi Jerome, *commMatt*, 28.19.

mdccxxxvii Origen, *Princ*, I.3.2.

mdccxxxviii Origen, *Princ*, I.3.5.

mdccxxxix Origen, *Princ*, I.3.7.

mdccxl Origen, *Princ*, I.4.2.

mdccxli Theodore of Heraclea, *frMatt*, fr. 133. The claim that this profoundly Nicene statement could have been written by this anti-Nicene leader and personal opponent of Athanasius would be just ridiculous. I should remind that the immediately preceding fragment which is attributed to this Theodore is but Origen's text itself about 'Phlegon, the Greek philosopher' quoted *supra*, folio 227v, and endnote mdclxxv.

mdccxlii Cf. Origen, *frJohn*, fr. 37: *Τὸ πνεῦμα ὅπου θέλει πνεῖ* [John, 3:8]. Σημαίνει δὲ τοῦτο καὶ οὐσίαν εἶναι τὸ πνεῦμα· οὐ γάρ, ὥς τινες οἴονται, ἐνέργειά ἐστι θεοῦ, οὐκ ἔχον κατ' αὐτοὺς ὑπάρξεως ἰδιότητα. ... εἰ δὲ θέλει καὶ ἐνεργεῖ καὶ διαιρεῖ, οὐσία γοῦν ἐστιν ἐνεργητική, ἀλλ' οὐκ ἐνέργεια. *Op. cit.* fr. 123: τὸ δὲ *Ὅπου θέλει πνεῖ* δείκνυσι οὐσίαν εἶναι τὸ πνεῦμα. Τινὲς γὰρ οἴονται ἐνέργειαν εἶναι θεοῦ, μὴ ἔχον ἰδίαν ὑπόστασιν.

mdccxliii Theodore of Heraclea, *frMatt*, fr. 134. J. Reuss cheerfully included this text under Theodore's name while declining to make room for even a slight bit of scepticism as to whether a conspicuous anti-Nicene theologian and personal opponent of Athanasius could have ever written such a profoundly Nicene statement.

mdccxliv John Chrysostom, *In Matthaeum*, PG.58.789.40-49.

mdccxlv *Catena in Matthaeum*, p. 242. Although Chrysostom was attributed lavishly numerous passages (most of which are either not his own or they were copied from Origen), this particular text and its wider context is anonymous. The portion immediately preceding this one (pp. 236-238) is designated 'Unattributed' ('Ἐξ ἀνεπιγράφου), whereas the preceding one (pp. 235-236) is ascribed to 'Cyril and Origen'. Actually though all of these passages are Origen's. In any event, Chrysostom paid his respects to Origen in deed, by standing up to Epiphanius' calumniation.

mdccxlvi Origen, *commMatt*, 12.34; cf. *commJohn*, X.10.43-44: Εἰκὸς δὲ οὐκ ἀλόγως ζητήσειν τινὰς εἰ μετὰ πάσας τὰς ἡμέρας τούτου τοῦ αἰῶνος οὐκέτι ἔσται ὁ εἰπών. *Ἰδοὺ ἐγὼ μεθ' ὑμῶν* μετὰ τῶν χωρησάντων αὐτὸν *ἕως τῆς συντελείας τοῦ αἰῶνος*. Τὸ γὰρ ἕως οἱονεὶ περιγραφήν τινα δηλοῖ χρόνου. Λεκτέον δὲ καὶ πρὸς τοῦτο, ὅτι ... *schLuc*, PG.17.341.25-29: Τὸ δὲ, *ἕως*, ἐνταῦθα δηλοῖ τὸν κατεπείγοντα περὶ τοῦ δηλουμένου χρόνον, οὐ περιοριζόμενον, ὥστε γενέσθαι μετὰ τὸ ἕως τὸ ἐν αὐτῷ τῷ δηλουμένῳ, ὡς τό· *Καὶ ἰδοὺ ἐγὼ μεθ' ὑμῶν εἰμι ἕως τῆς συντελείας τοῦ αἰῶνος*. The same, in *commMatt*, 12.34: παραστήσωμεν κατά τινα συνήθειαν τῆς γραφῆς τὸ ἕως δηλοῦν τὸν κατεπείγοντα περὶ τοῦ δηλουμένου χρόνον, οὐ περιοριζόμενον. See also Origen, part of fr. 22 (Klostermann), on Matt. 1:25: Τὸ *ἕως* ἐν τῇ γραφῇ πολλάκις ἐπὶ διηνεκοῦς εὑρίσκεται. In Cramer, this is attributed to 'Eusebius, Origen, Isidore of Pelusium' (*Catena in Matthaeum*, p. 13): (Εὐσεβίου. 'Ωριγένους. 'Ισιδώρου τοῦ Πηλουσιώτου.) Τὸ *ἕως* ἐν τῇ γραφῇ πολλάκις ἐπὶ διηνεκοῦς εὑρίσκεται (see full quotation *supra*, folio 4r). Yet again, in the same catena, this is preceded by joint attribution to both Chrysostom and Basil of Caesarea. *Op. cit.* pp. 12-13: (Βασιλείου. Τοῦ Χρυσοστόμου.) Τοῦτο ἀκούοντες μὴ ὑποπτεύσωμεν διὰ τὸ *ἕως*, ὅτι μετὰ ταῦτα αὐτὴν ἔγνω. Τὸ γὰρ *ἕως* ἔθος ἐστὶ τῇ γραφῇ πολλάκις τιθέναι δὲ εἰς τὸ διηνεκές. It could have been simpler and more instructive to explain that it was Origen who introduced the idea that critical scriptural usages of 'until' (ἕως) involve the notion of 'perpetuity' (ἐπὶ τοῦ διηνεκοῦς). Origen quoted Psalm 109:1, Isaiah, 46:4, Gen. 8:7, and Matthew 1:25, as examples of this. *Suda* (letter epsilon, entry 1904) reproduced his exegesis explaining the lemma 'until' (ἕως) quoting Origen's words along with his scriptural examples. In any event, those who copied from this commentary of Origen every now and then (John Chrysostom, Cyril of Alexandria, Apollinaris) could not have left this idea out of their attention. Cf. John Chrysostom, *In Matthaeum*, PG.58.594.8-10: *Παρέδωκε* γὰρ *αὐτόν, ἕως οὗ ἀποδῷ τὸ ὀφειλόμενον·* τουτέστι, διηνεκῶς· οὔτε γὰρ ἀποδώσει ποτέ. This is a replica from Origen's commentary (see *supra* folio 148r), which is also Apollinaris, fr. 92 (quoted *supra*, p. 261). Cyril of Alexandria, *frMatt*, fr. 138: τὸ δὲ *ἕως ἄρτι* τοῦτ᾽ ἔστιν ἕως τοῦ διηνεκοῦς. The same, Apollinaris, *frMatt*, fr. 60 (on Matt. 11:12): ἐπακολουθεῖ *ἕως ἄρτι* τὸ κηρυττόμενον, τοῦτ᾽ ἔστιν *ἕως* τοῦ διηνεκοῦς· τὸ γὰρ *ἕως ἄρτι* συμπαραπεμπτέον τῷ παντὶ χρόνῳ. No doubt, this is Origen's too; but commentary on that section of Matthew in not included in the present codex. Cf. Basil of Caesarea echoing Origen's exegesis. *In Sanctam Christi Generationem*, PG.31.1428.29-40: Πρὸς μὲν τό, ὅτι *Οὐκ ἐγίνωσκεν αὐτὴν ἕως οὗ ἔτεκε τὸν υἱὸν αὐτῆς*, ὅτι τὸ ἕως πολλαχοῦ χρόνου μέν τινα δοκεῖ περιορισμὸν ὑποφαίνειν, κατὰ δὲ τὴν ἀλήθειαν τὸ ἀόριστον δείκνυσιν. Ὁποῖόν ἐστι τὸ ὑπὸ τοῦ Κυρίου λεχθὲν τὸ *Καὶ ἰδοὺ ἐγὼ μεθ᾽ ὑμῶν εἰμι πάσας τὰς ἡμέρας ἕως τῆς συντελείας τοῦ αἰῶνος*. Οὐ γὰρ δήπου μετὰ τὸν αἰῶνα τοῦτον οὐκ ἔμελλε συνέσεσθαι τοῖς ἁγίοις ὁ Κύριος. ἀλλ᾽ ἡ ἐπαγγελία τοῦ παρόντος τὸ διηνεκὲς σημαίνει, οὐκ ἔστιν ἀποκοπὴ τοῦ μέλλοντος. Τὸν αὐτὸν δὴ τρόπον φαμὲν κἀνταῦθα παρειλῆφθαι τό, *ἕως*.

mdccxlvii Origen, *schLuc*, PG.17.341.25-29, commenting on the particle *ἕως* (= until, till) as in Matt. 16:28; Mark, 9:1; Luke, 9:27 in apposition with Matt. 20:20.

Bibliography

Achilles Tatius of Alexandria (astronomer, third century AD), ed. E. Vilborg, *Achilles Tatius. Leucippe and Clitophon*, Stockholm, 1955.

Acta Conciliorum Oecumenicorum (ACO), *Canones xv* (*contra Origenem et Origenistas*), eds. E. Schwartz – J. Straub, *Acta conciliorum oecumenicorum*, vol. 4.1, Berlin, 1971, pp. 248-249.

– *Concilium Lateranense a. 649 celebratum*, ed. R. Riedinger, *Acta conciliorum oecumenicorum. Series secunda, volumen primum: Concilium Lateranense anno 649*, Berlin, 1984.

– *Concilium Universale Chalcedonense anno 451*, ed. E. Schwartz, *Acta Conciliorum Oecumenicorum*, Berlin, 1933-1935 (repr. 1962-1965).

– *Concilium Universale Constantinopolitanum Tertium* (*680-681*), ed. R. Riedinger, *Acta Conciliorum Oecumenicorum*, Series secunda, volumen secundum: *Concilium universale Constantinopolitanum tertium*, Pars 1-2, Berlin, 1990, 1992.

– *Concilium Universale Ephesenum anno 431*, ed. E. Schwartz, *Acta Conciliorum Oecumenicorum*, vol. 1.5.1, Berlin, 1924-1925 (repr. 1963).

– *Sententia Synodica Contra Theodorum Mopsuestenum*, ed. E. Schwartz – J. Straub, *Acta conciliorum oecumenicorum*, vol. 4.1, Berlin, 1971, pp. 239-240.

– *Synodus Constantinopolitana et Hierosolymitana anno 536*, ed. E. Schwartz, *Acta Conciliorum Oecumenicorum*, vol. 3, Berlin, 1940 (repr. 1965).

Acta Joannis, ed. M. Bonnet, *Acta apostolorum apocrypha*, vol. 2.1, Leipzig, 1898 (repr. Hildesheim, 1972, pp. 151-215.

Acta Thomae, ed. M. Bonnet, *Acta apostolorum apocrypha*, vol. 2.2, Leipzig, 1903 (repr. Hildesheim, 1972, pp. 99-288.

Additamenta in Etymologicum Gudianum, ed. A. de Stefani, *Etymologicum Gudianum*, Amsterdam, 1965.

Aelius Aristides (rhetor, Mysia, second century AD), *Ῥώμης Ἐγκώμιον*, ed. W. Dindorf, *Aristides*, vol. 1, Leipzig, 1829 (repr. Hildesheim, 1964), pp. 321-370.

Aeschylus, *Fragmenta*, ed. H.J. Mette, *Die Fragmente der Tragödien des Aischylos*, Berlin, 1959.

Aesopus, *Proverbia*, ed. B.E. Perry, *Aesopica*, vol. 1, Urbana, 1952, pp. 265-291.

Aëtius of Amida (medical doctor, sixth century AD), *Iatricorum liber v*, ed. A. Olivieri, *Aëtii Amideni libri medicinales v-viii*, Corpus medicorum Graecorum 8.2, Berlin, 1950.

Aëtius (doxographer, first-second century AD), *De Placitis Reliquiae*, ed. H. Diels, *Doxographi Graeci*, Berlin, 1879 (repr. 1965).

Albinus, *Epitome Doctrinae Platonicae* (*Διδασκαλικός*), ed. P. Louis, *Albinos. Épitomé*, Paris, 1945.

Alexander of Aphrodisias (second-third century AD), *De Anima*, ed. I. Bruns, *Alexandri Aphrodisiensis praeter commentaria scripta minora*, Commentaria in Aristotelem Graeca suppl. 2.1, Berlin, 1887.

– *De Mixtione*, ed. I. Bruns, *Alexandri Aphrodisiensis praeter commentaria scripta minora*, Commentaria in Aristotelem Graeca suppl. 2.2, Berlin, 1892, pp. 213-238.

– *In Aristotelis Analyticorum Priorum Librum i Commentarium*, ed. M. Wallies, *Alexandri in Aristotelis analyticorum priorum librum i commentarium*, Commentaria in Aristotelem Graeca 2.1, Berlin, 1883.

– *In Aristotelis Metaphysica Commentaria*, ed. M. Hayduck, *Alexandri Aphrodisiensis in Aristotelis metaphysica commentaria*, Commentaria in Aristotelem Graeca 1, Berlin, 1891.

– *In Aristotelis Meteorologicorum Libros Commentaria*, ed. M. Hayduck, *Alexandri Aphrodisiensis in Aristotelis meteorologicorum libros commentaria*, Commentaria in Aristotelem Graeca 3.2, Berlin, 1899.

– *In Aristotelis Topicorum Libros Octo Commentaria*, ed. M. Wallies, *Alexandri Aphrodisiensis in Aristotelis topicorum libros octo commentaria*, Commentaria in Aristotelem Graeca 2.2, Berlin, 1891.

– *De Fato*, ed. I. Bruns, *Alexandri Aphrodisiensis praeter commentaria scripta minora*, Commentaria in Aristotelem Graeca, suppl. 2.2, Berlin, 1892, pp. 164-212.

– *In Librum De Sensu Commentarium*, ed. P. Wendland, *Alexandri in librum de sensu commentarium*, Commentaria in Aristotelem Graeca 3.1, Berlin, 1901, pp. 1-173.

Ammonius of Alexandria (*fortasse* fifth-sixth century), *In Aristotelis Librum De Interpretatione Commentarius*, ed. A. Busse, *Ammonius in Aristotelis de interpretatione commentarius*, Commentaria in Aristotelem Graeca 4.5, Berlin, 1897.

– *In Porphyrii Isagogen*, ed. A. Busse, *Ammonius in Porphyrii isagogen sive quinque voces*, Commentaria in Aristotelem Graeca 4.3, Berlin, 1891.

Ammonius of Alexandria (presbyter, *fortasse* fifth-sixth century), *Fragmenta in Joannem*, ed. J. Reuss, *Johannes – Kommentare aus der griechischen Kirche, Texte und Untersuchungen* 89, Berlin, 1966, pp. 196-358.

Amphilochius of Iconium, *Contra Haereticos*, ed. C. Datema, *Amphilochii Iconiensis opera*. Turnhout, 1978, pp. 185-214.

Analecta Hymnica Graeca)

– *Canones Januarii*, eds. A. Proiou – G. Schirò, *Analecta hymnica graeca e codicibus eruta Italiae inferioris*, vol. 5, Rome, 1971.

– *Canones Februarii*, eds. G. Schirò – E. Tomadakis, *Analecta hymnica graeca e codicibus eruta Italiae inferioris*, vol. 6, Rome, 1974.

– *Canones Martii*, eds. G. Schiro, – E. Tomadakis, *Analecta hymnica graeca e codicibus eruta Italiae inferioris*, vol. 7, Rome: Istituto di Studi Bizantini e Neoellenici, Università di Roma, 1971.

– *Canones Aprilis*, eds. C. Nicas – G. Schirò, *Analecta hymnica graeca e codicibus eruta Italiae inferioris*, vol. 8, Rome, 1970.
– *Canones Maii*, eds. C. Nicas – G. Schirò, *Analecta hymnica graeca e codicibus eruta Italiae inferioris*, vol. 9, Rome, 1973.
– *Canones Junii*, eds. A. Acconcia Longo – G. Schirò, *Analecta hymnica graeca e codicibus eruta Italiae inferioris*, vol. 10, Rome, 1972.
– *Canones Augusti*, eds. A. Proiou – G. Schirò, *Analecta hymnica graeca e codicibus eruta Italiae inferioris*, vol. 12, Rome, 1980.
– *Canones Septembris*, eds. A. Debiasi Gonzato – G. Schirò, *Analecta hymnica graeca e codicibus eruta Italiae inferioris*, vol. 1, Rome, 1966.
– *Canones Decembris*, eds. A. Kominis – G. Schirò, *Analecta hymnica graeca e codicibus eruta Italiae inferioris*, vol. 4, Rome, 1976.

Anastasius of Sinai, *In Hexaemeron Anagogicarum Contemplationum Libros Duodecim*, eds. J.D. Baggarly – C.A Kuehn, *Anastasius of Sinai Hexaemeron*, Orientalia Christiana Analecta 278, Rome, 2007.
– *Questiones et Responsiones*, ed. J.A. Munitiz – M. Richard, *Anastasii Sinaitae Questiones et Responsiones*, Corpus Christianorum Series Graeca 59, Turnhout, 2006.
– *Sermo i in Constitutionem Hominis Secundum Imaginem Dei*, eds. K.-H. Uthemann, *Sermones duo in constitutionem hominis secundum imaginem Dei necnon opuscula adversus Monotheletas*, Corpus Christianorum Series Graeca 12, Turnhout, 1985.
– *Sermo ii in Constitutionem Hominis Secundum Imaginem Dei*, ed. K.-H. Uthemann, *Sermones duo in constitutionem hominis secundum imaginem Dei necnon opuscula adversus Monotheletas* Corpus Christianorum Series Graeca 12, Turnhout, 1985.
– *Viae Dux*, ed. K.-H. Uthemann, *Anastasius Sinaïtae viae dux*, Corpus Christianorum Series Graeca 8, Turnhout, 1981.

Anaximenes of Lampsacus (rhetorician, historian, c. 380-320 BC), *Ars Rhetorica* (or, *Rhetorica ad Alexandrum*), ed. M. Fuhrmann, *Anaximenis ars rhetorica*, Leipzig, 1966.

Andreas of Caesarea, *Commentarii in Apocalypsin*, ed. J. Schmidt, *Studien zur Geschichte des griechischen Apokalypse – Textes*, 1. Text (und) Einleitung, Münchener theologische studien 1, Munich, 1955.

Andronicus Callistus (Constantinople, Italy, fifteenth century), *Defensio Theodori Gazae Adversus Michaelem Apostolium*, ed. L. Mohler, *Aus Bessarions Gelehrtenkreis: Abhandlungen, Reden, Briefe von Bessarion, Theodoros Gazes, Michael Apostolios, Andronikos Kallistos, Georgios Trapezuntinos, Niccolò Perotti, Niccolò Capranica* (*Kardinal Bessarion als Theologe, Humanist und Staatsmann. Funde und Forschungen* Band 3, Paderborn, 1942, pp. 171-203.

Andronicus Camaterus, *Sacrum Armamentarium*, ed. A. Bucossi, *Andronici Camateri Sacrum Armamentarium, pars prima*, Corpus Christianorum Series Graeca 75, Turnhout, 2014.

Anna Comnena, *Alexias*, eds. A. Kambylis – D.R. Reinsch, *Annae Comnenae Alexias*, Corpus Fontium Historiae Byzantinae, Series Berolinensis XL/1, Berlin – New York, 2001.

Anonymous (eighth-ninth century AD), *Συναγωγὴ Λέξεων Χρησίμων* (versio antiqua), ed. I.C. Cunningham, *Συναγωγὴ λέξεων χρησίμων*, Sammlung griechischer und lateinischer Grammatiker 10, Berlin – New York, 2003, pp. 73-523.

Anonymous (eighth-ninth century AD), *Συναγωγὴ λέξεων χρησίμων ἐκ διαφόρων σοφῶν τε καὶ ῥητόρων πολλῶν*, versio codicis B, ed. I.C. Cunningham, *Συναγωγὴ λέξεων χρησίμων ἐκ διαφόρων σοφῶν τε καὶ ῥητόρων πολλῶν*, Sammlung griechischer und lateinischer Grammatiker 10, Berlin – New York, 2003, pp. 527-701.

Anonymous, *Dialogus cum Judaeis (cod. Vatoped. 236)*, ed. J.H. Declerck, *Anonymus dialogus cum Iudaeis saeculi ut videtur sexti*, Corpus Christianorum Series Graeca 30, Turnhout, 1994.

Anonymous, *Dissertatio contra Judaeos*, ed. M. Hostens, *Anonymi auctoris Theognosiae dissertatio contra Iudaeos*, Corpus Christianorum Series Graeca 14, Turnhout, 1986.

Anonymous, *Dialogus Timothei et Aquilae*, ed. R.G. Robertson, *The Dialogue of Timothy and Aquila: A Critical Text, Introduction to the Manuscript Evidence, and an Inquiry into the Sources and Literary Relationships*, Cambridge Mass. 1986.

Anonymous, *Epimerismi Homerici*, ed. A.R. Dyck, *Epimerismi Homerici, pars prior epimerismos continens qui ad Iliadis librum A pertinent*, Sammlung griechischer und lateinischer Grammatiker 5.1, Berlin, 1983, pp. 55-256.

Anonymous, *Expositio Artis Rhetoricae*, ed. C. Walz, *Rhetores Graeci* 3, Stuttgart, 1834, pp. 725-748.

Anonymous, *Finis Alter* (cod. Iviron 381), *Epistula ad Theophilum Imperatorem De Imaginibus*, eds. J. Chrysostomides – Ch. Dendrinos – E. Harvalia – Crook – J.A. Munitiz, *The Letter of the Three Patriarchs to Emperor Theophilos and Related Texts*, Camberley, 1997, pp. 89-131.

Anonymous, *In Ethica Nicomachea Commentaria*, ed. G. Heylbut, *Eustratii et Michaelis et anonyma in ethica Nicomachea commentaria*, Commentaria in Aristotelem Graeca 20, Berlin, 1892, pp. 122-255.

Anonymous, *Lexicon de Atticis Nominibus* (*Περὶ Ἀττικῶν Ὀνομάτων*), ed. R. Pintaudi, "Lexicon quod Theaeteti vocatur," *Jahrbuch der Österreichischen Byzantinistik* 25, 1976, pp. 108-116.

Anonymous (medical doctor), *Περὶ Ἀττικῶν Ὀνομάτων*, eds. C. Daremberg – C.É. Ruelle, *Oeuvres de Rufus d'Éphèse*, Paris, 1879 (repr. Amsterdam, 1963), pp. 233-236.

Anonymous, *Papisci et Philonis Iudaeorum Cum Monacho Colloquium* (Ἀντιβολὴ Παπίσκου καὶ Φίλωνος Ἰουδαίων πρὸς μοναχόν τινα), ed. A.C. McGiffert, *Dialogue between a Christian and a Jew*, New York, 1889, pp. 51-83.

Anonymous, *Papyri Magicae* eds. A. Henrichs – K. Preisendanz, *Papyri Graecae magicae. Die griechischen Zauberpapyri*, vols. 1-2, second edition, Stuttgart, vol. 1, 1973; vol. 2, 1974.

Anonymous, *Prolegomena Philosophiae Platonicae*, ed. L.G. Westerink, *Anonymous prolegomena to Platonic philosophy*, Amsterdam, 1962, pp. 3-55.

Anonymous, *Sancti Pachomii Vita Tertia* (Τοῦ ὁσίου πατρὸς ἡμῶν Παχωμίου τοῦ μεγάλου βίος), ed. F. Halkin, *Sancti Pachomii vitae Graecae*, Subsidia hagiographica 19, Brussels, 1932, pp. 272-406.

Anonymous, *Scholia ad Hermogenis Librum Περὶ Στάσεων*, ed. C. Walz, Rhetores Graeci 4, Stuttgart, 1833.

Anonymous, *Scholia in Aristophanem*, Scholia in *Ranas* (scholia vetera) ed. F. Dübner, *Scholia Graeca in Aristophanem*, Paris, 1877 (repr. Hildesheim, 1969), pp. 273-314.

Anonymous, *Scholia in Euclidis Elementa* (*scholia vetera et recentiora*), ed. E.S. Stamatis (post J.L. Heiberg), *Euclidis opera omnia*, vols. 5.1-5.2, second edition, Leipzig, 1977.

Anonymous, *Scholia in Euripidem* (scholia vetera) (comm. on *Oresteia*), ed. E. Schwartz, *Scholia in Euripidem*, 2 vols, Berlin, vol. 1, 1887; vol. 2, 1891 (repr. 1966).

Anonymous, *Scholia in Euripides Andromacham*, ed. W. Dindorf, *Scholia Graeca in Euripidis tragoedias*, 4 vols. Oxford, 1863, vol. 4, pp. 120-209.

Anonymous, *Scholia in Euripidis Orestem*, ed. W. Dindorf, *Scholia Graeca in Euripidis tragoedias*, 4 vols. Oxford, 1863, vol. 2, pp. 3-347; vol. 4, pp. 254-259.

Anonymous, *Scholia in Iliadem* (scholia vetera et recentiora, cod. Genevensi gr. 44), ed. J. Nicole, *Les scolies genevoises de l'Iliade*, vol. 1, Geneva, 1891 (repr. Hildesheim, 1966).

Anonymous, *Scholia in Iliadem* (scholia vetera) (D scholia), ed. C.G. Heyne, *Homeri Ilias*, 2 vols, Oxford, 1834.

Anonymous, *Scholia in Iliadem* (scholia vetera) ed. H. Erbse, *Scholia Graeca in Homeri Iliadem* (scholia vetera) vols. 1-5, 7, Berlin, vol. 1, 1969; vol. 2, 1971; vol. 3, 1974; vol. 4, 1975; vol. 5, 1977; vol. 7, 1988.

Anonymous, *Scholia in Lucianum*, ed. H. Rabe, *Scholia in Lucianum*, Leipzig, 1906 (repr. Stuttgart, 1971).

Anonymous, *Scholia in Maximum Confessorem*, eds. C. Laga – C. Steel, *Maximi confessoris quaestiones ad Thalassium*, 2 vols. Corpus Christianorum Series Graeca 7 & 22, Turnhout, 1980; 1990.

Anonymous, *Scholia in Odysseam*, ed. W. Dindorf, *Scholia Graeca in Homeri Odysseam*, 2 vols. Oxford, 1855 (repr. Amsterdam, 1962).

Anonymous, *Synodicon Vetus* (ninth-tenth century), eds. M. Duffy – J. Parker, *The Synodicon Vetus*, Corpus Fontium Historiae Byzantinae, Series Washingtonensis 15, Washington, D.C. 1979, pp. 149-196.

Anonymous, *Synodicon Vetus* (versio altera) (ninth-tenth century), ed. M. Duffy – J. Parker, *The Synodicon Vetus* Corpus Fontium Historiae Byzantinae, Series Washingtonensis 15, Washington, D.C. 1979.

Anonymous, *Vita Sanctae Syncleticae*, ed. L. Abelarga, *The Life of Saint Syncletica*. Introduction – Critical Text – Commentary, Byzantine Texts and Studies 31, Thessaloniki, 2002, pp. 183-264.

Anonymous, *Vita Sancti Andreae Sali*, ed. L. Rydén, *The Life of St. Andrew the Fool*, vol. II, Studia Byzantina Upsaliensia 4, Uppsala, 1995.

Anonymous, *Vitae S. Alypii Stylitae* (*vita altera*) (sixth century), ed. H. Delehaye, *Les saints stylites*, Brussels, 1923, pp.170-187.

Anonymus (rhetor), *Progymnasmata*, ed. C. Walz, Rhetores Graeci 1. Stuttgart, 1832, pp. 597-648.

Anonymus, *Adversus Haereses* (cod. Coisl. 299, eleventh century), ed. G. Bardy, *Patrologia Orientalis* 15.2, Paris, 1920, pp. 277-284.

Anonymus, *Dialogus Cum Judaeis* (cod. Vatoped. 236), ed. J.H. Declerck, *Anonymus dialogus cum Iudaeis saeculi ut videtur sexti*, Corpus Christianorum Series Graeca 30, Turnhout, 1994.

Anonymous, *Vita Aristotelis*, Vita Marciana, ed. I. Düring, *Aristotle in the ancient biographical tradition*, Göteborg, 1957, pp. 96-106.

Anthologia Lyrica Graeca, ed. E. Diehl, fasc. 1, second edition, Leipzig, 1949, pp. 120-126.

Antiochus of Palestine (or Antiochus of Ancyra, seventh century), *Pandecta Scripturae Sacrae*, PG.80.1857-1866 & 1428-1849.

Antisthenes of Athens, *Fragmenta Varia*, ed. F.D. Caizzi, *Antisthenis fragmenta*, Milan, 1966, pp. 29-59.

Aphthonius, *Progymnasmata*, ed. H. Rabe, *Aphthonii progymnasmata*, Rhetores Graeci 10, Leipzig, 1926.

Apollinaris of Laodicea, *Fragmenta in Joannem*, ed. J. Reuss, *Johannes – Kommentare aus der griechischen Kirche, Texte und Untersuchungen* 89, Berlin, 1966.

– *Fragmenta in Matthaeum*, ed. J. Reuss, Matthäus – Kommentare aus der griechischen Kirche, Texte und Untersuchungen 61, Berlin, 1957.

Apollonius (sophist, first-second century AD), *Lexicon Homericum*, ed. I. Bekker, *Apollonii Sophistae lexicon Homericum*, Berlin, 1833 (repr. Hildesheim, 1967).

Apollonius Dyscolus, *De Pronominibus*, ed. R. Schneider, *Grammatici Graeci*, vol. 2.1, Leipzig, 1878 (repr. Hildesheim, 1965).

Apollonius of Perga, *Conica*, ed. J.L. Heiberg, *Apollonii Pergaei quae Graece exstant*, vols. 1&2, Leipzig, vol. 1: 1891; vol. 2: 1893.

Appendix Proverbiorum, eds. F.G. Schneidewin – E.L. von Leutsch, Corpus paroemiographorum Graecorum 1, Göttingen, 1839 (repr. Hildesheim, 1965), pp. 379-467.

Archimedes of Syracuse (third century BC), *De Planorum Aequilibriis*, ed. C. Mugler, *Archimède*, vol. 2, Paris, 1971, pp. 80-125.

– *De Sphaera et Cylindro*, ed. C. Mugler, *Archimède*, vol. 1, Paris, 1970, pp. 8-131.

Arethas of Caesarea, *Commentarius in Apocalypsin*, PG.106.493-785.

– *Scholia Arethae in Cyrilli Apologiam xii Anathematismorum contra Theodoretum et in Theodoreti Impugnationem*, ed. E. Schwartz, *Acta conciliorum oecumenicorum*, vol. 1.1.6, Berlin, 1928 (repr. 1960).
– *Scripta Minora* (cod. Mosq. Hist. Mus. gr. 315), ed. L.G. Westerink, *Arethae archiepiscopi Caesariensis scripta minora*, vol. 1-2, Leipzig, 1968-1972.
– *Scholia in Porphyrii Isagogen*, ed. M. Share, *Arethas of Caesarea's Scholia on Porphyry's Isagoge and Aristotle's Categories,* Corpus philosophorum Medii Aevi, Commentaria in Aristotelem Byzantina 1, Athens, Paris, Brussels, 1994.
Aristonicus (grammarian *De Signis Iliadis*, ed. L. Friedländer, *Aristonici Περὶ σημείων Ἰλιάδος reliquiae emendatiores*, Göttingen, 1853 (repr. Amsterdam, 1965).
Aristophanes, *Pax*, ed. N.G. Wilson, *Aristophanis Fabulae*, Oxford, 2007, pp. 283-338.
– *Plutus*, ed. N.G. Wilson, *Aristophanis Fabulae*, v. II, Oxford, 2007, pp. 273-326.
– *Ranae*, eds. V. Coulon – M. van Daele, *Aristophane*, vol. 4, Paris, 1928 (repr. 1967), pp. 85-157.
– *Thesmophoriazusae*, eds. V. Coulon – M. van Daele, *Aristophane*, vol. 4, Paris, 1928 (repr. 1967), pp. 17-71.
Aristotle, *Analytica Priora et Posteriora*, ed. W.D. Ross, *Aristotelis analytica priora et posteriora*, Oxford, 1964 (repr. 1968).
– *De Anima*, ed. W.D. Ross, *Aristotle. De Anima*, Oxford, 1961 (repr. 1967).
– *De Caelo*, ed. P. Moraux, *Aristote. Du ciel*, Paris, 1965.
– *De Coloribus*, ed. I. Bekker, *Aristotelis opera*, vol. 2, Berlin, 1831 (repr. Berlin, 1960).
– *De Generatione Animalium*, ed. H.J. Drossaart Lulofs, *Aristotelis de generatione Animalium*, Oxford, 1965 (repr. 1972).
– *De Generatione et Corruptione*, ed. C. Mugler, *Aristote. De la génération et de la corruption*, Paris, 1966.
– *De Insomniis*, ed. W.D. Ross, *Aristotle. Parva naturalia*. Oxford, 1955 (repr. 1970).
– *De Interpretatione*, ed. L. Minio – Paluello, *Aristotelis categoriae et liber de interpretation*, Oxford, 1949 (repr. 1966).
– *Divisiones Aristotelae*, ed. H. Mutschmann, *Divisiones quae vulgo dicuntur Aristoteleae*, Leipzig, 1906.
– *Ethica Eudemia*, ed. F. Susemihl, *Aristotelis ethica Eudemia*, Leipzig, 1884 (repr. Amsterdam, 1967).
– *Ethica Nicomachea*, ed. I. Bywater, *Aristotelis ethica Nicomachea*, Oxford, 1894 (repr. 1962).
– *Fragmenta Varia*, ed. V. Rose, *Aristotelis qui ferebantur librorum fragmenta,* Leipzig, 1886 (repr. Stuttgart, 1967).
– *Historia Animalium*, ed. P. Louis, *Aristote. Histoire des animaux*, vols. 1-3, Paris, 1, 1964; 2, 1968; 3, 1969.

- *Magna Moralia*, ed. F. Susemihl, *Aristotle*, vol. 18 (ed. G.C. Armstrong), Cambridge Mass. 1935 (repr. 1969).
- *Metaphysica*, ed. W.D. Ross, *Aristotle's metaphysics*, 2 vols, Oxford, 1924 (repr. 1970).
- *Meteorologica*, ed. F.H. Fobes, *Aristotelis meteorologicorum libri quattuor*, Cambridge Mass. 1919 (repr. 1967).
- *Physica*, ed. W.D. Ross, *Aristotelis physica*, Oxford, 1950 (repr. 1966).
- *Physiognomonica*, ed. I. Bekker, *Aristotelis opera*, vol. 2, Berlin, 1831 (repr. 1960).
- *Politica*, ed. W.D. Ross, *Aristotelis politica*, Oxford, 1957 (repr. 1964).
- *Problemata*, ed. I. Bekker, *Aristotelis opera*, vol. 2, Berlin, 1831 (repr. 1960).
- *Protrepticus*, ed. I. Düring, *Aristotle's protrepticus*, Stockholm, 1961.
- *Sophisticos Elenchos*, ed. W.D. Ross, *Aristotelis topica et sophistici elenchi*, Oxford, 1958 (repr. 1970).
- *Topica*, ed. W.D. Ross, *Aristotelis topica et sophistici elenchi*, Oxford, 1958 (repr. 1970).

Arius Didymus, *Liber De Philosophorum Sectis* (epitome from Stobaeus), ed. F.W.A. Mullach, *Fragmenta philosophorum Graecorum*, vol. 2), Paris, 1867, pp. 53-101.

Arsenius (or Aristobulus Apostolius, Bishop of Monembasia, paroemiographer, fifteen-sixteenth century), *Apophthegmata*, ed. E.L. von Leutsch, Corpus paroemiographorum Graecorum 2, Göttingen, 1851 (repr. Hildesheim, 1958), pp. 240-744.

Artemidorus, *Onirocriticon*, ed. R.A. Pack, *Artemidori Daldiani onirocriticon libri v*, Leipzig, 1963.

Asclepius of Tralles, *Commentaria in Nicomachi Introductionem Arithmeticam*, ed. L. Tarán, *Asclepius of Tralles. Commentary to Nicomachus' introduction to arithmetic*, Transactions of the American Philosophical Society n.s. 59.4, Philadelphia, 1969, pp. 24-72.
- *In Aristotelis Metaphysicorum Libros Commentaria*, ed. M. Hayduck, *Asclepii in Aristotelis metaphysicorum libros A-Z commentaria*, Commentaria in Aristotelem Graeca 6.2, Berlin, 1888.

Asterius of Amasea, *Homiliae*, ed. C. Datema, *Asterius of Amasea. Homilies i-xiv*, Leiden, 1970.

Asterius of Antioch, *Commentarii in Psalmos*, ed. M. Richard, *Asterii sophistae commentariorum in Psalmos quae supersunt*, Symbolae Osloenses, fasc. suppl. 16, Oslo, 1956.

Athanasius of Alexandria, *Apologia contra Arianos sive Apologia Secunda*, ed. H.G. Opitz, *Athanasius Werke*, vol. 2.1, Berlin, 1940, pp. 87-168.
- *Contra Gentes*, ed. R.W. Thomson, *Athanasius. Contra gentes and de incarnatione*, Oxford, 1971.
- *De Decretis Nicaenae Synodi*, ed. H.G. Opitz, *Athanasius Werke*, vol. 2.1, Berlin, 1940, pp. 1-45.
- *De Incarnatione Verbi*, ed. C. Kannengiesser, *Sur l'incarnation du verbe*, Sources chrétiennes 199, Paris, 1973, pp. 258-468.

– *De Sententia Dionysii*, ed. H.G. Opitz, *Athanasius Werke*, vol. 2.1, Berlin, 1940, pp. 46-67.
– *De Synodis Arimini in Italia et Seleuciae in Isauria*, ed. H.G. Opitz, Athanasius Werke, vol. 2.1, Berlin, 1940, pp. 231-278.
– *Epistula ad Afros Episcopos*, PG.26.1029-1048.
– *Epistula ad Episcopos Aegypti et Libyae*, eds. D.U. Hansen – K. Metzler, – K. Savvidis, *Athanasius Werke, Band I. Die dogmatischen Schriften*, Erster Teil, Berlin – New York, 1996, pp. 39-64.
– *Epistula ad Jovianum et Epistula Joviani ad Athanasium*, eds. H.C. Brennecke – A. von Stockhausen, *Athanasius Werke, Zweiter Band. Die "Apologien", 8. Lieferung*, Berlin – New York, 2006, pp. 352-357.
– *Epistula ad Maximum*, PG.26.1085-1089.
– *Epistula ad Monachos*, PG.26.1185-1188.
– *Epistulae Quattuor ad Serapionem*, PG.26.529-648 & K. Savvidis, *Athanasius Werke, Band I. Die dogmatischen Schriften, Erster Teil, 4. Lieferung*, Berlin, New York, 2010, pp. 449-600.
– *Expositiones in Psalmos*, PG.27.60-545 & 548-589.
– *In illud: Omnia Mihi Tradita Sunt*, PG.25.208-220.
– *In illud: Qui Dixerit Verbum in Filium*, PG.26.648-676.
– *Oratio i Contra Arianos*, eds. K. Metzler – K. Savvidis, *Athanasius Werke, Band I. Die dogmatischen Schriften*, Erster Teil, 2, Lieferung, Berlin – New York, 1998, pp. 109-175.
– *Oratio ii Contra Arianos*, eds. K. Metzler – K. Savvidis, *Athanasius Werke, Band I. Die dogmatischen Schriften*, Erster Teil, 2, Lieferung, Berlin – New York, 1998, pp. 177-260.
– *Oratio iii Contra Arianos*, eds. K. Metzler – K. Savvidis, *Athanasius Werke, Band I. Die dogmatischen Schriften,* Erster Teil, 3, Lieferung, Berlin – New York, 2000, pp. 305-81.
– *Orationes Tres Contra Arianos*, PG.26.PG.26.12-468.
– *Qui Dixerit Verbum In Filium*, PG.26.648-676.
– *Scholia in Job* (cod. Vat. Pii II), PG.27.1344-1348.
– *Vita Antonii*, ed. G.J.M. Bartelink, *Athanase d'Alexandrie, Vie d'Antoine*, Sources chrétiennes 400, Paris, 2004, pp. 124-376.

Athenaeus of Naucratis (sophist, second-third century AD), *Deipnosophistae*, ed. G. Kaibel, *Athenaei Naucratitae deipnosophistarum libri xv*, 3 vols, Leipzig, vols. 1-2, 1887; vol. 3, 1890 (repr. Stuttgart, vols. 1-2, 1965; vol. 3, 1966).
– *Deipnosophistae (epitome)*, ed. S.P. Peppink, *Athenaei dipnosophistarum epitome*, vols. 2.1-2.2, Leiden, vol. 2.1, 1937; vol. 2.2, 1939.

Athenagoras of Athens (apologist, second century), *Legatio*, ed. W.R. Schoedel, Athenagoras, *Legatio and De resurrectione*, Oxford, 1972.
– *De Resurrectione*, ed. W.R. Schoedel, *Athenagoras. Legatio and De resurrectione*, Oxford, 1972, pp. 88-148.

Bammel, C.P. "A New Witness to the Scholia from Origen in the Codex von der Goltz", in *Origeniana Rufiana*, Vetus Latina 29, Freiburg, 1996, pp. 137-138.

– "Die Pauluskommentare des Hieronymus: Die ersten wissenchaftlichen lateinnischen Bibelkommentare?", in *Christianesimo Latino e cultura Greca sino al sec. IV*, Studia Ephemeridis 'Augustinianum', 42, Rome, 1993, pp. 187-207.

Bardy, Gustave, "Saint Jérôme et ses maîtres hébreux", *Revue Bénedictine*, 46, 1934, pp. 145-164.

Barlaam of Calabria (monk, mathematician, theologian, Calabria, Constantinople, thirteenth-fourteenth century), *Λογιστική*, ed. P. Carelos, *Barlaam von Seminara, Logistiké*, Corpus philosophorum Medii Aevi, Philosophi Byzantini 8, Athens, 1996.

Barsanuphius and John (sixth century), *Quaestiones et Responsiones ad Coenobitas* (*Epistulae 224-616*), ed. F. Neyt – P. de Angelis – Noah, *Correspondance*, v. II, Aux cénobites: v. I, Lettres 224-398; v. II, Lettres 399-616, Sources chrétiennes 450, 451, Paris, 2000.

– *Quaestiones et Responsiones*, eds. F. Neyt – P. de Angelis – Noah, *Barsanuphe et Jean de Gaza, Correspondance, tome I-II,* Sources chrétiennes 426, 427, Paris, 1997-98.

Basil of Caesarea *Adversus Eos Qui per Calumniam Dicunt Dici a Nobis Tres Deos*, PG.31.1488-1496.

– *Adversus Eunomium*, PG.29: 497-669, 672-768.

– *Asceticon Magnum*, PG.31.901-1052.

– *Contra Sabellianos et Arium et Anomoeos*, PG.31.600-617.

– *De Baptismo*, PG.31.1513-1628.

– *De Jejunio*, PG.31.164-184.

– *De Legendis Gentilium Libris*, ed. by F. Boulenger, *Saint Basile. Aux jeunes gens sur la manière de tirer profit des lettres Helléniques*, Paris, 1935 (repr. 1965), pp. 41-61.

– *De Spiritu Sancto*, ed. B. Pruche, *Basile de Césarée. Sur le Saint – Esprit*, second edition, Sources chrétiennes 17, Paris, 1968, pp. 250-530.

– *Epistulae*, ed. Y. Courtonne, *Saint Basile. Lettres*, 3 vols, Paris, v. 1, 1957; v. 2, 1961; v. 3, 1966.

– *Homilia Adversus Eos Qui Irascuntur*, PG.31.353-372.

– *Homilia Dicta in Lacisis*, PG.31.1437-1457.

– *Homilia Exhortatoria Ad Sanctum Baptisma*, PG.31.424-444.

– *Homilia in martyrem Julittam*, PG.31.237-261.

– *Homilia in Principium Proverbiorum*, PG.31.385-424.

– *Homiliae in Hexaemeron*, ed. S. Giet, *Basile de Césarée. Homélies sur l'hexaéméron*, second edition, Sources chrétiennes 26, Paris, 1968, pp. 86-522.

– *Homiliae Super Psalmos*, PG.29.209-494.

– *In Ebriosos*, PG.31.444-464.

– *In illud: In Principio Erat Verbum*, PG.31.472-481.

– *In Quadraginta Martyres Sebastenses*, PG.31.508-525.

– *In Sanctam Christi Generationem*, PG.31. 1457-1476.

– *Quod Deus Non Est Auctor Malorum*, PG.31.329-53.

– *Regulae Morales*, PG.31.692-869.

– *Sermones De Moribus*, PG.32.1116-1381.

Basil of Seleucia, *Homilia in Pentecosten*, PG.52. 809-812.

– *Sermones*, PG.85.28-474.

Bessarion, Basil (Constantinople, Trapezus, Italy, cardinal, fifteenth century), *Ad Alexium Lascarem Philanthropenum De Processione Spiritus Sancti*, ed. M. Candal, *Ad Alexium Lascarem Philanthropenum De processione spiritus sancti*, Concilium Florentinum Documenta et Scriptores, Series B 7.2, Rome, 1961.

– *In Verbum Evangelii: Sic Eum Volo Manere, Quid Ad Te?*, ed. L. Mohler, *Aus Bessarions Gelehrtenkreis: Abhandlungen, Reden, Briefe von Bessarion, Theodoros Gazes, Michael Apostolios, Andronikos Kallistos, Georgios Trapezuntinos, Niccolò Perotti, Niccolò Capranica* (*Kardinal Bessarion als Theologe, Humanist und Staatsmann*, Funde und Forschungen Band 3, Paderborn, 1942, pp. 71-87.

– *De Sacramento Eucharistiae*, ed. L. Mohler, *Aus Bessarions Gelehrtenkreis: Abhandlungen, Reden, Briefe von Bessarion, Theodoros Gazes, Michael Apostolios, Andronikos Kallistos, Georgios Trapezuntinos, Niccolò Perotti, Niccolò Capranica* (Kardinal Bessarion als Theologe, Humanist und Staatsmann. Funde und Forschungen Band 3, Paderborn, 1942 (repr. Aalen, 1967).

– *In Calumniatorem Platonis*, ed. L. Mohler, *Bessarionis in calumniatorem Platonis libri IV* (Kardinal Bessarion als Theologe, Humanist und Staatsmann), Funde und Forschungen Band 2, Paderborn, 1927 (repr. Aalen, 1967).

Bethune – Baker, J.F., *The Meaning of Homoousios in the 'Constantinopolitan' Creed*, Cambridge, 1901.

Bigg, Charles, *The Christian Platonists of Alexandria*, Oxford, 1886.

Birdsall, J.N. "The Text and Scholia of the Codex von der Goltz and its Allies, and their bearing upon the Texts of the Words of Origen, especially the Commentary on Romans", in *Origeniana: Premier colloque international des études origeniennes*, Montserrat, 18-21 Septembre 1973, in H. Crouzel – G. Lomiento – J. Rius – Camps (eds), *Quaderni di Vetera Christianorum*, 12, Bari, 1975, pp. 215-222.

Blanc, C. *Origène, Commentaire sur saint Jean*, 5 vols. Sources chrétiennes 120, 157, 222, 290, 385, Paris, vol. 1: 1966; vol. 2: 1970; vol. 3: 1975; vol. 4: 1982; vol. 5: 1992.

Boylan, P. Thot, *The Hermes of Egypt*, London 1922.

Callistus I of Constantinople (Patriarch, died 1363), *Capitula De Puritate Animae*, ed. A. Rigo, "Callisto I patriarca, I 100 (109) Capitoli sulla purezza dell'anima," *Byzantion* 80, 2010, pp. 344-406.

Campenhausen, Hans von, *The Fathers of the Church*, Peabody, MA, 1999.

Carolidis, P., *Anubis, Hermes, Michael. Ein Beitrag zur Geschichte des religiös – philosophischen Synkretismus im grieschischen Orient*, Strasburg, 1913.

Cassian the Sabaite (c. 470-July 20, 548, abbot of the Laura of Sabas, Palestine), *Πρὸς Κάστορα ἐπίσκοπον περὶ διατυπώσεως καὶ κανόνων τῶν κατὰ τὴν Ἀνατολὴν καὶ Αἴγυπτον κοινοβίων*, ed. Panayiotis Tzamalikos, *A Newly Discovered Greek Father*, Leiden, 2012, pp. 19-75.

– *Περὶ τῶν η' λογισμῶν*, ed. Panayiotis Tzamalikos, *A Newly Discovered Greek Father*, Leiden, 2012, pp. 77-165.

– *Πρὸς Λεόντιον ἡγούμενον περὶ τῶν κατὰ τὴν Σκῆτιν ἁγίων πατέρων*, ed. Panayiotis Tzamalikos, *A Newly Discovered Greek Father*, Leiden, 2012, pp. 167-246.

– *Συνεισφορὰ τοῦ ἀββᾶ Σερήνου πρώτη*, ed. Panayiotis Tzamalikos, *A Newly Discovered Greek Father*, Leiden, 2012, pp. 247-309.

– *Συνεισφορὰ τοῦ ἀββᾶ Σερήνου Περὶ τῆς Παναρέτου*, ed. Panayiotis Tzamalikos, *A Newly Discovered Greek Father*, Leiden, 2012, pp. 311-372.

– *Scholia in Apocalypsin*, ed. Panayiotis Tzamalikos, *An Ancient Commentary on the Book of Revelation – A Critical edition of the Scholia in Apocalypsin*, Cambridge – New York, 2013.

Cassius Dio, *Historiae Romanae*, ed. U.P. Boissevain, *Cassii Dionis Cocceiani historiarum Romanarum quae supersunt*, 3 vols, Berlin, vol. 1: 1895; vol. 2: 1898; vol. 3: 1901 (repr. 1955).

Catena in Acta (catena Andreae), ed. J.A. Cramer, *Catenae Graecorum Patrum in Novum Testamentum*, vol. 3, Oxford, 1838 (repr. Hildesheim, 1967).

Catena in Epistulam ad Ephesios, ed. J.A. Cramer, *Catenae Graecorum Patrum in Novum Testamentum*, vol. 6. Oxford, 1842 (repr. Hildesheim, 1967), pp. 96-225.

Catena in Epistulam ad Hebraeos (catena Nicetae), ed. J.A. Cramer, *Catenae Graecorum Patrum in Novum Testamentum*, vol. 7, Oxford, 1843 (repr. Hildesheim, 1967), pp. 279-598.

Catena in Epistulam ad Romanos (typus Monacensis), ed. J.A. Cramer, *Catenae Graecorum Patrum in Novum Testamentum*, vol. 4, Oxford, 1844 (repr. Hildesheim, 1967), pp. 163-529.

Catena in Epistulam ad Romanos (typus Vaticanus), ed. J.A. Cramer, *Catenae Graecorum Patrum in Novum Testamentum*, vol. 4, Oxford, 1844 (repr. Hildesheim, 1967).

Catena in Epistulam i ad Corinthios (typus Vaticanus), ed. J.A. Cramer, *Catenae Graecorum Patrum in Novum Testamentum*, vol. 5, Oxford, 1841 (repr. Hildesheim, 1967).

Catena in Epistulam Jacobi, ed. J.A. Cramer, *Catenae Graecorum Patrum in Novum Testamentum*, vol. 8, Oxford, 1840 (repr. Hildesheim, 1967), pp. 1-40.

Catena in Epistulam Joannis i (catena Andreae), ed. J.A. Cramer, *Catenae Graecorum Patrum in Novum Testamentum*, vol. 8, Oxford, 1840 (repr. Hildesheim, 1967), pp. 105-145.

Catena in Joannem (catena integra), ed. J.A. Cramer, *Catenae Graecorum Patrum in Novum Testamentum*, vol. 2, Oxford, 1841 (repr. Hildesheim, 1967), pp. 177-413.

Catena in Joannem, ed. J.A. Cramer, *Catenae Graecorum Patrum in Novum Testamentum*, vol. 2. Oxford, 1841 (repr. Hildesheim, 1967), pp. 177-413.

Catena in Lucam, ed. J.A. Cramer, *Catenae Graecorum Patrum in Novum Testamentum*, vol. 2. Oxford, 1841 (repr. Hildesheim, 1967).

Catena in Marcum (*recensio ii*), ed. J.A. Cramer, *Catenae Graecorum Patrum in Novum Testamentum*, vol. 1, Oxford, 1840 (repr. Hildesheim, 1967), pp. 261-447.

Catena in Matthaeum (catena integra), ed. J.A. Cramer, *Catenae Graecorum Patrum in Novum Testamentum*, vol. 1, Oxford, 1840 (repr. Hildesheim, 1967).

Catena Palestinensis (Old Testament), ed. M. Harl, *La chaîne Palestinienne sur le Psaume 118 (Origène, Eusèbe, Didyme, Apollinaire, Athanase, Théodoret)*, Sources chrétiennes 189, Paris, 1972, pp. 182-472.

Catenae graecae in Genesim et Exodum, II. Collectio Coisliana in Genesim, ed. Françoise Petit, Corpus Christianorum Series Graeca, 15, Turnhout, 1986.

Catenae Graecorum Patrum in Novum Testamentum, ed. J.A. Cramer, v. 1, Oxford, 1840 (repr. Hildesheim, 1967).

Chronicon Paschale, ed. L. Dindorf, *Chronicon paschale*, vol. 1, Corpus scriptorum historiae Byzantinae, Bonn, 1832.

Chrysippus of Jerusalem (presbyter, fifth century), *Encomium in Joannem Baptistam*, ed. A. Sigalas, *Des Chrysippos von Jerusalem Enkomion auf den hl. Johannes den Täufer*, Texte und Forschungen zur Byzantinisch – Neugriechischen Philologie 20, Athens, 1937, pp. 29-48.

Clement of Alexandria, *Eclogae Propheticae*, eds. L. Früchtel – O. Stählin – U. Treu, *Clemens Alexandrinus*, vol. 3, second edition, GCS 17, Berlin, 1970, pp. 137-155.

– *Excerpta ex Theodoto*, ed. F. Sagnard, *Clément d'Alexandrie. Extraits de Théodote*, second edition, Sources chrétiennes 23, Paris, 1948 (repr. 1970), pp. 52-212.

– *Fragmenta*, eds. L. Früchtel – O. Stählin – U. Treu, *Clemens Alexandrinus*, vol. 3, second edition, GCS 17, Berlin, 1970, pp. 195-202, 212, 216-30.

– *Paedagogus*, eds. M. Harl – I. Marrou – C. Matray – C. Mondésert, *Clément d'Alexandrie. Le pédagogue*, 3 vols. Sources chrétiennes 70, 108, 158, Paris, vol. 1: 1960; vol. 2: 1965; vol. 3: 1970.

– *Protrepticus*, ed. C. Mondésert, *Clément d'Alexandrie. Le protreptique*, second edition, Sources chrétiennes 2, Paris, 1949, pp. 52-193.

– *Stromateis*, eds. L. Früchtel – O. Stählin – U. Treu, *Clemens Alexandrinus*, vol. 2, third edition, v. 3, second edition, GCS 52, Berlin, vol. 2: 1960; vol. 3: 1970.

Cleomedes, *Caelestia*, ed. R. Todd, *Cleomedis Caelestia* (*Μετέωρα*), Bibliotheca scriptorum Graecorum et Romanorum Teubneriana, Leipzig, 1990.

Constantine Manasses, *Monodia in Nicephorum Comnenum*, ed. E. Kurtz, "Εὐσταθίου Θεσσαλονίκης καὶ Κωνσταντίνου Μανασσῆ μονῳδίαι περὶ τοῦ θανάτου Νικηφόρρου Κομνηνοῦ", *Vizantijskij Vremennik* 17, 1910, pp. 302-322.

Constantine Porphyrogenitus, *De Legationibus*, ed. C. de Boor, *Excerpta historica iussu imp. Constantini Porphyrogeniti confecta*, vol. 1: *excerpta de legationibus*, parts 1-2, Berlin, 1903.

– *De Thematibus*, ed. A. Pertusi, *Costantino Porfirogenito. De thematibus*, Studi e Testi 160, Vatican City, 1952, pp. 59-100.

– *De Virtutibus et Vitiis*, eds. T. Büttner – Wobst & A.G. Roos, *Excerpta historica iussu imp. Constantini Porphyrogeniti confecta*, vol. 2: *Excerpta de virtutibus et vitiis*, parts 1 and 2, Berlin, vol. 2.1: 1906; vol. 2.2: 1910.

Constitutiones Apostolorum, ed. B.M. Metzger, *Les constitutions apostoliques*, 3 vols. Sources chrétiennes 320, 329, 336, Paris, vol. 1: 1985; vol. 2: 1986; vol. 3: 1987.

Cornutus, Lucius Annaeus (Stoic philosopher, Rome, first century AD), *De Natura Deorum*, ed. C. Lang, *Cornuti theologiae Graecae compendium*, Leipzig, 1881.

Corpus Hermeticum, *'Eκ τοῦ ὕμνου πρὸς τὸν παντοκράτορα*, eds. A.-J. Festugière – A.D. Nock, *Corpus Hermeticum*, vol. 4, Paris, 1954 (repr. 1972), p. 147.

– *Περὶ Νοῦ κοινοῦ πρὸς Τάτ*, eds. A.-J. Festugière – A.D. Nock, *Corpus Hermeticum*, vol. 1, Paris, 1946 (repr. 1972), pp. 174-183.

– *Poimandres*, eds. A.-J. Festugière – A.D. Nock, *Corpus Hermeticum*, vol. 1, Paris, 1946 (repr. 1972), pp. 7-19.

Cosmas Indicopleustes, *Topographia Christiana*, ed. W. Wolska – Conus, *Cosmas Indicopleustès. Topographie chrétienne*, 3 vols. Sources chrétiennes 141, 159, 197, Paris, vol. 1: 1968; vol. 2: 1970; vol. 3: 1973.

Crates of Thebes, *Fragmenta*, in E. Diehl (ed.), *Anthologia Lyrica Graeca*, fasc. 1, second edition, Leipzig, 1949, pp. 120-126.

Crouzel, H. "L'Hadès et la Géhenne selon Origène", *Gregorianum, Commentarii De Re Theologica et Philosophica*, 59, Roma, 1978, pp. 291-331.

Cyril of Alexandria, *Ad Calosyrium* (*epist. 83*), ed. E. Pusey, *Sancti patris nostri Cyrilli archiepiscopi Alexandrini in D. Joannis evangelium*, vol. 3, Oxford, 1872, pp. 603-607.

– *Ad Optimum Episcopum*, PG.77.365-372.

– *Commentarii in Joannem* (*additamenta*), ed. J. Reuss, *Johannes – Kommentare aus der griechischen Kirche, Texte und Untersuchungen* 89, Berlin, 1966, pp. 188-195.

– *Commentarii in Joannem*, ed. E. Pusey, *Sancti patris nostri Cyrilli archiepiscopi Alexandrini in D. Joannis evangelium*, 3 vols, Oxford, 1872, vol. 1: 1-728; vol. 2: 1-737; vol. 3: 1-171.

– *Commentarii in Joannem*, ed. P.E. Pusey, *Sancti patris nostri Cyrilli archiepiscopi Alexandrini in D. Joannis evangelium*, 3 vols, Oxford, 1872.

– *Commentarii in Lucam*, ed. J. Sickenberger, *Fragmente der Homilien des Cyrill von Alexandrien zum Lukasevangelium*, Texte und Untersuchungen 34, Leipzig, 1909, pp. 76-107.

– *Commentarii in Lucam*, PG.72.476-949.

- *Commentarii in Matthaeum* (in catenis), ed. J. Reuss, *Matthäus – Kommentare aus der griechischen Kirche*, Texte und Untersuchungen 61, Berlin, 1957, pp. 153-269.
- *Commentarius in Isaiam Prophetam*, PG.70.9-1449.
- *Commentarius in xii Prophetas Minores*, ed. P.E. Pusey, *Sancti patris nostri Cyrilli archiepiscopi Alexandrini in xii prophetas*, 2 vols, Oxford, 1868.
- *Contra Julianum*, eds. P. Burguière – P. Évieux, *Cyrille d'Alexandrie. Contre Julien*, v. 1, livres 1 et 2, Sources chrétiennes 322, Paris, 1985.
- *De Adoratione et Cultu in Spiritu et Veritate*, PG.68.132-1125.
- *De Exitu Animi*, PG.77.1072-1089.
- *De Incarnatione Unigeniti*, ed. G.M. de Durand, *Cyrille d'Alexandrie. Deux dialogues christologiques*, Sources chrétiennes 97, Paris, 1964, pp. 188-300.
- *De Sancta Trinitate Dialogi*, ed. G.M. de Durand, *Cyrille d'Alexandrie. Dialogues sur la Trinité*, 3 vols. Sources chrétiennes 231, 237, 246, Paris, vol. 1: 1976; vol. 2: 1977; vol. 3: 1978.
- *Encomium in Sanctam Mariam Deiparam*, PG.77.1029-1040.
- *Epistulae Paschales*, PG.77.401-981.
- *Expositio in Psalmos*, PG.69.717-1273.
- *Fragmenta in Acta Apostolorum et in Epistulas Catholicas*, PG.74.1008-1024.
- *Fragmenta in Canticum Canticorum*, PG.69.1277-1293.
- *Fragmenta in sancti Pauli epistulam ad Hebraeos*, ed. P.E. Pusey, *Sancti patris nostri Cyrilli archiepiscopi Alexandrini in D. Joannis evangelium*, vol. 3, Oxford, 1872, pp. 362-423.
- *Fragmenta in sancti Pauli epistulam ad Romanos*, ed. P.E. Pusey, *Sancti patris nostri Cyrilli archiepiscopi Alexandrini in D. Joannis evangelium*, vol. 3, Oxford, 1872, pp. 173-248.
- *Fragmenta in sancti Pauli Epistulam i ad Corinthios*, ed. P.E. Pusey, *Sancti patris nostri Cyrilli archiepiscopi Alexandrini in D. Joannis evangelium*, vol. 3, Oxford, 1872, pp. 249-318.
- *Fragmenta in sancti Pauli Epistulam ii ad Corinthios*, ed. P.E. Pusey, *Sancti patris nostri Cyrilli archiepiscopi Alexandrini in D. Joannis evangelium*, vol. 3. Oxford, 1872, pp. 249-318.
- *Glaphyra in Pentateuchum*, PG.69.9-677.
- *Homiliarum Incertarum Fragmenta*, ed. P.E. Pusey, *Sancti patris nostri Cyrilli archiepiscopi Alexandrini in D. Joannis evangelium*, vol. 3, Oxford, 1872, pp. 461-468, 470-475.
- *Quod Unus Sit Christus*, ed. G.-M. de Durand, *Cyrille d'Alexandrie. Deux dialogues christologiques*, Sources chrétiennes 97, Paris, 1964, pp. 302-514.
- *Responsiones ad Tiberium Diaconum Sociosque Suos*, ed. P.E. Pusey, *Sancti patris nostri Cyrilli archiepiscopi Alexandrini in D. Joannis evangelium*, vol. 3, Oxford, 1872 (repr. Brussels, 1965), pp. 577-602.

– *Thesaurus de Sancta Consubstantiali Trinitate*, PG.75.9-656.

Cyril of Jerusalem, *Catecheses ad Illuminandos*, eds. W.C. Reischl – J. Rupp, *Cyrilli Hierosolymorum archiepiscopi opera quae supersunt omnia*, 2 vols, Munich, vol. 1: 1848; vol. 2: 1860 (repr. Hildesheim, 1967).

– *Homilia in Paralyticum Juxta Piscinam Jacentem*, eds. W.C. Reischl – J. Rupp, *Cyrilli Hierosolymorum archiepiscopi opera quae supersunt omnia*, vol. 2. Munich, 1860 (repr. Hildesheim, 1967), pp. 405-426.

Cyril of Scythopolis, *Vita Euthymii*, ed. E. Schwartz, *Kyrillos von Skythopolis, Texte und Untersuchungen* 49.2, Leipzig, 1939, pp. 3-85.

– *Vita Sabae*, ed. E. Schwartz, *Kyrillos von Skythopolis, Texte und Untersuchungen* 49.2, Leipzig, 1939, pp. 385-200.

– *Vita Theodosii*, ed. E. Schwartz, *Kyrillos von Skythopolis, Texte und Untersuchungen* 49.2, Leipzig, 1939, pp. 235-241.

Damascenus Studites (monk, bishop, Constantinople, Thessaloniki, Naupactus, sixteenth century), *Thesaurus*, ed. E. Deledemou, *Θησαυρὸς Δαμασκηνοῦ τοῦ ὑποδιακόνου καὶ Στουδίτου*, New York, 1943.

Damascius, *De Principiis*, ed. C.É. Ruelle, *Damascii successoris dubitationes et solutiones*, vols. 1 & 2, Paris, vol. 1: 1889; (repr. Brussels, 1964).

– *In Parmenidem*, ed. C.É. Ruelle, *Damascii successoris dubitationes et solutiones*, vol. 2, Paris, 1899 (repr. Brussels, 1964).

– *In Phaedonem* (*versio 1*), ed. L.G. Westerink, *The Greek commentaries on Plato's Phaedo*, vol. 2, Amsterdam, 1977, pp. 27-285.

– *In Phaedonem* (*versio 2*), ed L.G. Westerink, *The Greek commentaries on Plato's Phaedo*, vol. 2. Amsterdam, 1977, pp. 289-371.

David Dishypatus (theologian, fourteenth century), *Ad Nicolaum Cabasilam contra Barlaam et Acindynum*, ed. D.G. Tsames, *Δαβὶδ Δισυπάτου λόγος κατὰ Βαρλαὰμ καὶ Ἀκινδύνου πρὸς Νικόλαον Καβάσιλαν*, Βυζαντινὰ Κείμενα καὶ Μελέται 10, Thessaloniki, 1976, pp. 39-107.

David of Alexandria (Neoplatonist, sixth century), *Prolegomena Philosophiae*, ed. A. Busse, *Davidis prolegomena et in Porphyrii isagogen commentarium*, Commentaria in Aristotelem Graeca 18.2, Berlin, 1904, pp. 1-79.

– *In Porphyrii Isagogen*, ed. A. Busse, *Davidis prolegomena et in Porphyrii isagogen commentarium*, Commentaria in Aristotelem Graeca 18.2, Berlin, 1904, pp. 80-219.

DeLater, James Albert, *Theory in the Age of Louis XIV: The 1683 De Optimo Genere Interpretandi* (on the Best Kind of Translating) by the cleric Pierre Daniel Huet (1630-1721), Oxford, 2002.

Demosthenes, *De Corona*, ed. S.H. Butcher, *Demosthenis orationes*, vol. 1. Oxford, 1903 (repr. 1966), pp. 225-332.

– *Olynthiaca 1*, ed. S.H. Butcher, *Demosthenis orationes*, vol. 1. Oxford, 1903 (repr. 1966), pp. 9-17.

Derchain, P. "L'authenticité De l'inspiration égyptienne dans la corpus Hermeticum", *Revue De l'Histoire des Religions*, 161, 1962, pp. 175-198.

Derchain, P. "La doctrine herméiste et l'influence de la religion égyptienne", résumé in *Revue De l'Histoire des Religions*, 163, 1963, pp. 126-127.

Dexippus (fourth century AD), *In Aristotelis Categorias Commentarium*, ed. A. Busse, *Dexippi in Aristotelis categorias commentarium*, Commentaria in Aristotelem Graeca 4.2, Berlin, 1888.

Diadochus of Photike, *Capita Centum De Perfectione Spirituali*, ed. J. Rutherford, *One hundred practical texts of perception and spiritual discernment from Diadochos of Photike*, vol. 8, Belfast Byzantine Texts and Translation, 2000, pp. 12-154.

Didymus, *Commentarii in Ecclesiasten 1.1-8*, eds. G. Binde – L. Liesenborghs, *Didymos der Blinde. Kommentar zum Ecclesiastes*, part 1, Papyrologische Texte und Abhandlungen 25, Bonn, 1979.

– *Commentarii in Ecclesiasten 11-12*, eds. G. Binder – L. Liesenborghs, *Didymos der Blinde. Kommentar zum Ecclesiastes*, part 6, Papyrologische Texte und Abhandlungen 9, Bonn, 1969.

– *Commentarii in Ecclesiasten 3-4.12*, ed. M. Gronewald, *Didymos der Blinde. Kommentar zum Ecclesiastes*, part 2, Papyrologische Texte und Abhandlungen 22, Bonn, 1977.

– *Commentarii in Ecclesiasten 7-8.8*, eds. J. Kramer – B. Krebber, *Didymos der Blinde. Kommentar zum Ecclesiastes*, part 4, *Papyrologische Texte und Abhandlungen* 16, Bonn, 1972.

– *Commentarii in Ecclesiasten 9.8-10.20*, ed. M. Gronewald, *Didymos der Blinde. Kommentar zum Ecclesiastes*, part 5, Papyrologische Texte und Abhandlungen 24, Bonn, 1979.

– *Commentarii in Job 1-4*, ed. A. Henrichs, *Didymos der Blinde. Kommentar zu Hiob*, part 1 (*Papyrologische Texte und Abhandlungen* 1, Bonn, 1968, pp. 24-308.

– *Commentarii in Job 12.1-16.8a*, eds. U. Hagedorn, D. Hagedorn – L. Koenen, *Didymos der Blinde. Kommentar zu Hiob*, part 4.1, Papyrologische Texte und Abhandlungen 33.1, Bonn, 1985.

– *Commentarii in Job* (5.1-6.29, ed. A. Henrichs, *Didymos der Blinde. Kommentar zu Hiob*, part 2, Papyrologische Texte und Abhandlungen 2, Bonn, 1968, pp. 14-194.

– *Commentarii in Job 7.20c-11*, eds. U. Hagedorn, D. Hagedorn – L. Koenen, *Didymos der Blinde. Kommentar zu Hiob*, part 3, Papyrologische Texte und Abhandlungen 3, Bonn, 1968.

– *Commentarii in Job*, PG.39.1120-1153.

– *Commentarii in Psalmos 20-21*, eds. L. Doutreleau, A. Gesché – M. Gronewald, *Didymos der Blinde. Psalmenkommentar*, part 1, Papyrologische Texte und Abhandlungen 7, Bonn, 1969.

– *Commentarii in Psalmos 22-26.10*, ed. M. Gronewald, *Didymos der Blinde. Psalmenkommentar*, part 2, Papyrologische Texte und Abhandlungen 4, Bonn, 1968.
– *Commentarii in Psalmos 29-34*, ed. M. Gronewald, *Didymos der Blinde. Psalmenkommentar*, part 3, Papyrologische Texte und Abhandlungen 8, Bonn, 1969.
– *Commentarii in Psalmos 35-39*, ed. M. Gronewald, *Didymos der Blinde. Psalmenkommentar*, part 4, Papyrologische Texte und Abhandlungen 6, Bonn, 1969.
– *Commentarii in Psalmos 40-44.4*, ed. M. Gronewald, *Didymos der Blinde. Psalmenkommentar*, part 5, Papyrologische Texte und Abhandlungen 12, Bonn, 1970.
– *Commentarii in Zachariam*, ed. L. Doutreleau, *Didyme l'Aveugle sur Zacharie*, 3 vols. Sources chrétiennes 83, 84, 85, Paris, 1962.
– *Fragmenta in Epistulam i ad Corinthios*, ed. K. Staab, *Pauluskommentar aus der griechischen Kirche aus Katenenhandschriften gesammelt*, Münster, 1933, pp. 6-14.
– *Fragmenta in Epistulam ii ad Corinthios*, ed. K. Staab, *Pauluskommentar aus der griechischen Kirche aus Katenenhandschriften gesammelt*, Münster, 1933, pp. 14-44.
– *Fragmenta in Joannem*, ed. J. Reuss, *Johannes – Kommentare aus der griechischen Kirche*, Texte und Untersuchungen 89, Berlin, 1966, pp. 177-186.
– *Fragmenta in Proverbia* PG.39.1621-1645.
– *Fragmenta in Psalmos Altera*, ed. E. Mühlenberg, *Psalmenkommentare aus der Katenenüberlieferung*, 2 vols. Patristische Texte und Studien 15 & 16, Berlin, vol. 1: 1975; vol. 2: 1977.
– *In Genesim*, eds. P. Nautin – L. Doutreleau, *Didyme l'Aveugle. Sur la Genèse*, vols. 1-2, Sources chrétiennes 233, 244, Paris, 1976; 1978.
Dio Chrysostom, *Orationes*, ed. J. von Arnim, *Dionis Prusaensis quem vocant Chrysostomum quae exstant omnia*, vols. 1-2, Berlin, 1962.
Diodore of Sicily, *Bibliotheca Historica*, eds. F. Vogel – K.T. Fischer, *Diodori bibliotheca historica*, 5 vols, Stuttgart, 1964.
Diodore of Sicily, *Bibliotheca Historica*, ed. F.R. Walton, *Diodorus of Sicily*, vols. 11-12, Cambridge Mass. 1968 (reprint), 12, 1967.
Diodore of Tarsus, *Fragmenta in Epistulam Ad Romanos*, ed. K. Staab, *Pauluskommentar aus der griechischen Kirche aus Katenenhandschriften gesammelt*, Münster, 1933, pp. 83-112.
Diogenes Laertius, *Vitae Philosophorum*, ed. H.S. Long, *Diogenis Laertii vitae philosophorum*, 2 vols, Oxford, 1964 (repr. 1966).
Diogenes of Sinope, *Epistulae*, in R. Hercher (ed.), *Epistolographi Graeci*, Paris, 1873 (repr. Amsterdam), 1965, pp. 235-258.
Dionysius of Halicarnassus (first century AD), *Antiquitates Romanae*, ed. K. Jacoby, *Dionysii Halicarnasei antiquitatum Romanarum quae supersunt*, 4 vols, Leipzig, vol. 1: 1885; vol. 2: 1888; vol. 3: 1891; vol. 4: 1905 (repr. Stuttgart, 1967).
– *De Thucidide*, eds. L. Radermacher – H. Usener, *Dionysii Halicarnasei quae exstant*, vol. 5, Leipzig, 1899 (repr. 1965), pp. 325-418.

Dioscorides (Anazarbus, Cilicia, c. 40-90 AD), *De Materia Medica*, ed. M. Wellmann, *Pedanii Dioscuridis Anazarbei de materia medica libri quinque*, 3 vols. Berlin; vol. 1: 1907; vol. 2: 1906; vol. 3: 1914 (repr. 1958).

Doctrina Patrum, ed. F. Diekamp, *Doctrina patrum de incarnatione verbi*, Münster, 1907.

Documenta Concilii Florentini, *Acta Graecorum concilii Florentini Pars II*, ed. J. Gill, *Quae supersunt actorum Graecorum Concilii Florentini Pars II*, Rome, 1953, pp. 241-472.

Documenta Concilii Secundi Lugduno, *Synopsis Canonum contra Latinos*, eds. J. Darrouzès – V. Laurent, *Dossier grec de l'Union de Lyon* (*1273-1277*), Archives de l'Orient Chrétien 16, Paris, Institut Français d'Études Byzantines, 1976, pp. 564-573.

– *Synodicon contra Joannem Beccum*, eds. J. Darrouzès – V. Laurent, *Dossier grec de l'Union de Lyon* (*1273-1277*, Archives de l'Orient Chrétien 16, Paris, Institut Français d'Études Byzantines, 1976, pp. 574-588.

Dodd, C.H., *The Bible and the Greeks*, London 1935.

Dorotheus of Gaza, *Doctrinae Diversae*, eds. J. de Préville – L. Regnault, *Dorothée de Gaza. Oeuvres spirituelles*, Sources chrétiennes 92, Paris, 1963, pp. 146-486.

Doutreleaux, L., *Didyme l'aveugle sur Zacharie*, vol. I, Paris, 1962.

Dositheus II, Patriarch (Dositheus Notaras, 1641-1707, Patriarch of Jerusalem), ed. E. Deledemos, *Δοσιθέου Πατριάρχου Ἱεροσολύμων Ἱστορία περὶ τῶν ἐν Ἱεροσολύμοις Πατριαρχευσάντων, ἄλλως καλουμένη Δωδεκάβιβλος Δοσιθέου*, vol. 4, Thessaloniki, 1983.

Drijvers, H.J.W., "Edessa und das jüdische Christentum", *Vigiliae Christianae*, 24,1, March, 1970, pp. 4-33.

Drijvers, H.J.W., *Bardaisan of Edessa and the Hermetica. The Aramaic philosopher and the philosophy of his time*, Jaarbericht Ex Oriente Lux 21, 1969-70.

Edwards, Mark, review of Panayiotis Tzamalikos, *Anaxagoras, Origen, and Neoplatonism, The Legacy of Anaxagoras to Classical and Late Antiquity*, vols. I and II, De Gruyter, 2016, *Journal of Ecclesiastical History*, v. 69 / 3, 2018, pp. 610-612.

Elias of Alexandria, *In Aristotelis Categorias Commentarium*, ed. A. Busse, *Eliae in Porphyrii isagogen et Aristotelis categorias commentaria*, Commentaria in Aristotelem Graeca 18.1, Berlin, 1900, pp. 107-255.

– *Commentarius in Aristotelis Analytica Priora*, ed. L.G. Westerink, "Elias on the prior analytics," *Mnemosyne* ser. 4, vol. 14, 1961, pp. 134-139.

Enchiridion Patristicum, ed. Marie Joseph Rouët de Journel, Freiburg, 1946.

Ephraem of Aenus (Thrace, thirteenth-fourteenth century), *Historia Chronica*, ed. O. Lampsides, *Ephraem Aenii Historia Chronica*, Corpus Fontium Historiae Byzantinae, Series Atheniensis 27, Athens, 1990.

Ephraem Syrus, *Adversus Improbas Mulieres*, ed. K.G. Phrantzoles, *Ὁσίου Ἐφραίμ τοῦ Σύρου ἔργα*, vol. 5, Thessaloniki, 1994, pp. 198-206.

– *Beati Ephraem Testamentum*, ed. K.G. Phrantzoles, *Ὁσίου Ἐφραίμ τοῦ Σύρου ἔργα*, vol. 7, Thessaloniki, 1998, pp. 395-432.

– *Beautitudines*, ed. K.G. Phrantzoles, *Ὁσίου Ἐφραίμ τοῦ Σύρου ἔργα*, vol. 2, Thessaloniki, 1989, pp. 252-266.
– *Consilium de Vita Spiritali; ad Monachum Novitium* (*capita xcvi*), ed. Konstantinos G. Phrantzoles, *Ὁσίου Ἐφραὶμ τοῦ Σύρου Ἔργα*, vol. 2, Thessaloniki 1989, pp. 209-51.
– *De Abstinendo ab Omni Consuetudine Perniciosa, et De Continentia*, ed. Konstantinos G. Phrantzoles, *Ὁσίου Ἐφραὶμ τοῦ Σύρου Ἔργα*, vol. 5, Thessaloniki 1989, pp. 231-238.
– *De Iudicio et Compunctione*, ed. Konstantinos G. Phrantzoles, *Ὁσίου Ἐφραὶμ τοῦ Σύρου Ἔργα*, vol. 2, Thessaloniki 1989, pp. 386-402.
– *De Locis Beatis*, ed. Konstantinos G. Phrantzoles, *Ὁσίου Ἐφραὶμ τοῦ Σύρου Ἔργα*, vol. 4, Thessaloniki 1992, pp. 298-302.
– *De Paenitentia*, ed. Konstantinos G. Phrantzoles, *Ὁσίου Ἐφραὶμ τοῦ Σύρου Ἔργα*, vol. 4, 1992, pp. 303-307.
– *De Panoplia, ad Monachos*, ed. Konstantinos G. Phrantzoles, *Ὁσίου Ἐφραὶμ τοῦ Σύρου Ἔργα*, vol. 6, 1995, pp. 9-41.
– *De Patientia et Compunctione*, ed. Konstantinos G. Phrantzoles, *Ὁσίου Ἐφραὶμ τοῦ Σύρου Ἔργα*, vol. 4, 1992, pp. 320-332.
– *De Recta Vivendi Ratione*, ed. Konstantinos G. Phrantzoles, *Ὁσίου Ἐφραὶμ τοῦ Σύρου Ἔργα*, vol. 3, 1990, pp. 11-35.
– *De Virtute, ad Novitium Monachum*, ed. Konstantinos G. Phrantzoles, *Ὁσίου Ἐφραὶμ τοῦ Σύρου Ἔργα*, vol. 2, 1989, pp. 77-110.
– *De Virtutibus et Passionibus*, ed. K.G. Phrantzoles, *Ὁσίου Ἐφραίμ τοῦ Σύρου ἔργα*, vol. 5, Thessaloniki, 1994, pp. 392-410.
– *Encomium in Magnum Basilium*, ed. K.G. Phrantzoles, *Ὁσίου Ἐφραίμ τοῦ Σύρου ἔργα*, vol. 7, Thessaloniki, 1998, pp. 338-355.
– *Encomium in Sanctos Quadraginta Martyres*, ed. K.G. Phrantzoles, *Ὁσίου Ἐφραίμ τοῦ Σύρου ἔργα*, vol. 7, Thessaloniki, 1998, pp. 131-162.
– *Fragmenta Paraenetica*, ed. K.G. Phrantzoles, *Ὁσίου Ἐφραίμ τοῦ Σύρου ἔργα*, vol. 7, Thessaloniki, 1995, pp. 255-261.
– *Hypomnesticon*, ed. K.G. Phrantzoles, *Ὁσίου Ἐφραίμ τοῦ Σύρου ἔργα*, vol. 2, Thessaloniki, 1989, pp. 46-58.
– *In Adventum Domini*, ed. K.G. Phrantzoles, *Ὁσίου Ἐφραίμ τοῦ Σύρου ἔργα*, vol. 4, Thessaloniki, 1992, pp. 180-184.
– *In illud: Attende Tibi Ipsi*, ed. K.G. Phrantzoles, *Ὁσίου Ἐφραίμ τοῦ Σύρου ἔργα*, vol. 2, Thessaloniki, 1989, pp. 142-198.
– *In Sermonem, Quem Dixit Dominus, Quod: In Hoc Mundo Pressuram Habebitis, et De Perfectione Hominis*, ed. K.G. Phrantzoles, *Ὁσίου Ἐφραίμ τοῦ Σύρου ἔργα*, vol. 2, Thessaloniki, 1992, pp. 333-398.
– *Institutio ad Monachos*, ed. Konstantinos G. Phrantzoles, *Ὁσίου Ἐφραὶμ τοῦ Σύρου Ἔργα*, vol. 5, Thessaloniki, 1994, pp. 300-370.

– *Paraenesis ad Ascetas*, ed. Konstantinos G. Phrantzoles, *Ὁσίου Ἐφραὶμ τοῦ Σύρου Ἔργα*, vol. 3, Thessaloniki, 1990, pp. 338-356.
– *Precationes ad Dei Matrem*, ed. Konstantinos G. Phrantzoles, *Ὁσίου Ἐφραὶμ τοῦ Σύρου Ἔργα*, vol. 6, Thessaloniki, 1995, pp. 354-413.
– *Quomodo Latro Ante Resurrectionem in Paradisum Intrauit*, ed. Konstantinos G. Phrantzoles, *Ὁσίου Ἐφραὶμ τοῦ Σύρου Ἔργα*, vol. 6, Thessaloniki, 1998, pp. 83-85.
– *Reprehensio Sui Ipsius atque Confessio*, ed. Konstantinos G. Phrantzoles, *Ὁσίου Ἐφραὶμ τοῦ Σύρου Ἔργα*, vol. 6, Thessaloniki, 1988, pp. 74-83.
– *Sermo Adversus Haereticos*, ed. Konstantinos G. Phrantzoles, *Ὁσίου Ἐφραὶμ τοῦ Σύρου Ἔργα*, vol. 6, Thessaloniki, 1995, pp. 131-172.
– *Sermo Animae Utilis*, ed. Konstantinos G. Phrantzoles, *Ὁσίου Ἐφραὶμ τοῦ Σύρου Ἔργα*, vol. 5, Thessaloniki, 1994, pp. 107-113.
– *Sermo De Communi Resurrectione*, ed. Konstantinos G. Phrantzoles, *Ὁσίου Ἐφραὶμ τοῦ Σύρου Ἔργα*, vol. 4, Thessaloniki, 1992, pp. 47-75.
– *Sermo De Passione Saluatoris*, ed. Konstantinos G. Phrantzoles, *Ὁσίου Ἐφραὶμ τοῦ Σύρου Ἔργα*, vol. 7, Thessaloniki, 1998, pp. 31-41.
– *Sermo De Virtutibus et Vitiis*, ed. Konstantinos G. Phrantzoles, *Ὁσίου Ἐφραὶμ τοῦ Σύρου Ἔργα* vol. 1, Thessaloniki, 1988, pp. 37-73.
– *Sermo in Adventum Domini*, ed. Konstantinos G. Phrantzoles, *Ὁσίου Ἐφραὶμ τοῦ Σύρου Ἔργα*, vol. 4, Thessaloniki, 1992, pp. 111-128.
– *Sermo in Pretiosam et Vivificam Crucem*, ed. Konstantinos G. Phrantzoles, *Ὁσίου Ἐφραὶμ τοῦ Σύρου Ἔργα*, vol. 4, Thessaloniki, 1992, pp. 129-154.
– *Sermo in Pulcherrimum Ioseph*, ed. Konstantinos G. Phrantzoles, *Ὁσίου Ἐφραὶμ τοῦ Σύρου Ἔργα*, vol. 7, Thessaloniki, 1998, pp. 260-300.
– *Sermo in Secundum Adventum Domini Nostri Jesu Christi*, ed. Konstantinos G. Phrantzoles, *Ὁσίου Ἐφραὶμ τοῦ Σύρου Ἔργα*, vol. 4, Thessaloniki, 1992, pp. 9-46.
– *Sermo in Transfigurationem Domini et Dei Salvatoris Nostri Jesu Christi*, ed. Konstantinos G. Phrantzoles, *Ὁσίου Ἐφραὶμ τοῦ Σύρου Ἔργα*, vol. 7, ed. Konstantinos G. Phrantzoles, *Ὁσίου Ἐφραὶμ τοῦ Σύρου Ἔργα*, vol. 7, Thessaloniki, 1998, pp. 13-30.
Epictetus, *Dissertationes ab Arriano Digestae*, ed. H. Schenkl, *Epicteti dissertationes ab Arriano digestae*, Leipzig, 1916.
Epiphanius of Salamis, *Ancoratus*, ed. K. Holl, *Epiphanius, Band 1: Ancoratus und Panarion*, GCS 25, Leipzig, 1915.
– *De Mensuris et de Ponderibus*, ed. E. Moutsoulas, *Τὸ Περὶ Μέτρων καὶ Σταθμῶν ἔργον τοῦ Ἐπιφανίου τοῦ Σαλαμῖνος*, in *Θεολογία*, 44, 1973, pp. 157-198.
– *Liturgia Praesanctificatorum*, ed. D.N. Moraites, *Ἡ λειτουργία τῶν προηγιασμένων*, Thessaloniki, 1955, pp. 53-77.
– *Panarion* (*Adversus Haereses*), ed. K. Holl, *Epiphanius, Bände 1-3: Ancoratus und Panarion*, GCS 25, 31, 37, Leipzig, vol. 1: 1915; vol. 2: 1922; vol. 3: 1933.

Etymologicum Genuinum (or, *Etymologicum Magnum Genuinum*, ninth century), eds. F. Lasserre – N. Livadaras, *Etymologicum magnum genuinum. Symeonis etymologicum una cum magna grammatica. Etymologicum magnum auctum*, vol. 1, Rome, 1976.

Etymologicum Genuinum, eds. F. Lasserre – N. Livadaras, *Etymologicum magnum genuinum. Symeonis etymologicum una cum magna grammatica. Etymologicum magnum auctum*, vol. 2, Athens, 1992.

Etymologicum Gudianum (α-ζ), ed. A. de Stefani, *Etymologicum Gudianum*, Amsterdam, 1965.

Etymologicum Gudianum (ζ-ω), ed. F.W. Sturz, *Etymologicum Graecae linguae Gudianum et alia grammaticorum scripta codices: manuscriptis nunc primum edita*, Hildesheim, 1973, pp. 229-584.

Etymologicum Gudianum, Additamenta in Etymologicum Gudianum, ed. F.W. Sturz, *Etymologicum Graecae linguae Gudianum et alia grammaticorum scripta codices: manuscriptis nunc primum edita*, Hildesheim, 1973, pp. 585-588.

Etymologicum Gudianum, ed. F.W. Sturz, *Etymologicum Graecae linguae Gudianum et alia grammaticorum scripta codices: manuscriptis nunc primum edita*, Hildesheim, 1973, pp. 595-600.

Etymologicum Magnum (twelfth century), ed. T. Gaisford, *Etymologicum magnum*, Amsterdam, 1967.

Etymologicum Symeonis (α-ἀμωσγέπως), eds. F. Lasserre – N. Livadaras, *Etymologicum magnum genuinum. Symeonis etymologicum una cum magna grammatica. Etymologicum magnum auctum*, vol. 1, Rome, 1976.

Etymologicum Symeonis (ἀνακωχῆς – βώτορες), eds. F. Lasserre – N. Livadaras, *Etymologicum magnum genuinum. Symeonis etymologicum una cum magna grammatica. Etymologicum magnum auctum*, vol. 2, Athens, 1992.

Etymologicum Symeonis (*Γ-Ε*), ed. D. Baldi, *Etymologicum Symeonis* (*Γ-Ε*), Corpus Christianorum Series Graeca 79, Turnhout, 2013.

Eubulus, *Fragmenta*, ed. T. Kock, *Comicorum Atticorum fragmenta*, vol. 2, Leipzig, 1884, pp. 164-214.

Euclides, *Elementa*, ed. E.S. Stamatis (post J.L. Heiberg), *Euclidis Elementa*, vols. 1-4, second edition, Leipzig, vol. 1: 1969; vol. 2: 1970; vol. 3: 1972; vol. 4: 1973.

Eudocia Augusta, *Homerocentones*, ed. A. Ludwich, *Eudociae Augustae, Procli Lycii, Claudiani carminum Graecorum reliquiae*, Leipzig, 1897, pp. 81-114.

Eunomius, *Apologia*, ed. R.P. Vaggione, *Eunomius The Extnant Works*, Oxford Early Christian Texts, Oxford, 1987.

Euripides, *Bacchae*, ed. J. Diggle, *Euripidis fabulae*, vol. 3, Oxford, 1994, pp. 291-351.

Eusebius of Caesarea, *Commentaria in Psalmos*, PG.23.66-1396; PG.24.9-76.

– *Commentarius in Isaiam*, ed. J. Ziegler, *Eusebius Werke*, Band 9, *Der Jesajakommentar*, GCS, Berlin, 1975.

– *Contra Marcellum*, eds. E. Klostermann – G.C. Hansen, *Eusebius Werke*, Band 4, *Gegen Marcell. Über die kirchliche Theologie. Die Fragmente Marcells*, GCS 14, Berlin, 1972.
– *De Ecclesiastica Theologia*, eds. E. Klostermann – G.C. Hansen, *Eusebius Werke*, Band 4, *Gegen Marcell. Über die kirchliche Theologie. Die Fragmente Marcells*, GCS 14, second edition, Berlin, 1972, pp. 61-182.
– *De Laudibus Constantini*, ed. I.A. Heikel, *Eusebius Werke*, vol. 1, GCS 7, Leipzig, 1902, pp. 195-259.
– *De Mensuris et Ponderibus* (*fragmenta*), ed. F. Hultsch, *Metrologicorum scriptorum reliquiae*, vol. 1, Leipzig, 1864, pp. 276-278.
– *De Solemnitate Paschali*, PG.24.693-706.
– *De Theophania* (*fragmenta*), ed. H. Gressmann, *Eusebius Werke*, Band 3.2, *Die Theophanie*, GCS 11.2, Leipzig, 1904.
– *Demonstratio Evangelica*, ed. I.A. Heikel, *Eusebius Werke*, Band 6, *Die Demonstratio evangelica*, GCS 23, Leipzig, 1913.
– *Eclogae Propheticae*, ed. T. Gaisford, *Eusebii Pamphili episcopi Caesariensis eclogae propheticae*, Oxford, 1842.
– *Epistula ad Caesarienses*, ed. H.G. Opitz, *Athanasius Werke*, vol. 2.1, Berlin, 1940, pp. 28-31.
– *Fragmenta in Lucam*, PG.24.529-605.
– *Generalis Elementaria Introductio*, ed. T. Gaisford, *Eusebii Pamphili episcopi Caesariensis eclogae propheticae*, Oxford, 1842.
– *Historia Ecclesiastica*, ed. G. Bardy, *Eusèbe de Césarée. Histoire ecclésiastique*, 3 vols. Sources chrétiennes 31, 41, 55, Paris, 1967.
– *In Isaiam*, ed. J. Ziegler, *Eusebius Werke, Band 9: Der Jesajakommentar*, GCS, Berlin, 1975.
– *Onomasticon*, ed. E. Klostermann, *Eusebius Werke*, Band 3.1, *Das Onomastikon*, GSS, 11.1, Leipzig, 1904.
– *Praeparatio Evangelica*, ed. K. Mras, *Eusebius Werke, Band 8, Die Praeparatio evangelica*, GCS 43.1 & 43.2, Berlin, vol. 43.1, 1954; vol. 43.2, 1956.
– *Quaestiones Evangelicae ad Marinum*, PG.22.937-957.
– *Quaestiones Evangelicae ad Stephanum*, PG.22.880-936.
– *Supplementa ad Quaestiones ad Stephanum*, PG.22.957-976.
– *Supplementa Minora ad Quaestiones ad Marinum*, PG.22.1008-1016.
– *Vita Constantini*, ed. F. Winkelmann, *Eusebius Werke*, Band 1.1, *Über das Leben des Kaisers Konstantin*, GCS, Berlin, 1975.

Eustathius (monk, Constantinople, sixth century), *Epistula ad Timotheum Scholasticum De Duabus Naturis Adversus Severum*, ed. P. Allen, *Diversorum postchalcedonensium auctorum collectanea* Corpus Christianorum Series Graeca 19, Turnhout, 1989, pp. 413-447.

Eustathius of Antioch, *De Engastrimytho Contra Origenem*, ed. M. Simonetti, *Origene, Eustazio, Gregorio di Nissa: La maga di Endor*, Florence, 1989, pp. 94-206.

Eustathius of Thessaloniki (bishop and scholar, c. 1115-1195/6), *Commentarii ad Homeri Iliadem*, ed. M. van der Valk, *Eustathii archiepiscopi Thessalonicensis commentarii ad Homeri Iliadem pertinentes*, vols. 1-4, Leiden, vol. 1: 1971; vol. 2: 1976; vol. 3: 1979; vol. 4: 1987.

– *Sermones*, ed. P. Wirth, *Eustathii Thessalonicensis opera minora* (*magnam partem inedita*, Corpus Fontium Historiae Byzantinae, Series Berolinensis 32, Berlin, 1999.

– *Commentarium in Dionysii Periegetae Orbis Descriptionem*, ed. K. Müller, Geographi Graeci minores, vol. 2, Paris, 1861 (repr. Hildesheim, 1965), pp. 201-407.

Eustratius of Constantinople (presbyter, sixth-seventh century), *De Statu Animarum Post Mortem*, ed. P. van Deun, *Eustratii Presbyteri Constantinopolitani Opera, De statu animarum post mortem*, Corpus Christianorum Series Graeca 60, Turnhout, 2006.

Eustratius of Nicaea (eleventh-twelfth century, a disciple of John Italus), *In Aristotelis Ethica Nicomachea vi Commentaria*, ed. G. *Heylbut, Eustratii et Michaelis et anonyma in ethica Nicomachea commentaria*, Commentaria in Aristotelem Graeca 20, Berlin, 1892, pp. 256-406.

– *Orationes*, ed. A. Demetrakopoulos, Ἐκκλησιαστικὴ Βιβλιοθήκη, vol. 1, Leipzig, 1866 (repr. 1965), pp. 47-198.

Eutecnius (sophist, third-fifth century), *Paraphrasis in Nicandri Theriaca*, ed. I. Gualandri, *Eutecnii paraphrasis in Nicandri theriaca*, Milan, 1968, pp. 21-70.

Euthymius Zigabenus, *Panoplia Dogmatica ad Alexium Comnenum*, PG.130.20-1360.

Eutocius of Ascalon, *Commentarii in Libros De Sphaera et Cylindro*, eds. J.L. Heiberg – E. Stamatis, *Archimedis opera omnia cum commentariis Eutocii*, vol. 3, Leipzig, 1915.

Evagrius of Pontus, *Chapitres des disciples d'Evagre*, Sources Chrétiennes, 514, Paris, 2007.

– *De Malignis Cogitationibus*, eds. P. Géhin – A. Guillaumont – C. Guillaumont, *Évagre le Pontique. Sur les pensées*, Sources chrétiennes 438, Paris, 1998, pp. 148-301.

– *De Octo Spiritibus Malitiae*, PG.79.1145-1164.

– *De Vitiis Quae Opposita Sunt Virtutibus*, PG.79.1140-1144.

– *Kefalaia Gnostica*, ed. J. Paramelle, "Évagre le Pontique, 'Chapitres des disciples d'Évagre' dans un manuscript grec du Musée Bénaki d'Athènes" (Greek title: *Κεφάλαια τῶν Μαθητῶν Εὐαγρίου*), in *Mélanges offerts au R. P. François Graffin, S. J Parole de l'Orient* 6-7 (1975-76), pp. 101-13.

– *Expositio in Proverbia Salomonis*, ed. C. Tischendorf, *Notitia editionis codicis bibliorum Sinaitici*, Leipzig, 1860, pp. 76-122.

– *Institutio sive Paraenesis ad Monachos*, PG.79.1235-1240.

– *Practicus*, eds. A. Guillaumont – C. Guillaumont, *Évagre le Pontique. Traité pratique ou le moine*, vol. 2, Sources chrétiennes 171, Paris, 1971.

– *Scholia in Proverbia (fragmenta)*, ed. P. Géhin, *Évagre le Pontique. Scholies aux Proverbes*, Sources chrétiennes 340, Paris, 1987.
– *Tractatus ad Eulogium*, PG.79.1093-1140.
Evagrius Scholasticus, *Historia Ecclesiastica*, eds. J. Bidez – L. Parmentier, *The ecclesiastical history of Evagrius with the scholia*, London, 1898.
Flinders Petrie, W.M., "Aspects of Egyptian Religion", in *Transactions of the Third International Congress of the History of Religions*, vol. I, Oxford 1908, pp. 185-200.
– "Historical References in Hermetic Writings", in *Transactions of the Third International Congress of the History of Religions*, vol. I, Oxford 1908, pp. 224-225.
– *Personal Religions in Egypt Before Christianity*, London, 1909.
Florilegium Cyrillianum, ed. R. Hespel, *Le florilège cyrillien réfuté par Sévère d'Antioche*, Bibliothèque du Muséon 37, Louvain, 1955, pp. 103-208.
Fragmenta in Matthaeum (in catenis)), ed. J. Reuss, *Matthäus – Kommentare aus der griechischen Kirche*, Texte und Untersuchungen 61, Berlin, 1957.
Fürst, Alfons, "Origen: exegesis and Philosophy in early Christian Alexandria", in Josef Löss – John W. Watt (eds.), *Interpreting the Bible and Aristotle in Late Antiquity: The Alexandrian Commentary tradition Between Rome and Baghdad*, Burlington, 2011.
Galen (second century AD), *Ad Glauconem De Medendi Methodo*, ed. C.G. Kühn, *Claudii Galeni opera omnia*, vol. 11, Leipzig, 1826 (repr. Hildesheim, 1965).
– *Adversus Ea Quae a Juliano in Hippocratis Aphorismos Enuntiata Sunt Libellus*, ed. E. Wenkebach, *Galeni adversus Lycum et adversus Iulianum libelli*, Corpus medicorum Graecorum 5.10.3, Berlin, 1951, pp. 33-70.
– *Alimentorum Facultatibus*, ed. G. Helmreich, *Galeni de alimentorum facultatibus libri iii*, Corpus medicorum Graecorum 5.4.2, Leipzig, 1923, pp. 201-386.
– *An In Arteriis Natura Sanguis Contineatur*, ed. F. Albrecht, *Galeni an in arteriis natura sanguis contineatur*, Marburg, 1911, pp. 1-21.
– *Ars Medica*, ed. C.G. Kühn, *Claudii Galeni opera omnia*, vol. 1, Hildesheim, 1964, pp. 305-412.
– *De Anatomicis Administrationibus*, ed. C.G. Kühn, *Claudii Galeni opera omnia*, vol. 2, Leipzig, 1821 (repr. Hildesheim, 1964), pp. 215-731.
– *De Animi Cuiuslibet Peccatorum Dignotione et Curatione*, ed. W. de Boer, *Galeni de animi cuiuslibet peccatorum dignotione et curatione*, Corpus medicorum Graecorum 5.4.1.1, Leipzig, 1937, pp. 41-68.
– *De Antidotis*, ed. C.G. Kühn, *Claudii Galeni opera omnia*, vol. 14, Leipzig, 1827 (repr. Hildesheim, 1965).
– *De Causis Pulsuum*, ed. C.G. Kühn, *Claudii Galeni opera omnia*, vol. 9, Leipzig, 1825 (repr. Hildesheim, 1965).
– *De Compositione Medicamentorum Per Genera*, ed. C.G. Kühn, *Claudii Galeni opera omnia*, vol. 13, Leipzig, 1827 (repr. Hildesheim, 1965), pp. 362-1058.

– *De Compositione Medicamentorum Secundum Locos*, ed. C.G. Kühn, *Claudii Galeni opera omnia*, vols. 12-13, Leipzig, vol. 12: 1826; vol. 13: 1827 (repr. Hildesheim, 1965).
– *De Crisibus*, ed. B. Alexanderson, *Galenos. Περὶ κρίσεων*, Studia Graeca et Latina Gothoburgensia 23, Göteborg, 1967, pp. 69-212.
– *De Diebus Decretoriis*, ed. C.G. Kühn, *Claudii Galeni opera omnia*, vol. 9, Leipzig, 1825 (repr. Hildesheim, 1965), pp. 769-941.
– *De Differentia Pulsuum*, ed. C.G. Kühn, *Claudii Galeni opera omnia*, vol. 8, Leipzig, 1824 (repr. Hildesheim, 1965), pp. 493-765.
– *De Difficultate Respirationis*, ed. C.G. Kühn, *Claudii Galeni opera omnia*, vol. 7, Leipzig, 1824 (repr. Hildesheim, 1965), pp. 753-960.
– *De Dignoscendis Pulsibus*, ed. C.G. Kühn, *Claudii Galeni opera omnia*, vol. 8, Leipzig, 1824 (repr. Hildesheim, 1965), pp. 766-961.
– *De Foetuum Formatione Libellus*, ed. C.G. Kühn, *Claudii Galeni opera omnia*, vol. 4, Leipzig, 1822 (repr. Hildesheim), 1964, pp. 652-702.
– *De Instrumento Odoratus*, ed. J. Kollesch, *Galeni de instrumento odoratus*, Corpus medicorum Graecorum suppl. 5, Berlin, 1964, pp. 30-64.
– *De Locis Affectis*, ed. C.G. Kühn, *Claudii Galeni opera omnia*, vol. 8, Leipzig, 1824 (repr. Hildesheim, 1965).
– *De Methodo Medendi*, ed. C.G. Kühn, *Claudii Galeni opera omnia*, vol. 10, Leipzig, 1825 (repr. Hildesheim, 1965).
– *De Morborum Temporibus*, ed. I. Wille, *Die Schrift Galens Περὶ τῶν ἐν ταῖς νόσοις καιρῶν und ihre Überlieferung*, part 2 (Diss.) Kiel, 1960.
– *De Musculorum Dissectione ad Tirones*, ed. C.G. Kühn, *Claudii Galeni opera omnia*, vol. 18.2, Leipzig, 1830 (repr. Hildesheim, 1965), pp. 926-1026.
– *De Naturalibus Facultatibus*, ed. G. Helmreich – J. Marquardt – I. Müller, *Claudii Galeni Pergameni scripta minora*, vol. 3, Leipzig, 1893 (repr. Amsterdam, 1967), pp. 101-257.
– *De Ossibus ad Tirones*, ed. C.G. Kühn, *Claudii Galeni opera omnia*, vol. 2, Leipzig, 1821 (repr. Hildesheim, 1964), pp. 732-778.
– *De Placitis Hippocratis et Platonis*, ed. P.H. De Lacy, *Galen. On the doctrines of Hippocrates and Plato*, Corpus medicorum Graecorum vol. 5.4.1.2, parts. 1-2, Berlin, 1978, 1, pp. 65-358; 2, pp. 360-608.
– *De Plenitudine*, ed. C.G. Kühn, *Claudii Galeni opera omnia*, vol. 7, Leipzig, 1824 (repr. Hildesheim, 1965), pp. 513-583.
– *De Praesagitione ex Pulsibus*, ed. C.G. Kühn, *Claudii Galeni opera omnia*, vol. 9, Leipzig, 1825 (repr. Hildesheim, 1965), pp. 205-430.
– *De Praenotione ad Posthumum*, ed. C.G. Kühn, *Claudii Galeni opera omnia*, vol. 14, Leipzig, 1827 (repr. Hildesheim, 1965), pp. 599-673.
– *De Pulsibus Libellus ad Tirones*, ed. C.G. Kühn, *Claudii Galeni opera omnia*, vol. 8, Leipzig, 1824 (repr. Hildesheim, 1965), pp. 453-492.

- *De Rebus Boni Malique Suci*, ed. G. Helmreich, *Galeni de rebus boni malique suci libellus*, Corpus medicorum Graecorum 5.4.2, Leipzig, 1923, pp. 389-429.
- *De Sanitate Tuenda*, ed. K. Koch, *Galeni de sanitate tuenda libri vi*, Corpus medicorum Graecorum, vol. 5.4.2, Leipzig, 1923.
- *De Semine*, ed. C.G. Kühn, *Claudii Galeni opera omnia*, vol. 4, Leipzig, 1822 (repr. Hildesheim, 1964), pp. 512-651.
- *De Simplicium Medicamentorum Temperamentis ac Facultatibus*, ed. C.G. Kühn, *Claudii Galeni opera omnia*, vols. 11-12, Leipzig, 1826 (repr. Hildesheim, 1965), vol. 11, pp. 379-892; vol. 12, pp. 1-377.
- *De Substantia Facultatum Naturalium Fragmentum* (*De Propriis Placitis fragmentum*, ed. C.G. Kühn, *Claudii Galeni opera omnia*, vol. 4, Leipzig, 1822 (repr. Olms, 1964), pp. 757-766.
- *De Temperamentis*, ed. G. Helmreich, *Galeni de temperamentis libri iii*, Leipzig, 1904.
- *De Theriaca ad Pisonem*, ed. C.G. Kühn, *Claudii Galeni opera omnia*, vol. 14, Leipzig, 1827 (repr. Hildesheim), 1965, pp. 210-294.
- *De Tremore, Palpitatione, Convulsione et Rigore*, ed. C.G. Kühn, *Claudii Galeni opera omnia*, vol. 7, Leipzig, 1824 (repr. Hildesheim, 1965), pp. 584-642.
- *De Usu Partium*, ed. G. Helmreich, *Galeni de usu partium libri xvii*, Leipzig, 1: 1907; 2: 1909 (repr. Amsterdam, 1968).
- *De Utilitate Respirationis*, ed. R. Noll, Galeni *Περὶ χρείας ἀναπνοῆς* libellus, Dissertation, Marburg, 1915.
- *De Venarum Arteriarumque Dissectione*, ed. C.G. Kühn, *Claudii Galeni opera omnia*, vol. 2, Leipzig, 1821 (repr. Hildesheim, 1964), pp. 779-830.
- *De Victu Attenuante*, ed. K. Kalbfleisch, *Galeni de victu attenuante*, Corpus medicorum Graecorum 5.4.2, Leipzig, 1923, pp. 433-451.
- *Dictionum Exoletarum Hippocratis Explicatio*, ed. C.G. Kühn, *Claudii Galeni opera omnia*, vol. 19, Leipzig, 1830 (repr. Hildesheim, 1965), pp. 62-157.
- *In Hippocratis Aphorismos*, ed. C.G. Kühn, *Claudii Galeni opera omnia*, vols. 17.2 & 18.1, Leipzig, 1829 (repr. Hildesheim, 1965).
- *In Hippocratis De Natura Hominis Librum Commentarii*, ed. J. Mewaldt, *Galeni in Hippocratis de natura hominis commentaria tria*, Corpus medicorum Graecorum 5.9.1, Leipzig, 1914.
- *In Hippocratis De Victu Acutorum Commentaria*, ed. G. Helmreich, *Galeni in Hippocratis de victu acutorum commentaria iv*, Corpus medicorum Graecorum, vol. 5.9.1, Leipzig, 1914.
- *In Hippocratis Librum De Articulis et Galeni in Eum*, ed. C.G. Kühn, *Claudii Galeni opera omnia*, vol. 18.1, Leipzig, 1829 (repr. Hildesheim, 1965), pp. 300-345, 423-767.
- *In Hippocratis Librum De Fracturis*, ed. C.G. Kühn, *Claudii Galeni opera omnia*, vol. 18.2, Leipzig, 1830 (repr. Hildesheim, 1965), pp. 318-628.
- *In Hippocratis Librum De Officina Medici*, ed. C.G. Kühn, *Claudii Galeni opera omnia*, vol. 18.2, Leipzig, 1830 (repr. Hildesheim, 1965), pp. 629-925.

– *In Hippocratis Librum iii Epidemiarum*, ed. E. Wenkebach, *Galeni in Hippocratis epidemiarum librum iii commentaria iii*, Corpus medicorum Graecorum 5.10.2.1, Leipzig, 1936.
– *In Hippocratis Librum Primum Epidemiarum*, ed. E. Wenkebach, *Galeni in Hippocratis epidemiarum librum i commentaria iii*, Corpus medicorum Graecorum 5.10.1, Leipzig, 1934.
– *In Hippocratis Librum vi Epidemiarum Commentarii VI*, ed. E. Wenkebach, *Galeni in Hippocratis sextum librum epidemiarum commentaria i-vi*, Corpus medicorum Graecorum, vol. 5.10.2.2, Leipzig, 1940.
– *In Hippocratis Prognosticum*, ed. J. Heeg, *Galeni in Hippocratis prognosticum commentaria iii*, Corpus medicorum Graecorum 5.9.2, Leipzig, 1915, pp. 197-378.
– *In Hippocratis Prorrheticum i*, ed. H. Diels, *Galeni in Hippocratis prorrheticum I commentaria iii*, Corpus medicorum Graecorum 5.9.2, Leipzig, 1915.
– *In Platonis Timaeum Commentarii Fragmenta*, ed. H.O. Schröder, *Galeni in Platonis Timaeum commentarii fragmenta*, Corpus medicorum Graecorum suppl. 1, Leipzig, 1934, pp. 9-26.
– *Institutio Logica*, ed. K. Kalbfleisch, *Galeni institutio logica*, Leipzig, 1896.
– *Linguarum Seu Dictionum Exoletarum Hippocratis Explicatio*, ed. C.G. Kühn, *Claudii Galeni opera omnia*, vol. 19, Leipzig, 1830 (repr. Hildesheim, 1965), pp. 62-157.
– *Quod Optimus Medicus Sit Quoque Philosophus*, ed. E. Wenkebach, "Der hippokratische Arzt als das Ideal Galens," Quellen und Studien zur Geschichte der Naturwissenschaften und Medizin 3.4, 1933, pp. 170-175.
– *Synopsis Librorum Suorum De Pulsibus*, ed. C.G. Kühn, *Claudii Galeni opera omnia*, vol. 9, Leipzig, 1825 (repr. Hildesheim, 1965), pp. 431-533.
– *Thrasybulus*, eds. G. Helmreich – J. Marquardt – I. Müller, *Claudii Galeni Pergameni scripta minora*, vol. 3, Leipzig, 1893 (repr. Amsterdam, 1967), pp. 33-100.
Gelasius of Cyzicus, *Historia Ecclesiastica*, eds. M. Heinemann – G. Loeschcke, *Gelasius. Kirchengeschichte*, GCS 28, Leipzig, 1918.
Gennadius I of Constantinople, *Fragmenta in Epistulam ad Romanos*, ed. K. Staab, *Pauluskommentar aus der griechischen Kirche aus Katenenhandschriften gesammelt*, Münster, 1933, pp. 352-418.
Gennadius Scholarius (c. 1400-c. 1473, Patriarch of Constantinople, 1454-1464), *Translatio commentarii Thomae Aquinae De anima Aristotelis*, eds. M. Jugie – L. Petit – X.A. Siderides, *Oeuvres complètes de Georges (Gennadios) Scholarios*, vol. 2, Paris, 1933, pp. 327-581.
– *De Prophetiis Principalibus Jesu Christi*, eds. M M. Jugie – L. Petit – X.A. Siderides, *Oeuvres complètes de Georges (Gennadios) Scholarios*, vol. 3, Paris, 1930, pp. 305-314.
– *De Quo Debet Sapere et Docere Sacerdos*, eds. M. Jugie – L. Petit – X.A. Siderides, *Oeuvres complètes de Georges (Gennadios) Scholarios*, vol. 4, Paris, 1935, pp. 190-197.

– *Tractatus De Processu Spiritus Sancti i*, eds. M. Jugie – L. Petit – X.A. Siderides, *Oeuvres complètes de Georges (Gennadios) Scholarios*, vol. 2, Paris, 1929, pp. 1-268.
– *Tractatus de Processu Spiritus Sancti ii*, eds. M. Jugie – L. Petit – X.A. Siderides, *Oeuvres complètes de Georges (Gennadios) Scholarios*, vol. 2, Paris, 1929, pp. 269-457.
– *De Unica Via ad Salutem Hominum*, eds. M. Jugie – L. Petit – X.A. Siderides, *Oeuvres complètes de Georges (Gennadios) Scholarios*, vol. 3, Paris, 1930, pp. 434-452.
– *Epistulae Contra Unionem Florentinam*, eds. M. Jugie – L. Petit – X.A. Siderides, *Oeuvres complètes de Georges (Gennadios) Scholarios*, vol. 3, Paris, 1930, pp. 117-165.
– *Epitome Summae contra gentiles Thomae Aquinae*, eds. M. Jugie – L. Petit – X.A. Siderides, *Oeuvres complètes de Georges (Gennadios) Scholarios*, vol. 5, Paris, 1931, pp. 1-338.
– *Epitome Primae Partis Summae Theologicae Thomae Aquinae, Epitome Summae Contra Gentiles Thomae Aquinae*, eds. M. Jugie – L. Petit – X.A. Siderides, *Oeuvres complètes de Georges (Gennadios) Scholarios*, vol. 5, Paris, 1931, pp. 338-510.
– *Expositio Brevis Fidei Christianae*, eds. M. Jugie – L. Petit – X.A. Siderides, *Oeuvres complètes de Georges (Gennadios) Scholarios*, vol. 3, Paris, 1930, pp. 453-458.
– *Fragmentum Exhortationis ad Peccatorem*, eds. M. Jugie – L. Petit – X.A. Siderides, *Oeuvres complètes de Georges (Gennadios) Scholarios*, vol. 4, Paris, 1935, pp. 284-295.
– *Orationes et Panegyrici*, eds. M. Jugie – L. Petit – X.A. Siderides, *Oeuvres complètes de Georges (Gennadios) Scholarios*, vol. 1, Paris, 1928, pp. 1-246.
– *Precatio ad Deum per Salutem Peloponnesi*, eds. M. Jugie – L. Petit – X.A. Siderides, *Oeuvres complètes de Georges (Gennadios) Scholarios*, vol. 4, Paris, 1935, pp. 385-389.
– *Responsiones Aliquorum Quaestionum in Scripturam Sacram*, eds. M. Jugie – L. Petit – X.A. Siderides, *Oeuvres complètes de Georges (Gennadios) Scholarios*, vol. 3, Paris, 1930, pp. 315-343.
– *Tractatus Contra Fautores Acindyni ad Joannem Basilicum De Verbis Theodori Grapti Interrogantem*, eds. M. Jugie – L. Petit – X.A. Siderides, *Oeuvres complètes de Georges (Gennadios) Scholarios*, vol. 3, Paris, 1930, pp. 204-228.
– *Tractatus De Uno Deo*, eds. M. Jugie – L. Petit – X.A. Siderides, *Oeuvres complètes de Georges (Gennadios) Scholarios*, vol. 4, Paris, 1935, pp. 172-189.
– *Adnotationes in Aristotelis Opera Diversa*, eds. M. Jugie – L. Petit – X.A. Siderides, *Oeuvres complètes de Georges (Gennadios) Scholarios*, vol. 7, Paris, 1936, pp. 349-509.
– *Contra Plethonis Ignorationem De Aristotele*, eds. M. Jugie – L. Petit – X.A. Siderides, *Oeuvres complètes de Georges (Gennadios) Scholarios*, vol. 4, Paris, 1935, pp. 1-116.
– *Quaestiones et Responsiones De Divinitate Domini Nostri Jesu Christi*, eds. M. Jugie – L. Petit – X.A. Siderides, *Oeuvres complètes de Georges (Gennadios) Scholarios*, vol. 3, Paris, 1930, pp. 458-475.
– *Disputationes Florentinae ad Quaestionem Religiosam*, eds. M. Jugie – L. Petit – X.A. Siderides, *Oeuvres complètes de Georges (Gennadios) Scholarios*, vol. 1, Paris, 1928, pp. 295-389.

George Acropolites (1217/1220-1282, *Laudatio Petri et Pauli*, ed. A. Heisenberg, *Georgii Acropolitae opera*, vol. 2, Leipzig, 1903, pp. 81-111.

– *In Gregorii Nazianzeni Sententias*, ed. A. Heisenberg, *Georgii Acropolitae opera*, vol. 2, Leipzig, 1903, pp. 70-80.

George Choeroboscus (deacon, grammarian, Constantinople, ninth century), *Prolegomena et scholia in Theodosii Alexandrini canones isagogicos de flexione nominum*, ed. A. Hilgard, *Grammatici Graeci*, vol. 4.1, Leipzig, 1894 (repr. Hildesheim, 1965), pp. 103-417.

– *De Orthographia*, ed. J.A. Cramer, *Anecdota Graeca e codd. manuscriptis bibliothecarum Oxoniensium*, vol. 2, Oxford, 1835 (repr. Amsterdam, 1963), pp. 167-281.

– *Epimerismi in Psalmos*, T. Gaisford, *Georgii Choerobosci epimerismi in Psalmos*, vol. 3, Oxford, 1842.

– *Scholia in Hephaestionem*, ed. M. Consbruch, *Hephaestionis enchiridion cum commentariis veteribus*, Leipzig, 1906, pp. 177-254.

George Monachus (monk, ninth century), Alexandria, *Chronicon*, ed. C. de Boor, *Georgii monachi chronicon*, 2 vols, Leipzig, 1904.

– *Chronicon Breve*, PG.110.41-1260.

George Pachymeres, *In Aristotelis Metaphysicam Commentarium* (*liber x*), ed. E. Pappa, *Kommentar zu Metaphysik des Aristoteles* (Buch 10), Corpus Philosophorum Medii Aevi, Commentaria in Aristotelem Byzantina 2, Athens, 2002, pp. 3-84.

– *Progymnasmata*, ed. C. Walz, *Rhetores Graeci* 1, Stuttgart, 1832, pp. 551-596.

– *Quadrivium* (*Σύνταγμα τῶν τεσσάρων μαθημάτων*), eds. R.P.E. Stephanou – P. Tannery, *Quadrivium de Georges Pachymère*, Studi e Testi 94, Vatican City, 1940.

George Syncellus (eighth-ninth century), *Ecloga Chronographica*, ed. A.A. Mosshammer, *Georgius Syncellus. Ecloga chronographica*, Leipzig, 1984.

Germanus I of Constantinople, *Historia Mystica Ecclesiae Catholicae*, ed. P. Meyendorff (*apud* N. Borgia, *St. Germanus of Constantinople on the Divine Liturgy*, Translation, Introduction and Commentary, Crestwood, New York, 1984, pp. 56-106.

– *Narratio De Haeresibus et Synodis ad Anthimum Diaconum*, PG.98.40-88.

Germanus II of Constantinople, *Orationes et Homiliae*, ed. S.N. Lagopates, *Γερμανὸς ὁ Β' Πατριάρχης Κωνσταντινουπόλεως – Νικαίας (1222-1240) Βίος συγγράμματα καὶ διδασκαλίαι αὐτοῦ*. Athens, 1913, pp. 214-349.

Gibbon, Edward, *The Decline and Fall of the Roman Empire*, New York, 1983.

Goltz, F. von der, *Eine textkritische Arbeit des zehnten bezw. sechsten Jahrbunderts*, TU 2.4, Leipzig, 1899.

Gottschalk, Hans B., "The earliest Aristotelian commentators", in R. Sorabji (ed.), *Aristotle Transformed: The Ancient Commentators and Their Influence*, Ithaca, NY, 1990, pp. 55-81.

Gregory Acindynus (Hesychast clergyman, fourteenth century), *Refutatio Magna*, ed. J.N. Cañellas, *Gregorii Acindyni Refutationes duae operis Gregorii Palamae cui titulus dialogus inter Orthodoxum et Barlaamitam*, Corpus Christianorum Series Graeca 31, Turnhout, 1995.

Gregory of Agrentium, *Commentarius in Ecclesiasten*, eds. G.H. Ettlinger – J. Noret, *Pseudo – Gregorii Agrigentini seu Pseudo – Gregorii Nysseni commentarius in Ecclesiasten*, Corpus Christianorum Series Graeca 56, Turnhout, 2007.

Gregory II (Cyprus, Patriarch, thirteenth century), *Tomus Fidei*, PG.142.233-246.

Gregory of Nazianzus, *Ad Cives Nazianzenos*, PG.35.964-981.

– *Ad Gregorium Nyssenum*, PG.35.832-841.

– *Ad Julianum Tributorum Exaequatorem*, PG.35.1044-1064.

– *Apologetica*, PG.35.408-513.

– *Apologeticus ad Patrem*, PG.35.820-825.

– *Carmina De Se Ipso*, PG.36.969-1029 &1166-1452.

– *Carmina Dogmatica*, PG.37.397-522.

– *Carmina Moralia*, PG.37.521-968.

– *Carmina Moralia*, PG.37.521-968.

– *Comparatio Vitarum*, ed. H.M. Werhahn, *Gregorii Nazianzeni Σύγκρισις βίων*, Klassisch – philologische Studien 15, Wiesbaden, 1953, pp. 22-29.

– *Contra Arianos et De Seipso*, PG.36.213-237.

– *Contra Julianum Imperatorem 1* (*orat. 4*), PG.35.532-664.

– *Contra Julianum*, PG.35.532-664.

– *De Dogmate et Constitutione Episcoporum* (*orat. 20*), PG.35.1065-1080.

– *De Filio* (*orat. 29*), ed. J. Barbel, *Gregor von Nazianz. Die fünf theologischen Reden*. Düsseldorf, 1963, pp. 128-168.

– *De Moderatione in Disputando* (*orat. 32*), PG.36.173-212.

– *De Pace 2* (*orat. 22*), PG.35.1132-1152.

– *De Pace 3* (*orat. 23*), PG.35.1152-1168.

– *De Spiritu Sancto*, ed. J. Barbel, *Gregor von Nazianz. Die fünf theologischen Reden*. Düsseldorf, 1963, pp. 218-276.

– *De Theologia*, J. Barbel, *Gregor von Nazianz. Die fünf theologischen Reden*. Düsseldorf, 1963, pp. 62-126.

– *Epistulae*, ed. P. Gallay, *Saint Grégoire de Nazianze. Lettres*, 2 vols, Paris, vol. 1: 1964; vol. 2: 1967.

– *Funebris Oratio in Laudem Basilii Magni Caesareae in Cappadocia Episcopi*, ed. F. Boulenger, *Grégoire de Nazianze. Discours funèbres en l'honneur de son frère Césaire et de Basile de Césarée*, Paris, 1908, pp. 58-230.

– *Funebris Oratio In Laudem Basilii Magni Caesareae* (*orat. 43*), ed. F. Boulenger, *Grégoire de Nazianze. Discours funèbres en l'honneur de son frère Césaire et de Basile de Césarée*, Paris, Picard, 1908, pp. 58-230.

– *In Aegyptiorum Adventum*, PG.36.241-256.

– *In Dictum Evangelii: Cum consummasset Jesus hos sermons* (*orat. 37*), PG.36. 281-308.

– *In Laudem Cypriani*, PG.35.1169-1193.
– *In Novam Dominicam*, PG.36.608-621.
– *In Pentecosten*, PG.36.428-452.
– *In Sanctum Baptisma*, PG.36.360-425.
– *In Sanctum Pascha*, PG.36.624-664.
– *In Theophania*, PG.36.312-333.

Gregory of Nyssa, *Ad Ablabium Quod Non Sint Tres Dei*, ed. F. Mueller, *Gregorii Nysseni opera*, vol. 3.1. Leiden, 1958, pp; 37-57.
– *Ad Eustathium De Sancta Trinitate*, ed. F. Mueller, *Gregorii Nysseni opera*, vol. 3.1. Leiden, 1958, pp. 3-16.
– *Ad Graecos ex Communibus Notionibus*, ed. F. Mueller, *Gregorii Nysseni opera*, vol. 3.1, Leiden, 1958, pp. 19-33.
– *Ad Simplicium De Fide*, ed. F. Mueller, *Gregorii Nysseni opera*, vol. 3.1. Leiden, 1958, pp. 61-67.
– *Ad Theophilum Adversus Apollinaristas*, ed. F. Mueller, *Gregorii Nysseni opera*, vol. 3.1. Leiden, 1958, pp. 119-128.
– *Adversus Arium et Sabellium De Patre et Filio*, ed. F. Mueller, *Gregorii Nysseni opera*, vol. 3.1. Leiden, 1958, pp. 71-85.
– *Adversus Macedonianos De Spiritu Sancto*, ed. F. Mueller, *Gregorii Nysseni opera*, vol. 3.1. Leiden, 1958, pp. 89-115.
– *Antirrheticus Adversus Apollinarium*, ed. F. Mueller, *Gregorii Nysseni opera*, vol. 3.1. Leiden, 1958, pp. 131-233.
– *Apologia in Hexaemeron*, PG.44.61-124.
– *Contra Eunomium*, ed. W. Jaeger, *Gregorii Nysseni opera*, vols. 1.1 & 2.2, Leiden, 1960.
– *Contra Fatum*, ed. J. McDonough, *Gregorii Nysseni opera*, vol. 3.2. Leiden, 1986, pp. 31-63.
– *Contra Usurarios*, ed. E. Gebhardt, *Gregorii Nysseni opera*, vol. 9.1. Leiden, 1967, pp. 195-207.
– *De Beneficentia*, ed. A. van Heck, *Gregorii Nysseni opera*, vol. 9.1, Leiden, 1967, pp. 93-108.
– *De Deitate Filii et Spiritus Sancti*, PG.46.553-76.
– *De Infantibus Praemature Abreptis*, ed. H. Hörner, *Gregorii Nysseni opera*, vol. 3.2. Leiden, 1986, pp. 67-97.
– *De Instituto Christiano*, ed. W. Jaeger, *Gregorii Nysseni opera*, vol. 8.1. Leiden, 1963, pp. 40-89.
– *De Mortuis Non Esse Dolendum*, ed. G. Heil, *Gregorii Nysseni opera*, vol. 9.1. Leiden, 1967, pp. 28-68.
– *De Opificio Hominis*, PG.44.124-256.

- *De Oratione Dominica*, ed. F. Oehler, *Gregor's Bischof's von Nyssa Abhandlung von der Erschaffung des Menschen und fünf Reden auf das Gebet*, Leipzig, 1859, pp. 202-314.
- *De Pauperibus Amandis ii* (*In illud: Quatenus uni ex his fecistis mihi fecistis*, ed. A. van Heck, *Gregorii Nysseni opera*, vol. 9.1. Leiden, 1967, pp. 111-127.
- *De Perfectione Christiana ad Olympium Monachum*, ed. W. Jaeger, *Gregorii Nysseni opera*, vol. 8.1. Leiden, 1963, pp. 173-214.
- *De Professione Christiana ad Harmonium*, ed. W. Jaeger, *Gregorii Nysseni opera*, vol. 8.1, Leiden, 1963, pp. 129-142.
- *De Sancto Theodoro*, PG.46.736-748.
- *De Virginitate*, ed. M. Aubineau, *Grégoire de Nysse. Traité de la virginité*, Sources chrétiennes 119, Paris, 1966.
- *De Vita Gregorii Thaumaturgi*, PG.46.893-957.
- *De Vita Mosis*, ed. J. Danielou, *Grégoire de Nysse. La vie de Moïse*, third edition, Sources chrétiennes 1, Paris, 1968.
- *Dialogus De Anima et Resurrectione*, PG.46.12-160.
- *Encomium in Sanctum Stephanum Protomartyrem i*, ed. O. Lendle, *Gregorius Nyssenus. Encomium in sanctum Stephanum protomartyrem*. Leiden, 1968, pp. 4-44.
- *Encomium in xl Martyres ii*, PG.46.773-788.
- *Epistulae*, ed. G. Pasquali, *Gregorii Nysseni opera*, vol. 8.2, Leiden, 1959, pp. 3-95.
- *In Basilium Fratrem*, ed. J. Stein, *Encomium of Saint Gregory Bishop of Nyssa on his brother Saint Basil*. Washington, D.C. 1928.
- *In Canticum Canticorum* (*homiliae 15*), ed. H. Langerbeck, *Gregorii Nysseni opera*, vol. 6, Leiden, 1960, pp. 3-469.
- *In Christi Resurrectionem oratio i*, ed. E. Gebhardt, *Gregorii Nysseni opera*, vol. 9.1, Leiden, 1967, pp. 273-306.
- *In Diem Luminum*, ed. E. Gebhardt, *Gregorii Nysseni opera*, vol. 9.1, Leiden, 1967, pp. 221-242.
- *In Ecclesiasten* (*homiliae 8*), ed. P. Alexander, *Gregorii Nysseni opera*, vol. 5, Leiden, 1962, pp. 277-442.
- *In Illud, Tunc et Ipse Filius*, ed. J.K. Downing, *Gregorii Nysseni opera*, vol. 3.2, Leiden, 1986.
- *In illud: Quatenus uni ex his fecistis mihi fecistis*, ed. A. van Heck, *Gregorii Nysseni opera*, vol. 9.1, Leiden, 1967, pp. 111-127.
- *In Inscriptiones Psalmorum*, ed. J. McDonough, *Gregorii Nysseni opera*, vol. 5, Leiden, 1962, pp. 24-175.
- *In Sanctum et Salutare Pascha*, ed. E. Gebhardt, *Gregorii Nysseni opera*, vol. 9.1. Leiden, 1967, pp. 309-311.
- *In Sanctum Pascha*, ed. E. Gebhardt, *Gregorii Nysseni opera*, vol. 9.1. Leiden, 1967, pp. 245-270.

– *Oratio Catechetica*, ed. J. Srawley, *The catechetical oratio of Gregory of Nyssa*, Cambridge, 1956.

– *Oratio in Diem Natalem Christi*, ed. F. Mann, *Die Weihnachtspredigt Gregors von Nyssa. Überlieferungsgeschichte und Text* (Dissertation) Münster, 1975, pp. 263-292.

– *Orationes viii De Beatitudinibus*, PG.44.1193-1301.

– *Refutatio Confessionis Eunomii*, ed. W. Jaeger, *Gregorii Nysseni opera*, vol. 2.2, Leiden, 1960, pp. 312-410.

– *Vita Sanctae Macrinae*, ed. P. Maraval, *Grégoire de Nysse. Vie de sainte Macrine*, Sources chrétiennes 178, Paris, 1971, pp. 136-266.

Gregory Palamas (Metropolitan of Thessaloniki, thirteenth-fourteenth century), *Homiliae* (*i-xx*), ed. P.K. Chrestou, *Γρηγορίου τοῦ Παλαμᾶ ἅπαντα τὰ ἔργα*, vol. 9, Ἕλληνες Πατέρες τῆς Ἐκκλησίας 72, Thessalonki, 1985, pp. 26-596.

– *Orationes Antirrheticae Contra Acindynum*, eds. L. Kontogiannes – B. Phanourgakes, *Ἀντιρρητικοὶ πρὸς Ἀκίνδυνον*, in P.K. Chrestou (series editor), *Γρηγορίου τοῦ Παλαμᾶ συγγράμματα*, vol. 3, Thessalonki, 1970, pp. 39-506.

– *Orationes Dogmaticae*, ed. G. Mantzarides, "Πραγματεῖαι" in P.K. Chrestou (series editor), *Γρηγορίου τοῦ Παλαμᾶ συγγράμματα*, vol. 2, Thessaloniki, 1966, pp. 69-277.

Gregory Thaumaturgus, *Fragmentum in Evangelium Matthaei 6.22-23*, PG.10.1189.

– *In Origenem Oratio Panegyrica*, ed. H. Crouzel, *Grégoire le Thaumaturge. Remerciement à Origène suivi de la lettre d'Origène à Grégoire*, Sources chrétiennes 148, Paris, 1969, pp. 94-182.

Greorge Cedrenus, *Compendium Historiarum*, ed. I. Bekker, *Georgius Cedrenus Ioannis Scylitzae ope*, 2 vols. Corpus scriptorum historiae Byzantinae, Bonn, vol. 1: 1838; vol. 2: 1839.

Grese, W.C., *Corpus Hermeticum XIII and Early Christian Literature*, Leiden, 1979.

Hadot, Ilsetraut, "Les Introductions aux commentaires exégétiques chez les Auteurs Néoplatoniciens et les auteurs chrétiens", in Michel Tardieu (ed.), *Les règles de l'interprétation*, Paris, 1989, pp. 99-122.

Hällström, Gunnar af, "More than initiation? Baptism according to Origen of Alexandria", in David Hellholm – Tor Vegge – Øyvind Norderval – Christer Hellholm (eds.), *Ablution, Initiation, and Baptism: Late Antiquity, Early Judaism, and Early Christianity*, Berlin, 2011.

Heine, Ronald, *Origen: Scholarship in the Service of the Church*, New York, 2010.

Heinrici, C.F.G., *Die Hermes – Mystik und das Neue Testament*, ed. E. v. Dobschütz, Leipzig 1918.

Hermas, *Pastor*, ed. M. Whittaker, *Die apostolischen Väter I. Der Hirt des Hermas*, Die griechischen christlichen Schriftsteller 48, second edition, Berlin, 1967.

Hermias of Alexandria (c. 410-450, *In Platonis Phaedrum Scholia*, ed. P. Couvreur, *Hermeias von Alexandrien. In Platonis Phaedrum scholia*, Paris, 1901 (repr. Hildesheim, 1971).

Herodian of Alexandria, *De Prosodia Catholica*, ed. A. Lentz, *Grammatici Graeci*, vol. 3.1, Hildesheim, 1965.

– *Περὶ Κλίσεως 'Ονομάτων*, ed. A. Lentz, *Grammatici Graeci*, vol. 3.2, Leipzig, 1870 (repr. Hildesheim, 1965), pp. 634-777.

– *Περὶ 'Ρημάτων*, ed. A. Lentz, *Grammatici Graeci*, vol. 3.2, Leipzig, 1870 (repr. Hildesheim, 1965), pp. 787-824.

– *Περὶ Παθῶν*, ed. A. Lentz, *Grammatici Graeci*, vol. 3.2, Leipzig, 1870 (repr. Hildesheim, 1965), pp. 166-389.

Heron of Alexandria, *Χειροβαλλίστρας Κατασκευὴ καὶ Συμμετρία*, ed. V. Prou, *La chirobaliste d'Héron d'Alexandrie* (Notices et extraits des manuscrits de la Bibliothèque Nationale 26.2, Paris, 1877, pp. 116-149.

– *De Mensuris*, ed. J.L. Heiberg, Heronis Alexandrini opera quae supersunt omnia, vol. 5, Leipzig, 1914, pp. 164-218.

– *Pneumatica*, ed. W. Schmidt, Heronis Alexandrini opera quae supersunt omnia, vol. 1, Leipzig, 1899.

Hesychius of Alexandria (lexicographer, fifth-sixth century probably a pagan, not to be confused with the homonymous Egyptian bishop, *c.* 300, or the Alexandrian exegete Hesychius, also *c.* 300), *Lexicon*, ed. K. Latte, *Hesychii Alexandrini Lexicon*, vols. 1, 2, Copenhagen, vol. 1: 1953; vol. 2: 1966.

Hesychius of Jerusalem *Homilia i De Hypapante*, ed. M. Aubineau, *Les homélies festales d'Hésychius de Jérusalem, vol. 1. Les homélies i-xv*, Subsidia hagiographica 59, Brussels, 1978, pp. 24-42.

– *Commentarius Brevis*, ed. V. Jagic, *Supplementum Psalterii Bononiensis. Incerti auctoris explanatio Graeca*. Vienna, 1917.

– *Commentarius in Odas*, ed. V. Jagic, *Supplementum psalterii Bononiensis. Incerti auctoris explanatio Graeca*. Vienna, 1917, pp. 301-320.

Hicetas of Syracuse (the Pythagorean), *Testimonia*, H. Diels – W. Kranz, *Die Fragmente der Vorsokratiker*, vol. 1, sixth edition, Berlin, 1951, pp. 441-442.

Hierocles of Alexandria (Neoplatonist philosopher, fifth century), *In Aureum Carmen*, ed. F.G. Köhler, *Hieroclis in aureum Pythagoreorum carmen commentaries*, Stuttgart, 1974.

Hierocles the Stoic (second century AD), *Fragmenta Ethica*, ed. J. von Arnim, *Hierokles. Ethische Elementarlehre (Papyrus 9780)*, Berliner Klassikertexte 4, Berlin, 1906, pp. 48-63.

Hippolytus, *Commentarium in Danielem*, ed. M. Lefèvre, *Hippolyte. Commentaire sur Daniel*, Sources chrétiennes 14, Paris, 1947, pp. 70-386.

– *Contra Haeresin Noeti*, ed. R. Butterworth, *Hippolytus of Rome. Contra Noetum*, London, 1977.

– *De antichristo*, ed. H. Achelis, *Hippolyt's kleinere exegetische und homiletische Schriften*, Die griechischen christlichen Schriftsteller 1.2, Leipzig, 1897, pp. 1-47.

– *De Benedictionibus Isaaci et Jacobi*, eds. M. Brière – L. Mariès – B.C. Mercier, *Patrologia Orientalis* 27, fasc. 1-2, Paris, 1954, pp. 2-114.

– *Fragmenta in Genesim*, ed. H. Achelis, *Hippolyt's kleinere exegetische und homiletische Schriften*, GCS 1.2, Leipzig, 1897, pp. 51-53; 55-71.

– *Fragmenta in Proverbia*, ed. H. Achelis, *Hippolyt's kleinere exegetische und homiletische Schriften*, GCS 1.2, Leipzig, 1897, pp. 157-167, 176-178.

– *Refutatio Omnium Haeresium* (*Philosophumena*), ed. M. Marcovich, *Hippolytus. Refutatio omnium haeresium*, Patristische Texte und Studien 25, Berlin, 1986.

Homer, *Ilias*, eds. D.B. Morno – T.W. Allen, *Homeri Opera: Ilias,* vols. I-II, Oxford (repr.) vol. I: 1969; vol. II: 1971.

– *Odyssea*, ed. T.W. Allen, *Homeri Opera: Odyssea.* vols. III-IV, Oxford (repr.) vol. III: 1967; vol. IV: 1966.

Iamblichus, *De Communi Mathematica Scientia*, ed. U. Klein (post N. Festa), *Iamblichi de communi mathematica scientia liber,* Leipzig, 1891 (repr. Stuttgart, 1975).

– *De Mysteriis*, ed. É. des Places, *Jamblique. Les mystères d'Égypte*, Paris, 1966.

– *De Vita Pythagorica*, ed. U. Klein (post L. Deubner), *Iamblichi de vita Pythagorica liber,* Leipzig, 1937 (repr. Stuttgart, 1975).

– *In Nicomachi Arithmeticam Introductionem*, ed. U. Klein, *Iamblichi in Nicomachi arithmeticam introductionem liber*, Stuttgart, 1975.

– *Protrepticus*, ed. H. Pistelli, *Iamblichi protrepticus ad fidem codicis Florentini,* Leipzig, 1888 (repr. Stuttgart, 1967).

Ignatius Diaconus (or, Ignatius Melodus, Nicaea, Constantinople, eighth-ninth century), *Vita Nicephori*, ed. C. de Boor, *Nicephori archiepiscopi Constantinopolitani opuscula historica*, Leipzig, 1880, pp. 139-217.

Ignatius Diaconus (or, Ignatius Melodus, Nicaea, Constantinople, eighth-ninth century), *Vita Gregorii Decapolitae*, ed. G. Makris, *Ignatios Diakonos und die Vita des Hl. Gregorios Dekapolites* (*Byzantinisches* Archiv 17, Stuttgart, 1997, pp. 56-152.

Ignatius of Antioch, *Epistulae*, ed. P.T. Camelot, *Ignace d'Antioche. Polycarpe de Smyrne. Lettres. Martyre de Polycarpe*, fourth edition, Sources chrétiennes 10, Paris, 1969, pp. 56-154.

Irenaeus, *Adversus Haereses* (*liber 4*, ed. A. Rousseau – B. Hemmerdinger – L. Doutreleau – C. Mercier, *Irénée de Lyon. Contre les hérésies, livre 4*, vol. 2, Sources chrétiennes 100, Paris, 1965.

– *Adversus Haereses*, W.W. Harvey, *Sancti Irenaei episcopi Lugdunensis libri quinque adversus haereses*, vol. 1, Cambridge, 1857.

Isidore Glabas, *Oratio ad Thessalonicenses ii*, ed. C. Tsirpanlis, *"Δύο ἀνέκδοτοι ὁμιλίαι Ἰσιδώρου ἀρχιεπισκόπου Θεσσαλονίκης"*, in *Θεολογία* 42, 1971, pp. 570-581.

Isidore of Pelusium (monk, fifth century), *Epistulae* (*1414-1700*), ed. P. Évieux, *Isidore de Péluse, Lettres* (*1414-1700*), Sources chrétiennes 454, Paris, 2000.

– *Epistulae De Interpretatione Divinae Scripturae*, PG.78.177-1048.

Jacob (Coccinobaphus, monk, twelfth century), *Epistulae*, eds. E. Jeffreys – M. Jeffreys, *Iacobi Monachi Epistulae* Corpus Christianorum Series Graeca 68, Turnhout, 2009, pp. 3-182, 203-208.

– *De Fide*, eds. E. Jeffreys – M. Jeffreys, *Iacobi Monachi Epistulae*, Corpus Christianorum Series Graeca 68, Turnhout, 2009, pp. 182-202.

Jerome, *De Viris Illustribus*, PL.23.597-720.

– *Eusebii Hieronymi Stridonensis Presbyteri Commentariorum in Evangelium Matthaei ad Eusebium libri quatuor*, PL.26.15-218.

– *Sancti Hieronymi Presbyteri. Commentariorum in Matthaeum libri iv*, eds. D. Hurst – M. Adriaen Corpus Christianorum Series Latina, Turnhout, 1969.

John Argyropulos, *Prolegomena Ad Progymnasmata Rhetoricae*, ed. S.P. Lampros, *Ἀργυροπούλεια*, Athens, 1910: 175-180.

Joel of Constantinople (chronographer, thirteenth century), *Chronographia Compendiaria*, ed. I. Bekker, *Ioelis chronographia compendiaria*, Corpus scriptorum historiae Byzantinae, Bonn, 1836.

John Carpathius (bishop, seventh century), *Capita Ad Monachos in India*, PG.85.1837-1860.

– *Capita Theologica*, eds. D. Balfour – M. Cunningham, *A Supplement to the Philocalia: The Second Century of Saint John of Karpathos*, The Archbishop Iakovos Library of Ecclesiastical and Historical Sources 16, Brookline, Mass. 1994.

John Chrysostom, *Ad Eos Qui Scandalizati Sunt*, ed. A. - M. Malingrey, *Jean Chrysostome. Sur la providence de Dieu*, Sources chrétiennes 79, Paris, 1961.

– *Ad Populum Antiochenum*, PG.49.15-222.

– *Adversus Judaeos*, PG.48.843-942.

– *Catecheses ad Illuminandos*, ed. A. Wenger, *Jean Chrysostome. Huit catéchèses baptismales*, second edition, Sources chrétiennes 50, Paris, 1970, pp. 108-260.

– *Commentarius in Job*, eds. D. Hagedorn – U. Hagedorn, *Johannes Chrysostomos. Kommentar zu Hiob*, Patristische Texte und Studien 35, Berlin, 1990.

– *Contra Eos Qui Subintroductas Habent Virgines*, ed. J. Dumortier, *Saint Jean Chrysostome. Les cohabitations suspectes*, Paris, 1955, pp. 44-94.

– *Contra Ludos et Theatra*, PG.59.263-270.

– *De Consubstantiali* (*Contra Anomoeos*), PG.48.755-768.

– *De Cruce et Latrone* (homily 1), PG.49.399-408.

– *De Diabolo Tentatore*, PG.49.241-276.

– *De Futurae Vitae Deliciis*, PG.51.347-354.

– *De Inani Gloria et De Educandis Liberis*, ed. A. - M. Malingrey, *Jean Chrysostome. Sur la vaine gloire et l'éducation des enfants*, Sources chrétiennes 188, Paris, 1972, pp. 64-196.

– *De Lazaro*, PG.48.963-1054.

– *De Paenitentia*, PG.49.277-350.

– *De Sancta Pentecoste*, PG.50.453-470.
– *De Sanctis Martyribus*, PG.50.645-654.
– *De Virginitate*, eds. B. Grillet – H. Musurillo, *Jean Chrysostome. La virginité*, Sources chrétiennes 125, Paris, 1966, pp. 92-394.
– *Encomium ad Maximum* (*Quales ducendae sint uxores*), PG.51.225-242.
– *Epistulae ad Olympiadem*, ed. A.-M. Malingrey, *Jean Chrysostome. Lettres à Olympias*, second edition, Sources chrétiennes 13, Paris, 1968, pp. 106-388.
– *Expositiones in Psalmos*, PG.55.39-498.
– *Fragmenta in Jeremiam*, PG.64.740-1037.
– *Fragmenta in Job*, PG.64.505-656.
– *Fragmenta in Proverbia*, PG.64.660-740.
– *In Acta Apostolorum*, PG.60.13-384.
– *In Epistulam ad Colossenses*, PG.62.299-392.
– *In Epistulam ad Ephesios*, PG.62.9-176.
– *In Epistulam ad Hebraeos*, PG.63.9-236.
– *In Epistulam Ad Titum*, PG.62.663-700.
– *In Epistulam i ad Corinthios*, PG.61.9-382.
– *In Epistulam i ad Timotheum*, PG.62.501-600.
– *In Epistulam ii ad Corinthios*, PG.61.381-610.
– *In Genesim* (*homiliae 1-67*, PG.53.21-385; PG.54.385-580.
– *In Genesim* (*sermones 1-9*, PG.54.581-630.
– *In illud: Filius ex Se nihil facit*, PG.56.247-256.
– *In Illud: Ne Timueritis Cum Dives Factus Fuerit Homo*, PG.55.499-518.
– *In illud: Pater, Si Possibile Est, Transeat*, PG.51.31-40.
– *In Isaiam*, ed. J. Dumortier, *Jean Chrysostome. Commentaire sur Isaïe*, Sources chrétiennes 304, Paris, 1983.
– *In Joannem* (*homiliae 1-88*), PG.59.23-482.
– *In Matthaeum* (*homiliae 1-90*), PG.57.13-472; PG.58.471-794.
– *In Principium Actorum*, PG.51.65-112.
– *In Psalmos 101-107*, PG.55.635-674.
– *In Psalmum 145*, PG.55.519-528.
– *In Sanctum Julianum Martyrem*, PG.50.665-676.
– *In Sanctum Pascha*, PG.52.765-772.
– *Quod Regulares Feminae Viris Cohabitare Non Debeant*, ed. J. Dumortier, *Saint Jean Chrysostome. Les cohabitations suspectes*, Paris, 1955, pp. 95-137.

John Climacus, *Scala Paradisi*, PG.88.631-1161.

John Cyparissiotes (c. 1310-1378, Kyparissia, Constantinople), *Expositio Materiaria*, ed. B.L. Dentakes, *'Ιωάννου τοῦ Κυπαρισσιώτου τῶν Θεολογικῶν 'Ρήσεων Στοιχειώδης Ἔκθεσις*, Ἡσυχαστικαὶ καὶ Φιλοσοφικαὶ Μελέται 5, Athens 1982, pp. 17-655.
– *Contra Tomum Palamiticum*, ed. K. Liakouras, *'Ιωάννου τοῦ Κυπαρισσιώτου κατὰ τῶν τοῦ Παλαμικοῦ Τόμου διακρίσεων καὶ ἑνώσεων ἐν τῷ Θεῷ*, Athens, 1991, pp. 137-480.

– *Orationes Antirrheticae Quinque contra Nilum Cabasilam*, ed. S. Th. Marangoudakis, *Ἰωάννου τοῦ Κυπαρισσιώτου κατὰ Νείλου Καβάσιλα λόγοι πέντε ἀντιρρητικοί*, Ἡσυχαστικαὶ καὶ φιλοσοφικαὶ μελέται 13, Athens, 1985, pp. 45-288.

John Doxapatres (eleventh century), Constantinople, *Prolegomena in Aphthonii Progymnasmata*, ed. H. Rabe, *Prolegomenon Sylloge*, Rhetores Graeci 14, Leipzig, 1931, pp. 80-155.

John Grammaticus (presbyter, theologian, grammarian, Palestine, sixth century), *Disputatio cum Manichaeo*, ed. M. Richard, *Iohannis Caesariensis presbyteri et grammatici opera quae supersunt*, Corpus Christianorum Series Graeca 1, Turnhout, 1977, pp. 117-128.

John Italus (Constantinople, Italy, eleventh century), *Quaestiones Quodlibetales*, ed. P.-P. Joannou, *Joannes Italos. Quaestiones quodlibetales* (*Ἀπορίαι καὶ Λύσεις*), Studia patristica et Byzantina 4, Ettal, 1956.

John Laurentius Lydus, *De Mensibus, De Mensibus*, ed. R. Wünsch, *Ioannis Lydi liber de mensibus*, Leipzig, 1898 (repr. Stuttgart, 1967).

John Malalas, *Chronographia*, ed. L. Dindorf, *Ioannis Malalae chronographia*, Corpus scriptorum historiae Byzantinae, Bonn, 1831.

John Mauropus, *Canones in Sanctum Nicolaum*, ed. A.D. Panagiotou, *Ὁ Ἰωάννης Μαυρόπους Ὑμνογράφος τοῦ Ἁγίου Νικολάου*, Βυζαντινὴ Γραμματεία 5, Athens, 2008, pp. 33-145.

John of Alexandria (medical doctor, seventh century), *Commentarii in Hippocratis Librum De Natura Pueri*, eds. T.A. Bell – D.P. Carpenter – D.W. Schmidt – M.N. Sham – G.I. Vardon – L.G. Westerink, *John of Alexandria: Commentary on Hippocrates' On the nature of the child*, Corpus medicorum Graecorum 11.1.4, Berlin, 1997, pp. 130-174.

John of Damascus, *Contra Manichaeos*, ed. B. Kotter, *Die Schriften des Johannes von Damaskos*, vol. 4, Patristische Texte und Studien 22, Berlin, 1981, pp. 351-398.

– *Contra Jacobitas*, ed. P.B. Kotter, *Die Schriften des Johannes von Damaskos*, vol. 4, Patristische Texte und Studien 22, Berlin, 1981, pp. 109-153.

– *Contra Nestorianos*, ed. P.B. Kotter, *Die Schriften des Johannes von Damaskos*, vol. 4, Patristische Texte und Studien 22, Berlin, 1981, pp. 263-288.

– *De Fide Contra Nestorianos*, ed. P.B. Kotter, Die Schriften des Johannes von Damaskos, vol. 4, Patristische Texte und Studien 22, Berlin, 1981, pp. 238-253.

– *De Haeresibus*, ed. B. Kotter, *Die Schriften des Johannes von Damaskos*, vol. 4, Patristische Texte und Studien 22, Berlin, 1981, pp. 19-67.

– *De Sancta Trinitate* (*fragmentum*), PG.95.9-17.

– *Dialectica* sive *Capita Philosophica* (recensio fusior), ed. B. Kotter, *Die Schriften des Johannes von Damaskos*, vol. 1, Patristische Texte und Studien 7, Berlin, 1969, pp. 47-95.

– *Epistula De Hymno Trisagio*, ed. P.B. Kotter, Die Schriften des Johannes von Damaskos, vol. 4, Patristische Texte und Studien 22, Berlin, 1981, pp. 304-332.

– *Expositio Fidei*, ed. B. Kotter, *Die Schriften des Johannes von Damaskos*, vol. 2, Patristische Texte und Studien 12, Berlin, 1973.
– *Homilia in Nativitatem Domini*, ed. P.B. Kotter, *Die Schriften des Johannes von Damaskos*, vol. 5, Patristische Texte und Studien 29, Berlin – New York, 1988, pp. 324-347.
– *Institutio Elementaris*, ed. P.B. Kotter, *Die Schriften des Johannes von Damaskos*, vol. 1, Patristische Texte und Studien 7, Berlin, 1969, pp. 20-26.
– *Laudatio Sanctae Martyris Barbarae*, ed. P.B. Kotter, *Die Schriften des Johannes von Damaskos*, vol. 5, Patristische Texte und Studien 29. Berlin – New York, 1988, pp. 256-278.
– *Laudatio Sancti Johannis Chrysostomi, Laudatio Sanctae Martyris Barbarae*, ed. P.B. Kotter, *Die Schriften des Johannes von Damaskos*, vol. 5, Patristische Texte und Studien 29. Berlin – New York, 1988, pp. 359-370.
– *Oratio Prima in Dormitionem Sanctae Dei Genitricis Mariae*, ed. P.B. Kotter, *Die Schriften des Johannes von Damaskos*, vol. 5, Patristische Texte und Studien 29. Berlin – New York, 1988, pp. 483-500.
– *Orationes De Imaginibus Tres*, ed. B. Kotter, *Die Schriften des Johannes von Damaskos*, vol. 3, Patristische Texte und Studien 17, Berlin, 1975, pp. 65-200.
– *Sacra Parallela* (*recensiones secundum alphabeti litteras dispositae, quae tres libros conflant*) (*fragmenta cod. Vat. gr. 1236*), PG.95.1040-1588; PG.96.9-441.
– *Sacra Parallela* (*recensiones secundum alphabeti litteras dispositae, quae tres libros conflant*) [*fragmenta cod. Berol. B.N. gr. 46* (= *parallela Rupefucaldina*)], PG.96.441-544.
– *Sacra Parallela*, PG.95.1040-1588; PG.96.9-544.
John of Sardis, *Commentarium in Aphthonii Progymnasmata*, ed. H. Rabe, *Ioannis Sardiani commentarium in Aphthonii progymnasmata*, Rhetores Graeci 15, Leipzig, 1928.
John of Sicily (eleventh century), *Commentarium in Hermogenis Librum Περὶ Ἰδεῶν*, ed. C. Walz, Rhetores Graeci 6, Stuttgart, 1834, pp. 80-504.
John Philoponus, *De Aeternitate Mundi*, ed. H. Rabe, *Ioannes Philoponus. De aeternitate mundi contra Proclum*, Hildesheim, 1963.
– *De Opificio Mundi*, ed. W. Reichardt, *Joannis Philoponi de opificio mundi libri vii*, Leipzig, 1897.
– *De Vocabulis Quae Diversum Significatum Exhibent Secundum Differentiam Accentus*, ed. L.W. Daly, *Iohannis Philoponi de vocabulis quae diversum significatum exhibent secundum differentiam accentus*, Philadelphia, 1983.
– *In Aristotelis Analytica Posteriora Commentaria*, ed. M. Wallies, *Ioannis Philoponi in Aristotelis analytica posteriora commentaria cum Anonymo in librum ii*, Commentaria in Aristotelem Graeca 13.3, Berlin, 1909.

– *In Aristotelis Analytica Priora Commentaria*, ed. M. Wallies, *Ioannis Philoponi in Aristotelis analytica priora commentaria*, Commentaria in Aristotelem Graeca 13.2, Berlin, 1905.
– *In Aristotelis Categorias Commentarium*, ed. A. Busse, *Philoponi (olim Ammonii) in Aristotelis categorias commentarium*, Commentaria in Aristotelem Graeca 13.1, Berlin, 1898.
– *In Aristotelis Libros De Anima Commentaria*, ed. M. Hayduck, *Ioannis Philoponi in Aristotelis de anima libros commentaria*, Commentaria in Aristotelem Graeca 15, Berlin, 1897.
– *In Aristotelis Libros de Generatione et Corruptione Commentaria*, ed. H. Vitelli, *Ioannis Philoponi in Aristotelis libros de generatione et corruptione commentaria*, Commentaria in Aristotelem Graeca 14.2, Berlin, 1897.
– *In Aristotelis Meteorologicorum Librum Primum Commentarium*, ed. M. Hayduck, *Ioannis Philoponi in Aristotelis meteorologicorum librum primum commentarium*, Commentaria in Aristotelem Graeca 14.1, Berlin, 1901.
– *In Aristotelis Physicorum Libros Commentaria*, ed. H. Vitelli, *Ioannis Philoponi in Aristotelis physicorum libros octo commentaria*, 2 vols. Commentaria in Aristotelem Graeca 16 & 17, Berlin, vol. 16: 1887; vol. 17: 1888.
– *In Libros De Generatione Animalium Commentaria*, ed. M. Hayduck, *Ioannis Philoponi (Michaelis Ephesii) in libros de generatione animalium commentaria*, Commentaria in Aristotelem Graeca 14.3, Berlin, 1903.
– *In Nicomachi Arithmeticam Introductionem*, ed. G. Giardina, *Giovanni Filopono matematico tra neopitagorismo e neoplatonismo*, Catania, 1999, pp. 105-181.

John Protospatharius (grammarian, thirteenth-fourteenth century), *Ἐξήγησις Φυσικὴ τῶν Ἡμερῶν Ἡσιόδου*, ed. T. Gaisford, *Poetae minores Graeci*, vol. 2, Leipzig, 1823, pp. 448-459.

John Tzetzes (grammarian, poet, Constantinople), *Chiliades*, ed. P.L.M. Leone, *Ioannis Tzetzae historiae*, Naples, 1968.

John XI Beccus (c. 1225-March 1297, Patriarch of Constantinople, 1275-1282), *In Andronici Camateri Animadversiones, In Andronici Camateri Animadversiones*, PG.141.396-613.

John Zonaras, *Epitome Historiarum*, ed. L. Dindorf, *Ioannis Zonarae epitome historiarum*, 3 vols, Leipzig, vol. 1: 1868; vol. 2: 1869; vol. 3: 1870.
– *Epitome Historiarum*, ed. T. Büttner – Wobst, *Ioannis Zonarae epitomae historiarum libri xviii*, vol. 3, Corpus scriptorum historiae Byzantinae, Bonn, 1897.

Joseph Bryennius (Byzantine monk and writer, c. 1350-1430), *Orationes*, ed. E. Boulgares, *Ἰωσὴφ τοῦ μοναχοῦ τοῦ Βρυεννίου τὰ Εὑρεθέντα*, vol. 1, Leipzig, 1768 (repr. 1991, pp. 29-345).

Josephus, *Antiquitas Judaica*, ed. B. Niese, *Flavii Iosephi opera*, vols. 1-4, Berlin, vol. 1: 1887; vol. 2: 1885; vol. 3: 1892; vol. 4: 1890 (repr. 1955).

– *Contra Apionem* (= *De Judaeorum Vetustate*), ed. B. Niese, Flavii Iosephi opera, vol. 5, Berlin, 1889 (repr. 1955), pp. 3-99.
– *De Bello Judaico*, ed. B. Niese, *Flavii Iosephi opera*, vol. 6, Berlin, 1955, pp. 3-628.
– *Josephi Vita*, ed. B. Niese, *Flavii Iosephi opera*, vol. 4, Berlin, 1890 (repr. 1955, pp. 321-389.
Julian, emperor, *Contra Galilaeos*, ed. C.J. Neumann, *Juliani imperatoris librorum contra Christianos quae supersunt*, Leipzig, 1880, pp. 163-233.
– *'Εγκώμιον εἰς τὸν αὐτοκράτορα Κωνστάντιον*, ed. J. Bidez, *L'empereur Julien. Oeuvres complètes*, vol. 1.1, Paris, 1932, pp. 10-68.
Julian the Arian, *Commentarius in Job*, D. Hagedorn, *Der Hiobkommentar des Arianers Julian*, Patristische Texte und Studien 14, Berlin, 1973.
Julius Africanus, *Chronographiae*, ed. M.J. Routh, *Reliquiae sacrae*, vol. 2. Oxford, 1846 (repr. Hildesheim, 1974), pp. 238-308.
– *Epistula ad Aristidem*, ed. W. Reichardt, *Die Briefe des Sextus Julius Africanus an Aristides und Origene*, Texte und Untersuchungen 34.3, Leipzig, 1909, pp. 53-62.
Julius Naucratites (or, Julius Pollux, or Julius Polydeuces, grammarian, second century AD), *Onomasticon*, ed. E. Bethe, *Pollucis onomasticon*, 2 vols. Lexicographi Graeci 9.1-9.2, Stuttgart, 1967.
Justin Martyr, *Apologia*, ed. E.J. Goodspeed, *Die ältesten Apologeten*, Göttingen, 1915, pp. 26-77.
– *Apologia Secunda*, ed. E.J. Goodspeed, *Die ältesten Apologeten*. Göttingen, 1915, pp. 78-89.
– *Dialogus cum Tryphone*, ed. E.J. Goodspeed, *Die ältesten Apologeten*. Göttingen, 1915, pp. 90-265.
Justinian, *Contra Monophysitas*, eds. M. Amelotti – R. Albertella – L. Migliardi (post E. Schwartz), *Drei dogmatische Schriften Iustinians*, second edition, Legum Iustiniani imperatoris vocabularium. Subsidia 2, Milan, 1973.
– *Contra Nestorianos*, M. Amelotti – L.M. Zingale, *Scritti teologici ed ecclesiastici di Giustiniano*. Milan, 1977, pp. 32-34.
– *Edictum contra Origenem*, in ACO, *Synodus Constantinopolitana et Hierosolymitana anno 536*, ed. E. Schwartz, *Acta conciliorum oecumenicorum*, vol. 3, Berlin, 1940 (repr. 1965), pp. 189-214.
– *Edictum Rectae Fidei*, eds. R. Albertella – M. Amelotti – L. Migliardi (post E. Schwartz), *Drei dogmatische Schriften Iustinians*, second edition, Legum Iustiniani imperatoris vocabularium Subsidia 2, Milan, 1973, pp. 130-168.
– *Epistula ad Synodum De Origene*, eds. M. Amelotti – L.M. Zingale, Scritti teologici ed ecclesiastici di Giustiniano, Milan, 1977, pp. 122-124.
– *Novellae*, eds. W. Kroll – R. Schöll, *Corpus iuris civilis*, vol. 3, Berlin, 1895 (repr. 1968).

Kettler, Franz Heinrich, *Der ursprüngliche Sinn der Dogmatik des Origenes*, Berlin, 1966.

Kirner, F. De Samaranch, *Elementos egipsios en el Corpus Hermeticum*, Madrid, 1970.

Lake, K. – New, S. (eds.), *Six Collections of New Testament Manuscripts*, Harvard Theological Studies, 17, Cambridge Mass. 1932.

Lampe, G.W.H., *A Patristic Greek Lexicon*. Oxford, 1984.

Leo Diaconus (Constantinople, Metropolitan of Caria, tenth century), *Historia*, ed. K.B. Hase, *Leonis diaconi Caloënsis historiae libri decem*, Corpus scriptorum historiae Byzantinae, Bonn, 1828.

Leo VI Sapiens, emperor, *Homiliae*, ed. Th. Antonopoulou, *Leonis VI Sapientis Imperatoris Byzantini Homiliae*, Corpus Christianorum Series Graeca 63, Turnhout, 2008.

Leontius (monk, Jerusalem, sixth century), *Testimonia Sanctorum*, ed. P.T.R. Gray, *Leontius of Jerusalem Against the Monophysites: Testimonies of the Saints and Aporiae*, Oxford Early Christian Texts, Oxford, 2006, pp. 46-160.

Lévy, I., "Statues divines et animaux sacrés dans l'apologétique gréco – égyptinenne", in *Melanges Capart, Annuaire De l'Institut De Philologie et d'Histoire Orientales 3*, 1935, pp. 295-301.

Lexica Segueriana, Collectio Verborum Utilium e Differentibus Rhetoribus et Sapientibus Multis (recensio aucta e cod. Coislin. 345), ed. L. Bachmann, Anecdota Graeca 1, Leipzig, 1828.

Lexica Segueriana, Collectio Verborum Utilium e Differentibus Rhetoribus et Sapientibus Multis (Συναγωγὴ λέξεων χρησίμων ἐκ διαφόρων σοφῶν τε καὶ ῥητόρων πολλῶν), ed. C. Boysen, Lexica Graeca minora, Hildesheim, 1965.

Lexica Segueriana, *Glossae Rhetoricae* (cod. Coislin. 345), ed. I. Bekker, Anecdota Graeca 1, Berlin, 1814, pp. 195-318.

Lexicon Vindobonense, ed. A. Nauck, *Lexicon Vindobonense*, Hildesheim, 1965.

Libanius (c. 314-392 or 393), *Declamationes*, ed. R. Foerster, *Libanii opera*, vols. 5-7, Leipzig, vol. 5: 1909; vol. 6: 1911; vol. 7: 1913 (repr. Hildesheim, 1997).

– *Epistulae 1-1544*, ed. R. Foerster, *Libanii opera*, vols. 10-11, Leipzig, vol. 10: 1921; vol. 11: 1922 (repr. Hildesheim, 1997).

– *Progymnasmata*, ed. R. Foerster, *Libanii opera*, vol. 8, Leipzig, 1915 (repr. Hildesheim, 1997), pp. 24-571.

Liddell, H.G. – Scott, R., *A Greek – English Lexicon*. Oxford, 1983.

Lloyd – Jones, H. – Parsons, P. (eds.) *Supplementum Hellenisticum*, Berlin, 1983, pp. 164-172.

Lommatzsch, Karl Heinrich Eduard, (ed.) *Origenes Opera Omnia*, V, Berlin, 1835.

Longinus, *De Sublimitate* (*Περὶ Ὕψους*), ed. D.A. Russell, *'Longinus' On the sublime*, Oxford, 1964.

Lucian of Samosata, *De Morte Peregrini*, ed. A.M. Harmon, *Lucian*, vol. 5, Cambridge Mass. 1936 (repr. 1972), pp. 2-50.

– *Dialogi Meretricii*, ed. M.D. Macleod, *Lucian*, vol. 7, Cambridge Mass. 1961, pp. 356-466.

– *Philopseudes sive Incredulous*, ed. A.M. Harmon, *Lucian*, vol. 3, Cambridge Mass. 1921 (repr. 1969), pp. 320-80.

– *Pro Imaginibus*, ed. A.M. Harmon, *Lucian*, vol. 4, Cambridge Mass. 1925 (repr. 1961), pp. 298-334.

– *Pseudologista*, ed. A.M. Harmon, *Lucian*, vol. 5, Cambridge Mass. 1936 (repr. 1972), pp. 372-414.

– *Quomodo Historia Conscribenda Sit*, ed. K. Kilburn, *Lucian*, vol. 6, Cambridge, Mas. 1959 (repr. 1968), pp. 2-72.

– *Revivescentes*, ed. A.M. Harmon, *Lucian*, vol. 3, Cambridge Mass. 1921 (repr. 1969), pp. 2-80.

– *Vitarum Auctio*, ed. A.M. Harmon, *Lucian*, vol. 2, Cambridge Mass. 1915, pp. 450-510.

Lysias, *Περὶ τῆς Εὐάνδρου Δοκιμασίας*, ed. C. Carey, *Lysiae orationes cum fragmentis*. Oxford, 2007, pp. 246-252.

Macarius Chrysocephalus (Metropolitan of Philadelphia, paroemiographer, fourteenth century), *Paroemiae*, ed. E.L. von Leutsch, Corpus paroemiographorum Graecorum 2. Göttingen, 1851 (repr. Hildesheim, 1958) pp. 135-227.

Macarius Macres, *Monodia in David Hieromonachum*, ed. A. Argyriou, *Μακαρίου τοῦ Μακρῆ συγγράμματα*, Βυζαντινὰ Κείμενα καὶ Μελέται 25, Thessaloniki, 1996, pp. 227-234.

Macarius of Magnesia (bishop, fourth-fifth century), *Μονογενής*, ed. R. Goulet, *Macarios de Magnésie, Le monogénès*, tome II, Paris, 2003.

Mansfeld, Jaap, *Prolegomena: Questions to Be Settled before the Study of an Author, or a Text*, Philosophia Antiqua 61, Leiden, 1994.

Manuel Calecas, *De Principiis Catholicae Fidei*, PG.152.429-661.

– *De Essentia et Operatione*, PG.152.284-428.

Manuel II Palaeologus (1350-1425, emperor, *Oratio in Dormitionem Deiparae*, ed. S. Eustratiades, *"Ὁ οἰκουμενικὸς πατριάρχης Κάλλιστος ὡς ἐκκλησιαστικὸς ῥήτωρ, Ἐκκλησιαστικὸς Φάρος*, 8, 1911, pp. 114-119.

Marcellus of Ancyra, *Fragmenta*, eds. E. Klostermann – G.C. Hansen, *Eusebius Werke*, vol. 4, second edition, GCS 14, Berlin, 1972, pp. 185–215.

Marcus Aurelius Antoninus (121-180 AD, emperor), *Τὰ εἰς Ἑαυτόν*, ed. A.S.L. Farquharson, *The meditations of the emperor Marcus Aurelius*, vol. 1, Oxford, 1944 (repr. 1968).

Marcus Eugenicus (Constantinople, Metropolitan of Ephesus, fourteenth-fifteenth century), *Epistulae*, ed. L. Petit, *Marci Eugenici Metropolitae Ephesi opera anti – unionistica*, 10/2, Concilium Florentinum documenta et scriptores, Rome, 1977, pp. 152-156; 162-175.

– *Libellus De Consecratione Eucharistica*, ed. L. Petit, *Marci Eugenici Metropolitae Ephesi opera anti – unionistica*, 10/2, Concilium Florentinum documenta et scriptores, Rome, 1977, pp. 118-126.
– *Testimonia Spiritum Sanctum ex Patre Procedere Probantia*, ed. L. Petit, *Marci Eugenici Metropolitae Ephesi opera anti – unionistica*, 10/2, Concilium Florentinum documenta et scriptores, Rome, 1977, pp. 34-59.
Marcus Monachus, *Florilegium*, ed. P. Roelli, *Marci Monachi opera ascetica: florilegium et sermones tres*, Corpus Christianorum Series Graeca 72, Turnhout, 2009.
Marinus of Neapolis (Samarea, a pupil of Proclus, fifth century), *Vita Procli*, ed. R. Masullo, *Marino di Neapoli. Vita di Proclo*, Naples, 1985, pp. 57-93.
Matthaeus Blastares (monk, theologian, Thessaloniki, fourteenth century), *Collectio Alphabetica*, eds. M. Potles – G.A. Rhalles, *Σύνταγμα τῶν θείων καὶ ἱερῶν κανόνων τῶν τε ἁγίων καὶ πανευφήμων ἀποστόλων, καὶ τῶν ἱερῶν οἰκουμενικῶν καὶ τοπικῶν συνόδων, καὶ τῶν κατὰ μέρος ἁγιῶν πατέρων*, Athens, 1859.
Maximus Confessor, *Ambigua Ad Joannem*, ed. N. Constas, *On Difficulties in the Church Fathers: The Ambigua*, vols. 1-2, Dumbarton Oaks Medieval Library, 2 vols, Cambridge Mass. 2014.
– *Ambigua ad Thomam*, ed. B. Janssens, *Maximi Confessoris Ambigua ad Thomam una cum Epistula secunda ad eundem*, Corpus Christianorum Series Graeca 48, Turnhout, 2002, pp. 37-49.
– *Epistula Secunda ad Thomam*, ed. B. Janssens, *Maximi Confessoris Ambigua ad Thomam una cum Epistula secunda ad eundem*, Corpus Christianorum Series Graeca 48, Turnhout, 2002, pp. 37-49.
– *Expositio in Psalmum lix*, ed. P. van Deun, *Maximi confessoris opuscula exegetica duo*, Corpus Christianorum Series Graeca 23, Turnhout, 1991, pp. 3-22.
– *Mystagogia*, ed. R. Cantarella, *S. Massimo Confessore. La mistagogia ed altri scritti*, Florence, 1931, pp. 122-214.
– *Quaestiones Ad Thalassium*, eds. C. Laga – C. Steel, *Maximi confessoris quaestiones ad Thalassium*, 2 vols. Corpus Christianorum Series Graeca 7 & 22, Turnhout, vol. 1: 1980; vol. 2: 1990.
– *Quaestiones et Dubia*, ed. J.H. Declerck, *Maximi confessoris quaestiones et dubia*, Corpus Christianorum Series Graeca 10, Turnhout, 1982.
Maximus of Tyre (sophist, second century AD), *Dissertationes*, ed. M.B. Trapp, *Maximus Tyrius Dissertationes*, Bibliotheca scriptorum Graecorum et Romanorum Teubneriana, Stuttgart – Leipzig, 1994.
Meletius of Tiberiopolis (medical doctor, probably, seventh to ninth century), *De Natura Hominis*, ed. J.A. Cramer, *Anecdota Graeca codices: manuscriptis bibliothecarum Oxoniensium*, vol. 3, Oxford, 1836 (repr. Amsterdam, 1963).
Menander, *Sententiae*, ed. S. Jäkel, *Menandri Sententiae*, Leipzig, 1964, pp. 33-83.

Methodius of Olympus, *Symposium*, eds. V.-H. Debidour – H. Musurillo, *Méthode d'Olympe. Le banquet*, Sources chrétiennes 95, Paris, 1963.

Michael Apostolius (paroemiographer, c. 1420, Constantinople; he died in 1474 or 1486, possibly in the Venetian Crete), *Collectio Paroemiarum*, ed. E.L. von Leutsch, Corpus paroemiographorum Graecorum 2, Göttingen, 1851 (repr. Hildesheim, 1958), pp. 233-744.

– *Collectio Paroemiarum*, ed. E.L. von Leutsch, Corpus paroemiographorum Graecorum 2, Göttingen, 1851 (repr. Hildesheim, 1958), pp. 233-744.

Michael Attaliates (patricius, Constantinople, eleventh century), *Historia*, ed. I. Bekker, *Michaelis Attaliotae historia* Corpus scriptorum historiae Byzantinae, Bonn, 1853.

Michael Choniates (or Michael Acominatus, Metropolitan of Athens, twelfth-thirteenth century), *Orationes*, ed. S.P. Lampros, *Μιχαὴλ 'Ακομινάτου τοῦ χωνιάτου τὰ σωζόμενα*, Athens, vol. 2, 1879-1880.

Michael Glycas (historian, astrologer, Constantinople, twelfth century), *Annales*, ed. I. Bekker, *Michaelis Glycae annales*, Corpus scriptorum historiae Byzantinae, Bonn, 1836.

– *Proverbia*, ed. S. Eustratiades, *Μιχαὴλ τοῦ Γλυκᾶ, Εἰς τὰς ἀπορίας τῆς Θείας Γραφῆς*, Athens, P.D. Sakellarios, 1906.

– *Quaestiones in Sacram Scripturam*, ed. S. Eustratiades, *Μιχαὴλ τοῦ Γλυκᾶ, Εἰς τὰς ἀπορίας τῆς Θείας Γραφῆς*, Alexandria, 1912.

– *Versus in Carcere Scripti*, ed. E.T. Tsolakes, *Μιχαὴλ Γλυκᾶ στίχοι, οὓς ἔγραψε καθ' ὃν κατεσχέθη καιρόν*, 'Επιστημονικὴ 'Επετηρὶς Φιλοσοφικῆς Σχολῆς, Παράρτημα 3, Thessaloniki, 1959, pp. 3-22.

Michael III of Anchialus (Patriarch of Constantinople, 1170-1178), *Epistula ad Alexandrum III Papam*, ed. G. Hofmann, "Papst und Patriarch unter Kaiser Manuel I. Komnenos. Ein Briefwechsel", *'Επετηρὶς 'Εταιρείας Βυζαντινῶν Σπουδῶν*, 23, 1953, pp. 77-80.

Michael of Ephesus (Aristotelian commentator, fl. early or mid – twelfth century), *In Ethica Nicomachea ix-x Commentaria*, ed. G. Heylbut, *Eustratii et Michaelis et anonyma in ethica Nicomachea commentaria*, in Commentaria in Aristotelem Graeca 20, Berlin, 1892, pp. 461-620.

– *In Aristotelis Sophisticos Elenchos Commentarius* (Pseudo – Alexander of Aphrodisias), ed. M. Wallies, *Alexandri quod fertur in Aristotelis sophisticos elenchos commentarium*, Commentaria in Aristotelem Graeca 2.3, Berlin, 1898.

– *In Librum De Animalium Incessu Commentarium*, ed. M. Hayduck, *Michaelis Ephesii in libros de partibus animalium, de animalium motione, de animalium incessu commentaria*, Commentaria in Aristotelem Graeca 22.2, Berlin, 1904, pp. 135-170.

– *In Librum Quintum Ethicorum Nicomacheorum Commentarium*, ed. M. Hayduck, *Michaelis Ephesii in librum quintum ethicorum Nicomacheorum commentarium*, Commentaria in Aristotelem Graeca 22.3, Berlin, 1901, pp. 1-72.

– *In Libros De Animalium Motione Commentarium*, ed. M. Hayduck, *Michaelis Ephesii in libros de partibus animalium, de animalium motione, de animalium incessu commentaria*, Commentaria in Aristotelem Graeca 22.2, Berlin, 1904, pp. 103-31.
– *In Libros De Partibus Animalium Commentaria*, ed. M. Hayduck, *Michaelis Ephesii in libros de partibus animalium, de animalium motione, de animalium incessu commentaria*, Commentaria in Aristotelem Graeca 22.2, Berlin, 1904.
– In Parva Naturalia Commentaria, ed. P. Wendland, *Michaelis Ephesii in parva naturalia commentaria*, Commentaria in Aristotelem Graeca 22.1, Berlin, 1903.
Michael Psellus, *Chronographia*, ed. É. Renauld, *Michel Psellos. Chronographie ou histoire d'un siècle de Byzance (976-1077)*, 2 vols, Paris, vol. 1: 1926; vol. 2: 1928 (repr. 1967).
– *De Omnifaria Doctrina*, ed. L.G. Westerink, *Michael Psellus, De omnifaria doctrina*, Nijmegen, 1948, pp. 17-108.
– *Encomium in Matrem*, ed. U. Criscuolo, *Michele Psello. Autobiografia: encomio per la madre*, Naples, 1989, pp. 85-153.
– *Epistulae*, ed. E.V. Maltese, "Epistole inedite di Michele Psello I-III," *Studi italiani di filologia classica* 3 (1987-88).
– *Historia Brevis*, ed. W.J. Aerts, *Michaelis Pselli Historia Syntomos*, Corpus Fontium Historiae Byzantinae, Series Berolinensis 30, Berlin – New York, 1990.
– *In Aristotelis Physicorum Libros Commentarium*, ed. G. Benakis, *Michael Psellos Kommentar zur Physik des Aristoteles*, Corpus Philosophorum Medii Aevi, Commentaria in Aristotelem Byzantina 5, Athens, 2008.
– *Opuscula Logica, Physica, Allegorica, Alia*, ed. J.M. Duffy, Michaelis Pselli philosophica minora, Leipzig, 1992.
– *Opuscula Psychologica, Theologica, Daemonologica*, ed. D.J. O'Meara, Michaelis Pselli philosophica minora, vol. 2, Leipzig, 1989.
– *Orationes Forenses et Acta*, ed. T. Dennis, *Michaelis Pselli orationes forenses et acta*, Stuttgart, 1994.
– *Orationes Funebres*, ed. J. Polemis, *Michael Psellus Orationes funebres*, vol. 1, Bibliotheca scriptorum Graecorum et Romanorum Teubneriana, Berlin – Boston, 2014.
– *Orationes Hagiographicae*, ed. E.A. Fisher, *Michaelis Pselli orationes hagiographicae*, Stuttgart, 1994.
– *Orationes Panegyricae*, ed. G.T. Dennis, *Michaelis Pselli orationes panegyricae.* Stuttgart, 1994.
– *Poemata*, ed. L.G. Westerink, *Michaelis Pselli poemata.* Stuttgart, 1992.
– *Theologica*, ed. P. Gautier, *Michaelis Pselli theologica*, vol. 1, Leipzig, 1989.
Nautin, Pierre, *Origène, Sa vie et son oeuvre*, Paris, 1977.
Nemesius of Emesa (bishop, fourth century AD), *De Natura Hominis*, M. Morani, *Nemesii Emeseni de natura hominis*, Leipzig, 1987.

Neophytus Inclusus (monk, presbyter, Cyprus, died in 1219), *Commentarius in Hexaemeron Genesim* (*Ἑρμηνεία εἰς τὴν ἑξαήμερον γένεσιν*), ed. Th. Detorakes, "Ἑρμηνεία τῆς ἑξαημέρου", in (series editors) D.G. Tsames – N. Zacharopoulos – C. Oikonomou – I. Karabidopoulos, *Ἁγίου Νεοφύτου τοῦ Ἐγκλείστου Συγγράμματα*, vol. 4, Πάφος: Ἱερὰ Βασιλικὴ καὶ Σταυροπηγιακὴ Μονὴ Ἁγίου Νεοφύτου, 2001, pp. 45-144.

– *Liber Catechesium*, ed. P. Sotiroudis, "Βίβλος τῶν κατηχήσεων", in (series editors) D.G. Tsames – N. Zacharopoulos – C. Oikonomou – I. Karabidopoulos, *ÔAgivou Neofuvtou tou` ΔEgkleivstou Suggravmmata*, vol. 2, Πάφος: Ἱερὰ Βασιλικὴ καὶ Σταυροπηγιακὴ Μονὴ Ἁγίου Νεοφύτου, 1998, pp. 189-431.

– *Decem Homiliae*, ed. I.E. Stephanes, "Δέκα λόγοι περί τοῦ Χριστοῦ ἐντολῶν", in (series editors) D.G. Tsames – N. Zacharopoulos – C. Oikonomou – I. Karabidopoulos, *Ἁγίου Νεοφύτου τοῦ Ἐγκλείστου Συγγράμματα*, vol. 2, Πάφος: Ἱερὰ Βασιλικὴ καὶ Σταυροπηγιακὴ Μονὴ Ἁγίου Νεοφύτου, 1996, pp. 35-212.

Neophytus Prodromenus (monk, Constantinople, Thessaloniki, Edessa, fourteenth century), *Contra Latinos*, ed. B. Kalogeropoulou – Metallinou, *Ὁ μοναχός Νεόφυτος Προδρομηνὸς καὶ τὸ θεολογικὸ του ἔργο*, Athens, 1996, pp. 213-335.

Neuschäfer, Bernard, *Origenes als Philologe*, Schweizerische Beiträge zur Altertumswissenschaft 18/1-2, Basel, 1987.

Nicander of Colophon (second century B.C.), *Theriaca*, eds. A.S.F. Gow – A.F. Scholfield, *Nicander. The poems and poetical fragments*, Cambridge, 1953, pp. 28-92.

Nicephorus (monk, philosopher, Constantinople, ninth-tenth century), *Encomium in Patriarcham Antonium II Cauleam*, ed. P.L.M. Leone, "L' 'Encomium in patriarcham Antonium II Cauleam' del filosofo e retore Niceforo," *Orpheus* n.s. 10 (1989), pp. 412-429.

Nicephorus Blemmydes (scholar and theologian, clergyman, 1197-1272), *Fragmentum ex Typico (cap. 4)*, ed. J.A. Munitiz, "A missing chapter from the typikon of Nikephoros Blemmydes", *Revue des études byzantines* 44 (1986), pp. 204-205.

– *Conspectus Geographiae*, ed. K. Müller, *Geographi Graeci Minores* 2, Paris, 1861 (repr. Hildesheim, 1965), pp. 458-468.

Nicephorus Callistus Xanthopulus (thirteenth-fourteenth century), *Historia Ecclesiastica*, PG.145.560–1332; 146.9-1273; 147.9-448.

Nicephorus Gregoras (Byzantine astronomer and historian, c. 1295-1360), *Historia Romana*, eds. I. Bekker – L. Schopen, *Nicephori Gregorae historiae Byzantinae*, 3 vols. Corpus scriptorum historiae Byzantinae, Bonn, vol. 1: 1829; vol. 2: 1830; vol. 3: 1855.

– *Explicatio in Librum Synesii De Insomniis*, ed. P. Pietrosanti, *Nicephori Gregorae explicatio in librum Synesii 'De insomniis'*, Bari, 1999.

Nicephorus I of Constantinople (Patriarch, c. 758-April 5, 828), *Eusebii Caesariensis Confutatio*, ed. J.B. Pitra, *Sancti Nicephori Antirrheticus liber quartus*, Spicilegium Solesmense 1, Paris, 1852, pp. 373-503.

– *Refutatio et Eversio Definitionis Synodalis anni 815*, ed. J. Featherstone, *Nicephori Patriarchae Constantinopolitani Refutatio et Eversio Definitionis Synodalis Anni 815*, Corpus Christianorum Series Graeca 33, Turnhout, 1997.

– *Adversus Iconomachos*, ed. J.B. Pitra, *Sancti Nicephori Antirrheticus liber quartus*, Spicilegium Solesmense 4, Paris, 1858, pp. 233-291.

– *Pseudo – Epiphanii sive Epiphanidis Confutatio*, ed. J.B. Pitra, *Sancti Nicephori Antirrheticus liber quartus*, Spicilegium Solesmense 4, Paris, 1858, pp. 292-380.

Nicetas David (or, Nicetas of Paphlagonia, Constantinople and Paphlagonia, philosopher, grammarian, theologian, 761/62-6 October 836), *Laudatio in Gregorium Theologum*, ed. J. Rizzo, *The Encomium of Gregory Nazianzen by Nicetas the Paphlagonian* Subsidia hagiographica 58, Brussels, 1976, pp. 19-79.

– *Encomium in Apostolum Petrum*, ed. A. Vogt, *Panégyrique de St. Pierre* (*Orientalia Christiana* 23, Rome, 1931, pp. 24-56.

Nicetas Seides (Constantinople, twelfth century), *Oratio Contra Eustratium Nicaeensem*, ed. Th. Zeses, “Νικήτα Σεΐδου Λόγος κατὰ Εὐστρατίου Νικαίας,” *Ἐπιστημονικὴ Ἐπετηρὶς Θεολογικῆς Σχολῆς*, 19 (Supplement), Thessaloniki, 1976, pp. 35-82.

Nicolas Hydruntinus, *Disputatio Contra Judaeos*, ed. M. Chronz, *Νεκταρίου, ἡγουμένου μονῆς Κασούλων Νικολάου Ὑδρουντίνου Διάλεξις κατὰ Ἰουδαίων*, Athens, 2009.

Nicolas of Methone (bishop, twelfth century), *Orationes*, ed. A. Demetrakopoulos, Ἐκκλησιαστικὴ Βιβλιοθήκη, vol. 1, Leipzig, 1866 (repr. 1965), pp. 219-380.

– *Ad Magnum Domesticum*, ed. A. Demetrakopoulos, Ἐκκλησιαστικὴ Βιβλιοθήκη, vol. 1, Leipzig, 1866 (repr. 1965), pp. 199-218.

– *Refutatio Institutionis Theologicae Procli*, ed. A.D. Angelou, *Nicholas of Methone. Refutation of Proclus' elements of Theology*, Corpus philosophorum Medii Aevi. Philosophi Byzantini 1, Athens, Academy of Athens, 1984.

Nicolas V (1397-1455, Pope 1447-1455, born Tommaso Parentucelli), *Epistula ad Imperatorum Romanorum Constantinum Translata De Voce Latina in Vocem Graecam Theodoro Gazae*, ed. S.P. Lampros, *Παλαιολόγεια καὶ Πελοποννησιακά*, Δ. Athens, 1930, pp. 49-63.

Nicomachus of Gerasa, *Introductio Arithmetica*, ed. R. Hoche, *Nicomachi Geraseni Pythagorei introductionis arithmeticae libri ii*, Leipzig, 1866.

– *Harmonicum Enchiridion*, ed. K. Jan, *Musici scriptores Graeci*, Leipzig, 1895 (repr. Hildesheim, 1962), pp. 236-265.

Nilus Cabasilas, *De Processione Spiritus Sancti*, ed. M. Candal, *Nilus Cabasilas et Theologia S. Thomae de Processione Spiritus Sancti*, Studi e Testi 116, Vatican City, 1945, pp. 188-384.

Nilus Cabasilas, *Orationes Quinque De Spiritu Sancto*, ed. Th. Kislas, *Nil Cabasilas sur le Saint – Esprit,* Paris, 2001, pp. 174-416.

Nilus of Ancyra (abbot, fifth century), *Commentarii in Canticum Canticorum*, ed. M.-G. Guérard, *Nil d'Ancyre. Commentaire sur le Cantique des cantiques*, Sources chrétiennes 403, Paris, 1994.

– *Εἰς τὸ τῶν Ἀσμάτων Ἆσμα*, ed. H.-U. Rosenbaum, *Nilus von Ancyra Schriften: Kommentar zum Hoehelid*, 1. Berlin – New York, 2004.

– *Epistulae*, PG.79.58-582.

– *Narrationes Septem De Monachis in Sina*, ed. F. Conca, *Nilus Ancyranus. Narratio*, *Leipzig*, 1983.

Nonnus of Panopolis (fifth century AD), *Dionysiaca*, ed. R. Keydell, *Nonni Panopolitani Dionysiaca*, 2 vols, Berlin, 1959.

Numenius of Apamea (second century AD), *Fragmenta*, ed. É. des Places, *Numénius. Fragments*, Paris, 1974.

Oecumenius, *Commentarius in Apocalypsin*, ed. H.C. Hoskier, *The Complete Commentary of Oecumenius on the Apocalypse*, Ann Arbor, 1928.

Olessner, M. "Hermes Trismegistus and Arab Science", *Studia Islamica* 2, 1954, pp. 44-59.

Olympiodorus, the deacon of Alexandria (sixth century), *Commentarii in Ecclesiasten*, PG.93.477-628.

– *Commentarii in Jeremiam*, PG.93.628-725.

– *Commentarii in Job*, eds. D. Hagedorn – U. Hagedorn, *Olympiodor Diakon von Alexandria. Kommentar zu Hiob*, Patristische Texte und Studien 24, Berlin, 1984.

Olympiodorus, the philosopher of Alexandria (sixth century), *In Aristotelis Meteora Commentaria*, ed. G. Stüve, *Olympiodori in Aristotelis meteora commentaria*, Commentaria in Aristotelem Graeca 12.2, Berlin, 1900.

– *In Platonis Alcibiadem Commentarii*, ed. L.G. Westerink, *Olympiodorus. Commentary on the first Alcibiades of Plato*, Amsterdam, 1956 (repr. 1982).

– *In Platonis Phaedonem Commentaria*, ed. L.G. Westerink, *The Greek commentaries on Plato's Phaedo*, vol. 1 [*Olympiodorus*], Amsterdam, 1976, pp. 39-181.

– *Prolegomena*, ed. A. Busse, *Olympiodori prolegomena et in categorias commentarium*, Commentaria in Aristotelem Graeca 12.1, Berlin, 1902, pp. 1-25.

Oribasius of Pergamum (c. 320-403), *Collectiones Medicae*, ed. J. Raeder, *Oribasii collectionum medicarum reliquiae*, vols. 1-4, Corpus medicorum Graecorum 6.1.1-6.2.2, Leipzig, 1928-1933.

– *Libri ad Eunapium*, ed. J. Raeder, *Oribasii synopsis ad Eustathium et libri ad Eunapium*, Corpus medicorum Graecorum 6.3, Leipzig, 1926 (repr. Amsterdam, 1964).

Origen, *Adnotationes in Deuteronomium*, PG.17.24-36.

– *Adnotationes in Genesim*, PG.17.12-16.

– *Adnotationes in Jesu Nave* (fragmenta), PG.17.36-37.

– *Adnotationes in Leviticum*, PG.17.17-22.

– *Adnotationes in Numeros*, PG.17.12-16.

– *Commentarii in Epistulam ad Romanos* (*cod. Athon. Laura 184 B64*), ed. O. Bauernfeind, *Der Römerbrieftext des Origenes nach dem codex von der Goltz*, Texte und Untersuchungen 44.3, Leipzig, 1923, pp. 91-119.

– *Commentarii in Epistulam ad Romanos (cod. Vindob. gr. 166)*, ed. K. Staab, "Neue Fragmente aus dem Kommentar des Origenes zum Römerbrief," *Biblische Zeitschrift* 18, 1928, pp. 74-82.
– *Commentarii in Epistulam ad Romanos (I.1-XII.21)*, ed. A. Ramsbotham, "Documents: The commentary of Origen on the epistle to the Romans," *Journal of Theological Studies* 13 & 14, 1912; v. 13, pp. 210-224, 357-368; v. 14, pp. 10-22.
– *Commentarii in Evangelium Joannis* (lib. I, II, IV, V, VI, X, XIII), ed. C. Blanc, *Origène. Commentaire sur saint Jean*, 3 vols, Sources chrétiennes 120, 157, 222, Paris, vol. 1: 1966; vol. 2: 1970; vol. 3: 1975.
– *Commentarii in Evangelium Joannis* (lib. XIX, XX, XXVIII, XXXII), ed. E. Preuschen, Origenes Werke, vol. 4, GCS 10, Leipzig, 1903, pp. 298-480.
– *Commentarii in Genesim* (fragmenta), PG.12.45-92.
– *Commentarii in Romanos (III.5-V.7)*, ed. J. Scherer, *Le commentaire d'Origène sur Rom. III.5-V.7*, Cairo, 1957, pp. 124-232.
– *Commentariorum Series in Matthaeum*, eds. E. Klostermann – E. Benz, Origenes Werke, vol. 11, GCS, 38.2, Leipzig 1933.
– *Commentarium in Evangelium Matthaei liri 12-17*, ed. E. Klostermann, Origenes Werke, v. 10.1-10.2, GCS 40.1-40.2. Leipzig. v. 10.1: 1935; v. 10.2: 1937.
– *Commentarium in Evangelium Matthaei*, eds. Ernst Benz – Erich Klostermann, *Origenes Matthauserklärung*, Leipzig, 1937. GCS 40: Origenes Werke X, *Commentarius in Matthaeum I* (Greek text of books 10-17). GCS 38: Origenes Werke XI, *Commentarius in Matthaeum II*. GCS 41.1, 41.2: Origenes Werke XII, *Commentarius in Matthaeum III* (quotations from other early Christians works, as well as fragments from catenae).
– *Commentary on Genesis*, ed. Karin Metzler, *Origenes – Die Kommentiergung des Buches Genesis*, Band 1/1, Berlin 2010.
– *Commentary on the Epistle to the Romans* 1-5 (Latin), English tr. Thomas P. Scheck, Washington D.C. 2001.
– *Commentary on the Epistle to the Romans* 6-10 (Latin), English tr. Thomas P. Scheck, Washington D.C. 2002.
– *Contra Celsum*, Books 1-4; P. Koetschau, GCS 1 (1899), pp. 51ff, PG.11.641f. Books 5-8, GCS 1, p. 1ff, PG.11.1181ff.
– *Contra Celsum*, ed. M. Marcovich, Leiden, 2001.
– *De Engastrimytho*, ed. E. Klostermann, Origenes Werke, vol. 3, GCS 6, Leipzig, 1901, pp. 283-294.
– *De Oratione*, ed. P. Koetschau, Origenes Werke, v. 2. GCS 3, Leipzig, 1899, pp. 297-403. PG.11.416f.
– *De Pascha*, ed. B. Witte, *Die Schrift des Origenes "Über das Passa"*, Arbeiten zum spätantiken und koptischen Ägypten 4, Altenberge, 1993, pp. 88-148.

- *De Principiis* (Lat. with Greek frs.), P. Koetschau, GCS 5, 1913. PG.11.115.
- *De Principiis*, eds. H. Crouzel – M. Simonetti, *Origène, Traité des Principes,* Paris, 5 vols. 1978-1984.
- *De Resurrectione Libri II* (fragmenta), PG.11.96.20 (rendered by Methodius of Olympus).
- *Dialogus cum Heraclide*, ed. J. Scherer, *Entretien d'Origène avec Héraclide*, Sources chrétiennes 67, Paris, 1960, pp. 52-110.
- *Epistula ad Africanum*, PG.11.48-85.
- *Epistula ad Gregorium Thaumaturgum*, ed. P. Koetschau, *Des Gregorios Thaumaturgos Dankrede an Origenes*, Freiburg, 1894, pp. 40-44.
- *Excerpta in Psalmos*, PG.17.105-149.
- *Exhortatio ad Martyrium*, ed. P. Koetschau, Origenes Werke, v. 1. GCS 2, Leipzig, 1899, pp. 3-47.
- *Expositio in Proverbia* (fragmenta ex commentariis in Proverbia e catenis), PG.13.17.161-252.
- *Fragmenta De Principiis*, eds. H. Görgemanns – H. Karpp, *Origenes vier Bücher von den Prinzipien*, Darmstadt, 1976.
- *Fragmenta Alia De Principiis*, eds. H. Görgemanns – H. Karpp, *Origenes vier Bücher von den Prinzipien*, Darmstadt, 1976.
- *Fragmenta ex Commentariis in Epistulam ad Ephesios*, ed. J.A.F. Gregg, "Documents: The commentary of Origen upon the epistle to the Ephesians," *Journal of Theological Studies* 3, 1902, pp. 234-244; 398-420.
- *Fragmenta ex commentariis in epistulam i ad Corinthios*, ed. C. Jenkins, "Documents: Origen on I Corinthians," *Journal of Theological Studies* 9 & 10 (1908); v. 9, pp. 232-47, 353-72, 500-14; v. 10: pp. 29-51.
- *Fragmenta ex commentariis in evangelium Matthaei*, eds. E. Benz – E. Klostermann, Origenes Werke, vol. 12, GCS 41.1, Leipzig, 1941.
  Origenes Matthäuserklärung III, (erste Hälfte: Fragmente und Indices), ed. E. Klostermann, (unter Mitwirkung von Ernst Benz), Origenes Werke *XII*, GCS 41.1, Leipzig, 1941.
- *Fragmenta ex commentariis in Exodum* (*In illud: Induravit dominus cor Pharaonis*), PG.12.281-297.
- *Fragmenta ex Commentariis in Genesim*, PG.12.45-92.
- *Fragmenta ex commentariis in Proverbia*, PG.13.17-33.
- *Fragmenta in Evangelium Joannis*, ed. E. Preuschen, Origenes Werke, v. 4. GCS 10, Leipzig, 1903, pp. 483-574.
- *Fragmenta in evangelium Matthaei*, ed. E. Klostermann, GCS, Origenes Werke, v. 12, Leipzig, 1941.
- *Fragmenta in Jeremiam*, ed. E. Klostermann, Origenes Werke, vol. 3, GCS 6, Leipzig, 1901, pp. 199-232.

– *Fragmenta in Lamentationes*, ed. E. Klostermann, Origenes Werke, vol. 3, GCS 6, Leipzig, 1901, pp. 235-278.
– *Fragmenta in Librum Primum Regnorum*, ed. E. Klostermann, Origenes Werke, vol. 3, GCS 6, Leipzig, 1901, pp. 295-303.
– *Fragmenta in Lucam*, ed. M. Rauer, Origenes Werke, vol. 9, second edition, GCS 49 (35), Berlin 1959, pp. 227-336.
– *Fragmenta in Matthaeum* (in catenis)), ed. J. Reuss, *Matthäus – Kommentare aus der griechischen Kirche*, Texte und Untersuchungen 61, Berlin, 1957.
– *Fragmenta in Matthaeum*, eds. E. Klostermann – E. Benz, Origenes Werke XII I. *Origenes Matthauserklarung III. Fragmente und Indices*, GCS 41, 1, Leipzig 1941. Revised edition of the Indices by E. Klostermann and L. Friichtel, GCS 41, 2; Berlin 1955.
– *Fragmenta in Psalmos 1-150*, ed. J.B. Pitra, *Analecta sacra spicilegio Solesmensi parata*, vols. 2 & 3.2, Farnborough, 1966; vol. 3, Venice, 1883.
– *Homiliae 1-16 in Genesim* (Lat.), W.A. Baehrens GCS 6 (1922, p. 1. PG.12.145; Greek fr. of *Hom. 2 in Gen.* GCS 6, p. 23. PG.12.161; *apud* Procopius of Gaza, *Commentarium in Octateuchum* (Gen. 5, 14-15), PG.87.273.
– *Homiliae in Exodum*, ed. W.A. Baehrens, Origenes Werke, vol. 6, GCS 29, Leipzig, 1920, pp. 217-218; 221-230.
– *Homilies on Genesis and Exodus*, tr. R.E. Heine, Washington, 1981.
– *Homiliae in Ezechielem*, ed. W.A. Baehrens, Origenes Werke, vol. 8, GCS 33, Leipzig, 1925.
– *Homiliae in Genesim*, ed. W.A. Baehrens, Origenes Werke, vol. 6, GCS 29, Leipzig, 1920, pp. 23-30.
– *Homiliae in Jeremiam* (*homiliae 1-11*), ed. P. Nautin, *Origène. Homélies sur Jérémie*, vol. 1, Sources chrétiennes 232, Paris, 1976.
– *Homiliae in Jeremiam* (*homiliae 12-20*, ed. E. Klostermann, Origenes Werke, vol. 3, GCS 6, Leipzig, 1901, pp. 85-194.
– *Homiliae in Jesu Nave*, ed. W.A. Baehrens, Origenes Werke, vol. 7, GCS 30, Leipzig, 1921.
– *Homiliae in Job* (fragmenta in catenis, typus I) (e codd. Paris.), PG.12.1032-1049.
– *Homiliae in Job* (*fragmenta in catenis, typus I+II*) (e codd. Vat.), ed. J.B. Pitra, *Analecta sacra spicilegio Solesmensi parata*, vol. 2, Paris, 1884, pp. 361-391.
– *Homiliae in Job* (fragmenta in catenis, typus II) (e codd. Marc. gr. 21, 538), PG.17.57-105.
– *Homiliae in Leviticum*, ed. W.A. Baehrens, Origenes Werke, vol. 6, GCS 29, Leipzig, 1920.
– *Homiliae in Lucam*, ed. M. Rauer, Origenes Werke, vol. 9, GCS 49 (35), Berlin, 1959.
– *Homélies sur Josué*, ed. and tr. Annie Jaubert, Sources Chrétiennes, 71, Paris, 1960.
– *Homiliae in Psalmos* (Psalms 15, 36, 67, 73, 74, 75, 76, 77, 80, 81), eds. L. Perrone – M. Molin Pradel – E. Prinzivalli – A. Cacciari, Origenes Werke, vol. 13, *Die neuen*

Psalmenhomilien. Eine kritische Edition des Codex Monacensis Graecus 314, GCS, Neue Folge 19, Berlin – Munich – Boston, 2015.
– *Homilies on Jeremiah, Homily 1 on Kings*, tr. by John Clark Smith, Washington, 1998.
– *Libri x in Canticum Canticorum* (fragmenta), W.A. Baehrens, Origenes Werke, vol. 8, GCS 33, Leipzig, 1925.
– *Philocalia*, ed. J.A. Robinson, *The Philocalia of Origen*, Cambridge, 1893.
– *Scholia in Canticum Canticorum*, PG.17.254-288.
– *Scholia in Lucam* (fragmenta), PG 17.312-369.
– *Scholia in Matthaeum*, PG.17.289-309.
– *Selecta in Deuteronomium* (fragmenta), PG.12.805-817.
– *Selecta in Ezechielem* (fragmenta), PG.13.768-825.
– *Selecta in Exodum*, PG.12. 281-297.
– *Selecta in Genesim* (fragmenta), PG.12.92-145.
– *Selecta in Jesu Nave* (fragmenta), PG.12.820-824.
– *Selecta in Numeros*, PG.12.576-584.
– *Selecta in Psalmos* (fragmenta), PG.12: 1053-1320; 1368-1369; 1388-1389; 1409-1685.
Oulton, J.E.L., "Rufinus's Translation of the Church History of Eusebius", *Journal of Theological Studies*, 30, 1929, pp. 150-174.
Palchus (Pseudo – ?) (Egyptian astrologer, fifth-sixth century), *Dodecaeteris Chaldaica*, ed. F. Cumont, *Codices Romani*, Catalogus Codicum Astrologorum Graecorum 5.1, Brussels, 1904, pp. 172-193.
Palladius of Alexandria (medical doctor, sixth century), *Scholia in Hippocratis De Fracturis*, ed. D. Irmer, *Palladius. Kommentar zu Hippokrates 'De fracturis' und seine Parallelversion unter dem Namen des Stephanus von Alexandria*, Hamburger philologische Studien 45, Hamburg, 1977, pp. 16-88.
– *Commentarii in Hippocratis Librum Sextum De Morbis Popularibus*, ed. F.R. Dietz, *Scholia in Hippocratem et Galenum*, vol. 2, Königsberg, 1834 (repr. Amsterdam, 1966).
Pamphilus (theologian, sixth/seventh century), *Difficultatum Solutio*, ed. J.H. Declerck, *Diversorum postchalcedonensium auctorum collectanea I: Pamphili theologi opus*, Corpus Christianorum Series Graeca 19, Turnhout, 1989, pp. 127-261.
Pamphilus of Caesarea (died 309 AD), *Apologia pro Origene*, PG.17.522-632.
Pappus of Alexandria, *Synagoge*, ed. F. Hultsch, *Pappi Alexandrini collectionis quae supersunt*, 3 vols, Berlin, vol. 1: 1876; vol. 2: 1877; vol. 3: 1878.
Pausanias (traveller and geographer, second century AD), *Graeciae Descriptio*, ed. F. Spiro, *Pausaniae Graeciae descriptio*, 3 vols, Leipzig, 1903.
Philagathus of Cerami (or, Philip Cerameus, or Theodore Cerameus, or Theophanes Cerameus, monk and preacher of Greco – Calabrian or Greco – Sicilian descent, twelfth century), *Homiliae*, ed. G. Rossi Taibbi, *Filagato da Cerami Omelie per i vangeli domenicali e le feste di tutto l'anno*, Istituto Siciliano di Studi Bizantini e Neoellenici. Testi e Monumenti 11, Palermo, 1969.

Philip of Side (presbyter, Side, Constantinople, fifth century), *Historia Christiana*, ed. G.C. Hansen, *Theodoros Anagnostes. Kirchengeschichte*, GCS, 1995, p. 160.

Philo, *De Abrahamo*, ed. L. Cohn, Philonis Alexandrini Opera quae supersunt, v. 4, Berlin, 1902 (repr. 1962), pp. 1-60.

– *De Aeternitate Mundi*, eds. L. Cohn – S. Reiter. Philonis Alexandrini Opera quae supersunt, v. 6, Berlin, 1915 (repr. 1962), pp. 72-119.

– *De Agricultura*, ed. P. Wendland, Philonis Alexandrini Opera quae supersunt, vol. 2, Berlin, 1897 (repr. 1962), pp. 95-132.

– *De Confusione Linguarum*, ed. P. Wendland, Philonis Alexandrini Opera quae supersunt, vol. 2, Berlin, 1897 (repr. 1962), pp. 229-267.

– *De Congressu Eruditionis Gratia*, ed. P. Wendland, Philonis Alexandrini Opera quae supersunt, vol. 3, Berlin, 1898 (repr. 1962), pp. 72-109.

– *De Decalogo*, ed. L. Cohn, Philonis Alexandrini Opera quae supersunt, vol. 4, Berlin, 1902 (repr. 1962), pp. 269-307.

– *De Ebrietate ii*, ed. P. Wendland, *Neu entdeckte Fragmente Philos nebst einer Untersuchung über die ursprüngliche Gestalt der Schrift de sacrificiis Abelis et Caini*, Berlin, 1891, pp. 22-25.

– *De Ebrietate*, ed. P. Wendland, Philonis Alexandrini Opera quae supersunt, vol. 2, Berlin, 1897 (repr. 1962), pp. 170-214.

– *De Josepho*, ed. L. Cohn, Philonis Alexandrini Opera quae supersunt, vol. 4, Berlin, 1902 (repr. 1962), pp. 61-118.

– *De Mutatione Nominum*, ed. P. Wendland, Philonis Alexandrini Opera quae supersunt, vol. 3, Berlin, 1898 (repr. 1962), pp. 156-203.

– *De Opificio Mundi*, ed. L. Cohn, Philonis Alexandrini Opera quae supersunt, vol. 1, Berlin, 1896 (repr. 1962), pp. 1-60.

– *De Posteritate Caini*, ed. P. Wendland, Philonis Alexandrini Opera quae supersunt, vol. 2, Berlin, 1897 (repr. 1962), pp. 1-41.

– *De Sacrificiis Abelis et Caini*, ed. L. Cohn, Philonis Alexandrini Opera quae supersunt, vol. 1, Berlin, 1896 (repr. 1962), pp. 202-257.

– *De Sobrietate*, ed. P. Wendland, Philonis Alexandrini Opera quae supersunt, vol. 2, Berlin, 1897 (repr. 1962), pp. 215-228.

– *De Somniis*, ed. P. Wendland, Philonis Alexandrini Opera quae supersunt, vol. 3, Berlin, 1898 (repr. 1962), pp. 204-306.

– *De Specialibus Legibus*, ed. L. Cohn, Philonis Alexandrini Opera quae supersunt, v. 5, Berlin, 1906 (repr. 1962).

– *De Virtutibus*, ed. L. Cohn, Philonis Alexandrini Opera quae supersunt, vol. 5, Berlin, 1906 (repr. 1962), pp. 266-335.

– *De Vita Mosis*, ed. L. Cohn, Philonis Alexandrini Opera quae supersunt, v. 4, Berlin, 1902 (repr. 1962).

– *Legatio ad Gaium*, eds. L. Cohn – S. Reiter, Philonis Alexandrini Opera quae supersunt, vol. 6, Berlin, 1915 (repr. 1962), pp. 155-223.

– *Legum Allegoriarum*, ed. L. Cohn, Philonis Alexandrini Opera quae supersunt, v. 1, Berlin, 1896 (repr. 1962).
– *Quaestiones in Genesim* (fragmenta), ed. F. Petit, *Quaestiones in Genesim et in Exodum. Fragmenta Graeca*, Les oeuvres de Philon d'Alexandrie 33, Paris, 1978, pp. 41-81, 83-153, 155-160, 162-183, 185-213, 216-228.
– *Quis Rerum Divinarum Heres Sit*, ed. P. Wendland, Philonis Alexandrini Opera quae supersunt, vol. 3, Berlin, 1898 (repr. 1962), pp. 1-71.
– *Quod Deterius Potiori Insidiari Soleat*, ed. L. Cohn, Philonis Alexandrini Opera quae supersunt, vol. 1, Berlin, 1896 (repr. 1962), pp. 258-298.
– *Quod Deus Sit Immutabilis*, ed. P. Wendland, Philonis Alexandrini Opera quae supersunt, vol. 2, Berlin, 1897 (repr. 1962), pp. 56-94.
– *Quod Omnis Probus Liber Sit*, ed. L. Cohn – S. Reiter, Philonis Alexandrini Opera quae supersunt, vol. 6, Berlin, 1915 (repr. 1962), pp. 1-45.

Philolaus, *Testimonia*, eds. H. Diels – W. Kranz, *Die Fragmente der Vorsokratiker*, vol. 1, sixth edition, Berlin, 1951, pp. 398-406.

Philostratus, Flavius, *Vita Apollonii*, ed. C.L. Kayser, *Flavii Philostrati opera*, vol. 1, Leipzig, 1870 (repr. 1964).

Philotheus Coccinus (Patriarch of Constantinople, fourteenth century), *Orationes et Homiliae*, ed. B.S. Pseftonkas, *Filoqevou Kokkivnou lovgoi kai; oJmilivai,* Thessalonian Byzantine Writers 2, Thessaloniki, 1981.

Photius (Patriarch of Constantinople, ninth century Constantinople, *Fragmenta in Epistulam ii ad Corinthios*, ed. K. Staab, *Pauluskommentar aus der griechischen Kirche aus Katenenhandschriften gesammelt*, Münster, 1933, pp. 583-604.
– *Bibliotheca*, ed. R. Henry, *Photius. Bibliothèque*, 8 vols, Paris, vol. 1: 1959; vol. 2: 1960; vol. 3: 1962; vol. 4: 1965; vol. 5: 1967; vol. 6: 1971; vol. 7: 1974; vol. 8: 1977.
– *Commentarii in Matthaeum* (in catenis), ed. J. Reuss, *Matthäus – Kommentare aus der griechischen Kirche*, Texte und Untersuchungen 61, Berlin 1957, pp. 270-337.
– *Commentarii in Joannem* (in catenis), ed. J. Reuss, *Johannes – Kommentare aus der griechischen Kirche, Texte und Untersuchungen* 89, Berlin, 1966, pp. 359-412.
– *De Spiritu Sancti Mystagogiae*, PG.102.153–191.
– *Epistula ad Arsenium De Manichaeis*, ed. W. Conus – Wolska, "Les sources grecques pour l'histoire des Pauliciens d'Asie Mineure. Vol. III. Photius. Récit de la réapparition des Manichéens," *Travaux et mémoires* 4 (1970), pp. 181-183.
– *Epistulae et Amphilochia*, eds. B. Laourdas – L.G. Westerink, *Photii patriarchae Constantinopolitani Epistulae et Amphilochia*, vols. 1-6.2, Bibliotheca Scriptorum Graecorum et Romanorum Teubneriana, Leipzig, vol. 1: 1983; vol. 2: 1984; vol. 3: 1985; vol. 4: 1986; vol. 5: 1986; vol. 6.1: 1987; vol. 6.2: 1988.
– *Epitome de Spiritu Sancti Mystagogiae*, ed. J. - P. Migne, "Κατὰ τῶν τῆς παλαιᾶς Ῥώμης ὅτι ἐκ τοῦ Πατρὸς μόνον ἐκπορεύεται τὸ Πνεῦμα τὸ ἅγιον", in J. Graves (ed.), *On the mystagogy of the Holy Spirit by Saint Photius patriarch of Constantinople*, Astoria, N.Y. 1983, pp. 193-196.

– *Fragmenta in Epistulam ad Romanos*, ed. K. Staab, *Pauluskommentar aus der griechischen Kirche aus Katenenhandschriften gesammelt*, Münster, 1933, pp. 470-544.
– *Fragmenta in Epistulam i ad Corinthios*, ed. K. Staab, *Pauluskommentar aus der griechischen Kirche aus Katenenhandschriften gesammelt*, Münster, 1933, pp. 544-583.
– *Fragmenta in Epistulam i ad Thessalonicenses*, ed. K. Staab, *Pauluskommentar aus der griechischen Kirche aus Katenenhandschriften gesammelt*, Münster, 1933, pp. 633-636.
– *Homiliae*, ed. B. Laourdas, *Ἑλληνικά* 12 Παράρτημα, Thessaloniki, 1966.
– *Lexicon (Α-Δ)*, ed. Chr. Theodoridis, *Photii patriarchae lexicon*, vol. 1 (A-D), Berlin, 1982.
– *Lexicon (Ε-Ω)*, ed. R. Porson, *Φωτίου τοῦ πατριάρχου λέξεων συναγωγή*, parts. 1-2, Cambridge, 1822, part 1: pp. 10-367; part 2: pp. 367-659.

Phrynichus of Bithynia (or Phrynichus Arabius, sophist, grammarian, and lexicographer of Attic language, second century AD), *Praeparatio Sophistica (epitome)*, ed. J. de Borries, *Phrynichi sophistae praeparatio sophistica*, Leipzig, 1911.

Pierret, P., *Hermès Trismégiste*, Mélanges d'archéologie égyptienne et assyriennne 1, 1872.

Pietschmann, R., *Hermes Trismegistos, nach ägyptischen, grieschischen und orientalischen Überlieferungen dargestellt*, Lepzig, 1875.

Plato, *Charmides*, ed. J. Burnet, Platonis opera, vol. 3, Oxford, 1903 (repr. 1968).
– *Cratylus*, ed. J. Burnet, Platonis opera, vol. 1, Oxford, 1900 (repr. 1967).
– *Critias*, ed. J. Burnet, Platonis opera, vol. 4, Oxford, 1902 (repr. 1968).
– *Epinomis*, ed. J. Burnet, Platonis opera, vol. 5, Oxford, 1907 (repr. 1967).
– *Gorgias*, ed. J. Burnet, Platonis opera, vol. 3, Oxford, 1903 (repr. 1968).
– *Leges*, ed. J. Burnet, Platonis opera, vol. 5, Oxford, 1907 (repr. 1967).
– *Phaedo*, ed. J. Burnet, Platonis opera, vol. 1, Oxford, 1900 (repr. 1967).
– *Phaedrus*, ed. J. Burnet, Platonis opera, vol. 2, Oxford, 1901 (repr. 1967).
– *Sophista*, ed. J. Burnet, Platonis opera, vol. 1, Oxford, 1900 (repr. 1967).
– *Philebus*, ed. J. Burnet, Platonis opera, vol. 2, Oxford, 1901 (repr. 1967).
– *Politicus*, ed. J. Burnet, Platonis opera, vol. 1, Oxford, 1900 (repr. 1967).
– *Respublica*, ed. J. Burnet, Platonis opera, vol. 4, Oxford, 1902 (repr. 1968).
– *Symposium*, ed. J. Burnet, Platonis opera, vol. 2, Oxford, 1901 (repr. 1967).
– *Theaetetus*, d. J. Burnet, Platonis opera, vol. 1, Oxford, 1900 (repr. 1967).
– *Timaeus*, ed. J. Burnet, Platonis opera, vol. 4, Oxford, 1902 (repr. 1968).

Plotinus, *Enneades*, ed. P. Henry – H. - R. Schwyzer, *Plotini opera*, 3 vols, Oxford, vol. 1:1964; vol. 2: 1977; vol. 3: 1982 (initially, Leiden, vol. 1: 1951; vol. 2: 1959; vol. 3: 1973).

Plutarch, *Aemilius Paullus*, ed. K. Ziegler, *Plutarchi vitae parallelae*, vol. 2.1, second edition, Leipzig, 1964, pp. 184-222.
– *Aetia Romana et Graeca*, ed. J.B. Titchener, *Plutarchi moralia*, vol. 2.1, Leipzig, 1935 (repr. 1971), pp. 273-366.

– *An Seni Respublica Gerenda Sit*, ed. H.N. Fowler, *Plutarch's moralia*, vol. 10, Cambridge Mass. 1936 (repr. 1969), pp. 76-152.
– *Antonius*, ed. K. Ziegler, *Plutarchi vitae parallelae*, vol. 3.1, second edition, Leipzig, 1971, pp. 60-148.
– *Aristides*, ed. K. Ziegler, *Plutarchi vitae parallelae*, vol. 1.1, fourth edition, Leipzig, 1969, pp. 249-287.
– *Cato Minor*, ed. K. Ziegler, *Plutarchi vitae parallelae*, vol. 2.1, second edition, Leipzig, 1964, pp. 32-92.
– *Cimon*, ed. K. Ziegler, *Plutarchi vitae parallelae*, vol. 1.1, fourth edition, Leipzig, 1969, pp. 332-359.
– *Comparatio Pelopidae et Marcelli*, ed. K. Ziegler, *Plutarchi vitae parallelae*, vol. 2.2, second edition, Leipzig, 1968, pp. 148-151.
– *Conjugalia Praecepta*, ed. F.C. Babbitt, *Plutarch's moralia*, vol. 2. Cambridge Mass. 1928 (repr. 1962), pp. 298-342.
– *De Animae Procreatione in Timaeo*, ed. C. Hubert, *Plutarchi moralia*, vol. 6.1, Leipzig, 1954 (repr. 1959), pp. 143-188.
– *De Facie in Orbe Lunae*, ed. M. Pohlenz, *Plutarchi moralia*, vol. 5.3, second edition, Leipzig, 1960, pp. 31-89.
– *De Genio Socratis*, W. Sieveking, *Plutarchi moralia*, vol. 3, Leipzig, 1929 (repr. 1972), pp. 460-511.
– *De Iside et Osiride*, ed. W. Sieveking, *Plutarchi moralia*, vol. 2.3, Leipzig, 1935 (repr. 1971), pp. 1-80.
– *De Pythiae Oraculis*, ed. W. Sieveking, *Plutarchi moralia*, vol. 3, Leipzig, 1929 (repr. 1972), pp. 25-59.
– *De Sera Numinis Vindicta*, ed. M. Pohlenz, *Plutarchi moralia*, vol. 3, Leipzig, 1929 (repr. 1972), pp. 394-444.
– *De Sollertia Animalium*, ed. C. Hubert, *Plutarchi moralia*, vol. 6.1, Leipzig, 1954 (repr. 1959), pp. 11-75.
– *De Stoicorum Repugnantiis*, ed. R. Westman (post M. Pohlenz), *Plutarchi moralia*, vol. 6.2, second edition, Leipzig, 1959, pp. 2-58.
– *De Virtute Morali*, ed. M. Pohlenz, *Plutarchi moralia*, vol. 3, Leipzig, 1929 (repr. 1972), pp. 127-156.
– *Fragmenta*, ed. F.H. Sandbach, *Plutarchi moralia*, vol. 7, Leipzig, 1967.
– *Marcellus*, ed. K. Ziegler, *Plutarchi vitae parallelae*, vol. 2.2, second edition, Leipzig, 1968, pp. 105-147.
– *Non Posse Suaviter Vivi sec Undum Epicurum*, ed. R. Westman (post M. Pohlenz), *Plutarchi moralia*, vol. 6.2, second edition, Leipzig, 1959, pp. 124-172.
– *Non Posse Suaviter Vivi Secundum Epicurum*, ed. R. Westman (post M. Pohlenz), *Plutarchi moralia*, vol. 6.2, second edition, Leipzig, 1959, pp. 124-172.

– *Non Posse Suaviter Vivi Secundum Epicurum*, ed. R. Westman (post M. Pohlenz), *Plutarchi moralia*, vol. 6.2, second edition, Leipzig, 1959, pp. 124-172.
– *Phocion*, ed. K. Ziegler, *Plutarchi vitae parallelae*, vol. 2.1, second edition, Leipzig, 1964, pp. 1-31.
– *Quaestiones Convivales*, ed. C. Hubert, *Plutarchi moralia*, vol. 4, Leipzig, 1938 (repr. 1971), pp. 1-335.
– *Quomodo Adolescens Poetas Audire Debeat*, ed. F.C. Babbitt, *Plutarch's moralia*, vol. 1. Cambridge, Mass. 1927 (repr. 1969), pp. 74-196.
– *Quomodo Adulator ab Amico Internoscatur*, ed. F.C. Babbitt, *Plutarch's moralia*, vol. 1. Cambridge Mass. 1927 (repr. 1969), pp. 264-394.
– *Tiberius et Gaius Gracchus*, ed. K. Ziegler, *Plutarchi vitae parallelae*, vol. 3.1, second edition, Leipzig, 1971, pp. 416-458.
– *Timoleon*, ed. K. Ziegler, *Plutarchi vitae parallelae*, vol. 2.1, second edition, Leipzig, 1964, pp. 222-255.

Polyaenus, *Strategemata* (Macedonian author and a rhetorician, second-century AD), ed. J. Melber and E. Woelfflin, *Polyaeni strategematon libri viii*, Leipzig, 1887.

Polybius, *Historiae*, ed. T. Büttner – Wobst, *Polybii historiae*, vols. 1-4, Leipzig, vol. 1: 1905; vol. 2: 1889; vol. 3: 1893; vol. 4: 1904 (repr. Stuttgart, vol. 1: 1962; vols. 2-3: 1965; vol. 4: 1967).

Porphyry, *Ad Marcellam*, ed. W. Pötscher, *Πορφύριος πρὸς Μαρκέλλαν*, Leiden, 1969.
– *Contra Christianos*, ed. A. von Harnack, *Porphyrius. Gegen die Christen*, Abhandlungen der preussischen Akademie der Wissenschaften, Philosoph. - hist. Kl. 1, Berlin, 1916.
– *De Abstinentia*, ed. A. Nauck, *Porphyrii philosophi Platonici opuscula selecta*, second edition, Leipzig, 1886 (repr. Hildesheim, 1963).
– *Εἰς τὰ Ἁρμονικὰ Πτολεμαίου Ὑπόμνημα*, ed. I. Düring, *Porphyrios. Kommentar zur Harmonielehre des Ptolemaios*, Göteborg, 1932 (repr. New York, 1980).
– *Epistula ad Anebonem*, ed. A.R. Sodano, *Porfirio. Lettera ad Anebo*, Naples, 1958, pp. 1-31.
– *In Aristotelis Categorias Commentarium*, ed. A. Busse, *Porphyrii isagoge et in Aristotelis categorias commentarium*, Commentaria in Aristotelem Graeca 4.1, Berlin, 1887, pp. 55-142.
– *In Aristotelis Categorias Expositio per Interrogationem et Responsionem*, ed. A. Busse, *Porphyrii isagoge et in Aristotelis categorias commentarium*, Commentaria in Aristotelem Graeca 4.1, Berlin, 1887.
– *In Platonis Parmenidem commentaria* (fragmenta), ed. P. Hadot, *Porphyre et Victorinus*, vol. 2, Paris, Études Augustiniennes, 1968, pp. 64-112.
– *In Platonis Timaeum commentaria* (fragmenta), ed. A.R. Sodano, *Porphyrii in Platonis Timaeum commentariorum fragmenta*, Naples, 1964.

– *Introductio in Tetrabiblum Ptolemaei*, eds. E. Boer – S. Weinstock, *Codices Romani* (*Catalogus Codicum Astrologorum Graecorum* 5.4), Brussels, 1940, pp. 190-228.
– *Περὶ Ἀγαλμάτων*, ed. J. Bidez, *Vie de Porphyre le philosophe néo – platonicien*, Leipzig, 1913 (repr. Hildesheim, 1964).
– *Quaestionum Homericarum ad Iliadem Pertinentium Reliquiae*, ed. H. Schrader, *Porphyrii quaestionum Homericarum ad Iliadem pertinentium reliquiae*, fasc. 1 & 2, Leipzig, vol. 1: 1880; vol. 2: 1882.
– *Quaestionum Homericarum ad Odysseam Pertinentium Reliquiae*, ed. H. Schrader, *Porphyrii quaestionum Homericarum ad Odysseam pertinentium reliquiae*, Leipzig, 1890.
– *Sententiae*, ed. E. Lamberz, *Porphyrii sententiae ad intelligibilia ducentes*, Leipzig, 1975.
– *Vita Plotini*, ed. P. Henry – H.R. Schwyzer, *Plotini opera*, vol. 1, Leiden, 1951, pp. 1-41.
– *Quaestiones Codicis Vaticani*, ed. H. Schrader, *Porphyrii quaestionum Homericarum ad Iliadem pertinentium reliquias*, Leipzig, 1882, pp. 281-335.
Posidonius, *Fragmenta*, ed. W. Theiler, *Posidonios. Die Fragmente*, vol. 1, Berlin, 1982.
Praechter, Karl "Die griechischen Aristotelescommentare" in *Byzantinische Zeitschirift*, 1909, pp. 516-538. This is a review of the Commentaria in Aristotelem Graeca published by the Berlin Academy in twenty-six volumes. See an English translation of Praechter's review by B. Caston in R. Sorabji (ed.), *Aristotle Transformed: The Ancient Commentators and Their Influence*, Ithaca, NY, 1990, pp. 31-54.
Preuschen, E., *Origenes, Commentarii in evangelium Joannis*, in Origenes Werke, vol. 4, Die griechischen christlichen Schriftsteller 10, Leipzig, 1903.
Proclus of Constantinople (bishop, fifth century), *Homilia Consolatoria ad Aegrotum*, ed. S.Y. Rudberg, "L'homélie pseudo – basilienne 'consolatoria ad aegrotum'," *Muséon* 72 (1959, pp. 310-322.
Proclus of Athens, *De Decem Dubitationibus Circa Providentiam*, ed. H. Boese, *Procli Diadochi tria opuscula*, Berlin, 1960, pp. 5-108.
– *De Providentia et Fato et Eo Quod in Nobis ad Theodorum Mechanicum*, ed. H. Boese, *Procli Diadochi tria Opuscula*, Berlin, 1960.
– *Hypotyposis Astronomicarum Positionum*, ed. C. Manitius, *Procli Diadochi hypotyposis astronomicarum positionum*, Leipzig, Stuttgart, 1974.
– *In Platonis Alcibiadem i*, ed. L.G. Westerink, *Proclus Diadochus. Commentary on the first Alcibiades of Plato*, Amsterdam, 1954.
– *In Platonis Cratylum Commentaria*, ed. G. Pasquali, *Procli Diadochi in Platonis Cratylum commentaria*, Leipzig, 1908.
– *In Platonis Parmenidem*, ed. V. Cousin, *Procli philosophi Platonici opera inedita*, part 3, Paris, 1864 (repr. Hildesheim, 1961) pp. 617-1244.
– *In Platonis Rem Publicam Commentarii*, ed. W. Kroll, *Procli Diadochi in Platonis rem publicam commentarii*, 2 vols, Amsterdam, 1965.

– *In Platonis Timaeum Commentaria*, ed. E. Diehl, *Procli Diadochi in Platonis Timaeum commentaria*, 3 vols. Leipzig, vol. 1: 1903; vol. 2: 1904; vol. 3: 1906 (repr. Amsterdam, 1965).
– *In Primum Euclidis Elementorum Librum Commentarii*, ed. G. Friedlein, *Procli Diadochi in primum Euclidis elementorum librum commentarii*, Leipzig, 1873.
– *Institutio Physica*, ed. A. Ritzenfeld, *Procli Diadochi Lycii institutio physica*, Leipzig, 1912.
– *Institutio Theologica*, ed. E.R. Dodds, *Proclus. The elements of theology*, second edition, Oxford, 1963 (repr. 1977).
– *Theologia Platonica*, eds. D. Saffrey – L.G. Westerink, *Proclus. Théologie platonicienne*, vols. 1-5, Paris, vol. 1: 1968; vol. 2: 1974; vol. 3: 1978; vol. 4: 1981; vol. 5: 1987; vol. 6: 1997.
Procopius of Caesarea (sixth century), *De Bellis*, ed. G. Wirth (post J. Haury), *Procopii Caesariensis opera omnia*, vols. 1-2, Leipzig, vol. 1: 1962; vol. 2: 1963.
– *De Aedificiis*, ed. G. Wirth (post J. Haury), *Procopii Caesariensis opera omnia*, vol. 4, Leipzig, 1964.
Procopius of Gaza (fifth-sixth century), *Catena in Canticum Canticorum*, PG.87(2).1545-1753.
– *Commentarii in Isaiam*, PG.87(2).1817-2717.
– *Commentarii in Genesim*, ed. K. Metzler, *Prokop von Gaza: Eclogarum in libros historicos Veteris Testamenti epitome, Teil 1: Der Genesiskommentar*, GCS, Neue Folge 22. Berlin – Munich – Boston, 2015.
– *Epistulae*, A. Garzya – R. - J. Loenertz (eds.), *Procopii Gazaei epistolae et declamationes*, Studia patristica et Byzantina 9, Ettal, 1963.
Pseudo – Alexander of Aphrodisias, *Ἀπορίαι καὶ Λύσεις*, ed. I. Bruns, *Alexandri Aphrodisiensis praeter commentaria scripta minora*, Commentaria in Aristotelem Graeca suppl. 2.2, Berlin, 1892, pp. 117-163.
– *Ἠθικὰ Προβλήματα*, ed. I. Bruns, *Alexandri Aphrodisiensis praeter commentaria scripta minora*, Commentaria in Aristotelem Graeca suppl. 2.2, Berlin, 1892, pp. 1-116.
– *De Anima Libri Mantissa*, ed. I. Bruns, *Alexandri Aphrodisiensis praeter commentaria scripta minora*, Commentaria in Aristotelem Graeca suppl. 2.1, Berlin, 1887, pp. 101-186.
– *Problemata* (*lib. 1-2*, ed. J.L. Ideler, *Physici et medici Graeci minores*, vol. 1, Berlin, 1841 (repr. Amsterdam, 1963).
– *Problemata* (*lib. 3-4*), ed. H. Usener, *Alexandri Aphrodisiensis quae feruntur problematorum liber iii et iiii*, Programm Gymnasium Joachimsthal 1859, pp. 1-37.
Pseudo – Amphilochius of Iconium, *Oratio in Mesopentecosten*, ed. C. Datema, *Amphilochii Iconiensis opera*. Turnhout, 1978, pp. 251-262.
Pseudo – Anastasius of Sinai, *Disputatio Adversus Judaeos*, PG.89.1204-1281.

– *Florilegium Adversus Monotheletas*, ed. K. - H. Uthemann, *Sermones duo in constitutionem hominis secundum imaginem Dei necnon opuscula adversus Monotheletas*, Corpus Christianorum Series Graeca 12, Turnhout, 1985, pp. 87-96.
Pseudo – Apollonius of Tyana, *Apollonii Epistulae*, ed. C.L. Kayser, *Flavii Philostrati opera*, vol. 1, Leipzig, 1870 (repr. Hildesheim, 1964), pp. 345-368.
Pseudo – Athanasius, *Contra Sabellianos*, PG.28.96-121.
– *De Sancta Trinitate*, PG.28: 1116-1173a, 1201c-1249b, 1265c-1285b.
– *Dialogus Athanasii et Zacchaei*, ed. F.C. Conybeare, *The dialogues of Athanasius and Zacchaeus and of Timothy and Aquila*. Oxford, 1898.
– *Homilia De Passione et Cruce Domini*, PG.28.185-249.
– *Liber De Definitionibus*, PG.28.533-553.
– *Quaestiones ad Antiochum Ducem*, PG.28.597-700.
– *Quaestiones Aliae*, PG.28.773-796.
– *Quaestiones in Evangelia*, PG.28.700-708.
– *Quaestiones in Scripturam Sacram*, PG.28.712-773.
– *Sermo Contra Omnes Haereses*, PG.28.501-524.
– *Sermo De Descriptione Deiparae*, PG.28.944-957.
– *Synopsis Scripturae Sacrae*, PG.28.284-437.
– *Syntagma ad Quendam Politicum*, PG.28.1396-1408.
– *Sermo in Annuntiationem Deiparae*, PG.28.917-940.
Pseudo – Basil of Caesarea (*forsan* Cassian the Sabaite), *Enarratio in Prophetam Isaiam*, ed. P. Trevisan, *San Basilio. Commento al profeta Isaia*, 2 vols, Turin, 1939.
Pseudo – Basil of Caesarea, *Consolatoria ad Aegrotum*, PG.31.1713-1722.
– *Sermo 11*, PG.31.625-648.
– *Sermo 12* (*De Ascetica Disciplina*), PG.31.648-652.
– *Orationes* (*Exorcismi*), PG.31.1677-1684.
Pseudo – Basil of Seleucia, *De Vita et Miraculis Sanctae Theclae*, ed. G. Dagron, *Vie et miracles de sainte Thècle* Subsidia hagiographica 62, Brussels, 1978, pp. 168-412.
Pseudo – Caesarius (= Cassian the Sabaite), *Quaestiones et Responsiones*, ed. R. Riendinger, *Pseudo – Kaisarios. Die Erotapokriseis*, GCS, Berlin, 1989.
Pseudo – Callisthenes, *Historia Alexandri Magni* (recensio), ed. W. Kroll, Historia Alexandri Magni, vol. 1, Berlin, 1926.
Pseudo – Clement of Rome, *Homiliae*, ed. B. Rehm, J. Irmscher and F. Paschke, *Die Pseudoklementinen I. Homilien*, GCS 42, Berlin, 1969.
– *Collectio Dictorum Veteris Testamenti*, PG.77.1176-1289.
– *De Sancta Trinitate*, PG.77.1120-1173.
– *De Synagogae Defectu* (fragmentum), PG.76.1421-1424.
Pseudo – David of Alexandria, *In Porphyrii Isagogen*, ed. L.G. Westerink, *Pseudo – Elias (Pseudo – David), Lectures on Porphyry's isagoge*, Amsterdam, 1967.

Pseudo – Demosthenes, *Eroticus*, ed. W. Rennie, *Demosthenis orationes*, vol. 3. Oxford, 1931 (repr. 1960), pp. 1400-1418.

Pseudo – Didymus (= Cassian the Sabaite), *De Trinitate* (*liber 1*), ed. J. Hönscheid, *Didymus der Blinde. De trinitate, Buch 1*, Beiträge zur klassischen Philologie, 44, Meisenheim am Glan, 1975.

– *De Trinitate* (*liber* 2.8-27), PG.39.600-769.

– *De Trinitate* (*liber* 3), PG.39.773-992.

Pseudo – Dionysius the Areopagite, *De Caelesti Hierarchia*, eds. G. Heil – A.M. Ritter, *Corpus Dionysiacum ii, Pseudo – Dionysius Areopagita. De coelesti hierarchia, de ecclesiastica hierarchia, de mystica theologia, epistulae*, Patristische Texte und Studien 36, Berlin, 1991, pp. 7-59.

– *De Divinis Nominibus*, ed. B.R. Suchla, *Corpus Dionysiacum i, Pseudo – Dionysius Areopagita. De divinis nominibus*, Patristische Texte und Studien 33, Berlin, 1990, pp. 107-231.

– *De Ecclesiastica Hierarchia*, eds. G. Heil – A.M. Ritter, *Corpus Dionysiacum ii, Pseudo – Dionysius Areopagita. De coelesti hierarchia, de ecclesiastica hierarchia, de mystica theologia, epistulae*, Patristische Texte und Studien 36, Berlin, 1991, pp. 63-132.

– *Epistulae*, eds. G. Heil – A.M. Ritter, *Corpus Dionysiacum ii, Pseudo – Dionysius Areopagita. De coelesti hierarchia, de ecclesiastica hierarchia, de mystica theologia, epistulae*, Patristische Texte und Studien 36, Berlin, 1991, pp. 155-210.

Pseudo – Epiphanius of Salamis, *Anacephalaeosis*, ed. K. Holl, *Epiphanius, Bände 1-3, Ancoratus und Panarion*, GCS 25, 31, 37, Leipzig, vol. 1: 1915; vol. 2: 1922; vol. 3: 1933.

– *Homilia in Assumptionem Christi*, PG.43.477-485.

– *Homilia in Christi Resurrectionem*, PG.43.465-477.

– *Homilia in Festo Palmarum*, PG.43.428-437.

– *Homilia In Laudes Mariae Deiparae*, PG.43.485-501.

– *Testimonia ex Divinis et Sacris Scripturis*, ed. R.V. Hotchkiss, *A Pseudo – Epiphanius testimony book*. Missoula, Montana, 1974, pp. 8-76.

Pseudo – Galen, *Ad Gaurum Quomodo Animetur Fetus*, ed. K. Kalbfleisch, "Die neuplatonische, fälschlich dem Galen zugeschriebene Schrift Πρὸς γαῦρον περὶ τοῦ πῶς ἐμψυχοῦνται τὰ ἔμβρυα", *Abhandlungen der königlichen Akademie der Wissenschaften zu Berlin*, Berlin, 1895.

– *De Affectuum Renibus Insidentium Dignotione et Curatione*, ed. C.G. Kühn, *Claudii Galeni opera omnia*, vol. 19, Leipzig, 1830 (repr. Hildesheim, 1965), pp. 643-698.

– *De Historia Philosophica*, ed. H. Diels, *Doxographi Graeci*, Berlin, 1879 (repr. 1965), pp. 597-648.

– *De Ponderibus et Mensuris*, ed. F. Hultsch, *Metrologicorum scriptorum reliquiae*, vol. 1, Leipzig, 1864 (repr. Stuttgart, 1971), pp. 218-244.

– *Definitiones Medicae*, ed. C.G. Kühn, *Claudii Galeni opera omnia*, vol. 19, Leipzig, 1830 (repr. Hildesheim, 1965), pp. 346-462.
– *Introductio*, ed. C.G. Kühn, *Claudii Galeni opera omnia*, vol. 14, Leipzig, 1827 (repr. Hildesheim, 1965), pp. 674-797.
– *Prognostica De Decubitu ex Mathematica Scientia*, ed. C.G. Kühn, *Claudii Galeni opera omnia*, vol. 19, Leipzig, 1830 (repr. Hildesheim, 1965), pp. 529-573.
Pseudo – Gregory of Nyssa, *Ad Imaginem Dei et ad Similitudinem*, PG.44.1328-1345.
– *De Occursu Domini*, PG.46.1152-1181.
– *Liber de Cognitione Dei* (Θεογνωσία) (fragmenta *apud* Euthymium Zigabenum, *Panoplia Dogmatica*), PG.130.28: 28-29; 257-276; 312-317.
– *Testimonia Adversus Judaeos*, PG.46.193-233.
Pseudo – Gregory Thaumaturgus, *Ad Tatianum De Anima Per Capita Disputatio*, PG.10.1137-1145.
– *Sermo in Omnes Sanctos*, PG.10.1197-1204.
Pseudo – Hermogenes, *Περὶ Εὑρέσεως*, ed. H. Rabe, *Hermogenis opera*, Leipzig, 1913 (repr. Stuttgart, 1969), pp. 93-212.
Pseudo – Hippolytus, *De Consummatione Mundi*, ed. H. Achelis, *Hippolyt's kleinere exegetische und homiletische Schriften*, GCS 1.2, Leipzig, 1897, pp. 289-309.
– *Fragmenta in Psalmos*, ed. H. Achelis, *Hippolyt's kleinere exegetische und homiletische Schriften*, GCS 1.2, Leipzig, 1897.
Pseudo – John Chrysostom, *De Jejunio*, PG.60.757-760.
– *De Occursu Domini, De Deipara et Symeone*, PG.50.807-812.
– *De Pseudoprophetis*, PG.59.553-568.
– *De Sancta Trinitate*, PG.48.1087-1096.
– *Eclogae i-xlviii ex Diversis Homiliis*, PG.63.567-902.
– *Epistula ad Caesarium*, ed. P.G. Nicolopoulos, *Αἱ εἰς τὸν Ἰωάννην τὸν Χρυσόστομον ἐσφαλμένως ἀποδιδόμεναι ἐπιστολαί*, Athens, 1973, pp. 513-518.
– *In illud: Exiit edictum*, PG.50.795-800.
– *In illud: Si qua in Christo Nova Creatura*, PG.64.25-34.
– *In illud: Verumtamen Frustra Conturbatur*, PG.55.559-564.
– *In Lazarum*, PG.62.771-776.
– *In Natale Domini Nostri Jesu Christi*, PG.61.763-768.
– *In Parabolam Samaritani*, PG.62.755-758.
– *In Psalmos 101-107*, PG.55.635-674.
– *In Psalmum 118*, PG.55.675-708.
– *In Psalmum 75*, PG.55.593-598.
– *In Ramos Palmarum*, PG.59.703-708.
– *In Sanctum Pascha*, ed. P. Nautin, *Homélies pascales*, vol. 2, Sources chrétiennes 36, Paris, 1953, pp. 55-75.

– *Interpretatio in Danielem Prophetam*, PG.56.193-246.
– *Oratio De Hypapante*, ed. E. Bickersteth, "Edition and translation of a hypapante homily ascribed to John Chrysostom," *Orientalia Christiana Periodica* 32, Rome, 1966, pp. 56-76.
– *Synopsis Scripturae Sacrae*, PG.56.313-386.
– *Visio Danielis*, ed. A. Vassiliev, *Anecdota Graeco – Byzantina*, vol. 1. Moscow, 1893, pp. 33-38.
Pseudo – John of Damascus, *Commentarii in Epistulas Pauli*, PG.95.441-1033.
– *Vita Barlaam et Joasaph*, eds. H. Mattingly – G.R. Woodward, [*St. John Damascene*]. *Barlaam and Joasaph*, Cambridge Mass. 1914 (repr. 1983).
Pseudo – Justin Martyr, *Quaestiones et Responsiones ad Orthodoxos*, ed. J.C.T. Otto, *Corpus apologetarum Christianorum saeculi secundi*, vol. 5, third edition, Jena, 1881.
– *Cohortatio ad Gentiles*, ed. J.C.T. Otto, *Corpus apologetarum Christianorum saeculi secundi*, vol. 3, third edition, Jena, 1879, pp. 18-126.
– *Epistula Ad Zenam et Serenum*, ed. J.C.T. Otto, *Corpus apologetarum Christianorum saeculi secundi*, vol. 4, third edition, Jena, 1880, pp. 66-98.
– *Expositio Rectae Fidei*, ed. J.C.T. Otto, *Corpus apologetarum Christianorum saeculi secundi*, vol. 4, third edition, Jena, 1880, pp. 2-66.
Pseudo – Lucian of Samosata, *Philopatris*, ed. M.D. Macleod, *Lucian*, vol. 8, Cambridge Mass. 1967, pp. 416-464.
– *Alexander*, ed. A.M. Harmon, *Lucian*, vol. 4, Cambridge Mass. 1925 (repr. 1961), pp. 174-252.
Pseudo – Macarius, *Epistula Magna*, ed. W. Jaeger, *Two rediscovered works of ancient Christian literature: Gregory of Nyssa and Macarius*, Leiden, 1954, pp. 233-301.
– *Homiliae Spirituales*, ed. H. Dörries, E. Klostermann – M. Krüger, *Die 50 geistlichen Homilien des Makarios*, Patristische Texte und Studien 4, Berlin, 1964.
– *Homiliae*, ed. G.L. Marriott, *Macarii anecdota*, Harvard Theological Studies 5, Cambridge Mass. 1918, pp. 19-48.
– *Sermo 28*, eds. H. Berthold – E. Klostermann, *Neue Homilien des Makarius/Symeon*, Texte und Untersuchungen 72, Berlin, 1961, pp. 160, 162, 164, 166-170.
– *Sermones 1-22, 24-27*, eds. H. Berthold – E. Klostermann, *Neue Homilien des Makarius/Symeon*, Texte und Untersuchungen 72, Berlin, 1961, pp. 1-113, 128-158.
– *Sermones 64* (*collectio B*), ed. H. Berthold, *Makarios/Symeon Reden und Briefe*, 2 vols. GCS, Berlin, 1973.
Pseudo – Martyrius, *Oratio Funebris in Laudem Iohannis Chrysostomi*, ed. M. Wallraff, *Oratio funebris in laudem sancti Iohannis Chrysostomi*, in *Quaterni della Rivista di Bizantinistica* 12, Spoleto, 2007.
Pseudo – Maximus Confessor, *Opusculum De Anima*, ed. R. Cantarella, *S. Massimo Confessore. La mistagogia ed altri scritti*. Florence, 1931, pp. 220-232.

Pseudo – Methodius, *Apocalypsis*, ed. A.C. Lolos, *Die Apokalypse des Ps. – Methodios*, Beiträge zur klassischen Philologie 83, Meisenheim am Glan, 1976, pp. 46-140.

Pseudo – Nonnus, *Scholia Mythologica*, ed. Nimmo Smith, *Pseudo – Nonniani in iv orationes Gregorii Nazianzeni commentarii*, Corpus Christianorum Series Graeca 27, Turnhout, 1992.

Pseudo – Palladius of Helenopolis, *De Gentibus Indiae et Bragmanibus*, ed. W. Berghoff, *Palladius. De gentibus Indiae et Bragmanibus*, Meisenheim am Glan, 1967.

Pseudo – Plato, *Definitiones*, ed. J. Burnet, Platonis opera, vol. 5. Oxford, 1907 (repr. 1967).

Pseudo – Plutarch, *Apophthegmata Laconica*, ed. W. Nachstädt, *Plutarchi moralia*, vol. 2.1, Leipzig, 1935 (repr. 1971), pp. 110-224.

– *Placita Philosophorum* ("pseudo" - by convention; ancient authors regarded this as a genuine work), ed. J. Mau, *Plutarchi moralia*, vol. 5.2.1, Leipzig, 1971, pp. 50-153.

Pseudo – Theodosius of Alexandria (grammarian, fourth-fifth century AD), *Περὶ Γραμματικῆς*, ed. K. Göttling, *Theodosii Alexandrini grammatica*, Leipzig, 1822.

Pseudo – Zonaras (thirteenth century), *Lexicon*, ed. J.A.H. Tittmann, *Iohannis Zonarae lexicon ex tribus codicibus manuscriptis*, 2 vols. Amsterdam, 1967.

Ptolemy, Claudius (mathematician, Alexandria, second century AD), *Apotelesmatica* (*Tetrabiblos*), eds. E. Boer – F. Boll, *Claudii Ptolemaei opera quae exstant omnia*, vol. 3.1, Leipzig, 1940 (repr. 1957).

– *Geographia*, ed. K. Müller, *Claudii Ptolemaei geographia*, vol. 1.1, Paris, 1883.

– *Harmonica*, ed. I. Düring, *Die Harmonielehre des Klaudios Ptolemaios*, Göteborgs Högskolas Arsskrift 36, Göteborg, 1930.

– *Syntaxis Mathematica*, ed. J.L. Heiberg, *Claudii Ptolemaei opera quae exstant omnia*, vols. 1.1-1.2, Leipzig, vol. 1.1: 1898; vol. 1.2: 1903.

Romanus Melodus (Constantinople, sixth century), *Cantica*, eds. P. Maas – C.A. Trypanis, *Sancti Romani Melodi cantica: cantica genuine*, Oxford, 1963.

Rufinus, *Apologia*, PL.21.559-560; 2.46-47; PL.21.621-624.

– *De Adulteratione Librorum Origenis*, PG.17.616-32.

– *Apologiae in sanctum Hieronymum libri duo*, PL.21.541-624.

Scott W. – Ferguson, A.S. (eds.) *Corpus Hermeticum*, Oxford 1936.

Scott, W., *Hermetica*, vol. I, Oxford 1924.

Scylax, *Periplus Scylacis*, ed. K. Müller, *Geographi Graeci minores*, vol. 1. Parisot, 1855 (repr. Hildesheim, 1965), pp. 15-96.

Secundus (second century AD), *Sententiae*, ed. B.E. Perry, *Secundus the silent philosopher*, American Philological Association Philological Monographs 22, Ithaca, New York, 1964, pp. 78-90.

Septuaginta, Editio altera, eds. A. Ralphs – R. Hanhart, Stuttgat, 2006.

Serapion of Thmuis (bishop, fourth century), *Contra Manichaeos*, ed. R.P. Casey, *Serapion of Thmuis: Against the Manichees*, Harvard Theological Studies 15, Cambridge Mass. 1931, pp. 29-78.

Serenus of Antinouplis (geometrician, fourth century), *De Sectione Coni*, ed. J.L. Heiberg, *Sereni Antinoensis opuscula*, Leipzig, 1896: 120-302.

Severian of Gabala, *Fragmenta in Epistulam ad Ephesios*, ed. K. Staab, *Pauluskommentar aus der griechischen Kirche aus Katenenhandschriften gesammelt*, Münster, 1933, pp. 304-313.

– *Fragmenta in Epistulam Ad Titum*, ed. K. Staab, *Pauluskommentar aus der griechischen Kirche aus Katenenhandschriften gesammelt*, Münster, 1933, pp. 344-345.

– *Fragmenta in Epistulam i ad Corinthios*, ed. K. Staab, *Pauluskommentar aus der griechischen Kirche aus Katenenhandschriften gesammelt*, Münster, 1933, pp. 225-277.

– *In Job*, PG.56.563-582.

Sextus Empiricus, *Adversus Mathematicos*, ed. H. Mutschmann – J. Mau, *Sexti Empirici opera*, vols. 2 & 3 (second edition), Leipzig, vol. 2: 1914; vol. 3: 1961. *Proemium;* Book 1: *Adversus Mathematicos et Grammaticos;* Book 2: *Adversus Rhetores;* Book 3: *Adversus Geometras;* Book 4: *Adversus Arithmeticos;* Book 5: *Adversus Astrologos;* Book 6: *Adversus Musicos;* Book 7: *Adversus Dogmaticos 1* (*Adversus Logicos 1*); Book 8: *Adversus Dogmaticos 2* (*Adversus Logicos 2*); Book 9: *Adversus Dogmaticos 3* (*Adversus Physicos 1*); Book 10: *Adversus Dogmaticos 4* (*Adversus Physicos 2*); Book 11: *Adversus Dogmaticos 5* (*Adversus Ethicos*).

– *Pyrrhoniae Hypotyposes*, ed. H. Mutschmann, *Sexti Empirici opera*, vol. 1, Leipzig, 1912.

Sextus, *Sententae Sexti* (second-third century AD), ed. H. Chadwick, *The sentences of Sextus*, Cambridge, 1959, pp. 12-72.

Schaff, Philip – Wallace, Henry, *Nicene and Post – nicene Fathers: Second Series* (*vol. III*): *Theodoret, Jerome*, Gennadius, Rufinus, New York, 2007.

Simplicius, *Commentarius in Epicteti Enchiridion*, ed. I. Hadot, *Simplicius Commentaire sur le Manuel d'Épictète*, Philosophia Antiqua 66, Leiden – New York – Köln, 1996, pp. 192-454.

– *In Aristotelis Categorias Commentarium*, ed. K. Kalbfleisch, *Simplicii in Aristotelis categorias commentarium*, Commentaria in Aristotelem Graeca 8, Berlin, 1907.

– *In Aristotelis Libros De Anima Commentaria* (cited by convention: attribution is currently considered dubious), ed. M. Hayduck, *Simplicii in libros Aristotelis de anima commentaria* Commentaria in Aristotelem Graeca 11, Berlin, 1882.

– *In Aristotelis Physicorum Libros Commentaria*, ed. H. Diels, *Simplicii in Aristotelis physicorum libros octo commentaria*, 2 vols. Commentaria in Aristotelem Graeca vols. 9 & 10, Berlin, vol. 9: pp. 1-800, 1882; vol. 10: pp. 801-1366, 1895.

– *In Aristotelis Quattuor Libros De Caelo Commentaria*, ed. J.L. Heiberg, *Simplicii in Aristotelis de caelo commentaria*, Commentaria in Aristotelem Graeca 7, Berlin, 1894.

Sirmond, Jacques (Jacobus Sirmundus, 1559-1651, French scholar and Jesuit priest), *Praedestinatus, seu Praedestinatorum haeresis et libris*, MDCXLV (1645, no place of publication).

Socrates Scholasticus (fourth-fifth century), *Historia Ecclesiastica*, ed. W. Bright, *Socrates' ecclesiastical history*, Oxford, 1893.

Sophonias (Byzantine monk, thirteenth-fourteenth century), *In Aristotelis De Anima Paraphrasis*, ed. M. Hayduck, *Sophoniae in libros Aristotelis de anima paraphrasis*, Commentaria in Aristotelem Graeca 23.1, Berlin, 1883.

Soranus of Ephesus (physician, Alexandria, Rome, first-second century AD), *Gynaeciorum*, ed. J. Ilberg, *Sorani Gynaeciorum libri iv, de signis fracturarum, de fasciis, vita Hippocratis secundum Soranum*, Corpus medicorum Graecorum 4, Leipzig, 1927.

Souter, A., "Notes on Incidental Gospel Quotations", *Journal of Theological Studies*, 42 (1941), pp. 12-18.

Sozomenus, *Historia Ecclesiastica*, ed. J. Bidez and G.C. Hansen, *Sozomenus. Kirchengeschichte*, GCS 50, Berlin, 1960.

Speusippus, *Fragmenta*, ed. L. Tarán, *Speusippus of Athens*, Philosophia Antiqua 39, Leiden, 1981.

Stead, Christopher, *Divine Substance*, Oxford, 1977.

– *Philosophy in Christian Antiquity*, Cambridge, 1994.

Steinmann, J., *Hieronymus: Ausleger der Bibel. Weg und Werk eines Kirchenvaters*, Leipzig, 1958.

Stephanus (philosopher, Athens, Alexandria, seventh century), *In Aristotelis Librum De Interpretatione*, ed. M. Hayduck, *Stephani in librum Aristotelis de interpretatione commentarium*, Commentaria in Aristotelem Graeca 18.3, Berlin, 1885.

– *Scholia in Hippocratis De Fracturis*, ed. D. Irmer, *Palladius. Kommentar zu Hippokrates 'De fracturis' und seine Parallelversion unter dem Namen des Stephanus von Alexandria*, Hamburger philologische Studien 45, Hamburg, 1977, pp. 17-89.

– *Scholia in Hippocratis Prognosticon*, ed. J.M. Duffy, *Commentary on Hippocrates' Prognosticon* (Dissertation, SUNY Buffalo 1975).

Stephanus Byzantius, *Ethnica* (epitome), ed. A. Meineke, *Stephan von Byzanz. Ethnika*, Berlin, 1849.

Stephanus Diaconus (deacon, Constantinople, eighth-ninth century), *Vita Stephani Iunioris*, ed. M.-F. Auzépy, *La Vie d'Étienne le Jeune par Étienne le Diacre*, Birmingham Byzantine and Ottoman monographs 3, Aldershot, 1997, pp. 87-177.

Stobaeus, *Anthologium*, eds. C. Wachsmuth – O. Hense, *Ioannis Stobaei anthologium*, 5 vols, Berlin, vols. 1-2: 1884; vol. 3: 1894; vol. 4: 1909; vol. 5: 1912 (repr. 1958).

Stoicorum Veterum Fragmenta, ed. J. von Arnim, *Stoicorum veterum fragmenta*, 4 vols, Leipzig, 1905 (repr. Stuttgart, 1968).

Strabo, *Geographica*, ed. A. Meineke, *Strabonis geographica,* 3 vols. Graz, 1969.

Suda, *Lexicon*, ed. A. Adler, *Suidae lexicon*, 4 vols. Lexicographi Graeci 1.1-1.4, Leipzig, vol. 1.1: 1928; vol. 1.2: 1931; vol. 1.3: 1933; vol. 1.4: 1935.

Supplementum et Varietas Lectionis ad Catenam in Evangelium Sancti Lucae (*cod. Oxon. Bodl. Laud. 33*), ed. J.A. Cramer, *Catenae Graecorum Patrum in Novum Testamentum*, vol. 2, Oxford, 1841 (repr. Hildesheim, 1967), pp. 415-430.

Supplementum et varietas lectionis ad commentarium Chrysostomi in evangelium sancti Matthaei (*cod. Oxon. Bodl. Auct. T.1.4*), ed. J.A. Cramer, *Catenae Graecorum Patrum in Novum Testamentum*, vol. 1. Oxford, 1840 (repr. Hildesheim, 1967), pp. 449-496.

Symeon Logothetes, *Chronicon*, ed. I. Bekker, *Leonis Grammatici chronographia,* Corpus scriptorum historiae Byzantinae, Bonn, 1842.

Symeon of Thessaloniki (Metropolitan, fifteenth century), *Epistulae*, ed. D. Balfour, *Ἁγίου Συμεὼν Θεσσαλονίκης 1416/1417-1429 ἔργα θεολογικά*, Ἀνάλεκτα Βλατάδων 34, Thessaloniki, 1981, pp. 84-184, 199-246.

– *Expositio De Divino Templo*, ed. S. Hawkes – Teeples, *St. Symeon of Thessalonika, The Liturgical Commentaries*, Studies and Texts 168, Toronto, 2011, pp. 80-162.

Symeon the New Theologian (tenth-eleventh century), *Orationes Ethicae*, ed. J. Darrouzès, *Syméon le Nouveau Théologien, Traités théologiques et éthiques,* Sources chrétiennes 122, 129; Paris, 1966, 1967.

– *Capita Theologica*, ed. J. Darrouzès, *Syméon le Nouveau Théologien, Chapitres théologiques, gnostiques et pratiques*, Sources chrétiennes 51, Paris, 1996, pp. 40-186; 191.

– *Catecheses*, eds. B. Krivochéine – J. Paramelle, *Syméon le Nouveau Théologien, Catéchèses*, Sources chrétiennes 96, 104, 113, Paris, vol. 1: 1963, vol. 2: 1964, vol. 3: 1965.

– *Hymni*, ed. A. Kambylis, *Symeon Neos Theologos, Hymnen*, Supplementa Byzantina 3, Berlin – New York, 1976.

– *Orationes Theologicae*, ed. J. Darrouzès, *Syméon le Nouveau Théologien, Traités théologiques et éthiques*, Sources chrétiennes 122, Paris, 1966, pp. 96-168.

Synesius of Cyrene (bishop, fourth-fifth century), *Dion*, ed. N. Terzaghi, *Synesii Cyrenensis opuscula*, Rome, 1944, pp. 233-278.

– *Epistulae*, ed. R. Hercher, *Epistolographi Graeci*, Paris, 1873 (repr. Amsterdam, 1965, pp. 638-739.

Synodicon Orthodoxiae, ed. J. Gouillard, "Le Synodikon de l'Orthodoxie," *Travaux et mémoires* 2, 1967, pp. 45-107.

Synodicon Vetus (ninth-tenth century), eds. J.M. Duffy – J. Parker, *The Synodicon Vetus,* Corpus Fontium Historiae Byzantinae, Series Washingtonensis 15, Washington, D.C. 1979.

Syrianus, *Commentarium in Hermogenis Librum Περὶ Στάσεων*, ed. H. Rabe, *Syriani in Hermogenem commentaria*, vol. 2, Leipzig, 1893.

– *In Aristotelis Metaphysica Commentaria*, W. Kroll, *Syriani in metaphysica commentaria*, Commentaria in Aristotelem Graeca 6.1, Berlin, 1902.

Tatian, *Oratio Ad Graecos*, ed. E.J. Goodspeed, *Die ältesten Apologeten*. Göttingen, 1915, pp. 268-305.

Testamenta XII Patriarcharum, ed. M. de Jonge, *The Testaments of the Twelve Patriarchs: A Critical Edition of the Greek Text*, Pseudepigrapha Veteris Testamenti Graece 1.2, Leiden, 1978.

Themistius (Constantinople, c. 317-390), *Δεκετηρικός*, eds. G. Downey – H. Schenkl, *Themistii orationes quae supersunt*, vol. 1, Leipzig, 1965, pp. 215-230.

– *In Aristotelis Libros De Anima Paraphrasis*, ed. R. Heinze, *Themistii in libros Aristotelis de anima paraphrasis*, Commentaria in Aristotelem Graeca 5.3, Berlin, 1899.

– *In Aristotelis Physica Paraphrasis*, ed. H. Schenkl, *Themistii in Aristotelis physica paraphrasis*, Commentaria in Aristotelem Graeca 5.2, Berlin, 1900.

Theoctistus Studites (monk, Constantinople, fourteenth century), *Vita Athanasii Archiepiscopi Constantinopolitani*, A. Papadopoulos – Kerameus, *Zitija dvuh Vselenskih patriarhov XIV v., svv. Afanasija I i Isidora I*, Zapiski istoriko – filologicheskogo fakul'teta Imperatorskago S. - Peterburgskago Universiteta 76, St. Petersburg, 1905, pp. 1-51.

Theodore Anagnostes (historian, fifth-sixth century), *Epitome Historiae Tripartitae*, ed. G.C. Hansen, *Theodoros Anagnostes. Kirchengeschichte*, second edition, GCS Neue Folge 3, Berlin, 1995.

Theodore Dexius (Constantinople, fourteenth century), *Appelatio Adversus Iohannem Cantacuzenum*, ed. J. Polemis, *Theodori Dexii Opera Omnia*, Corpus Christianorum Series Graeca 55, Turnhout, 2003.

Theodore II Ducas Lascaris (rhetor and theologian, Emperor of Nicaea from 1254 to 1258), *De Processione Spiritus Sancti*, ed. C.Th. Krikones, *Θεοδώρου Β' Λασκάρεως Περὶ Χριστιανικῆς Θεολογίας Λόγοι, Παράρτημα*, Ἀνάλεκτα Βλατάδων 49, Thessaloniki, 1988, pp. 161-182.

– *Epistula ad Georgium Acropolitam*, ed. L. Tartaglia, *Theodorus II Ducas Lascaris Opuscula Rhetorica*, Bibliotheca scriptorum Graecorum et Romanorum Teubneriana, Munich – Leipzig, 2000, pp. 2-22.

Theodore Metochites, *Στοιχείωσις Ἀστρονομική*, ed. B. Bydén, *Theodore Metochites' Stoicheiosis astronomike and the study of natural philosophy and mathematics in early Palaiologan Byzantium*, Göteborg, Acta Universitatis Gothoburgensis, 2003, pp. 417-474.

Theodore of Heraclea or Theodore of Mopsuestia, *Fragmenta in Matthaeum*, ed. J. Reuss, *Matthäus – Kommentare aus der griechischen Kirche*, Texte und Untersuchungen 61, Berlin, 1957, pp. 136-150.

Theodore of Heraclea, *Fragmenta in Joannem*, ed. J. Reuss, *Matthäus – Kommentare aus der griechischen Kirche*, Texte und Untersuchungen 89, Berlin, 1966, pp. 67-176.

– *Fragmenta in Matthaeum*, ed. J. Reuss, *Matthäus – Kommentare aus der griechischen Kirche*, Texte und Untersuchungen 61, Berlin, 1957, pp. 55-95.

Theodore of Mopsuestia, *Commentarii in Joannem*, ed. R. Devreesse, *Essai sur Théodore de Mopsueste*, Studi e Testi 141, Vatican City, 1948, pp. 305-419.

– *Commentarius in xii Prophetas Minores*, ed. H.N. Sprenger, *Theodori Mopsuesteni commentarius in XII Prophetas*, Wiesbaden, 1977.

– *Expositio in Psalmos*, ed. R. Devreesse, *Le commentaire de Théodore de Mopsueste sur les Psaumes (I-LXXX)*, Studi e Testi 93, Vatican City, 1939.

– *Fragmenta in Epistulam ad Hebraeos*, ed. K. Staab, *Pauluskommentar aus der griechischen Kirche aus Katenenhandschriften gesammelt*, Münster, 1933, pp. 200-212.

– *Fragmenta in Epistulam i Ad Corinthios*, ed. ed. K. Staab, Pauluskommentar aus der griechischen Kirche aus Katenenhandschriften gesammelt, Münster, 1933, pp. 172-196.

– *Fragmenta in Matthaeum*, ed. J. Reuss, *Matthäus – Kommentare aus der griechischen Kirche*, Texte und Untersuchungen 61, Berlin, 1957, pp. 96-135.

Theodore Prodromus (or, Ptochoprodromus, poet, polymath, Constantinople, eleventh-twelfth century), *Carmina Historica*, ed. W. Hörandner, *Theodoros Prodromos, Historische Gedichte*, Wiener Byzantinistische Studien 11, Vienna, 1974, pp. 177-553.

– *Epigrammata in Vetus et Novum Testamentum*, ed. G. Papagiannis, *Theodoros Prodromos – Jambische und hexametrische Tetrasticha auf die Haupterzaehlungen des Alten und Neuen Testaments*, vols. 1-2, Meletemata: Beiträge zur Byzantinistik und neugriechischen Philologie 7.2, Wiesbaden, 1997.

Theodore Studites (759-826, abbot), *Canon In Requiem Monachi*, M. Arco Magrì, "Il canone in requiem monachi di Teodoro Studita," *Helikon* 18/19 (1978/1979, pp. 280-292.

– *Epistulae*, ed. G. Fatouros, *Theodori Studitae Epistulae*, vol. 1-2, Corpus Fontium Historiae Byzantinae, Series Berolinensis 31, Berlin, 1992.

– *Μεγάλη Κατήχησις*, ed. A. Papadopoulos – Kerameus, *Theodoros Studites*, Μεγάλη Κατήχησις, St. Petersburg, 1904.

– *Epitaphius in Matrem Suam*, ed. A. Pignani, *Teodoro Studita Catechesi – epitafio per la madre (testo in parte edito per la prima volta, introduzione, traduzione e indici)*, Hellenica et byzantina neapolitana 22, Naples, 2007, pp. 67-148.

– *Parva Catechesis*, ed. E. Auvray, *Theodori Studitis Parva Catechesis*, Paris, 1891.

– *Sermo De Sancto Bartholomeo Apostolo*, ed. U. Westerbergh, *Anastasius Bibliothecarius. Sermo Theodori Studitae de Sancto Bartholomeo Apostolo*, Acta Universitatis Stockholmiensis. Studia Latina Stockholmiensia 9, Stockholm, 1963, pp. 41-48.

– *Sermones Catecheseos Magnae*, ed. J. Cozza – Luzi, *Nova Patrum Bibliotheca* 9/2: Catecheses 1-77; 10/1: Catecheses 78-111, Rome, 1888-1905.

Theodoret of Cyrrhus, *Commentarius in Isaiam*, ed. J. - N. Guinot, *Théodoret de Cyr. Commentaire sur Isaïe*, vols. 1-3, Sources chrétiennes 276, 295, 315, Paris, vol. 1: 1980; vol. 2: 1982; vol. 3: 1984.

– *De Incarnatione Domini*, PG.75.1420-1477.

– *De Providentia*, PG.83.556-773.

– *Epistulae: Collectio Sirmondiana* (*Epistulae 1-95*), ed. Y. Azéma, *Théodoret de Cyr. Correspondance II, Sources chrétiennes* 98, Paris, 1964.

– *Epistulae: Collectio Sirmondiana* (*epistulae 96-147*), ed. Y. Azéma, *Théodoret de Cyr. Correspondance III, Sources chrétiennes* 111, Paris, 1965.

– *Eranistes*, ed. G.H. Ettlinger, *Theodoret of Cyrus. Eranistes*, Oxford, 1975.

– *Explanatio in Canticum Canticorum*, PG.81.28-213.

– *Graecarum Affectionum Curatio*, ed. P. Canivet, *Théodoret de Cyr. Thérapeutique des maladies helléniques*, 2 vols. Sources chrétiennes 57, Paris, 1958.

– *Haereticarum Fabularum Compendium*, PG.83.336-556.

– *Historia Ecclesiastica*, eds. L. Parmentier – F. Scheidweiler, *Theodoret. Kirchengeschichte*, second edition, GCS 44, Berlin 1954.

– *Historia Religiosa* (*Φιλόθεος Ἱστορία*), eds. P. Canivet – A. Leroy – Molinghen, *Théodoret de Cyr. L'histoire des moines de Syrie*, 2 vols. Sources chrétiennes 234, 257, Paris, vol. 1: 1977; vol. 2: 1979.

– *In Epistulas Sancti Pauli*, PG.82.36-877.

– *Interpretatio in Danielem*, PG.81.1256-1546.

– *Interpretatio in Ezechielem*, PG.81.808-1256.

– *Interpretatio in Jeremiam*, PG.81.496-805.

– *Interpretatio in Psalmos*, PG.80.857-1997.

– *Interpretatio in xii Prophetas Minores*, PG.81.1545-1988.

– *Interpretatio in xiv Epistulas Sancti Pauli*, PG.82.36-877.

– *Quaestiones et Responsiones ad Orthodoxos*, ed. A. Papadopoulos – Kerameus, *Θεοδωρήτου ἐπισκόπου πόλεως Κύρρου πρὸς τὰς ἐπενεχθείσας αὐτῷ ἐπερωτήσεις παρά τινος τὸν ἐξ Αἰγύπτου ἐπίσκοπον ἀποκρίσεις*, St. Petersburg, 1895.

– *Quaestiones in Libros Regnorum et Paralipomenon*, PG.80.528-858.

– *Quaestiones in Octateuchum*, eds. N. Fernandez Marcos – A. Saenz – Badillos, *Theodoreti Cyrensis quaestiones in Octateuchum*, Textos y Estudios "Cardenal Cisneros" 17, Madrid, 1979.

Theodosius of Alexandria (grammarian, fourth century), *Περὶ Κλίσεως τῶν εἰς ων Ὀξυτόνων*, ed. A. Hilgard, *Excerpta ex libris Herodiani technici*, Leipzig, 1887, pp. 22-24.

Theodotus of Ancyra (fourth-fifth century), *In Domini Nostri Jesu Christi Diem Natalem*, ed. M. Aubineau, "Une homélie de Théodote d'Ancyre sur la nativité du Seigneur," *Orientalia Christiana Periodica* 26 (1960), pp. 224-232.

Theon of Alexandria (mathematician, Alexandria, fourth century AD), *Commentaria in Ptolemaei Syntaxin Mathematicam*, ed. A, Rome, *Commentaires de Pappus et de Théon d'Alexandrie sur l'Almageste*, vol. 1, Studi e Testi 54, Vatican City, 1931.

Theophanes Confessor (Θεοφάνης ὁ Ὁμολογητής, abbot, Constantinople, Samothrace, 758/760-817/818), *Chronographia*, ed. C. de Boor, *Theophanis chronographia*, vol. 1, Hildesheim, 1963.

Theophilus of Alexandria (in office, 384-412), *Fragmenta in Matthaeum*, ed. J. Reuss, *Matthäus – Kommentare aus der griechischen Kirche*, Texte und Untersuchungen 61, Berlin, 1957, pp. 151-152.

Theophilus of Antioch (apologist, second century AD), *Ad Autolycum*, ed. R.M. Grant, *Theophilus of Antioch. Ad Autolycum*, Oxford, 1970.

Theophrastus of Eresus (fourth-third century AD), *De Causis Plantarum*, ed. R.E. Dengler, *Theophrastus. De causis plantarum, book one*, Philadelphia, 1927.

Theosophorum Graecorum Fragmenta, *Textus Thesaurorum Minorum*, ed. H. Erbse, *Theosophorum Graecorum fragmenta*, Stuttgart – Leipzig, 1995, pp. 91-135.

Thrasyllus (historian, probably first century AD), *Fragmenta*, ed. Müller, *Fragmenta historicorum Graecorum, 3*, Paris, 1841-1870, pp. 502-504.

Thucydides, *Historiae*, eds. H.S. Jones – J.E. Powell, *Thucydidis historiae*, 2 vols. Oxford, vol. 1: 1942; vol. 2: 1942 (repr. vol. 1: 1970; vol. 2: 1967).

Timaeus (sophist, grammarian, a Neoplatonist, probably fourth century AD), *Lexicon Platonicum*, ed. F. Dübner, *Platonis opera quae feruntur omnia*, eds. J.G. Baiter – J.K. Orelli – A.W. Winckelmann, Zurich, 1839, pp. 971-1008.

Tzamalikos, Panayiotis, – *Anaxagoras, Origen, and Neoplatonism. The Legacy of Anaxagoras to Classical and Late Antiquity*, Berlin – New York, 2016.

– *An Ancient Commentary on the Book of Revelation*, Cambridge – New York, 2013.

– *Origen: Cosmology and Ontology of Time*, Leiden 2006.

– *Origen: Philosophy of History and Eschatology*, Leiden 2007.

– *A Newly Discovered Greek Father*, Leiden 2012.

– *The Real Cassian Revisited*, Leiden 2012.

– *The Concept of Time in Origen*, Bern, Frankfurt, Paris, New York, 1991.

– "Origen, The Source of Augustine's Theory of Time", in *Philosophia*, Yearbook of the Research Center for Greek Philosophy at the Academy of Athens, v. 17-18, 1989, pp. 396-418.

– "Creation *ex nihilo* in Origen, Rebuttal of a tragic historical bias". *Papers in Honour of Professor Emeritus G. Nitsiotas*, Aristotle University of Thessaloniki Press, Thessaloniki 1994, pp. 1157-1208.

– "Origen and the Stoic View of Time", *Journal of the History of Ideas*, v. 52 (4), 1991, pp. 535-561.

– "The concept of Accidental Being in Aristotle and its Significance for Patristic Thought". *Procceedings of the International Conference on Aristotle's Metaphysics*

(held at the Aristotle University of Thessaloniki, 9 & 10 October 1997, Thessaloniki 1999), pp. 171-185.
– "The Concept of Space – Time in Origen", *Diotima*, Review of Philosophical Research, 24, 1996, pp. 144 149.
– "The Concept of ὕλη ('matter') in Plato's *Timaeus*", in *Philosophia*, Yearbook of the Research Center for Greek Philosophy at the Academy of Athens, v. 27-28, 1997-98, pp. 131-141.

Vogt, H.J., *Origenes: Der Kommentar zum Evangelium nach Mattäus. Eingeleitet, übersetzt und mit Anmerkungen versehen.* Stuttgart, 1983-1993; Erster Teil: Buch X-XIII *Bibliothek der griechischen Literatur*, v. 18, Abt. Patristik, 1983. Zweiter Teil: Buch XIV-XVII (*Bibliothek der griechischen Literatur*, v. 30, Abt. Patristik, 1990. Dritter Teil: Die Commentariorum Series, Bibliothek der griechischen Literatur. v. 38, Abt. Patristik, 1993.
– *Origenes als Exeget*, Paderborn, 1999.

Wagner, Monica, *Rufinus the Translator. A Study of His Theory and Practice as Illustrated in His Version of the Apologetica of St. Gregory Nazianzen*, Washington DC, 1945.

Xenocrates, *Testimonia, Doctrina et Fragmenta*, in M.I. Parente (ed.), *Senocrate – Ermodoro. Frammenti*, Naples, 1982.

Xenophon, *Apologia Socratis*, ed. E.C. Marchant, *Xenophontis opera omnia*, vol. 2, second edition, Oxford, 1921 (repr. 1971).
– *Memorabilia*, ed. E.C. Marchant, *Xenophontis opera omnia*, vol. 2, second edition, Oxford, 1921 (repr. 1971).

Zosimus, *Historia Nova*, ed. F. Paschoud, *Zosime. Histoire nouvelle*, vols. 1-3.2, Paris, vol. 1: 1971; vols. 2.1-2.2: 1979; vol. 3.1: 1986; vol. 3.2: 1989.

Photos

Folia 1v-2r, "By Origen": Three *Homoousia* Persons.

Folia 18v-19r, "By Origen": There are three Hypostases, yet the ousia of the Three is one. The Holy Spirit is *homoousios* with the Son and the Father.

Folia 94v-95r: "By Origen": Homoousios Trinity. The text from folio 93v to folio 97r is continuous.

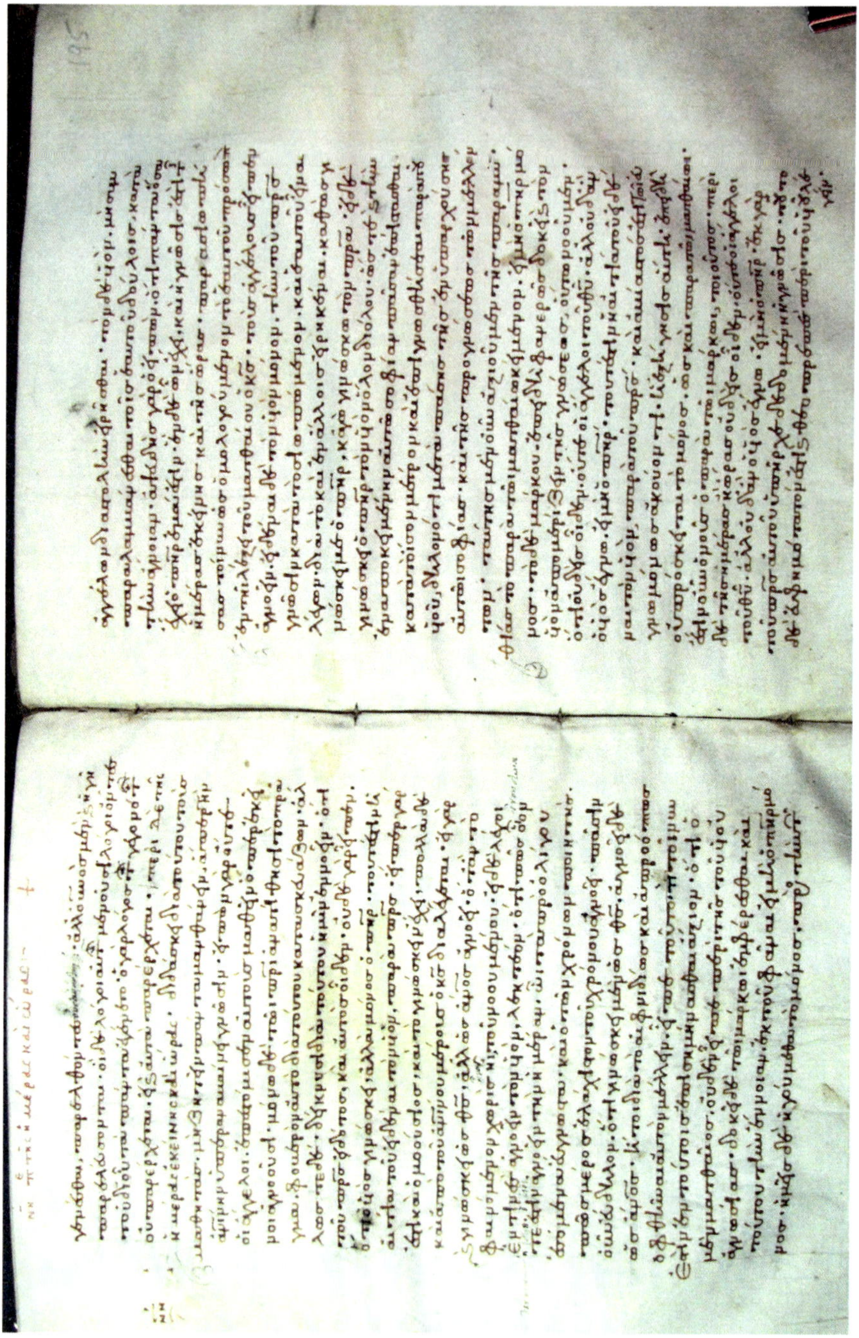

Folia 195v-196r. The Son is *homoousios* with the Father. The text 'By Origen' from 186v to 195v is continuous.

Folia 195v-196r. The Son is *homoousios* with the Father.

Folio 239v: "By Origen". One God in Three Hypostases. *Homoousios* Son. The text continues down to folio 240v (end of commentary).

Folio 240v (end of commentary). "By Origen". The Holy Spirit is a Hypostasis *homoousios* with the Father and the Son; He proceeds from the Father, and demonstrates Himself through the Son.

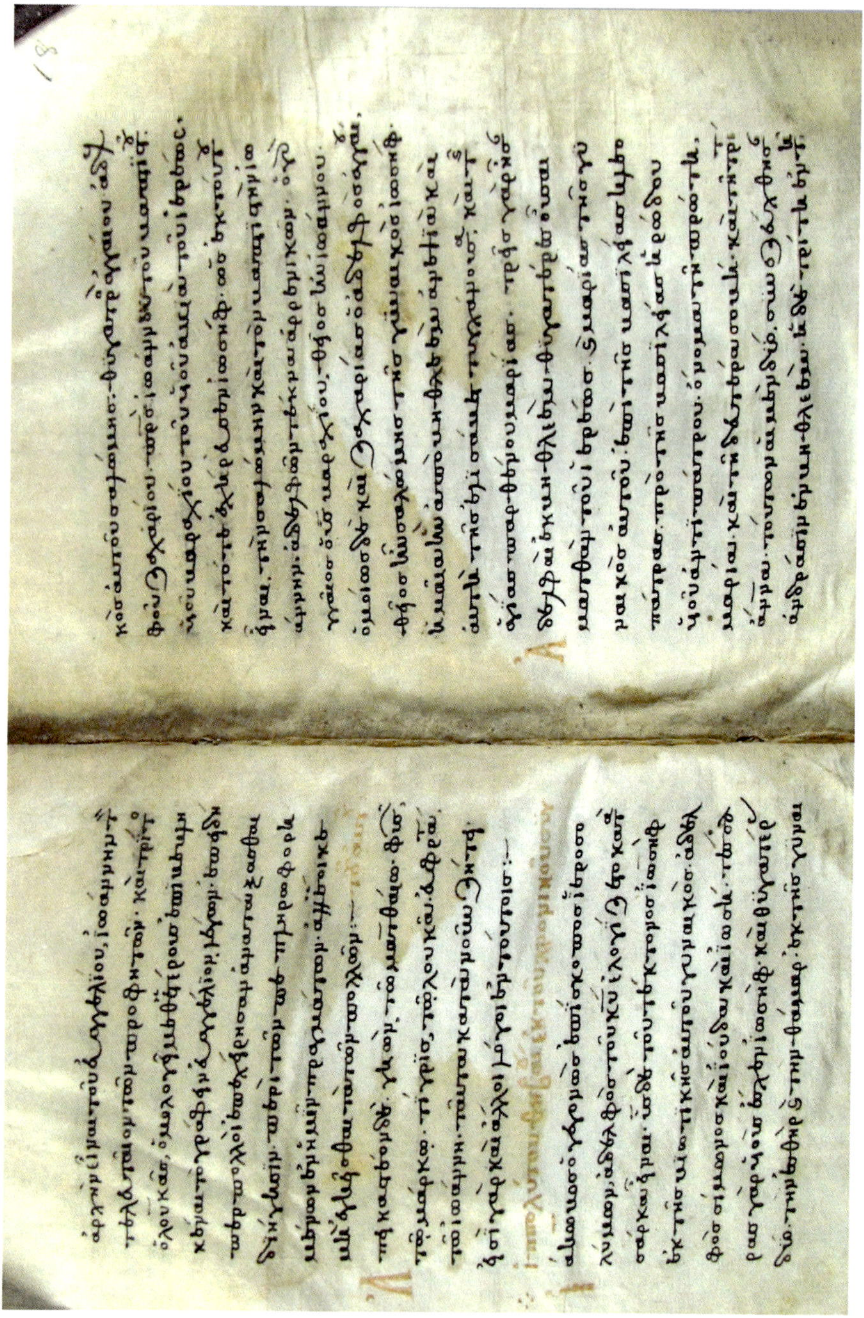

Codex Holy Cross 104, folio 17v: 'By the same" [Origen] [cont. from f. 16v-17r]: By the same [Origen, f. 16v)": a unique pictorialisation of the four Evangelists counterparting the four rivers of Gen. 2:14 (see p. CLXXX).

Index of Greek Terms

Index of Names

Index of Modern Names